Implementing
Tally.ERP 9

(Revised and Updated Edition)

Implementing

Tally.ERP 9

(Revised and Updated Edition)

By

Asok k. Nadhani

BPB PUBLICATIONS

20 Ansari Road, Darya Ganj, New Delhi-110002

Reprint 2017

SECOND REVISED & UPDATED EDITION 2015

FIRST EDITION 2007

ISBN : 978-81-8333-216-3

LIMITS OF LIABILITY AND DISCLAIMER OF WARRANTY

The information contained in this book is true and correct and the best of Author's & Publisher's knowledge. We are committed to serve students with best of our knowledge and resources. We have taken utmost care and attention while editing and printing of this book but Author and Publisher should not be held responsible for errors, omissions and any other unintentional mistake that might have crept in. However, errors brought to our notice shall be gratefully acknowledge and attend to.

Tally is registered trademark of Tally Solutions (P) Ltd. and is no way connected with this book. This is written solely for benefit and guidance of tally users and students.

Distributors:

COMPUTER BOOK CENTRE
12, Shrungar Shopping Centre,
M.G. Road, BENGALURU-560001
Ph: 25587923, 25584641

MICRO BOOKS
Shanti Niketan Building,
8, Camac Street, KOLKATA-700017
Ph: 22826518/22826519

MICRO MEDIA
Shop No. 5, Mahendra Chambers,
150 DN Rd. Next to Capital Cinema,
V.T. (C.S.T.) Station, MUMBAI-400 001
Ph: 22078296/22078297

DECCAN AGENCIES
4-3-329, Bank Street,
HYDERABAD-500195
Ph: 24756967/24756400

BPB PUBLICATIONS
B-14, Connaught Place,
NEW DELHI-110001
Ph:23325760/43526249

BPB BOOK CENTRE
376, Old Lajpat Rai Market,
DELHI-110 006,
Ph: 23861747

INFOTECH
G-2, Sidhartha Building,
96 Nehru Place,
NEW DELHI-110 019
Ph: 26438245

BPB PUBLICATIONS
20, Ansari Road, Darya Ganj,
NEW DELHI-110002
Ph: 23254990/23254991

Published by Manish Jain for BPB Publications, 20, Ansari Road, Darya Ganj, New Delhi- 110002 and Printed him at Rewa Printers, New Delhi.

To
Kanta

Books of the Author

Computer Programming

- Clipper Applications (1993)

Accounting Systems

- BI Financial Management & Accounting (1997)*
- Accounting with Tally 4.5 (1999)
- REAL Accounting Software (2000)*
- PURSE Payroll Software (2000)*
- Implementing Tally 5.4 (2000)
- Tally Tutorial 5.4 (2000)
- Implementing Tally 6.3 (2001)
- Tally Tutorial 6.3 (2001)
- Implementing FACT (2002)
- Implementing E.X.- NGN (2002)
- Simple Tally 6.3 (2005)
- Implementing Tally 7.2 (2005)
- Implementing Tally 7.2 – Hindi (2006)
- Simple Tally 7.2 (2006)
- Tally Instant Reference (2006)
- Simple Tally 7.2 Hindi - (2007)
- Tally Payroll (2007)*
- Implementing Tally 9 (2007)
- Managing VAT with Tally 9 (2008)
- Simple Tally 9 (2008)
- Tally 9 Training Guide (2009)
- Simple Tally.ERP 9 Hindi – (2011)
- Tally.ERP 9 Training Guide (2010, 2013)
- Tally.ERP 9 Made Simple (2012)
- Mastering Tally.ERP 9 (2012, 2013)

CA (CPT/ IPCC)

- Accounting Standards (2009)
- Business Ethics & Communications (2009)
- Business & Corporate Laws (2009)
- Information Technology (2009)
- Auditing & Assurance (2009)
- Mercantile Laws (2009)

Tutorial CDs

- Tally 6.3
- Learn Tally 9 (Basic Financial Accounting – Level 1)
- Learn Tally 9 (Traders Accounting – Level 2)

*With companion CD

Trademarks

Tally, Tally eis 5.4, Tally ees 6.3, Tally ies 7.2, Tally 8.1, Tally 9, Tally.ERP 9, TallyGold, TallySilver, Power of Simplicity are registered Trade marks of Tally Solutions P Ltd. Ali other trademarks are property of their respective owners and are hereby acknowledged.

Disclaimers

Though care is taken to provide correct information, neither the Author, nor the Publishers are responsible for any mistake or omission in the book.

The readers should, in their own interest, verify the usability of the software described in this book, in their context.

Readers should, in their own interest, confirm the availability / details of features of Tally.ERP 9 software, from Tally Solution Pvt Ltd., or their authorized dealers, or their website www.tallysolutions.com

Conventions Used in the book

Menu Path: Menu Path is shown with > indicator, like *Display>Account Books>Ledger* etc

Buttons: Buttons are indicated by the Function key or **Letter** and the Button Name, like F11:Features, P:Print etc

Sections & Parts: The book is divided **in 4 sections**, *Financial Accounting, Invoicing & Inventory, Taxation & Payroll.* Each section contains several Parts.

Chapters: Each Part contains several Chapters, identified by Part Number - Chapter Number: Chapter Name (e.g *02-03:Gateway of Tally*, indicates 3rd Chapter of Part 2 named *Gateway of Tally*). The Part Number & Chapter Number is separated by a hyphen, like 02-03.

Paragraphs: Paragraphs are sequentially numbered. Like 01, 02, (major paragraphs numbers), 04.01, 04.02, 05.02.01 (sub paragraphs) and so on, within each Chapter

Figures: Figures are identified by prefix F- and sequentially numbered with suffix A, B etc. (like F-5A, F-5B).

Cross Reference: Throughout the book, cross references are cited for related Topics & Figures, within parenthesis.

The *Paragraphs* are referred with §, followed by the Chapter Number (e.g §09). Topics of another chapter of the same *Section* are referred by adding a suffix of Part Number, after a slash (/), like §02/03- 02 indicates Paragraph Number 02 of Chapter 02 of Part 03 (03-02). For Topics of another *Section*, the Section number (S1 to S4), is added at the end, after a slash (/), like §02/03- 02/S2, referring to Paragraph Number 02 of Chapter 02 of Part 03 (03-02) of Section 2.

The Figures are referred with prefix F-, followed by the Figure Number (e.g F-2, F-3A etc). Figures of another chapter are referred by adding a suffix of Part Number – Chapter Number. For example, F-2A/02- 06) indicates Figure Number 2A of Chapter 06 of Part 02 (02-06). For figures of another Section (e.g Section 2), the section number is added with a slash at the end, like F-2A/02- 06/S2

Notes: Notes clarifying practical implications are briefly pointed out in the side boxes under the heading Notes.

For any query & clarification, the reader may e-mail to: sales@bpbonline.com

Preface

This book is the latest addition in *Implementing Tally* series of books of the author, starting from the year 2000. It is a comprehensive treatise for Learners as well as avid Users of Tally in business enterprises.

Tally.ERP 9 software encompasses a vast area. The book is organised into functional areas, so that each user can focus into the specified areas of his own application, instead of wading through all the features of Tally.ERP 9. Many organisations may use only a few of the functional areas covered by this book.

ERP means enterprise Resources Planning. This book is aptly organised to plan, manage & control the 3 primary Resources of any Business (known as 3 Ms): MONEY (Financial Accounting), MATERIALS (Inventory) & MANPOWER (Payroll Accounts). The book also deals with the statutory requirements of Tax (TAXATION), that any organisation is legally bond to comply to. So, the 4 sections cover the entire aspects of Accounting & Management of Resources, as well as Tax aspects & legal compliances.

Huge materials about Tally ERP are available in various forms and sources. The Help file that comes with the software describes the operational details in line with the structure (Menus) of the software. Other materials available in NET, scattered randomly, explains various specific aspects of that might be useful to users.

I have consciously avoided to replicate (and deviated from) the way as depicted in Help files of Tally and materials commonly available elsewhere. The approach of this book is to help the user to perform the desired business function. So, the book is organised according to business functions (rather than Tally's structure), loaded with practical examples and problems that the users encounter in their work, in relation to the specific aspects of the Business function. So, all the tasks related to a function (right from activation, set up, masters creation, transactions entries, reporting etc, along with all related configuration options), though scattered in Tally Software (and in the Help File), are compiled and placed together in logically sequence. For example all matters relating to Foreign Currency or all matters relating to Batch (normally NOT used by everyone) are assembled from various areas, scattered all over the software, and placed together. All configuration options are logically placed into Masters Entry, Transactions Entry, Display & Report Display/ Printing Configurations etc.

I hope that using this book, you do not have to wander, skimming entire literature (the Help Manual), when you activate and subsequently use the features in transactions & reporting. Similarly, the other way round, users NOT using specific functions may altogether skip the relevant chapters / topics of the functional areas, making their life simpler and easier. Most of the users, may thus skip many parts of this book, without losing continuity, while focusing more intently, the areas they are involved into.

Users naturally look at any functionality, problem & solution, in their own way, and often stumble if explained or depicted differently. So, the topics are arranged according to their domain areas, not as to how Tally sees them or shows them, through its own Technical structure. In Tally, all sorts of configuration of all functional areas, are placed together. So the readers have to go through all of them, even if many of them are not relevant to them.

In Tally's Help manual (or other Tally books), normally you have to wade through many aspects & options that might be irrelevant to you. Even from the very start, you ought to understand various options and implications of Company Creation, Company Features, Configuration and other aspects. You will often find setting them as per your requirements, quite intimidating (as many are irrelevant and look geek). In this book, you will find, right from Company Creation, how to start just from fewest bare essential things, and gradually uncover the specific aspects as per your choice and needs.

The book is also supplemented b an elaborate Table of Contents and an extensive Index of cross reference to the topics of the book, with key words in alphabetical order, to help the reader to locate desired topic and the linked materials easily.

However, even after writing about 20+ books on Tally for more than two decades, I must humbly submit that I am not expert in all functional areas. I am like a general physician, who knows the overall anatomy and functions of the human body, but not an expert to specific areas, like specialist. This book depicts the functionalities in general way, showing the solution to normal practical problems, as far as possible. But, it is the users, who only have experienced the varied and finer aspects of using and implementing a software system and know the intricate knots. The users are the real specialists in their own functional areas. I earnestly request the readers to share their rich experiences and innovative ideas with me. This book can be richer only on participation of the readers. Send your views through e-mail: (sales@bpbonline.com).

Asok K Nadhani

September 2014

Recent Updates of Tally.ERP 9 Series A

Significant New Features

New features from release 4.5 (14th Jan 2013) onwards of Tally.ERP 9 Series A, are listed below with brief comments. For more details, refer to HELP manual or visit www.tallysolutions.com

Release 4.9 (18th June 2014)

In Release 4.9, several issues have been resolved and some performance has been enhanced. No significant new feature added.

Release 4.8

Data / Migration: While migrating data from lower releases, a confirmation prompt, *Migrate?* is displayed. Further, upon opting to migrate data, the prompt *Backup before migrating?* is displayed, to enable users can take Data Backup before migration.

Voucher Display: The options to *Export, E-Mail,* and *Upload* are provided in *Voucher Display* screen.

Tally Update: If the Tally.NET subscription has expired, during *Auto Update* of Tally.ERP 9, a message denoting that their existing version cannot be upgraded, is displayed

Accounting Reports: The option *Exclude Particulars With Zero Closing Balance* is added to the *F12: Configure* options of the *Balance Sheet* and *Profit & Loss A/c*, to remove zero-valued items from these reports.

Accounting Vouchers

- Option to print the *Due Date* or *Credit Days,* is provided for *Payment, Receipt* and *Journal* Voucher Types.
- An option *Print Complete Mailing* details is provided in the *Invoice Printing Configuration* screen of Purchase order, Sales order, Receipt note, Delivery note, Rejection in, Rejection out, Purchase, Sales, Debit note, Credit note, Job work in order, Job work out order, Material in, Material out and Excise sales vouchers, to print the party's contact number(s), fax number(s), and e-mail ID.
- For ledgers grouped under *Bank Accounts* and *Bank OD A/c*, a new option, *Calculate Interest Based on* is provided to configure calculation of interest based on *Bank Reconciliation Date* or *Voucher Date.*
- An option *Default Jurisdiction* is provided in Voucher Type master, to be printed on Invoices.

Banking

- A new *Style of Date, dd mm yy,* is provided in the *Cheque Dimensions* screen of bank ledger master.
- Option is provided to enter Bank Details, like *Account Number, IFS Code, Name of Bank,* and *Transaction Type* in *Employee Masters, Cost Centres* and *Ledgers* grouped under Sundry Debtors, Sundry Creditors, Direct/Indirect Expenses etc.
- In *Cheque Register* report, a new button - *Alt+B: Alter Cheque Book* is provided to display *Cheque Book Management* screen to define details of *Cheque Range, Number of Cheques* and *Book Name.*
- In *Contra* voucher entry in Single Mode for Cash Withdrawal, the field *Favouring Name* in the *Bank Allocations* screen is prefilled with the text *Self.*
- The option *Transfer Mode* is provided in the *Bank Allocation* screen in Voucher Entry, to identify transactions of NEFT/RTGS.
- New Transaction Types - *ATM, Card* and *ECS* are added under Banking Features at *F11: Accounting Features.*
- In the Bank Allocations screen, a button *Reconcile All Unlinked* is provided in the *Bank Reconciliation* report, to link all transactions under *Amount not reflected in Company Books* with a single click.
- Forex details may be displayed at *Bank Reconciliation* while reconciling unlinked multi currency transactions.

CST: The option *Show Order Details* is provided at *F12: Configure* in the *Forms Receivable, Forms Issuable* Reports, and the Print Report for *Reminder Letters/Covering Letters* to print Buyer's Order Number and Date.

Excise for Manufacturers: Option to view and print *Excise Invoice Numbers* instead of Voucher Numbers is provided for the following reports:

- Ledger Vouchers report for Excise Sales invoices and Debit Note
- Confirmation of Accounts
- Columnar Register for Excise Sales invoices and Debit Note
- CST Forms Issuable
- CST Forms Receivable
- Outstanding Statement
- Sales Register
- Debit Note Register

Service Tax

- The option to specify *Allowable Expenses* at recording *Reverse Charge* transactions for *Tax Computation* is provided.
- Option to enable Service Tax for Ledgers created under listed *Primary Groups* is provided.

TDS

- Ledger grouped under *Provisions* may also be selected in Purchase Invoice (Accounting invoice and Item Invoice mode).
- Provision to pass separate entry, for calculation of *interest or penalty* Amount on delayed payment of TDS, is provided.

VAT: In *Voucher Class* configuration screen. the option to set *Default Accounting Allocations* on the basis of *Stock Items*, or on the basis of *Tariff/VAT Commodities* is provided

Release 4.7

E-mail

- Option to enter multiple e-mail addresses at To and CC fields is provided. to e-mail multiple recipients simultaneously.
- Option in the ledger account master, to enter *secondary e-mail id* is provided which will be shown in the *Exception Reports* under *F5: All Items.*
- **Printing Copy Type:** The provision to print any individual type of copy (like Duplicate, Triplicate, Quadruplicate and All, even without printing the original) have been provided,

Voucher Type

- An option *Use Defaults for Bill Allocations*, is added at *F12: Configure* options for *Journal Voucher Type.*
- A new method of Voucher Numbering called *Multi-user Auto,* is provided in *Voucher Type Creation/Alteration* , to ensure that the vouchers are numbered sequentially in multi user environment also, enabling the user to work smoothly without any hindrance or waiting.

Banking

- An option *Print Bank Transaction Details* is provided under *F12: Formal Receipt Printing Configuration* to print bank details on formal receipts
- For *Formal Receipts*, option to print details of *Bank* and *branch name* of the payer's bank, is provided.
- Only display rights for viewing/printing of the Bank Reconciliation report for Users may be set, if the option *Display/Print* is *Allowed* for them, although *Full Access* to *Create/Alter* is *Disallowed.*
- Option *S: Set Bank Date at Bank Reconciliation* report is provided (in place of *S: Set All Dates)* to perform *Auto Reconciliation* for *NEFT/RTGS* transactions. You may select *Bank Date Type* to set Dates as per the Instrument Date specified in the *Bank Allocations* screen for each voucher, or as per *Voucher Date*, for all transactions to be automatically filled as per the selected *Bank Date Type.*
- At *Cheque Dimensions* screen that appears when a Bank ledger is being configured for cheque printing, at *Style of Dates*, another option *d d m m _ _ y y* has been added to print only the last two digits of the year on cheques
- If the account holder's name has been specified in the ledger master of a bank, the same will be printed as the *Account Holder Name* on the *Cash Deposit Slips* for that bank. The Bank account number is validated ignoring the zeroes prefixed, while importing bank statements.
- An option, *Print Narration*, is included at Payment Advice Print Configuration, to print Voucher Narration will be printed in Payment advice.
- To create Journal Voucher using the option *C: Create Voucher*, for transactions listed under the section *Amounts not reflected in Company Books* in the *Bank Reconciliation* report.

Credit Limit: Control set for a party ledger will not be applied on sales orders. The warning message on the credit limit will appear and the voucher can still be saved.

CST: The *CST Forms details* entered in the invoice be printed in *Simple Format* also.

Excise for Manufacturers

- In Purchase and Sales, at invoice title, Order Reference will be printed as:
  - o *Supplier's Ref. /Order No.* for excise purchase order.
  - o *Buyer's Ref. / Order No.* for excise sales order.
- A New flag *CENVAT Reversal (Rule 6)*, is provided in Journal Voucher to account for reversal of CENVAT credit on inputs used for manufacturing *Exempted goods as per rule 6 CENVAT Credit Rules.*
- The Option for *Day Wise break up* (for *One Item, Multi Item*, and *Tariff Wise*) is added for Daily Stock Register, to track the movement of excise stock items on 'Daily Basis' and print the report for a particular period.
- The option *Use for Supplementary Invoice* is provided at *Purchase and Sales Voucher Type Creation / Alteration* when the option *Use for Excise* is enabled, to enable using as Supplementary Excise Invoice.
- *Excise Credit Note* now includes provision for recording *Sales Returns* and associated details to be printed in the Excise Reports.
- *Export Procedure* has been provided for direct exports and indirect exports through merchants. Sales can also be made to EOU and SEZ.

Inventory Vouchers

The option, *Print Name & Godown Address*, has been added at *F12: Configure* at Voucher screen of the following vouchers:

- Inventory Vouchers
- Order Vouchers

- All Accounting Vouchers except *Journal, Payment, Receipt, Contra* and *Reversing* Journal.

Multi Currency

At Sales *Invoice Printing Configuration*, the option *Print Base & Foreign currency for Total* is added for multi currency Invoices to print Total Invoice Amount, in both base and foreign currency, along with exchange rate.

Payroll

- Processing of salary deduction/contribution to the *National Pension Scheme* u/s 80 CCD(1)/(2) of the Income Tax Act is now enabled.
- Conforming to new changes in *E-TDS 24Q Returns*, the provision to enter late fee has been provided under *Payroll Auto Fill* in Payment.

Service Tax

- For Service Provider/Receiver Parties, new Types of Classifications, *Taxable* and *Input Credit*, have been provided.
- *Taxable Percentage, Taxable Amount & Notification Number*, will be displayed in the *Service Tax Details* screen of *Journal* vouchers.
- On using *S: Stat Payment* button (Alt+S) in Payment Voucher, *Payment Type, Late fee*, will also be displayed in the *Type of Payment* list. The *Late Fees* so entered will be printed in *G.A.R-7 challan, Form ST-3* & *Service Tax Computation* Reports.
- In the *Company Service Tax Details* screen, on selecting the *Type of Organisation* as Firm, Individual/Proprietary, Limited Liability Partnership or Partnership, a new field - *Compute Tax Liability on* will be displayed to select Basis of Computation (*Accrual* or *Realisation*) to compute Service Tax based on selected method

  This option acts in conjunction with the option *Allow to override Basis of Computation* during entry in F12: Invoice Configuration.
- To account for advance receipts in Journal Vouchers, the flags - *Money Equivalent of Consideration* and *Service Consideration Adjustments*, a new Type of reference, *Advance* has been provided.
- The *S: Service Tax* Helper button (Alt+S) is provided in Journal Voucher to facilitate auto adjustment of Service Tax Payable against Service Tax Input Credit and CENVAT.

TDS

- A new field, *TAN Registration Number*, is provided in the *TDS/TCS Details* screen under *F11: Statutory & Taxation Features* to be shown in *e-TDS for Form 26Q, Form 27Q* and *Form 27EQ*.
- In a payment voucher, if *S: Stat Payment* button is used disabling Auto-fill option to account for only the expenses, two new options - *Late Fee for Resident (Form 26Q)* and *Late Fee for Non-Resident (Form 27Q)* will be displayed in *Type of Payment* list. The option *Late Fee* is also added to the list of payment type, when Expense Ledger is selected along with TDS ledger.

  The amount thus entered for Late Fee Payment Type, the amount for *Late Fee for Resident (Form 26Q), Late Fee for Non-Resident (Form 27Q)* and *Late Fees* will be shown in *e-TDS/TCS Return, Form 26Q, 27Q and 27EQ* and *ITNS 281 Challan*.
- In the Deductee Account Master, the field *Country* is provided to select the Country of Residence of the Deductee Master for Deductee Type: *Company - Non Resident* or *Individual/HUF - Non Resident*. Accordingly, *Country Code* will be shown in *e-TDS Returns of Form 27Q*.
- The *e-TDS* for *Form 24Q, Form 26Q, Form 27Q* and *27EQ* have been enhanced to support the updated *e-TDS Validation* tool version 4.0.

VAT

- *MRP Value* is added at *F12: Configuration* of *VAT Purchases* and *VAT Sales Registers* to A section, *Default Accounting Allocations for selected Item in Invoice*, is provided in the *Voucher Type Class* screen of *Sales, Purchase, Debit Note* and *Credit Note* Voucher Types to configure a Voucher Class for recording multiple items with different VAT rates.
- An option *Show* show *MRP Value* column

Release 4.61 (4th Jun 2013)

TDS

From 01.06.2013,s. 206AA is no more applicable for section 194LC, implying whether or not a deductee' s PAN is furnished in the Party master. TDS on Income From Foreign Currency, Bonds Or Shares of Indian Company will be deducted at the normal rate (5%).

Release 4.6 (27 Apr 2013)

- **Print preview**:*Zoom In* is increased to 600%, for better visibility of Reports, using '+' and '-' keys, Ctrl+scroll wheel (mouse wheel) &Shift+scroll wheel (mouse wheel) for horizontal scrolling.
- **Accounting Reports:** *F7: Bill-Party wise*, is provided in Bills Receivable, Bills Payable, and Group Outstanding reports showing party-wise information on outstanding bills. Party-wise subtotals and age-wise details
- **Excise for Manufacturers**
  - o Invoice Printing Configuration of Excise Sales invoice, option Print Excise ED/SHE Cess in words separately added
  - o *Re-Processor* option added to the Nature of Purchase list in purchase invoice and in Excise Details screen of party ledger master, to record purchase of raw material from re-processors. The details will be shown in RG 23 A Part I.

- **Excise for Dealers**
  - o Print Company Logo option in excise debit note also
  - o Supplier Invoice No. captured in the Excise Details screen of excise purchase invoice when an excise purchase order is tracked.
- **Payroll**
  - o Tax Rebate U/s 87A added
  - o Surcharge of 10% upto taxable income Rs.1 crore per year.
  - o Income Tax Benefit on interest on Home Loan (First Time Buyer) U/s 80EE added
- **Service Tax**
  - o Using Auto Fill in Payment voucher, new Bank Ledger can be created through Cash/Bank field of the Statutory Payment screen.
  - o Print Category as Taxable Service option added at F12: Print Configuration for sales invoices, professional receipts, and advance receipts to print service category as "Taxable Service" on the invoice/ receipt
  - o List of Organisations in the Company Service Tax Details at F11: Features > F3: Statutory & Taxation includes:
    - Limited Liability Partnership
    - A Firm
    - Hindu Undivided Family
    - Government
    - An Association of Persons/Body of Individuals
    - Artificial Juridical Person
    - A Local Authority (74042)
    - *Taxable Service Category* will not be available for entries dated 1.4.2013 onwards.
- **TDS**
  - o The field *Tax Assessment Number* is changed to *Tax Deduction and Collection Account Number in F11: Features > F3: Statutory & Taxation* and the relevant *TDS* and *TCS* reports.
  - o *Cheque/DD Date*, added in the *Provide Details* screen under *S: Stat Payment* for TDS and TCS. The date entered is carried at *TDS Challan 281*. A new column *Cheque Date* has been added in *TDS Challan Reconciliation* report.
  - o *TAN* must be entered as 4 Alpha + 5 Num + 1 Alpha &*PAN* must be entered as 5 Alpha + 4 Num + 1 Alpha Check Digit (C, P, H, F, A, T, B, L, J, G).
  - o Option *Is Proprietorship Firm* is added in *TDS/TCS Details* screen of*F11: Features > F3: Statutory & Taxation* to carry *Name of person responsible from TDS/TCS Details* in *TDS Challans* and *Returns* as *Proprietor's Name.*
  - o *Name on PAN/IT No. is* added in *Ledger Creation/ Alteration* screen for party ledgers to print Name as per PAN on *TDS Certificate* and *Returns.*
  - o *Show Name on PAN/IT No.* is added in *F12: Configure* options of the following drilldown screens in *TDS Computation* report:
    - Expenses & Advances
    - Exempt in lieu of PAN available
    - Taxable Expenses & Advances
    - Deducted, Deducted at Normal rate, Deducted at Lower rate, Deducted at Higher Rate (No PAN)
    - Balance Deductable, Balance Deductable at Normal rate, Balance Deductable at Lower rate
  - o Following *Sorting Methods* are added under *F12: Configure* options, when drilled down to the *Party Wise* and *Expense Wise* screens from *TDS Computation* report:
    - Ref No (Decreasing)
    - Ref No (Increasing)
    - Nature of Payment (Decreasing)
    - Nature of Payment (Increasing) (61385)
    - Option Show *PAN Number* is added under *F12: Configure* of the drill down screen for *Exempt in lieu of PAN available* in *TDS Computation* report.

Release 4.51 (19th Mar 2013)

- **Cheque Printing:** Facility to print Amount in Foreign Currency
- **MCA Reports**: XBRL compliant MCA Reports, with new C & I Taxonomy Structure, Facility to map Tally's Chart of Accounts with MCA Taxonomy Elements and generate, validate & upload to MCA portal for filing.

Release 4.5 (14th Jan 2013)

- **64 Bit:**Release 4.5 is a 64-bit native application to enable larger volume of data faster.
- **Voucher Level Security:** Provides security control at the Voucher level for each type of Operation & Access Rights to enable better control on Voucher Creation and personalisation.
- **Group Company**: Users having rights of several associate companies of a Group Company may access all companies with single login.
- **Countries**: Maintenance of Accounts of Zimbabwe (in US Dollars) and for Mauritius (in Mauritian Rupees) is now supported.
- **Data Sessions**: New features for managing Data sessions to monitor Tally.NET users
- **License Management**: To view the Licensing & Configuration screen, based on Serial Number, Site ID, Email ID, or Site Status. Grouping of information displayed based on Products / Serial Number.
- **User Management**: To view the User details like Number of Users, Active & Inactive Users etc.

- **Sessions Management:** To display User session details at different points of time, manage & configure sessions.
- **Security Control**: Password strength indicator is incorporated.
- **Tally.NET**: Message notification on exceeding the limit of Tally.NET Users logging into Remote Companies,
- **CST Forms Issuable**: Enhancements in Covering Letter and additional info in the Report
- **Excise for Manufacturers**: Additional columns for period, Enhancements in Daily Stock Register, Excise Purchase Invoice and Excise Sales Invoice
- **Excise for Traders**: Enhancements in Excise Stock CENVAT Register report.
- **Service Tax**: Additional Info of Reverse Charge transactions. Facility to define Category/Service of a Ledger during Voucher entry in the Service Tax Details screen, to facilitate printing of correct Accounting Codes in GAR-7 Challan.
- **Financial Statements**: Company Name, Page Numbers in all pages of Schedule-VI. Balance Column in *Notes* to display balance of each Schedule-VI Group.

Organisation of the Book

Table of Contents

Section 1
Financial Accounting

Part 1

Basic Financial Accounting

In this section, we explain the entire process of Accounting with Tally.ERP 9, from Creation of Company, Accounts Masters, Accounts Vouchers, Viewing & Printing of various Books of Accounts to getting Final Accounts Statements (Profit & Loss Statement & Balance Sheet). Further, the process of finally closing of the current year accounts and creating next year's new set of accounts, carrying the Closing Balances of previous Financial Year, etc are elaborately explained. Finally, the steps of Backing up of Data are also explained to protect valuable data.

The entire chain of process are explained in the sequence of steps in which various tasks are performed.

Company Creation explains the process of creation of a Company in Tally.ERP 9 to enter data and manage accounts of an accounting entity.

Gateway of Tally explains the entry (and exit) point of each component & ancillary tasks to work with Tally.ERP 9.

Accounts Masters discusses about the Reserved Accounts Masters auto created by Tally.ERP 9 & about Creation of new Accounts Groups & Accounts Ledgers.

Accounts Vouchers explains the rules and steps of creation of various types of Accounts Vouchers, recording complete details of transactions. It also explains various novel short cut & quick methods of vouchers creation to save data entry time and ensure consistency & correctness of data.

Accounts Reports explains immediate display of reports on screen & seamlessly drill down & trace back through allied & subordinate areas of the entire system, and printing of reports & vouchers.

Cash / Bank Books explains the Display & Printing of Cash / Bank Books, the primary Books of Accounts, showing the details of daily Cash & Bank transactions. It also shows printing of Multi-Column combo Cash / Bank Books of several Cash / Bank Accounts in one Book, for convenience and better control.

Journal Books explains the Display & Printing of Journal Books of various types of Journals

Ledger Book shows the methods of Display & Printing of Ledger Accounts, Confirmation of Accounts etc and printing of Multiple Ledger Accounts in one shot.

Trial Balance shows Display & Printing of Trial Balance, with breakup of Opening, Transaction totals & Closing Balances, in organised structure.

Profit & Loss Statement shows Profit & Loss Statement, in various formats & contents.

Balance Sheet shows Balance Sheet, in various formats & contents

New Year Accounts describes various alternative methods to create the next year accounts and carry Ledger Accounts and Balances to New Financial Year accounts. It also explains ways to maintain several years data together. It also explains how to work with previous & next year data simultaneously, till accounts of previous year is closed.

Data Maintenance demonstrates the method of keeping Data Back Up, Restore Backed Up Data & Repair Damaged/ Re-Structure old Data

Part 1: Basic Financial Accounting, covers the root of the entire Accounting System, the complete needs of majority of Tally users. This Part is self encompassing, and users may skip the rest portion of the book, without any loss of continuity, unless they need specific or advanced features.

Company Creation

01-01

01 Starting Tally

Having installed Tally software in your computer, you may start (load)Tally in any of the following manner:

i. *Double click* the Tally shortcut on Desktop (if any shortcut is created)
ii. Select *Run* from Start Menu, enter the Drive, Path and the executable File Name, e.g. (*C:\Tally9\tally.exe*).
iii. At *Start Menu*, select *Programs*. From the Programs List, select *Tally.ERP 9* and then click *Tally ERP 9* (with Tally.ERP 9 icon) to launch Tally.ERP9.
iv. Explore the Tally Program folder (either through Windows Explorer or My Computer), double click the program file *Tally* (Application file)

The simplest way is to create a short cut of Tally Application file on Desktop and click on the Tally.ERP 9 shortcut on the desktop

02 Company Creation

On Starting Tally, you get the *Company Info* menu (F-1A) (with fewer option in first time), At *Company Info* menu (F-1A), click *Create Company* to get *Company Creation* Screen (F-2A)

02.01 Company Creation Screen

At *Company Creation* screen (F-2A), quite a number of Input appear to be filled Up. However, you may fill up only the essential info as discussed next, to create a Company, leaving others to be filled as & when required, to start the work quickly.

- **Name:** At *Name*, enter Name of the Enterprise (Company). The Company is identified and selected by this Name (called *Tally Company Name*).
- **Module:** At *Maintain*, select *Accounts Only* when you like to maintain Financial Accounts System only.
- **Financial Year Start Date:** At *Financial Year from*, enter beginning date of Financial Year (e.g 1-4-2013).

You may leave default values / blank (press <entre>) in other fields (like *Address* etc), to be filled / changed later on, as necessary.

Notes

- **Company data Folder:** At *Directory* field, the default data directory (where *Tally.exe* is installed) is shown and the field is skipped.
- **Company Name:** To identify the Company for each Year, you may add the FY after the Company name (like Info Consultants 12-13). So, in the next year, when you create separate Company for 13-14, you will name it like Info Consultants 13-14, to identify Accounts of the respective year from the *Tally Company Name*. Similarly, you may enter the Branch Suffix, like ABC Co (Delhi), ABC Co (Chennai), if you create separate Companies for Branches.

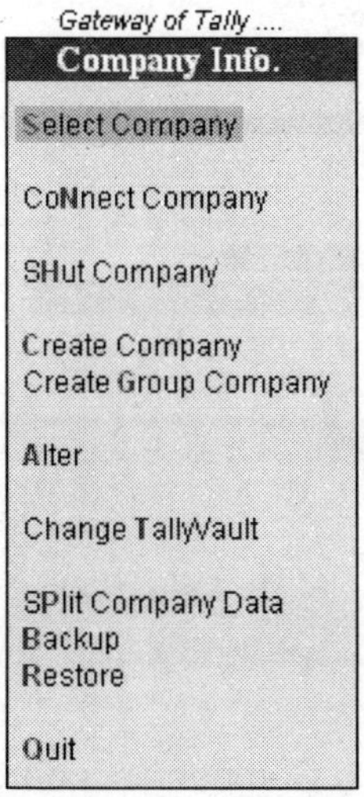

F-1A: Company Info Menu

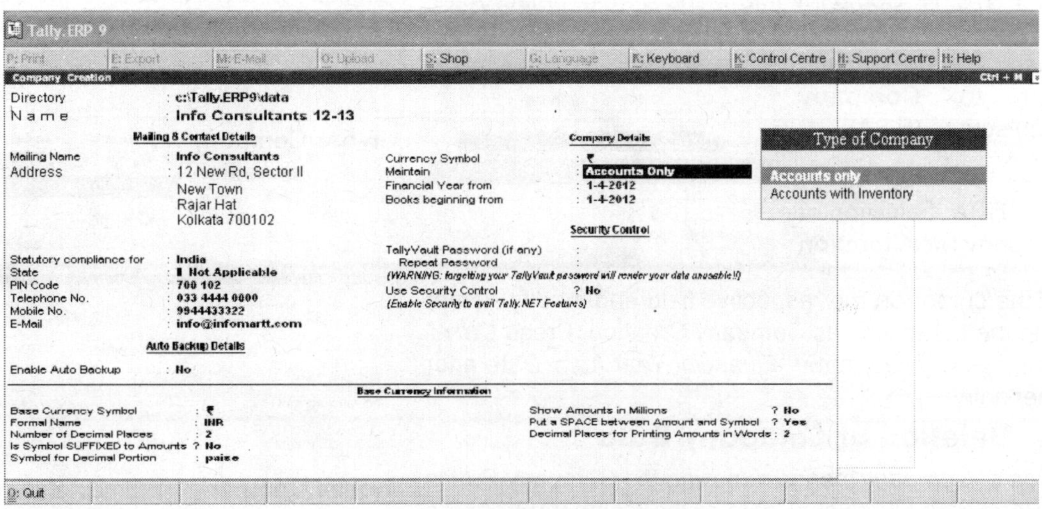

F-2A: Company Creation

- **Module:** At *Maintain*, when you select *Accounts Only,* Inventory System will not be maintained..The system remains simple, as the options related to Inventory systems do not get activated. Select *Accounts with Inventory* to maintain both Accounts & Inventory. Plan the System Module at the time of Company Creation. Don't change it after you have entered vouchers, otherwise your accounts may be incomplete / incompatible.
- **Financial Year:** Tally initially creates Accounting period of 1 year from *Financial Year from* date. For example, if you enter 14.10.2015 the accounting period would be upto 13.10.2016 (which you may extend). Do not change this date after voucher entry.

Saving the Company

After entering (or Altering through *Alteration* option) the data, Click *Yes* at *Accept* (at the bottom right) to save the Company profile. Alternatively, you may press *Ctrl+A* to save the Company profile directly (no confirmation required). Now a Tally Company gets created.

02.02 Creation of subsequent Companies

You may create several Tally Companies (as many as you like to) and maintain separate accounting records for each of them.

To create the next company, click *F3: Cmp Info* button at *Gateway of Tally* (F-1B/01-02), to get Company Info Menu (F-1A) and create another Company, as explained (§02).

03 Modification of Company

Company Profile: *Company Profile* refers to the info entered at *Company Creation* screen (F-2A). After Company Creation, you may modify the Company Profile at any time. You may also fill up the unfilled data fields in the Company Profile screen, as needed.

Modification of Company Profile: Click *F3: Company Info* button at *Gateway of Tally* (F-1B/01-02) to get *Company Info Menu* (F-1A). At *Company Info Menu* (F-1A). select *Alter,* select the Company Name from the list (F-3A), to get *Company Alteration* screen, similar to Company creation screen (F-2A).

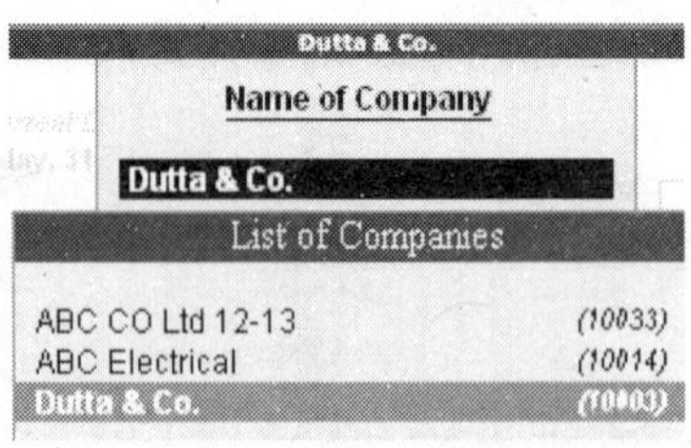

F-3A: Selection of Company for Alteration

Place the cursor on the respective field and modify / enter data, in the same way as Company Creation. Press *Ctrl+A* to save. Never change the '*Financial Year from*' Date after voucher entry.

04 Deletion of Company Data

Deletion of Company means removing the Company Profile data along with all voucher data of the Company from the Computer.

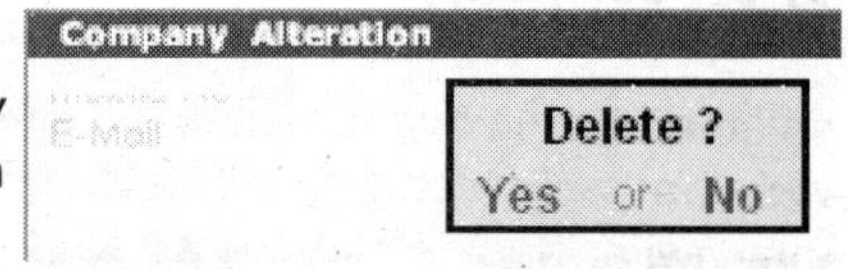

F-4A: Company Deletion Confirmation

You may Delete Company Profile through *Company Alteration* (§4). At *Company Info Menu* (F-1). select *Alter* (§04), Select the Company (F-3A) to be deleted to get the Company Alteration screen, similar to *Company Creation* screen (F-2). Now press *Alt+D* to get the *Company Deletion confirmation screen* (F-4A):

- At *Company Deletion confirmation screen* (F-4A),
  - o Click *Yes* (or type Y) to proceed to Delete, to further get *Company Deletion Re-confirmation screen* (F-4B)
  - o Click *No* to abort Deletion action (if you do not want to Delete the Company).
- At *Company Deletion Re-confirmation screen* (F-4B):
  - o Click Yes (or type Y) to confirm Deletion. The Company would be deleted
  - o Click *No* (or type N) to abort Deletion action (if you do not want to Delete the Company).

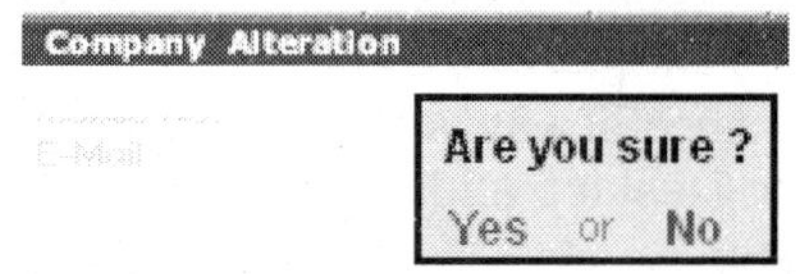

F-4B: Company Deletion re-confirmation

On Deletion of the Company, not only the particulars stored at the Company Creation screen goes, all the data that you have recorded for the Company, also get wiped out. So, be careful! before deletion.

05 Selection of Company

To work with a Company, you have to select (Open) the Company.

At Gateway of Tally (F-1B/01-02), Press *F1:Select Cmp* button to get the list of *Companies on Disk* at the current directory (F-5A). Now select the Company from the list (move the cursor on the Company Name and press <enter>

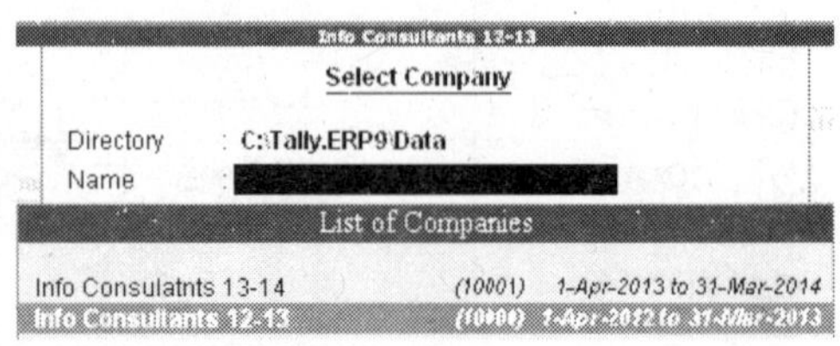

F-5A: Company Selection

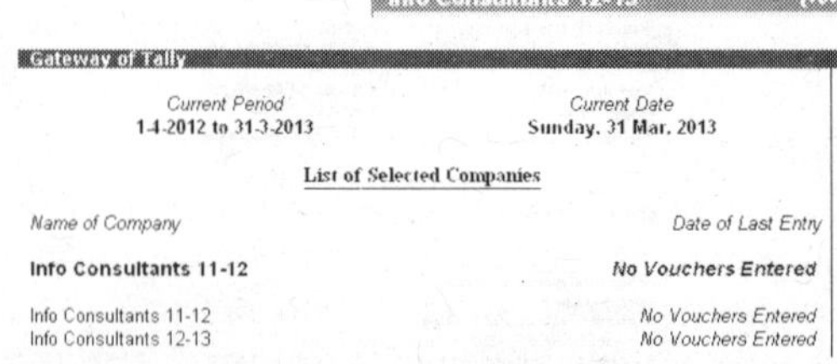

F-5B: Selected Company List

Active Company: You may *Select* multiple Companies, one by one. When you select another Company, the newly selected Company becomes the *Active* Company. You work with the (last selected) *Active* Company *only*. This way, you may switch selection between several Companies and work with the currently Active Company at any instance.

All currently selected Companies are listed at the left part of Gateway screen (F-5B). The Active Company Name is listed at the top in Bold separately.

05.01 Re-selection of Companies

When you select a Company, it becomes the *Active* Company. The previously selected Companies remain as *Selected* Company but no more remain Active. To re-select any previous selected company (not yet shut):

- **At Gateway of Tally:** At *Gateway of Tally*, click on the Company to be selected, from the list of Selected Companies at the left part (F-1A/01-02). The selected Company now becomes *Active* Company.
- **At other Places:** From other places, Click *F3:Company* button (this button gets activated only when more than ONE Company is created) to get the list of selected Companies (F-5A). Select the desired Company from the list of selected Companies.

> **Note:** *On re-selection, you get the same position in the next selected Company. For example, at* Display > Account Books Menu of the active Company, *when you re-select another Company, you will get the same Menu (*Display>Account Books) *of the next selected (Active) Company.*

06 Shutting of Company

When you select a Company, the Company remains selected, even if another Company is selected next. So, if you have selected several companies one after another, each of them remains selected.

Shutting a company means de-selecting (or un-selecting) the company. You cannot work with a Shut Company, until you select it again.

To *Shut* a Company, at Gateway, select *F1: Shut Cmp* (or click *Alt+F1*) and select the Company to Shut (if multiple Companies are selected). The Company will be *Shut* and will no more appear in the list of selected companies. To work with that Company next time, *Select* the Company again.

> **Note:** *Ideally, for no-frills fast work,* Select *a Company and work with that. To work with another company, it is often better to* Shut *the currently selected company and select the next company to work with. In this way, you normally keep only one Company selected at any point of time. You need to keep multiple companies selected to make Columnar Inter Company Reports (§06/02-13)*

FAQ: Frequently Asked Questions

FAQ-1: How you can maintain Financial Accounts only?

Ans: To maintain Financial Accounts only, at '*Maintain*', in Company Creation Screen (F-2A), select '*Accounts only*. In that case, some Inventory options will not be available and you will not be able to enter any data in respect of Inventory (Stock Items etc)..

You must conclusively decide that you like to maintain *Accounts only* for that Financial Year. You should not change from '*Accounts only*' to '*Accounts and Inventory*' in middle of a Financial Year. Your accounts may become partially incomplete and incompatible. So, if you decide to select '*Accounts only*', make sure that you will not cover Inventory during that financial year. Of course, you can opt for '*Accounts and Inventory*' for the next financial year, creating a new Company.

FAQ-2: What is Financial Year ? How do you set Financial Year ?

Ans: Financial Year is the 1 Year period (normally one year from 1st April to 31st March of the next year, but may be any other dates), for which the complete annual accounts are prepared. You may start from any date (other than 1st April) and may end at any date (other that 31st march). The Financial Year may be shorter than / or may be extended beyond one year (§04/02-26)

At '*Financial year from'* field (F-2A), enter the Beginning Date of Financial Year (§03). If you follow April- March Financial Year, enter 1st April of the beginning year (e.g. 1.4.2015). In fact, you may enter any date as *Financial Year From* Date (like 24.10.2014) and Tally would create the Financial Year exactly 12 months from the *Financial Year From* date (e.g. 23.10.2015).

FAQ-3: How to modify company profile (Company Particulars)

Ans: To modify Company Particulars, (NOT the voucher data), at Gateway of Tally, click *F3 Comp Info* (F1B/01-02), or press *Alt+F3*, to get Company Info menu (F-1A). Select *Alter* at Company Info menu and select the Company (F-3A) to get *Company Alteration* screen (similar to Company Creation screen:F-2A). Now, you can alter any data in the Company Alteration screen. You should not change *Books Beginning From* date after voucher entry. Normally, you may enter / change Address, Mailing Name, Telephone, e-mail address etc (or even change Company Name), or fill up any such field that remained unfilled at the time of Company Creation (§03).

FAQ-4: How to Delete a Company?

Ans: You may delete the company profile from *Company Alteration* (§04) screen.

- Click *F3 Comp Info* (or *Alt+F3*) to get Company Info menu (F-1A)
- Select *Alter* at *Company Info* menu (F-1A) and select the Company (F-3A) to get *Company Alteration* screen

(similar to Company Creation screen). Press *Alt+D*, at *Company Alteration* screen.

- A confirmation *'Delete ? Yes or No'* appears (F-4A). Type *Y* (Yes) to proceed to Delete the Company. A further Confirmation *'Are You Sure?'* would appear (F-4B). Type Y to Delete the Company

The Data files of the Company are Deleted (permanently removed) from computer. You cannot get back the Deleted Company (however, you may Restore data from *Back Up* (§03/01-13).

FAQ-5: How to select / re-select a Company to work for.

Ans: You may select / re-select a Company in following ways:

- **To select a Company**:At Gateway of Tally, Press *F1: Select Company* button to get the list of companies on disk. Now select the Company from the list (F-5A).
- **To reselect a selected company**: At the list of selected Companies appearing at the left Part of Gateway of Tally (F-1A/01-02), press the cursor on the Company to be re-selected and <enter> (or Double Click on the *Company Name*).

The selected / re-selected Company becomes the *Active* Company. Its name appears in bold at the top in the list of selected Companies. You can now work for the selected *Active* Company.

FAQ-6: How to Shut a Company

Ans: When you select a Company, that company remains selected, till you *Shut* it. So, if you work with multiple companies, each selected Company remains *Selected*, till you shut each of them separately.

To *Shut* a Company, at Gateway, click *F1: Shut Cmp* (or press *Alt+F1*) and select the company to shut. The company will be deselected and will no more appear in the list of selected companies. To work with that company next time, select the Company again.

Do not keep a Company selected, unless you want to work with it simultaneously, particularly, when you are making voucher entry. You may enter data in the wrong Company by mistake.

You may need to keep several companies selected to view reports from them, get Inter Company comparative reports (figures of several company in one report). Otherwise, Shut the inactive companies. Select the one as and when required.

FAQ-7: What is Tally Educational Mode? How to work with Educational Mode ?

Ans: Educational Mode is a restricted mode to use Tally for learning (no need to pay any License Fee). You can enter date 01, 02, and 31 only (and not other dates). Some other options (like Multi Account Printing etc), may not be activated (but such Reports are available through Display option in Educational Version also). But almost all features of Tally ERP.9 are available. Educational Version is quite suitable for learning Tally.ERP 9.

Before activation of Tally license, on loading Tally, you will get the *Startup* screen with various options. Click *W: Work in Educational Mode* (or press Alt+W) and then select *I: Silver Edition Mode (Single* User) to work with Tally Single User Educational Version

For commercial use, activate the License using the Serial Number of Tally.ERP 9. Tally.ERP 9 will be loaded directly (the *Startup* screen will get skipped) and all the options / features of Tally.ERP 9 will be available.

FAQ-8: What is Active Company?

Ans: *Active Company* is the last selected Company (which you are currently working with). It is shown at top (in bold face) in the *List of Selected Companies* (at the left Part of Gateway of Tally). Names of other selected Companies appear next in the list, shown in regular font (F-1A/01-02).

When you select / re-select another Company, that becomes the *Active Company*. You can do any work with the current *Active* Company only.

Gateway of Tally 01-02

01 Gateway of Tally (GoT)

The Gateway of Tally is the main entry point from where any part of the Tally can be accessed, to perform any task.

On Company Creation (§02/01-01) / Selection (§06/01-01), the Gateway of Tally (GoT) screen appears (F-1A). On entry to any operational screen from any Menu Item of Gateway of Tally, the respective screen appears *in place of* Gateway screen.

02 Components of Gateway of Tally

The *Gateway of Tally* (GoT) screen may be divided in following main sections,

- o **Horizontal Button Bar:** Contains various Buttons to perform allied tasks (F-1A/02-03),
- o **Main Area:** Tally Main area is divided into two parts (F-1A),
  - **Current Status**: Left Part is about the *Current status* (Current Period, Current Date, currently Active & Selected Companies
  - **Tally Menu**: Right part shows the current *Tally Menu.*
- o **Tally Product Info / Calculator Part:** This part shows Tally Product Info (F-2A) / Tally Calculator (F-2B)
- o **Current Path**: The Current Path appears (F-3A) at the bottom of the screen showing the position of current screen with respect to Main screen of Gateway.

Tally Product Info / Calculator Area

This part shows Product Info / Tally Calculator (F-2A) consisting of following parts (below the *Main Area*)

- **Tally Logo**: Shows the Tally Logo
- **Tally Product Info**: Information about the current Tally Product being used (Version, Release etc)
  - o **Version**: Show the current Version, Release Number, Edition, User etc
  - o **License.**: Details of Serials No, Registered ID, Tally Net Validity etc
  - o **Configuration:** Details of Proxy Server, Stat, ODBC etc
- **Calculator:** Here you perform Arithmetical calculations. Press *Ctrl+N* to activate Tally Calculator. The Calculator screen (F-2B) covers over the 3 Parts of Product Info Area.

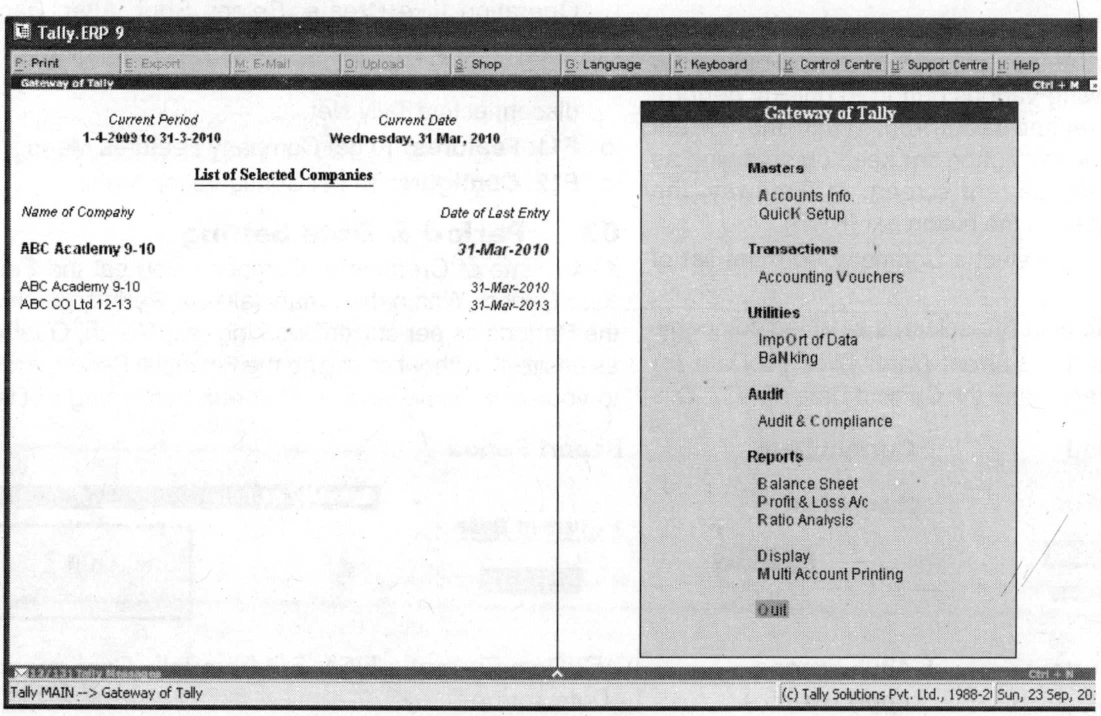

F-1A: Gateway of Tally

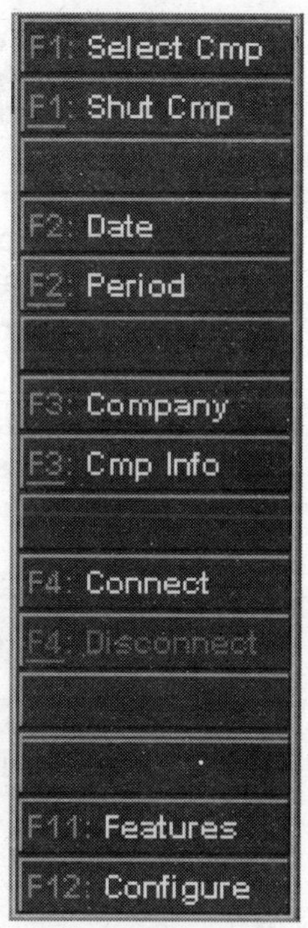

F-1B: Buttons

Hiding / Restoring Product Info part: The Info Panel (F-2A). may be optionally displayed / hidden.

- **Activating Calculator**: Press *Ctl+N* (or Click at the Calculator Area) to activate Calculator (hiding the 3 columns of Info Part, expanding Calculator Area- F-2B)

F-2A: Tally Info Panel -(all the parts visible)

F-2B: Info panel (Calulator Activated, 3 info cells hodden)

F-2C: Info panel hidden. The ^ handle to Restore Info Panel

F-3A: Current Path

- **Hiding Info Panel**: Click (x) button at the extreme right (F-2A) to hide the Info panel completely (F-2C).
- **Restoring Info Panel**: Click the ^ handle at the middle of the bottom panel to Restore the Info Panel (F-2A).

Current Path: At the last line of the Tally screen, the current path shows following (F-3A):

- The Path location of the current screen, from Gateway.
- Tally License notification
- Current Date & Time

Vertical Button Bar: At the right part, a vertical button bar (F-1B) appears showing various button to quickly perform some associated / related tasks from within the current screen. The buttons in the button bar keep on changing as per the context of the current screen. At Gateway, the following buttons appear in the button bar (F-1B)

- o **F1: Select Cmp**: To select a Company from the list of Companies
- o **F1: Shut Cmp**: To shut (de-select) a selected company
- o **F2: Date**: To set the *Current Date*. Click *F2:Date* (or press F2 button) and enter the Current Date (F-4C). This Date is carried as default current Date to the reports & vouchers being displayed / created The Current Date should lie within the Current Period.
- o **F2: Period**: To set the *Current Period*. Click F2:Period (or press Alt+F2 button) and enter the From & To Date of Current Period (F-4B). This Period is carried as default Current Period for the Report being displayed /Voucher being created.
- o **F3:Company**: To get the list of Companies on Disk, to select a Company (when multiple Companies are selected)
- o **F3: Cmp Info:** To get the Company Info Menu (F-1A/01-01) to select the desired tasks related to Company Operation (like Create, Select, Shut, Alter, Back Up, Restore etc)
- o **F4:Connect / F4: Disconnect**:Used for connecting / disconnecting Tally Net.
- o **F11: Features**: To get Company Features Menu
- o **F12: Configure:** To get Configuration Menu

03 Period & Date Setting

At the time of Creation of Company, you set the Financial Year Period. Within the Financial Year Period, you may set the Periods as per current working (e.g Month, Quarter etc, as desired), without changing the Financial Period, according to your own convenience. This reduces typing of Dates in

Current Period

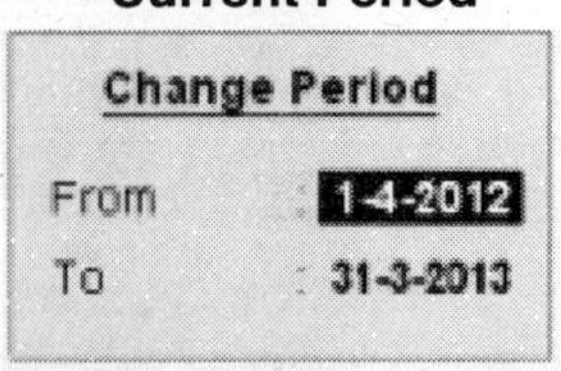

F-4A: *F2:Period* Current Period set up

Current Date

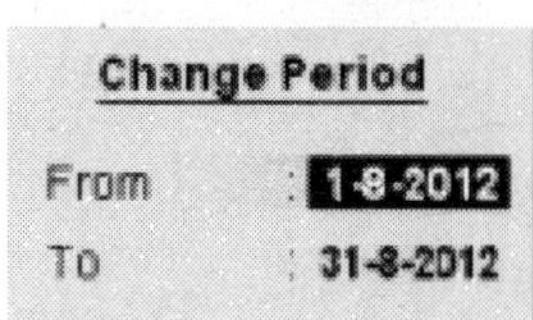

F-4B: *F2:Period* Report period set up

Report Period

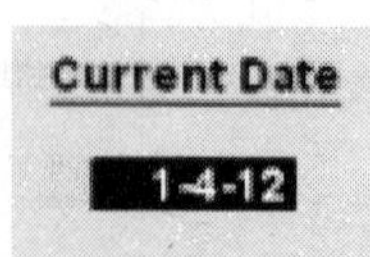

F-4C:*F2:Date* Current Date set up

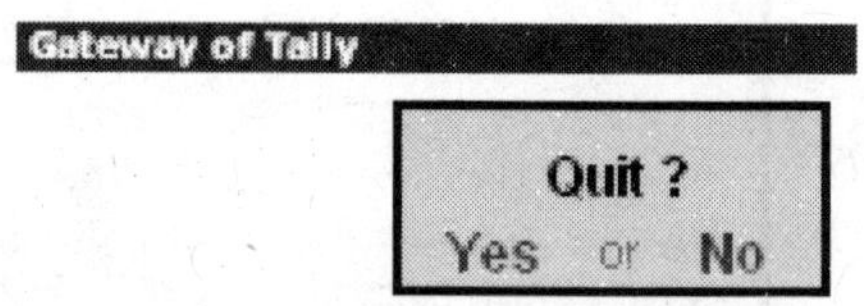

F:5A: Exit from Tally Confirmation

Period & Voucher every time, during working for a certain period, and reduces error.

You may set the Period & Dates through following buttons:

- **Voucher Date**: Click *F2:Date* (or press F2 button) during Voucher Entry. Enter the current Date (F-4C)
- **Current Period**: Click *F2:Period* (or press Alt+F2 button) at any *Menu screen* to get the *Change Period* screen. Enter the *Date From* & *Date To* (F-4A)
- **Report Period**: Click *F2:Period* (or press F2 button) at any *Display screen* to get the *Change Period* screen, and enter the *Date From* & *Date To* (F-4B)

03.01 Rules of Period & Date Setting

- **Current Period:** *Current Period* is the period for which you like to do any work in Tally (e.g enter voucher, display / print Report.). You cannot do any work for a period beyond the Current Period set.

  Click *F2:Period* button (or press Alt+F2 key) at Gateway (or at any Menu) to set the Current Period (F-4A).

  The *Current Period* is shown at the top line at the left part of *Gateway of Tally* (F-1A). The *Current Period* remains applicable to all the selected Companies, until you reset it again. So, after doing some work in FY 14-15 (setting the Current Period as 1-4-2014 to 31-3-2015), when you select another Company, starting Financial Year from 1-4-11, still the previous current period (1-4-2014 to 31-3-2015) remains active. To work for the period 11-12 of the selected Company, you have to reset Current period accordingly (like 1-4-11 to 31-3-12). So, check the current period and re-set it accordingly whenever you do any work. Otherwise, you may sometimes get surprises / shocks to find blank report (if the current period is not aligned to the period of the active company).
- **Report Period**: By default, the Report is set as per *Current Period.* At the *Display* screen (NOT at any Menu or Gateway), click *F2:Period* button (or press F2 key) and set the Start Date & End Date to set the *Report Period* to get the Display for the Report Period as set. The Report Period must be within the Current Period. So, the Report Period may be same as Current Period (by default), or may be part of the Current Period (when Report Period is re-set). However, the Report Period set through *F2: Period* does not affect the Current Period (set through *F2:Period*).
- **Current Date**: It is the Date which you have set while making voucher entry. This helps to make continuous voucher entry for the same date. At any Menu or Voucher Entry screen (NOT at Report Display screen), Click *F2:Date* button (or press F2 key) and re-set the current Date (by default, the next Date is proposed as Current Date), which you may *Accept* or *Change* (F-4B). *Current Date* applies to Voucher Date during new Voucher creation.

04 Exiting From Tally

From Gateway of Tally, you may exit Tally in any of the following ways:

- Click on the Rightmost Cross button, or
- *Select Quit* in the Main Menu (or type Q), or
- Press *Esc* key.

A confirmation screen 'Quit Yes or No' (F-5A) appears. Click *Yes (*Press *Y*) to exit from Tally, else press *N* to continue to work with Tally.

FAQ: Frequently asked Questions

FAQ-1: What is the difference between Current Period and Current Date?

Ans: Difference between Current Period & Current Date

Current Period: Current Period is the period for which you can perform any work from Tally. You may enter voucher and print reports within the current Period only. So re-set it accordingly as required during data entry and report printing.

Click *F2: Period* button (or press Alt+F2) to get the *Change Period* screen and enter the Start & End Date to specify the Current Period (F-4A)

You may extend the Current Period beyond 12 month Financial year:

- o If the financial year of the company is more than 12 months
- o To keep several financial year data together in one Company and enter voucher data for the re-set (extended) Current Period

Current Date: Current Date is carried as default Voucher Date during new voucher entry. You set the Current Date at any Menu or Voucher Entry screen (NOT at Report Display screen). To change it, during voucher entry, Click *F2: Date* button (or press F2) and enter the current Date (the next Date becomes the default Current Date). The *Current Date* must be within the *Current Period.*

FAQ-2: What is the difference between Current Period and Report period?

Ans: Difference between Current Period & Report Period

- **Current Period:** Current Period is the period for which you can perform any work from Tally. You may enter voucher and print reports within the current Period only.

  Current Period is universal. It applies to all the Tally Companies. It is set through F2:Period Button (Alt+F2).
- **Report Period:** Report Period applies to the current Display screen To set Report Period, at Display screen, press F2 function key (or click *F2:Period* button),

Report Period must be within Current Period

FAQ-3: How you can perform Arithmetic Computation in Tally?

Ans: At Gateway, click at the Calculator area (or press

Ctrl+N). The calculator area will get expanded (F-2B). Now type the computation expression and press <enter>. The result will be shown in the next line.

FAQ-4: How you can hide / restore product Info / Calculator area?

Click the cross (x) at the Calculator area. The lower band containing the Product Info / Calculator will get hidden, providing more space for Main Area (F-2B). To Restore, click on the ^ handle at the middle of the bottom panel (F-2C). Press *Ctrl+N* to get Calculator area activated (F-2B), which covers the bottom panels except the Tally Logo, giving extra space to enter arithmetical expressions.

Accounts Masters 01-03

01 Accounts Masters

Accounts Masters are the principal Accounting entities representing similar transactions (Account Ledgers) and similar Accounts (Account Groups) along which all transaction data are compiled, summarised and balanced, to be reflected in various Accounting Reports & Financial Statements (Profit & Loss Account & Balance Sheet).

On Company creation (§02/01-01), Tally.ERP 9 provides the means to organise and maintain Master data by user in their own way. To maintain the basic system, the following masters are to be initially planned and respective master data to be created.

- **Account Ledgers**: *Account Ledgers* (or *Ledger Accounts*) are entities representing similar transactions. For example Travelling Expenses *Ledger Account* contains all transactions (vouchers) related to Travelling Expenses. The transactions of a Ledger account are summed up (total Debit & Credit) and balanced (net Debit / Credit).
- **Account Groups**: Account Groups are just convenient & systematic grouping of Ledger Accounts of similar nature. Account Group helps to organise the Accounting Reports better and get Total & Net figures (of Debits & Credits) of the constituent Account Ledgers of each Account Group. The Account Group may be organised in multiple Levels to get accounting figures and report for each such sub level Groups.

02 Reserved Account Groups & Ledgers

During *Company Creation* (§02/01-01), Tally automatically creates 28 specified Accounts Groups (referred as *Reserved Account Groups*) & 2 Accounts Ledgers (referred as *Reserved Account Ledgers*), carrying some specific properties.

- **Reserved Accounts Groups:** Tally automatically creates 15 *Primary* Groups and 13 *Sub-Groups* to the *Primary* Groups (F-1A). The auto-created Groups for each Company are collectively referred as *Reserved Accounts Groups.*

  For a Company having few Ledger Accounts (like small Proprietary firm etc), the Tally created *Reserved Accounts Groups* (F-1A) may be adequate for organising the Accounts. However, for personalised organization of Accounts Ledgers and Groups, new Account Groups may need to be created.

  The *Reserved Accounts Groups* carry their own characteristics. The Ledger Accounts placed under these Groups inherit the properties of the respective Reserved Group. So, do not create new groups for these auto created Reserved Account Groups (if you do so, such newly created groups and their child groups will not behave / work properly). You may create new Account Groups under any of these auto created *Reserved* Account Groups.
- **Reserved Accounts Ledgers:** Apart from 28 *Reserved* Groups, Tally also auto creates 2 *Reserved Ledger Accounts*, viz *Cash* (under *Cash-in-Hand* Group) and *Profit & Loss* Account (F-1A). So, do not create any new Ledger for these 2 Ledger Accounts. All other Ledger Accounts are to be created.

Branch / Divisions
Capital Account
  Reserves & Surplus (Retained Earnings)
Current Assets
  Bank Accounts
  Cash-in-hand
    Cash
  Deposits (Asset)
  Loans & Advances (Asset)
  Stock-in-hand
  Sundry Debtors
Current Liabilities
  Duties & Taxes
  Provisions
  Sundry Creditors
Direct Expenses (Expenses (Direct))
Direct Incomes (Income (Direct))
Fixed Assets
Indirect Expenses (Expenses (Indirect))
Indirect Incomes (Income (Indirect))
Investments
Loans (Liability)
  Bank OD A/c (Bank OCC A/c)
  Secured Loans
  Unsecured Loans
Misc. Expenses (ASSET)
Purchase Accounts
Sales Accounts
Suspense A/c
Profit & Loss A/c
28 Group(s) and 2 Ledger(s)

F-1A: Alphabetical list of Reserved Account Masters

Reserved Groups(Liabilities)

Capital Account
  Reserves & Surplus (Retained Earnings)
Current Liabilities
  Duties & Taxes
  Provisions
  Sundry Creditors
Loans (Liability)
  Bank OD A/c (Bank OCC A/c)
  Secured Loans
  Unsecured Loans

Reserved Groups(Assets)

Branch / Divisions
Current Assets
  Bank Accounts
  Cash-in-Hand
  Deposits (Asset)
  Loans & Advances (Asset)
  Stock-in-Hand
  Sundry Debtors
Fixed Assets
Investments
Misc. Expenses (ASSET)

F-1B: Reserved Accounts Groups (Liabilities & Assets)

Reserved Groups (Income)

Direct Incomes (Income (Direct))
Indirect Incomes (Income (Indirect))
Sales Accounts

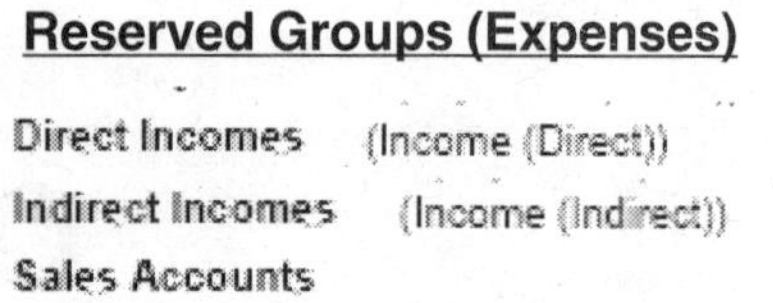

F-1C: Reserved Accounts Groups (Income & Expenses)

> **Note** *The Reserved Groups & Ledgers cannot be deleted. The parent Groups of these Groups / Ledgers cannot be changed.*

03 Account Master Creation

Reserved Accounts Masters are auto created at the time of Company Creation (§02/01-02). You can create new *Account Group* or *Account Ledger* in addition to the Pre-created *Reserved* Groups or Ledgers.

At *Gateway of Tally* (F-1A/01-02), select *Accounts Info* to get *Accounts Info* menu (F-2A).

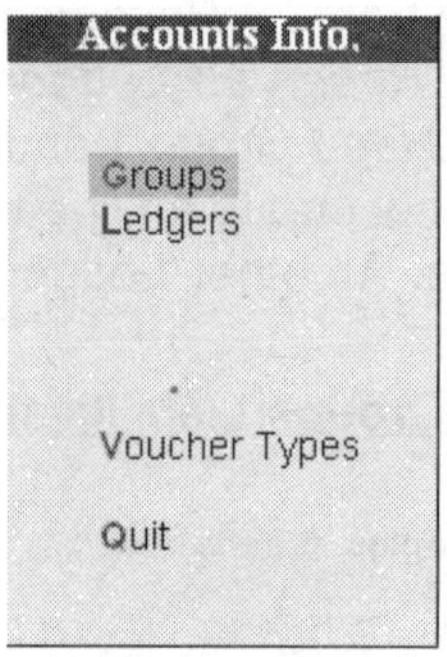

F-2A: Accounts Info Menu

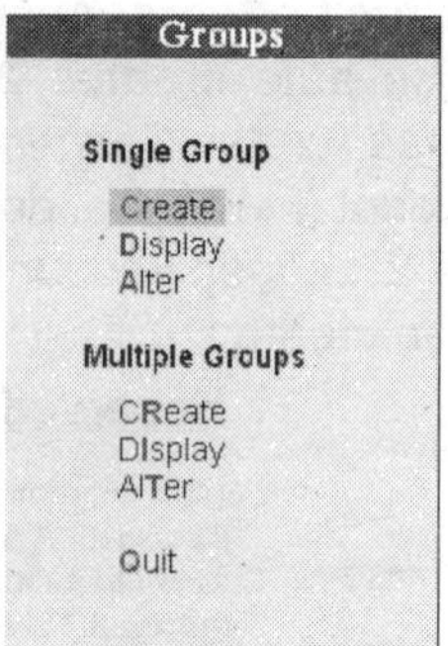

F-2B: Accounts Groups Menu

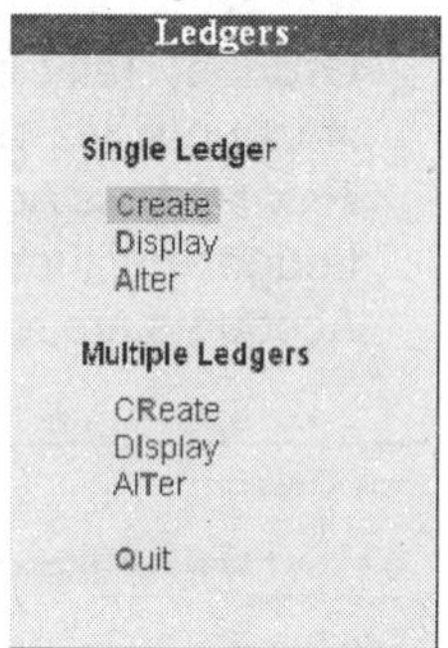

F-2C: Accounts Ledger Menu

03.01 Account Group Creation

At *Accounts Info Menu* (F-2A), select *Groups* to get *Account Groups Menu* (F-2B). Now select *Create* under *Single Group* (F-2B) to get *Account Group Creation* screen (F-3A).

At *Account Group Creation* Screen (F-3A), enter as follows:

- **Account Group Name:** At *Name*, enter unique Account Group Name.
- **Parent Group**: At *Under*, select the Parent Group from List of Groups already created. The new Group would be placed under the selected parent Group.

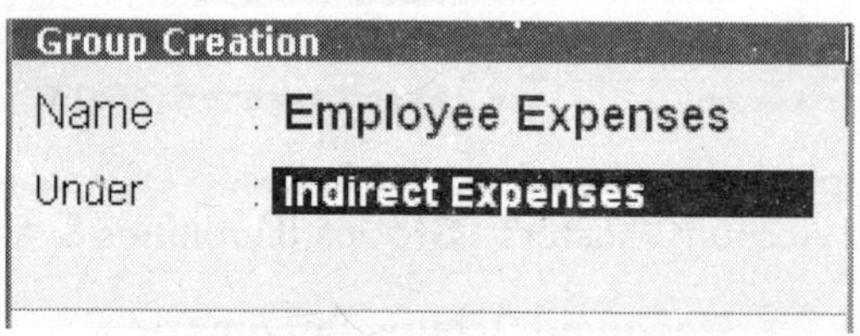

F-3A: Account Group Creation

03.02 Account Ledgers Creation

At *Accounts Info Menu* (F-2A), select *Ledgers* to get *Accounts Ledger* Menu (F-2C). Now select *Create* under *Single Ledger* (F-2C) to get *Account Ledger Creation* screen (F-3B).

At *Account Ledger Creation* Screen (F-3B), enter as follows:

- **Account Ledger Name:** At *Name*, enter the unique Name of the Ledger. This Name will be displayed / printed in all internal records (like Ledger, Trial Balance etc) and will be available in selection list of ledger.
- **Parent Group:** At *Under*, select the Parent Group of the Ledger from *List of Groups.*
- **Ledger Opening Balance:** At *Opening Balance*, you may enter Opening Balance (at the *Books Beginning Date*, as displayed) if any:
  - **Balance Amount**: Enter the figure of Opening Balance
  - **Balance Type**: The default Balance Type Dr. (for Debit) or Cr. (for Credit), as per Parent Group selected) appears, which you may change (Dr/ Cr) according to the nature of Opening Balance.

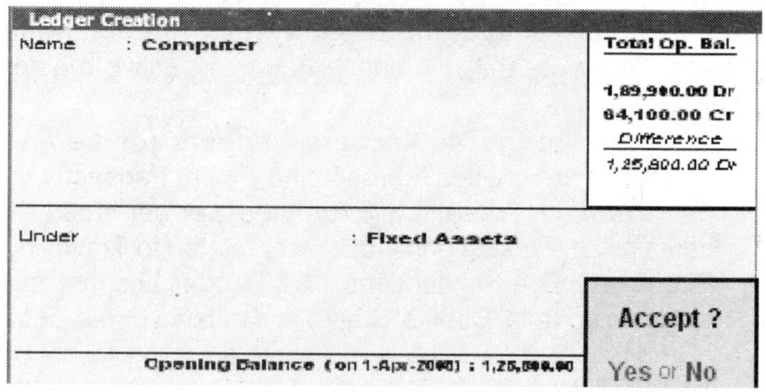

F-3B: Account Ledger Creation

When you start Accounts from the beginning of Financial Year, the Opening Balance of Nominal Ledger (Ledger Accounts appearing in Profit & Loss Account) may be zero. You may also enter Ledger Opening Balance later on, through Ledger *Alter* option (§05).

Finally, on entry of *Opening Balance* of Ledger of all Ledger Accounts, the Total of Debits & Credits of Opening Balance of all Ledger Accounts must be equal. At the time of Ledger creation, the Debit & Credit totals of Opening Balance of all ledger accounts is shown at the upper right part of Ledger entry screen (F-3B), to ensure completeness & correctness of entry of *Opening Balance* of Ledger Accounts.

03.03 Creation of New Parent Group During Ledger / Group entry

During Account Group or Ledger Account creation (F-3A/ F-3B), if you find that the Parent Group is not existing, press *Alt+C* at '*Under*' field to get *Account Group Creation (Secondary)* screen (like F-3A). Create the Parent *Account Group* and select the Parent Group at *Under* field in Group Entry (F-3A), at Ledger Entry (F-3B) as usual, without exiting the current Group / Ledger entry screen

04 Display of Account Master

To Display any of the existing Account Group / Ledger, at *Gateway of Tally*:

- **Account Group**: Select *Accounts Info>Group>Display* (F-2B) and select the desired Account Group
- **Account Ledger**: Select *Accounts Info>Ledger>Display* (F-2C), and select the desired Account Ledger

The respective Account Group / Account Ledger is displayed in the same way as entry screen (F-3A / F-3B). You can not Modify or Delete any Group or Ledger in Display Mode.

05 Alteration / Deletion of Account Master

To *Alter* or *Delete* any of the existing Account Group / Ledger, at Gateway of Tally:

- **Account Group**: Select *Accounts Info>Group>Alter* (F-2B) and select the desired Account Group
- **Account Ledger**: Select *Accounts Info>Ledger>Alter* (F-2C), and select the desired Account Ledger

The selected Master record (*Account Group* or *Account Ledger*) appears in *Alteration* mode (similar to Creation screen: F-3A / F-3B).

- o **Alteration:** To modify data, take the cursor at the desired field and Alter the data of any field of the Master record (Group or Ledger). You cannot alter the Parent Group of any Reserved Account. Master (Reserved Account Group or Reserved Account Ledger). Press *Alt+A* to save the changes made.
- o **Deletion:** To *Delete* the Master Record, Press Alt+D and press Y at '*Delete? Yes or No.*' to confirm Deletion.

05.01 Restriction on Deletion of Master

An Account Master (Group or Ledger) cannot be Deleted in following cases:

- **Deletion of Account Group**: An Account Group can not be Deleted, if there is any child Account Ledger of the Group (i.e, if the *Account Group* is specified at *Under* field of any Account Ledger).
- **Deletion of Account Ledger**: An Account Ledger can not be Deleted if it is transacted in a Voucher (i.e.,if the *Accounts Ledger* is specified in any Voucher).
- **Reserved Accounts:** The Tally created *Reserved Account Groups* & *Reserved Ledger Accounts* (Cash and P& L A/c) also cannot be Deleted.

06 Chart of Accounts

Chart of Accounts is the organized list of All Account Groups & Account Ledgers, represented in hierarchical structure (arranged according to level in a multi level structure: F-4).

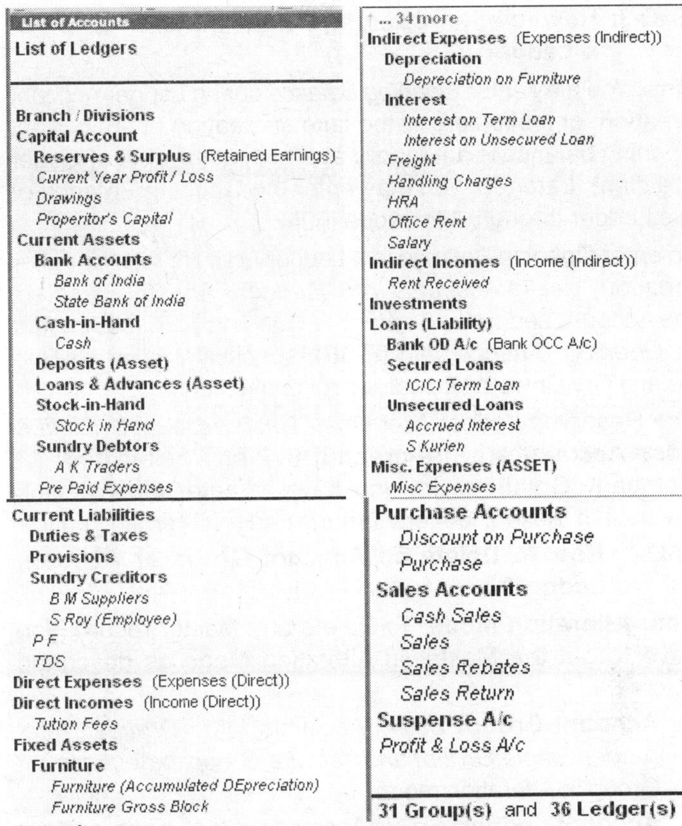

Contd ...

F-4: Chart of Accounts

FAQ: Frequently Asked Questions

FAQ-1: What are Pre-defined (or Reserved) Groups?

Ans: During Creation of a Company, Tally automatically creates 15 Primary Groups and 13 Sub-groups (known as *Reserved Groups*) for each Company (F-1A). These Groups carry specific properties which are inherited by the Child Groups created under the respective Groups.

- The Reserved Groups / Ledgers can not be Deleted
- Parent Group of Reserved Groups / Ledgers cannot be Altered (the cursor skips the *Under* Field at Alteration screen)

Through Account Group creation, you may create new child groups (called sub groups) under any of these Reserved Groups,

FAQ-2: How to create a new Parent group during Group / Ledger entry?

Ans: During *Account Group* or *Account Ledger* entry / edit, if you find that the Parent Group is not existing, press Alt+C at *Under* field to get Account Group Creation screen (referred as *Indirect Method* of Master Creation). Create the parent Account Group and select the parent Account Group at *Under* field, as usual.

FAQ-3: How to enter Opening Balance after creation of a Ledger

Ans: You may enter *Opening Balance* during Ledger Account creation, or leave zero at the time of creation (if the correct opening balance is not readily available at the time of ledger creation). Later on, you may enter the Opening Balance of the Ledger through *Alter* mode (§05).

To enter Opening Balance in a Ledger Account later on (after creation), select *Accounts Info> Ledger> Alter* (§05), select the Account Ledger and enter the Opening Balance Amount in *Opening Balance* field (F-3B), specifying Dr or Cr (the default Dr / Cr would be carried for convenience).

The Reserved Ledger Accounts - *Cash Account* & *Profit & Loss Account* are pre-created by Tally at the time of Company Creation. So, you have to enter the Opening Balance in these 2 ledgers through Ledger Alteration only.

FAQ-4: How to Delete an Account Group or Account Ledger?

Ans: Alteration Mode: To Delete any Master record, you have to get the Master in Alteration Mode as described below;

- **Account Group:** Select Accounts *Info >Groups> Alter (under Single Group) and select a Group* to get Account Group in Alteration mode.
- **Account Ledger:** Select Accounts *Info> Ledgers> Alter (under Single Ledger) and select a Ledger* to get Account Ledger in Alteration mode.

Deletion: Having opened the Master in Alteration Mode, as described above, press *Alt+D* and type 'Y' to Delete the selected Account Group / Account Ledger, at *Delete Yes / No* prompt, to confirm Deletion (§05)

FAQ-5: What is the Restriction in deletion of master Records?

Ans: Deletion is not permitted when you attempt to Delete a master record in the following cases (§05)

Account Group:

- Reserved Account Group (28 Reserved Account Groups)
- Account Group for which a Child Account Group or Ledger Account is created

Account Ledger:

- Reserved Account Ledger (*Cash* A/c & *Profit & Loss* A/c)
- Ledger Account which has been transacted in a Voucher.

FAQ-6: What are the Reserved Account Ledgers, automatically created by Tally

Ans: At the time of Company creation, Tally automatically creates two Ledger Accounts (§02)

- Cash (under *Cash-in-Hand* Group)
- Profit & Loss Account (*Primary* Account)

These ledger accounts cannot be deleted (and should not be created new). Besides these 2 auto created Ledgers, you have to create all other Ledger Accounts and place them under appropriate Account Group.

FAQ-7: How to enter Opening Balance of Account Group?

Ans: You do not have to enter Opening Balance of Account Groups. The Opening Balance of any Group is computed as net of sum of Opening Balance entered for subordinate Account Ledgers and shown in Reports.

FAQ-8: How to enter Opening Balance of Cash Account?

Ans: *Cash* Ledger Account is auto created (under the Account Group Cash-in-Hand) at the time of Company Creation. It is a reserved ledger account. So, do not create any Cash Ledger Account. To enter *Opening Balance* of Cash, select *Accounts Info>Ledger>Alter* and then enter the Opening Balance of Cash Account at *Opening Balance* field.

If you have multiple Cash Accounts, like Main Cash, Petty Cash, Branch Cash etc. then enter the Opening Balance of Main Cash Account in the pre-created *Cash* Account as stated above (you may change the name of *Cash* Account if necessary). Now create new Cash Ledger Accounts for other Cash Accounts, under the Group Cash-in-Hand and enter the Opening Balance as usual, as explained earlier.

FAQ-9: How to enter Opening Stock Value?

Ans: You should create a *Stock* Ledger Account under the pre created Account Group *Stock-in-Hand* and enter the Opening Stock Value at *Opening Balance* field of the created Ledger Account, as usual.

You may create multiple Stock Ledger Account (e.g Stock-Raw Materials, Stock-Finished Products, etc) and enter he Opening Balance for respective Stock Accounts.

Accounts Vouchers 01-04

01 Accounts Vouchers

All business transactions are recorded and fully described in Voucher. Voucher is a complete & comprehensive record of all important details related to the transaction. In fact, academically, all transactions (Cash or Non Cash) may be recorded in Journal Book.

However, for better control and division of accounting tasks to various persons, the Transactions are classified into several *Voucher Types*. So, different types of vouchers are used to record the transactions according to the nature of Transaction.

02 Basic Accounts Voucher Types

Voucher Types represent vouchers of a specific type of transaction (e.g *Payment* Voucher Type means all voucher in which payment of money is involved).

For convenience and error free entry, Tally provides following basic pre-created *Accounts Voucher Types*, according to nature of transactions. The specific type of Voucher is invoked through respective button (F-1), as described below.

- **Cash Vouchers:** Voucher in which Cash / Bank ledgers are transacted, indicating movement of Cash
  - o **Transfer of Cash**: Only movement of Cash but no real outflow / inflow of Cash
    - **F4:Contra:** Money transfer (Cash withdrawal, Cash Deposit) between two Cash/ Bank accounts.
  - o **Outflow / Inflow of Cash**: Entails Inflow / Outflow of Cash
    - **F5: Payment:** Money payment in Cash, Cheque, Bank Debit (Outflow of Cash)
    - **F6: Receipt:** Money Receipt in Cash, Cheque, Bank Credit (Inflow of Cash)
- **Journal Vouchers:** For recording Non Cash Transaction. For convenience, Journal Vouchers may be subdivided as:
  - **Journal Proper (F7:Journal)**: For various accounting adjustments (like Depreciation, Accrual of Interest etc)
  - **Trading Vouchers**: Trade Transactions (Sales & Purchase)
    - o **Sales Vouchers (F8: Sales):** All transactions of Sales
    - o **Purchase Vouchers (F9: Purchase)**: All transactions of Purchases

During voucher entry, Tally verifies that total of all Debits must be equal to the total of all Credits in each Voucher (the voucher cannot be saved if the total of debits is not equal to total of credits of the voucher).

03 Rules of Voucher Entry

To maintain consistency of basic accounting rules and to minimize gross errors of voucher entry, Tally checks up some basic rules for each Voucher Type, as explained below:

- **Contra Voucher:** Contra Voucher means transfer of fund from one Cash / Bank / Bank OCC to another Cash / Bank / Bank OCC a/c. So, in contra voucher, you can transact only Cash / Bank / Bank OCC a/c ledgers.

  The first entry is always Credit (Source of Funds transferred from). From 2nd entry onwards you may Debit (Destination of Funds transferred to) or Credit (Source of Funds transferred from) Accounts Ledger under Cash, Bank Accounts and Bank OCC group *only* (F-2A).
- **Payment Voucher:** Payment voucher records all transactions of Payment (Cash Outflow) through Cash or Bank. The Ledger Account paid to is Debited and the Cash / Bank / Bank OCC A/c (paid from) is Credited (F-2B).

  The first entry is always Debit (other than cash / bank/ bank occ a/c) and second entry onwards you may specify Debit or Credit. The Cash / Bank / Bank OCC A/c must be Credited (F-2B).
- **Receipt Voucher:** Receipt voucher records all transaction of receipt of money through Cash or Bank (Cash Inflow). The ledger account received from is Credited, and Cash / Bank/ Bank OCC A/c, which the money received is put into (received into) is Debited (F-2C).

  The first entry is always Credit and second entry onwards you may specify Debit or Credit. The Cash / Bank / Bank OCC A/c must be Debited (F-2C).
- **Journal Voucher:** Journal Voucher records all adjustments of any non-cash Ledger Accounts (Ledgers other than under Cash, Bank or Bank OCC group). The first entry is Debit (F-2D).
- **Sales Voucher**: Sales Voucher is created to record all sorts of Sales Transactions (Cash / Credit Sales). At first

ledger, select the *Customer Ledger* A/c (in case of Credit Sale) or *Cash / Bank* Account (in case of Cash Sale) to be Debited. The next ledger account would be a Ledger under *Sales* Group and must be Credited (F-3A). No ledger account under *Purchase* Group can be transacted

- **Purchase Voucher:** Purchase Voucher is created to record all sorts of Purchase Transactions (Cash / Credit Purchase). At first ledger, select *Supplier* Account (in case of Credit *Purchase*) or or *Cash / Bank* Account (in case of Cash Purchase) to be Credited. The next ledger account would be a Ledger under Purchase Group and must be Debited (F-3B). In a Purchase Voucher, a ledger account under Sales Group cannot be transacted.

The voucher entry of current Voucher is terminated when the total of all Debits is equal to total of all Credits.

04 Accounts Voucher Creation

Tally provides a standard Accounts Voucher Entry Form for all types of Accounts Vouchers. At Gateway (F-1A/01-02), select *Accounting Voucher* to get Accounts Voucher Entry

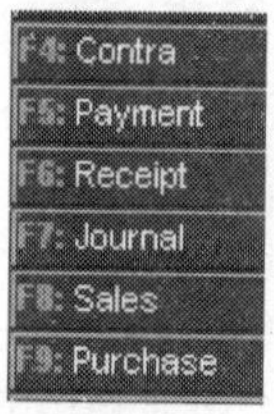

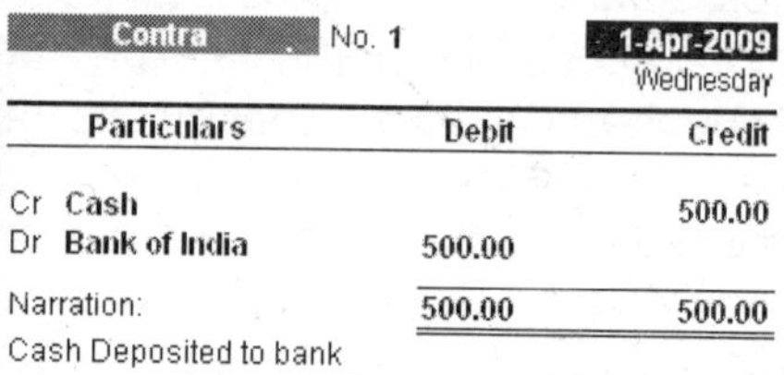

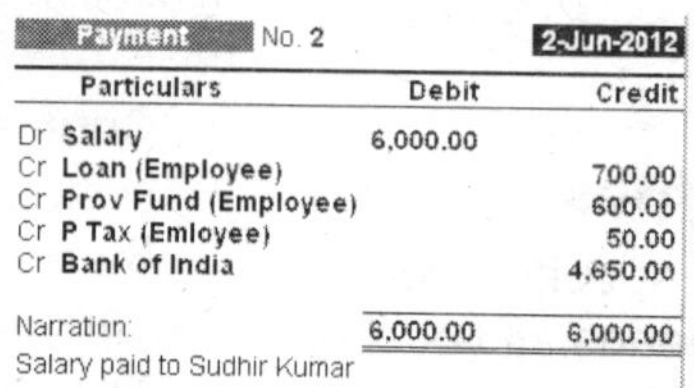

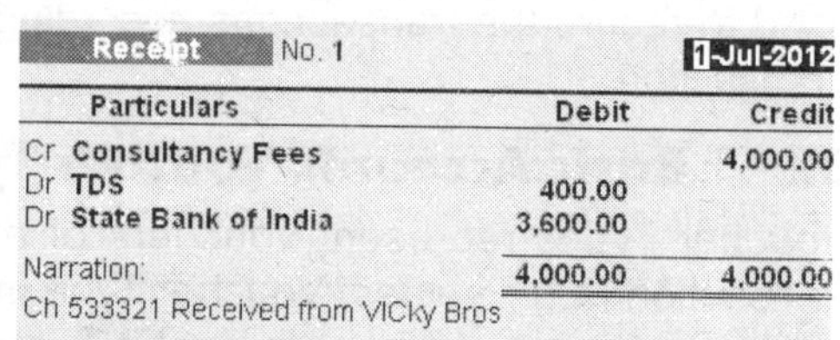

F-1:Buttons F-2A: Contra Voucher Creation F-2B Payment Voucher Creation F-2C:Receipt Voucher Creation

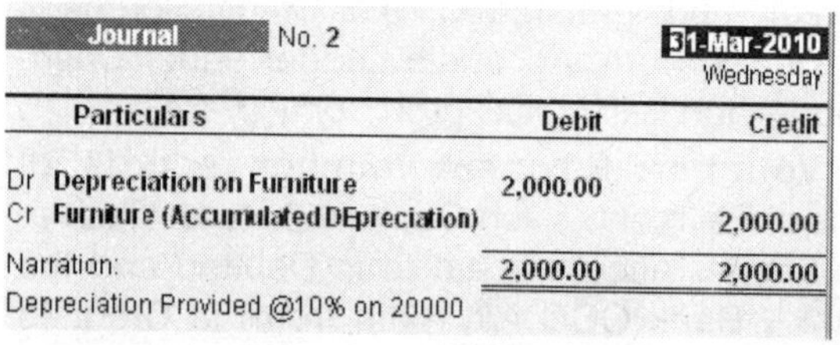

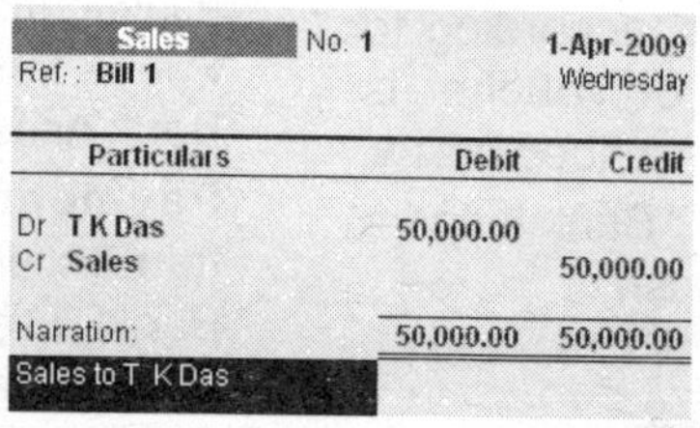

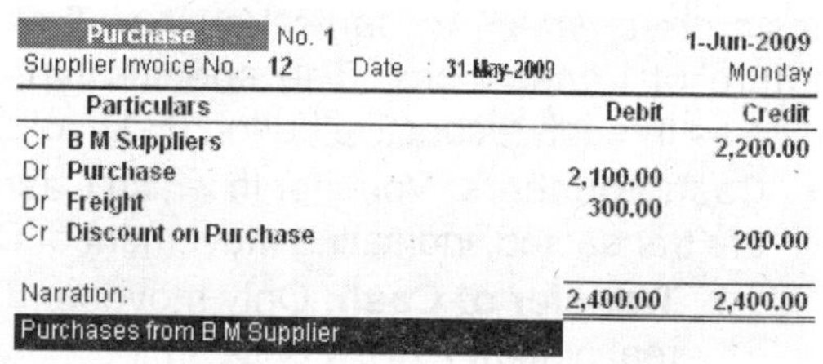

F-2D: Journal Voucher Creation F-3A: Sales Voucher Creation F-3B:Purchase Voucher Creation

Screen. Now click on the respective Voucher Type button (F-1) to invoke the specific type of Accounts Voucher.

> **Note**
>
> Payment / Receipt / Contra Voucher may be entered in Normal & Single Mode (§02/02-10). In this chapter, we discuss voucher entry in *Normal* Mode. We also use *Dr / Cr* to indicate Debit / Credit instead of *To /By*. At Voucher entry screen, click F12:Configure and set:
>
> - *No* at '*Use Single Mode at Pmt/Recp/Contra* ' to get Normal Mode Voucher Entry screen.
> - *Yes* at *'Use Dr/Cr instead of To/By during entry'* to use Dr / Cr at Transaction Sign

At Gateway of Tally (F-1A/01-02), select *Accounting Voucher* to get Voucher Entry screen.

We first discuss these common elements of each component and then discuss the specific details in respect of each Voucher Type Entry screen (F-2A to F-2D, F-3A to F-3B).

The Basic Accounts Voucher entry screen may be broadly divided into 3 areas:

Voucher Header	Ledger Details	Voucher Footer
• Voucher Type/ Number	• To/By(or Dr/Cr)	• Cheque Details
• Voucher Date/ Day	• Ledger Account	• Voucher Narration
	• Ledger Amount	• Voucher Amount

04.01 Voucher Header

At Voucher Header, enter the following.

- **Voucher Number**: Tally normally displays voucher number, serially generated in chronological order, for each Voucher type (under Automatic Voucher Numbering scheme). For example, if the last voucher number was 5, the next voucher number will be 6.
- **Voucher Date**: The Current Date (NOT *System* date) by default is carried for Voucher Date (at rightmost corner of first line at the voucher entry screen)
  - o **Change Current Date:** To change *Current* Date, click *F2: Date* button (the next Date is carried as default Current Date) and enter the Current Date (F-4C/01-02), which is carried as Voucher Date.
  - o **Change Voucher Date:** You may directly change Voucher Date. Press *Shift+Tab* to get back to the Date field and enter the Voucher Date, without changing the Current Date.

  Day of the Voucher Date (e.g., *Tuesday*) is displayed just below the Voucher Date (F-2A)

04.02 Voucher Ledger Account details

This is a tabular area where each Ledger Transaction data is entered.

- **Ledger Sign**: Press D (for Debit) or C (for Credit) at first column to indicate Debit / Credit sign for the Ledger Account that you select at *Particulars* Column. The Debit or Credit nature of the first Ledger Account in the Voucher is pre-determined according to Voucher Type. So, you have to enter *Dr/Cr*, only from second entry onwards.
- **Ledger Account**: At *Particulars* field, select the Ledger Account from List of Ledgers.
- **Ledger Amount**: As per Dr/Cr sign entry in the first column, the cursor goes to the respective column (Debit or Credit). Accordingly, enter the Ledger *Amount* in *Debit* or *Credit* column.

This way, you may enter many Debit and Credit entries in a voucher. The Ledger entries will be terminated as soon as the total of *Debit* and *Credit* is equal.

Here are some hot tips for quick ledger account entry in voucher:

- **Quick Ledger Account selection in voucher:** Sometimes you write several vouchers continuously of similar transaction involving same ledger account. In such case, at the first Ledger Entry (particulars) line, press *Ctrl+R* to repeat the same first ledger entered in previous voucher. This way, if you are entering several vouchers for Salary Payment for individual employees, Debiting Salary account, then after entering the first voucher for Salary, press *Ctrl+R*, the Salary account will be automatically carried, saving time for Ledger Account entry in Voucher.
- **New Ledger Accounts creation during voucher entry:** During voucher entry, if you need to create a new Ledger Account (the Ledger Account is not existing), press *Alt+C* at the ledger account (Particulars) field to get Ledger Accounts entry screen, without exiting from the current voucher. Now create the new ledger account as usual. Select the created Ledger account. You will get back to the voucher entry screen, at the same point.

04.03 Voucher Narration

After entry of all ledger accounts (when the Debit & Credit Totals are equal), enter *Voucher Narration*, describing the voucher transactions briefly but writing the essential details for future reference

To quickly rectify / insert words while entering Narration, use the following keys:

- **Home**: To reach beginning of the Narration.
- **End**: To reach end of the Narration.
- **Left & Right Arrow**: To move one character each time in the direction.
- **Cntl+ Left or Right Arrow**: To jump one word at a time Left or Right.
- **Insert**: To toggle between *Insert* (cursor is blinking line) and *Overwrite* (cursor is blinking block) mode.

Avoid redundant words like *Being the..* etc. Enter the important references in Narration. You must write the complete Narration in one continuous line (the line will spread itself to multiple lines). Do not press <enter> to break the Narration into multiple lines. You should press <enter> only at the end of Narration

Narration carried from previous Voucher

To save time and write Narration consistently & quickly, you may carry Voucher Narration entered in earlier voucher in the current voucher being entered, and just edit as required. At Voucher Narration field, press:

- **Carry Narration of Previous Voucher:** *Ctrl+R* to copy the voucher Narration entered in the previous voucher. Now instead of writing the full narration again, just modify the carried Narration as desired.
- **Carry Narration of Similar Voucher**: *Alt+R*. to copy Voucher Narration entered from earlier voucher having same first ledger account. This is quite helpful to quickly enter Voucher Narration of frequently occurred transactions, in a standard pattern (e.g, Narration of Conveyance Expenses will be of similar pattern). So, in Payment Voucher debiting Conveyance Expenses, press *Alt+R* at *Narration* field, the Narration of earlier Payment Voucher with Conveyance Expense as first ledger account, will be copied in the current voucher, which you may modify as required.

> ***Note:*** *Only Voucher Narration may be carried. Ledger Narration (05/02-09) cannot be carried.*

05 Alteration / Deletion of Accounts Voucher

To *Alter* or *Delete* any Accounts Voucher, select the Voucher (normally through Drill Down from any Report), and press <Enter>

The selected Voucher record (*Account Group* or *Account Ledger*) appears in *Alteration* mode (similar to Creation screen: F-2A to 2D, 3A to 3B).

- o **Alteration:** To *Modify* data, take the cursor at the desired field and Alter the data of any field of the Master record (Group or Ledger). Press *Alt+A* to save the changes made.
- o **Deletion:** To *Delete* the Master Record, Press *Alt+D* and press Y at '*Delete? Yes or No.*' to confirm Deletion.

06 Saving the Voucher

After complete entry of the voucher:

- **Save / Modify**: At the end of Entry / Modification, at *Accept Y/N* confirmation option (F-4A):
  - o **Saving:** Press <Enter> or type *Y* to save the voucher. The current voucher will be saved.
  - o **Modify**: To modify any data before saving, type *N* (or No) to go back to the top field, edit as desired and then save the voucher.

- o **Quick Saving**: To save the current voucher quickly (without confirmation), before reaching to the Save option (F-4A), press *A: Accept* button (or press Ctrl+A).

- **Quit without Saving:**
  - o **Quit with Prompt:** To close the voucher entry screen without saving the current voucher being saved, press <Esc> to get *Q: Quit* prompt (F-4B).
    - **Quit**: Set Yes to Quit,
    - **Continue**: Set No to continue the current Voucher screen),
  - o **Quick Quitting**: Ctrl+Q to Quit without saving, without any prompt.

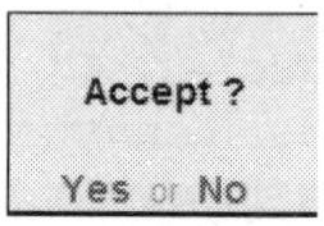

F-4A: Voucher Saving

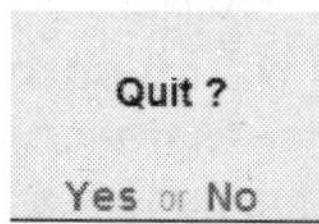

F-4B: Voucher Exiting

07 Terminating Voucher Entry

After saving the current voucher, a blank Voucher entry screen would appear to continue voucher entry:

To terminate voucher entry, press <Esc>. at the prompt, *Quit? Yes or No* (F-4B)

- **Exit from Voucher Entry session**: Type *Yes*. You get back to the *Main Menu*
- **Continue Voucher Entry session**: Type *No*, to continue Voucher entry (click the respective Voucher Type button - F4 to F7)

FAQ: Frequently asked Questions

FAQ-1: How to enter Voucher Date in Voucher.

Ans: To set Voucher Entry Modes, at Voucher Entry screen, click *F12:Configre* to get Voucher Entry Configuration screen. At Voucher Entry Configuration screen, at *Skip date Field in Create Mode (faster entry)*:

- **Automatic Voucher Date Carrying**: Set *Yes*, The cursor skips the Voucher Date field and the Current Date is automatically carried by default at Voucher Date, to save Voucher Date entry each time, as you have to consecutively enter same Voucher Date in all the vouchers of that Date.To change Voucher Date, just change the Current Date (Press F2:Date and enter current Date), which is again carried consecutively in all the vouchers entered, until you change it again.
- **Voucher Date entry in each Voucher**: Set *No*. Enter Voucher Date (cursor comes Voucher Date field). This method is useful when you enter Vouchers randomly (press <Shift> + <Tab> to get back the cursor to Voucher Date field, to enter the Voucher Date).

FAQ-2: How to carry Narration in the Current Voucher, during voucher entry, from another voucher

Ans: To speed up data entry, you may carry Narration from another voucher using following key combination at *Narration* field:

- **To Carry the Narration entered in the preceding voucher**: Press *Ctrl+R*. This is useful when you enter voucher of similar transactions consecutively.
- **To Carry the Narration entered from earlier similar voucher** (voucher with same first Ledger account):Press *Alt+R*. The Narration of a voucher having same first ledger account would be carried. This is quite helpful to quickly enter Narration of frequently occurred transactions, in a standard pattern (e.g, Narration of Conveyance Expenses Voucher will be of similar pattern). So, in Payment Voucher debiting Conveyance Expenses, press *Alt+R* at Narration field, the Narration of earlier Payment Voucher with Conveyance Expense as first ledger account, will be copied.

After getting the Narration copied from previous voucher, you may edit (modify) the Narration in the current voucher as desired. This helps you to enter consistent Narration text faster in all vouchers of similar nature of transactions.

FAQ-3: How to save a voucher after creation / modification

Ans: After you complete entry of the voucher, press <enter> or type at 'Accept*? Yes or No'* prompt,

To save the voucher instantly (without getting any prompt) after entry/modification, press Ctrl+A.

FAQ-4: What is effect of Voucher Number on insertion / deletion of back dated Voucher?

Ans: In automatic voucher numbering scheme, as soon as you Delete or Insert a back dated Voucher (or even modify the Date of a back dated voucher), all the voucher number of subsequent dates will automatically get renumbered chronologically. (§13/02-09).

So, if you have already printed the vouchers with Voucher Numbers, DO NOT Insert, or Delete (rather Cancel a Voucher), else your vouchers will get renumbered.

FAQ-5: How to convert a Voucher from one type to another?

Ans: If you have made the voucher entry in a wrong type of voucher, you may convert the voucher in the following way:

- Select the voucher in *Alteration* mode (drill down through the voucher record from any report)
- At Voucher Alteration screen, click the appropriate Voucher Type button on the Vertical Button Bar and press *Ctrl+A* to save the Voucher.

If some entries offend the voucher type to which you like convert to, you would be prompted to select appropriate Ledger from List of Ledgers. You may have to enter the Amount against the respective ledger again.

Accounts Reports 01-05

As soon as you enter a voucher, its effect is immediately reflected in the respective places and you may view any report on screen or print on paper at any point of time to get the updated figures.

01 Reports Display

Some top level reports like *Balance Sheet*, *Profit & Loss Statement* are normally available at *Main Menu* of Gateway of Tally, while other reports are available through *Display* option at Gateway of Tally Menu (F-1A/01-02), Here, we discuss about some common & salient features of reports displayed on screen.

01.01 Operations at Display Screen

Select the report from the respective menu to get the respective Reports Display screen

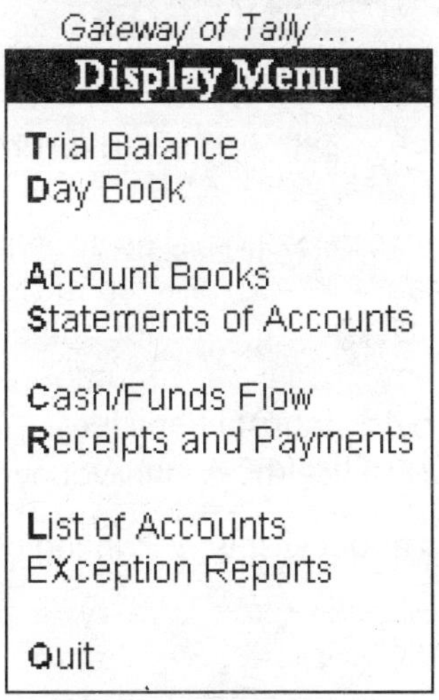

F-1: Display Menu

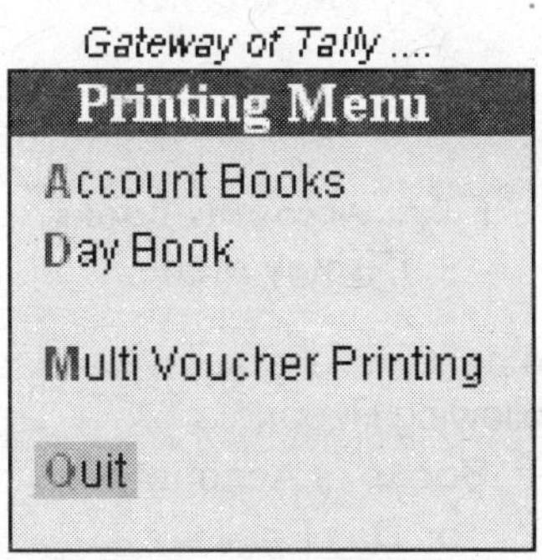

F-2A:Multi Account Printing Menu

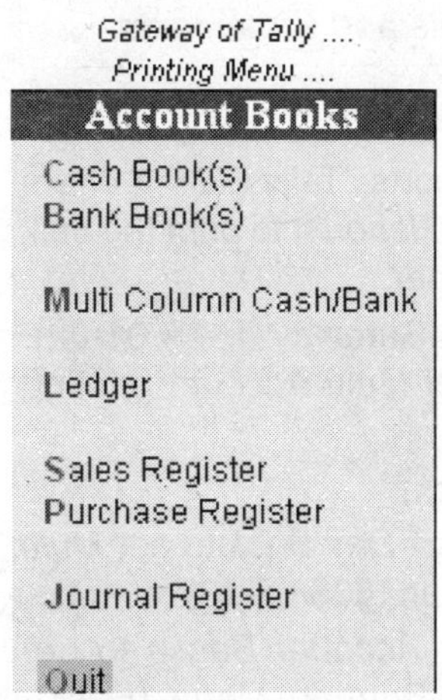

F-2B: Multi Account Books Printing Menu

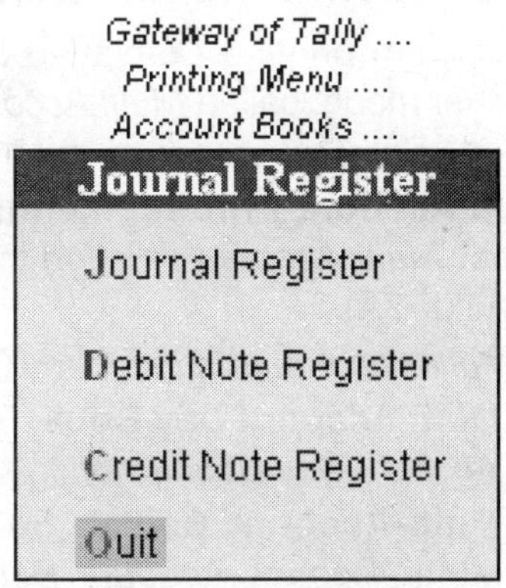

F-2C:Multi Account Journal Printing Menu

- **Drill Down**: From any on-screen report, press <enter> at any record to drill down, level-by-level to view the intermediary reports, and ultimately reach to the lowest level showing the list of vouchers constituting the Report.
- **Trace Back**: Press <Esc> key to trace back (to the higher level report) in the same path through which you drilled down.
- **Voucher in Alteration Mode:** At lowest level, you may select a Voucher to get the voucher in *Alteration* mode where you may carry out various operations (*Alteration/ Deletion/ Cancellation etc)* of voucher (§02/02-17).
- **Display Configuration**: At the *Report Display* screen, click *F12:Configure* to get the respective Report Configuration screen, showing the options to customize the contents of the report as desired. The Configuration options vary according to the Report.

02 Reports Printing

To Print the Report shown in Display, at Display screen, click *P:Print* button to get the respective *Report Printing Screen* (F-3A). The Report Printing screen contains the following major sections

- **Printing Info**: At the top part, the current Printing Info displayed. You may re-set these values through Configuration Options (F-3A)/ Printing Buttons (F-3B).
- **Report Title**: At the middle part, the Report Title (and the respective Title Options activated / deactivated) are displayed for information. You may re-set Report Title through *T:Titling* Button (F-3B),
- **Report Configuration**: At the lower Part, the default Report Printing Options are displayed (almost similar to the respective Display Configuration options). The report will be printed as per the options set as displayed (F-3A). To re-set the Options, click *No* (or Type *N*) at *Print Yes / No* option (the cursor goes to the first Configuration option) and change the options as desired.

Click *Yes* at *Print Yes / No* option (F-3A) to print the Report as per current options set

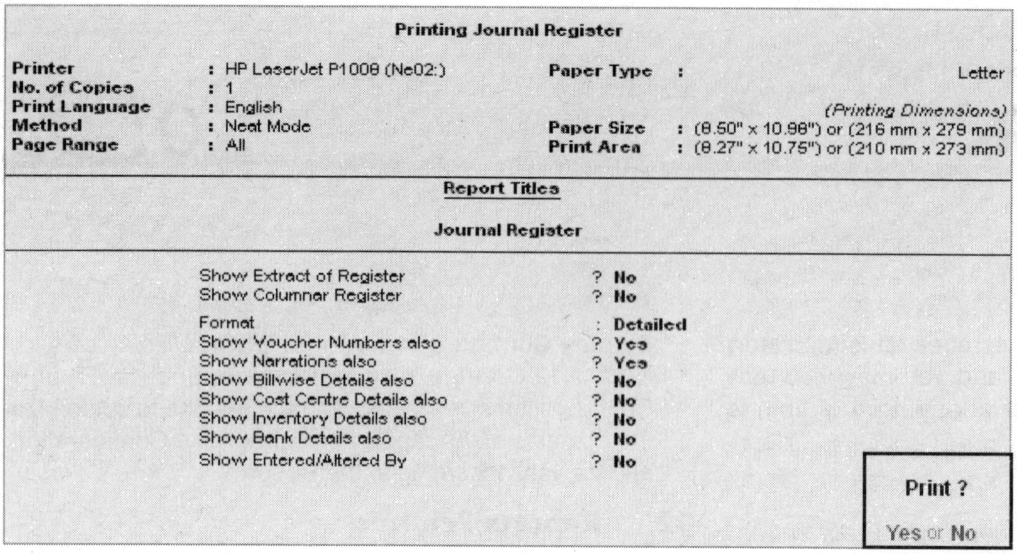

F-3A: Report Printing Screen

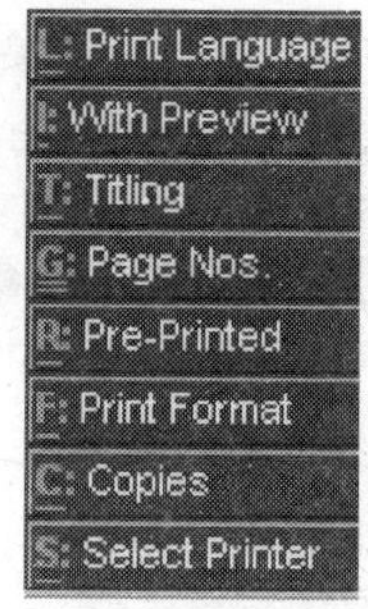

F-3B: Printing Buttons

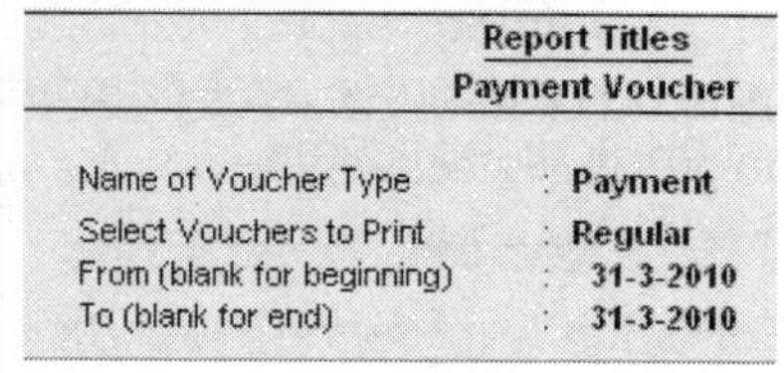

F-3C Multi Account Voucher Printing

Print Preview: You may see the exact replica of the report on screen through Print Preview option. Click *I: With Preview* toggle button (F-3B) to get the preview of the report on screen (F-8/02-14).

> **Note:** *Displayed Report is presented in a format to conveniently allow drill down, while the Report printed from Display is shown in the traditional format of Books of Accounts and Statements.*

02.01 Multi Account Reports

Apart from printing Displayed Reports, Tally.ERP 9 offers another mode, called *Multi Account Reports*, to print the bulk reports like Accounts Books, on paper.

Multi Account Printing menu: At Gateway (F-1A/01-02), select *Multi Account Printing* to get Multi-Account printing menu (F-2A).

At *Multi-Account printing menu* (F-2A):

- **Multi Account Day Book**: Select *Day Book* to get *Multi Account Day Book Printing* screen (§06/02-13)

  Multi-Account Books: Select *Account Books* to get Multi-Account *Account Books* Printing Menu (F-2B). Select the desired Account Book to get the respective printing screen. Enter the Report Period and Click *Yes* to print the Report on paper. This mode is suitable to print bulk Books of Account for a specified period, on paper.
- **Multi Vouchers**: Select *Multi Voucher Printing* to get *Multi Voucher Printing* screen (F-3C). Select the *Period, Voucher Type*. All the vouchers of the selected *Voucher Type* for the specified *Period* would be printed

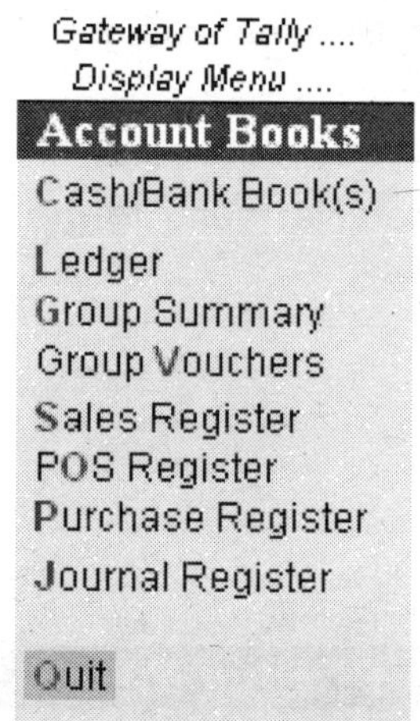

F-4A: Accounts Books Display Menu

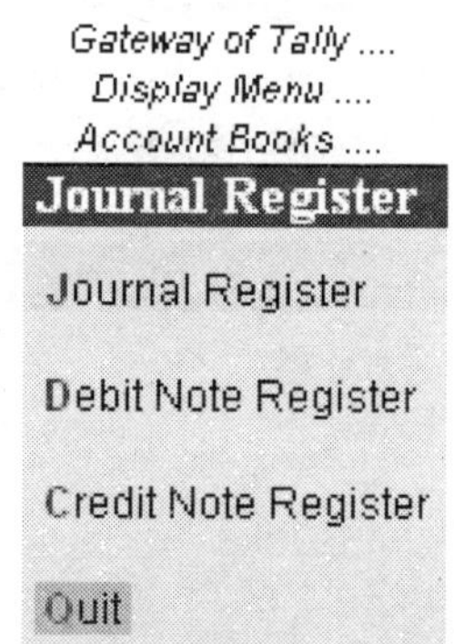

F-4B: Journal Register Display Menu

In next few chapters, we discuss about Display / Printing of following Reports

- **Books of Accounts**
  - o Day Book
  - o Cash / Bank Book
  - o Journal Proper
  - o Ledger
  - o Sales Register
  - o Purchase Register
- **Statement of Accounts**
  - o Trial Balance
  - o Profit & Loss Statement
  - o Balance Sheet

FAQ: Frequently Asked Questions

FAQ-1: How I can print report from Display screen?

Ans: At the respective Display screen, click *P:Print* button (or press Alt+P) to get Report Printing screen (like F-3A).

- Click *Y* to print with default printing options as shown in the printing screen.
- To change the options, type *N* and then change the options. Then type *Y* to print the report as per changed options

FAQ-2: How I can print Report from Multi Account option

Ans: At Gateway (F-1A/01-02), select *Multi Account Printing* to get *Multi Account Printing Menu* (F-2A). Select the Report to get the Multi Account Report printing screen for the Report. Set the Report Period and other options. Type Y to print the Report

FAQ-3: How I can print the current voucher from Voucher Entry screen

Ans: At Voucher entry screen, after voucher entry, click *P:Print* button (or press Alt+P) to get Voucher Printing screen. Set the period and other options and type *Y* to print the current voucher (F-1A/02-15)

FAQ-4: How I can print all vouchers entered for a specified period for a specified voucher type

Ans: At Gateway, select *Multi Account Printing* > *Multi Voucher Printing* to get *Multi Voucher Printing* screen (F-3C). Select the *Period*, *Voucher Type*. All the vouchers of the selected *Voucher Type* for the specified *Period* would be printed

Cash Bank Book 01-06

01 Cash / Bank Book

Cash / Bank Book is a special composite *Journal Book cum Ledger Book*:

It is a Journal Book: It contains chronological record of transaction entries (i.e vouchers) like a Journal Book

It is a Ledger Book: It shows Opening Balance, the details of all Receipts & Payments during the period & Closing Balance of Cash / Bank Account, like a Ledger Book

02 Cash / Bank Book Display

At Gateway of Tally, select *Display > Account Book > Cash & Bank Book*. However, at the first screen of the Cash Book, you get summary of transactions & Opening & Closing Balances. You get the Cash Bank Book through the following successive steps:

At *Cash Bank Summary* screen, click on (Drill down) any Cash or Bank Account to get *Ledger Monthly Summary* for the selected Cash / Bank account (*Ledger Monthly Summary*).

At *Ledger Monthly Summary*, select a month and set the period to get the *Cash Book* of the selected Cash/Bank Account for the selected month (*Ledger Vouchers*)

Click *F2:Period* and set the Period to get the Cash Book (*Ledger Vouchers*) for the selected period (F-1A)

The Cash Book Display (Ledger Voucher) shows the following main components and details (F-1A)

- **Voucher Details**: All Vouchers involving the selected cash / bank account (and complementary ledger accounts in detailed mode)
- **Total Voucher Amount**: Total of all Debit & Credit amounts separately, for the selected cash / bank account
- **Opening Balance**: Opening Balance of Cash & Bank Accounts for the specified period,
- **Current Total**: Total of Debits & Credits or the selected Period
- **Closing Balance**: Closing Balance for the end of the period, for the selected Cash / Bank account.9

02.01 Cash / Bank Book Configuration

At Cash / Bank Book Display screen (F-1A), click *F12:Configure* to get *Cash Book Configuration screen* (F-2) showing the options to customize the contents of the Report, as desired.

Ledger Vouchers | ABC Academy 9-10 | Ctrl + M

Ledger: Cash | 1-Feb-2010 to 28-Feb-2010

Date	Particulars		Vch Type	Vch No.	Debit	Credit
1-2-2010	A K Traders		Receipt	15	2,000.00	
1-2-2010	(as per details)		Receipt	16	2,850.00	
	Sales	3,000.00 Cr				
	Cash Discount	150.00 Dr				
20-2-2010	Bank of India		Contra	3		2,000.00
				Opening Balance :	19,189.50	
				Current Total :	4,850.00	2,000.00
				Closing Balance :	22,039.50	

F-1A: Cash Book in Dislplay Format

Cash Book
1-Feb-2010 to 28-Feb-2010

Date		Particulars		Vch Type	Vch No.	Debit	Credit
1-2-2010	Cr	Opening Balance				19,189.50	
1-2-2010	Cr	A K Traders		Receipt	15	2,000.00	
	Cr	(as per details)		Receipt	16	2,850.00	
		Sales	3,000.00 Cr				
		Cash Discount	150.00 Dr				
20-2-2010	Dr	Bank of India		Contra	3		2,000.00
						24,039.50	2,000.00
	Dr	Closing Balance					22,039.50
						24,039.50	24,039.50

F-1B: Cash / Bank Book in Print Format

Report Titles
Cash Book

Style of Report	: Normal Ledger
Select vouchers to show	: All Vouchers
Format	: Detailed
Show Billwise Details also	? No
Show Cost Centre Details also	? No
Show Inventory Details also	? No
Show Bank Details also	? No
Show Voucher Numbers also	? Yes
Show Narrations also	? No
Show Running Balance	? No
Include Opening Balances *(set as 'no' to remove from filtered reports)*	? Yes
Show Group Name	: No
Method of Balancing	: Monthly
Start fresh page for Balancing	? No

F-2: Cash / Bank Book Printing Screen

03 Cash Bank Book Printing

At Cash / Bank Book Display, Click *P:Print* Button to get Cash / Bank Book Printing screen (F-2). Set the options and Type Y at *Print Yes No* to print the Cash / Bank Book (F-1B).

In Print Form (F-1B), the Opening Balance is shown first, transactions are listed next. The Closing Balance is shown at the end, like the traditional Cash Book.

04 Multi Account Cash / Bank Book

At GoT, select *Multi Account Printing > Account Books* to get *Multi-Account Accounts Book Menu* (F-2B/01-05). At *Multi-Account Account Books Menu* (F-2B/01-05), select as follows:

Multi Account Cash Book

Select *Cash Book(s)* to get the list of all Cash Accounts (all Ledger accounts under the group Cash-in-Hand). Now select:

The desired *Cash Account*, to print the Cash Book for the selected Cash Account only

All Items to print the Cash Book for all the Cash Accounts (all Ledger accounts under the group Cash-in-Hand) one after another (in alphabetical order)

Multi Account Bank Book

Select *Bank Book(s)* to get list of All Bank Accounts (all Ledger accounts under the group *Bank Accounts* and *Bank OCC*).

Now select:

The desired *Bank Account*, to print the Bank Book for the selected Bank Account only

All Items to print the Bank Book for all the Bank Accounts (all Ledger accounts under the group Bank Accounts and Bank OCC) one after another (in alphabetical order)

to get Multi Account Cash / Bank Printing screen (F-4B). Set the printing options as desired to get Multi Account Cash / Bank Book in Print. The contents & format of Multi Account Cash / Bank Book is similar to Cash / Bank Book printed from Display (F-1B).

Multi Column Cash/ Bank Book

To Print composite Cash / Bank Book with separate column for each selected Cash / Bank Account. of selected Cash Account (s), at *Multi Account Books printing* menu (F-2B/01-05), select *Multi Column Cash Bank Book* to get *Multi Column Cash Bank Book* Printing screen (F-4A). At *Multi Column Cash Bank Book* Printing screen (F-4A), select upto 3 Cash / Bank Accounts, from the list of Cash / Bank Accounts (all Ledger accounts under the group Cash-in-Hand, Bank Accounts and Bank OCC), to include in the Multi Column Cash / Bank Book as follows:

Cash / Bank A/c for 1st column

Cash / Bank A/c for 2nd column

Cash / Bank A/c for 3rd column

Click *Yes* to print the Multi Column Cash / Bank Book (F-3)

Multi Column Cash/Bank Book

1-Apr-2010 to 1-May-2010

Page 1

Date	Particulars	Voucher Type	Number	*Cash* Dr	*Bank of India* Dr	*HDFC Bank S/B 1596* Dr	Date	Particulars	Voucher Type	Number	*Cash* Cr	*Bank of India* Cr	*HDFC Bank S/B 1596* Cr
1-Apr-2010	To Opening Balance			1,82,240.34	46,060.07	48,923.03							
							5-Apr-2010	By Reliance MF 7166	Pymt	1		1,000.00	
7-Apr-2010	To HDFC Bank S/B 1596	Ctra	1		40,000.00		7-Apr-2010	By DSP B Rock	Pymt	2		1,000.00	
							7-Apr-2010	By Bank of India	Ctra	1			40,000.00
				1,82,240.34	86,060.07	48,923.03	9-Apr-2010	By Bharti AXA Ins Prem 4760881	Pymt	3		2,100.00	
							9-Apr-2010	By ICICI Ins Prem 8849	Pymt	4		1,350.00	
				1,82,240.34	**86,060.07**	**48,923.03**	12-Apr-2010	By Reliance Reg Saving 1706	Pymt	5		1,050.00	
							16-Apr-2010	By UTI Oppor 505232161536	Pymt	6		1,000.00	
							16-Apr-2010	By Sund BNP 2708115/84	Pymt	7		1,000.00	
							16-Apr-2010	By ICICI Pru 12719117 (Prev Yr)	Pymt	8		3,050.00	
							16-Apr-2010	By ICICI LIC Ins Prem 13777794	Pymt	9		4,300.00	
							16-Apr-2010	By BOI FD	Pymt	10		49,000.00	
							19-Apr-2010	By Bank Charges	Pymt	11		725.00	
							21-Apr-2010	By Bank Charges	Pymt	12		725.00	
							21-Apr-2010	By Bank Charges	Pymt	13			110.30
							26-Apr-2010	By UTI Inf 505232161274	Pymt	14		1,000.00	
							26-Apr-2010	By HDFC Growth 5984/1100256	Pymt	15		1,000.00	
							26-Apr-2010	By ICICI Prem 10021319	Pymt	16		2,100.00	
							26-Apr-2010	By Sund BNP 27986714D014(New)	Pymt	17		1,150.00	
												71,550.00	40,110.30
								By Closing Balance			1,82,240.34	14,510.07	8,812.73
											1,82,240.34	**86,060.07**	**48,923.03**

F-3: Multi Column Cash / Bank Book (Detailed)

Report Titles

Cash Book

From (blank for beginning)	:	**1-4-2009**
To (blank for end)	:	**31-3-2010**
Cash/Bank A/c for 1st Column	:	**Cash**
for 2nd Column	:	**Bank of India**
for 3rd Column	:	**State Bank of India**
Format	:	**Detailed**
Show Billwise Details also	?	**No**
Show Cost Centre Details also	?	**No**
Show Inventory Details also	?	**No**
Show Bank Details also	?	**No**
Show Narrations also	?	**Yes**

F-4A: Multi Column Cash / bank Book printing screen

FAQ: Frequently Asked Questions

FAQ-1: Explain printing of Cash Book from Display and Multi Account Printing Options.

Ans: The steps of getting the reports in both the methods are described below:

Through Display:

For a month: At Gateway of Tally, Click on *Display > Account Books > Cash/Bank Book(s)* to get Cash/ Bank Summary. Select Cash A/c and then select a month to get Cash Book for the specified month.

For any Period: After selecting a month, press *F2: Period* button and set the period (e.g. 1-4-09 to 31-3-10), to get the Cash Book for specified period.

Printing from Display Screen: At Display screen, click *P:Print* button to get Cash Book Printing screen. Set *Yes* to Print the Cash book for the specified Period.

Through Multi A/c Printing:

At Gateway of Tally, select *Multi Account Printing> Account Books> Cash Book(s),* Select Cash Account to get the Multi Account Cash Book printing screen. Now set the period (e.g. 1-4-09 to 31-3-10) and other options to get Multi Account Cash Book for the selected Cash Account for the specified Period.

FAQ-2: How to print Cash Book from Display. What is the difference between Cash Book Display and Cash Book printed from Display screen.

Ans: At Cash Book Display (F-1A), click *P:Print* button to get Cash Boo Printing screen (F-2). Type Y to print to get Cash Book in Print (F-1B).

Report Titles

Cash Book

From (blank for beginning)	:	**1-4-2009**
To (blank for end)	:	**31-3-2010**
Style of Report	:	**Normal Ledger**
Select vouchers to show	:	**All Vouchers**
Format	:	**Condensed**
Show Billwise Details also	?	**No**
Show Cost Centre Details also	?	**No**
Show Inventory Details also	?	**No**
Show Bank Details also	?	**No**
Show Voucher Numbers also	?	**Yes**
Show Narrations also	?	**No**
Show Running Balance	?	**No**
Include Opening Balances	?	**Yes**
(set as 'no' to remove from filtered reports)		
Show Group Name	:	**No**
Method of Balancing	:	**Monthly**
Start fresh page for Balancing	?	**No**

F-4B: Multi Account Cash / bank Book printing screen

- In *Display* Format, the transactions are shown first in sequence of date. The Opening & Closing Balance for the specified period, at the end of Report. You may drill down through a Voucher to get the Voucher in Alteration Mode
- In *Print* Format, The Opening Balance is sown in the first line, followed by the transactions sequence of date. The Closing Balance is shown at the end of Report. like traditional Cash Book. You cannot drill down in Print Format.

FAQ-2: How to print Multi Column Cash Book.

Ans: To Print composite Cash / Bank Book with separate column for each selected Cash / Bank Account. selected Cash Account (s),

At *Multi Account Books printing* menu (F-2B/01-05), select *Multi Column Cash Bank Book* to get *Multi Column Cash Bank Book* Printing screen (F-4A). At *Multi Column Cash Bank Book* Printing screen (F-4A), select the Cash Bank Account, one by one, at each Cash / Bank Account (F-4A), from the list of Cash / Bank Accounts, upto 3 Cash / Bank Accounts

A column would be created for each selected Cash / bank Account will be created, at both Debit (for Receipts at left) & Credit Side (for Payments at ight) to include in the Multi Column Cash / Bank Book as follows:

Cash / Bank A/c for 1st column

Cash / Bank A/c for 2nd column

Cash / Bank A/c for 3rd column

Click *Yes* to print the Multi Column Cash / Bank Book (F-3)

Journal Book

01-07

01 Journal Book Display

Journal Book (also referred as *Journal Proper*) contains all Journal Vouchers in chronological order.

At Gateway of Tally Menu, select *Display > Account Book > Journal Register > Journal Register.* (F-4B/01-05) to get the Journal register Monthly Summary screen (showing number of Journal Vouchers for each Month). Select a Month and set the Period (Click *F2:Period* button) to get Journal Book (Voucher Register) for the specified Period (F-1A)

At Journal Book Display, click *F1: Condensed / Detailed* toggle button:

- **F1:Condensed:** Only the first ledger account of each voucher is shown with the corresponding amount in Debit Column (because in Journal voucher, the Debit Account is first written).
- **F1:Detailed:** The first ledger account of each voucher is shown with the corresponding amount in Debit Column. Other ledger transactions with corresponding amount, are shown in Inner column (under Particulars – F-1A).

The amount of first Debit Entry only is shown in Debit Column. Amount of complimentary Ledger Accounts are shown in inner column (at Particulars).

Voucher Register Ctrl + M

List of All Journal Vouchers — 1-Jan-2013 to 31-Mar-2013

Date	Particulars		Vch Type	Vch No.	Debit Amount	Credit Amount
1-1-2013	Pre Paid Expenses		Journal	1	1,500.00	
	Insurance Premia	1,500.00 Cr				
31-3-2013	Depreciation Account		Journal	2	32,000.00	
	Furniture Accounts	12,000.00 Cr				
	Building Account	20,000.00 Cr				
31-3-2013	P Kumar		Journal	3	2,300.00	
	Inerset Received	2,300.00 Cr				
31-3-2013	Interest Paid		Journal	4	1,250.00	
	D Sinha	1,250.00 Cr				
31-3-2013	Rent		Journal	5	2,500.00	
	Electricity Cahrges	1,250.00 Dr				
	Liablities for Expenses	3,750.00 Cr				
31-3-2013	Salary		Journal	6	24,000.00	
	Prov Fund (Employee)	2,200.00 Cr				
	P Tax (Emloyee)	210.00 Cr				
	Loan (Employee)	2,500.00 Cr				
	Outstanding Net Salary	19,090.00 Cr				
31-3-2013	Bonus		Journal	7	3,000.00	
	Leave Salary	3,400.00 Dr				
	Outstanding Net Salary	6,400.00 Cr				

F-1A Journal Book in Display Format (Detailed)

Journal Register

1-Jan-2013 to 31-Mar-2013

Page 1

Date	Particulars	Vch Type	Debit Amount	Credit Amount
1-1-2013	Pre Paid Expenses	Journal	1,500.00	
	Insurance Premia			1,500.00
	Proportionate Insurance Premia for 1.4.12 to 30.6.12 adjusted			
31-3-2013	Depreciation Account	Journal	32,000.00	
	Furniture Accounts			12,000.00
	Building Account			20,000.00
	Depreciation on Furniture @ 10% on 1,20,000=12000, Building @ 5% on 4,00,000			
31-3-2013	P Kumar	Journal	2,300.00	
	Inerset Received			2,300.00
	Interest Receivable from Borrower for the Q/e Jan - Mar debited to his account			
31-3-2013	Interest Paid	Journal	1,250.00	
	D Sinha			1,250.00
	Interst payable on Loan for Q/e Jan - Mar 2012 credited to lender's account			
31-3-2013	Rent	Journal	2,500.00	
	Electricity Cahrges		1,250.00	
	Liablities for Expenses			3,750.00
	Liabilty for Expenses for March 2012 provided			
31-3-2013	Salary	Journal	24,000.00	
	Prov Fund (Employee)			2,200.00
	P Tax (Emloyee)			210.00
	Loan (Employee)			2,500.00
	Outstanding Net Salary			19,090.00
	Salary paybale for he m/o March 2012			
31-3-2013	Bonus	Journal	3,000.00	
	Leave Salary		3,400.00	
	Outstanding Net Salary			6,400.00
	Liabilities for Bonus & unpaid Leave Salary provided			

F-1B: Journal Book Display in Print Format

Report Titles

Journal Register

Show Extract of Register	?	No
Show Columnar Register	?	No
Format	:	Condensed
Show Voucher Numbers also	?	Yes
Show Narrations also	?	No
Show Billwise Details also	?	No
Show Cost Centre Details also	?	No
Show Inventory Details also	?	No
Show Bank Details also	?	No
Show Entered/Altered By	?	No

F-1C Journal Book Printing screen

From (blank for beginning)	:	1-3-2010
To (blank for end)	:	31-3-2010
Show Extract of Register	?	No
Show Columnar Register	?	No
Format	:	Detailed
Show Voucher Numbers also	?	Yes
Show Narrations also	?	No
Show Billwise Details also	?	No
Show Cost Centre Details also	?	No
Show Inventory Details also	?	No
Show Bank Details also	?	No
Show Entered/Altered By	?	No

F-2A: Multi Account Journal Register Printing screen

Ledger Details in Journal Book
- **Display:** Only the first ledger account and the amount is shown in Debit Column (F-1A) - **Print from Display**: Each Ledger Account and amount is shown in respective Debit / Credit columns (F-1B). - **Multi-Account Print:** Each Ledger Account and amount is shown in respective Debit / Credit columns, lie Print from Display (F-1B)

02 Journal Book Printing

At *Journal Book Display* screen (F-1A), click *P:Print* button to get Journal Book Printing screen (F-1C).Set the options as desired and type *Y* to print the Journal Book (F-1B) as per options set.

03 Multi Account Journal Register Printing

At Gateway of Tally, select *Multi accounts Printing> Account Books* to get Multi-Account Account Books Printing Menu (F-2B/01-05).

At *Multi Account Printing* Menu (F-2B/01-05), select *Journal Register > Journal Register* (F-2C/01-05) to get Journal Register printing screen (F-2). Set the options to get Multi Account Journal Register, similar to Journal Book in print (F-1B)

FAQ: Frequently Asked Questions

FAQ-1: Explain printing of Journal Register from Display and Multi Account Printing Options.

Ans:

(i) **Through Display:**

(a) **For a Month:** At Gateway of Tally, Click on Display > Account Books > Journal register > Journal Register to get Monthly Journal Register. Select a Month to get the List of Journal Vouchers for the selected month.

(b) **For any Period:** After selecting a month, press *F2: Period* button and set the period (e.g. 1-4-09 to 31-3-10), to get the list of journal voucher for the selected period.

Printing from Display Screen: Now click *P:Print* button to get Journal Register printing screen (F-1C). Set Yes to Print the Journal Book.

(ii) **Through Multi A/c Printing:**

At Gateway of Tally, select *Multi Account Printing> Account Books > Journal register > Journal Register* to get Multi Account Journal Register Printing Screen (F-2A). Set the period (e.g. 1-4-09 to 31-3-10) and other options to print the Journal Register for the specified period.

Ledger Book

01-08

01 Ledger Book

Ledger Book shows assorted transactions related to a specified ledger account (F-2A). It shows Opening Balance, Transactions & Closing Balance of an Account Ledger, in chronological order, for the specified period.

02 Ledger Book Display

At Gateway of Tally, select *Display > Account Book > Ledger*. Select the Ledger Account to get Ledger Account (Ledger Vouchers) of the specified period. (F-1A).

Ledger Vouchers Ctrl + M

Ledger: **Salary** — 1-Apr-2012 to 31-Mar-2013

Date	Particulars		Vch Type	Vch No.	Debit	Credit
2-6-2012	(as per details)		Payment	3	6,000.00	
	Loan (Employee)	700.00 Cr				
	Prov Fund (Employee)	600.00 Cr				
	P Tax (Emloyee)	50.00 Cr				
	Bank of India	4,650.00 Cr				
1-7-2012	(as per details)		Payment	4	6,000.00	
	Loan (Employee)	800.00 Cr				
	Prov Fund (Employee)	600.00 Cr				
	P Tax (Emloyee)	75.00 Cr				
	Cash	4,525.00 Cr				
31-3-2013	(as per details)		Journal	6	24,000.00	
	Prov Fund (Employee)	2,200.00 Cr				
	P Tax (Emloyee)	210.00 Cr				
	Loan (Employee)	2,500.00 Cr				
	Outstanding Net Salary	19,090.00 Cr				
			Opening Balance :			
			Current Total :		36,000.00	
			Closing Balance :		36,000.00	

F-1A: Ledger Book Display

Ledger

All Accounts
One Account
Group of Accounts
Quit

F-1B: Multi Account Ledger Printing Menu

Configuration

Select vouchers to show	:	**All Vouchers**
Format	:	**Condensed**
Show Billwise Details also	?	**No**
Show Cost Centre Details also	?	**No**
Show Inventory Details also	?	**No**
Show Bank Details also	?	**No**
Show Narrations also	?	**No**
Include Opening Balances *(set as 'no' to remove from filtered reports)*	?	**Yes**
Appearance of Names	:	**Name Only**
Sorting Method	:	**Default**
Show Running Balance	?	**No**

F-1C: Ledger Display Configuration

Report Titles
ABC Supliers
Ledger Account

Style of Report	:	**Normal Ledger**
Select vouchers to show	:	**All Vouchers**
Format	:	**Condensed**
Show Billwise Details also	?	**No**
Show Cost Centre Details also	?	**No**
Show Inventory Details also	?	**No**
Show Bank Details also	?	**No**
Show Voucher Numbers also	?	**Yes**
Show Narrations also	?	**No**
Show Running Balance	?	**No**
Include Opening Balances *(set as 'no' to remove from filtered reports)*	?	**Yes**
Show Group Name	:	**No**
Method of Balancing	:	**Yearly**

F-1D Ledger Pritnting screen

Ledger Book Printing

- **Ledger Print from Display**: You may print the Ledge Account currently bein dislayed.
- **Multi Account Ledger Printing**: You may print several selected Ledger accounts together, in one shot. Youmay also print Index of Ledger.

The Format of Ledger Printed from Display & Mutli Account Printing is similar

Ledger Book shows the following main components and details (F-1A):

- **Opening Balance**: Opening Balance of Ledger Account for the specified period., if any:
  - o In *Display*, it is shown at the bottom at Total Part (F-1A)
  - o In *Print*, it is shown at the first line of the Ledger Account (F-2A)
- **Ledger Amount**: The Ledger Amount is shown in Debit / Credit column, as the case may be.
- **Complementary Ledger Account Details:** Under Particulars Column, the Complementary Ledger Accounts (Ledger Accounts Transacted in the voucher other than the current Ledger Accounts) are shown, as follows:
  - o In case of *Single complementary Ledger account* (Voucher with Single Debit & Single Credit), the Complementary Ledger Account is shown.
  - o *In case of Multiple complementary Ledger Accounts* (Voucher with more than one Debit or Credit), under

the head '*(as per details)*', all the Complementary Ledger Account & Amount with Dr/ Cr Sign are shown in inner column (under Particulars).

- **Amount Totals:** Total of Debit & Credit columns separately
- **Closing Balance**: Closing Balance for the end of the period, for the specified ledger account, at the last line, at the respective Debit or Credit column, as the case may be.
  - o In *Display*, it is shown at the last line of at the Ledger Account, at the respective Debit / Credit Column (the Debit Balance is shown in Debit Column and Credit Balance is shown in Credit Column: F-1A)
  - o In *Print*, it is shown after the current period Total, but before the Grand Total, at the *complementary* Dr/ Cr Columns (The Debit balance is shown in Credit Column and Debit balance is shown in Credit Column, to make the equal totals: F-2A).

02.01 Ledger Display Configuration

At Ledger Display screen (F-1A), click *F12:Config* to get *Ledger Display Configuration* screen (F-1C) to set the contents and format of the Ledger Book.

02.02 Ledger Display Format

Click *F1: Condensed / Detailed* toggle button to get the Ledger book in respective format as explained below:

- **F1:Condensed:** Only the first complementary Ledger account of the selected Ledger Accounts of the each voucher is shown with the corresponding amount in respective Debit / Credit column. So, one line is shown for each voucher.
- **F1:Detailed:** Details of all ledger accounts in the voucher are shown in multiple lines:
  - o If there is only one Complementary ledger account transaction (i.e voucher with 2 ledger accounts only) in the voucher, the complementary Ledger account is shown (at Particulars Column) with the corresponding amount in respective Debit / Credit
  - o If multiple ledger accounts are transacted in the voucher, the word '*(as per details)*' is shown in the first line and the ledger amount of the selected ledger is shown in respective Debit / Credit. All other ledger Accounts (all complementary ledger accounts) with corresponding amount are shown in Inner column (under Particulars), with Amount & Dr/ Cr sign.

03 Ledger Book Printing

At Ledger Book Display screen (F-1A), click *P:Print* button (or press Alt+P keys) to get Ledger Book printing screen (F-1D). Set *Yes* to get the Ledger in Print (F-2A).

04 Multi Account Ledger Book

Through Display, you can print only one Ledger Account at a time, whereas, through Multi Account Ledger option, you may print several Ledger Accounts of a Group (or all Ledger Account) at a time for the specified period

Salary
Ledger Account

1-Apr-2012 to 31-Mar-2013

Page 1

Date	Particulars		Vch Type	Vch No.	Debit	Credit
2-6-2012	Cr (as per details)		Payment	3	6,000.00	
		Loan (Employee)		700.00 Cr		
		Prov Fund (Employee)		600.00 Cr		
		P Tax (Emloyee)		50.00 Cr		
		Bank of India		4,650.00 Cr		
	Salary paid to Sudhir Kumar for the m/o May 12					
1-7-2012	Cr (as per details)		Payment	4	6,000.00	
		Loan (Employee)		800.00 Cr		
		Prov Fund (Employee)		600.00 Cr		
		P Tax (Emloyee)		75.00 Cr		
		Cash		4,525.00 Cr		
	Salary paid to Mohan Kumar for the m/o June 12					
31-3-2013	Cr (as per details)		Journal	6	24,000.00	
		Prov Fund (Employee)		2,200.00 Cr		
		P Tax (Emloyee)		210.00 Cr		
		Loan (Employee)		2,500.00 Cr		
		Outstanding Net Salary		19,090.00 Cr		
	Salary paybale for he m/o March 2012					
					36,000.00	
Dr	Closing Balance					36,000.00
					36,000.00	36,000.00

F-2A: Ledger Book in Print Form

Report Titles
Ledger Account

From (blank for beginning)	:	1-4-2009
To (blank for end)	:	31-3-2010
Style of Report	:	Normal Ledger
Select vouchers to show	:	All Vouchers
Format	:	Detailed
Show Billwise Details also	?	No
Show Cost Centre Details also	?	No
Show Inventory Details also	?	No
Show Bank Details also	?	No
Show Voucher Numbers also	?	Yes
Show Running Balance	?	No
Include Opening Balances	?	Yes
(set as 'no' to remove from filtered reports)		
Show Group Name	:	No
Sorting Method	?	Group
Method of Balancing	:	Yearly
Start fresh page for each Account	?	Yes
Start fresh page for Balancing	?	No
Allow Selection for Groups/Ledgers	?	No
Set Alphabetical print range	?	Yes
From (blank for beginning)	:	A To (blank for end) : B
Print index page	?	Yes

F-2B: Multi Account Ledger Printing Screen

Select *Multi Account Printing > Account Books > Ledger* (F-2B/01-05) to get Multi Account Ledger printing menu (F-1B) with following options:

- **All Ledgers**: Select *All Accounts* to print all Ledger Accounts. Each ledger accounts would be printed one after another, in alphabetical order
- **One Ledger Account**: Select *One* Ledger Account from the list of Ledger Accounts. The selected Ledger Account will be printed

- **All Ledgers of an Account Group**: Select *Group of Accounts* to print all Ledgers placed under selected Account Group, in alphabetical order, one after another.

On selection of the desired menu Item as above, you get the *Multi Account Ledger Printing* screen (F-2B). At *Multi Account Ledger Printing* screen (F-2B), set the printing options and the period for which you like to print the Ledger Book

The format of Multi Account Ledger is similar to Ledger printed from Display (F-2A). When All Ledgers or Group of Ledgers are printed, several Ledger Accounts are printed in the same Report, one after another, in alphabetical order, for the same period as specified at the *Multi Account Ledger Printing* screen (F-2B)

FAQ: Frequently Asked Questions

FAQ-1: Explain printing of Ledger from Display and Multi Account Printing Options.

Ans: Through Display, you get screenful of data in the report. You may scroll the long report up & down. It is useful for on screen viewing and drill down to subordinate reports / vouchers conveniently. Click *P:Print* button (or press Alt+P keys) to print the Ledger Account.

Through Multi Account printing option, you can print a hard copy of Ledger Books in proper formatted manner, in standard size stationery, for record and audit, to meet the statutory requirements of maintenance of Accounts Books.

The steps of getting the reports in both the methods are described below:

(a) **Through Display:**

At *Gateway of Tally> Display > Account Books > Ledger*, select a Ledger to Display the Ledger Account. At Ledger Display screen (F-1A), click *P:Print* to Print Ledger from Display (F-2A)

(b) **Through Multi A/c Printing:**

At Gateway of Tally > Multi Account Printing> Account Books > Ledger (F-1B), select any of the following options:

(i) **All Accounts:** To Print all the ledgers

(ii) **One Accounts:** To Print a specific ledger

(ii) **Group of Accounts:** To Print the ledgers of a selected group.

Set the period (e.g. 1-4-12 to 31-3-13) at Multi Account Printing screen to get the Ledger(s) for the period as per specified option.

The Format & Contents of Ledger Printed from Display & from Multi Account print is similar.

FAQ-2: What is Complementary Accounts of a Ledger Accounts in a voucher

Ans: Complementary Ledger Accounts are the rest of the ledger accounts transacted in a Voucher with reference to a ledger account in the voucher. Among the Complementary Accounts, the first Complementary Account of a Ledger is the first Account transacted in the Voucher (other than the Ledger Account), of a nature opposite to the current ledger Account

Multiple Account Vouchers

For example, in the following Multiple Account Voucher (Voucher with more than One Debit / Credit transactions, the Complimentary Ledger Accounts for each Ledger Account is shown below

Salary Dr 10000
HRA Dr 3000
PF Cr 1200
Cash Cr 11800

Ledger Account	First Complimentary Account	Other Complimentary Accounts
Salary	PF	HRA, Cash
HRA	PF	Salary, Cash
PF	Salary	HRA, Cash
Cash	Salary	HRA, PF

Single Account Vouchers

For example, in the following Single Account Voucher (Voucher with One Debit & One Credit transactions), the other ledger Account is the Complimentary Ledger Accounts for each Ledger Account is shown below

Depreciation Dr 1200
Furniture Cr 1200

The Ledger Accounts and the corresponding Complimentary Leger Accounts in Single Account Voucher s are shown below:

Ledger Account	Complimentary Account
Depreciation	Furniture
Furniture	Depreciation

FAQ-3: How the Complimentary Accounts are shown in Ledger Book Display

Ans: In case of Single Account Voucher (One Debit & One Credit), like

Depreciation Dr 1200
Furniture Cr 1200

The ledger are show as follows

Depreciation A/c

Particulars	Dr	Cr
Furniture	1200	

Furniture A/c

Particulars	Dr	Cr
Depreciation		1200

So, in Single Account Voucher, at the first line, the complementary Ledger Account name (e.g Furniture in case of Depreciation Ledger A/c & Depreciation in case of Furniture Ledger A/c), the Debit / Credit column (sign & Amount), represents to the current ledger A/c. (not the ledger account shown at Particulars column).

In Single Account Vouchers (One Debit & One Credit)

In Furniture Ledger Account, at Particulars column, the name of Depreciation Ledger A/c (the complimentary ledger a/c appears, but the Debit / Credit columns represent that of Furniture A/c (not of Depreciation A/c). You will see the Amount in Credit column (because the Furniture A/c is credited).

In Deprecation Ledger Account, at Particulars column, the name of Furniture Ledger A/c (the complimentary ledger a/c appears, but the Debit / Credit columns represent that of Depreciation A/c (not of Furniture A/c). You will see the Amount in Debit column (because the Furniture A/c is Debited).

The Account in Particulars column represent the Complimentary Account while the Debit / Credit column represent the Ledger Account

In Multiple Account Vouchers (More than One Debit or One Credit)

However, for Multiple Account Voucher, the presentation is different. For the following voucher:

Salary	Dr	10000
HRA	Dr	3000
PF	Cr	1200
Employee	Cr	11800

The corresponding Ledger Accounts would be shown as below:

In Condensed Mode

The first Complimentary Ledger Account (Account having first opposite transaction sign) is displayed.

Salary A/c			HRA A/c			PF A/c			Employee		
Particulars	Dr	Cr	Particulars	Dr	Cr	Particulars	Dr	Cr	Particulars	Dr	Cr
PF	10000		Salary	3000		Salary		1200	Salary		11800

In Detailed Mode

All the Complementary Ledger Accounts, transaction sign & corresponding Amount are shown in Inner Column

Salary A/c					HRA A/c				
Particulars			Dr	Cr	Particulars			Dr	Cr
(as per details)			10000		(as per details)			3000	
HRA	3000	Dr			Salary	10000	Dr		
PF	1200	Cr			PF	1200	Cr		
Employee	11800	Cr			Employee	11800	Cr		

PF A/c					Employee A/c				
Particulars			Dr	Cr	Particulars			Dr	Cr
(as per details)			1200		(as per details)				11800
Salary	10000	Dr			Salary	10000	Dr		
HRA	3000	Dr			HRA	3000	Dr		
Employee	11800	Cr			PF	1200	Cr		

Trial Balance

01 Trial Balance

Trial Balance is a summary Statement showing the Net Balance of all Ledger Accounts. In Double Entry System, every transaction causes equal Debit & Credit. Trial Balance is the account wise summary of all the Transactions (Vouchers) & Balances. So, the total of Debits & Credits in the Trial Balance would also be equal (F-1)

If the Trial Balance does not tally (i.e, the total of Debits & Credits of Trial Balance are not equal), there is mistake somewhere. As the equality of Debit / Credit in each voucher is ensured during voucher entry, the Trial Balance will not tally if the total Debits & Credits of *Opening Balance* of all Ledger Accounts are not equal. In such case, carefully check the *Opening Balance* to make sure the total debits & credits of all ledger accounts are equal.

Trial Balance serves 2 major objectives:

- **Ensuring Arithmetical Accuracy**: To check the arithmetic accuracy of totaling, casting, posting, balancing etc., of all figures ensuring Total Debits & Credits are equal (so the name Trial Balance),
- **Accounting Reports Preparation**: It shows the Accountwise Balance of each Ledger Account. These figures are used to prepare various Financial Statements and Final Accounts (Profit & Loss & Balance Sheet) Statements.

02 Trial Balance Display

At Display (*GoT>Display)* Menu (F-1/01-05), select *Trial Balance* to get *Trail Balance Display* Screen, showing the Closing Balance of Major Accounts Groups.

Format: Click F1: *Condensed / Detailed* toggle button to get the Trial Balance in respective format as explained below:

- **F1:Condensed:** The closing Balance of only the top Level Primary Group figures are shown. So, one line is shown for each Top Level Primary Group
- **F1:Detailed:** The next level Account Groups / Ledger Accounts under each top level Primary Group are shown, with the corresponding closing balance in Debit / Credit column as applicable. The Top level Primary Groups are shown in Bold, the Account Groups are shown in Normal Font and the Ledger Accounts are shown in Italics (F-1).

Configuration: At Trial Balance Display (F-1), click *F12:Configure* to get Trial Balance Configuration screen (F-2B) to set the contents of Trial Balance display.

Trial Balance | Info Consultants 12-13 | Ctrl + M

Particulars	Info Consultants 12-13 1-Apr-2012 to 31-Mar-2013 Closing Balance	
	Debit	Credit
Capital Account		**3,42,500.00**
Proprietor's Capital		*3,42,500.00*
Loans (Liability)		**15,845.00**
Bank OD A/c		14,720.00
D Sinha		*1,125.00*
Current Liabilities		**29,100.00**
Liabilties for Expenses		*3,750.00*
Outstanding Net Salary		*21,490.00*
Prov Fund (Employee)		*3,400.00*
P Tax (Emloyee)		*335.00*
TDS Deducted From Payments		*125.00*
Fixed Assets	**2,88,000.00**	
Building	*1,80,000.00*	
Furniture	*1,08,000.00*	
Current Assets	**1,06,655.00**	**4,000.00**
Loans & Advances (Asset)	25,300.00	4,000.00
Cash-in-hand	23,155.00	
Bank Accounts	52,120.00	
Pre Paid Expenses	*1,500.00*	
TDS Deducted From Receipts	*4,580.00*	
Direct Incomes		**79,800.00**
Consultancy Fees		*79,800.00*
Indirect Incomes		**2,300.00**
Inerset Received		*2,300.00*
Indirect Expenses	**78,890.00**	
Bonus	*3,000.00*	
		8 more ...
Grand Total	**4,73,545.00**	**4,73,545.00**

F-1 Trial Balance Display (Detailed)

Report Titles

Trial Balance

Scale Factor for Values	: **Default**
Show Opening Balances	? **Yes**
Show transactions	? **Yes**
Nett transactions only	? **No**
Show Closing Balances	? **Yes**
Show Percentages	? **No**
Method of information	: **Grouped**
Format	: **Detailed**
Expand all levels in Detailed Format	? **Yes**
Show ALL Accounts (incl. Empty A/cs)	? **No**

F-2A:Trial Balance Printing Screen

Configuration

Show Opening Balances	? No
Show transactions	? No
Show Closing Balances	? Yes
Show Percentages	? No
Appearance of Names	: Name Only
Scale Factor for Values	: Default
Sorting Method	: Default
Expand all levels in Detailed Format	? No

F-2B: Trial Balance Display Configuration

03 Trial Balance Printing

At Trial balance Display (F-1), Click *P:Print* (or press *Alt+P*) to get *Trial Balance Printing* screen (F-2A). Set the options to get Trial Balance in Print, similar to Trial Balance Display (F-1)

FAQ: Frequently Asked Questions

FAQ-1: What is Trial Balance

Ans: Trial Balance is a Statement showing net Balance (Net Debit or Net Credit) of all ledger accounts, as on a specified Date.

FAQ-2: Is Trial Balance a part of Books of Accounts

Ans: No, Journal, Cash Book etc, which record the Primary transactions (Vouchers) are Part of Books of Accounts. Ledger, which contain posting from these Books of Accounts & and net Balance, is also a part of Books of Accounts. Trial Balance is a Statement created for convenience to ensure arithmetic accuracy of the Balances of Ledger Accounts and to manually compile the P & L Statement and Balance Sheet easily.

You may even compile the P & L Statement and Balance Sheet from the Ledger Balance directly.

FAQ-3: Under what circumstances, the Trial Balance may not Tally. How you my detect and rectify the error?

Ans: In manual accounts, the Trial Balance may not tally due to errors in casting, posting etc. In Computerised system, these are done by the software (so the manual errors are eliminated). As each voucher contains equal Debit & Credit, the Trial balance must tally in Computerised system.

However, the Trial Balance will not Tally if the entry of Opening Balance in ledger accounts is not complete & correct. In that case the Balance Sheet and Trial Balance Statement shows a *Difference in Opening Balance*.

To check the correctness of Ledger Opening Balance entered:

- **Period Setting**: Click F2:Period and set the Period for Start and End of Financial Year
- **Configuration Set Up**: At Trial Balance Display Configuration (F-2B),:
  - o Set Yes at Show Opening Balance
  - o Set No at Show Transactions
  - o Set No at Show Closing Balance

FAQ-4: How the Account Groups & Ledger Accounts in Trial Balance is organized

Ans: The Primary Major Groups (Reserved Groups) appear in the order of Liability, Assets, Income & Expenses. The Subgroups & Ledger appear in hierarchical order under the respective parent Group. So, the Trial Balance shows the Group / Ledger Accounts in structured manner with Sub-Totals & Grand Totals at each group level.

FAQ-5: What you get when you drill down through a Group in Trial Balance Display

Ans: You get Group Summary showing the Balances of next Level Groups / Ledger Accounts of the selected Group

FAQ-6: What you get when you drill down through a Ledger Account in Trial Balance Display

Ans: You get Ledger Monthly Summary showing the break up figures (monthly summary figures) for each month of the selected Ledger Account

Profit & Loss Statement

01-10

01 Financial Statements

The objective of maintenance of Accounts is to prepare the following Statements of Final Accounts

- **Profit & Loss Statement**: It shows the performance of the enterprise showing *Income & Expenses* and the *Net Profit / Loss*, for the specified period (F-1)
- **Balance Sheet**: It shows the state of affairs of the enterprise showing *Liabilities* (what is *owed*) & *Assets* (what is *owned*), as on the specified *Date* (F-1/01-11).

02 Profit & Loss Statement

You may display P L Statement at any point of time, without any need to pass closing entries to transfer & close the balance of Nominal Accounts (normally done in traditional way of preparing Final Accounts).

> ***Note:*** *There is no need to enter Journal Voucher to transfer the Balances of Nominal Accounts to Profit & Loss Account.*
>
> *Tally dynamically constructs the P L Statement from the Ledger Balances of Nominal Accounts and Opening / Closing Stock Ledger Balances.*

At Gateway (F-1A/01-02), select Profit & Loss Account to get the *Profit & Loss Statement* (F-1). It contains 2 major parts, Expenses & Income, divided by a vertical line.

Profit & Loss A/c — ABC Academy 9-10 — Ctrl + M

Particulars	ABC Academy 9-10 1-Apr-2009 to 31-Mar-2010		Particulars	ABC Academy 9-10 1-Apr-2009 to 31-Mar-2010	
Opening Stock		1,000.00	**Sales Accounts**		60,800.00
Stock in Hand	1,000.00		*Cash Discount*	(-)150.00	
Purchase Accounts		7,050.00	*Cash Sales*	(-)2,000.00	
Discount on Purchase	(-)200.00		*Sales*	65,600.00	
Purchase	7,250.00		*Sales Rebates*	(-)650.00	
Gross Profit c/o		12,73,270.00	*Sales Return*	(-)2,000.00	
			Direct Incomes		12,18,520.00
			Tution Fees	12,18,520.00	
			Closing Stock		2,000.00
			Stock in Hand	2,000.00	
		12,81,320.00			12,81,320.00
Indirect Expenses		11,23,970.00	***Gross Profit b/f***		12,73,270.00
Depreciation	2,000.00		**Indirect Incomes**		3,000.00
Interest	5,400.00		*Rent Received*	3,000.00	
Conveyance Expenses					
Freight	20.00				
Handling Charges	700.00				
HRA	35,050.00				
Office Rent	7,800.00				
Salary	10,73,000.00				
Nett Profit		1,52,300.00			
Total		12,76,270.00	**Total**		12,76,270.00

F-1: Profit & Loss Account Display (Detailed)

- **Expenses Side (or Debit Side):** The Left Part shows the top level *Expenses* Groups (Direct & Indirect Expenses). The figures represent the total of Net Amount of all Ledger Accounts under the respective Group.
- **Incomes Side (or Credit Side):** The Right Part contains the top level *Income* Groups (Direct & Indirect Incomes). The figures represent the total of Net Amount of all Ledger Accounts under the respective Group.
- **Net Profit / Loss**: The *Net Profit / Loss* is computed as difference between Total of Income figures (Direct Income & Indirect Income) and the Total of Expenses figures (Direct Expense & Indirect Income).
  - o If the *Total of Income* figures is greater than *Total of Expense* figures, the difference is computed as *Net Profit* and is shown at *left* side of the Profit & Loss Statement
  - o If the *Total of Expense* figures is greater than *Total of Income* figures, the difference is computed as *Net Loss* and is normally shown at *right* side of the Profit & Loss Statement.

Format: At *Profit & Loss Statement* (F-1), Click *F1: Condensed / Detailed* toggle button:

- o **F1:Condensed:** Only the Primary Top Level Account Groups are displayed
- o **F1:Detailed:** The Next Level Groups / Ledger

Configuration

Show Vertical Profit & Loss	?	**No**
Show Percentages	?	**No**
Show with Gross Profit	?	**Yes**
Appearance of Names	:	**Name Only**
Scale Factor for Values	:	**Default**

F-2A: P L Statement Configuration

Report Titles
Profit & Loss A/c

Scale Factor for Values	:	**Default**
Format	:	**Detailed**
Show Vertical Profit & Loss	?	**No**
Show Percentages	?	**No**
Show with Gross Profit	?	**Yes**

F-2B:P L Satement Printing screen

Accounts are displayed, The Top Level Groups are shown in Bold. The Next Level Groups are shown in Normal Font while the Ledger Accounts are shown in Italics (F-1)

Initially, the P L statement is shown in Condensed Form, showing only the top level Reserved Groups are shown

P L Statement Printing: At the *P L Statement Display* screen (F-1), click *P:Print* button to get *P L Statement Printing Screen* (F-2B). Set the printing options as desired, to get the *P L Statement* in print, which is similar to Display (F-1)

Configuration: At the *P L Statement Display* screen (F-1), click *F12: Configure* to get P L Statement Configuration screen (F-2A) showing the options to customize the contents of the Report.

provisions for: Income Tax, Dividend, appropriation of Profit to Reserve / Capital Accounts etc.

These appropriation of Profit / Loss are to be entered through Journal Voucher. The entries of transfer of amount from / to Profit & Loss Account do not affect Net Profit but are reflected under the respective Reserves / Provisions / Profit & Loss Account

FAQ: Frequently Asked Questions

FAQ-1: In a Proprietorship firm, how to transfer the entire amount of Current Year loss to Capital Account

Ans: You have to transfer the net current year loss from Profit & Loss Account to Proprietor's Capital Account, through Journal Voucher as follows:

Ledger Alteration (Secondary)

Name : **Stock-In-Trade**

Under : **Stock-In-Hand** *(Current Assets)*

Opening Balance (on 1-Apr-2012) : 3,50,000.00 Dr

Closing Balance **31-Dec-2012 : 3,50,000.00 Dr**
31-Mar-2013 : 4,00,000.00 Dr

F-3A: Closing Stock value entry in Stock Ledger

Profit & Loss A/c — **ABC CO Ltd 12-13** — Ctrl + M

Particulars	ABC CO Ltd 12-13 1-Apr-2009 to 31-Mar-2013		Particulars	ABC CO Ltd 12-13 1-Apr-2009 to 31-Mar-2013	
Opening Stock		**3,80,000.00**	**Sales Accounts**		**36,70,000.00**
Stock-In-Trade	*3,50,000.00*		*Sale - Products*	*30,00,000.00*	
Stock In Transit	*30,000.00*		*Sale - Services*	*7,00,000.00*	
Purchase Accounts		**14,00,000.00**	*Excise Duty on Sales*	*(-)30,000.00*	
Purchases - Stock-in-Trade	*14,00,000.00*		**Direct Incomes**		**1,20,000.00**
Direct Expenses		**75,000.00**	*Other Operating Income*	*1,20,000.00*	
Job Contract Charges	*75,000.00*		**Closing Stock**		**4,30,000.00**
Gross Profit c/o		**23,65,000.00**	*Stock-In-Trade*	*4,00,000.00*	
			Stock In Transit	*30,000.00*	
		42,20,000.00			**42,20,000.00**
Indirect Expenses		**14,21,000.00**	***Gross Profit b/f***		**23,65,000.00**
Finance Cost	*2,00,000.00*		**Indirect Incomes**		**4,37,000.00**
Other Expenses	*6,03,000.00*		*Dividend Income*	*30,000.00*	
DEpreciation Current Year	*6,18,000.00*		*Interest Received*	*4,00,000.00*	
Nett Profit		**13,81,000.00**	*Profit on Sale of Fixed Asset*	*5,000.00*	
			Unclaimed Credit Balance Written Off	*2,000.00*	
Total		**28,02,000.00**	**Total**		**28,02,000.00**

F-3B; P L Statement showing Closing Stock values

03 Stock value in Final Accounts

The *Closing Stock* value is shown in *P L Statement* (F-1) as well as in *Balance Sheet* (F-1/01-11). In traditional system of accounting, you normally have to make a Journal entry for Closing Stock Adjustment. But in Tally, you do not have to make any Journal Entry. Just enter the Closing Stock Value for respective date in Stock Ledger Accounts.

Entry of Closing Stock Value: At Gateway of Tally, select *Accounts Info>Ledger>Alter*. Select the Stock Account (the Ledger Accounts under *Stock-in Hand* group in which you had entered Opening Stock Value at Opening Balance). Now enter Date & Value for Closing Stock for respective Date (F-3A). Consequently, the Closing Stock value for the respective date is shown in *P L Statement* (F-3B) and also in *Balance Sheet* (F-1/01-11)

> **Note:** *The Closing Stock Value do not appear in Trial Balance*

04 P & L Appropriation

At year end, you have to make various Journal entries for

- Proprietor's Capital Account Dr (Net Loss of current year)
- Profit & Loss Account Cr (Net Loss of current year)

In case of Profit, the above Journal Entry would be changed as follows:

- Dr Profit & Loss Account (Net Profit of current year)
- Cr Proprietor's Capital Account (Net Profit of current year)

This Journal Entry should be made only after finalization of Accounts. If there is any subsequent modification in accounts which affect the net Profit, the Journal Voucher has to be edited suitably changing the amount of voucher accordingly.

In the Balance Sheet, the amount transferred from Profit & Loss Account would be shown as a separate Item as *Transferred.*

FAQ-2: In a Partnership firm, how to transfer the entire amount of Profit for the current year to respective Partner's Capital Account in the agreed Profit Sharing Ratio

Ans: You have to transfer the net current year Profit from Profit & Loss Account to Proprietor's Capital Account, through Journal Voucher as follows

- Profit & Loss Account Dr (Amount of Net Profit)
  - Partner 1 Capital Account Cr (Share of Partner 1 of the Net Profit of current year)
  - Partner 2 Capital Account Cr (Share of Partner 2 of Net Profit of current year)

  (....... Like this for each Partner)

FAQ-3: In a Company, the Directors decided to transfer Rs 50000 from Profit for the current year to General Reserve Account. How to transfer the Amount to General Reserve.

Ans: You have to transfer Rs 50000 from current Profit & Loss A/c to General Reserves (create *General Reserve* Account under the Group *Reserves & Surplus*), through Journal Voucher as follows:

- Profit & Loss Account Dr 50000
  - General Reserve Account Cr 50000

FAQ-4: In a Company, the Directors decided to show the current year loss to Misc Expenses in Balance Sheet, instead of showing the loss amount under Profit & Loss Account

Ans: You have to transfer the current year loss to Misc Expenses (create an Account Misc Expenses under the Group Misc Expenses (Asset)), through Journal Voucher as follows:

- Misc Expenses Dr (Amount of current year loss)
- Profit & Loss Account Cr (Amount of current year loss)

FAQ-5: What you get when you drill down through a Group in P L Statement Display

Ans: You get Group Summary showing the Balances of next Level Groups / Ledger Accounts of the selected Group

FAQ-6: What you get when you drill down through a Ledger in P L Statement Display

Ans: You get Ledger Monthly Summary showing the monthly summary figures for each month of the selected Ledger Account

01 Balance Sheet

Balance Sheet shows the Assets & Liabilities at the close of the specified Date, in 2 Parts, divided by a vertical line.

- **Liabilities (or Credit Side):**The *Left* Part shows the top level Groups of *Capital & Liabilities* (Loans & Current Liabilities). The figures represent the total of Net Amount of all Ledger Accounts under the respective Group.
- **Assets (or Debit Side):** The *Right* Part contains the top *Assets* Groups (Fixed Assets, Investments & Current Assets). The figures represent the total of Net Amount of all Ledger Accounts under the respective Group.

Current Year Profit Loss: The Net Profit / Loss and appropriation therefrom are shown at Liabilities side (*Net Loss* is shown as negative figure)

Balance Sheet — ABC CO Ltd 12-13 — Ctrl + M

Liabilities	ABC CO Ltd 12-13 as at 31-Mar-2013	
Capital Account		20,00,000.00
Equity Shares	*8,70,000.00*	
Prefernce Shares	*50,000.00*	
Reserves & Surplus	*10,80,000.00*	
Share Application Money Pending Allotment		
Loans (Liability)		1,10,23,000.00
Bank OD A/c	*71,53,000.00*	
Secured Loans	*18,40,000.00*	
Unsecured Loans	*20,30,000.00*	
Current Liabilities		12,55,000.00
Provisions	*3,30,000.00*	
Sundry Creditors	*3,50,000.00*	
Duties & Taxes	*1,30,000.00*	
Deferred Tax Liability	*1,00,000.00*	
Other Current Liabilties	*3,45,000.00*	
Profit & Loss A/c		12,81,000.00
Opening Balance	*2,00,000.00*	
Current Period	*13,81,000.00*	
Less: Transferred	*3,00,000.00*	
Total		1,55,59,000.00

Assets	ABC CO Ltd 12-13 as at 31-Mar-2013	
Fixed Assets		1,10,07,000.00
Intangible Assets	*21,00,000.00*	
Tangible Assets	*74,07,000.00*	
Capital Work in Progress	*15,00,000.00*	
Investments		7,90,000.00
Non Trade Investment Non Current	*1,70,000.00*	
Non Trade Investments Current	*1,20,000.00*	
Trade Investment Non Current	*3,80,000.00*	
Trade Investments (Current)	*1,20,000.00*	
Current Assets		37,62,000.00
Closing Stock	*4,30,000.00*	
Deposits (Asset)	*70,000.00*	
Loans & Advances (Asset)	*2,70,000.00*	
Sundry Debtors	*21,50,000.00*	
Cash-in-Hand	*1,70,000.00*	
Bank Accounts	*6,72,000.00*	
Total		1.55,59,000.00

F-1: Balance Sheet Display (Detailed)

> ***Note:*** *The Closing Stock value entered in the Closing Stock Ledger (F-3A/01-10) is shown under the Current Asset (F-1)*

02 Balance Sheet Display

At Gateway (F-1A/01-02), click *Balance Sheet* to get Balance Sheet (F-1)

- **Format**: Click <u>F1</u>*: Condensed / Detailed* toggle button:
  - o **<u>F1</u>:Condensed:** Only the Primary Top Level Account Groups are displayed
  - o **<u>F1</u>:Detailed:** The Next Level Groups / Ledger Accounts are displayed, The Top Level Groups are shown in Bold. The Next Level Groups are shown in Normal Font while the Ledger Accounts are shown in Italics (F-1)

Initially, the Balance Sheet is shown in Condensed Form, showing only the top level Reserved Groups

- **Configuration**: At Balance Sheet Display screen (F-1), click *F12: Configure* to get *Balance Sheet Configuration* screen showing the options to customize the contents of the Report (F-2B)

03 Balance Sheet Printing

At *Balance Sheet Display* screen (F-1), click <u>P</u>*:Print* button to get Balance Sheet Printing screen (F-2A). The contents and options for both Print & Display Format of Balance Sheet are similar. Set the printing options (F-2A) as desired, to get the Balance Sheet in print (similar to Balance Sheet Display (F-1)

Report Titles
Balance Sheet

Scale Factor for Values	:	Default
Format	:	Detailed
Show Vertical Balance Sheet	?	No
Profit or Loss, both as Liability	?	No
Show Percentages	?	No
Show Working Capital figures	?	No
Method of showing Balance Sheet	?	Liabilities / Assets

F-2A:Balance Sheet Printing screen

Configuration

Show Vertical Balance Sheet	?	No
Profit or Loss, both as Liability	?	No
Show Percentages	?	No
Show Working Capital figures	?	No
Method of showing Balance Sheet	?	Liabilities / Assets
Appearance of Names	:	Name Only
Scale Factor for Values	:	Default

F-2B: Balance Sheet Configuration

FAQ: Frequently Asked Questions

FAQ-1: What is Balance Sheet

Ans: Balance Sheet is a Statement showing the Assets & Liabilities as on a specified Date

FAQ-2: After finalising the Accounts for FY 12-13 (1.4.12 to 31.3.13), you printed Balance Sheet for the Period 1.4.12 to 31.3.13 and another one for the period 1.10.12 to 31.3.13. In what respect the two Balance Sheets will differ?

Ans: Both the Balance Sheet would be similar as both of them depict the position of Liabilities & Assets as on 31.3.13.

FAQ-3: Does the Balance Sheet Display show Balance of Ledger Accounts also?

Ans: When you Display Balance Sheet (GoT>Balance Sheet), initially it is displayed in *Condensed* Form, showing only the Primary Major Groups are shown. Click *F1:Detailed* button (or Alt+F1 key) to show the next level details (next level Groups / Ledgers). So, if there is any ledger account placed immediately under any of the Major Group of Balance Sheet, that Ledger only would be displayed in Balance Sheet in *Detailed* Format.

FAQ-4: In Balance Sheet in detailed format, how do you identify, which one is Group and which one is Ledger Account

Ans: In Detailed Balance Sheet, the Group Names are shown in Normal Font, while Ledger Account Names are shown in *Italics*

FAQ-5: What you get when you drill down through a Group in Balance Sheet Display

Ans: You get Group Summary showing the Balances of next Level Groups / Ledger Accounts of the selected Group

FAQ-6: What you get when you drill down through a Ledger in Balance Sheet Display

Ans: You get Ledger Monthly Summary showing the break up figures (monthly summary figures) for each month of the selected Ledger Account.

New Year Accounts 01-12

01 New Year Accounts

After the Accounts of Current Year is closed, you have to create New Year Accounts, transferring the Balances (as per Balances Sheet of the current year) of Real & Personal Accounts to the Opening Balance of new Year Accounts.

> **Note:** *In Tally, you do not have to create Journal Entries for Opening Balance (as you do in traditional way)., bu t the Opening balance is entered in Ledger Account Masters*

02 *Starting New Year Accounts*

Create a New Company for the New Year (in the same way you created the first company- F-2/01-01). Having created the next year company, you may create the Masters as usual, in the same way you created the masters for the first company (and enter the Opening Balance of the new year from the Closing Balances of Previous Year).

> **Note:** *When you create separate Tally Company for each Year, to distinguish the respective Company, add the FY at the end of Name. For example, for the Company* ABC Academy, *enter the Company name ABC Academy 12-13 (for FY 12-13), ABC Academy 13-14 (for FY 13-14), to identify the Company Properly., as you cannot create multiple Companies of same name,. So, add the identifier at Name. However, you may enter same Name (ABC Academy) at Mailing Name for all the Financial Years.*

FAQ: Frequently Asked Questions

FAQ-1: How to create a Company for New Year (e.g creation of Company for FI 15-16 at the end of FY 14-15).

Ans: New Year Company Creation:Create a new Company for Accounts of next Financial Year (FY 15-16) in the same way as you created the Current Year Company for FY !4-15. At Gateway, click F3:Cmp Info (or press Alt+F3) to get *Company Info* menu (F-1A/01-01). At Company Info Menu (F-1A/01-01), select Create Company to get Company Creation screen (F-2/01-01).

At *Company Creation* screen (F-2A/01-01).

- **Company Name**: At *Name*, enter the Company name and suffix for the Financial Year to uniquely create and identify Companies for each Financial Year separately(e.g ABC 15-16)
- **Mailing Name:** At *Mailing Name*, the Company Name entered is carried. Remove the FY suffix (e,g ABC)
- **Financial Year From**: .Enter the Start date of the new Financial Year [e.g 1-4-2015]

Press Cntrl + A to save the new Financial Year Company

01 Accounts Data

Accounts Data are created with lot of efforts. It is the life of business. The business operation may get standstill if the data is lost or damaged.

A Computer System, after all, is a machine. At any time, the computer may fail functioning for some reason. The data in computer may get damaged due to disk failure, virus infection or any other reason. To mitigate the risk of losing data and keep the regular work going, you should regularly keep another set of data (a duplicate copy of the running data) in another place, so that you can use the copied set of data and continue working, if the original gets damaged or lost.

02 Data Backup

BACKUP means keeping a copy of working data at another place for safety, or for moving Data from one place to another.

- If the current working data is lost or damaged
- If you need to install data in another Computer

You can Restore the BACKUP data and continue working.

Back Up Process: At Gateway of Tally, click *F3: Cmp Info* button (or press Alt+F3 keys) to get *Company Info* Menu (F-1/01-01). Select *Backup* to get Back Up screen (F-1)

Data Locations for Back Up: At Data Back Up screen (F-1), specify the location of existing Data to be backed up and the location where the backed up data is to be stored, as follows:

- **Data Source Location:** At *Source*, the data directory of current company appears, from where data to be Backed Up. Change it if Back Up is to be taken from other place (normally you need not change it).
- **Data Destination Locations:** At *Destination*, enter the folder name (e.g c:\Tallydatabackup) where the backed up data would be stored (you may define a folder, a network drive or another drive (e.g to take Back up in Pen Drive / external disk). It is a good practice to keep data in external drive and store in another computer system.

> **Note:** *You may Back Up multiple Companies Data in one shot to keep a combined Back Up data file (named TBK900.001)*

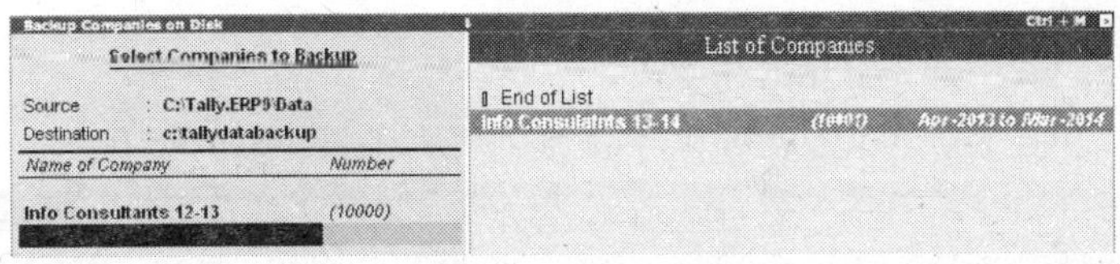

F-1: Data Back Up

Companies Selection: Now select the Company to be Backed Up, from the list of Companies in source directory, appearing at *List of Companies* at the right Part (F-1). As you select the Company for Back Up, the name of selected Company (selected for Back Up) is added in the list of Companies to be Backed Up (the Companies which will be backed up in the Back Up process) at the left part, and is removed from the List of Companies in the right Part (Companies which may be added in the list of Companies to be Backed up). Having selected the Companies to be Backed up, select *End of File* from the list of Companies.

This way, you may select several Companies to back up in one shot (F-1). Click *Yes* to start Back Up process.

All the selected Companies will be backed up one by one and placed together in ONE Back Up file (named TBK 900.001) in the destination drive (e.g c:\tallydatabackup)

During the process, the Name of the Company currently being Backed up is displayed showing the progress status.

> **Note:** *When you take Back Up, the older Back Up is overwritten. So, be careful when you take Back Up of several Companies together. You must take Back Up of all the Companies always, otherwise the Back Up of the left out Company would be lost. This is a serious risk of taking Back Up of Multiple Companies.*
>
> *For example, you have taken Back p of 3 companies, Comp A, Comp B, and Comp C. After you have done some work with Company C and take a Back Up of only Company C. The Back Up of Comp A and Comp B will be lost as the Back of C taken last will not contain any data of Comp A Comp B.*

03 Data Restoration

If the current working data gets damaged, you should restore the backed up data to get the data back in the current working directory, in functional condition. Only Backed Up data through Tally Back Up process (like TBK900.001, TABK900.001 etc) can be Restored.

Data Restoration Process: At Gateway of Tally click _F3: Cmp Info_ button to _Company Info_ screen (F-1/01-01). Select _Restore_ to get Restore screen (F-2).

03.01 Data Locations for Restoration

Now specify the location of Backed Up data to be restored and the location of the current working directory where the data is to be restored (F-2)

- At _Destination_ field, enter the current working data path where the Back Up data is to be copied (the current location is displayed).
- At _Source_ field, enter the data path from where the Backed Data is to be copied from.

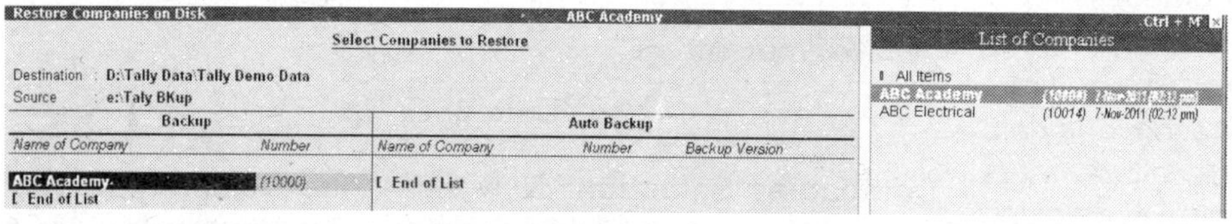

F-2: Data Restoration

The Source & Destination folder must be different, otherwise the existing data may be overwritten and get damaged. For your convenience, the Source & Destination drive of last Restoration process are populated in the respective fields, which you may change if necessary.

03.02 Data Restoration Process

At Name of Companies column, select the Companies whose data is to be restored, one by one. You may select _All Items_ to restore data of all available companies (F- 2)

Click _Yes_ at _Accept?_ to start Restoration process.

The Name of the Company being Restored is displayed showing the progress status during the process.

When you Restore data, you get the old backed up data in the current working directory. So, you lose the data entered / updated after the date of last Back Up. You have to enter / update those data again.

04 Data Rewriting

Rewriting means reconstructing inconsistent data. When any part of data gets damaged and Tally fails to open a company, you should repair the data through Rewrite Option.

You also need to re-write when you open a company created by older version or Release of Tally (e.g you open a company created in rel 1.x of Tally.ERP 9 with Rel 3.x).

At Gateway, press _Alt+Ctrl+R_ to get _Rewrite Company_ Screen (F-3). At _Rewrite Company_ Screen (F-3), select the Company which you wish to rewrite. Press _Yes_ to Rewrite

F-3: Data Re-writing

FAQ: Frequently Asked Questions

FAQ-1: How you can take current data Backup in a Pen drive?

Ans: Take Backup in a Pen drive (assuming your pen drive is F:\) of the following ways:

- At Gateway of Tally, click _F3: Cmp Info_ button (or press _Alt+F3_ keys) to get Company Info Menu (F-1A/01-01). Select _Backup_ to get Backup Screen (F-1)
    - o At _Source_, the source data directory where data of the company is stored, is displayed.
    - o At _Destination_ field enter the pen drive path (e.g. F:\) where the backed up data would be stored.
- Select the Companies to be Backed Up. Click _Yes_ to start Back Up process.

A Progress bar shows the Backup operation and you get back to Menu. A Backup file "TBK 900.001" is created in the specified Destination drive (e.g. F:\).

FAQ-2: How you can take Backup in a separate directory named "d:\Tally data Backup" in your hard Disk?

Ans: Take Backup in a separate directory "d:\Tally data Backup" as follows:

- At _Source_ field in Backup Screen, the source data directory (where the data is stored) is displayed.
- At _Destination_ field, enter the directory path name (e.g. "d:\Tally data Backup") where the backed up data would be stored.
- Select the Companies to be Backed Up. Click _Yes_ to start Back Up process.
- Click _Yes_ to start Back Up process.

A Progress bar shows the Backup operation and you get back to Menu. A Backup file "TBK 900.001" is created in the specified Destination drive.

FAQ-3: How you can take Backup of 3 Companies in separate files?

Ans: When you backup in same directory, previous Backup of any company would be over written every time, because Tally creates Backup file with name TBK900.001 for all files. So, you have to create 3 separate folders to store Back Up for each company.

For example, you have 3 companies (Binapani Bhander, B.K. Pvt. Ltd., ACC Corp. Pvt. Ltd.), Take separate backup as follows:

- At Backup screen (F-1), select a company (e.g. Binapani Bhander). The data directory name appears at source drive field
- At Destination drive, enter the directory path name for the first company (e.g. "D:\Tally data Backup\Binapani) where the Backed up data of Binapani Bhander would be stored. After selecting the Company to be Backed up, select *End of File* from the list of Companies. The Backup file of the Company, named TBK.900.001 will be stored in the specified Destination drive

In this way, select the second company (BK Pvt Ltd) and enter the respective directory name at Destination (e.g. D:\Tally data Back up\ BK Pvt Ltd)

Similarly, select the third company (ACC Corp Pvt Ltd) and enter the respective directory name at Destination (e.g. D:\Tally data Back up\ACC Corp Pvt Ltd)

A Backup file named TBK.900.001 will be created in each of the 3 directories. From the folder name, you will be able to identify the name of the respective Company (because each of the Back Up file will have same name (TBK.900.001)

Part 2

Advanced Accounting

In this Part, we discus about advanced Features and extended application areas of Financial Accounting.

Organisations desirous of using Advanced Accounting Features of Tally.ERP 9 (beyond the default Basic Accounting features), and to Customise the Input & Reporting as per their own needs, will find this Part useful.

- **Configuration Set Up** explains the various General options to customise and avail extended features of Financial Accounting to personalise and get more out of the System.
- **Company Creation** explains additional info for the Company & advanced features for storing data at desired places, Auto Back Up, Data Security, Base Currency properties set up, Multiple addresses & about Group Companies.
- **Gateway of Tally** gives details of various tools and facilities that can be invoked from Gateway, the Tally Main Menu and Help System.
- **Chart of Accounts** explains the hierarchy and properties of Reserved Groups & Ledgers, the Basic Structure of the Accounting System of Tally.
- **Accounts Masters** covers advanced features and configuration options of Account Groups & Ledgers
- **Multiple Accounts Masters creation** describes the alternate smarter way of creation & maintenance of Accounts Masters.
- **Voucher Types** explains creation of peer Voucher Types and configuration of its components & properties.
- **Voucher Class** explains creation of Voucher Types with advanced capabilities, customising the Voucher Type properties based on user specified parameters
- **Voucher Entry** describes the advanced features of voucher data entry process and ways of customisation of contents and display of Voucher data.
- **Single Mode Voucher Entry** describes an alternate & contemporary method of entry of Voucher data
- **Interest** elaborates the method of setting Interest Parameters for computation of Interest for Account Current. It also explains user specified multi rate over-riding Interest Computation methods.
- **Reports Display** explains the process of Display of Reports on screen, drill down, trace back and sideways traversing through related reports links, Reports customisation, defining & creation of Columnar Reports with user specified columns.
- **Reports Printing** explains the process of configuring the Report Contents & Printing of Reports from Screen Display. It also explains Multi Account printing of regular Books of Accounts and other Accounting Reports.

  The next few chapters explain several reports in various formats and contents. Each chapter explains report specific configuration options and buttons to set the report contents and layout.
- **Queries** explains how to get instant ad hoc info and filtered reports based on user specified query parameters.
- **Data Maintenance** explains advanced steps and processes of Data Back Up.
- **New Year Accounts explains** how to split a Company to create new New Year's Accounts transferring the Masters & carrying previous year closing balances.

Part 2: Advanced Accounting is addressed to users who intend to use the advanced features of Financial Accounting. Basic users may skip this Part.

Configuration Set Up

01 Configuration & Features

In previous section, we have discussed the operational methods with basic default options (pre-set at the time of Company Creation). To meet the requirements of wide section of users of various levels, Tally provides many Configuration options. You may re-set the respective Configuration options, as per your requirements and needs.

The following are various tools through which you may set various properties within Tally

- **General Configuration Set Up**: At Gateway of Tally (GoT), click *F12:Cofigure> General* to get Configuration Menu, which contains a host of Configuration options under each Menu Item. The Configuration options apply to all Companies whose data are placed in the same data folder
- **Features Set Up**: At Gateway of Tally (GoT), click *F11:Features* to get Company Features Menu. In the same way as Configuration Options, you may set the Features options, which apply to the respective Company for which it is set.
- **Current Configuration:** At the Current Entry/ Display / Printing screen, click *F12:Configure* to set Configuration options for the current task / operation being performed.
- **Buttons**: In the current screen, you may get a set of buttons to invoke various related current reports / actions

In this chapter, we discuss about common configuration options applicable in general. All other Master / Voucher / Report specific options are discussed at relevant topic, in respective chapters

02 General Configuration Set Up

At Gateway, Click *F12:Configure* button to get *Configuration Menu*. At *Configuration Menu*, select *General* to get *General Configuration* screen.

> **Note:** *The General Configuration Options apply by* Default *to all the Companies, whose data are placed under whose data are placed in the Data Directory specified at* Location of Data Files *specified at* GoT>F12:Configuration>Data Configuration. *However, most of the options may be re-set dynamically at Current Configuration screen (Configuration Options, applicable for that instance only).*

02.01 Country Configuration

To set the features applicable for the selected Country, Under the section *Country Details*, at the option *Use Accounting Terminologies of* (F-1A):

- Select *India / SAARC* (*default*) to select the Accounting Principles and Financial Statements as applicable to India (F-1B)
- Select *International* to select the International Accounting Principles and Financial Statements, for other countries

> **Note:** *Users of India need not change the default option (India/SAARC)*

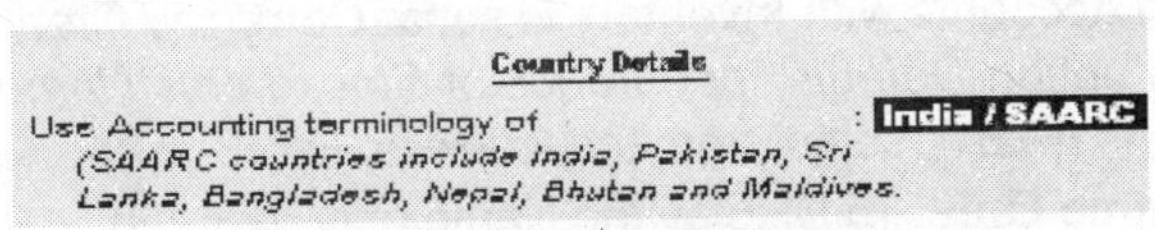

F-1A: Country Details option set up

F- 1B: Option list of Countries

02.02 Ledger Names Styles

In Reports and Documents, normally the Name of Master is printed. However, sometimes the *First Alias* Name (P-01/02-05), or the Name along with *First Alias* Name is shown.

> **Note:** *At General Configuration (*GoT>F12:Configuration> General), *you may set the default option which will be used in Reports Display & Printing as* Default. *However, you may change the default option at the specific Report Configuration. The changed option will be applicable for that specific instance only.*

To set the default format for appearance of Account Ledger Name. At the option *Default Appearance of Names in Report* (F-2A), select from the list (F-2B) as follows.:

- **Name Only**: To Display (default) the Name of the Ledger Account
- **Alias Only**: To Display the First Alias Name of the Ledger Account
- **Name (Alias)**: To Display the name followed by First Alias in parenthesis of the Account

- **Alias (Name)**: To Display the Alias Name followed by Name in parenthesis of the Account (where Alias is specified)

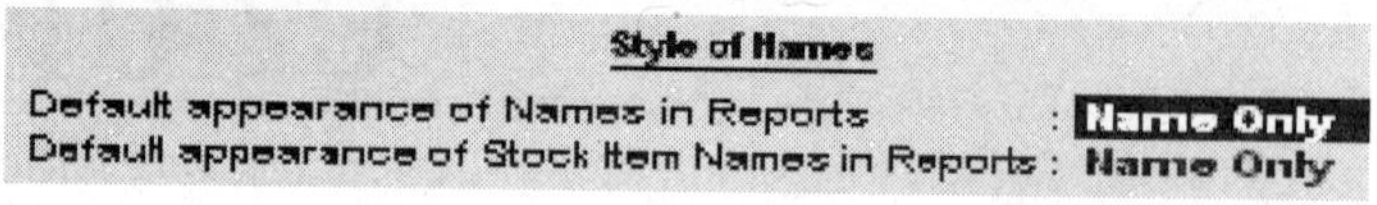

F- 2A: Names Styles set up options

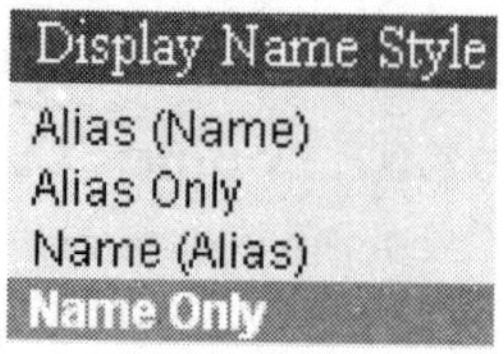

F-2B: Accounts Masters Names Styles List

> **Note:** *If you are using Accounts Codes through Alias, then you may set Name (Alias) or (Alias (names) as default Name Style so that the Accounts Codes are also printed alongwith Account Names, in all Reports*

02.03 Stock Item Names Styles

To set the default format for appearance of Stock Item Name (when Accounts with Inventory is set at Company Creation, at the option *Default Appearance of Stock Items Names in Reports* (F-2A), select from the following list (F-2C):

- **Name Only**: To Display the Name only (default)
- **Alias Only**: To Display the First Alias Name only
- **Name (Alias)**: To Display the name followed by First Alias in parenthesis
- **Alias (Name)**: To Display the Alias Name followed by Name in parenthesis (where Alias is specified)
- **Name (Description)**: To Display the Name followed by Description in parenthesis
- **Description (Name)**: To Display the Item Description (where specified) followed by Item Name in parenthesis
- **Part Number Alias Only**: To Display the First Part Number Alias only
- **Name (Part Number)**: To Display the name followed by First Part Number in parenthesis
- **Alias (Part No)**: To Display the First Alias Name followed by First Part Number in parenthesis (where Alias & Part Number, both are specified)
- **Part Number Alias (Part No)**: To Display the First Part Number Alias followed by First Part Number in parenthesis (where Part Number Alias & Part Number, both are specified)
- **Part Number (Description)**: To Display the First Part Number followed by Description in parenthesis (where Part Number & Description, both are specified)
- **Part Number Only**: To Display the First Part Number only
- **Part Number (Part No Alias)**: To Display the First Part Number followed by First Part Number Alias in parenthesis (where Part Number Alias & Part Number, both are specified).

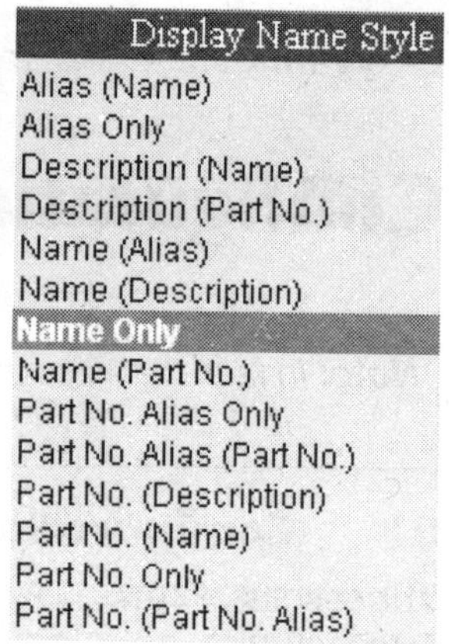

F- 2C:Inventory Masters Names Styles List

> **Note:** *If you are using Stock Item Codes through Alias, then you may set Name (Alias) or Alias (names) as default Name Style so that, in Reports, the Stock Item Codes are also printed alongwith Stock Item Names.*

02.04 Date Format

Date Format: Tally displays *Date* in 2 formats (also referred as *Date Mask*), as follows:

- **Long Format**: This Format is used in Report Header and Voucher Date. The Date is shown in dd-mmm-yyyy format (like 25 Jan 2013). The Date part is shown in 1 or 2 digits (e.g, 9, 19 etc). The Month part shows first 3 letters of the respective Month (e.g Jan), followed by 4 digit Year (e.g 2014). Each Part of the Date is separated by Date Part separator. The Long Format cannot be changed but its Date Part separator may be changed (explained below).
- **Short Format**: This Format is used to show Voucher Date in Display & Reports The Date part is shown in 1 or 2 digits (e.g, 9, 19 etc). The Month part shows 1 or 2 digit for Month (e. 4, 12, etc), followed by 4 digit Year (e.g 2013). Each Part of the Date is separated by Date Part separator. The short Format (Mask) & Date Part separator, may be changed.

Setting the Date Format: To set the Short Date Format & Date Part Separator, at *F12:Configure>General* (F-3A), at the section *Style of Dates* (recommended NOT to change he default settings)

Short Date Format: At the field *Style of Short Date*, select the desired Format from the list (F-3B)

- **Date Part Separator**: Normally hyphen (-) is used as Date Part Separator. At *Separator used in Short date*, you may type other characters (like Front Slash (/), Hyphen (-). Dot (.) etc), to separate each part of the Date.

Short date Format

- **dd-mm-yy**: 1/2 Digit Date, 1/2 Digit Month, 4 digit Year
- **mm-dd-yy**: 1/2 Digit Month, 1/2 Digit Date, 4 digit Year

- **yy-mm-dd**: 4 digit Year, 1/2 Month, 1/2 Digit Date

F-3A: Date set up options

> **Note:** *In fact, the Year part is always shown in 4 digits (yyyy Format)*

F-3B: Short Date Format List

The results of various Formats and separators are shown in F-3C o F-3I.

F-3C: dd-mm-yyyy format Separator (-)

F-3D: dd-mm-yyyy format Separator (-)

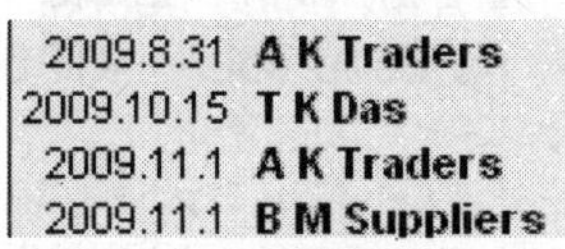

F-3E: yyyy-mm-dd format Separator (.)

F-3F: mm-dd-yyyy format Separator (/)

The Period is shown in Long Format (dd-mmm-yyyy), while in Reports & Vouchers, Date is shown in short Format.

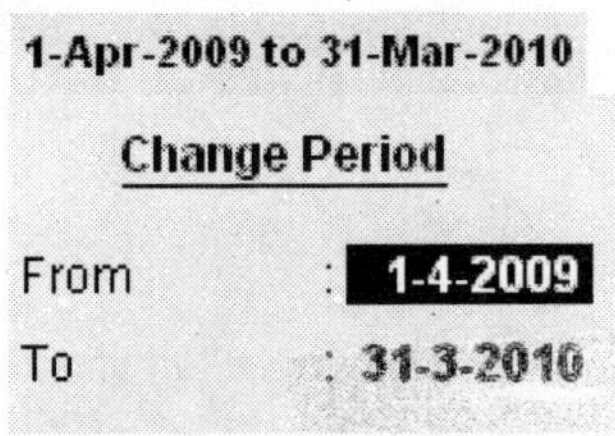

F-3G:dd-mm-yyyy format Separator (-)

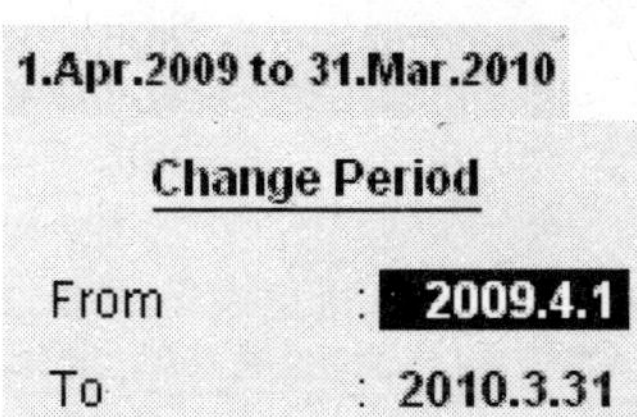

F-3H: yyyy-mm-dd format Separator (.)

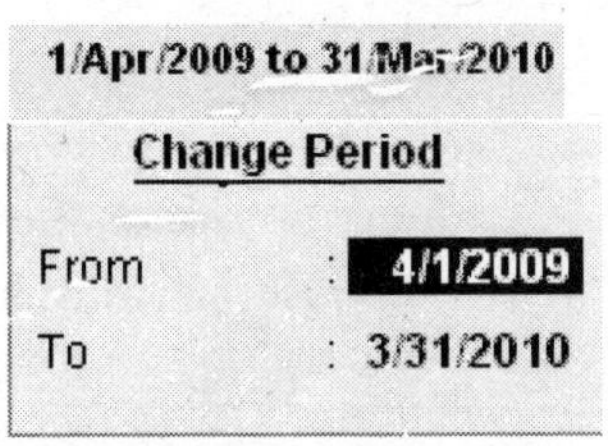

F-3I: mm-dd-yyyy format Separator (/)

> **Note**
>
> At General Configuration, you may set the Date Mask & Date Separator for Date Format, as follows:
>
> - Date Separator for Long Format (but not Date Mask)
> - Date Mask & Date Separator for Short Format
>
> The default Date Format cannot be changed during entry or in Report. You can set 3 letter Mont h Format (like Jan, Jun etc), in Long Format only in Report Headers but not for transaction date in shrt Format (Voucher Date).

02.05 Number Format

You may set the default options for formatting of Numbers. At *GoT>F12:Configure>General*, under the section *Configuration of Number (*F-4A*)*, set as follows:

- **Decimal Separator:** At the option *Decimal Character to use* (F-4A), Set the character to be used as decimal separator (to separate the mantissa and decimal part of a number). The default Decimal Separator is (. dot), which you may change (e.g – hyphen).
- **Thousands Separator:** At the option *Thousands Separator to use (*F-4A*)*, Set the character to be used as Thousands separator (to separate the position parts of a number). The default Decimal Separator is (, comma), which you may change.
- **Negative Amount Sign**: At the option *Put Sign before Currency / Unit Symbols (*F-4A*)*
  - o Set Yes to show the negative sign before the negative value (e.g (-'10))
  - o Set *No* to show the Negative sign after the currency symbol (e.g. '(-10)).

  However, for positive values, no sign symbol is shown.
- **Amount Format:** For better readability, figures are normally delimited by comma (e.g 32,734.59). Tally provides 2 types of Formatting, to represent figures of One Lac(100000) & above. To set the Amount Format, at the option *Show Numbers in Millions (*F-4A*)*,
  - o **Lacs Formatting**: Set *No* to express in Lacs (e.g 12,34,56,789, 1,23,456 etc). In India, traditionally Lacs format is widely used to represent figures in Rs One Lac & above (F-4C).
  - o **Millions Formatting**: Set *Yes* to express in Million format (e.g 123,456,789). Millions format is widely used Western Countries and by Foreign / Multinational Companies (F-4B).

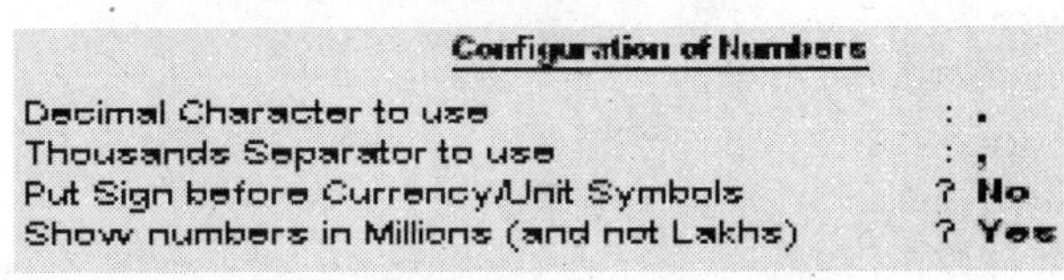

F-4A: Configuration of Numbers Formatting

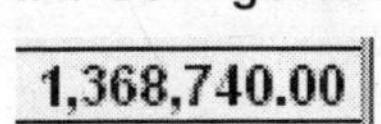

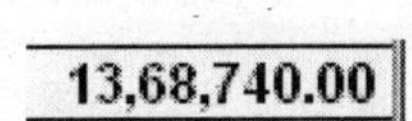

F-4B:Millions Formatting F-4C:Lacs Formatting

> **Note:** *You may set the Lakhs / Millions setting as per your choice. Do not change the other default settings.*

> **Note:** *After you change any configuration under* Style of Dates *or* Configuration of Numbers, *you have to reload Tally.ERP 9 to make the changes effective.*

02.06 Alert Beeps

Tally invokes various alert messages (e.g error encountered, non-permitted values entered etc to draw attention of the user), with beep sound. You may activate / disable the *Alert Beep* as follows.

At *GoT>F12:Configure>General*, under the section *Other Options*, at the option *Tally Alert using beeps* **(F-5)**

- Set Yes (default) to raise a beep sound at Alert Messages
- Set *No* to show Alert Messages without any beep sound

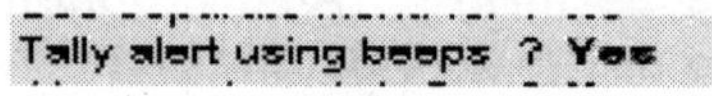

F-5: Alert Beep option set up

FAQ: Frequently Asked Questions

FAQ-1: I like to display / print amount figures in Lacs format (e.g.1,23,537). How do I set it?

Ans: At *GoT>F12:Configure>General*, under the section *Configuration of Number* (F-4A), at *Show Numbers in Millions (and not Lakhs):*

- Set Yes to show the amount in Millions (e.g 123,456,789, 123,456 etc).
- Set *No* to express in Lacs (e.g 12,34,56,789, 1,23,456 etc).

In India, traditionally Lacs format is widely used to represent figures in Rs One Lac & above (F-4C).

After making the changes, re-start Tally to get the effects of changes made.

FAQ-2: I like to display / print Date in dd/mm/yyyy format. How do I set it?

Ans: At *GoT>F12:Configure>General*, under the section *Style of Dates* (F-3A),

- At Style of Short Date, select dd-mm-yy
- At *Separator used in Short date*, type Front slash (/). Consequently, dates would be displayed (e.g 1st April 2013 as 1/4/2013).

After making the changes, You should re-start Tally to get the effects of changes made.

FAQ-3: I like to stop Alert Beeps How do I set it?

Ans: At *GoT>F12:Configure>General*, under the section *Other Options* (F-5), set *No* at *Tally Alert using beeps*. In case of error messages or Alerts, no beep sound will be heard (to work silently).

Company Creation 02-02

01 Company

The Term *Company* in Tally.ERP 9 means any Accounting Entity, for which a separate set of Accounting Records are maintained (referred as *Tally Company*). So, a Tally Company may be created for a Personal Accounts, a business organization of any form (Proprietorship, Partnership, Company), an Association, Trust or any entity for which a separate set of accounts are maintained.

- **Branches of same Legal Company**: When separate set of Accounting Records of a Company (called *Business Entity*) are maintained for its various branches, warehouses, Sales / Purchase depots, collection centres etc, each of these separate *Accounting entities* will be called a Company (technically referred as *Tally Company*), even if they are legally same Company or Organisation. Separate Tally Companies will be created for each of such Accounting Entity.
- **Financial Year of Same Company**: A Company may create separate Tally Companies for each Financial Year

So, a legal Company may have several separate *Tally Companies* for each of its distinct Accounting Entities for which separate Accounting records are maintained in Tally.ERP 9. For each Tally Company, Tally creates a separate reserved space to store all Data for the respective Company (Called *Tally Data Folder*)

01.01 Separate Company Name for same Legal Company

In such case, separate Companies are to be created in Tally.ERP 9. To identify the specific Company, add a suffix at the end of Company Name (you cannot create two companies with same name), at Company Name.

- ABC Company (HO)
- ABC Company (Patna)
- Info Consultants 12-13
- Info Consultants 13-14
- Info Consultants 12-13 (Patna)

and so on. However, you may use same Legal name at *Mailing Name* of the companies (§02.03)

02 Company Creation

We have explained entry of essential info for creation of Company (§02/01-01). Here, we discuss about entry of the rest of the data in Company Creation, which, you may optionally fill up at the time of Company Creation.

After Company Creation, you may change / enter info through

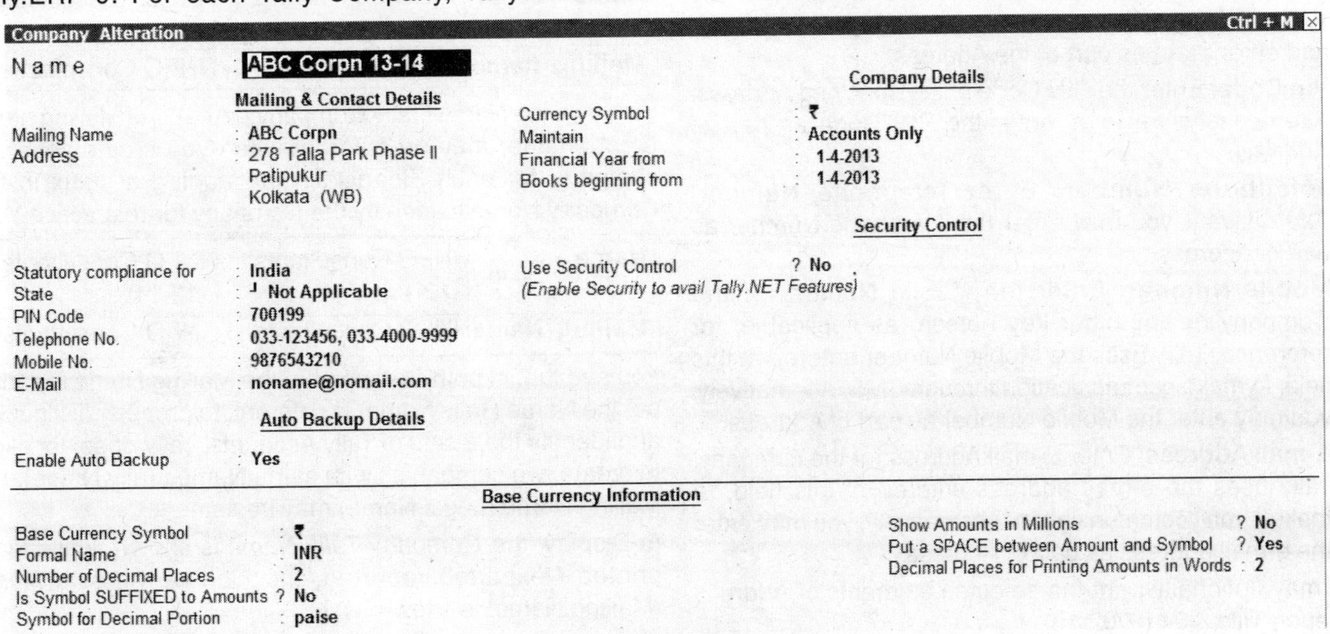

F-1A: Company Alteration

Company Alteration (§04/01-01). At Gateway, Click *F3:Comp Info* button (or press Alt+F3 keys) to get Company Info Menu (F-1A/01-01). Select *Alter* and select the Company to get *Company Alteration* Screen (F-1A). Now *Enter* (at blank fields) / *Alter* the respective info as desired.

The additional Info at Company Creation / Alteration are explained here.

02.01 Default Data Folder

At the time of creation of Company, at Company Creation screen (F-2A/01-01), at *Directory* field, the default Data folder name (F-1A/02-27) is shown and the field is skipped where the Company data would be placed (the cursor comes to *Name* Field), To keep Company data in any other data folder, press <Shift Tab> or <Up Arrow> to move the cursor to *Directory* field and enter the name of the Data folder (e.g d:tallydata\).

After creation of Company, you cannot change the name of Data Folder in Company Profile.

02.02 Mailing & Contact Details

Here you enter the Postal Address, Mailing Address, contact details like e-mail address, Phone Numbers etc, as follows. In Reports, you may print the selected data only, through the Report Configuration options.

Address: Enter the postal address for the Company in multiple lines. The address lines will be printed accordingly. So, break the lines as you like to print them in Reports. If you like to print the e-mail address, phone number etc., then enter them also as part of Address (in Reports, Documents)

You may enter the following as part of address, or may enter them at the respective separate fields

- **State**: Select State from the list (e.g. West Bengal). This is important when you maintain Statutory System like VAT with Tally. Otherwise you may select *Not Applicable* and enter State as part of the Address.
- **Pin Code**: Enter the PIN Code of the specified Address. Alternatively, you may enter the PIN Code as part of Address.
- **Telephone Number**: Enter Telephone Number. Alternatively, you may enter the Telephone Number as part of Address.
- **Mobile Number**: Enter the Mobile Number of the Company or any other key person, as applicable, for reference. Tally uses the Mobile Number entered at this field, to make communication through SMS. Alternatively, you may enter the Mobile Number as part of Address.
- **E-mail Address**: Enter E-mail Address for the company. Tally uses the e-mail address entered at this field, to make e-mail communication. Alternatively, you may enter the e-mail address as part of Address

You may optionally print the selected elements of Address in Report Title (§04.07/02-13)

Alternatively, you may enter all these data in Address field and leave all other fields blank.

When you enter the above components of address, in *Address* field, all the above elements would always be printed as part of the Address in all reports and documents. If you enter them in separate fields, you have to opt separately for each element to be printed in the document / report. So, make your plan accordingly.

02.03 Company Mailing Name

In *Company Creation* screen (F-1A/01-01), you get the field *Mailing Name* just after the *Name* (referred as *Company Legal Name* here for distinction). Internally Tally recognizes the Company by its *Name* (*Company Tally Name*). In all Data entry, Display screens, *Company Tally Name* is shown.

But sometimes, there may be several Tally Companies of same Legal Company. For example, separate Tally Companies may be created for each Financial Year or for each Branch, Warehouse etc. In such case, the *Company Legal Name* (Mailing Name) remains same, while the *Company Tally Name* is different.

Company Tally Name entered at *Name* field, is carried at *Mailing Name* (Legal Name).

You may change the carried Company name at Mailing Name field, when the Company Name is not the Legal Name (which you can print in external documents). For example, INFO Consultants maintains separate set of accounts for HO & its Patna Branch in the head office. Then it will create 2 separate Companies, for HO & Patna Branch. It will create 2 Tally Companies and enter the Name & Mailing Name as follows:

	Head Office	**Patna Branch**
Name	INFO Consultants (HO)	INFO Consultants (Patna)
Mailing name	INFO Consultants	INFO Consultants

Similarly, the Name (Tally Company name) and Mailing name (Legal name) may be different when you create separate company for each Financial Year, adding a suffix in the Company Name to identify the Company for respective Year

Name	INFO Consultants (12-13)	INFO Consultants (13-14)
Mailing Name	INFO Consultants	INFO Consultants

You see that in both Companies, the Mailing Name is same, but the Name (Tally Name) is different, to properly distinguish and identify the 2 sets of Tally Accounts. Tally does not allow to create two companies with same Name (Tally Name), but Mailing Name (Legal Name) may be same

In Display, the *Company Tally Name* is shown, while in all printed / exported reported, the *Company Legal Name* (Mailing Name) is shown.

> **Note:** *On Splitting of Company (§05/02-26, F-1A/02-26), the year beginning date is added in* Company Name *only but* Mailing Name *remains intact. Thus in* Mailing Name, *the legal Company Name (without Beginning Date suffix) is shown, while in Company Name is shown along with Beginning Date Suffix.*

02.04 Country Name

At the field**,** *Statutory Compliance for,* select *India* from the list (*India* is set as default), to apply rules applicable for the selected country.

03 Auto Back Up

To enable Auto Back Up feature (§02/02-25), set *Yes* at *Enable Auto Back Up,* else set *No*.

04 Company Details

In the upper Right part enter the following details

- **04.01 Currency Symbol:** The base currency symbol of Indian Rupee is displayed here. So, no need to change for new Indian Companies having ‘ as Base Currency).
- **04.02 Books Beginning Date:** It is the Date from which you start Accounting Work in the Tally Company created. By default, the *Date* as entered at *Financial Year From* (F-2A/01-01) is carried at the field *Books Beginning From* (as most of the time, accounting work starts from the beginning of Financial Year). However, if you start Tally Accounts from middle of a Financial Year, enter the Date from which you start Tally Accounts. For example, your Financial Year is 1.4.2014 to 31.3.2015, but you start Accounts in Tally from 1.8.2014, then at *Books Beginning from*, enter 1.8.2014. The books will however close on 31.3 2015 (one year from the date of Financial Year from). Tally does not allow to enter Voucher Date between Financial Year From (e.g.1.4.2014) and Books Beginning From (e.g. 31.7.2014)

05 Base Currency

Base Currency is the currency in which normally accounts are maintained for the Company. All other currencies are called Foreign Currency for that Company. Only ONE Base currency can be specified for a Company (F-1A).

At the bottom part of the Company Creation / Alteration screen, enter the particulars of Base Currency

Tally proposes the standard values for Base Currency for *Indian Rupee*. So, you do not need to change anything for Indian Rupee.

05.01 Base Currency Info

Following options are available for setting / formatting / presentation of Currency figures in Reports. At Company Creation / alteration screen (F-1A), set as follows:

Base Currency Symbol: At *Base Currency Symbol*, the new Indian Currency Symbol (₹) is shown as default.

Currency Name: At *Formal Name, Indian Rupees* (Indian Currency Name) is displayed by default. You may change (e.g INR), for better understanding & brevity. The currency name entered here is printed at Amount in Words (F-3A, F-4A).

Decimal Precision: At *Number of Decimal Places,* enter the decimal places to be used to represent the Base Currency Amount (default value 2) for Indian Rupees (to represent upto Paise).

Currency Symbol place: At *Is Symbol Suffixed to Amounts,*

- Set *Yes* to show the Amount with Symbol *suffixed* to (after) Amount. e.g 500 ₹ (F-4A)
- Set *No* (default) to show the Amount with Symbol *prefixed* to (before) Amount. e.g. ₹ 500. (F-3A)

Decimal Currency Name: Having set *No* at *Is Symbol Suffixed to Amount*, you may further set the Name of Decimal part of Currency as follows:

- **Decimal Part with Name**: At *Symbol for Decimal Portion*, enter the name of the decimal part of the currency (e.g Paise). This is printed at Amount in Words, in Invoice/ Receipt etc (F-3A).

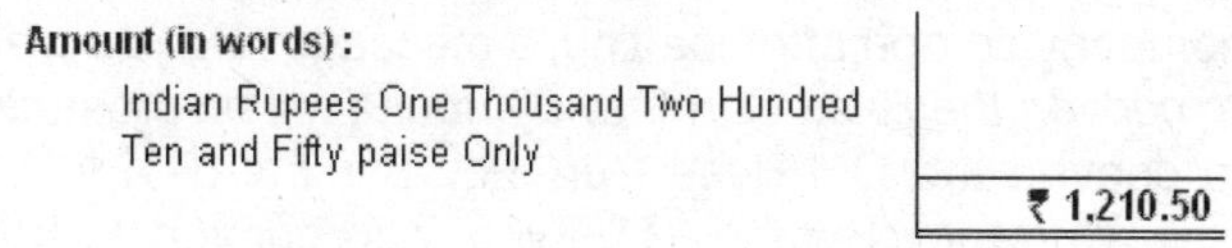

F-3A: Currency Symbol Prefixed.

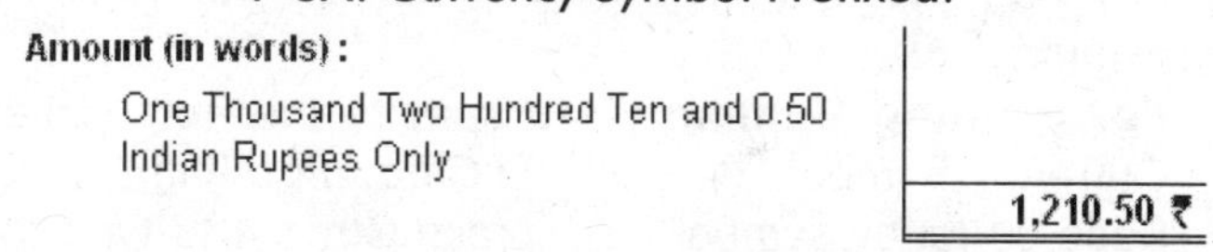

F-4A Currency Symbol Suffixed

Amount Format: For better readability, figures are normally delimited by comma (e.g 32,734.59). Tally provides 2 types of Formatting, to represent figures of One Lac (100000) & above. To set the Amount Format, at the option *Show Numbers in Millions,*

- **Lacs Formatting**: Set *No* (default) to express in Lacs (e.g 12,34,56,789, 1,23,456 etc). In India, traditionally Lacs format is widely used to represent figures in Rs One Lac & above (F-5A).
- **Millions Formatting**: Set *Yes* to express in Million format (e.g 123,456,789). Millions format is widely used Western Countries and by Foreign / Multinational Companies (F-5B).

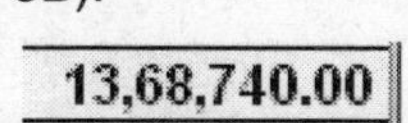

F-5A:Lacs Formatting

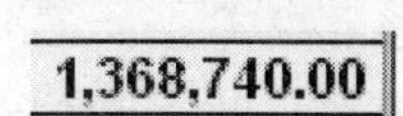

F-5B:Millions Formatting

Space between Amount & Symbol: You may optionally specify a space between Amount & Symbol (for better readability). At the field, *Put Space between Amount & Symbol:*

- Set *Yes* to show the amount with a space between Amount & Symbol, for better readability (e.g ' 500)
- Set *No* to show the Amount & Symbol concatenated (no space in between), to conserve space & provide better security (e.g '500)

Decimal Places in Amount in Words: At *Decimal Places for Printing Amount in Words*, specify the **number** of decimal places (not more than the number specified in *Number of Decimal places* field in company creation or currency master screen) for **printing the amount in words**. (e.g in Invoice and Cheque etc: F- 4A).

> **Note:** *The default options of Base Currency Symbol are properly set for INDIA. So, you normally do not need to re-set / change them*

05.02 Changing of Base Currency Symbol

You may set the New Indian Currency Symbol (₹) for Companies created earlier with older version, having Rs as Currency Symbol.

- **On conversion of Company from Old Version**: When you load your existing company in the latest version of Tally.ERP 9 Series A, for the first time, at the select company screen after loading, a message (*Do you want to convert the Base Currency Symbol?*) will be prompted to convert the Old Base Currency Symbol (Rs) to the New Currency Symbol (₹). Type *Y* to convert to new currency symbol, Type *N* to retain the old currency symbol (Rs).
- **For existing Company:** To specify the new Indian Currency Symbol (₹), Click *F3:Cmp Info >Alter*. At the Base currency symbol field, press Ctrl + 4 to type the new currency symbol and save the settings.

06 Company Auto Loading

We have explained how to load (select) a Company (§06/01-01). To automatically load (select) regular companies you work with, you may Auto Load the companies when Tally is loaded

Load Companies on startup	? Yes
Preload Companies on Startup	: 10000

F-6A: Company Auto Loading set up

List of Companies		
End of List		
Specific Company		
10000	ABC Academy 9-10	1-Apr-2008 to 31-Mar-2010
10001	ABC Softwares	1-Apr-2008 to 31-Mar-2009
10002	B. K. Traders	1-Apr-2008 to 31-Mar-2009

F-6B: Selection of Company for Auto Loading

> *Note: If you have set Pasword for autoloaded companies, you have to provide the Password for the respective Company, otherwise you cannot proceed.*

At Gateway, click *F12:Configure* to get Configuration Menu. At Configuration Menu, select *Data Configuration* to get *Data Configuration* screen. At *Data Configuration* screen (F-6A), set as follows:

- **Load Companies on Start Up**: Set *Yes* if you like to load (get selected) any company automatically when you load Tally.ERP9.
  - o **Pre-Load Companies on Start Up**: Having set Yes at the option *Load Companies on Start Up*, you may select the Company to be pre loaded (F-6B), from the list of Companies on Disk (all Companies created). So, when Tally.ERP 9 is loaded, the Company get loaded (you find them as selected Company at Gateway)

07 Company Multiple Addresses

When a Company maintains centralised accounts in its Head Office, including its branches in the same Tally Company, then the Company will like to print address for respective Branch in the Vouchers, Invoices, Reports etc.

Sometimes, the Customer / Supplier may have multiple offices, godowns, etc but you may maintain only one ledger account for the Party but print respective address in Invoice, Receipts etc.

Often legal provisions require to print the Registered / HO Office in the Invoice / Receipts

The Multi Address feature in Tally.ERP 9 allows you to maintain multiple mailing details for the Tally Company and Party / Branch Ledger Accounts created in the Company.

07.01 Activating Multiple Address

To activate Multi Address in Tally.ERP 9, select *GoT> F11: Features>Accounting Features* to get Accounting Features screen. At Accounting Features screen, under the Other Features section (F-7A), set Yes at *Maintain Multiple Mailing Details for Company & Ledgers* to activate the Multiple Address options.

Maintain Multiple Mailing Details for Company & Ledgers	? Yes
Set/Alter Company Mailing Details	? Yes

F-7A: Company Features option for Multiple Address

Having set Yes at *Maintain Multiple Mailing Details for Company & Ledgers* (F-7A), you may further set *Yes* at *Set/ Alter Company Mailing Details* (F-7A) to get *Company Address Type* entry screen (F-7B) to enter Company Branch names

At *Company Address Type* entry screen (F-7B), type the *Name* of the Branch/Location (e.g Kolkata Office). To enter more Branch/Location names, press <Down Arrow> key and add more name

To enter the address of the branch, at Address Type screen (F-7B), click on the respective Branch *Name* to get *Mailing Details* entry screen (F-7C). At, *Mailing Details* entry screen (F-7C), enter the Mailing Name, Address, PIN Code, etc. in the respective fields, in the same way as you enter Company Address etc (§02.02)

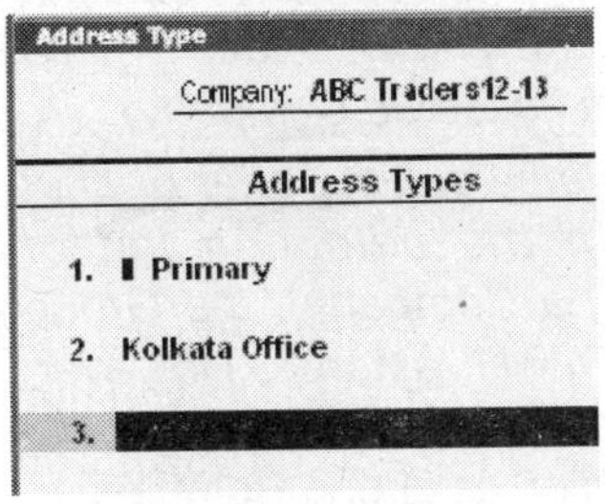

F-7B: Company Branch Names Entry screen

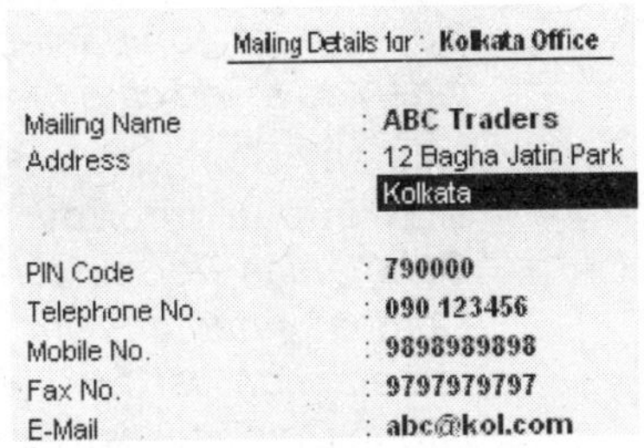

F-7C: Multiple Company Address Entry screen

07.02 Printing Multiple Addresses

Having entered mailing address for Branches (F-7C), you may print the respective in Invoices, Reports etc.

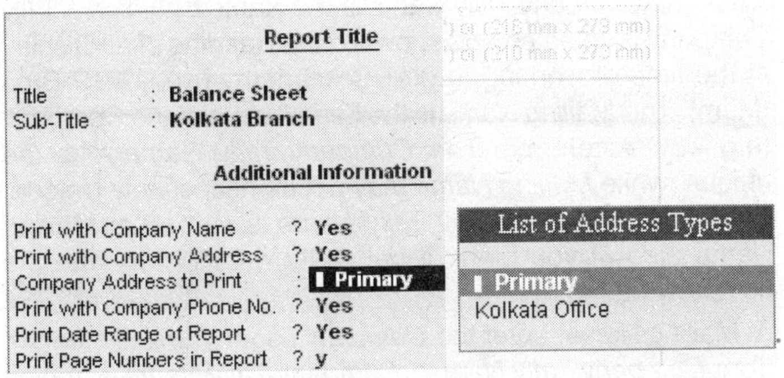

F- 8A: Company Address Printing at Report Title

In the respective Report Printing screen (Click *P:Print* button at the respective Reports Display to get Reports Printing screen), click *T: Titling* (or press Alt + T) to get *Report Title* screen (F-8A). At *Report Title* screen (F-8A), at *Company Address to print* (this field will appear only when you activate Multiple Address feature: F-7A), the list of all offices as entered (F-7B) will appear (F-8A). Now select the *Office Name* (select *Primary* to print the main Company address). In the Report, the address as entered for the selected *Office Name* would be printed

In the same way, you may print the respective Company Address at the Title of Voucher / Invoice etc

08 Group Company

Group Company is a virtual Company consisting of several constituent member companies, created to provide consolidated reports of member companies. So, you cannot enter data for Group Company. You can get reports of the Group Company showing the total figures of the constituent companies

Group Company is useful when several companies are owned by common owners. Since the owners manage several companies, they would be interested to see the information of all the companies managed by them together, to get the complete picture of the performance & state of affairs of all the member companies together

You may create a Group Company specifying the Member Companies. So, Member Companies must be created first. You may then open a Group Company and get any report showing the consolidated figures of member companies

You may get the report of Group Companies at Reserved Group Level only. Only Accounts figures are reported in Group Company Reports (even though the constituent companies may contain Inventory data)

When you select any option for Master / Voucher creation / display / alteration etc, the first constituent company gets selected. All actions are then performed for the first constituent company. For Example, if you have selected a Group Company **G** (having constituent Company **A** and **B**), then when you see a report for **G** (like Balance Sheet), it shows the combined report (of **A** & **B** for the current period). But when you select any data entry option (e.g Account Ledger Creation or Voucher Entry), the first Constituent single Company **A** only gets internally selected and all operations are performed in Company **A** (as if you have selected Company A), though **G** (the Group Company) is the currently active Company.

> *Note: In reports, you get the consolidated figures of Group / Ledger Accounts common to the Group & Member Companies. But when you drill down to individual voucher lists (Ledger Voucher), only the vouchers relating to the first member company (which gets selected internally), are shown (vouchers of other companies are not shown)*

08.01 Creation of Group Company

If you have created multiple Tally Companies, you may create Group Companies with specified constituent Tally Companies. For example, having created 3 Companies, *Company A, Company B* & *Company C,* you may create a Group *Company G* with 2 Constituent Companies *Company A* & *Company B.*

To create a Group Company, you must first select the constituent Companies. Now click *F3:Cmp Info* button to get Company Info Menu (F-9A). At Company Info Menu (F-9A). select *Create Group Company* (it appears only when you select more than one company) to get *Group Company Creation screen* (F-9B).

At *Group Company Creation screen* (F-9B), enter the following:

- **Directory**: Here enter the location of Data where you like to place the data of the Group Company. The Data Directory Name as specified in the active Company, is shown by default at Group Company creation (which you may change, if you like to).
- **Group Company Name**: Enter the distinct Group Company Name (it must be different from all the companies created)

- **Address:** Enter various address details as explained for Company Creation.
- **Members:** Select the Constituent (Member) Companies for the Group Companies. You may select several Member Companies for a Group Company.

The Group Company is then created.

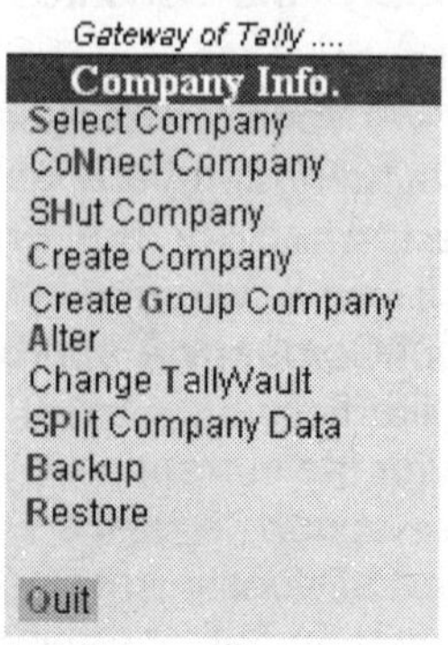

F-9A: Company Info Menu

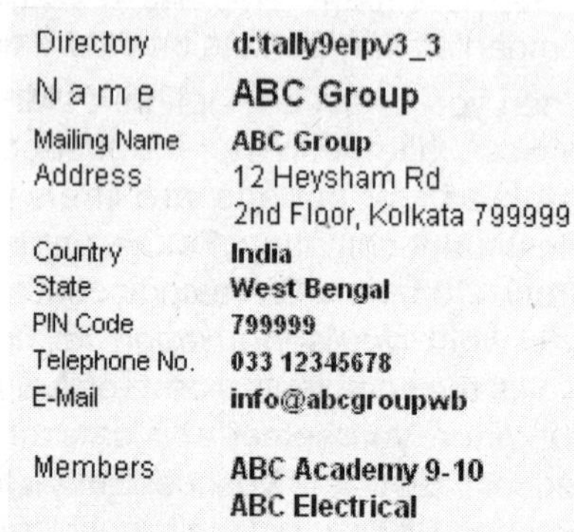

F-9B: Creation of Group Company

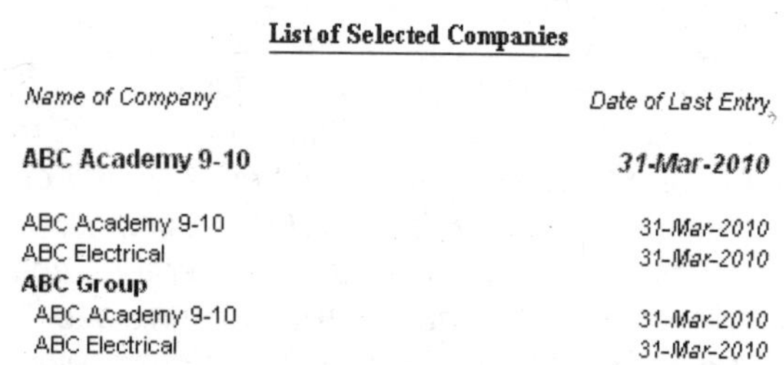

F-9C: List of selected Company (including Group Company)

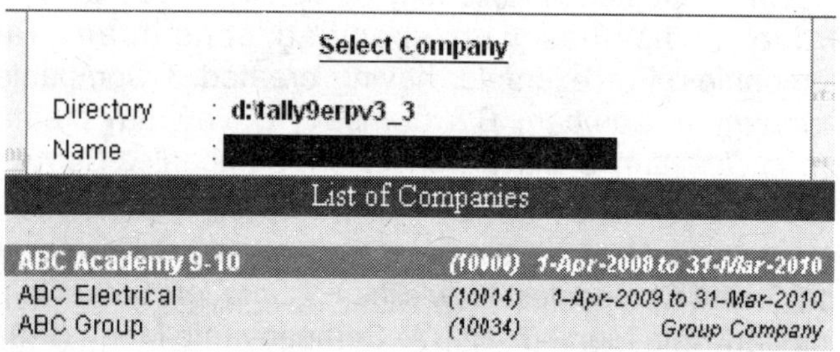

F-9D:Selection List of Company

Note: *A new Company Code is allotted to a Group Company also, like any other constituent single Company. The Company Code is shown in the selection list of Company (F-9D). Since no data is entered in the Group Company, there is no Financial Accounting period for Group Company (so no date is shown against Group Company in selection list (F-9D) or in the list of selected Companies in Gateway (F-9C).The created Group Company is shown in the list of selected Companies at the left part of Gateway of Tally (F-9C).*

The Group Company Name is shown in Bold (even if it is not the currently Active Company*) and the Constituent companies are shown under it (little indented to indicate them as Group Company).*

Like any Company, you may select / alter or shut a Group Company. In the selection list of Companies (for shutting a Company), the Group Company name is shown with Asterisk. However, in selection list for selection of Companies, the Group Company is identified as Group Company

FAQ: Frequently Asked Questions

FAQ-1: What is Company Mailing Name? How to create separate Tally Companies for One legal Company, at same place.

Ans: The Company Tally Name is the Name by which a Tally Company is selected and shown in the Heading of all Display at the time of working (e.g ABC Academy (Kol), ABC Bros (Mum). The *Mailing Name* is the Legal Name of the Company (e.g ABC Academy). The *Company Tally Name* must be unique, while *Mailing Name* may not be necessarily Unique. By default, the *Company Tally Name* is carried at Mailing Name also (if you blank it out, Tally will fill it up with the company name)

At Mailing Name, enter the *Company Legal Name* (if different from *Company Tally Name*). *Company Tally Name* is shown in all Display / data Entry etc., while *Mailing Name* is shown in Printed Reports.

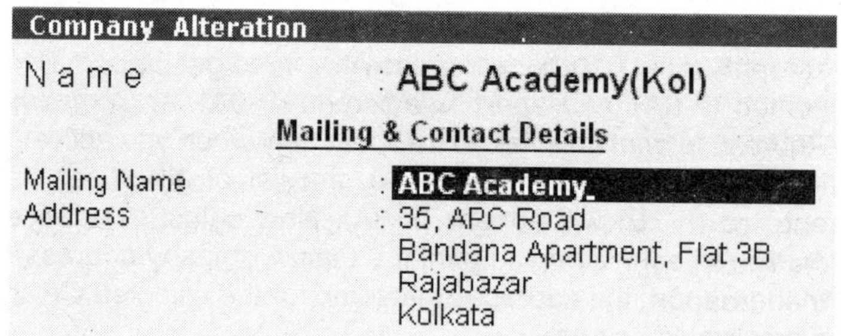

Changed Mailing Name

Different Tally Company may be created when separate set of accounts are maintained for each Tally Company (for the same Legal Company). So, in such case, for the Tally Company ABC Academy (Mum), enter ABC Academy (Mum), at Name and ABC Academy, at Mailing Name. Enter the respective addresses in each company.

Now, in the drop down list of company selection, you will get 2 distinct companies, ABC Academy (Kol), ABC Academy (Mum), In all Display screens, the respective Company name ABC Academy (Kol), and ABC Academy (Mum), as the case may be, will be displayed to distinguish each company. However, in Reports, legal company name ABC Academy will be printed, but the company addresses will be different, as entered by you for each Tally Company.

Different Name & Mailing Name may also be used to identify Accounts of each financial Year.

Name (Company Tally Name)	Mailing name (Legal Name)
Info Consultants 12-13 Info Consultants 13-14	Info Consultants Info Consultants

FAQ-2: How you can enter address in multiple lines?

Ans: At Address field, enter the postal address for the company. To enter address in several lines, Press <Enter> after each line to get a new line. Press <Enter> at last blank line to terminate address entry.

Now, in the documents, address will be printed as follows:

35, APC Road

Bandana Apartment, Flat 3B

Rajabazar

Kolkata

You may also enter the e-mail address & website address at the Address Line, to print them at the address line.

35, APC Road

Bandana Apartment, Flat 3B

Rajabazar

Kolkata – 700 017 (W.B)

Phone: 033 49998888, 09876543210

myname@mycompany.com

www.mycompany.com

This is convenient when you like to print e-mail & website address as part of the Address in all reports & documents. Otherwise, enter only the postal address at Address field and other info at the respective fields (like PINCODE, Telephone Number, e-mail address etc)

This way, break the address lines exactly in the way you like to appear in the external documents (like invoice, receipt etc). You may enter as many lines as you like (try to keep the address within 3-4 lines, otherwise the fonts would be too small to fit in the space)

FAQ-3: Can I write more than one phone number in Telephone Phone Number field?

Ans: You can enter more than one Phone Number, all in one line only.

Like 033-77771111, 033-88882222, or

like 033-77771111 (Accts), 033-88882222 (Sales) etc.

For Land Line phone number, preferably add the STD Code Numbers.

FAQ-4: Can I write more than one Mobile Phone number in Mobile Phone Number field?

Ans: You can enter more than one Mobile Phone Number, all in one line only.

Like 9898089898, 8989089098, or

like 9898089898 (Accts), 8989089098 (Sales) etc.

FAQ-5: Is it essential that I must enter Address, Phone Number, Mobile Phone Number, PINCODE, in Company Creation screen.

Ans: No. You may leave any or all of these fields blank. In that case, these data won't be printed at the respect place in Reports, but otherwise, you can do all work in Tally, as usual. You may enter these data gradually later on through Company Alter Option (*F3:Comp Info>Alter)*

FAQ-6: What is Book Beginning from date? How you start Account from Middle of Financial Year?

Ans: *Books Beginning from Date* is the Date from which you start Accounting Work in the Tally Company created. By default, the Date as entered at *Financial Year From* is carried at the field *Books Beginning From* (as most of the time, accounting work starts from the beginning of Financial Year). However, if you start Tally accounts from middle of a financial year, enter the date from which you start Tally Accounts. For example, your Financial Year is 1.4.2011 to 31.3.2012, but you start Accounts in Tally from 1.8.2011, then at *Books Beginning from*, enter 1.8.2011. The books will however close on 31.3 2013 (one year from the date of Financial Year from). Tally does not allow to enter Date between 1.4.2011 to 31.7.2011.

Maintain	: **Accounts Only**
Financial Year from	: **1-4-2011**
Books beginning from	: **1-4-2011**

Books starting from start of Financial year

When you start Accounts from Middle of Financial Year, then you enter the Date from which you enter voucher, at Books Beginning date.

Maintain	: **Accounts Only**
Financial Year from	: **1-4-2011**
Books beginning from	: **1-8-2011**

Books starting from mid Financial Year

The Books Beginning From date must be within the Financial Year (i.e 1 year from the *Financial Year From*

FAQ-7: Should the Financial Year specified for all the constituent companies of a Group Company be same ?

Ans: Though it is not essential that the Financial Accounting period of all the constituent companies be same, but it is useful to have same financial period to get consolidated report of Group Company constituting figures of all the constituent companies. For example, financial period of constituent companies Company A & Company B is same (1-4-12 to 31-3-13). Then when you specify current period as 1-4-12 to 31-3-13 for the Group Company, you get the consolidated report for (1-4-12 to 31-3-13). combining the figures of Company A and Company B. If the financial period is different, the consolidated statement will cover the specified period for the Group Company and it may produce illusive wrong result (data of one of the company may not get included in the Report).

Gateway of Tally 02-03

01 Gateway of Tally

We have explained the Basic Features & Components of Gateway of Tally (§02/01-02). Here we explain the components of Gateway of Tally in details.

At *Gateway of Tally* screen (F-1A/01-02), the Tally *Main Menu* appears, along with following other components

- Horizontal Button Bar (§02), at the top
- Current Status (§03), at the left part
- Product Info panel (§04), below the Menu
- Tally Calculator / Command line (§05), alongwith Product Info panel
- Vertical Button Bar (§06), at right Part
- Current Menu path (§07), at bottom line

When you perform any task (after finally selecting a menu option at Tally Menu), the Work Area takes the main screen area (in place of Tally Menu). The Vertical & Horizontal Button Bars, footer remain static and visible. Product Info / Calculator may remain visible (or may be hidden) while you work with Tally.

02 Horizontal Button Bar

The Horizontal Button Bar (F-1) appear at the top in all Tally screens to access / perform the relevant tasks from a broad range of tools.

Horizontal Button Bar (F-1) contains a set of Buttons, as follows

- o **P ; Print**: To print any Report from Display (§03/01-05)
- o **E: Export**: To get Tally data & tally Reports converted into specified format for use in other applications, out of Tally
- o **M: E-mail**: Send any Tally report by e-mail to any recipient
- o **O: Upload**: To upload any Tally report (like Balance Sheet) on the web so that other persons can see it from anywhere through Internet.
- o **S: Shop**: To buy other Tally Add-on Products
- o **G: Language**: To set up Language in which you like to work with Tally.
- o **K:** Keyboard: Set up keyboard for any specific language
- o **K:** Control Centre: To get the Control Centre to manage Tally
- o **H:** Support Centre: To get support from Tally Solutions. You need to login as remote Tally user to get support from Tally Solutions
- o **H:Help**: To get On-Line info about any Tally Topic (§09)

F-1 Horizontal Button Bar

03 Current Status

At the left part of Gateway (F-1A/01-02), you get the following information about current working:

- o **Current Period**: Shows the current period set through *F2: Period* button (F-4A/01-02).
- o **Current Date**: Shows the current date set through *F2: Date* button (F-4B/01-02).
- o **Active Company**: Shows the status of last selected company (the company you are currently working with (F-5B/01-01), at the top of list of selected Companies, in bold
- o **Selected Company**: Shows the list all the Companies currently selected (F-5B/01-01)

Current Period

It shows the Current Period set. Click *F2: Period* button (or press *Alt+F2*) to change the current period (F-2A/01-03). At *From* field, enter the Starting Date of the Current Period. It must not be earlier than *Books Beginning From* Date (F-2A/01-01). At *To* field, enter the Ending Date of the Current Period. It may be any date after 'Books Beginning From' Date. You can enter data or get reports for a period lying within the Current Period set. To get report or work for any date beyond the current period, click Alt+F2 and re-set the Current Period accordingly.

Current Date

Here the Current Date (the Date you worked last) is displayed. It is carried as Voucher Date (§04.01/01-04). Click *F2: Date* button (or press F2) to change *Current Date* (F-4B/01-02). The next Date appears by default. Now you may alter the Date (within the Current Period), which becomes the Current Date. When you create a Voucher, the Current Date is carried by default at Voucher Date.

Selected & Active Company

Active Company is the Company which you are currently working with (the last selected Company). Its name is shown in Gateway, at top (in bold face) in the list of Companies (F-1A/01-02). Names of other selected Companies appear next in the list, shown in regular font.

04 Product Info Panel

The components of Tally Info panel has been explained (§02.01/01-02). By default, the Info Panel appears at GoT (F-1A/01-02). To Hide / Restore the Info panel, Click *GoT>F12:Configure>General.* At the option, *Always Show info panel*,

- Set *Yes* to get the Info panel at all screens (the Display area reduces)
- Set *No* to get Info panel at Menu screens only

05 Tally Calculator

While viewing a Report or making data Entry, you may need to make some calculation mid way, You can perform any arithmetical computation (at Calculator area) without exiting from current Tally screen you are working with (you don't need to fetch your Calculator).

Making Arithmetic Calculation

Invoking the Calculator: Press Ctrl+N to activate Calculator to do arithmetical calculation (the Calculator screen will appear and the Calculator panel will get activated and expand, overlapping the Product Info Area (§02/01-02).

- **Arithmetic Expressions**: In Calculator area (F-2A), type the arithmetic expression and press enter. You may use +, -, * and / for addition, subtraction, multiplication, Division and properly paired parenthesis '( )'.
- **Calculation results**: The result of the arithmetic expression is shown in the next line (F-2B). You may continue to make more Calculations like this and get results of each calculations.

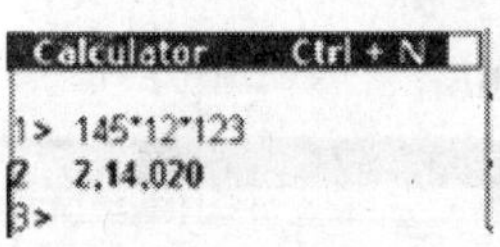

F-2A: Tally Calculator

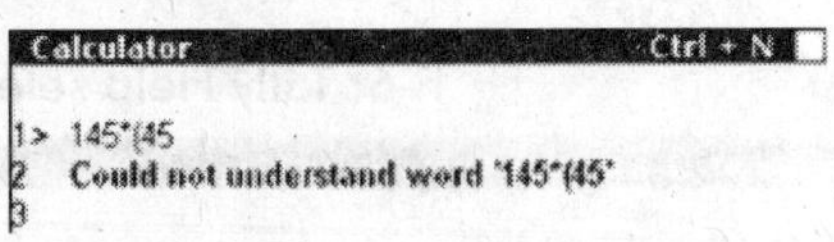

F-2B: Tally Calculator expression Error

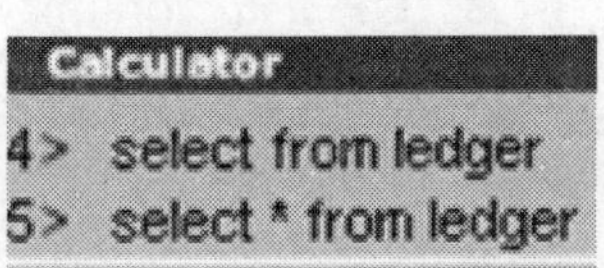

F-2C: Tally Commands entry

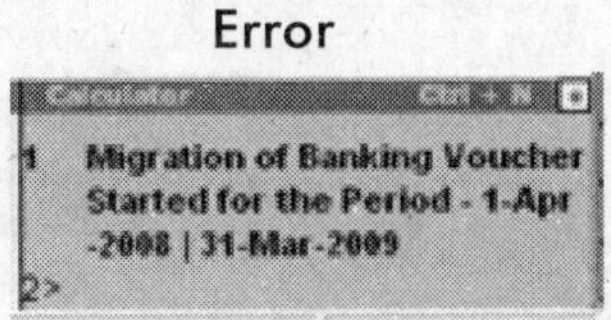

F-2D: Message displayed at Calcutor area

If there is any mistake in typing the arithmetic expression, Tally will show Error! Message (Error!) at the result line (F-2B)

After the Calculations are over, press at (▪) button at the right upper corner of Calculator area to hide the Calculator

Pasting Arithmetic Calculation Result

Sometimes you need to Calculate some value to be entered in any field during working (§12/02-09). In such case, apart from performing the desired calculation, you may also paste the result in Tally input field. It is useful when you like to enter some data that requires some numeric computation (e.g in a Voucher)

At the *Numeric Input*, where you like paste to enter some computed Data, press Alt+C. The Calculator will get invoked. Perform the Calculation as explained above. The result will be displayed in the numeric field where you invoked the calculator (Alt+C was pressed)

Executing Tally Commands: Apart from arithmetic expression, you may also type Tally commands at the Calculator Area (F-2C) and press <enter>. The result will appear in a window.

To exit from Calculator / Command line mode and return to work area, press Ctrl+M (or click on the Work Area bar).

Tally Messages: Sometimes, Messages are also displayed (F-2D) in Calculator area (of an action, error massages, etc).

06 Vertical Button Bar

At rightmost part of the Gateway, the Button Bar (F-1B/01-02) shows several buttons (the buttons vary according to current screen in work area) with Function Key / Hotkey, to provide quick and direct access to various options & tasks. Depending on various options set, some buttons may become inactive (the inactive buttons are dimmed).

Invoking a task through Button

You may invoke a button (in Horizontal or Vertical button bar) in 3 ways:

- **By Mouse**: Click the button at the button bar.
- **By Function Key**: Some buttons are named by Function keys (F1 to F12). Press the Function key to invoke (e.g F7). Use *Alt* combination key for underlined button (like Alt+F2 for F2:Period) and *Ctrl* combination key for double underlined button. (F-3)

Button	Function Key / Hotkey
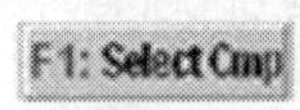	**Function Key**: Press the Function key (e.g. *F1:SelectCmp*, Press F1 Function Key).
	**Button with single underline:** Press Alt Key & Character/function key with single underline (e.g *H:Help*, press Alt+H).
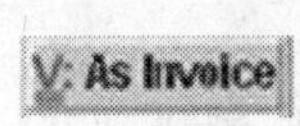	**Button with double underline:** Press Ctrl Key & Character/function key double underline (e.g *V:AsInvoice*,pressCtrl+V).

F-3: Buttons

> **Note:** *Selecting a Menu Item / Invoking a Task using Keyboard is much faster and easier than clicking Mouse*

07 Footer Line

At the bottom (Footer Line), you get the Current Screen Location bar (F-4) showing the following details about the current screen being displayed.

- **Current Screen Path**: It shows the complete path (form Gateway) of the current screen (e.g Gateway of Tally ->Balance Sheet->Group Summary).

F-4: Footer Line

- **Copyright Notice**: Shows the copyright notice [e.g.*(c) Tally Solutions Pvt Ltd., 1988-2013*]
- **Current System Date**: Shows the current System Day & Date (like Fri 10th Jun, 2005).
- **Current System Time**: Shows the current System Time in HH:MM:SS format (like 18:00:31).

08 Tally Menu

You may move between menus at various levels and invoke the menu tasks (i.e select menu options) in the following way:

F-5A: Current Wok Area Handle

08.01 Selecting a Menu Item

You can select an option in Tally Menu in any of the following ways:

- Press the highlighted character. For example, to select **B**alance Sheet, press ***B***(the highlighted character). This is the fastest way of selection.
- Move highlight bar on the option with ***Up/Dn arrow*** key and press <enter>
- Double click the option by the mouse [click twice, fast enough]

08.02 Moving to Upper Menu

Select *Quit* (or Press *Esc* key) at any Sub Menu (menus under Tally Main Menu) to return to the immediate upper level menu. Alternately, click on the rightmost *Cross* (X) at the current work area handle (F-5A).

This way, you may reach to the Tally main Menu (the uppermost level)

08.03 Exiting from Tally

You can Exit from Tally, only after reaching the Tally Main Menu (the uppermost level),. Now, you may finally Exit from Tally in the same way (select *Quit*, Press Esc key or click at the rightmost x handle) as you exit from Menu described above. A confirmation screen (F-5B) appears.

- Press *Y* or click at *Yes* button (F-5B) to exit from Tally
- Press *N* or click at *No* button (F-5B) to continue to work with Tally

09 Tally Help

Tally is an extensive software providing wide range of features, options and functionalities. Often the user will need to know more details and working steps regarding such features, options and functionalities.

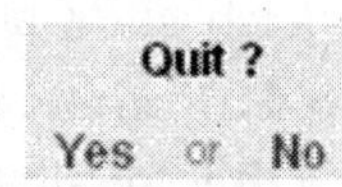

F-5B: Exit from Tally

To get *Help* about any topic, click *H:Help* button at the Horizontal Button Bar (F-1), or press Alt+H to get Help selection screen (F-6). Select from the following options

- **Local Help:** The *Tally Reference Manual* (tallyerp9ref – a compiled HTML file stored in the Tally software directory) is loaded. It is a Context-Sensitive Help System. Since the Local Help system is stored in your Computer alongwith Tally Software, you may load it anytime from inside Tally. Click *H:Help* button (or Type Alt+H, or click the *tallyerp9ref* file directly).
- **Online Help:** Through this option, get access to the *Online Help* available on the Knowledge Base. It provides Frequently Asked Questions, Trouble shooting articles on specific topics, Tips to quickly use Tally.ERP 9, Case Studies, Articles etc. You must be connected to Internet to get such Help.

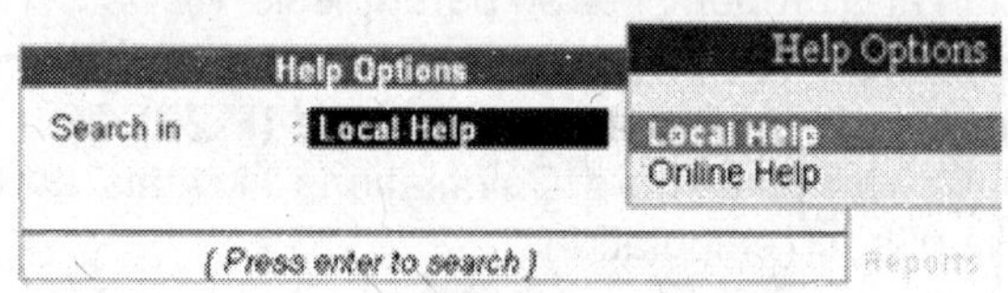

F-6: Tally Help selection

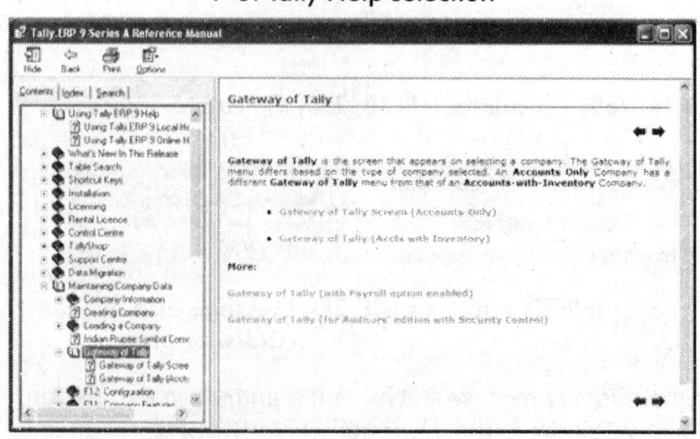

F-7A: Tally Local Help screen

09.01 Local Help

When you select *Local Help* option (F-6), the Local Help screen (F-7A) appears (the *Tally Reference Manual* - a Compiled help file, gets loaded)

The Tally Help screen shows 3 tabs as follows:

- **Contents:** A Tree Structured Expandable / Collapsible List (default) appears to show the details of the topic. Click at (+) node to expand the list showing underlying Topics and Click at (-) node to collapse, hiding the underlying topics to show the next upper level topic (F-7A)
- **Index:** Show this alphabetical list of Topics (F-7B)
- **Search**: To search the desired topic (F-7C)

> **Note:** *The file* tallyerp9ref *(a Compiled help file) must remain in the folder where Tally is installed, otherwise you get a message* Help file (tallyerp9ref.chm) is not available. Do you want to download it. *Click* Yes *to download the Help file from Tally website (*tallyssolutions.com*)*

Index Tab of the Help Manual: The alphabetical list of all Topics / Keywords appear (F-7B). Select the desired Topic / keyword and click *Display* button. The details of the selected Topic / keyword appears at the right part of the screen

Search Tab of the Help Manual: Type the desired Topic at the textbox *Type the Keyword to find* and click *Display* button (F-7B). All the topics related to the Search Topic entered at the Search textbox, are listed at the list box below. Now select the desired Topic in the list box and Click *List Topics* button (F-7C)

The details of the selected topic is displayed at the right Part showing the keyword highlighted in the details of the Topic part (F-7C)

09.02 On-line Help

When you select *On-Line Help* option at Tally Help selection screen (F-6), you get On-Line help Topic Search screen (F-8B). Enter the Topic to be searched. The topic is searched (you MUST be connected with Internet) from the Tally Knowledge base and shown in *On-Line Help* screen (F-8A)

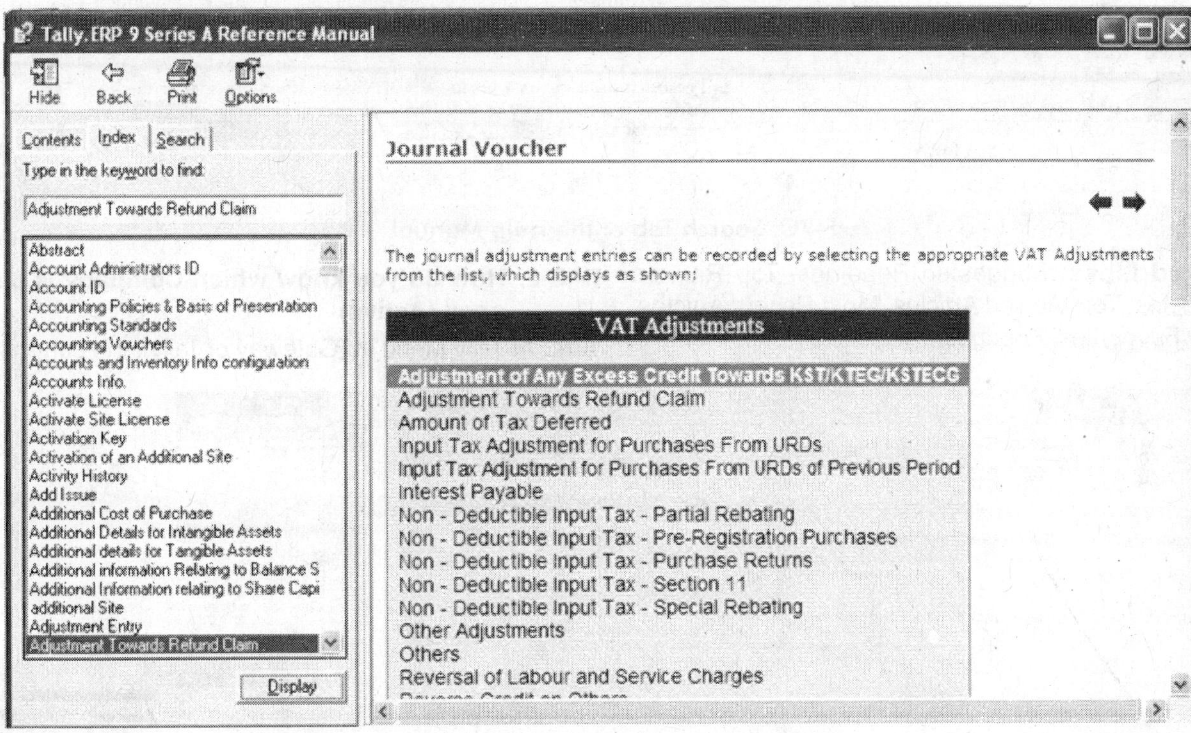

Fig 7B: Index Tab of Help Manual

Contents Tab of the Help Manual: Initially, the Contents Tab is shown, as follows (F-4A):

- **Main Help screen**: When you load Help (press at Alt+ H) at Gateway, the main menu of the Reference Manual appears, showing the first Page of Help manual
- **Context Sensitive:** When you load Help (press at Alt+ H) at any other screen, the context sensitive details (i.ethe details of the current topic where the Help system is invoked) is shown

The *On-Line Help* screen (F-8A) is divided into following sections:

- **Main Part**: Here the related topics searched from Knowledge base are listed. You may read them and further click related links.
- **Go To section**: In this section, links to more materials are made available under the following headings:
  - o **Search**: Links to Home, FAQs, Trouble Shooting & Case Studies

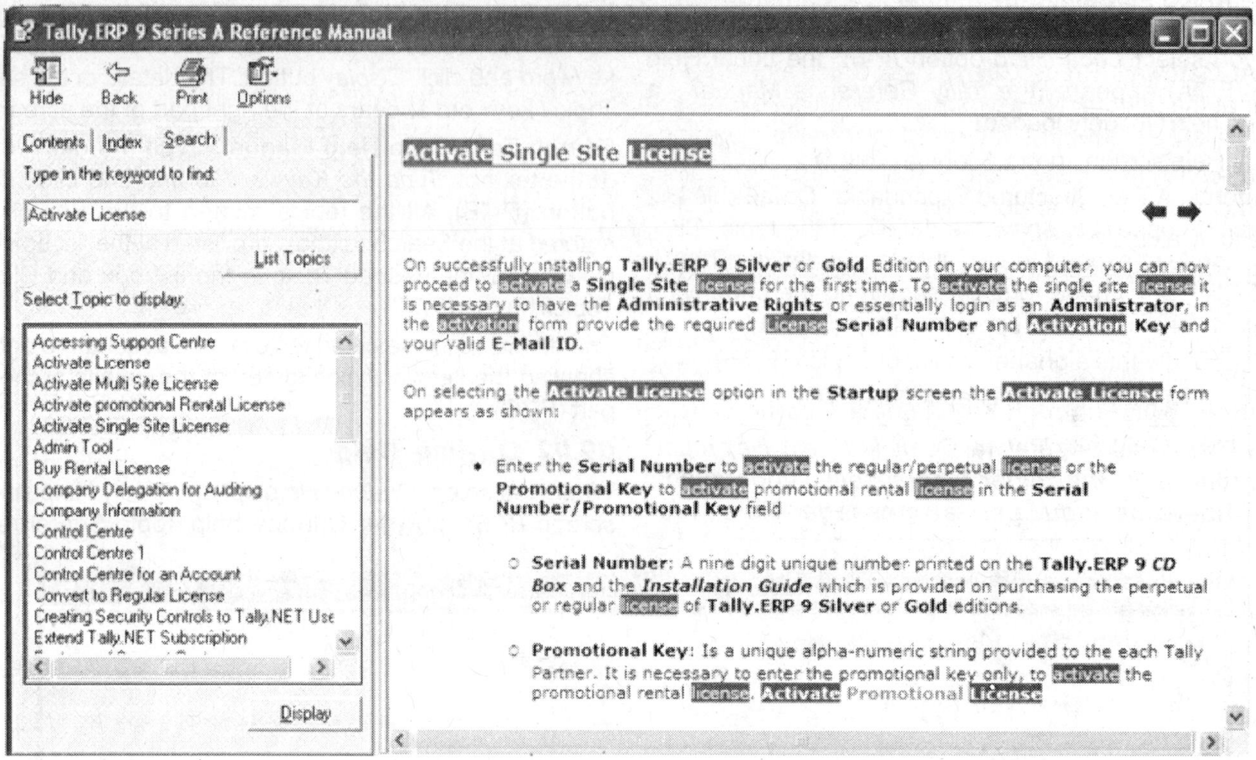

F-7C: Search Tab of the Help Manual

- o **Fixed Links**: Suggested Readings, Top Ranked Articles, Top Viewed Articles, Most Recent Articles, My Favourites, Feedback

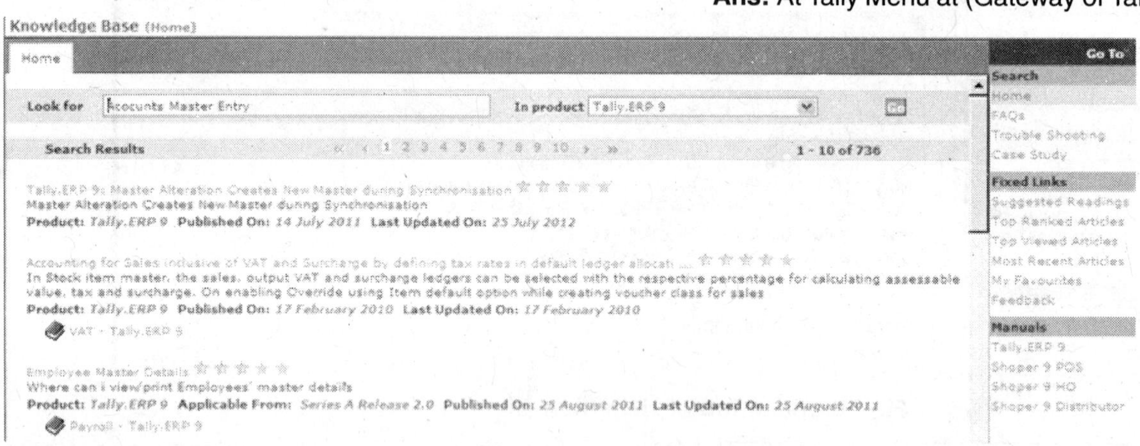

F-8A: On-Line Help screen

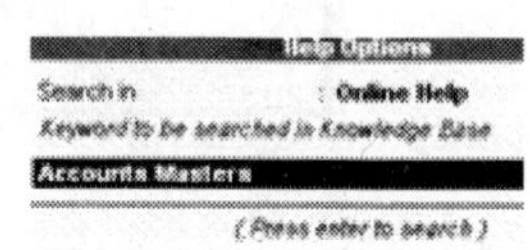

F-8B: Topic Search option

- o **Manuals**: Tally ERP9, Shoper 9 POS, Shoper 9 HO, Shoper 9 Distributor

FAQ: Frequently Asked Questions

FAQ-1: How you can hide the Product Info panel

Ans: At the right end of Info panel, click the (•) icon to hide the Info Panel. This will make more space or display of contents in the screen. To Restore the Info Panel, click on the (^) icon at the centre of bottom handle.

FAQ-2: How do you know which Company is currently open (Active)

Ans: At Tally Menu at (Gateway of Tally), the currently Active Company is shown at the top of list of selected Companies, at the left panel.

The name of the selected Company is shown at the Title of the screen.

FAQ-3: How do you know currently selected Companies & the Active Company

Ans. At Gateway of Tally, the list of selected Companies are shown at the left panel of. At all other places, the Active Company Name is shown at the top in Bold.

FAQ-4: How I can make Arithmetical Calculation while working in Tally

Ans: At Gateway, Press *Ctrl+N*. The Calculator area will appear at the bottom. Now type he arithmetical expression (formula like 10+(30/6.5)). The result is shown at next line.

You may continue to make more Calculations and get results of each calculation. After done with, you may press *Ctrl+M* to hide the Calculator area

FAQ-5: How I can select a Button or Menu Item using Keyboard (without using Mouse)

Ans: Selecting a Button or Menu Item from Keyboard is much faster than with Mouse.

- **Buttons with Function Key Name**: Press the Function key button (e.g *F2:Date*, press F2 key)
- **Buttons with Hot Key Name**: Press the hot key letter. The hot key letter in Menu Item is capitalized and shown Red (e.g **T**rial Balance, press T)

Many of the Buttons are lebelled with Underline or Double Underline. In that case, press the Function key / Hot Key with Alt Key for underlined Keys (e.g F3:Comp Info, press Alt+F3 key,) and with Ctrl Key for Double underlined Keys (e.g *V:AsInvoice*, press Ctrl+V)

FAQ-6: How I can get Local Help on any Topic

Ans: At any place, press click *H:Help* button (or press *Alt+H*), at the top line and then select *Local Help* from the list. The contextual Help topic (about the current task) will appear. However, you may move to any topic through the topic links at the left and find further details about any topic / task / operation

FAQ-7: How I can get On-Line Help on any Topic

Ans: At any place, press click *H:Help* button (or press *Alt+H*), at the top line and then select *Local Help* from the list (F-6). The On Line Help screen appears. Enter the Topic to be searched. The topic is searched (you MUST be connected with Internet) from the Tally Knowledge base and shown in *On-Line Help* screen (F-8A).

FAQ-8: How to make Arithmetic Calculations with Tally Calculator

Ans: Using Calculator

- **Invoking the Calculator**: Press Ctrl+N to activate Calculator to do arithmetical calculation (the Calculator screen will appear and the Calculator panel will expand & get activated, (F-2A)).
- **Typing Arithmetic Expressions**: In Calculator area (F-2A), type the arithmetic expression and press enter. You may use +, -, * and / for addition, subtraction, multiplication, Division and properly paired parenthesis '( )'.
- **Getting the Calculation results**: The result of the arithmetic expression is shown in the next line (F-2B). You may continue to make more Calculations like this and get results of each calculations.

After the Calculations are over, press at (▪) button at the right upper corner of Calculator area to hide the Calculator

Pasting Arithmetic Calculation Result: Sometimes you need to Calculate some value to be entered in any field during working. In such case, not only you make some calculation, you may also paste the result in Tally input field. It is useful when you like to enter some data that requires some numeric computation (e.g in a Voucher)

At the input field, Press Alt+C at the numeric field where you like paste the computed Data. The Calculator will get invoked. Perform the Calculation as explained above. The result will be displayed in the numeric field where you invoked the calculator (Alt+C was pressed).

Chart of Accounts 02-04

01 Chart of Accounts

The concept of Chart of Accounts (organization of Accounts Groups & Ledgers) and the pre-created *Accounts Groups* & *Accounts Ledgers* (called Reserved Groups & Ledgers) have been explained earlier (§02/01-03). Here, we explain the nature & properties of these pre created Groups to help you understand how to organise the Accounts Groups & Ledger Accounts, that you further create, under proper Reserved Groups.

02 Account Groups of Balance Sheet

We now describe the Accounts Groups that appear in Balance Sheet. Some common examples of Groups and underlying Ledger Accounts. Groups are shown in Normal Font while Ledger Accounts are shown Italics.

02.01 Account Groups of Liabilities

The Groups & common subgroups / Ledger Accounts of Liabilities of Balance Sheet are shown below:

Capital: This is a primary Group that contains the Capital and Reserves & Surplus of the Company.

- **Capital Account**: Ledger Accounts for Owners Capital may be placed under Capital Group (or its sub-group). Common example of Ledger Accounts under Capital Account group is Share (or Equity) Capital, Partners' Capital Accounts, Proprietors Capital Account. Members Capital A/c etc. Separate Ledgers may be created for Equity Capital, Preference Capital A/c etc.
- **Reserves & Surplus [Retained Earnings]:** It's a child-group to Capital Account. All Reserve Accounts (referred as Retained Earnings) are placed under this group. Common examples are: General Reserve, Capital Reserve, Investment Allowance Reserve, Share Premium Account etc.

Capital Account

Share Capital

Equity Shares

- *Equity Shares - paid up*

Preference Share

- *11% Redeemable Pref Share*

Reserves & Surplus (Retained Earnings)

- *Capital Redemption Reserve*
- *Capital Reserve*
- *General Reserve*
- *Investment Allowance Reserve*
- *Revaluation Reserve*
- *Share Premium*

> ***Note:*** *In case of Companies limited by shares (Limited & Private Limited Companies), though normally Credit Balance of P & L Account should go into Reserves & Surplus and Debit Balance should be shown under Misc Expenses (Assets), Tally shows under separate account – Profit & Loss account.*

Loans (Liabilities)*:* All loans taken by Company should be placed here. Tally creates 3 reserved sub-groups

- **Bank OD Accounts [Bank OCC A/c]**: While Current Bank A/c should be placed under Current Assets (explained later), Bank Overdraft and Cash/Credit Accounts availed under Hypothecation, Bill Discounting etc. operated on a day-to-day basis should be placed under this group, to allow transactions in Payment, Receipt and Contra Vouchers like normal Bank Accounts (although normally these are Secured Loan). The ledger accounts under this group participate in the Vouchers in same manner like ledgers placed under Bank Accounts (under Current Assets)
- **Secured Loans**: Debentures, Term Loans (Medium/Long term), Secured Loans taken from Banks, Financial Institutes etc. against security (like mortgage/hypothecation, pledge etc) should be placed under this group.
- **Unsecured Loans**: Loans taken (without any collateral security) from outside Parties, Directors, Friends and Relatives, Deposits etc, should be placed under this group.

Loans (Liabilities)

Bank OD Accounts

Overdraft A/c

- *SBI OD A/c*

Cash Credit Account

- *Bank of India C/C A/c*
- *Bank of India Bill Discounting A/c*

Secured Loans

Mid Term Loan

- *ICICI Term Loan*

Debentures

- *11% Redeemable Debentures*
- *9.5% Convertible Debentures*

Unsecured Loans

Public Deposits

Personal Loans

- *Mahesh Kumar*
- Brijmohan Shaw

Current Liabilities

This group normally constitutes a large number of Ledger Accounts and Sub Groups and is subdivided into 3 sub groups: Duties & Taxes, Provisions and Sundry Creditors.

- **Duties and Taxes**: This sub-group is for all Excise, Sales and other Trade Taxes. This head normally constitutes all the Duties & Taxes that you collect or pay through Sales & Purchase transactions, whose balance will appear in Balance Sheet, fro preparation of proper Statutory Returns, like Sales Tax (e.g., VAT, CST, Excise Duty,
  Taxes collected through other means (other than Invoice) like Marketing Fee, Purchase Tax and amount collected through Payroll (like TDS, PF, ESI, P Tax etc are not placed under this. Such accounts should be placed under Current Liabilities.
- **Provisions**: It is a place for all sorts of Provisions (like Provision for Bad Debts etc). Place similar Provisions as applicable (e. Provision for Bad & Doubtful Debts, Deferred Payment Liabilities etc). However Depreciation Provided should go under Fixed Assets (because Depreciation provided is *Diminution* in Book Value of Fixed Assets).
- **Sundry Creditors**: Place the ledger accounts of all Trade Creditors / suppliers (even if any ledger account has Debit Balance at some point of time due to advance payment etc). If you sell to or purchase from same party, create only one ledger account and place under Sundry Debtors or Sundry Creditors Group (as convenient).
- **Current Liabilities**: Place all other liability accounts (which are not candidates of any the above 3 groups), like Liabilities for Expenses, Employees contribution for ESI/PF or TDS realized from Contractors/Employees, etc.

Current Liabilities

Duties & Taxes

- *CST*
- *Excise Duty*
- *VAT*

Provision

- *Provision for Bad & Doubtful Debts*

Sundry Creditors

Suppliers- Raw Materials

- *A Bose & Co*

Suppliers – Other Materials

- *S Kumar Bros*
- *Premier Engg Co*

Current Liabilities

- *General Expenses*
- Government Dues
  - o *License Fees*
  - o *P F Payable*
  - o Excise Duty Payable
- *Interest Payable Accrued*
- *Liabilities for Expenses*
- Salary & Bonus Payable

02.02 Account Groups of Assets

Fixed Assets: This constitutes all the Fixed Assets like Immovable Properties, Patents, Trade Rights etc, Work-in-progress (Capital Projects) etc

Fixed Assets may have several subgroups for each type of assets if you wish to have separate Ledger Accounts for individual Asset. You may keep the figures of Original Cost and Accumulated Depreciation for Fixed Assets separately.

Fixed Assets

Leasehold Assets

- *Leasehold Land*

Free Hold Assets

- *Land*
- *Buildings*
- *Vehicles*
- Office Equipments
  - o *Computers*
  - o *Air Conditioners*
  - o *Misc Office Equipments*

Investments

Place here all Ledger Accounts related to Investments in Shares, Bonds, Govt. Securities and Investment in other companies

Investments

Equity Shares Quoted

Equity Shares UnQuoted

Mutual Funds

Government Securities

- *National Savings Certificates*
- *RBI Gold Bonds*

Current Assets

It constitutes 6 Reserved Sub Groups: Stock-in-hand, Deposits (Assets), Loans & Advances (Assets), Cash-in-hand, Bank Accounts, Sundry Debtors.

You should place individual Ledger Account under the appropriate subgroups and avoid placing any Ledger directly under primary group, i.e., Current Assets.

- **Stock-in-hand**: Create all Ledger Accounts for Closing Stock under this group. Normally, you should create separate Ledger Accounts for Raw Materials, Work-in-process and Finished Goods, as required.
- **Deposits (Assets)**: Place all the Deposits made by the Company (Deposits received by the Company should be placed under Unsecured Loans) like Fixed Deposits, Security Deposits, Deposits with Electricity, Telephone dept, Deposits in other companies, Rental Deposits etc. under this Group.
- **Loans and Advances (Assets)**: Place all Loans & Advances of non-trading nature given (Advances to Suppliers should be debited to the respective Supplier Ledger Account). Examples are: Advances against Salary, Loans to Employees, Advances to Fixed Assets Suppliers etc.
- **Sundry Debtors**: Place all the Trade Customer Ledger Accounts (even if Opening Balance is Credit). If you sell to or purchase from same party, create only one ledger account and place under Sundry Debtors or Sundry Creditors Group. Advances received from Customers also should also be Credited to the Customer's ledger under Sundry Debtors group. If the number of Debtors are more, you may create subgroups as per Region, Product Lines, Registered / Unregistered, etc, as per convenience in practical working & Debtors Control.
- **Cash-in-Hand**: Tally creates a Cash Ledger Account (Cash-in-Hand) and places under this group. You may create more Cash accounts (e.g., Petty Cash, Cash-at-Branch, Cash-in-Transit etc) and place under this group.
- **Bank Accounts**: All the Bank Accounts like Current Accounts, Savings Accounts etc. (except Cash Credit, Overdraft or Loan Accounts) should be placed here.

Stock-in-hand

- *Stock of Raw Materials*
- *Stock of Stores & Spares*
- *Work-in Process*
- *Stock of Packing Materials*
- *Stock of Finished Goods*

Deposits (Assets)

- *Deposit with CESC*
- *Deposit with Sales Tax*
- *Deposit with Excise Deptt*
- *Deposit with Office Landowner*

Loans and Advances (Assets)

Loan to Employees

Loan to Others

- *B K Mehra*
- *S Samaddar*

Sundry Debtors

Customers Kolkata

- *B K Stores*
- *M M Enterprises*

Customers Outside

- *Radha Govind Stores*
- *Krishna Stores*

Cash-in-Hand

- Main Cash
- Petty Cash

Bank Accounts

- *SBI Current Account*
- *Bank of India Current Account*

Branch / Divisions

Place Ledgers for Branch, Division, Affiliate, Sister Concern, Subsidiary etc under this Group. It may help Inter branch reconciliation & consolidation. Tally permits Sales/Purchase transactions also (like Party Accounts).

Branch / Division

- Bangalore Branch
- Vishakhapatnam Warehouse

Misc. Expenses (Asset)

For Limited Companies, Preliminary, Pre-operative and similar expenses (to the extent not written off to Profit & Loss A/cs) should be placed here. Though the accumulated Loss of a Company should also fall in this category, Tally treats it as negative Profit (Nett Loss) and carries to Profit & Loss a/c.

Misc Expenses (Asset)

- *Preliminary Expenses*
- *Profit & Loss A/c*

Suspense Account

This is a primary Group that appears in Balance Sheet. You may create a Suspense ledger to record money paid/received whose details are not yet known. Later on the transaction is posted to the appropriate account. Example: Advance paid for Travelling Expenses, an entry in Bank Statement not yet recorded in Bank Book, etc. details for which is not yet known, may be recorded in such ledger. As far as practicable, avoid using such Account.

Ultimately all the amounts of Suspense Account will be transferred to respective accounts and the Balance of Suspense Account would be NIL.

03 Account Groups of Profit & Loss Account

These groups are further classified as Direct Income & Direct Expenses (apart from Sales & Purchase) considered for

Gross Profit computation and Indirect Income & Indirect Expenses, considered for Net Profit computation.

Direct Income & Direct Expenses are relevant only when you wish to prepare separate Trading and Profit & Loss Account to get the figures of Gross Profit & Net Profit separately.

03.01 Account Groups of Income

Sales

All sorts of Sales should constitute this group. You may have multiple Sales Accounts. You may create separate accounts for Sales and Sales Returns or club up Sales and Sales Returns in one Account - the net effect in Accounts however remains same. You may create different Ledgers for Sales according to Tax Liability (e.g for VAT, CST etc) or Products or other criterion as per your reporting requirement.

Professionals or Servicing companies who do not have Sales income but have Income from Professional Fees & Services, may alter name of the Sales group to Service Income (or some suitable name) or place the Professional Service Charges or Servicing Charges under Direct Income (explained next).

Sales

- *Sales of Finished Goods*
- *Sales of Scrap*
- *Sales Returns*
- *Discount Allowed on Sales*

Direct Income

This Group holds Ledger Accounts for Income considered for computation of Gross Profit. Professionals may place Ledger Accounts like Professional Service Charges or Servicing Charges under this group.

Direct Income

- *Service Income*

Indirect Income

Normally, all non-major revenues like receipts on account of Rent, Interest, Commission, Dividend etc should be placed here. Ledger Accounts placed under this group are excluded for computation of Gross Profit but are considered for computation of Net Profit only.

Indirect Income

- *Rent Received*
- *Interest Received*
- *Dividend Received*
- *Profit on Sale of Fixed Asset*

03.01 Account Groups of Expenses

Purchase

This group holds all trade Purchases.

You may create separate Accounts for Purchases and Purchases Return or club up Purchases and Purchases Returns in one account – although net effect in accounts remains same. Most often, Purchases Bills include various additional charges like Freight, Delivery Charges, Postage, Sales Tax, Excise Duty, etc., required for computing additional cost on Purchase should be placed here.

Purchase

- *Raw Materials Purchase*
- *Stores Purchase*
- *Packing Materials Purchase*

Direct Expenses

Place all Ledger Accounts of Direct Expenses considered for computing Gross Profit/Loss, Example: Carriage Inwards, Wages etc

Direct Expenses

- *Power & Fuel*
- *Wages*
- *Freight Inwards*
- *Packing Charges*

Indirect Expenses

All expenses considered for computation of Net Profit/Loss only (and not considered for computation of Gross Profit) should be placed here

> ***Note:*** *Miscellaneous Expenses (Asset) is not an Expense Account – it's an Asset which appear under Balance Sheet and not in Profit & Loss Account.*

Indirect Expenses

Office Electricity

General Office Expenses

Repairs & maintenance

- *Building Repairs*
- *Electricity Repairs*
- *Computer Repairs*

License Fees & Local Taxes

Office Administration Expenses

Stationery & Postage

- *Stationery*
- *Postage*
- *Computer Consumables*

Internet Charges

Telephone & Mobile Expenses

Conveyance Expenses

Travelling Expenses

Advertisement Expenses

Depreciation

- *Depreciation on Building*
- *Depreciation on Machinery*
- *Depreciation on Vehicles*Interest Paid
- *Interest on Unsecured Loan*

- *Interest on Public Deposits*
- *Interest to Bank / FI*

Employee Expenses

- *Staff salary*
- *Bonus to Staff*
- *Leave Salary*
- *Incentive Salary*
- *Employer Contribution to PF / FPF*
- *Employer Contribution to ESI*
- *Staff Welfare*

Legal Expenses

04 Reserved Ledger Accounts

Tally automatically creates two Ledger Accounts:

- Cash (under Cash-in-Hand Group)
- Profit & Loss Account (Direct Primary Account)

Besides these 2 Ledgers, you have to create all other Ledger Accounts and place them under appropriate Group as explained above.

> **Note:** *Profit & Loss Account (ledger) can be transacted through Journal voucher only. Such voucher should contain transaction with Capital (Capital / Reserve) Account. Never make a Journal voucher to adjust the Revenue Accounts with P & L Account as Tally automatically computes Net Profit/Loss and reflects it in the Profit & Loss account.*

05 Organisation of Account Groups & Ledgers

In the above examples, we have shown how Accounts Groups & Ledgers may be organised in hierarchical way. There is no limit on depth of nesting, number of Group/sub Groups and number of Ledger Accounts that can be placed under a Group/sub-group.

The benefit of organisation of Accounts in several levels of Account Groups are that you get organised reports with control totals at each Group level.

Only Ledger Accounts are transacted in Vouchers. Account Groups do not participate in any voucher (they are used to organise the Ledger Accounts). You Debit or Credit a Ledger in any Voucher (but not any Group). So, you should be plan whether you will treat an Account as Account Group and create Ledgers under the Account Group to have detailed break up as per Account Ledgers, or you will create a Ledger only.

For example, a small organization will create a ledger account INTEREST (under Indirect Expenses).

Indirect Expenses

- *Interest Paid*

A large organisation who have taken loan from different sources may create several Interest accounts and place them under a Group Interest, as follows

Interest Paid

- *Interest on Unsecured Loan*
- *Interest on Debentures*
- *Interest to Banks*
- *Interest to Financial Institutions*

FAQ: Frequently Asked Questions

FAQ-1: What is Chart of Accounts

Ans: Chart of Accounts is the hierarchical multi level organised list of Account Groups & subordinate Ledgers.

On creation of Company, Tally automatically creates several Reserved Accounts Groups. New Account Groups are normally created subordinate to Reserved Accounts Groups.

FAQ-2: We have taken a secured loan from Bank of India. Under which Account Group we should place the Bank Ledger Account

Ans: If you make regular transactions from this Bank account (i.e deposit / issue cheques, then you should place the Bank Account under *Bank OCC* Group(to enable entry of its transactions in Payment / Receipt / Contra Vouchers). If you do not deposit / issue cheques, then you should place the Bank Account under *Secured Loans* Group.

FAQ-3: We Deduct TDS from Contractors Bill and for Payment of Interest. Under which group, we should place the Ledger Account *TDS Deducted from Parties*

Ans: If you maintain TDS system in Tally, then you should place TDS under Group Duties & Taxes, otherwise, you should place it under Current Liabilities.

FAQ-4: TDS is deducted from our Interest Bills by the Payee, at the time of payment, Under which group, we should place the Ledger Account *TDS Deducted by Parties*

Ans: You should place the Ledger Account *TDS Deducted by Parties* under Current Assets

FAQ-5: I made a gift to my son. Under which group, I should place the Gift Account, in my personal accounts

Ans: The *Gift* Account should be placed under *Capital* Account

Account Masters 02-05

We have earlier discussed Basic Accounts Master (§01/01-03). Now we explain Advanced Features of Accounts Masters.

01 Alias Names

Alias Names are additional Names / Identifiers for a Master record, used for Code / Mnemonics to select the Master record through *Alternate* Names.

Like the Name of the Master record, the Alias Names also appear in drop down list of master selection. You may select the Master by selecting either the *Name* or any of the *Alias* Names.

Configuration Set Up for Aliases

At Gateway, click *F12: Configuration > Accts/Inv Info* to get *Accounts Info Configuration* screen. At *Master Configuration* part, set *Yes* at *Allow Aliases along with Name* to enter Alias Names in any of the Master (F-1A). Consequently, you may enter Alias Name (or even Multiple Alias Names) in Masters, where applicable.

> **Note:** *At Master Configuration (F-1A), you may activate Alias feature. Consequently, at the respective Maser entry, you may selectively set Alias feature through Configuration for each Master Type, as explained at respective Master Creation. So, you may activate Alias for Ledger Account (F-6B) without activating Alias for Account Groups (F-3B).*

Master Configuration	
Allow ALIASES along with Names	? **Yes**
Allow Language ALIASES along with Names	? **Yes**

F-1A Masters General Configuration

Alias Name Entry in Masters

Having activated the *Alias* option, during master entry, you get a field *(alias)* to enter *Alias Names.* (F-2A / F-2B)

For example, you have one dealer at each city. You remember them by short name or place. So you can enter their short name as *Alias* and can select them by *Alias* Names.

Similarly, you may enter short Name, Code or Mnemonics as Alias name, e.g. for a Party G.C. Publishers, enter *Alias* as *GCP* (short Name) or *01125686* (Account Number). Now you can select the party from its Name (G.C. Publishers, GCP or 01125686)..

The First *Alias Name* may be displayed / printed at Name (in place of *Name* or *alongwith Name*) (§02.02/02-01)

The *Alias Names* cannot be created through *Multiple Masters Creation* mode (§01/02-06). Alias Names are to be entered through Single Masters option, as described earlier (§03/01-03)

> **Note:** *You may enter multiple Alias Names for any Master Record. But the Alias Name must be unique within the Master Type. For example, you cannot speciify same Aias name (e.g. AKB) to 2 ledger Accounts but can specify in one Ledger Account and one Account Group.*

Group Creation	
Name	: **Equity Share Capital**
(alias)	: EQCAP
	002
Under	: **Capital Account**

F-2A: Alias Name entry in Accounts Groups

Ledger Creation	
Name	: **Bank of Indal C/C A/c**
(alias)	: BOICC
	1205
Under	: **Bank OD A/c** *(Loans (Liability))*

F-2B: Alias Name entry in Ledger Accounts

02 Accounts Masters Advanced Features

At Master Configuration (*F12:Configure> Accts /Inventory Info*), set *Yes* at *Allow ADVANCED entries in Masters* (F-3A), to activate Advanced Configuration options for Masters

> **Note:** *To activate Advanced Mater entry option in respective Master Type (Account Group & Account Ledger), set Yes at* Allow ADVANCED entries in Masters *(F-3A). Then set up the individual options at respective Master Entry configuration (F-3B for Account Groups) & (F-6B for Account Ledgers)*

Accounts	
Allow ADVANCED entries in Masters	? **Yes**
Use ADDRESSES for Ledger Accounts	? **Yes**
Use CONTACT Details	? **Yes**
Add NOTES for Ledger Accounts	? **Yes**

F-3A: Advance Masters Entry Configuration screen

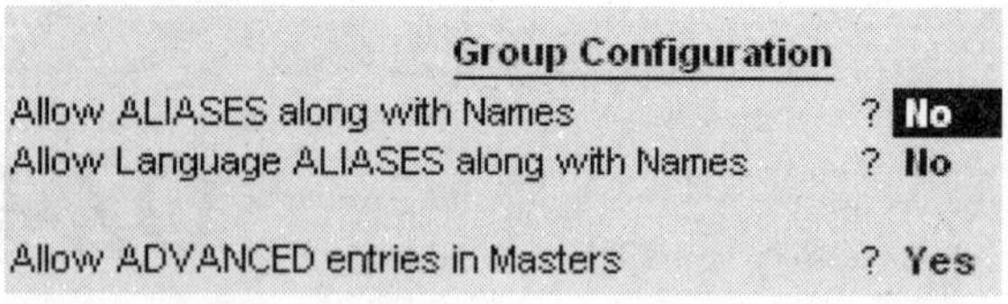

F-3B: Accounts Group Configuration screen

03 Accounts Groups Advanced Features

At Accounts Group creation / Alteration screen (§03.01/01-03 & §05/01-03), click *F12:Configure* to get Accounts Group Configuration screen (F-3B), to set the option for the current Group being entered / edited.

03.01 Primary Account Group

Tally organises Accounts Groups in hierarchical structure. The top level groups (called Primary Groups) do not have any higher parent group, while subordinate Groups are placed under some Group.

At the time of Company creation, Tally automatically creates some Primary Groups (called *Reserved Primary Groups*). All new groups created by are crated under some Groups (so they have a Parent group). The *Reserved Primary Groups* created by Tally carry some inherent properties (§01/02-04).

We have explained creation of Groups (§03.01/01-03) under some Reserved Primary Group (or its subordinate Groups). Normally you do not need to create new Primary Groups. However, in some special situations, you may need to create additional new Primary Groups (apart from Tally created *Reserved* Primary Groups) for organization of the Groups / Ledger Accounts in your own way.

To create new Primary Group, at Group Creation screen (F-4A), specify as follows:

- **Name:** At *Name*, Enter the Name of new Primary Group to be created
- **Parent Group**: At *Under*, select *Primary* from the list of Groups (F-4B)
- **Nature of Primary Group**: At *Nature of Group* field, select *the Nature of Group* list (F-4C)
- **Trading Account Applicability**: If you have selected *Income* or *Expense* at *Nature of Group*, you further get a prompt *Does it affect Gross Profit* (F-4A). At *Does it affect Gross Profit*,
    - o set *Yes* if the Group is to be included in Gross Profit / Loss (i.,e treated like *Direct Expense or Direct Income*),
    - o set *No*, if it is to be treated like *Indirect Income or Indirect Expense*.

This way you may create new important Primary Groups not provided by Tally (like Depreciation, Interest Paid etc.), for better presentation of Accounts.

Note: *Do not create Primary Groups for Sales, Purchase, Cash & Bank, Duties & Taxes. These groups carry special properties and the respective features will not work, if the related Ledger Accounts/ Account Groups are placed under any other user created Parent Group.*

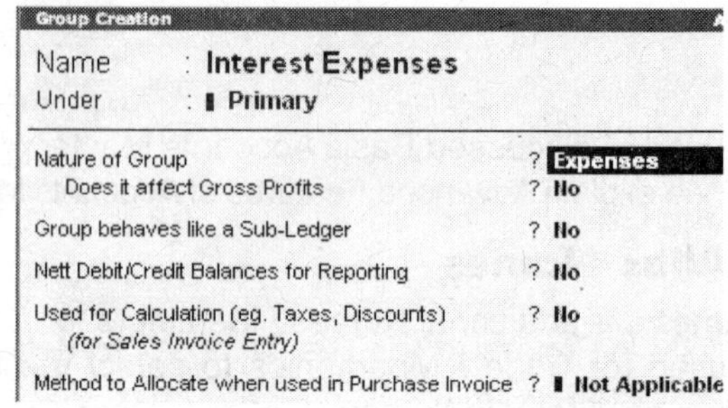

F-4A: Primary Group creation

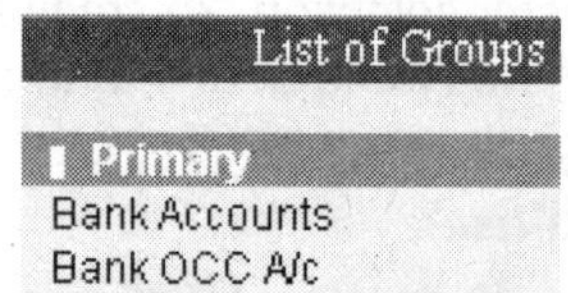

F-4B Parent Group selection

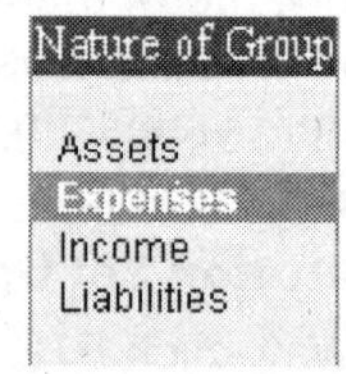

F-4C: Nature of Group list

03.02 Group Behaving like Ledger

There is no Sub Ledger concept in Tally. You have to create Account Groups & Ledgers. Often, under some Groups (like Sundry Debtors & Creditors, Employees, Advance etc), there are numerous Ledger Accounts. The Trial Balance and other reports showing the Ledger Accounts Details, become unmanageably long showing each Ledger Account.

To get a consolidated figures in Reports, you may create an Account Group showing the consolidated figures of all subordinate Ledgers under the Group (referred as *Group behaving as Ledger*).

However, in Voucher entry, you select Individual Ledgers, and you get separate Ledger Accounts as usual.

At Group Creation / Alteration (F-3A/01-03), set *Yes* at the field *Group Behaves like a sub Ledger* (F-4D).

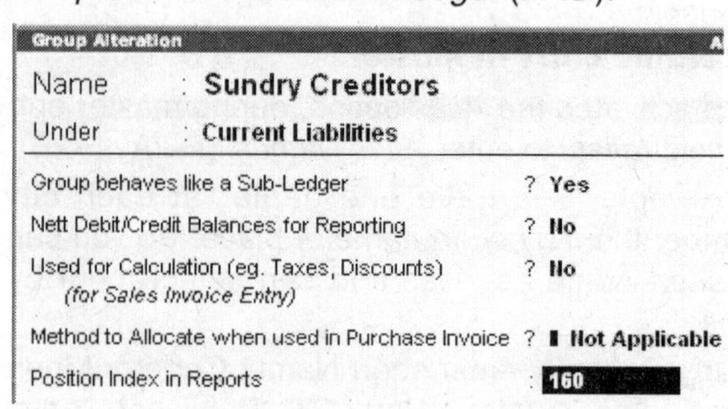

F-4D: Group behaving as Ledger

Trial Balance — Ctrl + M

Particulars	ABC Academy 9-10 1-Apr-2009 to 31-Mar-2010 Closing Balance	
	Debit	Credit
Current Liabilities		**9,79,490.00**
Sundry Creditors		8,78,880.00
P F		*1,00,590.00*
TDS		*20.00*
Grand Total	**25,07,710.00**	**25,07,710.00**

F-4E: Group figure instead of individual ledger figure

Trial Balance — Ctrl + M

Particulars	Debit	Credit
Current Liabilities		**9,79,490.00**
Sundry Creditors		8,78,880.00
B M Suppliers		7,170.00
S Roy (Employee)		8,71,710.00
P F		*1,00,590.00*
TDS		*20.00*
		40 more ...
Grand Total	**25,07,710.00**	**25,07,710.00**

F-4F: Individual ledger figure under the Group

Consequently, in Reports (e.g in Trial Balance), the total figure of the Group (e.g Sundry Creditors) is shown (F-4E), instead of individual ledger accounts which would have been shown (F-4F)

Note

- This feature only reduces the length of a Report, hiding individual ledger details. However, it makes no difference in voucher entry. All ledger accounts will be available in the selection list and all reports of the child Ledger Accounts of the Group will be printed as usual, without any effect.
- This feature is useful only for Lowest Level Group (Group having only child Ledger Accounts, but no child groups) containing a large number of Ledger Accounts.

03.03 Account Net Balance

Normally, in Reports showing the Transaction figures of Accounts Groups, the Net transaction is shown.

At Group Creation / Alteration (F-4D), at *Net Debit / Credit Balances for Reporting*:

- Set *No* to show both Debit & Credit figures total separately (under the respective Debit / Credit columns:F-5A)
- Set *Yes* to show the net of Debit / Credit figure only (under the respective Debit / Credit column:F-5B)

Consequently, the Group Balance of each Group is shown according to the option set for respective Group.

Group Summary — Ctrl + M

Particulars	Closing Balance	
	Debit	Credit
Loans & Advances (Asset)	**15,000.00**	
Sundry Debtors	**17,310.50**	**3,250.00**
Cash-in-Hand	**12,49,459.50**	
Bank Accounts	**32,100.00**	**83,730.00**
Pre Paid Expenses	1,800.00	
Opening Stock	**1,000.00**	
Grand Total	**13,16,670.00**	**86,980.00**

F-5A: Group Summary Showing both Dr/ Cr Figures

Group Summary — Ctrl + M

Particulars	Closing Balance	
	Debit	Credit
Loans & Advances (Asset)	**15,000.00**	
Sundry Debtors	**14,060.50**	
Cash-in-Hand	**12,49,459.50**	
Bank Accounts	**32,100.00**	**83,730.00**
Pre Paid Expenses	1,800.00	
Closing Stock	**2,000.00**	
Grand Total	**13,14,420.00**	**83,730.00**

F-5B:Group Summary Showing Net Figure

Note: *This feature is set for each Group separately. So, Balance of each Group is shown as per respective option set. So, in a report, one Group may show net Balance while another Group may show Debit & Credit figures separately.*

04 Ledger Accounts Configuration

We have shown Accounts Ledger Creation with default Features. At Ledger Account creation / Alteration, click *F12: Configure* to get Ledger Account Configuration screen (F-6B), to set the Options as follows:

- **Alias Name:** Alias have been explained earlier (§01). At *Allow Aliases for* Name, set Yes to enable entry for Alias entry for the current Ledger Account,
- **Ledger Account Notes:** At *Use Notes for Ledger Accounts*, Set *Yes* to get another field to enter Internal Notes about the ledger account, in one line (F-6A). The notes are for internal info only and is not shown in any report
- **Advanced Master Entries:** At *Advanced Entries in Master*, set *Yes* to get additional field 'Inventory Values are effected (except for Cash / Bank Ledger) & Tax Information section (F-6A).
- **Ledger Account Addresses:** At *Use Addresses for Ledger Account*, set *Yes* to get fields for Address Entry (Mailing Name, Address, State, PINCODE) to enter address for some Ledger Accounts (like Personal Ledger Accounts Bank Ledger Accounts etc), as described next (§04.01).
    - o **Contact Details:** Having set Yes at above option, at *Use Contact Details*, set *Yes* to get another filed to enter Contact details, in one line (F-6A)
    - o **Multiple Mailing Address:** To enter Multiple Address for the current Ledger Account, at *Use Multiple Mailing Address*, set *Yes* at *Use Multiple Mailing Address* (F-6B). Consequently, you will get a field *Set/Alter Multiple Mailing Address* at *Ledger Creation/ Alteration* screen (F-6A) to enter Multiple Address (§06/03-01).
- **Ledger Accounts Other info:** At *Use Other information for Ledger Accounts*, set *Yes* to get additional fields to enter other details, like related Party Info etc, normally applicable for Companies, for disclosure in the Notes in Financial Statements.

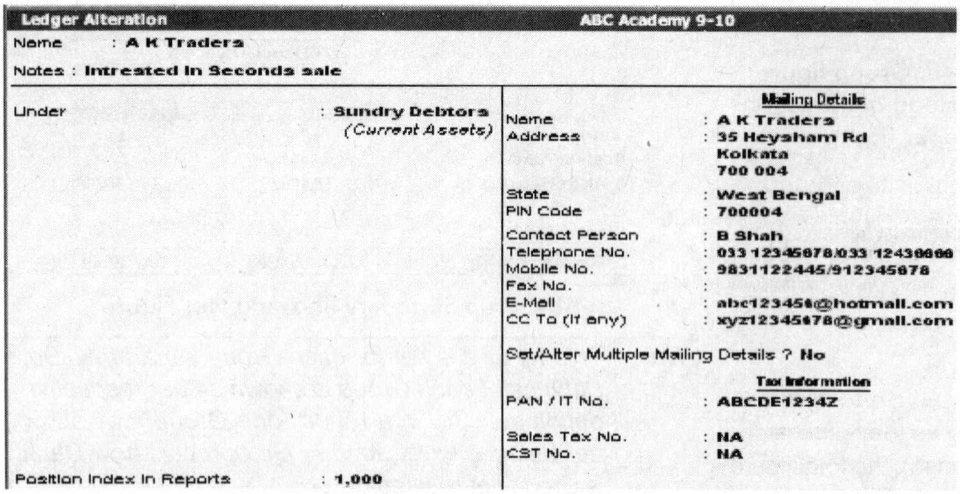

F-6A:Ledger Accounts creation with Advanced options

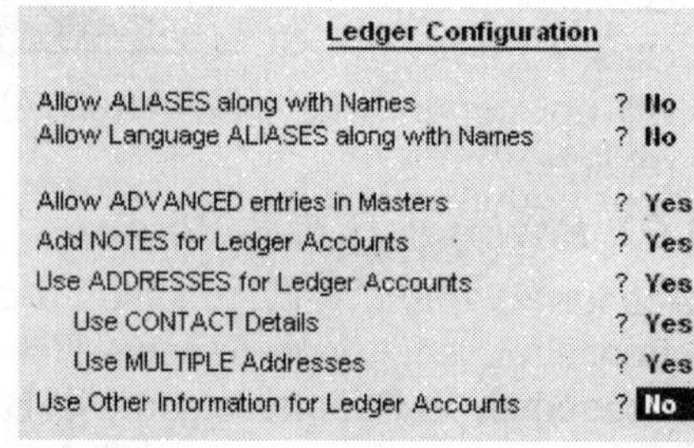

F-6B: Ledger creation configuration

04.01 Mailing Details / Tax Information

In case of personal ledger accounts placed under Loan, Advance, Branch, Sundry Debtors or Sundry Creditors, you may enter following additional Information (F-6A).

- **Name:** Enter here the Party's Mailing Name (i.e legal name). The ledger name is carried here. You may change the ledger name, The Mailing Name entered here will be printed in all external document
- **Mailing Details:** At the section, *Mailing Details*, enter following communication details as required (F-6A). You may leave any of the field, if not required.
  - **Address:** At *Address*, enter address in the same way as explained in Company creation. You may enter in multiple lines (normally 3-4 lines), in the way you want to print in the Invoices, Receipts etc.
  - **State:** At *State*, select State from the drop down list
  - **Pin Code:** At *Pin Code,* enter the PINCODE
  - **Contact Person:** At *Contact Person,* enter the name of the contact person of the organization.
  - **Telephone No:** At *Telephone No*, enter the Telephone / Mobile Number, if any. This helps you to keep the phone numbers of all parties at a central place (it serves as your ready phonebook/ address book). The phone numbers may be printed in Reports, as ready reference, without any need to look elsewhere,
  - **Fax:** At *Fax*, Enter the Fax Number, if any
  - **e-mail:** At *e-mail*, enter the e-mail address, if any. Reports may be e-mailed to the party even through Tally.ERP 9, It is good idea to fill the e-mail address even you do not send e-mail through Tally.ERP 9, as you can keep e-mail address of Parties at a centralized place, like phone numbers.
  - **e-mail copy:** At *c.c To (if any)*, enter the Copy to e-mail address. This is included in the copy to field in e-mail. This is relevant only when you enter main e-mail address.
  - **Ledger Multiple Mailing Address:** Having activated Multiple Mailing Address at Configuration (F-6B), at *Set Alter Multiple Address Details*, set *Yes* to enter Multiple Mailing Address for the Ledger Account in the same way as explained for Multiple Mailing Address for the Company (§07/02-02)

Tax Information: At *Tax Information* section, enter the following details:

i. PAN / IT No: Enter the I tax PAN, if any. This data is used in Accounts Confirmation Report etc.
ii. Sales Tax Number: Enter Sales Tax Number, if any.
iii. CST Number: Enter Central Sales Tax Number, if any.

You may leave any of these field blank at the time of Ledger Creation and enter later on through Ledger Alteration.

In Bank Ledger Accounts, you get some additional fields (F-2A/04-01), like:

- **Branch Name:** Name of the Bank Branch
- **BSR Code:** Enter the BSR Code of the Branch (as printed in the cheque book). This is useful for electronic transfer of fund.

05 Sort Position

Account Groups / Ledgers are listed in sequence of Sort (Index) Value and then in Alphabetical order having same Sort Value. The same default Sort Value is allotted to all subordinate Group / Ledger Accounts. So, the Groups / Ledgers are listed in alphabetical sequence within same parent Group (because sort values of all accounts under a common parent group are same)

However, sometimes, you may need to list important accounts in specific place, instead of default order. In that case, you need to change the Position Index value as desired.

At Account Groups (F-4D) & Ledger Account Masters (F-6A) creation / alteration, Click *F10:Skip Sort/ Edit Sort* toggle button:

- Click *F10:Edit Sort*, to get the field *Position Index in Reports*, showing the default value of Sort Sequence. (F-6A), which you may change to place the Account Group or Ledger in specific order with the Account Group.
- Click *F10:Skip Sort*. The Position Index in Reports field will not appear and the default value will be internally retained.

05.01 Position Index Values

In Account Groups, Tally specifies a default Sort value for Account Groups for each Reserved Group,as they appear in Balance Sheet & P L statements, the following order (F-7A & F-7B):

- Major Groups of Liabilities
- Major Groups of Assets
- Major Groups of Direct Income / Expenses
- Major Groups of Indirect Income / Expenses

Multi Group Alteration Ctrl + M

Under Group : All Items

S.No.	Name of Group	Under	Sorting Position
1.	Capital Account	Primary	10
2.	Loans (Liability)	Primary	20
3.	Current Liabilities	Primary	30
4.	Fixed Assets	Primary	40
5.	Investments	Primary	50
6.	Current Assets	Primary	60
7.	Branch / Divisions	Primary	70
8.	Misc. Expenses (ASSET)	Primary	80
9.	Suspense A/c	Primary	90

F-7A Primary Reserved Account of Balance Sheet Groups with default Sort:Position values

Multi Group Alteration Ctrl + M

Under Group : All Items

S.No.	Name of Group	Under	Sorting Position
... 9 more			
10.	Sales Accounts	Primary	230
11.	Purchase Accounts	Primary	240
12.	Direct Incomes	Primary	250
13.	Direct Expenses	Primary	260
14.	Indirect Incomes	Primary	270
15.	Indirect Expenses	Primary	280
16.	Reserves & Surplus	Capital Account	100
17.	Bank OD A/c	Loans (Liability)	110
18.	Secured Loans	Loans (Liability)	120
19.	Unsecured Loans	Loans (Liability)	130
20.	Duties & Taxes	Current Liabilities	140
21.	Provisions	Current Liabilities	150
22.	Sundry Creditors	Current Liabilities	160
23.	Stock-in-Hand	Current Assets	170
24.	Deposits (Asset)	Current Assets	180
25.	Loans & Advances (Asset)	Current Assets	190
26.	Sundry Debtors	Current Assets	200
27.	Cash-in-Hand	Current Assets	210
28.	Bank Accounts	Current Assets	220
29.	Share Capital	Capital Account	500
30.	A Burdhan	Unsecured Loans	500
31.	ICICI Term Loan	Secured Loans	500

F-7B Subordinate Reserved Account Group and user created Groups with default Sort Values

The user created Groups are given value of 500. All user created Ledgers are allotted value of 1000.

You may change the Order of appearance as per your own choice. So, the Ledger Accounts of ledgers under a Group will appear in Alphabetical Order. So, the following Groups under Sundry Debtors will appear in following alphabetical order:

Account Groups	Sort Value
Asansol	500
Durgapur	500
Kolkata	500
Siliguri	500

But, you may like the Groups to appear as follows according to the importance of each zone

To get that, you may allot Sort Sequence to each ledger as. So, you change the Sort Value accordingly, as shown in the following table:

Account Groups	Sort Value
Kolkata	500
Durgapur	501
Asansol	502
Siliguri	503

In the same way, you may change the Sort Value of Ledger Accounts of Kolkata Group as shown below

S Vaidya & Co	1000
A Zamir & Co	1001

In this case, the Ledger name S Vaidya will appear before A Zamir & Co.

The sort values are considered within the same Account Group for ordering the subordinate Group / Ledger Accounts. The sort values may be duplicate. In that case, the order will be alphabetical within the same sort value.

So, you can write the Sort Values as follows. The Ledger within the Parent Group will be sorted as per sort sequence.

S Vaidya & Co	1
A Zamir & Co	2

This way, you arrange the newly created Account Groups / Ledgers as per your own choice, defying the alphabetical sequence within a Group.

You may change the default Sort Value through Edit Mode of Account Groups & Ledgers (Single & Multiple).

FAQ: Frequently Asked Questions

FAQ-1: How I can print Ledger Accounts in my desired sequence

Ans: Normally the ledger accounts appear in alphabetical order in reports (like Trial Balance, Outstanding List etc). To print the Report as per user defined sequence, you may change the sort index of the ledger accounts.

At the time of creation of a Ledger, Tally allots a fixed Index Number (same value - 1000) to all Ledger Accounts. The ledgers appear in sequence of Index Number + Alphabet. As the Index value of all ledgers are same by default, the ledgers appear in alphabetical order.

To get the Ledger Account sin desired sequence, edit the Index Value as follows:

Select *Accounts Info>Ledger* and then select *Alter* under Multiple Ledgers. Click *F10:Edit Sort* to get the column *Sorting Position*. Now change the value of sorting position. For example to print the Ledger Accounts in following order, change the value of Sorting Position

Ledger Name	Sorting Position
V Traders	1001
A Traders	1002
T Traders	1003

FAQ-2: How can I list the Ledger Names of Sundry Debtors in respective Reports, in my own sequence (a few important parties at the top), not in Alphabetical sequence.

Ans: Get the Ledger Accounts of *Sundry Debtors* in Alter mode. (GoT>Accounts Info>Ledger >Alter (under Multiple). Select *Sundry Debtors* at *Under Group* field, All the Ledger Accounts of Sundry Debtors will be listed. At Sort Position field, you will see the value 1000 in all ledger Accounts. Now change the value of the respective ledger accounts, in sequence you want them to be listed. The ledger accounts will be listed in ascending order of Sort Values entered by you (instead of being listed in alphabetical order)

For example, you may enter 1,2 3 etc at the Sort Value. Even you may enter same value in multiple ledgers. They will be listed in alphabetical order within themselves. For example, you assign values 1,2,3,4 5 to 5 important ledger accounts. They will be listed as per the value. Other Ledger Accounts will be listed alphabetical order, after these 5 ledger accounts.

This way, you may order the sequence of Accounts Groups, Ledger Accounts, under any Group, in your desired sequence. You may also change the sequence of Primary Groups. The subordinate Groups / Ledgers will be listed under the respective parent group only.

FAQ-3: What is the difference between Ledger Name and Ledger Mailing Name?

Ans: Ledger Name is the unique identifying Name of the Ledger. You cannot create two Ledger Accounts of same Ledger Name. Ledger Name is printed in all internal books and statements.

Mailing Name is the Legal Name of the Organisation which is printed in the external documents. In most of the cases, both the Name & Mailing name are same. But in some cases, you may have to deal with multiple ledgers with same name (e.g different bank accounts of same bank, different parties with same name etc)

In such case, create distinctive ledger name (as ledger name must be unique), but give same legal name at Mailing Name, so that mailing name is printed in the documents / reports which are handed over to the Party.

For example, you have 3 different Customers named Binapani Pustakalalya at Malda, Bolpur & Siliguri. To keep 3 different ledgers, you must enter different ledger names (as ledger names cannot be duplicate), like Binapani Pustakalalya (Malda), Binapani Pustakalalya(Bolpur) & Binapani Pustakalalya(Siliguri), but enter the legal name of the Party (i.e Binapani Pustakalaya) at Ledger Mailing Name for all the 3 Parties (the Ledger Mailing Name may be duplicate). In all external documents (Bill, Receipt etc), Mailing name (i.e Binapani Pustakalaya) will be printed instead of Ledger name. So, in external documents (like invoice, receipt), only Binapani Pustakalalya will be printed in all the 3 cases, while in all internal records (ledger, cash book, Trial balance etc), the Ledger Name would be printed . At the time of selection of ledger name during working with Tally, the Ledger name, like Binapani Pustakalaya (Bolpur) will appear, to select the correct ledger.

Multiple Accounts Masters Creation 02-06

01 Multiple Account Masters Entry

We have so far seen entry of one master (Account Group / Account Ledger) at a time (referred as *Single Master Entry* mode). This mode is not very convenient to create large number of Masters, at a time.

In multiple masters mode, you may create / display / alter several masters in one screen. In case of large volume Masters creation / alteration, you may find using the multiple masters mode more convenient.

02 Multiple Account Group entry

At *Accounts Group Menu* (F-2B/01-03) select *Create* under *Multiple Group* section for creation of multiple Account Group in a single screen (F-1A)

Parent Group: At *Under Group* field (at the header):

- **Group Creation under Specific parent Group**: Select a the *Parent Group* under which you wish to create all the new Groups (press *Alt+C* to get Group Creation (secondary) screen, to create a New Group from within the current screen, and then select the newly created Group)
- **Group Creation under any parent Group**: Select *All Items*, to create new Groups under any existing parent Group

> ***Note:*** *At* Under Groups*, select* All Items *to create Group under any* Parent *Group (F-1A). However, select the specific* Parent *Group to create several Groups continuously under same parent Group (F-1B). You may change Parent Group at any point of time as desired.*

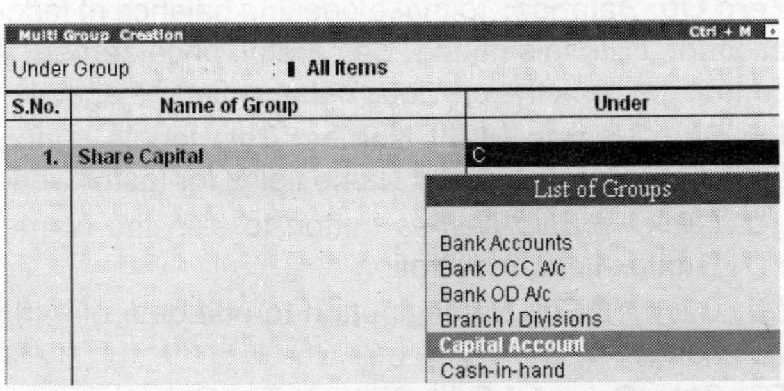

F-1A: Multiple Group creation (under any Parent Group)

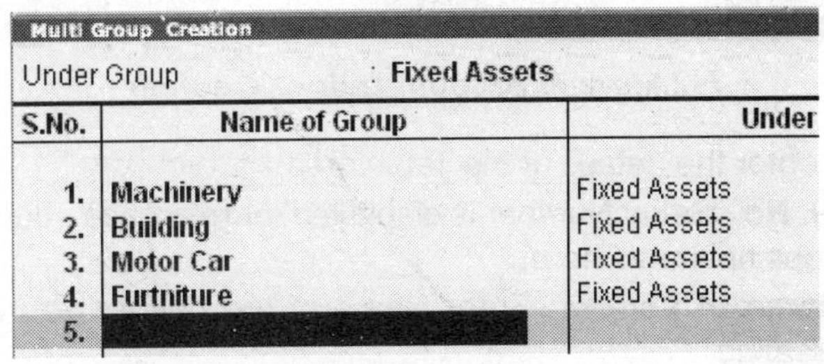

F-1B: Multiple Group creation (under one Group)

Now enter the details at the Table area (F-1B).

- **Sl. No.**: At *Sl. No*, Serial Number is displayed for reference - cursor does not move here.
- **Group Name**: At *Name of Group*, Enter Name of the Group you are creating.
- **Parent Group**: At *Under* field, select the Parent *Group* under which you wish to create Group.
  - If you have selected a Group at *Under Group*, the selected group (at Under Group field at the header) is carried as parent Group (at *Under* field, the cursor would not come at this field). This way you create several Groups under a Group much faster, as you do not to select the parent Group for each Group (F-1B)
  - If you had selected *All Items*, you have to select the parent Group at *Under* field for each ledger at this field from the *List of Groups* (F-1A)

This way, you can create multiple Groups in one entry screen. To terminate further entry, press <enter> on blank line and type *Yes* at *Accept? Yes or No* to save.

03 Multiple Account Ledger entry

At Accounts Ledger menu (F-2C/01-03), select *Create* under *Multiple Ledgers* section for creation of multiple Ledgers in a single screen (F-2A)

Parent Group: At *Under Group* field (at the header):

- **Ledger Creation under Specific parent Group**: Select the *Parent Group* under which you wish to create all the new Groups (press *Alt+C* to get Group Creation (secondary) screen, to create a New Group from within the current screen, and then select the newly created Group)
- **Ledger Creation any parent Group**: Select *All Items*, to create new Groups under any existing parent Group

> **Note:** *You may easily & quicky set the List of Ledger Names in your preffered order (rather than in Alphabetcal Order), using F10:Skip Sort through Multiple Mode, than through Single Mode entry.*

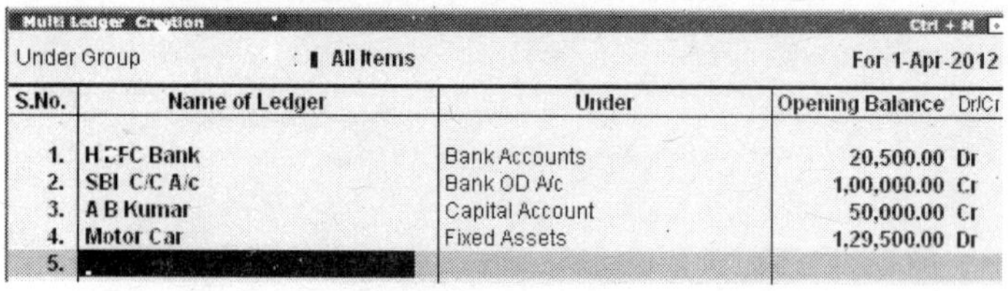

Multi Ledger Creation — Ctrl + M

Under Group : All Items — For 1-Apr-2012

S.No.	Name of Ledger	Under	Opening Balance	Dr/Cr
1.	H CFC Bank	Bank Accounts	20,500.00	Dr
2.	SBI C/C A/c	Bank OD A/c	1,00,000.00	Cr
3.	A B Kumar	Capital Account	50,000.00	Cr
4.	Motor Car	Fixed Assets	1,29,500.00	Dr
5.				

F-2A: Multi Account Ledger creation

Now enter the details at the Table area.

- **Sl. No.**: Serial Number is displayed for reference - cursor does not move here.
- **Name of Ledger**: Enter Name of the Ledger you are creating.
- **Parent Group**: At *Under*, select the Parent *Group* under which you wish to create the new Ledger Account.
  - If you have selected a Group at *Under Group*, the selected group (at Under Group field at the header) is carried as parent Group (at *Under* field, the cursor would not come at this field). This way you create several Ledger Accounts under a Group much faster, as you do not to select the parent Group for each Group.
  - If you had selected *All Items*, you have to select the Group at *Under* field for each ledger at this field from the *List of Groups* (F-2A).
- **Opening Balance**: Enter Opening Balance for the ledger, if any. At Dr/Cr field, enter ***D*** or ***C***.

This way, you can create multiple ledgers in one entry screen. To terminate further entry, press <enter> on blank line and type *Yes* at *Accept? Yes or No* to save.

04 Display of Multiple Masters

You may Display multiple Groups / Ledgers in one screen, in the same way as Multiple Masters Entry Screen

- **Groups Display:** Select (*GoT>Accounts Info>Group*. Select *Display* at Multiple section of Accounts Groups Menu. Now select the *Group* to be displayed (select All Items to display all Groups). The subordinate Groups are displayed
- **Ledger Display**: Select (*GoT>Accounts Info>Ledgers*. Select *Display* at Multiple section of Accounts Ledgers Menu and select the *Group* (select *All Items* to list all the Ledger Accounts). The subordinate Ledgers of the selected Groups are Displayed

05 Alteration / Deletion of Multiple Masters

You may get multiple Groups / Ledgers in *Alteration* Mode in one screen, in the same way as Multiple Masters Entry Screen

Selection of Master Record for Alteration / Deletion

- **Groups:** Select (*GoT>Accounts Info>Group >Alter* at Multiple section of Accounts Groups Menu. Now select the Group to be Altered / Deleted (select All Items to display all Groups). The subordinate Groups are listed
- **Ledger:** Select (*GoT>Accounts Info>Ledgers >Alter* at Multiple section of Accounts Ledgers Menu and select the Group / Deleted (select *All Items* to list all the Ledger Accounts). The subordinate Ledgers of the selected Groups are listed

Alteration of Master Record: Take the cursor at the desired field and edit the data, in similar way as entry.

Saving the changes: Press *Ctrl+A* to save the changes made. This way, you may make changes quickly in a number of items at a time.

The additional info of Accounts Group / Ledger Account (like Mailing Name, Address etc) cannot be Entered / Edited through Multiple entry mode. You may enter them though Create / Alter option of *Single Mode* option only. Master record *cannot* be Deleted through Multiple Mode.

06 Buttons at Multiple Master screen

The following buttons help quick operation at Multiple Master Creation / Alteration:

- **F4: Parent:** Click *F4:Parent* button to get to *Under Group* field at top part directly. Useful when you have entered few Groups / Ledgers in the columnar list and wish to change parent Group.
- **F8: Skip Details / Edit Details:** This toggle button is useful to select edit / skip specific fields mode for quicker work.
  - o Click *F8:Skip Details* button to skip the *Opening Balance* field (& some other fields) in ledger creation.
  - o Click *F8:Edit Details* button to edit data of various fields.
- **F4: New Parent:** To select another parent group, click this button (or press *Ctrl+F4*) which brings *List of Groups* to select from.
- **Zero Op. Balance:** To make opening balance of ledgers account, click this button. Be careful, once zeroed, you cannot get back the previous balance figures again.
- **F6: Skip Names / Edit Names:** This toggle button is useful to select edit / skip Name fields for faster work.
  - o Click *F6:Skip Names* button to skip the Name in Group / Ledger alteration
  - o Click *F6:Edit Names* button to edit data of various fields.
- **F7: Skip Parent / Edit Parent:** This toggle button is useful to select edit / skip specific fields for faster work.
  - o Click *F7:Skip Parent* Button to skip the parent Group

Name in Group / Ledger alteration

- o Click *F7:Edit Parent* Button to alter parent group name also

- **F10: Skip Sort / Edit Sort**:: This toggle button is useful to edit / skip sort value in Group / Ledgers (§05/02-05)
  - o Click *F10:Skip Sort* Button to skip the Sort field in Group / Ledger alteration (*Sorting Position* column is hidden)
  - o Click *F10:Edit Sort* Button to alter the value of Sort Field at *Sorting Position* column

The following Table (F-2) shows the buttons at the respective Master screen in Multiple Masters creation / Alteration

Other Optional fields: The optional fields of Masters (activated through F11:Features / F12: Configure) are not available in *Multiple Masters Creation / Alteration* mode. You can enter / edit such data through Alter under Single mode only.

Ledger Creation	Group Creation	Ledger Alteration	Group Alteration
F4: Parent F8: Skip Details	F4: Parent	F4: Parent F4: New Parent F6: Skip Names / Edit Names F7: Skip Parent / Edit Parent F8: Skip Details / Edit Details F10:Skp Sort/ Edit Sort Z: Zero op Bal	F4: Parent F4: New Parent F6: Skip Names / Edit Names F7: Skip Parent / Edit Parent F10:Edit Sort / Edit Details

F-2: Buttons at Multiple Masters

FAQ: Frequently Asked Questions

FAQ-1: Can you create account groups under different Groups in Multiple Groups entry in one screen

Ans: Yes, At Multiple Group creation screen (F-1A), you should select *All Items* at *Under Group* field and select the parent Group at *Under* field for each new Group created

FAQ-2: Can you create Ledger Accounts under different Groups in Multiple Ledger entry in one screen

Ans: Yes, At Multiple Ledger creation screen (F-2A), you should select *All Items* at *Under Group* field and select the Group at *Under* field for each new Ledger created.

FAQ-3: Can you create a new parent Group to a new Ledger Account being created in Multiple Ledgers entry

Ans: Yes. At Multiple Ledger creation screen (F-2A), when you select *All Items* at *Under Group* field, you may press Alt+C keys at *Under* field and create a New parent Group for the Ledger Account being created (like in Single Ledger entry mode).

Voucher Type

02-07

01 Voucher Type

We have explained the Voucher Types pre-created by Tally (called *Primary Voucher Types*) at the time of Company Creation (§02/01-04). The pre-created *Primary Voucher Types* carry inherent properties in respect of the nature of transaction that can be recorded through such Voucher Types

To organize the Transactions in a better manner as per requirements of the user, new Voucher Types of any the nature of any of the *Primary Voucher Types* may be created

02 Creation of new Voucher Type

Select *Accts Info > Voucher Type> Create* to create a new voucher type (F-1A) and enter the particulars as explained below:

Voucher Type Name: At *Name*, enter unique Name for the Voucher Type you are creating

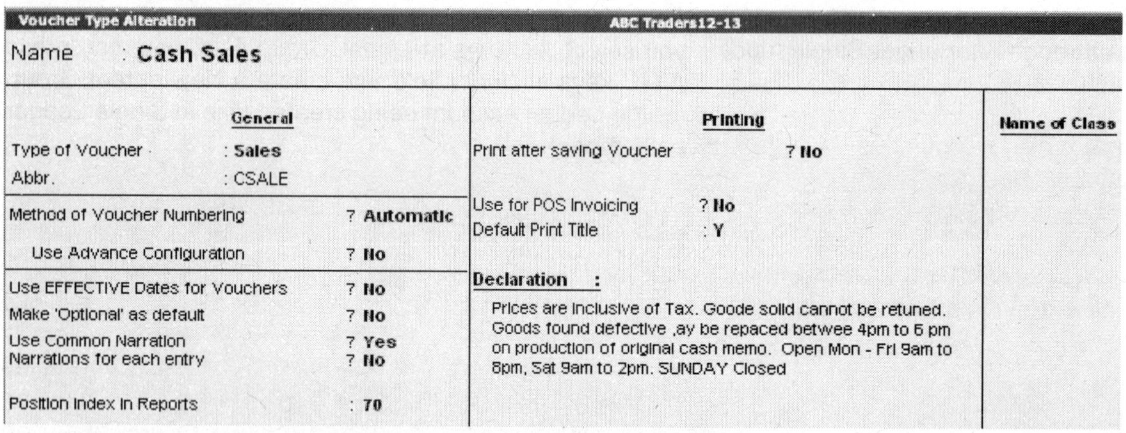

F-1A: Voucher Type Creation

Type of Voucher: At *Type of Voucher*, select the Voucher Type (F-2) from the list of voucher types (it shows all Tally Created Voucher Types, both Accounts & Inventory, even if you have set Accounts only). The new Voucher Type being created will inherit the properties of the Voucher Type you select here.

Voucher Type Abbreviation: At *Abbr*, enter a unique abbreviated (short) Voucher Name (different from Voucher Type Name) for the new type of Voucher, preferably within 5 letters. The abbreviated Name appears as Voucher Type in most of the Reports.

Voucher Numbering Method: At *Method of Voucher Numbering* field, select the Method from *Types of Numbering* list (F-1B), as follows:

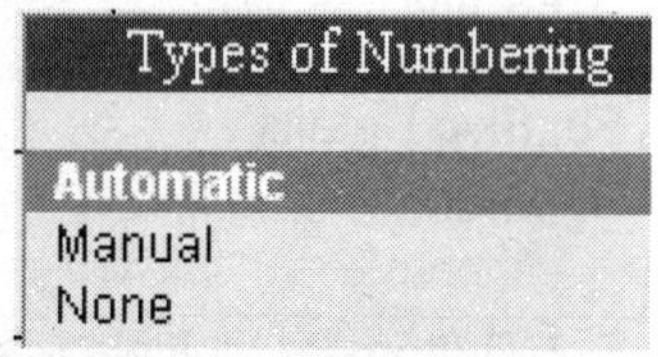

F-1B: Voucher Numbering Options

- **Manual Voucher Numbering Method**: *Manual.*to enter Voucher Numbers during Voucher Entry. Manual Voucher Numbering is useful when you enter voucher from a manual record, where Voucher Number is already given. For example, you write Voucher manually (and a voucher number is allotted when the voucher is written), and later on you enter the Voucher in Tally.ERP 9 system

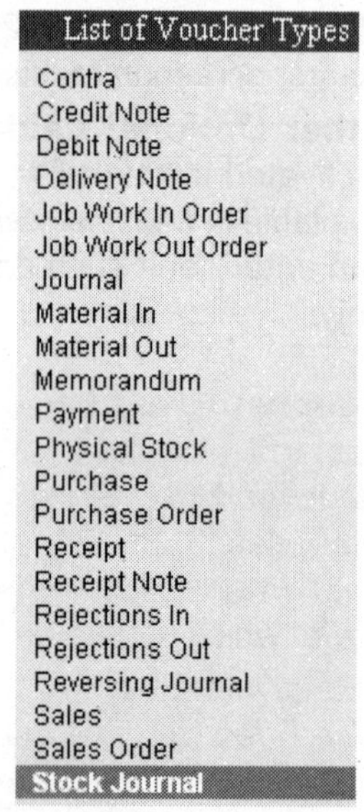

F- 2: List of Voucher Type

Duplicate Voucher Number: When you specify Manual Numbering System, you get another option *Prevent Duplicates.*

- Set *Yes* to prevent entry of Duplicate Voucher Number. (i.e you *cannot* create multiple voucher of same Voucher number of the same voucher type)
- Set *No* to allot a Voucher Number multiple times (i.e you *may* create multiple voucher of same Voucher number of the same voucher type)

In Manual Numbering scheme, Tally.ERP 9 will not trap any sequence violation or missing number. You can enter voucher number 4 after entry of voucher number 5. If you skip a voucher number, Tally will not trap any missing number (so there may not be a voucher number like 7)

- **No Voucher Numbering:** Select *None* from the Voucher Numbering List when Vouchers do not bear any number. Consequently, the voucher number field will not appear. This scheme is useful for small proprietorship firms where the Accounting Work is done by one man (normally the proprietor), who cannot enter Vouchers regularly. Normally he sits for voucher entry from various documents at certain interval (say at week end/ month end) and enters all the pending vouchers. The entry may be made randomly (not in chronological order). However, this scheme is not suitable in larger firms, where many people are working, as it may induce fraud and mistakes which may be untraceable.
- **Automatic Voucher Numbering:** Select *Automatic* at Types of Numbering List. In Automatic Numbering Scheme, you get another option *Use Advance Configuration*
    - o Set *Yes* to activate *Advanced Voucher Numbering Scheme* (§06). This is used to allot voucher numbers using a versatile automated voucher numbering scheme, as per user's own plan.
    - o Set *No* to get *Simple Automatic Numbering Scheme*, in which the Numbers are consecutively auto generated as in chronological order (as per Voucher Date

Voucher Effective Date: The Overdue Dates, Ageing Reports, Interest computation etc is done from the Date of Voucher. But, sometimes the Party may like to use some other date than Voucher Date (e.g from the Date of cheque, etc.). In such case you have to set the Date (called *Effective Date*) which should be considered for such purpose

To activate *Effective Date* feature in the Voucher, set *Yes* at *Use Effective Date* at the respective voucher type creation (F-1A),

Consequently, during voucher entry (§04/02-09), you will get a field for Effective Date in voucher entry. Effective Date is used to compute Due Date and Interest for Sales, Purchase, D/N & C/N voucher.

03 Display / Alteration / Deletion of Voucher Type

- **Display of Voucher Type:** Select *Accounts Info > Voucher Type > Display* and then select the Voucher type to view (but you cannot alter any data).
- **Alteration / Deletion of Voucher Type:** Normally you do not need to create new voucher types, though you may need to change some of the default properties of the pre-created voucher types.

To modify Voucher Type profile, Select *Accounts Info > Voucher Type > Alter* to get the *Voucher Type Alteration* screen. At *Voucher Type Alteration* screen (F-1A), select the Voucher Type:

- o **Alteration of Voucher Type**: Change any particulars / option as desired (this way, you may change any of the parameters in the pre-created Voucher Types).
- o **Deletion of Voucher Type**: Press Alt+D to Delete an user created Voucher Type (Tally Pre created voucher types cannot be deleted) and type *Yes* at '*Delete? Yes or No*' to confirm deletion (the voucher type cannot be deleted if any voucher exists for the Voucher Type).

04 Optional Voucher

Optional Vouchers are Provisional (inactive) Vouchers which reside as a dormant voucher without giving an effect (as if no voucher has been entered). Optional Vouchers are mostly used in following situations:

- To Create Scenarios
- To Create Proforma voucher for approval
- To Pre plan the transactions (create vouchers in advance)

To Create Scenarios

Scenarios are emulated virtual situations with different parameters, values, etc to dynamically see the changing effect. Scenarios are seen with emulated data. So, emulated transactions are to be created through Optional Voucher, which do not affect the actual report, but is considered for the scenario.

To create Proforma voucher for approval

A regular voucher gives immediate effects in the entire system. So, a voucher is entered only after the transaction has taken place.

In large organisation, a proforma voucher is first created (like an unsigned voucher), which does not affect the system. It just lies in the system for approval. The transaction takes place only after proper approval. In such case, first an *Optional* Voucher is created, which may be converted (regularized) to regular just by a click (data not be entered again). The advantage is that the voucher may be modified, deleted without any problem without affecting any area in the system.

A few such instances of Proforma Voucher are:

- The Cashier creates an Optional Payment Voucher. The voucher is checked by Accountant for correctness (Ledger Accounts and other details) and prints it. The printed voucher is then approved by appropriate authority (Accounts manager etc). The cashier then makes payment and converts the Optional Payment Voucher to Regular Payment Voucher (§16.01/02-09)
- Receipt Note (known as *Inspection Note*) may be created as optional Receipt Note Voucher. The stock is kept

separate and inspected. The Voucher is regularized on acceptance of materials and the stock gets updated only when the optional voucher is converted to regular voucher

- Delivery Note (known as *Packing Slip*) may be created as optional Delivery note Voucher. The materials are collected for packing & delivery. The Voucher is regularized only when the materials are packed for delivery and the stock gets updated only when the optional voucher is converted to regular voucher
- Rejection In Voucher (known as *Sales Returns*) may be created as optional Rejection In Voucher. The stock is kept separate and inspected. The Voucher is regularized on acceptance of returned materials in good saleable condition. The stock gets updated only when the optional voucher is converted to regular voucher
- Stock Transfer Voucher (known as *Requisition slip*, for issue of materials to jobber / production dept)

For this reason, companies make it a policy to create a voucher as *Optional* only and then to regularise it after proper verification & approval (called signing a voucher). This is a very sound method of internal control and implementing a robust on-line system (Manual Voucher writing is eliminated).

To pre plan the transactions: Optional Vouchers are also used by smaller organisations. as pre-planned / pre-approved voucher. For example, the Accountant may create advance optional voucher for anticipated transactions ensuring that the vouchers are created correctly (proper ledgers / narrations) and the transaction is made on the specified / planned date. Thus the Accountant is ensured that the transactions will be done as per plan and proper accounting record would be maintained even in his absence (in small organization, only one or two key persons manage the entire affairs, who are often out in business tours and not available to look after paper work). The optional voucher offers a neat way to do things in planned and controlled way.

Optional Voucher Creation: Optional voucher is created in 2 ways:

- **At Voucher Creation screen**: At the time of Voucher Creation, using the toggle button L:Optional /Regular (§16 / 02-09)
- **Automatic Optional Voucher Creation by default:** To automatically create optional voucher on voucher entry, at the respective Voucher Type creation / alteration screen (F-1A), set *Yes* at *Make optional as default.* Consequently, on Voucher entry, the new Voucher is created as *Optional* (§16/02-09), which you have to regularize later on.

05 Voucher Narration

You may enter voucher narration in 2 ways:

- *Common Narration* for the whole voucher
- *Ledger Narration* for each ledger entry

Voucher Common Narration

Common Voucher Narration is entered at the end of voucher data entry, describing the entire transaction details as a whole (§05.03/01-0). To allow entry of common Narration, at Voucher Type creation / alteration screen, at the option *Use Common Narration* Voucher (F-1A),

- Set *Yes* to enter Voucher Narration for the voucher,
- Set *No* to suppress common Narration entry in the voucher.

You should normally, set *Yes* at Receipt, Payment, Contra, Journal Voucher type to enter the description of the transaction in voucher. However, you may set *No* at Sales, Purchase, Debit & Credit Note (to save entry time), as normally the various voucher particulars are entered in the respective fields and Voucher Common Narration may not be needed.

Voucher Ledger Narration

Apart from Common voucher Narration, which describes the whole voucher, you may additionally enter Narration immediately after each Ledger Entry (called *Ledger Narration*) describing the transaction about that ledger entry only,

Ledger Narration is useful when you have to explain each entry separately. For example, while making a Salary voucher, you may make separate entry for each employee and enter the name of the employee and other details at each ledger entry

In *Single Mode* Voucher Entry (§03/02-10), you can enter ledger narration only for line accounts (not for header account).

Ledger Narration increases the Narration entry task as Narration has to be entered for each Ledger Account. So, you must plan properly to apply this feature only to those voucher types where separate details of each ledger transaction is to be maintained.

At Voucher Type Creation / Alter screen, at the option, *Narration for each entry* (F-1A):

- Set *Yes* to allow entry of Voucher Ledger Narration. Consequently, a Narration filed will appear after each entry in the Voucher, where you enter the details of that ledger transaction only (F-5B/02-09)
- Set *No* to suppress Voucher Ledger Narration. Consequently, no Narration field will appear after each Ledger Account (F-5A/02-09)

You may set Yes / No to either, both (Voucher Common & Ledger Narration) narration options. This means you may selectively activate Common Narration, Ledger Narration, or activate / deactivate both.

06 Advance Voucher Numbering

In Automatic voucher numbering scheme, you may even opt for advance configuration (F-1A), to customize the numbering features and properties in your own way.

On selecting *Automatic* at *Method of Voucher Numbering* (F-1A), you get an additional option *Use Advance Configuration.* Set Yes to get the Advance Voucher Number set up screen (F-3), else set *No.*

The Advance Voucher Number set up screen (F-3) is divided in 2 parts as follows

- **Voucher Number properties Specification**: At the upper part, you specify the Properties of Voucher Number
- **Voucher Numbering Scheme**: At the lower part, specify the various Voucher Number components, in the Table

Starting Number ? 1
Width of Numerical Part : 5
Prefill with ZERO ? Yes

Restart Numbering			Prefix Details		Suffix Details	
Applicable From	Starting Number	Particulars	Applicable From	Particulars	Applicable From	Particulars
1-Apr-2012	1	Monthly	1-Apr-2012	04/	1-Apr-2012	/12-13
1-May-2012	1	Monthly	1-May-2012	05/		

F-3: Advance Voucher Numbering Methods

Voucher Number Properties Specification: At Advance Voucher Number set up screen (F-3), at the upper part, you specify the Properties of Voucher Number as follows:

- **Starting Number**: Give Starting Number (normally 1) for the first Voucher of the first period. You may set any number and the voucher number will start from that number. For example, if your cash memo number ended at 7448 in the previous year and you like to continue that number in the current year, you may specify 7449 here to start the cash number from 7449.
- **Width of Numerical Part**: Specify width for fixed with voucher number to pad the smaller number with zero or blank at the left, to align the numbers properly in reports, else leave blank. For example, if you specify 5, the voucher number 2 will be padded with four zeros / spaces at the left. Leave blank to left align the number without any leading zero or space.
- **Prefill with Zero**: If you have set a value at *Width of Numerical Part*, at *Prefill with zero*:
  - o Set *Yes* to fill-up the numbers with zeros, (F-4A). For example, the voucher number 7, 12, 210 will appear as 0007, 0012, 0210 respectively, when the *Width of Numerical Part* is 4 and you set *Yes* at this field.
  - o Set *No* to show Voucher Numbers without any leading zeros (F-4B). However, if Width of Numerical Part is specified by a non-zero value, voucher number will appear with leading spaces

The effect of these options on appearance of voucher number is shown in the table below:

Width of Numerical Part	Prefill with zero	Appearance of Voucher Number
blank	-	7 (no leading zeros or spaces)
5	Yes	00007 (leading zeros)
5	No	7 (leading spaces)

F-4A: Voucher Number Pre-filled with zero

F-4B: Voucher Number without Pre-fill

06.01 Advance Voucher Numbering Methods

Next you get 3 columns (F-3) to set up the options for Voucher Numbering Methods as follows:

- **Re Start Numbering**: To set up the number re start period
- **Prefix details**: To set up voucher *Prefix* part
- **Suffix details:** To set up voucher *Suffix* part

Re-Start Numbering

In the first column (Re-Start Numbering), you set numbering scheme of each period as follows:

Numbering Period Start Date: At *Applicable from* column, enter the date from which numbering scheme is to apply.

Normally, it should be *Book Beginning From* Date. The start date must be the first date of a month. If the Book beginning date is from mid month, e.g 12-4-2006, the start date must be from 1st day of month (like 1-4-2006).

Period Starting Voucher Number: Enter the starting number for the period. For example, you may start from 1 or from any other number for the period.

Numbering period: At Particulars field, select the period as follows:

Type of Period	Renumbering rule
Yearly	The renumbering starts from 1st day of the month in every 12 months
Monthly	The renumbering starts from 1st day every month
Weekly	The renumbering starts from the same day of each week as the period starting date. For example, if the starting date is 1.11.2006 (Wed) then the renumber will be done from the first voucher of every Wednesday after that
Daily	When you select monthly, the renumbering starts everyday
Never	The number goes on continuously for ever

The Numbering scheme will continue till it is changed for subsequent period.

As you can specify only first day of Month at Applicable column, you will get vouchers with duplicate number when you specify Weekly / Daily renumbering scheme. For example, in case of Daily method, each day the voucher number will start from 1 (with same Prefix & Suffix). Also, in case of Weekly method, at the beginning of each week, the voucher number will start from 1 (with same Prefix & Suffix).

Example: Daily Renumbering

Applicable From	Staring Number	Particulars	Effect
1-4-2006	1001	Daily	The voucher number will start from 1001 from 1-4-2006. Every day, the voucher number will re start from 1001.
1-5-2006	5001	Daily	On 1-5-2006 the voucher number will start from 5001 and subsequently, it will re start as 5001 each day.

Example: Monthly Re Numbering

Applicable From	Staring Number	Particulars	Effect
1-4-2006	1001	Monthly	The voucher number will start from 1001 from 1-4-2006. On 1-5-2006, 1-6-2006 & 1-7-2006, the voucher will re start from 1001.
1-8-2006	5001	Monthly	On 1-8-2006 the voucher number will start from 5001 and will re start as 5001 from the 1st daya of evry month after that.

Renumbering Start Weekly	Day
1-11-2006	Wednesday
8-11-2006	Wednesday
15-11-2006	Wednesday
22-11-2006	Wednesday
29-11-2006	Wednesday

Example: Yearly Renumbering

Applicable From	Staring Number	Particulars	Effect
1-4-2006	1	Yearly	The voucher number will start from 1 from 1-4-2006. Subsequently, from 1st April of each year, the voucher number will re start from 1

Example: Continuous Numbering

Applicable From	Staring Number	Particulars	Effect
1-4-2006	1	Never	The voucher number will start from 1 from 1-4-2006 and will continue without any renumbering, until you specify to re start.

Example:

You have specified following for Payment Voucher Type (Company Financial Year starts from 1-4-2012. The company starts books in Tally from 13-10-2012 (F-2/01-01). So, the Books Beginning From is 13-10-2012. The last payment voucher number of Oct 2012 (12-10-2012) is 00128. The company wants to re start voucher number from 1 every month. So, the company wants to start payment voucher number as 00129 from 13-10-2012. Accordingly, it has specified as follows for Payment Voucher Type:

- Starting Number: 129
- Width of Numerical Part: 5
- Prefill with Zero:Yes

Applicable From	Staring Number	Particulars	Particulars
1-11-2012	1	Monthly	The number will start from 00129 from 13-10-2006 and will restart from 00001 from 1st day of each month from 1-11-2006 onwards.

Example: Prefix Numbers

From 1st May 06 the voucher number start from CsPmt/05/0001 and will continue as CsPmt/05/0002, CsPmt/05/0003, ... and so on.

Voucher Number Suffix Details

In the same way as Prefix Numbers, which is added *before* the numeric number, you may specify Suffix which will be added after the numeric number. This also helps to avoid duplicate numbers and add more clarity about the identification of type, origin etc of the voucher.

At *Suffix Details* column (F-3), enter the suffix number part as follows:

- **Voucher Number Suffix Applicable From**: At *Applicable From* field, enter Date from which the Suffix would be applicable.
- **Voucher Number Suffix**: At *Particulars* field, Enter the suffix of the voucher (e.g Bom/06-07), for the voucher re-numbering period.

Re Start Numbering			Prefix Details	
Applicable From	**Staring Number**	**Particulars**	**Applicable From**	**Particulars**
1-4-2006	1	Monthly	1-4-2006	CsPmt/04/
1-5-2006	1	Monthly	1-5-2006	CsPmt/05/

Voucher Number Prefix Details

Apart from numeric number, you may put some short identification in every voucher according to its type, location or other attribute to locate the voucher. In case of re numbering scheme, the voucher number may be repeated (for example voucher number starts from 1 from each month). In such case, it is always prudent to put Prefix in a voucher will automatically be added before the numeric part of the voucher number for better identification and prevention of duplicate numbers.

Example: Suffix Numbers

You see the suffix number is specified only in the 1st period. So, it will continue for all the periods until it is re specified again

With this scheme, the voucher number start from CsPmt/04/0001/ Bom/06-07 from 1st April 06 and will continue as CsPmt/04/0002/ Bom/06-07, CsPmt/04/0003/ Bom/06-07, ...

From 1st May 06 the voucher number start from CsPmt/05/0001/ Bom/06-07 and will continue as CsPmt/05/0002/ Bom/06-07, CsPmt/05/0003/ Bom/06-07, ... and so on.

So, using voucher number suffix & prefix, you can make very clear voucher numbering scheme to avoid duplicate numbering

Re Start Numbering			Prefix Details		Suffix Details	
Applicable form	**Starting Number**	**Particulars**	**Applicable form**	**Particulars**	**Applicable form**	**Particulars**
1-4-2006	1	Monthly	1-4-2006	CsPmt/04/	1-4-2006	Bom/06-07
1-5-2006	1	Monthly	1-5-2006	CsPmt/05/		

At *Prefix Details* column (F-3), enter the prefix number part as follows:

- **Voucher Number Prefix Applicable From**: At *Applicable From* field (Fig 4-3.19), enter Date from which the Prefix would be applicable.
- **Voucher Number Prefix**: At *Particulars* field, Enter the Prefix of the voucher (e.g 04/), for the voucher re-numbering period.

With this scheme, the voucher number start from CsPmt/04/0001 from 1st April 06 and will continue as CsPmt/04/0002, CsPmt/04/0003, ...

and avoid the ill effects of renumbering of voucher numbers on insertion/ deletion or date change for auto numbered vouchers.

It is better to create several types of voucher (user specified voucher types) to manage voucher numbers in better way. For example, you may create separate voucher types for Payment Vouchers as follows:

- CshPmt: For payment by Cash
- BoIPmt: Payment by cheque through Bank of India
- IoBPmt: Payment by cheque through Indian Overseas Bank

and specify separate prefix & suffix scheme for each voucher type.

Now while creating payment vouchers, use the specific Payment voucher type instead of general Payment Voucher type as created by Tally.

07 Change in Voucher Numbering scheme

After voucher entry, if you alter the voucher numbering method of any voucher type (through Alter option), all the voucher numbers for the voucher type will get affected as explained below:

Automatic to Manual	All voucher number will be blank. You will have to enter the voucher number again through Voucher Modification.
Automatic to None	All voucher number will be lost.
Manual to Automatic	Voucher Number will be automatically allotted as per Numbering Scheme set.
None to Automatic	Voucher Number will be automatically allotted as per Numbering Scheme set.
Manual to None	All voucher number will be lost.
None to Manual	All voucher number will be blank. You will have to enter the voucher number again through Voucher Modification.

08 On Line Voucher Printing option set up

To print each Voucher on-line after entry, at the respective Voucher type creation / alteration screen (F-1A), set *Yes* at *Print after saving Voucher* to get Voucher Printing screen immediately after Voucher entry (no need to click Print button) after each voucher entry.

09 Voucher Type Position Index

Tally allots a pre-set value (called *Position Index*) for each Voucher Type which determines the sequence of voucher in Reports.

You may change the Sort (Index) Value at GoT>Accts Info>Voucher Type > Alter and select the Voucher Type to get Voucher Type Creation / Alteration screen (F-1A). Click *F10:Edit Sort* toggle button to get the field *Position Index in Reports,* showing the default Sort Index Value. Now change the value as you need to show in the Reports, in the same way as explained for Position Value for Accounts Groups & Ledger Accounts (§05.01/02-05)

You may also change the Value by drill down through the respective Voucher Type at the Voucher Type List (F-6 §10) to get the Voucher Type Alteration screen (like F-1A) and change the value at the field *Position Index in Reports,*

Day Book — For 1-May-2006

Date	Particulars	Vch Type	Vch No.	Debit Amount Inwards Qty	Credit Amount Outwards Qty
1-5-2006	Mohan Lal	Receipt	5		12,000.00
1-5-2006	Mohan Lal	Receipt	6		3,000.00
1-5-2006	A K Corporation	Receipt	7		1,200.00
1-5-2006	A K Corporation	Payment	2	3,000.00	
1-5-2006	Salary	Payment	3	3,000.00	

F-5 Report showing changed Voucher Type position index

In the Reports, the Vouchers are listed according to the Position values of the respective Voucher Type (F-5 shows the Report where Payment Voucher has been changed from 20 (default value) to 31, higher than that of default value 30 of Receipt Voucher Type. So, Receipt Voucher appear over Payment Vouchers)

10 Voucher Type List

To get a list (F-6) of all existing Voucher Types, at *GoT>Display>List of Accounts* and the click V: *Voucher Type* (or press *Ctrl+V*) button.

List of Accounts

List of Voucher Types

Contra
Credit Note
Debit Note
Delivery Note
Job Work In Order
Job Work Out Order
Journal
Material In
Material Out
Memorandum
Payment
Physical Stock
PoS
Purchase
Purchase Order
Receipt
Receipt Note
Rejections In
Rejections Out
Reversing Journal
Sales
Sales Order
Stock Journal
VAT Adjt

24 Voucher Type(s)

F-6 Voucher Type List

The Voucher Type list (F-6). shows all existing Voucher Types, Primary (Pre-created by Tally and User Created), in alphabetical order, both of Accounts & Inventory, even if you have set *Accounts Only* system. The Tally pre-created Voucher Types are shown in Bold while user created Voucher Types are shown in Normal Font (F-6).

FAQ: Frequently Asked Questions

FAQ-1: How to set up Option for entering Ledger Narration in Payment Voucher

Ans: At GoT>*Accts Info > Voucher Type> Alter,* and then select *Payment* from the list of Voucher Type to get Voucher Type Alteration screen (F-1A). At *Narration for each entry,* set *Yes* to enter Narration against each Ledger Account during Payment Voucher entry (§05/02-09)

FAQ-2: I like to make salary payment to my employees (about 2 to 3 employees) and enter the amount separately for each Employee, in the same Voucher. How do I accomplish it.

Ans: Create a separate Payment Voucher Type for Salary Payment (e.g. SalPmt), as explained (§02/02-07). Set *Yes* at *Narration for Each Entry,* (F-1A) so that you may enter separate Narration for Each Employee Amount.

Now during voucher Entry, select the Voucher Type (e.g. SalPmt). After entry of Ledger Account (e.g Salary Account) and Ledger Amount for each Employee separately, you will get Narration Entry field, after each Ledger Account. Enter the Name of the employee and particulars of Payment. This way, select Salary Account each time, for each Employee and enter the Employee Name etc in Narration, separately for each Employee. Thus, you may keep record of salary payment in respect of each Employee. Finally enter the Voucher common Narration.

FAQ-3: How to set up Option for instant printing of Voucher after entry.

Ans: At GoT>*Accts Info > Voucher Type> Alter,* and then select *Payment* from the list of Voucher Type to get Voucher Alteration screen (F-1A). At *Print after saving Voucher*, set *Yes* to print voucher immediately before Saving. Consequently, you will get Voucher Printing Screen immediately after Voucher Entry (§05/02-15), to print the voucher immediately after saving

Voucher Class 02-08

01 Voucher Class

Voucher Class is a pre-defined Voucher Type Profile that helps to automate & expedite voucher entry and minimize errors. Voucher Class enables the administrator to set the controls on the operators.

Voucher Class is pre configured template with defined Accounting entities (like Account Groups, Ledgers, Cost Centres etc) & Allocation / Computation rules. Some of the uses of Voucher Class are:

- Automatically select a ledger account (or propose a specified ledger for quick selection) in voucher entry.
- Automatically round off figures as per rounding off rules.
- Automatically compute Tax, Duty and other allocations.
- Automatically allocate to Cost Centres as per pre-defined values

Voucher Class ensures fast and correct data entry, saves computations in vouchers, and provides more security (in some cases, the data modification is prevented).

Here, we show simple examples of using Voucher class for Payment, Receipt & Contra Voucher Types, to pre-set the Cash Bank Ledger Accounts, through Voucher Class. For each Voucher Type, you may create multiple voucher classes. Using the Voucher class, the entry screen appears in Single Mode only (even if you have set *No* at *Use Single Entry Mode for Payment, Receipt & Contra* at Voucher Entry Configuration).

For example, in payment Voucher, you may create separate Voucher Class for payments made from each Cash / Bank Account, viz. Petty Cash Payment Voucher, Cash Payment Voucher, SBI Payment Voucher, HDFC Payment Voucher etc., for faster, error free & in a standardized process, reflecting a certain type of transactions. The Payments tasks may be divided / distributed amongst several persons through separate Voucher Class, for better control and consistency.

In the same way, you may create several Receipt Vouchers, for each Cash / Bank Account or nature of transaction.

In contra voucher, you can specify voucher class for each transaction type, Cash Withdrawn from HDFC Bank, Cash Deposited to HDFC Bank etc.

02 Voucher Class Creation

Select *Accounts Info > Voucher Type* and select the Voucher Type from the list for which you like to create a Voucher Class. Enter the details of Voucher Type (F-1A).

At *Name of Class* enter the unique Voucher Class Name (F-1A) to get Ledger Account set up screen for the Voucher Class (F-1B).

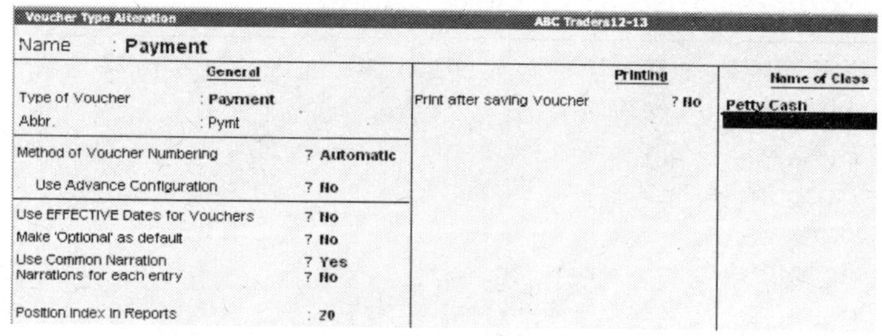

F-1A: Voucher Class Creation

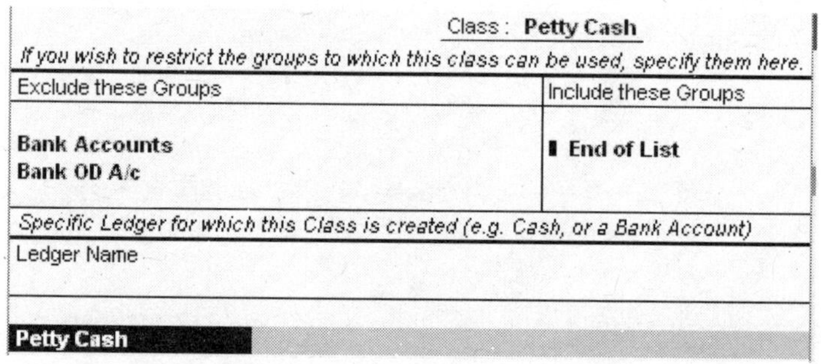

F-1B: Ledger set up in Voucher Class

In Payment, Receipt & Contra Voucher Class, to set rules for Cash Bank Accounts Groups (in upper part) and at Lower Bank, you may specify the Cash / Bank Ledger (F-1B)

03 Voucher Class Ledger Account set up

At Voucher Class Ledger Account set up screen (F-1B), you specify the Account Groups / Ledger Accounts, as follows:.

Account Groups: On the Upper 2 parts, you specify the *Account Groups* to be Excluded / Included. You may select Multiple Groups in each section. Select *End of List* to terminate selection of Groups.

- **Excluded Groups**: At the Upper Left Part, you specify the Cash / Bank Account Groups that you like to exclude in the Voucher Class. For example, if you want to create a Voucher Class for Cash Payments, you may specify the Bank Account Groups like Bank, Bank OOC etc.
- **Included Groups**: Having specified the Excluded Group, you may, if needed, include group some specific Group (among the sub groups of the Excluded Group).

Account Ledger: in the lower part, you may optionally specify the Ledger Account to be Included, or select Not Applicable

- **Selected Ledger Account:** The selected Ledger Accounts would be auto selected (carried) at the Header Account
- **No Ledger Account Selected:** When you set *Not Applicable* at Ledger Account, during voucher entry, at the header, you get the ledger accounts as per the Excluded / Included Groups (Ledger Accounts under Excluded Groups are not available for selection, but ledger accounts under the Included Groups are available.

Examples of Voucher Class Setting

Exclude Groups	Include Groups	Include Ledger	Effect
Bank Accounts Bank OD Accounts	None (End of List)	Petty Cash	The Petty Cash account will get auto selected at the Header
Bank Accounts Bank OD Accounts	None (End of List)	Not Applicable	No ledger account gets auto selected at header. Only the ledgers except under the Excluded Groups, but under the Included Groups are listed for selection, from which a ledger can be selected at the Header.
None (End of List)	None (End of List)	Petty Cash	The Petty Cash account will get auto selected at the Header

03.01 General Rules of Ledger Inclusion / Exclusion

The Ledger Exclusion / Inclusion in voucher class is explained above. The essence of General Rules of Exclusion / Inclusion in voucher class are described below:

- To set a specific Cash / Bank Ledger, do not select any Group at Exclude or Include at the upper part. Just select the Ledger at the Lower Part.
- To select a Cash / Ledger Account during Voucher Entry, specify the Exclude / Include groups at Upper portion but do not specify any ledger account at lower potion. The ledgers as per Rules set at the upper portion will be available for selection at Header during voucher entry. Now select the desired ledger from the list.

04 Voucher using Voucher Class

Voucher Class is just a way of voucher entry of a Voucher Type. The Voucher data is stored in the same way, and the Reports created are same whether you create a voucher through normal Voucher Type or through a Voucher Class. That does not make any difference in ultimate results or accounting process.

In Voucher Class, the properties specified for the Voucher Type (including advanced options of Automatic Voucher Numbering) are carried in the related Voucher Class also. So, they apply to all the Voucher Classes of the specified Voucher Type.

A Voucher Type may contain several Voucher Classes. So, a Voucher Class is a subset of the defining Voucher Type. For example, you may create 2 kinds of Voucher Class (Counter Sale 1 & Counter Sale 2) of Sales Voucher Type and specify different Cash Accounts (Cash A/c Counter -1) and Cash A/c Counter -2) under Cash Account Group, so that you can get separate reports of Cash Sales for the two Counters and separate Cash balances for the respective Counter.

FAQ: Frequently Asked Question

FAQ-1: Briefly explain the process of creation of Accounts Voucher Class

Ans: Through Voucher Class, you may set up the Cash / Bank Accounts for faster entry and to avoid mistake

The process of specifying Voucher Class constitute following major Steps:

Voucher Class Name: At Voucher Type creation of the Voucher class, at Name of Class, enter the Voucher Class Name. Next set up the Excude / Include Groups as follows:

- **Exclude Group**: Select the excluded Account Groups (the subordinate ledgers of the Selected Account groups will not be included in Ledger Account selection list during Voucher Entry).
- **Include Group**: Select sub set of excluded Account Groups (of the Groups which were selected at Exclude Group list), the subordinate ledgers of the Included Account groups will be included in Ledger Account selection list during Voucher Entry).

The combination of Exclude / Include section helps to precisely filter the desired Ledger Groups that could be allowed to be selected in the Voucher.

Voucher Entry

01 Voucher Entry General Configuration

We have seen Voucher Entry with basic features earlier (§05/01-04). Here we discuss about various Configuration options of Accounts Voucher Entry, to customise the contents and entry features.

The options set under General Voucher Configuration (F-1) are applied as default for all types of Voucher Entry. You may override the default option for the current voucher being entered, through Configuration of the Current Voucher.

Accounts	
Skip Date field in Create Mode (faster entry!)	? No
Use Single Entry mode for Pymt/Rcpt/Contra	? No
Use Payment/Receipt as Contra	? No
Use Cr/Dr instead of To/By during entry	? No
Use Cheque Printing for Contra	? No
Warn on Negative Cash Balance	? Yes
Pre-Allocate Bills for Payment/Receipt/Journal	? No
Allow Cash Accounts in Journals	? No
Allow Expenses/Fixed Assets in Purchase Vouchers	? No
Allow Income Accounts in Sales Vouchers	? No
Show Inventory Details	? Yes
Show Table of Bill Details for Selection	? Yes
Show Bill-wise Details	? Yes
Expand into multiple lines	? Yes
Show Ledger Current Balances	? No

F-1: Accounts Voucher Entry Configuration screen

Contra Configuration	
Skip Date field in Create Mode (faster entry!)	? No
Use Single Entry mode for Pymt/Rcpt/Contra	? No
Use Cr/Dr instead of To/By during entry	? Yes
Warn on Negative Cash Balance	? Yes
Show Ledger Current Balances	? Yes
Show Balances as on Voucher Date	? Yes
Confirm each Cheque before Print	? Yes
Use Default for Bank Allocations	? No
Show Remarks in Bank Allocation Details	? Yes

F-2A: Contra Voucher entry Configuration Screen

Payment Configuration	
Skip Date field in Create Mode (faster entry!)	? No
Use Single Entry mode for Pymt/Rcpt/Contra	? No
Use Payment as Contra	? No
Use Cr/Dr instead of To/By during entry	? Yes
Warn on Negative Cash Balance	? Yes
Pre-Allocate Bills for Payment/Receipt/Journal	? No
Show Inventory Details	? Yes
Show Table of Bill Details for Selection	? Yes
Show Bill-wise Details	? Yes
Expand into multiple lines	? Yes
Show Ledger Current Balances	? Yes
Show Balances as on Voucher Date	? Yes
Confirm each Cheque before Print	? Yes
Use Default for Bank Allocations	? No
Show Remarks in Bank Allocation Details	? Yes

F-2B: Payment Voucher entry

At *Gateway of Tally*, click *F12:Configure* to get Configuration Menu. Select *Voucher Entry* to get Voucher Entry Configuration screen (F-1), showing default Configuration options for Accounts Voucher Entry

02 Current Voucher Configuration Options

To set the Configuration option for current Voucher being entered, at the current entry screen, click *F12:Configure* to get the Voucher Entry Configuration screen for current Voucher, for the respective Voucher Type (F-2A to F-2D). Set the option which applies to the current voucher being entered.

Receipt Configuration	
Skip Date field in Create Mode (faster entry!)	? No
Use Single Entry mode for Pymt/Rcpt/Contra	? No
Use Receipt as Contra	? No
Use Cr/Dr instead of To/By during entry	? Yes
Warn on Negative Cash Balance	? Yes
Pre-Allocate Bills for Payment/Receipt/Journal	? No
Show Inventory Details	? Yes
Show Table of Bill Details for Selection	? Yes
Show Bill-wise Details	? Yes
Expand into multiple lines	? Yes
Show Ledger Current Balances	? Yes
Show Balances as on Voucher Date	? Yes
Use Additional Description(s) for Service Ledgers	? No
Use Default for Bank Allocations	? No
Show Remarks in Bank Allocation Details	? Yes

F-2C: Receipt Voucher entry Configuration screen

Journal Configuration	
Skip Date field in Create Mode (faster entry!)	? No
Use Cr/Dr instead of To/By during entry	? Yes
Warn on Negative Cash Balance	? Yes
Allow Cash Accounts in Journals	? No
Pre-Allocate Bills for Payment/Receipt/Journal	? No
Show Inventory Details	? Yes
Show Table of Bill Details for Selection	? No
Show Bill-wise Details	? Yes
Expand into multiple lines	? Yes
Show Ledger Current Balances	? Yes
Show Balances as on Voucher Date	? Yes
Confirm each Cheque before Print	? Yes
Use Default for Bank Allocations	? No
Show Remarks in Bank Allocation Details	? Yes

F-2D: Journal Voucher entry Configuration screen

The respective Configuration options (F-1 & F-2A to F-2D) and their effect in Voucher Entry screen / process are discussed next.

03 Voucher Date

Voucher Date may be entered in 2 ways by setting the way of Voucher Date entry. At *Skip Date Field in Create Mode (faster entry) (F-1 to F-2D),* set as follows:

- **Current Date carried by default**: Set *Yes* to automatically carry the current Date at Voucher Date field (the cursor skips the Voucher date field). To change the Voucher Date, at Voucher Entry screen:
    - o **Change Current Date**: Click *F2:Date* and enter the Current Date (F-4C/01-02), which is carried to Voucher Date (F-3A). This is useful when you like to enter several Vouchers of current Date so that you do not have to type Voucher Date in each Voucher. The Current Date is automatically carried in Voucher Date (F-3A).
    - o **Change Voucher Date**: Press *Shift+Tab* keys to go back to Voucher Date field and enter the Voucher Date. This is useful when you like to change the Voucher Date of the current Voucher (F-3B)
- **Voucher Date entry for each Voucher:** Set *No* to get the Cursor at Voucher Date at each Voucher Entry (F-3B). This is useful when you like to enter Vouchers of different Dates.

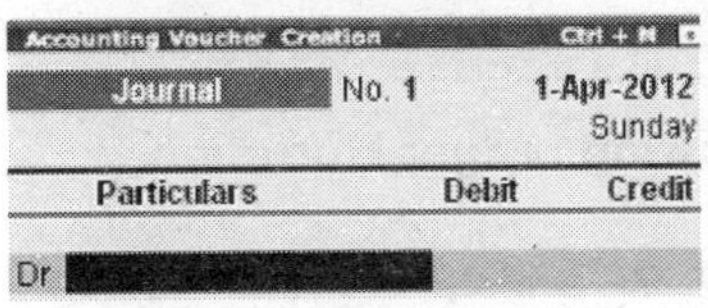

F-3A:Date skipped

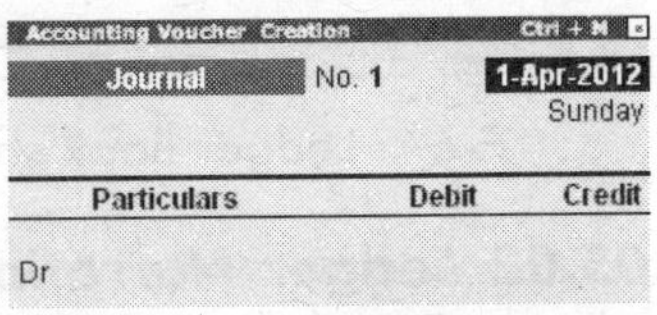

F-3B: Voucher Date Entry

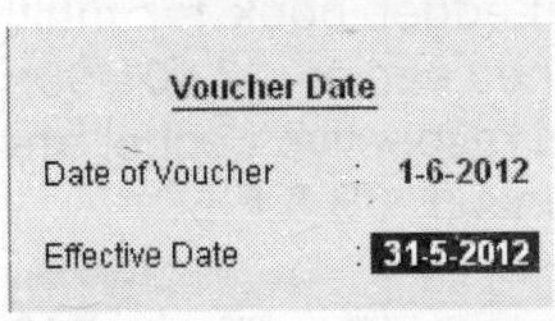

F-4A: Entry of Voucher Date & Effective Date

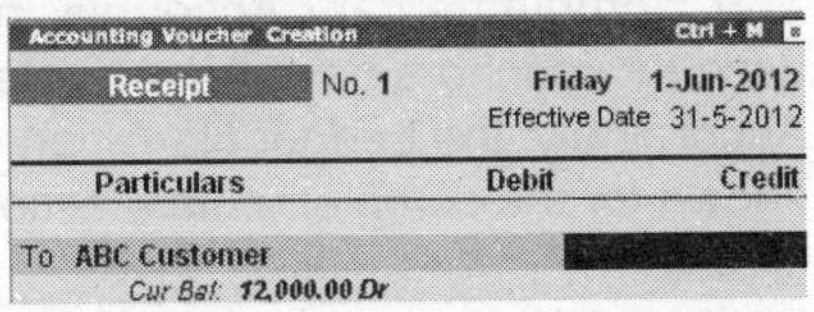

F:4B: Voucher entry with Effective Date

04 Voucher Effective Date

If you have set *Yes* at *Use Effective Date* at the respective Voucher Type (§02/02-07), during voucher entry, you will get a field for Effective Date in voucher entry (F-4A). Effective Date (F-4B) is used to compute Due Date and Interest for Sales, Purchase, D/N & C/N voucher. At the voucher entry screen Press *F2: Date* to enter Voucher Date & Effective Date (F-4A).

The next Date to current Date is carried at Voucher Date as well at Effective Date. Now you may change either or both of them. The effective Date may be earlier or later than Voucher Date but must lie within the Current Period.

Effective Date may be modified only though *F2:Date* (F-4B/ 01-02). If you alter Voucher Date in Voucher, the cursor does not move to Effective Date in the Voucher. To change it, press *F2:Date* and enter the Voucher Date & Effective Date of the voucher (F-4A), which is then carried to Voucher Date & Effective Date respectively, in the voucher (F-4B)

05 Voucher Narration

Voucher Narration is complete description of transaction details recorded in the voucher

Voucher Narration entry

At Voucher Type creation (§02/02-07), we have explained Voucher Common Narration & Voucher Ledger Narration set up (§05/02-07).

Here we explain the entry process of both types for Voucher Narration during Voucher Entry:

- **Common Narration entry in Voucher:** After entry of all particulars, the cursor goes to Voucher Common Narration field (if Voucher Common Narration is activated in for the respective Voucher Type). You have to enter voucher narration in one virtual continuous line within the Voucher Narration Text Box (F-5A). The Narration gets terminated where you press <Enter>. You may enter Cheque details also in Voucher Narration (instead of at Cheque details entry screen: (§ 06/04-01)

F-5A: Common Voucher Narration entry

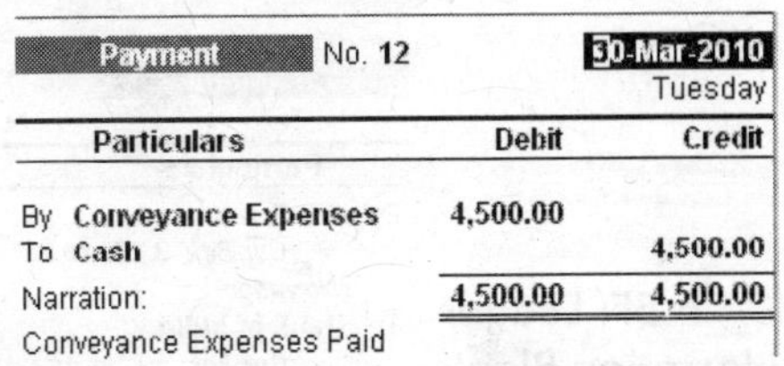

- **Ledger Narration entry in Voucher:** Having activated the Ledger Narration feature at respective Voucher Type, during voucher entry, you will get a prompt for Narration after entry of Ledger Account details (F-5B). Enter the Ledger Narration related to the ledger, after each Ledger account.

F-5B: Common & Ledger Narration entry in Voucher

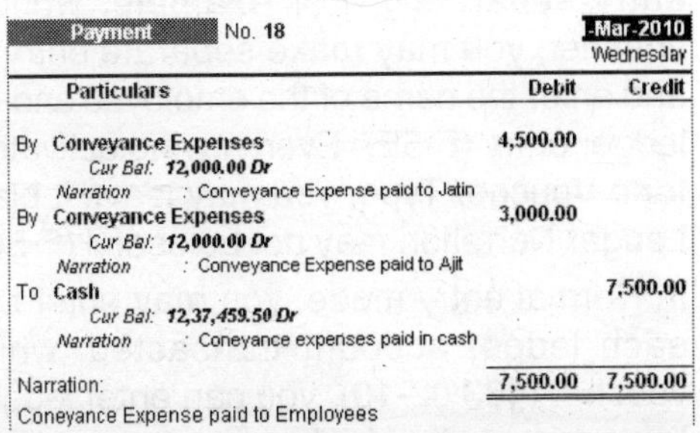

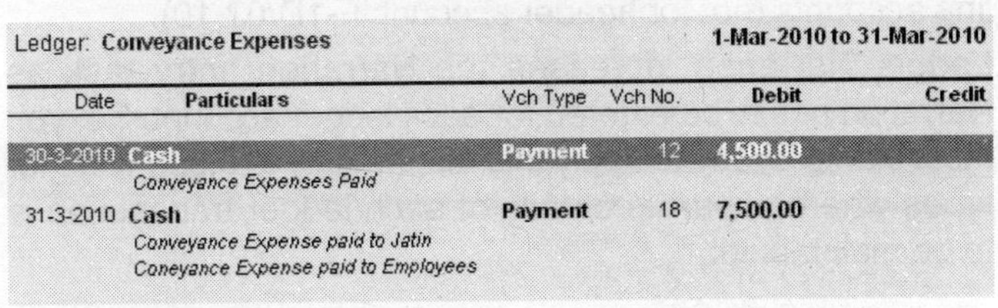

F-5C: Ledger Account showing Ledger Narration

If Ledger Narration is activated for the Voucher Type, you will get Ledger Narration field after each Ledger Entry.

Payment No. 18		31-Mar-2010 Wednesday
Particulars	**Debit**	**Credit**
By **Salary**	4,500.00	
Narration : Salary Paid to Ajit fot March 10		
By **Conveyance Expenses**	3,000.00	
Narration : Conveyance Expense paid to Ajit for Jan to Mar 10		
To **Cash**		7,500.00
Cur Bal: **12,37,459.50 Dr**		
Narration : Salary & Conv Exp paid to Ajit		
Narration:	7,500.00	7,500.00
Salary for March & Conv Exp for Jan to Mar paid to Ajit		

F-5D: Ledger & Common Narration

Payment No. 3		1-May-2009 Friday
Particulars	**Debit**	**Credit**
Dr **Salary**	12,300.00	
Narration : M pal for m/o April 09		
Dr **Conveyance Expenses**	470.00	
Narration : M Pal for Conveyance Expenses for April		
Dr **Salary**	11,400.00	
Narration : Niraj Mohta for April 09		
Dr **Travelling Expenses**	3,400.00	
Narration : Paid to Niraj Mohta for DEIhi Visit towrads Rail Fare / Hotel exp etc		
Cr **Bank of India**		27,570.00
Narration : Piad to M Pal 12770, & Niraj Mohta 14800		
	27,570.00	Accept ? Yes or No

F-5E: Ledger Narration entry in Voucher

Payment No. 17		31-Mar-2010 Wednesday
Particulars	**Debit**	**Credit**
By **A K Traders**	1,200.00	
Cur Bal: **3,250.00 Cr**		
Narration :		
To **Bank of India**		1,200.00
Cur Bal: **83,730.00 Cr**		
Narration :		
Narration:	1,200.00	1,200.00
Paid on Account		

F-5F: Ledger Narration Blank

Ledger Narration is useful when you have to explain each entry separately. For example, while making a salary voucher, you may make separate entry for each employee and enter the name of the employee and other details at each ledger entry (F-5E). Even having activated Ledger Narration for a Voucher Type, you may leave it blank where separate Ledger Narration may not be useful (F-5F).

In Normal entry mode, you may enter Ledger Narration for each ledger account transacted, while in single mode voucher (§03/02-10), you can enter ledger narration only for line accounts (not for header account: F-1D/02-10).

Ledger Narration increases the Narration entry task as Narration has to be entered for each ledger account. So, you must plan properly to apply this feature only to those voucher types where separate details of each ledger transaction is to be maintained.

05.01 Ledger Narration in Reports

To show Ledger Narration in Display / Print, at Reports Display / Printing Configuration option (§01/02-13, §02/02-14). set *Yes* at *Show Narration also.* For example, in Ledger Book, the Ledger Narration, if entered, will be printed just below in the first line, followed by voucher Narration, if any (F-6A).

In Ledger Account (Ledger Book), the *Ledger Narration* is shown after the respective complementary account, while the Common Narration is shown at the end of voucher.

> **Note:** *If multiple entries for same ledger account is entered in one voucher, the amount of all such entries for the ledger in the voucher is summed up and shown in the Report (Ledger / Cash Bank Journal Book) instead of each entry amount, and the Ledger Narration of first entry only is shown (the Narration of subsequent entries are NOT shown). The Common Narration is shown in the Ledger account, at the end of the voucher.*

Ledger: **Salary** — For 1-May-2009

Date	Particulars		Vch Type	Vch No.	Debit	Credit
1-5-2009	(as per details)		Payment	3	23,700.00	
	Conveyance Expenses	470.00 Dr				
	M Pal for Conveyance Expenses for April					
	Travelling Expenses	3,400.00 Dr				
	Paid to Niraj Mohta for DEIhi Visit towrads Rail Fare / Hotel exp etc					
	Bank of India	27,570.00 Cr				
	Piad to M Pal 12770, & Niraj Mohta 14800					
	M pal for m/o April 09					
				Opening Balance :		
				Current Total :	23,700.00	
				Closing Balance :	23,700.00	

F-6A: Ledger Book showing Ledger Narration

05.02 Ledger Narration of Complementary Accounts

The Complementary Accounts in Ledger book for multi account vouchers have been explained earlier (§02/01-08). Accordingly, the Ledger Narration of respective Ledger are shown for the complementary accounts (F-6B & F-6C)

Ledger: **Salary** — 1-Mar-2010 to 31-Mar-2010

Date	Particulars		Vch Type	Vch No.	Debit	Credit
31-3-2010	(as per details)		Payment	18	4,500.00	
	Conveyance Expenses	3,000.00 Dr				
	Conveyance Expense paid to Ajit for Jan to Mar 10					
	Cash	7,500.00 Cr				
	Salary & Conv Exp paid to Ajit					
	Salary Paid to Ajit fot March 10					
	Salary for March & Conv Exp for Jan to Mar paid to Ajit					

F-6B: Ledger Narration of Complementary Accounts in Ledger Accounts

Ledger: **Conveyance Expenses** — For 31-Mar-2010

Date	Particulars		Vch Type	Vch No.	Debit	Credit
31-3-2010	(as per details)		Payment	18	3,000.00	
	Salary	4,500.00 Dr				
	Salary Paid to Ajit fot March 10					
	Cash	7,500.00 Cr				
	Salary & Conv Exp paid to Ajit					
	Conveyance Expense paid to Ajit for Jan to Mar 10					
	Salary for March & Conv Exp for Jan to Mar paid to Ajit					

F-6C: Ledger Narration of Complementary Accounts in Ledger Accounts

06 Debit Credit sign in Voucher Entry

During Normal mode Voucher entry, the Debit / Credit sign of each entry has to be specified (by *Dr/Cr* pair or *To / By* Pair, as per personal choice). The voucher data is stored in same manner, whichever indicator you use. You may sw :h between these 2 options at any time as per your choice.

To set the (Dr/Cr or To/By) pair, at Voucher Configuration screen (F-1, F-2A to F-2D), at the option *Use Cr/Dr instead of To/By*,.set as follows:

- **Dr/Cr Setting**: Set *Yes* to indicate Debit / Credit through Dr/Cr at the first column in Voucher Entry Consequently, Type D (or Dr) for Debit, C (or Cr) for Credit during Voucher Entry (F-7A)
- **To/By Setting**: Set *No* to indicate Debit / Credit through To/By at the first column in Voucher Entry. Consequently, Type B (or By) for Debit, T (or To) for Credit during Voucher Entry (F-7B)

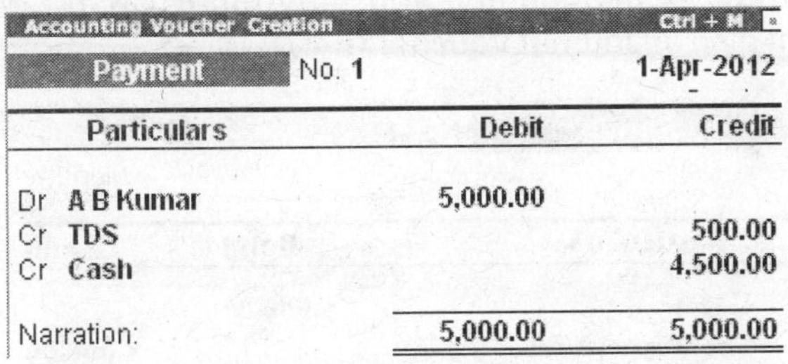

F-7A: Voucher Entry using Dr/ Cr Option

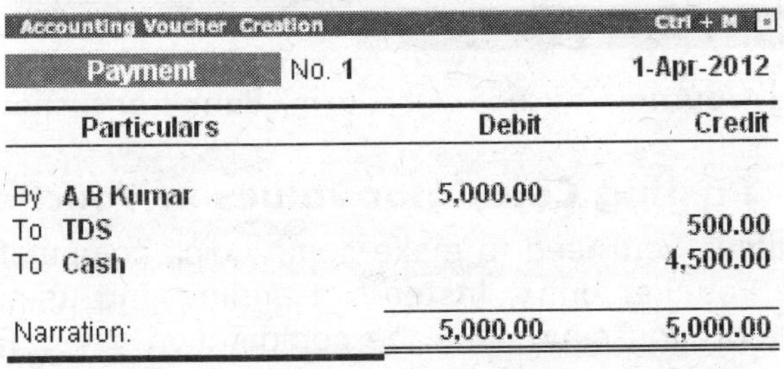

F-7B: Voucher Entry using To/By Option

It's a matter of personal preference. This option does not otherwise make any material effect on the system. As the Amount column headings are Debit and Credit, people prefer to use *Cr* & *Dr*, (in this book Dr / Cr would be used instead of To/By)

07 Negative Cash Balance Warning

Normally Tally would display the Ledger Balance on each voucher entry, from which you can view the balance (including negative cash balance in cash account). However, to make you specifically aware about negative cash balance, at *Warn on Negative Cash Balance* (F-1, F-2A to F-2D):

- Set *Yes,* to get the warning instantly at the point of entry to know immediately about the offending voucher that makes the cash balance negative (F-8), so that you can check up instantly Useful when you make voucher entries chronologically.
- Set *No*, you will not get any warning message during Vouchers entry when cash balance becomes negative (to avoid unnecessary warning message, when all vouchers may not be entered chronologically)

F-8: Voucher Entry Negative Cash Warning

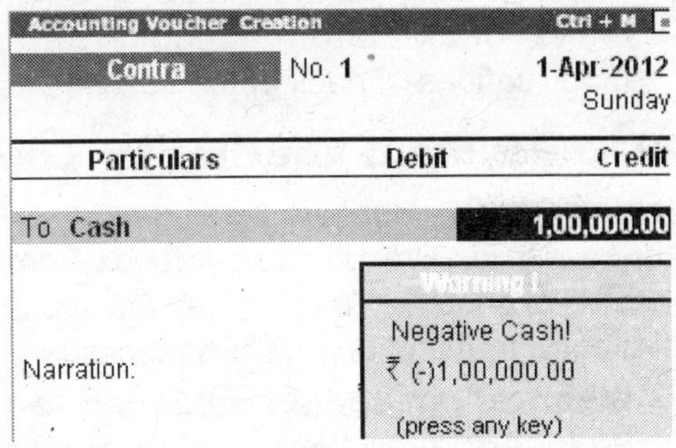

08 Ledger Balance Display

During Voucher Entry, you may view the current balance of each transacted ledger account prior to transaction and post-transaction.

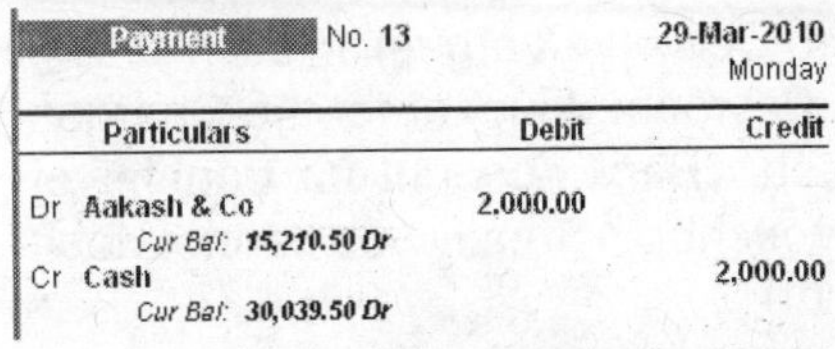

F-9A: Ledger Balance shown during Voucher Entry

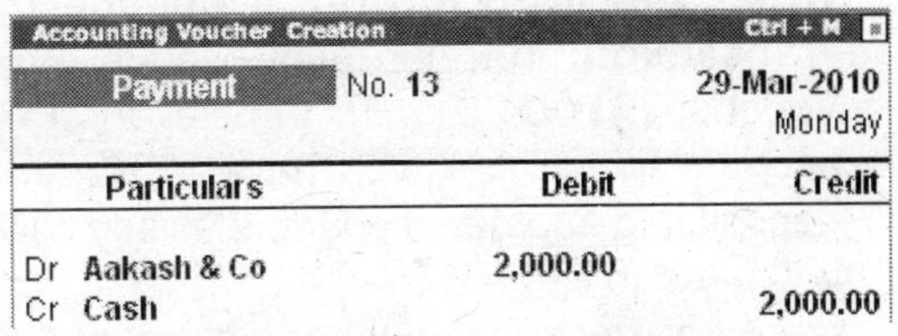

F-9B: Ledger Balance not shown during Voucher Entry

At *Show Ledger Current Balances* (F-1, F-2A to F-D):

- **Show Ledger Balance during voucher entry**: Set *Yes* to show the Current Balance of the selected Ledger Account, at the time of voucher entry (irrespective of voucher date). Just below the Ledger Account line (F-9A)
- **No Ledger Balance shown during voucher entry:** Set *No* to hide Ledger Balance (No Ledger Balance will appear at the time of entry) at the time of voucher entry (F-9B).
- **Type of Ledger Balance**: Having set for Ledger Balance Display (i.e when you set *Yes* at *Show Ledger Current Balances)*, you may further opt to show nature of Ledger Balance as follows:
  - o **Voucher Date Balance:** Set Yes at *Show balances as on Voucher Date* to display balance for the Ledger as at the Voucher Date instead of current balance. This may be helpful in case of Back dated Vouchers entry when you want display of balance for the Ledger as at the Voucher date instead of current balance
  - o **Current Balance:** Set *No* at *Show balances as on Voucher Date* to display Current Balance of Ledger at the time of entry (irrespective of Voucher Date)

for the Ledger as at the Voucher Date instead of current balance.

When you make voucher entry regularly and in chronological order, Current Balance is better option. Voucher Date Balance may be useful only when you make back dated voucher entry and frequent modifications of back dated voucher.

09 Payment Voucher for Contra

Sometimes Payment Voucher may also be used to make Contra entries like transfer of funds from one cash / bank account to another. You may need to use a Payment voucher for Contra transaction in following cases:

- **When other Ledger Accounts are transacted in Voucher:** When there is some additional ledger (other than cash / Bank) are also involved in the transfer of Fund (e.g you make a DD or advice Bank to transfer fund from one bank account to another and the Bank charges some Bank Charge for the services (F-10). Similarly, you direct the Bank to deliver Cash to your office / factory and the Bank charges the Cash Delivery Charges). In such cases, you have to create a Payment Voucher for the Charges and also Debit a Cash / Bank account for transfer of money (in Payment Voucher, normally you cannot debit a Cash / Bank Account).
- **When you need to print a Cheque for the Contra Transaction:** You can print cheque only for Payment Voucher (§11/04-01). To transfer fund from one bank account to another, you have to issue a cheque and deposit it to another account. Similarly, to withdraw cash, you need to issue a cheque. In such cases, you have to create a Payment Voucher instead of Contra Voucher, for Fund Transfer from One Cash / bank Account to another

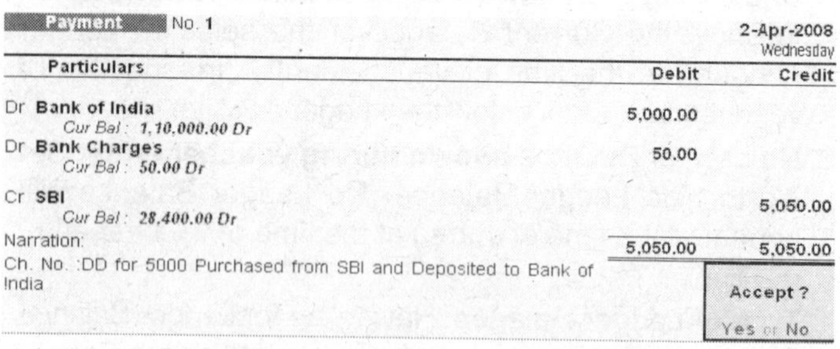

Payment No. 1 — 2-Apr-2008, Wednesday

Particulars	Debit	Credit
Dr **Bank of India** *Cur Bal : 1,10,000.00 Dr*	5,000.00	
Dr **Bank Charges** *Cur Bal : 50.00 Dr*	50.00	
Cr **SBI** *Cur Bal : 28,400.00 Dr*		5,050.00
Narration:	5,050.00	5,050.00

Ch. No. :DD for 5000 Purchased from SBI and Deposited to Bank of India

Accept ? Yes or No

F-10: Payment Voucher for Contra Transaction

At Payment Voucher entry Configuration (F-2B), set *Yes* at *Use Payment as Contra* to allow entry of Contra transaction (fund transfer from one cash / bank account to another) through a Contra Voucher also.

> **Note:** *When you create Payment / Receipt Voucher for Contra Transaction (Fund trasnfer from one cash / bank account to other), create only one voucher (DO NOT create two separate vouchers for Money Out & Money In. One voucher will affect two way entries (like a Contra Voucher).*

10 Receipt Voucher for Contra

Like Payment Voucher as discussed above, sometimes Receipt Voucher may also be used to make Contra entries like transfer of funds from one cash / bank account to another.

At Receipt Voucher Configuration (F-2C), set *Yes* at *Use Receipt as Contra* to allow entry of Contra transaction entry (fund transfer from one cash / bank account to another) through a Receipt Voucher also.

11 Cash / Bank Account in Journal Voucher

Normally, Cash / Bank Account transactions are not entered in Journal Voucher (entered in Contra / Payment / Receipt Voucher). However, some may prefer to enter data with Cash / Bank transactions also in Journal Voucher.

At Journal Voucher Configuration screen (F-2D), set Yes at *Allow Cash Accounts in Journal* to enter cash / bank account in Journal. Consequently, you may enter Cash / Bank Account also in Journal Voucher (F-11).

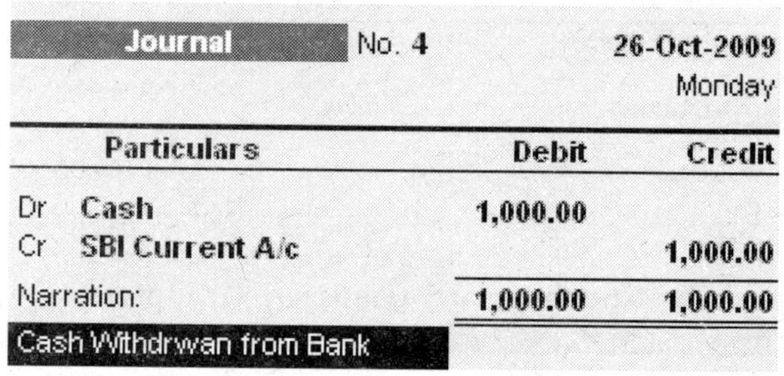

Journal No. 4 — 26-Oct-2009, Monday

Particulars	Debit	Credit
Dr **Cash**	1,000.00	
Cr **SBI Current A/c**		1,000.00
Narration:	1,000.00	1,000.00

Cash Withdrwan from Bank

F-11: Journal Voucher with Cash / Bank transaction

12 Pasting Calculator values in Voucher

Sometimes you need to make some quick computation during voucher entry. Instead of finding and using a Calculator, you may make the computation using Tally Calculator (§05/02-03) from the current screen and paste the result of an arithmetic calculation at a Numeric input field (like Amount in Voucher) without having to re-type it (and eliminate typing mistake)

- At Numeric Input Field, press *Alt+C* to invoke the Calculator (F-12)
- At Calculator Area, type the Arithmetic Expression (like 600*3)

The result (like 1800) will be shown in next line in the Calculator area and will also be pasted in the numeric field from where the Calculator was invoked (Alt+C was pressed).

> **Note:** *You may invoke Tally Calculator to compute & enter the computed value in any numeric input field. This is quite useful to compute-&-paste numeric figures in any entry screen, quickly and correctly, in one action. No need to use physical Calculator or invoke any other external Calculator Application to compute-copy- paste.*

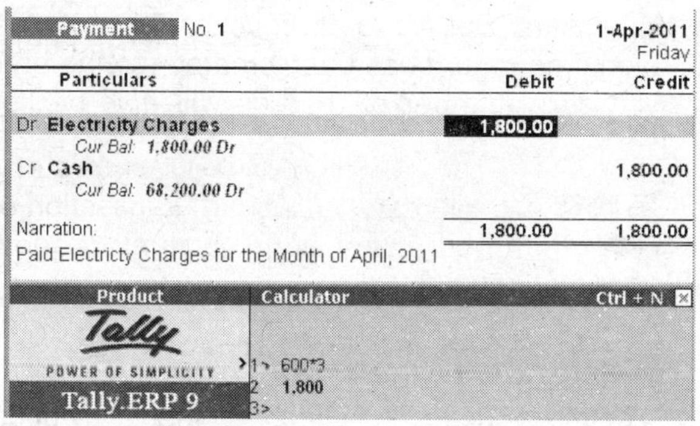

F-12: Pasting Computed Value from Tally Calculator

13 Automatic Voucher Numbers

When Automatic Voucher Numbering scheme is opted, subsequent effects of various operations on Automatically created voucher numbers are explained below:

- **Changing Voucher Date**: If the *Voucher Date* is changed to an earlier date, then voucher numbers of all the vouchers of subsequent date will be changed. For example you change the date of a payment voucher number 195 from 12 May to 12 April. Assuming that the last voucher number of payment Voucher date 12 April was 92, the changed voucher number will become 93 and the number of each payment voucher subsequent to date 12 April will get changed consecutively. The voucher number of vouchers dated 12 April and earlier will not be affected.
- **New back dated voucher entered**: If you enter a voucher of previous date, then voucher numbers of all the vouchers subsequent to the changed date will be changed. For example, after having entered payment voucher number 165 upto 12 May, you enter a payment voucher dated 12 April. Assuming that the last voucher number of payment Voucher date 12 April was 92, the newly entered voucher number will become 93 and the number of each payment voucher subsequent to date 12 April will increase by 1. The voucher number of vouchers dated 12 April and earlier will not be affected.
- **Back dated voucher Deleted**: If you delete a voucher of previous date, then voucher numbers of all the subsequent vouchers will be changed. For example, after having entered payment vouchers number 165 upto 12 May, you delete a payment voucher number 93 dated 12 April. Then the voucher number of all vouchers from 94 onwards will be reduced by 1. The voucher number of vouchers prior to 93 will not be affected.

The automated voucher numbering scheme is suitable in on-line Voucher Entry environment (when you strictly enter vouchers as per date and never change the voucher date nor enter or delete a back dated voucher). However, in many situations voucher entry are not done immediately at the time of transaction. So, practically, automated voucher numbering scheme is suitable only when you file the vouchers in chronological order but do not write the voucher numbers on the physical vouchers. The books of accounts should be printed after the finalization of accounts are over, for record keeping and auditing.

The Voucher Numbering scheme applies separately for each Voucher Type. So, the change affects only to the specific Voucher Type. So, you may create separate Voucher Types for various types of regular transactions, so that the effect of change in voucher remains restricted within that Voucher Type only, without disturbing the other Voucher Types.

14 Statistics

Statistics Report shows the Number of Masters records & Vouchers entered. Select *Display > Statement of Accounts > Statistics to get the* Statistics Report (F-13A)

In the left pane, you get the number of vouchers for each Voucher Type and in the right pane, you get the number of each master records.

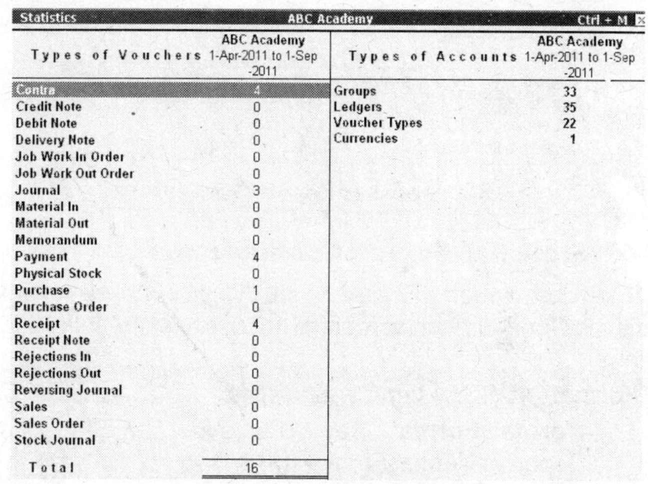

Statistics — ABC Academy — Ctrl + M

Types of Vouchers	ABC Academy 1-Apr-2011 to 1-Sep-2011	Types of Accounts	ABC Academy 1-Apr-2011 to 1-Sep-2011
Contra	4	Groups	33
Credit Note	0	Ledgers	35
Debit Note	0	Voucher Types	22
Delivery Note	0	Currencies	1
Job Work In Order	0		
Job Work Out Order	0		
Journal	3		
Material In	0		
Material Out	0		
Memorandum	0		
Payment	4		
Physical Stock	0		
Purchase	1		
Purchase Order	0		
Receipt	4		
Receipt Note	0		
Rejections In	0		
Rejections Out	0		
Reversing Journal	0		
Sales	0		
Sales Order	0		
Stock Journal	0		
Total	16		

F-13A: Statistics Report

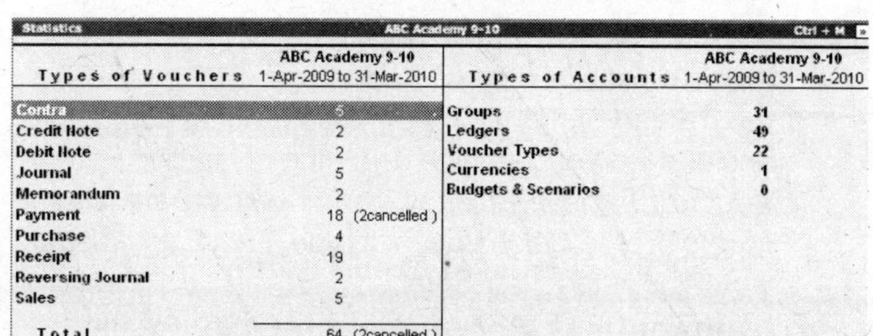

Statistics — ABC Academy 9-10 — Ctrl + M

Types of Vouchers	ABC Academy 9-10 1-Apr-2009 to 31-Mar-2010	Types of Accounts	ABC Academy 9-10 1-Apr-2009 to 31-Mar-2010
Contra	5	Groups	31
Credit Note	2	Ledgers	49
Debit Note	2	Voucher Types	22
Journal	5	Currencies	1
Memorandum	2	Budgets & Scenarios	0
Payment	18 (2cancelled)		
Purchase	4		
Receipt	19		
Reversing Journal	2		
Sales	5		
Total	64 (2cancelled)		

F-13B: Statstics Report (Created entries)

The number of Vouchers shown include Optional Voucher of the respective Type (number of Optional Vouchers are not revealed separately in the Report). Canceled Vouchers are indicated alongside (F-13B. F-13C)

Statistics

	1-Apr-2009 to 31-Mar-2010
Types of Vouchers :	
Contra	5
Credit Note	2
Debit Note	2
Delivery Note	0
Job Work In Order	0
Job Work Out Order	0
Journal	5
Material In	0
Material Out	0
Memorandum	2
Payment	18 (2cancelled)
Physical Stock	0
Purchase	4
Purchase Order	0
Receipt	19
Receipt Note	0
Rejections In	0
Rejections Out	0
Reversing Journal	2
Sales	5
Sales Order	0
Stock Journal	0
Total	64 (2cancelled)
Types of Accounts :	
Groups	31
Ledgers	49
Voucher Types	22
Currencies	1
Budgets & Scenarios	0

F-13C: Statistics Report (Vertical)

14.01 *Statistics Report Configuration*

At Statistics Report (F-13A), click *F12:Configure* to get Statistics Configuration screen (F-13D), to set the following options

- **Format:** At *Show Vertical Statistics*:
  - o **Normal Format**: Set *No* to show the Statistics Report in Normal Format (F-13A)
  - o **Vertical Format**: Set *Yes* to show the Statistics Report in Vertical Format (F-13C)
- **Sorting**: At *Sort by Parent Voucher Type:*
  - o **Parent Voucher Type Sequence**: Set *Yes* to list the Primary Voucher Type n alphabetical sequence and derived Voucher type under the respective Parent Voucher Type. For example, if you create *Cash Memo* of type *Sales* Voucher Type, then *Cash Memo* would be listed after Sales.
  - o **Alphabetical Sequence**: Set *No* to list in alphabetical sequence of Voucher Type Name. For example, if you create *Cash Memo* of type *Sales* Voucher Type, then *Cash Memo* would be listed in alphabetical order (i.e before *Sales*)
- **Usage**: At *Remove Voucher Type having No entries*:
  - o Created entities: Set *Yes* to list only those Voucher Types / Masters for which some record has ben created (so the entities with zero number of records will *not* be listed: F-13B)
  - o All entities: Set *No* to all Voucher Types / Master, even if no record has been created (so the entities with zero number of records will *also* be listed: F-13A)

Configuration	
Show Vertical Statistics	? No
Sort by Parent Voucher Type	? No
Remove Voucher Types having no entries	? No

F-13D: Statistics Report Configuration

15 Provisional Vouchers

When you enter a voucher, the effect is immediately updated in all related reports. However, in some situations, we need to defer the effect of the voucher in the system (keep the entered voucher dormant). Such Vouchers are called *Provisional* Vouchers

Tally.ERP 9 provides following kinds of Provisional vouchers, which do not impact the entire system immediately on entry of voucher

- Memorandum
- Optional
- Post Dated
- Reversing Journal

These are dormant vouchers and do not affect accounts on entry like regular vouchers.

15.01 *Activation for Provisional Voucher*

To activate Memorandum & Optional Voucher for the Company, at F11:Features>Accounting Features, set Yes at *Use Reversing Journals & Optional Vouchers*. Consequently, in voucher entry screen, you get following buttons (F-14C):

- L:Optional / Regular: To Create / Convert Optional / Regular Voucher
- F10:Memos: To Create Memorandum Voucher
- F10:Rev Jrnl: To create Reversing Journal Voucher
- T:Current / T: To Create / Convert Post dated Voucher

16 Optional Voucher

We have already explained Optional Voucher auto creation (§04/02-07). Here we explain creation of Optional Voucher and conversion between Optional / Regular Voucher through Voucher entry / alteration screen.

Creation of Optional Voucher: At the time of Voucher entry, click L:*Optional* button (F-14C) to create an Optional Voucher. An indicative tag *Optional* appears at the voucher header (F-14A)

Accounting Voucher Creation ABC Academy 9-10 Ctrl + M

Payment No. 1 1-Jun-2013 Saturday

Optional

Particulars	Debit	Credit
Dr Aakash & Co	1,000.00	
Cr Cash		1,000.00

F-14A: Optional Voucher Creation

Day Book — Ctrl + M

Day Book 1-Apr-2009 to 31-Mar-2010

Date	Particulars	Vch Type	Vch No.	Debit Amount	Credit Amount
1-4-2009	T K Das	Sales	1	50,000.00	
1-4-2009	Suspense	Memorandum	1	1,000.00	
1-5-2009	Salary	Payment	(Optional) 2	12,300.00	
5-5-2009	T K Das	Receipt	3		10,000.00
1-6-2009	Cash	Contra	(Optional) 2		500.00
1-6-2009	A K Traders	Payment	4	2,000.00	
1-6-2009	Aakash & Co	Payment	(Optional) 7	1,000.00	
1-6-2009	A K Traders	Credit Note	1		2,000.00
1-6-2009	B M Suppliers	Debit Note	1	2,500.00	

F:14B: Day Book showing Optional Voucher

F-14C: Buttons

Optional Voucher is shown in Day Book (F-14B) with Optional indicative tag shown beside the Voucher Type. But Optional Voucher is not shown in any other Accounting Reports (like Ledger, Cash Book etc)

> **Note:** Optional Voucher *is created when the transaction is anticipated to happen (before the transaction takes place). It is regularised after the transaton takes place. It may be deleted if the antcipated transaction does not take place. It is extensvely used in pefect on-line system, where manual paper voucher is* totally eliminated. *Optional Voucher is allotted numbers separately, within the voucher Type. So, if you create an* Optional Payment *Voucher after creating a* Regular Payment *Voucher number 2 (under automatic numbering scheme), the next created Regular as well as Optional voucher number will be allotted number 3. The regular voucher number will be consecutive but optional voucher get inserted wih a duplicate number that of Regular voucher of same Date (so Voucher Numbers may be skipped in Optional Voucher)*

16.01 Conversion of Optional / Regular Voucher

You may change Optional Voucher to Regular & Vice Versa:

- **From Optional to Regular**: At Voucher entry alteration screen of Optional Voucher, click L: *Regular* toggle button (F-14C). The tag *Optiona*l at the voucher header will be removed and the Voucher is converted to Regular.
- **From Regular to Optional**: At Voucher entry alteration screen, click L: *Optional* toggle button (F-14C). The tag Optional at the voucher header will appear and the Voucher is converted to Optional

17 Memorandum Voucher

Memorandum Vouchers (popularly called as *Memo Voucher*) are dormant vouchers and do not affect accounts until these are transformed into the any of the regular voucher type.

To enter Memorandum Voucher, select Voucher Entry and click F10: *Memos* to get Memorandum Voucher entry screen (F-15). The first ledger account must be Debit. The later accounts may be Debit / Credit

Memorandum Voucher will not be posted anywhere. Later on, when this voucher is converted to any kind of regular voucher (say a Payment Voucher), the voucher will get posted.

Memorandum No. 1 — 1-Apr-2009 Wednesday

Particulars	Debit	Credit
Dr Suspense	1,000.00	
Cr Cash		1,000.00
Narration:	1,000.00	1,000.00

Paid to Shakeel for Misc Payments / Expenses

F-15: Memorandum Voucher entry

> **Note:** Memorandum Voucher *is a Voucher Type, finally to be converted to the specific Voucher Type, while Optional Voucher is a special tag of the Voucher (it is not a separate Voucher* Type*). It is highly recommended* NOT to use Memorandum Voucher, *but use* Optional Voucher *instead.*

17.01 Conversion of Memorandum Voucher

To convert Memorandum Voucher to any Voucher Type, select the Memorandum Voucher in Day Book (F-15B) and press <enter>. to get the Memorandum Voucher in alteration mode. Now click the respective Voucher Type button to which the Memorandum Voucher is to be converted (e.g *F5:Payment* to convert the Memo Voucher to Payment Voucher).. You may have to change any offending ledger account to conform to the rules of the voucher type to which the Memorandum Voucher is being converted to. Press *Ctl+A* to save

Memorandum Voucher is much like Optional Voucher. The principal difference is that Memorandum Voucher is a common form of Voucher Type which can be converted to any Voucher Type, whereas Optional Voucher is of a specific Voucher Type which can be converted to Regular Voucher of that Voucher Type only

FAQ: Frequently Asked Question

FAQ-1: The voucher numbers are automatically generated as per Voucher Date. I find that a voucher of earlier date was wrongly entered. How do I delete the voucher without disturbing the voucher numbers of all the subsequent vouchers.

Ans: If you delete a voucher (in case of Auto Numbered Vouchers), the subsequent voucher of the deleted voucher type numbers will be renumbered (the number will be reduced by 1). To avoid that, do not delete the voucher but Cancel the voucher.

To cancel a voucher, select *Display > Day Book* and then set the period to include the voucher in the Day Book. Click

F4:Chg Vch and select the Voucher Type to get the Voucher list. Select the voucher to be *Cancelled* and click X:Cancel button (or press Alt+X). In Day Book, the *Cancelled* voucher will be shown as Cancelled with no figure in *Amount* column.

Once Cancelled, you cannot Restore the Cancelled voucher (Cancelled voucher may be Deleted).

FAQ-6: How to set Dr / Cr or By/To option for Ledger amount sign during Voucher Entry

To set the Ledger Sign, By/To to Dr / Cr:

- At Gateway, click *F12:Configure* and select *Voucher Entry* at the Configuration Menu to get Voucher Entry Configuration screen (F-1), or
- At Voucher Entry screen, click *F12:Configure* to get *Voucher Entry Configuration* screen (F-2A to F-2D)

At *Voucher Entry Configuration* screen (F-1, F-2A to F-2D), at the option *Use Cr/Dr instead of To / By during Voucher Entry:*

- Set *Yes* at to use Dr/Cr.
- Set *No* to get *To/By*

Single Mode Voucher Entry 02-10

01 Voucher Entry

You have seen that in Voucher, we record transactions as per standard accounting rules, in which we specify the ledger account involved, debit / credit sign and the corresponding amount. Each transaction must have 2 aspects, Debit & Credit.

To write a voucher, you have to know the ledger accounts which is be debited and which one to be credited and this has to be indicated in the Voucher. So, it requires a clear understanding of Debit & Credit

However, the concept of Debit / Credit is a bit technical matter. Some people, specially Non-Accountants do not feel comfortable with the terms *Debit* & *Credit.* They may find it a little bit difficult to understand and often commit mistake in writing voucher.

02 Single Mode Voucher Entry

To make ordinary people comfortable in writing voucher correctly, Tally.ERP 9 has evolved a new concept of voucher entry method (called *Single Mode* entry), where the user does not have to specify Debit / Credit during voucher entry. The rules of Debit/ Credit are embedded. In Single Mode entry, Tally intelligently understands the Debit / Credit nature from the position of ledger entry (header / table area), type of voucher (Payment, Receipt, Contra) and sign of the amount in Table Area (+, -). Tally internally assigns the debit / credit aspects to each transaction part,

This makes voucher entry rule simpler, faster and eliminates errors of Debit / Credit specification often committed during voucher creation.

The Single Mode entry method also allows to create Voucher Classes automatically carry ledger accounts to make voucher entry simpler, quicker and consistent. Internally, Tally keeps data in same way, whether entered in Single Mode or in Dual (Normal) mode.

In single entry also, aspects of debit & credit are internally maintained. Tally.ERP 9 stores the voucher in same manner irrespective of mode of entry. Tally only shields the confusing part of Debit & Credit from the user and provides an alternate no frills interface for voucher entry. You will get same results and reports. The way of entry is inly different, not the data.

However, some voucher types, like Voucher class etc, must be entered in Single Mode only

> **Note:** *Single Mode Voucher Entry (which is just a method of voucher entry), should not be confused with Single Entry accounting method (which is method of accounting system). They are completely two different aspects. Only the names look similar.*

02.01 Single Mode Voucher Entry Configuration

At Voucher Entry Configuration (F-1A/02-09 & F-2A to F-2C/ 02-09), set *Yes* at *Use Single mode for Payment/Receipt/ Contra* to get single entry mode for Contra(F-1A),, Payment (F-1B) & Receipt vouchers (F-1C),. However, Journal Vouchers must be entered in Normal (Dual) Mode only

03 Single Mode Voucher Entry Rules

In Single Entry mode, you enter Ledger Accounts data in 2 main areas:

- **Header Part**: Here you enter only one One Cash / Bank ledger account in Header (referred as *Header Account)* without any amount.
- **Line Area:** All other ledger accounts in Line Area, with amount are entered (negative amount for deductions)

Nowhere the user need to specify Dr/ Cr (or To/By). The debit/ credit aspect of the ledger Accounts are determined as follows:

- The debit/ credit aspect of the Header account is determined by the voucher type.
- The debit/ credit aspect of the Line Accounts are determined by the voucher type & the sign (positive / negative) of the amount entered in respect of each Ledger Account.

The amount for ledger account at header is computed as balancing amount of all other ledgers entered next, in the Line Area.

- In Header, select the Cash / Bank Ledger Account.
- In Line area, enter the other ledger accounts (one or more) and the amount (negative amount for deductions) for each ledger account (referred as *Line Accounts*).

The rules of entry of contra, payment & receipt voucher, and the nature of Debit / Credit for each Voucher Type in single entry mode are explained below:

Voucher Type	Header Account (Cash / Bank Accounts)	Dr/Cr	Line Accounts (Other Ledger Accounts)	Dr/ Cr
Payment	Cash / Bank account from which money is being paid. This account is Credited	**Cr**	Any ledger account other than cash / bank, bank occ. First ledger account must have positive figure. Net of all entries must be positive. These accounts are Debited (Credited if negative).	**Dr**
Receipt	Cash / Bank account to which money is being deposited. This account is Debited	**Dr**	Any ledger account other than cash / bank, bank occ.. First ledger account must have positive figure. Net of all entries must be positive. These accounts are Credited (Debited if negative).	**Cr**
Contra	Cash / Bank Account to which money is being transferred. This Account is Debited.	**Dr**	Any other Cash / Bank/ Bank OCC account from which money is being transferred. This account is Credited.	**Cr**

The Voucher Entry configuration options in Single Mode entry are same as Double Mode entry described in previous chapter (02/02-09).

04 Accounts Voucher Entry in Single Mode

The voucher entry sceen in Single Mode entyr for following transactions are shown next (F-1A to F-1C)

Account	Debit Amount	Credit Amount
Contra Voucher (F-1A)		
Cash	1000	
HDFC Bank		1000
Payment Voucher (F-1B)		
Salary	13000	
HRA	3000	
PF		1300
Bank Of India		14700
Receipt Voucher (F-1C)		
Tuition Fees		18000
Cash	18000	

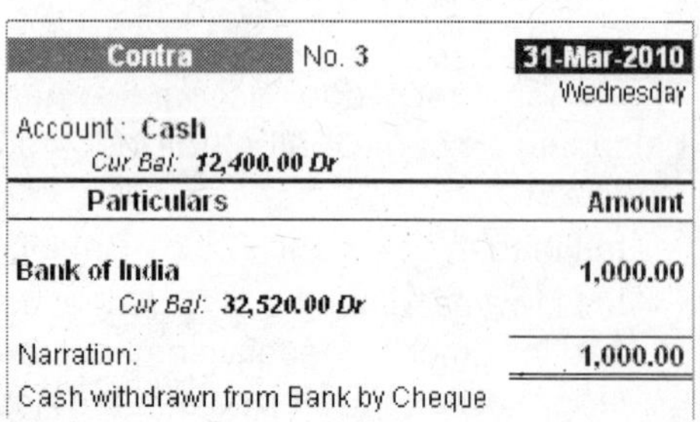
Contra No. 3 31-Mar-2010 Wednesday
Account: Cash
Cur Bal: 12,400.00 Dr

Particulars	Amount
Bank of India Cur Bal: 32,520.00 Dr	1,000.00
Narration:	1,000.00

Cash withdrawn from Bank by Cheque

F-1A Contra Voucher Entry in Single Mode

Narration Entry: The Voucher Narration & Ledger Narration entry in Single Mode entry (F-1D) is almost similar as Normal Voucher entry mode (P-05.03/01-04).

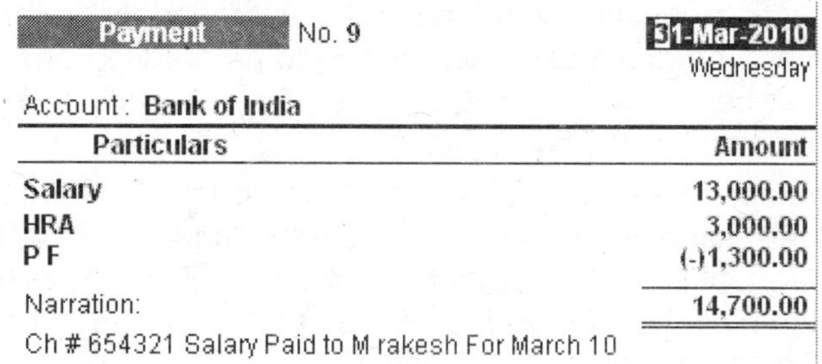
Payment No. 9 31-Mar-2010 Wednesday
Account: Bank of India

Particulars	Amount
Salary	13,000.00
HRA	3,000.00
P F	(-)1,300.00
Narration:	14,700.00

Ch # 654321 Salary Paid to M rakesh For March 10

F-1B Payment Voucher Entry in Single Mode

- **Common Narration**: Voucher Common Narration may be entered at the end of all Line Ledger accounts
- **Ledger Narration**: Ledger Narration may be entered at Line Area only, after each ledger account. However, Ledger Narration CAN NOT be entered for Header Account

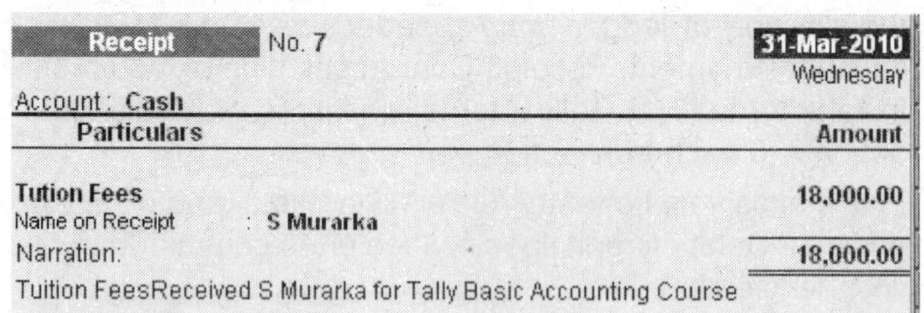
Receipt No. 7 31-Mar-2010 Wednesday
Account: Cash

Particulars	Amount
Tution Fees Name on Receipt : S Murarka	18,000.00
Narration:	18,000.00

Tuition FeesReceived S Murarka for Tally Basic Accounting Course

F-1C: Receipt Voucher Entry in Single mode

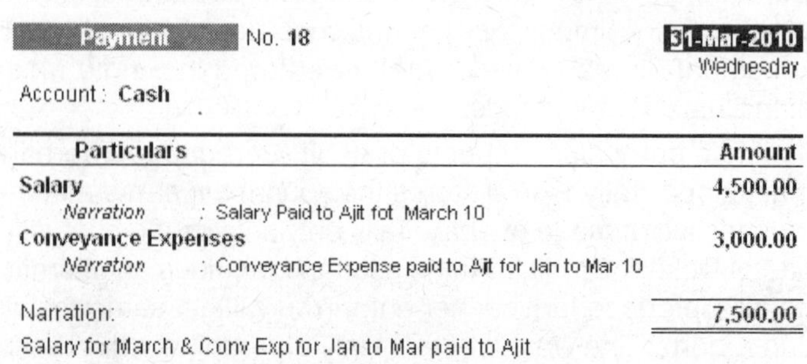
Payment No. 18 31-Mar-2010 Wednesday
Account: Cash

Particulars	Amount
Salary Narration : Salary Paid to Ajit fot March 10	4,500.00
Conveyance Expenses Narration : Conveyance Expense paid to Ajt for Jan to Mar 10	3,000.00
Narration:	7,500.00

Salary for March & Conv Exp for Jan to Mar paid to Ajit

F-1D: Common & Ledger Narration in Single Mode Voucher

FAQ: Frequently Asked Questions

FAQ-1: What is the difference between Single Entry Accounting method & Single Mode Voucher Entry

Ans: Single Entry Accounting method is a Method of Accounting, in which only one aspect of Double Entry is made. On the contrary, Single Mode Voucher Entry is just a method of data entry, the entry is made following the principle of Double Entry.

FAQ-2: In Cash Deposit into State Bank of India, which account would be entered in Header. Explain the accounting effect of he entry

Ans: Cash deposited to State bank of India Rs. 10000. So, the State bank of India would be entered Contra Voucher, in Header and this account would be *Debited* (Account where money is going to – i.e the Receiver Account)

Voucher Type	Header Accounts	Accounts	Amount
Contra	State Bank of India	Cash	10,000

The Accounting effect of the entry is:

Ledger Accounts	Debit Amount	Credit Amount
State Bank of India	10,000	
Cash		10,000

FAQ-3: In Cash Withdrawal from Bank of India for Rs 2500, which account would be entered in Header. Explain the accounting effect of the entry

Ans: *Cash Withdrawn from Bank of India Rs. 2500.* So, Cash would be entered in Header and this account would be *Debited* (Account where money is going to – i.e the Receiver Account)

Voucher Type	Header Accounts	Line Accounts	Amount
Contra	Cash	Bank of India	2500

The Accounting effect of the entry is:

Ledger Accounts	Debit Amount	Credit Amount
Cash	2,500	
Bank of India		2,500

FAQ-4: In Cash Deposit, into State Bank of India, which account would be entered in Line Area.

Ans: Cash Deposited to State bank of India Rs. 10000. So, Cash Account would be entered in Line Account area, as this account would be credited (Account from where money is going - i.e the Giver Account)

Voucher Type	Header Accounts	Line Accounts	Amount
Contra	State Bank of India	Cash	10,000

FAQ-5: In Cash Withdrawal from Bank of India, which account would be entered in Line Account Area. Explain the accounting effect of the entry

Ans: *Cash Withdrawn from Bank of India Rs. 2500* The money is taken from Bank of India Account (from where money is going - i.e the Giver Account)

Voucher Type	Header Accounts	Line Accounts	Amount
Contra	Cash	Bank of India	2500

FAQ-6: Salary (gross Rs 10,000) was paid by Cash after deducting P Tax (Rs 120). Specify the Accounts and corresponding Amounts in Header & Line Area. Explain the accounting effect of the entry

Voucher Type	Header Accounts	Line Accounts	Amount
Payment	Cash	Salary	10000
		P Tax	-120

Ans: Payment made from *Cash Account - Rs. 9880 (*10000-120) So, Cash Account is Credited (from where the money is going – i.e the Giver Account). The other accounts are entered in Ledger Area. Amount paid is entered in positive amount (which is debited) & amount deduced is entered in negative amount money (which is credited)

The Accounting effect of the entry is :

Ledger Accounts	Debit Amount	Credit Amount
Salary	10,000	
P Tax		120
Cash A/c		9,880

FAQ-7: Interest (gross Rs 10,000) was received in Cash, after deducting TDS (Rs 1000). Specify the Accounts and corresponding Amounts in Header & Line Area. Explain the accounting effect of the entry

Voucher Type	Header Accounts	Line Accounts	Amount
Receipt	Cash	Interest	10000
		TDS	-1000

Amount received in *Cash Account - Rs. 9000 (*10000-1000) So, Cash Account is Debited (where the money is going to – i.e the Receiver Account). The other accounts are entered in Ledger Area. Amount Received is entered in positive amount (which is Credited), while amount deducted is entered in negative amount money (which is Debited)

The Accounting effect of the entry is :

Ledger Accounts	Debit Amount	Credit Amount
Interest		10,000
TDS	1,000	
Cash A/c	9,000	

FAQ-8: I paid (in cash) Salary Rs 2500 (Net) after recovering Loan Rs 500 from Gross Salary Rs 3000, How do I make the Payment Voucher entry in Single Mode.

Ans: The above entry is :

Salary Dr 3000,

Loan A/c Cr 500,

Cash A/c Dr 2500

In single mode, Dr / Cr is not specified. In Payment Voucher, at the header, enter the Cash / Bank Account without specifying the Amount.

In Details line, enter the Ledger Accounts for which Payment is made and enter the Amount (this is debited). Next, enter the Ledger Accounts for which Deductions made and enter the Amount as negative (this is credited)

01 Interest

In business, Interest is paid / received for:

- **Ledger Interest on Monies Lent / Borrowed:** Interest is Paid / Payable by Borrower of money to the Lender

  Ledger Interest is computed on Ledger Balances at the end of the day, as per rates / period as specified in the Interest parameters for each ledger account.

  Ledger Interest is normally used to compute Interest on Loans, Deposits etc. In Ledger Interest, you have to specify Interest parameters for specific Ledger Account
- **Overdue Interest on Delayed Payments of Receivables / Payables:** Interest is Paid / Payable by Debtor to Creditor for delayed payment of due bills. It is computed for ledgers under Sundry Debtors, Sundry Creditors, on as specified for New Bill Reference

02 Activation of Interest Features

At *F11: Feature > Accounting Features,* under section Outstandings Management (F-1A), at *Activate Interest* Calculation:

- Set Yes to activate Interest computation features
- Set *No,* Interest features will not be activated

```
Activate Interest Calculation      ? Yes
   (use advanced parameters)       ? Yes
```

F-1A: Activation of Interest at Accounting Features

```
Ledger Alteration
Name      : A K Traders

Under                         : Sundry Debtors
                                 (Current Assets)
Set Credit Limit              : 30.00 Dr
Activate Interest Calculation ? Yes
```

F- 1B: Interest option set up at Ledger Accounts

> **Note:** *Simple Features of Interest means only one Rate of Interest is applicable for a specified Ledger / Bill Reference.. In Advanced Features of Interes, multiple Rate of Interest may be specfied for different period (e.g 12% forApr-June & 15% for Jul to Mar).*
>
> *Ledger Interest is computed on Daily balances of the Ledger, wile Bill Interst is computed on Bill Refernce Balance (§01/03-09)*

02.01 Interest Computation Levels

Having Set at the above options (i.e activating Interest features), at the option *Use Advanced Parameters*, set (F- 1A):

- **Simple Features**: Set *No* to activate only the simple features of computing Interest
- **Advanced Features**: Set *Yes* to also activate advanced features of computing Interest

> **Note:** *Don't confuse Simple / Advanced* Features *with Simple & Compound* computation *Method of Interest. These options are to activate some additional advanced & complex methods of Interest Computation (involving multiple rates & periods) in special cases.Here we discuss about Interest computation on Simple Method only (Interest may be computed on* Compound *Method through Voucher Class only: §09/03-09)*

Now we discuss about Simple Interest Options, i.e when you have set *No* at the option *Use Advanced parameters*, after having set *Yes* at Activate Interest Computation at *F11: Features > Accounting Features*

03 Ledger Interest (Account Current)

At Ledger Accounts entry/ alter screen (F-1B), set *Yes* at *Activate Interest Computation* to get Ledger Interest Rate entry screen (F-2A). At the option *Calculate Interest Transaction by Transaction* (F-2A), set *No* to compute Interest on running Ledger Balances (Account Current).

Interest Parameters Specification: Now specify the Interest Rate applicable for the Ledger Account (F- 2A & F- 2B)

- **Interest Rates**: At *Rate*, enter the Rate for Ledger in % (e.g 12)
- **Interest Rate Period:** At *Per*, select the Period from Interest Style list (F-2B) for which the Interest Rate (entered in the preceding field) would be applicable, from the following available Rate periods:
  - o **Monthly Interest Rates**: Monthly Interest Rate may be specified by selecting:
    - **30 day Month**: Select *30 Day Month* it to compute the Interest on 30 day month basis (so the Interest for Feb and Interest for March would be same for the same number of days),

- **Calendar Month**: Select *Calendar Month* to compute the Interest on number of days in the calendar (so the Interest For Feb and Interest for March would be different for the same number of days),

o **Yearly Interest Rates**: Yearly Interest Rate may be specified by selecting:

- **365 day Year:** Select *365 day Year* to compute the Interest on 365 day year (so the Interest for the year 2012 (366 days leap year) and Interest for the year 2013 (365 days year) would be same for the same number of days),
- **Calendar Year:** Select *Calendar Year* to compute the Interest on the basis of number of days in the Year (365/ 366) (so the Interest for the year 2016 (366 days leap year) and Interest for the year 2015 (365 days year) would be different for the same number of days),

F- 2A:Simple Interest Specification for Ledger Accounts

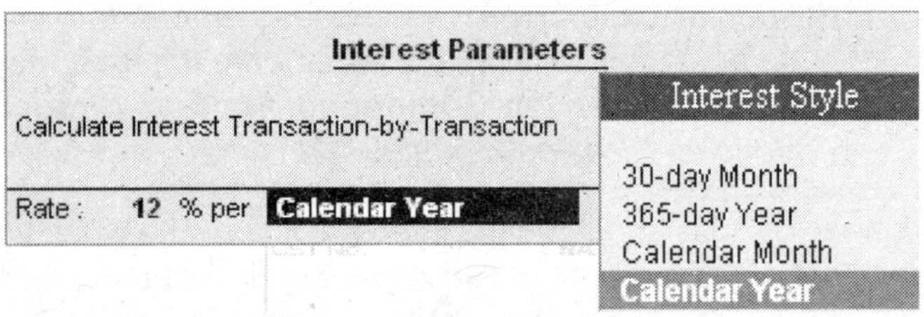

F- 2B: Simple Interest Method

In simple Ledger Interest method, you can apply a single rate for the Ledger Account in the Account Ledger. (you may set different Rates for each Ledger Account).

Example

A loan of Rs 25000 was paid on 1.5.2009 to A K Das.

Calculate Interest on the following Basis upto 31.8.09 – 1.5.09 to 31.8.09 – 122 Days (31+30+31+30). The date of payment is excluded in computation of chargeable days.

Interest Parameter	Computation	Interest Amount
12% per annum (Calendar Year)	25000x12x122/365	1002.74
1% per 30 day month	25000x122x1/30	1016.67
1% per Calendar Month	25000x1/100 (May = 250) + 25000x1/100 (June = 250) + 25000x1/100 (July = 250) +25000x1/100x(30/31) (Aug=241.94)	991.94

A loan of Rs 25000 was paid on 1.5.2009 to A K Das. He repaid Rs 10000 on 3.7.09

a. Calculate Interest @ 12% pa (calendar year) upto 31.8.09

Balance	From:	To:	Total Days	Rate %	Interest
25,000.00 Dr	1-May-2009	3-Jul-2009	63 days	12 %	517.81 Dr
15,000.00 Dr	3-Jul-2009	31-Aug-2009	59 days	12 %	290.96 Dr
				Grand Total	808.77 Dr

F-3A: Simple Ledger Interest @ 12% pa (calendar year)

F-3A shows the Interest computation details screen. The amount is computed as below:

i. 1-5-09 to 3-7-09 = 63 days (31+30+2). Interest = 25000x12x63/(365x100)=**517.81**

ii. 3-7-09 to 3-7-09 = 59 days (29+30). Interest = 25000x12x59/(365x100)=**290.96**

b. Calculate Interest @ 1% (30 day month) upto 31.8.09

Balance	From:	To:	Total Days	Rate %	Interest
25,000.00 Dr	1-May-2009	3-Jul-2009	63 days	1 %	525.00 Dr
15,000.00 Dr	3-Jul-2009	31-Aug-2009	59 days	1 %	295.00 Dr
				Grand Total	820.00 Dr

F-3B: Simple Ledger Interest @ 1% (30 day month)

Balance	From:	To:	Total Days	Rate %	Interest
25,000.00 Dr	1-May-2009	3-Jul-2009	63 days	1 %	516.13 Dr
15,000.00 Dr	3-Jul-2009	31-Aug-2009	59 days	1 %	285.48 Dr
				Grand Total	801.61 Dr

F- 3C: Simple Ledger Interest @ 1% (calendar month)

F-3B shows the Interest computation details screen. The amount is computed as below:

i. 1-5-09 to 3-7-09 = 63 days (31+30+2). Interest = 25000 x {(1/30)/100} x 63=**525.00**

ii. 3-7-09 to 3-7-09 = 59 days (29+30). Interest = 15000 x {(1/30/)/100} x 59=**295.00**

c. Calculate Interest @ 1% (calendar month) upto 31.8.09

Fig 3C shows the Interest computation details screen. The amount is computed as below:

i. 1-5-09 to 3-7-09 = 63 days (31+30+2). Interest = May (25000x 1/100) = 250 +June (25000x 1/100) = 250+ July (25000x 1/100 x 2/31) = 16.13= **516.13**

ii. 3-7-09 to 31-8-09 = 59 (29+30) days. Interest = July (15000x{(29/31/)/100}= 140.32 + Aug 15000x(30/31) = 145.16 = **285.48**

04 Advanced Ledger Interest Set Up

In Advanced Interest Method, you may specify multiple Interest Rates for different block of period (e.g 12% pa for Apl – June and then 15% for July onwards etc). You may further specify to round off the Interest amount (e.g to nearest rupee, nearest 10 rupee etc)

To set Advanced Interest Computation method, at *F11:Features>Accounting Features*, having set *Yes* at

Activate Interest Calculation (F- 1A), further set Yes at *Use Advanced parameters,* to get Advanced Ledger Interest parameters entry screen (F- 1A)

> **Note:** *When you set Mutiple Parameters, ensure that period for ecah period is distinct and not overlapping, otherwise the computaion would be wrong. You may specify different Account Balance Type for each In terest Rtaes.*

Interest Parameters

Calculate Interest Transaction-by-Transaction ? No

Rate: 12 % per 30-Day Month on All Balances
Applicable From: 1-Apr-2008 *To:* 30-Sep-2008
Rounding: Normal Rounding *Limit:* 1

Rate: 1.50 % per 30-Day Month on Debit Balances Only
Applicable From: 1-Oct-2008 *To:*
Rounding: Normal Rounding *Limit:* 1

Interest Balances
All Balances
Credit Balances Only
Debit Balances Only

F- 4:Advanced Interest Specification for Ledger Accounts

04.01 Advanced Interest Parameters set up

Now set the Advanced Interest Parameters as follows (F-4):

- **Interest Rates**: At *Rate*, enter the Rate and select the Rate Period (at *Per*) as described above (§03)
- **Balance Type:** At the field *On*, Select the Balance Type as follows:
  - o **All Balances**: Select it to take both Debit & Credit Balances into account for computation of Interest Consequently:
  - o **Credit Balances Only**: Select it to take Credit Balances only into account for computation of Interest
  - o **Debit Balances Only**: Select it to take Debit Balances only into account for computation of Interest
- **Interest Period:** Enter the Start & End date of the Period for which the Rate would be applicable at the field *Applicable* field
  - o At *From* Field, enter the Start Date of the period from which the specified Interest would be applicable
  - o At *To* Field, enter the End Date of the period for which the specified Interest would be applicable
- **Rounding Method:** At *Rounding* field, select the Rounding Method from the list and specify the Rounding Limit as follows:
  - o **No Rounding**: Select *Not Applicable* if no rounding is applicable. The computed Interest is auto rounded to nearest paise (equivalent to Normal Rounding to.01 Limit, as explained next).
  - o **Lower Rounding**: Select *Down ward Rounding* to Round off the amount to lower value. The rounded amount is lower than (or equal the computed) amount.
  - o **Higher Rounding**: To Round off the amount to higher value. The rounded amount is higher than (or equal to computed amount).
  - o **Normal Rounding**: To Round off to the nearest Value. The Rounded amount may be higher or lower than the computed amount, as per Rounding limit set (explained next).

  Rounding Limit: In any of the above 3 Rounding Methods, specify the Rounding limit (like.01,.10, 1.00, 10.00. ctc).

In case of Advanced Interest, you may specify multiple rates for different periods (their periods must not overlap), or you may have separate parameters for Debit & Credit Balances

Example

F-5A shows the Ledger Account showing the transaction details. F-5B shows the Advanced Interest Parameters setting with multiple Rates, for Debit & Credit Balances.

Ledger: A K Das — 1-Apr-2009 to 31-Mar-2010

Date	Particulars	Vch Type	Vch No.	Debit	Credit
1-5-2009	Cash	Payment	1	25,000.00	
1-6-2009	Cash	Receipt	3		30,000.00
3-7-2009	Cash	Receipt	6		10,000.00
4-8-2009	Cash	Payment	6	15,000.00	
		Opening Balance :			
		Current Total :		40,000.00	40,000.00
		Closing Balance :			

F- 5A: Ledger Account

Interest Parameters

Rate: 12 % per Calendar Year on Debit Balances Only
Applicable From: 1-Apr-2009 *To:*
Rounding: Not Applicable

Rate: 6 % per Calendar Year on Credit Balances Only
Applicable From: 1-Apr-2009 *To:*
Rounding: Not Applicable

F-5B:Advance Ledger Interest parameters

The Interest for Debit & Credit Balances for the respective period is computed separately at the specified Rate (F- 5C)

> *Note: You may set computation parameters at different Rates fro Debit & Credit Balances.*

Ledger Interest — ABC Academy 9-10

Ledger: A K Das — 1-Apr-2009 to 31-Mar-2010

Balance	From:	To:	Total Days	Rate %	Interest
25,000.00 Dr	1-May-2009	1-Jun-2009	31 days	12 %	254.79 Dr
5,000.00 Cr	1-Jun-2009	3-Jul-2009	32 days	6 %	26.30 Cr
15,000.00 Cr	3-Jul-2009	4-Aug-2009	32 days	6 %	78.90 Cr
				Grand Total	149.59 Dr

F- 5C: Ledger Interest Statement

Example

A loan of Rs 25000 was paid on 1.5.2009 to A K Das. He repaid Rs 10000 on 3.7.09

Calculate Interest @1.5.09 to 31.5.09 @ 12% p.a and from 1.6.09 to 31.8.09 @ 18% p.a

Interest Parameters

Rate : **12** % per **Calendar Year** on **All Balances**
Applicable From: ***1-Apr-2009*** *To:* ***31-May-2009***
Rounding : ***Not Applicable***

Rate : **18** % per **Calendar Year** on **All Balances**
Applicable From: ***1-Jun-2009*** *To:* ***31-Aug-2009***
Rounding : ***Not Applicable***

F- 6A: Advanced Ledger Interest parameter for multiple periods

Balance	From:	To:	Total Days	Rate %	Interest
25,000.00 Dr	1-May-2009	31-May-2009	30 days	12 %	246.58 Dr
25,000.00 Dr	31-May-2009	3-Jul-2009	33 days	18 %	406.85 Dr
15,000.00 Dr	3-Jul-2009	31-Aug-2009	59 days	18 %	436.44 Dr
				Grand Total	1,089.87 Dr

F- 6B: Advanced Ledger Interest

F- 6A shows the Advanced Interest parameters in the Ledger Account. F- 6B shows the Interest computation of Ledger Account as per parameters set in F- 6A

Example

A loan of Rs 25000 was paid on 1.5.2009 to A K Das. He repaid Rs 10000 on 3.7.09

Interest is chargeable from 1.5.09 to 31.5.09 @ 12% p.a (365 days), from 1.6.09 to 30.6.09 @ 1% (calendar Month) & 1.5% (30 days month) from 1.7.09 onwards.

Compute Interest from 1.4.09 to 31.8.09

Interest Parameters

Rate : **12** % per **Calendar Year** on **All Balances**
Applicable From: ***1-Apr-2009*** *To:* ***31-May-2009***
Rounding : ***Not Applicable***

Rate : **1** % per **Calendar Month** on **All Balances**
Applicable From: ***1-Jun-2009*** *To:* ***30-Jun-2009***
Rounding : ***Not Applicable***

Rate : **1.50** % per **30-Day Month** on **All Balances**
Applicable From: ***1-Jul-2009*** *To:*

F-7A: Advanced Ledger Interest parameter

Balance	From:	To:	Total Days	Rate %	Interest
25,000.00 Dr	1-May-2009	31-May-2009	30 days	12 %	246.58 Dr
25,000.00 Dr	31-May-2009	30-Jun-2009	30 days	1 %	250.00 Dr
25,000.00 Dr	30-Jun-2009	3-Jul-2009	3 days	1.50 %	37.50 Dr
15,000.00 Dr	3-Jul-2009	31-Aug-2009	59 days	1.50 %	442.50 Dr
				Grand Total	976.58 Dr

F- 7B: Advanced Ledger Interest

F-7A shows the Advanced Ledger Interest parameter. F-7B shows the Advanced Ledger Interest computation details as per Ledger Interest parameter set at F-7A

05 Interest Debit & Credit Notes

Interest Statements shows the Interest figures for information only and not posted to accounts. To post into accounts, you have to create a Debit / Credit Note (§08/03-02) or Journal Voucher (§04/01-04) for Interest.

- **Interest Debit Note:** You may create a Debit Note (F- 8A) for Interest Receivable from the Party (normally Customer) for delayed payments by the Party (Customer).
- **Interest Credit Note:** You may create a Credit Note for (F- 8B) for Interest Payable to the Party (normally Supplier) for delayed payments to the Party (Supplier).

> **Note:** *Create Debit & Credit Notes in usual way, as per the Interest computed shown in Interest Statement*

Debit Note No. 1 — 2-May-2006, Tuesday
Ref. :

Particulars	Debit	Credit
Dr Suduma Stores	460.70	
Cr Interest Received		460.70

F- 8A: Debit Note for Interest

Credit Note No. 1 — 1-Jun-2006, Thursday
Ref. :

Particulars	Debit	Credit
Cr A.K.Corporation		840.00
Dr Interest Paid	840.00	

F- 8B: Credit Note for Interest

06 Interest Journal Voucher

You may alternatively (instead of Interest Debit Note / Credit Note) create a Journal Voucher for (F- 9A) for Interest Payable to the Party (normally Lender) as well Interest Receivable from the Party (normally Borrower) for Interest Due (F- 9B) for a specified period.

- **Interest Receivable**: In such case, Debit The Party Account (normally Borrower) & credit Interest A/c by the amount of Interest Received / Receivable (F- 9A)
- **Interest Payable**: In such case, Debit Interest A/c & Credit Party Account (normally Lender) by the amount of Interest Paid/ Payable (F- 9B)

Journal No. 1 — 1-Jun-2006, Thursday

Particulars	Debit	Credit
Dr M N Shaw	480.00	
Cr Interest Received		480.00

Fig 9A: Journal Voucher for Interest Receivable

Journal No. 7 — 31-Mar-2010, Wednesday

Particulars	Debit	Credit
Dr Interst Paid	1,200.00	
Cr A K Das		1,200.00
Narration:	1,200.00	1,200.00

Interst Paybale for the period Jan - Mar 10

Fig 9B: Journal Voucher for Interest Payable

07 Interest Reports

Select *Display > Statement of Accounts > Interest Calculations* to get Interest Calculations menu (F-10) containing reports of Interest Receivable and Payable, for Ledger and Groupwise Interest.

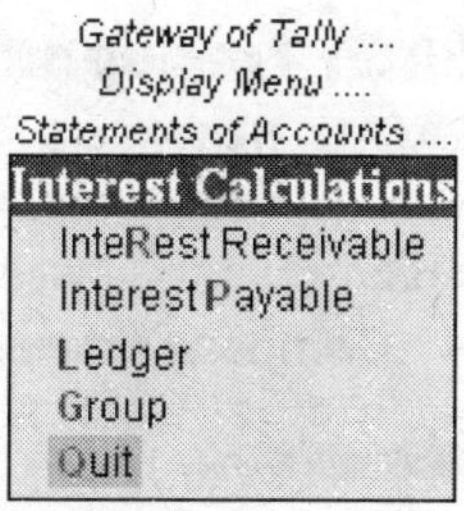

F-10: Interest menu

Interest Receivable ABC Academy 9-10	Ctrl + M	
Particulars	Sundry Debtors ABC Academy 9-10 1-Apr-2009 to 31-Dec-2009	
	Interest Calculation	
	Cl. Balance	Interest
B K Das	10,000.00 Dr	3,622.74 Dr
Grand Total	**10,000.00 Dr**	**3,622.74 Dr**

F-11A: Interest Receivables Statement

Group Interest Calculations	Ctrl + M	
Particulars	Sundry Debtors R.K.Traders 1-Apr-2008 to 31-Mar-2009	
	Interest Calculation	
	Cl. Balance	Interest
A.K.Das	95,800.00 Dr	23,157.35 Dr
P.Roy	1,000.00 Dr	1,825.09 Dr

F-12A: Group Interest Statement

The contents, format & buttons at Interest Receivables (F-11A) & Interest Payables Reports are similar

07.02 Ledger Interest

When you set *No* at *Calculate Interest Transaction by Transaction* at Interest parameters, Interest is calculated on daily ledger balances.

At Interest Reports Menu (F-10), select *Ledger* and select the Ledger (Loan, Supplier or Customer) to get Ledger Interest Report (F-13A)

You may also get Ledger Interest Statement by ultimately drilling down through a Ledger Account from Interest Receivable / Interest Payable Report (F-11A) or from Group Interest Statement (F-13A).

Buttons at Ledger Interest Statement

At *Ledger Interest Statement* (F-13A), you get following buttons (F-13B)

- **F4: Ledger**: To get the list of Ledger Accounts to select a Ledger Account to get Ledger Interest Statement for the selected Ledger Account
- **C:Contact**: To get Ledger Contact screen showing the complete details of Party Address, Contact person etc of the selected Ledger Account. The information is displayed in a pop up screen for reference only but not printed in any Interest report.

Ledger Interest — ABC Academy 9-10

Ledger: **A K Das** — **1-Apr-2009 to 31-Mar-2010**

Balance	From:	To:	Total Days	Rate %	Interest
10,000.00 Cr	3-Jul-2009	31-Mar-2010	**271 days**	1.50 %	**1,355.00 Cr**
				Grand Total	**1,355.00 Cr**

F-13A: Ledger Interest

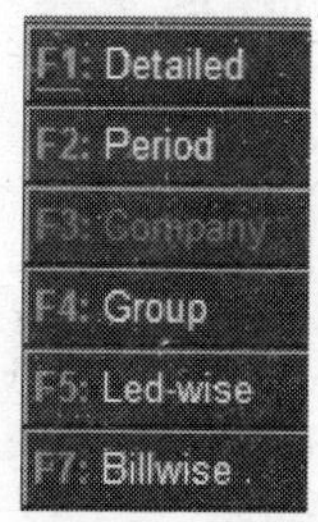

F-13B: Buttons Ledger Interest F-13C: Buttons Group Interest

07.01 Interest Receivables & Payables Statement

Interest Receivables / Payables report shows Interest computed as per Interest parameters set, for the specified period,

At *Interest* Menu (F-10):

- **Interest Receivables**: Select *Interest Receivables* to get *Receivables* Report (F-11A). It shows the Ledger wise details of Interest, when the Net Interest computed for the Ledger is Debit (Party A/c to be Debited & Interest A/c to be Credited)
- **Interest Payables:** Select *Interest Payables* to get *Payables* Report (like F-11A). It shows the Ledger wise details of Interest, when the Net Interest computed for the Ledger is Credit (Interest A/c to be Debited & Party A/c to be Credited)

07.03 Group Interest

Group Interest Statement shows Interest for all ledger accounts under the selected Group (listing all Sub-Groups and Ledgers). The Contents of the report is similar to Interest Receivables / Payables.

At Interest Reports Menu (F-10), select *Group and select the Account Group to get Group Interest Statement (F-12A) in respect of all ledgers under the selected Group.*

Buttons at Group Interest Statement

At *Group Interest Statement* (F-12A), you get following buttons (F-13C)

- **F4: Group:** Select this button to get the list of Account Groups to select an Account Group to get Group Interest Statement for the selected Account Group.
- **F5: Ledger / Group Interest**:

- o Click *F5:Led-wise* toggle button to see the figures of outstanding & accrued Interest of Ledger Accounts in alphabetical order.
- o Click *F5: Grouped* toggle button to see the figures of outstanding & accrued Interest of Accounts Groups / Ledger Accounts in hierarchical order.

Outstandings Management

Activate Interest Calculation ? **Yes**
(use advanced parameters) ? **Yes**

Interest Feature Activation

Ledger Alteration

Name : **A Bose & Co**

Under : **Loans & Advances (Asset)** *(Current Assets)*

Maintain balances bill-by-bill ? **No**

Activate Interest Calculation ? **Yes**

Interest Option set up in Ledger

Interest Parameters

Rate : **12** % per **Calendar Year** on **All Balances**
Applicable From: **1-Apr-2008** *To:* **31-Oct-2008**
Rounding : **Normal Rounding** *Limit :* **1**

Rate : **15** % per **365-Day Year** on **Debit Balances Only**
Applicable From: **1-Nov-2008** *To:* **31-Mar-2009**
Rounding : **Normal Rounding** *Limit :* **1**

Interest Parameters entry in Ledger

Project: 02-11 Interest

I charge Interest on Account Current on Ledger Balance @12% per Year, from 1st April, on all balances. Form 1st Nov, the Interest was increased to 15% pa (365 days), on Debit Balance only Set the Interest parameters for the Party.

Interest Style
30-day Month
365-day Year
Calendar Month
Calendar Year

Interest Style

Interest Balances
All Balances
Credit Balances Only
Debit Balances Only

Balance Type

Rounding Methods
Not Applicable
Downward Rounding
Normal Rounding
Upward Rounding

Rounding Option

FAQ: Frequently Asked Questions

FAQ-1: How you can activate Advanced Interest Features for Ledger Accounts

Ans:

- **Company Interest**: At *F11:Feature>Accounting Feature,* to activate Company Interest Features
  - o **Interest Feature Activation**: Set *Yes* at *Activate Interest* to activate Interest Features
  - o **Advanced Parameters**: Having Activated Interest Feature, set Yes at *Use Advanced Parameters*, to compute Interest at varied Interest rates, over-riding the default Rates
- **Party Ledger Interest**: At the respective Party Ledger entry / alteration screen (F-1B/02-12), set Yes at *Activate Interest Calculation* to get Interest Parameter screen (F-1A). At Interest Parameters screen of the Ledger Account, at *Calculate Interest Transaction by Transaction* set No. Now set the Advanced Interest Parameters for the Ledger Account.

Reports Display

02-12

01 Reports Display Operations & Configuration

Basic features of Reports Display have been discussed earlier (§01/05). Here we discuss about:

- **Common Operations at Display screen**:Various operations that you may perform at Display screen in general
- **Common Configuration options**: Common Configuration options available at Configuration screen of the reports, in general. The Report specific Configuration are discussed at respective Reports

02 Master / Voucher Alteration through Reports Display

- **Master Alteration**: To Alter the Master from Reports Display screen, position the Cursor on the name of the Master, e.g., Group, Ledger etc) and press *Ctrl + <enter>* to get the Master record in Alteration mode. Now carry out Alteration/ Deletion of the Master record as explained.
- **Voucher Alteration / Deletion**: To Alter / Delete Voucher from Reports Display screen, place the cursor on the Voucher record of the Report and press <enter> to get the Voucher in *Alteration mode*.
  - o **Voucher Alteration:** Now you may Alter the Voucher
  - o **Voucher Deletion / Cancellation**: Press Alt + D to *Delete* the Voucher, Press Alt + X to *Cancel* the Voucher
  - o **Master Alteration**: At Voucher in Alteration mode, place the cursor on Master record in the Voucher, and press <Ctrl+Enter> to get the Master in Alteration Mode. Now you may make Alteration in the Master also from the Voucher.

03 Exploding & Collapsing Report Lines

In Display, initially the top level Account (Account Group / Ledger) and the corresponding figures are displayed. The underlying details figures of any selected record may be exploded (shown) / collapsed (hidden) as follows, to show the report with details of specified data:

- **Exploding a record to show Details**: Press Shift + <enter> key (or right click) on a top level record, to show next level details (below the selected record), on same screen (F-1B)
- **Collapsing a record to hide details**: Press Shift + <enter>key (or right click) to collapse detailed records, showing only the corresponding top level record (F-1A)

Day Book — Ctrl + M

Day Book						For 31-Mar-2010
Date	Particulars		Vch Type	Vch No.	Debit Amount	Credit Amount
↑ ... 4 more						
31-3-2010	Pre Paid Expenses		Payment	8	1,800.00	
31-3-2010	Salary		Payment	11	13,000.00	
31-3-2010	ICICI Term Loan		Payment	12	14,500.00	
	Bank of India	14,500.00 Cr				
						4 more ...

F-1A: Collapsed Report

Day Book						For 31-Mar-2010
Date	Particulars		Vch Type	Vch No.	Debit Amount	Credit Amount
↑ ... 4 more						
31-3-2010	Pre Paid Expenses		Payment	8	1,800.00	
	Office Rent	1,800.00 Dr				
	Bank of India	3,600.00 Cr				
31-3-2010	Salary		Payment	11	13,000.00	
	HRA	3,000.00 Dr				
	P F	1,300.00 Cr				
	Bank of India	14,700.00 Cr				

F- 1B: Exploded Report

04 Hiding / Restoration Report Lines in Display

Sometimes, you may like to hide some lines in a Report.

- **Hiding Lines in Report**: To remove a line in the display screen (to hide the line), place the cursor on the record and press <space bar> to select the line to be removed (F-2B). This way, you may select several lines, one by one, to be removed, and press Alt+R. All the selected lines for removal are removed together from the Report (F-2A). However, no data gets deleted.
- **Restoring of Hidden Lines in Display:** To Restore (bring back) the removed lines, press Alt+U. The removed line is restored (F- 2B). If you have removed several lines and like to restore them all at a time, press Ctrl+U. All the removed lines would be restored.

Ledger Vouchers — Ctrl + M

Ledger: HDFC Bank				1-Apr-2011 to 31-Mar-2012	
Date	Particulars	Vch Type	Vch No.	Debit	Credit
2-5-2011	State Bank Of India	Contra	3		4,000.00
2-5-2011	Cash	Contra	4	3,000.00	
2-5-2011	Salary	Payment	4		11,450.00

F- 2A: Report after removing a line (with Alt+R)

The Report Totals also get changed as per records Removed / Restored.

Ledger Vouchers Ctrl + M

Ledger: HDFC Bank 1-Apr-2011 to 31-Mar-2012

Date	Particulars	Vch Type	Vch No.	Debit	Credit
2-5-2011	State Bank Of India	Contra	3		4,000.00
2-5-2011	Cash	Contra	4	3,000.00	
2-5-2011	Salary	Payment	3		7,335.00
2-5-2011	Cash	Contra	5		1,000.00
2-5-2011	Salary	Payment	4		11,450.00

F-2B: Original (and Restored with Alt+U) report

05 Reports Common Configuration Options

Each Display report provides various Configuration options to Configure the contents and format of the report. Press *F12:Configure* to get the Configuration options for the Report (F-3A). Some of the Configuration options are common to most of the reports, while other options are Report specific.

The common Configuration options are discussed here, while the Report specific options are discussed at the respective report.

05.01 Factored Figures

Sometimes factored Figures (e.g rounded Figures in Crores, Millions or Thousands), are shown to make it more readable, as the precise amount (accurate to Rs & Paise) is not so much relevant to top level people. Factored reports are more compact and meaningful.

Configuration

Show Opening Balances	? No
Show transactions	? No
Show Closing Balances	? Yes
Show Percentages	? No
Appearance of Names	: Name Only
Scale Factor for Values	: Default
Sorting Method	: Default
Expand all levels in Detailed Format	? No

Scale Factors

- New Number
- Crores
- Default
- Hundreds
- Lakhs
- Millions
- Ten Lakhs
- Ten Millions
- Ten Thousands
- Thousands

F- 3A: Configuration for factoring

New Scale

45.50

F-3B:To covert Rupee into Dollar equivalent (1$=Rs.45.50)

New Scale

0.90901

To inflate Figures by about 10%
F-3C: New Scale for factoring

To get reports in factored (scaled) Figures, at Reports Configuration screen, select the *Scale Factor for Values* to get the list of factoring options (F-3A):

- **Standard Factor values**: The list of options (F-3A) contain several standard scale factor from the list (like Crores, Lakhs, Thousands etc). Select the desired Scale Factor to show the factored Figures (rounded to 2 decimal places). For example, when you select Thousands, all the Figures of the report will be divided by 1000.
- **User Specified Factor Values**: To factor with any user specified value (other than the standard factor values listed, select *New Number* (F-3A) to get the *New Scale* input box (F-3B) to enter the user specified factor value. Enter your own scale factor (e.g 45.50 to show the amount in Rupees converted to equivalent US Dollars, when 1 USD = Rs 45.50 – F-3B).

This way, you may factor the Figures by some percent (e.g to increase the Figures by 10%, enter 0.90901 (=1/1.10) as the factor in New Scale (F-3C)

At the top of the report, the Scale Factor value (standard or user defined, as the case may be) is also shown for reference.

To restore to the Report with original value, select *Default* at the list of Scale Factor (F-3A)

Particulars	ABC Academy 9-10 1-Apr-2009 to 31-Mar-2010 Closing Balance	
	Debit	Credit
Capital Account	25,020.00	56,000.00
Loans (Liability)		51,900.00
Current Liabilities		20,490.00
Fixed Assets	30,000.00	12,000.00
Current Assets	85,220.00	
Sales Accounts	4,800.00	15,600.00
Purchase Accounts	7,250.00	200.00
Direct Incomes		18,000.00
Indirect Incomes		3,000.00
Indirect Expenses	44,920.00	
Profit & Loss A/c		20,020.00
Grand Total	1,97,210.00	1,97,210.00

F-3D: Report with Original Figure

F- 3D shows the Original Value (upper Part) and F-3E shows Factored Figures increased by appx 10% (*New scale =.90901*)

05.02 Sorting in Reports

Normally the report is displayed as per Default sort order. To get the data sorted in other sequence, at Report Configuration screen, select the option *Sorting Method* (F-4A) from the list of sorting options (F-4B)

Rules of Sorting

Initially, you get the default report sorted in ascending order of first column, as per following sequence:

Trial Balance — Ctrl + M

Particulars	ABC Academy 9-10 1-Apr-2009 to 31-Mar-2010 Closing Balance	
	Debit	Credit
Capital Account	**27,524.45**	**61,605.48**
Loans (Liability)		**57,095.08**
Current Liabilities		**22,541.01**
Fixed Assets	**33,002.94**	**13,201.17**
Current Assets	**93,750.34**	
Sales Accounts	**5,280.47**	**17,161.53**
Purchase Accounts	**7,975.71**	**220.02**
Direct Incomes		**19,801.76**
Indirect Incomes		**3,300.29**
Indirect Expenses	**49,416.40**	
Profit & Loss A/c		22,023.96
Grand Total	**2,16,950.31**	**2,16,950.31**

F-3E: Report with Factored Figure

- If the first column is Voucher Date (in case of report containing Vouchers, like Day Book etc), the default report appears as per Date
- If the first column is Name (Group Name / Account Name, like Trial Balance etc), the default report appears in alphabetical order of Account Name (Group Name / Ledger Name)

Some reports do not have any option to sort. These reports are sorted as per their own rules (like Balance Sheet, P & L Statement, etc)

Specifying Sorting Option

Now you can change the sort order (ascending / descending). Click F12:Configure to get Configuration screen (F- 4A). At the option *Sorting Method*, select the sort option (F-4B). The sort option list (F-4B) varies according to the Report. The sort option may be specified both in Ascending (Increasing) / Descending (Decreasing) on 3 attributes (F-4B):

- **Name**: Account Name, Group Name, Ref No, etc
- **Amount**: Account, Currency, etc
- **Date:** Voucher Date, Due Date, In sequence of entry etc

> **Note:** *The selected Sort option applies on the default column. For example, if a column is displayed through Configuration option, that will not be considered for Sort order. For example, in Trial Balance, the* Closing Balance *appears in default. So, if you specify the Sort option as Amount (Decreasing), the report will be sorted on Closing Balance (not on other columns displayed through Configuration options like Opening Balance, Transaction Dr / Cr etc).*

Configuration

Show Opening Balances	? No
Show transactions	? No
Show Closing Balances	? Yes
Show Percentages	? No
Appearance of Names	: Name Only
Scale Factor for Values	: 45.50
Sorting Method	: Default
Expand all levels in Detailed Format	? No

F-4A: Sort Option in Configuration

Sorting Methods

- Alphabetical (Decreasing)
- Alphabetical (Increasing)
- Amount-wise (Decreasing)
- **Amount-wise (Increasing)**
- Default

F-4B: List of Sorting Methods

The report gets sorted as per the sorting method selected.

05.03 Bar Graphs

Tally provides simple Bar Graphs in some selected Reports during Report Displays. like Summary Reports (Monthly / Quarterly / Half Yearly etc), as per specified Periodicity. Debit & Credit Figures are represented as Positive and Negative, according to the Report.

- **Default Setting for Graphs in General**: At *GoT>F12:Configure>General*, at the option (under the section Other Options) *Show Monthly Reports with Graph* (F-5C):

Ledger Monthly Summary — ABC Academy 9-10 — Ctrl + M

Particulars	A K Traders ABC Academy 9-10 1-Apr-2009 to 31-Mar-2010 Transactions		Closing Balance
	Debit	Credit	
Opening Balance			**1,000.00 Dr**
April			1,000.00 Dr
May		*1,100.00*	100.00 Cr
June	*4,800.00*	*2,000.00*	2,700.00 Dr
July	*2,150.00*		4,850.00 Dr
August	*1,000.00*		5,850.00 Dr
September			5,850.00 Dr
October			5,850.00 Dr
November		*500.00*	5,350.00 Dr
December			5,350.00 Dr
January		*4,000.00*	1,350.00 Dr
February	*1,200.00*	*2,000.00*	550.00 Dr
March	*2,200.00*	*6,000.00*	3,250.00 Cr
Grand Total	***11,350.00***	***15,600.00***	**3,250.00 Cr**

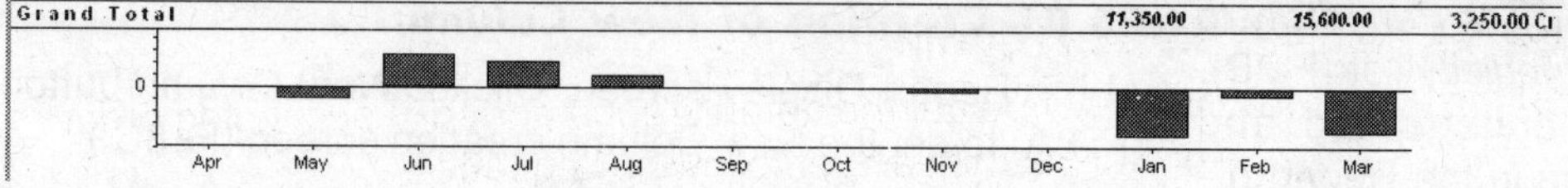

F-5A: Bar Graph

Configuration

Nett transactions only	? No
Show Closing Balances	? Yes
Show Percentages	? No
Appearance of Names	: Name Only
Scale Factor for Values	: Default
Periodicity to use	: Monthly
Show Average Details	? No
Graphs	
Show with Graph	? Yes

F- 5B: Report Configuration

Other Options

Show Monthly reports with Graphs	? Yes

F-5C: General Configuration for Graph

- o Set *Yes* to Display Graphs (for Monthly Figures for the Current Period) by default.
- o Set *No.* The Graph will not be shown in default (will be displayed only when you set Yes at the respective Configuration screen for the current Display screen:F-5B, as described below)

- **Specific Setting for Graphs for current Display**: Click *F12:Configure* at the Display screen to get Configuration screen of the current Report Display screen (F-5B). At the option *Show With Graph:*
  - o Set *Yes* to show the Graph
  - o Set *No* to suppress the Graph (Graph will not be shown)

The Graph scale appears according to the Periodicity set (Monthly / Quarterly etc)

05.04 Percentage Figures

In summary reports, sometimes, the % value on some base figures give a better meaning to the Management, than absolute values in Rupees.

To get column with % values of individual items (F-6), in respect the total (which is 100 %), at the Configuration screen (F-5B), set *Yes* at *Show Percentages.*

Group Summary — Ctrl + M

Particulars	Indirect Expenses ABC Academy 9-10 1-Apr-2009 to 31-Mar-2010 Transactions: Debit		Transactions: Credit		Closing Balance	
Depreciation	2,000.00	0.16%			2,000.00 Dr	0.16%
Depreciation on Furniture	2,000.00				2,000.00 Dr	
Interest	5,400.00	0.44%			5,400.00 Dr	0.44%
Interest on Term Loan	4,500.00				4,500.00 Dr	
Interest on Unsecured Loan	900.00				900.00 Dr	
Conveyance Expenses	7,500.00	0.61%			7,500.00 Dr	0.61%
Freight	780.00	0.06%	800.00	100.00%	20.00 Cr	0.00%
Handling Charges	700.00	0.06%			700.00 Dr	0.06%
HRA	35,050.00	2.84%			35,050.00 Dr	2.84%
Interest	30.00	0.00%			30.00 Dr	0.00%
Interst Paid	94,000.00	7.62%			94,000.00 Dr	7.63%
Office Rent	7,800.00	0.63%			7,800.00 Dr	0.63%
Penalty	100.00	0.01%			100.00 Dr	0.01%
Salary	10,79,700.00	87.56%			10,79,700.00 Dr	87.62%
Grand Total	**12,33,060.00**	**100.00%**	**800.00**	**100.00%**	**12,32,260.00 Dr**	**100.00%**

F-6: Group Summary with Percentage Figures

05.05 Periodicity

Normally, Monthly / Quarterly Summary Reports are shown (by default *Monthly* summaries are shown. To get such Summary Reports in smaller periods, sub-periods, Click *F12:Configure* at the Display screen to get Configuration screen of the current Report Display (F-5B). At Configuration screen, at Periodicity, select he Periodicity (e.g Weekly), to get the summary in selected periodicity. Tally provides the option to define the Periodicity of Report in some Periodic Reports.

At the Report Configuration screen (F-7B), at *Periodicity to Use,* select the *Periodicity* from the *Periodicity* list (F-7B). Accordingly, the sub periods are constructed and corresponding period Figures are shown in the Report (F-7A).

Ledger Monthly S — Ctrl + M

Particulars	Bank of India ABC Academy 11-Apr-2011 to 31-Mar-2012 Transactions: Debit	Transactions: Credit	Closing Balance
Opening Balance			**3,00,000.00 Dr**
1-Apr to 2-Apr	48,800.00	2,000.00	3,46,800.00 Dr
3-Apr to 9-Apr			3,46,800.00 Dr
10-Apr to 16-Apr			3,46,800.00 Dr
17-Apr to 23-Apr			3,46,800.00 Dr
24-Apr to 30-Apr			3,46,800.00 Dr
1-May to 7-May	34,200.00	19,000.00	3,62,000.00 Dr
8-May to 14-May			3,62,000.00 Dr
15-May to 21-May			3,62,000.00 Dr
22-May to 28-May			3,62,000.00 Dr
Grand Total	**1,01,200.00**	**1,03,800.00**	**2,97,400.00 Dr**

F-7A: Periodic (Weekly) Report

Configuration

Nett transactions only	? No
Show Closing Balances	? Yes
Show Percentages	? No
Appearance of Names	: Name Only
Scale Factor for Values	: Default
Periodicity to use	: Weekly
Show Average Details	? No
Graphs	
Show with Graph	? No

Periodicity

4 Week Month
Daily
Fortnightly
Half Yearly
Monthly
Quarterly
Weekly
Yearly

F-7B: Configuration option for Periodicity

06 Columnar Reports

Columnar Report is useful to show comparative data for multiple specified periods, within the Company (*Intra-Company Periodical* comparison) or different companies (*Inter-Company* comparison)

Tally provides a specific set of Buttons (F-8A) to create / alter / delete additional columns to get figures for other period or other selected company in one compact report for comparison, as explained below:

C: New Column — Button to create a New Column

A: Alter Column — Button to Alter a column

D: Del Column — Button to Delete a Column

N: Auto Column — Button to create Auto Column Reports

F- 8A: Buttons for Columnar Reports

06.01 Creation of New Column

At the Report Display screen, Click C:*New Column* button (F- 8A) to get the New Column creation screen (F- 8C)

Balance Sheet   Ctrl + M

	ABC Acac10 as at 30-9		ABC Acad-10 as at 31-110	
Sources of Funds :				
Capital Account		**51,000.00**		**30,980.00**
Current Year Profit / Loss			(-)20,020.00	
Drawings	(-)5,000.00		(-)5,000.00	
Properitor's Capital	56,000.00		56,000.00	
Loans (Liability)		**60,000.00**		**51,900.00**
Secured Loans	50,000.00		40,000.00	
Unsecured Loans	10,000.00		11,900.00	
Current Liabilities		**(-)1,930.00**		**20,490.00**
Sundry Creditors	1,950.00		17,970.00	
P F			2,500.00	
TDS	(-)20.00		20.00	
Profit & Loss A/c		**800.00**		**850.00**
Opening Balance			800.00	
Current Period	800.00		(-)19,970.00	
Total		**1,09,870.00**		**1,04,220.00**

F-8B: Columnar Report with Columns for 2 periods

Balance Sheet   Ctrl + M

	ABC Academy 9-10 as at 31-Mar-2010		ABC Electrical as at 31-Mar-2010	
Sources of Funds :				
Capital Account		**30,980.00**		**30,000.00**
Loans (Liability)		**51,900.00**		
Current Liabilities		**20,490.00**		**(-)466.90**
Profit & Loss A/c		**850.00**		**12,000.00**
Opening Balance				
Current Period	(-)19,170.00		12,000.00	
Less: Transferred	(-)20,020.00			
Diff. in Opening Balances				**(-)10,000.00**
Total		**1,04,220.00**		**31,533.10**
Application of Funds :				
Fixed Assets		**18,000.00**		
Current Assets		**86,220.00**		**31,533.10**
Misc. Expenses (ASSET)				
Total		**1,04,220.00**		**31,533.10**

F- 8E: Columnar report with columns for two companies

ABC Academy 9-10

Column Details

Name of Company : **ABC Academy 9-10**
From (blank for beginning) : **1-10-2009**
To (blank for end) : **31-3-2010**

F-8C: Column Specification

Auto Repeat Columns

Repeat Using : **Company**
Show Total Column ? **Yes**

Column Details
- 4 Week Month
- Company
- Daily
- Fortnightly
- Half Yearly
- Monthly
- Quarterly
- Weekly
- Yearly

F- 8D: Auto Repeat Column Specification

Column Definition at Multi Column Report: At the column definition screen (F-8C) specify as follows:

- **Period Specification for Inter-Period report:** At *From & To* fields (F-8C), specify the period for the New Column to get *Inter Period* Columnar Report (F-8B)
- **Company Specification for Inter-Company Report**: At the Name of the Company, select the Company Name (from the list of currently selected companies) for which data is to be shown in the new Column(F-8C), to get Inter Company columnar reports (F-8E).

> **Note:** *When you select a Company, you get a list of Selected Companies (so more than one Company must have been selected), from which you may select a Company for the new Column. The figures for each Company will be shown for the same period specified in respect of each company selected. When you select a periodicity (Monthly etc), columns will be auto created for the repeating periodicity for the specified period (e.g if you specify a period of 6 months and periodicity Monthly, then 6 columns will be created for 6 months)*

06.02 Modifying Column Definition

To modify the definition of any column, at the Report screen, select the column to be modified (use Left & Right Arrow keys to move the cursor over the columns) and Click A: *Alter Column* button (F-8A). You will get the column definition screen (F-8C), where you may change the column definition (like Period, Company etc). Having edited the column definition, press <enter> to get the report with changed figures as per changed column definition.

06.03 Deleting a Column

To Delete any column created by New Column button, at the columnar Report screen (F-8E), select the column to be deleted (use Left & Right Arrow keys to move the cursor over the columns) and Click D:*Del Column* button (F-8A). The selected Column will get removed in the Report.

06.04 Auto Columns

Apart from creation of specific defined column, you may auto-create multiple repeating periodical columns (e.g Monthly, Quarterly etc), to get compact report for Comparison of figures for multiple periods / companies.

Creation of Auto Repeating Columns: At the Report Display screen, Click N:*Auto Column* button to get Auto-Repeat column specification screen (F-8D), to auto-create multiple columns (for multiple periods / Companies). At the field *Repeat Using*, select the desired option from the list, as below:

- **Multiple Period Columns**: Select the auto repeating period (e.g. Monthly) to create a column for each component of the period.
- **Multiple Company Columns:** Select the option *Company* (F-8D), to create a column for each selected Company.

Total Column: At *Auto Repeat column specification screen* (F-8D), at the field *Show Total*:

- Set *Yes* to show the first Column for Total of all the columns displayed in the Report.
- Set *No* to show only the columns as per selected option (No *Total* Column is shown at the first column)

FAQ: Frequently Asked Questions

FAQ-1: How I can get:

Ans:

- **Detailed / Condensed Report of all Items**
- **Details / summary of selected Items in the report at the same time**

Detailed / Summary Report: Many of the reports contain *F1:Detailed / Condensed* toggle button to get the report in detailed / condensed mode.

- In *Condensed* mode *(click F1:Condensed toggle button)*, only the net Figures are displayed in one line for each top level Item in the report.
- In *Detailed* mode *(click F1:Detailed toggle button)*, the next level details are also displayed under the respective top level Items in the report.

Detailed / Summary of selected Items: While in detailed report, you get the details of ALL top level items in the report, you may selectively get the details of desired items in the report by exploding / collapsing the desired Items of the Report as explained below (§03):

- **Exploding a record to show Details**: Press the cursor on the desired top level Item and press Shift + <enter> key (or right click) to show next level details (below the selected record), on same screen
- **Collapsing a record to hide details**: Press the cursor on the desired exploded Item & press Shift + <enter>key (or right click) to collapse detailed records, showing only the corresponding top level record

You may explode / collapse the details to multiple levels (where any item is comprised of lower level Items). You may explode / collapse multiple Items in a report and see the detailed / summarized Figures of selected Items in the report, at the same time.

FAQ-2: How I can Remove / Restore selected Items in a Report

In Reports Display screen, you may remove certain specified Item (and Restore again) to temporarily manipulate / exclude some selected Items in a report, in some special cases (§04). Consequently, respective sub totals & grand totals also get changed (the Figure of the removed item gets excluded / restored Item gets included).

- **Removing an Item:** Place the cursor on the Item to be to be removed and press *R:Remove Line* button at the horizontal bottom bar at the bottom of the Report. The item will be removed from the display (but no data will be deleted). This way you may remove multiple items in the report (you cannot remove the sub level Items of an exploded Item)
- **Restoring the removed Item:** Press *U:Restore Line* button and the horizontal bottom bar at the bottom of the Report. The last Item removed will be restored. If you have removed multiple Items, press *U:Restore All* to restore all the removed lines in one go.

FAQ-3: How I can show the Figures of report (say Balance Sheet) rounded off to Rupees Lakhs

Ans: In the reports Display, click *F12:Configure* and select *Lakhs* at the option *Scale Factor for values* (§05.01). The Figures will be converted in Rs Lakhs (rounded off to 2 decimal places).

To get back the original Figures, again click *F12:Configure* and select *Default* at the option *Scale Factor for values.*

FAQ-4: I expect 10 % rise in my Sales / Purchase / Direct Income / Expenses / Gross Profit Figures. How I can get a report showing the sale / purchase (and underlying the detailed Figures) inflated by 10% (above the current Figures).

Ans: At Profit & Loss Account statement (Display > Profit & Loss Account), remove (press cursor on the lines to be removed and press *R:Remove Line*) the lines of Indirect Incomes & Indirect Expenses (§04). You will get the Trading Account only showing the Sales, Purchase, Direct Incomes & Direct Expenses & Gross Profit (as per current Figures).

To inflate the current Figures by 10%, Click *F1: Detailed* to get the detailed Figures of each Group. Click F12:Configure and select *New Number* at the option *Scale Factor for Values* (§05.01). At the input box *New Scale*, enter 0.90901 (divide by 1/1.10 to multiply by 1.10) at the input box. Now all the values in the report would be inflated by 10 %

FAQ-5: How I can get a columnar Report for comparison for different period / company in one report

Ans: In the report for a specified period, you may add more columns for different period / different columns side by side, for comparison.

- **Individual Columns**
  - o **Creation of New Column**: To create a new column, click *C: New Column* and set the period / select the company for the new column (§06.01).
- **Auto repeating Columns:** To create auto repeating multiple periodic / company columns, click *N: Auto Column* and select (§06.04):
  - o **Periodicity:** Select the desired periodicity (e.g Fortnightly) to get the multiple columns for each periodicity slab.
  - o **Company**: Select Company from the list to get a column for each selected Company

In the column definition screen, set *Yes* at *Show Total Column* to get an additional Total column showing the total of all displayed columns.

FAQ-6: How I can print Bar Graphs of periodical Figures in a Report

Ans: Some of the reports provide Bar Graphs at the bottom of the report (§05.03).

- Set *Yes* at the option *Show Monthly Reports with Graphs* at *GoT>F12:Configure > General*. Consequently, the Graph will be shown by default at all Monthly / Quarterly (or other periodical reports as per configuration).
- However, you may set the Graph option for the particular instance of the report through *Show with Graph option* at the specific report Configuration screen. Click *F12:Configure* at the Report Display Screen. Set *Yes* at *Show with Graph*.

The Bar Graph scale (X- axis with period scale & Y- axis with values) is dynamically created as per value range. If the values are both in debit & credit, the bar graph shows the values in *positive / negative* direction (above & below origin)

FAQ-7: How I can get percentage Figures of each Item in a Report

Ans: Some of the reports provide to optionally include a column showing percentage Figures for each top level Item (in respect of Total, which is considered as 100%).

To get the percentage figure, Click F12:Configuration at the Report Display Screen. Set *Yes* at *Show Percentages* (§05.04).

FAQ-8: How I can get reports with periodicity as per my choice

Ans: Some of the reports provide to set the periodicity. The standard periodicity (like Monthly / Quarterly) are often set by a toggle button (like F4:Monthly / Quarterly).

Apart from the standard period, the Configuration option provide for many additional standard period like 4 Week month, Daily, Fortnightly etc. Click *F12:Configuration* at the Report Display Screen (§05.05). Now select the desired periodicity option. The amount figures for each column of the report are split for each periodicity slab for the report period, even if the figure is blank for some specific periodicity slab. Such periodic reports are very useful for comparative figure over a longer period (F-7A)

Reports Printing

01 Accounting Reports

We have discussed some basic Accounting Reports, in default format, containing the basic particulars (§02/01-05).Tally provides enormous options to customize the contents and lay out of reports as per user's own choice & requirements, through various report printing configuration options.

In this chapter, we discuss about some common printing configuration options which are applicable to all reports in general. The report specific options are explained at the respective Report.

02 Report Printing General Configuration

At Gateway, click *F12:Configure >Printing >General* to get *Report Printing Common Configuration* screen (F-1A). Set the following default Report Printing options:

- o **Report Printing Date & Time:** At *Print Date & Time of Report*, set *Yes* to print Date of Time of printing the report, at Report Heading.. Set *No* (default) to suppress the Date & Time of printing
- o **Voucher Printing Date & Time:** At *Print Date & Time of Voucher Printing,* set *Yes* to print Date of Time in Vouchers. Set *No* (default) to suppress the Date & Time of printing (§03/02-15)
- o **State & PIN:** At *Print State & PIN with Address***,** set *Yes* to print State & PIN in address lines (just below the Company Name). So, you should not include the State & PIN in the address part of Company Profile. Set *No* (default) to suppress the State & PIN at address line (useful if you have included State & PIN at address line to avoid duplicate printing of State & PIN).
- o **Vertical Lines / Borders:** At *Stop Printing Vertical Lines / Borders*, set *Yes* to omit Vertical Lines & Borders so that the report looks better. Set *No* to suppress printing of Vertical Lines & Borders to print faster in Dot Matrix Printer. On omitting vertical lines, the speed will improve only in case of Impact Printer (e.g Dot Matrix Printer).In non-impact printer (like Ink Jet / Laser), there will be no appreciable change in speed. In such case, it is recommended to set *No* (default) at this option, to print Vertical Lines also to make the Report look better.
- o **Standard Top Space:** At *Standard Space in top of pages (inches)*, enter the value of top margin space (in inches) in report (default value 0.5 inch). This space is above the Top Margin as specified in Page Dimension.

F-1A: Report Printing Common Configuration

Configuration	
Print Date & Time of Report	? No
Print Date & Time of Voucher Printing	? No
Print State and PIN Code with Address	? No
Stop printing Vertical Lines/Borders *(for faster printing on dot-matrix printers)*	? No
Standard Space on Top of pages (inches)	: 0.50
Settings for 'Quick Format'	
Split long names into multiple lines	? No
Split long amts/numbers into multiple lines	? No
Print Party Name and Address from left margin in invoice	? No

Quick Format: Apart from the above, you may set the following options, relevant only in Quick format (normally used in Dot Matrix Printer),

- **Split Long names into multiple lines:** Sometimes, long text data may not fit into the available space.
  - o Set *Yes* to split the long text lines which do not fit into the specified space, into multiple lines (but the line looks odd).
  - o Set *No* to avoid splitting (but the values may get truncated).

  So, if you use Quick Format, set *Yes* to avoid truncation otherwise some important data may be truncated.
- **Split Long Numbers / Amount into multiple lines:** Sometimes, large numeric value may not fit into the available space.
  - o Set *Yes* to split the large numbers or amounts that do not fit into the specified space into multiple lines (but the line looks odd).
  - o Set *No* to avoid splitting (but the values may get truncated).

  So, if you use Quick Format, set *Yes* to avoid truncation otherwise amounts / numbers may be truncated.
- **Print Party Name & Address from Left Margin in Invoice:** Set *Yes* to Print Party Name & Address in Invoice from left Margin. Set *No* to print Name & Address centred)

03 Report Printing Screen

After you select any report from any of the report menu, you get the Report Printing screen (F-1B), through which you can set the various options of the Report

Report Printing screen (F-1B), may be divided into 3 major areas.

- At *top* part, you get the default general printer setting options of the Installed Printer (this remains same for all reports)
- At *middle* part, the default Report Title is shown (which you may change, for the current report)
- The *lower* part shows the default Report configuration options specific to the current report (which you may change)

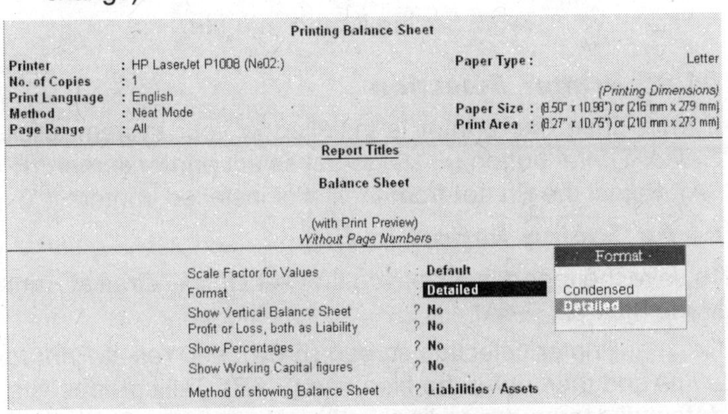

F-1B:Report Printing Screen

04 Report Printing Buttons

Through various buttons at the at the right button bar (F-1C) at report printing dialogue, you may to set the respective report printing option, as below:

- **L: Print Language:** To set the Print language of the printed Report
- **G: Page Number:** To set the Page Number range of the report to be printed (§04.01)
- **R: Pre Printed / Plain Paper:** To set the Stationery type of the Report (Plain / Pre printed - §04.02)
- **F: Print Format:** To set the Report Format (Neat / Quick / Dot Matrix - §04.03)
- **C: Copies:** To set Number of Copies of each report to be printed (§04.04)
- **S: Select Printer:** To select installed Printer for printing the current report (§04.05)
- **T: Titling:** To set the Report Title (§04.07)
- **I: With Preview / No Preview:** To see / suppress the Preview of the Report on screen (§04.08)
- **N: Auto Column:** To print auto repeating additional columns in Columnar reports (§04.09)

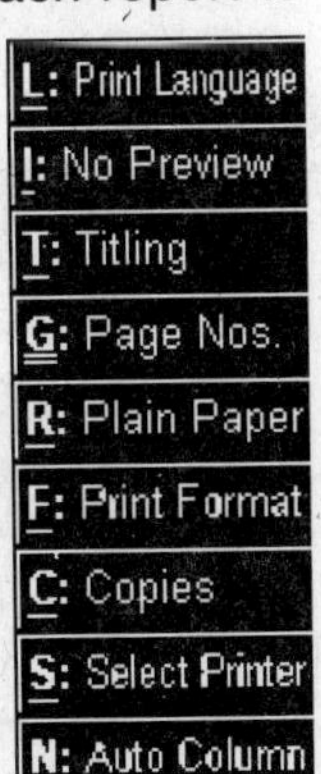

F-1C: Buttons

These options are explained below

04.01 Page Number / Range

By this option, you may specify the starting *Page Number* and the *Page Range* of the Report to be printed..

The page number in the printed Report is dynamically created during printing as per starting Page Number specified. So, page numbers depend on the options selected at the time of printing. So, next time when you print the report with different print options, the page number might change. So, when you re-print a report specifying page numbers, make sure that you specify same printing options otherwise you will get different part of the report than expected. To make sure that you are getting the pages that you want, first preview the report on screen before printing (§04.08)

Click *G: Page Nos* button (F-1C) to get Page Number / Range screen (F-2A & F-2B) to set:

- **Starting Page Number**: At *Page Number Starts From*, enter the starting page No (e.g. 5). Normally it is set to 1 to print from first page. This is useful to re-start from the middle even after being interrupted in a printing session of several pages, or print Running Page Numbers over successive print sessions.
- **Page Range**: At *Page Range*, enter a single page range (like 5-9) to print only a few selected pages, else select All (default Page No.) to print the entire report. You may omit the last page number to print upto the last page (e.g, you may enter 9- to print all pages from page number 9)

> **Note:** *You may print with continuous page number running over several print sessions, by specifying the starting page number.*

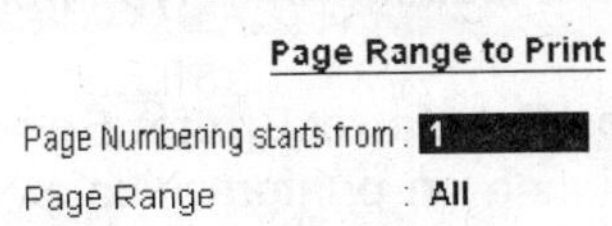

F-2A: Page Range to print from beginning

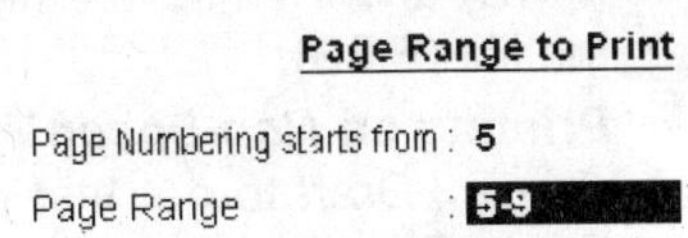

F-2B: Page Range to continue from last print.

04.02 Paper Type

Tally recognizes 2 types of stationery (paper type). Click *R:Plain Paper/ R:Pre- Printed* toggle button (F-1C), to select Paper Types as follows:

- **Plain Paper**: *R:Plain Paper* to print in Plain Paper format. In Plain Paper format, the paper is blank. So, Tally prints everything of the report (labels & data), like Company name, address etc., and data labels (F-3B).
- **Pre-Printed**: *R:Pre-Printed* to print on pre-printed stationery (headings not printed, only data printed: F-3A). The word Pre-Printed paper is added to the heading 'Method' at the Printing screen (F-1B), to indicate current setting of Paper Type.

Balance Sheet
1-Apr-2011 to 31-Mar-2012

F-3A Report Heading in Pre Printed Format (Co name etc not printed)

ABC Academy
35, APC Road
Bandana Appartment, Flat 3B
Rajabazar
Kolkata
Contact :5487952368,9999999999
Balance Sheet
1-Apr-2011 to 31-Mar-2012

F-3B Report Heading in Plain Paper

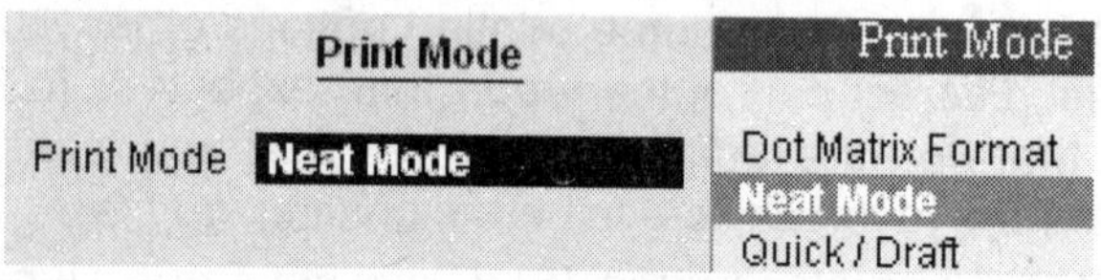

F-4A: Print Mode (print Format)

F-4B: Dot Matrix Printer selection

04.03 Print Format

Click *F: Print Format* button (F-1C) to get Print Format (Print Mode) set up screen (F-4A). At *Print Mode* field, select from the following options.

- **Neat Mode**: Select *Neat Mode* to print on non-impact printer like Ink Jet / Laser printer.
- **Fast Printing on *Epson* Type Dot Matrix Printer**: Select *Dot Matrix* to print through Dot Matrix Printer (F-4B) and then select the Dot Matrix Printer type from the list (F-4B).
- **Printing on *Non-Epson* Type Dot Matrix Printer**:Select *Quick / Draft* to get fast printing on printers (like Non Epson Dot Matrix) or to save report or file.

Note: *In Quick / Draft mode, large figures may get truncated or mis-aligned. This mode is useful to save the Report in a file. Now-a-days, with proliferation of Non-Impact Printer (Ink Jet / Laser Printer), and variety of Format available for Report Export option (allowing to save Report in file in various formats), the Quick Draft mode to save Report in File is not much relevant.*

04.04 Number of Copies

To print more than one copy of the report, click C:Copies button (F-1C) to get Number of Copies screen (F-5). Enter number of copies to print (initially it is set to 1)

F-5: Number of Copies

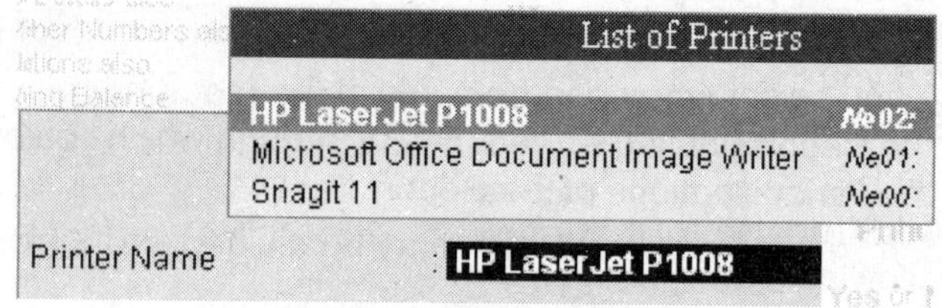

F-6A: Printer selection screen.

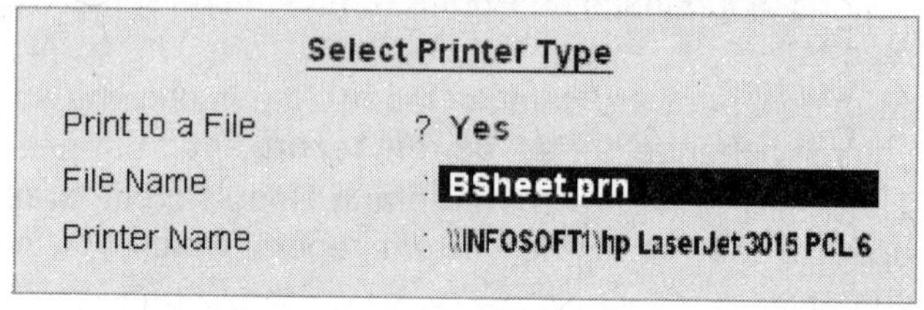

F-6B: Saving Report in a file

04.05 Printer Selection

If more than one printer is installed in your system, click *Select Printer* button (F-1C) to get select printer screen (F-6A). Select the Printer from the list of installed printers

04.06 Saving Report in file

To save the report in a file, you first set *Quick / Draft* at Print Mode (§04-02, F-4A).

Next, at Printer selection screen (F-6B), set *Yes* at *Print to a File* and then enter the filename (F-6B). Tally proposes a default filename depending on the selected report, Change the filename if you like to. The report will be saved in the designated file at the specified directory.

This report saved in file becomes independent and external to Tally and you may modify it as you like. You can send the report by e-mail to anyone, insert the report in any document, or print it without using Tally software.

04.07 Report Title

At the button bar, click *T:Titling* button (F-1C) to get Report Title set up screen (F-7). Now set up the Report Title options as follows:

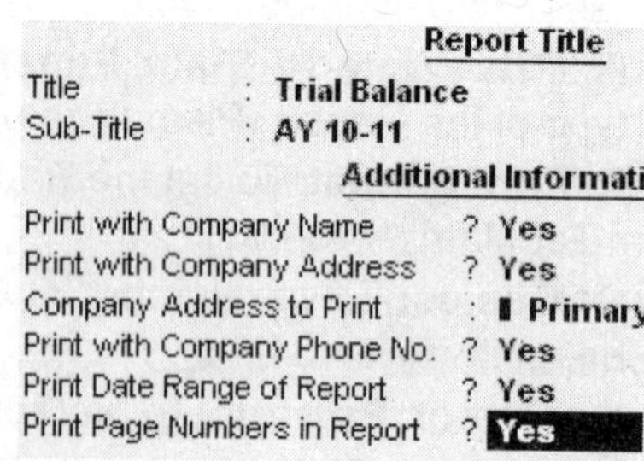

F-7: Report Title set up

Note: *Set the Report Title at the time of printing of each Report, at each session to get the Heading printed correctly.*

It is good practice to print Report & Voucher Printing Date & Time, through General Printing Configuration (§02). The Date Time is printed in Multi Account Reports as well as in Reports printed through Display.

- **Title**: Tally proposes a standard Report Title, which is printed at each Page Title, for the current report. Change it if you like
- **Sub-Title**: Enter sub title Report to be printed just below the Report Title, in 1st page only.
- **Additional Information**: Set *'Yes'* or *'No'* to print the following particulars at the Report Title.
    - o **Print with Company Name:** Set Yes to print Company Name, else set No
    - o **Print with Company Address:** Set Yes to print Company Address, else set No
    - o **Company Address to Print**: This option appears when you have set Multiple Address for the Company (§11/02-02). The list of multiple Address as specified appear, from which you may select the respective Address (select *Primary* to print the Company Address entered at the Company Creation screen: §04/02-02)
    - o **Print with Company Phone Number:** Set *Yes* to print Company Phone Number, else set No
    - o **Print Date Range of Report:** Set *Yes* to print Date Range as specified at Report Printing screen, else set No
    - o **Print Page Numbers in Report:** Set *Yes* to print Page Number at each Page, as per Page Number specification set through G:Page Number option (F-2A / F-2B), else set No (Page Number is not printed)

04.08 Report Preview

Before printing on paper, you may optionally see how the report will look like when printed. Click I:*Print Preview / No Preview* toggle button (this option does not appear if you set Quick / Draft at print format: F-4A) and set as follows (F-1C)

- **Direct Printing**: Click I:*No Preview*, the report is directly printed on Paper.
- **Print Preview**: Click I:*Print Preview* to see an exact replica of the Report on screen (F-8). The Report is not directly printed on Paper.

Scale at Print Preview: In *Print Preview* mode (also referred as Report Preview) of the Report (F-8), a scale at the Left & Bottom Edge to show the Report print area and layout of the Report, in respect of the paper size.

Buttons at Print Preview Screen:. You get following buttons at *Report Preview* screen (F-8), to quickly traverse through various part of the Report

- **Zoom**:Click *Zoom* button at Preview screen (F-8) to zoom in / out the preview display. In zoomed Report, use +/- keys (using keyboard), or Ctrl+Scroll (using Mouse), to further zoom the report upto 600%.
- **Pg Dn**: This button is activated when the Report extends to multiple pages. Click *PgDn* to move to successive pages, till you reach the last page of the Report.
- **Pg Up**: This button is activated to move backwards, Click *PgUp* when you have moved to successive pages, through *Pg Up* button, till you reach the first page of the Report.
- **Pg Right**: This button is activated in case of wide Report extending beyond the width of the Page. Click *PgRight* button to pan the report to the right till you reach the right edge current page.
- **Pg Left:** This button is activated when you have panned rightwards in a Report, through Pg Right button. Click *Pg Left* button to pan the report to the left till you reach the left edge current page
- **Home:** Click *Home* button to jump to the first page (start of the Report), from any position in the Report.
- **In MM/Inches:** Click *In MM* to show the scale in millimetres, Click *In Inches* to show the scale in Inches
- **Print:** To print the report from Print Preview screen

> **Note:** *It is a good practice to preview the Report before printing to ensure that you have specified correct period and printing options. To see print preview, click* I:Print Preview *to see the Report on screen. You flip / pan the report through the Pg Up Pg Dn / PgRight PgLeft buttons at the bottom of the Print Preview. Press <esc> to exit from Print Preview,*
> *To change print option, set No at Print and then change the printing options. See the review again.*
> *Having ensured that the Report is alright as shown in the preview, Click* I:No Preview *button and print the Report on printer.*

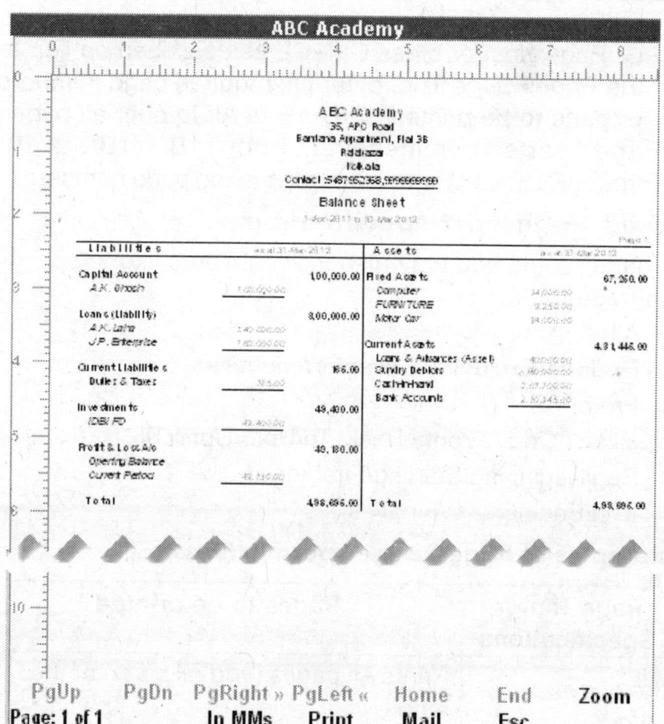

F-8: Print Preview

04.09 Auto Column

To get *Auto Columnar* report (§06.04/02-13), Click *N:Auto Column* button (F-1C), and then select the Period at the field *Repeat Using* (§06.04/02-13).

05 Multi-Part Printing

In some wide reports, the entire line does not fit the specified page width/ page length. In such case, you may print the entire report into several parts, and paste the parts together side by side. This way, you may print a report of any width even with a smaller width paper (e.g in standard A-4 stationery)

05.01 Viewing multiple Parts

In Print Preview (F-8), the Part Number of Multi Part report is shown at right upper corner.

- **Identifying the Parts**: Each part is identified with an alphabet and associated to the respective page number (like cells of a spreadsheet), Each page can have parts commencing with the alphabet A and ending with Z, in case the number of parts for a page are exceeding the alphabet Z, the fresh parts commence with a combination of alphabets AA, AB, AC……AZ, BA, BB, BC…..BZ and so on.
- **Parts Printing Sequence:** In multiple parts report, printing commences by printing all the pages from part A,, i.e., 1A, 2A, 3A, 4A, …….nA, followed by printing all the pages for part B and then prints all pages for part C and so on.
- **Printing Specific Parts**: To print specific parts of the report, select the required report that you want to print, G: Page Nos (or press Ctrl+G), as described earlier. In the *Page Range* field, enter the required page numbers or parts to be printed. E.g.: 1B to All to print all pages and parts commencing from 1B (1B……nB, 1c….nC,……….) where n is the ending page number.

05.02 Page Part specification

In page range, you may also include words like to specify the Page Parts:

- All
- Exclude/Excluding/Except/Without/Not,
- From, To,
- Even / Odd / Front / Back, To/Upto/Uptill/Till,
- Beg/Beginning/Starting/First/Initial,
- End/Ending/Last/Final etc,

Examples of Page Range specifications

Page Range Specifications	Pages to be printed
All	Prints All pages (and all parts) of the report
5,8,10	Prints the pages 5, 8 & 9 (all the Parts)
4A, 6B, 7C	Prints the part of page 4, par B of Page 6, & part C of Page 7 only
7C to 9D	Starts Printing from Part C of Page 7 and continues printing as per default print sequence (7C, 7D…8A, 8B..; 9A, 9B, 9C, 9D) and stops after printing part 9D.
1-5, exclude 3A	Prints all parts of pages 1,2,3,4 & 5 except Part A of page 5
2-6 Even	Prints pages, 2,4 & 6 (all parts)
Upto 3A	Prints page 1,2 (all parts) and part A of page 3.
Front	Prints odd pages
Back	Prints Even pages

You may re-set the Printer's Page Layout through the option of the Printer, to contain the Report in the current page size. The Report Scale in Print Preview (F-8) will help you to re-set page layout

- **Paper Size**: Increase the size of the stationery (Length / Width)
- **Margin**: Reduce the left, right, top, bottom Margin of the Page Layout
- **Orientation**: Set Landscape mode for Wide Report
- **Font Type & Font Size:** Set more compact Font and reduce Font Size to pack more materials in a page

Collation of Multi part Report: When a report spills beyond the width of paper, depending on the Report Type:

- **Paste the Report Parts**:The stripped contents in successive right part pages are printed. In such case, you have to paste the Report side by side, to get the full report
- **Tile the Report Parts:**The First column of the Report is repeated in successive Right parts. In such case you may place the parts successively and use the Report without pasting all the parts together (as the first column is printed in each printed part)

06 Multi Account Printing Menu

From Display, you can print the report of currently selected Account only (e.g the current Ledger Account) at a time. Through Multi Account Printing, you may print for a specified range. For example you may print off line Static reports (but cannot drill down through such report) of multiple accounts in one stroke through Multi Account Printing Menu.

At Gateway of Tally, Select *Multi Account Printing* to get *Multi Account Printing Menu* (F-9A).

> ***Note:*** *In Multi Account Printing, you have to specify the Report Period at prinitng screen. You set the Printing Options & Buttons in the same way as Printing from Display.*

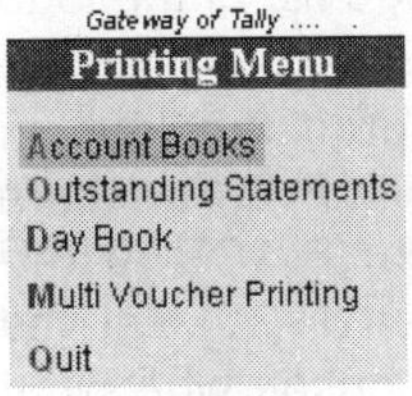

F-9A: Multi Account Printing Menu

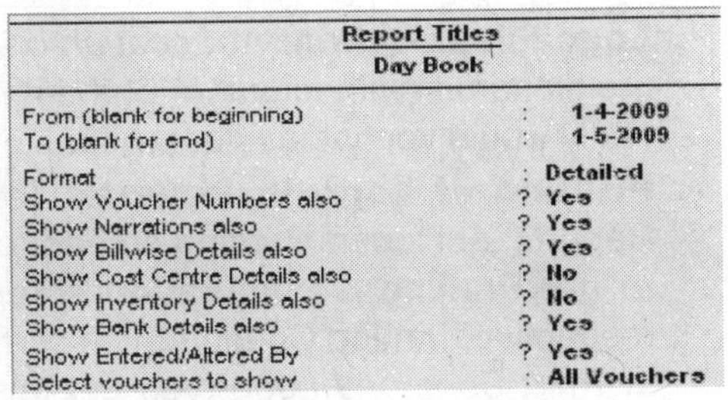

F-9B: Multi Account Report Printing Configuration

Select the appropriate menu option and finally select the desired report to be printed from the menu.

07 Print Configuration

Having selected the report, the Print Configuration screen appears showing the prompt *Print? Yes or No* (F-9B). At the Y/N option:

- **Printing with currently set Configuration**: Type *Y* to print the report as per currently set configuration options.
- **Changing the Configuration options**: Type *N* to change the desired option. Having re-set the desired option, press Ctrl+A to save the changed option and then type Y at *Print Yes / No* option to print the report.

All buttons at button bar (of F-1C, except *Print Preview*) as discussed earlier (§04), work in the same way in Multi Account Printing also.

Company Logo: You may print Company Logo in some vouchers, Invoices & Reports. The logo file should be in.bmp or.jpeg format and should have maximum size of 96x80 pixels (width x height)

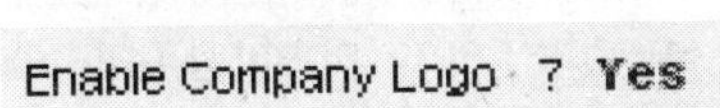

F-10A: Company Logo set up option

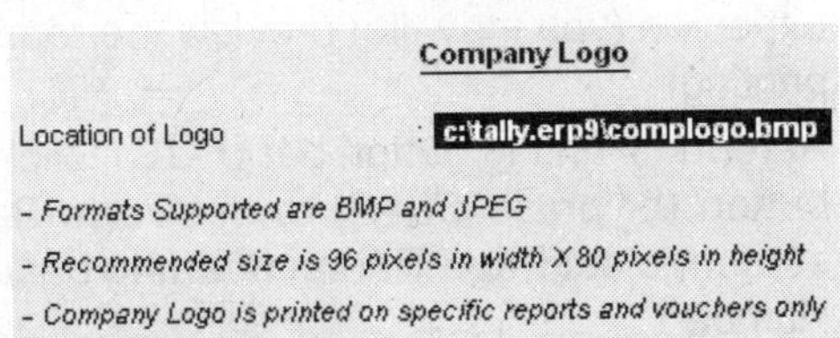

F-10B Company Logo Import

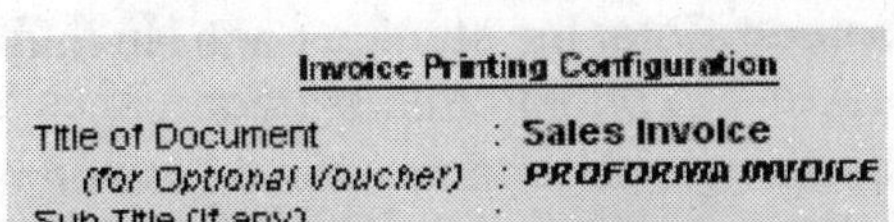

F-10C Option to print Logo in Report Printing Configuration

- **Logo set up Option**: At *F11:Features>Accounting Features*, under the section *Other Features,* at *Enable Company Logo* (F-10A)
    - o Set *Yes* to get the option to import Logo Image file, which may be printed in specified vouchers, Invoices & Reports. Set *No* (default).
    - o Set *No,* No logo can be set / printed in reports
- **Setting the Logo Image file**: When you set *Yes* at the option *Enable Company Logo,* you get Company Logo import screen (F-10B), to import the Company Logo (an image file), which is printed in the reports.
- **Logo File Location:** At the field *Location of Logo* (F-10B), enter the filename (with location) of the image file of the logo.
- **Printing Logo in Reports**: To print the logo in Reports, at the respective Printing Configuration screen (F-10C), set Yes at *Print Company Logo*

Report Printing Configuration Options: We have discussed the common configuration options & features of Report Printing. Apart from these common properties, each report has its own set of configuration options to customize the Report Contents. These report specific Configuration Options are discussed at the respective Reports, in later chapters

Projects: Report Printing

P-01 Multi-Part Printing: To divide wide & long reports which do not fit in to printer page size, into Multiple defined Parts and print the Parts separately

Steps of printing Multi Part Report

Viewing multiple Parts: In Print Preview (F-8), the Part Number of Multi Part report is shown at right upper corner.

Identifying the Parts: Each part is identified with an alphabet and associated to the respective page number (like cells of a spreadsheet), Each page can have parts commencing with the alphabet A and ending with Z, in case the number of parts for a page are exceeding the alphabet Z, the fresh parts commence with a combination of alphabets AA, AB, AC......AZ, BA, BB, BC.....BZ and so on.

Parts Printing Sequence: In multiple parts report, printing commences by printing all the pages from part A,, i.e., 1A, 2A, 3A, 4A, ...nA, followed by printing all the pages for part B and then prints all pages for part C and so on.

Printing Specific Parts: To print specific parts of the report, select the required report that you want to print, click G: Page Nos (or press Ctrl+G**),** as described earlier. In the *Page Range* field, enter the required page numbers or parts to be printed. E.g.: 1B to All to print all pages and parts commencing from 1B (1B......nB, 1c....nC,.........) where n is the ending page number.

P-02 Project: Date / Time Printing at Reports / Documents

I like to print the Date & Time of Priting of the Report / Document for reference.

To print date / Time, you have to set the option at Report General Configuration. You cannot set the option at individual Report Printing screen. So, you must plan whether you like to print Date / Time in general n every report / document.

At Gateway, click *F12:Configure >Printing >General* to get

Report Printing Common Configuration screen (P-1A). Set the following default Report Printing options:

- **Date & Time Printing on 1st page of Report:** At *Print Date & Time of Report*, set *Yes* to print Date of Time of printing the report in the 1st Page of Report (P-1B), else set *No* (default) to suppress the Date & Time of printing.
- **Date & Time Printing on all pages of Report:** Having set *Yes* at *Print Date & Time of Report,* stated above, at (on al Pages of Report), set:
    - o *Yes* to print the Date & Time of Printing on all pages of the Report
    - o *No* to print the Date & Time of Printing only on 1st Page of the Report
- **Voucher Printing Date & Time on 1st page of Voucher:** At *Print Date & Time of Voucher Printing,* set *Yes* to print Date of Time in 1st Page of the Voucher. Set *No* (default) to suppress the Date & Time of printing (P-1C)
- **Date & Time Printing on all pages of Voucher:** Having set *Yes* at *Print Date & Time of Report,* stated above, at (on al Pages of Report), set:
    - o *Yes* to print the Date & Time of Printing on all pages of the Report (P-1C)
    - o *No* to print the Date & Time of Printing only on 1st Page of the Report

P-1A Date / Time Printing set up

Configuration	
Print Date & Time of Report	? Yes
(on all pages of report)	? Yes
Print Date & Time of Voucher Printing	? Yes
(on all pages of voucher)	? Yes

Printed on 18-Oct-2013 at 02:40

Dr ABC

Trial Balance

1-Apr-2014 to 31-Mar-2015

P-1B: Date / Time Printing in Report Heading

Printed on 18-Oct-2013 at 02:44

Dr ABC

Journal Voucher

P-1C: Date / Time Printing in Voucher Heading

P-03 Printing Company Logo in Reports & Documents

You may print Company Logo vouchers, Invoices & Reports. For that, you have to store the Logo File in.bmp or.jpeg format. The logo image should have maximum size of 96x80 pixels (width x height)

- **Logo Option set up:** At *F11:Features>Accounting Features*, at the option *Enable Company Logo*, under the section *Other Features* (P-1A), set *Yes* to get the option to import Logo Image file, which may be printed in specified vouchers, Invoices & Reports. Set *No* (default).
- **Logo Image file Set Up**: When you set *Yes* at the option *Enable Company Logo* (P-1A), you get Company Logo import screen (P-1B), to import the Company Logo (an image file), which is printed in the reports.
- **Logo File Location:** At *Location of Logo* (P-1B), enter the filename (with location) of the image file of the logo (Tally would verify the File location)
- **Printing of Logo in Reports**: To print the logo in Reports, at Report Printing screen, click *F12:Configure* to get Printing Configuration screen (P-1C). At the respective Printing Configuration screen (P-2C), set Yes at *Print Company Logo* (you get this option when you have activated Logo Printing Option (P-1A) and have imported a Logo image file (P-2C).

P-1A: Company Logo set up option

Enable Company Logo ? **Yes**

Company Logo

Location of Logo : **c:\tally.erp9\complogo.bmp**

- Formats Supported are BMP and JPEG
- Recommended size is 96 pixels in width X 80 pixels in height
- Company Logo is printed on specific reports and vouchers only

P-1B Company Logo Import

P-1C Option to print Logo in Report Printing Configuration

Invoice Printing Configuration	
Title of Document	: **Sales Invoice**
(for Optional Voucher)	: ***PROFORMA INVOICE***
Sub Title (if any)	:
Print Company Logo	? **Yes**

FAQ: Frequently Asked Questions

FAQ-1: How I can print Page Number in Report

Ans: Tally does not store page number in the data. The page number is dynamically created during printing. So, page numbers depend on the options selected at the time of printing. So, next time when you print the report with different print options, the page number might change. So, when you re-print a report specifying staring page numbers & page range, make sure that you specify same printing options otherwise you will get different part of the report than expected (you may first preview the report on screen before printing)

At report Printing button bar (F-1C), click Click G: *Page Nos* button (or press *Ctl+G*) to get Page Range screen to set screen to set Page Range (starting page number and page Number)

- **Starting Page Number**: Enter the starting page No (e.g. 5). Normally it is set to 1 to print from first page.
- **Page Range**: Enter a single page range (like 5-9) to print only a few selected pages, else select All (default Page No.) to print the entire report.

You may omit the last page number to print upto the last page. For example, 9- to print all pages from page number 9.

FAQ-2: How I can use Pre-Printed / Palin Paper Stationery for Reports Printing

Ans: At report Printing button bar (F-1C),, Click *R:Plain Paper / Pre Printed* toggle button (or press *Alt+R*) to set the Paper Types as follows:

- **Plain Paper**: In Plain Paper format, the paper is blank and nothing is printed. So, Tally prints everything of the report, like Company name, address etc
- **Pre-Printed**: To print on pre-printed stationery. The Company Name / Address etc are not printed by Tally (as these are pre - printed on the stationery).. The word Pre-Printed paper is added to the heading 'Method' at the Print Dialogue, to indicate the selection of Paper Type.

FAQ-3: How I can print multiple Number of Copies of a Report

Ans: To print more than one copy of the report, At report Printing button bar (F-1C),, click *C:Copies* button (or press Alt+C) to get Number of Copies screen. Enter number of copies to print (initially it is set to 1)

FAQ-4: Multiple Printers are installed in my Computer. How I can print the Report in the desired Printer.

Ans: At report Printing button bar (F-1C),, click *S:Select Printer* button (or press *Alt+S*) to get list of installed printers. Select the Printer from the list for the current report being printed.

FAQ-5: How I can print Company Name, Address etc at Report Title

Ans: To set the Report Title options, At report Printing button bar (F-1C), click *T:Titling* button (or press *Alt+T*) and set as follows:

- **Title**: Tally proposes a standard Report Title for the current report. Change it if you like
- **Sub-Title**: Enter sub title Report to be printed just below the Report Title, in 1st page only.
- **Additional Information**: Set *'Yes'* or *'No'* at the following options, to print / omit the desired particulars at the Report Title,
  - **Print with Company Name**
  - **Print with Company Address**
    - o **Company Address to Print:** Select the Address Type (if Multiple Address are entered through the option *Set / Alter Company mailing Details* at *F11:Features>Company Features*), else select *Primary*
  - **Print Date Range of Report:** Set *Yes* to print the Report Period (just below the Report Title)
  - **Print Page Number of Report:** Set Yes to print Page Number of the Report.

FAQ-6: How I can see (preview) the Report on screen

Ans: At report Printing button bar (F-1C), click *I:Print Preview / No Preview* toggle button (or press *Alt+I*) to get the Report Preview on screen to see how the report will look like when printed. Click *Zoom* button at Preview screen to zoom in / out the preview display. If you find the Report OK, then click on Print option at the Report Preview screen to print the report.

The print Preview also shows a scale around the Report showing the Report Dimension (in mm). This helps you to decide paper size.

Account Masters List

01 Account Masters List

After entry of Accounts Masters (Account Groups, Accounts Ledgers, Voucher Types etc), you may display / print the lists in Hierarchical / Alphabetical order.

02 Account Masters List Display

Select *Display > List of Accounts* to get the list of all Accounts Masters

Buttons

At Account Master list (F-1A, F-2A), you get buttons (F-3A) to show the list of each type of Accounts Master

- **List of Account Groups:** Click *G: Groups* button at the button bar to get the list of Account Groups only in hierarchical structure (F-2A).
- **List of Account Ledgers:** List of Ledgers shows the Account Groups and the underlying Ledger Accounts in hierarchical structure (F-1A)

  Click *L: Ledgers* button to show the List of Account Groups & Ledgers, the complete chart of accounts (F-1A)

- **List of Voucher Types**: Click *V: Voucher Types* button to show the List of Voucher Types in alphabetical sequence of Voucher Type Name. The Tally created Primary Voucher Type is shown in Bold, while user created new voucher types are shown in Normal Font

List of Ledgers
1-Apr-2008 to 31-Mar-2010

Branch / Divisions
Capital Account
  Reserves & Surplus (Retained Earnings)
  Current Year Profit / Loss
  Drawings
  Properitor's Capital
Current Assets
  Bank Accounts
    Bank of India
    State Bank of India
  Cash-in-Hand
    Cash
  Deposits (Asset)
  Loans & Advances (Asset)
    A K Das
  Stock-in-Hand
    Stock
    Stock in Hand
  Sundry Debtors
    Aakash & Co (0571)
    A Bose & Co (AB)
    A K Traders
    B K Das
    T K Das
    XYZ Traders (X1)
  Pre Paid Expenses
Current Liabilities
  Duties & Taxes
  Provisions
  Sundry Creditors
    B M Suppliers
    S Roy (Employee)

F-1A: List of Accounts Ledgers

List of Groups
1-Apr-2008 to 31-Mar-2010

Branch / Divisions
Capital Account
  Reserves & Surplus (Retained Earnings)
Current Assets
  Bank Accounts
  Cash-in-Hand
  Deposits (Asset)
  Loans & Advances (Asset)
  Stock-in-Hand
  Sundry Debtors
Current Liabilities
  Duties & Taxes
  Provisions
  Sundry Creditors
Direct Expenses (Expenses (Direct))
Direct Incomes (Income (Direct))
Fixed Assets
  Furniture
Indirect Expenses (Expenses (Indirect))
  Depreciation
  Interest
Indirect Incomes (Income (Indirect))
Investments
Loans (Liability)
  Bank OD A/c (Bank OCC A/c)
  Secured Loans
  Unsecured Loans
Misc. Expenses (ASSET)
Purchase Accounts
Sales Accounts
Suspense A/c

31 Group(s)

F- 2A: List of Account Groups

List of Accounts
List of Voucher Types

Cash Sales
Cons
Contra
Credit Note
Debit Note
Delivery Note
Job Jrnl
Job Work In Order
Job Work Out Order
Journal
Manufacturing Journal
Material In
Material Out
Mat In FG
Mat In (RM)
Mat Out Trf_FG
Memorandum
Mfg Jrnl (Mfg Jnl)
M Out RM
Payment
Physical Stock
POS
Purchase
Purchase Order
Receipt
Receipt Note
Rejections In
Rejections Out
Reversing Journal
Sales
Sales Order
Stock Journal

F-3A: List of Vouchr Types

- **Accounts Group List**: Initially, the List shows Primary Major Account Groups in Alphabetical Order, with subordinate Account Groups / Ledger in hierarchical structure (F-1A). The Account Groups are shown in bold and the ledger accounts are shown in Italics.
- **Other Masters Lists**: At the Button Bar (F-4A), you get the buttons for each Master type activated. Select the button (F-4A) to get respective List of Accounts (F-1A, F-2A, F-3A).

F-4A: Buttons

F-5A: Printing screen

F-5B: Master Type List

F-6: Button Bar at the bottom of the Account Master List

03 Account Masters List Printing

At Account Master List Display (F-1A, F-2A), click *P:Print* button to get *Accounts Master Printing* screen (F-5A).

At Accounts Master Printing screen (F-5A), at *Type of Master*, select the type of Master from Account Master Type list, to print the respective list of Master

04 Operations from Account Master List

You may make following operation of any Account Master record, from any of the Account Master list, from the options appearing at the button bar at the bottom of the Report (F-6)

- **Create New Account Master record:** At Accounts Groups / Ledgers list (F-1A, F-2A etc), Click *C:Create Mst* button (F-6) to create new Account Master record from the Master List display.
- **Selection of Master:** Move the cursor on the Master record and press *Spacebar* to select it (the colour band will change to indicate that the record has been selected).
  - o **Alteration of Master:** Press <enter> on the selected Master to get it in *Alteration mode* to make the desired modification of any data in the selected master record
    - **Deletion of Master:** To Delete the Masters, click *D:Delete* button (or press Alt+D), the selected Account Groups / Ledgers would be Deleted (subject to rules of Deletion of Account Groups / Accounts Ledgers – §05.01/01-03)
- **Remove / Restore Lines**: You may even select multiple Masters at a time to Remove / Restore Masters as explained (§04/02-13).
  - o **Remove Lines**: Select Master records (place the cursor& press space bar) to be removed from the current list. Now press *R:Remove* line button (or Alt+R) to remove the selected (Marked) lines from the list (the master records do not get deleted, they only disappear from the current list)
  - o **Restore Lines**: To Restore the last removed line, press *U:Restore* Line (or press *Alt+U*). To restore all the removed lines (when you have removed multiple lines in one go), press *U: Restore All* (or press Ctrl+U). The removed lines are shown back in the list.

First Alias Name is also shown (where specified) beside the Master Name. Alias Name of Reserved Groups are also shown.

05 E-mail IDs

The e-mail IDs may be entered in Ledger Accounts under Bank Accounts, Branch, Capital A/c, Deposits, Loans & Advances (Asset), Loans (Liability), Reserves & Surplus, Retained Earnings, Secured Loans, Unsecured Loans, Sundry Creditors and Sundry Debtors Account Groups. Using e-mail IDs, you may directly e-mail reports to the respective parties.

To manage entry of e-mail ID, you may print a list of Ledger to view / update e-mail IDs.

05.01 E-Mail ID List Display

At Exception Report Menu (*GoT>Display>Exception Reports*), select *e-mail IDs*. By default, you get a list of Ledger Accounts (F-7) for which e-mail ID is not yet entered (e-mail ID is blank)

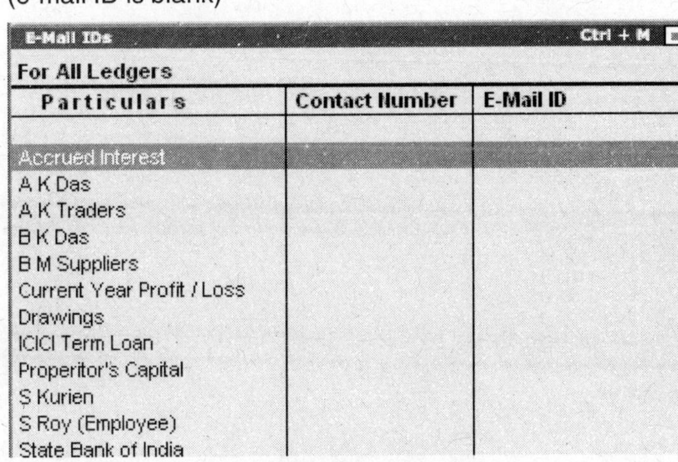

F-7: e-mail ID List (blank IDs)

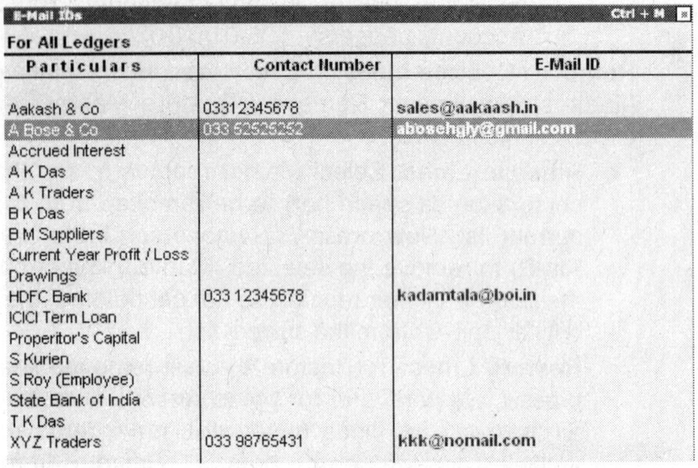

E-Mail IDs

For All Ledgers

Particulars	Contact Number	E-Mail ID
Aakash & Co	03312345678	sales@aakaash.in
A Bose & Co	033 52525252	abosehgly@gmail.com
Accrued Interest		
A K Das		
A K Traders		
B K Das		
B M Suppliers		
Current Year Profit / Loss		
Drawings		
HDFC Bank	033 12345678	kadamtala@boi.in
ICICI Term Loan		
Properitor's Capital		
S Kurien		
S Roy (Employee)		
State Bank of India		
T K Das		
XYZ Traders	033 98765431	kkk@nomail.com

F-8: e-mail ID List (All)

Buttons: At e-mail ID Display screen (F-7), you get following buttons (F-9):

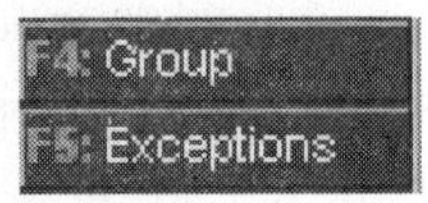

F-9: Buttons

- **F4:Group:** To select a Group to get list of Ledger names (in alphabetical sequence) under the selected Group (select Primary to get List of All Ledgers)
- **F5:All Items / Exceptions:** Click this toggle button to:
  - o **All Ledger Accounts**: *F5:All Items* toggle button to list all ledger accounts with e-mail IDs (F-8). This helps to see the entered e-mail Ids for each Ledger Accounts
  - o **Blank e-mail ID**: *F5:Exceptions* toggle button to list all ledger accounts with blank e-mail IDs (F-7). This helps to see the Ledger Accounts for which e-mail ID has not yet been entered.

05.02 E-Mail ID List Printing

At e-mail ID Display screen (F-7), click *P:Print* button to print the e-mail ID list

05.03 Alteration of Ledger Accounts Master

At e-mail ID Display screen (F-7), drill down through any Ledger Name to get the Ledger Account Master in Alteration mode. Now you may modify any data (and fill up / change address, e-mail Id and other info)

FAQ: Frequently Asked Questions

FAQ-1: I have created one group wrongly and also created some ledger accounts under the Group. How I can delete the Account Group & Ledger Accounts under it.

Ans: You cannot delete a Group if it contains subordinate ledgers under it. So, you have to first delete the wrongly created Ledger Accounts under the Group

Select Display>List of Accounts.

- **Deletion of Ledger Accounts:** Click *L:Ledgers* button at the vertical button bar. Now select the ledger accounts to be deleted. Click *D:Delete* button at the bottom button bar. Type *Yes* at the Delete? Y/N prompt to confirm Deletion.

  Having deleted the Ledger Accounts, delete the Parent Account Group as follows:
- **Deletion of Account Group:** Click *G:Groups* button at the vertical button bar. Now select the Account Group to be deleted. Click *D:Delete* button at the bottom button bar. Type *Yes* at the *Delete? Y/N* prompt to confirm Deletion.

Accounts Voucher Printing

01 Accounts Voucher Printing

Vouchers are basic documents of transactions, containing the complete records of the transaction. Naturally, every organization must keep the voucher for records, audit, evidence and to keep the supporting documents alongwith the voucher. So, the voucher is printed to keep a hard copy of it as record.

The voucher may be printed in 2 stages:

- **Individual Voucher printing at Voucher Entry/ Alteration:** During Voucher Entry / Alteration, the current voucher may be printed.

  Instant Printing at Voucher creation: If you have set *Yes* at *Print after Saving Voucher* at the respective *Voucher Type creation / alteration*, as explained earlier (§02/02-07), the Voucher printing screen (F-1A) appears. Type:

  - o Y to print the current voucher being entered, as per current configuration setting
  - o N to skip printing

  After saving the Voucher: You may print the saved voucher (after voucher entry session), at Voucher alteration screen (§02/02-17).Click *P:Print* button (or press *Alt+P*) at the voucher alteration screen to get Voucher Printing screen (F-1A), showing the printing screen. Type:

  - o Y to print the current Voucher as per as per current configuration setting.
  - o N and change the current configuration setting and then Type Y at Voucher Printing screen to print the voucher as per changed configuration setting.

- **Multiple Voucher printing:** You may print saved (already entered) vouchers for a specific period in one shot through *GoT>Multi Account Printing>Multi Voucher Printing* (§12)

02 Accounts Voucher Printing Configuration

The Vouchers are printed as per default Configuration Options set. You may set the contents and layout of printed voucher by setting the Voucher Printing Configuration options.

At Gateway, click *F12:Configure >Printing* to get *Voucher Printing Configuration* Menu (F-1), which contains options for printed voucher layout set up.

Gateway of Tally ....
Configuration ....

Printing

General
PUrchase Transactions
Payment Voucher
Sales Transactions
Receipt Voucher
Journal / Contra
Debit / Credit Note
REminder Letters
Confirmation Statements
PAyment Advice Configuration
PaYroll
Quit

F-1: Voucher Printing Configuration Menu

Voucher Printing

Report Titles

Contra Voucher

F-1A: Voucher Printing screen

Receipt Printing Configuration

Print Company Logo	? Yes
Height of Voucher (inches)	: 7
Width of Voucher (inches)	: 7
Space to leave on top (default 0.25)	: 0.25
Space to leave on left (default 0.75)	: 0.25
Receipt Mode on Top of Voucher	? Yes
Print Bill-wise Details	? No
Print Bill Due Date also	? No
Print Inventory Details	? No
Print Bank Transaction Details	? No
Space for Checked/Verified initials	? No
Print Base Currency Symbol for Total	? Yes

Formal Receipt Printing Configuration

Print Company Logo	? Yes
Height of Receipt (inches)	: 6
Width of Receipt (inches)	: 5
Space to leave on top (default 0.25)	: 0.25
Print Narration	? Yes
Print Narration for each entry	? Yes

F- 2A: Receipt Voucher Printing Configuration

Payment Printing Configuration	
Height of Voucher (inches)	: 7
Width of Voucher (inches)	: 7
Space to leave on top (default 0.25)	: 0.25
Space to leave on left (default 0.75)	: 0.75
Payment Mode on Top of Voucher	? Yes
Print Bill-wise Details	? No
Print Bill Due Date also	? No
Print Inventory Details	? No
Print Bank Transaction Details	? No
Space for Checked/Verified initials	? No
Print Narration	? Yes
Print Narration for each entry	? Yes
Print Base Currency Symbol for Total	? Yes

F-2B: Payment Voucher Printing

Journal / Contra Printing Configuration	
Height of Voucher (inches)	: 7
Width of Voucher (inches)	: 5
Space to leave on top (default 0.25)	: 0.25
Space to leave on left (default 0.75)	: 0.75
Print Bill-wise Details	? Yes
Print Bill Due Date also	? No
Print Inventory Details	? Yes
Space for Checked/Verified initials	? Yes
Print Narration	? Yes
Print Narration for each entry	? Yes
Print Base Currency Symbol for Total	? Yes

F-2C: Journal & Contra Voucher Printing

At Voucher Printing screen (F-1A), you may click F12: Configure to change the Voucher Printing Configuration (F-2A, F-2B, F-2C) for the current voucher being printing.

03 Voucher Printing Date & Time

We have explained the option to print Date & Time of Report in Reports Printing (02/02-13). In same way, you may set option to print date & Time in Voucher also

At Gateway, click *F12:Configure >Printing >General* to get Report Printing options (F-1A/02-13). At the option *Print Date & Time of Voucher Printing*, set *Yes* to print Date & Time of Voucher, else Set *No* (default) to suppress the Date & Time of printing in Voucher.

At Printing Configuration Menu (F-1), select the desired Voucher Type to get the respective Voucher Printing Configuration screen, as shown below:

- Receipt Voucher & Formal Receipt (F-2A)
- Payment Voucher (F-2B)
- Journal / Contra Voucher (F-2C)
- Payment Advice (F-4B)

04 Voucher Dimensions

Through the voucher printing configuration options (F-2A to F-2C), the Height, Width & Top Margin may be specified. The standard values in the printing option screen are pre set to fit voucher in standard size. However, you may change them to adjust according to the size of stationery you use.

The spaces of each column / field are proportionately adjusted by Tally, as per voucher dimension set in the configuration (Height, Width).

You may view the Voucher Dimension in Print Preview (§04.08/02-13) and adjust the Dimension Values in Voucher Printing Configuration accordingly.

However, Tally.ERP 9 internally specifies minimum size for each component of voucher (header, details, footer etc). So, you cannot control the size of each component (or the overall dimension) completely. For example, a voucher will take some minimum space in details portion, even if the details are very few. So, you will find a large amount of space in the voucher, which you can not reduce or adjust, just be setting the dimensions in the Configuration (if you reduce the dimension too much, even a small voucher will spill in 2 pages, leaving a lot of space in each page)

Through the following options in Voucher Configuration screen (F- 2A to 2C), set the dimensions of the voucher. The dimensions values are to be set in inches, to specify Dimension & Margins (in inches) of the printed Voucher (including margins). The default dimension values for each type of voucher are displayed as follows, which you may change as required.

- **Voucher Height:** At *Height of Voucher,* enter the height of the voucher (print area in inches including top & bottom margin). Default value is 7 (inches). If you reduce the height of voucher, the voucher may take up 2 pages (even if there is one entry) with a lot of blank space in the first page.
- **Voucher Width:** At *Width of Voucher*, enter the width of the voucher (print area in inches including left & right top & bottom margin). Default value is 7 (inches). If you reduce the Width of voucher, the vertical lines and the header columns & data columns may not align properly.

If you specify zero at Height of the voucher, the Height of Voucher will increase to take up the entire voucher. Similarly, if you set zero at Width, the Width of the voucher will increase to take up the entire page size. So, if you are using standard A4 size stationary to print Voucher, you may specify zero to get the full space of the stationary, to avoid chance of extending the voucher to next page in some long vouchers.

- **Top Margin:** At *space to leave at top,* enter the value of top margin (in inches). Default value (.25)
- **Left Margin:** *At space to leave on left,* enter the value of left margin (in inches). Default value (.75)

05 Voucher Printing Configuration Options

The following options are available to all Accounts Voucher Types (Receipt, Payment, Contra & Journal Voucher Type).

- **Signatories:** At *space for Checked / Verified initials*, set:
  - o Set *Yes* to print a guide (*Checked / Verified by*) for space for putting signature
  - o *No* (default value) to omit it. This is useful when the authorities sign on the computer printed voucher (no manual voucher is used).
- **Voucher Narration:** At *Print Narration,* set:
  - o *Yes* (default value) to print Voucher common Narratio (under the head '*On Account of*'.
  - o *No* to omit Voucher Common narration (it may sometimes be useful when separate ledger narration is printed).
- **Ledger Narration:** At *Print Narration for each entry*, set:
  - o *Yes* (default value) to print separate Ledger Narration for each ledger account transacted.

  - o *No* to omit separate ledger narration (it may sometimes be useful when Common Narration is printed).
- **Currency Symbol:** At *Print Base Currency Symbol for Total*, set:
  - o *Yes* (default value) to print Base Currency Symbol before the total voucher amount (F-3A),
  - o *No* to omit the currency symbol
- **Bank details:** At *Pint Bank Transaction details,* set:
  - o *Yes* to print details of Cheque (Cheque Number & Cheque Dt),
  - o *No* (default value) to omit Cheque details (the Bank details are printed if any Bank Account is transacted in the voucher and the Bank details are entered in the voucher).

05.01 Voucher Specific Printing Options

The following options are available for Receipt (F-2A), Payment (F-2B) & Journal (F-2C) Vouchers:

- **Bill Ref details:** At *Print Billwise details*, set:
  - o *Yes* (default value) to print the bill reference details (if available in the voucher)
  - o *No* to omit Bill Reference details.
    - **Bill Due Date:** If *Yes* is set at the above option for Bill Reference, at *Print Bill Due Date Details also*, you may further:
      - Set *Yes* to print Bill Due Date
      - Set *No* to omit Bill Due Date
- **Inventory Details:** At *Print Inventory Details,* set *Yes* to print Inventory details (if available in the voucher, when Accounts with Inventory System is activated), else set *No* (default value) to omit Inventory details. This is normally applicable in Receipt / Payment Voucher for Cash Purchase / Sales.

The following options are available for Receipt Voucher only

Receipt Mode: At *Receipt mode on top of voucher* (F-2A, set:

- o *Yes* to print the Cash / Bank Ledger Account at the top (with the word *Through*) of Receipt Voucher
- o *No* (default value) to omit it.

The following options are available for Payment Voucher only

Payment Mode: At *Payment mode on top of voucher (F-2B),* set:

- o *Yes* to print the Cash / Bank Ledger Account at the top (with the word *Through*) of Payment Voucher,
- o *No* (default value) to omit it.

06 Format of Printed Vouchers

Irrespective of mode of Voucher entry mode (entered in Single or Double mode), the vouchers are printed in following Format:

Receipt & Payment Voucher:Receipt & Payment vouchers are always printed in *Single Mode* format (there is no separate Debit & Credit columns for Amount:F-3A & 3B).

- The Cash / Bank Account are printed in Header, with a word '*Through*' (if the option is set)
- Under the Particulars column, all the Ledger accounts with positive amount are printed first, under the head '*Accounts*'
- If the voucher contains Deduction accounts, they are printed with the word 'Less, the amounts are shown in negative
- The Cheque Details of Bank Account are printed, if available.
- The Voucher Narration is Printed under the head '*On Account of*'
- The Net Voucher Amount in word is printed under the head 'Amount in Words', with the Base Currency symbol (like ₹).
- The signature space is printed at bottom as follows:
  - o Receiver's Signature & Authorised Signatory are printed in Payment Voucher
  - o Authorised Signatory are printed in Receipt & Contra Voucher

Journal & Contra voucher: Journal & Contra voucher are printed showing figures of each ledger account is separate Debit & Credit Columns, like in Double mode (F-3C & 3D)

07 Voucher dimension scale

To see the voucher dimension, get the Print Preview of the voucher (04.08/02-13). The horizontal & vertical scale shows the voucher dimension. Accordingly you may adjust the dimension in Voucher Printing Configuration.

08 Basic Accounts Vouchers

Here we will discuss about the following Basic Accounting Voucher Types. Specimen samples of various type of Basic Accounts Voucher are shown below (F-3A to F-3D)

At Voucher Entry screen, click *P:Print* button to get the Voucher Printing screen (F-1A).

- Set *Yes* to print the voucher with default options as shown
- Set *No* and change the options as desired. Then set *Yes* to print with changed option

Receipt Voucher

No. : 8 Dated : 31-May-2011
Through : Cash

Particulars	Amount
Account :	
SS Computer	10,000.00
Less: Cash Discount	(-)100.00
On Account of :	
Received from SS Computer after allowing Cash Discount	
Amount (in words) :	
INR Nine Thousand Nine Hundred Only	
	₹ 9,900.00

Authorised Signatory

F-3A: Receipt Voucher

Payment Voucher

No. : 10 Dated : 1-Jul-2011

Through : HDFC Bank

Particulars	Amount
Account :	
Salary	8,000.00
Dearness Allowance	1,500.00
Less. Contribution to PF	(-)800.00
Less. Contribution to ESI	(-)500.00
On Account of :	
Ch. No. 445468 Salary paid to A Mitra by Cheque for the Month of June 2011	
Amount (in words) :	
INR Eight Thousand Two Hundred Only	
	₹ 8,200.00

Receiver's Signature : Authorised Signatory

F-3B: Payment Voucher

The contents of each Voucher Type are shown as example (F-3A to F-3D). The figures are not to scale (excess spaces are stripped off to save space).

Voucher Title: The Voucher Title may be configured in same way as Report Title (04.07/-2-13)

Contra Voucher

No. : 4 Dated : 2-May-2011

Particulars		Debit	Credit
To Cash			7,000.00
HDFC Bank	*Dr*	3,000.00	
State Bank Of India	*Dr*	4,000.00	
On Account of :			
Cash Deposited in Two Bank Account			
		₹ 7,000.00	₹ 7,000.00

Authorised Signatory

F-3C: Contra Voucher

Journal Voucher

No. : 2 Dat 2-Jun-2011

Particulars		Debit	Credit
Depreciation	*Dr*	17,000.00	
To FURNITURE			5,000.00
To Motor Car			6,000.00
To Computer			6,000.00
On Account of :			
Depreciatiois on Furniture, M, Computer			
		₹ 17,000.00	17,000.00

F-3D: Journal Voucher

F-3A shows a printed Receipt Voucher with deduction account. The Deduction amounts are shown in negative amount at the end (after printing all the positive amounts with a word *'Less'*.

The text Authorised Signatory is printed at the end (the word Authorised Signatory cannot be changed).

09 Money Receipt (Formal Receipt)

Formal Receipt (popularly known as *Money Receipt*) is a receipt voucher printed in Money Receipt format which is handed over to the payer as a document and evidence of the money having been received (it does not show ledger Account head, as that is internal for the organization).

09.01 Option to set up Formal Receipt

To print Formal Receipt, you should set the configuration option at Receipt Voucher Type, as follows:

At Gateway, select *Account Info>Voucher Type>Alter* and select *Receipt* from the list of Voucher Types. Under the Printing section, at the option, *Print Formal Receipt after Entry*, set *Yes* to activate Formal Receipt Printing option for Receipt Voucher.

Money Receipt (*Formal Receipt*) in Print (F-4A):

- *Voucher Number* is printed at '*No*'
- *Voucher Date* is printed at '*Dated*'
- *Payer's Name* (from whom the money is received) is printed after the word '*Received with thanks from*'
- *Mode of payment* (Cash / Bank Account) is printed after the word '*By*'
- *Net Amount received* is printed in words after the words '*The sum of*' & '*Indian Rupees*' (Base Currency Forma Name as set F-2A/02-02).
- *Voucher Narration* is printed after the word '*Remarks*'
- *Net Amount* is printed in figures with the Base Currency Symbol (₹)

No.: 3 Dated 31-Mar-2010

RECEIPT

Received with thanks from : **Bikash Ganguly**

The sum of : **Indian Rupees Eighteen Thousand Only**

By : **Cash**

Remarks : **Tuition FeesReceived for Tally ERP 9 Advanced Course 2010-11 session**

₹ 18,000.00/- Authorised Signatory

F-4A: Formal Receipt (Money Receipt)

09.02 Configuration option for Formal Receipts

Enter the following specific options to print Formal Receipt (money receipt given to the payer). Other options are applicable as specified for Receipt Voucher (F-2A)

- **Receipt Height:** At *Height of Receipt,* enter the height of the voucher (print area in inches including top & bottom margin). Default value is 6 (inches)

- **Receipt Width:** At *Width of Receipt*, enter the width of the voucher (print area in inches including left & right top & bottom margin). Default value is 5 (inches)
- **Top Margin:** At *Space to leave at top,* enter the value of top margin (in inches). Default value (.25 inch)
- **Voucher Narration:** At *Print Narration*, set *Yes* (default value) to print Voucher common Narration. Set *No* to omit Voucher Common narration (it may sometimes be useful when separate ledger narration is printed)
- **Ledger Narration:** At *Print Narration for each entry*,set *Yes* (default value) to print separate Ledger Narration for each ledger account transacted. Set *No* to omit separate ledger narration (it may sometimes be useful when Common Narration is printed).

10 Payment Advice

Payment advice is a letter that is sent to the Payee while enclosing the cheque. It contains a standard Text, which may be modified through the Payment Advice Configuration

10.01 Payment Advice Text Set Up

At *Voucher Printing Configuration Menu* (F-1), select *Payment Advice Configuration* to get *Payment Advice Configuration* screen (F-4B).

Payment Advice Configuration

Payment Advice Salute : The cheque per details below is enclosed

Payment Advice Acknowledgement : Kindly acknowledge the receipt.

F-4B: Payment Advice Standard Text set up

At *Payment Advice Configuration* screen (F-4B), you set the text of the Payment Advice letter as follows. The text, as entered here is printed in Payment Advice. You may modify the Text later on, at any time.

- **Salutation Text**: At *Payment Advice Salute*, enter the Text that is printed in the first line (after address etc) *before* Payment details. A standard text (*Please find below the Payment details*) is shown, which you may modify.
- **Acknowledgement Text**: At *Payment Advice Acknowledgement*, enter the Text that is printed after the Payment details A standard text (*Kindly Acknowledge the Receipt*) is shown, which you may modify (F-4B).

The Payment advice details (the voucher data) are printed between these two texts specified (F-5B)

10.02 Payment Advice Printing Options

At Payment Voucher Printing screen (F-5A), you get following additional options for Payment Advice printing (F-5B). Set the options:

- **Advice Print:** At *Print Payment Advice,* set *Yes* to Print Payment Advice after printing Payment Voucher.
- **Advice Date:** At *Payment Advice Date*, enter the Payment Advice Date in Payment Voucher.
- **Due Date:** At *Print Due Date,* set *Yes/No* to print / omit due Date in Payment Voucher.
- **IT PAN:** At *Print Company's PAN/IT Number,* set *Yes* to Print Company's PAN/ IT Number in Payment Advice

Report Titles

Payment Voucher

Print Payment Advice : Yes
Payment Advice Date : 2-May-2011
Print Due Date ? Yes
Print Company's PAN/IT Number ? Yes

F-5A: Payment Advice Printing Screen

10.03 Contents of Payment Advice

Contents of Payment Advice (F-5B) are described below:

- The Voucher Number is printed at No
- Payment Advice Date is printed at 'Date'
- Payee's Name (whom the money is paid to, the First Ledger Account of the voucher) is printed
- The ledger Accounts and the amount are printed. Deduction Accounts are shown after the word 'Less' and the amount is shown in negative.
- The Net Amount in figures is printed with the Word 'Net Amount'. The net Amount in words is not printed.
- The Bank details (details of cheques) are printed in a Table

Payment Advice

M/s Salary Date : 2-May-2011

Dear Sir/Madam,

Please find below the payment details.

Particulars	Amount
Salary	6,000.00
Overtime	1,500.00
Less : P. Tax	(-)45.00
Less : I. Tax	(-)120.00
Nett Amount	7,335.00

Payment Detail(s)				
Mode of Payment	Bank Name	Instrument No.	Instrument Date	Amount
Cheque	HDFC Bank	25	2-May-2011	7,335.00
			Total	7,335.00

Kindly acknowledge the receipt.

Thanking You

Authorised Signatory Rver's Signature

F-5B: Payment Advice

11 Printing Company logo on Voucher / Invoice

You may print Company Logo in Voucher / Invoice as described at Reports Printing (§07/02-03). The Company Logo is printed at the top left of the Voucher. To do that, you must load the image file (in.bmp or.jpeg format) and set options for printing Company Logo.

At Receipt voucher printing configuration option (F-2A), Set *Yes* at *Print Company Logo* to print the Logo in the Voucher / Invoice (else set *No*). The default Location of Company Logo as set is carried as default, which you may change at the time of printing (to print different logo).

12 Multi Voucher Printing

At Multi Account printing Menu (F-2A/01-05), select *Multi Voucher printing* to get *Multi Account Voucher Printing* screen (F-7A)

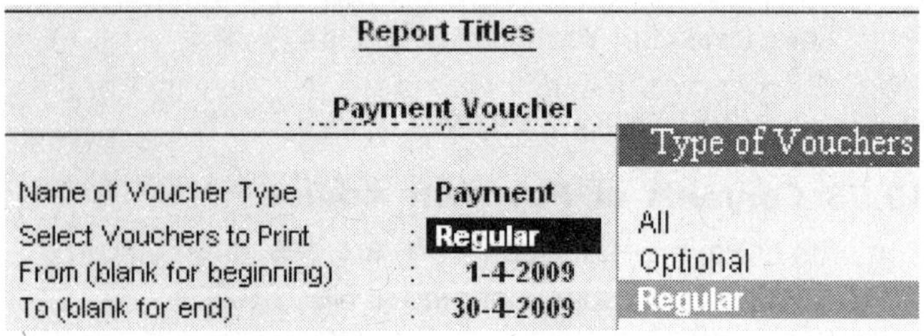

F-7A: Multi Account Voucher Printing screen

At *Multi Account Voucher Printing* screen (F-7A), set as follows:

- **Voucher Type Name:** At *Name of Voucher Type,* select the Voucher Type from the list of Voucher Types
- **Voucher Selection:**At *Select Vouchers to print*, select as follows:
  - o **All**: To Print *Regular* as well as *Optional* Vouchers of the selected voucher type
  - o **Optional**: To Print only *Optional* Vouchers of the selected voucher type
  - o **Regular**: To Print only Regular Vouchers of the selected voucher type
- **Period Start Date**: At *From,* enter the Voucher Date from which the voucher to be printed (leave blank to print from the first voucher of the current period
- **Period End Date**: At *To*: enter the Voucher Date upto which the voucher to be printed (leave blank to upto the last voucher of the current period)

Click *Yes* to print the vouchers. All the voucher of the specified type for the specified period will be printed.

FAQ: Frequently Asked Questions

FAQ-1: The default size of Receipt / Payment / Contra / Journal Voucher is shorter (in width / height) than the A4 Stationery I use. So, a lot of blank space is wasted. Moreover, vouchers containing more data sometimes takes 2 pages. How I can set the page dimension to get the full page space for the voucher.

Ans: You can adjust the dimension and set the default at the Printing Configuration through Voucher Printing Configuration options

You may find that there is ample blank space in the default voucher (if there is normally one or two entries in voucher), but reducing the height may cause the voucher to spill over 2 pages. Reducing the height, may cause dis-alignment of the header and the data in the columns. So, check and try the dimension that suits you most.

If you cannot reduce the stationary size of a voucher (so you will use a full page of standard stationery for each voucher, leaving a lot of unutilised space in the voucher stationery. In such case it will be prudent to change the dimension so that it uses the full stationary size. The added advantage that longer voucher with more entries even will be accommodated in one page, due to increased print area.

To set the maximum size of the voucher, at Gateway, click *F12:Configure >Printing* to get Voucher Printing Configuration Menu. Now select the Voucher type from the menu, and set the voucher dimension (in inches) for Height & Width, as follows:

- Height of Voucher (in inches): 0
- Width of Voucher (in inches): 0

When you print the voucher, you will find that the contents are spread over the occupying the full page size. The voucher looks standard and balanced. Due to availability of more space, longer voucher (with more entries, Journal Voucher, Receipt & Payment Voucher with Bank details etc, will now be accommodated in one page, instead of spilling over to 2 pages)

FAQ-2: How to print a money Receipt just on entering a Receipt Voucher

Ans: Activate the Money Receipt / Payee Name option: At gateway, select *Accounts Info>Voucher Type >Alter* and then select Receipt from the list of Voucher Types to get the Voucher Type. Now set *Yes* at *Print Formal receipt after Saving* to activate the Money Receipt printing option (§09).

Receipt Voucher / Money Receipt Printing: To print the current Receipt Voucher / Money Receipt, At Voucher Entry screen, Click P:Print button (or press Alt + P) to get the Receipt Voucher printing screen.

Printing of Receipt Voucher / Money receipt: Now you will see the Title of the Voucher and the prompt *Print Yes / No?* to print Receipt Voucher, or Money Receipt or both, as desired, in the following way:

- **Receipt Voucher**: First you get *Receipt Voucher* at the *Voucher Title,* to print the *Receipt Voucher.* Click *Yes* (or Type Y) to print the Receipt Voucher, else Click *No* (or Type N) to skip Receipt Voucher printing (you may not print Receipt Voucher if you have written a manual Receipt Voucher, as normally done)

- **Money Receipt**: Next you get *Receipt* at the *Voucher Title*, to print the *Money Receipt.* Click *Yes* (or Type Y) to print the Money Receipt Voucher (normally Money Receipt is printed to hand it over to the payer of the money, as evidence of having received the money), else Click *No* (or Type N) to skip Money Receipt printing (you may not print Money Receipt if you have written a manual Receipt Voucher, in special pre numbered book, as followed by some organisations)

At the bottom of the Receipt Voucher / Money Receipt, a label Authorised Signatory appears where the Authorised Officer may sign the Receipt Voucher

If the money is received through Cheque / DD, a note *'Subject to Realisation'* appears to indicate that the receipt is valid only after the instrument received is encashed (it is a standard practice to put such note to defend / protect the receiver, in case of dishonor of the instrument against which the Money Receipt is issued)

FAQ-3: How to print a Payment Advice immediately on creation of Payment Voucher

Ans: Payment Advice Configuration: At Gateway Click F12:Configure and select Printing >Payment Advice Configuration to get the payment Advice Configuration screen (F-4B). Set up the Text for:

- **Salutation Text**: At *Payment Advice Salute*, enter the standard text that will appear at the first paragraph before the Payment details (§10.01)

Acknowledgement Text: At *Payment Advice Acknowledgement*, enter the standard text that will appear at the end after the Payment details.

You may change the default texts appearing in these two fields. One set up, these configuration are

used in Printing of all subsequent Payment Advices, until you change them.

Printing of Payment Voucher / Advice: After entry of Voucher, Click P:Print button (or press Alt + P). and set the Printing options as follows (§10.2):

- **Print Payment Advice:** Set Yes to Print Payment Advice after printing of Payment Voucher,
- **Payment Advice Date:** Enter the Payment Advice Date (the Voucher Date is carried, which you may change)
- **Print Due Date:** Set Yes/No to print Due Date
- **Print Company's PAN/IT Number:** Set Yes to Print Company's PAN/ IT Number

When the Payee's representative personally comes to collect the Payment, normally 2 copies of Payment Advice is printed.

- One copy is handed over to the Payee as record of payment made.
- The second copy is signed by payee and retained by the Payer as evidence of having received the payment by the Payee.

So, you can either choose to print Payment Voucher or Payment Advice (which also contains all details of Payment Voucher, except the Voucher Number) in one shot. To print both, you have to print in 2 steps. First, print the Payment Voucher, and next the Payment Advice, by changing the Print options.

Account Voucher Lists 02-16

01 Account Voucher Lists

Account Voucher List refers to following reports that show the voucher data, in various formats. Account Voucher lists are first level Accounts Reports showing individual voucher transactions.

- Voucher Register
    - Day Book
    - Group Voucher
    - Ledger Voucher

There is great deal of similarity in all these reports. The Report Configuration options are quite similar in these reports. A voucher may be selected from any of such report to get the voucher in Modification (Alteration) mode and carry out various operations on the selected voucher

02 Operations at Account Vouchers Lists

There are two ways to reach a voucher in Voucher Lists.

- Drill down Through Display
- Get any of the Voucher List as Listed above

In Voucher Lists, you get a set of buttons (F-1) at the bottom of the screen, to perform various operations of voucher.

At the Voucher List screen, select the voucher (place cursor on the voucher and click) and then click the respective button at the bottom button bar (F-1) to perform the respective operation, as described below:

- **A: Add Voucher (to create a new Voucher):** To create a new voucher from the existing screen press Alt+A on the selected voucher. A blank voucher entry screen of the same voucher type (of the selected voucher) appears to create a new voucher. Useful to directly create a new voucher from the report, without leaving the current screen.
- **<Enter>: Alter (to Modify a Voucher)**: Place the cursor on the desired record and press <enter> to get the voucher in alteration mode and change any data in the voucher in the same way as you enter data in voucher.
    - o **D:Delete (to Delete Voucher)**: To physically de ete a voucher. On Deletion of a voucher, the voucher number of all subsequent vouchers may get changed (in case of auto numbered voucher)

      Press Alt+D, and click *Yes* at *Delete? Yes or No* to confirm Deletion.
    - o **X:Cancel (to Cancel Voucher)**: To nullify the voucher (but the cancelled voucher physically remains with zero values). So, the voucher numbers do not change. The cancelled voucher has no impact in accounts. From audit principles, it is a good policy to cancel a voucher instead of deleting. Cancellation does not disturb the numbering scheme of any voucher.

      Press *Alt+X,* and click *Yes* at *Cancel? Yes or No* to confirm Cancellation. Once Cancelled, you cannot Restore the Cancelled voucher (but the Cancelled voucher may be Deleted). The Cancelled Voucher is shown in Voucher list (like Day Book), as *Cancelled* without any amount figure

The following toggle butons are used to select/unselect the desired voucher(s) to perform the above operations

- **Space (press spacebar): Select (to select a voucher):** To select a voucher, move the cursor over the desired voucher and press <space bar>. The voucher gets selected (and highlighted – colour changes)
- **Space (press Ctrl+spacebar): Select All (to select all vouchers of the report):** To select all vouchers in the report, move the cursor to the record and press Ctrl + <space bar>. All the vouchers get selected (and highlighted colour changes)

The following buttons are used to perform on selected Voucher

- **2: Duplicate (to Duplicate a voucher):** To create another voucher copying from a selected voucher, press Alt+2. This is useful when you like to create another similar type of voucher. Now change the desired data (e.g, Date, Amount, Narration etc) of the duplicated voucher and save it as a new voucher. This eliminates entry of all data of the voucher as a substantial portion of data carried from the previous voucher is re-used.
- **I: Insert Voucher (to Insert a Voucher at specific place):** To create a new voucher at a specific position,

F-1: Bottom Button Bar at various Account Voucher Lists

press Alt+I to insert a voucher at a specific position. Insertion of Voucher is useful for manual numbered (or unnumbered) voucher. In auto numbered voucher, the voucher number is controlled by voucher date.

- **R: Remove Line (to remove a line):** To remove the line in the display screen (to hide the line), place the cursor on the record and press *Alt+R*. The record is removed from the Report (but no data gets deleted). Thus you may get an edited report on screen, deleting some lines.
- **U: Restore (to restore the removed line)**: To Restore (bring back) all the removed lines, press Alt+U. The removed line is restored.
- **U: Restore All (to restore all the removed line)**: Press *Ctrl+U* To Restore (bring back) the removed lines, press *Ctrl+U*. All the removed lines are restored.

Q (to quit from the screen): Press *Ctrl+ Q* to exit from the screen.

Buttons at Report Configuration: The following Table shows the buttons available at the respective reports Account Vouchers List Display screen:

Additional Buttons at Button Bar

In case of Ledger Voucher, some additional buttons appear according to the Ledger Account selected, as follows:

- **Bank Accounts:**
  - o F5: Reconcile: To reconcile the entries of the Bank for Bank Reconciliation
  - o F6: Multi Ch. Print: To get Cheque Printing Report to facilitate Multiple Cheques printing in one shot.
  - o F6: Deposit Slip Print: To print deposit slips of the deposits made into the bank account
  - o C: Contact: To show the contact details of the selected Bank account

Button	Description	Voucher Register	Day Book	Group Voucher	Ledger Voucher
F1: Detailed / Condensed	To show the lowest level details	✓		✓	✓
F4:Chg Vch	To select a Voucher Type (or select All Voucher Types)	✓		✓	
F5: Columnar	To define columns to create a columnar report	✓			
F6: Extract	To get Group / Ledger wise summary of transactions	✓			
F4:Group	To select a an Account Group			✓	
F6: Monthly	To get monthly break up for the selected period			✓	
F7:Summary/ Voucher	To get Ledger wise summary / Voucher wise detail Report			✓	
F4:Ledger	To select a Ledger Account				✓
F6: Dly Brk-up	To get daily totals of the ledger				✓
F7: Monthly	To get monthly totals of the ledger				✓
F8: Columnar	To define columns to create a columnar report				✓
C: Contact	To show Contact details of the selected Personal Ledger account				✓

03 Buttons at Account Vouchers Lists

The vertical button bar also contains buttons for some tasks. The following table shows a compact summary of buttons in all these reports.

Date, Current Period & Report Period buttons

- At Gateway of Tally, you get *F2:Period* (Alt+F2) button to set the Current Period (F2 for Date)
- In Reports, you normally get *F2:Period* button to set the Report Period for the current Report. In some reports, where both Date & Period buttons are available (like Sales / Purchase Register), you get *F2:Date* & *F2:Period* buttons

- **Debtor / Creditor Ledger**
  - o C: Contact: To show the contact details of the selected Party account
  - o B: Billwise: To get Ledger Voucher Outstanding report with Bill details
- **Sales Register** (Voucher Register of Sales Voucher)
  - o **F7**: Show Profit / Hide Profit: To show additional columns for Gross profit in respect of each Sales voucher (F-3D)

04 Account Voucher Lists Configuration

The options of Configuration screen of various Accounts Voucher Lists are shown in the following Table:

Option	Description	Voucher Register	Day Book	Group Voucher	Ledger Voucher
Show Extract of Register	Group / Ledgerwise Summary of vouchers	✓			
Show Columnar Register	Define Columns to get Columnar Register	✓			
Format	To set condensed / detailed format	✓	✓	✓	✓
Show Narrations also	To show /hide voucher Narrations	✓	✓	✓	✓
Show Bank details also	To show cheque Particulars	✓	✓		✓
Show Entered / Altered by	To show user name of voucher writer	✓	✓	✓	✓
Select Vouchers to Show	Select Debit / Credit / All Vouchers		✓	✓	✓
Show All Ledger Details	To show all Ledgers in Detail Format			✓	
Include Opening Balance				✓	✓
Show Running Balance	To show balance against each entry				✓

05 Voucher Register

Voucher Register normally shows a list of a specific type of voucher for a period (F- 2A)

Select *Display > Account Books* (F-2B/01-05) and then select the Register Type (like *Journal Register* (F-4A/01-05, F-4B/01-05) *)* to get the monthly breakup of vouchers (F-4B/ 02-19). Drill down through a month to get the Voucher Register for the selected month. Press *F2: Period* and select the period to get the Voucher Register for the selected period.

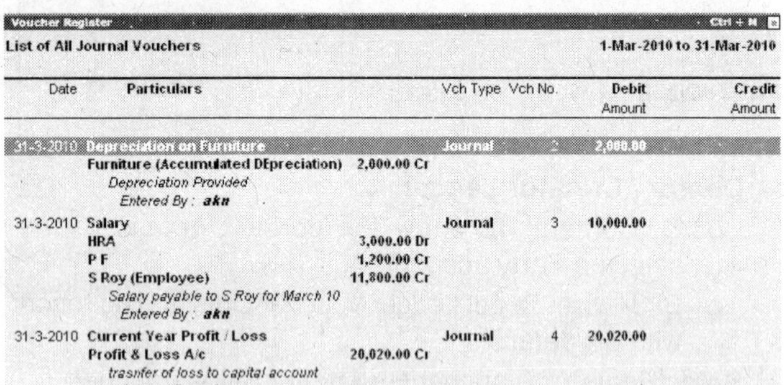

F- 2A: Voucher Register

Buttons at Voucher Register

At Voucher Register, you may set options through following buttons (F-3C):

- ***F1: Detailed/ Condensed**: To* toggle between *Detailed* & Condensed Voucher Register
- ***F4:Chg Vch***: To select the Voucher Type to get Voucher Register for the selected Voucher Type (or select *All Items* to show all Types of Accounts Vouchers)
- ***F5: Columnar*** to define columns to create a columnar report (§02/02-18)
- ***F6: Extract /Vouchers:*** To toggle between Group / Ledger wise summary (*Extract*) of transactions (F-3A) / List of Vouchers (*Vouchers: F-2A*)

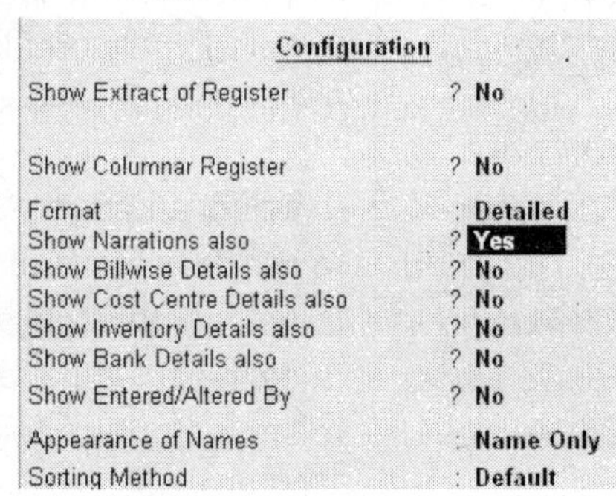

F-2B: Voucher Register Configuration

In case of Sales Voucher Register: *F7: Show Profit / Hide Profit* (F-3D) to get an additional column. Click *F7:Show Profit / Hide Profit* toggle button (and additional option *Show Gross Profit Estimates* in Configuration screen) to show additional columns for Gross Profit / Loss for each Sales Voucher (F-1D/03-04)

Voucher Register Configuration

At Voucher List Screen (F-2A). Click *F12: Configure* to get the *Voucher Register Configuration* screen (F-2B).

At *Voucher Register Configuration* screen (F-2B), set the options as desired to Configure the report (only the options related to Basic Accounts are explained here. Other options are explained at relevant place)

- **Account Summary / Voucher List:** At *Extract of Register* (or click *F6: Extract/ Summary* toggle button), type:

- o *Yes* to get the Account Group / Ledger wise summary (Extract) of the transactions for the specified period (F-3A).
- o *No* to get the Voucher Lists (F-2B)

- **Columnar Register Format**: At *Show Columnar Register* (or click F5: Columnar), type:
  - o *Yes* to get the Column specification screen to set the Columnar Report (§02/02-18)
  - o *No* to get Voucher Register (F-2A)
- **Format**: At Format:
  - o Select *Condensed* to get only the top level figures (Account Group / Ledger).
  - o Select *Detailed* to get the lowest level details
- **Voucher Narration**: At *Show Narration also*, type:
  - o *Yes* to show the voucher Narration also for each voucher.
  - o No to omit voucher Narration.
- **Bank Details**: At *Show Bank details also*, type
  - o *Yes* to show the Bank Details (Payee, Bank etc)
  - o *No* to omit voucher Bank details.
- **User Name:** At *Show Altered / Entered By*, type:
  - o Yes to show the name of the user who created / last modified the voucher (F-2A)
  - o No. User Name is NOT shown

Voucher Register | ABC Academy 9-10 | Ctrl + M

Extract of All Journal Vouchers | 1-Mar-2010 to 31-Mar-2010

Particulars	Debit Amount	Credit Amount
Capital Account	**20,020.00**	
Current Year Profit / Loss	*20,020.00*	
Current Liabilities		**13,000.00**
Sundry Creditors		11,800.00
S Roy (Employee)		*11,800.00*
P F		*1,200.00*
Fixed Assets		**2,000.00**
Furniture		2,000.00
Furniture (Accumulated DEpreciation)		*2,000.00*
Indirect Expenses	**20,400.00**	
Depreciation	2,000.00	
Depreciation on Furniture	*2,000.00*	
Interest	5,400.00	
Interest on Term Loan	*4,500.00*	
Interest on Unsecured Loan	*900.00*	
HRA	*3,000.00*	
Salary	*10,000.00*	
Loans (Liability)		**5,400.00**
Secured Loans		4,500.00
ICICI Term Loan		*4,500.00*
		3 more ...
	40,420.00	**40,420.00**

F-3A: Voucher Register Extract

Voucher Register Extract

Voucher Register Extract (F-3A) is Accountwise Summary of Vouchers. This report is useful to get the Transaction Summary for a specified Account voucher type (or all Accounts voucher types), for a specified period.

Configuration

Show Extract of Register	? **Yes**
Show Inventory-wise Extract	? **No**
Format	: **Detailed**
Appearance of Names	: **Name Only**

F-3B: Voucher Extract Configuration

F1: Condensed
F2: Date
F2: Period
F3: Company
F4: Chg Vch
F5: Columnar
F6: Extract

F-3C: Buttons at Voucher Regsiter

F1: Detailed
F2: Date
F2: Period
F3: Company
F4: Chg Vch
F5: Columnar
F6: Extract
F7: Show Profit

F-3D: Buttons at Voucher Regsiter of Sales Voucher

To get Voucher Register Extract (F-3A):

- At Voucher Register Display screen (F-2A), Click *F6:Extract* toggle button (F-3C)
- At Voucher Register Configuration (F-3B), set *Yes* at the option *Show Extract of Register*

06 Day Book

While Voucher Register normally shows list of specific Vouchers, Day Book normally shows list of all types of Vouchers. Select *Display > Day Book to get the list of all vouchers for the Current Date. Click F2:Period and set the Period to get the Day Book for the desired period (F-4A)*

Buttons at Day Book Display

The following buttons are shown at Day Book

- ***F1: Detailed/ Condensed:*** *To* toggle between Detailed & Condensed Voucher Register
- ***F4:Chg Vch:*** To select the Voucher Type to get Voucher Register for the selected Voucher Type (or select All Items to show all Types of Accounts Vouchers)

Day Book Display Configuration

At Day Book screen (F-4A), click *F12: Configuration* to get Day Book Configuration screen (F-4B). Set the options as follows:

- **Format**: At Format:
  - o Select *Condensed* to get only the top level figures (Account Group / Ledger).
  - o Select *Detailed* to get the lowest level details
- **Voucher Narration**: At *Show Narration also*, type:
  - o *Yes* to show the voucher Narration also for each voucher.

- o No to omit voucher Narration.
- **Bank Details**: At *Show Bank details also*, type
  - o *Yes* to show the Bank Details (Payee, Bank etc)
  - o *No* to omit voucher Bank details.
- **Voucher Nature**: At *Select Vouchers to Show*, Select:
  - o **All Vouchers:** To show al Vouchers
  - o **Debit Entries only:** To Show Vouchers having Debit Entries only
  - o **Credit Entries only:** To Show Vouchers having Credit Entries only
- **User Name:** At *Show Altered / Entered By*, type:
  - o Yes to show the name of the user who created / last modified the voucher (F-2A)
  - o No. User Name is NOT shown

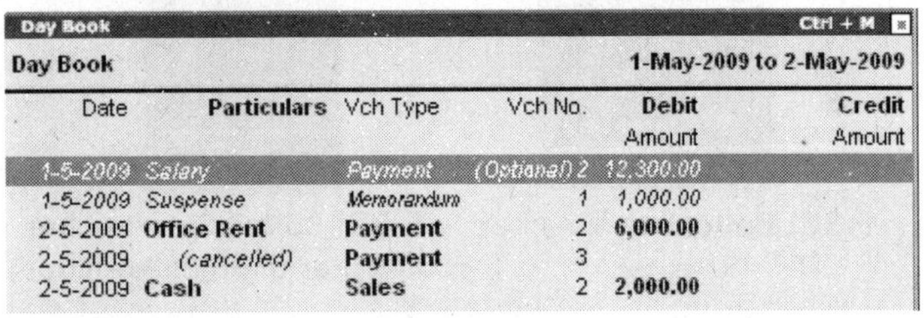

F-4A: Day Book

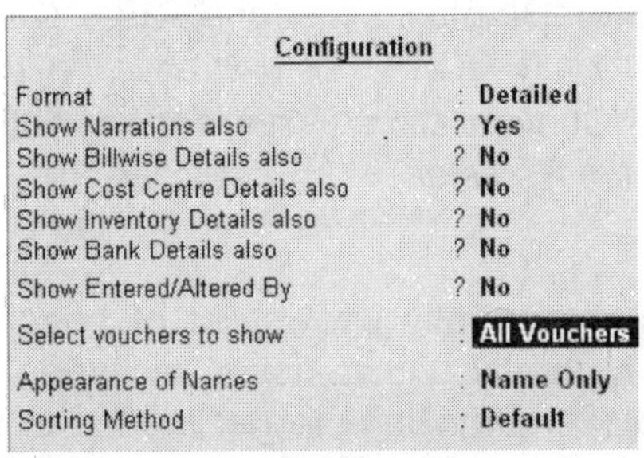

F-4B: Day Book Configuration

F-4C: Voucher Types List

06.01 Multi Account Day Book

You may print Day Books through Multi Account Printing option. This is more convenient method to get hard copy reports (printed on paper). At *GoT> Tally > Multi-Account Printing,* select *Day Book* to get *Multi Account Day Book Printing* screen (F-5B). At Print *Yes/ No* option:

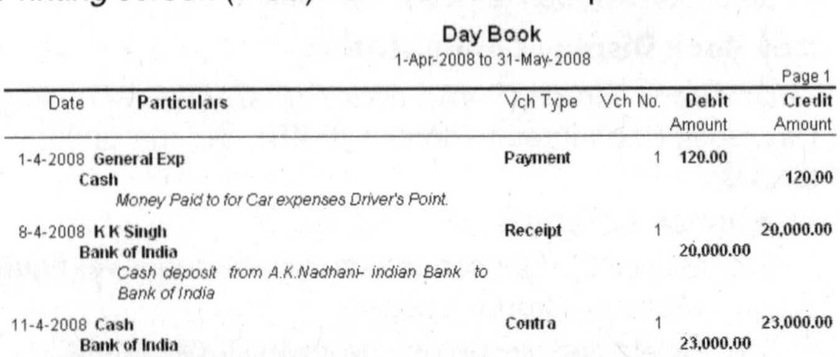

F-5A: Multi Account Day Book

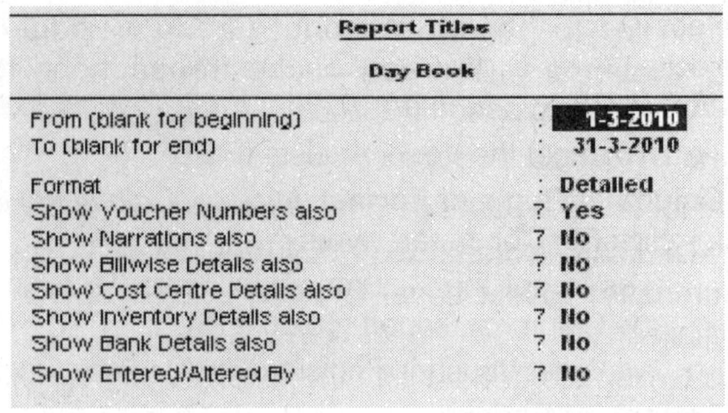

F-5B: Multi Account Day Book Printing

- Type *Yes* at to print the Day Book as per current options set, as shown in the screen (F-5B)
- Type *No* to change the Report Period and other Configuration options at the Printing screen (F-5B). Then type Y to print the Day Book (F-5A) as per changed Configuration options.

07 Group Vouchers List

Group Vouchers List (F-6A) shows the list of Vouchers for a selected Account Group.

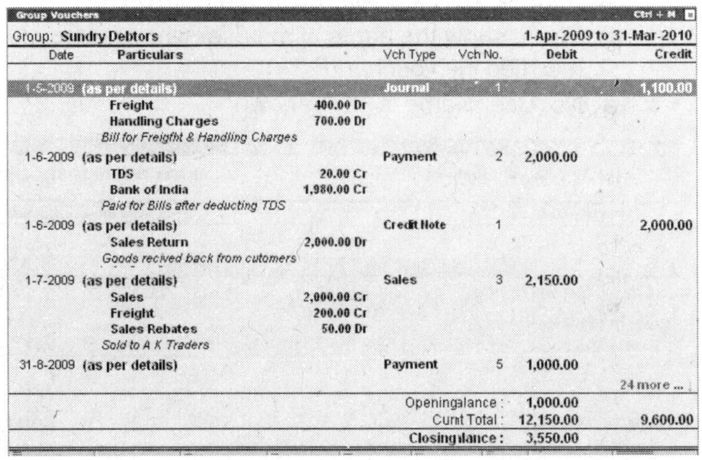

F-6A: Group Vouchers List

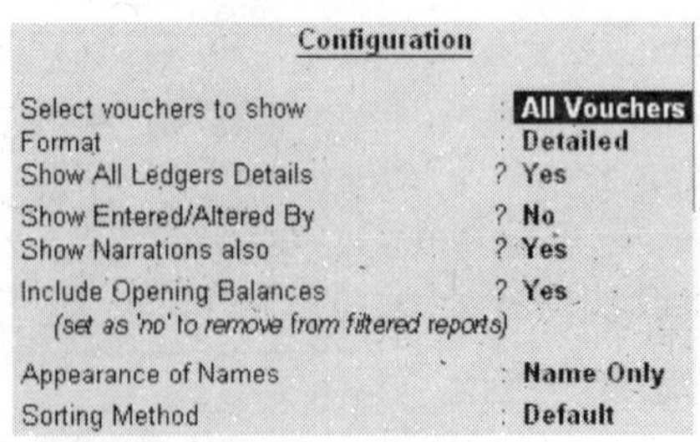

F-6B: Group Vouchers List Configuration

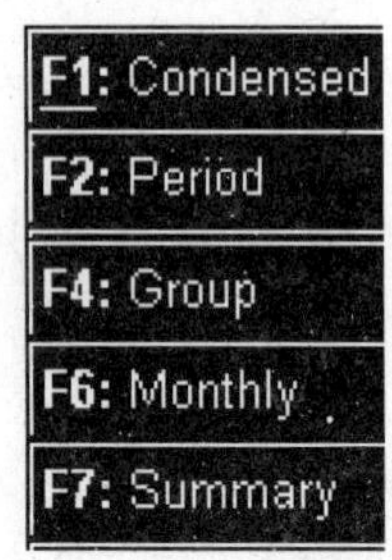

F-6C: Buttons at Group Vouchers List

You may get this report in any of the following ways:

- Select *Display > Account Books > Group Vouchers* and select the Account Group to get the list of all Vouchers (for the current period) relating to the selected Account Group.

- Select *Display > Account Books > Group Summary.* Select a Group *to get Group Summary.* Click *F7: Voucher* button at *Group Summary* to get *Group Voucher* List.

Buttons at Group Voucher List

You get following Buttons (F-6C) at Group Voucher Report

- **F1: Detailed / Condensed**: To get Top Level Groups only (Summary) / Next Level Group / Ledger details also (Detailed)
- **F4: Group**: To get the list of Account Group to select a Group for which you like to get Group Voucher Report.
- **F6: Monthly**: To get Monthly Summary of Group Vouchers
- **F7: Summary**: To get Group Summary Report

Group Voucher List Configuration

At Group Voucher list (F-6A), click *F12: Configuration* to get Group Voucher Configuration screen (F-6B) to set the option as follows:

- **Voucher Nature**: At *Select Vouchers to Show,* Select:
  - o **All Vouchers:** To show al Vouchers
  - o **Debit Entries only:** To Show Vouchers having Debit Entries only
  - o **Credit Entries only:** To Show Vouchers having Credit Entries only
- **Format**: At Format:
  - o Select *Condensed* to get only the top level figures (Account Group / Ledger).
  - o Select *Detailed* to get the lowest level details
- **Ledger Details**: If *Details* is selected, at the above option, you get another option *Show All Ledger Details.* At *Show All Ledger Details*, type:
  - o Yes to get the details of each ledger account of the voucher.
  - o No, to show the all ledger accounts except the ledger account of the selected Group.
- **Voucher Narration**: At *Show Narration also*, type:
  - o *Yes* to show the voucher Narration also for each voucher.
  - o No to omit voucher Narration.
- **Opening Balance:** At *Include Opening Balances*, type:
  - o *Yes* to show Opening Balances also in the Report
  - o *No* to omit the Opening Balance

08 Ledger Vouchers List

Ledger Vouchers List (F-7A) shows the transaction for the selected Account Ledger:

You get this report from:

- Ledger [*Display > Account Books > Ledger > Ledger Account*].
- Ledger Monthly Summary
  - o *Display > Account Books > Group Summary > Account Group > Ledger Account.* Select a Month.
  - o *Display > Account Books > Cash / Bank Book -> Account Group -> Ledger Account.*

  Select a Month. Click *F2:Period* to set the Report period

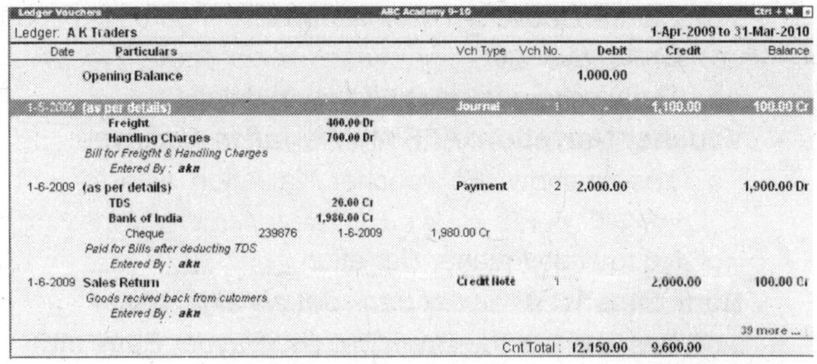

F-7A: Ledger Voucher List

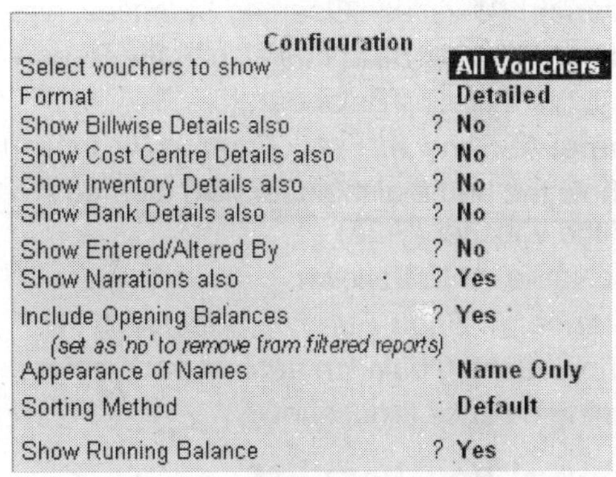

F-7B: Ledger Voucher List Configuration

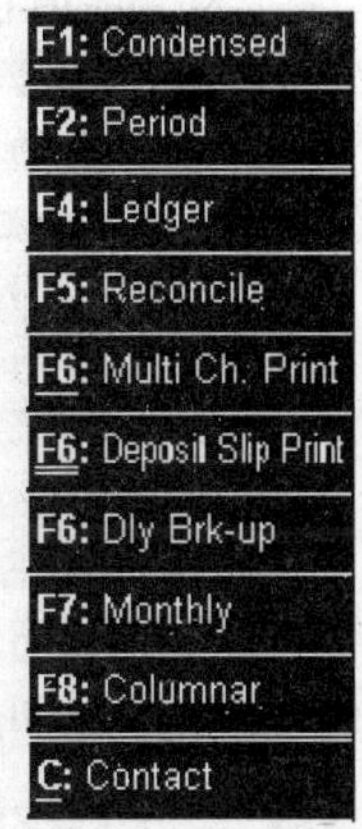

F-7C: Buttons

Buttons at Ledger Voucher List

The following buttons are available at Ledger Voucher list (F-7C)

- **F4: Ledger**: To select another Ledger Account
- **F6: Daily Break up**: To get Daly summary & balance
- **F7: Monthly:** To show monthly break up figures
- **F8: Columnar**: To specify column definition to get Columnar Register
- **C: Contact:** To show the Contact details of the ledger account

Apart from the above the following additional buttons related to Banking Transactions are available in case of Bank Ledger Account (F-7C)

- **F5: Reconcile**: To tag cleared cheques for Bank Reconciliation
- **F6: Mult Ch. Print**: To print cheques
- **F6: Deposit Slip Print**: To print Deposit Slips

Ledger Voucher List Configuration

At Ledger Voucher List (F-7A), click *F12: Configuration* to get Ledger Configuration screen (F-7B) to set the options.

- **Voucher Nature**: At *Select Vouchers to Show,* Select:
  - o **All Vouchers:** To show al Vouchers
  - o **Debit Entries only:** To Show Vouchers having Debit Entries only

- o **Credit Entries only:** To Show Vouchers having Credit Entries only
- **Format**: At Format, Select
  - o *Condensed* to get only the top level figures (Account Group / Ledger).
  - o *Detailed* to get the lowest level details
- **Voucher Narration**: At *Show Narration also*, type:
  - o *Yes* to show the voucher Narration also for each voucher.
  - o No to omit voucher Narration.
- **Bank Details**: At *Show Bank details also*, type
  - o *Yes* to show the Bank Details (Payee, Bank etc)
  - o *No* to omit voucher Bank details.
- **Opening Balance:** At *Include Opening Balances*, type:
  - o *Yes* to show Opening Balances also in the Report
  - o *No* to omit the Opening Balance
  - **User Name:** At *Show Altered / Entered By*, type:
  - o Yes to show the name of the user who created / last modified the voucher (F-2A)
  - o No. User Name is NOT shown
- **Running Balance**: At *Show Running Balance*, type:
  - o Yes to show running balance against each entry
  - o No. Running balance is not shown

09 Provisional Vouchers list

For list of Provisional voucher which has not yet been regularized, select *Display >Exception* Report to get *Exception Reports* Menu (F-8). At *Exception Reports* Menu (F-8):

- **Memorandum Voucher List**: Select *Memorandum Voucher* to get Memorandum Voucher List (F-9A)
- **Optional Voucher List**: Select *Optional Voucher* to get Memorandum Voucher List (F-9B)
- **Post Dated Voucher List**: Select *Post Dated Voucher* to get Post Dated Voucher List (F-9C)

First you get the Monthly statement of Number of Vouchers. Select the month and set the Period to get the Voucher Register for the specified period.

The contents & configuration options (F-2B) and buttons (F-3C) are similar to Voucher Register discussed earlier.

Gateway of Tally ....
Display Menu ....

Exception Reports

Negative Ledgers

OveRdue Receivables
Overdue Payables

Memorandum Vouchers
REversing Journals
Optional Vouchers
PoSt-Dated Vouchers

E-MAil IDs

Quit

F-8: Exception Reports Menu

Voucher Register Ctrl + M

List of All Memorandum Vouchers 1-Apr-2009 to 1-Feb-2010

Date	Particulars		Vch Type	Vch No.	Debit Amount	Credit Amount
1-5-2009	Suspense		Memorandum	1	1,000.00	
	Cash	1,000.00 Cr				
	Paid to Shakeel for Misc Payments / Expenses					
1-2-2010	Suspense		Memorandum	2	2,100.00	
	Cash	2,100.00 Cr				
	given to abc for some petty expenses					

F-9A: Memeorandium Voucher List

Voucher Register Ctrl + M

List of All Optional Vouchers 1-Apr-2009 to 31-Mar-2010

Date	Particulars	Vch Type	Vch No.	Debit Amount	Credit Amount
1-5-2009	Salary	Payment	2	12,300.00	
1-6-2009	Cash	Contra	2		500.00
1-6-2009	Aakash & Co	Payment	7	1,000.00	
1-3-2010	A K Traders	Payment	9	2,000.00	
31-3-2010	Accrued Interest	Journal	6	2,000.00	

F-9B: Optional Voucher List

Voucher Register Ctrl + M

List of All Post Dated Vouchers 1-Apr-2009 to 31-Mar-2010

Date	Particulars		Vch Type	Vch No.	Debit Amount	Credit Amount
1-6-2009	A K Traders		Payment	4	2,000.00	
	TDS	20.00 Cr				
	HDFC Bank	1,980.00 Cr				

F-9C: Post Dated Voucher List

FAQ: Frequently Asked Questions

FAQ-1: I prepare Payment Voucher for payment of salary to Staff. The voucher details are almost similar for each Month. How can enter the voucher quickly and in consistent way

Ans: Having created the first voucher, next time in each month, you can conveniently duplicate the voucher as explained below:

Select *Display > Day Book* and then set the period from the beginning of the year till the current date upto which you like to enter the voucher (e.g 1-4-2012 to 2-5-2012). Click *F4:Chg Vch* and select payment Voucher from the list to show all the Payment Vouchers for the selected period.

Now place the cursor on the last Payment Voucher for Salary and click on *2:Duplicate* button (or press Alt+2) at the bottom button bar. You get a voucher Duplication screen carrying the selected voucher to be duplicated. Now change the voucher Date and any other data (like Amount, a small part of Voucher Narration etc) as required. As most of the data remain same, you will need to modify only a few data. The voucher is now ready for saving (without entering everything afresh). The Narration pattern also becomes standard (as it is carried from previous voucher)

Click *A;Accept* (or press Alt + A) at the duplicate voucher entry screen. The new voucher is created and saved as if you have entered it as new voucher

The advantage of duplicating a voucher (than creating a new one from an existing similar voucher) are:

- You don't have to enter all data in the voucher. Just modify a few data only (Voucher Date, Amount, Narration etc), but normally do not have to enter ledger accounts
- Any person ignorant of ledger accounts may enter the voucher correctly from the previous one. So, even non-accounting persons or persons with limited accounting knowledge can correctly create such voucher using the previous voucher as template
- The Narration pattern in all such vouchers remain standard and comprehensive

FAQ-2: I want to get Group / Ledger Account wise summary of transaction of each voucher type separately for any specified period

Ans: Select *Display > Account Books* and then select the Register Type (like *Journal Register)* to get the monthly breakup of the selected voucher Type. Drill down through a month to get the Voucher Register for the selected month. Press *F2: Period* and select the period to get the Voucher Register for the selected period, for which you like to get the Ledger Accountwise summary

Click *F6:Extract* button to get the Account Group / Ledger wise summary. The groups are shown at the top level with subordinate Groups / Ledgers and the corresponding net Debit / Credit figure for each Ledger Account and the corresponding Account Group wise figure of the parent group.

This report is useful to get the accountwise summary of transaction of any selected Voucher Type

Books of Accounts

01 Books of Accounts Display & Printing Features

We have explained the Basic Features of Books of Accounts with default options. In this chapter, we discuss about various Configuration options to customize the contents & Format of the Books of Accounts.

02 Display & Printing Configuration Chart

At the respective Report Display screen, click *F12:Configure* to get Configuration screen for the respective report. The options among each of the Report are quite common. The following Table shows the summarized position of the availability of each of the options (Ö tick indicates the feature / option is available). The details of each feature / option is described later.

Features	Display*				Print*				Multi Account Print*			
	C/B	J/B	L/B		C/B	J/B	L/B		C/B	J/B	L/B	MC/B
Show Extract of Register		√				√				√		
Show Columnar Register		√				√				√		
Style of Report					√		√		√		√	
Select Voucher to Show	√		√		√		√		√		√	
Format	√	√	√		√	√	√		√	√	√	
Show Billwise Details also	√	√	√		√	√	√		√	√	√	
Show Cost Centre Details also	√	√	√		√	√	√		√	√	√	√
Show Inventory Details also	√	√	√		√	√	√		√	√	√	√
Show Bank Details also	√	√	√		√	√	√		√	√	√	√
Show Narrations also	√	√	√		√	√	√		√	√	√	√
Show Entered / Altered by	√	√			√	√						√
Include Opening Balances	√		√		√		√		√	√	√	
Show Running Balance	√		√		√		√		√	√	√	
Show Voucher Number also							√		√	√	√	√
Appearance of Name	√		√		√							
Sorting Method	√		√		√						√	
Show Group Name					√		√		√		√	
Method of Balancing					√		√		√		√	
Start Fresh page for Balancing					√		√		√		v	
Show Fresh page for Accounts											√	
Allow Selection for Groups/ Ledgers											√	
Set Alphabetical Print Range											√	
Print Index Page											√	
Cash / Bank Account												√

*C/B: Cash / Bank Book, J/B: Journal Book, L/B: Ledger Book, MC/B: Multi Column Cash / Bank Book

03 Reports Display Buttons Chart

At the respective Report Display screen, you get a set of buttons to perform various ancillary tasks from within the current Display screen. The Buttons among each of the Report are quite common. The following Table shows the summarized position of the availability of each of the options (Ö tick indicates the feature / option is available). The details of each the Button is described later.

Buttons	C/B	J/B	L/B
F1:Ledger	√		√
F6:Dly Break up	√		√
F8:Columnar	√		√
C:Contact		√	
F4:Chg Vch		√	
F5:Columnar		√	√
F6:Extract / Vouchers		√	
F7:Monthly			√
B:Billwise		√	

Buttons in Ledger Display screen, related to Banking System: You get following additional buttons in Bank Ledger Display. These are relevant only when you activate Cheque maintenance / Bank Reconciliation. These buttons are discussed in relevant place at Chapter 04-01:Banking.

- **F5:Reconcile**: To get Bank Reconciliation screen
- ***F6*:Multi Chq Printing**: To get Cheque Printing screen
- **F6:Deposit Slip Print:** To get Deposit Slip Printing screen

04 Cash & Bank Book

Cash / Bank Book is described earlier (§01/01-06). Here we describe various formats of the Cash / Bank Book using the Configuration options & Buttons available at Cash / Bank Book.

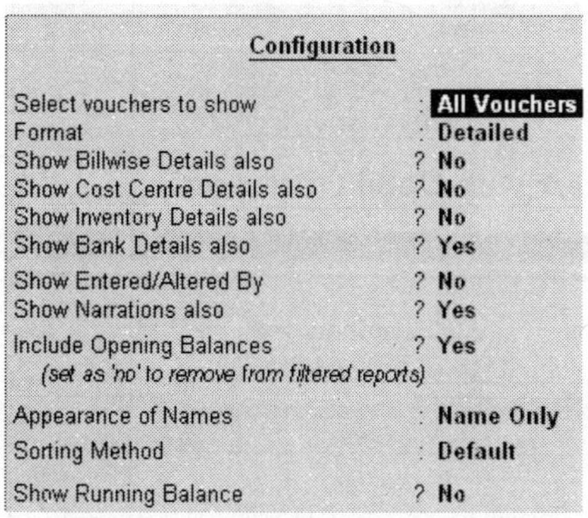

F-1A: Cash / Bank Book Display Configuration

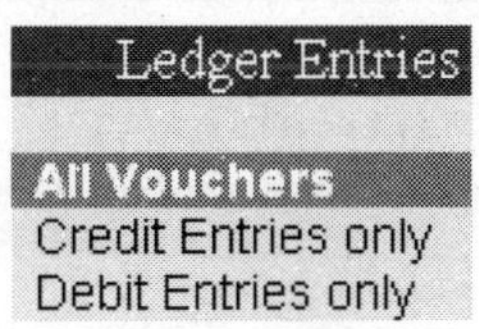

F-1B: List of Voucher Type

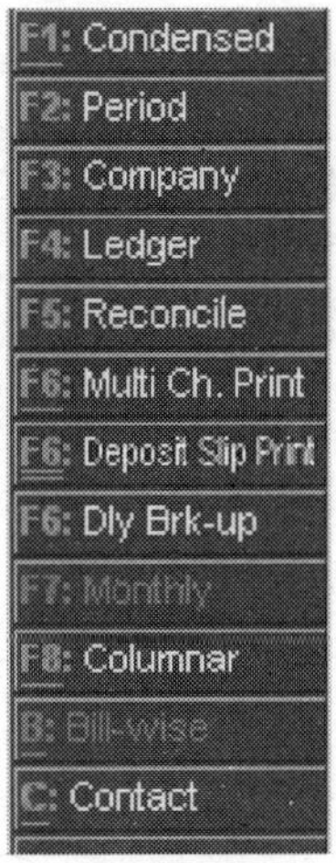

F-1C: Buttons

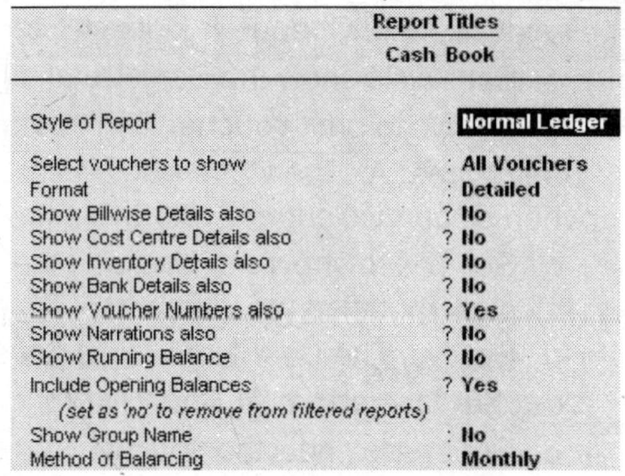

F-1D: Cash / Bank Book Printing screen

Cash / Bank Book Configuration

At Cash / Bank Book Display (Ledger Voucher screen of Cash / Bank Account: F-2A, F-2B), click *F12: Configuration* to get Cash Bank Book Display Configuration screen (F-1A) to set the options.

- **Vouchers Types**: At *Select Vouchers to Show*, select the option vouchers to show from the list (F-1B), as follows:
  - o **Credit Entries:** Select *Credit Entries only* to show only the entries for Credit of Cash / Bank Account (i.e Payment & Contra Vouchers), in condensed form only
  - o **Debit Entries:** Select *Debit Entries only* to show only the entries for Debit of Cash / Bank Account (i.e Receipt & Contra Vouchers), in condensed form only
  - o **All Vouchers:** Select *All Vouchers* to show all transactions involving Cash / bank Accounts (i.e Receipt, payment & Contra Vouchers)
- **Format**: At *Format,*
  - o Select *Condensed* to get only the top level figures (Account Group / Ledger: F-2B).
  - o Select *Detailed* to get the lowest level ledger details (you may also use *F1:Detailed / Condensed* toggle button): F-2A

  Bill Ref Details: At *Show Billwise Details also* (relevant only when Bill Reference is activated: §05.01/03-07)
  - o Set *Yes* to show the Bill Reference details.
  - o Set *No* to omit Bill Reference details
- **Cost Centre Details**: At *Show Cost Centre Details also* (relevant only when Cost Centre is activated)
  - o Set *Yes* to show Cost Center details.
  - o Set *No* to omit Cost Center details
- **Inventory Details**: At *Show Inventory Details also* (relevant only when *Accounts with Inventory* module is activated §03/01-01)

  - o Set *Yes* to show Inventory details.
  - o Set *No* to omit Inventory details
- **Bank Details**: At *Show Bank details also* (useful for Bank Reconciliation, Cheque & Deposit Slip Printing)
  - o Set *Yes* to show the Bank Details (Payee, Bank etc),
  - o Set *No* to omit voucher Bank details.
- **User Name:** At *Show Altered / Entered By* (relevant only when *Security Control* System is activated)
  - o Set *Yes* to show the Name of the user who created / last modified the voucher.
  - o Set *No*. The User Name to is not shown
- **Voucher Narration**: At *Show Narration also*
  - o Set *Yes* to show the voucher Narration also for each voucher (F-2B).
  - o Set *No* to omit voucher Narration (F-2A).
- **Opening Balance:** At *Include Opening Balance also*
  - o Set *Yes* to show Opening balance, to show Opening Balance in the Report (F-2A)
  - o Set *No* to omit the Opening Balance (only Transactions & Closing Balance is shown: F-2G)
- **Running Balance**: At *show running balance*
  - o Set Yes to show running balance of Cash / Bank Ledger against each entry (F-2F)
  - o Set *No*. No Running balance after each entry is shown

Buttons at Cash Bank Book

Following Buttons are available for Cash / Bank Books (F-1C)

- **F4:Ledger:** To select a Cash / Bank Ledger Account
- **F6: Daily Break up**: To show Daily summary & Balance (F-2E)
- **F8: Columnar**: To set column definition for columnar report (§02/02-18)

Apart from the above, the following additional buttons related to Banking Transactions are available in case of Bank Ledger Account (Cash Bank Book is a kind of Ledger Account of specified Cash / Bank Ledger)

- **F5: Reconcile**: To tag cleared cheques for Bank Reconciliation (§17.1/02-1)
- **F6: Mult Ch. Print**: To print multiple Cheques (§11.1/02-11)

Ledger Vouchers — Ledger: Cash — 2-May-2009 to 4-May-2009

Date	Particulars		Vch Type	Vch No.	Debit	Credit
2-5-2009	Office Rent		Payment	2		6,000.00
2-5-2009	(as per details)		Sales	2	2,000.00	
	Sales	2,100.00 Cr				
	Sales Rebates	100.00 Dr				
3-5-2009	Properitor's Capital		Receipt	1	1,900.00	
4-5-2009	T K Das		Receipt	2	6,000.00	
				Opening Balance :	289.50	
				Current Total :	9,900.00	6,000.00
				Closing Balance :	4,189.50	

F-2A: Cash Book in Display Format (Detailed)

Ledger Vouchers — Ledger: Cash — 2-May-2009 to 4-May-2009

Date	Particulars		Vch Type	Vch No.	Debit	Credit
2-5-2009	Office Rent		Payment	2		6,000.00
	Rent Paid to Landlord M M Seth for April to June 09, @ 2000 p.m					
2-5-2009	(as per details)		Sales	2	2,000.00	
	Sales	2,100.00 Cr				
	Sales Rebates	100.00 Dr				
	Goods sold in cash after allowing rebates					
3-5-2009	Properitor's Capital		Receipt	1	1,900.00	
	Cash contributed by Proprietor towards Capital					
4-5-2009	T K Das		Receipt	2	6,000.00	
				Opening Balance :	289.50	
				Current Total :	9,900.00	6,000.00
				Closing Balance :	4,189.50	

F-2B: Cash Book in Display Format (Condensed)

- **F6: Deposit Slip Print**: To print Deposit Slips (§10.5/02-11)
- **C: Contact**: To show Contact details (F-3B) of the selected Bank Account

Ledger Vouchers — Ledger: Cash — 1-Apr-2009 to 30-Jun-2009

Date	Particulars	Vch Type	Vch No.	Debit	Credit
1-4-2009	Aakash & Co	Payment	1		1,210.50
1-4-2009	HDFC Bank	Contra	1		500.00
2-5-2009	Office Rent	Payment	2		6,000.00
1-6-2009	Drawings	Payment	5		5,000.00
1-6-2009	Cash Sales	Payment	6		2,000.00
1-6-2009	HDFC Bank	Contra	2		1,000.00
		Opening Balance :		2,000.00	
		Current Total :			15,710.50
		Closing Balance :			13,710.50

F-2C: Cash Book with Credit Entries only

Ledger Vouchers — Ledger: Cash — 1-Apr-2009 to 30-Jun-2009

Date	Particulars		Vch Type	Vch No.	Debit	Credit
2-5-2009	(as per details)		Sales	2	2,000.00	
	Sales	2,100.00 Cr				
	Sales Rebates	100.00 Dr				
3-5-2009	Properitor's Capital		Receipt	1	1,900.00	
4-5-2009	T K Das		Receipt	2	6,000.00	
5-5-2009	T K Das		Receipt	3	10,000.00	
1-6-2009	A K Traders		Receipt	4	3,000.00	
6-6-2009	T K Das		Receipt	5	4,000.00	
9-6-2009	T K Das		Receipt	6	7,000.00	
				Opening Balance :	2,000.00	
				Current Total :	33,900.00	
				Closing Balance :	35,900.00	

F-2D: Cash Book with Debit Entries only

Daily Breakup of Ledger

Particulars	Cash ABC Academy 9-10 2-May-2009 to 4-May-2009		
	Transactions		Closing Balance
	Debit	Credit	
Opening Balance			289.50 Dr
2-May	2,000.00	6,000.00	3,710.50 Cr
3-May	1,900.00		1,810.50 Cr
4-May	6,000.00		4,189.50 Dr
Grand Total	**9,900.00**	**6,000.00**	**4,189.50 Dr**

F-2E: Cash Book Daily Break up

Ledger Vouchers — ABC Academy 9-10 — Ctrl + M

Ledger: **Cash** — 2-May-2009 to 4-May-2009

Date	Particulars	Vch Type	Vch No.	Debit	Credit	Balance
	Opening Balance			289.50		
2-5-2009	Office Rent	Payment	2		6,000.00	5,710.50 Cr
2-5-2009	(as per details)	Sales	2	2,000.00		3,710.50 Cr
	Sales 2,100.00 Cr					
	Sales Rebates 100.00 Dr					
3-5-2009	Properitor's Capital	Receipt	1	1,900.00		1,810.50 Cr
4-5-2009	T K Das	Receipt	2	6,000.00		4,189.50 Dr
			Current Total :	9,900.00	6,000.00	
			Closing Balance :	4,189.50		

F-2F: Cash Book with Running Balance

Ledger Vouchers — Ctrl + M

Ledger: **Cash** — 1-Apr-2009 to 4-May-2009

Date	Particulars	Vch Type	Vch No.	Debit	Credit
1-4-2009	Aakash & Co	Payment	1		1,210.50
1-4-2009	HDFC Bank	Contra	1		500.00
2-5-2009	Office Rent	Payment	2		6,000.00
2-5-2009	Sales	Sales	2	2,000.00	
3-5-2009	Properitor's Capital	Receipt	1	1,900.00	
4-5-2009	T K Das	Receipt	2	6,000.00	
			Opening Balance :		
			Current Total :	9,900.00	7,710.50
			Closing Balance :	2,189.50	

F-2G: Cash Book Display without Opening Balance

Ledger Vouchers — Ctrl + M

Ledger: **Cash** — 1-Apr-2009 to 30-Jun-2009

Date	Particulars	Vch Type	Vch No.	Debit	Credit
1-4-2009	HDFC Bank	Contra	1		500.00
1-6-2009	HDFC Bank	Contra	2		1,000.00
1-4-2009	Aakash & Co	Payment	1		1,210.50
3-5-2009	Properitor's Capital	Receipt	1	1,900.00	
2-5-2009	Sales	Sales	2	2,000.00	
1-6-2009	Cash Sales	Payment	6		2,000.00
1-6-2009	A K Traders	Receipt	4	3,000.00	
6-6-2009	T K Das	Receipt	5	4,000.00	
1-6-2009	Drawings	Payment	5		5,000.00
2-5-2009	Office Rent	Payment	2		6,000.00
4-5-2009	T K Das	Receipt	2	6,000.00	
9-6-2009	T K Das	Receipt	6	7,000.00	
5-5-2009	T K Das	Receipt	3	10,000.50	
			Opening Balance :		
			Current Total :	33,900.00	15,710.50
			Closing Balance :	18,189.50	

F-2H: Cash Book Display (Amountwise increasing)

Cash Book

2-May-2009 to 4-May-2009

Date		Particulars		Vch Type	Vch No.	Debit	Credit
2-5-2009	Cr	Opening Balance				289.50	
2-5-2009	Dr	Office Rent *Rent Paid to Landlord M M Seth for April to June 09, @ 2000 p.m*		Payment	2		6,000.00
	Cr	(as per details)		Sales	2	2,000.00	
		Sales	2,100.00 Cr				
		Sales Rebates *Goods sold in cash after allowing rebates*	100.00 Dr				
3-5-2009	Cr	Properitor's Capital *Cash contributed by Proprietor towards Capital*		Receipt	1	1,900.00	
4-5-2009	Cr	T K Das		Receipt	2	6,000.00	
						10,189.50	6,000.00
	Dr	Closing Balance					4,189.50
						10,189.50	**10,189.50**

F-3A: Cash Book in Print Format (with Voucher Narration)

04.01 Cash / Bank Book Printing

At Cash Book Display (F-1A) click P:Print to get Cash / Bank Book printing screen (F-1D). The options are similar to Cash Book Display Configuration (F-1A) / Multi Account Cash Book Printing screen (F-10A).

Ledger Contact Details

*Ledger: **HDFC Bank***

Mailing Name	:	HDFC Bank
Address	:	33 Haskar Rd Badamtala Kolkata
State	:	West Bengal
PIN Code	:	799999
Contact	:	B Bhadra
Phone No.	:	033 12345678
Mobile No.	:	9998887771
Fax No.	:	033 12345679
E-Mail	:	kadamtala@[illegible]
Notes	:	9-30am to 3-30 pm

F-3B: Bank Ledger Contact details

05 Journal Book

Journal Book has been explained earlier (§01/01-07). Here we describe various formats of Journal Book using the Configuration options & Buttons available at Journal Book Display.

Journal Book Configuration: At Journal Book Display (F-5A), click *F12:Configure* to get *Journal Book Configuration* screen (F-4A), to set the Configuration options as below:

- **Voucher Register Extract:** Voucher Register Extract is Account Group / Account Ledgerwise Summary of Vouchers for the Period. At *Show Extract of Register*,
  - o Set Yes to get Voucher Register Extract of Journal Vouchers for the selected Period (§04/02-20).
  - o Set *No* to get Journal Register in Normal Format (F-5A)
- **Columnar Register:** Columnar Register shows Accountwise Column figures in a specified Tabular Format. At *Show Columnar Register*,
  - o Set *Yes* to set Column Definition screen (02/02-18) to set Column definitions to get Columnar Register, else set *No*.
  - o Set *No* (default)to get the report in Normal Format.
- **Format**: At *Format*:
  - o Select *Condensed* to get only the top level figures (Account Group / Ledger).
  - o Select *Detailed* to get the lowest level ledger details
- **Voucher Narration**: At *Show Narration also*
  - o Set *Yes* to show the voucher Narration also for each voucher.
  - o Set *No* to omit voucher Narration.

  Bill Ref Details: at *Show Billwise Details also* (relevant only when Bill Reference is activated: §05.01/03-01)
  - o Set *Yes* to show the Bill Reference details.
  - o Set *No* to omit Bill Reference details
- **Cost Centre Details**: At *Show Cost Centre Details also* (relevant only when Cost Centre is activated (§01/05-01))

  - o Set *Yes* to show Cost Center details.
  - o Set *No* to omit Cost Center details
- **Inventory Details**: At *Show Inventory Details also* (relevant only when *Accounts with Inventory* module is activated: §02/01-01)
  - o Set *Yes* to show Inventory details.
  - o Set *No* to omit Inventory details
- **Bank Details**: At *Show Bank details also* (useful for Bank Reconciliation, Cheque & Deposit Slip Printing)
  - o Set *Yes* to show the Bank Details (Payee, Bank etc),
  - o Set *No* to omit voucher Bank details.
- **User Name:** At *Show Altered / Entered By* (relevant only when *Security Control* System is activated)
  - o Set *Yes* to show the Name of the user who created / last modified the voucher.
  - o Set *No.* The User Name to is not shown

Show Extract of Register	?	No
Show Columnar Register	?	No
Format	:	Condensed
Show Narrations also	?	No
Show Billwise Details also	?	No
Show Cost Centre Details also	?	No
Show Inventory Details also	?	No
Show Bank Details also	?	No
Show Entered/Altered By	?	No
Appearance of Names	:	Name Only
Sorting Method	:	Default

F-4A: Journal Book Display Configuration

Report Titles
Journal Register

Show Extract of Register	?	No
Show Columnar Register	?	No
Format	:	Condensed
Show Voucher Numbers also	?	Yes
Show Narrations also	?	No
Show Billwise Details also	?	No
Show Cost Centre Details also	?	No
Show Inventory Details also	?	No
Show Bank Details also	?	No
Show Entered/Altered By	?	No

F-4B: Journal Book Printing

F1: Detailed
F2: Date
F2: Period
F3: Company
F4: Chg Vch
F5: Columnar
F6: Extract

F-4C: Journal Book Display Buttons

Buttons at Journal Book

At Journal Book Display (F-5A), you get following buttons (F-4C):

- **F4: Ch Vch**: To select the Voucher Type to be included in the Report. Select the specific Voucher Type to get Voucher Register for selected Voucher Type (or select *All Items* to get Voucher Register including all types of Voucher for the current period.
- **F5:Columnar:** To get Column definition set up screen (§02/02-18) to set get Columnar Journal Register as per Column specification set.
- **F6:Extract:** To get Voucher Register Extract of Journal Vouchers (§04/02-19)

05.01 Journal Book Printing

At Journal Book Display (F-4A), click *P:Printing* to get Journal Book printing screen (F-4B). The options are similar to *Journal Book Configuration* screen (F-4A). Type *Y* to print the Journal Book (F-5B) as per default printing options set as shown in the screen, else type N to change the printing options. Type Y to print as per changed Printing options

Voucher Register Ctrl + N
List of All Journal Vouchers 1-Apr-2009 to 31-Mar-2010

Date	Particulars		Vch Type	Vch No.	Debit Amount	Credit Amount
4-5-2009	Freight		Journal	1	400.00	
	Handling Charges	700.00 Dr				
	A K Traders	1,100.00 Cr				
	Bill for Freigfht & Handling Charges					
28-2-2010	Salary		Journal	2	9,30,000.00	
	HRA	32,050.00 Dr				
	P F	90,340.00 Cr				
	S Roy (Employee)	8,71,710.00 Cr				
	Salary payable to S Roy for March 10					
31-3-2010	Depreciation on Furniture		Journal	3	2,000.00	
	Furniture (Accumulated DEpreciation)	2,000.00 Cr				
	Depreciation Provided					
31-3-2010	Interest on Term Loan		Journal	4	4,500.00	
	ICICI Term Loan	4,500.00 Cr				
	Interest paybale upto 31.3.10 credited to the account of ICICI Term Loan					
31-3-2010	Interest on Unsecured Loan		Journal	5	900.00	
	Accrued Interest	900.00 Cr				
	Intersr Accrued upto 31.3.10 in respect of unsecured Loan from S Kurien					

F-5A: Journal Register Display (Detailed with Voucher Narration)

Journal Register
1-Apr-2009 to 31-Mar-2010
Page 1

Date	Particulars	Vch Type	Debit Amount	Credit Amount
4-5-2009	Freight	Journal	400.00	
	Handling Charges		700.00	
	A K Traders			1,100.00
	Entered By : akn			
28-2-2010	Salary	Journal	9,30,000.00	
	HRA		32,050.00	
	P F			90,340.00
	S Roy (Employee)			8,71,710.00
	Entered By : akn			
31-3-2010	Depreciation on Furniture	Journal	2,000.00	
	Furniture (Accumulated DEpreciation)			2,000.00
	Entered By : akn			
31-3-2010	Interest on Term Loan	Journal	4,500.00	
	ICICI Term Loan			4,500.00
	Entered By : akn			
31-3-2010	Interest on Unsecured Loan	Journal	900.00	
	Accrued Interest			900.00
	Entered By : akn			

F-5B: Journal Register in Print (Detailed without Voucher Number, with User Name)

06 Ledger Book

Ledger Book has been discussed earlier (01/01-08). Here we discuss about various configuration option of Ledger Book

Ledger Book Configuration

At Ledger Display (F-7A), click *F12:Configure* to get Ledger Display Configuration screen (F-6A), similar to Cash / Bank Account Configuration screen (F-1A), as Cash / Bank Book is also a type of Ledger Book (of Cash / Bank Account).

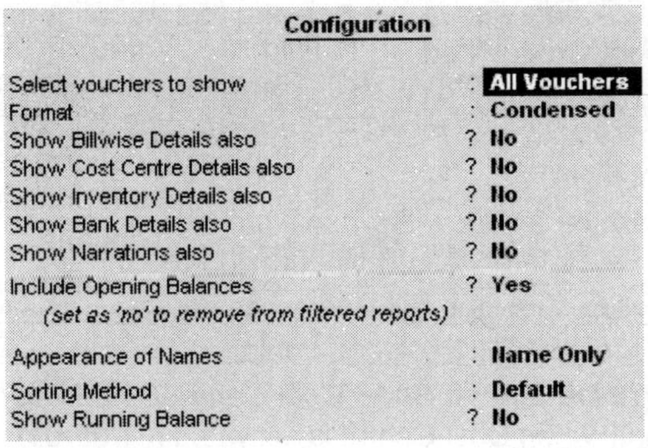

F-6A: Ledger Book Display Configuration

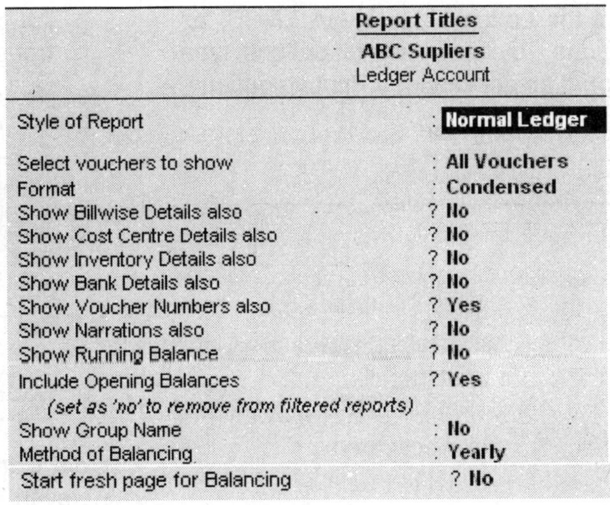

F-6B: Ledger Book Printing screen

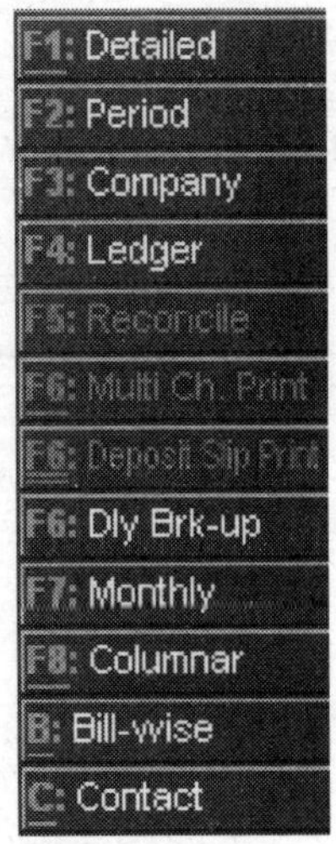

F-6C: Buttons at Ledger Book Display

Buttons at Ledger Book

At Ledger Book Display (F-7A), you get following buttons (F-6C):

- **F4: Ledger**: Click *F4:Ledger* (or press F4 button) to select the Ledger Account (from the list of Ledger Accounts) for which you like to get the Ledger Book.

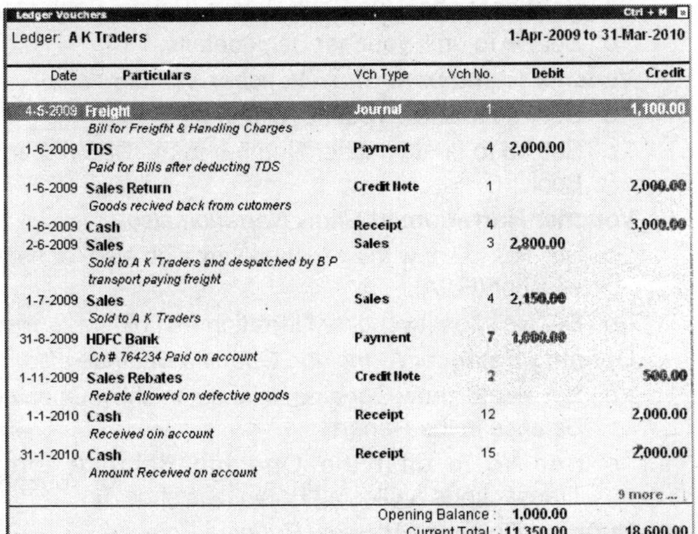

Ledger Vouchers — Ledger: A K Traders — 1-Apr-2009 to 31-Mar-2010

Date	Particulars	Vch Type	Vch No.	Debit	Credit
4-5-2009	Freight *Bill for Freigfht & Handling Charges*	Journal	1		1,100.00
1-6-2009	TDS *Paid for Bills after deducting TDS*	Payment	4	2,000.00	
1-6-2009	Sales Return *Goods recived back from cutomers*	Credit Note	1		2,000.00
1-6-2009	Cash	Receipt	4		3,000.00
2-6-2009	Sales *Sold to A K Traders and despatched by B P transport paying freight*	Sales	3	2,800.00	
1-7-2009	Sales *Sold to A K Traders*	Sales	4	2,150.00	
31-8-2009	HDFC Bank *Ch # 764234 Paid on account*	Payment	7	1,000.00	
1-11-2009	Sales Rebates *Rebate allowed on defective goods*	Credit Note	2		500.00
1-1-2010	Cash *Received oin account*	Receipt	12		2,000.00
31-1-2010	Cash *Amount Received on account*	Receipt	15		2,000.00
					9 more ...
		Opening Balance :		1,000.00	
		Current Total :		11,350.00	18,600.00
		Closing Balance :			6,250.00

F-7A: Ledger Book Display with Narration (condensed)

- **F6:Daily Break up**: Click *F6:Dly Brk- up* (or press F6 button) to get *Daily Breakup of Ledger* Report showing the *Transaction* & *Closing Balance* for each date for the current period. The Report will show for each Date even if there is no transaction for a Date.
- **F7:Monthly Break up**: Click *F7: Monthly* (or press F7 button) to get *Monthly Breakup of Ledger* Report showing the *Transaction* & *Closing Balance* for each month for the current period. The Report will show for each Month even if there is no transaction for a Month.
- **F8:Columnar:** Click *F8:Columnar* button (or press *Alt+F8*), to get Column definition set up screen (like §02.02/02-18) to set for Columnar Ledger Book for the select Ledger Account, as per Column specification set.
- **B:Billwise**: Click B:Billwise (or press Alt+B keys) to get Ledger Voucher Outstanding report showing the details of pending Bills (like §05/03-05). This is relevant only when you have set up Bill Reference feature (§03/03-07)
- **C: Contact**: Click *C:Contact* button (or press *Alt+C keys*) to get all the Contact Details & Notes as entered in the Ledger Account Master, for the selected Ledger Account.

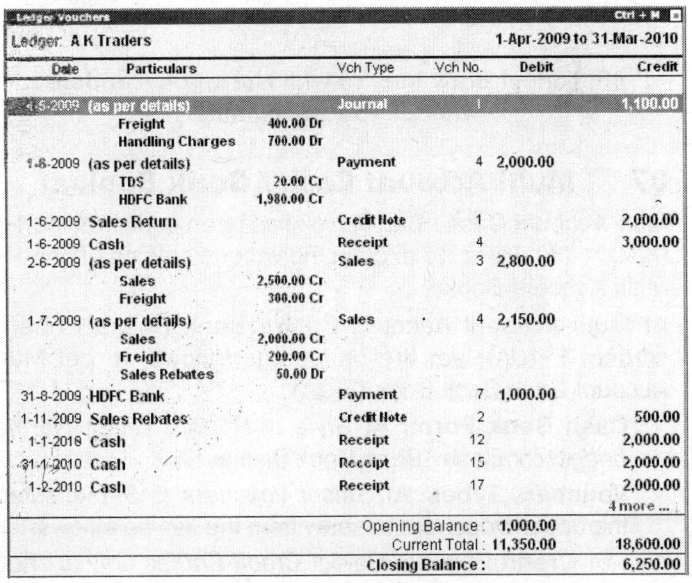

Ledger Vouchers — Ledger: A K Traders — 1-Apr-2009 to 31-Mar-2010

Date	Particulars		Vch Type	Vch No.	Debit	Credit
4-5-2009	(as per details)		Journal	1		1,100.00
	Freight	400.00 Dr				
	Handling Charges	700.00 Dr				
1-6-2009	(as per details)		Payment	4	2,000.00	
	TDS	20.00 Cr				
	HDFC Bank	1,980.00 Cr				
1-6-2009	Sales Return		Credit Note	1		2,000.00
1-6-2009	Cash		Receipt	4		3,000.00
2-6-2009	(as per details)		Sales	3	2,800.00	
	Sales	2,500.00 Cr				
	Freight	300.00 Cr				
1-7-2009	(as per details)		Sales	4	2,150.00	
	Sales	2,000.00 Cr				
	Freight	200.00 Cr				
	Sales Rebates	50.00 Dr				
31-8-2009	HDFC Bank		Payment	7	1,000.00	
1-11-2009	Sales Rebates		Credit Note	2		500.00
1-1-2010	Cash		Receipt	12		2,000.00
31-1-2010	Cash		Receipt	15		2,000.00
1-2-2010	Cash		Receipt	17		2,000.00
						4 more ...
			Opening Balance :		1,000.00	
			Current Total :		11,350.00	18,600.00
			Closing Balance :			6,250.00

F-7B: Ledger Book Display (Detailed)

06.01 Ledger Book Printing

At *Ledger Book Display* (F-7A), click *P:Printing* to get Ledger Book printing screen (F-6B). The Ledger printing options (F-6B) are similar to *Cash/Bank Book Printing* screen

(F-1A). Type *Y* to print the Ledger Book (F-8A / F-8B) as per default printing options. To change default options, type N, and then type Y to print as per changed Printing options

A K Traders
Ledger Account
1-Apr-2009 to 30-Jun-2009
Page 1

Date		Particulars	Vch Type	Debit	Credit
1-4-2009	Cr	**Opening Balance**		**1,000.00**	
4-5-2009	Dr	**Freight** *Bill for Freigfht & Handling Charges*	Journal		1,100.00
1-6-2009	Cr	**TDS** *Paid for Bills after deducting TDS*	Payment	2,000.00	
	Dr	**Sales Return** *Goods recived back from cutomers*	Credit Note		2,000.00
	Dr	**Cash**	Receipt		3,000.00
2-6-2009	Cr	**Sales** *Sold to A K Traders and despatched by B P transport paying freight*	Sales	2,800.00	
				5,800.00	6,100.00
	Cr	**Closing Balance**		300.00	
				6,100.00	**6,100.00**

F-8A: Ledger Book in Print with Narration (condensed)

A K Traders
Ledger Account
1-Jun-2009 to 30-Jun-2009

Date		Particulars		Vch Type	Debit	Credit
1-6-2009	Dr	**Opening Balance**				**100.00**
1-6-2009	Cr	**(as per details)**		Payment	2,000.00	
		TDS	**20.00 Cr**			
		HDFC Bank	**1,980.00 Cr**			
		Paid for Bills after deducting TDS				
	Dr	**Sales Return** *Goods recived back from cutomers*		Credit Note		2,000.00
	Dr	**Cash**		Receipt		3,000.00
2-6-2009	Cr	**(as per details)**		Sales	2,800.00	
		Sales	**2,500.00 Cr**			
		Freight	**300.00 Cr**			
		Sold to A K Traders and despatched by B P transport paying freight				
					4,800.00	5,100.00
	Cr	**Closing Balance**			300.00	
					5,100.00	**5,100.00**

F-8B: Ledger Book in Print with Narration (condensed, without Voucher Number)

07 Multi Account Cash / Bank Book(s)

Multi Account Cash / Bank Book has been explained earlier (§04/01-06). Here we explain the various options of printing Multi Account Books.

At Multi-Account Account Cash / Bank Books Printing screen (F-10A), set the options as follows, to get Multi Account Cash Bank Book (F-9A)

- **Cash Book Form:** At *Style of Report,* select *Normal Ledger* for Cash / Bank Book Display
- **Vouchers Types**: At *Select Vouchers to Show*, select the option vouchers to show from the list, as follows:
    - o **Credit Entries:** Select *Credit Entries only* to show only the entries for Credit of Cash / Bank Account (i.e Payment & Contra Vouchers), in condensed form only
    - o **Debit Entries:** Select *Debit Entries only* to show only the entries for Debit of Cash / Bank Account (i.e Receipt & Contra Vouchers), in condensed form only
    - o **All Vouchers:** Select *All Vouchers* to show all transactions involving Cash / bank Accounts (i.e Receipt, payment & Contra Vouchers)
- **Format**: At *Format,*
    - o Select *Condensed* to get only the top level figures (Account Group / Ledger: F-11B).
    - o Select *Detailed* to get the lowest level ledger details (you may also use *F1:Detailed / Condensed* toggle button: F-9A)
- **Bill Ref Details**: at *Show Billwise Details also* (relevant only when Bill Reference is activated: §03/03-07)
    - o Set *Yes* to show the Bill Reference details.
    - o Set *No* to omit Bill Reference details
- **Cost Centre Details**: At *Show Cost Centre Details also* (relevant only when Cost Centre is activated (01/05-01))
    - o Set *Yes* to show Cost Center details.
    - o Set *No* to omit Cost Center details
- **Inventory Details**: At *Show Inventory Details also* (relevant only when Accounts with Inventory module is activated §02/01-01)
    - o Set *Yes* to show Inventory details.
    - o Set *No* to omit Inventory details
- **Bank Details**: At *Show Bank details also*
    - o Set *Yes* to show the Bank Details (Payee, Bank etc),
    - o Set *No* to omit voucher Bank details.
- **Voucher Number**: at *Show Voucher Numbers also*
    - o Set *Yes* to show Voucher Number,
    - o Set *No* to omit voucher Number in the Cash / Bank Book
- **Voucher Narration**: At *Show Narration also*
    - o Set *Yes* to show the voucher Narration also for each voucher (F-9A).
    - o Set *No* to omit voucher Narration (F-11B).
- **Opening Balance:** At *Include Opening Balance also*
    - o Set *Yes* to show Opening balance, to show Opening Balance in the Report,
    - o Set *No* to omit the Opening Balance (only Transactions & Closing Balance is shown)
- **Running Balance**: At *Show Running Balance*
    - o Set Yes to show running balance of Cash / Bank Ledger against each entry
    - o Set No. No Running balance after each entry is shown
- **Group Name:** At *Show Group Name,*
    - o Set *Yes* to show Account Group Name of the Ledger Account
    - o Set *No.* Group Name will not be shown
- **Method of Balancing:** At Method of Balancing, select the Balancing period from the list (F-10B), to print the Debit Credit Total sand the period end Closing balance,

which is carried as Opening balance for next period (or at the end of Report)

- o **Yearly:** To Balance at the end of Financial Year End Date
- o **Monthly:** To Balance at the end of each month (F-11A)
- o **Weekly:** To Balance at the end of each week (starting from the period beginning Date)
- o **Daily**: To Balance at the end of each Date (F-11B)

- **New Page:** At *Start Fresh page for Balancing*,
  - o Set *Yes* to skip to a new page start the next period from the beginning of page (skipping the page),
  - o Set No to continue next period in the same page.

ABC Academy 9-10
99, Airport Rd
Kolkata 700 098
W Bengal

Cash Book
1-Apr-2009 to 31-May-2009

Page 1

Date	Particulars	Vch Type	Vch No.	Debit	Credit
1-4-2009	To **Opening Balance**			**2,000.00**	
1-4-2009	By **Bank of India** *Cash deposited to bank*	Contra	1		500.00
				2,000.00	500.00
	By **Closing Balance**				1,500.00
				2,000.00	**2,000.00**
1-5-2009	To **Opening Balance**			**1,500.00**	
1-5-2009	To **Properitor's Capital** *Cash contributed by Proprietor towards Capital*	Receipt	1	1,900.00	
2-5-2009	By **Office Rent** *Rent Paid to Landlord M M Seth for April to June 09, @ 2000 p.m*	Payment	1		6,000.00
	To **(as per details)**	Sales	1	2,000.00	
	Sales 2,100.00 Cr				
	Sales Rebates 100.00 Dr				
	Goods sold in cash after allowing rebates				
				5,400.00	6,000.00
	To **Closing Balance**			600.00	
				6,000.00	**6,000.00**

F-9A: Multi Account Cash Book

Report Titles
Cash Book

From (blank for beginning)	:	**1-4-2009**
To (blank for end)	:	**31-5-2009**
Style of Report	:	**Normal Ledger**
Select vouchers to show	:	**All Vouchers**
Format	:	**Detailed**
Show Billwise Details also	?	**No**
Show Cost Centre Details also	?	**No**
Show Inventory Details also	?	**No**
Show Bank Details also	?	**No**
Show Voucher Numbers also	?	**Yes**
Show Narrations also	?	**Yes**
Show Running Balance	?	**No**
Include Opening Balances *(set as 'no' to remove from filtered reports)*	?	**Yes**
Show Group Name	:	**No**
Method of Balancing	:	**Monthly**
Start fresh page for Balancing	?	**No**

F-10A: Multi Account Cash / Bank Book Printing

Balancing
Daily
Monthly
Weekly
Yearly

F-10B: Method of Balancing List

Bank of India Book
1-Apr-2009 to 30-Jun-2009

Page 1

Date	Particulars	Vch Type	Vch No.	Debit	Credit
1-4-2009	By **Opening Balance**				**2,000.00**
1-4-2009	To **Cash**	**Contra**	1	500.00	
	Cheque/DD 1-4-2009 500.00 Dr				
	Cash deposited to bank				
				500.00	2,000.00
	To **Closing Balance**			1,500.00	
				2,000.00	**2,000.00**
1-6-2009	By **Opening Balance**				**1,500.00**
1-6-2009	By **(as per details)**	**Payment**	2		1,980.00
	A K Traders 2,000.00 Dr				
	TDS 20.00 Cr				
	Cheque 239876 1-6-2009 1,980.00 Cr				
	Paid for Bills after deducting TDS				
					3,480.00
	To **Closing Balance**			3,480.00	
				3,480.00	**3,480.00**

F-11A: Multi Account Bank Book (Monthly Balancing)

Cash Book
3-Jun-2009 to 9-Jun-2009

Date	Particulars	Vch Type	Debit	Credit
3-6-2009	Cr **Opening Balance**		**11,189.50**	
3-6-2009	Dr **Cash Sales**	**Payment**		2,000.00
			11,189.50	2,000.00
	Dr **Closing Balance**			9,189.50
			11,189.50	**11,189.50**
6-6-2009	Cr **Opening Balance**		**9,189.50**	
6-6-2009	Cr **T K Das**	**Receipt**	4,000.00	
			13,189.50	
	Dr **Closing Balance**			13,189.50
			13,189.50	**13,189.50**
9-6-2009	Cr **Opening Balance**		**13,189.50**	
9-6-2009	Cr **T K Das**	**Receipt**	7,000.00	
			20,189.50	
	Dr **Closing Balance**			20,189.50
			20,189.50	**20,189.50**

F-11B: Multi Account Cash Book (Condensed, Daily Balancing, without Voucher Number)

08 Multi-Column Cash/Bank Book

Multi Column Cash / Bank Book have been discussed earlier (04.01/01-06). Here we discuss about Configuration & Button Options to customize the contents of Cash / Bank Book

At Multi Column Cash / Bank Book Printing screen (F-12B), set the options as follows, to get Multi Column Cash bank Book (F-12A):

- **Cash Bank Account**: Here you may select Cash Bank Account from the list of Cash / Bank Accounts, defined for each Cash / bank column. This way, you may select upto 3 Cash / Bank Accounts to be shown in Multi Column Cash Bank Book (You may select lesser accounts than 3 (leave unused columns blank)
  - o 1st Column: Select the Cash / Bank Account to be shown in 1st Column

- o 2nd Column: Select the Cash / Bank Account to be shown in 1st Column
- o 3rd Column: Select the Cash / Bank Account to be shown in 1st Column

- **Format**: At *Format*:
  - o Select *Condensed* to get only the top level figures (Account Group / Ledger).
  - o Select *Detailed* to get the lowest level ledger details
- **Voucher Narration**: At *Show Narration also*
  - o Set *Yes* to show the voucher Narration also for each voucher.
  - o Set *No* to omit voucher Narration.
- **Bill Ref Details**: at *Show Billwise Details also* (relevant only when Bill Reference is activated: §03/03-07)
  - o Set *Yes* to show the Bill Reference details.
  - o Set *No* to omit Bill Reference details
- **Cost Centre Details**: At *Show Cost Centre Details also* (relevant only when Cost Centre is activated)
  - o Set *Yes* to show Cost Center details.
  - o Set *No* to omit Cost Center details
- **Bank Details**: At *Show Bank details also*
  - o Set *Yes* to show the Bank Details (Payee, Bank etc),
  - o Set *No* to omit voucher Bank details.
- **Inventory Details**: At *Show Inventory Details also* (relevant only when Accounts with Inventory module is activated §02/01-02)
  - o Set *Yes* to show Inventory details.
  - o Set *No* to omit Inventory details

Report Titles

Multi Column Cash/Bank Book

From (blank for beginning)	:	**1-4-2009**
To (blank for end)	:	**30-6-2009**
Cash/Bank A/c for 1st Column	:	**Cash**
for 2nd Column	:	**Bank of India**
for 3rd Column	:	**State Bank of India**
Format	:	**Detailed**
Show Billwise Details also	?	**No**
Show Cost Centre Details also	?	**No**
Show Inventory Details also	?	**No**
Show Bank Details also	?	**Yes**
Show Narrations also	?	Yes

F-12B: Multi Column Cash Bank Book printing

09 Multi Account Journal Register

Multi Account Journal Register has been explained earlier (§03/01-07). At Multi Account Journal Book printing screen (F-13B), set the options as follows to get Multi Account Journal Book (F-13B):

- **Register Type:** At *Show Extract of Register*
  - o Set Yes to get Voucher Register Extract of Journal Vouchers for the selected Period (§04/02-20).
  - o Set *No* to get Journal Register in Normal Format (F-13A)
- **Columnar Register:** Columnar Register shows Accountwise Column figures in a specified Tabular Format. At *Show Columnar Register*,
  - o Set *Yes* to set Column Definition screen (§02/02-19) to set Column definitions to get Columnar Register (§04/02-19), else set *No*.
  - o Set *No* (default) to get the report in Normal Form (F-13A).
- **Format**: At *Format*:
  - o Select *Condensed* to get only the top level figures (Account Group / Ledger).
  - o Select *Detailed* to get the lowest level ledger details

Multi Column Cash/Bank Book

1-Apr-2009 to 30-Jun-2009

Page 1

Date	Particulars	Voucher Type	Number	Cash Dr	Bank of India Dr	State Bank of India Dr
1-Apr-2009	To **Opening Balance**			2,000.00		32,100.00
1-Apr-2009	To **Cash** *Cash deposited to bank*	Ctra	1		500.00	
1-May-2009	To **Properitor's Capital** *Cash contributed by Proprietor towards Capital*	Rcpt	1	1,900.00		
2-May-2009	To **(as per details)** Sales 2,100.00 Cr Sales Rebates 100.00 Dr *Goods sold in cash after allowing rebates*	Sale	1	2,000.00		
				5,900.00	500.00	32,100.00
	To Closing Balance			7,600.00	3,480.00	
				13,500.00	**3,980.00**	

Date	Particulars	Voucher Type	Number	Cash Cr	Bank of India Cr	State Bank of India Cr
1-Apr-2009	By **Opening Balance**				2,000.00	
1-Apr-2009	By **Bank of India** *Cash deposited to bank*	Ctra	1	500.00		
2-May-2009	By **Office Rent** *Rent Paid to Landlord M M Seth for April to June 09, @ 2000 p. m*	Pymt	1	6,000.00		
1-Jun-2009	By **(as per details)** A K Traders 2,000.00 Dr TDS 20.00 Cr Bank of India 1,980.00 Cr Cheque 239876 1-6-2009 1,980.00 Cr *Paid for Bills after deducting TDS*	Pymt	2		1,980.00	
1-Jun-2009	By **Drawings** *Cash withdrawn by Properitor for personal use*	Pymt	3	5,000.00		
1-Jun-2009	By **Cash Sales** *Cash sales*	Pymt	4	2,000.00		
				13,500.00	3,980.00	
	By Closing Balance					32,100.00
				13,500.00	**3,980.00**	**32,100.00**

F-12A: Multi Column Cash Bank Book

- **Voucher Narration**: At *Show Narration also*
  - o Set *Yes* to show the voucher Narration also for each voucher.
  - o Set *No* to omit voucher Narration.
- **Bill Ref Details**: at *Show Billwise Details also* (relevant only when Bill Reference is activated: §02/03-07)
  - o Set *Yes* to show the Bill Reference details.
  - o Set *No* to omit Bill Reference details
- **Cost Centre Details**: At *Show Cost Centre Details also* (relevant only when Cost Centre is activated)
  - o Set *Yes* to show Cost Center details.
  - o Set *No* to omit Cost Center details
- **Inventory Details**: At *Show Inventory Details also* (relevant only when Accounts with Inventory module is activated §02/01-01)
  - o Set *Yes* to show Inventory details.
  - o Set *No* to omit Inventory details
- **Bank Details**: At *Show Bank details also*
  - o Set *Yes* to show the Bank Details (Payee, Bank etc),
  - o Set *No* to omit voucher Bank details.
- **User Name:** At *Show Altered / Entered By* (relevant only when *Security Control* System is activated)
  - o Set *Yes* to show the Name of the user who created / last modified the voucher.
  - o Set *No.* The User Name to is not shown

Journal Register
1-Apr-2009 to 31-Mar-2010

Page 1

Date	Particulars	Vch Type	Vch No.	Debit Amount	Credit Amount
1-5-2009	**Freight**	Journal	1	400.00	
	Handling Charges			700.00	
	A K Traders				1,100.00
	Bill for Freight & Handling Charges				
31-3-2010	**Depreciation on Furniture**	Journal	2	2,000.00	
	Furniture (Accumulated DEpreciation)				2,000.00
	Depreciation Provided				
31-3-2010	**Salary**	Journal	3	10,000.00	
	HRA			3,000.00	
	P F				1,200.00
	S Roy (Employee)				11,800.00
	Salary payable to S Roy for March 10				
31-3-2010	**Interest on Term Loan**	Journal	5	4,500.00	
	ICICI Term Loan				4,500.00
	Interest paybale upto 31.3.10 credited to the account of ICICI Term Loan				

F-13A: Multi Account Journal Register

From (blank for beginning)	:	**1-3-2010**
To (blank for end)	:	**31-3-2010**
Show Extract of Register	?	**No**
Show Columnar Register	?	**No**
Format	:	**Detailed**
Show Voucher Numbers also	?	**Yes**
Show Narrations also	?	**No**
Show Billwise Details also	?	**No**
Show Cost Centre Details also	?	**No**
Show Inventory Details also	?	**No**
Show Bank Details also	?	**No**
Show Entered/Altered By	?	**No**

F-13B: Multi Account Journal Register printing

10 Multi Account Ledger Book

Multi Account Ledger Book printing has been discussed earlier (04/01-08).Select *Multi Account Printing > Account Books > Ledger* to get Multi Account Ledger printing menu. At Multi Account Ledger printing menu, select:

- **All Ledgers**: Select *All Accounts* to print all Ledger Accounts. The Ledgers would be printed in one after another (F-15A)

Report Titles
Ledger Account

From (blank for beginning)	:	**1-4-2009**
To (blank for end)	:	**31-3-2010**
Style of Report	:	**Normal Ledger**
Select vouchers to show	:	**All Vouchers**
Format	:	**Detailed**
Show Billwise Details also	?	**No**
Show Cost Centre Details also	?	**No**
Show Inventory Details also	?	**No**
Show Bank Details also	?	**Yes**
Show Voucher Numbers also	?	**Yes**
Show Narrations also	?	**Yes**
Show Running Balance	?	**No**
Include Opening Balances *(set as 'no' to remove from filtered reports)*	?	**Yes**
Show Group Name	:	**No**
Sorting Method	?	**Default**
Method of Balancing	:	**Yearly**
Start fresh page for each Account	?	**No**
Start fresh page for Balancing	?	**No**
Allow Selection for Groups/Ledgers	?	**Yes**
Set Alphabetical print range	?	**No**
From (blank for beginning)	:	To (blank for end)
Print index page	?	**Yes**

F-14A: Multi Account Ledger Printing screen

Office Rent

Date		Particulars			Vch Type	Vch No.	Debit	Credit
2-6-2009	To	Cash			[illegible]	1	6,000.00	
		Rent Paid to Landlord M M Seth for April to June 09, @ 2000 p.m						
31-3-2010	To	(as per details)			[illegible]	8	1,800.00	
		Pre Paid Expenses	1,800.00 Dr					
		Bank of India		3,600.00 Cr				
		Cheque/DD 123456 31-3-2010 3,600.00 Cr						
		Ch # 876543 Rent paid for 6 months for Jan 10 to Jun 10 @ 600 p.m						
							7,800.00	
	By	Closing Balance						7,800.00
							7,800.00	7,800.00

P F

Date		Particulars			Vch Type	Vch No.	Debit	Credit
31-3-2010	By	(as per details)			[illegible]	3		1,200.00
		Salary	10,000.00 Dr					
		HRA	3,000.00 Dr					
		S Roy (Employee)		11,800.00 Cr				
		Salary payable to S Roy for March 10						
	By	(as per details)			[illegible]	9		1,300.00
		Salary	13,000.00 Dr					
		HRA	3,000.00 Dr					
		Bank of India		14,700.00 Cr				
		Cheque 31-3-2010 14,700.00 Cr						
		Ch # 654321 Salary Paid to M rakesh For March 10						
								2,500.00
	To	Closing Balance					2,500.00	
							2,500.00	2,500.00

F-15A: Multi Account Ledger (Multiple Ledgers range)

- **One Ledger Account**: Select *One* Ledger Account from the list of Ledger Accounts to print the selected Ledger Account (F-18A)

- **All Ledgers of an Account Group**: Select *Group of Accounts* to print all Ledgers placed under selected Account Group.

to get Multi Account Ledger printing screen (F-14A).

At Multi Account ledger printing screen (F-14A), set as follows:

- **Ledger Book Form:** At *Style of Report* (F-17A)
  - o Select *Normal Ledger* for Cash / Bank Book Display
  - o Select *Confirmation of Accounts* to print *Confirmation of Accounts*
- **Vouchers Types**: At *Select Vouchers to Show*, select the option vouchers to show from the list (F-1B), as follows:
  - o **Credit Entries:** Select *Credit Entries only* to show only the entries for Credit of Cash / Bank Account (i.e Payment & Contra Vouchers), in condensed form only
  - o **Debit Entries:** Select *Debit Entries only* to show only the entries for Debit of Cash / Bank Account (i.e Receipt & Contra Vouchers), in condensed form only
  - o **All Vouchers:** Select *All Vouchers* to show all transactions involving Cash / bank Accounts (i.e Receipt, payment & Contra Vouchers)
- **Format**: At *Format,*
  - o Select *Condensed* to get only the top level figures (Account Group / Ledger).
  - o Select *Detailed* to get the lowest level ledger details (you may also use *F1:Detailed / Condensed* toggle button)
- **Bill Ref Details**: At *Show Billwise Details also* (relevant only when Bill Reference is activated: §03/03-07)
  - o Set *Yes* to show the Bill Reference details.
  - o Set *No* to omit Bill Reference details
- **Cost Centre Details**: At *Show Cost Centre Details also* (relevant only when Cost Centre is activated)
  - o Set *Yes* to show Cost Center details.
  - o Set *No* to omit Cost Center details
- **Inventory Details**: At *Show Inventory Details also* (relevant only when Accounts with Inventory module is activated §02/01-01)
  - o Set *Yes* to show Inventory details.
  - o Set *No* to omit Inventory details
- **Bank Details**: At *Show Bank details also*
  - o Set *Yes* to show the Bank Details (Payee, Bank etc),
  - o Set *No* to omit voucher Bank details.
- **Voucher Number**: at *Show Voucher Numbers also*
  - o Set *Yes* to show Voucher Number,
  - o Set *No* to omit voucher Number in the Cash / Bank Book
- **Voucher Narration**: At *Show Narration also*
  - o Set *Yes* to show the voucher Narration also for each voucher.
  - o Set *No* to omit voucher Narration.
- **Opening Balance:** At *Include Opening Balance also*
  - o Set *Yes* to show Opening balance, to show Opening Balance in the Report,
  - o Set *No* to omit the Opening Balance (only Transactions & Closing Balance is shown)
- **Running Balance**: At *show running balance*
  - o Set Yes to show running balance of Cash / Bank Ledger against each entry
  - o Set No. No Running balance after each entry is shown
- **Group / Ledger Selection**: When you select All Accounts, at *Allow Selection of Ledgers*, you may further set:
  - o **Inclusion / Exclusion**: Set *Yes* to get Include / Exclude Ledger screen to further set Include / Exclude Account Groups / Ledgers (F-19A)
  - o **Alphabetical Range**: Set *No.* to get Alphabetical Range setting screen to further set Alphabetical Range of Ledger Names to print (F-16A)
- **Sorting Method**: When you select All Ledgers or Group of Ledgers at Ledger Printing Menu, at *Sorting Method*, select from the list (F-17B):
  - o Select *Default* to print Ledgers in Alphabetical Order of Ledger Name
  - o Select *Group* to print Ledgers in Alphabetical Order of Parent Group Name (and then in alphabetical order of Ledger Name within the parent Group Name)
- **Group Name:** At *Show Group Name,*
  - o Set *Yes* to show Account Group Name of the Ledger Account (F-18B) just below the Ledger Account Name in parenthesis
  - o Set *No*. Group Name will not be shown (F-15A)

  Method of Balancing: At *Method of Balancing*, select the Balancing period from the list, to print the Debit Credit Total sand the period end Closing balance, which is carried as Opening balance for next period (or at the end of Report)
  - o **Yearly:** To Balance at the end of Financial Year End Date (F-15A)
  - o **Monthly:** To Balance at the end of each month
  - o **Weekly:** To Balance at the end of each week (starting from the period beginning Date)
  - o **Daily**: To Balance at the end of each Date
- **New Page:** At *Start Fresh page for Balancing,*
  - o Set *Yes* to skip to a new page start the next period from the beginning of page (skipping the page),
  - o Set No to continue next period in the same page.

Alphabetical Range of Ledgers: To print several ledgers in selective lots, at *Allow selection of Ledger Accounts*, Set

Yes to get to get options to further set Alphabetical Range as follows (F-16A), to print ledgers in alphabetical order of Ledger Names

At *Alphabetical Print Range* (F-16A), set as follows:

- Set *Yes* and then specify the Starting & Ending Alphabetical Range (of parent Group Name & Ledger Name within Group, or Ledger Name, as per Sort Option selected) at From & To fields (e.g A to C, AA to AB etc).
- Set *No.* The Range fields would be skipped (to print All Ledgers)

Allow Selection for Groups/Ledgers	? **No**	
Set Alphabetical print range	? **Yes**	
From (blank for beginning)	: **A**	To (blank for end) **B**
Print index page	? **No**	

F-16A: Selection of Alphabetical Range of Ledgers

Style of Report
Confirmation of A/cs
Normal Ledger

F-17A: Report Style List

Sorting Met
Default
Group

F-17B: Sorting Method List

A K Traders
Ledger Account
1-Apr-2009 to 30-Jun-2009

Page 1

Date	Particulars	Vch Type	Vch No.	Debit	Credit
1-4-2009	To Opening Balance			1,000.00	
1-5-2009	By (as per details)	Journal	1		1,100.00
	Freight	400.00 Dr			
	Handling Charges	700.00 Dr			
	Bill for Freigtht & Handling Charges				
1-6-2009	To (as per details)	Payment	2	2,000.00	
	TDS		20.00 Cr		
	Bank of India		1,980.00 Cr		
	Cheque 239876 1-6-2009	1,980.00 Cr			
	Paid for Bills after deducting TDS				
	By Sales Return	Credit Note	1		2,000.00
	Goods recived back from cutomers				
2-6-2009	To (as per details)	Sales	2	2,800.00	
	Sales		2,500.00 Cr		
	Freight		300.00 Cr		
	Sold to A K Traders and despatched by B P transport paying freight				
				5,800.00	3,100.00
	By Closing Balance				2,700.00
				5,800.00	5,800.00

F-18A: Multi Account Ledger for a selected Ledger Account

Properitor's Capital
(Capital Account)

3-5-2009	Dr **Cash**	**Receipt**		1,900.00
				1,900.00
	Cr **Closing Balance**		1,900.00	
			1,900.00	1,900.00

Pre Paid Expenses
(Current Assets)

31-3-2010	Cr **HDFC Bank**	**Payment**	1,800.00	
			1,800.00	
	Dr **Closing Balance**			1,800.00
			1,800.00	1,800.00

F-18B: Multi Account Ledger (with Group Name)

Group Selection	
Include these Groups	**Exclude these Groups**
▮ End of List	**Sundry Debtors** **Indirect Expenses**
Ledger Selection	
Include these Ledgers	**Exclude these Ledgers**
A K Traders **Depreciation on Furniture** **Freight**	

F-19A: Include/ Exclude Selection of Multiple Ledgers for Printing

10.01 Selected Ledgers Printing

To print selected ledgers at a time, at Multi Account Ledger printing (F-16A), you may filter the selected Accounts Groups / Accounts Ledgers.

At Multi Account Ledger printing (F-16A), at *Allow Selection of Ledgers*, set Yes to get Account Group / Ledger Account Exclude / Include screen (F-19A). The screen is divided in two major sections- Groups & Ledgers. Each section contain 2 columns – Exclude & Include, to filter a selected bunch of ledgers to be printed, as per Exclude / Include parameters set. The list of Items will be managed by the selection of Items in the previous sections, to avoid conflicts / duplication.

Selection of Groups: At the top section, select the Groups as follows:

- **Include Groups:** At *Include these Groups*, select the Groups from the List of Groups to include the parent of the Ledgers to be printed.
- **Exclude Groups:** Having selected the Groups under Include these Groups, at *Exclude these Groups*, you may select the sub groups of the selected groups (at Include these Groups) that you like to be excluded from your selection of Groups. The ledgers under these Groups will NOT be printed. For exclusion of Groups, only the subgroups of the Groups selected under the *Include these Groups* will be listed. If no Group is selected under *Include these Groups*, all groups will be listed at *Exclude these Groups* for selection of excluded Groups.

Selection of Ledgers: At the next section, select the Ledgers as follows:

- **Include Ledgers:** At *Include these Ledgers,* select the specific Ledgers that you like to be printed (these were not included / excluded under Include / Exclude Groups) as mentioned above. Only the ledgers not belonging to the Groups placed under Include these Groups will be listed (to prevent double selection).
- **Exclude Ledgers:** At *Exclude these Ledgers*, select the specific Ledgers that you do not like to print but belonging to the Groups placed under Include these Groups). The specified ledger Accounts will NOT be printed. For

exclusion of Ledgers, only the ledgers of the Groups selected under the Include these Groups will be listed. If any group is selected under Exclude these Groups, then the ledger under such selected groups will be listed for specific selection of Ledgers from the excluded Groups.

10.02 Ledger Index Printing

You may also print Index Page (like the Index of Manual Ledgers) to find a Ledger Account easily from the heap of pages quickly

Having selected *All Ledgers* or *Group of Ledgers* at Ledger printing Menu, at the Ledger Printing screen (F-14A), set *Yes* at the option *Print Index Page* to print Index of Ledgers (F-19).

The Index (F-19) shows the list of Ledgers printed and the corresponding page numbers at which the ledger is printed.

10.03 Confirmation of Accounts Printing

Confirmation of Accounts is basically a Ledger Account report, in the form of a letter. It is used for Audit / supporting evidence of transaction with another Party.

At *Multi Account Ledger Printing* Screen (F-14A), at *Style of Report*, select *Confirmation of Accounts* to print *Confirmation of Accounts* (F-20).

Index
1-Apr-2009 to 31-Mar-2010

Sl. No.	Particulars	Page No.
1	Accrued Interest	1
2	A K Traders	1
3	Bank of India	1
4	B M Suppliers	1
5	Cash	2
6	Cash Sales	2
7	Current Year Profit / Loss	2
8	Depreciation on Furniture	2
9	Discount on Purchase	2
10	Drawings	3
11	Freight	3
12	Furniture (Accumulated DEpreciation)	3
13	Handling Charges	3
14	HRA	3
15	ICICI Term Loan	3
16	Interest on Term Loan	4
17	Interest on Unsecured Loan	4
18	Office Rent	4
19	P F	4
20	Pre Paid Expenses	4
21	Profit & Loss A/c	4
22	Properitor's Capital	4
23	Purchase	5
24	Rent Received	5
25	Salary	5
26	Sales	5
27	Sales Rebates	5
28	Sales Return	5
29	S Kurien	6
30	S Roy (Employee)	6
31	Stock in Hand	6
32	TDS	6
33	Tution Fees	6

F-19:Ledger Index

To : A K Traders
30 Heysham Rd
Kolkata
700 004

From : ABC Academy
99, Airport Rd
Kolkata 700 096
W Bengal

Dear Sir/Madam,

Dated : 1-Apr-2010

Sub: Confirmation of Accounts
1-Apr-2009 to 31-Mar-2010

Given below is the details of your Accounts as standing in my/our Books of Accounts for the above mentioned period.

Kindly return 3 copies stating your I.T. Permanent A/c No., duly signed and sealed, in confirmation of the same. Please note that if no reply is received from you within a fortnight, it will be assumed that you have accepted the balance shown below.

Date	Particulars	Debit Amount	Date	Particulars	Credit Amount
1-Apr-2009	**Opening Balance**	1,000.00			
			4-May-2009	Freight	1,100.00
3-Jun-2009	TDS	2,000.00	1-Jun-2009	Sales Return	2,000.00
4-Jun-2009	Sales - 3	2,800.00	1-Jun-2009	Cash	3,000.00
1-Jul-2009	Sales - 4	2,150.00			
31-Aug-2009	Bank	1,000.00			
			1-Nov-2009	Sales Rebates	500.00
			1-Jan-2010	Cash	2,000.00
			31-Jan-2010	Cash	2,000.00
28-Feb-2010	Bank	1,200.00	1-Feb-2010	Cash	2,000.00
3-Mar-2010	Bank	1,000.00	1-Mar-2010	Bank	6,000.00
31-Mar-2010	Bank	1,200.00			
		12,350.00			18,600.00
	Closing Balance	6,250.00			
		18,600.00			18,600.00

I/We hereby confirm the above

Yours faithfully,

Accountant

I.T. PAN No. : ABCDE1234Z

Our I.T. PAN No. : ACDPE3456V

F-20: Confirmation of Accounts

FAQ: Frequently Asked Questions

FAQ-1: How to Print Confirmation of Accounts of all Ledger Accounts under a specific Account Groups?

Ans: At Gateway of Tally > Multi Account Printing> Account Books > Ledger > All Accounts.

Set period (e.g. 1-4-08 to 31-3-09). Select "Confirmation of A/cs " from "Style of Report". Select the Group at *Exclude / Include* options to get the confirmation of accounts of ledgers of specified Group

FAQ-2: How to Print Ledger Accounts under a specific Account Group, excluding some specific Ledger Accounts

At Gateway of Tally, select Multi Account Printing> Account Books > Ledger > All Ledger Accounts

Set Yes at the option Allow Selection of Groups Ledgers to get the Exclude / Include Group / Ledger screen, and select the Groups / Ledgers in the respective sections as follows:

- **Include these Groups:** Select the Group from the List of Groups for which the Ledger Accounts are to be printed.
- **Exclude these Ledgers:** Select the Ledgers from the List of Ledgers under the selected Group, for which the Ledger Accounts are not to be printed.

FAQ-3: How you can set PAN No. of the Party and the Company and print Company & Party PAN, Company & Party's Address in Confirmation of Accounts?

i. To set PAN of the party, at Gateway of Tally > Account Info > Ledger > Alter, select the Party Account. At Tax Information, enter the PAN No. of the party.

ii. To set PAN of the Company, Click F11: Features Button, Click F3: Statutory options button. At Tax Information enter Company's PAN No. at "PAN / Income - Tax No" field.

iii. Click P:Print (or press Alt+P) to get Ledger Account Printing screen

iv. Click T:Titling button and set Yes at
   - Print with Company Name
   - Print with Company Address

At Ledger Printing Configuration options:

- Set Yes at Company's PAN / IT Number
- Set Yes at Party Address to print
- Set Yes at Show Party's PAN / IT Number

Columnar Register

02-18

01 Columnar Voucher Register

We have seen various types of Accounts Voucher Lists in which each Ledger Account transaction is printed in separate line, showing debit or credit figures, as applicable, in a common column. To get the account wise details, you have to look into Ledger Book, a separate report

However, businessmen sometimes prefer both these reports (listing like Journal & Accountwsie figure like a Ledger) in a compact single report. The columnar Voucher register shows the voucher details like any Account Voucher List, and simultaneously it shows the amount in separate columns for Ledger Accounts / Account Group, to give the figures like a Ledger. So, it is combination of a Journal & Ledger,

Columnar Voucher Register gives detailed (each voucher detail) as well as summary figures (column totals for each ledger / group), provide more information at a glance, are compact in format conserving space and simpler to apprehend.

Further, the Ledger Account columns and Report contents may be defined by the user to print various types of columnar reports. Such facility makes the columnar report a great tool to get customized reports.

02 Voucher Register Column Definitions

You get Column Definition screen (F-1A) through the following reports

Columnar Reports are defined and viewed through a set of buttons, available in some reports

- Voucher Register (*Display > Account Books' > Journal Register >* select a month, Click *F5: Columnar* button or set *Yes* at *Show Columnar Register* at Voucher Register configuration option.
- Day Book (*Display > Day Book Click F4:Chg Vch* and select a Voucher Type, Click *F5: Columnar* button or set *Yes* at *Show Columnar Register* at List of Voucher Configuration option.
- Ledger Vouchers (*Display > Account Books > Ledger ->* select a Ledger, Click *F8: Columnar* button (or press *Alt+F8*).

Columnar Register Alteration screen (F-1A), contains 2 parts, to set column definitions:

- **Voucher Particulars**: In the first part (Voucher Particulars), you specify the Voucher Particulars (particulars of the entire voucher).
- **Ledger Accounts**: In the second part (Ledger Amount), you specify the Ledger / Groups (Ledger / Groups for which the amount is shown in the column).

02.01 Voucher Particulars Columns Definition

At *Columnar Register Alteration* screen (F-1A), at upper part of the *Columnar Register Alteration* screen, set *Yes / No* to create the columns to show the respective data in each column. These columns appear first in the report.

- **Voucher Type**: At *Show Voucher Type,* set *Yes* to show the Voucher Type. This column is useful when you print the Report for all types of Voucher, else set *No* to omit this column
- **Voucher Number**: At *Show Voucher Number* set *Yes* to show the Voucher No. else set *No* to omit this column (when Voucher Number is not maintained)
- **Voucher Ref:** At *Show Voucher Ref* set *Yes* to show the Voucher Ref No. else set *No* to omit this column
- **Party's Tax Regn No**: At *Show Party's Tax Regn No,* set *Yes* to show the Party's Tax Regn Number (VAT), Useful when VAT is also implemented in the system, else set *No* to omit this column
- **Service Tax Regn No**: At *Show Service Tax Regn No,* set *Yes* to show the Party's Service Tax Regn Number Useful when Service Tax is also implemented in the system, else set *No* to omit this column
- **IT PAN:** At *Show PAN No,* set *Yes* to show the Party's Income Tax PAN, else set *No* to omit the column.
- **CST No**: At *Show CST No,* set *Yes* to show the Party's Central Sales Tax Regn Number Useful when CST is also implemented in the system, else set *No* to omit this column
- **Voucher Narration**: At *Show Voucher Narration*, set *Yes* to show the Voucher Narration. else set *No* to omit this column (to conserve space)
- **Quantity Details:** At *Show Quantity Details,* Set *Yes* to show Quantity details of the Item. This is useful when Inventory System is also implemented, else set *No* to omit this column
    - o **Rate details**: If you have set Yes at *show Quantity details*, you may further Set *Yes* to at *Show Rate details,* to show Rate details of the Item, else set

No to omit this column. Item Rate column useful when Inventory System is also implemented,

- **Item Value**: At *Show Item Value*, set *Yes* to show Value of the Item. This is useful when Inventory System is also implemented, else set *No* to omit this column

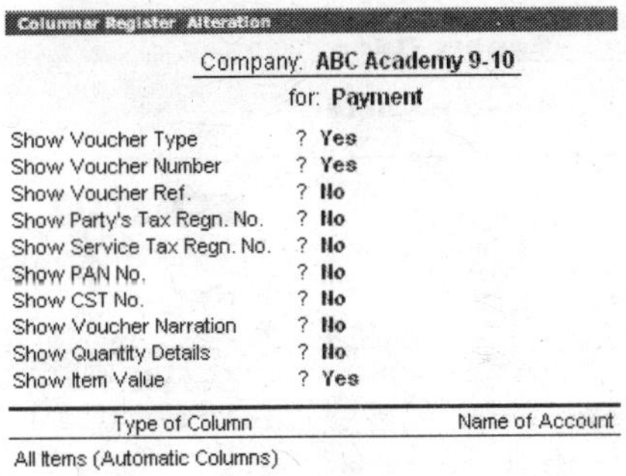

F-1A: Columnar Register column definition

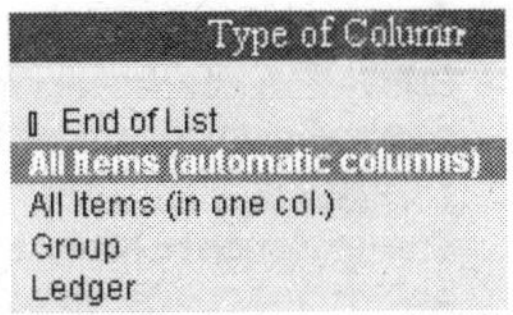

F-1B: Column Type List

F-1C: Group Column Selection

F-1D:Ledger Column Selection

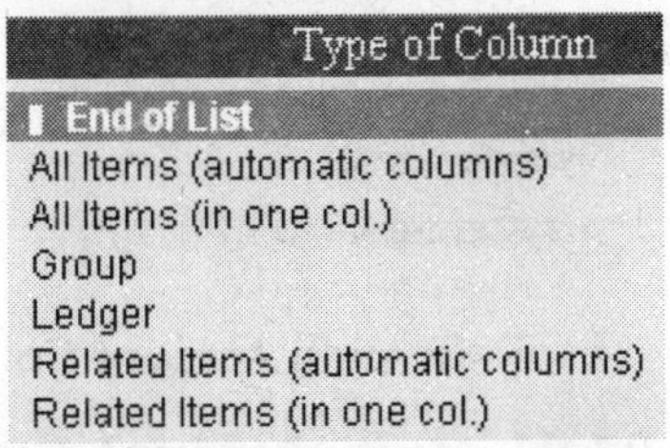

F-1E:Group/Ledger Column Selection list

For versatility, several sets of definition scheme, to show columns for Ledger Amounts, Group Amounts or a combination of them are provided,

At *Type of Columns* field, select the Column Type (F-1B), as explained below:

02.02.01 Individual Group / Ledger Columns

At *Type of Column* (F-1A), select *All Items (Automatic Columns-)*, from the Column type list (F-1B), to automatically create individual column for each Ledger Account transacted in the Vouchers for the period, to produce the Columnar Register (F 2A).

02.02.02 Specific Group / Ledger Column

To create column for Account Group / Account Ledger, at Type of Column (F-1A), select the respective option from the column type list (F-1B), as follows:

- Select *Group* to create column for the summed up figures of all subordinate ledgers of an Account Group (F-1C)
- Select *Ledger* to create column for specific Ledger Accounts (F-1E)
- Select *All Items (in One column)* to combine the remaining Ledgers (Items which are not selected individually) in one Column only.

  Now specify the column definition for Group / Ledger columns (F-1E)
- Select *Related Items (Automatic Columns).* Related Item means the Complementary / Left out transacted Accounts, other than specifically selected Accounts.
  - o When you select *Ledger*, a column will be auto created for each selected ledger account transacted in the Vouchers (F-1D)

Ledger Vouchers — ABC Academy 9-10 — Ctrl + M

Ledger: **Salary** — **1-Apr-2009 to 31-Mar-2010**

Date	*Particulars*	Voucher Type	Vch No.	Narration	Gross Total	Salary	HRA	P F
31-Mar-2010	**S Roy (Employee)**	Journal	3	Salary payable to S Roy for March 10	**11,800.00**	10,000.00	3,000.00	(-)1,200.00
31-Mar-2010	**Bank of India**	Payment	11	Ch # 654321 Salary Paid to M rakesh For March 10	**14,700.00**	13,000.00	3,000.00	(-)1,300.00
	Grand Total				**26,500.00**	23,000.00	6,000.00	(-)2,500.00

F-2A: Columnar Register

02.02 Account Groups / Ledgers Columns Definition

At the lower part of the *Columnar Register Alteration* screen, define the Amount columns, where the amount of respective Account Group / Ledger Accounts are shown

  - o When you select *Group*, a column will be created for each Account Group in which the figures of all subordinate ledgers accounts transacted in the voucher, falling under the selected Account Group (F-1C)
  - o When you select *Related Items (in One Column)*, figures of related Ledgers will be clubbed together into one column named *Others* (F-1E)

03 Multi Account Columnar Register

You may print Multi Account Columnar Register for various Account Books.

- At Gateway of Tally, select *Multi Account Printing > Account Books to get Multi-Accounts Accounts Books* printing menu (F-2B/01-05), and then select the respective Account Books, as follows to get the Multi Account Register printing screen.
    - o *Sales Register* to print Multi Account Columnar Sales Register (F-4A)
    - o *Purchase Register* to print Multi Account Columnar Purchase Register (F-5A)
    - o *Journal>Debit Note Register* to print Multi Account Columnar Debit Note Register (F-6A)
    - o *Journal>Credit Note Register* to print Multi Account Columnar Credit Note Register (F-7A)
    - o *Journal>Journal Register* to print Multi Account Columnar Journal Register (F-8A)
- At the respective Multi Account Register printing screen (F- 3A), set *Yes* at *Show Columnar Register* to get the Column Definition screen (F-1A).

At *Column Definition screen* (F-1A), set the column definition as described (§02.01).

- Having set the Column definitions (F-1A), you get the Multi Account Columnar Register printing screen (F-3B). Set the printing options and type Y to print the Columnar Register (F-4A),as per options set at *Multi Account Columnar Register printing screen* (F-3B).

04 Columnar Sales / Purchase Register

This way, you may define the columns and print the Multi-Account columnar register for:

- Sales Register (F-4A)
- Purchase Register (F-5A)
- Debit Note Register (F-6A)
- Credit Note Register (F-7A)
- Journal Register (F-8A)

Report Titles

Sales Register

From (blank for beginning)	:	1-3-2010
To (blank for end)	:	31-3-2010
Show Extract of Register	?	No
Show Columnar Register	?	No
Format	:	Detailed
Show Voucher Numbers also	?	Yes
Show Narrations also	?	No
Show Billwise Details also	?	No
Show Cost Centre Details also	?	No
Show Inventory Details also	?	No
Show Bank Details also	?	No
Show Entered/Altered By	?	No

F-3A: Multi Account Register printing screen

Report Titles

Sales Register

From (blank for beginning)	:	1-4-2009
To (blank for end)	:	31-3-2010
Show Extract of Register	?	No
Show Columnar Register	?	Yes
Format	:	Detailed
Show Entered/Altered By	?	y

F-3B: Multi Account Columnar Register printing

04.01 Multi Account Columnar Sales Register

Sales Register

1-Apr-2009 to 31-Mar-2010

Page 1

Date	Particulars	Voucher Type	Vch No.	Narration	Gross Total	Sales	Sales Rebates	Freight
2-May-2009	Cash *Entered By : akn*	Sales	1	Goods sold in cash after allowing rebates	**2,000.00**	2,100.00	(-)100.00	
2-Jun-2009	A K Traders *Entered By : akn*	Sales	2	Sold to A K Traders and despatched by B P transport paying freight	**2,800.00**	2,500.00		300.00
1-Jul-2009	A K Traders *Entered By : akn*	Sales	3	Sold to A K Traders	**2,150.00**	2,000.00	(-)50.00	200.00
	Grand Total				**6,950.00**	6,600.00	(-)150.00	500.00

F- 4A: Multi Account Columnar Sales Register

04.02 Multi Account Columnar Purchase Register

Date	Particulars	Voucher Type	Vch No.	Sales Tax No.	PAN No.	Narration	Gross Total	Purchase on Purchase	Freight	Discount
01/06/2009	**B M Suppliers**	Purchase	1	WB 3790	ACFBT 3457D	Purchases from B M Suppkier a sper their Bill # 12 Dt 31.5.09	**2200.00**	2100.00	300.00	-200.00
01/11/2009	**B M Suppliers**	Purchase	2	WB 3790	ACFBT 3457D	Materials purchased ag party's Inv No 12 dt 3110.11	**3040.00**	3000.00	40.00	
01/11/2009	**B M Suppliers**	Purchase	3	WB 3790	ACFBT 3457D	Materials purchased ag party's Inv No 14 dt 3110.11	**3040.00**	3000.00	40.00	
01/12/2009	**B M Suppliers**	Purchase	4		ACFBT 3457D	Materials purchased ag party's Inv No 12 dt 3110.11	**3040.00**	3000.00	40.00	
	Grand Total						**11320.00**	11100.00	420.00	-200.00

F-5A:Multi Account Columnar Purchase Register

04.03 Multi Account Columnar Debit & Credit Note Register

Like Columnar Sales & Purchase Register, you may set up columns for Debit Note Register (F-6A) & Credit Note Register (F-7A) also, and print the Register as per columns options set, as described.

04.04 Multi Account Columnar Journal Register

At Gateway, select *Multi Account Printing>Account Books> Journal Register>Journal* to get Multi Account Journal Register printing screen. Select the options & set the Columnar Register column definitions (Fig 1) to get the Multi Account Columnar Journal Register (F-8A).

Debit Note Register

1-May-2008 to 31-May-2008

Page 1

Date	*Particulars*	Voucher Type	Vch No.	Gross Total	Purcha-se
2-May-2008	**D K Enterprises**	Debit Note	1	**600.00**	600.00
	Grand Total			**600.00**	600.00

F-6A: Multi Account Columnar Debit Note Register

Credit Note Register

1-May-2008 to 31-May-2008

Page 1

Date	*Particulars*	Voucher Type	Vch No.	Gross Total	Sales
2-May-2008	**A K Traders**	Credit Note	1	**250.00**	250.00
	Grand Total			**250.00**	250.00

F-7A: Multi Account Columnar Credit Note Register

Journal Register
1-Apr-2008 to 31-May-2008

Page 1

Date	Particulars	Voucher Type	Vch No.	Narration	Gross Total	Basant Kr. Chithangia	Interest Receiv-ed on Loan	Interest Paid	Kamala Devi Patwari
14-May-2008		Journal	1	Money received from Basant kumar chitangia. (1, 01,880 - 1,00493)= Rs. 1387.00	**0.00**	(-)1,387.00	1,387.00		
21-May-2008		Journal	2	Interest for the period provided @12% pa	**0.00**			(-)1,198.00	1,198.00
	Grand Total					(-)1,387.00	1,387.00	(-)1,198.00	1,198.00

F-8A: Multi Account Columnar Journal Register

04.05 Columnar Petty Cash Book

Using the columnar feature of Ledger, you may print Petty Cash Book in columnar format. To maintain Petty Cash:

- Create a Petty Cash Ledger Account and Main Cash Account (under Cash -in -Hand).
- To transfer money from Main cash to Petty Cash, create a Contra voucher as usual.
- In all payments from Petty Cash, create payment voucher. Select Petty Cash Account.

To print Columnar Petty Cash Book, select *Display > Account Book > Ledger*, select Petty cash Account. Click *columnar* button and set the columns.

All the vouchers having a transaction with Petty Cash Ledger account are listed (F-2)

Jounal Register
1-Jan-2009 to 31-Mar-2009

Page 1 (A)

Date	Particulars	Voucher Type	Vch No.	Narration	Gross Total	Ritesh Nadhani	Interest Received on Loan	A.K. Nadhani	Medical Insurance Claim
31-Mar-2009		Journal	4	Interet received on loan @ 12%.	**0.00**	(-)12,000.00	12,000.00		
31-Mar-2009		Journal	5		**0.00**			(-)60,000.00	60,000.00
31-Mar-2009		Journal	6		**0.00**		7,200.00	(-)7,200.00	
31-Mar-2009		Journal	7	Interest on HDFC FD (42106) of Rs. 80,000@11 %	**0.00**				
31-Mar-2009		Journal	8		**0.00**		100.00	(-)100.00	
31-Mar-2009		Journal	9		**0.00**		100.00	(-)100.00	
	Grand Total					(-)12,000.00	19,400.00	(-)67,400.00	60,000.00

Page 1 (B)

HDFC FD	Interest on FD
(-)2,989.59	2,989.59
(-)2,989.59	2,989.59

F-9A: Multi Part Register - Part 1A

Part 1B

05 Multipart Columnar Register Printing

When you select too many columns during Display, you may pan the report (left & right) to see the columns.

When you print such wide report, the report is broken into multiple parts (F- 9A) and you may print the specific part, specifying the page range, as explained under Multi part Reports (§05/02-13). You may view the specific Part in Print Preview. In the first few columns the specified voucher info are shown, followed by the defined amount columns are shown. Such reports are useful to paste the parts together, to get a wider report than what the printer allows to print. The 2nd part onwards, the Voucher info columns are not printed. So, you need to paste the parts together to make use of the report.

FAQ: Frequently Asked Questions

FAQ-1: How I can print columnar Sales Register with columns for specified info and Amount for each Ledger Account in separate column

Ans: Select *Display > Account Books > Ledger* and select *Sales* from the list of Ledger to get Ledger Vouchers for Sales Ledger. Click *F8: Columnar* button (or press *Alt+F8*).

At the upper Part, set Yes to those Info columns which you like to print in the Sales Register

At the lower part, at *Type of Column,* select *All Items (Automatic Columns)*

Now you get the Columnar Sales Register (list of vouchers in which a ledger account under *Sales* Group has been transacted) with selected Info columns and separate Amount column for each Ledger Account. The Debit Amounts (Amount Charged) are shown in negative, while Credit Amounts (Deductions) are shown positive

FAQ-2: How I can print a Salary Register with columns for each ledger account and employee Names.

Ans: The recommended way is to create Voucher Type for Salary. The Voucher Type can be of Journal or Payment, depending on your approach to create the Ledger Accounts of Employees

At Gateway, select *Accounts Info>Voucher Type > Create*. At name, enter *Salary*. At Type of Voucher, select Journal or Payment, as the case may be, as explained below.

Case 1: You create a ledger Account for each Employee

In such case, you create a Journal Voucher debiting / crediting the expenses / deduction and crediting the net Pay to Employee's personal account. At the time of payment, you create a Payment voucher debiting the Employee's personal account (crediting Cash / Bank)

In such case, create a new Journal Voucher Type *Salary* (at Type of Voucher in Voucher Type creation, select Journal)

The Voucher would be like this:

1. Salary Voucher Type at the end of month

   Salary A/c Dr

   HRA A/c Dr

   PF A/c Cr

   ESI A/c Cr

   Employee A/c Cr (by Net Salary Payable)

(Through this voucher, all the ledger accounts are charged, even if no payment is made to the employees. To get the Salary Register for each employee details, separate voucher is to be created for each employee)

2. Payment Voucher at the time of Payment

   Employee A/c Dr

   Cash / Bank Cr A/c

(One voucher may be created debiting the respective employee ledger accounts)

This is better approach as each employee ledger accounts show complete details of transaction for the respective employee.

Columnar Salary Register: To get Salary Register, select Day Book (*Display > Day Book Click F4:Chg Vch* and select Salary Voucher Type, Click *F5: Columnar* button (or set *Yes* at *Show Columnar Register* at List of Voucher Configuration option.

- At Columnar Register Alteration screen, Set *Yes* at the respective Info Column which you like to print in Salary Register.
- At Type of Column, select *All Items (Automatic Columns)*

Now you will get the Salary Register showing the Salary details of each Employee. Debit Accounts (payments) are shown as negative, while Credit Accounts (Deductions) are shown as positive. The Employee Ledger Name appears at the Particulars column and the net Salary is shown at Gross Total columns

Case 2: You do not create separate ledger Accounts for each Employee

In such case, you create a Payment Voucher debiting / crediting the expenses / deduction and crediting the net Pay to Cash / Bank Account. Create a new Payment Voucher Type *Salary*

Salary A/c Dr

HRA A/c Dr

PF A/c Cr

ESI A/c Cr

Cash / Bank A/c Cr

The Name of the Employee, Pay Month etc are to be entered at Voucher Narration.

(Through this voucher, all the ledger accounts are charged, only at the time of payment. To get the Salary Register for each employee details, separate voucher is to be created for each employee)

Columnar Salary Register: To get Salary Register, select Day Book (*Display > Day Book Click F4:Chg Vch* and select Salary Voucher Type, Click *F5: Columnar* button. At Columnar Register Alteration screen, set as follows

- Set Yes at the respective Info Column which you like to print in Salary Register (like Voucher Type, Voucher Number, Voucher Narration). or set *Yes* at *Show Columnar Register* at List of Voucher Configuration option.
- At Type of Column, select *All Items (Automatic Columns)*

Now you will get the Salary Register showing the Salary details of each Employee. Debit Accounts (payments) are shown as negative, while Credit Accounts (Deductions) are shown as positive. The Cash /Bank Account appears at the Particulars and the net Salary is shown at Gross Total columns. Employee names are shown in Narration

The first method is superior from Accounting point of view.

This way, you may create separate Journal Voucher type for regular bulk types of transaction (like Salary, Travelling & Conveyance, Contractors Charges). In this way, you can have a subsidiary Journal Book with compact and complete details of a particular nature of transaction. This will help to maintain better organized books of accounts. The number of entries in main books of accounts (Cash Bank Book, Ledger etc) will also get reduced (as one payment voucher can cover payment to several Employees paid in one day) This type of columnar register is quite useful where multiple ledger accounts are involved in a voucher.

Account Summaries 02-19

01 Account Summaries

Earlier we have explained Voucher Lists type of Reports (P-1/02-16), which are the first level report of Vouchers, showing the vouchers. In voucher list, a voucher may be directly selected.

Account Summaries comprise of summary reports of Vouchers in various formats. These are immediate higher level Reports of Voucher Lists. On drill down from Account Summaries, you get the next level report of the Voucher List (P-1/02-17).

02 Account Summaries Configuration Table

The following Reports comprise Account Summaries:

- Account Group Summary
- Cash Bank Summary
- Periodic Summaries
- Ledger Daily Break Up
- Voucher Register Extract

03 Account Summaries Buttons Table

The buttons & configuration options of these reports are quite similar. The following table shows the button bars available in the respective report

Option	Description	Account Group Summary	Periodic Summaries	Ledger Daily Break Up	Cash Bank Summary
Show Opening Balances	To include Opening Balance in the report	✓			
Show Transactions	To show transaction figures (Debit & Credit amounts) for the selected period	✓			✓
- Show Net Transactions only	To show the net of Transactions (debit or credit)	✓	✓	✓	✓
Show Closing balance	To show closing balance for each account group / ledger	✓	✓	✓	✓
Show Percentage	To show % figures in respect of each Account Group / Ledger	✓	✓	✓	✓
- Type of %	To specify the basis of % computed as above	✓	✓	✓	✓
Expand all Level in detail Format	To show all subordinate groups / ledger accounts	✓			
Periodicity to Use	Select the periodicity for the Periodic Report		✓	✓	✓
Show Average Details	Show Period Average figures			✓	✓
Show High/Low Details	Show Highest / Lowest periodic balances		✓	✓	✓
Show Graph	Show Bar graph for the periodical figures		✓	✓	✓

Button	Description	Account Group Summary	Periodic Summaries	Ledger Summary	Cash Bank Summary
F1: Detailed / Condensed	To show all subordinate groups / ledger accounts	√		√	√
F4: Group / Ledger	To select an Account Group / Ledger	√	√	√	√
F5:Ledgwise	To show ledger wise report	√			√
F6: Monthly	To show Monthly figures for a specific selected Group	√			
F7:Vouchers	To show voucher wise details	√			
F5:Qrtly/Mnthly	To show Quarterly / Monthly Break up		✓		✓
Columnar Report Buttons Reports	Column specification to get columnar	√	✓	✓	√

In case of Cash Ledger Account, an additional toggle button *X:Exception/ All* appears to show all figures / only Negative Cash Balance figures (Exceptions)

04 Account Group Summary

Account Group Summary shows the figures of Account Groups and underlying Account Groups / Ledgers (F-1A)

Select *Display > Account Books > Group Summary.*

- Select *Primary* to get figures of next level Groups / Ledgers
- Select a Group to get the report of selected Account Group

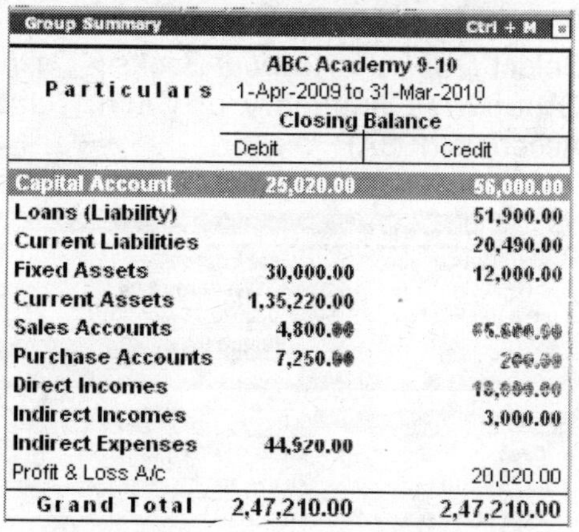

Group Summary — Ctrl + M

Particulars	ABC Academy 9-10 1-Apr-2009 to 31-Mar-2010 Closing Balance Debit	Credit
Capital Account	25,020.00	56,000.00
Loans (Liability)		51,900.00
Current Liabilities		20,490.00
Fixed Assets	30,000.00	12,000.00
Current Assets	1,35,220.00	
Sales Accounts	4,800.00	65,600.00
Purchase Accounts	7,250.00	200.00
Direct Incomes		18,000.00
Indirect Incomes		3,000.00
Indirect Expenses	44,920.00	
Profit & Loss A/c		20,020.00
Grand Total	2,47,210.00	2,47,210.00

F-1A: Account Group Summary(default)

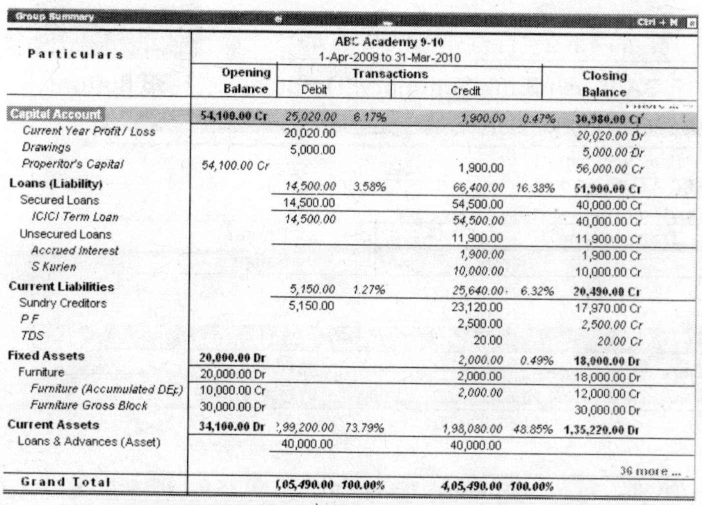

Group Summary — Ctrl + M

ABC Academy 9-10, 1-Apr-2009 to 31-Mar-2010

Particulars	Opening Balance	Transactions Debit		Credit		Closing Balance
Capital Account	54,100.00 Cr	25,020.00	6.17%	1,900.00	0.47%	30,980.00 Cr
Current Year Profit / Loss		20,020.00				20,020.00 Dr
Drawings		5,000.00				5,000.00 Dr
Properitor's Capital	54,100.00 Cr			1,900.00		56,000.00 Cr
Loans (Liability)		14,500.00	3.58%	66,400.00	16.38%	51,900.00 Cr
Secured Loans		14,500.00		54,500.00		40,000.00 Cr
ICICI Term Loan		14,500.00		54,500.00		40,000.00 Cr
Unsecured Loans				11,900.00		11,900.00 Cr
Accrued Interest				1,900.00		1,900.00 Cr
S Kurien				10,000.00		10,000.00 Cr
Current Liabilities		5,150.00	1.27%	25,640.00	6.32%	20,490.00 Cr
Sundry Creditors		5,150.00		23,120.00		17,970.00 Cr
P F				2,500.00		2,500.00 Cr
TDS				20.00		20.00 Cr
Fixed Assets	20,000.00 Dr			2,000.00	0.49%	18,000.00 Dr
Furniture	20,000.00 Dr			2,000.00		18,000.00 Dr
Furniture (Accumulated DEp)	10,000.00 Cr			2,000.00		12,000.00 Cr
Furniture Gross Block	30,000.00 Dr					30,000.00 Dr
Current Assets	34,100.00 Dr	2,99,200.00	73.79%	1,98,080.00	48.85%	1,35,220.00 Dr
Loans & Advances (Asset)		40,000.00		40,000.00		
						36 more ...
Grand Total		4,05,490.00	100.00%	4,05,490.00	100.00%	

F-1B: Account Group Summary with various Configuration options set

Account Group Summary Buttons

At Account Group Summary (F-1A), you get following buttons (F-2B):

Button	Description
F1: Detailed / Condensed	F1: *Detailed*: To show next level groups / ledger detailsF1: *Condensed*: To show only top level Accounts
F4: Group	To select an Account Group
F5:Grouped / Ledgwise	To show Group / Ledger wise report
F6: Monthly / Quarterly	To show Monthly / Quarterly figures for a specific selected Group
F7:Vouchers	To show voucher wise details
Columnar Report Buttons	Column specification to get columnar Reports

Account Group Summary Configuration

> **Note:** *When Transactions are shown, Closing balance (both Debit & Credit) is shown in one column only (Debit & Credit Totals are not available).*Expand All Level Details *(in Configuration) is applicable only in Detailed mode (*F1:Detailed*)*

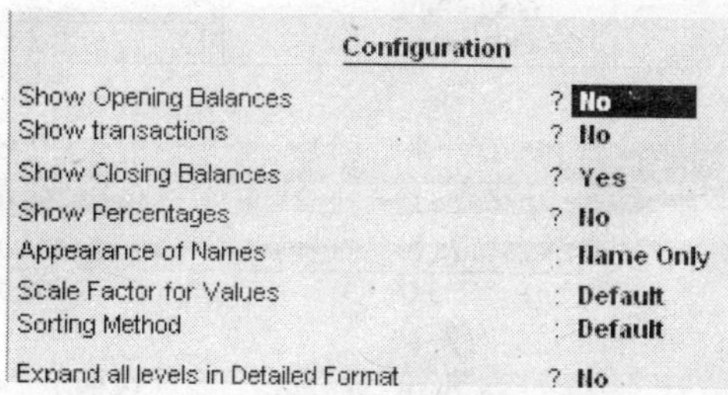

Configuration

Show Opening Balances	? No
Show transactions	? No
Show Closing Balances	? Yes
Show Percentages	? No
Appearance of Names	: Name Only
Scale Factor for Values	: Default
Sorting Method	: Default
Expand all levels in Detailed Format	? No

F-2A: Configuration Options at Group & Ledger Summary (default)

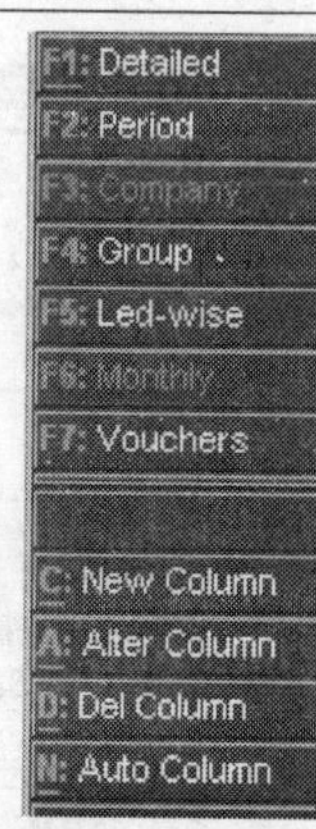

F-2B: Buttons

At Account Group Summary (F-1A), Click *F12: Configure* to get the Account Group Summary configuration screen (F-2A) to set the report options, as follows:

Option	Description
Opening Balance	At *Show Opening Balances*: - Set *Yes* to include Opening Balance in the report (F-1B) - Set *No* to exclude the Opening balance (only the transaction figures for the selected period are considered)
Transaction Details	At *Show Transactions*: - Set *Yes* to show transaction figures (Debit & Credit amounts) for the selected period (F-1B) - Set *No* to suppress the Transaction columns
- Net Transactions	Having set Yes at *Show Transactions*, At *Show Net Transactions only* - Set *Yes* to show the Net Transactions (Net debit or credit), - Set *No* to show both Debit & Credit figures in separate columns (F-1B)
Closing balance	At *Show Closing Balance* - Set *Yes* to show closing balance for each account group / ledger (F-1B) - Set *No* to suppress Closing Balance column **Note:** - You must set *Yes* in at least one of the above 3 options (Opening Balance, Transaction, Closing Balance).
Show Percentage	At *Show Percentage* - Set *Yes* to show % figures (F-1B) in respect of each Account Group / Ledger (on the basis of Total Amount), - Set *No* to suppress % column
Type of %	If *Yes* is set to above options, the Basis of computation *On Total Amount* is displayed (you do not have any option for selection)
Details Levels	Having set *F1:Detailed* button, at *Expand all Level in detail Format* - Set *Yes* to show all subordinate groups ledger accounts to the lowest level (F-1B) - Set *No* to show only the next level Groups/ Ledgers

05 Cash/Bank Summary

Cash / Bank Summary is a specific type of Account Group Summary for Cash / Bank Accounts. The contents, buttons and configuration options of Cash Bank Summary are quite similar to Account Group Summary. In Account Group Summary, you can select only one Cash / Bank Account group, while in Cash Bank summary, all the Cash / Bank Account Group figures appear in the default report. When you select a Cash / Bank Group in Cash / Bank Summary, it works like Account Group Summary

Select *Display > Account Books > Cash/Bank Books* to get GroupWise summary of Cash, Bank and Bank OCC Accounts (F-3A)

Cash/Bank Summary Ctrl + M

Particulars	Bank Accounts ABC Academy 9-10 1-Apr-2009 to 31-Mar-2010 Closing Balance	
	Debit	Credit
Cash-in-Hand	68,250.00	
Cash	*68,250.00*	
Bank Accounts	60,620.00	
Bank of India	*28,520.00*	
State Bank of India	*32,100.00*	
Grand Total	1,28,870.00	

F-3A: Cash Bank Summary (Default)

- F1: Condensed
- F2: Period
- F3: Company
- F4: Group
- F5: Led-wise
- F6: Monthly
- C: New Column
- A: Alter Column
- D: Del Column
- N: Auto Column

F-3B Buttons

Cash/Bank Summary ABC Academy 9-10 Ctrl + M

Particulars	Bank Accounts ABC Academy 9-10 1-Apr-2009 to 31-Mar-2010 Opening Balance		Transactions				Closing Balance	
			Debit		Credit			
Cash-in-Hand	2,000.00 Dr	1.29%	10,19,750.00	92.77%	32,810.50	16.91%	9,88,939.50 Dr	93.23%
Cash	*2,000.00 Dr*		10,19,750.00		32,810.50		*9,88,939.50 Dr*	
Bank Accounts	1,53,556.78 Dr	98.71%	79,500.00	7.23%	1,61,230.00	83.09%	71,826.78 Dr	6.77%
HDFC Bank	*1,21,456.78 Dr*		79,500.00		1,61,230.00		*39,726.78 Dr*	
State Bank of India	*32,100.00 Dr*						*32,100.00 Dr*	
Grand Total	1,55,556.78 Dr	100.00%	10,99,250.00	100.00%	1,94,040.50	100.00%	10,60,766.28 Dr	100.00%

F-3C: Cash Bank Summary (Detailed) with configuration options set

Buttons at Cash Bank Summary

The buttons at Cash Bank Summary (F-3B) are mostly similar to Account Group Summary (F-2B), as shown in the following Table

Button	Description
F1: Detailed / Condensed	To show all subordinate groups / ledger accounts
F4: Group	To select an Account Group
F5: Grouped / Ledgwise	To show Grouped Ledger wise report
Columnar Report Buttons	Column specification to get columnar Reports

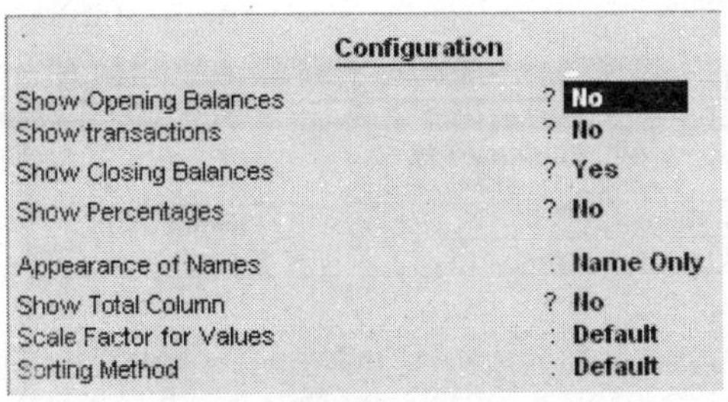

F-3D: Cash Bank Summary Configuration

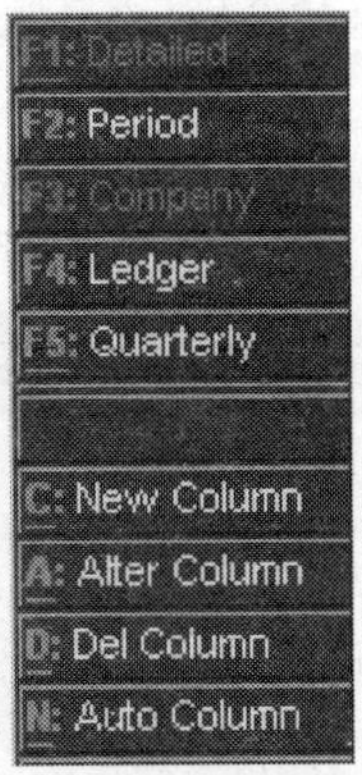

F-4A: Periodic Summary Buttons

Cash / Bank Summary Configuration

At *Cash / Bank Summary* (F-3A), click *F12: Configure* button to get Cash Bank Summary Configuration screen (F-3D), to set the options as desired.

The Cash Bank Summary Configuration options (F-3D) are explained below:

Option	Description
Opening Balance	At *Show Opening Balances*: - Set *Yes* to include Opening Balance in the report (F-3C) - Set *No* to exclude the Opening balance (only the transaction figures for the selected period are considered)
Transaction Details	At *Show Transactions:* - Set *Yes* to show transaction figures (Debit & Credit amounts) for the selected period (F-3C) - Set *No* to suppress the Transaction columns
- Net Transactions	Having set Yes at *Show Transactions*, At *Show Net Transactions only* - Set *Yes* to show the Net Transactions (Net debit or credit), - Set *No* to show both Debit & Credit figures in separate columns (F-3C)
Closing balance	At *Show Closing Balance* - Set *Yes* to show closing balance for each account group / ledger (F-3C) - Set *No* to suppress Closing Balance column **Note:** - You must set *Yes* in at least one of the above 3 options (Opening Balance, Transaction, Closing Balance). - When all the Amount Columns are selected (Opening, Transaction & Closing Balance), the Opening & Closing balances are shown in one columns (Dr/Cr), instead of separate columns (F-3C)
Show Percentage	At *Show Percentage* - Set *Yes* to show % figures (F-3C) in respect of each Account Group / Ledger (on the basis of Total Amount), - Set *No* to suppress % column
Type of %	If *Yes* is set to above options, the Basis of computation *On Total Amount* is displayed (you do not have any option for selection)
Details Levels	Having set F1:Detailed button, at *Expand all Level in detail Format* - Set *Yes* to show all subordinate groups ledger accounts to the lowest level (F-3C) - Set *No* to show only the next level Groups/ Ledgers

06 Periodic Summaries

Periodic Summaries show the periodic break up (Quarterly, Monthly, 4 week month, Weekly, Daily). The period is selected in the Monthly Group / Ledger Summary from the Configuration option *Periodicity to use*, as follows

06.01 Account Group Periodic Summary

This report shows the periodic break up break up of selected Account Group.

Select *Display > Account Books > Group Summary*. Select a Group, Click *F6: Monthly* to get Monthly Group Summary (4-B), with default options

Group Summary Ctrl + M

Particulars	Current Assets ABC Academy 9-10 1-Apr-2009 to 31-Mar-2010		
	Transactions		Closing Balance
	Debit	Credit	
Opening Balance			**34,100.00 Dr**
April	60,500.00	10,500.00	84,100.00 Dr
May	34,900.00	38,100.00	80,900.00 Dr
June	45,800.00	51,980.00	74,720.00 Dr
July	25,150.00	10,000.00	89,870.00 Dr
August	67,000.00	17,000.00	1,39,870.00 Dr
September			1,39,870.00 Dr
October	3,000.00	3,000.00	1,39,870.00 Dr
November		500.00	1,39,370.00 Dr
December	3,000.00	4,000.00	1,38,370.00 Dr
January	12,000.00	12,000.00	1,38,370.00 Dr
February	6,000.00		1,44,370.00 Dr
March	41,850.00	51,000.00	1,35,220.00 Dr
Grand Tota	**2,99,200.00**	**1,98,080.00**	**1,35,220.00 Dr**

F-4B: Account Group Summary (Default)

Group Summary -1 Ctrl + M

Particular	Current Assets ABC Academy 9-10 1-Apr-2009 to 31-Mar-2010				
	Transactions				Closing Balance
	Debit		Credit		
April	60,500.00	20.22%	10,500.00	5.30%	84,100.00 Dr
May	34,900.00	11.66%	38,100.00	19.23%	80,900.00 Dr
June	45,800.00	15.31%	51,980.00	26.24%	74,720.00 Dr
July	25,150.00	8.41%	10,000.00	5.05%	89,870.00 Dr
August	67,000.00	22.39%	17,000.00	8.58%	1,39,870.00 Dr
September					1,39,870.00 Dr
October	3,000.00	1.00%	3,000.00	1.51%	1,39,870.00 Dr
November			500.00	0.25%	1,39,370.00 Dr
December	3,000.00	1.00%	4,000.00	2.02%	1,38,370.00 Dr
January	12,000.00	4.01%	12,000.00	6.06%	1,38,370.00 Dr
February	6,000.00	2.01%			1,44,370.00 Dr
March	41,850.00	13.99%	51,000.00	25.75%	1,35,220.00 Dr
Grand Tot	**2,99,200.00**	**100.00%**	**1,98,080.00**	**100.00%**	**1,35,220.00 Dr**
Average	24,933.33		16,506.67		1,20,408.33 Dr

F-4C: Account Group Summary (with %)

Group Summary ABC Academy 9-10 Ctrl + M

Particulars	Current Assets ABC Academy 9-10 1-Apr-2009 to 31-Mar-2010				
	Transactions				Closing Balance
	Debit		Credit		
... 1 more					
April	60,500.00	20.22%	10,500.00	5.30%	84,100.00 Dr
May	34,900.00	11.66%	38,100.00	19.23%	80,900.00 Dr
June	45,800.00	15.31%	51,980.00	26.24%	74,720.00 Dr
July	25,150.00	8.41%	10,000.00	5.05%	89,870.00 Dr
August	67,000.00	22.39%	17,000.00	8.58%	1,39,870.00 Dr
September					1,39,870.00 Dr
October	3,000.00	1.00%	3,000.00	1.51%	1,39,870.00 Dr
November			500.00	0.25%	1,39,370.00 Dr
December	3,000.00	1.00%	4,000.00	2.02%	1,38,370.00 Dr
January	12,000.00	4.01%	12,000.00	6.06%	1,38,370.00 Dr
February	6,000.00	2.01%			1,44,370.00 Dr
March	41,850.00	13.99%	51,000.00	25.75%	1,35,220.00 Dr
Grand Total	**2,99,200.00**	**100.00%**	**1,98,080.00**	**100.00%**	**1,35,220.00 Dr**
Average	24,933.33		16,506.67		1,20,408.33 Dr

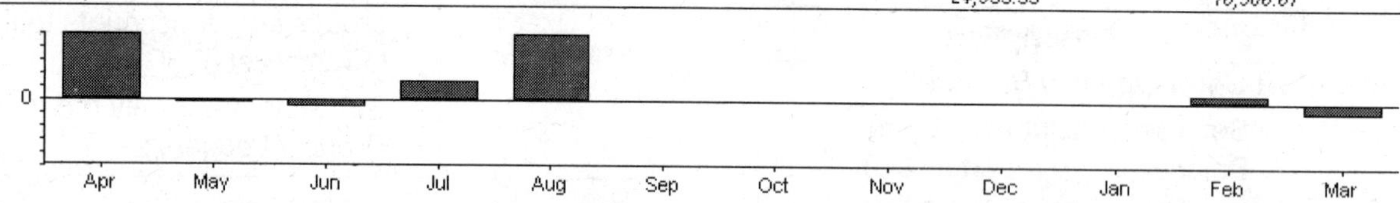

F-4D: Account Group Summary (with Graph)

F-4C shows Monthly Group Summary with detailed configuration options set. F-4D shows Monthly Group Summary with Graph and other configuration options set

06.02 Account Ledger Periodic Summary

This report shows the periodic break up of a Ledger (F-5A)

Select *Display > Account Books > Group Summary.* Select a Group and then select a Ledger (at Group summary, you may click *F5:Grouped/ Ledgwise* button (F-2B) to select a ledger / Group account)

Ledger Monthly Summary-1 Ctrl + M

Particulars	Bank of India **ABC Academy 9-10** 1-Apr-2009 to 31-Mar-2010				
	Transactions				Closing Balance
	Debit		Credit		
↑ ... 10 more					1 more ...
16-Aug to 31-Aug			*1,000.00*	*2.38%*	59,520.00 Dr
1-Sep to 15-Sep					59,520.00 Dr
16-Sep to 30-Sep					59,520.00 Dr
1-Oct to 15-Oct					59,520.00 Dr
16-Oct to 31-Oct					59,520.00 Dr
1-Nov to 15-Nov					59,520.00 Dr
16-Nov to 30-Nov					59,520.00 Dr
1-Dec to 15-Dec			*4,000.00*	*9.53%*	55,520.00 Dr
16-Dec to 31-Dec					55,520.00 Dr
1-Jan to 15-Jan					55,520.00 Dr
16-Jan to 31-Jan					55,520.00 Dr
1-Feb to 15-Feb	*6,000.00*	*8.28%*			61,520.00 Dr
16-Feb to 28-Feb					61,520.00 Dr
1-Mar to 15-Mar					61,520.00 Dr
16-Mar to 31-Mar	*2,000.00*	*2.76%*	*35,000.00*	*83.37%*	28,520.00 Dr
Grand Total	***72,500.00***	***100.00%***	***41,980.00***	***100.00%***	**28,520.00 Dr**
Average	*3,020.83*		*1,749.17*		38,141.67 Dr
Highest Balance	*(dt. 1-Aug-2009)* **50,000.00**		*(dt. 31-Mar-2010)* **35,000.00**		*(dt. 1-Feb-2010)* ***61,520.00 Dr***
Lowest Balance	*(dt. 1-Apr-2009)* **500.00**		*(dt. 31-Aug-2009)* **1,000.00**		*(dt. 1-Jun-2009)* ***3,480.00 Cr***

F-5A Account Ledger Periodic (Fortnight) Summary with %, Highest / Lowest / Average figures

Configuration

Nett transactions only	?	**No**
Show Closing Balances	?	**Yes**
Show Percentages	?	**No**
Appearance of Names	:	**Name Only**
Scale Factor for Values	:	**Default**
Periodicity to use	:	**Fortnightly**
Show Average Details	?	**No**
Show High/Low Details	?	**No**

Graphs

Show with Graph	?	**No**

F-5B: Periodic Summary Configuration

Buttons for Periodic Summaries

At Periodic Summary (F-4B, F-5A), you get following buttons (F-4A):

Button	Description	Periodic Group Summary	Periodic Ledger Summary
F1: Detailed	To show all subordinate groups / ledger accounts	√	
F4: Group / Ledger	To select an Account Group / Ledger	√	√
F5:Ledgwise	To show ledger wise report	✓	
F7:Vouchers	To show voucher wise details	✓	
F5:Qrtly/ Mnthly	To show Quarterly / Monthly Break up	✓	✓
Columnar Report Buttons	Column specification to get columnar Reports	✓	✓

Periodic Summary Configuration

At Group or Ledger Monthly summary, click *F12: Configure* button to get Monthly Summary Configuration screen (F-5B), to set the options as desired. When you set the options for Average /Highest / Lowest Balance, you cannot get the Graph (F-5A)

Configuration options for Periodic Summaries

Option	Description
Net Transactions	At *Show Net Transactions only* - Set *Yes* to show the Net Transactions (Net debit or credit), - Set *No* to show both Debit & Credit figures in separate columns (F-5A)
Closing balance	At *Show Closing Balance* - Set *Yes* to show closing balance for each account group / ledger (F-5A) - Set *No* to suppress Closing Balance column **Note:** - You must set *Yes* in at least one of the above 3 options (Opening Balance, Transaction, Closing Balance). - When all the Amount Columns are selected (Opening, Transaction & Closing Balance), the Opening & Closing balances are shown in one columns (Dr/Cr), instead of separate columns (F-5A)
Show Percentage	At *Show Percentage* - Set *Yes* to show % figures (F-5A) in respect of each Account Group / Ledger (on the basis of Total Amount), - Set *No* to suppress % column
Periodicity	At *Periodicity to Use,* select the Periodicity from the list, to show the periodic break up (default period *Monthly*)
Average Details	At *Show Average Details*: - Set *Yes* to Show period Average figures (F-5A) - Set *No* (default). Average figures are not shown

High/Low Details	At *Show High / Low Details*: - Set *Yes* to Show period High & Low figures (F-5A) - Set *No* (default). High & Low figures are not shown
Show with Graph	At Show with Graph - Set *Yes* to show Bar Graph (F-4B) for the periodical figures (when High Low details are not set) - Set *No*. The Graph is not shown

07 Voucher Extract

Voucher Extract is obtained from Voucher List of Journal, Sales, Purchase, Debit Note & Credit Notes. It shows Account Group / Account Ledger wise summary of Vouchers transacted for a specific Voucher Type

At Voucher Register (§05/02-16), Click *F6:Extract* Button (or set Yes at Show Extract of Register at Voucher Register Configuration) to get Voucher Register Extract (F-6A).

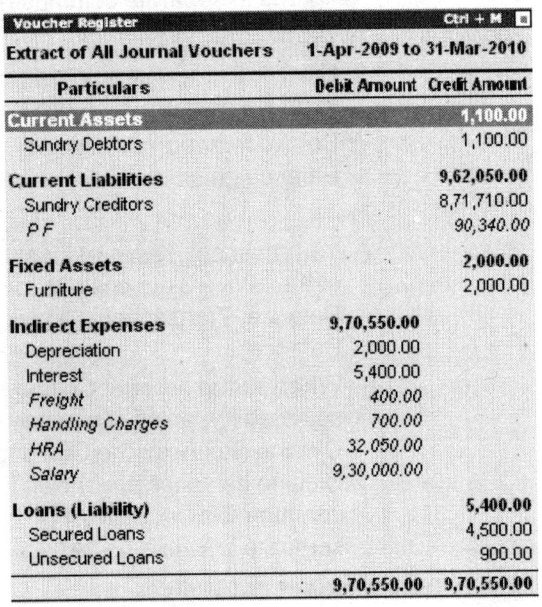

Voucher Register — Ctrl + M

Extract of All Journal Vouchers — 1-Apr-2009 to 31-Mar-2010

Particulars	Debit Amount	Credit Amount
Current Assets		**1,100.00**
Sundry Debtors		1,100.00
Current Liabilities		**9,62,050.00**
Sundry Creditors		8,71,710.00
P F		*90,340.00*
Fixed Assets		**2,000.00**
Furniture		2,000.00
Indirect Expenses	**9,70,550.00**	
Depreciation	2,000.00	
Interest	5,400.00	
Freight	*400.00*	
Handling Charges	*700.00*	
HRA	*32,050.00*	
Salary	*9,30,000.00*	
Loans (Liability)		**5,400.00**
Secured Loans		4,500.00
Unsecured Loans		900.00
	9,70,550.00	**9,70,550.00**

F-6A: Voucher Extract

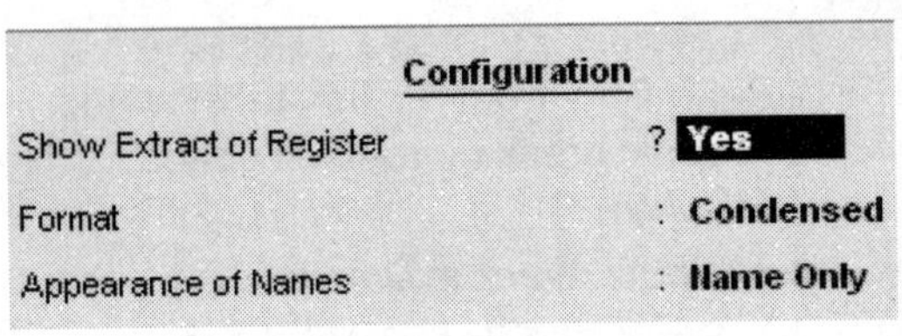

F-6B: Voucher Extract Configuration

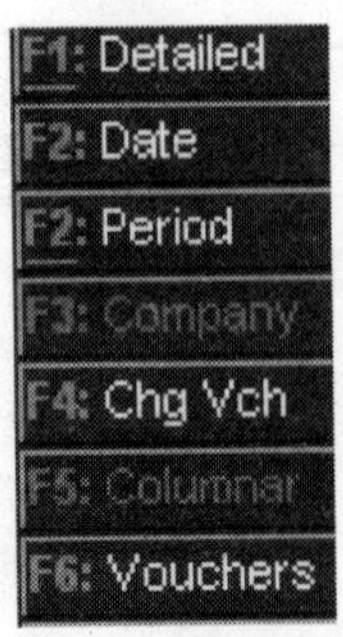

F-6C: Voucher Extract Buttons

Configuration Options at Voucher Extract

At *Voucher Extract* (F-6A), click *F12:Configure* to get *Voucher Extract Configuration* (F-6B), to set the options as follows:

- **Form:** At *Show Extract of Register*.
  - o Set *Yes* to show Extract (F-6A)
  - o Set *No* to show Voucher details
- **Format**: At *Format*:
  - o Select *Detailed* (or Click *F1:Detailed* toggle button) to show lowest level Ledger details
  - o Select *Condensed* (or Click *F1:Condensed* toggle button)to show next level Group / Ledger details (F-6A)

Buttons at Voucher Extract

At *Voucher Extract* (F-6A), you get buttons (F-6C), as follows:

- o **F1:Detailed / Condensed:** To get Detailed / Condensed report as explained above.
- o **F4:Chg Vch**: To select a Voucher Type to get the Voucher Extract for the selected Voucher Type

FAQ: Frequently Asked Questions

FAQ-1: How I can print columnar Monthly figures of Sales Group with details

Ans: Select *Display > Account Books > Group Summary* and select *Sales Accounts* (Primary Group) from the list of Groups to get the Group Summary report of Sales Accounts Group

Click and then select *Primary* from the list of Groups to get the Group Summary of all the top level Primary Groups.

a. Click *F1:Detailed* toggle button to get the next level details of each Group in the report
b. Click *F12:Configure* button and set *Yes* at the option *Expand All Levels in detailed format* to get detailed figures of all underlying sub groups / ledger accounts
c. Click *N:Auto Column* button and set as follows:
   i. At *Repeat Using* field, select Monthly from the list to get columns for monthly figures
   ii. At *Show Total Columns*, set Yes to get a column showing the total figures of all the monthly columns shown

Now you will get the columnar report of *Sales Accounts* Group with details, for each month, along with a column for Total figures

FAQ-2: How I can print Daily Closing Balance of Cash, highlighting Negative Cash Balances

a. Select *Display > Account Books>Cash Bank Book* to get the Cash Bank Summary Report. Select Cash Account to get the month summary of Cash Account
b. Click *F2:Period* button and set the period for which you like to get the Daily Balance of Cash Account

c. Click *F12:Configure* button and select *Daily* at the field *Periodicity to Use* to get the Daily Cash Balance at the column *Closing Balance*. The negative Cash Balances (Credit Balance) are indicated in Red to highlight the Negative Cash Balances.

You may also get the Daily Cash Balance in following way:

a. Select *Display > Account Books>Ledger and* select *Cash* Account to get the ledger vouchers report.

b. Click *F2:Period* button and set the period for which you like to get the Daily Balance of Cash Account

c. Click *F6:DlyBrk up* button and set the period for which you like to get the Daily Balance of Cash Account

FAQ-3: How I can print the Dates and Amount of Negative Cash Balances only

Ans:

a. Select *Display > Account Books>Ledger and* select *Cash* Account to get the ledger vouchers report of Cash Accounts

b. Click *F6:DlyBrk up* button and set the period for which you like to get the Daily Balance of Cash Account

c. Click *F2:Period* button and set the period for which you like to get the Negative Balance of Cash Account

d. Click *X:Exceptions* toggle button to list the Dates & Amount of Negative Closing Cash Balance

Trial Balance 02-20

01 Trial Balance

We have discussed about Account Summaries of Account Groups & Account Ledgers (§01/02-20). Trial Balance is the topmost level Summary report of Account Groups & Account Ledgers

We have discussed the default Trial Balance earlier (§01/01-09). Here, we explain various configuration options of Trial Balance to configure the format & contents of Trial Balance

02 Trial Balance Configuration

The Configuration & Buttons of Trial Balance is similar to Group Summary. In fact, Trial Balance is Group Summary of all Accounts Groups.

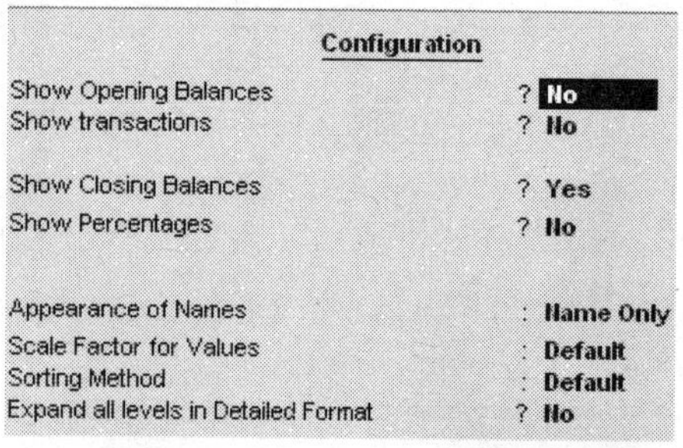

Configuration

Show Opening Balances	?	No
Show transactions	?	No
Show Closing Balances	?	Yes
Show Percentages	?	No
Appearance of Names	:	Name Only
Scale Factor for Values	:	Default
Sorting Method	:	Default
Expand all levels in Detailed Format	?	No

F-1A: Trial Balance Display Configuration

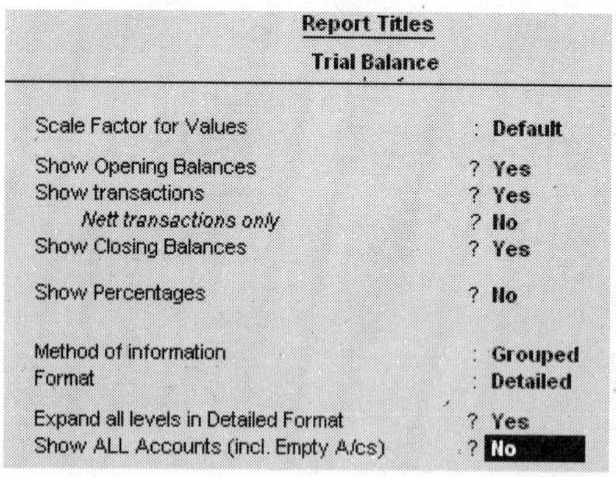

Report Titles

Trial Balance

Scale Factor for Values	:	Default
Show Opening Balances	?	Yes
Show transactions	?	Yes
Nett transactions only	?	No
Show Closing Balances	?	Yes
Show Percentages	?	No
Method of information	:	Grouped
Format	:	Detailed
Expand all levels in Detailed Format	?	Yes
Show ALL Accounts (incl. Empty A/cs)	?	No

F-1B: Trial Balance Printing screen

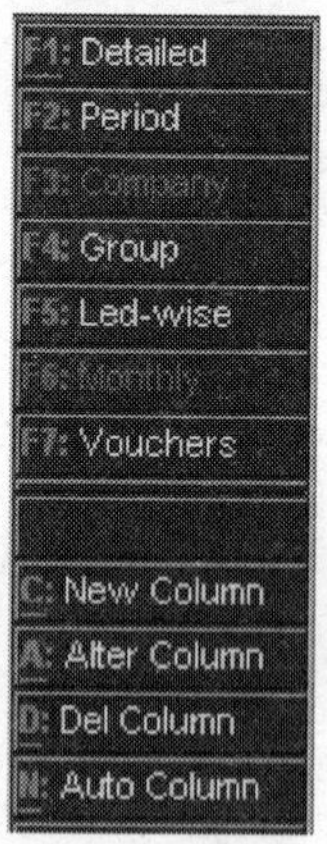

F1: Detailed
F2: Period
F3: Company
F4: Group
F5: Led-wise
F6: Monthly
F7: Vouchers
C: New Column
A: Alter Column
D: Del Column
N: Auto Column

F-1C Buttons

At Trial Balance Display (F-2A), click *F12: Configure* to get configuration screen (F-1A). Set up the following options as required.

Opening Balance	At *Show Opening Balances*: - Set *Yes* to include Opening Balance in the report (F-2B) - Set *No* to exclude the Opening balance (only the transaction figures for the selected period are considered)
Transaction Details	At *Show Transactions*: - Set *Yes* to show transaction figures (Debit & Credit amounts) for the selected period (F-2B) - Set *No* to suppress the Transaction columns
- Net Transactions	Having set Yes at *Show Transactions*, At *Show Net Transactions only* - Set *Yes* to show the Net Transactions (Net debit or credit), - Set *No* to show both Debit & Credit figures in separate columns (F-1B)
Closing balance	At *Show Closing Balance* - Set *Yes* to show closing balance for each account group / ledger (F-2B) - Set *No* to suppress Closing Balance column **Note:** - You must set *Yes* in at least one of the above 3 options (Opening Balance, Transaction, Closing Balance). - When all the Amount Columns are selected (Opening, Transaction & Closing Balance), the Opening & Closing balances are shown in one columns (Dr/Cr), instead of separate columns (F-2B)
Details Levels	Having set *F1:Detailed* button, at *Expand all Level in detail Format* - Set *Yes* to show all subordinate groups ledger accounts to the lowest level (F-2B) - Set *No* to show only the next level Groups/ Ledgers

Particulars	ABC Academy 9-10 1-Apr-2009 to 31-Mar-2010 Closing Balance Debit	Credit
Capital Account	**5,000.00**	**50,000.00**
Loans (Liability)		**62,900.00**
Current Liabilities		**9,79,490.00**
Fixed Assets	**1,20,000.00**	**2,000.00**
Current Assets	**10,87,626.78**	
Suspense A/c		**20,000.00**
Sales Accounts	**5,300.00**	**65,600.00**
Purchase Accounts	**7,250.00**	**200.00**
Direct Incomes		**9,54,500.00**
Indirect Incomes		**3,000.00**
Indirect Expenses	**11,35,970.00**	
Grand Total	**23,61,146.78**	**23,61,146.78**

F-2A: Trial Balance (Default)

Particulars	Opening Balance	Transactions Debit		Transactions Credit		Closing Balance
Capital Account	**48,100.00 Cr**	5,000.00	0.21%	1,900.00	0.08%	**45,000.00 Cr**
Drawings		5,000.00				*5,000.00 Dr*
Properitor's Capital	*48,100.00 Cr*			1,900.00		*50,000.00 Cr*
Loans (Liability)		*14,500.00*	*0.62%*	*77,400.00*	*3.29%*	**62,900.00 Cr**
Secured Loans		14,500.00		54,500.00		40,000.00 Cr
ICICI Term Loan		*14,500.00*		*54,500.00*		40,000.00 Cr
Unsecured Loans				12,900.00		12,900.00 Cr
Accrued Interest				*2,900.00*		2,900.00 Cr
S Kurien				*10,000.00*		10,000.00 Cr
A K Das				10,000.00		*10,000.00 Cr*
Current Liabilities		*4,150.00*	*0.18%*	*9,83,640.00*	*41.76%*	**9,79,490.00 Cr**
Sundry Creditors		4,150.00		8,83,030.00		8,78,880.00 Cr
B M Suppliers		*4,150.00*		*11,320.00*		7,170.00 Cr
S Roy (Employee)				*8,71,710.00*		8,71,710.00 Cr
P F				1,00,590.00		*1,00,590.00 Cr*
TDS				20.00		*20.00 Cr*
						39 more ...
Grand Total		**23,55,530.50**	***100.00%***	**23,55,530.50**	***100.00%***	

F-2B Trial Balance with various details

03 Buttons at Trial Balance

AT Trial Balance screen (F-2A), following buttons are available at (F-1C)

- **F1: Detail / Condensed:** Normally the Trial Balance shows the top level groups figures only (F-2A). Click *F1:Detail* button to show the next level details (F-2B)
- **F4: Group:** To get the Trial Balance for a selected Group, click *F4; group* and select the desired Group. Select *Primary* to get the report of complete Trail Balance of all Primary Groups (F-2A).
- **F5: Led-wise / Grouped:** Toggle button to get Ledgerwise Trial Balance in alphabetical order of Ledger Names (F-2C) / Groupwise with next level ledger Accounts (F-2B)
- **F7:Vouchers:** To get Group Vouchers report showing the vouchers of selected Group / Ledger
- **Column Definition Buttons:** To set column definition to get Columnar Report with other periods / Companies

Particulars	Opening Balance	Transactions Debit		Transactions Credit		Closing Balance
Opening Stock	**1,000.00 Dr**					**1,000.00 Dr**
Aakash & Co	12,000.00 Dr	*7,310.50*	*0.31%*			19,310.50 Dr
Accrued Interest				*2,900.00*	*0.12%*	2,900.00 Cr
A K Das				*10,000.00*	*0.42%*	10,000.00 Cr
A K Traders	1,000.00 Dr	*11,350.00*	*0.48%*	*18,600.00*	*0.79%*	6,250.00 Cr
B M Suppliers		*4,150.00*	*0.18%*	*11,320.00*	*0.48%*	7,170.00 Cr
Cash	2,000.00 Dr	*10,28,750.00*	*43.67%*	*32,810.50*	*1.39%*	9,97,939.50 Dr
Cash Discount		*650.00*	*0.03%*			650.00 Dr
Cash Sales		*2,000.00*	*0.08%*			2,000.00 Dr
Conveyance Expenses		*7,500.00*	*0.32%*			7,500.00 Dr
Depreciation on Furniture		*2,000.00*	*0.08%*			2,000.00 Dr
Discount on Purchase				*200.00*	*0.01%*	200.00 Cr
Drawings		*5,000.00*	*0.21%*			5,000.00 Dr
Freight		*820.00*	*0.03%*	*800.00*	*0.03%*	20.00 Dr
Furniture (Accumulated DEpreciation)				*2,000.00*	*0.08%*	2,000.00 Cr
Furniture Gross Block	1,20,000.00 Dr					1,20,000.00 Dr
Handling Charges		*700.00*	*0.03%*			700.00 Dr
HDFC Bank	1,21,456.78 Dr	*79,500.00*	*3.38%*	*1,61,230.00*	*6.84%*	39,726.78 Dr
HRA		*35,050.00*	*1.49%*			35,050.00 Dr
ICICI Term Loan		*14,500.00*	*0.62%*	*54,500.00*	*2.31%*	40,000.00 Cr
Interest on Term Loan		*4,500.00*	*0.19%*			4,500.00 Dr
						20 more ...
Grand Total		**23,55,530.50**	***100.00%***	**23,55,530.50**	***100.00%***	

F-2C:Trial Balance - Ledger wise Alphabetical

FAQ: Frequently Asked Questions

FAQ-1: How I can print the Opening Balance of all Ledger Accounts in alphabetical order

Ans: Select Display>Trial Balance. Click F12:Configure and:

- Set Yes at Show Opening balance
- Set No at Show Transactions
- Set No at Show Closing Balance

Click *F5:Led-wise* to get the Trial Balance showing all ledger accounts in alphabetical order. This report is useful to check the Opening Trial Balance figures with the Final Closing Balance figures (of Personal & Real Accounts) of previous year.

FAQ-2: How I can print the Closing Balance of Trial Balance with Amountwise Decreasing order.

Ans: Select Display>Trial Balance. Click *F12:Configure* and select *Amountwise Decreasing* at Sorting Method. Sorting Method is applied on the columns of default report only. The Trial Balance with Debit & Credit Columns are shown. So, the sorting will be applied primarily on *Debit* Column value of Primary Groups.

If you click *F1:Detailed,* the next level details of the Primary Group would be shown, with the same sorting order (descending on Debit column values of top level Primary Groups)

If you click *F5:Ledgwise* and select *Amountwise Decreasing at Sorting Method,* no specific pattern is found in the order of ledger accounts (as Sorting applies only on default report)

FAQ-3: How I can get the Extended Trial Balance in alphabetic sequence of Primary Groups with details of all subordinate Groups / Ledgers, with Opening Balance (Debit & Credit separate columns), Transaction break up with Debit & Credit columns & Closing Balance with Debit & Credit Columns

Ans: Select *Display>Trial Balance*. Click *F1:Detailed* button.

Click *F12:Configure* button and set as follows:

- **Show Opening Balance**: Set *Yes* to get the column showing Opening Balance as at the report period start date.
- **Show Transactions:** Set *Yes* to get the transaction figures for the specified report period.
    - o **Nett Transaction only:** On specifying *Yes* to *Show Transactions* Option as above, *Set No* to get separate figures of debit / credit of each ledger / group in the report in both the columns
- **Show Closing Balance**: Set Yes to get the column of showing Closing Balance as at the report period end date.
- **Expand all levels in Detail Format**: Set Yes to get the report showing all subordinate Groups / Ledgers upto the lowest level.

FAQ-4: How I can print Trial Balance of Closing Balance of 4 quarters in one report, with details of all Sub Groups / Ledger accounts

Ans: Select Display>Trial Balance. Click *F1:Detailed* button.

Click *F12:Configure* button and set as follows:

- **Show Opening Balance**: Set *No*
- **Show Transactions:** Set *No*
- **Show Closing Balance**: Set Yes to get the column of showing Closing Balance as at the report period end date.
- **Expand all levels in Detail Format**: Set Yes to get the report showing all subordinate Groups / Ledgers upto the lowest level.

Now click *N:Auto* Column button and set as follows:

- **Repeat Using:** Select *Quarterly*
- **Show Total Column:** Set *No*

Now you will get the Trial balance with Quarterly Closing Balance, in alphabetical sequence of top level Primary Groups with details of subordinate Groups / Ledger Accounts.

FAQ-5: Under what circumstances, the Trial Balance may not tally. How to detect and rectify the mistake quickly?

Ans: In manual accounts, the Trial Balance may not tally due to errors in casting, posting etc. In Computerised system, these are done by the software. As each voucher contains equal Debit & Credit, the Trial balance must tally in In Computerised system.

However, the Trial Balance will not tally if the entry of opening balance in ledger accounts are not complete & correct. In that case the Balance Sheet and Trial Balance Statement shows a like Difference in Opening Balance. To help you detect that the Ledger Opening Balance is correct and complete, the till date Totals of opening balance is shown on line at the time of Opening Balance entry. If the total Debit & Total Credit as shown during Ledger Opening balance entry is not equal even after entry of Opening Balance of all ledger, you know that the Opening Balance entry is not correct.

To check that the Opening Balances has been entered correctly for all Ledger Accounts and that the Total of Opening balance of all Debit Balances is equal to the Total of all Credit Balance in respect of Opening Balance of all Ledger Accounts, print the Opening Balance of all ledger accounts in the Trial balance and check them thoroughly with the Closing Balance of previous financial Year.

To print Opening Balance in trial balance, at the Trial balance Configuration (F-1A), set *Yes* at *Show Opening Balances*, set *No* at *Show Transactions* & Set *No* at *Show Closing balances*. The Trial balance Statement will show Opening Balance of all ledgers accounts. Now check them manually, track the mistake and rectify the mistake.

FAQ-6: How Trial Balance may be printed showing all Ledger Accounts in Alphabetical Order, in one level.

Ans At Trial Balance screen, click *F5:Ledgwise*. The Opening Stock figure will appear at the top followed by all ledger accounts in alphabetical order

Receipts & Payments

01 Receipts & Payments Statement

Receipts and Payments Account is a report of Cash and Bank transactions during a period. Normally, It is used in place of an Income and Expenditure Statement where accounts are based on Cash Transactions, without distinguishing between Capital and Revenue & without considering Accruals.

Special Features of Receipts and Payments Statement

- It is a consolidated summary of Cash / Bank transactions, along with Opening & Closing Balances of Cash & Bank Accounts
- It does not take Accruals into account. Only current period Payments & Receipts are considered irrespective of the Period it relates to. In fact, it is account headwise summary of Cash Inflows & Cash Outflows.
- It shows reports based on the default Primary Groups.

Receipts and Payments — ABC Academy 9-10 — Ctrl + M

Receipts	ABC Academy 9-10 1-Apr-2009 to 31-Mar-2010	Payments	ABC Academy 9-10 1-Apr-2009 to 31-Mar-2010
Opening Balance	34,100.00	Opening Balance	2,000.00
Capital Account	1,900.00	Capital Account	5,000.00
Loans (Liability)	61,000.00	Loans (Liability)	14,500.00
Current Liabilities	1,320.00	Current Liabilities	1,000.00
Current Assets	96,000.00	Current Assets	49,000.00
Sales Accounts	11,100.00	Sales Accounts	2,250.00
Direct Incomes	18,000.00	Indirect Expenses	23,800.00
Indirect Incomes	3,000.00	Closing Balance	1,28,870.00
Total	2,26,420.00	Total	2,26,420.00

F-1A: Receipts and Payments (Primary Group – Default)

Receipts and Payments — ABC Academy 9-10 — Ctrl + M

Receipts	ABC Academy 9-10 1-Apr-2009 to 31-Mar-2010	Payments	ABC Academy 9-10 1-Apr-2009 to 31-Mar-2010
Opening Balance	34,100.00	Opening Balance	2,000.00
Accrued Interest	1,000.00	A K Das	40,000.00
A K Das	40,000.00	A K Traders	7,200.00
A K Traders	6,000.00	B M Suppliers	1,000.00
ICICI Term Loan	50,000.00	Cash Discount	150.00
P F	1,300.00	Cash Sales	2,000.00
Properitor's Capital	1,900.00	Drawings	5,000.00
Rent Received	3,000.00	HRA	3,000.00
Sales	11,100.00	ICICI Term Loan	14,500.00
S Kurien	10,000.00	Office Rent	7,800.00
TDS	20.00	Pre Paid Expenses	1,800.00
T K Das	50,000.00	Salary	13,000.00
Tution Fees	18,000.00	Sales Rebates	100.00
		Closing Balance	1,28,870.00
Total	2,26,420.00	Total	2,26,420.00

F-1B: Receipts and Payments (Ledgerwise)

02 Receipts and Payments Statement Display

Select *GoT > Display > Receipts and Payments* to get the Receipt & Payments Statement (F-1A).

03 Receipts & Payment Configuration

At Receipts & Payment display (F-1A), click *F12:Configure* (or press F12 key) to get *Receipts & Payment Configuration* (F-2A).

Configuration

Show Vertical Receipts & Payments	?	No
Show Nett Opening & Closing Balance only	?	No
Show Nett balance for Ledgers	?	No
Appearance of Names	:	Name Only
Scale Factor for Values	:	Default
Expand all levels in Detailed Format	?	No

F-2A: Receipts & Payment

- F1: Detailed
- F2: Period
- F3: Company
- F5: Led-wise
- C: New Column
- A: Alter Column
- D: Del Column
- N: Auto Column

F-3A: Buttons

> **Note:** *The Receipts & Payments Report shows Transaction as per Ledger Accounts transacted in Voucher. So, if any Personal Account is transacted, the Receipt Payment statement shows the Personal Account instead of the corresponding REAL Account. For example, if you have debited* Fixed Asset *Account and Credited a* Supplier *Account for purchase of Fixed Asset, in the current year, the transaction will not be reflected in Receipts & Payments Report in the current year (as no cash payment is made). In the next year, when the payment is made debiting the supplier's Account (a personal account), it will show the Supplier Account (the Personal Account) in the Receipt Payment Statement, instead of showing the Fixed Asset Account (the corresponding REAL Account for which the Payment is made) So, the Fixed Asset Account do not get reflected in any of the Receipt Payment Account.*

At Receipts & Payment Configuration (F-2A), set the options as follows:

- **Form**: At *Show Vertical Receipts & Payment:*
  - o **Vertical Form**: Set *Yes* to get Receipts & Payment in Vertical format in which details of Receipts, followed by details of Payments are shown in one column in vertical form
  - o **Normal Form**: Set *No* to get two columnar report showing Receipts & Payments in separate columns
- **Balances Type**: At *Show Nett Opening & Closing Balances only*:
  - o Set *Yes* to show the net Opening & Closing Balance of Cash & Bank Account.
  - o Set *No* to show net of Debit & Credit Balances of Cash & Bank Accounts (to reveal the current & overdrawn amounts in Bank)
- **Show Nett Balance for Ledgers**: At *Show Nett Balance for Ledgers*:
  - o Set *Yes* to show the net balance of each account (either in Receipt or Payment, whichever is greater).
  - o Set *No* to show both Receipts & Payments separately.
- **Details Levels:** Having set *F1:Detailed* button, at *Expand all Level in detail Format*
  - o Set *Yes* to show all subordinate groups ledger accounts to the lowest level (F-2B)
  - o Set *No* to show only the next level Groups/ Ledgers

04 Receipts & Payment Summary Buttons

Following Buttons appear at Receipts & Payment Summary Display screen (F-3A):

- **F4: Group**: To select a Group to get the Receipts & Payments Summary of the selected Group (you may also drill down through the Group in Receipts & Payments Statement to get the Receipts & Payments Summary of the selected Group). This option is useful to get Receipts & Payments Summary of a specified Group under the Primary Groups
- **F5: Ledgwise / Grouped:** Click the Toggle button F5:Grouped to get the Group figures of Receipts & Payments Statement. Click the Toggle button F5:Ledgwise to get the Ledger figures of Receipts & Payments Statement.
- **F7 Vouchers**: Click to get the Group Voucher list of all the vouchers (Contra, Receipt & Payment) related to the Current Group / Ledger Account selected

05 Vertical Receipts & Payment Statement

At *Receipts & Payment Configuration* (F-2A), set *Yes* at *Show Vertical Receipts & Payments* Statement to get *Vertical Receipts & Payments Statement* (F-4A)

Receipts & Payments
1-Apr-2009 to 31-Mar-2010

Page 1

		1-Apr-2009 to 31-Mar-2010	
Opening Balance			32,100.00
Bank Accounts		*30,100.00*	
Cash-in-Hand		*2,000.00*	
Receipts:			
Capital Account		1,900.00	
Propentor's Capital	*1,900.00*		
Loans (Liability)		61,000.00	
Secured Loans	*50,000.00*		
ICICI Term Loan	*50,000.00*		
Unsecured Loans	*11,000.00*		
Accrued Interest	*1,000.00*		
S Kurien	*10,000.00*		
Current Liabilities		1,320.00	
P F	*1,300.00*		
TDS	*20.00*		
Current Assets		96,000.00	
Loans & Advances (Asse	*40,000.00*		
A K Das	*40,000.00*		
Sundry Debtors	*56,000.00*		
A K Traders	*6,000.00*		
T K Das	*50,000.00*		
Sales Accounts		11,100.00	
Sales	*11,100.00*		
Direct Incomes		18,000.00	
Tution Fees	*18,000.00*		
Indirect Incomes		3,000.00	
Rent Received	*3,000.00*		
Nett Receipts			1,92,320.00
			2,24,420.00

F-4A: Receipts and Payments (Vertical) - Receipt Part 1

Payments:			
Capital Account		5,000.00	
Drawings	*5,000.00*		
Loans (Liability)		14,500.00	
Secured Loans	*14,500.00*		
ICICI Term Loan	*14,500.00*		
Current Liabilities		1,000.00	
Sundry Creditors	*1,000.00*		
B M Suppliers	*1,000.00*		
Current Assets		49,000.00	
Pre Paid Expenses	*1,800.00*		
Loans & Advances (Asset)	*40,000.00*		
A K Das	*40,000.00*		
Sundry Debtors	*7,200.00*		
A K Traders	*7,200.00*		
Sales Accounts		2,250.00	
Cash Discount	*150.00*		
Cash Sales	*2,000.00*		
Sales Rebates	*100.00*		
Indirect Expenses		23,800.00	
HRA	*3,000.00*		
Office Rent	*7,800.00*		
Salary	*13,000.00*		
Nett Payments			95,550.00
Closing Balance			1,28,870.00
Bank Accounts		*60,620.00*	
Cash-in-Hand		*68,250.00*	

Receipts and Payments (Vertical) - Payments Part 2

In *Vertical Receipts & Payments Statement* (F-4A), the Opening Cash & Bank balances are shown first, successively followed by the details of Receipts (Part 1) & Payments and then the Closing Cash & Bank Balances (Part 2)

06 Drill Down from Receipts & Payment Summary

At Receipts & Payment Summary, drill down as follows:

- **Account Group**: Drill down through an Account Group to get next level details of Account Group / Ledger Account (F-5B).
- **Account Ledger**: Drill down through an Account Ledger to get Monthly Summary of the Ledger (§06.02/02-20).

Cash/Bank Opening Summary — Ctrl + M

Particulars	ABC Academy 9-10 1-Apr-2009 to 31-Mar-2010			
	Opening Balance		Closing Balance	
	Debit	Credit	Debit	Credit
Bank Accounts	**1,53,556.78**		**71,826.78**	
HDFC Bank	*1,21,456.78*		*39,726.78*	
State Bank of India	*32,100.00*		*32,100.00*	
Cash-in-Hand	**2,000.00**		**9,97,939.50**	
Cash	*2,000.00*		*9,97,939.50*	
Grand Total	**1,55,556.78**		**10,69,766.28**	

F-5A: Cash / Bank Balance Opening / Closing Summary

- **Closing & Opening Balance**: Drill down through Opening Balance or Closing Balance to get the Account Group wise figures Opening & Closing Figures Cash / Bank ledger accounts (F-5A).

Receipts and Payments Summary — Ctrl + M

Particulars	*Current Assets* ABC Academy 9-10 1-Apr-2009 to 31-Mar-2010	
	Transactions	
	Receipts	Payments
Loans & Advances (Asset)	**40,000.00**	
A K Das	*40,000.00*	
Sundry Debtors	**56,000.00**	
Grand Total	**96,000.00**	

F-5B: Receipts & Payment Group Summary

07 Receipts & Payment Statement Printing

At Receipt & Payment Display (F-1A), click P:*Print* button to get *Receipt & Payment Printing* screen (F-6B). Set the options (similar to Configuration Options: F-2A) and print the Receipt & Payment Statement (F-6A)

Receipts & Payments
1-Apr-2009 to 31-Mar-2010

Page 1

Receipts	1-Apr-2009 to 31-Mar-2010		Payments	-Apr-2009 to 31-Mar-2010	
Opening Balance		**34,100.00**	**Opening Balance**		**2,000.00**
Bank Accounts	*32,100.00*		Bank Accounts	*2,000.00*	
Cash-in-Hand	*2,000.00*		**Capital Account**		**5,000.00**
Capital Account		**1,900.00**	*Drawings*	*5,000.00*	
Properitor's Capital	*1,900.00*		**Loans (Liability)**		**14,500.00**
Loans (Liability)		**61,000.00**	Secured Loans	*14,500.00*	
Secured Loans	*50,000.00*		*ICICI Term Loan*	*14,500.00*	
ICICI Term Loan	*50,000.00*		**Current Liabilities**		**1,000.00**
Unsecured Loans	*11,000.00*		Sundry Creditors	*1,000.00*	
Accrued Interest	*1,000.00*		*B M Suppliers*	*1,000.00*	
S Kurien	*10,000.00*		**Current Assets**		**49,000.00**
Current Liabilities		**1,320.00**	*Pre Paid Expenses*	*1,800.00*	
PF	*1,300.00*		Loans & Advances (Asset)	*40,000.00*	
TDS	*20.00*		*A K Das*	*40,000.00*	
Current Assets		**96,000.00**	Sundry Debtors	*7,200.00*	
Loans & Advances (Asset)	*40,000.00*		*A K Traders*	*7,200.00*	
A K Das	*40,000.00*		**Sales Accounts**		**2,250.00**
Sundry Debtors	*56,000.00*		*Cash Discount*	*150.00*	
A K Traders	*6,000.00*		*Cash Sales*	*2,000.00*	
T K Das	*50,000.00*		*Sales Rebates*	*100.00*	
Sales Accounts		**11,100.00**	**Indirect Expenses**		**23,800.00**
Sales	*11,100.00*		*HRA*	*3,000.00*	
Direct Incomes		**18,000.00**	*Office Rent*	*7,800.00*	
Tution Fees	*18,000.00*		*Salary*	*13,000.00*	
Indirect Incomes		**3,000.00**	**Closing Balance**		**1,28,870.00**
Rent Received	*3,000.00*		Bank Accounts	*60,620.00*	
			Cash-in-Hand	*68,250.00*	
Total		**2,26,420.00**	**Total**		**2,26,420.00**

F-6A: Receipt & Payments Print (Details)

Report Titles
Receipts & Payments

Scale Factor for Values	: **Default**
Format	: **Detailed**
Show Vertical Receipts & Payments	? **No**
Show Nett balance for Ledgers	? **No**

F-6B: Receipts & Payments Printing screen

FAQ: Frequently Asked Questions

FAQ-1: How to print Receipt & Payment Statement in vertical format

Ans: At *Receipts & Payment* Display, click P:Print to get Receipts & Payment printing screen. Set Yes at *Show Vertical Receipts & Payments* Statement to print *Vertical Receipts & Payments Statement*

Profit & Loss Statement 02-22

01 Profit & Loss Statement

We have already discussed Profit & Loss Statement (§01/01-10). The *Profit & Loss Statement* & *Balance Sheet* may be placed in the Tally Menu as follows:

At *GoT>F12:Configure>General,* at the option *Use Separate Menu for Final Accounts Statement* (F-1E), set:

- *Yes* to get another Item *Final Accounts* in Main menu (F-1D). The various management reports are placed under *Final Accounts* menu (F-1F). In that case, you select *GoT>Final Accounts>Profit & Loss A/c* to get the Profit & Loss Statement.
- *No* to show *Profit & Loss Statement*, Balance Sheet & *Ratio Analysis* at Main Menu (Fig 1C) instead of being placed under Final Accounts Menu. In that case, you select *GoT>Profit & Loss A/c* to get the Profit & Loss Statement.

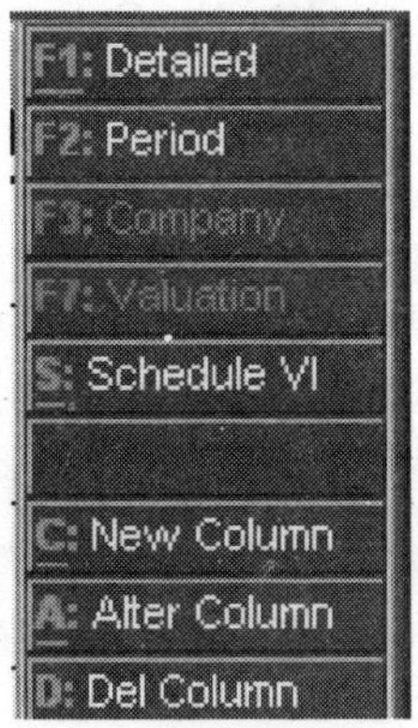

F- 1B: Buttons at P L Statement

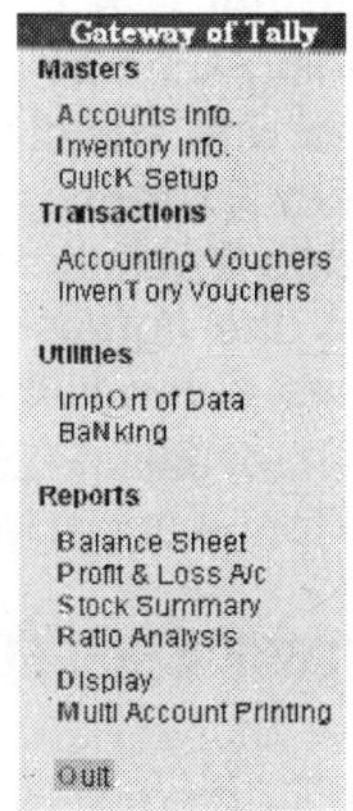

F-1C: BS & PL in Main Menu

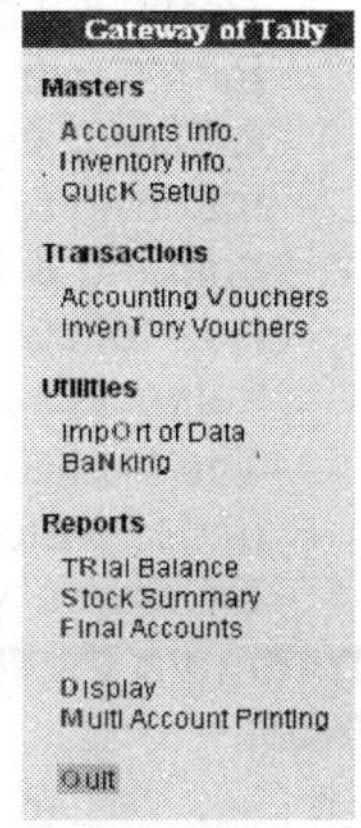

F-1D: Separate Menu Item for Final Accounts

Use separate Menu for Final A/c Statements ? Yes

F-1E: Final Accounts Menu option1

Configuration		
Show Vertical Profit & Loss	?	No
Show Percentages	?	No
Show with Gross Profit	?	Yes
Appearance of Names	:	Name Only
Scale Factor for Values	:	Default

F-1A: P L Statement Configuration

02 Profit & Loss Statement Configuration

At Profit & Loss Display (F-2A), click *F12: Configuration* to get Profit & Loss Configuration screen (F- 1A).

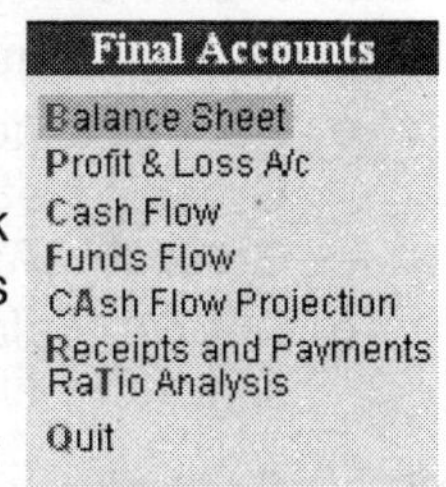

F-1F: Final Accounts Menu

Profit & Loss A/c — ABC Academy 9-10 — Ctrl + M

Particulars	ABC Academy 9-10 1-Apr-2009 to 31-Mar-2010			Particulars	ABC Academy 9-10 1-Apr-2009 to 31-Mar-2010		
Opening Stock		**1,000.00**	1.64 %	**Sales Accounts**		**60,800.00**	100 %
Stock in Hand	1,000.00			*Cash Discount*	(-)150.00		
Purchase Accounts		**7,050.00**	11.60 %	*Cash Sales*	(-)2,000.00		
Discount on Purchase	(-)200.00			*Sales*	65,600.00		
Purchase	7,250.00			*Sales Rebates*	(-)650.00		
Gross Profit c/o		**72,750.00**	119.65 %	*Sales Return*	(-)2,000.00		
				Direct Incomes		**18,000.00**	29.61 %
				Tution Fees	18,000.00		
				Closing Stock		**2,000.00**	3.29 %
				Stock in Hand	2,000.00		
		80,800.00				**80,300.00**	
Indirect Expenses		**44,920.00**	73.88 %	***Gross Profit b/f***		**72,750.00**	119.65 %
Depreciation	2,000.00			**Indirect Incomes**		**3,000.00**	4.93 %
Interest	5,400.00			*Rent Received*	3,000.00		
Freight	20.00						
Handling Charges	700.00						
HRA	6,000.00						
Office Rent	7,800.00						
Salary	23,000.00						
Nett Profit		**30,830.00**	50.71 %				
Total		**75,750.00**		**Total**		**75,750.00**	

F-2A: Profit & Loss Statement (with Gross Profit)

Profit & Loss A/c — ABC Academy 9-10 — Ctrl + M

Particulars	ABC Academy 9-10 1-Apr-2009 to 31-Mar-2010		
Trading Account :			
Sales Accounts		**60,800.00**	100 %
Cash Discount	(-)150.00		
Cash Sales	(-)2,000.00		
Sales	65,600.00		
Sales Rebates	(-)650.00		
Sales Return	(-)2,000.00		
Direct Incomes		**18,000.00**	29.61 %
Tution Fees	18,000.00		
		78,800.00	129.61 %
Cost of Sales :		**6,050.00**	9.95 %
Opening Stock	1,000.00		
Add: Purchase Accounts	7,050.00		
Less: Closing Stock	2,000.00		
Gross Profit :		**72,750.00**	119.65 %
Income Statement :			
Indirect Incomes		**3,000.00**	4.93 %
Rent Received	3,000.00		
		75,750.00	124.59 %
Indirect Expenses		**44,920.00**	73.88 %
Depreciation	2,000.00		
		7 more ...	

F-2B: Profit & Loss Statement (Vertical)

At P L Statement Configuration screen (F-1A), set the Options as follows:

- **Profit & Loss Format**: You may get Profit & Loss Statement in 2 formats:
    - o **Normal Format (T Form)**: Set *No* at *Show Vertical Profit & Loss* to get Normal Profit & Loss Account Statement (in T Form) showing Expenses at Left side Income at Right side (F-2A).
    - o **Vertical Format (I Form)**: Set Yes *at Show Vertical Profit & Loss* to get P & L statement in vertical format with Trading Account at Top, showing Sales & Direct Income with subtotal, followed by Direct Income & Direct Expenses with adjustment of opening & Closing Stock to show the Gross Profit. It is followed by the figures of Indirect income & Indirect Expenses, showing the Net Profit (F-2B).

      The Vertical form reveals (F-2B) operational results and is preferred for Financial Management, Analysis & Control.
- **Trading & Profit & Loss Account**: At *Show with Gross Profit*:
    - o set Yes to get Trading & Profit & Loss Account showing Gross Profit / Loss with Sales, Direct Income, Purchases, Direct Expenses and all other accounts showing the Net Profit / Loss (F-2A)
    - o Set *No*, to get only Net Profit / Loss considering all Income & Expenses (No break up of Gross / Net Profit / Loss)
- **Percentage Figures**: At *Show Percentage*,
    - o Set *Yes* to get the % figures of each Account Group, Gross / Net Profit Loss based on Total of Sales Group (F-2A)
    - o Set *No* (default). No percentage figures would be shown

03 Buttons at P L Statement

Ans: At P L Statement Display (F-2A), you get following buttons

- **Format:**
    - o **Detailed:** Click *F1:Detailed* button to show the next level details (F-2B)
    - o **Condensed**: Click *F1:Condensed* button (default) to show figures of Top Level Primary Groups only (F-2B)
- **Schedule VI:** Click *S:Schedule VI* button to get Schedule VI of P L Statement
- **Columnar Report Buttons:** Buttons to create Columnar Report

FAQ: Frequently Asked Questions

FAQ1: How I may get Sales / Cost of Sales with % figures

Ans: At Gateway of Tally, (F-1A/01-02) select *Profit & Loss Account* to get *Profit & Loss Statement* Display screen. Set the Period as desired (Click *F2:Period* button or Press *Alt+F2* keys). At *Profit & Loss Statement* Display, click *F12:Configure* to get *Profit & Loss Statement Configuration* screen (F-1A).

FAQ-3: Profit & Loss Statement with Cost of Sales

At *Profit & Loss Statement Configuration* screen (F-1A):

- **Cost of Sales**: Set *Yes* at *Show Vertical Profit & Loss* to show P L *Statement* in Vertical form (F-3A) showing segregated figures of Sales / Cost of Sales.
- **Percentage Figures**: Set *Yes* At *Show Percentage* to show the % figures with respect to Sales to get *Profit & Loss Statement* showing *Sales / Cost of Sales* with *Percentage* figures

FAQ-2: How to print Profit & Loss Statement in Vertical format without Gross Profit

Ans: At *Profit & Loss Statement* Display (F-2A), click *P:Print* to get Receipts & Payment printing screen.

- Set Yes at *Show Vertical Profit & Loss* Statement to print *Vertical Receipts & Payments Statement*
- Set No at *Show with Gross Profit*

Balance Sheet 02-23

01 Balance Sheet Display

We have explained the default Balance Sheet (P-01/01-11). Here, we discuss about various configuration options to customise the format & contents of Balance Sheet

02 Balance Sheet Configuration

At Balance Sheet Display screen (F-2A), click *F12:Coniguration* to get Balance Sheet Configuration screen (F-1A). Set the following options as desired.

Format: The Balance Sheet may be shown in following 2 formats. At *Show Vertical Balance Sheet*

- **T Format:** Set *No* to show Balance Sheet in T (Normal) Format showig Liabilities / Assets in two separate sides (F-2A).
  - o **Loss Display:** If you have set *No* at *Show Vertical Balance Sheet,* at option *Profit or Loss both,* set
    - ▪ *Yes* at *Profit or Loss both as Liability* to display Loss even in Liability side.
    - ▪ Set *No* to show Profit at Liability side & Loss at Asset Side
- **Vertical Format**: Set *Yes* to show Balance Sheet in Vertical format (showing Sources & Application of Funds, one after another: F-2C/F-2D)

Working Capital: At *Show Working Capital Figures*:

- Set Yes to show the Balance Sheet in the format of Application of Funds & Sources of Fund with Working Capital figures (Net of Current Liabilities & Current Assets).
- Set *No* to show the figures of Current Assets & Current Liabilities separately

Form: The Liabilities & Assets parts may be shown in desired side as follows. At *Method of Showing Balance Sheet,* set as follows:

- o Select *Liabilities & Assets* to show Liabilities in left side and Assets at right side (popularly used by Indian organizations: F-2A).

Configuration

Show Vertical Balance Sheet	? **No**
Profit or Loss, both as Liability	? **Yes**
Show Percentages	? **No**
Show Working Capital figures	? **No**
Method of showing Balance Sheet	? **Liabilities / Assets**
Appearance of Names	: **Name Only**
Scale Factor for Values	: **Default**

F-1A: Balance Sheet Configuration

Report Titles

Balance Sheet

Scale Factor for Values	: **Default**
Format	: **Detailed**
Show Vertical Balance Sheet	? **No**
Profit or Loss, both as Liability	? **No**
Show Percentages	? **No**
Show Working Capital figures	? **No**
Method of showing Balance Sheet	? **Liabilities / Assets**

F-1B: Balance Sheet Printing

- F1: Detailed
- F2: Period
- F3: Company
- F7: Valuation
- S: Schedule VI

F-1C: Buttons

Balance Sheet — ABC CO Ltd 12-13 — Ctrl + M

Liabilities		ABC CO Ltd 12-13 as at 31-Mar-2013	
Capital Account		**20,00,000.00**	12.85 %
Equity Shares	8,70,000.00		
Preference Shares	50,000.00		
Reserves & Surplus	10,80,000.00		
Share Application Money Pending Allotment			
Loans (Liability)		**1,10,23,000.00**	70.85 %
Bank OD A/c	71,53,000.00		
Secured Loans	18,40,000.00		
Unsecured Loans	20,30,000.00		
Current Liabilities		**12,55,000.00**	8.07 %
Provisions	3,30,000.00		
Sundry Creditors	3,50,000.00		
Duties & Taxes	1,30,000.00		
Deferred Tax Liability	1,00,000.00		
Other Current Liabilties	3,45,000.00		
Profit & Loss A/c		**12,81,000.00**	8.23 %
Opening Balance	2,00,000.00		
Current Period	13,81,000.00		
Less: Transferred	3,00,000.00		
Total		**1,55,59,000.00**	100 %

Assets		ABC CO Ltd 12-13 as at 31-Mar-2013	
Fixed Assets		**1,10,07,000.00**	70.74 %
Intangible Assets	21,00,000.00		
Tangible Assets	74,07,000.00		
Capital Work in Progress	15,00,000.00		
Investments		**7,90,000.00**	5.08 %
Non Trade Investment Non Current	1,70,000.00		
Non Trade Investments Current	1,20,000.00		
Trade Investment Non Current	3,80,000.00		
Trade Investments (Current)	1,20,000.00		
Current Assets		**37,62,000.00**	24.18 %
Closing Stock	4,30,000.00		
Deposits (Asset)	70,000.00		
Loans & Advances (Asset)	2,70,000.00		
Sundry Debtors	21,50,000.00		
Cash-in-Hand	1,70,000.00		
Bank Accounts	6,72,000.00		
Total		**1,55,59,000.00**	100 %

F-2A: Balance Sheet

- o Select Assets / Liabilities to show in the reverse direction, i.e Assets in left side and Liabilities at right side (popularly used by American organizations: F-2B).

03 Buttons at Balance Sheet

At Balance Sheet Display screen F-2A), you get the following Buttons (F-1C)

- **Format:**
  - o Click *F1:Detail* button to show the next level details (F-2B)
  - o Click *F1:Condesned* button (default) to show figures of Top Level Primary Groups only (F-2B)
- **Schedule VI:** Click *S:Schedule VI* button to get Schedule VI of Balance Sheet

04 Balance Sheet Printing

At Balance Sheet Display (F-2A), click *P:Print* button to get Balance Sheet printing (F-1B). Set the printing options (like Configuration options) to get Balance Sheet in Print (F-3)

Balance Sheet — ABC CO Ltd 12-13 — Ctrl + M

Assets		ABC CO Ltd 12-13 as at 31-Mar-2013		Liabilities		ABC CO Ltd 12-13 as at 31-Mar-2013	
Fixed Assets		**1,10,07,000.00**	*70.74 %*	**Capital Account**		**20,00,000.00**	*12.85 %*
Intangible Assets	*21,00,000.00*			Equity Shares	*8,70,000.00*		
Tangible Assets	*74,07,000.00*			Prefernce Shares	*50,000.00*		
Capital Work in Progress	*15,00,000.00*			Reserves & Surplus	*10,80,000.00*		
Investments		**7,90,000.00**	*5.08 %*	Share Application Money Pending Allotment			
Non Trade Investment Non Current	*1,70,000.00*			**Loans (Liability)**		**1,10,23,000.00**	*70.85 %*
Non Trade Investments Current	*1,20,000.00*			Bank OD A/c	*71,53,000.00*		
Trade Investment Non Current	*3,80,000.00*			Secured Loans	*18,40,000.00*		
Trade Investments (Current)	*1,20,000.00*			Unsecured Loans	*20,30,000.00*		
Current Assets		**37,62,000.00**	*24.18 %*	**Current Liabilities**		**12,55,000.00**	*8.07 %*
Closing Stock	*4,30,000.00*			Provisions	*3,[illegible]000.00*		
Deposits (Asset)	*70,000.00*			Sundry Creditors	*3,50,000.00*		
Loans & Advances (Asset)	*2,70,000.00*			Duties & Taxes	*1,30,000.00*		
Sundry Debtors	*21,50,000.00*			Deferred Tax Liability	*1,00,000.00*		
Cash-in-Hand	*1,70,000.00*			Other Current Liabilties	*3,45,000.00*		
Bank Accounts	*6,72,000.00*			**Profit & Loss A/c**		**12,81,000.00**	*8.23 %*
				Opening Balance	*2,00,000.00*		
				Current Period	*13,81,000.00*		
				Less: Transferred	*3,00,000.00*		
Total		**1,55,59,000.00**	100 %	**Total**		**1,55,59,000.00**	100 %

F-2B: Balance Sheet (Assets/ Liabilities Format)

Balance Sheet — Ctrl + M

		ABC CO Ltd 12-13 as at 31-Mar-2013	
Sources of Funds :			
Capital Account		**20,00,000.00**	*12.85 %*
Equity Shares	*8,70,000.00*		
Prefernce Shares	*50,000.00*		
Reserves & Surplus	*10,80,000.00*		
Share Application Money Pending Allotment			
Loans (Liability)		**1,10,23,000.00**	*70.85 %*
Bank OD A/c	*71,53,000.00*		
Secured Loans	*18,40,000.00*		
Unsecured Loans	*20,30,000.00*		
Current Liabilities		**12,55,000.00**	*8.07 %*
Provisions	*3,30,000.00*		
Sundry Creditors	*3,50,000.00*		
Duties & Taxes	*1,30,000.00*		
Deferred Tax Liability	*1,00,000.00*		
Other Current Liabilties	*3,45,000.00*		
Profit & Loss A/c		**12,81,000.00**	*8.23 %*
Opening Balance	*2,00,000.00*		
Current Period	*13,81,000.00*		
Less: Transferred	*3,00,000.00*		
Total		**1,55,59,000.00**	100 %

F-2C: Vertical Balance Sheet (Source of Fund part)

Application of Funds :			
Fixed Assets		**1,10,07,000.00**	*70.74 %*
Intangible Assets	*21,00,000.00*		
Tangible Assets	*74,07,000.00*		
Capital Work in Progress	*15,00,000.00*		
Investments		**7,90,000.00**	*5.08 %*
Non Trade Investment Non Current	*1,70,000.00*		
Non Trade Investments Current	*1,20,000.00*		
Trade Investment Non Current	*3,80,000.00*		
Trade Investments (Current)	*1,20,000.00*		
Current Assets		**37,62,000.00**	*24.18 %*
Closing Stock	*4,30,000.00*		
Deposits (Asset)	*70,000.00*		
Loans & Advances (Asset)	*2,70,000.00*		
Sundry Debtors	*21,50,000.00*		
Cash-in-Hand	*1,70,000.00*		
Bank Accounts	*6,72,000.00*		
Total		**1,55,59,000.00**	100 %

F-2D: Vertical Balance Sheet (Application of Fund part)

Balance Sheet 1-Apr-2009 to 31-Mar-2013								
Liabilities	as at 31-Mar-2013			**Assets**		as at 31-Mar-2013		
Capital Account		**20,00,000.00**	13.98 %	**Fixed Assets**			**1,10,07,000.00**	76.95 %
Equity Shares	*8,70,000.00*			Intangible Assets		*21,00,000.00*		
Prefernce Shares	*50,000.00*			Tangible Assets		*74,07,000.00*		
Reserves & Surplus	*10,80,000.00*			Capital Work in Progress		*15,00,000.00*		
Loans (Liability)		**1,10,23,000.00**	77.06 %	**Investments**			**7,90,000.00**	5.52 %
Bank OD A/c	*71,53,000.00*			Non Trade Investment Non Current		*1,70,000.00*		
Secured Loans	*18,40,000.00*			Non Trade Investments Current		*1,20,000.00*		
Unsecured Loans	*20,30,000.00*			Trade Investment Non Current		*3,80,000.00*		
				Trade Investments (Current)		*1,20,000.00*		
Profit & Loss A/c		**12,81,000.00**	8.96 %					
Opening Balance	*2,00,000.00*			**Working Capital**			**25,07,000.00**	17.53 %
Current Period	*13,81,000.00*			**Current Assets**		37,62,000.00		
Less: Transferred	*3,00,000.00*			Closing Stock	4,30,000.00			
				Deposits (Asset)	70,000.00			
				Loans & Advances (Asset)	2,70,000.00			
				Sundry Debtors	21,50,000.00			
				Cash-in-Hand	1,70,000.00			
				Bank Accounts	6,72,000.00			
				Less :Current Liabilities		12,55,000.00		
				Provisions	3,30,000.00			
				Sundry Creditors	3,50,000.00			
				Duties & Taxes	1,30,000.00			
				Deferred Tax Liability	1,00,000.00			
				Other Current Liabilities	3,45,000.00			
Total		**1,43,04,000.00**	100 %	**Total**			**1,43,04,000.00**	100 %

F-3: Balance Sheet in Print (Detailed with Working Capital & % figures)

FAQ: Frequently Asked Questions

FAQ-1: How to print Balance Sheet in Vertical format showing Working Capital

Ans: At *Balance Sheet* Display (F-2A), click *P:Print* to get *Balance Sheet* printing screen.

- Set *Yes* at *Show Vertical Balance Sheet*
- Set *Yes* at *Show working Capital Figures*

At *Print Yes/No*, Type *Y* to print

01 Queries

So far, we have discussed about various standard Reports. Apart from such laid out formatted reports, you may also need ad hoc information on various parameters provided by you, popularly known as *Queries.*

Through Tally, you may get such ad hoc information 2 types of Queries:

- **Range Based Queries**: At Display screens, click F12: Range button.

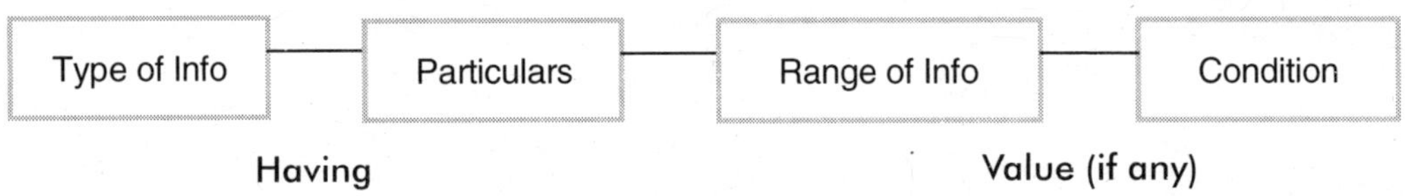

- **Value Based Queries**: At Display screens, click F12: Value button.

We discuss about how you may get such info using these two buttons.

02 Range Based Queries

At Report Display screen, click *F12: Range* to get Query screen (F-1A). Here, you get a series of drop down list of specified query conditions The sequence of lists for the can be query parameters may be presented as under:

Thus the Query pattern in case of single condition:-

<Type of Info> having <Particulars> <Range of Info> value (if any)

In case of multiple conditions:-

<Type of Info> having <Particulars> <Range of Info> value (if any) and/or

<Type of Info> having <Particulars> <Range of Info> value (if any) and/or (in case of further conditions) and so on ....

At Periodical Summary Reports (Group / Ledger) etc, F12:Range button is not available

02.01 Data Tables

At *Type of Info* column (F-1A), according to the current display screen, select one of the following Data Tables from which the Query would extract the information:

- Groups
- Ledgers
- Vouchers
- Bills
- Voucher Types

> ***Note:*** *Through Query, you get a quick shot info based on the specified Query Parameters.*

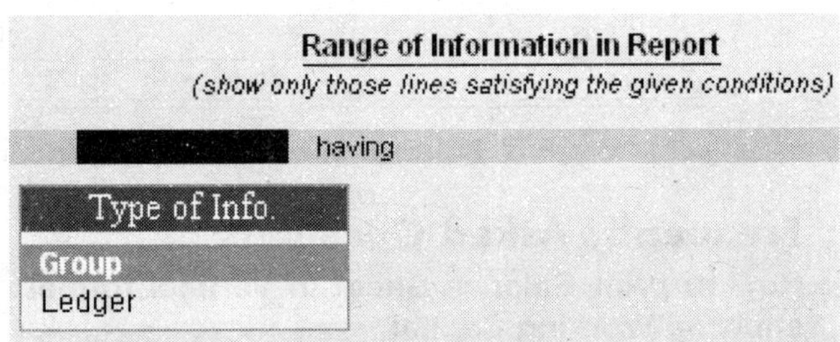

F-1A: Selection of Type of Info (Masters) for Query

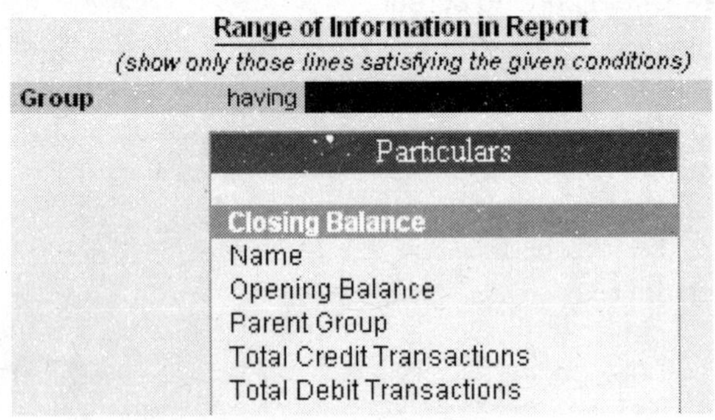

F-1B:Selection of Data Range

02.02 Query Data Range

Depending on the Data Table selected, a list of valid Query options appear at *Particulars* column to select from (F-1B).

Depending on the Query Particulars options selected, at *Range of Info* column, a list of valid Data Range options appear to select from (F-2A).

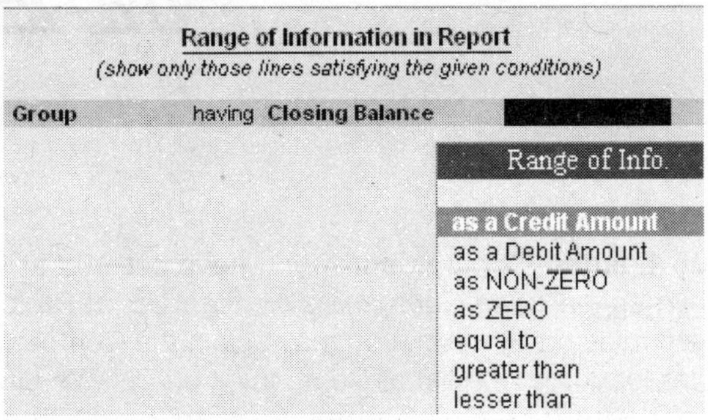

F-2A:Selection of Query Particulars

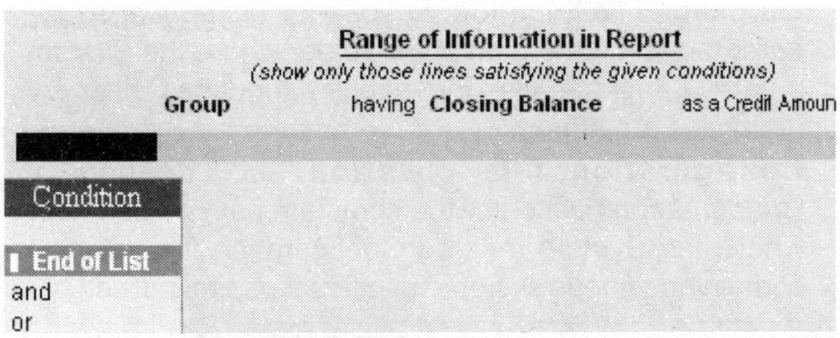

F-2B: Selection of Query Condition

02.03 Query Conditions

At *Conditions* column, select the Condition concatenation options from the list to execute single query (F-2B) or build up a multiple condition query.

- ***Single Condition Query:*** At Condition column, after selecting one set of Query, select End of List to get the result set on the Single Query.
- **Multiple Condition Query:** At Condition column, after selecting one set of Query, select And / Or to specify more query conditions (F-2B) to build up the result set:
    - o **Exclusive Query**: Select *And* to set up more Query conditions that must also be satisfied to get the Query result set (when you select AND, *All* the conditions must be satisfied)
    - o **Inclusive Query**: Select *Or* to set up more Query conditions when any of the satisfied condition may produce the Query result set (when you select OR, *Any* of the conditions may be satisfied

03 Value Based Queries

In Reports built from Voucher Data, normally All *Vouchers* are considered. Through Value Query, you may give filter parameters to set up conditions for inclusion of the participating vouchers to get a filtered report.

Click *F12: Value* button to get the Value Filter specification screen. At Ledger Vouchers, F12:Value button is not available

Like *Range* filter, you get a screen to build up query. The query pattern is like:

Using Voucher having <Particulars> <Range of Info> <value, if any> <Condition>

At *Particulars* column select the filter option from the list (F-3A).

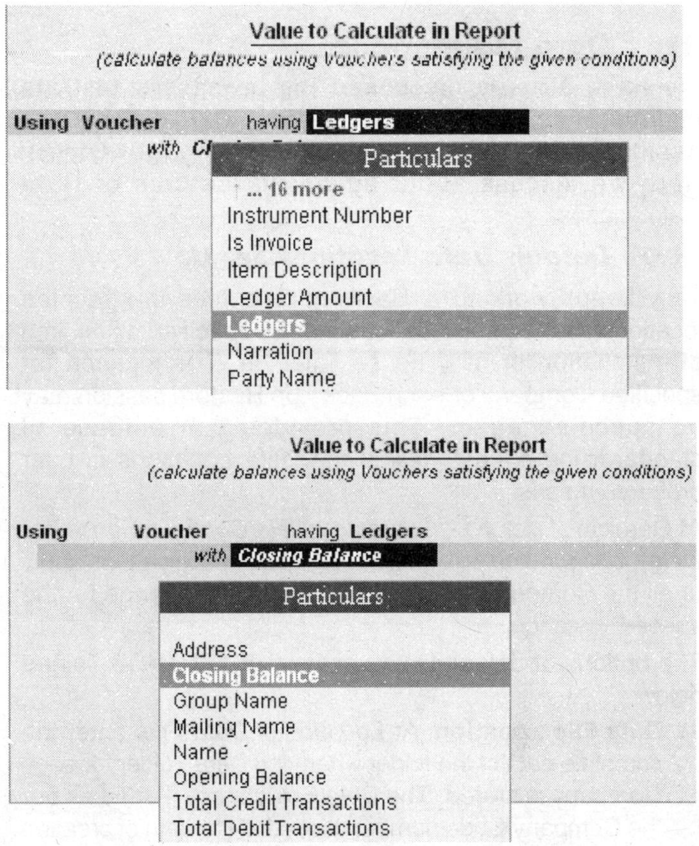

F-3A: Selection of Query Particulars in Value Filter

FAQ: Frequently Asked Questions

FAQ-1: How to get list of Vouchers in which Bill Ref No 5 is entered at Ref Number

Ans: To get the list of vouchers having Bill Name (Bill Reference) 5

- At any Voucher List Type Display (§01/02-16), click *F12:Range* to get Query screen. At *Type of Info*, Select *Bill Name*
- At *Range of Info*, Select *Equal to*
- At the input prompt, enter *5*
- Select *End of List*

01 Data Maintenance

We have already discussed the processes of Data Maintenance, like Data back Up (§02/01-13), Data Restoration (§03/01-13) & Data Re-writing (§04/01-13). Here we discuss about advanced features of Data Maintenance

01.01 Default Data Locations Set Up

Tally keeps working & Back up data files in specified locations. The default locations may be specified at the time of installation or may be set later on. The location for specified Company or each Back / Up Restore session may be specified again. This provides convenience of standardising & customising the Data Locations in user preferred means.

At Gateway, Click *F12:Configure>Data Configuration* to get *Data Configuration* screen (F-1A). These specifications apply to all the Companies by default, unless you change for the specific instance.

The options of default Data Location (F-1A) are explained below:

- **Data File Location**: At *Location of Data File*, enter the complete path of the folder where the Data Folder for each Company is stored. The Data Folders are named as per the Company Code number allotted at the time of creation of each Company.
- **Auto Back Up:** At *Enable Auto Back Up Copy*,Set Yes to activate Auto Back Up feature (§02), else set *No*.
- **Auto Back Up File Location**: At *Location of Auto Back File (TABK)*, enter the complete path of the folder where the Auto Back Up Data Folder is stored. The TABK.900 file is created for Multiple Companies and stored in the specified folder (§02)
- **Export File Location:** At Location of Export File, enter the complete path of the folder where the Exported Data File (when you click *E:Export* (§02/02-03) at Report Display screen) is stored.
- **Company Auto Load:** You may specify the Company which you like to be auto loaded at the time of Loading Tally. To activate the feature of Auto Loading of Companies, set *Yes* at *Load Companies on Start Up* (to enable selection of Companies to Auto Load), else set *No*.
- **Auto Loaded Companies:** If you have set *Yes* at the above option *Load Companies on Start Up*, at Preload Companies on Start Up, you may select the Companies to pre-load from the list of Companies on Disk You may select Multiple Companies to auto load. These Companies are listed in the list of selected Companies.
- **Language File Location**: At *Location of Language File*, enter the complete path of the folder where the System created Language files for various Language Dictionary (.dct) files are stored.
- **Configuration File Location**: At *Location of Configuration File*, enter the complete path of the folder where the System created Configuration file (tally.ini) containing various system specifications are stored.

> **Note:** *It is better to store data in Drive oher than C (drive where the operating system is loaded), as you may have to sometime format th drive de to some problem. If Data is kept in C: drive, that would be wiped out.*

Data Configuration

Location of Data files	:	d:\tally9erpv3_3
Enable Auto Backup Copy	?	Yes
Location of Auto Backup file (TABK)	:	d:\tally9erpv3_3
Location of Export files	:	d:\tallyrel_37
Load Companies on startup	?	No
Preload Companies on Startup	:	
Location of Language files	:	d:\tallyrel_37\Lang
Location of Configuration file	:	d:\tallyrel_37

Note: Tally.ERP 9 will confirm and restart for the changes to have effect.

F-1A: Data Configuration

Auto Backup Details

Enable Auto Backup	: Yes

F-1B:Auto Back Up set up at Company Creation

> **Note:** *When you maintain Auto Back Up, you do not lose anything when data is lost. Even if Auto Back Up is activated, you should religiously take Manual Back Up (§02/01-13) in some removable media.*

02 Auto Back Up

Auto Back Up means data Back Up internally & automatically taken by Tally, without intervention of User. Through Backup, you take Back Up through Back Up process as discussed above. The Data of that instance is copied in another specified place. Through Auto Back Up, Tally.ERP 9 automatically takes a Back Up in the background, at the end of the Day, keeping a copy of working data at another place for safety. If the current working data is lost or damaged, you can Restore the Backed up data and continue working.

03 Auto Back Up Set Up

- **Auto Back Activation**: At Gateway of Tally, click *F12:Configure* to get Configuration Menu. At Configuration menu, select Data Configuration to get Data Configuration Screen (F-1A). At *Data Configuration Screen* (F-1A), at the option *Enable Auto Back Up Copy* (F-1A), set Yes to activate the Auto Back Up feature.
- **Default Location of Auto Back File (TABK)**: If you set Yes at the option *Enable Auto Back Up Copy (*F-1A*)*, then at the option *Location of Auto Back Up File (TABK)*, enter the location of *Auto Back Up* file (F-1A). The location of Data File as entered at the field *Location of Data File* is carried by default at the field *Location of Auto Back Up File (TABK)*, which you may change.
    - o *Multiple Auto Back Up* (of several companies together) would be kept in a file TABK.900 at the folder as specified at *Location of Auto Back Up File (TABK)*, at Data Configuration (F-1A)
    - o *Single Auto Back Up* file of each Company, for which Auto Back is activated, ABK.900 would be stored in the respective data folder of the Company Data (like 10000 under the Data folder), as specified at Company Creation screen (F-02/01-01)

  The folder for Data Location & Folder for Auto Back Up location may be same or different
- **Company Auto Back Up Activation:** Having activated to Back up at Data Configuration (F-1A), set *Yes* at *Enable Auto Back Up* at Company Creation screen (F-2/01-01, F-1B)

10040		Folder	1/1/2013 1:54 PM
10041		Folder	1/11/2013 4:04 PM
abk.lck	0 KB	LCK File	1/12/2013 4:44 PM
TABK.900	15,320 KB	900 File	1/11/2013 4:27 PM

F-2A: Multiple Auto Back File TABK

04 Special Features of Auto Back Up

Auto back is optional. It helps you to have Back Up takes automatically in the background. So, Auto Back Up keeps the latest Back Up. Some of the features, differentiating Regular back Up and Auto Back are listed below:

ABK.900	2,337 KB	900 File	1/11/2013 4:27 PM
AddlCmp.900	40 KB	900 File	1/10/2013 2:05 PM
CmpSave.900	4 KB	900 File	1/11/2013 4:27 PM
Company.900	4 KB	900 File	1/11/2013 4:27 PM
LinkMgr.900	1 KB	900 File	1/11/2013 4:27 PM
Manager.900	1,299 KB	900 File	1/11/2013 4:27 PM
TACCESS.TSF	0 KB	TSF File	1/5/2013 10:00 AM
TEXCL.TSF	0 KB	TSF File	1/5/2013 10:00 AM
TranMgr.900	4 KB	900 File	1/11/2013 4:27 PM
TSTATE.TSF	1 KB	TSF File	1/11/2013 4:27 PM

F-2B: ABK.900 in respective Data Folder

- By default, the backup is stored in ABK.900 file for each Company and is stored in the respective company folder.
- Even if you have enabled Auto Back Up, you should take Regular Back Up, as a matter of safely. Data restored from Regular Back Up is more reliable
- If the Auto Backup file is deleted from data folder, it is recreated whenever the company is loaded.
- While loading a company, if you get a 'Failed to Setup Auto Backup, manually remove ABK.900 file and load the company once again to recreate the Auto Backup file.
- While taking a backup of the company data, the auto backup file (ABK.900) is excluded from the data backup process. However, when you Restore Data, a new Auto Backup file is created. So, a backup of data is always available.

05 Auto Back Up Files

- When Auto Back Up is activated for one company, a ABK.900 file is created in the same data folder of the respective Company. When Auto Back Up is activated for multiple Companies, TABK.900 is stored in user defined location, as specified at *Location of Auto Back Up File (TABK),* The TABK.900 file contains auto back up of all the Companies for which Auto Back feature is enabled.
- The Auto Back Up path may be specified in Data Configuration (F-1A)
- If no Auto Back Up path is specified, Auto Back up file is saved in ABK.900 in respective folder
- Multiple Company auto back is taken when Auto Back is specified in Multiple Companies
- Multiple Company auto backed data may be Restored if the location of auto back file is specified

06 Auto Back Up Restoration

When Auto Back up is activated, several versions of data are preserved (of various dates). You may Restore the desired version.

The process of Auto Back up is similar to Data Restore process as explained.

At Company Info menu (At gateway, Click F3:Company Info), select Restore to get *Restore Companies on Disk* screen (F-2A).

- **Destination Folder:** At Destination, the working data folder name is carried
- **Source Folder:** At Source, enter the name of the path where from the Back Up Data are to be restored. Select the Company to be restored at Auto Back Up section (right part). All the Back Up data versions of the selected Company are displayed (F-3A). Now select the version to be Backed up. This way, you may even restore the older version of data if required.

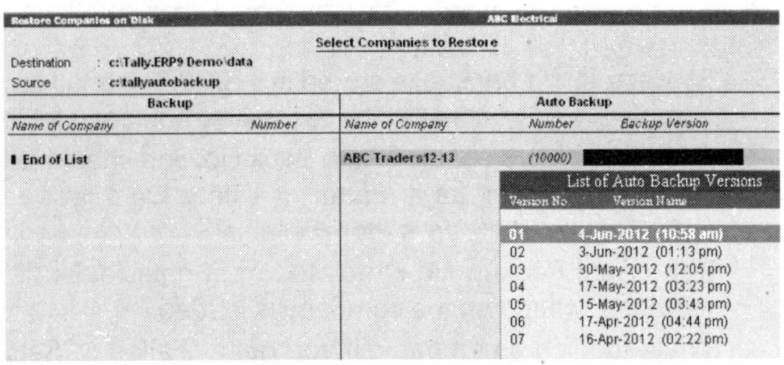

F-3A: Restoration from Auto Back Up

The data is copied and overwritten in the folder starting with number 9 (e.g data of Company 10000 is restored in folder 90000).

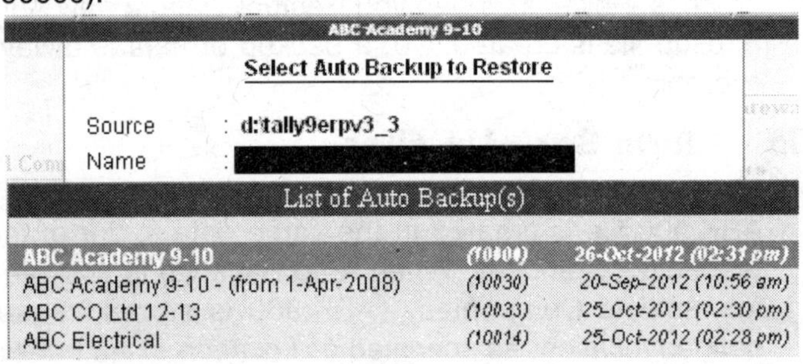

F-4A: Selection of Company for Auto Back Up Restoration

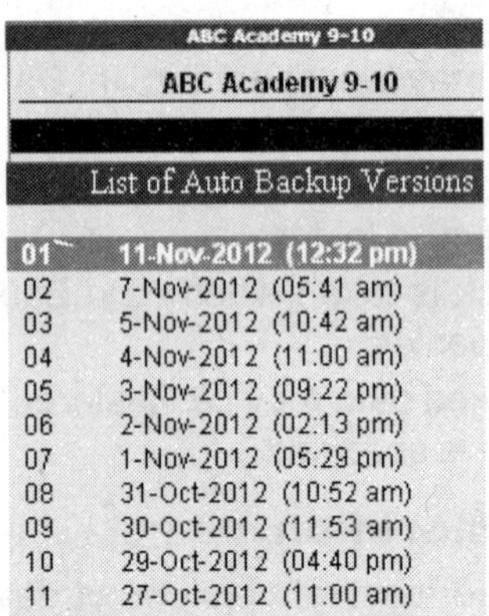

F-4B: Selection of Data Version for Auto Back

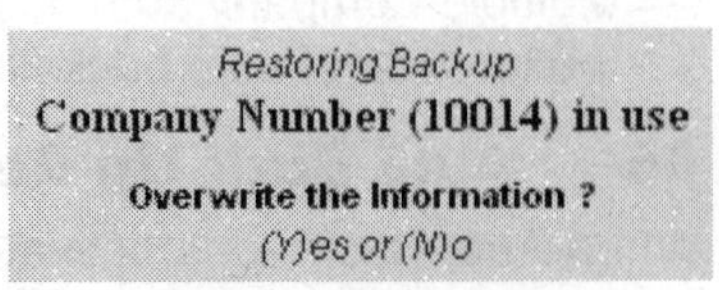

F-4C: Message on restoration of Data Up Restoration

Alternatively, at Gateway, you press Ctl+Alt+K to get Auto Back Up Restoration screen (F-4A). Select the Company for which data is to be Restored (F-4A). Now select the Back Up data version to be Restored (F-4B). A message of overwriting of Data (when the Restored Company is already existing in Destination data older) is shown (F-4C). Type *Yes* to overwrite older data with the Restored Data.

07 Auto Back Up Status

To know the Status of Auto Back up data, at Company Info screen (At Gateway, Click *F3:Cmp Info*), click *U:Auto Back Up Status* button (F-6) at the Button Bar (or press *Alt+U* keys) to get *Auto Back Up status* screen (F-5A). It shows the status of currently selected companies (showing the Number of entries not yet backed up) and list of Other Companies (for which Auto Back is activated but currently not selected).

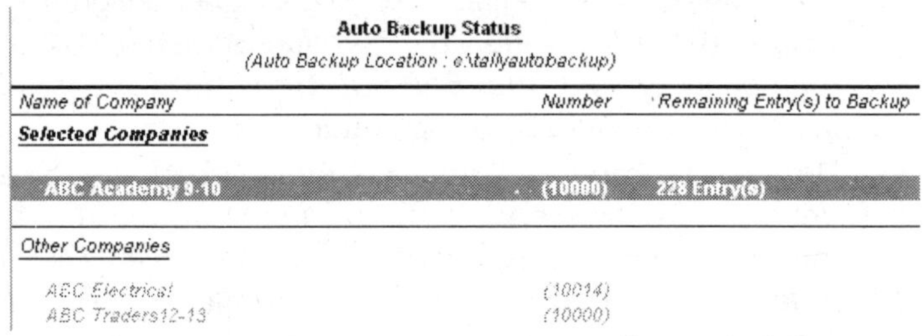

F-5A: Auto back Up Status

F-6: Auto Back Status Button

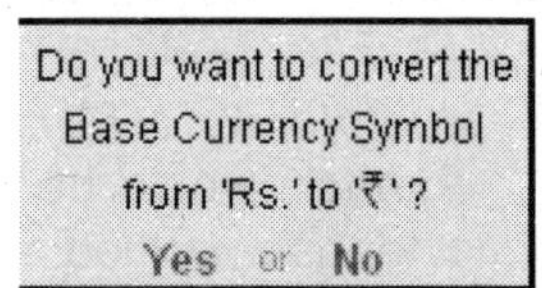

F-7: Message for Base Currency symbol change

Extra Space in Data folder: Auto Back up requires extra space in Data folder, as it continuously creates restoration points which are stored in incremental backup file, which is stored with the same company folder.

08 Re-writing of New Currency Symbol

We have explained Re-writing of data earlier (04/01-13). During Re-writing of data of older version, you get a prompt (F-7) to change the old 'Rs' currency symbol to new currency Symbol (₹)

At the prompt '*Do you want to convert the Base Currency Symbol from old currency symbol 'Rs'.to '₹'* (F-3)*:*

- Click *Yes* to change to the new currency symbol (₹)
- Click *No* to retain the old currency symbol Rs.

FAQ: Frequently Asked Questions

FAQ-1: How to Activate Auto Back Up feature

Ans: At Gateway of Tally, click *F12:Configure* to get Configuration Menu. At Configuration menu, select Data Configuration to get Data Configuration Screen (F-1A). At *Data Configuration Screen* (F-1A), at the option *Enable Auto Back Up Copy* (F-1A), set Yes to activate the Auto Back Up feature.

New Year Accounts 02-26

01 New Year Accounts

We have discussed about extension of Financial Accounting period for the next year to keep next year accounts also in the same Company.

However, for operational convenience & better security, organizations normally prefer to keep separate Data for each Financial Year. You may temporarily extend the Financial Year to enter data of the new Financial Year also in the same Company, till completion of voucher entry of previous year.

02 Extension of Financial Year

Tally creates the Financial Year for 12 Months from the *Financial Year From* (F-2A/01-01). If you enter 01.04.12 at *Financial Year From* in Company Creation screen (F-2A/01-01), the year end is 31.03.13. Having entered the data for 12-13, you may extend the financial year for 13-14, i.e from 01.04.13 to 31.03.14, by changing Current Period.

Click *F2: Period* button (or press Alt+F2) to change current period (F-4A / 01-02). At *To* field, enter the next year closing date 31.03.14

Now you can enter voucher data for the next Financial Year. At any point of time, you may change the Current Period through *F2: Period* button and work for that period.

This way, you can start working for new year (e.g FY 13-14), even before the accounts of previous year (FY 12-13) are closed. So, you can enter data in both years simultaneously.

02.01 Multi Year Company

This way, you can work for both the years simultaneously and you do not have to create new Account Masters (Ledger / Groups). You also do not have to carry the closing balances of previous financial year to Opening Balance of next Financial year, as data for both the financial years are contained in same Tally Company. This way, you may keep data of all the years in ONE Tally Company

03 Splitting of Company

After having completed the accounts finally for the current year (i.e. FY 12-13), you may split the Company into 2 years (FY 12-13 & FY 13-14) to make separate new Company for the next Financial Year Company (FY 13-14) with Opening Balances carried from the Closing Balances of previous year (FY 12-13), as described below:

- Click *F3: Cmp Info* button to get *Company Info Menu* (F-1A/01-01) and select *Split Company Data* to get *Split Company Data Menu* (F-2A).
- At *Split Company Data Menu* (F-2A), select *Select Company* to get *Split Company Data screen* (F-1A). At *Split Company Data* screen (F-1A), at *Split From* field, enter the Date (i.e 1-4-2013) from which the next year Company (FY 13-14) is to be created (i.e First Date of New Year Company,

On splitting, Tally creates 2 new Company (F-2A) Data files, showing the progress status (do not interrupt till the process is over). The original company data (combined data before splitting) is also retained.

The Closing Balance (of Real & Personal Accounts, except the Nominal Accounts) of the first part Company is carried to Opening Balance of the 2nd Part Company

F-1A: Company Splitting screen

F-2A: Company Split Menu

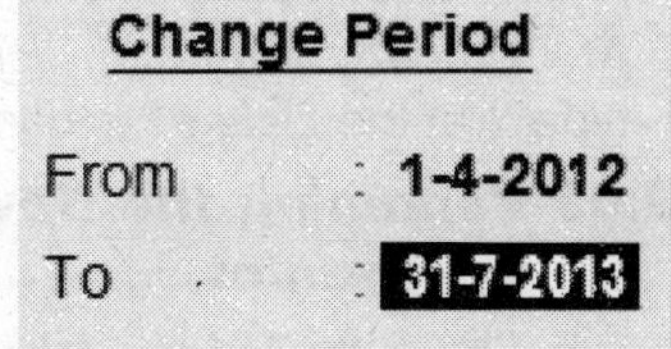

F-2B: Extension of Period

Financial Year From date is added (suffixed) to the Company Name of the respective Split Company for identification (F-1A).

The newly created Companies as well as the old extended Company is shown in the list of selected Companies (F-4A)

03.01 Verification of Split Data

Having split the data, you should check both the split companies to make sure there is no error in any voucher.

- **At** *Company Split Menu* (F-2A). select *Verify Company Data* to get *Verify Company Data* screen (F-3A)
- At *Verify Company Data* screen (F-3A), at *Company Name*, select the *Split Company* to be verified. Tally checks each voucher and lists vouchers where there may be some error or inconsistency in data.

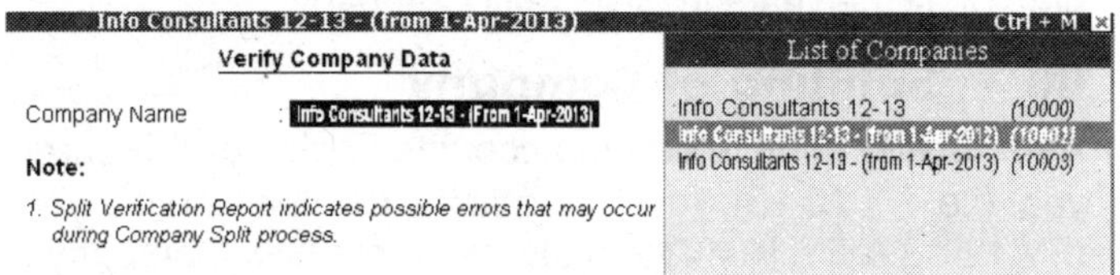

F-3A: Split Company data Verification screen

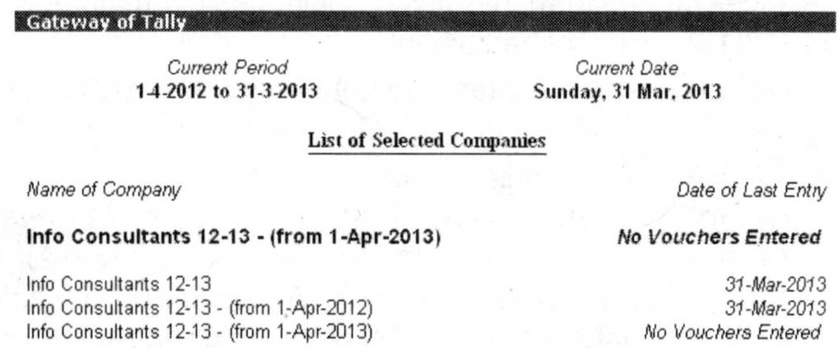

F-4A: List of Companies (Old & Split)

After verifying the split Companies, edit the vouchers listed and rectify error, if any.

03.02 Deletion of Original Company

Now you have to Delete the Original Company which contained complete data of previous year (e.g FY 12-13) and some data of next year also (e.g FY 13-14), entered before splitting

- Click *F3:Cmp Info* button at Gateway of Tally to get *Company Info* Menu (F-1A/01-01)
- At *Company Info Menu* (F-1A/01-01), select *Alter* and select the Company to be Deleted (e.g Info Consultants) to get the Company Alteration screen.
- At *Company Alteration screen*, press Alt+D and then type Y at the *Delete?* to confirm Deletion.

03.03 Renaming the Newly Created Split Companies

Now you have to *Rename* (change the Company Name) of the newly created split companies (remove the suffixed Period from the name)

- Select the 1st Company - Info Consultants (from 1-4-2011) to get Gateway of Tally of the selected Company
- Click *F3:Cmp Info* button (or press Alt+F3 keys) at Gateway of Tally, to get Company Info Menu (F-1A/01-01)

Split Company name	Rename as
Info Consultants 12-13 (from 1 Apr 21012)	Info Consultants 12-13
Info Consultants 12-13 (from 1 Apr 21013)	Info Consultants 13-14

At *Company Info* Menu (F-1A/01-01), select *Alter*, select the Company to be renamed, At *Name* field, change the Company name (e.g from *Info Consultants (from 1-4-2011)* to *Info Consultants 11-12).*

In the same way, change the Company name of 2nd Company (e.g from *Info Consultants (from 1-4-2012)* to *Info Consultants 12-13*)

Entry of Opeing Balances in the New Year Company: At the

03.04 Transfer of Balances between Split Companies

The Closing Balance of all Balance Sheet Accounts (Real & Personal) only of the 1st Part of the Split Company (e.g FY 12-13) will be carried as Opening Balance of 2nd Part of the Split Company (e.g FY13-14). But the Closing Balance of Nominal Accounts will not be carried (Closing Balances of Real & Personal Accounts, appearing in Balance Sheet only will be carried). So, the Balance of all Nominal Accounts in the 2nd split Company (accounts appearing in Profit & Loss Statement) will be zero.

FAQ: Frequently Asked Questions

FAQ-1: How you continue to enter Voucher for next Financial Account in the same Company?

Ans: Tally initially creates a Financial Period of 12 months from the "*Financial Year From* date", So, if *Financial Year From* Date is 1-4-2011, the FY is 1-4-2011 to 31-3-2012. When next financial year (FY 12-13) starts, you may extend the financial period to 31-3-2013 and continue working without closing the FY 12-13. To do that, click *F2: Period* button (or press Alt+F2 keys) and enter the Date 31-03-2013 at 'To' field (F-2B). This way, you may keep more than one year's data (FY 11-12 & FY 12-13) in one company by extending Financial Year (and continue to keep data of successive years in one Company).

FAQ-2: How to continue working for next financial year and then Split data for each financial year in the same Tally Company?

Ans: After extending the Financial Year, you continue working for both the years simultaneously. After completing the Accounts of Previous Year, you may split the Company into 2 years to make separate Company for the each Financial

Year. The closing balances of Balance Sheet Accounts previous year is carried to Opening Balances of next year.

- Click F3: *Cmp Info* button to get Company Info Menu (F-1/02-01) and select *Split Company Data* to get *Split Company Data* Menu (F-2A).
- Select Split Company to get *Split Company Data screen* (F-1). Enter the Date from which you like to split the Data (e.g 1-4-2012).
- Press *Yes* to confirm splitting.

Tally creates 2 new companies data files, showing the progress status (do not interrupt till the process is over). The original company data is also retained. *Financial Year From* date is added (suffixed) to the Name of the Split Company for identification.

Tally, adds the year beginning date in *Name* only but *Mailing Name* remains intact.

Select *Alter* at *Company Info Menu* (F-1A/01-01) and change the Company Name to remove the Year suffix in the Name, through *Company Alteration* (§04/01-01)

Now verify data for both the split companies. After verifying the split Companies, you may delete the original Company.

FAQ-3: The Financial Year ends on 31st March. Till the Accounts of previous year are completed and finalized, I like to continue voucher entry for both the years in the existing Company. Later on, when the accounts of previous year are finalized. I like to split the combined company into two separate companies for each Financial Year. How I should plan and proceed.

a. On 1st April, extend the Period of the current Company, to next Financial Year (§02).
b. Set the current period for the respective year (§02) and enter voucher for both the respective years
c. After the accounts of previous year are finalized (voucher entry is complete), split the company into two financial years from the date of beginning from the new financial year (§03)
d. Verify the data of both the split companies (§03.01) and rectify reported errors, if any.
e. Delete the old company (§03.02)
f. Rename (§03.03) both the newly created split companies (remove year beginning suffix in the Company Name)
g. Continue working in the new year company and shut the old year company

FAQ-4: After splitting, the Company Start Date is added in the Company name. How I rename (change the Company name) after splitting and delete the old combined company

Ans: After splitting, the Company, Financial Beginning Date is added to the Company name of both the newly created split Companies. For example, when you split the Company Info Consultants (having data from 1.4.11), from 1-4-2012, two split Companies will be created as follows

- Info Consultants (from 1-4-2011)
- Info Consultants (from 1-4-2012)

Deletion of Company

Now you have to *Delete* the old extended Company (Info Consultants) which contained data of FY 11-12 and some data of FY 12-13 also, entered before splitting (for safety, keep a Back Up of the Company (§02/01-13)

- Click F3:*Cmp Info* button at Gateway of Tally, to get Company Info Menu (F-1A/01-01)
- At Company Info Menu (F-1A/01-01), select *Alter* and select the Company to be Deleted (the original extended Company, to get the Company Alteration screen.
- Press *Alt+D* and then type Y at the Query *Delete?* to confirm Deletion.

Renaming Company (Changing Company name)

Now you have to Rename (change the *Company Name*) the newly created split companies

- Select the 1st Company - Info Consultants (from 1-4-2011), to get Gateway of Tally of the selected Company (A-01)
- Click F3:*Cmp Info* button (or press Alt+F3 keys) at *Gateway of Tally*, to get Company Info Menu (F-1/01-01)
- At *Company Info* Menu, select *Alter* and select the new year split Company to be Renamed (Info Consultants *(from 1-4-2012)* to get the Company Alteration screen
- At *Name* field, change the Company name from *Info Consultants (from 1-4-2011)* to *Info Consultants 11-12* (delete the end portion of Starting date from Company Name). At *Mailing Name*, enter *Info Consultants.*
- In the same way, change the Company name of 2nd Company from *Info Consultants (from 1-4-2012)* to *Info Consultants 12-13*. At *Mailing Name*, enter *Info Consultants.*

Part 3
Accounts Receivables & Payables

Sales & Purchase constitute the major bulk of business transactions. Gradual expansion of trade alongwith control of Receivables & Payables is the main concern for sustenance & growth of any Business Entity. This Part exclusively deals with Business Trade Transactions with Suppliers & Customers and maintenance of detailed records of transactions and Party Accounts for Party Analysis & Performance, constant tracking & control of Receivables & Payables

Party Ledger Accounts explains additional features & info for maintenance & control of Accounts Receivables & Payables.

Sale / Purchase Voucher explains the advanced features and entry of additional details in Sales & Purchase transactions.

Invoice Printing explains configuration of Invoice Formats and its contents as per specific needs and printing of Invoices on-line and post entry in bulk.

Bill Register explains printing of Sales, Purchase Transactions details (and Debit & Credit Notes) in various formats and contents

Columnar Bill Register explains printing of Sales, Purchase, Debit & Credit Notes particulars in compact columnar format with user defined column parameters.

Sale Purchase Summary describes various summary reports derived from Sales & Purchase transactions for better management control.

Accounts Receivables & Payables explains Bill Reference, the unique identifier to track transactions trails for each distinct transaction.

Outstanding Bills Statements explains various reports for control & tracking of Open Accounts, like *Age Analysis,* reminder letters for overdues, final settlement of multiple Open Accounts of a Party, etc

Overdue Interest explains computation of Interest on overdue bills. It vividly covers Interest computed on complex terms of Payment & varied Interest rates for each transaction, where open accounts are settled through multiple payments.

Closing Stock Value explains entry of Closing Stock Value in Stock Ledger Account Master.

Part 3: Accounts Receivables & Payables describes how to implement better control on Debtors & Creditors accounts. Traders / Retailers doing mostly Cash Sales / Purchase, where tracking of Open Accounts is not so crucial, may skip this Part.

Party Ledger Accounts

01 Party Ledger Accounts

So far, we have discussed about various types of Accounting Transactions in general. However, in business, transactions with Buyers & Suppliers (referred as Parties) form the bulk of the business transactions. Here we discuss about Advanced Features of Ledger Accounts related to Parties (Buyers / Debtors & Vendors / Creditors)

02 Activation of Advanced Features of Ledger Accounts

To Activate Advanced Features of Ledger Accounts, set the options at:

- **Configuration:** At Gateway of Tally, click *F12:Configurtaion >Accts/Inventory Info* (F-1A)
- **Company Accounting Features**: *Click F11: Features > F1:Accounting Features* and set the options(F-1B, F-1C & F-1D) discussed next (§04)

F-1A: Accts / Inventory Info Configuration

Accounts	
Allow ADVANCED entries in Masters	? Yes
Use ADDRESSES for Ledger Accounts	? Yes
Use CONTACT Details	? Yes
Add NOTES for Ledger Accounts	? Yes

Maintain Multiple Mailing Details for Company & Ledgers	? No
Set/Alter Company Mailing Details	? No

F-1B: Multiple Mailing Address set Up

Budgets & Scenario Management	
Maintain Budgets and Controls	? Yes

F-1C: Accounting Features set up – Credit period

F-1D: Accounting Features set up – AR/AP & Interest

Outstandings Management	
Maintain Bill-wise Details	? No
(for Non-Trading A/cs also)	? No
Activate Interest Calculation	? Yes
(use advanced parameters)	? Yes

03 Ledger Accounts Configuration set up

Ledger Accounts creation is discussed earlier (§03.02/01-03). Here, we discuss about advanced options of Party Ledger Accounts.

At Gateway, Click *F12:Configure > Accts / Inventory Info* to get *Accts / Inventory Info Configuration* screen (F-1A). At Accounts section of *Accts / Inventory Info Configuration* screen (F-1A), set the Advanced options for Accounts Masters (Accounts Groups & Accounts Ledgers), as follows:

- **Advanced Features**:Set *Yes* at Allow *Advanced Entries in Masters* (under section *Accounts*: F-1A) to activate Advanced Features in Account Group (§03/02-05) & Ledger Accounts (§04/02-05)
- **Ledger Address**: Set *Yes* at *Use Address for Ledger Accounts* (F-1A) to enable entry of Mailing Address in Ledger Account (F-2A)

  Having set *Yes* for Ledger Address as above, you may further set as follows:
  - o **Contact Details**: Set Yes at *Use Contact Details* (F-1A) to enable enter Contact Person details (F-2A) in Ledger Account master.
- **Ledger Notes**: Set Yes at Add Notes at Ledger Accounts entry (§02/02-05)
- **Multiple Mailing Addresses:** At *F11:Features> Accounting Features*, set Yes at *Maintain Multiple Mailing Details for Company & Ledgers* to activate option for Multiple Mailing Address in Ledger Accounts (§06)

04 Accounts Masters Features set up

Having activated the Advanced Accounts Master Configuration option (Set *Yes* at *Allow Advanced Entries in Masters*: F-1A), set the following options:

- **Bill Reference & Credit Features Activation ;** Set the Bill Reference options as follows (F-1D):
  - o **Bill Reference Feature for Traders' Ledger Accounts**: Set *Yes* at *Maintain Bill By Bill* to activate Bill Reference Feature (§05/03-07) for Ledger Accounts under Sundry Debtors, Sundry Creditors, Loans & Advance and Branch Accounts (F-1D)
  - o **Bill Reference Feature for Other ledger accounts**: Having set *Yes* at *Maintain Bill By Bill* (F-1D), further set Yes at *(for Non Trading Accounts also)* to activate Bill Reference Feature for other Ledger Accounts Ledger Accounts also (Like Ledgers under Loans & Advances, Loans Liabilities Groups etc)
- **Interest:** Set the options for Interest on delayed payments, as follows
  - o **Activate Simple Mode Interest Feature:** Set *Yes* at *Activate Interest Calculation* to activate Simple

Mode Interest Computation (F-1D, §02/02-11),

- o **Activate Advance Mode Interest Feature:** Having set *Yes* at *Activate Interest Calculation*, further set Yes at *Use Advanced parameters* to activate Advanced Interest Feature (F-1D, §02/03-09)

- **Credit Limit:** To set Credit Limit for Customers (§05), at *F11:Features>Accounting Feature*, set *Yes at Maintain Budgets & Control*, under Budgets & Scenarios section (F-1C).

05 Advanced Entries at Accounts Ledger

We have explained the options to activate the Advanced Configuration & Features in for Party Ledger Account Master. Having set the respective options, you may enter the respective data in Ledger Account master (F-2A), as follows:

- **Credit Limit**: Credit Limit is used to control receivables. It denotes the maximum credit limit that the Party may be allowed. If the dues of the Party exceeds the limit, further sales to the Party is restricted (no voucher will be allowed to create which makes the Balance dues form the Party to exceed the Credit Limit set.

  Having activated the feature of Credit Limit entry (F-1C), at Party Ledger Entry screen (F-2A). you get the field *Set Credit Limit.* Enter the Credit Limit for the Party (if you like to set any), else leave zero (no limit set). Consequently, when you attempt to enter a Sales Voucher, if the new voucher being entered causes to exceed the outstanding dues cross the specified credit limit (NOT Zero), a warning message will be prompted and you will not be allowed to enter the Voucher (§06.03/03-02, F-8A/03-02). In that case, you have to exit from the voucher, change Credit Limit and again come back to voucher entry).

- **Ledger Account Notes:** If you have activated *Notes for Ledger Accounts* (F-1A), at Ledger Accounts entry screen (F-2A), at *Notes* field, you may write notes about the Party, for internal info. The Ledger Note is not printed in any report, but may be displayed on screen in some reports.

- **Default Credit Period**: *Default Credit Period* means the standard credit period that you normally allow to the Party. This credit Period is carried in the voucher (which you may change in the specific voucher) so that you do not have to type it in each voucher again. You get the field *Default Credit Period* at Party Ledger creation (F-2A), when you have set *Yes at Maintain Bill By Bill* option at Company Features set up (F-1E),

  At *Default Credit Period* field, enter the Number of Days. You may enter the credit period in other time units also, by typing the respective unit letter after the number like Week (type w), Month (type m) or Year (type Y), If you do not specify unit, Day is assumed, e.g 3 means 3 days). So, 30d (or 30) indicates 30 Days, 2w indicates 2 weeks, 2 m indicates 2 Months and 1y indicates 1 Year.

  The Due Date of a Bill is computed from the Invoice Date / Effective Date of the Bill and the Credit Period entered (§09.03/ 04-07)..

- **Mailing Details:** At the right part of the Ledger Accounts entry screen, (F-2A) you enter the mailing & related details as follows:

  - o **Mailing Address**: You get the field *Address* to enter Address (F-2A) when you set *Yes* at *Use Address for Ledger Accounts at Accts/Inventory Masters Configuration* screen (F-1A) under Accounts section.

    Here enter the Party's Main office address and other details for communication (F-2A) This address is normally printed in vouchers & reports.

  - o **Tax Information**: At Party Master entry screen (F-2A), under the section *Tax Information*, you enter the IT PAN, Sales Tax & CST Number of the Party (as described for Company Creation / Alteration – F-2/01-01). These info are used to print the details in Vouchers (like Invoice etc) and *Confirmation of Accounts*.

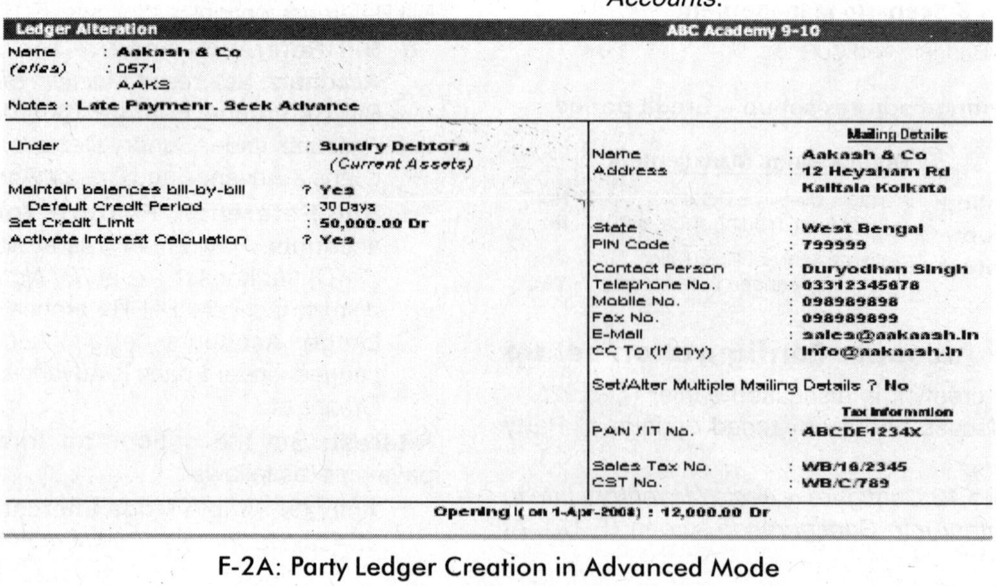

F-2A: Party Ledger Creation in Advanced Mode

06 Multiple Mailing Details

When you set *Yes* at *Set / Alter Multiple Mailing Details for Company & Ledgers* (F-1B), you get *Multiple Address Type Entry* screen (F-2B) to enter multiple *Address Type* of a Party Ledger Account. At the *Party Master multiple address Type entry* screen (F-2B). You may enter name of each of its offices (if there are multiple Branches / offices of the Party: §06.01), in the same way as multiple address of Company is entered (§11/02-02). So, only ONE ledger account is created for the Party but addresses of its branches may be entered. You may selectively print the Main office Address or respective Branch address in the Documents / Reports (§04.07/02-14)

F-2B: Multiple Office Type entry screen

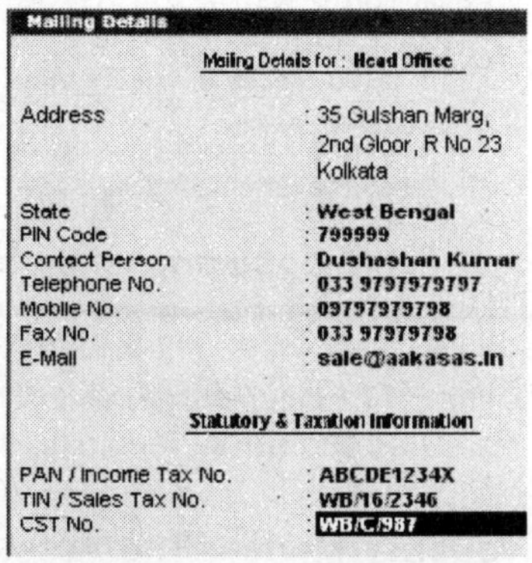

F-2C: Address Entry for Ledger A/c Address Types

06.01 Multiple Address Type Entry

At Multiple Address Type entry screen (F-2B) to enter the Names of each Branch / Office, enter the *Address Type* names first (F-2B) and then,

- Press <Dn Arrow> key to successively enter all the Address Types (F-2B). Now select the Address type & press <Enter> to get the Mailing Details screen (F-2C) and then enter the details for each address type, n he same way as Ledger Address & Other Details
- Press <Enter> to enter the address details of the respective Address Type entered at Mailing Details screen (F-2C) simultaneously.

06.02 Statutory & Tax Info

Having entered the Mailing Details (F-2A) and Multiple Mailing Details, if any (F-2B & F-2C), next enter the Statutory Tax Info at (F-2A) for Main Office & F-2C for respective Offices), as described for Company Creation / Alteration (§04/02-02)

FAQ: Frequently Asked Questions

FAQ-1: How to set up Address in Party Ledger Accounts

Ans: Party Address& Contact Details: At Accounts section of *Accts / Inventory Info Configuration* screen (F-1A), set *Yes* at *Use Address for Ledger Accounts* (F-1A) to enable entry of Mailing Address in Ledger Account (F-2A). To enter Contact Details also, set Yes at *Use Contact Details* (F-1A) to enable enter Contact Person details (F-2A).

Multiple Mailing Addresses: At *F11:Features>Accounting Features*, set Yes at *Maintain Multiple Mailing Details for Company & Ledgers* to activate option for Multiple Mailing Address in Ledger Accounts (P-06), if there are multiple Branches / offices of the Party (§06.01)

On activating Multiple Mailing Address for a Party, at *Party Master multiple address Type entry* screen (F-2B), enter name of each of its in the same way as multiple address of Company is entered (§11/02-02). So, only ONE ledger account is created for the Party but addresses of its branches may be entered. You may selectively print the Main office Address or respective Branch address in the Documents / Reports (§04.07/02-14)

Sale & Purchase Vouchers

03-02

01 Sale / Purchase Vouchers

Basic Accounting Vouchers (Contra, Receipt, Payment, have been discussed earlier (P-05/01-05). Here we discuss about Sales & Purchase transactions for an organisation in which Inventory (materials) has not been activated. So, we discuss about entry of vouchers with Accounting Transactions only (only Ledger Accounts, no Stock Item), like:

- **Sale / Purchase of Pure Services**: Consultancy, Labour Services etc, where materials are not normally involved, but Sales Purchase Voucher / Invoice is created.
- **Sale / Purchase of Materials cum Services**: Repairs, Contract Services, etc., where Composite charges are billed in respect of Labour Charges and Materials consumed. In such case, though materials are purchase and their cost are included in the Invoice, no stock records (Stock Item Ledgers) are maintained. So the vouchers do not contain transaction of Stock Items, but the materials cost are merged/ compounded in the Vouchers / Invoice
- **Sale / Purchase Voucher of Accounts Part only:** Accounts details of Sale / Purchase are only entered (but Stock details are not recorded when Inventory System is not activated). This is common for small retailers where Invoices are created manually (at the small & busy sales counters) and only amounts are recorded in Computers System from the Invoices, to maintain Accounts.

It is recommended that all sorts of Sales / Purchase (Cash / Credit) should be entered through Sales / Purchase Voucher only (as explained in this chapter), so that Sales Purchase register shows complete records of all Sales / Purchases.

Sale / Purchase transactions for trade only are recorded through Sale / Purchase voucher, Sale / Purchase of Non Trading goods (e.g., Furniture, Motor Car etc for own use) should be entered through Journal Voucher.

02 Sales / Purchase Voucher Entry

We have explained Basic options of Sales / Purchase Voucher Entry (§05/01-04). Here we discuss about advanced features of Sales / Purchase Voucher / Invoice Entry

> **Note:** *In* Invoice *Mode, Party Ledger is entered in Header, other ledger accounts are entered in line area, No separate Debit / Credit column appears in Voucher entry screen.In* Voucher *Mode, All Ledger Accounts are entered in respective Debit or Credit column.*

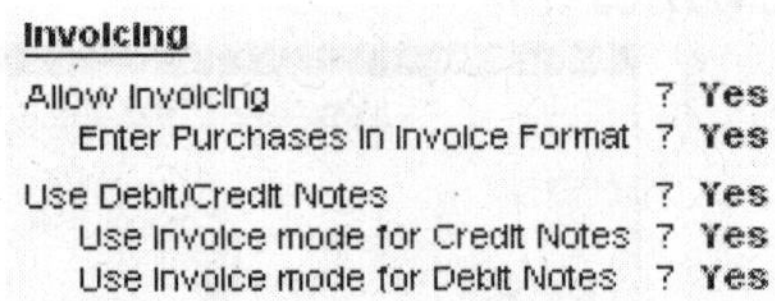

F-1A: Company set up for Invoice entry

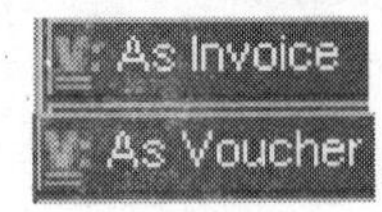

F-2A: Buttons

Click *F11:Features> Accounting Features* to get *Accounting Features* screen. At Invoicing section (F-1A), set the following options:

Voucher Modes: The Accounting transactions may in 2 modes as follows. At *Allow Invoicing* (F-1A):

- **Accounts Voucher Mode**: Set *No* to enter the Sales / Purchase Accounting Transaction in Voucher Mode only.
- **Accounting Invoice Mode** To enter Sales / Purchase voucher in Accounts Invoice Mode as follows (F-1A):
  - o **Accounts Invoice Mode of Sales Voucher**: Set *Yes* at *Allow Invoicing* to enter the Sales Accounting Transaction in Invoicing Mode also.
  - o **Accounts Invoice Mode of Purchase Voucher**: Having set *Yes* at *Allow Invoicing* to enter Invoicing Mode for Sales Voucher, you may further set Yes at *Enter Purchases in Invoice format.* to enter the Purchase Accounting Transaction in Invoicing Mode also.

02.01 Voucher Mode Buttons

Consequently, you get toggle buttons *V:As Voucher /As Invoice* (F-2A) at the vertical button bar. Select Voucher Mode (click *V:As Voucher* button) or Invoice Mode (Click *V:As Invoice* button)

- **Accounting Voucher:** Click *V: As Voucher* button (F-2A) to enter the accounts transaction in Accounting Voucher Mode. In this mode, you select all the Ledger Accounts at Particulars columns and enter the Ledger Amount at Debit / Credit columns as per rules stated.
- **Accounting Invoice:** Click *V: As Invoice* button (F-2A) to enter the sales accounts transaction in Accounting Invoice Mode.

In *Accounting Invoice* mode, you select the Party Ledger Accounts at Header without specifying Dr / Cr and Amount All other ledger accounts are selected in Particulars column and the Ledger amount is entered (in *Negative* figure if the amount is *Deducted)*

V: As Voucher / As Invoice is a toggle button (same button switches to either of the modes). The button (F-2A) shown indicates that you are currently in complimentary mode (other mode), and will take you to the mode shown in the button, as explained below:

V: As Invoice — When you see this button, you are currently in Invoice mode, click *V: As Voucher* button to get Voucher Mode

V: As Voucher — When you see this button, you are currently in Voucher Mode. Click *V: As Invoice* to get Invoice Mode

03 Sales / Purchase Entry Mode

- **Voucher Mode**: Voucher Mode is mostly useful for Individuals and small organisations, who do not normally print Sales Invoice (§05/01-04).. It is also useful where Invoices are manually created first and then only Accounting Entries only in computer, to maintain accounts (common for small traders who can not keep computer inn their small and busy counter)
- **Accounting Invoice**: Accounting Invoice mode is useful for Consultants and professionals (who do not use Inventory Module as they do not sell materials), to enter and print Invoices (Service Bills), instead of using Voucher Mode. In Invoice mode, they can enter additional particulars relating to Invoice and can print them in better formatted manner

03.01 Components of Accounting Invoice Entry screen

- **Header Part**
  - o Voucher Date
  - o Voucher Number
  - o Supplier Invoice Number & Date (in case of Purchase Invoice) / Reference Number (in case of Sales)
  - o Party Accounts Name (select Customer for sales / Supplier for Purchase).
  - o *Supplementary details*, where opted (in separate subscreen:§07).
- **Other Ledgers Part**
  - o Ledger Account at Particulars field
  - o Ledger Amount at Amount field (in positive number for amount to be added/ as negative number for amount to be deducted)
- **Voucher Narration**
  - o Voucher Narration at Narration field, where applicable

04 Sales / Purchase Voucher Entry Configuration

You may set the Configuration options in following ways:

04.01 Sales / Purchase Voucher Entry General Configuration set up

At *GoT,* Click *F12:Configure* to get Configuration Menu (F-1/02-01). Now select:

- o **Voucher Mode:** *Voucher Entry* to get *Voucher Entry Configuration* screen (F-3A). You may set the options under Accounts section in the Configuration screen (F-3A).
- o **Invoice Mode:** *Invoice / Orders Entry* to get Invoice Configuration screen (F-4A). You may set the options under General section in the Configuration screen (F-4A).

Accounts	
Skip Date field in Create Mode (faster entry!)	? No
Use Single Entry mode for Pymt/Rcpt/Contra	? No
Use Payment/Receipt as Contra	? No
Use Cr/Dr instead of To/By during entry	? No
Use Cheque Printing for Contra	? No
Warn on Negative Cash Balance	? Yes
Pre-Allocate Bills for Payment/Receipt/Journal	? No
Allow Cash Accounts in Journals	? No
Allow Expenses/Fixed Assets in Purchase Vouchers	? No
Allow Income Accounts in Sales Vouchers	? No
Show Inventory Details	? Yes
Show Table of Bill Details for Selection	? Yes
Show Bill-wise Details	? Yes
Expand into multiple lines	? Yes
Show Ledger Current Balances	? No

F-3A: General Voucher Configuration screen

General	
Accept Supplementary Details	? No
(Address Details, Despatch Details etc.)	
Print Default Name & Address of Party	? Yes
Allow Separate Buyer and Consignee Names	? No
Allow modification of ALL fields during entry	? No
Use Defaults for Bill Allocations	? No
Use Additional Description(s) for Item Name	? No
Use Additional Description(s) for Ledger Name	? No
(for Accounting Invoice.)	
Consolidate Stock Items with same rates	? No
Show Compound Unit of Item based on Rate	? No
Show Full Details of Compound Unit	? No
Show turnover achieved with Customer	? No

F-4A: General Invoice Configuration screen

04.02 Sales / Purchase Current Voucher Configuration screen

At the current Voucher / Invoice entry screen, click *F12:Configure* button to get the *Current Sales Voucher Configuration* screen (F-5A) & *Current Purchase Voucher Configuration* screen (F-5B)

> **Note:** *The default Configuration options set (F-4A) are carried at Current Voucher Configuration (F-5A & F-6A), screen (when you click F12:Configuration at Voucher entry screen). You may change them for the current voucher entry session.*

Sales Configuration

Accept Supplementary Details	?	No
Skip Date field in Create Mode (faster entry!)	?	No
Use Cr/Dr instead of To/By during entry	?	Yes
Warn on Negative Cash Balance	?	Yes
Allow Income Accounts in Sales Vouchers	?	No
Show Inventory Details	?	Yes
Show Table of Bill Details for Selection	?	Yes
Show Bill-wise Details	?	Yes
Expand into multiple lines	?	Yes
Use Voucher No. as Bill Ref. No. for Bill Allocations	?	No
Show Ledger Current Balances	?	No
Use Default for Bank Allocations	?	No
Show Remarks in Bank Allocation Details	?	No

F-5A: Current Sales Voucher Entry configuration screen

Purchase Configuration

Accept Supplementary Details	?	No
Skip Date field in Create Mode (faster entry!)	?	No
Use Cr/Dr instead of To/By during entry	?	Yes
Warn on Negative Cash Balance	?	Yes
Allow Expenses/Fixed Assets in Purchase Vouchers	?	No
Show Inventory Details	?	Yes
Show Table of Bill Details for Selection	?	Yes
Show Bill-wise Details	?	Yes
Expand into multiple lines	?	Yes
Show Ledger Current Balances	?	No
Confirm each Cheque before Print	?	Yes
Use Default for Bank Allocations	?	No
Use Auto Cheque Numbering	?	Yes
Allow Selection of Cheque Range	?	Yes
Show Remarks in Bank Allocation Details	?	No

F-5B: Current Purchase Voucher Entry Configuration screen

04.03 Sales / Purchase Voucher Mode Entry Configuration

Most of options in both types of Configuration screens (General & Current) for both types of Voucher (Sales & Purchase) are similar. The options specifically related to Sales / Purchase Vouchers are discussed below:

- **Pre Allocate Bills for Payment / Receipt / Journal:** When money is received from, or paid to Parties against open Bills (Outstanding Bills), To make the allocation easier and automatic, set *Yes* at *Pre Allocate Bills for Payment / Receipt / Journals* (F-4A), to allocate the amount Received (in Receipt Voucher / Paid (in Payment Voucher) / Adjusted (in Journal Voucher), as per Bill Due Date (and treat the extra amount if any, as *On Account*) in the Bill Allocation screen, otherwise set No (the Bill Allocation is to be done by the user in Bill Allocation screen, as usual (§09/03-07)
- **Expenses / Fixed Asset in Purchase Voucher:** Normally only Trade Purchases should be entered in Purchase Voucher (§05). Purchase for Fixed Assets (.e.g Vehicles For own use) / Expenses (e.g Stationery etc) are entered through Payment / Journal Voucher (§05/01-04).

  To allow entry of Purchases relating to *Expenses / Fixed Assets* also in Purchase Voucher, at *Allow Expenses / Fixed Asset in Purchase Vouchers* (F-5B), set:
  - o *Yes*, to allow selection of Fixed Assets (and other ledger Accounts) at Purchase Account
  - o *No* to allow selection of Ledger Accounts under Purchases Group only
- **Allow Income Accounts in Sales Voucher:** Normally only voucher for Sales should be entered in Sales Voucher. Income from other activities (e.g Consultancy Fees) are normally entered through Receipt / Journal Voucher.

  To allow entry of Income also in Sales Voucher, at *Allow Income Accounts in Sales Voucher* (F-5A), set:
  - o *Yes*, to allow selection of Other Income Ledger Accounts also at Sales Accounts.
  - o *No* to allow entry for Trade Sales only in Sales Account.

04.04 Sales / Purchase Invoice Mode Entry Configuration

At Sales / Purchase Voucher Entry screen with Accounting Invoice mode, click *F12: Configure* to get *Current Sales Invoice Configuration Screen* (F-6A) & *Current Purchase Invoice Configuration Screen* (F-6B).

> **Note:** *Most of the options of Current Sales / Purchase Invoice configuration (F-6A / F-6B) & Voucher configuration (F-5A / F-5B) are similar. In Purchase Voucher configuration (F-6B), you get additional option for Cheque Printing for Payment to Creditors.*

Sales Invoice Configuration

Accept Supplementary Details *(Address Details, Despatch Details etc.)*	? **No**
Print Default Name & Address of Party	? **Yes**
Allow Separate Buyer and Consignee Names	? **No**
Use Defaults for Bill Allocations	? **No**
Use Voucher No. as Bill Ref. No. for Bill Allocations	? **No**
Use Additional Description(s) for Ledger Name	? **No**
Use Default for Bank Allocations	? **No**
Show Remarks in Bank Allocation Details	? **No**
Other Options	
Show turnover achieved with Customer	? **No**
Allow modification of ALL fields during entry	? **No**
Warn on Negative Stock Balance	? **Yes**

F-6A: Current Sales Invoice Entry Configuration

Purchase Invoice Configuration

Accept Supplementary Details *(Address Details, Despatch Details etc.)*	? **No**
Print Default Name & Address of Party	? **Yes**
Allow Separate Buyer and Consignee Names	? **No**
Use Defaults for Bill Allocations	? **No**
Use Additional Description(s) for Ledger Name	? **No**
Confirm each Cheque before Print	? **Yes**
Use Default for Bank Allocations	? **No**
Use Auto Cheque Numbering	? **Yes**
Allow Selection of Cheque Range	? **Yes**
Show Remarks in Bank Allocation Details	? **No**
Other Options	
Show turnover achieved with Customer	? **No**
Allow modification of ALL fields during entry	? **No**
Warn on Negative Stock Balance	? **Yes**

F-6B: Current Purchase Invoice Entry Configuration

Now set the configuration options as follows (F-6A, F-6B):

- **Supplementary Details**:To keep such additional info, set Yes at *Accept supplementary Details* (F-6A, F-6B) to get the Supplementary Details screen (F-8B, F-8C) to enter the various details related to the transaction.
- **Default Address**: When you set *No*, at *Accept supplementary Details* (F-6A, F-6B), the supplementary Details screen is not available even in Invoice Mode (the supplementary details screen is not activated in Voucher Mode). In such case, at the subsequent option *Print Default Name & Address of the Party* (F-6A, F-6B), you may further set:
  - o Yes to print the Name & address as per Mailing Name / Address of the Party as entered in Party Ledger Account Master entry.
  - o *No* to suppress Party Name in Invoice (the party Name / Address is not printed.
- **Consignee Details:** Sometimes, good are shipped to different Party (called Consignee) as per advise of the Buyer. At the option, *Allow Separate Buyer & Consignee Name* (F-6A, F-6B):
  - o Set Yes to specify the details of consignee
  - o Set *No* (when there is no separate Consignee specified by Buyer
- **Bill Reference:** Normally, the Bill Number (Voucher Number) is carried as Bill Reference Number (used to track Open Bills). At the option, *Use Defaults for Bill Allocation* (F-6A, F-6B)
  - o Set Yes at to carry the Bill Number at Bill Reference Number to make the Bill Allocation entry faster
  - o Set *No* to enter Bill Reference number (you get blank field to enter Bill Ref Number, Voucher Number is not carried by default)
- **Party Turnover in Invoice Entry**

  To see Turnover (Total of Net Bill Value till date) with the Party during voucher entry (excluding the current invoice being entered), at Invoice Configuration, *Yes* at *Show Turnover achieved with Customer.*

  Consequently, during Invoice Entry, you will get the cumulative turnover till date at the field *Turnover* (F-6C). Such info help you to evaluate the current performance to decide further transaction with the Party

Sales No. 13 **31-Mar-2010** Wednesday
Ref.:
Party's A/c Name : **B.K.Services**
Turnover : ***3,170.30 Dr*** *Current Balance* ***8,753.21 Cr***
Sales Ledger : **Sales**

Name of Item	**Quantity**	**Rate**	per	**Amount**

F-6C: Party Turnover / Ledger Balance Display in Invoice Entry

04.01 Sales Invoice Declaration Text

In *Sales Voucher Type* (F-1A/02-07), you may also specify *Declaration* (F-6D), which will be printed in place of Standard Declaration in Invoice.

Declaration :

Goods sold will not be taken back. Defective goods may be exchnaged, when available, between 2pm tp 5pm except on Saturdays/ Sundays.

F-6D: Declaration text

05 Purchase entry

When goods are purchased by buyer from the vendor, the buyer receives the goods from the vendor. Sometimes, the byer makes the payment to the vendor immediately (Called Cash Purchase). Often, the buyer pays later on, in due course of time, as agreed (Called Credit Purchase).

All Purchases (Credit & Cash) are entered in Purchase Voucher.

At GoT>Accounts Voucher entry screen, click *F9:Purchase* button to get *Purchase* Entry screen,

- Click *V:As Voucher* button to get Purchase Entry screen in *Voucher* Mode (F-7A)
- Click *V:As Invoice* button to get Purchase Entry screen in I*nvoice* Mode (F-7B)

Credit Purchase

	Particulars	Dr	Cr
Cr	Name of Vendor		(Amount)
Dr	Purchase Account	(Amount)	

Cash Purchase

	Particulars	Dr	Cr
Cr	Cash /Bank / bank OCC A/c		(Amount)
Dr	Purchase Account	(Amount)	

The rules & process of Purchase Voucher entry both in Voucher & Invoice mode are described below:

05.01 Purchase Entry in Voucher Mode

At Purchase Entry screen in *Voucher Mode* (F-7A), first entry should always be a Credit involving any Creditor (in case of Credit Purchase), or Cash, Bank or Bank OCC Account (in case of Cash Purchase) and second entry should be a Debit to a Ledger placed under *Purchase Account* group. Rest of the Accounts may be any Revenue Account (except Sales) or any Account under the Group *Current Liabilities* (other than Sundry Creditors). Thus you can include *Duties & Taxes* or other billing terms from 3rd entry onwards.

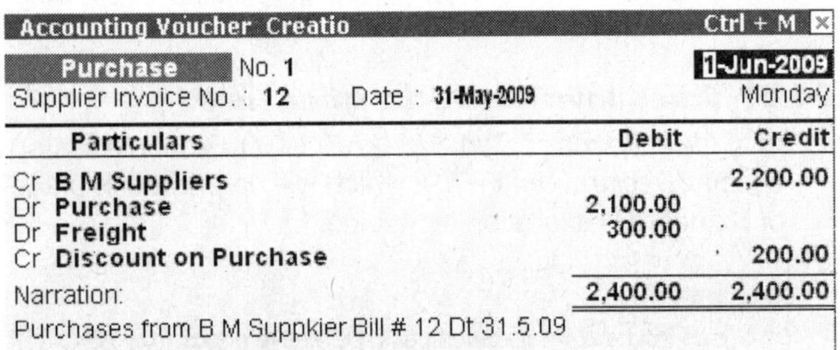
Accounting Voucher Creatio Ctrl + M
Purchase No. 1 1-Jun-2009
Supplier Invoice No. : 12 Date : 31-May-2009 Monday

Particulars	Debit	Credit
Cr **B M Suppliers**		2,200.00
Dr **Purchase**	2,100.00	
Dr **Freight**	300.00	
Cr **Discount on Purchase**		200.00
Narration:	2,400.00	2,400.00

Purchases from B M Suppkier Bill # 12 Dt 31.5.09

F-7A: Purchase voucher Entry in Voucher Mode

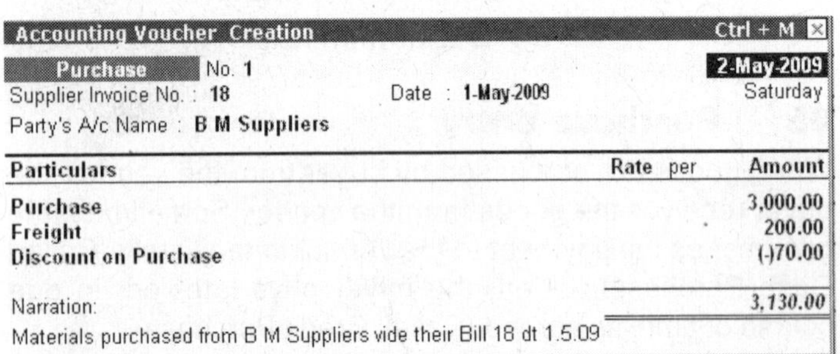
Accounting Voucher Creation Ctrl + M
Purchase No. 1 2-May-2009
Supplier Invoice No. : 18 Date : 1-May-2009 Saturday
Party's A/c Name : B M Suppliers

Particulars	Rate per	Amount
Purchase		3,000.00
Freight		200.00
Discount on Purchase		(-)70.00
Narration:		3,130.00

Materials purchased from B M Suppliers vide their Bill 18 dt 1.5.09

F-7B: Purchase voucher Entry in Accounting Invoice Mode

Rules:

1. The 1st entry is Credit (Sundry Debtors/ Creditors, Cash/ Bank /Bank OCC, Branch & Divisions).
2. The 2nd entry is Debit (Purchase)
3. The 3rd entry onward may be Debit (for Addition in Bill)/ Credit (for Deduction in Bill)/ of any revenue account (except Sales)

05.02 Purchase Entry in Invoice Mode

At Purchase Entry screen in Accounting Invoice Mode (F-7B). At Header, select Sundry Creditor Ledger (in case of Credit Purchase) or Cash / Bank Account (in case of Cash Purchase).

At ledger Account areas, select other ledger accounts and the corresponding amount (amount deducted are entered in negative).

06 Sales Entry

When goods are sold by the vendor to the buyer, the vendor delivers the goods to the buyer. Sometimes, the vendor gets the payment from the buyer immediately (Called Cash Sales). Often, the vendor gets payment later on, in due course of time, as agreed (Called Credit Sales).

All Trade *Sales* (in Cash or Credit) should be entered through Sales voucher.

At GoT>Accounts Voucher entry screen, click *F8:Sales* button to get sales Voucher Entry screen,

- Click *V:As Voucher* button to get Sales Entry in *Voucher* Mode (F-7C)
- Click *V:As Invoice* button to get Sales Entry in *Invoice* Mode (F-7D)

Sale Voucher Accounting Entry

Credit Sales

	Particulars	Debit	Credit
Dr	Name of Buyer	(Amount)	
Cr	Sales Account		(Amount)

Cash Sales

	Particulars	Debit	Credit
Dr	Cash/ Bank/Bank OCC	(Amount)	
Cr	Sales Account		(Amount)

06.01 Sales Entry in Voucher Mode

At sales Entry screen in Voucher Mode (F-7C), first entry must be a Debit involving any Debtor (the Buyer, in case of Credit Sales), or a Cash, Bank or Bank OCC Account (in case of Cash Sales). Second entry should be Credit to a ledger placed under Sales Account group. Rest of the accounts may be any Revenue Account (except Purchase) or Accounts under the Group Current Liabilities (other than Sundry Creditors). Thus you can include Duties & Taxes or other billing terms from 3rd entry onwards.

Additional Charges like Freight / Handling / Insurance Charges may be entered as follows:

Particulars		Debit	Credit
Dr	Name of Buyer (or Cash / Bank / Bank OCC account)	(Net Bill Amount)	
Cr	Sales Account		(Sale Amount)
Cr	Expenses / Income Account (e.g realization of expenses like Delivery / Packing / Handling Charges etc, or some Income Account)	(Rebates etc deducted in the bill)	(Additional Charges added Amount)

Rules:

1. The 1st entry is Debit (Sundry Debtors/ Creditors, Cash/ Bank /Bank OCC, Branch & Divisions).
2. The 2nd entry is Credit (Sales)
3. The 3rd entry onward may be sales, any revenue account (except purchase), Credit (for addition in the bill), or Debit (for deduction in the bill)

> **Note:** *In* Voucher Mode, *second ledger entry must be a ledger under respective Sales / Purchase Group - In* Invoice mode, *you may enter any revenue account in place of sales / purchase account*

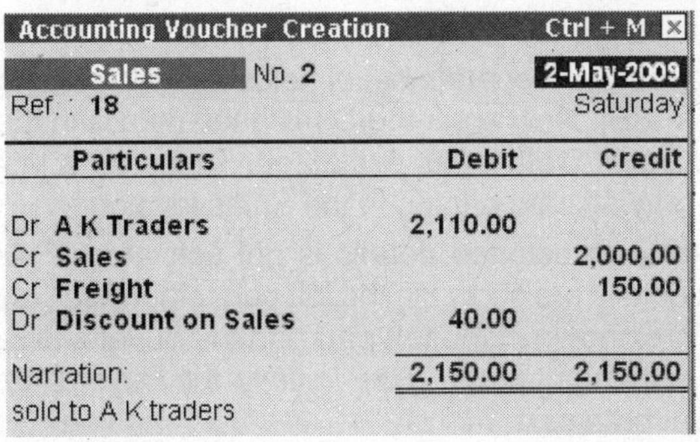

F-7C: Sales Entry in Voucher Mode

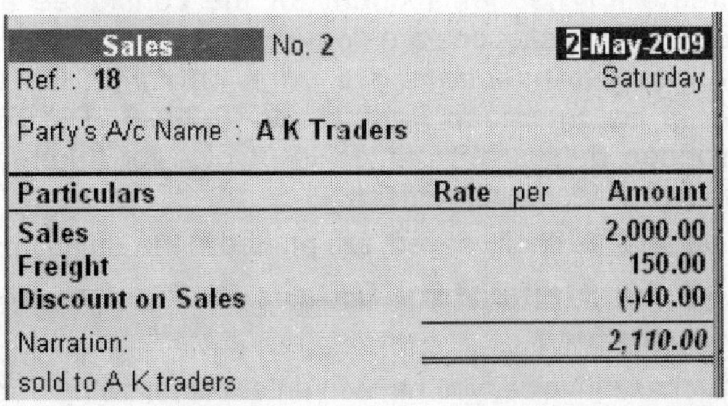

F-7D: Sales Entry in Accounting Invoice Mode

06.02 Sales Entry in Invoice Mode

At Sales Entry screen in Accounting Invoice Mode (F-7D). At Header, select Sundry Creditor Ledger (in case of Credit Purchase) or Cash / Bank Account (in case of Cash Purchase).

At ledger Account areas, select other ledger accounts and the corresponding amount (amount deducted are entered in negative).

06.03 Credit Limit Warning

If you have set Credit Limit (NOT Zero), at Party Ledger (F-8A), when you attempt to create a new *Sales* Voucher (not any other voucher type), if the current voucher causes to exceed the outstanding dues cross the specified credit limit, a warning message 'Eh? *Credit Limit of ....Exceeded (Current ...)'* showing the *allowable limit* and *current balance* will be prompted (F-8A) and you will not be allowed to enter the Voucher (in that case you have to exit from the voucher, reduce Credit Limit and again come back to voucher entry)This ensures that Credit Limit set by you for the Party can not be by-passed.

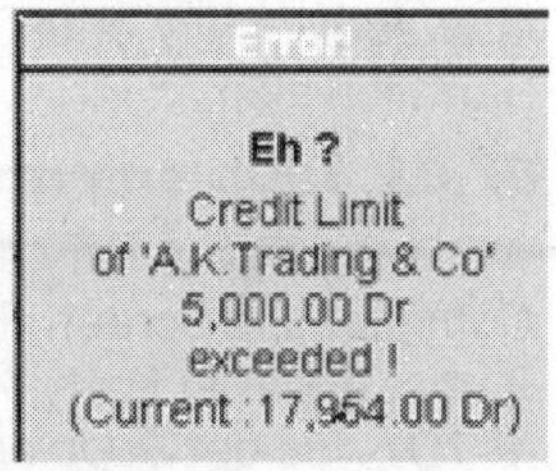

F-8A: Sales Voucher entry-Credit Limit Warning on exceeding limit

07 Supplementary Details Entry

Normally supplementary details contain the details of various documents related to the transaction. These details are entered in Invoice, where goods are despatched.

However, in Service Bills, often here are related documents like Work Orders and reference of other documents, that need to be included in the Accounting Invoice, for complete records and Party's Reference.

Even if you do not maintain Delivery Challans & Goods Receipt notes in Tally (but do it manually or some other external system), you may set the options to enter the references of these documents to be printed in the Invoice.

To record various other details like Despatch, Receipt, Order or other important related reference in Invoice entry. At *Invoice Configuration* screen (F-4A, F-5A, F-5B, F-6A, F-6B), set Yes at *Accept Supplementary Details.*

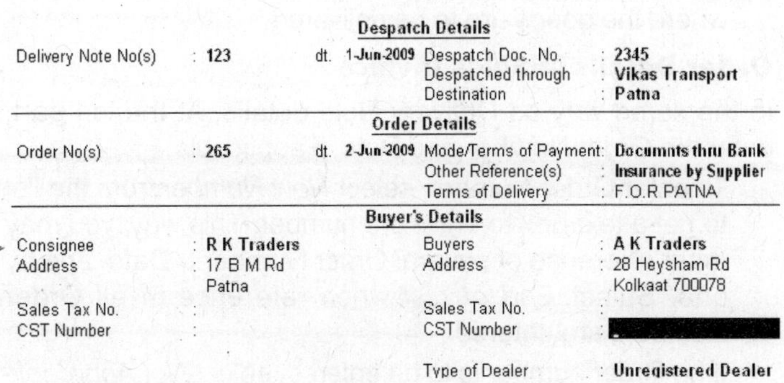

F-8B: Supplementary Details Entry in Sales Accounting Invoice

Receipt Details

Receipt Note No.(s) : 4567	dt. 31-May-2009			

Order Details

Order No(s)	: 114	dt. 1-Apr-2009		

Supplier's Details

Consignee	: **ABC Academy**	Supplier	: **B M Suppliers**
Address	: 18 Hesham Rd Kolkata 700 028	Address	: 23, Ring Rd Patna 800 011
Sales Tax No.	:	Sales Tax No.	:
CST Number	:	CST Number	:
		Type of Dealer	: **Unregistered Dealer**

F-8C: Supplementary Details in Purchase Accounting Invoice

Consequently, you will get Supplementary screen entry screen to enter the details of the Voucher (F-8B, F-8C). You may additionally enter the Voucher Particulars at Voucher Narration also.

07.01 Supplementary Details in Sales Invoice

When Supplementary details (§04.04) is activated at *Invoice Configuration* screen (F-4A, F-5A, F-5B), on selection of a Party Ledger at Party A/c Name field in Sales Invoice entry (F-7D), you get *Supplementary Details* sub screen (F-8B) to enter the following details in respective section

- Despatch Details
- Order Details
- Buyers Details

Despatch Document details in Sales Invoice

At the left part, enter the *Delivery Note Number* and *Date*, Enter reference of several Delivery Note Number & Date, one by one. Finally press <Enter>

Despatch Particulars in Sales Invoice

At the right part, enter the following details

- **Consignment Note Number**: At *Despatch Doc No*, you may enter Consignment Note Number like L/R, R/R (and may enter Date also).
- **Carrier**: At *Despatched thru*, enter Carrier like Transporter, Rail, Air, Courier etc.
- **Destination**: At *Destination* field, enter the name place where the goods are to be delivered.

Order Details in Sales Invoice

In the same way as Delivery Note details, At the left part, enter the Order Number and Date, if applicable

- To enter Order Number, select *New Number* from the list to get a text box to enter the number. This way, you may enter reference of several Order Number & Date, one by one. Select *End of List* when reference of all Order Numbers are entered.
- If no Order number is to be entered, select *Not Applicable* from the list

Order Particulars in Sales Invoice

At the right part, enter the following details

- **Payment terms**: At *Mode/Terms of Payment*, you may enter Terms of Payment (this is for information only, the Bill Due Date is not affected).
- **Other References**: At *Other Reference*, you may enter any other reference related to the order, for your reference.
- **Delivery Terms**: At *Terms of Delivery*, you may enter Terms of Delivery (this is for information only. the Delivery Due Date is not affected).

Buyer's Details in Sales Invoice

- **Buyer Name**: The Buyer's Name from the selected Party Ledger Account is shown, which you may change
- **Buyer Address**: The Address for the selected Party Ledger A/c is shown, which you may change. Buyer Sales Tax Number. The Sales Tax Number entered in the Party ledger, if any, is carried, which you may change.

Consignee Details in Sales Invoice

Sometimes, the Buyer may advice to send the gods to some other Party (called Consignee) on his behalf. In such case, it is necessary to record the consignee details in the document. To enter Consignee details also (when Consignee is different from Buyer), at Invoice Configuration set *Yes* (F-4A) at *Allow Separate Buyer & Consignee Name*.

Consequently, a separate set of fields appear for Consignee details (F-8B). Now enter the Consignee details in the same way as Buyer Details, as explained. These data, as finally saved, may also be printed in the Sales Invoice.

If Separate Consignee details is not activated (F-4A), the buyer's details are shown in the left part, otherwise consignee details are shown in the left part and the buyer's details are shown in the right part (F-8B). Initially, the Buyer Details are carried at both part.

Now, type the Consignee name and details. There is no need to create any ledger account for the consignee as no accounting transactions are dome with the Consignee. The accounting transactions are done only with Buyer or Supplier, as entered at Party Name (F-7B, F-7D). Buyer / Consignee details are printed in Invoice for Information, without any Accounting Effect.

These data, as finally saved, are printed in the Sales Invoice.

07.02 Supplementary Details in Purchase Invoice

In Purchase Invoice, you have to enter the following Supplier Details (F-8C).

- Receipt Details
- Order Details
- Supplier's Details

Receipt Details in Purchase Invoice

At the left part, at the Receipt Note Nos, you may enter the Receipt Note Number and Date, if applicable, Enter reference of several Receipt Note Number & Date, one by one. Finally press <enter>

Order Details Purchase Invoice

At Order Nos, you may enter the Order Number and Date, if applicable

- To enter Order Number, select *New Number* from the list to get a text box to enter the number. This way, you may enter reference of several Order Number & Date, one by one. Select *End of List* when reference of all Order Numbers are entered.
- If no Order Number is to be entered, select *Not Applicable* from the list.

Supplier's Details

Consignee Details in Purchase Invoice

At the *Left* part, you may enter Consignee details (when you have set *Yes* at *Allow Separate Buyer & Consignee Name* at *Invoice Configuration*: F-4A*)*, as follows:

- **Consignee Name**: At *Consignee* field, the Party Name is carried, field, which you may change where applicable
- **Consignee Address**: At *Address*, enter the address of the Consignee, as applicable.
- **Sales Tax Number**. At sales Tax Number, enter the Sales Tax Number of the Consignee, if any,
- **CST Number**. At *CST Number*, enter the CST Number of the Consignee, if any,

Supplier Details in Purchase Invoice

At the *Right* Part, at *Supplier* details, enter as follows:

- **Supplier Name**: At *Supplier*, the Party Name is carried, field, which you may change, where applicable
- **Supplier Address**: At *Address*, enter the address of the Supplier, as applicable.
- **Sales Tax Number**. At Sales Tax Number, enter the Sales Tax Number of the Supplier, if any,
- **CST Number**. At *CST Number*, enter the CST Number of the Supplier, if any,
- **Type of Dealer:** At *Type of Dealer*, select the Dealer Type from the list. In case of unregistered dealer, select *Not Applicable* from the list.

08 Debit & Credit Notes

Debit & Credit Notes are issued by Customer to Supplier, or by Supplier to Customers for Accounting Adjustments due to return of goods, Supplementary Charges / discount / rebates offered / rate difference or any another adjustments with customer / supplier. One party's Debit Note corresponds to the other Parety's Credit Note to bring the accounts of both parties in sync.

For Goods Retuned

Debit Note	Credit Note
The Party returning the goods (original Buyer), issues a Debit Note on the Party to whom the goods are returned	The Party receiving back the returned goods (original seller), issues a Credit Note on the Party who returned the goods.

For other Adjustments

Debit Note	Credit Note
The supplier issues to Buyer for supplementary (additional) charges (like additional rate difference, expenses incurred by supplier on behalf of Buyer)	The Buyer issues to Supplier for supplementary (additional) charges (like additional rate difference, expenses incurred by supplier on behalf of Buyer)
The Buyer issues to Supplier for Rebate allowed by Supplier on goods purchased from the supplier	The Supplier issues to Buyer for Rebate allowed by Supplier on goods purchased from the supplier

Debit & Credit Notes entry in the books of Customers / Suppliers

The buyer & seller makes the entry of Debit & Credit Note as reverse document.

The Debit Note Issued by Buyer on Seller corresponds to Credit Note issued i by Seller to Buyer. Similarly, the Credit Note Issued by Buyer to Seller corresponds to Debit Note is by Seller on Buyer.

Debit Note	Credit Note
The Debit Note Issued by Buyer on Seller corresponds to the Credit Note issued by Seller - The Buyer Debits the account of Supplier in his books of Accounts - The Supplier Credits the account of Buyer in his books of Accounts	The Credit Note Issued by Buyer on Seller corresponds to the Debit Note issued by Seller - The Buyer Credits the account of Supplier in his books of Accounts - The Supplier Debits the account of Buyer in his books of Accounts
The Debit Note Issued by Seller on Buyer corresponds to the Credit Note issued by Buyer - The Seller Debits the account of Buyer in his books of Accounts - The Buyer Credits the account of Supplier in his books of Accounts	The Credit Note Issued by Seller on Buyer corresponds to the Debit Note issued by Buyer - The Supplier Credits the account of Buyer in his books of Accounts - The Buyer Debits the account of Supplier in his books of Accounts

08.01 Debit / Credit Note Activation

At Gateway of Tally, Click *F11: Features*, select *Accounting Features* and set Yes at *Use Debit/Credit Notes.* to activate Debit & Credit Note for the Company

Consequently, during Voucher Entry, the buttons *F8: Credit Note & F9: Debit Note* would be available at the vertical button bar at the right.

Having set *Yes* at *Use Debit/Credit Notes* (F-1A)

- At the option *Use Invoice Mode for Credit Note*
  - o Set *No* to enter Credit Note in Accounting Voucher format (F-9B)
  - o Set *Yes* to enter Credit Note also in Accounting Invoice format (F-10B)
- At the option *Use Invoice Mode for Debit Note* (F-1A)
  - o Set *No* to enter Debit Note in Accounting Voucher format (F-9A)
  - o Set *Yes* to enter Debit Note also in Accounting Invoice format (F-9B)

At GoT>Accounting Vouchers screen:

- Click *F8:Credit Note* button to get Credit Note Voucher entry screen
- Click *F9:Debit Note* button to get Debit Note Voucher entry screen

At Debit / Credit Note Voucher entry screen:

- Click *V:As Voucher* button to get the Debit / Credit Note entry screen in *Voucher* Mode (F-9A & F-9B)
- Click *V:As Invoice* button to get the Debit / Credit Note entry screen in Accounting I*nvoice* Mode (F-10A & F-10B)

09 Debit / Credit Note Entry Accounting Rules

Debit Note: At Accounting Voucher Creation screen, Press Ctrl+F9 function key (or click *F9: Debit Note* button) to get *Debit Note* entry screen.

Rules:

Particulars	Dr	Cr
Dr Party Account (Supplier)	(Amount)	
Cr Purchase Returns (Purchase)		(Amount)

The following entry shows a typical Debit Note (in the books of customer) for goods returned by the customer to the supplier,:

Particulars	Dr	Cr
Dr Party Account (Supplier)	500.00	
Cr Purchase Returns (Purchase)		500.00

The following entry shows a typical Debit Note (in the books of buyer) in respect of Rebate received from the supplier.

Particulars	Dr	Cr
Dr Party Account (Supplier)	500.00	
Cr Rebate on Purchase		500.00

Credit Note: At Accounting Voucher Creation screen, Press Ctrl+F8 key (or click *F8: Credit Note* button) to get *Credit Note* entry screen. Normally Credit Note is issued when a Buyer returns some goods (Sales Returns) or when the supplier grants him credit due to rate difference or discount / rebate etc

Rules:

Particulars	Dr	Cr
Cr Party Account (Customer)	(Amount)	
Dr Sales Returns (Sales)		(Amount)

Credit Note Entry Accounting

The following entry shows a typical Credit Note (in the books of seller) in respect of goods returned by the customer to the seller,

Particulars	Dr	Cr
Dr Party Account (Customer)	500.00	
Dr Sales Returns (Sales)		500.00

The following entry shows a typical Credit Note (in the books of seller), in respect of Rebate allowed by the seller to the buyer,

Particulars	Dr	Cr
Cr Party Account	500.00	
Dr Rebate on Sales		500.00

10 Debit / Credit Note Entry in Voucher Mode

The data entered in Debit / Credit Note in voucher format (F-9A & F-9B) are listed below:

Header Part

- Voucher Date
- Voucher Number
- Reference

Ledgers Part

- Ledger Account at Particulars field
- Ledger Amount at Amount field in Debit / Credit column, as the case may be
  - o **Debit Note:**
    - The 1st entry must be Debit involving any Party (or Branch / Division, Cash or Bank Account)
    - The 2nd entry should be a credit to any Nominal ledger Account.
    - The 3rd entry onward, you can debit or Credit any Account.

- o **Credit Note**
  - The 1st entry must be Credit involving any Party (or Branch & Division, Cash or Bank Account)
  - The 2nd entry should be a Debit to any Nominal Ledger Account.
  - The 3rd entry onward, you can Debit or Credit any Account.

Voucher Narration

- Enter Voucher Narration at Narration field, where applicable

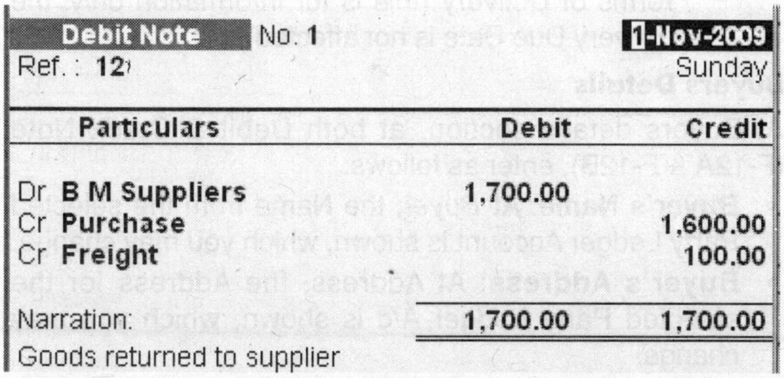

F-9A: Debit Note entry (Voucher Mode) for Return of Purchase Goods to Suppliers

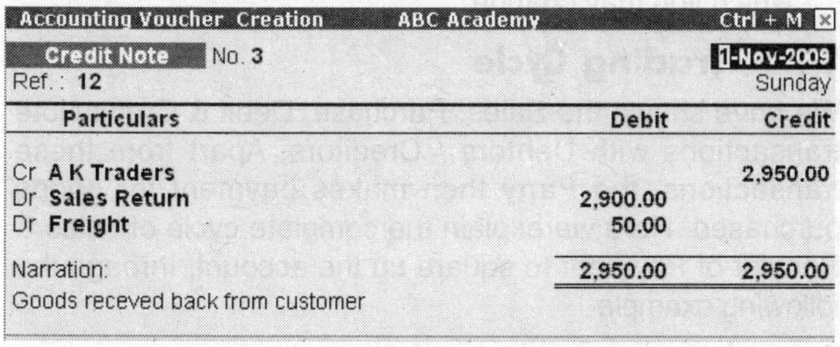

F-9B: Credit Note Entry in Voucher Mode for goods returned by Customers to Suppliers

11 Debit / Credit Note entry in Invoice Mode

The entry screen of Debit Note (F-10A) & Credit (F-10B) Notes in Invoice Mode are similar to Sales (§05.02) & Purchase (§06.02) Accounting Invoice entry.

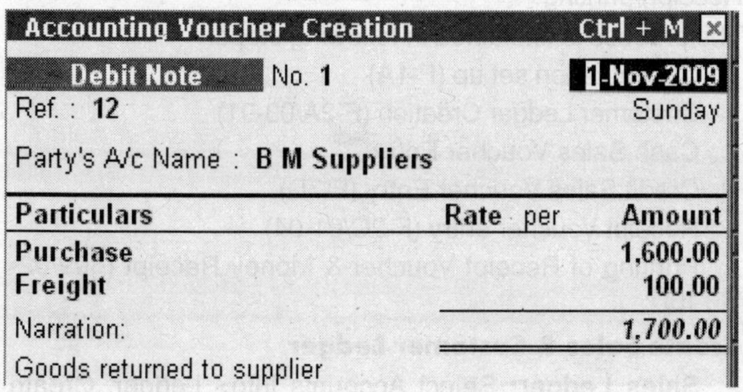

F-10A: Debit Note entry (Invoice Mode) for Return of Purchase Goods to supplier

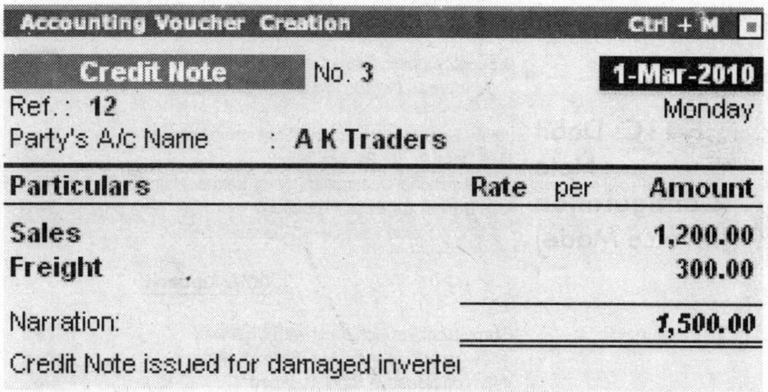

F-10B: Credit Note entry (Invoice Mode) for Return of sold Goods by customers

12 Debit / Credit Note Voucher Entry Configuration

In Voucher Mode (i.e when you select *V:As Voucher Button*), click *F12:Configure*:

- At Debit Note entry screen (F-9A), you get Debit Note Configuration screen (F-11A)
- At Credit Note entry screen (F-9B), you get Credit Note Configuration screen (F-11B)

> **Note:** *The voucher entry configuration options are similar for both Debit (F-11A) & Credit (F-11B) Notes.In Credit Note (F-11B), additional options for printing of Cheque in payment of Credit Notes are available*

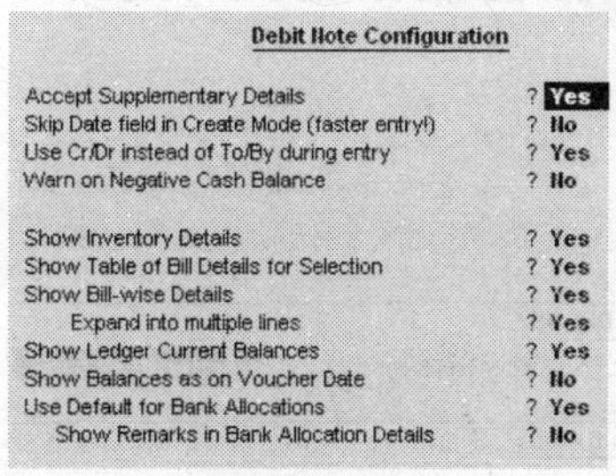

F-11A: Debit Note Configuration (Voucher Mode)

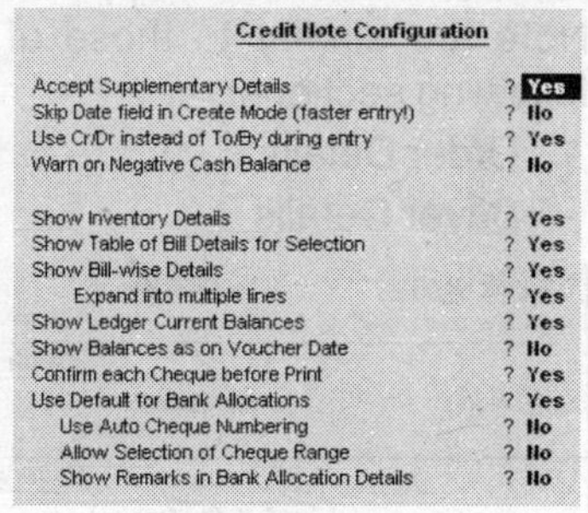

F-11B: Credit Note Configuration (Voucher Mode)

In Invoice Mode (i.e when you select *V:As Invoice Button*), click *F12:Configure*:

- At Debit Note entry screen (F-9A), you get Debit Note Configuration screen (F-11C)
- At Credit Note entry screen (F-9B), you get Credit Note Configuration screen (F-11D)

> **Note:** *The Supplementary details entry fields are similar for both Debit (F-12A) & Credit (F-12B) Notes.In Credit Note (F-12B), additional options for entry of Order Details are available*

Debit Note Configuration

Accept Supplementary Details *(Address Details, Despatch Details etc.)*	? Yes
Allow Separate Buyer and Consignee Names	? No
Use Defaults for Bill Allocations	? Yes
Use Additional Description(s) for Ledger Name	? No
Use Default for Bank Allocations	? Yes
Show Remarks in Bank Allocation Details	? No
Other Options	
Show turnover achieved with Customer	? Yes
Allow modification of ALL fields during entry	? Yes
Warn on Negative Stock Balance	? No

F-11C: Debit Note Configuration (Invoice Mode)

Credit Note Configuration

Accept Supplementary Details *(Address Details, Despatch Details etc.)*	? Yes
Allow Separate Buyer and Consignee Names	? No
Use Defaults for Bill Allocations	? Yes
Use Additional Description(s) for Ledger Name	? No
Confirm each Cheque before Print	? Yes
Use Default for Bank Allocations	? Yes
Use Auto Cheque Numbering	? No
Allow Selection of Cheque Range	? No
Show Remarks in Bank Allocation Details	? No
Other Options	
Show turnover achieved with Customer	? Yes
Allow modification of ALL fields during entry	? Yes
Warn on Negative Stock Balance	? No

F-11D: Credit Note Configuration (Invoice Mode)

13 Supplementary Details of Debit / Credit Note

Most of the fields in supplementary details of Debit / Credit Note are similar to those of Sales Purchase Invoice, in following sections:

- Order Details
- Buyer Details

Tracking No(s) : [Not Applicable dt.

Order Details

Order No(s) : [Not Applicable   Other Reference(s) : Letter dt 19.5.06

Buyer's Details

Consignee : A K Traders
Address : 35 Heysham Rd
Kolkata
700 004
Sales Tax No. :
CST Number :

Type of Dealer : [Not Applicable

F-12A: Supplementary Details in Debit Note

Receipt Details

Tracking No(s) : 8 dt. 31-May-2009

Order Details

Order No(s) : 6 dt. 1-May-2009 Mode/Terms of Payment :
Other Reference(s) :
Terms of Delivery :

Buyer's Details

Consignee : A K Traders
Address : 12 Heysham Rd
Kolkata 700078

Sales Tax No. :
CST Number :

F-12B: Supplementary Details in Credit Note

Order Details

- At Debit Note (F-12A), enter Order Number
- At Credit Note (F-12B), enter the following details (F-12B).
  - **Payment terms**: At *Terms of Payment*, you may enter Terms of Payment (this is for information only, the Bill Due Date is not affected).
  - **Order References**: At *Other Reference*, you may enter any other reference related to the order, for your reference.
  - **Delivery Terms**: At *Terms of Delivery*, you may enter Terms of Delivery (this is for information only. the Delivery Due Date is not affected).

Buyers Details

At Buyers details section, at both Debit & Credit Note (F-12A & F-12B), enter as follows:

- **Buyer's Name**: At *Buyer*, the Name from the selected Party Ledger Account is shown, which you may change.
- **Buyer's Address**: At Address, the Address for the selected Party Ledger A/c is shown, which you may change.
- **Buyer's Sales Tax Number**: At Sales Tax No., the Sales Tax Number entered in the Party ledger, if any, is carried, which you may change.

14 Trading Cycle

We have shown the Sales, Purchase, Debit & Credit Note transactions with Debtors / Creditors. Apart from these transactions, the Party then makes payment for goods purchased. Here we explain the complete cycle of sales & Receipt of Payment to square up the account, through the following example

Example

A K Textiles sells in Cash as well as Credit. For some customers, who pay cash, cheque or draft, no customer ledger account is created, cheque details are entered. Those who do not pay immediately, or make part payment, a customer ledger account is maintained (with Party Name & address) and sales bill prepared in the customer name. Also explain Receipt Voucher & Money Receipt (Formal Receipt) printing

The process is explained in following steps:

- Configuration set up (F-1A)
- Customer Ledger Creation (F-2A/03-01)
- Cash Sales Voucher Entry
- Credit Sales Voucher Entry (F-7D)
- Receipt Voucher entry (F-2C/01-04)
- Printing of Receipt Voucher & Money Receipt (§09/02-16)

Create Sales & Customer Ledger

- **Sales Ledger:** Select Accounts Info> Ledger. Create Sales Ledger (under *Sales* Group). Set *No* at *Inventory*

Values are affected (because we are not maintaining Inventory System in this case)

- **Customer Ledger:** Select Accounts Info> Ledger. Click *F12: Configure* and set *Yes* at *Addresses for Ledger Accounts,* to get the fields to enter Party Address.

Set Voucher & Money Receipt Printing options:

To print Voucher, select *Accounts Info> Voucher Type> Alter.* Now select the respective Voucher Type (Sales, Receipt) to get the Voucher Alteration screen of the respective voucher type:

- Set *Yes* at *Print after saving voucher* to enable voucher printing option for the respective voucher type
- To print Money Receipt (formal Receipt) also for Receipt Voucher, set Yes at *Print Formal Receipt after saving* at Receipt Voucher Type

At gateway, Select *Accounting Voucher.* Click *F8:Sales.* Click *V:As Invoice* and *I:Acct Invoice* buttons.

Create Sales Voucher receiving Cash (in Accounting Invoice mode)

At Party Account Name, select Cash. At Ledger Account, select Sales and enter the Amount n credit column.

Create Sales Voucher receiving Cheque (in Voucher mode)

Select *Accounting Vouchers.* Click *F8:Sales.* Click *V:As Voucher.* Click *F12: Configure* and set *No* at *Use Defaults for Bank Allocations* to get Cheque Details screen after entry of Bank Ledger Accounts.

At first ledger, select Bank. Ledger Account and the amount in Debit Column. The Bank Details (Bank Allocation) screen appears. Now enter the cheque details as follows:

- **Payer Name:** Enter the Name of the Party (i.e Customer) from whom the cheque was received
- **Transaction Type:** Select Cheque / DD from the list at *Transaction Type* field
- **Cheque Amount:** The Bank Ledger amount is carried at *Amount* field
- **Cheque Number:** Enter the Cheque Number at *Instrument* field
- **Cheque Date:** Enter the Cheque Date at *Instrument Date* field
- **Drawee Bank Name:** Enter the Bank Name on which the cheque is drawn at *Bank Name* field
- **Drawee Bank Branch Name:** Enter the Branch Name of the Bank on which the cheque is drawn at *Branch Name* field

At *Narration* field, enter the complete Name and Address of the Party so that you can contact him later on

Create Credit Sales Voucher (in Accounting Invoice mode)

Select Accounting Voucher. Click F8:Sales. Click V:As Invoice and I:Acct Invoice buttons.

At Party Account Name, select the Customer Ledger. At Ledger Account, select Sales and enter the Amount in credit column.

Payment Received from Customer by Cheque:

Select *Accounting Vouchers.* Click *F6:Receipt.* Click F12: Configure and set *Yes* at *Use Defaults for Bank Allocations* to get Cheque Details screen after entry of Bank Ledger Accounts.

At first ledger, select Customer Ledger Account and the amount in Credit Column. Enter the amount of cheque received

At second ledger, select Bank Ledger Account and enter the amount in Debit Column. The Bank Details (Bank Allocation) screen appears. Now enter the cheque details as explained above.

Payment Received from Customer by Cash

Select *Accounting Vouchers.* At first ledger, select Customer Ledger Account and the amount in Credit Column. Enter the amount of Cash received

At second ledger, select Cash Ledger Account and enter the amount in Debit Column.

Print Receipt Voucher & Money Receipt for money Received from Customer

During entry of Receipt Voucher, after entry of all Receipt Voucher data, press Alt+P

- **Receipt Voucher Printing**: First you get Receipt Voucher printing screen (at Report Title, *Receipt Voucher* appears). Type Y to point the Receipt Voucher, The Receipt Voucher would be printed. Else, type N to skip the Receipt Voucher printing.
- **Money Receipt (Formal Receipt) Printing**: Next you get Receipt Voucher printing screen (at Report Title, *Receipt* appears). Type Y to point Money Receipt, The Money Receipt would be printed. Else, type N to skip the Money Receipt printing

FAQ: Frequently Asked Questions

FAQ-1: I like to enter Sales / Purchase Voucher in Voucher mode, with ledger accounts and amount in Debit / Credit Columns like a Journal Voucher. How I should enter

Ans: At Gateway, select Accounts Vouchers, Click *F7:Sales* and click *V:As Voucher* toggle button. In such situation, the toggle button *I:Accounting Invoice / Item Invoice* toggle button has no effect

FAQ-2: I like to enter Sales / Purchase Voucher in Invoice mode, with Party / Cash /Bank accounts at header and other ledger accounts in the line area. No Debit & Credits are specified. Deduction are entered in negative figure like Single Mode entry Voucher. How I should enter

Ans: At Gateway, select Accounts Vouchers, Click *F7:Sales*

and click V:As Invoice & I:Accounting Invoice toggle button.

FAQ-3: How I can enter Cash Sales to maintain Sales Register?

Ans: Enter the Cash Sales memos through Sales Voucher (enter Cash Account at Party Ledger). Now the Sales Register will include the Cash Sales Bills also. If you enter Cash Sales in Receipt Voucher, the Cash Sales transactions entered through Receipt Voucher will not be shown in Sales Register. However, the final accounting effect remains same, whether you enter Cash Sales trough Sales Voucher or through Receipt Voucher.

FAQ-4: How I can maintain separate Cash Sales Registers for each Cash Counter?

Ans: Method 1

Create a separate Voucher Type for each Cash Sales Counter (Select Accounts Info>Voucher Type. Create the two new Voucher Types: Cash Sale Counter 1 & Cash Sale Counter 2) under Sales Voucher Type. Now the respective Sales Vouchers at the counters should enter using and enter Sales Voucher for Cash Sales, using these two separate voucher type.

While printing Sales Register / Multi column Sales Register (at Gateway > Display or Multi Account printing > Account Books > Sales Register) select the voucher type for each Cash Sales Counter (for Cash A/c - Cash Sale counter 1 & Cash Sale counter 2 separately)

Method 2

Create 2 additional cash ledger accounts (Cash Sale counter 1 & Cash Sale counter 2)

Enter the cash sales memos through Sales Voucher. At the day end, create a contra voucher to transfer the Cash for each Cash Counter cash account to main cash account. Print Ledger selecting appropriate Cash Account (e.g Cash Sale counter 1), or Cash Book for each cash ledger account, to get the list of all vouchers for the specific cash ledger (Sales Counter). The cash transferred from cash Counter accounts to main Cash is also shown in the ledger.

Method 1 is preferred.

FAQ-5: I have a retail shop with very small place. There are numerous customers in the day. It is not possible to issue Cash Memos to every buyer. The sales value is written in a note book. I want to keep sales voucherwise entry. In what form I should enter the sales Voucher. Sometimes, there are credit sales, for which a Sales Invoice is prepared manually and delivered to Customer.

Ans: As no inventory details are maintained, you should enter the voucher in Accounts Voucher Mode

At Gateway, select Accounts Voucher and click *F8:Sales* button to get the Sales Voucher entry screen. Click V: *As Voucher* button to enter the ledger accounts and the amount in Voucher format to quickly enter the Sales Voucher.

- In case of Credit Sales, enter the Customer's ledger Account at the first entry.
- In case of Cash Sales, enter the Cash Account at the first entry.

FAQ-6: The customer returned some goods. How I should enter the voucher for retuned goods

Ans: On receiving back the goods returned by customer, a credit note should be issued in favour of the Party returning the goods, for the value of goods returned

At gateway, select Accounting Voucher. Click *F8: Credit Note*. Click *V:As Voucher* button and enter the Credit Note Voucher as follows:

- Select Party Account at Particulars columns and enter the value of goods returned at Credit Column
- Select Sales Returns Account at Particulars columns and enter the value of goods returned at Debit Column

FAQ-7: Some of the goods purchased were returned to supplier. How I should the voucher for retuned goods

Ans: On returning the goods to Supplier, a Debit Note (for the value of goods returned) should be issued on the Party to whom the goods were returned.

At gateway, select Accounting Voucher. Click *F9: Debit Note*. Click *V:As Voucher* button and enter the Debit Note Voucher as follows:

- Select Party Account at Particulars columns and enter the value of goods returned at Debit Column
- Select Purchase Returns Account at Particulars columns and enter the value of goods returned at Credit Column

FAQ-8: Y, after receiving the goods bought from X, found some goods defective. Y complained to X. X then allowed Rebate of Rs 2000 to Y for the goods.

Ans: How both the parties X & Y should make the entries in their respective Accounts.

Y should issue a Debit Note of Rs 2000 on X, as follows:

At gateway, select Accounting Voucher. Click *F9: Debit Note*. Click *V:As Voucher* button and enter the Debit Note Voucher as follows:

- Select X Account at Particulars columns and enter Rs 2000 at Debit Column
- Select Purchase Account at Particulars columns and enter Rs 2000 Credit Column

X should issue a Credit Note of Rs 2000 in favour of Y, as follows:

At gateway, select Accounting Voucher. Click *F8: Credit Note*. Click *V:As Voucher* button and enter the Credit Note Voucher.as follows:

- Select Y Account at Particulars columns and enter Rs 2000 at Credit Column
- Select Sales Account at Particulars columns and enter Rs 2000 Debit Column

FAQ-9: X sold some goods to Y and issued a Sales Invoice for Rs 4000. Y, on receiving the Invoice, found that the Sales Invoice was overcharged by Rs 1000 by mistake. Y informed to X about the mistake. How X would adjust in his books of accounts.

Ans: X has already created a Sales Invoice of Rs 4000, for actual Sales of Rs 3000 (Invoice overcharged by Rs 1000). So, X should issue a Credit Note in favour of Y, as follows:

At gateway, select Accounting Voucher. Click *F8: Credit Note*. Click *V:As Voucher* button and enter the Credit Note as follows:

- Select Y Account at Particulars columns and enter Rs 1000 at Credit Column
- Select Sales Account at Particulars columns and enter Rs 1000 Debit Column

Invoice Printing 03-03

01 Invoice Printing

In previous chapter we have discussed about Sale/ Purchase & Debit / Credit Note entry (§02/03-02). After voucher entry, the Voucher / Invoice is to be printed, showing the relevant details of the transaction. Sales Invoice, Debit Note & Credit Note are normally printed to hand over a copy to the Party (and a copy is kept for internal record), while Purchase Invoice are received from suppliers and may not be printed.

In this chapter, we discus about printing of Sale / Purchase & Debit / Credit Note in Voucher & Invoice format. Normally, these documents are printed in Invoice Format to be handed over to the Party. But sometimes, they may be printed in Voucher Format (like Purchase Voucher for keeping internal record)

02 Invoice Printing Configuration

The format & contents of Sales / Purchase Invoice may be set through Sales / Purchase printing Configuration options (F-1A, F-1B)

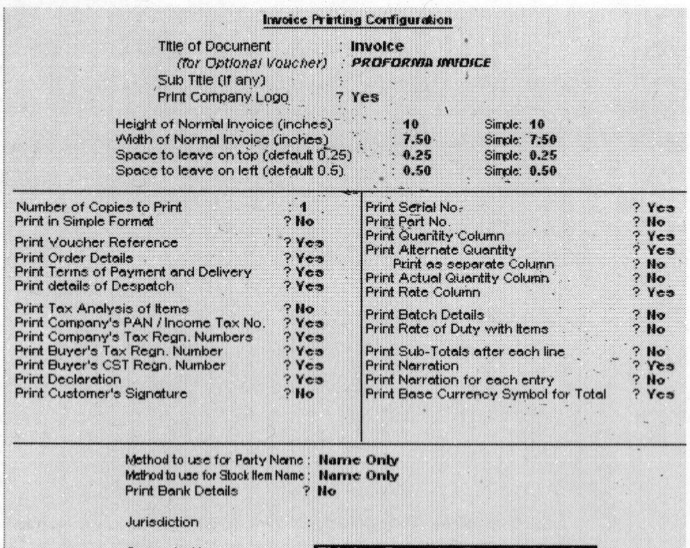

Invoice Printing Configuration

Title of Document : Invoice
(for Optional Voucher) : PROFORMA INVOICE
Sub Title (if any) :
Print Company Logo ? Yes

Height of Normal Invoice (inches) : 10 Simple: 10
Width of Normal Invoice (inches) : 7.50 Simple: 7.50
Space to leave on top (default 0.25) : 0.25 Simple: 0.25
Space to leave on left (default 0.5) : 0.50 Simple: 0.50

Number of Copies to Print	: 1	Print Serial No.	? Yes
Print in Simple Format	? No	Print Part No.	? No
Print Voucher Reference	? Yes	Print Quantity Column	? Yes
Print Order Details	? Yes	Print Alternate Quantity	? Yes
Print Terms of Payment and Delivery	? Yes	Print as separate Column	? No
Print details of Despatch	? Yes	Print Actual Quantity Column	? No
Print Tax Analysis of Items	? No	Print Rate Column	? Yes
Print Company's PAN / Income Tax No.	? Yes	Print Batch Details	? No
Print Company's Tax Regn. Numbers	? Yes	Print Rate of Duty with Items	? No
Print Buyer's Tax Regn. Number	? Yes	Print Sub-Totals after each line	? No
Print Buyer's CST Regn. Number	? Yes	Print Narration	? Yes
Print Declaration	? Yes	Print Narration for each entry	? No
Print Customer's Signature	? No	Print Base Currency Symbol for Total	? Yes

Method to use for Party Name : Name Only
Method to use for Stock Item Name : Name Only
Print Bank Details ? No

Jurisdiction :

Generated by : This is a Computer Generated Invoice

F-1A: Sales Invoice Configuration screen

At Gateway, click *F12: Configure* to get Configuration menu (F-1/02-01). Select *Printing* to get Printing Configuration Menu (F-1/02-15)

At Printing Configuration Menu (F-1/02-15), select:

- **Sales Invoice**: *Sales Transactions> Sales Invoice* to get the Sales Invoice Printing Configuration screen (F-1A)
- **Purchase Voucher / Invoice:** *Purchase Transactions> Purchase Invoice / Voucher* to get the Purchase Voucher / Invoice Printing Configuration screen (F-1B).

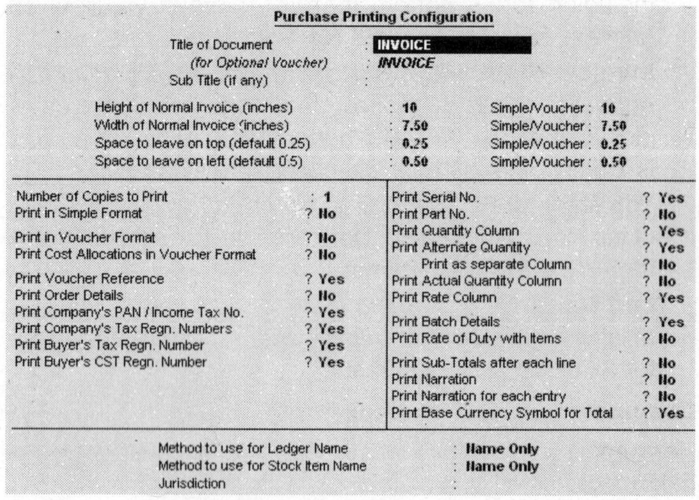

Purchase Printing Configuration

Title of Document : INVOICE
(for Optional Voucher) : INVOICE
Sub Title (if any) :

Height of Normal Invoice (inches) : 10 Simple/Voucher : 10
Width of Normal Invoice (inches) : 7.50 Simple/Voucher : 7.50
Space to leave on top (default 0.25) : 0.25 Simple/Voucher : 0.25
Space to leave on left (default 0.5) : 0.50 Simple/Voucher : 0.50

Number of Copies to Print	: 1	Print Serial No.	? Yes
Print in Simple Format	? No	Print Part No.	? No
Print in Voucher Format	? No	Print Quantity Column	? Yes
Print Cost Allocations in Voucher Format	? No	Print Alternate Quantity	? Yes
Print Voucher Reference	? Yes	Print as separate Column	? No
Print Order Details	? No	Print Actual Quantity Column	? No
Print Company's PAN / Income Tax No.	? Yes	Print Rate Column	? Yes
Print Company's Tax Regn. Numbers	? Yes	Print Batch Details	? Yes
Print Buyer's Tax Regn. Number	? Yes	Print Rate of Duty with Items	? No
Print Buyer's CST Regn. Number	? Yes	Print Sub-Totals after each line	? No
		Print Narration	? No
		Print Narration for each entry	? No
		Print Base Currency Symbol for Total	? Yes

Method to use for Ledger Name : Name Only
Method to use for Stock Item Name : Name Only
Jurisdiction :

F-1B: Purchase Invoice / Voucher Configuration screen

The options for Configuration are almost similar for both Sales & Purchase Invoice / Voucher printing, as explained below:

02.01 Components of Invoice Configuration

At Invoice Configuration (F-1A, F-1B), set the following major components

Invoice Titles

Specify the default Invoice Title & Sub Titles as follows:

- **Document Title:** At *Title of Document*, enter the default Title of Document (default – INVOICE), e.g Tax Invoice
- **Optional Voucher Title**: At *For Optional Voucher*, enter the default Title of optional Voucher
  - o For Sales Invoice, enter the Title for Optional Invoice at *For Optional Voucher* field (the default is shown as – PROFORMA INVOICE), like Quotation, Proforma Invoice etc. Normally Proforma Invoice / Quotation are entered as optional voucher as they do not affect Accounts /Inventory
  - o For Purchase Invoice, enter the Title for Optional Invoice at *For Optional Voucher* field (the default is shown as INVOICE), like Enquiry, Proforma Invoice etc. Normally Proforma Invoice / Enquiry etc are

entered as optional voucher as they do not affect Accounts /Inventory

- **Sub Title (if any)**:. Enter the document sub title to be printed just below the document title, if any. This is printed only in first page of document

Invoice Dimensions

Enter the following default values to specify Dimension & Margins (in inches) of the printed Voucher (including margins). Specify two sets of values. First for Neat Invoice and the second for Simple Invoice (if invoice is also printed in simple format)

- **Invoice Height:** At *Height of Normal Invoice (Inches),* enter the height of the voucher (print area in inches including top & bottom margin). Default value is 10 (inches), both for Simple & Normal format
- **Invoice Width:** At *Width of Normal Invoice (Inches),* enter the width of the voucher (print area in inches including left & right top & bottom margin). Default value is 7.5 (inches), both for Simple & Normal format
- **Top Margin:** At *Space to leave on top*, enter the value of top margin (in inches). Default value is.25 (inches) both for Simple & Normal format.
- **Left Margin:** At *Space to leave on left*, enter the value of left margin (in inches). Default value is.75 (inches) both for Simple & Normal format.

Document contents print options

Here specify the following components of Invoice (F-1A, F-1B):

- Invoice Header
- Item details (for Invoice with Inventory Details)
- Ledger Account details
- Invoice Footer

a. **Invoice Header Particulars:** Set ***Yes / No to print /*** suppress the specific contents in the **voucher**
   - **Number of Copies:** At *Number of Copies to Print*, enter the Number of copies to be printed for each document (default value is 1). So, to print 4 copies of each Invoice, enter 4 here.
   - **Voucher Reference:** At *Print Voucher Reference*:
     - o Set *Yes* (default value) to print the Sales Voucher reference number.
     - o Set *No*, Voucher Reference is not printed
   - **Order Details:** At *Print Order Details:*
     - o Set *Yes* (default value) to print Order details (if available in the voucher)
     - o Set *No* to omit Orders details.
   - **Format:** At *Print in Simple Format:*
     - o Set *Yes* to print in *Simple* Format (the individual cells for each particulars of supplementary details are not printed). It takes lesser space leaving more space for header, leaving more space for Item details (useful for invoices with too many Items / Item details).
     - o Set *No* (default) to print in *Normal* Format (more space taken for Invoice header for supplementary details)

b. Ledger Account Details

Here set the options (Yes / No) for printing ledger account details entered in the Invoice

- **Ledger Narration:** At *Print Narration for each entry*, set:
  - o *Yes* (default value) to print separate Ledger Narration for each ledger account transacted.
  - o *No* to omit separate ledger Narration (it may sometimes be useful when Common Narration is printed).
- **Subtotals:** At *Print Subtotals after each line,* set:
  - o *Yes* (default value) to print Sub Total after each ledger amount,
  - o *No*, the intermediate Sub Totals are not printed (only Net Invoice amount is printed)

d. **Voucher Footer details**

Set the options for the particulars for the whole voucher, printed at footer after the Item details

- **Company Tax Regn:** At *Print Company's Tax Registration Number*, set:
  - o *Yes* (default value) to print Company's Local Sales Tax Number if entered at *F11: Features > Statutory & Taxation*
  - o *No* to omit these details from Invoice printing.
- **Buyer Tax Regn:** At *Print Buyer's Tax Registration Number,* set
  - o *Yes* (default value) to print Customer's TIN/Sales Tax Number if entered at the Customer's Ledger Account
  - o *No* to omit these details from Invoice printing.
- **Buyer's CST Regn:** At *Print Buyer's CST Registration Number*, set
  - o *Yes* (default value) to print Customer's TIN/Sales Tax Number if entered at the Customer's Ledger Account
  - o *No* to omit these details from Invoice printing.
- **Voucher Narration:** At *Print Narration,* set:
  - o *Yes* (default value) to print Voucher common Narration
  - o *No* to omit Voucher Common narration (it may sometimes be useful when separate ledger narration is printed).
- **Currency Symbol:** At *Print Base Currency Symbol for Total,* set
  - o *Yes* (default value) to print Base Currency Symbol before the Total Amount

  o *No* to print only amount figure without any currency symbol
- **Jurisdiction:** At *Jurisdiction*, enter Jurisdiction Name to print Jurisdiction at the bottom of the Invoice. The text *Subject to < Jurisdiction Name >* is printed (like *Subject to Kolkata Jurisdiction*) in Invoice. Leave blank to omit Jurisdiction

Additional Options for Sales Voucher / Invoice printing configuration

Apart from the general options explained above, you may set the following options at *Sales* Invoice Printing Configuration (F-1A):

- **Logo:** At *Company Logo* (F-10C/ 02-14, F-6B/02-16)
  o Set Yes at *Print Company Logo* at the header (useful to print in plain paper stationery). The Logo is set at the option *Enable Company Logo* at *F11:Features>Accounting Features*
  o Set *No*, no logo would be printed.
- **Payment / Delivery:** At *Print Terms of Payment & Delivery details* (F-1A, F-1B):
  o Set *Yes* to print Terms of Payment & Delivery details as entered under supplementary details section in Invoice entry.
  o Set *No* (default value) to omit these details from Invoice printing. Normally these are applicable in case of Sale of Materials only
- **Despatch:** At *Print details of Despatch*, set
  o *Yes* to print details as entered under supplementary details section in Invoice entry
  o *No* (default value) to omit these details from Invoice printing. Normally these are applicable in case of Sale of Materials only.
- **Declaration:** At *Print Declaration*, set
  o *Yes* (default value) to print declaration as specified in Sales Voucher Type
  o *No* to omit the declaration
- **Message:** At *Generated By*, enter the text (default *This is a Computer Generated Invoice)* to be printed at the last line (otherwise leave blank)

Additional Options for Purchase Voucher / Invoice printing configuration

Apart from the general options explained above, you may set the following options at Purchase Invoice Printing Configuration (F-1B)

- **Format:** At *Print in Voucher Format* set
  o *Yes* to print the Purchase Transaction in Voucher Format
  o *No* to print in Invoice Format
- **Cost Allocation:** At *Print Cost Allocation in Voucher Format,* set:
  - *Yes* to print the Cost Allocation of Items when printed in Voucher Format
  - *No.* The Cost allocation will not be printed in Voucher Format

02.02 Printing of Invoice

As described for Voucher Printing earlier (P-01/ 02-16), at Voucher entry screen click *P:Print* button to get Invoice Printing screen (F-2A).

At Invoice Printing configuration screen (F-2A):

- **Print as per default configuration**: Type Y to print the Invoice as per default configuration set

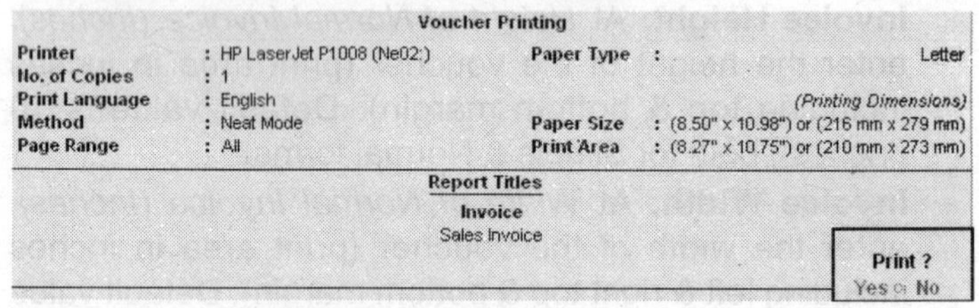

F-2A: Invoice Printing screen

- **Change Options**: Click *F12:Configure* (F-2B) to get the respective Printing Configuration screen (F-1A / F-1B). Change the Configuration options as described. You may also click respective buttons (F-2B) and set the printing options as explained.

  Type Y to print the Invoice as per changed Configuration

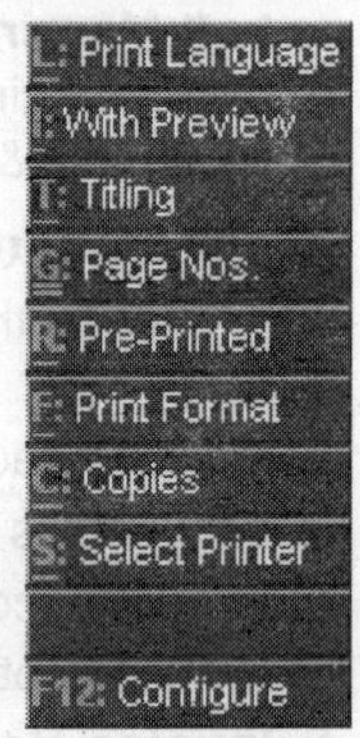

F-2B: Buttons

03 Sales Invoice Printing

The Sales Invoice may be printed in following Formats. At *Sales Invoice Printing Configuration* (F-1A), at *Print in Simple Format,*

- **Normal Format**: Set No to print in Normal Invoice Format (F-3A)
- **Simple Format**: Set Yes at to print in Simple Invoice Format (F-3B)

04 Purchase Voucher / Invoice Printing

The Purchase Voucher / Invoice may be printed in following Formats. At *Purchase Invoice Printing Configuration* (F-1B): At *Print in Simple Format*:

- **Normal Format**: Set No to print in *Normal* Invoice Format (F-4A)
- **Simple Format**: Set Yes at to print in *Simple* Invoice Format (F-4B)

Voucher Format: at *Print in Voucher Format*, set Yes to print in *Voucher* Format (F-4C)

INVOICE

ABC Academy 99, Airpot Rd Kolkata 700 098 Contact :651234,9876523409 E-Mail :abc@tmail.com	Invoice No. 3	Dated 1-Jul-2009
	Delivery Note 12	Mode/Terms of Payment Through Bank
	Supplier's Ref.	Other Reference(s) Letter Dt 12.5.09
Consignee A K Traders 18 , Hysham Rd KOlkata 700 08	Buyer's Order No. 75	Dated 1-Jul-2009
	Despatch Document No. 234	Dated
	Despatched through B N Couriers	Destination Patna
Buyer (if other than consignee) A K Traders	Terms of Delivery Th Courier	

Particulars	Amount
Sales	2,000.00
Freight	200.00
Less : Discount on Sales	(-)50.00
Total	₹ 2,150.00

Amount Chargeable (in words) *E. & O.E*
Indian Rupees Two Thousand One Hundred Fifty Only

Inter State Sales Tax No. : CST 23456

for ABC Academy

Authorised Signatory

SUBJECT TO KOLKATA JURISDICTION

This is a Computer Generated Invoice

F-3A: Sales Invoice in Normal Format

SUBJECT TO KOLKATA JURISDICTION

Invoice No. 3 Dated 1-Jul-2009
Ref. No. :

ABC Academy
99, Airpot Rd
Kolkata 700 098
Contact :651234,9876523409
E-Mail :abc@tmail.com

INVOICE

Party : A K Traders

Order No.	Payment Terms	Despatch Document	Delivery Note
75 1-Jul-2009	Through Bank	234 dt. Through : B N Couriers	12 To Patna

Particulars	Amount
Sales	2,000.00
Freight	200.00
Less : Discount on Sales	(-)50.00
Total	₹ 2,150.00

Amount Chargeable (in words) *E. & O.E*
Indian Rupees Two Thousand One Hundred Fifty Only

Inter State Sales Tax No. CST 23456

for ABC Academy

Authorised Signatory

This is a Computer Generated Invoice

F-3B: Sales Invoice in Simple Format

05 Debit / Credit Note Printing

The Debit / Credit Note may be printed in following Formats. At Debit / Credit Note Voucher Entry screen, click P:Print button to get *Debit / Credit Note printing screen* (like F-2A)

F-6A shows Debit Note in Voucher Format & F-5B shows Debit Note (in Voucher Format) without Ledger details (when you set *No* at the configuration option *Print with Full Ledger Details)*

INVOICE

B M Suppliers	Invoice No. 1	Dated 1-Jun-2009
	Supplier's Ref. 12	Other Reference(s)
	Buyer's Order No.	Dated
Consignee ABC Academy 99, Airpot Rd Kolkata 700 098 Contact :651234,9876523409 E-Mail :abc@tmail.com		

Particulars	Amount
Purchase	2,100.00
Freight	300.00
Less : Discount on Purchase	(-)200.00
Total	₹ 2,200.00

Amount Chargeable (in words) *E. & O.E*
Indian Rupees Two Thousand Two Hundred Only

Remarks:
Purchases from B M Suppkier a sper their Bill # 12 Dt 31.5.09

Company's Sales Tax No. :
Buyer's Sales Tax No. :
Company's CST No. :
Buyer's Inter State Sales Tax No. : CST 23456

for B M Suppliers

Authorised Signatory

SUBJECT TO KOLKATA JURISDICTION

F-4A: Purchase Invoice in Normal Format

SUBJECT TO DURGAPUR JURISDICTION

Invoice No. 1 Dated 1-Jun-2009
Ref. No. : 12

M P Traders
12 Heysham Rd
Asansol 712121
Contact Person : A Barua
Contact : 0345-67123 , 9990990000
Fax : 9990101010
E-Mail : inf0@mptrd.com

INVOICE
Purchase Invoice

Party : ABC Academy
99, Airpot Rd
Kolkata 700 098
Contact :651234,9876523409
E-Mail :abc@tmail.com

Sl No.	Description of Goods	Amount
	Purchase	2,100.00
	Freight	300.00
	Less : *Discount on Purchase*	(-)200.00
	Total	₹ 2,200.00

Amount Chargeable (in words) *E. & O.E*
Indian Rupees Two Thousand Two Hundred Only

Company's Sales Tax No. : DURG1234 dt 12.5.81
Buyer's Sales Tax No. :
Company's CST No. : DURG(C)872 dt 18.5.81
Buyer's Inter State Sales Tax No. : CST 23456

for M P Traders

Authorised Signatory

F-4B: Purchase Invoice in Normal Format

ABC Academy
99, Airpot Rd
Kolkata 700 098
E-Mail :abc@tmail.com

Purchase Voucher

No. : **1** Dated : **1-Jun-2009**
Ref. : **12**

Party's Name : **M P Traders**

Particulars		Amount
Purchase	*2,100.00*	**₹ 2,200.00**
Freight	*300.00*	
Discount on Purchase	*(-)200.00*	
On Account of :		
Purchases from B M Suppkier a sper their Bill # 12 Dt 31.5.09		
Amount (In words) :		
Indian Rupees Two Thousand Two Hundred Only		

Authorised Signatory

F-4C: Purchase Voucher

05.01 Debit / Credit Note Printing Configuration

Like Sales / Purchase Invoice, you may pre-set the default format & contents of Debit / Credit Note in Voucher / Invoice Format.

At Gateway, click *F12: Configure > Printing > Debit / Credit Note* to get Debit / Credit Note Voucher Configuration screen (F-5A)

Debit / Credit Note Printing Configuration

Print Company Logo	?	**No**
Height of Voucher (inches)	:	**6**
Width of Voucher (inches)	:	**5**
Space to leave on top (default 0.25)	:	**0.25**
Space to leave on left (default 0.75)	:	**0.75**
Print full Ledger details	?	**Yes**
Print Inventory details	?	**Yes**
Print with Narrations	?	**Yes**
Print Narration for each entry	?	**Yes**
Print Bill-wise Details	?	**Yes**
Print Bill Due Date also	?	**No**
Space for Checked/Verified initials	?	**Yes**
Print Base Currency Symbol for Total	?	**Yes**

F-5A: Debit / Credit Note printing Configuration

ABC Academy
99, Airpot Rd
Kolkata 700 098
Contact :651234,9876523409
E-Mail :abc@tmail.com

Debit Note

No. : **1** Dated : **1-Jun-2009**
Ref.: **12**

Party's Name: **B M Suppliers**

Particulars		Amount
Purchase	*2,200.00*	**₹ 2,500.00**
Freight	*300.00*	
On Account of :		
Purchased goods returned to supplier		
Amount (in words) :		
Indian Rupees Two Thousand Five Hundred Only		

Authorised Signatory

Checked by: Verified by

F-6A: Debit Note in Voucher Format

ABC Academy
99, Airport Rd
Kolkata 700 098
W Bengal
Contact :651234,9876523409
E-Mail :abc@tmail.com

Debit Note

No.: 2 Dated: **01/08/2009**
Ref.: **34**
Party's Name: **B M Suppliers**

Particulars	Amount
	? 1650.00
On Account of :	
Rebate allowed due to defective goods	
Amount (in words) :	
Indian Rupees One Thousand Six Hundred Fifty Only	

Authorised Signatory
Checked by: Verified by

F-7A: Debit Note without Ledger Account name

F-7B shows printed Credit Note in Invoice format

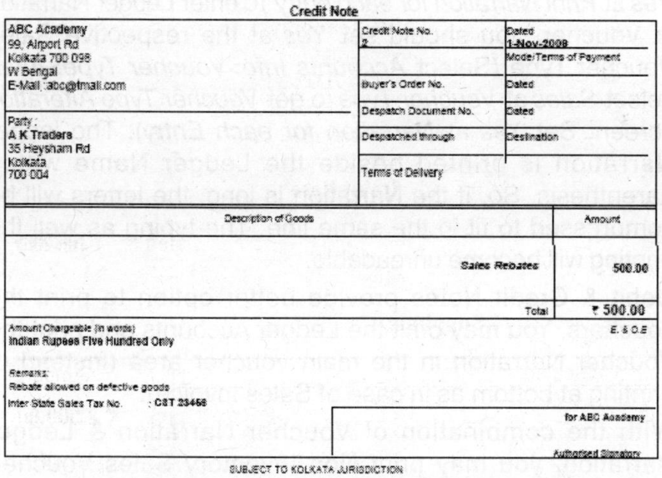

Credit Note

ABC Academy
99, Airport Rd
Kolkata 700 098
W Bengal
E-Mail :abc@tmail.com

Credit Note No. 2 | Dated 1-Nov-2008
Mode/Terms of Payment
Buyer's Order No. | Dated
Despatch Document No. | Dated
Despatched through | Destination
Terms of Delivery

Party :
A K Traders
35 Heysham Rd
Kolkata
700 004

Description of Goods	Amount
Sales Rebates	500.00
Total	₹ 500.00

Amount Chargeable (in words) E. & O.E
Indian Rupees Five Hundred Only

Remarks:
Rebate allowed on defective goods
Inter State Sales Tax No. : CST 23458

for ABC Academy

Authorised Signatory

SUBJECT TO KOLKATA JURISDICTION

F-7B: Credit Note in Invoice (Normal) Format

At Debit / Credit Note printing Configuration screen (F-5A), set the options as follows:

Company Logo: At *Print Company Logo*, Set:

- *Yes* at the header (useful to print in plain paper stationery).
- *No*, no logo is printed.

Dimensions: Enter the following default values to specify Dimension & Margins (in inches) of the printed Voucher (including margins)

- **Voucher Height:** At *Height of Voucher,* enter the height of the voucher (print area in inches including top & bottom margin). Default value is 6 (inches)
- **Voucher Width:** At *Width of Voucher,* enter the width of the voucher (print area in inches including left & right top & bottom margin). Default value is 5 (inches)
- **Top Margin:** At *Space to leave at top,* enter the value of top margin (in inches). Default value (.25)
- **Left Margin:** At *Space to leave on left*, enter the value of left margin (in inches). Default value (.75)

  Print Options: Set Yes / No top print / suppress the specific contents in the voucher
- **Ledger Details:** At *Print Full ledger details,* set:
  - o *Yes* to print Ledger details alongwith Inventory details
  - o *No* (default value) to omit ledger details printing (F-7A).
- **Full Details**:Having set Yes at *Print Full ledger details*, you may further set Yes / No at the following options (F-5A):
  - o **Inventory Details:** At *Print Inventory Details,* set
    - ▪ *Yes* to print Inventory details (if Inventory System is activated)
    - ▪ *No* (default value) to omit Inventory details.
  - o **Voucher Narration:** At *Print with Narration*, set
    - ▪ *Yes* (default value) to print Voucher common Narration.
    - ▪ *No* to omit Voucher Common narration (it may sometimes be useful when separate ledger narration is printed).
  - o **Ledger Narration:** At *Print Narration for each entry,* set
    - ▪ *Yes* (default value) to print separate Ledger Narration for each ledger account transacted.
    - ▪ *No* to omit separate ledger narration (it may sometimes be useful when Common Narration is printed). The voucher Narration is printed under the caption: *On Account of.*
- **Initials:** At *Space for Checked / Verified initials,* set:
  - o *Yes* to print a guide (Checked / Verified by) for space for putting signature,
  - o *No* (default value) to omit the tag. This is useful when the authorities sign on the computer printed voucher (no manual voucher is used).
- **Currency Symbol:** At *Print Base Currency Symbol for Total*, set
  - o *Yes* (default value) to print Base Currency Symbol before the Total Amount.
  - o *No* to print only amount figure without any currency symbol

FAQ: Frequently Asked Questions

FAQ-1: I do not maintain Inventory. I enter sales transaction in Voucher format only. How to print Sales Voucher in Voucher format

Ans: Having entered the voucher, at voucher entry screen, click P:Print button (or press Alt+P) to get Invoice Printing Screen.

Sales Voucher without Inventory data is useful for Service / Professional Invoice where no materials are traded.

FAQ-2: The contents of my Sales Invoice are few. How I can use smaller stationery to print Invoice

Ans: The size of stationery may be changed at the Invoice Printing Configuration

At Gateway, click F12:Configure>Printing> Sales Transaction > Sales Invoice. Now reduce the Height / Width / Top Margin & Bottom Margin

Now see the Print Preview of some Invoice check a few Invoices (Click *F12:Configure*, click *I:With Preview)* to see the Print Preview of the Invoice on screen. It shows an exact replica of Invoice alongwith a scale at the top & left margin, to see the length & height of Invoice (click at *In Inches* at the print preview to see the scale in inches, because you have to specify the dimension of voucher in Inches in Printing configuration). Viewing few Invoices on screen, you will get an idea of the average printing space taken by the Invoice.

To reduce the height of Invoice. You may use Pre Printed stationery and print Company Name, Address and other fixed info at strategic position within the planned Invoice stationery Size.

To design the pre printed stationery, At Print Configuration, click *R:Pre-Printed* toggle button to print only the data items in the Invoice (without any heading). When you specify Pre Printed stationery, Tally will print only the voucher data contents (no headings). Now plan the design of the pre-printed stationary (headings and fixed info) keeping the overall stationary size in mind.

In case of Cash Memo, you may print the Cash Memo at the heading and omit printing Party Name (as it is Cash Account). This will considerably reduce the height of Invoice.

When you print Accounting Voucher, the ledger accounts & corresponding Amount are printed. For explanation of Invoice contents, you may print Voucher Narration (where you enter the details of voucher), at the last line (set *Yes* at *Print Narration*).

To print the details just beside each ledger Narration, set *Yes* at *Print Narration for each entry* To enter Ledger Narration in Voucher, you should set *Yes* at the respective Sales Voucher Type (Select *Accounts Info>Voucher Type>Alter*, select *Sales* at *Voucher Type* to get *Voucher Type Alteration* screen. Set *Yes* at *Narration for each Entry*). The ledger Narration is printed beside the Ledger Name within parenthesis. So, if the Narration is long, the letters will be compressed to fit in the same line. The typing as well the printing will become unreadable.

Debit & Credit Notes provide better option to print the vouchers. You may omit the Ledger Accounts and print the Voucher Narration in the main voucher area (instead of printing at bottom as in case of Sales Invoice).

With the combination of Voucher Narration & Ledger Narration, you may print Non Inventory Sales Voucher, particularly for Consultancy & Service Invoice, where no goods are traded.

Bill Registers 03-04

01 Bill Registers

Bill Registers represent a set of subsidiary Journal Books of Sales & Purchase and Debit & Credit Note Vouchers (Voucher Registers) showing transactions of Sales / Purchase and the Debit & Credit Notes with Customers & Suppliers. Normally, separate Bill Register is printed for each type of Voucher.

Apart from the Bill Registers, Group Vouchers (§07/02-16) & Ledger Vouchers (§08/02-16) also show list of Vouchers related to subordinate ledger Accounts of specified Account Group / Ledger. Hence, Group Vouchers & Ledger Vouchers may also be considered as type of Bill Register.

01.01 Bill Registers Display

At Gateway of Tally, select *Display> Accounts Book* to get Account Book Menu (F-4A/01-05)

At Accounts Book Menu (F-4A/01-05):

- **Purchase Register**: Select *Purchase Register* to get Purchase Register (F-4B)
- **Sales Register**: Select *Sales Register* to get Sales Register (F-2B)
- **Journal Register**: Select *Journal Register* to get Journal Register Menu (F-4B/01-05)

At **Journal Register** Menu (F-4B/01-05)

- **Debit Note Register**: Select *Debit Note* to get Debit Note Register. (F-6A)
- **Credit Note Register**: Select *Credit Note* to get Credit Note Register (F-8A)

Initially, you get Monthly total figures. Select a month to get Bill Register (Voucher Register) for the month. Click *F2: Period* and enter the period (Date From & Date To) to get Bill Register for specified Period.

There are 2 types of Bill Register Reports

- **Bill Register (Voucher Register)**: This shows the details of each Voucher for the specified Voucher type for a specified period.
- **Bill Register Extract**: This shows Summary as per Accounts Group / Accounts Ledger (or Stock Group / Stock Ledger). In fact, it is Voucher Summary (§07/02-19) rather than Voucher Register.

02 Bill Register Display Configuration

The contents of Bill Registers may be configured trough Configuration options for each Voucher type

At the respective Bill Register screen, click *F12:Configure* to get the Configuration screen and set the Configuration options (F-1A to F-1C)

Most of the Bill Register Display Configuration options of Sales / Purchase of Bill Registers (F-1A & F-1B) are similar. The Configuration options of Debit & Credit Note are same (F-1C).

02.01 Bill Register Configuration Table

The following table shows the options in each type of Bill Register

Options	Sales	Purchase	Debit Notre	Credit Note
Show Extract of Register	√	√	√	√
Show Columnar Register	√	√	√	√
Show Gross Profit Estimates	√			
Format	√	√	√	√
Show Narrations Also	√	√	√	√
Show Billwise details also	√	√	√	√
Show Entered / Altered By	√	√	√	√

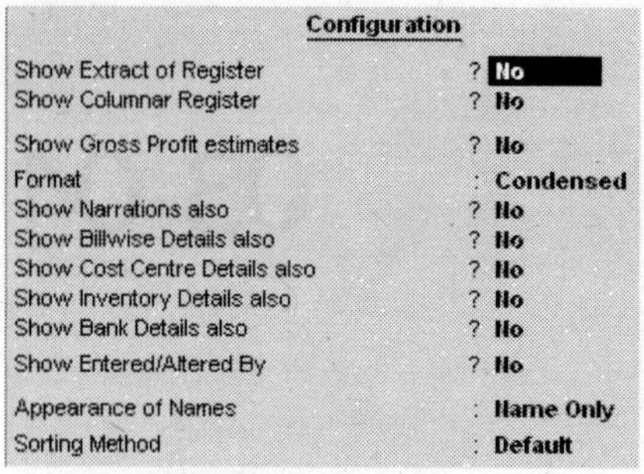

F-1A: Sales Register Configuration

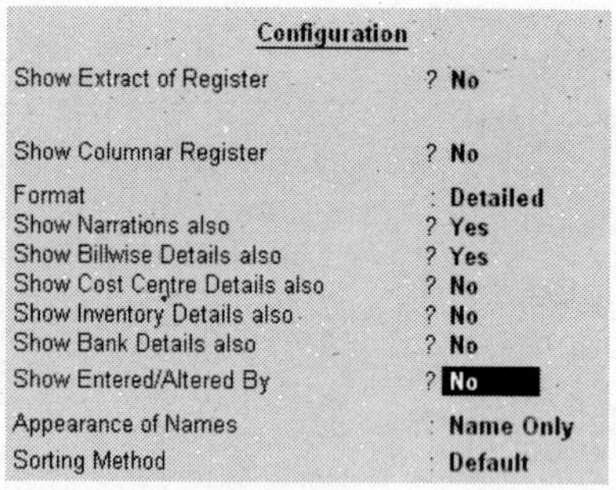

F-1B: Purchase Register Configuration

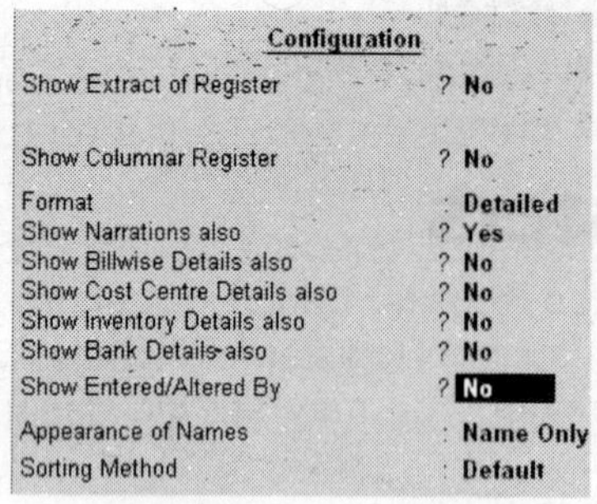

F-1C: Debit / Credit Note Register Configuration

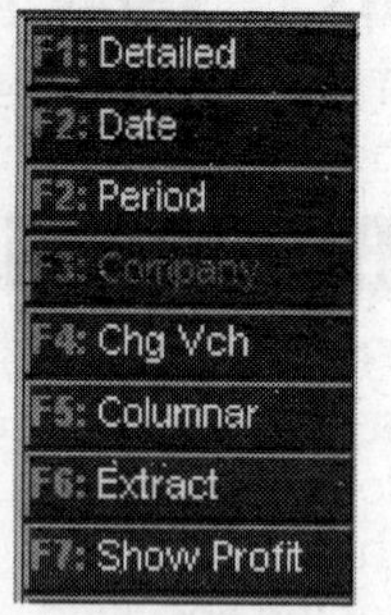

F-1D: Buttons

02.02 Bill Register Display Configuration Options

- **Extract / Register:** At *Show Extract of Register:*
  - o **Register**: Set *No* to get the Register with each voucher details.
  - o **Extract**: Set *Yes* to get Bill Register Extract, showing Ledger Accountwise summary of vouchers for the selected period
- **Columnar / Regular Register**: At *Show Columnar Register*
  - o **Columnar:** Set *Yes* To define Columns and get Sales Register in Columnar format
  - o **Regular:** Set *No* to get Regular Register
- **Format:** At *Format*
  - o Select '*Detailed*' to view all ledger accounts of each voucher,
  - o Select '*Condensed*' to get only the first ledger account (Party / Cash bank) and the net amount of the voucher.

  You may also set the Format using F1: *Detailed / Condensed* toggle button at Button Bar
- **Voucher Narration:** At *Show Narrations Also*
  - o Set Yes to show Voucher Narration for each Voucher (if entered),
  - o Set *No* to suppress Narration (Narration is not shown)
- **Billwise details:** This is relevant only when the Bill Ref is activated for the Company (you have *Yes* at Maintain Billwise Details at *F11:Features>Accounting Features.* At *Show Billwise details also*:
  - o Set *Yes* to show the Bill Reference Details
  - o Set *No.* Bill Reference is not shown (If Voucher Number & Bill Ref is same, you may suppress it)
- **Show Cost Centre Details also:** This is relevant only when Cost Centre is activated
- **Show Inventory Details also:** This is relevant only when Inventory System is also activated
- **Bank Details:** This is relevant only in case of Cash Sales where the payment is received by Cheque. At *Show Bank Details also,* set *Yes,* to show Cheque Particulars, else set *No.*
- **User Name**: At *Show Entered / Altered By* Set *Yes* to show user name of voucher writer, else set *No.*
- **Sales Contribution (Gross Profit)**: To get the Sales contribution (Sales Value – Cost of Sales) for each *Sales* Voucher (this option is not available for other Voucher Types) with Profit % in respect of each sales voucher. This is relevant only when you maintain Inventory system also, where the Itemwise Data of Cost & Sale Value is available.

  At *Show Gross Profit Estimates:*
  - o Set Yes to get a new column showing the Gross Profit % of each Voucher
  - o Set *No.* The Gross Profit % columns is not shown

02.03 Bill Register Display Buttons

The buttons at the vertical button bar at all Bill Registers are quite similar (F-1D), as described below:

Button	Description
F1: Detailed / Condensed	Set *Detailed* to show all subordinate groups / ledger accounts. Set *Condensed* to show only top level groups / ledger accounts.
F4: Chg Vch	Click to select desired Voucher Type.to show the list of voucher of selected Voucher Type
F5:Columnar	Click to get the Column definition screen to define Columnar Register
F6 Extract / Vouchers	Toggle button to get voucher register Extract / Voucher Register
F7: Show Profit / Hide Profit	This toggle button is available for Sales Register only - Click Toggle button *F7: Show Profit* to show the figures of Gross Revenue, Cost & Gross Profit / Loss (based on Cost) in respect of each Sales Voucher (Show Profit), - Click Toggle button *F7: Hide Profit* suppress these columns of Cost & Net Profit, in respect of Sales Voucher.

03 Sales Register

The Sales Register (Voucher Register) is a subsidiary Journal book, which shows the Sales Vouchers in chronological order.

At Gateway of Tally, select *Display> Accounts Book > Sales Register* to get Sales Register (Monthly Summary), Select a month to get the Voucher Register (of all Sales Vouchers) for the specified month. You may set the desired Period through *F12: Period* button to get the list of all Sales Voucher for the specified period (F-2B)

Voucher Register — Ctrl + M

List of All Sales Vouchers — 1-Jun-2009 to 31-Mar-2010

Date	Particulars			Vch Type	Vch No.	Debit Amount	Credit Amount
2-6-2009	**A K Traders**			Sales	3	2,800.00	
	On Account		2,800.00 Dr				
	Sales		2,500.00 Cr				
	Freight		300.00 Cr				
	Sold to A K Traders and despatched by B P transport paying freight						
	Entered By : **akn**						
1-7-2009	**A K Traders**			Sales	4	2,150.00	
	New Ref 3		2,150.00 Dr				
	Sales		2,000.00 Cr				
	Freight		200.00 Cr				
	Sales Rebates		50.00 Dr				
	Sold to A K Traders						
	Entered By : **akn**						
1-9-2009	**Aakash & Co**			Sales	5	4,000.00	
	New Ref 5	3 Days	4,000.00 Dr				
	Tution Fees		4,500.00 Cr				
	Cash Discount		500.00 Dr				
	Tution Fees for CPT Course Oct- Apr 2009						
	Entered By : **akn**						
					:	8,950.00	

F-2A: Sales Register Display (Configured)

Voucher Register — Ctrl + M

List of All Sales Vouchers — 1-Apr-2009 to 31-Mar-2010

Date	Particulars	Vch Type	Vch No.	Debit Amount	Credit Amount
1-4-2009	T K Das	Sales	1	50,000.00	
2-5-2009	Cash	Sales	2	2,000.00	
2-6-2009	A K Traders	Sales	3	2,800.00	
1-7-2009	A K Traders	Sales	4	2,150.00	
1-9-2009	Aakash & Co	Sales	5	4,000.00	
			Total:	60,950.00	

F-2B: Sales Register Display (Default)

Sales Register

1-May-2009 to 31-Mar-2010

Page 1

Date	Particulars		Vch Type	Vch No.	Debit Amount	Credit Amount
2-5-2009	Cash		Sales	2	2,000.00	
	Sales					[illegible],100.00
	Sales Rebates				100.00	
	Goods sold in cash after allowing rebates					
	Entered By :	akn				
2-6-2009	A K Traders		Sales	3	2,800.00	
	Sales					[illegible],500.00
	Freight					300.00
	Sold to A K Traders and despatched by B P transport paying freight					
	Entered By :	akn				
1-7-2009	A K Traders		Sales	4	2,150.00	
	Sales					[illegible],000.00
	Freight					200.00
	Sales Rebates				50.00	
	Sold to A K Traders					
	Entered By :	akn				
1-9-2009	Aakash & Co		Sales	5	4,000.00	
	Tution Fees					[illegible],500.00
	Cash Discount					[illegible]500.00
	Tution Fees for CPT Course Oct- Apr 2009					
	Entered By :	akn				
					Total: 10,950.00	

F-3A: Sales Register (in Print Form)

Report Titles

Sales Register

Show Extract of Register	?	No
Show Columnar Register	?	No
Format	:	Condensed
Show Voucher Numbers also	?	Yes
Show Narrations also	?	No
Show Billwise Details also	?	No
Show Cost Centre Details also	?	No
Show Inventory Details also	?	No
Show Bank Details also	?	No
Show Entered/Altered By	?	No

F-3B: Sales Register Printing Screen

At Sales Register Display (F-2B), Click P:Print to get the Printing screen (F-3B). Set the option (similar to Display Configuration options:F-1A), to get the Sales Register in Print Form (F-3A). The Printed Report (F-3A) is similar to Display (F-2A).

04 Purchase Register

The Purchase Register (Voucher Register) is a subsidiary Journal book, showing the Purchase Vouchers

At Gateway of Tally, select *Display> Accounts Book > Purchase Register* to get Purchase Register (Monthly Summary), Select a month to get the Voucher Register (of Purchase Vouchers) for the specified month. You may set the desired Period through *F12: Period* button to get the list of all Purchase Voucher for the specified period (F-4B)

Voucher Register — Ctrl + M

List of All Purchase Vouchers — 1-Nov-2009 to 30-Nov-2009

Date	Particulars			Vch Type	Vch No.	Debit Amount	Credit Amount
2-11-2009	**B M Suppliers**			Purchase	2		3,040.00
	New Ref 12	30 Days	3,040.00 Cr				
	Purchase		3,000.00 Dr				
	Freight		40.00 Dr				
	Materials purchased ag party's Inv No 12 dt 3110.11						
	Entered By : **akn**						
2-11-2009	**B M Suppliers**			Purchase	3		3,040.00
	New Ref 16/25	30 Days	3,040.00 Cr				
	Purchase		3,000.00 Dr				
	Freight		40.00 Dr				
	Materials purchased ag party's Inv No 12 dt 3110.11						
	Entered By : **akn**						
						Total:	6,080.00

F-4A: Purchase Register Display (Configured)

Voucher Register — Ctrl + M

List of All Purchase Vouchers — 1-Apr-2009 to 31-Mar-2010

Date	Particulars	Vch Type	Vch No.	Debit Amount	Credit Amount
1-6-2009	B M Suppliers	Purchase	1		2,200.00
2-11-2009	B M Suppliers	Purchase	2		3,040.00
2-11-2009	B M Suppliers	Purchase	3		3,040.00
1-12-2009	B M Suppliers	Purchase	4		3,040.00
				Total:	11,320.00

F-4B: Purchase Register Display (Default)

At Purchase Register Display (F-4B), Click P:Print to get the *Purchase Register Printing* screen (F-5B), similar to Purchase Register Display Configuration options (F-1B), At *Purchase Register Printing Configuration* (5B), set the options to get the Purchase Register in Print Form (F-5A). The Purchase Register in Print Form (F-5A) is similar to Purchase Register in Display Form (F-4A)

Purchase Register
1-Nov-2009 to 30-Nov-2009

Page 1

Date	Particulars	Vch Type	Vch No.	Debit Amount	Credit Amount
2-11-2009	**B M Suppliers**	Purchase	2		3,040.00
	New Ref 12 30 Days 3,040.00 Cr				
	Purchase			3,000.00	
	Freight			40.00	
	Materials purchased ag party's Inv No 12 dt 3110.11				
	Entered By : akn				
2-11-2009	**B M Suppliers**	Purchase	3		3,040.00
	New Ref 16/25 30 Days 3,040.00 Cr				
	Purchase			3,000.00	
	Freight			40.00	
	Materials purchased ag party's Inv No 12 dt 3110.11				
	Entered By : akn				
			Total:		6,080.00

F-5A: Purchase Register (in Print Form)

Purchase Register

Show Extract of Register	? **No**
Show Columnar Register	? **No**
Format	: **Detailed**
Show Voucher Numbers also	? **Yes**
Show Narrations also	? **Yes**
Show Billwise Details also	? **Yes**
Show Cost Centre Details also	? **No**
Show Inventory Details also	? **No**
Show Bank Details also	? **No**
Show Entered/Altered By	? **Yes**

F-5B: Purchase Register Printing Screen

05 Debit Note Register

The Debit Note Register (Voucher Register) is a subsidiary Journal book, showing the Debit Notes.

At *Gateway of Tally > Display> Accounts Book> Journal Register >Debit Note Register* to get Debit Note Register, showing monthly counts of Debit Note Vouchers.

Select a month to get the Voucher Register of Debit Note Vouchers for the month. Click *F2: Period* and set the period to get the list of Debit Note Vouchers for the specified period (F-6A)

Voucher Register Ctrl + M

List of All Debit Note Vouchers **1-Apr-2009 to 31-Mar-2010**

Date	Particulars	Vch Type	Vch No.	Debit Amount	Credit Amount
1-6-2009	**B M Suppliers**	**Debit Note**	1	**2,500.00**	
1-8-2009	**B M Suppliers**	**Debit Note**	2	**1,650.00**	

F-6A: Debit Note Register Display (Default)

Voucher Register Ctrl + M

List of All Debit Note Vouchers **1-Apr-2009 to 31-Mar-2010**

Date	Particulars		Vch Type	Vch No.	Debit Amount	Credit Amount
1-6-2009	**B M Suppliers**		**Debit Note**	1	2,500.00	
	Purchase	2,200.00 Cr				
	Freight	300.00 Cr				
	Purchased goods returned to supplier					
1-8-2009	**A K Traders**		**Debit Note**	2	1,650.00	
	Purchase	1,650.00 Cr				
	Rebate allowed due t dfective goods					

6B: Debit Note Register Display (Detailed)

At Debit Note Register Display (F-6B), Click P:Print to get the Printing Configuration screen (F-7B). Set the option (similar to Display Configuration options – F- 1C), to get the Debit Note Register in Print Form (F-7A), similar to Display Form (F-6A).

Debit Note Register
1-Apr-2009 to 31-Mar-2010

Page 1

Date	Particulars	Vch Type	Vch No.	Debit Amount	Credit Amount
1-6-2009	**B M Suppliers**	Debit Note	1	2,500.00	
	New Ref DN/6 30 Days 2,500.00 Dr				
	Purchase				2,200.00
	Freight				300.00
	Purchased goods returned to supplier				
	Entered By akn				
1-8-2009	**B M Suppliers**	Debit Note	2	1,650.00	
	New Ref DN/15 30 Days 1,650.00 Dr				
	Purchase				1,650.00
	Rebate allowed due t dfective goods				
	Entered By akn				

F-7A: Debit Note Register (in Print Form)

Report Titles

Debit Note Register

Show Extract of Register	? **No**
Show Columnar Register	? **No**
Format	: **Condensed**
Show Voucher Numbers also	? **Yes**
Show Narrations also	? **No**
Show Billwise Details also	? **No**
Show Cost Centre Details also	? **No**
Show Inventory Details also	? **No**
Show Bank Details also	? **No**
Show Entered/Altered By	? **No**

F-7B: Debit / Credit Note Register Printing Screen

06 Credit Note Register

The Credit Note Register (Voucher Register) is a subsidiary Journal book, showing the Credit Notes.

At Gateway of Tally, select *Display> Accounts Book> Journal Register >Credit Note Register* to get Credit Note Register, showing monthly counts of Credit Note Vouchers. Select a month to get the Voucher Register of Debit Note Vouchers for the month. Click *F2: Period* and set the period to get the list of Credit Note Vouchers for the specified period (F-8A)

Voucher Register Ctrl + M

List of All Credit Note Vouchers **1-Apr-2009 to 31-Mar-2010**

Date	Particulars	Vch Type	Vch No.	Debit Amount	Credit Amount
1-6-2009	**A K Traders**	**Credit Note**	1		**2,000.00**
1-11-2009	**A K Traders**	**Credit Note**	2		**500.00**

F-8A Credit Note Register Display

At Credit Note Register Display (F-8A), Click *P:Print* to get the Debit / Credit Note Printing screen (F-7B). (similar to Display Configuration options – F-1C). Set the options to print Credit Note Register (F-9A), which is quite similar to Credit Note Register in Display Form (F-8A).

Voucher Register — Ctrl + M

List of All Credit Note Vouchers — 1-Apr-2009 to 31-Mar-2010

Date	Particulars		Vch Type	Vch No.	Debit Amount	Credit Amount
1-6-2009	**A K Traders**		Credit Note	1		2,000.00
	New Ref 1	2,000.00 Cr				
	Sales Return	**2,000.00 Dr**				
	Goods recived back from cutomers					
1-11-2009	**A K Traders**		Credit Note	2		500.00
	New Ref 2	500.00 Cr				
	Sales Rebates	**500.00 Dr**				
	Rebate allowed on defective goods					

F-8B: Credit Note Register Display (Detailed)

> **Note:** *In Display, the amount is shown in Debit (for Debit Note) / Credit (for Credit Note) column for the first ledger account and in inner (Particulars) column for other accounts, with Dr / Cr sgn.In Print from, the amount is shown in respective Debit / Credit column.In Debit / Credit Note Register, the Report Grand Total is not shown.*

Credit Note Register
1-Apr-2009 to 31-Mar-2010

Page 1

Date	Particulars		Vch Type	Vch No.	Debit Amount	Credit Amount
1-6-2009	**A K Traders**		Credit Note	1		2,000.00
	New Ref 1	2,000.00 Cr				
	Sales Return				2,000.00	
	Goods recived back from cutomers					
1-11-2009	**A K Traders**		Credit Note	2		500.00
	New Ref 2	500.00 Cr				
	Sales Rebates				500.00	
	Rebate allowed on defective goods					

F-9A: Credit Note Register (in Print Form)

07 Multi Account Registers

The printing of Sales (§03) & Purchase (§04) Register and Debit (§05) & Credit (§06) Note Register from Display screen have been explained (F-2B/01-05)

You may print Sales & Purchase Register and Debit & Credit Note Register from Multi Account Printing menu. This is more convenient for regular bulk printing.

At Gateway, select *Multi Account Printing >Account Books* to get *Multi-Account Account Printing Menu* (F-2B/01-05).

07.01 Multi Account Sales / Purchase Register

At Multi-Account Account Printing Menu (F-2B/01-05), select:

- **Multi-Account Purchase Register***: Purchase Register* to get Purchase Register printing screen (F-10B). Set the options to get *Multi Account Purchase Register* (F-11B), similar to *Purchase Register* printed from Display (F-5A)
- **Multi-Account Sales Register***: Sales Register* to get Sales Register printing screen (F-10A). Set the options to get *Multi Account Sales Register* (F-11A), similar to *Sales Register* printed from Display (F-3A)

Report Titles

Sales Register

From (blank for beginning)	:	**1-3-2010**
To (blank for end)	:	**31-3-2010**
Show Extract of Register	?	**No**
Show Columnar Register	?	**No**
Format	:	**Detailed**
Show Voucher Numbers also	?	**Yes**
Show Narrations also	?	**No**
Show Billwise Details also	?	**No**
Show Cost Centre Details also	?	**No**
Show Inventory Details also	?	**No**
Show Bank Details also	?	**No**
Show Entered/Altered By	?	**No**

F-10A: Multi Account Sales Register Printing

Report Titles

Purchase Register

From (blank for beginning)		**1-3-2010**
To (blank for end)		**31-3-2010**
Show Extract of Register	?	**No**
Show Columnar Register	?	**No**
Format	:	**Detailed**
Show Voucher Numbers also	?	**Yes**
Show Narrations also	?	**No**
Show Billwise Details also	?	**No**
Show Cost Centre Details also	?	**No**
Show Inventory Details also	?	**No**
Show Bank Details also	?	**No**
Show Entered/Altered By	?	**No**

F-10B: Multi Account Purchase Register Printing

Sales Register
1-Apr-2009 to 31-Mar-2010

Page 1

Date	Particulars	Vch Type	Vch No.	Debit Amount	Credit Amount
1-4-2009	**T K Das**	**Sales**	1	**50,000.00**	
	Sales				**50,000.00**
2-5-2009	**Cash**	**Sales**	2	**2,000.00**	
	Sales				**2,100.00**
	Sales Rebates			**100.00**	
2-6-2009	**A K Traders**	**Sales**	3	**2,800.00**	
	Sales				**2,500.00**
	Freight				**300.00**
1-7-2009	**A K Traders**	**Sales**	4	**2,150.00**	
	Sales				**2,000.00**
	Freight				**200.00**
	Sales Rebates			**50.00**	
1-9-2009	**Aakash & Co**	**Sales**	5	**4,000.00**	
	Tution Fees				**4,500.00**
	Cash Discount				**(-)500.00**
			Total:	**60,950.00**	

F-11A Multi Account Sales Register

07.02 Multi Account Debit / Credit Note Register

At Multi-Account Account Printing Menu (F-2B/01-05), select *Journal Register* to get *Multi Account Journal Register Printing* menu (F-2C/01-05). At *Multi Account Journal Register Printing* menu (F-2C/01-05), select

Purchase Register
1-Apr-2009 to 31-Mar-2010

Date	Particulars	Vch Type	Debit Amount	Credit Amount
1-6-2009	**B M Suppliers**	Purchase		2,200.00
	Purchase		2,100.00	
	Freight		300.00	
	Discount on Purchase			200.00
	Purchases from B M Suppkier a sper their Bill # 12 Dt 31.5.09			
2-11-2009	**B M Suppliers**	Purchase		3,040.00
	Purchase		3,000.00	
	Freight		40.00	
	Materials purchased ag party's Inv No 12 dt 3110.11			
2-11-2009	**B M Suppliers**	Purchase		3,040.00
	Purchase		3,000.00	
	Freight		40.00	
	Materials purchased ag party's Inv No 12 dt 3110.11			
1-12-2009	**B M Suppliers**	Purchase		3,040.00
	Purchase		3,000.00	
	Freight		40.00	
	Materials purchased ag party's Inv No 12 dt 3110.11			
		Total:		11,320.00

F-11B Multi Account Purchase Register (with Narration, without voucher number)

- **Multi-Account Debit Note Register**: *Debit Note Register* to get *Debit Note Register* printing screen (F-12A). Set the options to get *Multi Account Debit Note Register* (F-13A), similar to *Debit Note Register* Sales / Purchase Register printed from Display (F-7A)
- **Multi-Account Credit Note Register**: *Credit Note Register* to get *Credit Note* Register printing screen (F-12B). Set the options to get *Multi Account Credit Note Register* (F-13B), similar to Credit Note Register printed from Display (F-9A)

Report Titles

Debit Note Register

From (blank for beginning)	:	**1-3-2010**
To (blank for end)	:	**31-3-2010**
Show Extract of Register	?	**No**
Show Columnar Register	?	**No**
Format	:	**Detailed**
Show Voucher Numbers also	?	**Yes**
Show Narrations also	?	**No**
Show Billwise Details also	?	**No**
Show Cost Centre Details also	?	**No**
Show Inventory Details also	?	**No**
Show Bank Details also	?	**No**
Show Entered/Altered By	?	**No**

F-12A: Multi Account Debit Note Register Printing

Report Titles

Credit Note Register

From (blank for beginning)	:	**1-3-2010**
To (blank for end)	:	**31-3-2010**
Show Extract of Register	?	**No**
Show Columnar Register	?	**No**
Format	:	**Detailed**
Show Voucher Numbers also	?	**Yes**
Show Narrations also	?	**No**
Show Billwise Details also	?	**No**
Show Cost Centre Details also	?	**No**
Show Inventory Details also	?	**No**
Show Bank Details also	?	**No**
Show Entered/Altered By	?	**No**

F-12B: Multi Account Credit Note Register Printing

Debit Note Register
1-Apr-2009 to 31-Mar-2010

Page 1

Date	Particulars	Vch Type	Debit Amount	Credit Amount
1-6-2009	**B M Suppliers**	Debit Note	2,500.00	
	Purchased goods returned to supplier			
1-8-2009	**B M Suppliers**	Debit Note	1,650.00	
	Rebate allowed due t dfective goods			

F-13A: Multi Account Debit Note Register (Condensed, With Narration, Without Voucher Number)

Credit Note Register
1-Apr-2009 to 31-Mar-2010

Date	Particulars	Vch Type	Debit Amount	Credit Amount
1-6-2009	**A K Traders**	Credit Note		2,000.00
	Sales Return		2,000.00	
1-11-2009	**A K Traders**	Credit Note		500.00
	Sales Rebates		500.00	

F-13B: Multi Account Credit Note Register (Detailed, without Narration & Voucher Number)

08 Group Vouchers

Group Vouchers Report shows all the Vouchers (of any Voucher Type) in which any ledger subordinate to the selected Account Group is transacted, as explained earlier (§07/02-16). This Report does is not specifically related to Sales / Purchase, but selecting Sales / Purchase Group, you may get the list of all Vouchers related to Sales / Purchase Accounts (F-14A).

So, if Cash Sales & Purchases transactions are entered through Receipt / Payment Vouchers or Credit Sales / Purchase are entered through Journal Vouchers, then such Vouchers will not be listed in Sales / Purchase Register, but will be listed in Group Voucher Report of Sales / Purchase Group. So, Group Voucher list of Sales Group is more comprehensive and covers all sorts of Vouchers in respect of any ledger account transacted (in any voucher type), under a specified Account Group.

At Gateway of Tally, select *Display >Account Books > Group Vouchers* and then select the Account Group:

Group Vouchers Ctrl + M

Group: **Sales Accounts** — **1-Apr-2009 to 31-Mar-2010**

Date	Particulars		Vch Type	Vch No	Debit	Credit
2-5-2009	**(as per details)**		Sales	1		2,100.00
	Cash	2,000.00 Dr				
	Discount on Sales	100.00 Dr				
	Sales	2,100.00 Cr				
	Cash Sales					
1-6-2009	**(as per details)**		Credit Note	1	2,000.00	
	A K Traders	2,000.00 Cr				
	Sales Return	2,000.00 Dr				
	Goods recived back from cutomers					
1-7-2009	**(as per details)**		Sales	3		2,000.00
	A K Traders	2,150.00 Dr				
	Freight	200.00 Cr				
	Discount on Sales	50.00 Dr				
	Sales	2,000.00 Cr				
	Sold to A K Traders					
1-11-2009	**(as per details)**		Credit Note	2	500.00	
	A K Traders	500.00 Cr				
	Sales Rebates	500.00 Dr				
	Rebate allowed on defective goods					
			Opening Balance :			
			Current Total :		2,500.00	6,600.00
			Closing Balance :			4,100.00

F-16A: Group Voucher Display

- *Sales Accounts* to get Group Vouchers Report for Sales Group (F-16A)
- *Purchase Accounts* to get Group Vouchers Report for Purchase Group (F-16G)

Configuration

Select vouchers to show	:	**All Vouchers**
Format	:	**Condensed**
Show All Ledgers Details	?	**No**
Show Entered/Altered By	?	**No**
Show Narrations also	?	**No**
Include Opening Balances *(set as 'no' to remove from filtered reports)*	?	**Yes**
Appearance of Names	:	**Name Only**
Sorting Method	:	**Default**

F-16B: Group Voucher Display Configfuration

Ledger Entries

All Vouchers
Credit Entries only
Debit Entries only

F-16C: Voucher Nature List

F1: Condensed
F2: Period
F3: Company
F4: Group
F5: Led-wise
F6: Monthly
F7: Vouchers

F-16D: Buttons

Group Voucher Configuration

At Group Voucher Display (F-16A), click *F12:Configure* to get *Group Voucher Display Configuration* screen (F-16B), as explained earlier (§07/02-16).

Group Voucher Display Buttons

At Group Voucher Display (F-16A), you get the following Buttons (F-16D)

- **F1: Detailed / Condensed**: To get Top Level Groups only (Summary) / Next Level Group / Ledger details also (Detailed)
- **F4: Group**: To select a Group to display Group Vouchers for the selected Group

Group Vouchers Ctrl + M

Group: **Purchase Accounts** 1-Jun-2009 to 30-Jun-2009

Date	Particulars		Vch Type	Vch No.	Debit	Credit
1-6-2009	(as per details)		Purchase	1	2,100.00	200.00
	B M Suppliers	2,200.00 Cr				
	Freight	300.00 Dr				
	Purchase	2,100.00 Dr				
	Discount on Purchase	200.00 Cr				
1-6-2009	(as per details)		Debit Note	1		2,200.00
	B M Suppliers	2,500.00 Dr				
	Freight	300.00 Cr				
	Purchase	2,200.00 Cr				
			Opening Balance :			
			Current Total :		2,100.00	2,400.00
			Closing Balance :			300.00

F-16F: Group Voucher with all ledger accounts details (Yes at Show All Ledger details)

- **F6: Monthly**: To get Monthly Summary of Group Vouchers (F-16H)
- **F7:Summary**: To get Accountwise Summary of Vouchers listed in Group Voucher Statement (F-16I)

Group Vouchers Ctrl + M

Group: **Purchase Accounts** 1-Jun-2009 to 30-Jun-2009

Date	Particulars		Vch Type	Vch No.	Debit	Credit
1-6-2009	(as per details)		Purchase	1	2,100.00	200.00
	B M Suppliers	2,200.00 Cr				
	Freight	300.00 Dr				
1-6-2009	(as per details)		Debit Note	1		2,200.00
	B M Suppliers	2,500.00 Dr				
	Freight	300.00 Cr				
			Opening Balance :			
			Current Total :		2,100.00	2,400.00
			Closing Balance :			300.00

F-16G: Group Voucher (Details)

F-16F shows Group Voucher with all ledger accounts details (Yes at *Show All Ledger details*), showing all ledger accounts including Accounts under the selected Group (Sales / Purchase), while F-16G shows when you set No, ledger accounts including Accounts under the selected Group (Sales / Purchase) are not shown.

Group Monthly Summary Ctrl + M

Particulars	*Purchase Accounts* **ABC Academy 9-10** 1-Apr-2009 to 31-Mar-2010		
	Transactions		**Closing Balance**
	Debit	Credit	
Opening Balance			
April			
May			
June	*2,100.00*	*2,400.00*	300.00 Cr
July			300.00 Cr
August		*1,650.00*	1,950.00 Cr
September			1,950.00 Cr
October			1,950.00 Cr
November	*6,000.00*		4,050.00 Dr
December	*3,000.00*		7,050.00 Dr
January			7,050.00 Dr
February			7,050.00 Dr
March			7,050.00 Dr
Grand Total	***11,100.00***	***4,050.00***	**7,050.00 Dr**

F-16H: Group Voucher Monthly Break up

Group Summary Ctrl + M

Particulars	*Purchase Accounts* **ABC Academy 9-10** 1-Apr-2009 to 31-Mar-2010		
	Transactions		**Closing Balance**
	Debit	Credit	
Discount on Purchase		*200.00*	200.00 Cr
Purchase	*11,100.00*	*3,850.00*	7,250.00 Dr
Grand Total	***11,100.00***	***4,050.00***	**7,050.00 Dr**

F-16I: Group Voucher Summary

Group Voucher Report Printing

At Group Voucher Display (F-16F etc), click *P:Print* Button to get Group Voucher Printing screen (F-17A), showing printing options (similar to Group Voucher Display Configuration options F-16B). Set the options and Type Y to print the Group Voucher Statement (almost similar to Group Voucher Display).

Report Titles

Sales Accounts

Select vouchers to show	: **All Vouchers**
Format	: **Condensed**
Show Billwise Details also	? **No**
Show Cost Centre Details also	? **No**
Show Inventory Details also	? **No**
Show Bank Details also	? **No**
Show Voucher Numbers also	? **Yes**
Show Narrations also	? **No**
Show Running Balance	? **No**
Include Opening Balances	? **Yes**
(set as 'no' to remove from filtered reports)	
Method of Balancing	: **Monthly**
Start fresh page for Balancing	? **No**

F-17A: Group Voucher Printing Screen

Sales Accounts
1-May-2009 to 30-Jun-2009

Date		Particulars		Vch Type	Debit	Credit
1-5-2009	Dr	**Opening Balance**				**50,000.00**
2-5-2009	Cr	**(as per details)**		Sales	100.00	2,100.00
		Cash	**2,000.00 Dr**			
					100.00	52,100.00
	Cr	**Closing Balance**			52,000.00	
					52,100.00	**52,100.00**
1-6-2009	Dr	**Opening Balance**				**52,000.00**
1-6-2009	Cr	**(as per details)**		Credit Note	2,000.00	
		A K Traders	**2,000.00 Cr**			
3-6-2009	Cr	**(as per details)**		Payment	2,000.00	
		Cash	**2,000.00 Cr**			
4-6-2009	Dr	**(as per details)**		Sales		2,500.00
		A K Traders	**2,800.00 Dr**			
		Freight	**300.00 Cr**			
					4,000.00	54,500.00
	Cr	**Closing Balance**			50,500.00	
					54,500.00	**54,500.00**

F-17B: Group Voucher Statement in Printing

At Group Voucher Display, the opening & Closing Balance is shown at the bottom part (F-16F)

At Group Voucher in Print, the Opening balance is shown at the beginning, followed by transactions and the Closing Balance is printed at last line (F-17B)

FAQ: Frequently Asked Questions

FAQ-1: How I can get ledger Accountwise summary of Sales Vouchers for a specified period

Ans: At gateway, select *Display> Account Books>Sales Register*. Select any month and then set the period (Click *F2:Period* and enter the Period) for which you like to get the summary figures, to get the Voucher Register (Sales). Click *F6:Extract* (or Click *F12:Configure* and set *Yes* at *Show Extract of Register*) to get the Ledger Accountwise transaction figures of Sales Vouchers for the specified period.

FAQ-2: Various types transactions related to Indirect Income (like Interest, Rent etc, placed under the Group Miscellaneous Income) are entered through different type of voucher (e.g Journal Voucher, Receipt Voucher etc). How I can get the list of all vouchers which contain transaction with any ledger account placed under the Group Miscellaneous Income

Ans: At Gateway, select *Display> Account Books>Group Vouchers* and then select the Account Group *Miscellaneous Income.* All the vouchers (of any voucher type) in which a any ledger account under the Group *Miscellaneous Income* (like Interest Received, Dividend Received, Misc Receipts) etc are transacted,

While Sales Register, Purchase Register, Debit Note Register, Credit Note Register & Journal Register shows the Vouchers of a specific voucher type, the Group Voucher Register, shows vouchers of any voucher type, related to ledgers of a specific Account Group.

Columnar Bills Register

03-05

01 Columnar Register

We have already explained Columnar Voucher Register for Payment, Receipt, Contra & Journal Vouchers (01/02-18), In this chapter, we show Columnar Bill Registers for Sales, Purchase, Debit Note & Credit Note.

The contents, Format, Column definition as well as Display / Printing of Columnar Bill Register discussed in this chapter for are quite similar to Columnar Voucher Register discussed earlier (01/02-18).

02 Columnar Sales / Purchase Register

To display the respective columnar Register of Sales (F-1A), Purchase (F-1B), at the respective Bill Register (Voucher Register) Display screen (§01.01/03-04):

Voucher Register — **ABC Academy** — Ctrl + M

List of All Sales Vouchers — **1-Apr-2009 to 31-Mar-2010**

Date	Particulars	Voucher Type	Vch No.	Narration	Gross Total	Sales	Discount on Sales	Freight
2-May-2009	**Cash**	Sales	1	Cash Sales	**2,000.00**	2,100.00	(-)100.00	
2-Jun-2009	**A K Traders**	Sales	2	Sold to A K Traders and despatched by B P transport paying freight	**2,800.00**	2,500.00		300.00
1-Jul-2009	**A K Traders**	Sales	3	Sold to A K Traders	**2,150.00**	2,000.00	(-)50.00	200.00
	Grand Total				**6,950.00**	6,600.00	(-)150.00	500.00

F-1A: Columnar Sales Register (Detailed)

- Click *F5:Columnar* button
- At Bill Register Display configuration screen (F-1C), set Yes at *Show Columnar Register* to get Columnar Register specification screen, to set Columnar Register specification (P-02/02-18)

Having set the options for Sales / Purchase Register, you get the respective columnar register for Sales (F-1A) & Purchase (F-1B).

Voucher Register — Ctrl + M

List of All Purchase Vouchers — **1-May-2008 to 31-May-2008**

Date	Particulars	Voucher Type	Vch No.	Gross Total	Purchase
2-May-2008	**D K Enterprises**	Purchase	1	**18,513.21**	18,513.21
27-May-2008	**HDFC Bank (A/c No.151065)**	Purchase	2	**5,589.80**	5,589.80
	Grand Total			**24,103.01**	24,103.01

F-1B: Columnar Purchase Register Display (condensed)

At Columnar Resister Display screen (F-1A, F-1B), click *F12:Configure* to get Columnar Resister Display *Configuration* screen (F-1C) as explained earlier (§02/02-18).

Configuration

Show Extract of Register	?	**No**
Show Columnar Register	?	**Yes**
Show Gross Profit estimates	?	**No**
Format	:	**Condensed**
Show Entered/Altered By	?	**No**
Appearance of Names	:	**Name Only**
Sorting Method	:	**Default**

F-1C: Columnar Register Display Configuration screen

In Columnar Sales / Purchase Register:

- **Sales Register**: In *Sales* Register. Debits (like Sales Discount) are shown as negative figure, while credits (like Sales) are shown in Positive figures.
- **Purchase Register**: In *Purchase* Register. Credits (like Purchase Discount) are shown as negative figure, while Debits (like Purchase) are shown in Positive figures.

03 Columnar Debit / Credit Note Register

To display the respective columnar Register of Debit & Credit Note, at the respective Register (Voucher Register) Display screen (§01.01/03-04):

- Click *F5:Columnar* button
- At respective Register Display configuration screen (F-1C), set Yes at *Show Columnar Register* to get Columnar Register specification screen, to set Columnar Register specification (§02/02-18)

Voucher Register — ABC Academy 9-10 — Ctrl + M

List of All Debit Note Vouchers — 1-Apr-2009 to 31-Mar-2010

Date	*Particulars*	Voucher Type	Vch No.	Narration	Gross Total	Purchase	Freight
1-Jun-2009	**B M Suppliers**	Debit Note	1	Purchased goods returned to supplier	**2,500.00**	2,200.00	300.00
1-Aug-2009	**B M Suppliers**	Debit Note	2	Rebate allowed due t dfective	**1,650.00**	1,650.00	
	Grand Total				**4,150.00**	3,850.00	300.00

F-2A: Columnar Debit Note Register

Voucher Register — Ctrl + M

List of All Credit Note Vouchers — 1-Apr-2009 to 31-Mar-2010

Date	*Particulars*	Voucher Type	Vch No.	Narration	Gross Total	Sales Rebates
1-Jun-2009	**A K Traders**	Credit Note	1	Goods recived back from cutomers		
1-Nov-2009	**A K Traders**	Credit Note	2	Rebate allowed on defective goods	**500.00**	500.00
	Grand Total				**500.00**	500.00

F-2B: Columnar Credit Note Register

F1: Detailed
F2: Date
F2: Period
F3: Company
F4: Chg Vch
F5: Columnar
F6: Extract
F7: Show Profit

F-2C: Buttons for Columnar Register

Having set the options for Debit Note / Credit Note Register, you get the respective columnar register for Debit Note (F-2A) & Credit Note (F-2B).

Columnar Debit Note / Credit Note Register contains the defined columns for Debit / Credit Note Register and total of the each defined Amount columns

In Columnar Debit / Credit Note Register

- **Debit Note Register**: In *Debit Note* Register. Debits are shown as negative figure, while credits (like Purchase Returns) are shown in Positive figures.
- **Credit Note Register**: In *Credit Note* Register. Credits are shown as negative figure, while Debits (like Sales Returns) are shown in Positive figures.

04 Columnar Register Printing

Columnar Register Printing has been explained earlier (§01/02-18).

- At respective Columnar Register Display Configuration screen (F-1C), set Yes at Show Columnar Register, or
- At respective Columnar Register Display screen, click *F5:Columnar* button (F-2C) to get column set up screen as described earlier (§02/02-18).

At Column Register set up screen, set the Column specifications as described earlier (§02/02-18).

Having set the Column specifications, at Register Printing screen, type Y to print the Columnar Register. The contents of Columnar Register in print, is similar to Multi Account Columnar Register (F-4A, F-4B)

> ***Note:*** F7: Show Profit *button at Button Bar (F-2C) and* Show Gross Profit Estimate *option (F-1C) is available only in Sales Register.*

05 Multi Account Columnar Register

Now, we discuss about. Columnar Register in multi accounts printing mode. The options and Report Formats are quite similar to Display Mode.

At Gateway, select *Multi Account printing> Account Books* to get *Multi- Account Accounts Books Printing* Menu (F-2B/01-05)

At *Multi- Account Accounts Books Printing* Menu (F-2B/01-05):

- **Multi- Account Sales / Purchase Register Printing**: Select::
  - o Sales Register to print Sales Register (F-4A)
  - o Purchase Register to Purchase Register (F-4B)
- **Multi- Account Debit / Credit Note Register Printing**: Select *Journal Register* to get *Multi- Account Journal Register Printing Menu* (F-2C/01-05). At *Multi- Account Journal Register Printing Menu* (F-2C/01-05), select:
  - o Debit Note Register: To print Debit Note Register (F-4C)
  - o Credit Note Register: To print Credit Note Register (F-4D)

To get the respective Multi- Account Register printing screen (like F-3A)

At respective Multi- Account Register printing screen (like F-3A), Set Y at shown Column Register

Report Titles		
Sales Register		
From (blank for beginning)	:	1-3-2010
To (blank for end)	:	31-3-2010
Show Extract of Register	?	No
Show Columnar Register	?	No
Format	:	Detailed
Show Voucher Numbers also	?	Yes
Show Narrations also	?	No
Show Billwise Details also	?	No
Show Cost Centre Details also	?	No
Show Inventory Details also	?	No
Show Bank Details also	?	No
Show Entered/Altered By	?	No

F-3A: Multi Account Register Printing screen

Report Titles		
Sales Register		
From (blank for beginning)	:	1-3-2010
To (blank for end)	:	31-3-2010
Show Extract of Register	?	Yes

F-3B: Multi Account Register Extract Printing screen

Sales Register

1-May-2008 to 2-May-2008

Page 1

Date	Particulars	Voucher Type	Vch No.	Gross Total	Sales
1-May-2008	**A K Traders**	Sales	5	**18,933.53**	18,933.53
1-May-2008	**HDFC Bank (A/c No.151065)**	Sales	6	**6,384.94**	6,384.94
2-May-2008	**A K Traders**	Sales	7	**4,066.36**	4,066.36
2-May-2008	**HDFC Bank (A/c No.151065)**	Sales	8	**11,346.00**	11,346.00
	Grand Total			**40,730.83**	40,730.83

F-4A: Multi Account Columnar Sales Register

Purchase Register

1-May-2008 to 31-May-2008

Page 1

Date	Particulars	Voucher Type	Vch No.	Gross Total	Purchase
2-May-2008	**D K Enterprises**	Purchase	1	**18,513.21**	18,513.21
27-May-2008	**HDFC Bank (A/c No.151065)**	Purchase	2	**5,589.80**	5,589.80
	Grand Total			**24,103.01**	24,103.01

F-4B: Multi Account Columnar Purchase Register

Debit Note Register

1-May-2008 to 31-May-2008

Page 1

Date	Particulars	Voucher Type	Vch No.	Gross Total	Purcha-se
2-May-2008	**D K Enterprises**	Debit Note	1	**600.00**	600.00
	Grand Total			**600.00**	600.00

F-4C: Multi Account Columnar Debit Note Register

Credit Note Register
1-Apr-2008 to 31-May-2008

Page 1

Date	Particulars	Voucher Type	Vch No.	Gross Total	Sales
2-May-2008	**A K Traders**	Credit Note	1	**250.00**	250.00
	Grand Total			**250.00**	250.00

F-4D: Multi Account Columnar Credit Note Register

FAQ: Frequently Asked Questions

FAQ-1: Following ledger accounts are transacted in sales vouchers

Ans:

- **Ledger Accounts:** Fabric Sales, & Apparel Sales & Accessories Sales under 'Sales' Group
- **Ledger Accounts:** Freight, Insurance under Invoicing Charges Group. These amounts are added in the Sales Bill.

Column Heading	Fabric Sales	Apparel Sales	Accessories Sales	Freight	Insurance	Discount	Net Bill Amount

- **Ledger Account:** Discount Under Sales Expenses Group. It is deducted in the Sales Bill.

How I can set the columns in following ways:

Case A: Sales Register showing each ledger account in separate column

Case B: Columnar Sales Register with Group Column

How I can print Sales Register with following columns

Column Heading ->	Sales	Other Charges	Discount	Net Bill Amount
Contents ->	Total of all 3 types of Sales	Total of Invoicing Charges	Discount	

Solution

Solution (Case A): At Bills Register screen, click *F5: Columnar* button (or set *Yes* at *Show Columnar Register* at Voucher Register Configuration screen) to get Columnar Register Alteration screen to define the following Columns contents

Show Voucher Type	Yes
Show Voucher Number	Yes
Type of column	**Name of Accounts**
All items (Automatic Columns)	

Solution (Case B): At Bills Register screen, click *F5: Columnar* button or set *Yes* at *Show Columnar Register* at Voucher Register Configuration screen to get Columnar Register Alteration screen (Fig 1). Now define the following Columns contents. to get Sales Register showing total sales in one column, total tax in one column and other ledger accounts in separate columns,

Account Group / Ledger Column Definition Set Up

Show Voucher Type	Yes
Show Voucher Number	Yes
Type of column	**Name of Accounts**
Group	Sales Accounts
Group	Invoicing Charges
All items (Automatic Columns)	

FAQ-2: We enter Petty Cash expenses / Misc Receipts in Petty Cash Vouchers. About 6 ledger expenses / Income ledger accounts (and one main cash account) are transacted in Petty Cash Vouchers. How I can print Petty Cash Register with following details

Ans: Voucher Date, Voucher Number & Voucher Narration and the ledger wise amount in separate columns for ledger accounts.

You may print columnar Petty Cash Ledger which shows all ledger transactions complementary to Petty Cash Account in the vouchers. So it will show columns for each ledger account and the man cash account as negative / positive figures for Debi / Credit)

At gateway, select Display >Account Books>Ledger

- Click F2:Period:
- Click F5:Columnar and set the column definition as follows:
  - o Set *Yes* at the columns to be printed
  - o At Type of Column, select *All Items (Automatic Columns)*

Now you get the Columnar Petty Cash Book Register, with ledger amount in separate columns for each ledger account and a column total at bottom for each ledger account.

FAQ-3: How I can get the Account Group / ledgerwise summary of transactions of Petty Cash Payment Vouchers

Ans: At Gateway, Select Display> Day Book.

- Click *F4: Chg Voucher* and select the Petty Cash Payment Voucher (of Payment Voucher Type).
- Click *F2:Period*
- Click *F6 Extract* to get the Account Group / Ledger Accountwise transaction summary pf Petty Cash Vouchers.
- Click *F2:Detailed* to get lowest level ledger details

Sale Purchase Summary

03-06

01 Sales & Purchase Summary

In previous chapters, we have discussed about Bill Registers, in Normal (§01/03-04) & Columnar (§01/03-05) Format. In this chapter, we explain various periodical summary reports of Sales, Purchase, Debit Note & Credit Notes. These reports are derived from the Vouchers listed in Bill Register.

02 Sales & Purchase Summary Display

At Gateway, Select *Display > Account Books* to get Accounts Books Menu (F-4A/01-05)

At Account Books Menu, select

- *Sales Register* to get Monthly Summary (F-1A)
- *Purchase Register* to get Monthly Purchases Summary

Sales / Purchase Summary initially shows the monthly total of net Voucher Amount of Sales / Purchase Vouchers, Debit / Credit Notes for each month. Click *F2:Period* button and set the Period (From & To) to get the Monthly Summary for desired period (F-1A)

Sales Register Ctrl + M

Particulars	Sales ABC Academy 1-Apr-2009 to 31-Jul-2009			
	Transactions			Closing Balance
	Debit	Credit		
May		2,000.00	28.78%	2,000.00 Cr
June		2,800.00	40.29%	4,800.00 Cr
July		2,150.00	30.94%	6,950.00 Cr
Grand Total		**6,950.00**	**100.00%**	**6,950.00 Cr**
Average		1,737.50		3,437.50 Cr

F-1A: Periodic Sales Summary (Monthly)

Purchase Register Ctrl + M

Particulars	Purchase ABC Academy 9-10 1-Apr-2009 to 31-Mar-2010			
	Transactions			Closing Balance
	Debit		Credit	
Apr - Jun	2,200.00	19.43%		2,200.00 Dr
Jul - Sep				2,200.00 Dr
Oct - Dec	9,120.00	80.57%		11,320.00 Dr
Jan - Mar				11,320.00 Dr
Grand Total	**11,320.00**	**100.00%**		**11,320.00 Dr**
Average	2,830.00			6,760.00 Dr

F-1B:Periodic Purchase Summary (Quarterly)

Sales Register — ABC Academy 9-10 — Ctrl + M

Particulars	Sales ABC Academy 9-10 1-Apr-2009 to 30-Sep-2009			
	Transactions			Closing Balance
	Debit	Credit		
April		50,000.00	82.03%	50,000.00 Cr
May		2,000.00	3.28%	52,000.00 Cr
June		2,800.00	4.59%	54,800.00 Cr
July		2,150.00	3.53%	56,950.00 Cr
August				56,950.00 Cr
September		4,000.00	6.56%	60,950.00 Cr
Grand Total		**60,950.00**	**100.00%**	**60,950.00 Cr**
Average		10,158.33		55,275.00 Cr

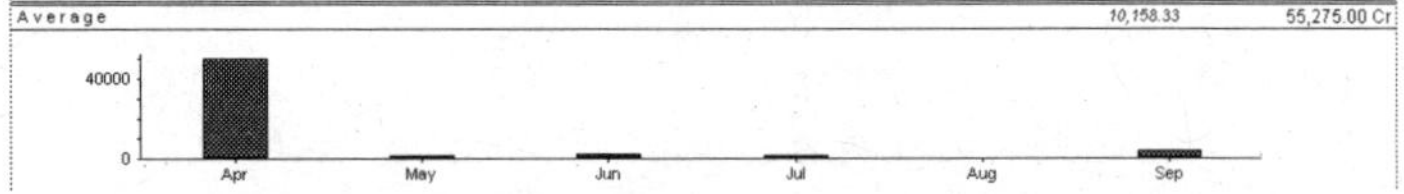

F-1C: Monthly Sales Summary with Graph, Average & % figures

Sales Register Ctrl + M

Particulars	Sales ABC Academy 9-10 1-Apr-2009 to 30-Sep-2009		
	Nett Transactions		Closing Balance
April	50,000.00 Cr	82.03%	50,000.00 Cr
May	2,000.00 Cr	3.28%	52,000.00 Cr
June	2,800.00 Cr	4.59%	54,800.00 Cr
July	2,150.00 Cr	3.53%	56,950.00 Cr
August			56,950.00 Cr
September	4,000.00 Cr	6.56%	60,950.00 Cr
Grand Total	**60,950.00 Cr**	**100.00%**	**60,950.00 Cr**

F-1D: Periodic Sales Summary (Monthly) with % figures

03 Sales / Purchase Summary Display Configuration

At Sales Register Summary (F-2A) / Purchase Register Summary (F-2B) screen. Click *F12:Configure* to get Sales / Purchase Register Summary Configuration screen (F- 2A)

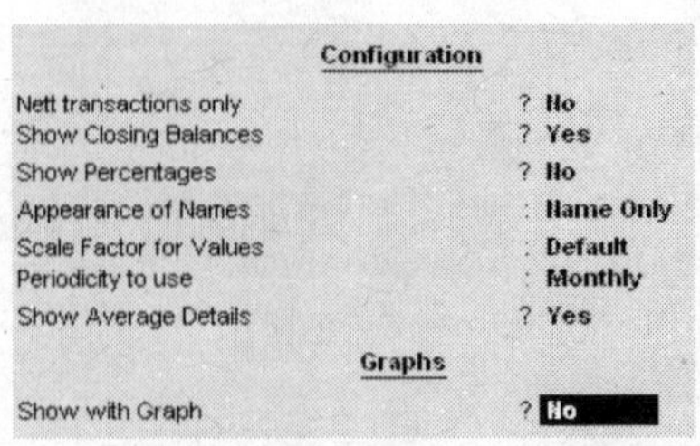

F-2A: Periodical Summary Configuration

F-2B: Period List

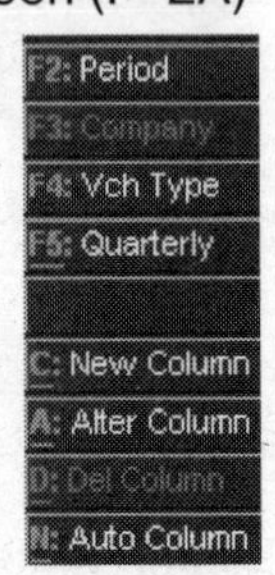

F-2C: Buttons

At Sales Register Configuration screen (F- 2A), set the options as below. The options are quite similar to Periodic Summary Configuration (§06/02-20).

Option	Description
Transaction Columns	At *Net Transactions only*: - Set *Yes* to show the Net of Transactions (Net of Debit or credit), - Set *No* to show both Debit & Credit amount in separate columns
Closing Balance	At Show Closing Balance: - Set *Yes* to show closing balance for each account group / ledger, - Set *No* to omit the Closing Balance Column
Percentage on Sales	At *Show Percentage* - Set *Yes* to show % figures (of the Total figures for the selected period), At *Show Percentage*, The basis of *%: Of Total appears* in the next line - Set *No*, the Percentage column does not appear
Periodicity to Use	At *Periodicity to Use*, select the desired Periodicity from the list (F-2B). The figures are shown according to the period selected
Periodic Average	When you set *No* at *Net Transactions only*, at *Show Average Details*, you may further: - Set *Yes* to show period Average values of each column in a line. - Set *No*, the line containing the Average Figures does not appear.
Show Graph	AT Show Graph - Set *Yes* to show Bar graph for the periodical figures, at the bottom of the report (the area for the report get reduced). - Set *No*, the Graph does not appear

04 Sales / Purchase Summary Display Buttons

The following Table describes Sales / Purchase Register Summary Buttons (F-2C)

Button	Description
F4: Vch TYpe	To get list of Voucher Type to select Voucher Type, to get the Report of selected specific Voucher Type.
F5:Qrtly/Monthly	Toggle button to show Quarterly / Monthly Break up
Column Buttons	Buttons for Columnar Reports –:New Column, A: Alter Column, D:/Delete Column, N:Auto Column

05 Bill Register Extracts

Bill Register Extract (F-3A, F-3B) shows account group / ledger wise summary of all transactions of a specified voucher type (Sales, Purchase, Debit Note, Credit Note, Journal), for a specified period

05.01 Bill Register Extract Display

Voucher Register — Ctrl + M

Extract of All Sales Vouchers 1-Apr-2009 to 31-Mar-2010

Particulars	Debit Amount	Credit Amount
Sundry Debtors	**4,950.00**	
A K Traders	*4,950.00*	
Cash-in-hand	**2,000.00**	
Cash	*2,000.00*	
Sales Accounts		**6,600.00**
Sales		*6,600.00*
Indirect Expenses		**350.00**
Discount on Sales		*(-)150.00*
Freight		*500.00*
:	**6,950.00**	**6,950.00**

F-3A: Sales Register Extract Display

Voucher Register — Ctrl + M

Extract of All Purchase Vouchers 1-Apr-2009 to 31-Mar-2010

Particulars	Debit Amount	Credit Amount
Sundry Creditors		**5,240.00**
B M Suppliers		*5,240.00*
Purchase Accounts	**4,900.00**	
Discount on Purchase	*(-)200.00*	
Purchase	*5,100.00*	
Indirect Expenses	**340.00**	
Freight	*340.00*	
:	**5,240.00**	**5,240.00**

F-3B: Purchase Register Extract Display

At *Register Extract* (F-3A, F-3B), Click *P:Print* to get the Register Extract Printing screen (F-4B). Set the option (similar to Display Configuration options: F-4A), to get the Register Extract in Print Form (F-5A), similar to Display Form (F-3A to F-3D)

Voucher Register — Ctrl + M

Extract of All Debit Note Vouchers 1-Apr-2009 to 31-Mar-2010

Particulars	Debit Amount	Credit Amount
Current Liabilities	**4,150.00**	
Sundry Creditors	4,150.00	
B M Suppliers	*4,150.00*	
Indirect Expenses		**300.00**
Freight		*300.00*
Purchase Accounts		**3,850.00**
Purchase		*3,850.00*
:	**4,150.00**	**4,150.00**

F-3C: Debit Note Register Extract Display

Voucher Register Ctrl + M

Extract of All Credit Note Vouchers 1-Apr-2009 to 31-Mar-2010

Particulars	Debit Amount	Credit Amount
Current Assets		**2,500.00**
Sundry Debtors		2,500.00
A K Traders		*2,500.00*
Sales Accounts	**2,500.00**	
Sales Rebates	*500.00*	
Sales Return	*2,000.00*	
:	**2,500.00**	**2,500.00**

F-3D: Credit Note Register Extract Display

05.02 Bill Register Extract Configuration

At Bill Register (Voucher Register) Configuration screen (of Sales / Purchase / Debit Note or Credit Note – F-1A, F-1B, F-1C), set *Yes* at *Show Extract of Configuration*. Consequently, several options of the Configuration screen will be deactivated to show *Bill Register Extract Configuration* (F-4A).

At *Bill Register Extract Configuration* (F-4A), set the options as follows:

- **Show Inventory wise Extract**: Se *No* to get Accounts Group / Accounts Ledger wise Summary, Set *Yes* to get Stock Group / Stock Ledger wise Summary (this is relevant only when Inventory System is activated)
- **Format:** Select '*Detailed*' to view all ledger accounts of each voucher (F-5A), Select '*Condensed*' to get only the first ledger account (Party / Cash bank) and the net amount of the voucher. You may also toggle through *F1: Detailed / Condensed* toggle button.

Configuration

Show Extract of Register	? **Yes**
Show Inventory-wise Extract	? **No**
Format	: **Detailed**
Appearance of Names	: **Name Only**

F-4A: Bill Register Extract Configuration

Report Titles

Sales Register

Show Extract of Register ? **Yes**

F-4B: Extract Report printing screen

F1: Condensed
F2: Date
F2: Period
F3: Company
F4: Chg Vch
F5: Columnar
F6: Vouchers

F-4C: Extract Report Buttons

05.03 Bill Register Extract Buttons

At Extract Report, you get the following buttons (F-4C):

Button	Description
F1: Detailed / Condensed	Click *Detailed* Toggle button to show all subordinate groups / ledger accounts) Click *Condensed* to show only top level groups / ledger accounts of each Voucher.
F4: Chg Vch	Click to select desired Voucher Type.to show the Register of selected Voucher Type
F6 Voucher / Extract	Click F6: Voucher Toggle button to show the Bill Register (Voucher Register). Click F6: Extract Bill Register Extract

05.04 Bill Register Extract Printing

At Extract Register Display (F-3A to F-3D), click *P:Print* button (or press *Alt+P*) to get *Extract Register* printing screen (F-4B), Set *Yes* to print the Extract Report (F-5A) similar to Extract Register Display.

Sales Register
1-Apr-2009 to 31-Mar-2010

Page 1

Particulars	Debit Amount	Credit Amount
Sundry Debtors	**58,950.00**	
Aakash & Co	*4,000.00*	
A K Traders	*4,950.00*	
T K Das	*50,000.00*	
Cash-in-Hand	**2,000.00**	
Cash	*2,000.00*	
Sales Accounts		**55,950.00**
Cash Discount		*(-)500.00*
Sales		*56,600.00*
Sales Rebates		*(-)150.00*
Direct Incomes		**4,500.00**
Tution Fees		*4,500.00*
Indirect Expenses		**500.00**
Freight		*500.00*
Grand Total :	**60,950.00**	**60,950.00**

F-5A: Register Extract in print

06 Multi Account Register Extract

At the respective Multi Account Register Printing screen (F-10A/03-04, F-10B/03-04, F-12A/03-04, F-12B/03-04), set *Yes* at *Show Extract of Register*. Consequently, all subsequent options are hidden, showing Multi Account Register Extract Printing screen (F-4B). Type Y to print the Extract Report for the specified period (F-6)

Sales Register
1-Apr-2008 to 31-Mar-2009

Page 1

Particulars	Debit Amount	Credit Amount
Sundry Debtors	**24,899.89**	
A K Traders	*24,899.89*	
Bank Accounts	**98,785.48**	
HDFC Bank (A/c No.151065)	*98,785.48*	
Sales Accounts		**1,23,685.37**
Sales		*1,23,685.37*
Grand Total :	**1,23,685.37**	**1,23,685.37**

F-6: Multi Account Register Extract

FAQ: Frequently Asked Questions

FAQ-1: How you can get Sales Summary showing Daily Net Sales figures?

Ans: Display Sales Summary (*Display > Account Books > Sale Register*). Press *F12: Configure* & set as follows:

- Set Yes at *Net Transactions* only, to show Net Sales figures.
- Select *Daily* at periodicity to use to show Daily sales figures.

FAQ-2: How you can get Sales Summary showing Monthly Net Sales figures?

Ans: Display Sales Summary (Display > Account Books > Sale Register). Press *F12: Configure* & set as follows:

- Set Yes at *Net Transactions* only, to show Net Sales figures
- Select *Monthly* at periodicity to use to show monthly sales figure

FAQ-3: How you can get Sales Summary showing Monthly Net Sales & YTD Sales figures

Ans: Display Sales Summary (Display > Account Books > Sale Register). Press *F12: Configure* & set as follows:

- Set Yes at *Net Transactions* only, to show Net Sales figures
- Set Yes at *Closing Balance*, (to get YTD figures)
- Select *Monthly* at Periodicity to use to show monthly Sales figures.

FAQ-4: How you can get monthly summary of Sales for a specific Sales Voucher Type

Ans: At Sales Summary (Display > Account Books > Sale Register)., click F4:Vch Type and select the Voucher Type (of type Sales) to get the Sales Summary in respect of the selected Voucher Type only.

FAQ-5: How you can get break of Cost & Profit / Loss figures of Sales Value

Ans: At sales Summary, click F7:Show Profit toggle button to get the break of Cost & Profit / Loss figures of Sales Value

FAQ-6: How you can get the monthly Average of Sales for a specified period.

Ans: At Sales Summary, Click *F12: Configure*

- Select *Monthly* at *Periodicity to use*
- Select *Yes* at *Show Average Details*

FAQ-07: How I can get the Daily Average of Sales for a specified period.

Ans: At Sales Summary, Click F12: Configure:

- Select *Daily* at *Periodicity to use*
- Select *Yes* at *Show Average Details*

Accounts Receivables & Payables 03- 07

01 Trade Cycle

When Trade is done on credit, the transaction (Sale / Purchase) happens first and then the payment is made (by Debtor to Creditor) to clear up the dues. The complete payment of dues on account of the transaction by the debtor to creditor closes the trade cycle and the ledger account balances of the Party (Customer / Supplier) in their books become zero. So, when the trade cycle is completed (closed), the Party Ledger balance become zero, indicating that no amount is payable or receivable on account of the transaction.

02 Open Account

Open Account means there is some balance still receivable or payable, on account of a specific transaction

Often there are numerous transactions and open balance amounts in respect of multiple deals. To avoid dispute, maintain complete details of transactions, make payment in time and to charge Interest / penalty for delayed payments, it is necessary to keep details of each Transaction and the Open Balance in respect of each such deal.

03 Bill Reference

Bill Reference is the unique Identity Number to link all the transactions in respect of a deal (Invoice Number, Order Number, Contract Number or any other reference initiating the transaction). The Bill Reference Number is used to link all the transactions chronologically and to compute the Balance due (Payable / Receivable) against the Reference Number.

04 Accounts Receivables & Payables (A/R & A/P)

Accounts Receivables & Payables are the statements of all *Open Accounts* with details of transactions and the balance amount Payable & Receivable, in respect of each Bill Reference

A/R & A/P. Vs. Ledger Account

The Party (Debtor / Creditor) Ledger balance also reflects the total amount of Open Bills in respect of all transactions with the Party. So, the Ledger Balance and the total amount of Dues in respect of the Party in the accounts Receivable / Payable statement should match.

So, the Accounts Receivables & Payables statement is the billwise details of open amount of the Ledger Account Balance of the Party.

The ledger account is the chronological statement of each transaction (irrespective of Bill Reference). So, the ledger balance does not show the Bill Reference wise breakup. In ledger, the pivot point is date of transaction, while in Accounts Receivable & Payable, the pivot point is Bill Reference. The Closing Balance Amount of Ledger gives the net balance, but does not give the billwise details of Balance, The Ledger is part of Statutory Books of Accounts, while Accounts Receivable & Payable is just an Accounting statement, used for control of Receivables & Payables by the management, to tackle and manage accounts of multiple transactions.

Here we explain how to enter & maintain Bill Reference details and various reports for Billwise Outstanding of Accounts Receivable & Payables, Age Analysis of open bills etc.

05 Activation of Bill Reference

To maintain Accounts Receivables, first you have to activate the feature for the Company, and then enable the feature for the respective Party Ledger Accounts for which you like to set AR/ AP system. Thus you may enable AR/ AP for selected Parties only with whom you have regular transactions.

05.01 Activation of Bill Reference for Company

To activate Bill Reference feature, at *F11:Features> Accounting Features*, under the section Outstanding Management, at *Maintain Bill by Details* (F-1A)

- **Bill Reference for Traders**:
  - o Set *Yes* to activate Bill Reference for Ledger Accounts under Customer / Supplier and Branch Account Groups
  - o Set *No* (the Bill Reference feature will not be activated for the Company)
- **Bill Reference for Non-Traders:** Having set *Yes* at the above option, you may further set, at *(for Non Trading Accounts also)*:
  - o Set *Yes* to activate Bill Reference for Ledger Accounts for other Ledger Accounts also

- Set *No,* to activate Bill Reference for Ledger Accounts under Customer / Supplier and Branch Account Groups only.

> **Note:** *You may also mainain Bill Ref for Non Trading Account (Like Loan A/c) to manain sevaral open accounts with different due date & interest parameters, of same ledger account*

F-1A: Company Features Set Up

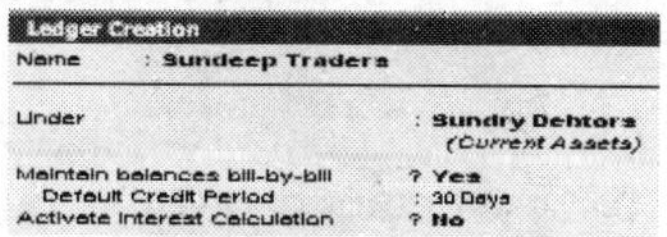

F-1B: Ledger Accounts Set Up

05.02 Activation of Bill Reference for Party Ledger Accounts

Having activated Bill Reference for Company (§05-01, F-1A), you may selectively activate Bill Reference for respective Ledger Accounts for which you like to maintain Bill Reference details

At Ledger creation / alteration screen (§03.02/01-03), at *Maintain Balances Bill* (F-1B)

- Set Yes to enable entry of Bill Reference details (Ref Number & Due Date) in Voucher
- Set *No,* to omit the Bill Reference details in Voucher ((Bill Reference will not be activated for the specific Party)

06 Effective Date entry in Voucher

The Due Date is normally considered from Voucher Date. However, you may opt to compute due date from any other date (other than voucher date like L/R Date, Delivery Challan date, GRN Date, Order Date, Hundi Date, Bank Advice Date etc),

To activate the feature of Effective Date entry in Voucher, at Gateway, select *Accounts Info>Voucher Type >Alter,* select the Voucher Type and set *Yes* at *Use Effective Date for Vouchers* (01/02-07).

In voucher entry, the Voucher Date is first carried in Effective Date field (§04/02-09). To change the Effective Date, F2:Date at Voucher entry to get a subscreen to enter Voucher Date and Effective Date (F-3C). Now you can change the Effective Date.

The Effective Date is shown just blow the Voucher Date in place of Day of Vocher Date (F-3C)

07 Accounting Vouchers Configuration

At Gateway, Click *F12: Configure.* Select Voucher Entry to get *Voucher Entry configuration* screen (§01/02-09). At Accounting Voucher section, set the following options, to enter Bill Reference details in Voucher (F-1/02-09, F-2B/02-09, F-2C/02-09, F-2D/02-09)

Bill Reference Selection: At *Show Table of Bill Details for Selection*:

- Set *Yes* to get the list of open bill references for selection in Bill Reference entry screen (F-2A)
- Set *No*, you will have to enter the Bill Reference (no list will be displayed)

Bill Reference Details: At *Show Bill-wise Details*:

Set *Yes* to get Bill Allocation Table in Voucher entry screen

Set *No* (you will not get the Bill Allocation table).

- **Due Date in Multiple Lines:** Having set *Yes* at *Show Billwise Details*, further at, *Expand into Multiple Lines*
  - Set *Yes* to get multiple lines Bill Allocation screen (e.g. Due Date is also shown in main screen in second line: F-3A)
  - Set *No* to get only one line details for each bill reference (Due Date entered is not shown in main screen, leaving more space)

08 Party Ledger Opening Balance

When you enter the Ledger Opening Balance (§03.02/01-03) of a Party Ledger, for which you have set Bill by Bill Option (F-1B) you get a screen to enter Bill Reference wise break-up of the Opening Balance amount as follows (F-2A)

Date	Enter Date of Bill (Prior to *Books Beginning From* date).
Name	Enter Bill Reference (normally Bill No.) or Advance (as the case be)
Due Date, or Credit Days	Enter the *Due Date* of the Bill or *Credit Days* – Bill Due Date would be arrived at by adding the Credit Days from Date of Bill.
Amount	Enter the Opening Outstanding Bill Amount (not original bill amount, if part paid).
Dr / Cr	Enter the sign, *D* (for Debit Balance) or *C* (for Credit Balance).

The Opening Balance may contain multiple references of several voucher types (like Bills, Debit Notes, Credit Note, etc). and may comprise of Bill References of Open Bills, Advance, On Account also. Each reference would be entered in separate row.

On Account in Opening Balance: If there is any difference between the Ledger opening balance & net of all Billwise break up, that will be treated as *On Account* (F-2A). This amount (difference) is auto computed and carried by Tally (you do not have to enter the *On Account* Amount. (e.g in F- 2A, 12000-9000=3000 is treated as *On Account*).

> **Note:** *In Opening Balance, you do not have to enter amount for* On Account. *It is auto computed as difference between Ledger Balance & Total Balances against Bills & Advances.However, in Voucher, you may enter* On Account *amount..*

Bill-wise Breakup of : **Aakash & Co**
Upto: **₹ 12,000.00 Dr**

Date	Name	Due Date, or Credit Days	Amount	Dr/ Cr
1/3/2008	B/1	1-May-2009	5,000.00	Dr
5/3/2008	C/4		1,000.00	Cr
8/3/2008	B/16	15-May-2009	5,000.00	Dr
			9,000.00	Dr
		On Account:	3,000.00	Dr
			12,000.00	Dr

F-2A: Billwise details Opening Balance entry

09 Vouchers Entry

During Voucher entry, you should enter following Bill Details for transaction (F-3A)

- **Bill Ref Type**: Select the Bill Ref Type from the List (F-3B), as discribed next (§09.01)
- **Bill Reference Number**: Enter / Select the Reference Number, as described next
- **Credit Period / Due Date**: Enter Credit Period or Due Date for New Reference (when Credit Period is entered, the Due date is computed from the Voucher Date & Credit Period and shown)
- **Bill Reference Amount**: Enter the Amount for the respective Bill Reference Number. In case of Against Reference, the Balance amount of Reference is auto carried (which may be changed)

The entry process of each of these elements are explained below in details

09.01 Bill Reference Type

Select the relevant Type of Bill Reference at *Type of Adjustment field*, from the following list (F-3B):

- **New Ref.**: Select it when a new Ref is created (normally a Sales or Purchase Voucher). Consequently, At *Name* field, the Ref Number from the voucher would be auto carried, which you may change.
- **Against Ref.**: Select it when the transaction is for adjustment of an existing reference (like payment is received or made against any existing Ref). All existing references are listed from which select the *Ref* to which the current entry relates.
- **Advance**: Select it when you make a Receipt or Payment as Advance (which would be adjusted against a reference later on).
- **On Account**: Select it (this option does not appear in Sales / Purchase Voucher) when payment is received or made but not against specific Bill or Advance (or Bill reference is not known). *On Account* amounts are not reflected in Interest Statement, Outstanding (Open Bills) Statements or Age Analysis Statement.

Receipt No. 4 — Tuesday 2-Jun-2009, Effective Date 3-6-2009

Particulars		Debit	Credit
Cr **A K Traders**			3,000.00
Agst Ref 1	3,000.00 Cr		
Dr **Cash**		3,000.00	
Name on Receipt : A K Traders			
Narration:		3,000.00	3,000.00
Received ag Bills			

F-3A: Voucher Entry with Bill Details

Method of Adj.
Advance
Agst Ref
New Ref
On Account

F-3B: Reference Type List

Voucher Date
Date of Voucher : 2-6-2009
Effective Date : 3-6-09

F-3C: Effective Date Entry

Usually, a Sale or Purchase Bill contains *New Reference* and Receipt & Payment Voucher contains *Against Reference* (though sometimes it may differ according the flow of business transaction or on Account).

09.02 Bill Due Date / Credit Days

When you select *New ref.* or *Advance*, you can enter Credit Days (carried by default from Ledger account, which you may change in the voucher) in terms of Days, Weeks, Months or Years, or enter Due Date directly (F-4A), as explained next (§09.03).

Sales No. 1 — 1-Apr-2009, Wednesday
Ref. :

Particulars		Debit	Credit
Dr **M P Traders**			22,000.00 (Debit)
New Ref M1	30 Days (1-May-2009)	5,000.00 Dr	
New Ref D30	10 Weeks (10-Jun-2009)	4,000.00 Dr	
New Ref M2	2 Months (1-Jun-2009)	7,000.00 Dr	
New Ref D 60	60 Days (31-May-2009)	4,000.00 Dr	
New Ref 1Y	1 Years (1-Apr-2010)	1,000.00 Dr	
Advance Ad	20 Days (21-Apr-2009)	500.00 Dr	
On Account		500.00 Dr	
Cr **Sales**			22,000.00

F-4A: Credit Days / Due Dates for various period units

You may even enter multiple due dates against same reference, as per different due date. F-4A shows amount due on different dates and entry of Credit Period in different period units (Days, Weeks, Months, Years).

09.03 Due Date Computation Rule

Credit Period may be specified in 4 units: Days, Weeks, Months & Years. The Due date is computed as per following rules, according to the units of Credit Period specified (in whole numbers only)

- **Days**: To enter credit period in days, just type the number of days (e.g 3). You may add d after the credit days (e.g 1d), but that is not necessary for days (if no period unit is given, tally takes it as days). The number of days are added to effective date. So, the Due date will vary according to the number of days in the calendar month in the intervening period. If the credit days is 3 and Effective Date is 28 Feb 2008, then Due date is 2nd March 2008. But if the Effective Date is 28 Feb 2009, the Due date is 3rd March 2009. If the Effective Date is 28 Mar 2009, Due date is 31st March 2009.

- **Weeks**: To enter credit period in weeks, type w after the credit period (e.g 1w to indicate credit period of 1 week, 2w to indicate credit period of 2 weeks The due date would be computed as same day of the following number of weeks. For example, if Effective Date is 26th Feb 2009 (Thu), and the credit period is 1w (1 week), the due date would also be on Thu, 5th March 2009. Similarly, if Effective Date is 28th Feb 2009 (Sat), and the credit period is 2w (2 weeks), the due date would be on Sat, 14th March.
- **Months**: To enter credit period in months, type m after the credit period (e.g 1m to indicate credit period of 1 month, 2m to indicate credit period of 2 months The due date would be computed as same date of the following number of months, irrespective the number of days in the calendar month in the intervening period. For example, if Effective Date is 26th Feb 2009, and the credit period is 1m (1month), the due date would be on 26th Mar 2009. If Effective Date is 26th Feb 2009, and the credit period is 2m (2months), the due date would be on 26th Apr 2009.
- **Years**: To enter credit period in Years, type y after the credit period (e.g 1y to indicate credit period of 1 year, 2y to indicate credit period of 2 Years. The due date would be computed as same date of the following number of years, irrespective the number of days in the year in the intervening period (365 or 366). For example, if Effective Date is 26th Feb 2008, and the credit period is 1y (1year), the due date would be on 26th Feb 2009. If Effective Date is 26th Feb 2008, and the credit period is 2y (2years), the due date would be on 26th Feb 2010.

The following table shows the example of Due Date computation from Voucher Date or Effective Date.

Voucher Date / Effective Date	Credit Period	Due Date
1-4-2008	1 week	8-April-2008
1-2-2008	1 month	1-Mar-2008
1-3-2008	1 month	1-April-2008
1-3-2008	30 days	31-Mar-2008
25-2-2008	7 days	3 Mar-2008
25-3-2008	7 days	1- April-2008
31-3-2009	1 year	31-Mar-2010
31-3-2007	365 days	31 Mar-2008
31-3-2008	365 days	30 Mar-2009
31-3-2009	365 days	31 Mar-2010

- In case of *New* Ref / Advance, you may enter Reference Number and Due Date / Credit Days (or change the default date carried).
- In case of *Agnst Ref,* Due date of selected reference is shown
- In case of *On Account*, due date is not applicable, so it is shown blank.

09.04 Bill Reference Amount

Enter the Amount of each reference and specify *D* for Debit, *C* for Credit for each reference amount.

As soon as the net total (net of all Debits and Credits) of Amount is equal to the amount entered in the Voucher, the bill details entry (F-4A) is terminated and cursor returns to Voucher entry screen to continue Voucher entry.

Example

We show examples of Billwise details entry as follows:

Date	Transaction
10-6-2008	Goods sold to T Pal Bill No. 08-09/110 for 1,500 on 30 days credit
22-8-2008	Goods returned by T.Pal under CN 08-09/010 for Rs 1,850 (from earlier paid purchases)
11-9-2008	Rs 350 paid to T Pal to square up the C/N and Bill by payment voucher

Now the Sale Bill & Credit Notes are adjusted fully

1st Transaction is entered in Sales Voucher (F-5A)

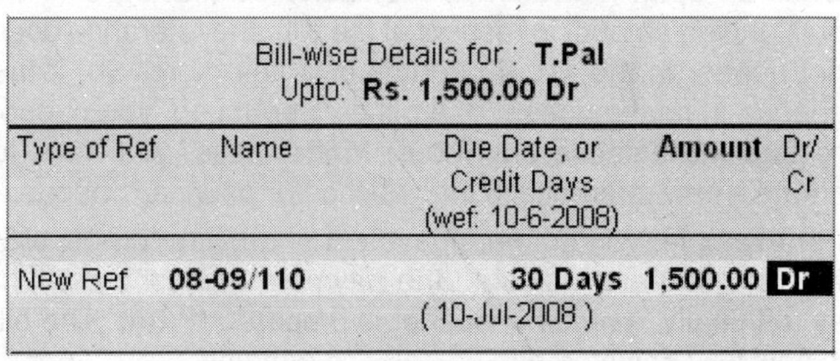

F-5A: Bill Allocation Entry (New Reference)

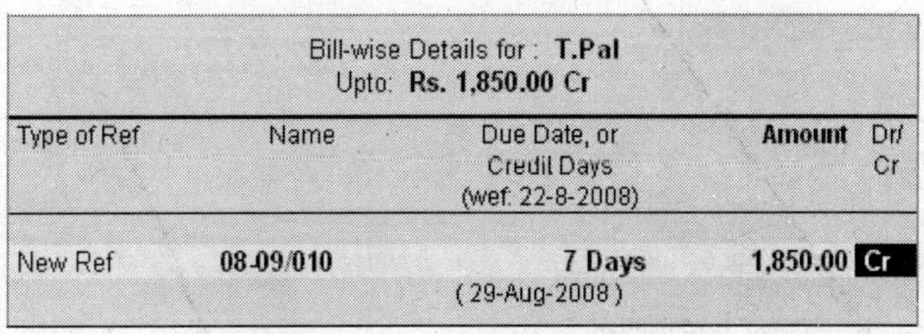

F-5B: C/N entry for goods returned

2nd Transaction is entered in Credit Note Voucher (F-5B) for Goods returned (the goods were purchased' by them earlier)

3rd Transaction is entered in Payment Voucher (F-5C) for the balance payment of Rs 350 is made to square up the Credit Note and the Sales Bill. So, both the references have been selected in the Voucher (F-5C). Otherwise, though the Ledger Balance would show Nil Balance, the Outstanding (Open) Bills Statement would show the Bill and the Credit Note as outstanding.

> **Note:** *In final Payment / Receipt voucher, you should adjust al previous open balances, advance & on accounts to clear the open balances.*

Payment No. 6				11-Sep-2008 Thursday
Particulars			**Debit**	**Credit**
Dr **T.Pal**			350.00	
Cur Bal: 12,250.00 Cr				
Agst Ref 08-09/010	7 Days (29-Aug-2008)	1,850.00 Dr		
Agst Ref 08-09/110	30 Days (10-Jul-2008)	1,500.00 Cr		
Cr **Cash**				350.00
Cur Bal: 1,24,850.00 Dr				
Narration:			350.00	350.00
Money refunded to T Pal after adjusting CN 08-09/010 Bill No. 08-09/110				

F-5C: Payment Voucher Entry with Bill Adjustments

The account of T Pal is squared up. The ledger will show no Balance and the pending Bill statement will also show no Balance.

10 Reversal of Adjusted Reference

Once an open reference is fully adjusted (i.e. there is no outstanding amount in respect of the bill), the reference does not appear in the list of pending bills any more. So, if the cheque in final payment of a bill gets bounced, you cannot restore the balance any more. In that case, you have to create a new reference in the voucher for bounced cheque.

For example, you got final payment of a bill ref 08-09/105, for Rs 1,500 and adjusted the payment against the bill to set off finally. A receipt voucher is prepared (F-6A). The bill is now fully adjusted and no balance remains.

Receipt No. 2			20-Jun-2008 Friday
Particulars		**Debit**	**Credit**
Cr **Kiran Trading Ltd.**			1,500.00
Cur Bal: 0.00 Cr			
Agst Ref 08-09/105	1,500.00 Cr		
Dr **HDFC Bank**		1,500.00	
Cur Bal: 66,500.00 Dr			
Narration:		1,500.00	1,500.00
Ch. No. :352410 Money full received from Kiran Trading Ltd. against the Bill No.:08-09/105			

F-6A: Receipt Voucher entry in respect of a bill paid in full

Now you get back the cheque from bank as it got bounced. So, you have to debit the Customer Account (from whom you got the cheque). So, you have to create a payment voucher in respect of the returned cheque (F-6B). In Reference entry sub screen, you cannot select 'Agnst Ref' as the old Reference number (i.e 08-09/105) will no longer be available in the list.

Payment No. 4			8-Jul-2008 Tuesday
Particulars		**Debit**	**Credit**
Dr **Kiran Trading Ltd.**		1,500.00	
Cur Bal: 1,500.00 Dr			
New Ref Ch. Ret.	1,500.00 Dr		
Cr **HDFC Bank**			1,500.00
Cur Bal: 65,000.00 Dr			
Narration:		1,500.00	1,500.00
Ch. No. :210541 Cheque return from Bank.			

F-6B: Payment Voucher entry in respect of cheque returned

So, you have to select *New Reference* (F-6B) at Bill Reference allocation screen and enter 'Ch. Ret.' (you cannot enter Ref 08-09/105 as *New Reference* again, you may, however, enter the returned cheque number at New Ref).

Receipt No. 6			13-Aug-2008 Wednesday
Particulars		**Debit**	**Credit**
Cr **Kiran Trading Ltd.**			1,500.00
Cur Bal: 0.00 Cr			
Agst Ref Ch. Ret.	1,500.00 Cr		
Dr **HDFC Bank**		1,500.00	
Cur Bal: 66,500.00 Dr			
Narration:		1,500.00	1,500.00
Ch. No. : 253101 Received against returned cheque 210541			

6C: Receipt Voucher entry in respect of fresh cheque received in lieu of the returned cheque

When you get a new cheque, enter a Receipt Voucher and select Against Ref at Bill Allocation screen. Select the pending Reference 'Ch. Ret (F-6C).

Ledger: **Kiran Trading Ltd.**						1-Apr-2008 to 31-Mar-2009
Date	**Particulars**		Vch Type	Vch No.	**Debit**	**Credit**
12-6-2008	**Sales**		**Sales**	08-09/105	1,500.00	
	New Ref 08-09/105 *Goods sales to Kiran Trading Ltd. of Rs.1,500*	1,500.00 Dr				
20-6-2008	**HDFC Bank**		**Receipt**	2		1,500.00
	Agst Ref 08-09/105 *Ch. No. : 210541 Money full received from Kiran Trading Ltd. against the Bill No.:08-09/105*	1,500.00 Cr				
8-7-2008	**HDFC Bank**		**Payment**	4	1,500.00	
	New Ref Ch. Ret. *Ch. No. :210541 Cheque return from Bank.*	1,500.00 Dr				
13-8-2008	**HDFC Bank**		**Receipt**	6		1,500.00
	Agst Ref Ch. Ret. *Ch. No. :253101 Money received against returned Cheque # 210541*	1,500.00 Cr				
			Opening Balance :			
			Current Total :		3,000.00	3,000.00
			Closing Balance :			

F-6D: Ledger account with bill-wise details

Now the account gets squared up. The Customer Ledger (F-6D) shows the entries of cheque return and replaced cheque.

11 Post-Dated Vouchers

You can post-date a Current voucher during entry so that Tally would not update the accounts until the date has arrived and you convert it as Current Voucher. This is useful when you issue or receive post dated cheques, to defer the reflection until made current, but reflect immediately as Post Dated in Party Outstanding Statements (§09/03-08) for tracking.

When the cheque gets matured, at Voucher Alteration screen, convert the Post -Dated Voucher to Current

11.01 Creation / Conversion of Post Dated Voucher

- **Creation of Post Dated Voucher**: To enter an Post Dated Voucher, at Voucher Entry screen, click *T:Post Dated toggle* button: F-7C (or press Ctrl+T). The Voucher would be marked as *Post Dated* as indication (F-7A)
- **Conversion of Post Dated Voucher**: To convert a Post Dated / Current Voucher, get the Voucher in Alter Mode (02/02-17). At Voucher Alteration screen (F-7B)
  - o **Conversion from Current to Post Dated**: Click *T:Post-Dated* toggle button (or press Ctrl+T). The Voucher would be marked as *Post-Dated*
  - o **Conversion from Post Dated to Current**: Click *T:Current* toggle button (or press Ctrl+T). The Post-Dated tag in the voucher would be removed

F-7A: Post Dated Voucher entry

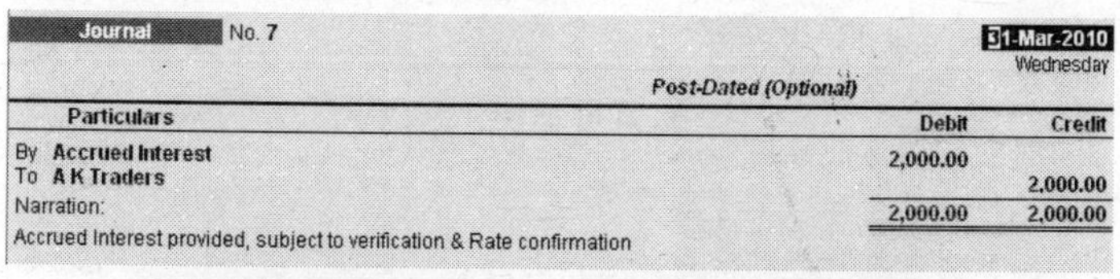

F-7B: Post Dated / Optional Voucher entry

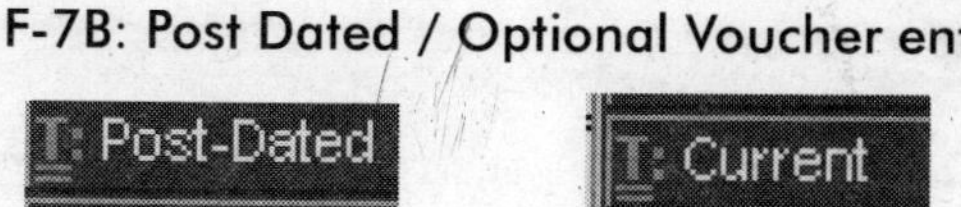

F-7C: Current / Post dated Toggle button in Voucher Entry

The outstanding receivable & payables report shows Post Dated Cheque (06/03-09) until the Post Dated Cheque is regularized.

You may even create a Post dated Optional Voucher (click *L:Optional* & *T:Post Dated toggle button*), to pre plan receipt & issue of post dated cheques.

FAQ: Frequently Asked Questions

FAQ-1: How I can maintain Bill by Bill details to get Billwise Outstanding & Age Analysis Reports for Customers & Suppliers?

Ans:

- Click *F11:Features* and set *Yes* at *Maintain Bill-wise* details to activate Bill by Bill feature for the Company (§05).
- During Creation / Alteration of Ledger Accounts (*Accounts Info>Ledger>Create or Accounts Info>Ledger>Alter*), set *Yes* at *Maintain Balance Bill by Bill* for those ledger accounts for which you like to maintain Bill-wise details (F-1B).

Next, At *Default Credit Period* field, enter the Credit Period (in Days / Month / Weeks/ Years) that you normally offer to Customers. This will be carried to Credit Days for all new bill references entered subsequently (F-1B), which you may change only when required. The default credit days entered substantially reduces data entry time for Credit Days in all subsequent Credit Days / Due Date entry in voucher. You may also enter 0 if you normally do not allow credit (or there is no standard credit period policy).

- Enter the Bill Reference for Opening Balance in Party Ledger Account, with Billwise details (F-2A)
- At Voucher Configuration (At gateway click *F12:Configure >Voucher entry* or at Sales Voucher (F-1/02-09) entry screen click *F12:Configure*), you may set *Yes* at *Show Bill-wise details* (you may further set *Yes* at *Expand into multiple lines* to get a subscreen for Bill Reference details) for convenience of entry of Bill Reference in Voucher.
- Enter Bill Reference in and all vouchers in which such ledger is transacted (F-4A)

Now you can print Open Bills Statements & Age Analysis Reports (discussed in next chapter)

FAQ-2: How to enter *On Account* figures in Bill Reference details?

Ans:

- **In Ledger Opening Balance:** You need not enter *On Account* details of Opening Balance, The difference of Ledger Opening Balance and the sum of all bill reference details entered for of Opening Balance, would be automatically taken as *On Account* (§08)

For example, the Ledger Opening Balance of a Customer Ledger is Rs 5000 Dr. You have entered Bill details for the Opening Balance of Rs 4000 Dr. Then Tally will automatically consider Rs 1000 Dr as *On Account* in Opening Balance details, which you may adjust later against any other outstanding bill of the customer.

- **In Voucher:** During Voucher entry, at Bill Reference screen, select *On Account* (F-3B) and enter the amount in respect of On Account payment / receipt and the corresponding amount of *On Account*.

FAQ-3: How I can maintain Credit period / Due Dates of each Bill ?

Ans:

- At Party Ledger ((*Accounts Info>Ledger>Create or Accounts Info>Ledger>Alter*), set *Yes* at *Maintain Balances Bill by Bill* (F-1B).
- At *Default Credit Period* field, enter the standard Credit Period (in Days / Month / Weeks/ Years) that you normally offer to Customers. This will be carried to Credit Period for all new bill references entered subsequently, which you may change only when required.

  The default credit period entered substantially reduces data entry time for Credit period in all subsequent Credit period entry in voucher. You may also enter 0 if you normally do not allow credit (or there is no standard credit period policy).
- When you select *New Ref* at Reference details entry sub screen in a voucher (or in Opening Balance entry of a Party Ledger Account), the default credit period is carried in Credit period field (F-4A), which you may change. The Due Date would be computed from voucher effective date as per Credit period entered.

FAQ-4: How the Due Date is computed from Voucher Date & Credit Days?

Ans:

a. **Due Date:** In Voucher, the Due Date specified in 2 ways:

   i. **Due Date entry:** You enter the Due Date in the Due Date field

   ii. **Due Date derived:** Due Date is computed by adding the Credit Days to the Effective Date of the voucher.

b. **Effective Date:** In Bills Receivable Reports / Interest computation etc, you may select the option Effective Date to compute the Due Date for Age Analysis, Due Date, Interest computation etc, from effective date instead of Voucher Date.

FAQ-5: How to restore a closed bill (fully paid bill) as Open (outstanding) on cheque dishonour

Ans: When the cheque in respect of a fully paid bill (e.g sale bill against which final payment is received by cheque and the balance is NIL) is returned by the banker unpaid, you create a payment voucher against the bill paid for (F-5A). But in the bill allocation screen, in selection of *Agnst Ref* option, you do not get the bill, as its balance is NIL.

- To create an open bill (outstanding), you have to create a new Ref (instead of *Agnst Ref:* F-6B*)*. You cannot enter the same bill number, as Tally does not allow to create duplicate references (that Ref was created when the original bill was created).
- Enter the returned cheque number in the New Ref (instead of Bill Number: F-6B). In all outstanding report, the returned cheque would be shown outstanding. Next time, when you receive payment against the returned cheque, select *Agnst Ref*, select the returned cheque number and enter the amount received against the cheque (F-6C).

Outstanding Bills Statements

01 Outstanding Bills Statements

We have discussed about Bill Reference (§03/03-07), to track open accounts (Bill References which has not yet squared up). A NEW Reference is created when a new Bill is created, All subsequent transactions related to the Reference are marked as AGAINST Ref, linking the earlier reference created. Until the reference gets squared up, the Balance against the reference is tracked (Open account)

Outstanding Bills Statement lists the details of *Open* Bills (Receivables & Payables). This is very useful to track and manage the *Open Bills*.

We have discussed about the Set Up options (§05.01/03-07, §05.02/03-07) and data entry procedure (§09/03-07) to maintain Bill Reference details to track Open Bills.

Here we discuss the reports relating to Outstanding Bills (Open Bills), commonly referred as *Statement of Outstanding Bills* (§06), which comprise of Statement of Accounts *Receivables* (Open Bills for which amount is receivable by Creditor from Debtor) & *Payables* (Open Bills for which amount is Payable by Debtor to Creditor).

02 Outstanding Reports Menu

All the reports related to Open Bills and their summary / analysis reports are placed under *Outstandings Menu* (F-1)

Select *Display > Statement of Accounts> Outstandings* to get Party *Outstandings Menu* (F-1)

The Outstanding Menu (F-2A) shows option for following outstanding Reports.

- *Receivables* menu gives you Reports for all Accounts receivables (from Customers)
- *Payables* menu gives you Reports for all Accounts Payables (to Suppliers).
- *Ledger menu* gives reports of outstanding reports of a selected Ledger Account of Customer/Supplier.
- *Group* menu gives reports showing consolidated figures all ledger accounts of a selected Group Customer/ Supplier.

03 Outstanding Reports Configuration Table

The following Table shows the various Display Configuration & Printing Options among various Reports.

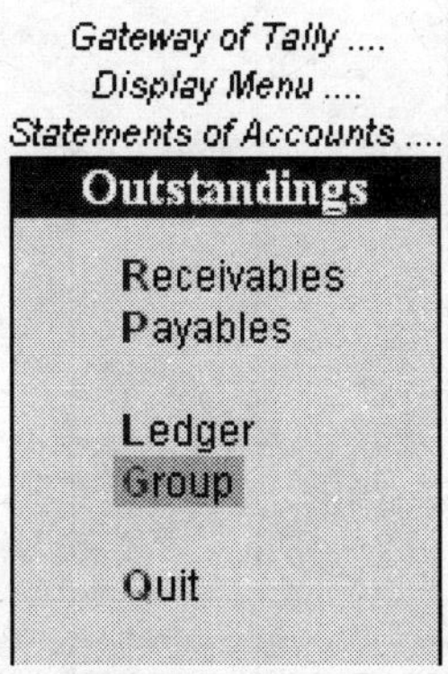

F-1: Outstanding Reports Menu

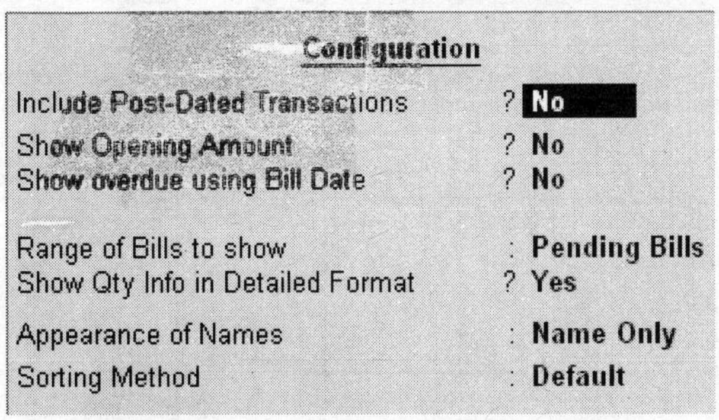

F-2A: Outstanding Reports Configuration

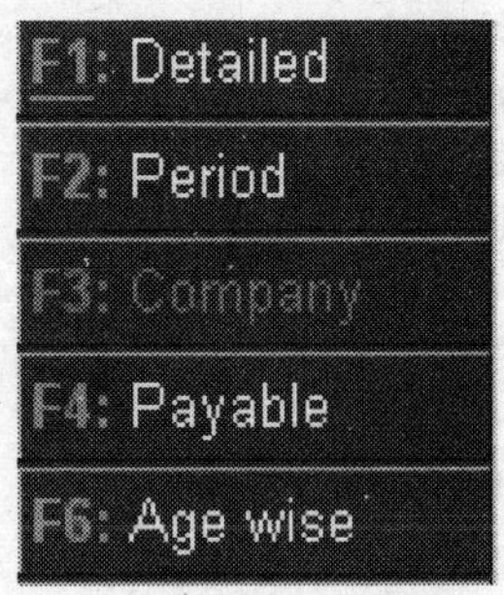

F-2B: Buttons

	Display								Muti Account Pritnting		
Options	**Outstadings /Age Analysis Configuration**	**Outstadings Printing**	**Party Outstadings Configuration**	**Party Outstadings Printing**	**Party Age Analysis Configuration**	**Party Age Analysis Printing**	**Group Outstadings Configuration**	**Group Outstadings Printing**	**Outstadings Printing**	**Party Outstadings**	**Group Outstadings**
	F-2A	**F-3C**	**F-6B**	**F-6D**	**F-7B**	**F-7D**	**F-9B**	**F-9D**	**F-11B**	**F-11C**	**F-16A**
Format	-	-	-	√	-	√	-	√	√	√	√
Include Post dated Transactions	√	√	√	√	√	√	-	-	√	√	-
Show Opening Amount	√	√	-	-	-	-	-	-	-	-	-
Show Overdue using Bill date	√	√	√	√	√	√	-	-	√	√	-
Range of Bills to Show	√	√	√	√	√	√	√	√	√	√	√
Show Quantity Info in Detailed Format	√	-	-	-	-	-	-	-	-	-	-
Show Bills of Type	-	-	√	√	√	-	-	-	-	-	-
Print Reminder Letter	-	-	-	√	-	√	-	-	-	-	-
Show Group Name	-	-	-	√	-	√	-	-	-	√	-
Show Contact Details	-	-	-	√	-	√	√	√	-	√	√
Start Fresh page for each Account	-	-	-	√	-	√	-	-	-	√	-
Show Nett Balances	-	-	-	-	-	-	√	√	-	-	√
Expand all Levels in Details							√	√	-	-	√
Method								√			√
Party Address to Print										√	-

Buttons

The following Table shows the Buttons at Various Report Display screen

Options	Outstadings / Age Analysis	Party Outstadings	Party Age Analysis	Group Outstadings
F-2B	F-6C	F-7C	F-9C	
F1:Detailed / Condensed	√	-	√	√
F2:Period	√		√	√
F4:Payable / Receivable	√			
F6:Age Wise	√	√	√	√
F4:Ledger -	√	√	-	
C:Contact -	√	√	-	
B:Bill Settlement	-	√	√	-
F4:Group -	-	-	√	
F5:Led-wise	-	-	-	√
F7:Billwise	-	-	-	√

04 Outstanding Reports Display Configuration

The contents of Receivables & Payables Reports may be configured through their respective Configuration screen. Click *F12:Configure* at the respective report to get the corresponding configuration screen (F-2A).

At Outstanding Bills Reports Configuration (F-2A), set the options as described below.

- **Post Dated Cheques**: To show / hide the Post dated Cheques not yet deposited to Bank (mostly the dealers pay post dated cheques – cheques dated on due date of the Bill / mutually agreed date of payment. The post dated cheques are banked on the cheque date only). Though in the books, the post dated cheques are not accounted for, this is important from the view of reminding the Debtor for payment. By paying a post dated cheque, though no real payment is made, but the Debtor is not expected for reminding in respect of outstanding appearing in the books, for which the post dated cheques are received.

At *Include Post dated Transactions:*

- o Set *Yes* at to show the amount of post-dated vouchers also in a separate column (Post Dated Amount), against the related reference. Having set Yes at *Include Post dated Transactions*, you get the following column
    - **Final Balance**: It shows the amount due after considering the Post dated Cheques
- o Set *No* to omit the Post dated column. Consequently you get the following columns
    - **Due date:** Shows the Due Date of the Bill as per Bill date / effective Date and the credit days
    - **Age of Bill in Days:** Number of days elapsed from the Due Date till the Report End Date

- **Opening Amount**: At *Show Opening Amount*
    - o Set *Yes* to show the original bill amount (opening balance in case of previous year's open bill) in a separate column, apart from the Pending Amount.
    - o Set *No* to hide the Opening Amount of the Bill.
- **Overdue Basis:** At *Show Overdue using Bill date*:
    - o Set *Yes* to compute overdue days from the bill date (without considering the due date / credit days)
    - o Set *No* to compute overdue days from due date (Bill Date + Credit days)
- **Open Bills Type**: At *Range of Bills to Show*, select:
    - o *Pending Bills* to list all outstanding bills (whether due or not).
    - o *Overdue Bills* to list only overdue bills (outstanding bills whose due date is within the report period)
- **Quantity Details**: This is relevant only when Inventory is activated and Stock Item quantity are entered in the Invoice. At *Show Quantity Info at Detailed Format*,:
    - o Set *Yes* to show the Quantity figures in *Detailed* format (i.e when *F1:Detailed* button is clicked at vertical button bar in the report display screen).
    - o Set No to omit Quantity details

05 Outstanding Reports Display Buttons

The following buttons are available at Outstanding Reports (F-2B)

- **F1: Detailed / Condensed**: To switch between Condensed / Detailed mode. Click *Detailed* button to see all the vouchers related to the reference
- **F4: Payable/ Receivable:** To switch between Payable / Receivable Report
- **F6: Agewise**: To show Age Analysis Report
- **F7:** Billwise/Bill Partywise

06 Outstanding Reports Display

The Report shows following columns depending upon the various configuration options set (F-3A & F-3B):

- ***Opening Amount:*** Shows original bill amount (opening balance in case of previous year's open bill) in a separate column, apart from the Pending Amount. This column appears when you set Yes at *Show Opening Amount.* Set No to hide the Opening Amount of the Bill.

- ***Pending Amount:*** This column shows outstanding balance of the bill, as on the report end date.
- **Due Date**: This column shows the Due Date of the Bill as per Credit days (Bill Date + Credit Days).
- **Age of Bill in Days**: Shows the Number of days elapsed from the Due Date (when *No* is set at *Show Overdue using Bill Date)* / Bill Date (when Yes is set at *Show Overdue using Bill date)*
- **Final Balance**: It shows the amount due after considering the Post dated Cheques. This column appears when Yes is set at *Include Post dated Transactions*

Bills Outstanding — Ctrl + M

Bills Receivable — 1-Apr-2009 to 31-Mar-2010

Date	Ref. No.	Party's Name		Opening Amount	Pending Amount	Due on	Age of Bill in Days
1-Feb-2009	S/5	M P Traders		12,000.00 Dr	5,000.00		423
	1-Feb-2009 Opening Balance		12,000.00 Dr				
	1-Jun-2009 Receipt	1	7,000.00 Cr				
31-Mar-2009	Advance	M P Traders		4,000.00 Dr	2,000.00	31-Mar-2009	365
	31-Mar-2009 Opening Balance		4,000.00 Dr				
	1-Jun-2009 Receipt	1	2,000.00 Cr				
2-Jun-2009	2	A K Traders		2,800.00 Dr	2,300.00	2-Jul-2009	302
	2-Jun-2009 Sales	2	2,800.00 Dr				
	1-Nov-2009 Credit Note	2	500.00 Cr				
1-Jul-2009	3	A K Traders		2,150.00 Dr	2,150.00		273
	1-Jul-2009 Sales	3	2,150.00 Dr				
1-Nov-2009	4	M P Traders		42,000.00 Dr	42,000.00	31-Dec-2009	150
	1-Nov-2009 Sales	4	42,000.00 Dr				
				62,950.00 Dr	53,450.00		

F-3A: Outstanding Bills (Receivables)

Bills Outstanding — Ctrl + M

Bills Payable — 1-Apr-2009 to 31-Mar-2010

Date	Ref. No.	Party's Name		Opening Amount	Pending Amount	Due on	Age of Bill in Days
1-Jun-2009	1	A K Traders		2,000.00 Cr	2,000.00	1-Jun-2009	303
	1-Jun-2009 Credit Note	1	2,000.00 Cr				
1-Jun-2009	12	M P Traders		2,200.00 Cr	5,240.00	31-Jul-2009	303
	1-Jun-2009 Purchase	1	2,200.00 Cr				
	1-Nov-2009 Purchase	2	3,040.00 Cr				
				4,200.00 Cr	7,240.00		

F-3B: Outstanding Bills (Payables)

07 Outstanding Reports Printing

At Outstanding Reports Display (F-3A, F-3B), click P:Print button to get Outstanding Reports Printing screen (F-3C) showing printing options similar to Display Configuration options (F-2A). Set the options and type Y to get the Outstanding Statement in Print (F-3D)

Report Titles
Bills Receivable

Include Post-Dated Transactions ? **No**
Show Opening Amount ? **Yes**
Show overdue using Bill Date ? **Yes**

Range of Bills to show : **Pending Bills**
Format : **Detailed**

F-3C: Outstanding Statement Printing

Bills Receivable
1-Apr-2009 to 31-Mar-2010

Date	Ref. No.	Party's Name		Opening Amount	Pending Amount	Due on	Age of Bill in Days
1-Jun-2009	DN/6	B M Suppliers		2,500.00 Dr	2,500.00	1-Jul-2009	303
	1-Jun-2009 Debit Note	1	2,500.00 Dr				
4-Jun-2009	4	A K Traders		2,800.00 Dr	2,800.00	4-Jul-2009	300
	4-Jun-2009 Sales	3	2,800.00 Dr				
1-Jul-2009	3	A K Traders		2,150.00 Dr	2,150.00	1-Jul-2009	273
	1-Jul-2009 Sales	4	2,150.00 Dr				
1-Aug-2009	DN/15	B M Suppliers		1,650.00 Dr	1,650.00	31-Aug-2009	242
	1-Aug-2009 Debit Note	2	1,650.00 Dr				
1-Sep-2009	5	Aakash & Co		4,000.00 Dr	4,000.00	4-Sep-2009	211
	1-Sep-2009 Sales	5	4,000.00 Dr				
				13,100.00 Dr	13,100.00		

F-3D: Outstanding Statement (Receivables) in Print

08 Age Analysis

Agewise Analysis Report (F-4A) is a compact view of Outstanding Bills, analysing the Outstanding into several convenient age slab, for better control and management of Receivables & Payables, as per Aging Slab set (§08.02)

Bills Receivable — 1-Apr-2008 to 22-Aug-2008

Date	Ref. No.	Partys' Name	Pending Amount	(< 30 days)	30 to 45 days	45 to 60 days	60 to 90 days	(> 90 days)
15-Feb-2008	07-08/009	A.K.Das	3,000.00					3,000.00
22-Mar-2008	07-08/012	P.Roy	1,000.00					1,000.00
31-Mar-2008	07-08/014	Susma Stores	10,000.00					10,000.00
18-Jun-2008	08-09/014	P.Roy	7,000.00				7,000.00	
18-Jun-2008	08-09/008	Susma Stores	5,000.00				5,000.00	
23-Jun-2008	08-09/005	A.K.Das	12,000.00			12,000.00		
15-Aug-2008	08-09/023	Susma Stores	4,040.00	4,040.00				
			42,040.00	4,040.00		12,000.00	12,000.00	14,000.00

F-4A: Age Analysis Display (Receivables)

Bills Outstanding — Ctrl + M

Bills Payable — 1-Apr-2009 to 31-Mar-2010

Date	Ref. No.	Party's Name		Pending Amount	(< 180 days)	(> 180 days)
1-Jun-2009	1	A K Traders		2,000.00		2,000.00
	1-Jun-2009 Credit Note	1	2,000.00 Cr			
1-Nov-2009	2	A K Traders		500.00	500.00	
	1-Nov-2009 Credit Note	2	500.00 Cr			
2-Nov-2009	12	B M Suppliers		3,040.00	3,040.00	
	2-Nov-2009 Purchase	2	3,040.00 Cr			
2-Nov-2009	16/25	B M Suppliers		3,040.00	3,040.00	
	2-Nov-2009 Purchase	3	3,040.00 Cr			
				8,580.00	6,580.00	2,000.00

F-4B: Age Analysis Display (Payables)

08.01 Ageing Method

At Outstanding Bills Receivables (F-4A) / Payables (F-4B) report, Click *F6: Agewise* button to first specify the Ageing Method as follows (F-5A)

- **Ageing by Bill Date:** Select *Ageing by Bill Date* to compute due / overdue days are computed from the voucher date.
- **Ageing by Due Date**: Select *Ageing by Due Date* to compute due / overdue days are computed from the due date (Voucher date + credit period)

Ageing Analysis

Method of Ageing :

Ageing Methods
Ageing by Bill Date
Ageing by Due Date

F-5A: Ageing Method

Company Ageing Alteration

Company: **Agni Computers1**

From	: **0**	To	: **30**
From	: **30**	To	: **60**
From	: **60**	To	: **90**
From	: **90**	To	: **0**

F-5B: Ageing Slab

08.02 Ageing Slab

After selecting the method of ageing (F-5A), the *Company Ageing Analysis* screen (F-5B) appears, to create multiple age slabs for better control of outstanding.

At *Company Ageing Analysis* screen (F-5B), set as follows:

- **Slab beginning value**: At *From* field, enter the start value of the Slab. The first slab will start from zero value

- **Slab end value**: At *To* field, enter the end value of the Slab. The last slab will have zero value (but represents any higher value) to indicate termination of Age Slab

This way, create multiple slabs for each slab range (e.g. From 0 to 30, 30-45, 45-60, 60-90, 90 to rest of days.). At last line enter 0 to end and Press Yes to show the Bill Receivable Report with specified columns for each slab (F-5B)

The Ageing period as specified applies to all Parties for both Receivable/Payables, until you change again. So, next time, when you print any Age Analysis report, the Age period as set by you will be carried as default, which you may change again. This helps you to set a standard Ageing period

Restrict the Ageing Periods in 3-4 slabs only, otherwise the Ageing report will be too wide to view in one screen and you will have to pan the screen sideways to see all the slabs.

08.03 Age Analysis Report Display

Having set the Aging Method & Age Slab, you get the Age Analysis Display (F-4A, F-4B), as per Aging Method & Age Slab set.

08.07 Multi Part Age Analysis Statement Printing

If too many slabs are specified, the report may be too wide and extend to multiple parts (see Report Print Preview for each part), as explained below:

- If you set *Yes* at *Include Post dated Transactions*, then the columns for Opening Amount (if set Yes), Pending Amount, Post dated Amount & Final Balance for each Bill is repeated (shown) in each Part, while the Agewise slabs are spread over multiple Parts.
- If you set *No* at *Include Post dated Transaction,* then the columns for Opening Amount (if set Yes), & Pending Amount for each Bill is repeated (shown) in each Part, while the Agewise slabs are spread over multiple Parts.

Printing of Multiple Part Report has been described earlier (05/02-14)

09 Party Outstanding Statement

The Age analysis Report shows separate statement of Receivables or Payables in respect of all Parties. This is

Bills Payable
1-Apr-2009 to 31-Mar-2010

Date	Ref. No.	Party's Name		Pending Amount	(< 180 days)	(> 180 days)
1-Jun-2009	1	**A K Traders**		**2,000.00**		**2,000.00**
	1-Jun-2009 Credit Note	*1*	*2,000.00 Cr*			
1-Nov-2009	2	**A K Traders**		**500.00**	**500.00**	
	1-Nov-2009 Credit Note	*2*	*500.00 Cr*			
2-Nov-2009	12	**B M Suppliers**		**3,040.00**	**3,040.00**	
	2-Nov-2009 Purchase	*2*	*3,040.00 Cr*			
2-Nov-2009	16/25	**B M Suppliers**		**3,040.00**	**3,040.00**	
	2-Nov-2009 Purchase	*3*	*3,040.00 Cr*			
				8,580.00	**6,580.00**	**2,000.00**

F-5C: Age Analysis Statement in Print

08.04 Age Analysis Report Configuration

At Age Analysis Statement Display (F-4A, F-4B), click *F12:Configure* to get *Age Analysis Configuration* screen, similar to *Outstanding Reports Configuration* (F-2A) to set the Configuration options.

08.05 Age Analysis Report Buttons

At Age Analysis Statement Display (F-4A, F-4B), you get Buttons similar to Outstanding Reports (F-2B).

08.06 Age Analysis Statement Printing

At Age Analysis Statement Display (F-4A, F-4B), click *P:Print* button to get Age Analysis Printing screen, showing printing options similar to Outstanding Report Printing screen (F-3C).

Set the options and type Y to get the Age Analysis Report in Print (F-5C)

useful to the status of Receivables / Payables form all Parties for Financial Management.

Party Outstanding Report (or Ledger Outstanding Report) *shows the Receivables & Payables (both) in respect of a selected Party (F-6A). So, it is more useful to track a Party for outstanding Bills, Party and follow up to clear the open accounts.*

09.01 Party Outstanding Statement Display

Ledger : **A.K.Das** — **1-Apr-2008 to 31-Mar-2009**

Date	Ref. No.			Opening Amount	Pending Amount	Due on	*Age of Bill in Days*
15-Feb-2008	07-08/009			30,000.00 Dr	**3,000.00 Dr**	21-Mar-2008	*410*
	15-Feb-2008 Opening Balance		*30,000.00 Dr*				
	12-Jul-2008 Receipt	*4*	*12,000.00 Cr*				
	12-Aug-2008 Receipt	*5*	*15,000.00 Cr*				
23-Jun-2008	08-09/005			20,000.00 Dr	**12,000.00 Dr**	8-Jul-2008	*281*
	23-Jun-2008 Sales	*08-09/005*	*20,000.00 Dr*				
	12-Jul-2008 Receipt	*4*	*8,000.00 Cr*				
13-Jul-2008	08-09/016			200.00 Cr	**200.00 Cr**	13-Jul-2008	*261*
	13-Jul-2008 Credit Note	*08-09/016*	*200.00 Cr*				
				49,800.00 Dr	**14,800.00 Dr**		

F-6A: Party Outstanding Statement

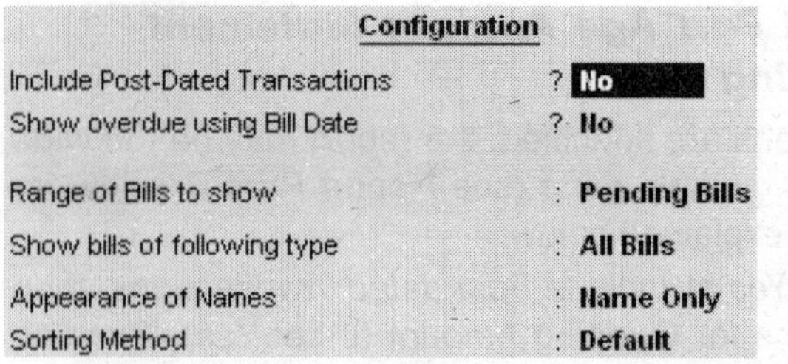

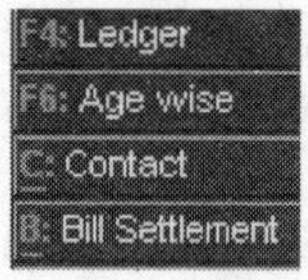

F-6B: Party Outstanding Configuration F-6C: Buttons

At Outstanding Menu (F-1), select *Ledger and then select a Party Ledger Account to get the* Ledger Outstanding Report for the selected Party (F-6A).

09.02 Party Outstanding Configuration

At *Party Outstanding Display* (F-6A), click F12:Configure to get *Party Outstanding Configuration* screen (F-6B), to set the following options:

- **Post Dated Cheques:** At *Include Post dated Transaction*:
  - o Set Yes to show Post dated Cheque also,
  - o Set No to omit Post Dated Cheques
- **Overdue Bills:** At *Show Overdue using Bill date*
  - o Set Yes to compute the Overdue Days from Bill date,
  - o Set No to compute the Overdue Days from Due Date (Bill date + Credit Period).
- **Open Bill Types:** At *Range of Bills to Show*, select
  - o *Outstanding Bills: Pending Bills* to show all Outstanding Bills (whether overdue or not)
  - o *Overdue Bills: Overdue Bills* to show only Overdue Bills.
- **Bills Type:** At *Show Bills of Following Type*, select:
  - o *All Bills:* To Show all Open Bills (whether due or not)
  - o *Due Bills only:* To show Open Bills which has become Due
  - o *Over Due Bills*: To show Open Over due Bills (Bill date has creased)

09.03 Party Outstanding Statement Buttons

At *Party Outstanding Display* (F-6A), you get following buttons (F-6C)

- **F1: Detailed / Condensed**: To switch between Condensed / Detailed mode. Click *F1:Detailed* button to see all the vouchers related to the reference (F-6A). Click *F1: Condensed* to show the net outstanding of each open reference
- **F4: Ledger**: To select a Party Ledger Account from the list of Party Ledgers (§09.01)
- **F6: Agewise**: To set up Age Slab and get Age Analysis Report (§08.01)
- **C: Contact**: To view Contact details of the Party
- **B:Bills Settlement**: To create Receipt / Payment voucher for Final payment (§11)

09.04 Party Outstanding Printing

At *Party Outstanding Display* (F-6A), click *P: Print* button to get *Party Outstanding Printing* screen (F-6D), showing the following printing options, similar to *Party Outstanding Configuration options* (F-6B). Set the printing options (F-6D) and type *Y* to get the *Party Outstanding Report* in print (F-6E)

- **Post dated Cheques:** At *Include Post dated Transaction*:
  - o Set Yes to show Post dated Cheque also,
  - o Set No to omit Post Dated Cheques
- **Report Form:** At *Print Reminder Letter,*
  - o Set Yes to print the Outstanding Report in the form of Reminder letter,
  - o Set No to print in Normal Outstanding Report Form
- **Parent Group:** At *Show Group Name,*
  - o Set Yes to print the Parent Group Name (just bemow the Ledger Name in parenthesis).
  - o Set *No* to omit the Group Name.
- **Overdue Method:** At *Show Overdue using Bill date,*
  - o Set Yes to compute the Overdue Days from Bill date,
  - o Set No to compute the Overdue Days from Due Date (Bill date + Credit Period).
- **Contact Details:** At *Show Contact Details,*
  - o Set Yes to print the Contact details of each Party just below the Ledger name (useful for follow up)
  - o Set No, the contact details are not printed in the Report.
- **Open Bill Types:** At *Range of Bills to Show*, select
- **Outstanding Bills:** *Pending Bills* to show all Outstanding Bills (whether overdue or not)
- **Overdue Bills:** *Overdue Bills* to show only Overdue Bills.
- **Format:** At *Format:*
  - o Select *Condensed* to show the net amount of the Bill,
  - o Select *Detailed* to show all the transaction related to the Bill.
- **Bills Type:** At *Show Bills of Following Type*, select:
  - o *All Bills:* To Show all Open Bills (whether due or not)
  - o *Due Bills only:* To show Open Bills which has become Due
  - o *Over Due Bills*: To show Open Over due Bills (Bill date has creased)
- **Page Break:** At *Start fresh page for Each Account*
  - o Set *Yes* to start each ledger account in a new page only (leaving the blank space of the page). This is useful when you distribute the Ledger Outstanding report to Parties / Sales People.
  - o Set *No*, to continue next ledger in the same page, if space is available, to save paper space.

Report Titles

T K Das

Bill-wise Details

Include Post-Dated Transactions	? **Yes**
Print Reminder Letter	? **No**
Show Group Name	: **No**
Show overdue using Bill Date	? **Yes**
Show Contact Details	? **No**
Range of Bills to show	: **Pending Bills**
Format	: **Detailed**
Show bills of following type	: **All Bills**
Start fresh page for each Account	? **Yes**

F-6D: Party Outstanding Printing

T K Das

Bill-wise Details

1-Apr-2009 to 30-Sep-2009

Date	Ref. No.	Opening Amount	Pending Amount	*Post-Dated Amount*	Final Balance
1-Apr-2009	1st Inst	10,000.00 Dr	6,000.00 Dr		6,000.00 Dr
	1-Apr-2009 Sales 1 10,000.00 Dr				
	6-Jun-2009 Receipt 4 4,000.00 Cr				
1-Apr-2009	2nd Inst	10,000.00 Dr	3,000.00 Dr		3,000.00 Dr
	1-Apr-2009 Sales 1 10,000.00 Dr				
	9-Jun-2009 Receipt 5 7,000.00 Cr				
1-Apr-2009	4th Inst	10,000.00 Dr	10,000.00 Dr	*10,000.00 Cr*	
	1-Apr-2009 Sales 1 10,000.00 Dr				
	1-Mar-2010 Receipt 17 10,000.00 Cr Post-Dated				
1-Apr-2009	3rd Inst	10,000.00 Dr	10,000.00 Dr	*10,000.00 Cr*	
	1-Apr-2009 Sales 1 10,000.00 Dr				
	3-Jan-2010 Receipt 12 10,000.00 Cr Post-Dated				
		40,000.00 Dr	29,000.00 Dr	*20,000.00 Cr*	9,000.00 Dr

F-6E: Party Outstanding in Print

10 Party Age Analysis

Like Age Analysis Report (F-4A, F-4B), which shows Age Analysis of all Parties, Party Age Analysis shows Age Analysis Statement of a selected Party

So, Party Agewise Analysis Report is another view of Party Outstanding Bills, analysing the Outstanding into several convenient age slab for better control and management of Receivables & Payables

10.01 Party Age Analysis Display

At Party Outstanding Statement (F-6A), click *F6: Age-wise* to get the Age Analysis report (F-7A). You may set Ageing Method (F-5A), Ageing Slab (F-5B) as described for Age Analysis, to get the Party Age Analysis Report (F-7A)

Ledger Outstandings — ABC Academy 9-10 — Ctrl + M

Ledger : **A K Traders** — **1-Apr-2009 to 31-Mar-2010**

Date	Ref. No.	Opening Amount	Pending Amount	(< 180 days)	180 to 270 days	(> 270 days)	On Account
1-Jun-2009	1	2,000.00 Cr	2,000.00 Cr			2,000.00 Cr	
4-Jun-2009	4	2,800.00 Dr	2,800.00 Dr			2,800.00 Dr	
1-Jul-2009	3	2,150.00 Dr	2,150.00 Dr			2,150.00 Dr	
1-Nov-2009	2	500.00 Cr	500.00 Cr	500.00 Cr			
	Sub Total	*2,450.00 Dr*	*2,450.00 Dr*				
31-Mar-2010	*On Account*	*8,700.00 Cr*	*8,700.00 Cr*				*8,700.00 Cr*
		6,250.00 Cr	6,250.00 Cr	500.00 Cr		2,950.00 Dr	8,700.00 Cr

F-7A: Party Age Analysis Display

Configuration

Include Post-Dated Transactions	? **No**
Show overdue using Bill Date	? **Yes**
Range of Bills to show	: **Pending Bills**
Show bills of following type	: **All Bills**
Appearance of Names	: **Name Only**
Sorting Method	: **Default**

F-7B: Party Age Analysis Configuration

F1: Detailed
F2: Period
F3: Company
F4: Ledger
F6: Age wise
C: Contact
B: Bill Settlement

F-7C: Buttons

10.02 Party Age Analysis Configuration

At Party Age Analysis Report (F-7A), click *F12:Configure* to get *Party Age Analysis Configuration* screen (F-7B) to set the following options:

- **Post dated Cheques:** At *Include Post dated Transaction*:
  - o Set Yes to show Post dated Cheque also,
  - o Set No to omit Post Dated Cheques
- **Overdue Method:** At *Show Overdue using Bill date*,
  - o Set Yes to compute the Overdue Days from Bill date,
  - o Set No to compute the Overdue Days from Due Date (Bill date + Credit Period).
- **Open Bill Types:** At *Range of Bills to Show*, select
  - o *Outstanding Bills: Pending Bills* to show all Outstanding Bills (whether overdue or not)
  - o *Overdue Bills: Overdue Bills* to show only Overdue Bills.
- **Bills Type:** At *Show Bills of Following Type*, select:
  - o *All Bills:* To Show all Open Bills (whether due or not)
  - o *Due Bills only:* To show Open Bills which has become Due
  - o *Over Due Bills*: To show Open Over due Bills (Bill date has creased)

10.03 Party Age Analysis Configuration Buttons

At Party Age Analysis Report (F-7A), you get following Buttons (F-7C):

- **F1: Detailed / Condensed**: To switch between Condensed / Detailed mode. Click *F1:Detailed* button to see all the vouchers related to the reference (F-6A). Click *F1: Condensed* to show the new outstanding of each open reference
- **F4: Ledger**: To select a Party Ledger Account from the list of Party Ledgers
- **F6: Agewise**: To set up Age Slab (F-5B) and get Age Analysis Report
- **C: Contact**: To view Contact details of the Party
- **B:Bills Settlement**: To create Receipt / Payment voucher for Final payment for the Bill as explained later (§11)

10.04 Party Age Analysis Printing

At *Party Age Analysis Report* (F-7A), click *P:Print* button to get *Party Age Analysis Printing* screen (F-7D), showing printing option similar to *Party Age Analysis Configuration* screen (F-7B). Set the printing options and type Y to get *Party Age Analysis Report* in print (F-7E)

Report Titles
Aakash & Co
Bill-wise Details

Include Post-Dated Transactions	? **No**
Print Reminder Letter	? **No**
Show Group Name	: **No**
Show overdue using Bill Date	? **No**
Show Contact Details	? **No**
Range of Bills to show	: **Pending Bills**
Format	: **Condensed**
Show bills of following type	: **All Bills**
Start fresh page for each Account	? **Yes**

7D: Party Age Analysis Printing screen

displayed at the top of the Ledger Outstanding Report. This way, you may select one or more open bills for which you like to make settlement.

11.01 Bill Settlement Entry

You enter Receipt Voucher (to settle Bills Receivable), or enter Payment Voucher (to settle Bills Payable), and enter the details of Bill Reference of the Bills settled.

However, there is an alternate method to create Payment / Receipt Voucher in respect of settlement of open Bills, through Bills Settlement option, as described below:

At Party Outstanding statement (F-6A), Click *B:Bills Settlement* button (or press Alt+B) to get the Bill Settlement screen (F-8A), showing the Party Name & the outstanding amount. Now create a voucher (F-8B) to settle the open Bills, as follows:

A K Traders
Bill-wise Details
1-Apr-2009 to 30-Sep-2009

Date	Ref. No.				Opening Amount	Pending Amount	(< 120 days)	120 to 150 days	(> 150 days)	On Account
1-Jun-2009	1				2,000.00 Cr	**2,000.00 Cr**		**2,000.00 Cr**		
	1-Jun-2009	*Credit Note*	*1*	*2,000.00 Cr*						
4-Jun-2009	4				2,800.00 Dr	**2,800.00 Dr**	**2,800.00 Dr**			
	4-Jun-2009	*Sales*	*3*	*2,800.00 Dr*						
1-Jul-2009	3				2,150.00 Dr	**2,150.00 Dr**	**2,150.00 Dr**			
	1-Jul-2009	*Sales*	*4*	*2,150.00 Dr*						
Sub Total					*2,950.00 Dr*	*2,950.00 Dr*				
30-Sep-2009	*On Account*				*100.00 Cr*	***100.00 Cr***				***100.00 Cr***
	31-Mar-2008	*Opening Balance*		*1,000.00 Dr*						
	4-May-2009	*Journal*	*1*	*1,100.00 Cr*						
	1-Jun-2009	*Receipt*	*3*	*3,000.00 Cr*						
	2-Jun-2009	*Payment*	*5*	*2,000.00 Dr*						
	31-Aug-2009	*Payment*	*7*	*1,000.00 Dr*						
					2,850.00 Dr	**2,850.00 Dr**	**4,950.00 Dr**	**2,000.00 Cr**		**100.00 Cr**

7E: Party Age Analysis in Print (Detailed)

> **Note:** *You may Print Reminder Letter with all details of Ledger Outstanding in the Form of Letter, to be sent to the concerned Party.*

11 Bills Settlement

Bills settlement is a feature to conveniently create a voucher to clear up the pending balance of open bill of a Party. The voucher may be created conveniently through Outstanding Display screen.

At Party Outstanding statement, select the Bills to be settled (move the cursor over the Bill and press Space bar – the colour of the selected Bills will change). As you select the Bills, the total pending amount of the selected Bills is

- **Voucher Type:** The voucher type Payment / Receipt is shown as follows:
  - o *Payment*: If the Bill is payable, the Voucher Type *Payment* is shown (as a Payment voucher is to be created to settle the Bill)
  - o *Receipt*: If the Bill is Receivable the Voucher Type Receipt is shown(as a Receipt voucher is to be created to settle the Bill)
- **Voucher Date:** The current date is shown by default (which you may change if necessary)
- **Account:** Select the desired Cash / Bank Account through which the transaction is carried out
- **Narration**: Enter the Voucher Narration

Bill Settlement

(for : A K Traders Amount : ₹ 2,000.00 Cr)

Voucher Type	: **Payment**
Voucher Date	: **31-Mar-2010**
Account	: **Bank of India**
Narration	: Final payment of all bills due

F-8A: Bill Settlement Entry

Accounting Voucher Creation Ctrl + M

Payment No. **17** **31-Mar-2010**

Account : **Bank of India**

Particulars		Amount
A K Traders		**2,000.00**
Agst Ref **1**	**2,000.00 Dr**	
Narration:		**2,000.00**

Final payment of all bills due

F-8B: Bill Settlement Voucher

You get the voucher entry screen (F-8B) for full settlement, showing the outstanding balance in respect of each Bill Reference for the selected Ledger.

- **Full Settlement**: To make full settlement of the outstanding of the Party, set Yes at *Accept (Y/N)* prompt to save the voucher, (or press *Ctrl+A)*
- **Part Settlement**: If only a part payment is received or you like to make any amendment in the voucher, type N and change the Amount in the voucher. Now set Yes at *Accept (Y/N)* prompt to save the voucher, (or press *Ctrl+A)*

This is an alternative & quicker way to create voucher for final settlement of dues of Party, to square up the open accounts.

During voucher entry you may enter the Bank Details (if transaction is made through Bank), print the Receipt Voucher and the Formal Receipt (with Bank details where applicable) as explained for Receipt Voucher printing, in earlier chapter.

You may enter Receipt / payment Vouchers in usual way selecting the Bill Reference, as described earlier (§09/03-07). The resulting voucher is created in same manner irrespective the method how you create the voucher.

12 Account Group Outstanding

In Outstanding Report, you get the Outstanding Statements in respect of All Parties. In Ledger Outstanding Report, you get the Outstanding Statements in respect of a selected Party (F-9A). The *Account Group Outstanding report gives report for Parties for a selected Account Group*

If the Parties are numerous, then often the Parties are divided into several Groups / Sub Groups. For example, Area / Zone wise (viz North Zone, South Zone, District A, District B, etc), Registration status wise, e/.g Registered parties, Unregistered Parties, etc, or a combination of them.

The advantage is that you can control them in a better way and get separate outstanding Reports for each such Group / Sub Group created, while getting report for a Group comprising of several sub groups at different levels

Account Group Outstanding Reports gives the collective reports in respect of the Parties belonging to the selected section (Group / Sub Group).

12.01 Account Group Outstanding Display

Select Display > Statement of Accounts > Outstandings > Group. Select a Customer / Supplier Group from a list of Customer / Supplier Account Groups to get outstanding list in respect of all subordinate Groups & Party Ledgers for a selected Accounts Group (F-9A)

Group Outstandings Ctrl + M

Particulars	*Sundry Debtors* **ABC Academy 9-10** 1-Apr-2009 to 31-Mar-2010 **Pending Bills**	
	Debit	Credit
Aakash & Co	19,310.50	
A K Traders	4,950.00	11,200.00
T K Das	9,000.00	
A Bose & Co	2,000.00	
Grand Total	**35,260.50**	**11,200.00**

F-9A: Account Group Outstanding Display

Configuration

Range of Bills to show	: **Pending Bills**
Show Nett Balances	? **No**
Show Contact Details	? **Yes**
Appearance of Names	: **Name Only**
Scale Factor for Values	: **Default**
Sorting Method	: **Default**
Expand all levels in Detailed Format	? **Yes**

F-9B: Account Group Outstanding Report Configuration

F1: Detailed
F2: Period
F3: Company
F4: Group
F5: Led-wise
F6: Age wise
F7: Billwise

F-9C Button

12.02 Account Group Outstanding Configuration

At *Account Group Outstanding* report (F-9A), click *F12: Configure* to get *Account Group Outstanding* Configuration screen (F-9B). Now, set the options as follows:

- **Open Bill Types:** At *Range of Bills to Show*, select
  - o *Outstanding Bills: Pending Bills* to show all Outstanding Bills (whether overdue or not)
  - o *Overdue Bills: Overdue Bills* to show only Overdue Bills.

- **Balance Type**: At *Show Nett Balances:*
  - o Set *Yes* to show the net balance (Net Dr / Cr) of all child ledger accounts of the selected Group.
  - o Set *No* to show both the Debit & Credit Balance separately in respect of the subordinate Parties / Groups
- **Contact Details:** At *Show Contact Details,*
  - o Set Yes to print the Contact details of each Party just below the Ledger name (useful for follow up)
  - o Set No, the contact details are not printed in the Report.
- **Expand all levels into Detailed Format**: At *Expand all levels into Detailed Format,*
  - o Set *Yes* (in Detailed Format) to show all the transactions in respect of the Open Bill.
  - o Set *No* to show Baalnce Amount only in respect of the Open Bill.

12.03 Accounts Group Outstanding Buttons

At *Account Group outstanding* report (F-9A), you get the following buttons (F-9C):

Report Titles
Sundry Debtors
Group Outstandings

Range of Bills to show	:	**Pending Bills**
Show Nett Balances	?	**No**
Scale Factor for Values	:	**Default**
Method of information	:	**Grouped**
Format	:	**Condensed**
Expand all levels in Detailed Format	?	**No**
Show Contact Details	?	**No**

F-9D: Group Outstanding printing

- **F1: Condensed / Detailed:** Select Condensed to show the net figures for each Group. Select Detailed to *show the details of each Party.*
- **F4: Group:** To select an Account Group
- **F5: Ledgwise / Groupwise:** Toggle button to show Groupwise / Alphabetical Ledger Name wise report.
- **F6: Agewise:** To define Age Slabs and print the Age Analysis Report for the Account Group
- **F7:Billwise / Summary:** Toggle button to get Report in sequence of Bill Numbers / Partywise Net figures
  - o *Column Options:* When *F7:Summary* option is selected,, the various buttons to create columns are also available, to create columnar report with Multiple Period / Multiple Companies, for comparison.

12.04 Accounts Group Outstanding printing

At Account Group outstanding report (F-9A), click *P:Print* button to get *Account Group Outstanding Printing* screen (F-9D), showing printing option similar to *Account Group Outstanding Configuration* screen (F-9B). Set the printing options and type Y to the *Account Group Outstanding Report* in print (F-9E)

13 Account Group Age Analysis

Like Age Analysis Reports (§08), Accounts Group Age Analysis Report shows the outstanding bills in respect of all Account Groups / Ledger Accounts under the selected Account Group.

Sundry Debtors
Group Outstandings
1-Apr-2009 to 31-Mar-2010

Page 1

Particulars			Pending Bills	
			Debit	Credit
Aakash & Co	Duryodhan Singh	03312345678	19,310.50	
A K Traders			4,950.00	11,200.00
T K Das			9,000.00	
A Bose & Co	B Bose	033 52525252	2,000.00	
Grand Total			**35,260.50**	**11,200.00**

F-9E: Group Outstanding in Print

13.01 Account Group Age Analysis Display

At Account Group Outstanding report (F-9A), Click *F6: Agewise* button. Set the *Method of Age Analysis* and *Age Analysis Slab* as explained in Age Analysis Report (F-5A/ fB) to get Account Group Age Analysis report (F-10A).

Group Outstandings **ABC Academy** Ctrl + M

Particulars	*Sundry Debtors* **ABC Academy** 1-Apr-2009 to 31-Mar-2010 **Pending Bills**		Sundry Debtors *ABC Academy* *1-Apr-2009 to 31-Mar-2010* **(< 270 days)**		*Sundry Debtors* **ABC Academy** 1-Apr-2009 to 31-Mar-2010 **270 to 365 days**	
	Debit	Credit	Debit	Credit	Debit	Credit
A K Traders	10,550.00	2,000.00			4,450.00	2,000.00
M P Traders	57,650.00	5,240.00	*42,000.00*		2,000.00	5,240.00
Grand Total	**68,200.00**	**7,240.00**	**42,000.00**		**6,450.00**	**7,240.00**

F-10A: Account Group Outstanding Age Analysis

13.02 Group Age Analysis Configuration

At Account Group Age Analysis Report (F-10A), click *F12: Configure* to get Account Group Age Analysis Configuration screen, similar to Account Group Outstanding Report Configuration screen (F-9B)

13.03 Group Age Analysis Buttons

At Age Analysis Report (F-10A), you get buttons similar to Account Group Outstanding Report Buttons (F-9C)

13.04 Accounts Group Outstanding printing

At Account Group Analysis Report (F-10A), click *P:Print* button to get *Account Group Age Analysis Printing* screen, showing printing option similar to *Account Group Outstanding Configuration* screen (F-9D). Set the printing options and type Y to the *Account Group Age Analysis Report* in print, with contents similar to *Account Group Age Analysis Display* (F-10A).

14 Multi Account Outstanding Statements

We have discussed Outstanding Bills Statements from Display, for one account (Ledger / Group).

Multi Account Outstanding Statement menu provides printing of Outstanding (F-3A & F-3B) & Age Analysis (F-4A & F-4B) Reports more conveniently

Select *Multi Account Printing > Outstanding Statements* to get *Multi Account Outstanding Reports Printing* Menu (F-11A), with options similar to Outstanding Reports under Display (F-1).

Gateway of Tally ....
Printing Menu ....

Outstandings

Receivables
Payables

Ledger
Group

Quit

F-11A: Multi Account Outstanding Menu

Report Titles
Bills Receivable

From (blank for beginning)	:	**1-4-2009**
To (blank for end)	:	**31-3-2010**
Include Post-Dated Transactions	?	**Yes**
Show Opening Amount	?	**Yes**
Show overdue using Bill Date	?	**Yes**
Range of Bills to show	:	**Pending Bills**
Format	:	**Detailed**

F-11B: Multi Account Outstanding Receivables/ Payables Printing screen

Report Titles
Aakash & Co
Bill-wise Details

From (blank for beginning)	:	**1-4-2009**
To (blank for end)	:	**31-3-2010**
Include Post-Dated Transactions	?	**No**
Print Reminder Letter	?	**No**
Party Address to Print	:	**Primary**
Show Group Name	:	**No**
Show overdue using Bill Date	?	**No**
Show Contact Details	?	**No**
Range of Bills to show	:	**Pending Bills**
Format	:	**Condensed**
Show bills of following type	:	**All Bills**
Start fresh page for each Account	?	**Yes**

F-11C: Multi Account Ledger Outstanding Printing screen (All Accounts)

Range of Bills

All Bills
Overdue Bills
Pending Bills

F-11D: Bills Range List

Types of Bills

All Bills
Credit Bills
Debit Bills

F-11E: Bills Types List

Bills Receivable
1-Apr-2009 to 31-Mar-2010

Page 1

Date	Ref. No.	Party's Name		Opening Amount	Pending Amount	Due on	Age of Bill in Days
1-Apr-2009	1st Inst	**T K Das**		10,000.00 Dr	**6,000.00**	1-Apr-2009	*364*
1-Apr-2009	*Sales*	*1*	*10,000.00 Dr*				
6-Jun-2009	*Receipt*	*4*	*4,000.00 Cr*				
1-Apr-2009	2nd Inst	**T K Das**		10,000.00 Dr	**3,000.00**	1-Apr-2009	*364*
1-Apr-2009	*Sales*	*1*	*10,000.00 Dr*				
9-Jun-2009	*Receipt*	*5*	*7,000.00 Cr*				
1-Jun-2009	DN/6	**B M Suppliers**		2,500.00 Dr	**2,500.00**	1-Jul-2009	*303*
1-Jun-2009	*Debit Note*	*1*	*2,500.00 Dr*				
4-Jun-2009	4	**A K Traders**		2,800.00 Dr	**2,800.00**	4-Jul-2009	*300*
4-Jun-2009	*Sales*	*3*	*2,800.00 Dr*				
1-Jul-2009	3	**A K Traders**		2,150.00 Dr	**2,150.00**	1-Jul-2009	*273*
1-Jul-2009	*Sales*	*4*	*2,150.00 Dr*				
1-Aug-2009	DN/15	**B M Suppliers**		1,650.00 Dr	**1,650.00**	31-Aug-2009	*242*
1-Aug-2009	*Debit Note*	*2*	*1,650.00 Dr*				
1-Sep-2009	5	**Aakash & Co**		4,000.00 Dr	**4,000.00**	4-Sep-2009	*211*
1-Sep-2009	*Sales*	*5*	*4,000.00 Dr*				
				33,100.00 Dr	**22,100.00**		

F-12: Multi Account Receivables Report

14.01 Multi Account Receivables

At *Multi Account Outstanding Reports Printing* Menu (F-11A), select *Receivables* to get *Multi Account* Receivables printing screen (F-11B). Set the options to get *Multi Account Receivables* Report (F-12)

of Reminder letter,

- o Set No to print in Normal Outstanding Report Form
- **Parent Group:** At *Show Group Name,*
  - o Set Yes to print the Parent Group Name (just bemow the Ledger Name in parenthesis).

Bills Payable

1-Apr-2009 to 31-Mar-2010

Date	Ref. No.	Party's Name		Opening Amount	Pending Amount	Due on	Age of Bill in Days
1-Jun-2009	1	**A K Traders**		2,000.00 Cr	**2,000.00**	1-Jun-2009	303
	1-Jun-2009	*Credit Note 1*	*2,000.00 Cr*				
1-Nov-2009	2	**A K Traders**		500.00 Cr	**500.00**	1-Nov-2009	150
	1-Nov-2009	*Credit Note 2*	*500.00 Cr*				
2-Nov-2009	12	**B M Suppliers**		3,040.00 Cr	**3,040.00**	2-Dec-2009	149
	2-Nov-2009	*Purchase 2*	*3,040.00 Cr*				
2-Nov-2009	16/25	**B M Suppliers**		3,040.00 Cr	**3,040.00**	2-Dec-2009	149
	2-Nov-2009	*Purchase 3*	*3,040.00 Cr*				
				8,580.00 Cr	**8,580.00**		

F-13 Multi Account Payables Report

14.02 Multi Account Payables

At *Multi Account Outstanding Reports Printing* Menu (F-11A), select *Receivables* to get *Multi Account* Receivables printing screen (F-11B). Set the options to get *Multi Account Payables* Report (F-13)

14.03 Multi Account Party Outstanding

As explained for Ledger Outstanding (§09), you may print Party Leger Outstanding of a number of selected Parties in one go.

At *Multi Account Outstanding Reports Printing* Menu (F-11A), select *Ledger* to get *Multi Account Ledger Printing* Menu with following options:

- **One Account:** To select a ledger Account
- **All Accounts:** To select All Ledger Accounts or multiple selected Accounts as desired
- **Group of Accounts:** To select All Ledger Accounts or multiple selected Ledger Accounts as desired, from one Account Group

At *Party Ledger Accounts Printing screen* (F-11C), set options as follows:

- **Period:** Enter the Report period:
  - o *From*: Enter the starting date of Report (leave blank to start from the Accounts beginning date)
  - o *To:* Enter the Ending date of Report (leave blank to report upto the last date)
- **Post dated Cheques:** At *Include Post dated Transaction*:
  - o Set Yes to show Post dated Cheque also,
  - o Set No to omit Post Dated Cheques
- **Report Form:** At *Print Reminder Letter,*
  - o Set Yes to print the Outstanding Report in the form
  - o Set *No* to omit the Group Name.
- **Overdue Method:** At *Show Overdue using Bill date,*
  - o Set Yes to compute the Overdue Days from Bill date,
  - o Set No to compute the Overdue Days from Due Date (Bill date + Credit Period).
- **Contact Details:** At *Show Contact Details,*
  - o Set Yes to print the Contact details of each Party just below the Ledger name (useful for follow up)
  - o Set No, the contact details are not printed in the Report.
- **Open Bill Types:** At *Range of Bills to Show*, select
  - o Outstanding Bills: *Pending Bills* to show all Outstanding Bills (whether overdue or not)
  - o Overdue Bills: *Overdue Bills* to show only Overdue Bills.
- **Format:** At *Format:*
  - o Select *Condensed* to show the net amount of the Bill,
  - o Select *Detailed* to show all the transaction related to the Bill.
- **Quantity Details:** This is relevant only when you implement Inventory system. At *Show Quantity in detailed Format*:
  - o Set *Yes* to show the Inventory details of the Bill
  - o Set No, Inventory details wil not be shown
- **Bills Type:** At *Show Bills of Following Type*, select:
  - o *All Bills:* To Show all Open Bills (whether due or not)
  - o *Due Bills only:* To show Open Bills which has become Due
  - o *Over Due Bills*: To show Open Over due Bills (Bill date has creased)

- **Foreign Currency Details:** This is relevant only when foreign currency is also implemented. At *Show Bills in Foreign Exchange*:
  - o Set *Yes* to show the Inventory details of the Bill
  - o Set No, Inventory details wil not be shown
- **Page Break:** At *Start fresh page for Each Account*
  - o Set *Yes* to start each ledger account in a new page only (leaving the blank space of the page). This is useful when you distribute the Ledger Outstanding report to Parties / Sales People.
  - o Set *No*, to continue next ledger in the same page, if space is available, to save paper space.

A K Traders
Bill-Wise Details
(Sundry Debtors)
1-Apr-2009 to 31-Mar-2010

Date	Ref. No.	Opening Amount	Pending Amount	Due on	Age of Bill in Days
1-Jun-2009	1	2,000.00 Cr	2,000.00 Cr	1-Jun-2009	303
4-Jun-2009	4	2,800.00 Dr	2,800.00 Dr	4-Jul-2009	300
1-Jul-2009	3	2,150.00 Dr	2,150.00 Dr	1-Jul-2009	273
1-Nov-2009	2	500.00 Cr	500.00 Cr	1-Nov-2009	150
	Sub Total	2,450.00 Dr	2,450.00 Dr		
31-Mar-2010	On Account	8,700.00 Cr	8,700.00 Cr		
		6,250.00 Cr	6,250.00 Cr		

F-14 Multi Account Party Ledger

To : **Abc Computers Ltd.**
810 Bangur

From : **Agni Computers1**
21, Lenin Sarani
Kolkata-700013

Dear Sir/Madam,

Dated: **1-Apr-2009**

Sub : Outstandings

Given below is the detail of amounts outstanding against your name in our books till today.

We request you to take immediate steps for settling the overdue bills and oblige.

Date	Particulars	Due on	Overdue by	(< 700 days)	700 to 900 days	(> 900 days)
1-Apr-2006	3	1-Apr-2006	(1095 days)			3,180.00
1-Apr-2006	4	1-Apr-2006	(1095 days)			250.00
1-Jul-2006	37	1-Jul-2006	(1004 days)			1,000.00
1-Aug-2006	69	5-Sep-2006	(938 days)			2,000.00
1-Sep-2006	72	1-Oct-2006	(912 days)			4,000.00
1-Sep-2006	74	9-Jan-2007	(812 days)			12,000.00
2-Nov-2006	110	2-Nov-2006	(880 days)		18,200.00	
31-Mar-2007	111	31-Mar-2007	(731 days)		50,000.00	
					68,200.00	22,430.00

On Account	**49,971.00 Cr**
Total	**40,659.00 Dr**

Yours faithfully,
Accountant

F-15: Reminder Letter of Outstanding Bills

14.04 Party Outstanding Reminder

To follow up the customers to pay their outstanding dues, you may print Outstanding Reminder, which is letter like report for a Party (F-15). The contents are similar to party Age Analysis with some text embedded in it. This letter is then sent to respective Party urging them to pay outstanding bills.

At Multi Account Ledger Printing screen (F-11C), set Yes at *Print Reminder Letter*) to print *Party Outstanding Reminder* (F-15).

14.05 Multi Account Group Outstanding

At *Multi Account Outstanding Reports Printing* Menu (F-11A), select *Group* to get *Multi Account Group Printing* screen (F-16A). Set the printing options to print Multi Account Group Outstanding Report (F-16B).

Report Titles

Sundry Debtors
Group Outstandings

From (blank for beginning)	:	**1-4-2009**
To (blank for end)	:	**31-3-2010**
Range of Bills to show	:	**Pending Bills**
Show Nett Balances	?	**No**
Scale Factor for Values	:	**Default**
Method of information	:	**Grouped**
Format	:	**Detailed**
Expand all levels in Detailed Format	?	**Yes**
Show Contact Details	?	**Yes**

F-16 A: Multi Account Group Outstanding printing

Sundry Debtors
Group Outstandings
1-Apr-2009 to 31-Mar-2010

Page 1

Particulars	Pending Bills	
	Debit	Credit
Aakash & Co	19,310.50	
A K Traders	4,950.00	11,200.00
T K Das	9,000.00	
A Bose & Co	2,000.00	
Grand Total	35,260.50	11,200.00

F-16 B: Multi Account Group Outstanding Report

FAQ: Frequently Asked Questions

FAQ-1: I want to get the list of all outstanding Bills Receivable.

Ans: *Select Display > Statement of Accounts > Outstanding > Receivables. Now select the Account Group (All Items / Sundry Debtors) to get the outstanding list.*

FAQ-2: I want to get the list of all outstanding bills receivable from all Customers also showing the Post Dated Cheques Received.

Ans: *Display > Statement of Accounts > Outstanding > Receivables. Now select the Account Group (All Items / Sundry Debtors) to get the outstanding list. Click F12:Configuration and:*

- Set Yes at Post Dated Transactions
- Select Pending Bills at Range of Bills to show

FAQ-3: I want to get the list of all overdue bills receivable.

Ans: *Display > Statement of Accounts > Outstanding > Receivables. Now select the Account Group (All Items / Sundry Debtors) to get the outstanding list.*

Click F12:Configuration and set Yes at Overdue Bills at Range of Bills to show, To get the overdue bills as per Bill Date, *else set No* To get the overdue bills as per Effective Date (e.g L/R Date, Delivery Date, Oder Date, Hundi Date, etc).

FAQ-4: How I can get Age Analysis of all pending Bills of a Party as per my own Ageing Period and Method?

Ans: At gateway, select *Display > Statement of Accounts > Outstanding > Ledger*),Select the Party Ledger Account. click *F6: Agewise* button. Select the *Method of Aging* as follows:

- To get the Aging as per Bill date, select *Aging by Bill Date*
- To get the Aging as per Due date, select *Aging by Due Date*

Having selected the Method of Aging, you get a screen to set up the Aging Period for the Company. This Ageing period applies to all parties (Receivables & Payables) until you change again.

FAQ-5: How I can get outstanding Bills showing original bill amount?

Ans: To see the original bill amount (of current year bills or Opening balance for previous year bills), at *Display > Statement of Accounts > Outstanding > Receivable. Select the Account Group (All Items / Sundry Debtors) to get the outstanding list. Click F12:Configuration and set Yes at Show Opening Amount*

FAQ-6: How I can get outstanding Bills of a specific Party?

Ans: *At Display > Statement of Accounts > Outstandings > Ledger. Select a Party Ledger Account to get the* Ledger Outstandings Report for the selected Party.

FAQ-7: How I can get outstanding Bills of a specific Party with Party Contact details & special Notes?

Ans:

- *At Display > Statement of Accounts > Outstandings > Ledger, select a Party Ledger Account to get the* Ledger Outstandings Report for the selected Party.
- Click C: *Contact* button at button bar to view Mailing Name, Address, S T Regn. No and Contact Details (Contact Person, Phone, Fax but not e-mail) and Notes entered if any, for the Ledger.

FAQ-8: How I get the list of all outstanding bills of all Customers of a selected Account Group?

Ans: *Select Display > Statement of Accounts > Outstandings > Group.* Select the desired Account Group (Under Sundry Debtor/Creditor). *Click F12: Config* and select *Pending Bills at Range of Bills to show*

FAQ-9: How I can print reminder for Parties for Outstanding bills?

Ans: At *Multi Account Printing > Outstanding statements>Ledger* to get Ledger menu, select *All Accounts,* to print for all ledger Accounts.

Set Yes at *Print Reminder Letters.* Next set the Aging period. The reminder letters will be printed only for those Parties having Pending Bill Amount (In Receivables, the reminder letter will not be printed where the pending amount is zero or there is credit balance).

Overdue Interest

01 Interest on overdue Trade Bills

We have already discussed Ledger Interest, normally applicable for Loans, Customers & Supplier (§01/02-11). Such Interest are of the nature of Finance Cost, for using money.

Apart from Interest on use of Money, Interest is also charged when Payment is not made by Debtors on scheduled dates. Here, we discuss about Overdue Interest for Customers & Suppliers Bills, in respect of each Trading Transaction (Sales / Purchase Bills and payments thereon), as per terms (from due date / Invoice Date / Effective date).

02 Activation for overdue Interest feature

As explained earlier (§02/02-11), you have to activate Interest Feature at *F11:Feature>Accounting Feature*:

- **Activate Interest Feature using Simple Parameters**: Set *Yes* at *Activate Interest* to activate Computation Features
- **Enable Interest Feature using Advanced Parameters**: Having Activated Interest Feature, at *Use Advanced Parameters*, set *Yes* to compute Interest at varied Interest rates, over-riding the default rates for any transaction. To use the feature, you must have activated Bill Reference Feature both at Company Feature (§05.01/03-07) and at the respective Party Ledger Account (e g.§05.02/03-07), and also have set the default Credit Period for Party Ledger (F-2A/03-01).

03 Bill by Bill Interest Specification

For Sale / Purchase bills, Interest is computed on each transaction (against each Bill). So, even within one ledger account, different Interest parameters may be applied for each transaction. For example in one Bill Interest may be @ 12% pa, while in another Bill Interest Rate may be staggered with increasing rates for advanced periods (e.g 12% for first 30 days, 15% or next 30 days and 24% thereafter)

For Bill by Bill Interest computation, you may specify the Interest Rate for each voucher, during voucher entry. The default Voucher Interest parameters specified in the Ledger Account is carried for the Voucher, which may be overwritten during voucher entry.

04 Simple Interest Parameters Specification

Interest is computed on Simple Parameters when you have Set *No* at *Use Advanced parameters,* at *F11:Compnay features >Accounting Features*, (§02/02-12),

Voucher Interest Specification: At Ledger Account entry / alteration screen (F-1B/02-12), set Yes at *Activate Interest Calculation* to get Interest Parameter screen (F-1A). At Interest Parameters screen of the Ledger Account, set Yes at *Calculate Interest Transaction by Transaction* to specify Bill by Bill Simple Interest parameters (F-1A).

- **Interest Rate Method**: At the Interest Parameter screen (F-1A), at option *Over-ride parameters for each Transaction*:
  - o **Uniform Rate Interest**: Set *No* to apply same parameter rates in each voucher (F-1A). The Rates are carried from the parameter, which cannot be modified during voucher entry. So, same parameter is applied as per *Ledger Specified* Rate (Rate specified in *Ledger* Account).
  - o **Variable Rate Interest**: Set *Yes* to apply variable parameter rates in each voucher (F-1B). During voucher entry, the rates are carried from the Interest parameter specified in Ledger Account, which may be modified during voucher entry. So, different parameter may applied in vouchers of the same Ledger Account, as per *Voucher Specified* Rate (Rate specified in *Voucher*).

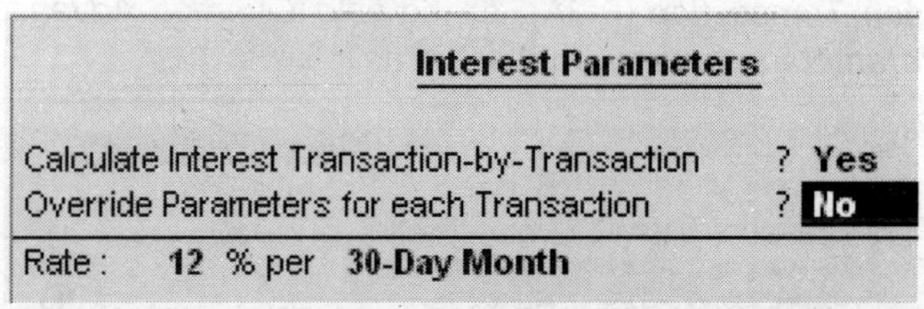

F-1A: Voucher Simple Interest Rate Specification

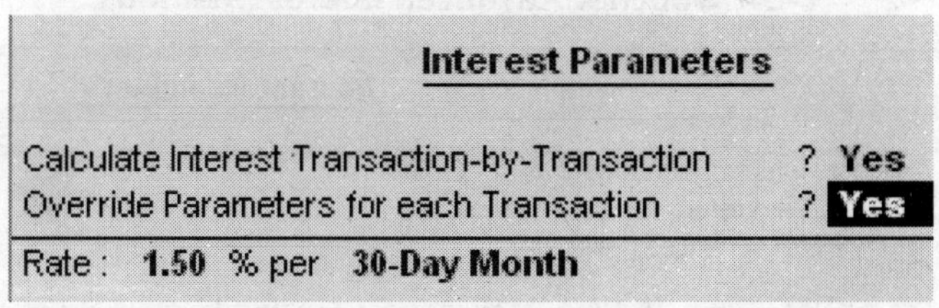

F-1B:Voucher Simple Interest Rate – over riding

- **Interest Rate**: At *Rate* field, (F-1A & F-1B), enter the Interest Rate (e.g 1.5%) and the applicable period (e.g 30 day Month) for Rate, as explained earlier (§03/02-12).

Example

Sold to B K Das on 3-4-09 for Rs 25000 ag Bill No 1. Payment received against Bill – Rs 10000 on 12/5/09, Rs 5000 on 12/6/09 & finally Rs 10000 on 29/6/09.

Interest computed at various Rates, from the date of bill to date of payment, is shown below (F-1A to F-1C)

3-Apr-2009 1						25,000.00 Dr	529.32 Dr
25,000.00 Dr	3-Apr-2009	12-May-2009	39 days	12 %	320.55 Dr		
15,000.00 Dr	12-May-2009	12-Jun-2009	31 days	12 %	152.88 Dr		
10,000.00 Dr	12-Jun-2009	29-Jun-2009	17 days	12 %	55.89 Dr		

F-2A: Voucher Interest Simple – Interest @12% pa (Calendar Year)

Compute Interest @1% pa (Calendar Month) from 1-4-09 to 30-6-09

3-Apr-2009 1						25,000.00 Dr	529.25 Dr
25,000.00 Dr	3-Apr-2009	12-May-2009	39 days	1 %	322.58 Dr		
15,000.00 Dr	12-May-2009	12-Jun-2009	31 days	1 %	150.00 Dr		
10,000.00 Dr	12-Jun-2009	29-Jun-2009	17 days	1 %	56.67 Dr		

F-2B: Voucher Interest Simple – Interest @1% pa (Calendar Month)

Compute Interest @1% pa (30 day Month) from 1-4-09 to 30-6-09

3-Apr-2009 1						25,000.00 Dr	536.67 D
25,000.00 Dr	3-Apr-2009	12-May-2009	39 days	1 %	325.00 Dr		
15,000.00 Dr	12-May-2009	12-Jun-2009	31 days	1 %	155.00 Dr		
10,000.00 Dr	12-Jun-2009	29-Jun-2009	17 days	1 %	56.67 Dr		

F-2C: Voucher Interest Simple –Interest @1% pa (30 day Month)

05 Advanced Interest Parameters Specification

Interest is computed on Advanced Parameters when you have Set *Yes* at *Use Advanced parameters,* at *F11:Compnay features >Accounting Features*, (§1A/02-11).

Consequently, when you set Yes at *Over-ride parameters for each Transaction* (F-3A), at the field *Override Advanced Parameters*, you may further set as follows:

Interest Parameters

Calculate Interest Transaction-by-Transaction	? Yes
Override Parameters for each Transaction	? Yes
Override advanced parameters	? No

F-3A: Voucher Advanced Interest Methods

Interest Parameters

Calculate Interest Transaction-by-Transaction	? Yes
Override Parameters for each Transaction	? Yes
Override advanced parameters	? Yes

F-3B: Voucher Advanced Interest Methods over riding

- Set *No* (F-3A), to apply the Default Advanced Interest Parameters set in Ledger Account, which cannot be overwritten in voucher.
- Set Yes (F-3B), to get the Default Advanced Interest Parameters set in Ledger Account, carried in voucher, which may be overwritten in voucher

In Voucher Interest, the period may be different for each voucher, as the vouchers are added later on after creation of ledger Account. So, the parameters are mostly unknown at the time of creation of Ledger Account. So, you may specify default parameters with option to override the parameters during voucher entry.

If you specify multiple parameters in Voucher Interest, you must make sure that they are for different non overlapping period or non-overlapping Balance Types (Debit / Credit Balances only), else there will be double interest computation.

Now set the advanced interest parameters as follows (F-4)

- **Interest Rates**: At the field *Rate*, enter the Rate for Ledger in % (e.g 12)
- **Interest Rate Period:** At *Per* field, select the Period from Interest Style pop-up (F-2B/02-11) for which the Interest Rate (entered in the preceding field) would be applicable, from the following available Rate periods:
  - **Monthly Interest Rates**: When Monthly Interest Rate is specified:
    - o **30 day Month**: Select it to compute the Interest on 30 day month basis (so the interest Interest for Feb and Interest for March would be same for the same number of days),

Interest Parameters

Calculate Interest Transaction-by-Transaction ? **Yes**
Override Parameters for each Transaction ? **Yes**
Override advanced parameters ? **Yes**

Rate : **1.50** % per **30-Day Month** on **Debit Balances Only**
*Applicability : **Past Due Date** by* **0** *days Calculate From : **Date Specified During Entry***
*Rounding : **♦ Not Applicable***

Rate : **2** % per **Calendar Month** on **Debit Balances Only**
*Applicability : **Past Due Date** by* **30** *days Calculate From : **Date Specified During Entry***
*Rounding : **♦ Not Applicable***

F-4: Voucher Advanced Interest Parameters entry screen

- o **Calendar Month**: Select it to compute the Interest on number of days in the calendar (so the Interest For Feb and Interest for March would different for the same number of days),

- **Yearly Interest Rates**: When Yearly Interest Rate is specified:
  - o **365 day Year:** Select it to compute the Interest on 365 day year (so the Interest for the year 2012 (366 days leap year) and Interest for the year 2013 (365 days year) would be same for the same number of days),
  - o **Calendar Year:** Select it to compute the Interest on the basis of number of days in the Year (365/366) (so the Interest for the year 2012 (366 days leap year) and Interest for the year 2013 (365 days year) would be different for the same number of days),

- **Balance Type:** At the field *On*, Select the Balance Type as follows (F-4/02-11):
  - **All Balances**: Select it to consider both Debit & Credit Balances into account for computation of Interest Consequently:
  - **Credit Balances Only**: Select it to consider Credit Balances only into account for computation of Interest
  - **Debit Balances Only**: Select it to consider Debit Balances only into account for computation of Interest
- **Applicability Rule:** At the field *Applicability*, select the following Due Period option from the list. This option is only for viewing and is not considered for Interest computation
  - Always:
  - Past Due Date:
- **Applicability Date:** At the field *Calculate From*, select the Interest Applicable Date option from the following
  - **Due date of Invoice / Ref**: To compute Interest from Due date of the Invoice / Ref
  - **Date of Applicability**: To compute interest from due date of the invoice / ref
  - **Effective Date of transaction**: To compute interest from Effective Date of transaction (§06/03-07)
- **Rounding Method:** At Rounding field, select the Rounding Method (or *Not Applicable)* from the list and specify the Rounding Limit as follows (F-4A/02-11):
  - o **No Rounding**: Select *Not Applicable* if no rounding is applicable. The computed Interest is auto rounded to nearest paise (equivalent to Normal Rounding to.01 Limit, as explained next).
  - o **Lower Rounding**: Select *Down ward Rounding* to Round off the amount to lower value. The rounded amount is lower than (or equal the computed) amount.
  - o **Higher Rounding**: To **Up ward Rounding** Round off the amount to higher value. The rounded amount is higher than (or equal to computed amount).
  - o **Normal Rounding**: To Round off to the nearest Value. The Rounded amount may be higher or lower than the computed amount, as per Rounding limit set (explained next).

  Rounding Limit: In any of the above 3 Rounding Methods, specify the Rounding limit (like.01,.10, 1.00, 10.00. etc).

You may enter such multiple definitions for different Interest applicable Periods

Example

Sold to B K Das on 3-4-09 for Rs 25000 ag Bill No 1. Credit Period 30 Days. Payment received against Bill – Rs 10000 on 12/5/09, Rs 5000 on 12/6/09

Interest @1.5% pm (30 day) past due date from Bill date &

2% / Calendar Month past due date by 90 days from Bill date.

Compute Interest for the period 1-4-09 to 30-9-09

Interest Parameters

Rate : **1.50** % per **30-Day Month** on **Debit Balances Only**
*Applicability : **Past Due Date** by* **0** *days*
*From: **Date Specified During Entry*** *Date:* **2-May-2009** *To:* **2-Aug-2009**
*Rounding : **♯ Not Applicable***

Rate : **2** % per **Calendar Month** on **Debit Balances Only**
*Applicability : **Past Due Date** by* **90** *days*
*From: **Date Specified During Entry*** *Date:* **2-Aug-2009** *To:*
*Rounding : **♯ Not Applicable***

F-5A: Interest parameter in Voucher

The Interest parameters are set in Ledger (F-5A). The rates set in Ledger (F-5A) are carried from Ledger Interest

Ledger Interest — ABC Academy 9-10 — Ctrl + M

Ledger : **B K Das** — **1-Apr-2009 to 30-Sep-2009**

Date	Ref. No.						Opening Amount	Pending Amount	Interest
3-Apr-2009	1						25,000.00 Dr	**10,000.00 Dr**	999.17 Dr
	25,000.00 Dr	*2-May-2009*	*12-May-2009*	*10 days*	*1.50 %*	*125.00 Dr*			
	15,000.00 Dr	*12-May-2009*	*12-Jun-2009*	*31 days*	*1.50 %*	*232.50 Dr*			
	10,000.00 Dr	*12-Jun-2009*	*2-Aug-2009*	*51 days*	*1.50 %*	*255.00 Dr*			
	10,000.00 Dr	*2-Aug-2009*	*30-Sep-2009*	*59 days*	*2 %*	*386.67 Dr*			
							25,000.00 Dr	**10,000.00 Dr**	999.17 Dr

F-5B: Voucher Interest - Advanced

parameters which you have to edit and put the correct applicable period in each Voucher parameter to compute the Interest (F-5B)

F-5A shows the Interest computed as per parameters set as shown in F-5A

Interest parameters entry for Billwise Opening Balance

We have discussed the Interest Parameters for current period transactions. There may be some outstanding Bills of pervious year being carried, on which Interest may be chargeable.

While entering each Bill Reference Details of Party Opening Balance (§08/03-07), you should also enter the Interest Rate & Period unit for each outstanding Bill, as explained.

06 Interest Receivables & Payables Statement

Interest Receivables / Payables report shows Interest on Receivables (from Debtors) and Payables (to Creditors), computed as per Interest parameters set, for the specified period,

At *Interest Calculations* Menu (F-10/02-11), select

Interest Receivable — Ctrl + M

Particulars	*Sundry Debtors* **ABC Academy 9-10** 1-Apr-2009 to 31-Mar-2010 **Interest Calculation**	
	Cl. Balance	Interest
Aakash & Co	19,310.50 Dr	2,197.48 Dr
A K Traders	6,250.00 Cr	420.00 Dr
T K Das	9,000.00 Dr	5,354.58 Dr
A Bose & Co	2,000.00 Dr	240.00 Dr
Grand Total	**24,060.50 Dr**	**8,212.06 Dr**

F-6A: Interest Receivables Report

Interest Payable — Ctrl + M

Particulars	*Sundry Creditors* **ABC Academy 9-10** 1-Apr-2009 to 31-Mar-2010 **Interest Calculation**	
	Cl. Balance	Interest
B M Suppliers	7,170.00 Cr	301.98 Cr
Grand Total	**7,170.00 Cr**	**301.98 Cr**

F-6B: Interest Payables Report

- **Interest Receivables Report**: *Receivables* to get *Interest Receivables* Report (F-6A), showing accrued Interest on Receivables
- **Interest Payables Report**: *Payables* to get Interest *Payables* Report (F-6B) showing accrued Interest on Payables

The contents, format & buttons at Interest Receivables & Interest Receivables Reports are similar

06.01 Interest Receivables / Payables Configuration

At *Interest Receivables or Interest Payables* reports (F-6A, F-6B), click *F12: Configure* to get the *Interest Report*

Configuration screen (F-6C). At *Interest Report Configuration* screen (F-6C), set as follows:

- **Due Bill Types**: At *Range of Bills to show*, select:
  - o **Overdue Bills**: *Overdue Bills* to show the Balance & Interest accrued on Overdue Bills only, as at the end of current period.

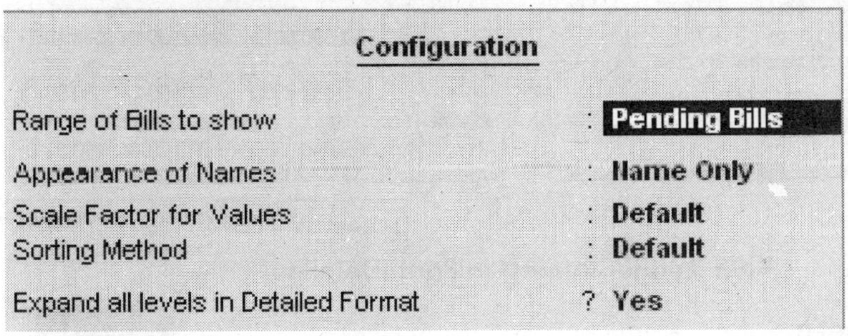

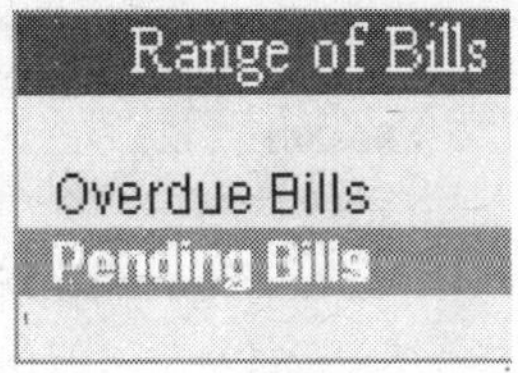

F-6C: Interest Receivables / Payables Configuration

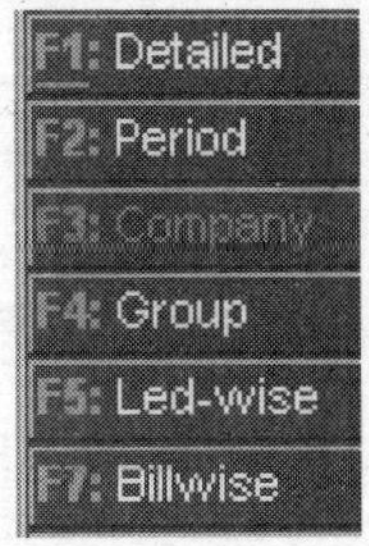

F-6D: Buttons

  - o **Outstanding Bills**: *Pending Bills* to show the Balance & Interest accrued on all Outstanding (Open) Bills as at the end of current period.
- **Details**: Set *Yes* at *Expand all levels to show* the Party Ledger balances of each party in detailed mode (when F1:Details toggle button is clicked)

06.02 Interest Receivables & Payables Statement Buttons

At *Interest Report Configuration* screen (F-6B), you get the following buttons (F-6D)

F1: Detailed / Condensed:

- Set the *Detail* toggle button to see the next level details of outstanding & accrued Interest of Groups / Ledgers.
- Set the *Condensed* toggle button to see the top level figures of outstanding & accrued Interest of Groups / Ledgers.

F4 Group:

- To select Group from list of Groups

F5 Ledger / Group Interest:

- Set the *F5:Led-wise* toggle button to see the figures of outstanding & accrued Interest of Ledger Accounts in alphabetical order.
- Set the *F5: Grouped* toggle button to see the figures of outstanding & accrued Interest of Accounts Groups / Ledger Accounts in hierarchical order.

F7 Billwise Details / Summary:

- Set the *F7:Billwise* toggle button to see the figures of outstanding (like Outstanding Statement) & accrued Interest of each outstanding Bill. The Configuration screen (when you press F12:Configurtaion button ta Billwise Statement) is similar to Outstanding Statement discussed n previous chapter
- Set the *F7: Summary* toggle button to see the figures of outstanding & accrued Interest of Accounts Groups / Ledger Accounts in hierarchical order.

07 Ledger Interest

We have discussed Ledger Account computed on Ledger Balances (§07.02/02-11). Here, we discuss about Ledger Interest on delayed payments, computed on each Bill.

07.01 Ledger Interest Display

At *Interest Calculations* Menu (§07.02/02-11), select *Ledger* and select the Ledger Account to get *Ledger Interest Report* Display (F-7A) for the selected Ledger Account

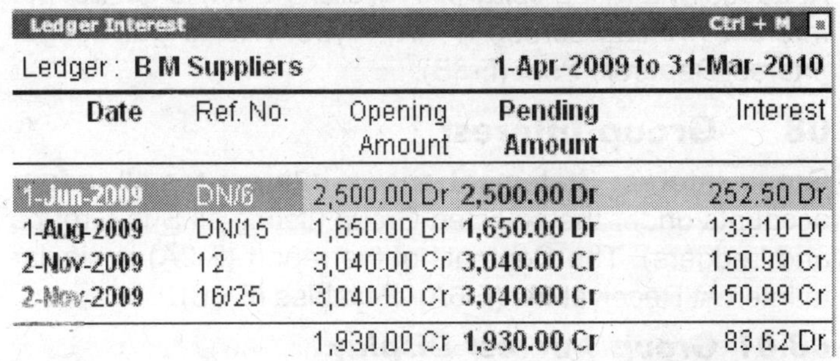

Ledger Interest — Ctrl + M

Ledger : B M Suppliers — 1-Apr-2009 to 31-Mar-2010

Date	Ref. No.	Opening Amount	Pending Amount	Interest
1-Jun-2009	DN/6	2,500.00 Dr	2,500.00 Dr	252.50 Dr
1-Aug-2009	DN/15	1,650.00 Dr	1,650.00 Dr	133.10 Dr
2-Nov-2009	12	3,040.00 Cr	3,040.00 Cr	150.99 Cr
2-Nov-2009	16/25	3,040.00 Cr	3,040.00 Cr	150.99 Cr
		1,930.00 Cr	1,930.00 Cr	83.62 Dr

7A Ledger Interest

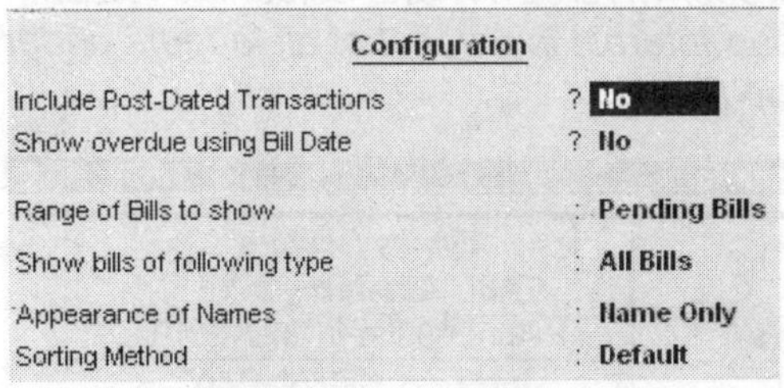

7B Ledger Interest Configuration

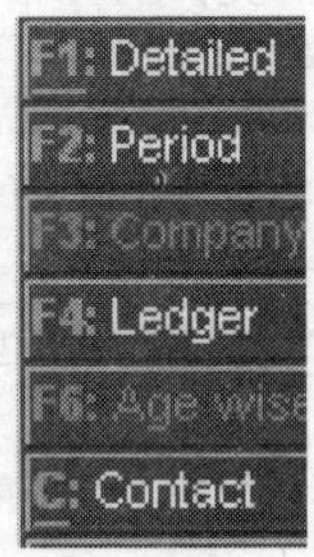

7C Ledger Interest Buttons

07.02 Ledger Interest Configuration

At *Ledger Interest Display* (F-7A), click F12:Configure to get *Ledger Interest Configuration screen* (F-7B)

07.03 Ledger Interest Buttons

At *Ledger Interest Report* (F-7A), you get buttons (F-7C), as described below:

- **F4: Ledger**: Select this button to get the list of Ledger Accounts to select a Ledger Account to get Ledger Interest Statement for the selected Ledger Account

B M Suppliers
Interest Details
1-Apr-2009 to 31-Mar-2010

Page 1

Date	Ref. No.						Opening Amount	Pending Amount	Interest
1-Jun-2009	DN/6						2,500.00 Dr	2,500.00 Dr	252.50 Dr
	2,500.00 Dr	*1-Jun-2009*	*31-Mar-2010*	*303 days*	*1 %*	*252.50 Dr*			
1-Aug-2009	DN/15						1,650.00 Dr	1,650.00 Dr	133.10 Dr
	1,650.00 Dr	*1-Aug-2009*	*31-Mar-2010*	*242 days*	*1 %*	*133.10 Dr*			
2-Nov-2009	12						3,040.00 Cr	3,040.00 Cr	150.99 Cr
	3,040.00 Cr	*2-Nov-2009*	*31-Mar-2010*	*149 days*	*1 %*	*150.99 Cr*			
2-Nov-2009	16/25						3,040.00 Cr	3,040.00 Cr	150.99 Cr
	3,040.00 Cr	*2-Nov-2009*	*31-Mar-2010*	*149 days*	*1 %*	*150.99 Cr*			
							1,930.00 Cr	1,930.00 Cr	83.62 Dr

F-8B: Ledger Interest in Print (Detailed)

Report Titles

B M Suppliers
Interest Details

F-8A: Ledger Interest Printing screen

- C:Contact: Click *this* button to get Ledger Contact screen showing the complete details of Party Address, Contact person etc of the selected Ledger Account. The information is displayed in a pop up screen for reference only but not printed in any Interest report.

07.04 Ledger Interest Printing

At *Ledger Interest Display* (F-7A), click *P:Print* to get *Ledger Interest Printing screen* (F-8A), Type Y to to get *Ledger Interest* Report in Print (F-8B).

08 Group Interest

Group Interest Statement shows Interest for all ledger accounts under the selected Group (listing all Sub-Groups and Ledgers). The Contents of the report (F-9A) is similar to Interest Receivables (F-6A)/ Payables (F-6B).

08.01 Group Interest Display

Select *Display > Statement of Accounts > Interest Calculations > Group (F-10/02-11) and select the Account Group to get Group Interest in respect of all ledgers under the selected Group (F-9A).*

Group Interest Calculations Ctrl + M

Particulars	*Sundry Debtors* **ABC Academy 9-10** 1-Apr-2009 to 31-Mar-2010 **Interest Calculation**	
	Cl. Balance	Interest
Aakash & Co	19,310.50 Dr	1,697.75 Dr
A K Traders	6,250.00 Cr	420.00 Dr
T K Das	9,000.00 Dr	5,354.58 Dr
A Bose & Co	2,000.00 Dr	240.00 Dr
Grand Total	**24,060.50 Dr**	**7,712.33 Dr**

F-9A: Group Interest Statement

Configuration

Range of Bills to show	: **Pending Bills**
Appearance of Names	: **Name Only**
Scale Factor for Values	: **Default**
Sorting Method	: **Default**
Expand all levels in Detailed Format	? **Yes**

F-9B: Group Interest Configuration

F1: Detailed
F2: Period
F3: Company
F4: Group
F5: Led-wise
F7: Billwise

F-9C Buttons

Group Interest Calculations Ctrl + M

Group : **Sundry Debtors** 1-Apr-2009 to 31-Mar-2010

Date	Ref. No.	Party's Name	Opening Amount	Pending Amount	Interest
1-Mar-2008	3	Aakash & Co	2,000.00 Cr	2,000.00 Cr	499.73 Cr
31-Mar-2008	12	Aakash & Co	8,000.00 Dr	8,000.00 Dr	1,920.00 Dr
1-Apr-2009	1st Inst	T K Das	10,000.00 Dr	6,000.00 Dr	885.78 Dr
1-Apr-2009	2nd Inst	T K Das	10,000.00 Dr	3,000.00 Dr	1,305.31 Dr
4-Jun-2009	4	A K Traders	2,800.00 Dr	2,800.00 Dr	420.00 Dr
1-Sep-2009	5	Aakash & Co	4,000.00 Dr	4,000.00 Dr	277.48 Dr
			32,800.00 Dr	:1,800.00 Dr	4,308.84 Dr

F-9D: Group Interest Statement (Billwise)

Group Interest Calculations ABC Academy 9-10 Ctrl + M

Group : **Sundry Debtors** 1-Apr-2009 to 31-Mar-2010

Date	Ref. No.					Party's Name	Opening Amount	Pending Amount	Interest
1-Mar-2008	3					Aakash & Co	2,000.00 Cr	2,000.00 Cr	499.73 Cr
2,000.00 Cr	*1-Mar-2008*	*31-Mar-2010*	*760 days*	*12 %*	*499.73 Cr*				
31-Mar-2008	12					Aakash & Co	8,000.00 Dr	8,000.00 Dr	1,920.00 Dr
8,000.00 Dr	*31-Mar-2008*	*31-Mar-2010*	*730 days*	*12 %*	*1,920.00 Dr*				
1-Apr-2009	1st Inst					T K Das	10,000.00 Dr	6,000.00 Dr	885.78 Dr
10,000.00 Dr	*1-Jun-2009*	*6-Jun-2009*	*5 days*	*12 %*	*16.44 Dr*				
6,000.00 Dr	*6-Jun-2009*	*30-Jan-2009*	*24 days*	*12 %*	*47.34 Dr*				
6,000.00 Dr	*30-Jan-2009*	*31-Mar-2010*	*274 days*	*1.50 %*	*822.00 Dr*				
1-Apr-2009	2nd Inst					T K Das	10,000.00 Dr	3,000.00 Dr	1,305.31 Dr
10,000.00 Dr	*1-Apr-2009*	*9-Jun-2009*	*69 days*	*12 %*	*226.85 Dr*				
3,000.00 Dr	*9-Jun-2009*	*31-Mar-2010*	*295 days*	*12 %*	*290.96 Dr*				
10,000.00 Dr	*1-Apr-2009*	*9-Jun-2009*	*69 days*	*1.50 %*	*345.00 Dr*				
3,000.00 Dr	*9-Jun-2009*	*31-Mar-2010*	*295 days*	*1.50 %*	*442.50 Dr*				
4-Jun-2009	4					A K Traders	2,800.00 Dr	2,800.00 Dr	420.00 Dr
2,800.00 Dr	*4-Jun-2009*	*31-Mar-2010*	*300 days*	*1.50 %*	*420.00 Dr*				
1-Sep-2009	5					Aakash & Co	4,000.00 Dr	4,000.00 Dr	277.48 Dr
4,000.00 Dr	*1-Sep-2009*	*31-Mar-2010*	*211 days*	*12 %*	*277.48 Dr*				
							32,800.00 Dr	21,800.00 Dr	4,308.84 Dr

F-9E:Group Interest Statement (Billwise Detailed)

08.02 Group Interest Configuration

At Group Interest Statement (F-9A), click *F12: Configure* to get the *Group Interest Configuration* screen (F-9B), similar to *Interest Receivable / Payable Statement Configuration* (F-6B). Now set the options as below:

- **Due Bill Types**: At *Range of Bills to show*, select:
    - o **Overdue Bills**: Select *Overdue Bills* to show the

Balance & Interest accrued on Overdue Bills only, as at the end of current period.

- o **Outstanding Bills**: Select *Pending Bills* to show the Balance & Interest accrued on all Outstanding (Open) Bills as at the end of current period.

- **Details**: Set *Yes* at *Expand all levels to show* the Party Ledger balances of each party in detailed mode (when F1:Details toggle button is clicked:F-7E)

08.03 Group Interest Buttons

At Group Interest Statement (F-9A), you get buttons (F-9C), similar to Interest Receivable / Interest Payable Statement (F-6D), as described below:

- **F1: Detailed / Condensed**
  - o Set the *Detail* toggle button to see the next level details of outstanding & accrued Interest of Groups / Ledgers. (F-9D)
  - o Set the *Condensed* toggle button to see the top level figures of outstanding & accrued Interest of Groups / Ledgers. (F-9A)
- **F4: Group:** To get the list of Account Groups to select an Account Group to get Group Interest Statement for the selected Account Group.
- **F5 Ledger / Group Interest:**
  - o Click *F5:Led-wise* toggle button to see the figures of outstanding & accrued Interest of Ledger Accounts in alphabetical order.
  - o Click *F5: Grouped* toggle button to see the figures of outstanding & accrued Interest of Accounts Groups / Ledger Accounts in hierarchical order.
- **F7 Billwise Details / Summary:**
  - o Click *F7:Billwise* toggle button to see the figures of outstanding (like Outstanding Statement) & accrued Interest of each outstanding Bill. The Configuration screen (F-9F: when you press *F12:Configuration* button at Billwise Statement: F-9E) is similar to Outstanding Statement (F-6D)
  - o Click *F7: Summary* toggle button to see the figures of outstanding & accrued Interest of Accounts Groups / Ledger Accounts (F-9A).

08.04 Group Interest Printing

At Group Interest Statement (F-9A), click *P:Print* to get the *Group Interest Printing* screen (F-9F). Set the printing options to get Group Interest Statement in Print (F-9G).

Report Titles

Sundry Debtors

Group Interest

Range of Bills to show	:	**Pending Bills**
Scale Factor for Values	:	**Default**
Method of information	:	**Grouped**
Format	:	**Detailed**
Expand all levels in Detailed Format	?	**Yes**

F-9F: Group Interest Printing Screen

Sundry Debtors

Group Interest

1-Apr-2009 to 31-Mar-2010

Page 1

Date	Ref. No.	Party's Name				Opening Amount	Pending Amount	Interest
1-Mar-2008	3	Aakash & Co				2,000.00 Cr	2,000.00 Cr	499.73 Cr
2,000.00 Cr	*1-Mar-2008*	*31-Mar-2010*	*760 days*	*12 %*	*499.73 Cr*			
31-Mar-2008	12	Aakash & Co				8,000.00 Dr	8,000.00 Dr	1,920.00 Dr
8,000.00 Dr	*31-Mar-2008*	*31-Mar-2010*	*730 days*	*12 %*	*1,920.00 Dr*			
1-Apr-2009	1st Inst	T K Das				10,000.00 Dr	6,000.00 Dr	885.78 Dr
10,000.00 Dr	*1-Jun-2009*	*6-Jun-2009*	*5 days*	*12 %*	*16.44 Dr*			
6,000.00 Dr	*6-Jun-2009*	*30-Jun-2009*	*24 days*	*12 %*	*47.34 Dr*			
6,000.00 Dr	*30-Jun-2009*	*31-Mar-2010*	*274 days*	*1.50 %*	*822.00 Dr*			
1-Apr-2009	2nd Inst	T K Das				10,000.00 Dr	3,000.00 Dr	1,305.31 Dr
10,000.00 Dr	*1-Apr-2009*	*9-Jun-2009*	*69 days*	*12 %*	*226.85 Dr*			
3,000.00 Dr	*9-Jun-2009*	*31-Mar-2010*	*295 days*	*12 %*	*290.96 Dr*			
10,000.00 Dr	*1-Apr-2009*	*9-Jun-2009*	*69 days*	*1.50 %*	*345.00 Dr*			
3,000.00 Dr	*9-Jun-2009*	*31-Mar-2010*	*295 days*	*1.50 %*	*442.50 Dr*			
4-Jun-2009	4	A K Traders				2,800.00 Dr	2,800.00 Dr	420.00 Dr
2,800.00 Dr	*4-Jun-2009*	*31-Mar-2010*	*300 days*	*1.50 %*	*420.00 Dr*			
1-Sep-2009	5	Aakash & Co				4,000.00 Dr	4,000.00 Dr	277.48 Dr
4,000.00 Dr	*1-Sep-2009*	*31-Mar-2010*	*211 days*	*12 %*	*277.48 Dr*			
						32,800.00 Dr	21,800.00 Dr	4,308.84 Dr

F-9G: Group Interest in Print

09 Interest Voucher Class

For Interest Payable, you may create a *Credit Note* in favour of the Creditor. Similarly, for Interest Receivable, you may create a *Debit Note* on the Debtor To create Debit / Credit Note for Interest (F-12A). There are 2 ways to create Interest Debit & Credit Notes:

- Get the Interest Payable / Receivable from the Interest Payable / Receivable Report, discussed earlier. Then Create the Debit / Credit Note for the respective Party, for the Interest Amount (§05/02-11)
- Create Interest Voucher class which would compute the Interest and auto create the Interest Debit / Credit Note (§10)

09.01 Interest Voucher Class creation

To create a Interest Voucher class, first create a Voucher Type for Interest Debit / Credit. Note (F-10A),as discussed earlier (§01/02-07).

To create Voucher Class, select *Accounts Info > Voucher Type > Create* (§02/02-07) to get Voucher type creation screen (F-10A). Now enter as follows:

- **Name**: Enter Voucher Type Name (e.g IntCls)
- Type of Voucher: Select Debit Note (to create Debit Note Voucher Class) or select Credit Note (to create Credit Note Voucher Class)
- **Abbn:** Enter a short abbreviation of Voucher Class that would be printed in all reports

Enter other information (F-10A). At *Voucher Class* (F-10A), enter the name of Voucher Class to get *Voucher Class Specification* screen (F-10B)

At *Voucher Class Specification* screen (F-10B), specify the following in respect of *Interest Voucher Class.*

- **Interest Class**: Set *Yes* at *Use Class for Interest Accounting* to create Interest Voucher Class. The process of setting up Debit & Credit Note Voucher is similar to Voucher Class explained earlier (§03/02-07).

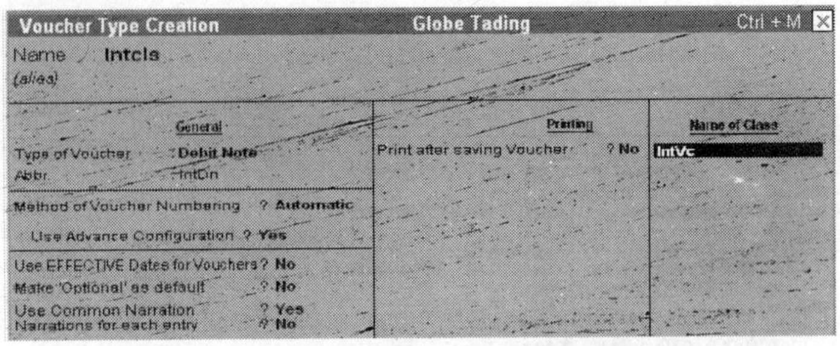

F-10A: Interest Class Debit Note Voucher creation

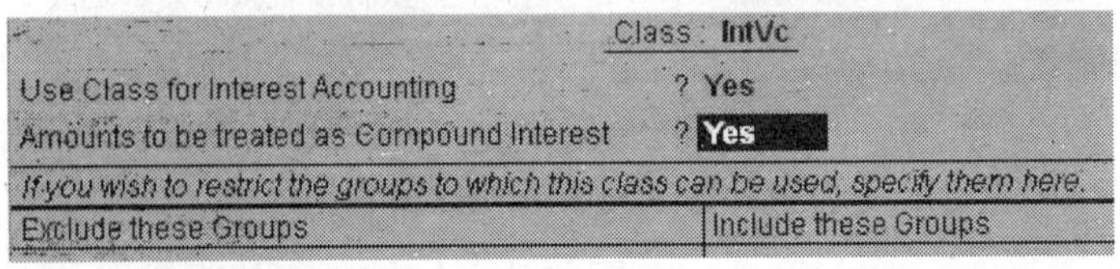

F-10B: Interest Voucher Class for Debit Notes

- **Interest Method**: Having set *Yes* at *Use Class for Interest Accounting* (F-10B), at *Amounts to be treated as Compound Interest*:
  - o **Compound Interest**: Set *Yes* to compute the Interest by *Compound Interest* Method
  - o **Simple Interest**: Set *No* to compute the Interest by *Simple Interest* Method

10 Debit / Credit Note Interest Voucher Class

Having created Interest Voucher class as explained (§09), you may create Debit / Credit Note voucher using the voucher class, as explained next

Voucher entry using voucher class has been explained earlier (§04/02-08). At Voucher entry screen:

- **Credit Note Entry**: Click F8: *Credit Note* button
- **Debit Note Entry**: Click F9: *Debit Note* button

and then the select the *Voucher Type* (F-11A) and *Voucher Class* (F-11B) to get Interest Debit Note / Credit Note voucher entry screen (F-12A)

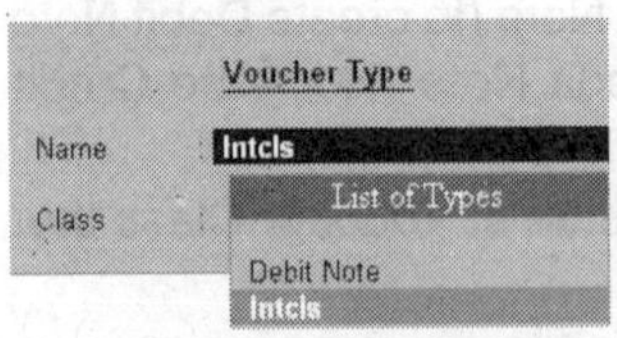

F-11A: Interest Voucher Type selection

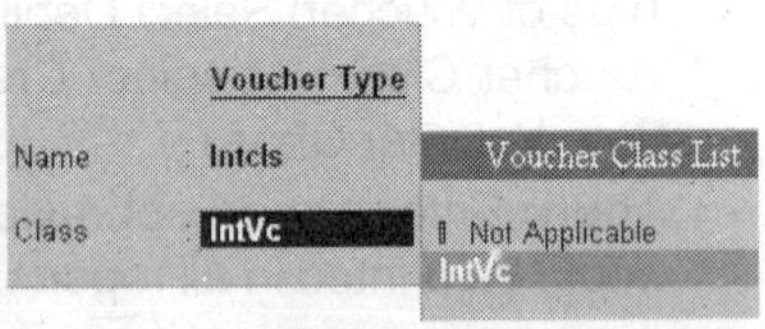

F-11B: Interest Voucher Class selection

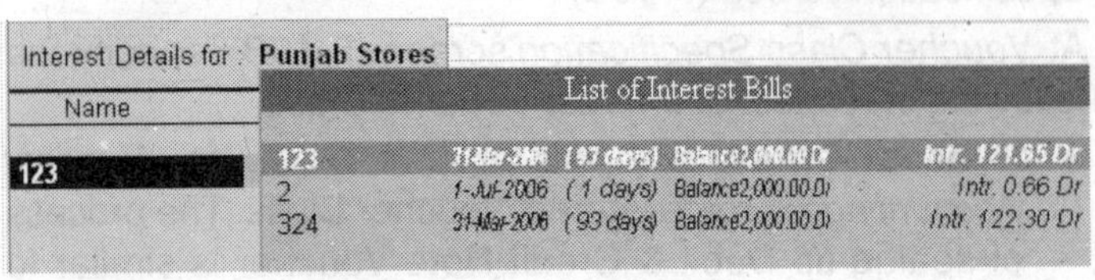

F-11C: Selection of Bill in Interest Voucher Class

At Voucher Entry screen (F-12A), after selecting the Party, you get the Bill allocation screen (F-11C)

At Bill allocation screen (F-11C), select the Open Bills for which you like to prepare Interest Debit Note, from the list of Interest Bills.

On selection of the open bill references, the Interest is computed as per parameters set in the Party Ledger and the Interest Computation Method (Simple or Compound) as set in Voucher Class (F-10B), and gets reflected in the Party Ledger (F-12B)

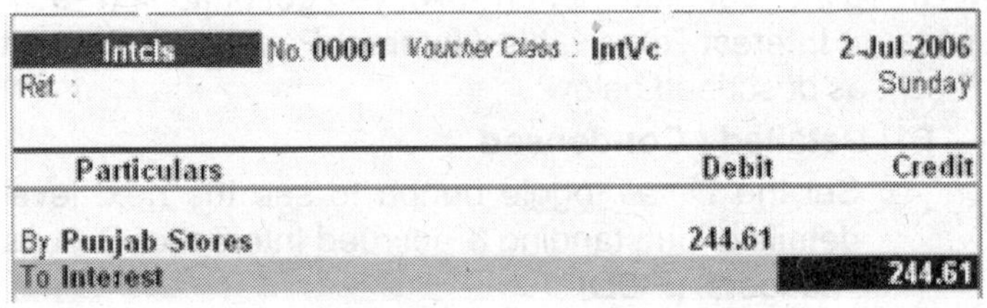

F-12A: Interest Debit Note creation

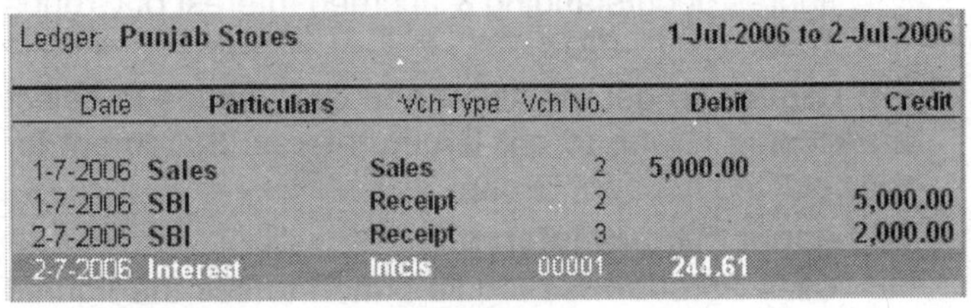

F-12B: Interest Debit Note in Party Ledger

11 Installment Payments / Hire Purchase

In case of Sale under Installment Payment / Hire Purchase, a series of payment is to be made in instalments in subsequent period, on specified dates. Interest is to be paid for delayed payments. Punitive rate of Interest is charged as the delayed period increases. So, variable rate of Interest is charged for each slab of delay.

The following example demonstrates case of Installment Payments and computation of Interest on different rates according to the slab of delayed payments.

ABC Traders machine seller sold a Machine to B K for Rs 50,000, on installment on 1.4.09. The installment amounts are payable on 1.4.09 – Rs 10000 and then balance amount of Rs 40,000 in 4 in quarterly installment of Rs 10,000 each on 1st June, 1st Sep, 1st Dec and 1st Mar. Interest is payable on overdue balance @ 12% pa (calendar Year) and @ 1.5% / 30 day month for overdue beyond 30 days. He will be entitled to credit of 12% pa on early payments before due Date

B K Traders paid Rs 10000 on 4.4.09 Against Reference *Dn Pmt*, Rs 6000 on 4.5.09 & Rs 4000 on 6.6.09 against 1st Installment, Rs 7000 on 9.9.09 and Rs 3000 on 15.10.09 against 2nd Installment, Rs 10000 on 3.1.10 ag 3rd Installment and Rs 10000 on 31.3.09 towards final payment.

The Interest Set up, entry in Masters, Vouchers and computation of Interest payable from 1.4.09 to 31.3.10 is explained next.

As there are multiple rates applicable, you have to set *Advanced* Interest option. As there are separate installment payments with different due dates, you have to maintain Transaction by Transaction details.

- **Interest Features Set Up**: Set Advanced Interest option (§05) at Accounting Features screen (F-1A / 02-11)
- **Party Ledger**: At Party Ledger (§04/02-11), set the Interest parameters (F-13A)
- **Sales Voucher Entry:** During Voucher entry (F-4A), set Interest parameters (Reference, Due Date & Amount) in respect of each installment payable (F-13B)
- **Receipt Voucher Entry:** During Voucher entry, set Interest parameters in respective voucher (over-riding the default Interest Parameters: F-14B)

Each of the steps are explained next

Accounting Features: Set Advanced Accounting Features as explained earlier. At *F11:Features >Accounting Features* (F-1A/02-12), *set Yes at Activate Interest calculation* and then set Yes at *use Advanced Parameters.*

Interest Parameters in Party Ledger: Set default Interest Parameters in Party Ledger (F-13A), which would be carried by default during Voucher Entry (F-13B)

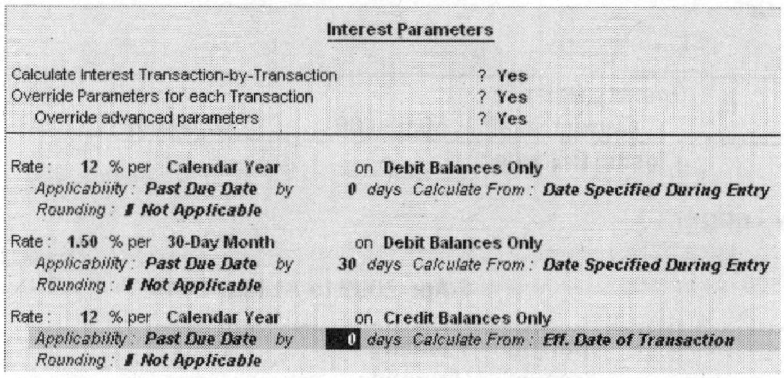

F-13A: Default Interest parameters in Party Ledger

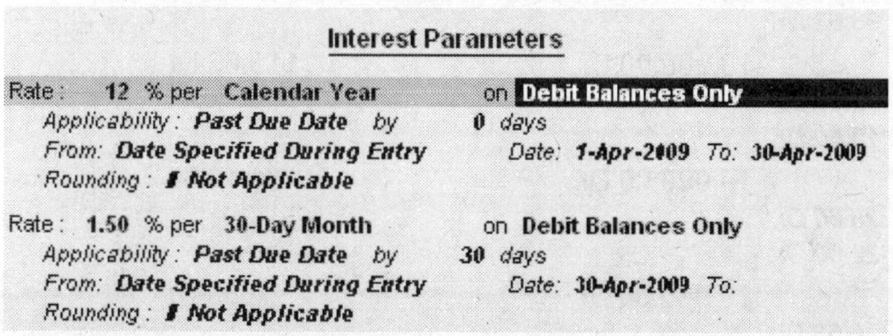

F-13B: Interest Parameters in Sales Voucher for Bill Ref Dn Pmt

Sales Voucher Entry: Having set the Interest Parameters in Party Ledger, create the Sales Voucher (F-14A). As described earlier (§03/03-07), create *New Reference* for each installment Payable Bill Reference at Bill Allocation screen, set Interest parameter for each Installment. F-13B shows the screen of Interest Parameter for 1st installment.

The following Table shows the values to be set in Interest parameters for next 4 references for each Installment Payment

Bill Ref #	Rate	Date from	Date To	Balance Type
1st Inst	12%/Cal Yr	1-6-09	30-6-09	Dr Bal
	1.5%/30D		30-6-09	Dr Bal
	12%/Cal Yr	1-6-09	30-9-09	Cr Bal
2nd Inst	12%/Cal Yr	1-9-09	30-9-09	Dr Bal
	1.5%/30D	30-9-09		Dr Bal
	12%/Cal Yr	1-9-09	31-12-10	Cr Bal
3rd Inst	12%/Cal Yr	1-12-09	31-12-09	Dr Bal
	1.5%/30D	31-12-09		Dr Bal
	12%/Cal Yr	1-12-09	31-3-10	Cr Bal
4th Inst	12%/Cal Yr	1-3-10	31-3-10	Dr Bal
	1.5%/30D	31-3-10	31-3-10	Dr Bal
	12%/Cal Yr	1-3-10	31-3-10	Cr Bal

Enter Interest parameters for the next 4 Installments as the 1st installment entry shown above (F-13B) to complete the Sales Voucher entry (F-14A).

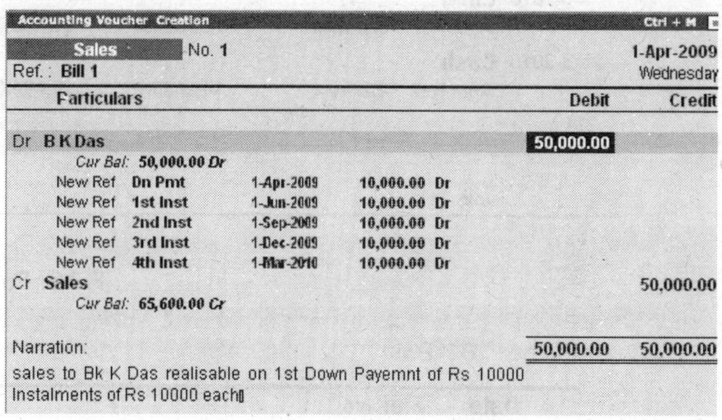

F:14A: Sales Voucher Entry

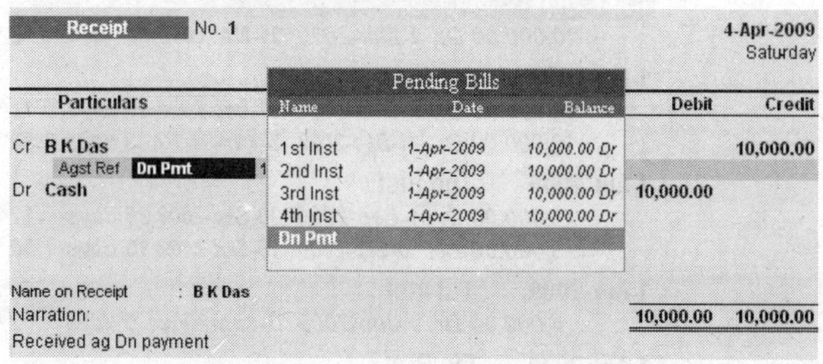

F-14B: Receipt Voucher Entry

Receipt Voucher Entry

Create Receipt Voucher (F-14B) when money is received against an Installment. Select the respective pending Reference. F-14B shows the Receipt Voucher entry for Down payment. In the same way, make entry of the next Receipt Vouchers against balance installment payments.

Party Ledger

On entry of all receipt vouchers in respect of all installment payments, the Party Ledger (F-15) shows the vouchers (Sales & Receipt Vouchers)

Interest Statement: After entry of all receipt vouchers, print the Interest statement (F-16) as described earlier (§07)

Ledger: **B K Das** — **1-Apr-2009 to 31-Mar-2010**

Date	Particulars				Vch Type	Vch No.	Debit	Credit
1-4-2009	**Sales**				**Sales**	1	**50,000.00**	
	New Ref	**Dn Pmt**	1-Apr-2009	**10,000.00 Dr**				
	New Ref	**1st Inst**	1-Jun-2009	**10,000.00 Dr**				
	New Ref	**2nd Inst**	1-Sep-2009	**10,000.00 Dr**				
	New Ref	**3rd Inst**	1-Dec-2009	**10,000.00 Dr**				
	New Ref	**4th Inst**	1-Mar-2010	**10,000.00 Dr**				
4-4-2009	**Cash**				**Receipt**	1		**10,000.00**
	Agst Ref	**Dn Pmt**	1-Apr-2009	**10,000.00 Cr**				
4-5-2009	**Cash**				**Receipt**	3		**6,000.00**
	Agst Ref	**1st Inst**	1-Jun-2009	**6,000.00 Cr**				
6-6-2009	**Cash**				**Receipt**	5		**4,000.00**
	Agst Ref	**1st Inst**	1-Jun-2009	**4,000.00 Cr**				
9-6-2009	**Cash**				**Receipt**	6		**7,000.00**
	Agst Ref	**2nd Inst**	1-Sep-2009	**7,000.00 Cr**				
15-10-2009	**Cash**				**Receipt**	11		**3,000.00**
	Agst Ref	**2nd Inst**	1-Sep-2009	**3,000.00 Cr**				
3-1-2010	**Cash**				**Receipt**	12		**10,000.00**
	Agst Ref	**3rd Inst**	1-Dec-2009	**10,000.00 Cr**				
31-3-2010	**Cash**				**Receipt**	20		**10,000.00**
	Agst Ref	**4th Inst**	1-Mar-2010	**10,000.00 Cr**				
					Opening Balance :			
					Current Total :		**50,000.00**	**50,000.00**
					Closing Balance :			

F-15: Party Ledger

Ledger : **B K Das** — **1-Apr-2009 to 31-Mar-2010**

Date	Ref. No.	Opening Amount	**Pending Amount**	Interest
1-Apr-2009	4th Inst	10,000.00 Dr		98.63 Dr
	10,000.00 Dr 1-Mar-2010 31-Mar-2010 30 days 12 % 98.63 Dr			
1-Apr-2009	3rd Inst	10,000.00 Dr		113.63 Dr
	10,000.00 Dr 1-Dec-2009 31-Dec-2009 30 days 12 % 98.63 Dr			
	10,000.00 Dr 31-Dec-2009 3-Jan-2010 3 days 1.50 % 15.00 Dr			
1-Apr-2009	2nd Inst	10,000.00 Dr		51.10 Dr
	3,000.00 Dr 1-Sep-2009 30-Sep-2009 29 days 12 % 28.60 Dr			
	3,000.00 Dr 30-Sep-2009 15-Oct-2009 15 days 1.50 % 22.50 Dr			
1-Apr-2009	1st Inst	10,000.00 Dr		6.58 Dr
	4,000.00 Dr 1-Jun-2009 6-Jun-2009 5 days 12 % 6.58 Dr			
1-Apr-2009	Dn Pmt	10,000.00 Dr		9.86 Dr
	10,000.00 Dr 1-Apr-2009 4-Apr-2009 3 days 12 % 9.86 Dr			
		50,000.00 Dr		279.80 Dr

F:16: Interest Statement

Interest Debit Note

Now create the Interest Debit Note for Interest Receivable (F-12A). For example, for the case described above, you may create separate Interest Debit Note for the Interest Receivable in respect of each installment payment (Rs 9.86 dt 4.4.09, Rs 6.58 dt 6.6.09, Rs.51.10 dt 15.10.09, Rs 113.63 dt 3.1.10 & Rs 98.63 dt 31.3.10) to charge Interest for each delayed payment) or may create one Debit Note for Rs 279.80 for total Interest on delayed payment.

FAQ: Frequently Asked Questions

FAQ-1: How to set up Interest parameters for Overdue Bills

- **Company Interest Computation**: At *F11:Feature> Accounting Feature*, to activate Company Interest Features:
  - o **Simple Parameters**: Set *Yes* at *Activate Interest* to activate Computation Features
  - o **Advanced Parameters**: Having Activated Simple Interest Feature, set Yes at *Use Advanced Parameters*, to compute Interest at varied Interest rates, over-riding the default rates for any transaction.
  - o **Bill Reference:** To activate Overdue Interest Features, at *Maintain Bill by Bill details*, set Yes to compute Overdue Interest on Customer / Supplier Bills
- **Party Interest Activation:** Having Activated Interest & Bill Reference, at the respective Party Ledger entry / alteration screen (F-1B/02-11), set Yes at *Activate Interest Calculation* to get Interest Parameter screen (F-1A). At Interest Parameters screen of the Ledger Account, set Yes at *Calculate Interest Transaction by Transaction* to specify Bill by Bill to activate Interest parameters (F-1A) for Overdue Bills for the Party.
- **Advanced Party Interest Activation:** You may further set Yes at Override Advanced Parameters (if advanced Interest parameters is set up at Company Features: P-02/02-11)

Closing Stock Value 03-10

01 Closing Stock Value

So, far we have entered all data of all sorts business transactions. We have also discussed various Books of Accounts & Accounting Reports. You are now ready to get Final Accounts Statements (PL Statement & Balance Sheet) as discussed earlier (§01/01-11).

For a pure service organnisation (like Consultancy Firm), who do not trade in any materials, there may not be any tradable stock involved. In that case, the Profit & Loss Statement and the Balance Sheet may be readily obtained after voucher entry. However, for organiastions having trade materials in stock, the Closing Stock Value must be entered, to get Final Accounts Statements,

In traditional method, the Closing Stock is entered through Journal Voucher, at the end of Financial Year. However, to facilitate Final Accounts Reporting for mid period (in middle of Financial Year – i.e Month end, Quarter end, Half Year end etc), Tally provides a novel and flexible means of entry of Closing Stock value for multiple dates. This, in fact, amounts to several Journal Entries for respective dates, which remain dormant in the system and the specific Journal Entry as per the report period selected. gets activated and considered for the report, So, you can get the Final Accounts of any period, without having to enter / edit Journal Voucher for Closing Stock, each time you print the reports.

To get Final Accounts instantly for any period (including past mid periods for comparison), you do not enter Journal Voucher for closing stock at the end of Financial Year (as traditionally done by Accountants). Instead, you just enter the Closing Stock value (F-1) for the respective date at Stock-in-Hand Ledger (the Ledger Account in which the Opening Stock value, if any, is also entered as Ledger Opening Balance)

02 Closing Stock in Tally

The difference in entry process in traditional Journal Voucher for Closing Stock Entry and the method of Closing Stock Entry in Stock-in-Hand Ledger Master, are:

So, Tally provides a dynamic method of entry of *Closing Stock Value* to enable display of Final Accounts statement (P L statement & Balance Sheet) for any mid period and a comparative / composite statement for any past periods.

Journal Voucher entry in Traditional Method	Entry at Stock-in-Hand Ledger Account in Tally
A Journal Voucher is created for the Closing Stock Value for the Financial Period end Date	No Journal Voucher is created for the Closing Stock Value. Instead, Closing Stock value for respective Date is entered in Stock-in-Hand Ledger Account through Ledger Alteration
Only one Journal Voucher may be created for the respective period end. Ledger.	Closing Stock value for multiple dates (e.g for each month, or for each quarter etc) may be entered in Stock-in-Hand
For Final Accounts Report, for each period end (monthly, Quarterly etc), you have to delete the previous voucher and create another voucher for the respective Date. So, the voucher for previous period gets deleted and only one closing stock value remains in the data, at any point of time.	Just add the date & closing stock value for the respective date, at the Stock-in-Hand Ledger Account. So, the closing stock value for all the periods may simultaneously remain (the previous values do not get deleted) in the data, at all point of time.
To get Final Accounts for previous period (or for ant period), you have delete the Journal Voucher and create a new Journal Voucher for the Closing Stock Value for the respective period	At any point of time, you may instantly print the Final Accounts for any period end (even the pervious period, if required) for which Closing Stock Value has been entered in Stock-in-Hand Ledger.

03 Closing Stock Value Entry

Select *GoT>Accounts Info>Alter* and select the respective Closing Stock Ledger Accounts to get Ledger Alteration screen (F-1). At *Closing Balance* field (this field apperas only in Alteration of Ledger Accounts under Stock-in-Hand Group), enter the *Date* and *Value* of Closing Stock on the Specified Date, for the respective Closing Stock Ledger Account.

You may enter Closing Stock Value for several Dates (e.g for each month end, quarter end, H/Y end, Year end etc). In fact, you should enter the Closing Stock Value for the Date for which you print the Balance Sheet / Profit & Loss Statement.

The respective value of closing stock would be shown according to the reporting period.

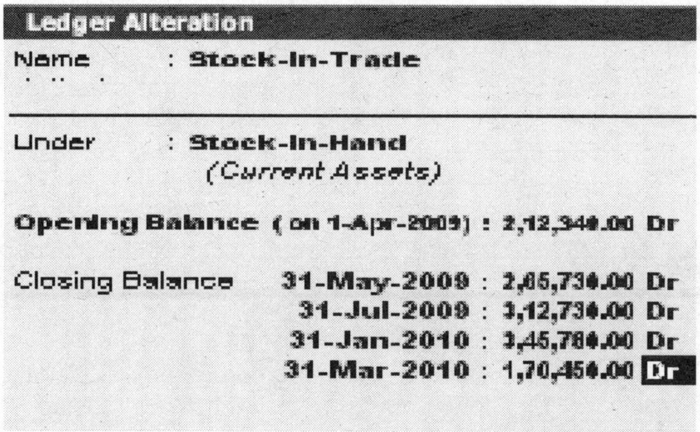

F-1: Closing Stock value entry in Stock Ledger Account

> **Note:** *You may enter the Closing Stock Value through Ledger Alteration mode only (NOT during Stock Ledger Account creation). At the time of Stock Ledger creation, you may enter the Opening Stock Value at Opening Balance field – §03.03/01-03)*

After you enter the Closing stock value, you get the final Profit & Loss A Statement (F-1/01-10) & Balance Sheet (F-1/01-11) as per The Closing Stock value entered in Stock-in-Hand Ledger Account (F-1)

FAQ: Frequently Asked Questions

FAQ-1: How to enter Closing Stock Value for Final Accounts

Ans: At Closing Stock Ledger Accounts Alteration (*GoT>Accounts Info>Alter*) and select the respective Closing Stock Ledger Accounts) screen (F-1). At *Closing Balance* field (this field appears only in Alteration of Ledger Accounts under Stock-in-Hand Group), enter the *Date* and *Value* of Closing Stock on the Specified Date, for the respective Closing Stock Ledger Account.

You may enter Closing Stock Value for several Dates (e.g for each month end, quarter end, H/Y end, Year end etc). In fact, you should enter the Closing Stock Value for the Date for which you print the Balance Sheet / Profit & Loss Statement.

The respective value of closing stock would be shown according to the reporting period.

Part 4
Banking

Any enter prise, even small, is likely to make Financial transaction with bank. Banking is an essential part of business activities. A lot of clerical work is involved for Banking tasks

In this Part, we discuss about the various Banking Tasks that an enter prise has to perform for transactions with Bank and guide how to do those tasks using Tally ERP 9, instead of doing manually. Banking using Tally ERP 9 may save time and ease the tasks of Cheque Printing, Bank Reconciliation etc., where Banking Transactions of the Organisation is of substantial volume

Banking explains activation and set up of Banking features, creation of Masters, design & printing of Cheques, entry of Cheque details in voucher, entry & printing of Bank Deposit slips etc

Bank Reconciliation explains matching / tagging of cleared bank transactions to get Bank Reconciliation Statement.

Auto Bank Reconciliation explains downloading the e-bank statements from the website of the Bank and auto-matching / tagging of cleared bank transactions to get Bank Reconciliation Statement

Organisations not having substantial Banking Transactions may do the Banking part manually and skip this chapter.

Banking

01 Banking

Every business organisation keeps at least one bank account for its business transactions. Tally.ERP 9 exclusively provides certain operation & features related to banking, like Cheque printing, Deposit Slip Printing, Bank Reconciliation etc. These are optional tasks that you can do through Tally.ERP 9, than doing manually.

Banking Tasks

- **Enabling Cheque Activities:** Set Up options to activate & Cheque entry & printing (§02)
- **Bank Ledger set up for Cheque options and Bank details** (§03)
  - o Enabling Cheque Printing options
  - o Entering Cheque Book Range
  - o Designing Cheque Templates conforming to Bank's cheque stationery (§04)
- **Cheque details entry in Voucher:** Entry of cheque details (of cheques issued & received) in Vouchers (§06)
- **Cheque Printing**: Printing Cheques and daily reports for cheques issued (§11)
- **Bank Deposit slips**: Printing Deposit slips for depositing money into bank account and daily reports of monies deposited into bank account (§10)
- **Bank Reconciliation:** Entry of Bank Clearing dates of cheques and reconciling the Pass Book & Bank Book Balances (§01/04-02)

At Gateway, Select Banking to get Banking Menu (F-3)

02 Activate Cheque Printing

To activate Cheque Printing Feature, *Click F11:Features >F1: Accounting Features* to get *Accounting Features screen. At Other Features* section, set *Yes* at *Enable Cheque Printing* (F-1)

F-1: Cheque Printing Feature Activation

Cheque Range for : **Bank of India**

From Number	To Number	Number of Cheques	Book Name
123401	123500	100	Book 1
345651	345700	50	Book 2

F-2B: Cheque Book Range entry

03 Bank Ledger Creation / Alteration

At Account Ledger Creation / Alteration screen (F-2A) of a Bank Ledger, you have to specify some additional information relating to Cheques, as below:

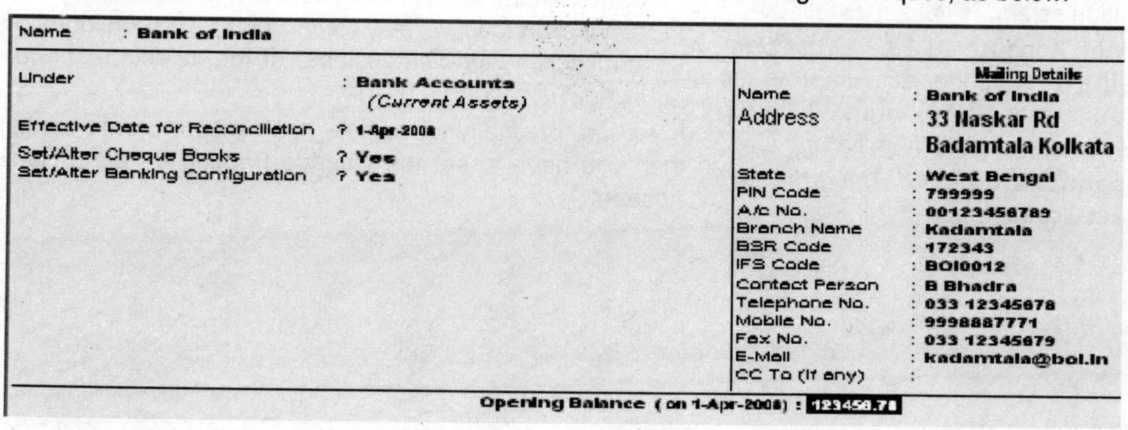

F-2A: Bank Ledger Creation

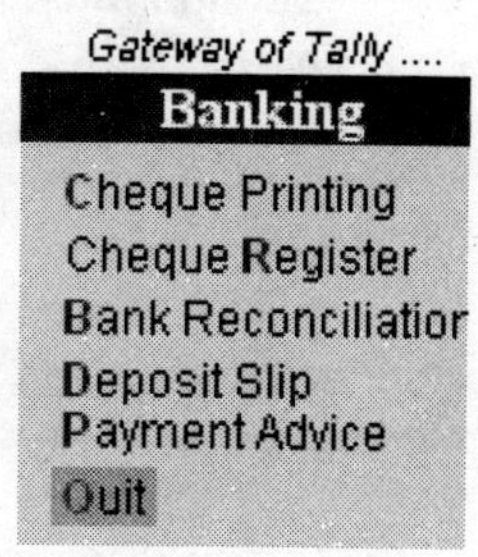

F-3:Banking Menu

- **Bank Reconciliation Effective Date:** It is the Date upto which the Bank Reconciliation is already done. Normally, the Books Beginning date is carried by default (which you may change, if required).
- **Cheque Book Details:** Bank issues a blank cheque book, containing certain number of cheque leaves (25, 50 100 etc). At the Bank Ledger Entry / Alter screen (F-2A), set *Yes* at *Set Alter Cheque Books* to get *Cheque Range* entry screen (F-2B) to enter the details of each Blank Cheque Book issued by the Bank to the Company, as below:
  - o **Starting Cheque Number**: *At From Number* column, enter the serial number of the first cheque in the book
  - o **Ending Cheque Number:** *At To Number* column, enter the serial number of last cheque in the book
  - o **Number of Cheques:** The number of cheques are computed from the Starting & Ending Number and displayed. As a cheque book contains specified standard number of cheque leaves, any mistake in entry of Starting & Ending Cheque number can be easily located here.

  As a Cheque book contains specified standard number of Cheque leaves, any mistake in entry of Starting & Ending Cheque number can be easily located here.

  Alternatively, instead of entering Ending Cheque Number, you may specify the number of cheque leaves in the book (e.g.50). The Ending Number will be computed from the Starting Number and displayed.
  - o **Book Name:** Enter here Book Name for identification (like Book – 1, Book 2, or Suppliers, Other Payments etc)
- **Banking Configuration:** At *Set Alter Banking Configuration* (F-2A), set *Yes* to get *Banking Configuration* screen (F-4) to download the Cheque Configuration from the Net, This requires Internet Connection and valid Tally Net Subscription

  At Banking Configuration screen (F-4), set as follows:
  - o **Selection for Bank Acocunt**: At *Select Your Bank Account*, select the Bank Ledger Account from the List of Ledger Accounts (F-5A) whose Cheque Configuration can be downloaded from Net.
  - o **Auto Bank Reconciliation**: At *Activate Auto Reconciliation*, set *Yes* to Import Bank Statements to match the entries in Bank Book, to perform Auto Bank Reconciliation
  - o **Setting Cheque Configuration:** At the field *Set / Alter Banking Configuration*, set Yes to get the list of Cheque Formats available for the Bank (F-6). Often, several Formats of the Cheque Stationery are available. As you roll over each cheque Format in the list, the image of the Cheque Leaf is shown beside. On viewing the image of each Format, select the right Format which matches the Cheque Leaf used by you

> ***Note:*** *You may copy the Cheque Dimension Configuration instead of designing yourselves., saving a lot of time, well matching the Cheque Format.*

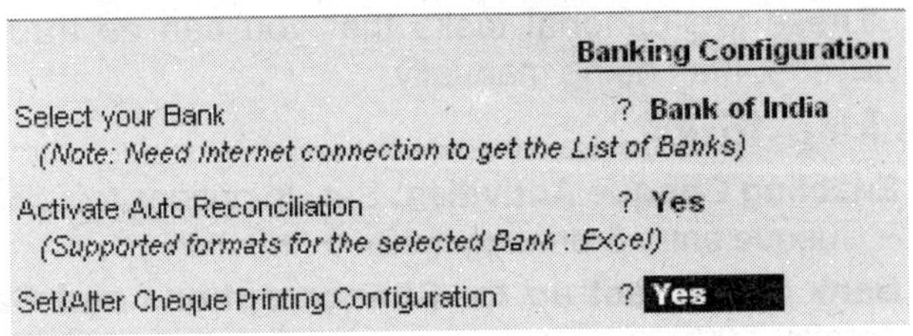

F-4 Banking Configuration

04 Cheque Configuration

A Cheque is printed on Bank's Cheque stationery (Cheque Books issued by Bank). The layout of cheque stationery for each Bank is not same. The position of each element of cheque (like Drawee Name, Amount etc) differs. So, to print cheque correctly, you have to specify the position of each element of the cheque (distance from Top / Left edge). This can be done in ways:

- **Entering the Cheque Specification for respective Bank Account**: Enter the values of Cheque Configuration as per respective Bank Cheque Stationery (§04.02)
- **Importing the Cheque Specification for respective Bank Account:** Instead of entering the specification, download the specification from Net (it requires Internet connection & active Tally Net Account). The configuration values (Cheque Dimensions) of the selected Cheque Format is imported. (F-4)

If you are maintaining multiple bank accounts with banks, then you have to set the Cheque Printing for each Bank Account

List of Banks

Not Applicable
Abhyudaya Co-Op. Bank Ltd.
ADCB (UAE)
Allahabad Bank
Andhra Bank
Arab Bank (UAE)
Axis Bank
Bank Asia Limited (Bangladesh)
Bank of Baroda
Bank of Baroda (UAE)
Bank of India
Bank of Maharashtra
Bharat Co-Operative Bank (Mumbai) Ltd
BNP Paribas
Bombay Mercantile Co-Operative Bank Limited
BRAC Bank (Bangladesh)
Canara Bank
Central Bank of India
Citi Bank
Citizen Credit Co-Op. Bank Ltd.
City Union Bank Limited
Commercial Bank of Ceylon PLC (Bangladesh)
Commercial Bank of Dubai
Corporation Bank
DBS (Hongkong)
DBS (Singapore)
DCB Bank
Dena Bank
Deutsche Bank
Dhaka Bank Limited (Bangladesh)
Dhanlaxmi Bank
DNS BANK
Dutch-Bangla Bank Limited (Bangladesh)
Emirates NBD (UAE)
Federal Bank
First Bank of Nigeria Plc.
GMCB
Guaranty Trust Bank (Nigeria)
Habib Bank AG Zurich (UAE)
HDFC Bank
HSBC Bank
HSBC Bank (Bangladesh)
HSBC Bank (Hongkong)
HSBC Bank (UAE)
ICICI Bank
IDBI Bank
Indian Bank
Indian Overseas Bank
IndusInd Bank
Ing Vysya Bank
Islami Bank Bangladesh Limited
Jammu and Kashmir Bank
Jamuna Bank Limited (Bangladesh)
Janaseva Sahakari Bank Ltd Pune
Janata Sahakari Bank Ltd
JNS Bank
Karnataka Bank Ltd.
Karur Vysya Bank
Kotak Mahindra Bank
Lakshmi Vilas Bank
Lokmangal Co-Op Bank Ltd. Solapur
Lokseva Sahakari Bank Ltd., Pune
Mashreq Bank (UAE)
M.D.Pawar People's Co-Operative Bank Ltd., Urun
Mizuho Corporate Bank Ltd
National Bank of Abu Dhabi (UAE)
National Bank of Fujairah
NBS (Malawi)
NCC Bank (Bangladesh)
New India Co-Op Bank Ltd
NKGSB Co-Op Bank Ltd
Nutan Nagarik Sahakari Bank Ltd.
ONE Bank (Bangladesh)
Oriental Bank of Commerce
Pavana Sahakari Bank Limited, Pune
Premier Bank (Bangladesh)
Prime Cooperative Bank Limited
Punjab and Sind Bank
Punjab & Maharashtra Co-Op. Bank Ltd.
Punjab National Bank
Rajarambapu Sahakari Bank Ltd.,Peth.
RAK Bank (UAE)
Ratnakar Bank
RHB (Malaysia)
Rupee Co-Op. Bank Ltd.
Sangli Urban Co-Op. Bank Ltd
Saraswat Bank
Sardar Vallabhbhai Sahakari Bank Ltd
Shree Sharada Sahakari Bank Ltd., Pune
Shri Arihant Co-Op. Bank Limited
Social Islami Bank Limited (Bangladesh)
South Indian Bank
Standard Bank of Malawi
Standard Chartered Bank
Standard Chartered Bank (BGD)
Standard Chartered Bank (Hongkong)
Standard Chartered Bank (UAE)
State Bank of Bikaner and Jaipur
State Bank of Hyderabad
State Bank of India
State Bank of Mysore
State Bank of Patiala
State Bank of Travancore
Syndicate Bank
Tamilnad Mercantile Bank
The Ahmedabad Mercantile Co-Operative Bank Ltd.
The A.P. Mahesh Co-Operative Urban Bank Ltd.
The Bank of Tokyo-Mitsubishi UFJ, Ltd.
The Baramati Sahakari Bank Ltd.
The Catholic Syrian Bank Ltd
The C.K.P. Co-Op. Bank Ltd.
The Cosmos Co-Operative Bank Ltd
The Gadhinglaj Urban Co-Op. Bank Ltd
The Gandhinagar Urban Co-Op. Bank Ltd.
The Goa State Co-Operative Bank Ltd.
The Greater Bombay Co-Operative Bank Ltd.
The Jamnagar Peoples Co-Op. Bank Ltd
The Kalupur Commercial Co-Op Bank Ltd.
The Kapol Co-Op Bank Ltd.
The Karad Urban Co-Op. Bank Ltd.
The Mehsana Urban Co-Op. Bank Ltd.
The Muslim Cooperative Bank Ltd, Pune
The Nawanagar Co-Operative Bank Ltd
The Royal Bank of Scotland
The Seva Vikas Co-Operative Bank Ltd
The Shamrao Vithal Co-Op. Bank Ltd.
The Thane Janata Sahakari Bank Ltd.
The Vaish Cooperative New Bank Ltd
The Vishweshwar Sahakari Bank Ltd., Pune
The Zoroastrian Co-Operative Bank Ltd
Trust Bank Limited (Bangladesh)
UCO Bank
Union Bank of India
Union Bank of Nigeria Plc
Union National Bank (UAE)
United Bank of Africa
United Bank of India
United Commercial Bank Ltd (Bangladesh)
Vasai Vikas Sahakari Bank Ltd
Vijaya Bank
Vishwas Co-Op Bank Ltd., Nashik
Yes Bank
Zenith International Bank (Nigeria)

F-5A:List of Banks of Downloadable Cheque Configuration

> **Note:** *A large number of Banks are listed whose cheque diemnsions are provided by Tally. So, it is likely your banker is also listed. You should activate Auto Reconciliation only when you can download the Bank Account Statement from the Banker's site.*

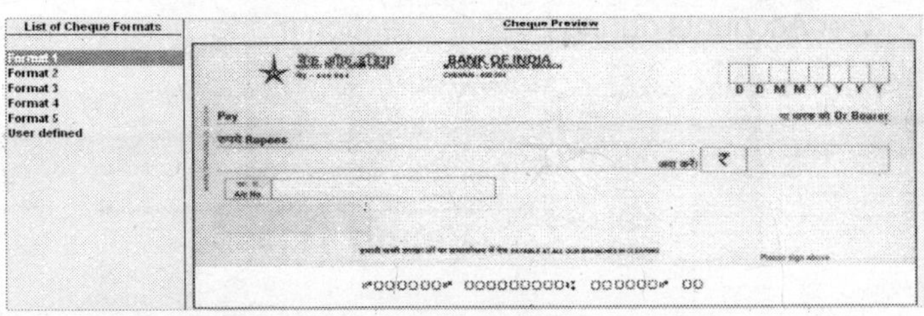

F-6 Cheque Format Import selection

> **Note:** *Check that your printer can properly print on the cheque stationery. You may need to change the printer set up for cheque paper size.*

4.01 User Defined Cheque Template

If the Cheque Stationery used by you is not available in the Format, select *User Defined* in the list of Cheque Formats (F-6). Press *Al;t+U* to get *Cheque Dimensions Configuration* screen (F-7) to specify the Cheque Template for the Bank Account

At *Cheque Dimensions Configuration* screen (F-7), you specify the size, margins, print area, position of cheque amount in words & numbers etc.,among various banks.

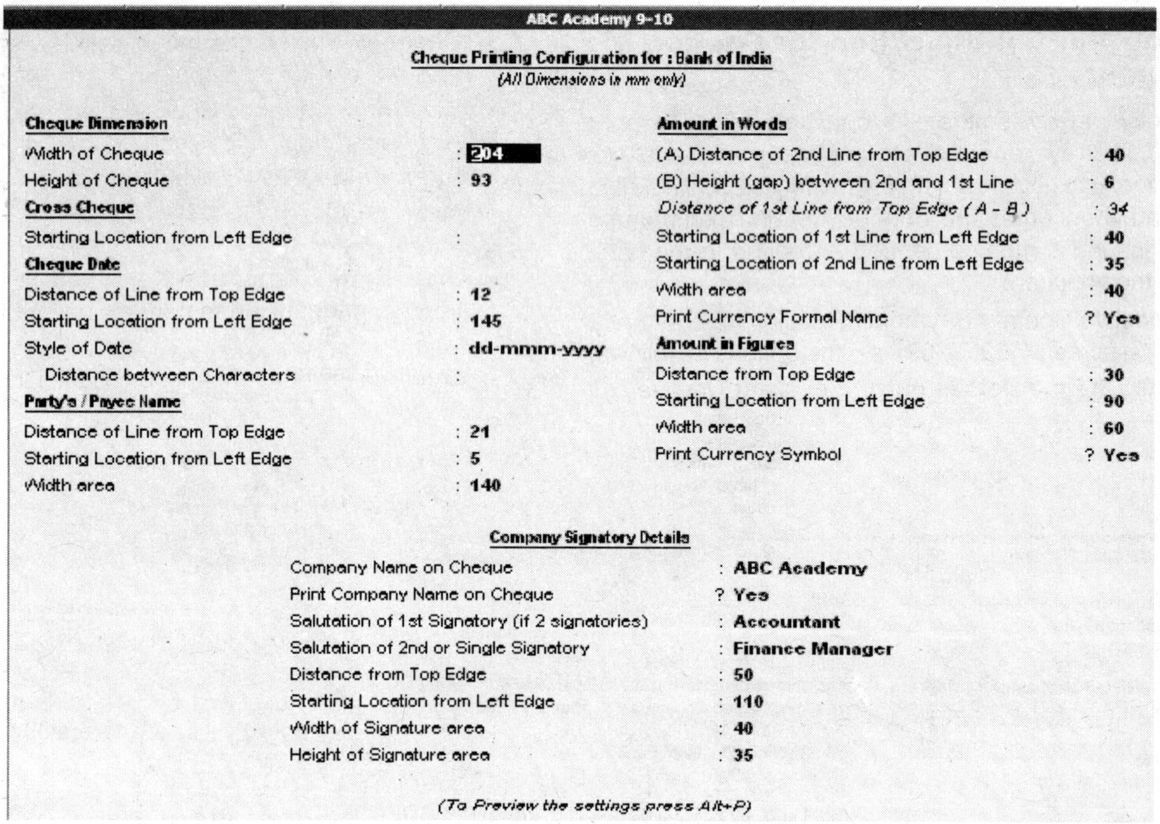

F-7: Cheque Dimensions Configuration

First, you measure these values, specify the respective values in Cheque Printing Configuration and print some dummy cheques in plain paper (semi transparent see-through paper will be more useful) as Trial. Impose the printed paper over a bank cheque leaf and see if the elements are properly placed. If not, change the value for the respective element and re print on paper. After a few trials, you will be able to set the cheque printing specifications perfectly as per the cheque stationery of the bank

04.02 Cheque Dimension Configuration

In the *Cheque Dimension Configuration (F-7),* enter each dimension & position to fill up the specifications correctly.

04.03 Sample Cheque Printing

After setting the values at *Cheque Dimension Configuration (F-7),* press *Alt+P* to get the Cheque printing screen (F-8B), to print the Test Cheque Template with dummy values (F-8A).

Now check the template to ensure that it matches with your cheque stationery (you may use photocopies of cheque stationery as dummy).

Now measure the dimensions and positions of the printed sample cheque and adjust the dimension values accordingly. With some trials, you will be able to configure it properly. Once it is set, you will be able to print cheque in the Bank's Cheque stationery

In this way, set the dimension for each Bank's cheque stationery.

You may later on change the values at *Cheque Dimension Configuration* in the same way, as you set the values

This way, you may set the Cheque Dimension for new Bank Ledger Accounts during Ledger Creation mode

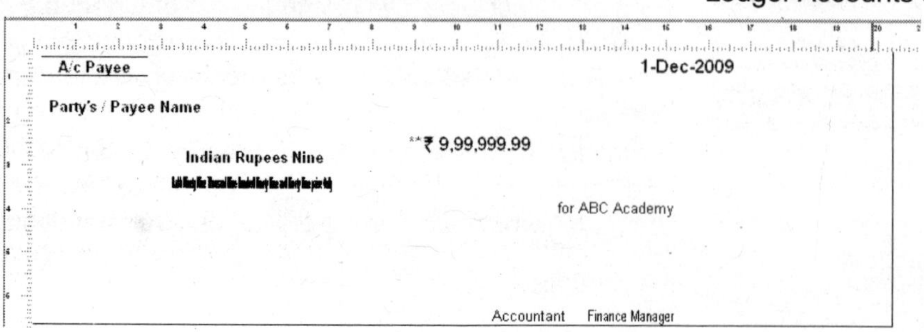

F-8A: Test (sample) Cheque Template

F-8B Sample Cheque Printing

05 Voucher Configuration for Cheque Details

Creation of Cheque template is one time task. To print cheques / money receipts etc and to perform Bank Reconciliation, you have to set up the respective configuration options and then enter the cheque details (of cheques received / issued & monies debited / credited in the bank account in the voucher)

At the respective Contra / Payment / Receipt voucher entry Configuration screen (§02/02-09), set the options as follows:

- **Activate Cheque Details entry**: Set *No* at *Use Default for Bank Allocations* to get the Cheque details entry screen after selection of Bank account in the voucher
- **Remarks**: Set *Yes* at *Show Remarks at Bank Allocation details* to enter details of the cheque / transaction at Remark column (this helps matching at the time of Bank Reconciliation)

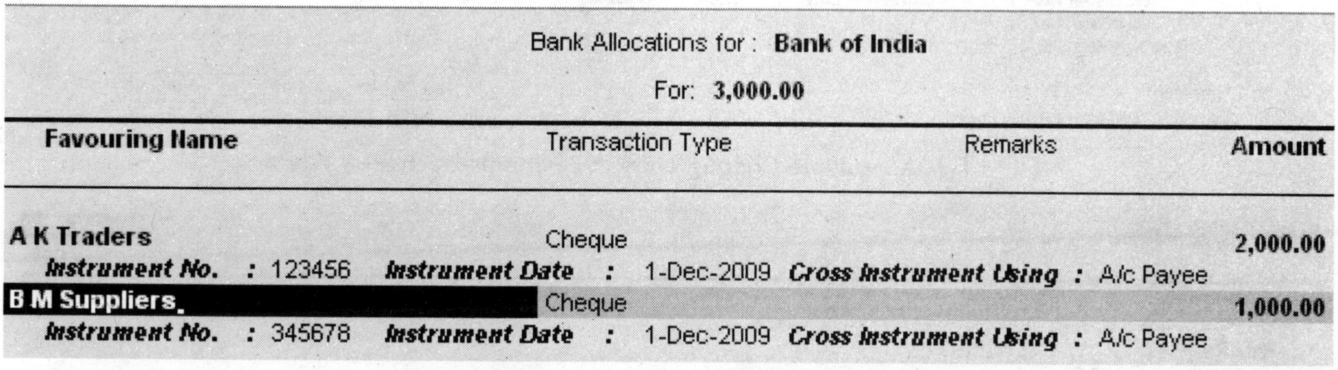

F-9A: Cheque details in Voucher Entry (bank Details sub-screen)

06 Cheque Details Entry in Voucher

Having set the Configuration as stated above at the respective voucher entry screen, on selection of a Bank Account, you get the Cheque details entry screen **(F-9A)**

Common Details: At the cheque details entry screen (F-9A), enter the following details:

- **Party Name:** Enter the Name of the Payee (in Payment Voucher)/ Payer (in Receipt Voucher). For convenience, the first account name of the voucher is carried, which you may change. This name would be printed in the cheque. So, if the ledger name is different from payee's name, overwrite the correct Payee Name.
- **Transaction Type**: Select the transaction type from the list (F-9B) as follows:

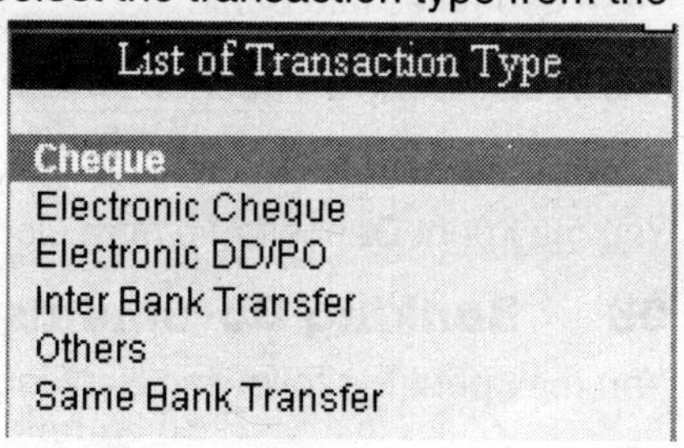

F-9B: List of valid Transaction Types in Bank details sub-screen in Voucher entry

  - **Cheque:** When a cheque is issued / received (this option is carried by default)
  - **Electronic Cheque:** When an electronic transaction is done through net banking or other digital means
  - **Electronic DD/PO:** When the bank is asked to issue an electronic DD/ PO advise the payee's banker
  - **Inter Bank Transfer:** When fund is transferred through net banking to payee's account in another bank
  - **Others:** Any other means, e.g Bank Debits etc.
  - **Same Bank Transfer:** Bank transfer to payee's account in same bank.
- **Cheque Amount**: Enter the Cheque Amount. The amount of the respective Bank Ledger Account in the voucher is carried, which you may change
- **Instrument Number**: Enter the Instrument Reference Number (Cheque Number / other debit reference number for electronic transaction). Tally does not automatically carry the cheque numbers consecutively. You have to enter it (keep a note manually). If any cheque is cancelled and another cheque is issued, you have to edit the voucher to change the cheque number.
- **Instrument Date**: The voucher date is carried by default. Change the instrument date (if different from voucher date) where necessary.
- **Crossing Type**: Enter the Crossing Type. This will be printed on the cheque. Leave blank for uncrossed cheque. If the crossing is pre printed on cheque, leave blank at this field

You may enter multiple cheques breaking up the amount of Bank Ledger (F-10A). The cheque date may be different from Voucher Date. This way, you may make entry for Post Dated cheques issued / received. You may also enter cheques issued to / received from different parties in one voucher. The total amount must match with the Bank Ledger Amount in the voucher.

Payment No. 7 — 1-Dec-2009, Tuesday

Particulars	Debit	Credit
Dr **A K Traders**	2,000.00	
Cur Bal: **5,550.00 Dr**		
Dr **B M Suppliers**	1,000.00	
Cur Bal: **6,170.00 Cr**		
Cr **Bank of India**		3,000.00
Cur Bal: **28,520.00 Dr**		
A K Traders — Cheque — 1,200.00		
Instrument No. : 123456 ***Instrument Date*** : 2-Dec-2009 ***Cross Instrument Using*** : A/c Payee		
Bank Date :		
A K Traders — Cheque — 800.00		
Instrument No. : 123457 ***Instrument Date*** : 3-Dec-2009 ***Cross Instrument Using*** : A/c Payee		
Bank Date :		
B M Suppkliers — Cheque — 1,000.00		
	3,000.00	**3,000.00**

Narration:
Cheques issued to various credtor:

F-10A: Multiple Cheque entry in Payment Voucher

Receipt No. 3 — 31-Jul-2009, Friday

Particulars	Debit	Credit
Cr **Rent Received**		3,000.00
Cur Bal: **3,000.00 Cr**		
Dr **Bank of India**	3,000.00	
Cur Bal: **28,520.00 Dr**		
A K Traders — Cheque/DD — 2,000.00		
Instrument No. : 234567 ***Instrument Date*** : 31-Jul-2009 ***Bank Name*** : SBI ***Branch*** : Burrabazar		
Bank Date :		
A K Traders — Cheque/DD — 1,000.00		
Instrument No. : 238761 ***Instrument Date*** : 3-Aug-2009 ***Bank Name*** : HDFC ***Branch*** : Salt Lake		
Bank Date :		
Name on Receipt : **A K Traders**		
	3,000.00	**3,000.00**

Narration:
Received from A K Traders, Rent for the m/o July 09

F-10B; Multiple Cheque entry in Receipt Voucher

Cheque Details Entry in Receipt Voucher: In the same way, you enter the details of Cheque Received, in Receipt Voucher. You have to additionally enter the Bank Name & Branch (F-10B).on which the received cheque is drawn, to keep complete details of Cheque Received.

07 Cash Deposit into Bank

When Cash is deposited into Bank, in the *Contra* Voucher (F-10D), when you select the Bank Account, the Cash deposit denominations screen appear in which you have to enter the details of Cash for each denomination (F-10C).

HDFC Bank
Denominations For: **20,000.00**

Denominations		Amount
1000 X	6	6,000.00
500 X	23	11,500.00
100 X	25	2,500.00
50 X		
20 X		
10 X		
5 X		
2 X		
1 X		
Others		
Total		20,000.00
Difference		

F-10C: Cash deposit Note dimension entry

Accounting Voucher Creation — Ctrl + M

Contra No. 6 — 31-Mar-2010, Wednesday

Particulars	Debit	Credit
Cr **Cash**		20,000.00
Dr **HDFC Bank**	20,000.00	
	20,000.00	**20,000.00**

Narration:
Cash deposited into Bank

F-10D: Contra Voucher for Cash Deposit into Bank Account

You may print Deposit Slip from Contra Voucher entry (§10).

08 Banking Documents Printing

You may print the following Banking Documents

In respect of Cheques Received

- Deposit Slip

In respect of Cheques Issued

- Chqeue
- Cheque Register
- Payment Advice

At gateway of Tally, select *Banking* to get the Banking menu (F-3) to perform the above operations

09 Cheque Register

At Banking Menu (F-3), select *Cheque Register* to get *Cheque Register Summary,* showing number of Cheques of different Status (F-11B, F-11C).

Buttons at Cheque Register:

- **F1:Detailed / Condensed**:
  - o Click *F1:Detailed* toggle button to get the details of Cheques within the specified Cheque Book Range and outside the Cheque Book range (F-11C),
  - o Click *F1:Condensed* toggle button to get the number of cheque for each status (F-11B),
- **F2:Period**: To Set the Period of the Report
- **F5: Reconcile**: To get Bank Reconciliation screen (F-20)
- **S: Quick Search**: To Quickly Search a Cheque (instrument). Click *S: Quick Search* button (or press Alt +S) to get instrument search screen (F-11D). At Enter Instrument Number field, enter the cheque number to be searched. As you type the number, the instruments with matching numbers are listed (when you type the full cheque number, only the respective cheque record is shown)
- **S:Show All**: Click *S: Show All* button (or press Ctrl +S) to get the Cheque Status list (F-11A) to show the cheques of selected Status (F-12A & F-12B).

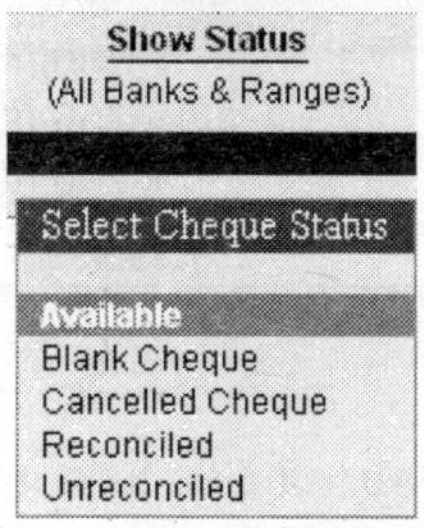

F-11A: Cheque Status selection List

Cheque Register — ABC Academy 9-10 — Ctrl + M

Bank Wise Report

Particulars	Available	Unreconciled	Reconciled	Blank	Cancelled	Out of Period	Total Cheques
		1-Apr-2008 to 31-Mar-2010					
Bank of India	100	4					104
Total	100	4					104

F-11B:Cheque Register (Summary)

Cheque Register — ABC Academy 9-10 — Ctrl + M

Bank Wise Report

Particulars		Available	Unreconciled	Reconciled	Blank	Cancelled	Out of Period	Total Cheques
			1-Apr-2008 to 31-Mar-2010					
Bank of India		100	4					104
123501-123600	*(Book 1)*	*100*						*100*
Not in Range			*4*					*4*
Total		100	4					104

F-11C:Cheque Register (Detail)

Instrument Number

Enter Instrument Number :

List of Cheque Numbers

Instrument Number	Bank Name	Cheque Status	Transaction Date	Cheque Range
123501	***Bank of India***	***Available***		***123501-123600***
123502	*Bank of India*	*Available*		*123501-123600*
123503	*Bank of India*	*Available*		*123501-123600*
123504	*Bank of India*	*Available*		*123501-123600*

F-11D: Quick Search of Cheque (S:Quick Search)

Instrument Wise — ABC Academy 9-10 — Ctrl + M

Ledger: **Bank of India** — 1-Apr-2008 to 31-Mar-2010

Cheque Range: **123501-123600**

Cheque No.	Status	Date	Particulars	Vch Type	Vch No.	Instrument Date	Amount
123501	Available						
123502	Available						
123503	Available						
123504	Available						
123522	Available						

78 more ...

F-12A: Cheque Details (Available Cheques)

Instrument Wise — ABC Academy 9-10 — Ctrl + M

Ledger: **All Items** — **(Unreconciled)** — 1-Apr-2008 to 31-Mar-2010

Cheque Range: **All Items**

Cheque No.	Status	Date	Particulars	Vch Type	Vch No.	Instrument Date	Amount
189743	Unreconciled	31-8-2009	A K Traders	Payment	7	31-8-2009	1,000.00
239876	Unreconciled	1-6-2009	A K Traders	Payment	4	1-6-2009	1,980.00
345678	Unreconciled	31-3-2010	Salary	Payment	15	31-3-2010	1,35,750.00
345765	Unreconciled	28-2-2010	A K Traders	Payment	8	28-2-2010	1,200.00
Total	:						**1,39,930.00**

F-12B: Cheque Details (Unreconciled Cheques)

10 Deposit Slip

When you Deposit Cash or Cheques received, in your Bank Account, you have to fill up up a Deposit Slip form giving the details of Cheques (in case of *Cheque* Deposit) and denominationwise details of Cash (in case of *Cash* Deposit) and submit it to the Bank.

You may print the Deposit Slips from the Contra Vouchers entered for Cash Deposit and Contra / Receipt Vouchers for Cheque Deposits, eliminating the task of writing manual deposit slips, saving time and eliminating errors.

Deposit Slip Report

At Banking menu (F-3), select Deposit Printing (GoT>Banking >Deposit Slip) to get *Deposit Slip* menu (F-13A). At *Deposit Slip* menu (F-13A):

- **Cheque Deposit Slip**: Select *Cheque Deposit* Slip to enter the details of cheques to be deposited into the Bank.
- **Cash Deposit Slip**: Select *Cash Deposit Slip* to enter the details of Cash denominations of Cash to be deposited into the Bank.

Next select the bank Account into which Cheque / Cash is to be deposited, from the list of the Bank accounts.

10.1 Cheque Deposit Report

When you select *Cheque Deposit Slip*, the Receipt Vouchers for the specified Bank Account are listed in the Report (F-13B)

10.2 Cash Deposit Report

When Cash is Deposited into Bank, in the *Contra Voucher*, when you select the Bank Account, the Cash Deposit Denominations screen appear in which you have to enter the details of Cash for each Denomination (F-13D).

When you select *Cash Deposit Slip*, the Contra Vouchers for the specified Bank Account are listed in the Report (F-13E)

Gateway of Tally ....
Banking ....

Deposit Slip

Cheque Deposit Slip
Cash Deposit Slip
Quit

F-13A Depsoit Sip Menu

Cheque Deposit Slip — ABC Academy 9-10 — Ctrl + M

Ledger: **Bank of India** — 1-Mar-2010 to 31-Mar-2010

Date	Particulars	Instrument No.	Instrument Date	Printed ?	Amount
1-3-2010	A K Traders	123567	1-3-2010	No	6,000.00
Selected Total					
Grand Total					6,000.00

F-13B:Cheque Deposit Slip

F2: Period
F3: Company
F4: Bank
F5: Cash
F6: Show All
F7: Edit Ch. Details
P: Mark as Printed

13C Buttons

Bank of India
Denominations For: **1,000.00**

Denominations		Amount
1000 X		
500 X	2	1,000.00
100 X		
50 X		
20 X		
10 X		
5 X		
2 X		
1 X		
Others		
Total		1,000.00
Difference		

F-13D: Denomination entry for Cash Deposit

Cash Deposit Slip Ctrl + M

Ledger: **Bank of India** **1-Mar-2010 to 31-Mar-2010**

Date	Particulars	Instrument Date	Printed ?	Amount
31-3-2010	Cash	31-3-2010	No	1,000.00
Selected Total				
Grand Total				1,000.00

F-13E: Cash Deposit Slip

At *Cash Deposit Slip* screen (F-13E), click *P:Print* (or press Alt+P) to get *Cash Deposit Slip printing* Configuration screen (13F).

10.3 Cash Deposit Slip printing Configuration

At *Cash Deposit Slip printing* Configuration screen (13F), you may set the options as follows:

- **Print Cash Deposit Slip**: Set *Yes* to print Cash Deposit Slip, else set *No*
- **Date of Printing**: Enter the Date of Deposit of Cash to Bank. The current Date is carried, which you may change
- **Space to leave at Top**: Enter the top margin (in inches-default value 0.5 inch)
- **Print Company's Telephone Number**: Set *Yes* to print Company's Telephone Number, as entered in Company creation screen (§04/02-02), else set *No* (Company's Telephone Number is not printed in Deposit Slip)
- **Print Company's PAN/IT Number**: Set *Yes* to print PAN/ IT Number, as entered in Company's Statutory Info screen ((§04/02-02)), else set *No* (Company's PAN is not printed in Deposit Slip). As per IT Rules, the PAN/ IT Number must be mentioned in Cash deposit slip of Rs 50000 or above

On setting the *Cash Deposit Slip printing Configuration* options (F-13F), you get Deposit Slip Printing screen (F-13G) showing the details of Cash being deposited to Bank. Check the correctness of details Click Yes at *Print Yes / No* to print the *Cash Deposit Slip.*

10.4 Cash Deposit Slip Printing

When you click *Yes* at Print Yes / No at *Cash Deposit Slip* printing screen (F-13G), 2 copies of *Cash Deposit Slip* is printed (F-13H), one for Bank (Banker's Copy) and another for the Company, with same details., for submitting to bank alongwith the Cash at the time of deposit. The bank retains the Banker's copy and signs & returns the Customer copy as receipt of Cash deposited into the Bank.

Report Titles
HDFC Bank
Cash Deposit Slip

Print Cash Deposit Slip	? **Yes**
Date of Printing	: **6-Jan-2013**
Space to leave on Top(default 0.5 inches)	? **0.50**
Print Company's Telephone Number	? **No**
Print Company's PAN/IT Number	? **No**

F-13F: Cash Deposit Slip Printing Configuration

Report Titles
HDFC Bank
Cash Deposit Slip

Cash Deposit Slip Details
Date : **1-Jun-2009** Particulars : **Cash** Instrument Date : **1-Jun-2009** Amount : **1,000.00**

Cash Denomination

Denominations		Amount
1000 X	1	1,000.00
500 X		
100 X		
50 X		
20 X		
10 X		
5 X		
2 X		
1 X		
Others		
Total		1,000.00
Difference		

Print ?
Yes or No

F-13G:Cash Deposit Slip Printing screen

(Banker's Copy)
Cash Deposit Slip/Pay-in-Slip

Bank Name	: HDFC Bank		
Branch Name	: Salt Lake		
Account No.	: 00181000103968	Date	: 6-Jan-2013
Account Holder Name	: ABC Academy		

Denominations		Amount
1000 X	1	1,000.00
500 X		
100 X		
50 X		
20 X		
10 X		
5 X		
2 X		
1 X		
Others		
Total		₹ 1,000.00

Amount (in words) : Indian Rupees One Thousand Only

Deposited by   Received by

F-13H: Deposit Slip

By default, the Report for current date is displayed. Click *F2:Period* and specify the Period for which the Deposit slip is to be printed.

Deposit slip can also be printed from Ledger Voucher List of Bank Ledger A/c (§08/02-16, F-7C)

10.5 Buttons at Deposit Slip report

At Deposit Slip Display screen you get the buttons (F-13C), as follows:

- **F2: Period**: To change the period.
- **F4: Bank**: To select other required Bank from the list.
- **F5: Cash:** To select Cash Account
- **F6: Show All** To show Cheques of all Banks
- **F7: Edit Ch Details**: To edit/update Payer's Name Instrument No, & Instrument Date
- **P: Mark as Printed**: To mark the Selected Voucher as Deposit-slip Printed

10.6 Cheque Deposit Slip Printing

At *Cheque Deposit Slip Display screen (F-13B),* click *P:Print* or (Press Alt+P) to get *Print Deposit slip* Printing screen (F-14A) to print as per options set as displayed (F-14C).

- **Print Deposit Slip**: Set *Yes* to print the Deposit Slip, else set *No*
- **Space to leave on Top** (default 0.5 inches): Set the required space.
- **Cheque Details:** Now set options (Yes / No) for following details to be printed (as entered in the respective Receipt Voucher) in the Deposit Slip
  - o **Show Received From**: Set Yes to print the Payer's Name (when it is different from Party / Ledger Name)
  - o **Show Bank/Branch Name also**: Set Yes to display the Bank and Branch columns in the report.
  - o **Show Remarks also**: Set Yes to display the Cheque Remarks (as entered in the in the Cheque details screen at the respective Voucher entry) in the report in text line.

Report Titles
Bank of India
Deposit Slip

Print Deposit Slip	? **No**
Space to leave on Top(default 0.5 inches)	? **0.50**
Show Received From	? **Yes**
Show Bank/Branch Name also	? **Yes**
Show Remarks also	? **Yes**

F-14A: Deposit Slip Printing Options

Configuration

Show Forex Transactions only	? **No**
Show Received From	? **Yes**
Show Bank/Branch Name also	? **No**
Show Remarks also	? **No**
Appearance of Names	: **Name Only**
Scale Factor for Values	: **Default**
Sorting Method	: **Default**

F-14B: Deposit Slip Configuration

10.7 Cheque Deposit Slip Printing Configuration

At *Deposit Slip Display screen* (F-13B*),* Click *F12:Configuration* to get the *Deposit Slip Configuration* screen (F-14B), At *Deposit Slip Configuration* screen (F-14B), set the options as follows:

Bank of India
Deposit Slip
1-Apr-2009 to 31-Mar-2010
Page 1

Date	Particulars	Received From	Bank	Branch	Instrument No.	Instrument Date	Amount
1-4-2009	**Cash**				Cash	1-4-2009	**500.00**
1-7-2009	**S Kurien**				875432	1-7-2009	**10,000.00**
31-7-2009	**Rent Received**	A K Traders	SBI	Burrabazar	234567	31-7-2009	**2,000.00**
31-7-2009	**Rent Received**	A K Traders	HDFC	Salt Lake	238761	3-8-2009	**1,000.00**
1-8-2009	**ICICI Term Loan**				345876	1-8-2009	**50,000.00**
2-8-2009	**Cash**	Disha Infotech			Cash	2-8-2009	**1,000.00**
1-2-2010	**Sales**				Cash	1-2-2010	**6,000.00**
31-3-2010	**Cash**	ABC Academy 9-10			Cash	31-3-2010	**2,000.00**
Grand Total							**72,500.00**

F-14C: Deposit Slip Report

- **Payer's Name:** At *Show Received From,* set *Yes* to print the *Payer's Name* as entered in the Receipt Voucher (at Received From column), else set *No* to omit Payer's Name details
- **Bank / Branch Name**: At *Show Bank / Branch Name,* set *Yes* to print the Bank Name & Branch Name of the Drawee Bank (at Bank & Branch Column) of the cheque being deposited into the Bank (Drawee Bank details are necessary to be printed in the Deposit Slip submitted to bank to deposit the cheques into bank), else set *No* to omit the Drawee Bank details

to print cheques (F-15C). The Cheque Printing screen, showing the list of pending cheques (the Bank Account must be configured for Cheque Printing) appears (F-15A for *All Banks,* F-15B for *Selected Bank)*

11.1 Buttons at Cheque Printing Screen

At Cheque Printing Screen (F-15A, F-15B), you get flowing Buttons:

- **F2: Period**: To change the period.
- **F4: Bank**: To select the Bank Account (or select *All* to select All Bank Accounts for which Cheque Configuration is set)

Cheque Printing | ABC Academy 9-10 | Ctrl + M

Ledger: **All Items** | 1-Apr-2009 to 31-Mar-2010

(Cheque Printing - Pending Cheques)

Date	Particulars	Favouring Name	Bank Name	Instrument No.	Instrument Date	Printed ?	Amount
1-12-2009	A K Traders	A K Traders	Bank of India	123567	3-12-2009	No	800.00
1-12-2009	A K Traders	A K Traders	Bank of India	456789	5-12-2009	No	200.00
1-12-2009	A K Traders	A K Traders	Bank of India	123456	2-12-2009	No	1,200.00
1-12-2009	A K Traders	A K Traders	Bank of India	123457	3-12-2009	No	800.00
1-12-2009	A K Traders	A K Traders	Bank of India	123458	4-12-2009	No	1,000.00
Selected Total							
Grand Total							4,000.00

F-15A: Cheque Printing List (Cheques for all Banks)

Cheque Printing | ABC Academy 9-10 | Ctrl + M

Ledger: **Bank of India** | 1-Mar-2010 to 31-Mar-2010

Date	Particulars	Instrument No.	Instrument Date	Printed ?	Amount
31-3-2010	Salary	345678	31-3-2010	No	1,35,750.00
31-3-2010	ICICI Term Loan		31-3-2010	No	14,500.00
31-3-2010	A K Traders		31-3-2010	No	1,200.00
3-3-2010	A K Traders		3-3-2010	No	1,000.00
Selected Total					
Grand Total					1,52,450.00

F-15B: Cheque Printing List for a selected Banks

- **Cheque Remarks**: At *Show Remarks also*, set Yes to print the Remarks as entered in the cheque details for the respective cheque in the Receipt Voucher, else set *No* to omit Remarks.

F-15C: Bank Selection

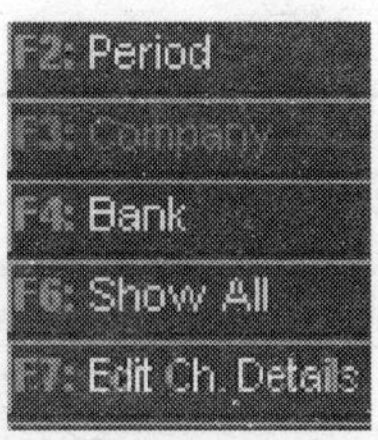

F-15D: Buttons at Cheque Printing

11 Cheque Printing

At Banking menu (F-3), select Cheque Printing (*GoT>Banking >Cheque printing).* Select the Bank Account (or select *All Items* for all Bank Accounts) for which you like

- **F6: Show All / Hide Printed**: Toggle button to show all cheques (Show All) / show unprinted Cheques (Hide Printed)
- **F7: Edit Ch Details**: To edit/update the *Favouring Name, Instrument No* and *Instrument Date* columns (F-15E), as required (when only one Bank is selected)

11.2 Cheque Printing Configuration

At Cheque Printing screen (F-16B), click *F12:Configure* to get *Cheque Printing Configuration* (F-16A) to set the options as follows:

- **Cheque Printing Confirmation**: At *Confirm each Cheque Before Print,* set Yes to stop printing after printing each cheque (takes more printing time but allows to check the printed Cheque or correctness), else set No (all the selected cheques wll be printed) at one stroke
- **Include Printed Cheque**: At *Include Printed Cheques also:* set *Yes* to display the printed cheques also in the report.

Cheque Printing ABC Academy 9-10 Ctrl + M

Ledger: **HDFC Bank** **1-Mar-2010 to 31-Mar-2010**

(Cheque Printing - Pending Cheques)

Date	Particulars	Favouring Name	Instrument No.	Instrument Date	Printed ?	Amount
31-3-2010	**Salary**	K Kumar	345678	31-3-2010	**No**	**1,35,750.00**
31-3-2010	**ICICI Term Loan**	ICICI Bank	345679	31-3-2010	**No**	**14,500.00**
31-3-2010	**Cash**	Ourselves	345680	31-3-2010	**No**	**1,000.00**
Selected Total						
Grand Total						**1,51,250.00**

F-15E: Edit Cheque Details

- **Payee Name:** At *Show Payment Favouring*, set *Yes* to display *Payee's Name* as entered in the Cheque details in the voucher, in the report.
- **Remarks**: At *Show Remarks also*, set *Yes* to display the Remarks (as entered in the Cheque details in the voucher) in the report.

Configuration

Confirm each Cheque before Print	? **No**
Include Printed Cheques also	? **No**
Show Payment Favouring	? **Yes**
Show Remarks also	? **No**
Appearance of Names	: **Name Only**
Scale Factor for Values	: **Default**
Sorting Method	: **Default**

F-16A: Cheque Printing Configuration

Bank of India
Cheque Printing

Print Cheque	? **Yes**
Include Printed Cheques also	? **No**
Show Payment Favouring	? **No**
Show Remarks also	? **No**

F-16B: Cheque Printing screen

11.3 Cheque Printing

- **Selection of Voucher for Cheque Printing**: At Cheque Printing screen (F-16B), select the Vouchers for which Cheques to be printed. To select the vouchers, place the cursor on the voucher record and press <spacebar>. This way, you may select several vouchers for cheque printing (press <space bar> again to unselect a selected Voucher)
- **Printing of Cheques of selected Voucher**: At Cheque Printing screen (F-16B), having selected the Vouchers for which Cheques to be printed, Click *P:Print* (or Press *Alt+P)*.to get the *Cheque Details* screen (F-16C)
- **Printed Cheque Template**: At *Cheque Details* screen (F-16C), click Yes at Print Yes / No prompt, to print the Cheque. The cheque is printed on the cheque leaf, as per the dimension configuration set for the Bank (F-16D shows the template of the printed matter on the cheque leaf)

Cheque Details

Favouring Name: **A K Traders** Inst. No.: Inst. Date: **3-3-2010** Amount: **1,000.00**

Print ?
Yes or No

F-16C: Cheque Details screen

A/c Payee 0 3 0 3 2 0 1 0

A K Traders

One Thousand Only

****1,000.00**

for ABC Academy

F-16D: Printed Cheque Template

Cheque Printing

1-Dec-2009 to 31-Dec-2009

Page 1

Date	Particulars	Favouring Name	Instrument No.	Instrument Date	Printed ?	Amount
1-12-2009	**A K Traders**		123567	3-12-2009	**No**	**800.00**
1-12-2009	**A K Traders**		456789	5-12-2009	**No**	**200.00**
1-12-2009	**A K Traders**		123456	2-12-2009	**No**	**1,200.00**
1-12-2009	**A K Traders**		123457	3-12-2009	**No**	**800.00**
1-12-2009	**A K Traders**		123458	4-12-2009	**No**	**1,000.00**
Grand Total						**4,000.00**

F-16E: Cheque Printing report

12 Cheque Printing Report

At cheque printing screen (F-16B), select Yes to print the cheques as per options set as shown. (select *No* to change the following default options as desired):

- **Print Cheque**: Set *Yes* to print the cheque as per configuration option set
- **Include Printed Cheques also**: Set *Yes* to display the printed cheques also in the report.
- **Show Payment Favouring**: Set *Yes* to display Favouring Name (*Payee's Name* as entered in the Cheque details in the voucher) details in the report.
- **Show Remarks also**: Set *Yes* to display the Remarks (as entered in the Cheque details in the voucher) in the report, in next line.

13 Payment Advice

At Banking Menu (F-3), select *Payment Advice.* Then Select the Ledger Account (e.g Party Ledger Account) to get the Payment Advice List showing pending Advices List for the selected ledger (F-17A)

Payment Advice — Ctrl + M

Ledger: A K Traders — 1-Apr-2009 to 31-Mar-2010

Date	Particulars	Vch Type	Vch No.	Debit	Credit
1-6-2009	TDS	Payment	2	2,000.00	
31-8-2009	Bank of India	Payment	5	1,000.00	
1-12-2009	Bank of India	Payment	6	1,000.00	
1-12-2009	Bank of India	Payment	7	2,000.00	
31-3-2010	Bank of India	Payment	10	1,200.00	
	Opening Balance :			1,000.00	
	Current Total :			7,200.00	
	Closing Balance :			8,200.00	

F-17A: Payment Advice List

Report Titles

Payment Voucher

Print Payment Advice : Yes
Payment Advice Date : 2-Apr-2010
Print Due Date ? Yes
Print Company's PAN/IT Number ? Yes

Print ?
Yes or No

F-17B: Payment Advice Printing Screen

At Payment Advice List (F-17A), select the Vouchers for which Payment Advice to be printed (select the required rows from the Payment Advice list and press spacebar on the row)

Click *P:Print* (or Press *Alt+P).*to get the *Payment Advice Printing* screen (F-17B)

Payment Advice Printing

At *Payment Advice Printing* screen (F-17B), select Yes to print the Payment Advice as per options set as shown (select *No* to change the following default options as desired):

- **Advice Printing**: At *Print Payment Advice*, set *Yes* to print Payment Advice
- **Advice Date**: At *Payment Advice Date* (by default, the current date is displayed here). enter the Payment Advice Date (it may be different from Voucher Date)
- **Due Date**: At *Print Due Date* Set *Yes* to print the due date in the payment advice.
- **Company PAN**: At *Print Company's PAN/IT Number*, set *Yes* to Print PAN / IT Number in the Payment Advice

Now the Payment Advice will be printed one by one (F-17C).

ABC Academy
99, Airport Rd
Kolkata 700 098
W Bengal
E-Mail :abc@tmail.com
Our PAN / I.T. No. : ACDRE3456V

Payment Advice

M/s A K Traders
35 Heysham Rd
Kolkata
700 004

Date : 2-Apr-2010

Dear Sir/Madam,

Please find below the payment details.

Bill Ref.	Bill Date	Due Date	Amount
A K Traders			
			1,200.00
		Nett Amount	1,200.00

Payment Detail(s)				
Mode of Payment	Bank Name	Instrument No.	Instrument Date	Amount
Cheque	Bank of India	345765	31-Mar-2010	1,200.00
			Total	1,200.00

Kindly acknowledge the receipt.

Thanking You

Authorised Signatory

Receiver's Signature

F-17C: Payment Advice

FAQ: Frequently Asked Questions

FAQ-1: How I can enter Cheque details in Voucher during voucher entry

You may enter the cheque details (of cheques received / issued / monies debited / credited in the bank account in Payment / Receipt / Contra Voucher and print the cheque details in Voucher, Money Receipt, payment Advice and also in Reports voucher)

At the respective Contra / Payment / Receipt voucher entry screen, click F12:Configure to get the configuration screen. Now set the options as follows:

- **Activate Cheque Details:** Set *No* at *Use Default for Bank Allocations* to get the Cheque details entry screen after selection of Bank account in the voucher
- **Remarks**: Set *Yes* at *Show Remarks at Bank Allocation details* to enter details of the cheque / transaction at Remark column

Having set the options as above, during Contra / Payment / Receipt voucher entry screen, on selection of the Bank Account, you get the cheque details entry screen to enter the details in voucher.

FAQ-2: How I can print cheques of my Bank Account from Tally ERP 9

If the cheque stationery is printed on fanfold continuous paper (this is old style), then you should use a Dot Matrix Printer having a tractor. Some Inkjet printers also provide attachment for fan fold continuous stationery. You may use such printer for cheque printing

If the cheque stationery is on cut sheet (you may tear the regular cheque leaves from the Cheque Books and place the cut sheets on InkJet or Laser printer Tray. The Printer tray must have arrangement to fix such stationery and the printer should be able to set the paper size to print on such special size stationary. First check the specification of the printer and get demonstration of the printer before buying. Only few printer models provide easy & seamless process of cheque printing on standard cheque leaves of cheque books that Banks normally provide.

Bank Reconciliation

01 Bank Reconciliation

The Bank Book shows all transactions with the Bank. The Banker also keeps a ledger account of the transactions with its customer (called Pass Book). The Bank Book and the Pass Book contains same transaction details. So, ideally, the Bank Book Balance and Pass Book should match.

Even after entering all transactions with bank correctly, you may find that the Closing Balance of your Bank Book does not tally with the Bank Pass Book. This may happen due to various reasons.

- **Float Time**: When you issue Cheque to any Party, you credit Bank's Ledger (in your books) on the date of issue, but normally it is not debited in the Bankers Books (i.e., in your account) on the same date. Similarly, when you deposit a cheque into your Bank Account, you debit Bank's ledger on the date of deposit, but it is normally not credited by your Bankers on same date. So, the Bank Balance as per your books and Bank Balance as per Bank Pass Book normally differs. You need to track that all the transactions entered in your books are also reflected in your Banker's books.
- **Direct Entry at Bank**: Apart from that, Bank may charge Interest, Bank Charges, debit / credit for Interest, Standing payment instructions etc. Similarly, There may be direct collection by Bank / Direct credit into Bank Account. These may not have been entered in Bank Book and are traced at the time of Bank Reconciliation.

Bank Reconciliation is the process of matching the entries between Bank Book & Pass Book) with Bank Pass Book) and tracing the unmatched entries in either of the books (Bank Book or the Pass Book), It is essential to ensure correctness of Bank Accounts.

The main reason of the reconciliation arises due to difference in balance caused by the time gap between debit and credit entries in the books of drawee and drawer bank, due to the time to get the money moved from one bank account to another bank account (called *Float Time*). As electronic banking spreads, the Float Time will minimize as these transactions get instantly reflected simultaneously in both the drawee & drawer bank accounts. In such case, the bank book and bank statement will mostly tally.

However, due to direct transfers in the Bank Account through electronic modes, and other kind of entries directly into Bank Pass Book (Interest, Bank Charges etc), Bank reconciliation would be necessary to trace such entries.

02 Bank Reconciliation process

Bank Reconciliation is the process to reconcile the apparent differences between the Bank *Pass Book* balance (balance as per the banker) and *Bank Book* balance (balance as per your books of accounts). Bank Reconciliation process ensures that the numerical figures of bank ledger account (Debit Amounts & Credit Amount) are in agreement with the Bankers Account.

An entry for Bank transaction will be reflected in Bank's Pass Book (Banker's ledger account for its customer's account), when the transaction passes through the Bank. So, for an entry in Bank Book, the Bank Pass would also show a corresponding entry.

Bank Reconciliation is the process to find out the one way entries in either of these books (Bank Book or Pass Book) which remained unmatched in the other counterpart book, normally due to time lag (float time) between the transactions at both ends (customer & bank), or entries missing at the other end.

Bank Reconciliation is done by matching the entries in both the books to filter out the rest entries (unmatched entries). The entry of Voucher (Bank Book) is matched with the Pass Book (Bank Statement). In the matched entries, the date of clearance in the Pass Book is recorded. Untagged (Undated) items can then be traced to compile the Reconciliation Statement.

02.01 Modes of Banks Reconciliation

Tally ERP.9 provides 2 modes of Bank Reconciliation:

- **Manual Bank Reconciliation**: In this process the Bank Pass Book date is marked into the respective voucher for Reconciliation. It is a tedious & time consuming process for organisations having vast banking transactions.
- **Auto Bank Reconciliation:** In this process, the e-Bank Statement (in digital from) is imported, from which entries are matched by Tally ERP 9 and Bank Reconciliation is prepared. This is possible only for selected Banks which provides import of Bank Statement in compatible form.

We first discuss about Manual Process and then will explain the Auto Reconciliation in next chapter

02.02 Bank Reconciliation Screen

You make Bank Reconciliation at Bank Reconciliation screen (F-3A), which you may access in the following ways, from:

- **Banking Menu**: At Gateway of Tally, select *Banking > Bank Reconciliation* and select a *Bank Account* from the list
- **Bank Ledger Account**: Select *Display>Account Books>Ledger*, select the Bank Ledger Account and click *F5:Reconcle* button at Ledger Account of bank to get Bank Reconciliation screen.
- **Cash Book**: Select *Display > Account Books > Cash Bank Books*, select a Bank Ledger (Click *F1: Detailed* if required, to get Bank Ledgers displayed), to get Ledger Monthly Summary. At Ledger Monthly Summary, select a month (for which you like to make Bank Reconciliation) to get Ledger Vouchers showing the list of Vouchers related to the selected Bank. Click *F5: Reconcile* button to get Bank Reconciliation screen

03 Opening Reconciliation entries

When you start accounting in Tally from a date when there are some unreconciled entries on Books Beginning from date, you have to create unreconciled entries relating to period prior to books beginning date, at Opening Reconciliation screen

- **Accounting from Mid Year**: You start Accounting in Tally from middle of Financial Year

Start Date of Bank Reconciliation: For each Bank Account, you have to enter the Start date of Bank Account. It is presumed that all bank entries prior to that date have been reconciled. You should not enter any instrument prior to the Start Date

To enter the Start date of Reconciliation for each Bank Account, at the respective Bank Ledger Account Creation/ Alteration (F-2A/04-01), at the field *Effective Date of Reconciliation,* enter the Start Date of Bank Reconciliation (normally the first date of Opening Bank Reconciliation entries (F-1A)

03.01 Opening BRS Entry screen

At Bank Reconciliation screen, click *U: Opening BRS* button (F-2C) to get the Opening BRS screen (F-1A)

Now enter the data for Opening BRS, at the respective columns (F-1A) as follows:

- **Date**: Enter the transaction Date at *Date* field. This must be prior to the Date of Effective Bank Reconciliation Date as entered in the respective Bank Ledger Account Master
- **Particulars**: Enter the brief Particulars of entry / Instrument Number for memorandum. This will facilitate

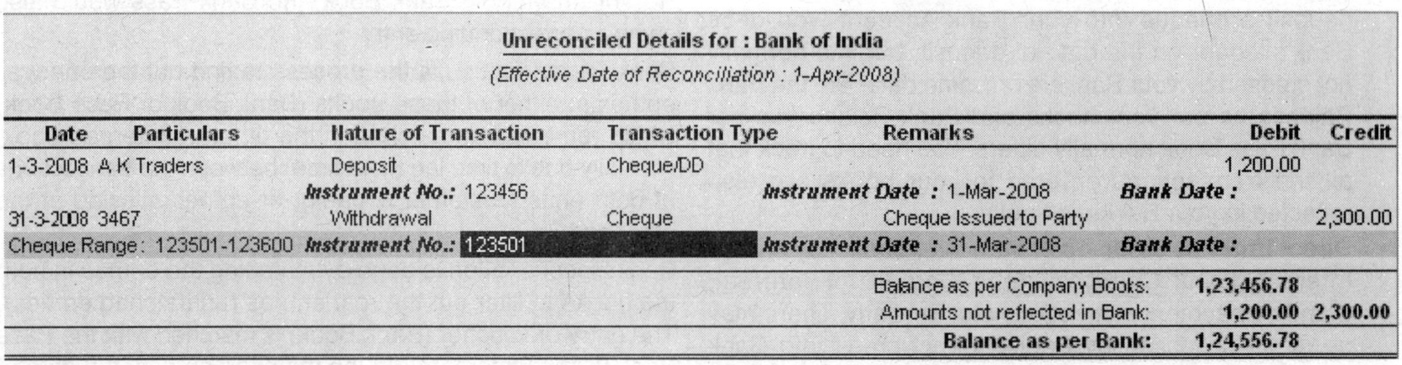

F-1A: Opening BRS Screen

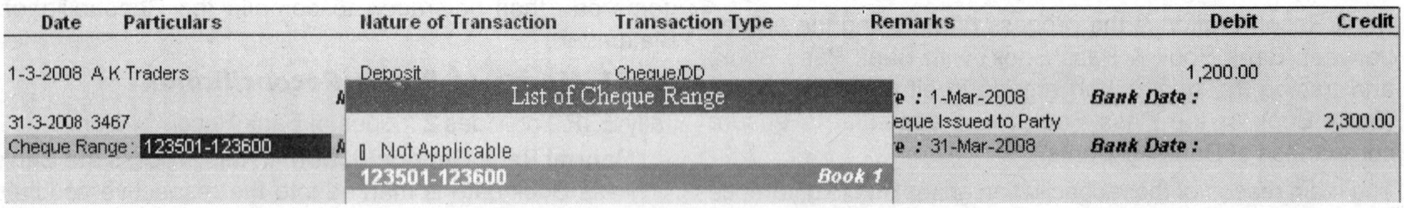

F-1B: Selection of Cheque Book for Withdrawals

Entries in Opening Reconcilitaion need to be created in the following cases:

- **Opening Entries**: You start Accounts in Tally of an existing company, which has some unreconciled bank entries, at the start of Books Beginning from date, related to the period prior to Books Beginning from date
- **BRS from Mid Year**: You activate BRS feature from middle of Financial Year, and there are some unreconciled entries on Books Beginning from date

identification & reconciliation of the entry at a later stage.

- **Nature of Transaction**: Select as follows:
  - o **Withdrawal:** For amount withdrawn from Bank. You get a subscreen to select the respective Cheque Book from the list (F-1B)
  - o **Deposit**: For amount deposited into Bank.
- **Transaction Type**: Select the appropriate Transaction type (Cheque/ DD etc) from the Transaction Type list.

This is only for memorandum and the selection does not affect the reconciliation:

- **Remarks**: Enter Remarks as memorandum of the entry. This will facilitate reconciliation of the entry at a later stage.
- **Amount:** Enter the transaction amount in Debit / Credit columns as follows:
  - o **Debit**: In case of Deposit (i.e Bank Account Debit in Bank Book / Credit in Pass Book)
  - o **Credit**: In case of Withdrawal (i.e Bank Account Credit in Bank Book / Debit in Pass Book

The total of both columns and the balance as per Bank Book are shown at the end of the report for reference and quick check up with Bank Book and Pass Book as on Books Beginning Date. Proceed to Bank Reconciliation for current period only after these figures agree to your Bank Book / Bank Pass Book (otherwise you will not get the reconciliation correct)

The entries made in Opening BRS are included in the BRS statement and are reconciled in the same way as regular entries for the accounting period.

04 Bank Reconciliation Configuration

At Bank Reconciliation screen (F-3A), click *F12: Configure* to get *Bank Reconciliation configuration* screen (F-2A). Here you can set the options to configure the contents of the Bank Reconciliation screen (F-3A), as described below:

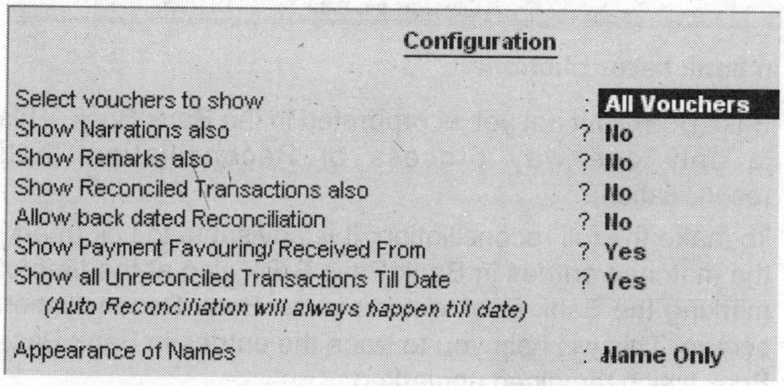

F-2A Bank Reconcilitaion Configuration screen

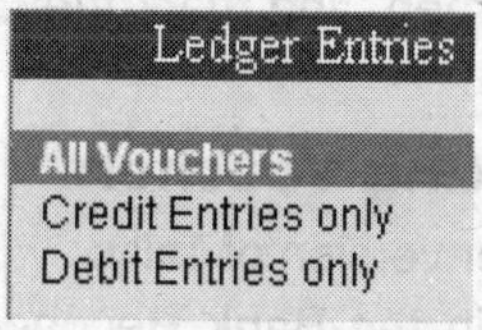

F-2B: Selection List of Voucher to show

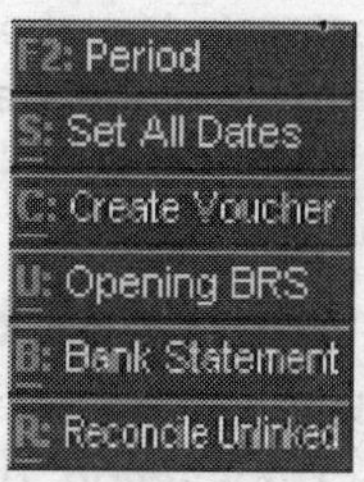

F-2C Buttons at Bank Reconciliation screen

- **Selection of Voucher**: For convenience of operation, you may filter the entries for reconciliation as below (F-2B),
  - o **All Vouchers:** When you like to match both Debt & Credit Transactions (payment & Receipt Vouchers) simultaneously
  - o **Credit Entries only:** When you like to match only Credit Transactions (e.g, In Payment Vouchers, & Withdrawals from Bank in Contra voucher, Bank Account is *Credited*).
  - o **Debit Entries only:** When you like to match only Debit Transactions (e.g In Receipt Vouchers & Deposits to Bank, Bank Account is *Debited*).
- **Voucher Narration**: Set *Yes* at *Show Narrations also* to see the Voucher Narrations also.
- **Voucher Remarks**: Set *Yes* at *Show Remarks also* to see the Voucher Remarks also. This may be useful to facilitate matching of records
- **Reconciled Transactions**: Set *Yes* at *Show Reconciled Transactions also* to show the Reconciled entries also, else set *No* to filter out the reconciled entries for convenience of matching
- **Back Dated Reconciliation**: Set *Yes* at *Allow back dated Reconciliation* to get the unreconciled entries earlier than the current period, to reconcile older entries also. Else set *No* to filter out the entries for convenience of reconciliation of vouchers of current period only
- **Payee / Payer's' Name**: Set *Yes* at *Show Payment favouring / Received From* to show the Payee / payer's name. This is quite helpful to quickly identify the entries for matching as the Payer's / Payee's Name is normally mentioned in Bank Pass Book.
- **Past unreconciled transactions**: Set *Yes* at *Show all unreconciled transactions till date* to show older unreconciled entries also to help reconciliation of earlier unreconciled vouchers

04.01 Buttons at Bank Reconciliation Screen

The following buttons are available at Bank Reconciliation screen (F-2C)

- **S: Set All Dates**: To quick post a single Date at Bank Date column of all the records at a time,
- **C; Create Voucher:** To create a Receipt / Payment / Contra voucher from within the Reconciliation screen. It is useful to create voucher for the corresponding missing entries on the other end.
- **U: Opening BRS:** To make Opening BRS entry

05 Bank Date Entry

Through this process, the entries for which the bank transaction has been cleared by the bank (the matched entries) are marked.

At Bank Reconciliation screen (F-3A), the vouchers for which the Bank Date has not been filled up (unmarked entries till the last date of the current month) are listed. Now enter the Date of clearing (referred as Marking of entries) of the cheque as per Bank Statement (Bank Pass Book) at the blank *Bank Date* field against the voucher record. After entering Bank Dates (marking) for the respective entries, press *Ctrl+A* to save.

Quick Entry of Bank Date: If you have to enter same Date at Bank Date field in all the entries in the screen (if all the entries have been cleared through Bank Pass Book on the same date), you may click *S: Set All Dates* (F-2C) button, enter the Date of clearing and press *<enter>*. The Date entered will be posted in the Blank Bank Date column of all the records in the screen (be careful!)

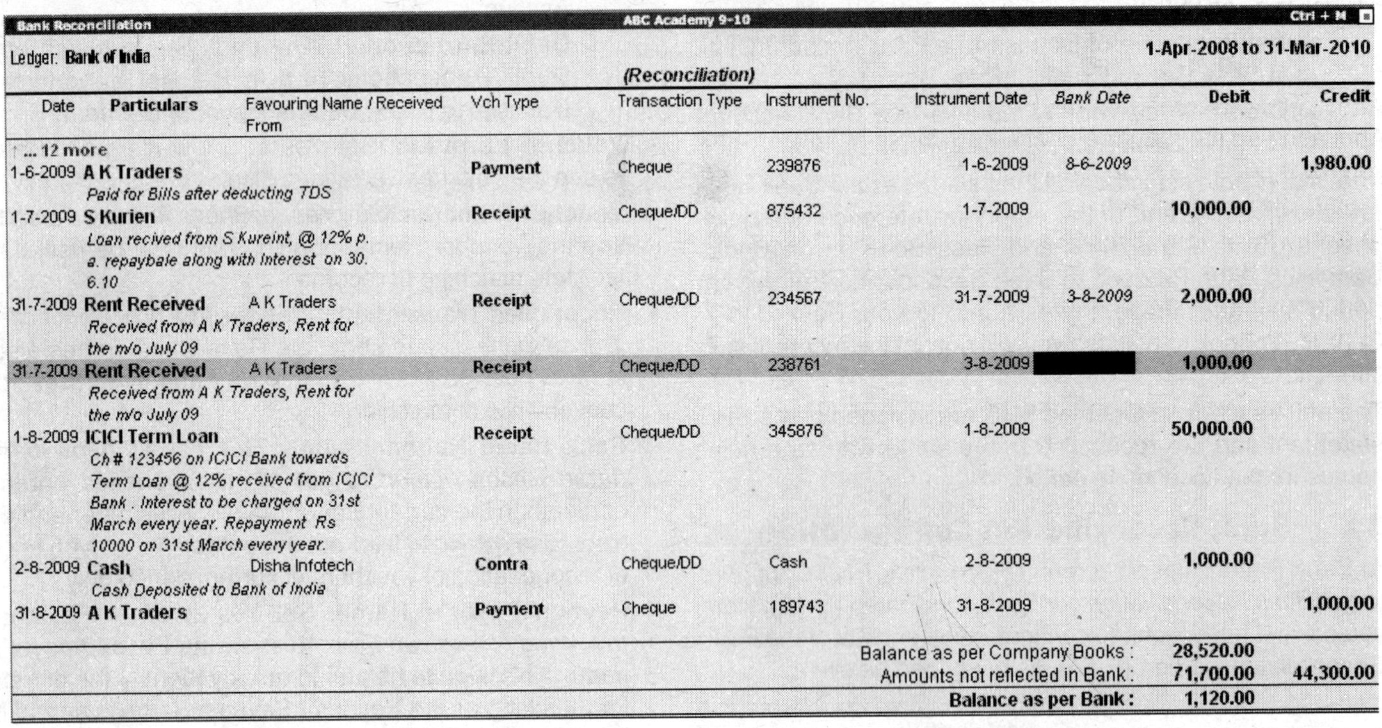

Bank Reconciliation | ABC Academy 9-10 | Ctrl + M

Ledger: **Bank of India** | 1-Apr-2008 to 31-Mar-2010

(Reconciliation)

Date	Particulars	Favouring Name / Received From	Vch Type	Transaction Type	Instrument No.	Instrument Date	Bank Date	Debit	Credit
↑ ... 12 more									
1-6-2009	**A K Traders** *Paid for Bills after deducting TDS*		**Payment**	Cheque	239876	1-6-2009	8-6-2009		**1,980.00**
1-7-2009	**S Kurien** *Loan recived from S Kureint, @ 12% p. a. repaybale along with Interest on 30. 6.10*		**Receipt**	Cheque/DD	875432	1-7-2009		**10,000.00**	
31-7-2009	**Rent Received** *Received from A K Traders, Rent for the m/o July 09*	A K Traders	**Receipt**	Cheque/DD	234567	31-7-2009	3-8-2009	**2,000.00**	
31-7-2009	**Rent Received** *Received from A K Traders, Rent for the m/o July 09*	A K Traders	**Receipt**	Cheque/DD	238761	3-8-2009		**1,000.00**	
1-8-2009	**ICICI Term Loan** *Ch # 123456 on ICICI Bank towards Term Loan @ 12% received from ICICI Bank . Interest to be charged on 31st March every year. Repayment Rs 10000 on 31st March every year.*		**Receipt**	Cheque/DD	345876	1-8-2009		**50,000.00**	
2-8-2009	**Cash** *Cash Deposited to Bank of India*	Disha Infotech	**Contra**	Cheque/DD	Cash	2-8-2009		**1,000.00**	
31-8-2009	**A K Traders**		**Payment**	Cheque	189743	31-8-2009			**1,000.00**
							Balance as per Company Books :	**28,520.00**	
							Amounts not reflected in Bank :	**71,700.00**	**44,300.00**
							Balance as per Bank :	**1,120.00**	

F-3A: Bank Date entry in Bank Reconciliation

At the bottom, you get the following figures as per entry of Bank Date.

- **Amounts not reflected in Bank**: The total figures of unreconciled entries (total amount of Debit and Credit entries against which Bank Date has not been marked) are displayed here.
- **Balance as per Bank**: This shows the net effect of Balance as per your Books offset by the Amounts not reflected in Bank. Arithmetically this should be the balance in the Bank Statement (Pass Book).

06 Pending Bank Book Entries

If the Balance as per Bank in the Reconciliation Statement does not match with the pass book balance, there is a possibility of some bank transactions (Bank Charges, Interest etc) that have not been incorporated in Bank Book. Find out the entries that are appearing in Bank Statement but not in your books (e.g, Interest, Incidental Charges, Collection Charges debited by Bank). Make such entries in your Books and then enter the Bank Date as stated to get the matched balance.

The Bank Reconciliation process helps you to mark and trace unmarked entries in Bank Book, but cannot readily trace the entries that have been passed by Bank (appearing in Bank Pass Book) but not yet incorporated in the Bank Book. This is only one way process of Reconciliation (half reconciliation).

To make the full reconciliation, it is advisable to tick (mark) the matched entries in Bank Pass Book also at the time of marking the Bank Book entries in the Bank Reconciliation screen. This will help you to trace the entries in Bank Pass Book which remained unmarked.

New Voucher Entry from Bank Reconciliation screen: Click *C:Create Voucher* button (F-2C) at the Reconciliation screen to enter the transaction of such missing voucher, through Bank Reconciliation screen, and mark the Date of Pass Book entry in the vouchers

07 Migration of Banking Vouchers

When data is migrated from older version of Tally:

- The Transaction Type row in the Bank Reconciliation screen will be blank. You may, if required, alter the vouchers and select the appropriate transaction type (Cheque/DD) in the Bank Allocation Table
- The Instrument Date displayed in the Bank Reconciliation screen will be the Voucher Date (the reconciliation is based on Instrument Date, not on the Voucher date)

- The Bank Reconciliation screen lists the transactions on the basis of each transaction type (eg. Cheque, DD etc) selected. A voucher with multiple transaction type will be split and shown for each transaction type

FAQ: Frequently Asked Questions

FAQ-1: My Accounts are entered in Tally from Beginning of Financial Year, but BRS was done manually. How I can start Bank Reconciliation in Tally from middle of the Year

Ans: Let us assume that the Financial Year starts from 1st April and you have entered data upto 31st July. Till 31st July you have done Bank Reconciliation manually. Now you like to start BRS from 1st Aug

At Gateway of Tally, select Banking > Bank Reconciliation. Select the Bank Account for which you like to make Bank Reconciliation, to get the Bank Reconciliation screen

At Bank Reconciliation screen Click *U: Opening BRS*, and enter the Closing Bank Reconciliation entries as on 31st July as Opening Bank Reconciliation entries of 1st Aug.

FAQ-2: After Reconciliation of voucher entries, I find that the Bank Book Balance does not tally with the Bank Reconciliation statement, as vouchers for some entries appearing in Bank Statement (like Bank Charges, Interest, Bills collected by Bank, Payments made by Bank on standing instructions etc) are still not made. How can I make those Voucher entries from within the Bank Reconciliation & make final Bank Reconciliation

Ans: During Reconciliation process, the pending entries in Bank Book not matched in Bank Pass Book are shown. During this process, you have to scrutinize & locate the entries found in Bank Pass Book but not entered in Bank Book (Vouchers not entered).

At Bank Reconciliation screen, *C:Create Voucher* button to get the Voucher Entry screen. Now enter the missing Voucher corresponding to the entry found in Bank Pass book. On entry of the voucher, you will get the Bank Reconciliation screen with the new voucher appearing in the Bank Reconciliation screen. Now enter the corresponding Bank Date (from the Bank Pass Book) of the Voucher to get the voucher entered reconciled.

This way, crate all the missing vouchers and get them reconciled. Now the Balance as per Bank shown in the Bank Reconciliation Statement will Tally with the Bank Pass Book.

Auto Bank Reconciliation 04-03

01 Auto Bank Reconciliation

As the entry in Bank Book corresponds to entries in Bank Pass Book, they can be digitally matched if the Bank Pass Book is also available in digital Form.

In Auto Bank Reconciliation, Bank Pass Book data in digital form (e-Bank Pass Book) are imported into Tally ERP 9 to perform matching through the common reference (Cheque Number etc)

Here we discuss about the tasks related to Auto Bank Reconciliation (i.e digital matching of records) between Bank Ledger Account as recorded in Tally ERP with imported Record of Bank Pass Book.

02 Auto Bank Reconciliation Configuration

At Gateway of Tally, click F12:Configure>Banking Configuration to get *Banking Configuration* screen (F-1A). Now set as follows:

- **Unreconciled Transaction:** At *Show all Unreconciled Transaction in BRS Till Date*, set *Yes* to show the Opening Unreconciled Entries (P-16). You may also see it from Configuration Option of Bank Reconciliation (F-2A / 03-02)
- **Bank Date Removal on altered Voucher**: At *Remove Bank Date on Altering Reconciled Voucher* (Bank Ledger / Amount), set *Yes* to remove the manual tags, on alteration of any voucher. A message '*Altering Reconciled Voucher will remove the Bank Date as it may not match the Bank Balance on Reconciliation*' appears to make the user aware of the consequences of activating this option.
- **Location of Bank Statement files**: Here enter the location where the downloaded Bank Statement will be stored. By default, the location of Configuration File as specified in Data Configuration (F-1A/02-27) is shown, which you may change.

Type *Yes* at the prompt Continue Yes / No to save the configuration settings

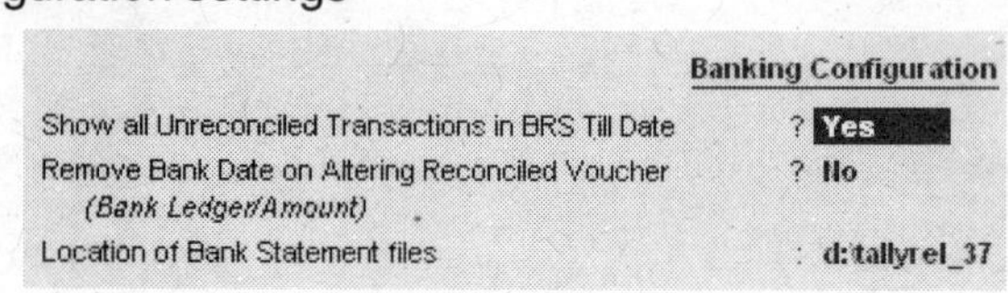

F-1A Configuration Set Up for Banking

> ***Note:*** *Auto Bank Reconciliation may be helpful in case of Companies having large number of Bank Transactions. It helps reduce manual matching considerably. However, you have to manually match the entries left out in Auto Bank Reconciliation process. You have to first download the digital copy of Bank Statement from Bank Site, through Net Banking Account.*

03 Activation of Auto Reconciliation

At Bank Ledger Account (F-2A/04-01) *Yes* at the field *Set / Alter Banking Configuration*, to get Banking Configuration screen (F-4/04-01), set *Yes* at *Activate Auto Reconciliation* to activate Auto Bank Reconciliation feature for the selected Bank Account (you must have selected a Bank Account from the list:F-5A), otherwise, the field *Activate Auto Reconciliation* would be skipped.

At *GoT>Banking>Bank Reconciliation* screen, select the Bank for which you need to perform Auto Bank Reconciliation to get the Bank Reconciliation Screen (F- 3A/03-02). Now you will find Button (B:Bank Statement: F -2C/03-02) to import digital Bank Pass Book from the website of Bank.

04 Downloading Bank Statement

At Bank Reconciliation screen (F-3A/03-02), Click *B:Bank Statement* button (F-2C/04-02) to get *Select File* screen to import Bank Statement (F-2A)

- **Directory:** At the field *Directory*, the Bank File Location specified at *Banking Configuration screen* is displayed.
- **File Type**: Select the File Type (e.g Excel, CSV etc) from the list of supported file types for the Bank
- **File Name**: Now a list of File names of the selected File Type would appear. Click *I: With View* button (or press *Alt+I* keys) to view the Bank statement to be imported.

05 Display of Imported Statement

When importing the e-bank statement, the statement which is already imported will also appear. To hide the imported statement, click *S: Hide Imported* toggle button to import only the statement which is not yet imported gets displayed (F-2B)

ABC Academy 9-10

Directory : **d:\tallyrel_37**
(Supported format(s) for selected Bank: Excel)
File Type : **Excel**
File Name :

List of Files : d:\tallyrel_37

File Name	System Date	Size	Type	Is Imported ?
1354770729292_2219963.xls	6-Dec-2012	25.50 KB	xls	No

F-2A: Bank Statement Import File selection screen

Bank Statement — ASOK KUMAR NADHANI 12-13 — Ctrl + M

Bank Ledger : **HDFC Salt Lake 103968**
Account Number : **00181000103968**
Statement Number :
Statement till: **30-Apr-2012**

Sl. No.	Date	Particulars	Instrument No.	Debit	Credit	Balance
		Opening Balance				
1	2-4-2012	ATW-5264190151162152 -BANGUR AVENUE	0004536	10,000.00		1,80,171.48 Cr
2	3-4-2012	ATW-5264190151162152 -BANGUR AVENUE	0004733	10,000.00		1,70,171.48 Cr
3	9-4-2012	ECS DR TP ICICI PRULIFE-2076179367	6179367	2,500.00		1,67,671.48 Cr
4	9-4-2012	ISAQMC-ST-EC Jan-Mar12-162279 250112	0000000	110.30		1,67,561.18 Cr
5	11-4-2012	Chq Paid-MICR INW CLG-KOLKATA	0786765	1,000.00		1,66,561.18 Cr
6	13-4-2012	ATW-5264190151162152 -BANGUR AVENUE	0006538	5,000.00		1,61,561.18 Cr
7	16-4-2012	Chq Paid-INWARD TRAN-HDFC	0786772	1,874.42		1,59,686.76 Cr
8	17-4-2012	ECS DR TP ICICI PRULIFE-2076382115	6382115	1,500.00		1,58,186.76 Cr
9	25-4-2012	REVERSAL OF ISA CHARGES			882.10	1,59,068.86 Cr
10	25-4-2012	Chq Paid-INWARD TRAN-SUSMA SOMANI	0786774	37,692.00		1,21,376.86 Cr
			Current Total :	69,676.72	882.10	
			Closing Balance :		1,21,376.86	

F-2B Imported e-Bank Statement

Success !!
Total Entries in Bank Statement: 10
Reconciled: 4
Additional Bank Entries: 6
(press any key)

F-2C: Message on Import of e-Bank Statement

06 Import of Bank Statement

Click *F12:Configure* and set *Yes* at the Option *Show Imported Statement*, to re-import the viewed imported Bank Statement. The list of Bank Statement files are displayed in Alphabetical order showing the Import Status.

- **File Import**:To Import the file, click *I:Import* button (or press Alt+I)
- **Abandon Import**: To abandon the Import, press *<Esc>* key or click *Q:Quit* (the file will not be re-imported)

Bank Reconciliation — ASOK KUMAR NADHANI 12-13 — Ctrl + M

Ledger: **HDFC Salt Lake 103968** — **1-Apr-2012 to 25-Apr-2012**

(Reconciliation)

Date	Particulars	Favouring Name / Received From	Vch Type	Transaction Type	Instrument No.	Instrument Date	*Bank Date*	Debit	Credit
2-4-2012	Cash	ASOK KUMAR NADHANI	Contra	Others	ATM	2-4-2012			10,000.00
3-4-2012	Cash	ASOK KUMAR NADHANI	Contra	Others	ATM	3-4-2012			10,000.00
9-4-2012	ICICI Prulife #5585		Payment	Others	ECS	9-4-2012			2,500.00
9-4-2012	Bank Charges		Payment	Others	BK DEbit	9-4-2012	*9-4-2012*		110.30
11-4-2012	Legal Expenses		Payment	Cheque	786765	11-4-2012	*11-4-2012*		1,000.00
11-4-2012	Cash	ASOK KUMAR NADHANI	Contra	Others	ATM	11-4-2012			5,000.00
16-4-2012	Personal Expenses		Payment	Cheque	786772	16-4-2012	*16-4-2012*		1,874.42
17-4-2012	ICICI Life Ins Premia 3556		Payment	Cheque	ECS	17-4-2012			1,500.00
17-4-2012	Bank Charges		Receipt	Same Bank Transfer	Reversal	17-4-2012		882.10	
25-4-2012	Susma Somani		Payment	Cheque	786774	25-4-2012	*25-4-2012*		37,692.00
	Amounts not reflected in Company Books								
	ATW-5264190151162152 -BANGUR AVENUE			Withdrawal	0004536	2-4-2012	*3-4-2012*		10,000.00
	ATW-5264190151162152 -BANGUR AVENUE			Withdrawal	0004733	3-4-2012	*3-4-2012*		10,000.00
	ECS DR TP ICICI PRULIFE-2076179367			Withdrawal	6179367	9-4-2012	*9-4-2012*		2,500.00
	ATW-5264190151162152 -BANGUR AVENUE			Withdrawal	0006538	13-4-2012	*13-4-2012*		5,000.00
									2 more ...
							Balance as per Company Books :	1,21,376.86	
							Amounts not reflected in Bank :	882.10	29,000.00
							Amounts not reflected in Company Books :	882.10	29,000.00
							Balance as per Bank :	1,21,376.86	
							Balance as per Imported Bank Statement :		1,21,376.86
							Difference :		

F-3A: Bank Reconciliation Statement showing Auto Matched entries

If the file has been Edited or changed in any way, a message '*Not a valid Format*' appears

During Import, a progress bar appears and on completion of Import process, the *Success* message appears, showing:

- Total entries in the Imported Bank Statement
- Number of Reconciled Entries
- Number of extra Entries in Bank Statement

If the file is already Imported, on attempting to Import again by mistake, an error message *Bank Statement already imported Continue Yes / No* will be displayed.

During Import, the entries with same cheque number & Amount are matched and the Bank Date as per imported Bank Statement is posted in the Voucher, and shown in the Bank Voucher. Now the Bank Reconciliation Statement appears (F-3A) with Bank Date filled in (in Bank Date column) for Matched (reconciled entries).

07 Extra Entries in Bank Statement

The entries found in imported Bank Statement, for which no corresponding entries are found in Bank Ledger Accounts, are shown under the head '*Amount Not reflected in Company Books*' (F-3A).

08 Reconciliation Summary

At the end of the Bank Reconciliation Statement (F-3A), the Balance as Per Company Books, Entries not reflected in Company Books (Debit & Credit figures shown separately) and the Balance as per Imported Bank Statement is shown.

09 Reconciliation of Unreconciled Entries

During Import, the entries with same cheque number & Amount are matched and the Bank Date as per imported Bank Statement is posted in the Voucher, and shown in the Bank Voucher. The Bank Reconciliation Screen shows following unreconciled entries. The Bank Reconciliation at this stage is in unfinished state, showing unreconciled entries as follows, that are to be further matched (reconciled):

- **Unreconciled entries in Company Bank Book**: The are unreconciled entries in the Bank Reconciliation screen, in which the Bank Date is not posted (the field in *Bank Date* column for the entry is blank) as no matching entries are found in imported Bank Statement. It includes:
    - **Entries which have not been cleared at Bank.** Cheques issued but not yet presented to Bank and Cheques deposited not yet collected by Bank. These will be automatically cleared in subsequent Reconciliation process.
    - **Unlinked entries:** Corresponding entries may exist in Imported Bank statement but did not get reconciled as the common reference number is not found between the Company Bank Book and Imported Bank Statement. These are to be traced by further scrutinising both types of Unreconciled Entries
- **Unreconciled entries in Imported Bank Statement:** The are unreconciled entries appearing under the head *Amount Not reflected in Company Books.* These are entries appearing in Imported Bank Statement but no corresponding entry found in Company Bank Book. It includes:
    - **Entries not yet entered in Company Bank Book:** Entries appearing in Imported Bank Statement for which the corresponding entries has not been entered in Company Bank Book. These include Bank Charges, Interest etc. debited, amount paid by Bank under standing instruction, Interest Credited, Amount directly credited to bank account etc

  For such entries, corresponding Vouchers are to be entered and these will get reconciled in subsequent Reconciliation Statement.

However the entries which has not been yet cleared by Bank (Cheques Drawn on Bank / Cheques deposited with Bank), will remain in the Bank Reconciliation at the end of the current period, which will get auto reconciled at subsequent next Reconciliation processes, when these instruments are cleared.

10 Unlinked Entries

To reconcile an Unlinked enrty in Company Books with Unreconciled Entry in Imported Bank Statement (not reflected in Company Books), Click *R:Reconcile Unlinked* button (or press *Alt+R*). The corresponding entry to an unreconciled amount would be highlighted. Select the correct entry and press <Enter>. The status *Reconciled Successfully* would displayed and the Date of corresponding record in Imported Bank Statement would be posted in Bank Date column.

11 Creation of Missing Voucher

The entries under *Amount Not reflected in Company Books* are not entered in Company Books. Click *C:Create Voucher* button (or press *Alt+C*) to create a new Voucher to get Voucher Creation screen. Create the new Voucher. Now the entry will no ore appear in the Reconciliation screen.

12 Difference in Bank Balance

Sometimes, the Bank Balance as reported in Bank Reconciliation may not match with Imported Bank Statement (F-3B). To see the difference, at Bank Reconciliation Configuration screen, set Yes at the option *Show Bank Balance Difference* to show the amount of difference between Bank Balance as per Bank (computed Bank Balance as per Bank Book and the unreconciled entries) and the Bank Balance as per Imported Bank Statement is shown separately at the Reconciliation Summary, at the end of Reconciliation Statement. Now you have to scrutinise the Imported Bank statement and locate the difference.

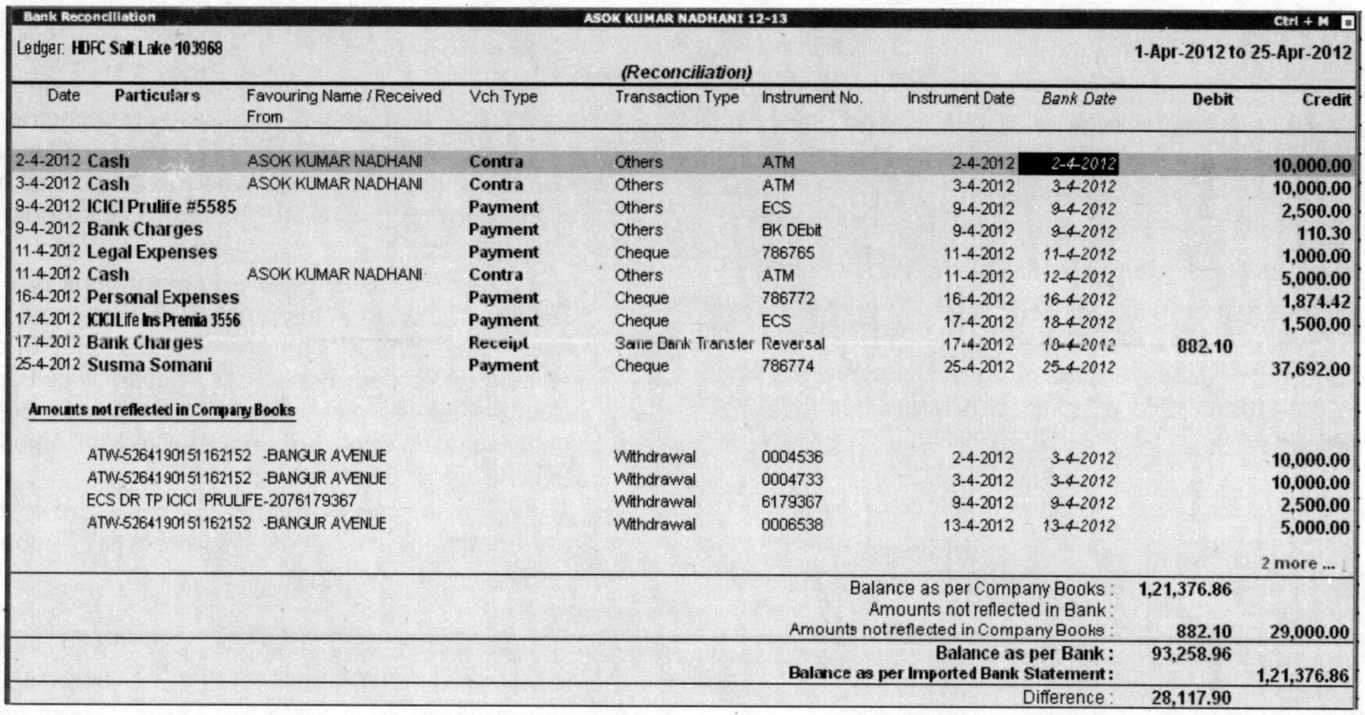

Bank Reconciliation — ASOK KUMAR NADHANI 12-13 — Ctrl + M

Ledger: **HDFC Salt Lake 103968** — **1-Apr-2012 to 25-Apr-2012**

(Reconciliation)

Date	Particulars	Favouring Name / Received From	Vch Type	Transaction Type	Instrument No.	Instrument Date	*Bank Date*	Debit	Credit
2-4-2012	**Cash**	ASOK KUMAR NADHANI	**Contra**	Others	ATM	2-4-2012	*2-4-2012*		**10,000.00**
3-4-2012	**Cash**	ASOK KUMAR NADHANI	**Contra**	Others	ATM	3-4-2012	*3-4-2012*		**10,000.00**
9-4-2012	**ICICI Prulife #5585**		**Payment**	Others	ECS	9-4-2012	*9-4-2012*		**2,500.00**
9-4-2012	**Bank Charges**		**Payment**	Others	BK DEbit	9-4-2012	*9-4-2012*		**110.30**
11-4-2012	**Legal Expenses**		**Payment**	Cheque	786765	11-4-2012	*11-4-2012*		**1,000.00**
11-4-2012	**Cash**	ASOK KUMAR NADHANI	**Contra**	Others	ATM	11-4-2012	*12-4-2012*		**5,000.00**
16-4-2012	**Personal Expenses**		**Payment**	Cheque	786772	16-4-2012	*16-4-2012*		**1,874.42**
17-4-2012	**ICICI Life Ins Premia 3556**		**Payment**	Cheque	ECS	17-4-2012	*18-4-2012*		**1,500.00**
17-4-2012	**Bank Charges**		**Receipt**	Same Bank Transfer	Reversal	17-4-2012	*10-4-2012*	**882.10**	
25-4-2012	**Susma Somani**		**Payment**	Cheque	786774	25-4-2012	*25-4-2012*		**37,692.00**
Amounts not reflected in Company Books									
	ATW-526419015162152 -BANGUR AVENUE			Withdrawal	0004536	2-4-2012	*3-4-2012*		**10,000.00**
	ATW-526419015162152 -BANGUR AVENUE			Withdrawal	0004733	3-4-2012	*3-4-2012*		**10,000.00**
	ECS DR TP ICICI PRULIFE-2076179367			Withdrawal	6179367	9-4-2012	*9-4-2012*		**2,500.00**
	ATW-526419015162152 -BANGUR AVENUE			Withdrawal	0006538	13-4-2012	*13-4-2012*		**5,000.00**
									2 more ...
							Balance as per Company Books :	**1,21,376.86**	
							Amounts not reflected in Bank :		
							Amounts not reflected in Company Books :	**882.10**	**29,000.00**
							Balance as per Bank :	**93,258.96**	
							Balance as per Imported Bank Statement :		**1,21,376.86**
							Difference :	**28,117.90**	

F-3B: Bank Reconciliation screen after matching

FAQ: Frequently Asked Questions

FAQ-1: How I may activate Auto Bank Reconciliation

Ans: At Bank Ledger Account, set *Yes* at *Set / Alter Banking Configuration*, to get Banking Configuration screen. Set *Yes* at *Activate Auto Reconciliation* to activate Auto Bank Reconciliation feature for the selected Bank Account

At *GoT>Banking>Bank Reconciliation* screen, select the Bank for which you need to perform Auto Bank Reconciliation to get the Bank Reconciliation Screen (F-3A/03-02). Now you will find Button (B:Bank Statement: (F -2C/03-02) to import digital Bank Pass Book from the website of Bank.

Part 5

Cost Centre

Cost Centre is an additional dimension of Financial Analysis of Transactions, independent of Account Ledgers and Account Groups.

Like Account Groups / Ledgers, Cost Centres can also be organised into Multi Level hierarchical structure to provide structured analytic reports.

Cost Category further allows another dimension in Cost Centre analysis by providing multiple sets of Cost Centres, to which the amounts can be independently allocated in multiple parallel ways, enabling the user to create a complex multi dimensional analytic system to review the financial status and operations for better analysis.

Cost Centre Class is pre defined set of parameters to auto allocate ledger accounts into multiple Cost Centres

Cost Centre

05-01

Cost Centre is used to analyse Ledger Accounts in another dimension. For example, to get Branchwise analysis of expenses (like Conveyance Expenses, Car Expense etc), Cost Centres (for each Branch) may be created to allocate the respective Expenses entered in Vouchers to the Cost Centres (i.e Branches). For example, Travelling Expenses may be allocated to the respective Cost Centres (Branches), to get Cost Centrewise (Branchwise) analysis of Travelling Expenses at each level. Cost Centre gives another dimension for analysis of ledger accounts for management information.

01 Cost Centre Activation

To activate Cost Centre feature, at Company Operations screen (*F11: Features* >Accounting Feature), set *Yes* at *Maintain Cost Centre* (F-1A). Consequently, the Cost Centre option will get activated at *GoT>Accounts Info* to create Cost Centres for the Company (F-2A).

Cost/Profit Centres Management

Maintain Payroll	? No
Maintain Cost Centres	? Yes
Use Cost Centre for Job Costing	? No
More than ONE Payroll / Cost Category	? Yes
Use Pre-defined Cost Centre Allocations during Entry	? Yes
Show Opening Balance for Revenue Items in Reports	? No

F-1A: Cost Centre Activation

Example of Multi Level Cost Centre

- West Bengal
    - o South Bengal
- Hooghly
- 24Prgns
- Howrah
    - o North Bengal
- Siliguri
- Jalpaiguri
- Bihar

......

....

Note: *The amount allocated to Upper Level Cost Centres (like Account Group) includes the amount allocated to its subordinate Cost Centres (like Sub Group / Ledgers). For example, the amount allocated to South Bengal would constitute the total of amount allocated to its subordinate Cost Centres (viz Hooghly, 24 Prgns & Howrah) and also the direct amount allocated to South Bengal.*

Cost Centre somewhat behaves like a Ledger Account, as Ledger Amount may be allocated to a Cost Centre. It also behaves somewhat like an Account Group, as a Child Cost Centre may be created under any Cos Centre.

Note: *In the voucher, allocation to Cost Center may be done to any Cost Centre of any level. For example, amount may be allocated to lowest level Cost Centre (viz Howrah) or to upper level Cost Centres, like South Bengal, West Bengal, etc., or a combination of some or all of them.*

02 Cost Centre Master

Like Ledger Accounts, you need to first create Cost Centres to which the amount of ledger accounts in the voucher are to be allocated. The Cost Centres are independent of Ledger Accounts. That means amount of any Ledger Account may be allocated to any Cost Centre. So, a Cost Centre may contain amount allocated from various ledger accounts.

Like Account Groups & Stock Group, Cost Centres may be created in a multi level hierarchical structure. So, a Cost Centre may be created under another Cost Centre and so on.

Cost Centre Master Creation: To create Cost Centre Master, at Gateway, select *Accounts Info* to get Accounts Info Menu (F-2A). At Accounts Info menu (F-2A), select *Cost Centre* to get *Cost Centre Menu* (F-2B). At *Cost Centre Menu* (F-2B), select *Create* (under Single Cost Centre) to get *Cost Centre Creation* screen (F-3A). Now enter as follows:

- **Cost Center Name**: At *Name*, enter Cost Centre Name.
- **Parent Cost Centre**: At *Under*, select the parent Cost Centre (or select Primary) under which you like to place the Cost Centre (for the first Cost Centre created, you must select *Primary* only).

If *Alias* is activated, you may enter *Cost Centre Alias Names* also, as explained for other Masters.

Cost Centre Master Alteration: To Alter a Cost Centre Master, at Cost Centre Menu (F-2B), select *Alter* (under

Single Cost Centre) and then select the Cost Centre to be Altered, from the List, to get The Cost Centre Alteration screen, displaying the Cost Center, similar to Cost Centre creation screen (F-3A). Place the cursor to the desired field and make necessary alteration in the same way as Creation of Cost Centre, explained above.

Cost Centre Master Display: To Display a Cost Centre Master, at Cost Centre Menu (F-2B), select *Display* (under Single Cost Centre) and then select the Cost Centre to be Displayed, from the List, to get the Cost Centre Display screen, displaying the Cost Center, similar to Cost Centre creation screen (F-3A). You may view the details but you cannot change any data from Display screen.

Creation of Parent Cost Centre during Cost Centre entry: If the Parent Cost Centre is not existing, during Cost Centre creation (F-3A), at *Under*, press *Alt+C* to get Cost Centre Creation (Secondary) screen. Create the new Cost Centre and select it as Parent Cost Centre at *Under* field.

F-2A: Accounts Info Menu

F-2B: Cost Centre Menu

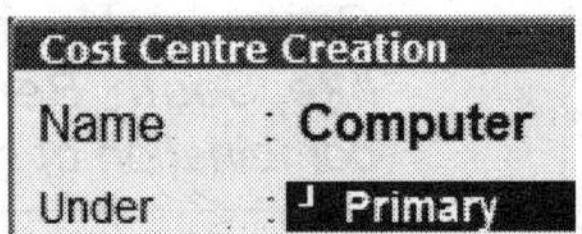

F-3A: Cost Centre Creation

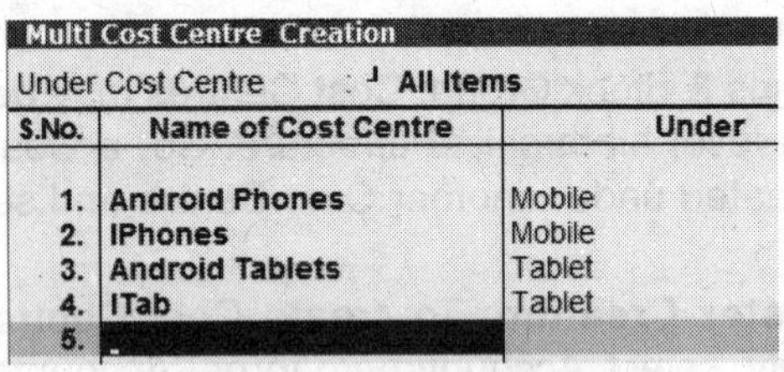

F-4A: Cost Centre Creation (Multi Mode)

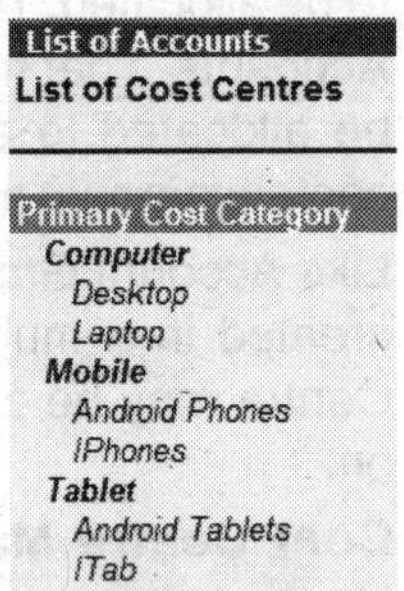

F-5: Cost Centre List

03 Cost Centre creation in Multiple Mode

As explained for Ledger Accounts, you may create Multiple Cost Centres through Multi Mode. The *Multi Mode* is more convenient to create / alter / display a number of Cost Centres at a time, in one screen.

Cost Centre Master Creation: To create Cost Centre Master, At Cost Centre Menu (F-2B), select *Create* (under Multiple Cost Centre) to get *Multi Mode Cost Centre Creation* screen (F-4A). Now enter following:

- **Parent Cost Centre**: At *Under Cost Centre*:
  - o To create a Cost Centre under any Cost Centre, select *All Items* at *Under Cost Centre* and then select the Parent Cost Centre at *Under* column, for each Cost Centre creation.
  - o To Create a Cost Centre under a specified Parent Cost Centre, select the Parent Cost Cenre at *Under Cost Centre*. This would be carried at *Under* column and the Parent Cost entre would be auto selected.
- **Cost Center Name**: At *Name*, enter Cost Centre Name.
- **Parent Cost Centre:** At *Under*, select the Cost Centre from the list.

Cost Centre Master Alteration: To Alter Cost Centre Master, at Cost Centre Menu (F-2B), select *Alter* (under Multiple Cost Centre) to get Cost Centre Alteration screen, displaying the Cost Center, similar to Cost Centre creation screen (F-4A). Place the cursor to the desired field and make necessary alteration in the same way as Creation of Cost Centre, explained above.

Cost Centre Master Display: To Display a Cost Centre Master, at Cost Centre Menu (F-2B), select *Display* (under Multiple Cost Centre), to get the Cost Centre Display screen, displaying the Cost Center, similar to Cost Centre creation (F-4A) screen. You may view the details but you cannot change any data from Display screen.

04 Cost Allocable Ledger Accounts

Ledger Creation has been explained earlier. For Cost Allocable Ledger Accounts (Ledger Accunts for which you like to enter Cost Centre allocation in Voucher), at Ledger Creation/Alter screen (F-6A), set *Yes* at *Cost Centres are Applicable*. Consequently, in Voucher Entry (F-7A), you will get Cost Cenre Allocation screen (F-7B), to allocate the ledger account amount for in the voucher to Cost Centres., as described next.

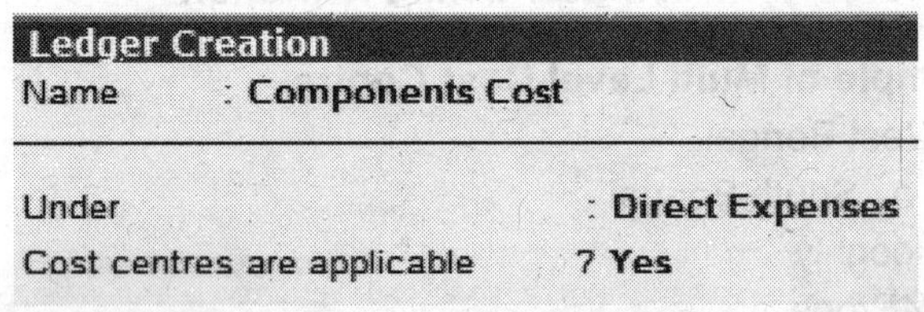

F-6A: Cost Centre activation in Ledger Accounts

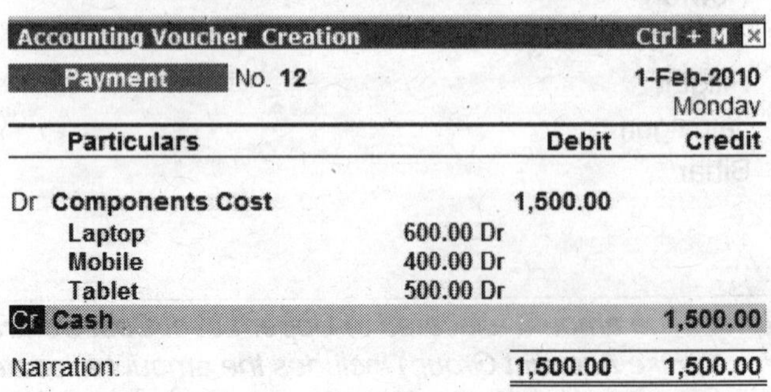

F-7A: Voucher Entry with Cost Allocations

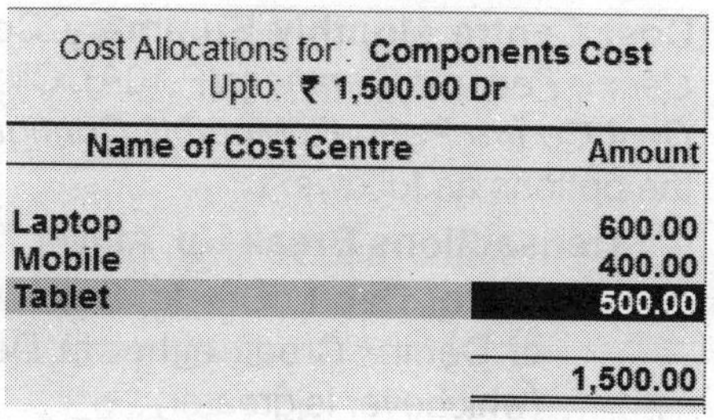

F-7B: Cost Allocations in Voucher Entry

05 Cost Centre Allocation in Accounts Voucher

During voucher entry, on entry of a Cost Allocable Ledger (Ledger Accounts for which Cost entre has been activated (F-6A), and entering the Ledger amount (F-7A), Cost Allocation screen appears to enter the Cost Centre Allocation for the Ledger Amount (F-7B). At Cost Allocation screen (F-7B), enter as follows:

- **Cost Centre Name**: At *Name of Cost Centre*, select the Cost Center.
- **Cost Centre Amount**: At *Amount*, Tally proposes the balance amount allocable to Cost Centre. Press <enter> to allocate the balance amount or enter the amount allocated to Cost Centre.

This way, Ledger Amount is allocated may be allocated to Cost Centre. If the amount is to be allocated to multiple cost centres, continue to enter successive Cost Centres and allocate the amount, on by one, till the ledger amount is fully allocated to the Cost Centres.

06 Cost Centre Reports

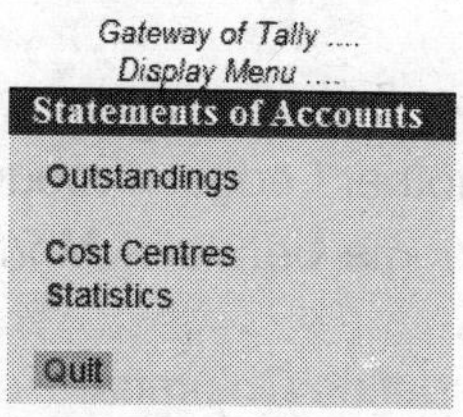

F-8A: Statement of Accounts Menu

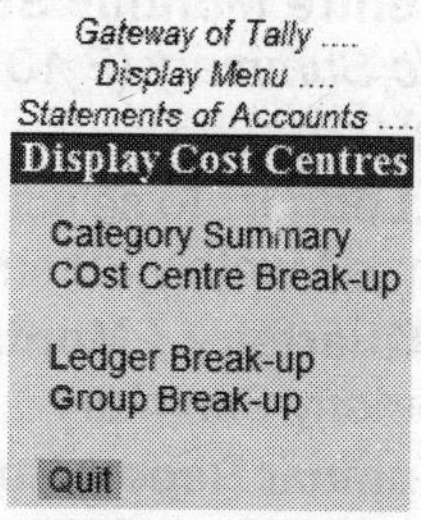

F-8B: Cost Centre Reports Menu

At *GoT>Display,* select *Statement of Accounts* to get *Statement of Accounts* menu (F-8A). At *Statement of Accounts* menu (F-8A). select *Cost Centres* to get Cost Centres Reports menu (F-8B), to Display following Reports relating to Cost Centre Analysis

- Cost Centre Break Up (§07)
- Group Break Up (§08)
- Ledger Break Up (§09)

These Reports are discussed next.

07 Cost Centre Break Up

Cost Centre Break Up Report shows Ledger Account wise break up of selected Cost Centre. At Cost Centre Reports Menu (F-8B), select *Cost Centre Break Up* and select a Cost Centre to get Cost Centre Break Up Display (F-9A).

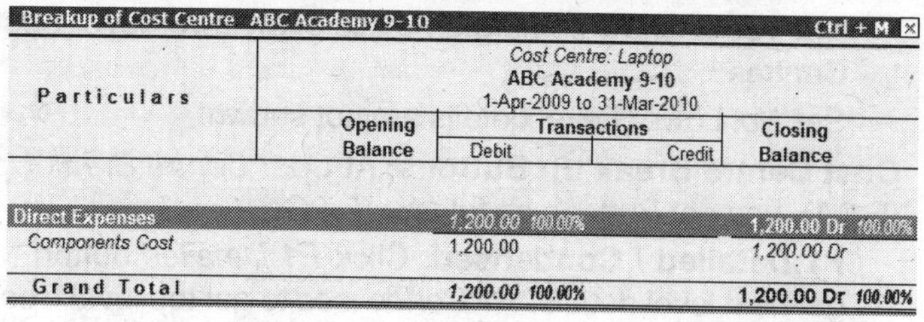

F-9A: Cost Centre Break Up (with all columns, %)

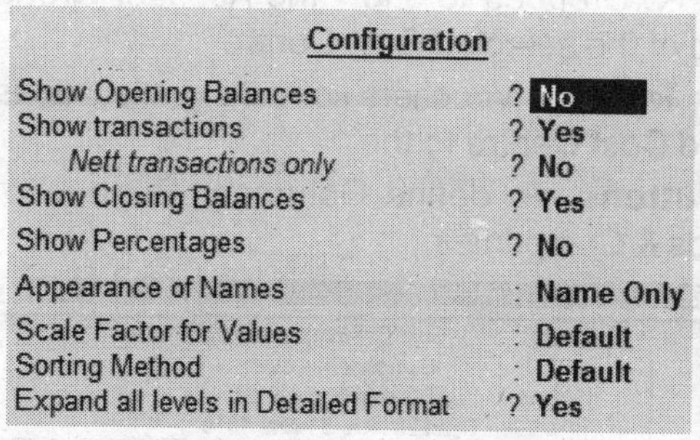

F-9B: Cost Centre Break Up Configuration

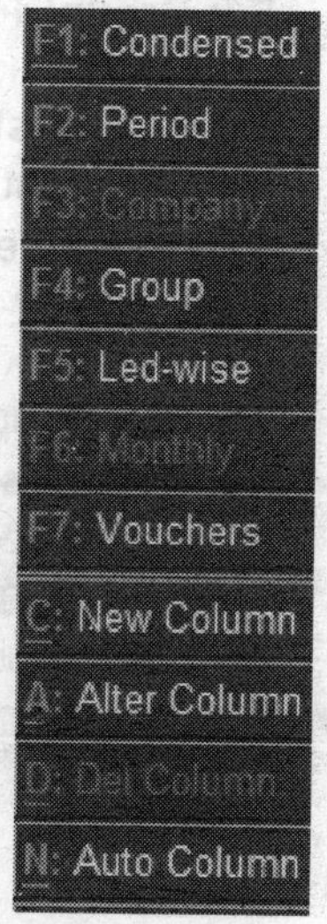

F-9C: Buttons

Cost Centre Break Up Configuration: At *Cost Centre Break Up* Display (F-9A), click *F12:Configure* to get Cost Centre Configuration screen (F-9B), to set up following options:

- **Opening Balances:** At *Show Opening Balances*:
  - o Set Yes to show Opening Balance of the Cost Centre
  - o Set *No*. The Opening Balance of the Cost Centre is not shown
- **Transactions Break Up**: At *Net Transaction only*:
  - o **Net of Debit / Credit**: Set Yes to show only he Net of Debit / Credit either in Debit or Credit Column (whichever is greater)
  - o **Debit / Credit Break Up**: Set *No* to show both Debit & Credit amount separately, in respective Debit or Credit Column (whichever is greater)
- **Closing Balances:** At Show *Closing Balances*:
  - o Set Yes to show Closing Balance of the Cost Centre
  - o Set *No*. The Closing Balance of the Cost Centre is not shown
- **Percentage:** At Show Percentages:
  - o Set Yes to show the % of amount of each Cost Centre in respect of Total for that column
  - o Set No. % column is shown

- **All Details**: Having set *F1:Detailed* button, at *Expand all Levels in Details Format,*
- Set *Yes* to show complete details of all lower level Cost Centres
- Set *No*. Lower Level details are not shown

Cost Centre Break Up Buttons: At *Cost Centre Break Up* (F-9A), you get Buttons as follows (F-9C):

- **F1:Detailed / Condensed**: Click *F1:Detailed* button to get next level details. *F1:Condensed* to get top level Cost Centre only
- **F4: Group**: To select the Account Group to get the Cost Centre Break Up of the selected Group in respect of selected Cost Centre select Primary to show Break Up of all Account Groups of the selected Cost Centre)
- **F5:Ledgwise / Grouped**: Click *F5:Ledgewise* to show the Ledger Account wise Break up o the selected Cost Centre. Click *F5:Grouped* to show the Account Group wise Break up of the selected Cost Centre
- **F7:Vouchers**: To list the Vouchers containing allocations to the selected Cost Centre ro the
- **Columnar Buttons**: To define Columnar Reports of various Periods & Companies

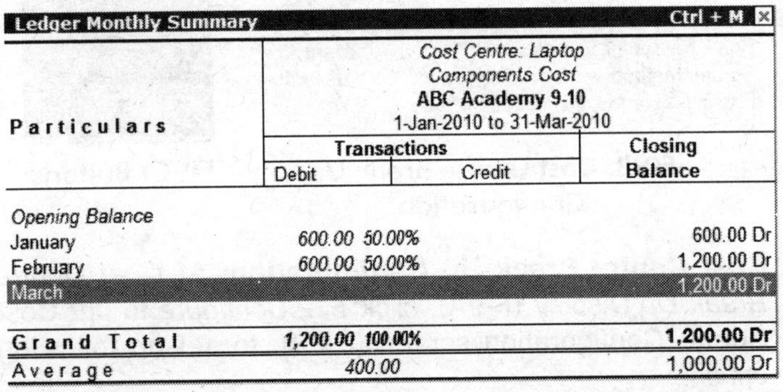

Ledger Monthly Summary — Ctrl + M

Cost Centre: Laptop
Components Cost
ABC Academy 9-10
1-Jan-2010 to 31-Mar-2010

Particulars	Transactions Debit	Transactions Credit	Closing Balance
Opening Balance			
January	600.00 50.00%		600.00 Dr
February	600.00 50.00%		1,200.00 Dr
March			1,200.00 Dr
Grand Total	1,200.00 100.00%		1,200.00 Dr
Average	400.00		1,000.00 Dr

F-10A: Cost Centre Periodic Summary (with Average, %)

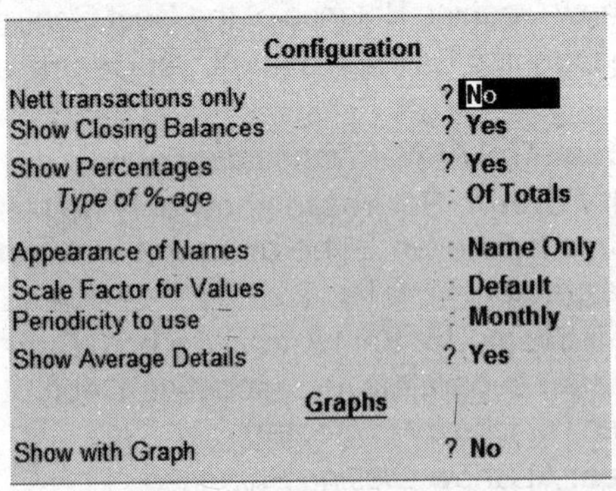

F-10B: Cost Centre Periodic Summary Configuration

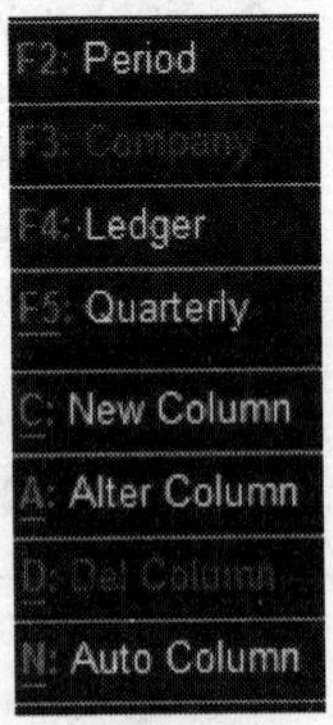

F-10C: Buttons

Cost Centre Monthly Summary

Drill down through a Cost Centre in the *Cost Centre Break Up* (F-9A), to get *Cost Centre Monthly Summary* (F-10A) showing the Monthly Break Up of the Cost Centre.

Cost Centre Monthly Summary Configuration: At *Cost Centre Periodic Summary* (F-10A), Click F12:Configure to get *Cost Centre Periodic Monthly Configuration* (F-10B), to set the options as follows:

- **Transactions Break Up**: At *Net Transaction only*:
  - o **Net of Debit / Credit**: Set *Yes* to show only he Net of Debit / Credit either in Debit or Credit Column (whichever is greater)
  - o **Debit / Credit Break Up**: Set *No* to show both Debit & Credit amount separately, in respective Debit or Credit Column (whichever is greater)
- **Closing Balances:** At Show *Closing Balances*:
  - o Set *Yes* to show Closing Balance of the Cost Centre
  - o Set *No*. The Closing Balance of the Cost Centre is not shown
- **Percentage:** At *Show Percentages*:
  - o Set *Yes* to show the % of amount of each Cost Centre in respect of Total for that column
  - o Set *No*. % column is shown
- **Averages**: At *Show Average Details*:
- Set *Yes* to show Periodic Average figures of the respective columns, at the bottom of the Report
- Set *No*. The Average details line is now shown
- **Periodicity:** Select the Periodicity from the list
- **Graph:** At *Show Graph*:
  - o Set *Yes* to show Bar Graph of the Transactions of each period.
  - o Set *No*. The Graph is not shown

Cost Centre Monthly Summary Buttons: At *Cost Centre Periodic Summary* (F-10A), you get the buttons as follows (F-10C):

- **F4: Ledger**: To select the Ledger Account to get the Cost Centre Monthly Summary of another Ledger Account
- **F5:Quartelry / Monthly:** To toggle between Monthly / Quarterly Summary
- **Columnar Report Buttons**: To define Columnar Reports of various Periods & Companies

Cost Centre Voucher List

At *Cost Centre Periodic Summary*(F-10A), drill down through a period to get *Cost Centre Voucher List* (F-11A), showing the Vouchers related to the Cost Centre for the selected Period.

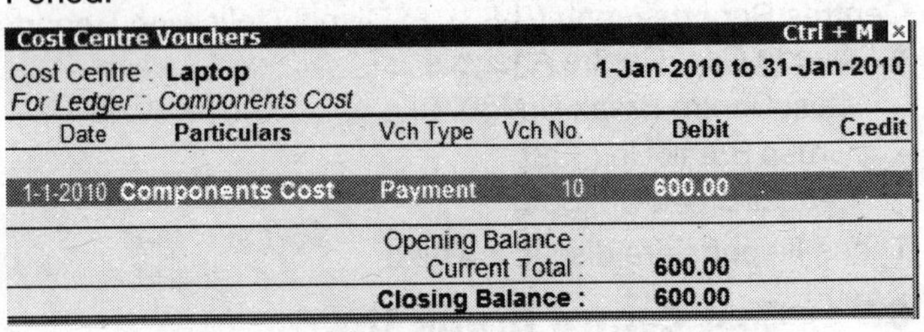

Cost Centre Vouchers — Ctrl + M

Cost Centre : **Laptop** — **1-Jan-2010 to 31-Jan-2010**
For Ledger : Components Cost

Date	Particulars	Vch Type	Vch No.	Debit	Credit
1-1-2010	Components Cost	Payment	10	600.00	
	Opening Balance :				
	Current Total :			600.00	
	Closing Balance :			600.00	

F-11A: Cost Centre Voucher List

Configuration

Select vouchers to show	:	All Vouchers
Show Narrations also	?	No
Include Opening Balances *(set as 'no' to remove from filtered reports)*	?	Yes
Appearance of Names	:	Name Only
Sorting Method	:	Default

F-11B: Cost Centre Voucher List Configuration.

- F1: Detailed
- F2: Period
- F3: Company
- F4: Cost Centre
- F6: Dly Brk-up

F-11C: Buttons

You may further drill down through any voucher to get the Voucher in Alteration Mode to perform various operations on the voucher.

Cost Centre Voucher List Configuration: At *Cost Centre Voucher List* (F-11A), Click F12:Configure to get *Cost Centre Voucher List Configuration* (F-11B).

- **Transaction Type:** At *Select Vouchers to show*, select Transaction Type from the list to show Vouchers of the selected Transaction Type, as follows:
    - o **All Transactions**: Select *All Vouchers* to show Vouchers of all types of transaction (debits & Credits)
    - o **Debit Allocations only**: Select *Debit Entries only* to show vouchers of allocation of Debit Transactions only
    - o **Credit Allocations only**: Select *Credit Entries only* to show vouchers of allocation of Credit Transactions only
- **Voucher Narration:** At *Show Voucher Narration also*:
    - o Set Yes to Show Voucher Narration of the listed Voucher
    - o Set No. Voucher Narration is not shown
- **Opening Balance:** At *Include Opening Balances*:
    - o Set Yes to Opening Balance of Cost Centre.
    - o Set No. Opening Balance of Cost Centre. is not shown

Cost Centre Voucher List Buttons: At *Cost Centre Voucher List* (F-11A), you get the buttons (F-11C) as follows:

- **F1:Detailed / Condensed**: Click *F1:Detailed* toggle button to get next level details. *F1:Condensed* to get top level Cost Centre only
- **F4: Cost Centre**: To select the Cost Centre to get Voucher List of another Cost Centre
- **F6: Daily Break Up**: To get daily figures (transactions and balances for each day for the selected period) of the selected Cost Centre for the selected Ledger Account

08 Cost Centre Account Group Break Up

Cost Centre Account Group Break Up shows Cost Centre wise break up of all vouchers in which the Ledger Accounts of the selected Account Group is transacted.

At Cost Centre Reports Menu (F-8B), select *Group Break up* and then select the Account Group to get *Cost Centrewise Break up* of the selected Account Group (F-12A).

Cost Breakup of Group ABC Academy 9-10 Ctrl + M

Particulars	Opening Balance	Transactions Debit	Transactions Credit	Closing Balance
	Group: Direct Expenses ABC Academy 9-10 1-Apr-2009 to 31-Mar-2010			
Primary Cost Category		3,000.00 100.00%		,000.00 Dr 100.00%
Computer		1,200.00		,200.00 Dr
Computer				
Laptop		*1,200.00*		,200.00 Dr
Mobile		800.00		800.00 Dr
Mobile		*800.00*		*800.00 Dr*
Tablet		1,000.00		,000.00 Dr
Tablet		*1,000.00*		*',000.00 Dr*

F-12A: Cost Centre Account Group Break Up

Configuration

Show Opening Balances	?	Yes
Show transactions	?	Yes
Nett transactions only	?	No
Show Closing Balances	?	Yes
Show Percentages	?	Yes
Type of %-age	:	Of Totals
Appearance of Names	:	Name Only
Scale Factor for Values	:	Default
Expand all levels in Detailed Format	?	Yes

F-12B: Cost Centre Account Group Break Up Configuration

- F1: Condensed
- F2: Period
- F3: Company
- C: New Column
- A: Alter Column
- D: Del Column
- N: Auto Column

F-12C: Buttons

Cost Centre Account Group Break Up Configuration: At *Cost Centre Account Group Break Up* (F-12A), click *F12:Configure* to get *Cost Centre Account Group Break Up Configuration* screen (F-12B), to set the options as described below (similar to Cost Centre Break Up: F-9B)

- **Opening Balances:** At *Show Opening Balances*:
    - o Set Yes to show Opening Balance of the Cost Centre
    - o Set *No.* The Opening Balance of the Cost Centre is not shown
- **Transactions Break Up**: At *Net Transaction only*:
    - o **Net of Debit / Credit**: Set Yes to show only he Net of Debit / Credit either in Debit or Credit Column (whichever is greater)
    - o **Debit / Credit Break Up**: Set *No* to show both Debit & Credit amount separately, in respective Debit or Credit Column (whichever is greater)
- **Closing Balances:** At Show *Closing Balances*:
    - o Set Yes to show Closing Balance of the Cost Centre
    - o Set *No.* The Closing Balance of the Cost Centre is not shown
- **Percentage:** At Show Percentages:
    - o Set Yes to show the % of amount of each Cost Centre in respect of Total for that column
    - o Set No. % column is shown

- **All Details**: Having set *F1:Detailed* button, at *Expand all Levels in Details Format*,
- Set *Yes* to show complete details of all lower level Cost Centres
- Set *No*. Lower Level details are not shown

Cost Centre Account Group Break Up Buttons: At *Cost Centre Break Up* (F-12A), you get Buttons (F-12C), as follows:

- **F1:Detailed / Condensed**: Click *F1:Detailed* toggle button to get next level details. *F1:Condensed* to get top level Cost Centre only
- **Columnar Report Buttons**: To define Columnar Reports of various Periods & Companies

Drill Down: Drill down from various elements at *Cost Centre Account Group Break Up* (F-12A) to get reports as follows:

- **Cost Center Summary**: From the Higher level Cost Centre (Cost Centre having subordinate Cost Centre), you get *Cost Centre Summary* (F-13A) showing the summary figures of each Cost Centre under the selected Cost Centre / Category, for the specified period.
- **Cost Centre Monthly break up**: From the lowest level Cost Centre (Cost Centre having no subordinate Cost Centre), you get *Cost Centre Monthly Summary* (F-14A) giving the monthly figures of the selected Cost Centre, for the specified period. You may set the Period & Periodicity of the Report.

Cost Centre Summary ABC Academy 9-10 Ctrl + M

Particulars	Opening Balance	Transactions Debit	Transactions Credit	Closing Balance
	Group: Direct Expenses ABC Academy 9-10 1-Apr-2009 to 31-Mar-2010			
Computer		1,200.00 40.00%		1,200.00 Dr 40.00%
Mobile		800.00 26.67%		800.00 Dr 26.67%
Tablet		1,000.00 33.33%		1,000.00 Dr 33.33%
Grand Total		3,000.00 100.00%		3,000.00 Dr 100.00%

F-13A: Cost Centre Summary

Configuration

Show Opening Balances	? Yes
Show transactions	? Yes
Nett transactions only	? No
Show Closing Balances	? Yes
Show Percentages	? Yes
Type of %-age	: Of Totals
Appearance of Names	: Name Only
Scale Factor for Values	: Default
Expand all levels in Detailed Format	? Yes

F1: Detailed
F2: Period
F3: Company
F4: Cost Centre
C: New Column
A: Alter Column
D: Del Column
N: Auto Column

F-13B: Cost Centre Summary Configuration

F-13C: Buttons

Cost Centre Monthly Break Up Configuration: At *Cost Centre Monthly Break Up* (F-14A), click *F12:Configure* to get *Cost Centre Account Monthly Summary Configuration* screen (F-14B), to set the options as below:

- **Opening Balances:** At Show *Opening Balances*:
  - o Set Yes to show Opening Balance of the Cost Centre
  - o Set *No*. The Opening Balance of the Cost Centre is not shown
- **Transactions Break Up**: At *Net Transaction only*:
  - o **Net of Debit / Credit**: Set Yes to show only he Net of Debit / Credit either in Debit or Credit Column (whichever is greater)
  - o **Debit / Credit Break Up**: Set *No* to show both Debit & Credit amount separately, in respective Debit or Credit Column (whichever is greater)
- **Closing Balances:** At Show *Closing Balances*:
  - o Set Yes to show Closing Balance of the Cost Centre
  - o Set *No*. The Closing Balance of the Cost Centre is not shown
- **Percentage:** At Show Percentages:
  - o Set Yes to show the % of amount of each Cost Centre in respect of Total for that column
  - o Set No. % column is shown
- **All Details**: Having set *F1:Detailed* button, at Expand all Levels in Details Format,
- Set *Yes* to show complete details of all lower level Cost Centres
- Set *No*. Lower Level details are not shown

Cost Centre Monthly Break Up Buttons: At *Cost Centre Monthly Summary* (F-13A),, you get Buttons (F-13C), as follows:

- **F1:Detailed / Condensed**: Click *F1:Detailed* toggle button to get next level details. *F1:Condensed* to get top level Cost Centre only
- **F4: Cost Centre**: To select the Cost Centre to get Voucher List of another Cost Centre
- **Columnar Report Buttons**: To define Columnar Reports of various Periods & Companies

CC Monthly Summary Ctrl + M

Particulars	Transactions Debit	Transactions Credit	Closing Balance
	Group: Direct Expenses Laptop ABC Academy 9-10 1-Jan-2010 to 31-Mar-2010		
Opening Balance			
January	600.00 50.00%		600.00 Dr
February	600.00 50.00%		1,200.00 Dr
March			1,200.00 Dr
Grand Total	1,200.00 100.00%		1,200.00 Dr
Average	400.00		1,000.00 Dr

F-14A: Cost Centre Monthly Summary

Cost Centre Monthly Summary Configuration: At *Cost Centre Periodic Summary (F-14A),* Click F12:Configure to get *Cost Centre Periodic Monthly Configuration* (F-14B).

- **Transactions Break Up**: At *Net Transaction only*:

- o **Net of Debit / Credit**: Set *Yes* to show only Net of Debit / Credit either in Debit or Credit Column (whichever is greater)

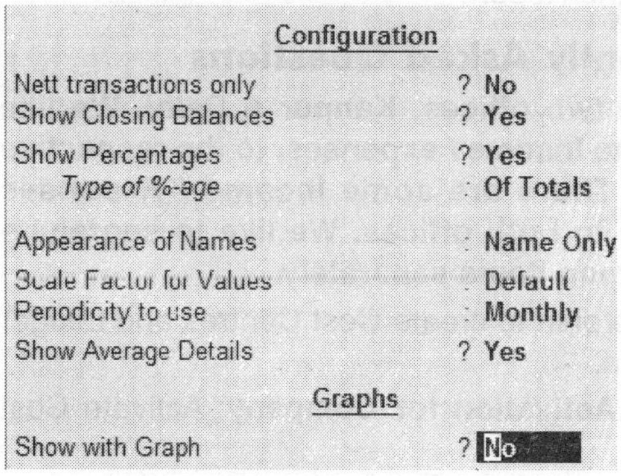

F-14B: Cost Centre Monthly Summary Configuration

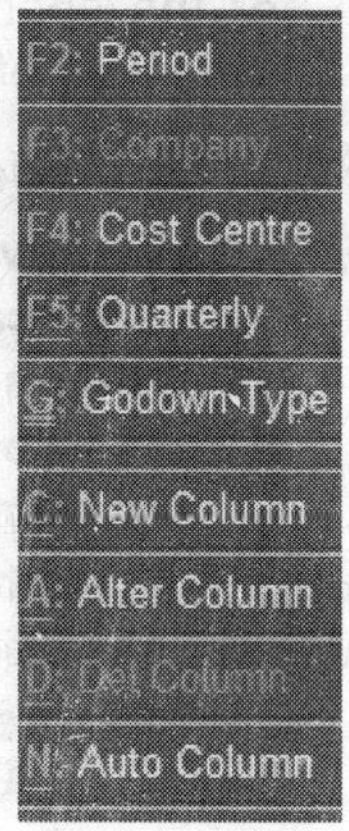

F-14C: Buttons

- o **Debit / Credit Break Up**: Set *No* to show both Debit & Credit amount separately, in respective Debit or Credit Column (whichever is greater)
- **Closing Balances:** At Show *Closing Balances*:
  - o Set *Yes* to show Closing Balance of the Cost Centre
  - o Set *No*. The Closing Balance of the Cost Centre is not shown
- **Percentage:** At *Show Percentages*:
  - o Set *Yes* to show the % of amount of each Cost Centre in respect of Total for that column
  - o Set *No*. % column is shown
- **Averages**: At *Show Average Details*:
  - Set *Yes* to show Periodic Average figures of the respective columns, at the bottom of the Report
- Set *No*. The Average details line is now shown
- **Graph:** At *Show Graph*:
  - o Set *Yes* to show Bar Graph of the Transactions of each period.
  - o Set *No*. The Graph is not shown

  Cost Centre Monthly Summary Buttons: At *Cost Centre Periodic Summary (F-14A)*, you get the buttons as follows (F-14C):
- **F4: Ledger**: To select the Ledger Account to get the Cost Centre Monthly Summary of another Ledger Account
- **F5:Quartelry / Monthly:** To toggle between Monthly / Quarterly Summary

Cost Centre Voucher List

At *Cost Centre Monthly Summary* (F-14A), drill down through a period to get *Cost Centre Voucher List*, (F-11A) showing the Vouchers related to the Cost Centre for the selected Period. You may further drill down through any voucher to get the Voucher in Alteration Mode to perform various operations on the voucher.

09 Cost Centre. Ledger Account Break Up

Cost Centre. Ledger Account Break Up (F-15A) shows the Cost Centrewise breakup of the selected Ledger Account. At Cost Centre Reports Menu (F-8B), select *Ledger Break Up* and select the Ledger Account to get *Cost Centre Ledger Break Up* of the selected Ledger Account (F-15A).

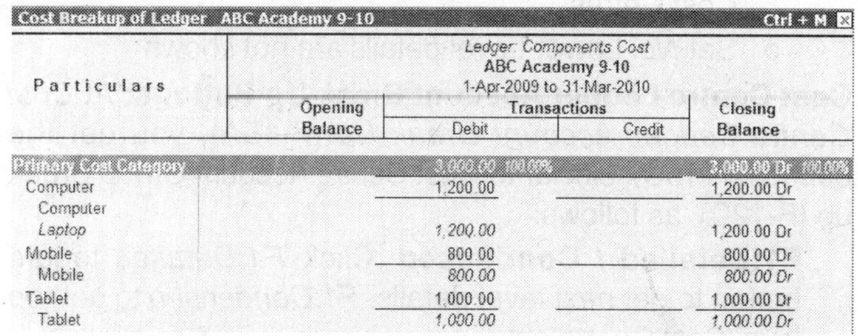

F-15A: Cost Centre. Ledger Account Break Up

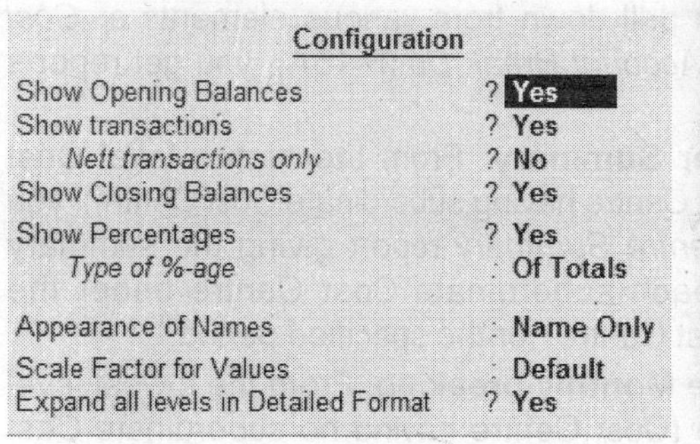

F-15B: Cost Centre. Ledger Account Break Up Configuration

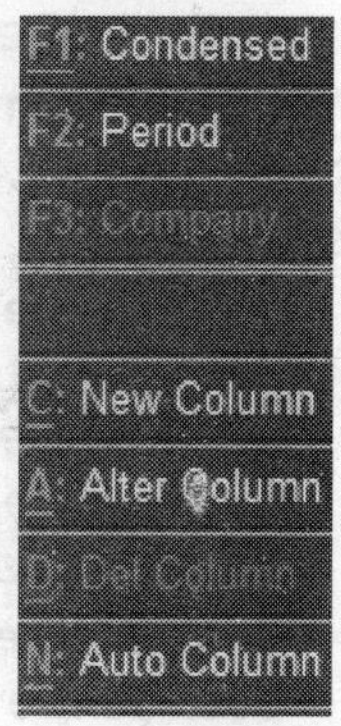

F-15C: Buttons

Cost Centre Ledger Account Break Up Configuration: At *Cost Centre Ledger Account Break Up* (F-15A), Click F12:Configure to get *Cost Centre Ledger Account Break Up Configuration* (F-15B), similar to Cost Centre Account Group Configuration (F-12B).

- **Opening Balances:** At Show *Opening Balances*:
  - o Set Yes to show Opening Balance of the Cost Centre
  - o Set *No*. The Opening Balance of the Cost Centre is not shown
- **Transactions Break Up**: At *Net Transaction only*:
  - o **Net of Debit / Credit**: Set Yes to show only he Net of Debit / Credit either in Debit or Credit Column (whichever is greater)
  - o **Debit / Credit Break Up**: Set *No* to show both Debit & Credit amount separately, in respective Debit or Credit Column (whichever is greater)
- **Closing Balances:** At Show *Closing Balances*:
  - o Set Yes to show Closing Balance of the Cost Centre
  - o Set *No*. The Closing Balance of the Cost Centre is not shown

- **Percentage:** At Show Percentages:
  - o Set Yes to show the % of amount of each Cost Centre in respect of Total for that column
  - o Set No. % column is shown
- **All Details**: Having set *F1:Detailed* button, at Expand all Levels in Details Format,
  - o Set *Yes* to show complete details of all lower level Cost Cetres
  - o Set *No*. Lower Level details are not shown

Cost Centre Ledger Account Break Up Buttons: At *Cost Centre Ledger Account Break Up* (F-15A), you get the buttons (F-15C), similar to Cost Centre Account Group Break up (F-12C), as follows:

- **F1:Detailed / Condensed**: Click *F1:Detailed* toggle button to get next level details. *F1:Condensed* to get top level Cost Centre only
- **Columnar Report Buttons**: To define Columnar Reports of various Periods & Companies

Drill Down: On drill down from various elements at *Cost Centre Ledger Account Break Up* (F-15A), you get reports as follows:

- **Cost Center Summary**: From the higher level Cost Centre (Cost Centre having subordinate Cost Centre), you get *Cost Centre Summary* report giving the summary figures of each subordinate Cost Centre under the selected Cost Centre, for the specified period.
- **Cost Centre Monthly break up**: From the lowest level Cost Centre (Cost Centre having no subordinate Cost Centre), you get *Cost Centre Monthly breakup* report giving the monthly figures of the selected Cost Centre, for the specified period. You may set the Period & Periodicity of the Report.

FAQ: Frequently Asked Questions

FAQ-1: We have two offices, Kanpur & Delhi. We like to allocate Income / expenses, to the respective Offices. There are some Income / Expenses common to both offices. We like to segregate the common items separately.

Ans: Suggest the plan to create Cost Centres and Ledger Account Allocation.

- **Cost Centre Activation for Company**: Activate Cost Centre (F-1A).
- **Cost Centre Activation for Ledger Accounts**: As you like to allocate to Cost Centres of Income / Expenses (accounts of P & L), set *Yes* at *Cost Centre Applicable* (F-6A), at Ledger Account Creation / Alteration for the respective Ledger Accounts of Income & Expenses (and set *No* to all other Ledger Accounts),
- **Cost Centre Creation**: Create Cost Centre as below:
  Offices (Primary)
  - o Kanpur (under Offices)
  - o Delhi (under Offices)

In voucher entry, you should allocate the Ledger Amount to the respective Cost Centre (Kanpur, Delhi) which are exclusively related to the respective Office and allocate the common amounts to Offices Cost Centre.

Cost Categories 05-02

01 Cost Categories

Cost Categories are parallel sets of Cost Centre used to allocate ledger accounts of same transactions to Cost Centres under each Cost Category simultaneously. For example, you may allocate ledger accounts of a voucher to Cost Centres under Cost Categories as follows:

- Products Type (Mobile, Tablet, Note Book, Laptop)
- Service Type (Board, Memory Card, AMC)

The allocation of Ledger Amount to Cost Centres under multiple Cost Categories simultaneously, are distinct and independent of each other.

Ledger Account Transactions in Voucher are allocated to Cost Centres only (NOT to Cost Categories). The Cost Category organizes the allocation to respective Cost Category

02 Activation of Cost Categories

Having activated Cost Centre (set *Yes* at *Maintain Cost Centre*: F-1A/05-01*)*, also set *Yes* at *More than one Payroll / Cost Category* at Company Operations screen, to enable entry of Cost Categories. Consequently, the option Cost Categories also appear at Accounts Info Menu (F-2A/05-01) to create & maintain Cost Categories.

Even when Cost Category is not activated (when you set No at *More than one Payroll / Cost Category*, as explained above), a Primary Cost Category is internally created and all Cost Centres created are placed under this internally created Primary Cost Category (but you cannot create any new Cost Category).

> **Note:** *When Cost Category is activated. Cost Centre must be placed under a specific Cost Category (F-3A)*

F-1A: Cost Category menu

F-2A: Cost Category creation

F-3A: Cost Centre creation

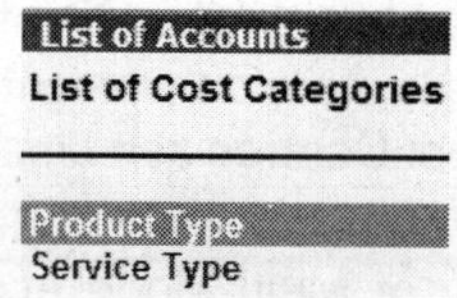

F-4A: List of Cost Categories

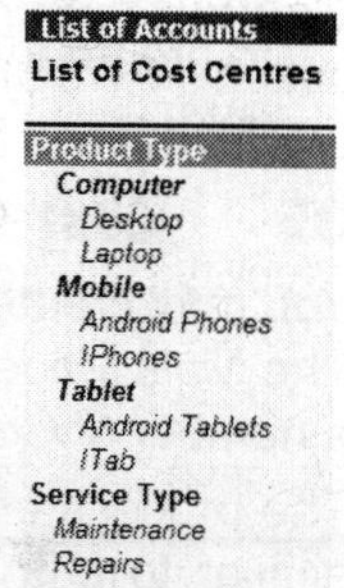

F-4A: List of Cost Centres

03 Cost Category Creation

At *Accounts Info Menu* (F-2A/05-01), select *Cost Category* to get *Cost Category Menu* (F-1A). At Cost Category Menu (F-1A), select *Cost Category* to get Cost Category creation screen (F-2A). Now enter as follows:

- **Cost Category Name**: At *Name*, enter Cost Category Name.
- **Cost Allocation Type**: You may specify the Ledger Account Types for Allocation to Cost Centres, as follows:
  - **Allocation of Revenue Accounts Items:** At *Allocate Revenue Items*, set *Yes* to allocate amount of Nominal Ledger Accounts only (i. e. Ledger Accounts of Income / Expenses), else set *No* (Non Revenue Ledger Account cannot be allocated to the Cost Category).
  - **Allocation of Non Revenue Accounts Items:** At *Allocate Non-Revenue Items* field, set *Yes* to allocate Non Revenue Ledger Account (i. e, Ledger Accounts of Assets / Liabilities) to the Cost Category, else set *No* (Non Revenue Ledger Accounts can not be allocated to the Cost Category

You may set *Yes* at either of the option (to allocate for selected type of Ledger Accounts, or both (to allocate all ledger accounts). Do not set *No* to both the option (No Ledger account would be allocated)

04 Cost Centre creation under Cost Category

Cost Centre creation has been explained earlier (F-3A/05-01). However, After you have created Cost Category (F-2A), you have to create a Cost Centre under a Cost Category only. During Cost Centre creation / alteration (F-3A), enter as follows:

- **Parent Cost Category**: At *Category*, select the Parent Cost Category (if the cursor has skipped to next field, press Shift+Tab (or Up Arrow) to get to Category field and select the parent Category from the list.
- **Cost Centre Name**: At *Name*, enter the Cost Centre Name.
- **Parent Cost Centre**: At *Under*, select the Parent Cost Centre (or select *Primary*) from the list (or press Alt+C to create the parent Cost Centre and select it at Under field)

05 Cost Category creation in Multi Mode

You may create Multiple Cost Centres through Multi Mode. The *Multi Mode* is more convenient to create / alter / display a number of Cost Centres at a time, in one screen.

The process of Entry of Multi Mode Cost Category entry is similar to entry of Multi Mode Accounts Ledger, Account Group & Cost Centres (§03/05-01), described earlier.

Select Create under Multiple Cost Categories at Cost Categories Menu (F-1A), to get Must Cost Categories creation screen (F-5A), to enter as follows:

- **Cost Category Name**: At *Name of Cost Category* column, enter Cost Category Name.
- **Cost Category Account Type**: You may specify the Ledger Type for Allocation as explained earlier (§03).
- **Allocation of Revenue Accounts Items:** At *Revenue Items* column, set *Yes* to allocate amount of Nominal Ledger Accounts only (i. e. Ledger Accounts of Income / Expenses), else set *No* (Non Revenue Ledger Account cannot be allocated to the Cost Category).
- **Allocation of Non Revenue Accounts Items:** At *Non-Revenue Items* column, set *Yes* to allocate Non Revenue Ledger Account (i. e, Ledger Accounts of Assets / Liabilities) to the Cost Category, else set *No* (Non Revenue Ledger Accounts can not be allocated to the Cost Category

You may set *Yes* at either of the option (to allocate for selected type of Ledger Accounts, or both (to allocate all ledger accounts). Do not set *No* to both the option (No Ledger account would be allocated)

Multi Cost Category Alteration Ctrl + M

S.No.	Name of Category	Allocations for	
		Revenue Items	Non-Revenue Items
1.	Product Type	Yes	Yes
2.	Service Type	Yes	No

F-5A: Multi ModeCost Category creation

F6: Skip Names
F8: Skip Details

F-5B: Buttons

Cost Category Master Alteration: To Alter a Cost Centre Master, at Cost Centre Menu (F-1A), select *Alter* (under Multiple Cost Centre) to get Cost Centre Alteration screen, displaying the Cost Category, similar to Cost Category creation screen (F-5A). Place the cursor to the desired field and make necessary alteration in the same way as Creation of Cost Centre, explained above.

Cost Centre Master Display: To Display a Cost Centre Master, at Cost Centre Menu (F-1A), select *Display* (under Multiple Cost Centre), to get the Cost Category Display screen, displaying the Cost Category, similar to Cost Category creation (F-5A) screen. You may view the details but you cannot change any data from Display screen.

06 Multi Mode Cost Centre Creation under Cost Category

We have explained Multi Mode Cost Centre Creation earlier (F-4A/05-01). However, on Cost Category creation, you have to create Cost Centres under Cost Category (F-3A). You may create Cost Category under Multi Mode. As described, at Cost Centre Menu (F-2B/05-01), select *Create* under Multiple Cost Centre to get Multi Mode Cost Center creation under Cost Category entry screen (F-6A, F-6B).

Multi Cost Centre Alteration ABC Academy

Under Cost Centre : ┘ All Items

S.No.	Category	Name of Cost Centre	Under
1.	Product Type	Computer	┘ Primary
2.	Service Type	Maintenance	┘ Primary
3.	Product Type	Mobile	┘ Primary
4.	Service Type	Repairs	┘ Primary
5.	Product Type	Tablet	┘ Primary
6.	Product Type	Android Phones	Mobile
7.	Product Type	Android Tablets	Tablet
8.	Product Type	Desktop	Computer
9.	Product Type	IPhones	Mobile
10.	Product Type	ITab	Tablet
11.	Product Type	Laptop	Computer

F-6A: Multi Mode Cost Center creation under any Cost Category

Multi Cost Centre Alteration ABC Academy

Under Cost Centre : Computer

S.No.	Category	Name of Cost Centre	Under
1.	Product Type	Computer	Computer
2.	Product Type	Maintenance	Computer
3.	Product Type	Mobile	Computer
4.	Product Type	Repairs	Computer
5.	Product Type	Tablet	Computer
6.	Product Type	Android Phones	Computer
7.	Product Type	Android Tablets	Computer
8.	Product Type	Desktop	Computer
9.	Product Type	IPhones	Computer
10.	Product Type	ITab	Computer
11.	Product Type	Laptop	Computer

F-6B: Multi Mode Cost Center creation under specified parent Cost Category

F4: Parent
F4: New Parent
F5: Skip Category
F6: Skip Names
F7: Skip Parent

F-6C: Buttons

Now enter as follows (F-6A, F-6B):

Parent Cost Centre: At *Under Cost Centre*, select the parent Cost Centre (or select *Primary*) under which you like to place the Cost Centre (for the first Cost Centre created, you can select *Primary* only).

- o To create a Cost Centre under any Cost Centre, select *All Items* at *Under Cost Centre* (F-6A).
- o To Create a Cost Centre under a specified Parent Cost Group, select the Parent Cost Centre at *Under Cost Centre* (F-6B).

Now enter the Cost Centres as follows:

- **Cost Category Name**: At *Category* column, select the Cost Category from the list.
- **Cost Centre**: Enter the Name of the new Cost Centre to be created
- **Parent Cost Centre:** At *Under* column, select as follows:
  - o If *All Items* is specified at *Under Cost Centre*, then select the Parent Cost Centre from the list of Cost Centres (F-6A)
  - o If a specified Cost Centre was selected at *Under Cost Centre*, then the selected Cost Centre is auto carried at *Under* column and you do not have to select the Parent Cost Centre at Under column (F-6B)

07 Multiple Cost Category allocation in Voucher

We have seen Cost Centre Allocation of Ledger Account in Voucher (§05/05-01). On creation of Cost Categories, you may allocate the Cost Allocable Ledger Amount to Multiple set of Cost Categories.

During voucher entry, on entry of Cost Allocable Ledger & Amount (F-7A), you get Cost Allocation screen to allocate the Ledger Amount to Cost Category / Cost Centre (F-7B).

- **Cost Category**: Select the Cost Category
- **Cost Centres**: Now allocate to the Cost Centres under the selected Cost Category, one by one, till the entire ledger amount is fully allocated. Select the Cost Centre. Enter the amount (you may enter amount in negative, in case of deduction or reverse adjustment). The net of total amount allocated must match with the Ledger Amount.

After allocation of Ledger Amount to the selected Cost Category (and underlying Cost Centres), you may again select another Cost Category and allocate the edger Amount to another set of Cost Category/ Cost Centres, in the same way.

Press <enter>at Cost Category field to terminate allocation to Cost Category for the Ledger Amount.

Allocation details in Voucher:You get back to the main voucher entry screen (F-7A) showing the allocation details to the Cost Categories & Cost Centres (Amount with Dr/Cr sign) as entered in Cost Centre allocation screen (F-7B).

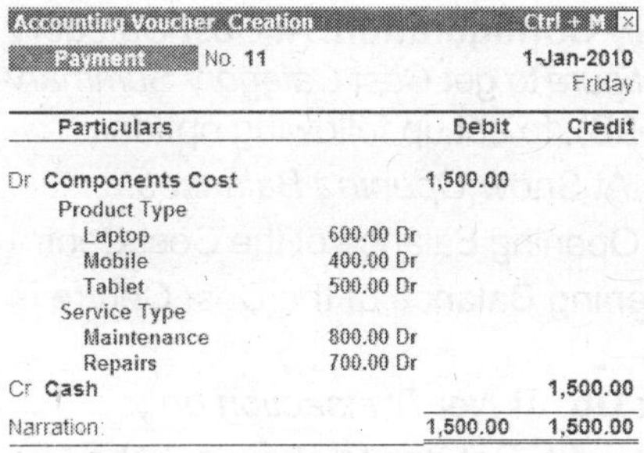

F-7A: Multi Cost Category Voucher entry

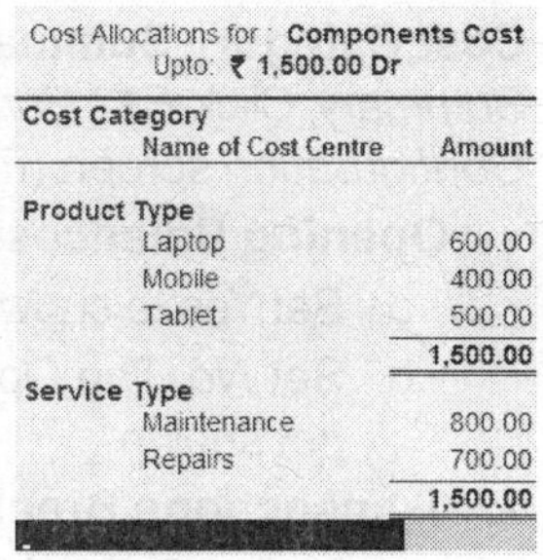

F-7B: Multi Cost Category allocation

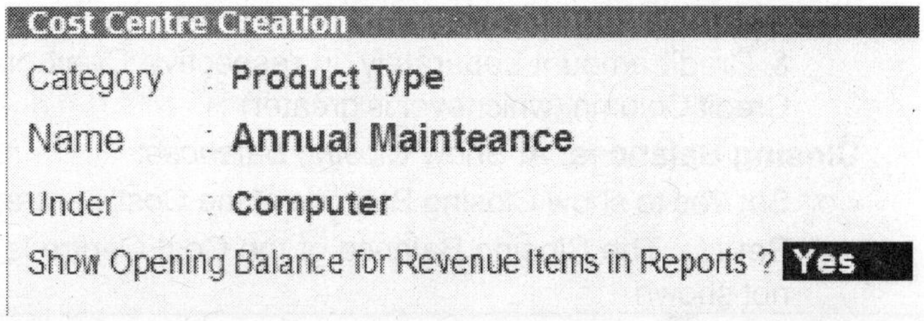

F-8A: Cost Centre Opening Balance option set Up

The sign of positive allocation (F-7B) is same (Dr/Cr) as the sign of allocated Ledger Amount (F-7A), while the sign the sign of negative allocation (Dr/Cr) is opposite.

08 Cost Category Summary

Select *Display > Statement of Accounts > Cost Centres > Category Summary* to get Cost Category. It shows summary of all Cost Categories, displaying figures for underlying Cost Centres..

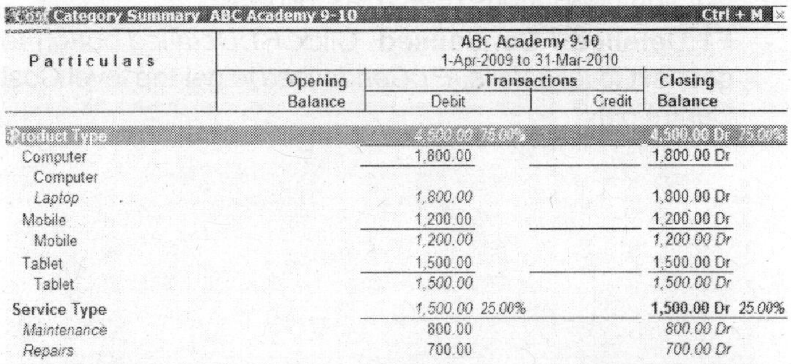

Cost Category Summary ABC Academy 9-10 Ctrl + M

Particulars	ABC Academy 9-10 1-Apr-2009 to 31-Mar-2010 Opening Balance	Transactions Debit	Transactions Credit	Closing Balance
Product Type		4,500.00 75.00%		4,500.00 Dr 75.00%
Computer		1,800.00		1,800.00 Dr
Computer				
Laptop		*1,800.00*		1,800.00 Dr
Mobile		1,200.00		1,200.00 Dr
Mobile		*1,200.00*		*1,200.00 Dr*
Tablet		1,500.00		1,500.00 Dr
Tablet		*1,500.00*		*1,500.00 Dr*
Service Type		*1,500.00 25.00%*		**1,500.00 Dr** 25.00%
Maintenance		800.00		*800.00 Dr*
Repairs		700.00		*700.00 Dr*

F-9A: Cost Category Summary

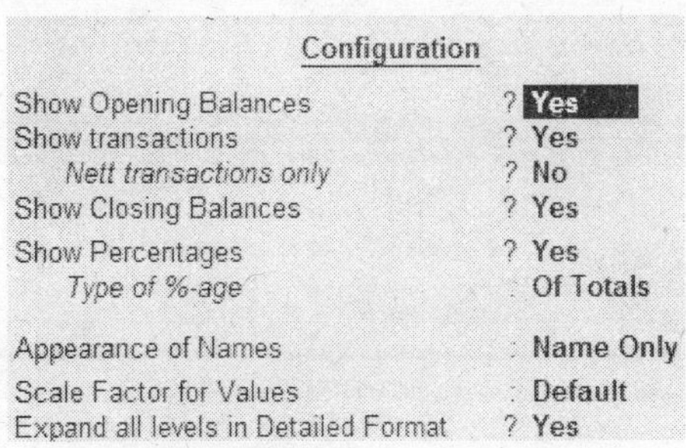

F-9B: Cost Category Summary Configuration

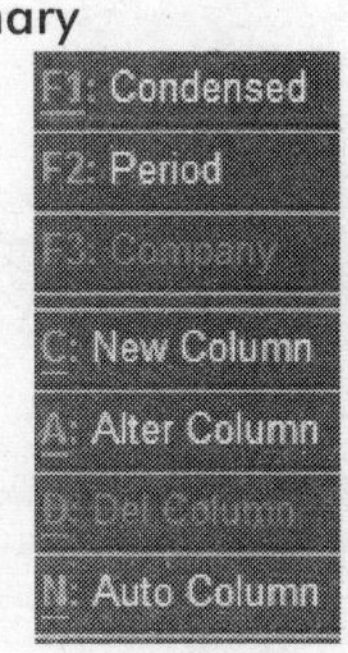

F-9C: Buttons

Cost Category Summary Configuration: At *Cost Category Summary,* Click *F12:Configure* to get *Cost Category Summary Configuration* screen (F-9B), to set up following options:

- **Opening Balances:** At Show *Opening Balances*:
  - o Set Yes to show Opening Balance of the Cost Centre
  - o Set *No.* The Opening Balance of the Cost Centre is not shown
- **Transactions Break Up**: At *Net Transaction only*:
  - o **Net of Debit / Credit**: Set Yes to show only he Net of Debit / Credit either in Debit or Credit Column (whichever is greater)
  - o **Debit / Credit Break Up**: Set *No* to show both Debit & Credit amount separately, in respective Debit or Credit Column (whichever is greater)
- **Closing Balances:** At Show *Closing Balances*:
  - o Set Yes to show Closing Balance of the Cost Centre
  - o Set *No.* The Closing Balance of the Cost Centre is not shown
- **Percentage:** At Show Percentages:
  - o Set Yes to show the % of amount of each Cost Centre in respect of Total for that column
  - o Set No. % column is shown
- **All Details**: Having set *F1:Detailed* button, at Expand all Levels in Details Format,
- Set *Yes* to show complete details of all lower level Cost Cetres
- Set *No.* Lower Level details are not shown

Cost Category Summary Buttons: At *Cost Centre Summary* (F-9A), you get Buttons (F-9C), as follows:

- **F1:Detailed / Condensed**: Click *F1:Detailed* button to get next level details. *F1:Condensed* to get top level Cost Centre only
- **Columnar Buttons**: To define Columnar Reports of various Periods & Companies

Drill Down: On drill down from various elements at *Cost Category Summary,* you get reports as follows:

- **Cost Center Summary**: From the top level Cost Category (or higher level Cost Centre having subordinate Cost Centre), you get *Cost Centre Summary* report giving the summary figures of each Cost Centre under the selected Cost Centre / Category, for the specified period
- **Cost Centre Monthly break up**: From the lowest level Cost Centre (Cost Centre having no subordinate Cost Centre), you get *Cost Centre Monthly breakup* report giving the monthly figures of the selected Cost Centre, for the specified period. You may set the Period & Periodicity of the Report.

09 Opening Balance of Revenue Items in Reports

To show Opening Balance of Revenue Items, at Cost Centre creation screen, set *Yes* at *Show Opening Balance in Revenue Accounts in Reports* (F-8A)

FAQ: Frequently Asked Questions

FAQ-1: What is the special advantage of Cost Category

Ans: Using Cost Centre, you may allocate the ledger account to Cost Centres. Using Cost Category, you may allocate the ledger account to multiple sets of Cost Centres under multiple Cost Categories. For example, Ledger Amount (e.g Wages) can be analysed according to Product Types as well as Locations of manufacturing.

For example, Sales may be analysed according to Product Types, Brands, Supplier, etc

Cost Centre Class 05-03

01 Cost Centre Class

In voucher entry, the allocation of ledger account to Cost Centre are to be entered in each Voucher. Often, the ledger amount is allocated to Cost Centres as per stipulated %. In such case, Cost Centre allocation may be automatically done on the basis of pre fixed ratio, using Cost Centre Class, instead of entering the allocation for each voucher.

A defined Cost Centre Class may be used in any Accounting Voucher.

Upon voucher entry, the amount of the transaction for the related Cost Allocable Ledger accounts are auto allocated to the Cost Centres in the background, as per allocation parameters set in the selected Cost Centre Class and the allocation screen does not appear during voucher entry.

Cost Centre Class enables allocation in voucher entry extremely fast and accurate.

02 Cost Centre Class set Up

At *F1:Features>Accounting Features* screen (F-1A / 05-01), having activated Cost Centre, set *Yes* at *Use Pre-defined Cost Centre Allocations during Entry*, to get *Auto Cost Allocation* screen (F-1A).

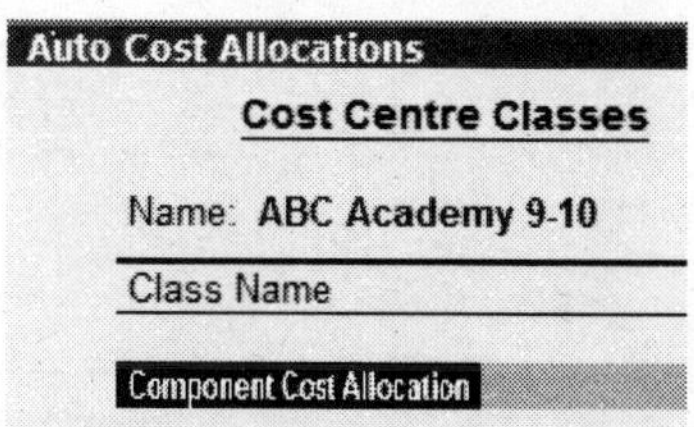

F-1A: Cost Class creation

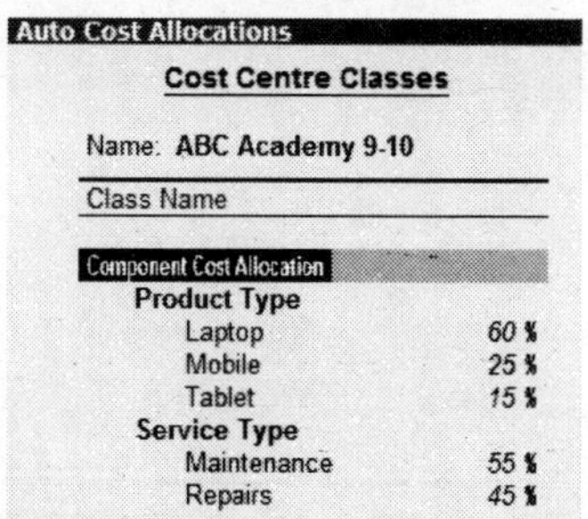

F-1B: Cost Centre Allocation Values

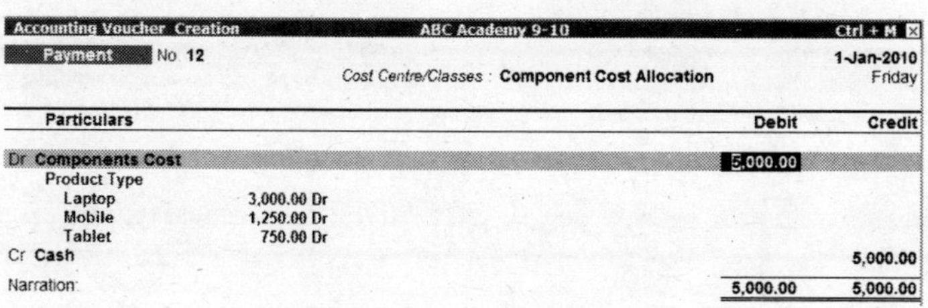

F-1E: Voucher Configuration

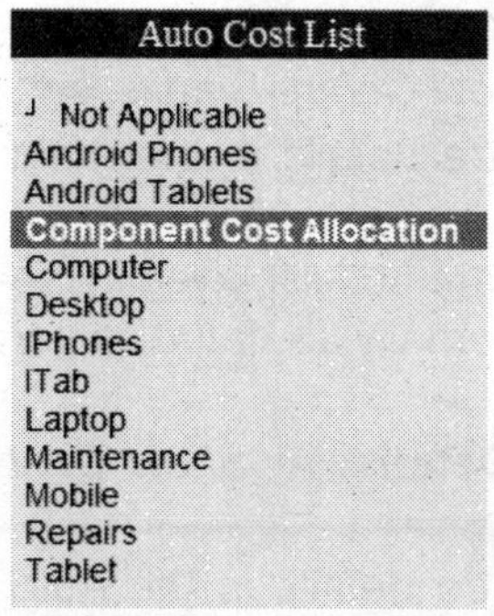

F-1C: Voucher entry with Cost Class

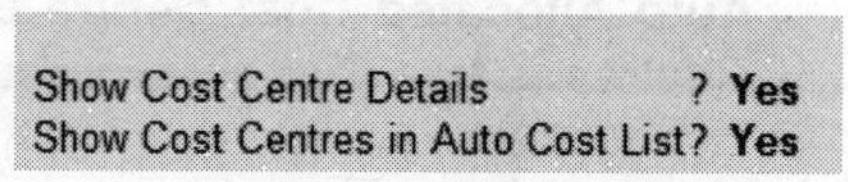

F-1D: Cost Class selection list

At *Auto Cost Allocations Screen* (F-1A), at *Class Name*, enter the *Cost Centre Class Name* to get Cost Centre Allocation Values entry screen (F-1B).

Cost Centre Allocation Values Entry

At *Cost Centre Allocation Values* entry screen (F-1B), enter as follows:

Cost Category / Cost Centre: Select the Cost Category / Cost Centre as follows:

- **Cost Category** At first column, select the Cost Category. Next select the Cost Centre form the list of child Cost Centres of the selected Category
- **Cost Centre Allocation Rate**: Against a selected Cost Centre, enter the Rate (in %) to be allocated to the Cost Centre.

This way continue to create the desired Cost Classes and specify the Auto Cost Allocation % for each Cost Class / Cost Category, until you fully allocate (100%) to the Cost Centre under the selected Cost Category.

Press <enter> at blank line to terminate Cost Class Name entry.

This way, you may create more Cost Centre Class and make allocation to The Cost Categories & underlying Cost Centres

02 Voucher Entry using Cost Centre Class

Having entered the auto cost allocation for Cost Classes, during Accounts Voucher entry (F-1C), at the voucher header, a field *Cost Centre / Class* appears to select the Cost Centre Class from the list (F-1D),

After you enter a Ledger Account and amount (F-1D) of any Cost Allocable Ledger Account (Ledger Account for which Cost Centre is activated), the Ledger Amount is auto allocated to the respective Cost Category / Cost Centres (F-1D) as per allocation % set in the selected Cost Centre Class.

03 Voucher Entry Configuration

At Voucher entry screen (F-1C), click F12:Configure to get *Voucher Entry configuration* screen. At *Voucher Entry configuration* screen (F-1E), set the option as follows:

- **Cost Centre Details**: At *Show Cost Centre Details*, set:
  - o *Yes* to show the Cost Centre details in the main voucher screen
  - o *No*. The Cost Centre details are not displayed in the main voucher screen (but internally allocated as per Voucher Class)
- **Auto Allocated Cost Centre Details:** At *Show Cost Centres in Auto Cost screen*, set:
  - o *Yes* to show the Cost Centre details in the Auto Allocation list
  - o *No*. The Cost Centre in Auto Allocation screen are not displayed in the main voucher screen (but internally allocated as per Voucher Class)

FAQ: Frequently Asked Questions

FAQ-1: What is the special Advantage of Cost Class

Ans: A. Cost Class is useful only when Multiple Cost Category is activated and tne the Ledger Amounts are allocated to Cost Centres as per pre-specified %. The amount is allocated in the background as per Cost Class definition and no need to manually enter the allocation fro each Cost Centre.

FAQ-2: What happens when having activated Cost Centre Class, in some voucher the allocation are to be done in different way than specified in Cost Class

Ans: A. In such cases, do not select the Cost Class (select *Not Applicable*) from the list of Cost Class (F-1D), select he Cost Centres one by one and manually enter the amount to be allocated to them

Part 6
Financial Management

This part deals with financial plans, tools & controls to be implemented to run the business efficiently and optimize the business operations.

Financial Budgets discusses about presentation of various Budget Plans for overall and sectional Budgets, & Budget Variance Analysis, for management actions

Scenarios help you to model Business Scenarios in different conditions for evaluation.

Cost Centre Budget discusses about preparation of Cost & Revenue Budget Plans to plan the operational activities of each Cost Centre

Cash Flow shows the periodical Cash inflow & outflow of past periods throwing light for planning better cash management

Funds Flow shows the net movement of Working Capital for better operational planning

Cash Flow Projections: *Cash Flow Projections* show adequacy of available liquid fund to meet the Payment Liabilities (Payables) in time, to avoid liquidity crisis and better cash management

Performance Analysis highlights some important analytical values to measure & evaluate various conditions, focusing on strengths & weaknesses of the enterprises

Financial Management 06-01

01 Financial Management

Every Business has its objectives and goals. It must have an efficient mechanism to set its targets and appraisal of achievements in respect to the target. To exercise the important management controls, Tally provides several management tools like:

- **Budgets:** Budgets are Future plan and tools for managing business & industry in a planned manner. Budgets are usually set up in the light of past experience after considering the changes that are expected to occur in the future.

  Tally provides tools to set up independent Budgets for Account Groups, Ledger Accounts & Cost Centres, with an efficient reporting and analysis of Actuals, Budgets & Variances.

- **Scenarios:** Scenarios are Financial Models to evaluate *What If* situations by emulating various hypothetical scenarios.

  Tally provides innovative method of creating flexible scenarios with dormant vouchers to emulate Scenarios of any conceivable situation, evaluate each scenario and re model s per changing situations

- **Performance Analysis**: Key Financial Ratios give snapshot of all key Financial Ratios & figures at a keystroke

  Tally provides one screen dash board showing all ke Financial Ratios for quick glance to evaluate the performance of the Company.

- **Cash & Funds Flow**: Cash & Funds Flow statements help to evaluate the liquidity position and manage Working Capital efficiently

  Tally provides Cash Flow statement showing the periodical Cash Inflows & Outflows to quick locate periodical Cash shortfalls and idle Cash for better and efficient Cash Management.

  Tally also provides Funds Flow statements showing Working Capital positions for better Financial Management.

- **Cash Projections:** *Cash Flow Projections* show adequacy of available Cash (Cash and Free Bank Balance / OD Limit) to meet the Cash Payment Liabilities (Payables) in time, to avoid payment defaults.

  Tally provides a comprehensive report of Cash & Bank Balances, Overdrafts, Cash receivables & payables and available Fund, or better Cash planning and management

Financial Budgets 06-02

01 Activation of Budgetary System

In Tally, you may set independent Budgets for Account Groups, Ledger Accounts & Cost Centres and to track Budget Variance.

At Gateway, click *F11: Features* >Accounting Features to get Accounting Features screen. At Budgets & scenario Management section of Accounting Features screen (F-1A), set *Yes* at *Maintain Budgets and Controls* to activate Budgets. Consequently you get *Budgets* & *Scenarios* options at *Account Info* menu (F-1B).

Budgets & Scenario Management	
Maintain Budgets and Controls	? Yes
Use Reversing Journals & Optional Vouchers	? Yes

F-1A: Activation of Budgets

Gateway of Tally ....
Accounts Info.
Groups
Ledgers
COst Categories
Cost Centres
Budgets
Scenarios
Voucher Types
Quit

F-1B: Accounts Info Menu

Budget Creation
Name : **Primary Budget**
Under : **Primary**

Period of Budget		Set / Alter Budgets of	
From:	To:	Groups	Ledgers
1-Apr-2013	31-Jul-2013	Yes	Yes

F-1C: Budgets Entry

ABC Corpn 13-14
Group Budgets Under 'Primary Budget'
(From 1-Apr-2013 to 31-Jul-2013)

Account Name	Type of Budget	Amount
Employee Expenses	On Nett Transactions	3,00,000.00
Interest	On Nett Transactions	45,000.00
General Expenses	On Nett Transactions	36,000.00

F-1F: Balance Type List

ABC Corpn 13-14
Ledger Budgets Under 'Primary Budget'
(From 1-Apr-2013 to 31-Jul-2013)

Account Name	Type of Budget	Amount
Salary	On Nett Transactions	2,00,000.00
Employee Bonus	On Nett Transactions	25,000.00
Employee Perquisites	On Nett Transactions	75,000.00

F-1D: Group Budget Creation

Budget Transaction Table
On Closing Balance
On Nett Transactions

F-1E: Ledger Budget Creation

02 Budget Entry

Select *GoT>Accts Info* to get *Accounts Info Menu (F-1B)*. At *Accounts Info Menu (F-1B)*, select *Budget* to get *Budget* Menu. At Budget Menu, select *Create* to get Budget *Creation* screen (F-1C).

At Budget Table Entry screen (F-1C), enter as follows:

- **Budget Name**: At *Name*, enter *Budget* Name.
- **Parent Budget**: At *Under*, select the parent Budget, else select *Primary* (you must select *Primary* for the first Budget record created).
- **Periodical Budget Details:** Enter the following details for each Budget Period
    - o **Budget Period**: Enter the Start and End Date of the Budget period at *From* & *To* column, respectively.
    - o **Budget Account Type**: At *Set Alter / Budgets of* column, set:
        - ▪ **Group Budget:** *Yes* at *Groups* column to get Group Budget Creation screen (F-1D), else set *No*
        - ▪ **Ledger Budget:** *Yes* at *Ledgers* column to get Ledgers Budget Creation screen (F-1E), else set *No*

03 Account Group Budget

At Budget Table entry screen (F-1C), on setting *Yes* at Groups column, you get Accounts Groups Budget entry screen (F-1D) to enter Group Budget for each Account Group, as explained below:

- **Account Group Name**: At *Account Name* field, select the Account *Group* for which you like to enter the Budget figures (press Alt+C to create new Account Group)
- **Balance Type**: At *Type* of *Budget* column, select the Balance Type from the list (F-1F), as follows:
    - o **Budget for Closing Balance**: Select *On Closing Balance* to create Budget for Closing Balances (normally used for Liabilities & Assets types for accounts, like Loans, Debtors / Creditors accounts).
    - o **Budget for Transaction**: Select *On Net Transactions* to create Budget for Net transactions (normally used for Income & Expenses Account, like Expenses, Sales, Purchase etc).

- **Budget Amount**: At *Amount* field, enter the Budget Amount for the selected Account Group

This way, continue to enter Budget Figures for each Account Group successively. To terminate entry, press <Enter> at the blank Account Name field (do not select any Account Group).

04 Account Ledger Budget

At Budget Table entry screen (F-1C), on setting *Yes* at Ledgers column, you get Accounts Ledgers Budget entry screen (F-1E) to enter Ledger Budget for Ledger Account

- **Account Ledger Name**: At *Account Name*, select the Account *Ledger* for which you like to enter the Budget figures (press Alt+C to create new Ledger Account)
- **Balance Type**: At *Type* of *Budget* column, select the Balance Type from the list (F-1F), as follows:
  - o **Budget for Closing Balance**: Select *On Closing Balance* to create Budget for Closing Balances (normally used for Liabilities & Assets types for accounts, like Loans, Debtors / Creditors accounts).
  - o **Budget for Transaction**: Select *On Net Transactions* to create Budget for Net transactions (normally used for Income & Expenses Account, like Expenses, Sales, Purchase etc).
- **Budget Amount**: At *Amount* column, enter the Budget Amount for the selected Account Ledger

This way, continue to enter Budget Figures for each Account Ledger successively. To terminate entry, press <Enter> at the blank Account Name field (do not select any Ledger Account). The total of Budget Amounts for all Ledger Accounts under a Group, *normally* equals to the Budget Amount for the corresponding Group.

05 Budget Variance Statements

Having set the Budgets and entering Vouchers as usual (which constitutes the *Actuals*), you may get Budget Variance Statements showing figures of *Budgets*, *Actuals* & *Variance,* from the following reports:

- Trial Balance (*Display>Trial Balance*)
- Group Summaries (*Display > Account Books > Group Summary*).

At the Report *Display* screen, click the *B:Budget Variance* button (F-2B) from the button bar and select the Budget Master record from List of Budgets at Budget screen (F-2A) to get the Budget Variance Report.

05.01 Trial Balance with Budget & Variance details

Trial Balance (*Display > Trial Balance*) has been explained earlier (§02/01-09). You may set the important options:

- **Details**: At Trial Balance with Budget Report (F-2C), click *F1:Detailed* button to get next level details.
- **Full Details**:In Detailed Format (with *F1:Detailed* button), at Trial Balance Configuration screen (F-2B/01-09), set Yes at *Expand All Levels in detailed format* to show details (of Budget, Actual & Variance) of all underlying Ledger Accounts of each Account Group (F-2D)
- **Percentage Figures**: At Trial Balance Configuration screen (F-2B/01-09), set *Yes* at *Show Percentages* to get % of Variances and other figures (F-2D)

Other Buttons (F-1C/02-21) & Configuration (F-1B/02-21) options of Trial Balance are explained earlier.

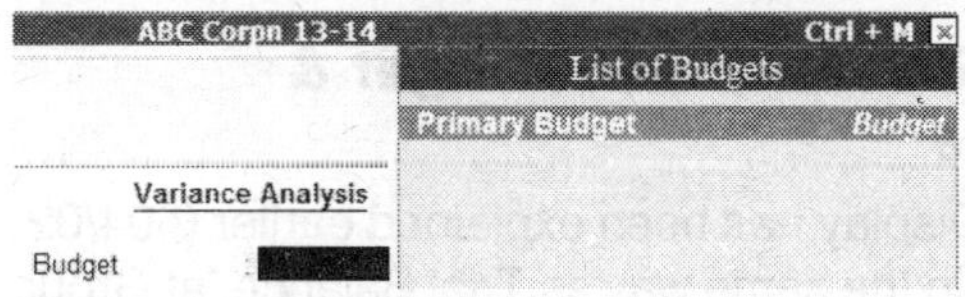

F-2A: Budget Name selection

F-2B: Budget Variance Button

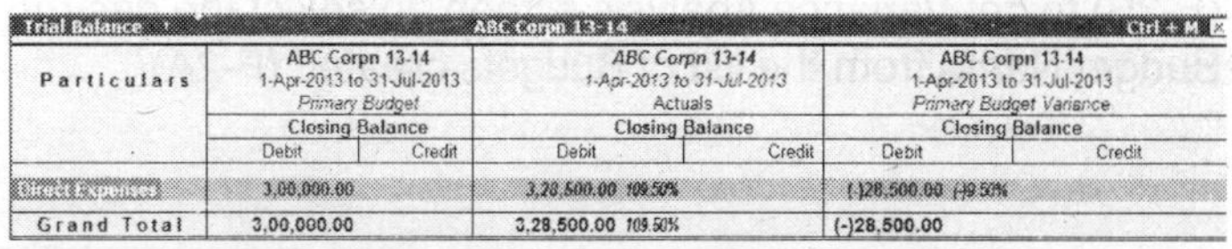

F-2C: Trial Balance with Budget Variance

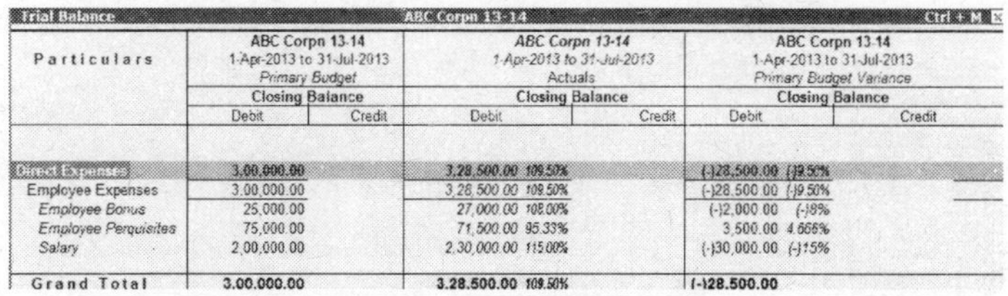

F-2D: Trial Balance with Budget Variance (detailed)

05.02 Trial Balance with Comparative Budget Report

Columnar Report with Comparative figures for various Periods / Companies have been discussed earlier (§06/02-13). Here, we explain the additional steps relating to Budget Report.

Specified New Columns: To get comparative columnar Budget Reports, at Budget Report Display, Click *C:New Column* button (F-8A/02-13), to get Column Definition screen (F-3A). Now set as follows:

- o **Budget Figures**: At *Type of Value to Show* prompt, select the Budget Name from list of Budgets. The Budget figures would be shown in a new Column, to get a new columns for specified period / specified Company
- o **Variance Figures**: At *Show Variance*, set *Yes* to show Variance Figures also.

Auto Columns: Auto Repeat Columnar Reports has been explained earlier (§06/02-13, F-8C/F-8D/02-13). To get comparative columnar Budget Reports, at Budget Report Display, Click *N:Auto Column* button to get Auto Repeat Columns set up screen (F-3B). At *Repeat Using*, Select the Period / Company as follows:

- o **Periodical Report:** Select the repeating period frequency from the list to get Periodical break up of the figures
- o **Inter Company Report:** Select *Company* from the list to get columns of each currently selected Companies,

ABC Corpn 13-14	
Column Details	
Name of Company	: **ABC Corpn 13-14**
From (blank for beginning)	: **1-4-2013**
To (blank for end)	: **31-7-2013**
Types of Value to show	: **Primary Budget**
(Show Variance)	? ***Yes***
Name of Group	: **Employee Expenses**

F-3A: Budget Report Column Definition

05.03 Group Summary with Budget & Variance

Group Summary Display has been explained earlier (§04/02-20,, F-1A/02-20). In the same way as Trial Balance, at Group Summary Display (*Display > Account Books > Group Summary: F-1A/02-20*), click *B:Budget Variance* button (F-2B) to get Variance Analysis screen, to select the desired Budget Name from the list of Budgets created (F-2A).

Auto Repeat Columns

Repeat Using	: **Company**
Show Total Column	? **n**

Column Details

- 4 Week Month
- Company
- Daily
- Fortnightly
- Half Yearly
- Monthly
- Quarterly
- Weekly
- Yearly

F-3B: Budget Report Auto Column Definition

In the same way, you may get the Budget Figures using the Budget Variance Button (F-2B) in other Reports (where available) and the respective Configuration Options.

Scenarios

01 Scenarios

Scenarios are simulated models like Forecast, Projection or Estimation with different parameters and conditions.

02 Scenario Activation

Click *F11: Features* > Accounting Features to get Accounting Features screen. Under the section Budges & Scenario Management, Set *Yes* at *Use Reversing Journals and Optional Voucher* (F-1A/06-02), to activate Scenario Features for the Company. Consequently, the option *Scenario* gets activated at Accounts Info Menu (F-1B/06-02).

03 Scenario Creation

Select *Accts Info > Scenarios* to get *Scenario* Menu. At *Scenario* Menu, select *Scenario* to get *Scenario creation* screen (F-1A)

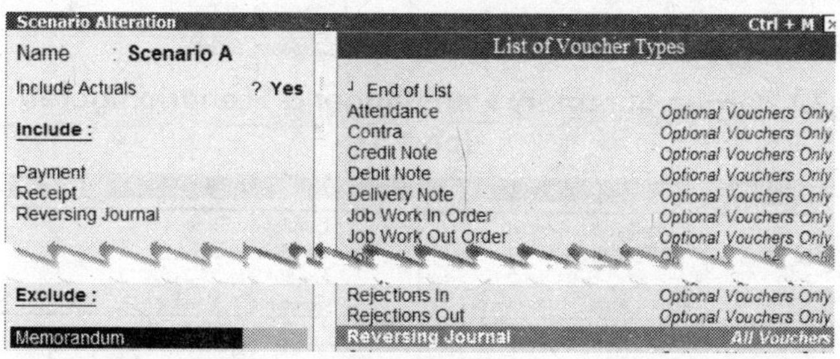

F-1A: Scenario Creation

At Scenario creation screen (F-1A), enter as follows

- **Scenario Name**: At *Name*, enter the Scenario Name.
- **Actuals:** At *Include Actuals*:
  - o Set Yes to *Include* the Regular Vouchers also in Scenario Report (apart from Voucher Types selected under Include Head)
  - o Set *No* to *Exclude* the Regular Vouchers Voucher Types. Only *Optional / Memorandum Voucher* Types as selected under *Include* Head, will be considered in Scenario Report.
- **Voucher Types:** Select the Voucher Types for exclusion / inclusion of Scenario. Except for *Memorandum* and *Reversing Journals*, only *Optional* voucher types will be available in Voucher Type selection list.
  - o **Include Voucher Types:** At *Include*, select the voucher types (one after another) from the list of Voucher Types, that you like to include in the scenario.
  - o **Exclude Voucher Types:** At *Exclude*, select the voucher types that you like to exclude in the scenario.

04 Reversing Journal

Creation of Provisional Voucher has been explained earlier (§15/02-09). Here, we explain entry of Reversing Journal in light of creation of scenario.

To create Reverse Journal Voucher (F-2A), select Accounts Vouchers and click *F10:Rev.Jrnl* button to get Reverse Journal entry screen (F-2A). The process of Reverse Journal Voucher Entry is similar to Journal Voucher Entry.

At *Applicable Upto* field (F-2A), enter the date upto which the reverse Journal would be included in scenario reports, explained next.

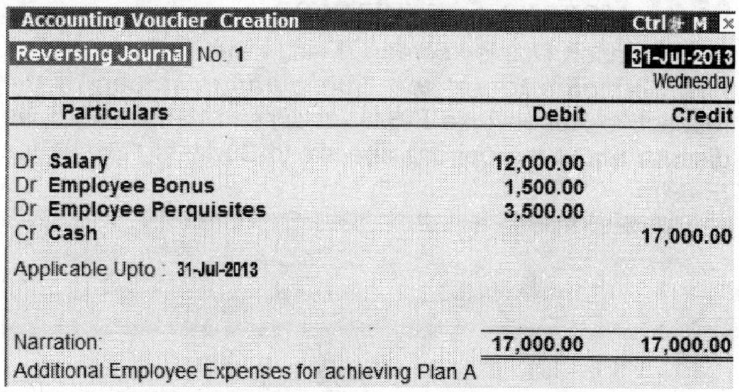

F-2A: Reversing Journal for Scenario creation

05 Scenario Reports

Having created Scenario (F-1A) & Vouchers (including Memorandum Vouchers, Reversing Journal, Optional Vouchers etc) to be included in Scenario (F-1A), you may get the scenario figures in a new column in a Report (where available) for comparison.

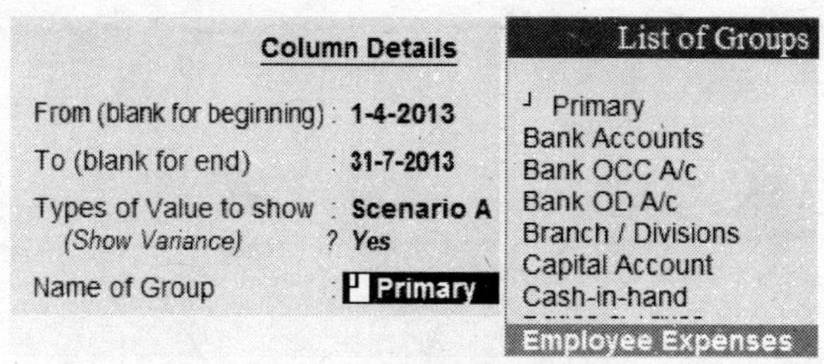

F-3A: Scenario Column Definition

Type of Value	
Actuals	
Primary Budget	*Budget*
Scenario A	*Scenario*

F-3B: Scenario Selection

Trial Balance Ctrl + M

Particulars	ABC Corpn 13-14 1-Apr-2013 to 31-Jul-2013 *Actuals*		Employee Expenses *ABC Corpn 13-14* *1-Apr-2013 to 31-Jul-2013* Scenario A Variance	
	Closing Balance		**Closing Balance**	
	Debit	Credit	Debit	Credit
Direct Expenses	**3,28,500.00**			
Employee Expenses	3,28,500.00		*17,000.00 4.92%*	
Employee Bonus			*1,500.00 5.263%*	
Employee Perquisites			*3,500.00 4.666%*	
Salary			*12,000.00 4.958%*	
Grand Total	**3,28,500.00**		**17,000.00**	

F-4A: Trial Balance Display with Scenario columns

At the respective Report Display screen, click *New Column* button to get column details screen (F-3A). At Column Details screen (F-3A), at *Type of Values to Show*, select the scenario from the list (F-3B). Next select the Account Group (F-3A)

The figures as per parameters selected in the scenario (F-3A) and configuration options set (F-6A) are shown in the Scenario columns (F-5A, F-7A).

05.01 Scenario Configuration

At the Report Display screen (F-4A, F-5A, F-7A etc), click *F12:Configure* to get the *Configuration* screen of the respective Report (like F-6A), discussed earlier. Here we discuss about the options specific to Budgets / Scenarios (F-6A)

Group Summary ABC Corpn 13-14 Ctrl + M

Particulars	*Direct Expenses* ABC Corpn 13-14 1-Apr-2013 to 31-Jul-2013 *Scenario A*		Direct Expenses *ABC Corpn 13-14* *1-Apr-2013 to 31-Jul-2013* Actuals		*Direct Expenses* ABC Corpn 13-14 1-Apr-2013 to 31-Jul-2013 *Scenario A Variance*	
	Closing Balance		**Closing Balance**		**Closing Balance**	
	Debit	Credit	Debit	Credit	Debit	Credit
Employee Expenses	**3,45,500.00**		**3,28,500.00 95.08%**		**17,000.00 4.92%**	
Employee Bonus	*28,500.00*		27,000.00 94.74%		*1,500.00 5.263%*	
Employee Perquisites	*75,000.00*		71,500.00 95.33%		*3,500.00 4.666%*	
Salary	*2,42,000.00*		2,30,000.00 95.04%		*12,000.00 4.958%*	
Grand Total	**3,45,500.00**		**3,28,500.00 95.08%**		**17,000.00**	

F-5A: Group Summary Display with Scenario figures

Configuration	
Show Opening Balances	? **No**
Show transactions	? **Yes**
Nett transactions only	? **No**
Show Closing Balances	? **No**
Show Percentages	? **Yes**
Type of %-age	: **Of Totals**
Appearance of Names	: **Name Only**
Type of Values to Show	? ┘ **All Items**
Show Total Column	? **No**
Scale Factor for Values	: **Default**
Sorting Method	: **Default**
Expand all levels in Detailed Format	? **Yes**

F-6A: Group Summary Configuration

%-age Type
Of First Column
Of Totals

F-6B: % age Type

Types of Values
┘ **All Items**
Values exceeding Budgets
Values within Budgets

F-6C: Value Type

- **Percentage Type**: At *Type of %*, select the percentage Base, from the list (F-6B)
- **Value Type**: At *Type of Value to Show*, select the Value Type from the list (F-6C)

Group Summary ABC Corpn 13-14 Ctrl + M

Particulars	*Employee Expenses* ABC Corpn 13-14 1-Apr-2013 to 31-Jul-2013 *Primary Budget*		Employee Expenses *ABC Corpn 13-14* *1-Apr-2013 to 31-Jul-2013* Actuals	
	Transactions		**Transactions**	
	Debit	Credit	Debit	Credit
Employee Bonus	*25,000.00 8.33%*		27,000.00 8.22%	
Employee Perquisites	*75,000.00 25.00%*		71,500.00 21.77%	
Salary	*2,00,000.00 66.67%*		2,30,000.00 70.02%	
Grand Total	***3,00,000.00 100.00%***		**3,28,500.00 100.00%**	

F-7A: Group Summary with Budget & Scenario figures (part 1)

ABC Corpn 13-14 Ctrl + M

Employee Expenses ABC Corpn 13-14 1-Apr-2013 to 31-Jul-2013 *Primary Budget Variance*		Employee Expenses *ABC Corpn 13-14* *1-Apr-2013 to 31-Jul-2013* Scenario A Variance	
Transactions		**Transactions**	
Debit	Credit	Debit	Credit
(-)2,000.00 (-)8%		**1,500.00 5.263%**	
3,500.00 4.666%		3,500.00 *4.666%*	
(-)30,000.00 (-)15%		12,000.00 *4.958%*	
(-)28,500.00		**17,000.00**	

(part 2)

Cost Centre Budget 06-04

01 Cost Centre Budget

Budgets of Accounts Groups & Account Ledgers have been discussed earlier (§02/06-02). Cost Centre also have been discussed earlier (§02/05-01).

Budget Alteration

Name : **Primary Budget**

Under : **Primary**

Period of Budget		Set / Alter Budgets of		
From:	To:	Groups	Ledgers	Cost Centres
1-Apr-2013	31-Jul-2013	Yes	Yes	Yes
1-Aug-2009	31-Dec-2009	Yes	Yes	Yes
1-Jan-2014	31-Mar-2014	Yes	Yes	Yes

F-1A: Cost Centre Budget Entry Set Up

ABC Corpn 13-14

Cost Centre Budgets Under 'Primary Budget'
(From 1-Apr-2013 to 31-Jul-2013)

Cost Centre	Expenses	Income	Closing Balance
HO	3,00,000.00	4,00,000.00	
Patna Branch	1,00,000.00	1,50,000.00	

F-1B: Cost Centre Budget Entry

When Cost Centre is activated (§01/05-01), at Budget Entry set up, you get another column *Cost Centre* to include Cost Centre figures also, apart from Group & Ledger (F-1A). At Cost *Centres* column (F-1A), Set Yes to get Cost Centre Budget entry screen (F-1B). Now enter as follows:

- **Cost Centre Name: At** Cost Centre column, select the Cost Centre (Pres *Alt+C* to create a new Cost Centre)
- **Cost Centre Budget Amount**: Enter the Budget Amount as below
    - o **Cost Centre Expenses Budget**: At *Expenses* column, enter the *Expenses Budget* Amount for the selected Cost Centre.
    - o **Cost Centre Income Budget**: At *Income* column, enter the *Income Budget* Amount for the selected Cost Centre.

This way continue to enter Cost Centre Budget Figures for other Cost Centres successively. To terminate entry, press <enter> at the blank Cost Centre Name field (do not select any Cost Centre).

02 *Cost Centrewise Budget of Account Groups*

To enter Cost Centrewise Account Group Budget, at Budget Entry set up (F-1A), set *Yes* at *Group* to get *Account Group / Cost Centre Budget* entry screen (F-2A).

Group Budgets Under 'Primary Budget'
(From 1-Apr-2013 to 31-Jul-2013)

Account Name	Cost Centre	Type of Budget	Amount
Employee Expenses	HO	On Nett Transactions	2,50,000.00
Employee Expenses	Patna Branch	On Nett Transactions	50,000.00

F-2A: Cost Centrewise Group Budget

ABC Corpn 13-14

Ledger Budgets Under 'Primary Budget'
(From 1-Apr-2013 to 31-Jul-2013)

Account Name	Cost Centre	Type of Budget	Amount
Salary	HO	On Nett Transactions	1,50,000.00
Salary	Patna Branch	On Nett Transactions	25,000.00
Employee Bonus	HO	On Nett Transactions	60,000.00
Employee Perquisites	Patna Branch	On Nett Transactions	20,000.00
Employee Perquisites	HO	On Nett Transactions	32,000.00

F-3A: Cost Centrewise Ledger Budget

Now Enter Cost Centrewise break up of *Account Group* Budget, as follows (F-2A):

- **Account Group**: At *Account Name*, select the Account Group (or pres Alt+C) to create a new *Account Group*
- **Cost Centre**: At *Cost Centre*, select the Cost Centre (pres Alt+C to create a new Cost Centre)
- **Balance Type**: At *Type* of *Budget* column, select the Balance Type from the list (F-1F/ 06-02), as follows:
    - o **Budget for Closing Balance**:, Select *On Closing Balance* to create Budget for Closing Balances (normally used for Liabilities & Assets types for accounts, like Loans, Debtors / Creditors accounts).
    - o **Budget for Transaction**: Select *On Net Transactions* to create Budget for Net transactions (normally used for Income & Expenses Account, like Expenses, Sales, Purchase etc).
- **Budget Amount**: At *Amount* field, enter the Budget Amount for the selected Account Group

This way, continue to enter Budget Figures for each

combination of Account Group & Cost Centre successively. To terminate entry, press <Enter> at the blank Account Name field (do not select any Account Group).

03 Cost Centrewise Budget of Ledgers

In the same way as Cost Centrewise Account Groups Budget Entry (§02), you may enter Cost Centrewise Budget of Ledger Accounts.

To enter Cost Centrewise Ledger Budget, set *Yes* at Ledger and Cost Centre column (F-1A) to get Account Ledger / Cost Centre Budget entry screen (F-3A).

Now Enter Cost Centrewise break up of Account *Ledger* Budget, as follows (F-3A):

- **Ledger Account**: At *Account Name*, select the Ledger Account (pres Alt+C) to create a new *Account Ledger*
- **Cost Centre**: At *Cost Centre*, select the Cost Centre (pres *Alt+C* to create a new *Cost Centre*)
- **Balance Type**: At *Type* of *Budget* column, select the Balance Type from the list (F-1F/ 06-02), as follows:
    - o **Budget for Closing Balance**: Select *On Closing Balance* to create Budget for Closing Balances (normally used for Liabilities & Assets types for accounts, like Loans, Debtors / Creditors accounts).
    - o **Budget for Transaction**: Select *On Net Transactions* to create Budget for Net transactions (normally used for Income & Expenses Account, like Expenses, Sales, Purchase etc).
- **Budget Amount**: At *Amount* field, enter the Budget Amount for the selected Account Group

This way, continue to enter Budget Figures for multiple Account Ledger successively. To terminate entry, press <Enter> at the blank Account Name field (do not select any Account Group).

You may also select *Not Applicable* at Cost Centre, in that case, it becomes a Group / Ledger Budget (§03/06-02, §04/ 06-02)

04 Vouchers entry with Cost Centre Details

In Voucher entry, you have to enter the Cost Centre wise allocation for each Ledger Account in the Voucher (§05/05-01, F-7A/05-01), which constitute the *Actuals* figures in the Budget Reports (F-5A/ F-5B).

Accounting Voucher Alteration (Secondary) Ctrl + M

Payment No. **1** — 31-Jul-2013 Wednesday

Particulars		Debit	Credit
Dr **Salary**		2,30,000.00	
HO	1,85,000.00 Dr		
Patna Branch	45,000.00 Dr		
Dr **Employee Bonus**		27,000.00	
HO	16,500.00 Dr		
Patna Branch	10,500.00 Dr		
Dr **Employee Perquisites**		71,500.00	
HO	52,000.00 Dr		
Patna Branch	19,500.00 Dr		
Cr **Cash**			3,28,500.00
Narration:		3,28,500.00	3,28,500.00

Employee Expenses with Cost Centre allocation

F-4A: Voucher with Cost centrewise allocation

Reversing Journal No. **1** — 31-Jul-2013 Wednesday

Particulars		Debit	Credit
Dr **Salary**		12,000.00	
HO	9,500.00 Dr		
Patna Branch	2,500.00 Dr		
Dr **Employee Bonus**		1,500.00	
HO	850.00 Dr		
Patna Branch	650.00 Dr		
Dr **Employee Perquisites**		3,500.00	
HO	3,100.00 Dr		
Patna Branch	400.00 Dr		
Cr **Cash**			17,000.00
Applicable Upto : 31-Jul-2013			
Narration:		17,000.00	17,000.00

Additional Employee Expenses for achieving Plan A

F-4B: Reversing Voucher with Cost centrewise allocation

05 Cost Centre Budget / Scenario Report

As explained for Account Group / Account Ledger Report, you may get the Cost Centre Budget figures from *Category Summary* (F-9A/05-02).

Cost Category Summary ABC Corpn 13-14 Ctrl + M

Particulars	ABC Corpn 13-14 1-Apr-2013 to 31-Jul-2013 *Primary Budget* Transactions		*ABC Corpn 13-14* *1-Apr-2013 to 31-Jul-2013* Actuals Transactions		ABC Corpn 13-14 1-Apr-2013 to 31-Jul-2013 *Primary Budget Variance* Transactions	
	Debit	Credit	Debit	Credit	Debit	Credit
Primary Cost Category	*3,28,500.00*		3,28,500.00 *100.00%*			
HO	3,00,000.00	4,00,000.00	*2,53,500.00 84.50%*		46,500.00 *15.50%*	(-)4,00,000.00 *(-)100%*
Patna Branch	1,00,000.00	1,50,000.00	*75,000.00 75.00%*		25,000.00 *25%*	(-)1,50,000.00 *(-)100%*

F-5A: Cost Category Summary with Budget Figures

Cost Category Summary — ABC Corpn 13-14 — Ctrl + M

Particulars	ABC Corpn 13-14 1-Apr-2013 to 31-Jul-2013 *Primary Budget* Transactions		ABC Corpn 13-14 1-Apr-2013 to 31-Jul-2013 Actuals Transactions		ABC Corpn 13-14 1-Apr-2013 to 31-Jul-2013 *Primary Budget Variance* Transactions		ABC Corpn 13-14 1-Apr-2013 to 31-Jul-2013 *Scenario A Variance* Transactions	
	Debit	Credit	Debit	Credit	Debit	Credit	Debit	Credit
Primary Cost Category	*4,00,000.00*	*5,50,000.00*	4,00,000.00 *100.00%*	5,50,000.00 *100.00%*				
HO	3,00,000.00	4,00,000.00	*2,53,500.00 84.50%*		46,500.00 *15.50%*	(-)4,00,000.00 *(-)100%*	13,450.00 *5.038%*	
Patna Branch	1,00,000.00	1,50,000.00	*75,000.00 75.00%*		25,000.00 *25%*	(-)1,50,000.00 *(-)100%*	3,550.00 *4.519%*	

F-5B: Cost Category Summary with Budget / Scenario Figures

05.01 Cost Category Summary with Cost Centre Budget Details

Cost Category Summary has been explained earlier (F-9A/05-02).

At *Cost Category Summary* (*Display>Statement of Accounts>Cost Ceres>Category Summary*), click B:*Budget Variance* button to select the Budget from the list (F-2A/06-02) to get Budget Variance Report (F-5A, F-5B)

Cash Flow

01 Cash & Funds flow

Cash & Funds flow reports indicate the movement of resources into various forms of Assets & Liabilities.

- **Cash Flow**: Cash flow indicate the inflow & outflow from cash (cash, Bank OCC & Bank OD Accounts)
- **Funds Flow**: Funds flow shows movement of resources into various forms of Assets & Liabilities.

> ***Note:*** *Normally, by Cash & Funds Flow, we understand operation wise analysis of Cash (e.g Cash Flow from Operations, Cash Flow from Investments, etc. in Direct & Indirect Methods, etc) & changes in Assets & Liabilities (Refer to* Cash & Funds Flow *Statements as shown in Financial statements of Companies). On the other hand, in Tally, Cash Flow just shows the summary of Debits & Credits of Cash / Bank Accounts in terms of Account Groups / Ledger Accounts. This is quite different from the perception of Cash / Funds Flow in academic & professional Terms.*

Select *Display > Cash / Funds Flow* to get Cash & Funds flow menu (F-1A)

Gateway of Tally ....
Display Menu ....
Cash/Funds Flow
Cash Flow
Funds Flow
Cash Flow Projection
Quit

F-1A: Cash & Funds flow menu

Cash Flow Ctrl + M

Particulars	ABC Academy 9-10 1-Apr-2009 to 31-Mar-2010		
	Cash Movement		Nett Flow
	Inflow	Outflow	
April		2,410.50	(-)2,410.50
May	14,000.00	72,780.00	(-)58,780.00
June	14,520.00	20,300.00	(-)5,780.00
July	43,000.00	1,320.00	41,680.00
August	50,000.00	1,000.00	49,000.00
December		24,890.00	(-)24,890.00
January	9,64,000.00	14,500.00	9,49,500.00
February	11,000.00	2,850.00	8,150.00
March	28,250.00	1,80,400.00	(-)1,52,150.00
Grand Total	**11,24,770.00**	**3,20,450.50**	**8,04,319.50**
Average	93,730.83	26,704.21	

F-2A: Cash Flow Statement

02 Cash Flow

At Cash Flow Menu (F-1A), select *Cash Flow* to get *Cash Flow Statement* (F-2A) showing periodical movement of money In and Out (Cash Inflow & Outflow) into the business.

Cash Flow Configuration

At Cash Flow statement (F-2A), *click F12:Configuration to get Cash Flow configuration screen (F-2B)*

Configuration	
Appearance of Names	: **Name Only**
Scale Factor for Values	: **Default**
Periodicity to use	: **Monthly**
Show Average Details	? **Yes**
Graphs	
Show with Graph	? **No**

F-2B: Cash Flow Configuration

F2: Period
F3: Company
F5: Quarterly
G: Godown Type
C: New Column
A: Alter Column
D: Del Column
N: Auto Column

F-2C: Cash Flow Buttons

Periodic Average: At Show Average Details:

- Set Yes to show Average (as per selected Periodicity) at the last line of the Report (F-2A)
- Set No, the Average line is not shown.

Cash Flow Statement Buttons

At Cash Flow Display (F-2A), you get following Buttons:

- **F5:Quarterly / Monthly:** To get Quarterly / Monthly break up of In & Out figures

03 Cash Flow Summary

At Cash Flow statement (F-2A), drill down through any month to get Cash Flow Summary statement for the specified period (F-3A). It shows Account Group/ Ledgerwise figures of Cash Inflow (*Left* part) & Cash Outflow (*Right* part) and net of Inflow /Outflow at bottom (net Outfow is show as negative value). The Inflow & Outflow of an Account (Group/ Ledger) are shown separately at respective side.

03.01 Cash Flow Summary Configuration

At Cash Flow Summary (F-3A), click *F12:Configure* to get Cash Flow Summary Configure screen (F-4A), to set the following options

- **Format**: At *Show Vertical Cash Flow Summary*,
  - o Set *Yes* to show Cash Flow Summary in Vertical format (F-4C) as explained next (§03.02)
  - o Set *No* to show Cash Flow Summary in Normal format (F-3A)
- **Percentage Figures**: At *Show Percentage*,
  - o Set *Yes* to show Percentage against each Account Group (of the Total)

- o Set *No.* The % column is not shown

Cash Flow Summary — ABC Academy 9-10 — Ctrl + M

Inflow		ABC Academy 9-10 1-Apr-2009 to 31-Mar-2010	
Capital Account		**1,900.00**	*0.17%*
Properitor's Capital	*1,900.00*		
Loans (Liability)		**82,000.00**	*7.29%*
Secured Loans	*50,000.00*		
Unsecured Loans	*12,000.00*		
A K Das	*20,000.00*		
Current Liabilities		**10,770.00**	*0.96%*
Duties & Taxes	*500.00*		
P F	*10,250.00*		
TDS	*20.00*		
Current Assets		**66,000.00**	*5.87%*
Loans & Advances (Asset)	*10,000.00*		
Sundry Debtors	*56,000.00*		
Sales Accounts		**11,100.00**	*0.99%*
Sales	*11,100.00*		
Direct Incomes		**9,50,000.00**	*84.46%*
Tution Fees	*9,50,000.00*		
Indirect Incomes		**3,000.00**	*0.27%*
Rent Received	*3,000.00*		
Total		**11,24,770.00**	100%

Outflow		ABC Academy 9-10 1-Apr-2009 to 31-Mar-2010	
Capital Account		**5,000.00**	*1.56%*
Drawings	*5,000.00*		
Loans (Liability)		**50,800.00**	*15.85%*
Secured Loans	*14,500.00*		
A K Das	*36,300.00*		
Current Liabilities		**48,260.00**	*15.06%*
Duties & Taxes	*8,080.00*		
Sundry Creditors	*40,180.00*		
Current Assets		**36,510.50**	*11.39%*
Loans & Advances (Asset)	*25,000.00*		
Sundry Debtors	*9,710.50*		
Pre Paid Expenses	*1,800.00*		
Sales Accounts		**2,250.00**	*0.70%*
Cash Discount	*150.00*		
Cash Sales	*2,000.00*		
Sales Rebates	*100.00*		
Direct Expenses		**9,500.00**	*2.96%*
Components Cost	*9,500.00*		
Indirect Expenses		**1,68,130.00**	*52.47%*
Conveyance Expenses	*7,500.00*		
HRA	*3,000.00*		
Interest	*30.00*		
Office Rent	*7,800.00*		
Penalty	*100.00*		
Salary	*1,49,700.00*		
Total		**3,20,450.50**	100%

F-3A: Cash Flow Summary

Configuration

Show Vertical Cash Flow Summary ?	**No**
Show Percentages ?	**Yes**
Appearance of Names :	**Name Only**
Scale Factor for Values :	**Default**

F-4A: Cash Flow Summary Configuration

- F1: Condensed
- F2: Period
- F3: Company
- F4: Daily Flow
- C: New Column
- A: Alter Column
- D: Del Column
- N: Auto Column

F-4B: Cash Flow Buttons

03.02 Cash Flow Summary (Vertical)

At Cash Flow statement Configuration (F-4A), set *Yes* at *Show Vertical Cash Flow Summary* to get *Vertical Cash Flow Summary* (F-4C).

It shows Account Group/ Ledgerwise figures of Cash Inflow & Cash Outflow and net of Inflow /Outflow at bottom (net Outfow is show as negative value). The Inflow & Outflow of an Account (Group/Ledger) are shown separately under the respective head.

04 Groupwise Cash Flow

At *Cash Flow Summary* (F-3A), drill down through any Account Group to get Group Cash Flow Statement (F-5A) showing details of Cash Inflow and Outflow of subordinate Groups & Ledgers of the selected Group.

Cash Flow Summary
1-Apr-2009 to 31-Mar-2010

		1-Apr-2009 to 31-Mar-2010	
Inflow of Cash :			
Capital Account		**1,900.00**	*0.17%*
Properitor's Capital	*1,900.00*		
Loans (Liability)		**82,000.00**	*7.29%*
Secured Loans	*50,000.00*		
Unsecured Loans	*12,000.00*		
A K Das	*20,000.00*		
Current Liabilities		**10,770.00**	*0.96%*
Duties & Taxes	*500.00*		
P F	*10,250.00*		
TDS	*20.00*		
Current Assets		**66,000.00**	*5.87%*
Loans & Advances (Asset)	*10,000.00*		
Sundry Debtors	*56,000.00*		
Sales Accounts		**11,100.00**	*0.99%*
Sales	*11,100.00*		
Direct Incomes		**9,50,000.00**	*84.46%*
Tution Fees	*9,50,000.00*		
Indirect Incomes		**3,000.00**	*0.27%*
Rent Received	*3,000.00*		
Total		**11,24,770.00**	100%
Outflow of Cash :			
Capital Account		**5,000.00**	*1.56%*
Drawings	*5,000.00*		
Loans (Liability)		**50,800.00**	*15.85%*
Secured Loans	*14,500.00*		
A K Das	*36,300.00*		
Current Liabilities		**48,260.00**	*15.06%*
Duties & Taxes	*8,080.00*		
Sundry Creditors	*40,180.00*		
Current Assets		**36,510.50**	*11.39%*
Loans & Advances (Asset)	*25,000.00*		
Sundry Debtors	*9,710.50*		
Pre Paid Expenses	*1,800.00*		
Sales Accounts		**2,250.00**	*0.70%*
Cash Discount	*150.00*		
Cash Sales	*2,000.00*		
Sales Rebates	*100.00*		
Direct Expenses		**9,500.00**	*2.96%*
Components Cost	*9,500.00*		
Indirect Expenses		**1,68,130.00**	*52.47%*
Conveyance Expenses	*7,500.00*		
HRA	*3,000.00*		
Interest	*30.00*		
Office Rent	*7,800.00*		
Penalty	*100.00*		
Salary	*1,49,700.00*		
Total		**3,20,450.50**	100%
Nett Inflow		**8,04,319.50**	100%

F-4C: Cash Flow Summary (Vertical)

Group Cash Flow ABC Academy 9-10 Ctrl + M

Particulars	Current Assets ABC Academy 9-10 1-Apr-2009 to 31-Mar-2010			
	Opening Balance	Cash Movement		Nett Flow
		Inflow	Outflow	
Loans & Advances (Asset)			25,000.00 68.47%	(-)15,000.00 (-)50.87%
A Bose & Co			25,000.00	(-)15,000.00
Sundry Debtors	13,000.00 Dr 100.00%		9,710.50 26.60%	46,289.50 156.97%
Pre Paid Expenses			1,800.00 4.93%	(-)1,800.00 (-)6.10%
Grand Total	13,000.00 Dr 100.00%		36,510.50 100.00%	(-)36,510.50 (-)123.81%

F-5A: Group Cash Flow

Configuration

Show Opening Balances	? Yes
Show transactions	? Yes
Nett transactions only	? No
Show Closing Balances	? Yes
Show Percentages	? Yes
Type of %-age	: Of Totals
Appearance of Names	: Name Only
Scale Factor for Values	: Default
Sorting Method	: Default
Expand all levels in Detailed Format	? Yes

F-6A: Group Cash Flow Configuration

F1: Condensed
F2: Period
F3: Company
F4: Group
F5: Led-wise
F7: Vouchers
C: New Column
A: Alter Column
D: Del Column
N: Auto Column

F-6B: Buttons

04.01 Group Cash Flow Summary Configuration

At Group Cash Flow summary (F-5A), click *F12: Configure* to get Cash Flow Configuration (F-6A).to set up following options:

- **Opening Balances:** At *Show Opening Balances*:
  - o Set Yes to show Opening Balance at Opening Balance Column
  - o Set *No*. The Opening Balance column is not shown
- **Transactions Break Up**: At *Net Transaction only*:
  - o **Net of Debit / Credit**: Set Yes to show only the Net of Debit / Credit either in Inflow or Outflow Column (whichever is greater)
  - o **Debit / Credit Break Up**: Set *No* to show both Inflow & Outflow amount separately, in respective Column (whichever is greater)
- **Net Flow:** At *Show Closing Balances*:
  - o Set Yes to show Net Flow
  - o Set *No*. The Net Flow column is not shown
- **Percentage:** At *Show Percentages*:
  - o Set Yes to show the % of amount of each column displayed for each Account Group, of the total amount of respective columns
  - o Set *No*. % column is not shown
- **All Details**: Having set *F1:Detailed* button, at *Expand all Levels in Details Format*,
  - Set *Yes* to show complete details of all lower level Accounts
  - Set *No*. Lower Level details are not shown.

04.02 Group Cash Flow Buttons

At *Group Cash Flow summary* (F-5A), you get Buttons as follows:

- **F1:Detailed / Condensed**: Click *F1:Detailed* button to get next level details. *F1:Condensed* to get top level Cost Centre only
- **F4: Group**: To select the Account Group to get the Cash Flow of the selected Group (select Primary to show all Account Groups)
- **F5:Ledgwise / Grouped**: Click *F5:Ledgewise* to show the Ledger Account wise Cash Flow Click *F5:Grouped* to show the Account Group wise report with subordinate Group Ledger
- **F7:Vouchers**: To list the Vouchers containing transaction of Ledgers under the selected Account Group
- **Columnar Buttons**: To define Columnar Reports of various Periods & Companies

FAQ: Frequently Asked Questions

FAQ-1: How I may get Cash Flow Summary in Vertical Format

Ans: At Cash Flow statement Configuration (F-4A), set *Yes* at *Show Vertical Cash Flow Summary* to get Vertical Cash Flow Summary report (F-4C).

Funds Flow

01 Funds Flow

In Tally, Funds Flow provides the information of Movement of Funds (i.e., source and utilization), showing the increase /decrease in Working Capital.

At Cash & Funds Flow menu (F-1A/06-05), select *Funds Flow* to get the Funds Flow statement showing monthwise Opening and Closing Balance of Working Capital and the flow of Funds (i.e difference in Opening & Closing Working Capital (F-1A).

Funds Flow — Ctrl + M

Particulars	ABC Academy 9-10 1-Apr-2009 to 31-Mar-2010 Working Capital Opening	 Closing	 Funds Flow
April	1,69,556.78	1,98,356.78	28,800.00
May	1,98,356.78	1,72,656.78	(-)25,700.00
June	1,72,656.78	1,52,756.78	(-)19,900.00
July	1,52,756.78	1,74,906.78	22,150.00
August	1,74,906.78	2,26,556.78	51,650.00
September	2,26,556.78	2,30,556.78	4,000.00
October	2,30,556.78	2,30,556.78	
November	2,30,556.78	1,98,976.78	(-)31,580.00
December	1,98,976.78	1,92,346.78	(-)6,630.00
January	1,92,346.78	11,34,346.78	9,42,000.00
February	11,34,346.78	1,79,646.78	(-)9,54,700.00
March	1,79,646.78	8,346.78	(-)1,71,300.00
Grand Total	**1,69,556.78**	**8,346.78**	**(-)1,61,210.00**
Average	2,71,768.45	2,58,334.28	

F-1A: Funds Flow Display

Configuration

Appearance of Names	: Name Only
Scale Factor for Values	: Default
Periodicity to use	: Monthly
Show Average Details	? Yes

Graphs

Show with Graph	? No

F-1B: Funds Flow Configuration

F2: Period
F3: Company
F5: Quarterly
G: Godown Type
C: New Column
A: Alter Column
D: Del Column
N: Auto Column

F-1C: Buttons

Fund Flow Configuration

At Fund Flow statement (F-1A), click F12:Configuration to get Fund Flow configuration screen (F-1B)

Average Details: At Show Average Details:

- Set Yes to show the Average figures of each column shown (as per selected Periodicity), at the Average line (last line after Grand Total: F-1A)
- Set No. Average line at the bottom of the Report is not shown

Fund Flow Display Buttons

At Fund Flow statement (F-1A), click F12:Configuration to get Fund Flow configuration screen (F-1C)

02 *Funds Flow Summary*

At *Funds Flow* statement (F-1A), drill down through the respective period record, to get Funds Flow Summary (F-2A) showing details of *Source* and *Application* of Funds, for the selected period.

Funds Flow Summary — ABC Academy 9-10 — Ctrl + M

Sources		ABC Academy 9-10 1-Apr-2009 to 31-Mar-2010		Applications		ABC Academy 9-10 1-Apr-2009 to 31-Mar-2010	
Loans (Liability)		1,20,900.00	98.37%	Capital Account		3,100.00	1.09%
Secured Loans	40,000.00			*Drawings*	5,000.00		
Unsecured Loans	12,900.00			*Propentor's Capital*	(-)1,900.00		
A K Das	58,500.00			Nett Loss		2,81,010.00	98.91%
Small & Co	9,500.00						
Fixed Assets		2,000.00	1.63%				
Furniture	2,000.00						
Total		1,22,900.00	100%	**Total**		2,84,110.00	100%

Particulars	*Opening Balance*	*Closing Balance*	*Wkg Cap Increase*
Current Assets	1,69,556.78 Dr	10,00,736.78 Dr	8,31,180.00
Current Liabilities		9,92,390.00 Cr	(-)9,92,390.00
Working Capital	1,69,556.78 Dr	8,346.78 Dr	(-)1,61,210.00

F-2A: Funds Flow Summary

Configuration

Show Vertical Funds Flow Summary	? No
Show Percentages	? Yes
Appearance of Names	: Name Only
Scale Factor for Values	: Default

F-2B: Funds Flow Configuration

F1: Condensed
F2: Period
F3: Company
C: New Column
A: Alter Column
D: Del Column
N: Auto Column

F-2C: Buttons

Funds Flow Summary			Ctrl + M
	ABC Academy 9-10 1-Apr-2009 to 31-Mar-2010		
Sources of Funds :			
Loans (Liability)		1,20,900.00	98.37%
Secured Loans	40,000.00		
Unsecured Loans	12,900.00		
A K Das	58,500.00		
Small & Co	9,500.00		
Fixed Assets		**2,000.00**	1.63%
Furniture	2,000.00		
Total		**1,22,900.00**	100%
Application of Funds :			
Capital Account		**3,100.00**	1.09%
Drawings	5,000.00		
Properitor's Capital	(-)1,900.00		
Nett Loss		**2,81,010.00**	98.91%
Total		**2,84,110.00**	100%
Wkg Capital Details :			
Chg in Current Assets		**8,31,180.00**	292.56%
Opening Balance	1,69,556.78		
Closing Balance	10,00,736.78		
Chg in Current Liabilities		**(-)9,92,390.00**	(-)349.30%
Opening Balance			
Closing Balance	9,92,390.00		
Chg in Wkg Cap		**(-)1,61,210.00**	(-)56.74%
Opening Balance	1,69,556.78		
Closing Balance	8,346.78		

F-3A: Funds Flow Summary (Vertical)

Funds Flow Summary Configuration

At Fund Flow Summary statement (F-2A), click F12:Configuration to get Fund Flow Configuration screen (F-2B), to set the following options:

Vertical Funds Flow: At Show Vertical Funds Flow Summary:

- Set Yes to show Funds Flow Statement in Vertical Format (F-3A)
- Set No (Default) to show Funds Flow Statement in Normal Format (F-2A)

02.01 Funds Flow Summary (Vertical)

At Funds Flow Summary Configuration (F-2B), set *Yes* at *Show Vertical Funds Flow Summary*, to get *Vertical Funds Flow Summary* Statement (F-3A).

FAQ: Frequently Asked Questions

FAQ1: How I may get Funds Flow Summary in Vertical Format

Ans: At Funds Flow Summary Configuration (F-2B), set *Yes* at *Show Vertical Funds Flow Summary*, to get *Vertical Funds Flow Summary* Statement (F-3A).

Cash Flow Projections

01 Cash Flow Projections

Cash Flow Projections show adequacy of available Cash (Cash and Free Bank Balance / OD Limit) to meet the Payment Liabilities (Payables) in time, in future period, for better cash management.

Display > Cash & Funds Flow>Cash Flow Projections (F-1A/ 06-05) to get Cash Flow Projection Report (F-1A). Click *F2:Period* to set the Period (F-1D). By default the Cash Flow Projection would be shown for the date of last voucher entered), as this is a Projection Report (Report for a future Period). So, the Start Date of the Period to set (F-1D) should be higher than the last Voucher entered, otherwise an error message (F-1E) would elicit and you will not be able to proceed.

Cash Flow Projection — Ctrl + M

Particulars	1-Apr-2010 to 30-Apr-2010	1-May-2010 to 31-May-2010
A. Current Balance	12,59,876.28	3,38,856.78
Bank Accounts	3,17,136.78	
HDFC Bank	*85,036.78*	
State Bank of India	*2,32,100.00*	
Cash-in-Hand	9,42,739.50	
Cash	*9,42,739.50*	
B. Receivables	95,310.50	
Overdue Receivables	95,310.50	
Total (A+B)	13,55,186.78	3,38,856.78
C. Payables	10,16,330.00	
Overdue Payables	10,16,330.00	
Nett Balance (A+B-C)	3,38,856.78	3,38,856.78

F-1A: Cash Flow Projection Display

Configuration

Expand all levels in Detailed Format	? Yes
Include Cash Account	? Yes
Include Scenarios	? Yes
Include Overdues	? Yes
Appearance of Names	: Name Only

F-1B: Cash Flow Projection Configuration

F1: Detailed
F2: Period
F3: Company
S: Set OD Limit
N: Auto Column

F-1C: Buttons

Change Period

From	: 1-4-2010
To	: 31-5-10

F-1D: Period Set Up

Eh ?
Date below
Date of Last Entry
(31-Mar-2010)

F-1E: Error message for Period

S.No:	Name of Bank OD Ledger	Under	OD Limit
1.	HDFC Bank	Bank Accounts	1,00,000.00
2.	State Bank of India	Bank Accounts	2,00,000.00

F-2A: OD Limit Set Up

01.01 Cash Flow Projections Configuration

At *Cash Flow Projection Display* (F-1A), click *F12:Configure* to get Cash Flow Projection Configuration (F-1B) to set up the Configuration options

- **All Details**: Having set *F1:Detailed* button, at Expand all Levels in Details Format,
  - o Set *Yes* to show complete details of all lower level Accounts
  - o Set *No*. Lower Level details are not shown
- **Cash Account**: At *Include Cash Account*,
  - o Set *Yes* to Include Cash Account also in the Report
  - o Set *No* to exclude Include Cash Account in the Report (Bank Accounts are included)
- **Scenarios**: At *Include Scenarios*,
  - o Set *Yes* to Include Scenarios also in the Report
  - o Set *No* to exclude Scenarios in the Report
- **Overdues**: At *Include Overdues*,
  - o Set *Yes* to Include Overdues (Receivables & Payables) also in the Report
  - o Set *No* to exclude Overdues in the Report (only Dues till the report date are included)

01.02 Cash Flow Projections Display Buttons

At Cash Flow Projection Display (F-1A), you get the following buttons (F-1C)

- **S:Set OD Limit:** To set Bank OD Limit, as described next

01.03 Bank OD Limit Set Up

At *Cash Flow Projection* Display (F-1A), click S*:Set OD Limit* to get OD Limit Set Up screen (F-2A) to set the OD limit of Bank Accounts (under Bank Accounts, Bank OCC/ OD Group).

Against each of the Bank Account, enter the OD Limit sanctioned / available.

Performance Analysis 06-08

01 Performance Analysis

Various Accounting Reports & Financial statement show varieties of Reports with enormous amount of figures. Often, it is difficult to for th tp executives to go through al these reports and evaluate the operational efficiency and status of the financial health of the organization, sing these bulky reports.

To get the intrinsic view about the health, liquidity or earning capability of an enterprise, financial analysts look for some key figures & ratios to quickly assess the health & performance of an enterprise.

Ratio Analysis — ABC Academy 9-10 — Ctrl + M

Principal Groups	ABC Academy 9-10 1-Apr-2009 to 31-Mar-2010
Working Capital *(Current Assets-Current Liabilities)*	99,136.78 Dr
Cash-in-Hand	9,97,939.50 Dr
Bank Accounts	71,826.78 Dr
Bank OD A/c	
Sundry Debtors	15,060.50 Dr
Sundry Creditors	8,78,880.00 Cr
Sales Accounts	60,300.00 Cr
Purchase Accounts	7,050.00 Dr
Stock-in-Hand	2,000.00 Dr
Nett Loss	1,24,220.00 Dr
Wkg. Capital Turnover *(Sales Accounts / Working Capital)*	0.61
Inventory Turnover *(Sales Accounts / Closing Stock)*	30.15

Principal Ratios	ABC Academy 9-10 1-Apr-2009 to 31-Mar-2010
Current Ratio *(Current Assets : Current Liabilities)*	1.10 : 1
Quick Ratio *(Current Assets-Stock-in-Hand : Current Liabilities)*	1.10 : 1
Debt/Equity Ratio *(Loans (Liability) : Capital Account + Nett Profit)*	0.67 : 1
Gross Profit %	1,672.89 %
Nett Profit %	(-)206.00 %
Operating Cost % *(as percentage of Sales Accounts)*	306.00 %
Recv. Turnover in days *(payment performance of Debtors)*	80.06 days
Return on Investment % *(Nett Profit / Capital Account + Nett Profit)*	156.80 %
Return on Wkg. Capital % *(Nett Profit / Working Capital) %*	(-)125.30 %

F-1A: Ratio Analysis screen

02 Ratio Analysis Display

At Tally Main menu (F-1C/02-23), or at Final Accounts Menu (F-1F/02-23), select *Ratio Analysis* to get *Ratio Analysis* (F-1A).

The *Ratio Analysis* (F-1A) is divided into 2 panes. Left pane displays figures of Principal Groups and right pane lists Principal Ratios, computed for the specified period.

You may drill down through any figure to get related details. The meaning and computation of each of these figures are now explained.

02.01 Principal Groups

At the left part of *Ratio Analysis* screen (F-1A), the figures of some Principal groups are shown.

- ***Working Capital:*** It is computed as [Current Assets - Current Liabilities]. Current Assets consists of the 6 Reserved Groups namely, Stock-in-Hand, Cash-in-Hand, Bank Accounts, Loans & Advances (Asset), Deposits (Asset) and Sundry Debtors while Current Liabilities consists of 3 Reserved Groups namely, Duties & Taxes, Provisions and Sundry Creditors.

Normally, Working Capital balance of a running concern has a positive figure. Low level of Working Capital may be indicator of insolvency while high level is indicator of insufficiency of liquid funds (or too much burden of Liabilities)

- ***Cash-in-Hand & Bank Accounts:*** It shows the total of all current bank accounts and cash accounts, showing the free cash available. This figure helps Cash management and payment decision.
- **Bank OCC**: It indicates Overdraft as on the period end Date.
- ***Sundry Debtors & Creditors:*** Reveals balance as on the date alongwith current dues. It helps Credit Management.

- ***Sales and Purchases:****Shows the net value of Sales & Purchase, at a glance*
- ***Stock-in-Hand:*** *Reveals fund blocked in Stock Items*
- ***Net Profit or Loss:*** Shows the overall results for the period.
- ***Working Capital Turnover:*** Indicates number of times Working Capital has been rolled over. It is arrived by dividing Sales with Working Capital (Current Assets- Current Liabilities). This is an indicator how good the working capital has been deployed into productive return. Higher figure indicates efficient utilisation of available resources.
- ***Inventory Turnover:*** Indicates number of times Stock has been rolled over. It is arrived by dividing Sales with Stock –in -hand. Higher figure indicates better management of Inventory.

02.02 Principal Ratios

At the right part of *Ratio Analysis* screen (F-1A), you get the Principal Ratios.

- **Current Ratio*:*** Computation Formula: Current Assets / Current Liabilities.

  This ratio speaks about health of the organisation and measures the relative ability to pay Short-term debts.
- **Quick Ratio*:*** *Computation Formula: [Current Assets - Stock] / Current Liabilities.*

  It is also termed as Acid Test Ratio. The Assets which can be quickly converted into liquid assets are considered for computation of this ratio and is considered a better tool to measure financial strength of an organisation from the liquidity perspective
- **Debt/Equity Ratio*:*** Computation Formula: Loans (Liability) / Net Capital Employed (Capital + Reserves)

  This Ratio is the proportion of Long Term Debts to Net owned Capital (Capital + Reserves + Profit/Loss). This Ratio is indicator of Financial structure of the Company. Higher the Ratio, higher the risk of failure to repay Loan (Principal and Interest).
- **Gross Profit %*:*** Computation Formula: [Gross Profit / Net Sales] * 100

  Expresses Gross Profit Margin which serves as an index of overall efficiency of main business of the organization.
- **Net Profit %:** *Computation Formula: [Net Profit / Net Sales] * 100 Expresses Net Profit Margin which is an indicator of overall performance of the Organisation.*
- ***Operating Cost %:*** Shows the component of expenses incurred on productive activities. Lower it is, higher the profitability. Computation Formula: 100- Net Profit Ratio
- ***Receivables Turnover in days:*** Computation Formula: [Sundry Debtors / Net Sales] * Number of Calendar Days Some call it *Collection Ratio* also which is an indicator of average collection period of debts. Higher value calls for stringent control on Receivables.
- ***Return on Investment %:*** Computation Formula: Net Profit / Capital Employed (Capital + Reserves) * 100

  An important indicator for utilisation of resources to generate earnings.
- ***Return on Working Capital %:***Computation Formula: [Net Profit / Working Capital] * 100

  Indicates rate of return on the Working Capital (Current Assets - Current Liabilities) employed by the organization.

Thus Principal Group figures coupled with Ratio analysis throws light on the performance of the organisation to exercise proper control at appropriate time for better performance and return.

03 Ratio Analysis Configuration

At *Ratio Analysis* screen (F-1A), click *F12:Configure* to get *Ratio Analysis Configuration* screen (F-2). Set the options as follows:

- **Analysis Report Style**: At *Show Vertical Analysis*:
  - o Set Yes to show Analysis Report in Vertical format (F-5A)
  - o Set No to show Analysis Report in Normal format (F-1A)
- **Explanatory Lines**: At *Show Explanatory Lines:*
  - o Set *Yes* to Show Explanatory Lines below each Ratio (F-1A)
  - o Set *No*. The Explanatory lines will not be shown (F-5A)

Buttons

At *Ratio Analysis* screen (F-1), you get the following buttons (F-3):

- **F2:Period:** Click *F2:Period* to set the period for Ratio Analysis Report.
- **Columnar Buttons**: Use the columnar buttons (F-3A) to create comparative columnar Reports for different Period / Companies (F-6A).

04 Ratio Analysis Printing

At Ratio Analysis Display (F-1A), click *P:Print* to get Ratio Analysis Printing screen (F-4A). Type *Y* at *Print? Yes / No prompt* to print the Report

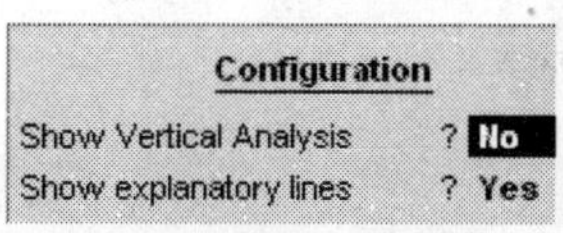

F-2A: Ratio Analysis Configuration

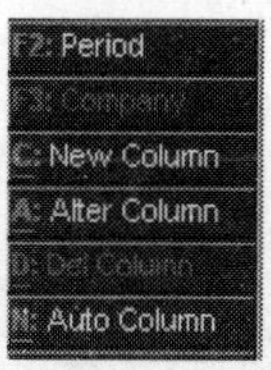

F-3A: Buttons

F-4A: Ratio Analysis Printing screen

04 Ratio Analysis (Vertical)

At *Ratio Analysis Configuration* screen (F-2A), set *Yes* at *Show Vertical Analysis* to get Analysis Report in Vertical format (F-5A). In vertical format (F-5A), the Principal Groups are shown first, followed by Principal Ratios.

> **Note:** *Columnar Report can be seen in Vertical format only.Ratio Analysis figures are computed as per Reserved Groups. User created* Primary *Groups may not be considered for Ratio Analysis.*

Ratio Analysis
1-Apr-2009 to 31-Mar-2010

	1-Apr-2009 to 31-Mar -2010
Principal Groups :	
Working Capital	99,136.78 Dr
Cash-in-Hand	9,97,939.50 Dr
Bank Accounts	71,826.78 Dr
Bank OD A/c	
Sundry Debtors	15,060.50 Dr
Sundry Creditors	8,78,880.00 Cr
Sales Accounts	60,300.00 Cr
Purchase Accounts	7,050.00 Dr
Stock-in-Hand	2,000.00 Dr
Nett Loss	1,24,220.00 Dr
Wkg. Capital Turnover	0.61
Inventory Turnover	30.15
Principal Ratios :	
Current Ratio	1.10 : 1
Quick Ratio	1.10 : 1
Debt/Equity Ratio	0.67 : 1
Gross Profit %	1,672.89 %
Nett Profit %	(-)206.00 %
Operating Cost %	306.00 %
Recv. Turnover in days	80.06 days
Return on Investment %	156.80 %
Return on Wkg. Capital %	(-)125.30 %

F-5A: Ratio Analysis (Vertical Format, without explanation)

05 Ratio Analysis Columnar Report

At *Ratio Analysis* screen (F-1A), at the button bar (F-3A) click the respective buttons for Columnar Report, to get Columnar comparative reports (F-6A) for Multiple Period / Multiple Companies.

Ratio Analysis

	1-Apr-2009 to 30-Sep -2009	1-Oct-2009 to 31-Mar -2010
Principal Groups :		
Working Capital	2,83,256.78 Dr	99,136.78 Dr
Cash-in-Hand	29,189.50 Dr	9,97,939.50 Dr
Bank Accounts	2,16,076.78 Dr	71,826.78 Dr
Bank OD A/c		
Sundry Debtors	45,060.50 Dr	15,060.50 Dr
Sundry Creditors	1,950.00 Dr	8,78,880.00 Cr
Sales Accounts	51,950.00 Cr	8,350.00 Cr
Purchase Accounts	1,950.00 Cr	9,000.00 Dr
Stock-in-Hand	1,000.00 Dr	2,000.00 Dr
Nett Profit	54,800.00 Cr	1,79,020.00 Dr
Wkg. Capital Turnover	0.18	0.08
Inventory Turnover	51.95	4.18
Principal Ratios :		
Current Ratio	145.77 : 1	1.10 : 1
Quick Ratio	145.25 : 1	1.10 : 1
Debt/Equity Ratio	0.60 : 1	0.39 : 1
Gross Profit %	112.42 %	11,381.44 %
Nett Profit %	105.49 %	(-)2,143.95 %
Operating Cost %	(-)5.49 %	2,243.95 %
Recv. Turnover in days	130.56 days	498.37 days
Return on Investment %	54.91 %	133.58 %
Return on Wkg. Capital %	19.35 %	(-)180.58 %

F-6A: Columnar Ratio Analysis Statement

FAQ: Frequently Asked Questions

FAQ-1: How to print Ratio Analysis with explanatory statement

Ans: At Tally Main Menu, select *Ratio Analysis* (*GoT>Ratio Analysis*) to get Ratio Analysis Display (F-1A). Click F12:Configure to get Ratio Analysis Configuration screen (F-2A). At *Show Explanatory Lines,* set *Yes* to Show Explanatory Lines below each Ratio. Click *P:Print* to get *Ratio Analysis* printing screen (F-4A). Type Y to print he Report

Part 7

Foreign Currency

This part shows the process of maintenance of Accounts of multiple currencies, by Importers, Exporters, and multinational companies who trade and maintain accounts in Foreign Currency.

Foreign Currency explains activation of Foreign Currency features of the Company, creation of different Currencies, Exchange Rates etc

Foreign Currency Transactions explains the entry of transactions in Foreign Currency

Forex Gain Loss explains accounting adjustment of Currency Exchange Gain / Loss

Foreign Currency

01 Foreign Currency

Normally organizations maintain accounts in currencies of that country (called *Base Currency*). However, Importers, Exporters, Money Exchangers, etc, who buy / sell or pay/ receive in foreign currency are required to enter transactions in Foreign currency also.

02 Base Currency

For every Company, you must define a *Base Currency* at Company Creation screen. This is normally the Native Currency (the Currency of the Country where the Accounts are maintained), for example, Rupees in India.

02.01 Company Base Currency Symbol

At Company Creation screen, at Currency symbol field (F-1A), enter Symbol for the Base Currency in which Books of Accounts for the company is to be maintained (Tally proposes '₹', do not change it for Indian Companies maintaining Accounts in Indian Currency).

02.02 Base Currency Particulars

The particulars of Base Currency are shown at the bottom part of the Company creation screen (F-1C).

Tally proposes the standard values for *Indian Rupee* as Base Currency. So, you do not need to change default values for Base Currency '₹' as shown. However, organisations maintaining accounts in other Base Currency may change as follows:

Currency Symbol At *Base Currency Symbol*, the currency symbol entered in top section is displayed here for information.

Currency Name At *Formal Name* Enter the full Name for the currency. Example: INR(for Indian Rupee), USD (for US Dollar), HKD (for Hong Kong Dollar) etc, as commonly used by International Trading Community & Bankers.

Decimal Places At *Number of Decimal Places,* enter here the number of decimal places to represent fraction part of the currency. For Dollar, Pound, Rupees etc, enter 2 (e.g Rs 1245.74), for Dinars, enter 3.

Amount Format For better readability, figures are normally delimited by comma (e.g 32,734.59). set: - *Yes* at *Show Amount in Millions*, to express in Millions (e.g 123,456,789), - *No* to express in *Lacs / Crores* format (12, 34, 56,789). For India, it is set as *No* by default, to express figures in Crores / Lacs

Symbol Place At *Is Symbol suffixed to Amounts*, set:- *No* to show symbol first (default), followed by the *Amount* (e.g $ 1000, £1000, '1000 etc.). -*Yes* to show *Amount* first, followed symbol (e.g., 1000¥),

Symbol Spacing At *Put a space between amount and Symbol*, set:-*Yes* to insert one letter space between the Currency Symbol and the Amount (like 152 $ or $ 152), - *No* to concatenate the Foreign Currency Symbol and the Amount ((like $152 or 152$).

Company Details

Currency Symbol : ₹

F-1A: Base Currency Symbol

Allow Multi-Currency ? Yes

F-1B: Foreign Currency Activation

Base Currency Information

Base Currency Symbol	: ₹	Show Amounts in Millions	? No
Formal Name	: INR	Put a SPACE between Amount and Symbol	? Yes
Number of Decimal Places	: 2	Decimal Places for Printing Amounts in Words	: 2
Is Symbol SUFFIXED to Amounts	? No		
Symbol for Decimal Portion	: paise		

F-1C: Base Currency Information

03 Activation of Foreign Currency

All currencies created in Tally, other than the Base Currency, are considered as Foreign Currency for the Company.

To activate foreign currency (to maintain amount in currencies other than base currency also), click *F11:Features>Accounting Features* to get Accounting Features screen. At Accounting Features screen, under section *General*, set *Yes* at *Allow Multi Currency* (F-1B). Consequently, at *Accounts Info menu* (*GoT>Accounts Info*), *Currencies* option gets activated (F-2A).

> ***Note:*** *Do not use a symbol for Foreign Currency for which there is no convenient key in Key Board. You may not be able to type it in Voucher. For example, Use Y (or Yen), or E for Euro) (instead of ¥ or , if a key is not available for ¥ or).*

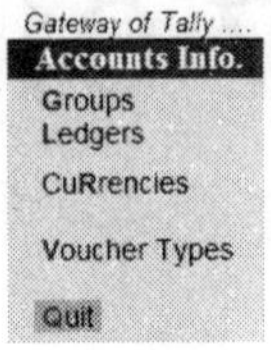

F-2A: Accounts Info Menu

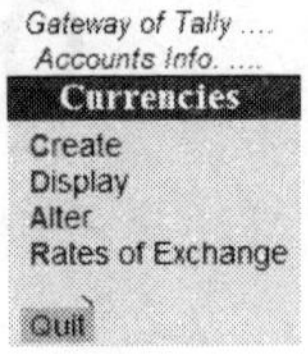

F-2B: Currencies Menu

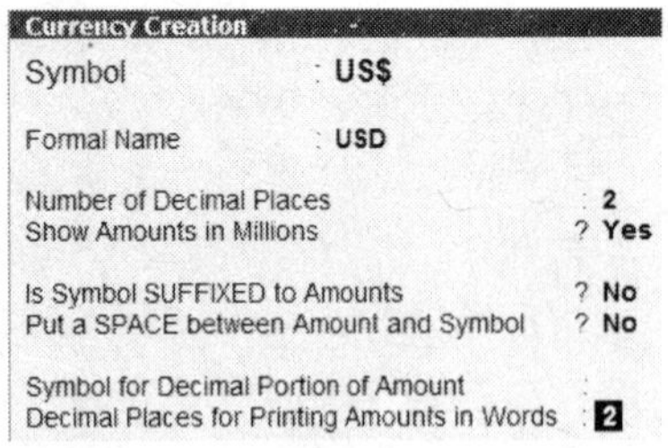

F-3A: Foreign Currency creation

04 Foreign Currency Master Entry

At *Accounts Info menu* (F-2A), select *Currencies* to get *Currencies Menu* (F-2B), for creation of Foreign Currency master.

At Currency Menu (F-2B), select *Create* to get Currency Creation screen (F-3A). Now enter as follows:

- **Currency Symbol**: At *Symbol*, enter the Foreign Currency Symbol of the Currency.
- **Currency Name**: At *Formal Name*, enter the Complete Name of the Foreign Currency (it must be different from Foreign Currency Symbol), as commonly used by International Trading Community & Bankers.
- **Currency Decimal Places**: At *Number of Decimal Places*, enter the number of decimal places required to express the amount in Foreign Currency (e.g 2 for Dollars, Pounds etc, 3 for Dinars etc).
- **Currency Amount Format**: At *Show Amount in Millions*, set:
    - o *Yes* to show the Foreign Currency Amount formatted in Million Figures (like 9,999,999)
    - o *No* to show the amount in Lacs format (like 99, 99,999).
- **Currency Symbol position**: At *Is Symbol Suffixed to Amounts*, set:
    - o *Yes* to show the Foreign Currency Symbol after the Amount figure (like 152 $),
    - o *No* to show the Foreign Currency Symbol prefixed to Amount ((like $152).
- **Currency Symbol Spacing**: At *Put a Space between Amount & Symbol,* set:
    - o *Yes* to insert one letter space between the Foreign Currency Symbol and the Amount (like 152 $ or $ 152)
    - o *No* to concatenate the Foreign Currency Symbol and the Amount ((like $152 or 152$).
- **Amount Delimiter**: At *Symbol for Decimal Portion of Amount* enter the delimiter for the decimal portion. Normally dot (.) is used. However, you may use any other symbol like (,).

05 Currency Exchange Rate Entry

Having created the new currency Master (§04), enter the Daily Exchange Rate of the currency with Base Currency. At Currencies Menu (F-2B), select *Rate of Exchange*, to get *Exchange Rate Entry* screen (F-4A). Enter the Exchange Rate (with Base Currency) on the specified date, for the respective Currencies (F-4A):

Date of Exchange Rate: At *Date of Exchange Rate,* enter the *Date* for which you enter the Exchange Rate.

Exchange Rate Details: Now enter the Exchange Rate details with base currency, in respect of each foreign currency, for the specified date, as follows:

- **Foreign Currency Name:** At *Currency* column, select the Foreign currency from the list of Currencies
- **Standard Exchange Rate:** At *Std Rate* column, enter the Exchange Rate (normally published by RBI), which is used to compute the Foreign Exchange Gain / Loss.
- **Currency Selling Rate:** At *Last Voucher Rate* column, the Rate is carried from the last *Receipt* Voucher, if entered. At *Specified Rate* column, enter your Selling Rate, i.e, Rate in Base currency at which the Bank pays you in conversion of the Foreign Currency received by you.
- **Currency Buying Rate:** At *Last Voucher Rate* column, the Rate is carried from the last *Payment* Voucher, if entered. At *Specified Rate* column, enter your Buying Rate, i.e, Rate in Base currency at which you pay to Bank for remitting in Foreign Currency.

Enter the *Exchange Rate* for each Date whenever there is any change in any of the element of Rate entered. The Rate for the Date entered or immediately prior Date (if no Rate is entered for that Date) is applied to the voucher as default. For example for Date 5 Jun 2013, the Rate entered for 5 Jun 13 or immediately prior to that (e.g 1June 13) would be applied.

Currency Buying & Selling Rates are also used for calculating foreign exchange variances where there is no Standard Rate. Tally automatically calculates Forex Gain or Loss for foreign exchange transactions using the Standard Rates (or Specified Rates) and Actual transaction Rates as applicable,

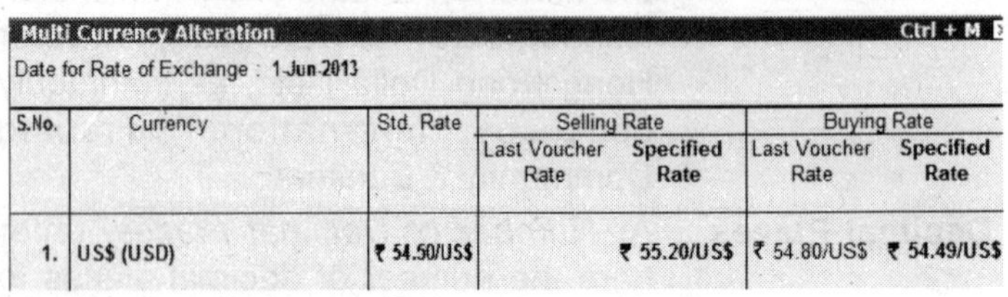

F-4A: Exchange Rate Entry

05.01 Currency Display

At Currency Menu (F-2B), select *Display* and then select the Currency to be displayed from the list of Currencies:

- **Foreign Currency Details**: On selection of Foreign Currency, you get the details of Currency & Exchange Rates as entered (F-5A).
- **Base Currency Details**: On selection of Base Currency, you get the details of Base Currency as entered at Base

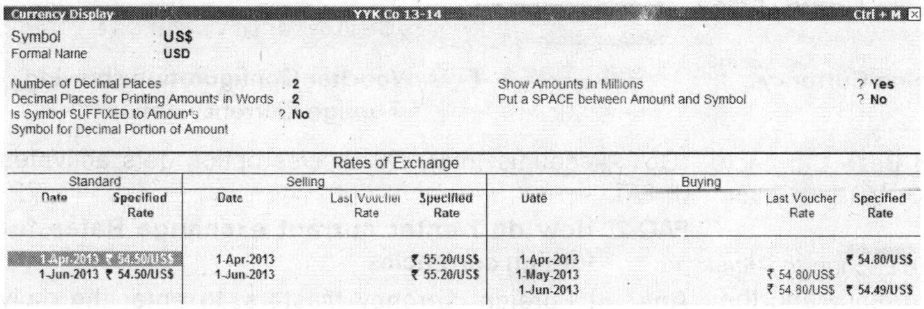

F-5A: Foreign Currency Display

Currency (F-5B), at Company Creation / Alteration screen. However, in Display screen, you just view the details, but you cannot make any alteration in the screen.

05.02 Currency Alteration

At Currency Menu (F-2B), select *Alter* and then select the Currency to be Altered. You get similar screen as Display (F-4A). Now, you can make any alteration in any field in the screen (take the cursor on the field by keyboard or click on the field by Mouse) and make alteration in the data as desired. After changing, Type Yes (at Yes No) or press Alt+A to save the changes made.

06 Currency Specification in Ledger Accounts

Accounts Ledger Creation has been explained earlier. Having activated Foreign Currency (§03), at *Ledger Creation* screen, you get an additional Field *Currency of Ledger* (F-6A). At *Currency of Ledger*, select the Currency in which you like to maintain for the ledger account, from the list of Currencies. Normally, you should specify the respective foreign Currency for Parties with whom you deal in Foreign Currencies. In all other ledgers, you should specify Base Currency. Similarly, for Bank Accounts, you should select the respective Currency in which the account is maintained.

F-6A: Currency set up at Ledger Account Master Creation

07 Accounts Voucher entry in Foreign Currency

Accounts Voucher Entry has been explained earlier. Here we discuss about the entry of Amount in Foreign Currency.

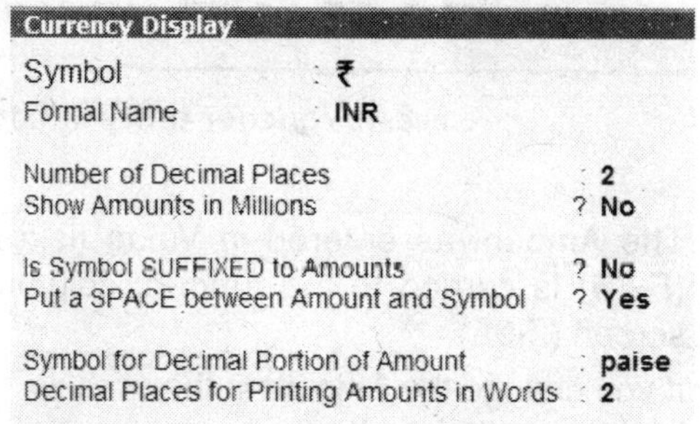

F-5B: Base Currency Display

Having selected the Ledger Account in Voucher entry, enter the Ledger Amount details as follows:

- **Amount in Foreign Currency**: To enter an amount in any Foreign Currency, at amount field enter currency symbol as specified in the respective currency master (e.g $, US$ etc: F-6A) before the amount (like $1200.00, US$2000: F-7A).
- **Amount in Base Currency:** To enter amount in Base Currency, just enter the Amount as usual without any Currency prefix

F-7A: Foreign Currency Symbol letter in Amount entry

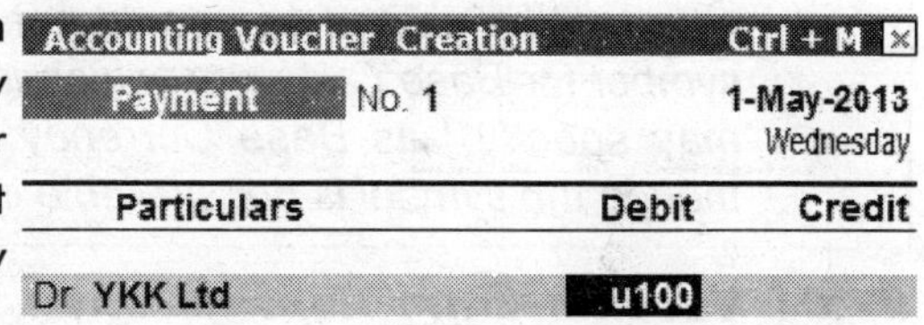

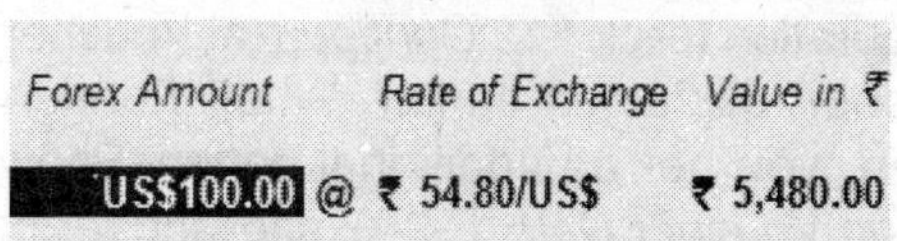

F-7B: Foreign Currency details entry

Foreign Currency Details: On entering Ledger Amount in Foreign currency, you will get *Forex Rate of Exchange* subscreen (F-7B), to enter the following details.

- **Forex Amount**: The Amount entered in Foreign currency is carried (you may change it in the window).
- **Rate of Exchange**: Tally proposes the Currency Rate (Selling Rate in Receipt Voucher, Buying Rate in Payment voucher or the Standard Rate), as the case may be, which you may change.
- **Value**: The computed value in Base Currency as per Exchange Rate entered is displayed, which you may change.

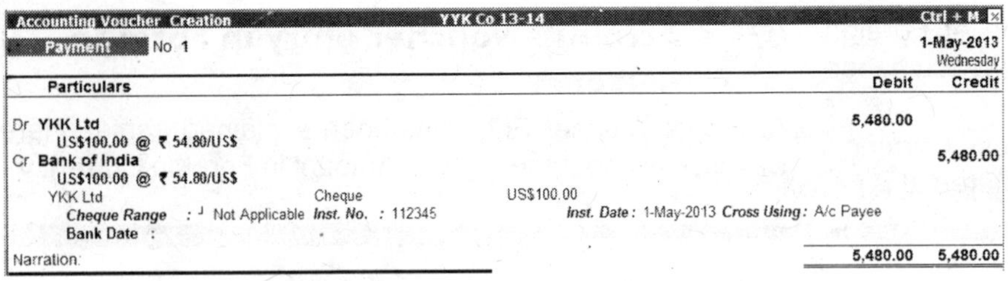

F-8A: Voucher entry in Foreign Currency

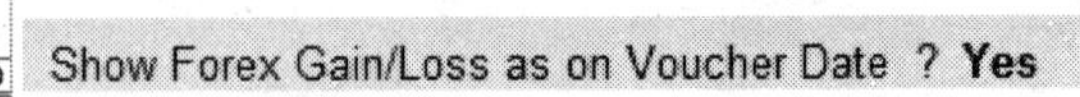

F-9A: Voucher Configuration showing Foreign Currency option

The Amount as entered in Value field in Base Currency (F-7B) is carried to the Amount column in Voucher Main screen (F-9A)

If you change the Amount in the window, the Exchange Rate is back calculated as per the foreign currency and the Amount.

> **Note:** *If the symbol does not match with existing Currency Master, cursor would not move to next field. If the currency symbol is not available at your keyboard, you may be able to enter it in conjunction with* Alt *key. For example, to enter £, hold down* Alt *key and type 156 at numeric keypad. You may be able to enter ¥ by holding down* Alt *and pressing 157 from numeric keypad (you may try if it works). So, avoid such currency symbols (you may use normal keyboard characters for initials for Symbol (e.g* **Y** *instead of ¥ as currency symbol), otherwise data entry will be painful.As you do not have to enter symbol for Base Currency (which is default), you may specify ' as Base Currency Symbol even though the symbol is not available in keyboard.*

07.01 Voucher Entry Configuration

Voucher Entry Configuration (click *F12:Configure* at Voucher Entry screen) has been explained earlier. When Foreign Currency is activated, you get an additional option *Show Forex Gain Loss as on Voucher Date* (F-9A), showing forex Gain Loss (§01/07-03).

FAQ: Frequently Asked Questions

FAQ-1: How do I activate Forighn currency features in the Company

Ans: To activate foreign currency (to maintain amount in currencies other than base currency also), click *F11:Features>Accounting Features* and set *Yes* at *Allow Multi Currency* (F-1A). Consequently, at *Accounts Info menu* (GoT>Accounts Info), *Currencies* option gets activated (F-2A).

FAQ-2: How do I enter current exchange Rates for foreign currencies

Ans: At Foreign currency Masters, to enter the daily Exchange Rate, at *Currencies* Menu (F-2B), select *Rate of Exchange*, to get Exchange Rate Entry screen (F-4A). Enter the Exchange Rate (with Base Currency) on the specified date, for the respective Currencies

Date of Exchange Rate: At *Date of Exchange Rate,* enter the *Date* for which you enter the Exchange Rate.

Exchange Rate Details: Now enter the exchange rate details with base currency, in respect of each foreign currency, for the specified date, as follows

- **Foreign Currency Name:** At *Currency* column, select the Foreign currency from the list of Currencies
- **Standard Exchange Rate:** At *Std Rate* column, enter the Exchange Rate (normally published by RBI), which is used to compute the Foreign Exchange Gain / Loss.
- **Currency Selling Rate:** At *Last Voucher Rate* column, the Rate is carried from the last *Receipt* Voucher, if entered. At *Specified Rate* column, enter your Selling Rate, i.e, Rate in Base currency at which the Bank pays you in conversion of the Foreign Currency received by you.
- **Currency Buying Rate:** At *Last Voucher Rate* column, the Rate is carried from the last *Payment* Voucher, if entered. At *Specified Rate* column, enter your Buying Rate, i.e, Rate in Base currency at which you pay to Bank for remitting in Foreign Currency.

Enter the Exchange Rate for each Date whenever there is any change in any of the element of Rate entered. The Rate for the Date entered or immediately prior Date (if no Rate is entered for that Date) is applied to the voucher as default. For example for Date 5 Jun 2103, the Rate entered for 5 Jun 13 or immediately prior to that (e.g 1June 13) would be applied.

Foreign Currency Transactions

07-02

01 Foreign Currency Transaction

We now show a complete chain of related entries in foreign Currency (Sales and Receipt), outstanding dues, resulting forex Gain/Loss and Adjustment of forex Gain Loss.

Voucher entry in Foreign Currency has been explained earlier (F-7A/07-01).Here, we show some specific vouchers and the effect in the Reports.

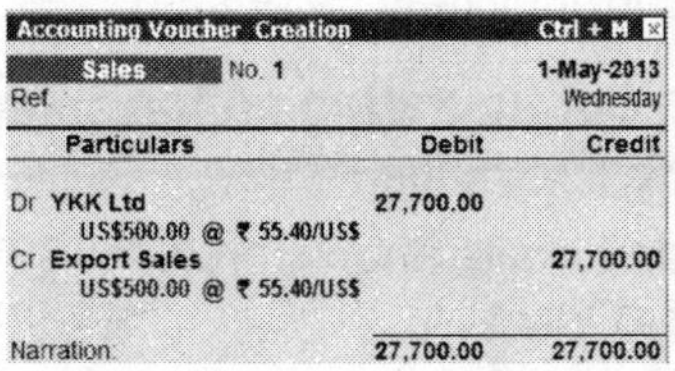

F-1A: Sales Voucher

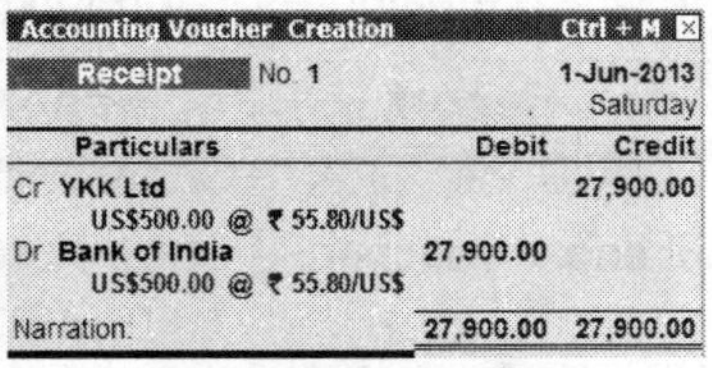

F-1B: Receipt Voucher

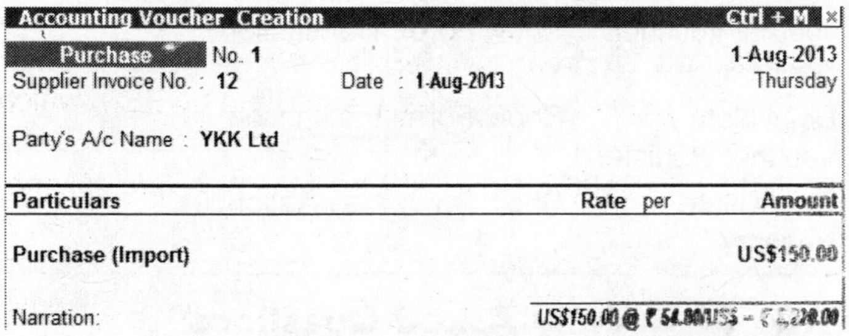

F-1C: Purchase Voucher (Accounting Invoice Mode)

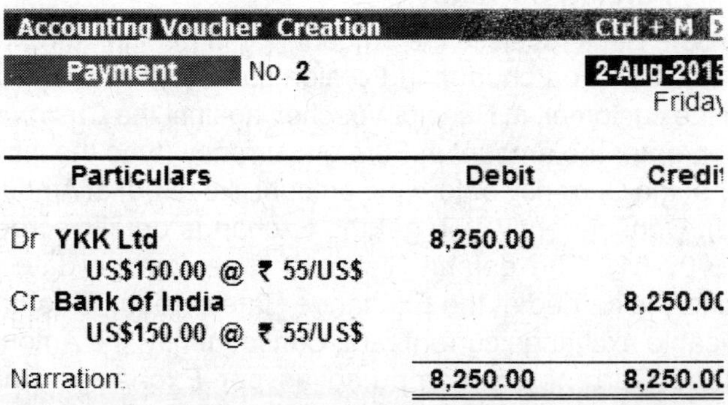

F-1D: Purchase Voucher (Voucher Mode)

02 Sales Voucher entry in Foreign Currency

Enter the Sales Voucher as explained. Against the Customer ledger, enter the amount in Foreign currency (e.g, type u for US$ before the amount- like u500 at Amount Field). Consequently, you get the Exchange details screen (F-7B/ 07-01). The default standard rate is carried at the Exchange Rate screen. Enter the applicable exchange current rate. Consequently, the Amount in Base Currency is computed as per Exchange Rate entered and shown. This amount is carried in the Amount column in the voucher.

In the same way, enter other ledger accounts (like Sales Accounts) and enter the amount (F-1A)

03 Receipt Voucher entry Foreign Currency

When the Bank receives the amount of Sales Bill in foreign Currency, from the customer, enter the Receipt Voucher in the same manner. Against the Customer ledger, enter the amount in Foreign currency (type u for US$ before the amount- like u500 at Amount Field). Consequently, you get he Exchange details screen (F-1B). The default Standard Rate (on the date of voucher) is carried at the Exchange Rate screen. Enter the applicable exchange current rate. Consequently, the Amount in Base Currency is computed as per Exchange Rate entered and show. This amount is carried in the Amount column in the voucher.

In the same way, enter other ledger accounts (like Bank Account) and enter the amount (F-1B). This way, enter Purchase Vouchers (F-1C / F-1D)

Having entered the Voucher with Foreign Currency details, you may see the relevant info in Reports

04 Reports with Foreign Currency details

In most of the reports, you will get Configuration options to show Foreign Currency details, as follows:

- Accounts Ledger (§05)
- Outstanding Statement (§06)
- Other Reports (§07)

05 Ledger Account

Ledger Account has been explained earlier. Here, we discus exclusively about Foreign Currency related points.

At Gateway, select *Display > Account Book > Ledger* and then select the Party Ledger to get Ledger Voucher screen of the Party Ledger Account. (F-3A)

Click *F12: Configure* to get Ledger Configuration screen (F-2A). The following Configuration options relate to Foreign Currency:

Sho.. Forex details also	? Yes
Show Forex Transactions only	? Yes

F-2A: Ledger Configuration

Show Bills in Foreign Exchange	? No

F-2B: Outstanding Configuration

Ledger Vouchers Ctrl + M

Ledger: **YKK Ltd** **1-Apr-2013 to 1-Jun-2013**

Date	Particulars	Vch Type	Vch No.	Debit	Credit
1-5-2013	**Export Sales** US$500.00 @ ₹ 55.40/US$	Sales	1	27,700.00	
1-6-2013	**Bank of India** US$500.00 @ ₹ 55.80/US$	Receipt	1		27,900.00
	Opening Balance :				
	Current Total :			27,700.00	27,900.00
	Closing Balance :				200.00

F-3A: Ledger

- *Show Forex Transaction only:*
  - o Set *Yes* to show the amount in Foreign currency only (The amount in Base Currency would not be shown).
  - o Set *No*. The Amount in Base Currency would also be shown
- *Show Forex Details also:*
  - o Set *Yes* to show the amount in Foreign currency also.
  - o Set *No*. The amount in Foreign Currency will not be shown (However, Amount in Base Currency would be shown)

06 Ledger Outstanding

Ledger Outstanding Statement has been explained earlier. Here, we discus exclusively about Foreign Currency related points.

Select *Display > Statement of Accounts > Outstanding > Ledger* and then select the Party Ledger Account to get Ledger Outstanding report (F-4A).

Ledger Outstandings Ctrl + M

Ledger : **YKK Ltd** **1-Apr-2013 to 31-Jul-2013**

Date	Ref. No.	Opening Amount	Pending Amount	Due on	Age of Bill in Days
31-Jul-2013	On Account	200.00 Cr	200.00 Cr		
	1-May-2013 Sales 1 27,700.00 Dr				
	1-Jun-2013 Receipt 1 27,900.00 Cr				
		200.00 Cr	200.00 Cr		

F-4A: Ledger Outstanding (In Base Currency)

Click *F12: Configure* to get Ledger Outstanding Configuration screen (F-2B). The following Configuration option relates to Foreign Currency:

Show Bills in Foreign Exchange:

- Set *Yes* to show pending amount in Foreign currencies. The Bills for which the amount in Foreign Currency is pending, will only be shown. For example, if 90 $ has been paid of a Bill of 100$, then the Bill will be shown in Outstanding irrespective of amount pending in Base Currency
- Set *No*. The Bills for which the amount in Foreign Currency is fully paid, will not be shown, irrespective of amount pending in Base Currency.

07 Other Reports with Foreign Currency Details

In several reports configuration options, you will get option for showing the report in Foreign Currency. Set the respective option to show the figures in foreign currency.

Consequently, the Foreign currency figures (where applicable) will also be shown in report.

The following table shows the reports & the respective options in which the figures in foreign currency may be printed.

Report	Report Configuration option
Day Book	Show Forex Transaction
Ledger Voucher	Show Forex Details/Show Forex Transaction Only
Group Voucher	Show Forex Details/Show Forex Transaction Only
Journal Voucher Register	Show Forex Transaction
Debit Note Voucher Register	Show Forex transaction
Credit Note Register	Show Forex transaction

FAQ: Frequently Asked Questions

FAQ-1: How I may enter Receipt Voucher in entry Foreign Currency

When the Bank receives the amount, e.g in foreign currency, of Sales Bill (or a cheque in Foreign currency is received) from the customer, in Receipt Voucher, against the Customer ledger, enter the amount in Foreign currency (type the initial letter of the Currency before the amount like u500) at Amount Field). Consequently, you get the Exchange details screen (F-7B/07-01). The default Standard Rate (on the date of voucher) is carried at the Exchange Rate screen. Enter the applicable exchange current rate. Consequently, the Amount in Base Currency is computed as per Exchange Rate entered and show. This amount is carried in the Amount column in the voucher.

In the same way, enter other ledger accounts (like Bank Account) and enter the amount (F-1B).

Forex Gain / Loss

01 Forex Gain / Loss

Forex Gain Loss arises when any amount received / paid in foreign currency at different Rate than the original transaction, difference resulting in Gain / Loss (Called Forex Gain Loss) arises. This amount is to be adjusted through Forex Gain Loss account and respective ledger accounts squared up.

Some instances of Forex Gain Loss

- Amount received from Customer against Sales Bill at a different Rate of Exchange that at the time of Sale
- Amount paid to Supplier against Purchase Bill at a different Rate of Exchange that at the time of Purchase.
- Amount re-paid to Lender against money borrowed at a different Rate of Exchange that at the time of Loan taken..
- Amount received from Borrower against money lent at a different Rate of Exchange that at the time of Loan given..

01.01 Forex Gain / Loss Adjustment

Sales / Purchase & Party Ledger account shows figures in Base currency at the Exchange Rates entered in the voucher. Subsequently, at the time of payment, Due to variation in exchange Rate, some Forex Gain / Loss might arise. This is reflected in Party Ledger Account (F-3A/07-02).

When the Bill is settled in Foreign Currency, balance lying in Party Account, due to the difference in Exchange Rate (F-3A/07-02), is to be adjusted to square off the Party Account and transferred to Forex Gain Loss, through a Journal Voucher.

In Journal Voucher, first entry should be Debit. So:

- **Adjustment of Forex Gain**: Select the Party Account an enter the Forex Gain in Debit Column. Next select Forex Gain / Loss Account and enter the Amount in Credit Column (F-1A)
- **Adjustment of Forex Loss**: Select the Forex Gain Loss Account and enter the Forex Loss in Debit Column. Next select Party Account and enter the Amount in Credit Column

F-1A: Journal Voucher for Forex Gain / Loss Adjustment

Journal No. **1** — **31-Jul-2013** Wednesday

Particulars	Debit	Credit
Dr **YKK Ltd**	**200.00**	
Cr **Forex Gain Loss**		**200.00**
Narration:	**200.00**	**200.00**
Forex gain adjsuted		

02 Forex Gain/Loss Journal Voucher Class Creation

Instead of Journal Voucher, you may also create a Journal Voucher Class (§02/02-08)to auto adjust the Forex Gain Loss. Journal Voucher Class creation has been explained earlier. Here we explain points related to creation of Forex Journal Voucher Class

At Voucher Type creation of Journal Voucher Type, enter the Journal Voucher Class Name to create a Forex Journal Voucher Class to get *Voucher Class set up* screen (F-2A)

At *Voucher Class Set Up* screen, enter as follows (F-2B).

- Set *Yes* at *Use Class for Forex Gain/Loss adjustments.*
- At *Ledger Name*, select the Forex Gain Loss Accounts. These ledger accounts will be available in Forex Journal Voucher Entry for adjustment of Forex Gain / Loss.

Voucher Type Creation — YYK Co 13-14

Name : **FxAdj**

General		Printing		Name of Class
Type of Voucher	: Journal	Print after saving Voucher	? No	ExJrn
Abbr.	: FxJv			
Method of Voucher Numbering	? Automatic			
Use Advance Configuration	? No			
Use EFFECTIVE Dates for Vouchers	? No			
Make 'Optional' as default	? No			
Use Common Narration	? Yes			
Narrations for each entry	? No			

F-2A: Journal Voucher class creation

F-2B: Journal Voucher class set Up

Class : **FxJrn**

Use Class for Forex Gain/Loss Adjustments ? **Yes**

Forex Gain/Loss Ledger Account to use :

Ledger Name

Forex Gain Loss

03 Forex Adjustment Journal Voucher Entry

Journal Voucher entry using Voucher Class has been explained earlier (§04/02-08). Here we explain entry of Journal Voucher Class elated to adjustment of Forex Gain / Loss. At Voucher entry, select the respective Voucher Type (F-3A) and then the Voucher Class (F-3B)

> **Note:** *It is recommended that you create Journal Voucher to adjust Forex Gain Loss instead of Journal Voucher Class. You get more flexibility.*

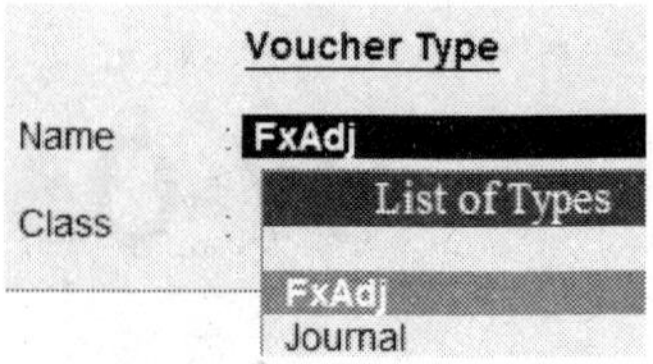

F-3A: Voucher Type selection

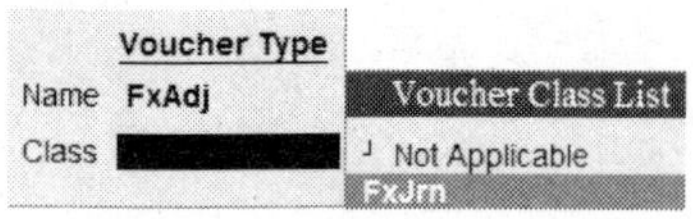

F-3B: Voucher Class selection

At Forex JV entry, select the Party Ledger Account. At the *Amount* field, the foreign gain/loss due to exchange variation is carried (loss is displayed as Credit and profit as Debit, you can change this figure also). Save the journal voucher. The Forex gain/loss is now adjusted.

Having made the Forex Adjustment through Journal Voucher (or Journal Voucher Class)

At Ledger Voucher List (*GoT>Display>Account Books>Ledger*) select the Party Ledger Account to see the effect of the Forex Adjustment Journal Voucher.

Ledger Vouchers Ctrl + M

Ledger: **YKK Ltd** **1-Apr-2013 to 31-Jul-2013**

Date	Particulars	Vch Type	Vch No.	Debit	Credit
1-5-2013	**Export Sales**	Sales	1	27,700.00	
1-6-2013	**Bank of India**	Receipt	1		27,900.00
31-7-2013	**Forex Gain Loss**	Journal	1	200.00	
		Opening Balance :			
		Current Total :		27,900.00	27,900.00
		Closing Balance :			

F-4A: Party Ledger Display

Ideally the unadjusted profit / loss due to foreign transaction should be transferred to Forex Gain/Loss a/c on the completion of a transaction to square off the account. A sale transaction would be complete when the full receipts have been received. A purchase transaction is treated closed on making full payment.

Even a single JV can be used to adjust the forex gain / loss of several parties. For example, you may create a single forex JV at the month-end (or periodic interval) to adjust the gain or loss of all the Parties.

FAQ: Frequently Asked Questions

FAQ-1: How to create Journal Voucher to make Accounting Adjustment of Forex Gain / Loss.

Ans: After Receipt / Payment against transactions in foreign currency, the Ledger Balance may not reflect the actual balance due, on account of difference in exchange Rates between the transactions and its settlement..

Sales / Purchase & Party Ledger account shows figures in Base currency at the Exchange Rates entered in the voucher. Subsequently, at the time of payment, Due to variation in exchange Rate, some Forex Gain / Loss might arise in Party Ledger Account (F-1A).

When the Bill is settled in Foreign Currency fully, balance lying in Party Account (sometimes even when Part of the Bill is settled), the amount due to the difference in Exchange Rate (F-1A), is to be adjusted and transferred to Forex Gain Loss, through a Journal Voucher.

In Journal Voucher (GoT>Accounts Voucher), first entry should be Debit. So:

- **Adjustment of Forex Gain**: Select the Party Account an enter the Forex Gain in Debit Column. Next select Forex Gain / Loss Account and enter the Amount in Credit Column (F-1A).
- **Adjustment of Forex Loss**: Select the Forex Gain Loss Account and enter the Forex Loss in Debit Column. Next select Party Account and enter the Amount in Credit Column

Section 2

Invoicing & Inventory

Part 1

Basic Invoicing & Inventory

So far we discussed about Financial Accounting (Accounting of Money). In this section, we discuss about Accounting of Materials, covering creation of Masters, Entry of Transactions, Printing of Invoices and various Inventory Reports.

- **Introduction to Inventory** explains Basic Concept & Features of System, Trading Activities, various types of Inventory Transactions and linking of Inventory System with Financial Accounting System.
- **Inventory Masters** explains creation of the Basic Inventory Masters, like UoM, Stock Group & Stock Items, essential to maintain Inventory System
- **Inventory Vouchers** describes various types of transactions of materials. It describes how the Accounting & Inventory transactions (like in Sales, Purchase, Debit & Credit Notes) are entered and synched in one voucher. It also describes Stock Journal Vouchers (pure Inventory Voucher which may not affect financial accounting part.

  Invoicing explains entry of Invoice data, the most important task of Inventory system, taking most of the time and volume of Inventory work. The finer aspect of data Entry & Configuration of Invoice as per personal preferences, are explained.
- **Invoice Printing** explains the process of configuring the contents of Invoice and printing the Invoice in various formats
- **Inventory Reports** describes scores of Inventory reports Display & Printing,
- **Multi-Account Inventory Reports** describes Printing of Regular bulk Reports of Inventory
- **Point of Sales** describes quick entry & instant printing of Retail Invoices on-line.

Organisations not maintaining Inventory (Materials Accounts) in Tally, may skip this Part

Basic Inventory System

01 Inventory System

So far we have explained maintenance of Financial Accounting System for accounting of money only. However, in a business system, materials is another important component of business transactions. So, a businessman need to maintain records of transactions of Stock Items also (called *Inventory* System)

Here, we discuss about following activities to maintain a *Basic Inventory* System:

- **Inventory Master**: To create Unit of Measure, Stock Group & Stock Item Masters
- **Inventory Voucher / Invoice / Point of Sales**: To enter Inventory voucher / Invoice in respect of Purchase, Sales & transfer of stock, Sales & Purchase Returns. Adjustment of Party Accounts due to Rate Difference, Rebates, Claims etc
- **Voucher / Invoice Printing**: Printing of Inventory Voucher / Invoice
- **Inventory Reports**: To print various Inventory reports (Day Books of Sales, Purchases, Debit & Credit Notes, Customer & Supplier Ledgers, Stock Item Ledgers, Stock Statements etc)

02 Activation of Inventory System

To maintain Inventory system, first you have to activate Inventory features for Company. At *Company Creation / Alteration* (F-2/02-01), select *Accounts with Inventory* at *Maintain* field. Consequently, various options relating to Inventory get activated at Menu, Company Operations options, Configuration options and Button Bar and other places.

03 Trading transactions

The trading transactions may classified in the following major activities in respect of movement & stock of materials

Activity	Related Voucher
Buying of Goods	Purchase Invoice
Selling of Goods	Sales Invoice
Return of Bought Goods to Supplier	Debit Note
Return of Sold Goods from Customers	Credit Note
Other Adjustments / Stock transfers	Stock Journal

04 Sales & Purchase

- From the point of view of maintaining Customers & Suppliers Accounts, Sales & Purchase activities may be broadly classified as:
  - Cash Sale & Cash Purchase
  - Credit Sale & Credit Purchase
  - Sales & Purchase Returns

04.01 Cash Sale & Cash Purchase

- **Cash Sale:** The simplest case of Sale is to sell from showroom. The customers come to showroom and buys goods. The seller makes a Sales Voucher (normally referred as Cash Memo). The seller collects the money & delivers the goods.

  The Cash Sales transaction updates both Inventory (stock is updated) and the Accounts (Sales & related Accounts) are updated.

  In case of Cash Sales, accounting becomes simpler as records for Debtors need not be maintained.
- **Cash Purchase:** The simplest case of Purchase is to purchase from showroom. The buyer goes to showroom and buys goods. The seller makes Cash Memo for goods sold, The buyer pays the money & collects the goods. The Cash memo given by the seller becomes the Purchase Voucher for the buyer. The buyer records the Purchase Voucher in his accounts.

In case of Cash Purchase, accounting becomes simpler as the buyer does not have to maintain records for Creditors.

The Cash Purchase transaction updates both Inventory (stock is updated) and the Accounts (Purchase & related Accounts) are updated.

04.02 Credit Sale & Credit Purchase

However, in business, most of the trade transactions are done on Credit. The Sale / Purchase transaction and the related Payments occur at different stages.

On sale of goods, the seller issues a Sales Invoice on the buyer. The buyer records the Invoice issued by the seller in his books as Purchase Invoice.

Subsequently. the buyer makes payment of the Invoice to the seller, creating a *Payment Voucher*. On receiving the payment from buyer, the seller records it in *Receipt Voucher* in his books.

04.03 Sales & Purchase Returns

- Sometimes, the Buyer may return the goods to the seller (due to defect or some other reasons). In such case, the Buyer, who returns the goods makes a Debit Note on the seller whom the goods are retuned to, and the seller, who receives back the sold goods, makes a Credit Note on the Buyer who returned the goods.

05 Stock Journal

Stock Journal is used to make rectification or other adjustments in Stock (e.g to make adjustments for shortage, breakage, damage, evaporation, melting/moisture loss/gain, shrinkage and other shortfall/ gains). It does not affect Customer, Supplier or any other ledger account. It only affects the book stock (stock ledgers)

06 Integration of Inventory & Accounts

Accounts may be optionally Integrated with Inventory. When Accounts and Inventory is integrated, the computed value of stock as per Inventory records is automatically & dynamically carried to Financial Accounts Statements (*P & L Statement* and *Balance Sheet*) and no entry for Closing Stock Value is needed in accounts. If not integrated, the closing stock vale has to be entered (F-1/03-10) for the Final Accounts (which may be different from the closing stock value as per inventory records).

These options may be interchanged as required, offering the benefit of either option at any stage.

07 Inventory Masters

Masters reflect the plan how the transaction data are linked to a central entity to track all the related information resulted from the transaction. So, to get the information related to a Stock Item (say a TV), an entity called *Stock Item* is to be created which would contain the particulars of the Stock Item. The data of all regular business transactions are linked to Masters so that any info may be obtained with reference to the Master. For example, to get the information of Stock Item, we would create an entity called Stock Item master.

So, in a business system, the Masters are to be created first and all the transactions would refer to a Master.

So, planning the Masters and entering necessary initial info about the Master, are the crucial point of maintaining the Inventory System. Where there are large Number of Maters, the Masters data need to be organized according to the reporting needs of the business. In such case, a well thought out plan of organising the masters is to be made (e.g Groups / Categories). Accordingly, the entities of the Groups / Categories are to be planned, organised to get the reports in a way required by the business entity. So, planning and creation of master data is entirely organisation specific and varies from one organisation to another.

Tally ERP 9 prides the means to organise and maintain Master data in multilevel hierarchical structure, by user, in their own way. To maintain the basic inventory system, the following masters are to be initially planned and respective master data to be created.

- Unit of Measure
- Stock Groups
- Stock Items

08 Units of Measure

As money is measured in terms of Currency, Stock Item is measured in terms of Unit of Measurement (popularly called as *Unit* or *UoM*). Various Units (UoMs) are used for Stock Items.

Normally, a Stock Item is measured in one Unit (Unit of Measure). While creating master for Stock Item, you need to specify unit for the item. So, before creating stock items, the applicable Units for each Item must be ascertained.

Value of Unit of measure may be expressed in fraction also, in specified precision, upto 4 places to decimal (e.g 3.492 Kg).

In some special cases (like Service Items), a Stock Item may not have any Unit associated with it.

09 Stock Groups

For better organisation of the hundreds & thousands of Stock Items that are stocked & traded by an enterprise, you may organise the stock items into appropriate Stock Groups, to get the summarized and organised reports for each level of Stock Group. So, Stock Group is Master of Masters (a higher level Master)

The relationship between Stock Item and Stock Group is similar to that of Accounts Ledger and Accounts Groups. So, only Stock item *moves in* or *moves out* and stock group never participates in any Inventory voucher, Stock Groups merely help to organise the Stock Items.

10 Stock Items

Stock Item is the identity of *traded* goods, for which quantitative details of Materials transactions (materials In & Out) & Stock-in-hand are maintained in the Inventory System. If a book is purchased by bookseller for trading, or by a Library for Lending (and the stock accounts are maintained), it is Stock Item. If the book is purchased for study and no stock is maintained in the stock accounts, it is not a Stock Item for our discussion in this book.

However, sometimes, a Stock Item (called Service Items) may be created for Billing / Accounting, even if no Stock is maintained.

Stock Items are the actual items that are transacted (received, issued or produced) and take part in any Inventory Voucher. For better organisation of large number of Stock Items, Stock Items are organized into Stock Groups in an hierarchical structure (parent – child structure)

Example of Stock Group / Stock Item hierarchical Structure

The following example explains the concept of Stock Groups & Stock Items. A Paints & Hardware Dealer may organise the Stock Groups and Stock Items in the following manner:

Paints
- *Berger*
  - *Dulux*
    - Dulux Shade 101
    - Dulux Shade 102
    - Dulux Shade 103
  - *Duco*
    - Duco Shade 501
    - Duco Shade 502
    - Duco Shade 503
- *Snowcem*
  - Snowcem Shade 1201
  - Snowcem Shade 1202
  - Snowcem Shade 1203
- *Asian*
  - *Apcolite*
    - Apcolite Shade 2302
    - Apcolite Shade 2303
    - Apcolite Shade 2304
  - *Gattu*
    - Gattu Shade 7101
    - Gattu Shade 7202

The items in *italics* are Stock Groups, Stock Items are shown in normal. In the above example, when we view a report for *Berger* group, we get total of all items under *Dulux* and *Duco* group while report for *Duco* will show total of items under *Duco* group only.

As Accounts Ledger participates in Accounts transactions (voucher), Similarly, *Stock Items* take part in all Inventory Transactions (Vouchers).

FAQ: Frequently Asked Questions

FAQ-1: How I can integrate Accounts & Inventory. What is its effect on Final Accounts

Ans: Click *F11:Features* to get Company features Menu Select *Accounting Features* to get Accounting features set up screen. Under the *General* section, at the option, *Integrate Accounts & Inventory,* set as follows:

- **Integrated System**: Set *Yes* to Integrate Accounts with Inventory. In that case, the stock value as per specified valuation method is automatically posted to the Accounts and reflected in all accounting statement. You do not need to compute and enter the Stock Value.

  In Integrated system, when you drill down from the Stock Value figures (from Balance Sheet, P & L Statement or any other report), you get the Inventory Stock Report.
- **Non Integrated System**: Set *No* to delink the Accounts with Inventory. In that case, you have to manually compute and enter the Closing Stock value for the specified date, at the Closing Stock Ledger Account. The entered stock value is reflected in all accounting statements.

  In Non Integrated system, when you drill down from the Closing Stock ledger account (from Balance Sheet, P & L Statement or any other report), you get the Accounting Reports with figures of closing stock value as entered in the Closing Stock Ledger (but not the Inventory Stock Statements).

  In Non Integrated system also, the entire Inventory System (Transactions & Stock) are maintained as usual (in the same way as Integrated System). However, the Stock value as per Inventory system is not linked to the Accounting System. So, the current period Profit / Loss may be different in Integrated & Non Integrated System (if the stock entered in Non Integrated system is different from the Stock Value computed as per Inventory System)

  You may, at any time, change the option at *F11:Features > Accounts* and see the effect in both the systems.

FAQ-2: List the Voucher Types which affect both Accounts & Inventory

Ans: The transaction in following voucher types may contain data of both Accounts & Inventory:

- Sales Voucher
- Purchase Voucher
- Debit Note
- Credit Note
- Journal Voucher

FAQ-3: List the Voucher Types which affect Inventory but do not affect Accounts directly

Ans: The transaction in following voucher types directly affect Inventory System only:

- Stock Journal Voucher
- Physical Stock Voucher

FAQ-4: I run a service business providing consultancy services. I like to maintain only one Income Account Ledger but like to get the details of Income for each Service and also print Service Vouchers to Parties.

Ans: To get the facility of printing Service Vouchers in nice way, you should create Stock Items for each type of Service without UoM (in the UoM of the Stock Item, set *Not Applicable* (§05/04-02).

Now, you will be able to enter and print Service Vouchers (of Sales Voucher type) and get various reports with details of each Service, yet maintaining a single Service Income Ledger Account.

Basic Inventory Masters 01-02

01 Basic Inventory Masters

In previous chapter, we have disused the concept about the following 3 Basic Inventory Masters that you need to create in an Inventory System

- Unit of Measure (§08/04-01)
- Stock Group (§09/04-01)
- Stock Item (§10/04-01)

02 Inventory Masters creation

F- 1A: Inventory Info Menu

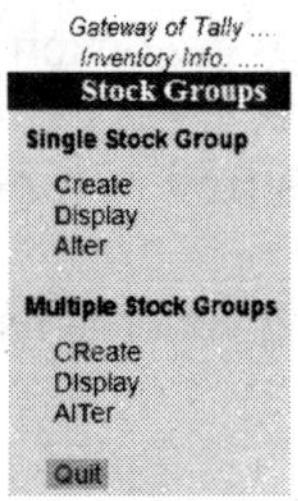

F- 1B: Stock Group Menu

F- 1C: Stock Item Menu

F- 1D: UoM Group Menu

At Gateway of Tally, select *Inventory Info* to get *Inventory Info* Menu (F-1A) containing menu options to create various Inventory Masters.

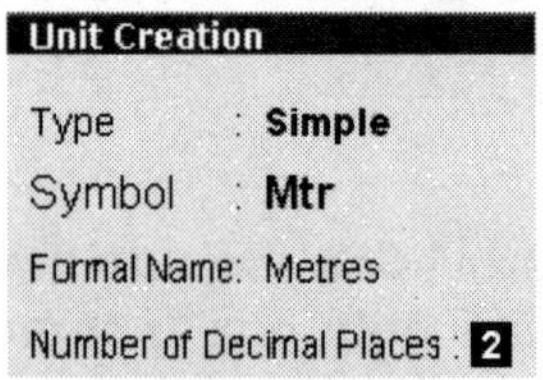

F-2: Simple UoM Creation

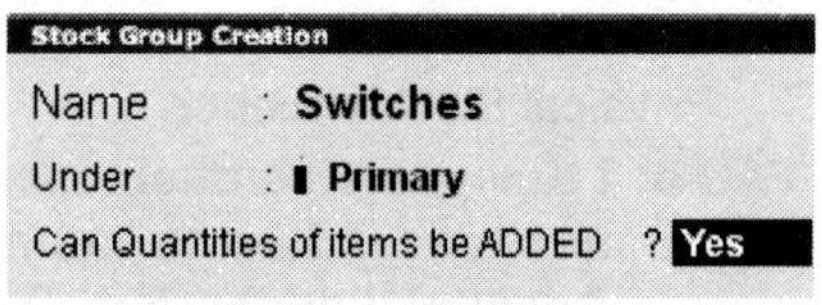

F-3: Stock Group Entry

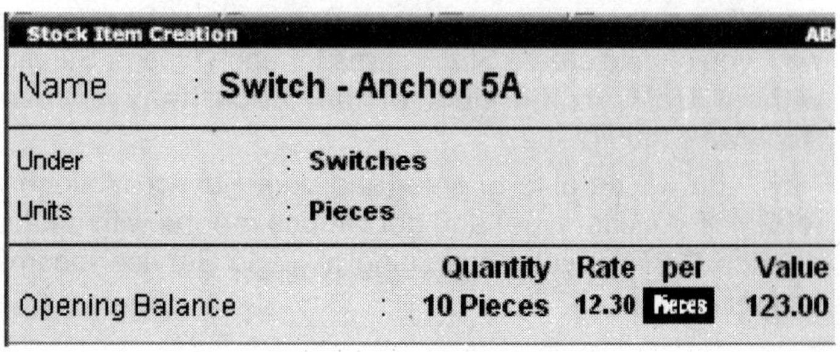

F-4: Stock Item Entry

03 Simple Unit of Measure

At Gateway, select *Inventory Info* > *Unit of Measure* > *Create* to get Unit (UoM) Creation Screen (F-2)

Now enter the following Particulars.

- **Type**: Cursor normally skips showing at *Type* field, with *Simple* as selected, to create a Simple Unit. Otherwise press <shift+Tab> or <backspace> to get the cursor at Type field and select *Simple*.
- **Symbol**: At *Symbol* field, enter the Short Name of the Unit (e.g., Kg. Ltr.). In all reports, the Unit Symbol appears alongwith Quantity, to indicate the UoM of the Quantity. The bare Quantity figure (e.g 15) does not carry any meaning unless associated with Unit Symbol (like Pcs). The symbol must be distinct and unique. Duplicate symbols are not accepted.
- **Formal Name**: Enter full Name of the Unit (e.g., Kilogram, Litre etc) different from UoM Symbol, for internal Info about the UoM. The Formal name is displayed in UoM selection list (in parenthesis), beside the UoM symbol, to identify the correct Unit record. The Formal Name must be distinct and unique. Duplicate Formal name is not accepted. The Formal Name must be distinct from Symbol (e.g Kilograms & Kgs). Same name cannot be used as Symbol & Formal Name
- **Number of Decimal Places**: Decimal places refer to the precision upto which the Quantity value may be shown. Decimal part beyond the decimal value specified would be dropped. This may cause rounding errors in computed value (particularly in large values) as the extra decimal places are dropped. Specify maximum number of decimal places (between 0 to 4) in which reporting is required (e.g 3 to show upto 3 places of decimals in Quantity, like 1.234 MT, 0 to omit the decimal values in Quantity, like 29 Pcs). The higher decimal place values in Quantity figures are truncated (for example if decimal places is 3, then 1.2344 will be truncated to 1.234). So, specify adequate decimal places to avoid truncation. Maximum 4 decimal places may be set.

One Unit may be used to measure many Sock Items. For example, Kg may be used as UoM in many Stock Items. In bulk Item (like Coal), Kg may be used without decimal place, while for smaller & costlier Items (e.g Cinnamon), the weight in Kg may be expressed upto 3 decimal places (e.g 12.125).

In such case, you must set the decimal places keeping in mind the requirement of higher decimal place to avoid errors resulting from truncation.

The decimal places apply to all Items using the specified UoM. So, if you set 3 at Decimal place for Kg, then quantity of all Items having Kg as UoM will be shown with the specified decimal place (i.e 3). So, 200 Kg of Coal will be shown as 200.000 (and NOT as 200).

The number of decimal place in UoM cannot be modified later. So plan it properly before you create the UoM record.

04 Stock Group

Creation of *Stock Group* is optional. If you maintain a few Stock Items only (e.g Sugar), you may place the Stock Items under a Tally created Stock Group called *Primary* without any need to create new Stock Groups (Primary Stock Group is created by Tally when you create a Company). However, on most cases, creation of Stock Group is necessary to get organized reports with figures for each Stock Group

Select *Inventory Info > Stock Group > Create* under Single Stock Group to get Stock Group Creation screen (F-3). Enter the following Particulars:

- **Stock Group Name**: Enter Name of Stock Group (e.g Suitings)
- **Parent Stock Group**: At *Under* field, select the parent Stock Group for the Stock Group being created (select *Primary* to create top level Group). The first Group created must be placed under Primary. To create a new parent Group (if the Parent Stock Group is not existing, press Alt+C to create the parent Stock Group).
- **Stock Group Quantity**: At the *Can Quantities of Items be Added*, set *Yes* to get Total Stock Quantity of the child Stock Items under the Stock Group (if all child Stock Items are measured in same UoM), else set *No* (Stock Group Quantity is not computed).

05 Stock Items

Stock Item is the primary inventory entity and is the lowest level of information in inventory system. You have to create a Stock Item in Tally.ERP 9 for each inventory item that you want to account for.

At *Inventory Info* Menu, select *Stock Item > Create* under Single Stock Item to get Stock Item Creation screen (F-4)

Now enter the following particulars.

- **Stock Item Name**: At *Name* field, enter a unique Name of the Stock Item.
- **Parent Stock Group**: At *Under* field, select the Parent Stock Group (if the Parent Stock Group is not existing, press Alt+C at this field and create the Parent Stock Group).
- **Stock Item UoM**: At *Units* field, select the Unit of Measurement (from pop-up) in which the Item would be measured (if the UoM is not existing, press ***Alt+C*** at this field and create the new UoM). Select *Not Applicable* if no UoM is applicable (e.g, for Service Item) and quantity details will not be maintained for such Item.

After entry of the above details, the cursor moves to *Opening Balance* field, where you have to enter the Opening Stock details.

05.01 Entry of Opening Stock Details

At *Opening Balance* field, enter Opening Stock details for the Item as on the *Books Beginning From Date* (F-2/01-01), as explained below.

- **Opening Stock Quantity**: At *Quantity* field, enter the Opening Stock Quantity
- **Opening Stock Rate**: At *Rate* field, enter the Opening Stock Rate (if you do not know the Rate, leave it blank, and enter the Opening Stock value, Tally will compute & fill up the Rate).
- **Opening Stock Value**: The Opening Stock value is computed from the Opening Stock Quantity & Opening Stock Rate as entered and displayed at Value field. However, you may change the Amount. The Rate will get changed accordingly.

If the details of Opening Stock is readily not available at the time of Stock Creation, Press <Enter>at Opening Balance (to leave blank). You may enter the Opening Stock later on (if the Opening Stock figure is not readily available at the time of Stock Item master entry) through Stock Item Alteration mode (§07).

After completing the Opening Stock entry for the Stock Item (F-4), a blank screen appears to enter for another Stock Item. Continue to enter more Stock Items. Press Esc to *Quit*.

06 Display of Inventory Masters

To Display Inventory Masters as discussed above, select Display from the respective Menu in the same way. All the records will be displayed. Now select the record to get complete details displayed. In Display mode, you cannot modify the record.

- **Display of Stock Group**: Select *Inventory Info > Stock Group > Display*, choose the Group you wish to view, from *List of Stock Group*.
- **Display of Stock Item**: Select *Inventory Info > Stock Item > Display* and select the Stock Item to Display.
- **Display of Unit of Measure**: Select *Inventory Info > Units > Display* and select the Unit to Display.

07 Alteration / Deletion of Inventory Masters

To Alter / Delete Inventory Masters as discussed above, select *Alter* from the respective Menu in the same way. All the records will be displayed. Now select the record to *Alter* or *Delete*.

- **Alteration / Deletion of Stock Group**: Select *Inventory Info > Stock Group > Alter. Select the* Stock Group.

- o **Alteration:** Make necessary modification and press Ctrl+A to save.
- o **Deletion:** To Delete the Group, press Alt+D and click *Yes* to confirm.

- **Alteration / Deletion of Units of Measure**: Select *Inventory Info > Units > Alter* and select the Unit.
  - o **Alteration** Carry out the Alteration (if the unit has been referred in any voucher, number of decimal places cannot be changed) and press Ctrl+A to save.
  - o **Deletion** To Delete any Unit, press Alt+D and click *Yes* at *Delete Yes or No?* to confirm Deletion.
- **Alteration / Deletion of Stock Item**: Select *Inventory Info > Stock Items > Alter* and select the Stock Item to Alter.
  - o **Alteration**: Carry out the Alteration (if the unit has been referred in any voucher, UoM cannot be changed). Alteration is also used to fill up the fields left blank at the time of Master Creation (like Opening Stock details). Press Ctrl+A to save.
  - o **Deletion**: To Delete any Stock Item, press *Alt+D* and click *Yes* at *Delete Yes or No?* to confirm Deletion.

07.01 Restriction in Deletion of Inventory Masters

In following cases, the Inventory Master Record cannot be Deleted.

- **Stock Group**: The Group would not be deleted if it is parent of any Stock Group or Stock Item. *Primary* Stock Group created by Tally also cannot be deleted.
- **Stock UoM**: The Stock UoM cannot be deleted if is has been referred in any Stock Item.
- **Stock Item**: The Stock Item cannot be deleted if it has been referred in any Voucher.

In such case, when you press *Alt+D*, the record remains visible (it does not get dimmed) and the Deletion Confirmation screen does not appear.

FAQ: Frequently Asked Questions

FAQ-1: I want to maintain Accounts with Inventory. How do I set up Inventory Option?

Ans: At time of creation of Company (F-2/02-01), at *Maintain* field, select *Accounts with Inventory.* Now you will get all options of Inventory in the respective Menu

FAQ-2: How to show Stock Group Quantity in Reports?

Ans: In Reports, the Stock Group Quantity, represents the total of quantity of Stock Items under the Stock Group. At Stock Group creation screen (Inventory Info>Stock Groups>Create), to get the quantity of Stock Group, set Yes at *Can Quantities of Items be added,* to get the Stock Group Quantity where the UoM of all the Items under the Group is same.

> ***Note:*** *The Stock Quantity of Items having different UoM are not added even if they are under same Stock Group and you have specified Yes at Can Quantities of Items be added.*

FAQ-3: At the time of creation of Stock Items, the Opening Stock Quantity is not known. How I can enter the Opening Stock Quantity later on.

Ans: At the time of creation of Stock Item (Inventory Info>Stock Items>Create), press <enter> at the *Opening Balance* field

Later on, to enter the Opening Stock Balance, select *Inventory Info>Stock Items>Alter*, Under Single or Multiple Option.

- In Single Stock Item Alteration Option, select the Stock Item to get it in alteration mode and then enter or modify the Opening Stock Quantity anytime (P-07)
- In Multiple Stock Item Alteration Option, select *All Items* to get all Items in alteration mode. Now enter or modify the Opening Stock Quantity anytime (P-19.01/05-01)

It is easier to enter Opening Stock Value in many Items through *Multiple* options. Click Skip Parent to easily reach the *Opening Quantity* column.

FAQ-4: We undertake service jobs of various kinds and like to know the amount of service done for each kind but maintain only one Service Income Ledger Account. What is the preferred way?

Ans: Create Stock items for each type of Service (.g Repairing Charges, Cleaning Charges etc). If you like, you may set *Not Applicable* at UoM for some or all service Items where you do not have any quantity. During voucher entry, enter the respective Stock Item. Quantity will not be asked when you select the Item in any voucher (but Amount is to be entered).

You may rename the *Sales* Account Group to *Service Income.*, create a Service ledger Account (§03.02/01-03) under it.

This way, you will get Service Income figures (in amount) for each type of service, even maintaining one Service Income ledger account.

Inventory Voucher 01-03

01 Accounts Voucher with Inventory Transactions

Having created Inventory Masters, you may start Inventory transaction (Vouchers) entry. Since, the trading transactions involving Inventory (like Sales, Purchase) affect Inventory & Financial Accounts, Inventory details are also entered in corresponding Accounts Voucher.

Now we discuss about Accounting Vouchers like Sales, Purchase, Debit Note, Credit Note & Stock Journal vouchers with inventory details.

02 Invoice & Voucher Entry Mode

Inventory Transactions may be entered in Voucher mode and in Invoice Mode. In Voucher mode, the Ledger Amount is entered first and then the corresponding Item wise details are entered. In Invoice mode, the Item details are entered first, the computed Item value is posted into Ledger amount.

So, in voucher mode entry, you enter the Net Amount of Bill first in the Party Account and then the amount for each Ledger Account (Like Sales Account etc). This means that you must have all the Amounts computed first. So, voucher mode is suitable when you have got all the amounts already computed (e.g you enter sales voucher from manual sales bills). Tally will not compute anything.

In Invoice mode entry of Sales Voucher, you enter the Stock Item Data first (Rate, Quantity etc). Tally computes the Item Value etc and posts into Sales Ledger. You then enter Tax Rates etc. Tally computes Taxes etc and posts into the respective ledger. Finally, Tally computes the Net Bill Amount and posts to the Party Ledger Account. So, Invoice mode is suitable for on-line billing (i.e you prepare the invoices from Tally only).

The process of Voucher entry of Sales, Purchase, Debit Note & Credit Note (in Voucher & Invoice mode) have been discussed earlier (§02/03-02). Here, we explain only the additional steps for entry of Stock Items in Voucher

03 Inventory linked Accounts Ledger

To enter Item details and for linking of Item Value to respective Sales / Purchase Ledger Account (§03.02/01-03), at ledger entry /alteration, set *Yes* at *Inventory Values are affected* at the respective ledger account (F-1). This way, you may link Sales / Purchase Ledger Account with Stock Items as follows:

So, you should set *Yes at* ledgers like Sales, Purchase, Sales Return & Purchase Return ledger accounts, where you have to associate a stock Item to the transaction entered in the voucher.

Whenever you enter a voucher involving transaction with such ledger account, you will be prompted to enter the inventory details also (like Quantity, Amount etc).

04 Inventory Voucher Entry

We have already explained the entry process of Sales / Purchase Voucher entry in voucher mode (§02/03-02). Select the Voucher Type, click *V: As Voucher* button, as explained in Sales Purchase Voucher entry (F-3). Here we explain the additional steps for Stock Item details entry.

Inventory Linked Ledger Accounts Entry in Voucher

As explained, at the second line of Voucher entry in voucher mode (F-3), when you select an Inventory Linked Ledger Account (Ledger Account for which you have set *Yes* at *Inventory Values are affected –like Sales, Purchase etc.)*, you get the Item Allocation screen to enter the Item Details (F-2)

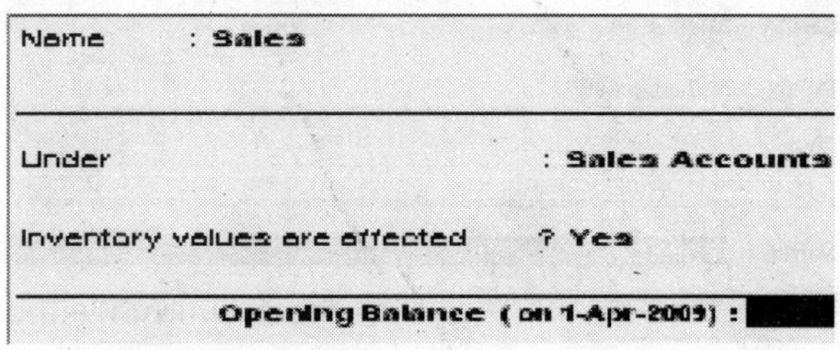

F-1: Invetory Linked Ledger Account creation

Inventory Allocations for : **Sales**

Name of Item	Quantity	Rate	per	Amount
Philips CFL Lamp 20W	5 Pieces	135.00	Pieces	675.00
Switche Anchor 15A	5 Pieces	60.00	Pieces	300.00
	10 Pieces			975.00

F-2 Item Allocation for Sale / Purchase Ledger in voucher entry

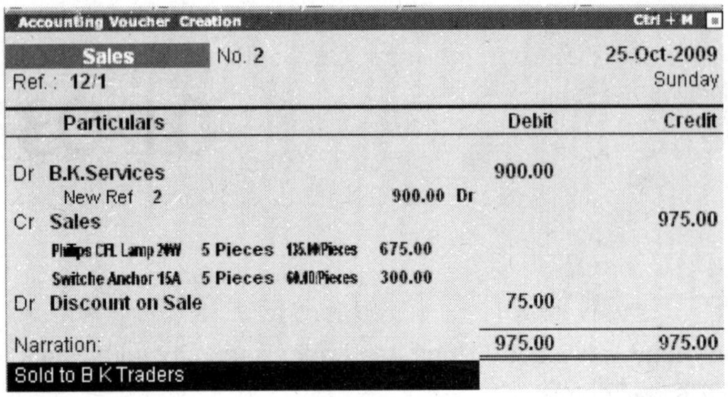

F- 3: Accounts Voucher Entry in Voucher mode with Inventory details

Voucher Item Details

At Item Allocation screen (F-2), enter the Item details, as explained below

- **Item Name**: At *Name of Item* field, select the Stock Item (Press *Ctl+C* to create new Stock Item).
- **Quantity**: Enter the Quantity. The UoM of the Item is displayed at *Per* field
- **Rate**: Enter the Rate per Unit (you may leave the Rate column and enter amount directly)
- **Item Value**: At *Amount* field, the computed Amount (as per Quantity & Rate) is displayed, which you may change.

This way, enter the Items to complete the Ledger allocation. The total Item Value must match the entered Ledger Amount.

This way you may enter multiple ledger accounts and the Item allocations for each Inventory linked Ledger Accounts.

The ledger entries are terminated, when the total of Debits equals to total of Credits.

05 Stock Journal Voucher Entry

Stock Journal Voucher is used to make internal stock adjustments Stock Adjustment, e.g., due to shortage, wastage, excess or any other increase or decrease in stock, At Gateway, select *Inventory Vouchers* (F-1A/01-02) and Click *F7:Stk Jrnl*) to get Stock Journal Voucher entry screen (F-4)

Item Details in Stock Journal Voucher: Enter the Voucher Date. At the left part, you enter the Source (Consumption) Item details (i.e Items OUT), while at the right part, you enter the Destination (Consumption) Item details (i.e Items IN), in the same way as explained for Sale / Purchase Voucher.

You may enter the Item details in both Source & Destination, or in any of the column. The quantity as entered for the Item in Source column is reduced from Stock and the quantity as entered for the Item in Destination column is increased.

So, for shortage etc, you enter in Source (Consumption) side only. For excess etc, enter in Destination (Production) side only.

In a Stock Journal (F-4), the Item, Quantity & Value may differ between Source (Consumption) & Destination (Production)

You may perform Voucher Alteration, Deletion & Cancellation at Voucher in Alteration Mode (§02/02-16)

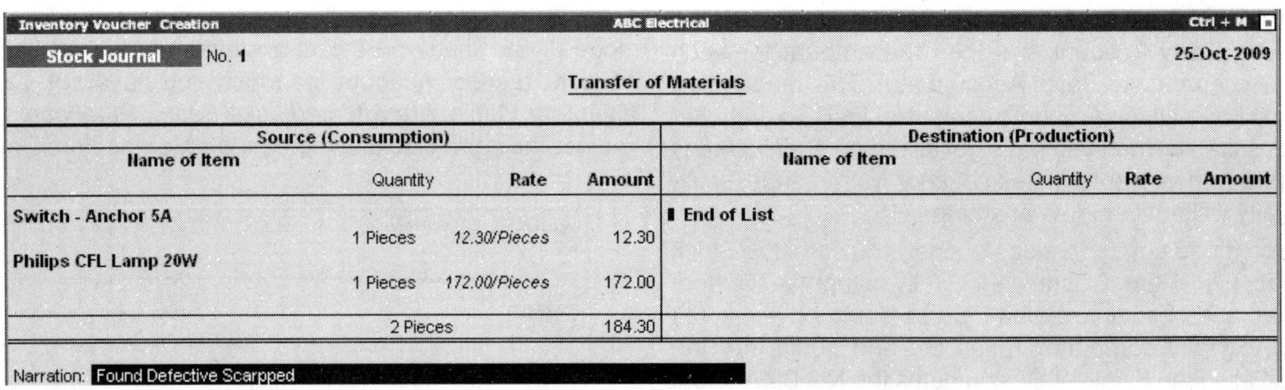

F- 4: Stock Journal without value (for adjustment of Stock)

FAQ: Frequently Asked Questions

FAQ-1: My Sales bills are prepared manually at my shop, where I cannot keep computer due to space constraints and rush. But I like to maintain accounts and inventory in computer so that I can get stock figures and all reports upto date. How do I enter the Sales and Purchase Bill quickly

Ans: In this case, as all the figures of sales bill (product value, tax discount, net bill amount) etc are already available in manual bill, you may enter the bill in voucher mode, instead of invoice mode for faster and accurate entry. At Sale voucher (*Gateway>Accounts Voucher>F8: Sales)* or purchase voucher entry (*Gateway>Accounts Voucher>F9: Purchase*), click V:*As Voucher* button. Now enter the ledger accounts. When you enter an Inventory linked ledger account (like Sales, Purchase), you get the Inventory allocation screen, where you enter the Stock Item details (Item name, Quantity, UoM,

Value) from the manual sales voucher and supplier's purchase voucher.

FAQ-2: I bought Himani Compo pack of Tooth Paste & Tooth Brush (1 Toothpaste & 1 Tooth Brush) @ Rs 40 per set. Toothpaste & Toothbrush are bought & sold separately. The stock of Tooth Brush exhausted. So, I dismantled 3 sets of Combo Pack to get the Tooth Paste & Tooth Brush separately. How to adjust the Stock & Sales Account (the proportionate cost of 1 Toothpaste is Rs 28 & that of 1 Pc Toothbrush is Rs 12)

Source (Consumption)				Destination (Production)			
Stock Item	**Quantity**	**Rate**	**Value**	**Stock Item**	**Quantity**	**Rate**	**Value**
Himani Combopack	3	40	120	Himani Toothpaste	3	28	84
				Himani ToothBrush	3	12	36

Ans: Create a Stock Journal Voucher and enter as follows:

In a Stock Journal, the Item, Quantity & Value may differ between Source (Consumption) & Destination (Production)

FAQ-3: I created 50 Christmas Gift Packs with 1 Pc Cake (Rs 50), 1 Pc Pastry (Rs 10) and 1 Pc Choco Bar (Rs 20) to sell the Gift Pack @ 100 per Gift Pack. How do I adjust the stock of Items used in Gift pack and the Gift Packs produced

Create a Stock Journal Voucher and enter as follows:

In stock journal, the value of item produced would be as per cost (not Sale Price)

Source (Consumption)				Destination (Production)			
Stock Item	**Quantity**	**Rate**	**Value**	**Stock Item**	**Quantity**	**Rate**	**Value**
Cake	50	50	2500	Christmas Gift Pack	50	80	4000
Pastry	50	10	500				
Choco Bar	50	20	1000				

Invoice

01 Invoice

Invoice is the most important document of a Trader in which details of transactions and all related information are recorded. Invoice contain many additional details in well organized formatted manner for clarity.

In Invoice entry, only the basic data of computation (Rate, Quantity, Discount % etc) is entered. The computation of Invoice automatically gets done during entry.

We have explained Inventory Voucher Entry in Voucher form (§04/04-03). In this chapter, we discuss Invoice Entry (Inventory Voucher in Invoice Mode).

02 Company Features set up for Invoicing

To enter Inventory Vouchers in Invoice form, Click *F11: Features*, and select Inventory Features. to get *Inventory Features screen* (F-1A/03-02). At Inventory Features screen (F-2), set as follows:

- **Sales transaction in Invoice Format**: Set *Yes* at *Allow Invoicing* to enter Sales Invoice in Invoice Format.
- **Purchase transaction in Invoice Format**: Having set Yes at *Allow Invoicing*, further set *Yes* at *Enter Purchases in Invoice Format* in the next line.

So, Purchases transaction can be entered in Invoice format, only when Sales Invoice format is activated

Having activated Invoice mode for Sales / Purchase, you should click the V:*As Invoice* (F-2A/03-02) & I:*Item Invoice* Toggle Buttons from the vertical button bar, during Sales, Purchase entry

03 Discount Entry in Invoice

Discount means some reduction in price offered by seller to loyal customer. Discount may be offered in 2 ways:

- **Item Discount**: Such Discount is treated as normal Trade Discount offered against respective Item. Such Discount is entered against each Item and such Discount is reduced from the gross sales value and the net Sales Value is posted to Sales Value for the Item. No discount ledger appears in the books.

  Item Discount Features Set Up: To allow Discount against each Item in Invoice, at *Inventory Features screen* (F11:Features > Inventory Features), set *Yes* at *Separate Discount Column in Invoice* (F-2). During Invoice entry, enter Itemwise Discount Rate (in %) at *Discount* column in Sales, Debit & Credit Note entry in Invoice entry. The Net Amount (Product value less Discount) would be posted in the respective Sales Ledger Account.
- **Invoice Discount**: Item Discount is allowed against the respective Item, Invoice Discount does not relate to any specific Item and so the Discount amount is NOT reduced from value of Item. Invoice Discount allowed in an Invoice is entered at the end of all Items, on the whole of the Invoice. The amount of such Discount is posted to a separate Discount Account

  Such Invoice Discount Account should be placed under Sales Group, but set *No* at *Inventory Values are affected* (F-1A)

04 Invoice Entry

At Gateway, select *Accounts Voucher* and click the respective Voucher button from the button bar, to get the Voucher entry screen (F-7C/03-02). Click *V:As Invoice* & *I:Item Invoice* buttons (if you are in Voucher mode) to get to Invoice Mode.

At Sales / Purchase Ledger Account creation / alteration (F-1/01-03), set *Yes* at *Inventory Values are affected* (F-1A).

Sales / Purchase Accounting Voucher Entry (without Stock Item Details) has been explained earlier. Here we explain additional steps for Item Details entry

Sales / Purchase Ledger: You enter common Sales Purchase Ledger Account at the header (when you set Yes at *Use Common Account for Item* Allocation at Invoice Configuration screen:F-1). Here you select Sales Ledger (For Sales Invoice) or Purchase Ledger (For Purchase Invoice), The Item value of all the Items in the Invoice is allocated to the specified sales / Purchase Ledger Account.

Item Details Entry: Now enter the Item details (F-3, F-4) as explained below:

- **Item Name**: Select the Item Name
- **Item Quantity**: Enter the Item Quantity. The Item UoM is displayed along side.
- **Item Rate**: The Item Rate per UoM as entered in Item Master, if any, is carried, which you may change.
- **Item Discount Rate**: If Discount column has been activated, enter the Discount Rate (in %).

- **Item value**: The computed Item value (after Discount. If any) is displayed, which you may change.

  This way, enter Item details for all the Items. To terminate Items entry, press <enter> at *Name of Item* to enter Accounting Allocations (Ledger Account details), as explained below:

Ledger Account details:Now you may enter details of other ledger accounts (like Discount, Freight etc):

- o **Ledger Account**: Select the Ledger Account from the list.
- o **Ledger Amount**: Enter the Amount (to reduce the amount, enter in negative figure).

Accept Supplementary Details *(Address Details, Despatch Details etc.)*	? No
Print Default Name & Address of Party	? No
Allow Separate Buyer and Consignee Names	? No
Allow modification of ALL fields during entry	? No
Use Common Ledger A/c for Item Allocation	? Yes
Use Defaults for Bill Allocations	? Yes
Use Additional Description(s) for Item Name	? No
Use Additional Description(s) for Ledger Name *(for Accounting Invoice.)*	? No
Consolidate Stock Items with same rates	? No
Show Compound Unit of Item based on Rate	? No
Show Full Details of Compound Unit	? No
Show turnover achieved with Customer	? No

F-1 Invoice Entry Configuration

F-2: Inventory Features

Invoicing	
Allow Invoicing	? Yes
Enter Purchases in Invoice Format	? Yes
Use Debit/Credit Notes	? No
Use Invoice mode for Credit Notes	? No
Use Invoice mode for Debit Notes	? No
Separate Discount column in Invoices	? Yes

Sales No. 1 — 1-Apr-2009, Wednesday
Ref.
Party's A/c Name : **Anil Agencies**
Current Balance : *9,788.00 Dr*

Name of Item	Quantity	Rate	per	Disc %	Amount
Add Gel Pens	10.0 stp	120.00	stp	5 %	1,140.00
Implementing Tally 9	3 Pcs	500.00	Pcs		1,500.00
Discount on Sale					(-)100.00
Narration:					*2,540.00*

F-3: Sale Invoice Entry

Supplementary Details

At *Invoice / Orders Configuration* screen (F-1B), at the option *Accept Supplementary Details* (§07/03-02/S1)

- Set *Yes* to enter relevant Invoice Information to be printed in the Invoice
- Set *No,* if you do not have any such details to be to be printed in the Invoice

Purchase No. 1 — 1-Sep-2009, Tuesday
Supplier Invoice No. : 12 Date : 31-Aug-2009
Party's A/c Name : **A K Traders**

Name of Item	Quantity	Rate	per	Amount
Headphone Large Frontech	1 Nos	2,200.00	Nos	2,200.00
Mobile Phone LG 3210	1 Nos	3,600.00	Nos	3,600.00
DElivery Charges				200.00
Narration:	2 Nos			*6,000.00*

F-4: Purchase Invoice Entry

FAQ: Frequently Asked Questions

FAQ-1: Sometimes, I allow discount in respect of specific Items only. How do I enter and print discount in invoice against each Item. The net amount of sale or purchase for each item after discount should be posted to respective sales purchase account (there will be no discount ledger account).

Ans: To create a separate column of discount in sales / purchase voucher, click F11: Features > Inventory Features and set Yes at *Separate Discount Column in Invoices* (F-2)

FAQ-2: I trade in Paints & Hardware Items. To get separate accounts figures in respect of sales & purchase for paints & hardware, I like to maintain 2 sales accounts, paints sale & hardware sales. Similarly, I like to maintain paints purchase & hardware purchase accounts. However one sales or purchase bill may contain both paints & hardware item. How do I make entry in the bill so that sales and purchase accounts get properly reflected?

Ans: To post the value of sale / purchase of a voucher in multiple sales / purchase ledger accounts, click F12: Configure > Invoice / Order entry. Set *No* at *Use Common Ledger A/c in Item Allocation* (F-1B). Now for every Item in the sale purchase voucher, you may select the respective sales / purchase account.

FAQ-3: The company has announced 5% price raise in some of its products. However, the Company still likes to charge at old rates to some specified parties. How to enter the invoices.

Ans: One way is to specify negative Discount of 5% (i.e -5%) in the invoices in which it likes to charge the escalated new rates charging 5% extra. This method mat be used also where the Company wants to charge at extra rates (to include taxes, or other expanse, on specified Items (Discount may be charged on selected Items in the Invoice).

01 Invoice Printing

We have described how you can configure the contents and layout of Accounts Vouchers for printing (§03/03-03). Here, we show the contents and layout of Invoice with Stock Item details.

By Invoice Printing, we normally mean Sales Invoice. Sales Invoice is printed by the seller (a copy of which is given to Buyer), becomes Purchase Invoice for the Buyer. So, Purchase Invoice is normally not printed. However, Tally provides option to print a copy of Purchase Invoice, for internal reference, if required, in the same way as Sales Invoice.

Sometimes, a Debit / Credit Note is also printed which also become the reverse document for the other Party (a Debit note Issued by a Party becomes a Credit note for the other Party & Vice versa). In such case, only one party may print the Debit Note / Credit Note and other Party uses it as the complementary document (Credit Note / Debit Note)

02 Invoice Formats

Invoice may be printed in 2 formats as follows. At Invoice Printing Configuration, at the option *Print in Simple Format* (F-1A/03-03, F-1B/03-03):

- **Simple Format**: Set *Yes* to print in *Simple* Format (F-2B). The various particulars of Invoice are all put in one place in the header, leaving more space for Item details (F-2B). This format is used when number of Items in the Invoice are more.
- **Normal Format**:: Set *No* to print in In *Normal* Format (F-2A). The various particulars of Invoice are printed in separate cells. So, the header takes more space, leaving less space for Item details (F-2A). This format is used when number of Items in the Invoice are less (otherwise the Invoice would spread to multiple pages

03 Invoice Printing Configuration

To print Invoice with complete details of Invoice Info:

- At Gateway, click *F12:Configure*, select Invoice / Orders Entry to get *Invoice / Orders Configuration screen*, or
- At the respective Voucher Entry screen (Sales, Purchase, D/N & C/N), click *F12:Configure*, to get *Invoice / Orders Configuration screen* (F-1A/03-03, F-1B/03-03)

04 Invoice Printing Methods

Invoice may be printed in 2 ways:

- On-line during Invoice entry session
- Off-line after an Invoice is saved, through Invoice Alteration mode

04.01 On-line Invoice Printing

To print Invoice on-line during Invoice entry session, immediately on completion of data entry of the Invoice.

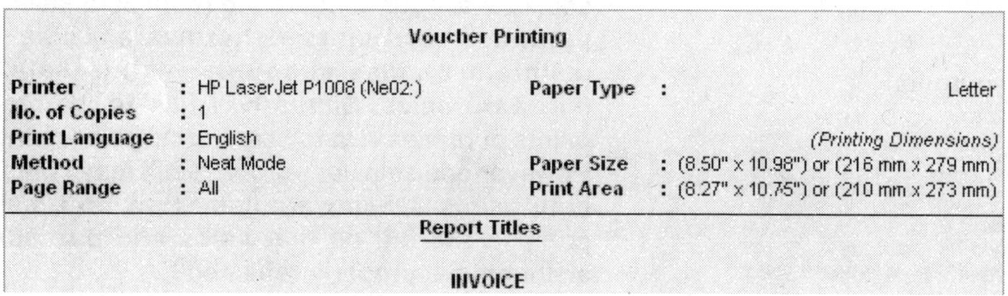

F-1A: Current Voucher Printing screen during Entry

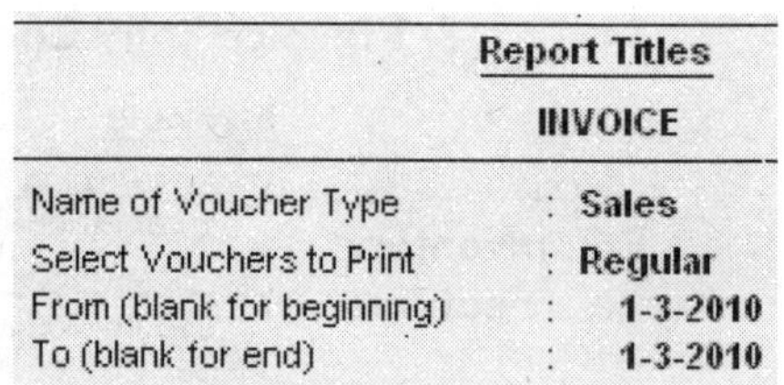

F-1B: Multi Voucher Printing screen

On-Line Voucher Printing set Up: At Inventory Info> Voucher Type, select the Voucher Type>Alter and then select the desired Voucher Type (Sales, Purchase, D/N & C/N) to get the respective Voucher Type Alteration screen (F-1A/02-07). Under the heading Printing, set *Yes* at the option *Print After Saving*?. Consequently, after entry of Voucher, you will get the Voucher Printing Screen. Type Y to print the current voucher entered.

04.02 Off-line Voucher / Invoice Printing

After you have saved an voucher and exited from the Voucher entry session, you may get any saved voucher through Voucher Alteration mode, reaching through Drill Down from any Voucher List or other reports. Click *P:Print* button (or press *Alt+P*) to get the voucher printing screen, showing the current configuration options set to print the Invoice (§02.02/03-03).

04.03 Voucher / Invoice Printing Process

At Voucher Alteration screen (reached during voucher entry session or through Display), click P:Print button (or press Alt+P) to get the voucher printing screen, showing the current configuration options set (F-1A/03-03, F-1B/03-03).

INVOICE

B. K. Traders 103 R. N. Road Kolkata-700 102	Invoice No. **1**	Dated **1-Sep-2009**
	Delivery Note **12, 16**	Mode/Terms of Payment **30 Days**
	Supplier's Ref. **12**	Other Reference(s) **Ltter dt 12.8.09**
Consignee B. K. Traders 103 R. N. Road Kolkata-700 102	Buyer's Order No. **34**	Dated **1-Aug-2009**
	Despatch Document No. **34**	Dated **31-Aug-2009, 1-Sep-2009**
	Despatched through **Adarsh Carrier**	Destination **Burdwan**
Buyer (if other than consignee) **A K Traders** 12 A B Kalam Rd Burdwan	Terms of Delivery **By Road**	

Sl No.	Description of Goods	Quantity	Rate	per	Amount
1	**Headphone Large Frontech**	**1 Nos**	2,200.00	Nos	**2,200.00**
2	**Mobile Phone LG 3210**	**1 Nos**	3,600.00	Nos	**3,600.00**
					5,800.00
	Less : ***DElivery Charges***				(-)200.00
	Total	**2 Nos**			**₹ 5,600.00**

Amount Chargeable (in words) *E. & O.E*
Indian Rupees Five Thousand Six Hundred Only

Declaration
We declare that this invoice shows the actual price of the goods described and that all particulars are true and correct.

for B. K. Traders

Authorised Signatory

SUBJECT TO KOLKATA JURISDICTION

This is a Computer Generated Invoice

F-2A: Sales Invoice (Normal Format)

SUBJECT TO KOLKATA JURISDICTION

Invoice No. 1 Dated **1-Sep-2009**
Ref. No. : 12

B. K. Traders
103 R. N. Road
Kolkata-700 102

INVOICE

Party : **A K Traders**
12 A B Kalam Rd
Burdwan

Order No.	Payment Terms	Despatch Document	Delivery Note
34 1-Aug-2009	30 Days	34 dt. 31-Aug-2009, 1-Sep-2009 Through : Adarsh Carrier	12, 16 To Burdwan

Sl No.	Description of Goods	Quantity	Rate	per	Amount
1	**Headphone Large Frontech**	**1 Nos**	2,200.00	Nos	**2,200.00**
2	**Mobile Phone LG 3210**	**1 Nos**	3,600.00	Nos	**3,600.00**
					5,800.00
	Less : ***DElivery Charges***				(-)200.00
	Total	**2 Nos**			**₹ 5,600.00**

Amount Chargeable (in words) *E. & O.E*
Indian Rupees Five Thousand Six Hundred Only

Declaration
We declare that this invoice shows the actual price of the goods described and that all particulars are true and correct.

for B. K. Traders

Authorised Signatory

This is a Computer Generated Invoice

F-2B: Sales Invoice (Simple Format)

- **Print the voucher / Invoice with current Configuration options**: Type *Y* at *Print Yes or No* option to print the voucher with current configuration option
- **Modify the current Printing options and then print:** Type N at *Print Yes or No* option to get the cursor at the first Configuration option of the Printing Configuration screen. Now change the option as desired. Now type *Y* at *Print Yes or No* option to print the voucher with changed configuration options

04.04 Purchase Voucher Printing

Purchase Invoice is an Internal document, often it is printed in Voucher Mode for Internal record. There is an additional option to print Purchase Invoice in Voucher Mode (Sales Invoice can be printed in Invoice Format only)

At Invoice Printing Configuration (F-1B), set *No* at the option *Print in Simple Format* and then set Yes at *Print in Voucher Format* to print the Purchase Invoice in Voucher Format

Debit Note

B. K. Traders 103 R. N. Road Kolkata-700 102	Debit Note No. **1**	Dated **1-Nov-2009**
	Supplier's Ref. **12**	Other Reference(s) **12**
Party : **A K Traders** 12 A B Kalam Rd Durgapur		

Sl No.	Description of Goods	Quantity	Rate	per	Amount
1	**Headphone Large TechCom**	**1 Nos**	900.00	Nos	**900.0**
	Total	**1 Nos**			**₹ 900.0**

Amount Chargeable (in words) *E. & O.*
Indian Rupees Nine Hundred Only

for B. K. Traders

Authorised Signatory

F-3A: Debit Note (Normal format)

SUBJECT TO DURGAPUR JURISDICTION

Invoice No. 1 Dated **1-Sep-2009**
Ref. No. : 12

A K Traders
12 A B Kalam Rd
Durgapur

INVOICE

Party : **B. K. Traders**
103 R. N. Road
Kolkata-700 102

Sl No.	Description of Goods	Quantity	Rate	per	Amount
1	**Headphone Large Frontech**	**1 Nos**	2,200.00	Nos	**2,200.00**
2	**Mobile Phone LG 3210**	**1 Nos**	3,600.00	Nos	**3,600.00**
					5,800.00
	DElivery Charges				**200.00**
	Total	**2 Nos**			**₹ 6,000.00**

Amount Chargeable (in words) *E. & O.E*
Indian Rupees Six Thousand Only

for A K Traders

Authorised Signatory

F-3B: Credit Note (Simple Format)

In Voucher Format, the Ledger Accounts are shown and the Item details are shown under the Sales / Purchase Ledger Accounts (for which you have set Yes at Inventory Values are affected at the respective ledger account master)

04.05 Multiple Voucher / Invoice Printing

You may print several vouchers in a range, through Multi Account Voucher Printing (§12/02-15). At Gateway, select *Multi Account printing > Multi Voucher printing (*F-1A/04-07) to get the Voucher printing screen (F-7A/02-15). Now select the period and Voucher Type to print the vouchers / Invoices in one shot.

FAQ: Frequently Asked Questions

FAQ-1: What is the difference between Simple Invoice format and Normal Invoice Format

Ans: In *Normal Invoice* format (F-2A), the data elements of Invoice Particulars and Supplementary details are printed in separate cell. The Invoice looks smart and conforms to International Format. It takes more space for Invoice headers leaving less space for Item data. So, it is suitable for Invoice with few Items and is more suitable for printing in Standard Format.

In *Simple Invoice* format (F-2B), Invoice Particulars and Supplementary details take lesser space. Simple Format is useful to print more number of Items / Item details.

Invoice formats are independent of voucher entry format. The Invoice format is decided at the time of printing of Invoice, not at the time of invoice entry.

To set the Invoice printing format, at gateway, select *F12:Configure>Printing* to get Voucher printing Menu. Now select:

- *Sales Transactions > Sales Invoice* to get the Invoice configuration screen for *Sales Invoice* (F-1A/03-03)
- *Purchase Transactions > Purchase Voucher / Invoice* to get Purchase Printing configuration screen for Purchase Voucher / Invoice (F-1B/03-03)

At the respective printing Configuration screen, at option *Print in Simple Format*:

- Set *No* to print in Normal Format
- Set *Yes* to print in Simple Format

Inventory Reports

01-06

01 Inventory Reports

Having entered the transaction vouchers (of Purchase & Sales Voucher, Invoice) with Inventory Details, you may get various inventory reports instantly. Such Inventory Reports range from various Registers, Day Books to Summary Statements.

02 Inventory Masters Lists

The following reports belong to the first Category: *Lists of Inventory Masters.*

- **Stock Groups List:** Select *Display > List of Accounts.* Click the button *T:Stock Groups* to get the List of Stock Groups in hierarchical order (F-1A). The list appears in alphabetical order of Primary Stock Groups. The Stock Group list shows the hierarchical structure Stock Groups & Sub Groups, as per reporting needs and better Inventory management.
- **Stock Items List:** Select *Display > List of Accounts.* Click the button *I: Stock Items* to get the List of Stock Groups & Stock Items in hierarchical order (F-1B). The list appears in alphabetical order of Primary Stock Groups with sub groups and stock items in hierarchical order.
- **Units of Measure List:** Select *Display > List of Accounts.* Click the button *N:Units* to get the List of UoM (F-1C) in alphabetical order.

List of Stock Groups

Cables & Wires
  Cables
  Wires
Lamp
  CFL Lamp
  Glow Lamp
Switches
  Combo Switches
  Single Switches

9 Stock Group(s)

F-1A: List of Stock Groups

List of Stock Items

Cables & Wires
  Cables
    Armoured Cables ARCO 5/12
  Wires
    Wire 3/20
    Wire 4mm
Lamp
  CFL Lamp
    Philips CFL Lamp 20W
  Glow Lamp
    Glow Lamp Philips 100W
Switches
  Combo Switches
    Combo Switch JACO 15A
  Single Switches
    Switch Anchor 15A
    Switch - Anchor 5A

9 Stock Group(s) and 8 Stock Item(s)

F-1B List of Stock Items

List of Units

Mtrs (Metres)
Pieces (Pc)

2 Unit(s)

F-1C: List of Units

Day Book 1-Apr-2009 to 2-Apr-2009

Date	Particulars				Vch Type	Vch No.	Debit Amount / Inwards Qty	Credit Amount / Outwards Qty
1-4-2009	**Anil Agencies**				Sales	1	2,600.00	
	Sales		2,700.00 Cr					
	Add Gel Pens	10.0 stp	120.00/stp	1,200.00				
	Implemnting Tally 9	3 Pcs	500.00/Pcs	1,500.00				
	Discount on Sale		100.00 Dr					
2-4-2009	**Praveen Traders**				Sales	2	1,520.00	
	Sales		1,470.00 Cr					
	White Paper Sheet	5 Pcs	300.00/Pcs	1,470.00				
	Delivery Charges		50.00 Cr					

F-2: Day Book with Inventory Details

03 Inventory Voucher Registers

Inventory Voucher Lists comprise the collectively set of Reports containing Voucher Data. These Reports constitute the lowest level of Inventory Reports and contain data of a voucher. On drill down from any voucher data in any type Inventory Voucher list, you get the selected Voucher in Alteration mode.

Here we discuss the following reports of the type Inventory Voucher List.

- **Day Book**: *Display>Day Book.* (§04)
- **Voucher Registers:** These Reports show the Accounts Voucher Registers with Inventory details (§06)
  - o **Sales Register:** *Display> Account Books > Sales Register*
  - o **Purchase Register:** *Display> Account Books > Purchase Register*
  - o **PoS Register:** *Display> Account Books > PoS Register*
  - o **Journal Register:** *Display> Account Books > Journal Register*
  - o **Debit Note Register:** *Display> Account Books > Journal Register > Debit Note Register*
  - o **Credit Note Register:** *Display> Account Books > Journal Register > Credit Note Register*
  - o **Stock Journal Registers:** *Display> Inventory Books >Stock Transfers* (§07)
- **Stock Voucher Register**: The Stock Voucher Registers are obtained through successive drill down from any Summary Report, reaching upto a Stock Item / Month

and then drill down through the Stock Item / Month to get voucher lists of the selected Item / Month, like:

- o *Display > Inventory Books > Stock Item*
- o *Display > Inventory Books > Group Summary*. Select a Stock Group
- o *Display > Inventory Books > Ageing Analysis*. Select a Stock Group
- o *Stock Summary*. Select a Stock Group

04 Day Book

Day Book is a datewise list of all types of Voucher. In Sales / Purchase Vouchers may contain Inventory details.

Select *Display>Day Book* to get Day Book the Day Book for the current Date (F-2). Click F12:Configure to get *Day Book Configuration* screen (F-4B/02-16). At Day Book Configuration screen (F-4B/02-16), set *Yes* at *Show Inventory Details also* to get Day Book with inventory details. Click *F1:Detailed* to see the ledger account details for each voucher

- The Item details are shown under the Sales Purchase Ledger Account (net of Item Discount, if any), the Item Level Discount % & Discount amount is not shown in Day Book, as Item level Discount is reduced from the Sales Value.
- The Dr / Cr against the Ledger Account indicates whether the amount is added /reduced in the Voucher.
  - o In *Sales Voucher*, Cr indicates the amount is added, while Dr indicates the amount is reduced in the voucher.
  - o In *Purchase Voucher*, Dr indicates the amount is added, while Cr in Purchase Voucher indicates the amount is reduced.
  - o In *Debit Note*, Cr indicates the amount is added, while Dr indicates the amount is reduced in the voucher.
  - o In Credit Note, Dr indicates the amount is added, while Cr indicates the amount is reduced.

To get Day Book for a selected Voucher Type, Click *F4: Chng Voucher* (§06/02-16), and select the Voucher Type (Sales, Purchase, Debit Note & Credit Note).

05 Stock Voucher Lists

Stock Voucher Lists (F-3A) are linked Reports to various Inventory Monthly summary statements, for a selected Item, as described below. Drill Down from Monthly summary to get the Voucher List for the selected Month. Click *F2:Period* and specify the period to get the Stock Voucher list for the specified period

- Select *Display > Inventory Books > Stock Item* and then select an Item to get Item Monthly Summary. Now select a month to get Stock Vouchers for the selected Month.
- Select *Display > Inventory Books > Group Summary*. Select a Stock Group / Stock Item to get *Stock Item Monthly Summary*. Now select a month to get Stock Vouchers for the selected Period.
- Select *Display > Inventory Books > Ageing Analysis*. Select a Stock Group / Stock Item to get Stock Item Monthly Summary. Now select a month to get Stock Vouchers for the selected Period
- Select *Display > Inventory Books > Exception Report > Negative Stock*. Select an Item to get Item Monthly Summary. Now select a month to get Stock Vouchers for the selected Period.
- Select *Stock Summary*. Select a Stock Group / Stock Item to get Item Monthly Summary. Now select a month to get Stock Vouchers for the selected Period.

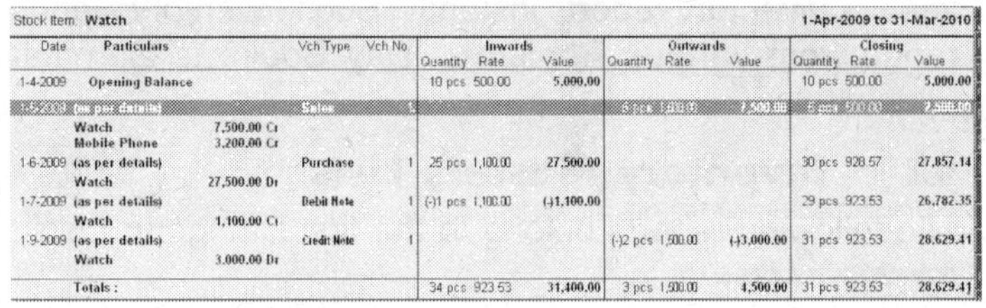

Stock Item: Watch — 1-Apr-2009 to 31-Mar-2010

Date	Particulars		Vch Type	Vch No	Inwards Quantity	Rate	Value	Outwards Quantity	Rate	Value	Closing Quantity	Rate	Value
1-4-2009	Opening Balance				10 pcs	500.00	5,000.00				10 pcs	500.00	5,000.00
1-5-2009	(as per details)		Sales	1				5 pcs	1,500.00	7,500.00	5 pcs	500.00	2,500.00
	Watch	7,500.00 Cr											
	Mobile Phone	3,200.00 Cr											
1-6-2009	(as per details)		Purchase	1	25 pcs	1,100.00	27,500.00				30 pcs	928.57	27,857.14
	Watch	27,500.00 Dr											
1-7-2009	(as per details)		Debit Note	1	(-)1 pcs	1,100.00	(-)1,100.00				29 pcs	923.53	26,782.35
	Watch	1,100.00 Cr											
1-9-2009	(as per details)		Credit Note	1				(-)2 pcs	1,500.00	(-)3,000.00	31 pcs	923.53	28,629.41
	Watch	3,000.00 Dr											
	Totals :				34 pcs	923.53	31,400.00	3 pcs	1,500.00	4,500.00	31 pcs	923.53	28,629.41

F-3A: Stock Vouchers List for an Item

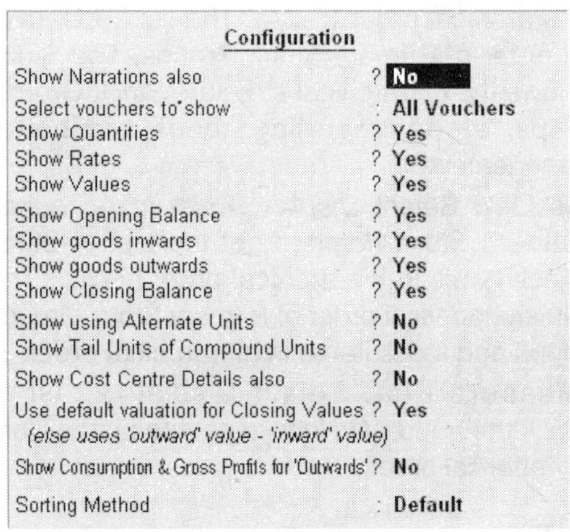

Configuration

Show Narrations also	? No
Select vouchers to show	: All Vouchers
Show Quantities	? Yes
Show Rates	? Yes
Show Values	? Yes
Show Opening Balance	? Yes
Show goods inwards	? Yes
Show goods outwards	? Yes
Show Closing Balance	? Yes
Show using Alternate Units	? No
Show Tail Units of Compound Units	? No
Show Cost Centre Details also	? No
Use default valuation for Closing Values (else uses 'outward' value - 'inward' value)	? Yes
Show Consumption & Gross Profits for 'Outwards'	? No
Sorting Method	: Default

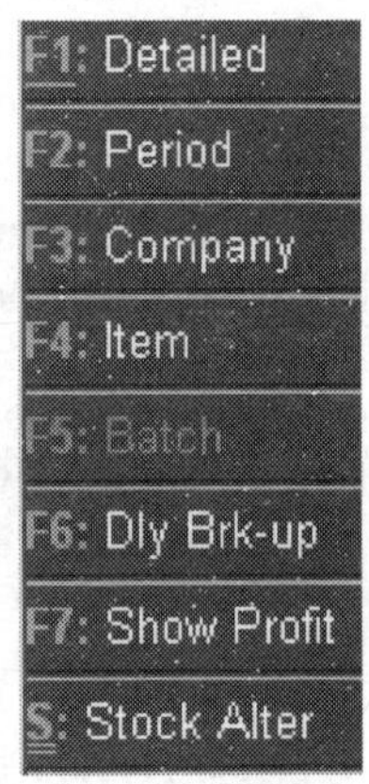

F-3B Stock Vouchers List Configuration F-3C Buttons

The Stock Voucher list in Condensed format (Click *F1:Condensed* toggle button – F-3C) shows the Inward / Outward & Stock column in respect of the selected Item. So, it is like a columnar Stock Ledger of the selected Stock Item.

The Stock Voucher list in Detail format (Click F1:Detail toggle button – F-3C) shows the details of all Items transacted in a voucher, but the Inward /Outward & Stock column shows the quantity in respect of the selected Item (F-3A). So, it is like a composite Journal & Ledger of all the vouchers in which the Item is transacted.

06 Accounts Voucher Register with Inventory details

Voucher Registers are list of Vouchers. Voucher like Sales,

Purchase, Debit & Credit Note may also contain Inventory details (F-4A). Select the desired Register as described below. Select a month to get Monthly Register. Click *F2:Period* and set the desired period to get the Voucher Register for selected Period.

- **Sales Voucher Register**: Select *Display > Account Books > Sales Register.*
- **Purchase Voucher Register**: Select *Display > Account Books > Purchase Register.*
- **Debit Note Register**: Select *Display > Account Books > Journal Register > Debit Note Register.*
- **Credit Note Register**: Select *Display > Account Books > Journal Register > Credit Note Register.*
- **Journal Register**: Select *Display > Account Books > Journal Register > Journal Register.*

Inventory Details: At Voucher Register, click *F12: Configure* to get Voucher Register Configuration screen (F-2B/02-16),. At Voucher Register configuration screen (F-2B/02-16), Set *Yes* at *Show Inventory Details also* to get the Inventory details (when you set *No* at *Show Extract of Vouchers*). The Item details (Name, Quantity, Value etc) is displayed under the respective ledger for which Inventory details are entered (F-4A)

List of All Sales Vouchers — 1-Apr-2009 to 2-Apr-2009

Date	Particulars				Vch Type	Vch No.	Debit Amount	Credit Amount
1-4-2009	**Anil Agencies**				**Sales**	1	**2,600.00**	
	Sales		**2,700.00 Cr**					
	Add Gel Pens	10.0 stp	120.00/stp	1,200.00				
	Implemnting Tally 9	3 Pcs	500.00/Pcs	1,500.00				
	Discount on Sale		**100.00 Dr**					
2-4-2009	**Praveen Traders**				**Sales**	2	**1,520.00**	
	Sales		**1,470.00 Cr**					
	White Paper Sheet	5 Pcs	300.00/Pcs	1,470.00				
	Delivery Charges		**50.00 Cr**					

F-4A: Voucher Register with Inventory details

Extract of All Sales Vouchers — 1-Oct-2009 to 31-Oct-2009

Particulars	Inwards Qty	*Rate*	Amount	Outwards Qty	*Rate*	Amount
Lamp				**5 Pieces**	**135.00**	**675.00**
CFL Lamp				5 Pieces	135.00	675.00
Philips CFL Lamp 20W				*5 Pieces*	*135.00*	*675.00*
Switches				**5 Pieces**	**60.00**	**300.00**
Single Switches				5 Pieces	60.00	300.00
Switch Anchor 15A				*5 Pieces*	*60.00*	*300.00*
Grand Total :				**10 Pieces**	*97.50*	**975.00**

F-4B: Inventory Extract of Sales Voucher Register

07 Stock Journal Voucher Register

Select *Display > Inventory Books > Stock Transfer* to get a list showing the number of Stock Journal vouchers in each month.

List of All Stock Journal Vouchers — 1-Apr-2009 to 31-Mar-2010

Date	Particulars		Vch Type	Vch No.	Inwards Quantity	Outwards Quantity
1-4-2009	**Cello Ball Pens**		Stock Journal	1		1 Pcs
	White Paper Sheet	(-)1 Pcs				
	Items damaged					

F-5A: Stock Journal Voucher Register

Drill down through a month to get Stock Journal Voucher List. Click F2:Period and set the desired period to get the Stock Journal Voucher Register for selected Period (F-5A). Click *F12:Config* to get Voucher Register Configuration screen (F-5B) and F-5C shows the buttons at Voucher Register Display.

Configuration

Show Extract of Register	? **No**
Show Columnar Register	? **No**
Format	: **Detailed**
Show Narrations also	? **Yes**
Show Billwise Details also	? **No**
Show Cost Centre Details also	? **No**
Show Inventory Details also	? **No**
Show Bank Details also	? **No**
Appearance of Names	: **Name Only**
Sorting Method	: **Default**

F-5B:Stock Journal Voucher Register Configuration

F1: Detailed
F2: Date
F2: Period
F3: Company
F4: Chg Vch
F5: Columnar
F6: Extract

F-5C Buttons at Stock Journal Voucher Register

Negative Stock Exclusion

Sometimes Negative Stock may appear due to mistake in entry, wrong measurements etc. Such negative value wrongly affects the Stock Value (the Negative Value will be deducted in the Stock Value Report). To ignore the negative value (its value will not be considered while adding up stock value of Items in Stock report), at behaviour section of Stock Item entry (F-4A/02-01), set *Yes* at *Ignore Negative Balances.*

08 Closing Stock value in Final Accounts

The Closing Stock Value is shown in P L Statement (§06/04-01) as well as in Balance Sheet. When Accounts & Inventory are Integrated (At F11:Features > Inventory Features, when you set Yes at *Integrate Accounts with Inventor)*, no entry is made for Closing Stock. Closing Stock Value as per Inventory System, as shown in Stock Summary, is automatically posted in P Statement and in Balance Sheet.

When Accounts & Inventory are NOT Integrated (At *F11:Features > Inventory Features*, when you set *No* at *Integrate Accounts with Inventor)*, you have to manually enter the Closing Stock Value in Closing Stock Ledger Account.

At Gateway of Tally, select *Accounts Info>Ledger>Alter* & select the Stock Account (under *Stock-in Hand* group). Now enter Date & Value for Closing Stock for respective Date (§03/03-10)).

Drill Down

- **Integrated mode**: When you drill down for the *Closing Stock* from Balance Sheet (under Current Assets) or Profit & Loss Account, (at Credit Side), you get the Stock Summary Report as per Inventory System.
- **Non-integrated mode**: When you drill down for the *Closing Stock* from Balance Sheet (under Current Assets)

or Profit & Loss Account, (at Credit Side), you get the Stock Values as per values entered at Closing Stock Ledger (under Stock-in-Hand Group under Current Assets) Account (F-1/03-10). At the respective Ledger Account under Stock-in-Hand, enter the Date and the corresponding Closing Balance Value for each Date

You may change the option at *Integrate Accounts with Inventory* at *F11:Features > Accounts Features* at any time to get the Accounts as per Integrated (as per Inventory System Closing Stock Value) or Non Integrated (as per Book Stock Value) system, for comparison.

FAQ: Frequently Asked Question

FAQ-1: I am a trader. I like to get the gross profit in respect of each sale transaction

Ans: Select *Display>Account Books>Sales Register*, select a month (or set the period), to get Sales Voucher Register. Click *F12: Configure* and set *Yes* at *Show Consumption & Gross Profit for Outwards.* Against each Sale Bill, the Gross Profit would also be shown.

FAQ-2: I like to get comparative sales realization from different customers and purchase cost from different supplier of an Item

Ans: Select Display>Inventory Books>Movement Analysis> Stock Item Analysis and select the Item for which you want the comparative Analysis of Sales & Purchase (§07/05-08). You get Partywise Sales & Purchase summary figures of the selected Item, showing quantity, basic & effective rate and value in respect of each Supplier & Customer

FAQ-3: I like to get a summary of all Items Produced & Consumed in my factory for a specified period

Ans: Select Display>Inventory Books > Movement Analysis> Transfer Analysis and select Stock Journal Voucher Type to get the Production & Consumption of Items in separate columns, showing the Quantity, Effective Rate & Value in respect of Production & Consumption (§10/05-08).

FAQ-4: How I can get Gross Profit figures with value of Sales / Cost of Sales

Ans: At Profit & Loss Account Statement (F-1). Click *F12:Configure* & set *Yes* at *Show Vertical Profit & Loss.* You will get the Trading Account at Top, showing Sales, Direct Income & Cost of Sales (Purchases adjusted with Opening & Closing Stock values) & Direct Expenses, showing the Gross Profit, followed by the figures of Indirect income & Indirect Expenses, showing the net Profit.

Multi Account Inventory Reports 01-07

01 Multi Accounts Inventory Reports Printing

So far, we have discussed Reports through Display, to view the Report on screen. Drill down & trace Back, Print the Report on paper/ or Preview the Report on screen, from the current screen (without leaving the current screen)

Through Display, you may get report from the current screen. So, you get the Report for the selected Item only. It is useful to view a desired report quickly on screen for information.

Multi Account Reports provide better facility print reports for a selected period. You may select one or many Stock Items (under Stock Group / Stock Category) at a time. It is useful to print the Report on Paper for Record keeping / Distribution. The printing configuration options are almost similar to Display Configuration discussed earlier. The format & contents of the Multi Account Report are mostly similar to Display (or Reports printed from Display).

Multi Account Inventory Reports may be broadly classified as follows

- **Inventory Bocks**: Stock Item, Stock Transfer, Physical Stock Register
- **Multi Account Reports with Inventory details**
    - o **Day Book:** List of Vouchers for all Voucher Types, or a selected Voucher Type
    - o **Account Books**: Sales Register, Purchase Register, Debit Note, Credit Note, Journal Book, Cash Book, Bank Book
    - o **Outstandings:** Outstandings, Party Outstandings, Age Analysis

Tally has unique capability to include Inventory details also in Accounting Reports. For example, in Cash / Bank Book, Party Ledger or Outstanding Bills Statement, you can also get the details of Item details of Sales / Purchase, Debit / Credit Note. So, when talking with Parties regarding some disputes, you can immediately find out the complete details of the Items involved in the same statement. You do not have to look and flip through several reports together. Normally Inventory details are separated from Accounting Reports.

02 Multi Account Inventory Reports Printing Menu

At Gateway, select *Multi Account printing* to get Multi Account printing menu (F-1A). At Multi Accounts Printing menu, select *Inventory Books* to get Multi Account Inventory Books Printing menu (F-1B), providing for Printing of:

- **Stock Item:** To print Stock Item Ledger
- **Stock Transfer:** To print Stock Journal Register

We now discuss each option under the Multi Account Inventory Books Printing Menu (F-1A).

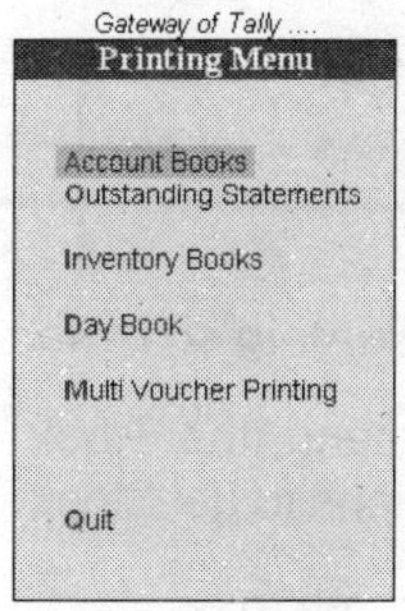

F-1A: Multi Account Printing menu

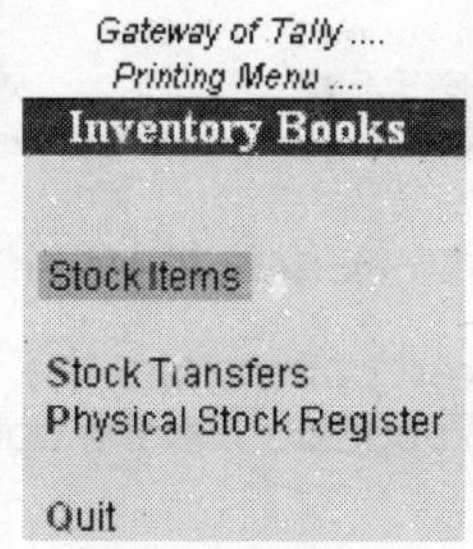

F-1B Multi Account Inventory Books Printing menu

F-1C Multi-Account Books Printing menu

03 Multi Account Stock Item Ledger printing

This report shows the Stock Item ledger for selected Stock Items (F-2A)

Select *Multi Account Printing > Inventory Books > Stock Item* (F-1B) to get Stock Item menu.

The Stock Item menu, contains following options:

- **All Items**: To print the report for All Stock Items.
- **One item**: To print report for ne selected Stock Item Select the Stock Item from the list of Stock Items.
- **Group of Items**: Select the Stock Group from the list of Stock Groups, to print the report for all Items under the selected Group.

Hard Disk
Item Register
1-Oct-2009 to 31-Oct-2009

Date	Particulars	Vch Type	Vch No.	Inwards			Outwards			Closing		
				Quantity	Rate	Value	Quantity	Rate	Value	Quantity	Rate	Value
1-10-2009	Opening Balance			10 pcs	3,000.00	30,000.00				10 pcs	3,000.00	30,000.00
12-10-2009	Raj & Computer Ltd.	Sales	1				7 pcs	3,500.00	24,500.00			
	Raj & Computer Ltd.	Credit Note	1				(-)2 pcs	3,500.00	(-)7,000.00	5 pcs	3,000.00	15,000.00
25-10-2009	Matrix Computer	Debit Note	1	(-)2 pcs	3,000.00	(-)6,000.00				3 pcs	3,000.00	9,000.00
	Totals :			8 pcs	3,000.00	24,000.00	5 pcs	3,500.00	17,500.00	3 pcs	3,000.00	9,000.00

F-2A: Multi Account Stock Item Register

Report Titles

Item Register

From (blank for beginning)	: 1-4-2009
To (blank for end)	:
Format	: Condensed
Show Voucher Numbers also	? Yes
Show Narrations also	? No
Select vouchers to show	: All Vouchers
Show Quantities	? Yes
Show Rates	? No
Show Values	? Yes
Show Opening Balance	? Yes
Show goods inwards	? Yes
Show goods outwards	? Yes
Show Closing Balance	? Yes
Show using Alternate Units	? No
Show Tail Units of Compound Units	? No
Use default valuation for Closing Values (else uses 'outward' value – 'inward' value)	? Yes
Show Consumption & Gross Profits for 'Outwards'	? No
Method of Balancing	: Yearly
Start fresh page for each Account	? Yes
Start fresh page for Balancing	? No
Set Alphabetical print range	? No
From (blank for beginning)	: To (blank for end)
Print index page	? Yes

F-2B: Multi Account Stock Item Register Printing screen

On selecting the desired option from the menu, the Stock Printing screen (F=2B) appears. Set the options to get Stock Item Register (F-2A).

04 Multi Account Stock Journal Register

This report shows the list of Stock Journal Vouchers only for a specified period (F-3A)

Select *Multi Account Printing > Inventory Books > Stock Transfers* (F-1B) to get Stock Journal Register printing screen (F-3B). Set the options as desired to get Stock Journal Register (F-3A).

Stock Journal Register

1-May-2008 to 2-May-2008

Page 1

Date	Particulars	Vch Type	Vch No.	Inwards Quantity	Outwards Quantity
1-5-2008	**Mobile Phone LG 1210** *1 Pc damaged,*	Stock Journal	1		1 Nos

F-3A: Multi Account Stock Journal Register

Report Titles

Stock Journal Register

From (blank for beginning)	: 1-4-2009
To (blank for end)	: 31-3-2010
Show Extract of Register	? No
Show Columnar Register	? No
Format	: Detailed
Show Voucher Numbers also	? Yes
Show Narrations also	? Yes
Show Billwise Details also	? Yes
Show Cost Centre Details also	? No
Show Inventory Details also	? Yes
Show Bank Details also	? No

F-3B: Multi Account Stock Journal Register Printing screen

05 Multi Account Day Book with Inventory Details

At gateway, select *Multi Account Printing>Day Book* (F-1A) to get the Day Book printing screen (F-5B/02-16/S1). Set *Yes* at *Show Inventory Details also.* Consequently, the Inventory details in the respective Vouchers (Sales, Purchase, Debit Note, Credit Note, Journal, Stock Journal), are also included (F-4)

Day Book

1-May-2008 to 31-May-2008

Page 1

Date	Particulars				Vch Type	Vch No.	Debit Amount / Inwards Qty	Credit Amount / Outwards Qty
1-5-2008	**A K Traders**				**Sales**	6	**18,933.53**	
	Sales							**18,933.53**
	VCR TT LG	25 Nos	193.60/Nos	4,839.89				
	VCR TT LG	25 Nos	194.60/Nos	4,864.89				
	Mobile Phone LG 2220	3 Nos	1,746.30/Nos	5,238.89				
	Headphone Earpad TechCom	5 Nos	797.97/Nos	3,989.86				
1-5-2008	**Headphone Large I Ball**				**Physical Stock**	1	1 Nos	
	Headphone Large Microtech						199 Nos	
	Mobile Phone Nokia 2210						29 Nos	
1-5-2008	**Mobile Phone LG 1210**				**Stock Journal**	1		1 Nos
2-5-2008	**A K Traders**				**Sales**	7	**4,066.36**	
	Sales							**4,066.36**
	Headphone Earpad TechCom	5 Nos	813.27/Nos	4,066.36				
2-5-2008	**HDFC Bank (A/c No.151065)**				**Sales**	8	**11,346.00**	
	Sales							**11,346.00**
	VCR Portable Philips	100 Nos	42.08/Nos	4,208.00				
	Mobile Phone LG 2220	4 Nos	1,784.50/Nos	7,138.00				
2-5-2008	**D K Enterprises**				**Purchase**	1		**18,513.21**
	Purchase						**18,513.21**	
	Transistor Pocket Bush	25 Nos	202.38/Nos	5,059.55				
	Mobile Phone Nokia 3220	100 Nos	48.35/Nos	4,834.55				
	Transistor TT Star	50 Nos	100.19/Nos	5,009.55				
	Headphone Earpad TechCom	5 Nos	721.91/Nos	3,609.56				

F- 4: Multi Account Day Book with Inventory Details

In Accounts Voucher (Sales, Purchase, Debit Note, Credit Note), Stock Item quantity details are shown in Particulars column (Amount figures are shown in Debit / Credit Column), while for Inventory Voucher (Stock Journal, Physical Stock) the Stock Item quantity details are shown in Inward / Outward columns.

06 Multi-Account Accounts Books with Inventory Details

We have seen various accounting reports containing only financial figures in respect of Sales / Purchase transactions (like Sales Register, Purchase Register, Debit Note, Credit Note, Journal Book).

Multi Account Printing of Account Books have been described earlier. At gateway, select *Multi Account Printing>Account Books* to get Multi-Account Account Books Menu (F-1C)

To print Inventory details also contained in Accounts Voucher (Sales, Purchase, Debit Note, Credit Note, Journal) in the following books, set *Yes* at the configuration option *Show Inventory Details also* of the respective account books (F-1A/02-17/S1, F-1D/02-17/S1, F-4A/02-17/S1, F-4B/02-17/S1, F-6A/02-17/S1, F-6B/02-17/S1, F-10A/02-17/S1, F-12B/02-17/S1, F-13B/02-17/S1, F-14A/02-17/S1)

06.01 Multi Account Sales Register with Inventory details

Sales Register
1-May-2008 to 2-May-2008

Date	Particulars				Vch Type	Vch No.	Debit Amount	Credit Amount
1-5-2008	**A K Traders**				**Sales**	5	**18,933.53**	
	Sales							**18,933.53**
	VCR TT LG	25 Nos	193.60/Nos	4,839.89				
	VCR TT LG	25 Nos	194.60/Nos	4,864.89				
	Mobile Phone LG 2220	3 Nos	1,746.30/Nos	5,238.89				
	Headphone Earpad TechCom	5 Nos	797.97/Nos	3,989.86				
1-5-2008	**HDFC Bank (A/c No.151065)**				**Sales**	6	**6,384.94**	
	Sales							**6,384.94**
	VCR Portable Philips	100 Nos	41.37/Nos	4,137.47				
	Transistor Pocket LG	20 Nos	112.37/Nos	2,247.47				
2-5-2008	**A K Traders**				**Sales**	7	**4,066.36**	
	Sales							**4,066.36**
	Headphone Earpad TechCom	5 Nos	813.27/Nos	4,066.36				
2-5-2008	**HDFC Bank (A/c No.151065)**				**Sales**	8	**11,346.00**	
	Sales							**11,346.00**
	VCR Portable Philips	100 Nos	42.08/Nos	4,208.00				
	Mobile Phone LG 2220	4 Nos	1,784.50/Nos	7,138.00				
							Total: 40,730.83	

F- 5A: Multi Account Sales Register with Inventory details

Purchase Register
1-May-2008 to 31-May-2008

Page 1

Date	Particulars				Vch Type	Vch No.	Debit Amount	Credit Amount
2-5-2008	**D K Enterprises**				**Purchase**	1		**18,513.21**
	Purchase						**18,513.21**	
	Transistor Pocket Bush	25 Nos	202.38/Nos	5,059.55				
	Mobile Phone Nokia 3220	100 Nos	48.35/Nos	4,834.55				
	Transistor TT Star	50 Nos	100.19/Nos	5,009.55				
	Headphone Earpad TechCom	5 Nos	721.91/Nos	3,609.56				
27-5-2008	**HDFC Bank (A/c No.151065)**				**Purchase**	2		**5,589.80**
	Purchase						**5,589.80**	
	VCR Portable Philips	150 Nos	37.27/Nos	5,589.80				
						T		**24,103.01**

F-5B: Multi Account Purchase Register with Inventory details

At gateway, select *Multi Account Printing>Account Books> Sales Register* to get the Multi Account Sales Register printing screen (F-10A/03-04/S1). Enter the period & set the options to get the Sales Register (F-5A).

06.02 Multi Account Purchase Register with Inventory details

At Gateway, select *Multi Account Printing>Account Books> Purchase Register* to get the Multi Account Purchase Register printing screen. Enter the period. Now set the Period & set the options (F-10B/03-04/S1) to get Multi Account Purchase Register (F-5B)

06.03 Multi Account Debit Note Register with Inventory details

At Gateway, select *Multi Account Printing>Account Books> Journal Register>Debit Note Register* to get the Multi Account Debit Note Register printing screen. Enter the period & set the options (F-12A/03-04/S1) to get Multi Account Debit Note Register (F-6A)

Debit Note Register
1-May-2008 to 31-May-2008

Date	Particulars				Vch Type	Vch No.	Debit Amount	Credit Amount
2-5-2008	**D K Enterprises**				**Debit Note**	1	**600.00**	
	Purchase							**600.00**
	Transistor TT Star	1 Nos	600.00/Nos	600.00				

F-6A: Multi Account Debit Note Register with Inventory details

F-6B: Multi Account Credit Note Register with Inventory details

Credit Note Register
1-May-2008 to 31-May-2008

Date	Particulars				Vch Type	Vch No.	Debit Amount	Credit Amount
2-5-2008	**A K Traders**				**Credit Note**	1		**250.00**
	Sales						**250.00**	
	VCR TT LG	1 Nos	250.00/Nos	250.00				

06.04 Multi Account Credit Note Register with Inventory details

At Gateway, select *Multi Account Printing>Account Books> Journal Register>Credit Note Register* to get the Multi Account Credit Note Register printing screen. Enter the period & set the options (F-12B/03-04/S1) to get Multi Account Credit Note Register (F-6B)

06.05 Multi Account Journal Register with Inventory details

At Gateway, select *Multi Account Printing>Account Books> Journal Register>Journal Register* to get the Multi Account Journal Register printing screen. Enter the period & set the options (F-1C/01-07,F-2/01-07/S1) to get Multi Account Journal Register (F-7)

Journal Register
1-Jul-2008 to 31-Jul-2008

Date	Particulars	Vch Type	Vch No.	Debit Amount	Credit Amount
1-7-2008	**A K Traders**	**Journal**	3	**1,500.00**	
	Sales				**1,500.00**
	VCR TT LG 1 Nos 1,500.00/Nos 1,500.00				

F-7: Multi Account Journal Register with Inventory details

Sales
Ledger Account
1-May-2008 to 2-May-2008

Date	Particulars	Vch Type	Vch No.	Debit	Credit
1-5-2008	By **Opening Balance**				**19,651.99**
1-5-2008	By **A K Traders**	**Sales**	5		18,933.53
	VCR TT LG 25 Nos 193.60/Nos 4,839.89				
	VCR TT LG 25 Nos 194.60/Nos 4,864.89				
	Mobile Phone LG 2220 3 Nos 1,746.30/Nos 5,238.89				
	Headphone Earpad TechCom 5 Nos 797.97/Nos 3,989.86				
	By **HDFC Bank (A/c No.151065)**	**Sales**	6		6,384.94
	VCR Portable Philips 100 Nos 41.37/Nos 4,137.47				
	Transistor Pocket LG 20 Nos 112.37/Nos 2,247.47				
2-5-2008	By **A K Traders**	**Sales**	7		4,066.36
	Headphone Earpad TechCom 5 Nos 813.27/Nos 4,066.36				
	By **HDFC Bank (A/c No.151065)**	**Sales**	8		11,346.00
	VCR Portable Philips 100 Nos 42.08/Nos 4,208.00				
	Mobile Phone LG 2220 4 Nos 1,784.50/Nos 7,138.00				
	To **A K Traders**	**Credit Note**	1	250.00	
	VCR TT LG 1 Nos 250.00/Nos 250.00				
				250.00	60,382.82
	To **Closing Balance**			60,132.82	
				60,382.82	**60,382.82**

F-8: Multi Account Ledger Account with Inventory details

06.06 Multi Account Ledger with Inventory Details

Inventory details in Ledger are available only for Sales / Purchase Account Ledgers (for which you have set Yes at *Inventory Values are affected* in the Ledger Creation).

At Gateway, select *Multi Account Printing>Account Books>Ledger* to get the Multi Account Ledger printing screen (F-2B/01-08/S1)

Enter the period & set the options (F-1C/01-08, F-1D/01-08, F-2B/01-08) to get Multi Account Ledger (F-8)

FAQ: Frequently Asked Questions

FAQ-1: What are the difference in characteristics of Reports printed through Display & Multi Account Reports

Ans: Report Printing Modes

You may print all reports in paper through *P:Print* option in Reports Display. The Display provides more reports (All reports in Display may be printed). Though the Report printing configuration options are quite similar in Display & Multi Account printing, Display provides a little more versatile configuration options.

- **Printing through Display**: At the Report Display screen, click *P:Print* button (or press Alt+P) to get Report printing screen, showing the current configuration options set. The Report is printed for the current period set.
- **Multi Account Printing:** Multi Account printing is available only for a selected reports available under Multi Account printing menu.

  Though the principal contents of the reports in both the methods are similar, the detailed contents and layout of the Report may differ in both the reports. So, select the desired method as per suitability of the contents and layout in your own context.

Report printing

- **Print the Report with current Configuration options:** Type *Y* at *Print Yes or No* option to print the Report for the current period & current configuration options set.
- **Modify the current Printing options and then print:** Type N at *Print Yes or No* option to get the cursor at the first Configuration option (Report Period) of the Printing Configuration screen. Now change the Report Period & other options as desired.

You may also set the respective options using the buttons at vertical button bar at the report printing scree.

Now type *Y* at *Print Yes or No* option, to print the Report with changed configuration options. Multi Account printing is more suitable for large volume and routine reports to be kept as part of Books of Accounts.

Point of Sales 01-08

01 Point of Sales (PoS)

PoS is an acronym for point-of-sale. Point of Sale can be a retail outlet, a checkout counter in a shop, or any other location where a sale transaction takes place with full payment made at counter.

The PoS system involves:

- Creation of PoS Voucher Type
- Creation of PoS Voucher Class

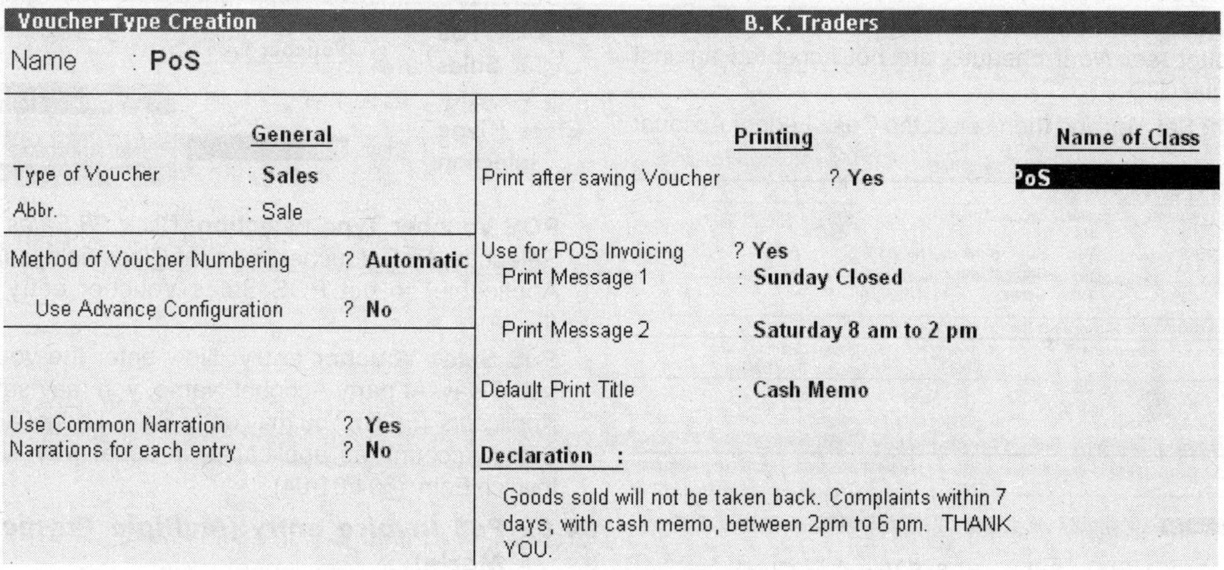

F- 1: PoS Voucher Type Creation

- PoS Invoice Entry
- PoS Invoice Printing
- PoS Register Printing

PoS Voucher is a special type of Sales Voucher type for preparation of quick Cash Memo at retail counters.

02 PoS Voucher Type creation

At *Accounts Info>Voucher Types>Create* to get Voucher Type creation screen (F-1)

Now set the options as follows (F-1)

- **Voucher Type:** At *Type of Voucher*, select *Sales* (as PoS is a Sales type Voucher)
- **Abbreviation:** At *Abbr*, enter short name (Abbreviation) of the Voucher Type. This is printed in all Books of Accounts, for the Voucher Type
- **Method of Numbering:** At *Method of Numbering*, select *Automatic* (§02/02-07/S1). The voucher numbers will be automatically posted serially as per Date
- **Mode:** At the field, *Use Advance Configuration,* set *No*
- **Common Narration:** At the field *Use Common Narration*, set *No* (In PoS, normally no Narration is entered for faster entry)
- **Ledger Narration:** At the field *Narration for each entry,* set *No* (In PoS, normally no Ledger is entered for faster entry)
- **Use for PoS Invoicing**: Set *Yes* to define it as PoS Type voucher, to inherit special characteristics of PoS voucher
- **Print Message 1 & Print Message 2**:Enter the messages texts that you like to print at the bottom of each Invoice.
- **Default Print Title**, Enter the Title of the Document to be printed.
- **Declaration**, Enter the text that would be printed at the end of each Bill after Voucher Narration.

03 PoS Voucher Class creation

Using PoS Voucher type, you can enter payment of one invoice in one mode only (like entire payment of the invoice made in cash). To accept payment in multiple mode in respect one invoice (e.g combination of Cash, Cheque, Credit Card, Gift Voucher etc), create a voucher class

To create a voucher class, enter the Voucher Class Name in Voucher Type Creation screen (F-1), as described above, to get the *Voucher Class definition* screen (F-2),otherwise press <enter>.

Default Ledger Accounts for Payment

At Voucher class definition screen (F-2), set *Yes* against the type of payment you like to include in the PoS voucher class and specify the Sales & other ledger accounts

- **Gift Voucher**: Set *Yes* and then select the Ledger Account (under Sundry Debtors), else set *No* (if Gift Voucher system is not implemented).
- **Credit / Debit Card Payment**: Set *Yes* and then select the Bank Ledger Account through which Credit / Debit Card accounts are managed, else set *No* (if Credit / Debit Card system is not implemented)
- **Cheque / DD**: Set *Yes* and then select the Bank Ledger Account, set *No* if cheques are not accepted against Cheque / DD
- **Cash:** Set *Yes* and then select the Cash Ledger Account

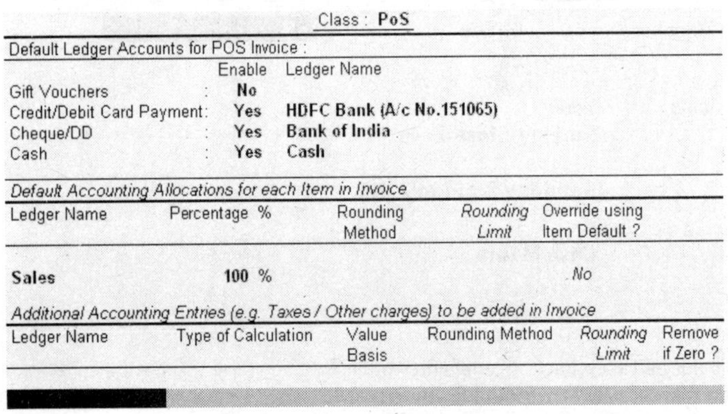

F-2: Ledger Set up in PoS Voucher Class

Next enter Sales Ledger & then enter accounting allocation ledgers in usual way, as applicable

04 PoS Invoice Entry

Having created PoS Voucher Type / Voucher Class, you may create *PoS Sales Invoice*. PoS Sales invoice is a special type of invoice, having following exclusive features

- No Customer ledger to be entered.
- Quick selection of Item manually from drop down list or through other input device like Bar Code
- Acceptance of multi mode payment in one invoice (like combination of Cash, Cheque, Credit / Debit Card, Gift Voucher etc).
- Entry of Tendered Amount and computation of refundable amount
- Small Invoice format, user defined massages in invoice
- Advanced Features of Sales Voucher class

04.01 PoS Invoice entry (Single Payment Mode)

Now we describe the PoS Voucher entry using PoS Voucher Type (when you select a Voucher Type in which PoS Voucher class has not been specified).

At Gateway, Select *Accounting Voucher.*

F- 3A: PoS Sales Voucher type selection (No Voucher Class)

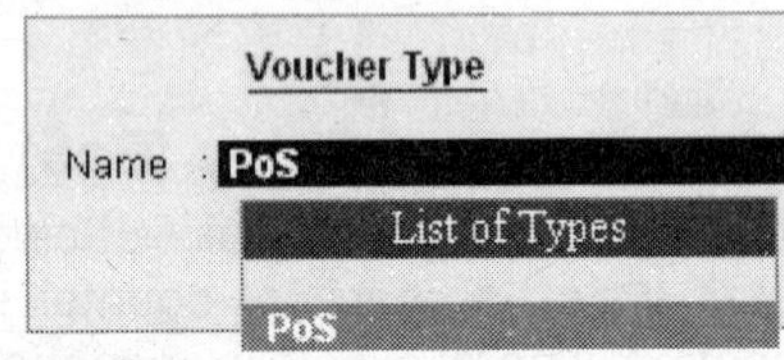

F-3B:PoS Sales Voucher entry header (No Voucher Class)

F-3C PoS Sales Voucher Class / Type selection

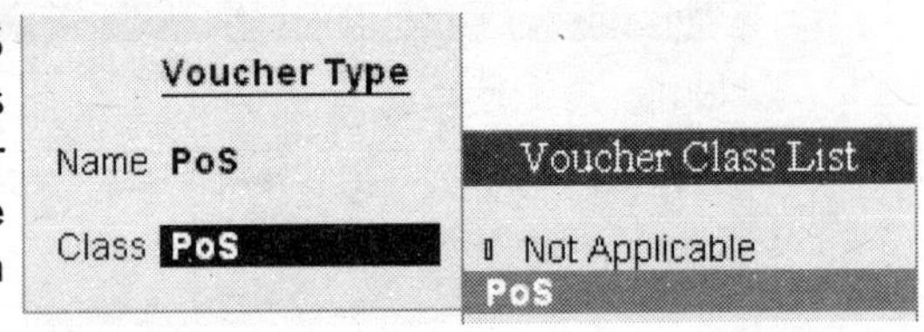

- **POS Voucher Type selection**: Click *F8:Sales* Button. Select the PoS Voucher Type (at Class field, select Not Applicable) to get POS Sales Voucher entry screen (F- 3A)
- **PoS Sales Voucher entry:** Now enter the voucher in usual way. At party Account Name, you may select *Not Applicable.* (F-3B). You may enter Sales Ledger and other Sales Account, as applicable, in usual way, likeSales Invoice Entry (§04/01-04)

04.02 PoS Invoice entry (Multiple Payment Mode)

At Gateway, Select Accounts Voucher.

- **POS Voucher Type selection**: Click *F8:Sales* Button. Select the PoS Voucher Type (at Class field, select the PoS Voucher Class) to get POS Sales Voucher entry screen (F-3C)
- **PoS Sales Voucher entry:** Now enter the voucher in usual way. At party Account Name, you may select *Not Applicable* You may enter Sales Ledger and other Sales Account, as applicable, in usual way.

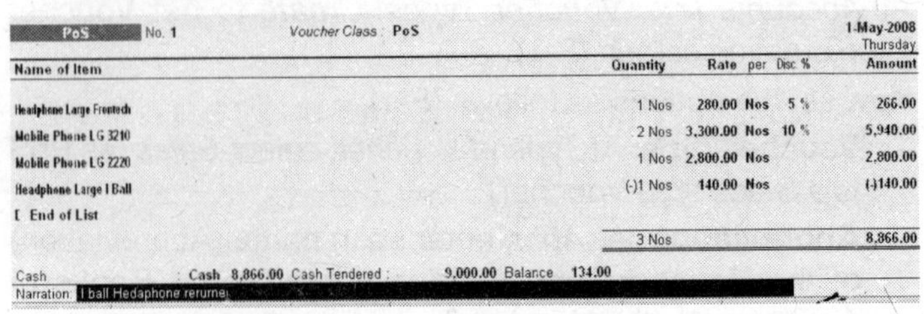

F-4: PoS Voucher entry (Single Payment Mode)

F-5 Single / Multi Account buttons in PoS

Payment Mode selection: You may enter Invoice in 2 modes as per modes of payment.

- **Single Mode Payment PoS Invoice**: Normally, you get the PoS voucher entry in single mode (or click P:Single Pymt button of the P:Single Pymt/ Multi Mode Pymt toggle button – F-5), in which you can enter only one mode of payment (like Cash). Having entered the Item details and Accounting Allocation, select the Cash / Bank Account (F-4)
- **Multi Mode Payment PoS Invoice**: If the payment of one invoice is received in multiple mode (like combination of Cash, Cheque, Credit / Debit Card, Gift Voucher etc), then click P:Mulit Mode Pmt button (of the P:Single Pymt/ Multi Mode Pymt toggle button – F-5) and you will get the prompts to enter multi mode payments received against the invoice (F-6)

Payment Entry:Now the Cash / Bank ledger accounts set in the PoS Voucher Class are available

- **Single mode entry**: Only the Cash Ledger Account would appear. Enter the amount of Cash Tendered (it cannot be less than the Bill Amount).
- **Multiple mode entry**: All the defined Ledger Account would appear. Enter the amount received in respect of each Ledger Account. The balance bill amount (Bill Amount - total amount received other than cash) will be shown at Cash Ledger Account.

Now enter the amount of Cash tendered (cash tendered cannot be less than amount shown n Cash Account)

The excess amount received & refundable to the customer (Cash Tendered – Cash Account) would be shown at the *Balance* field (fF-6). This makes it convenient to quickly refund the balance cash without mistake.

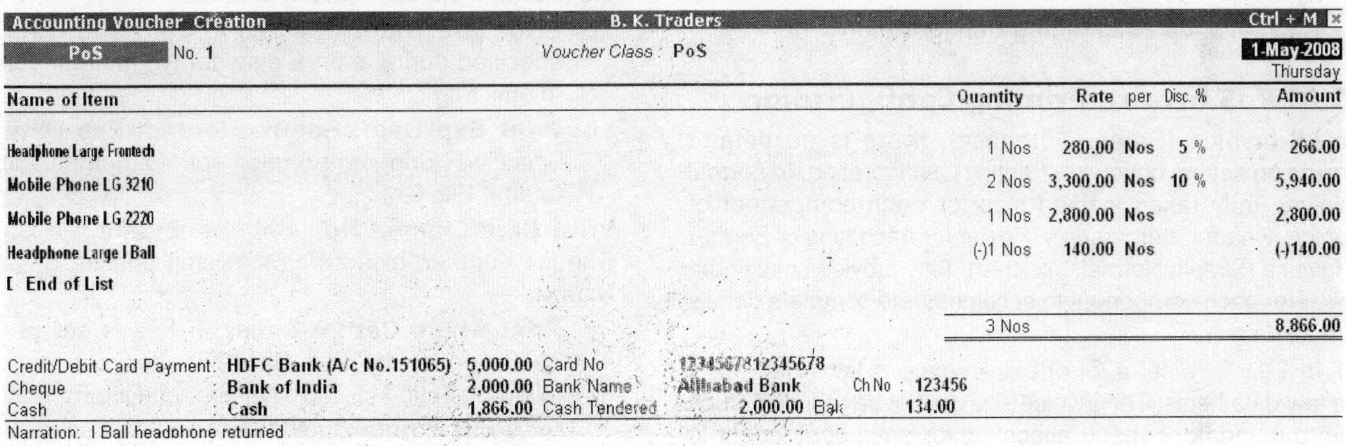

F-6: PoS Voucher entry (Multiple Payment Mode)

PoS Invoice Printer Selection

Normally PoS invoice are printed on line during entry. After the invoice data entry is over, click Print button (or press Alt+P) to get PoS Invoice printing dialogue. To select a different printer, click on Select Printer button (or press Alt+S) and select the printer from the list of Installed Printer (§04.05/02-14)

If necessary, select Print Format (§04.03/02-14) and select Print Mode (e.g Neat).

05 PoS Invoice Printing

Normally PoS invoice are printed on line during entry. After the PoS voucher entry is over, you get PoS Voucher printing screen (if you have set *Yes* at *Print after saving voucher* at the respective voucher Type creation screen: F-1). You may set the Printing Options (F-7B).

Having set the printing options at *PoS Invoice printing screen* (F-7B), set Yes at *Print Yes / No* to print the PoS Invoice (F-7A). At the bottom, the details of payment in each payment mode, cash tendered & refunded, if any are printed. At the end, the message line 1 & line 2 as specified in the PoS voucher type, if any, are printed (F-7A).

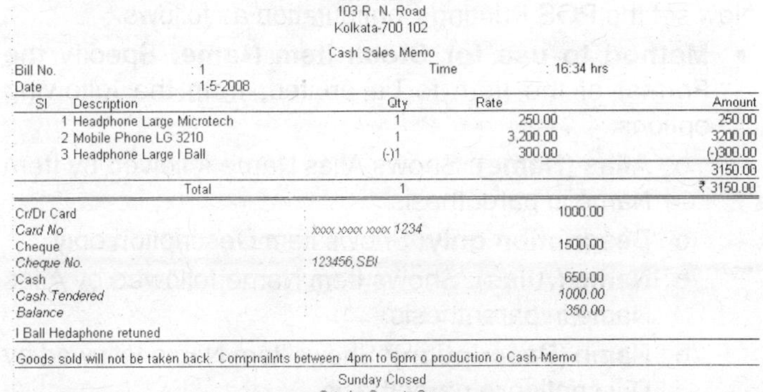
B. K. Traders
103 R. N. Road
Kolkata-700 102

Cash Sales Memo

Bill No. : 1 Time : 16:34 hrs
Date : 1-5-2008

Sl	Description	Qty	Rate	Amount
1	Headphone Large Microtech	1	250.00	250.00
2	Mobile Phone LG 3210	1	3,200.00	3200.00
3	Headphone Large I Ball	(-)1	300.00	(-)300.00
				3150.00
	Total	1		₹ 3150.00

Cr/Dr Card		1000.00
Card No	*xxxx xxxx xxxx 1234*	
Cheque		1500.00
Cheque No.	*123456,SBI*	
Cash		650.00
Cash Tendered		*1000.00*
Balance		*350.00*

I Ball Hedaphone retuned

Goods sold will not be taken back. Compnailnts between 4pm to 6pm o production o Cash Memo

Sunday Closed
Satuday 8 am to 2 pm

F-7A: Printed PoS Invoice

POS Invoice Printing Configuration

Title of Document	:	**Sales Memo**
Method to use for Stock Item Name	:	**Name Only**
Print Item Name in one line	?	**No**
Print Serial No.	?	**Yes**
Print Part No.	?	**No**
Print Quantity Units	?	**No**
Print Rate Column	?	**Yes**
Print Rate Units	?	**No**
Print Additional Description(s) for Item Name	?	**No**
Print Batch Details	?	**Yes**
Print Mfg Date	?	**Yes**
Print Card / Cheque No.	?	**Yes**
Print whole Card Number	?	**No**
Print Tax Analysis of Items	?	**No**
Print Narration	?	**No**
Print Default Name & Address of Party	?	**No**
Print Base Currency Symbol for Total	?	**Yes**

F-7B PoS Printing Configuration

05.01 PoS Invoice Printing Configuration

Unlike Invoice (Sales, Purchase), there is no default dimension setting options in Printing Configuration. In normal invoice, Tally takes a fixed size for each component of Invoice, Header, Item details, Footer for each type of Format of Invoice (Simple Normal, Voucher). Tally provides maximum space for each component to accommodate complete details with all data.

So, in Tally Invoice, a lot of blank space is left when there are few data Items. The invoice size cannot be reduced much due to mandatory space allocation for each component in the Invoice.

In PoS, very few Info are printed a header and the space in Item area are taken as per the number of Items (F-7A). So, the printed area of the length of Invoice may vary (convenient for Roll Paper invoice with variable length)

Now set the POS Printing Configuration as follows

- **Method to use for Stock item Name:** Specify the Format of the Item to be printed, from the following options:
  - o **Alias (Name)**: Shows Alias Name followed by Item Name in parenthesis
  - o **Description only**: Shows Item Description only
  - o **Name (Alias)**: Shows Item Name followed by Alias Name in parenthesis
  - o **Name (Description)**: Shows Item Name followed by Description in parenthesis
  - o **Name only**: Shows Item Name only. This is the default format shown in all reports
  - o **Name (Part No)**: Shows Item Name followed by Part Number in parenthesis
  - o **Part No (Name)**: Shows Part No followed by Item Name in parenthesis
- **Print Item Name in One Line:** Set *Yes* to print the Item details in a single line In *Neat Mode*, Tally will compress the letters to fit into one line, In *Quick Draft Mode*, Tally truncates the text and prints in multiple lines.
- **Print Serial Number:** Set *Yes* (default value) to print the running Serial Number for each Item (starting from 1), else set *No* to omit Serial Number in Invoice
- **Print Rate Column**: Set *Yes* to print the Rate column.
- **Print Additional Description of Item Name:** Set *Yes* to print the Item Additional Description (if entered in voucher input), else set *No* (default value) to omit Item Additional Description in the Invoice
- **Print Batch details:** Set *Yes* to print Batch Number (if specified during entry), else set *No* (default value) to omit Batch details.

  Having set Yes at the Batch details option, you may set the following options relating to Batch
  - o **Print Mfg Date:** Set *Yes* to print Mfg Date (if specified during entry), else set *No* (default value) to omit Mfg Date.
  - o **Print Exp Date:** Set *Yes* to print Exp Date (if specified during entry), else set *No* (default value) to omit Exp Date.
- **Print Card/Cheque No**.: Set Yes to print the Card/ Cheque number, else set yes to omit printing of Card Number
  - o **Print whole Card Number**: If Yes is set to the above option to print Card Number, set, set the following option for Card Number printing Format:
    - ***Print Whole Card Number:*** Set *Yes* at *Print Whole Card Number,* to print entire (16 digit) card number on the POS Invoice,
    - ***Print Last 4 digits of Card Number.*** Set *No* at *Print Whole Card Number,* to print only last 4 digit of card number (to conserve space and maintain secrecy of card number).
- **Print VAT Analysis of Items:** Set *Yes* to print Itemwise break up of Sales Values & VAT amounts, else set *No* (default value) to omit these details from Invoice printing.
- **Print Narration:** Set *Yes* (default value) to print Voucher common Narration. Set *No* to omit Voucher Common narration
- **Print Default Name & Address of Party**: Set *Yes* to print Party Name & Address as per Party Master, set *No* to omit Party Name from Invoice printing.
- **Print VAT Analysis of Items:** Set *Yes* to print Itemwise break up of Sales Values & VAT amounts, else set *No* (default value) to omit these details from Invoice printing.
- **Print Narration:** Set *Yes* (default value) to print Voucher common Narration. Set *No* to omit Voucher Common narration

- **Print Default Name & Address of Party**: Set *Yes* to print Party Name & Address as per Party Master, set *No* to omit Party Name from Invoice printing.

At printing screen, click *S:Select Printer* and select the Printer form the list of Installed Printers, to get the Printer set Up screen of the selected (which varies according to the printer model). Now set the paper Size and other options as desired. This way, you may customize the Paper size exclusively for PoS Invoice. It is recommended that you install dedicated printer for PoS.

At PoS print screen, set *Yes* at *Print Yes / No* to print the Invoice with current printing configuration set.

06 PoS Register

Having entered the PoS Invoice, you may print the PoS Register listing the PoS Invoices. Select *Display>Account Books>PoS Register* to get PoS Register for the current period (F-8). This report is similar to Sales Register (§05/02-16)

To view the inventory details in POS Register, at POS Register (F-8), click *F12:Configure* to get ***POS Register Configuration*** (F-4B/05-08). and set *Yes* at ***Show Inventory Details also***

PoS Register shows the list of PoS Invoice with separate column for each payment type (viz, Cash, cheque, gift voucher & Credit / Debit Cards).

List of All POS Vouchers								1-Apr-2008 to 31-Mar-2009
Date Vch Type		Vch No.		Gift Vouchers	Credit/Debit Card Pymt	Cheque	Cash	Total
1-5-2008 PoS		1			1,000.00	1,500.00	650.00	**3,150.00**
Sales			**3,150.00**					
Headphone Large Microtech	1 Nos		250.00					
Mobile Phone LG 3210	1 Nos		3,200.00					
Headphone Large I Ball	(-)1 Nos		(-)300.00					
Total:					1,000.00	1,500.00	650.00	**3,150.00**

F-8: PoS Register with Inventory Details

FAQ: Frequently Asked Questions

FAQ-1: How you create a PoS Voucher Type.

Ans: You may alter Sales Voucher Type to PoS Voucher Type or Create a New PoS Voucher Type (F-1)

- **Alteration of Sales Voucher Type**: If you use only PoS voucher for sale (like in Retail Store), you do not need to create a New Voucher Type. Select Sales to Alter the Sale Voucher Type as PoS Voucher Type. At *GoT>Accounts Info>Voucher Type>Alter* to get Voucher Type Alteration screen
- **Creation of PoS Voucher Type**: If you need to create a separate voucher type for PoS (apart from Sales Voucher), create a New Sales Voucher Type for PoS. At *GoT>Accounts Info>Voucher Type>Create, select Sales* to get Voucher Type Creation screen, to create a new PoS Voucher Type (od Type Sales)

Now make necessary entry / alteration at the Voucher Entry / Alterations screen (both look similar: F-1) and set the options, as explained earlier (§02).

Part 2

Advanced Inventory

We have already discussed about the default and Basic Features of Invoicing & Inventory. In this Part we discuss about various configuration options to customise data entry form, documents & Report to users requirements and advanced features of Invoicing & Inventory Reports.

- **Inventory Master** explains set up of configuration options and advanced features of Stock Groups & Stock Items. It also explains various additional identities & particulars of Stock Items, standard prices & costs and fast creation of multiple Inventory Masters in one entry screen.
- **Units of Measure** explains advanced features of *Alternate* and *Compound* Units of Measure (UoM).
- **Stock Categories** explains the parallel classification of Stock Items and various Inventory Reports analysed as per Stock Category.
- **Invoicing** describes various advanced aspects and entry of additional data in Invoice, configuration of Invoice Layout & contents as per user preferences.
- **Invoice Voucher Class** describes the process of pre-setting a customised Invoice Template with defined Account Ledgers and Computation methods for secured, fast and accurate Invoice Entry.
- **Point of Sales** explains customisation of Point of Sales Invoice features, layout & contents for Multi Mode Payment facilities and advanced features.
- **Price List** explains creation of various classes of Price Lists, Price updation of Individual or Group of Items together and printing of historical prices of any Item, and Invoicing using Price Lists.
- **Inventory Reports** explains the Display & Printing of massive set of Inventory reports with varied contents and formats.
- **Stock Query** shows the Stock Item Dash Board to get classified info of any selected Stock Item instantly at finger tip.

Organisations using only Basic Features of Inventory as covered in Part 4, may skip this Part.

Inventory Masters 02-01

01 Inventory Masters Configuration

Basic Options of Inventory Masters are explained earlier (§01/ 01-02). In this chapter, we describe additional Advanced Options.

At Gateway Click *F12: Configure* and select *Accts/ Inv Info* to get Masters Configuration screen (F-1A) to set the default Configuration options for Inventory Masters, applicable in general for all the companies having data residing in same directory.

> ***Note:*** *To activate Aliases, set* Yes *at* Allow Aliases along with Names *at Masters Configuration (F-1A).*
> *To activate Alias name at respective Master, further set* Yes *at* Allow Aliases along with Names *at respective Masters Configuration (F-2A, F-3A etc).*

Master Configuration		
Allow ALIASES along with Names	?	Yes
Allow Language ALIASES along with Names	?	No
Inventory		
Allow ADVANCED entries in Masters	?	Yes
Use PART NUMBERS for Stock Items	?	Yes
Use Description for Stock Items	?	Yes
Use REMARKS for Stock Items	?	Yes
Use ALTERNATE UNITS for Stock Items	?	Yes
Allow Std. Rates for Stock Items	?	Yes
Specify Default Ledger Allocation for Invoicing	?	Yes
Allow Component list details (Bill of Materials)	?	No
Use ADDRESSES for Godowns	?	No

F-1A: Inventory Masters Configuration

02 Alias Names

Alias Names for Accounts Master are explained earlier (§01/ 02-05).

At *F12:Configure > Accts/Inventory Info,* under *Master Configuration* section (F-1A), set *Yes* at *Allow ALIASES along with Names* to activate Alias Names for various Masters (both Accounts & Inventory).

Consequently, at the respective Master entry Configuration screen (F-2A, F-3A), you will further get an option to enable Alias entry in respective Inventory Master Entry screen (Stock Item, Stock Group, Stock Category, Godown, Voucher Type etc and also of Stock Item Part Number)

Alias are Alternate Names for Master Names (all types of Masters). Alias Names also appear In the selection list of Masters. So, you may select an Item by Alias Names also. So, Alias Name is used where Codes are used (for Stock Item etc) or Masters are selected through mechanical devices (like Bar Code, QR Code scanners etc)

You may use Alias Names as short names or other alternate names for quick selection of Inventory Masters (like Stock Item, Stock Category, Stock Groups, Godowns, Voucher Types etc). You may enter multiple distinct Alias Names for each Master record.

03 Advanced Entries of Inventory Masters

At Inventory masters Configuration (F-1A), set Yes at *Allow Advanced Entries in Masters,* to activate Advanced Entries in various Inventory Masters (like Sock Group, Stock Item, Unit of measure etc). Consequently, some additional fields become activated and available in various Inventory Masters, as explained at respective Masters entry.

04 Stock Group Advanced Features

Basic features of Stock Group entry has been explained earlier (§04/01-02). Having activated Advanced Entries for Inventory Masters (F-1A), you get additional entry fields in Stock Group Master Entry (F-3A), as explained here,

Stock Group Configuration		
Allow ALIASES along with Names	?	Yes
Allow Language ALIASES along with Names	?	No

F-2A: Stock Group Entry Configuration

Stock Item Configuration		
Allow ALIASES along with Names	?	No
Allow Language ALIASES along with Names	?	No
Allow ADVANCED entries in Masters	?	No
Use PART NUMBERS for Stock Items	?	No
Use Description for Stock Items	?	No
Use REMARKS for Stock Items	?	No
Specify Default Ledger Allocation for Invoicing	?	Yes
Use ALTERNATE UNITS for Stock Items	?	No
Allow Std. Rates for Stock Items	?	No
Allow Component list details (Bill of Materials)	?	No

F-2B: Stock Item Entry Configuration

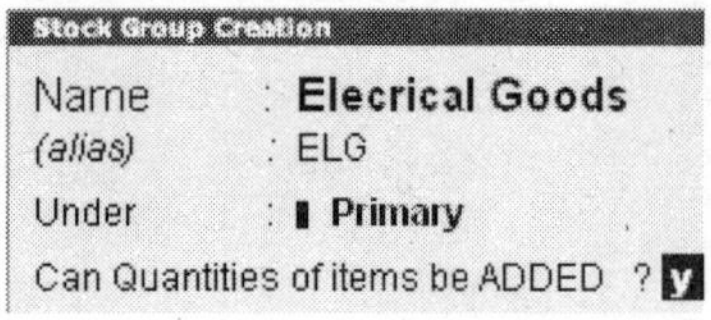

F-3A: Stock Group Entry

- **Stock Group Alias:** If you have set *Yes* at *Allow Aliases with Names* at Masters Configuration screen (F-1B), at *Stock Group Configuration* screen (F-2A), at the option *Allow ALIASES along with Names*:
  - o Set Yes to get the field *(alias)* at Stock Group Entry screen (F-3A)
  - o Set *No*, the field *(alias)* at Stock Group Entry screen will not appear. So, you would not be able to enter any Alias Name for Stock Group.
- **Stock Group Quantity:** At the field, *Can Quantities be added*, (F-3A) set:
  - o *Yes* to add up the Quantity of Subordinate Stock Items having same UoM and show against the Stock Group in Display/ Reports
  - o *No*, the Stock Group Quantity is not shown (as the quantity of subordinate Stock Group is not added)

The Quantity of Stock Items under a parent Stock Group is added only when the UoM of all such Stock Items are same. Otherwise, the Quantity is not added even if you set Yes at this option. So, it is preferred to always set *Yes* at *Can Quantities be added*, to get quantity of Stock Group when the UoM of all subordinate Stock Items are same (total quantity of Items of different UoM is meaningless and deceiving).

05 Stock Item Advanced Entries

Basic features of Stock Item entry has been explained earlier (§05/01-02). At Stock Item creation / alteration screen, click *F12:Configure* to get Stock Item Entry Configuration screen (F-2B), to set the following option:

Stock Item Alias Names: If you have set *Yes* at *Allow Aliases with Names* at Masters Configuration screen (F-1B), at *Stock Item Configuration* screen (F-2B), at the option *Allow ALIASES along with Names*:

- Set *Yes* to get the field *(alias)* at Stock Item Entry screen (F-4A) for:
  - o *Stock Item Alias Name*: Enter *Stock Item Alias Name* at *(alias)* just below the Stock Item name
  - o *Part Number Alias Name*: Enter *Part Number Alias Name* at *(alias)* just below the Part Number
- Set *No*, the field *(alias)* below Stock Item and Part Number, at Stock Item Entry screen (F-4A) will not appear. So, you would not be able to enter any Alias Name for Stock Item or Part Number.

You may enter multiple unique Stock Item Alias names and Part Number Alias names for each Stock Item (F-4A).

Having set *Yes* at *Allow Advanced Entries in Master* at *Masters Configuration screen* (F-2B), you get additional fields at Stock Item Masters entry (F-4A) as described next

06 Stock Item Behaviour

During entry / alteration of Stock Item (F-4A), at the right part of the Stock Item screen, you get the Stock *Behaviour* default options:

i. **Costing Method**: At *Costing Method* select the default Computation methods of Consumption & Stock in Hand, from the list of Costing methods (F-5A), as described next (§07)
ii. **Market Valuation Method**: At *Market Valuation Method*, select the default computation methods of Market Value of Stock in Hand, from the list of *Market Valuation Methods* (F-5B), as described next (§08)
iii. **Physical Stock Discrepancy:** At *Ignore Diff due to physical counting*, set up the options to reflect the effect of Physical Stock Voucher (for adjustment of Physical & Book stock difference) in reporting of stock figures, as described next (§09)

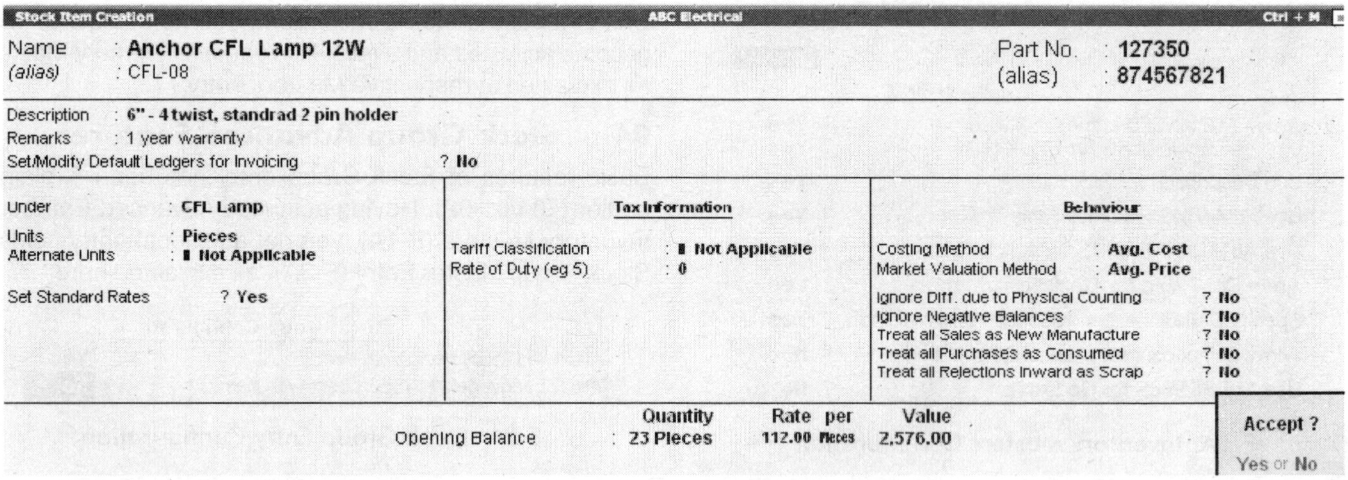

F-4A: Advance entry in Stock Item Master

iv. **Negative Stock Balances:** At *Ignore Negative Stock Balances* set the option of the effect of Negative Stock Balances (due to omission / mistake of Stock Accounting) in or non-adjustment of Balances, as described next (§10).

v. **Purchased Items Consumption**: At *Treat all Purchases as Consumed*, set the option for consumption of Purchased Items, as described next (§11).

vi. **Sales Items Production**: At *Treat All Sales as New Manufacture*, set the option for treatment of sold Items, as described next (§12).

vii. **Returned Items:** At *Treat all rejection inward a Scrap*, set the option of treatment of sold Items returned by the customers, as described next (§13).

Note: *Check the effect of the Behavious options in your context before changing the defaults.*

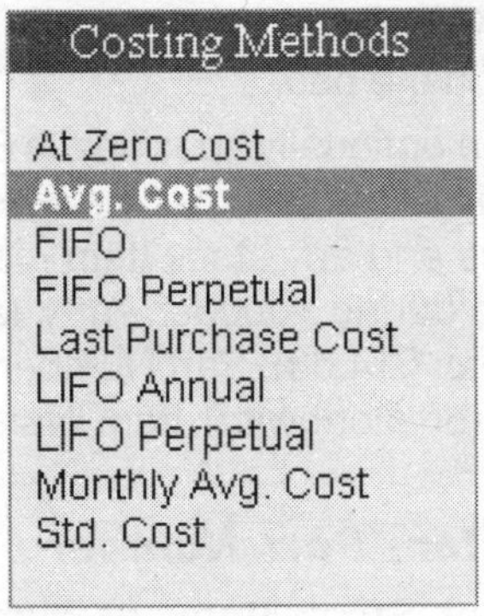

F-5A: Costing Methods List

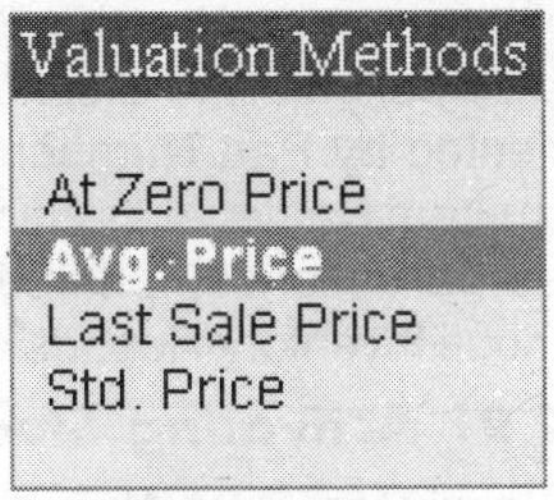

F-5B: Market Valuation Methods List

07 Costing Method

Select the default computation method to compute cost of Consumption & Stock in Hand, from the options available (F-5A). By default, the specified method would be applied to show the values in various Inventory Reports. However, alternate method may still be applied at the time of printing any specific report offering the option to specify valuation method

- o **At Zero Cost**: The Item value would be valued at Zero Cost (normally rejected / scrap having no realizable value, or FREE Items) are computed at zero cost
- o **Average Cost**: The Item would be valued at Weighted Average Cost for the current year
- o **FIFO**: The consumption would be valued at First In First Out method during the current year. So, the Stock-in-Hand would be valued at Latest Purchase Costs
- o **FIFO Perpetual**: The consumption would be valued at First In First Out method from the purchase time of oldest stock. So, the Stock-in-Hand would be valued at Latest Purchase Costs
- o **Last Purchase Cost**: The Item would be valued at Last Purchase Cost
- o **LIFO Annual**: The consumption would be valued at Last In First Out method during the current year. So, the Stock-in-Hand would be valued at Oldest Purchase Costs
- o **LIFO Perpetual**: The consumption would be valued at Last In First Out method from the earliest period. So, the Stock-in-Hand would be valued at Oldest Purchase Costs
- o **Monthly Average Cost**: The Item would be valued at Weighted Average Cost for the current month
- o **Standard Cost**: The Item would be valued at Standard Cost specified in Stock Item Master

08 Market Valuation Method

Market Valuation Method allows you to determine the realisable value of an Item (potential disposable value). The unrealised Profit / Loss (to be realized on sale) of an Item = Closing value as per Market valuation method - Closing value as per Costing Method. Costing Method is normally relevant for Consumable / Tradable Items, while Market Valuation Method is normally relevant for Manufactured Tradable Products.

Here you select the default computation methods of Market Value of Stock- in- Hand from the following methods:

- o **At Zero Price**: The Item would be valued at Zero Value (normally rejected / scrap having no realizable value, or FREE Items) are computed at zero cost
- o **Average Price**: The Item would be valued at Weighted Average Cost for the current year
- o **Last sales Price**: The Item would be valued at Last sale Price
- o **Standard Price**: The Item would be valued at Standard Sale Price specified in Stock Item Master

As per Accounting Standard, in Financial Statements (P & L Statement & Balance Sheet), the value of Inventory is to be taken as lower of the value as computed under Costing Method & Market Valuation Method

09 Stock Difference

Ideally, the Book Stock (Stock as per Stock Item Ledgers & Stock Statements) should match with the Physical Stock lying in Stores. However, due to some reasons, the Physical Stock may not exactly tally with the Book Stock found on measurement & counting.

At *Ignore Difference Due to Physical Counting:*

- Set *Yes* to consider the Book Stock in the Stock Reports (ignoring Physical Stock Voucher)
- Set *No* to consider the Physical Stock in the Stock Reports (as per Physical Stock Voucher)

10 Negative Stock

Ideally, there should never be Negative Stock as no one can

give more than one what is available in stock. Negative Stock Balances often result from missing entry of some voucher, mistake in quantity or entry of wrong stock Item (e.g Issue posted to another Item due to mistake in entry). This causes differences in Inventory Reports.

- Set *Yes* at *Ignore Negative Stock Balances* to get the figures of Stock in Inventory Reports ignoring the negative Stock Balances (due to omission / mistake of Stock Accounting).
- Set *No* at *Ignore Negative Stock Balances* to consider the effect of negative Stock Balances in Inventory Reports.

You may change the *Yes / No* options at any time to get the net effect of Negative Stock Balances of all the Stock Items.

11 Treatment of Purchases

Often small items are bought as and when required for immediate use and no issue voucher is created for its use (e.g maintenance items, office stationery etc), or in case of highly perishable goods (like Milk etc), where the Stock is completely sold on the same day.

To adjust the stock of such Items, at Stock Item creation / alteration screen, at *Treat all Purchases as Consumed* (F-4A),

- Set Yes to treat the purchases as consumption and adjust the stock accordingly. This avoids the entry of consumption,
- Set *No* (default) and make entry of consumption as usual

12 Treatment of Sales

Sometimes the goods bought or manufactured are sold immediately through numerous sales transactions. This is useful in case of manufacture of highly perishable goods (like Milk, Bakery Products etc). In such case, the day's Sales may be considered as Production / Purchase (he cannot keep the Item in stock as it will get spoilt). In such cases, Production / Purchase can be practically considered as equal to Sales,

To adjust the stock of such Items, at Stock Item creation / alteration screen, at *Treat all Sales as New Manufacture* (F-4A),

- Set *Yes* so that the Production / Purchase is automatically computed from Sales and the stock is adjusted accordingly. This avoids the entry of Production / Purchase. Otherwise,
- Set *No* (Default) and make entry of Production / Purchase as usual

13 Treatment of Rejection

Some organisations have a policy not to take back sold goods unless there is some manufacturing defects. In such case, the returned goods are not included in regular Stock

To treat Returned Goods as Rejected Items with no value, at *Treat all Rejection Inward at Zero Value*

- Set *Yes* so that goods returned are not accounted in Stock In Hand.
- Set *No* (default) to treat returned goods as normal Stock Item and included in Stock In Hand.

14 Stock Item Part Number

Many manufacturers use Part Number to precisely identify an Item.

Most manufacturers use their own Item ID (popularly known as Part Number). These IDs are referred by the manufacturers to precisely identify a product in their documents (price list, Invoices, Orders),

For example, a Book may be identified and referred in a catalogue by following:

- o Retailers own Publishers Item ID
- o Publisher's Own Item ID
- o ISBN
- o Library of Congress Catalogue
- o Bar Code Number printed on the book

Like Alias, *Part Number* may be optionally specified in Stock Item Consequently, the Part Number will also be listed in the selection list of Stock Items and any stock Item may be selected by Part Number also during voucher entry (apart from Item Name, Alias Name etc: §14.03). Part Number may also be optionally printed at (or alongwith) Item Name in various Inventory Reports.

14.01 Activating Stock Item Part Number

To activate Part Numbers at Stock Item, at Masters Configuration screen (F-2B), set *Yes* at *Use Part Numbers for Stock Items*

Consequently, during Stock Item Master entry (F-4A), you may enter Part Number. Consequently, you get the Part Number also at selection list of Items in voucher entry. Part Number may also be printed in Inventory Reports and Invoices / Orders / Challans)

14.02 Part Number Alias

If you have activated Alias Names (i.e Set *Yes* at *Use Aliases along with Names* at Masters Configuration – F-2B), then in Stock Item Master entry screen (F-4A), you will get field for Part Number Alias. You may enter multiple Part Number Alias Names one by one. To terminate part Number Alias Entry, press <enter> at Blank line at Part Number Alias Name.

The Part Numbers are also listed in the selection list of Masters in Inventory Voucher entry and you can select any Item by the Part Number.

Part Number Alias is useful when same Item is referred by different Part Number of different manufacturer. In such case, all the Part Number may be used through multiple Aliases

14.03 Stock Item Identities

There may be multiple name Alias & part Number Alias. So, you may create numerous Stock Item Identity for uniquely selecting an Item. This flexibility of setting user defined multiple identities is very useful to select Items in Voucher using any of such Stock Item identity. For example, each authority (Government, Statutory Bodies, manufacturers, Distributors attach their own identity for an Item. So, an Item may be referred by any of these Identities)

So, in Voucher or Item selection list of Stock Item, an Item may be selected by any of the following Identity of Stock Item, specified in Stock Item Name:

- Stock Item Name:
- Item Name Alias
- Part Number
- Part Number Alias

15 Stock Item Remarks

Apart from Stock Item Description, you may enter *Remarks* about any Stock Item for your internal information. Stock Item Remark does not get printed or shown in any Inventory Document or Report, but may only be viewed in Stock Query (§02/02-09)

15.01 Activation of Stock Item Remarks

At Inventory master Configuration (F-1A), set Yes at *Use Remarks for Stock Items* to activate Stock Item Remarks option. Consequently, at *Stock Item Configuration* screen (F-2B), you get the option *Use Remarks for Stock Items*, where you set *Yes* to activate Remarks option at Stock Item entry screen (F-4A)

Consequently, during Stock Item entry / alteration (F-4A), at *Remarks* field, you get may enter some internal remarks / private Info, regarding the Stock Item.

16 Stock Item Description

For Items having technical information & specification, it may be necessary to specify complete details in all documents (like Enquiry, Quotation, Delivery Notes, Invoice etc), for complete information and avoid litigation. For such Items, Item Description may be entered at *Description* field in Item Master.

Description entered in Item Master is carried in Inventory Voucher during entry, where it may be changed in the specific Inventory Voucher during entry (and may be optionally printed in the Inventory Report)

16.01 Activation of Stock Item Description

To activate the Item Description entry in Stock Item, at Accts/ Inv Info configuration screen (F-1A), set *Yes* at *Use Description for Stock Items.*

At Inventory master Configuration (F-1B), set Yes at *Use Description for Stock Items* to activate Stock Item Description option. Consequently, at Stock Item Configuration screen (F-2B), you get the option *Use Description for Stock Items*, where you set *Yes* to activate Description option at Stock Item entry screen (F-4A)

Consequently, during Stock Item entry / alteration (F-4A), at *Description* field, Stock Item Description is carried by default at Voucher entry screen (§03/02-04), where it may be changed, if needed. You get a limited space for Stock Item Description in a Part of input line (you cannot enter a Description longer than the permitted length).

> *[Tip: Plan about the contents of Description, how you like to Item Name / Description in Documents / Reports. Enter Description in Item master accordingly].*

17 Stock Item selection List Configuration

During Voucher Entry/ Reports Display etc, you select a specific Stock Item from a drop down list of Stock Item. To customize the property of drop down list as per your convenience, set the Configuration as explained below:

At *Gateway of Tally*, click *F12:Configure* to get *Configuration Menu.* At *Configuration Menu* select *General* to get *General Configuration screen.*

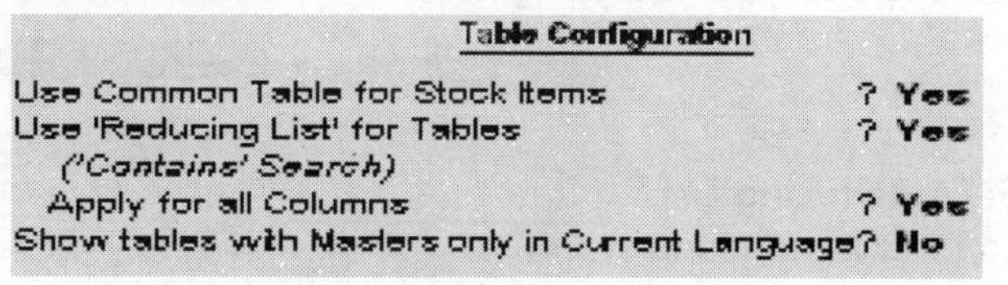

F-6A: Tables Configuration

F-6B: List showing Stock Item names only

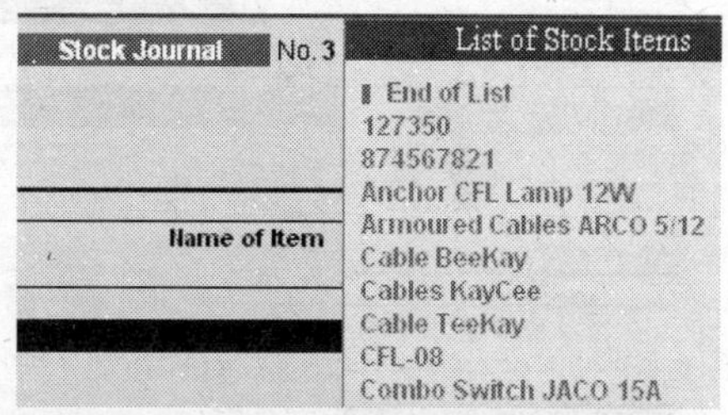

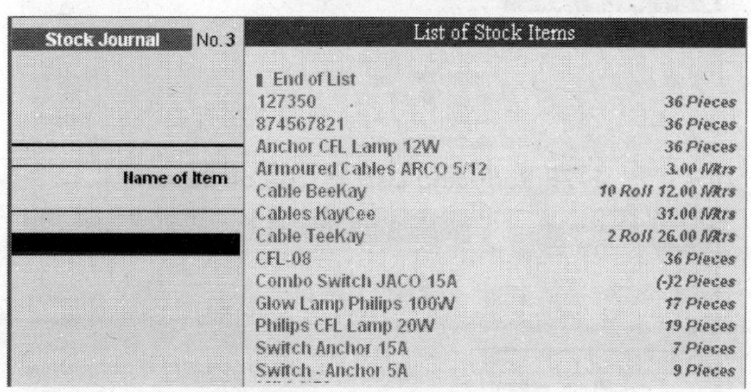

F-6C: List showing other columns of Stock Item name

At *General Configuration screen, under* the section Table Configuration (F-6A) set the method of Display of drop down list for selection of Stock Item from List of Stock Items (e.g in Voucher Entry, selection of Stock Item in Report etc), as follows:

At *Use Common Table for Stock Items* (F-6A)

- Set *Yes* to list only Stock Item Names are listed in the list of Stock Items (F- 6B)
- Set *No* to list other columns also of Stock Item (like Current Stock Quantity) are listed in the list of Stock Items (F-6C).

17.01 Reducing List of Matching Items

For quicker selection, you may set the option to shorten the list of Stock Items showing only the Items matching to the characters typed at Item Name column, as described below:

At *Use 'Reducing List' for Tables* (F-6A):

- Set Yes to get the reducing list starting from matching names (F-7A)
- Set No to get the complete list. The Items of matching characters are highlighted (F-7B)

Having set Yes at the option *Use 'Reducing List' for Tables*, at the next option *Apply for all columns*, set:

- Yes to show the matching Items in all the Columns (F-7C)
- No to show the matching Items in 1st Column only

F-7A:Reducing List, 1st Col, matching Items

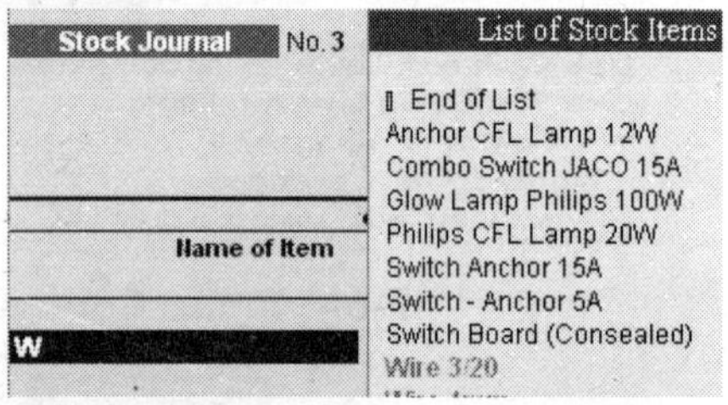

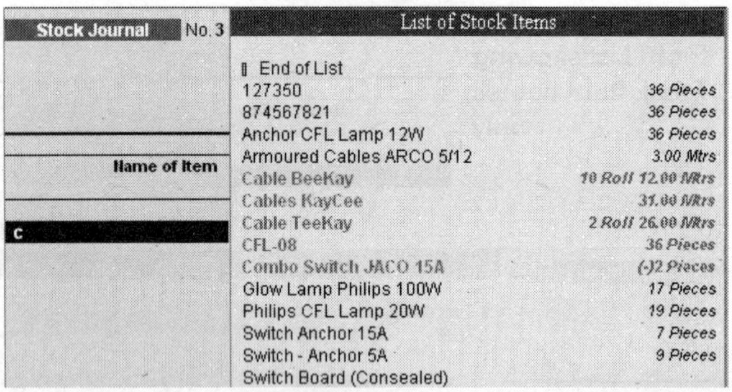

F-7B:Reducing List, 1st Col, all Items

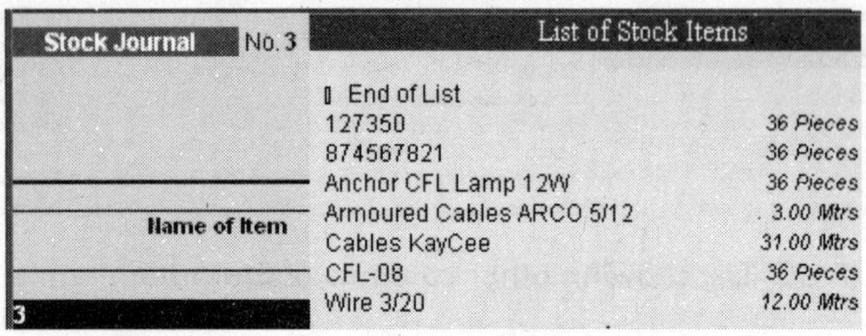

F-7C: Reducing List on all Columns

Table Configuration screen can also be invoked by pressing *Ctrl + Alt + F12* from Gateway of Tally

18 Stock Item Standard Price

Businessmen normally follow a *Standard Price* for sale of Stock Items, as fair business policy. To avoid repeated entry of price, avoid mistake and enable faster Invoice Entry, you may set the Standard Sale / Purchase price in Item master. During Invoice entry, the Standard Price will be carried in Sale / Purchase Invoice for the respective Item (the carried standard price may be modified in any Invoice, as necessary). This greatly helps in quick & correct Invoice entry, yet maintaining flexibility of entering different price in any Invoice.

18.01 Activation of Stock Item Standard Price

At *Inventory Master Configuration* (F-1B), set Yes at *Use Std. Rates for Stock Items* to activate Stock Item *Standard Price* option. Consequently, at Stock Item Configuration screen (F-2B), you get the option *Use Std. Rates for Stock Items*, where you set *Yes* to activate Standard Price option at Stock Item entry screen (F-4A)

Consequently, during Stock Item entry / alteration (F-4A), you get the option *Set (or Alter) Standard Rates* to activate Standard Sales & Cost Price entry in respective Stock Item Master.

18.02 Standard Price Entry

At *Set (or Alter) Standard Rates* (F-4A), set Yes to get *Standard Rates entry screen* (F-8), to enter Standard Sales / Purchase Rate for the Item.

At *Standard Rates entry screen* (F-8),:

- **Standard Cost**: At the left part, enter the Standard Cost (proposed Purchase Rate)
- **Standard Sale Price**: At the Right Part enter the Standard Selling Price (proposed Sale Rate).

At the respective columns, as follows:

- **Applicable Date**: At *Applicable From*, enter the Date from which the Rate is effective.
- **Rate**: At *Rate*, enter the Rate per unit as per Unit specified
- **Unit:** At Per field, enter the Unit at which the Rate is specified

> ***Note:*** *The Standard Cost is carried by default at Purchase Voucher entry, while the Standard Selling Price is carried as default at Sales Voucher entry (you may change them in current voucher being entered).The Standard Selling Price may differ from Pice List Price (§02/02-07)*

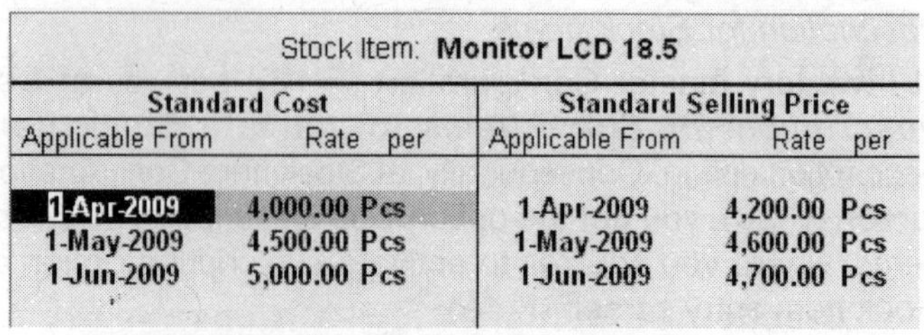

F-8: Stock Item Standard Rates entry

Change in Rate: When rate of any Item is changed, at Standard Price screen, enter the Effective date of new Rate and enter new Rates (for Purchase / Sale) as applicable (Do not edit the previous rate). This way, the chronological changes in Rates are readily available, which shows valuable historical info of changes in Standard Cost & Selling Price, over time.

19 Inventory Masters Entry in Multiple Mode

You have seen Entry of Stock Groups and Stock Items in single entry mode, where you may create only one record at a time. To create large numbers of Stock Groups and Stock Items takes a lot of time to enter individual record in the entry screen.

In such case, you may take advantage to Create, Alter or Display many Stock Groups and Stock Items in one screen more conveniently through Multiple Options in respective Master creation Menu.

Groups > CReate (under Multiple Stock Groups) to create multiple Stock Groups in one screen (F-9A)

- **Creation of Multiple Stock Items:**Select *Stock Items > CReate* (under Multiple Stock Items) to create many Stock Items in one screen (F-10A).

The process of creation of *Multiple Inventory Masters* are similar to creation of *Multiple Accounts Masters,* described earlier (§01/02-06)

F-9A & F-9B show Multiple Stock Group Creation screen & Button bar at the screen

F-10A & F-10B show Multiple Stock Item Creation screen & Button bar at the screen

19.02 Inventory Masters Display in Multiple Mode

Like Display of Multiple Accounts Masters (§04/02-06), you may Display the following Inventory Masters in multiple modes:

Select *Inventory Info > Stock Groups > Display* (under

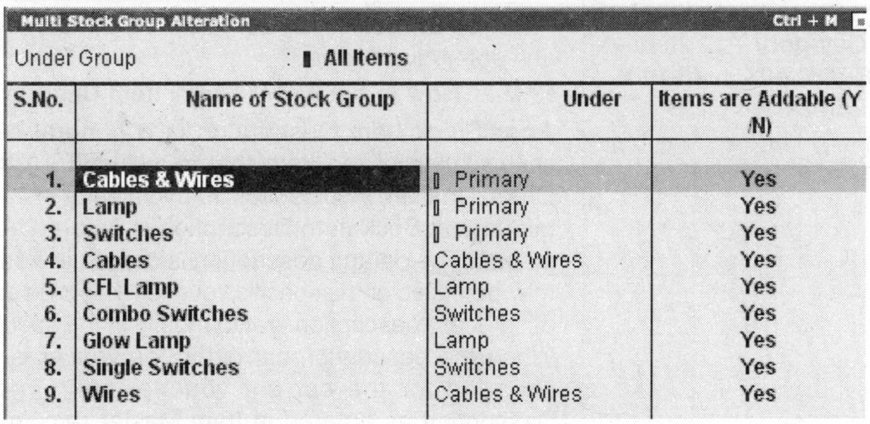

F-9A Multiple Stock Group creation / alteration

F-9B Buttons

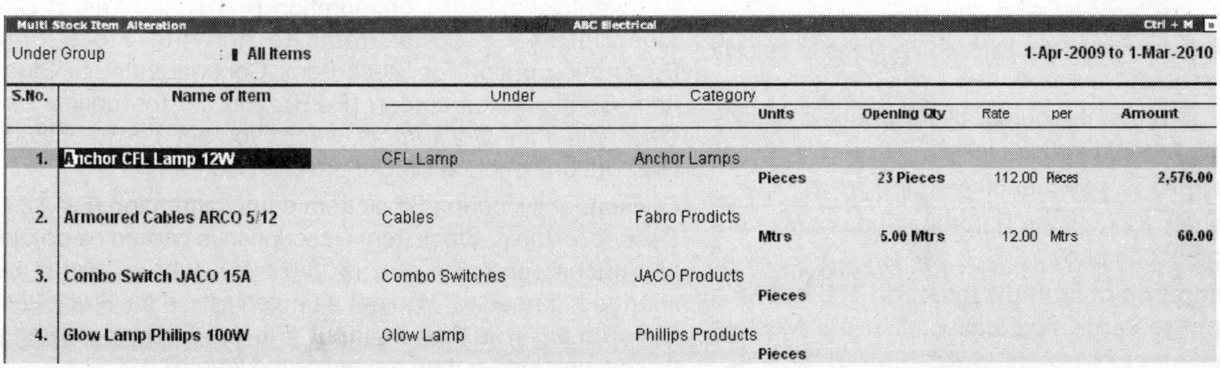

F-10A: Multi Stock Item Creation

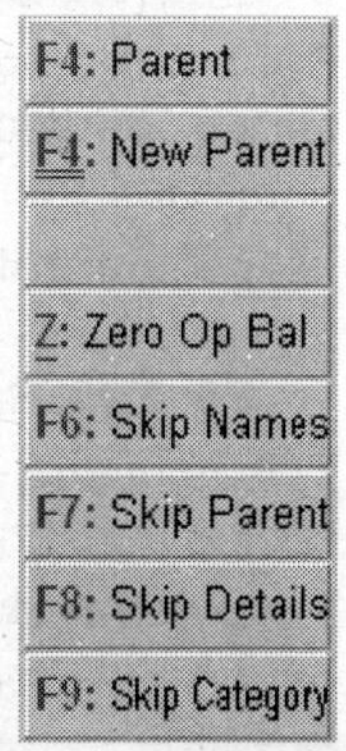

F-10B: Buttons

19.01 Inventory Masters Creation in Multiple Mode

Like Multiple Accounts Masters (§01/02-06), you may create the following Inventory Masters in multiple mode. At *GoT>Inventory Info* (F-1A/01-02):

- **Creation of Multiple Stock Groups**: Select *Stock*

Multiple Stock Groups) and select the Stock Group (select *All Items* (to display All Groups) to get Multiple Stock Groups screen, similar to Stock Group Entry screen (F-9A)

19.03 Inventory Masters Alteration in Multiple Mode

The process of Multiple Stock Item Master is similar to

creation screen, as described above (§19.01), and explained earlier (§05/02-06).

- Select *Inventory Info > Stock Groups > Alter* (under Multiple Stock Groups) and select *All Items* (to alter any Stock Group) or select the Group to list the child Stock Groups, carry out the desired alteration and press Ctrl+A to save.
- Select *Inventory Info > Stock Items > Alter* (under Multiple Stock Items) and select *All Items* (to alter any Item) or select the Category / Group to list the Stock Items for a Category / Group, carry out the desired alteration and press *Ctrl+A* to save.

19.04 Multiple Masters Multiple Mode Buttons

At Multiple Inventory Masters entry / display / alter screens, you may use the buttons as explained next. The following Table shows the appearance of buttons at the respective screen, which are similar to Multiple Accounts Masters discussed earlier (§06/02-06)

Buttons	Stock Group (F-9B)			Stock Category (F-7D/02-03, 7E/02-03)			Stock Item (F-10B)		
	C	D	A	C	D	A	C	D	A
F4: Parent:	√		√	√		√	√		√
F4: New Parent		√	√		√	√		√	√
F6: Skip Names			√			√			√
F7: Skip Parent			√			√			√
F8: Skip Details			√				√		√
F9:Skip Category							√		√
Z: Zero Balance									√

C=Creation, D=Display, A=Alter.

Changing Parent Stock Group: During Stock Item or Stock Group Alteration screen, use the following buttons to quickly enter the Parent Group:

- **F4: Parent**: To move the cursor to Parent field quickly and select the parent Group quickly.
- **F4: New Parent**: To select another stock group.

This is useful when you change Parent Groups of Masters copied from another company.

Fast & Bulk Alteration of multiple masters: The following buttons are helpful for quick modification of several Masters at a time

- **F6: Skip Names**: To skip Stock Item Name field in Stock Item entry for faster alteration of other data (other than Name. e.g when you enter or modify the Opening Stock in Stock Items).
- **F7: Skip Parent**: To skip Stock Group Name field for faster alteration of other data (other than Stock Group).
- **F8: Skip Details**: To skip the Opening Qty. field for faster alteration of data (other than Opening Balance).
- **Z: Zero Balance:** To make the opening Balance of the Stock Items as zero.

FAQ: Frequently Asked Questions

FAQ-1: How to set up for Alias Name

Ans: First activate the Alias name feature in general and then set Alias Name for respective Master record.

Alias name feature in General: At *F12:Configure > Accts/ Inventory Info,* under *Master Configuration* section (F-1A), set *Yes* at *Allow ALIASES along with Names* to activate Alias Names for various Masters (both Accounts & Inventory).

Set Alias Name for respective Master record: At respective Inventory Master Entry screen (Stock Item, Stock Group, Stock Category, Godown, Voucher Type etc, for which you like to activate Alias Name. At he respective Master entry / alteration screen, click F12:Configure and set *Yes* at *Allow Aliases with Names.*

Consequently, at Master enyr screen, set enter Alias names at Alias filed of the Master entry screen.

Thus you can selectively activate Alias for each Master record and enter Alias Name

FAQ-2: How to set up for Stock Item Description

Ans: Stock Item Description is a general description / specification of the Item that is included in Voucher (like Order, Challan, Invoice etc). To avoid entry in each voucher, the default Sock Item Description is entered at Stock Item master. The default description is carried in Voucher, which may be edited or the specific voucher. This plan enables entry of standard description, yet to modify in the specific voucher. When the description carried in the voucer is edited, it is changed for the current voucher only. The Standard Description as entered in Item Master remain unchanged (you can change it through Alteration of the Stock Item).

At Inventory master Configuration (F-1B), set Yes at *Use Description for Stock Items* to activate Stock Item Description option for Stock Item. Consequently, at Stock Item Configuration screen (F-2B), you get the option *Use Description for Stock Items*, where you set *Yes* to activate Description option at Stock Item entry screen (F-4A)

Consequently, during Stock Item entry / alteration (F-4A), at *Description* field, Stock Item Description is carried by default at Voucher entry screen (§03/02-04), where it may be changed, if needed. You get a limited space for Stock Item Description in a Part of input line (you cannot enter a Description longer than the permitted length).

FAQ-3: How to enter Standard Price for each Stock Item

Ans: To avoid repeated entry of price, avoid mistake and enable faster Invoice Entry, you may set the Standard Sale / Purchase price in Item master. During Invoice entry, the Standard Price will be carried in Sale / Purchase Invoice for the respective Item (the carried standard price may be modified in any Invoice, as necessary). This greatly helps in quick & correct Invoice entry, yet maintaining flexibility of entering different price in any Invoice.

Activation of Stock Item Standard Price

At *Inventory Master Configuration* (F-1B), set Yes at *Use Std. Rates for Stock Items* to activate Stock Item *Standard Price* option. Consequently, at Stock Item Configuration screen (F-2B), you get the option *Use Std. Rates for Stock Items*, where you set *Yes* to activate Standard Price option at Stock Item entry screen (F-4A)

Entry of Stock Item Standard Price

Consequently, during Stock Item entry / alteration (F-4A), you get the option *Set (or Alter) Standard Rates* appear to activate Standard Sales & Cost Price entry in respective Stock Item Master.

At *Set (or Alter) Standard Rates* (F-4A), set Yes to get *Standard Rates entry screen* (F-8), to enter Standard Sales / Purchase Rate for the Item (F-8)

Units of Measure 02-02

01 Units of Measure

We have discussed *Simple Unit of Measure*, where on item is measured in one Unit of Measure only (§03/01-02). However, sometimes, an Item may be measured in multiple *Units of Measure* (UoM).

- **Alternate Unit of Measure**: When a stock Item Quantity is expressed in any of two units, (like Bags or Kg, Box or Pcs). One is called *Base* Unit and another is called *Alternate* Unit.
- **Compound Unit of Measure**: When a stock Item is expressed in combination of two Units (like Hr-Min, Strip-Tabs, Box-Pcs etc). The larger one is called *Main* Unit and the smaller one is called *Tail* Unit

02 Alternate Units of Measure

Sometimes, an Item may be measured in either of 2 alternate units, For example, Nuts & Bolts may be measured in Pcs as well as in Kg. Hessian cloth may be measured in Metres & in Kg. Cables & Wires may be measured in Coils / Rolls & Mtrs. Here, the first unit is called the *Base* Unit and the second unit is referred as *Alternate* Unit, through a relationship between them (e.g 1 Pc = 25 Grams, 3.23 Kg = 17 Pcs, 480 Sheets = 23.5 Kg, 1 Roll = 25 Mtrs etc).

02.01 Alternate Units Set Up

- o **Activation for Alternate Unit:** At Gateway, click *F12: Configure* and select Accts /Inv Info to get Accounts / Inv Info Configuration screen (F-1A/05-01). Set *Yes* at *Use Alternate Units for Stock Items*, to activate Alternate Unit feature for the Company.
- o **Creation of Alternate Unit**: First create an Alternate Unit in the same way as creation of Simple Unit (§03/01-02). Alternatively, you may also create the Alternate Unit from within the Stock Item Entry screen, as explained next.
- o **Alternate Unit set up in Stock Item Master:** Having activated Alternate Unit feature for the Company (F-1A/02-01), In Item Master Entry / Alteration screen, you get following fields to enter details of Alternate Units (F-1A):
- o **Alternate Unit**: At Item Master Entry / Alteration screen (F-1A), after entry of Base Unit (e.g Mtrs), at *Alternate Units* field:
    - Select the Alternate Unit (e.g Roll) from the list of Units defined, or
    - Click *Alt+C* at Alternate Units field to get Unit creation screen and create the Alternate Unit as explained (§08/01-01). Select the Alternate Unit
- o **Conversion Factor**: At *where* field, enter the conversion factor between the Base Unit & Alternate Unit. Enter the value of Alternate Unit (e.g Roll) and then enter the equivalent quantity in Base Unit (Mtrs). [e.g 1 Roll (Alternate Unit) = 25 Mtrs (Base Unit].
- o **Standard Rates entry for alternate units in Stock Item master:** If Standard Rates is activated (§18.01/02-01), you get at Standard Rate entry screen (F-1B). At Standard Rate entry screen (F-1B), you may enter Rates of the Item either in Base Unit, Alternate Unit or in both, as explained earlier (§18.02/02-01)

02.02 Quantity & Price entry for Alternate Units

In Inventory Voucher you may enter Quantity in Base Unit and Rate in Base or in Alternate Unit (F-2A). The unit at which the Rate (Price) is entered is called the Rate Unit.

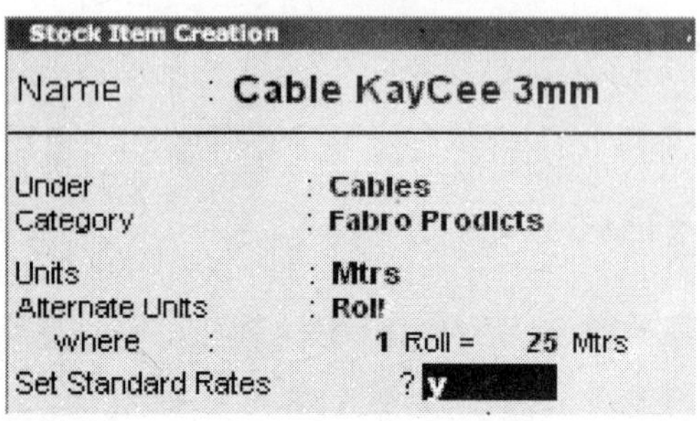
Stock Item Creation

Name : Cable KayCee 3mm

Under : Cables
Category : Fabro Prodicts
Units : Mtrs
Alternate Units : Roll
where : 1 Roll = 25 Mtrs
Set Standard Rates ? y

F-1A: Alternate Unit in Stock Item master

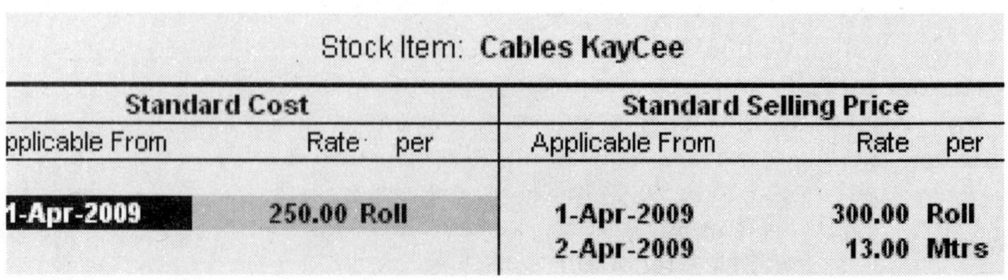
Stock Item: Cables KayCee

Standard Cost			Standard Selling Price		
pplicable From	Rate	per	Applicable From	Rate	per
1-Apr-2009	250.00	Roll	1-Apr-2009	300.00	Roll
			2-Apr-2009	13.00	Mtrs

F-1B: Entry of Quantity Rate in Basic and Alternate unit

> **Note:** *Quantity is entered in Main Unit, the corresponding Quantity in Alternate Unit is shown just below it. The Quantity is to be entered in Main Unit, while the Rate may be entered in Alternate Unit. The value is computed as per Rate Unit and the Quantity in the corresponding Rate Unit.*

Accounting Voucher Creation — Ctrl + M

Sales No. 5 — 1-Mar-2010, Monday

Ref. :

Party's A/c Name : **P.K.Motors**

Sales Ledger : **Sales**

Name of Item	Quantity	Rate	per	Amount
Cables KayCee	13.00 Mtrs *(0.52 Roll)*	13.00	Mtrs	169.00
Cables KayCee	26.00 Mtrs *(1.04 Roll)*	300.00	Roll	312.00
				481.00

F-2A: Item quantity & rate entry in Base & Alternate unit

- **Quantity:** In Inventory Voucher, the Base Unit may be entered at Quantity field. The equivalent Quantity in *Alternate* unit would be displayed in parenthesis, just below the Base Quantity, as per the conversion factor specified in the Item master. To specify the *Unit* for the quantity entered, type the quantity and then type the first letter (or letters) of the Unit. For example to enter 5 Mtrs, type 5m. To enter 2 Rolls, type 2r. If the Base & Alternate Unit Name starts with same letter, type more letters to make both distinctive [for e.g for Pc (pieces) & Pk (packets), both starting with P, type 2Pk, 5Pc]
    - o **Quantity in Base Unit**: When you enter quantity in *Base* unit (specify the Base Unit), the computed quantity in *Alternate* unit would be displayed in parenthesis as per the conversion factor specified in the Item master.
    - o **Quantity in Alternate Unit**: When you attempt to enter quantity in Alternate unit, Tally will instantly replace it with the equivalent quantity in Base unit (as per the conversion factor) and show at Quantity field. The Quantity entered in Alternate Unit would be shown below (in parenthesies).
- **Rate** You may enter Rate in either unit.
- **Amount:** The value is computed as per Rate Unit specified. So, if the *Rate* in both units does not correspond as per conversion factor, differences will result.

Normally, the price of larger unit is comparatively lower than smaller unit (e.g Rs 300 / Roll of 25 Mtrs, Rs 13 per Mtr). Keeping in mind that you can enter quantity in Base unit only (equivalent quantity in alternate unit will be displayed for info). you should decide the Base Unit & Alternate Unit. There is no hard & fast rule that Base Unit should be larger or smaller (but computation will be simpler when smaller unit is base unit). You can have in any way as convenient to you. If you sell mostly in Mtrs, then Mtrs should be Base unit and Rolls should be alternate unit, with relationship as 1mtr =.04 Rolls. Remember to set sufficient places of decimals for larger unit to avoid error due to fractions.

03 Compound Unit of Measure

Normally, the Unit of Measure contain only one element of Unit (like Pc, Kg- called Simple Unit of Measure), But sometimes an Item may be expressed in a Unit which is composed of two component units. For example, a Box of 10 Pcs, Strip of 20 Tablets, Tin of 4 Kgs. Traders like to maintain such units as trade is normally done in both units (whole sale / large trades in bigger unit & small / retail trades in smaller unit).

In such case, 2 units are created and the quantity in one unit (e.g Box) is defined in terms of the other unit (e.g Pcs). Compound units show the quantity two components - Main Unit (the bigger unit) and the Tail unit (the smaller unit)

Several compound units composed of same simple unit may even be created (like Bottle of 100 Tabs, Bottle of 20 Tabs, Tin of 2 kg, Tin of 4 kg etc).

The following table shows some examples of Compound Units and how the Quantity is expressed in Compound Units]

1st Unit (Basic unit)	2nd Unit (Tail unit)	Compound UoM	Relationship	Quantity	Representing
Tin	Kg	Tin of 4 Kg	1 Tin=4Kg	1-2 2-0 0-2	1 Tin 2 Kg= 6 Kg Kg2 Tin = 8 2 Kg
Strip	Tab	Strip of 20 Tabs	1 Strip=20 Tab	1-92-00-12	1 Strip 9 Tab = 291 Tab 2 Strip = 40 Tab 12 Tab

03.01 Creation of Compound Unit of Measure

To create Compound Unit of Measure, at Gateway, select *Inventory Info> Unit of Measure* to get Unit Creation screen.

- **Creation of Constituent Simple Units**: First, the constituent simple units are to be created as usual (§03/01-02). For example, to create Unit of *Strip of 20 Tablets*, both the Units – Roll & Mtrs, must be created first, as Simple Units, as explained earlier (§03/01-02) At larger unit (e.g Roll), provide sufficient number of decimal places to express fractional values (e.g 3).

- **Creation of Compound Unit**: To create compound unit, at Unit Creation screen (F-3A), select *Compound* at Type field (press Backspace at the first field to get the cursor at Type field) to get Compound Unit creation screen (F-4A)

  At Compound Unit creation screen (F-4A), at First Unit field, select the Main unit from the list of Units and enter the conversion factor (relationship) between Main & Tail unit. Next, select the Tail Unit. Now the Compound Unit (which is another Unit distinct from the 2 constituent Simple Units) is created (F-4A).

  So, for Compound unit, (Roll of 25 Mtrs) 3 units are to be created, 2 Simple Units (Roll & Mtrs) and 1 Compound unit (Roll of 25 Mtrs). In the respective Item Master, the Compound Unit (F-3A) should be specified as the UoM of the Item (not the constituent simple units). During voucher entry, the compound unit would be specified for Quantity & Rate (not the constituent Simple Units).

03.02 Inventory Voucher Entry with Compound Unit

In Inventory Voucher entry (F-5A), against the Stock Item, enter the Quantity in Compound Unit (in Main & Tail Unit),

Stock Item Creation

Name	: **Cable BeeKay**
Under	: Cables
Category	: Fabro Prodicts
Units	: Roll of 25 Mtrs
Alternate Units	: ▮ Not Applicable

F-3A: Compound Unit in Stock Item master

Unit Alteration

Type : Compound

Units with Multiplier Factors
(example: Kgs of 1000 gms)

First Unit	Conversion	Second Unit
Roll	of 25	Mtrs

F-4A: Compound Unit Creation

Accounting Voucher Creation Ctrl + M

Sales No. 4 **1-Feb-2010** Monday

Ref. :
Party's A/c Name : **BDF**
Sales Ledger : **Sales**

Name of Item	Quantity	Rate	per	Amount
Cable BeeKay *Roll of 25 Mtrs*	2-13.00 Roll	300.00	Roll	756.00
Cable BeeKay *Roll of 25 Mtrs*	0-20.00 Roll	325.00	Roll	260.00
				1,016.00
Narration:	3- 8.00 Roll			*1,016.00*

F-5A: Voucher showing Stock Item transaction with Compound Unit

In voucher using Compound Unit, you may set the display & computation of Quantity in Compound Unit as follows:

Quantity & Rate: In voucher using Compound Unit, to set the display of Quantity & Rate entered, at Invoice Entry Configuration screen (*GoT>F12:Configure>Invoice / Orders Entry*), at *Show Compound Unit Based on Rate* (F-6A)

- Set *Yes* to convert the Quantity entered in terms of Rate entered. In that case, the Quantity is converted in terms of Rate. For example when you enter Quantity in Roll, e.g 1-3 Roll (when 1 Roll =25 Mtrs), then at Rate & Unit:

Show Compound Unit of Item based on Rate	? Yes
Show Full Details of Compound Unit	? Yes

F-6A: Configuration Options related to Compound UoM

  - o Enter Rate / Roll, 250/Roll, then the computation will be @250 per Roll =Rs.280 (F-6A)
  - o Enter Rate / Mtr, 11/Mtr, then the Quantity will be converted in terms of Rate Unit, i.e Mtrs. So, 1-3 Roll will be converted into 28 Mtrs and amount would be computed as computation will be @28per Mtr =Rs.308 (F-6B)

- Set *No*, the Quantity and Rate would be shown as entered and amount would be computed as per Rate unit (without converting the Quantity as per Rate Unit)

Name of Item	Quantity	Rate	per	Amount
Cable BeeKay	1- 3.00 Roll	250.00	Roll	280.00

F-7A: Quantity & Rate entry

Name of Item	Quantity	Rate	per	Amount
Cable BeeKay	28.00 Mtrs	11.00	Mtrs	308.00

F-7B: Converted Quantity as per Rate Unit

Name of Item	Quantity	Rate	per	Amount
Cable BeeKay	1 Roll 3.00 Mtrs	250.00	Roll	280.00

F-8: Full details of Quantity

Quantity Details: Having set *Yes* at *Show Compound Unit Based on Rate* (F-6A), at *Show Full Details of Compound Unit*:

- Set *Yes* to show the full details of Compound unit showing the Name of Constituent Units. For example 1-3 Roll is shown as 1 Roll 3 Mtrs (F-8)
- Set *No* to show the Quantity of Compound Unit as entered (F-7A) in Compound Unit (e.g 1-3 Roll)

03.03 Fractional Quantity in Compound Unit

If you have specified number of decimal places in First Unit of the compound unit (e.g in Stp), you may enter the Quantity in fractions also. Tally will instantly replace it with equivalent quantity in terms of main and tail unit. So, when you enter 10.50 Stp, it will be converted to 10-6 indicating 10 Strip and 6 Tabs (0.5 Stp=6 Tabs).

You cannot have any constituent Unit of a Compound Unit as Alternate Unit. For example, you can not have Roll of 25 Metres and Metres as Base Unit & Alternate Unit as Mtr is also a constituent unit of Roll.

You may have several compound unit of same constituent units, For example Tin of 4 kg, Tin of 20 Kg. Roll of 25 Mtrs, Roll of 91 Mtrs, but in the UoM, in both cases, Roll will be displayed. To clarify, it is better to give the value of the compound unit in the description for clarification.

You cannot use numeric numbers as part of name or Short Name of Simple Unit. For example, Tin4 (to indicate 4 kg Tin, Tin12 etc) are not accepted in Name or Short Name of an UoM.

04 Compound & Alternate Unit in Stock Item

You may even use Compound Unit in main unit while using Alternate unit simultaneously, as explained through following example of trade of Yarn.

In wholesale trade, Yarn is normally sold in Bales. A Bale contains several Bundles (a bundle contains several hanks). Special Yarns are sold in bundles also (like Dyed Yarn). So, normally the Yarn traders use compound unit like Bales-Bundle as selling unit. For example, if one Bale consists of 40 Bundles (1 Bundle =4.54 kg), they will specify like:

- 2-20 (2 Bales, 20 Bundles) instead of 100 Bundles
- 0-20 (0 Bales, 20 Bundles) instead of 20 Bundles
- 1-30 (1 Bale, 30 Bundles) instead of 70 Bundles

However, the Sale Rate is expressed in Rs./ Kg, irrespective of UoM of Quantity. In such case, a combination of Units, Alternate Unit and Compound is to be used, as explained below:

- Create the constituent simple units
- Create the compound unit
- Specify the Units in Item master
- Enter quantity in compound Units in Invoice

Create the constituent simple units

Create the following three Simple Units:

- Bales (Bale)
- Bundles (Bdl)
- Kilogram (Kg)

Create the compound unit

Now create the Compound Unit *Bale of 40 Bundles* (F-9A)

First Unit (Main Unit)	Conversion (Tail Unit)	Second Unit
Bale	40	Bdl

Specify the Units in Item Master

Through Item master creation / alteration (F-9A), specify the compound unit (Bale of 40) as *Basic* Unit and Kg as *Alternate* unit at the Stock Item Master and specify the conversion factor (1 Bdl=4.54 kg).

In Description field (F-9A), you may enter the details for Bale / Bundle for reference. This may optionally be printed in Invoice (§16/05-04).

Invoice Entry using Compound Unit

Now enter the quantity in compound unit, in 2 components (F-9B). The details (like weight of Bale etc) is entered in Description field in Stock Item is displayed in entry screen for reference.

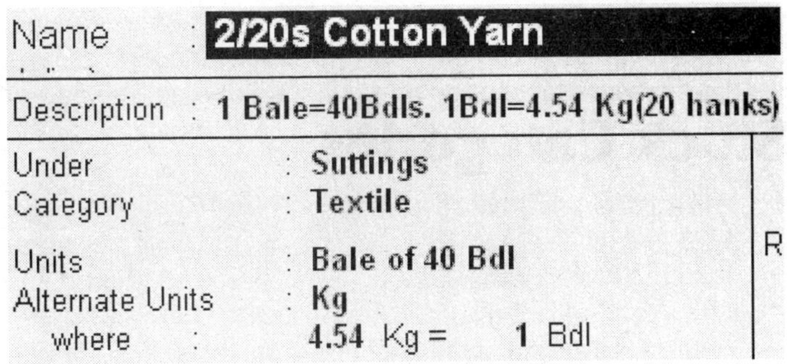

Name : 2/20s Cotton Yarn
Description : 1 Bale=40Bdls. 1Bdl=4.54 Kg(20 hanks)
Under : Suttings
Category : Textile
Units : Bale of 40 Bdl
Alternate Units : Kg
where : 4.54 Kg = 1 Bdl

F-9A: Compound Unit in Stock Items

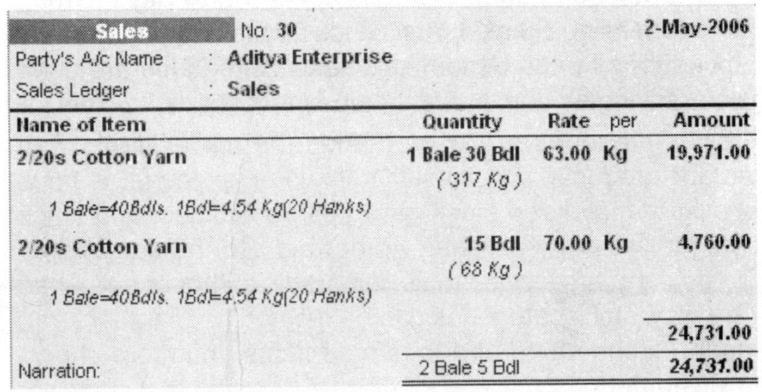

Sales No. 30 2-May-2006
Party's A/c Name : Aditya Enterprise
Sales Ledger : Sales

Name of Item	Quantity	Rate	per	Amount
2/20s Cotton Yarn	1 Bale 30 Bdl (317 Kg)	63.00	Kg	19,971.00
1 Bale=40Bdls. 1Bdl=4.54 Kg(20 Hanks)				
2/20s Cotton Yarn	15 Bdl (68 Kg)	70.00	Kg	4,760.00
1 Bale=40Bdls. 1Bdl=4.54 Kg(20 Hanks)				
				24,731.00
Narration:	2 Bale 5 Bdl			24,731.00

F-9B: Invoice showing Compound & Alternate Unit

FAQ: Frequently Asked Questions

FAQ-1: How to enter Alternate Unit of Measure in Stock Item

Ans: Sometimes, an Item may be measured and invoiced in either of 2 alternate units (like Pcs & Kg).

- **Activation for Alternate Unit:** At Gateway, click *F12: Configure* and select Accts /Inv Info to get Accounts / Inv Info Configuration screen (F-1A/05-01). Set *Yes* at *Use Alternate Units for Stock Items*, to activate Alternate Unit feature for the Company.
- **Alternate Unit set up in Stock Item Master:** Having activated Alternate Unit feature for the Company (F-1A/ 05-01), In Item Master Entry / Alteration screen, set up Alternate Units (F-1A):
  - **Alternate Unit**: At Item Master Entry / Alteration screen (F-1A), (after entry of Base Unit), at *Alternate Units* field, select the Alternate Unit from the list of Units defined
  - **Conversion Factor**: At *where* field, enter the conversion factor between the Base Unit & Alternate Unit. Enter the value of Alternate Unit (e.g Roll) and then enter the equivalent quantity in Base Unit (Mtrs). [e.g 11 Pcs (Alternate Unit) = 2.8 Kg (Base Unit].
- **Standard Rates entry for alternate units in Stock Item master:** If Standard Rate is activated (P-18.01/05-01), at Standard Rate entry screen (F-1B), you may enter Rates of the Item either in Base Unit, Alternate Unit or in both (18.02/05-01)

Stock Categories

02-03

01 Stock Categories

Stock Categories are parallel classification to Stock Group for categorising Stock Items. Stock Group helps to classify Stock Items in one dimension. Stock Categories are used to classifying an Item in another independent dimension.

Stock Categories are useful when the trader deals with variant products with similar utility. For example, a book publisher may keep stock group as per Subject and stock category as per Publisher, Author etc. So, he can find all the books of a specified topic, language, author or publisher. This way, stock categories can be created for manufacturer, model, brand etc to offer alternate Items and more choice to customers. So, if one book of a specific author is not available, he may find all other books on similar subject.

Stock Category Activation: To activate Stock categories features for the Company, Click *F11: Features > Inventory Features* and set *Yes at Maintain Stock Categories*

02 Stock Category Creation

We have discussed Stock Group (§04/01-02). In the same way, you may create Stock Categories.

Select *GoT>Inventory Info > Stock Category > Create* at Single Stock Category to get Stock category creation screen (F-1A & F-2A). Now enter the particulars as described below:

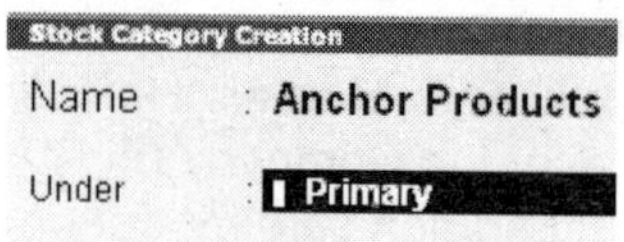

F-1A: Primary Stock Category creation

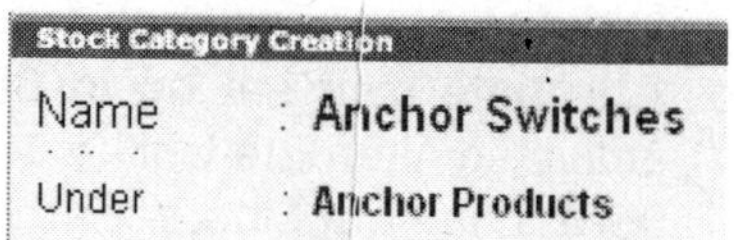

F-1B: Subordinate Stock Category creation

F-1C Stock Category (with Alias Name)

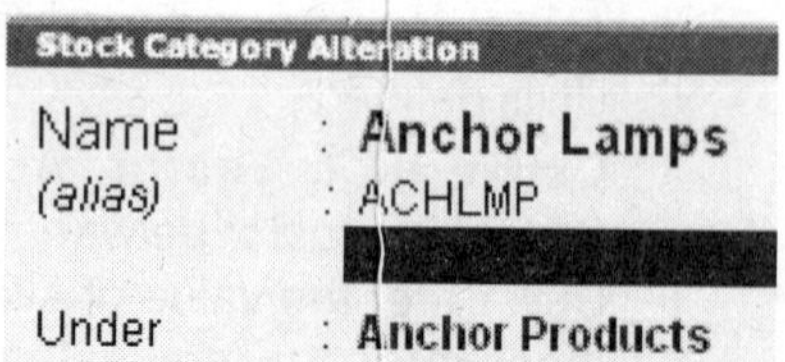

- **Stock Category Name**: At *Name* field, enter Name of Stock Category (F-1A)
- **Stock Category Alias**: At Alias (if activated), you may enter Stock Category Alias (F-1C)
- **Parent Stock Category**: At *Under* field, select the Parent Stock Category (F-1B) from List of Categories (or select *Primary* to create top level Stock Category – F1A). The first Stock Category created must be Primary (F-1A)

If the Parent Stock Category does not exist, press *Alt+C* at Under Field, to create a new Parent Stock Category in the same way as creation of new Stock Category

03 Stock Categories Alteration / Deletion

- Select *Inventory Info > Stock Category > Alter* and select the Stock Category to Alter. Carry out necessary alteration and Press Ctrl+A to save. To *Delete* the Stock Category press Alt+D, and set *Yes* at *Delete Yes or No?*
- Select *Inventory Info > Stock Category > Display* at Single Stock Category and select Stock Category to be displayed. You can view but cannot Alter.

03.01 Stock Category linking in Stock Item

At Stock Item creation / alteration (§05/02-01). You may specify the parent Stock Category of the Stock Item (F-1E). At Stock Item creation, At *Category* select the Parent Stock Category (like Parent Group)

04 Stock Categories List

At *GoT>Display>List of Accounts*, click *K;Stock Categories* to get the List of Stock Categories (F-1D)

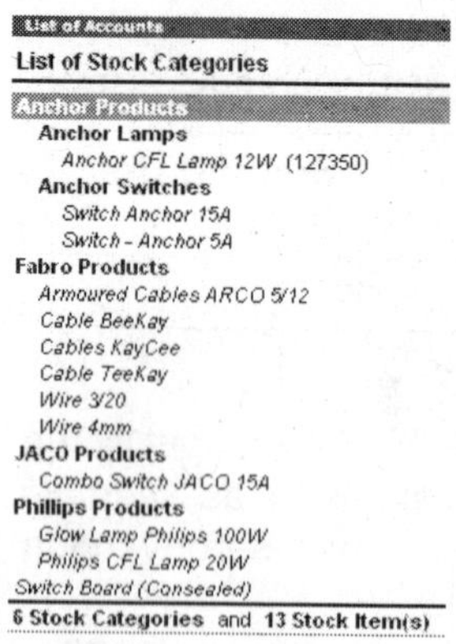

F-1D: Stock Category List

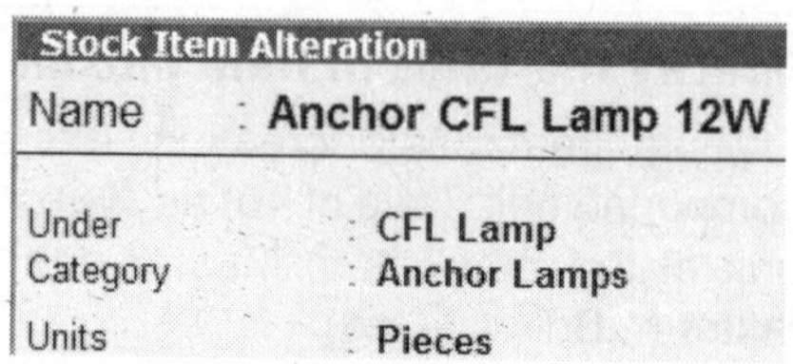

F-1E: Stock Catgory at Stock Item

05 Stock Category Summary

Stock Category Summary shows the Transaction & Stock Summary of all Items placed under the Stock Category.

Stock Category Summary — Ctrl + M

Particulars	ABC Electrical 1-Apr-2009 to 31-Mar-2010 Closing Balance		
	Quantity	Rate	Value
Anchor Products	52 Pieces	93.70	4,872.45
Fabro Products	516.00 Mtrs	10.38	5,355.47
JACO Products	(-)2 Pieces		
Phillips Products	36 Pieces	160.88	5,791.78
Grand Total			16,019.70

F-2A: Stock Category Summary (Default)

Configuration

Show Quantities	?	Yes
Show Rates	?	Yes
Show Values	?	Yes
Show Opening Balance	?	Yes
Show goods inwards	?	Yes
Show goods outwards	?	Yes
Show Closing Balance	?	Yes
Show All Items (incl. zero balance)	?	No
Show Consumption & Gross Profits	?	No
Show using Alternate Units	?	No
Show Tail Units of Compound Units	?	No
Appearance of Stock Item Names	:	Name Only
Appearance of Names	:	Name Only
Scale Factor for Values	:	Default
Sorting Method	:	Default
Expand all levels in Detailed Format	?	Yes

F-3A: Stock Category Summary Configuration

- F1: Condense
- F2: Period
- F3: Company
- F4: Category
- F6: Monthly
- F7: Hide Profit
- C: New Colum
- A: Alter Colum
- D: Del Column
- N: Auto Colum

F-3B Buttons

05.01 Stock Category Summary Display

Select *Display > StatEment Of Inventory > Categories* and select a Stock Category to (select Primary to get all top level Stock Categories & Stock Items) get Stock Category Summary for the selected Category (F-2A)

F-4A shows various columns as per Configuration options (F-3A), F-4B shows report in detail format (when you click *F1:Detailed* toggle button)

F-4C shows details at all levels (set Yes at *Expand All Levels in Detailed Format* at Configuration screen – F-3A)

Stock Category Summary — ABC Electrical — Ctrl + M

Particulars	ABC Electrical 1-Apr-2009 to 1-Mar-2010 Opening Balance			Inwards			Outwards			Closing Balance		
	Quantity	Rate	Value	Quantity	Rate	Value	Quantity	Rate	Value	Quantity	Rate	Value
Anchor Products	45 Pieces	72.51	3,263.00	12 Pieces	131.67	1,580.00	8 Pieces	76.29	610.30	49 Pieces	88.77	4,349.70
Fabro Products	656.00 Mtrs	10.25	6,725.80	155.00 Mtrs	10.48	1,624.12	294.00 Mtrs	12.62	3,709.00	517.00 Mtrs	10.38	5,367.47
JACO Products												
Phillips Products	6 Pieces	172.00	1,032.00				5 Pieces	227.40	1,137.00	1 Pieces	172.00	172.00
Grand Total			11,020.80			3,204.12			5,456.30			9,889.17

F-4A: Stock Category Summary (Condensed)

Stock Category Summary — ABC Electrical — Ctrl + M

Particulars	ABC Electrical 1-Apr-2009 to 1-Mar-2010 Opening Balance			Inwards			Outwards			Closing Balance		
	Quantity	Rate	Value	Quantity	Rate	Value	Quantity	Rate	Value	Quantity	Rate	Value
Anchor Products	45 Pieces	72.51	3,263.00	12 Pieces	131.67	1,580.00	8 Pieces	76.29	610.30	49 Pieces	88.77	4,349.70
Anchor Lamps	23 Pieces	113.04	2,600.00	12 Pieces	131.67	1,580.00	2 Pieces	149.00	298.00	33 Pieces	118.91	3,924.00
Anchor Switches	22 Pieces	30.14	663.00				6 Pieces	52.05	312.30	16 Pieces	26.61	425.70
Fabro Products	656.00 Mtrs	10.25	6,725.80	155.00 Mtrs	10.48	1,624.12	294.00 Mtrs	12.62	3,709.00	517.00 Mtrs	10.38	5,367.47
Armoured Cables ARCO 5/12	5.00 Mtrs	12.00	60.00				1.00 Mtrs	15.00	15.00	4.00 Mtrs	12.00	48.00
Cable BeeKay	15 Roll	255.33	3,830.00	2 Roll	250.00	500.00	6 Roll 13.00 Mtrs	309.20	2,016.00	10 Roll 12.00 Mtrs	257.63	2,700.00
Cables KayCee	30.00 Mtrs	10.00	300.00	25.00 Mtrs	9.80	245.00	24.00 Mtrs	12.50	300.00	31.00 Mtrs	9.92	307.40
Cable TeeKay	2 Roll 52.00 Mtrs	951.61	2,447.00	80.00 Mtrs	1,000.00	879.12	1 Roll 15.00 Mtrs	1,183.00	1,378.00	2 Roll 26.00 Mtrs	972.68	2,223.27
Wire 3/20	12.00 Mtrs	7.40	88.80							12.00 Mtrs	7.40	88.80
Wire 4mm												
JACO Products												
Combo Switch JACO 15A												
Phillips Products	6 Pieces	172.00	1,032.00				5 Pieces	227.40	1,137.00	1 Pieces	172.00	172.00
Glow Lamp Philips 100W												
Philips CFL Lamp 20W	6 Pieces	172.00	1,032.00				5 Pieces	227.40	1,137.00	1 Pieces	172.00	172.00
Grand Total			11,020.80			3,204.12			5,456.30			9,889.17

F-4B: Stock Category Summary (Detailed)

Stock Category Summary | ABC Electrical | Ctrl + M

Particulars	ABC Electrical 1-Apr-2009 to 1-Mar-2010											
	Opening Balance			**Inwards**			**Outwards**			**Closing Balance**		
	Quantity	*Rate*	Value	Quantity	*Rate*	Value	Quantity	*Rate*	Value	Quantity	*Rate*	Value
Anchor Products	**45 Pieces**	*72.51*	**3,263.00**	**12 Pieces**	*131.67*	**1,580.00**	**8 Pieces**	*76.29*	**610.30**	**49 Pieces**	*88.77*	**4,349.70**
Anchor Lamps	23 Pieces	113.04	2,600.00	12 Pieces	131.67	1,580.00	2 Pieces	149.00	298.00	33 Pieces	118.91	3,924.00
Anchor CFL Lamp 12W	23 Pieces	*113.04*	2,600.00	12 Pieces	*131.67*	1,580.00	2 Pieces	*149.00*	298.00	33 Pieces	*118.91*	3,924.00
23 Main Location	15 Pieces	112.00	1,680.00							15 Pieces	112.00	1,680.00
37 *Despatch Room*	8 Pieces	115.00	920.00	2 Pieces	150.00	300.00				10 Pieces	122.00	1,220.00
Primary Batch Main Location				10 Pieces	128.00	1,280.00	2 Pieces	149.00	298.00	8 Pieces	128.00	1,024.00
Anchor Switches	22 Pieces	30.14	663.00				6 Pieces	52.05	312.30	16 Pieces	26.61	425.70
Switch Anchor 15A	12 Pieces	*45.00*	540.00				5 Pieces	*60.00*	300.00	7 Pieces	*45.00*	315.00
Main Location	12 Pieces	45.00	540.00				5 Pieces	60.00	300.00	7 Pieces	45.00	315.00
Switch - Anchor 5A	10 Pieces	*12.30*	123.00				1 Pieces	*12.30*	12.30	9 Pieces	*12.30*	110.70
Main Location	10 Pieces	12.30	123.00				1 Pieces	12.30	12.30	9 Pieces	12.30	110.70
Fabro Products	**656.00 Mtrs**	*10.25*	**6,725.80**	**155.00 Mtrs**	*10.48*	**1,624.12**	**294.00 Mtrs**	*12.62*	**3,709.00**	**517.00 Mtrs**	*10.38*	**5,367.47**
Armoured Cables ARCO 5/12	*5.00 Mtrs*	12.00	*60.00*				*1.00 Mtrs*	15.00	*15.00*	*4.00 Mtrs*	12.00	*48.00*
Main Location	5.00 Mtrs	*12.00*	60.00				1.00 Mtrs	*15.00*	15.00	4.00 Mtrs	*12.00*	48.00
Cable BeeKay	*15 Roll*	255.33	*3,830.00*	*2 Roll*	250.00	*500.00*	*6 Roll 13.00 Mtrs*	309.20	*2,016.00*	*10 Roll 12.00 Mtrs*	257.63	*2,700.00*
Despatch Room	1 Roll	*260.00*	260.00							1 Roll	*260.00*	260.00
Main Location	10 Roll	*250.00*	2,500.00	2 Roll	*250.00*	500.00	6 Roll 13.00 Mtrs	*309.20*	2,016.00	5 Roll 12.00 Mtrs	*250.00*	1,370.00
Siliguri Godown	2 Roll	*270.00*	540.00							2 Roll	*270.00*	540.00
Warehouse	2 Roll	*265.00*	530.00							2 Roll	*265.00*	530.00
Cables KayCee	*30.00 Mtrs*	10.00	*300.00*	*25.00 Mtrs*	9.80	*245.00*	*24.00 Mtrs*	12.50	*300.00*	*31.00 Mtrs*	9.92	*307.40*
Despatch Room	5.00 Mtrs	*10.00*	50.00							5.00 Mtrs	*10.00*	50.00
												14 more ...
Grand Total			**11,020.80**			**3,204.12**			**5,456.30**			**9,889.17**

F-4C: Stock Category Summary (All Levels Details)

The Contents of Stock Summary are described below:

i. Multi Column Options

Set Yes / No to the following options as required. Each option affects multiple set of columns (*Opening / Inward / Outwards/ Closing)*

a. **Quantity / Rate / Value**: The following columns appear for Opening Balance, Goods Inwards, Goods outwards & Closing Balance. The option is applicable for all these columns, if activated (e.g if *Yes* is set at Show Quantity, Quantity column will appear in the activated columns (Goods Inwards, Goods outwards & Closing balance, and like that for Rate & Value column)
   - o **Quantity**: At *Show Quantities*, set
     - *Yes* to show the Quantity column (and the base unit)
     - *No* to suppress the Quantity column
   - o **Rate**: At *Show Rates,* set:
     - *Yes* to show the Rate column (as per the base UoM displayed with Quantity figure)
     - *No* to suppress the Rate column.
   - o **Values**: At *Show Values*, set:
     - *Yes* to show the Value column
     - *No* to suppress the Value column

b. **Opening/ Inwards / Outwards / Closing**: Set Ye- to show the figures for the respective 3 columns activated (Quantity, Rate, Value)
   - o **Opening:** At *Show Opening Balance*, set Yes to show the figures of Opening Balance for the respective columns activated (Quantity, Rate, Value).
   - o **Inwards**: At *Show Goods Inwards,* set Yes to show the figures of Goods Inwards for the respective column activated (Quantity, Rate, Value)
   - o **Outwards**: At *Show Goods Outwards*, set Yes to show the figures of Goods Outwards for the respective column activated (Quantity, Rate, Value)
   - o **Closing:** At *Show Closing Balance*, set Yes to show the figures of Closing balance for the respective column activated (Quantity, Rate, Value)

The values (Quantity, Rate, Amount) of each of the column (Opening, Inwards, Outwards, Closing) are displayed according to *Report Period* (set through F2: period button) for the respective columns:

ii. Set Yes / No to the following options to show / suppress the columns as required

- **Items Types:** At *Show All Items*:
  - o Set Yes to show the Item even if all the displayed figures for the Item is zero.
  - o Set No to suppress the Items where the values of all the displayed column are zero. (if value of any of the displayed column for the Item is non zero, the Item will be displayed)
- **Cost / Contribution**: At *Show Consumption & Gross Profit*,

- o Set *Yes* to show the Consumption Value (Cost) & Gross Profit (Contribution)for Sales / Outwards column (F-4D). Groos is compted as (Sales Value – Cost)
- o Set No, the Consumption Value & Gross Profit column is not shown.

- **Alternate Unit**: At *Show using Alternate units*:
  - o Set *Yes* to show the quantity in *Alternate units* also (for Items having Dual Units),
  - o Set No, only the Base Unit is shown.
- **Tail Unit**: At *Show Tail units of Compound Units,*
  - o Set *Yes* to show the tail units of compound unit,
  - o Set *No.* the base unit is shown (with fraction values, where applicable)
- **Format**: At *Expand all levels in Detailed Format,*
  - o Set *Yes* to show the Items upto the lowest level details (in detail mode- i.e, when F1: Detail is selected),
  - o Set No. Only next level detail (Item Group / Stock Items) are shown in detail mode.

At Stock Category Summary, drill down through any Stock Category to get the Stock Category Summary for the next level (showing next level Stock Category / Stock Items)

At Stock Category Summary, select any Stock Item to get Item Monthly Summary (Ref??)

05.02 Stock Category Summary with Consumption & Gross Profit details

To get the Stock Itemwise gross profit details of Sale (shown in Outwards column) under each Stock Category, at Stock Category Summary Configuration (F-A), set Yes at *Show Consumption & Gross Profit.* Consequently, in the consumption column, the following new columns appear:

- o **Consumption:** The computed cost of godds sold / consumed as per valuation method specified for the stock Item
- o **Gross Profit:** The gross profit, i.e the difference of value of consumption / sale is shown. If the cost is more than the consumption / sale value, the profit is shown in negative.
- o **Perc %:** The percentage of gross profit on the consumption / sale value is shown (Gross Profit / Consumption) x 100

The Gross Profit & Perc % is shown only when Sale Quantity & Value is entered in the voucher

05.03 Drill Down from Stock Category Summary

On drill down from any Stock Category / Stock Item, the next level reports appear as follows:

- o **From Stock Category:** The Stock Summary for the selected Stock Category appears showing the next level Stock Category / Stock Items
- o **From Stock Items:** The Stock Item Monthly Summary for the selected Stock Item appears showing the monthwise figures for each month for the current period.

Stock Category Summary — ABC Electrical — Ctrl + M

Particulars	ABC Electrical 1-Apr-2009 to 1-Mar-2010														
	Opening Balance			Inwards			Outwards						Closing Balance		
	Quantity	*Rate*	Value	Quantity	*Rate*	Value	Quantity	*Rate*	Value	Consumption	Gross Profit	Perc %	Quantity	*Rate*	Value
Anchor Products	**45 Pieces**	*72.51*	**3,263.00**	**12 Pieces**	*131.67*	**1,580.00**	**8 Pieces**	*76.29*	**610.30**	**493.30**	**117.00**	**19.17 %**	**49 Pieces**	*88.77*	**4,349.70**
Anchor Lamps	23 Pieces	113.04	2,600.00	12 Pieces	131.67	1,580.00	2 Pieces	149.00	298.00	256.00	42.00	14.09 %	33 Pieces	118.91	3,924.00
Anchor Switches	22 Pieces	30.14	663.00				6 Pieces	52.05	312.30	237.30	75.00	24.02 %	16 Pieces	26.61	425.70
Fabro Products	**656.00 Mtrs**	*10.25*	**6,725.80**	**155.00 Mtrs**	*10.48*	**1,624.12**	**294.00 Mtrs**	*12.62*	**3,709.00**	**2,982.45**	**726.55**	**19.59 %**	**517.00 Mtrs**	*10.38*	**5,367.47**
Amoured Cables ARCO 5/12	*5.00 Mtrs*	12.00	*60.00*				*1.00 Mtrs*	15.00	*15.00*	*12.00*	*3.00*	*20.00 %*	*4.00 Mtrs*	12.00	*48.00*
Cable BeeKay	*15 Roll*	255.33	*3,830.00*	*2 Roll*	250.00	*500.00*	*6 Roll 13.00 Mtrs*	309.20	*2,016.00*	*1,630.00*	*386.00*	*19.15 %*	*10 Roll 12.00 Mtrs*	257.63	*2,700.00*
Cables KayCee	*30.00 Mtrs*	10.00	*300.00*	*25.00 Mtrs*	9.80	*245.00*	*24.00 Mtrs*	12.50	*300.00*	*237.60*	*62.40*	*20.80 %*	*31.00 Mtrs*	9.92	*307.40*
Cable TeeKay	*2 Roll 52.00 Mtrs*	951.61	*2,447.00*	*80.00 Mtrs*	1,000.00	*879.12*	*1 Roll 15.00 Mtrs*	1,183.00	*1,378.00*	*1,102.85*	*275.15*	*19.97 %*	*2 Roll 26.00 Mtrs*	972.68	*2,223.27*
Wire 3/20	*12.00 Mtrs*	7.40	*88.80*										*12.00 Mtrs*	7.40	*88.80*
Wire 4mm															
JACO Products															
Combo Switch JACO 15A															
Philips Products	**6 Pieces**	*172.00*	**1,032.00**				**5 Pieces**	*227.40*	**1,137.00**	**860.00**	**277.00**	**24.36 %**	**1 Pieces**	*172.00*	**172.00**
Glow Lamp Philips 100W															
Philips CFL Lamp 20W	*6 Pieces*	172.00	*1,032.00*				*5 Pieces*	227.40	*1,137.00*	*860.00*	*277.00*	*24.36 %*	*1 Pieces*	172.00	*172.00*
Grand Total			**11,020.80**			**3,204.12**			**5,456.30**	**4,335.75**	**1,120.55**	**20.54 %**			**9,889.17**

F-4D: Stock Category Summary with Gross Profit Details

05.04 Stock Category Summary Columnar Display

To get corresponding Stock Category Summary figures in adjacent columns for better comparison, at Stock Category Summary Report, click as follows:

- *C: New Column*: To create a new columns as per specified column definition, to get the corresponding figures in adjacent columns for better comparison.

- N: Auto Column: To create multiple columns (as per specified period frequency or for various Stock Valuation methods)

Column definitions for Columnar Stock Category Summary

At Stock Category Summary, click the button as follows:

Single New Column: Click *C: New Column* to create an adjacent new column, to get corresponding figures for better comparison. Set the column definition as follows, for:

- **Another Company:** At Name of Company, select a Company from the list of selected Company
- **Another Period:** At *From* & *To* field respectively, specify the Start & End Date of the report
- **Another Stock Category:** At *Name of Stock Category* field, select another Stock Category
- **Another Valuation Method:** At Valuation Method, select the Valuation Method. It is useful for comparison of consumption / stock values in different methods for management decisions (like price fixing / quotation, make buy decisions etc and to get Stock value to be entered manually in the Accounts System.

This way you may create several adjacent new columns in any manner as desired.

Automatic Multiple Columns: Click *N: Auto Column* to create repeating multiple columns for:

- **Regular Period interval:** Select a period interval (e.g weekly, monthly, quarterly etc), to get automatically created columns for each period, showing comparative periodical figures
- **Stock Valuation Methods:** Select Stock Valuation Methods to get automated columns for each of the Stock Valuation Methods specified by Tally.

05.05 Stock Category Summary Configuration

At Stock Category Summary (F-2A), click *F12: Configuration* to get Stock Category Summary Configuration (F-3A). The options are similar to Stock Summary Report (F-2A/05-08)

05.06 Stock Category Summary Buttons

At Stock Category Summary, you get the following buttons (F-3B)

- **F1: Condensed / Detailed**: Toggle button (*Condensed* – To show the top level Stock Category info only. *Detailed* - to show next level details of Stock Categories)
- **F4: Category**: To select another Stock Category from the list of Stpck Category to show the Report for other Stock Category
- **F7: Show Profit / Hide Profit**: To show Stock Itemwise Contribution (Gross Profit) in respect of Outwards (F-4D)

06 Stock Category Analysis

Stock Category Analysis (F-5A) shows Details of Inwards & Outwards as per Items under same Stock Category.

Category Analysis — Ctrl + M

Particulars	ABC Electrical 1-Apr-2009 to 1-Mar-2010 Inward			Outward		
	Quantity	*Eff. Rate*	Value	Quantity	*Eff. Rate*	Value
Anchor Products	**12 Pieces**	*131.67*	**1,580.00**	**8 Pieces**	*76.29*	**610.30**
Fabro Products	**155.00 Mtrs**	*10.48*	**1,624.12**	**294.00 Mtrs**	*12.62*	**3,709.00**
Phillips Products				**5 Pieces**	*227.40*	**1,137.00**
Grand Total			3,204.12			5,456.30

F-5A: Stock Category Analysis (Summary)

Configuration

Format	:	Detailed
Expand all levels in Detailed Format	?	No
Show Inwards Column	?	Yes
Show Outwards Column	?	Yes
Show Quantities	?	Yes
Show using Alternate Units	?	No
Show Tail Units of Compound Units	?	No
Show Rates	?	Yes
Show Values	?	Yes

F-5B: Stock Category Analysis

F1: Detailed
F2: Period
F3: Company
F4: Category
F5: Item-wise
F6: By Ledgers
C: New Column
A: Alter Column
D: Del Column
N: Auto Column

F-5C: Buttons

Category Analysis — Ctrl + M

Particulars	ABC Electrical 1-Apr-2009 to 1-Mar-2010 Inward			Outward		
	Quantity	*Eff. Rate*	Value	Quantity	*Eff. Rate*	Value
Anchor Products	**12 Pieces**	*131.67*	**1,580.00**	**8 Pieces**	*76.29*	**610.30**
Anchor Lamps	12 Pieces	131.67	1,580.00	2 Pieces	149.00	298.00
Anchor Switches				6 Pieces	52.05	312.30
Fabro Products	**155.00 Mtrs**	*10.48*	**1,624.12**	**294.00 Mtrs**	*12.62*	**3,709.00**
Armoured Cables ARCO 5/12				*1.00 Mtrs*	15.00	*15.00*
Cable BeeKay	*2 Roll*	*250.00*	*500.00*	*6 Roll 13.00 Mtrs*	309.20	*2,016.00*
Cables KayCee	*25.00 Mtrs*	*9.80*	*245.00*	*24.00 Mtrs*	12.50	*300.00*
Cable TeeKay	*80.00 Mtrs*	*1,000.00*	*879.12*	*1 Roll 15.00 Mtrs*	1,183.00	*1,378.00*
Phillips Products				**5 Pieces**	*227.40*	**1,137.00**
Philips CFL Lamp 20W				*5 Pieces*	227.40	*1,137.00*
Grand Total			3,204.12			5,456.30

F-5C: Stock Category Analysis (Detailed)

Category Analysis						Ctrl + M
Particulars	**ABC Electrical** 1-Apr-2009 to 1-Mar-2010					
	Inward			**Outward**		
	Quantity	*Eff. Rate*	Value	Quantity	*Eff. Rate*	Value
Anchor Products	**12 Pieces**	*131.67*	**1,580.00**	**8 Pieces**	*76.29*	**610.30**
Anchor Lamps	12 Pieces	*131.67*	1,580.00	2 Pieces	149.00	298.00
Anchor CFL Lamp 12W	12 Pieces	*131.67*	1,580.00	2 Pieces	*149.00*	298.00
37 *Despatch Room*	2 Pieces	*150.00*	300.00			
Primary Batch *Main Location*	10 Pieces	*128.00*	1,280.00	2 Pieces	149.00	298.00
Anchor Switches				6 Pieces	52.05	312.30
Switch Anchor 15A				5 Pieces	*60.00*	300.00
Main Location				5 Pieces	60.00	300.00
Switch - Anchor 5A				1 Pieces	*12.30*	12.30
Main Location				1 Pieces	12.30	12.30
Fabro Products	**155.00 Mtrs**	*10.48*	**1,624.12**	**294.00 Mtrs**	*12.62*	**3,709.00**
Armoured Cables ARCO 5/12				*1.00 Mtrs*	15.00	*15.00*
Main Location				1.00 Mtrs	*15.00*	15.00
Cable BeeKay	*2 Roll*	*250.00*	*500.00*	*6 Roll 13.00 Mtrs*	309.20	*2,016.00*
Main Location	2 Roll	*250.00*	500.00	6 Roll 13.00 Mtrs	*309.20*	2,016.00
Cables KayCee	*25.00 Mtrs*	*9.80*	*245.00*	*24.00 Mtrs*	12.50	*300.00*
Main Location	25.00 Mtrs	*9.80*	245.00	24.00 Mtrs	*12.50*	300.00
Cable TeeKay	*80.00 Mtrs*	*1,000.00*	*879.12*	*1 Roll 15.00 Mtrs*	1,183.00	*1,378.00*
Main Location	80.00 Mtrs	*1,000.00*	879.12	1 Roll 15.00 Mtrs	*1,183.00*	1,378.00
						3 more ...
Grand Total			3,204.12			5,456.30

F-5D: Stock Category Analysis (with Complete Details)

06.01 *Stock Category Analysis Display*

At *Display > Inventory Books> Movement Analysis* menu (F-15A/02-08), select *Category Analysis* and select a Stock Category (select *Primary* to get Analysis Report for all Stock Categories) to get Stock Category Analysis report (F-5A)

F-5C shows Stock Category Analysis (Detailed), when you select *Detailed* at Format option.

F-5D shows Stock Category Analysis (Detailed) report, when you select *Expand All Levels in Detailed Format* at Detailed Format (F-5B).

06.02 *Stock Category Analysis Configuration*

At Stock Category Analysis display (F-5A), click F12:Configure to get Stock Category Analysis Configuration screen (F-5B). Set the options to get Stock Category Analysis Report as per configuration set (F-5C & F-5D)

- **Format:** At *Format*, Select
  - o *Condensed* to get the top level primary category only
  - o *Detailed* to get the next level details (Item category / Stock Items - F-5C),
- **Detail Level**: At *Expand All Levels in Detailed Format* (at Detailed Format Report) Set:
  - o *Yes* to show details to the lowest level (F-5D)
  - o *No* to show only the next level details (F-5D)
- **Inwards:** At *Show Inward column* (showing quantity, rate, value as specified), Set:
  - o *Yes* to show the goods Inward column
  - o *No.* The goods Inward column will NOT be shown
- **Outwards:** At *Show Outward column* (showing quantity, rate, value as specified), Set:
  - o *Yes* to show the goods Outwards column
  - o *No.* The goods Outwards column will NOT be shown
- **Quantity**: At *Show Quantities,* set:
  - o *Yes* to show quantity figures (with UoM),
  - o *No* to suppress Quantity column
- ***Rates***: Set Yes to show Rates (Value / Quantity), else set No to suppress Rate column
- ***Values***: At ***Show Values***, Set:
  - o Yes to show value (where value has been specified)
  - o No to suppress value column

06.03 *Stock Category Analysis Buttons*

At Stock Category Analysis display (F-5A), you get buttons (F-5C) like Stock Group Analysis:

07 Stock Categories in Multiple Mode

We have described Stock Category entry in Single entry mode (§02), in which you may create / alter / display ONE

Stock Category in one screen. As described for entry of Multiple Stock Group / Stock Item ((§19.01/02-01)), you may create, alter & delete Stock Categories, through Multiple Stock Categories option of Stock Categories Menu (GoT>Inventory Info>Stock Categories>Create) in same way.

07.01 Stock Categories Creation in Multiple Mode

Select *Inventory Info > Stock Categories > CReate* (under Multiple Stock Groups) to get Multiple Stock Entry screen create multiple Stock Categories in one screen (F-6A)

Parent Category: At *Under Category* field, select the parent Category to place the new Stock Items under one Stock Category, else select *All Items* to select parent Stock for each Stock Item.

Stock Category Name: At *Name of Category*, enter the Stock Category Name

Parent Category: The Parent Category entered at *Under Category* is carried at *Under* field and this filed is skipped. Else enter the Parent Stock category of the Stock Category being created. If the Parent Stock Category is not yet created, press *Alt+C* at *Under* to create a new Stock Category and select it at *Under* field.

Multi Stock Category Creation Ctrl + M

Under Category : ▮ All Items

S.No.	Name of Category	Under
1.	Anchor CFL	Anchor Lamps
2.		

F-6A: Multiple Stock Categories creation

Multi Stock Category Alteration

Under Category : ▮ All Items

S.No.	Name of Category	Under
5.	Anchor Lamps	Anchor Products
6.	Anchor Switches	Anchor Products

F-6B: Multiple Stock Categories Alteration

Buttons: At Multiple Stock Category creation screen (F-5A), you get the buttons (F-6D), as described for multiple entry of Stock Group / Stock Items.

07.02 Stock Categories Alteration / Deletion in Multiple Mode

To alter / delete Stock Category, select *Inventory Info > Stock Category > Alter* (under Multiple Stock Category) and select a Stock Category (or select *All Items*) to list the Stock Categories under the selected Stock Category (all *Stock Categories* when *All Items* is selected). Now you may make alteration of Stock category as explained for Stock Groups / Stock Items, using the buttons (F-6E)

07.03 Stock Categories Display in Multiple Mode

To Display Stock Category, select *Inventory Info > Stock Category > Display* (under Multiple Stock Category) and select a Stock Category (or select *All Items*) to list the Stock Categories under the selected Stock Category (all *Stock Categories* when *All Items* is selected).

You may just view the data, but cannot alter.

Multi Stock Category Display

Under Category : ▮ All Items

S.No.	Name of Category	Under
1.	Anchor Products	Primary
2.	Fabro Products	Primary
3.	JACO Products	Primary
4.	Phillips Products	Primary

F-6C: Multiple Stock Categories Display

F3: Company
F3: New Cmp
F4: Parent
F4: New Parent

F-6D: Buttons Multiple Stock Category Creation / Display

F4: Parent
F4: New Parent
F6: Skip Names
F7: Skip Parent

F-6E: Buttons Multiple Stock Category Alteration

08 Stock Category Movement Analysis

At *Movement Analysis* Menu (F-15A / 02-08), select *Stock Category Analysis* to get *Stock Category Movement* Analysis (F-7A), showing the figures for top level (Primary) Stock Categories. The contents of *Stock Category Movement Analysis* (F-7A) is similar to *Stock Group Movement Analysis* (F-19A/02-08)

Category Analysis Ctrl + M

Particulars	ABC Electrical 1-Apr-2009 to 31-Mar-2010					
	Inward			Outward		
	Quantity	Eff. Rate	Value	Quantity	Eff. Rate	Value
Anchor Products	20 Pieces	135.23	2,704.64	17 Pieces	124.72	2,120.30
Fabro Products	155.00 Mtrs	10.48	1,624.12	346.00 Mtrs	18.14	6,276.40
JACO Products				2 Pieces	25.00	50.00
Phillips Products	54 Pieces	160.59	8,672.08	36 Pieces	176.06	6,338.24
Switch Board (Concealed)						90.00
Grand Total			13,000.84			14,874.94

F-7A: Stock Category Movement Analysis

Stock Category Movement Analysis Buttons

At *Stock Category Movement Analysis* (F-7A), you get Buttons similar to *Stock Group Movement Analysis* (F-18A/ 02-08). Instead of *F4:Group*, you get *F4:Category* to select a *Stock Category* to get *Stock Category Movement Analysis* of the selected Stock Catgory (selecte Primary to get Pimary Level Stock Category Analysis.

Category Analysis						Ctrl + M
Particulars	ABC Electrical 1-Apr-2009 to 31-Mar-2010					
	Inward			Outward		
	Quantity	*Eff. Rate*	Value	Quantity	*Eff. Rate*	Value
Anchor Products	**20 Pieces**	*135.23*	**2,704.64**	**17 Pieces**	*124.72*	**2,120.30**
Anchor Lamps	20 Pieces	*135.23*	2,704.64	11 Pieces	164.36	1,808.00
Anchor Switches				6 Pieces	52.05	312.30
Fabro Products	**155.00 Mtrs**	*10.48*	**1,624.12**	**346.00 Mtrs**	*18.14*	**6,276.40**
Armoured Cables ARCO 5/12				*12.00 Mtrs*	177.62	*2,131.40*
Cable BeeKay	*2 Roll*	*250.00*	*500.00*	6 Roll 13.00 Mtrs	305.52	*1,992.00*
Cables KayCee	*25.00 Mtrs*	*9.80*	*245.00*	*65.00 Mtrs*	11.92	*775.00*
Cable TeeKay	*80.00 Mtrs*	*1,000.00*	*879.12*	1 Roll 15.00 Mtrs	1,183.00	*1,378.00*
JACO Products				**2 Pieces**	*25.00*	**50.00**
Combo Switch JACO 15A				*2 Pieces*	*25.00*	*50.00*
Phillips Products	**54 Pieces**	*160.59*	**8,672.08**	**36 Pieces**	*176.06*	**6,338.24**
Glow Lamp Philips 100W	*28 Pieces*	**126.67**	*3,546.67*	*23 Pieces*	149.02	*3,427.44*
Philips CFL Lamp 20W	*26 Pieces*	**197.13**	*5,125.41*	*13 Pieces*	223.91	*2,910.80*
Switch Board (Concealed)						90.00
Despatch Room						90.00
Grand Total			13,000.84			14,874.94

F-7B: Stock Category Movement Analysis (Detailed)

FAQ: Frequently Asked Questions

FAQ-1: How to set up Stock Category

Ans: Stock Categories are parallel classification to Stock Group for categorising Stock Items.

Stock Category Activation: To activate Stock Category features for the Company, Click *F11: Features > Inventory Features* and set *Yes at Maintain Stock Categories*

Stock Category Creation: Having activated Stock Category, at *GoT>Inventory Info > Stock Category,* select *Create* at Single Stock Category to get Stock category creation screen (F-1A & F-2A). Now enter the particulars (§02/05-03)

Invoicing 02-04

01 Advanced Invoicing Features

We have described Invoice entry earlier (§04/01-04). Here, we describe advanced options relating to entry of Stock Item in Sales / Purchase Invoice, Debit & Credit Notes.

02 Stock Items Selection using Alias, Part Number

We have described Alias Name (§02/02-01) of Inventory Masters. Having activated Alias Names and having entered Alias Names in respective Masters, you may select the Master in any selection list (e.g Voucher Entry, Master Entry, Report Printing etc, by Part Number, Alias Name of the Master, in the same way as Name.

We have also discussed about Part Number & its Alias Names (§14/02-01). During Inventory Voucher entry, the following appears in Item selection list from which any one may be selected to select an Item (F-1A)

- Stock Item Name
- All Alias of Stock Item Name
- Stock Item Part Number
- All Alias of Part Number of the Stock Item

An Item may be referred by any of these IDs in a document, or selected during voucher entry.The facility of selection of Item Name through multiple IDs allow to make selection of Item using varied types of IDs by which the Item may be referred by different types of organizations (manufacturer's code, agent's code, trade name, bar codes etc). There is no limit in number of such alias of Stock Item Names and its Part Number.

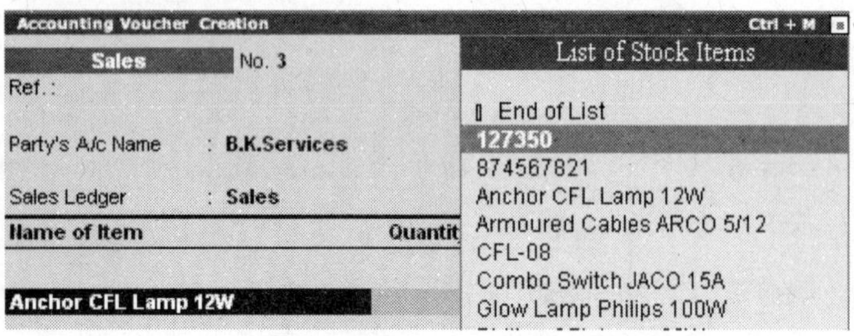

F-1A: Item selection through Item Name Alias, Part Number / Part Number Alias

Note: *You may select an Item by any of the Stock Item Identities as described. However, all of them must be Unique among all the Stock Items (so, Alias of Stock Itm annot be a Part number of a Stock Item or Part Number Alias, etc).*

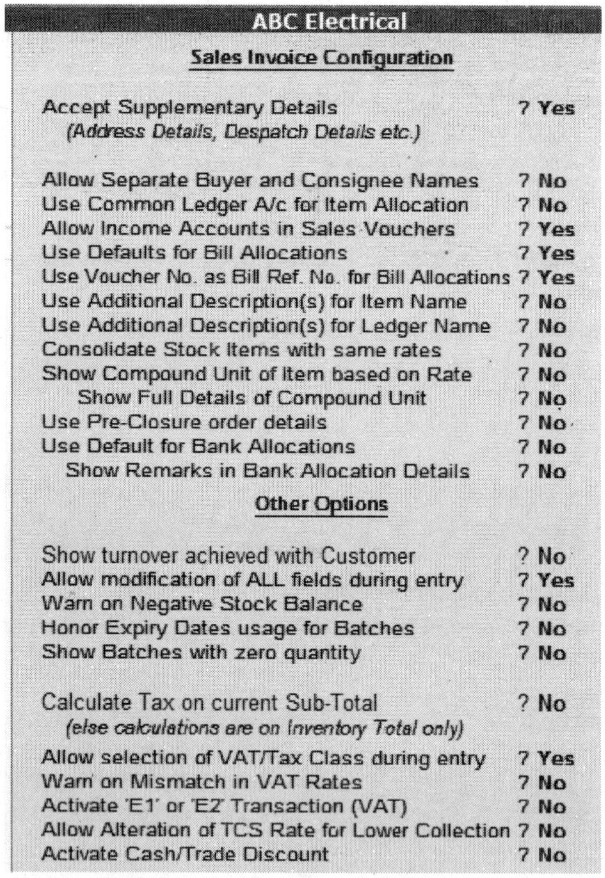

ABC Electrical

Sales Invoice Configuration

Accept Supplementary Details (Address Details, Despatch Details etc.)	? Yes
Allow Separate Buyer and Consignee Names	? No
Use Common Ledger A/c for Item Allocation	? No
Allow Income Accounts in Sales Vouchers	? Yes
Use Defaults for Bill Allocations	? Yes
Use Voucher No. as Bill Ref. No. for Bill Allocations	? Yes
Use Additional Description(s) for Item Name	? No
Use Additional Description(s) for Ledger Name	? No
Consolidate Stock Items with same rates	? No
Show Compound Unit of Item based on Rate	? No
Show Full Details of Compound Unit	? No
Use Pre-Closure order details	? No
Use Default for Bank Allocations	? No
Show Remarks in Bank Allocation Details	? No

Other Options

Show turnover achieved with Customer	? No
Allow modification of ALL fields during entry	? Yes
Warn on Negative Stock Balance	? No
Honor Expiry Dates usage for Batches	? No
Show Batches with zero quantity	? No
Calculate Tax on current Sub-Total (else calculations are on Inventory Total only)	? No
Allow selection of VAT/Tax Class during entry	? Yes
Warn on Mismatch in VAT Rates	? No
Activate 'E1' or 'E2' Transaction (VAT)	? No
Allow Alteration of TCS Rate for Lower Collection	? No
Activate Cash/Trade Discount	? No

F-1B: Invoice Entry Configuration

03 Stock Item Description in Voucher

Description entered in Item Master (F-2A & F-2B) as described earlier (§16/02-01) is carried in Inventory Voucher during entry (F-2C), where it may be changed in the specific Inventory Voucher during entry (and may be optionally printed in the Inventory Report)

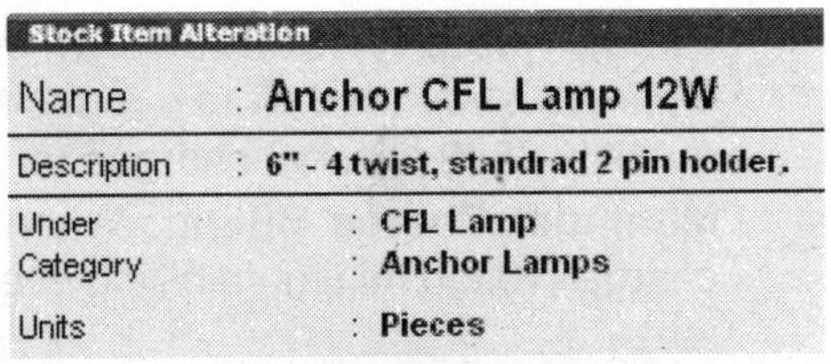

F-2A: Description in Stock Item Master

F-2B: Description entry in Stock Item Master

F-2C: Stock Item Description entry in Voucher

At *Invoice Configuration* (F-1B), set *Yes* at *Use Additional Description for Item Name.*

Consequently, during Invoice entry, you get a screen showing the Stock Item Description carried (F-3A) You may change the Item Description carried and also enter the Additional Description for the Voucher (F-2C). The additional Description may be entered in Multiple lines. After the first line, a blank line appears. Continue entering additional description line by line Press <enter> at a blank line to terminate.

Having entered the Additional Description (F-2C), it is carried at the main entry screen (F-3A). You may make further modification of Additional Description only in Main Entry screen (you do not get back to the Additional Description entry sub-screen).

Item Description entered at Stock Item Master is carried (F-2A, F-2B).at Additional Description in Voucher (F-3A). You may modify/ add more details into it. The description entered is specific to that voucher only (F-2C, 3A). Thus you may enter different description (e.g Item Serial Number) of same Item in different Voucher.

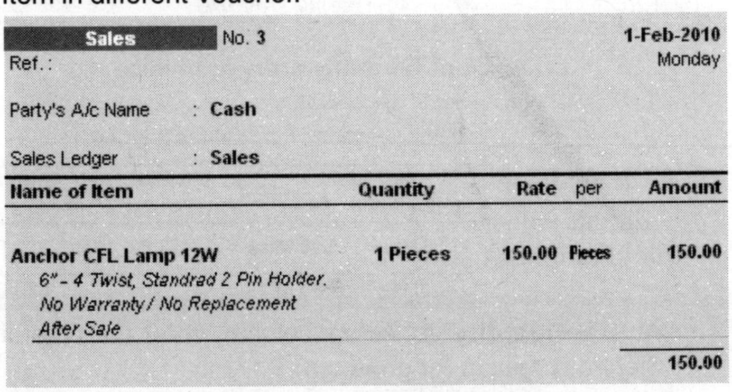

F-3A: Additional Description in Voucher

04 Standard Price Entry in Invoice

We have described entry of Standard Sales / Cost Price in Stock Item Master (§18/02-01), During Sales / Purchase Voucher entry, the Standard Selling Rate (in Sales Voucher) / Standard Cost (in Purchase Voucher) as applicable on the voucher date will be carried as default Item Rate. The Standard Rate as carried in Voucher may optionally be changed during voucher entry (the change will be in that voucher only but Standard Rates in the Item Master will not change). Thus Standard Rate enables much faster and accurate sales / purchase voucher entry.

> **Note:** *At Invoice Entry, the linked price list (F-5A/02-07) gets selected by default (F-4A). You may select another Price List (or select Not Applicable to enter Price as desired).*

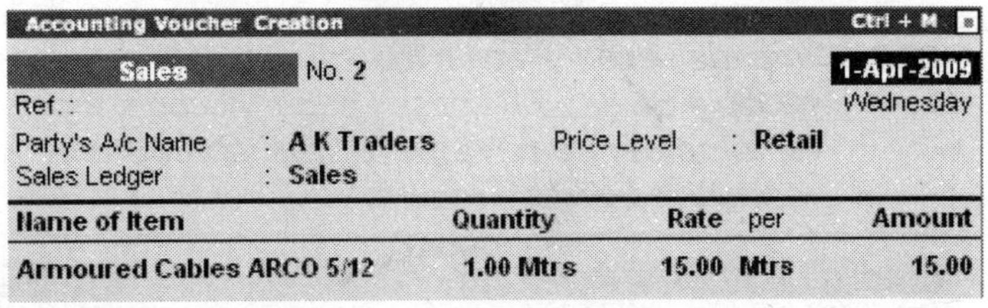

F-4A: Invoice Entry using Price List

05 Negative Stock Warning

In Inventory system, Stock cannot go negative unless there is some mistake in entry. To prevent such mistake at the point of entry itself, at Invoice Configuration (F-1A), at *Warn on Negative Stock Balance*:

- Set *Yes* to get Warning of negative Stock during Voucher Entry, if the current voucher would cause stock to go negative (F-5A)
- Set No, No Warning would be displayed during Invoice entry

If you still like to enter the Inventory Voucher allowing the stock to go negative, press any key and go ahead to enter the Inventory Voucher.

> **Note:** *Negative Stock is just an Warning (information). It does not trap Voucher Entry. You may bypass it and still enter the Voucher to go the quantity negative. Often, the Negative Stock occurs if the Receipts / transfers are not entered properly.*

F-5A: Negative Stock Warning

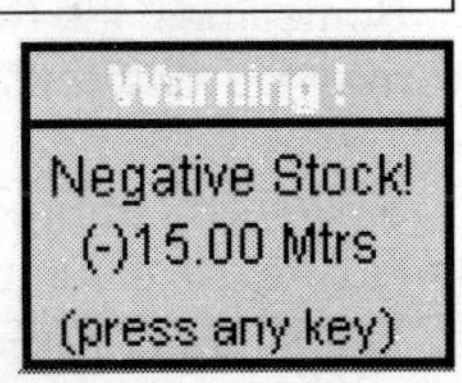

06 Sales / Purchase Ledger

Entry of common Sales / Purchase Ledger in Invoice at header is explained earlier (§04/01-04). The total value of all the Items are posted to the common Sales / Purchase Ledger Account specified.

To allocate the Sales / Purchase Value to different Sales / Purchase Ledger (e.g different Sales / Purchase Ledger), at

Invoice Configuration (F-1B), at *Use Common Ledger A/c for Item Allocation*,

- **Common Ledger**: Set *Yes* to allocate total sales / Purchase Value to one account specified at Header (F-6A)
- **Separate Ledger**: Set *No* so that you can specify the Sales Ledger (one or more) separately for each Item in the Invoice,

Consequently (when you set *No*), the Sales / Purchase Account field will not appear at Header. Instead, the Ledger allocation sub-screen (F-6B) will appear after entry of each Item, where you can select the respective Sales / Purchase Ledger Account

> ***Note:*** *You may even allocate the amount of one Item to multiple Sales / Purchase Ledger Account (useful to allocate Item Value & Tax component to respective Ledger Accounts)*

Sales No. 5 | 1-Jul-2009 Wednesday
Ref.: **16**
Party's A/c Name : **A K Traders**

Name of Item	Quantity	Rate	per	Amount
Anchor CFL Lamp 12W	2 Pieces	155.00	Pieces	310.00
Switch Board (Consealed)				90.00
				400.00
	2 Pieces			400.00

Narration: Sales & SErvice

F-6A: Multi Account Invoice

Accounting Details for: **Anchor CFL Lamp 12W**
Upto: ₹ **310.00 Cr**

Particulars	Amount
Sales	310.00

Accounting Details for: **Switch Board (Consealed)**
Upto: ₹ **90.00 Cr**

Particulars	Amount
Service Income	90.00

F-6B: Multiple Sales/ Purchase Ledger Account allocation of Item Value

07 Dual Quantity in Invoice

Sometimes, the Billing Quantity in Sales or Purchase Invoice may be different from the actual Received or Delivered Quantity. Common examples of such instances are Receipt or Delivery of Free Items, Samples. Allowances for Defects (e.g Textile or Timber dealers give some allowance in quantity for minor defects).

Normally, the Billing Quantity is same as Delivery Quantity. It means, the bill is raised for the quantity Purchased / Sold. But, sometimes, it may differ. Some instances are:

- **Free Items:** When some items are given Free. For example, 200 gm packet given free on sale of 1 Kg packet of a washing powder, or a 200 gm packet of biscuit given free on sale of 1 Kg packet of a washing powder.
- **Billing quantity rounded off:** Sometimes the Billing Quantity is rounded off to a rounding figure (e.g delivery quantity 9879 pcs, but charged for 10000 pcs)
- **Minimum Charge Billing:** When there is a minimum charge (10 ton minimum billing even if the quantity is 9.8 ton).
- **Allowances for Defectives:** Sometimes the billing quantity may be less for defective portions, like Timber, Leather, Textiles (10 metre textile sold, but charged for 9 metres due to some defects in some portion).
- **Rate Difference Adjustments:** To make supplementary Invoice, Debit / Credit Note for Rate Difference, Rebates, the Actual Quantity would be zero (as no more quantity is delivered) but the Billed quantity be entered to compute the supplementary charges / rebates etc at the specified adjustment Rate (e.g Rate Difference charged on sales during a specified period, due to rate increase)

The Actual Quantity entered in Invoice is updated in Stock and Billed quantity is used for computation of Item value in the Invoice.

07.01 Dual Quantity Activation in Invoice

To allow entry for the dual quantity (Billed Quantity and Actual Quantity) in Inventory voucher, click *F11: Features>Inventory Features* and set *Yes* at *Use Different Actual & Billed Quantity.*

Dual Quantity Entry in Invoice: Consequently, you get 2 columns for Quantity (Actual & Billing) instead of one Quantity column in Invoice entry. Enter the *Actual* & *Billed* Quantity in the respective columns (F-7B)

Sales No. **12** | 1-Feb-2010 Monday
Ref.:
Party's A/c Name : **A K Traders**
Sales Ledger : **Sales**

Name of Item	Quantity		Rate	per	Amount
	Actual	Billed			
Cables KayCee *Roll of 25 Mtrs*	11.00 Mtrs	10.00 Mtrs	13.00	Mtrs	130.00
					130.00
Narration:	11.00 Mtrs	10.00 Mtrs			130.00

F-7A: Dual Quantity entry in Invoice

Item Allocations for: **Cables KayCee**

Quantity		Rate	per	Amount
Actual	Billed			
11.00 Mtrs	10.00 Mtrs	13.00	Mtrs	130.00
11.00 Mtrs	10.00 Mtrs			130.00

F-7B: Item details with Dual Quantity

- **Actual Quantity**: At *Actual* column, enter the Quantity that has come in (or gone out)
- **Billed Quantity**: At *Billed* column, enter the Quantity on which the Item Value is computed.

For example, you sell 11 mtrs of cloth, but charge for 10metres metres (as some portion of cloth is defective). In such case, you should enter 11 Mtrs at Actual column and 10 Mtrs at Billed column (F-7A).

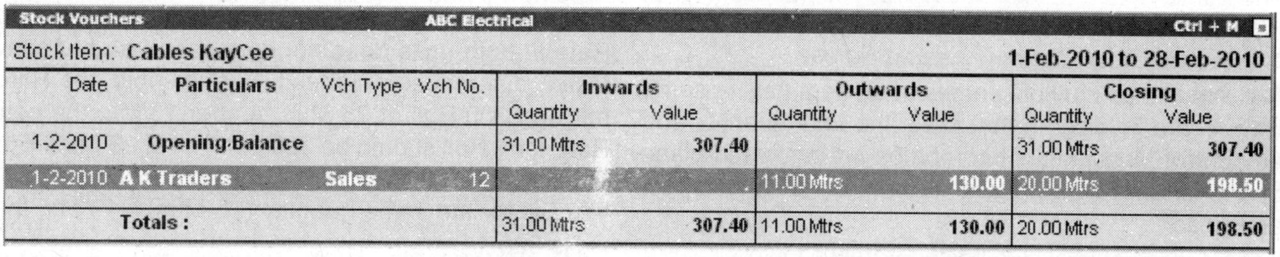

Stock Vouchers — ABC Electrical — Ctrl + M

Stock Item: Cables KayCee — 1-Feb-2010 to 28-Feb-2010

Date	Particulars	Vch Type	Vch No.	Inwards Quantity	Inwards Value	Outwards Quantity	Outwards Value	Closing Quantity	Closing Value
1-2-2010	Opening Balance			31.00 Mtrs	307.40			31.00 Mtrs	307.40
1-2-2010	A K Traders	Sales	12			11.00 Mtrs	130.00	20.00 Mtrs	198.50
	Totals :			31.00 Mtrs	307.40	11.00 Mtrs	130.00	20.00 Mtrs	198.50

F-7C: Posting of actual quantity in Stock Item Ledger

If you give free along with some other Items, then you enter the Free Quantity at Actual column and Zero at Billed Quantity column. For example, when you give 2 Pcs of Lux Soap free on sale of 2 Boxes of Surf, then you should make 2 entries for Items, as follows:

- Surf: Actual Quantity - 6 Box, Billed Quantity- 6 Box
- Lux: Actual Quantity 2, Billed Quantity- zero

The Item value is computed as per Billed Quantity while the Item Stock is updated as per Actual Quantity (F-7C)

A few instances of use of different Actual & Billed Quantity are listed below:

Type of Transaction	Item Name	Actual Quantity	Billed Quantity
Sell 2 Pcs of Lux Soap and give 1 Pc Free	Lux Soap	3	2
Give 2 Pcs of Wallet sample Free	Wallet	2	0
Sell 1 Box Surf Excel and give 1 Pc Lux Soap Free	Surf Excel Lux Soap	11	10
Sell 2 Mtrs of defective cloth and charge for 1.75 Mtrs	Cloth	2.00	1.75
Rebate of Rs 2/- per Mtr on sale of 200 Mtrs, sold earlier	White Cambric 80x20, 56cm width	0	200

The effect of such entry is that the transaction has taken place for the quantity transacted as mentioned in Actual Quantity column for value as specified in the amount column. The stock ledgers are updated accordingly. The quantity specified in the billing quantity column is used only for computation of Amount. The Billing Quantity has no other relevance or effect in any part of the stock accounts.

08 Zero Valued Voucher Entry

Sometimes, Stock Item is received or delivered without value (e.g Samples, Free Items etc). In such case, the Quantity is entered in Invoice, without Value.

To enable entry of such Zero Valued transaction, at *F11:Features> Inventory Features*, at *Allow Zero Valued Entries*:

- Set Yes to allow entry of Invoice with Zero Value.
- Set No. Zero Valued Invoice cannot be saved.

Such entries may also be entered through Stock Journal

You may enter such transaction, in 2 ways:

- Enter the Actual Quantity but enter zero at Billed Quantity (F-8A), as explained at Dual Quantity entry (§07.01). So, the stock will be updated but Invoice value (Amount column) will be zero (Zero Valued)
- Enter the Actual Quantity at Quantity column, but enter zero at Rate / Amount column (F-8B). So, the stock will be updated but Invoice Value will be zero (Zero Valued)

> ***Note:** At* Inventory Features, *set Yes at Allow Zero Valued Entries to enter zero valued voucher. The Stock will be updated as pe voucher.*

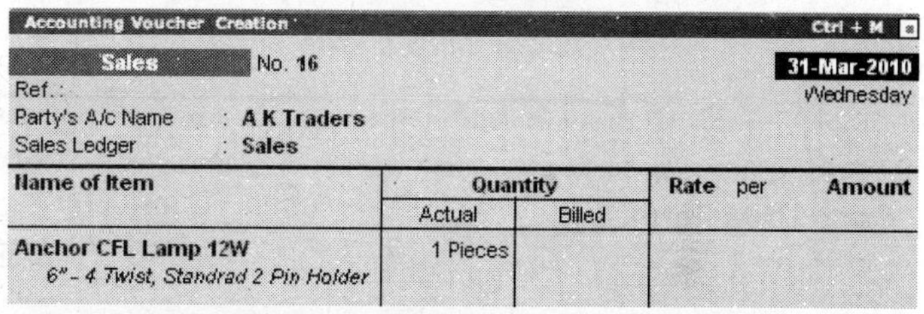

F-8A: Zero Valued Entry with Dual Quantity

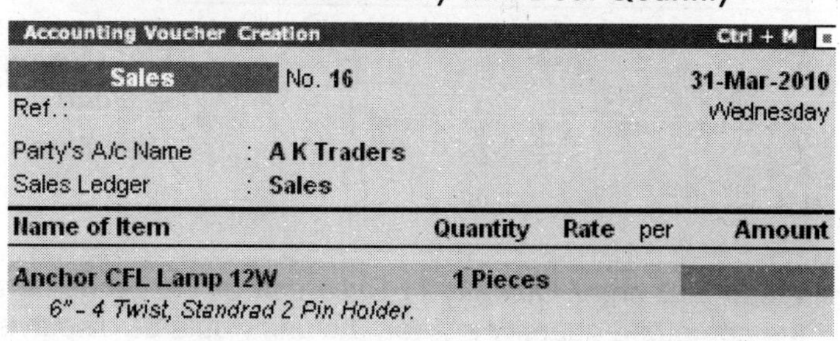

F-8B: Zero Valued Entry in Invoice

09 Consolidation of Same Rate Items in Invoice

Sometimes different Batch Number or Godown (with same Rate) of ONE Item are entered in an Invoice (they are entered as separate entry for each Godown / Location). This makes the Invoice long and total quantity of an Item in the Invoice with same Rate is not readily available.

Activating consolidation of same Rate entries: At *Invoice*

Configuration (*GoT>F12:Configure>Invoice / Orders Entry*), at *Consolidate Stock Items with same Rates*:

- Set *Yes* to club multiple entries of an Item having same Rate in the Invoice. In that case, the total quantity and amount of all such clubbed entries are shown in place of each individual entry and the Invoice looks compact and clean.
- Set *No*, each entry would be separately shown

10 Dual Unit & Price entry in Invoice

If you have set Dual Unit (Alternate Unit) for any Item in Stock Item Master (§02/02-02), then in Inventory Voucher, you may enter quantity in Base Unit and Rate in Base or in Alternate Unit (F-9A). The UoM at which the Rate is entered is called the Rate Unit.

Accounting Voucher Creation — Ctrl + M

Sales No. 5 — 1-Mar-2010, Monday

Ref. :
Party's A/c Name : **P.K.Motors**
Sales Ledger : **Sales**

Name of Item	Quantity	Rate	per	Amount
Cables KayCee	13.00 Mtrs (0.52 Roll)	13.00	Mtrs	169.00
Cables KayCee	26.00 Mtrs (1.04 Roll)	300.00	Roll	312.00
				481.00

F-9A: Dual UoM & Rate entry

F-9B: Billing in one UoM Rate

Name of Item	Quantity	Rate	per	Amount
Cables KayCee	30.00 Mtrs (1.20 Roll)	300.00	Roll	360.00
Roll of 25 Mtrs				
				360.00

Name of Item	Quantity	Rate	per	Amount
Cables KayCee	25.00 Mtrs (1.00 Roll)	300.00	Roll	300.00
Roll of 25 Mtrs				
Cables KayCee	5.00 Mtrs (0.20 Roll)	13.00	Mtrs	65.00
Cut From Roll				
				365.00

F-9C: Billing in Dual UoM Rate

When you enter Quantity in *Base* unit of the Stock Item, the computed quantity in Alternate unit would be displayed in parenthesis as per the conversion factor specified in the Item master (F-9A). You may enter Rate in either Base or Alternate UoM. The value (Amount) would be computed as per Rate and Rate unit specified.

When you attempt to enter Quantity of the Stock Item in Alternate unit, Tally will instantly replace it with the equivalent quantity in base unit (convert as per the conversion factor). For example, if you type 1r (to enter 1 Roll in Alternate unit), automatically the quantity will get converted to Base Un it (25 Mtrs) and the quantity in Alternate Unit (1 Roll) will be shown in parenthesis just below the Base Quantity (F-9C)

The value is computed as per Rate Unit specified. So, if the Rate in both units does not correspond as per conversion factor, differences will result. For example, the Rate is 13/ mtr and 300/Roll of 25 Mtrs. As per 13/Mtr, the equivalent Rate for 1 Roll should be 325 per Roll of 25 Mtrs. So, now if you bill for 1 Roll @ 300/Roll, the amount is Rs 300, while if you Bill for the same quantity (25 Mtrs)@13/Mtr, the value is Rs 325.

In such case, normally it is practice to split the quantity in Larger & Smaller Packs and charge at the corresponding rate. For example, the figures below show 2 different Bills for a sale bill of 1 Roll 5 Metres (1 Roll = 25 Mtrs), with Rate of 13/Mtr & 300/Roll

To Bill in different Rates, you have to select the Item separately (F-9C). In the Item details subscreen, you cannot make entry in different UoM Rates.

11 Discount

Often Discount is allowed by vendors in sales Invoice, to customers to induce loyal customers. Here we discuss about how you can enter Discount in Invoice.

You may enter Discount in Invoice at 2 levels (F-10C):

- **At Item Level**: Different Discount (Rate or Amount) for each Item (F-10C)
- **At Invoice Level**: Total Discount (Rate or Amount) for the whole Invoice, as negative Charges. This is explained at Additional Charges (P-14) in Invoice as negative amount (F-10C)

Discount may be allowed in Sales Invoice, or may be earned in Purchase Invoice

11.01 Item Level Discount

Item Level discount is useful when the Rate of discount is not same for all Items in the invoice (or Discount is allowed only for some specified Items). You should enter the Discount Rate (or Discounted Amount) for the specific Item sold in the invoice (F-10C). The Amount of Discount allowed is not reflected in Invoice, nor posted to any ledger account. The net value after discount is shown at Amount column and is treated as Sale / Purchase Value.

11.02 Item Level Discount set up

At Inventory Features (F11:Features>Inventory Features), at *Separate Discount Column on Invoice*:

- Set *Yes* at to enable Item Discount entry in Sales / Purchase Invoice (the additional *Disc%* column appears)
- Set *No*. No additional Discount column appears in Sales / Purchase Invoice (so you cannot enter Discount against an Item)

11.03 Item Level Discount Entry in Invoice

Consequently, during Voucher entry, after entry of Item Quantity & Rate, you get a column to enter the Rate in Discount (*Disc%)* column for each Item (F-10C). Enter the Discount rate as applicable

Tips: *You cannot enter lump sum amount in Discount for each Item, but can edit the net amount. So, you can use this trick to enter zero at Discount Rate and discounted value at Amount column.*

Note: *You may selecively speciffy different rates for Items. You may inflate the Rates by entering negative Discount Rate. This is useful when the Rate is charged at some % above some Base Rate.*

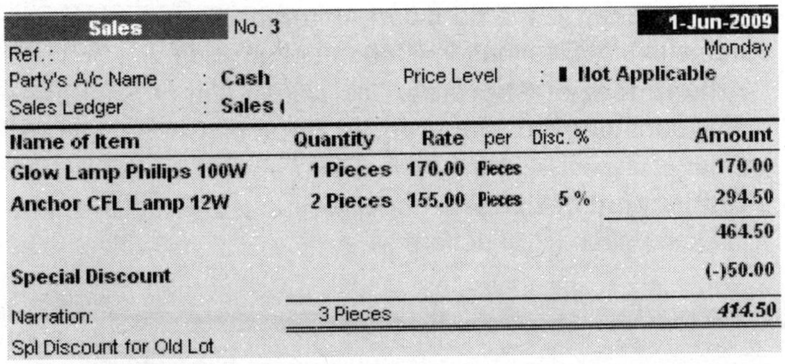

F-10C: Item / Invoice Level Discount Entry in Invoice

Tally does not store the value of Discount separately but internally reduces it from the Item Value. Separate Discount Rate may be allowed for respective Items in an Invoice.

12 Additional Charges in Invoice

Apart from Item Values, you may need to add or reduce (.e.g Discount, Rebates) etc. in Invoice.

There are 2 ways of adding / subtracting such amount in Invoice

- **Lump Sum amount:** The amount is input by the user
- **Computed Amount**: The Rate is input, amount is computed as per some pre set rules (%, quantity etc)

12.01 Lump Sum Additional Charges

In such case, after entering the Item details (select <end of

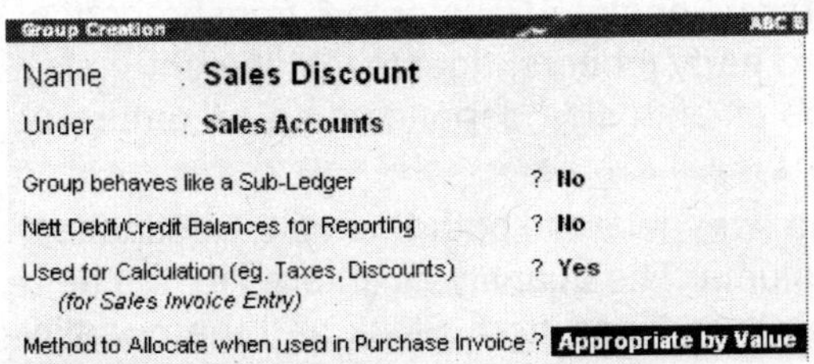

F-11A: Additional Charges Group creation

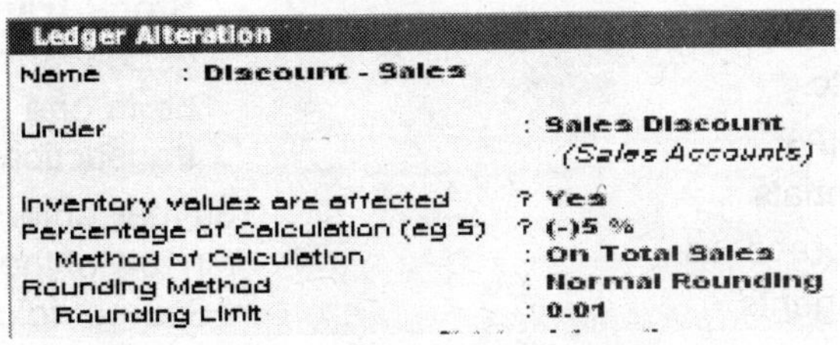

F-11B: Additional Charges Ledger creation

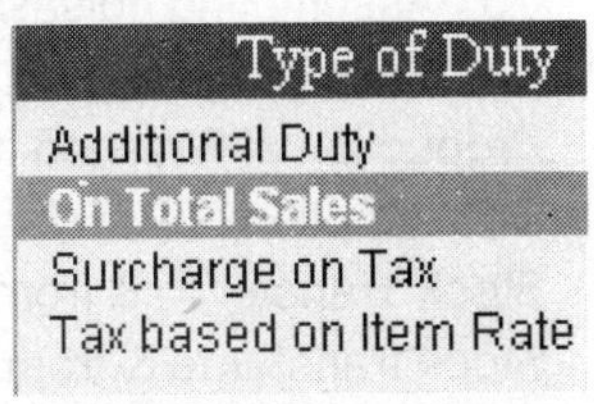

F-11C: Calculation Method List

list>), you may select a ledger account and enter the Amount. To add a charge (like Freight, Insurance Charges, Handling Charges,) enter the amount to be added in the Invoice. To allow rebate etc (amount to be reduced in Invoice), enter the amount in negative value (like – 200).

12.02 Additional Charges Computation Parameters Setting

To enable Tally to compute the amount in Purchase Invoice on the basis of Item Value, you have to set the parameters and specify the rules of Computation

Account Group:In the Parent Account Group of the respective ledger account creation / alteration, set *Yes* at *Used for Computation.* (at the option *Methods to Allocate when used in Purchase Account*, select *Not Applicable* (F-11A), as the option relates to Purchase Cost Allocation, not for Charges in Sales Invoice)

Ledger Account: In the respective Ledger Account creation / alteration, set as follows:

At *Under* field, select the Parent Group (for which computation is activated as explained above).

- **Inventory Values are affected**: Set *No* at this option.
- **Percentage of Calculation**: Enter the standard Rate of Charges in % (e.g 5). For Amount to be deducted enter the % as negative number (e.g -5).
- **Method of Calculation**: After entering the Percentage of Calculation, select the method (e.g *On Total Sales* to compute Amount on Sales value) as Method of Calculation from the list of Type of Duty.

Computation Base ; At *F12: Configuration > Invoicing / Orders, at Calculate Tax on current sub-total* (F-1B)

- **On Item Value only**: Set No to compute the amount on Item Value only
- **On Cumulative Value**: Set Yes to compute the additional charges amount on cumulative Bill amount (e.g after considering the Item value and other prior additional charges)

12.03 Additional Charges Entry in Invoice

During Invoice entry, after entry of Item details, select the respective Additional Charges Ledger. The Rate (in %), if entered in the ledger account at *Percentage of Calculation,* is carried which you may change (for Deduction, the Rate would be negative). The computed value, as per Calculation Method (F-11C) is shown in Amount column, Such computed amount may again be changed as desired, in voucher,

> ***Note:*** *The Voucher Level Discount is to be entered as negative Charge, to be deducted in the Invoice.*

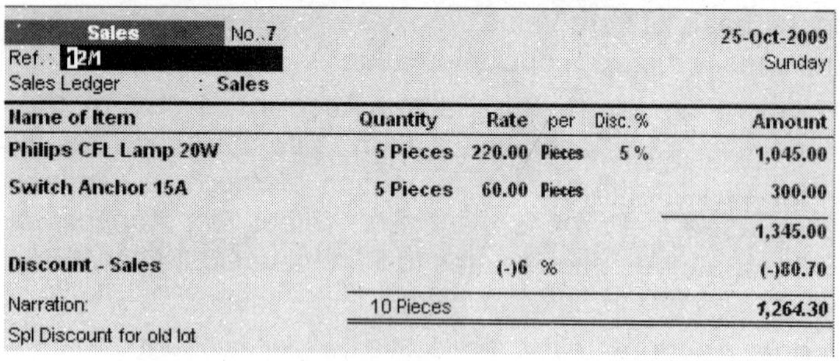

Sales No. 7					25-Oct-2009 Sunday
Ref.: 12M					
Sales Ledger : Sales					
Name of Item	Quantity	Rate	per	Disc. %	Amount
Philips CFL Lamp 20W	5 Pieces	220.00	Pieces	5 %	1,045.00
Switch Anchor 15A	5 Pieces	60.00	Pieces		300.00
					1,345.00
Discount - Sales		(-)6 %			(-)80.70
Narration:	10 Pieces				1,264.30
Spl Discount for old lot					

F-12A: Additional Charges in Invoice

13 Stock Journal Voucher

So far, we have discussed about Inventory Transactions on account of Sales & Purchase. Apart from that, several other Inventory transactions occur, for instance:

- Issue of materials to third party jobber and receipt back of jobbed items
- Adjustment of book stock due to
    - o Leakage, shortage evaporation etc
    - o Mistake in Item in any prior voucher
    - o Transfer from one godown to another
    - o Assembling / disassembling of items
    - o Scrapping of Items etc.
- Production of Finished Items
- Consumption of Raw Materials
- Stock Transfer to & from Branches
- Stock transfer to & from Agents

In all such cases, a Stock Journal Voucher is created to adjust the stock (and stock value) properly.

13.01 Stock Journal Voucher Entry

At Gateway, select Inventory Voucher and then Click *F7: Stk Jrn* to get Stock Journal Voucher entry screen (F-13)

Item Details

After entry of Voucher Number & Date, you enter the Item details as follows (F-13):

The Stock Journal has 2 sections:

- Source (Consumption)
- Destination (Production)

The following types of entries are made:

- **Consumption:** At the left part, enter the Item details (i.e Items OUT) at Source (Consumption) side.
- **Production**: At the right part, enter the Item details (i.e Items IN), at Destination (Consumption) side.
- **Adjustment of Shortage**: For adjustment of Shortage etc, consumption etc, enter in Source (Consumption) side.
- **Adjustment of Excess**: For adjustment of Excess, enter in Destination (Production) side

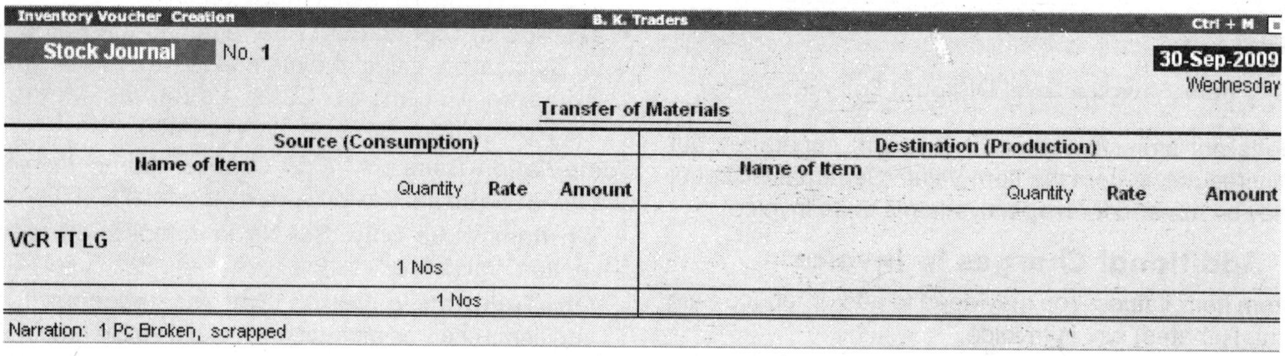

Inventory Voucher Creation — B. K. Traders — Ctrl + M

Stock Journal No. 1 — 30-Sep-2009 Wednesday

Transfer of Materials

Source (Consumption)				Destination (Production)			
Name of Item	Quantity	Rate	Amount	Name of Item	Quantity	Rate	Amount
VCR TT LG	1 Nos						
	1 Nos						

Narration: 1 Pc Broken, scrapped

F-13: Stock Journal entry

- **Rectification of Mistake**: For rectification of any mistake (in quantity, Stock Item Name) in some Inventory Voucher earlier entered, a stock Journal Voucher is created to bring the sock in sync. Depending on the type of mistake, adjustment, entry may be in Consumption side, Production Side or in both sides.
- **Stock Transfers**: For stock transfer to & from branches, godowns, third party jobbers, agents, etc the entry may be in one side or both side depending on he nature of transaction.

You may enter the Item details in both Source & Destination, or in any of the column. The quantity as entered for the Item in Source column is reduced from Stock and the quantity as entered for the Item in Destination column is increased.

The following Table shows some common types of entries in Stock Journal

Nature of Transaction	Consumption	Production
Adjustment of Shortage	√	
Adjustment of Excess		√
Adjustment between two Items	√	√
Issue / Consumption of Materials	√	
Receipt / Production of Items		√
Production-cum-Consumption	√	√
Transfer of Stock	√	√

14 Default Invoice Printing Configuration

We have described Invoice Printing Configuration (§02/03-03/S1). Here we describe the options related to Inventory details in Invoice. At the respective Printing Configuration menu, you may set the default options. At the time of printing respective documents from Display or Multiple Voucher printing, you may re-set the printing options at the respective Invoice printing session

Invoice Printing Options: The default Invoice Printing Configuration options (F-1B) are described earlier (§02/03-03/S1)

Stock Items Details Printing in Invoice:The default Invoice Printing Configuration options (F-1B) for Sales & Purchase Invoice, related to Stock Item details are described below:

- **Serial Number:** At *Print Serial Number, set:*
  - o *Yes* to print a column showing running Serial Number (F-14A)
  - o *No.* Running Serial Number is not printed (so save space, useful in Narrow Stationery: F-14B)
- **Part No.:** At *Print Part No, set:*
  - o *Yes* to print Part No of the Item (as entered in Stock Item Master: (F-14C)
  - o *No.* Part No is not printed (F-14A)
- **Quantity:** At *Print Quantity column*, set
  - o *Yes* (default value) to print Quantity (i.e Billed Quantity)
  - o *No* to omit Quantity column
- **Actual Quantity column:** At *Print Actual Quantity column*, set:
  - o *Yes* (default value) to print Actual Quantity (if specified), for each Item (F-14B)
  - o *No* to omit Actual Quantity column (F-14A)
- **Alternate Quantity column:** At *Print Alternate Quantity column,* set:
  - o *Yes* (default value) to print Alternate Quantity (if specified: F-14E)
  - o *No* to omit Alternate Quantity column (F-14A)

  Alternate Quantity in separate column: If you set Yes at Print Alternate Quantity column, further, at *Print as Separate Column*, set
  - ▪ *Yes* to print Alternate Quantity in separate column (F-14E)
  - ▪ *No* to print Alternate Quantity in same column, to save column space (F-14F)
- **Item Rate:** At *Print Rate column,* set:
  - o *Yes* (default value) to print Rate for the Item (F-14A)
  - o *No.* Rate column is not printed (useful to print Challan / Transporter Copy etc, where Rate need not be disclosed: F-14G)
- **Batch Details:** This is relevant only when Batch is activated for the Company. At *Print Batch Details*, set:
  - o *Yes* to Print Batch Details (Batch Number, Mg Exp Date etc).
  - o *No* to Batch Details NOT printed.
- **Rate with Duty for Items:** This is relevant only when Excise Duty is activated for the Company. At *Print Rate with Duty for Items,* set,
  - o *Yes* to print Excise Duty Details
  - o *No.* Excise Duty Details will NOT be printed
- **Ledger Narration:** At *Print Narration for each Entry,* set:
  - o *Yes* to Print Voucher Narration at the end of Voucher
  - o *No.* No Voucher Narration is printed
- **Sub Totals after each Item:** At Print Sub Totals after each Item, *set*
  - o *Yes* to print Sub Total after each Ledger Account (F-14D)
  - o *No* Sub Total is printed. Only Net Invoice Amount is prited at the end of all amounts in the Amount column (F-14A)
- **Print Base Currency Symbol for Total:** At *Print Base Currency Symbol for Total*, set:
  - o *Yes* to print Base Currency Symbol (like ': F-14A).
  - o No. No Base Currency Symbol is printed (F-14D)
- **Method to use for Ledger Name:** Specify the Format of the Ledger name to be printed, from the list, as explained earlier (§02/03-03/S1).
- **Method to use for Stock item Name:** Specify the Format of the Item to be printed, from the following options. These are applicable in case of Sale of Materials.
  - o **Alias (Name)**: Shows Alias Name followed by Item Name in parenthesis
  - o **Description (Name)**: Shows Description followed by Item Name in parenthesis
  - o **Description only**: Shows Item Description only
  - o **Description (Part No)**: Shows Description followed by Part No in parenthesis
  - o **Name (Alias)**: Shows Item Name followed by Alias Name in parenthesis (F-14C)

- o **Name (Description)**: Shows Item Name followed by Description in parenthesis
- o **Name only**: Shows Item Name only. This is the default format shown in all reports
- o **Name (Part No)**: Shows Item Part Number also (F-14C)
- o **Part No Alias only**: Shows Part No Alias only
- o **Part No Alias (Part No)**: Shows Part No Alias followed by Part No in parenthesis
- o **Part No (Description)**: Shows Part No followed by Description in parenthesis
- o **Part No (Name)**: Shows Part No followed by Item Name in parenthesis
- o **Part No only**: Shows part No only
- o **Part No (Part No Alias)**: Shows Part No followed by Part No Alias in parenthesis
- o In DN/ CN Voucher

- **Voucher Narration:** At *Print Narration,* set:
  - o *Yes* to print Voucher Narration (F-14D)
  - o *No.* Voucher Narration not printed (F-14A)
- **Jurisdiction:** At *Jurisdiction*, enter the name of the Court Jurisdiction under which disputes are to be settled, to be printed, as Notice to the Customer. The line *Subject to < Jurisdiction > Jurisdiction* is printed with the Name of the Jurisdiction (F-14B)

Invoice No. 4 Dated 30-Jun-2009
Ref. No.

ABC Electrical
27/C, Rasbihari Road
3rd Floor, Suit No.305
Kolkata-700019
E-Mail :nomail@kmail.com

INVOICE

Party : G V Motots
12 Beliaghat Rd
Kolkata 700 078

Order No. 13 25-Jun-2009	Payment Terms 30 days from delivery	Despatch Document 234 dt 28.6.09 dt. 28-Jun-2009 Through : VAN WB 02 P 2328	Delivery Note 12 To Customer Godown

Sl No.	Description of Goods	Quantity	Rate	per	Disc. %	Amount
1	Glow Lamp Philips 100W	18 Pieces	160.00	Pieces		2,880.00
2	Anchor CFL Lamp 12W	4 Pieces	180.00	Pieces		720.00
						3,600.00
	Output VAT 12.5%		12.50	%		450.00
	Goshala Donation		0.50	%		18.00
	Total	22 Pieces				₹ 4,118.00

Amount Chargeable (in words) E. & O.E
Indian Rupees Four Thousand One Hundred Eighteen Only

Local Sales Tax No. : ST8624870
Inter State Sales Tax No. : 86581240
Company's Service Tax No. : WB8672054
Buyer's Local Sales Tax No. : WB 123468
Buyer's CST No. : WB (C) 5129
Company's PAN : ABPN5866K

Declaration
We declare that this invoice shows the actual price of the goods described and that all particulars are true and correct.

for ABC Electrical

Authorised Signatory

This is a Computer Generated Invoice

F- 14A:Sales Invoice in Simple Format

INVOICE

ABC Electrical 27/C, Rasbihari Road 3rd Floor, Suit No.305 Kolkata-700019 E-Mail :nomail@kmail.com	Invoice No.	Dated
	Delivery Note 12	Mode/Terms of Payment 30 days from delivery
	Supplier's Ref.	Other Reference(s) [illegible]
Buyer G V Motots 12 Beliaghat Rd Kolkata 700 078	Buyer's Order No. 13	Dated 25-Jun-2009
	Despatch Document No. 234 dt 28.6.09	Dated 28-Jun-2009
	Despatched through VAN WB 02 P 2328	Destination Customer Godown
	Terms of Delivery By VAN to customer godwon at owners cost	

Description of Goods	Quantity Shipped	Quantity Billed	Rate	per	Disc %	Amount
Glow Lamp Philips 100W	18 Pieces	18 Pieces	160.00	Pieces		2,880.00
Anchor CFL Lamp 12W	4 Pieces	4 Pieces	180.00	Pieces		720.00
						3,600.00
Output VAT 12.5%			12.50	%		450.00
Goshala Donation			0.50	%		18.00
Cess						
Total	22 Pieces	22 Pieces				₹ 4,118.00

Amount Chargeable (in words) E. & O.E
Indian Rupees Four Thousand One Hundred Eighteen Only

Local Sales Tax No. : ST8624870
Inter State Sales Tax No. : 86581240
Buyer's Local Sales Tax No. : WB 123456
Buyer's CST No. : WB (C) 5129
Company's PAN : ABPN5866K

Declaration
We declare that this invoice shows the actual price of the goods described and that all particulars are true and correct.

Customer's Seal and Signature for ABC Electrical

Authorised Signatory

SUBJECT TO KOLKATA JURISDICTION

F-14B: Sales Invoice in Normal Format

- **Message:** At *Generated By*, enter the Message to be printed at last line (F-14A). A default message '*This is a Computer Generated Invoice*' is shown, which you may change. You may leave blank if no message line is to be printed at the bottom of the Invoice (F-14B).

Invoice No. 4 Dated 1-Jun-2009

ABC Electrical
27/C, Rasbihari Road
3rd Floor, Suit No.305
Kolkata-700019
E-Mail :nomail@kmail.com

INVOICE

Party : G V Motots
12 Beliaghat Rd
Kolkata 700 078

Description of Goods	Part No.	Quantity	Rate	per	Disc. %	Amount
Glow Lamp Philips 100W (127286)	GL6783	18 Pieces	160.00	Pieces		2,880.00
Anchor CFL Lamp 12W (CFL-12)	127962	4 Pieces	180.00	Pieces		720.00
						3,600.00
Output VAT 12.5%			12.50	%		450.00
Goshala Donation			0.50	%		18.00
Total		22 Pieces				₹ 4,068.00

Amount Chargeable (in words) E. & O.E
Indian Rupees Four Thousand Sixty Eight Only

for ABC Electrical

Authorised Signatory

F- 14C:Sales Invoice in Simple Format (With Part Number / Alias Names)

Invoice No. 4 Dated 1-Jun-2009

ABC Electrical

INVOICE

Party : G V Motots
12 Beliaghat Rd
Kolkata 700 078

Description of Goods	Part No.	Quantity	Rate	per	Disc. %	Amount
Glow Lamp Philips 100W (127286)	GL6783	18 Pieces	160.00	Pieces		2,880.00
Anchor CFL Lamp 12W (CFL-12)	127362	4 Pieces	180.00	Pieces		720.00
						3,600.00
Output VAT 12.5%			12.50	%		450.00
						4,050.00
Goshala Donation			0.50	%		18.00
						4,068.00
Total		22 Pieces				4,068.00

E. & O.E

Amount Chargeable (in words)

Indian Rupees Four Thousand Sixty Eight Only

Remarks:

Old Lots. Non Returnable

for ABC Electrical

Authorised Signatory

F- 14D:Sales Invoice in Simple Format (with Simple Format. Without Company Address. With Voucher Narration. Without Currency Symbol)

INVOICE

Party : A K Traders

Description of Goods	Alt.Quantity	Quantity	Rate	per	Disc. %	Amount
Cables KayCee	1.00 Roll	25.00 Mtrs	300.00	Roll		300.00
Cables KayCee	0.20 Roll	5.00 Mtrs	13.00	Mtrs		65.00
Total	1.20 Roll	30.00 Mtrs				365.00

E. & O.E

Amount Chargeable (in words)

Indian Rupees Three Hundred Sixty Five Only

Buyer's Service Tax No. : WB/35210

for ABC Electrical

Authorised Signatory

F-14E: Sales Invoice in Simple Format (Alternate Quantity in Separate Column)

Invoice No. 17 Dated 31-Mar-2010

ABC Electrical

INVOICE

Party : A K Traders

Description of Goods	Quantity	Rate	per	Disc. %	Amount
Cables KayCee	25.00 Mtrs (1.00 Roll)	300.00	Roll		300.00
Cables KayCee	5.00 Mtrs (0.20 Roll)	13.00	Mtrs		65.00
Total	30.00 Mtrs				365.00

E. & O.E

Amount Chargeable (in words)

Indian Rupees Three Hundred Sixty Five Only

Buyer's Service Tax No. : WB/35210

for ABC Electrical

Authorised Signatory

F-14F: Sales Invoice in Simple Format (Alternate Quantity in Quantity Column)

Invoice No. 17 Dated 31-Mar-2010

ABC Electrical

INVOICE

Party : A K Traders

Sl No.	Description of Goods	Quantity	Disc. %	Amount
1	Cables KayCee	25.00 Mtrs (1.00 Roll)		300.00
2	Cables KayCee	5.00 Mtrs (0.20 Roll)		65.00
	Total	30.00 Mtrs		365.00

E. & O.E

Amount Chargeable (in words)

Indian Rupees Three Hundred Sixty Five Only

Buyer's Service Tax No. : WB/35210

for ABC Electrical

Authorised Signatory

F-14G: Sales Invoice in Simple Format (Without Rate)

FAQ: Frequently Asked Questions

FAQ-1: How I can enter multiple Sales / Purchase Ledger in Invoice

Ans: To allocate the Sales / Purchase Value to any Sales / Purchase Ledger for each Item (e.g different Sales / Purchase Ledger for each Item), at Invoice Configuration screen (F-1B), set *No* at *Use Common Ledger A/c for Item Allocation.* Consequently, you have to specify the Sales Ledger (one or more) separately for each Item in the Invoice at Item Allocation screen (instead of at Voucher Header)

01 Voucher Class

Inventory Vouchers creation requires lot of data entry, involving repetitive steps and process. We have explained Voucher Class for Basic Accounting Vouchers (Receipt, Payment, Contra) earlier (§02/02-08). Here, we discuss Invoice Class for Sales, Purchase, Debit & Credit Notes.

Through Voucher Class, the recurring tasks and standard values may be pre set to make voucher entry process faster, accurate and secure. Voucher Class helps to automate transaction entries, minimize errors and manipulations. For example, *Sales* Account, Prices, Discounts, Tax computations, Account Allocations etc., may be pre-defined in the Voucher Class and need not be entered each time in Invoice. The Voucher Class (for Sale/ Purchase Invoice, Debit / Credit Notes) internally provides all the values as per parameters set for.

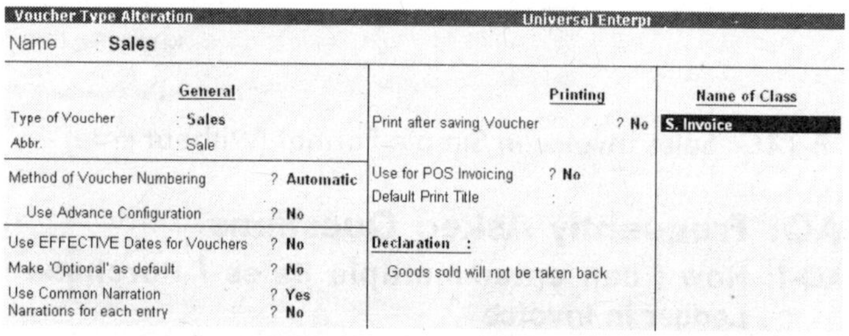

F-1A: Voucher Class creation

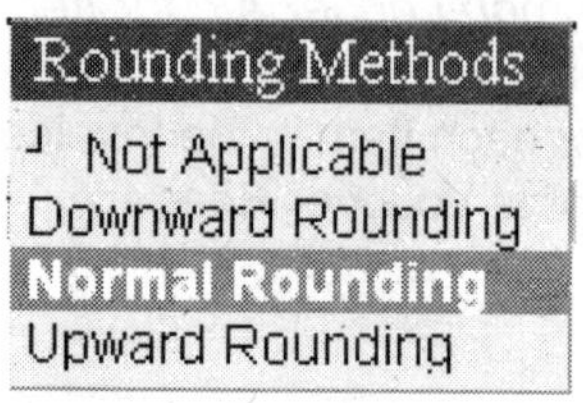

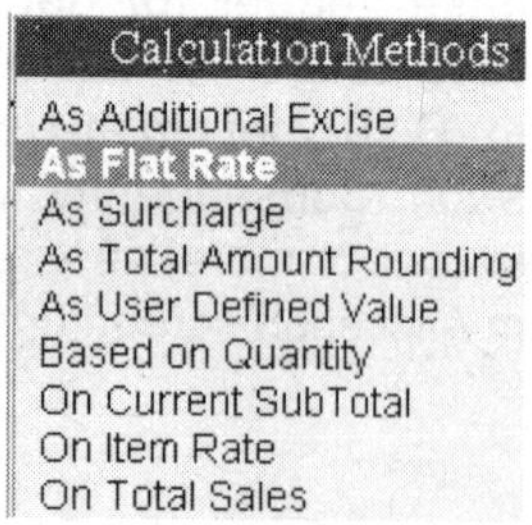

F-1B: Rounding Method List F-1C: Calculation Method List

Voucher class can be used in Invoice Mode only. So, at Company Features, set the Voucher entry in Invoice Mode (§03/ 03-02/S1)

02 Voucher Class Creation

Voucher Class is created through Voucher Type creation screen described earlier (§02/02-08). At Gateway, select *Accounts Info>Voucher Type>Create* (or *Inventory Info>Voucher Type>Create)* to get Voucher Type creation screen (F-1A). Fill up all information to create a voucher type. as described (§02/02-08).

At *Name of Class* (F-1A), type Voucher Class Name to be created, to get the Voucher Class set up screen for the respective Voucher Type, Sales (F-2A), Purchase (F-2B), Debit Note (F-3A) & Credit Note (F-3B), as specified at Voucher Type creation screen (F-1A)

The voucher Class creation screen (F-2A to F-2B, F-3A to F-3B) contain following components

- Excluded Groups
- Included Groups
- Default Accounting Allocation for Items
- Additional Accounting Allocation for other ledger accounts

At the Exclude / Included Group, for the Party Accounts. Specify the respective Account Groups. Ledgers under Excluded Group will not be listed in Party Accounts, while Ledgers under Excluded Group will be listed in Party Accounts

Specify as follows:

- **Excluded Groups in Voucher Class:** Here, select the Groups to be excluded for Party Ledger Accounts. Consequently, in the Party Ledger field in Sales Voucher entry, the ledgers under the selected Group will not be available.
- **Included Group in Voucher Class:** Here, the Group for inclusion.

For example, to create a Sales Voucher class for Credit Customers, select Sundry Creditors (to exclude Suppliers), Cash & Bank Account Groups (to exclude Cash Sales) and select Sundry Debtors & Branch Divisions in the included Groups. However, if you have several Groups of Customers, Local and several other groups for each territory, for a sales voucher class exclusively for Local Customers, select Sundry Debtors at Excluded Group and select Local Customers Group at Included section (F-2A)

Accordingly, enter Account Groups in Excluded / Included section, for Purchase Voucher Class (F-2B)

Accounting Allocations

In the next part, specify accounting allocations of Item Value to ledger under Sales / Purchase Group (F-2A, F-2B).

- o **Ledger Name:** At *Leger Name* column, select the Ledger Accounts The first ledger should be a Sales / Purchase Account (an Inventory linked ledger account).

  If the Item Value is to be allocated into multiple Ledgers, you may select other accounts (other than Inventory Linked Accounts) in the next lines.
- o **Percentage:** At *Percentage %* column, enter the allocation percentage for each Ledger Accounts entered in this area.

  For example, to allocate the Sales value into Sales Account and Sales Tax (8%), select Sales Account and enter 92.59 % (1/1.08).

  In the next Account, select Sales Tax A/c and enter 7.41% (.08/1.08).

  The total percentage of all allocated Ledgers must be 100
- o **Rounding Method & Rounding Limit:** This is applicable when Item Value is allocated to more than one ledger account. You can specify Rounding method from the list and then specify the corresponding limit

  Rounding Method: At Rounding Method columns, select
  - *Normal*: To round off to nearest amount of the limit,
  - *Upward*: To round off to next higher rounding,.
  - *Lower*: To round off to next lower rounding,
  - *Not Applicable*: Not to apply any rounding

  Rounding Limit

  If you selected any Rounding method, at *Rounding Limit*, specify the corresponding rounding limit to be rounded to.

  You cannot specify Rounding Methods for the last ledger account specified. Its value will be computed as the balancing figure.

Item Default Overriding: This is applicable only to the first Inventory linked Ledger account (i.e. the Sales Ledger Account). At the column *Override using Item Default*, set:

- *Yes* to post to the Sales Ledger Account linked with the stock Item as default,.
- *No* to enter Ledger Account during Voucher entry,

For example, Sales Ledger A/c 4% is linked with Item A and Sales Ledger A/c 12% is linked with ledger B. you like to select the Ledger Account linked with the Item. In such case, at Default Item Allocation of Item part, you may select any Ledger Account (either Sales Ledger A/c 4% or Sales Ledger A/c 12% and set Yes at the option *Override using Item default.* Consequently, The ledger account as specified in Item Master will get selected irrespective of the ledger account specified in the voucher class.

> ***Tips:*** *At the column* Override using Item Default *(F-4A), set:*
> - Yes *when the Item Value is to be posted to a specified ledger accounts for every type of Sale (i.e the Item value for the respective Item is to be posted to a specified Sales Ledger Account in respect of every type of Sale)*
> - *Set* No *when the Item Value is to be posted to different Ledger Accounts in different Sales Voucher*

Additional Accounting Entries

At this part, specify Duties, Taxes and Other Charges levied in the Invoice. Select the Ledger Account. Now specify:

Type of Calculation

Select a Method of Calculation from the following

- On Item Rate
- On Total Sales
- As Surcharge
- As Additional Excise
- On Current Sub Total

And any of the following methods available exclusively in Voucher Class only

- **As a Flat Rate**: Here you may specify a fixed amount which will be included in the invoice irrespective Sales value or any other amount.
- **Based on Quantity**: Select it when the value is to be computed on total quantity of all the Items in the invoice (irrespective of UoM of the Items).
- **As User Defined Value**: Select it when the amount is to be entered in the Invoice (no computation by Tally).
- **As Total Amount Rounding**: This is selected as a last Item to allocate the fractional figure of the Total Invoice value to round off the Net Amount of the Invoice.

Value Basis

Here enter the Rate (or ser defined value) as specified in the *Method of Calculation*, specified in the previous column.

- **Rounding Method & Rounding Limit:** You may also specify the *Rounding Method* and *Rounding limit* as explained above.
- **Remove if Zero:** Set *Yes* to suppress printing of ledger account name in the invoice, for which the amount is zero, else set *No*, to print the ledger name even for zero amount (useful when preprinted stationary is used).

03 Credit Note Voucher Class

Credit Note class can be created in relation to Rate Difference, Rebates, Sales Returns and also for Interest Accounting.

In Credit Note Class screen, set *No* at *Use Class for Interest Accounting* (F-3A)

The rest part of the Credit Note Class screen is similar to Sales Invoice Class. Like Sales Invoice Class, you may allocate Sales Value to multiple Accounts in the Voucher Class.

Class : **S. Invoice**

If you wish to restrict the groups to which this class can be used, specify them here.

Exclude these Groups	Include these Groups
Sundry Creditors **Bank Accounts** **Bank OD A/c** **Cash-in-Hand**	**Sundry Debtors** **Branch / Divisions**

Default Accounting Allocations for each Item in Invoice

Ledger Name	Percentage %	Rounding Method	*Rounding Limit*	Override using Item Default ?
Sales	92.59 %	Normal Rounding	1	Yes
Sales Tax	7.41 %			

Additional Accounting Entries (e.g. Taxes / Other charges) to be added in Invoice

Ledger Name	Type of Calculation	Value Basis	Rounding Method	*Rounding Limit*
Freight	As Flat Rate	200	Normal Rounding	1

F-2A: Sales Voucher Class creation set up

Class : **P Invoice**

If you wish to restrict the groups to which this class can be used, specify them here.

Exclude these Groups	Include these Groups
Sundry Debtors **Bank Accounts** **Bank OD A/c** **Cash-in-Hand**	**Sundry Creditors**

Default Accounting Allocations for each Item in Invoice

Ledger Name	Percentage %	Rounding Method	*Rounding Limit*	Override using Item Default ?
Purchase	100 %			Yes

Additional Accounting Entries (e.g. Taxes / Other charges) to be added in Invoice

Ledger Name	Type of Calculation	Value Basis	Rounding Method	*Rounding Limit*
Freight	As User Defined Value			

F-2B: Purchase Voucher Class creation set up

Universal Enterprises

Class : **C. Note**

Use Class for Interest Accounting ? **No**

If you wish to restrict the groups to which this class can be used, specify them here.

Exclude these Groups	Include these Groups
End of List	**Sundry Debtors** **Sundry Creditors**

Default Accounting Allocations for each Item in Invoice

Ledger Name	Percentage %	Rounding Method	*Rounding Limit*	Override using Item Default ?
Sales Return	92.59 %	Normal Rounding	1	Yes
Sales Tax	7.41 %			

Additional Accounting Entries (e.g. Taxes / Other charges) to be added in Invoice

Ledger Name	Type of Calculation	Value Basis	Rounding Method	*Rounding Limit*	Remove if Zero ?
Freight	As User Defined Value				Yes
Handling Charges	As User Defined Value				Yes

F-3A: Credit Note Voucher Class set up

04 Debit Note Voucher Class

Debit Note class can be created in relation to Rate Difference, Rebates, Purchase Returns and also for Interest Accounting (§10/03-09/S1).

In Debit Note Class screen, for other than Interest, set *No* at *Use Class for Interest Accounting.* (F-3B)

The rest part of the Debit Note Class screen is similar to Purchase Invoice Class. Like Purchase Invoice Class, you can not allocate Purchase Value to multiple Accounts in the Voucher Class.

Class : **D. Note**

Use Class for Interest Accounting ? **No**

If you wish to restrict the groups to which this class can be used, specify them here.

Exclude these Groups	Include these Groups
End of List	**Sundry Creditors** **Sundry Debtors**

Default Accounting Allocations for each Item in Invoice

Ledger Name	Percentage %	Rounding Method	*Rounding Limit*	Override using Item Default ?
Purchase	100 %			Yes

Additional Accounting Entries (e.g. Taxes / Other charges) to be added in Invoice

Ledger Name	Type of Calculation	Value Basis	Rounding Method	*Rounding Limit*	Remove if Zero ?
Freight	As User Defined Value				Yes

F-3B: Debit Note Voucher Class set up

05 Ledger allocation for Item value

Sometimes, the Item Sales value may be allocated to more than one account. For example, if the sales value includes local Tax (for example a certain % is charged for local trade association, whose rate differs from Item to Item), then the amount may be split among multiple ledger accounts like Sales Account & Tax Account. In such case, the Sales Value may need to be allocated to Sales & Sales Tax ledgers.

Activating Item Allocation to Ledger Accounts: To enable the feature of specifying the default ledger allocation in Stock Item Master, at *Accts / Inv Info configuration*, set Yes at the option. *Specify Default Ledger allocation for Invoicing*

Consequently, during Item Master entry, you get an option *Set Modify Default Ledgers* for Invoicing to specify default ledger allocation for such Inventory linked Sales / Purchase Ledger Accounts, to set:

- Default Accounting Allocations for Sales Invoice
- Default Accounting Allocations for Purchase Invoice

Now specify the allocation percentage in the respective area, as follows (F-4A):

- **Ledger Account**: At Ledger Name, select the Ledger Account (Sales / Purchase) to which the Stock value will be allocated.
- **Allocation Percentage**: At Percentage % column, enter the percentage allocated to the Ledger Account.
- **Rounding Method:** Select the Rounding Method
- **Rounding Limit:** If Rounding Method is selected, enter the Rounding Limit.

This way, enter all the ledger accounts to which the Item Value to be allocated. The Total allocable percentage should be 100. In the last ledger account, the Rounding Method is not asked. The balance amount is posted to the last account to avoid rounding of errors.

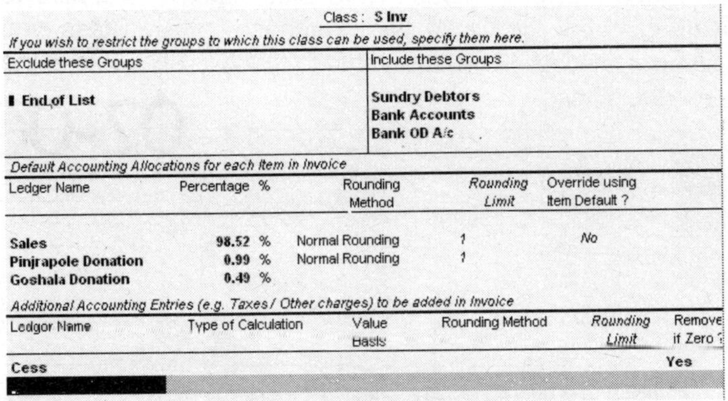

Class : S Inv

If you wish to restrict the groups to which this class can be used, specify them here.

Exclude these Groups	Include these Groups
■ End of List	Sundry Debtors Bank Accounts Bank OD A/c

Default Accounting Allocations for each Item in Invoice

Ledger Name	Percentage %	Rounding Method	*Rounding Limit*	Override using Item Default ?
Sales	**98.52** %	Normal Rounding	1	*No*
Pinjrapole Donation	**0.99** %	Normal Rounding	1	
Goshala Donation	**0.49** %			

Additional Accounting Entries (e.g. Taxes / Other charges) to be added in Invoice

Ledger Name	Type of Calculation	Value Basis	Rounding Method	*Rounding Limit*	Remove if Zero ?
Cess					**Yes**

F-4A: Default Ledger Allocation for Stock Item value in Voucher Class

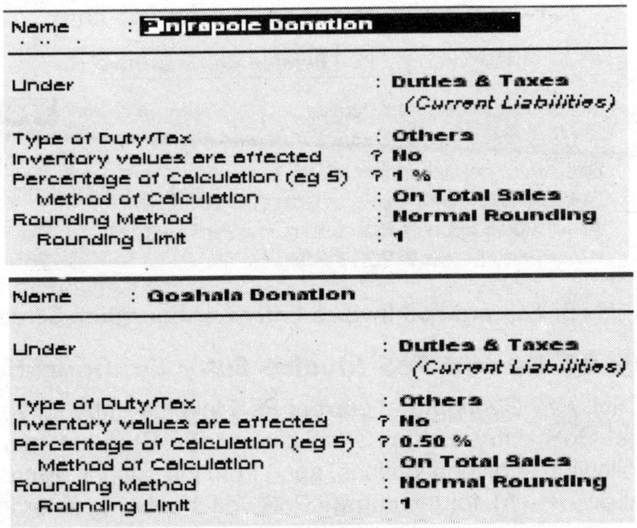

Name	: **Pinjrapole Donation**
Under	: **Duties & Taxes** *(Current Liabilities)*
Type of Duty/Tax	: **Others**
Inventory values are affected	? **No**
Percentage of Calculation (eg 5)	? **1 %**
Method of Calculation	: **On Total Sales**
Rounding Method	: **Normal Rounding**
Rounding Limit	: **1**

Name	: **Goshala Donation**
Under	: **Duties & Taxes** *(Current Liabilities)*
Type of Duty/Tax	: **Others**
Inventory values are affected	? **No**
Percentage of Calculation (eg 5)	? **0.50 %**
Method of Calculation	: **On Total Sales**
Rounding Method	: **Normal Rounding**
Rounding Limit	: **1**

F-4B: Allocable Ledger Accounts

This option is useful to allocate sales / purchase value to product value, Local Tax, Agency Commission, or other amount included in Sales / Purchase Value..

FAQ: Frequently Asked Questions

FAQ-1: Briefly explain the process of creation of Invoice Voucher Class

Ans: Through Voucher Class, the recurring tasks and standard values may be pre set to make voucher entry process faster, accurate and secure. Voucher Class helps to automate transaction entries, minimize errors and manipulations. For example, *Sales* Account, Prices, Discounts, Tax computations, Account Allocations etc., may be pre-defined in the Voucher Class and need not be entered each time in Invoice. The Voucher Class (for Sale/ Purchase Invoice, Debit / Credit Notes) internally provides all the values as per parameters set.

The entire process of specifying Voucher Class constitute following major Steps:

Voucher Class Name: At Voucher Type creation of the Voucher class, at Name of Class, enter the Voucher Class Name. Next set up the Voucher Class as follows:

- Account Groups
- Default Accounting Allocation for Items
- Additional Accounting Allocation for other ledger accounts

Account Groups: Specify the Accounts Groups to filter allowable ledger accounts in the Voucher:

- **Exclude Group**: Select the excluded Account Groups (the subordinate ledgers of the Selected Account groups will not be included in Ledger Account selection list during Voucher Entry).
- **Include Group**: Select sub set of excluded Account Groups (of the Groups which were selected at Exclude Group list), the subordinate ledgers of the Included Account groups will be included in Ledger Account selection list during Voucher Entry).

The combination of Exclude / Include section helps to precisely filter the desired Ledger Groups that could be allowed to be selected in the Voucher.

Default Accounting Allocation for Items: Specify the allocated % of the total Sales /Purchase Value to respective ledger accounts and related details.

Additional Accounting Allocation for other Ledger Accounts: Specify other ledger Accounts to be included in the Invoice and related details.

Point of Sales 02-06

01 Point of Sales

POS (or PoS) has been described earlier (§01/01-08). Here we discuss about advanced features of PoS.

02 PoS Invoice Entry Configuration

At GoT, click *F12:Configure>Invoice/Orders Entry*, under the section POS (F-1A) set the following options for Point of Sale:

- **Faster POS Invoicing:** In retailing, normally 1 unit is billed for most of the Items. At *Skip Qty field during POS Invoicing (faster entry)*, set:
  - o Yes to carry 1 automatically at quantity field (so quantity need not be typed in 1 unit item sale)
  - o *No* (Quantity figure is to be entered every time for each Item)
- **Modification of Rate in Invoice**: The Rates carried are automatically picked as per the Standard Rates defined in the Stock Item master or from the selected Price List. At *Allow modification of Rate field during POS Invoicing*, set:
  - o *Yes* to allow modification of Rates carried during PoS Invoice entry
  - o *No* to prevent change of Rates
- **Party Details in POS Invoice**: Normally ledgers are not created for customers for PoS as payments are made at the counter at the time of sale and no balance remains outstanding. However, sometime, you may need to keep Customer details. At *Allow Party Details in POS Invoice*, set:
  - o *Yes*, to select the Customer's Ledger in PoS entry
  - o *No*. Party Details are not to be entered in PoS Invoice for faster entry

To enter Party details without selecting a Party Ledger, during PoS entry, select *Not Applicable* at Party Ledger and enter Party Name & Address at Buyers Details.

POS	
Skip Qty field during POS Invoicing (faster entry!)	? Yes
Allow modification of Rate field during POS Invoicing	? No
Allow Party Details in POS Invoice	? Yes

F-1A: Configuration options for PoS Entry

POS Invoice Configuration	
Accept Supplementary Details *(Address Details, Despatch Details etc.)*	? Yes
Use Additional Description(s) for Item Name	? Yes
Skip Qty field during POS Invoicing (faster entry!)	? Yes
Allow modification of Rate field during POS Invoicing	? No
Allow Party Details in POS Invoice	? Yes

F-1B: Current PoS Invoice Entry Configuration Screen

02.01 Current PoS Invoice Entry Configuration

Click *F12:Configure* at current PoS Invoice entry screen to get PoS entry configuration screen (F-1B). Here you get following additional options, apart from the options discussed above (F-1A), for the current PoS Voucher being entered:

- ***Accept Supplementary Details***: Set *Yes* to enter supplementary details as described earlier (§07/03-02/S1).
- ***Use Additional Description for Item Name***: Set *Yes* to enter Additional Item Description as described earlier (§03/02-04).

Additional Charges in POS

You may also specify the other charges (F-2A) and its computation / rounding methods (F-2B) in the Voucher Class. Consequently, you may enter the Additional Charge in the PoS Voucher (F-3B)

Buyers Details in PoS

When you set *Yes* at *Accept Supplementary details* at *PoS Voucher Entry configuration* (F-1B), you may enter Buyer's details (F-3A)

Additional Accounting Entries (e.g. Taxes/ Other charges) to be added in Invoice

Ledger Name	Type of Calculation	Value Basis	Rounding Method	*Rounding Limit*	Remove if Zero ?
Carry Bag	As Flat Rate	2	Normal Rounding	1	**Yes**

F-2A: Additional Charges specification in Voucher Class

Calculation Methods
As Additional Excise
As Flat Rate
As Surcharge
As Total Amount Rounding
As User Defined Value
Based on Quantity
On Current SubTotal
On Item Rate
On Total Sales

F-2B: Calculation Methods List

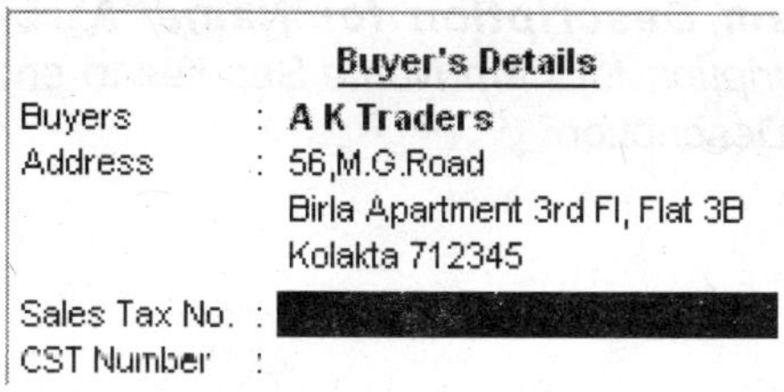

F-3A: Entry of Buyer details

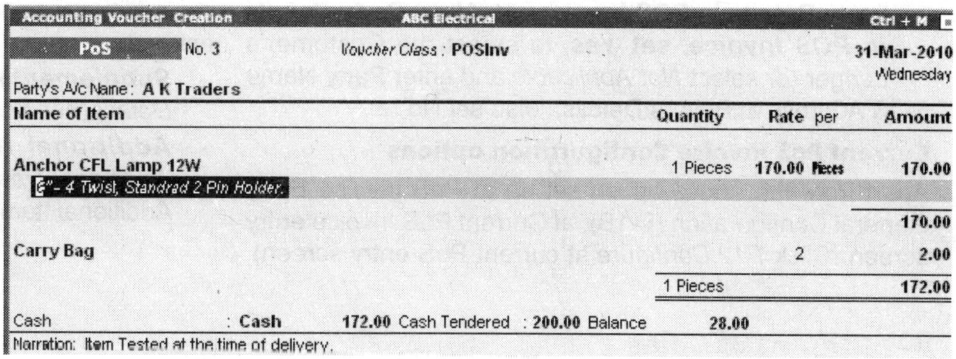

F-3B: PoS Invoice using Voucher Class, with fixed additional amount, Item description.

You may also enter Narration (Ledger / Voucher) in PoS Voucher (F-3B), if specified in the Voucher Type / Class (F-1/01-08).

03 PoS Register

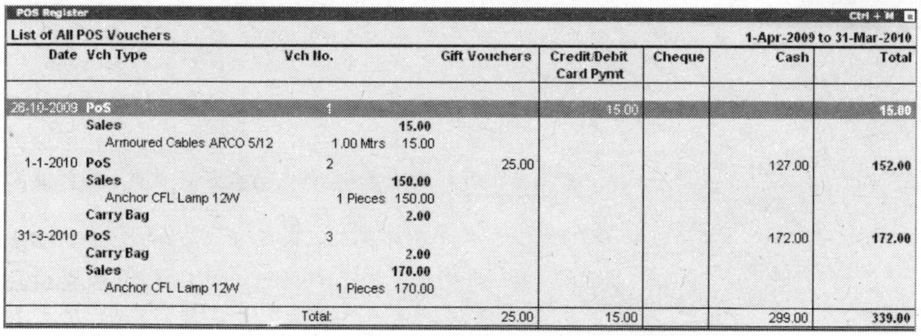

POS Register — List of All POS Vouchers — 1-Apr-2009 to 31-Mar-2010

Date	Vch Type	Vch No.		Gift Vouchers	Credit/Debit Card Pymt	Cheque	Cash	Total
26-10-2009	PoS	1			15.00			15.00
	Sales		15.00					
	Armoured Cables ARCO 5/12	1.00 Mtrs	15.00					
1-1-2010	PoS	2		25.00			127.00	152.00
	Sales		150.00					
	Anchor CFL Lamp 12W	1 Pieces	150.00					
	Carry Bag		2.00					
31-3-2010	PoS	3					172.00	172.00
	Carry Bag		2.00					
	Sales		170.00					
	Anchor CFL Lamp 12W	1 Pieces	170.00					
	Total:			25.00	15.00		299.00	339.00

F-4A: PoS Register Display

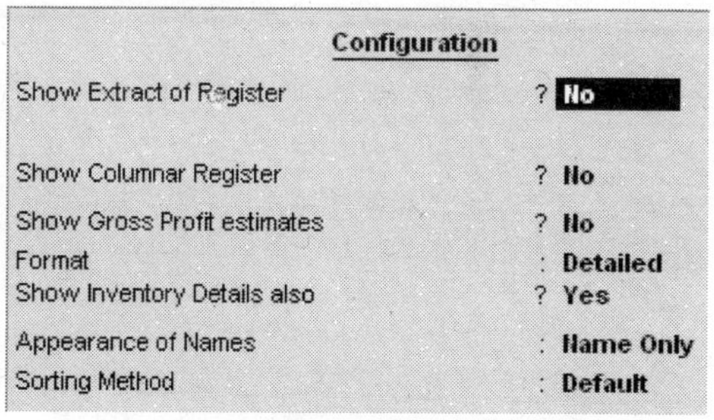

F:4B: PoS Register Configuration

Having entered the PoS Invoice, you may print the PoS Register listing the PoS Invoices. Select *Display>Account Books>PoS Register* to get PoS Register for the current period (F-4A)

This report is similar to Voucher Register (F-4A/01-06)

03.01 PoS Register Configuration

At POS Register Display (F-4A), click *F12:Configure* to get PoS Register Configuration (F-4B), similar to Sales Register Configuration (§02/03-04). Set the options as desired

F-4A shows. PoS Register with separate column (viz, Cash, cheque, gift voucher & Credit / Debit Cards) for each payment type (when you set *Yes* at *Show Inventory Details also*: F-4B)

FAQ: Frequently Asked Questions

FAQ-1: How you create a PoS Voucher Type.

Ans: You may alter Sales Voucher Type to PoS Voucher Type or Create a New PoS Voucher Type

- **Alteration of Sales Voucher Type**: If you use only PoS voucher for sale (like in Retail Store), you do not need to create a New Voucher Type. Select Sales to Alter the Sale Voucher Type as PoS Voucher Type. At *GoT>Accounts Info>Voucher Type>Alter* to get Voucher Type Alteration screen
- **Creation of PoS Voucher Type**: If you need to create a separate voucher type for PoS (apart from Sales Voucher), create a New Sales Voucher Type for PoS. At *GoT>Accounts Info>Voucher Type>Create select Sales* to get Voucher Type Creation screen, to create a new PoS Voucher Type (od Type Sales)

Now make necessary entry / alteration at the Voucher Entry / Alterations screen (both look similar: F-1) and set the options, as explained earlier (§02).

FAQ-2: How to set up POS Invoicing

Ans: At GoT, click *F12:Configure>Invoice/Orders Entry*, under the section POS (F-1A) set the following General Configuration options for Point of Sale:

- **Faster POS Invoicing:** At ***Skip Qty field during POS Invoicing (faster entry),*** **set** Yes to carry 1 automatically at quantity field (so quantity need not be typed in 1 unit item sale), else set No
- **Modification of Rate in Invoice**: The Rates carried are automatically picked as per the **Standard Rates** defined in the **Stock Item master** or from the selected **Price List.** At ***Allow modification of Rate field during POS Invoicing,*** set *Yes* to allow modification of Rates carried during PoS Invoice entry, else set *No* to prevent change of Rates

- **Party Details in POS Invoice: At *Allow Party Details in POS Invoice,* set *Yes***, to select the Customer's Ledger (or select *Not Applicable* and enter Party Name & Address at Buyers Details), else set No

Current PoS Invoice Configuration options

Apart from the above option set up at PoS Invoice Entry General Configuration (F-1B), at Current PoS Invoice entry screen (Click *F12:Configure* at current PoS entry screen), set additional options, for the current PoS Voucher being entered:

- ***Supplementary Details***: At *Accept Supplementary Details*, set *Yes* to enter supplementary details.
- ***Additional Item Description for Name***: At *Use Additional Description for Item Name* Set *Yes* to enter Additional Item Description.

Price List

02-07

01 Price List

A Business Organisation may follow a standard Sale Price for all its Parties, or follow different sets of Price Lists for different class of Parties.

We have already explained entry of Standard Sale Rate in Stock Item Master (§18/02-01), which is carried in Invoice entry. However, some organizations use separate Price Lists for different customer type, e.g Registered & Unregistered dealers, Wholesalers, Retailers, Government bodies, Institutions etc (or for specified Party).

02 Stock Item Price List

Stock Item Price List is a collection of applicable Sales Rates & Discounts for specified volume slabs.

The prices in Price List may be changed over time.

As the Price / Discount Rate changes, the revised prices may be added in the Price List. So, the past prices are also maintained in the Price List for reference and record During Invoice entry, prices are carried from the selected price list, saving time and ensuring consistency & accuracy.

For example, a Price List may contain Uniform Price for any volume, variable price for different volume range, uniform Discount Rate or variable Discount for different volume range.

Advantages of Price List

- Keeps historical rates for each item to refer to in future.
- Allows to use several Price Lists concurrently for various customer types, sales campaign, schemes etc.
- Allows to set graded Prices & Discount for various volume slabs.
- Prices carried from Price List cannot be modified in the Invoice, so manipulation can be avoided and invoice accuracy is ensured.

Steps to set up Price Level / Price List

- Set up Company Features option to create Price Levels (§03.01)
- Create Price List for each Price Levels (§03.02, §04)
- Link default price level for each Party (§05)
- Select Price List in Invoice entry to carry Price & discount data from Price List (§06)

03 Price Level

Price Level is a term used in Tally ERP9 to indicate specific Price:List applicable for a specific type of Parties. For example, separate Price Levels may be created for Retailers, Wholesalers, Registered Dealers, Unregistered Dealers, Agents etc.

03.01 Price Level Activation

At Gateway, Click *F11: Features* and select *Inventory Features* to get Inventory Features screen (F-1A)

At Inventory Features screen (F-1A), set *Yes* at *Use Multiple Price Levels* to get Company Price levels screen (F-1C). Enter the name of Price list (like wholesale, retail etc).

F-1A: Inventory Feature setup for Price List

F-1B; Price List Menu

F-1C: Price Levels Creation

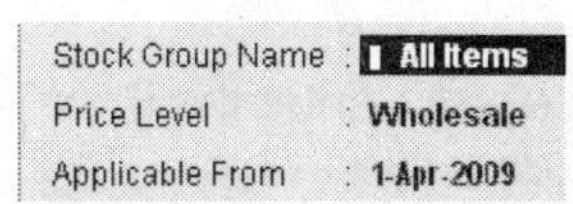

F-1D: Price List Creation for Stock Group

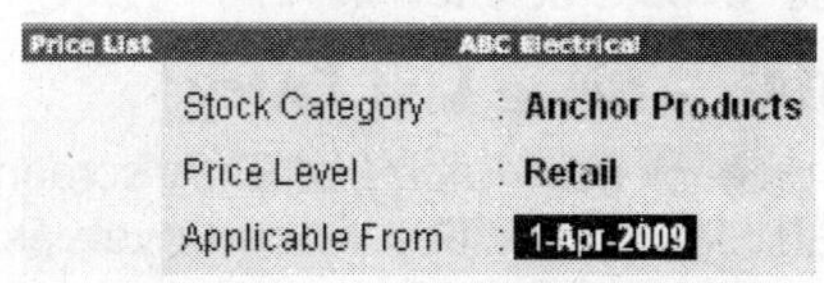

F-1E: Price List Creation for Stock Category

> **Note:** *You may create several Price Levels. You may link any Price List to a Party.as default. However, you may select any other Price List (or select no Price List at all) giving complete flexibility to adhere to or bypass a Price List, as desired.*

Consequently, at *Inventory Info* menu, *Price List* option gets activated to enter Price List for each Price Level (F-1B)

03.02 Price Level Creation

After setting Price Levels at Company Features, create Price List (enter Sales Prices for Items) for each Price Level

At Gateway of Tally, select *Inventory Info > Price List* to get to get Price List Menu (F-1B). At Price List Menu (F-1B), select:

- **Stock Group Price List**: Select Stock Group to create Price Level / Price List (§04) to get Stock Group Price List creation screen (F-1D)

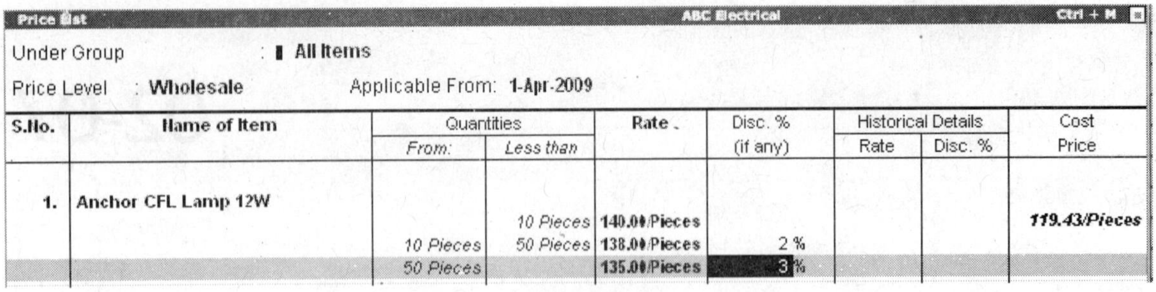

F-2A: Price List Entry for Stock Item

F-2B: Buttons

- **Stock Category Price List**: Select Category to create Price Level / Price List (§04) to get Stock Category Price List creation screen (F-1E)

At Price Group (F-1D) / Price Category (F-1E) creation screen, set as follows:

- **Stock Group**: At Stock Group Name (F-1D), select the Stock Group for which you like to create the Price List for Stock Items under the selected Stock Group, and then select the Stock Item
- **Stock Category**: At Stock Category Name (F-1E), select the Stock Category for which you like to create the Price List for Stock Items under the selected Stock Category, and then select the Stock Item

At Price Group (F-1D) / Price Category (F-1E) creation screen, you may select *All Items* to create Price List for All Stock Items. Having selected a Stock Item from the list of Stock Items, you get the Price List entry screen for the selected Stock Item (F-2A).

04 Price List Entry

At *Stock Item Price List Entry* screen (F-2A), enter the Price List for a specified Price Level, as described below. The screen is divided in 2 sections,:

Header Part: Here enter the particulars of the price list (F-2A, F-3B):

- **Stock Item Group / Category**: At *Under Group / Category* field, select the Item Group / Category for which you like to enter Price List. If the number of Items are not very large, you may select *All Items* (instead of any Item Group) to enter price for all Items in one shot. If you have selected any specific Group / Category, you will get Stock Items under the selected Group / Category and you may enter Price List for respective Stock Items
- **Price List Type**: At *Price Level* field, select the Price Level from the drop down list of Price Levels
- **Price List Effective Date**: At *Applicable From* field, enter the Date from which the rates are applicable.

Item details Part: The list of Items for the selected *Group / Category* (or All Stock Items) are displayed. Now enter the Price details / Discount for each Item as follows:

Quantities	From	The first line is blank (indicating starting from 1). In the next line enter the highest quantity value in slab range. Quantity at *Less Than* field of previous is carried in this field.
	Less than	Enter the Quantity upto which the quantity slab is applicable.
Rate		Enter the applicable Sale Rate for the Quantity block.
Discount %		Enter the Discount Rate in %, if applicable, for the Quantity Block,
Historical Details	Rate	The corresponding Rate of the previous price list (if existing) is displayed for reference. This helps as guideline to set up current prices and as reference of historical prices (F-3B).
	Disc %	The corresponding Discount Rate of the previous price list, if any, is displayed for reference.
Cost Price		The Standard Cost as entered in the Item master is displayed for reference and guidelines to set up current price.

05 Party Price List

For each Party ledger Entry / Edit screen, at *Price Level Applicable* (F-3A), select the applicable default Price Level from the list. Consequently, at the time of creation of Sales Order / Delivery Note, Sales Invoice, the default Price List for the Customer will get auto selected. This helps to charge appropriate price to the customer as per management policy.

To associate the default Price Level with the Party Account, at Party Ledger creation, at the field *Price Level Applicable* (F-3A), select the Price List to be linked.

F-3A: Linking of price list with Customer Ledger Master

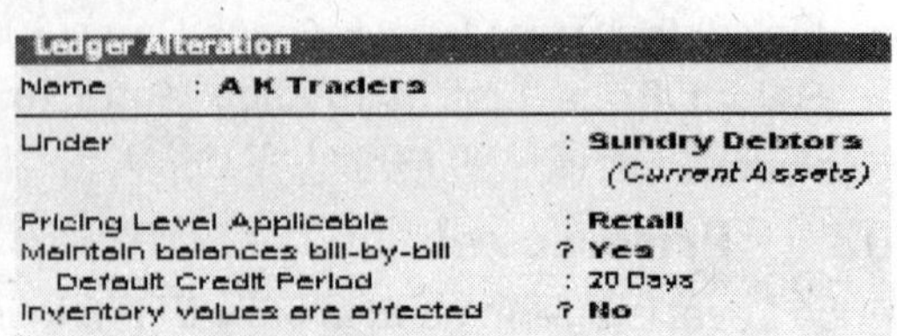

Price List — ABC Electrical — Ctrl + M

Under Group : All Items

Price Level : Wholesale Applicable From: 1-Oct-2009

S.No.	Name of Item	Quantities From:	Quantities Less than	Rate	Disc. % (if any)	As on : 22-Jun-2009 Rate	As on : 22-Jun-2009 Disc. %	Cost Price
1.	Anchor CFL Lamp 12W							
			10 Pieces	155.00/Pieces		150.00/Pieces		123.36/Pieces
		10 Pieces	50 Pieces	155.00/Pieces	5 %	148.00/Pieces	2 %	
		50 Pieces		150.00/Pieces	5 %	146.00/Pieces	3 %	

F-3B: Price List Revision

When you select the Party in Order/ Delivery Note/ Invoice entry (§07), Tally proposes the linked price list for selection (but you may select another Price Level during Invoice entry)

06 Price List Revision

Revision of Price List is like entry of a new set of Rates for the New Effective Date. You do not overwrite on the old prices, rather enter the Revised Prices, in the same manner as entry of Price List.

You may Revise the Prices in 2 ways:

- **Revised Price**: Enter new price effective from specified date, in the Price List entry screen, as explained. This is useful to enter specific revised Price for specified Item.
- **General Price Revision**: Specify general revision in Price (increase / decrease) as per specified quantum in Prices of a specified Group / Category. This is useful for general price by specifying the price revision parameters, to cause revision in bulk.

Entry of Revised Price

At Price:List Creation screen for Stock Group (F-1D)/ Category (F-1E):

- **Stock Group / Category Name** ; At *Group / Category Name,* select the *Stock Group/ Category* (or select *All Items*) as explained for Price List creation (§04)
- **Price Level**: At *Price Level,* select the Price Level for which Revised Rates would be effective
- **Effective Date**: At *Applicable From* enter the Date from which the revised price would be effective

Now select the Stock Item to get Price List entry screen for the Stock Item. The selected Price Level & Effective Date entered is displayed at the Price List screen (F-3B)

At Price List entry screen (F-3B), enter the new Price / Discount Rates as described earlier (§04). The Prices & Discounts of previous price list is now shown alongside (with Date of earlier Price List).

General Price Revision

Often prices are increased in bulk by specified amount / percentage over all the Items of a Specified Group / Category. To effect such bulk change, through a single parameter specification, at Price List entry screen, click R:Revise Price button (F-2B), to get *Revise Price* screen (F-4A). Enter the Parameters to automatically revise the Prices as per specified rule.

- **Revised Price Change Type**: At *Revise Price*, select the *Price Revision Type* from the *Type of Revise Price* List (F-4B) and then enter the Rate (in Amount or % as per Type selected)
- **Revised Discount Change Type:** At *Revise Discount*, select the *Discount Revision Type* from the *Type of Revise Discount* List (F-4C) and then enter the Rate in %

F-4A: Price Revision parameters

ABC Electrical

Revise Price

Stock Group Name : Glow Lamp

Price Level : Retail

Applicable From : 1-Nov-2009

Revise Price : Increase By Percentage 5 %

Revise Discount : Decrease By Percentage 1 %

Type of Revise Price

- Not Applicable
- Decrease By Amount
- Decrease By Percentage
- Increase By Amount
- Increase By Percentage

F-4B: Price Revision Type

Type of Revise Discount

- Not Applicable
- Decrease By Percentage
- Increase By Percentage

F-4C: Discount Revision Type

07 Invoice Entry using Price List

Sales Invoice entry has been explained earlier (§04/01-04). Here we explain the steps specific to selection of Price List and carrying Price from the selected Price List.

At Invoice Entry screen (F-5A), after entry of Party Name, at the field *Price Level*, select the Price Level, as explained next

> **Note:** *At Invoice Entry, the linked price list gets selected by default. You may select another Price List (or select Not Applicable to enter Price as desired).*

Accounting Voucher Creation — Ctrl + M

Sales	No. 2		1-Apr-2009 Wednesday
Ref. :			
Party's A/c Name : A K Traders		Price Level : Retail	
Sales Ledger : Sales			

Name of Item	Quantity	Rate per	Amount
Armoured Cables ARCO 5/12	1.00 Mtrs	15.00 Mtrs	15.00

F-5A: Invoice Entry using Price List

Selection of Price Level

- **When no default Price Level is linked with the Customer Ledger**: If no default Price List is set in Customer ledger,the list of Price Levels appear at the field Price Level. Select the desired Price Level. Applicable for the Customer
- **When a default Price List is already linked with the Customer Ledger:** If any default Price List is already linked to the selected Customer, the linked price list level gets auto selected internally and the prices are carried from the selected Price Level

Report Titles

Price List
All Items

Show Historical Details ? Yes

F-6A: Price List Printing Screen

Entry of Item Details

Now select the Item to get Item details subscreen and enter the Item details (Quantity etc). The appropriate price is carried from the selected Price Level. The computed value (as per Price) is displayed at Amount column. The Rate carried from price List or the computed amount (Value) cannot be changed.

This ensures that the Invoice is created applying correct price / discount and the Price / Discount Rates cannot be manipulated.

08 Price List Printing

At Price List entry Screen (F-3B), click P:Print Button to get the Price List printing screen (F-6A)

Historical Price: At Price List Printing screen (F-6A), at *Show Historical Details*,

- Set Yes at to print Past Prices also (F-6B),
- Set *No*. The past prices would not be shown

FAQ: Frequently Asked Questions

FAQ-1: Briefly explain the process of creating & using Price List

Ans: A Business Organisation may follow a standard sale / purchase price for all its Parties, or follow different sets of prices list for different class of parties. Item Price List is a collection of applicable Sales / Purchase Rates & Discounts for specified volume slabs.

The major steps of Price List set up are described below:

- **Price Level Activation:** At Inventory Features screen (F-1A), set *Yes* at *Use Multiple Price Levels* to get Company Price levels screen (F-1C). Enter the name of Price list (like wholesale, retail etc).

Price List
All Items

Page 1

Price Level : Wholesale — Applicable From : 22-Jun-2009

S.No.	Name of Item	Quantities From:	Quantities Less than	Rate	Disc. % (if any)	As on : 1-Apr-2009 Rate	As on : 1-Apr-2009 Disc. %	Cost Price
1.	Anchor CFL Lamp 12W							
			10 Pieces	150.00/Pieces		140.00/Pieces		119.43/Pieces
		10 Pieces	50 Pieces	148.00/Pieces	2 %	138.00/Pieces	2 %	
		50 Pieces		146.00/Pieces	3 %	135.00/Pieces	3 %	

F-6B: Price List in Print

- **Price Level Creation:** After setting Price Levels, create Price List (enter Sales Prices for a Group / Category of Items) for each Price Level.
- **Price List Entry:** Having created Price Level, At *Stock Item Price List Entry* screen (F-2A), enter the Price List for a specified Price Level (F-2A, F-3B)
- **Party / Price List Link:** Having set up prices for Price Levels (creation of Price List), at *Price Level Applicable* (F-3A), select the applicable default Price Level to link he Price Levels for each Party ledger Entry. Consequently, at Voucher Entry (Sales Order / Delivery Note, Sales Invoice), the default Price List for the Customer will get auto selected. This helps to charge appropriate price to the customer as per management policy.

Inventory Reports 02-08

01 Stock Value in Final Accounts

Various methods of valuation of Stock have been discussed earlier (§07/02-01) So, the value of Closing Stock would depend on the methods adopted. Apart from that, there are other considerations for valuation of stock depending on types of materials (devaluation due to obsolescence, quality defects, market fluctuations etc, technological changes etc).

In normal trade, the stock value is usually taken on Cost Basis. In such case, the Accounts & Inventory are Integrated and the stock value as per Inventory System is automatically carried to Accounts System. So, there is no need to enter Stock Value in the Accounts System.

- **Integrated System**: If Inventory System is maintained and if it the Accounting & Inventory System is integrated (at *F11:Features>Accounting Features* or *F11:Features> Inventory Features*, set *Yes* at *Integrate Accounts with Inventory*), the Closing Stock Value may is carried to the Accounting System and the Final Accounts Statements show the Stock Value based on the value computed in the Inventory System, In such case, when you drill down through Stock Value from Accounts Reports, you get Stock Summary (F-3B)
- **Non-Integrated System**: If Inventory System is not integrated with Accounts (at *F11:Features>Accounting Features* or *F11:Features>Inventory Features*, set *No* at *Integrate Accounts with Inventory*)or the Inventory System is not maintained in Tally, the value of Closing Stock as at the end of the accounting period, is to be entered manually to prepare the Final Accounts Statements (§03/01-10, F-1/01-10), In such case, when you drill down through Stock Value from Accounts Reports, you get Group / Ledger details under the Group Stock-in-Hand.

We have discussed various Inventory Reports (P-01/04-06). Here we discuss about Stock Reports, which depict the effect of all transactions and Stock-in-Hand

02 Stock Summary

Stock Summary is the most comprehensive Report of Stock movement, giving the summarized position of Opening Stock, Movement of Stock and Stock In hand.

02.01 Stock Summary Display

At Gateway of Tally, select *Stock Summary*, to get Stock Summary Display (F-1A)

F-1A: Stock Summary (Default)

Stock Summary — Ctrl + M

Particulars	ABC Electrical 1-Apr-2009 to 31-Mar-2010		
	Closing Balance		
	Quantity	Rate	Value
Cables & Wires	465.00 Mtrs	10.64	4,946.57
Lamp	68 Pieces	142.05	9,659.45
Switches	17 Pieces	25.04	425.70
Grand Total			15,031.72

Configuration

Show Quantities	? Yes
Show Rates	? Yes
Show Values	? Yes
Show Opening Balance	? No
Show goods inwards	? No
Show goods outwards	? No
Show Closing Balance	? Yes
Show All Items (incl. zero balance)	? No
Exclude Items With No Transactions	? No
Show Consumption & Gross Profits	? No
Show using Alternate Units	? No
Show Tail Units of Compound Units	? No
Appearance of Stock Item Names	: Name Only
Appearance of Names	: Name Only
Scale Factor for Values	: Default
Sorting Method	: Default
Expand all levels in Detailed Format	? No

F1: Detailed
F2: Period
F3: Company
F4: Group
F5: Item-wise
F6: Monthly
F7: Show Profit
F7: Orders
G: Godown Type
C: New Column
A: Alter Column
D: Del Column
N: Auto Column

F-2A: Stock Summary Configuration F-2B Buttons

02.02 Stock Summary Configuration

At Stock Summary Display (F-1A), click *F12:Configure* to get Configuration screen (F-2A) to set the options as follows:

The Configuration options of Stock Summary (F-2A) are described below:

i. Multi Column Options

Set Yes / No to the following options as required. Each option affects multiple set of columns (*Opening / Inward / Outwards/ Closing*)

a. **Quantity / Rate / Value**: The following columns appear for Opening Balance, Goods Inwards, Goods outwards & Closing Balance. The option is applicable for all these columns, if activated (e.g if *Yes* is set at Show Quantity, Quantity column will appear in the activated columns (Goods Inwards, Goods outwards & Closing balance, and like that for Rate & Value column)

   o **Quantity**: At *Show Quantities*, set *Yes* to show the

Quantity column (and the base unit), Set *No* to suppress the Quantity column.

- o **Rate**: At *Show Rates,* set *Yes* to show the Rate column (as per the base UoM displayed with Quantity figure), Set *No* to suppress the Rate column.
- o **Values**: At *Show Values*, set *Yes* to show the Value column, Set *No* to suppress the Value column

b. **Opening/ Inwards / Outwards / Closing**: Set Yes to show the figures for the respective 3 columns activated (Quantity, Rate, Value)

- o **Opening:** At *Show Opening Balance*, set Yes to show the figures of Opening Balance for the respective columns activated (Quantity, Rate, Value).
- o **Inwards**: At *Show Goods Inwards,* set Yes to show the figures of Goods Inwards for the respective column activated (Quantity, Rate, Value)
- o **Outwards**: At *Show Goods Outwards*, set Yes to show the figures of Goods Outwards for the respective column activated (Quantity, Rate, Value)
- o **Closing:** At *Show Closing Balance*, set Yes to show the figures of Closing balance for the respective column activated (Quantity, Rate, Value)

The values (Quantity, Rate, Amount) of each of the column (Opening, Inwards, Outwards, Closing) are displayed according to the current period (referred as *Report Period* – set through F2: period button) for the respective columns:

ii. Set *Yes* / *No* to the following options to show / suppress the columns as required

- **Items Types:** At *Show All Items*:
  - o Set *Yes* to show the Item even if all the displayed figures for the Item is zero.
  - o Set *No* to suppress the Items where the values of all the displayed column are zero. (if value of any of the displayed column for the Item is non zero, the Item will be displayed).

    Items Movement: Having set *Yes* at *Show All Items*, at *Exclude Items with No Transaction*, further set:
    - ▪ *Yes.* The Items which are not transacted (No In / Out) are not shown(excluded)
    - ▪ *No.* Al Items are shown (even if there is no In / Out).
- **Cost / Contribution**: At *Show Consumption & Gross Profit*,
  - o Set *Yes* to show the Consumption Value (Cost) & Gross Profit (Contribution)for Sales / Outwards column (F-4D). Gross is computed as (Sales Value – Cost), F-3E
  - o Set No, the Consumption Value & Gross Profit column is not shown.
- **Alternate Unit**: This is relevant only when Alternate Unit is activated. At *Show using Alternate units*:
  - o Set *Yes* to show the quantity in *Alternate units* also (for Items having Dual Units), F-3F
  - o Set No, only the Base Unit is shown.
- **Tail Unit**: This is relevant only for Items with Compound Unit. At *Show Tail units of Compound Units,*
  - o Set *Yes* to show the tail units of compound unit,
  - o Set *No.* the base unit is shown (with fraction values, where applicable), F-3F
- **Format**: At *Expand all levels in Detailed Format,*
  - o Set *Yes* to show the Items upto the lowest level details (in detail mode- i.e, when *F1: Detail* button is clicked: F-3D),
  - o Set No. Only next level detail (Item Group / Stock Items) are shown in detail mode.

At Stock Summary, drill down through:

- Any Stock Group to get the Stock Group Summary for the next level (showing next level Stock Group / Stock Items)
- Any Stock Item to get the Stock Item Monthly Summary

02.03 Stock Summary Buttons

At Stock Summary Display (F-2A), you get following buttons (F-2B):

Button	Description
F1: Detailed / Condensed	- F1: *Detailed*: To show next level Stock Groups / Stock Item details - F1: *Condensed*: To show only top level Stock Groups.
F4: Group	To select a Stock Group to get Stock Group Report of a selected Stock Group (select *Primary* to get Report of Top Level Stock Groups)
F5:Itemwise / Grouped	F5:Itemwise: To show Stock Item wise report.F5:Gouped: To show Stock Group wise report
F7: *Show Profit* / *Hide Profit*	- F7: *Show Profit*: To show the details of Consumption, Gross Profit & % of Outwards - F7: *Hide Profit*: Monthly figures for a specific selected GroupNote: You may also set Yes / No at *Show Consumption & Gross Profit* at *Configuration* (F-2A).
G:Godown type	To select the Godown,. Relevant only when Multiple Godown is activated
Columnar Report Buttons	Column specification to get columnar Reports

Stock Summary Ctrl + M

Particulars	ABC Electrical 1-Apr-2009 to 31-Mar-2010			
	Opening Balance Quantity	Inwards Quantity	Outwards Quantity	Closing Balance Quantity
Cables & Wires	**656.00 Mtrs**	**155.00 Mtrs**	**346.00 Mtrs**	**465.00 Mtrs**
Cables	644.00 Mtrs	155.00 Mtrs	346.00 Mtrs	453.00 Mtrs
Wires	12.00 Mtrs			12.00 Mtrs
Lamp	**41 Pieces**	**74 Pieces**	**47 Pieces**	**68 Pieces**
CFL Lamp	29 Pieces	46 Pieces	24 Pieces	51 Pieces
Glow Lamp	12 Pieces	28 Pieces	23 Pieces	17 Pieces
Switches	**22 Pieces**		**5 Pieces**	**17 Pieces**
Combo Switches			(-)1 Pieces	1 Pieces
Single Switches	22 Pieces		6 Pieces	16 Pieces
Grand Total				

F-3A: Stock Summary (Detail) showing Quantity only

Stock Summary Ctrl + M

Particulars	ABC Electrical 1-Apr-2009 to 31-Mar-2010 Opening Balance Quantity	Rate	Value
Cables & Wires	**656.00 Mtrs**	*10.25*	**6,725.80**
Cables	644.00 Mtrs	10.31	6,637.00
Armoured Cables ARCO 5/12	5.00 Mtrs	*12.00*	60.00
Despatch Room			
Main Location	5.00 Mtrs	12.00	60.00
Cable BeeKay	15 Roll	*255.33*	3,830.00
Despatch Room	1 Roll	260.00	260.00
Main Location	10 Roll	250.00	2,500.00
Siliguri Godown	2 Roll	270.00	540.00
Warehouse	2 Roll	265.00	530.00
Cables KayCee	30.00 Mtrs	*10.00*	300.00
Despatch Room	5.00 Mtrs	10.00	50.00
Main Location	25.00 Mtrs	10.00	250.00
Cable TeeKay	2 Roll 52.00 Mtrs	*951.61*	2,447.00
Despatch Room	52.00 Mtrs	1,001.00	572.00
Main Location	1 Roll	900.00	900.00
Siliguri Godown	1 Roll	975.00	975.00
Wires	12.00 Mtrs	7.40	88.80
Wire 3/20	12.00 Mtrs	*7.40*	88.80
Main Location	12.00 Mtrs	7.40	88.80
Wire 4mm			
			25 more ...
Grand Total			**12,460.80**

F-3B: Stock Summary (Detail) showing Opening Balance only

Stock Summary ABC Electrical Ctrl + M

Particulars	ABC Electrical 1-Apr-2009 to 31-Mar-2010											
	Opening Balance			Inwards			Outwards			Closing Balance		
	Quantity	*Rate*	Value	Quantity	*Rate*	Value	Quantity	*Rate*	Value	Quantity	*Rate*	Value
Cables & Wires	**656.00 Mtrs**	*10.25*	**6,725.80**	**155.00 Mtrs**	*10.48*	**1,624.12**	**346.00 Mtrs**	*18.14*	**6,276.40**	**465.00 Mtrs**	*10.64*	**4,946.57**
Cables	644.00 Mtrs	10.31	6,637.00	155.00 Mtrs	10.48	1,624.12	346.00 Mtrs	18.14	6,276.40	453.00 Mtrs	10.72	4,857.77
Wires	12.00 Mtrs	7.40	88.80							12.00 Mtrs	7.40	88.80
Lamp	**41 Pieces**	*123.71*	**5,072.00**	**74 Pieces**	*153.74*	**11,376.72**	**47 Pieces**	*173.32*	**8,146.24**	**68 Pieces**	*142.05*	**9,659.45**
CFL Lamp	29 Pieces	125.24	3,632.00	46 Pieces	170.22	7,830.05	24 Pieces	196.62	4,718.80	51 Pieces	147.85	7,540.12
Glow Lamp	12 Pieces	120.00	1,440.00	28 Pieces	126.67	3,546.67	23 Pieces	149.02	3,427.44	17 Pieces	124.67	2,119.33
Switches	**22 Pieces**	*30.14*	**663.00**				**5 Pieces**	*57.46*	**287.30**	**17 Pieces**	*25.04*	**425.70**
Combo Switches							(-)1 Pieces	25.00	(-)25.00	1 Pieces		
Single Switches	22 Pieces	30.14	663.00				6 Pieces	52.05	312.30	16 Pieces	26.61	425.70
Grand Total			**12,460.80**			**13,000.84**			**14,709.94**			**15,031.72**

F-3C: Stock Summary Detail (with all columns)

Stock Summary ABC Electrical Ctrl + M

Particulars	ABC Electrical 1-Apr-2009 to 31-Mar-2010											
	Opening Balance			Inwards			Outwards			Closing Balance		
	Quantity	*Rate*	Value	Quantity	*Rate*	Value	Quantity	*Rate*	Value	Quantity	*Rate*	Value
Cables & Wires	**656.00 Mtrs**	*10.25*	**6,725.80**	**155.00 Mtrs**	*10.48*	**1,624.12**	**346.00 Mtrs**	*18.14*	**6,276.40**	**465.00 Mtrs**	*10.64*	**4,946.57**
Cables	644.00 Mtrs	10.31	6,637.00	155.00 Mtrs	10.48	1,624.12	346.00 Mtrs	18.14	6,276.40	453.00 Mtrs	10.72	4,857.77
Armoured Cables ARCO 5/12	5.00 Mtrs	*12.00*	60.00				12.00 Mtrs	*177.62*	2,131.40	(-)7.00 Mtrs	*5.14*	36.00
Despatch Room							10.00 Mtrs	200.00	2,000.00	(-)10.00 Mtrs		
Main Location	5.00 Mtrs	12.00	60.00				2.00 Mtrs	65.70	131.40	3.00 Mtrs	12.00	36.00
Cable BeeKay	15 Roll	*255.33*	3,830.00	2 Roll	*250.00*	500.00	6 Roll 13.00 Mtrs	*305.52*	1,992.00	10 Roll 12.00 Mtrs	*257.63*	2,700.00
Despatch Room	1 Roll	260.00	260.00							1 Roll	260.00	260.00
Main Location	10 Roll	250.00	2,500.00	2 Roll	250.00	500.00	6 Roll 13.00 Mtrs	305.52	1,992.00	5 Roll 12.00 Mtrs	250.00	1,370.00
Siliguri Godown	2 Roll	270.00	540.00							2 Roll	270.00	540.00
Warehouse	2 Roll	265.00	530.00							2 Roll	265.00	530.00
Cables KayCee	30.00 Mtrs	*10.00*	300.00	25.00 Mtrs	*9.80*	245.00	65.00 Mtrs	*11.92*	775.00	(-)10.00 Mtrs	*10.15*	(-)101.50
Despatch Room	5.00 Mtrs	10.00	50.00				30.00 Mtrs	12.17	365.00	(-)25.00 Mtrs	10.00	(-)250.00
Main Location	25.00 Mtrs	10.00	250.00	25.00 Mtrs	9.80	245.00	35.00 Mtrs	11.71	410.00	15.00 Mtrs	9.90	148.50
Cable TeeKay	2 Roll 52.00 Mtrs	*951.61*	2,447.00	80.00 Mtrs	*1,000.00*	879.12	1 Roll 15.00 Mtrs	*1,183.00*	1,378.00	2 Roll 26.00 Mtrs	*972.68*	2,223.27
Despatch Room	52.00 Mtrs	1,001.00	572.00							52.00 Mtrs	1,001.00	572.00
Main Location	1 Roll	900.00	900.00	80.00 Mtrs	1,000.00	879.12	1 Roll 15.00 Mtrs	1,183.00	1,378.00	65.00 Mtrs	946.78	676.27
Siliguri Godown	1 Roll	975.00	975.00							1 Roll	975.00	975.00
Wires	12.00 Mtrs	7.40	88.80							12.00 Mtrs	7.40	88.80
Wire 3/20	12.00 Mtrs	*7.40*	88.80							12.00 Mtrs	*7.40*	88.80
Main Location	12.00 Mtrs	7.40	88.80							12.00 Mtrs	7.40	88.80
Lamp	**41 Pieces**	*123.71*	**5,072.00**	**74 Pieces**	*153.74*	**11,376.72**	**47 Pieces**	*173.32*	**8,146.24**	**68 Pieces**	*142.05*	**9,659.45**
												21 more ...
Grand Total			**12,460.80**			**13,000.84**			**14,709.94**			**15,031.72**

F-3D: Stock Summary with complete Detail (with all columns)

Stock Summary — ABC Electrical — Ctrl + M

Particulars	ABC Electrical 1-Apr-2009 to 31-Mar-2010														
	Opening Balance			Inwards			Outwards						Closing Balance		
	Quantity	*Rate*	Value	Quantity	*Rate*	Value	Quantity	*Rate*	Value	Consumption	Gross Profit	Perc %	Quantity	*Rate*	Value
Cables & Wires	**656.00 Mtrs**	*10.25*	**6,725.80**	**155.00 Mtrs**	*10.48*	**1,624.12**	**346.00 Mtrs**	*18.14*	**6,276.40**	**3,403.35**	**2,873.05**	**45.78 %**	**465.00 Mtrs**	*10.64*	**4,946.57**
Cables	644.00 Mtrs	10.31	6,637.00	155.00 Mtrs	10.48	1,624.12	346.00 Mtrs	18.14	6,276.40	3,403.35	2,873.05	45.78 %	453.00 Mtrs	10.72	4,857.77
Armoured Cables ARCO 5/12	5.00 Mtrs	*12.00*	60.00				12.00 Mtrs	*177.62*	2,131.40	24.00	2,107.40	98.87 %	(-)7.00 Mtrs	*5.14*	36.00
Despatch Room							10.00 Mtrs	200.00	2,000.00		2,000.00	100.00 %	(-)10.00 Mtrs		
Main Location	5.00 Mtrs	12.00	60.00				2.00 Mtrs	65.70	131.40	24.00	107.40	81.74 %	3.00 Mtrs	12.00	36.00
Cable BeeKay	15 Roll	*255.33*	3,830.00	2 Roll	*250.00*	500.00	6 Roll 13.00 Mtrs	*305.52*	1,992.00	1,630.00	362.00	18.17 %	10 Roll 12.00 Mtrs	*257.63*	2,700.00
Despatch Room	1 Roll	260.00	260.00										1 Roll	260.00	260.00
Main Location	10 Roll	250.00	2,500.00	2 Roll	250.00	500.00	6 Roll 13.00 Mtrs	305.52	1,992.00	1,630.00	362.00	18.17 %	5 Roll 12.00 Mtrs	250.00	1,370.00
Siliguri Godown	2 Roll	270.00	540.00										2 Roll	270.00	540.00
Warehouse	2 Roll	265.00	530.00										2 Roll	265.00	530.00
Cables KayCee	30.00 Mtrs	*10.00*	300.00	25.00 Mtrs	*9.80*	245.00	65.00 Mtrs	*11.92*	775.00	646.50	128.50	16.58 %	(-)10.00 Mtrs	*10.15*	(-)101.50
Despatch Room	5.00 Mtrs	10.00	50.00				30.00 Mtrs	12.17	365.00	300.00	65.00	17.81 %	(-)25.00 Mtrs	10.00	(-)250.00
Main Location	25.00 Mtrs	10.00	250.00	25.00 Mtrs	9.80	245.00	35.00 Mtrs	11.71	410.00	346.50	63.50	15.49 %	15.00 Mtrs	9.90	148.50
Cable TeeKay	2 Roll 52.00 Mtrs	*951.61*	2,447.00	80.00 Mtrs	*1,000.00*	879.12	1 Roll 15.00 Mtrs	*1,183.00*	1,378.00	1,102.85	275.15	19.97 %	2 Roll 26.00 Mtrs	*972.68*	2,223.27
Despatch Room	52.00 Mtrs	1,001.00	572.00										52.00 Mtrs	1,001.00	572.00
Main Location	1 Roll	900.00	900.00	80.00 Mtrs	1,000.00	879.12	1 Roll 15.00 Mtrs	1,183.00	1,378.00	1,102.85	275.15	19.97 %	65.00 Mtrs	946.78	676.27
Siliguri Godown	1 Roll	975.00	975.00										1 Roll	975.00	975.00
Wires	12.00 Mtrs	7.40	88.80										12.00 Mtrs	7.40	88.80
Wire 3/20	12.00 Mtrs	*7.40*	88.80										12.00 Mtrs	*7.40*	88.80
Main Location	12.00 Mtrs	7.40	88.80										12.00 Mtrs	7.40	88.80
Lamp	**41 Pieces**	*123.71*	**5,072.00**	**74 Pieces**	*153.74*	**11,376.72**	**47 Pieces**	*173.32*	**8,146.24**	**6,789.27**	**1,356.97**	**16.66 %**	**68 Pieces**	*142.05*	**9,659.45**
															21 more ...
Grand Total			**12,460.80**			**13,000.84**			**14,709.94**	**10,429.[illegible]2**	**4,280.02**	**29.10 %**			**15,031.72**

F-3E: Stock Summary with Profit Loss details of Outwards

Stock Summary — ABC Electrical — Ctrl + M

Particulars	ABC Electrical 1-Apr-2009 to 31-Mar-2010							
	Opening Balance		Inwards		Outwards		Closing Balance	
	Quantity	*(Alt. Units)*	Quantity	*(Alt. Units)*	Quantity	*(Alt. Units)*	Quantity	*(Alt. Units)*
Cables & Wires	**656.00 Mtrs**		**155.00 Mtrs**		**346.00 Mtrs**		**465.00 Mtrs**	
Cables	644.00 Mtrs		155.00 Mtrs		346.00 Mtrs		453.00 Mtrs	
Armoured Cables ARCO 5/12	5.00 Mtrs				12.00 Mtrs		(-)7.00 Mtrs	
Despatch Room					10.00 Mtrs		(-)10.00 Mtrs	
Main Location	5.00 Mtrs				2.00 Mtrs		3.00 Mtrs	
Cable BeeKay	15 Roll		2 Roll		6 Roll 13.00 Mtrs		10 Roll 12.00 Mtrs	
Despatch Room	1 Roll						1 Roll	
Main Location	10 Roll		2 Roll		6 Roll 13.00 Mtrs		5 Roll 12.00 Mtrs	
Siliguri Godown	2 Roll						2 Roll	
Warehouse	2 Roll						2 Roll	
Cables KayCee	30.00 Mtrs	*(1.20 Roll)*	25.00 Mtrs	*(1.00 Roll)*	65.00 Mtrs	*(2.60 Roll)*	(-)10.00 Mtrs	*((-)0.40 Roll)*
Despatch Room	5.00 Mtrs	*(0.20 Roll)*			30.00 Mtrs	*(1.20 Roll)*	(-)25.00 Mtrs	*((-)1.00 Roll)*
Main Location	25.00 Mtrs	*(1.00 Roll)*	25.00 Mtrs	*(1.00 Roll)*	35.00 Mtrs	*(1.40 Roll)*	15.00 Mtrs	*(0.60 Roll)*
Cable TeeKay	2 Roll 52.00 Mtrs		80.00 Mtrs		1 Roll 15.00 Mtrs		2 Roll 26.00 Mtrs	
Despatch Room	52.00 Mtrs						52.00 Mtrs	
Main Location	1 Roll		80.00 Mtrs		1 Roll 15.00 Mtrs		65.00 Mtrs	
Siliguri Godown	1 Roll						1 Roll	
Wires	12.00 Mtrs						12.00 Mtrs	
Wire 3/20	12.00 Mtrs						12.00 Mtrs	
Main Location	12.00 Mtrs						12.00 Mtrs	
Lamp	**41 Pieces**		**74 Pieces**		**47 Pieces**		**68 Pieces**	
								21 more ...
Grand Total								

F-3F: Stock Summary with Compound & Alternate Units

02.04 Stock Summary Printing

At Stock Summary Display (F-2A), click P:Print to get Stock Summary Printing screen (F-4A). Set the print options to get Stock Summary in Print (F-4B).

03 Sales / Purchase Register with Inventory Details

At Sales / Purchase / Debit / Credit Note Register Configuration (§02/03-04), set *Yes* at *Show Inventory Details also* to get Sales Register (F-5A) / Purchase Register (F-6A) / Debit Note (F-7A) / Credit Note Register (F-8A) with Item details.

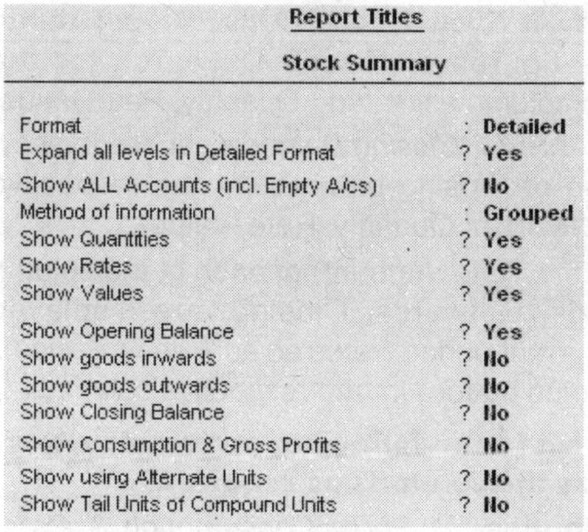
Report Titles

Stock Summary

Format	:	**Detailed**
Expand all levels in Detailed Format	?	**Yes**
Show ALL Accounts (incl. Empty A/cs)	?	**No**
Method of information	:	**Grouped**
Show Quantities	?	**Yes**
Show Rates	?	**Yes**
Show Values	?	**Yes**
Show Opening Balance	?	**Yes**
Show goods inwards	?	**No**
Show goods outwards	?	**No**
Show Closing Balance	?	**No**
Show Consumption & Gross Profits	?	**No**
Show using Alternate Units	?	**No**
Show Tail Units of Compound Units	?	**No**

F-4A: Stock Summary Printing screen

Stock Summary
1-Apr-2009 to 31-Mar-2010

Page 1

Particulars	Opening Balance			Inwards			Outwards			Closing Balance		
	Quantity	*Rate*	Value	Quantity	*Rate*	Value	Quantity	*Rate*	Value	Quantity	*Rate*	Value
Cables & Wires	**656.00 Mtrs**	*10.25*	**6,725.80**	**155.00 Mtrs**	*10.48*	**1,624.12**	**346.00 Mtrs**	*18.14*	**6,276.40**	**465.00 Mtrs**	*10.64*	**4,946.57**
Cables	644.00 Mtrs	10.31	6,637.00	155.00 Mtrs	10.48	1,624.12	346.00 Mtrs	18.14	6,276.40	453.00 Mtrs	10.72	4,857.77
Wires	12.00 Mtrs	7.40	88.80							12.00 Mtrs	7.40	88.80
Lamp	**41 Pieces**	*123.71*	**5,072.00**	**74 Pieces**	*153.74*	**11,376.72**	**47 Pieces**	*173.32*	**8,146.24**	**68 Pieces**	*142.05*	**9,659.45**
CFL Lamp	29 Pieces	125.24	3,632.00	46 Pieces	170.22	7,830.05	24 Pieces	196.62	4,718.80	51 Pieces	147.85	7,540.12
Glow Lamp	12 Pieces	120.00	1,440.00	28 Pieces	126.67	3,546.67	23 Pieces	149.02	3,427.44	17 Pieces	124.67	2,119.33
Switch Boards									**90.00**			
Switch Board (Cor									*90.00*			
Switches	**22 Pieces**	*30.14*	**663.00**				**5 Pieces**	*57.46*	**287.30**	**17 Pieces**	*25.04*	**425.70**
Combo Switches							()1 Pieces	25.00	(-)25.00	1 Pieces		
Single Switches	22 Pieces	30.14	663.00				6 Pieces	52.05	312.30	16 Pieces	26.61	425.70
Grand Tota			**12,460.80**			**13,000.84**			**14,799.94**			**15,031.72**

F-4B: Stock Summary in Print

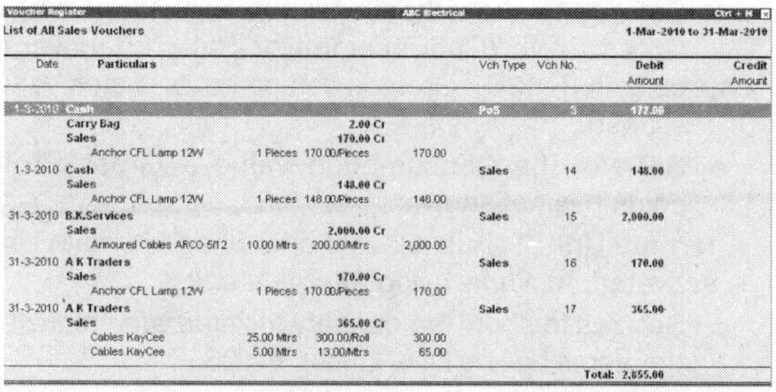
Voucher Register — ABC Electrical — Ctrl + M

List of All Sales Vouchers — 1-Mar-2010 to 31-Mar-2010

Date	Particulars					Vch Type	Vch No.	Debit Amount	Credit Amount
1-3-2010	Cash					PoS	3	172.00	
	Carry Bag			2.00 Cr					
	Sales			170.00 Cr					
	Anchor CFL Lamp 12W	1 Pieces	170.00/Pieces		170.00				
1-3-2010	Cash					Sales	14	148.00	
	Sales			148.00 Cr					
	Anchor CFL Lamp 12W	1 Pieces	148.00/Pieces		148.00				
31-3-2010	B.K.Services					Sales	15	2,000.00	
	Sales			2,000.00 Cr					
	Armoured Cables ARCO 5/12	10.00 Mtrs	200.00/Mtrs		2,000.00				
31-3-2010	A K Traders					Sales	16	170.00	
	Sales			170.00 Cr					
	Anchor CFL Lamp 12W	1 Pieces	170.00/Pieces		170.00				
31-3-2010	A K Traders					Sales	17	365.00	
	Sales			365.00 Cr					
	Cables KayCee	25.00 Mtrs	300.00/Roll		300.00				
	Cables KayCee	5.00 Mtrs	13.00/Mtrs		65.00				
							Total:	2,855.00	

F -5A: Sales Register with Inventory details

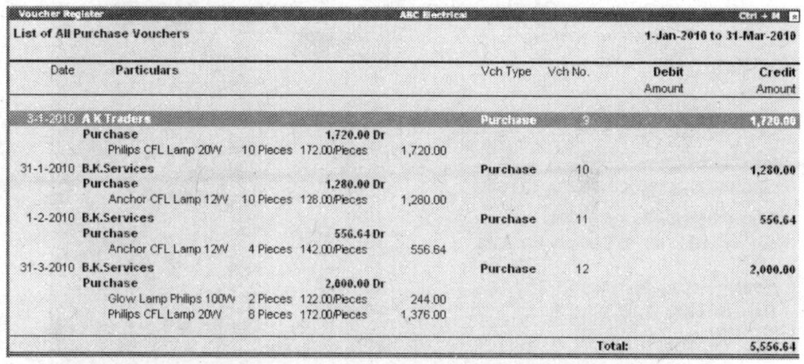
Voucher Register — ABC Electrical — Ctrl + M

List of All Purchase Vouchers — 1-Jan-2010 to 31-Mar-2010

Date	Particulars					Vch Type	Vch No.	Debit Amount	Credit Amount
3-1-2010	A K Traders					Purchase	9		1,720.00
	Purchase			1,720.00 Dr					
	Philips CFL Lamp 20W	10 Pieces	172.00/Pieces		1,720.00				
31-1-2010	B.K.Services					Purchase	10		1,280.00
	Purchase			1,280.00 Dr					
	Anchor CFL Lamp 12W	10 Pieces	128.00/Pieces		1,280.00				
1-2-2010	B.K.Services					Purchase	11		556.64
	Purchase			556.64 Dr					
	Anchor CFL Lamp 12W	4 Pieces	142.00/Pieces		556.64				
31-3-2010	B.K.Services					Purchase	12		2,000.00
	Purchase			2,000.00 Dr					
	Glow Lamp Philips 100W	2 Pieces	122.00/Pieces		244.00				
	Philips CFL Lamp 20W	8 Pieces	172.00/Pieces		1,376.00				
							Total:		5,556.64

F -6A Purchase Register with Inventory details

> **Note:** *In Voucher Register (Sales, Purchase, Debit & Credit Notes), the Inventory details show Item Name, Billed Quantity (in Base UoM) and Item value for each Stock Item.*

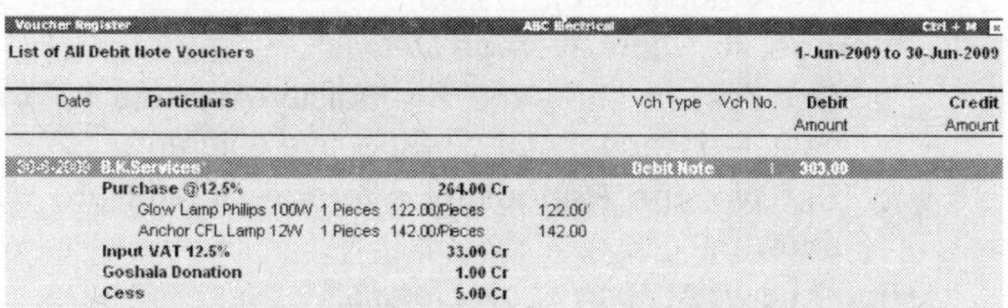
Voucher Register — ABC Electrical — Ctrl + M

List of All Debit Note Vouchers — 1-Jun-2009 to 30-Jun-2009

Date	Particulars					Vch Type	Vch No.	Debit Amount	Credit Amount
30-6-2009	B.K.Services					Debit Note	1	303.00	
	Purchase @12.5%			264.00 Cr					
	Glow Lamp Philips 100W	1 Pieces	122.00/Pieces		122.00				
	Anchor CFL Lamp 12W	1 Pieces	142.00/Pieces		142.00				
	Input VAT 12.5%			33.00 Cr					
	Goshala Donation			1.00 Cr					
	Cess			5.00 Cr					

F -7A Debit Note Register with Inventory details

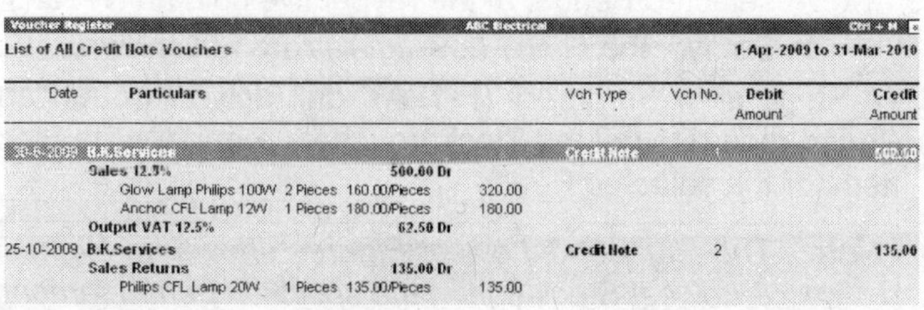
Voucher Register — ABC Electrical — Ctrl + M

List of All Credit Note Vouchers — 1-Apr-2009 to 31-Mar-2010

Date	Particulars					Vch Type	Vch No.	Debit Amount	Credit Amount
30-6-2009	B.K.Services					Credit Note	1		562.50
	Sales 12.5%			500.00 Dr					
	Glow Lamp Philips 100W	2 Pieces	160.00/Pieces		320.00				
	Anchor CFL Lamp 12W	1 Pieces	180.00/Pieces		180.00				
	Output VAT 12.5%			62.50 Dr					
25-10-2009	B.K.Services					Credit Note	2		135.00
	Sales Returns			135.00 Dr					
	Philips CFL Lamp 20W	1 Pieces	135.00/Pieces		135.00				

F -8A Credit Note Register with Inventory details

04 Ledger Account with Inventory Details

Ledger Voucher Display has been discussed earlier (§08/02-16). At Ledger Account Configuration (§08/02-16), set Yes at *Show Inventory Details also* to get Ledger Account (of Inventory Linked Ledger Accounts – like Sales, Purchase etc) with Item details (F-9A).

> **Note:** *In Ledger Voucher, the Inventory details of Inventory Linked Leger Accounts, show Item Name, Billed Quantity (in Base UoM) and Item value for each Stock Item.*

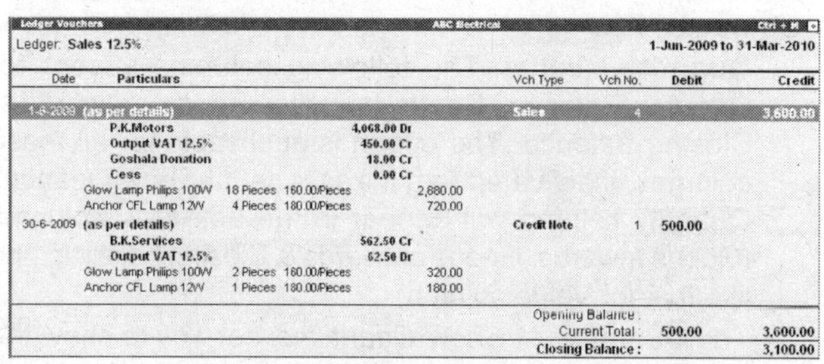
Ledger Vouchers — ABC Electrical — Ctrl + M

Ledger: Sales 12.5% — 1-Jun-2009 to 31-Mar-2010

Date	Particulars					Vch Type	Vch No.	Debit	Credit
1-6-2009	(as per details)					Sales	4		3,600.00
	P.K.Motors			4,068.00 Dr					
	Output VAT 12.5%			450.00 Cr					
	Goshala Donation			18.00 Cr					
	Cess			0.00 Cr					
	Glow Lamp Philips 100W	18 Pieces	160.00/Pieces		2,880.00				
	Anchor CFL Lamp 12W	4 Pieces	180.00/Pieces		720.00				
30-6-2009	(as per details)					Credit Note	1	500.00	
	B.K.Services			562.50 Cr					
	Output VAT 12.5%			62.50 Dr					
	Glow Lamp Philips 100W	2 Pieces	160.00/Pieces		320.00				
	Anchor CFL Lamp 12W	1 Pieces	180.00/Pieces		180.00				
							Opening Balance :		
							Current Total :	500.00	3,600.00
							Closing Balance :		3,100.00

F-9A: Sales Ledger with Inventory details

05 Stock Item Monthly Summary

You get *Stock Item Monthly Summary* (F-10A) when you drill down though any Stock Item in a report showing Stock Item details.

Stock Item Monthly Summary Configuration

At *Stock Item Monthly Summary* (F-10A), click *F12:Configure* to get *Stock Item Monthly Summary*

Stock Item Monthly Summary — ABC Electrical — Ctrl + M

Particulars	Anchor CFL Lamp 12W ABC Electrical 1-Apr-2009 to 31-Mar-2010					
	Inwards		**Outwards**		**Closing Balance**	
	Quantity	Value	Quantity	Value	Quantity	Value
Opening Balance					**23 Pieces**	**2,600.00**
April					23 Pieces	2,600.00
May					23 Pieces	2,600.00
June	6 Pieces	868.00	4 Pieces	710.00	25 Pieces	2,988.89
July			2 Pieces	310.00	23 Pieces	2,749.33
August					23 Pieces	2,749.33
September					23 Pieces	2,749.33
October					23 Pieces	2,749.33
November	4 Pieces	556.64			27 Pieces	3,305.97
December			1 Pieces	150.00	26 Pieces	3,163.97
January	10 Pieces	1,280.00	1 Pieces	150.00	35 Pieces	4,335.19
February					35 Pieces	4,335.19
March			3 Pieces	488.00	32 Pieces	3,945.42
Grand Total	**20 Pieces**	**2,704.64**	**11 Pieces**	**1,808.00**	**32 Pieces**	**3,945.42**

F-10A: Stock Item Monthly Summary

Configuration	
Show Quantities	? **Yes**
Show Values	? **Yes**
Show goods inwards	? **Yes**
Show goods outwards	? **Yes**
Show Closing Balance	? **Yes**
Show Consumption & Gross Profits	? **No**
Show using Alternate Units	? **No**
Show Tail Units of Compound Units	? **No**
Scale Factor for Values	: **Default**
Periodicity to use	: **Monthly**
Show Average Details	? **No**
Show High/Low Details	? **No**
Graphs	
Show with Graph	? **No**

F-11A:Stock Item Monthly Summary Configuration

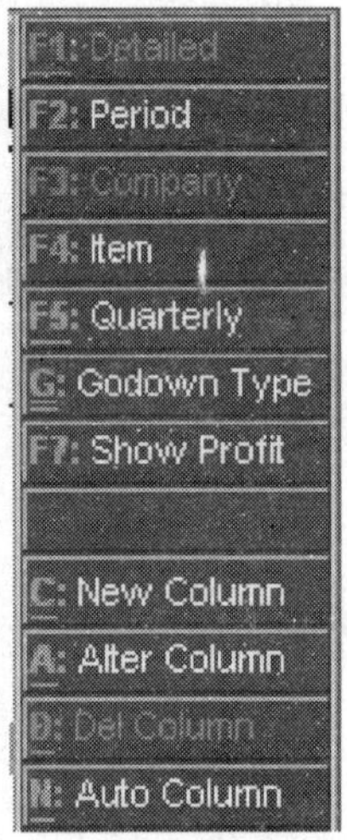

F-11B: Buttons

Configuration (F-11A) to set the options as follows:

i. Multi Column Options

Set Yes / No to the following options as required. Each option affects multiple set of columns (*Opening / Inward / Outwards/ Closing)*

- **Quantity / Value**: The following columns appear for Opening Balance, Goods Inwards, Goods outwards & Closing Balance. The option is applicable for all these columns, if activated (e.g if *Yes* is set at Show Quantity, Quantity column will appear in the activated columns (Goods Inwards, Goods outwards & Closing balance, and like that for Value column)
  - o **Quantity**: At *Show Quantities,* set *Yes* to show the Quantity column (and the base unit), Set *No* to suppress the Quantity column.
  - o **Values**: At *Show Values,* set *Yes* to show the Value column, Set *No* to suppress the Value column
- **Inwards / Outwards / Closing**: Set Yes to show the figures for the respective 3 columns activated (Quantity, Rate, Value)
  - o **Inwards**: At *Show Goods Inwards,* set Yes to show the figures of Goods Inwards for the respective column activated (Quantity, Rate, Value)
  - o **Outwards**: At *Show Goods Outwards,* set Yes to show the figures of Goods Outwards for the respective column activated (Quantity, Rate, Value)
  - o **Closing:** At *Show Closing Balance,* set Yes to show the figures of Closing balance for the respective column activated (Quantity, Rate, Value)

The values (Quantity, Rate, Amount) of each of the column (Opening, Inwards, Outwards, Closing) are displayed according to the current period (referred as *Report Period* – set through F2: period button) for the respective columns:

ii. Set Yes / No to the following options to show / suppress the columns as required

- **Cost / Contribution**: At *Show Consumption & Gross Profit,*
  - o Set *Yes* to show the Consumption Value (Cost) & Gross Profit (Contribution) for Sales / Outwards column (F-12C). Gross is computed as (Sales Value – Cost).
  - o Set No, the Consumption Value & Gross Profit column is not shown.
- **Alternate Unit**: This is relevant only when Alternate Unit is activated. At *Show using Alternate units*:
  - o Set *Yes* to show the quantity in *Alternate units* also (for Items having Dual Units), F-12B
  - o Set No, only the Base Unit is shown.
- **Tail Unit**: This is relevant only for Items with Compound Unit. At *Show Tail units of Compound Units,*
  - o Set *Yes* to show the tail units of compound unit (F-12C)
  - o Set *No.* the base unit is shown (with fraction values, where applicable),
- **Average:** At *Show Average Details*:
  - o Set Yes, to show the Periodicity Average for the selected Period, at the respective column
  - o Set *No,* the Periodicity Average details are not shown.
- **High / Low:** At *High / Low Details*:
  - o Set Yes to show the *High / Low figures* for the selected Period, at the respective column (F-12A)
  - o Set *No.* the *High / Low figures* are not shown.

At *Stock Item Summary* (F-12A), drill down through any Period record to get the Stock Vouchers report for the Stock Item for the selected Period.

> ***Note:*** *The Highest & Lowest Figures shows he Highest & Lowest Stock during the specified period (among the non-zero stock figures)The average Inwards / Outwards show the Average figures of Inwards / Outwards for the selected period. For example, if the total for 6 months is 12, then the average would be 2, even if there are no transactions in some months.*

Stock Item Monthly Summary — ABC Electrical — Ctrl + M

Particulars	Cable BeeKay ABC Electrical 1-Nov-2009 to 31-Mar-2010					
	Inwards		Outwards		Closing Balance	
	Quantity	Value	Quantity	Value	Quantity	Value
Opening Balance					**15 Roll**	**3,830.00**
November	2 Roll	500.00			17 Roll	4,330.00
December			3 Roll 5.00 Mtrs	976.00	13 Roll 20.00 Mtrs	3,530.00
January					13 Roll 20.00 Mtrs	3,530.00
February			3 Roll 8.00 Mtrs	1,016.00	10 Roll 12.00 Mtrs	2,700.00
March					10 Roll 12.00 Mtrs	2,700.00
Grand Total	**2 Roll**	**500.00**	**6 Roll 13.00 Mtrs**	**1,992.00**	**10 Roll 12.00 Mtrs**	**2,700.00**
Average	10.00 Mtrs	100.00	1 Roll 7.60 Mtrs	398.40	13 Roll 2.80 Mtrs	3,358.00
Highest Balance	(dt. 1-Nov-2009) **2 Roll**	**500.00**	(dt. 1-Feb-2010) **3 Roll 8.00 Mtrs**	**1,016.00**	(dt. 1-Nov-2009) **17 Roll**	**4,330.00**
Lowest Balance	(dt. 1-Nov-2009) **2 Roll**	**500.00**	(dt. 1-Dec-2009) **3 Roll 5.00 Mtrs**	**976.00**	(dt. 1-Feb-2010) **10 Roll 12.00 Mtrs**	**2,700.00**

F-12A: Stock Item Monthly Summary (with High, Low & Average values)

06 Stock Journal Register

At Gateway, select *Display>Inventory Books > Stock Transfers* to get monthly break up of Stock Journal Vouchers.

Select a month to get the *Stock Journal Voucher Register* for the selected Month. Click *F2:Period* button and set the period to get *Stock Journal Voucher Register* for the specified period (F-13A).

Stock Journal Voucher Register Configuration

At *Stock Journal Voucher Register*, click *F12:Configure* to get *Stock Journal Voucher Register Configuration* screen (F-14A), similar to Bill Register Display Configuration (§02.02/03-04/S1).

Here, we discuss about Configuration Options relating to Inventory

- **Extract:** At *Show Extract of Register*:
  - o Set *Yes* to get Stock Group / Stock Item summary of Inwards / Outwards of the Stock Items for the selected Period (F-14A, F-14B)

Stock Item Monthly Summary — ABC Electrical — Ctrl + M

Particulars	Cables KayCee ABC Electrical 1-Dec-2009 to 31-Mar-2010								
	Inwards			Outwards			Closing Balance		
	Quantity	(Alt. Units)	Value	Quantity	(Alt. Units)	Value	Quantity	(Alt. Units)	Value
Opening Balance							**30.00 Mtrs**	***(1.20 Roll)***	**300.00**
December	25.00 Mtrs	*(1.00 Roll)*	245.00	24.00 Mtrs	*(0.96 Roll)*	280.00	31.00 Mtrs	*(1.24 Roll)*	307.40
January							31.00 Mtrs	*(1.24 Roll)*	307.40
February				11.00 Mtrs	*(0.44 Roll)*	130.00	20.00 Mtrs	*(0.80 Roll)*	198.50
March				30.00 Mtrs	*(1.20 Roll)*	365.00	(-)10.00 Mtrs	*((-)0.40 Roll)*	(-)101.50
Grand Total	**25.00 Mtrs**	***(1.00 Roll)***	**245.00**	**65.00 Mtrs**	***(2.60 Roll)***	**775.00**	**(-)10.00 Mtrs**	***((-)0.40 Roll)***	**(-)101.50**

F-12B: Stock Item Monthly Summary (with Alternate Units)

Stock Item Monthly Summary — ABC Electrical — Ctrl + M

Particulars	Cables KayCee ABC Electrical 1-Dec-2009 to 31-Mar-2010								
	Inwards		Outwards					Closing Balance	
	Quantity	Value	Quantity	Value	Consumption	Gross Profit	Perc %	Quantity	Value
Opening Balance								**30.00 Mtrs**	**300.00**
December	25.00 Mtrs	245.00	24.00 Mtrs	280.00	237.60	42.40	15.14 %	31.00 Mtrs	307.40
January								31.00 Mtrs	307.40
February			11.00 Mtrs	130.00	108.90	21.10	16.23 %	20.00 Mtrs	198.50
March			30.00 Mtrs	365.00	300.00	65.00	17.81 %	(-)10.00 Mtrs	(-)101.50
Grand Total	**25.00 Mtrs**	**245.00**	**65.00 Mtrs**	**775.00**	**646.50**	**128.50**	**16.58 %**	**(-)10.00 Mtrs**	**(-)101.50**

F-12C: Stock Item Monthly Summary (with Gross Profit details & Tail Units)

Voucher Register — Ctrl + M

List of All Stock Journal Vouchers — 1-Apr-2009 to 31-Mar-2010

Date	Particulars		Vch Type	Vch No.	Inwards Quantity	Outwards Quantity
25-10-2009	**Switch - Anchor 5A**		**Stock Journal**	1		**1 Pieces**
	Philips CFL Lamp 20W	**(-)1 Pieces**				
31-3-2010	**Glow Lamp Philips 100W**		**Stock Journal**	2	**7 Pieces**	
	Philips CFL Lamp 20W	**8 Pieces**				
	Glow Lamp Philips 100W	**(-)7 Pieces**				
	Philips CFL Lamp 20W	**(-)8 Pieces**				

F-13A: Stock Journal Register

Configuration

Show Extract of Register	? **No**
Show Columnar Register	? **No**
Format	: **Detailed**
Show Narrations also	? **No**
Show Billwise Details also	? **No**
Show Cost Centre Details also	? **No**
Show Inventory Details also	? **Yes**
Show Bank Details also	? **No**
Appearance of Names	: **Name Only**
Sorting Method	: **Default**

F-14A: Stock Journal Register Configuration

- F1: Condensed
- F2: Date
- F2: Period
- F3: Company
- F4: Chg Vch
- F5: Columnar
- F6: Extract
- F7: Show Profit

F-14B: Stock Journal Register Buttons

- o Set *No* to get Voucher list of Stock Journals for the selected Period (F-13A)
- **Format**: At *Format:*
  - o Select *Condensed* to show top level Stock Group only
  - o Select *Detailed* to show next level Stock Group / Stock Items (F-13A)

Voucher Register Ctrl + M
Extract of All Stock Journal Vouchers — 1-Mar-2010 to 31-Mar-2010

Particulars	Inwards Qty	Rate	Amount	Outwards Qty	Rate	Amount
Lamp	15 Pieces	175.61	2,634.08	15 Pieces	179.75	2,696.24
CFL Lamp	8 Pieces	213.33	1,706.64	8 Pieces	228.60	1,828.80
Philips CFL Lamp 20W	*8 Pieces*	*213.33*	*1,706.64*	*8 Pieces*	*228.60*	*1,828.80*
Glow Lamp	7 Pieces	132.49	927.44	7 Pieces	123.92	867.44
Glow Lamp Philips 100W	*7 Pieces*	*132.49*	*927.44*	*7 Pieces*	*123.92*	*867.44*
	15 Pieces	175.61	2,634.08	15 Pieces	179.75	2,696.24

F-14C: Stock Journal Register Extract (Detailed)

Voucher Register Ctrl + M
Extract of All Stock Journal Vouchers — 1-Mar-2010 to 31-Mar-2010

Particulars	Inwards Qty	Rate	Amount	Outwards Qty	Rate	Amount
Lamp	15 Pieces	175.61	2,634.08	15 Pieces	179.75	2,696.24
CFL Lamp	8 Pieces	213.33	1,706.64	8 Pieces	228.60	1,828.80
Glow Lamp	7 Pieces	132.49	927.44	7 Pieces	123.92	867.44
	15 Pieces	175.61	2,634.08	15 Pieces	179.75	2,696.24

F-14D: Stock Journal Register Extract (Condensed)

Stock Journal Voucher Register Buttons

At *Stock Journal Voucher Register*, you get Buttons (F-14B), similar to Bill Register (§02.03/03-04)

07 Movement Analysis

At Gateway of Tally, select *Display>Inventory Books > Movement Analysis* to get *Movement Analysis* Menu (F-15A).

Gateway of Tally ....
Display Menu ....
Inventory Books ....

Movement Analysis

Stock Group Analysis
Category Analysis
Stock Item Analysis

Group Analysis
Ledger Analysis

Transfer Analysis

Quit

F: 15A: Movement Analysis Menu

Configuration

Format	:	Condensed
Expand all levels in Detailed Format	?	No
Show Inwards Column	?	Yes
Show Outwards Column	?	Yes
Show Quantities	?	Yes
Show using Alternate Units	?	No
Show Tail Units of Compound Units	?	No
Show Rates	?	Yes
Show Values	?	Yes

F:16A: Stock Group & Stock Category Movement Analysis Configuration

Configuration

Show 'Suppliers' Section	?	Yes
Show 'Job Work Transfer Inward' Section	?	No
Show 'Transfers Inward (Production)' Section	?	Yes
Show 'Buyers' Section	?	Yes
Show 'Job Work Transfer Out' Section	?	No
Show 'Transfers Outward (Consumption)' Section	?	Yes
Show Quantities	?	Yes
Show using Alternate Units	?	No
Show Tail Units of Compound Units	?	No
Show Rates	?	Yes
Show Values	?	Yes

F-17A: Stock Item Movement Analysis Configuration

F-18A: Stock Group	F-18B: Stock Item	F-18C: Stock Category	F-18D: Columnar Report Buttons
F1: Detailed	F1: Detailed	F1: Detailed	C: New Column
F2: Period	F2: Period	F2: Period	A: Alter Column
F3: Company	F3: Company	F3: Company	D: Del Column
F4: Group	F4: Item	F4: Category	N: Auto Column
F5: Item-wise		F5: Item-wise	
F6: By Ledgers		F6: By Ledgers	

F-18A: Stock Group F-18B: Stock Item F-18C: Stock Category F-18D: Columnar Report Buttons

07.01 Stock Group Movement Analysis

At *Movement Analysis* Menu (F-15A), select *Stock Group Analysis* to get *Stock Group Movement Analysis* (F-19A).

Movement Analysis Ctrl + M
ABC Electrical — 1-Apr-2009 to 31-Mar-2010

Particulars	Inward Quantity	Inward Eff. Rate	Inward Value	Outward Quantity	Outward Eff. Rate	Outward Value
Cables & Wires	155.00 Mtrs	10.48	1,624.12	346.00 Mtrs	18.14	6,276.40
Lamp	74 Pieces	153.74	11,376.72	47 Pieces	173.32	8,146.24
Switch Boards						90.00
Switches				8 Pieces	45.29	362.30
Grand Total			13,000.84			14,874.94

F-19A: Stock Group Movement Analysis (Condensed)

Movement Analysis Ctrl + M
ABC Electrical — 1-Apr-2009 to 31-Mar-2010

Particulars	Inward Quantity	Inward Eff. Rate	Inward Value	Outward Quantity	Outward Eff. Rate	Outward Value
Cables & Wires	155.00 Mtrs	10.48	1,624.12	346.00 Mtrs	18.14	6,276.40
Cables	155.00 Mtrs	10.48	1,624.12	346.00 Mtrs	18.14	6,276.40
Lamp	**74 Pieces**	153.74	**11,376.72**	**47 Pieces**	173.32	**8,146.24**
CFL Lamp	46 Pieces	170.22	7,830.05	24 Pieces	196.62	4,718.80
Glow Lamp	28 Pieces	126.67	3,546.67	23 Pieces	149.02	3,427.44
Switch Boards						**90.00**
Switch Board (Consealed)						*90.00*
Switches				**8 Pieces**	45.29	**362.30**
Combo Switches				2 Pieces	25.00	50.00
Single Switches				6 Pieces	52.05	312.30
Grand Total			13,000.84			14,874.94

F-19B: Stock Group Movement Analysis (Detailed)

Stock Group Movement Analysis Configuration

At *Stock Group Movement* Analysis (F-19A), click *F12:Configure* to get *Stock Group Movement Analysis* Configuration (F-16A) to set the Configuration options as follows:

- **Format**: At *Format:*
  - o Select *Condensed* to show top level Stock Group only (F-19A)
  - o Select *Detailed* to show top level Stock Group / Stock Items (F-19B)
- **Form**: Having set Detailed at Format, At *Expand all levels in Detailed Format,* you may further set:
  - o Set *Yes* to show the Items upto the lowest level details (in detail mode- i.e, when *F1: Detail* button is clicked: F-19C),
  - o Set No. Only next level detail (Item Group / Stock Items) are shown in detail mode.

- **Quantity**: At *Show Quantities*:
  - o Set *Yes* to show the Quantity column (and the base unit), if the Base Unit of all the Items under the Stock Group is same
  - o Set *No* to suppress the Quantity column.
- **Rate**: At *Show Rates*,
  - o Set *Yes* to show the Rate column (and the base unit),
  - o Set *No* to suppress the Rate column.
- **Values**: At *Show Values*,:
  - o Set *Yes* to show the Value column,
  - o Set *No* to suppress the Value column

ii. Set Yes / No to the following options to show / suppress the columns as required

- **Alternate Unit**: This is relevant only when Alternate Unit is activated. At *Show using Alternate units*:
  - o Set *Yes* to show the quantity in *Alternate units* also (for Items having Dual Units: F-19F)
  - o Set No, only the Base Unit is shown.
- **Tail Unit**: This is relevant only for Items with Compound Unit. At *Show Tail units of Compound Units,*
  - o Set *Yes* to show the tail units of compound unit (F-19D)
  - o Set *No.* the base unit is shown (with fraction values, where applicable)

At *Stock Group Movement Analysis*, drill down through:

- Any Stock Group to get next level details of Stock Group / Stock Items
- Any Stock Item to get *Stock Item Movement Analysis*

Movement Analysis — Ctrl + M

Particulars	ABC Electrical 1-Apr-2009 to 31-Mar-2010					
	Inward			Outward		
	Quantity	*Eff. Rate*	Value	Quantity	*Eff. Rate*	Value
Cables & Wires	155.00 Mtrs	10.48	1,624.12	346.00 Mtrs	18.14	6,276.40
Cables	155.00 Mtrs	*10.48*	1,624.12	346.00 Mtrs	18.14	6,276.40
Armoured Cables ARCO 5/12				12.00 Mtrs	*177.62*	2,131.40
Despatch Room				10.00 Mtrs	200.00	2,000.00
Main Location				2.00 Mtrs	65.70	131.40
Cable BeeKay	2 Roll	*250.00*	500.00	6 Roll 13.00 Mtrs	*305.52*	1,992.00
Main Location	2 Roll	*250.00*	500.00	6 Roll 13.00 Mtrs	305.52	1,992.00
Cables KayCee	25.00 Mtrs	*9.80*	245.00	65.00 Mtrs	*11.92*	775.00
Despatch Room				30.00 Mtrs	12.17	365.00
Main Location	25.00 Mtrs	*9.80*	245.00	35.00 Mtrs	11.71	410.00
Cable TeeKay	80.00 Mtrs	*1,000.00*	879.12	1 Roll 15.00 Mtrs	*1,183.00*	1,378.00
Main Location	80.00 Mtrs	*1,000.00*	879.12	1 Roll 15.00 Mtrs	1,183.00	1,378.00
Lamp	**74 Pieces**	*153.74*	**11,376.72**	**47 Pieces**	*173.32*	**8,146.24**
CFL Lamp	48 Pieces	*170.22*	7,830.05	24 Pieces	196.62	4,718.80
Anchor CFL Lamp 12W	20 Pieces	135.23	2,704.64	11 Pieces	*164.36*	1,808.00
1 *Despatch Room*				1 Pieces	170.00	170.00
23 *Main Location*	9 Pieces	*140.74*	1,266.64	1 Pieces	150.00	150.00
37 *Despatch Room*	1 Pieces	*158.00*	158.00	7 Pieces	170.00	1,190.00
Primary Batch *Main Location*	10 Pieces	*128.00*	1,280.00	2 Pieces	149.00	298.00
Philips CFL Lamp 20W	26 Pieces	***197.13***	5,125.41	13 Pieces	*223.91*	2,910.80
						17 more ...
Grand Total			13,000.84			14,874.94

F-19C: Stock Group Movement Analysis (with all level details)

> ***Note:*** *In Stock Group / Stock Category Movement Analysis, the Effective Rate (Rate including other costs) are shown, while in Stock Item Analysis, both* Basic & Effective *Rates are shown separately. In Stock Item Movement Analysis, the Basic Rate for Outwards (F-21C) is not shown (only Effective Rate is shown), even though the figure is available for Basic Rate (you get Basic Rate when you drill down through any Stock Item to get Item Voucher Analysis).*

Stock Group Movement Analysis Buttons

At *Stock Group Movement Analysis* (F-19A), you get following Buttons (F-18A):

Button	Description
F1: Detailed / Condensed	- F1: *Detailed*: To show next level Stock Groups / Stock Item details (F-19B) - F1: *Condensed*: To show only top level Stock Groups (F-19A)
F4: Group	To select a Stock Group to get Stock Group Report of a selected Stock Group (select *Primary* to get Report of Top Level Stock Groups)
F5:Itemwise / Grouped	- F5:Itemwise: To show Stock Item wise report. - F5:Gouped: To show Stock Group wise report (F-19C)
F6: By Ledgers / Items	- F6: By Ledgers: To get Account Group Movement Analysis (F-22A) - F6: By Items: To get Stock Group Movement Analysis (F-19C)
Columnar Report Buttons	Column specification to get columnar Reports

07.02 Stock Item Movement Analysis

At *Movement Analysis* Menu (F-15A), select *Stock Item Analysis* and select a Stock Item from the list to get to get *Stock Item Movement Analysis* (F-21A).

The *Stock Item Movement Analysis* (F-21A) shows the Supplier & Buyer wise summary figures of Sales & Purchase of the selected Stock Item. The Report shows average Basic Rate and Effective Rate of the Stock Item in respect of each Party. This is a valuable comparative statement to compare the Basic & Effective Rate of sales realization & purchase cost of the Item.

Movement Analysis	ABC Electrical							Ctrl + M
Particulars	*Cables* **ABC Electrical** 1-Apr-2009 to 31-Mar-2010							
	Inward				**Outward**			
	Quantity	*(Alt. Units)*	*Eff. Rate*	Value	Quantity	*(Alt. Units)*	*Eff. Rate*	Value
Armoured Cables ARCO 5/12					12.00 Mtrs		*177.62*	2,131.40
Despatch Room					10.00 Mtrs		200.00	2,000.00
Main Location					2.00 Mtrs		65.70	131.40
Cable BeeKay	50.00 Mtrs		*250.00*	500.00	163.00 Mtrs		*305.52*	1,992.00
Main Location	50.00 Mtrs		*250.00*	500.00	163.00 Mtrs		305.52	1,992.00
Cables KayCee	25.00 Mtrs	*(1.00 Roll)*	*9.80*	245.00	65.00 Mtrs	*(2.60 Roll)*	*11.92*	775.00
Despatch Room					30.00 Mtrs	*(1.20 Roll)*	12.17	365.00
Main Location	25.00 Mtrs	*(1.00 Roll)*	*9.80*	245.00	35.00 Mtrs	*(1.40 Roll)*	11.71	410.00
Cable TeeKay	80.00 Mtrs		*1,000.00*	879.12	106.00 Mtrs		*1,183.00*	1,378.00
Main Location	80.00 Mtrs		*1,000.00*	879.12	106.00 Mtrs		1,183.00	1,378.00
Grand Total	155.00 Mtrs		**10.48**	1,624.12	346.00 Mtrs		*18.14*	6,276.40

F-19D: Movement Analysis of a selected Stock Group (with Tail Unit & Alternate Unit)

Movement Analysis			Ctrl + M
Particulars	ABC Electrical 1-Apr-2009 to 31-Mar-2010		
	Outward		
	Quantity	*Eff. Rate*	Value
Anchor CFL Lamp 12W	11 Pieces	*164.36*	1,808.00
Armoured Cables ARCO 5/12	12.00 Mtrs	*177.62*	2,131.40
Cable BeeKay	6 Roll 13.00 Mtrs	*305.52*	1,992.00
Cables KayCee	65.00 Mtrs	*11.92*	775.00
Cable TeeKay	1 Roll 15.00 Mtrs	*1,183.00*	1,378.00
Combo Switch JACO 15A	2 Pieces	*25.00*	50.00
Glow Lamp Philips 100W	23 Pieces	*149.02*	3,427.44
Philips CFL Lamp 20W	13 Pieces	*223.91*	2,910.80
Switch Anchor 15A	5 Pieces	*60.00*	300.00
Switch - Anchor 5A	1 Pieces	*12.30*	12.30
Switch Board (Concealed)			90.00
Grand Total			14,874.94

F-19E: Movement Analysis (Itemwise, Condensed, Outwards only)

Movement Analysis								Ctrl + M
Particulars	*Cables* **ABC Electrical** 1-Apr-2009 to 31-Mar-2010							
	Inward				**Outward**			
	Quantity	*(Alt. Units)*	*Eff. Rate*	Value	Quantity	*(Alt. Units)*	*Eff. Rate*	Value
Armoured Cables ARCO 5/12					12.00 Mtrs		*177.62*	2,131.40
Despatch Room					10.00 Mtrs		200.00	2,000.00
Main Location					2.00 Mtrs		65.70	131.40
Cable BeeKay	2 Roll		*250.00*	500.00	6 Roll 13.00 Mtrs		*305.52*	1,992.00
Main Location	2 Roll		*250.00*	500.00	6 Roll 13.00 Mtrs		305.52	1,992.00
Cables KayCee	25.00 Mtrs	*(1.00 Roll)*	*9.80*	245.00	65.00 Mtrs	*(2.60 Roll)*	*11.92*	775.00
Despatch Room					30.00 Mtrs	*(1.20 Roll)*	12.17	365.00
Main Location	25.00 Mtrs	*(1.00 Roll)*	*9.80*	245.00	35.00 Mtrs	*(1.40 Roll)*	11.71	410.00
Cable TeeKay	80.00 Mtrs		*1,000.00*	879.12	1 Roll 15.00 Mtrs		*1,183.00*	1,378.00
Main Location	80.00 Mtrs		*1,000.00*	879.12	1 Roll 15.00 Mtrs		1,183.00	1,378.00
Grand Total	155.00 Mtrs		**10.48**	1,624.12	346.00 Mtrs		*18.14*	6,276.40

F-19F: Movement Analysis of a selected Stock Group (with Alternate Unit)

Movement Analysis			Ctrl + M
Particulars	ABC Electrical 1-Apr-2009 to 31-Mar-2010		
	Inward		
	Quantity	*Eff. Rate*	Value
Anchor CFL Lamp 12W	20 Pieces	*135.23*	2,704.64
Armoured Cables ARCO 5/12			
Cable BeeKay	2 Roll	*250.00*	500.00
Cables KayCee	25.00 Mtrs	*9.80*	245.00
Cable TeeKay	80.00 Mtrs	*1,000.00*	879.12
Combo Switch JACO 15A			
Glow Lamp Philips 100W	28 Pieces	***126.67***	3,546.67
Philips CFL Lamp 20W	26 Pieces	***197.13***	5,125.41
Switch Anchor 15A			
Switch - Anchor 5A			
Switch Board (Concealed)			
Grand Total			13,000.84

F-20A: Movement Analysis (Itemwise, Condensed, Inwards only)

Item Movement Analysis			Ctrl + M
Particulars	*Cable BeeKay* **ABC Electrical** 1-Apr-2009 to 31-Mar-2010		
	Movement Values		
	Quantity	*Basic Rate* *Effective Rate*	Value
Movement Inward :			
Suppliers :			
B.K.Services	2 Roll	*250.00* *250.00*	500.00
	2 Roll	**250.00**	500.00
Movement Outward :			
Buyers :			
A K Traders	3 Roll 8.00 Mtrs	306.02	1,016.00
P.K.Motors	3 Roll 5.00 Mtrs	305.00	976.00
	6 Roll 13.00 Mtrs	**305.52**	1,992.00

F-21A: Stock Item Movement Analysis

Item Movement Analysis			Ctrl + M
Particulars	*Anchor CFL Lamp 12W* **ABC Electrical** 1-Apr-2009 to 31-Mar-2010		
	Movement Values		
	Quantity	*Basic Rate*	*Effective Rate*
Movement Inward :			
Suppliers :			
A K Traders	2 Pieces	*150.00*	*150.00*
B.K.Services	18 Pieces	*133.59*	*133.59*
	20 Pieces		**135.23**

F-21B: Stock Item Movement Analysis (Inwards, Quantity & Rate)

Item Movement Analysis			Ctrl + M
Particulars	*Cables KayCee* **ABC Electrical** 1-Apr-2009 to 31-Mar-2010		
	Movement Values		
	Quantity	*Basic Rate*	*Effective Rate*
Movement Outward :			
Buyers :			
A K Traders	41.00 Mtrs		12.07
P.K.Motors	24.00 Mtrs		11.67
	65.00 Mtrs		**11.92**

F-21C: Stock Item Movement Analysis (Outwards, Quantity & Rate)

Stock Item Movement Configuration

At *Stock Item Movement Analysis* (F-21A), click F12:Configure to get *Stock Item Movement Configuration* (F-17A), to set Configuration options as follows:

- **Supplier Section**: At *Show Supplier Section*, set:
  - o *Yes* to show the Supplier section showing the Purchases details from each Supplier under *Movement Inward* section
  - o *No*. The Supplier section is not shown
- **Buyer Section**: At *Show Buyer Section*, set:
  - o *Yes* to show the Buyer section showing the Sales details to each Buyer under *Movement Outward* section
  - o *No*. The Buyer section is not shown (F-21B)
- **Quantity**: At *Show Quantities*:
  - o Set *Yes* to show the Quantity column (and the base unit), if the Base Unit of all the Items under the Stock Group is same

Group Analysis						Ctrl + M
Particulars	*Sundry Creditors* **ABC Electrical** 1-Apr-2009 to 31-Mar-2010					
	Purchases			**Sales**		
	Quantity	*Eff. Rate*	Value	Quantity	*Eff. Rate*	Value
Anchor CFL Lamp 12W	18 Pieces	*133.59*	2,404.64	3 Pieces	*180.00*	540.00
Armoured Cables ARCO 5/12				10.00 Mtrs	*200.00*	2,000.00
Cable BeeKay	2 Roll	*250.00*	500.00	3 Roll 5.00 Mtrs	*305.00*	976.00
Cables KayCee	25.00 Mtrs	*9.80*	245.00	24.00 Mtrs	*11.67*	280.00
Cable TeeKay	80.00 Mtrs	*1,000.00*	879.12	1 Roll 15.00 Mtrs	*1,183.00*	1,378.00
Combo Switch JACO 15A				2 Pieces	*25.00*	50.00
Glow Lamp Philips 100W	21 Pieces	*124.73*	2,619.23	16 Pieces	*160.00*	2,560.00
Philips CFL Lamp 20W	8 Pieces	*212.35*	1,698.77	4 Pieces	*227.50*	910.00
Switch Anchor 15A				5 Pieces	*60.00*	300.00
Grand Total			8,346.76			8,994.00

F-22A: Account Group Movement Analysis (Sundry Creditors)

  - o Set *No* to suppress the Quantity column.
- **Rate**: At *Show Rates*,
  - o Set *Yes* to show the Rate column (and the base unit),
  - o Set *No* to suppress the Rate column.
- **Values**: At *Show Values*,:
  - o Set *Yes* to show the Value column,
  - o Set *No* to suppress the Value column (F-21B)
- **Alternate Unit**: This is relevant only when Alternate Unit is activated. At *Show using Alternate units*:
  - o Set *Yes* to show the quantity in *Alternate units* also (for Items having Dual Units), F-3F
  - o Set No, only the Base Unit is shown.
- **Tail Unit**: This is relevant only for Items with Compound Unit. At *Show Tail units of Compound Units,*
  - o Set *Yes* to show the tail units of compound unit,
  - o Set *No*. the base unit is shown (with fraction values, where applicable)

Stock Item Movement Analysis Buttons

At *Stock Item Movement Analysis* (F-18B), you get the following buttons

F4: Item	To select a Stock Item to get Stock Item Movement Report of the selected Stock Item
Columnar Report Buttons	Column specification to get columnar Reports

08 Account Group Movement Analysis

At *Movement Analysis* Menu (F-15A), select *Group Analysis* and then select any Account Group as follows:

- **Sundry Debtor**: To get Stock Item Transaction Analysis of Sales (& Purchase) with all Parties under Sundry Debtor Account Group (F-23C)
- **Sundry Creditor**: To get Stock Item Transaction Analysis of Purchase (& Sales) with all Parties under Sundry Creditor Account Group

Configuration	
Show Purchases Column	? Yes
Show Sales Column	? Yes
Show Quantities	? Yes
Show using Alternate Units	? No
Show Tail Units of Compound Units	? No
Show Rates	? Yes
Show Values	? Yes

F-23A: Group / Ledger MovementAnalysis Configuration

Buttons
F2: Period
F3: Company
F4: Group
C: New Column
A: Alter Column
D: Del Column
N: Auto Column

F-23B: Buttons

- **Cash Bank:** To get Stock Item Transaction Analysis of Cash Purchase & Cash Sales through all Cash Bank transaction of Sales / Purchase Voucher
- **Branch**: To get Stock Item Transaction Analysis of transaction with Ledger Accounts under Branch /

Divisions through all Cash Bank transaction of Sales / Purchase Voucher.

Group Analysis Ctrl + M

Particulars	Sundry Debtors ABC Electrical 1-Apr-2009 to 31-Mar-2010					
	Purchases			Sales		
	Quantity	*Eff. Rate*	Value	Quantity	*Eff. Rate*	Value
Anchor CFL Lamp 12W	2 Pieces	*150.00*	300.00	4 Pieces	*157.50*	630.00
Armoured Cables ARCO 5/12				1.00 Mtrs	*116.40*	116.40
Cable BeeKay				3 Roll 8.00 Mtrs	*306.02*	1,016.00
Cables KayCee				41.00 Mtrs	*12.07*	495.00
Philips CFL Lamp 20W	10 Pieces	*172.00*	1,720.00			
Switch Board (Concealed)						90.00
Grand Total	12 Pieces	168.33	2,020.00			2,347.40

F-23C: Account Group Movement Analysis (Sundry Debtors)

Item Voucher Analysis Ctrl + M

Stock Item: **Anchor CFL Lamp 12W** — **1-Apr-2009 to 31-Mar-2010**

Under Group: **Sundry Debtors**

Date	Particulars	Quantity	Basic Rate	Basic Value	*Addl. Cost*	Total Value	Eff. Rate
	Purchases						
1-Jun-2009	A K Traders	2 Pieces	150.00/Pieces	300.00		300.00	150.00/Pieces
	Total	2 Pieces	150.00/Pieces	300.00		300.00	150.00/Pieces
	Sales						
1-Jul-2009	**A K Traders**	2 Pieces	155.00/Pieces	310.00			
1-Jan-2010	**Gift Voucher**	1 Pieces	150.00/Pieces	150.00			
31-Mar-2010	**A K Traders**	1 Pieces	170.00/Pieces	170.00			
	Total	4 Pieces	157.50/Pieces	630.00			

F-24A: Item Voucher Analysis (of an Item / Account Group)

Account Group Movement Analysis Buttons

At Account Group Movement Analysis (F-22A, F-23A, F-24A), you get following buttons (F-23B):

Button	Description
F4: Group	To select an Account Group to get Account Group Movement Analysis Report of the selected Account Group
Columnar Report Buttons	Column specification to get columnar Reports

09 Account Ledger Movement Analysis

At *Movement Analysis* Menu (F-15A), select *Ledger Analysis* and then select any Account Ledger as follows:

- **Customer Ledger:** To get Stock Item Transaction Analysis of Sales (& Purchase) with the selected Ledger Account.
- **Supplier Ledger:** To get Stock Item Transaction Analysis of Purchase (&Sales) with the selected Ledger Account.
- **Cash Bank Account**: To get Stock Item Transaction Analysis of Cash Purchase & Cash Sales through the selected Cash / Bank Ledger Account of all transaction through Sales / Purchase Voucher
- **Branch Account**: To get Stock Item Transaction Analysis of transaction with the selected Ledger Accounts under Branch / Divisions through all Cash Bank transaction of Sales / Purchase Voucher.

> **Note:** *In Account Ledger / Account Group Movement Analysis (F-23C, 25A), you get Basic & Effective Rates both for Outwards (Sales) and Inwards (Purchase), for each Stock Item.*

Ledger Analysis Ctrl + M

Particulars	A K Traders ABC Electrical 1-Apr-2009 to 31-Mar-2010					
	Purchases			Sales		
	Quantity	*Eff. Rate*	Value	Quantity	*Eff. Rate*	Value
Anchor CFL Lamp 12W	2 Pieces	*150.00*	300.00	3 Pieces	*160.00*	480.00
Cable BeeKay				3 Roll 8.00 Mtrs	*306.02*	1,016.00
Cables KayCee				41.00 Mtrs	*12.07*	495.00
Philips CFL Lamp 20W	10 Pieces	*172.00*	1,720.00			
Switch Board (Concealed)						90.00
Grand Total	12 Pieces	168.33	2,020.00			2,081.00

F-25A: Party Ledger Account Movement Analysis

Account Ledger Movement Analysis Buttons

At Account Ledger Movement Analysis (F-25), you get following buttons (F-26A):

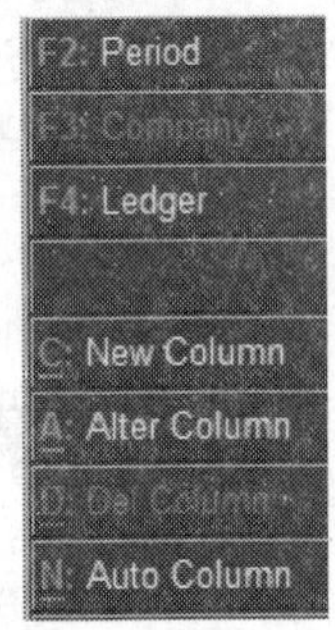

F-26A: Button

Button	Description
F4: Ledger	To select an Account Ledger to get Account Ledger Movement Analysis Report of the selected Account Ledger.
Columnar Report Buttons	Column specification to get columnar Reports

09.01 Account Group / Ledger Movement Analysis Configuration

At Account Group Movement Analysis (F-22A) / Account Ledger Movement Analysis (F-25A), click F12:Configure to get Account Movement Analysis Configuration (F-23A) to set the following options:

- **Purchases**: At *Show Purchases Column*:
  - o Set *Yes* to show the Purchases section columns (Quantity, Rate, Value etc)
  - o Set *No* to suppress the Purchases section columns
- **Sales**: At *Show Sales Column*:
  - o Set *Yes* to show the Sales section columns (Quantity, Rate, Value etc)
  - o Set *No* to suppress the Sales section columns
- **Quantity**: At *Show Quantities*:
  - o Set *Yes* to show the Quantity column (at Purchase / Sales section)

- o Set *No* to suppress the Quantity column (at Purchase / Sales section)
- **Alternate Unit**: This is relevant only when Alternate Unit is activated. At *Show using Alternate units*:
  - o Set *Yes* to show the quantity in *Alternate units* also (for Items having Dual Units),
  - o Set No, only the Base Unit is shown.
- **Tail Unit**: This is relevant only for Items with Compound Unit. At *Show Tail units of Compound Units,*
  - o Set *Yes* to show the tail units of compound unit,
  - o Set *No.* the base unit is shown (with fraction values, where applicable),
- **Rate**: At *Show Rates,*
  - o Set *Yes* to show the Rate column (at Purchase / Sales section)
  - o Set *No* to suppress the Rate column (at Purchase / Sales section)
- **Value**: At *Show Values*:
  - o Set *Yes* to show the Value column (at Purchase / Sales section)
  - o Set *No* to suppress the Value column (at Purchase / Sales section)

10 Stock Journal Movement Analysis

At *Movement Analysis* Menu (F-15A), select *Transfer Analysis* and then select any Stock Journal Type to get *Stock Journal Movement Analysis* (F-27A).

Transfer Analysis — Ctrl + M

Stock Journal
ABC Electrical
1-Apr-2009 to 31-Mar-2010

Particulars	Goods In (Production)			Goods Out (Consumption)		
	Quantity	*Eff. Rate*	Value	Quantity	*Eff. Rate*	Value
Glow Lamp Philips 100W	7 Pieces	*132.49*	927.44	7 Pieces	*123.92*	867.44
Philips CFL Lamp 20W	8 Pieces	*213.33*	1,706.64	9 Pieces	*222.31*	2,000.80
Switch - Anchor 5A				1 Pieces	*12.30*	12.30
Grand Total	15 Pieces	175.61	2,634.08	17 Pieces	*169.44*	2,880.54

F-27A: Stock Journal Movement Analysis

Configuration

Show 'Goods In (Production)' Column	?	Yes
Show 'Goods Out (Consumption)' Column	?	Yes
Show Quantities	?	Yes
Show using Alternate Units	?	No
Show Tail Units of Compound Units	?	No
Show Rates	?	Yes
Show Values	?	Yes

F-28A: Stock Journal Movement Configuration

F2: Period
F3: Company
F4: Vch Type
C: New Column
A: Alter Column
D: Del Column
N: Auto Column

F-28B: Buttons

Stock Journal Movement Analysis Configuration

At Stock Journal Movement Analysis (F-27A), click *F12:Configure* to get *Stock Journal Movement Analysis* Configuration (F-28A) to set the following options:

- **Goods In**: At *Show Goods In (Production) Column*:
  - o Set *Yes* to show the *Goods In (Production)* section columns (Quantity, Rate, Value etc)
  - o Set *No* to suppress the *Goods In (Production)* section columns
- **Goods Out**: At *Show Goods In (Consumption) Column*:
  - o Set *Yes* to show the *Goods In (Consumption)* section columns (Quantity, Rate, Value etc)
  - o Set *No* to suppress the *Goods In (Consumption)* section columns
- **Quantity**: At *Show Quantities*:
  - o Set *Yes* to show the Quantity column (at Purchase / Sales section)
  - o Set *No* to suppress the Quantity column (at Purchase / Sales section)
- **Alternate Unit**: This is relevant only when Alternate Unit is activated. At *Show using Alternate units*:
  - o Set *Yes* to show the quantity in *Alternate units* also (for Items having Dual Units),
  - o Set No, only the Base Unit is shown.
- **Tail Unit**: This is relevant only for Items with Compound Unit. At *Show Tail units of Compound Units,*
  - o Set *Yes* to show the tail units of compound unit,
  - o Set *No.* the base unit is shown (with fraction values, where applicable), F-3F
- **Rate**: At *Show Rates,*
  - o Set *Yes* to show the Rate column (at Purchase / Sales section)
  - o Set *No* to suppress the Rate column (at Purchase / Sales section)
- **Value**: At *Show Values*:
  - o Set *Yes* to show the Value column (at Purchase / Sales section)
  - o Set *No* to suppress the Value column (at Purchase / Sales section)

Stock Journal Movement Analysis Buttons

At Stock Journal Movement Analysis (F-27A), you get following buttons (F-28B):

Button	Description
F4: Voucher Type	To select a Stock Journal Voucher Type to get Stock Journal Movement Analysis Report of the selected Voucher Type.
Columnar Report Buttons	Column specification to get columnar Reports

11 Stock Item Voucher Analysis

Stock Item Voucher Analsyis is a class of Reports showing the Itemwise Sumary of Transactions of a selected Stock Group, Account Group, Account Ledger or StockJounal Voucher Type, obtained on drill down of any record inany of the Movement Analyss Reports discussed above.

You get the resepctive *Stock Item Voucher Analysis* as follows:

11.01 Stock Item / Account Ledger Voucher Analysis

At *Stock Item Movement Analysis* (F-21A), drill down through any Party record under Buyer / Supplier section to get Item Voucher Analysis Report (F-29A) showing the details of Purchase / Sale transactions of the selected Item with the selected Party

Item Voucher Analysis — Ctrl + M

Stock Item: **Cable BeeKay** — **1-Apr-2009 to 31-Mar-2010**
InwardsUnder Ledger : **B.K.Services**

Date	Particulars	Quantity	Basic Rate	Basic Value	*Addl. Cost*	Total Value	Eff. Rate
	Purchases						
1-Nov-2009	B.K.Services	2 Roll	250.00/Roll	500.00		500.00	**250.00/Roll**
	Total	2 Roll	250.00/Roll	500.00		500.00	**250.00/Roll**

F-29A: Stock Voucher Analysis of a Supplier of Stock Item Analysis (Condensed) of Stock Item

Item Voucher Analysis — Ctrl + M

Stock Item: **Cable BeeKay** — **1-Apr-2009 to 31-Mar-2010**
OutwardsUnder Ledger : **A K Traders**

Date	Particulars	Quantity	Basic Rate	Basic Value	*Addl. Cost*	Total Value	Eff. Rate
	Sales						
1-Feb-2010	A K Traders *1-Feb-2010 Sales 11*	2 Roll 13.00 Mtrs	300.00/Roll	756.00			
1-Feb-2010	**A K Traders** *1-Feb-2010 Sales 11*	20.00 Mtrs	325.00/Roll	260.00			
	Total	3 Roll 8.00 Mtrs	306.02/Roll	1,016.00			

F-29B: Stock Voucher Analysis of a Customer of Stock Item Analysis (Detailed)

Configuration

Show Addl. Cost Column	? **Yes**
Show full Addl. Cost Details	? **No**
Format	: **Condensed**
Show Billed Qty Column	? **Yes**
Show using Alternate Units	? **No**
Show Tail Units of Compound Units	? **No**
Show Base Rate Column	? **Yes**
Show Base Value Column	? **Yes**
Show Total Value Column	? **Yes**
Show Eff. Rate Column	? **Yes**

F-30A: Stock Voucher Analysis Configuration

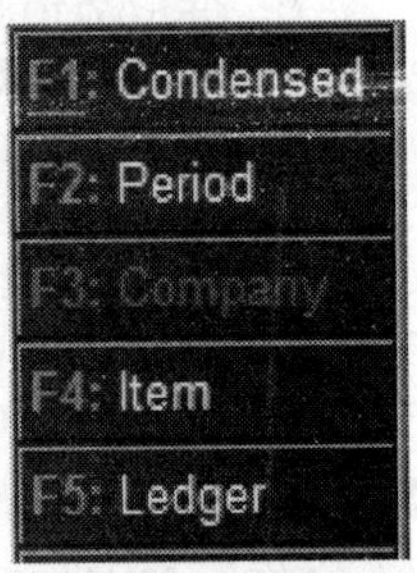

F-31A: Buttons of Customer / Supplier Ledger

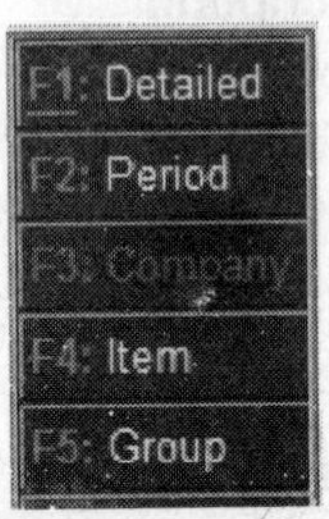

F-31B: Stock Voucher Analysis Buttons of Account Group

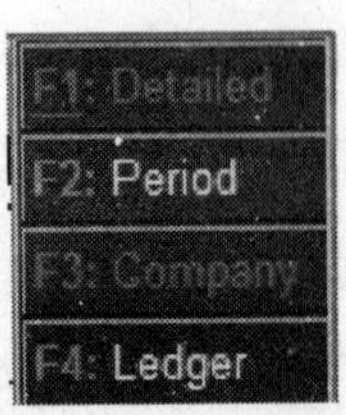

F-31C: Stock Voucher AnalysisButtons of Account Ledger

11.02 Stock Item / Account Group Voucher Analysis

At *Account Group Movement Analysis* (F-22A), drill down through any Stock Item record under to get *Item Voucher Analysis* showing (F-32A) the details of Purchase / Sale transactions of the selected Item with the Parties under the selected Group.

11.03 Stock Item / Account Ledger Voucher Analysis

At *Account Ledger Movement Analysis* (F-25A), drill down through any Stock Item record under to get *Item Voucher Analysis* (F-33A)showing the details of Purchase / Sale transactions of the selected Item with the selected Ledger Account.

Item Voucher Analysis — Ctrl + M

Stock Item: **Tendu Leaves** — **1-Apr-2009 to 31-Mar-2010**
Under Group: **Sundry Debtors**

Date	Particulars	Quantity	Basic Rate	Basic Value	*Addl. Cost*	Total Value	Eff. Rate
	Sales						
2-Oct-2009	P R Produce	1,000 Kgs	12.00/Kgs	12,000.00			
2-Oct-2009	**A K Traders**	1,200 Kgs	12.00/Kgs	14,400.00			
	Total	2,200 Kgs	12.00/Kgs	26,400.00			

F-32A: Item Voucher Analysis (of an Item / Account Group)

Item Voucher Analysis — Ctrl + M

Stock Item: **Anchor CFL Lamp 12W** — **1-Apr-2009 to 31-Mar-2010**
Under Ledger : **A K Traders**

Date	Particulars	Quantity	Basic Rate	Basic Value	*Addl. Cost*	Total Value	Eff. Rate
1-Jun-2009	A K Traders	2 Pieces	150.00/Pieces	300.00		300.00	**150.00/Pieces**
	Total	2 Pieces	150.00/Pieces	300.00		300.00	**150.00/Pieces**
	Sales						
1-Jul-2009	**A K Traders**	2 Pieces	155.00/Pieces	310.00			
31-Mar-2010	**A K Traders**	1 Pieces	170.00/Pieces	170.00			
	Total	3 Pieces	160.00/Pieces	480.00			

F-33A: Item Voucher Analysis (of an Item / Account Ledger)

11.04 Stock Item / Stock Journal Voucher Analysis

At *Stock Journal Movement Analysis* (F-27A), drill down through any Stock Item record to get Item Voucher Analysis Report (F-34A) showing the details of Goods In (Production) / Goods Out (Consumption) of the Stock Journal transactions of the selected Item through the selected Stock Journal Voucher Type

Item Voucher Analysis — Ctrl + M

Stock Item: **Glow Lamp Philips 100W** — **1-Apr-2009 to 31-Mar-2010**
Under Transfer : **Stock Journal**

Date	Particulars	Quantity	Basic Rate	Basic Value	*Addl. Cost*	Total Value	Eff. Rate
	Goods In (Production)						
31-Mar-2010	Stock Journal	7 Pieces	128.21/Pieces	897.44	*30.00*	927.44	**132.49/Pieces**
	Total	7 Pieces	128.21/Pieces	897.44	*30.00*	927.44	**132.49/Pieces**
	Goods Out (Consumption)						
31-Mar-2010	**Stock Journal**	7 Pieces	123.92/Pieces	867.44			
	Total	7 Pieces	123.92/Pieces	867.44			

F-34A: Item Voucher Analysis of Stock Journal Movement Analysis

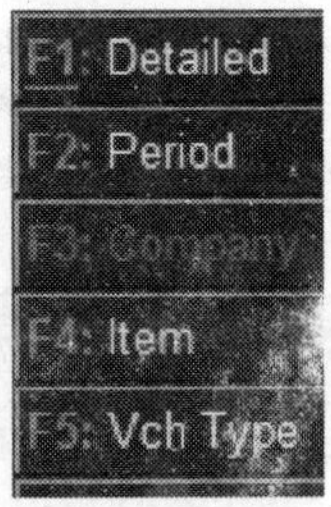

F-35A: Item Voucher Analysis Buttons of Stock Journal

11.05 Stock Item Voucher Analysis Configuration

At any *Stock Item Voucher Analysis* report described above, click *F12:Configure* to get *Stock Voucher Analysis Configuration* (F-30A), to set following options:

- **Additional Cost**: At *Show Addl. Cost Column*:
  - o Set *Yes* to get the *'Addl Cost'* column for Additional Cost (Apportioned / Allocated Other per Unit, apart from the Item Basic Cost
  - o Set *No*. The *Addl Cost'* column is not shown
- **Full Additional Cost:** Having set *Yes* at *Show Addl. Cost Column,* at *Full Additional Cost,:*
  - o Set *Yes* to get the column 'Others' in place of *Addl Cost'* to show full Additional Cost apart from the Item Basic Cost
  - o Set *No*. The '*Others'* column is not shown
- **Format**: At *Format:*
  - o Select *Condensed* to show top level Stock Group only
  - o Select *Detailed* to show top level Stock Group / Stock Items
- **Quantity**: At *Show Billed Qty Column*:
  - o Set *Yes* to show the Quantity column (and the base unit), if the Base Unit of all the Items under the Stock Group is same
  - o Set *No* to suppress the Quantity column.
- **Alternate Unit**: This is relevant only when Alternate Unit is activated. At *Show using Alternate units*:
  - o Set *Yes* to show the quantity in *Alternate units* also (for Items having Dual Units),
  - o Set No, only the Base Unit is shown.
- **Tail Unit**: This is relevant only for Items with Compound Unit. At *Show Tail units of Compound Units,*
  - o Set *Yes* to show the tail units of compound unit,
  - o Set *No*. the base unit is shown (with fraction values, where applicable),
- **Rate**: At *Show Base Rate Column,*
  - o Set *Yes* to show the Base Rate column (and the base unit),
  - o Set *No* to suppress the Base Rate column.
- **Base Value**: At *Show Base Value Column*:
  - o Set *Yes* to show the Base Value column
  - o Set *No* to suppress the Base Value column
- **Total Value**: At *Show Total Value Column*:
  - o Set *Yes* to show the Total Value column (Base Value + Other Charges)
  - o Set *No* to suppress the Total Value column
- **Effective Rate:** At *Show Eff. Rate Column*:
  - o Set *Yes* to show Effective Rate column (Rate per unit on Total Value)
  - o Set *No* to suppress the *Eff. Rate* column

11.06 Item Voucher Analysis Buttons

At *Stock Voucher Analysis* Report of Customer / Supplier Ledger, you get following Buttons (F-31A):

Button	Description
F1: Detailed / Condensed	- F1: *Detailed*: To show next level Stock Groups / Stock Item details - F1: *Condensed*: To show only top level Stock Groups.
F4: Item	To select a Stock Item to get Stock Voucher Analysis of transactions of the selected Stock Item with the currently selected Party.
F5:Ledger	To select a Party Ledger to get Stock Voucher Analysis of transactions of the selected Party Ledger with the currently selected Stock Item.

At *Stock Voucher Analysis* Report of Account Ledger, you get following Buttons (F-31B):

Button	Description
F4:Ledger	To select a Account Ledger to get Stock Voucher Analysis of transactions of the selected Account Ledger with the currently selected Stock Item.

At *Stock Voucher Analysis* Report of Account Group, you get following Buttons (F-31C):

Button	Description
F1: Detailed / Condensed	- F1: *Detailed*: To show next level Stock Groups / Stock Item details - F1: *Condensed*: To show only top level Stock Groups.
F4: Item	To select a Stock Item to get Stock Voucher Analysis of transactions of the selected Stock Item with the currently selected Party.
F5:Group	To select an Account Group to get Stock Voucher Analysis of transactions of the selected Account Group with the currently selected Stock Item.

FAQ: Frequently Asked Questions

FAQ-1: How to link Closing Stock Value with Accounts

Ans: At *F11:Features>Accounting Features* or *F11:Features>Inventory Features*, set *Yes* at *Integrate Accounts with Inventory*) to Integrate Accounts with Inventory. Consequently, the computed Closing Stock Value as per Inventory System is automatically carried to Final Accounts. In Integrated System, when you drill down through Stock Value from Accounts Reports, you get Stock Summary (F-3B).

FAQ-2: How to get Inventory Details in Party Ledger

Ans: At Party Ledger Display, click F12:Configure and set Yes at *Show Inventory Details also* to get Ledger Account (of Inventory Linked Ledger Accounts – like Sales, Purchase etc) with Item details (F-9A).

Stock Query 02-09

01 Stock Query

The Stock Query shows various information of a stock item (like Alias, Part No., Stock Group, Stock Category, Closing Stock, Remarks, Cost Price, Std. Selling Price, Costing & Market Valuation Method etc), at one centralized place for viewing

03 Stock Query Configuration

At Stock Query (F-1), click F12:Configure to get Stock Query Configuration screen (F-2A). Now set the Configuration as follows:

- **Show related Items of same Group**: Set *Yes* to show other Items under the same Stock Group, Set *No* to show other Items under the same Stock Category
- **Show All Aliases**: Set *Yes* to show all Aliases (otherwise Alias name are not shown)
- **Show using Alternate Units:** Set *Yes* to display Alternate Units information, where applicable
- **Show Tail Units of Compound Units:** Set *Yes* to display Tail units (if the Stock Item is expressed in Compound Unit)
- **Show Remarks of the Item**: Set *Yes* to display Remarks (as entered in the Stock Item master)
- **Show Description of the Item:** Set *Yes* to show Item Description (as specified in the Stock Item master)
- **Show Last Nos. of Transactions** Set *Yes* to display the last transaction Voucher Number & date
- **Show All Godown / Batches (incl. zero balance)**: Set *Yes* to show Godwnwise / Batchwise details of current stock

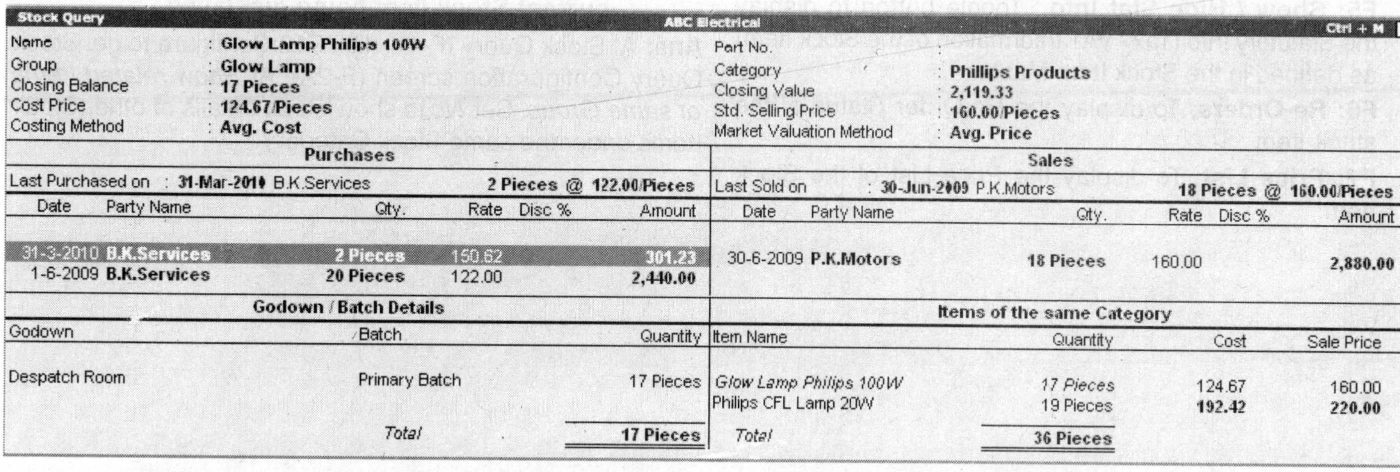

Stock Query | ABC Electrical | Ctrl + M

Name	: Glow Lamp Philips 100W	Part No.	:
Group	: Glow Lamp	Category	: Phillips Products
Closing Balance	: 17 Pieces	Closing Value	: 2,119.33
Cost Price	: 124.67/Pieces	Std. Selling Price	: 160.00/Pieces
Costing Method	: Avg. Cost	Market Valuation Method	: Avg. Price

Purchases

Last Purchased on : 31-Mar-2010 B.K.Services 2 Pieces @ 122.00/Pieces

Date	Party Name	Qty.	Rate	Disc %	Amount
31-3-2010	B.K.Services	2 Pieces	150.62		301.23
1-6-2009	B.K.Services	20 Pieces	122.00		2,440.00

Sales

Last Sold on : 30-Jun-2009 P.K.Motors 18 Pieces @ 160.00/Pieces

Date	Party Name	Qty.	Rate	Disc %	Amount
30-6-2009	P.K.Motors	18 Pieces	160.00		2,880.00

Godown / Batch Details

Godown	Batch	Quantity
Despatch Room	Primary Batch	17 Pieces
	Total	17 Pieces

Items of the same Category

Item Name	Quantity	Cost	Sale Price
Glow Lamp Philips 100W	*17 Pieces*	124.67	160.00
Philips CFL Lamp 20W	19 Pieces	192.42	220.00
Total	36 Pieces		

F-1: Stock Query showing Items under same Stock Group

02 Stock Query Display

At Gateway of Tally, select *Display > Statements of Inventory > Stock Query* and then select the Item from List of Items to view the *Stock Query* screen (F-1) of the selected Stock Item.

Major components of Stock Query

Stock Query screen (F-1)contains following major Parts:

- **Stock Item Particulars:** In this part, various important info of the Stock Item like Group, current closing stock, Stock Item remarks, details of last Purchase & Sale (Date, Party, Quantity & Rate) etc are shown.
- **Godown/Batch Detail:** In this part, godownwise detail of the current available stock (with Batch details, where applicable) are displayed
- **Items of the same Group / Category:** In this part, details of other Items (Stock Quantity, Cost & sale Price) in the same Group / Category are displayed

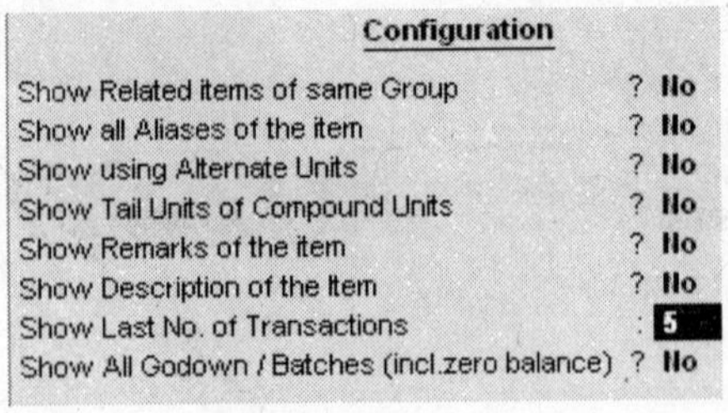

F-2A: Stock Query Configuration screen

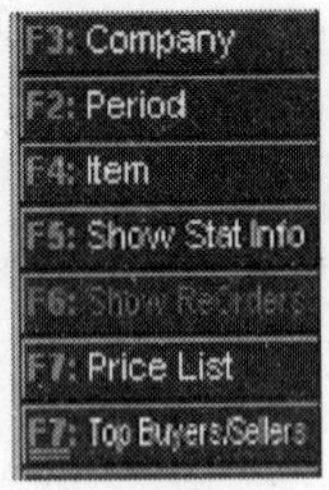

F-2B: Buttons

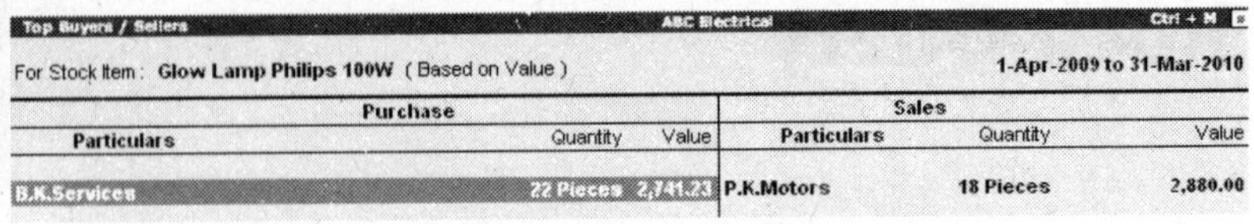

F-3: List of Top Buyers / Seller of the Item in Stock Query

04 Buttons in Stock Query

Following special buttons are (F-2B) available in Stock Query screen (F-1)

- **F4:Item**: To select another Stock Item to show the Stock Query for the selected Stock Item
- **F5: Show / Hide Stat Info.**: Toggle button to display the Statutory Info (Tax / VAT Information of the Stock Item) as defined in the Stock Item Master.
- **F6: Re-Orders**: To display the Re-Order Status of the stock item.
- **F7: Price List**: To display the Price List of the Stock Item.
- **F7: Top Buyers/Sellers**: To display the Top buyers and sellers for the Stock Item (F-3).

FAQ: Frequently Asked Questions

FAQ-1: In Stock Query, how to get he details of all Stock Items of the same Stock Category of the current Stock Item being displayed.

Ans: At Stock Query (F-1), click F12:Configure to get Stock Query Configuration screen (F-2A). At *Show related Items of same Group*, Set *No* to show stock details of other Stock Items under the same Stock Category

Part 3

Challans

This part explains Pure Inventory Voucher like Delivery Notes, Receipt Notes & Materials Returns, for organisations who prepare separate documents for Deliveries & Invoice

Challans explains the concept of separate Delivery Documents (Delivery / Receipt Notes & Returns / Rejection Notes)

Challans Entry explains entry of various Challans & Return Notes creation of Sales / Purchase Invoice, Debit / Credit Notes against the respective Challan / Return Documents.

Challans Invoice Processing explains matching of the Challas / Returns, with corresponding Sales / Purchase Invoice, Debit / Credit Notes and creation of Invoices, Debit & Credit Notes.

Challans 03-01

01 Challans

So far we have discussed Invoice entry (Sales/ Purchase Invoice & Debit / Credit Notes) in which Stock and Financial Accounts are simultaneously updated. This is the normal case when Sales / Purchase Invoice or Debit / Credit Notes are entered when goods are delivered or received. In such case, both Inventory and Accounts are updated through ONE voucher (Invoice)

Sometimes, only movement of goods (Goods In & Goods Out) are recorded in a voucher (commonly called Challan) to update the stock but accounting entries are done subsequently at a later date.

In such case, Delivery / Receipt of materials (i.e preparation of Delivery / Receipt Note & Rejection Notes) & Invoices entry (Sales / Purchase Invoice and Debit / Credit Note) entry are done separately. Normally Challans (materials Delivery / Receipt Notes) are made first and then the corresponding Invoices (Sales / Purchase Invoice), are created, but reverse may occur.

> **Note**
>
> As per terms commonly used in Trade, we use the term:
>
> - *Challan* to indicate Delivery Challans & Goods Receipt note. Sales Return & Purchase Return are also a kind of Challan, as only Inventory are effected through these types of Vouchers.However, Tally uses it own Terminilogy for these types of Documents:
>   - o *Delivery Challan* is referred by *Delivery Notes* (earlier *Delivery Out*)
>   - o *Goods Receipt Note* is referred by *Receipt Notes* (earlier *Delivery In*)
>   - o *Sales Return* is referred by *Rejection Out*
>   - o *Purchase Return* is referred by *Rejection In*
> - *Invoice* indicates Sales Invoice & Purchase Invoice. Debit Note & Credit Note are also a kind of Invoice, as Accounts are also effected through these types of Vouchers

Sometimes sold goods are returned by buyer to seller and a document is created by both parties. The original Buyer makes a Purchase Return (referred by Tally as *Rejection Out*), and the original Seller makes Sales Return (referred by Tally as *Rejection In*)

02 Tracking Number

When the Accounting Transaction (Invoice) & Inventory Transaction (Challans) are recorded at different stages, a common reference is used to *Track & Link* separate Accounting Transaction (Invoice) & Inventory Transaction (Challans), This common reference is referred as *Tracking Number* and is created recording the first event (e.g Delivery / Receipt Note entry). The subsequent matching entry (the second event) is recorded linking the first entry through the *Tracking Number* created in the corresponding first transaction. Thus Delivery Note / Receipt Note, Rejection In (Sales Return) / Rejection Out (Purchase Return) Notes may be created first and then corresponding Sales / Purchase Invoices (and Debit / Credit Notes) entered against the earlier Delivery Note / Receipt Note, Rejection In (Sales Return) / Rejection Out (Purchase Return) Notes, at later stage.

Sometimes, the transactions may even occur in reverse way. The *Invoice* may be first created, creating a *new Tracking Number* and the *Challan* is created later linking the *earlier Tracking Number*

02.01 Advantages / Disadvantages of Tracking Number

Tracking Number is an additional layer of activity, separate Vouchers (Inventory Voucher to affect Stock & Accounts Voucher to affect Accounts), relating to the same set of transactions. When you create an Accounts Voucher (Sale/ Purchase / Debit Note/ Credit Note), without Tracking Number, both Inventory & Accounts are simultaneously affected through One Voucher. No linking / adjustment is needed.

So, you should use Tracking Number only when you have to create Inventory & Accounts Voucher at different point of time. A few such instances are cited below:

- You create one Sales or Purchase Voucher at the end of a period or contract for multiple Inventory Vouchers
- You create a Sales / Purchase Voucher at month end for multiple deliveries made during the month, or create a final Sales / Purchase Voucher for multiple deliveries against a contract
- You receive goods without receiving an Invoice from supplier
- You deliver goods without issuing an Invoice (for some reason, Rate not finalized or other reason)

- You get Sales Returns (create *Rejection In* Voucher), but do not issue a Credit Note immediately
- You make Purchase Returns (create *Rejection Out* Voucher), but do not issue a Debit Note immediately

Except in such compelling situations, create an Accounts Voucher (Sale/ Purchase / Debit Note/ Credit Note), without Tracking Number, so that both Inventory & Accounts are simultaneously affected through one Voucher. No linking / adjustment is needed.

03 Creation & Linking of Tracking Numbers

Before we discuss about creation of Voucher with Tracking Numbers, let us understand the concept of Tracking Number, creation of subsequent Voucher linking the previous Tracking Number and the effects of such linking. In the next chapter, we explain the process of creation of Voucher, with new Tracking Number and linking Pending Tracking Numbers.

03.01 Creation of Separate Inventory & Accounts Vouchers of same Transaction

Tracking Number is used to create separate Voucher for Inventory & Accounts Transactions, at different point of time, viz

- **Inventory Voucher**: Delivery Challan (or Delivery Note), Goods Receipt Note (Receipt Note), Sales Return (Rejection Out) Purchase Return (Rejection In) etc.
- **Accounts Voucher**: Sales Invoice, Purchase Invoice, Debit Note, Credit Note, etc

Normally, the Inventory Voucher is created first, the Accounts Voucher is created next and matched with the corresponding Inventory voucher linking both the vouchers. If both the transactions are done simultaneously (goods delivered and invoice created, *Tracking Number is NOT involved*, as seen in case of Sales & Purchase Invoice Entry, discussed in earlier chapters. So, Tracking Number is involved only when these transactions occur as separate events.

The *First* voucher (Challan or Invoice) is created in which a *new* tracking number is originated (normally Delivery or Rejection Note). The matching second voucher is later created (normally Sales / Purchase Invoice or Debit / Credit Note) linking (adjusting) the Tracking Number created in the first voucher (no *New* Tracking Number is created). These sets of matching vouchers, when fully linked (adjusted), constitute the complete Accounting & Inventory Transactions. Sometimes, multiple vouchers with different tracking number may be mutually matched (creating *implicit link*).

03.02 Some instances of Creation & Matching of Tracking Numbers

Inventory Voucher created first, subsequently matched with Accounts Voucher

o *Delivery Note* created first (Positive Voucher) with New Tracking Number, subsequently matched with Sales Invoice created later (Negative Voucher).
  - **Example:** Delivery Note 1 dt 1.4.12 for 40 Pcs created with Tracking Number 1. A Sales Voucher No 8 dt 5.4.12 for 40 Pcs is created adjusting the Tracking Number 1, The transaction is now complete.
  - **Example:** Delivery Note 1 dt 1.4.12 for 40 Pcs created with Tracking Number 1. A Sales Voucher No 8 dt 5.4.12 for 25 Pcs is created adjusting the Tracking Number 1. At this stage, there is a balance of Sales Bills to be made for 15 Pcs. Later on, a Sales Invoice No 11 dt 12.4.12 for 15 Pcs is created adjusting the Tracking Number 1. The transaction is now complete and there is no balance of Sales Bills to be made.
  - **Example:** Delivery Note 1 dt 1.4.12 for 40 Pcs created with Tracking Number 1. Later on, Delivery Note 8 dt 12.4.12 for 20 Pcs created with Tracking Number 6. A Sales Voucher No 15 dt 30.4.12 for 60 Pcs is created adjusting the both Tracking Numbers 1 & 6, The transaction is now complete.

o *Receipt Note* created first with New Tracking Number, subsequently matched with Purchase Invoice created later
  - **Example:** Receipt Note 1 dt 1.4.12 for 40 Pcs created with Tracking Number 1. A Purchase Invoice No 5 dt 5.4.12 for 40 Pcs is created adjusting the Tracking Number 1, The transaction is now complete.
  - **Example:** Receipt Note 1 dt 1.4.12 for 40 Pcs created with Tracking Number 1. A Purchase Invoice No 5 dt 5.4.12 for 25 Pcs is created adjusting the Tracking Number 1. At this stage, there is a balance of Purchase Invoice to be made for 15 Pcs. Later on, a Purchase Invoice No 8 dt 12.4.12 for 15 Pcs is created adjusting the Tracking Number 1. The transaction is now complete and there is no balance of Purchase Invoice to be entered.
  - **Example:** Receipt Note 1 dt 1.4.12 for 40 Pcs created with Tracking Number 1. Later on, Receipt Note 8 dt 12.4.12 for 20 Pcs created with Tracking Number 6. A Purchase Invoice No 15 dt 30.4.12 for 60 Pcs is created adjusting the Tracking Number 1 & 6, The transaction is now complete.

o *Rejection In (Sales Return)* created first with New Tracking Number, subsequently matched with Credit Note created later
  - **Example:** Rejection In (Sales Return) # 1 dt 1.4.12 for 40 Pcs created with Tracking Number 1. A Credit Note Voucher No 5 dt 5.4.12 for 40 Pcs is created adjusting the Tracking Number 1, The transaction is now complete.

- **Example:** Rejection In (Sales Return) # 1 dt 1.4.12 for 40 Pcs created with Tracking Number 1. A Credit Note Voucher No 5 dt 5.4.12 for 25 Pcs is created adjusting the Tracking Number 1. At this stage, there is a balance of Credit Note to be made for 15 Pcs. Later on, a Credit Note No 8 dt 12.4.12 for 15 Pcs is created adjusting the Tracking Number 1. The transaction is now complete and there is no balance of Credit Note to be made
- **Example:** Rejection In (Sales Return) # 1 dt 1.4.12 for 40 Pcs created with Tracking Number 1. Later on, Rejection In (Sales Return) # 8 dt 12.4.12 for 20 Pcs created with Tracking Number 6. A Credit Note No 15 dt 30.4.12 for 60 Pcs is created adjusting the Tracking Number 1 & 6, The transaction is now complete.

o *Rejection Out (Purchase Return)* created first with New Tracking Number, subsequently matched with Debit Note created later

- **Example:** Rejection Out (Purchase Return) # 1 dt 1.4.12 for 40 Pcs created with Tracking Number 1. A Debit Note Voucher No 5 dt 5.4.12 for 40 Pcs is created adjusting the Tracking Number 1, The transaction is now complete.
- **Example:** Rejection Out (Purchase Return) # 1 dt 1.4.12 for 40 Pcs created with Tracking Number 1. A Debit Note Voucher No 5 dt 5.4.12 for 25 Pcs is created adjusting the Tracking Number 1. At this stage, there is a balance of Debit Note to be made for 15 Pcs. Later on, a Debit Note No 8 dt 12.4.12 for 15 Pcs is created adjusting the Tracking Number 1. The transaction is now complete and there is no balance of Debit Note to be made
- **Example:** Rejection Out (Purchase Return) # 1 dt 1.4.12 for 40 Pcs created with Tracking Number 1. Later on, Rejection In (Sales Return) # 8 dt 12.4.12 for 20 Pcs created with Tracking Number 6. A Debit Note No 15 dt 30.4.12 for 60 Pcs is created adjusting the Tracking Number 1 & 6, The transaction is now complete.

03.03 Multiple Inventory Vouchers mutually adjusted & linked with Accounts Voucher

Following examples show how Multiple Inventory Vouchers (Challans) are first mutually adjusted among themselves and then adjusted against Accounts Voucher (Invoice):

- **Delivery Note / Rejection In & Sales Invoice**: Delivery Note is created first with New Tracking Number. Subsequent Rejection In (Sales Return) is adjusted against the Delivery Note. The adjusted Delivery Note is subsequently matched with Sales Invoice created for Net Quantity.
  - o **Example:** Delivery Note 1 dt 1.4.12 for 40 Pcs created with Tracking Number 1. Subsequently Rejection In (for Sales Return by the customer) # 5 dt 5.4.12 for 25 Pcs is created adjusting the Tracking Number 1. At this stage, there is a balance of Sales Invoice to be made for 15 Pcs. Later on, a Sales Invoice No 8 dt 12.4.12 for 15 Pcs is created adjusting the Tracking Number 1. The transaction is now complete and there is no balance of Sales Bills to be made
  - o **Example:** Delivery Note 1 dt 1.4.12 for 30 Pcs created with Tracking Number 1. Rejection In (Sales Return) # 5 dt 5.4.12 for 12 Pcs is created with new Tracking Number 9.Further, Rejection In (Sales Return) # 8 dt 5.4.12 for 8 Pcs is created with new Tracking Number 12. At this stage, there is a balance of Sales Bills to be made for 10 Pcs. Later on, a Sales Invoice No 8 dt 12.4.12 for 10 Pcs is created adjusting the Tracking Number 1 with Tracking Number 9 & 12. The transaction is now complete and there is no balance of Sales Bills to be made. This shows that several Tracking Numbers may be mutually linked & adjusted.
- **Receipt Note / Rejection Out & Purchase Invoice:** Receipt Note is created first with New Tracking Number. Subsequent Rejection In (Sales Return) is adjusted against the Receipt Note. The adjusted Receipt Note is subsequently matched with Purchase Invoice created for Net Quantity.
  - o **Example:** Receipt Note 1 dt 1.4.12 for 40 Pcs created with Tracking Number 1. Rejection Out (Purchase Return) # 5 dt 5.4.12 for 25 Pcs is created adjusting the Tracking Number 1. At this stage, there is a balance of Purchase Bills to be made for 15 Pcs. Later on, a Purchase Invoice No 8 dt 12.4.12 for 15 Pcs is created adjusting the Tracking Number 1. The transaction is now complete and there is no balance of Purchase Bills to be made
  - o **Example:** Receipt Note 1 dt 1.4.12 for 30 Pcs created with Tracking Number 1. Rejection Out (Purchase Return) # 5 dt 5.4.12 for 12 Pcs is created with new Tracking Number 9.Further, Rejection Out (Purchase Return) # 8 dt 5.4.12 for 8 Pcs is created with new Tracking Number 12. At this stage, there is a balance of Purchase Bills to be made for 10 Pcs. Later on, a Purchase Invoice No 8 dt 12.4.12 for 10 Pcs is created adjusting the Tracking Number 1 with Tracking Number 9 & 12. The transaction is now complete and there is no balance of Sales Bills to be made. This shows that several Tracking Numbers may be mutually linked & adjusted.

The above instances show creation of Inventory Voucher First and then matching with Accounts Voucher. However, the reverse may also happen. Accounts Voucher created first may be matched with Inventory Voucher, as explained later through examples

04 Tracking Numbers Linking

When a transaction is recorded through Delivery Note, it effects stock only but not accounts.

We now explain general concept & process of how to link Challans (Delivery, Receipt, Sales Return, Purchas Return) having pending tracking numbers against the respective Invoice (Sales & Purchase Invoice, Debit or Credit Note) and vice versa.

During Invoice entry, in the Party Details sub-screen at *Delivery Note No.* prompt, you get the *List of Tracking Numbers* showing:

- All pending tracking numbers for the selected Party & Item showing the balance quantity not yet adjusted
- *New Number,*
- *Not Applicable.*

To terminate entry of Tracking Numbers, select *End of List*

When you create a voucher, the pending Tracking Numbers for the Party will be listed. The current voucher number will be carried as default at Tracking Number. Now you may:

- **Pending Tracking Number**: Select a pending Tracking Number from the list, to adjust the current voucher to the already existing pending tracking number. For example, the first new tracking number 5 was for 6 Pcs Delivery In. The current voucher is for:
  - o 4 Pcs Delivery In, you may select the pending Tracking Number 5. Then the pending quantity against Tracking Number 5 will become 10Pcs (6+4).
  - o 1 Pcs Delivery Out, you may select the pending Tracking Number 5. Then the pending quantity against Tracking Number 5 will become 5 Pcs (6-1).
  - o 1 Pcs Sales Return (Rejection In), you may select the pending Tracking Number 5. Then the pending quantity against Tracking Number 5 will become 7 Pcs (6+1).
  - o 1 Pcs Purchase Return (Rejection Out), you may select the pending Tracking Number 5. Then the pending quantity against Tracking Number 5 will become 7 Pcs (6-1).
- **New Tracking Number**: You may create a New Tracking Number for the current voucher in 2 ways:
  - o **Default Number**: The current Voucher Number is carried as default Tracking Number. Press <enter> to select it. A new tracking number with the current voucher number is created. This is the recommended method as it will be easier to link the pending Tracking Number through the common Voucher Number.
  - o **Your own new Tracking Number**: Select *New Number* and the enter an unique new Tracking Number. In such case, the Tracking Number is different from Voucher Number. This is useful when you cross link any pending tracking number.

    A new Tracking number is created which is to be adjusted against Pending Tracking Number in later voucher, as explained above.

Now, we explain the concept of creation of new Tracking Numbers & matching of Pending Tracking Numbers, through a few examples.

04.01 Challan first, Invoice later

Often, Challan (Delivery Note) is created first, which affects only Inventory (and not Accounts). At the time of preparation of Challan, a *New Reference* of Tracking Number is created when the goods move out.

Later on, when the corresponding Sales Invoice is entered, the tracking Number (earlier created in the Challan) is selected. This affects accounts also and links the two documents through the common Tracking Number. The transaction is now complete in respect of Stock & Inventory and both documents are linked properly.

This is the normal procedure of using Delivery Out voucher and making Sales Invoice later on (One Invoice may be linked with several Delivery Out vouchers). In the same way, Delivery In vouchers may be created with *New* Tracking Number and then linked with Purchase Voucher.

In the same way, Rejection In (Sales Return) / Rejection Out (Purchase Return) vouchers may be created with New Tracking Number and then linked with Credit Note and Debit Notes.

Example:

10 Nos. of Maxell CD @ 110/- are sold to Ramamurthy Computers on 30th June. A *Delivery Note* is entered, and a *New Tracking Number* (say T/133) is entered at the *Tracking No.* field. This will reflect stock out (but will not affect accounts, i.e., neither Ramamurthy Computers account will be debited nor Sales account will be credited).

On 5th July, Sales Invoice for the above delivery (to effect accounts only) is entered. At Tracking No. field, the pending Tracking Number (T/133) is selected to update accounts only (stock already updated on 30th June).

These two documents make the entry complete in respect of stock movement & accounts linking each other.

Note

If, at Tracking Number, instead of selecting the earlier Tracking No.(T/133 in this instance), if you select

- o *Not Applicable*, Tally will once again effect the stock (so there will be double stock out) and the Tracking No T/133 will remain pending.

- o *New Number*, Tally will create another Sales Invoice (without affecting Stock) and the Tracking No T/133 and the new Sales Invoice will remain pending for adjustment.

So, clearly understand the implications and select the correct option as perthe nature of transaction. Otherwise serious accounting / stock mistakes might occur.

Instead of creating a Sales Invoice for the entire quantity of pending Challan, you may create a Sales Invoice for part quantity and then another Invoice for balance quantity. You may continue creating Invoices until the entire quantity of pending tracking number is adjusted.

For example, in Sales Invoice of 5th July, you may enter 6 Nos against Tracking Number T/133 (select Tracking Number T/133 and enter 6 Pcs at Quantity). In such case, 4 Pcs will remain as pending to be billed. You may create another Sales Invoice later against Tracking No T/133 (select Tracking Number T/133 and enter 4 Pcs at Quantity) to create the Sales Invoice for 4 Pcs. This way, 2 invoices of Quantity 6 Pcs & 4 Pcs respectively will be created for the 10 Pcs delivered.

In the same way, you may create one Sales Invoice against several Pending Tracking Numbers. For example, you create Delivery Challans on different dates in July, for 10 Pcs, 12 Pcs & 8 Pcs. On 31st July, you create an Invoice and select the 3 pending tracking numbers, to create an Invoice of 30 Pcs, adjusting all the 3 pending tracking numbers.

Let us assume, you create Delivery Challan with Tracking # 12 on 3rd July, for 10 Pcs. When you create next Delivery Challan dt 5th July for 12 Pcs, for the same Party, in the selection list, the pending Tracking Number 12 will be listed. Now you may:

- **Select the Pending Tracking # 12:** In that case the pending quantity for Tracking Number will become 22 Pcs
- **Enter new Tracking Number (say 21):** In that case, two pending Tracking Number will be shown, Tracking # 12 for 10 Pcs & Tracking # 21 for 12 Pcs (Total Pending Quantity 22 Pcs)

Now, you may create Sales Invoice linking the pending Delivery Challans as follows:

- Select Pending Tracking # 12 for 22 Pcs, or
- Select the Pending Tracking # 12 for 10 Pcs & Tracking # 21 for 12 Pcs, as the case may be

04.02 Invoice first, Challan later

Likewise, you can create Invoice first, creating a new Tracking Number. This affects Account only (but not Inventory),. Later, enter Delivery Challan to effect Inventory and link the pending Tracking Number that was created in Invoice. This affects Inventory also and links the two documents through the linking Tracking Number. The transaction is now complete in respect of Stock & Inventory and both documents are linked properly.

Example:

Hanooman Mills sells varieties of Jute Goods. They first enter Sales Invoice and give a copy of the Invoice to the customer (goods are to be delivered later on). The customer produces the Invoice at the company's godown to take delivery of goods. A Delivery Note is created which is linked to the tracking number created in the related Invoice.

Let us explain the entry through an example.

First create a Sales Invoice (say G/15 dt 1st June). Select *New Number* at Tracking Numbers and select the current Invoice Number (G/15) from the list of tracking number and enter Item details. Print the Invoice.

The customer now presents the Invoice to Godown keeper, who creates a Delivery Note (D/98 dt 3rd June). At Tracking number, select the pending tracking number (G/15). In this way, several Delivery Notes (even of different dates) may be linked against the Invoice, through Tracking Number G/15.

04.03 Delivery Quantity Different from Invoice

When Delivery is made first, the invoice is made for the quantity delivered matching the invoice & delivery quantity. But when Invoice is made first and delivery is made later in one stage or in multiple stages), the delivery quantity may differ due to various reasons:

- The pack quantity is different. For example the Invoice is for 50 Kg but the bale delivered weighs 48.5 kg or 51.2 kg (the bale cannot be unpacked and the packed bale must be delivered).
- There is not enough stock to deliver the quantity, so lesser quantity is delivered.

We explain the process in such situation. First the invoice is prepared for 50 Kg (Rs 100 per Kg – Rs 5000), with a new tracking number (e.g D/95).

Now the delivery is made. Two situations may arise:

- **Delivery is less than Invoice and no further delivery can be made:** In such case, create the delivery note for actual quantity delivered (e.g 48.5 kg) and link the delivery note with tracking number (D/95). Now there will be a Delivery Note of 48.5kg (the actual delivery quantity. So, the stock properly adjusted by the actual quantity delivered, but the sale is overstated by 1.5 Kg (50- 48.5). So, we have to adjust the sale without further affecting the Stock. To do that, create a Credit Note Voucher for the value of 1.5 Kg (Accounts voucher without Inventory) for Rs 150 (1.5 kg @ 100). adjusting the Tracking Number D/95. No Inventory details are to be entered (Credit Note voucher in Voucher mode without Inventory details), as explained earlier

  Consequently the Party is debited with Rs. 48500 (Sale Invoice 50000 & Credit Note Rs 1500), for 48.5 Kg @ Rs. 100 / Kg and the Tracking Number is fully adjusted.
- **Delivery is more than the Invoice Quantity:** Let us assume that the Bale delivered weighs 51.2 Kg. Now create a Delivery Note (for 51.2 Kg) and adjust against

the earlier Invoice of 50 Kg (G/15). Now create another Sales Invoice (G/21) for 1.2 Kg (51.2 – 50) for Rs 1200 (1.2 Kg @ 100), selecting *the same Tracking Number* D/95. The stock is adjusted by 51.2 kg through the delivery challan and is adjusted against the Invoice of 50 kg and another Sales Vocher of 1.2 Kg (Tracking Number D/95) is also fully adjusted. The Party account will be debited by Rs 51200 (Rs 50000 + 1200)

04.04 Inter Challan linking

Tracking Number is also used to link one type of challan with another type of pending challan(s). For example, Purchase Return (Rejection Out) linking pending goods Receipt Note, Sales Return (Rejection In) linking Delivery Note, etc, to mutually offset the deliveries & returns of goods.

A K Paper purchases 10 Pcs of Ball Bearings from P K Stores and creates a Receipt Note 10 Pcs.. Later on it returns 3 Pcs defective under Rejection Out Note. Now he enters Purchase Invoice for 7 Pcs. and links the Receipt Note (10 Pcs) and Rejection Out (Purchase Return) for 3 Pcs

The entry can be made in 2 ways, with different way of adjustment of tracking number, though the result will be same

Method 1: Adjust the Rejection Out (Purchase Return) against the original Receipt Note through the same tracking number.

In this method, first create the Receipt Note (Voucher Number & Tracking Number REC/53), for 10 Pcs.

Next create the Rejection Out (Voucher Number R/58) and select the Pending Tracking Number of the earlier Receipt Note (REC/53). So, one Receipt Note voucher for 10 Pcs and one Rejection Out (Purchase Return) voucher for 3 Pcs is created. The pending unbilled quantity for the Receipt voucher REC/53 is 7 Pcs (not 10 Pcs, as 3 Pcs has already been adjusted.)

Now, create a Purchase Voucher (for 7 Pcs) and select the pending Tracking number REC/ 53). Thus, the Receipt Note and the Rejection Out (Purchase Return) voucher gets adjusted against the Purchase Invoice.

Method 2: Adjust the pending documents in the Invoice.

In this method, first create the Receipt Note (Voucher Number & Tracking Number REC/53, for 10 Pcs). Next create the Rejection Out (Voucher Number & Tracking Number RET/68) for 3 Pcs. Now there are 2 pending Tracking Number, REC/53 for 10 Pcs Receipt Note and RET/68 for 3 Pcs Rejection Out.

Now, create a Purchase Voucher P/127 and select both the pending Tracking Numbers REC/53 for 10 Pcs Receipt Note and RET/68 for 3 Pcs Rejection Out (Purchase Return). i.e Net 7 Pcs Receipt. Now both the Pending Tracking Numbers will be adjusted and a Purchase Voucher P/127 for 7 Pcs will be created.

04.05 Rej. In/Out voucher first, Credit / Debit Note later

A K Paper has purchased Ball Bearings from P K Stores, from time to time. Purchase Invoices has been duly entered and there is no pending Tracking Number. Now it returns 3 Pcs of defective Bearings. Now, you may:

Using Tracking Number: Create a Rejection Out (Purchase Return) Voucher with Voucher & New Tracking Number (REJ/13). Later on, it creates a Debit Note (D/12) and selects the pending tracking number (REJ/13) to link with the Rejection Note. So, a Debit Note D/12 on P K Stores in the books of A Paper is created. There is no pending Tracking Number Tracking Number REJ/13 is fully adjusted). In such case, 2 Vouchers are created, One Rejection Out (Purchase Return) Voucher REJ/13 and a Debit Note D/12

05 Invoicing without Tracking Number

If the Invoice (Purchase/ Sales Invoice, DN/CN) is being created at the time of movement of Goods (Delivery In/Out, Rejection In (Sales Return)/Out), select *Not Applicable* at Tracking Number field. This happens when you create an Invoice at the time of sale.

By this process, stock and ledger accounts are simultaneously updated. So, no pending tracking numbers is created. This is similar as Invoice entry when Tracking Number is NOT activated, as explained in earlier chapters so far.

Let us look at the cases described above.

Case 1: Purchase for 10 Pcs and subsequent Purchase Return for 3 Pcs.

Create Purchase Bill P/127 for 10 Pcs (at Tracking Number, select *Not Applicable*) when goods are received. Later on, Create Debit Note D/91 for 3 Pcs (at Tracking Number, select *Not Applicable*). You get a Purchase Bill P/127 for 10 Pcs & Debit Note D/91 for 3 Pcs. There are no pending Tracking Number.

Now you may make accounting adjustment of Purchase Bill P/127 & Debit Note D/91 at the time of entering Payment Voucher for the net amount of Purchase Bill & Debit Note

Case 2: Purchase Return for 3 Pcs. No pending Tracking Number exists

Create a Debit Note D/12 (select Not Applicable at Tracking Number). So, a Debit Note D/12 on P K Stores in the books of A Paper is created. There is no pending Tracking Number (No Tracking Number created). In such case, only Voucher (Debit Note D/12) is created.

FAQ: Frequently Asked Questions

FAQ1: For a regular Customer, we make one monthly Invoice at the end of month, for all the deliveries made during the month. How we create Challan for each Delivery and the Final Invoice in respect of all the Deliveries during the month.

Ans: First, you must activate Delivery Note (Tracking Number) feature for the Company to create Delivery Notes. At the time of delivery of goods, do not make any Sales Invoice, but create a Delivery Challan (Delivery Note). Each of the Delivery Note will bear distinct Delivery Note Numbers (with new tracking numbers).

At the month end, after all deliveries for the month, create a Sales Invoice (against Tracking Numbers) and select all the Pending Tracking Numbers of the Challans created during the month. The Items details of all the selected challan will be carried in the new Invoice. The Invoice will be linked with the challans selected.

Example: Delivery Note 1 dt 1.4.12 for 40 Pcs created with Tracking Number 1. Later on, Delivery Note 8 dt 12.4.12 for 20 Pcs created with Tracking Number 6. A Sales Voucher No 15 dt 30.4.12 for 60 Pcs is created adjusting the both Tracking Numbers 1 & 6, The transaction is now complete.

Challans Entry

03-02

01 Activation of Tracking Numbers

In previous chapter, we have described the concept and use of Tracking Number.

Click *F11: Features>Inventory Features*, to get *Inventory Features* Screen. At *Inventory Features* Screen, set *Yes* at *Use Tracking Numbers (Delivery / Receipt Notes)* to activate Tracking Numbers.

Consequently, the buttons *F8: Dely Note* & *F9: Recpt Note* get activated in Inventory Voucher entry screen (F-4A) and the related options in Entry Forms & Reports are made available.

The process of Delivery Note entry is similar to Invoice Entry, explained earlier

- *Receipt* Note entry screen is quite similar to *Purchase* Invoice Entry
- *Delivery* Note entry screen is quite similar to *Sales* Invoice Entry

Here we describe points exclusively related to Delivery Notes (Tracking Number)

02 Tracking Number Entry in Challans

In *Delivery Notes* (F-5A) / *Receipt Notes* (F-6A) entry, after selection of Stock Item at *Name of Item* Column, you get Item allocation screen to enter the transaction details of the selected Item:

Tracking Number: At *Tracking Number*, select the option from *List of Tracking Number* (F-2B), to enter Tracking Number as follows:

- **When a Tracking Number is to be created**: This is relevant when the current tracking number is to be linked with another voucher later on. This is the normal way of creating multi-step transaction like Challan – Invoice process.
    - o **Default Tracking Number**: The Voucher Number of current Voucher (Receipt Note/ Delivery Note/ Rejection In / Rejection Out) being entered is carried as default Tracking Number. Select it from the list (a new tracking number is created having the similar number as Challan number). This is usual and most convenient way to maintain same Reference Number for Voucher & Tracking.
    - o **New Tracking Number**: Sometimes, you may use some other number (other than Challan Number), through which you may track the Challans & Invoices (like Contract Number, Job Number etc). In such case, select *New Number* option from the list (F-2B) to get New Number entry box (F-2A) to enter the new Tracking Number. Enter the new Tracking Number in the New Number input box (F-2A). The new Tracking Number cannot be an existing tracking number)
- **When no Tracking Number is to be created**: This is relevant when the Challan is NOT to be linked with any Invoice (like Samples Receipt / Delivery). In such case, select *Not Applicable*.

F-1A: Activation of Tracking Number

F-2A: New Tracking Number

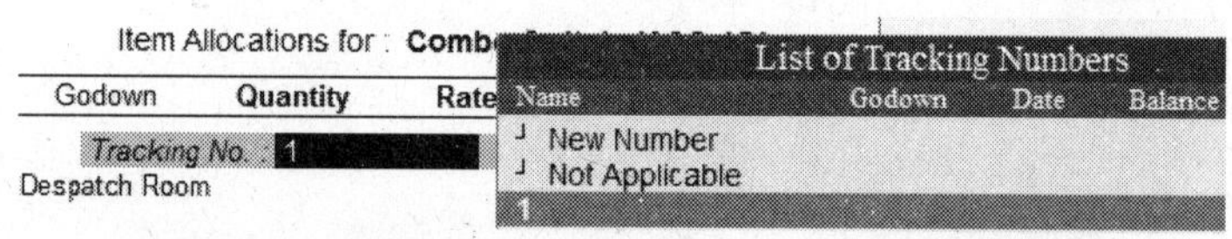

F-2B: Default Tracking Number selection

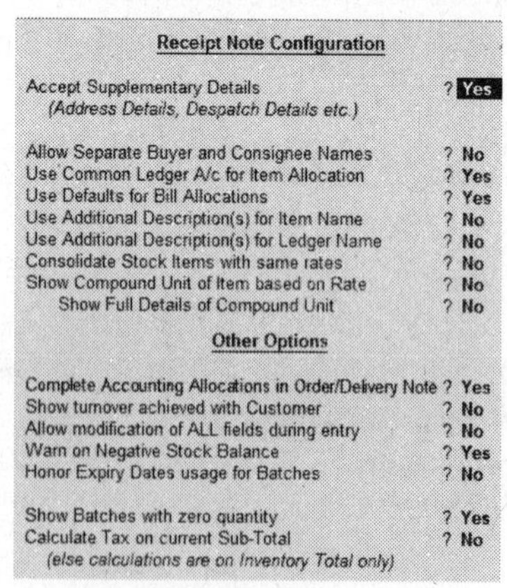

F-3A: Challan Configuration

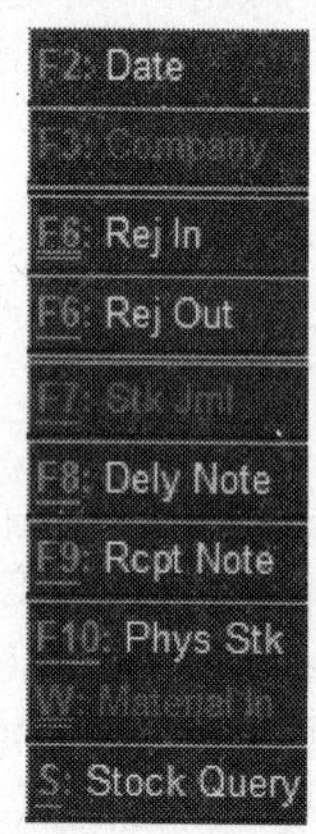

F-4A: Buttons

03 Delivery Note / Goods Receipt Note Entry

At *Delivery Note* entry screen (F-5A), enter as follows:

Item Name: Select the Item and enter the following details in the Item Details subscreen

Tracking Number: A pop up window appears to enter the Tracking Number (F-5B). Select the default tracking number or enter new number, as applicable, as explained (§02), to get Item Allocation screen (F-5C)

- **Item Allocation Details**: At *Item Allocation* screen (F-5C), enter the following details, as activated and applicable
    - o **Tracking Number**: The selected Tracking Number is shown.
    - o **Order:** Enter the Order Number, where applicable.
    - o **Godown Details**: Select the Godown (if Multiple Godown is activated)
    - o **Batch Details**: Select the Batch (if Batch is activated)

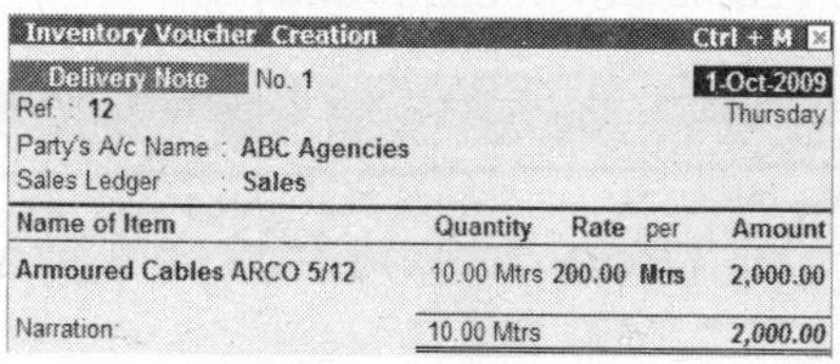

F-5A: Delivery Note Entry

F-5B: Tracking Number entry

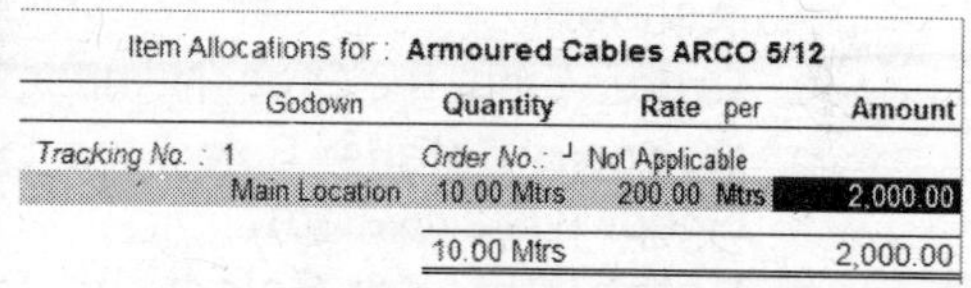

F-5C: Item allocation screen

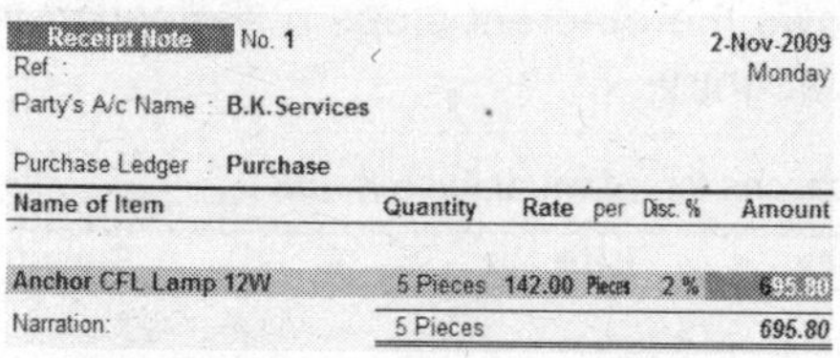

F-6A: Receipt Note Entry

F-6B: Tracking Number entry

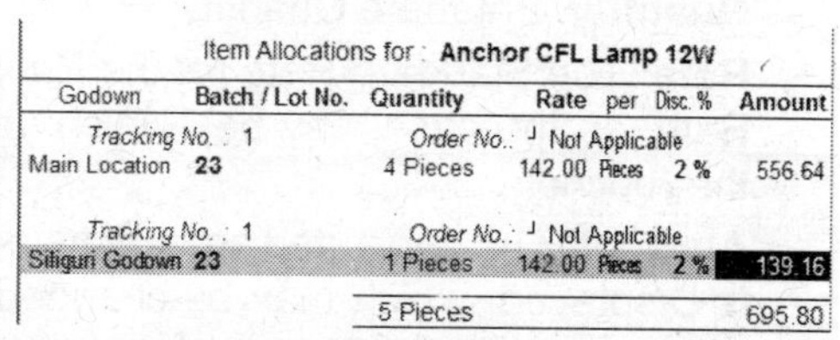

F-6C: Item allocation screen

- **Quantity**: Enter the Quantity
- Rate: The Standard Rate (or the Price List Rate, Order Rate, as the case may be), which you may change in the voucher.
- **Amount**: The computed amount as per Quantity & Rate is displayed, which may be changed (in case of lump sum value, the Amount may be entered without entering the Rate)

In Challans, the Rate & Amount (F-5C) may be skipped if desired, to be filled up later on at the time of creation of corresponding Credit Note.

Rest of the entries are similar to Sales Invoice Entry as explained earlier. Fig F-5A to F-5C shows the different steps of Delivery Note Entry.

Entries of Receipt Note are similar to Purchase Invoice Entry as explained earlier (F-6A to F-6C)

Challan Entry Configuration: At Challan Entry (Delivery Notes & Receipt Notes) screen, click *F12:Configure* to get Configuration screen (F-3A), through which you may set options for the voucher entry. The Configuration Options both for *Delivery Notes* & *Receipt Notes* are similar (F-3A)

04 Sales Return / Purchase Return Entry

Goods returned by customers to suppliers are entered in Rejection Notes. The Customer returning the bought goods prepares a Purchase Return (*Rejection Out*) voucher on the supplier whom the goods are returned to. On the other hand, the supplier receiving back the retuned sold goods from the customer, prepares a Sales Return (*Rejection In)* Voucher on the Customer from whom the returned goods are received back.

04.01 Activation for Rejection Notes

At Gateway, click *F11:Fetaures >Inventory Features* (F-1A) and set Yes at *Use Rejection Inward / Outward Voucher* to activate Rejection Vouchers (Tracking Number must have been activated). Consequently, you get the following buttons (F-4A) activated in Inventory Voucher entry.

- *F6: Rej In* for Rejection In Voucher (Sales Returns)
- *F6: Rej Out* for Rejection Out Voucher (Purchase Returns)

At Gateway, click Inventory Voucher and then click the respective button to get *Rejection Note* entry screen

04.02 Sales Return Entry

At the button bar (F-4A), click *F6: Rej In* button to get *Rejection In* voucher entry screen (F-7A). The entry process is similar to *Delivery Out / Receipt Note* entry

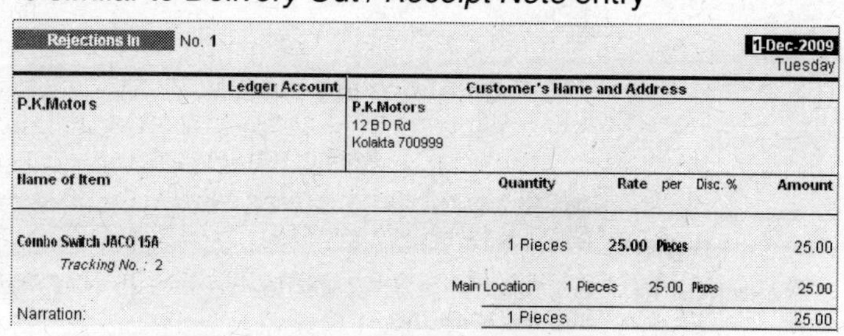

F-7A: Rejection In (Sales Return) Voucher entry

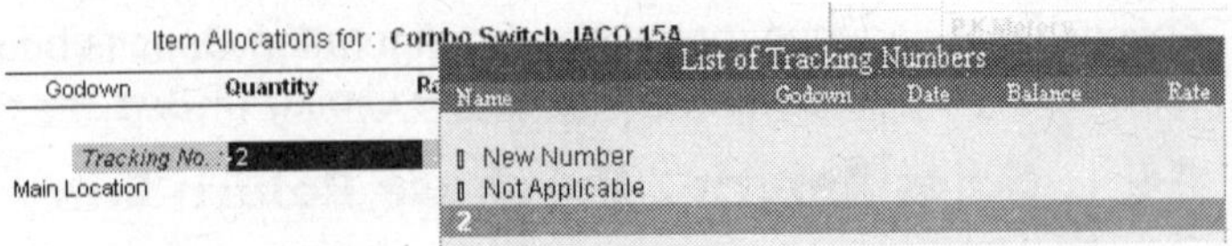

F-7B: Tracking Number entry in Rejection In Note

At Rejection In Voucher entry scren (F-7A) enter as follows:

Item Name: Select the Item and enter the following details in the Item Details subscreen

Tracking Number: A pop up window appears to enter the Tracking Number (F-7B). Select the default tracking number or enter new number, as applicable, as explained earlier, to get Item Allocation screen (F-7C)

- **Item Allocation Details**: At *Item Allocation* screen (F-7C), enter the following details, as activated and applicable
  - o **Tracking Number**: The selected Tracking Number is shown.
  - o **Order:** Enter the Order Number, where applicable.
  - o **Godown Details**: Select the Godown (if Multiple Godown is activated)
  - o **Batch Details**: Select the Batch (if Batch is activated)
- **Quantity**: Enter the Quantity
- **Rate:** The Standard Rate (or the Price List Rate, Order Rate, as the case may be), which you may change in the voucher.
- **Amount**: The computed amount as per quantity & Rate is Displayed, which may be changed (in case of lump sum value, the Amount may be entered without entering the Rate).

In Rejection Note, the Rate & Amount (F-7C) may be skipped if desired, to be filled up later on at the time of creation of corresponding Credit Note.

Fig F-7A to F-7C shows the different steps of Rejection In (Sales Return) Voucher entry.

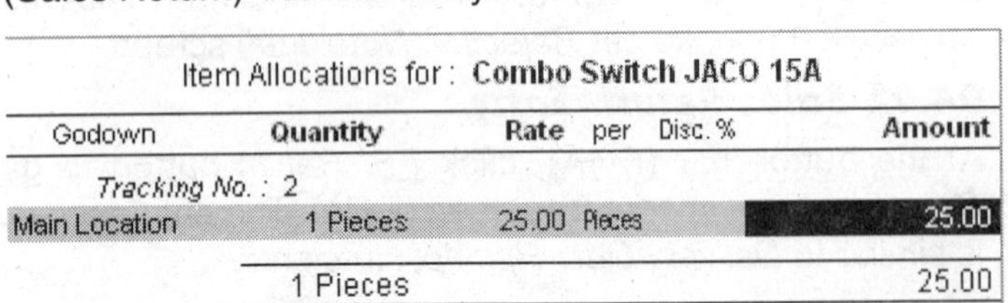

F-7C: Item Allocation details

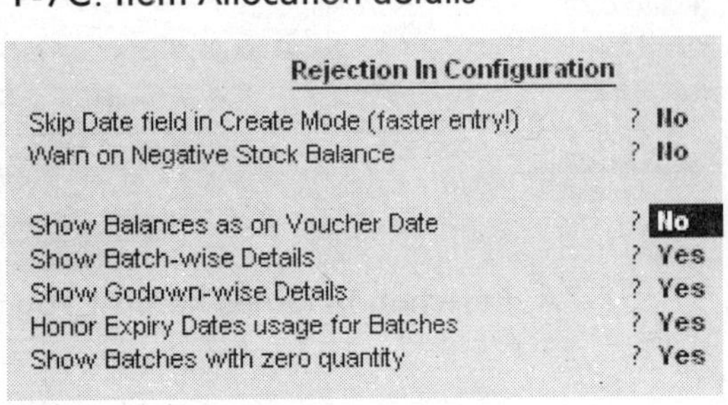

F-8A: Rejection In entry Configuration

The Rejection In voucher thus entered affects stock only but does not affect Accounts (e.g Sales & Customer's Accounts), until it is linked to a Credit Note Voucher.

04.03 Purchase Return Voucher Entry

At the button bar, click <u>*F6*</u>*: Rej Out* button to get *Rejection Out* voucher entry screen (F-9A). The entry process is similar to Delivery In / Rejection In entry

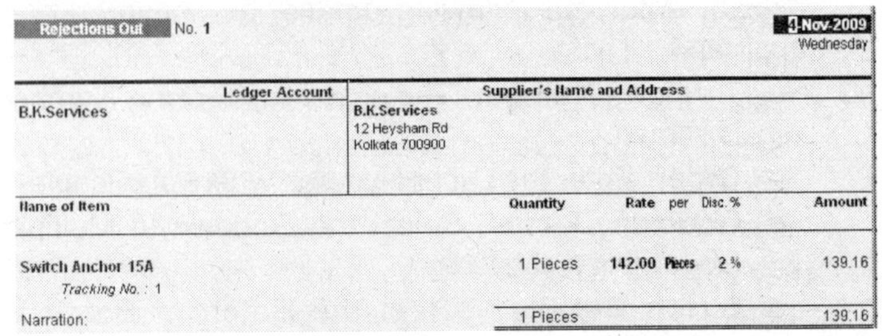

F-9A: Rejection Out Voucher entry

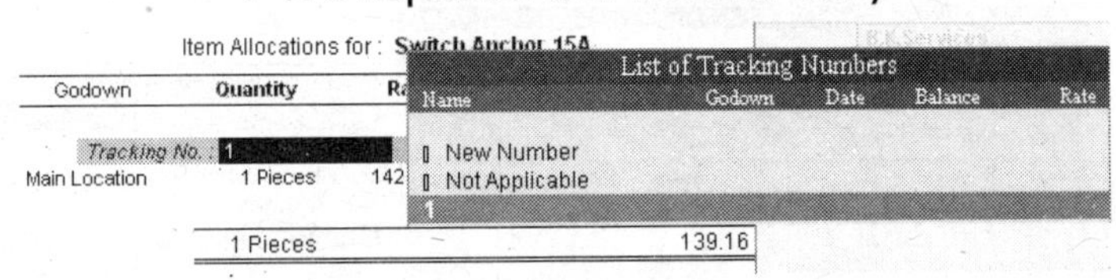

F-9B: Tracking Number entry

Fig F-9A to F-9C shows the different steps of Rejection In (Sales Return) Voucher entry

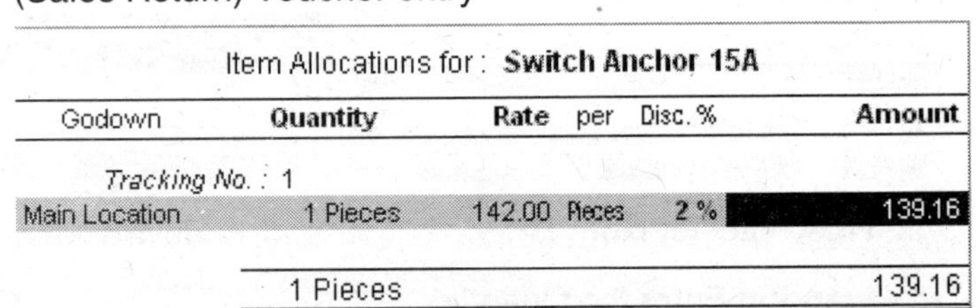

F-9C: Item details subscreen

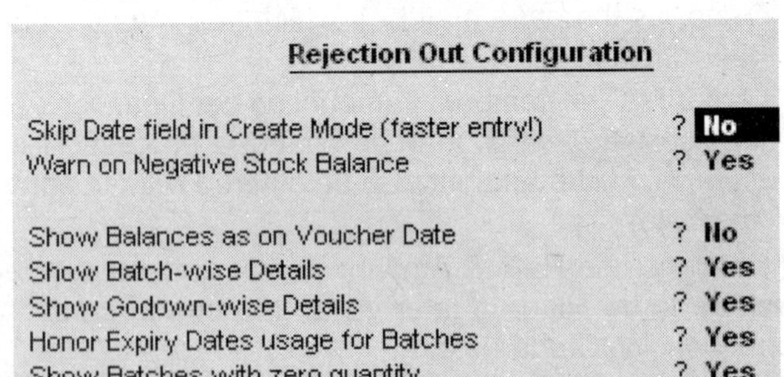

F-10A: Rejection In / Out Entry Configuration

The Rejection Out voucher thus entered affects stock only but does not affect Accounts (e.g Purchase & Supplier's accounts), until it is linked to a Credit Note Voucher.

04.04 Purchase / Sales Return entry Configuration

At Rejection In or Rejection Out entry screen Click *F12: Config* at Rejection Voucher entry screen (F-7A / F-9A) to get Rejection Voucher Configuration screen (F-8A). The Configuration options for both Rejection In & Rejection Out is similar.

- **Voucher Date:** At *Skip Date field in create mode (faster entry)*, set Yes to skip the Date field, the current Date is carried as default voucher date enabling voucher entry (press Shift + tab to go back to Date field and change voucher date)
- **Stock Warning:** At *Warn on Negative Stock Balance*, set *Yes* to get warning if the current voucher causes stock balance go negative (in case of Rejection Out voucher)
- **Stock Balance:** At *Show Balance as on Voucher Date*, set *Yes* to show current stock balance of the Item during voucher entry.

Other options: You may further set the following options if activated:

- **Batch Details**: At *Show Batchwise Details*, set Yes to enter Batch details (if Batch is activated for the Item)
- **Godown Details**: At *Show Godownwise Details*, set Yes to enter Godown details (if Multiple Godown is activated)
- **Expired Batches:** *At Honor Expiry dates usage for Batches*, set Yes to prevent in / out of expired batches (if Batch Expiry is activated for the Item).

Voucher Narration

If you set *Yes* at *Use Common Narration* at the respective Voucher Type creation (§02/02-07), then you may also enter Voucher Narration, giving more details. The Voucher Narration so entered may be optionally printed in Delivery Note / Day Book.

05 Challans Printing

Having entered Challan (Delivery Note / Receipt Note / Rejection In / Rejection Out), you may print the Challan. The process of Challan Printing is similar to Invoice Printing explained earlier (for immediate voucher Printing, at the respective Voucher Type creation screen, set Yes at Print After Saving he Voucher:§01/02-15, F-1A/02-07)

Having entered the voucher, Click *P:Print* button to get Printing screen. At Printing screen, click *F12:Configure* to get Configuration screen to set the Configuration options (F-11A). Having set the Configuration options (F-11A), set *Yes* to print the Voucher (F-11B).

Receipt Note Printing Configuration

Title of Document	: **Receipt Note**		
(for Optional Voucher)	: ***Receipt Note***		
Sub Title (if any)	:		
Height of Normal Invoice (inches)	: **10**	Simple:	**10**
Width of Normal Invoice (inches)	: **7.50**	Simple:	**7.50**
Space to leave on top (default 0.25)	: **0.25**	Simple:	**0.25**
Space to leave on left (default 0.5)	: **0.50**	Simple:	**0.50**

Print in Simple Format	? **No**	Print Serial No.	? **Yes**
Print Voucher Reference	? **Yes**	Print Part No.	? **No**
Print Order Details	? **No**	Print Quantity Column	? **Yes**
Print Company's PAN / Income Tax No.	? **No**	Print Alternate Quantity	? **No**
Print Company's Tax Regn. Numbers	? **No**	Print as separate Column	? **No**
Print Supplier's Tax Regn. Numbers	? **No**	Print Actual Quantity Column	? **No**
Print Supplier's CST Regn. Numbers	? **No**	Print Rate Column	? **No**
		Print Amount Column	? **No**
		Print Batch Details	? **No**
		Print Rate of Duty with Items	? **No**
		Print Sub-Totals after each line	? **No**
		Print Narration	? **No**
		Print Base Currency Symbol for Total	? **No**

Method to use for Ledger Name	: **Name Only**
Method to use for Stock Item Name	: **Name Only**
Jurisdiction	: **Kolkata**

F-11A: Receipt Note Printing Configuration

Receipt Note

ABC Electrical 27/C, Rasbihari Road 3rd Floor, Suit No.305 Kolkata-700019 E-Mail :nomail@kmail.com	Receipt Note No. 1 Supplier's Ref.	Dated **2-Nov-2009** Other Reference(s)
Supplier **B.K.Services**		

Sl No.	Description of Goods	Quantity
1	**Anchor CFL Lamp 12W**	**5 Pieces**
	Total	**5 Pieces**

E. & O.E

for ABC Electrical

Authorised Signatory

SUBJECT TO KOLKATA JURISDICTION

F-11B: Receipt Note in Print

FAQ: Frequently Asked Questions

FAQ-1: How do I activate Challans (Delivery Note / Receipt Note)

Ans: To activate Challans Features (Delivery Note / Receipt Note for the Company, Click *F11: Features>Inventory Features*, to get *Inventory Features* Screen (F-1A). At *Inventory Features* Screen, At *Use Tracking Numbers (Delivery/ Receipt Notes)*, set *Yes* to activate (Delivery Note / Receipt Note). Consequently, the buttons *F8: Dely Note* & *F9: Recpt Note* get activated in Inventory Voucher entry screen (F-4A) and the related options in Entry Forms & Reports are made available.

FAQ-2: How do I activate Sales / Purchase Returns (Rejection In / Rejection Out Note) also

Ans: Having activated Tracking Numbers (for Delivery Note / Receipt Note) as explained, further, at *Use Rejection Inward / Outward Notes,* set Yes to activate *Rejection In* (for *Sales Returns*) & *Rejection Out* (for *Purchase Returns*). Consequently, the buttons *F6: Rej In Note* & *F6: Rej Out Note* get activated in Inventory Voucher entry screen (F-4A) and the related options in Entry Forms & Reports are made available.

Challans Processing

03-03

01 Challans Invoice Linking

We have discussed use of Tracking Number and linking of various documents through Tracking Number. Here we discuss about complete cycle of entry of Challans (Delivery Note / Receipt Note. Rejection In /Rejection Out) / Invoice (Sales / Purchase / Debit Note / Credit Note) and matching them against each other.

Normally, Challans (Delivery / Receipt / Rejection In / Rejection Out Notes) are created first at the time of Receipt / Delivery of materials, without corresponding Invoice, using a new tracking number. Later on, the Invoice (Sales / Purchase/ Debit Note / Credit Note) may be created using the same Tracking Number to link the pending Challan created earlier.

However, the reverse sequence may also happen. Sometimes, an Invoice (Purchase / Sales / Debit Note / Credit Note) may be created first using a Tacking Number. Later on, the pending Invoice is adjusted against a Challan using the same Tracking Number to link the pending Challan created earlier.

Here, we explain the process of creating an Invoice (Sales / Purchase) using a Tracking Number.

02 Sales Invoice Entry with Tracking Number

Sales Invoice may be entered with Tracking Number. In such case, only an Accounting Entry is created but no Inventory Entry (Stock is not affected). Later on, a Delivery Note may be created against the Sale Invoice.

In the Sales Invoice entry (F-1A), after selection of Stock Item, you get Tracking Number entry screen (F-1B). Either you create a New Tracking Number (Click *New Number* (F-1B),from the list and enter New Number, as explained earlier) or select one from the list of Tracking Number to add the quantity of the current Invoice to the selected Tracking Number)

Fig F-1A to F-1C shows the entry of Sales Invoice with a new Tracking Number.

03 Purchase Invoice Entry with Tracking Number

In the same way, Purchase Invoice may be entered with Tracking Number. In such case, only an Accounting Entry is created but no Inventory Entry (Stock is not affected). Later on, a Receipt Note may be created against the Purchase Invoice.

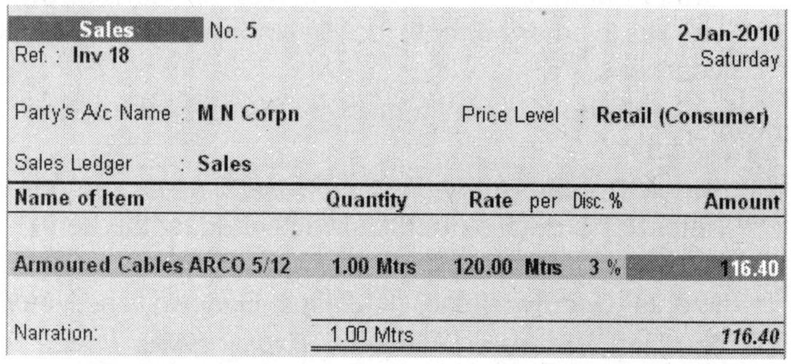

F-1A: Sales Invoice entry with Tracking Number

F-1B: Tracking Number entry

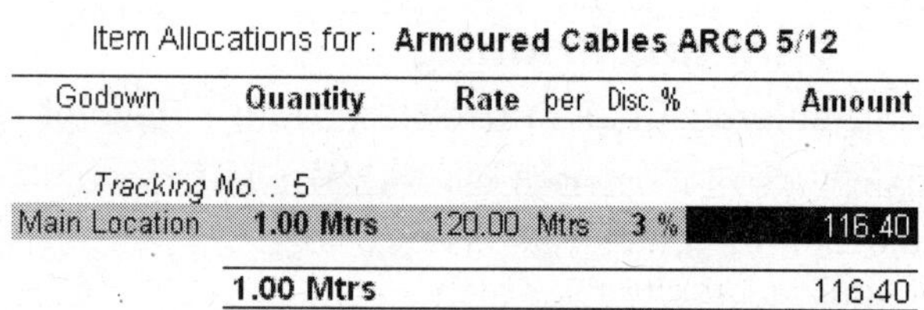

F-1C: Sales Invoice - Item Allocation details

In the Purchase Invoice entry (F-2A), after selection of Stock Item, in the same way, either you select the Current Purchase Invoice Number as Tracking Number (F-2B), or select *New Number* and enter a New Tracking Number

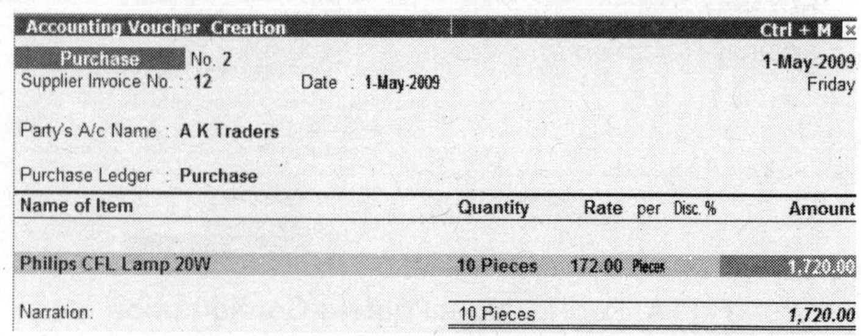

F-2A: Purchase Invoice with Tracking Number

Item Allocations for : Philips CFL Lamp 20W

Godown	Quantity	Rate	per	Disc. %	Amount
Tracking No. : 12					
Despatch Room	10 Pieces	172.00	Pieces		1,720.00
	10 Pieces				1,720.00

F-2B: Item Allocation for Purchase Invoice

Fig F-1A to F-1C shows he entry of Sales Invoice with a new Tracking Number.

If you select *Not Applicable* at Tracking Number screen (e.g F-1B), No new Tracking Number is created (hence there will be no pending Tracking Number) and both Accounts and Inventory is affected on entry of the Invoice.

04 Open Tracking Number List

Having entered the Vouchers with Tracking Number (e. F-1A, F-2A), you may get the Pending Reports of Open Tracking Number (Vouchers in which there is a balance against the Tracking Number)

Select *Display > StatEment Of Inventory* to get *Statement Of Inventory* Menu (F-3A) from where Pending Tracking Reports may be displayed.

04.01 Sales Bills Pending Report

At *Statement Of Inventory* Menu (F-3A), select *Sales Bills Pending* to print list of Pending Tracking references (F-4A).

Sales Bills Pending (F-4A) shows 2 sections:

Goods Delivered but Bills not made

These constitute the Open Sales *Inventory* Vouchers

- *Delivery Out* voucher created but not completely set off against *Sales* Voucher.
- *Rejection In* voucher is created but completely not set off against *Credit Note* voucher.

Bills Made but Goods not Delivered

These constitute the Open Sales *Accounts* Vouchers

- *Sales* voucher created but not completely set off against *Delivery Note*
- *Credit Note* Voucher created but completely not set off against *Rejection In* voucher.

Gateway of Tally ....
Display Menu ....

Statements of Inventory

- Godowns
- STock Query
- COst Estimation
- Item Cost Analysis
- PUrchase Bills Pending
- Sale Bills Pending
- Statistics
- Quit

F-3A: Statement of Inventory Menu

04.02 Purchase Bills Pending Report

At *Statement Of Inventory* Menu (F-3A), *select Purchase Bills Pending* to print list of Pending Tracking references (F-6A)

Sales Bills Pending 1-Apr-2009 to 31-Mar-2010

Date	Tracking Number	Name of Item	Initial Quantity	Pending Quantity	Rate (Disc %)	Value
Goods Delivered but Bills not Made :						
15-Nov-2009	1	Combo Switch JACO 15A To: P.K.Motors	3 Pieces	3 Pieces	25.00	75.00
1-Dec-2009	2	Combo Switch JACO 15A To: P.K.Motors	(-)1 Pieces	1 Pieces	25.00	25.00
			2 Pieces	2 Pieces		50.00
Bills Made but Goods not Delivered :						
2-Jan-2010	5	Armoured Cables ARCO 5/12 To: M N Corpn	(-)1.00 Mtrs	(-)1.00 Mtrs	120.00 (3 %)	(-)116.40
			(-)1.00 Mtrs	(-)1.00 Mtrs		(-)116.40

F-4A: Pending Sales Bill (Detailed)

Configuration

Show Outstanding Sales Bills	? Yes
Show Cleared Sales Bills	? No
Show Bills Made but Goods not delivered	? Yes
Show Outstanding Purchase Bills	? No
Show Cleared Purchase Bills	? No
Show Bills Recd. but Goods not Recd	? No
Show Batch Details	? No
Show Location Details	? No
Show using Alternate Units	? No
Show Tail Units of Compound Units	? No
Appearance of Stock Item Names	: Name Only
Appearance of Names	: Name Only
Sorting Method	: Default

F-5A: Pending Sales / Purchase Bill Configuration

Purchase Bills Pending (F-6A) shows 2 sections:

Goods Received but Bills not Received

These constitute the Open Purchase *Inventory* Vouchers

- *Delivery In* voucher created but not completely set off against *Purchase* Voucher.
- *Rejection Out* voucher created but completely not set off against *Debit Note* voucher.

Purchase Bills Pending 1-Apr-2009 to 31-Mar-2010

Date	Tracking Number	Name of Item	Initial Quantity	Pending Quantity	Rate (Disc %)	Value
Goods Recd. but Bills not Recd. :						
2-Nov-2009	1	Anchor CFL Lamp 12W From: B.K.Services	5 Pieces	5 Pieces	142.00 (2 %)	695.80
4-Nov-2009	1	Anchor CFL Lamp 12W From: B.K.Services	(-)1 Pieces	1 Pieces	142.00 (2 %)	139.16
			4 Pieces	4 Pieces		556.64
Bills Recd. but Goods not Recd. :						
3-Jan-2010	12	Philips CFL Lamp 20W From: BDF	(-)10 Pieces	(-)10 Pieces	172.00	(-)1,720.00
			(-)10 Pieces	(-)10 Pieces		(-)1,720.00

F-6A: Pending Purchase Bill Report

F-7A	F-7B
F1: Detailed	F1: Condensed
F2: Period	F2: Period
F3: Company	F3: Company
F4: Item	F4: Item
F5: Ledger	F5: Ledger
F6: Outward	F6: Inward

F-7A: Buttons at Pending Purchase Bill Report

F-7B: Buttons at Pending Sales Bill Report

Bills Received but Goods not Received

These constitute the Open Purchase *Accounts* Vouchers

- *Purchase* Voucher created but not completely set off against *Receipt Note* voucher.
- *Debit Note* created but completely not set off against *Rejection Out* voucher.

04.03 Pending Bills Statement Configuration

At pending Bills Report (F-4A / F-6A), click *F12: Configure* to get pending Bills Configuration screen (F-5A), to set the. Configuration options as follows:

- **Pending Sales Inventory Vouchers**: At *Show Outstanding Sales Bills*, set:
    - o *Yes* to show Pending Sales Inventory Vouchers (with Balance in Tracking Number)
    - o *No*. The Pending Sales Inventory Vouchers are not shown
- **Cleared Sales Inventory Vouchers**: At *Show Cleared Sales Bills*, set:
    - o *Yes* to show the details of fully adjusted Sales Inventory Vouchers for which Balances have been completely adjusted (No Balance against Tracking Numbers)
    - o *No*. The fully adjusted Sales Inventory Vouchers are not shown
- **Pending Sales Accounts Vouchers**: At *Bills Made but Goods not Delivered*, set:
    - o *Yes* to show Pending Sales Accounts Vouchers (with Balance in Tracking Number)
    - o *No*. The Pending Sales Accounts Vouchers are not shown
- **Pending Purchase Inventory Vouchers**: At *Show Outstanding Purchase Bills*, set:
    - o *Yes* to show Pending Purchase Inventory Vouchers (with Balance in Tracking Number)
    - o *No*. The Pending Purchase Inventory Vouchers are not shown
- **Cleared Purchase Inventory Vouchers**: At *Show Cleared Purchase Bills*, set:
    - o *Yes* to show the details of fully adjusted Purchase Inventory Vouchers for which Balances have been completely adjusted (No Balance against Tracking Numbers)
    - o *No*. The fully adjusted Purchase Inventory Vouchers are not shown
- **Pending Purchase Accounts Vouchers**: At *Bills Recd but Goods not Recd*, set:
    - o *Yes* to show Pending Sales Accounts Vouchers (with Balance in Tracking Number)
    - o *No*. The Pending Sales Accounts Vouchers are not shown

You may further se the following options, where activated

- **Batch Details**: At *Show Batch Details*, set
    - o *Yes* to show Batch details for Items for which Batch Number is activated (applicable only when Batch Number is activated for the Company)
    - o *No*. Batch details are not shown
- **Godown Details**: At *Show Location Details*, set
    - o *Yes* to show Godown Details (applicable only when Godown is activated for the Company)
    - o *No*. Godown details are not shown
- **Alternate Unit Details**: At *Show Using Alternate Unit Details*, set
    - o *Yes* to Show Quantity details in Alternate Unit also for Items for which Alternate Unit is specified
    - o *No*. Quantity details in Alternate Unit are not shown
- **Tail Unit Details**: At *Show Tail Units of Compound Unit*, set
    - o *Yes* to Show Quantity details in Tail Unit also for Items for which Compound Unit is specified
    - o *No*. Quantity details in Tail Unit are not shown

05 Pending Invoice figures in P & L Statement

The figures of Pending Purchase Bills and Pending Sale Bills will also be reflected in Profit & Loss Account (in *Detailed* Mode). Pending Tracking number for goods received / delivered but invoice not entered, is shown in P L Statement (F-8A) to reflect the Sales & Purchase value properly (when Accounts & Inventory are Integrated, i.e you must have set *Yes* at *Integrate Accounts with Inventory* at *F11:Featues >Accounting Features*).

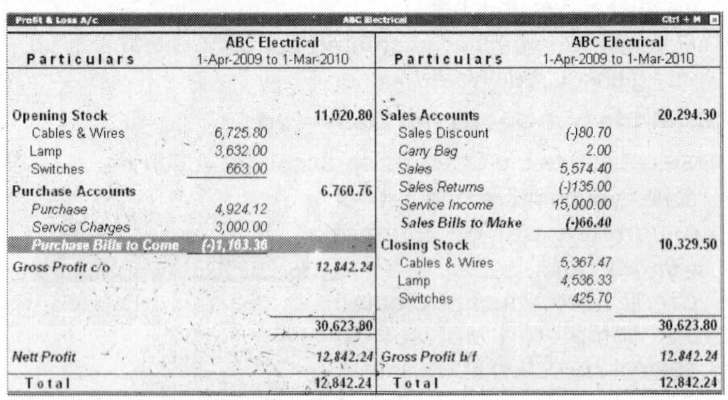

Profit & Loss A/c — ABC Electrical — Ctrl + M

Particulars	ABC Electrical 1-Apr-2009 to 1-Mar-2010		Particulars	ABC Electrical 1-Apr-2009 to 1-Mar-2010	
Opening Stock		11,020.80	**Sales Accounts**		20,294.30
Cables & Wires	6,725.80		Sales Discount	(-)80.70	
Lamp	3,632.00		*Carry Bag*	2.00	
Switches	663.00		*Sales*	5,574.40	
Purchase Accounts		6,760.76	*Sales Returns*	(-)135.00	
Purchase	4,924.12		*Service Income*	15,000.00	
Service Charges	3,000.00		***Sales Bills to Make***	(-)66.40	
Purchase Bills to Come	(-)1,163.36		**Closing Stock**		10,329.50
Gross Profit c/o		12,842.24	Cables & Wires	5,367.47	
			Lamp	4,536.33	
			Switches	425.70	
		30,623.80			30,623.80
Nett Profit		12,842.24	*Gross Profit b/f*		12,842.24
Total		12,842.24	Total		12,842.24

F-8A: P L Account showing the figures for pending purchase/ Sales invoice

Drill down from Pending Bills in P & L Statement (F-8A)

- **Purchase Bills to Come**: To get Pending Purchase Bills Statement (F-6A)
- **Sales Bills to Make**: To get Pending Sales Bills Statement (F-4A)

06 Accounts Voucher Entry against Pending Inventory Voucher

We have discussed entry of Inventory Voucher with tracking number. The pending Tracking Number is to be linked and matched with corresponding Accounts voucher to update both Inventory & Accounts to complete the transaction

- **Purchase Invoice / Debit Note Entry Against Receipt Note / Rejection Out Note**
  - o Purchase Invoice entry against Pending Receipt Note
  - o Debit Note entry against Rejection Out Note.
  - o Purchase Invoice entry for Net Quantity Received against Pending Receipt Note & Rejection Out Note.
- **Sales Invoice / Credit Note Entry Against Delivery Challan / Rejection In Note**
  - o Purchase Invoice entry against Pending Receipt Note
  - o Debit Note entry against Rejection Out Note.
  - o Purchase Invoice entry for Net Quantity Received against Pending Receipt Note & Rejection Out Note.

Here we show linking of Inventory Vouchers created earlier, with Accounts Voucher

06.01 Purchase Invoice entry against Pending Tracking Number

At Gateway, select Accounting Vouchers, click *F9:Purchase* to get Purchase Voucher Entry screen (F-9A)

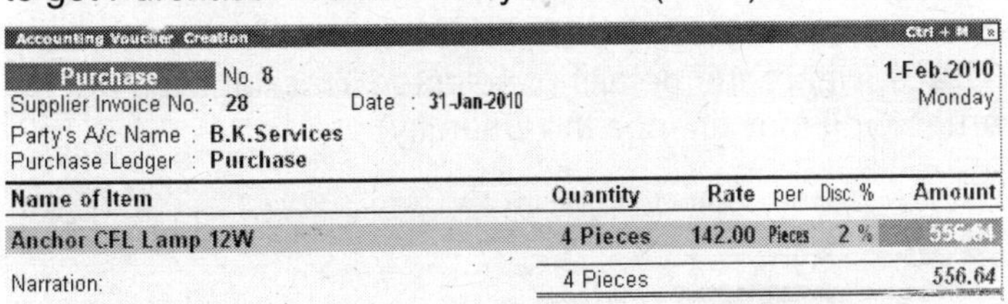

F-9A: Purchase Invoice against Pending Tracking Numbers

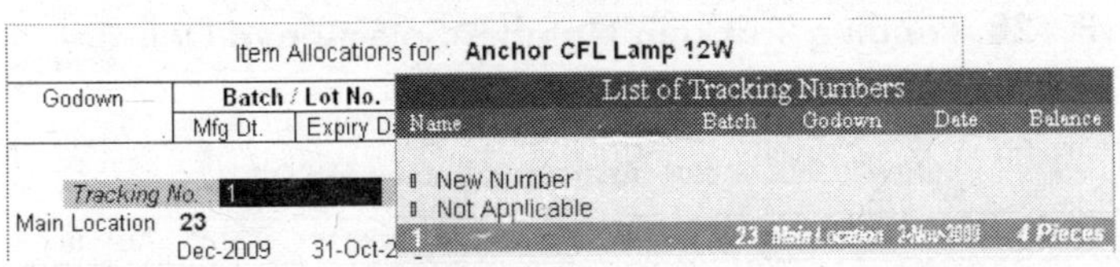

F-9B: Pending Tracking Number selection at Purchase Invoice entry

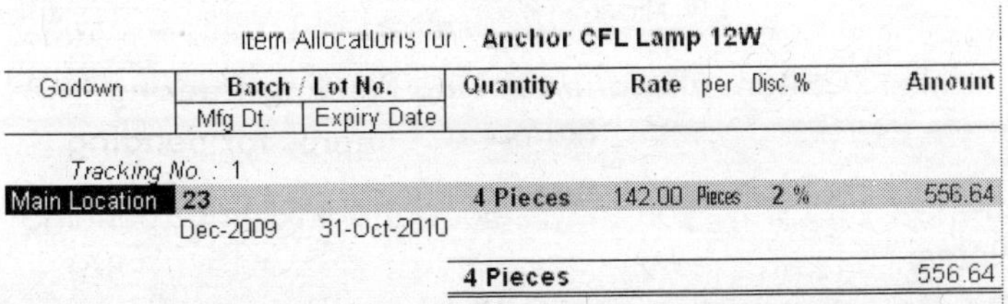

F-9C: Item allocation linking Pending Tracking Numbers

After you select a Stock Item at name of Item column (F-9A), you get Tracking Number entry screen (F-9B) in which all Pending Receipt Notes / Rejection In Notes are shown. Select the Pending Note against which the Current Purchase Invoice is to be created (F- 9B). Now you get the Item Allocation screen (F-9C) showing the selected Tracking Number (you may overwrite the Quantity).

In the same way, you may select and link more Items / Pending Tracking Number.

On adjusting the pending tracking numbers of the Invoice being entered, save the Purchase Invoice

06.02 Sales Invoice entry against Pending Tracking Number

At Gateway, select Accounting Vouchers, click *F8:Sales* to get Sales Voucher Entry screen (F-10A)

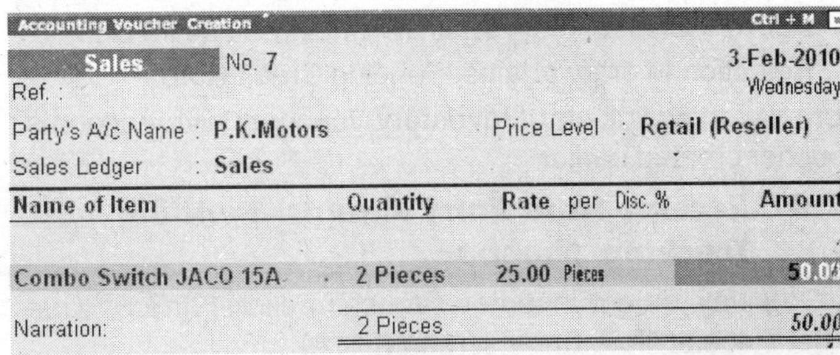

F-10A: Sales Invoice against Pending Tracking Number

F-10B: Pending Tracking Number selection at Sales Invoice entry

After you select a Stock Item at *Name of Item* column (F-10A), you get Tracking Number entry screen (F-10B) showing Pending Tracking Numbers. Select the Pending Note against which the Current Sales Invoice is to be created (F-10B)

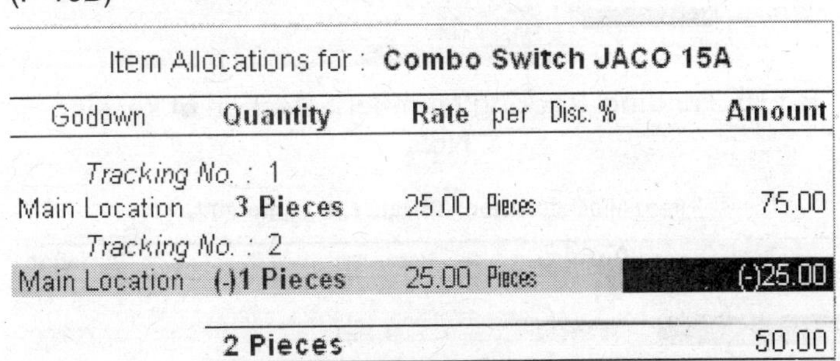

F-10C: Item allocation linking Pending Tracking Numbers

Now you get the Item Allocation screen (F-10C) showing the selected Tracking Number (you may overwrite the Quantity).

In the same way, you may select and link more pending Notes.

On entry of all the Items of the Sales Invoice in this manner, you may save the Purchase Invoice

07 Inventory Voucher Entry against Pending Accounts Voucher

We have discussed entry of Accounts Voucher with tracking number. The pending Tracking Number is to be linked and matched with corresponding Inventory voucher to update both Inventory & Accounts to complete the transaction

Receipt Note / Rejection Out Note Entry Against Purchase Invoice / Debit Note

- Receipt Note entry against Pending Purchase Invoice
- Rejection Out entry against Pending Debit Invoice

Delivery Challan / Rejection In Note Entry Against Sales Invoice / Credit Note

- Delivery Challan entry against Pending Sales Invoice
- Rejection In entry against Pending Credit Note

Here we show linking of Inventory Vouchers with Accounts Voucher created earlier

07.01 Receipt Note Entry Against Pending Tracking Number

At Gateway, select Inventory Voucher, click *F9:Rcpt Note* to get Receipt Note Entry screen (F11A)

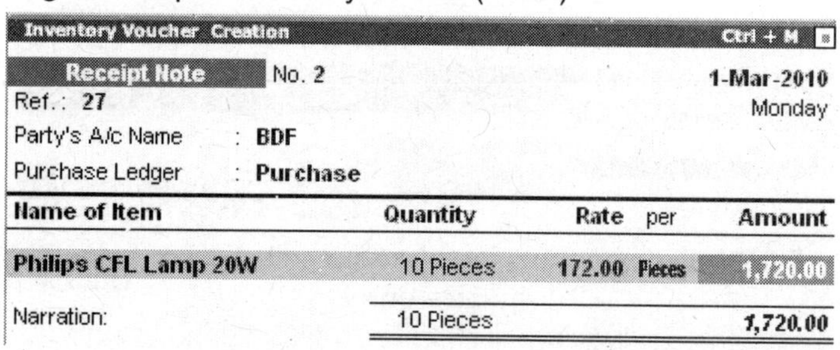

F-11A: Receipt Note Entry Against Pending Tracking Number

F-11B: Pending Tracking Number Selection at Receipt Note

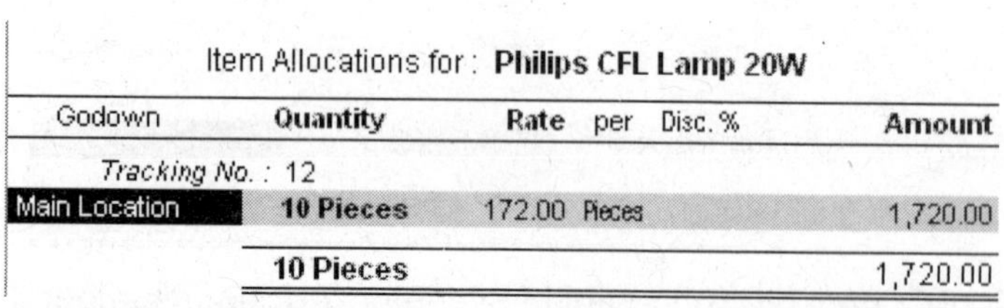

F-11C: Item allocation linking Pending Tracking Numbers

After you select a Stock Item at *Name of Item* column (F-11A), you get Tracking Number entry screen (F-11B) showing all Pending Tracking Numbers. Select the Pending Tracking Number (F-11B) against which the Current Receipt Note is to be created to get Item Allocation Screen (F-11C), where the details of selected Tracking Number is carried (you may change the Quantity).

In the same way, you may select and link more pending Notes.

On entry of all the Items of the Receipt Note in this manner, you may save the Receipt Note (F-11A)

07.02 Delivery Note Entry Against Pending Sales Invoice

At Gateway, select Inventory Voucher, click *F8:Dely Note* to get Delivery Note Entry screen (F-12A)

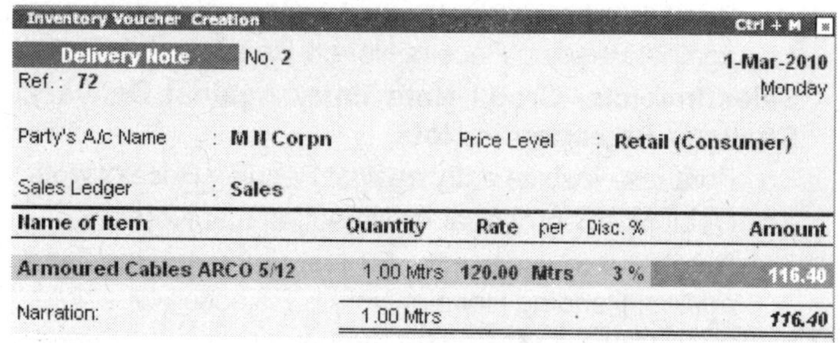

F-12A: Delivery Note Entry linking Pending Tracking Number

After you select a Stock Item at *Name of Item* column, you get Tracking Number entry screen (F-12B). Select the Pending Tracking Number against which the Current Delivery Note is to be created (F-12B) to get *Item Allocation* Screen (F-12C), where the details of selected Tracking Number is carried (you may change the Quantity)

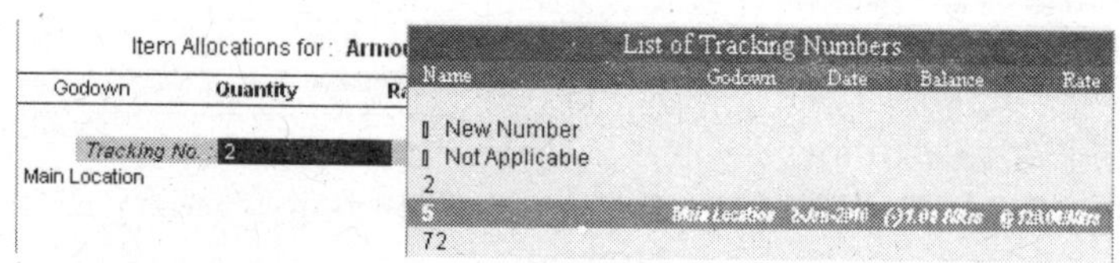

F-12B: Pending Tracking Number Selection at Delivery Note

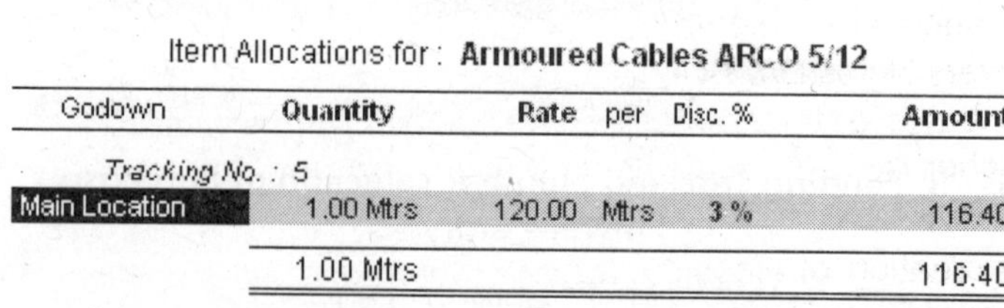

F-12C: Item allocation linking Pending Tracking Numbers

In the same way, you may select and link more pending Notes.

On entry of all the Items of the Delivery Note in this manner, you may save the Delivery Note

After the Pending Inventory Vouchers and Accounts Vouchers are linked fully, the Pending Balances in P & L Statement would be NIL (F-13A).

Profit & Loss A/c	ABC Electrical	Ctrl + M			
Particulars		ABC Electrical 1-Apr-2009 to 1-Mar-2010	**Particulars**		ABC Electrical 1-Apr-2009 to 1-Mar-2010
Opening Stock		**11,020.80**	**Sales Accounts**		**20,410.70**
Cables & Wires	6,725.80		Sales Discount	(-)80.70	
Lamp	3,632.00		*Carry Bag*	2.00	
Switches	663.00		*Sales*	5,624.40	
Purchase Accounts		**8,480.76**	*Sales Returns*	(-)135.00	
Purchase	5,480.76		*Service Income*	15,000.00	
Service Charges	3,000.00		***Sales Bills to Make***		
Purchase Bills to Come			**Closing Stock**		**12,036.09**
Gross Profit c/o		***12,945.23***	Cables & Wires	5,355.47	
			Lamp	6,254.92	
			Switches	425.70	
		32,446.79			**32,446.79**
Nett Profit		***12,945.23***	***Gross Profit b/f***		***12,945.23***
Total		**12,945.23**	**Total**		**12,945.23**

F-13A: P & L Statement after full linking of all Pending Balances of Accounts & Inventory Vouchers

08 Challans Processing

Often, the Supplier sends goods under their Delivery Note, but sends the corresponding Invoice later on. Sometimes, they send one Invoice against multiple Delivery Notes.

In such case, the Customer creates a Receipt Note on receipt of goods, corresponding to the Delivery Note of the supplier. The supplier then creates a Purchase Invoice corresponding to the supplier Invoice and links the Purchase Invoice to the Receipt Notes already created.

This process is illustrated with the following example

Example

Let us assume, the supplier sends goods under Delivery Note No D/5 Dt 1.9. The buyer receives the goods on 5.9 and creates his own Receipt Note No 1 dt 5.9 (Tracking No 1)

The supplier again sends goods under Delivery Note No D/16 Dt 12.9. The buyer receives the goods on 15.9 and creates his own Receipt Note 2 dt 15.9 (Tracking No 2)

The supplier sends an Invoice S/15 dt 31.12 in respect of Delivery Notes D/5 Dt 1.9. & Delivery Note No D/16 Dt 12.9. The buyer enters the Supplier's Invoice under Purchase Voucher No 9 dt 15.9, linking the Receipt Notes 1 dt 5.9 & 2 dt 15.9.

The creation of Receipt Notes & Purchase Invoice in the books of Buyer are now explained

First the Receipt Notes (1 dt 5.9 & 2 dt 15.9) are entered as and when goods are received

Later on, the corresponding Purchase Invoice (9 dt 15.9) is entered against the Receipt Notes 1 & 2 created earlier

08.01 Sales Invoice entry against Delivery Note

Often, the Vendor sends goods under their Delivery Note. Subsequently, the Vendor creates corresponding Invoice linking the delivery Note (sometimes one Invoice is created against multiple Delivery Notes).

This process s illustrated with the following example

Example

Let us assume, the supplier sends goods under Delivery Note No 1 Dt.4.10 & again by Delivery Note No 2 Dt. 3.11 and then creates a Sales Invoice 5 dt 15.11. against these 2 Delivery Notes

The creation of Delivery Notes & Sales Invoice in the books of Vendor are now explained

The Delivery Note 1 Dt 4.10 (Tacking Number1) & Delivery Note No 2 Dt. 3.11 (Tacking Number 2) are first entered.

Later on, Sales Invoice No 5 dt 15.11 against the linking Tracking No 1 (Delivery Note1 Dt 4.10.2010) & Tracking No 2 (Delivery Note No 2 Dt. 3.11.2010) is entered.

08.02 Debit Note entry against Rejection Out Note

Often, the Customer returns goods under Rejection Out Note and then creates a Debit Note against the Rejection Out Note

This process is illustrated with the following example.

Example

C returns bought goods to S, under Rejection Out Note No 1 Dt 15.9 and then C creates a Debit Note No 1 dt 15.10. on S, against the Rejection Out Note

The creation of Rejection Out Note & subsequent creation of Debit Note linking the Rejection Out Note is now explained

First, C creates Rejection Out Note No 1 Dt 15.9 (Tracking No 12). Later on, C creates Debit Note No 1 dt 15.10.against Tracking No 12 (Rejection Out Note No 1 Dt 15.9)

08.03 Credit Note entry against Rejection In Note

In the above paragraph, we have explained the entries in the books of Customer (C) who returns the Goods to Supplier S. Here, we explain the corresponding entry in the books of Supplier S, who receives back the returned goods from Customer C.

On receiving the returned goods from C (who sends a Rejection Out Note to S), the Supplier S creates Rejection In Voucher on C, on receipt of returned goods from C. Subsequently, the Supplier S creates corresponding Credit Note (on receiving Debit Note from the C) linking the Rejection In Note (one Credit Note may be created against multiple Rejection In Notes)

This process s illustrated with the following example

Example

S, on receiving Returned goods from C (sent by C under Rejection Out # 1 dt 15.9) under Rejection In voucher 1 dt 8.10 and later on creates Credit Note No 5 dt 15.12. The creation of Rejection In Note & Credit Note in the books of S are now explained

First the Rejection In Note No 1 dt 8.10 (Tracking No 12) is created.

Later on, the Credit Note No 5 dt 15.12 is created against the Tracking No 12 (Rejection In Note 1 dt 4.10)

09 Sale under Buy or Return scheme

Under this scheme, goods (like Books) are delivered by Seller to customers (Buyer) with an option to buy (nad test on trial) or return the item intact, within a specified period. The Items accepted or retained are then billed.

The versatile facility of Tally of creating Delivery Notes independently (without creating sale bill simultaneously) and inter adjustment of Pending Challans provide excellent mechanism for maintaining complete system of such type of trade.

Delivery on Buy-or-Return Basis: At the time of delivery of book, a *Delivery Note* is to be prepared with a new tracking number, in the name of the customer. Now the following cases may arise:

- **Customer Retains / Accepts all Items:** A Sale Bill (S/9) is created linking the Delivery Note (D/5). So, the all the items delivered are properly billed. The customer now pays for the sale bill (S/9).
- **Customer Retains / accepts some Items and returns the rest of the Items:** This involves 2 steps
  - o **Creation of Rejection In Note for the goods returned:** Create a Rejection In Note for the Items returned (R/7).
  - o **Creation of Sale Bill after adjusting the Rejection Note from the Delivery Note:** A Sale Bill (S/9) is created linking the Delivery Note D/5 and Rejection Note R/7. So, all the items delivered / retained are properly billed (the item returned gets adjusted through the rejection Note). The customer now pays for the sale bill (S/9).
- **Customer Returns all the Items:** In this case, the Delivery Note D/5 remains pending. A rejection note R/7 is created for the all the returned Item, linking the Delivery Note D/5. Now the Delivery Note is completely set off leaving a zero Balance

10 Sale through Agents (Consignment Sales)

In case of sale through Agents, the gods are merely transferred to Agent. It is not sale. When the agent, in turn, sells the goods to its customers, the sale invoice is created by the principal on the customer. There is no sale transaction between the Agent and the customer.

The trade of sale through Agent may be implemented by using the combined features of Godown (the Agent is treated as Godown) and the features of Delivery Challan, Rejection Note and linking of these documents to Sale Invoice.

The basic concepts of Sale through Agent are:

- Create a Godown for each Agent. So, Agents become godown of the organization. Consequently, godownwise transactions and stock give the nécessary records and statements for Agents
- Create a Stock Journal for goods delivered to Agent. Within Tally, it is treated as stock Transfer to a godown. So, the stock lying with Agent is treated as stock lying in a godown and is part of the inventory of the organization.(perfectly complying to the principle of Accountancy).
- The Agent submits a sales statement for Items sold. A sales invoice is created in the name of actual customer (whom the goods are sold by the agent), using the goods from the respective godown (the agent). This way, the godown stock (stock with the agent) are properly accounted for.
- All the accounting transactions with agent are dome through account ts voucher as usual. This way, any organization trading through agents may maintain complete accounting & inventory system and tracking of stock lying with agents

FAQ: Frequently Asked Questions

FAQ-1: How do I print Sales Bills Pending Report

Ans: At *Statement Of Inventory* Menu (F-3A), select *Sales Bills Pending* to print list of Pending Tracking references (F-4A). *Sales Bills Pending* (F-4A) shows 2 sections:

Goods Delivered but Bills not made

These constitute the Open Sales *Inventory* Vouchers

- *Delivery Out* voucher created but not completely set off against *Sales* Voucher.
- *Rejection In* voucher is created but completely not set off against *Credit Note* voucher.

Bills Made but Goods not Delivered

These constitute the Open Sales *Accounts* Vouchers

- *Sales* voucher created but not completely set off against *Delivery Note*
- *Credit Note* Voucher created but completely not set off against *Rejection In* voucher.

Part 4
Orders

Orders are contract for Sales & Purchase. The Orders are pre planned as per availability of materials, orders procured, Current and forthcoming stocks etc. This Part explains the nuances of Order Planning, Ordering & Order execution processes

Orders explains the concept of Ordering System, from creation of Order to its execution

Order Execution explains the various steps of Order Execution process

Orders Reports explains various Reports of Orders at various stages until complete execution

Orders Outstandings explains various types of Reports displaying the current status of Open Orders

Order Levels explains the process of building plans for Materials Purchase based on Current Stock & forthcoming materials arrivals & consumptions

Order Processing explains the complete life cycle process of Order, right from creation to its final execution

Orders

01 Order

Orders are Trade Contracts for transactions between the Seller & Buyer. Ordering System helps better inventory control & impart better planning and control for Sales & Purchase Activities,

Orders are pre-Invoice documents. You may prepare Invoices even without incorporating ordering system. Orders do not affect Inventory (i.e., have no effect on stock) or Accounts.

The Order issued by Customer on Supplier is called Purchase Order, while the Order issued by Supplier on Customer is called Sales Order. Normally, Purchase Order is issued by Customer on Supplier (customer enters as Purchase Order). The Supplier accepts it and records the Customer's Purchase Order as its own Sales Order (Supplier enters as Sales Order). However, the sequence may happen in reverse order (the Supplier issues Sales Order on Customer. Customer accepts it and records as its Purchase Order).

01.01 Ordering System

- Ordering System facilitates better control on procurement & sales activities & Inventory management
- Ordering System ensures implementation of production / purchase & Sale Plan, as the sale / purchase contracts (Orders) are guided and followed by such plans
- Order system ensures proper Invoicing as the Rates & Order Quantity is specified and authorised by proper authority.

01.02 Activating Ordering System

To activate Order System, Click *F11:Feature>Inventory Feature* and set the options as follows (F-1A):

- Set Yes at *Allow Purchase Order processing* to activate Purchase Orders. Consequently, *F4: Purchase Order* button would also appear at Inventory Voucher Entry screen to enter Purchase Orders (F-3A)
- Set Yes at *Allow Sales Order processing* to activate Sales Orders. Consequently, *F5: Sales Order* button would also appear at Voucher Entry screen to enter Sales Orders (F-3A)

You may set *Yes* at either, both or at none of the above two order processing options (F-1A), as required. On activating Order, *Order Vouchers* option appears in Main Manu of Gateway of Tally (F-2A), to enter Sales / Purchase Order.

02 Orders Entry Configuration

At Order entry screen (F-5A), click *F12:Configure* to get respective Order Entry Configuration screen (F-4A, F-4B), to set the Configuration options, which are quite similar to Challan / Invoice Entry discussed earlier.

Order Processing

Allow Purchase Order Processing	? Yes
Allow Sales Order Processing	? Yes

F-1A: Order System Activationwith

Transactions

Accounting Vouchers
InvenTory Vouchers
OrdEr Vouchers

F-2A: Main Menu Orders Option

F5: Sales Order
F4: Purc. Order

F-3A: Order Entry buttons

Purchase Order Configuration

Accept Supplementary Details *(Address Details, Despatch Details etc.)*	? No
Print Default Name & Address of Party	? No
Allow Separate Buyer and Consignee Names	? No
Use Common Ledger A/c for Item Allocation	? Yes
Use Additional Description(s) for Item Name	? No
Use Additional Description(s) for Ledger Name	? No
Complete Accounting Allocations in Order/Delivery Note	? No
Show turnover achieved with Customer	? No
Allow modification of ALL fields during entry	? No
Show Compound Unit of Item based on Rate	? No
Show Full Details of Compound Unit	? No
Warn on Negative Stock Balance	? No
Honor Expiry Dates usage for Batches	? Yes
Show Batches with zero quantity	? Yes
Calculate Tax on current Sub-Total *(else calculations are on Inventory Total only)*	? No

F-4A: Purchase Order Entry Configuration

Sales Order Configuration

Accept Supplementary Details *(Address Details, Despatch Details etc.)*	? No
Print Default Name & Address of Party	? No
Allow Separate Buyer and Consignee Names	? No
Use Common Ledger A/c for Item Allocation	? Yes
Use Additional Description(s) for Item Name	? No
Use Additional Description(s) for Ledger Name	? No
Complete Accounting Allocations in Order/Delivery Note	? No
Show turnover achieved with Customer	? No
Allow modification of ALL fields during entry	? No
Show Compound Unit of Item based on Rate	? No
Show Full Details of Compound Unit	? No
Warn on Negative Stock Balance	? No
Honor Expiry Dates usage for Batches	? Yes
Show Batches with zero quantity	? Yes
Calculate Tax on current Sub-Total *(else calculations are on Inventory Total only)*	? No

F-4B: Sales Order Entry Configuration

The Configuration options for Sales (F-4A) & Purchase orders (F-4B) are similar

03 Purchase Order Entry

At Main Menu, select Order Vouchers (F-2A), Click *F4: Purc. Order* button (F-3A) to get Purchase Order entry screen (or press Alt+F4), quite similar to Purchase Invoice Entry screen (F-4/01-04).

Purchase Order No. **1** **1-Jul-2009** Wednesday

Party's A/c Name : **Digitech Infosys** Order No. : **17**
Current Balance : ***25,025.00 Cr***
Purchase Ledger : **Purchase**

Name of Item	Quantity		Rate	per	Disc. %	Amount
	Actual	Billed				
Fax with Scan C-T45	15 Pcs	15 Pcs	8,000.00	Pcs		1,20,000.00
Freight						300.00
Handling Charges						500.00
	15 Pcs	15 Pcs				*1,20,800.00*

Narration:
Purchased Order Placed

F-5A:Purchase Order entry

Supplier's Details

Supplier	: **Digitech Infosys**
Address	: 67, BC/2 SB. Road Bangalore
Sales Tax No.	: **DHFGF6453**

Order Details

Mode/Terms of Payment	: **30 days**
Other Reference(s)	: **L-13/06-06-09**
Terms of Delivery	: By Rail

Receipt Details

Despatch through	: **By Rail**
Destination	: **Kolkata**

F-5B: Supplementary Details

The Purchase Order entry screen (F-5A) may be divided in following components:

- Header Part
  - o Party A/c Name
  - o Order Number
  - o Supplementary Details
  - o Purchase Account
- Item Details
  - o Item Name
  - o Item Allocation
  - - Other Ledger Accounts
  - - Voucher Narration

a. Header Part

In Header Part (F-5A), enter the details common to the entire Purchase Order, as follows:

- **Party's A/c**: At *Party's A/c Name*, select the Supplier Name from the list of Supplier Ledger Accounts
- **Order Ref:** At *Order No.* enter your Purchase Order Reference (or Party's Reference) as Order Reference (the Order Voucher Number is carried as default, which you may change). All the subsequent documents (like Receipt Note, Invoice etc) are linked through Order Reference Number (not the Order Voucher Number) and pending Order Reports are listed as per the Order Reference Number so entered.
- **Supplementary Details:** If you have set Yes at *Accept Supplementary Details* at Delivery Note / Orders / Invoice configuration (F-4A), then the *Supplementary entry* screen appears to enter the following details (F-5B):
  - i. Supplier Details
  - ii. Order Details
  - iii. Receipt Details

i. **Supplier Details:** Enter the following Supplier's Details.
  - **Supplier Name**: The Party Name is carried by default, which you may change
  - **Address**: The Party Address is carried as default, which you may change
  - **TIN / Sales Tax Number**: The TIN / Sales Tax Number entered in Party Master, if any, is carried which you may change
  - **Type of Dealer**: If the dealer is registered under Central Excise / VAT etc., then select the Dealer Type (you may select *Not Applicable*)

ii. **Order Details**: Enter the following Order details (normally the Order Instructions & Terms)
  - **Mode / Terms of Payment**: Enter the Terms of Payment (Credit / Cash etc) and mode of Payment (Cheque, through Bank collection etc).
  - **Other References**: Any other references (correspondence reference, etc. if any)
  - **Terms of Delivery**: Terms of Delivery (like FOR Destination, CIF etc)

iii. **Receipt Details:** Enter the following Despatch details (normally the Despatch Instructions & Terms in the Order)
  - **Despatch through**: Enter the Name of carrier etc.
  - **Destination**: Enter the Destination of goods to be despatched
  - **Purchase Ledger:** Select the Purchase Ledger from the list of Purchase Ledger Accounts (Ledger Accounts under the *Purchase Group*). If you have set *No* at *Use Common Ledger Account for Item Allocation*, then the Purchase Ledger A/c is to be selected for each Item after Item entry (provided you have set Yes at *Complete Accounting Allocation in Delivery Note / Orders* at Invoice / Delivery Note / Orders Configuration screen)

b. Item Details

After entry of Header details, the following Item Details are entered, as explained:

i. Item Name
ii. Item Allocation Details

i. **Item Name**: Select The Item

ii. **Item Allocation Details**: After entry of Item Name, a pop up window appears (F-5C) to enter the Item details as follows:

- **Delivery Due Date**: At *Due on* field, enter the Delivery Due Date of the Item. In case of staggering delivery plan (Item to be delivered in parcel on different dates), you have to enter the Item details separately for each Delivery Date.
- **Batch / Godown**:Enter the following details if the respective features are activated:
  - o **Godown Details**: Under *Godown* column, select the Godown (if Multiple Godown is activated). If the Godown is not known at the time creation of Order, you may select *Any* (and later specify the Godown at the time of Receipt of Goods).
  - o **Batch Details**: Select the Batch (if Batch is activated). If the Batch is not known at the time creation of Order, you may select *Any* (and later specify the Batch at the time of Receipt of Goods).
- **Quantity**: Enter the Order Quantity for the Item.
- **Rate**: The Standard Rate (or the price list Rate) is carried, which you may change in the Order
- **Discount**: Enter the Discount Rate (in %), if Discount / Price List option is activated.
- **Amount**: The computed amount as per Quantity & Rate (& Discount) is displayed, which may be changed (in case of lump sum value, the Amount may be entered without entering the Rate)

Item Allocations for : **Fax with Scan C- T45**
For Order Number : **17**

Godown	Quantity Actual	Quantity Billed	Rate per Disc. %	Amount
Due on 5-Jul-2009				
Main Location	15 Pcs	15 Pcs	8,000.00 Pcs	1,20,000.00

F-5C: Purchase Order Entry – Item Allocation

This way, enter the details of each Item in the Purchase Order.

c. Other Ledger Details

After completing the entry of all Item details at voucher entry screen (F-5A), enter the details for other ledger accounts (like Freight, Tax etc, if any). The process is similar to Purchase Invoice Entry (F-4/01-04).

- **Ledger Account**: Select the Ledger Account
- **Rate**: Enter the Rate in % (or may leave zero and fill up amount figure directly)
- **Amount**: The computed amount as per Rate specified (according to rule specified in the Ledger Account), is displayed which you may change.

This way, enter the details of each ledger account.

d. Voucher Narration

If you set *Yes* at *Use Common Narration* at the Delivery Note voucher type, then you may also enter Narration for the voucher, giving more details. The Narration entered may be optionally printed in Purchase Order / Day Book.

04 Sales Order Entry

At Main Menu (F-2A), select Inventory Vouchers to get Inventory Voucher entry screen. Click *F4: Sales Order* button (F-3A) to get Sales Order entry Screen (or press Alt+F4), quite similar to Sales Invoice Entry screen (F-6A).

Sales Order No. 1 — 4-Jul-2009 Saturday

Party's A/c Name : **Digitech Infosys** — Order No. : **09**
Current Balance : ***25,025.00 Cr***
Sales Ledger : **Sales**

Name of Item	Quantity Actual	Quantity Billed	Rate per Disc. %	Amount
FAX (Jx-201)	10 Pcs	10 Pcs	400.00 Pcs	4,000.00
Freight				200.00
Narration:	10 Pcs	10 Pcs		*4,200.00*

Sale order plased by P.K. Paul

F-6A: Sale Order Entry

Buyer's Details
Despatch To : **Digitech Infosys**
Address : 12, N.S. Bose Road
Kolkata 700125

Sales Tax No. : **SGSFDD45**

Order Details
Mode/Terms of Payment : **By Bus**
Other Reference(s) :
Terms of Delivery : 30 days

Despatch Details
Despatch through : **By Bus**
Destination : **Bangalore**

F-6B: Supplementary Details

The Sales Order entry screen (F-6A) may be divided in following components:

- a.Header Part
  - i. Party A/c Name
  - ii. Order Number
  - iii. Supplementary Details
  - iv. Sales Ledger
- b.Item Details
  - i. Item Name
  - ii. Item Allocation
- c.Other Ledger Accounts
- d. Voucher Narration

These elements of Sales Order Entry are described below:

a. Header Part

In Header Part, you enter the details common to the entire Sales Order, as follows:

i. **Party's A/c**: At *Party's A/c Name*, select the Customer Name from the list of Customer Ledger Accounts

ii. **Order Reference:** At *Order No,* the Sales Order Voucher Number is carried. You may change it and enter your Sales Order Reference (or Party's Reference) as Order Reference. All the subsequent documents (like Delivery Note, Invoice etc) are linked through Order Number (not the Voucher Number) and pending Order Reports are listed as per the Order Number so entered.

iii **Supplementary Details:** If you have set Yes at *Accept Supplementary Details* at Delivery Note / Orders / Invoice configuration, then the Supplementary entry screen appears to enter the following details (F-6B)

- Buyer's Details
- Order Details
- Despatch Details

1. **Buyer's Details:** At *Buyer's Details* section (F-6B), enter as follows:
   - **Consignee:** At *Despatch to*, enter the consignee name (whom the gods are sent to). The Party Name is carried by default, which you may change (if the consignee is different from Buyer)
   - **Consignee Address**: At *Address*, enter the Consignee Address. The Buyer Address is carried as default, which you may change (if the consignee address is different from Buyer Address)
   - **Sales Tax Number**: At *Sales Tax Number*, the TIN / Sales Tax Number entered in Party Master, if any, is carried, which you may change
2. **Order Details**: At *Order Details* section (F-6B), enter as follows:
   - **Mode / Terms of Payment**: At *Mode / Terms of Payment,* enter the Terms of Payment (Credit / Cash etc) and mode of Payment (Cheque, through Bank collection etc)
   - **Other References**: At *Other References*, enter any other important references (correspondence reference, etc. if any)
   - **Terms of Delivery**: At *Terms of Delivery,*enter Terms of Delivery, (like FOR Destination, CIF etc), if any.
3. **Despatch Details:** At *Despatch Details* section (F-6B), enter as follows:
   - **Transport**: At *Despatch through*, enter the Name of Carrier etc.
   - **Destination**: At *Destination*, enter the Destination of goods despatched

iv. **Sales Ledger:** Select the Sales Ledger from the list of Sales Ledger Accounts (Ledger Accounts under the *Sales Group*). If you have set *No* at *Use Common Ledger Account for Item Allocation*, then the Sales Ledger A/c is to be selected for each Item after Item entry (provided you have set *Yes* at *Complete Accounting Allocation in Delivery Note / Orders* at Invoice / Delivery Note / Orders Configuration screen)

b. **Item Details:** After entry of Header details, enter the following Item Details (F-6A), as explained:

- Item Name
- Item Allocation Details

i. **Item Name**: At main voucher entry screen (F-6A), select the Item ordered, from the list of Stock Items to get Item Allocation screen (F-6C).

ii. **Item Allocation Details**: On entry of Item Name (F-6A), Allocation screen (F-6C) appears to enter the Item details as follows (F-6C):

- **Delivery Due Date**: At *Delivery Due Date*, Enter the Delivery Due Date of the Item. In case of staggering delivery plan (Item to be delivered in parcel on different dates), you have to enter the details separately for each Delivery Date.
- **Batch / Godown**:Enter the following details if the respective features are activated:
  - o **Godown Details**: Under *Godown* Column, select the Godown (if Multiple Godown is activated). If the Godown is not known at the time creation of Order, you may select *Any* (and later specify the Godown at the time of Delivery of Goods).
  - o **Batch Details**: Select the Batch (if Batch is activated). If the Batch is not known at the time creation of Order, you may select *Any* (and later specify the Batch at the time of Delivery of Goods).
- **Order Quantity:** At *Quantity* column, enter the Quantity Ordered
- **Sales Rate**: At *Rate*, enter the Item Sales Rate. The Standard Rate (or the Price list Rate) is carried, which you may change.
- **Discount %:** At Discount column, enter the Discount Rate in %, if any (if Discount / Price List option is activated
- **Item value:** At *Amount* column, the computed amount as per Quantity & Rate / Discount is displayed, which may be changed (in case of lump sum value, the Amount may be entered without entering the Rate)

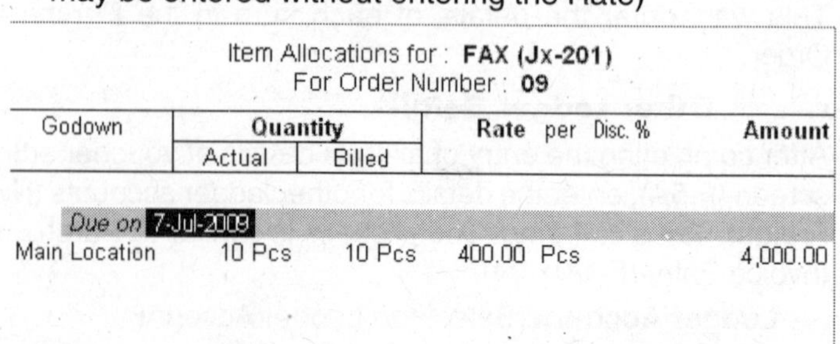

F-6C. Sales Order entry – Item Allocation Sales Order Entry Configuration

This way, enter the details of each Item in the Purchase Order.

c. Other Ledger Details

After completing the entry of all Item details (F-6C), at main voucher screen (F-6A), enter the details for other ledger accounts (like Freight, Tax etc, if any)

- **Ledger Account**: Select the Ledger Account
- **Rate**: Enter the Rate in % (or may leave zero and fill up amount figure directly)
- **Amount**: The computed amount as per Rate specified (according to rule specified in the Ledger Account), is displayed which you may change (or enter amount figure directly)

This way, enter the details of each ledger account.

d. Voucher Narration

If you have set *Yes* at *Use Common Narration* at the Sales Order voucher type, at main voucher screen (F-6A), you may also enter Narration for the voucher, giving more details. The Narration entered may be optionally printed in Sales Order / Day Book.

05 Order Printing

Having entered Order, you may print the Order (currently being entered) on-line immediately after entry (while saving). The process of Order Printing is similar to Invoice Printing explained earlier (§01/01-05)

FAQ: Frequently Asked Questions

FAQ-1: How do I activate Ordering System

Ans: To activate Order System, Click *F11:Feature>Inventory Feature* and set the options as follows (F-1A):

- Set *Yes* at *Allow Purchase Order processing* to activate Purchase Orders. Consequently, *F4: Purchase Order* button would also appear at Inventory Voucher Entry screen to enter Purchase Orders
- Set *Yes* at *Allow Sales Order processing* to activate Sales Orders. Consequently, *F5: Sales Order* button would also appear at Voucher Entry screen to enter Sales Orders

You may set *Yes* at either, both or at none of the above two order processing options, as required. On activating Order, the Option *Order Vouchers* appears in Main Manu of Gateway of Tally (F-2A), to enter Sales / Purchase Order.

Order Execution 04-02

01 Order Execution

Order Execution means transaction of goods as per Order (Order Fufilment). After issue of Order, the Order is executed. The vendor supplies the goods against their Sales Order and the buyer receives the goods against their Purchase Orders. So when the goods are received / delivered, the Delivery / Receipt Note or the Sales / Purchase Invoice are to be created by the Buyer / Seller, against the respective Order.

The entry process of Sales / Purchase Order have been explained earlier. Now the additional part of Execution of Order (Creation of Challan / Invoice linking Orders) are explained:

Sales Order Execution

- Creation of Delivery Note against Sales Order (§02)
- Creation of Sales Invoice against Sales Order (§03)

Purchase Order Execution

- Creation of Receipt Note against Purchase Order (§04)
- Creation of Purchase Voucher against Purchase Order (§05)

02 Delivery Note entry against Sales Order

Delivery Note entry has been explained earlier (§03/03-02). Here we explain the additional process of linking the Delivery Note against Order.

During Delivery Note entry, at Order Details section of the Supplementary Details subscreen (F-1A), the list of all pending order numbers appear at *Order Number* field. Now enter as follows for Delivery Note:

- **Against existing Pending Order**: Select the Order number against which the Delivery Note is being created, from the list of Pending Orders. You may select several Orders one by one in one Delivery Note.
- **Against Order to be issued**: Sometimes, the Delivery Note is created first and the respective Order is to be created later. In such case, select *New Number*, and enter the Order Number (that would be created for the delivery note). Later on, create the Order (with he specified Order Number) which will get linked with the Delivery Note.
- **Without Order**: Select *Not Applicable*.

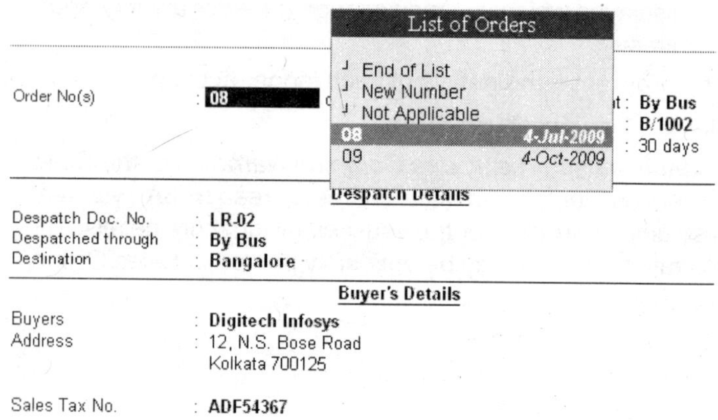

F-1A: Delivery Notes against Sales Order

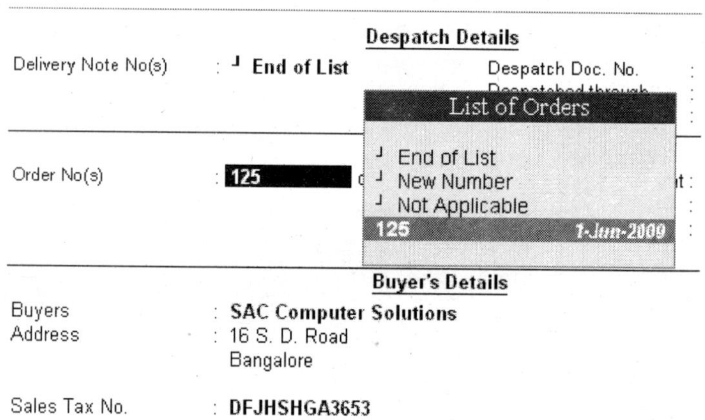

F-1B: Sales Invoice against Sales Order

03 Sales Invoice entry against Sales Order

Sales Invoice may be directly entered against Order (no Delivery Note is created). Sales Invoice entry has been explained earlier (F-3/01-04). Here we explain the additional process of linking the Delivery Note against Order.

During Sales Invoice entry, at Order Details section of the Supplementary Details subscreen (F-1B), the list of all pending order numbers appear at *Order No(s)* field. Now enter as follows for Sales Invoice:

- **Against existing Pending Order**: Select the Order number against which the Sales Invoice is created, from the list of Pending Order. You may select several Orders one by one in one Sales Invoice.

- **Against Order to be issued**: Sometimes, the Sales Invoice is created first and the respective Sales Order is to be created later. In such case, select *New Number*, and enter the Sales Order Number (that would be created for the Sales Invoice). Later on create the Order which will get linked with the Sales Invoice.
- **Without Order**: Select *Not Applicable*.

04 Receipt Note entry against Purchase Order

Receipt Notes entry has been explained earlier (§03/03-02). Here we explain the additional process of linking the Receipt Note against Order.

During Receipt Note entry, at Order Details section of the Supplementary Details subscreen (F-2A), the list of all pending order numbers appear at *Order Number* field. Now enter as follows for *Receipt Note*:

- **Against existing Pending Order**: Select the Order number against which the *Receipt* Note is created from the list. You may select several Orders one by one in one *Receipt* Note.
- **Against Order to be issued**: Sometimes, the *Receipt* Note is created first and the respective Purchase Order is to be created later. In such case, select *New Number*, and enter the Purchase Order Number (that would be created for the Receipt Note). Later on create the Order which will get linked with the Receipt Note.
- **Without Order**: Select *Not Applicable*.

F-2A: Receipt Notes entry against Purchase Order

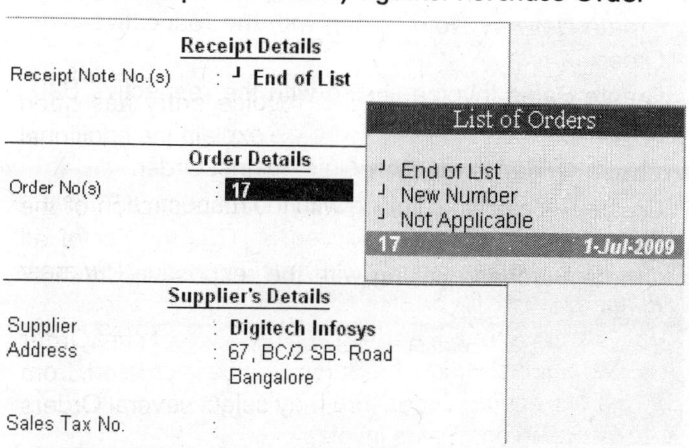

F-2B: Purchase Invoice against Purchase Order

05 Purchase Invoice entry against Purchase Order

Purchase Invoice may be directly entered against Order (no Receipt Note is created). Purchase Invoice entry has been explained earlier (F-4/01-04). Here we explain the additional process of linking the Purchase Invoice against Order.

During Purchase Invoice entry, at Order Details section of the Supplementary Details subscreen (F-2B), the list of all pending order numbers appear at *Order Number* field. Now enter as follows for Purchase Invoice:

- **Against existing Pending Order**: Select the Purchase Order number against which the Purchase Invoice is created, from the list of Pending Order. You may select several Purchase Orders one by one in one Purchase Invoice.
- **Against Order to be issued**: Sometimes, the Purchase Invoice is created first and the respective Purchase Order is to be created later. In such case, select *New Number*, and enter the Purchase Order Number (that would be created for the Purchase Invoice). Later on create the Order which will get linked with the Purchase Invoice.
- **Without Order**: Select *Not Applicable*.

> **Note:** *Orders do not affect any Ledger Accounts. So, the ledger accounts specified in Orders entry, do not impact any ledger account, but helps entry of corresponding subsequent stage vouchers (e.g Delivery / Receipt Note against orders, Sales / Purchase Invoice entry against Delivery / Receipt Note & Sales / Purchase Invoice entry against Sales / Purchase Orders as the respective details are carried from he previous documents o the next level linked documents.*

06 Pre-Closure of Order

An Order is an accepted contract between Buyer & Seller. So, in natural course, the contract would be executed in full. That means, the Seller would deliver full quantity of Ordered goods and the Buyer would accept the full quantity of Ordered goods.

However, sometimes, Buyer / Seller may decide that the balance undelivered quantity of an order (full or partial) will not be further delivered by Seller and the Balance Order Quantity be cancelled. The order be treated as fully executed.

> **Note:** *Sometimes, a part of the Balance Order may be-pre closed. In such case, the entire order is not closed, but the Balance Order Quantity gets reduced.*

Pre Closure of Order may be done at during Voucher Entry or at Order Details screen:

Use Pre-Closure order details ? **Yes**

F-3A: Order Pre Closing Configuration option

C: Pre-Close

F-3B: Pre Closure button at Order Entry screen

Item Allocations for : **Biostar 945gc-M7 Te**

Godown	Quantity	Pre-Close Quantity	Rate	per	Disc. %	Amount
Due on 1-Jun-2009						
Main Location	5 Pcs	3 Pcs	3,500.00	Pcs		17,500.00
Reason for Pre-Close		: Order Reduced				

F-4A: Item Level Pre Closing from Order

Pre-Close Order Completely?

Reason Balance Order Cancelled As Mutually Agreed Closed on 2-Mar-2010

F-4B: Entire Order Pre Closing

06.01 Pre Closure at Order Alteration

You may pre close order (before Order Completion), in following ways:

You may Pre Close an Order in 2 ways:

- **Pre Close the entire Order**: At Order Alteration screen, click *C:Pre Close* (or pres *Ctrl+C*) button (F-3B) to get Pre Closure screen (F-4B).
  - o **Pre Closure Reason**: At Reason, specify the Reason.
  - o **Pre Closure Date**: At *Closed On*, enter the Date of Pre Closure

The entire Order (in respect of all the Items) is closed.

- **Pre Close Balance of selected Item**: To get Pre Close Order at Item Level, at *Order Configuration* screen (Click *F12:Configure* at Orders Alteration screen), set *Yes* (F-3A) at *Use Pre Closure Order details.* Consequently, at *Item Allocation* screen (F-4A), the column *Pre – Close Quantity* appears. Now, enter as follows:
  - o **Pre Closure Quantity:** At *Pre Close Quantity Column*, enter the Quantity to be reduced from the Balance Order
  - o **Reason:** At *Reason for Pre Closure*, enter the Reason

The Balance of Order of the Item gets reduced by the specified Pre Closure Quantity.

06.02 Pre Closure from Voucher Entry

If during Orders Entry, it is decided that Balance Order (full or Partial) will not be fully executed, the Pre Closure Quantity may be entered at respective Voucher Entry screen.

At Voucher Entry (Delivery Note / Receipt Note / Purchase Invoice / Sales Invoice), you may pre –close Order at Item Level. At Voucher Entry Configuration (at current Voucher entry / Alteration screen, click *F12:Configure* to get respective Voucher Entry Configuration screen), set *Yes* at *Use Pre Closure Orders Details* (F-3A).

Item Allocations for : **PrinterSamsung ML-3561ND**

Godown	Quantity: Actual	Quantity: Billed	Pre-Close Quantity	Rate	per	Disc. %	Amount
Tracking No. : 2		*Order No.*: 12		*Due on* 1-Jan-2010			
Main Location	3 Pcs	3 Pcs	1 Pcs	38,500.00	Pcs		1,15,500.00
Reason for Pre-Close		Orde for 2 Pcs Cancelled					
	3 Pcs	3 Pcs	1 Pcs				1,15,500.00

F-5A: Pre Closing of Order

Consequently, at Item Allocation screen, a new Column Pre Close Quantity appears (F-5A). At the Item Allocation screen of the Item for which Order to be cancelled, enter as follows:

- **Pre Closure Quantity:** At *Pre Close Quantity Column*, enter the Quantity to be reduced from the Balance Order.
- **Reason:** At *Reason for Pre Closure*, enter the Reason.

The Balance of Order for the Item gets reduced by the specified Pre Closure Quantity.

FAQ: Frequently Asked Questions

FAQ-1: What is the process of Order Execution?

Ans: Order Execution means transaction of goods as per Order (Order Fufilment). After issue of Order, the Order is executed. The vendor supplies the goods against their Sales Order and the buyer receives the goods against their Purchase Orders. So when the goods are received / delivered, the Delivery / Receipt Note or the Sales / Purchase Invoice are to be created by the Buyer / Seller, against the respective Order.

At Challans / Invoices entry, select the respective Order Number, to carry the Item details from the selected Orders and link the current challan / Ivoice being created with the respective Orders, as described below:

Sales Order Execution

- Create Delivery Note linking with the respective Sales Order
- Create Sales Invoice linking with the respective Sales Order

Purchase Order Execution

- Create Receipt Note linking with the respective Purchase Order
- Create Purchase linking with the respective Purchase Order

Order Reports

Having created the Orders, you may print various reports related to Orders and its Status, as described next.

01 Orders Books

Order Book shows the chronological list of Orders for a specified period. Select *Display > Inventory Books* to get *Inventory Books* Menu (F-5A).

The Inventory Book Menu contains Order Reports while Outstanding Order Reports are placed under Outstanding menu discussed in next chapter.

01.01 Sales Orders Book

Sales Order book shows the chronological list of Sales Orders for a specified period. At *Inventory Books* Menu (F-5A), select *Sale Orders Books* to get *Sales Orders Book Display (F-1A)*

01.02 Purchase Orders Book

Purchase Order book shows the chronological list of Purchase Orders for a specified period. At *Inventory Books* Menu (F-5A), *select Purchase Orders Book.* to get *Purchase Orders Book Display (F-3A)*

01.03 Order Book Configuration

At Purchase / Sales Order Book (F-1A, F-3A), click *F12: Configure* to get *Order Book Configuration screen* (F-2A). At *Order Book Configuration screen* (F-2A), set as follows:

- **Columnar Register**: At *Show Columnar Register*, set *Yes* to get Columnar Register Definition screen to set up columns & contents of Columnar Register, as described earlier

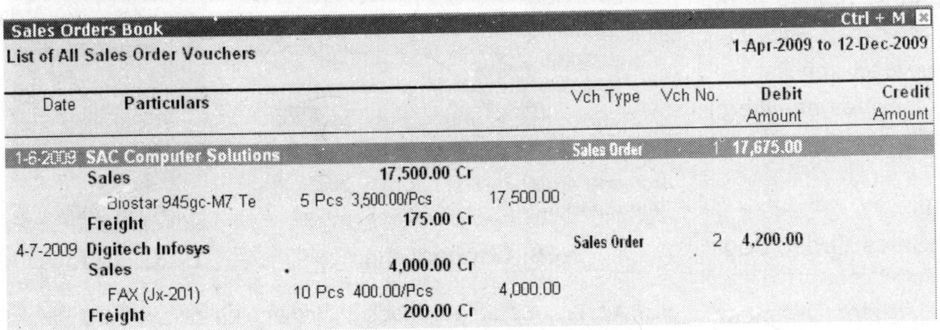

F-1A: Sales Order Book

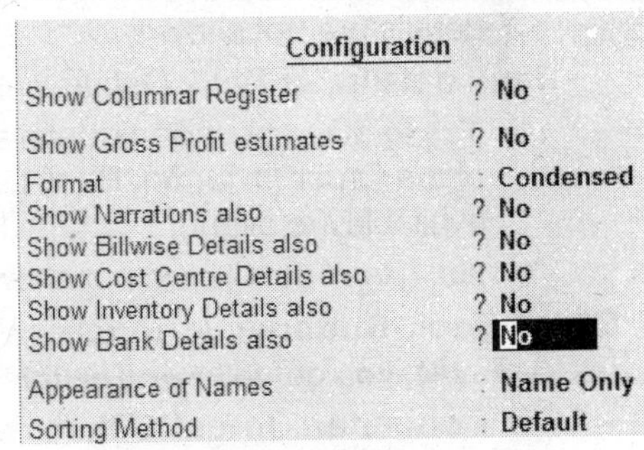

F-2A: Order Book Configuration

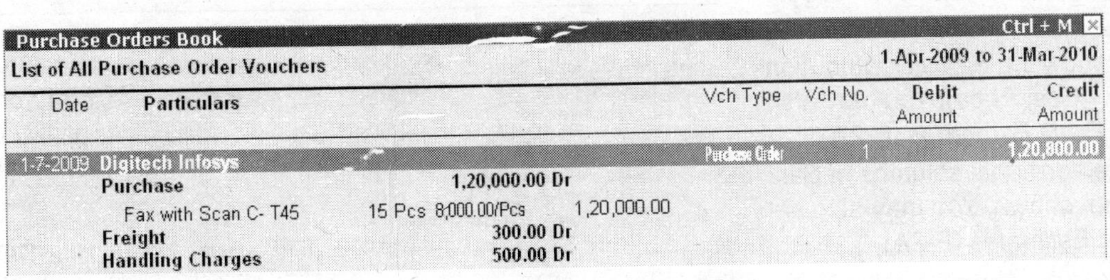

F-3A: Purchase Order Book

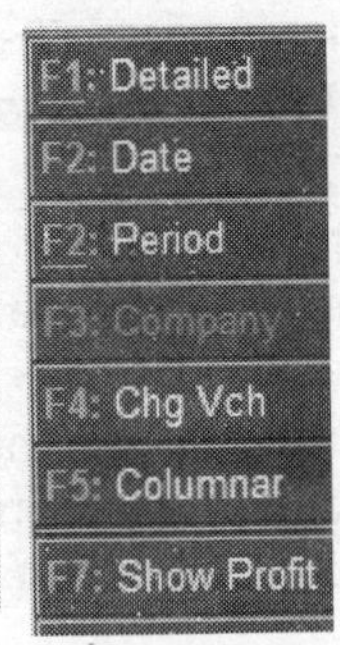

F-4A: Buttons F-5A: Inventory Books Menu

- **Sales Contribution**: At *Show Gross Profit Estimates*, set:
  - o *Yes* to display the profitability of the selected Sales Order (or click *F7: Show Profit* button)
  - o *No*. The columns for profitability are not shown (or click *F7: Hide Profit* button)

This option is available only at Sales Order Book (not available at Purchase Order Book)

- **Format:** At *Format*, select:
    - o *Detailed* to get all the Accounts details
    - o *Condensed* to get the Party Account and the net Order value
- **Voucher Narration:** At *Show Narration also*, set
    - o *Yes* to also show Voucher Narration the Order, if any
    - o *No*. Voucher Narration is not shown
- **Bill Details:** At *Bill Details also*, set
    - o *Yes* to show Bill Details the Order also, if any (in Order, Bill Details are normally not available / relevant)
    - o *No*. Bill Details is not shown
- **Cost Details:** At *Cost Centre Details also*, set
    - o *Yes* to also show Cost Centre Details the Order, if any (in Order, Cost Centre Details are normally not available / relevant)
    - o *No*. Bill Details is not shown
- **Inventory details:** At *Show Inventory details also*, set
    - o *Yes* to also show the Item details of the Order
    - o *No* to get only the Ledger Accounts details (Item details are not shown)
- **Bank details:** At *Bank Details details also*, set
    - o *Yes* to also show Bank details (Cheque details etc) of the Order (in Order, Bank Details are normally not available / relevant)
    - o *No*. (Bank details are not shown)

Order Book Buttons: At Purchase / Sales Order Book (F-1A, F-3A), you get following Buttons:

- **F5: Columnar**: To get Columnar Register Definition screen to set up columns & contents of Columnar Register, as described earlier. You may also set Yes at Show Columnar Register (F-2A)
- **F7: Profitability**: At *F7:Show Profit /Hide Profit*, toggle button:
    - o Click, *F7:Show Profit* to show the Sales Contribution of the Item (Sales Price – Cost Price). You may also set *Yes* at *Show Gross Profit Estimates* (F-2A)
    - o Click, *F7:Hide Profit*. The additional columns of Sale Value Gross Profit are not shown, You may also set *No* at *Show Gross Profit Estimates* (F-2A)

02 Orders Statement

The *All Orders* options of Order Outstanding (F-1B/04-04) shows Order Statement showing details of Sales / Purchase Order in various contents & formats..

At *Sales Order Outstanding Menu* (*GoT>Display>Sales Order*), select *All Orders* to get *Sales Orders Details* Statement (F-6A)

Order Details — Ctrl + M

Sales Orders(Due Only) — 1-Apr-2009 to 31-Mar-2010

Date	Order Number	Name of Item	Ordered Quantity	Balance Quantity	Rate (Disc %)	Value	Due on (overdue)
Sales Orders Outstanding:							
1-Apr-2009	1	Desktop Server	1 Pcs	1 Pcs	2,000.00	2,000.00	1-Apr-2009
		From: Desire Infotech					(364 days)
	1-Apr-2009 Sales Order	1 Pcs					
4-Jul-2009	08	FAX (Jx-201)	10 Pcs	10 Pcs	400.00	4,000.00	7-Jul-2009
		From: Digitech Infosys					(267 days)
	4-Jul-2009 Sales Order	10 Pcs					
			11 Pcs	11 Pcs		6,000.00	

F-6A: Sales Order Details (Due Orders)

Configuration

Show Outstanding Sales Orders	? Yes
Show Cleared Sales Orders	? No
Show Goods delivered but Orders not Recd.	? No
Show Outstanding Purchase Orders	? No
Show Cleared Purchase Orders	? No
Show Goods received but Orders not sent	? No
Show Pre-Closure order details	? No
Show Reason	? No
Show Pre-Closed orders only	? No
Show Batch Details	? No
Show Location Details	? No
Show using Alternate Units	? No
Show Tail Units of Compound Units	? No
Show Actual and Billed Quantity details	? No
Appearance of Stock Item Names	: Name Only
Appearance of Names	: Name Only
Sorting Method	: Default

F-6B: Configuration

- F1: Condensed
- F2: Period
- F3: Company
- F4: Item
- F5: Ledger
- F6: Purchase
- F7: All Orders
- F6: Age wise
- C: Pre-Close

F-6C: Buttons

Similarly. st *Purchase Order Outstanding Menu* (*GoT>Display>* Purchase *Order* (F-1C/04-04)) select *All Orders* to get *Purchase Orders Details* Statement (F-7A).

Order Details — Ctrl + M

Purchase Orders(Due Only) — 1-Apr-2009 to 31-Mar-2010

Date	Order Number	Name of Item	Ordered Quantity	Balance Quantity	Rate (Disc %)	Value	Due on (overdue)
Purchase Orders Outstanding:							
9-Sep-2009	08	Intel BLKDG45SG P45 X-Fire/DDR3/S/V		1 Pcs	1,670.00	1,636.60	10-Oct-2009
		To: G.S. Computers			(2 %)		(172 days)
1-Nov-2009	PO/0001	Keyboard 544	3 Pcs	3 Pcs	1,500.00	4,500.00	26-Nov-2009
		To: Digitech Infosys					(125 days)
3-Nov-2009	PO/0002	Monitor LCD 18.5	2 Pcs	2 Pcs	4,000.00	8,000.00	25-Nov-2009
		To: Digitech Infosys					(126 days)
12-Dec-2009	12	HD 250 Gb Seagate Barracuda SATA	5 Pcs	5 Pcs	4,129.37	20,646.85	26-Jan-2010
		To: Desire Infotech					(64 days)
			10 Pcs	11 Pcs		34,783.45	
Goods received but Orders not Sent :							
15-Sep-2009	08	Biostar 945gc-M7 Te		(-)2 Pcs	1,670.00	(-)3,273.20	10-Oct-2009
		To: G.S. Computers			(2 %)		(172 days)
				(-)2 Pcs		(-)3,273.20	

F-7A: Purchase Order Details (Due, Pending)

02.01 Orders Statement Configuration

At *Orders Details* (F-6A, F-7A), click *F12:Configure* to get *Orders Details Configuration* (F-6B), to set the following options:

Order Details — Ctrl + M

Purchase Orders(Due Only) — 1-Apr-2009 to 31-Mar-2010

Date	Order Number	Name of Item	Ordered Quantity	Balance Quantity	Rate (Disc %)	Value	Due on (overdue)
Purchase Orders Outstanding:							
9-Sep-2009	08	Intel BLKDG45SG P45 X-Fire/DDR33/S/V		1 Pcs	1,670.00	1,636.60	10-Oct-2009
		To: G.S. Computers			(2 %)		(172 days)
1-Nov-2009	PO/0001	Keyboard 544	3 Pcs	3 Pcs	1,500.00	4,500.00	26-Nov-2009
		To: Digitech Infosys					(125 days)
3-Nov-2009	PO/0002	Monitor LCD 18.5	2 Pcs	2 Pcs	4,000.00	8,000.00	25-Nov-2009
		To: Digitech Infosys					(126 days)
12-Dec-2009	12	HD 250 Gb Seagate Barracuda SATA	5 Pcs	5 Pcs	4,129.37	20,646.85	26-Jan-2010
		To: Desire Infotech					(64 days)
			10 Pcs	11 Pcs		34,783.45	
Purchase Orders Cleared :							
1-Jul-2009	17	Fax with Scan C. T45	15 Pcs		8,000.00	1,20,000.00	10 Jul 2009
		To: Digitech Infosys					
2-Jul-2009	PO/01	Biostar 945gc-M7 Te	1 Pcs		3,000.00	3,000.00	20-Jul-2009
		To: Digitech Infosys					
3-Jul-2009	PO/02	CCTV (Panasonic ,Yoko,Avancar)	1 Pcs		5,000.00	5,000.00	25-Jul-2009
		To: Digitech Infosys					
4-Jul-2009	PO/3	HD 250 Gb Seagate Barracuda SATA	1 Pcs		780.00	780.00	25-Jul-2009
		To: Digitech Infosys					
9-Sep-2009	08	Asus P5KPL SE G31 V/PCI-E/S/L/1333FSB			1,000.00	(-)1,000.00	10-Oct-2009
		To: G.S. Computers					
			18 Pcs			1,27,780.00	

F-7B: Purchase Order Details (Due, Executed)

Order Details — Ctrl + M

Order Analysis(Due Only) — 1-Apr-2009 to 31-Mar-2010

Date	Order Number	Name of Item	Ordered Quantity	Balance Quantity	Rate (Disc %)	Value	Due on (overdue)
Sales Orders Outstanding:							
1-Apr-2009	1	Desktop Server	1 Pcs	1 Pcs	2,000.00	2,000.00	1-Apr-2009
		From: Desire Infotech					(364 days)
4-Jul-2009	08	FAX (Jx-201)	10 Pcs	10 Pcs	400.00	4,000.00	7-Jul-2009
		From: Digitech Infosys					(267 days)
			11 Pcs	11 Pcs		6,000.00	
Purchase Orders Outstanding:							
9-Sep-2009	08	Intel BLKDG45SG P45 X-Fire/DDR33/S/V		1 Pcs	1,670.00	1,636.60	10-Oct-2009
		To: G.S. Computers			(2 %)		(172 days)
1-Nov-2009	PO/0001	Keyboard 544	3 Pcs	3 Pcs	1,500.00	4,500.00	26-Nov-2009
		To: Digitech Infosys					(125 days)
3-Nov-2009	PO/0002	Monitor LCD 18.5	2 Pcs	2 Pcs	4,000.00	8,000.00	25-Nov-2009
		To: Digitech Infosys					(126 days)
12-Dec-2009	12	HD 250 Gb Seagate Barracuda SATA	5 Pcs	5 Pcs	4,129.37	20,646.85	26-Jan-2010
		To: Desire Infotech					(64 days)
			10 Pcs	11 Pcs		34,783.45	

F-7C: Order Details (Sales & Purchase – Due)

- **Outstanding Sales Orders**: At *Show Outstanding Sales Orders*, set:
    - o *Yes* to show Outstanding Sales Orders (Orders which have not been fully *executed*)
    - o *No.* Unexecuted Orders are not shown
- **Cleared Sales Orders**: At *Show Cleared Sales Orders*, set:
    - o *Yes* to show Cleared Sales Orders (Orders which are fully *executed*)
    - o *No.* Fully executed Orders are not shown
- **Unordered Delivery Notes**: At *Goods Delivered but Order Not Received*, set
    - o Yes to show Items details of Delivery Notes, which has not been linked with any Sales Order
    - o No. The Unordered Items details of Delivery Notes are not shown
- **Outstanding Purchase Orders**: At *Show Outstanding Purchase Orders*, set:
    - o *Yes* to show Outstanding Purchase Orders (Purchase Orders which have not been fully *executed*)
    - o *No.* Unexecuted Purchase Orders are not shown
- **Cleared Purchase Orders**: At *Show Cleared Purchase Orders*, set:
    - o *Yes* to show Cleared Purchase Orders (Purchase Orders which are fully *executed*)
    - o *No.* Fully executed Purchase Orders are not shown
- **Unordered Receipt Notes**: At *Goods Received but Order Not sent*, set,
    - o Yes to show Items details of Receipt Notes, which has not been linked with any Purchase Order
    - o *No.* The Unordered Items details of Receipt Notes are not shown
- **Pre Closing of Order:** At *Show Pre Closure Order Details*, set
    - o *Yes* to enter Pre Closure Order Details at Item Allocation screen
    - o *No.* The Pre Closure details entry column do not appear
        - ▪ **Pre Closure Reason**: Having Set Yes at *Show Pre Closure Order Details* as above, at *Show Reason*, you may further set:
- Yes to get a field *Reason for Pre Close* to enter Pre Closure Reason
- No. The field *Reason for Pre Close* dos not appear
- **Pre Closure Order Details:** At *Show Pre Closed Orders only*, set:
    - o *Yes* to show the Item details of Orders for which Pre Closure have been entered
    - o *No.* The Item details for which Pre Closure have been entered are not shown

You may further set the following options if the respective features are activated

- **Batch Details:** This is applicable only when Batch is activated for the Company. At *Show Batch Details*, set:
    - o Yes to further show the Batch Details of the Items shown in the Report
    - o *No.* Batch Details of Items are not shown
- **Godown Details:** This is applicable only when Godown is activated for the Company. At *Show Location Details*, set:
    - o Yes to further show the Godown Details of the Items shown in the Report
    - o *No.* Godown Details of Items are not shown
- **Alternate Unit Quantity**: This is applicable only when Alternate UoM is set for the Stock Items. At *Show Using Alternate Units*, set:
    - o Yes to further show the Quantity in Alternate Units also (where applicable) of the Items shown in the Report

   - o *No.* Alternate Quantity of Items is not shown
- **Tail Unit Quantity**: This is applicable only when Compound Unit is set up for the Items. At *Show Tail Unit of Compound Units*, set:
   - o Yes to further show the Quantity in Tail Units of Compound Unit also (where applicable) of the Items shown in the Report
   - o *No.* Alternate Quantity of Items is not shown
- **Actual & Billed Quantity**: This is relevant only when Different *Actual & Billed Quantity* is activated for the Company. At *Show Actual & Billed Quantity Details*, set:
   - o Yes to further show the Quantity in Tail units of Compound Unit (where applicable) of the Items shown in the Report
   - o *No.* Quantity in Tail units of Compound Unit of Items is not shown

02.02 Orders Details Buttons

At *Orders Details* (F-6A, F-7A), you get the following Buttons at button bar (F-6C):

- **Voucher Type:** Click *F6:Purchase / F6:Purchase* Toggle Button,
   - o *F6:Sales* Toggle Button to get Sales Order Details
   - o *F6:Purchase* Toggle Button to get Purchase Order Details
- **Order Status:** Click *F7:All Orders / F7:Due Only* Toggle Button,
   - o *F7:All Orders* Toggle Button to show All Order Details (Executed & Outstanding)
   - o *F7:Due Only* Toggle Button to Show only Due Order Details
- **Ageing Analysis Method:** Click *F6:Agewise* to select Ageing Method from the List (F-8B):
   - o Ageing by Voucher Date: Select *Ageing by Bill Date* to set Ageing Slab to show Age Analysis of Due Orders as per Order Date
   - o Ageing by Due Date: Select *Ageing by Due Date* to set Ageing Slab to show Age Analysis of Due Orders as per Order Due Date
- **Order Pre Closure:** Click *C:Pre Close* to get Pre Closure screen to enter Order Pre Closure Details, as explained next.

03 Outstanding Order Ageing

Like Bills / Batch, you may set the Age Slab of Orders to get Ageing Analysis of Outstanding Orders

At *Orders Statement* screen (F-6A, F-7A), Click *F6:Agewise* Button to get *Age Analysis Method* selection screen (F-8B). At *Age Analysis Method* selection screen (F-8B). select the Method from the list to get *Age Analysis Slab Set Up* screen (F-8C). At *Age Analysis Slab Set Up* screen (F-8C), set the Age Slabs to get Orders Age Analysis Report (F-8A) as per Ageing Slab set up

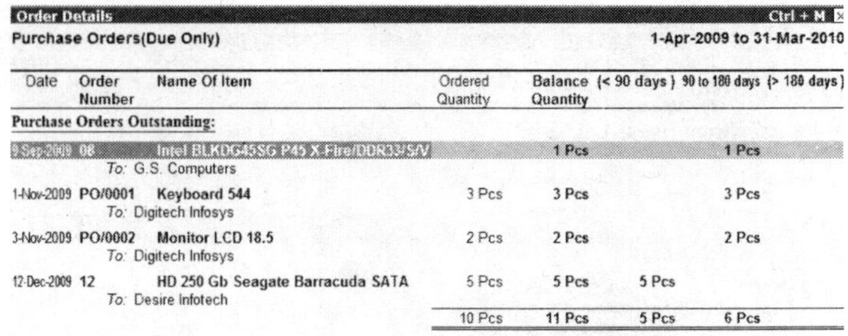

F-8B: Age Analysis Method

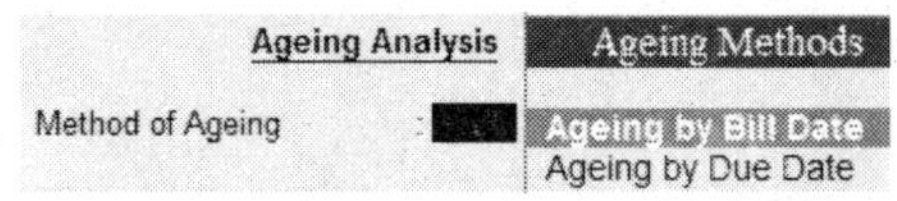

F-8A: Purchase Order Ageing Report

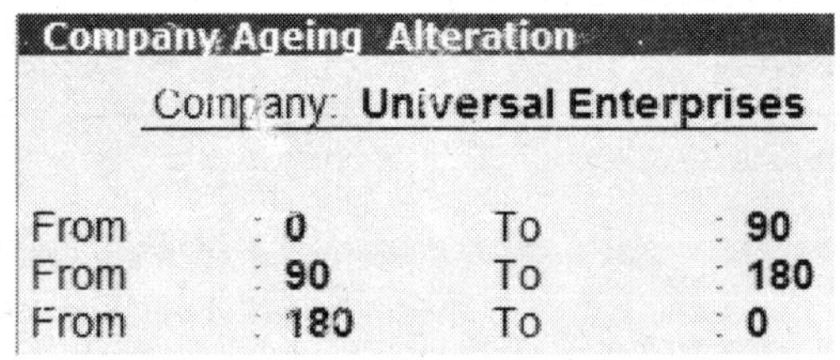

F-8C: Age Analysis Slab

FAQ: Frequently Asked Questions

FAQ-1: What is Outstanding Order Ageing Report? How I can print various Outstanding Purchase Order Reports

Ans: Order Outstanding Report: Order Outstanding Report is a list of Open Orders (in sequence of Date, Party, Item etc), used by Clerical staff, normally for tracking and regular accounting work of Order Processing.

Outstanding Order Ageing Report: Outstanding Order Ageing Report is a statement of Open Orders in which the Orders are segregated according to Age of the Order (or Overdue time of Order). This report is extremely helpful for intense tracking of Pending Orders and follow up

Orders Ageing Slabs Set Up: At *Orders Statement* screen (F-6A / F-7A), Click *F6:Agewise* Button to get *Age Analysis Method* selection screen (F-8B). At *Age Analysis Method* selection screen (F-8B). select the Method from the list to get *Age Analysis Slab Set Up* screen (F-8C). At *Age Analysis Slab Set Up* screen (F-8C), set the Age Slabs

Orders Outstanding Ageing Display: On setting the Age Slab, you to get Orders Age Analysis Report (F-8A) as per Ageing Slab set up

Order Outstanding

In previous chapter, we have discussed various Order reports. Here we discuss exclusively about Open Orders (Orders which have not yet been fully executed) for intense tracking of pending orders.

01 Order Outstanding

Order Outstanding Reports show the Open Order Statement (Orders which has not been fully executed) for:

- Sales Order Outstanding
- Purchase Order Outstanding

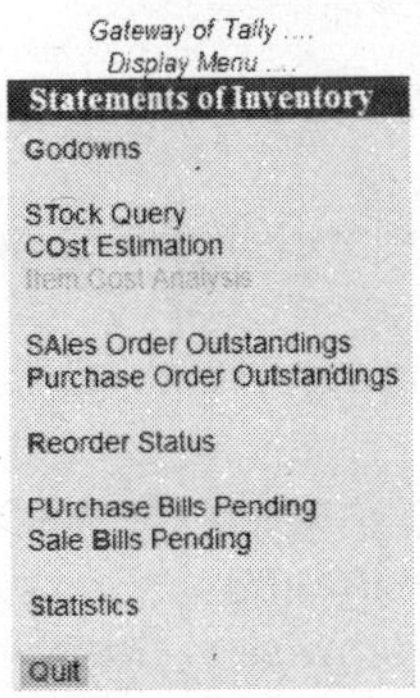

F-1A: Statement Inventory Menu

F-1B: Sales Order OutstandingMenu

F-1C: Purchase of Order Outstanding Menu

At Gateway of Tally, select *Display> Statement of Inventory* to get *Statement of Inventory* Menu (F-1A). At *Statement of Inventory* Menu (F-1A), select:

- *Sales Order Outstanding* to get *Sales Order Outstanding Menu*, (F-1B)
- *Purchase Order Outstanding* to get *Purchase Order Outstanding Menu*, (F-1C)

02 Stock Group Sales Order Outstanding

At *Sales Order Outstanding Menu* (F-1B), select *Stock Group* and then select a *Stock Group* (or select *Primary* for Reports of all Primary Stock Groups) to get *Stock Group Sales Order Outstanding* report for selected Stock Group (F-2A).

02.01 Stock Group Sales Order Outstanding Configuration

At *Stock Group Sales Order Outstanding* (F-2A), click *F12:Configure* to get *Stock Group Sales Order Outstanding Configuration* (F-2B), to set the options as follows:

Common Options for sections: The following options apply to the activated column sections (Opening Orders / Orders Booked / Orders Cleared / Pending Orders).

- **Item Quantity**: At *Show Quantities* (at *F1:Detailed* Format):

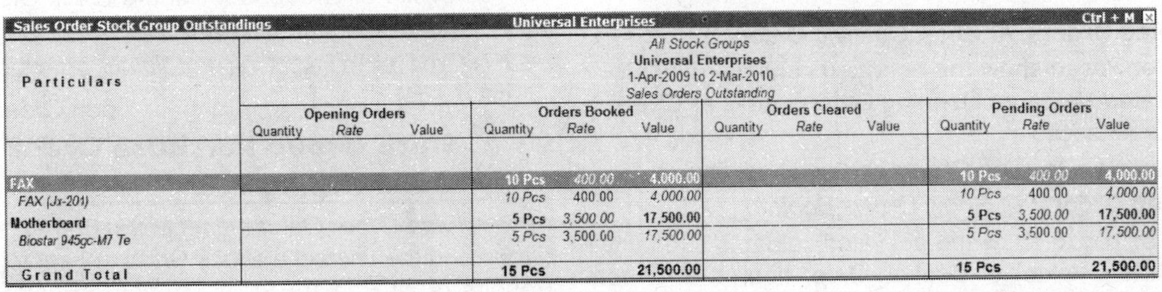
Sales Order Stock Group Outstandings — Universal Enterprises — Ctrl + M

All Stock Groups
Universal Enterprises
1-Apr-2009 to 2-Mar-2010
Sales Orders Outstanding

Particulars	Opening Orders			Orders Booked			Orders Cleared			Pending Orders		
	Quantity	Rate	Value	Quantity	Rate	Value	Quantity	Rate	Value	Quantity	Rate	Value
FAX				10 Pcs	400.00	4,000.00				10 Pcs	400.00	4,000.00
FAX (Jx-201)				10 Pcs	400.00	4,000.00				10 Pcs	400.00	4,000.00
Motherboard				5 Pcs	3,500.00	17,500.00				5 Pcs	3,500.00	17,500.00
Biostar 945gc-M7 Te				5 Pcs	3,500.00	17,500.00				5 Pcs	3,500.00	17,500.00
Grand Total				15 Pcs		21,500.00				15 Pcs		21,500.00

F-2A: Stock Group Sales Order Outstanding

F-2D: Order Type selection

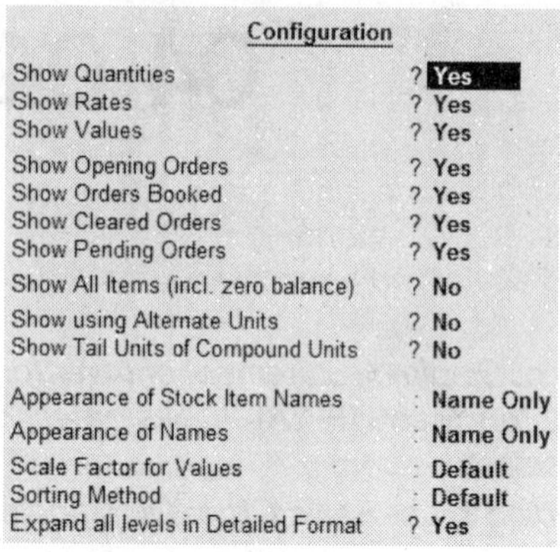

F-2B: Order Outstanding Configuration

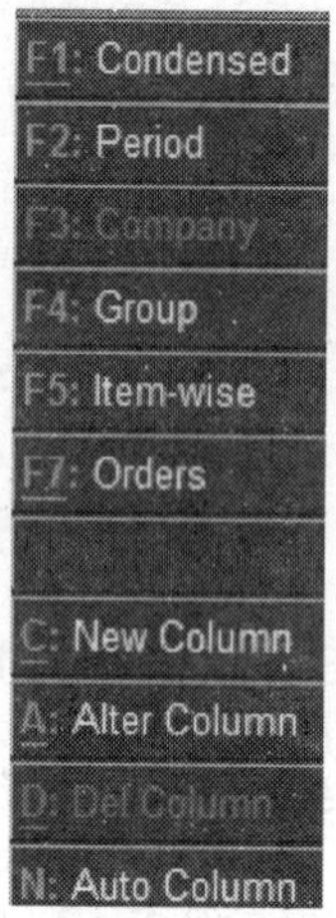

F-2C: Order Outstanding Buttons

- Set *Yes* to show Quantity of Items (at Quantity column) of Sales Order,
- Set *No* Quantity column is not shown

- **Item Rates**: At *Show Rates* (at *F1:Detailed* Format):
  - Set *Yes* to show Rate of Items (at Rate column) of Sales Order
  - Set *No* Rate column is not shown
- **Item Value**: At *Show Value* (at *F1:Detailed* Format):
  - Set *Yes* to show Value of Items (at Rate column) of Sales Order
  - Set *No.* Value column is not shown

Quantity, Rate & Value details are not shown in Condensed Format (when *F1:Condensed* Button is clicked)

Column section Activation: Set the option for respective section. You must activate (set *Yes*) at least one of the following sections (Pending Orders section get activated by default).

- **Opening Orders**: At *Show Opening Orders*,
  - Set *Yes* to show the activated columns (Quantity / Rate / Value) of Opening Order figures at *Opening Order* section
  - Set *No. Opening Orders* section is not shown.
- **Booked Orders:** At *Show Orders Booked*,
  - Set *Yes* to show the activated columns (Quantity / Rate / Value) of Booked Order figures at *Orders Booked* section
  - Set *No. Order Booked* section is not shown.
- **Executed Orders:** At *Show Cleared Orders*,
  - Set *Yes* to show the activated columns (Quantity / Rate / Value) of Executed Order figures at *Cleared Orders* section
  - Set *No. Cleared Orders* section is not shown.
- **Pending Orders:** At *Show Pending Orders*,
  - Set *Yes* to show the activated columns (Quantity / Rate / Value) of Executed Order figures at *Pending Orders* section
  - Set *No. Pending Orders* section is not shown.
- **All Item Details**: At *Show All Items (incl zero balance)*,
  - Set *Yes* to show the details of all orders booked even if the order has been fully executed (zero pending order)
  - Set *No.* Particulars of fully exerted orders (No Pending Order) are not shown

02.02 Stock Group Sales Order Outstanding Buttons

At Stock Group Sales Order Outstanding, you get the following buttons (F-2C),

- **F1:Detailed / Condensed**: At *F1:Detailed / Condensed* toggle button:
  - Click *F1:Detailed* to show next level Item / Group Details
  - Click *F1:Condensed* to show top level Item / Group Details
- **F4: Group**: To select an Item Group from the list of Groups (select *Primary* for All Stock Groups)
- **F5: Itemwise / Grouped**: At *F5: Itemwise / Grouped*, toggle button
  - Click *F5: Itemwise* to list the Items I alphabetical order
  - Click *F5: Grouped* to list the Stock Groups / Stock Items in hierarchical order
- **F7: Orders**: To select *Type of Values* from the Order Type list (F-2D).

03 Stock Group Purchase Order Outstanding

At *Purchase Order Outstanding Menu* (F-1C), select *Stock Group* and then select a *Stock Group* (or select *Primary* for Reports of all Primary Stock Groups) to get *Stock Group Purchase Order Outstanding* report (F-3A) for selected Stock Group.

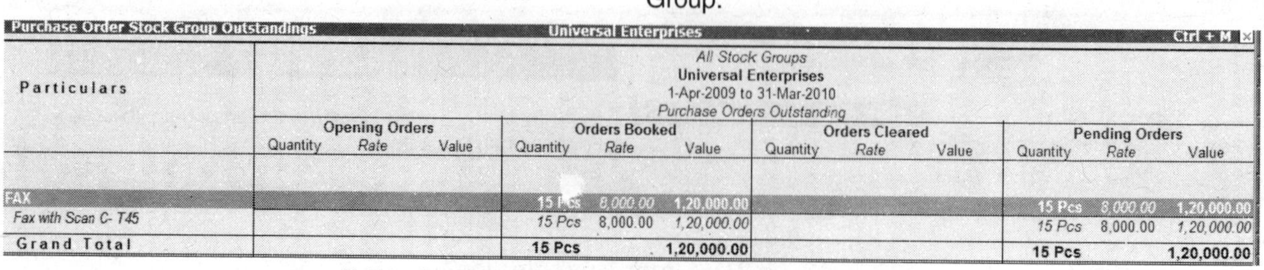

Purchase Order Stock Group Outstandings — Universal Enterprises — Ctrl + M

All Stock Groups
Universal Enterprises
1-Apr-2009 to 31-Mar-2010
Purchase Orders Outstanding

Particulars	Opening Orders			Orders Booked			Orders Cleared			Pending Orders		
	Quantity	Rate	Value	Quantity	Rate	Value	Quantity	Rate	Value	Quantity	Rate	Value
FAX				15 Pcs	8,000.00	1,20,000.00				15 Pcs	8,000.00	1,20,000.00
Fax with Scan C- T45				*15 Pcs*	8,000.00	*1,20,000.00*				*15 Pcs*	8,000.00	*1,20,000.00*
Grand Total				**15 Pcs**		**1,20,000.00**				**15 Pcs**		**1,20,000.00**

F-3A: Stock Group Purchase Order Outstanding

- **Stock Group Purchase Order Outstanding Configuration**: At Stock Group Purchase Order Outstanding (F-3A), Click *F12:Configure* to get *Stock Group Purchase Order Outstanding* Configuration, similar to *Stock Group Sales Order Outstanding* Configuration (§02.01, F-2B).
- **Stock Group Purchase Order Outstanding Buttons:** At *Stock Group Purchase Order Outstanding* (F-3A), you get he buttons to that of *Stock Group Sales Order Outstanding* (§02.02, F-2C).

04 Stock Category Sales Order Outstanding

At *Sales Order Outstanding Menu* (F-1B), select *Stock Category* and then select a *Stock Category* (or select *Primary* for Reports of all Primary Stock Category) to get *Stock Category Sales Order Outstanding* report (F-4A) for selected Stock Category.

buttons similar to *Stock Group Outstanding* (§02.02, F-2C).

05 Stock Category Purchase Order Outstanding

At *Purchase Order Outstanding Menu* (F-1C), select *Stock Category* and then select a *Stock Category* (or select *Primary* for Reports of all Primary Stock Category) to get *Stock Category Purchase Order Outstanding* report (F-5A) for selected Stock Category.

- **Stock Category Purchase Order Outstanding Configuration**: At *Stock Category Purchase Order* Outstanding (F-5A), Click *F12:Configure* to get *Stock Category Purchase Order Outstanding* Configuration similar to Stock Group Sales Order Outstanding (§02.01, F-2B).
- **Stock Category Purchase Order Outstanding Buttons:** At *Stock Category Purchase Order* Outstanding (F-5A), you get buttons similar to Stock Group Outstanding (§02.02, F-2C).

Sales Order Stock Category Outstandings — Universal Enterprises — Ctrl + M

All Stock Categories
Universal Enterprises
1-Apr-2009 to 2-Mar-2010
Sales Orders Outstanding

Particulars	Opening Orders			Orders Booked			Orders Cleared			Pending Orders		
	Quantity	Rate	Value	Quantity	Rate	Value	Quantity	Rate	Value	Quantity	Rate	Value
Biostar				5 Pcs	3,500.00	17,500.00				5 Pcs	3,500.00	17,500.00
Biostar 945gc-M7 Te				*5 Pcs*	3,500.00	*17,500.00*				*5 Pcs*	3,500.00	*17,500.00*
Canon				**10 Pcs**	*400.00*	**4,000.00**				**10 Pcs**	*400.00*	**4,000.00**
FAX (Jx-201)				*10 Pcs*	400.00	*4,000.00*				*10 Pcs*	400.00	*4,000.00*
Grand Total				**15 Pcs**		**21,500.00**				**15 Pcs**		**21,500.00**

F-4A: Stock Category Sales Order Outstanding

Purchase Order Stock Category Outstandings — Universal Enterprises — Ctrl + M

All Stock Categories
Universal Enterprises
1-Apr-2009 to 2-Mar-2010
Purchase Orders Outstanding

Particulars	Opening Orders			Orders Booked			Orders Cleared			Pending Orders		
	Quantity	Rate	Value	Quantity	Rate	Value	Quantity	Rate	Value	Quantity	Rate	Value
Canon				15 Pcs	8,000.00	1,20,000.00				15 Pcs	8,000.00	1,20,000.00
Fax with Scan C- T45				*15 Pcs*	8,000.00	*1,20,000.00*				*15 Pcs*	8,000.00	*1,20,000.00*
Grand Total				**15 Pcs**		**1,20,000.00**				**15 Pcs**		**1,20,000.00**

F-5A: Stock Category Purchase Order Outstanding

- **Stock Category Sales Order Outstanding Configuration**: At *Stock Category Sales Order Outstanding* (F-4A), Click *F12:Configure* to get *Stock Category Sales Order Outstanding* Configuration similar to *Stock Group Sales Order Outstanding* (§02.01, F-2B)
- **Stock Category Sales Order Outstanding Buttons:** At *Stock Category Sales Order Outstanding*, you get you get buttons similar to Stock Group Outstanding (§02.02, F-2C).

06 Stock Item Sales Order Outstanding

At *Sales Order Outstanding Menu* (F-1B), select *Stock Item* and then select a *Stock Item* from the list of Stock Items to get *Stock Item Sales Order Outstanding* report for selected Stock Item.

Sales Order Stock Item Outstandings — Universal Enterprises — Ctrl + M

FAX (Jx-201)
Universal Enterprises
1-Apr-2009 to 2-Mar-2010
Sales Orders Outstanding

Particulars	Opening Orders			Orders Booked			Orders Cleared			Pending Orders		
	Quantity	Rate	Value	Quantity	Rate	Value	Quantity	Rate	Value	Quantity	Rate	Value
FAX (Jx-201)				10 Pcs	400.00	4,000.00				10 Pcs	400.00	4,000.00
Grand Total				**10 Pcs**		**4,000.00**				**10 Pcs**		**4,000.00**

F-6A: Stock Item Sales Order Outstanding

- F1: Condensed
- F2: Period
- F3: Company
- F4: Item
- F7: Orders

F-6B: Buttons

Stock Item Sales Order Outstanding Configuration: At Stock Item Sales Order Outstanding (F-6A), Click *F12:Configure* to get *Stock Item Sales Order Outstanding* Configuration, similar to *Stock Group Sales Order Outstanding* (§02.01, F-2B).

Stock Item Sales Order Outstanding Buttons: At *Stock Item Sales Order Outstanding* (F-6A), you get following buttons (F-6B)

- **F4: Item**: To select an Item from the list of Items to show the Stock Item Sales Order Outstanding for the selected Stock Item.

Purchase Order Stock Item OutStandings — Universal Enterprises — Ctrl + M

Fax with Scan C- T45
Universal Enterprises
1-Apr-2009 to 2-Mar-2010
Purchase Orders Outstanding

Particulars	Opening Orders			Orders Booked			Orders Cleared			Pending Orders		
	Quantity	*Rate*	Value	Quantity	*Rate*	Value	Quantity	*Rate*	Value	Quantity	*Rate*	Value
Fax with Scan C- T45				15 Pcs	*8,000.00*	1,20,000.00				15 Pcs	*8,000.00*	1,20,000.00
Grand Total				**15 Pcs**		**1,20,000.00**				**15 Pcs**		**1,20,000.00**

F-7A: Stock Item Sales Order Outstanding

Sales Order Group Outstandings — Universal Enterprises1 — Ctrl + M

Sundry Debtors
Universal Enterprises1
1-Apr-2009 to 31-Mar-2010
Sales Orders Outstanding

Particulars	Opening Orders			Orders Booked			Orders Cleared			Pending Orders		
	Quantity	*Rate*	Value	Quantity	*Rate*	Value	Quantity	*Rate*	Value	Quantity	*Rate*	Value
Desktop Server				1 Pcs	*2,000.00*	2,000.00				1 Pcs	*2,000.00*	2,000.00
Grand Total				**1 Pcs**		**2,000.00**				**1 Pcs**		**2,000.00**

F-8A: Account Group Sales Order Outstanding

F1: Condensed
F2: Period
F3: Company
F4: Group

F-8B: Buttons

- **F7: Orders**: To select type of Values from the list (F-2D).

07 Stock Item Purchase Order Outstanding

At *Purchase Order Outstanding Menu* (F-1C), select *Stock Item* and then select a *Stock Item* from the list of Stock Items to get *Stock Item Purchase Order Outstanding* report (F-7A) for selected Stock Item.

Stock Item Purchase Order Outstanding Configuration: At *Stock Item Purchase Order Outstanding* (F-7A), Click *F12:Configure* to get Stock Item *Stock Item Purchase Order Outstanding Configuration*, similar to Stock Group Sales Order Outstanding (§02.01, F-2B).

Stock Item Sales Order Outstanding Buttons: At *Stock Item Purchase Order Outstanding* (F-7A), you get following buttons (F-6B)

- **F4: Item**: To select an Item from the list of Items to show the Stock Item Sales Order Outstanding for the selected Stock Item.
- **F7: Orders**: To select type of Values from the list (F-2D).

08 Account Group Sales Order Outstanding

It shows all the Sales Order Outstanding related to Parties under the selected Account Group. At *Sales Order Outstanding Menu* (F-1B), select *Group* and then select an Account Group (Sundry Debtor / Creditor / Cash / Bank) to get Account Group *Sales Order Outstanding* report (F-8A) for selected Account Group.

Account Group Sales Order Outstanding Configuration: At Account Group Sales Order Outstanding (F-8A), Click *F12:Configure* to get *Account Group Sales Order Outstanding Configuration*, similar to Stock Group Sales Order Outstanding Configuration (§02.01, F-2B) explained above.

Account Group Sales Order Outstanding Buttons: At Account Group Sales Order Outstanding, you get the following buttons:

- **F4:Group**: To select an Account Group to get Account Group Sales Order Outstanding for the selected Group

09 Account Group Purchase Order Outstanding

It shows all the Sales Order Outstanding related to Parties under the selected Account Group. At *Purchase Order Outstanding Menu* (F-1C), select *Group* and then select an Account Group (Sundry Debtor / Creditor / Cash / Bank) to get Account Group *Purchase Order Outstanding* report (F-9A) for selected Account Group.

Account Group Purchase Order Outstanding Configuration: At Account Group Purchase Order Outstanding (F-9A), Click *F12:Configure* to get *Account Group* Purchase *Order* Outstanding *Configuration*, similar to Stock Group Sales Order Outstanding *Configuration* (§02.01, F-2B) explained above.

Account Group Purchase Order Outstanding Buttons: At Account Group Purchase Order Outstanding, you get the following buttons:

- **F4:Group**: To select an Account Group to get Account Group Purchase Order Outstanding for the selected Group.

10 Account Ledger Sales Order Outstanding

It shows all the Sales Order Outstanding related to selected

Purchase Order Group OutStandings — Universal Enterprises — Ctrl + M

Particulars	Sundry Creditors Universal Enterprises 1-Apr-2009 to 2-Mar-2010 Purchase Orders Outstanding											
	Opening Orders			Orders Booked			Orders Cleared			Pending Orders		
	Quantity	Rate	Value	Quantity	Rate	Value	Quantity	Rate	Value	Quantity	Rate	Value
Fax with Scan C T45				15 Pcs	8,000.00	1,20,000.00				15 Pcs	8,000.00	1,20,000.00
Grand Total				15 Pcs		1,20,000.00				15 Pcs		1,20,000.00

F-9A: Account Group Purchase Order Outstanding

Sales Order Ledger Outstandings — Universal Enterprises1 — Ctrl + M

Particulars	Desire Infotech Universal Enterprises1 1-Apr-2009 to 31-Mar-2010 Sales Orders Outstanding											
	Opening Orders			Orders Booked			Orders Cleared			Pending Orders		
	Quantity	Rate	Value	Quantity	Rate	Value	Quantity	Rate	Value	Quantity	Rate	Value
Desktop Server				1 Pcs	2,000.00	2,000.00				1 Pcs	2,000.00	2,000.00
Grand Total				1 Pcs		2,000.00				1 Pcs		2,000.00

F-10A: Account Ledger Sales Order Outstanding

F1: Detailed
F2: Period
F3: Company
F4: Ledger

F-10B: Buttons

Party. At *Sales Order Outstanding Menu*, select *Ledger* and then select an Account Ledger (Sundry Debtor / Creditor / Cash / Bank) to get Account Ledger *Sales Order Outstanding* report (F-10A) for selected Account Ledger (Party).

Account Ledger Sales Order Outstanding Configuration: At Account Ledger Sales Order Outstanding (F-10A), Click *F12:Configure* to get *Account Ledger Sales Order Outstanding Configuration*, similar to Stock Group Sales Order Outstanding Configuration (§02.01, F-2B) explained above.

Purchase Order Ledger OutStandings — Universal Enterprises — Ctrl + M

Particulars	Digitech Infosys Universal Enterprises 1-Apr-2009 to 2-Mar-2010 Purchase Orders Outstanding											
	Opening Orders			Orders Booked			Orders Cleared			Pending Orders		
	Quantity	Rate	Value	Quantity	Rate	Value	Quantity	Rate	Value	Quantity	Rate	Value
Fax with Scan C- T45				15 Pcs	8,000.00	1,20,000.00				15 Pcs	8,000.00	1,20,000.00
Grand Total				15 Pcs		1,20,000.00				15 Pcs		1,20,000.00

F-11A: Account Ledger Purchase Order Outstanding

Account Ledger Sales Order Outstanding Buttons: At Account Ledger Sales Order Outstanding (F-10A), you get the following buttons:

- **F4:Ledger**: To select a Ledger Account to get Account Ledger Purchase Order Outstanding for the selected Ledger Account.

11 Account Ledger Purchase Order Outstanding

It shows all the Purchase Order Outstanding of selected Party. At *Purchase Order Outstanding Menu* (F-1C), select *Ledger* and then select an Account Ledger (Sundry Debtor / Creditor / Cash / Bank) to get Account Ledger *Purchase Order Outstanding* report (F-11A) for selected Account Ledger (Party)

Account Ledger Purchase Order Outstanding Configuration: At Account Ledger Purchase Order Outstanding (F-11A), Click *F12:Configure* to get *Account Ledger Sales Order Outstanding Configuration*, similar to Stock Group Sales Order Outstanding Configuration (§02.01, F-2B), explained above.

Account Ledger Purchase Order Outstanding Buttons: At Account Ledger Purchase Order Outstanding (F-1A), you get the following buttons:

- **F4:Ledger**: To select a Ledger Account to get Account Ledger Purchase Order Outstanding for the selected Ledger Account (Party)

FAQ: Frequently Asked Questions

FAQ-1: How I can get Open Purchase Orders for a selected Purchase Ledger (we have several Purchase Ledger Accounts for each line of Product, like Raw Materials Purchase, Stores Purchase, Scraps Purchase etc)

Ans. At *Purchase Order Outstanding Menu* (F-1C), select *Ledger* and then select an Account Ledger (Sundry Debtor / Creditor / Cash / Bank) to get Account Ledger *Purchase Order Outstanding* report (F-11A) for selected Account Ledger.

01 Re-Order Level

Re-order level is the pre set Inventory Stock Levels at which replenishment action should be taken. It is plan for Scientific Inventory Management System. The objective is minimum investment in Inventory (minimum Inventory Carrying Cost) avoiding stock-outs.

Re-Order levels are normally set for Stock Control Items like:

- Items which are regularly consumed / Sold
- Items whose sale / consumption trend is predictable
- Items whose non-availability in time may cause loss of Sales/ Production

02 Re-order Level Set Up

The Reorder Level may be set up in 2 ways:

- **Estimated**: The level fixed is based is set on past experience or rough estimate based on normal activity level of the organization (herein referred as *Simple* Re-order Level).
- **Computed:** The level is computed on the basis of consumption and the inventory replenishment period (herein referred as *Advanced* Re-order Level)

At *Gateway of Tally > Inventory Info. > Reorder Levels*, select the Group (or select *All Items*) to get *Specify Re-Order level* screen (F-1A) to enter / alter Re-Order Level for the Items of the selected Group (or All Items). Here you get following Toggle Buttons to set Re-Order Level screen Modes (F-1B):

- **Re-Order Stock Level Entry**: *R: Simple Re-Order / R: Adv. Re-Order* Toggle button. *Re-Order Level* means the stock level at which new order should be placed for replacement of Stock
- **Minimum Quantity Entry**: *M: Simple Min Qty / M Adv. Min Quantity* Toggle button. *Minimum Order Quantity* means the optimum Re-Order quantity to be ordered when the stock reaches the Re-Order Level.

03 Simple Re-Order Level Entry

This is convenient when you know the Re-Order Level & Re-Order Quantity for each Item, upon your own judgment or computation.

To enter Re-Order levels in Simple Mode, click the Toggle button (F-1B):

- *R: Simple Re-Order* to get Re Order Quantity column
- *M: Simple Min Qty* to get Minimum Order Quantity column

Now enter the Re Order Quantity & Minimum Order Quantity as follows:

- **Re Order Quantity**: Enter the Stock Level (Re-Order level) at which new Purchase Order is to be placed (New Purchase Order to be placed when Stock reaches this level)
- **Min Order Quantity**: Enter the Re-Order Quantity (Order Quantity of the new order to be placed, when stock reaches the Re-Order Level)

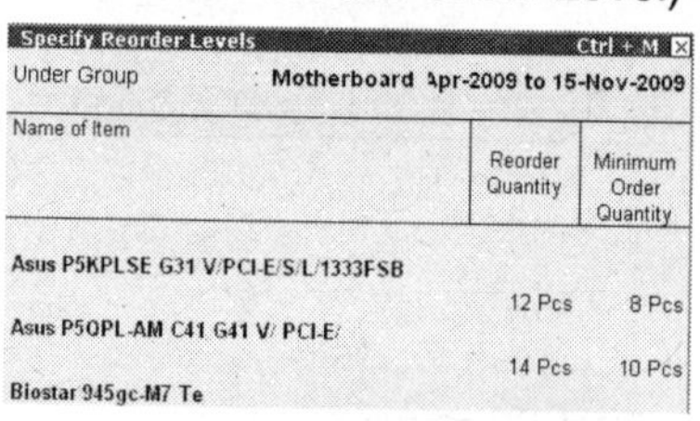

F-1A: Simple Re-Order level Entry

F-1B:Re-Order level Entry buttons

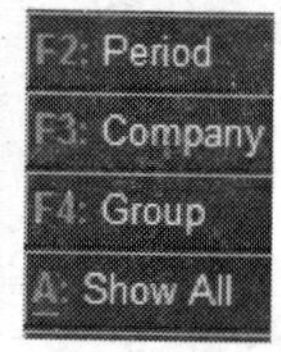

F-1C: Re-Order level Display buttons

Inventory Reorder Status — Universal Enterprises

Items Under : **Motherboard** (all items)

Name of Item	Closing Stock	Purc Orders Pending	Sale Orders Due	Nett Available	Re-order Level	Short fall	Min Reorder Qty	Order to be Placed
Asus P5KPLSE G31 V/PCI-E/S/L/1333FSB	15 Pcs			15 Pcs	*12 Pcs*		*8 Pcs*	
Asus P5QPL-AM C41 G41 V/ PCI-E/	4 Pcs			4 Pcs	*14 Pcs*	10 Pcs	*10 Pcs*	10 Pcs

F-2A: Re-Order Status Report

04 Re-Order Status Report

Having entered Re-Order data (F-1A), select *Display > Statement of Inventory > Reorder Status* and then select the Group (for All Items, select *Primary*) to get Re-Order Status report (F-2A) for all underlying Stock Group / Stock Item for the selected Stock Group.

Drill Down: From *Re Order Status* Report (F-2A), you may drill down from different columns of the Report, to get related detailed reports. You can move cursor sideways to different fields (except for computed figures like *Nett Available*, *Shortfall* or *Order to be placed*) and drill down to respective underlying report (press *Enter* on respective column), as explained below:

- o *A: Show All*: To get the list showing Inventory Re-Order Status of all Items

05 Party-wise Movement of Re-order Item

At *Re-Order Status* Report (F-2A), drill down through any Item to get *Item Movement Analysis* (F-3A) showing Party wise breakup of Sale / Purchase of the Item (Item Movement Analysis has een explained earlier).

Thus Reorder Status Report shows various critical information related to Orders at a central place from where you may get related figures by moving around through various columns to get finer details.

Column	Description	Drill Down
Name of Item:	Shows Name of the Item	Stock Item Movement Analysis (F-3A) showing Name of Suppliers Basic Rate & Effective Rate. You can further drill down to Item Voucher Analysis
Closing Stock	Shows Stock of the Item at the report period end date	Monthly Summary You may further drill down to get Stock Vouchers
Purchase Orders Pending:	Shows Quantity of Pending Purchase Order of the Item at the report period end date	Outstanding Purchase Order Report from where you can further drill down to selected Purchase Order.
Sale Orders Due	Shows Quantity of Pending Sales Order of the Item at the report period end date	Outstanding Sales Order Report from where you can further drill down to selected Sales Order.
Net Available	Shows the quantity for Free Sale (Nett Available = Closing Stock + Order pending – Sales Order Due	
Re Order level	Shows the Re – Order Level as entered	Re Order Level entry for the Item
Shortfall	Shows the Shortfall (Quantity for which further Purchase Order to be placed). Shortfall = Reorder Level - Nett Available where Nett Available is lower than Re Order Level	
Min Re-Order Quantity	Shows the Minimum Re Order Quantity for the Item as entered	Re Order Level entry for the Item
Order to be Placed	Shows the Quantity of Order to be placed based on Re Order Quantity	

04.01 Re Order Level Report Buttons

At *Order Level Report*, you get following Buttons (F-1C):

- **Stock Group:** Click *F4:Group* to select the Stock Group (or select All Items) for which Re-Order Stock Report is to be displayed
- **Re- Order Stock Items:** Click *A: Re-order Only / A: Show All* toggle button as follows:
  - o *A: Re-order Only*: To get the list for only those Items whose stock has gone below the Re-Order level

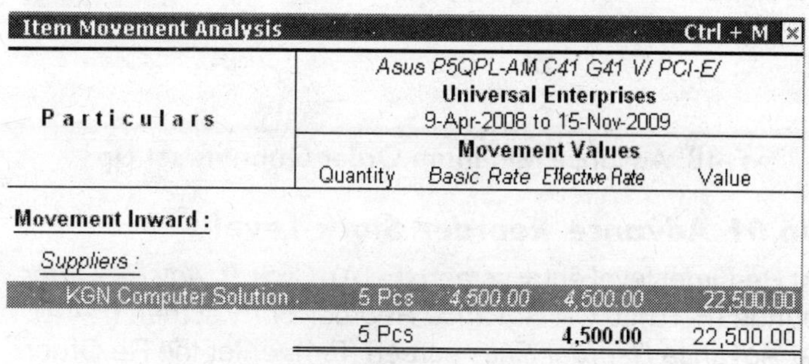
Item Movement Analysis — Ctrl + M

Particulars	Asus P5QPL-AM C41 G41 V/ PCI-E/ Universal Enterprises 9-Apr-2008 to 15-Nov-2009			
	Movement Values			
	Quantity	Basic Rate	Effective Rate	Value
Movement Inward :				
Suppliers :				
KGN Computer Solution	5 Pcs	4,500.00	4,500.00	22,500.00
	5 Pcs		**4,500.00**	22,500.00

F-3A: Item Movement Analysis Report

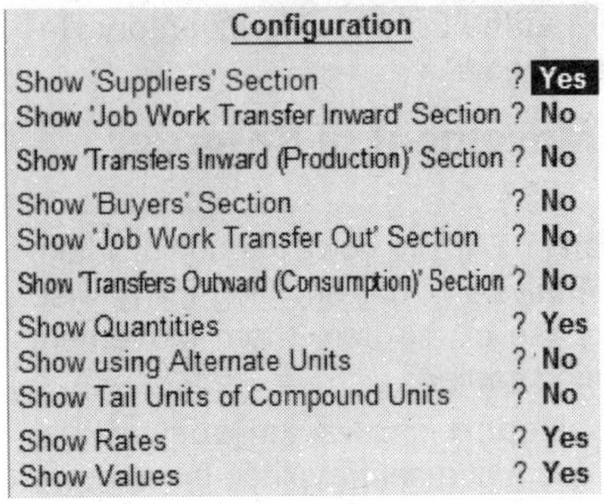

F-3B: Item Movement Analysis Configuration

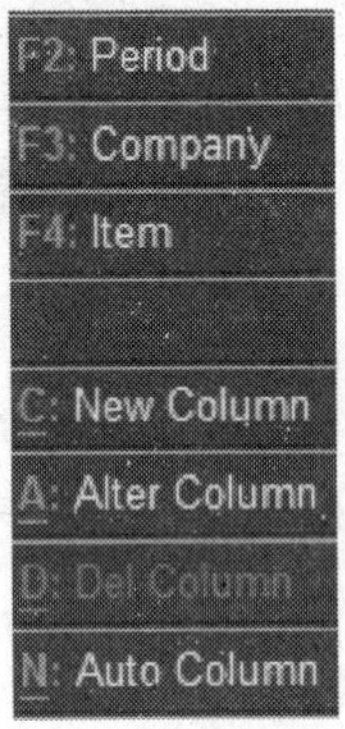

F-3C: Re-Order item Analysis Buttons

06 Advanced Reorder Parameters entry

In simple re-order entry (F-1A), the estimated value of Re-Order Level & Minimum Order Quantity is entered

In advanced mode, instead of making estimates, the values are computed through formula for using scientific Inventory Control methods.

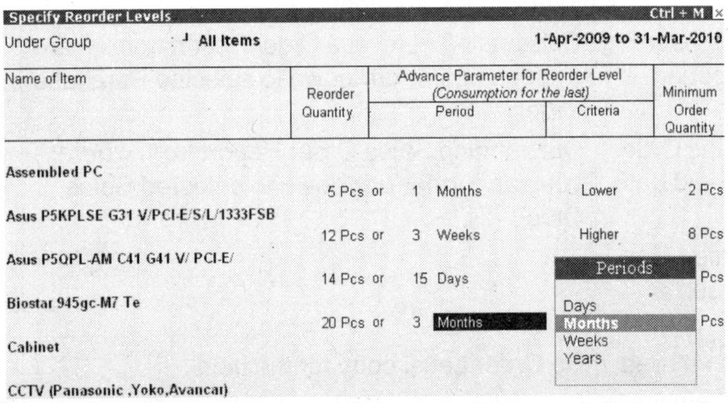

F-4A: Advance Reorder Level parameters entry

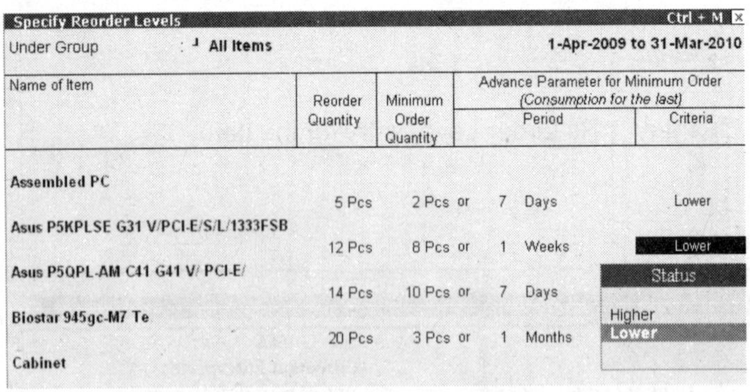

F-4B: Advance Minimum Order Quantity set Up

06.01 Advance Reorder Stock Level

At Re-Order level entry screen (F-1A), Click *R: Adv Re-Order* button (F-1B) to get *Advance Reorder Entry* screen (F-4A). At *Advance Reorder Entry* screen (F-4), enter the Re Order Quantity as follows:

- **Reorder Quantity**: Enter the estimated (maximum / minimum) Re-Order Quantity (this should be according to standard pack size of the Item, if any).
- **Advance Parameters**: Set the following under the section *Advance Parameter for Re-Order level* to compute the alternate value of Re-Order Quantity for more accurate computation based on consumption parameters (in 2 components)
  - o **Period**: At *Period*, Select the period for which stock should be maintained (e.g day, week, month, year)
  - o **Criterion**: At *Criteria*, select the criterion (lower/ higher)

The Re-order level would first be computed as per consumption for the specified period and then subjected to the limit specified at Criteria. For example, Re-Order Quantity, 1000, Consumption – 10 days (@60 per day) and criteria – Higher, The Re order level would be computed as 1000 (higher of 1000 or 10x60). If the criteria is specified as Lower, then the Re order level would be computed as 600 (lower of 1000 or 10x60).

06.02 Advance Minimum Quantity

Minimum Order Quantity means the Optimum Quantity that should be ordered when the stock reaches Re Order level.

At ReOrder Entry screen (F-1A), Click *M:Adv Min Qty* button (F-1B) to set for Advanced Minimum Quantity (F-4B)

- **Minimum Order Quantity**: Enter the estimated Minimum Order Quantity (this should be according to standard pack size of the Item, if any).

  Set the following under the section *Advance Parameter for Minimum Order* to compute the alternate value of Minimum Order Quantity for more accurate computation based on consumption parameters (in 2 components)
  - o **Period**: Select the period for which stock should be maintained (e.g day, week, month, year)
  - o **Criterion**: Select the criterion (lower/ higher)

The Minimum Order Quantity would first be computed as per consumption for the specified period and then subjected to the limit specified at Criteria. For example, Minimum Order Quantity, 500, Consumption – 5 days (@60 per day) and criteria – Higher, The Minimum Order Quantity would be computed as 500 (higher of 500 or 5x60). If the criteria is specified as Lower, then the Minimum Order Quantity would be computed as 300 (lower of 500 or 5x60).

06.03 Combined Advanced Mode Entry

You may also set up Advanced option both for Re Order Level and for Minimum Order Quantity, At Re-Order screen (F-1A), Click both the toggle buttons as follows (F-1B) to get Advance Re-order / Min Quantity entry screen (F-5A):

- *R:Adv Re-order* to set for Advanced Re-order Level
- *M:Adv Min Qty* to set for Advanced Minimum Quantity.

Now set both the parameters as described above.

Specify Reorder Levels — Universal Enterprises — Ctrl + M

Under Group : All Items — 1-Apr-2009 to 31-Mar-2010

Name of Item	Reorder Quantity	Advance Parameter for Reorder Level (*Consumption for the last*)		Minimum Order Quantity	Advance Parameter for Minimum Order (*Consumption for the last*)	
		Period	Criteria		Period	Criteria
Assembled PC	5 Pcs or	1 Months	Lower	2 Pcs or	7 Days	Lower
Asus P5KPLSE G31 V/PCI-E/S/L/1333FSB	12 Pcs or	2 Weeks	Higher	8 Pcs or	1 Weeks	Lower
Asus P5QPL-AM C41 G41 V/ PCI-E/	14 Pcs or	15 Days	Lower	10 Pcs or	7 Days	Higher
Biostar 945gc-M7 Te	20 Pcs or	3 Months	Lower	3 Pcs or	1 Months	Higher

F-5A:Advance Re-Order level & Advance Minimum Order Quantity set Up

FAQ: Frequently Asked Questions

FAQ-1: On the basis of past experience, we have enumerated the Re-Order Level (the stck Level at which the Item should be Re-Ordered & Re-Order Quantities (Standrad Order Quantity for Re-Order) for important Stock Control Items. How I can enter Simple Re-Order Values for each Purchase Item.

Ans: To enter Re-Order levels in Simple Mode, click the Toggle button (F-1B):

- R: *Simple Re-Order* to get Re Order Quantity column
- M: *Simple Min Qty* to get Minimum Order Quantity column

Now enter the Re Order Quantity & Minimum Order Quantity as follows (F-1A):

- **Re Order Quantity**: Enter the Stock Level (Re-Order level) at which new Purchase Order is to be placed (New Purchase Order to be placed when Stock reaches this level)
- **Min Order Quantity**: Enter the Re-Order Quantity (Order Quantity of the new order to be placed, when stock reaches the Re-Order Level)

01 Order Processing

Order Processing refers to the complete chain of linked transactions from Orders, Challans to Invoices

We have explained the steps of creation of each of these documents, in earlier chapters. Now we discuss about some advanced aspects of Ordering System & steps of Order Processing

02 Consignee Details in Vouchers

Normally the goods are delivered to the Buyer. But, sometimes goods are to be despatched to a specified third party (called Consignee), as per instruction of the Buyer.

In the books of the supplier, though the goods may be consigned to Consignee, still, the Invoice is to be created on the Buyer and the Buyer remains responsible for Payment for the Invoice. So, only the Buyer's Ledger Account is created in the books of Seller and all transactions are recorded in the name of Buyer. Consignee name is recorded for the purpose of information only, to book the goods with the carrier, in the name of consignee,.

To record the consignee name at the entry screen (Order / Despatch Note / Invoice), at respective Configuration (F12:Config>Invoice / Orders Entry) screen, set *Yes* at *Allow Separate Buyer & Consignee Name*. Consequently, during Orders / Delivery Note / Invoice entry, at supplementary details screen (F-1A, F-2A, F-3A), you get two fields for Buyer's name (Despatch To / Consignee Name & Buyers Name). The Buyer's Name & Address are carried as default at the Consignee Name, where you may change the Consignee Name if different from the Buyer, as described next.

02.01 Consignee Name Entry in Vouchers

For each Voucher Type, the field where the Consignee Name may be entered are described in the following Table. Consequently, the Party Name, Company Name & Consignee Name are printed in the respective document as described.

Voucher Type	Default	Consignee name entered at	Company name is printed at	Consignee Name is printed at	Party Name is printed at
Sales Order	Party Name is carried as default both at *Despatch To* & *Buyers* Field at Buyer's section	Despatch To	Document Header	Despatch To	Invoice To
Delivery Note	Party Name is carried as default both at *Consignee* & *Buyers Field* at Buyer's section	Consignee	Document Header	Consignee	Buyer (if other than consignee)
Sales Invoice	Party Name is carried both at *Consignee* field and *Buyers* Field at Buyer's Section	Consignee	Document Header	Consignee	Buyer (if other than consignee)
Purchase Order	Company Name is carried at *Despatch To* field & Party Name is carried *Supplier* field at Supplier section	Despatch To	Invoice To field	Despatch To	Supplier
Receipt Note	Company Name is carried at *Consignee* field & Party Name is carried at *Supplier* field at Supplier section		Header	Consignee	Supplier
Purchase Invoice	Party Name is carried at *Consignee* and *Supplier* fields at Supplier section	Consignee	Consignee	Not Printed in the Purchase Invoice	Document Header

02.02 Consignee Particulars entry in Vouchers

The entry of Consignee name in supplementary section in various voucher types are shown below.

Buyer's Details

Despatch To	: S. BOSE	Buyers	:	S P Technologies
Address	: 71 D. F. C Road Kolkata 700127	Address	:	12/c AJC Bose Road Kolkata 700124
		Sales Tax No.	:	

Order Details

Mode/Terms of Payment	:
Other Reference(s)	:
Terms of Delivery	:

Despatch Details

Despatch through	:
Destination	:

F-1A: Consignee Details in Sales Order

Order Details

Order No(s)	: OR/01	dt. 1-Jun-2009	Mode/Terms of Payment	: 30 Days
			Other Reference(s)	:
			Terms of Delivery	: By train

Despatch Details

Despatch Doc. No.	: JF4653
Despatched through	: TRAIN
Destination	: KOLKATA

Buyer's Details

Consignee	: S. BOSE	Buyers	:	S P Technologies
Address	: 71 D. F. C Road Kolkata 700127	Address	:	12/c AJC Bose Road Kolkata 700124
		Sales Tax No.	:	ABPNFGHTHKJ

F-2A: Consignee Details in Delivery Note

Consignee name in supplementary section in respective document is shown in the entry screen:

- Sales Order (F-1A):
- Delivery Note (F-2A).
- Sales Invoice (F-3A).

If the goods are to be dispatched to a different Party on behalf of the buyer (called Consignee), you may overwrite the Consignee Name at *Despatch To* field (F-1A /F-3A). The Consignee details may be printed in the respective document.

Despatch Details

Delivery Note No(s)	: 1	dt. 10-Jun-2009	Despatch Doc. No.	: JF4653
			Despatched through	: TRAIN
			Destination	: KOLKATA

Order Details

Order No(s)	: OR/01	dt. 1-Jun-2009	Mode/Terms of Payment	: 30 Days
			Other Reference(s)	:
			Terms of Delivery	: By train

Buyer's Details

Consignee	: S. BOSE	Buyers	:	S P Technologies
Address	: 71 D. F. C Road Kolkata 700127	Address	:	12/c AJC Bose Road Kolkata 700124
		Sales Tax No.	:	ABPNFGHTHKJ

F-3A: Consignee Details in Sales Invoice

Linked Documents: When the Sales Order is selected in any Delivery Note / Sales Invoice (or Purchase Order is selected in any Receipt Note /Purchase Invoice) the Consignee details are also carried as default in the respective Delivery Note / Sales Invoice (or Receipt Note /Purchase Invoice), which may be changed if desired, and also printed in the Delivery Note / Sales Invoice (or Receipt Note / Purchase Invoice)

In case of Sales Order / Delivery Note / Sales Invoice, the Party Name (Buyer) is carried as default both at Buyer Name & at Despatch To / Consignee Name. You may overwrite the Consignee Name at Despatch To / Consignee Name field.

03 Sales & Purchase against Multiple Orders

Sometimes, thee may be multiple pending orders in respect of same party, for some Item. Such case, a Challan / Invoice may be created against multiple Orders, such as:

In respect of Purchases:

- Creation of Receipt Note against Multiple Purchase Orders (§04)
- Creation of Purchase Invoice against Multiple Receipt Notes (§05)
- Creation of Purchase Invoice against Multiple Purchase Orders (§06)

In respect of Sales:

- Creation of Delivery Notes against Multiple Sales Orders (§07)
- Creation of Sales Invoice against Multiple Delivery Notes (§08)
- Creation of Sales Invoice against Multiple Sales Orders (§09)

The process of creating such documents against multiple orders are explained next:

04 Receipt Note entry against Multiple Purchase Order

Sometimes, Goods against several Purchase Orders may be received at a time from a supplier in one lot. In such case, a Receipt Note is to be created against multiple Purchase orders, the Order Numbers are entered in the Receipt Note (F-4A), as described below.

Receipt Note No. 2 — 5-Jul-2009 Sunday

Ref. :

Party's A/c Name : Digitech Infosys

Name of Item	Quantity Actual	Quantity Billed	Rate	per	Disc. %	Amount
Biostar 945gc-M7 Te	1 Pcs	1 Pcs	3,000.00	Pcs		3,000.00
CCTV (Panasonic,Yoko,Avancar)	1 Pcs	1 Pcs	5,000.00	Pcs		5,000.00
						8,000.00

F-4A: Receipt Note

Order No(s)	: PO/01 PO/02			
Consignee	: P Biswas	Supplier	:	Digitech Infosys
Address	: 201-202, Phase III SIDCO Industrial Estate Kolkata	Address	:	
		Sales Tax No.	:	

List of Orders

- End of List
- New Number
- Not Applicable
- PO/01 2-Jul-2009
- PO/02 3-Jul-2009

F-4B: Multiple Purchase Order selection in Receipt Note entry

Item Allocations for : **Biostar 945gc-M7 Te**

Godown	Quantity		Rate	per	Disc. %	Amount
	Actual	Billed				
Tracking No. : 2		Order No.: PO/01			Due on 20-Jul-2009	
Main Location	1 Pcs	1 Pcs	3,000.00	Pcs		3,000.00

F-4C: Item allocation entry for Receipt Note

Order Number Selection: During Receipt Note entry (F-4A), after entry of Party Name, at Supplementary details screen (F-4B), at the Orders field, all the pending order numbers of the selected Suppliers are listed. Now select the Order Numbers one by one, against which goods are received in the current Receipt Note.

Next, on selection of Stock Item, at the Item Allocation screen (F-4C), all the pending orders Items against the selected orders are carried (with pending quantity, rates, discount and the computed value) as default.

To change any data in any Item, press <enter> and change the Quantity as well as Rate / Discount etc (if permitted). You may also enter other details like Godown, Batch etc, for the Item (F-4C).

This way, select / enter data in respect of Items in the Receipt Note (F-4A) and save the Receipt Note.

The Quantity entered in the Receipt Note for each Item is adjusted against the respective pending Purchase orders selected (F-4B) for each Item.

05 Purchase Invoice entry against Multiple Receipt Notes

Sometimes, supplier delivers goods in several lots. Consequently, the buyer creates several Goods Receipt Notes each time the goods are received. Finally, the buyer enters one Purchase Invoice linking multiple Receipt Notes, as described below:

Receipt Note Number Selection: During Purchase Invoice entry (F-5A), after entry of Party Name, at the Receipt Notes field in the Supplementary Details subscreen (F-5B), all the pending Tracking Numbers of the selected Supplier are listed. Now select the Tracking Numbers one by one, against which current Purchase Invoice is being entered (F-5B).

Purchase No. **10** — **7-Jul-2009**, Tuesday

Ref. :

Party's A/c Name : **Digitech Infosys**

Name of Item	Quantity		Rate	per	Amount
	Actual	Billed			
Biostar 945gc-M7 Te	1 Pcs	1 Pcs	3,000.00	Pcs	3,000.00
CCTV (Panasonic, Yoko, Avancar)	1 Pcs	1 Pcs	5,000.00	Pcs	5,000.00
HD 250 Gb Seagate Barracuda SATA	1 Pcs	1 Pcs	780.00	Pcs	780.00
					8,780.00

F-5A: Invoice Entry against Multiple Receipt Notes

Receipt Note No.(s) 2, 3

List of Tracking Numbers
- End of List
- New Number
- Not Applicable
- 1 — 5-Jul-2009
- 3 — 6-Jul-2009

Order No(s) 09, PO/02 dt. 3-Jul-2009

Supplier's Details

Consignee	**P Biswas**	Supplier	: **Digitech Infosys**
Address	201-202, Phase III SIDCO Industrial Estate Kolkata	Address	:
		Sales Tax No.	: **ADF54367**

F-5B: Multiple Receipt Note selection in Purchase Invoice entry

To change any carried data of any Item in the Purchase Invoice, select the Item and press <enter> to get the respective data in Item details screen. Change the data (Quantity) as well as Rate / Value (if permitted), as required.

This way, you may change the desired data of any Item and save the Purchase Invoice.

This way, select the Tracking Number in respect of each order for each of the Stock Item entered in the Receipt Voucher.

Other Ledger Account details in Purchase Invoice: The other ledger accounts data, as entered in the selected Receipt Notes, are carried at the supplementary screen (F-5B), which you may change for the current Invoice, as necessary.

Alternately, to enter data for any ledger account (if not entered at Order), select the Ledger Account and enter the Rate / Amount.

This way, change / enter data in respect of ay ledger account. Now save the Invoice.

06 Purchase Invoice entry against Multiple Purchase Orders

Sometimes, supplier delivers goods against several Orders. Consequently, the buyer creates one Purchase Invoice linking multiple Purchase Orders, as described below:

Purchase Order Numbers Selection: During Purchase Invoice entry (F-6A), after entry of Party Name, at the Order Number field in the Supplementary Details subscreen (F-6B), all the pending Order numbers (for which Purchase Invoice are not fully prepared) of the selected Suppliers are listed. Now select the Purchase Order Numbers one by one, against which current Purchase Invoice is being entered.

Item Details in Purchase Invoice: Consequently, In the Item details screen, all the pending Items against the selected Purchase Orders are carried (with pending quantity, rates, discount and the computed value) as default.

To change any carried data of any Item in the Purchase Invoice, select the Item and press <enter> to get the respective data in Item details screen. Change the data (Quantity / Rate / Value) as required.

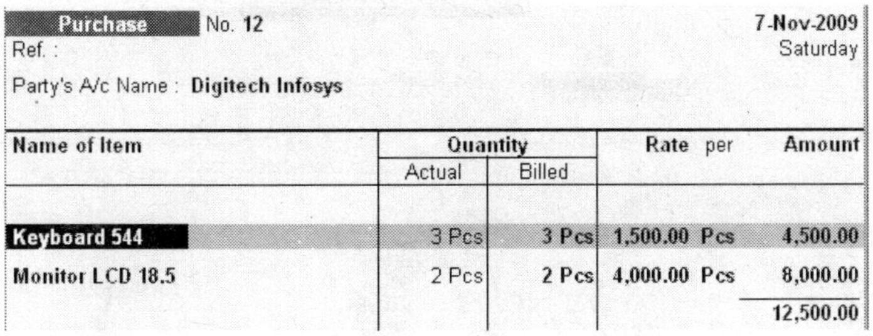

Purchase No. 12 — 7-Nov-2009, Saturday
Ref. :
Party's A/c Name : Digitech Infosys

Name of Item	Quantity Actual	Quantity Billed	Rate per	Amount
Keyboard 544	3 Pcs	3 Pcs	1,500.00 Pcs	4,500.00
Monitor LCD 18.5	2 Pcs	2 Pcs	4,000.00 Pcs	8,000.00
				12,500.00

F-6A: Invoice entry against Multiple Orders

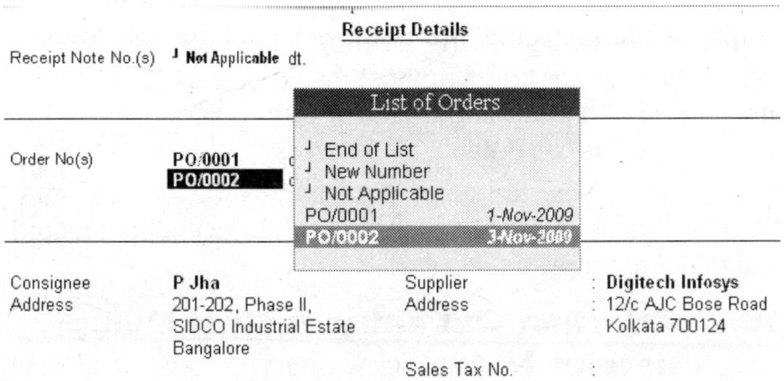

Receipt Details
Receipt Note No.(s) : Not Applicable dt.
Order No(s) PO/0001, PO/0002
List of Orders: End of List; New Number; Not Applicable; PO/0001 1-Nov-2009; PO/0002 3-Nov-2009
Consignee Address: P Jha, 201-202, Phase II, SIDCO Industrial Estate, Bangalore
Supplier Address : Digitech Infosys, 12/c AJC Bose Road, Kolkata 700124
Sales Tax No. :

F-6B: Multiple Order Number selection in Purchase Invoice entry

This way, you may change the desired data of any Item (F-6B)

Other Ledger Account details in Purchase Invoice: The ledger accounts data, if entered in the selected Purchas Order are carried. To change data of any ledger account, select the ledger account and change the data.

To enter new data for of ledger account, select the Ledger Account and enter the Rate / Amount.

This way, change / enter data in respect of any ledger account. Now save the Purchase Invoice (F-6A)

07 Delivery Note entry against Multiple Sales Order

Sometimes, goods are delivered at a time under one Delivery Note, against several Sales Orders. Consequently, the vendor creates one Delivery Note linking multiple Sales Orders (F-7A), as described below:

Order Number Selection: During Delivery Note entry (F-7A), after entry of Party Name, at the Orders field in the subscreen at supplementary details screen (F-7B), all the pending order numbers of the selected customer are listed. Now select the Sales Orders Numbers one by one, against which goods are delivered in the current Delivery Note

Item Details Entry: In the Item details screen (F-7B), all the pending orders Items against the selected orders are carried (with pending quantity, rates, discount and the computed value) as default.

Select any Item and press <enter> to change any carried data like Quantity, Rate, Discount, Value etc., (if permitted).

You may need to enter other details like Godown, Batch etc, in this screen (F-7B).

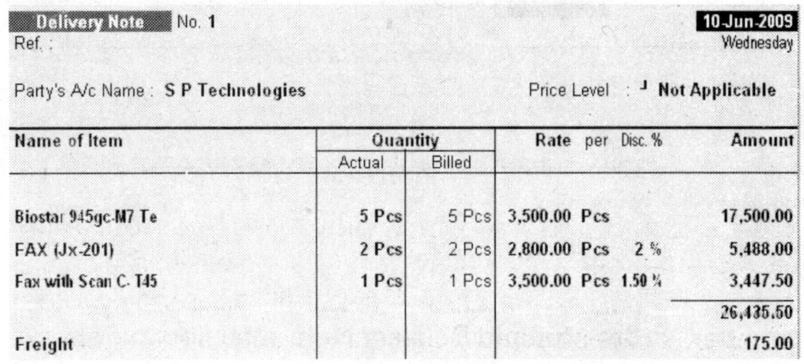

Delivery Note No. 1 — 10-Jun-2009, Wednesday
Ref. :
Party's A/c Name : S P Technologies — Price Level : Not Applicable

Name of Item	Quantity Actual	Quantity Billed	Rate per	Disc. %	Amount
Biostar 945gc-M7 Te	5 Pcs	5 Pcs	3,500.00 Pcs		17,500.00
FAX (Jx-201)	2 Pcs	2 Pcs	2,800.00 Pcs	2 %	5,488.00
Fax with Scan C-T45	1 Pcs	1 Pcs	3,500.00 Pcs	1.50 %	3,447.50
					26,435.50
Freight					175.00

F-7A: Delivery Note creation against multiple orders

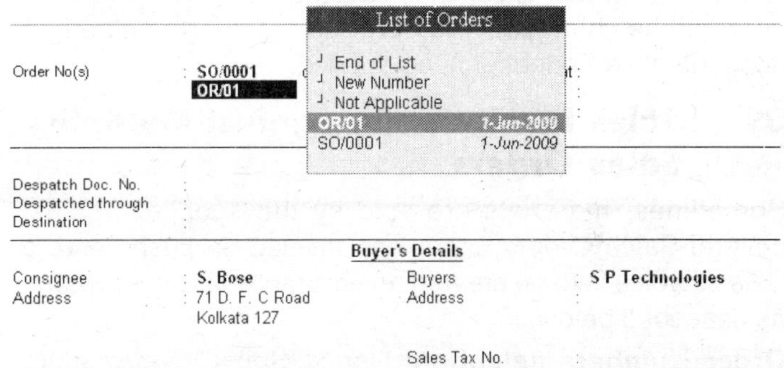

Order No(s) SO/0001, OR/01
List of Orders: End of List; New Number; Not Applicable; OR/01 1-Jun-2009; SO/0001 1-Jun-2009
Despatch Doc. No. :
Despatched through :
Destination :
Buyer's Details
Consignee Address : S. Bose, 71 D. F. C Road, Kolkata 127
Buyers Address : S P Technologies
Sales Tax No. :

F-7B: Multiple Order selection in Delivery Note entry

08 Sales Invoice entry against Multiple Delivery Notes

Sometimes, goods are delivered at several stages. At the time of each delivery, a Delivery Note is created. Subsequently, the Sales Invoice is created linking multiple Delivery Notes, as described below:

Delivery Note Number Selection: During Sales Invoice entry, after entry of Party Name, at the Delivery Note field in the subscreen, all the pending Delivery Note numbers. Now select the Delivery Note Numbers one by one, against which current Sales Invoice is being entered.

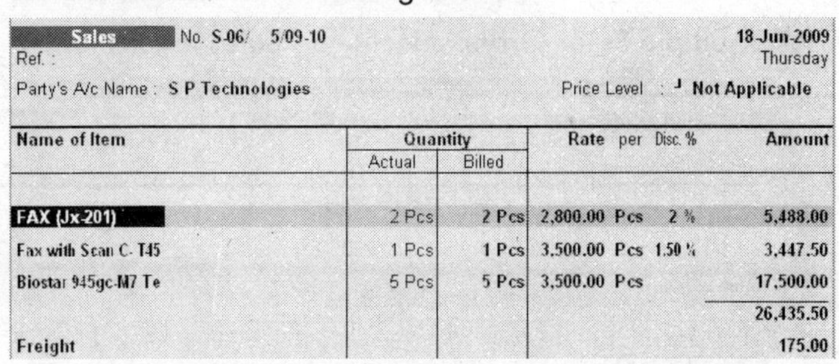

Sales No. S-06/ 5/09-10 — 18-Jun-2009, Thursday
Ref. :
Party's A/c Name : S P Technologies — Price Level : Not Applicable

Name of Item	Quantity Actual	Quantity Billed	Rate per	Disc. %	Amount
FAX (Jx-201)	2 Pcs	2 Pcs	2,800.00 Pcs	2 %	5,488.00
Fax with Scan C-T45	1 Pcs	1 Pcs	3,500.00 Pcs	1.50 %	3,447.50
Biostar 945gc-M7 Te	5 Pcs	5 Pcs	3,500.00 Pcs		17,500.00
					26,435.50
Freight					175.00

F-8A: tem details entry in Sales Invoice

Item Details Entry: In the Item details screen, all the Items under the selected Delivery Note are carried (with quantity, rates, discount and the computed value) as default.

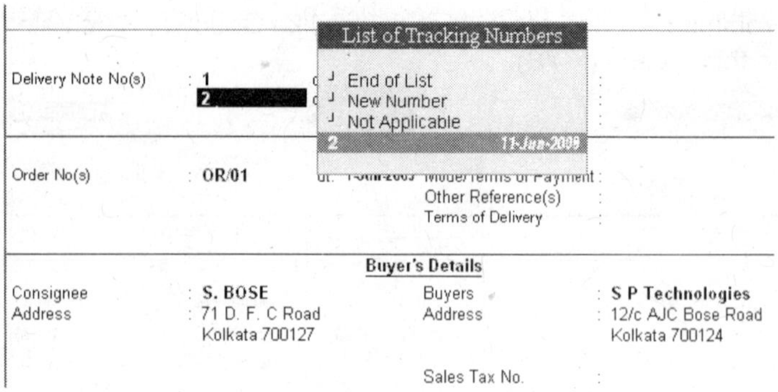

F-8B: Multiple Delivery Note selection in Sales Invoice entry

Now press <enter> to save the data (normally, the particulars need not be changed). You may add entry for other ledger accounts (like Freight etc), as needed.

09 Sales Invoice entry against Multiple Sales Orders

Sometimes, materials are sold by the supplier against several Sales Orders under one Invoice. In such case, a Sales Invoice is to be created against multiple Sales Orders, as described below:

Order Numbers selection: During Sales Invoice entry (F-9A), after entry of Party Name, at the Order Number field at supplementary details subscreen (F-9B), all the pending Order numbers of the selected customer are listed. Now select the Sales Order Numbers one by one, against which current Sales Invoice is being entered (F-9B).

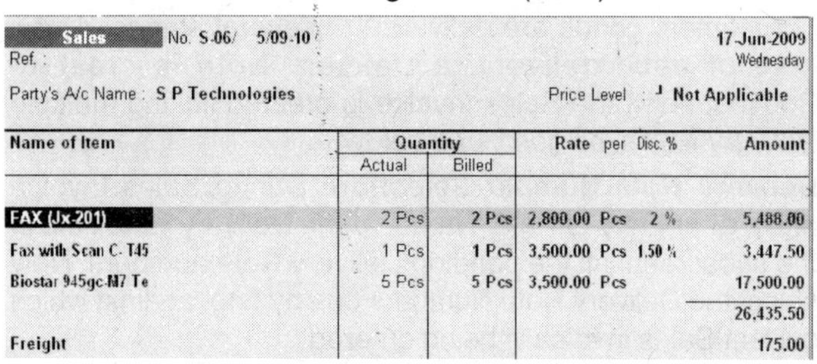

F-9A; Multiple Sales Order selection in Sales Invoice entry

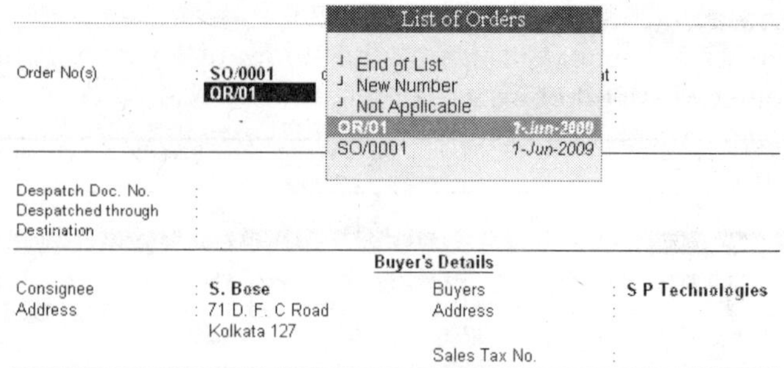

F-9B: Sales Invoice entry linking multiple Orders

Item Details Entry: In the Item details screen (F-9B), all the pending Order Items against the selected Sales Orders are carried (with pending quantity, rates, discount and the computed value) as default.

To change any carried data, like Quantity, as well as Rate, Discount, Value (if permitted), pres <enter> at the Item record and make changes as required.

10 Rejection Out entry against Multiple Receipt Notes

On receipt of goods from supplier, the buyer creates a GRN. Sometimes, the buyer may return goods originally supplied under several Receipt Notes earlier, making a Rejection Out Voucher against multiple Receipt Notes.

Rejection Out voucher entry has been explained earlier. The steps of adjustment against the GRN are explained here.

Receipt Note Number Selection: During Rejection Out voucher entry (F-10A), in the Item details screen, after entry of Item Name of the returned Stock Item, the Item allocation screen appears. At the Item allocation field, all pending Tracking Numbers (for the selected Item) appear. Select the tracking number of the Receipt Notes against which the current Rejection Out note is being issued.

Item Details Entry: On selection of Tracking Number, the Item details are carried from the selected document. You may change Quantity (if only a part of the Items of the Receipt Note are returned), or change other values (like Rate, Discount etc) as required. The computed value of the Item is shown (which may also be changed).

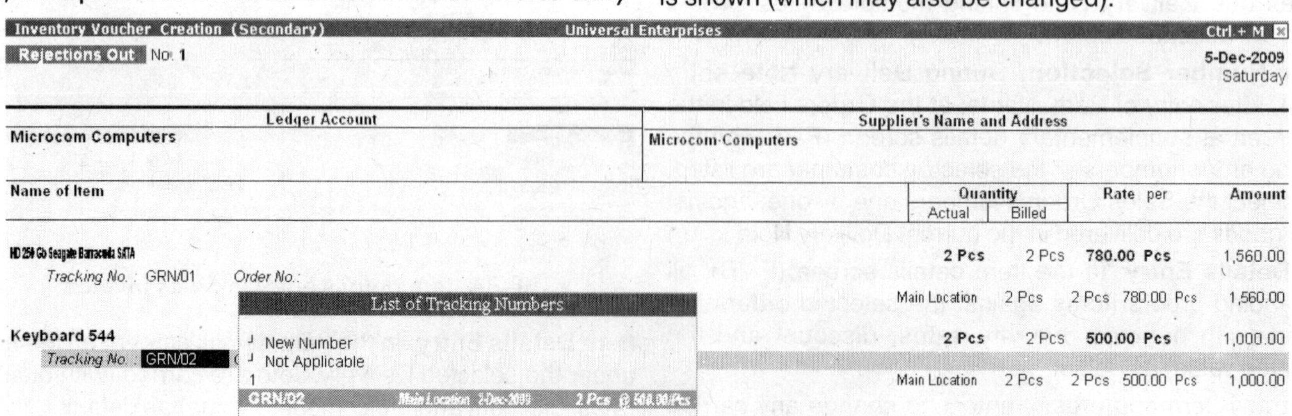

F-10A: GRN selection in Rejection Out Voucher entry

This way, at Tracking Number, select the respective Tracking Number in respect of the all the Items of Receipt Notes against which goods are returned, one by one, to enter the details of each Item returned in the Rejection Out Voucher (F-10A).

11 Rejection In entry Voucher against Multiple Delivery Note

On delivery of goods to customer, the supplier creates a Delivery Note. Sometimes, the buyer returns goods to the supplier (for defects etc) delivered under several Delivery Notes. When the Rejection In (Sales Return) voucher is issued against Delivery Note, the Item details (Rate etc) are earlier. The steps of issuing against the Delivery are explained here.

Delivery Note Number selection: During Rejection In voucher entry (F-10B), in the Item details screen, after entry of Item Name of the returned Stock Item, the Item allocation screen appears. At the Item allocation field, all pending Tracking Numbers (for the selected Item) appear in the list. Select the Tracking Number of the Delivery Note against which the current Rejection In voucher is being issued.

Item Details Entry: On selection of Tracking Number, the Item details are carried from the Delivery Note. You may change Quantity (if only a part of the Items of the Delivery Note are returned), or other values (like Rate, Discount etc)

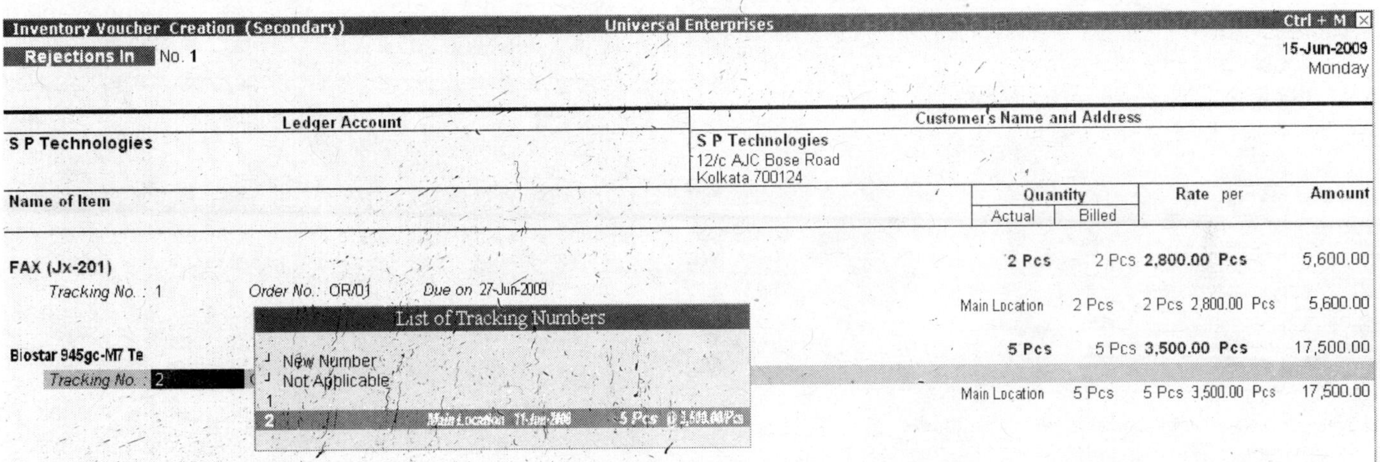

F-10B: Delivery Note selection in Rejection In Voucher entry

carried from the linked Delivery Note for accurate pricing of the goods returned under the Rejection In voucher.

Rejection In (Sales Return) voucher entry has been explained as required. The computed value of the Item is shown (which you may also be changed).

This way, you may enter the details of each Item returned in the Rejection In Voucher (F-10B)

Part 5
Batch

This Part explains the Concept & implementation of Batches for Products

Batch explains the Concept and setting up of Bach Features for the Company and the selective Stock Items, and entry of Batch details in vouchers.

Batch Reports gives the details of Stock & Transactions with Batch details

Batch

01 Batch

Batch means a lot of similar Items. Each lot is separately identified by an Identifier called Batch ID or Batch Number.

- In case of small Items (like Medicines), all the items in a lot may be identified by the same Batch ID.
- In case of larger Items (like Machinery), each Item may be separately identified by an unique Batch ID.

02 Batch Numbers

Stock Item Batch Numbers are physical identifiers (Batch ID) to specifically identify an Item (e.g a Machine) or a lot of similar Items (e.g a lot of medicine).

- In case of single identifiable Item (e.g a Machine) Batch Numbers are Physically placed on the Item to identify the specific piece.
- In case of lot of similar Items, Batch Numbers are normally Physically placed on the Item or on the packing (e.g Medicine, Food Items) to identify the specific lot

Batch Number maintains next level details of an Item. It is normally used for perishable / service warranty Items (using Mfg & Exp Dates in food & medicine items, warranty period for durable items, etc.).

Batch Number may be further associated with Manufacturing & Expiry Date, as commonly used for perishable Items like Food, Medicine and other Items with limited shelf – life (must be sold within Expiry Date), and for Item with limited Guarantee / Warrantee period (can be serviced within Service Contract period)

Utility of Batch Number: Batch Numbers are used for following purposes:

- **To physically identify an Item:** Through Batch Number, any Item (or a lot of similar Items) is specifically identified for Inventory transaction, service, warranty
- **To record expiry date of the Item:** Through Batch Expiry date, delivery / consumption of perishable Item or servicing of Items under specified period of guarantee / warrantee is controlled.
- **Stock Age:** To know the time period since when an Item is lying in Stock

Batch numbers may also be sometimes used for other attributes of Item (like Model, Colour, Size etc

03 Activating Batch Numbers for the Company

At GoT, Click *F11: Features*>select Inventory Features to get Inventory Features screen. At Inventory Features screen, Under *Storage & Classification section*, at *Maintain Batchwise Details* (F-1A), set:

- *Yes* to activate the Batch option for the Company
- *No*. The Batch Features will not be activated for the Company

03.01 Batch Expiry Dates

Sometimes, apart from the physical ID (the Batch Number), the Expiry Date (e.g Date within which the Item may be sold or serviced under guarantee / warrantee terms) is also to be maintained.

Activating Batch Expiry Dates: Having activated Batch Feature, at *Set Expiry Dates for Batches,* set (F-1A)

- *Yes* to Activate Expiry dates also for the Company. Consequently, at Stock Item creation / alteration (Inv Info>Stock Items), you get additional option to set *Manufacturing / Expiry Date* for the Stock Item. For such Items, apart from Batch Number, Mfg / Expiry Dates are also to be entered in vouchers.
- *No.* The Expiry Date field in Transactions will not be available, however, Batch Numbers may be entered. This is useful for on perishable goods where Expiry Date is not important.

04 Batch Activation for Stock Item

Having Activated Batch for the Company, you may selectively activate Batch for each Stock Item. Consequently at Stock Item Master, you may set the Batch option for any Item for which you like to get Batch/Lot-wise transaction and Stock details.

Stock Item creation has been explained earlier. At Stock Item creation / alteration screen (F-2A), at *Maintain In Batches*:

- Set Yes to activate Batch feature for the Stock Item. Consequently, you will get another option *Track Date of Mfg*:
    - o Set Yes to activate Mfg Date for the Stock Items. Consequently, at the option, *Use Expiry Dates*:
- Set *Yes,* to activate Expiry Date also for the Stock Item

- Set *No,* Expiry Date will not be activated for the Stock Item. However, Mfg Date will remain activated as per options set
  - o Set *No.* Mfg Date for the Stock Items will not be activated (however Batch Number feature will remain activated as set for the Stock Item). Consequently, you will also not get option to set Expiry date.
- Set *No.* Batch feature for the Stock Item will not be activated

Maintain Batch-wise Details	? Yes
(set Expiry Dates for Batches)	? Yes

F-1A: Batch Activation for the Company

Name	: Glow Lamp Phillips 100W		
Under	: Electrical Goods	**Tax Information**	
Units	: Pcs	Tariff Classification	: Not Applicable
Maintain in Batches	? Yes	Rate of Duty (eg 5)	: 0
Track Date of Mfg	? Yes		
Use expiry dates	? Yes	Rate of VAT (%)	: 4

	Quantity	Rate per	Value
Opening Balance	20 Pcs	12.40 Pcs	248.00

F-2A: Batch Activation at Stock Item

Allocations of : **Glow Lamp Phillips 100W**
for: **20 Pcs**

Batch	Mfg Dt.	Expiry Date	Quantity	Rate	per	Amount
12	Dec-2012	1-Jun-2013	12 Pcs	12.00	Pcs	144.00
18	Jan-2013	1-Aug-2013	8 Pcs	13.00	Pcs	104.00
			20 Pcs			248.00

F-2B: Opening Stock Batch details Entry

05 Opening Stock Batch details entry

After you have activated Batch options for a Stock Item, on entry of Opening Stock (at Opening Balance field) for the Item (F-2A), you get a sub screen to enter Batchwise details of the Opening Stock (F-2B).

At Opening Stock entry screen (F-2B), at the top, the Item Name and the Opening Stock Quantity is displayed. Depending on options set, you get the following fields in the Item Allocation sub screen to enter batch details of Opening Stock (F-2B):

- **Batch Number**: Select *New Batch* and enter the Batch Number.
- **Batch Manufacturing Date**: At *Mfg Dt* column (appears If you have set *Yes* to *Track Date of Mfg* for the Item at Item Master) enter the Batch Manufacturing Date.
- **Batch Expiry Date**: At *Expiry Date* column (appears If you have set *Yes* at *Use Exp Date* for the Item at Item Master) enter the Batch Expiry Date.
- **Batch Quantity**: At *Quantity* column, enter the Batch Quantity (and UoM) in the Opening Stock.
- **Batch Rate**: At *Rate* column, enter the Rate (and Rate UoM).
- **Batch Value**: At *Amount* column, the computed Batch Value is displayed (If Rate is entered), which you may change, else enter the Batch Value.

06 Voucher Entry Configuration set up for Batch details

Having Activated Batch Feature for the Company (F-1A), you have to set Batch option at

Voucher Configuration

General Voucher Configuration: At *GoT>F12: Configure>Voucher Entry*, set Yes at *Show Batch-wise Details* (F-3A) to enable entry of Batch Details in Voucher.

07 Voucher Entry with Batch details

Various types of Voucher Entry with Inventory details have been explained earlier. Here we describe the steps of entry of Batch details in Voucher for a Stock Item, After selection of a Stock Item in the Voucher (F-4A), in Item allocation screen (F-4B), enter the Batch Details (for Item for which Batch Details has been activated), as follows:

Batch Entry: Depending on options set, you get the following fields in the Item Allocation sub screen to enter batch details (F-3B):

- **Batch Number**: You mat create a New Batch or select from an existing Batch, as follows:
  - o **New Batch:** In case of *New Batch* (normally in Purchase), select *New Batch* and enter the Batch Number in the Box.
  - o **Existing Batch**: In case of existing Batch (Normally in Sales), select the Batch Number from the list of Batches.

Batch Allocation Details: After entry / selection of Batch Number (F-4B), enter the following details at *Batch Allocation* screen (F-4C)

- **Batch Manufacturing Date**: In case of New Batch, at *Mfg Date* (this prompt appears if you have set *Yes* to *Track Date of Mfg* for the Item at Item Master) enter the Batch Manufacturing Date. In case of existing Batch selected, the Batch Manufacturing Date is carried, which you may change in the Batch Allocation screen in the Voucher.
- **Batch Expiry Date**: In case of New Batch, at *Mfg Date* (this prompt appears if you have set *Yes* to *Track Date of Mfg* for the Item at Item Master) enter the Batch Expiry Date. In case of existing Batch selected, the Batch Expiry Date is carried, which you may change in the Batch Allocation screen in the Voucher.
- **Batch Quantity**: At *Quantity* field, enter the Batch Quantity (and UoM).

- **Batch Rate**: At *Rate* field, enter the Rate (and Rate UoM).
- **Batch Value**: At *Amount* field, the computed Batch Value is displayed, which you may change.

This way, you may select Multiple entries for different Batches, with same or different prices, Godowns etc.

F-3A: Voucher Entry Configuration

Show Batch-wise Details ? **Yes**

Accounting Voucher Creation Ctrl + M

Sales No. **1** 1-Apr-2013
Ref. Monday
Party's A/c Name : **B B Traders**
Sales Ledger : **Sales @12.5%**

Name of Item	Quantity	Rate per	Amount
Glow Lamp Phillips 100W	2 Pcs	16.00 Pcs	32.00
Narration:	2 Pcs		32.00

F-4A: Voucher Entry

Item Allocations for : **Glow Lamp Phillips 100W**

Batch / Lot No.
Mfg Dt. | Expiry Date

List of Active Batches

Name	Expiry	Balance
New Number		
12	*1-Jun-2013*	*12 Pcs*
18	*1-Aug-2013*	*8 Pcs*

F-4B: Batch Number entry / selection at Item Allocation screen

Item Allocations for : **Glow Lamp Phillips 100W**

Batch / Lot No. (Mfg Dt. / Expiry Date)	Quantity	Rate per	Amount
12	2 Pcs	16.00 Pcs	32.00
Dec-2012 / 1-Jun-2013			
	2 Pcs		32.00

F-4C: Batch Details entry in Item allocation screen

Note

You may set Expiry Date only after you have activated Mfg Date. When Expiry date is activated, in voucher, you may either:

- o Enter the Expiry Date, or
- o Enter the useful life of the Item (jn days / weeks/ months/ Year etc) to compute the Expiry date (Expiry Date = Mfg date + Useful Life)
  - To select / enter a Batch having zero quantity in Invoice, at *GoT>Configure>Invoice / Orders Entry*, (F-1B/02-04) set Yes at *Show Batches with Zero Quantity*

08 Transaction of Expired Batches

Normally, expired item should not be sold / purchased. To control transaction of Expired Items, you need to set up the option as desired at Configuration / Stock Item.

Configuration Set Up for Expired Batches: At *GoT>Configure>Voucher* or *GoT> Configure> Invoice Order Entry*, at *Honour Expiry Dates Usage for Batches* (or Click F12:Configure at current voucher entry screen):

- Set *Yes* to prevent issue of Expired Batches in General in Inventory Vouchers
- Set *No*. Expired Batches will not appear in selection list of Batches

Stock Item Set Up for Expired Batches: At Stock Item entry, at *Behaviour* section (when Advanced Entry is set for the Stock Item), set

- *No* at *Allow Use of Expired Batches* to prevent entry of Expired Batch of the Item Inventory Voucher.
- *Yes* to allow entry of expired batches in Inventory Vouchers.

09 Batch details in Reports

When you have entered Batch details in Vouchers, you may get the details of Batch in various reports showing Stock Item details. At the Report Display screen Click *F12:Configure* to get the respective Report Configuration screen. Set *Yes* at the respective Batch option (like *Show Batch Details also*) to get Batch Details (Batch Number, Quantity, date of Mfg & Expiry dates etc as entered in the voucher. Sometimes, at Configuration Screen, you get specific options to selectively show Mfg / Exp date of the respective Batch. Set *Yes* at the respective options (like *Show Mfg Date also*, *Show Exp Date also*, etc).

10 Use of Batch for other attributes

Though Batch is normally used to physically identify each piece/ lot of Item, Batch Number may also be used for various attributes of Item (like Colour, Size, Model, Brand etc), to classify Items & maintain separate stock accounts for Items with distinct attributes

For example, textile and apparel dealers may use Batch for Model, Colour etc to maintain record of Stock Item according to colour, model (Mfg & Exp Date may be deactivated if not needed in such cases).

Example: A computer dealer likes to keep stock of Lamps (which come in various shades) as per shades. So, he uses Shade Name as Batch Number to get Shadewise (Batchwise) Stock.

Item Allocations for : **Glow Lamp Phillips 100W**

Batch / Lot No.		Quantity	Rate	per	Amount
Mfg Dt.	Expiry Date				
Pink		**10 Pcs**	12.00	Pcs	120.00
Apr-2013	1-Jun-2013				
		10 Pcs			120.00

F-5A: Colour as Batch Number

New Number

Pink

F-5B:New Batch Entry

At the time of first time entry of a Batch (Colour), select New Batch and enter Colour at Batch Number (F-5B, F-5C). Later on, for any sort of transaction (Receipt/ Delivery), select the Colour at Batch Number screen (do not enter a new Batch). This way, you get details of Colour in transaction as well as Stock Reports

11 Stock control for Items of obsolescence

In case of Items of changing model, fashion, where the realizable value of the Item diminishes with passage of time, normally control is maintained through Mfg Date / Purchase Date to know the age of the Item, so that old Items may be quickly sold through discount sale / sales campaign to realize best possible value avoiding loss.

In such case, the Mfg Date / Purchase Date is entered in the purchase voucher. The stock Age Analysis Report shows the age range wise analysis of stock. In Expiry Date, you may write the date after which the stock should be sold at Discount Price, if still lying till that date, to avoid further loss on the Item.

Case Studies

Batch Aging Analysis

Case 1: An apparel distributor maintains Batch as per buyer's invoice number (Buyers invoice number is batch number). He buys directly from manufacturer, so one item is bought from one vendor only). He likes to get stock in the age of 3 months, 6 months and more than 6 months from the date of purchase. Explain how he should maintain batches, enter the Batch Numbers in purchase & sales invoices, configure the batch ageing report and print the batch aging report.

Case 2: A Medicine dealer likes to know the batches expiring in next 3 months so that he can return the batches to the distributor. He also wants to ensure that that no expired batches are sold.

Recommendation

He should Activate only Expiry date (Date Of Mfg is not to be entered). Set the option to prevent sale of expired batches.

Now enter the batch number as 'New Batch' in Purchase Invoice. Select Batch Number as 'Against Batch' in sale invoice. Print Age Report of Batches

Batch as Product Attribute

Case 3: A hosiery dealer uses Size for each product as Batch Number to maintain stock for each size (J = Junior, S=Standard, L=Large, XL=Xtra Large, XXL = Xtra Xtra Large, The prices of J/S/L are same while for XL XXL are higher. Explain how he should maintain batches so that he can maintain stock for each size for proper inventory control. enter the Batch Numbers in purchase & sales invoices, configure the batch ageing report and print the batch aging report.

Recommendation

As there are 2 types of prices and 5 types of sizes, he may create The Products Stock Items in two ways depending on his convenience how he maintains price lists:

Method 1: Create 2 Product Masters for each Item e.g Vests (Std) & Vests (Lrg).

He should create 3 batches for:

- **Vests (Std):** J, S & L. In the sale price, enter the sale price in stock Item or in Price List (the sale price is same for these sizes)
- **Vests (Large):** XL & XXL. In the sale price, enter the sale price in stock Item or in Price List (the sale price is same for these sizes)

In sale / purchase invoice, select the proper batch (i.e size) so that he can maintain sizewise stock of each product. The advantage is that he has to enter sale prices only in the Item Master and the prices will be carried in the invoice. This will save substantial time in price entry in Invoice and also eliminate error /manipulation in Invoice

Method 2: Alternately, he can create only one master for each Product (e.g Vests) and 5 batches (J, S, L, XL & XXL). But he has to enter the price in each invoice as the prices differ for sizes. He cannot enter Sale Price in Stock Item or in Price List

Case 4: A Paint dealer sells Paints. He has different Pack Size (1/2 ltr, 1 Ltr, 2 Ltr, 4 Ltr, 10 Ltr etc) for each product and about 12 shades (Blue, Red etc). The prices (per Tin) differ as per size but is same for each shade. Explain how he should create the Stock Items so that he can make proper invoices & maintain stock for each size & shade and get the batch aging report.

Recommendation

In this case, since the prices differ as per pack size, you should create separate stock Item for each Pack Size (1 Ltr, 2 Litre etc) for each product (e.g Asian Acrylic 1 Ltr, Asian Acrylic 2 Ltr, JN Acrylic 1 Ltr, BP Acrylic 1 Ltr, etc).

Specify the Sale Price in Stock Item or Price List. Now enter Batch Number (Colour) in Sales Invoice (select 'New Batch' in the first purchase Invoice of that Batch (Colour) and enter the Colour, select Against Batch in all subsequent Purchases and all sales) and select the Batch (Colour). This way, you can maintain stock for each Size & Colour.

FAQ: Frequently Asked Questions

FAQ-1: How I may Activate Batch Features for the Company

Ans. Activate Batch Features for the Company: At GoT, Click *F11: Features* button, select *Inventory Features.* Under Storage & Classification section, at *Maintain Batchwise Details* (F-1A), set *Yes* to activate the Batch option for the Company

- **Batch Expiry Dates**: Having activated Batch Feature, at *Set Expiry Dates for Batches*(F-1A), set *Yes* to Activate Expiry dates also for the Company. Consequently, at Stock Item creation / alteration (Inv Info>Stock Items), you get additional option to set Manufacturing / Expiry Date for the Stock Item. For such Items, apart from Batch Number, Mfg / Expiry Dates are also to be entered in vouchers.

Batch Activation for Stock Item: Having Activated Batch for the Company, you may selectively activate Batch for each Stock Item. Consequently at Stock Item Master, you may set the Batch option for any Item for which you like to get Batch/Lot-wise transaction and Stock details.

At Stock Item creation / alteration screen (F-2A), at *Maintain In Batches*, set Yes to activate Batch feature for the Stock Item. Consequently, you will get another option *Track Date of Mfg*:

- o **Manufacturing Date**: Set Yes to activate Mfg Date for the Stock Items. Consequently, at the option, *Use Expiry Dates*:
- o **Expiry Date**: Set *Yes,* to activate Expiry Date also for the Stock Item
  - Set *No,* Expiry Date will not be activated for the Stock Item. However, Mfg Date will remain activated as per options set
- o Set *No*. Mfg Date for the Stock Items will not be activated (however Batch Number feature will remain activated as set for the Stock Item. Consequently, you will also not get option to set Expiry date.

Batch Reports

05-02

01 Batch Ageing

Ageing Analysis of Batches helps to identify Expired Batches and Aged Batches (Batches soon to expire) for perishable goods (food products, pharmaceuticals etc.) lying in Stock. It also gives trend of shelf stay time of stock (average time an Item is lying in stock before disposal) and helps to compute *Inventory Carrying Cost* more precisely.

Select *Display > Inventory Books > Ageing Analysis* and select Stock Group (*Primary* to select All Stock Groups) to get Stock Ageing Analysis for the related Stock Items.

At Batch Analysis Report, you get the following buttons (F-1D):

- **F1:Detailed / Condensed**
  - o Click *F1:Detailed* to get next level details (F-1C) of each Stock Item (like Batch, Godown)
  - o Click *F1:Condensed* to get Itemwise total figures of stock (without Batch, Godown details: F-1A)
- **F4: Group:** To select Stock Item Group (select Primary for All Stock Items) to show the Age Analysis of the Stock Items under the selected Group)
- **F6: Ageing Period**: To set the Age Analysis Slab (§02, F-2A)
- **F7: Valuation**; To select the Valuation Method for valuation of Stock in Hand (F-1B)
- **A: Hide Amount / Show Amount:**
  - o Click *A: Show Amount* to show the Amount at Value columns
  - o Click *A: Hide Amount* to suppress the Value Columns (Amount figure will not be shown)
- **S: Ageing Style**: To set the Ageing Style Parameters (§02.02, F-2B)
- **B: Expired Batches / All Batches**
  - o Click *B: Expired Batches* to show only those Batches which have been expired
  - o Click *B: All Batches* to show all the Batches (all stock- Regular as well as Expired)

The Batch Ageing report is divided into 3 major sections, Particulars, Total Quantity and Agewise break-up. Stock Item with Total quantity is shown in bold in first row with agewise break-up, followed by batchwise (and godownwise) details. You can move cursor between Total Quantity and Agewise break-up columns with left / right arrow keys, and press <enter>at the respective column to get further detailed reports:

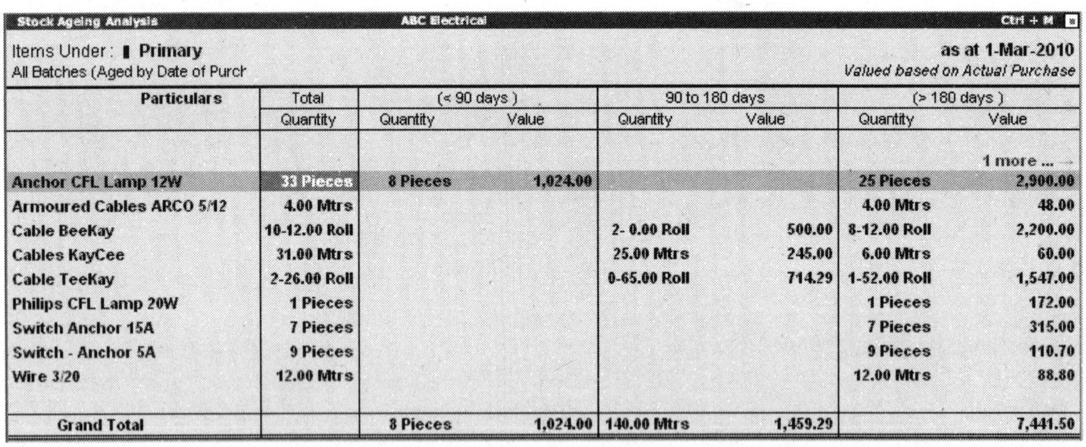

Stock Ageing Analysis — ABC Electrical — Ctrl + M

Items Under : Primary — as at 1-Mar-2010

All Batches (Aged by Date of Purch — Valued based on Actual Purchase

Particulars	Total	(< 90 days)		90 to 180 days		(> 180 days)	
	Quantity	Quantity	Value	Quantity	Value	Quantity	Value
							1 more ... →
Anchor CFL Lamp 12W	33 Pieces	8 Pieces	1,024.00			25 Pieces	2,900.00
Armoured Cables ARCO 5/12	4.00 Mtrs					4.00 Mtrs	48.00
Cable BeeKay	10-12.00 Roll			2- 0.00 Roll	500.00	8-12.00 Roll	2,200.00
Cables KayCee	31.00 Mtrs			25.00 Mtrs	245.00	6.00 Mtrs	60.00
Cable TeeKay	2-26.00 Roll			0-65.00 Roll	714.29	1-52.00 Roll	1,547.00
Philips CFL Lamp 20W	1 Pieces					1 Pieces	172.00
Switch Anchor 15A	7 Pieces					7 Pieces	315.00
Switch - Anchor 5A	9 Pieces					9 Pieces	110.70
Wire 3/20	12.00 Mtrs					12.00 Mtrs	88.80
Grand Total		8 Pieces	1,024.00	140.00 Mtrs	1,459.29		7,441.50

F-1A: Batch Ageing Summary

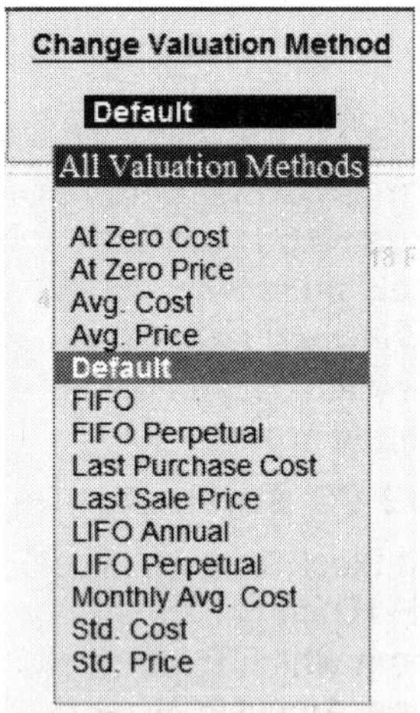

F-1B: Valuation Method List

- **Total Quantity**: To get Item Monthly Summary.
- **Age Column**: At any break-up column to get Item Inward Details for relevant period

02 Ageing Slab

At Batch Ageing Analysis (F-1C), click *F6: Ageing Periods* button (F-1D) to re-define the Ageing Slab (i.e columns for Ageing Analysis). To terminate, enter 0 at last field (F-2A).

Stock Ageing Analysis Ctrl + M

Items Under : Primary
All Batches (Aged by Date of Purchase)

as at 1-Mar-2010
Valued based on Actual Purchase

Particulars	Expiry Date	Total	(< 90 days)	90 to 180 days	(> 180 days)	Negative Stock
		Quantity	Quantity	Quantity	Quantity	Quantity
Anchor CFL Lamp 12W		**33 Pieces**	**8 Pieces**		**25 Pieces**	
23 (Main Location)	*31-Oct-2010*	*15 Pieces*			*15 Pieces*	
37 (Despatch Room)	*1-Dec-2010*	*10 Pieces*			*10 Pieces*	
Primary Batch (Main Location)	*31-Jan-2010*	*8 Pieces*	*8 Pieces*			
Armoured Cables ARCO 5/12		**4.00 Mtrs**			**4.00 Mtrs**	
Main Location		*4.00 Mtrs*			*4.00 Mtrs*	
Cable BeeKay		**10-12.00 Roll**		**2- 0.00 Roll**	**8-12.00 Roll**	
Despatch Room		*1- 0.00 Roll*			*1- 0.00 Roll*	
Main Location		*5-12.00 Roll*		*2- 0.00 Roll*	*3-12.00 Roll*	
Siliguri Godown		*2- 0.00 Roll*			*2- 0.00 Roll*	
Warehouse		*2- 0.00 Roll*			*2- 0.00 Roll*	
Cables KayCee		**31.00 Mtrs**		**25.00 Mtrs**	**6.00 Mtrs**	
Despatch Room		*5.00 Mtrs*			*5.00 Mtrs*	
Main Location		*26.00 Mtrs*		*25.00 Mtrs*	*1.00 Mtrs*	
Cable TeeKay		**2-26.00 Roll**		**0-65.00 Roll**	**1-52.00 Roll**	
Despatch Room		*0-52.00 Roll*			*0-52.00 Roll*	
Main Location		*0-65.00 Roll*		*0-65.00 Roll*		
Siliguri Godown		*1- 0.00 Roll*			*1- 0.00 Roll*	
Philips CFL Lamp 20W		**1 Pieces**			**1 Pieces**	
Main Location		*1 Pieces*			*1 Pieces*	
Switch Anchor 15A		**7 Pieces**			**7 Pieces**	
						5 more ...
Grand Total			**8 Pieces**	**140.00 Mtrs**		

F-1C: Batch Ageing Details

- F1: Detailed
- F2: Period
- F3: Company
- F4: Group
- F6: Ageing Periods
- F7: Valuation
- A: Hide Amounts
- S: Ageing Style
- B: Expired Batches

F-1D: Batch Ageing Buttons

Stock Ageing Alteration

Company: **ABC Electrical**

From	: **0**	To	: **90**
From	: **90**	To	: **180**
From	: **180**	To	: **0**

F-2A: Ageing Slab Set Up

Ageing Style

Ageing Style : **By Date of Purchase**
Show only Expired Batches ? **No**

Ageing Styles

- By Date of Purchase
- By Expiry Date
- By Mfg. Date
- To be Expired

F-2B: Ageing Style selection

02.01 Removing an Age Slab column

To remove any age slab column (useful when any specific age slab column shows no figure), place the cursor on the column to be removed (use Left / Right arrow keys to move sideways between the columns) and click *D:Del Column*. The deleted column cannot be restored (you will have to view the report again).

02.02 Batch Ageing Style

At Stock Ageing Analysis (F-1C), click *S:Ageing Style* button (F-1D) to get Ageing Style screen (F-2B), to specify the Date from which the Age would be computed for the purpose of Age Analysis Report and select the option as explained below.

- **Age as per Expiry Date**: Select *By Expiry Date* to show Agewise break-up on the basis of Expiry Date of each batch.
- **Unexpired Batches**: Select *To be Expired* to show Agewise break-up for batches that would expire in future.
- **Age as per Manufacturing Date**: Select *By Manufacturing Date* to get Agewise break-up as per Manufacturing Date for each Batch.
- **Age as per Date of Purchase**: Select *By Date of Purchase* to get Agewise break up as per Voucher Date (Date of Voucher in which the Batch was created as New Batch).

02.03 Filtering of Batches

To filter the Ageing Report (F-1C), click *B:Expired Batches* / All Batches toggle button:

- *B:Expired Batches*, or at *Ageing Style* (F-2B) set *Yes* at *Show only Expired Batches* to show the Batches which have been expired at the end of the period set
- B:All Batches, or at *Ageing Style* (F-2B), set *No* at *Show only Expired Batches* to show all the Batches in Stock

FAQ: Frequently Asked Questions

FAQ-1: How I can set up slabs for Batch Stock Aged Analysis

Ans. At Stock Ageing Analysis Report, click *F6: Ageing Periods* button to re-define the Ageing Slab (i.e columns for Ageing Analysis). To terminate, enter 0 at last field (F-2A).

Part 6

Godowns

In this Part, we discuss about Godowns (Storage places of materials) and storages of materials at different locations, and movements of materials to & from each storage places. We also discuss about Virtual Godown and other applications of Godown Features.

Godown explains the concept of Godown and activation of Godown Features in Tally.ERP 9.

Godown Masters explains creation of Physical & Virtual Godowns

Godown Reports describes various reports giving details of Location for Stock & Materials movements.

Godowns

06-01

01 Godowns

Godowns are location of materials storage. When Stock Items are stored in different locations, you may maintain the transactions and stock of Items with location (Godownwise) details.

Like Stock Item Groups, Godowns may be organized into different levels.

Any storage space may be treated as a separate Godown to maintain separate stock reports. The Storage spaces (i.e Godowns) may be logically organized into Warehouses, Sheds, Godowns, Racks, BINs, etc. in a multi-tier hierarchy for better organization, to systematically manage storage & handling of Stocks and prepare Stock Reports.

Normally, a Godown is part of the Company's organisation, where Company's Goods are stored. However, any location where Company's Goods (owned or held in Custody) is stored, is called the Godown of the Company. So, the storage place where goods of Third Party held by Company or the storage place where Company's Goods are held by Third Party will also be treated as Company's Godown, irrespective of location. So, a third Party Warehouse or goods held by carrier (e.g Goods-in-Transit) etc, are also treated as Company's Godown.

02 External Agencies as Godowns

Sometimes the goods may lie at other places. For example, goods despatched to Selling Agents, Branches or third party Jobbers are in fact company's property. So, these may be conveniently treated as Godown to get Stock & transaction report with Godownwise details.

Where goods are sold trough Agents, Goods are delivered to Agent, who sells to the Buyers and send us a statement of sale. A sale Invoice is drawn on the buyers.

To track transactions & stock lying with Agents, create a Godown for each Agent. Create Delivery Challan for goods delivered to Agent. Create Sales Invoice selecting the respective Agent (from Godown list).

03 Godown for other attributes

Apart from Storage Place, Godown may alternatively be used for other attributes (instead of storage locations). For example, a Company may use Godown for Grades (like Fresh, Seconds, Defectives), Colour (White Black), Size (22, 18, 16 etc) etc

Example: TVs sets of different brands to be classified as per Size. Each brand has different models (with different price). TVs come in several sizes (like 16, 20, 24, 28, & 30 inches size). The size is common for all the brands. The following scheme to maintain Stock as per Size All Items are stored in Showroom.

To have only one Product Master for each Brand (for all the Models & Sizes). you may treat Brand as Product, Godown as Size (as Size is common for each Brand & Model) & Model as Batch (as Model vary for each Brand). Activate Multiple Godown (as explained)

List of Sizes (Godowns)

TV 16"

TV 20"

....

List of Products

Samsung TV

LG TV

....

Now enter Purchase Voucher for the product and select Size (from Godown). In Sales Voucher, similarly select the Godown after selecting the Product. Now in Godown Summary, you will get Sizewise details of each TV Brand. You may also get columnar Report with columns for each Size.

04 Activation of Godown Features

Click *F11: Features* > *Inventory Features* to get *Inventory Features* screen. At *Inventory Features* screen (F-1A), set *Yes* at *Maintain Multiple Godowns / Excise Units* to enable creation of new Godowns (consequently the option *Godown /Excise Units* will get activated at Inventory Masters Menu to create New Godowns. A Reserved Godown named *Main Location* will be internally auto created by Tally.

Storage & Classification

Maintain Multiple Godowns / Excise Units ? **Yes**

F-1A: Godown Activation

FAQ: Frequently Asked Questions

FAQ-1: How I may activation Godown Features for a Company

Ans: At Click *F11: Features> Inventory Features,* set *Yes* at *Maintain Multiple Godowns / Excise Units* (F-1A) to enable creation of new Godowns. Consequently the option *Godown /Excise Units* will get activated at Inventory Masters Menu to create New Godowns. A Reserved Godown named *Main Location* will be internally auto created by Tally.

Godown Master

06-02

01 Creation of Godown Master

Select *Inventory Info > Godowns* to get Godown Master Menu (F-1A). Select *Create at Single Godown* to get Godown Entry screen (F-2A) and enter the following particulars.

- **Godown Name:** At *Name*, enter Name of the Godown.
- **Parent Godown:** At *Under,* select the Parent Godown (select *Primary* to create a top level Godown and the first Godown). Like Stock Groups, Godowns may be organized into various levels.

Advanced Entries in Godown Master: If you have set *Yes* at *Allow Advanced Entries in Master* under Inventory section, at Masters Configuration (At GoT>F12:Configue>Accts Inventory Info), you may enter the following additional details (advanced options) also at Godown entry screen (F-2A)

- **Godown Address:** At Godown Master Configuration screen (F-2B), set Yes at *Use Godown Address.* Consequently, at Godown Entry screen (F-2A), you may enter the Godown Address in multiple lines.
- **Godown Type:** At *Allow Storage of Materials*:
    - o **Physical Godown:** Set *Yes* when materials are stored in the Godown (to select the Godown in Inventory Voucher entry).
    - o **Virtual Godown:** Set *No* if no materials are not stored in the Godown directly (it is used to Organise Godowns, like Godown Group) and the Godown will not appear in the selection list during voucher entry.

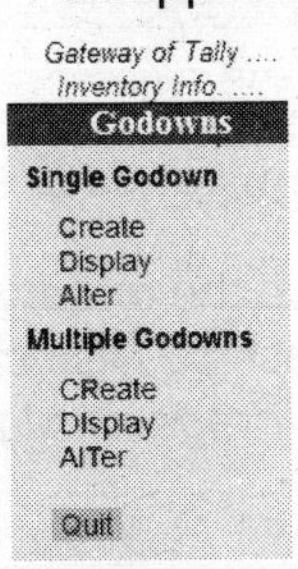

F-1A: Godown Master Menu

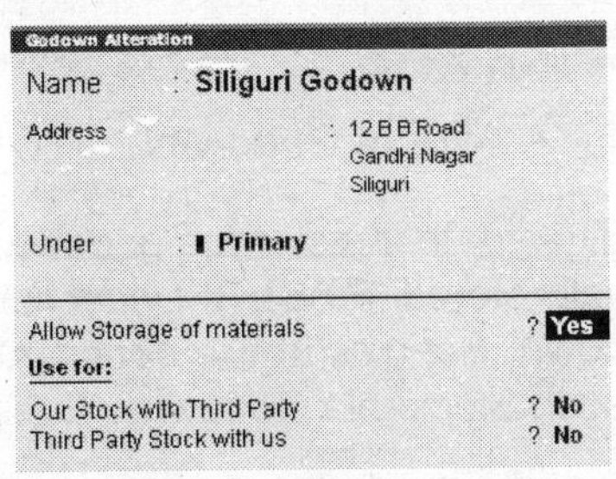

F-2A: Godown Creation

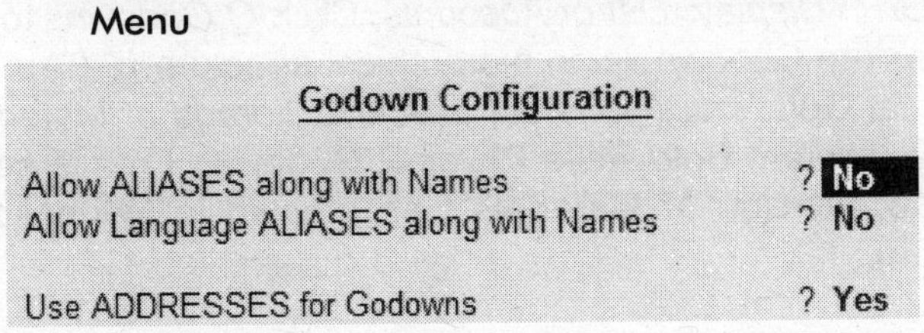

F-2B: Godown Master Configuration

- **Third Party Stock:** According to the purpose of keeping third party stock in Physical Godown, set as follows:
    - **Own Stock with Third Party:** If own stock is kept with third Party, then set *Yes* at *Our Stock with Third party,* else set *No*
    - **Third Party Stock in Own Godown:** If third Party stock is kept in own Godown, then set *Yes* at *Third Party Stock with Us,* else set *No*

02 Godown details in Opening Stock

We have explained entry of Opening Stock Details at Stock Item Master. When Godown is activated, on entry of Opening Stock Quantity for an Item, you get a sub screen to enter Godownwise details of Opening Stock as follows (F-3A):

- **Godown Name**: At *Godown* column, select the Godown from the list of Stockable Godowns (F-3B).
- **Godown Quantity**: At Quantity column, enter the Quantity (and Quantity UoM) of Opening Stock for the Godown.
- **Godown Stock Rate**: At Rate column, enter the Rate (and Rate UoM at *per field*) of Opening Stock for the Godown.
- **Godown Stock Value**: At Amount column, the computed value (Rate X Quantity) is shown (which you may change).

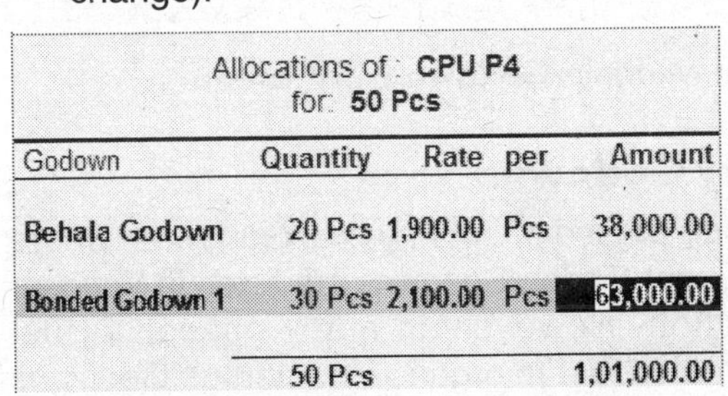

F:3A: Godownwise Opening Stock details

F-3B: List of Godowns

03 Godown Master Display

Select *Inventory Info > Godowns > Display at Single Stock Godown* to view details of any Godown Master. Select the Godown from List to view (like Godown Entry screen, but you can not modify any data).

04 Godown Master Alteration / Deletion

Select *Inventory Info > Godowns > Alter at Single Stock*

Godown to alter any Godown Master data. Select the Godown to alter from List. Carry out the Alteration and press Ctrl+A to save. To *Delete* the Godown, press *Alt+D,* and click *Yes* at *Delete Yes or No?* to confirm Deletion (the Godown cannot be deleted if it has a child Godown or it has been referred in any Voucher or Opening Stock details.

05 Multiple Mode Godown Entry

In Single Mode entry, you can enter only one Godown record at a time, in one screen. To create several Godown records in on screen, select Create at Godown Master Menu (F-1A) at Multiple section to get *Multiple Godown Entry screen* (F-4A).

The process of Godown Entry in Multiple Mode is smilar to Stock Item, Stock Category etc.

Parent Godown: At *Under Godown*,

- Select the Parent Godown under which you like to create new Godowns (useful to create new Godown under same Parent Godown), or
- Select *All Item* (useful to create new Godown under any parent Godown)

Now enter for each new Godown to be created, as follows:

- **Godown Name**: At *Name* column, enter the Godown Name
- **Parent Godown:** At *Under* column, select the Parent Godown (or select *Primary* to create new Godown at Primary level).

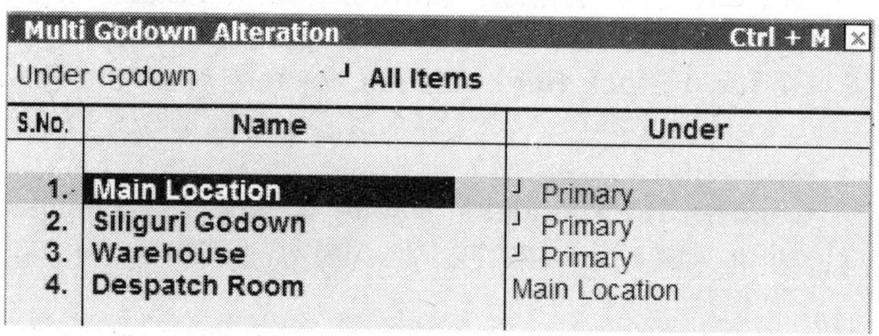

F-4A: Multiple Godown Entry screen

06 Virtual Godowns

So far, we have discussed about Physical Godowns, where Stock is actually kept. These Godowns are listed in Voucher Entry for selection. However, in many cases, Virtual Godowns are created just to organise numerous Godowns at different Levels (Like Stock Group / Stock Category is used to organize Sock Items

For example, A Company has Godowns / Warehosues in different parts of the country. It likes to maintain Godown stock of the Items organised according to State, District & City. First Organise the Godown according to States, Districts & Cities.

- Now first create Top Level Godown (Primary) for each State (e.g Orissa, Bihar etc). At under field, select *Primary* (F-5A).
- Now create second level Godown for each District (F-5B). At *Under* field, select the State Level Godown.
- Next create third level Godown for each City (F-5C). At under field, select the District Level Godown.

Set *No* (F-5A, F-5B, F-5C) at *Allow Storage of Materials* for such Godowns (as these Godowns are Virtual Godown used to organise the actual Godown as per District).

F-5A: State Level Primary Godown

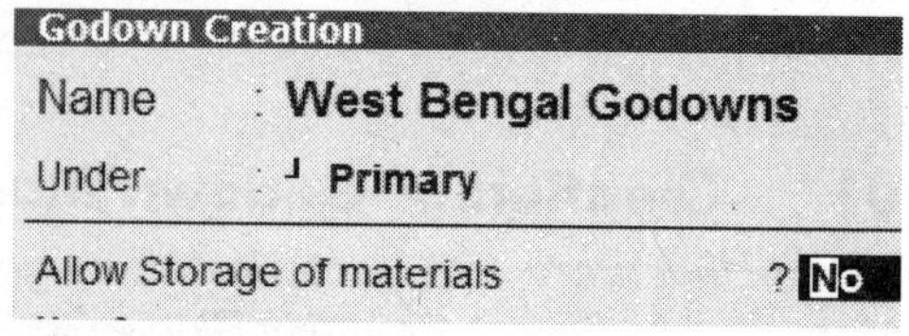

F-5B: District Level Virtual Godown

F-5C: City Level Storage Godown

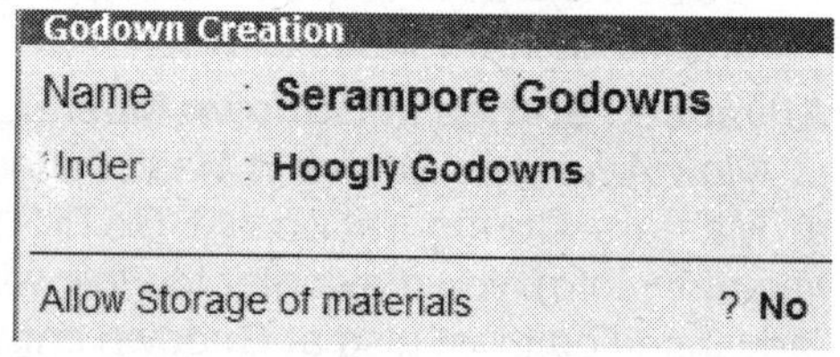

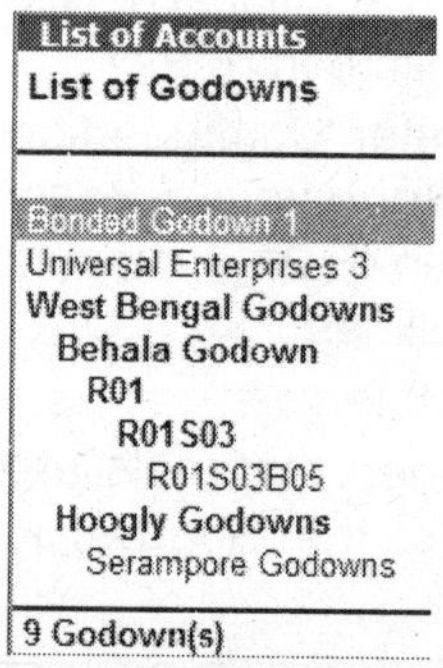

The virtual Godowns may be created in a single physical location with Virtual Godown as identifier of individual section of Godown F-7A). Set *No* at *Allow Storage of Materials* (F-7A), as goods are not stored in such Godowns).

F-6A: Godowns List

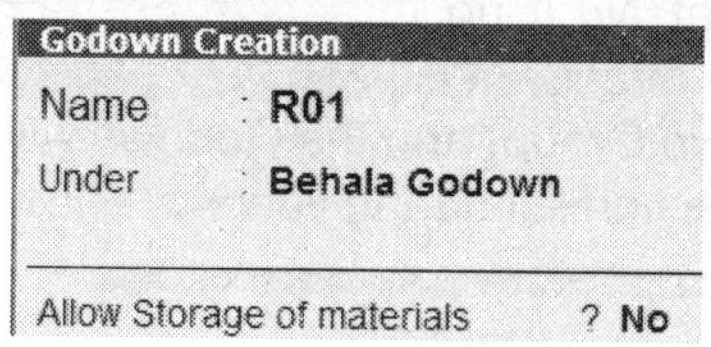

F-7A: Virtual Godowns

F-8B: Physical Godowns

Finally create the storage godowns where the materials are actually stored (F-8B). At *Under* field, select the District Level Godown. Set *Yes* at the option *Allow Storage of Materials* for such Stockable Godowns (F-8B)

07 List of Godowns

At *GoT>Display>List of Accounts*, Click *O:Godowns* to get complete Godown list in hierarchical structure (F-9A). The Virtual Godowns *(No is set at Allow Storage of Materials)* are shown in Bold while Physical Godowns (*Yes* is set at *Allow Storage of Materials*) are shown in Normal font (F-6A).

FAQ: Frequently Asked Questions

FAQ-1: A Company has godwns at differ locations throughout the country. How it can organise the Godown so that it can get Stocks as per State, District, Town etc.

Ans: First Organise the Godown according to States, Districts & Cities.

- Now first create Top Level Godown (Primary) for each State (e.g Orissa, Bihar etc). At under field, select *Primary* (F-5A).
- Now create second level Godown for each District (F-5B). At *Under* field, select the State Level Godown.
- Next create third level Godown for each City (F-5C). At under field, select the District Level Godown.

Set *No* (F-5A, F-5B, 5C) at *Allow Storage of Materials* for such Godowns (as these Godowns are Virtual Godown used to organise the actual Godown as per District).

Godown Reports

06-03

01 Godown details entry in Inventory Voucher

Having created Godown Masters, while entering Stock Item transaction details in Voucher, you may enter Godown details alongwith.

Stock Item details entry in Voucher has been explained earlier. Here we explain the additional process of Godown Details entry at Stock Item allocation screen (F-1B).

At Voucher Entry (F-1A), on selection of Stock Items, you get Item Allocation screen (F-1B), to enter Godownwise details of the stock Item transaction, as follows:

- **Godown**: At *Godown* column, select the Godown from the list of stockable Godowns.
- **Quantity**: At *Quantity* column, Enter the Quantity of transaction of the Item for the Godown.

Purchase No. | 2-Apr-2009 Thursday

Supplier Invoice No. : B001

Party's A/c Name : **Anil Computers**

Purchase Ledger : **Purchase**

Name of Item	Quantity	Rate	per	Amount
Monitor17" AOC Black	3 Pcs	7,500.00	Pcs	22,500.00
Printer Samsung CLX-3175FN	2 Pcs	40,000.00	Pcs	80,000.00
				1,02,500.00
Freight		1.50	%	1,537.50
Trade Discount		(-)2	%	(-)2,050.00
Handling Charges		1.80	%	1,845.00
Narration:	5 Pcs			*1,03,832.50*

F-1A: Voucher Entry

Item Allocations for : **Monitor17" AOC Black**

Godown	Quantity	Rate	per	Amount
Behala Godown	**2 Pcs**	7,500.00	Pcs	15,000.00
Bonded Godown 1	**1 Pcs**	7,500.00	Pcs	7,500.00
	3 Pcs			22,500.00

F-1B: Godown details in Voucher Entry

- **Godown Item Rate**: At *Rate* column, enter the Rate (and Rate & Rate UoM at Per field)
- **Godown Item Value**: At *Amount* column, the computed value (Rate X Quantity) is shown, which you may change.

02 Godown Reports

Having entered the Godown Masters and voucher data, you may now print various reports with Godown data, like:

- Godown Summary
- Godownwise Profitability
- Godown Stock Details
- Columnar Godown Reports

03 Godown Summary

Godown Summary (F-2A) shows the Summary of Transaction & Stock figures of Stock Items in Godowns

At Gateway of Tally, select *Display > Statements of Inventory > Godowns* to get Godown Summary (F-2A)

Godown Summary | ABC Manufacturing | Ctrl + M

ABC Manufacturing
1-Apr-2009 to 1-Mar-2010

Particulars	Opening Balance			Inwards			Outwards						Closing Balance		
	Quantity	*Rate*	Value	Quantity	*Rate*	Value	Quantity	*Rate*	Value	Consumption	Gross Profit	Perc %	Quantity	*Rate*	Value
Bonded Godown 1	40 Pcs	*1,887.50*	75,500.00	13 Pcs	*5,391.72*	70,092.40	140 Pcs	*345.29*	48,340.00	57,457.42	(-)9,117.42	(-)18.86 %	(-)87 Pcs	*1,013.05*	88,134.98
CPU	30 Pcs	2,100.00	63,000.00	9 Pcs	2,293.60	20,642.40	8 Pcs	1,900.00	15,200.00	17,157.42	(-)1,957.42	(-)12.88 %	31 Pcs	2,144.68	66,484.98
CPU P4	30 Pcs	*2,100.00*	63,000.00	9 Pcs	*2,293.60*	20,642.40	8 Pcs	*1,900.00*	15,200.00	17,157.42	(-)1,957.42	(-)12.88 %	31 Pcs	*2,144.68*	66,484.98
Desktop PC							1 Pcs	5,000.00	5,000.00		5,000.00	100.00 %	(-)1 Pcs		
Assembled PC							1 Pcs	*5,000.00*	5,000.00		5,000.00	100.00 %	(-)1 Pcs		
LCD							2 Pcs	12,000.00	24,000.00		24,000.00	100.00 %	(-)2 Pcs		
LCD 18.5							2 Pcs	*12,000.00*	24,000.00		24,000.00	100.00 %	(-)2 Pcs		
Monitor				2 Pcs	3,950.00	7,900.00							2 Pcs	3,950.00	7,900.00
Monitor				1 Pcs	*400.00*	400.00							1 Pcs	*400.00*	400.00
Monitor17" AOC Black				1 Pcs	*7,500.00*	7,500.00							1 Pcs	*7,500.00*	7,500.00
Motherboard	10 Pcs	1,250.00	12,500.00	1 Pcs	1,250.00	1,250.00	128 Pcs	30.00	3,840.00		3,840.00	100.00 %	(-)117 Pcs	117.52	13,750.00
Mother Board	10 Pcs	*1,250.00*	12,500.00	1 Pcs	*1,250.00*	1,250.00							11 Pcs	*1,250.00*	13,750.00
Mother Board Port							128 Pcs	*30.00*	3,840.00		3,840.00	100.00 %	(-)128 Pcs		
															42 more ...
Grand Total	**532 Pcs**		**54,64,740.00**	**150 Pcs**		**2,91,442.40**	**165 Pcs**		**1,53,090.00**	**1,75,328.85**	**(-)22,238.85**	**(-)14.53 %**	**517 Pcs**		**55,80,853.55**

F-2A: Godown Summary (Details)

03.01 Godown Summary Configuration

By default, the Godown Summary initially shows the Godowns under the selected Godown (Select *Primary* to show top level Godowns)

At *Godown Summary* (F-2A), click *F12:Configure* to get the Godown Summary configuration screen (F-3A) to set up options to configure the contents of the Report as follows:

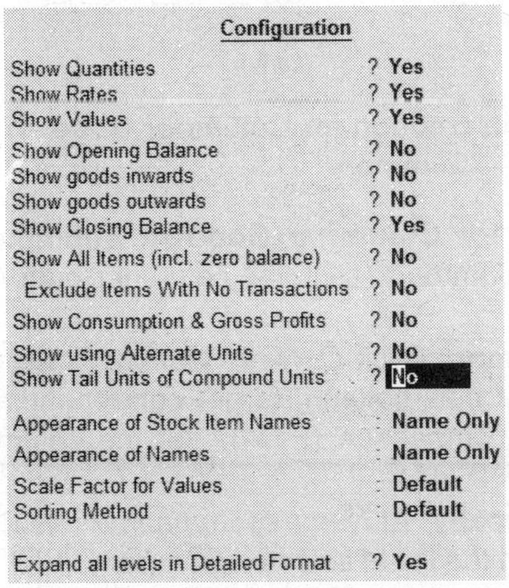

F-3A: Godown Summary Configuration

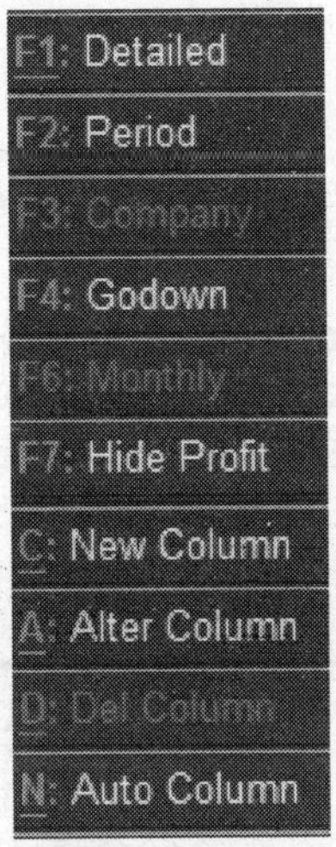

F-3B: Godown Summary Buttons

i. Multi Column Options

Set Yes / No to the following options as required. Each option affects multiple set of columns (*Opening / Inward / Outwards/ Closing)*

a. **Quantity / Rate / Value**: The following columns appear for Opening Balance, Goods Inwards, Goods Outwards & Closing Balance. The option is applicable for all these columns, if activated (e.g if *Yes* is set at Show Quantity, Quantity column will appear in the activated columns (Goods Inwards, Goods outwards & Closing balance, and like that for Rate & Value column)
   - o **Quantity**: At *Show Quantities*, set *Yes* to show the Quantity column (and the base unit), Set *No* to suppress the Quantity column
   - o **Rate**: At *Show Rates*, set *Yes* to show the Rate column (as per the base UoM displayed with Quantity figure), Set *No* to suppress the Rate column.
   - o **Value**: At *Show Values*, set *Yes* to show the Value column, Set *No* to suppress the Value column

b. **Opening/ Inwards / Outwards / Closing**: Set Yes to show the figures for the respective 3 columns activated (Quantity, Rate, Value)
   - o **Opening Balance**: At *Show Opening Balance*, set *Yes* to show the figures of Opening Balance for the respective column activated (Quantity, Rate, Value)
   - o **Goods Inwards**: At *Show Goods Inwards,* set *Yes* to show the figures of Goods Inwards for the respective column activated (Quantity, Rate, Value)
   - o **Goods Outwards**: At *Show Goods Outwards*, set Yes to show the figures of Goods Outwards for the respective column activated (Quantity, Rate, Value)
   - o **Closing Balance**: At *Show Closing Balance*, set Yes to show the figures of Closing balance for the respective column activated (Quantity, Rate, Value)

The values (Quantity, Rate, Amount) of each of the column (Opening, Inwards, Outwards, Closing) are displayed according to the current period (referred as *Report Period* – set through F2: period button) for the respective column:

ii. Set *Yes* / *No* to the following options to show / suppress the columns as required

- **Stock Items**: At *Show All Items,* set:
  - o *Yes* to show the Item even if all the displayed figures for the Item is zero.
  - o *No* to suppress the Items where the values of all the displayed column are zero.
- **Consumption & Gross Profit**: At *Show Consumption & Gross Profit* Set:
  - o *Yes* to show the Consumption Value & Gross Profit figures also, for Sales / Outwards column (explained next),
  - o No. the Consumption Value & Gross Profit columns are not shown.
- **Alternate Units**: At *Show using Alternate units*, set
  - o *Yes* to show the quantity also in *Alternate units* (for Items having Dual Units),
  - o *No* to show the quantity only the Base Unit
- **Tail Units**: At *Show Tail units of Compound Units*, set:
  - o *Yes* to show Quantity in Tail units of Compound unit
  - o *No* to show only in terms of Base (Major) unit (with fraction values, where applicable)
- **Detail Levels**: At *Expand all levels in Detailed Format*, set *Yes* to show the Items upto the lowest level details (in detail mode- i.e, when *F1: Detail* is selected), otherwise only next level detail (Item Group / Stock Items) are shown in detail mode.

03.02 Godownwise Profitability / Contribution

Godownwise Profitability report shows the Itemwise Contribution (Sale Amount – Cost) against outward transaction (normally sales) for each Godown.

To get the gross profit details of Sale (shown in Outwards column: F-2A),

- At Godown Summary Configuration screen (F-3A), set *Yes* at *Show Consumption & Gross Profit.*, or
- At Godown Summary buttons (F-3B), Click *F7:Show Profit* toggle button

Consequently, at Outwards section of Stock Summary, in the consumption column (F-2A), the following new columns appear:

- o **Consumption**: The computed cost of Goods sold / consumed as per valuation method specified for the stock Item
- o **Gross Profit**: The gross profit, i.e the difference of value of consumption / sale is shown. If the cost is more than the consumption / sale value, the profit is shown in negative.
- o **Perc %**: The percentage of gross profit on the consumption / sale value is shown (Gross Profit / Outwards Value) x 100

The Gross Profit & Perc % is shown only when Sale Value is entered in the voucher. If Cost data is not available, the Profit Percentage would be shown as 100% (as Cost is treated as Zero). So, this report is reliable only when correct and complete Sales & Cost Data are entered in respect of each transaction, otherwise the figures would be erroneous and misleading.

03.03 Godown Details report

Initially, the report shows the Primary Godown (with subordinate Godowns / Stock Items in detail format). On drill down from any Godown / Stock Item, the next level reports appear as follows:

- o **From Godown:** The Stock Summary for the selected Godown appears showing the next level Godown / Stock Items
- o **From Stock Items:** The Stock Item Monthly Summary for the selected Stock Item appears showing the monthwise figures for each month for the current period.

03.04 Columnar Godown Summary

Columnar Report creation as per defined new column has been explained earlier. To get corresponding Godown Summary figures in adjacent columns for better comparison, at Godown Summary Report (F-2A), click the columnar buttons (F-3B) as follows:

- *C: New Column*: To create a new columns as per specified column definition, to get the corresponding figures in adjacent columns for better comparison.
- N: Auto Column: To create multiple columns (as per specified period frequency or for various Stock Valuation methods)

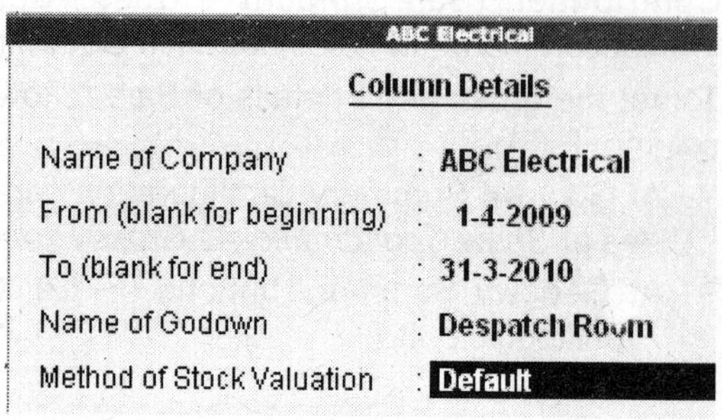

F-4A: New Column creation for Columnar Godown Summary

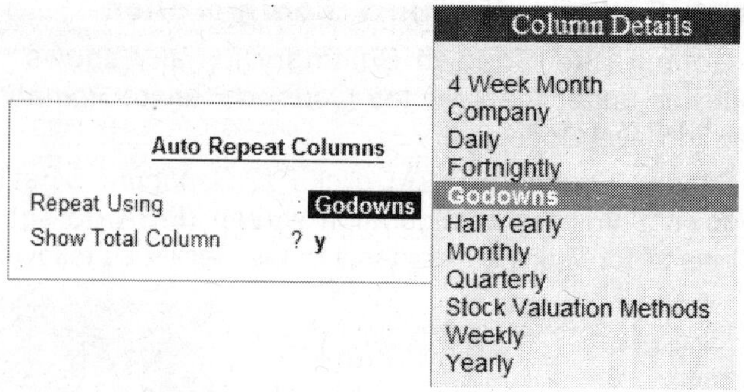

F-4B: Auto r Column creation for Columnar Godown Summary

Column definitions for Columnar Godown Summary Report: At Godown Summary, click the columnar buttons as follows (F-3B):

- **Single New Columns:** Click *C: New Column* (F-3B) to create an adjacent new column, to get corresponding figures for better comparison (F-5A). Set the column definition as follows (F-4A)
  - o **Another Company:** At *Name of Company*, select a Company from the list of selected Company
  - o **Another Period:** At *From* & *To* field respectively, specify the Start & End Date of the report
  - o **Another Godown:** At *Name of Godown* field, select another Godown
  - o **Another Valuation Method:** At *Method of Stock Valuation*, select the Valuation Method. It is useful for comparison of consumption / stock values indifferent methods for management decisions (like price fixing / quotation, make buy decisions, stock value to be entered manually in Accounts, etc

  This way you may create several adjacent new columns in any manner as desired.
- **Automatic Multiple Columns**: Click *N: Auto Column* to get Auto Column set up screen (F-4B) to create repeating multiple columns. At *Repeat Using* (F-4B), select as follows from the list
  - o **Regular period interval:** Select a Repeating period interval (e.g weekly, monthly, quarterly etc), to get automatically created columns for each period, showing comparative periodical figures
  - o **Godown:** Select *Godown* to get automated columns for each Godown.
  - o **Stock Valuation Methods:** Select *Stock Valuation Methods* to get automated columns for each of the Stock Valuation Methods specified by Tally.

At *Show Total Columns* (F-4B), set Yes to get a new Column for Totals of the corresponding figures of all the Auto Columns created.

On setting the columns, you get the Columnar Godown Report as per columns defined (F-5A).

Godown Summary **ABC Electrical** Ctrl + M

Particulars	Despatch Room **ABC Electrical** 1-Jan-2010 to 31-Mar-2010				Main Location ***ABC Electrical*** *1-Jan-2010 to 31-Mar-2010*			
	Opening Balance Quantity	**Inwards** Quantity	**Outwards** Quantity	**Closing Balance** Quantity	**Opening Balance** Quantity	**Inwards** Quantity	**Outwards** Quantity	**Closing Balance** Quantity
Despatch Room					*82.00 Mtrs*			*82.00 Mtrs*
Cables & Wires	82.00 Mtrs			82.00 Mtrs	***327.00 Mtrs***		***83.00 Mtrs***	***244.00 Mtrs***
Lamp					***24 Pieces***	***10 Pieces***	***2 Pieces***	***32 Pieces***
Switches					***16 Pieces***			***16 Pieces***
Grand Total	82.00 Mtrs			82.00 Mtrs		10 Pieces		

F-5A: Columnar Godown Summary

FAQ: Frequently Asked Questions

FAQ-1: How I can get a columnar report for Stock & transactions for each Godown in separate columns

Ans: To get Stock figures for each Gowon in adjacent columns, in compact tabular format, at Godown Summary Report (F-2A), click *C: New Column* buttons (F-3B), and select the Godown & Period (F-4A), to create a new column for each Godown. Thus you get the corresponding figures in adjacent column.

Part 7

Production

In this Part, we discuss abut Bill of Materials of a Manufactured Item and the recording of materials transformation in Production Process.

Bill of Materials describes how to create alternate sets of consumable Materials for Production of an Item

Manufacturing explains creation of Manufacturing Journal and recording of Raw Materials Consumed & Finished Materials produced in each stage of Production process.

Bill of Materials

07-01

01 Bill of Materials (BoM)

Often, standard products are manufactured in which specified consumable (Raw) materials are used to produce specified quantity of Finished Products (alongwith Bye Product / Joint Product in some cases).

Bill of Materials (BoM) is a profile of a Manufactured / Assembled product showing the standard consumption of each Raw Materials / Components to produce Standard Assembled / Finished product. For any Manufactured / Assembled Item, where some materials are consumed to produce a different product (finished or semi-finished), the BoM may be created specifying the standard quantity for Production & Consumption. This profile is used to create Manufacturing Journals used for control of materials issue & consumption in a production system.

02 BoM Activation

At GoT> *F12: Configure> Accts/Inv Info*, set *Yes* at *Allow Component List Details (Bill of Materials)* to activate BoM features (F-1A).

03 BoM Masters Entry

Having activated BoM feature at Configuration (F-1A), set the BoM for the Stock Item (Manufactured / Assembled Product). Before creation of BoM, you should have already created the Stock Item Masters for component Stock Items, which would be used to produce the Finished Product for which the BoM is being created.

Stock Item creation has already been explained. Here we explain additional features related to BoM.

At Stock Item Creation / Alteration screen (*GoT>Inventory Info>Stock Items>Create*), set *Yes* at *Set Components (BoM)* (F-1B), to get BoM List entry screen (F-1C).

F-1A: Inventory Master Configuration

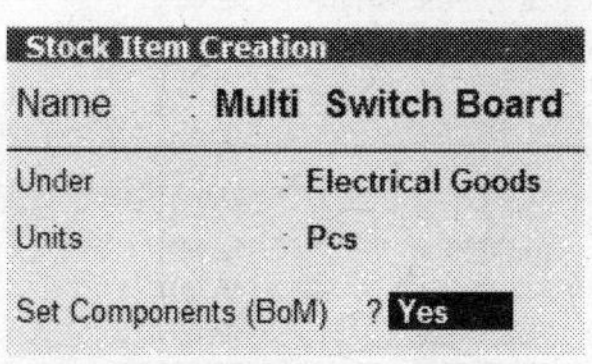

F-1B: Stock Item (BoM) Entry

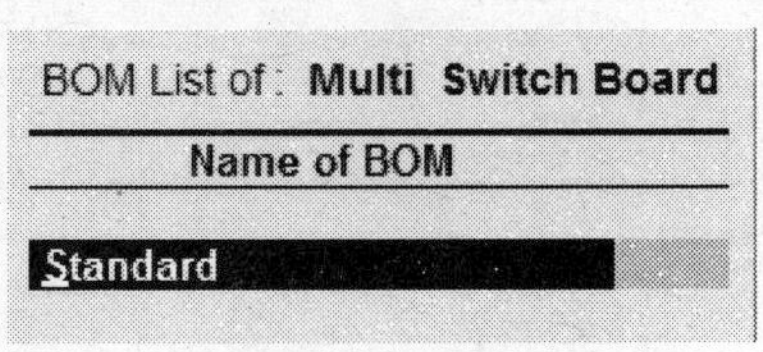

F-1C: BoM List entry

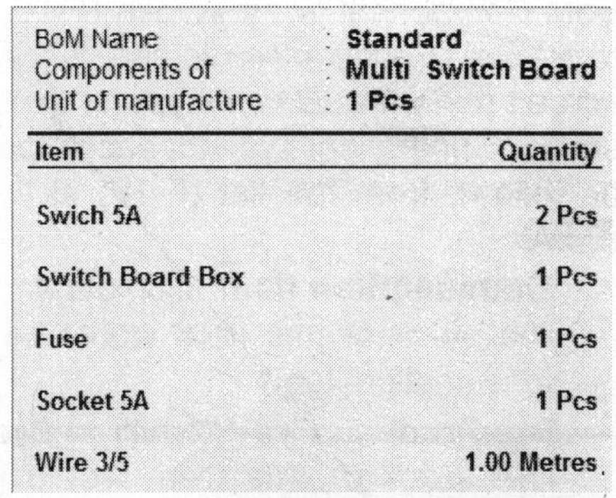

F-1D: BoM Component list entry

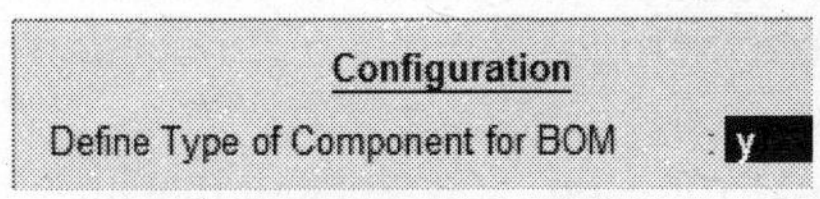

F-1E: BoM Configuration

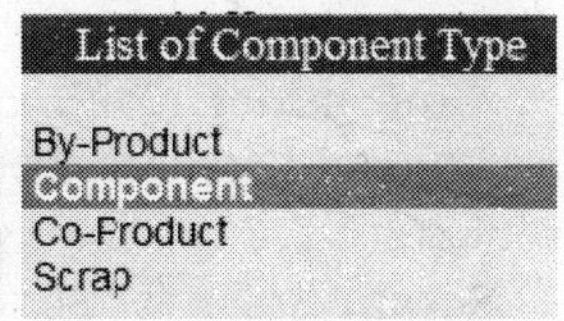

F-1F: Component Type List

At BoM List entry screen (F-1C), at *Name of BoM* column, enter the Name of BoM to get BoM Entry screen (F-1D)..

BoM entry screen (F-1D) has 2 main component. At the upper part, enter the details of Finished Product (Production part), while in Lower Part (Consumption part), enter the details of Standard Components used to produce the Item specified in Production part

Through BoM List, you may create multiple BoM as explained later (§04).

03.01 BoM Production Details Entry

At the upper part at of BoM entry screen (F-1D), enter the details of Production Item, as follows:

- **BoM Name**: At *BoM Name*, the BoM Name as entered in BoM List is carried for reference
- **Produced Item Name**: At *Components of*, name of Produced Item is displayed for reference.
- **Standard Quantity:** At *Unit of Manufacture*, enter the standard quantity of the Finished Goods for which you wish to enter List of Components. For example, if you have Component List for making 100 Pcs Wallets, enter here 100 Pcs.

03.02 BoM Consumption Details Entry

After the entry of Production Item (F-1D), enter the details of Consumption items.

- **Item Name**: At *Item* column, select the Item consumed (pres Alt+C to create a new Item and then select the Item)
- **Item Quantity**: At *Quantity* column, enter standard quantity of the materials that would be consumed to manufacture the quantity of finished goods as specified at *Unit of Manufacture*.

03.03 Joint / Bye Products Details in BoM

To enter the details of Bye-Product / Joint Product also, at BoM Component entry screen (F-1D), click *F12:Configure* to get *BoM Configuration* screen (F-1E). At *BoM Configuration* screen (F-1E), at *Define Type of Component*, set *Yes* at to specify Component Type for each Stock Item entered, select as follows from the list (F-1F) at the BoM Entry screen (F-2A).

- **Consumption Item**: *Component* for Items consumed. The stock of this Item would be reduced. (as it is a consumption Item)
- **Bye-Product:** *Bye-Product* for Bye-Products Produced. The stock of this Item would increase (as it is a Production Item)
- **Co-Product**: *Co-Product* for Joint Product Produced. The stock of this Item would increase (as it is a Production Item)
- **Scrap:** *Scrap* for Scrap Produced. The stock of this Item would increase (as it is a Production Item).

03.04 Expenses for Additional Items Production

In case of additional Items produced (Scrap / Bye Product / Co-Product), at BoM Entry screen (F-2A), at Rate % column, you may enter the expenses (if any), in terms of % of total cost to recover the additional produced Item. For example, if some Scrap is produced, you may enter the % of value that would be spent to recover the Scrap / Bye Product (enter zero if there is no additional cost to recover the Bye Product / Joint Product / Scrap Item).

BoM Name : **Standard**
Components of : **Multi Switch Board**
Unit of manufacture : **1 Pcs**

Item	Type of Item	Quantity	Rate (%)
Swich 5A	Component	2 Pcs	
Switch Board Box	Component	1 Pcs	
Fuse	Component	1 Pcs	
Socket 5A	Component	1 Pcs	
Wire 3/5	Component	1.00 Metres	
Wood Scrap	Scrap	0.10 Kilograms	0.50 %

F-2A: BoM entry with additional product

BOM List of : **Multi Switch Board**

Name of BOM
Standard
Dual

F-2B: BoM Name List

BoM Name : **Dual**
Components of : **Multi Switch Board**
Unit of manufacture : **1 Pcs**

Item	Type of Item	Quantity	Rate (%)
Swich 5A	Component	1 Pcs	
Switch 15A	Component	1 Pcs	
Socket 5A	Component	1 Pcs	
Wire 3/5	Component	1.00 Metres	
Fuse	Component	1 Pcs	
Wood Scrap	Scrap	0.15 Kilograms	0.50 %
Switch Board Box	Component	1 Pcs	

F-2C: Additional BoM Entry

04 Multiple BoM Entry

Sometimes, Alternate versions / models of same Item may be produced in which the components used may differ to some extent. In such case, you create separate BoM (multiple BoMs) for each version (model) of the Item.

To enter additional BoM, at Stock Item entry/ alteration screen, at explained above, at BoM Name list screen (F-1C), enter the name of another BoM (press down arrow to get next line). Enter the name of BoM (F-2B) to get BoM Component List entry as explained earlier. Now enter the Item details for the BoM (F-2C) in the same way as explained earlier.

05 Cost Estimation

Having created the BoM, you may display the Materials Cost of the Finished Products, as per BoM set.

At *GoT>Display>Statement of Inventory>Cost Estimation*, select the Stock Item Group. The Cost Item Report for the Stock Items (for which BoM have been entered) under the selected Stock Group are displayed (F-3B). If there are multiple BoMs set for an Item, details of each BoM will be listed (F-3B).

Item Estimates Ctrl + M

Items Under : **Electrical Goods** **as at 22-May-2013**
BoM Type : **Default**

Particulars	Qty	Cost	Amount
Multi Switch Board	1 Pcs	90.00/Pcs	90.00
Swich 5A	*2 Pcs*	*15.00/Pcs*	*30.00*
Switch Board Box	*1 Pcs*	*25.00/Pcs*	*25.00*
Fuse	*1 Pcs*	*2.00/Pcs*	*2.00*
Socket 5A	*1 Pcs*	*18.00/Pcs*	*18.00*
Wire 3/5	*1.00 Metres*	*15.00/Metres*	*15.00*

F-3A: Default BoM Cost

Item Estimates Ctrl + M

Items Under : **Electrical Goods** **as at 22-May-2013**
BoM Type : **All Items**

Particulars	Qty	Cost	Amount
Multi Switch Board			
Standard	*1 Pcs*	*90.00/Pcs*	*90.00*
Swich 5A	*2 Pcs*	*15.00/Pcs*	*30.00*
Switch Board Box	*1 Pcs*	*25.00/Pcs*	*25.00*
Fuse	*1 Pcs*	*2.00/Pcs*	*2.00*
Socket 5A	*1 Pcs*	*18.00/Pcs*	*18.00*
Wire 3/5	*1.00 Metres*	*15.00/Metres*	*15.00*
Dual	*1 Pcs*	*117.45/Pcs*	*117.45*
Swich 5A	*1 Pcs*	*15.00/Pcs*	*15.00*
Switch 15A	*1 Pcs*	*40.00/Pcs*	*40.00*
Socket 5A	*1 Pcs*	*18.00/Pcs*	*18.00*
Wire 3/5	*1.00 Metres*	*15.00/Metres*	*15.00*
Fuse	*1 Pcs*	*2.00/Pcs*	*2.00*
Switch Board Box	*1 Pcs*	*25.00/Pcs*	*25.00*

F-3B: Multiple BoM Cost

Buttons

At *Cost Estimate* Report (F-3A/ F-3B), you get following Buttons (F-3C)

- **F4: Group:** To select he Stock Group of the Parent Group of the Stock Items for which the Cost Estimate is to be displayed

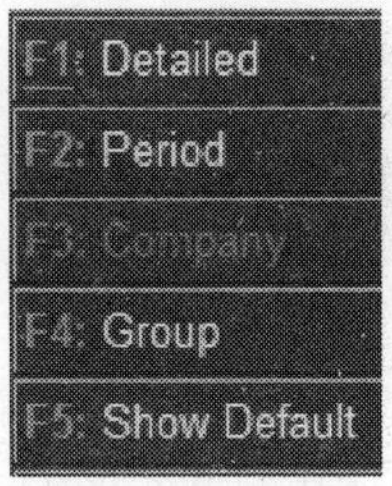

F-3C: Buttons

- **F5:Show Default / Show All BoM**
    - o Click *Show Default* to show the Cost Estimate as per the first BoM specified for the Stock Item
    - o Click *Show All BoM* to show the Cost Estimate of all the BoMs specified for the Stock Item

FAQ: Frequently Asked Questions

FAQ-1: How to activate Bill of Materials Features for the Company & Stock Items

Ans:

a. **Activation for Company**: At GoT> *F12: Configure> Accts/Inv Info*, set *Yes* at *Allow Component List Details (Bill of Materials)* to activate BoM (P-1A).

b. **Bill of Materials set up for Stock Item:** At Stock Item Creation / Alteration screen (*GoT>Inventory Info>Stock Items>Create*) of the Manufactured / Assembled Item, set *Yes* at *Set Components (BoM)* (F-1B), to get BoM List entry screen.

Manufacturing 07-02

01 Manufacturing

In Trading Business, the Items bought are sold in the same state. In Manufacturing, Items bought (Raw Materials) are consumed to produce the Finished Products. The Finished Goods produced are then sold. So, the Items bought (Raw Materials & components) are different from Items sold (Finished Product).

In this Chapter, we explain the Inventory Vouchers relating to consumption of Raw Materials and components to produce Finished Products during the Manufacturing Process.

02 Manufacturing Journal Type

The consumption of consumable materials and production of Finished Product in a manufacturing process are recorded in *Manufacturing Journal*. Unlike Sales (Materials *Out)* or Purchase (Materials *In*), in Manufacturing Journal, both way transactions (consumables Materials *Out* & produced materials *In*) are recorded in same voucher.

02.01 Manufacturing Journal Type Creation

To create a *Manufacturing Journal Type*, create a Stock Journal Voucher Type (F-1A) and then specify it as *Manufacturing Journal Type*

Voucher Type creation has been explained earlier. Here we explain the points specific to Manufacturing Journal Voucher Type creation. At Voucher Type creation screen (GoT>Inventory Info>Voucher Type – F-1A)):

- **Voucher Type:** At *Type of Voucher*, select Stock Journal.
- **Manufacturing Journal**: Set *Yes* at *Use as a Manufacturing Journal*

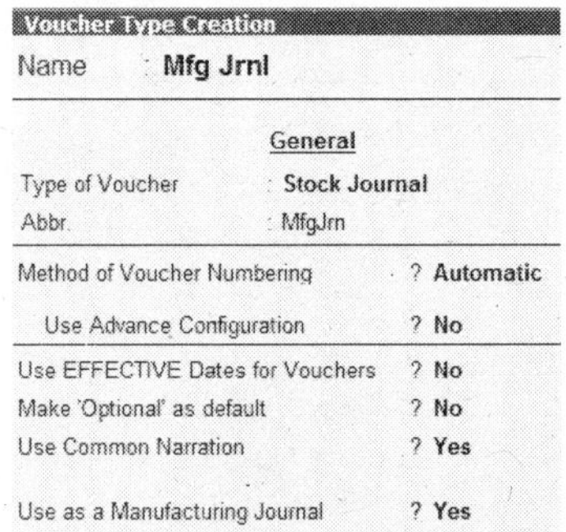

Save the *Manufacturing Journal* Voucher Type

F-1A: Manufacturing Journal Creation

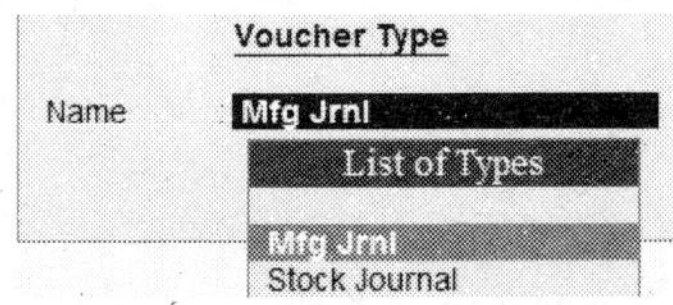

F-2A: Manufacturing Journal Type selection

03 Manufacturing Journal Entry

Manufacturing Journal is the record of Materials Produced and the corresponding materials consumed for the Production, in a manufacturing process.

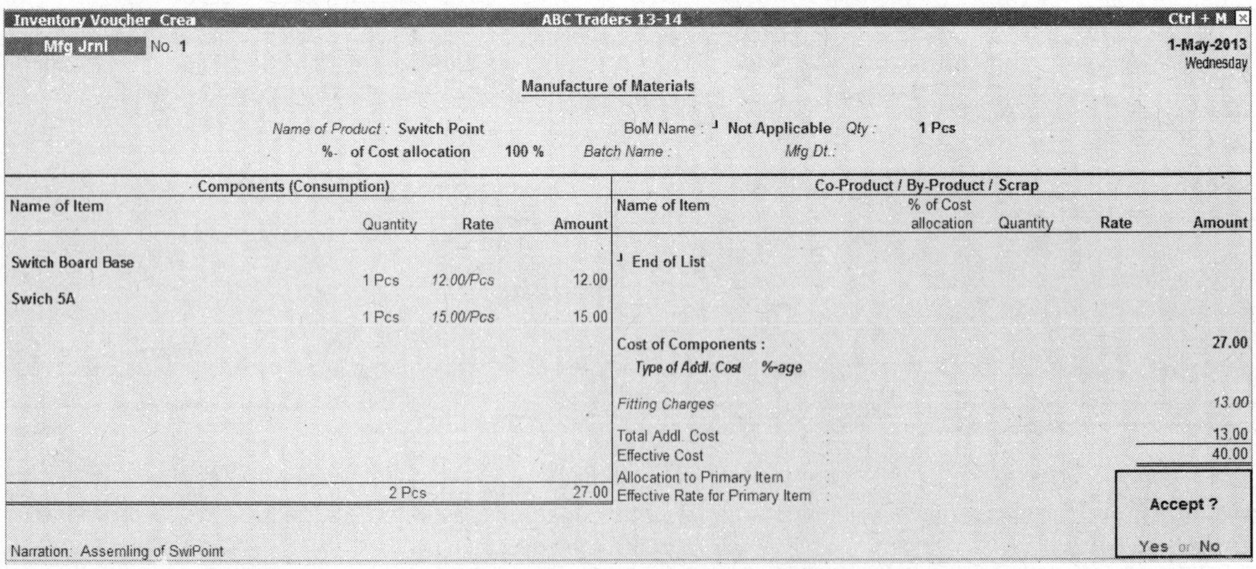

F-2B: Manufacturing Journal Entry

At Gateway, select Inventory Voucher, click *F7: Stk Journal* button and then select Manufacturing Journal from the list of Voucher Types (F-2A), to get Manufacturing Journal entry screen (F-2B).

At Manufacturing Journal entry screen (F-2B), after entry of Voucher Number & Date as usual, enter the Production & Consumption details as follows:

- Production Item Details
- Consumption Items Details
- Bye / Joint Products / Scrap Details
- Manufacturing / Additional Expenses

03.01 Production Item Details

At top part enter details of Manufactured Item (F-2B)

- **Produced Item Name**: At *Name of Product*, select the Item Produced.
- **Production Quantity**: At *Quantity*, enter the Quantity Produced.
- **Allocation %:** At *% of Cost Allocation*, enter the % of total cost to be allocated to the Product (In case of single product, normally 100% Cost is allocated to the Product).
- **Other Details:** Enter other details as follows, as activated and applicable
  - o **Batch**: If Batch number is activated for the Item produced, enter the Batch Number, Mfg Date & Expiry Date, as applicable.
  - o **Godown**: If Multiple Godown is also activated, enter the Godown Name
  - o **BoM**: If BoM is specified for the Item, select the BoM Name

The stock of the Item produced will increase by the Production quantity entered here.

03.02 Consumption Item Details

On entry of the Production details, enter the details of Consumption Items as below (F-2B):

- **Item Name**: If BoM is selected, at *Name of Item* column, the Item consumed as per BoM is displayed. You may also select a new Item consumed to add in the list. If no BoM is specified, select the Item.
- **Consumption Quantity**: If BoM is selected, at Quantity column, the computed Standard Consumption Quantity is displayed, which you may change. If no BoM is specified, enter the Item Quantity.
- **Rate**: At Rate column, the Standard Cost as entered in the Item (if any) is carried, which you may change. Otherwise, enter the Rate (Cost) of the Item.
- **Item Cost**: The computed cost of the Item is displayed at *Amount* Column, which you may change.

The stock of the Items consumed will be reduced from the bt the quantity specified against the respective Stock Item in consumption side.

03.03 Manufacturing / Cost Expenses

The Total Cost is composed of two main components. Cost of Material Consumed and Manufacturing Expenses. The Costs are shown at the Right Part (F-2C).

Cost of Components: The total cost of components consumed, as shown at the left part, is carried at the at the right part.

Manufacturing Expenses: Apart from Cost of Components, additional expenses (like manufacturing direct expenses, overheads etc) are also incurred for the manufacturing

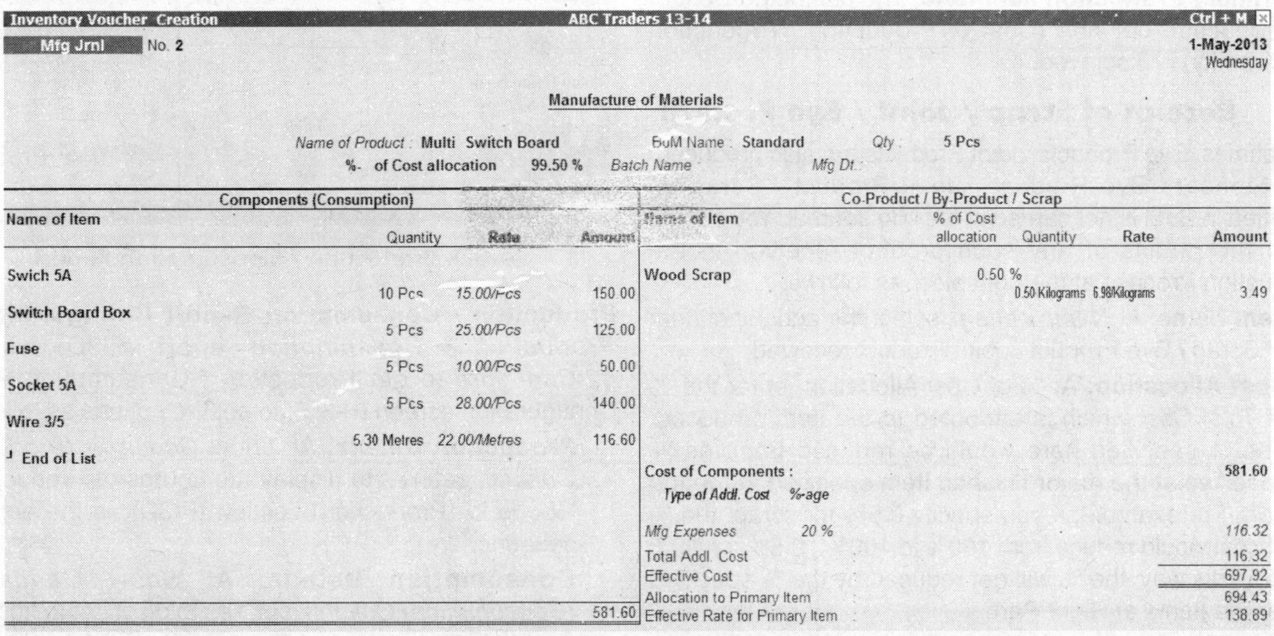

F-2C: Manufacturing Jounal using BoM (with scrap production)

process. Enter these expenses as % of the Cost of Components so arrived.

Enter the details of each Expenses Ledger as explained below:

- **Expense Ledger Account**: At *Name of Item* column, select the Expenses Ledger Account (or press *Alt+C* to get Ledger Creation screen, create the Ledger Account and select it)
- **Expense Rate**: At next field, enter the expenses Rate in % (or you leave it blank)
- **Expense Amount**:
  - o If Expenses Rate is specified, the computed amount of Expenses (Total Component Cost x Expense Rate / 100) is shown at Amount column, which you may change.
  - o If Expenses Rate is not specified, enter the Expense Amount at Amount column

This way, enter for all the expenses.

Manufacturing Journal is a pure Inventory Voucher. Only stock if the Items get affected. The Ledger Accounts (Expenses Accounts) entered in the Mfg Journal are not affected.

The following figures as computed from the Item details as entered are shown:

- **Effective Cost**: The Total Cost (Cost of Components & Manufacturing Expenses) is shown at *Effective Cost*
- **Primary Production Item Rate**: The computed Cost of production per unit (Cost of Production / Production Quantity) is displayed.

04 Receipt of Scrap / Joint / Bye Product

Sometimes, Bye Products, Joint Products are also produced. The Standard Bye Product / Joint Product / Scrap as specified in BoM is not carried in the Mfg Journal. You should enter the details of any such product received in the Production Process at the right side, as follows:

- **Item Name**: At *Name of Item*, select the additional Item of Scrap / Bye Product / Joint Product received.
- **Cost Allocation:** At % of Cost Allocation, enter the % of Total Cost which is attributed to the Item produced. The % specified here would be reduced from the % specified at the major finished Item specified at the top part. For example, if you specify 0.5% for scrap, the % of cost would reduce from 100% to 100% - 0.5%, i.e 99.5 %). This way, the % will get reduced by the % specified for the Items at Right Part.
- **Quantity**: Enter the Quantity of the Item Received
- **Rate / Amount:** If any % allocation is specified, then the amount is computed accordingly and shown at *Amount* column. The Rate is computed from the Amount and the Quantity and shown at Rate column. If no Cost Allocation % is specified, the Rate and Amount remains zero

Primary Production Item Cost: The Total Cost less the Cost Allocated to Joint /Bye Product / Scrap is Cost, is allocated to the Primary Item produced, as shown at the header. This is shown at *Allocation to Primary Item.*

05 Production & Consumption Report

We have already explained Stock Journal Report. If you have created Manufacturing Journal also, you may get the report of Production & Consumption, as entered in Manufacturing Journal

Select *Display > Inventory Books > Movement Analysis > Transfer Analysis* and select the Manufacturing Journal Type (F-3A) to get Production & Consumption report (F-3D)

F-3A: Selection of Voucher Type

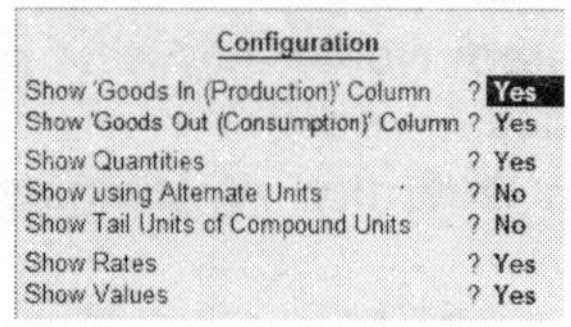

F-3B: Configuration

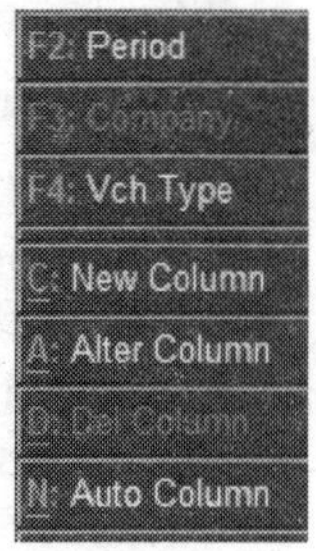

F-3C: Buttons

Transfer Analysis — Ctrl + M

Mfg Jrnl
ABC Traders 13-14
1-Apr-2013 to 22-May-2013

Particulars	Goods In (Production)			Goods Out (Consumption)		
	Quantity	*Eff. Rate*	Value	Quantity	*Eff. Rate*	Value
Fuse				5 Pcs	10.00	50.00
Multi Switch Board	5 Pcs	***138.89***	694.43			
Socket 5A				5 Pcs	*28.00*	140.00
Swich 5A				11 Pcs	*15.00*	165.00
Switch Board Base				1 Pcs	*12.00*	12.00
Switch Board Box				5 Pcs	*25.00*	125.00
Switch Point	1 Pcs	***40.00***	40.00			
Wire 3/5				5.30 Metres	*22.00*	116.60
Wood Scrap	0.50 Kilograms	***6.98***	3.49			
Grand Total			737.92			608.60

F-3D: Production / Consumption Report

Production / Consumption Report Configuration: At *Production & Consumption* report (F-3D), click *F-12:Configure* to get Production / Consumption Report Configuration screen (F-3B), to set the options as follows:

- **Production Details**: At *Show Goods In (Production) Column*, set *Yes* to display the figures of Production at Goods In (Production) section (F-3D), in the activated columns.
- **Consumption Details**: At *Show Goods Out (Consumption) Column*, set *Yes* to display the figures of Consumption at Goods Out (Consumption) section (F-3D), in the activated columns

06 Item Voucher Analysis Report

Item Voucher Analysis Report of Transfer Voucher has been explained earlier (§11/02-08, F-29A/02-08). To get Item Voucher Analysis of Production / Consumption Items, at Production / Consumption Report (F-3D), drill down through a Stock Item to get Item Analysis Report (F-4A / F-4B).

Item Voucher Analysis Ctrl + M

Stock Item: **Multi Switch Board** 1-Apr-2013 to 22-May-2013
Under Transfer : **Mfg Jrnl**

Date	Particulars	Quantity	Basic Rate	Basic Value	Addl. Cost	Total Value	Eff. Rate
	Goods In (Production)						
1-May-2013	Mfg Jrnl	5 Pcs	115.74/Pcs	578.69	115.74	694.43	138.89/Pcs
	Total	5 Pcs	115.74/Pcs	578.69	115.74	694.43	138.89/Pcs

F-4A: Production Item Analysis (Condensed)

Item Voucher Analysis Ctrl + M

Stock Item: **Socket 5A** 1-Apr-2013 to 22-May-2013
Under Transfer : **Mfg Jrnl**

Date	Particulars	Quantity	Basic Rate	Basic Value	Addl. Cost	Total Value	Eff. Rate
1-May-2013	Mfg Jrnl	5 Pcs	28.00/Pcs	140.00			
	1-May-2013 Mfg Jrnl 2						
	Total	5 Pcs	28.00/Pcs	140.00			

F-4B: Consumption Item Analysis (Detailed)

Item Voucher Analysis Report Configuration (F-4C) & Buttons (F-4D) has been explained earlier (F-30A/02-08, F-31B/02-08)

Configuration

Show Addl. Cost Column	? Yes
Show full Addl. Cost Details	? Yes
Format	: Detailed
Show Narrations	? No
Show Billed Qty Column	? Yes
Show using Alternate Units	? No
Show Tail Units of Compound Units	? No
Show Base Rate Column	? Yes
Show Base Value Column	? Yes
Show Total Value Column	? Yes
Show Eff. Rate Column	? Yes

F-4C: Item Analysis Configuration

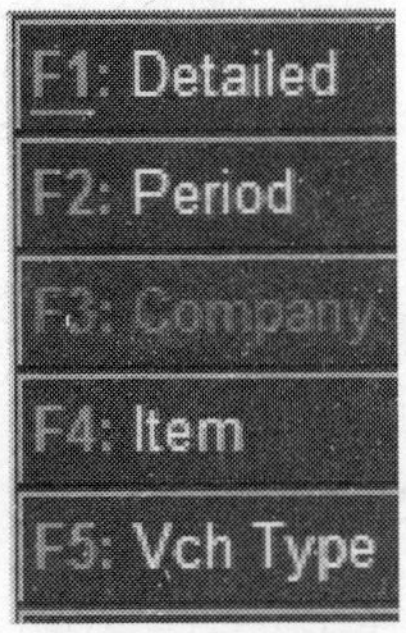

F-4D: Buttons

FAQ: Frequently Asked Questions

FAQ-1: How I may create Manufacturing Journal Type

Ans: To create a *Manufacturing Journal Type*, create a Stock Journal Voucher Type (F-1A) and then specify it as *Manufacturing Journal Type*

Voucher Type creation has been explained earlier. Here we explain the points specific to Manufacturing Journal Voucher Type creation. At Voucher Type creation screen (GoT>Inventory Info>Voucher Type – F-1A)):

- **Voucher Type:** At *Type of Voucher*, select Stock Journal.
- **Manufacturing Journal**: Set *Yes* at *Use as a Manufacturing Journal*

Save the *Manufacturing Journal* Voucher Type

Part 8
Job Cost

In this Part we discuss about Job Cost Centres, allocation of resources & revenues to Job Cost Centres and enumeration of Materials Consumption, Expenses, Revenues & Profit for each Job Cost Centre

Job Costing explains the concept of Job Cost Centres, Job Costing, Activation & Set Up for Job Costing Features for the Company. Job Transactions recording allocation of Materials & Expenses to Job Cost Centres

Job Costing Report describes the details of Jobs executed and Revenue, Expenses & Contribution in respect of each Job

Job Costing

08-01

01 Job Costing

Job Costing means allocation of all expenses relating o a Job. Job is a generic term here which may mean a Project, a Product, a Contract or any identifiable entity for which the revenue & costs can be allocated or apportioned.

Job Costing involves tracking of each element of cost and revenue to ascertain the actual costs incurred for each job. Each Job is a distinct entity, identified by a distinct Job Number or Job name.

A Job may be done in house in its own workshop, or may be sub contracted to external Jobber. In some cases, a combination of both process are used. Some parts of the Job are given to external agencies whiles some processes are done internally within the organization.

02 *Job Costing Activation*

To activate Job Costing feature, at *Gateway of Tally,* Click *F11: Features* to get *Company Features* Menu. At *Company Features* Menu:

- *Accounting Features set up*: Select *Accounting Features* to get Accounting Features screen (F-1A). At Accounting Features screen (F-1A), set:
    - o *Yes* at *Maintain Cost Centres*
    - o *Yes* at *Use Cost Centre for Job Costing*
- *Inventory Features Set up*: Select *Inventory Features* to get Inventory Features screen (F-1B). At Inventory Features screen (F-1B), set:
    - o *Yes* at *Maintain Multiple Godown / Excise Units,* to activate Projects as Godowns

Maintain Cost Centres	? **Yes**
Use Cost Centre for Job Costing	? **Yes**

F-1A: Accounting features set up for Job Costing

Storage & Classification	
Maintain Multiple Godowns / Excise Units	? **Yes**

F-1B: Inventory features set up for Multiple Job Cost

03 Job Cost Masters

For Job Costing System, create the following types of Masters

- Ledger Accounts for:
    - o Jobber
    - o Sales / Purchase
    - o Income / Expenses
- Cost Centres for Job Costs
- Godowns for Jobber
- Job Cost Voucher Class

04 Ledger Accounts for Job Costs.

Create following Ledger Accounts for Job Costing (F-2A).:

- o **Jobber Ledger:** Create Jobber Ledger in usual way, like Supplier Ledger Account.
- o **Job Sales & Purchases Ledger:** Create Job Sales Ledger (F-2B) under Sales Account and Job Purchase Ledger (F-2C) under Purchase Account group, as usual.
- o **Job Income and Expenses Ledger:** Apart from Sales & Purchase, for all Income & Expenses directly attributable or indirectly allocable to Job Costs, create Income & Expenses Ledger (F-2D) under Direct Income & Expenses Group.

Ledger Alteration	
Name	: S.K. Lal
Under	: Sundry Creditors (Current Liabilities)
Maintain balances bill-by-bill	? Yes
Default Credit Period	: 30 Days
Inventory values are affected	? No
Cost centres are applicable	? No
Activate Interest Calculation	? No

F-2A: Jobber Ledger

Ledger Alteration	
Name	: Job Sales
Under	: Sales Accounts
Inventory values are affected	? Yes
Cost centres are applicable	? Yes
Allow Cost allocation (Stock Item)	? No
Activate Interest Calculation	? No

F-2B: Job Sales

Ledger Alteration	
Name	: Purchase
Under	: Purchase Accounts
Inventory values are affected	? Yes
Cost centres are applicable	? Yes
Allow Cost allocation (Stock Item)	? No
Activate Interest Calculation	? No

F-2C: Purchase

To get Job Cost analysis, you may set *Yes* at *Cost Centres Applicable* for all such Ledgers.

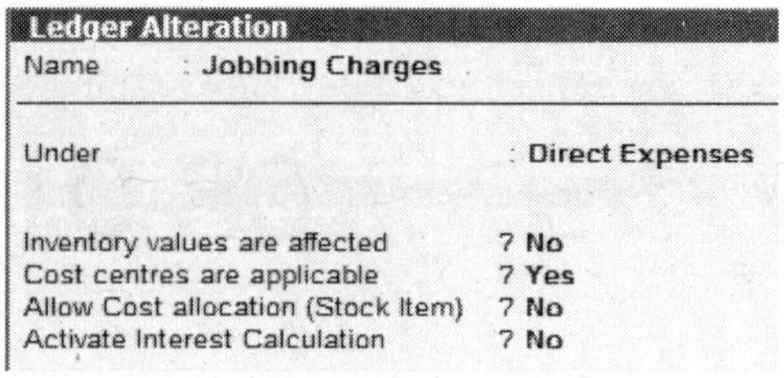

F-2D: Jobbing Charges

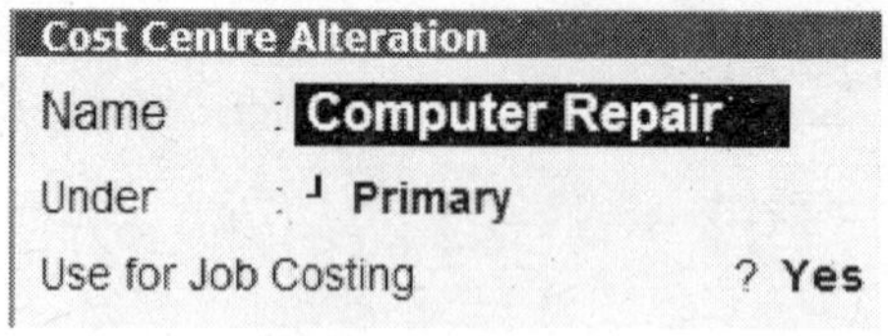

F-3A: Job Cost Centre

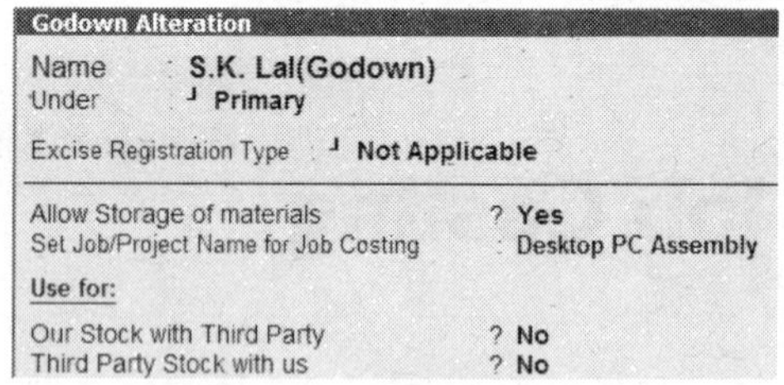

F-4A: Jobber Godown

05 Cost Centre Master for Job Costing

Cost Centre creation has been explained earlier (§02/05-01/S1). Create Cost Centre for each Job to which the Income & Expenses will be allocated. At *Gateway of Tally,* select *Accounts Info > Cost Centres > Create* to create Job Cost Centre (F-3A). Normally, a work order number, or an Item/work order number combination may be used as Cost Centre, to get Cost/Profit Analysis in respect of a work order or each Item of work order.

06 Jobber Master Godown for Job Costing

Raw materials are issued to workshop / process department. So, create a Godown for each of these departments where the materials for the job are transferred to & transferred from Job process.

Sometimes, materials are issued to third party Jobber, In such case, create a Godown for each Jobber, as the transferred materials are property of the organisation. So Jobber's place is treated as Godown.

Godown Creation has been explained earlier. At *Gateway of Tally,* select *Inventory Info > Godowns > Create* to get Godown Creation screen. Create the Godown (F-4A). At *Set Job / Project Name,* select the associated default Job Cost Centre (from the list of Cost Centres for which you have set *Yes* at *Use for Job Costing* associated with the Godown).

07 Job Cost Voucher Class Creation

All Issue & Receipt of materials relating to Job are to be entered through Job Cost Vouchers.

To get Jobwise Analysis and cost of materials issued to and received from respective Jobs, you should create Job Cost Stock Journal Voucher classes. You must have created at least two Job Cost Godowns to activate Job Cost Stock Journal class.

Voucher Class creation has been explained earlier. At *Gateway of Tally*, select *Accounts Info>Voucher Type>Create* and create Stock Journal Voucher Type as usual (F-5A).

At the *Name of the Class*, write the class name (F-5A).

Now set the options to create a voucher class for Jobber as follows:

Job Class Voucher for Inter-Godown Transfer: At *Use Class Voucher for Inter-Godown Transfer*

- Set *Yes* to get only one column for details of Items transferred (F-5C). This option is useful when the Items, Quantity and their value of source and destination is same, so that you do not have to type the Items both for Source & Destination. This is useful for internal department or Godown transfer.
- Set *No* to get different columns for Source & Destination (F-5B). This is useful when the Items, Quantity or value may be different (due to conversion, shortage, excess etc), additional expenses.

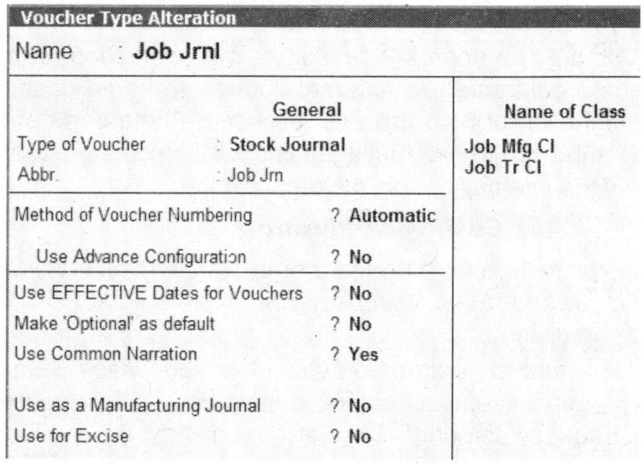

F-5A: Job Cost Stock Journal Voucher Class creation

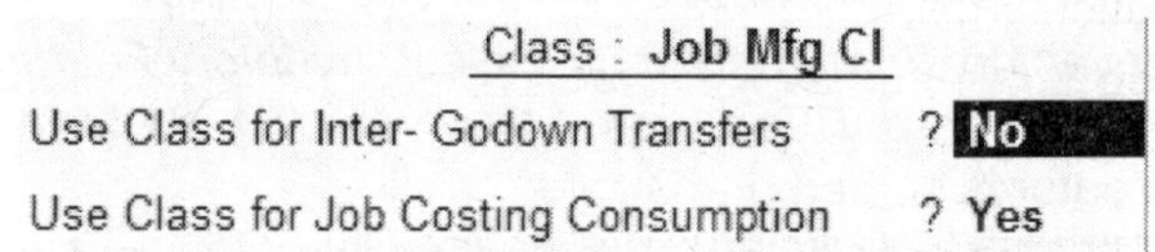

F-5B: Job Cost Class set up for Consumption

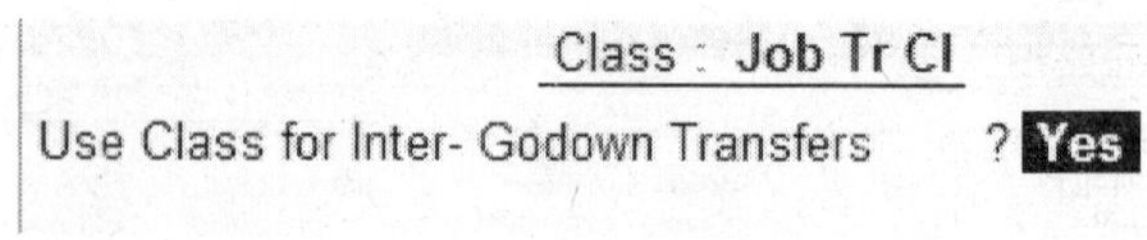

F-5C: Job Cost Class set up for Inter Godown Transfer

Job Class Voucher for Consumption: Set Yes at *Use Class Voucher for Job Costing Consumption* (F-5B).This option is available only of you set *No* at *Use Class Voucher for Inter-Godown Transfer.*

08 Manufacturing Journal Voucher Type

Stock Journal Voucher Class has been explained earlier. At *Gateway of Tally,* select *Accounts Info>Voucher Type>Create* to create *Stock Journal Voucher* Type (F-6A).

Voucher Type Alteration

Name : **Manufacturing Journal**

General

Type of Voucher	: **Stock Journal**
Abbr.	: Mfg
Method of Voucher Numbering	? **Automatic**
Use Advance Configuration	? **No**
Use EFFECTIVE Dates for Vouchers	? **No**
Make 'Optional' as default	? **No**
Use Common Narration	? **Yes**
Use as a Manufacturing Journal	? **Yes**

F-6A: Manufacturing Journal V Type creation

Set *Yes* at *Use as a Manufacturing Journal* (F-6A)

09 Job Cost Voucher entry

Having created the Masters, you may now enter the vouchers for:

- **Job Purchase**: Enter Purchase Voucher for Materials Purchased for use in the Job (§09.01, F-7A)
- **Job Charges:** Enter expense Voucher (or Purchase Voucher) for expenses / Jobber Charges for a Job. (§09.02, F-8A)
- **Job Issue**: Enter Stock Journal Voucher for materials purchased for use in the Job (§09.03, F-9A)
- **Job Manufacturing Voucher**: Enter Manufacturing Journal Voucher for Raw Materials consumed and Finished Products Manufactured, alongwith manufacturing costs incurred (§09.04, F-10A)
- **Job Expenses Payment Voucher:** Enter Payment Voucher for Payment for Job Expenses (§09.05, F-12A)
- **Job Sales Voucher**: Enter Sales Voucher for the Jobbing Charges (§09.06, F-11A)

Accounting Voucher Alteration (Secondary) Ctrl + M

Journal No. 1 — **2-Feb-2010** Tuesday

Particulars			Debit	Credit
Dr **Jobbing Charges**			500.00	
Desktop PC Assembly		500.00 Dr		
Cr **S.K. Lal**				500.00
New Ref 12	30 Days (4-Mar-2010)	500.00 Cr		

F-8A: Cost Centre in Journal Voucher for Jobber Charges

The steps for each type of voucher entry are now discussed.

09.01 Job Purchase Voucher Entry

Purchase Voucher entry has been explained earlier. Enter Purchase Voucher (F-7A) as usual with Godown details (F-7B)

At Item allocation screen (F-7B), select the Godown in which the received materials are stored and enter the Quantity & Rate / Amount.

Accounting Voucher Alteration (Secondary) Ctrl + M

Purchase No. 13 — **15-Dec-2009** Tuesday

Supplier Invoice No. : Date :

Party's A/c Name : **Desire Infotech**

Name of Item	Quantity Actual	Quantity Billed	Rate	per	Amount
Asus P5KPLSE G31 V/PCI-E/S/L/1333F SB	1 Pcs	1 Pcs	5,000.00	Pcs	5,000.00
Narration:	1 Pcs	1 Pcs			*5,000.00*

F-7A: Job Purchase Voucher entry

Item Allocations for : **Asus P5KPLSE G31 V/PCI-E/S/L/1333FSB**

Godown	Quantity Actual	Quantity Billed	Rate	per	Disc. %	Amount
Tracking No. : 15	*Order No.* : Not Applicable					
Main Location	1 Pcs	1 Pcs	5,000.00	Pcs		5,000.00

F-7B: Item Allocation details

09.02 Jobber Charges Voucher Entry

Journal Voucher entry has been explained earlier. Create Journal Voucher (you may create a Purchase Voucher also) for the Jobber Charges (F-8A), debiting the Job Expenses Account and crediting the Jobber Ledger Account, recording the details of expenses incurred

On entering the Job Expense Ledger in the voucher, enter the Cost Centre allocation for the Ledger Account (F-8A)

09.03 Job Issue Voucher Entry

As Jobbers are treated a Godown, Materials issued to jobber should be recorded through a Stock Transfer Voucher (F-9A).

For materials issued to Jobbers, create a Stock Journal voucher by selecting the respective Voucher Class (e.g Job Issue)

Inventory Voucher Alteration (Secondary) Universal Enterprises2 Ctrl + M

Stock Journal No. 5 — **12-Nov-2009** Thursday

Transfer of Materials

Source (Consumption) Name of Item	Godown	Quantity	Rate	Amount	Destination (Production) Name of Item	Godown	Quantity	Rate	Amount
Cabinet	Main Location	1 Pcs	400.00/Pcs	400.00	Cabinet	S.K. Lal(Godown)	1 Pcs	400.00/Pcs	400.00
[illegible]	Main Location	1 Pcs	1,950.00/Pcs	1,950.00	[illegible]	S.K. Lal(Godown)	1 Pcs	1,950.00/Pcs	1,950.00
SMPS	Main Location	1 Pcs	350.00/Pcs	350.00	SMPS	S.K. Lal(Godown)	1 Pcs	350.00/Pcs	350.00
Mother Board (845)	Main Location	1 Pcs	1,600.00/Pcs	1,600.00	Mother Board (845)	S.K. Lal(Godown)	1 Pcs	1,600.00/Pcs	1,600.00

F-9A: Materials Issue to Jobber

- At *Source* side, select the Items issued and select the Godown from where the materials are issued (e.g Main Location).
- At *Destination* side, select the Items issued and select the Jobber at Godown field whom the materials are issued.

09.04 Manufacturing Journal Voucher Entry

After the materials are issued to Jobber, Jobber does the manufacturing Job. In this process, the Jobber consumes raw materials given to him and produces finished products. He then delivers the finished products to the principals and submits the consumption statement in respect of materials consumed to produce the materials delivered to the principals

At Gateway, Select Inventory Voucher to get Inventory Voucher entry screen. Click *F7: Stock Journal* and Select *Manufacturing Journal Voucher* type as created (§08, F-6A) from the list, to get *Manufacturing Journal Voucher* Creation screen (F-10A)

Enter the Manufacturing Journal voucher in respect of Finished Item produced, materials consumed to produce the Finished Item and Manufacturing expenses incurred (F-10A), as follows:

- **Top Part: Produced Item Details:**
  - o **Produced Item Name:** At *Name of Product,* Enter the finished Product produced by the Jobber
  - o **Godown**: At *Godown*, select the Godown at which the Produced Item is stored
  - o **Quantity**: Enter the Quantity of Item Produced

    You may further enter Batch details as follows, if the respective options are activated
    - o **Batch Number**: At *Batch Name*, enter the Batch Reference of the Item Produced
    - o **Mfg Date**: At *Mfg Dt.,* enter the Date of Manufacturing
    - o **Expiry Date**: At Expiry, enter the Date of Expiry
- **Left Part: Raw materials consumed:** Now enter the details of each Item consumed to manufcature the Item produced, as follows
  - o **Item Name***:* At *Item Name* column, select he Name of the Item consumed,
  - o **Godown:** At *Godown* column, enter the Godown where the produced Item is stored..
  - o **Quantity**: At *Quantity* column, enter the Quantity of Item produced
  - o **Rate**: At *Rate* column, the Rate (Cost) of the Item (with Rate UoM) is displayed
  - o **Item Cost**: At *Amount*, the cost of the Item consumed (Quantity x Rate) is displayed

  Total Cost of Components: The Total Cost of materials consumed and unit cost of production (Total Cost of Components per unit of Item produced) is shown at the right part at *Cost Of Components*, as explained next
- **Right Part: Cost Details**: Here the the details of Cost of Product is shown
  - o **Cost of Components**: Total Cost of materials consumed entered at the left part is displayed at Cost of Components.
  - o **Manufacturing Cost**: Now enter the additional Manufacturing Cost details as follows:
    - **Expenses Account**: At *Type of Cost*, select the Expenses Ledger Account
    - **Expenses %**: Enter the Percentage of the Expenses
    - **Expenses Amount**: The computed amount as per % entered on Total Component Cost is displayed, which you may change. In this way, you may enter the exact amount of Cost incurred for each type of Expenses.

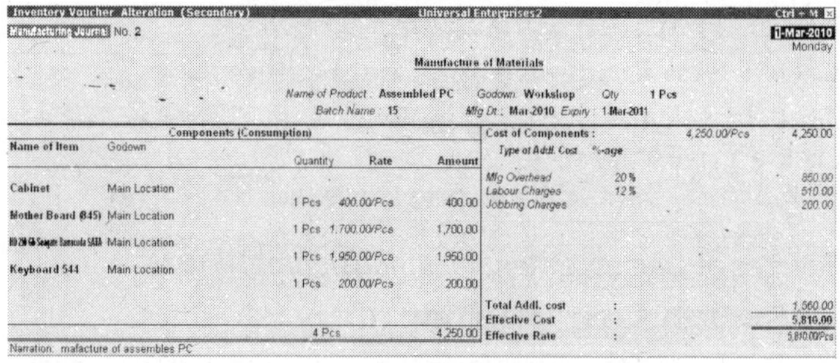

F-10A: Manufacturing Journal

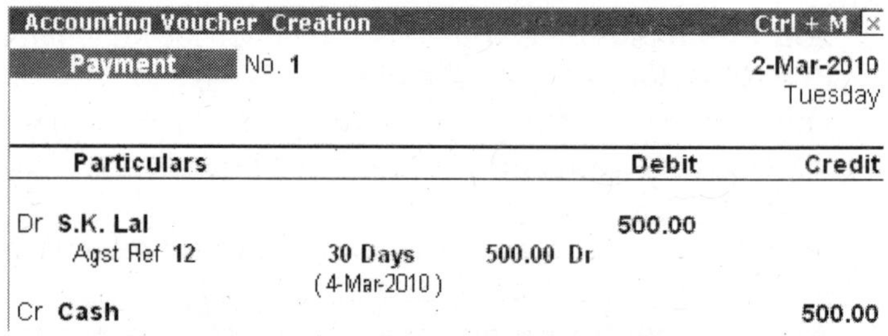

F-11A: Jobber payment Voucher

09.05 Jobber payment Voucher

Payment Voucher has been explained earlier. After entry of Job Expenses Journal Voucher (F-8A), create Payment Voucher in respect of payment of Jobber charges (F-12A)

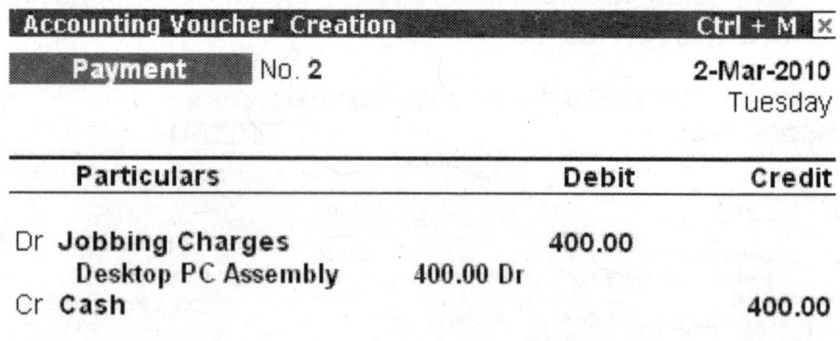

F-12A: Job Expenses Payment Voucher

Job Expenses Voucher

Apart from Jobber Charges, payment for other expenses for the Job are made through Payment Voucher, debiting the Job Expenses Account

09.06 Job Sales Voucher

Sales Voucher has been explained earlier. Enter Sales Voucher for the Jobbing Charges (F-13A).

At Item allocation screen, select the Godown from which the Item is sold (F-13B).

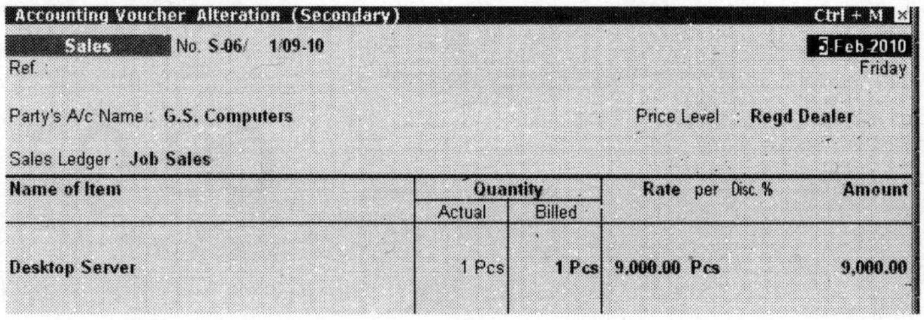

Accounting Voucher Alteration (Secondary)				Ctrl + M
Sales No. S-06/ 1/09-10				3 Feb 2010 Friday
Ref :				
Party's A/c Name : G.S. Computers			Price Level : Regd Dealer	
Sales Ledger : Job Sales				
Name of Item	Quantity Actual	Billed	Rate per Disc. %	Amount
Desktop Server	1 Pcs	1 Pcs	9,000.00 Pcs	9,000.00

F-13A: Job Sales Voucher

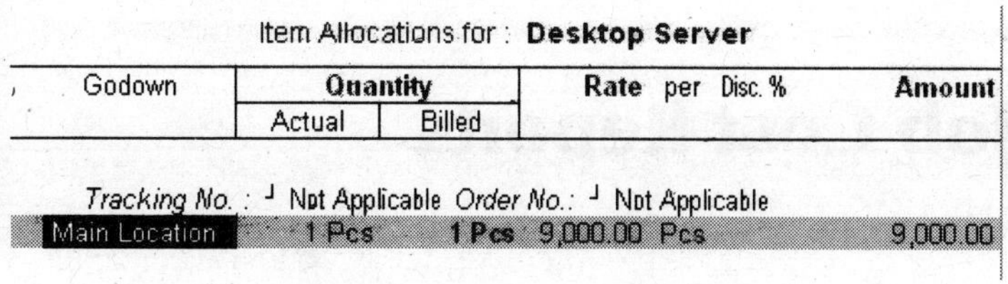

Item Allocations for : **Desktop Server**

Godown	Quantity Actual	Billed	Rate per Disc. %	Amount
Tracking No. : Not Applicable Order No.: Not Applicable				
Main Location	1 Pcs	1 Pcs	9,000.00 Pcs	9,000.00

F-13B: Job Sales Voucher – Item allocation

FAQ: Frequently Asked Question

FAQ-1: How to activate Job Cost Feature

Ans: To activate Job Costing feature, at *Gateway of Tally* click *F11: Features* to get *Company Features* Menu. At *Company Features* Menu, set as follows:

- *Accounting Features Set Up*: Select *Accounting Features* to get Accounting Features screen. At *Accounting Features* screen (F-1A), set:
  - o *Yes* at *Maintain Cost Centres*
  - o *Yes* at *Use Cost Centre for Job Costing*
- *Inventory Features Set up*: Select *Inventory Features* to get *Inventory Features screen.* At *Inventory Features* screen (F-1B), set:

Yes at *Maintain Multiple Godown / Excise Units,* to activate Projects as Godowns

Job Cost Reports 08-02

01 Job Cost Reports

Having created the vouchers as explained above, you may get the following reports related to Job Costs:

- Job Work Analysis (§02)
- Material Consumption Summary (§03)

02 Job Work Analysis Report

At Gateway of Tally, select *Display > Statements of Accounts > Job Work Analysis, or Display > Statements of Inventory > Job Work Analysis.*

Select the Cost Centre (from the list of Cost Centres for which you have set *Yes* at *Use for Job costing*) to get *Job Work Analysis* Report (F-1A), showing details of Revenue, Cost for Materials Consumed and Expenses Incurred and the Profit for the selected Job (Cost Centre).

Job Work Analysis — Ctrl + M

Particulars	Desktop PC Universal Enterprises 1-Aug-2009 to 31-Aug-2009		
A. Revenue (Income) :			
B. Cost (Expenses) :			
Consumption			**6,500.00**
Cost of Sales			
Job Consumption	400.00		
Opening Stock			
Add: Inwards		14,650.00	
Purchase			
Manufacturing Journal			
Inter Project Transfer	6,500.00		
Other Transfer	8,150.00		
Less: Outwards		8,150.00	
Manufacturing Journal			
Inter Project Transfer	8,150.00		
Other Transfer			
Less: Closing Stock		100.00	
			6,500.00
Nett Profit: (A - B)			**(-)6,500.00**

F-1A: Job Work Analysis Report (In Detail Format)

Job Work Analysis Configuration: At *Job Work Analysis Report* (F-1A), click F12:Configure to get Job Work Analysis Report Configuration (F-1B), to set the options as follows:

Configuration

Format	: **Detailed**
Show Percentages	? **No**
Appearance of Names	: **Name Only**
Scale Factor for Values	: **Default**

Format

- Condensed
- **Detailed**

F-1B: Job Work Analysis Report Configuration

- F1: Detailed
- F2: Period
- F3: Company
- F4: Job / Project

F-1C: Job Work Analysis Report Buttons

- **Format:** At *Format*:
  - o *Detailed*: select *Detailed* to get the Report in Detailed Format (F-1A) showing details of each major element (Opening Stock, Inwards, Outwards etc),
  - o *Condensed*: Select Condensed to get net figures of each major element
- **Percentage:** At *Show Percentage* set *Yes* to show the percentage of each major head figures with respect to Revenue (when Revenue Figure is available)

Job Work Analysis Buttons: At Job Work Analysis Report (F-1A), you get following Buttons (F-1C)

- **F4:Job / Project:** To select a Job / Project to get Work Analysis for the selected Job / Project

03 Material Consumption Summary

At Job Work Analysis Report (F-1A), drill down through Consumption line to get *Material Consumption Summary* (F-2A), showing details of Opening, Voucher Type wise breakup of Inwards & Outwards and Closing Stock figures for each Job Cost Godown.

Material Consumption Summary Configuration

At Material Consumption Summary (F-2A), click *F12:Configure* to get Material Consumption Summary Configuration screen (F-2B) to configure the columns of the Report. Set *Yes / No* to show / suppress the respective columns in the report.

- **Opening Balance:** At *Show Opening Balance*, set *Yes* to show the Opening Balance Column, else set *No* (the Opening Balance Column is not shown).
- **Goods Inwards:** At *Show Goods Inwards* set Yes to show the *Goods Inwards* Column, else set No (the *Goods Inwards* Column is not shown).

Material Consumption Summary — Universal Enterprises — Ctrl + M

Desktop PC / Universal Enterprises / 1-Aug-2009 to 31-Aug-2009

Particulars	Inwards				Consumption		Outwards		
	Purchase	Manufacturing Journal	Inter Project Transfer	Other Transfers	Cost of Sales	Job Consumption	Manufacturing Journal	Inter Project Transfer	Other Transfers
S.K. Lal(Godown)									
Workshop			6,500.00	8,150.00		6,500.00		8,150.00	

F-2A: Material Consumption Summary

o **Goods Inwards Details:** Having shown Goods Inwards, at *Show Goods Inwards* in details, set *Yes* to show the break up columns of *Goods Inwards* (F-2A), else set *No* (the Details break up columns are not shown).

Configuration

Show Opening Balance	? No
Show goods inwards	? Yes
Show goods inwards in details	? Yes
Show Consumption	? Yes
Show goods Consumption in details	? Yes
Show goods outwards	? Yes
Show goods outwards in details	? Yes
Show Closing Balance	? No
Appearance of Names	: Name Only
Scale Factor for Values	: Default

F-2B: Configuration

- **Consumption:** At *Show Consumption* set Yes to show the *Consumption* Column, else set No (the *Consumption* Column is not shown).
  - o **Consumption Details:** Having shown Consumption, at *Show Goods Consumption in details*, set *Yes* to show the break up columns of *Consumption* (F-2A), else set *No* (the Details break up columns are not shown).
- **Goods Outwards:** At *Show Goods Outwards* set *Yes* to show the *Goods Outwards* Column, else set No (the *Goods Outwards* Column is not shown).
  - o **Goods Outwards Details:** *Having shown Goods Outwards*, at *Show Goods Outwards* in details, set *Yes* to show the break up columns of *Goods Outwards* (F-2A), else set *No* (the Details break up columns are not shown).
- **Closing Balance:** At *Show* Closing *Balance*, set *Yes* to show the Closing Balance Column, else set *No* (the Closing Balance Column is not shown).

Material Consumption Stock Summary — Universal Enterprises — Ctrl + M

Godown : Workshop / Desktop PC / Universal Enterprises / 1-Aug-2009 to 31-Aug-2009

Particulars	Inwards				Consumption		Outwards		
	Purchase	Manufacturing Journal	Inter Project Transfer	Other Transfers	Cost of Sales	Job Consumption	Manufacturing Journal	Inter Project Transfer	Other Transfers
All HD			1,950.00			1,950.00			
Desktop PC			400.00	8,150.00		400.00		8,150.00	
Keyboard			200.00			200.00			
Motherboard			3,950.00			3,950.00			

F-3A: Material Consumption Stock Summary

F1: Detailed
F2: Period
F3: Company
F4: Godown
F5: Item-wise
F7: Show Prof

F-3B: Configuration

04 Material Consumption Stock Summary

At Material Consumption Summary (F-2A), drill down through a Job Godown to get *Material Consumption Stock Summary* (F-3A) showing details for the selected Job Godown

Material Consumption Stock Summary Configuration

At Material Consumption Stock Summary (F-3A), click *F12:Configure* to get Material Consumption Stock Summary Report configuration screen, with options similar to *Material Stock Summary* Configuration (F-2B). Set *Yes / No* to show / suppress the respective columns in the report.

Complete Details: At Material Consumption Stock Summary Report configuration screen (like F-2B), at *Expand at All Levels in detailed Format*, set *Yes* to get details upto lowest level in Detailed Format.

Material Consumption Stock Summary Buttons

At Material Consumption Stock Summary (F-3A), you get following buttons (F-3B)

- **F4: Godown:** To select a Job / Project Godown to get the Report for selected Godow**n**
- **F5:Itemwsie / Grouped:** To get the Report for each Stock Item Name / Stock Item Group
- **F7: Show Profit / Hide Profit:** To get additional columns for Gross sales / Cost / Contribution (Profit columns)

FAQ: Frequently Asked Questions

FAQ-1: How I can print Job Work Analysis Report, showing the Revenue, Cost & Contribution for each Job.

Ans: At Gateway of Tally, select *Display > Statements of Accounts > Job Work Analysis, or Display > Statements of Inventory > Job Work Analysis.*

Select the Job Cost Centre (from the list of Cost Centres for which you have set *Yes* at *Use for Job costing*) to get Job Work Analysis Report (F-1A), showing details of Revenue, Cost for Materials Consumed and Expenses Incurred and the Profit for the selected Job (Cost Centre).

Part 9
Job Work

This Part describes the entire cycle of Job Work Order, in respect of Job Work given to Third Party Jobber and execution of Jobs received from Customers.

Job Work describes the basic concept of Third Party Jobbing, by receiving materials from Principals, Execution of Job and delivery of Job to the Principals.

Job Work Out describes the transactions in respect of Job Work given out to third party. It describes the Work Order, issue of Raw Materials to Third Party Jobber, Receipt of Jobbed Materials from Third Party Jobber and creation of Jobbing Bill to te Customer.

Job Work In describes the transactions in respect of Job Work ordered by Principals. It describes the Work Order, Receipt of Raw Materials from Principals, Delivery of Jobbed Materials to Principals and creation of Jobbing Bill on the Principals for the Job executed.

Job Work 09-01

01 Job Work

Job is a generic term which may represent a distinctly identifiable Project, Item, Job, Process etc). A Job may constitute several smaller Jobs. In such case, each component Job is considered as separate Job for Job Costing.

Job Work Order is a pre plan of materials movement between Principal & Jobber. Job Work accounting (also referred as Job Costing) involves allocation and analysis of all transactions (e.g Materials and Expenses/ Income) identifiable with a Job

Job Work constitutes a series of activities & transactions, and involves tracking of each cost & revenue element in connection with each Job. All direct materials cost and expenses related to labour and other costs, all Expenses / Income are allocated to Jobs to find the total income & contribution attributed to a Job.

To collect the attributable Costs & Revenues for each job, each job is assigned a unique *Job Name* (or Job Identifiers). Job costing system accumulates costs / revenues for each Job.

02 Job Work Activation

Accounting Features Activation: At *F11: Features >Accounting Features*, set *Yes* at (F-1A)

- **Maintain Cost Centres**: To activate Job Cost, you must first activate Cost Centre
- **Use Cost Centre for Job Costing**: To Activate Job Cost

Inventory Features Activation: At *F11: Features >Inventory Features*, set Yes at

- *Allow Job Order Processing* to activate Job Order Feature (F-1C). Consequently:
    - o Option *Use Materials In / Out* would be automatically set to Yes (F-1D)
        - ▪ Consequently, Materials In & Materials Out Voucher Type will get activated to record materials transfers
    - o Menu option *Order Vouchers* will get activated at Main Menu (F-1E) and two *Order Voucher Types* viz, *Job Work In Order* and *Job Work Out Order* will get enabled.
    - o *Use Cost Tracking for Stock Item* would be automatically set to *Yes* (F-1D).
- *Maintain Multiple Godown* (F-1B) to store / transfer Materials from to Jobbers / Shop Floor for Jobbing work (F-1B)

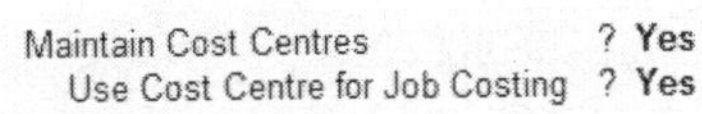

F-1A: Job Cost Activation

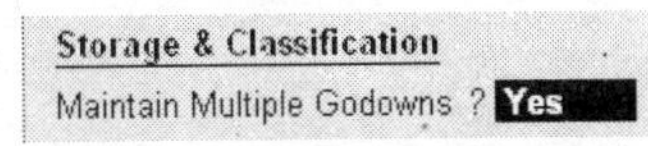

F-1B: Multiple Godown Activation

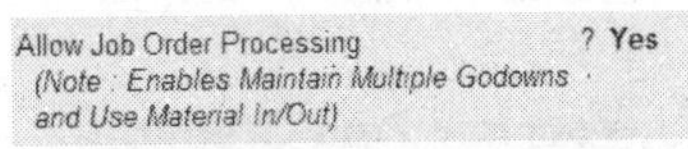

F-1C: Job Cost Set Up

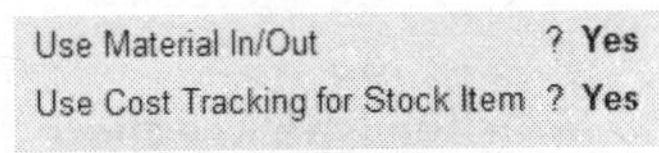

F-1D: Item Cost Tracking set Up

F-1E: Work Order option in Main Menu

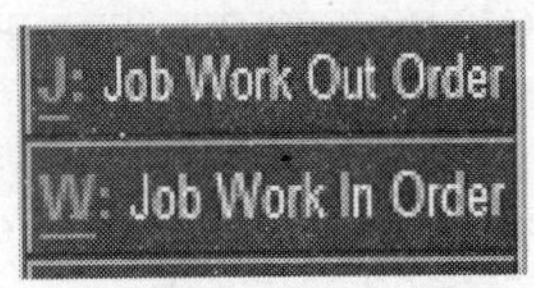

F-1F: Job Work Voucher Type Buttons

The effect of each these options set (F-1D) are elaborated below:

- **Use Material In/Out**: This option, though associated with Job order Processing, you may enable only Material Transfer In/Out feature without enabling *Allow Job Order Processing. Use Material In/Out* feature may be enabled to create Material Transfer vouchers for other purposes (other than Job Work)., like transfers related to consignee/ consignor, Inter Godown Transfers etc
- **Track Stock Item Cost**: The option *Use Cost Tracking for Stock Items* (F-1D) may be enabled to track the cost of stock item from purchase of stock till sale. On enabling this option, in *Stock Item* Master, *Enable Cost Tracking* option will be activated.
- **Job Work Voucher Type Buttons:** Consequently, at Order Voucher entry screen, you get 2 additional buttons *J:Job Work Out Order* & *J:Job Work In Order* (F-1F).

03 Job Work Order Type

Job Work Order are of 2 Types:

- **Job Work In Order:** When the Company itself works as Jobber, i.e it takes up Job Work of other Principals, it issues Job Work In Order (corresponding to Job Work

Out Order of its Principals). It is like Service Sales Order (F-2A).

- **Job Work Out Order:** When the Company itself works as Principal, i.e it gives Job Work to Third Party Jobbers, it issues Job Work Out Order to Jobbers (corresponding to Job Work In Order of its Jobbers). It is like Service Purchase Order (F-2B).

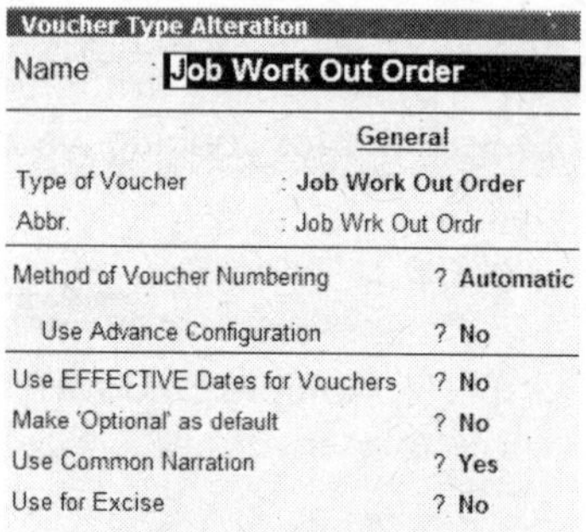

F-2A: Job Work Out Voucher Type Creation

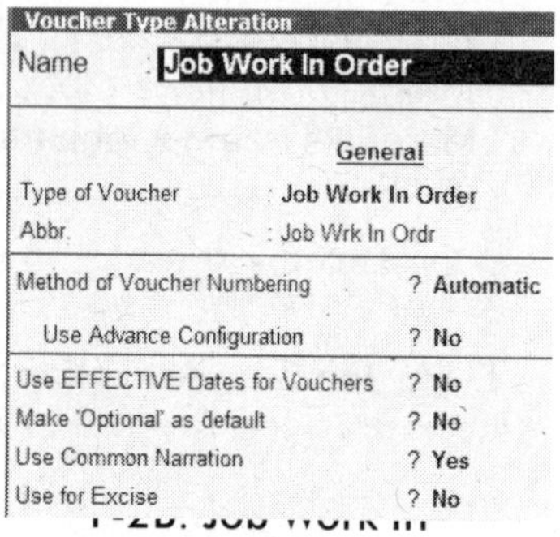

F-2B: Job Work In Voucher Type Creation

04 Materials Transfer Voucher Type

Material transfer transactions between Jobber & Principals are to be recorded through

Material Out/In vouchers. These Voucher Types are activated when *Use Material In/Out option* is set to Yes (and auto activated when Job Order Processing is activated), as explained earlier (F-1D).

- **Material Out**: This voucher type can be used to record the *material transfer OUT* for:
  - o Raw Materials for *Job Work Out* (when the Company is Principal). *Principal Manufacturer* may use this Voucher Type to transfer the Raw Materials to the Job Worker
  - o Finished Goods for *Job Work In* (when the Company is Jobber). *Job Worker* may use this Voucher Type to transfer the Finished goods to the principal Manufacturer
- **Material In**: This voucher type can be used to record the material transfer IN for
  - o Raw Materials for *Job Work Out* (When Company is Principal). *Principal Manufacturer* can use this Voucher to record the receipt of Finished Goods / Scrap /By-Product/ Co-Product from the Job Worker.
  - o Finished Goods for Job Work In (When Company is Jobber). *Jobber* can use this voucher to account the receipt of Raw Material from the Principal Manufacturer.

Sometimes, a Party may be acting as *Principal Manufacturer* as well as *Jobber*. In that case

it must maintain separate sets of Material In/Out *vouchers for* Job Work Out *and* Job Work In *Processes.*

Material In / Material Out voucher can also be used by Manufacturer (In Manufacturing Process)

04.01 Material Out Voucher Types

These Voucher Types are used for Delivery of Materials

- **Material Out (RM):** This Voucher Type (Materials Out) will be used by the *Principal Manufacturer* in *Job Work Out* process for *Transfer of Raw Materials* to the *Job Worker* **(F-**3A).
  - o Set *Materials Out* at *Type of Voucher*
  - o Set Yes at *Use for Job Work* to use the voucher type to record Job work transactions.
  - o Set *No* at *Use for Job Work In*
- **Material Out (Transfer/FG):** This Voucher Type (Materials Out) is used by the Jobber in *Job Work In* process for Transfer Out of Finished Goods, Scrap, By-Products, Co-Products to the *Principal Manufacturer.* **(F-**3B).
  - o Set *Materials Out* at *Type of Voucher*
  - o Set Yes at *Use for Job Work*
  - o *Set Yes at* Use for Job Work In

04.02 Material In Voucher Types

These Voucher Types are used for Receipt of Materials

- ***Material In (RM):*** *This voucher Type (Materials In) is used by the* Jobber *for Receipt of Raw Materials from* Principal *(F-4A).*
  - o Set *Materials In* at *Type of Voucher*
  - o Set Yes at the option Use for Job Work
  - o Set Yes at *Use for Job Work In*
  - o Set No at *Allow Consumption*
- **Material In (FG):** This voucher Type is used by the *Principal Manufacturer for Receipt of Finished Goods, Scrap, By-Products, Co-Products* from the Job Worker **(F-**4B).
  - o Set *Materials In* at *Type of Voucher*
  - o Set *Yes* at the option *Use for Job Work*
  - o Set *No* at *Use for Job Work In*
  - o Set *Yes* at *Allow Consumption*

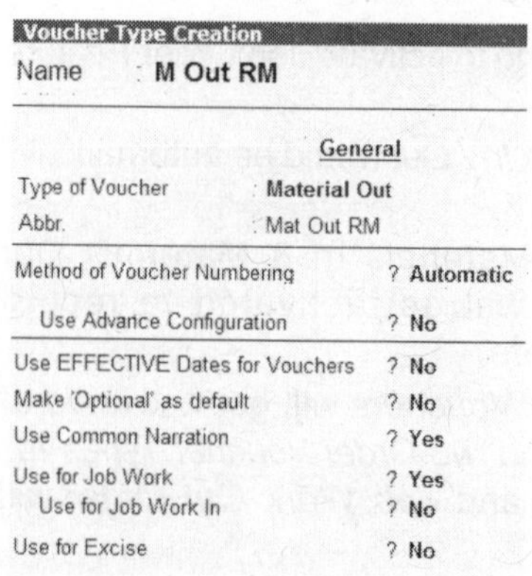

F-3A: Mat Out RM V Type

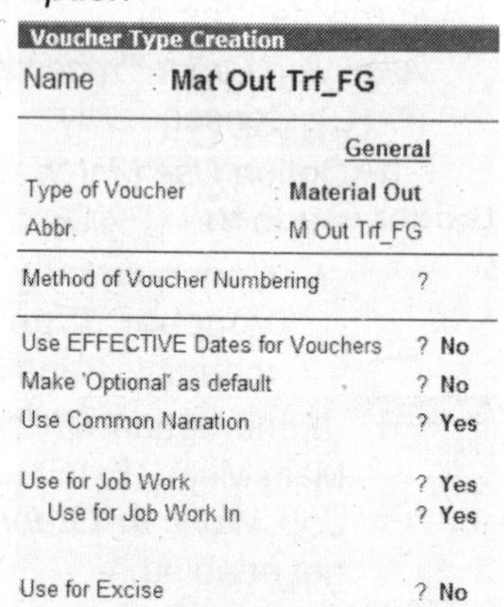

F-3B: Mat Out Trf_FG V Type

Voucher Type Creation	
Name	: Mat In (RM)
General	
Type of Voucher	: Material In
Abbr.	: Mat IN RM
Method of Voucher Numbering	? Automatic
Use Advance Configuration	? No
Use EFFECTIVE Dates for Vouchers	? No
Make 'Optional' as default	? No
Use Common Narration	? Yes
Use for Job Work	? Yes
Use for Job Work In	? Yes
Allow Consumption	? No
Use for Excise	? No

F-4A: Mat In RM V Type

Voucher Type Creation	
Name	: Mat In FG
General	
Type of Voucher	: Material In
Abbr.	: M In FG
Method of Voucher Numbering	? Automatic
Use Advance Configuration	? No
Use EFFECTIVE Dates for Vouchers	? No
Make 'Optional' as default	? No
Use Common Narration	? No
Use for Job Work	? Yes
Use for Job Work In	? No
Allow Consumption	? Yes
Use for Excise	? No

F-4B: Mat In FG V Type

At *Use for Excise* (appears when Excise Duty has been activated for the Company), set Yes if the Finished Product attracts Excise Duty provisions (in that case, Excise Details are to be entered), else set *No*

Note:

- Set Yes at the option *Allow Consumption* in *Material In* voucher types, to be used by the *Principal Manufacturer* to account the receipt of Finished Goods from the Job Worker.
- When *Allow Consumption* is set to *Yes*, on creation of *Material In* voucher, Raw Materials used in the manufacture of Finished goods will be considered as Consumed and stock will be reduced accordingly.

05 Party Ledger Account

Party Ledger Creation has been explained earlier. Create Party Ledger Account for:

- **Jobber Party:** Jobber Party Account (F-5A) whom Input Materials are delivered for Jobbing and Processed Materials are received from.
- **Principal Party:** Principal Party Account (F-6A) from whom Input Materials are received for Jobbing and Processed Materials are delivered to.

Ledger Creation	
Name	: ABC Jobber
Under	: Sundry Creditors (Current Liabilities)
Maintain balances bill-by-bill	? Yes
Default Credit Period	:
Inventory values are affected	? No
Cost centres are applicable	? No
Activate Interest Calculation	? No

F-5A: Jobber Ledger Creation

Ledger Creation	
Name	: ABC Principals
Under	: Sundry Debtors (Current Assets)
Maintain balances bill-by-bill	? No
Inventory values are affected	? No
Cost centres are applicable	? No
Activate Interest Calculation	? No

F-6A: Principal Ledger Creation

06 Job Work Materials Godown

Separate Godown are to be created for materials received for:

- **Job Work In:** Materials received from Principals for Jobbing and Processed Goods to be delivered back to Principals (F-7A)
- **Job Work Out:** Materials delivered to Jobbers for Jobbing and Processed Goods to be received back from Principals (F-8A)

Godown Creation	
Name	: Job Work In
Under	: Primary
Excise Registration Type	: Not Applicable
Allow Storage of materials	? Yes
Set Job/Project Name for Job Costing	: Not Applicable
Use for:	
Our Stock with Third Party	? No
Third Party Stock with us	? Yes

F-7A: Job Work In Godown

Godown Creation	
Name	: Job Work Out
Under	: Primary
Excise Registration Type	: Not Applicable
Allow Storage of materials	? Yes
Set Job/Project Name for Job Costing	: Not Applicable
Use for:	
Our Stock with Third Party	? Yes
Third Party Stock with us	? No

F-8A: Job Work Out Godown

Godown creation has been explained earlier. Set as follows (F-7A / F-8A):

- **Excise Registration:** At *Excise Registration Type* (appears when Excise Duty has been activated for the Company), select
  - o **Not Applicable**: If the Job Work does not attract provisions of Excise Duty (consequently Excise Records / details are to be maintained)
  - o **Dealer**: If the Company is registered as *Dealer* under Excise Rules
  - o **Manufacturer**: If the Company is registered as *Manufacturer* under Excise Rules
- **Materials Storage**: At *Allow Storage of Materials*, set *Yes* as materials would be stored at the Job Work Godown.
- **Materials Ownership**: Materials at Job Godown do not affect Stock Account as the ownership of the stock remains with the Principal, though the Stock may be stored at Jobber's place for processing and subsequent delivery. Set as follows:
  - o **Our Stock with Third Party**: Set *No* for *Job Work In* & set *Yes* for *Job Work Out*, as the Company is Principal
  - o **Third Party Stock with** us: Set *Yes* for *Job Work In* & set *No* for Job Work Out, as the Company is Jobber

FAQ: Frequently Asked Questions

FAQ 1: How I may activate Job Work features for the Company

Ans: To Activate Job Work features for the Company

At F11: Features >Accounting Features, set *Yes* at (F-1A)

- *Maintain Cost Centres*: To activate Job Cost, you must first activate Cost Centre
- *Use Cost Centre for Job Costing*: To Activate Job Cost

At F11: Features >Inventory Features, set Yes at

- *Allow Job Order Processing* to activate Job Order Feature (F-1C). Consequently:
  - o Options *Use Materials In / Out* would be automatically set to Yes (F-1D)
    - ▪ Consequently, Materials In & Materials Out Voucher Type will get activated to record materials transfers
  - o Menu option *Order Vouchers* will get activated at Main Menu (F-1E) and two *Order Voucher Types* viz, *Job Work In Order* and *Job Work Out Order* will get enabled.
  - o *Use Cost Tracking for Stock Item* would be automatically set to Yes (F-1D).
- *Maintain Multiple Godown* to store / transfer Materials from to Jobbers / Shop Floor for Jobbing work (F-1B)

Job Work Out

01 Job Work Out Vouchers

Having created the Masters as explained in previous chapter, you may now enter *Job Work Out Order* and then Materials Transfer (In/Out) Vouchers against *Job Work Out Order*.

02 Job Work Out Order

The Principal issues *Job Work Out Order* on Jobber, specifying the details of Input materials (materials to be delivered by Principal to Jobber) and Out Put Materials (Processed Materials, including Joint / Bye Products / Scrap) to be received by Principal from Jobber after processing)

02.01 Job Work Out Order Entry

At *GoT>Order Voucher*, click *J:Job Work Out Order* to get Job Work Out Order entry screen (F-1A).

Order Voucher Alteration (Secondary) — Ctrl + M

Job Work Out Order No. 1 — 1-Oct-2009, Thursday

Party's A/c Name : **Omnisoftware India** — Order No. : 10

Name of Item	Quantity	Rate	per	Amount
Assembled PC	5 Pcs	5,000.00	Pcs	25,000.00
Narration:	5 Pcs			*25,000.00*

F-1A: Job Work Out Order Voucher creation

screen (F-1C). The Item Name & Order Number is shown. At *Track Components* (F-1C), set *Yes* to get the Component entry screen (F-1E), else set *No* (Component entry screen will not appear).

Despatch Details

Despatched through : Cart 3456 — Mode/Terms of Payment: 30 Days
Destination : Factory

Process Instruction

Duration of Process : 30 Days
Nature of Processing : Machining

Party Details

Sub Contractor : **Omnisoftware India**
Address : 34 Hesham Rd, Kidderpore Kolkata

Sales Tax No. : NA
CST Number : NA

F-1B: Party (Supplementary) Details screen

Item Allocations for : **Assembled PC**
For Order Number : **10**
Track Components ? **Yes**

Godown	Batch / Lot No. / Mfg Dt.	Quantity	Rate	per	Amount
Due on 1-Oct-2009					
Main Location	**Primary Batch** / 31-Mar-2009	5 Pcs	5,000.00	Pcs	25,000.00
		5 Pcs			25,000.00

F-1C: Item Allocation

Type of Component
Pending to Issue
Pending to Receive

F-1D: Component Type List

Components Allocations for : **Assembled PC**
For Godown : **Main Location**
For Batch : **Primary Batch**
Quantity : **5 Pcs**

Name of Item	Track	Godown	Batch / Lot No. / Mfg Dt.	Quantity	Rate	per	Amount
Cabinet	Pending to Issue			5 Pcs			
	Due on : *1-Oct-2009*	Main Location	**Primary Batch**	5 Pcs	1,600.00	Pcs	8,000.00
CPU P4	Pending to Issue			**5 Pcs**			
	Due on : *1-Oct-2009*	Main Location	**Primary Batch**	3 Pcs	1,900.00	Pcs	5,700.00
	Due on : *1-Oct-2009*	Koramongala Godown	**Primary Batch**	2 Pcs	1,900.00	Pcs	3,800.00

F-1E: Component Allocation screen

The Job Work Out Order Entry (F-1A) is similar to Order Entry. If supplementary details is set on, you get supplementary details screen (F-1B), where you enter the details as shown in the screen, if desired.

Out Put Products: At Main Order Entry screen (F-1A), select the Output Product (the Processed Item that would be received by Principal from Jobber) to get Item Allocation screen (F-1C). The Item Name & Order Number is shown.

Components Entry: At Components entry screen (F-1E), which appears when *Track Components* is set to *Yes* (F-1C), enter the details of each Component, delivered to the Jobber, as follows:

- **Header**: The name of the Output Product selected, Godown and Quantity, as entered at Item Allocation screen (F-1C), is shown at the header (F-1E).

- **Component Details**: In the Table area, enter the Component details as follows (F-1E):
  - o **Component Name**: At *Name of Item* column, select the Component.
  - o **Component Type**: At *Track* column, select the Component Type from the list (F-1D):
- *Pending to Issue* for Component to be Issued to Jobber
- *Pending to Receive* for Joint Product, Bye Product, Scrap etc receivable from Jobber after the process
- **Delivery Details:** Next enter the delivery details as follows:
  - o **Due Date:** At *Due on*, enter the Delivery Due Date
  - o **Godown:** At *Godown* column, select the Godown Name from where the Components would be issued
  - o **Batch Details:** At *Batch, Mfg / Expiry* columns, enter the respective details, if Batch is activated for the Company
  - o **Quantity:** At *Quantity* column, enter the Quantity of the Item to be issued
  - o **Rate:** At *Rate* column, the Rate (and Rate UoM) of the Item is displayed
  - o **Item Cost:** At *Amount* column, the Item Cost (Quantity x Rate) **is** displayed

This way, enter the details of each of the Components to be issued, Joint Product, Bye Product, Scrap etc to be received (F-1E)

After entry of all Component Details, save the Job Work Out Voucher (F-1A).

02.02 Job Work Out Order with BoM

In the above example, the component details has been entered in the Job Work Out Order. If any BoM for Out Put Stock Item is already created, at Components Entry screen, the default BoM Name will appear (you may select Alternate BoM from the list, if multiple BoM are created for the Item) and the Component details as per BoM a the column as per BoM will be carried as default. Now modify the respective data as required.

02.03 Transfer Out of Input Materials to Jobber against Job Work Out Order

The Principal will issue Materials against the Work Order.

At *GoT>Inventory Voucher*, click *J:Materials Out* button to get Materials Out Voucher Type selection screen (F-2A).

At Materials Out Voucher Type selection screen (F-2A), select the Materials Out (Raw Materials) Voucher Type, as explained earlier, to get Materials Out (Raw Materials) Voucher entry screen (F-2B).

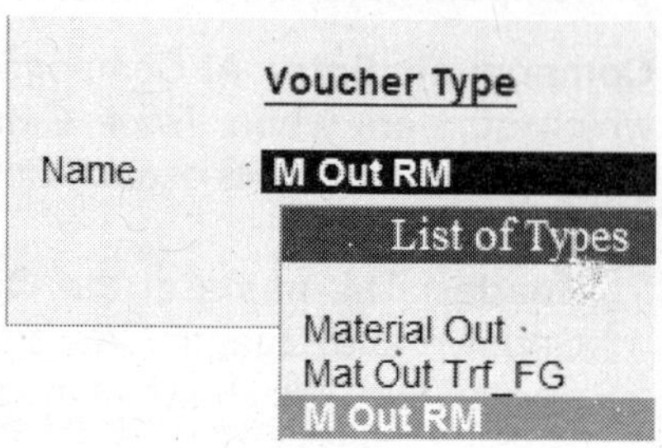

F- 2A: V Type selection

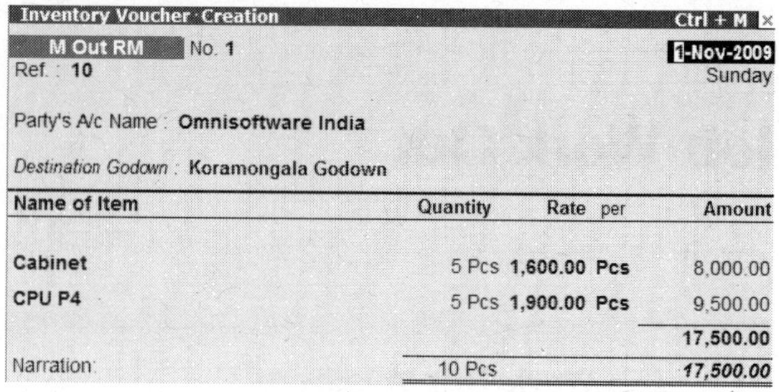

F-2B: Materials Out (RM) Voucher against Job Work Out Order

At Materials Out (Raw Materials) Voucher entry screen (F-2B), select the Party to get the list of Pending Work Orders for the Party (F-2D). Select the Item / Work Order from the list, against which Materials are being issued to Jobber (F-2D), to get Item allocation screen (F-2E). At Item allocation screen (F-2E), enter the Quantity (pending values are carried by default). You may also enter Rate / Value (For Job Costing).

At Supplementary details screen (F-2C), enter requisite details. Most of these are carried by default from the selected Job Work, which you may change.

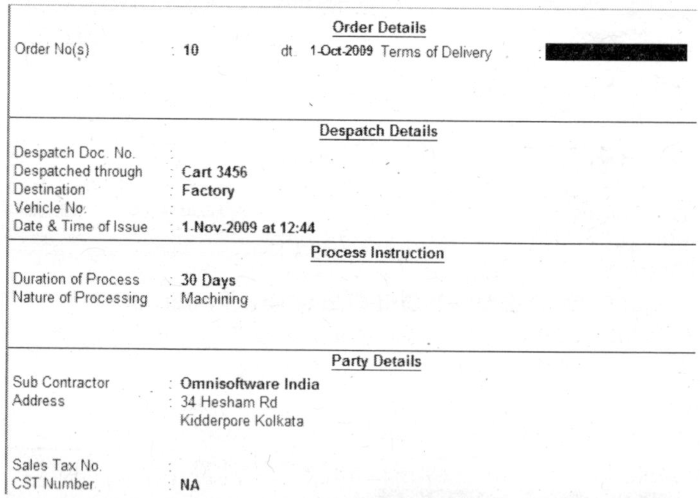

F-2C: Supplementary Details

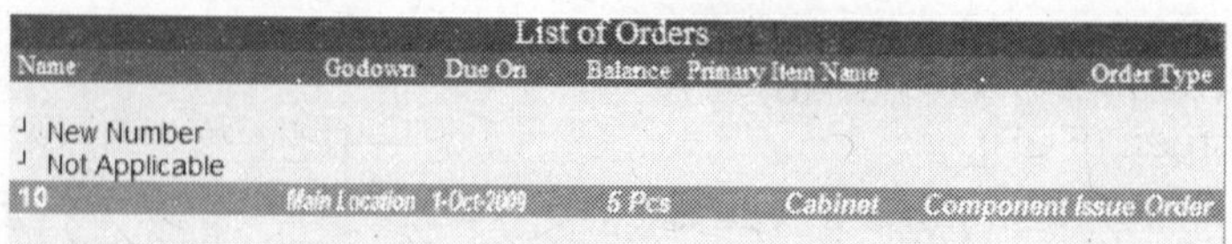

F-2D: Work Order / Item Selection

03 Printing of Materials Out Voucher

At Materials Out (Raw Materials) Voucher entry screen (F-2B), click *P:Print* button to get the Voucher in Print (F-2G).

Item Allocations for : **Cabinet**

Godown	Quantity	Rate	per	Amount
Order No.: 10 *Due on* 1-Oct-2009 *Component of* : Cabinet				
Main Location	5 Pcs	1,600.00	Pcs	8,000.00
	5 Pcs			8,000.00

F-2E: Work Order details at Item Allocation screen.

MATERIAL OUT

Universal Enterprises Kolaghata Kolkata E-Mail :nomail@univ.com	Challan No. **1**	Dated **1-Nov-2009**
		Mode/Terms of Payment **30 Days**
	Supplier's Ref. **10**	Other Reference(s)
Party **Omnisoftware India** 34 Hesham Rd Kidderpore Kolkata	Buyer's Order No. **10**	Dated **1-Oct-2009**
	Despatch Document No.	Dated
	Despatched through **Cart 3456**	Destination **Factory**
	Date & Time of Issue **1-Nov-2009 at 12:44**	Duration of Process **30 Days**
	Nature of Processing **Machining**	

Sl No.	Description of Goods	Quantity	Rate	per	Amount
1	**Cabinet**	**5 Pcs**	1,600.00	Pcs	**8,000.00**
2	CPU P4	**5 Pcs**	1,900.00	Pcs	**9,500.00**
	Total	**10 Pcs**			₹ **17,500.00**

Amount Chargeable (in words) E. & O.E
Indian Rupees Seventeen Thousand Five Hundred Only

Buyer's CST No. : **NA**

for Universal Enterprises

Authorised Signatory

F-2G: Materials Out (RM) Voucher in print

04 Receipt of Finished Goods against Job Work Order

Upon receiving the Raw materials from Principal, the Job Worker will Produce the agreed goods, and deliver to the Principal manufacturer. On Receiving the Finished Goods from Jobber, the Principal will create a Finished Goods Receipt Voucher against Job Work Order.

At *GoT>Inventory Voucher*, click *W:Materials In* button to get *Materials In* Voucher Type selection screen (F-3A).

At Materials In Voucher Type selection screen (F-3A), select the Materials In (Finished Products) Voucher Type, as explained earlier, to get Materials In (Finished Products) Voucher entry screen (F-3B).

Voucher Type

Name : **Mat In FG**

List of Types

Material In
Mat In FG
Mat In (RM)

F-3A: Voucher Type selection

At Materials In (Finished Products) Voucher entry screen (F-3B), select the Party to get the list of Pending Work Orders for the Party (F-3C). Select the Item / Work Order from the list, against which Materials are being issued to Jobber (F-3C), to get *Item allocation* screen (F-3E). At *Item Allocation* screen (F-3E), enter the Quantity (pending values are carried by default). You may also enter Rate / Value (For Job Costing).

Inventory Voucher Creation Ctrl + M

Mat In FG No. **1** **2-Mar-2010**
Ref. : **10** Tuesday

Party's A/c Name : **Omnisoftware India**

Consumption Godown : **Koramongala Godown**

Name of Item	Quantity	Rate	per	Amount
Assembled PC	5 Pcs	**5,000.00**	**Pcs**	25,000.00
Enter Consumption Details ? **Yes** *(Auto)*				
	5 Pcs			***25,000.00***

F-3B: Materials In (Finished Goods) Voucher Entry

List of Orders

Name	Due On	Order Type
End of List		
New Number		
Not Applicable		
10	1-Oct-2009	Material Receipt Order

F-3C: Selection of Job Work Order

At Item Allocation screen (F-3E), set:

- Yes at *Consider as Primary Item*, for Receipt of Finished Goods
- No at *Consider as Scrap* for Finished / Joint / Bye Products (set *Yes* in case of Receipt of Scrap)

If BoM exists for the Finished Item, at BoM name, select the applicable BoM (else select *Not Applicable*)

Next enter the Item details as follows:

- **Godown**: At *Godown* column, select the Godown
- **Batch**: At *Batch / Lot No* column, select the Batch (if Batch is activated for the Item).
- **Quantity**: At *Quantity* column, enter the Quantity
- **Rate**: At *Rate* column, the Item Rate & Rate Unit is displayed
- **Item Value**: At *Amount* column, the Item Value (Quantity x Rate) is displayed.

Order Details

Order No(s) : **10** dt. 1-Oct-2009 Terms of Delivery :

Party's Document Details

Challan No(s) : Despatched through : **Cart 3456**
Destination : **Factory**

Party Details

Sub Contractor : **Omnisoftware India**
Address : 34 Hesham Rd
Kidderpore Kolkata

Sales Tax No. :
CST Number : **NA**

F-3D: Supplementary Details screen

Item Allocations for : **Assembled PC**
Consider as Primary Item ? **Yes**
BoM Name : ┘ **Not Applicable**
Consider as Scrap ? **No**

Godown	Batch / Lot No.	Quantity	Rate per	Amount
Order No.: 10	*Due on* 1-Oct-2009 *Component of* : ┘ Not Applicable			
Main Location	**Primary Batch**	4 Pcs	5,000.00 Pcs	20,000.00
		4 Pcs		20,000.00

F-3E: Item Allocation

At Supplementary details screen (F-3D), enter requisite details. Most of these are carried by default from the selected Job Work Order (F-2C), which you may change.

04.01 Consumption of Materials

At *Materials In* voucher entry screen (F-3B), click *F12:Configure* to get *Materials In Configuration screen.* At *Materials In* Configuration screen, at *Allow Auto Consumption*

- Set Yes to automatically treat the Materials issued as consumed (Enter Consumption Details will be shown as Auto, the cursor skips this field (F-3B)
- Set *No.* The field will turn to Manual. Press <Enter> to get the Components Consumption Details screen (F-3F). At Components Consumption Details screen (F-3F), first select the Component and enter the details (F-3F) to get *Item Allocation screen* (F-3G). At *Item Allocation screen* (F-3G), select the Finished Gods for which the Components are consumed (F-3G). This way, enter for each Component (F-3F)

Component Consumption Details

Name of Item	Quantity	Rate per	Amount
Cabinet	4 Pcs		
CPU P4	5 Pcs		
	9 Pcs		

F-3F: Component Consumption Entry

Item Allocations for : **CPU P4**

Component of	Godown	Quantity	Rate per	Amount
Assembled PC	Job Work Out	**4 Pcs**		

F-3G: Finished Product details in Component Consumption Entry

Save the Materials In Voucher (F-3B).

04.02 Printing of Materials In Voucher

At *Materials In* (Finished Products) Voucher entry screen (F-3B), click *P:Print* button to get the Voucher in Print / Print Preview (F-3H).

MATERIAL IN

Universal Enterprises Kolaghata Kolkata E-Mail :nomail@univ.com	Voucher No. **1**	Dated **2-Mar-2010**
	Supplier's Ref. **10**	Other Reference(s)
	Challan No.	Dated
Party **Omnisoftware India** 34 Hesham Rd Kidderpore Kolkata	Challan Document No.	Destination **Factory**
	Despatched through **Cart 3456**	
	Terms of Delivery	

Sl No.	Description of Goods	Quantity
1	**Assembled PC** *Consumption :* *Cabinet* *CPU P4*	**4 Pcs** *4 Pcs* *5 Pcs*
	Total	**4 Pcs**

E.& O.E

for Universal Enterprises

Authorised Signatory

UJECT TO KOLKATA JURISDICTION

F-3H: Finished Products In Entry

05 Job Work Service Bill

After delivery of processed goods (and Scrap/By-Product/Co-Product) to Principal, the Principal has to pay Bills for Materials & Labour Charges, raised by the Jobber.

Masters Creation: The Principal need to create Ledger Accounts for Labour Charges & Material Cost (under Direct Expenses Group). Set *Yes* at *Allow Cost Allocation (Stock Item)* at the respective Ledger Accounts (F-4A & F-4B).

Ledger Alteration
Name : **Job Work Charges**
Under : **Direct Expenses**
Inventory values are affected ? **No**
Cost centres are applicable ? **No**
Allow Cost allocation (Stock Item) ? **Yes**
Activate Interest Calculation ? **No**

F-4A: Job Work Charges Ledger

Ledger Creation
Name : **Cost of Materals Consumed**
Under : **Direct Expenses**
Inventory values are affected ? **No**
Cost centres are applicable ? **No**
Allow Cost allocation (Stock Item) ? **Yes**
Activate Interest Calculation ? **No**

F-4B: Materials Cost Ledger

Accounting Voucher Creation Ctrl + M

Purchase No. **14** — **2-Mar-2010** Tuesday
Supplier Invoice No. : **14** Date : **2-Mar-2010**

Party's A/c Name : **Omnisoftware India**

Particulars	Rate per	Amount
Job Work Charges		**2,000.00**
Cost of Materals Consumed		**3,000.00**
Narration:		***5,000.00***

F-4C: Purchase

Purchase Bill Entry: Purchase Bill Entry (in Accounting Voucher Mode) has been described earlier. At Purchase Bill Entry screen (F-4C), at Particulars column, enter as follows:

- **Job Work Charges:** Select the Job Work charges Ledger Account and enter the Amount.

- **Materials Expenses:** Select the Materials Expenses Ledger Account and enter the Amount.

Save the Purchase Voucher.

FAQ: Frequently Asked Questions

FAQ-1: I like to give out a Job to a third party Jobber. How should I plan each stage of the entire Process from creation of Work Order, Issue of Raw Materials & Receipt of Jobbed Materials and Billing for the executed Job to my customer

Ans: The steps may be broadly listed as follows:

- Set Up of Job Work Feature for the Company
- Creation of Job Work Out Order
- Entry of Job Work Out Voucher for Issue of Raw materials to Jobber against Job Work Out Order
- Entry of Job Work.In Voucher for Receipt of Jobbed materials from Jobber against Job Work Order
- Entry of Purchase / Journal Voucher for Jobbing Bill of the Third Party Jobber
- Payment of Jobbing Bill of the Third Party Jobber
- Entry of Service Bill on Customer for Job Work Done
- Receipt of Money from Custmer in respect of Jobbing Bill issued

Job Work In

01 Job Work In Vouchers

Having created the Masters as explained in previous chapter, you may now enter Job Work In Order and then Materials Transfer (In/Out) Vouchers against Job Work In Order.

02 Job Work In Order

The Jobber issues Job Work In Order on Principal, specifying the details of Input materials (materials to be Received by Jobber from Principal) and Out Put Materials (Processed Materials, including Joint / Bye Products / Scrap) to be delivered to Principal after processing)

02.01 Job Work In Order Entry

At *GoT>Order Voucher*, click *W:Job Work In Order* to get Job Work In Order entry screen (F-1A)

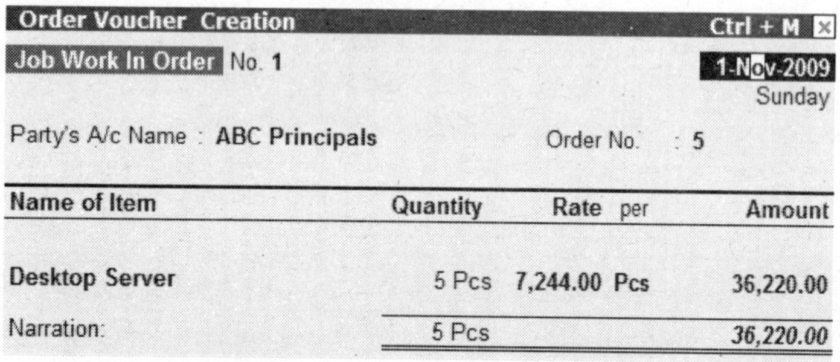

F-1A: Job Work In Order creation

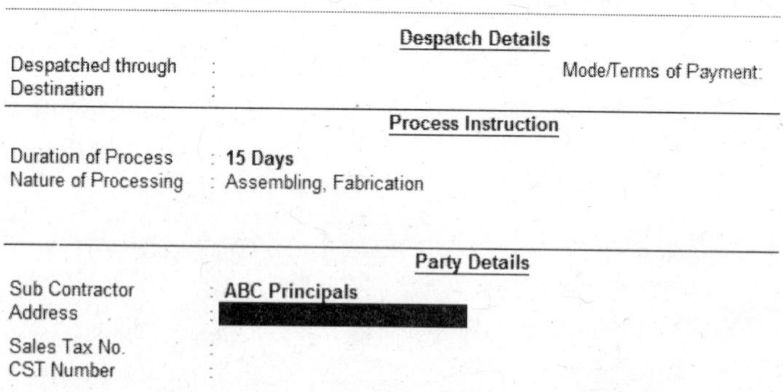

F-1B: Party (Supplementary) Details screen

The Job Work In Order Entry (F-1A) is similar to Order Entry. If supplementary details is set on, you get supplementary details screen (F-1B), where you enter the details as shown in the screen, if desired.

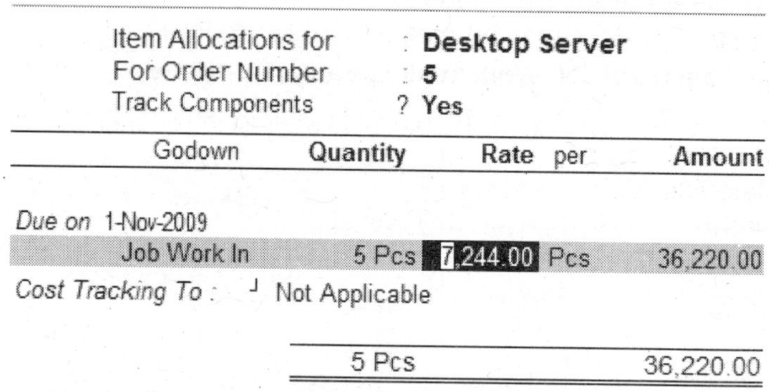

F-1C: Item Allocation

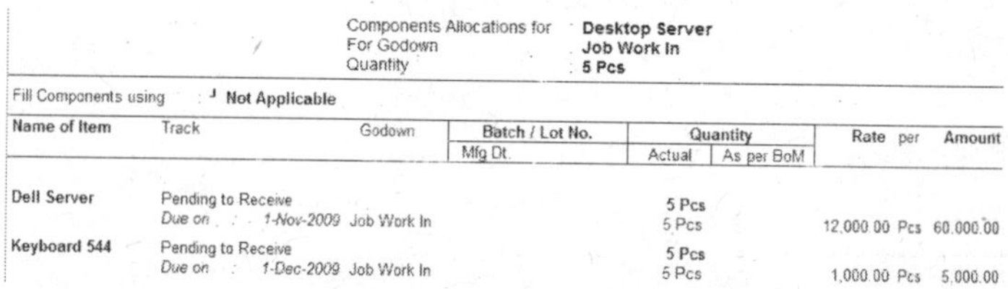

F-1D: Component Allocation screen

Out Put Products: At Main Order Entry screen (F-1A), select the Output Product (the Processed Item that would be delivered by Jobber to Principal) to get Item Allocation screen (F-1C). The Item Name & Order Number is shown. At Track Components, set *Yes* to get the Component entry screen (F-1D), else set *No* (Component entry screen will not appear).

Components Entry: At Components entry screen (F-1D), enter the details of each Component, delivered to the Jobber, by the Principal, as follows:

- **Header**: The name of the Output Product selected, Godown and Quantity, as entered at Item Allocation screen (F-1C), is shown at the header.
- **Component Details**: In the Table area, enter the Component details as follows (F-1D):
  - o **Component Name:** At *Name of Item column*, select the Component to be received.
  - o **Component Type:** At *Track* column, select the Component Type from the list:
    - *Pending to Issue* for Jobbed Articles to be Issued to Principals
    - *Pending to Receive* for Component to be Received by Jobber

This way, enter the details of all Components to be Received, (F-1D)

After entry of all Component Details (else set Not Applicable). Save the Job Work In Voucher (F-1A).

02.02 Transfer In of Input Materials from Principal to Jobber against Job Work In Order

The Jobber will Receive Materials against the Work Order. Materails In & Materials Out Voucher Type has been explained earlier.

At *GoT>Inventory Voucher*, click W:*Materials In* button to get Materials In Voucher Type selection screen (F-2A).

At Materials In Voucher Type selection screen (F-2A), select the Materials In (Raw Materials) Voucher Type, as explained earlier, to get Materials In (Raw Materials) Voucher entry screen (F-2B).

Voucher Type

Name : **Mat In (RM)**

List of Types

Material In
Mat In FG
Mat In (RM)

F- 2A: V Type selection

Inventory Voucher Creation — Ctrl + M

Mat In (RM) No. **1** — **2-Mar-2010**, Tuesday

Ref. : **5**

Party's A/c Name : **ABC Principals**

Source Godown : **Job Work In**

Name of Item	Quantity	Rate	per	Amount
Dell Server	4 Pcs	**12,000.00**	**Pcs**	48,000.00
Keyboard 544	3 Pcs	**1,000.00**	**Pcs**	3,000.00
				51,000.00
Narration:	7 Pcs			***51,000.00***

F-2B: Materials In (RM) Voucher against Job Work In Order

At Materials In (Raw Materials) Voucher entry screen (F-2B), select the Party to get the list of Pending Work Orders for the Party (F-2D). Select the Item / Work Order from the list, against which Materials are being received by Jobber (F-2D), to get Item allocation screen (F-2E). At *Item Allocation* screen (F-2E), enter the Quantity (pending values are carried by default). You may also enter Rate / Value (For Job Costing).

Order Details

Order No(s) 5 dt. 1-Nov-2009 Terms of Delivery

Party's Document Details

Challan No(s) — Despatched through, Destination

Party Details

Sub Contractor **ABC Principals**
Address

Sales Tax No.
CST Number

F-2C: Supplementary Details

List of Orders

Name	Godown	Due On	Balance	Primary Item Name	Order Type
New Number					
Not Applicable					
5	Job Work In	1-Nov-2009	5 Pcs	Desktop Server	Component Receipt Order

F-2D: Work Order / Item Selection

Item Allocations for : **Dell Server**

	Godown	Quantity	Rate	per	Amount
Order No.: 5	*Due on 1-Nov-2009*	*Component of : Desktop Server*			
	Job Work In	4 Pcs	12,000.00	Pcs	48,000.00
Cost Tracking To Not Applicable					
		4 Pcs			48,000.00

F-2E: Work Order details at Item Allocation screen.

Supplementary details: At Supplementary details screen (F-2C), enter requisite details. Most of these are carried by default from the selected Job Work Order (F-1B), which you may change.

03 Printing of Materials In Voucher

At Materials In (Raw Materials) Voucher entry screen (F-2B), click P:*Print* button to get the Voucher in Print (F-2G).

MATERIAL IN

Universal Enterprises
Kolaghata
Kolkata
E-Mail :nomail@univ.com

Voucher No. 1	Dated 2-Mar-2010
Supplier's Ref. 5	Other Reference(s)
Challan No.	Dated
Challan Document No.	Destination
Despatched through	
Terms of Delivery	

Party
ABC Principals

Sl No.	Description of Goods	Quantity
1	**Dell Server**	**4 Pcs**
2	**Keyboard 544**	**3 Pcs**
	Total	**7 Pcs**

E.& O.E

for Universal Enterprises

Authorised Signatory

SUBJECT TO KOLKATA JURISDICTION

F-2G: Materials In (RM) Voucher in print

04 Delivery of Finished Goods against Job Work Order

Upon receiving the Raw materials from Principal, the Job Worker will Produce the finished goods, and deliver to the Principal, creating a Materials Out (Finished Goods) Voucher against Job Work In Order.

At *GoT>Inventory Voucher*, click J: *Material Out* button to get Materials Out Voucher Type selection screen (F-3A).

At Materials Out Voucher Type selection screen (F-3A), select the Materials Out (Finished Products) Voucher Type, as explained earlier, to get Materials Out (Finished Products) Voucher entry screen (F-3B).

At Materials Out (Finished Products) Voucher entry screen (F-3B), select the Party to get the list of Pending Work Orders for the Party (F-3C). Select the Item / Work Order from the list, against which Materials are being issued to Jobber (F-3C), to get Item allocation screen (F-3E). At Item allocation screen (F-3E), enter the Quantity (pending values are carried by default). You may also enter Rate / Value (For Job Costing).

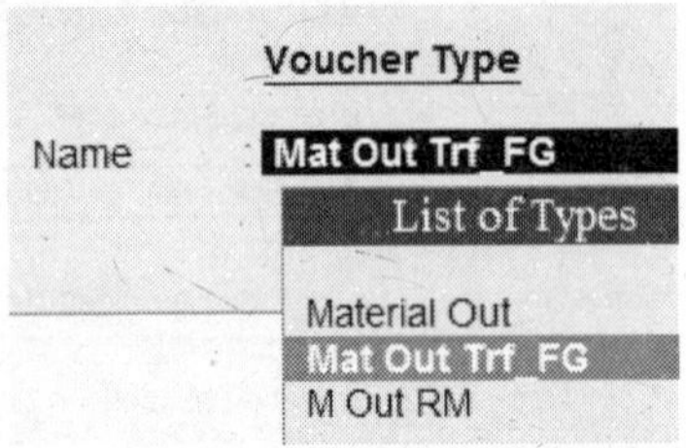

F-3A: Voucher Type selection

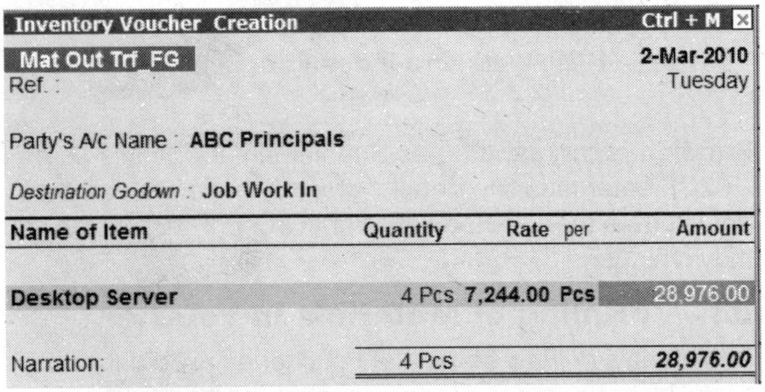

F-3B: Materials Out (Finished Goods) Voucher Entry

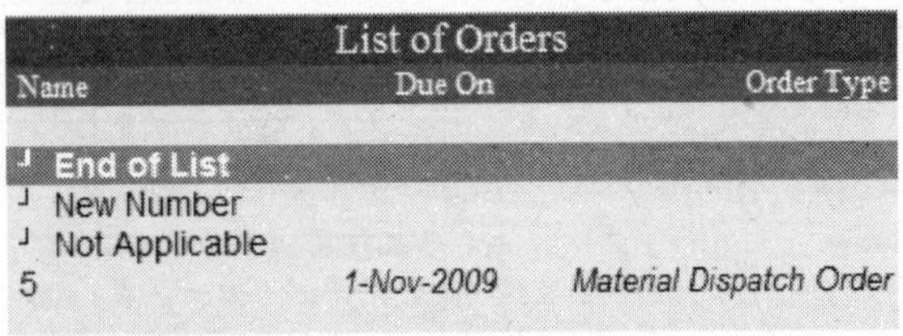

F-3C: Selection of Job Work Order

At Item Allocation screen (F-3E), set:

- Yes at *Consider as Primary Item*, for Receipt of Finished Goods
- No at *Consider as Scrap* for Finished / Joint / Bye Products (set Yes in case of Receipt of Scrap)

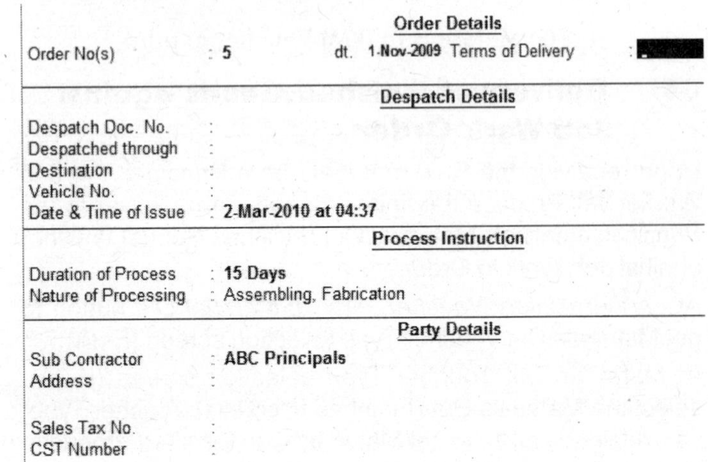

F-3D: Supplementary Details screen

At *Supplementary details* screen (F-3D), enter requisite details. Most of these are carried by default from the selected Job Work Order (F-1B), which you may change.

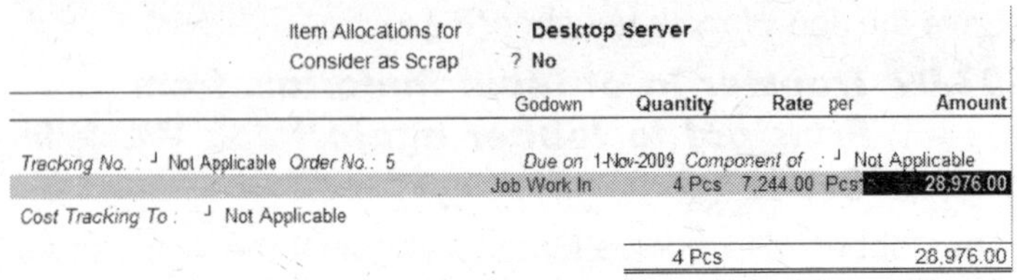

F-3E: Item Allocation

Save the Materials Out Voucher (F-3B)

05 Printing of Materials Out Voucher

At *Materials Out* (Finished Goods) Voucher entry screen (F-3B), click *P:Print* button to get the Voucher in Print (F-3F).

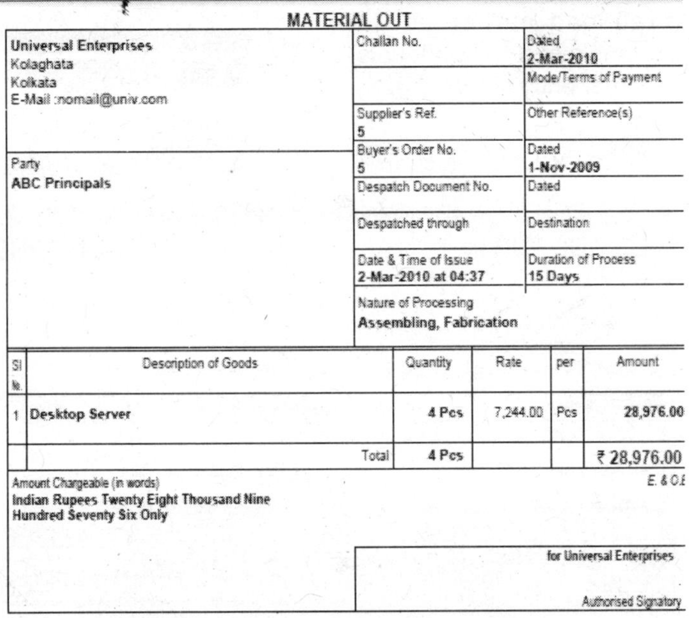

F-3F: Materials Out Voucher in print

FAQ: Frequently Asked Questions

FAQ-1: I have received a Job Work Order from Principal, to execute a Job How should I plan each stage of the entire Process from creation of Work Order, Receipt of Raw Materials from Principal, Issue of Jobbed Materials Principal and Billing for the executed Job.

Ans: The steps may be broadly listed as follows:

- Set Up of Job Work Feature for the Company
- Creation of Job Work In Order
- Entry of Job Work In Voucher for Receipt of Raw materials from Principals against Job Work In Order
- Entry of Job Work Issue Voucher for Delivery of Jobbed materials to Principals against Job Work Order
- Entry of Sale / Journal Voucher for Jobbing on the Principal
- Receipt of Money from Principal against Jobbing Bill

Job Work Reports

09-04

01 Job Work Reports

Having entered voucher data relating to Job Work, you may get various reports related to Job Work. At *GoT>Display>Statement of Inventory*:

- **Job Work In Reports**: Select *Job Work In Reports* to get Job Work In report Menu (F-1A)
- **Job Work Out Reports**: Select *Job Work Out Reports* to get Job Work Out report Menu (F-1B)

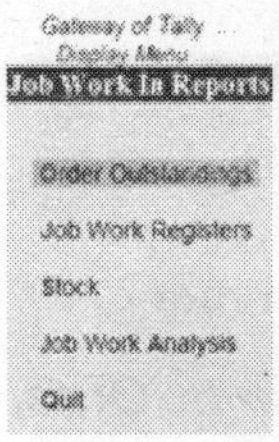

F-1A: Job Work In Reports Menu

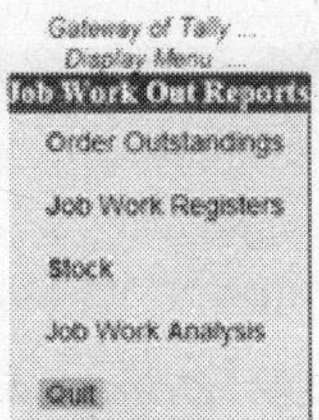

F-1B: Job Work Out Reports Menu

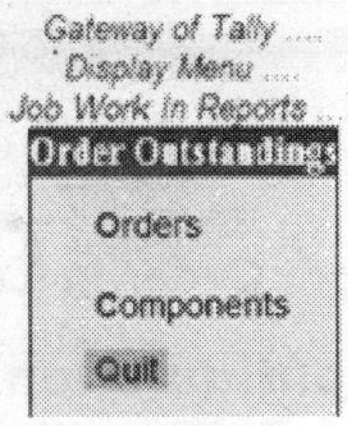

F-2A: Job Work In Order Outstanding Reports Menu

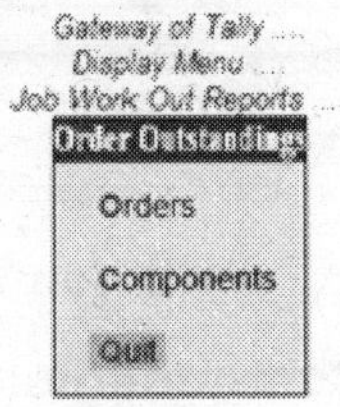

F-2B: Job Work Out Order Outstanding Reports Menu

02 Order Outstanding Reports

Order Outstanding Menu contains following Reports relating to Outstanding Job Orders:

- **Job Work In Outstanding**: At *Job Work In Reports Menu* (F-1A), select *Order Outstanding* to get *Job Work In Order Outstanding* Report Menu (F-2A)
- **Job Work Out Outstanding**: At *Job Work Out Reports Menu* (F-1B), select *Order Outstanding* to get *Job Work Out Order Outstanding* Report Menu (F-2B)

03 Job Work Order Outstanding Summary Reports

The Reports show the list of Outstanding Job Orders.

- **Job Work In Outstanding Summary**: At *Job Work In Orders Outstanding Reports Menu* (F-2A), select *Order* to get *Job Order In Summary* Report (F-3A). *Job Order In Summary* report displays Summary of all Outstanding Job work In orders (Job Order In raised on Principal Manufacturer towards which the raw materials are pending to receive from Principals & Finished Materials to be issued to Principals).
- **Job Work Out Outstanding Summary**: At *Job Work Out Orders Outstanding Reports Menu* (F-2B), select *Order* to get *Job Order Out Outstanding Summary* Report (F-3B). *Job Order Out Summary* report displays Summary of all Outstanding Job work Out orders (Job Order Out raised on Job Workers towards which the raw materials are pending for Issue to Jobbers and Finished Materals to be received from Jobbers).

Job Orders Summary — Ctrl + M

Particulars	Universal Enterprises 1-Apr-2009 to 2-Mar-2010 Orders	
	Ordered Quantity	Balance Quantity
Job Work Orders Outstanding :		
Desktop Server	5 Pcs	1 Pcs
ABC Principals	*5 Pcs*	*1 Pcs*

F-3A: Job Work Order In Outstanding Summary

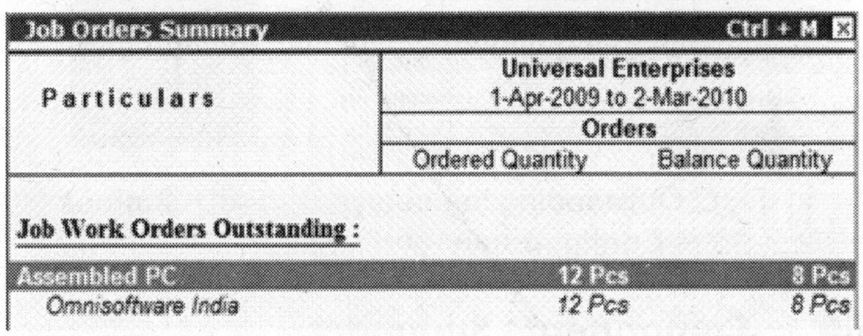

Job Orders Summary — Ctrl + M

Particulars	Universal Enterprises 1-Apr-2009 to 2-Mar-2010 Orders	
	Ordered Quantity	Balance Quantity
Job Work Orders Outstanding :		
Assembled PC	12 Pcs	8 Pcs
Omnisoftware India	*12 Pcs*	*8 Pcs*

F-3B: Job Work Order Out Outstanding Summary

Report Contents: *Job Order Outstanding Summary* Reports (F-3A / F-3B) display the summary of all the Job work orders which are outstanding. The contents and format of both the *Job Order Outstanding Summary* reports (F-3A / F-3B) referred above are similar, as described below:

- **Stock Item:** At *Particulars*, the Stock Item Name is displayed
- **Order Quantity**: At Ordered Quantity, the Order Quantity is shown
- **Balance Quantity**: At Balance Quantity, the Order Balance Quantity as on the Report end date (by default, the Current Balance Quality as) is shown

Report Configuration: At *Job Order Outstanding Summary* Reports, click *F12:Configure* to get *Job Order Outstanding*

Summary Configuration screen (F-3C), to set the Configuration Options as follows

- Outstanding Orders: At *Show Outstanding Orders*, set:
  - o Yes to show only Balance Outstanding Order details
  - o No. to show Order & Balance Outstanding Order details
- Cleared Orders: At *Show* Cleared *Orders*, set:
  - o Yes to show the details of Cleared Order (orders which have been fully executed and here is no Balance are also shown)
  - o No. to show Outstanding Orders only (orders which have been fully executed and here is no Balance are NOT shown)

Buttons: At *Job Order Outstanding Summary* Reports, you get following buttons (F-3D):

- **F1:Detailed / Condensed**: Click *F1: Detailed* toggle button to get the Report in Detailed Format (complete details with Due / Overdue Days)
- ***F5:Partywise / Itemwise****:* Click *F5:partywise / Itemwise* toggle button to get the Report in Partywise / Item wise sequence (default)
- ***C:Components***: Click *C:Components* button (F-3D) to get the (F-4A, F-4B) Components Summary

Configuration

Show Outstanding Job Orders	?	Yes
Show Cleared Job Orders	?	No
Show using Alternate Units	?	No
Show Tail Units of Compound Units	?	No
Appearance of Stock Item Names	:	Name Only
Appearance of Names	:	Name Only
Sorting Method	:	Default

F-3C:Outstanding Summary Configuration

F1: Detailed
F2: Period
F3: Company
F5: Party Wise
C: Components

F-3D: Buttons

04 Components Summary

The Reports (F-4A / F-4B) display the Components Outstanding (for issue) for Job Orders raised.

- **Components In Outstanding Summary**: At *Job Work In Orders Outstanding Reports Menu* (F-2A), select Components to get *Components In Summary* Report (F-4B). This Report displays Summary of all Components of Job Work Order In (Components pending to receive from Principals).
- **Components Out Outstanding Summary**: At *Job Work Out Orders Outstanding Reports Menu* (F-2B), select *Components* to get *Job Order Out Outstanding Summary* Report (F-4A). This Report displays Summary of all Components of Job work Out orders (Components pending for Issue to Jobbers).

You may also get the Components Reports (F-4A, F-4B) when you Click *C:Components* button (F-3D) at Job Order Outstanding Summary Reports (F-3A, F-3B).

Components Order Summary Ctrl + M

Particulars	Universal Enterprises 1-Apr-2009 to 2-Mar-2010 Components	
	Ordered Quantity	Balance Quantity
Job Work Orders Outstanding :		
Cabinet	7 Pcs	7 Pcs
Omnisoftware India	*7 Pcs*	*7 Pcs*
Job Work Orders Cleared :		
Cabinet	**5 Pcs**	
Omnisoftware India	*5 Pcs*	
CPU P4	**5 Pcs**	
Omnisoftware India	*5 Pcs*	

F-4A: Job Work Order Out Components Summary

Components Order Summary Ctrl + M

Particulars	Universal Enterprises 1-Apr-2009 to 2-Mar-2010 Components	
	Ordered Quantity	Balance Quantity
Job Work Orders Outstanding :		
Dell Server	5 Pcs	1 Pcs
ABC Principals	*5 Pcs*	*1 Pcs*
Keyboard 544	**5 Pcs**	**2 Pcs**
ABC Principals	*5 Pcs*	*2 Pcs*

F-4B: Job Work Order In Components Summary

Components Configuration: At *Components Order Summary* (F-4A, F-4B), click *F12:Configure* to get Components Configuration screen, similar to Outstanding Summary Reports Configuration (F-3C), to set the Configuration options

Components Buttons: At *Components Order Summary*, you get Buttons, similar to Outstanding Summary Reports Buttons (F-3D).

05 Job Work Registers

These Reposts show the details of Job Work Orders, Materials In & Out against the Job Work and Materials Movement.

- o **Job Work In Materials Menu:** At *Job Work In Reports Menu* (F-1A), select *Job Work Register* to get *Job Works In Registers menu* (F-5A), containing various reports of *Job Work In Registers.*
- o **Job Work Out Materials Menu:** At *Job Work Out Reports Menu (*F-1B), select *Job Work Register* to get *Job Works Out Registers menu* (F-5B), containing various reports of *Job Work Out Registers*

Gateway of Tally ....
Display Menu ...
Job Work In Reports ...
Job Work Registers
Job Work In Orders Book
Material Out Register
Material In Register
MateRial Movement Register
Quit

F-5A: Job Work In Register Menu

Gateway of Tally ....
Display Menu ...
Job Work Out Reports ...
Job Work Registers
Job Work Out Orders Book
Material Out Register
Material In Register
MateRial Movement Register
Quit

F-5B: Job Work Out Register Menu

05.01 Job Work Order Books

These Reports gives lists of Job Work Orders.

- **Job Work In Orders Book:** At *Job Woks In Registers Menu* (F-5A), select *Job Work In Order Book* to get *Job Work In Orders Book* Display screen (F-6A).
- **Job Work Out Orders Book:** At *Job Woks Out Registers Menu* (F-5B), select *Job Work Out Orders Book* to get to get *Job Work Out Order Book* Display screen (F-6B).

Job Work Order Books Configuration: At *Job Work In Orders Book (F-6A) / Job Work Out Orders Book (F-6B)*, click F12:Configure to get *Job Work Order Books Configuration* screen, similar to Registers Configuration screen (F-14A/02-08), described earlier.

Job Work Order Books Buttons: At *Job Work In Orders Book / Job Work Out Orders Book*, you get Buttons similar to Registers (F-14B/02-08), described earlier.

Job Work In Orders Book — Ctrl + M

List of All Job Work In Order Vouchers — 1-Apr-2009 to 2-Mar-2010

Date	Particulars	Vch Type	Vch No.	Order Ref.No.	Order Amount
1-11-2009	ABC Principals	Job Work In Order	1	5	36,220.00

F-6A: Job Work In Order Book

Job Work Out Orders Book — Ctrl + M

List of All Job Work Out Order Vouchers — 1-Apr-2009 to 2-Mar-2010

Date	Particulars	Vch Type	Vch No.	Order Ref.No	Order Amount
1-10-2009	Omnisoftware India	[illegible]	1	10	25,000.00
	Assembled PC 5 Pcs				
1-1-2010	Omnisoftware India	[illegible]	2	11	84,000.00
	Assembled PC 7 Pcs				
				Total:	1,09,000.00

F-6B: Job Work Out Order Book

05.02 Materials Out Registers

These Reports show lists of Materials Out Vouchers for transfer of Consumption stock to Jobbers and the Finished goods transferred to the Principal Manufacturer

- **Materials Out Register for Job Work In:** At *Job Woks In Registers Menu* (F-5A), select *Materials Out Register* to get *Materials Out Registers* (for Job Work In) Display screen (F-7B).

Material Out Register — Ctrl + M

List of All Material Out Vouchers — 1-Apr-2009 to 2-Mar-2010

Date	Particulars		Vch Type	Vch No.	Inwards Quantity	Outwards Quantity
1-11-2009	Cabinet		Ml Out RM	1		5 Pcs
	Omnisoftware India					
	CPU P4	5 Pcs				
	Cabinet	(-)5 Pcs				
	CPU P4	(-)5 Pcs				

F-7A; Material Out (Job Work Out) Register

Material Out Register — Ctrl + M

List of All Material Out Vouchers — 1-Apr-2009 to 2-Mar-2010

Date	Particulars		Vch Type	Vch No.	Inwards Quantity	Outwards Quantity
2-3-2010	Desktop Server		[illegible]			4 Pcs
	ABC Principals					
	Desktop Server	(-)4 Pcs				

F-7B: Material Out (Job Work In) Register

- **Materials Out Register for Job Work Out:** At *Job Woks Out Registers Menu* (F-5B), select *Materials Out Registers* to get to get *Materials Out Registers* (for Job Work Out) Display screen (F-7A).

05.03 Materials In Registers

These Reports (F-8A / F-8B) show lists of Materials In Vouchers, for receipt of Raw Materials/Components from the Principal / Manufacturer.

- **Materials In Register for Job Work In:** At *Job Woks In Registers Menu* (F-5A), select *Materials In Register* to get *Materials In Registers* (for Job Work In) Display screen (F-8A).
- **Materials In Register for Job Work Out:** At *Job Woks Out Registers Menu* (F-5B), select *Materials In Registers* to get to get *Materials In Registers* (for Job Work Out) Display screen (F-8B).

Material In Register — Ctrl + M

List of All Material In Vouchers — 1-Apr-2009 to 2-Mar-2010

Date	Particulars		Vch Type	Vch No.	Inwards Quantity	Outwards Quantity
2-3-2010	Dell Server		[illegible]	1	4 Pcs	
	ABC Principals					
	Keyboard 544	3 Pcs				
	Dell Server	(-)4 Pcs				
	Keyboard 544	(-)3 Pcs				

F-8A: Material In (Job Work In) Register

Material In Register — Ctrl + M

List of All Material In Vouchers — 1-Apr-2009 to 2-Mar-2010

Date	Particulars		Vch Type	Vch No.	Inwards Quantity	Outwards Quantity
2-3-2010	Assembled PC		Mat In FG	1	4 Pcs	
	Omnisoftware India					
	Cabinet	(-)4 Pcs				
	CPU P4	(-)4 Pcs				

F-8B: Material In (Job Work Out) Register

Materials Registers Configuration: At *Materials Out Registers* (for Job Work In: F-7A) / *Materials Out Registers* (for Job Work Out: F-7B), click *F12:Configure* to get *Materials Out Registers Configuration* screen (F-8C)

Configuration

Format	Condensed
Show Narrations also	? No
Appearance of Names	: Name Only
Sorting Method	: Default

F-8C: Material Register Configuration

F1: Detailed
F2: Date
F2: Period
F3: Company
F4: Chg Vch

F-8D: Material Register Buttons

Materials Registers Buttons: At *Materials Out Registers* (for Job Work In) / *Materials Out Registers* (for Job Work Out), you get Buttons (F-8D).

05.04 Material Movement Register

These Reports (F-9A) show the details of Movement of Material (Raw Materials and Finished Goods) of Orders.

- **Materials Movement Register for Job Work In:** At *Job Woks In Registers Menu* (F-5A), select *Materials Movement Register* to get *Materials Movement Register* (for Job Work In) Display screen (F-9A).

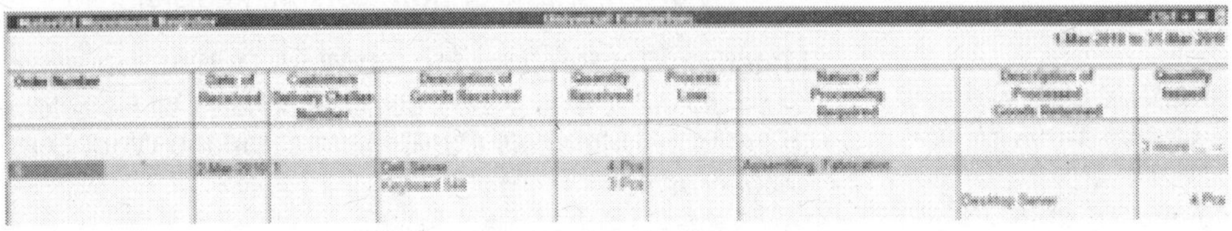

F- 9A: Materials Movement Register (Job Work In) Part 1

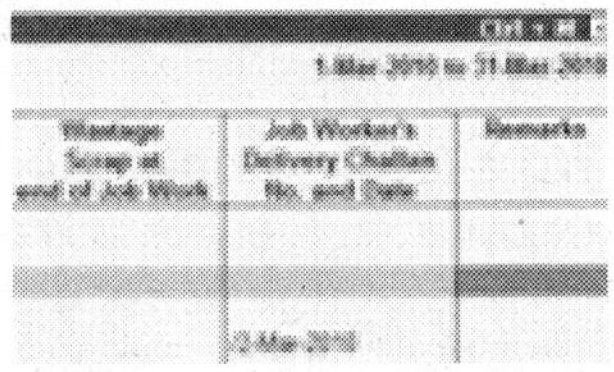

Materials Movement Register (Job Work In) Part 2

- **Materials Movement Register for Job Work Out:** At *Job Woks Out Registers Menu* (F-5B), select *Materials Movement Registers* to get to get *Materials Movement Register* (for Job Work Out) Display screen.

Contents of Materials Movement Registers (F-9A)

- **Order Number**: Job Order number towards which the material movement (Out/In) Voucher is recorded.
- **Delivery Challan Number**: Voucher number of the Material out voucher through which the materials are transferred against the Job Order.
- **Date of Dispatch**: Date of materials movement voucher.
- **Description of Goods dispatched**: Name of the stock items in the movement voucher
- **Quantity Dispatched to Job Worker: Quantity** of each goods transferred
- **Name and Address of Job Worker**: Job worker Name on whom the order is raised.
- **Nature of Processing Required**: Nature of Processing required, as entered in Party Details of Material In / Out voucher.
- **Goods Received from Job Worker**: Finished Goods/ Scrap/By-Products/Co- Products) received from the Job Worker
- **Quantity Received form Job Worker**: This column displays the Quantity of Finished Goods received.
- **Job Worker's Delivery Challan No. and Date**: Job worker's Delivery Challan Number and Date entered in the Material In Voucher.
- **Factory GRN/GRRNo. and Date**: Shows the Voucher Number and Date of **Material In / Out** voucher.
- **Shortages if any**: Shows the details of Shortages recorded in Voucher
- **Wastage/Scrap at the end of Job worker**: Quantity of wastage and scrap produced during the manufacture of Finished Goods.
- **Duty Paid on Shortages/Scrap/Wastage**: Displays the details of Excise Duty paid (on Excisable Goods, if any) on the Shortage/ scrap/Wastage
- **Remarks**: Remark as the Job Order is closed.

06 Job Work Stock Reports

These Reports show the Materials lying with Jobbers / Principals and the period since when the Stock is lying

- o **Stock Against Materials In Menu:** At *Job Work In Reports Menu* (F-1A), select *Stock* to get *Stock Against Materials In Menu* (F-10A) containing various reports of *Stock against Job In Orders*
- o **Stock Against Materials Out Menu:** At *Job Work Out Reports Menu* (F-1B), select *Stock* to get *Stock Against Materials Out Menu* (F-10B) containing various reports of *Stock against Job Out Orders*

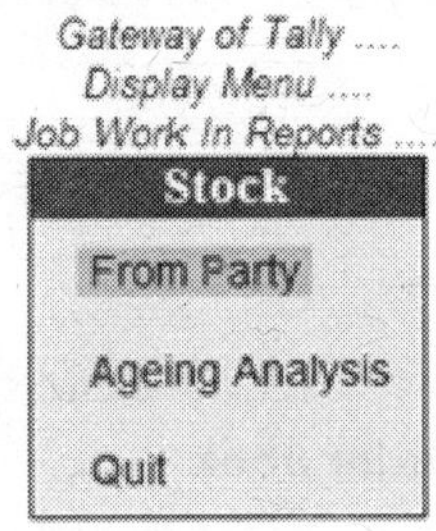

F-10A: Stock Menu (Job Work In)

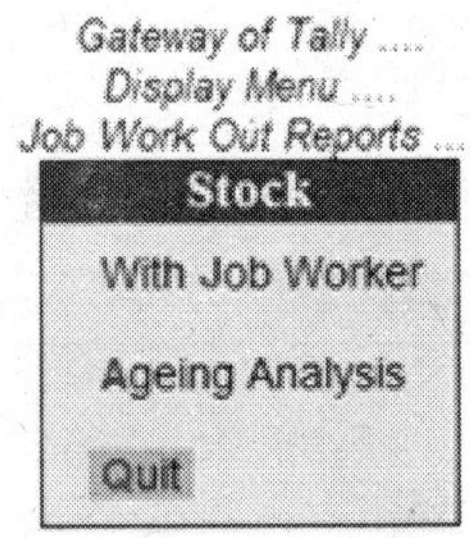

F-10B: Stock Menu (Job Work Out)

F-11A: Stock with Job Worker

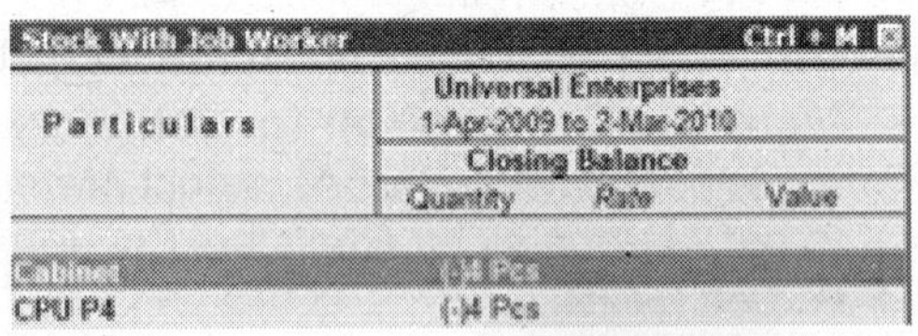

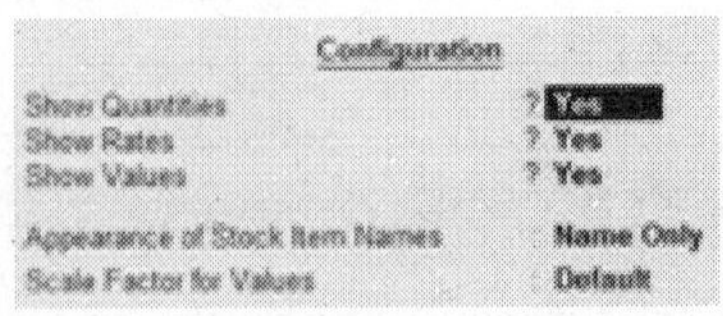

F-11B: Stock with Job Worker Configuration

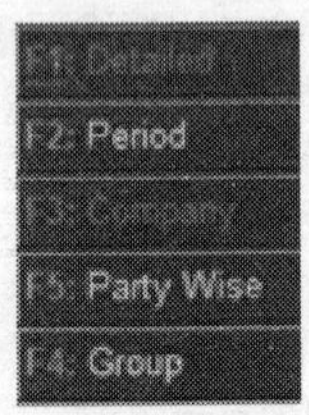

F-11C: Stock with Job Worker Buttons

The Stock menus (F-10A) / (F-10B) contain following Reports:

07 Stock Reports

These Reports show Stock of Third party / Stock with Third party

- o **Stock of Party**: This Report displays the details of stock received from different Principal Manufacturer. At *Stock (Job Work In) Menu* (F-10A), select *From Party* to get Stock From Party Report. It shows the details of stock received from different Principal Manufacturer.
- o **Stock with Job Worker**: This Report displays the details of stock lying with different Jobbers. At *Stock Against (Job Work Out) Menu (F-10B),* select *With Job Worker* to get Stock With Jobber Report (F-11A)

Configuration: At *Stock From Party* / Stock With Jobber Reports (F-11A), click F12:Configure to get Configuration screen (F-11B), to set the following Options:

- **Quantity**: At *Show Quantities*, set *Yes* to show Quantity column, else set *No* (Quantity column is not shown)
- **Rate**: At *Show Rates*, set *Yes* to show Rate column, else set *No* (Rate column is not shown)
- **Value**: At *Show Value*, set *Yes* to show Value column, else set *No* (Value column is not shown)

You must set *Yes* at least one of the above options

Buttons: At *Stock* Reports, you get following Buttons (F-11C)

On selecting the option, select the *Stock Group* from the list of Stock Group (select *All Items* for all Stock Items). The Age Analysis Report for the Stock Items under the selected Stock Group will be displayed (F-12A), as per *Ageing period* set.

Buttons: At *Age Analysis* Reports (F-12A), you get following Buttons (F-12B)

- **F4:Group:** To select Account Group (Sundry Debtor / Sundry Creditor). The Age Analysis Report for Parties under the selected Group will be listed
- **F5:Paty Wise / Itemwise:** To get the Stock Report in Partywise / Stock Itemwise sequence
- **F6: Ageing Periods**: To set the Ageing Slabs as discussed earlier
- **A:Hide Amounts / Show Amounts:** Toggle button to Hide / Show Amount columns

09 Job Work Analysis

- **Job Work In Analysis**: At *Job Work In Reports Menu* (F-1A), select *Job Work Analysis* to get *Job Work In Analysis* Menu (F-13A)
- **Job Work Out Analysis**: At *Job Work Out Reports Menu* (F-1B), select *Job Work Analysis* to get *Job Work Out Analysis* Menu (F-13B)

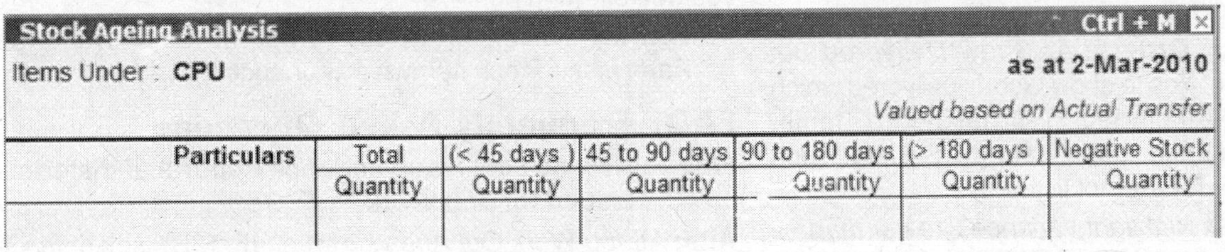

F-12A: Age Analysis

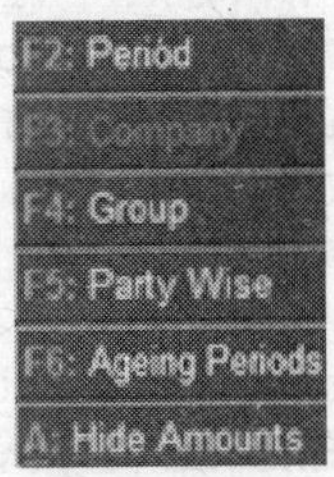

F-12B: Buttons (Age Analysis)

- **F5:Paty Wise / Itemwise:** To get the Stock Report in Partywise / Stock Itemwise sequence
- **F4:Group:** To select Account Group (Sundry Debtor / Sundry Creditor). Th Parties under the selected Group will be listed (this option is available for when F5:Partywise option is selected)

08 Ageing Analysis

These Reports (F-12A) show the Age of Stock (period of stock lying)

- **Ageing Analysis of Job Work In**: This Report shows the time period of each Stock Item of Principals lying with the Jobber. At *Stock (Job Work In) Menu* (F-10A), select *Ageing Analysis* to get Ageing Analysis of *Stock Against Job Work In.*
- **Ageing Analysis of Job Work Out**: This Report shows the time period of each Stock Item lying with Jobber. At At *Stock (Job Work Out) Menu* (F-10B), select *Ageing Analysis* to get Ageing Analysis of *Stock Against Job Work Out.*

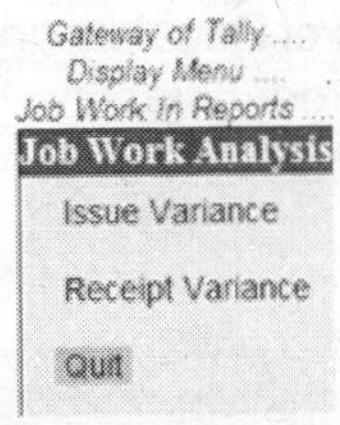

F-13A: Job Work In Analysis Menu

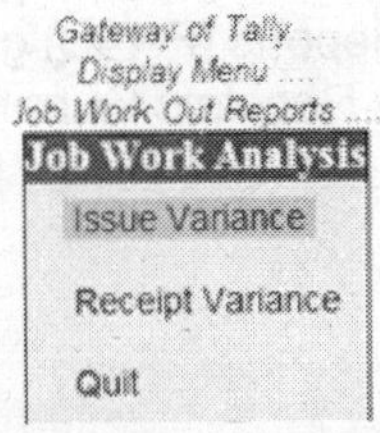

F-13B: Job Work Out Analysis Menu

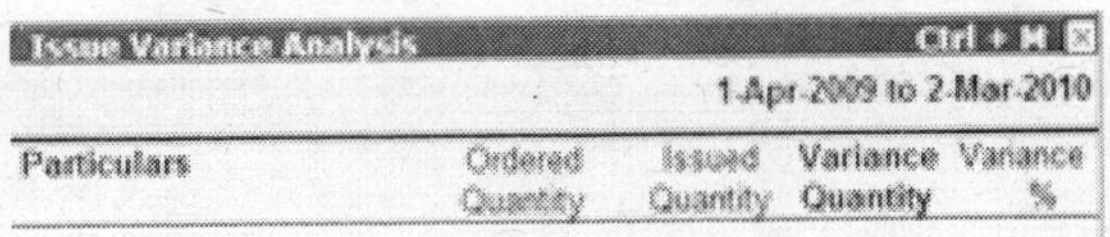

F-14A: Issue Variance Analysis

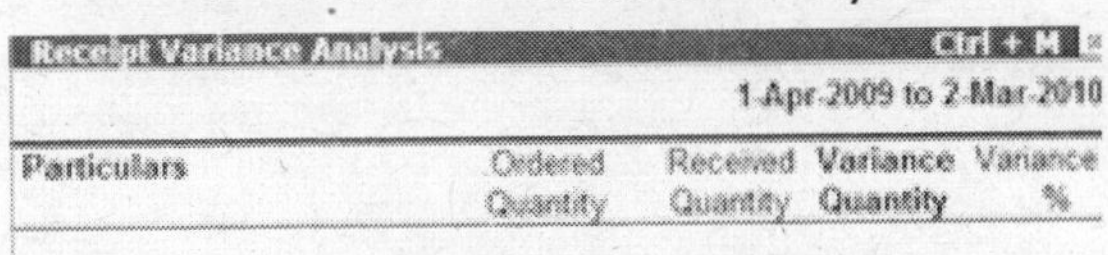

F-14B: Receipt Variance Analysis

F-14C: Variamce Analysis Configuration

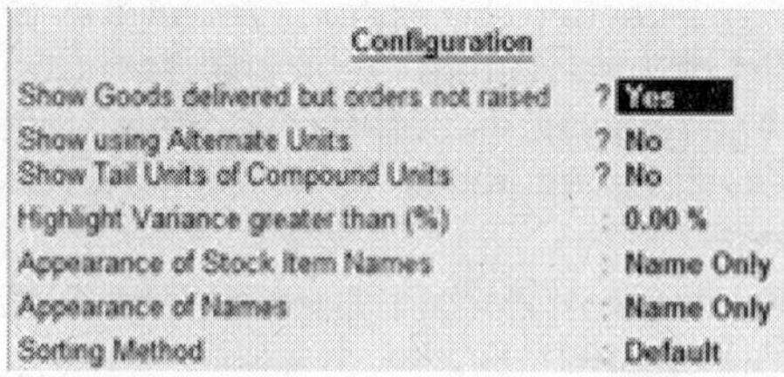

09.01 Issue Variance Reports

These Reports give details of issues and variance (in %) of Issue Quantity with Order Quantity:

- **Job Work In Issue Variance Report:** At *Job Work In Analysis* Menu (F-13A), select Issue Variance to get *Job Work In Issue Variance* Report (F-14A). This Report shows the Issues against Job Work In Orders, Ordered Quantity, Issue Quantity, Variance %, separately for Primary Items, Bye Products & Scrap
- **Job Work Out Issue Variance Report:** At *Job Work Out Analysis* Menu (F-13B), select Issue Variance to get *Job Work Out Issue Variance* Report. This Report shows the Issues against Job Work Out Orders, Ordered Quantity, Issue Quantity, Variance %, separately for Primary Items, Bye Products & Scrap

Issue Variance Configuration*:* At *Issue Variance Report* (F-14A), click *F12:Configure* to get *Configuration* (F-14C), screen to set options as follows:

- **Deliveries without Orders**: At *Show Delivered but Orders not raised*, set Yes to show Goods delivered which were not originally included in Order (extra items, replacement / substitute items issued). Set *No*, such issues (without Orders) are not listed.
- **Excess Variance**: At *Highlight Variance Greater than %*, enter the higher limit of %, to highlight issues having higher Variance.

09.02 Receipt Variance Reports

These Reports (F-14B) give details of Receipts and variance (in %) of Receipts Quantity with Order Quantity:

- **Job Work In Receipt Variance Report:** At *Job Work In Analysis* Menu, select *Receipt Variance* to get *Job Work In Receipt Variance* Report (F-14B). This Report shows the Receipts against Job Work In Orders, Ordered Quantity, Receipt Quantity, Variance %, separately for Primary Items, Bye Products & Scrap
- **Job Work Out Receipt Variance Report:** At *Job Work Out Analysis* Menu, select *Receipt Variance* to get *Job Work Out Receipt Variance* Report. This Report shows the *Receipt* against Job Work Out Orders, Ordered Quantity, Receipt Quantity, Variance %, separately for Primary Items, Bye Products & Scrap

Receipt Variance Configuration*:* At *Receipt Variance Report*, click *F12:Configure* to get *Configuration* screen to set options as follows:

- **Deliveries without Orders**: At *Show Received but Orders not raised*, set Yes to show Goods delivered which were not originally included in Order (extra items, replacement / substitute items issued). Set No, such issues (without orders) are not listed.
- **Excess Variance**: At *Highlight Variance Greater than %*, enter the higher limit of %, to highlight issues having higher Variance.

Variance Analysis Buttons: At *Variance Analysis Reports*, you get following buttons

- **F5:Paty Wise / Itemwise:** To get the Stock Report in Partywise / Stock Itemwise sequence

FAQ: Frequently Asked Questions

FAQ-1: How do I get Issue Variance Reports of materials Issued for Job Work

Ans: At *Job Work Out Analysis* Menu (F-13B), select *Issue Variance* to get *Job Work Out Issue Variance* Report. This Report shows the Issues against Job Work Out Orders, Ordered Quantity, Issue Quantity, Variance %, separately for Primary Items, Bye Products & Scrap

Section 3

Taxation

Part 1

Tax Deducted at Source (TDS)

In this Part, we discuss about the compliance of TDS (Tax Deducted at Source), deduction of TDS from Payment, deposit of TDS to Government and filing of Statutory Returns of TDS.

- **TDS Set Up** describes activation of TDS features for the Company and set up of various Ledger accounts related to TDS.
- **TDS Voucher Entry** describes the Voucher Entry for Deduction of TDS & net Payment to Deductee, after deduction of TDS.
- **TDS Deposit** describes Voucher entry for Deposit of TDS to Government and printing of TDS Challan
- **TDS Reports** explains various Reports related to TDS as well as Statutory Reports to be filed with the Income Tax Department
- **TDS Special Cases** explains some special cases of lower deduction / exemption of TDS

TDS Set Up 01-01

01 TDS

TDS (Tax Deducted at Source) is a mode of collection of advance Income Tax. While making certain kinds of payment, the payer deducts Income Tax from the payee and deposits with Income Tax authority. The payer (i.e Deductor), later on issues a certificate to the payee (i.e Deductee), in respect of deduction of TDS and deposits to the government. The TDS deducted and deposited to Government (by the deductor) is treated as advance payment of Income Tax on behalf the deductee.

02 TDS Process

- **Service Seller** (including Lender of Money) submits Services (or Interest) Bill to the Service Receiver (or Borrower)
- Service Buyer (TDS Deductor) deducts TDS from the Service Bill and makes the balance payment to Seller (TDS Deductee)
- **Deductor** remits the Deducted TDS amount into Bank (Treasury). Bank (Treasury) remits the amount to the Government Account.
- **Deductor** Issues Form 16A to Deductee for the TDS amount deducted
- Deductor Files the e-TDS to NSDL.
- NSDL uploads the e-TDS information to Income Tax Department.
- Deductee Files the Return with Form 16A to Income tax Department

03 TDS Set up for the Company

At Accounting Features screen (*F11: Features* >Accounting Features) set as follows:

- **TDS Activation**: At *Enable Tax Deducted at Source*, set *Yes* to Activate TDS Features for the Company (F-1A)
- **TDS Details**: At *Set / Alter TDS Details*, set *Yes* (F-1A), to get *Company TDS Deductor Details* screen (F-2A), to enter the Company TDS Details as described next (§04).'
- **PAN**: At *Accounting Features* screen, at *PAN / Income Tax Number*, enter the Company PAN (F-1B)

Enable Tax Deducted at Source (TDS)	? **Yes**
Set/Alter TDS Details	? **Yes**

F-1A: Activation of TDS

PAN / Income - Tax No.: ACDRE3456V

F-1B: PAN Details Entry

Company TDS Deductor Details

Tax Deduction and Collection Account Number	: **ACFG12345A**
Head Office TAN Number	: **DSFG67890G**
Income Tax Circle/Ward (TDS)	: **24(3)**
Deductor Type	: **Others**
Is Proprietorship Firm	? **Yes**
Name of person responsible	: **S K Chandra**
Son/daughter of	: **P K Chandra**
Designation	: **Proprietor**

(Note: All the above details will be used in Challan, Forms & Returns)

F-2A: TDS Deductor Details entry

List Of Company Type
Government
Others

F-2B: Deductor Type List

Eh ?
Invalid TAN Structure.
(Format should be of
4 Alpha, 5 Numeric and 1 Alpha)
E.g.: AAAA12345A

F2C:Invalid TAN Format error

04 Company TDS Details

At *TDS Deductor Details* entry screen (F-2A), enter the following details:

- **Company TAN:** At *Tax Deduction & Collection Account Number*, enter the 10 digit TAN (in the form of AAAA99999A, A represents an Alpha letter [A-Z] and 9 represents numeric digit [0-9]) of the Company allotted by the Income Tax Department. An error message will appear (F-2C), if the TAN is not entered in proper Format
- **Company HO TAN:** At *Head Office TAN Number*, enter the head office TAN, if any (else leave blank)
- **Income Tax Circle / Ward**: At *Income Tax Circle / Ward*, enter the Income Tax Circle / Ward Number where the Company is being assessed.
- **Deductor Type**: At *Deductor Type*, select the Organisation constitution type (Government / Others) from the list (F-2B).
- **Proprietorship Firm:** At *Is Proprietorship Firm*, set *Yes*, if it is Proprietorship Firm, else set *No*
- **Officer Name:** At *Name of the Person Responsible*, enter the name of the deductor Company official
- **Officer Father Name:** At *Son / Daughter of,* enter the N*ame of the Father of the* deductor Company official (as

entered above) responsible for deduction & deposit of TDS.

- **Officer Designation**: At *Designation*, enter the Deductor Company Designation of the official.

These details are printed in TDS Challan and other Reports.

05 TDS Statutory Masters

On activation of TDS (§03). Tally internally uploads TDS related Statutory Masters. At *GoT>Display*, select *Statutory Info* to get *Statutory Master* Menu (F-3A).

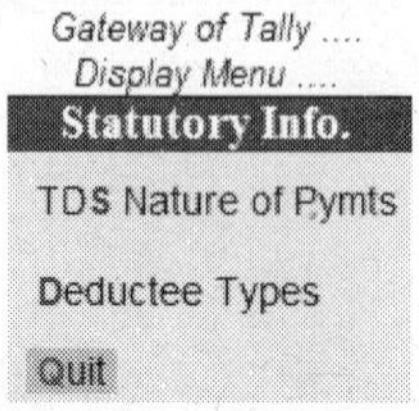

F-3A: Statutory Info Menu

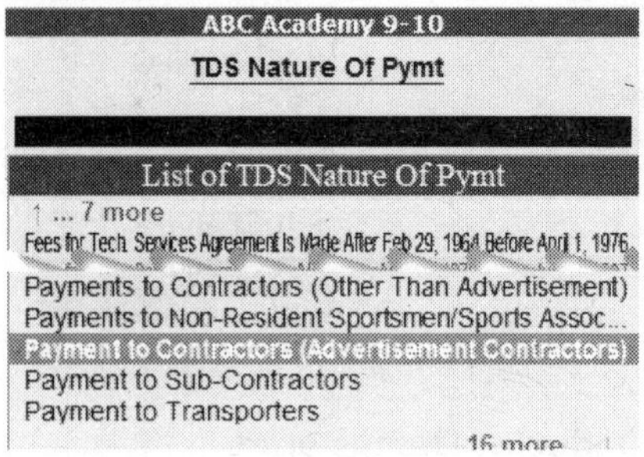

F-3B: TDS nature of Payment List

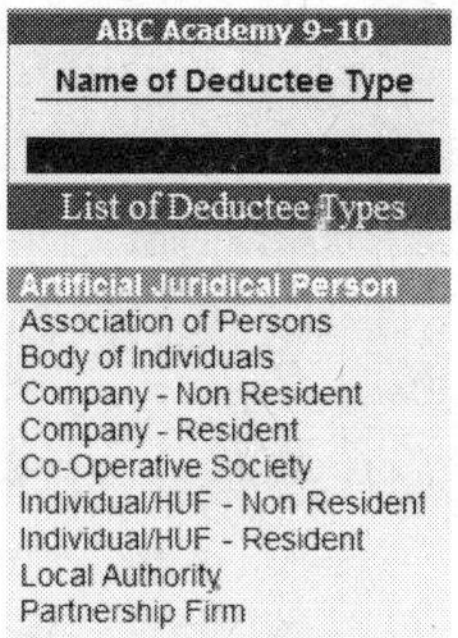

F-3C: TDS Deductee Type

- **TDS nature of Payment List**: At *Statutory Master* Menu (F-3A), select *TDS nature of Payment* to view TDS nature of Payment List (F-3B), showing the various Nature of Payment as classified by I Tax Department.
- **Deductee Type List**: At *Statutory Master* Menu (F-3A), select *Deductee Types* to get TDS Deductee Type List (F-3C), showing the various Type of Deductee as classified by I Tax Department.

05.01 Statutory Info Details

You may further view the details of any selected Item from the list TDS Nature of Payment & TDS Deductee Type, as described below:

- **TDS Nature of Payment Details:** At *TDS nature of Payment List* (F-3B), drill down from a record to view the details of the selected Payment Nature (F-4A), as follows:
  - o Full Name: At *Full Name*, the full Name of the Nature of Payment, as per I Tax Act / Rule, is displayed
  - o Section: At *Section*, the Applicable Section Number of Income Tax Act, 1961 is shown for information
  - o Payment Code: At *Payment Code*, the Payment Code, as specified by Income Tax Department, is shown, for information
  - o **Single Bill Value Limit**: At *Single Bill Value Limit*, the Limit over which a TDS is to be Deducted for Single Bill Value, is shown
  - o Section Name: At *Section Name*, the relevant Section Head of TDS deduction is shown, for information

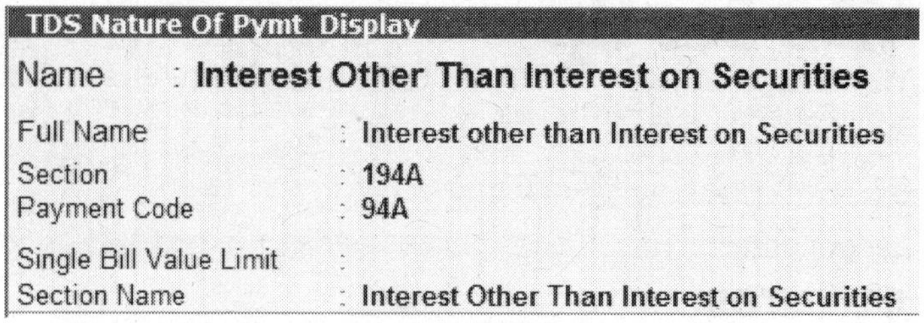

F-4A: TDS Nature of Payment Display

- **TDS Deductee Type Details:** At *TDS Deductee Type List* (F-3C), drill down from a record to view the details of the selected Deductee Type (F-4B), as follows:
  - o **Name**: At *Name*, the Name of the Deductee Type is shown
  - o **Residential Status**: At ***Residential Status***, Residential Status of the Deductee is shown (Resident / Non-Resident).
  - o **Deductee Status**: At ***Deductee Status***, Deductee Status is shown (Company/ Non Company).
  - o **Deductee TDS Details**: The Table section displays following details in respect of each Nature of Payment:

> ***Note:*** *The fields* Active & Module Type *is internal info of Tally*

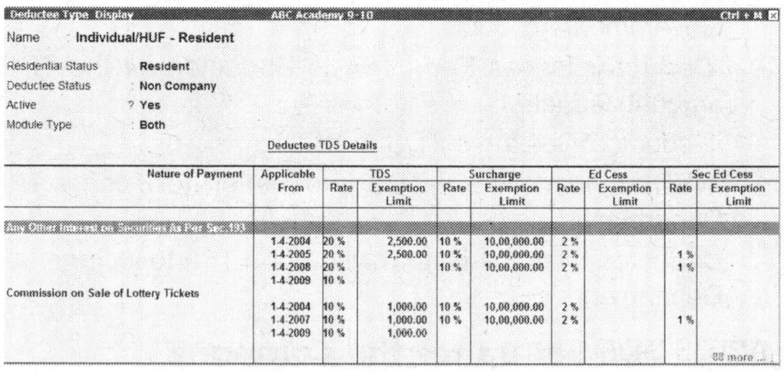

F-4B: Deductee Type Display

- **Nature of Payment**: At ***Nature of Payment* column**, the Nature of Payments heading, applicable for the Deductee is listed
- **Applicability**: At ***Applicable From* column**, the respective dates of applicability for each Nature of Payment is shown.
- **TDS**: At *TDS* section, the applicable *TDS Rate* and *TDS Exemption limit* (ceiling of exemption) is shown
- **Surcharge**: At *Surcharge* section,the applicable Surcharge Rate and corresponding Surcharge Exemption limit is shown

- **Ed Cess:** At *Ed Cess* section,the applicable Education Cess Rate is shown
- **Sec Ed Cess:** At *Sec Ed Cess* section,the applicable Secondary Education Cess Rate is shown

This way, the details of each Nature of Payment, as applicable for the Deductee are listed

06 TDS Ledger Accounts creation

Ledger creation has been explained earlier. Here we describe the features exclusively related to TDS Ledger Account Master. At *Ledger Account Configuration* screen (Click F12:Configure at Ledger Account creation screen), you must have set *Yes* at *Allow Advanced entries for Masters (F-8A/ 02-05/51)* & *Allow Advanced Entries in TDS Master,* at Ledger Account Configuration (F-6D) to activate advanced Features of Ledger Accounts & TDS.

Create separate ledger account for each type of TDS under the Group Duties & Taxes (or you may create a group TDS under duties and taxes and place the individual TDS ledger account under it).

Ledger Creation
Name : TDS on Interest
Under : Duties & Taxes (Current Liabilities)
Type of Duty/Tax : TDS
Nature Of Payment : Interest Other Than Interest on Securities

F-5A: TDS Ledger creation

Types of Duty/Tax
Excise
Others
TDS

F-5B:Duty Type List

List of TDS Nature Of Pymt

Any	
Interest on 8% Savings (Taxable) Bonds, 2003	193
Interest on Infrastructure Debt Fund	194LB
Interest on Securities	193
Interest Other Than Interest on Securities	194A
Interest Payable by Government Or Indian Concem in Foreign Currency	195
	14 more ...

F-5C:TDS Nature Type List

At TDS Ledger Account creation / alteration screen (F-5A), enter the following details:

- **Parent Group**: At *Under*, select Duties & Taxes (or a Group created under Duties & Taxes)
- **Type of Duty /Tax**: At *Type of Duty /Tax*, select *TDS* from the list (F-5B)
- **Nature of Payment**: At *Nature of Payment*, select the from the list (F-5C), for the TDS Ledger Account

07 Party Ledger Account creation

Party Ledger creation has been explained earlier. We describe points exclusively related to

Ledger Creation / Alteration of the Party from whom TDS is deducted.

Ledger Alteration
Name : A K Das
Under : Loans (Liability)
Maintain balances bill-by-bill ? Yes
Default Credit Period : 30 Days
Activate Interest Calculation ? Yes
Statutory Information
Is TDS Deductable ? Yes
Treat as TDS Expenses ? No
Deductee Type : Individual/HUF - Resident
Use Advanced TDS Entries ? Yes

F-6A: Party Ledger Entry

At *Statutory Information* section of the Party Ledger (F-6A), enter as follows:

List of Deductee Types
Unknown
Artificial Juridical Person
Association of Persons
Body of Individuals
Company - Non Resident
Company - Resident
Co-Operative Society
Individual/HUF - Non Resident
Individual/HUF - Resident
Local Authority
Partnership Firm

F-6B: List of Deductee Type

Tax Information
PAN / IT No. : SFER23451N
(PAN / IT No. is mandatory for eTDS, should be of 10 Characters)

F-6C: Party PAN

Allow ADVANCED entries in TDS Master ? Yes

F-6D: Configuration option set up

TDS Applicability: At *Is TDS Applicable*, set *Yes* for the Party from whom TDS is deductible (else *No* for the Parties from whom TDS is not to be deducted). Now further enter as follows (for the Parties for which you have set *Yes*):

- **TDS Nature**: At *Treat TDS as Expenses*, set:
  - o *No* where TDS Amount is deducted from the amount Payable to the Party. So, TDS is not company's expenses
  - o *Yes* where the TDS is to be borne by the Company and paid to Government
- **Organisation Type**: At *Deductee Type,* select the *Deductee Type* from the list (F-6B), according to the nature of constitution of the Party.
- **Party PAN:** At Tax Information section of the Party Ledger, enter the Party PAN (F-6C)

08 TDS Expense Ledger Accounts

Expense Ledger creation has been explained earlier. We describe points exclusively related to TDS, for Creation / Alteration of Expense Ledger from which TDS is deducted.

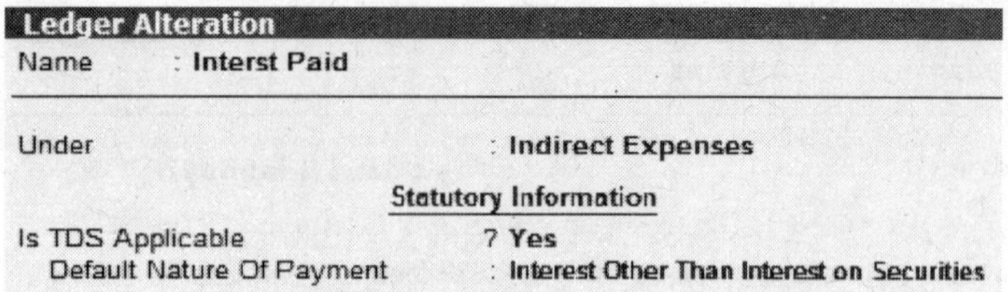

F-7A: Expense Ledger Account Creation

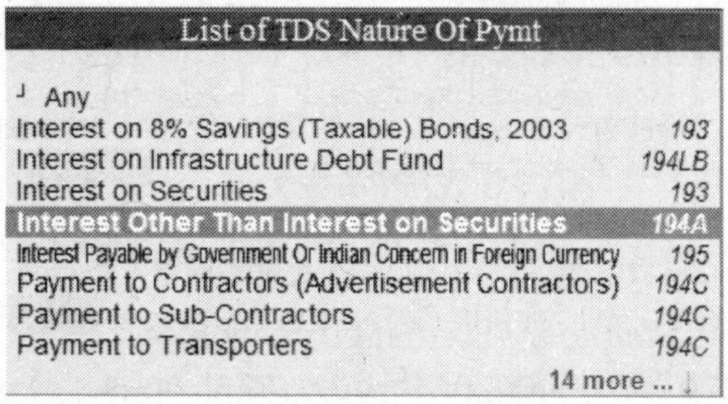

F-7B: Nature of Payment List

At *Statutory Information* section of the Expense Ledger Account creation / alteration screen (F-7A), enter as follows:

- **TDS Applicability**: At *Is TDS Applicable*, set *Yes* for the Expense Ledger Account from whom TDS is deductible (F-7A)
- **Payment Nature**: At *Default Nature of Payment* (F-7A), select the Nature of Payment from the list of TDS Nature of Payment (F-7B), like (F-3B).

Having set up the TDS options in Company Features, TDS

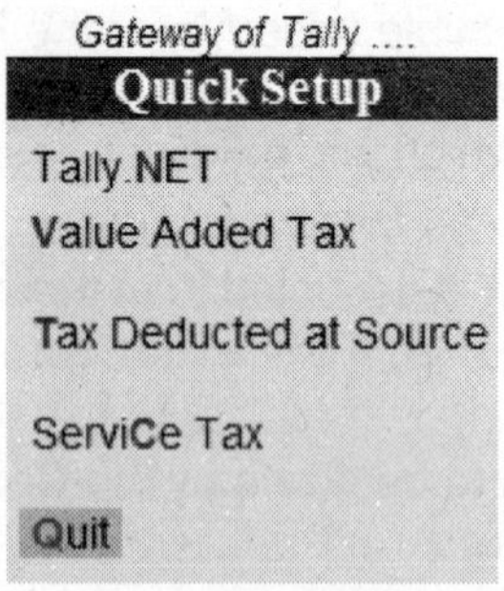

F-8A: Quick Set Up Menu

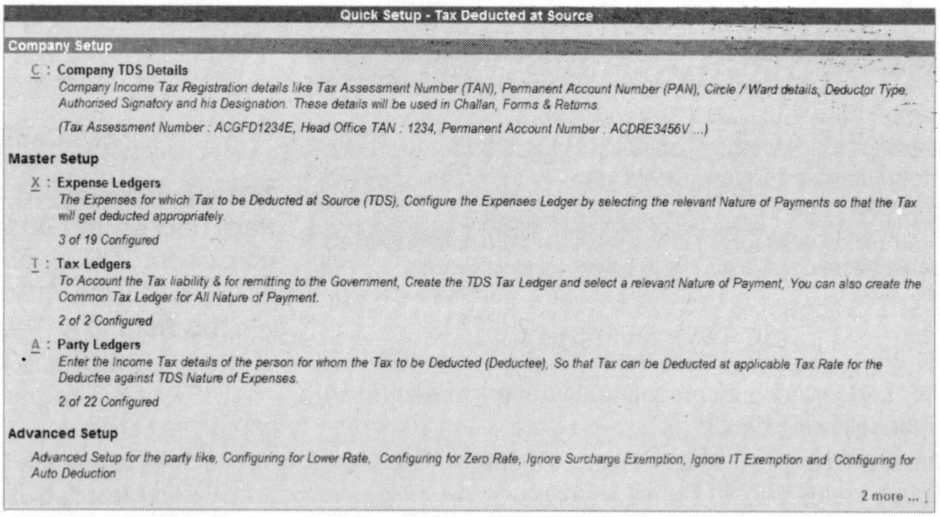

F-8B: TDS Quick Set Up screen

& Party Ledgers, you may start voucher entry involving TDS.

09 Quick set Up for TDS

We have described the initial set up for:

- Company Set Up
- TDS related Ledger Creation
  - o Expense Ledger
  - o Party Ledger
  - o TDS Ledger

Instead of set up from the respective Features / Configuration options and Ledger Creation, you may set up these through a special Quick Set up menu option. This helps you to first create the environment correctly before you enter transactions related to TDS.

At Gateway, select *Quick Set Up* to get *Quick Set Up* menu (F-8A). At *Quick Set Up* menu (F-8A)., select *Tax Deducted at Source* to get *Quick Set Up-Tax Deducted at Source* screen (F-8B).

> ***Note:*** *Quick Set Up is only an alternate gateway for Statutory Info. You get the same screen if you select the individual options as explained earlier. So, if you set up through Individual options, you do not need to set up from Quick Option (and vice versa). Through Quick Set Up, you may set up the Ledger Accounts through Multiple Mode only*

Now we discuss about the set Up through Quick Set Up screen (F-8B). At *Quick Set Up* screen (F-8B), click at the respective option to get the same screen that you get from respective options, as discussed earlier

- **C: Company TDS Details:** To get *Company TDS Deductor Details* screen (F-2A),to set the *Deductor Particulars* as explained.
- **X: Expense Ledgers**: To get *Expense Ledger* set up screen showing the list of all Expense Ledgers already created (Ledger Accounts under Direct / Indirect Expenses), like a multi mode Ledger Accounts creation screen (F-9A). Select the Ledger Account for which TDS is to be deducted. Set *Yes* at *Is TDS Applicable*. Next at *Default Nature of Payment*, select the applicable Nature of Payment from the list.

This way, set the *Default Nature of Payment* for the respective Ledger Accounts. Press Ctrl+A to save the settings

- **T:Tax Ledger Set Up**: To get TDS Ledger set up screen showing the list of all Ledgers (under Duties & Taxes) already created, like a multi mode Ledger Accounts creation screen. Select the Ledger Account for which TDS is to be deducted (F-9B). Next at *Nature of Payment* column, select the applicable Nature of Payment from the list of TDS Nature of Payment

  This way, set the *Nature of Payment* for the respective Ledger Accounts. Press Ctrl+A to save the settings
- **A: Party Ledgers**: To get Party Ledger set up screen showing the list of all Party Ledger Accounts (under Sundry Debtors/ Creditors), like a multi mode Ledger Accounts creation screen in a tabular format. Select the Party Ledger Account for which TDS is to be deducted (F-9C). Set *Yes* at *Is TDS Applicable*. Next at *Deductee Type column*, select the applicable Deductee Type from the list of Deductee Types. Next enter the PAN of the Party at PAN /IT No column.

  This way, set the *Deductee Type* and PAN for the respective Ledger Accounts. Press *Ctrl+A* to save the settings.

Expense Ledgers Setup — ABC Academy 9-10 — Ctrl + M

Under Group : All Items — 1-Apr-2008 to 31-Mar-2010

S.No.	Name of Ledger	Under	Is TDS Applicable	Default Nature of Payment
1.	A K Das	Loans (Liability)	Yes	Interest Other Than Interest on Securities
2.	Components Cost	Direct Expenses	No	
3.	Conveyance Expenses	Indirect Expenses	No	
4.	Depreciation on Furniture	Depreciation	No	
5.	Discount on Purchase	Purchase Accounts	No	
6.	Freight	Indirect Expenses	No	
7.	Handling Charges	Indirect Expenses	No	
8.	HRA	Indirect Expenses	No	
9.	Interest on Term Loan	Interest	No	
10.	Interest on Unsecured Loan	Interest	No	
11.	Interst Paid	Indirect Expenses	Yes	Interest Other Than Interest on Securities
12.	Job Work Charges	Purchase Accounts	Yes	Payments to Contractors (Other Than Advertisement)
13.	Misc Expenses	Misc. Expenses (ASSET)	No	

F-9A:TDS Expense Ledgers Quick Set Up

Tax Ledgers Setup — ABC Academy 9-10 — Ctrl + M

Under Group : All Items — 1-Apr-2008 to 31-Mar-2010

S.No.	Name of Ledger	Under	Nature of Payment
1.	TDS From Contractors	Duties & Taxes	Payments to Contractors (Other Than Advertisement)
2.	TDS on Interest	Duties & Taxes	Interest Other Than Interest on Securities

F-9B:TDS Ledger Accounts Quick Set Up

Party Ledgers Setup — ABC Academy 9-10 — Ctrl + M

Under Group : All Items — 1-Apr-2008 to 31-Mar-2010

S.No.	Name of Ledger	Under	Is TDS Deductable	Deductee Type	PAN / IT No.
1.	Aakash & Co	Sundry Debtors	No		ABCDE1234X
2.	Accrued Interest	Unsecured Loans	No		
3.	A K Traders	Sundry Debtors	No		ABCDE1234Z.
4.	B K Das	Sundry Debtors	No		
5.	B M Suppliers	Sundry Creditors	No		
6.	Current Year Profit / Loss	Capital Account	No		
7.	D D Contractor	Sundry Creditors	Yes	Partnership Firm	SDFHK1234X

F-9C:TDS Party Accounts Quick Set Up

Now the initial set up are complete and the TDS environment is ready to enter TDS related transactions

FAQ: Frequently Asked Questions

FAQ-1: How do I activate TDS System for the Company

Ans: TDS Activation: At Company Operations screen (*F11: Features* >Accounting Features), set as follows:

- **TDS Activation**: At *Enable Tax Deducted at Source*, set Yes to Activate TDS Features for the Company (F-1A)
- **TDS Details**: At *Set / Alter TDS Details*, set Yes (F-1A), to get *Company TDS Deductor* screen to enter the TDS Particulars of the Company
- **PAN**: At *PAN / Income Tax Number*, enter the Company PAN (F-1B)

TDS Voucher Entry

01-02

01 Expenses Voucher

If TDS is deductible, you should not make a direct Payment voucher for expenses. You should first enter, either:

- Journal Voucher (e.g for Interest)
- Purchase Voucher (e.g for Purchase of Service).

02 Expenses Journal Voucher

Create a Journal Voucher to book the expense (F-1C). We have explained entry of Journal Voucher earlier. Here we describe the points exclusively related to TDS in the voucher entry.

a. **Expense Ledger**: At 1st Ledger Account entry at main Voucher entry screen (F-1C), enter the Expenses Ledger Account and the Gross Expense amount, to get the sub screen for *TDS Nature entry* (F-1B). The default TDS Nature for the Expense appears, which may be changed by selecting from the list of TDS Nature. You get back to the main voucher entry screen (F-1C).

   - **TDS Nature of Payment for Expense Ledger**: At Voucher entry screen (F1C), On entry of Expense Ledger Amount, you get the default TDS nature of Payment screen (F-1B). Select the Nature of Payment from the list (you may change the Amount to enter lower TDS Chargeable Amount if TDS is not chargeable on whole amount). TDS would be computed on the Assessable Value entered. Next you get another entry line for the Balance Amount. For this, at *Nature of Payment*, select *Not Applicable* from the list. So, the TDS would not be computed on the balance amount

b. **Party Ledger**: At 2nd entry, select the Party Ledger Account (F-1C) to be credited to get the *Bill Allocation / TDS Details* screen (F-1A). At *Bill Allocation / TDS Details* (F-1A), enter as follows:

   - **Reference Type**: At *Type of Ref* column, select the Ref Type (Normally *New Ref*)
   - **Reference ID:** At *Name* column, the default Ref ID is carried, which you may change
   - **Nature of Payment**: At *Nature of Payment*, the Nature of Payment selected (at first entry) will be carried
   - **TDS Ledger**: At TDS Ledger, the list of all *TDS Ledger Accounts* (for which you have set TDS), will appear, from which select the TDS Ledger Account
   - **Assessable Amount**: The Amount for the Expense Ledger Account will be carried, which you may change (if TDS is not chargeable on entire Amount). Enter the Amount on which TDS is to be deducted
   - **TDS Deductability**: At *Deduct Now*, set:
     - o Yes to Deduct TDS in the current voucher
     - o No. TDS will not be deducted and the screen will be closed
   - **TDS Amount:** If TDS is Deducted, the total TDS Amount including Surcharge / Cess / SE Cess(with detailed breakup) is shown
   - **Net Payable:** At *Payable Amount*, the Net Amount Payable (Ledger Amount - TDS Deduction) is shown

c. **TDS Ledger:** At main voucher screen (F-1C), select the TDS Ledger Account (if TDS is Deducted. The TDS deducted (as shown at F-1A), is carried at the Credit column.

At Main voucher screen (F-1C), enter Other Ledger Accounts (if any). Save the Voucher.

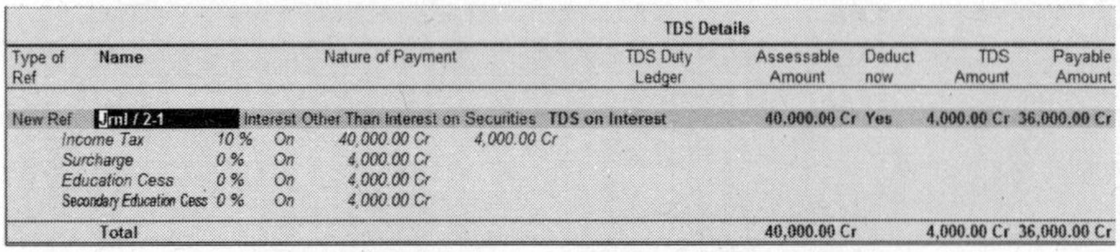

F-1A: Bill Allocation / TDS Deduction Entry

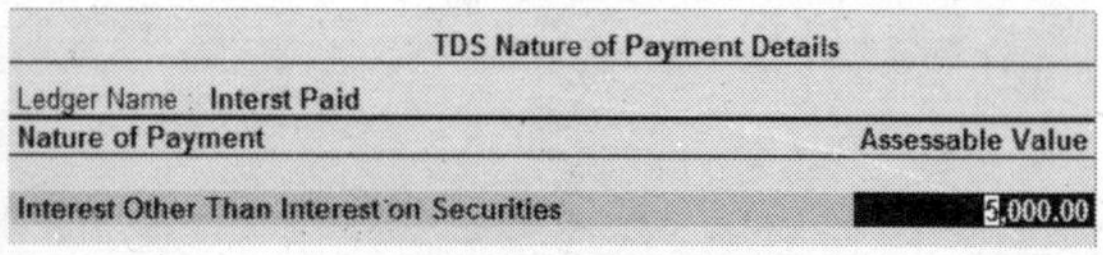

F-1B: TDS Nature Entry

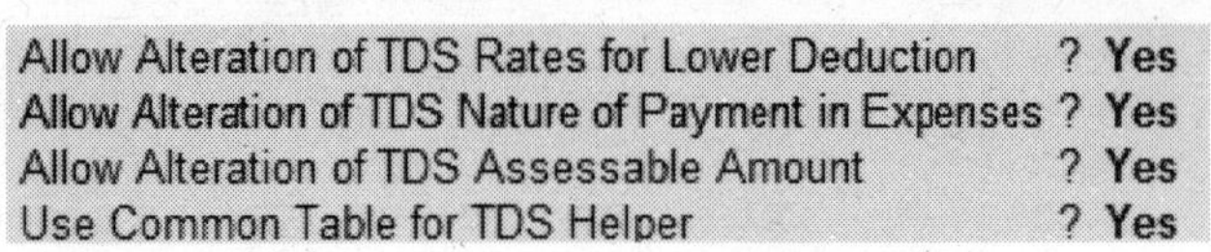

F-1D: Voucher Entry Configuration

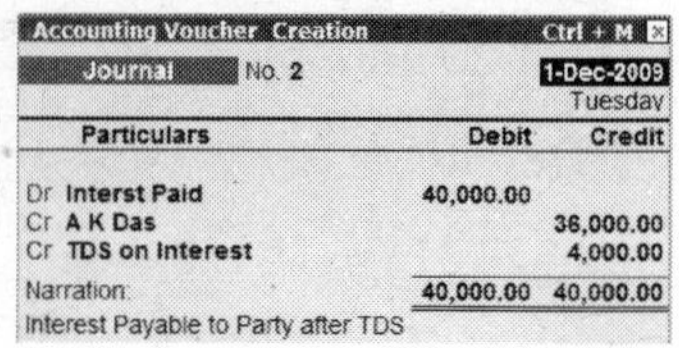

F-1C: Expense Voucher with TDS

02.01 TDS Journal Voucher Entry Configuration

At Journal Voucher entry screen (F-2A), click *F12:Configure* to get Voucher Entry Configuration screen (F-1D), to change the default options, as follows, as required.

- **TDS Deduction on Lower Amount:** Sometimes, TDS Expense may include some amount on which TDS is not to be deducted. In such case, you change the Assessable Value. At *Allow Alteration of TDS Rates for Lower Amount*, set Yes to enable change TDS Rate)
- **TDS Assessable Amount Alteration**: At *Allow Alteration of TDS Assessable Amount*, set Yes to enable change TDS Assessable Value) and also set Yes at *Allow Alteration of TDS Nature of Payment* (to enable change of TDS Payment Nature)

03 TDS Purchase Voucher

We have seen Journal Voucher entry for booking of expenses, through which TDS is deducted at the time of booking the expenses, before payment is made. In such case, the organization is to deposit TDS within the specified period as per Journal Voucher entry date even if the payment is not made for the expense. However, normally Parties prefer to deduct TDS at the time of payment.

In such case, you have to create a Purchase Voucher for the booking of expenses, instead of Journal Voucher, as explained next.

03.01 Purchase Voucher entry

Purchase Voucher entry in Accounting Invoice Mode (Click *I:As Invoice* button at Purchase Voucher entry) has been explained earlier. Here, we explain specific points relating to TDS entry.

TDS Nature of Payment Details

Ledger Name : Job Work Charges

Nature of Payment	Assessable Value
Payments to Contractors (Other Than Advertisement)	25,000.00

F-3A: TDS Nature of Payment

TDS Details

Type of Ref	Name	Nature of Payment	TDS Duty Ledger	Assessable Amount	TDS Amount
New Ref	Purc / 2-1	Payments to Contractors (Other Than Advertisement)	TDS From Contractors	25,000.00 Cr	
	Income Tax 2 % On			25,000.00 Cr	
	Surcharge 0 % On			500.00 Cr	
	Education Cess 0 % On			500.00 Cr	
	Secondary Education Cess 0 % On			500.00 Cr	
Total				25,000.00 Cr	

F-3B:TDS Details

Bill-wise Details for : D D Contractor
Upto: ₹ 25,000.00 Cr

Type of Ref	Name	Due Date, or Credit Days (wef: 1-Nov-2009)	Amount	Dr/Cr
New Ref	12	30 Days (1-Dec-2009)	25,000.00	Cr
			25,000.00	Cr

F-3C:Bill Reference Details

After entry of Expenses Ledger (for which TDS Feature has been activated) in Purchase Voucher (F-3D), you get the TDS nature of Payment screen (F-3A). Enter the details.

Press <enter> again (after the cursor goes into Total Amount field) to get the TDS details entry screen (F-3B). Enter the details as explained earlier.

Next you get the Bill Allocation screen (F-3C). Enter the details.

> **Note:** *in Purchase Voucher, though you enter TDS details, the TDS Account is not selected in main voucher. So, TDS is not deducted (though internally computed) and the related TDS nature of Payment /TDS Ledger Account etc properly linked.*

Accounting Voucher Creation Ctrl + M

Purchase No. 2 1-Nov-2009 Sunday

Supplier Invoice No. : 12 Date : 31-Oct-2009

Party's A/c Name : D D Contractor

Particulars	Rate	per	Amount
Job Work Charges			25,000.00
Narration:			25,000.00

F-3D: Purchase Voucher for TDS Expenses

You get back to the main Voucher screen. Enter Narration and save the Voucher.

03.02 TDS Purchase Voucher Entry Configuration

At Purchase Voucher entry screen (F-3D), click *F12:Configure* at Purchase Voucher Entry screen to get Purchase Voucher Entry Configuration screen and set *No* at the following configuration options:

- At *Use Common Ledger Accounts*, set *No* (to select Ledger Account for Purchase Accounts)
- At *Defaults Ledger Accounts*, set No (to assign Bill Reference Number).

04 TDS Deduction Journal Voucher

Having created the Purchase Voucher (without deducting TDS), you should next create a Journal Voucher (F-4D) for Entry for TDS Deduction on the Expenses booked.

At Journal voucher entry (F-4D), click the *TDS deduction* button (F4A). Select the Party Ledger (F-4D). You get TDS Accounts, computation details and amount for each head as per standard Rates (F-4D).

S: TDS Deduction

F-4A: TDS Deduction Button

TDS Deductions

Till Date : 1-Dec-2009
Party : D D Contractor
Nature of Payment :

F-4B: TDS Details

List of Nature of Pymt(s)

Payments to Contractors (Other Than Advertisement)

F-4C: TDS Nature of Payment List

Accounting Voucher Creation				Ctrl + M
Journal No. **4**				**1-Dec-2009**
				C Tuesday
Account : **D D Contractor**				
Particulars				**Amount**
TDS From Contractors				**500.00**
Agst Ref **Purc / 2-1**		**500.00 Cr**		
Income Tax	*2 %*	*On*	*25,000.00 Cr*	*500.00 Cr*
Surcharge	*0 %*	*On*	*500.00 Cr*	
Education Cess	*0 %*	*On*	*500.00 Cr*	
Secondary Education Cess	*0 %*	*On*	*500.00 Cr*	

F-4D:TDS Deduction Voucher

Save the voucher. This Voucher has the accounting effect of:

- Party A/c (as entered at the header) Dr (amount of TDS Deducted)
- TDS A/c (as entered at Particulars) Cr (amount of TDS Deducted)

05 Party Payment voucher with TDS Deduction

Now you have to make payment to the Party after deduction of TDS. So, create a payment voucher (F-5A). Here we discuss exclusively regarding Payment to a Party against out standing Purchase Bill. This is entered in same way described earlier. There is nothing special related to TDS in such Payment Voucher as all the entries relating to TDS have been already made in Purchase / Journal Vouchers.

Accounting Voucher Creation				Ctrl + M
Payment No. **10**				**2-Dec-2009**
				Wednesday
Particulars			**Debit**	**Credit**
Dr **D D Contractor**			**24,500.00**	
Agst Ref **12**	**30 Days** (1-Dec-2009)	**24,500.00 Dr**		
Cr **HDFC Bank**				**24,500.00**
Narration:			**24,500.00**	**24,500.00**

F-5A: Payment Voucher to Party after TDS

Bill-wise Details for : **D D Contractor**
Upto: **₹ 24,500.00 Dr**

Type of Ref	Name	Due Date, or Credit Days (wef: 2-Dec-2009)	Amount	Dr/ Cr
Agst Ref	**12**	**30 Days** (1-Dec-2009)	**24,500.00**	**Dr**
			24,500.00	**Dr**

F-5B: Bill Allocation details

At Particulars column, (F-5A), first select the Party Ledger account to get the Bill Allocation screen (F-5B) with details all open bills of the Party, showing the outstanding balance after deduction of TDS. Select the Bills to be paid. You may change the amount if full payment is not made against the outstanding bill.

You get back to the main voucher entry screen. Select Bank Ledger Account. The net amount payable is carried. Now enter the Narration and save the Voucher.

FAQ: Frequently Asked Question

FAQ-1: I have to pay Bill to Contractor for a Job Done. How do I enter Voucher with TDS Deduction.

Ans: Like normal expense voucher, you can not create a payment voucher directly to pay for the expenses, deducting TDS. Instead, you have to perform following accounting entries:

- Create the liability (e.g Journal Voucher or Purchase Voucher) Debiting expenses (Gross Amount), Crediting Party Account (Net Payable to Party after Deducting TDS) and crediting TDS (TDS Deducted)
- Create Payment Voucher to make payment of net amount payable to Party

We explain the process of Journal Voucher Entry

Journal Voucher Entry: Create a Journal Voucher to book the expense (F-1C). Here we describe the points exclusively related to TDS in the voucher entry.

a. **Expense Ledger**: At 1st Ledger Account entry at main Voucher entry screen (F-1C), enter the Expenses Ledger Account and the Gross Expense amount. A sub screen for TDS Nature entry will appear (F-1B). The default TDS Nature for the Expense would appear, which may be changed by selecting from the list of TDS Nature. You get back to the main voucher entry screen (F-1C).
   - **TDS Nature of Payment for Expense Ledger**: On entry of Expense Ledger Amount, you get the default *TDS nature of Payment* screen. Select the *Nature of Payment* from the list

b. **Party Ledger**: At 2nd entry, select the Party Ledger Account (F-1C) to be credited to get the *Bill Allocation / TDS Details* screen (F-1A). At *Bill Allocation / TDS Details* (F-1A), enter as follows:
   - **Reference Type**: At *Type of Ref* column, select the Ref Type (Normally *New Ref*)
   - **Reference ID:** At *Name* column, the default Ref ID is carried, which you may change
   - **Nature of Payment**: At *Nature of Payment*, the Nature of Payment selected (at first entry) will be carried

c. **TDS Ledger**: At TDS Ledger, the list of all *TDS Ledger Accounts* (for which you have set TDS), will appear, from which select the TDS Ledger Account

- **Assessable Amount**: The Amount for the Expense Ledger Account will be carried

.o **TDS Deductability**: At *Deduct Now*, type Yes to Deduct TDS in the current voucher

- **TDS Amount:** The total TDS Amount including Surcharge / Cess / SE Cess(with detailed breakup) is shown
- **Net Payable:** At *Payable Amount*, the Net Amount Payable (Ledger Amount - TDS Deduction) is shown

d. **TDS Ledger:** At main voucher screen (F-1C), select the TDS Ledger Account (F-1A).The TDS deducted is carried at the Credit column.

At Main voucher screen (F-1C), enter Other Ledger Accounts (if any). Save the Voucher.

TDS Deposit

01-03

01 TDS Deposit to Government

After deducting TDS, you have to deposit the TDS to Bank / Treasury. You should make separate challan for each type of Deductee & Nature of Payment

So, you make separate payment voucher according to each Challan for deposit of TDS to Govt. Such payment voucher must also be made in single mode.

We have explained Payment Voucher entry in Single Mode. Here, we discuss about points exclusively related to TDS.

01.01 TDS payment using S:Stat Payment buttons.

You may automate the TDS Payment using *S:Stat Payment* (available in Single Mode payment voucher entry) button.

At *Payment Voucher* entry screen (F-1B), Click *F12:Configure* and set *Yes* at *Use Single Entry Mode for Pymt/Rcpt/Contra*). Click *S:Stat Payment* button to get Statutory Payment Screen (F-1A). Now enter as follows:

Duty / TaxType: At *Type of Duty/Tax*, select TDS from the list of Duty / Tax Type

Mode of Entry: At *Auto Fill Statutory Payment*, select *Yes* to get the fields to fill up the Payment details as below:

- **Period End**: At *Deducted Till Date*, enter he Date upto which the TDS deducted is being deposited through the current voucher. Accordingly the amount of TDS deducted would be carried in the voucher, for TDS Deposit.
- **I Tax Section**: At *Section*, select the I Tax section under which the TDS is being deposited from the list (showing the sections under which TDS deducted is to be deposited)
- **Payment Nature**: At *Nature of Payment*, select the Nature of Payment from the list, for which TDS is being deposited.

Statutory Payment

Type of Duty/Tax	: TDS
Auto Fill Statutory Payment	? Yes
Deducted Till Date	: 31-12-2009
Section	: 194A
Nature of Payment	: Interest Other Than Interest on Securities
Deductee Status	: Non Company
Cash/Bank	:

F-1A:Statutory Payment details

- **Company Type**: At *Deductee Status*, select the Status (Company / Non Company) from the list, as per constitution of the Company)
- **Cash / Bank Account**: At *Cash / Bank*, select the Account from which the TDS is being paid, from the list of Cash / Bank Accounts

Accounting Voucher Creation — ABC Academy 9-10 Ctrl + M

Payment No. 14 — 1-Jan-2010

Statutory Payment for : TDS

Account : **HDFC Bank**

Particulars		Amount
TDS on Interest		6,500.00
Agst Ref Jrnl / 2-1	**4,000.00 Dr**	
Income Tax	*4,000.00 Dr*	
Surcharge		
Education Cess		
Secondary Education Cess		
Agst Ref Jrnl / 3-1	**2,500.00 Dr**	
Income Tax	*2,500.00 Dr*	
Surcharge		
Education Cess		
Secondary Education Cess		
Provide Details : Yes		
Narration:		6,500.00

F-1B: TDS payment Voucher

Payment Details

From Date	: 1-Oct-2009
To Date	: 31-Dec-2009
(Note: This payment belongs to the above Quarter)	
Cheque/DD No	: 123456
Name of Bank	: HDFC Bank
Bank Account Number	: 123456789
Branch Name	: Bowbazar
BSR Code	: 700123456
Challan No.	: 12
Challan Date	: 1-1-10
(Note: All the above details will be used in Challan, Forms & Returns)	

F-1C: TDS Payment Details

Consequently, the Ledger Account and corresponding Amount would be auto filled in the Main Voucher Entry screen (F-1B). At Main Voucher Entry screen (F-1B), set Yes at *Provide Details* to get TDS payment Details screen (F-1C)

At *Payment Details screen* (F-1C), enter the details of TDS payment being made in the current Payment voucher (F-1B):

- **Period**: At *From & To*, enter the period for which the TDS is being deposited
- **Cheque Number**: At *Cheque / DD No*, enter the number of the Cheque / DD, by which the pyment is being deposited to the bank / treasury
- **Bank Name**: At *Name of the Bank*, enter the Bank Name on which the Cheque / DD s drawn
- **Bank Account Number**: At *Bank Account Number*, enter he Account Number of the Bank from which the cheque is issued
- **Branch Name:** At *Branch Name*, enter the Bank Branch name on which the Cheque is drawn
- **Bank BSR Code**: At BSR Code, enter the Bank BSR Code on which the Cheque is drawn
- **Bank Challan Number**: At *Challan Number*, enter the Bank Challan Number as alloted by the Bank on the Challan after receipt of Cheque
- **Bank Challan Date**: At *Challan Date*, enter the Bank Challan Date on which the challan was deposited to Bank.

02 TDS Challan Printing

On entry of TDS payment voucher (F-1B), click *P:Print* button to get the *Payment Voucher Printing* screen (F-2A), to print *TDS Challan* (F-2C) / *Payment Advice* (F-2B).

Report Titles

Payment Voucher

Print as TDS Challan	? Yes
TDS/TCS Regular Assessment (Raised by I.T. Dept.)	? No
Filing Date	: 1-Jan-2010
Print Payment Advice	: No
Payment Advice Date	: 1-Jan-2010
Print Due Date	? No
Print Company's PAN/IT Number	? No

F-2A: TDS Payment Voucher printing screen

Payment Advice

M/s TDS on Interest Date : 1-Jan-2010

Dear Sir/Madam,

Please find below the payment details.

Particulars	Amount
TDS on Interest	6,500.00
Nett Amount	₹ 6,500.00

Payment Detail(s)

Mode of Payment	Bank Name	Instrument No.	Instrument Date	Amount
Cheque	HDFC Bank	123507	1-Jan-2010	6,500.00
			Total	₹ 6,500.00

Kindly acknowledge the receipt.

Thanking You

Authorised Signatory Receiver's Signature

F-2B: TDS Payment Advice

02.01 Challan / Payment Advice Printing

At *Payment Voucher printing* screen (F-2A), to Print TDS Challan (F-2C) / Payment Advice (F-2B), set as follows:

T.D.S. TAX CHALLAN Single Copy (to be sent to ZAO)

CHALLAN No./ITNS 281

Tax Applicable (Tick one)*
TAX DEDUCTED AT SOURCE FROM
(0020) COMPANY DEDUCTEES ☐ (0021) NON-COMPANY DEDUCTEES ☑

Assessment Year 2010-11

Tax Deduction Account No. (T.A.N.) A C G F D 1 2 3 4 E

Full Name A B C ACADEMY

Complete Address with City & State
99, Airport Rd, Kolkata 700 098, W Bengal
West Bengal

Tel. No. 651234 Pin 700 098

Type of Payment Code * 9 4 A

TDS Payable by Taxpayer (200) ☑

TDS Regular Assessment (Raised by I.T. Deptt.) (400) ☐

FOR USE IN RECEIVING BANK

Debit to A/c / Cheque credited on

D D M M Y Y

DETAILS OF PAYMENTS Amount (in Rs. Only)

Income Tax	6,500.00
Surcharge	
Education Cess	
Interest	
Penalty	
Total	6,500.00

SPACE FOR BANK SEAL

Total (in words)

CRORES	LACS	THOUSANDS	HUNDREDS	TENS	UNITS
Zero	Zero	Six	Five	Zero	Zero

Paid in Cash/ Debit to A/c /Cheque No. 123456 Dated 1-Jan-2010

Rs. 6,500.00

Drawn on HDFC Bank - Salt Lake
(Name of the Bank and Branch)

Date : 1-Jan-2010 Signature of person making payment

Tear Here

Taxpayers Counterfoil (To be filled up by taxpayer)

TAN A C G F D 1 2 3 4 E

Received from A B C ACADEMY
(Name)

Cash/ Debit to A/c /Cheque No. 123456 For Rs. 6,500

Rs. (in words) Six Thousand Five Hundred Only.

Drawn on HDFC Bank - Salt Lake
(Name of the Bank and Branch)

Non Company(0021) Deductees

on account of Tax Deducted at Source (TDS) from 9 4 A for the Assessment Year 2010-11

SPACE FOR BANK SEAL

Rs. 6,500.00

F-2C: TDS Challan

- o **Challan Printing**: At *Print as TDS Challan* (F-2A):
  - Set Yes to print Challan (else set *No*, Challan would not be printed)

  When you set *Yes* at *Print as TDS Challan,* you may further set following options (F-2A)
  - o TDS / TCS Regular Assessment (raised y IT Deptt): Set *Yes* to print for Challan relating to Regular Assessment as ordered by I Tax authority, else set *No.*
- o **Payment Advice Printing**: You get to the field *Print Payment Advice*, when you set *No* at Print TDS Challan. Set *Yes* at *Print Payment Advice*, to Print Payment Advice, else set *No* (Payment Advice is not printed).

  When you set *Yes* at *Print Payment Advice,* you may further set / enter (F-2A):
  - **Payment Advice Date**: At *Payment Advice Date*, you may enter the Date of Payment Advice (Voucher Date is carried, which you may change).

- At *Print Due Date*, set *Yes* to print Due Date in Advice, else set *No* to omit Due Date in Payment Advice
- At *Print Company PAN*, set *Yes* to print *Company PAN* at Payment Advice,else set *No* to omit Company PAN in Payment Advice

FAQ: Frequently Asked Questions

FAQ-1: How do I deposit TDS to Government with Auto Fill

Ans: You may automate the TDS Payment using *S:Stat Payment* (available in Single Mode payment voucher entry) button.

Auto Fill: At *Payment Voucher* entry screen, Click *F12:Configure* and set *Yes* at *Use Single Entry Mode for Pymt/ Rcpt/Contra*),

Click *S:Stat Payment* button to get Statutory Payment Screen (F-1A). Now enter as follows:

Duty / TaxType: At *Type of Duty/Tax*, select TDS from the list of Duty / Tax Type

Mode of Entry: At *Auto Fill Statutory Payment*, select *Yes* to get the fields to fill up the Payment details as below:

- **Period End**: At *Deducted Till Date*, enter he Date upto which the TDS deducted is being deposited through the current voucher. Accordingly the amount of TDS deducted would be carried in the voucher, for TDS Deposit.
- **I Tax Section**: At *Section*, select the I Tax section under which the TDS is being deposited from the list (showing the sections under which TDS deducted is to be deposited)
- **Payment Nature**: At *Nature of Payment*, select the Nature of Payment from the list, for which TDS is being deposited.
- **Company Type**: At *Deductee Status*, select the Status (Company / Non Company) from the list, as per constitution of the Company)
- **Cash / Bank Account**: At *Cash / Bank*, select the Account from which the TDS is being paid, from the list of Cash / Bank Accounts

Consequently, the Ledger Account and corresponding Amount would be auto filled in the Main Voucher Entry screen (F-1B). At Main Voucher Entry screen (F-1B), set Yes at *Provide Details* to get TDS Payment Details screen (F-1C)

At *TDS Payment Details screen* (F-1C), enter the details of TDS payment being made in the current Payment voucher (F-1B):

- **Period**: At *From & To*, enter the period for which the TDS is being deposited
- **Cheque Number**: At *Cheque / DD No*, enter the number of the Cheque / DD, by which the pyment is being deposited to the bank / treasury
- **Bank Name**: At *Name of the Bank*, enter the Bank Name on which the Cheque / DD s drawn
- **Bank Account Number**: At Bank Account Number, enter he Account Number of the Bank from which the cheque is issued
- **Branch Name**: At *Branch Name*, enter the Bank Branch name on which the Cheque is drawn
- **Bank BSR Code**: At BSR Code, enter the Bank BSR Code on which the Cheque is drawn
- **Bank Challan Number**: At *Challan Number*, enter the Bank Challan Number as alloted by the Bank on the Challan after receipt of Cheque
- **Bank Challan Date**: At *Challan Date*, enter the Bank Challan Date on which the challan was deposited to Bank.

TDS Reports

01-04

01 TDS Reports

After entry of Vouchers relating to TDS, you may print various TDS Reports.

Select *Display>Statutory Reports>TDS* to get TDS Reports Menu to get TDS Reports menu

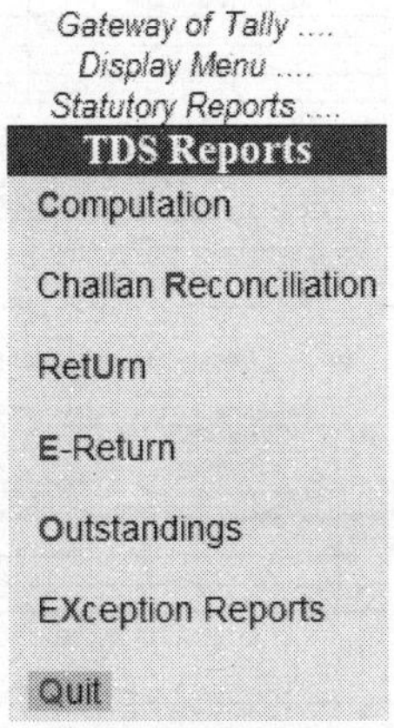

F-1A: TDS Reports Menu

Page 1

TDS Computation	1-Apr-2009 to 31-Mar-2010	
	Amount	**Tax**
Deduction Details		
Expenses & Advances	**95,000.00**	**7,000.00**
TDS Not Applicable	5,000.00	
Under Exemption Limit		
Zero Rated		
Exempt in lieu of PAN available		
Taxable Expenses & Advances	90,000.00	7,000.00
Deducted		**7,500.00**
at Normal rate		*7,500.00*
at Lower rate		
at Higher Rate (No PAN)		
Balance Deductable		
at Normal rate		
at Lower rate		
Excess Deducted		**500.00**
at Normal rate		*500.00*
at Lower rate		
at Higher Rate (No PAN)		
Payment Details		
Paid		**6,500.00**
Previous Month(s)		*6,500.00*
Current Month		
Balance Payable		**1,000.00**
Previous Month(s)		*1,000.00*
Current Month		

F-2A: TDS Computation

F-3A: Challan Reconciliation Statement

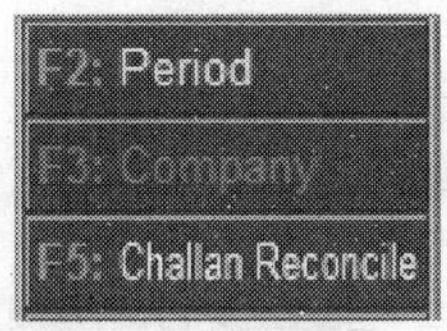

F-3B: Chalan Reconciliation Buttons

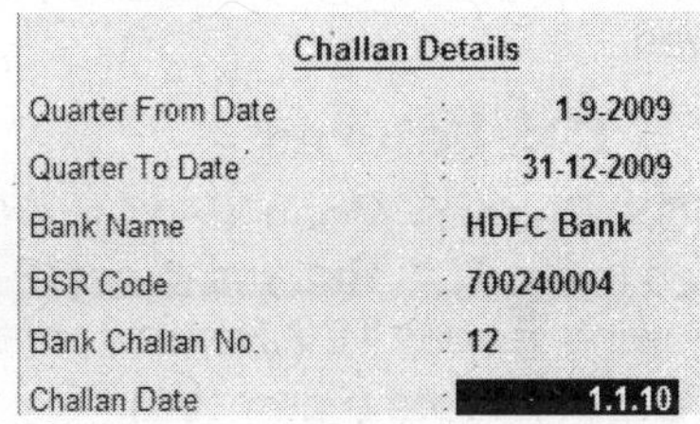

F-3C: Challan Details entry

F-3D: Chalan Details button

02 TDS Computation Report

At TDS Reports Menu (F-1A). select *Computation* to get TDS Computation Statement (F-2A) showing the details of TDS Deducted, Paid, Payable etc.

Buttons: At TDS Computation Report (F-2A), you get following buttons

- **F2:Period**: To set the period of the report

03 TDS Challan Reconciliation

After printing of Challan (§02/01-03), you should enter the details of Challan through Challan Reconciliation, for reconciliation of Challans with Tax Deposit Vouchers.

At TDS Reports Menu (F-1A). select *Challan Reconciliation* to get *Challan Reconciliation Statement* (F-3A).

Buttons: At Challan Reconciliation Statement, you get following Buttons:

- **F2:Period:** To set the Period of the Report
- **F5:Challan Reconcile**: To Reconcile the challans (the indicator Reconciliation appear at the heading of *Challan Reconciliation Statement* for info)

Challan Details: At *Challan Reconciliation Statement* (F-3A), Click *S:Set Challan Details* button (F-3D), to get *Challan Details entry* screen (F-3C).

At *Challan Details entry* screen (F-3C), enter the respective details as follows:

- **Period:** At *Quarter From Date* & *Quarter To Date*, enter the Start Date and End Date of the period for which the Tax is being deposited under the Challan.
- **Bank:** At *Bank Name*, enter the Bank Name at which the Tax is being deposited
- **Bank BSR Code**: At *BSR Code*, enter the Bank BSR Code of the Bank Branch at which the Tax is being deposited
- **Bank Challan No**: At *Bank Challan No*, enter the Bank Challan Number of the TDS Deposit Challan
- **Bank Challan Date**: At *Challan Date*, enter the Date of Bank Challan of TDS Deposit.

Press *Alt+A* to save the details entered to get back the *Challan Reconciliation Statement*, showing the details entered.

04 TDS Returns

At TDS Reports Menu (F-1A), select *Return* to get TDS Returns Menu (F-4A) to showing various TDS Returns printing.

- TDS Certificate (Form 16A)
- Quarterly Returns
- Annual Returns

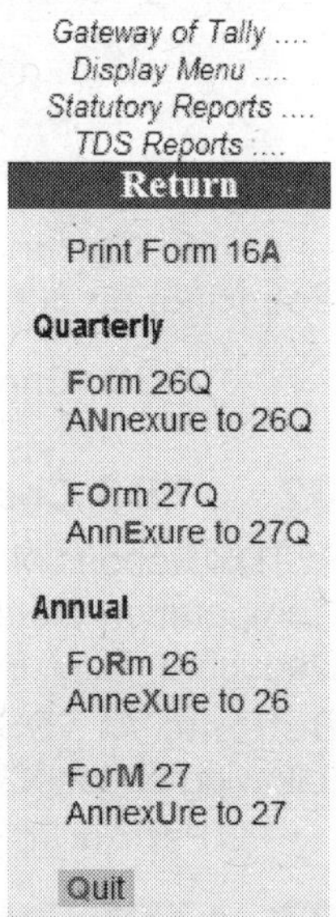

F-4A: TDS Returns menu

04.01 Form 16A

Form 16Ais the certificate of Deduction ad deposit of TDS to government. The deductor has to submit Form 16A to the deductee.

At TDS Returns Menu (F-4A), select *Print Form 16A* to get TDS Form 16A Printing screen (F-6A). Fill up the data to print the Form 16A (F-5A & F-5B).

Form 16A Printing Configuration: At *Form 16A Printing screen* (F-6A) click *F12:Configure* to get *Form 16A Printing Configuration* screen (F-6B) to set the printing configuration options.

- **Second Page Title**: At *Print Form Title on subsequent pages (if applicable)*:
  - o Set *Yes* to print Form Title in subsequent pages also (when the Form extends to multiple pages)
  - o Set *No*. Form Title is printed in First Page only (not in subsequent pages)
- **Government Treasury Details**: At *Print Government Details also*:
  - o Set *Yes* to print the section of details of Government Treasury (useful when payment is made through Government treasury also) also (apart from section of Bank Deposits)
  - o Set *No* to omit the section of details of Government Treasury (useful when payment is made only through Bank only)

Fig F-5A & F-5B shows Form 16A in multiple pages

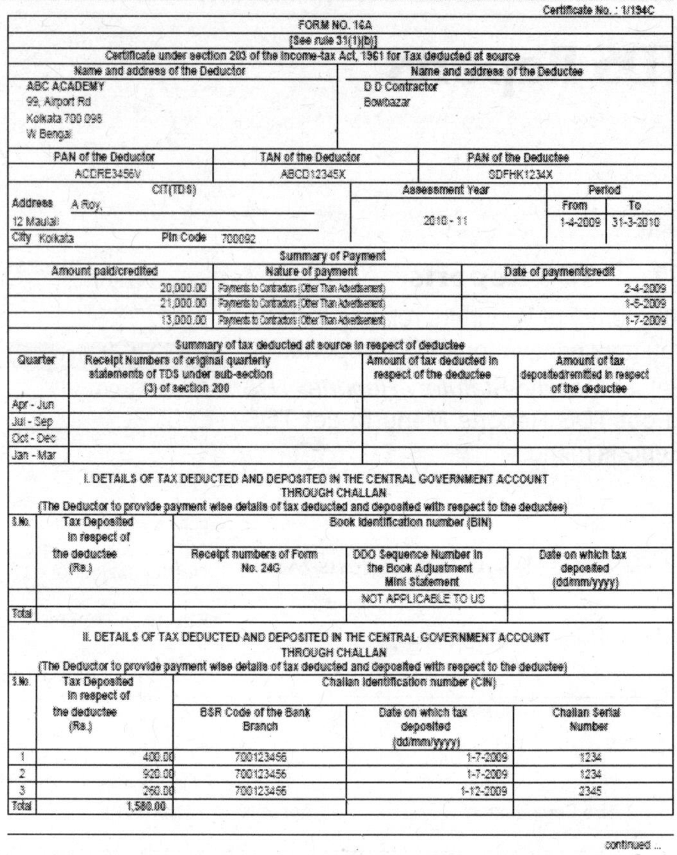

Certificate No. : 1/194C

FORM NO. 16A
[See rule 31(1)(b)]
Certificate under section 203 of the Income-tax Act, 1961 for Tax deducted at source

Name and address of the Deductor	Name and address of the Deductee
ABC ACADEMY 99, Airport Rd Kolkata 700 096 W Bengal	D D Contractor Bowbazar

PAN of the Deductor	TAN of the Deductor	PAN of the Deductee
ACDRE3456V	ABCD12345X	SDFHK1234X

CIT(TDS)	Assessment Year	Period From	Period To
Address A Roy, 12 Maulali City Kolkata Pin Code 700092	2010 - 11	1-4-2009	31-3-2010

Summary of Payment

Amount paid/credited	Nature of payment	Date of payment/credit
20,000.00	Payments to Contractors (Other Than Advertisement)	2-4-2009
21,000.00	Payments to Contractors (Other Than Advertisement)	1-5-2009
13,000.00	Payments to Contractors (Other Than Advertisement)	1-7-2009

Summary of tax deducted at source in respect of deductee

Quarter	Receipt Numbers of original quarterly statements of TDS under sub-section (3) of section 200	Amount of tax deducted in respect of the deductee	Amount of tax deposited/remitted in respect of the deductee
Apr - Jun			
Jul - Sep			
Oct - Dec			
Jan - Mar			

I. DETAILS OF TAX DEDUCTED AND DEPOSITED IN THE CENTRAL GOVERNMENT ACCOUNT THROUGH CHALLAN
(The Deductor to provide payment wise details of tax deducted and deposited with respect to the deductee)

S.No.	Tax Deposited in respect of the deductee (Rs.)	Book Identification number (BIN)		
		Receipt numbers of Form No. 24G	DDO Sequence Number in the Book Adjustment Mini Statement	Date on which tax deposited (dd/mm/yyyy)
			NOT APPLICABLE TO US	
Total				

II. DETAILS OF TAX DEDUCTED AND DEPOSITED IN THE CENTRAL GOVERNMENT ACCOUNT THROUGH CHALLAN
(The Deductor to provide payment wise details of tax deducted and deposited with respect to the deductee)

S.No.	Tax Deposited in respect of the deductee (Rs.)	Challan Identification number (CIN)		
		BSR Code of the Bank Branch	Date on which tax deposited (dd/mm/yyyy)	Challan Serial Number
1	400.00	700123456	1-7-2009	1234
2	920.00	700123456	1-7-2009	1234
3	260.00	700123456	1-12-2009	2345
Total	1,580.00			

continued ...
Page 1

F-5A: TDS Deduction Certificate (Form 16A)(1st page)

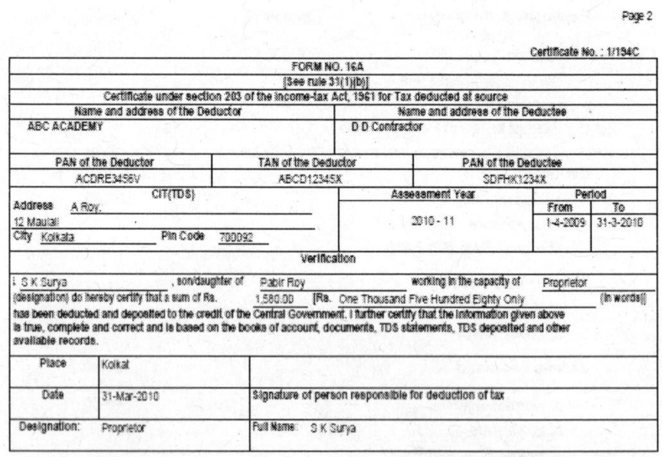

Page 2

Certificate No. : 1/194C

FORM NO. 16A
[See rule 31(1)(b)]
Certificate under section 203 of the Income-tax Act, 1961 for Tax deducted at source

Name and address of the Deductor	Name and address of the Deductee
ABC ACADEMY	D D Contractor

PAN of the Deductor	TAN of the Deductor	PAN of the Deductee
ACDRE3456V	ABCD12345X	SDFHK1234X

CIT(TDS)	Assessment Year	Period From	Period To
Address A Roy, 12 Maulali City Kolkata Pin Code 700092	2010 - 11	1-4-2009	31-3-2010

Verification

I S K Surya , son/daughter of Pabir Roy working in the capacity of Proprietor (designation) do hereby certify that a sum of Rs. 1,580.00 [Rs. One Thousand Five Hundred Eighty Only (in words)] has been deducted and deposited to the credit of the Central Government. I further certify that the information given above is true, complete and correct and is based on the books of account, documents, TDS statements, TDS deposited and other available records.

Place	Kolkat	
Date	31-Mar-2010	Signature of person responsible for deduction of tax
Designation:	Proprietor	Full Name: S K Surya

F-5B: TDS Deduction Certificate (Form 16A)(2nd page)

04.02 TDS Quarterly Returns

At *TDS Returns* Menu (F-4A), you get the option to print Quarterly Returns under the section *Quarterly*, as explained next.

TDS Form 26Q

At TDS Returns Menu (F-4A), under *Quarterly* section, select *Form 26Q* to get Form 26Q Printing screen (F-9A). Fill up the required data to print Form 26Q (F-7A)

Report Titles

TDS Form16A

Name	: S K Surya	Place	: KOLKATA
Son/Daughter of	: P K Chandra	Date	: 31-Jul-2009
Designation	: Proprietor	**Quarter**	**Acknowledgement**
Print as Previous Format	: No	Apr-Jun	: APL-JUN
Nature of Payment	: Interest Other Than Interest on Securities	Jul-Sep	:
From (blank for beginning)	: 1-4-2009	Oct-Dec	:
To (blank for end)	: 31-7-2009	Jan-Mar	:
Challan Date Till	: 31-7-2009		
Type of Copy	: Default	**CIT(TDS) Details**	
Certificate No	: 12345	Name	: A B BARDHAN
Print Total	: No	Address	: BOWBAZAR
		City	: KOLKATA
		Pin Code	: 700012

F-6A: TDS Form 16A Printing

F-6B: Form 16A Printing Configuration

Configure

Print Form Title on Subsequent pages (if applicable) : Yes

Print Government Details also : Yes

Form No. 26Q

[See sections 193, 194, 194A, 194BB, 194C, 194D, 194EE, 194F, 194G, 194H, 194-I, 194J, 194LA and rule 31A]

Quarterly statement of deduction of tax under sub-section (3) of section 200 of the Income-tax Act, 1961 in respect of payments other than Salary for the quarter ended June/September/December/March (tick whichever applicable) 2009 - 10 (Year)

1. (a) Tax Deduction Account No. : ACGFD1234E
   (b) Permanent Account No. : ACDRE3456V
   (c) Financial year : 2009 - 10
   (d) Assessment year : 2010 - 11
   (e) Has any statement been filed earlier for this quarter (Yes/No) : No
   (f) If answer of (e) is 'Yes' then Provisional Receipt No. of original statement :

2. Particulars of the deductor
   (a) Name : ABC Academy
   (b) Type of deductor : Others
   (c) Branch / Division (if any) :
   (d) Address :
   Flat No. : 99, Airport Rd
   Name of premises / building : Kolkata 700 098
   Road / Street / Lane : W Bengal
   Area / Location :
   Town / City / District : W Bengal
   State : West Bengal
   Pin code : 700 098
   Telephone No. : 651234
   E-mail : abc@tmail.com

3. Particulars of the person responsible for deduction of tax
   (a) Name : S K Surya
   (b) Address :
   Flat No. : 99, Airport Rd
   Name of premises / building : Kolkata 700 098
   Road / Street / Lane : W Bengal
   Area / Location :
   Town / City / District :
   State : West Bengal
   Pin code : 700 098
   Telephone No. :
   E-mail : abc@tmail.com

F-7A: TDS Form 26Q

ANNEXURE - DEDUCTEE WISE BREAK-UP OF TDS

(Please use seperate Annexure for each line-item in the table at S.No. 4 of main Form 26Q)

Details of amounts paid/credited during the quarter ended 31-Mar-2010 (DD-MM-YYYY) and of tax deducted at source

BSR Code of the branch where tax is deposited	700123456	Name of Deductor	ABC Academy
Date on which tax deposited (dd-mm-yyyy)	1-Jan-2010		
Challan Serial No.	12		
Section under which payment made	94A	TAN	ACGFD1234E
Total TDS to be allocated among deductees as in the vertical total of col. 425	6,500.00		
Interest			
Others			
Total of the above	6,500.00		

Sr. No.	Dedutee Code (01-Company 02-Other than Company)	PAN of the Deductee	Name of Deductee	Date of Payment / Credit	Amount Paid / credited Rs.	Paid by book entry or otherwise	TDS
414	415	416	417	418	419	420	421
1	02	SDFGC3456B	A K Das	1-Dec-2009	40,000.00	No	4,000.00
2	02	SDFGC3456B	A K Das	1-Dec-2009	25,000.00	No	2,500.00
Total					65,000.00		6,500.00

F-8A: TDS Form 26Q Annexure

Report Titles

TDS Form26 Quartely

Person Responsible Details		Other Details	
Flat No	: 99, Airport Rd	Category (deductor/collector)	: Individual/HUF
Name	: S K Surya	From (blank for beginning)	: 1-4-2009
Designation	: Proprietor	To (blank for end)	: 31-3-2010
Name of the premises/building	: Kolkata 700 098	Challan Date Till	: 31-3-2010
Road/Street/Lane	: W Bengal	Place	: Kolkata
Area/Location	:	Date	: 31-Mar-2010
Town/City/District	:		
State	: West Bengal		
Pin code	: 700 098		
Mobile No.	: 9876523409		
STD Code	:		
Telephone	:		
E-mail	: abc@tmail.com		

F-9A: Form 26Q Printing

Report Titles

Form26Q ANNEXURE

Person Responsible Details		Other Details	
Flat No	: 99, Airport Rd	Category (deductor/collector)	: Individual/HUF
Name	: S K Surya	From (blank for beginning)	: 1-4-2009
Designation	: Proprietor	To (blank for end)	: 31-3-2010
Name of the premises/building	: Kolkata 700 098	Challan Date Till	: 31-3-2010
Road/Street/Lane	: W Bengal	Place	: Kolkata
Area/Location	:	Date	: 31-Mar-2010
Town/City/District	:		
State	: West Bengal		
Pin code	: 700 098		
Mobile No.	: 9876523409		
STD Code	:		
Telephone	:		
E-mail	: abc@tmail.com		

F-10A: Form 26Q Annexure Printing

TDS Form 26Q Annexure

Form No. 27Q

[See sections 194E, 195, 196A, 196B, 196C, 196Dand rule 31A and 37A]

Quarterly statement of deduction of tax under sub-section (3) of section 200 of the I.T. Act, 1961 in respect of payments other than Salary made to non-residents for the quarter ended June/September/December/March (tick whichever applicable) 2009 - 10 (Year)

1. (a) Tax Deduction and collection Account No.(TAN) : ACGFD1234E
   (b) Permanent Account No.(PAN) : ACDRE3456V
   (c) Financial year : 2009 - 10
   (d) Assessment year : 2010 - 11
   (e) Has any statement been filed earlier for this quarter (Yes/No) : No
   (f) If answer of (e) is 'Yes' then Provisional Receipt No. of original statement :

2. Particulars of the deductor
   (a) Name : ABC Academy
   (b) Type of deductor : Others
   (c) Branch / Division (if any) :
   (d) Address :
   Flat No. : 99, Airport Rd
   Name of premises / building : Kolkata 700 098
   Road / Street / Lane : W Bengal
   Area / Location :
   Town / City / District : W Bengal
   State : West Bengal
   Pin code : 700 098
   Telephone No. : 651234
   E-mail : abc@tmail.com

3. Particulars of the person responsible for deduction of tax
   (a) Name : S K Surya
   (b) Address :
   Flat No. : 99, Airport Rd
   Name of premises / building : Kolkata 700 098
   Road / Street / Lane : W Bengal
   Area / Location :
   Town / City / District :
   State : West Bengal
   Pin code : 700 098
   Telephone No. :
   E-mail : abc@tmail.com

F-11A: Form 27Q

At *TDS Returns* Menu (F-4A), under *Quarterly* section, select Annexure to Form *26Q* to get *Form 26Q Annexure Printing* screen (F-10A). Fill up the required data to print *Form 26Q Annexure* (F-8A)

TDS Form 27Q

At *TDS Returns* Menu (F-4A), under *Quarterly* section, select Form 27Q to get Form 27Q Printing screen (F-12A). Fill up the required data to print Form 27Q (F-11A)

Report Titles

TDS Form27 Quarterly

Person Responsible Details		Other Details	
Flat No	: 99, Airport Rd	Category (deductor/collector)	: Individual/HUF
Name	: S K Surya	From (blank for beginning)	: 1-4-2009
Designation	: Proprietor	To (blank for end)	: 31-3-2010
Name of the premises/building	: Kolkata 700 098	Challan Date Till	: 31-3-2010
Road/Street/Lane	: W Bengal	Place	: Kolkata
Area/Location	:	Date	: 31-Mar-2010
Town/City/District	:		
State	: West Bengal		
Pin code	: 700 098		
Mobile No.	: 9876523409		
STD Code	:		
Telephone	:		
E-mail	: abc@tmail.com		

F-12A: TDS Form 27Q Printing

Report Titles

TDS Form27Q Annexure

Person Responsible Details		Other Details	
Flat No	: 99, Airport Rd	Category (deductor/collector)	: Individual/HUF
Name	: S K Surya	From (blank for beginning)	: 1-4-2009
Designation	: Proprietor	To (blank for end)	: 31-3-2010
Name of the premises/building	: Kolkata 700 098	Challan Date Till	: 31-3-2010
Road/Street/Lane	: W Bengal	Place	: Kolkata
Area/Location	:	Date	: 31-Mar-2010
Town/City/District	:		
State	: West Bengal		
Pin code	: 700 098		
Mobile No.	: 9876523409		
STD Code	:		
Telephone	:		
E-mail	: abc@tmail.com		

F-12B: Form 27Q Annexure Printing

TDS Form 27Q Annexure

At TDS Returns Menu(F-4A), under *Quarterly* section, select Form 27Q to get *Form 27Q Annexure Printing* screen (F-12B). Fill up the required data (similar to Form 27Q Printing) to print Form 27Q Annexure

04.03 TDS Annual Returns

At TDS Returns Menu (F-4A), under *Annual* section, you get the option to print following Annual Returns

Annexure

Details of **Interest Other Than Interest on Securities** paid / credited during the financial year and of tax deducted at source under Section 194A of Income Tax Act, 1961 :-

Deductee Code	Permanent Account Number (PAN) of Deductee	Name and Address of Deductee (Address need not be given if PAN is mentioned)	Amount of payment (Rs.)	Date on which amount paid / credited	Paid by book entry or otherwise	Rate at which tax deducted	Amount of tax [illegible] (Rs.)	Date on which tax deducted	Bank Branch Code(5)	Date on which tax paid to the credit of Central Government	Challan number [illegible] bank	Date of furnishing Tax [illegible] Certificate	Reason for non -deduction / lower deduction if any
108	109	110	111	112	113	114	115	116	117	118	119	120	121
(1)	(2)	(3)	(4)	(5)	(6)	(7)	(8)	(9)	(10)	(11)	(12)	(13)	(14)
02	SDFGC3456B	A K Das	40,000.00	1-Jan-2010	No	10 %	4,000.00	1-Dec-2009	70123456	1-Jan-2010	12	1-Jan-2010	
02	SDFGC3456B	A K Das	25,000.00	1-Jan-2010	No	10 %	2,500.00	1-Dec-2009	70123456	1-Jan-2010	12	1-Jan-2010	

F-14A: Form 26 Annexure (Top Part)

TDS Form 26

At *TDS Returns* Menu (F-4A), under Annual section, select *Form 26* to get Form 26 Annual Return Printing screen, similar to Form 26Q (Quarterly) Printing Screen (F-6A). Fill up the required data to print Form 26 (F-13A to F-13C).

TDS Form 26 Annexure

At TDS Returns Menu (F-4A), *under Annual section*, select *Annexure to Form 26* to get Annexure to Form 26 Annual Return Printing screen, similar to Form 26Q (Quarterly) Annexure Printing screen (F-10A). Fill up the required data to print Form 26 Annexure (F-14A & F-14B).

Form No. 26

(See sections 193, 194, 194A, 194B, 194BB, 194C, 194D, 194EE, 194F, 194G, 194H, 194-I, 194J, 194LA and rule 37)

Annual Return of deduction of tax under section 206 of I.T. Act, 1961 in respect of all payments other than 'Salaries' for the year ending 31st March'10

1 Particulars of the person making deduction of tax

(a) Name	:	S K Surya
(b) Address : Flat / Door / Block No.	:	99, Airport Rd
Name of Premises / Building	:	Kolkata 700 098
Road / Street / Lane	:	W Bengal
Area / Locality	:	
Town / District / City	:	
PIN	:	700 098
State	:	West Bengal
(c) Tax Deduction Account Number	:	ACGFD1234E
(d) Permanent Account Number	:	ACDRE3456V

2. Has address of the person making deduction of tax changed(1) Tick 'X' as applicable Yes [ ] No [ ]

3. Status as defined within the meaning of Section 204 read with Rule 30 Tick 'X' as applicable Central Govt. [ ] Others [X]

(a) Please tick the boxes below indicating the section and type of payment (other than 'Salaries') made during the year from which tax was required to be deducted at source by you under the Income Tax Act, 1961

193	194	194A	194B	194BB	194C	194D	194EE	194F	194G	194H	194I	194J	194LA

(b) Please furnish information in seperate Annexures as per the enclosed proforma for each type of payment indicated in item(a) above viz. interest, rent, commission etc

F-13A: Form 26 Annual (Top Part)

Details of tax deducted and paid to the credit of the Central Government

S.No	Section Code	TDS Rs.	Surcharge Rs.	Educaton Cess Rs.	Interest Rs.	Others Rs.	Total tax deposited	Cheque / DD No. (if any)	BSR Code	Date on which tax deposited	Transfer voucher/ Challan serial Number(2)	Whether TDS deposited by book entry
(09-5)	(096)	(097)	(098)	(099)	(100)	(101)	(102)	(103)	(104)	(105)	(106)	(107)
(1)	(2)	(3)	(4)	(5)	(6)	(7)	(8)	(9)	(10)	(11)	(12)	(13)
1	194A	6,500.00					6,500.00	123456	70012-3456	1-Jan-2010	12	No
	Total	6,500.00					6,500.00					

F-13B: Form 26 Annual (Tax Details Part)

VERIFICATION

I, S K Surya, hereby certify that all the particulars furnished above are correct and complete.

Place: Kolkata Signature of the person responsible for deducting tax at source ________

Date: 31-Mar-2010 Name and designation of person responsible for deducting tax at source S K Surya, Proprietor

Notes :- 1. If address has changed give changed address in column 1(b).
2. Where deduction is made by or on behalf of the Government to give particulars of transfer vouchers; other deductors to give particulars of challan no. regarding deposit into bank.
3. Column is relevant only for Government deductors.

F-13C: Form 26 Annual (Verification Part)

Notes :-

1. Please state the nature of payment viz. interest, rent, contract payment etc.
2. Please use seperate Annexures for deductions made under different sections.
3. Please enter Deductee Code 01 for companies, 02 for 'other than companies'.
4. Write B if paid by book entry, write C otherwise.
5. Where deduction is made by or on behalf of the Government, transfer voucher number may be entered in column (10).
6. Write A if the 'lower deduction' or 'no deduction' is on account of a certificate under Section 197.
   Write B if no deduction is on account of declaration under Section 197A
7. If necessary, please use additional sheets to give full details of payment in the above format. Please also give running serial number to all pages.

Signature of person responsible for deducting tax at source ________

Name and designation of person responsible for deducting tax at source S K Surya, Propnetor

F-14B: Form 26 Annexure (Bottom Part)

TDS Form 27

At TDS Returns Menu (F-4A), *under Annual section*, select Form 27 (Annual) to get *Form 27 Printing* screen, similar to Form 2Q Printing screen (F-12A). Fill up the required data to print Form 27 (F-15A to F-15C).

TDS Form 27Q Annexure

At TDS Returns Menu (F-4A), *under Annual section*, select *Annexure to Form 27* to get *Form 27 Annexure* Printing screen, similar to Form 27Q Annexure Printing screen (F-12B). Fill up the required data to print Form 27 (F-15A to F-15C).

Form No. 27
(See rule 37A)

Statement of deduction of tax from interest, dividends or any other sum payable to (i) persons, not being companies, who are non-residents or residents but not ordinarily residents, and (ii) companies which are neither Indian companies nor companies which have made the prescribed arrangements for the declaration and payment of dividends within

1 Particulars of the person making deduction of tax

(a) Name	:	S K Surya
(b) Address : Flat / Door / Block No.	:	99, Airport Rd
Name of Premises / Building	:	Kolkata 700 098
Road / Street / Lane	:	W Bengal
Area / Locality	:	
Town / District / City	:	
PIN	:	700 098
State	:	West Bengal
(c) Tax Deduction Account Number	:	ACGFD1234E
(d) Permanent Account Number	:	ACDRE3456V

2. Has address of the person making deduction of tax changed(1) Tick 'X' as applicable Yes [ ] No [ ]

3. Status as defined within the meaning of Section 204 read with Rule 30 Tick 'X' as applicable Central Govt. [ ] Others [X]

(a) Please tick the boxes below indicating the section and type of payment (other than 'Salaries') made during the year from which tax was required to be deducted at source by you under the Income Tax Act, 1961

194E	195	196A	196B	196C	196D

Please furnish information in seperate Annexures as per the enclosed proforma for each type of payment indicated above. viz, interest, dividends etc. including the payments on which no tax has been deducted on the basis of certificate issued by a

F-15B: Form 27 Annual – Tax Details Part

Details of tax deducted and paid to the credit of the Central Government

S.No	Section Code	TDS Rs.	Surcharge Rs	Education Cess Rs.	Interest Rs.	Others Rs.	Total tax deposited	Cheque / DD No. (if any)	BSR Code	Date on which tax deposited	Transfer voucher/ Challan serial Number(2)	Whether TDS deposited by book ent
(09-5)	(096)	(097)	(098)	(099)	(100)	(101)	(102)	(103)	(104)	(105)	(106)	(107)
(1)	(2)	(3)	(4)	(5)	(6)	(7)	(8)	(9)	(10)	(11)	(12)	(13)
	Total											

F-15A: Form 27 Annual – Top Part

VERIFICATION

I, S K Surya, hereby certify that all the particulars furnished above are correct and complete.

Place: Kolkata Signature of the person responsible for deducting tax at source

Date: 31-Mar-2010 Name and designation of person responsible for deducting tax at source S K Surya, Proprietor

Notes - 1. If address has changed give changed address in column 1(b).
2. Where deduction is made by or on behalf of the Government to give particulars of transfer vouchers; other deductors to give particulars of challan no. regarding deposit into bank
3. Column is relevant only for Government deductors.

F-15C: Form 27 Annual – Verification Part

05 TDS Outstanding Reports

At TDS reports Menu (F-4A), select *Outstandings* to get *TDS Outstanding Reports* Menu (F-16A)

05.01 TDS Payables

At *TDS Outstanding Menu* (F-16A), select *TDS Payables* to get *TDS Payables* report (F-17A)

Buttons: The buttons of Outstanding Statement have been described earlier. Here we describe buttons exclusively related to TDS.

Gateway of Tally ....
Display Menu ....
Statutory Reports ....
TDS Reports ....

Outstandings

Payables

TDS Payables
Ledger
Nature of Payment

TDS Not Deducted

Quit

F-16A: TDS

TDS Outstanding Ctrl + M

TDS Payable 1-Apr-2009 to 31-Mar-2010

Date	Ref. No.	Nature of Payment	Opening Amount	Pending Amount	Due on	Overdue days
1-May-2009	Pymt / 4-1	Interest Other Than Interest on Securities	500.00 Cr	500.00 Cr		297
1-Dec-2009	Purc / 2-1	Payments to Contractors (Other Than Advertisement	1,000.00 Cr	1,000.00 Cr		83
1-Jun-2009	Jrnl / 4-2	Interest Other Than Interest on Securities	700.00 Cr	700.00 Cr		267
1-May-2009	Jrnl / 1-1	Interest Other Than Interest on Securities	500.00 Cr	500.00 Cr		297
			2,700.00 Cr	2,700.00 Cr		

F-17A: TDS Payables (Condensed)

TDS Outstanding Ctrl + M

TDS Payable 1-Apr-2009 to 31-Mar-2010

Date	Ref. No.		Nature of Payment	Opening Amount	Pending Amount	Due on	Overdue days
1-May-2009	Pymt / 4-1		Interest Other Than Interest on Securities	500.00 Cr	500.00 Cr		297
	1-May-2009 Payment	*4*	*500.00 Cr*				
	1-Jun-2009 Journal	*4*	*700.00 Cr*				
1-Dec-2009	Purc / 2-1		Payments to Contractors (Other Than Advertisement	1,000.00 Cr	1,000.00 Cr		83
	1-Nov-2009 Purchase	*2*					
	1-Dec-2009 Journal	*7*	*1,000.00 Cr*				
1-Jun-2009	Jrnl / 4-2		Interest Other Than Interest on Securities	700.00 Cr	700.00 Cr		267
	1-Jun-2009 Journal	*4*	*700.00 Cr*				
1-May-2009	Jrnl / 1-1		Interest Other Than Interest on Securities	500.00 Cr	500.00 Cr		297
	1-May-2009 Journal	*1*	*500.00 Cr*				
				2,700.00 Cr	2,700.00 Cr		

F-18A: TDS Payables (Detailed)

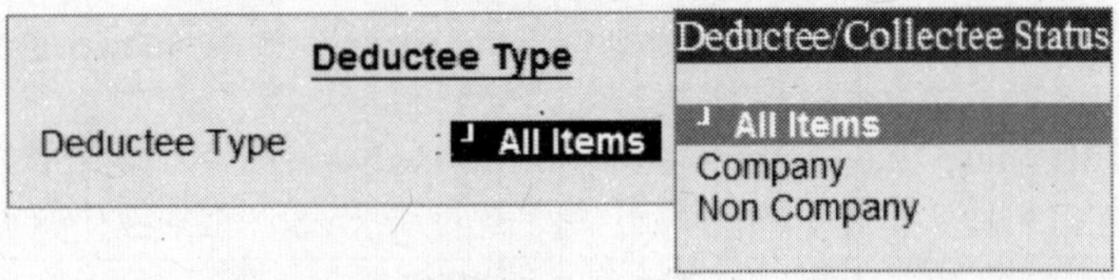

F-19A: Deductee Type selection screen

- **F7:Deductee Type**: Click *F7: Deductee Type*, to get Deductee Type selection screen (F-19A) to select the Deductee Type form the list (F-19A)

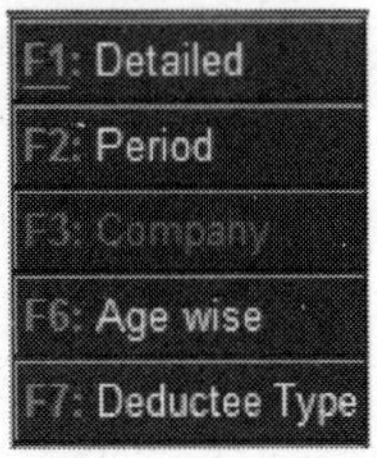

F-20A: Buttons

05.02 TDS Ledger Outstandings

At TDS Outstandings menu (F-16A), select *Ledger* to get *TDS Ledger Outstanding* Menu (F-21A).

At TDS Ledger Outstanding Menu (F-21A), select:

- *Al Items* to get TDS Ledger Outstandings of all Parties (F-22A).
- *One Item* and then select the Party Leger Account to get TDS Ledger Outstanding of the selected Party Ledger (F-22B)

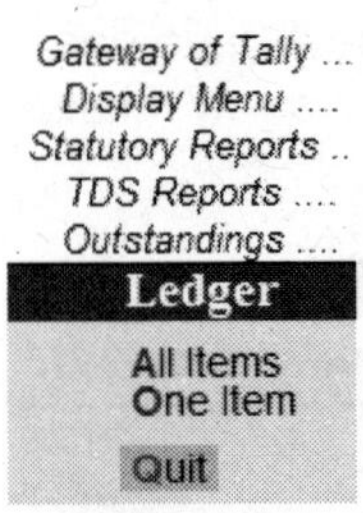

F-21A: TDS Ledger Menu

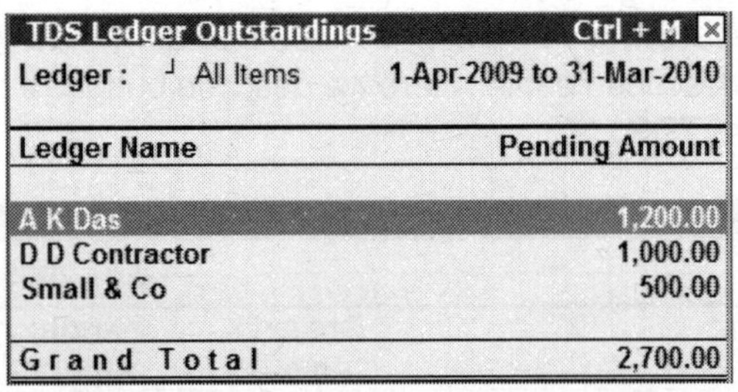

TDS Ledger Outstandings — Ctrl + M

Ledger : All Items — 1-Apr-2009 to 31-Mar-2010

Ledger Name	Pending Amount
A K Das	1,200.00
D D Contractor	1,000.00
Small & Co	500.00
Grand Total	2,700.00

F-22A:TDS Ledger Outstandings

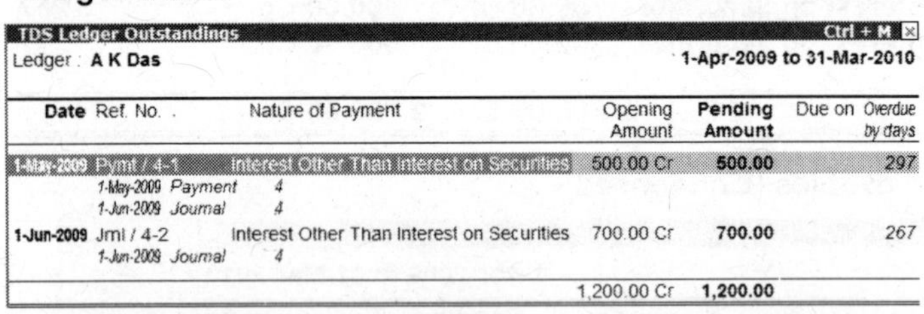

TDS Ledger Outstandings — Ctrl + M

Ledger : A K Das — 1-Apr-2009 to 31-Mar-2010

Date	Ref. No.	Nature of Payment	Opening Amount	Pending Amount	Due on	Overdue by days
1-May-2009	Pymt / 4-1	Interest Other Than Interest on Securities	500.00 Cr	500.00		297
	1-May-2009 Payment	4				
	1-Jun-2009 Journal	4				
1-Jun-2009	Jrnl / 4-2	Interest Other Than Interest on Securities	700.00 Cr	700.00		267
	1-Jun-2009 Journal	4				
			1,200.00 Cr	1,200.00		

F-22B:TDS Ledger Outstandings of a selected Ledger

The Buttons and Configuration options of *Ledger Outstandings* have been described earlier.

05.03 TDS Nature of Payments Outstandings

At TDS Outstandings menu (F16A), select *Nature of Payments* to get TDS Nature of Payments Menu (F-23A).

At TDS *Nature of Payments* Menu (F-23A), select:

- *All Items* to get TDS Outstandings of all types of Nature of Payments (F-24A).
- *One Item* and then select the Nature of Payment to get TDS Nature of Payment Outstandings of the selected Nature of Payment (F-25A).

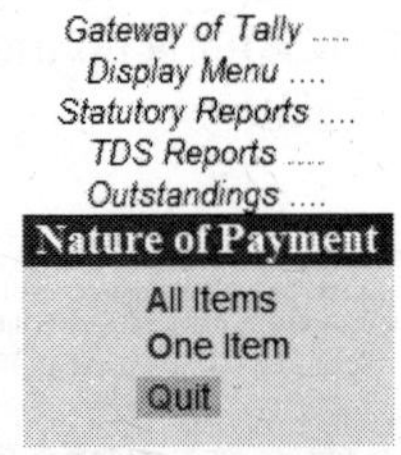

F-23A TDS Nature of Payments Menu

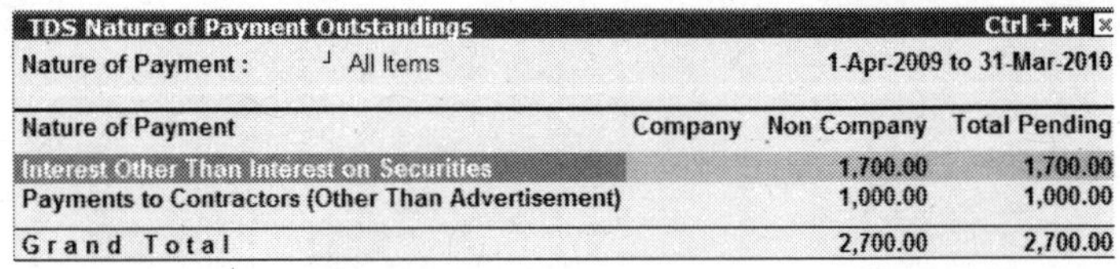

TDS Nature of Payment Outstandings — Ctrl + M

Nature of Payment : All Items — 1-Apr-2009 to 31-Mar-2010

Nature of Payment	Company	Non Company	Total Pending
Interest Other Than Interest on Securities		1,700.00	1,700.00
Payments to Contractors (Other Than Advertisement)		1,000.00	1,000.00
Grand Total		2,700.00	2,700.00

F-24A: TDS Nature of Payments Outstanding

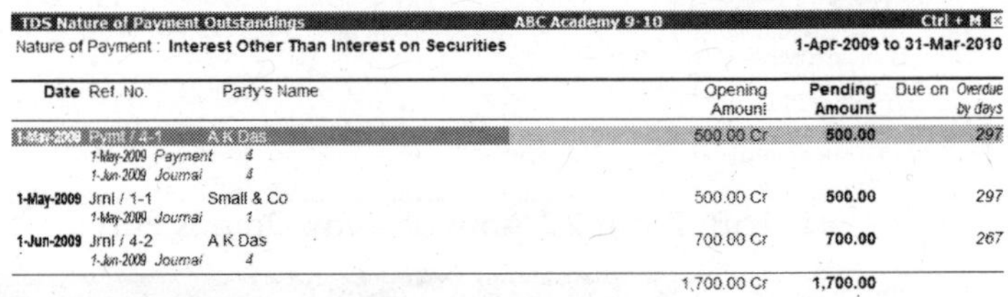

TDS Nature of Payment Outstandings — ABC Academy 9-10 — Ctrl + M

Nature of Payment : Interest Other Than Interest on Securities — 1-Apr-2009 to 31-Mar-2010

Date	Ref. No.	Party's Name	Opening Amount	Pending Amount	Due on	Overdue by days
1-May-2009	Pymt / 4-1	A K Das	500.00 Cr	500.00		297
	1-May-2009 Payment	4				
	1-Jun-2009 Journal	4				
1-May-2009	Jrnl / 1-1	Small & Co	500.00 Cr	500.00		297
	1-May-2009 Journal	1				
1-Jun-2009	Jrnl / 4-2	A K Das	700.00 Cr	700.00		267
	1-Jun-2009 Journal	4				
			1,700.00 Cr	1,700.00		

F-25A: TDS Nature of Payments Outstanding of a Ledger

The buttons at Nature of Payments are similar to those of TDS Outstandings (F-20A)

05.04 TDS Not Deducted Report

This Report shows the payments made to parties without deduction of TDS.

At TDS Outstandings menu (F-16A), select *TDS Not Deducted* to get *TDS Not Deducted* Report (F-27A)

Buttons: At *TDS Not Deducted* Report (F-27A), the following buttons are available related to TDS (F-28A)

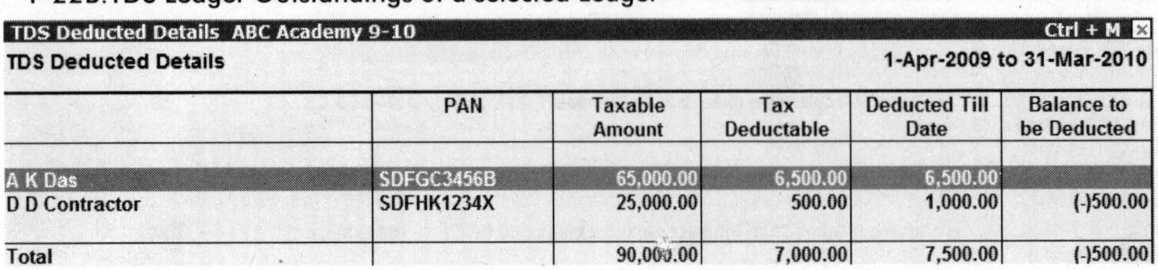

TDS Deducted Details ABC Academy 9-10 — Ctrl + M

TDS Deducted Details — 1-Apr-2009 to 31-Mar-2010

	PAN	Taxable Amount	Tax Deductable	Deducted Till Date	Balance to be Deducted
A K Das	SDFGC3456B	65,000.00	6,500.00	6,500.00	
D D Contractor	SDFHK1234X	25,000.00	500.00	1,000.00	(-)500.00
Total		90,000.00	7,000.00	7,500.00	(-)500.00

F-27A: TDS Not Deducted Report

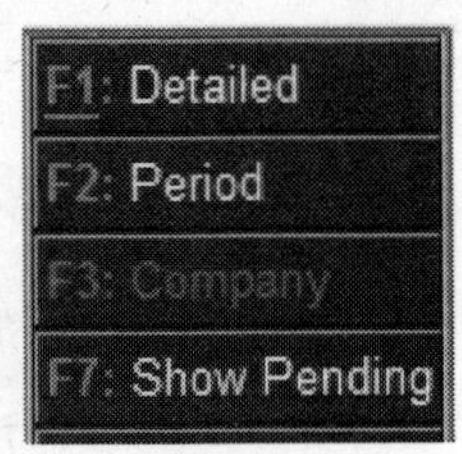

F-28A: Buttons

- **F7:Show Pending / Show All**: Click the toggle Button
  - o **F7: Show Pending**: To show only the Pending Items for which TDS is not deducted
  - o **F7: Show All**: To show all Items for which TDS was not deducted

FAQ: Frequently Asked Questions

FAQ-1: How do I get a comprehensive summary statement of TDS

Ans: At TDS Reports Menu (F-1A). select *Computation* to get TDS Computation Statement (F-2A) showing the details of TDS Deducted, Paid, Payable etc.

TDS Special Features 01-05

01 TDS Special Features

We have explained TDS Set Up, creation of TDS related Leger Accounts, TDS Vouchers, Deposit of TDS to Government and various Statutory and other TDS Tracking Reports, These cover the entire topic of TDS management for most of the users.

However, there are special instances where some special treatment is required. Here, we cover such exclusive special instances which require elaboration for proper operation of handling such situations

02 TDS at Lower / Zero Rates

Sometimes, a Party may be allowed to get TDS Deducted at lower Rate by the *Assessing Officer*. In such case, the Assessing Officer issues a certificate for deduction of Tax at Lower Rate (herein referred as *Concession Certificate*) than the aplicable rate specified under the section.

The *Concession Certificate* granted would be valid for the specified assessment year and the person named therein.

Now we discuss the exclusive steps of Deduction of TDSat Lower / Zero Rate

Ledger Account Master: First you have to set the configuration option at the Ledger Account creation / alteration of the Party in favour of whom a Concession Certificate has been issued.

Ledger Account creation of Party for which TDS is to be deducted has been explained earlier. Here we discuss abut points exclusively related to TDS deduction at Lower Rate.

At Ledger Account creation (F-2A) of the Party (Account s Info>Ledger), click *F12: Configure* to get *Party Ledger Account Configuration* screen (F-1A). At *Party Ledger Account Configuration* screen (F-1A), set *Yes* at *Allow Advanced Entries in TDS master.*

Consequently, at Ledger creation screen (F-2A), you get another option *Use Advanced TDS Entries.* Set *Yes* at *Use Advanced TDS* to get *Advanced TDS Entry screen* (F-2B).

At *Advanced TDS Entry screen* (F-2B), set:

- **Zero /Lower Rate***:* At *Zero Lower Deduction* (F-2B), set *Yes* to get Zero/ Lower Deduction Details screen (F-3B), to set the required information as explained next.
- **TDS in same voucher**: For Deduction of TDS in same voucher (for lower rate deduction), set Yes at *Deduct TDS in same Voucher if applicable* (F-2B), and select the *TDS nature of Payment* from the list.

Ledger Configuration

Allow ALIASES along with Names	? Yes
Allow Language ALIASES along with Names	? No
Allow ADVANCED entries in Masters	? Yes
Allow ADVANCED entries in TDS Master	? Yes
Add NOTES for Ledger Accounts	? No
Use ADDRESSES for Ledger Accounts	? Yes
Use CONTACT Details	? Yes
Use Other Information for Ledger Accounts	? No

F-1A: Party Ledger Configuration

Ledger Creation

Name	: Small & Co
Under	: Loans (Liability)
Statutory Information	
Is TDS Deductable	? Yes
Treat as TDS Expenses	? No
Deductee Type	: Partnership Firm
Use Advanced TDS Entries	? Yes

F-2A: Party Ledger Creation

Advanced TDS Entries

Ignore Surcharge Exemption Limit	? No
Set Ignore Income Tax Exemption Limit	? No
Set Zero / Lower Deduction	? Yes
Deduct TDS in Same Voucher If applicable	? No

F-2B: Advance TDS details in Party Ledger Creation

02.01 Setting for TDS with Zero / Lower Rate

At *Zero / Lower Rate Details* screen (F-3B), set as follows:

- **Nature of Payment**: At *Nature of Payment* column, select the applicable Nature of Payment from the list

Zero / Lower Rate

197	Lower Deduction
197A	Zero Rate (Form 15G/ 15H)

F-3A: Zero / Lower Rate option list

Zero / Lower Deduction Details

Nature of Payment	Section Number	Certificate No. / Date	Applicable From	Applicable To	TDS	Surcharge	Ed Cess	Sec Ed Cess
Interest Other Than Interest on Securities								
	197	123	1-4-2009	31-3-2010	5 %	0 %	0 %	0 %

F-3B: Zero / Lower Rate Deduction screen

- **ITax Section**: At *Section Number* column, select from the list of Section / I Tax Rate (F-3A)
- **Certificate Number / Date**: At *Certificate Number / Date* column,
  - o **Lower Rate:** Enter the Certificate Number & date issued by I Tax authority allowing Lower Rate Deduction.
  - o **Zero Rate:** Enter the reference number of receipt of Form 15G/15H from the Party
- **Date of Applicability**: Enter the Start Date (at *Applicable From* column) & End Date (at *Applicable To* column) of the I Tax Previous Year of Concession Certificate / Form 15G/15H
- **Applicable Rate**: At *TDS*, enter the Rate as follows:
  - o **Lower Rate**: Enter the Applicable Lower Rate of TDS (and also for Ed Cess & S. Ed Cess, if applicable)
  - o **Zero Rate**: The Zero Rates are auto carried in all columns and cursor do not move to these fields and returns to main entry screen (F-4A).

02.02 Journal Voucher with Zero / Lower TDS

Journal Voucher entry with TDS deduction in same voucher has been explained earlier. Here we explain the points exclusively related to Zero / Lower Rate

Accounting Voucher Creation		Ctrl + M
Journal No. 1		1-May-2009 Friday
Particulars	**Debit**	**Credit**
Dr **Interst Paid**	10,000.00	
Cr **Small & Co**		9,500.00
Cr **TDS on Interest**		500.00
Narration:	10,000.00	10,000.00

F-4A: Journal Voucher entry with Lower TDS

TDS Nature of Payment Details	
Ledger Name : Interst Paid	
Nature of Payment	**Assessable Value**
Interest Other Than Interest on Securities	10,000.00

F-5A:TDS Nature of Payment Entry

Type of Ref	Name	Nature of Payment	Is Zero/ Lower Rate	TDS Duty Ledger	Assessable Amount	Deduct now	TDS Amount	Payable Amount
New Ref	Jrnl / 1-1	Interest Other Than Interest on Securities	197	TDS on Interest	10,000.00 Cr	Yes	500.00 Cr	9,500.00 Cr
	Income Tax 5 % On 10,000.00 Cr	*500.00 Cr*						
	Surcharge 0 % On 500.00 Cr							
	Education Cess 0 % On 500.00 Cr							
	Secondary Education Cess 0 % On 500.00 Cr							
	Total				10,000.00 Cr		500.00 Cr	9,500.00 Cr

F-5B: TDS Details entry for Lower Rate

At Journal Voucher entry screen (F-4A), enter as follows:

- **Expense Ledger Account**: Select the *Expense Ledger* Account and enter the Amount to get TDS nature of Payment screen (F-5A). Select the applicable TDS nature from the list.
- **Party Ledger Account**: Next select the *Party Ledger* Account to get TDS Details screen (F-5A).
- **Lower Rate:** You get TDS Details entry screen (F-5B). The default values as entered at Party Ledger are carried. The Net Amount Payable to Party after TDS, is carried at the credit column in the main voucher screen (F-4A).
- **Zero Rate:** The TDS subscreen does not appear. The full amount (entered at Expense) is carried to the Party Ledger Account at Credit column in the man voucher entry screen (F-4A).
- **TDS Ledger Account**: At main voucher screen (F-4A),
  - o **Lower Rate:** Select the *TDS Ledger* Account. The computed amount of TDS is carried and shown at Credit Column
  - o **Zero Rate:** The Ledger entry is complete and you do not have to enter any TDS Ledger account / amount

03 TDS on Advance Payments

So far we have discussed TDS deduction on Expense. Sometimes, Advance is paid to supplier of service etc, before the expense has been incurred. Normally this is in form of some lump sum amount in advance. As per rules, TDS is to be deducted on Advance payment also. Later on when the final payment is made, the balance TDS is deducted.

03.01 Payment of Advance with TDS Deduction

You have to create a Payment Voucher in Single Mode as explained earlier. Here we explain points exclusively related to TDS in Payment Voucher.

Bill-wise Details for : A K Das Upto ₹ 5,000.00 Dr			
Type of Ref	Name	Due Date, or Credit Days (wef: 1-May-2009)	Amount Dr/ Cr
Advance	4	30 Days (31-May-2009)	5,000.00 Dr
			5,000.00 Dr

F-6A: Bill Allocation details

Type of Ref	Name	Nature of Payment	Assessable Amount	TDS Amount
New Ref	Pymt / 4-1	Interest Other Than Interest on Securities	5,000.00 Dr	500.00 Cr
	Income Tax 10 % On 5,000.00 Cr	*500.00 Cr*		
	Surcharge 0 % On 500.00 Cr			
	Education Cess 0 % On 500.00 Cr			
	Secondary Education Cess 0 % On 500.00 Cr			
	Total		5,000.00 Dr	500.00 Cr

F-6B: TDS Details

Accounting Voucher Creation			Ctrl + M
Payment No. 4			1-May-2009 Friday
Account : **Cash**			
Particulars			**Amount**
A K Das			5,000.00
Advance 4	30 Days (31-May-2009)	5,000.00 Dr	
TDS on Interest			(-)500.00
Narration:			4,500.00

F-6C: Advance Payment with TDS

At Payment Voucher Entry screen in single entry mode (F-6C), after entry of Cash / Bank Account, enter the Ledger Accounts details at Particulars column, as follows (F-6C):

- **Party Ledger**: At the first ledger (at *Particulars* column), select the Party Ledger Account whom advance payment is being made to (Bill by Bill must be se for the Party). Enter the amount paid to get the Bill Allocation screen (F-6A). At *Type Ref*, select *Advance*. At Due Date / Credit Days, the Due Date / Credit Days is carried from Party Master, which you may change.
- **TDS Ledger Account**: Next select TDS Ledger Account to get TDS Details screen (F-6B). The figures are carried as default. The amount of TDS is carried against TDS Ledger account as negative figure in the voucher main screen (F-6C).

Enter Voucher Narration and save the voucher (F-6C).

03.02 Advance Adjustment against Bill

Later on, the expense is to be booked and the Advance is to be adjusted through Journal Voucher. TDS is deducted on Balance Amount paid after adjustment of Advance, and TDS already deducted from Advance Payment is also adjusted. The net Amount payable (after TDS adjustment) is credited to the Party Account.

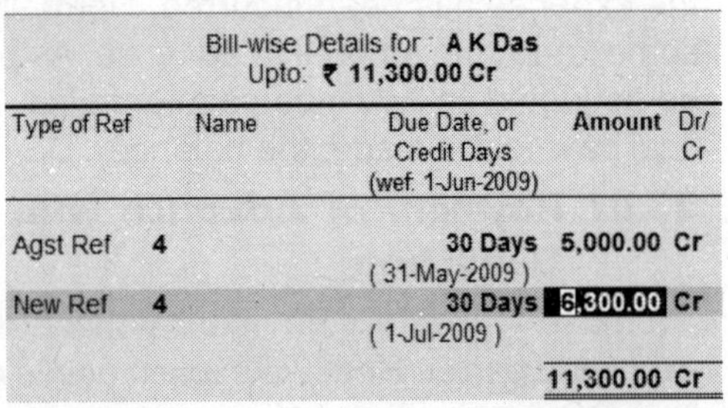

Bill-wise Details for : A K Das
Upto: ₹ 11,300.00 Cr

Type of Ref	Name	Due Date, or Credit Days (wef: 1-Jun-2009)	Amount	Dr/ Cr
Agst Ref	4	30 Days (31-May-2009)	5,000.00	Cr
New Ref	4	30 Days (1-Jul-2009)	6,300.00	Cr
			11,300.00	Cr

F-7A: Bill Allocation screen

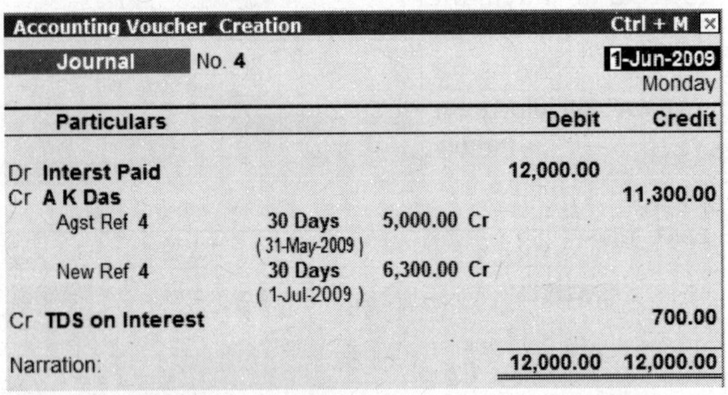

Accounting Voucher Creation — Ctrl + M

Journal No. 4 — 1-Jun-2009, Monday

Particulars			Debit	Credit
Dr **Interst Paid**			12,000.00	
Cr **A K Das**				11,300.00
Agst Ref 4	30 Days (31-May-2009)	5,000.00 Cr		
New Ref 4	30 Days (1-Jul-2009)	6,300.00 Cr		
Cr **TDS on Interest**				700.00
Narration:			12,000.00	12,000.00

F-7B: Journal Voucher for Advance Adjustment & Expense Booking

At Journal entry screen (F-7B), enter as follows:

- **Expense Ledger**: Select the *Expense Ledger* to get *TDS Nature of Payment* screen (F-7C). At *TDS Nature of Payment* screen (F-7C), select the applicable nature of Payment and enter the total amount of expense. This is carried at the main voucher screen (F-7B) at Debit Column against the Expense Ledger Account
- **Party Ledger**: Select Party Ledger to get *TDS Details* screen (F-7D). At *TDS Details* screen (F-7D):
    - o Select *Agst Ref* and select the Ref of Advance paid to adjust the advance.
    - o Next select *New Ref* and create the new Ref for the Balance Amount of the Bill after adjustment of Advance

The default TDS Ledger, Amount etc are auto carried.

Bill Allocation

Next you get the Bill Allocation screen (F-7A), At *Bill Allocation screen* (F-7A), enter the Bill details in the same way as entered at TDS Details screen (F-7D)

- o Select *Agst Ref* and select the Ref of Advance paid to adjust the advance.
- o Next select *New Ref* and create the new Ref for the Balance Amount of the Bill after adjustment of Advance.
    - **TDS Ledger**: At Main Voucher screen (F-7A), select TDS Ledger. The TDS deducted in the voucher (on the balance amount paid after advance adjustment, as shown in F-7D) is auto carried at the Credit Column.

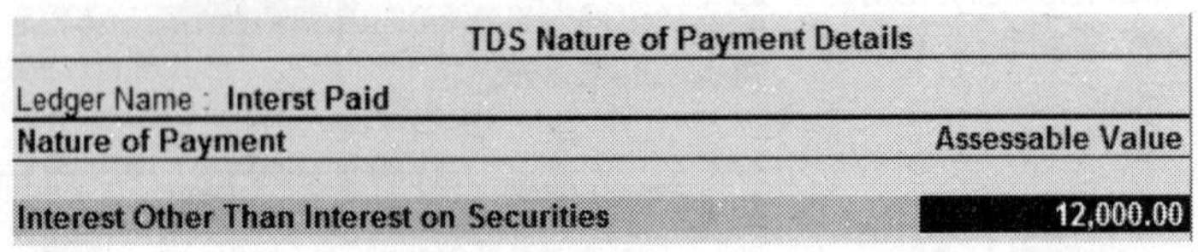

TDS Nature of Payment Details

Ledger Name : Interst Paid

Nature of Payment	Assessable Value
Interest Other Than Interest on Securities	12,000.00

F-7C: TDS nature of Payment

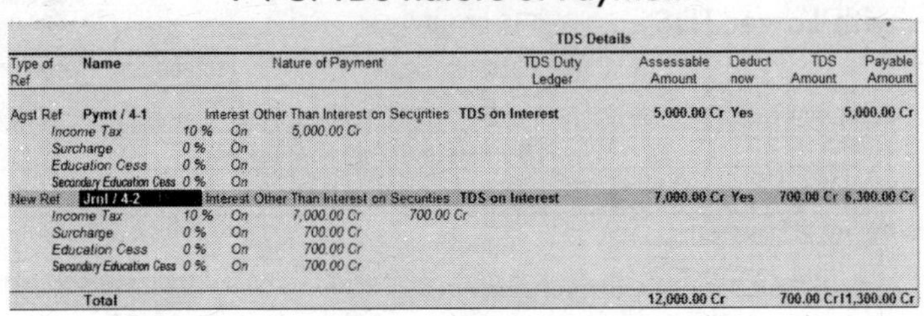

TDS Details

Type of Ref	Name	Nature of Payment	TDS Duty Ledger	Assessable Amount	Deduct now	TDS Amount	Payable Amount
Agst Ref	Pymt / 4-1	Interest Other Than Interest on Securities	TDS on Interest	5,000.00 Cr	Yes		5,000.00 Cr
	Income Tax 10 % On 5,000.00 Cr						
	Surcharge 0 % On						
	Education Cess 0 % On						
	Secondary Education Cess 0 % On						
New Ref	Jrnl / 4-2	Interest Other Than Interest on Securities	TDS on Interest	7,000.00 Cr	Yes	700.00 Cr	6,300.00 Cr
	Income Tax 10 % On 7,000.00 Cr 700.00 Cr						
	Surcharge 0 % On 700.00 Cr						
	Education Cess 0 % On 700.00 Cr						
	Secondary Education Cess 0 % On 700.00 Cr						
	Total			12,000.00 Cr		700.00 Cr	11,300.00 Cr

F-7D: TDS Details

Enter Voucher Narration and save the Voucher.

03.03 Final Payment Voucher

Having booked the final expenses / TDS Deduction through Journal Voucher and having adjusted the Advance Paid, you may now make payment of Balance payable through Payment Voucher. The summary of Amount Paid and Payable is shown below for refernce

	Amount Paid		TDS Deducted	Net Amount Paid
Advance		5000	500	4500
Final	(12000-5000) =	7000	700	6300
Total		**12000**	**1200**	**10800**

At Payment Voucher, enter as follows (F-8A):

- **Party A/c**: Select Party Account and enter the Net Amount Payable to get *Bill Allocation* screen (F-8B). At *Bill Allocation* screen (F-8B), select *Agst Ref* and select the Bill Reference showing the Balance Amount payable for the Reference.
- **Cash / Bank A/c**: Select the Cash / bank A/c through which the Payment is being made. The Net Amount payable is carried at Credit column

Enter the Voucher Narration and save the Voucher

Accounting Voucher Creation Ctrl + M

Payment No. 8 — 1-Jun-2009, Monday

Particulars			Debit	Credit
Dr **A K Das**			6,300.00	
Cur Bal: 0.00 Dr				
Agst Ref 4	30 Days (31-May-2009)	6,300.00 Dr		
Cr **HDFC Bank**				6,300.00
Narration:			6,300.00	6,300.00

F-8A: Final Payment Voucher

Bill-wise Details for : **A K Das**
Upto: ₹ **6,300.00 Dr**

Type of Ref	Name	Due Date, or Credit Days (wef. 1-Jun-2009)	Amount	Dr/Cr
Agst Ref	4	30 Days (31-May-2009)	6,300.00	Dr
			6,300.00	Dr

F-8B: Bil Allocation of Final Payment

04 Reversal of Expenses

Sometime a Bill which is already entered may be cancelled (Job not done), or the final Bill may be reduced (Less Job not done). In such case, the Buyer who entered a TDS Journal Voucher for the full bill amount earlier having deducted TDS thereon, would issue a Debit Note on the Party and adjust the Expenses Amount as well as TDS deducted on it.

04.01 Expenses Booking

First a Journal Voucher is created for the Booking of Expenses, TDS Deduction thereon and Net Amount Credit to the Party, as explained below:

At Journal Voucher entry screen (F-9A), enter as follows:

- **Expense Ledger**: Select Expense Account to get *TDS Type of payment.* Screen (F-9C).
  - o At *TDS Type of payment.* Screen (F-9C), select the TDS Type of payment and enter the Amount of Expenses. The amount is carried in voucher in Debit Column (F-9A)
- **Party Ledger**: Select Party Account to get. *TDS Details screen* (F-9D). At *TDS Details screen* (F-9D)., enter TDS Details.
  - o Next you get Bill Allocation screen (F-9B). At *Bill Allocation screen* (F-9B), enter Bill Allocation Details.
- Select *New Ref* and enter the Gross Amount of Bill as Credit.
- Select *New Ref* and enter the TDS Amount of Bill as Debit
  - o The Net amount after TDS deduction is carried in main voucher entry screen (F-9A) in Credit Column
- **TDS Ledger**: Select TDS Account. The TDS deducted as shown in TDS details screen is carried

Save the Journal Voucher (F-9A).

Accounting Voucher Creation Ctrl + M

Journal No. 1 — 2-Apr-2009, Thursday

Particulars			Debit	Credit
Dr **Job Work Charges**			20,000.00	
Cr **D D Contractor**				19,600.00
New Ref 1	30 Days (2-May-2009)	20,000.00 Cr		
New Ref 1	30 Days (2-May-2009)	400.00 Dr		
Cr **TDS From Contractors**				400.00
Narration:			20,000.00	20,000.00

F-9A: Journal Voucher for Expense Booking

Bill-wise Details for : **D D Contractor**
Upto: ₹ **19,600.00 Cr**

Type of Ref	Name	Due Date, or Credit Days (wef. 2-Apr-2009)	Amount	Dr/Cr
New Ref	1	30 Days (2-May-2009)	20,000.00	Cr
New Ref	1	30 Days (2-May-2009)	400.00	Dr
			19,600.00	Cr

(Note: 'Breaking of above bills helps to identify the original bill amount in the outstanding statement')

F-9B: Bill Allocation of Party Ledger

TDS Nature of Payment Details

Ledger Name : **Job Work Charges**

Nature of Payment	Assessable Value
Payments to Contractors (Other Than Advertisement)	20,000.00

F-9C: TDS Nature of Payment entry

TDS Details

Type of Ref	Name	Nature of Payment	TDS Duty Ledger	Assessable Amount	Deduct now	TDS Amount	Payable Amount
New Ref	Jrnl / 1-1	Payments to Contractors (Other Than Advertisement)	TDS From Contractors	20,000.00 Cr	Yes	400.00 Cr	19,600.00 Cr
	Income Tax 2 % On 20,000.00 Cr 400.00 Cr						
	Surcharge 0 % On 400.00 Cr						
	Education Cess 0 % On 400.00 Cr						
	Secondary Education Cess 0 % On 400.00 Cr						
	Total			20,000.00 Cr		400.00 Cr	19,600.00 Cr

F-9D: TDS Details

04.02 Debit Note

Later on, a Debit Note (of Rs 4000) was issued on the Party as Part of the Job was not done (Job for Rs 16,000 out of 20,000 was only done).

TDS Nature of Payment Details	
Ledger Name : Job Work Charges	
Nature of Payment	**Assessable Value**
Payments to Contractors (Other Than Advertisement)	**4,000.00**

F-10A: Nature of Payment

TDS Details						
Type of Ref	Name		Nature of Payment		Assessable Amount	TDS Amount
Agst Ref	Purc / 2-1		Payments to Contractors (Other Than Advertisement)		4,000.00 Dr	80.00 Dr
	Income Tax	*2 %*	*On*	*4,000.00 Cr*	*80.00 Dr*	
	Surcharge	*0 %*	*On*	*80.00 Cr*		
	Education Cess	*0 %*	*On*	*80.00 Cr*		
	Secondary Education Cess	*0 %*	*On*	*80.00 Cr*		
	Total				4,000.00 Dr	80.00 Dr

F-10B: TDS Details

Accounting Voucher Creation		Ctrl + M
Debit Note No. 1		1-May-2009
Ref. : 12		Friday
Party's A/c Name : D D Contractor		
Particulars	Rate per	**Amount**
Job Work Charges		4,000.00
TDS From Contractors		(-)80.00
Narration:		*3,920.00*

F-10C: Debit Note Entry

At Debit Note entry screen in Accounting Invoice mode, (F-10C), enter as follows:

- **Party Account**: Select the party Account at the Header
- **Expenses Account**: Select the Expenses Account at Particulars column to get *Nature of Payment Details* screen (F-10A).
    - o At *Nature of Payment Details* (F-10A), select the Nature of Payment and enter the expenses amount of Debit Note, which is then carried at the debit column in the main voucher entry screen (F-10D)
- **TDS Account**: Next select the TDS Ledger to get *TDS Details* screen (F-10B). The TDS Amount is carried at the Main Voucher entry screen (F-10C) as negative amount.

04.03 Final Payment to Party

Now make the Final Payment of the net Payable Amount through Payment Voucher after adjusting the Debit Note.

In Payment Voucher (F-11A), enter as follows:

- **Party Account**: Select Party Account to get Bill Allocation screen (F-11B). At *Bill allocation* screen, select *Agst Ref* and select the pending reference. The amount (19600-3920=15680) is carried against Party Account at Debit Column.
- **Cash / Bank Account**: Select Cash Bank Account. The Net amount payable is carried at Credit Column.

Enter Narration and save the Voucher.

Accounting Voucher Creation			Ctrl + M
Payment No. 7			2-May-2009 Saturday
Particulars		**Debit**	**Credit**
Dr **D D Contractor**		15,680.00	
Agst Ref **1**	30 Days (2-May-2009) 15,680.00 Dr		
Cr **HDFC Bank**			15,680.00
Narration:		15,680.00	15,680.00

F-11A: Payment Voucher

Bill-wise Details for : **D D Contractor** Upto: ₹ 15,680.00 Dr			
Type of Ref	Name	Due Date, or Credit Days (wef. 2-May-2009)	Amount Dr/Cr
Agst Ref	1	30 Days (2-May-2009)	15,680.00 Dr
			15,680.00 Dr

F-11B: Bill Allocation of Payment

05 Deposit of Tax to Government

Having deducted TDS, you have to deposit the TDS to government within stipulated time. TDS deposit has been explained earlier. Here we describe the Payment Voucher of Deposit of Balance Tax.

At Payment Voucher entry screen (F-12C), enter as follows:

- **Statutory Details**: Click *S:Stat Payment* button (and select TDS) to get *Statutory Payment* Screen (F-12A). At *Statutory Payment* Screen (F-12A), enter the details as explained earlier.
- **Bank Account**: At Header (F-12C), select the Bank Account through which the Payment is made
- **TDS Account**: At Particulars column (F-12C), select the TDS Account to get TDS Details screen (F-12D). The Pending Reference details would be shown. Select them one by one as explained earlier. The Bills selected at *TDS Details* screen (F-12D) would be carried and shown in Main voucher screen (F-12C)
- **Payment Details**: At *Provide Details* (F-12C), set *Yes* to get the Payment Details screen (F-12B). Enter the details as explained earlier (F-1C/01-03).

Statutory Payment	
Type of Duty/Tax	: TDS
Auto Fill Statutory Payment	? Yes
Deducted Till Date	: 1-7-2009
Section	: 194C
Nature of Payment	: Payments to Contractors (Other Than Advertisement)
Deductee Status	: Non Company
Cash/Bank	:

F-12A: Statutory Details

Payment Details

From Date : 1-Apr-2009
To Date : 1-Jul-2009

(Note: This payment belongs to the above Quarter)

Cheque/DD No : 123456

Name of Bank : HDFC Bank
Bank Account Number : 001234567890
Branch Name : Bowbazar
BSR Code : 700123456

Challan No. : 1234
Challan Date : 1-7-09

(Note: All the above details will be used in Challan, Forms & Returns)

F-12B: Payment Details

Accounting Voucher Creation — ABC Academy 9-10 — Ctrl + M

Payment No. 12 — 1-Jul-2009

Statutory Payment for : TDS

Account : **HDFC Bank**

Particulars		Amount
TDS From Contractors		**1,320.00**
Agst Ref Jrnl / 1-1	400.00 Dr	
Income Tax	*400.00 Dr*	
Surcharge		
Education Cess		
Secondary Education Cess		
Agst Ref Purc / 2-1	920.00 Dr	
Income Tax	*920.00 Dr*	
Surcharge		
Education Cess		
Secondary Education Cess		

Provide Details : Yes

Narration: — 1,320.00

F-12C: Tax Deposit Payment Voucher

TDS Details

Type of Ref	Name	Nature of Payment	Paid Amount
Agst Ref	**Jrnl / 1-1**	Payments to Contractors (Other Than Advertisement)	**400.00 Dr**
	Income Tax	*400.00 Dr*	
	Surcharge		
	Education Cess		
	Secondary Education Cess		
Agst Ref	**Purc / 2-1**	Payments to Contractors (Other Than Advertisement)	**920.00 Dr**
	Income Tax	*920.00 Dr*	
	Surcharge		
	Education Cess		
	Secondary Education Cess		
(Note: Part bill payment will be considered as lower deduction in the E-returns)			
Total			**1,320.00 Dr**

F-12D: TDS Details

06 Challan Printing

Having entered the Payment Voucher for TDS desposit to Government (F-12C), you may print Challan as explained earlier

On entry of TDS payment voucher (F-12C), click P:*Print* button to get the *Payment Voucher Printing* screen (like F-2A / 08-03), to print TDS Challan (F-13A) / Payment Advice (if required), as explained earlier

T.D.S. TAX CHALLAN — Single Copy (to be sent to ZAO)

CHALLAN No./ITNS 281

Tax Applicable (Tick one)*
TAX DEDUCTED AT SOURCE FROM
(0020) COMPANY DEDUCTEES [ ] (0021) NON-COMPANY DEDUCTEES [✓]

Assessment Year 2010-11

Tax Deduction Account No. (T.A.N.): ACGFD1234E

Full Name: ABC ACADEMY

Complete Address with City & State: 99, Airport Rd, Kolkata 700 098, W Bengal

West Bengal

Tel. No. 551234 — Pin 700 098

Type of Payment — Code * 94C

TDS Payable by Taxpayer (200) [✓]

TDS Regular Assessment (Raised by I.T. Dept.) (400) [ ]

FOR USE IN RECEIVING BANK
Debit to A/c / Cheque credited on
DD MM YY

DETAILS OF PAYMENTS — Amount (in Rs. Only)

	Amount
Income Tax	1,320.00
Surcharge	
Education Cess	
Interest	
Penalty	
Total	1,320.00

SPACE FOR BANK SEAL

Total (in words):

CRORES	LACS	THOUSANDS	HUNDREDS	TENS	UNITS
Zero	Zero	One	Three	Two	Zero

Rs. 1,320.00

Paid in Cash/ Debit to A/c /Cheque No. 123456 — Dated

Drawn on HDFC Bank - Salt Lake
(Name of the Bank and Branch)

Date : — Signature of person making payment

Tear Here

Taxpayers Counterfoil (To be filled up by taxpayer)

TAN ACGFD1234E

Received from ABC ACADEMY
(Name)

Cash/ Debit to A/c /Cheque No. 123456 — For Rs. 1,320

Rs. (in words) One Thousand Three Hundred Twenty Only.

Drawn on HDFC Bank - Salt Lake
(Name of the Bank and Branch)

Non Company(0021) Deductees

on account of Tax Deducted at Source (TDS) from 94C for the Assessment Year 2010-11

SPACE FOR BANK SEAL

Rs. 1,320.00

F-13A: Tax Deposit Challan

07 Form 16A

Having deposited the TDS, you may print Form 16A as explained earlier

At TDS Returns Menu (F- 4A / 08-04), select *Print Form 16A* to get TDS Form 16A Printing screen (F-14A). Fill up the data to print the Form 16A (F-14B).

Report Titles

TDS Form16A

Name : S K Surya
Son/Daughter of : P K Chandra
Designation : Proprietor
Print as Previous Format : No
Nature of Payment : Payments to Contractors (Other Than Advertisement)
From (blank for beginning) : 1-4-2009
To (blank for end) : 1-7-2009
Challan Date Till :
Type of Copy : Default
Certificate No : 12345
Print Total : No

Place : KOLKATA
Date : 1-Jul-2009

Quarter — **Acknowledgeme**
Apr-Jun : Apr - Jun
Jul-Sep :
Oct-Dec :
Jan-Mar :

CIT(TDS) Details
Name : A B BARDHAN
Address : BOWBAZAR
City : KOLKATA
Pin Code : 700012

F-14A: Form 16 A Printing screen

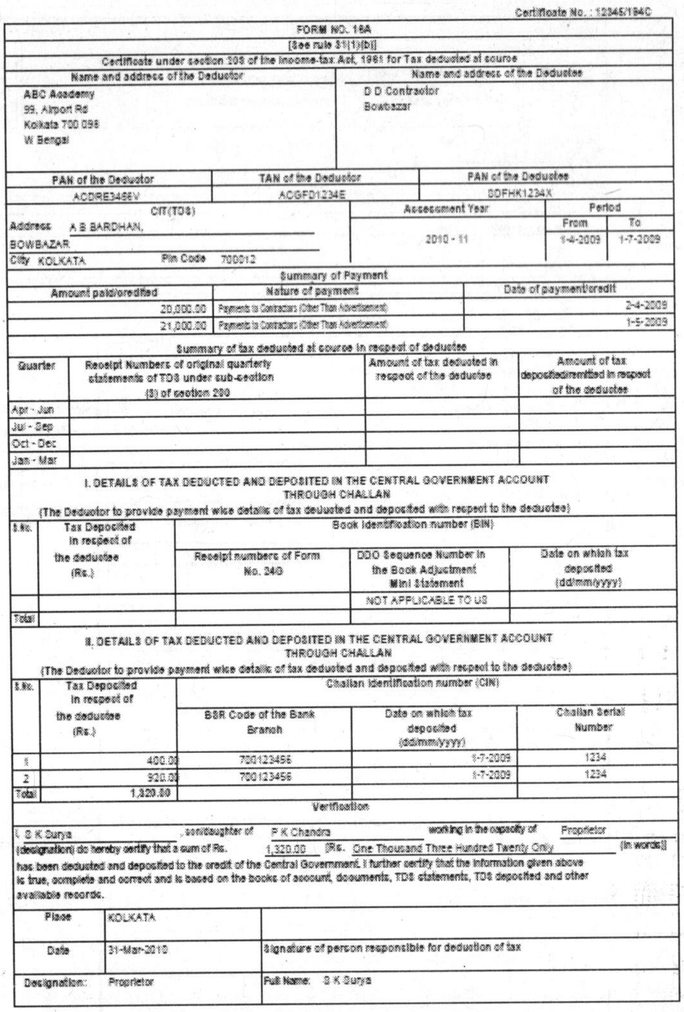

Certificate No. : 12345/194C

FORM NO. 16A				
[See rule 31(1)(b)]				
Certificate under section 203 of the Income-tax Act, 1961 for Tax deducted at source				
Name and address of the Deductor		Name and address of the Deductee		
ABC Academy 99, Airport Rd Kolkata 700 098 W Bengal		D D Contractor Bowbazar		
PAN of the Deductor	TAN of the Deductor	PAN of the Deductee		
ACDRE3456V	ACGFD1234E	SDFHK1234X		
CIT(TDS)		Assessment Year	Period	
Address A B BARDHAN, BOWBAZAR City KOLKATA Pin Code 700012		2010 - 11	From 1-4-2009	To 1-7-2009

Summary of Payment

Amount paid/credited	Nature of payment	Date of payment/credit
20,000.00	Payments to Contractors (Other Than Advertisement)	2-4-2009
21,000.00	Payments to Contractors (Other Than Advertisement)	1-5-2009

Summary of tax deducted at source in respect of deductee

Quarter	Receipt Numbers of original quarterly statements of TDS under sub-section (3) of section 200	Amount of tax deducted in respect of the deductee	Amount of tax deposited/remitted in respect of the deductee
Apr - Jun			
Jul - Sep			
Oct - Dec			
Jan - Mar			

I. DETAILS OF TAX DEDUCTED AND DEPOSITED IN THE CENTRAL GOVERNMENT ACCOUNT THROUGH CHALLAN

(The Deductor to provide payment wise details of tax deducted and deposited with respect to the deductee)

S.No.	Tax Deposited in respect of the deductee (Rs.)	Book Identification number (BIN)		
		Receipt numbers of Form No. 24G	DDO Sequence Number in the Book Adjustment Mini Statement	Date on which tax deposited (dd/mm/yyyy)
			NOT APPLICABLE TO US	
Total				

II. DETAILS OF TAX DEDUCTED AND DEPOSITED IN THE CENTRAL GOVERNMENT ACCOUNT THROUGH CHALLAN

(The Deductor to provide payment wise details of tax deducted and deposited with respect to the deductee)

S.No.	Tax Deposited in respect of the deductee (Rs.)	Challan Identification number (CIN)		
		BSR Code of the Bank Branch	Date on which tax deposited (dd/mm/yyyy)	Challan Serial Number
1	400.00	700123456	1-7-2009	1234
2	920.00	700123456	1-7-2009	1234
Total	1,320.00			

Verification

I, S K Surya, son/daughter of P K Chandra working in the capacity of Proprietor (designation) do hereby certify that a sum of Rs. 1,320.00 [Rs. One Thousand Three Hundred Twenty Only (in words)] has been deducted and deposited to the credit of the Central Government. I further certify that the information given above is true, complete and correct and is based on the books of account, documents, TDS statements, TDS deposited and other available records.

Place	KOLKATA	
Date	31-Mar-2010	Signature of person responsible for deduction of tax
Designation:	Proprietor	Full Name: S K Surya

F- 14B: Form 16A: TDS Certificate of the Party

08 Form 26Q Return

Form 26Q Return has been explained earlier. At TDS Returns Printing Menu, select Form 26Q and Form 26Q Annexure to print Form 26Q and Form 26Q Annexure (F-15A).

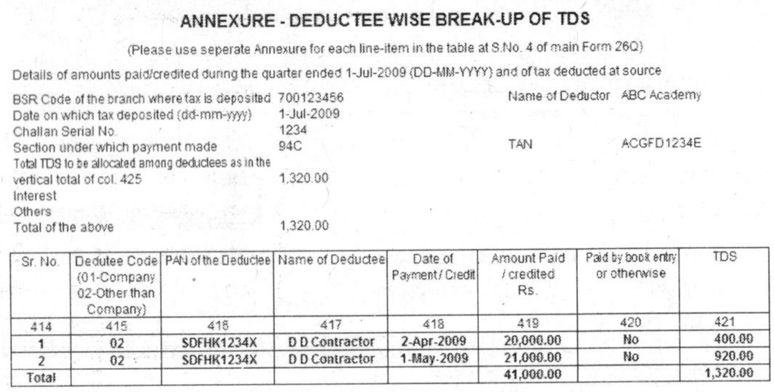

ANNEXURE - DEDUCTEE WISE BREAK-UP OF TDS

(Please use seperate Annexure for each line-item in the table at S.No. 4 of main Form 26Q)

Details of amounts paid/credited during the quarter ended 1-Jul-2009 (DD-MM-YYYY) and of tax deducted at source

BSR Code of the branch where tax is deposited 700123456 — Name of Deductor ABC Academy
Date on which tax deposited (dd-mm-yyyy) 1-Jul-2009
Challan Serial No. 1234
Section under which payment made 94C — TAN ACGFD1234E
Total TDS to be allocated among deductees as in the vertical total of col. 425 1,320.00
Interest
Others
Total of the above 1,320.00

Sr. No.	Dedutee Code (01-Company 02-Other than Company)	PAN of the Deductee	Name of Deductee	Date of Payment / Credit	Amount Paid / credited Rs.	Paid by book entry or otherwise	TDS
414	415	416	417	418	419	420	421
1	02	SDFHK1234X	D D Contractor	2-Apr-2009	20,000.00	No	400.00
2	02	SDFHK1234X	D D Contractor	1-May-2009	21,000.00	No	920.00
Total					41,000.00		1,320.00

F-15A: Form 26Q Annexure

This shows a complete cycle of TDS Deduction from Bill, Payment of Service Provider, Deposit of TDS to Government and Printing of related Returns.

09 Payment of Interest / Penalty along with TDS

If the TDS deposit is delayed (or remain unpaid), in addition to the TDS, Interest & Penalty is also to be made alongwith TDS Deposit.

09.01 Interest / Penalty Ledger Accounts

Expense Leger Account creation has been explained earlier. In the same way, create Interest (F-16A) / & Penalty (F-16B) Ledger Accounts.

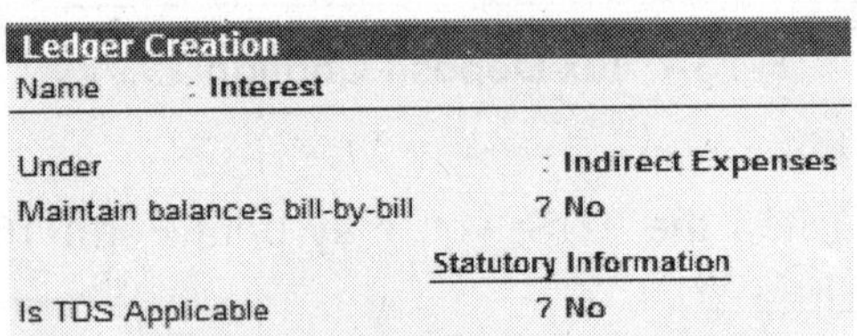

Ledger Creation
Name : Interest
Under : Indirect Expenses
Maintain balances bill-by-bill ? No
Statutory Information
Is TDS Applicable ? No

F-16A: Interest Ledger Account cretaion

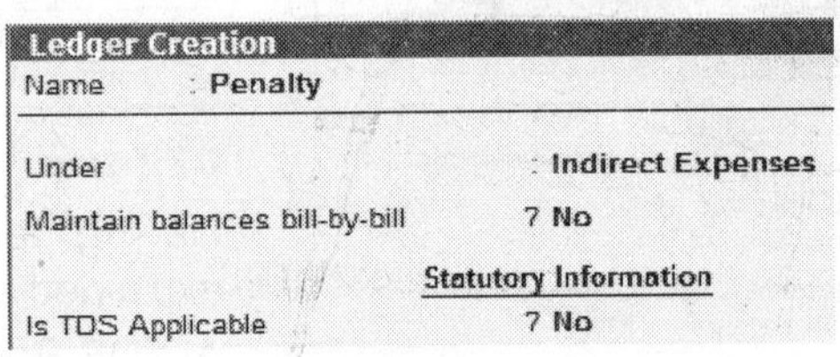

Ledger Creation
Name : Penalty
Under : Indirect Expenses
Maintain balances bill-by-bill ? No
Statutory Information
Is TDS Applicable ? No

F-16B: Penalty Ledger Account cretaion

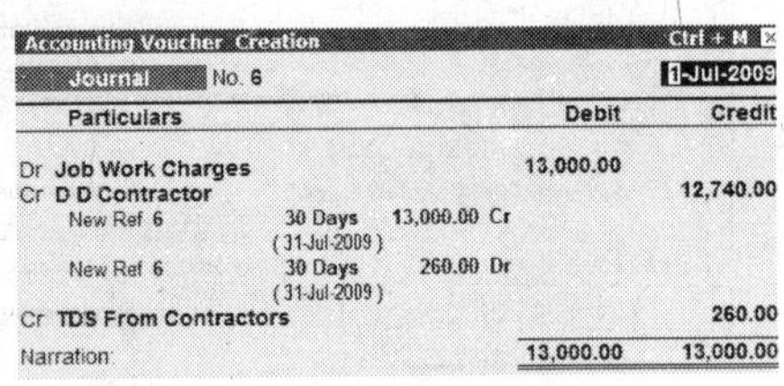

Accounting Voucher Creation — Ctrl + M
Journal No. 6 — 1-Jul-2009

Particulars			Debit	Credit
Dr Job Work Charges			13,000.00	
Cr D D Contractor				12,740.00
New Ref 6	30 Days (31-Jul-2009)	13,000.00 Cr		
New Ref 6	30 Days (31-Jul-2009)	260.00 Dr		
Cr TDS From Contractors				260.00
Narration:			13,000.00	13,000.00

F-17A: Expenses Booking Journal Voucher

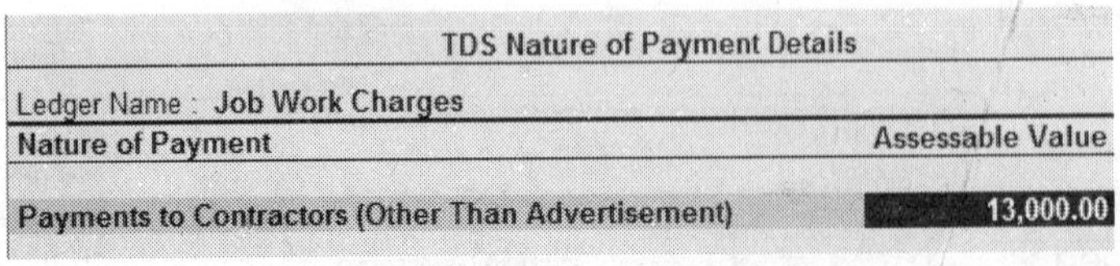

TDS Nature of Payment Details
Ledger Name : Job Work Charges

Nature of Payment	Assessable Value
Payments to Contractors (Other Than Advertisement)	13,000.00

F-17B: TDS Nature of Payment

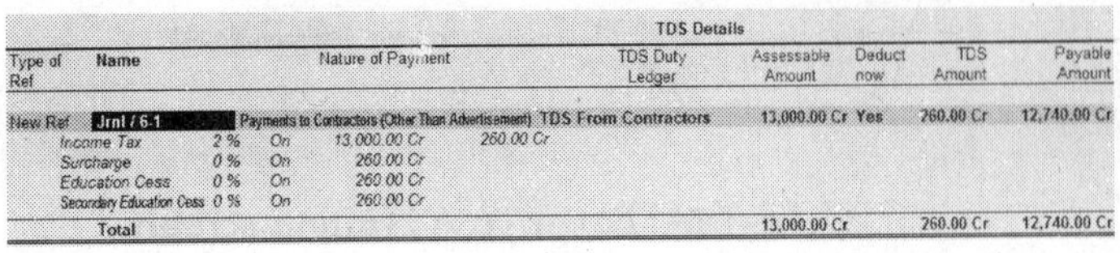

TDS Details

Type of Ref	Name	Nature of Payment	TDS Duty Ledger	Assessable Amount	Deduct now	TDS Amount	Payable Amount
New Ref	Jrnl / 6-1	Payments to Contractors (Other Than Advertisement)	TDS From Contractors	13,000.00 Cr	Yes	260.00 Cr	12,740.00 Cr
	Income Tax 2 % On 13,000.00 Cr 260.00 Cr						
	Surcharge 0 % On 260.00 Cr						
	Education Cess 0 % On 260.00 Cr						
	Secondary Education Cess 0 % On 260.00 Cr						
	Total			13,000.00 Cr		260.00 Cr	12,740.00 Cr

F-17C: TDS Details

09.02 Expense Booking /TDS Deduction voucher

Create the Journal Voucher for Expense Booking & corresponding deduction of TDS, as explained (F-17A to F-17D)

09.03 Payment Voucher for TDS Deposit

Now enter the Payment Voucher for Deposit of TDS alongwith Interest & Penalty, for late deposit

At Payment Voucher entry (in single mode entry) screen (F-18F), enter as follows:

Cash Bank Account: At the header, select the Cash / Bank A/c from which payment made.

Bill-wise Details for : **D D Contractor** Upto: ₹ **12,740.00 Cr**				
Type of Ref	Name	Due Date, or Credit Days (wef: 1-Jul-2009)	Amount	Dr/ Cr
New Ref	6	30 Days (31-Jul-2009)	13,000.00	Cr
New Ref	6	30 Days (31-Jul-2009)	260.00	Dr
(Note: 'Breaking of above bills helps to identify the original bill amount in the outstanding statement')			12,740.00	Cr

F-17D: Bill Allocation details

Ledger Account details: At *Particulars column,* enter as follows*:*

- **TDS Ledger**: Select *TDS* Account to get *TDS Details* screen (F-18A). At *TDS Details* (F-18A), select Agst Ref. The pending Ref & corresponding details are shown at Tax Details (F-18C). Select the respective details from *Tax Details* screen (F-18C), The TDS Amount is carried at Tax Details screen (F-18A) and at the main voucher entry screen (F-18F).
- **Interest Ledger**: Select *Interest* Account. Select *Interest* at payment Type list (F-18D). Enter Interest Amount
- **Penalty Ledger**: Select *Penalty* Account. Select *Penalty* at payment Type (F-18E). Enter Penalty Amount

Payment Details: After entry of Ledger Accounts, at main voucher entry screen (F-18F), at *Provide Details*, set Yes to get Payment details screen (F-18B). Enter the Payment Details and then get back to the main voucher entry screen (F-18F)

Enter Voucher Narration. Save the Payment Voucher.

TDS Details			
Type of Ref	Name	Nature of Payment	Paid Amount
Agst Ref	**Jrnl / 6-1**	Payments to Contractors (Other Than Advertisement)	
	Income Tax	*260.00 Dr*	
	Surcharge		
	Education Cess		
	Secondary Education Cess		
(Note: Part bill payment will be considered as lower deduction in the E-returns)			
	Total		260,00 Cr

F-18A: TDS Details

Payment Details

From Date	: 1-Apr-2009
To Date	: 1-Jul-2009
(Note: This payment belongs to the above Quarter)	
Cheque/DD No	: 345678
Name of Bank	: HDFC Bank
Bank Account Number	: 00675483456
Branch Name	: Bowbazar
BSR Code	: 700453234
Challan No.	: 345
Challan Date	: 1-12-09

(Note: All the above details will be used in Challan, Forms & Returns)

F-18B: Payment Details

Tax Details					
Ref. Name	Nature of Payment	Party Name	Deductee Status	Deduction Date	Pending Amount
Jrnl / 6-1	Payments to Contractors (Other Than Advertisement)	*D D Contractor*	*Non Company*	*1-Jul-2009*	*260.00*

F-18C: Tax Details

Payment Type : **Interest**

Payment Type
- Not Applicable
- Interest
- Others
- Penalty
- Upward Rounding

F-18D: Interest Payment Type

Payment Type : **Penalty**

Payment Type
- Not Applicable
- Interest
- Others
- Penalty
- Upward Rounding

F-18E: Penalty Payment Type

Accounting Voucher Creation Ctrl + M

Payment No. 14 **1-Dec-2009**

Account : **HDFC Bank**

Particulars	Amount
TDS From Contractors	260.00
Interest	30.00
Penalty	100.00
Provide Details : **Yes**	
Narration:	390.00
Ch. No. : 345678	

F-18F: TDS Payment Voucher with Interest & Penalty

T.D.S. TAX CHALLAN Single Copy (to be sent to ZAO)

CHALLAN No./ITNS 281

Tax Applicable (Tick one)*
TAX DEDUCTED AT SOURCE FROM
(0020) COMPANY DEDUCTEES ☐ (0021) NON-COMPANY DEDUCTEES ☑

Assessment Year 2010-11

Tax Deduction Account No. (T.A.N.) A C G F D 1 2 3 4 E

Full Name: A B C A C A D E M Y

Complete Address with City & State: 9 9 , Airport Rd, Kolkata 700 098, W Bengal

West Bengal

Tel. No. 651234 Pin 700 098

Type of Payment Code * 9 4 C

TDS Payable by Taxpayer (200) ☑

TDS Regular Assessment (Raised by I.T. Dept.) (400) ☐

FOR USE IN RECEIVING BANK

Debit to A/c / Cheque credited on

D D M M Y Y

DETAILS OF PAYMENTS

	Amount (in Rs. Only)
Income Tax	260.00
Surcharge	
Education Cess	
Interest	30.00
Penalty	100.00
Total	390.00

Total (in words)

CRORES	LACS	THOUSANDS	HUNDREDS	TENS	UNITS
Zero	Zero	Zero	Three	Nine	Zero

SPACE FOR BANK SEAL

Rs. 390.00

Paid in Cash/ Debit to A/c /Cheque No. 123456 Dated 1-Dec-2009

Drawn on H D F C Bank - Bowbazar
(Name of the Bank and Branch)

Date : 1-Dec-2009 Signature of person making payment

Tear Here

Taxpayers Counterfoil (To be filled up by taxpayer)

TAN A C G F D 1 2 3 4 E

Received from A B C A C A D E M Y
(Name)

Cash/ Debit to A/c /Cheque No. 123456 For Rs. 390

Rs. (in words) Three Hundred Ninety Only.

Drawn on H D F C Bank - Bowbazar
(Name of the Bank and Branch)

Non Company(0021) Deductees

on account of Tax Deducted at Source (TDS) from 9 4 C for the Assessment Year 2 0 1 0 - 1 1

SPACE FOR BANK SEAL

Rs. 390.00

F-19A: TDS Challan with Interest & Penalty Payment

09.04 TDS Challan Printing for Payment with Interest & Penalty

Having created the Payment Voucher of TDS, Penalty & Interest to government, you may print the Challan as described earlier.

On entry of TDS payment voucher, click *P:Print* button to get the *Payment Voucher Printing* screen (like F-2A / 08-03), to print TDS Challan (F-19A) / Payment Advice (if required), as explained earlier

This shows a complete cycle of TDS Deduction from Bill, Payment of Service Provider, Deposit of TDS to Government and Printing of Challan.

FAQ: Frequently Asked Questions

FAQ-1: What are the steps & process of TDS Deduction at Lower rate / Zero Rate

Ans: Sometimes, a Party may be allowed to get TDS Deducted at lower Rate by the *Assessing Officer.* In such case, the Assessing Officer issues a certificate for deduction of Tax at Lower Rate (herein referred as *Concession Certificate*) than the relevant rate specified under the section

- Set the Option at Party Ledger Configuration (F-1A)
- Set the Option at Party Ledger (F-2A)
- Set the Option at Advanced TDS Entries (F-2B)
- Enter he deals at Zero / Lower Deduction rates screen (F-3B)
- Enter Journal Voucher with Zero / Lower Rate (F-4A, 5A / 5B)

Part 2

Tax Collected at Source (TCS)

In this Part, we discuss about the compliance of TCS (Tax Collected at Source), regarding charging of TCS in Bills, deposit of TCS to Government and filing of Statutory Returns of TCS.

TCS Set Up describes the steps of activation / set up of TCS, and creation of Masers relating to TCS

Sales Invoice describes creation / Printing of Invoice charging TCS

TCS Deposit describes voucher for deposit of TCS and TCS Challan Printing

TCS Reports describes reports relating to TCS Payable, TCS Challan Reconcilliation and various Statutory Returns relating to TCS.

TCS Set Up

01 Tax Collected at Source (TCS)

TCS means *Tax Collected at Source* by the seller (or lessor, licensor – commonly referred as *Collector*) from the buyer/ lessee (collectee/ payee), on sale of specified goods (defined u/s 206C of the Income Tax Act, 1961).

01.01 Goods on which TCS is Applicable

TCS is applicable on following kinds of goods:

Alcoholic liquor for human consumption including Indian Made Foreign Liquor (IMFL), Tendu leaves, Timber obtained under a forest lease, Timber obtained by any mode other than under a forest lease, Any other forest produce not being Timber or Tendu, Scrap (usable materials from manufacture process)), Licensing or leasing of Parking Lot, Toll Plaza, Mining and Quarrying.

01.02 Types of Collector

For the purpose of TCS, the Sellers (or Collectors) are classified as

- Central Government
- State Government
- Local Authority
- Statutory Corporation or Authority
- Company
- Partnership Firm
- Co-operative Society
- Individual/HUF (whose turnover exceeds the threshold limits specified u/s 44AB (a) / 44AB (b) of I Tax Act, 1961, during the previous year.

01.03 Excluded Buyers

The following types of Buyers are excluded from TCS

- Public Sector Companies
- Central Government
- State Government
- Embassy of High Commission, Consulate and other Trade Representation of a Foreign State
- Any Club, such as social clubs, sports clubs and the like

01.04 Payment of TCS to the Government

The seller, lessor or licensor charges the tax from the buyer (lessee/ licensee) and deposits with the Government Account.

01.05 TCS Certificate

The collector of Tax must submit a certificate of collection of TCS in Form No-27D within 7th of the following half year (30th Sep & 31st Mar), within one month.

01.06 TCS Exemptions

TCS may be totally or partly exempted in following cases:

- **Full Exemption**: TCS may not be collected on goods used for manufacturing or processing and not trading, on submitting a declaration by the buyer in Form 27C. A copy of the declaration has to be given to the collector of TCS, who will submit the copy to the authorities concerned on or before the seventh day of the following month.
- **Lower Rate**: If the Total Income of the buyer is lower than the applicable limit of TCS, the buyer (Collectee) may apply to the Assessing Officer (AO) for a lower rate (in Form No.13). The AO on being satisfied, may issue a certificate, specifying the lower rate of TCS. On submitting a copy of such certificate to the collector, the collector will charge TCS at the lower rate as specified in the certificate.

02 Filing of TCS Return

TCS Returns are to be filed as follows:

- **Quarterly Returns**: The Quarterly returns for first 3 quarters (i.e Q/e June, September & December) are to be filed in Form 27EQ within 15th of following month of the Quarter. For the last quarter (i.e Q/e March), the Returns are to be filed on or before April 30.
- **Annual Returns**: Annual Returns are to be filed in Form 27E by June 30 of the following financial year.

02.01 Electronic Filing of TCS Return

Every Corporate and Government collector must file TCS returns in electronic form (referred as e-TCS). Other Collectors may file TCS Returns either in electronic or in physical form. NSDL collects the e-TCS returns from the Collectors on behalf of the Income Tax Department.

03 TCS Activation

Click *F11: Features> Statutory and Taxation* to get *Statutory & Taxation* screen.

At *Statutory & Taxation screen* (F-1A), set:

- **Activate TCS**: At *Enable Tax Collect at source*, set Yes
- **TCS Details**: Having set Yes at *Enable Tax Collect at source, at* set *Yes* at *set/Alter TCS Details* (F-1A), set Yes to get *Company Deductor/ Collector Details* (F-1B)

Enable Tax Collected at Source (TCS) ? **Yes**
Set/Alter TCS Details ? **Yes**

F-1A: TCS Statutory details

Company Deductor/Collector Details

Tax Deduction and Collection Account Number	: **ABCD12345X**
Head Office TAN Number	:
Income Tax Circle/Ward (TDS/TCS)	: **KOL 67(9)**
Deductor/Collector Type	: **Others**
Is Proprietorship Firm	? **No**
Name of person responsible	: **Mohan Roy**
Son/daughter of	: **Pabir Roy**
Designation	: **Manager**

(Note: All the above details will be used in Challan, Forms & Returns)

F-1B: TCS Details entry

List Of Company Type
Government
Others

F-1C: Company Type List

Error
Eh ?
Invalid TAN Structure.
(Format should be of
4 Alpha, 5 Numeric and 1 Alpha)
E.g.: AAAA12345A

F-1D: TAN Error Message

03.01 Deductor / Collector Details

At *Company Deductor/ Collector Details* screen (F-1B), enter the following details:

- **Tax Collection No (TAN)**: At *Tax Deduction & Collection Account Number*, Enter the 10 digit TCS Number (4 Alpha, 5 Numeric, 1 Alpha) allotted by the I Tax Deptt. In case of wrong number pattern entry, an error message will be displayed (F-1D).
- **Head Office TAN**: At *Head Office TAN Number*, enter the Head Office TAN, if any, else leave blank
- **Income Tax Circle / Ward (TDS/TCS)**: At *Income Tax Circle / Ward (TDS/TCS),* enter the Income Tax Circle / Ward # to which the organisation is being assessed under I Tax Act.
- **Collector Type**: At *Deduction / Collector Type,* select the Type of the organisation from the list (F-1C)
- **Officer Name**: At *Name of the Person Responsible*, enter the name of the officer in the organisation responsible for filing the return under Income Tax Act
    - o **Father Name:** At *Son / Daughter of*, enter the Officer's Father's name as stated above
- **Designation**: At *Designation*, enter the Designation of the named officer.

The data entered in the Form will be carried and printed in Reports / Challans etc

04 TCS Statutory Lists

At *GoT>Display*, select *Statutory Info* to get *Statutory Info Menu* (F-2A), showing the Statutory Details, for information (you do not need to enter /modify anything)

Gateway of Tally ....
Display Menu ....
Statutory Info.
TCS Nature of Goods
Collectee Types
Quit

F-2A: Statutory Info menu

List of Collectee Types
Artificial Juridical Person
Association of Persons
Body of Individuals
Company - Non Resident
Company - Resident
Co-Operative Society
Individual/HUF - Non Resident
Individual/HUF - Resident
Local Authority
Partnership Firm

F-3A:TCS Collectee Type List

Collectee Type Display ABC

Name	: **Individual/HUF - Resident**
Residential Status	: **Resident**
Collectee Status	: **Non Company**
Active	? **Yes**
Module Type	: **Both**

Collectee TCS Details

Applicable From	Surcharge Exemption Limit	Surcharge	Addl Surcharge (Cess)	Addl Education (Cess)
1-4-2004	10,00,000.00	10 %	2 %	0 %
1-4-2007	10,00,000.00	10 %	2 %	1 %
1-4-2009		0 %	0 %	0 %

F-3B:Collectee Type Details

At *Statutory Info* Menu (F-2A), select:

- **TCS Goods**: *TCS Nature of Goods* to get *TCS Goods Type List* (F-4A).
    - o **TCS Rates**: Drill down through any Item at any Goods at *TCS Goods List* (F-4A), to get TCS Goods Rate List (F-4B) showing the TCS Rate applicable for the respective Good, for each type of Collectee
- **TCS Collectee:** *Collectee Type* to get *TCS Collectee Type* List (F-3A).
    - o **TCS Surcharge Rates**: Drill down through any Collectee Type at *TCS Collectee Type List* (F-3A), to get *Collectee Type Details* (F-3B), showing the TCS Surcharge Rate applicable for the respective Collectee Type.

List of TCS Types
Alcoholic Liquor for Human Consumption
Any Other Forest Produce (Not Being Tendu Leaves)
Bullion Or Jewellery
Contractors/Licensee/Lease Relating to Mine/Quarry
Contractors/Licensee/Lease Relating to Parking Lots
Contractors/Licensee/Lease Relating to Toll Plaza
Minerals, Being Coal Or Lignite Or Iron Ore
Scrap
Tendu Leaves
Timber Obtained by Any Mode Other Than Forest Lease
Timber Obtained Under Forest Lease

F-4A: TCS Goods Type List

TCS Nature Of Goods Display		
Name : **Tendu Leaves**		
Section : 206C		
Payment Code : 6CI		
Tax Rate Details		
Collectee Type	Applicable From	Rate
Association of Persons	1-4-2004	5 %
Body of Individuals	1-4-2004	5 %
Company - Non Resident	1-4-2004	5 %
Company - Resident	1-4-2004	5 %
Co-Operative Society	1-4-2004	5 %
Individual/HUF - Non Resident	1-4-2004	5 %
Individual/HUF - Resident	1-4-2004	5 %
Local Authority	1-4-2004	5 %
Partnership Firm	1-4-2004	5 %

F-4B: TCS Goods Rate List

05 Collectee Ledger creation

Customer Ledger creation has been explained earlier. Here we discuss about features relating to TCS for ledger creation of Customer (Collectee).

At *Gateway of Tally* select *Accounts Info > Ledgers > Create* to get Ledger Creation screen (F-5A). Here we discuss about additional info to be entered, if any, relating to TCS.

Ledger Alteration	
Name	: **A K Traders**
Under	: **Sundry Debtors** *(Current Assets)*
Maintain balances bill-by-bill	? **Yes**
Default Credit Period	: 20 Days
Inventory values are affected	? **No**
	Statutory Information
Is TCS Applicable	? **Yes**

F-5A: Collectee Ledger Creation

TCS Details	
Buyer/Lessee	: **Individual/HUF - Resident**
Is Lower/No Collection Applicable	? **Yes**
Section Number	: 206C
TCS Lower Rate (%)	: 2 %
Ignore Surcharge Exemption Limit	? **No**

F-5B: TCS Details Entry of Collectee

05.01 Collectee Ledger TCS Activation

At Collectee Ledger creation screen (F-5A), set *Yes* at *Is TCS Applicable* to get TCS details screen for the Collectee (F-5B). At *TCS details* screen (F-5B), enter as follows:

- **Collectee Type**: At *Buyer / Lessee*, select the appropriate Collectee Type from the list (F-3A)
- **Tax Relief**: At *Is Lower / No Tax Rate applicable:*
  - o **Relief**: Set *Yes* where Lower Rate Tax or Tax Exemption (No Tax) is applicable
  - o **No Relief**: Set *No* if Tax is collected at Normal Rate

  In case of *Tax Relief* (where *Yes* is set at *Is Lower / No Tax Rate applicable)*, enter the following details further:
  - o **Section Number**: At *Section Number*, enter the relevant section number of Income Tax Act 1961, under which the Relief is made available to the Party
  - o **Lower Rate**: At *Rate of TCS*, Enter the applicable TCS Rate for the Party (0 in case of total exemption)
- **Surcharge Limit**: *At Ignore Surcharge Limit* (it appears for a few specified Collectee Types only), set,
  - o *Yes* to ignore the threshold limit of Surcharge
  - o *No* to Consider the threshold limit of Surcharge

06 TCS Ledger

We have discussed Ledger Creation earlier. Create a TCS Ledger (Ledger Account to which TCS charged in Sales Invoice is booked) under Duties & Taxes Group (like TDS Ledger). Crerate separate ledger for each type of TCS Goods as the ledger is to be linked with specific TCS Goods Type

Here, we discuss about specific points relating to TCS Ledger.

Ledger Creation	
Name	: **TCS (Tendu Leaves)**
Under	: **Duties & Taxes** *(Current Liabilities)*
Type of Duty/Tax	: **TCS**
Nature Of Goods/Contract/License/Lease	: **Tendu Leaves**
Inventory values are affected	? **No**

F-6A: TCS Ledger Creation

At Ledger Creation screen (F-6A), enter as follows:

- **Parent Group**: At *Under*, select Duties & Taxes Account Group or its sub Group from the list of Groups
- **Duty Type**: At *Type of Duty / Tax*, select TCS from the list (F-6B)

Types of Duty/Tax
Excise
Others
TCS

F-6B: Duty Type List

- **TCS Type**: At *Nature of Goods/Contact/License/Lease*, select *TCS Type* from the list (F-4A)
- **Inventory Values Link**: At *Inventory Values are affected*, set *No*

> **Note:** ***Sales & Purchase Ledger***: *Create Sales & Purchase Ledger as usual. There is no special information required to be given specifically for TCS in Sales & Purchase Ledger*

07 TCS Applicable Stock Item Creation

Stock Item creation has been discussed earlier.

At Stock Item Creation screen (F-7A), at Tax *Information* section, at *TCS Nature of Goods*, select the Goods Type from the *TCS Goods Type* list (F-4A).

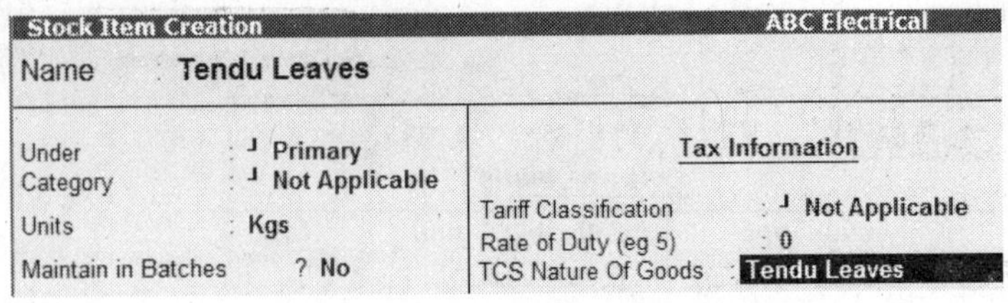

F-7A: TCS Stock Item creation

01 Sales Invoice Entry with TCS details

Sales Invoice Entry has been discussed earlier. Here, we discuss points specific to Sales with TCS,

Accounting Voucher Creation Ctrl + M

Sales No. 8 2-Oct-2009

Ref. : Friday

Party's A/c Name : **A K Traders**

Sales Ledger : **Sales**

Name of Item	Quantity	Rate	per	Amount
Tendu Leaves	1,200 Kgs	12.00	Kgs	14,400.00
TCS (Tendu Leaves)		5	%	720.00
Narration:	1,200 Kgs			*15,120.00*

F-1A: TCS Sales Voucher entry

TCS Details

TCS Party Ledger : A K Traders

Gross Amount : 14,400.00

Income Tax	: @	5 %	720.00
Surcharge	: @	0 %	
Cess	: @	0 %	
Addl Ed Cess	: @	0 %	
Total TCS	:		720.00

TCS - Bill Wise Detail for : TCS (Tendu Leaves)

Type of Ref	Name	Due Date, or Credit Days	Amount	Dr/ Cr
New Ref	Sale/8		720.00	Cr

F-1B: Invoice TCS Details

Allow Alteration of TCS Rate for Lower Collection ? **Yes**

F-1C: Invoice Entry Configuration

At Sales Invoice Entry screen (F-1A), having entered Party & Sales Ledger and the Stock Item details, as usual, select the TCS ledger to get the TCS details sub screen (F-1B). By default the Gross Amount and the default Rates of TCS are shown. However, you may change the Assessable Value. The Duty would be computed accordingly and carried to main screen in the Invoice against the TCS Ledger. To change TCS Rate, at Invoice Entry screen, click *F12:Configure* to get Invoice Entry Configuration screen. Set *Yes* at *Allow Alteration of TCS Rate for Lower Collection* (F-1C).

02 Invoicing with Lower / Zero TCS Rate

Some Parties (Collectee) are entitled to be charged at lower Rate (or Zero Rate). Here we explain the process of creation of Ledgers & Invoice with Tax Relief (Lower / Zero Rate).

Ledger Creation

Name : **P R Produce**

Under : **Sundry Debtors** *(Current Assets)*

Maintain balances bill-by-bill ? **Yes**
Default Credit Period : 30 Days
Inventory values are affected ? **No**

Statutory Information

Is TCS Applicable ? **Yes**

F-2A: Collectee Ledger creation

TCS Details

Buyer/Lessee : **Individual/HUF - Resident**
Is Lower/No Collection Applicable ? **Yes**
Section Number : **206C**
TCS Lower Rate (%) : **1 %**
Ignore Surcharge Exemption Limit ? **No**

F-2B: Collectee Ledger with Tax Relief

Ledger Alteration (Secondary)

Name : **TCS 1% (Tendu Leaves)**

Under : **Duties & Taxes** *(Current Liabilities)*

Type of Duty/Tax : **TCS**
Nature Of Goods/Contract/License/Lease: **Tendu Leaves**
Inventory values are affected ? **No**

F-3A: TCS Ledger with Lower Rate

Ledger Creation: Create the following Ledger Accounts

- **Collectee Ledger**: Party (Collectee) Ledger creation / alteration screen has been explained earlier (§05/02-01, F-5B/02-01). For Parties having been sanctioned Tax Relief ((Lower / Zero Rate), at TCS Details sub screen (F-2B) of Party (Collectee) Ledger creation / alteration screen (F-2A), at *Is Lower / No Tax Rate applicable*, set Yes and then enter the following details in respect of Lower Rate Applicable:
  - o **I Tax Section Number:** At *Section Number*, enter the *I Tax Section Number* and applicable *TCS Lower Rate* for the Party (enter zero at Rate if no TCS is to be charged).
  - o **Applicable TCS Rate:** At *TCS Lower Rate*, enter the applicable TCS Rate

- **TCS Ledger:** We have discussed TCS Ledger Creation earlier. Create a separate TCS Ledger for Lower Rate (F-3A), apart from the TCS Ledger for Normal Rate.

03 Sales Invoice Entry

Sales Invoice Entry with TCS has been explained earlier (§01). At Sales Invoice Entry (F-4A), after entry of Item details, select TCS Ledger Account to get TCS details screen (F-4B), which shows Tax Computation as per TCS Rates specified for Collectee Ledger.

Accounting Voucher Creation Ctrl + M

Sales No. 9 — 2-Oct-2009, Friday

Ref. :

Party's A/c Name : **P R Produce**

Sales Ledger : **Sales**

Name of Item	Quantity	Rate	per	Amount
Tendu Leaves	1,000 Kgs	12.00	Kgs	12,000.00
TCS 1% (Tendu Leaves)		1	%	120.00
Narration:	1,000 Kgs			*12,120.00*

F-4A: Sales with Tax Relief

TCS Details

TCS Party Ledger : P R Produce

Gross Amount : 12,000.00

Income Tax	@	1 %	120.00
Surcharge	@	0 %	
Cess	@	0 %	
Addl Ed Cess	@	0 %	
Total TCS			120.00

TCS - Bill Wise Detail for : TCS 1% (Tendu Leaves)

Type of Ref	Name	Due Date, or Credit Days	Amount	Dr/Cr
New Ref	Sale/9		120.00	Cr

F-4B: TCS details of Sales Invoice with lower TCS Rate

04 TCS Sales Invoice Printing

Sales Invoice Printing has been explained earlier. On entry of Sales Invoice, click P: *Print* button to get *Invoice Printing* Screen. At *Invoice Printing* screen, click *F12:Configure* to get *Invoice Printing Configuration* screen (F-5A). At *Invoice Printing Configuration* screen (F-5A), at *Print TCS details*, set *Yes*, to get TCS Invoice in Print (F-6A).

> **Note:** *At Printing screen Configuration (F-5A), at* Print TCS details, *set* Yes *to get TCS Invoice in Print (F-6A).*

Invoice Printing Configuration

Title of Document : **Excise Invoice**
(for Optional Voucher) : ***PROFORMA INVOICE***
Sub Title (if any) :

Height of Normal Invoice (inches)	: 10	Simple: 10
Width of Normal Invoice (inches)	: 7.50	Simple: 7.50
Space to leave on top (default 0.25)	: 0.25	Simple: 0.25
Space to leave on left (default 0.5)	: 0.50	Simple: 0.50

Print in Simple Format	? No	Print Serial No.	? No
Print Voucher Reference	? Yes	Print Part No.	? No
Print Order Details	? Yes	Print Quantity Column	? Yes
Print Terms of Payment and Delivery	? Yes	Print Alternate Quantity	? No
Print details of Despatch	? Yes	Print as separate Column	? No
Print TCS Details	? Yes	Print Actual Quantity Column	? No
Print Tax Analysis of Items	? Yes	Print Rate Column	? Yes
Print Company's PAN / Income Tax No.	? Yes	Print Batch Details	? No
Print Company's Tax Regn. Numbers	? Yes	Print Rate of Duty with Items	? No
Print Buyer's Tax Regn. Number	? Yes	Print Sub-Totals after each line	? No
Print Buyer's CST Regn. Number	? Yes	Print Narration	? No
Print Declaration	? Yes	Print Narration for each entry	? No
Print Customer's Signature	? No	Print Base Currency Symbol for Total	? Yes

Method to use for Party Name : **Name Only**
Method to use for Stock Item Name : **Name Only**
Print Bank Details ? **No**

Jurisdiction : **Kolkata**

Generated by : **This is a Computer Generated Invoice**

F-5A: Invoice Printing Configuration

Excise Invoice

ABC Electrical
27/C, Rasbihari Road
3rd Floor, Suit No.305
Kolkata-700019
E-Mail :nomail@kmail.com

Invoice No. 8	Dated 2-Oct-2009
Delivery Note	Mode/Terms of Payment 20 Days
Supplier's Ref.	Other Reference(s)
Buyer's Order No.	Dated
Despatch Document No.	Dated
Despatched through	Destination
Terms of Delivery	

Buyer
A K Traders
56,M.G.Road
Birla Apartment

Description of Goods	Quantity	Rate	per	Amount
Tendu Leaves	**1,200 Kgs**	12.00	Kgs	**14,400.00**
TCS (Tendu Leaves)		5	%	**720.00**
				15,120.00
Total	**1,200 Kgs**			**₹ 15,120.00**

Amount Chargeable (in words) *E & O.E*
Indian Rupees Fifteen Thousand One Hundred Twenty Only

Local Sales Tax No. : **ST8524970**
Inter State Sales Tax No. : **86531240**
Buyer's Local Sales Tax No. : **WB5864LD**
Buyer's CST No. : **123(C)**
Company's PAN : **ABPN5865K**

Declaration
We declare that this invoice shows the actual price of the goods described and that all particulars are true and correct.

for ABC Electrical

Authorised Signatory

SUBJECT TO KOLKATA JURISDICTION

This is a Computer Generated Invoice

F-6A: TCS Invoice in Print

05 TCS on Right to Use

We have discussed Invoice by Collector charging TCS in Sale Invoice of Goods. In the same way, A Collector granting Lease or License or transferring any right or interest (e.g in a parking lot, Toll plaza, Mine, Quarry etc) to another person, for Business, is liable to collect tax at source from the licensee or lessee at prescribed Rate.

The exclusive steps for TCS Invoice on Right to Use is explained next

05.01 Ledger Creation

Here we discuss about Ledger Creation related to TCS Voucher

- **TCS Ledger Creation:** We have already explained TCS Ledger Creation (§06/02-01). At TCS Ledger creation / alteration for Contracts (F-7A), enter as follows:
  - o **TCS Types**: At *Nature of Goods / Contract /License / Lease*, select the TCS Type from the list of TCS Types (F-4A/01-01).
- o **Inventory Link**: At *Inventory Values are Affected*, set *No* (as no Stock Item is involved)
- **TCS Collectee Ledger Creation:** We have already explained TCS Collectee Creation (F-5A/01-01),). In the same way, create Collectee Ledger (F-7B) and set the TCS details (F-7C), as explained earlier
  - o **Direct Income Ledger:** Instead of Sales Ledger creation, create Direct Income Ledger (F-7D). At *Inventory Values are Affected*, set *No* (as no Stock Item is involved)

Ledger Creation
Name : TCS 2% (Parking Lot)

Under : Duties & Taxes
(Current Liabilities)

Type of Duty/Tax : TCS
Nature Of Goods/Contract/License/Lease : Contractors/Licensee/Lease Relating to Parking Lots
Inventory values are affected ? No

F-7A: TCS Ledger (Contracts)

Ledger Creation
Name : ABC Agencies

Under : Sundry Debtors
(Current Assets)

Maintain balances bill-by-bill ? Yes
Default Credit Period : 30 Days
Inventory values are affected ? No

Statutory Information
Is TCS Applicable ? Yes

F-7B: Collectee Ledger for Contracts

TCS Details

Buyer/Lessee : Individual/HUF - Resident
Is Lower/No Collection Applicable ? No

Ignore Surcharge Exemption Limit ? No

F-7C: TCS details of Collectee Ledger for Contracts

Ledger Creation
Name : Parking Lot License

Under : Direct Incomes
Inventory values are affected ? No

F-7D: Direct Income Ledger

05.02 Sales Voucher Configuration

At *Sales Voucher Configuration* screen (*GoT >F12:Configure> Voucher,* click *F12:Configure,* or at Sales Voucher Entry screen, click *F12:Configure*), as described earlier (F-1/02-09/S1). Set Yes at *Allow Income Accounts in Sales Voucher* (F-8A), to enable selection of Direct Income Accounts at Sales Accounts

05.03 Sales Voucher Creation

We have explained Sales Voucher creation in Accounting Invoice Mode. Here we explain TCS Sales Voucher creation in Accounting Mode. At Sales Voucher entry screen. Click *I:Acct Invoice* toggle button (F-8B) to get *Accounting Voucher Entry* screen (F-8C).

Allow Income Accounts in Sales Vouchers ? Yes

F-8A: Sales Voucher Configuration

F-8B: Accounting Invoice Button   I: Acct Invoice

Accounting Voucher Creation Ctrl + M

Sales No. 1 2-Nov-2009
Ref. : Tuesday
Party's A/c Name : ABC Agencies

Particulars	Rate	per	Amount
Parking Lot License			2,000.00
TCS 2% (Parking Lot)	2	%	40.00
Narration:			2,040.00

F-8C: Sales Voucher in Accounting Invoice Mode

TCS Details

TCS Party Ledger : ABC Agencies

Gross Amount : 2,000.00

Income Tax	: @	2 %	40.00
Surcharge	: @	0 %	
Cess	: @	0 %	
Addl Ed Cess	: @	0 %	
Total TCS	:		40.00

TCS - Bill Wise Detail for : TCS 2% (Parking Lot)

Type of Ref	Name	Due Date, or Credit Days	Amount	Dr/ Cr
New Ref	Sale/1		40.00	Cr

F-8D: TCS Details of Sales Voucher

At *Accounting Voucher Entry* screen (F-8C), enter as follows:

- At the *Header*, select the Licensee (Collectee) Ledger
- Under *Particulars* column, enter as follows:
    - **Direct Income Ledger**: Select the Direct Income Ledger and enter the amount of License Fees at Amount Column.
    - **TCS Ledger**: Select the TCS Ledger to get the *TCS Details* screen (F-8D), showing the *Assessable Amount* and computed *TCS* Amount. The *TCS* Amount is carried at the main voucher screen (F-8C)

Enter other Ledger account details, if any. Enter Voucher Narration and save the Voucher

TCS Deposit

02-03

01 Deposit of TCS with Government

After collection of TCS through Sales Invoice, the TCS collected has to be deposited with government within specified period. For Deposit of TCS, create a Payment Voucher (in Single Entry Mode), as explained earlier. At Payment Voucher entry screen (F-1A), click S:*Stat Payment* button (F-1D) to get *Statutory Payment Screen* (F-1C).

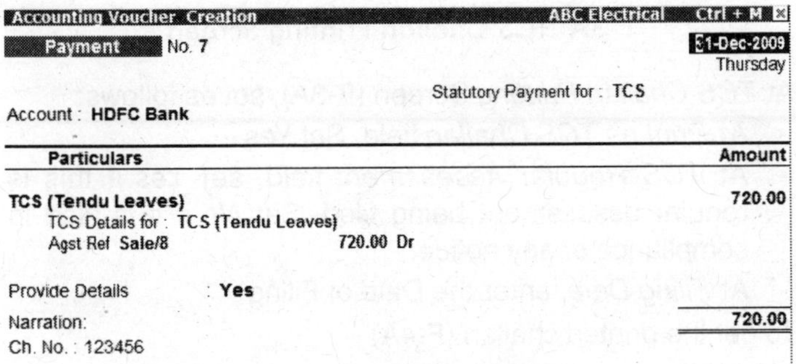

F-1A: TCS Payment Voucher Entry

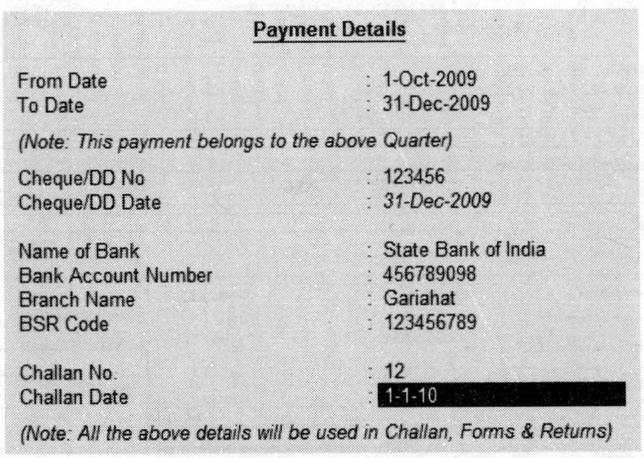

F-1B: TCS Payment Details screen

At *Statutory Payment Screen* (F-1C), enter as follows:

- **Duty/Tax Type**: At *Type of Duty /Tax*, select TCS
- **Entry Method**: At *Auto Fill Statutory Payment*, set:
  - o **Manual Method**: *No* to create voucher manually (not using Auto Fill)
  - o **Auto Fill Method**: *Yes* to create voucher using Auto Fill

02 TCS Payment Voucher Entry (Manual Method)

After you set *No* at *Auto Fill Statutory Payment* at *Statutory Payment Screen* (F-1C), you get the Main Voucher Entry screen (F-1A). At Particulars column, select the TCS Ledger Account to get Tax Bill Ref selection screen (F-1E). Select the Bill Ref of the Sale Voucher (F-1E) for which Tax to be deposited to get Tax Bill Ref Entry screen showing the selected Bill Ref (F-1F). The Tax Amount to be deposited against the selected Bill is shown (F-1F). This way, select all the References of Bills for which Tax to be deposited.

F-1C: Statutory payment screen

F-1D: Statutory Payment Button

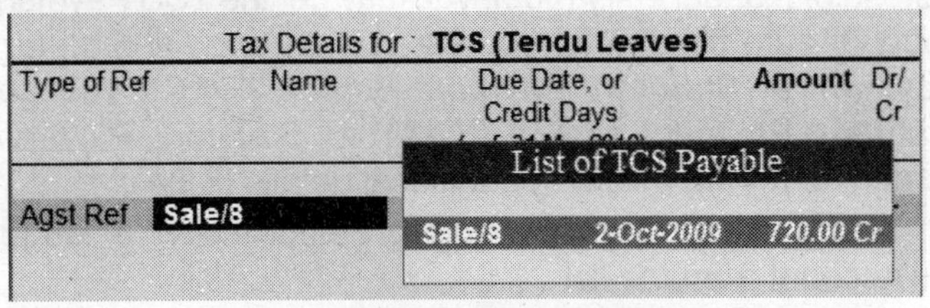

F-1E: Tax Bill Ref selection

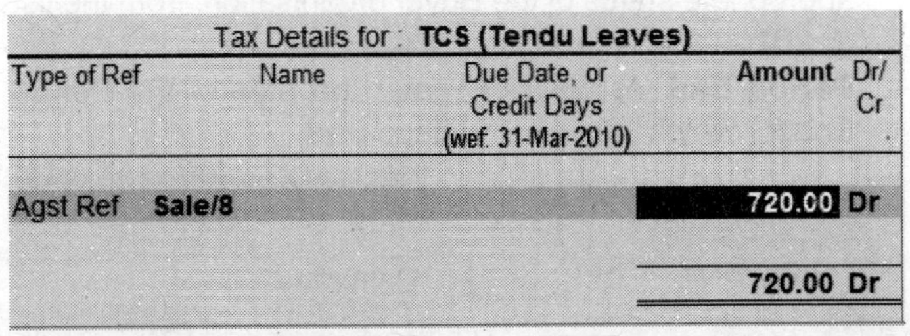

F-1F: Tax Bill Ref Entry

02.01 TCS Payment Details

After entry of Bill References (F-1F), you get back to the main voucher entry screen (F-1A). At main voucher entry screen (F-1A), type *Yes* at *Provide details*, to get *Payment Details entry* screen (F-1B). At

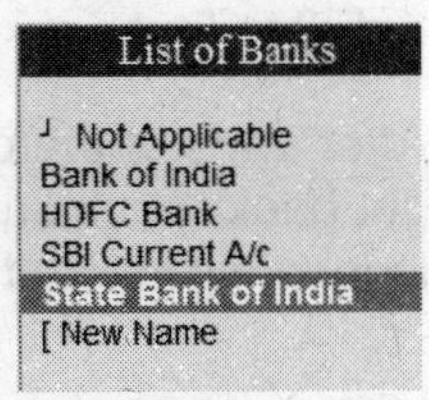

F-1G:Bank List

Payment Details entry screen (F-1B). enter the following details:

- **Period:** Enter the Period for which TCS is being deposited at *From Date* & *To Date* fields
- **Cheque Number**: At *Cheque / DD No*, enter the Cheque / DD No by which the Payment is deposited to designated Bank
- **Cheque Date**: At *Cheque / DD Date*, enter the Date of the Cheque / DD being deposited
- **Bank Name**: At *Name of Bank*, select the Name of Designated Bank (or select New Bank and enter Bank Name, if the name of the Bank is not listed: F-1G)
- **Bank Account Number**: At *Bank Account Number*, enter the Bank Account Number into which the Cheque is being deposited
- **Bank Branch Name**: At *Branch Name,* enter the Branch Name of the Bank into which the Cheque is being deposited
- **Bank BSR Code**: At *BSR Code,* enter the BSR Code of the Bank into which the Cheque is being deposited.
- **Challan Number**: At *Challan Number*, enter the Challan Number as allotted by Bank (if available)
- **Challan Date**: At Challan Date, enter the Bank Challan Date (if available)

These info are printed in the Bank Challan, Forms & Return

03 TCS Payment Voucher Entry (using Auto Fill)

Instead of manual entry (§02), you may get the TCS Payment voucher auto filled. After you set *Yes* at *Auto Fill Statutory Payment* at *Statutory Payment Screen* (F-1C), you get Statutory Payment screen (F-2A). At *Statutory Payment* screen, enter the following additional details (F-2A):

- **TCS Ledger**: At *TCS Ledger*, Select the TCS ledger Account from the list
- **Collectee Status**: At *Buyer / Lessee Status*, select the appropriate status of the Buyer organisation, from the list (F-2B)
- **Period End**: At *To Date*, enter the date of the Period End for which Tax is being deposited

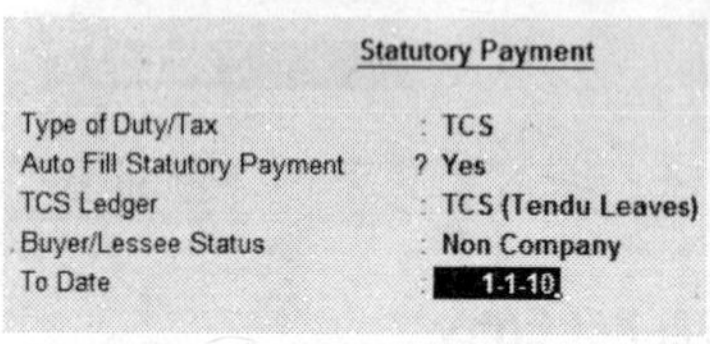

F-2A: Statutory Payment

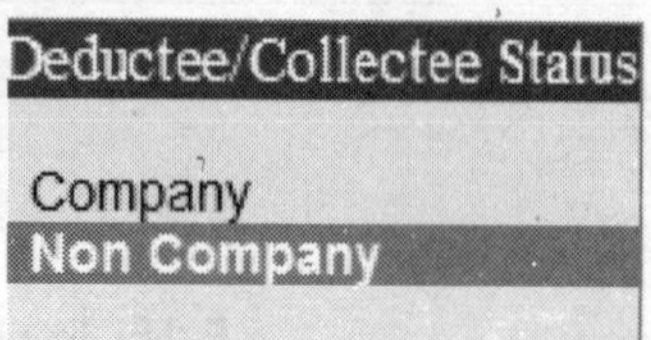

F-2B: Collectee Status List

After entry of the details at *Statutory Payment* screen, you get back the main voucher entry screen with the TCS Tax ledger and amount auto carried. This saves the onerous task of selecting each Bill Reference that you had to do otherwise as explained (F-1E, F-1F) and the exact amount payable is auto carried for quick entry.

As explained (§02.01), at Payment Voucher entry screen, set *Yes* at *Provide Details* to get the *Payment Details* entry screen (F-1B). Enter the details.

04 TCS Challan Printing

To print TCS Challan (F-4A), at Payment voucher screen (F-1A), click *P:Print* button to get *TCS Challan Printing* screen (F-3A).

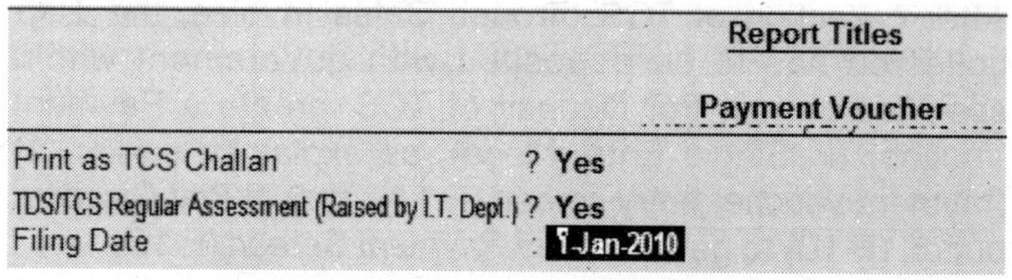

F-3A: TCS Challan Printing Screen

At *TCS Challan Printing* Screen (F-3A), set as follows:

- At *Print as TCS Challan* field, Set Yes
- At *TCS Regular Assessment* field, set *Yes* if this is regular assessment being filed. Set *No* if it is filed in compliance of any notice.
- At *Filing Date*, enter the Date of Filing

To get the printed challan (F-4A)

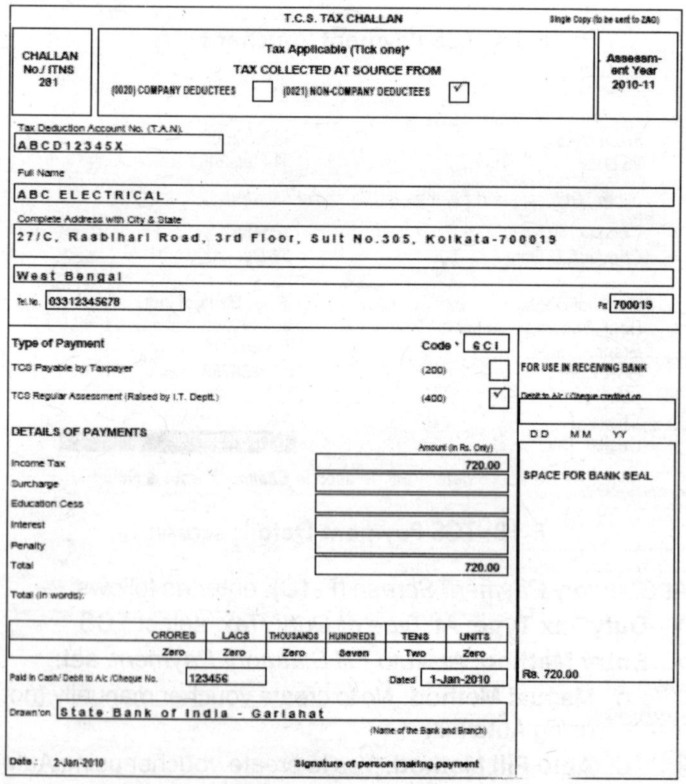

T.C.S. TAX CHALLAN — Single Copy (to be sent to ZAO)

CHALLAN No./ ITNS 281

Tax Applicable (Tick one)*
TAX COLLECTED AT SOURCE FROM
(0020) COMPANY DEDUCTEES ☐ (0021) NON-COMPANY DEDUCTEES ☑

Assessment Year 2010-11

Tax Deduction Account No. (T.A.N.) ABCD12345X

Full Name: ABC ELECTRICAL

Complete Address with City & State: 27/C, Rasbihari Road, 3rd Floor, Suit No.305, Kolkata-700019
West Bengal

Tel.No. 03312345678 Pin 700019

Type of Payment — Code * 6CI
TCS Payable by Taxpayer (200) ☐
TCS Regular Assessment (Raised by I.T. Deptt.) (400) ☑

FOR USE IN RECEIVING BANK
Debit to A/c / Cheque credited on
DD MM YY

DETAILS OF PAYMENTS — Amount (in Rs. Only)

Income Tax	720.00
Surcharge	
Education Cess	
Interest	
Penalty	
Total	720.00

Total (in words):

CRORES	LACS	THOUSANDS	HUNDREDS	TENS	UNITS
Zero	Zero	Zero	Seven	Two	Zero

SPACE FOR BANK SEAL

Rs. 720.00

Paid in Cash/ Debit to A/c /Cheque No. 123456 Dated 1-Jan-2010

Drawn on State Bank of India - Gariahat (Name of the Bank and Branch)

Date : 2-Jan-2010 Signature of person making payment

F-4A: TCS Deposit Challan in Pri

Having created the Vouchers for TCS Sales & Tax Deposit, you may print various periodical Reports & Returns of TCS.

01 TCS Payables

Select *GoT > Display >Statements of Accounts > TCS Outstandings* to get TCS Outstandings Menu (F-1A)

At TCS Outstandings Menu (F-1A), select *TCS Payables* to get TCS Payables Report (F-2A)

TCS Payable Configuration

At *TCS Payable* Display (F-2A), click *F12:Configure* to get TCS Payable Configuration screen (F-2B) to set the Configuration similar to *Outstandings Payable* discussed earlier

TCS Payable Buttons

At TCS Payable Display (F-2A), you get the buttons as shown at F-3C, similar to Buttons shown at *Outstandings Payable* explained earlier

02 TCS Ledger Outstanding

At TCS *Outstandings Menu* (F-1A), select *Ledger* to get *TCS Ledger Outstanding Display* (F-3A)

TCS Ledger Outstandings Display Configuration

At *TCS Ledger Outstanding Display* (F-3A), click *F12:Configure* to get *TCS* Ledger Outstanding Display Configuration screen (F-3B) to set the Configuration similar to Ledger Outstanding Display Configuration discussed earlier

TCS Payable Display Buttons: At TCS Payable Display (F-2A), you get the buttons (F-3C), similar to Buttons shown at *Outstandings Payable* explained earlier

03 Challan Reconciliation

Ledger Voucher has been discussed earlier. Reconciliation of Challan Payments to the assigned Bank for TCS is done in the Ledger Voucher report (F-4A). At *GoT>Display > Accounts Book > Ledger*, select the *TCS Ledger* Account from the list of Accounts Ledger to get Ledger Voucher List of the selected TCS Ledger Account (F-4A).

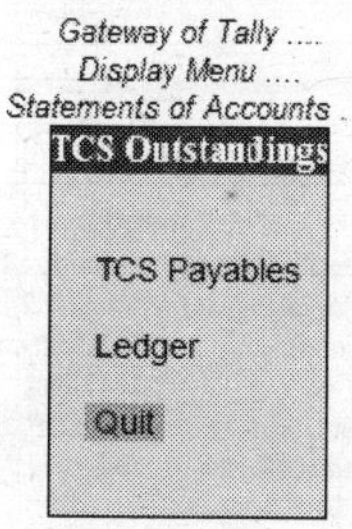

F-1A:TCS Reports Menu

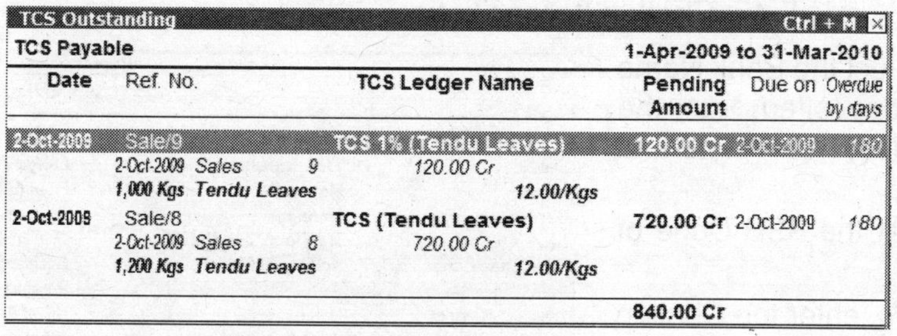

F-2A:TCS Payable Display

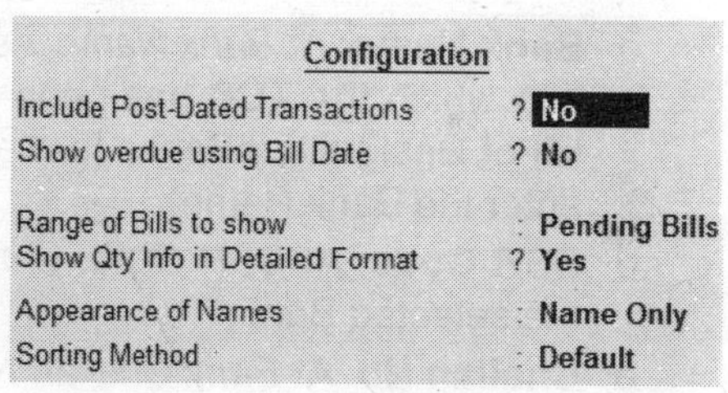

F-2B:TCS Payable Configuration

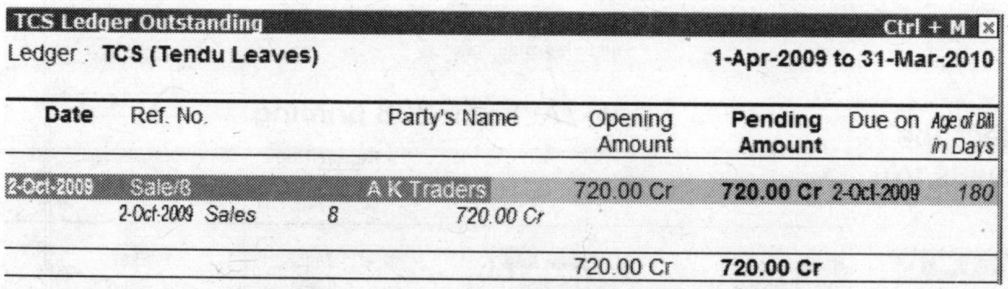

F-3A:TCS Ledger Outstanding Display

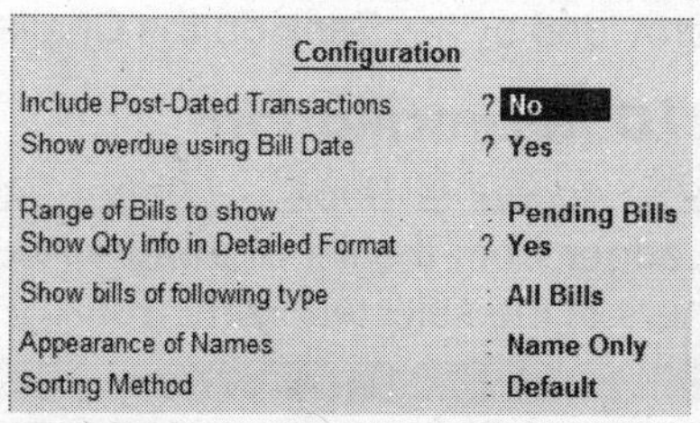

F-3B:TCS Ledger Outstanding Configuration

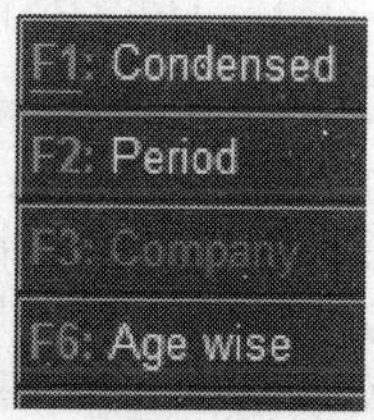

F-3C Buttons

- **Challan Reconciliation**: At *Ledger Voucher Display* of TCS Ledger (F-4A), click *F5: Challan Reconcile* Button (F-4B) to get TCS *Challan Reconciliation* screen (F-4E).
- **Challan Details Entry**: At *TCS Challan Reconciliation* screen (F-4E), click *S:Set Challan Details* button (F-4C) to get *Challan Details* screen (F-4D). At *Challan Details* screen (F-4D), enter the details as follows:

Ledger Vouchers Ctrl + M

Ledger: **TCS (Tendu Leaves)** **1-Oct-2009 to 31-Mar-2010**

Date	Particulars	Vch Type	Vch No.	Debit	Credit
2-10-2009	A K Traders	Sales	8		720.00
		Opening Balance :			
		Current Total :			720.00
		Closing Balance :			720.00

F-4A: Ledger Voucher for TCS Ledger

F5: Challan Reconcile

F-4B: Reconcile Button

S: Set Challan Details

F-4C: Challan Details Button

Challan Details

Bank Name	:	HDFC Bank
BSR Code	:	123456789
Bank Challan No.	:	12
Challan Date	:	1.1.10

F-4D: Challan Details

TCS Challan Reconcilation **ABC Electrical** Ctrl + M

TCS Challan Reconcilation **1-Oct-2009 to 31-Dec-2009**

(Reconciliation)

Date	Particulars	Cheque/DD No.	Name of Bank	BSR Code	Challan No.	Challan Date	Vch No.	Amount
		123456	HDFC Bank	123456789	12	1-1-2010		

F-4E: Challan Reconciliation

- **Bank Name**: At *Bank Name*, select the Bank Name into which the TCS has been deposited, from the list of Designated Banks (or select *New Name* and enter the Bank Name).
- **BSR Code**: At *BSR Code*, enter the BSR Code of the selected Bank.
- **Challan No**: At *Bank Challan No.* enter the Challan Number as allotted by the Bank on the Challan
- **Challan Date:** At *Challan Date*, enter the Challan Date as provided by the Bank on the Challan.

04 Form 27D Reconciliation

At *GoT> Display > Accounts Book > Ledger*, select the *Collectee Party* Ledger from the list of Ledger Accounts to get Ledger Vouchers of the selected Party (F-5A).

Ledger Vouchers Ctrl + M

Ledger: **A K Traders** **1-Oct-2009 to 31-Dec-2009**

Date	Particulars	Vch Type	Vch No.	Debit	Credit
2-10-2009	Sales	Sales	8	15,120.00	

F-5A: Party Ledger Voucher

At Ledger Vouchers screen of the Collectee Party (F-5A), click *F5:Form 27D Reconcile* button (F-5B) to get *Form 27 D Reconcile screen* (F-5D) At *Form 27 D Reconcile screen* (F-5D), click *S:Set All Dates* (F-5C) to auto update the Date of Form 27D Issue Date against each Voucher record.

F5: Form27D Reconcile

F-5B: Form 27D Reconciliation Button

S: Set all Dates

F-5C: Date Setting Button

Form 27D Reconciliation Ctrl + M

Ledger: **A K Traders** **1-Oct-2009 to 31-Dec-2009**

Date	Particulars	*Form27D Issue Date*	Vch Type	Vch No.	Debit	Credit
2-10-2009	Sales	1-1-10	Sales	8	15,120.00	

F-5D: Form 27D Reconcilliation

05 TCS Form 27B Printing

At Gateway, select *Display>Statutory Report>TCS Reports* to get the *TCS Reports* menu (F-1A).

At *TCS Reports* menu (F-6A), select *Print Form 27B* to get *Form 27B printing* screen (F-7A).

Gateway of Tally ....
Display Menu ....
Statutory Reports ....

TCS Reports

PrinT Form 27D
ETCS Forms
Print Form 27B
Quit

F-6A: TCS Reports Menu

Report Titles
TCSForm27B

Person Responsible Details

Flat No	:	27/C, Rasbihari Road
Name	:	Mohan Roy
Designation	:	Manager
Name of the premises/building	:	3rd Floor, Suit No.305
Road/Street/Lane	:	Kolkata-700019
Area/Location	:	
Town/City/District	:	
State	:	West Bengal
Pin code	:	700019
Mobile No.	:	9876543210
STD Code	:	033
Telephone	:	12345678
E-mail	:	nomail@kmail.com

Other Details

Category (deductor/collector)	:	Individual/HU
From (blank for beginning)	:	1-10-2009
To (blank for end)	:	31-12-2009
Challan Date Till	:	31-12-2009
Enclosed Form Type	:	Form 27E
Previous Receipt No.	:	234
No. of Annexures enclosed	:	5
Other Information	:	
Place	:	Kolkata
Date	:	1-Jan-2010

F-7A: Form 27B printing

Report Titles
TCS Form27D

Name	:	Mohan Roy
Son/Daughter of	:	Pabir Roy
Designation	:	Manager
Print as Previous Format	:	No
TCS Ledger	:	TCS 1% (Tendu Leaves)
From (blank for beginning)	:	1-10-2009
To (blank for end)	:	31-12-2009
Challan Date Till	:	
Type of Copy	:	Default
Certificate No	:	1

Place	:	Kolkat
Date	:	31-Mar-2010
Quarter		**Acknowledgement**
Apr-Jun	:	
Jul-Sep	:	
Oct-Dec	:	Oct-Dec/1
Jan-Mar	:	
CIT(TDS) Details		
Name	:	
Address	:	
City	:	
Pin Code	:	

F-7B: Form 27D printing

At Form *27B Printing* screen (F-7A) specify the following:

- **Person Responsible details:** At the left part, enter the address and Contact details of collector (Authorised Person), signing the Form.
  - o **Flat No**: At *Flat No*, enter the Flat Number / Door Number
  - o **Name:** At *Name*, enter the Name of the Person
  - o **Designation:** At *Designation*, enter the Designation of the Person.
  - o **Premises Name**: At *Name of the Premises/ Building*, enter the Name of the Building
  - o **Road:** At *Road / Street /Lane*, enter the Name of the Road / Street /Lane
  - o **Location:** At *Area/ Location*, enter the Area/ Location Name of the premises.
  - o **Town / City /District**: At *Town / City /District*, enter the Town /City & District Name of the location of premises
  - o **State**: At *State*, enter the State where the premises is situated.
  - o **Telephone**: At *Telephone*, enter the Telephone Number (Land line with STD Code / Mobile Number) of the signatory.
  - o **e-Mail**: At *E-Mail*, enter the e-mail address of the Person (if any)
- **Other details:** At the right part, enter the Particulars of the Form 27 Report, as follows:
  - o **Collector Category**: At *Category (Deductor / Collector)*, enter the Category of the Deductor Oganisation.
  - o **Report Start Date:** At *From*, enter the Start Date of the Return (leave blank to start from beginning of FY)
  - o **Report End Date**: At *To*, enter the End Date of the Return (leave blank for upto end of FY)
  - o **Last Challan Period**: At *Challan Date Till*, enter the last challan date considered in the report
  - o **Form Type**: At *Enclosed Form Type*, select the enclosed Form Number from the list (e.g 27E)
  - o **Previous Receipt Reference**: At *Previous Receipt No.* enter the previous Return submission acknowledgement number, if any
  - o **Annexures**: At *Number of Annexures enclosed*, enter Number of annexed documents enclosed.
  - o **Other information**: At *Other information*, enter any other important note you like to record
  - o **Place**: At *Place*, enter the Place of filing the return
  - o **Date**: At *Date*, enter Date of filing the return

Type Y to get the printed Form 27B (F-8A)

Form No. 27B

Form for furnishing information with the statement of collection of tax at source filed on computer media for the period (From 1/4/2009 to 31/3/2010)

1 (a) Tax Deduction and Collection Account Number: ABCD12345X

(b) Permanent Account No.: ABPN5865K

(c) Financial Year: 2009-10

(d) Assessment Year: 2010-11

(f) Previous receipt number: 234

(In Case return / statement has been filed earlier)

2 Particulars of the collector

(a) Name	ABC Electrical
(b) Type of Collector*	Others
(b) Branch / Division (if any)	
(c) Address	
Flat No.	27/C, Rasbihari Road
Name of the premises / building	3rd Floor, Suit No.305
Road / Street / Lane	Kolkata-700019
Area / Location	
Town / City / District	
State	West Bengal
Pin code	700019
Telephone	03312345678
E-mail	nomail@kmail.com

3 Name of the person responsible for collection of tax

(a) Name	Mohan Roy
(b) Address	
Flat No.	27/C, Rasbihari Road
Name of the premises / building	3rd Floor, Suit No.305
Road / Street / Lane	Kolkata-700019
Area / Location	
Town / City / District	
State	West Bengal
Pin code	700019
Telephone	12345678
E-mail	nomail@kmail.com

4 Control totals

Sr.No.	No. of party records	Amount paid ₹	Tax Collected ₹	Tax deposited (Total challan amount) ₹
Total	0	26,400.00		

5 Total Number of Annexures enclosed: 5

6 Other Information:

F-8A: From 27B in Print

06 TCS Form 27D Printing

At *TCS Reports* menu (F-6A), select *Print Form 27D* and select the Collectee (Customer) to get Form 27D printing screen (F-7B), to print Form 27D (F-9A)

At Form 27D printing screen (F-7B), at the left Part, enter as follows:

- **Name:** At *Name*, enter the Name of the Person
- **Designation:** At *Designation*, enter the Designation of the Person.
- **Format**: At *Print in Previous Format*, set *Yes* to print in Previous Format, else set *No*
- **Report Start Date:** At *From*, enter the Start Date of the Return (leave blank to start from beginning of FY)
- **Report End Date**: At *To*, enter the End Date of the Return (leave blank for upto end of FY)
- **Last Challan**: At *Challan Date Till*, enter the last challan date considered in the report
- **Copy Type**: At *Type of Copy*, select from the list as follows:
  - o **User Defined**: To use User Defined Format. Further, at *Copy Type Txt* Box, enter the Form Type.
  - o **Default**: To use Standard Format
- **Certificate No.**: At *Certificate No*, enter the Certificate Reference Number

At Form 27D printing screen (F-7B), at the Right Part, enter the Particulars of the Return as follows:

- **Place**: Place of filing the Return
- **Date**: Date of filing the Return
- **Acknowledgement Reference**: Under *Acknowledgement*, enter the Return Acknowledgement Reference & Dates against each Quarter
- **CIT (TDS) Details**: Under *CIT (TDS) Details*, enter the details of the Commissioner as follows
  - o **Name**: At Name, enter the Name of the Commissioner
  - o **Address**: At Address, enter the address of the commissioner office
  - o **City**: At City Enter City name of the commissioner office
  - o **Pin Code**: At Pin Code, enter the PIN Code of the commissioner office

Original

Certificate No. : 1234/206C

FORM NO. 27D

[See rule 37D]

Certificate under section 206C of the Income-tax Act, 1961 for Tax collected at source

Name and address of the Collector	Name and address of the Collectee
ABC ELECTRICAL 27/C, Rasbihari Road 3rd Floor, Suit No. 305 Kolkata-700019	P R Produce

PAN of the Collector	TAN of the Collector	PAN of the Collectee
ABPN5865K	ABCD12345X	

CIT(TDS)

Address A K Ghosh,

Beliaghata

City Kolkata Pin Code 700085

Assessment Year	Period From	Period To
2010 - 11	1-4-2009	31-3-2010

Summary of receipt

Amount received/debited	Nature of receipt	Date of receipt/debit
12,000.00	Tendu Leaves	3-10-2009

Summary of tax collected at source

Quarter	Receipt Number of original quarterly statements of TCS under proviso to sub-section (3) of section 206C	Amount of tax collected in respect of the collectee	Amount of tax deposited/remitted in respect of the collectee
Apr - Jun			
Jul - Sep			
Oct - Dec	2345	120.00	120.00
Jan - Mar			

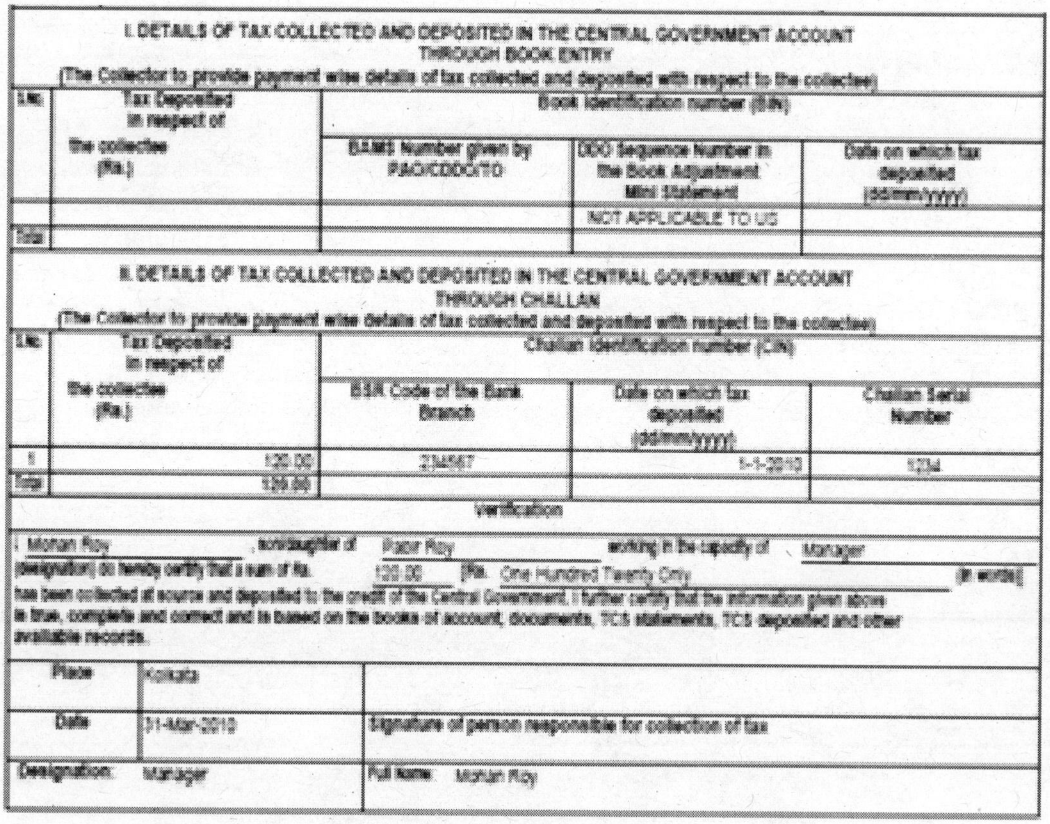

I. DETAILS OF TAX COLLECTED AND DEPOSITED IN THE CENTRAL GOVERNMENT ACCOUNT THROUGH BOOK ENTRY
(The Collector to provide payment wise details of tax collected and deposited with respect to the collectee)

S.No.	Tax Deposited in respect of the collectee (Rs.)	Book Identification number (BIN)		
		BAMS Number given by PAO/CDDO/TO	DDO Sequence Number in the Book Adjustment Mini Statement	Date on which tax deposited (dd/mm/yyyy)
			NOT APPLICABLE TO US	
Total				

II. DETAILS OF TAX COLLECTED AND DEPOSITED IN THE CENTRAL GOVERNMENT ACCOUNT THROUGH CHALLAN
(The Collector to provide payment wise details of tax collected and deposited with respect to the collectee)

S.No.	Tax Deposited in respect of the collectee (Rs.)	Challan Identification number (CIN)		
		BSR Code of the Bank Branch	Date on which tax deposited (dd/mm/yyyy)	Challan Serial Number
1	120.00	234567	1-1-2010	1234
Total	120.00			

Verification

I, Mohan Roy, son/daughter of Pabir Roy working in the capacity of Manager (designation) do hereby certify that a sum of Rs. 120.00 [Rs. One Hundred Twenty Only (in words)] has been collected at source and deposited to the credit of the Central Government. I further certify that the information given above is true, complete and correct and is based on the books of account, documents, TCS statements, TCS deposited and other available records.

Place	Kolkata	
Date	31-Mar-2010	Signature of person responsible for collection of tax
Designation: Manager		Full Name: Mohan Roy

F-9A:Form 27D in Print

07 Multi Account TCS Form 27D Printing

To print Form 27D of all Customers, select *GoT>Multi-Account printing> Multi-Form 27D printing* at to get the Form 27D Printing screen. Set up the options as above for Form 27D printing.

Part 3

Service Tax

So far we have discussed about the entire process of Financial Accounting, Invoicing & Inventory. However, some registered Service Providers have to maintain statutory records of Transactions, collection of Service Tax, deposit of Service Tax and filing various Statutory Returns to Government. In this part, we describe the additional features for Statutory compliance of Service Tax related functions.

- **Service Tax** explains the basic concepts of Service Tax and related terminologies.
- **Service Tax Set Up** explains the initial set up for Service Tax registration of the Company and scheduled Service Categories.
- **Service Tax Masters** explains creation & configuration of Masters related to Service Tax.
- **Service Tax Bill Entry** explains entry of Service Tax particulars in the Service Bills for providing Taxable Services by Registered Service Providers.
- **Service Tax Deposit** explains the process of creation of Payment Voucher for deposit of appropriate amount of Net Service Tax payable, to the Government.
- **Input Service Tax Credit** explains entry of Service Purchase Bill and adjustment of Service Tax paid thereon, from the Service Tax Payable.
- **Special Features** explains exclusive cases of some special types of Service Providers, like Importers, Exporters, Exempte©d Organisation, Exempted Services, Taxes on Advances and Final Service Bills, Service at Lower Tax Rates etc, with examples.

Organizations not registered under Service Tax rules, or Service Tax registered organisations who maintain and file Statutory Returns under Service Tax Rules manually, may skip this Part.

Service Tax

03-01

01 Service Tax

Service Tax is a tax imposed on services provided in India (except in Jammu & Kashmir). The service provider collects the tax (and is ultimately borne by the Customers) and pays the same to the government. It is charged on all services except the services in the negative list of services.

01.01 Applicability of Service Tax

With effect from 1 April 2011, the *Point of Taxation Rule* was introduced for effective collection of Service Tax (in place of earlier Collection Basis Rule).

According to the new *Point of Taxation* Rule, Date of Issue of Invoice, or Date of receipt of Payment, whichever is earlier, shall be reckoned.

With effect from 1 July, 2012, *Negative List-based System of Tax on Services* was introduced. As per this system, the Term Service refers to *Any Activity Carried out by a person for another, for consideration, and includes a declared service*

02 Liability to Pay Service Tax

The liability of paying tax to the Government is on the service provider i.e. the person providing service (in some cases, on the service receiver).

Generally it is the service provider who is liable to collect Service Tax from his customer/client and pay the same to the Government. But in some cases (as cited below), the service receiver is liable to pay Service Tax (as per Notification 36/2004 ST dated 31.12.2004 as amended from time to time)

- Goods Transport Agency service
- Business auxiliary service of distribution of mutual fund by a mutual fund distributor or agent
- Sponsorship service provided to any Body Corporate / Firm
- Taxable services received by any person in India from abroad
- Insurance auxiliary service by an insurance agent

03 Rate of Service Tax

Currently, Service Tax would be charged as:

- Service Tax (ST): @ 12% of the value of taxable service
- Education Cess (EC):@ 2% on Service Tax
- Higher Education Cess (HEC): @ 1% on Service Tax.

Thus, total Service Tax is 12.36% [12% + (2%+1%, i.e 3% on 12%) =.36%]

04 Taxable Percentage

Abatement has been replaced by *Taxable Percentage*, w.e.f. 1.7.12

Taxable Percentage refers to the specified percentage of the value of Service on which Service Tax can be levied (*Abatement* was a deduction allowed on the value considered for Service Tax.). So, if Taxable % is 30%, then on Taxable Service of Rs. 1000, Service Tax would be charged on Rs 300 only.

05 Pure Agent

Pure agent means a person who incurs expenditure or costs in the course of providing taxable services, acting as pure Agent:

- Not to hold the title to goods or services provided
- Not to use the procured goods or services
- Only the actual amount incurred to procure the services or goods, is received by Agent

Expenses (or Costs) incurred by Agent may be deducted from the Total Service Charge to compute the Taxable Amount.

06 Input Tax Credit

Service Tax is payable by Service Provider. So, the Service Tax paid on Purchase of Service (called *Input Service Tax*) may be adjusted on Service Tax payable on sale of services (Output Service Tax)

The deduction of Input Service Tax is called adjusting credit against service tax (popularly known as *Input Tax Credit*). The difference between the service tax payable on sale of service and Input Service Tax (Service Tax paid on purchase of Service) becomes the net service tax payable.

The Input Service Tax can be adjusted only when the Service Purchased is required for providing the Service Sold.

For Example, S provides Taxable Service on which Tax of Rs 1000 is collected. S purchased Service (for providing the

Taxable services rendered) on which he paid Rs 400 as Service Tax. So, S is liable to pay Rs 600 (1000-400) to the Government (instead of Rs 1000).

07 Service Tax Payment

Service Tax is to be paid by:

- **Individual, Proprietorship / Partnership firms**: Quarterly within 5th day of the month following the end of respective Quarter. However, for Quarter ending 31st March, the Tax would be paid by 31st March itself (i.e 5th July, 5th Oct, 5th Jan & 31st Mar).
- **Others**: Monthly within 5th day of the next month. However, for Quarter ending 31st March, the Tax would be paid by 31st March itself (i.e 5th of each month & 31st Mar).

08 Service Tax Returns

Every Service Tax Assessee would submit Return in Form ST-3 half-yearly by 25th day of the month following the half-year (i.e 25th April / 25th October) alongwith copies of TR-6 Challans in respect of Service Tax deposited

Any assesse making provisional assessment should submit Return in Form ST-3A

FAQ: Frequently Asked Questions

FAQ-1: What is the rate of Service Tax and how it computed

Ans: Currently, Service Tax would be charged as:

- Service Tax (ST): @ 12% of the value of taxable service
- Education Cess (EC):@ 2% on Service Tax
- Higher Education Cess (HEC): @ 1% on Service Tax.

Thus, total Service Tax is 12.36% [12% + {(2%+1%) of 12%, i.e 3% on 12%)}] = [12%+.36%]

FAQ-2: In which cases, the Customer of Service is to deposit Service Tax with Government

Ans: In following cases, the Customer of Service is to deposit Service Tax with Government

- Goods Transport Agency service
- Business auxiliary service of distribution of mutual fund by a mutual fund distributor or agent
- Sponsorship service provided to any Body Corporate / Firm
- Taxable services received by any person in India from abroad
- Insurance auxiliary service by an insurance agent

Service Tax Set Up

01 Service Tax Quick Set Up

For convenience of user, Tally provides all the essential starting steps for Activation, Set Up and Master entry in one place. You may either perform the tasks through the options of Quick Steps (F-1B) or perform the tasks from the respective options directly.

For Quick Set Up, at Gateway of Tally, select *Quick Set Up* to get *Quick Set Up* Menu (F-1A). At Quick Set Up Menu (F-1A), select Service Tax to get Service Tax Quick Set Up screen (F-1B), describing the steps of initial set up for Service Tax, for convenience.

We explain the operational steps and simultaneously explain how you can use the alternate options from Quick Steps screen (F-1B).

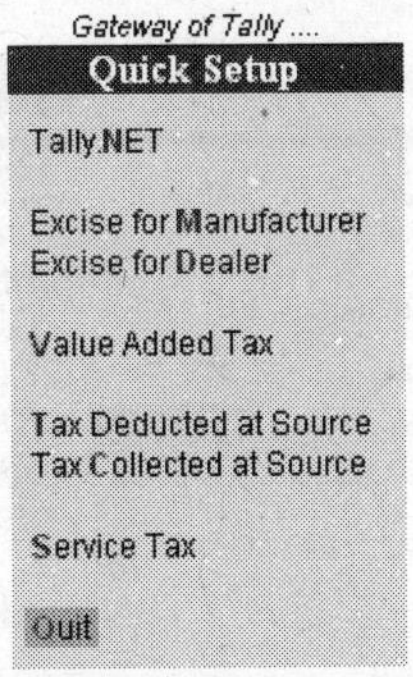

F-1A: Quick Set Up Menu

02 Service Tax Activation

To maintain Service Tax system in Tally, you should first activate Service Tax for the Company. At Gateway, *Click F11:Features* to get the *Company Features Menu* (F-2A).

- At *Company Features* Menu (F-2A), select *Statutory & Taxation* to get Statutory & Taxation features set up screen (F-3A).
- At *Statutory & Taxation* features set up screen (F-3A),
  - o Set *Yes* at *Enable Service Tax* to activate Service Tax Features for the Company.
  - o Set Yes at *Set / Alter Service Tax details* to get *Company Service Tax details* screen to enter the Company's Service Tax Registration Number & Jurisdictional Authority details (F-4A).

Alternately, you may click *C:Company* Service Tax details at Service Tax Quick Set up screen (F-1B), to get the Company Service Tax details screen (F- 4A), directly.

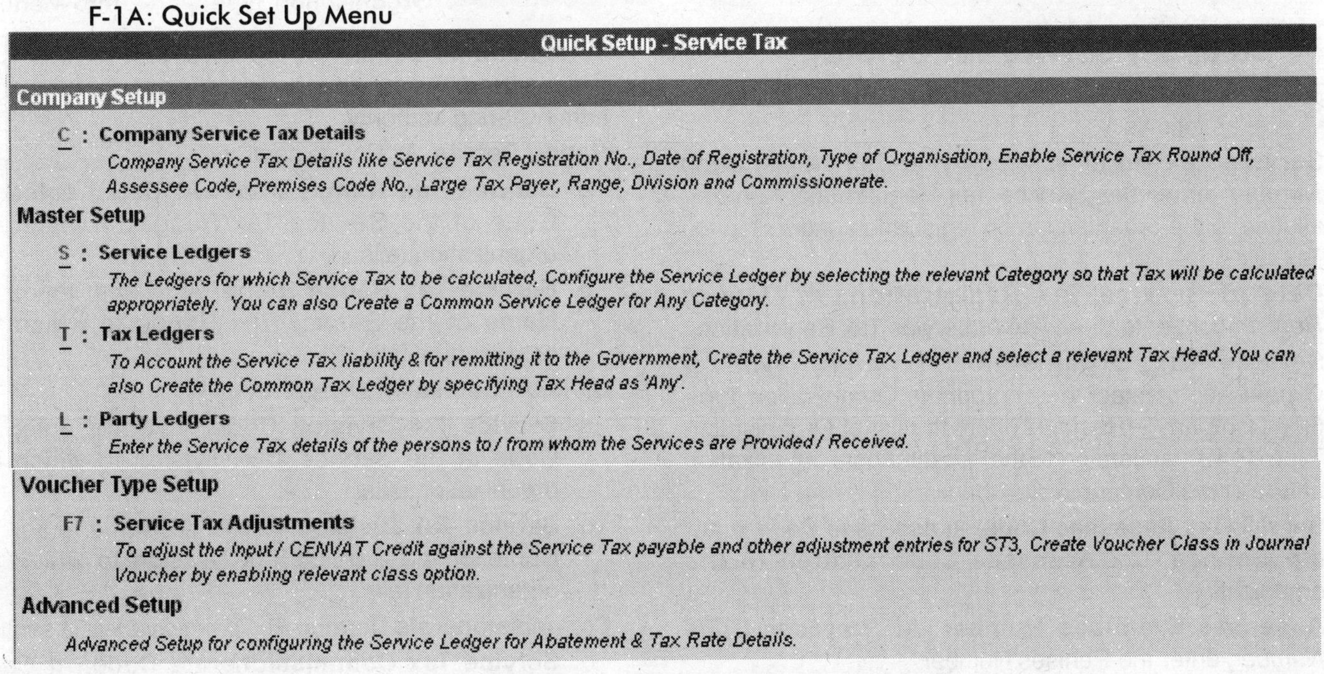

F-1B: Service Tax Quick Set Up screen

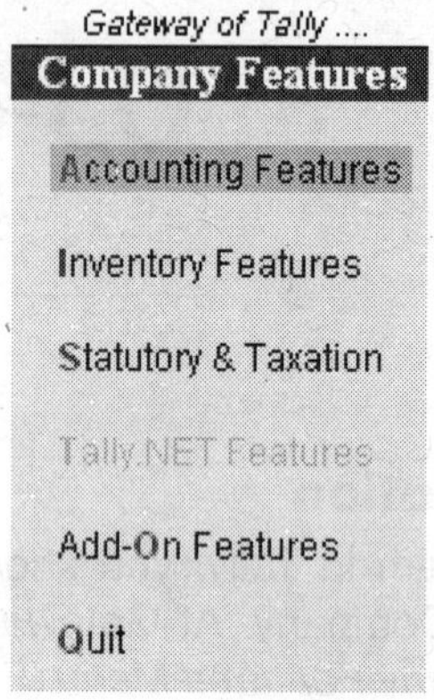

F-2A: Company Features Menu

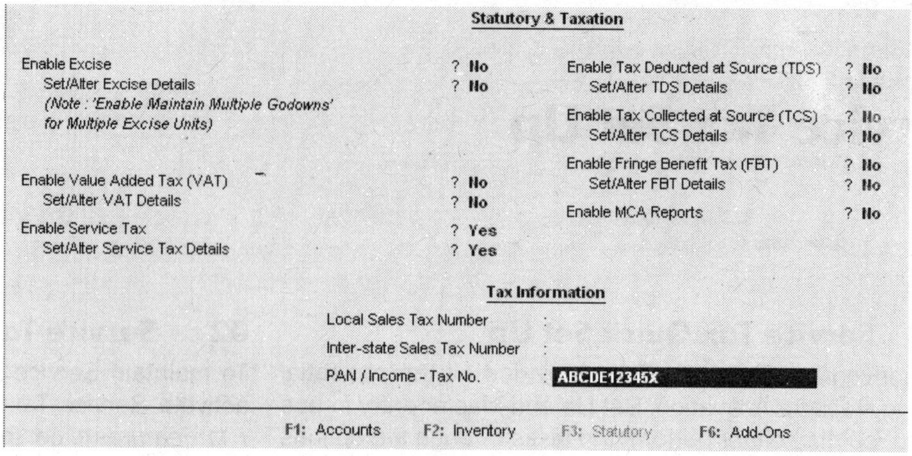

F-3A: Statutory & Taxation screen

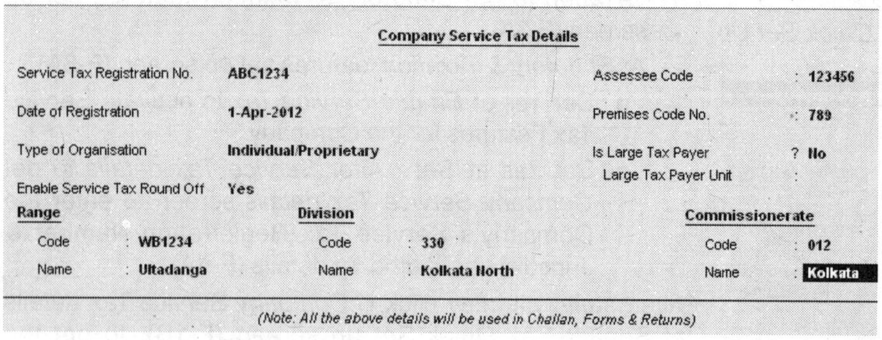

F-4A: Service Tax Set Up Screen

F-4B: Selection list of Organisation Type

F-5A: Statutory Info Menu

03 Company Service Tax Details

At Company Service Tax details screen (F-4A), at the left part, enter as follows

- **Service Tax Regn #**: *At Service Tax Registration Number*, enter the Service Tax Registration Number, allotted to the organisation on registration under Service Tax rules.
- **Date of Service Tax Registration**: *At Date of Registration,* enter the Date of Service Tax Registration
- **Service Tax Organisation Type**: At *Type of Organisation*, select the appropriate Organisation Type (like Company – Resident) from the list of Organisation Type (F-4B), according to the constitutional organization nature of the Company.
- **Service Tax Assessee Code**: *At Assessee Code***,** enter the Service Tax Assessee code allotted to the organization.
- **Assessee Premises Number**: At *Premises Code Number*, enter the Penises Number
- **Tax Payer Type:** At *Is Large Tax Payer*, set Yes (for Large Tax Payer) or No (Not Large Tax Payer) as applicable
  - o **Large Tax Payer Unit:** If you have set Yes at *Is Large Tax Payer*, then enter the applicable Large Tax Payer Unit Number at the field *Large Tax Payer Unit*

Jurisdictional Details: At the lower part (F-4A), enter the particulars of the jurisdictional Service Tax administering authority:

Range Details: At *Range* section:

- o **Service Tax Range Code**: At *Code*, enter the Code of the Service Tax Range to which the organization falls.
- o **Service Tax Range Name**: At *Name*, enter the Name of the Service Tax Range to which the organization falls.

- **Division Details**: At *Division* section:
  - o **Service Tax Division Code**: At *Code*, enter the Code of the Service Tax Division to which the organization falls.
  - o **Service Tax Division Name**: At *Name*, enter the Name of the Service Tax Division to which the organization falls.
- **Commissionerate Details**: At *Commissionerate* section:
  - o **Service Tax Commissionerate Code**: At *Code*, enter the Code of the Service Tax Commissionerate to which the organization falls.
  - o **Service Tax Commissionerate Name**: At *Name*, enter the Name of the Service Tax Commissionerate to which the organization falls.

04 Taxable Services

From time to time, Government notifies the specific categories of Services which are subject to Service Tax rules. Tally provides an updated profile of such Taxable Services

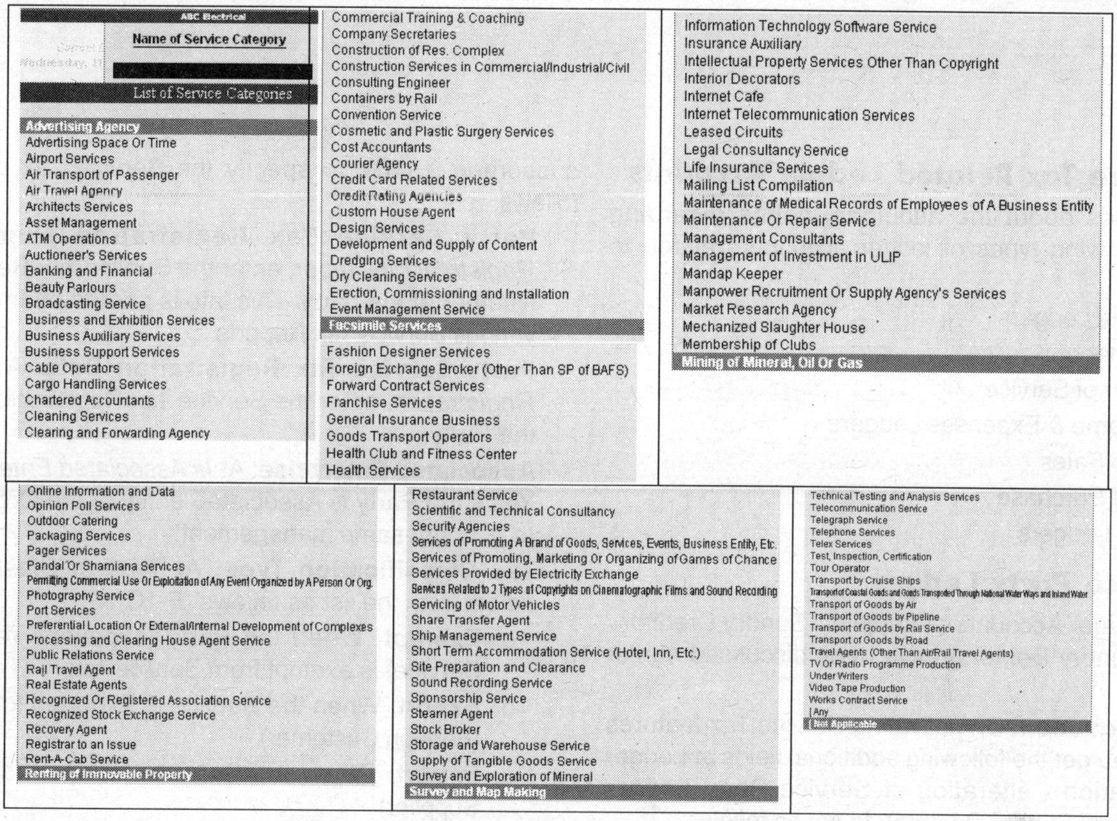

F-6A: List of Service Categories

(called *Service Categories*), their applicability date, Rates of Service Tax and Surcharge etc.

Select *GoT>Display > Statutory Info* to get Statutory Info menu (F-5A). At *Statutory Info* menu (F-5A). select *Service Categories* to get list of Service Categories List (F-6A)

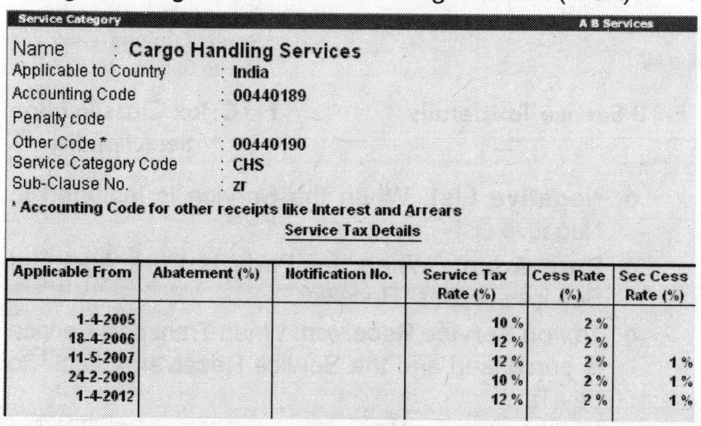

Service Category — A B Services

Name : **Cargo Handling Services**
Applicable to Country : India
Accounting Code : 00440189
Penalty code
Other Code * : 00440190
Service Category Code : CHS
Sub-Clause No. : zr
* Accounting Code for other receipts like Interest and Arrears

Service Tax Details

Applicable From	Abatement (%)	Notification No.	Service Tax Rate (%)	Cess Rate (%)	Sec Cess Rate (%)
1-4-2005			10 %	2 %	
18-4-2006			12 %	2 %	
11-5-2007			12 %	2 %	1 %
24-2-2009			10 %	2 %	1 %
1-4-2012			12 %	2 %	1 %

F-7A:Service Category details

05 Service Category details

To get the details of any Service Category, at Service Category List (F-6A), press <enter> on the selected Service Category, to get *Service Category Details* screen (F-7A), showing the Code Numbers and applicable Service Tax Rates.

> **Note:** *w.e.f 1.7.12, as per new* Negative List system, *services not included in Negative List are chargeable to Tax.*

FAQ: Frequently Asked Questions

FAQ-1: How do I activate Service Tax features for the Company

Ans: To activate Service Tax for the Company, at Gateway, *Click F11:Features* to get the *Company Features Menu* (F-1A).

- At Company Features Menu (P-1A), select *Statutory & Taxation* to get Statutory & Taxation features set up screen (F-2A).
- At *Statutory & Taxation* features set up screen (F-2A),
  - o Set *Yes* at *Enable Service Tax* to activate Service Tax Features for the Company.

At *Set / Alter Service Tax details*, set *Yes* to get *Company Service Tax details* screen (F-3A) to enter the Company's Service Tax Registration Number & Jurisdictional Authority details.

Service Tax Masters 03-03

01 Service Tax Related Ledger Accounts

We now discuss about the additional points regarding creation of following types of ledger accounts, related to Service Tax

- Service Party Ledgers
    - o Customer of Service
    - o Supplier of Service
- Service Income & Expenses Ledgers
    - o Service Sales
    - o Service Purchase
- Service Tax Ledgers

02 Service Party Ledger

Creation of Ledger Accounts of Supplier (Sundry Creditor / Customers (Sundry Debtors) have been discussed earlier (§01/03-01/S1

Statutory Information: On activating Service Tax features (§02/03-02), you get the following additional fields at Ledger Accounts creation / alteration of Service Party Ledger (Sundry Creditor / Sundry Debtors), to set as follows:

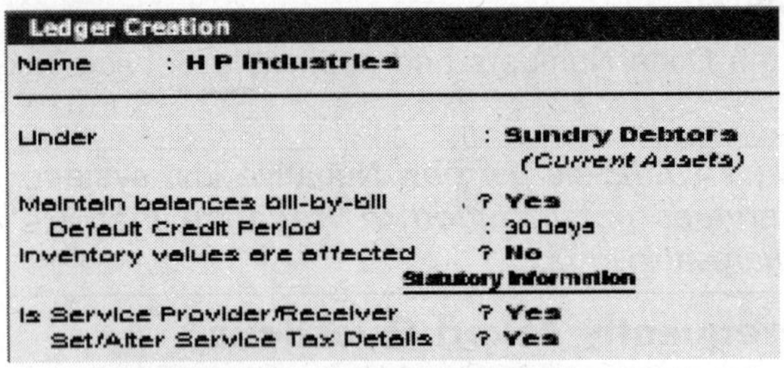

F-1A Service Party Ledger Creation

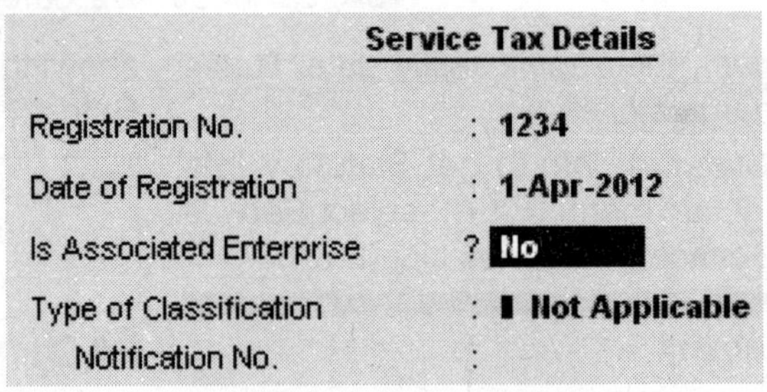

F-1B Service Tax details

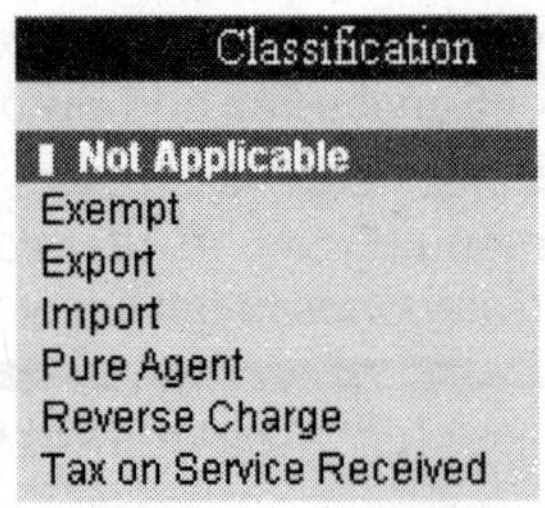

F-1C:Tax Classification Selection list

Service Tax Applicability: At *Is Service Tax Applicable* (F-1A), set:

- *Yes* for Customers whom you charge Service Tax in your bills.
- *Yes* for Suppliers who charges you service tax that you claim for credit.
- *No* for other ledger accounts.

Party Ledger Service Tax Details

Having set *Yes* at *Is Service Tax Applicable* at Service Party Ledger creation screen (F-1A), you get additional option *Set Alter Service Tax.* Set *Yes* to get *Service Tax Details* subscreen (F-1B), to specify the Service Tax details as follows:

- **Party Service Tax Registration Number**: At *Registration Number*, enter the Service Tax Registration Number of the party. This info is printed on Invoice and various Service Tax Reports.
- **Party Service Tax Registration Date**: At *Date of Registration*, enter the Service Tax Registration Date of the Party.
- **Associated Enterprise**: At *Is Associated Enterprise* Set Yes if the Party is Associated entity of the Organisation (e.g, under same management)
- **Tax Classification Type:** At *Type of Classification*, select from the list as follows (F-1C):
    - o **Exempt**: When the Party (supplier / receiver of Service) is exempt from Service Tax
    - o **Export**: When the Service is Exported to the Party (Foreign Customer)
    - o **Import:** When the Service is Imported (Foreign Supplier)
    - o **Negative List**: When the Service is included in Negative List
    - o **Pure Agent**: When the Party is Pure Agent of Service supplier / Receiver
    - o **Tax on Service Received**: When Transport Service is purchased and the Service Receiver is liable to pay Tax.
    - o **Not Applicable:** When Service Tax is applicable (no exemption is applicable) This is the most common option applicable.

- **Notification Number**: On selection of the *Type of Classification* (except *Not Applicable*), enter the applicable Notification Number of the Government

03 Service Income / Expense Ledger

We have discussed Ledger Creation earlier (§03.02/01-03). Here we discuss about specific features related to Service Income / Expense accounts

At *Service Income / Service Expense Ledger* Creation (F-2A), for each Service Income / Expense on which Service Tax is chargeable, set as follows:

- **Ledger Name**: At *Name* field, enter the appropriate Ledger Name:
  - o **Service Sales / Service Income**: Service Income, Professional Fees, Consultancy Fees, etc)
  - o **Service Purchase / Service Expenses:** Service Charges etc.
- **Parent Group:** At *Under* field, select the parent Group, such as:
  - o **Service Sales / Service Income**: Under *Sales* or *Direct Income* Group (or subgroup)
  - o **Service Purchase / Service Expenses**: Under *Purchase* or *Direct Expenses*
- **Inventory Link**: Since service income / expense are not related to materials (it is about manpower), at *Inventory Values are Affected,* select *No* (set *Yes* for linking with *Stock Item* for Services).

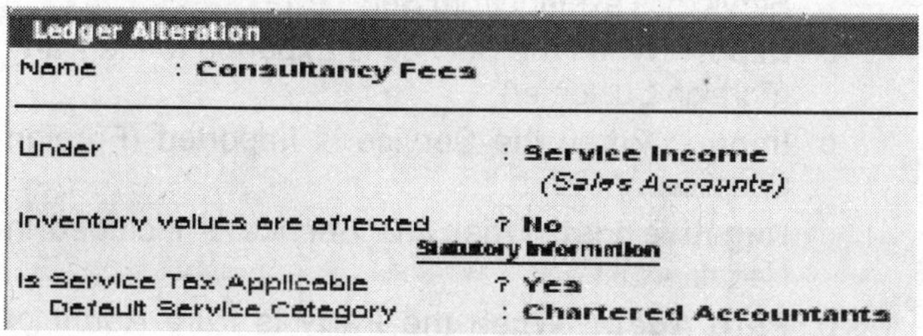

F-2A: Service Income Ledger Creation

F-2B:Service Category Selection List

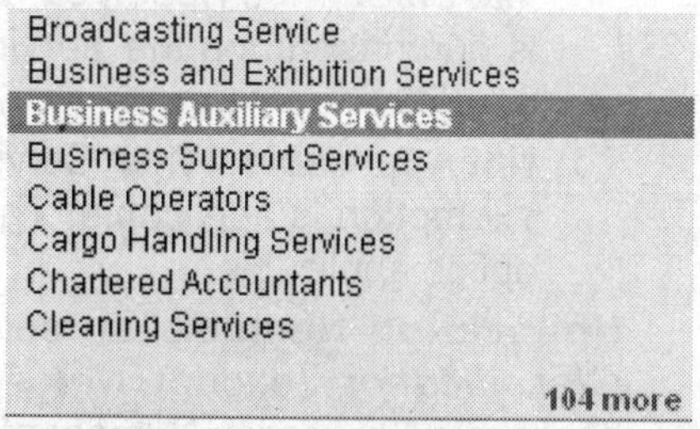

Now enter the details under *Statutory Information* as follows (F-2A):

Applicability of Service Tax: At *Is Service Tax Applicable* set as follows, set *Yes* if the Service Sales / Purchase Account is for *Taxable* Service, else set *No* (for *Non Taxable* Services).

- **Principal Service Category**: For Taxable Service Accounts (when you have set Yes at *Is Service Tax Applicable)*, you get another field *Default Service Category* (F-2A) to select the Service Category from the list (F-2B):
  - o Select the Main Service Category of the organization (if the Services rendered by the Organisation falls under multiple Service Category, select the Service Category in respect of principal Services offered by the Organisation).
  - o You may also select *Taxable Service* (instead of any specific Item) from the list

04 Service Tax Ledgers

Here we explain the options to be set up for the following types of Ledger Accounts, for Service Tax:

- **Service Tax Account**: One common Service Tax Account, or separate
  - o Input Service Tax Account (for Service Tax on Service Purchase)
  - o Output Service Tax Account (for Service Tax on Service Sales)
- **Cess Accounts**: For each of the above accounts, you may create separate Service Tax Cess Account as follows (or create a combo account for Service Tax & Cess)
  - o *Service Tax Education Cess* Account
  - o *Service Tax Secondary Education Cess* Account

04.01 Service Tax Ledger Accounts Creation

At the Ledger Account creation / alteration (F-3A), set as follows:

- At *Name* enter the appropriate Name of the Ledger Account
- At *Under*, select *Duties & Taxes* (as all the above accounts are Tax Accounts). Input Tax Ledger Accounts may alternatively be placed under *Current Asset* Group (or its subgroup), instead of Duties & Taxes, as it is deductible from Output Tax. However, such ledger account must be used for Input Tax Credit.

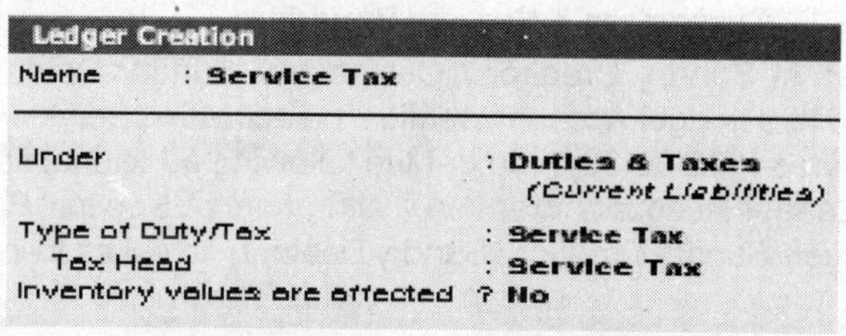

F-3A: Service Tax Ledger Creation

- At *Type of Duty Tax*, select *Service Tax* from the list (F-3B)(as all the above accounts relate to Service Tax)
- At *Tax Head,* select from the list (F-3C) as follows
  - o *Service Tax* for Service Tax Ledger Account
  - o *Service Tax Education Cess* for Service Tax Education Cess Account

   - o *Service Tax Secondary Education Cess* for Service Tax Secondary Education Cess Account
- At the *Inventory Values are affected*, set *No*

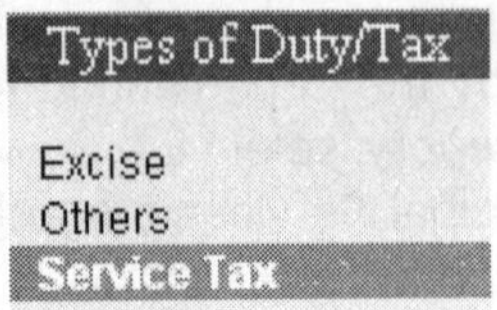

F-3B: Duty Type selection List

F-3C: Tax Head selection list

You may create one Service Tax Ledger for Service Tax & Cess Accounts. However, if you adjust Input Tax Credit, separate Output & Input Service Tax accounts may be helpful. Accordingly, you have to select the option at the field *Tax Head* of the respective Ledger Account (F-3A), as follows:

So, you may create:

- One Common Service Tax Ledger Account (combining Service Tax & Cess Accounts). Select *Any* at the field *Tax Head*
- One *Input* Service Tax Ledger Account & another *Output* Service Tax Ledger Account (combining Service Tax & Cess Accounts), i.e 2 Tax Ledger Accounts. Select *Any* at the field *Tax Head*
- Separate Ledger Accounts for Service Tax, Educational Cess & Higher Educational Cess, separately for Input & Output Tax. i.e 6 Tax Ledger Accounts. At the field *Tax Head*, select as follows:
   - o *Service Tax* at both the Input & Out Put Service Tax accounts
   - o *Education Cess* at both the Input & Out Put Education Cess accounts
   - o *Secondary Education Cess* at both the Input & Out Put Secondary Education Cess accounts.

FAQ: Frequently Asked Questions

FAQ-1: How to create Party Ledger Accounts of Service Customers & Service Providers

Ans: At Sundry Creditor / Customers (Sundry Debtors / Creditors Ledger Account creation, on activating Service Tax features (§02/06-02), you get the following additional fields at Ledger Accounts creation / alteration of Service Party Ledger (Sundry Creditor / Sundry Debtors), to set as follows:

Service Tax Applicability: At *Is Service Tax Applicable* (F-1A), set:

- *Yes* for Customers whom you charge Service Tax in your bills.
- *Yes* for Suppliers who charges you service tax that you claim for credit.
- *No* for other ledger accounts.

Party Ledger Service Tax Details

Having set *Yes* at *Is Service Tax Applicable* at Service Party Ledger creation screen (F-1A), you get additional option *Set Alter Service Tax*. Set *Yes* to get *Service Tax Details* subscreen (F-1B), to specify the Service Tax details as follows:

- **Party Service Tax Registration Number**: At *Registration Number*, enter the Service Tax Registration Number of the party. This info is printed on Invoice and various Service Tax Reports.
- **Party Service Tax Registration Date**: At *Date of Registration*, enter the Service Tax Registration Date of the Party.
- **Associated Enterprise**: At *Is Associated Enterprise* Set Yes if the Party is Associated entity of the Organisation (e.g, under same management)
- **Tax Classification Type:** At *Type of Classification*, select from the list as follows (F-1C):
   - o **Exempt**: When the Party (supplier / receiver of Service) is exempt from Service Tax
   - o **Export**: When the Service is Exported to the Party (Foreign Customer)
   - o **Import:** When the Service is Imported (Foreign Supplier)
   - o **Negative List**: When the Service is included in Negative List
   - o **Pure Agent**: When the Party is Pure Agent of Service supplier / Receiver
   - o **Tax on Service Received**: When Transport Service is purchased and the Service Receiver is liable to pay Tax.
   - o **Not Applicable:** When Service Tax is applicable (no exemption is applicable) This is the most common option applicable.
- **Notification Number**: On selection of the *Type of Classification* (except *Not Applicable*), enter the applicable Notification Number of the Government

Service Bill Entry

03-04

01 Service Bill Entry

Having set up the Company and having created the Ledger Accounts as explained earlier (§01/03-03), you are now ready to start entry of Sales Voucher in respect of Sales of Service

The Service Tax is to be charged by the service provider, in the service bill, when any taxable service is provided (i.e. for Sale of Service).

As discussed earlier, you may enter Service Sales Voucher either in:

- Voucher Mode (§02)
- Accounts Invoice Mode (§03)

Here we explain the steps which are exclusively related to Sales Voucher entry in respect of Sales of Service

02 Service Bill Entry in Voucher Mode

To Enter the Service Sales Voucher, create a Sales Voucher (Accounts Voucher>F8:Sales:F-1A) in Accounts Voucher (click V:*As Voucher* button) Mode (F-1A)

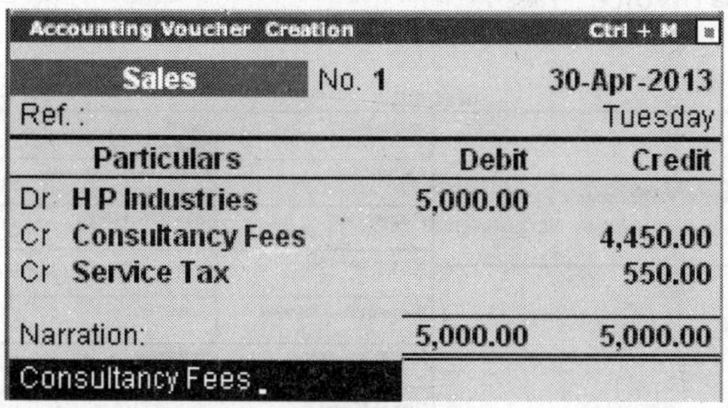

F-1A: Sales Voucher with Service Tax

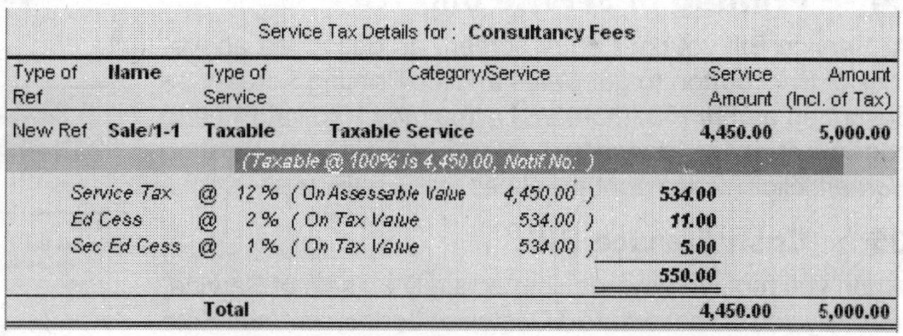

F-1B: Service Tax details entry in Sales Voucher

Now enter as follows:

- In first ledger entry (Fig 1A), select the Party Ledger (or Cash / Bank Account when the payment is immediately received in Cash / Cheque) and enter the Net Amount of the Service Bill (inclusive of Tax etc) at Debit column, to get the Bill Allocation window.
- At Bill Allocation Window, enter Bill Ref No, Due Date and Net Bill Amount of respective reference, as usual.
- At second ledger entry, select Service Income Ledger to get *Service Tax details* screen (F-1B). Enter the details as described next.
- At third ledger, select Service Tax Ledger to get the Service Tax Details entry screen showing the computation details (F-1A)
- Next enter other ledger accounts details, if any, one by one.
- Finally, enter Voucher Narration (F-1A), if any, and Press *Ctrl +A* to save the Voucher quickly.

Service Tax Details: At *Service Tax Details screen* (F-1B), enter as follows:

At *Service Tax details for* (at the Header), the ledger name as selected in main voucher (F-1A) is displayed for reference.

Now enter the Bill Details as follows:

- At *Name* column, the Voucher Number is carried (by default a subscript like /1 is added to the Voucher Number as Reference Number), which you may change.
- At category / Service column, the default Service Category is carried (*Taxable Service* is carried if you have set *Not Applicable* at Type of Classification at the Party Master (F-3C/06-03) and the field is skipped.
- At *Service Amount*, enter the Service Account Ledger Amount. Consequently, the computed amount inclusive of Service Tax is shown in *Amount Incl of Tax* column (Service Income amount is shown at the Credit Column in the main voucher screen (F-1A)
- The various components of Service Tax is shown next. Accept the Service the Tax Details Screen (press <enter>) to get back the Main voucher entry screen (F-1A).

03 Service Bill Entry in Invoice Mode

Entry of Sales Transaction in Accounting Invoice Mode has been explained earlier (§06.02/03-06). In the same way as explained for entry in Voucher Mode (§02), you may enter

Service Sales Invoice in Accounting Invoice Mode (F-2A & F-2B).

Enter the Party (or Cash / Bank Account) ledger at the header (F-2A). The Service Tax details screen entry for Invoice Mode (F-2B) is similar to that for Voucher Mode (F-2A)

Accounting Voucher Creation Ctrl + M

Sales No. 2 **31-May-2013**
Ref.: 12 Friday
Party's A/c Name : **H P Industries**

Particulars	Rate	per	Amount
Consultancy Fees			3,000.00
Service Tax			371.00
Narration:			3,371.00

Consultancy Fees

F-2A: Sales Voucher with Service Tax in Invoice Mode

Service Tax Details for : **Consultancy Fees**

Type of Ref	Name	Type of Service	Category/Service	Service Amount	Amount (Incl. of Tax)
New Ref	Sale/12-1	Taxable	Taxable Service	3,000.00	3,371.00

Service Tax	@	*12 % (On Assessable Value*	*3,000.00)*	360.00
Ed Cess	@	*2 % (On Tax Value*	*360.00)*	7.00
Sec Ed Cess	@	*1 % (On Tax Value*	*360.00)*	4.00
				371.00

Total	3,000.00	3,371.00

F-2B:Service Tax details entry screen

04 Printing of Service Bill

At Service Bill voucher entry screen, as described above, click P:*Print* button to get *Sales Invoice* Printing Screen, as described earlier (§03/03-03/S1). You may also set Printing configuration as described (§03/03-03/S1). At *Printing Screen*, click *Yes* to print the Sales Invoice (F-3A).

05 Cash Service Bill

When you receive payment immedialtely on sale of Service, normally you do not create a Customer Ledger. In Cash Sale Invoice, in which you may select the Cash / Bank Account, instead of Customer Ledger Account.

Buyer Details: At Invoice Entry screen, clcik *F12:Configure* to get *Invoice Entry Configurtaion screen* (§04.04/03-02/S1). At *Invoice Entry Configurtaion* screen (§04.04/03-02/S1). at *Accept Supplementary Details:*

- *Buyer's Details*: Set *Yes* to get *Supplemntray Details entry* screen (F-3B).

  At *Supplementary details* screen (F-3B), enetr the Buyer dtails. Now print the Cash Sales Invoice in the same way as described for sales Invoice.The Buyer's details (as entered at Supplementary Details: F-3B) would also be printed in the Sales Invoice (F-3C).
- *Without Buyer Details*: Set *No* for quick entry & printing of sales invoice without buye'rs details. Print the Invoice after entry, as described. At Buye's Name in the Invoice, *CASH* would be shown

INVOICE

A B Services
12 Heysham Rd
Kolkata 700999
Contact :033 12345678,9876543210

Invoice No. 1	Dated 30-Apr-2013
Delivery Note	Mode/Terms of Payment 30 Days
Supplier's Ref.	Other Reference(s)
Buyer's Order No.	Dated
Despatch Document No.	Dated
Despatched through	Destination
Terms of Delivery	

Buyer
H P Industries
34 Dharmatalla St
Kolakta 799999

Sl No.	Particulars	Quantity	Rate	per	Amount
	Consultancy Fees (Service : Taxable Service)				4,450.00
	Service Tax (On Assessable Amount 4,450.00)		12	%	534.00
	Education Cess		2	%	11.00
	Secondary and Higher Education Cess		1	%	5.00
	Total				₹ 5,000.00

Amount Chargeable (in words) E. & O.E
INR Five Thousand Only

Remarks:
SErvice Bill

Company's Service Tax No. : ABC1234
Buyer's Service Tax No. : ABCDE1234X
Company's PAN : ABCDE12345X

for A B Services

Authorised Signatory

F-3A: Sales Invoice

Buyer's Details

Buyers : **Manick Das**
Address : 12 Dharmatolla St
Kolakta 799999
Sales Tax No :
CST Number :

F-3B: Buyer's details in Cash Sale Invoice

INVOICE

A B Services
12 Heysham Rd
Kolkata 700999
Contact :033 12345678,9876543210

Invoice No. 1	Dated 30-Apr-2013
Delivery Note	Mode/Terms of Payment 30 Days
Supplier's Ref.	Other Reference(s)
Buyer's Order No.	Dated
Despatch Document No.	Dated
Despatched through	Destination
Terms of Delivery	

Buyer
Manick Das
12 Dharmatolla St
Kolakta 799999

Sl No.	Particulars	Quantity	Rate	per	Amount
	Consultancy Fees (Service : Taxable Service)				4,450.00
	Service Tax (On Assessable Amount 4,450.00)		12	%	534.00
	Education Cess		2	%	11.00
	Secondary and Higher Education Cess		1	%	5.00
	Total				₹ 5,000.00

Amount Chargeable (in words) E. & O.E
INR Five Thousand Only

Remarks:
SErvice Bill

Company's Service Tax No. : ABC1234
Company's PAN : ABCDE12345X

for A B Services

Authorised Signatory

This is a Computer Generated Invoice

F-3C: Cash Sales Invoice

FAQ: Frequently Asked Questions

FAQ1: Explain the steps of entry of Service Sales Voucher

To enter the Service Sales Voucher (F-1A), create a Sales Voucher (Accounts Voucher>F8:Sales), as follows:

- In first ledger entry (F-1A), select the Party Ledger (or Cash / Bank Account when the payment is immediately received in Cash / Cheque) and enter the Net Amount of the Service Bill (inclusive of Tax etc) at Debit column, to get the Bill Allocation window.
- At Bill Allocation Window enter Bill Ref No, Due Date and Net Bill Amount of respective reference, as usual.
- At second ledger entry, select Service Income Ledger to get *Service Tax details* screen (F-1B), enter the Tax details. The Service Income Ledger amount is shown at th Credit Column of the main voucher screen (F-1A)
- At third ledger, select Service Tax Ledger to get the Service Tax Details entry screen showing the computation details (F-1A)
- Enter Voucher Narration (F-1A), if any, and Press *Ctrl +A* to save the Voucher.

Service Tax Payable 03-05

01 Service Tax Payable

On creation of Service Bill for Taxable Service, charging Service Tax, Service Tax becomes payable (even if the payment of the Bill is not received).

To View / Print the Service Tax Payable statement (or other Service Tax related reports), At Gateway, select *Display > Statutory Reports* to get *Statutory Reports* Menu (F-1A). At *Statutory Reports* Menu, (F-1A), select *Service Tax Reports* to get *Service Tax Reports Menu* (F-1B).

F-1A: Statutory Reports Menu

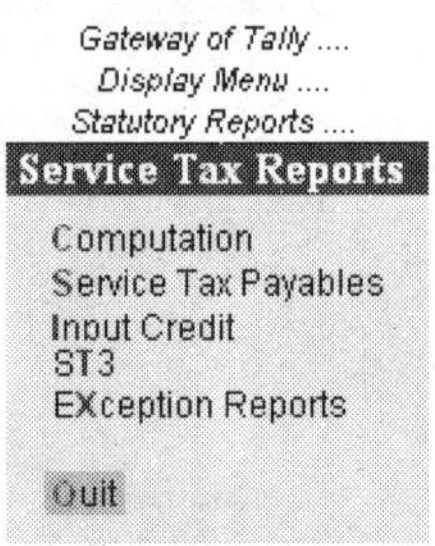

F-1B:Service Tax Reports Menu

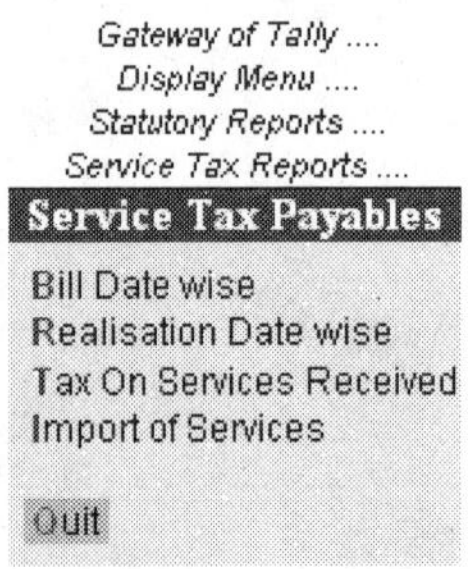

F-1C: Service Tax Payables Menu

Service Tax Computation — Ctrl + M

Particulars	A B Services 1-Apr-2013 to 30-Jun-2013		
	Total Amount	Assessable Value	Tax Amount
A. Input Credit			
Current Period			
Previous Period			
B. Service Tax Payable	8,371.00	7,450.00	921.00
Current Period	8,371.00	7,450.00	921.00
Previous Period			
C. Service Tax Payments / Credit Adjustments			
D. Balance Service Tax Payable (B-C)			921.00
E. Refund of Service Tax Input Credit			
F. Balance Available Credit			
G. Service Tax Adjusted Towards Excise Payabl			
H. Other Payments			

F-2 Computation Statement

02 Computation Statement

The Computation statement shows the summary of Tax Payable.

At *Service Tax* Menu (F-1B), select *Computation* to get Computation screen.(F-2). Click *F2:Period* button (or press F2) and set the period for the Report to get the Computation Report for the specified period (F-2).

The *Computation Statement* (F-2) shows the summary figures of Total Bill Amount, Assessable Value and Net Tax Payable at one glance. Tax as shown in Computation Statement is to be deposited to Govt. (§01/02-06)

03 Service Tax Payables Statements

While the Computation Statement shows the summary figures of Bills & Tax payable, The Service Tax Payable Reports show the details of Bills for which Tax is to be deposited.

At *Service Tax* menu (F-1B), select *Service Tax Payables* to get Service Tax Payable Report Menu (F-1C), showing the list of Reports related to Service Tax Payables

04 Bill Datewise Service Tax Payable Reports

At *Service Tax Payable* Report Menu (F-1C), select *Bill Datewise* to Display list of Bills for which Service Tax is still payable (F-3A).

04.01 Bill Date wise Service Tax Payables Statement Configuration

At *Service Tax Payables* Report (F-3A), Click *F12: Configuration* to get *Service Tax Payables Configuration* screen (F-3C), to set Cnfigurtaion options as below:

Service Tax Registration Number: At *Show Service Tax Registration Number,* set *Yes* to show the column of Service Tax Registration Number of the Party (Service Receiver), else set *No* (Service Tax Registration Number column will not be shown)

Service Tax Payable (Bill Date - wise) — A B Services — Ctrl + M

Type of Bills : Realised Bills — 1-Apr-2013 to 30-Jun-2013

Date	Ref. No.	Category	Bill Amount	Total Tax	Realised Amount	Total Tax Payable	Balance to be Paid
30-Apr-2013	Sale/1-1	Taxable Service	5,000.00	550.00	5,000.00	550.00	550.00
31-May-2013	Sale/12-1	Taxable Service	3,371.00	371.00	3,371.00	371.00	371.00
Total			8,371.00	921.00	8,371.00	921.00	921.00

F-3A:Service Tax Payable Statement Bill date wise (Condensed)

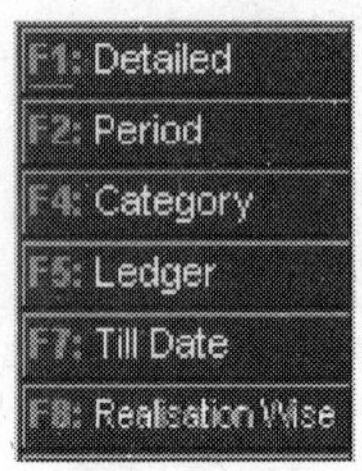

F-3B Buttons

Assessable Value: At *Show Assessable Value*, set Yes to show Assessable Value figures, else set No (the options for display of Assessable Value figures will not be shown)

Having set Yes at *Show Assessable Value,* you may set the following options

- **Billed Assessable Value:** At *Show Billed Assessable Value,* set *Yes* to show the Assessable Value of Billed Amount, else set No (the Billed Assessable Value figure will not be shown)
- **Realised Assessable Value:** At *Show Realised Assessable Value,* set *Yes* to show the Assessable Value of Realised Amount, else set No (the Realised Assessable Value figure will not be shown)

04.02 Bill Date wise Service Tax Payable Report Buttons

At *Bill Datewise Service Tax Payable* Statement Display (F-3A), you get following buttons (F-3B)

- **F4:Category:** To select a Service Tax Category to get the Report for selected Category (or select *All Items* to show for all Tax Categories)
- **F5:Ledger**: To select a Customer (Service Receiver) Ledger Account to get the Report for selected Ledger (or select *All Items* to show for all Customer Ledgers)

A B Services

Service Tax Payable

Bill Date - wise

1-Apr-2013 to 3-Jun-2013

Page 1 (A)

Type of Bills : All Bills

Date	Ref. No.			Party's Name	Category	Bill Amount	Service Tax	Ed Cess	Sec Ed Cess	Total Tax	Realised Amount	Service Tax Payable
30-Apr-2013	Sale/1-1			H P Industries	Taxable Service	5,000.00	534.00	11.00	5.00	550.00	5,000.00	534.00
30-Apr-2013	Sales	1	5,000.00									
31-May-2013	Sale/12-1			H P Industries	Taxable Service	3,371.00	360.00	7.00	4.00	371.00	3,371.00	360.00
31-May-2013	Sales	2	3,371.00									
Total						8,371.00	894.00	18.00	9.00	921.00	8,371.00	894.00

F-4A:Service Tax Payable Statement Bill date wise (detailed – Part A)

- **F7:Monthly/ Till date**: Toggle button to get Monthwise / uptodate list of Bills
- **F8:Realisation Datewise**: To get Realsiation Datewise Report – F-4A (you may also get it by selecting Realsiation Datewise option at Service Tax Paybales Reports Menu (F-1C)

04.03 Bill Date wise Service Tax Payable Report Printing

At *Bill Datewise Service Tax Payable* Statement Display (F-3A), click *P:Print* button to get *Bill Date wise Service Tax Payable Printing* screen (F-3D). Type Y to print get the report in print (F-4A), as per Configuration options set (F-3C)

This report provides options to print many columns. So, the Report may extend to multiple parts (F-4A), if a number of columns are selected at the configuration option (F-3C).

The first column (Bill Reference) is repeated in all the parts for reference (F-4A)

Page 1 (B)

Type of Bills : All Bills

Date	Ref. No.			Ed Cess Payable	Sec Ed Cess Payable	Total Tax Payable	Balance to be Paid
30-Apr-2013	Sale/1-1			11.00	5.00	550.00	550.00
30-Apr-2013	Sales	1	5,000.00				
31-May-2013	Sale/12-1			7.00	4.00	371.00	371.00
31-May-2013	Sales	2	3,371.00				
Total				18.00	9.00	921.00	931.00

Service Tax Payable Statement - Bill date wise (detailed – Part B)

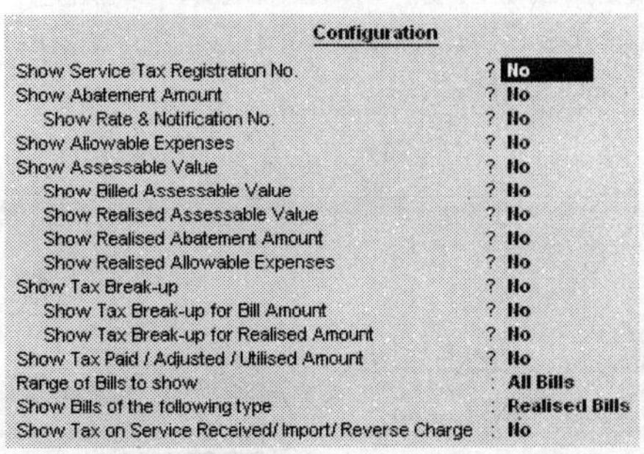

F-3C: Bill Date wise Service Tax Display Configuration

F-3D: Bill Date wise Service Tax Printing

05 Realisation Date wise Service Tax Payable

Realisation date is the actual Date of Receipt of money by the Service Provider. For example, Payment of Bill No 5 Dt 25.2.14. is received on 1.3. 14. Then for Bill No 5, Bill Date is 25.2.14 and Realisation Date is 1.3.14.

At Service Tax Payable Report Menu (F-1C), select *Realisation Datewise* to get *Realisation Date wise Service Tax Payable Display* (F-5A), showing list of Bills for which Service Tax is still payable, as per Date of Realisation

The contents of *Realisation Date wise Service Tax Payable Report* (F-5A) is similar to Bill Datewise report (F-3A). The Bills appear as per date of realization. However, the Import Bills / Tax on Service Received Bills are excluded from the Report.

Service Tax Payable (Realisation Date-wise) — A B Services 13-14 — Ctrl + M

1-Apr-2013 to 31-Mar-2014

Date	Vch Type	Vch No.	Party's Name	Category	Realised Amount	Realised Assessable Value	Total Tax Payable
							2 more ... →
2-Jul-2013	Receipt	1	K B Enterprise	Taxable Service	3,001.00	2,671.00	330.00
2-Aug-2013	Sales	3	K B Enterprise	Taxable Service	7,000.00	6,230.00	770.00
9-Aug-2013	Sales	4	H P Industries	Taxable Service	3,371.00	3,000.00	371.00
20-Aug-2013	Sales	6	B R Traders	Taxable Service	7,865.00	7,000.00	865.00
26-Aug-2013	Sales	7	M N Agencies	Taxable Service	1,11,124.00	90,000.00	11,124.00
	Total				1,32,361.00	1,08,901.00	13,460.00

F-5A: Realisation Datewise Payable Part 1

Ctrl + M

1-Apr-2013 to 31-Mar-2014

Paid / Adjusted	Balance To Be Paid
	330.00
	770.00
	371.00
	865.00
	11,124.00
	13,460.00

Part 2

05.01 Realisation Date wise Service Tax Payable Configuration

At *Service Tax Payable Report (Realisation Datewise*: F-5A), Click *F12:Configure* to get Configuration screen (F-5B), to set the Configuration options of the Report as below:

- **Service Tax Registration Number**: At *Show Service Tax Registration Number,* set *Yes* to show the column of Service Tax Registration Number of the Party (Service Receiver), else set *No* (Service Tax Registration Number column will not be shown)
- **Tax Details:** At *Tax Break Up*, set *Yes* to show the Tax & Cess figures separately, else set *No* (combined Tax & Cess figures are shown).
- **Paid / Adjusted Bils**: At *Show Tax paid / Adjusted Bills,* set *Yes* to show the Bills for which Tax has been adjusted / paid also, else set *No* to show only Bills for which Tax has not been paid yet.

Configuration

Show Service Tax Registration No.	? **No**
Show Tax Break-up	? **No**
Show Tax Paid/Adjusted Bills also	? **No**

(Note: This report excludes Tax on Service Recd/Import Tax Bills)

F-5B: Configuration screen for Realisation Datewise Payable Report

F2: Period
F4: Category
F5: Ledger

F-5C Realisation Datewise Report Buttons

05.02 Realisation Date wise Service Tax Payable Buttons

At *Service Tax Payable Report (Realisation Datewise)* Report, you get buttons (F-4C)

- **F4:Category:** To select Service Tax Category to get the Report for selected Category (or select *All Items* to show for all Tax Categories)
- **F5:Ledger**: To select Customer (Service Receiver) Ledger Account to get the Report for selected Ledger (or select *All Items* to show for all Customer Ledgers)

05.03 Realisation Date wise Service Tax Payable Printing

At *Realisation Datewise Service Tax Payable* Display (F-5A), click *P:Print* button to get Realisation Date wise Service Tax Payable Printing screen (F-6A). Type Y to print get the report in print (F-6B), as per Configuration options set (F-5B)

The Report may extend to multiple parts (F-6B), if a number of columns are selected at the *Configuration* option (F-5B).

Report Titles

Service Tax Payable
Realisation Date-wise

F-6A: Service Tax Payable (Realisation Datewise) printing

FAQ: Frequently Asked Question

FAQ-1: How to get figures of Output / Input Service Tax and Service Tax Payable

Ans: Print the Service Tax Computation Statement (§02), which shows the summary figures of Total Bill Amount, Assessable Value and Net Tax Payable at one glance. Tax as shown in Computation Statement is to be deposited to Govt. (§01/06-06).

At *Service Tax* Menu (F-1B), select *Computation* to get Computation screen.(F-2). Click *F2:Period* button (or press F2) and set the period for the Report to get the Computation Report for the specified period (F-2).

Service Tax Payable
Realisation Date-wise
1-Aug-2013 to 31-Aug-2013

Page 1 (A)

Date	Vch Type	Vch No.	Party's Name	Category	Realised Amount	Realised Assessable Value	Total Tax Payable	Paid / Adjusted
2-Aug-2013	Sales	3	K B Enterprise	Taxable Service	7,000.00	6,230.00	770.00	
9-Aug-2013	Sales	4	H P Industries	Taxable Service	3,371.00	3,000.00	371.00	
20-Aug-2013	Sales	6	B R Traders	Taxable Service	7,865.00	7,000.00	865.00	
26-Aug-2013	Sales	7	M N Agencies	Taxable Service	1,11,124.00	90,000.00	11,124.00	
	Total				1,29,360.00	1,06,230.00	13,130.00	

F-6B: Service Tax Payable (Realisation Datewise) in Print – part 1

Page 1 (B)

Balance To Be Paid
770.00
371.00
865.00
11,124.00
13,130.00

part 2

Service Tax Deposit 03-06

01 Service Tax Deposit

The Service Tax is to be paid Quarterly / Monthly (depending on constitution of Organisation - §07/01-01), as per Computation Statement discussed earlier (§02/03-05).

02 Service Tax Payment Voucher

To deposit Service Tax, create a Payment voucher (F-1A). At Payment Voucher entry screen, on selection of *Service Tax Ledger* Account, the *Bill Allocation* screen for Service Tax Ledger appears (F-1C).

At *Bill Allocation* screen (F-1C), at *Type of Ref* column, select *Against Ref* to get the list of Bills for which Tax is Payable (F-1B). The amount payable appears as default (which you may change). This way, select all the Bills for which Service Tax to be paid. The total of amount entered for the selected Bills at Bill Allocation screen (F-1C) is carried in the Voucher at Amount column (F-1A).

Accounting Voucher Creation — Ctrl + M

Payment No. 1 — **5-Jun-2013** Wednesday

Account : **HDFC Bank**

Particulars		Amount
Service Tax		**921.00**
Provide Details	: **Yes**	
Narration:		**921.00**
Service Tax for Apr13-Jun13		

F-1A Service Tax Payment Voucher

F-1B Lisit of Pending Bills for selection for Tax Payment

Pending Tax Bills					
Tax Name	Date	PartyName	Category	Total Tax	PendingTax
Sale/1-1	***30-Apr-2013***	***H P Industries***	***Taxable Service***	***550.00***	***550.00***
Sale/12-1	*31-May-2013*	*H P Industries*	*Taxable Service*	*371.00*	*371.00*

Service Tax Payment Details

Service Tax Details for : **Service Tax**

Type of Ref.	Name	Category/Service	Amount
Agst Ref	**Sale/1-1**	**Taxable Service**	**550.00**
Agst Ref	**Sale/12-1**	**Taxable Service**	**371.00**
			921.00

F-1C Bill Allocation screen for Tax Payment

At the voucher entry screen (F-1A), at *Provide Details*, set Yes to get *Service Tax Payment Details* screen (F-1D) to enter the following details:

- **Period**: At *From* & *To* field, enter the *Start Date* & *End Date* of the Period (Quarter / Month) for which Tax is being deposited.
- **Cheque Details**: Now enter the details of Payment (Cheque Details / Challan Details), by which the Tax is deposited to Bank as follows:
  - o **Cheque / DD Number**: At *Cheque / DD No*, enter the Cheque / DD Number
  - o Bank Name: At *Name of Bank*, enter the Bank Name
  - o **Bank Account Number**: At *Bank Account No*, enter the Bank Account Number from which the Cheque is drawn
  - o **Cheque Date**: At *Cheque Date*, enter the date of Cheque being deposited
- **Challan Details:** Now enter the details of Challan, by which the Tax is deposited to Bank as follows:
  - o **Challan Number:** At *Challan No*, enter the Challan Number
  - o **Challan Date:** At *Challan Date*, enter the Date of Challan
  - o **ePayment No**: Reference of e-Payment (if paid through electronic transfer)

03 Service Tax Challan Printing

At *Payment Voucher entry* screen (F-1A), click *P:Print* button to get Challan printing screen (F-2A), to print GAR 7 Challan / Payment Advice. Set the options a sfollows:

- **GAR 7 Challan**: At *Print GR 7 Challan,* set *Yes* to Print GAR-7 Challan to print the G.A.R 7 Challan (F-2B), else st No (GAR -7 Challan is not printed)
- **Payment Advice**: At *Print Payment Advice*, set *Yes* to Print *Payment Advice*, else set No (*Payment Advice* is not printed).

Service Tax Payment Details

From	:	1-Apr-2013
To	:	30-Jun-2013

(Note : This Payment Belongs to the Above Period)

Cheque / DD No.	:	123456
Name of Bank	:	*HDFC Bank*
Bank Account No.	:	12345678
Branch Name	:	Kanjurgachi
Cheque Date	:	5-Jun-2013
Challan No.	:	123
Challan Date	:	5-Jun-2013
ePayment No.	:	

(Note : All the Above Details Will Be Used in Challan, Forms & Returns)

F-1D Service Tax Payment Details

F-2A: Challan Printing Screen

Print G.A.R.-7 Challan	:	Yes
Print Payment Advice	:	**No**
Payment Advice Date	:	**5-Jun-2013**
Print Due Date	?	**No**
Print Company's PAN/IT Number	?	**No**

- **Payment Advice Date**: At *Print Payment Advice Date*, set *Yes* to Print *Payment Advice Date* also at Payment Advice, else set No (*Payment Advice Date* is not printed).
- **Due Date**: At *Print Due Date*, set Yes to pint Due Date also else set No (*Due Date* is not printed).
- **PAN**: At *Print Company's PAN / IT Number,* set Yes to print Company's PAN, else set No (Company's PAN is not printed).

04 ST- 3 Form Printing

Form ST-3 is a Half yearly Return of Service Tax (Apr-Sep/ Oct-Mar), to be filed within 25th of the month following the Half Year Ending (§08/01-01), alongwith the respective GR-7 Challans

At *ST-3 Menu* (F-3A), select *Report* to get ST-3 Printing screen (F-3B) to print ST-3 Report (F-4A). Set as follows:

- **Period**: Select the respective Half Year period from the list
- **Place**: Enter the place of filing the report.
- **Date**: Enter the Date of Report

The above data entered are printed in the S-3 Return.

For payments from April 2007 onwards **G.A.R.-7 Proforma for Service Tax Payments** (Receipts & Payment Rules 26)

Full Name	A B Services
Complete Address	12 Heysham Rd. Kolkata 7 00999
Telephone No.	033 123456
Pincode	700 09
Assessee Code No.	123456
Commissionerate Name	Kolkata
Commissionerate Code	01
Division Code	33
Range Code	WB

Accounting Code of the Service	Amount Tendered in Rupees
00441089	894
00440298	18
00440426	9
Total	921

RECEIVING BANK BRANCH STAMP

(In words) Rupees Nine Hundred Twenty One Only. tendered by

Cash/Cheque/Draft/Pay Order No. 123456 Dated 5-Jun-2013 Drawn on HDFC Bank

Signature of the Tenderer with date

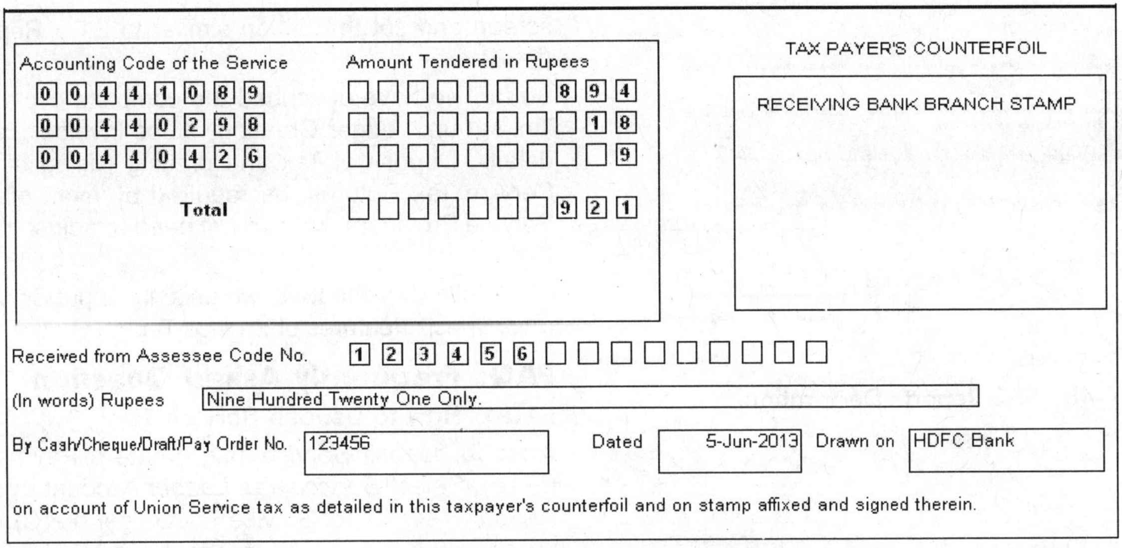
Accounting Code of the Service | Amount Tendered in Rupees | TAX PAYER'S COUNTERFOIL

Accounting Code of the Service	Amount Tendered in Rupees
00441089	894
00440298	18
00440426	9
Total	921

RECEIVING BANK BRANCH STAMP

Received from Assessee Code No. 123456

(In words) Rupees Nine Hundred Twenty One Only.

By Cash/Cheque/Draft/Pay Order No. 123456 Dated 5-Jun-2013 Drawn on HDFC Bank

on account of Union Service tax as detailed in this taxpayer's counterfoil and on stamp affixed and signed therein.

F-2B: G.A.R-7 Challan

ST-3 Form Contents

ST-3 Form (F-4A) is a long report running into several pages. The first 2 pages which contain the basic info of the Organisation and Tax Deposit details for the respective Half Year are shown here (F-4A).

At the end, the report contains Declaration in respect of Self Assessment (F-4B) to be signed by authorized signatory and Acknowledgement Part (F-4C) which would be signed by the Tax Authority on Receipt of ST-3 Form.

Gateway of Tally ....
Display Menu ....
Statutory Reports ....
Service Tax Reports ....

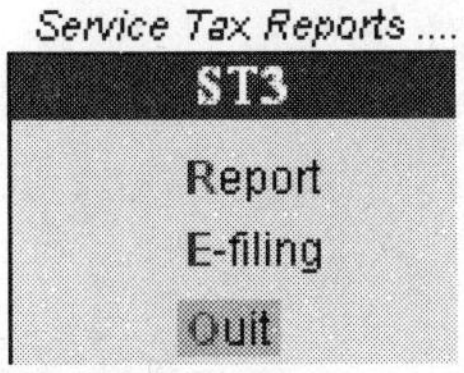

F-3A:ST-3 Menu

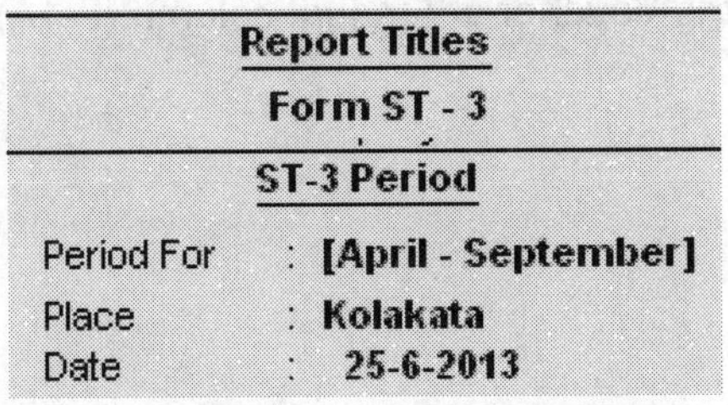

F-3B:ST-3 Form Printing/ e-filing

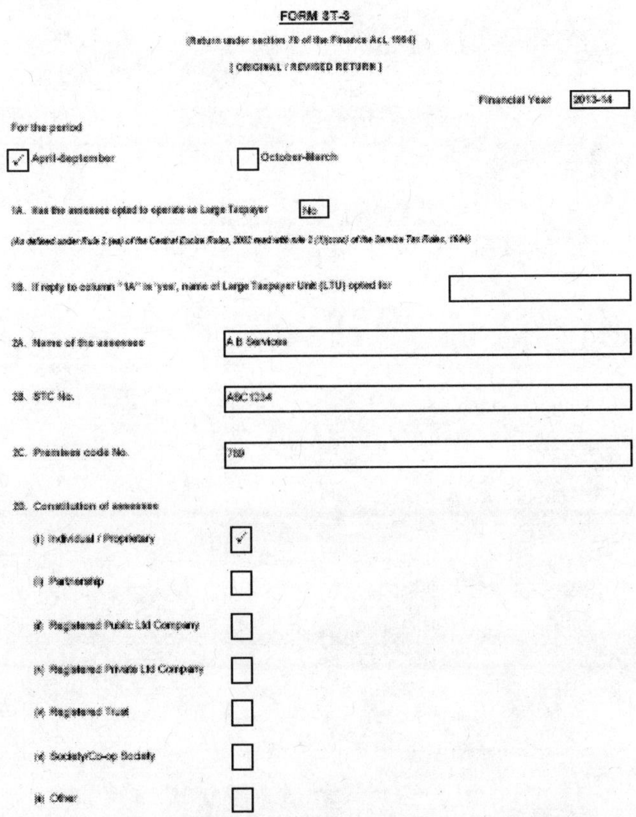
FORM ST-3

(Return under section 70 of the Finance Act, 1994)

[ORIGINAL / REVISED RETURN]

Financial Year 2013-14

For the period

☑ April-September ☐ October-March

1A. Has the assessee opted to operate as Large Taxpayer: No

(As defined under Rule 2 (ea) of the Central Excise Rules, 2002 read with rule 2 (1)(cccc) of the Service Tax Rules, 1994)

1B. If reply to column "1A" is 'yes', name of Large Taxpayer Unit (LTU) opted for

2A. Name of the assessee: A B Services

2B. STC No.: ABC1234

2C. Premises code No.: 789

2D. Constitution of assessee

(i) Individual / Proprietary ☑

(ii) Partnership ☐

(iii) Registered Public Ltd Company ☐

(iv) Registered Private Ltd Company ☐

(v) Registered Trust ☐

(vi) Society/Co-op Society ☐

(vii) Other ☐

F-4A: ST-3 Form : Page 1

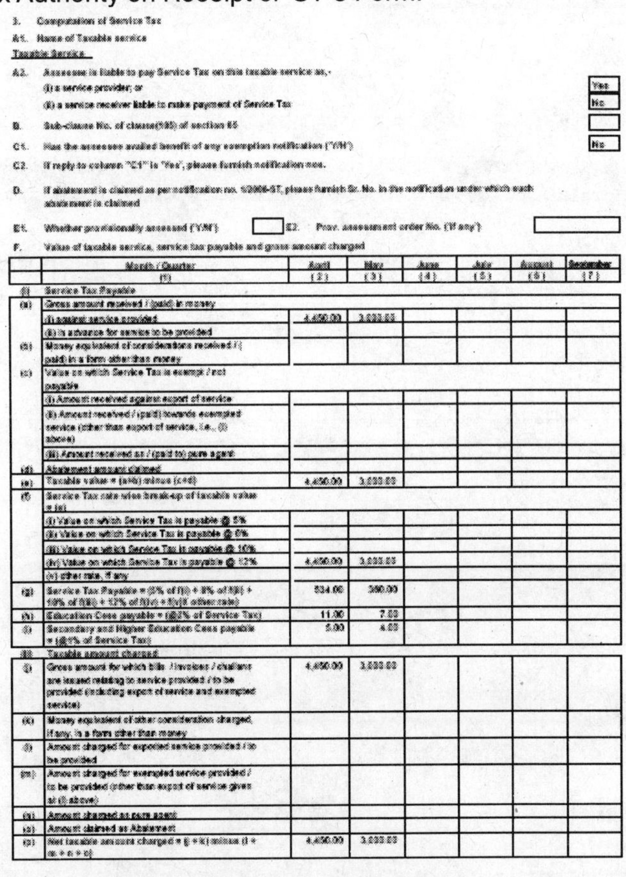
3. Computation of Service Tax

A1. Name of Taxable service

Taxable Service

A2. Assessee is liable to pay Service Tax on this taxable service as,-

(i) a service provider; or: Yes

(ii) a service receiver liable to make payment of Service Tax: No

B. Sub-clause No. of clause(105) of section 65

C1. Has the assessee availed benefit of any exemption notification ('Y/N'): No

C2. If reply to column "C1" is 'Yes', please furnish notification nos.

D. If abatement is claimed as per notification no. 1/2006-ST, please furnish Sr. No. in the notification under which such abatement is claimed

E1. Whether provisionally assessed ('Y/N') E2. Prov. assessment order No. ('If any')

F. Value of taxable service, service tax payable and gross amount charged

	Month / Quarter (1)	April (2)	May (3)	June (4)	July (5)	August (6)	September (7)
(I)	Service Tax Payable						
(a)	Gross amount received / (paid) in money						
	(i) against service provided	4,450.00	3,033.03				
	(ii) in advance for service to be provided						
(b)	Money equivalent of considerations received / (paid) in a form other than money						
(c)	Value on which Service Tax is exempt / not payable						
	(i) Amount received against export of service						
	(ii) Amount received / (paid) towards exempted service (other than export of service, i.e., (i) above)						
	(iii) Amount received as / (paid to) pure agent						
(d)	Abatement amount claimed						
(e)	Taxable value = (a+b) minus (c+d)	4,450.00	3,033.03				
(f)	Service Tax rate wise break-up of taxable value = (e)						
	(i) Value on which Service Tax is payable @ 5%						
	(ii) Value on which Service Tax is payable @ 8%						
	(iii) Value on which Service Tax is payable @ 10%						
	(iv) Value on which Service Tax is payable @ 12%	4,450.00	3,033.03				
	(v) other rate, if any						
(g)	Service Tax Payable = (5% of f(i) + 8% of f(ii) + 10% of f(iii) + 12% of f(iv) + f(v)X other rate)	534.00	360.00				
(h)	Education Cess payable = (@2% of Service Tax)	11.00	7.00				
(i)	Secondary and Higher Education Cess payable = (@1% of Service Tax)	5.00	4.00				
(II)	Taxable amount charged						
(j)	Gross amount for which bills / invoices / challans are issued relating to service provided / to be provided (including export of service and exempted service)	4,450.00	3,033.03				
(k)	Money equivalent of other consideration charged, if any, in a form other than money						
(l)	Amount charged for exported service provided / to be provided						
(m)	Amount charged for exempted service provided / to be provided (other than export of service given at (l) above)						
(n)	Amount charged as pure agent						
(o)	Amount claimed as Abatement						
(p)	Net taxable amount charged = (j + k) minus (l + m + n + o)	4,450.00	3,033.03				

ST-3 Report : Page 2

7. Self Assessment memorandum

(a) I / We declare that the above particulars are in accordance with the records and books maintained by me / us and are correctly stated.

(b) I / We have assessed and paid the Service Tax and / or availed and distributed CENVAT credit correctly as per the provisions of the Finance Act, 1994 and the rules made thereunder.

(c) I / We have paid duty within the specified time limit and in case of delay, I / We have deposited the interest leviable thereon.

8. If the return has been prepared by a Service Tax Return Preparer (STRP), furnish further details as below:

(a) Identification No. of STRP

(b) Name of STRP

(Signature of Service Tax Return Preparer)

Place : Kolkata
Date : 25-Jun-2013

(Name and Signature of Assessee or Authorised Signatory)

F-4B : ST-3 Report : Declaration

ACKNOWLEDGEMENT

Date : 25-Jun-2013
Place : Kolkata

I hereby acknowledge the receipt of your ST-3 return for the period April 2013 - September 2013

(Signature of the Officer of Central Excise & Service Tax)

(With Name & Official Seal)

F-4C : ST-3 Report : Acknowledgement

05 ST-3 E-filing

At ST-3 Menu (F-3A), select *E-filing* to get ST-3 Printing screen and set the option similar to ST-3 Report Printing (F-3B)

So far, we have described the complete cycle of Service Tax set up, Ledger Creation, Sales Invoice, Tax Payables details, Deposit of Tax and printing / filing of Half Yearly Service Tax Returns, as required by most of the smaller Service Providers, who do not need to adjust Input Service Tax.

In the following chapters, we describe Input Service Tax and other special features of Service Tax.

FAQ: Frequently Asked Question

FAQ-1: How to Deposit Service Tax

Ans: To deposit Service Tax, create a Payment voucher (F-1A). Select *Service Tax Ledger* Account to get the *Bill Allocation* screen for Service Tax Ledger (F-1C).

At *Bill Allocation* screen (F-1C), select Bills one by one for which Tax is payable (F-1B). The total of amount for the selected Bills at Bill Allocation screen (F-1C) is carried in the Voucher at Amount column (F-1A).

Input Service Tax Credit

01 Input Service Tax

We have discussed Service Tax in Sales voucher (§01/06-04) for services provided and deposit of Service Tax with Government (§02/03-06)

Some organizations also buy Taxable Services paying service tax, to provide Taxable Services, If Taxable service is bought to render a Taxable Service sold, then the service tax paid on services purchased (called *Input Tax Credit*) may be adjusted from the service tax payable on services rendered.

02 Input Service Tax related Ledger Accounts

To enter data for Service Purchase, first create the ledger accounts related to Purchase of Taxable Service, for which Input Credit is to be claimed

Accounts Ledger creation is explained earlier (§03.02/01-03/S1). Create the ledger accounts of:

- Service Purchase (F-1A),
- Input Service Tax (F-1B),
- Service Supplier (F-1C),

Creation of Ledger Accounts related to Service Sale Bill has been explained earlier (§02/03-03). In the same way, create Ledger Accounts related to purchase of Service

02.01 Service Purchase Ledger

At Service Purchase Ledger creation screen (F-1A), set as follows:

Ledger Name: At *Name* field, enter the appropriate Ledger Name:

- **Service Purchase / Service Expenses:** Enter the Name of the Ledger Account, like Professional Fees Paid etc. Service Charges Paid etc.

Parent Group: At *Under* field, select the parent Group, such as:

- **Service Purchase / Service Expenses**: *Purchase* or *Direct Expenses*

Inventory Link: Since service expense are not related to materials (it is about manpower), at the field *Inventory Values are Affected,* select *No* (set *Yes* when you create *Stock Item* for Services)

Statutory Information: Now enter the details under *Statutory Information* as follows:

- **Applicability of Service Tax**: At *Is Service Tax Applicable* set as follows, set *Yes* If the Service Sales / Purchase Account is for *Taxable* Service, else set *No* (for *Non Taxable* Services).
  - o **Principal Service Category**: For Taxable Service Accounts (when you have set Yes at *Is Service Tax Applicable)*, you get another field *Default Service Category* to select the Service Category from the list (F-2B/03-03). Select the Main Service Category of the organisation. You may also select *Taxable Service* (instead of any specific Item) from the list

02.02 Input Service Tax Ledger

At the Input Service Tax Ledger Account creation / alteration (F-1B), set as follows:

- At *Name*, enter the appropriate Name of the Ledger Account
- At *Under*, select *Duties & Taxes* (as all the above accounts are Tax Accounts). Input Tax Ledger Accounts may alternatively be placed under *Current Asset* Group (or its subgroup), instead of Duties & Taxes, as it is deductible from Output Tax. However, such ledger account must be used for Input Tax Credit.
- At *ype of Duty Tax*, select *Service Tax* from the list (as all the above accounts relate to Service Tax)
- At the field *Tax Head,* select from the list (F-3C/03-03) as follows
  - o *Service Tax* for Service Tax Ledger Account
  - o *Service Tax Education Cess* for Service Tax Education Cess Account
  - o *Service Tax Secondary Education Cess* for Service Tax Secondary Education Cess Account
  - o *Any* for combined Tax / Cess Service Tax Account
- At *Inventory Values are affected*, set *No*

You may create one consolidated Input Tax Ledger Account comprising for Service Tax, Education Cess & Secondary Education Cess, or create 3 separate ledger accounts for them as explained earlier (§04/03-03)

02.03 Service Supplier Party Ledger

Creation of Ledger Accounts of Supplier have been discussed earlier (§01/03-01). On activating Service Tax features (§02/03-02), you get the additional field *Is Service Provider / Receiver* (F-1C), in Ledger Accounts creation / alteration of

Service Party Ledger (Sundry Creditor / Sundry Debtors). At the field *Is Service Provider / Receiver* (F-1C):

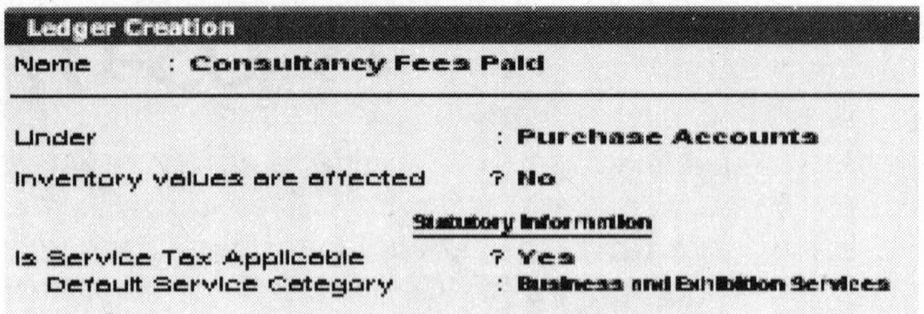

F-1A: Service Purchase Account

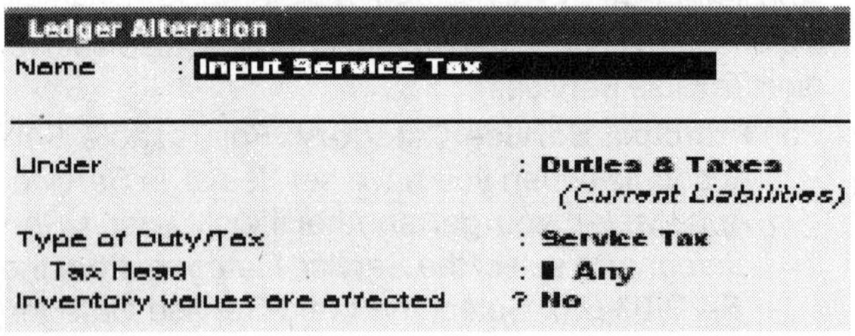

F-1B Input Service Tax Ledger Account

- *Set Yes* for Customers whom you charge Service Tax in your bills.
- *Set Yes* for Suppliers who charges you service tax that you claim for credit.
- *Set No* for other ledger accounts.

Party Ledger Service Tax Details

Having set *Yes* at *Is Service Provider / Receiver* at Service Party Ledger creation screen (F-1C), you get additional option *Set Alter Service Tax*. Set *Yes* to get *Service Tax Details* subscreen (F-1D), to specify the Service Tax details as follows:

- **Party Service Tax Registration Number**: At the field *Registration Number*, enter the Service Tax Registration Number of the party. This info is printed on Invoice and various Service Tax Reports.
- **Party Service Tax Registration Date**: At the field *Date of Registration*, enter the Service Tax Registration Date of the Party.
- **Associated Enterprise**: At the field *Is Associated Enterprise* Set Yes if the Party is Associated entity of the Organisation (e.g, under same management), else set *No*
- **Tax Classification Type:** At the field *Type of Classification*, select from the list as follows (F-1C/03-03):
    - o **Exempt**: When the Party (supplier / receiver of Service) is exempt from Service Tax
    - o **Export**: When the Service is Exported
    - o **Import:** When the Service is Imported
    - o **Negative List**: When the Service is included in Negative List
    - o **Pure Agent**: When the Party is Pure Agent of Service supplier / Receiver
    - o **Tax on Service Received**: When Transport Service is purchased and the Service Receiver is liable to pay Tax.
    - o **Not Applicable:** Select when Service Tax is applicable (no exemption is applicable)
- **Notification Number**: On selection of the *Type of Classification* (except *Not Applicable*), enter the applicable Notification Number of the Government

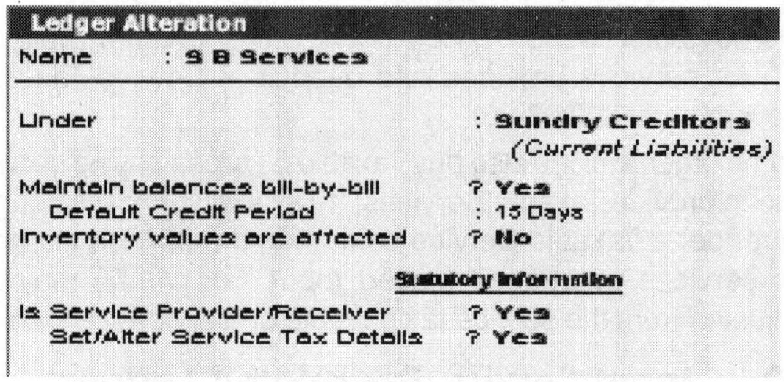

F-1C: Service Supplier Ledger Account

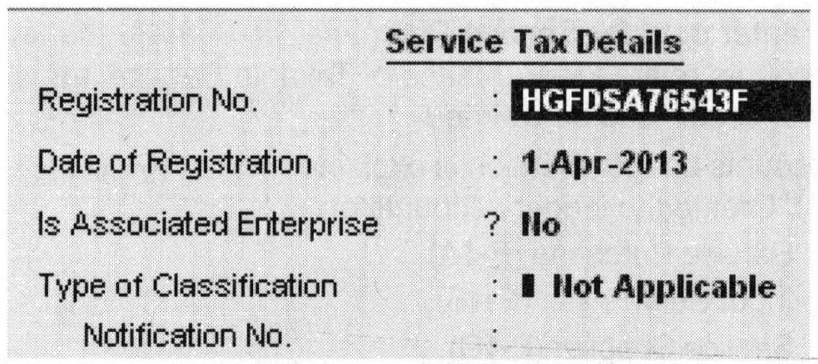

F-1D: Service Supplier Tax details

03 Service Purchase Voucher creation

Having created the Ledger Accounts, you create a Purchase voucher (F-2A) for Taxable Service Purchased. We have explained Purchase Voucher entry earlier (§05/03-02). Here we explain the process related to Service Tax only.

- **Party Ledger Account**: At Voucher entry screen (F-2A), at *Particulars* column, on selecting Party Ledger Account (supplier of Service), enter the net Bill amount (inclusive of Service Tax) in Credit column (F-2A) to get the Bill Allocation screen (F-.2C). At Service Bill Allocation screen (F-.2C), select *New Reference* (the voucher number is carried as Reference Number, by default, which you may change.
- **Service Purchase Account**: At Voucher entry screen (F-2A), at *Particulars* column, next enter the Taxable Service Purchase Leger Account to get *ServiceTax Details* screen (F-2B).
- **Bil Refernce**: Enter the Bill Reference details as follows:
    - o **Ref Type:** At *Type of Ref* column, select *New Ref* & enter the New Reference Number (the Purchase

Ref Number prefixed by *Purc/* & suffixed by *-1*, is carried by default, which you may change).

- o **Amount**: You may enter the Basic Amount / Tax Inclusive Amount, as follows (F-2B):
  - **Basic Amount**: You may enter Basic Amount (excluding Service Tax) at *Service Amount* column. Consequently, the Tax Inclusive Amount would be auto computed and filled at the *Amount Inclusive of Tax* column
  - **Tax Inclusive Amount**: Otherwise, you may enter the Tax inclusive amount (including Service Tax) at *Amount Inclusive of Tax* column. The Basic Amount would be auto computed and filled at the *Service Amount* column

  The amount of each component of Tax (Basic, Cess etc), are displayed next

The Basic Purchase Amount is carried to Service Purchase Account at Debit Column at the main voucher screen (F-2A).

- **Service Tax Account:** At Voucher entry screen (F-2A), at *Particulars* column, next enter the Input Service Tax Account and the Service Tax Amount in Debit Column (F-2A).

Accounting Voucher Creation — Ctrl + M

Purchase No. **1** — **31-May-2013** Friday

Ref.: **15**

Particulars				Debit	Credit
Cr **S B Services**					**2,200.00**
New Ref **15**	**15 Days** (15-Jun-2013)	**2,200.00**	**Cr**		
Dr **Consultancy Fees Paid**				**1,958.00**	
Dr **Input Service Tax**				**242.00**	
Narration:				**2,200.00**	**2,200.00**

Service Purchased

F-2A: Taxable Service Purchase Voucher

Service Tax Details for : **Consultancy Fees Paid**

Type of Ref	Name	Type of Service	Category/Service			Service Amount	Amount (Incl. of Tax)
New Ref	**Purc/15-1**	**Input Credit**	**Taxable Service**			**1,958.00**	**2,200.00**
			(Taxable @ 100% is 1,953.00, Notif.No:)				
Service Tax	@	12 %	*(On Assessable Value*	*1,958.00)*	**235.00**		
Ed Cess	@	2 %	*(On Tax Value*	*235.00)*	**5.00**		
Sec Ed Cess	@	1 %	*(On Tax Value*	*235.00)*	**2.00**		
					242.00		
		Total				**1,958.00**	**2,200.00**

F-2B: Service Tax details on Service Purchase

Bill-wise Details for : **S B Services**
Upto: **₹ 2,200.00 Cr**

Type of Ref	Name	Due Date, or Credit Days (wef: 31-May-2013)	**Amount**	Dr/ Cr
New Ref	15	15 Days (15-Jun-2013)	**2,200.00**	**Cr**
			2,200.00	Cr

F-2C: Bill Allocation details in Purchase Voucher

04 Payment of Service Purchase Bill

Now enter the Payment Voucher for Payment of the Service Purchase Invoice (F-3A), in single entry mode. At Payment Voucher entry screen (F-3A), at *Particulars* column, select the Payee Account to get the *Tax details* screen (F-3B).

At *Tax details* screen (F-3B). at *Type of Ref*, select *Agnst Ref.* At Name column, select the Bill for which Payment is being made. Tthe balance amount of he Bill is carried at Amount column. Enter the Net Amount Received against the Bill at *Amount (Inclusive of Tax)* column. The proportionate Service Amount is computed and shown at *Service Amount* column. The tax details are auto computed and shown (F-3B)

The amount paid is shown at Debit column in the Payment Voucher (F-3A).

Enter *Voucher Narration* & save the Voucher.

Payment No. **1** — **1-Jun-2013** Saturday

Account : **HDFC Bank**

Particulars				Amount
S B Services				**1,500.00**
Agst Ref **15**	**15 Days** (15-Jun-2013)	**1,500.00**	**Dr**	
Narration:				**1,500.00**

Payment for Service Purchase

F-3A: Part payment of Service Purchase Bill.

Service Tax Details for : **S B Services**

Type of Ref	Name	Type of Service	Category/Service			Amount (Incl. of Tax)	Service Amount
Agst Ref	**Purc/15-1**	**Input Credit**	**Taxable Service**			**1,500.00**	**1,335.00**
			(Taxable @ 100% is 1,335.00, Notif.No:)				
Service Tax	@	12 %	*(On Assessable Value*	*1,335.00)*	*160.00*		
Ed Cess	@	2 %	*(On Tax Value*	*160.20)*	*3.00*		
Sec Ed Cess	@	1 %	*(On Tax Value*	*160.20)*	*1.00*		
					164.00		
		Total				**1,500.00**	**1,335.00**

F-3B: Tax details of Payment of Service Purchase Bill.

05 Service Tax Input Credit Statement

After entry of Taxable Service Purchase Bill, the full amount of Tax in the Purchase Bill would be available for Input Credit, whether an payment (full or part) is made for the Service Purchased.

Having entered Purchase Service Bill, print the Input Credit Statement. At Service Tax Reports menu (*GoT>Display> Statutory Reports>Service Tax Reports*: F-1B/03-05), select *Input Credit* to get the Input Credit Menu (F-4A).

05.01 Service Tax Input Credit Summary

At *Input Credit* Menu (F-4A), select *Summary* to get Input

Credit Summary Statement (F-5A) in respect of Input Credit available to adjust against the Service Tax Payable (§03/03-05).

Gateway of Tally ....
Display Menu ....
Statutory Reports ....
Service Tax Reports ....

Input Credit

Summary
Reversal Details
Quit

F-4A Input Credit Menu

Configuration

Show Service Tax Registration No.	?	No
Show Abatement Amount	?	No
Show Rate & Notification No.	?	No
Show Allowable Expenses	?	No
Show Assessable Value	?	No
Show Billed Assessable Value	?	No
Show Realised Assessable Value	?	No
Show Realised Abatement Amount	?	No
Show Realised Allowable Expenses	?	No
Show Tax Break-up	?	No
Show Tax Break-up for Bill Amount	?	No
Show Tax Break-up for Realised Amount	?	No
Show Tax Paid / Adjusted / Utilised Amount	?	No
Range of Bills to show	:	All Bills
Show Bills of the following type	:	Paid Bills
Show Tax on Services Received / Import Tax Bills	:	No

F-4B: Input Credit Summary Configuration

Type of Bills

Adjusted Bills
All Bills
Paid Bills
Unpaid Bills

F-4C: Type of Bills List

Type of Bills

All Bills
Cash Bills
Credit Bills

F-4D: Range of Bills List

F1: Detailed
F2: Period
F4: Category
F5: Ledger
F7: Till Date
F8: Payment Wise

F-4E: Buttons at Input Credit Satement

- **Bill Amount**: Shows Total Amount of Service Bill (including Tax)
- **Total Tax**: Shows Total Service Tax (including Cess)
- **Paid Amount**: Shows the Amount Paid to he supplier against the Service Bill
- **Total Input Credit:** Shows the amount of Service Tax
- **Balance Input Credit:** Shows balance amount of Tax to be adjusted

05.02 Input Credit Summary Configuration

At *Input Credit Summary Display* (F-5A), click *F12:Configure* to get the Configuration screen (F-4B). Set the following Basic options (F-4B)

- **Service Tax Registration No:** At *Show Service Tax Registration No,* set *Yes* to show service tax registration number of the Service Receivers, else set No (this column will not be shown)
- **Assessable Value:** At *Show Assessable Value*, set *Yes* to show the Billed/Realised/Abatement/ Allowable Expenses Assessable Value of Service Bill, else set No (this column will not be shown).
    - o **Billed Assessable Value:** At *Show Billed Assessable Value* (activated only when the above option *Show Assessable Value* is set to Yes), set Yes to view the Billed Assessable value of the Service Bill, else set *No* (this column will not be shown).
    - o **Realised Assessable value**: At *Show Realised Assessable value* (activated only when *Show Assessable Value* is set to Yes), set Yes to show the Realised Assessable Value, else set No (this column will not be shown).
- **Tax break-up:** At *Show Tax break-up* set **Yes** to show the Tax Break up of Bill/Realised Amount, else set *No* (this column will not be shown).

Input Credit Summary — **A B Services** — Ctrl + M

Type of Bills : All Bills — 1-Apr-2013 to 30-Jun-2013

Date	Ref. No.	Party's Name	Category	Bill Amount	Total Tax	Paid Amount	Total Input Credit	Balance Input Credit
31-May-2013	Purc/15-1	S B Services	Taxable Service	2,200.00	242.00	1,500.00	242.00	242.00
Total				2,200.00	242.00	1,500.00	242.00	242.00

F-5A: Input Credit Summary

Contents of Input Credit Summary

The Input Credit Summary Report (F-5A) contains following Columns

- **Date**: Shows Service Bill Date (Voucher Date).
- **Ref. No.**: Shows Service Bill Reference (Bill Number / Ref Number)
- **Party's Name**: Shows the Party Name
- **Category**: Shoes the Service Category

- o **Tax break-up for Bill Amount**: At *Show Tax break-up for Bill Amount* (activated only when the above option *Show Tax break -up* is set to Yes). Set *Yes* this to show the Tax Break up of Service bill amount, else set *No* (this column will not be shown).
- o **Tax break-up for Realised Amount**: At *Show Tax break-up for Realised Amount* (activated only when the above option *Show Tax break -up* is set to Yes).

Set *Yes* this to show the Tax Break up of Realised amount, else set *No* (this column will not be shown).

- **Range of Bills:** At *Range of Bills to show*, select the options from the list as follows (F-4D):
  - o **All Bills**: To show both cash and Credit bills (by default All Bills are shown)
  - o **Cash Bills**: To show only Cash Bills
  - o **Credit Bills**: To show only Credit bills
- **Type of Bills:** *At Show bills of the following Type*, select the options from the list as follows (F-4C):
  - o **All Bills**: To show all the bills i.e. paid, realised and unrealised bills
  - o **Paid Bills**: To show only the bills for which service tax is already paid to the government
  - o **Unpaid Bills**: To show only those bills for which the payment is realised from the customers and on which tax is payable

05.03 Input Credit Summary Buttons

At Input Credit Summary Display (F-5A), you get buttons (F-4E), similar to buttons at Tax Payable Summary (§03/03-05)

- **F1:Detailed / Condensed:** Click *F1:Detailed* button to get the next level details of the Bill showing the Bill Amount & Paid Amount (F-6C) in multiple lines.. Click *F1:Condensed* button to get the net figure at the respective columns, in one line (F-6B)
- **F4:Category:** Click *F4:Catgory* and then select a Service Tax Category to get the Report for selected Category (or select All Items to show for all Tax Categories)
- **F5:Ledger**: Click *F5:Ledger* and then select a Customer (Service Receiver) Ledger Account to get the Report for selected Ledger (or select All Items to show for all Customer Ledgers)
- **F7:Monthly/ Till date**: Click *F7:Monthly /Till Date* toggle button to get Monthlwise / Uptodate list of Bills
- **F8:Payment/Bill Datewise**: Click *F8 Realisation Date* button to get Realisation Datewise Report – F-4A (you may also get it by selecting *Realisation Datewise* at Service Tax Payables Reports Menu (F-1C/06-05)

05.04 Input Credit Summary Printing

At Input Credit Summary Display (F-5A), click *P:Print* to get Input Credit Summary Printing screen (F-6A). Type Y to get the Input Credit Summary in print (F-6B), as per Configuration options set.

The Report may extend to multiple parts (F-6C), depending on the columns selected at Configuration (F-4B)

Report Titles

Input Credit Summary

F-6A: Input Credit Summary Printing

Input Credit Summary

(See Sub-rule(4) of rule 5)

Return under rule 5 of the Service Tax Credit Rules, 2002

1-Aug-2013 to 31-Aug-2013

Page 1

Type of Bills All Bills

Date	Ref. No.	Party's Name	Category	Bill Amount	Total Tax	Paid Amount	Total Input Credit	Balance Input Credit
4-Aug-2013	Jrnl/1-1	AB C Courier Service	Taxable Service	1,123.00	123.00		123.00	123.00
6-Aug-2013	Purc/15-1	AB C Courier Service	Taxable Service	224.00	24.00		24.00	24.00
30-Aug-2013	Purc/24-1	B R Traders	Works Contract Service	10,165.00	165.00		165.00	165.00
	Total			11,512.00	312.00		312.00	312.00

F-6B: Input Credit Summary (Condensed) in Print

Input Credit Summary

(See Sub-rule(4) of rule 5)

Return under rule 5 of the Service Tax Credit Rules, 2002

1-Aug-2013 to 31-Aug-2013

Page 1 (A) Page 1 (B)

Type of Bills : All Bills

Date	Ref. No.			Party's Name	Category	Bill Amount	Assessable Value	Total Tax	Paid Amount	Total Input Credit	Balance Input Credit
4-Aug-2013	Jrnl/1-1			AB C Courier Service	Taxable Service	1,123.00	1,000.00	123.00		123.00	123.00
4-Aug-2013	*Journal*	1	*1,000.00*								
6-Aug-2013	Purc/15-1			AB C Courier Service	Taxable Service	224.00	200.00	24.00		24.00	24.00
6-Aug-2013	*Purchase*	2	*12,224.00*								
30-Aug-2013	Purc/24-1			B R Traders	Works Contract Service	10,165.00	4,000.00	165.00		165.00	165.00
30-Aug-2013	*Purchase*	5	*10,165.00*								
Total						11,512.00	5,200.00	312.00		312.00	312.00

F-6C: Input Credit Summary (Detailed) in Print – Part 1 Part 2

06 Service Tax Computation Statement with Input Credit

The computation statement (F-7A), as discussed earlier (§02/03-05), shows the effect of Input Tax Credit, after entry of Service Purchase Bills.

Service Tax Computation — Ctrl + M

Particulars	A B Services 1-Apr-2013 to 30-Jun-2013		
	Total Amount	Assessable Value	Tax Amount
A. Input Credit	**2,200.00**	**1,958.00**	**242.00**
Current Period	*2,200.00*	*1,958.00*	*242.00*
Previous Period			
B. Service Tax Payable	**8,371.00**	**7,450.00**	**921.00**
Current Period	*8,371.00*	*7,450.00*	*921.00*
Previous Period			
C. Service Tax Payments / Credit Adjustments			
D. Balance Service Tax Payable (B-C)			**921.00**
E. Refund of Service Tax Input Credit			
F. Balance Available Credit			**242.00**
Service Tax Credit			*242.00*
G. Service Tax Adjusted Towards Excise Payable			
H. Other Payments			

F-7A: Computation Summary (after input credit)

07 Service Tax Deposit after Input Credit Adjustment

We have explained Payment Voucher for Service Tax Deposit (§02/02-06). In the same way, create Payment Voucher for deposit of Service Tax, adjusting the Input Credit from the Tax Payable In the Payment Voucher (F-8A), enter as follows:

- **Output Tax Account**: Select the *Output Service Tax Account* to get the Bill Allocation screen (F-8B) for the selected Ledger Account and select the References for which you are making the payments (F-8B). The total Tax amount of the selected Bills is carried at the main voucher screen (F-8A) at *Debit* Column.

Payment No. 2 — **5-Jul-2013** Friday

	Particulars	Debit	Credit
Dr	**Output Service Tax**	**921.00**	
Cr	**Input Service Tax**		**242.00**
Cr	**HDFC Bank**		**679.00**
	Provide Details : **Yes**		
	Narration:	**921.00**	**921.00**

Payment of Tax for Apr13-Jun13

F-8A: Service Tax Payment after adjusting Input Credit

- **Input Tax Account**: Select the Input Credit Tax Account to get the Bill Allocation screen (F-8C) for the selected Ledger Account and select the References of Input Service Tax which you like to adjust. The total Tax amount of the selected Bills is carried at the main voucher screen (F-8A) at *Credit* Column.

> ***Note:*** *If you use a common ledger account for Input & Output Tax (not recommended), then you select the common ledger account and select the Sales Bills & the Purchase Bills respectively.*

- **Bank Ledger Account**: Now select the Bank Account. The Net Amount Payable (Output Tax – Input Tax) is carried at main screen (F-8A) and shown at Credit Column

Service Tax Details for : **Output Service Tax**

Type of Ref.	Name	Category/Service	Amount
Agst Ref	**Sale/1-1**	**Taxable Service**	**550.00**
Agst Ref	**Sale/12-1**	**Taxable Service**	**371.00**

F-8B: Bill allocation of Output Service Tax

Service Tax Details for : **Input Service Tax**

Type of Ref.	Name	Category/Service	Amount
Agst Ref	**14/1-1**	**Taxable Service**	**242.00**
			242.00

F-8C: Bill allocation of Input Service Tax

Payment Details: At *Provide Details*, set Yes (F-8A) and enter the Payment details as explained (02/03-06). On entry of Payment Voucher for Service Tax paid, click *P:Print* button and print the Deposit Challan as explained (§03/03-06).

08 Service Tax Adjustment Journal Voucher Class

Various adjustment of Service Tax are to be done through Voucher Class. We have explained creation of Voucher Class earlier (§02/02-08/S1). Here we explain how to create a voucher class for Service Tax Adjustments

Name : **Serrvice Tax Adjustment**

General		Printing		Name of Class
Type of Voucher	: **Journal**	Print after saving Voucher	? **No**	**STAdj**
Abbr.	: STax Adj			
Method of Voucher Numbering	? **Automatic**			
Use Advance Configuration	? **No**			
Use EFFECTIVE Dates for Vouchers	? **No**			
Make 'Optional' as default	? **No**			
Use Common Narration	? **Yes**			
Narrations for each entry	? **No**			
Position Index in Reports	: **40**			

F-9A: Journal Voucher Class creation for S Tax adjustments

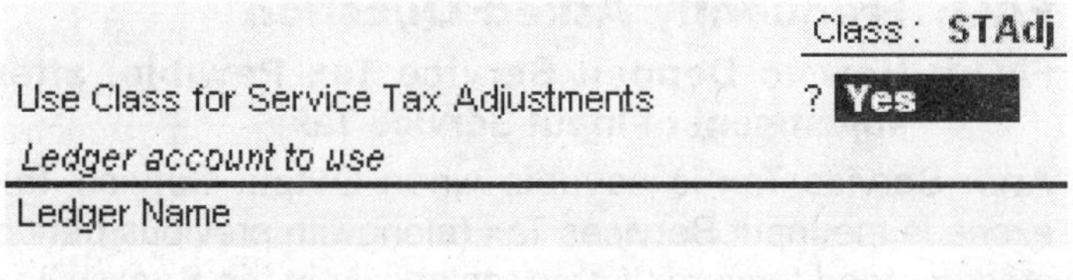

F-9B: Journal Voucher Class set up for S Tax adjustments

Create a Journal Voucher Type for Service Tax Adjustment (F-9A), as explained (§02/02-07/S1). At *Name of Class*, enter the Name of Voucher class to be created (F-8A) to get *Journal Voucher Class Set Up* screen (F-8B).

At *Journal Voucher Class Set Up* screen (F-9B), set Yes at *Use Class for Service Tax Adjustments* to create a *Service Tax Adjustment Journal Voucher Class* for adjustment of Service Tax. Save the Journal Voucher Class.

09 Reversal of Utilised Input Credit

The Input Service Tax is adjusted irrespective of the amount of Payment made for the Service Purchase Bill (whether paid partly or fully unpaid). However, the Input Credit has to be reversed if the payment for the Service Purchase Bill is not made within 3 months of Date of Service Purchase Bill.

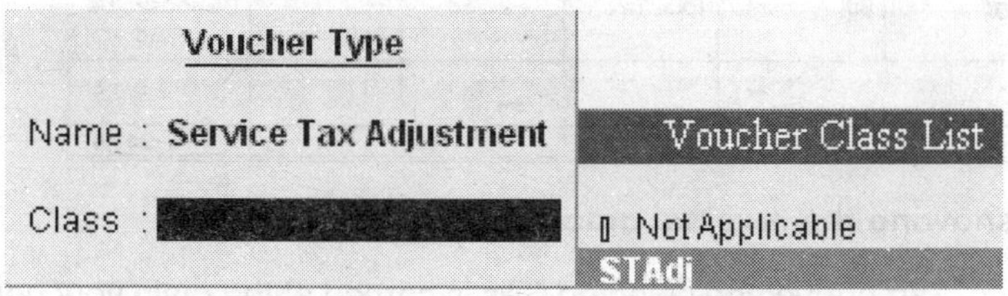

F-10A: S Tax Journal Voucher Class selection

For Reversal of Input Tax Credit, create a Service Tax Adjustment Journal Voucher (F-10C), using Service Tax Adjustment Journal Voucher Class (§08). Journal Voucher entry is explained earlier (§05/01-04/S1). Here we discuss additional steps for entry for Service Tax Adjustment Journal Voucher entry.

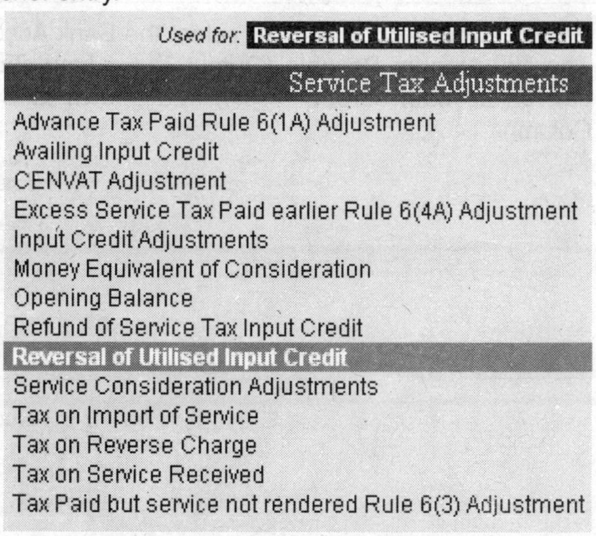

F-10B: S Tax Journal Voucher Class selection

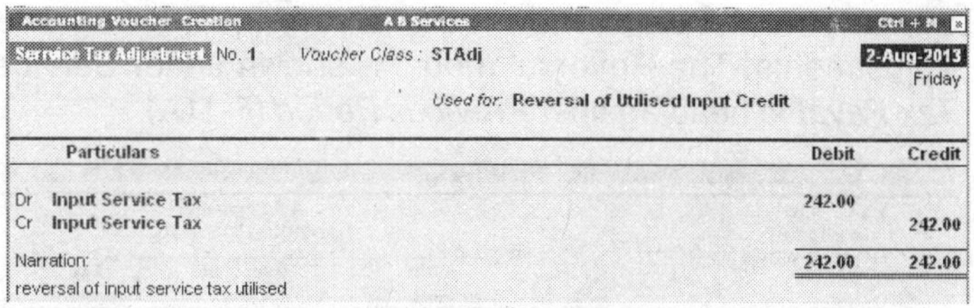

F-10C:Service Tax Input credit reversal Journal entry

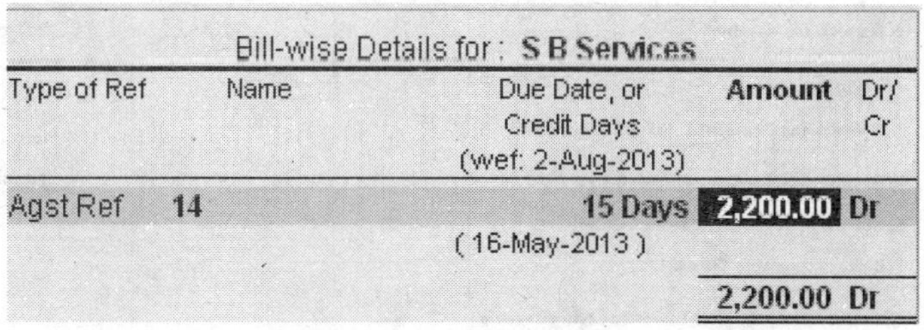

F-10D:Bill allocation for Tax reversal (for Debit) – Ag Ref

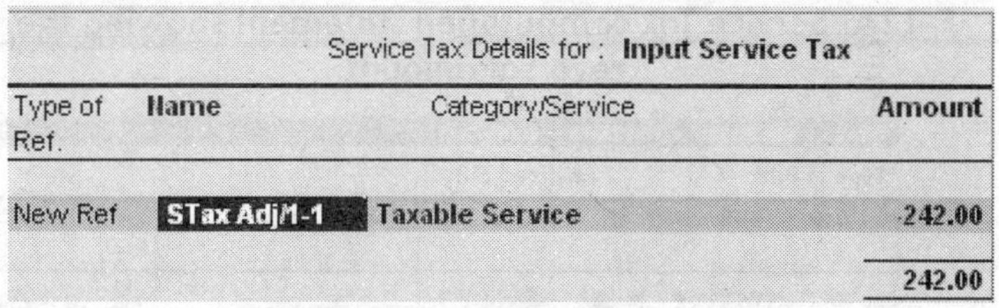

F-10E:Bill allocation for Tax reversal (for Debit) – New Ref

For Journal Voucher entry, at Voucher entry screen, click *F7:Journal* and select the Service Tax Adjustment Journal Voucher class (F-10A), to get *Service Tax Adjustment Journal Voucher* entry screen (F-10C).

At *Service Tax Adjustment Journal Voucher* entry screen (F-10C), at *Used for*, select *Reversal of Utilised Input Credit* from the list (F-10B) to create a Journal Voucher for Reversal of Utilised Input Credit

At Journal Voucher entry screen (F-10C), at *Particulars* column:

- **Adjustment entry of earlier Input Credit**: Select Input Service Tax Account to get *Bill Allocation* screen (F-10D). At *Type of Ref* column, select *Agst Ref* and at *Name* column, select the Bill Reference of (Purchase Bill) Input Credit (the Amount is carried). to reverse the previous Input Tax credit entry.
- **Creation of Tax Payable entry**: Next, again Select Input Service Tax Account to get *Service Tax* Details screen (F-10E). At *Type of Ref* column (F-10E), select *New Ref* to create the entry for Service Tax payable for the reversed Input Credit. At *Name*, a new Reference number with prefix *S Tax Adj* is carried (which you may change), to create the reversed Entry.

09.01 Service Tax Computation Report after Adjustment

After entry of Adjustment Journal Voucher, you get the

Service Tax Computation Statement, reflecting the Adjustments. The Reversal mount is shown under *Service Tax Payable* head against *Previous Period* (F-11A)

Service Tax Computation — Ctrl + M

Particulars	A B Services 1-Jul-2013 to 30-Sep-2013		
	Total Amount	Assessable Value	Tax Amount
A. Input Credit			
Current Period			
Previous Period			
B. Service Tax Payable			242.00
Current Period			
Previous Period			*242.00*
C. Service Tax Payments / Credit Adjustments			
D. Balance Service Tax Payable (B-C)			242.00
E. Refund of Service Tax Input Credit			
F. Balance Available Credit			
G. Service Tax Adjusted Towards Excise Payable			
H. Other Payments			

F-11A: Service Tax computation statement showing the reversal amount

FAQ: Frequently Asked Question

FAQ-1: How to Deposit Service Tax Payable, after adjustment of Input Service Tax

Ans: Service Tax is payable when Output Service Tax exceeds the Input Services Tax (alongwith previous period credit carried forward, if any), as shown in the Service Tax Computation Statement.

Create Payment Voucher for deposit of Net Service Tax paybale, adjusting the Input Credit In the Payment Voucher (F-8A), enter as follows:

- **Output Tax Account**: Select the Output Service Tax Account to get the Bill Allocation screen (F-8B) for the selected Ledger Account and select the References for which you are making the payments (F-8B). The total Tax amount of the selected Bills is carried at the main voucher screen at *Debit* Column
- **Input Tax Account**: Select the Input Credit Tax Account to get the Bill Allocation screen (F-8C) for the selected Ledger Account and select the References of Input Service Tax which you like to adjust. The total Tax amount of the selected Bills is carried at the main voucher screen at *Credit* Column

> **Note:** *If you use a common ledger account for Input & Output Tax (not recommended), then select the same ledger account for Output Tax (Debit) & Output Tax (Credit) separately as described, and select the Sales Bills & the Purchase Bills respectively.*

- **Bank Ledger Account**: Now select the Bank Account. The Net Amount Payable (Output Tax – Input Tax) is carried at main screen (F-8A) and shown at Credit Column

Service Tax Payable (Bill Date - wise) — A B Services — Ctrl + M

Type of Bills : Realised Bills — 1-Jul-2013 to 30-Sep-2013

Date	Ref. No.	Party's Name	Category	Bill Amount	Total Tax	Realised Amount	Total Tax Payable	Balance to be Paid
2-Aug-2013	STax Adj/1-1		Taxable Service					242.00
	Total							242.00

F-11B: Service Tax Pauable summary showing the reversal amount paybale

09.02 Service Tax Payable Report after Adjustment

After the Journal Voucher Entry, you get the Service Tax Paybale Report (§03/06-05) reflecting the Service Tax Paybale Report for the corresponding period (F-11B).

So far, we have described the complete cycle of Service Tax Set up, Ledger Creation, Sales & Purchase Invoices & payments thereof, Tax Payables details, Adjustment of Input Credit, Deposit of Tax and printing of Half Yearly Service Tax Returns. We have also described and Reversal of Input Credit on account of non-payment / delayed payment of Taxable Service Purchase Bills

In next chapter, we describe some special treatments relating to Service Tax

01 Service Tax Special Features

So far, we have described the complete cycle of Service Tax Set up, Ledger Creation, regular process of Service Sales Invoicing, Purchase Invoices entry & Payments thereof, Tax Payables details, Adjustment of Input Credit, Reversal of Input Credit on account of non-payment / delayed payment of Taxable Service Purchase Bills, Deposit of Tax, Half Yearly Service Tax Returns, normally applicable for all Registered Service providers in general.

Here, we describe some special treatments relating to Service Tax, arising in some special situations

02 Advance Received from Customers

Sometimes customer pay advance for some service to be provided. In such case, the final Bill is created only after the service is performed. As per rules, Service Tax is to be paid as per Sales Bill or Payment received, whichever is earlier. So, Service Tax is to be paid as per date of Advance Received, even if the Sales Bill is not created.

02.01 Receipt Voucher creation for Advance Received

On receipt of advance (before the Service Provider has created Service Bill), from Customer (Service Receiver), a Receipt Voucher (F-1A) is to be created by Service Provider, for Advance received. We have explained creation of Receipt Voucher in Single Mode (§02/02-10/S1). Here we explain the steps specific to Service Tax. Enter as follows (F-1A):

- **Cash / Bank Account**: At the header, select the Cash / Bank Account
- **Customer (Payer) Account**: Select the ledger account of the customer who pays the advance to get *Service Tax allocation* screen (F-1B).
- **Service Tax Allocation:** At *Service Tax Details* screen (F-1B), enter as follows:
  - o **Type of Reference**: At *Type of Ref.* column, select *Advance*
  - o **Bill Reference**: At *Name* column, the Reference Number (the Voucher Number with subscript /-1, like Rcpt/1-1) will be auto assigned.
  - o **Type of Service**: At *Type of Service* column, the *Type of Classification* as set at Customer Ledger will be carried (*Taxable* will be carried if you have set *Not Applicable* at *Type of Classification* at Customer Ledger: §02/02-03).
  - o **Category / Service**: At *Category / Service* column, the default Category specified is carried and the field is skipped (to change the category, click *F12:Configure* to get the Tax *Configuration* screen (F-11C) and set *Yes* at *Allow to override Service Category during Entry*. Now at the Tax allocation screen, press <Shift+Tab> to get the back to the Category field and change the Category).
  - o **Tax Inclusive Amount:** At *Amount Inc. of Tax* column, enter the Amount Received
  - o **Amount Details:** The Service Amount (basic amount exclusive of Service Tax) is back computed from Amount Received, then the respective component of the amount inclusive of Tax is computed and shown (e.g, if Rs 5000 is amount received, Service Amount would be Rs 4450, Service Tax – Rs 534 (12% on 4450 rounded off), Education Cess Rs 11 (2% on 534 rounded off), and Secondary Education Cess Rs 5 (1% on 534 rounded off). The component wise break up of chargeable amount and the corresponding tax component is shown (F-1B). Press <enter> to move to next screen.
- **Bill Allocation**: After entry in Tax details screen (F-1B), you get the *Bill Allocation* screen (F-1C) to enter the Bill Reference details. Tally splits up the amount Received into 2 components:
  - o **Total Amount Received**: In the first reference, the Amount Received is carried (as Credit)
  - o **Tax Amount**: in the 2nd Reference, the Tax Amount is carried as Debit).

In both the Reference, the Voucher Number is accrued as default at the *Name* column as *Reference* Number.

- **Customer Ledger**: The net Amount after deduction of Tax from the amount received, is shown and is carried in the *Amount* column against the Customer Ledger Account at the main voucher entry screen (F-1A).
- **Tax Ledger Account**: Now select Tax Ledger Account, the amount of Tax is auto carried in the *Amount* column (F-1A)

Now enter other ledger accounts, if any, in the voucher (F-1A).

Accounting Voucher Creation Ctrl + M

Receipt No. 1 — **2-Jul-2013** Tuesday

Account : **HDFC Bank**

Particulars				Amount
K B Enterprise				2,671.00
Advance 1	15 Days (17-Jul-2013)	3,001.00 Cr		
Advance 1	15 Days (17-Jul-2013)	330.00 Dr		
Output Service Tax				330.00
Narration:				3,001.00

Adv recd ag service to be provided. SErvice Tax realised

F-1A: Receipt Voucher Entry for Advance Received

Service Tax Details for : **K B Enterprise**

Type of Ref	Name	Type of Service	Category/Service			Amount (Incl. of Tax)	Service Amount
Advance	Rcpt/1-1	Taxable	Taxable Service			3,001.00	2,671.00
			(Taxable @ 100% is 2,671.00, Notif.No:)				
	Service Tax	@	*12 % (On Assessable Value*	*2,671.00)*	321.00		
	Ed Cess	@	*2 % (On Tax Value*	*321.00)*	6.00		
	Sec Ed Cess	@	*1 % (On Tax Value*	*321.00)*	3.00		
					330.00		
	Total					3,001.00	2,671.00

F-1B: Tax details screen for Advance Received

Finally, enter the Cheque details / Voucher Narration etc, as usual (F-1A) and save the voucher.

Bill-wise Details for : **K B Enterprise**

Type of Ref	Name	Due Date, or Credit Days (wef: 2-Jul-2013)	Amount	Dr/Cr
Advance	1	15 Days (17-Jul-2013)	3,001.00	Cr
Advance	1	15 Days (17-Jul-2013)	330.00	Dr
			2,671.00	Cr

(Note: 'Breaking of above bills helps to identify the original bill amount in the outstanding statement')

F-1C:Bill Allocation screen for Adv Received

02.02 Sale Voucher Creation adjusting Advance Received

Accounting Voucher Creation Ctrl + M

Sales No. 3 — **2-Aug-2013** Friday

Ref. :

Party's A/c Name : **K B Enterprise**

Particulars	Rate	per	Amount
Consultancy Fees			8,901.00
Output Service Tax			770.00
Narration:			9,671.00

Final Sale Bill. Tax charged on additional amt

F-2A: Final Sales Bill

Service Tax Details for : **Consultancy Fees**

Type of Ref	Name	Type of Service	Category/Service			Service Amount	Amount (Incl. of Tax)
Agst Ref	Rcpt/1-1	Taxable	Taxable Service			2,671.00	3,001.00
			(Taxable @ 100% is 2,671.00, Notif.No:)				
	Service Tax	@	*12 % (On Assessable Value*	*2,671.00)*	321.00		
	Ed Cess	@	*2 % (On Tax Value*	*321.00)*	6.00		
	Sec Ed Cess	@	*1 % (On Tax Value*	*321.00)*	3.00		
					330.00		
New Ref	Sale/3-2	Taxable	Taxable Service			6,230.00	7,000.00
			(Taxable @ 100% is 6,230.00, Notif.No:)				
	Service Tax	@	*12 % (On Assessable Value*	*6,230.00)*	748.00		
	Ed Cess	@	*2 % (On Tax Value*	*748.00)*	15.00		
	Sec Ed Cess	@	*1 % (On Tax Value*	*748.00)*	7.00		
					770.00		
	Total					8,901.00	10,001.00

F-2B: Final Sale Bill Tax details screen

After the Job is completed, Sales Bill for the Service rendered is to be created. Now you know the amount of Service Charge for which bill to be made. The Amount of Final Bill may be more than the amount received.

You create a Sales Voucher (F-2A) in Accounting Invoice Mode (§06.02/03-02/S1) as follows:.

Party Account: At the header, at *Party's A/c Name*, select the Customer (Service Receiver) Ledger Account.

Now enter other ledger account details as follows:

- **Service Ledger Account**: At *Particulars* column, select the Service Ledger Account to get the Tax details screen (F-2B).
- **Tax Details:** At *Tax Details screen* (F-2B), to adjust the Advance Amount received earlier (as *Against Reference*), in the current Service Bill. enter as follows (F-2B):
  - o **Type of Reference**: At *Type of Ref* column, select *Agst Ref*
  - o **Name**: At *Name* column, select the Reference Number as entered in the earlier Receipt Voucher (F-1B), from the list. The data as entered in the Receipt Voucher, for the selected Reference, is carried in the respective columns
- **Additional Service Charges:** If the Service Charges is more than that received in the Advance, you have to create a New Reference and enter the additional amount of Service Charges as *New Reference* (F-2B), in the next entry (if the service bill is exactly equal to the amount of advance received, then no *New Reference* need to be created, the advance would fully adjusted against the Service Bill of equal amount). Enter the additional amount against *New Ref* as follows:
  - o **Type of Reference**: At type of *Ref column,* select *New Ref*
  - o **Name**: At *Name* column, the sale Voucher Number with a subscript would be auto created and carried (which you may change).
  - o **Type of Service**: At *Type of Service,* the *Type of Classification* is carried (as explained under the Receipt Voucher entry explained above)

- o **Category / Service**: At *Category / Service*, the Category is carried (as explained under the Receipt Voucher entry explained above)
- o **Amount:** At *Service Amount* column, enter the additional Basic Service Amount (total service amount less what was adjusted in Receipt Voucher in the previous entry)
- o **Tax Inclusive Amount:** At *Amount Inc. of Tax* column, the amount inclusive of Tax as per amount entered at Service Amount column is shown

Having entered the Tax details, you get back to the main voucher screen to make entry (F-2A), for entry of Tax Accounts and other ledger accounts, if any.

- **Tax Account**: Now select the Service Tax Ledger Account, the Tax Amount for the additional Service Charges (over the advance received) is carried in the *Amount* column in the main voucher entry screen (F-2A).

Now enter Voucher Narration etc. as usual (F-2A) and save the voucher.

02.03 Service Tax Computation Statement after Advance Adjustments

Now get the Service Tax Computation Statement (§02/02-05) after Advance Adjustments (F-3)

It shows the Service Tax Computation summary reflecting the Tax on Advance & Final Bill.

02.04 Service Tax payable Summary after Advance Adjustments

Now get the Service Tax payable Summary (§03/03-05) after Advance Adjustments (F-4)

The Report (F-4) shows the amount pertaining to the Advance Received and Service Bill, and Service Tax payable thereon separately, according to the respective Voucher Dates.

03 Service Expense

So, far we have shown entry of Service purchased in *Purchase* Voucher, in respect of Taxable Services Purchased to provide (sell) Taxable Services. However, sometimes Payment is made for using Taxable Services (§03/03-07).

You have to create the related Accounts as explained earlier for Service Purchase (§01/03-03):

- **Service Providers Ledger Account**: Service Provider's Ledger Account (like ABC Courier Service – F-5A). At *Type of Classification*, select *Not Applicable*, as explained (§02/03-03)
- **Expense Ledger Account**: Expense Ledger Account (F-5B) for the Taxable Service (e.g Courier Charges). It is recommended to select *Any* at *Default Service Category*, as explained (§03/03-03)
- **Service Tax Ledger Account**: Service Tax Ledger Account (e.g Service Tax – F-5C), as explained (§03/03-03)

Service Tax Payable (Bill Date - wise) — A B Services — Ctrl + M

Type of Bills : Realised Bills — 1-Jul-2013 to 30-Sep-2013

Date	Ref. No.	Party's Name	Category	Bill Amount	Total Tax	Realised Amount	Total Tax Payable	Balance to be Paid
2-Jul-2013	Rcpt/1-1	K B Enterprise	Taxable Service	3,001.00	330.00	3,001.00	330.00	330.00
2-Aug-2013	Sale/3-2	K B Enterprise	Taxable Service	7,000.00	770.00	7,000.00	770.00	770.00
2-Aug-2013	STax Adj/1-1		Taxable Service					242.00
Total				10,001.00	1,100.00	10,001.00	1,100.00	1,342.00

F-4: Service Tax Payable Summary (after advance adjustments)

Service Tax Computation — Ctrl + M

Particulars	A B Services 1-Jul-2013 to 30-Sep-2013		
	Total Amount	Assessable Value	Tax Amount
A. Input Credit			
Current Period			
Previous Period			
B. Service Tax Payable	**10,001.00**	**8,901.00**	**1,342.00**
Current Period	*10,001.00*	*8,901.00*	*1,100.00*
Previous Period			*242.00*
C. Service Tax Payments / Credit Adjustments			
D. Balance Service Tax Payable (B-C)			**1,342.00**
E. Refund of Service Tax Input Credit			
F. Balance Available Credit			
G. Service Tax Adjusted Towards Excise Payable			
H. Other Payments			

F-3A: Computation Statement

Ledger Creation

Name	: **AB C Courier Service**
Under	: **Sundry Creditors** *(Current Liabilities)*
Maintain balances bill-by-bill	? **Yes**
Default Credit Period	: **7 Days**
Inventory values are affected	? **No**
Statutory Information	
Is Service Provider/Receiver	? **Yes**
Set/Alter Service Tax Details	? **Yes**

F-5A: Service Provider Ledger Account Creation

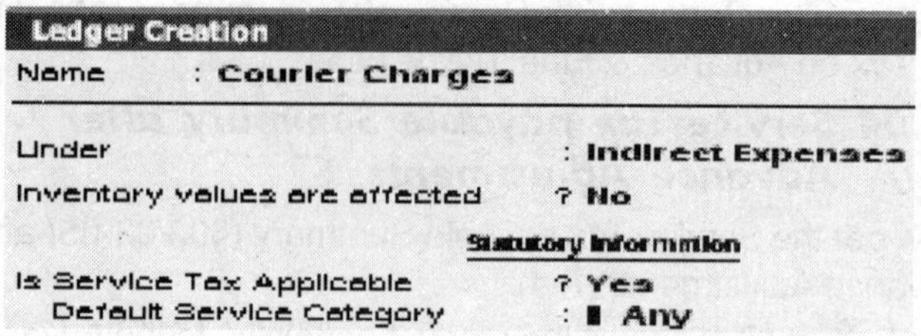

F-5B: Service Expense Ledger Account Creation

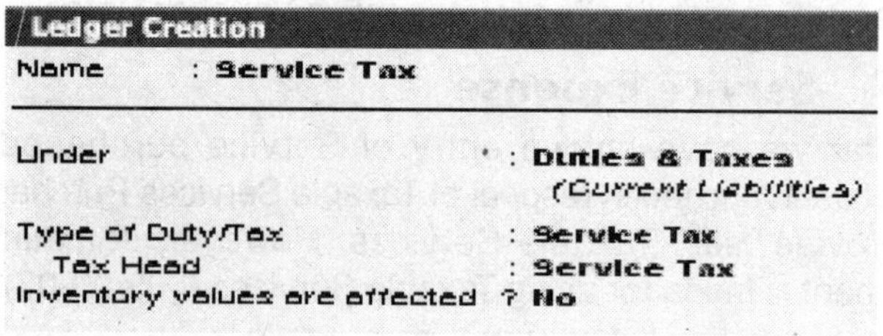

F-5C: Service Tax Ledger Account Creation

03.01 Service Expense Journal Voucher

Journal Voucher entry has been explained earlier (§05/01-04/S1). Here, we explain the process related to Service Tax. In Journal Voucher creation screen (F-6A).

- **Expense Ledger Account**: At *Particulars* column, first ledger account, select the *Taxable Expense* account, to get *Tax Details* screen (F-6B).
  - o **Tax Details**: At *Tax Details* screen (F-6B), enter the details (as *New Reference*- select New Ref at Type of Reference), as explained for Purchase (§03/03-07). At *Type of Service* column (F-6B), select *Input Credit* from the list of Service Types (F-6C). Enter the Service Charges at *Service Amount* (F-6B). The Tax inclusive amount is shown in *Amount Incl of Tax* column (F-6B), as explained earlier. The break up of Tax details are shown in the next lines, as explained earlier. You get back to the main entry screen (F-6A). The basic Service Expense Amount (exclusive of Tax) is shown in the Debit Column in the main voucher screen (F-6A).
- **Tax Ledger Account:** At Main entry screen (F-6A), at *Particulars* column, next select the *Tax Ledger* Account. The Tax Amount is auto carried and shown in the Debit Column.
- **Service Provider's Ledger Account:** At Main entry screen (F-6A), at *Particulars* column, next select the *Service Provider's Ledger* Account to get the Service Tax details screen (F-6B). At Service Tax details screen (F-6B), at *Name* column, the voucher number is carried as Reference Number as default (which you may change). At *Service Amount* column, the Service Charges (exclusive of Tax).- is carried. At *Amount inclusive* of Tax, amount is shown, which is carried in the main entry screen (F-6A) against the Service Provider's ledger account, at Credit column.

Now enter other ledger accounts details, Voucher Narration etc, as usual.

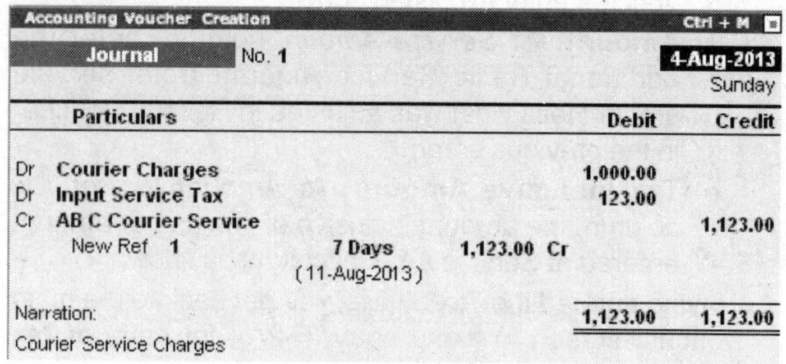

F-6A: Service Expense Journal Voucher

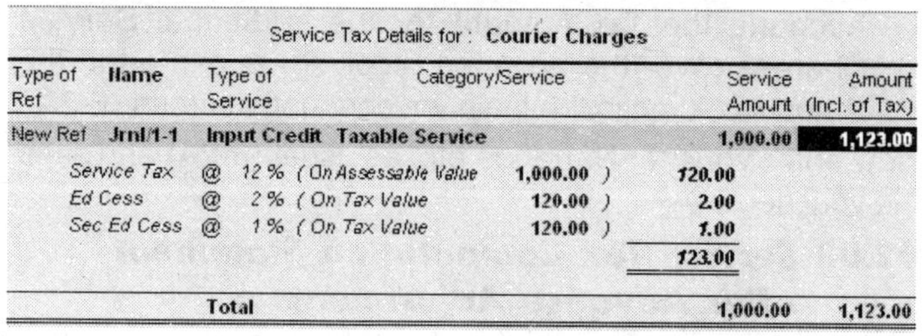

F-6B: Tax details of Service Expense Journal Voucher

04 Partly Taxable Service Purchase

Sometimes, a Purchase Bill may contain part of Non Taxable Amount and Part Taxable Amount. For example, vendor may submit a Bill in respect of materials provided (Non Taxable) and Taxable Service in one Bill.

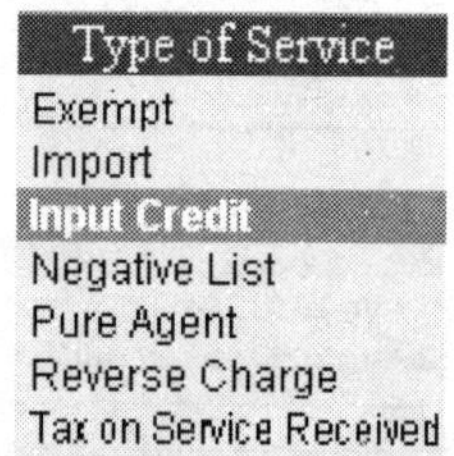

F-6C: Service Type list

Expense Ledger Account creation: First, you must create the respective Expense ledger account as described earlier (§03/03-03)

- **Non-Taxable Expense Ledger Account Creation**: Create the Ledger Account (e.g Stores Purchase). At *Is Service Tax Applicable*, set *No*
- **Taxable Expense Ledger Account Creation**: Create the Ledger Account (e.g Courier Charges). At *Is Service Tax Applicable*, set *Yes*

Purchase Bill Entry: Now create a Purchase Bill comprising of Taxable & Non Taxable Accounts (F-7A).

Party Ledger Account: At Purchase Voucher, at header, select the Party Ledger Account.

Other Ledger Accounts: Next enter the other Ledger Account details as follows:

- **Non Taxable Ledger Account**: At *Particulars* column (F-7A), select the Non Taxable Account (Expense / Purchase ledger account) and enter the amount for the ledger account as usual.

Accounting Voucher Creation Ctrl + M

Purchase No. 2 **6-Aug-2013**

Ref.: **15** Tuesday

Party's A/c Name : **AB C Courier Service**

Particulars	Rate per	Amount
Stores Purchase		**12,000.00**
Courier Charges		**200.00**
Input Service Tax		**24.00**
		12,224.00

Narration:
Materials & Courier Ch Cost

F-7A: Purchase Bill for Taxable & Non Taxable Items

Service Tax Details for : **Courier Charges**

Type of Ref	Name	Type of Service	Category/Service		Service Amount	Amount (Incl. of Tax)
New Ref	**Purc/15-1**	**Input Credit**	**Taxable Service**		**200.00**	**224.00**
	Service Tax	@ 12 %	(On Assessable Value 200.00)	24.00		
	Ed Cess	@ 2 %	(On Tax Value 24.00)			
	Sec Ed Cess	@ 1 %	(On Tax Value 24.00)			
				24.00		
		Total			**200.00**	**224.00**

F-7B: Tax details screen for Purchase Bill

- **Taxable Ledger Account**: Next, at *Particulars* column (F-7A), select the Taxable (Expense / Service Charges) Account to get the *Service Tax details* screen (F-7B).
  - o **Service Tax Details:** At *Tax details* screen (F-7B), enter the Tax details (F-7B) as explained in Purchase Voucher entry (§03/03-07). The Basic Expense Amount (exclusive of Tax) is carried in main voucher screen (F-7A), against the Taxable Service Ledger Account.
- **Tax Ledger Account:** At *Particulars* column (F-7A), select the *Service Tax Ledger* Account. The Tax Amount will be auto carried and shown in main voucher screen (F-7A).

Enter other ledger accounts (if any), Voucher Narration etc, as usual, at the main voucher screen (F-7A).

05 Taxable & Non Taxable composite Service Sales Voucher

Sometimes, a Service Provider may render multiple types of Services of which some are taxable while some are exempt.

For example, a coaching institute provides Coaching Tutorials (Taxable) and Sports Coaching (Exempt) and submits a combined bill.

Service Income Ledger Account creation: The Service Provider would create Service Income Ledger accounts for Taxable & Non Taxable services (F-8A & F-8B), as described earlier (§03/03-03)

- **Non-Taxable Service Ledger Account Creation**: Create the Service Ledger Account (e.g Sports Coaching Services). At *Is Service Tax Applicable*, set *No* (F-8A)
- **Taxable Service Ledger Account Creation**: Create the Ledger Account (e.g Coaching Services). At *Is Service Tax Applicable*, set *Yes* (F-8B)

Ledger Display

Name : **Coaching Services**

Under : **Direct Incomes**

Inventory values are affected ? **No**

Statutory Information

Is Service Tax Applicable ? **Yes**

Default Service Category : **[Any**

F-8A: Ledger Account of Taxable Service Income

Ledger Display

Name : **Sports Coaching Fees**

Under : **Direct Incomes**

Inventory values are affected ? **No**

Statutory Information

Is Service Tax Applicable ? **No**

F-8B: Ledger Account of Non-Taxable Service Income

Sales Voucher Entry: Now create the Sales Voucher for both type of Services rendered. In Sales Voucher creation screen (F-9A):

- **Non Taxable Service Account Ledger**: Select the Non Taxable Service Account and enter the amount. The amount is carried in the main voucher against the ledger account (F-9A)
- **Taxable Service Account Ledger:** Select the Taxable Service Account to get the service Tax entry screen (F-9B) and enter the details as explained in Sales Voucher entry (F-1B/02-04).The basic amount (excluding the Tax) is carried in the main voucher against the ledger account (F-9A).
- **Service Tax Ledger:** At main screen (F-9A), select the Output Service Tax Ledger. The Tax amount is carried at the amount column.

Now enter other Ledger Account details if any and then enter Voucher Narration etc. (F-9A). Save the Sales Voucher

Accounting Voucher Creation Ctrl + M

Sales No. 4 **9-Aug-2013**

Ref.: **17** Friday

Party's A/c Name : **H P Industries**

Particulars	Rate per	Amount
Sports Coaching Fees		**2,000.00**
Coaching Services		**3,000.00**
Output Service Tax		**371.00**
		5,371.00

Narration:
Service Fees

F-9A: Sales Voucher Entry for Taxable & Non Taxable Services

Service Tax Details for : **Coaching Services**

Type of Ref	Name	Type of Service	Category/Service	Service Amount	Amount (Incl. of Tax)
New Ref	Sale/17-1	Taxable	Taxable Service	3,000.00	3,371.00
	Coaching Services	0% is 3,000.00, Notif.No.)			
	Service Tax @ 12 % (*On Assessable Value* 3,000.00)			360.00	
	Ed Cess @ 2 % (*On Tax Value* 360.00)			7.00	
	Sec Ed Cess @ 1 % (*On Tax Value* 360.00)			4.00	
				371.00	
	Total			3,000.00	3,371.00

F-9B: Tax Details screen for Taxable Service

06 Transactions with Exempted Organisations

Sometimes, government grant exemption of Service Tax (Partial or Complete) to certain organisations through a Notification (the reference of the Notification & Date is called Notification Number & Notification Date). This Notification Number must be informed to the provider of service to issue Service Bill without charging Service Tax.

06.01 Taxable Service Sale to Exempted Organisation

Customer Ledger Creation: At the Customer Ledger creation screen (F-10A) of Exempted Organisation, set as follows:

- At *Is Service Provider / Receiver*, set *Yes*
- At *Set / Alter Service Tax details*, set *Yes* to get *Service Tax details screen* (F-10B)

At *Service Tax details screen* (F-10B):

- At *Type of Classification*, select *Exempt* from the *Classification List* (F-10C).
- At *Notification Number*, enter the Exemption Notification Number (F-10B)

Ledger Creation

Name : **Pintoo's Corner**

Under : **Sundry Debtors** *(Current Assets)*

Maintain balances bill-by-bill ? **Yes**
Default Credit Period :
Inventory values are affected ? **No**

Statutory Information

Is Service Provider/Receiver ? **Yes**
Set/Alter Service Tax Details ? **Yes**

F-10A: Exempted Customer Ledger

Service Tax Details

Registration No.	:	**ABCDE9876X**
Date of Registration	:	**1-Apr-2011**
Is Associated Enterprise	?	**No**
Type of Classification	:	**Exempt**
Notification No.	:	**345678 dt 1.7.12**

F-10B: Exempted Customer Tax Details

Classification

- Not Applicable
- Exempt
- Export
- Import
- Pure Agent
- Reverse Charge
- Tax on Service Received

F-10C List of Tax Classification

Sales Voucher Entry: Now enter the Sales Voucher (F-10D). Select the Customer Ledger to get *Tax Details screen* (F-10E).

At *Service Tax details* screen (F-10E), at *Type of Service* column, *Exempt* is auto carried as default & *Exempted Service* is carried as default at *Category/Service* column. The Notification Number as entered in the Party Ledger is carried. Press <enter> to get back to the voucher entry main screen (F-10D).

Accounting Voucher Creation Ctrl + M

Sales No. **5** **15-Aug-2013** Thursday

Ref. :
Party's A/c Name : **Pintoo's Corner**

Particulars	Rate per	Amount
Coaching Services		**1,200.00**
Narration:		**1,200.00**
Service to Exmept Orgn		

F-10D: Service sale Bill to Exempt Organisation

Service Tax Details for : **Coaching Services**

Type of Ref	Name	Type of Service	Category/Service	Service Amount	Amount (Incl. of Tax)
New Ref	Sale/5-1	Exempt	Exempted Service	1,200.00	1,200.00
	(Exempt Notification No. : 345678 dt 1.7.12)				
				1,200.00	1,200.00

F-10E:Tax details for Service sale Bill to Exempt Organisation

At voucher entry main screen (F-10D), enter details of ledger accounts. Enter Voucher Narration etc as usual

06.02 Taxable Service Purchase from Exempted Organisation

As described (§06.01), sale of Taxable Service by exempted service provider, would be without charging Service Tax. So, Purchase of Taxable Service from Exempted Service Provider would be without Service Tax.

In the Purchase Voucher entry (F-11A), select the Taxable Service Purchase Account to get the Service Tax details screen (F-11B). Since it is Taxable Service defined in the Purchase Ledger Account, you will get default values carried in the columns *Type of Service* & *Category / Service* (F-11B). To change them, type *F12:Configure* to get the *Service Tax entry Configuration* screen (F-11C).

Accounting Voucher Creation Ctrl + M

Purchase No. **3** **12-Aug-2013** Monday

Ref. : **16**
Party's A/c Name : **S B Services**

Particulars	Rate per	Amount
Coaching Fees Purchased		**2,000.00**
Narration:		**2,000.00**
Service purchased from Exempt Orgn		

F-11A: Service Purchase from Exempted Organisation

Service Tax Details for : **Coaching Fees Purchased**

Type of Ref	Name	Type of Service	Category/Service	Service Amount	Amount (Incl. of Tax)
New Ref	**Purc/16-1**	**Exempt**	**Exempted Service**	**2,000.00**	**2,000.00**
		(Exempt Notification No. : 1234 dt 1.7.12)			
		Total		**2,000.00**	**2,000.00**

F-11B: Service Tax details entry screen

At *Service Tax entry Configuration* screen (F-11C), set *Yes* at *Allow Override Service Category during Entry.* Now get to the field *Type of Service* (press *Shift+Tab* to go back to previous field), to get the selection list of Service Type (F-11B). At the field *Type of Service*, select *Exempt* from the Service Type list (F-11D). At *Category / Service* column, *Exempted Service* is carried. Now you get the *Exempt Notification Number* screen (F-11E). Enter the respective Exemption Notification Number. This number is then carried in the Tax Details entry screen (F-11B) also.

As there is no Tax, the Service Amount would be carried to Amount inclusive of Tax and no Tax Details will be shown (F-11B).

Configuration

Allow to override Service Category during entry	? **Yes**
Allow alteration of Abatement Rate during entry	? **No**
Allow alteration of Tax Rate	? **No**
Allow alteration of Taxable Percentage	? **No**

F-11C: Configuration for Service Tax entry in Voucher

Type of Service

Exempt
Import
Input Credit
Negative List
Pure Agent
Reverse Charge
Tax on Service Received

F-11D:Selection list Service Tax Type

Exempt Notification No.

1234 dt 1.7.12

F-11E:Exemption Notification of entry

After entry of Tax Details, you get the main screen (F-10A). Now enter Voucher Narration etc.

07 Service Bill of Professionals

Professionals like Chartered Accountants, Legal Firms etc, normally issues a Receipt for money received for Services, instead of issuing Bills.

Here we decsribe how to enter the Service Fees received in Receipt Voucher and issue a Receipt to the person making the payment for Service received (alongwith Tax).

Taxbale Income Ledger Account: Create the Taxbale Income Ledger Account (e.g Consultancy Fees) and set the Service Tax details as described (§03/03-03)

Receipt Voucher: When the money for Service is Received, a Receipt Voucher is created (F-12A)

Accounting Voucher Creation Ctrl + M

Receipt No. 2 **12-Aug-2013**
Monday

Account : **Cash**

Particulars	Amount
Consultancy Fees	**1,335.00**
Output Service Tax	**165.00**
	1,500.00

Narration:
Professional Fees Received

F-12A: Receipt Voucher for Professional Fees

Service Tax Details for : **Consultancy Fees**

Type of Ref	Name	Party Ledger	Type of Service	Category/Service	Amount (Incl. of Tax)	Service Amount
New Ref	**Rcpt/2-1**	**Cash**	**Taxable**	**Taxable Service**	**1,500.00**	**1,335.00**
	(Taxable @ 100% is 1,335.00, Notif No:)					
	Service Tax @ 12 % (On Assessable Value 1,335.00)			*160.00*		
	Ed Cess @ 2 % (On Tax Value 160.00)			*3.00*		
	Sec Ed Cess @ 1 % (On Tax Value 160.00)			*2.00*		
				165.00		
			Total		**1,500.00**	**1,335.00**

F-12B: Receipt Voucher for Professional Fees

In Receipt Voucher entry screen (F-12A), enter as follows:

- **Cash / Bank Ledger Account**: First select the Cash (when money is received in cash) or Bank Account (when money is Received by Cheque, etc).
- **Professional Fees Ledger Account**: Now select the Professional Fees Ledger Account to get the *Tax Details* screen (F-12B).
- **Tax Details**: At Tax Details screen (F-12B), enter as follows:
  - o **Reference:** Select *New Reference*, the Voucher Number with subscript is carried by default. The default *Type of Service* & *Category / Service* are also carried.
  - o **Amout**: You may enter the Amount in either way as follows:
    - **Amount Inclusive of Tax**: Enter the Amount Received (inclusive of Service Tax) in Amount Inclusive of Tax column. The Basic Service Amount is back computed and shown in Service Amount Column
    - **Service Amount (exclusive of Tax)**: Enter the basic Service Amount (exclusive of Service Tax) in Service Amount column. The Amount *inclusive of Tax* is computed and shown in *Amount Inclusive of Tax* column

The Tax details (break up of each element of Service Tax / Cess are shown next

07.01 Professional Receipt Printing

Having entered the Receipt Voucher (F-12A), at Receipt Voucher entry screen (F-12A), click P:Print button (or press Alt+P keys) to get the Receipt Voucher Pritnting screen (F-13A)

At Voucher Pritnting screen (F-13A), set *Y* at the option *Print Service Tax Professional Receipt cum Challan* to get Receipt (F-13B) giving the details of Service and receipt of money (you may enter the Name & Other details of the Party in Voucher Narration which would be printed in the Receipt.

A B Services
12 Heysham Rd
Kolkata 700999

Professional Receipt Cum Challan

Party :	No. : Dated :

Particulars	Rate	per	Amount
Consultancy Fees *(Service : Taxable Service)*			**1,335.00**
Service Tax (On Assessable Amount 1,335.00)	**12**	%	**160.00**
Education Cess	**2**	%	**3.00**
Secondary and Higher Education Cess	**1**	%	**2.00**
Total			**₹ (-)1,500.00**

Amount Chargeable (in words) *E. & O.E*

INR One Thousand Five Hundred Only

Service Tax Payable (in words)

INR One Hundred Sixty Five Only

Remarks:
Professional Fees Received

Company's Service Tax No. : **ABC1234**

for A B Services

Authorised Signatory

This is a Computer Generated Invoice

F-13B: Money Receipt for Professional Service Fees

Report Titles

Receipt Voucher

Print Service Tax Professional Receipt Cum Challan : y

F-13A:Receipt Printing screen

08 Service Export

Service rendered outside India is exepmt from Tax, similar to Sale of Service to exempted Organsiation discussed (§06.01).

Customer Ledger Creation: At the Customer Ledger creation screen (F-14A) of Foreign Customer set as follows:

- At *Is Service Provider / Receiver*, set *Yes*
- At *Set / Alter Service Tax details*, set *Yes* to get *Service Tax details screen* (F-14B)

At *Service Tax details screen* (F-14B):

- At *Type of Classification (F-14B)*, select *Export* from the *Classification Type List* (F-10C).
- At *Notification Number (F-14B)*, enter the Exemption Notification Number

Service Export Bill: Now create the Sales Invoice (F-14C) in the same way as Sale to Exempted Customer (§06.01).

Ledger Alteration

Name : **A B (Japan)**

Under : **Sundry Debtors** *(Current Assets)*

Maintain balances bill-by-bill ? **Yes**
Default Credit Period :
Inventory values are affected ? **No**

Statutory Information

Is Service Provider/Receiver ? **Yes**
Set/Alter Service Tax Details ? **Yes**

F-14A: Foreign Customer Ledger Account

Service Tax Details

Registration No. :
Date of Registration :
Is Associated Enterprise ? **No**
Type of Classification : **Export**
Notification No. : **12345 dt 1.4.12**

F-14B: Tax details set up Foreign Customer Ledger

At *Service Tax details* screen (F-14D), *Export* is auto carried as default at *Type of Service* & *Taxable Service* is carried as default at *Category/Service*. The Notification Number as entered in the Party Ledger is carried. Press <enter> to get back to the voucher entry main screen (F-14D).

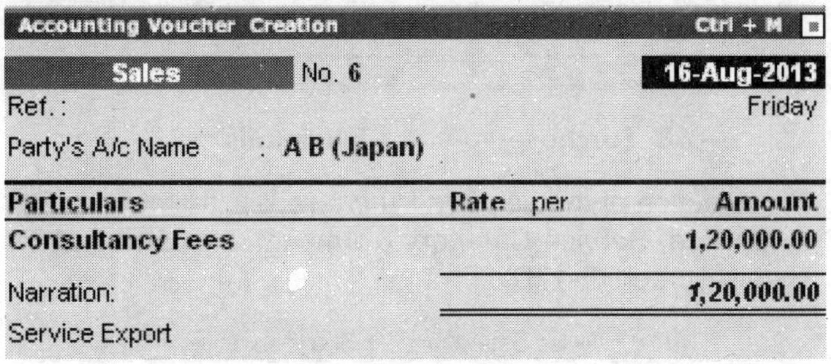
Accounting Voucher Creation Ctrl + M
Sales No. 6 16-Aug-2013
Ref.: Friday
Party's A/c Name : A B (Japan)

Particulars	Rate per	Amount
Consultancy Fees		1,20,000.00
		1,20,000.00

Narration:
Service Export

F-14C: Service Export Bill

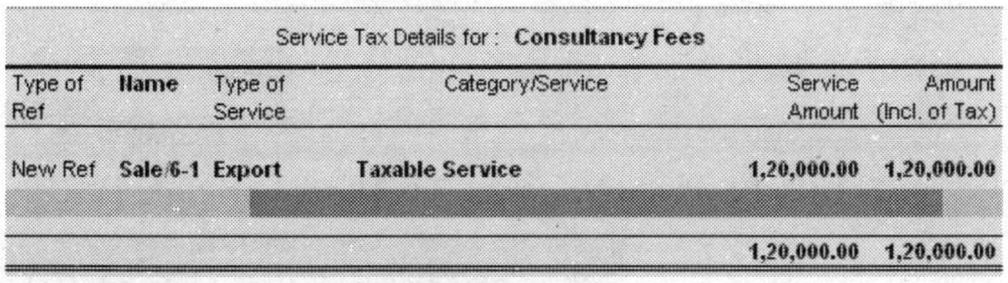
Service Tax Details for : Consultancy Fees

Type of Ref	Name	Type of Service	Category/Service	Service Amount	Amount (Incl. of Tax)
New Ref	Sale/6-1	Export	Taxable Service	1,20,000.00	1,20,000.00
				1,20,000.00	1,20,000.00

F-14D: Service Export Bill

At Voucher entry main screen (F-14D), enter other ledger details, if any and finally enter Voucher Narration, if any.

09 Service Import

On *Import of Service* (Service provided from outside India and received in India), *Service Receiver in India* is liable to pay Service Tax (§06/03-01).

The service tax paid on imports, normally can not be considered for availing the Input Credit (except in certain special cases, as allowed). Purchase of Imported Service is recorded through Purchase Voucher (like Purchase from Exempted Service Provider). No Service Tax is entered in Purchase Voucher (as no Service Tax is charged by Foreign Service Provider). The Liability of Tax Payable is created separately through Journal Voucher.

09.01 Service Provider's Ledger Account Creation

Create the Ledger Account of Foreign Service Supplier (F-15A).

- At *Is Service Provider / Receiver*, set *Yes*
- At *Set / Alter Service Tax details*, set *Yes* to get *Service Tax details screen* (F-15B)

At *Service Tax details screen* (F-15B):

- At *Type of Classification (F-15B)*, select *Import* from the *Classification Type List* (F-10C).
- At *Notification Number (F-15B)*, enter the Notification Number

09.02 Service Tax on Imports Ledger Account Creation

Create the Ledger Account of Service Tax Imports (F-15C), which should be placed under Indirect Expenses. Under Statutory section, at *Is Service Tax Applicable*, set *No* (as the Service Provider is not a Registered Service Provider in India).

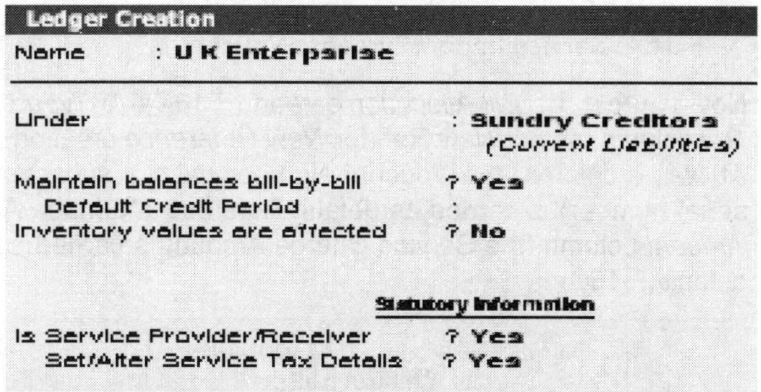
Ledger Creation
Name : U K Enterparise
Under : Sundry Creditors
(Current Liabilities)
Maintain balances bill-by-bill ? Yes
Default Credit Period :
Inventory values are affected ? No
Statutory Information
Is Service Provider/Receiver ? Yes
Set/Alter Service Tax Details ? Yes

F-15A: Foreign Service Provider Ledger Creation

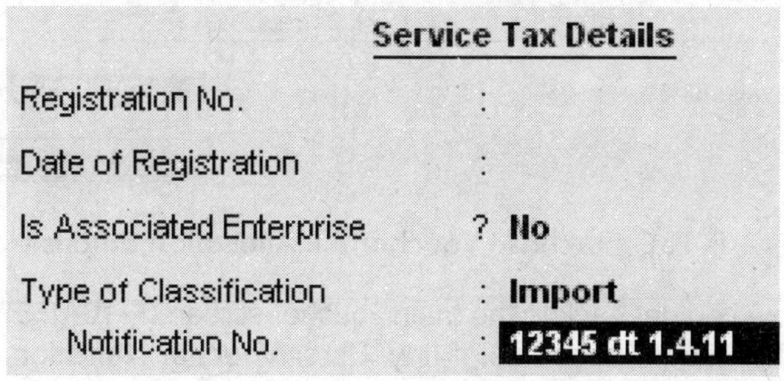
Service Tax Details
Registration No. :
Date of Registration :
Is Associated Enterprise ? No
Type of Classification : Import
Notification No. : 12345 dt 1.4.11

F-15B: Foreign Service Provider Tax details

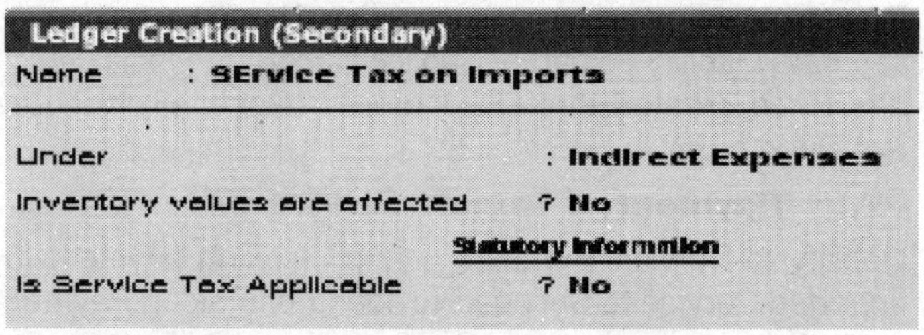
Ledger Creation (Secondary)
Name : SErvice Tax on Imports
Under : Indirect Expenses
Inventory values are affected ? No
Statutory Information
Is Service Tax Applicable ? No

F-15C: Service Tax on Imports Ledger Creation

09.03 Service Import Purchase Voucher

At Purchase Voucher entry screen (F-16A) for Service rendered by foreign Service Provider, select the Foreign Service Provider Ledger Account to get the Service Tax details screen (F-16B). The Type of Service & Category/Service as entered at Party Ledger (F-15B) is carried by default at Service Tax details screen at Voucher entry (F-16B). At *Service Amount* column, enter the Service Amount, which is carried to Amount Inclusive of Tax column also.

Accounting Voucher Creation Ctrl + M

Purchase No. 4 19-Aug-2013
Ref.: 19 Monday

Particulars		Debit	Credit
Cr U K Enterpsrise			1,00,000.00
New Ref 19	1,00,000.00 Cr		
Dr Consultancy Fees Paid		1,00,000.00	
		1,00,000.00	1,00,000.00

Narration:
Import of Service

F-16A: Service Import Purchase Voucher

Service Tax Details for : **Consultancy Fees Paid**

Type of Ref	Name	Type of Service	Category/Service	Service Amount	Amount (Incl. of Tax)
New Ref	Purc/19-1	Import	Taxable Service	1,00,000.00	1,00,000.00
				1,00,000.00	1,00,000.00

F-16B: Purchase Voucher Tax details

Now you get the *Bill Allocation* screen (F-16C). At *Type of Ref* column, select *New Ref* (for *New Reference* creation). At *Name* column, the Voucher Number (with a subscript serial number) is carried as default Reference Number. At *Amount* column, the Service Charge Amount is carried as default (F-16C)

Bill-wise Details for : **U K Enterpsrise**
Upto: **₹ 1,00,000.00 Cr**

Type of Ref	Name	Due Date, or Credit Days (wef: 19-Aug-2013)	Amount	Dr/ Cr
New Ref	19		1,00,000.00	Cr
			1,00,000.00	Cr

F-16C:Purchase Voucher Bill Allocation details

Now you get back to the main voucher screen (F-16A). Enter other ledger accounts, if any. Enter Voucher Narration etc and save the voucher.

You do not need to enter Service Tax as the foreign Service Provider does not charge service Tax. The Service Tax is a separate Liability on part of Service Receiver in India, which has to be created through Journal Voucher (F-18D), as explained next.

09.04 Payment of Import Service Bill

Liability to Service Tax arise only on making payment for Imported Service to Service Provider. For making Payment to Service Provider, enter a Payment Voucher like Payment of Service Purchase Bill of an Exempted Service Provider.

In Payment Voucher entry screen (F-17A), select the Service Provider Account, to get the Bill Allocation screen (F-17B). At Bill Allocation screen (F-17B), select the pending Purchase Bill from the list (F-17C).

F-17A: Payment Voucher for Payment to Foreign Service Provider

Accounting Voucher Creation Ctrl + M

Payment No. 3 20-Aug-2013
Tuesday

Account : **HDFC Bank**

Particulars		Amount
U K Enterpsrise		1,00,000.00
Agst Ref 19	1,00,000.00 Dr	
		1,00,000.00

Narration:
Payment for Service Import

On selection of the pending Purchase Bill, the default Type of Service, Service Category & Amount are carried at Tax Details screen (F-17D).

Bill-wise Details for : **U K Enterpsrise**

Type of Ref	Name	Due Date, or Credit Days (wef: 20-Aug-2013)	Amount	Dr/ Cr
Agst Ref	19		1,00,000.00	Dr
			1,00,000.00	Dr

F-17B: Payment Voucher Bill Allocation details

F-17C: Pending Bill Selection

Pending Bills

Name	Date	Balance
19	19-Aug-2013	1,00,000.00 Cr

At Tax details screen (F-17D), select the pending Bill (F-17E). The details of selected Bill are carried in the main voucher screen (F-17A)

Service Tax Details for : **U K Enterpsrise**

Type of Ref	Name	Type of Service	Category/Service	Amount (Incl. of Tax)	Service Amount
Agst Ref	Purc/19-1	Import	Taxable Service	1,00,000.00	1,00,000.00
	Total			1,00,000.00	1,00,000.00

F-17D: Payment Voucher Tax details entry

Pending Tax Bills

Name	Date	Type of Service	Category	Amount	Service Amount
Purc/19-1	19-Aug-2013	Import	Taxable Service	1,00,000.00	1,00,000.00

F-17E: Pending Purchase Bill Selection

At main voucher screen (F-17A), enter other ledger accounts details, if any and enter Voucher Narration etc. Save the Voucher.

09.05 Import Service Tax Liability Journal

Having paid the Money for Service Bill Import, you have to create the corresponding Tax Liability, through Journal Voucher (F-18D) using Voucher Class (F-18A) as explained earlier (§03.01)

To enter Journal Voucher, At GoT>Accounts Voucher, Click *F7:Journal* and then select the Journal Voucher Class (F-18A), which is carried at the Journal Voucher entry screen (F-18D). At *Used For* field (F-18D), select *Tax on Import of*

Service from the list (F-18B) to get *Service Tax Liability* entry screen (F-18C)

At *Service Tax Liability* screen (F-18C), enter as follows:

- **Date**: At *Till Date* field, the Payment Voucher Date is carried by default.
- **Service Category**: At *Service Category* field, select the Service Category (or you may select *Taxable Service,* or *Any*).
- **Input Credit**: At *Avail Input Credit*, set *No*, if Input Credit is not to be availed (only in some special cases, Input Credit may be availed).
- **Service Tax Ledgers**: At *Output Ledgers* field, select the Service Tax Ledger. If you have created a single Ledger for Service Tax, Education Cess & Secondary Education Cess, the same ledger account would be shown for all these Tax components (F-18C).
- **Tax on Service Import Ledger**: At *Input / Expense Ledgers*, Select the *Tax on Import* Ledger Account created (F-18C), as explained (F-15C). If this ledger is not created, press *Ctrl+C* to get Ledger Creation screen and create the Ledger Account (F-15C).

F-18A: Selection of Journal Voucher Type

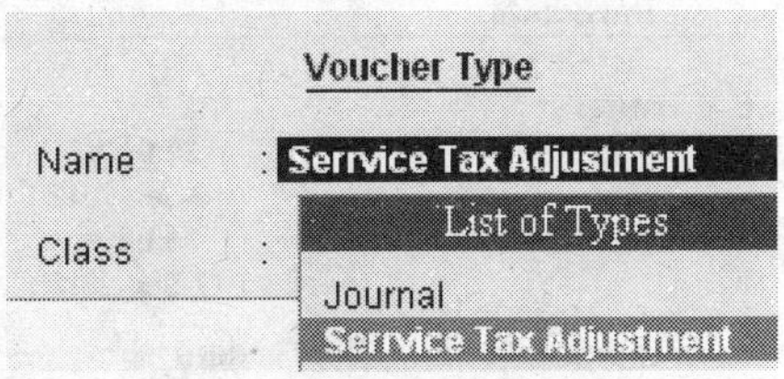

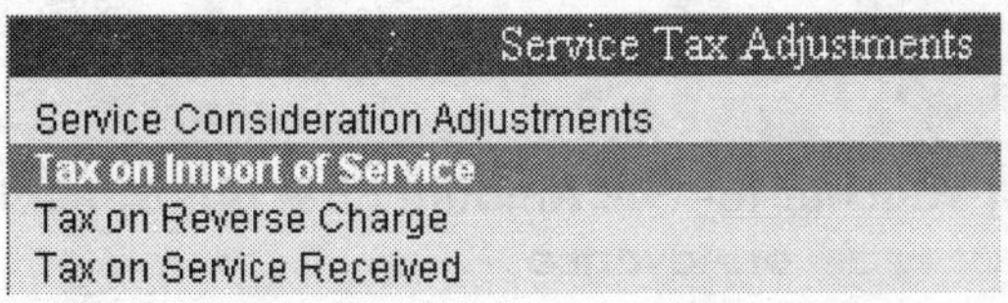

F-18B: Selection of Tax Type at Used For

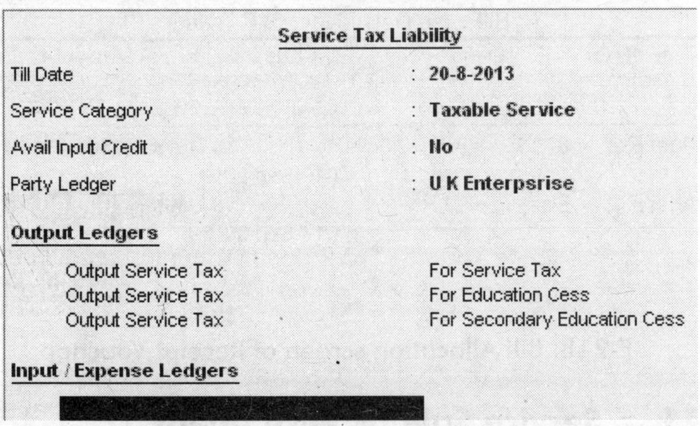

F-18C: Service Tax Liability Entry screen

Journal Voucher Entry Service Import Liability: Now you get back to the main Journal Voucher Entry screen (F-18D) showing the Tax on Import ledger carried at Debit and the Service Tax Ledger selected (F-18C) at Credit Column for the amount of Tax on Import. Enter Voucher Narration (F-18D) and save the voucher.

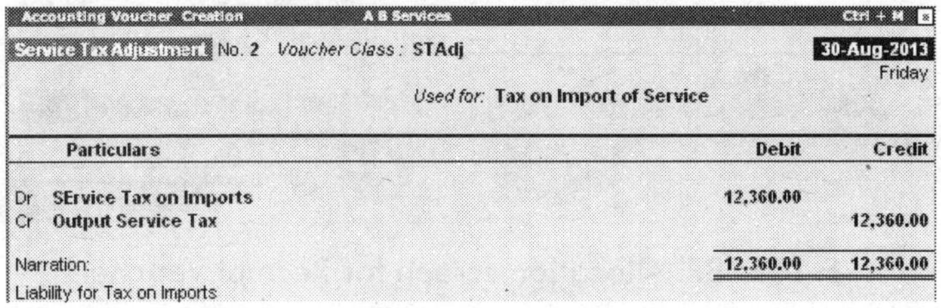

F-18D: Journal Voucher creation for Service Tax Liability

10 General Advances

Service Tax is payable on preparing the Service Bill (i.e on rendering the service), or receipt of money for the service, whichever is earlier. So, service tax is to be deducted on receipt of advance against services rendered (or to be rendered), as explained earlier (§02.01).

However, sometimes organisation may receive general advances, which is not specifically related to any job. They may adjust the advance against the subsequent service bills. In such case, Service Tax is not deducted at the time of receipt of advance. Service Tax is charged in the Service Bill and the Advance received is adjusted from the Bill.

Entries for such Advances received and subsequent adjustment against service bill are now explained.

10.01 General Advance Receipt

When Advance is received, a Receipt Voucher is created In Receipt Voucher entry (F-19A), At Receipt Voucher entry screen (F-19A), on selecting the Party Ledger, you get *Tax Details* screen. At *Type of Reference*, select *End of List* to skip the Tax details screen. Now you get *Bill Allocation* Screen (F-19B). At *Bill Allocation* screen (F-19B), the Receipt Voucher Number is carried as Reference Number (which you may change). Now enter the Net Amount Received at *Amount* Column (F-19B).

Now you get the Voucher entry main screen (F-19A), with the Amount carried from the *Bill Allocation* screen. Enter the *Narration* etc and save the Receipt Voucher

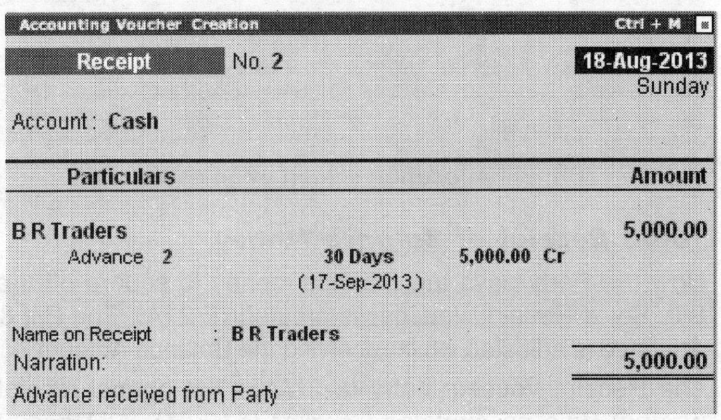

F-19A: Receipt Voucher Entry for Advance

Bill-wise Details for : **B R Traders**				
Type of Ref	Name	Due Date, or Credit Days (wef: 18-Aug-2013)	**Amount**	Dr/ Cr
Advance	2	30 Days (17-Sep-2013)	5,000.00	Cr
			5,000.00	Cr

F-19B: Bill Allocation screen for Receipt Voucher

10.02 *Service Bill*

After the service is provided, create the Service Sales Bill (F-20A) as explained earlier (§03/03-04). At Tax details screen (F-20B), at *Service Amount* column, enter the Base Service Amount excluding the Tax. The amount including the Service Tax is computed and shown in *Amount incl. of Tax* column. The details of Tax components are shown in the next lines (F-20B).

After Tax details entry, you get back to the voucher main entry screen (F-20A). The Base Service Amount is carried against the Service Ledger account. Now select the Tax ledger account. The amount of Tax is carried against the Tax Ledger.

Enter Voucher Narration etc (F-20A) and save the Voucher.

Accounting Voucher Creation Ctrl + M

Sales No. 6 20-Aug-2013 Tuesday

Ref.: 28

Party's A/c Name : **B R Traders**

Particulars	Rate	per	Amount
Consultancy Fees			7,000.00
Output Service Tax			865.00
Narration:			7,865.00

F: 20A: Sales Voucher entry

Service Tax Details for : **Consultancy Fees**

Type of Ref	Name	Type of Service	Category/Service		Service Amount	Amount (Incl. of Tax)
New Ref	Sale/28-1	Taxable	Taxable Service		7,000.00	7,865.00
Service Tax	@	12 % (On Assessable Value	7,000.00)	840.00		
Ed Cess	@	2 % (On Tax Value	840.00)	17.00		
Sec Ed Cess	@	1 % (On Tax Value	840.00)	8.00		
				865.00		
Total					7,000.00	7,865.00

F: 20B: Bill Allocation screen of Sales Voucher

10.03 *Receipt of Balance Money*

Now the Party pays the Balance money to square off the Bill. So, a Receipt Voucher is created (F-21A). The Bill & Advance is adjusted while receiving the Balance Amount.

The Receipt Voucher entry (F-21A) is like normal receipt against Bills as explained earlier (§10.01). At Receipt Voucher, select the Payer's Ledger Account to get *Bill Allocation* screen (F-21B). At *Bill Allocation* screen (F-21B), Select *Agst Ref* (because you like to Adjust the References of Advance & Sales Bill). The pending references of Advance (Cr balance) & and Sale Bill (Debit Balance) are listed. Select them one by one (F-21B).

Now the selected references (F-21B) are adjusted fully. The balance payable (difference between the Sale Bill Amount with Tax and the Advance Received) is then carried to Party Account (F-21B) and shown in the main screen at *Amount* Column (F-21A)

At Main Voucher entry screen (F-21A), at *Name on Receipt* enter the Payees Name (this will be printed in the Money Receipt (Formal Receipt).

You may also print the Money Receipt (Formal Receipt) from the Receipt Voucher (§09/02-15/S1), which shows complete details of Adjustment of Bill & Advance and the net Amount received.

Accounting Voucher Creation Ctrl + M

Receipt No. 3 25-Aug-2013 Sunday

Account : **HDFC Bank**

Particulars					Amount
B R Traders					2,865.00
Agst Ref	6	30 Days (19-Sep-2013)	7,865.00	Cr	
Agst Ref	2	30 Days (17-Sep-2013)	5,000.00	Dr	

Name on Receipt : **B R Traders**

Narration: 2,865.00

Amt rceived after adjustment of advance

F-21A: Receipt Voucher for Net Amount after adjustment of Advance

Bill-wise Details for : **B R Traders**				
Type of Ref	Name	Due Date, or Credit Days (wef: 25-Aug-2013)	**Amount**	Dr/ Cr
Agst Ref	6	30 Days (19-Sep-2013)	7,865.00	Cr
Agst Ref	2	30 Days (17-Sep-2013)	5,000.00	Dr
			2,865.00	Cr

F-21B: Bill Allocation screen of Receipt Voucher

11 Service Sale by Pure Agent

Often Services are sold through Agent. The expenses incurred by Pure Agent (an agent who is a liaison between *Principal Service Provider* and the *Service Receiver*), is exempt from Service Tax.

11.01 *Pure Agent Ledger Account Creation*

Create the Ledger Account of Pure Agent (F-22A) in the same way as Service Provider, as explained. At *Under* field, select

Sundry Creditors (as the agent incurs expenses on behalf of the principals).

- At *Is Service Provider / Receiver*, set *Yes* (F-22A)
- At *Set / Alter Service Tax details* (F-22A), set *Yes* to get *Service Tax details screen* (F-22B)

At *Service Tax details screen* (F-22B),:

- At *Type of Classification (F-22B)*, select *Pure Agent* from the *Classification Type List* (F-10C).
- At *Notification Number (F-22B)*, enter the Notification Number.

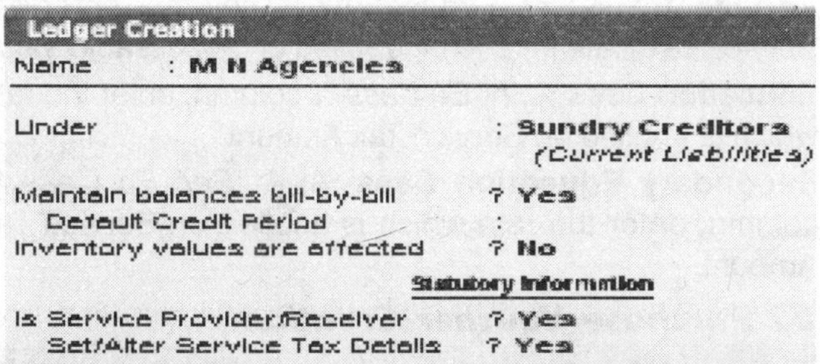

F-22A: Pure Agent Ledger Account Creation

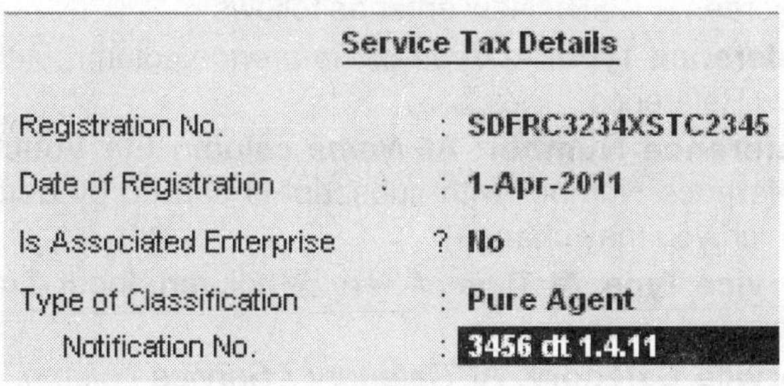

F-22B: Pure Agent Ledger Account Tax Details

11.02 Pure Agent Service Sale Voucher Creation

Now create the Sales Voucher for Service Charges (F-23A) including the expenses incurred (e.g Service Charges: 90000 + Agents Expenses: 10000).

On selecting the Service Income Ledger Account (F-23A), you get the Tax details screen (F-23B).

Tax Details: At Tax details screen (F-23B), at *Service Amount* column, enter the Service Amount (Own Service Charge & Agents Expenses). At *Type of Service* column (F-23B), select *Pure Agent* from the list to get *Expenses Amount* Entry screen (F-23C).

At *Expenses Amount* Entry screen (F-23C), enter the Expenses incurred by the Agent (which is not Taxable). The Amount including Service Tax is shown in *Amount inclusive of Tax* column. The component of Tax details are shown below. It will be seen that Tax is computed on Service Charges entered – Expenses (e.g 100000-10000=90000). *At Type of Ref* at next entry line (F-23B), select <End of List> to get back to main voucher screen (F-23A).

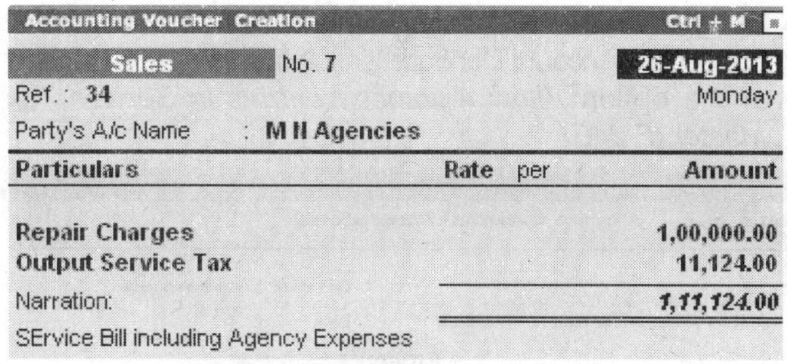

F-23A: Pure Agent Service Bill

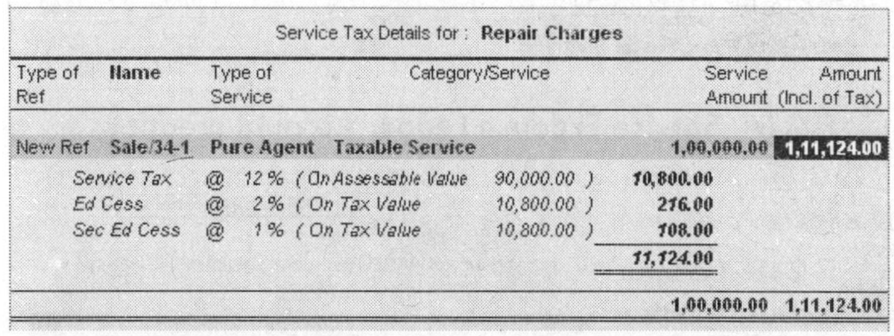

F-23B: Pure Agent Service Bill Tax details

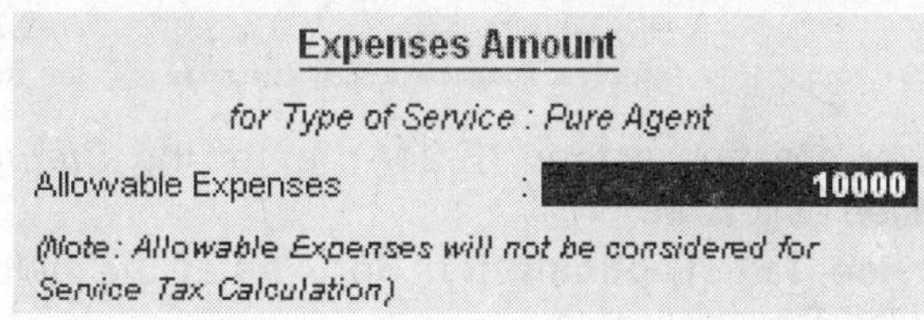

F-23C: Pure Agent Service Bill Expenses details

At main voucher entry screen (F-23A), select the Service Tax Ledger account. The Service Tax as shown in Tax Details screen (F-23B) is carried and shown in Amount Column in main screen (F-23A)

Finally, enter *Voucher Narration* etc (F-23A) and save the Voucher.

12 Service Purchase at Lower Tax Rate

In some cases, there may be provision under law to charge Service Tax for some specified service, at a Lower Rate [lower than 12%+ (2%+1% on 12% = 12.36%].

For such Taxable Service Purchase Ledger account, set the applicable lower rates in the respective ledger account master. During Voucher entry, the applicable Rates as entered would be carried by default and the Tax would be calculated accordingly.

12.01 Service Charges Account Ledger Creation

Taxable Service Ledger Account creation has been explained (§03/03-03). At the respective Service Charges Ledger Account entry screen (F-24A), enter as follows:

- **Ledger Account Name**: At *Name, e*nter Ledger Account Name
- **Parent Account Group**: At *Under* field, select the Account Group (Direct / Indirect Expenses)

- **Ledger Account Configuration**: Click *F12:Configure* to get Ledger Account Configuration screen (F-24B). Set *Yes* at the option *Allow Advanced entries in Service Tax Master (F-24B)*

Ledger Creation

Name : **Works Contract Services**

Under	: **Direct Expenses**
Inventory values are affected	? **No**
Statutory Information	
Is Service Tax Applicable	? **Yes**
Default Service Category	: **Works Contract Service**
Set/Alter Abatement Details	? **No**
Set/Alter Tax Rate Details	? **Yes**

F-24A: Service Expense Ledger Account creation

Ledger Configuration

Allow ALIASES along with Names	? No
Allow Language ALIASES along with Names	? No
Allow ADVANCED entries in Masters	? Yes
Allow ADVANCED entries in Service Tax Master	? **Yes**
Add NOTES for Ledger Accounts	? No
Use ADDRESSES for Ledger Accounts	? Yes
Use CONTACT Details	? Yes
Use Other Information for Ledger Accounts	? No

F-24B: Ledger Accounts entry configuration

At Ledger creation screen (F-24A), enter the *Statutory Information* as follows:

- **Service Tax Applicability**: Set *Yes* at the field *Is Service Tax Applicable,*
- **Service Category**: At *Default Service Category*,select the specific *Service Category* from the list, for which you like to re-set the Tax Rates Service Category (Do not select *Taxable Service* or *Any*).

Tax Rate Details

Category	Applicable From	Service Tax %	Ed Cess %	Sec Ed Cess %
Works Contract Service	1-Apr-2012	4 %	2 %	1 %

Note : Specifying Tax Rate percentage will override default percentages

F-24C: Tax Rate details entry

- **Abatement**: At *Set Alter Abatement details*, set *No* (Abatement is now withdrawn and Taxable Percentage is replaced in its place)

- **Tax Rate Details Set Up**: At *Set/ Alter Tax Rate Details*, set *Yes* to get *Tax Rate Details entry screen* (F-24C).

Tax Rates Entry: At *Tax Rate Details entry screen* (F-24C), enter the Tax Rates components:

- **Service Category**: At *Category* column, Select the Service Category for which you like to set the applicable Tax Rates
- **Applicable From**: At *Applicable From* column, Enter the Date from which the new Rate being entered becomes Applicable
- **Service Tax %**: At *Service Tax %* column, enter the Service Tax Rate in % to be applied on Assessable Value
- **Education Cess %**: At *Ed Cess %* column, enter the rate which is applied on Service Tax Amount
- **Secondary Education Cess %**: At *Sec Ed Cess %* column, enter the rate which is applied on Service Tax Amount

12.02 Purchase Voucher Creation

At Purchase Voucher entry screen (F-25A), select the Service Expenses Ledger Account to get the Tax Details entry screen (F-25B). Now enter as follows:

- **Reference Type**: At *Type of Reference* column, select New Reference
- **Reference Number**: At *Name* column the Voucher Reference Number with subscript is carried by default (which you may change)
- **Service Type**: At *Type of Service* column, Input Credit is carried by default
- **Service Category**: At *Category / Service column*, the default Service Category is carried. Press Shift+Tab keys to get back to the Service Category column and select the applicable Service Category.
- **Basic Service Amount**: At *Service Amount* column, enter the Basic Service Amount (excluding Tax).
- **Tax Inclusive Amount**: At *Amount Incl. of Tax column*, the Tax Inclusive Amount is computed at the applicable Rate as entered for the Service Tax Category (F-24C), and shown

Next, the details of each component of Tax are shown (F-25B)

Accounting Voucher Creation Ctrl + M

Purchase No. 5 **30-Aug-2013**

Ref.: **24** Friday

Party's A/c Name : **B R Traders**

Particulars	Rate per	Amount
Works Contract Services		**10,000.00**
Input Service Tax		**165.00**
		10,165.00

Narration:

Works Contrcat Charges

F-25A: Service Purchase at Lower Tax Rates

Service Tax Details for : **Works Contract Services**

Type of Ref	Name	Type of Service	Category/Service	Service Amount	Amount (Incl. of Tax)
New Ref	**Purc/24-1**	**Input Credit**	**Works Contract Service**	**10,000.00**	**10,165.00**
	Service Tax	@	*4 % (On Assessable Value 4,000.00)*	**160.00**	
	Ed Cess	@	*2 % (On Tax Value 160.00)*	**3.00**	
	Sec Ed Cess	@	*1 % (On Tax Value 160.00)*	**2.00**	
				165.00	
		Total		**10,000.00**	**10,165.00**

F-25B: Service Tax details for Purchase at Lower Tax Rates

Input Service Tax: After entry of Tax details (F-25B), you get back to main voucher entry screen (F-25A). Select the Input Service Tax Account. The Amount of Tax is carried from the Tax details screen and shown in the Amount Column against the Tax Ledger Account (F-25A)

Enter the Voucher Narration etc. (F-25A) and save the Voucher.

FAQ: Frequently Asked Questions

FAQ-1: How to enter Receipt Voucher for Final Adjustment of Bill, against which some advance were received earlier, without deducting Service Tax.

Ans: As Advance was received earlier without deducting Service Tax, the Tax on whole amount of Bill would be deducted at the time of Final Payment, after adjusting the Advances received earlier.

The Receipt Voucher entry (F-21A), select the Party (Payer's Ledger Account to get *Bill Allocation* screen (F-21B). At *Bill Allocation* screen (F-21B), Select *Agst Ref* (because you like to Adjust the References of Advance & Sales Bill). The pending references of Advance (Cr balance) & and Sale Bill (Debit Balance) are listed. Select them one by one (F-21B)

Now the selected references (F-21B) are adjusted fully. The balance payable (difference between the Sale Bill Amount with Tax and the Advance Rcceived) is then carried to Party Account (F-21B) and shown in the main screen at *Amount* Column (F-21A)

At Main Voucher entry screen (F-21A), at *Name on Receipt* enter the Payees Name (this will be printed in the Money Receipt (Formal Receipt).

Part 4
Value Added Tax (VAT)

Registered Dealers have to prepare Invoice as per VAT Rules, showing details of VAT charged, maintain complete records of transactions, Deposit VAT and file Statutory Returns.

In this Part, we discuss about additional features related to VAT and Statutory Compliance of VAT related functions.

- **Value Added Tax** explains the basic concepts of VAT and related terminologies.
- **VAT Set Up** explains initial set for VAT activation & registration, VAT Classifications, VAT Commodity & VAT related Ledger Accounts creation.
- **VAT Invoice** explains entry of VAT Purchase & Sales Invoice details
- **VAT Report** explains of generation of various VAT Related transaction Registers, Summaries & Analytical Reports.
- **VAT Deposit** describes the process of deposit of VAT to the Government.
- **Special Features** discusses about various special instances like Multi VAT Class Invoice, VAT on MRP etc.
- **VAT Composition** explains the special features for set up for activation of VAT Composition, Invoice related Ledger Accounts, Voucher for VAT Composition Tax Liability, Payment of VAT Composition and submission of VAT Return.

Organizations not registered under VAT rules, or VAT registered organisations who maintain and file Statutory Returns under VAT Rules manually, may skip this Part.

Value Added Tax

04-01

01 Value Added Tax

VAT (Value Added Tax) is a *Consumption Tax*. As value addition takes place, tax on the value added is paid at that stage. For example, a raw material is converted to semi-finished goods by one organization and another organization converts the semi-finished goods to finished products. In first stage, tax on value addition made over the raw materials to make semi-finished goods are paid by the first organization. Likewise the second organisation pays tax on the value addition made by them from semi-finished products to finished goods. The entire tax is ultimately borne by the consumer. The following example clarifies the concept.

Organization A bought raw materials of Rs 1000 and paid VAT @ 4% and sold the semi-finished products at Rs 2000 to Organization B on which VAT was charged @ 4%.

Organization B sold the finished products at Rs 4000 to the end customer on which VAT was charged @ 12.5%.

The following table depicts the transactions and VAT payable at each stage:

As can be seen in the above table, Organization A while buying raw materials within the state paid Rs 40 as VAT which was set-off as *Input VAT* against their *Output VAT* liability of Rs 80 on account of sales to Organization B and net VAT (Output – Input) of Rs 40 was paid by them. Likewise Organization B paid a net VAT of Rs 420 upon setting of the Input VAT paid by them whereas the Customer borne the entire VAT of Rs 500 (@12.5% on 4000).

Seller	Buyer	Sale Price	Rate of VAT	Invoice Value	VAT Payable	Input VAT	Nett VAT Payable
Vendor	A	1000	4%	1040	40		40
A B	2000	4%	2080	80	40	40	
B Customer	4000	12.5%	4500	500	80	420	

02 Input & Output VAT

VAT = Tax Collected on Sale (Output Tax) – Tax Paid on Purchase (Input Tax)

So, the VAT depends on 2 distinct activities (Sale & Purchase). It is immaterial when the sold goods was purchased (or when the Purchased Goods was sold (or still remaining unsold). It considers only the periodical Output Tax Collected & Input Tax paid.

April

Item	Purchase Qty	Purchase Value	Input VAT @4%	Sale Qty	Sales Value	Output VAT @4%
Color TV	100	200000	8000	-	-	-
Washing Mch	50	150000	6000	20	80000	3200
Micro Wave	100	100000	4000	40	60000	2400
Total			**18000**			**5600**

April: VAT carried forward = 18000 (Input VAT) -5600 (Output VAT) = 12400

May

Item	Purchase Qty	Purchase Value	Input VAT @4%	Sale Qty	Sales Value	Output VAT @4%
Color TV	-			70	210000	8400
Washing Mch	10	30000	1200	30	80000	3200
Micro Wave	-		-	40	60000	2400
Total			**1200**			**14000**
Grand Total			**19200**			**19600**

May: VAT Payable = 14000 (Output VAT) – [(1200 (Input VAT)+12400 (VAT Carried forward)] = 14000- 13600= 400

You find that dealer has not sold any Colour TV in April. So, no VAT is payable in April for Colur TV. So, it sold Micro Wave in May but did not purchase in May. So, in May, it paid VAT on Micro Wave sold in May.

03 Types of Dealers

In a VAT-enacted state, a trader having turnover less than the threshold limit is exempted from registration under the state VAT Act and can maintain normal accounts. However, such traders can optionally get themselves registered under the state VAT Act to issue Tax Invoice and claim set-off for Input VAT paid by them.

Organizations having turnover exceeding the threshold limit (fixed by each state) are required to get registered under the state VAT Act. They may opt for composite scheme and pay composite tax (normally at a lower rate). But composite dealers are not allowed to issue Tax Invoice nor can claim benefit of Input Tax paid by them (only VAT registered dealers can issue Tax Invoice and set off Input Tax paid by them on purchases).

Thus the Dealers can be classified as under:

- **Unregistered Dealers**: Dealers having turnover below threshold limit are exempted from the purview of VAT Act.
- **Dealers registered under VAT Act**: Dealers registered under VAT Act may have either of the following status:
    - o ***Composition Dealers***: Dealers having turnover less than the limit determined for composition and have opted for composition scheme.
    - o ***Registered Dealers***: Dealers registered under state VAT Act are eligible to issue Tax Invoice and claim set-off for Input tax paid by them.

For unregistered dealers, no special step is required for VAT compliance; they only need to maintain proper accounts, as usual.

Composite Dealers need not to maintain VAT accounts but are required to maintain proper accounts to derive at the turnover figure for computation of composite tax and also to establish that their turnover have not exceeded the upper ceiling limit fixed for composition.

Registered Dealers are required to maintain proper accounts and records as required under state VAT Act.

FAQ: Frequently Asked Question

FAQ-1: What is output VAT

Ans: Output VAT is the VAT charged by Seller in the Sales Bill

FAQ-2: What is Input VAT

Ans: Input VAT is the VAT paid by Customer in the Purchase Bill

FAQ3: How the VAT is deposited by VAT dealer to Government Account

Ans: A Registered VAT dealer pays VAT to the Government (for the respective Accounting Period), an amount equal to total Output VAT charged in Sales Bill, LESS, total amount of Input VAT paid on Prchase Bill, if any

FAQ-4: What are the types of Dealer under VAT Rules

Ans: Dealership status under VAT Rules are as under:

- **Unregistered Dealers**: Dealers having turnover below threshold limit are exempted from the purview of VAT Act.
- **Dealers registered under VAT Act**: Dealers registered under VAT Act may have either of the following status:
    - o ***Composition Dealers***: Dealers having turnover less than the limit determined for composition and have opted for composition scheme.
    - o ***Registered Dealers***: Dealers registered under state VAT Act are eligible to issue Tax Invoice and claim set-off for Input tax paid by them.

VAT Set Up

01 Location Set Up

At *Company Creation / Alteration* screen (§02/01-01/S1), set as follows:

- **Country:** At *Statutory Compliance for*, select *India*.
- **State**: At *State,* select the respective State under which the VAT is applicable for the organisation.

02 VAT Activation

Having set the Location (§01), first you have to activate VAT Features for the Company. Click *F11:Features* and select *Statutory & Taxation* to get *Statutory & Taxation features* screen (F-1A).

At *Statutory & Taxation features* screen (F-1A). set as follows:

- **Activation of VAT**: At *Enable Value Added Tax (VAT)*:
    - o Set *Yes* to activate VAT (when VAT is applicable for the Company). Consequently, the features & options related to VAT will be available.
    - o Set *No* (default), when VAT is not applicable for the Company). The features & options related to VAT will not be available.
- **VAT Details**: Having Set *Yes* at *Enable Value Added Tax,* at *Set Alter / VAT*, set:
    - o *Yes* to get VAT details screen (F-1B), to set Up VAT details for the Company (and subsequently change the Details as necessary). These details are printed in VAT Challan, Returns etc
    - o *No*. The VAT details for the Company can not be entered

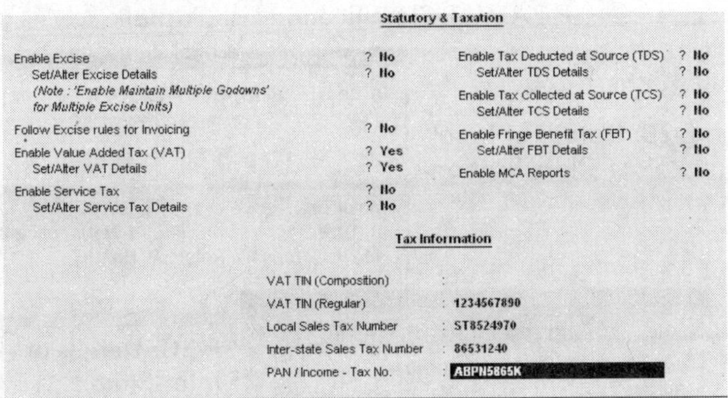

F-1A: Activation of VAT at Company Features – Statutory

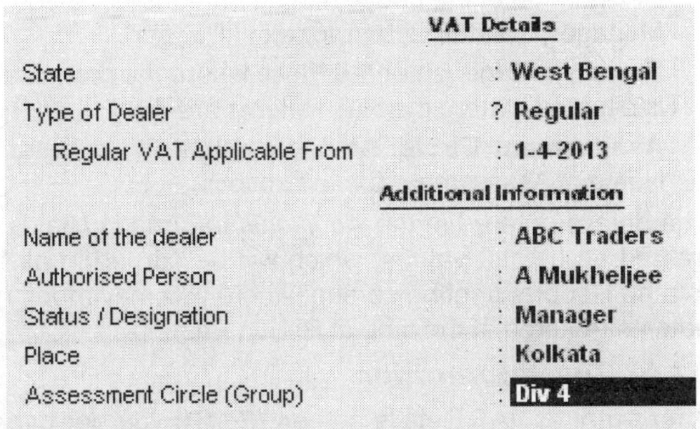

FeaturesF-1B: VAT Details Entry

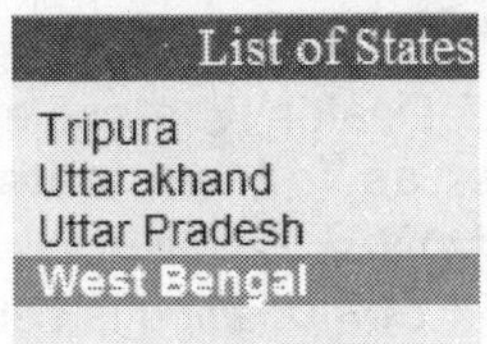

F-1C: List of States

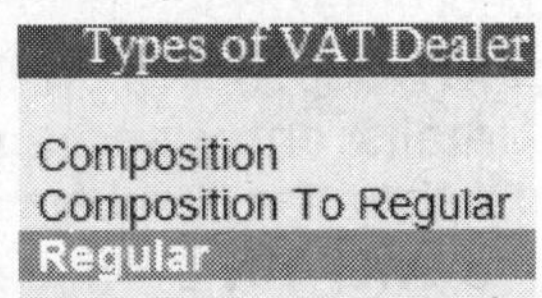

F-1D: VAT Dealer Type List

At VAT Details Entry screen (F-1B), enter as follows:

a. VAT Details

- **State**: At *State*, select the State (in which the organization is registered as VAT Dealer) from the list of States (F-1C). The VAT Returns will be generated as per applicable rules of the selected STATE.
- **Dealer Type:** At *Type of Dealer,* select the applicable option from the list (F-1D):
    - o *Regular:* When the dealer is registered as Regular VAT dealer
    - o *Composition*: When the dealer is registered as Composition VAT dealer
    - o *Composition to Regular*. When a Composition dealer is converted to Regular
- **VAT Applicability:** At *VAT Applicable from*, enter the Date of applicability of VAT for the dealer (the *Books Beginning From* date is carried as default, which you may change as necessary)

In case of an existing Company, on activation of VAT as described above, the VAT *Applicable Date* will be treated as cut-off date for VAT compliance, and for prior period, the Company will be treated as Non-VAT Company.

b. Additional Information

Now enter the following Information:

- **Dealer Name:** At *Name of Dealer*, enter the Name of the Business Organisation as per VAT Registration Certificate
- **Authorised Person**: At *Authorised Person*, enter Name of the Authorised Person who is responsible for compliance of VAT on behalf of the Organisation
- **Status / Designation**: At *Status / Designation,* enter the Designation of the above named Authorised Person (e.g Manager) / Status (e.g Proprietor / Partner)
- **Place**: At *Place*, enter the Place where the organisation is situated (where the VAT Returns are filed).
- **Assessment Circle:** At *Assessment Circle,* enter the Name of Assessment Circle Group

The details entered in the *Additional Information* fields are treated as default values, which will be carried in all VAT related Reports printing screen, where you may modify the data as required at the time of Report Printing.

02.01 Tax Information

After entry at VAT Details screen (F-1B), you get back to the *Statutory & Taxation* screen (F-1A) to enter further details at *Tax Information* section at the bottom part (F-1A), in respect of Tax Registration Numbers, as follows:

- **VAT:** Depending on the VAT Dealer type set at VAT details entry screen, enter as follows, enter the Registration Numbers related to VAT, as follows:
    - o **VAT TIN Composition:** If *Composition* is selected at VAT Dealer Type (F-1B), at *VAT TIN (Composition)*, enter the VAT TIN (Composition) registration number (otherwise this field is skipped)
    - o **VAT TIN Regular:** If *Regular* is selected at VAT Dealer Type, at *VAT TIN (Regular)*, enter the 10 digit VAT TIN (Regular) registration number (otherwise this field is skipped)
- **Sales Tax**: Enter the Registration Numbers related to Sales Tax, as follows:
    - o **Local Sales Tax Number**: At *Local Sales Tax Number*, enter the State Sales Tax Registration Number, if any (or leave blank)
    - o **Central Sales Tax Number**: At *Inter State Sales Tax Number*, enter the Central Sales Tax Registration Number, if any (or leave blank)
- **Income Tax**: At PAN/Income Tax, enter the Income Tax PAN / Registration Number, if any (or leave blank)

03 VAT Classification

VAT Class is a segregation of various Taxable Items into specified classes by the respective State VAT authorities, as per applicable State VAT Rules. For classifying the sales and purchase transactions under appropriate VAT Class and various filing Statutory Reports under VAST Rules, Tally provides system-created VAT classification for respective State.

At the time of creation of Company, on selection of State at VAT Details screen (F-1B), the respective VAT Classifications are automatically loaded. To see the corresponding system created VAT Classification, at Gateway, select *Display>Statutory Info > VAT Classifications* to get the list of VAT Classifications (F-2A). These are system generated and you cannot make changes in them. You have to select the respective Classification during Voucher entry.

03.01 VAT Classification Details

At *VAT Classification List* (F-2A), select a Classification Item to get the details of the selected Classification (F-2A, F-2B, F-2C), showing the related detailed Info. Such info are internally stored and used by Tally and cannot be changed by user.

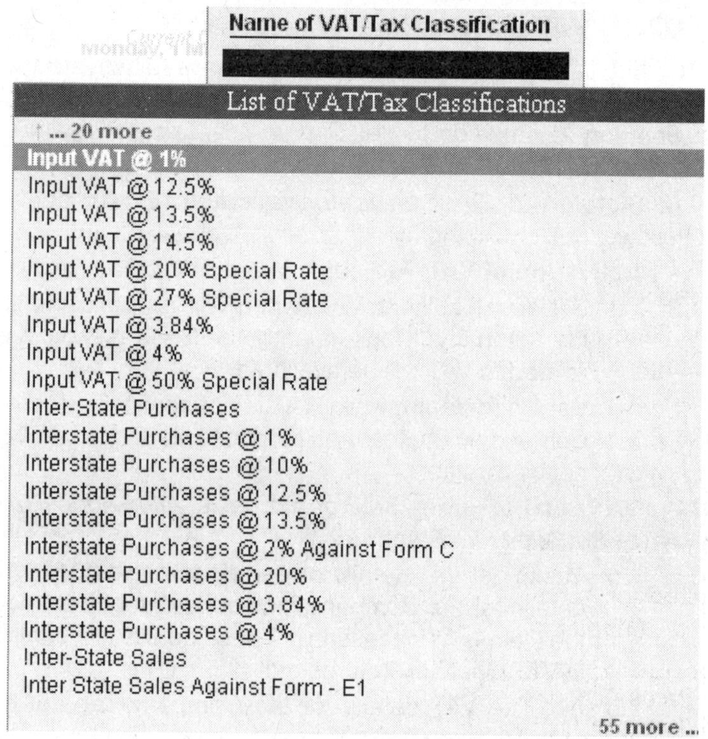

F-2A: VAT Classification List (Partial)

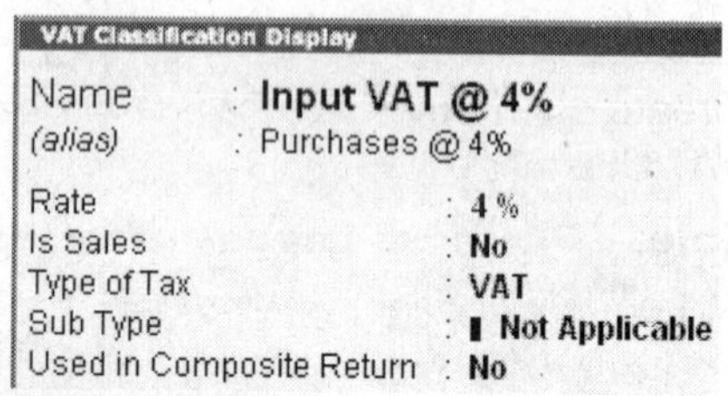

F-2B: Details of Input VAT Classification

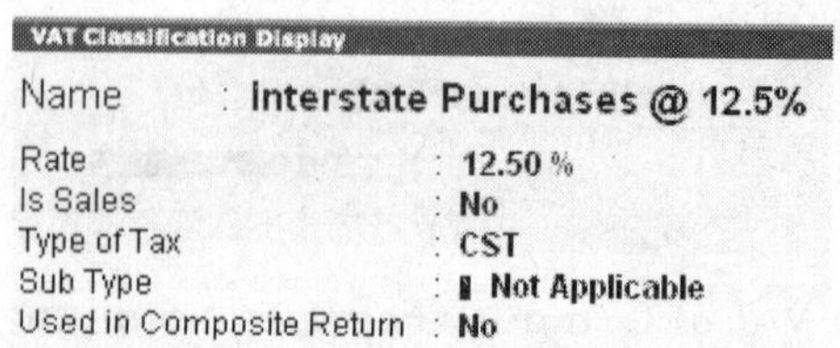

F-2C: Details of Inter-State Purchase VAT Classification

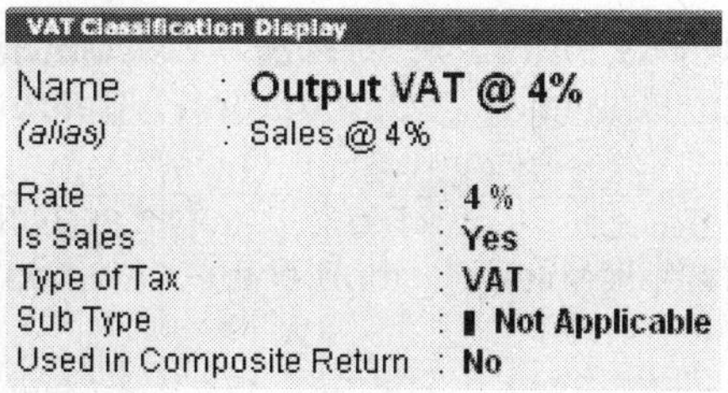

F-2D: Details of Output VAT Classification

In VAT Classification related to VAT Accounts, the related default Sale / Purchase Account is shown in the field *Alias* (F-2B & F-2D).

04 VAT related Ledger Accounts

Having set up the VAT features as explained (§02), you have to create Ledger Accounts related to VAT as follows, in respect of each VAT Classification, as applicable:

- Sales Ledgers
- Purchase Ledgers
- Output VAT Ledgers (VAT Ledger related to Sales)
- Input VAT Ledgers (VAT Ledger related to Purchases)
- Any Other ledgers related with VAT Computation

Ledger creation has been explained earlier (§03.02/01-03/S1). Here we describe the respective applicable parameters in respect of each type of such Ledger Accounts related to VAT. The following Table summarises the values to be entered in respective type of Ledger Accounts, to be entered in respective Ledger creation screen

At Gateway, select *Accounts Info>Ledger>Create* to get Ledger Creation screen. The entry process of each type of Ledger Account is described next.

04.01 Sales / Purchase Ledger Accounts

Set the values at respective fields for Sales Ledger Accounts (F-3A & F-3B) and for Purchase Ledger Accounts (F-4A & F-4B), as described in the following Table

Ledger Account (Name)	Group (Under)	Inventory Values (Inventory Values are affected)	Type of Ledger (Type of Ledger)	VAT Return (Used in VAT Return)	VAT Class
Sales Account (F-3A)	Sales	Yes	Not Applicable	Yes	Select the Applicable VAT Class for Sales
Purchase Account (F-4A)	Purchase	Yes	Not Applicable	Yes	Select the Applicable VAT Class for Purchases

Create such separate Sales / Purchase Account for each VAT Class

Sales / Purchase Ledger Accounts creation

At *Ledger Creation / Alteration* screen (F-3A, F-4A):

- **Ledger Name**: At *Name*, enter the Ledger Name (add the Rate % in the ledger name for clear identification, like Sales 4%, Sales 12%, Purchase 4%, Purchase 12% etc)
- **Parent Group**: At Under, select the parent Group (e.g Sales, Purchase etc)
- **Type of Ledger**: Select *Not Applicable*
- **VAT Class**: At *Used in VAT Returns*, set *Yes* to get VAT Class selection list (F-3B, F-4B). Select the respective Sales Account from the VAT Class. The selected VAT Class is not displayed in Ledger Entry / Alter / Display screen, but remain internally linked and you get back to the Ldger Creation screen (F-3A, F-4A)

F-3A: Sales Ledger creation

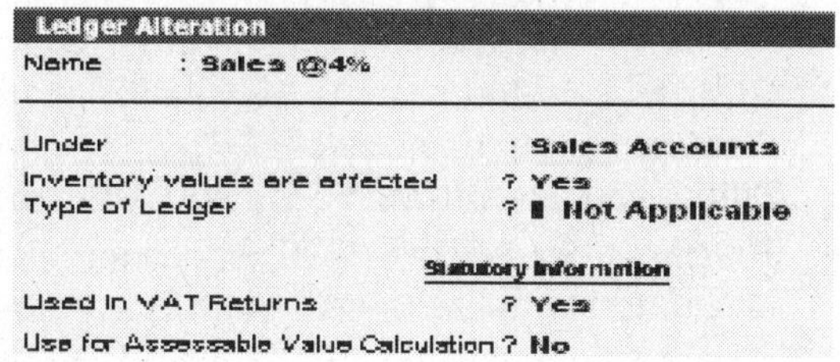

- **Assessable Value Calculation**: At *Use for Assessable Value Calculation*, set *No* (F-3A, F-4A).

F-3B:Sales VAT Class List

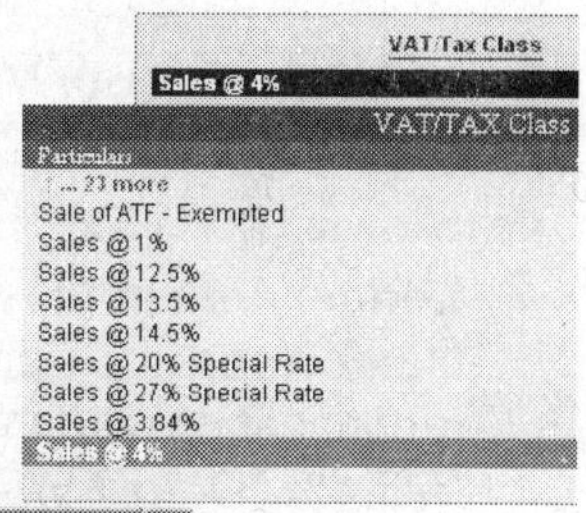

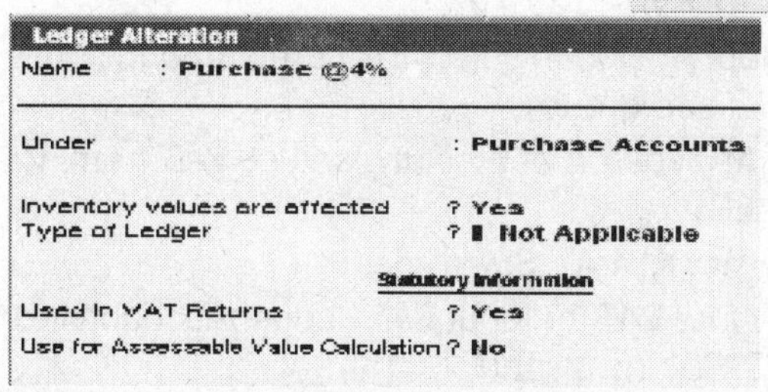

F-4A: Purchase Ledger creation

04.02 Input VAT / Output VAT Ledger Accounts

Set the values at respective fields for Output VAT Ledger Accounts (F-5A & F-5B) and for Purchase Ledger Accounts (F-6A, F-6B), as described in the following Table

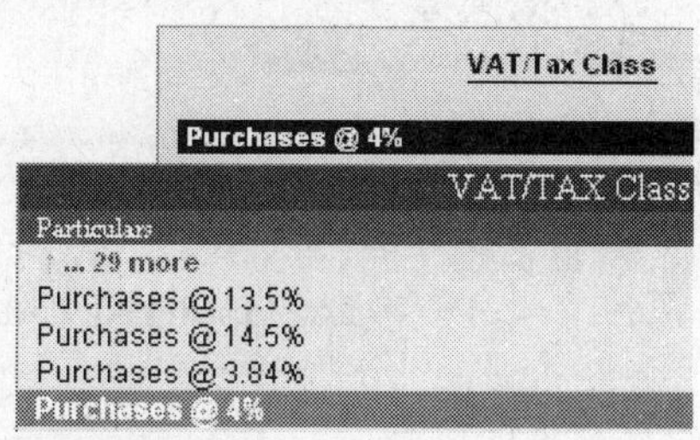

F-4B: Purchase VAT Class List

Ledger Account (Name)	Group (Under)	Type of Duty/Tax	VAT Sub Type	VAT / Tax Class	% of Calculation	Method of Calculation	Rounding Method
Input VAT (F-5A)	Duties & Taxes	VAT	Input VAT	Select Applicable Input VAT Class from the List	The applicable Rate will be carried as per VAT Class selected	On VAT Rate (carried)	Select the Rounding Method. In case of *Not Applicable*, computed VAT will be rounded to nearest paise
Output VAT (F-6A)	Duties & Taxes	VAT	Output VAT	Select Applicable Input VAT Class from the List	The applicable Rate will be carried as per VAT Class selected	On VAT Rate (carried)	

Input VAT / Output VAT Ledger Accounts creation

At *Ledger Creation / Alteration* screen (F-5A, F-6A), enter as follows:

- **Ledger Name**: At *Name*, enter the VAT Account Ledger Name (add the Rate % in the ledger name for clear identification, like Input VAT 4%, Input VAT 12%, Output VAT 4%, Output VAT 12%, etc)
- **Parent Group**: At *Under*, select the parent Group (Duties & Taxes or its sub group)
- **VAT Type:** At *Type of VAT / Duty,* select *VAT* from *VAT Type* list (F-6B)
- **VAT Sub Type:** At *VAT Sub Type*,
  - o Select *Input VAT* for Input VAT Ledger Accounts from the *VAT Sub type* list (F-6C)
  - o Select *Output VAT* for Output VAT Ledger Accounts, from the *VAT Sub type* list (F-6C)
- **VAT Class:** At *VAT / Class,* select the respective VAT Class from *VAT Class* list (F-3B, F-4B). The selected VAT Class is displayed alongside (F-5A & F-6A).
- **Tax Rate %**: At *Percentage of Calculation*, enter the VAT Rate (%) applicable for the respective VAT Ledger Account.

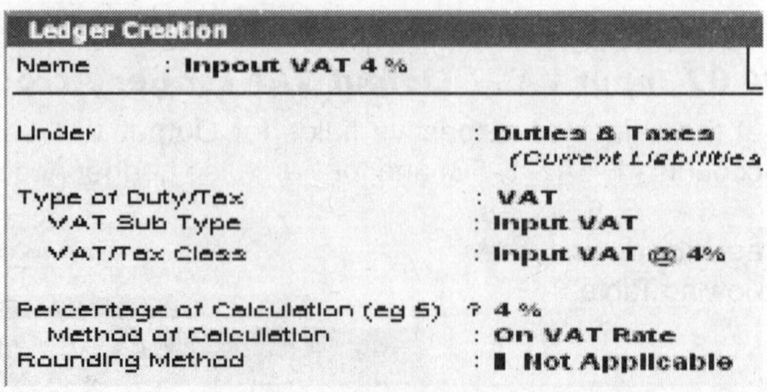

F-5A: Input VAT Ledger Creation

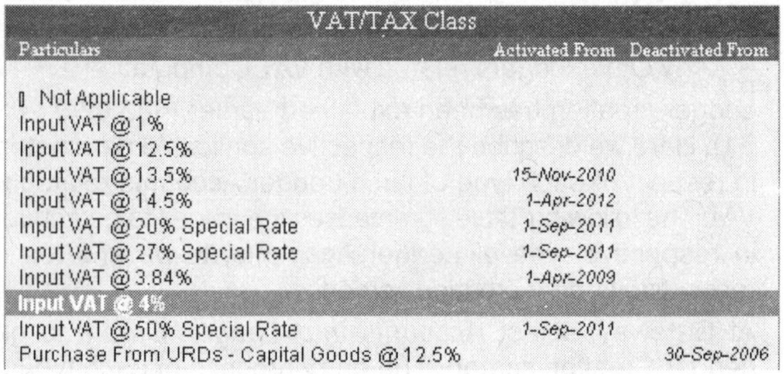

F-5B: Voucher Class selection for Input VAT Ledger Creation

- **Method of Calculation**: Select *On VAT Rate* (it is auto displayed) from list.
- **Rounding Method:** Select the Rounding Method from *Rounding Methods* list (F-6D)

F-5A shows the *VAT Ledger* creation for an *Input VAT* Account and F-6A shows the *VAT Ledger* creation for an *Output VAT* Account.

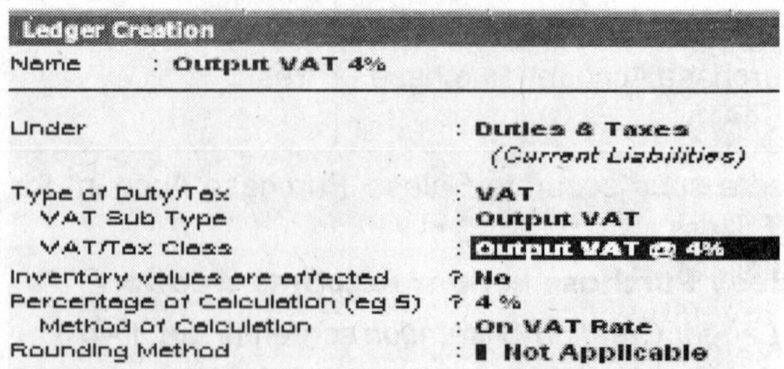

F-6A: Output VAT Ledger Creation

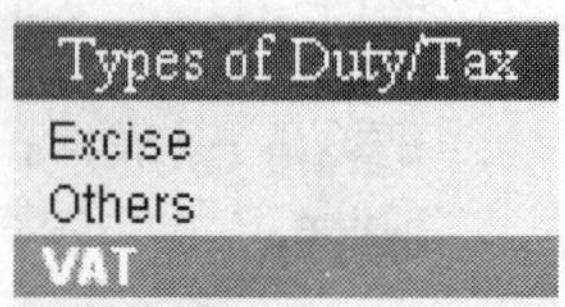

F-6B: VAT Type List

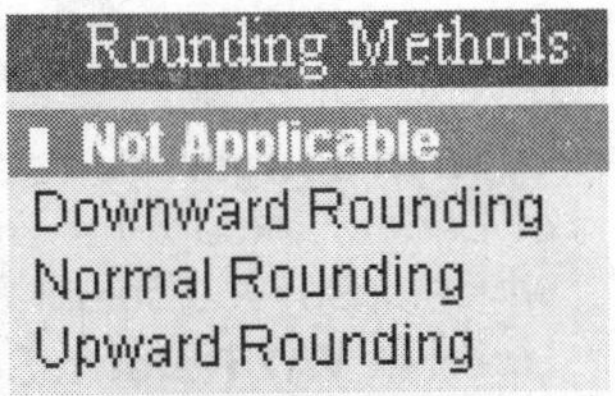

F-6C: VAT Sub Type List F-6D: Rounding Method List

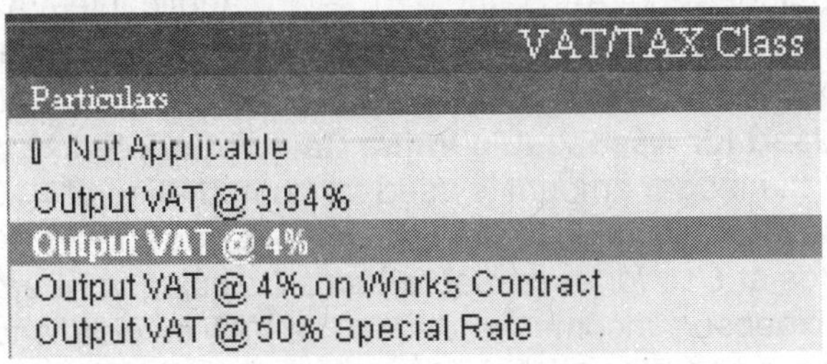

F-6E: VAT Tax / Class List

04.03 VAT Dealer Ledger Accounts

We have discussed Customer / Supplier Ledger Account creation (§05/03-01). Here we describe creation of Ledger Accounts of Parties (Customer: F-7A & Supplier: F-8A) registered under VAT.

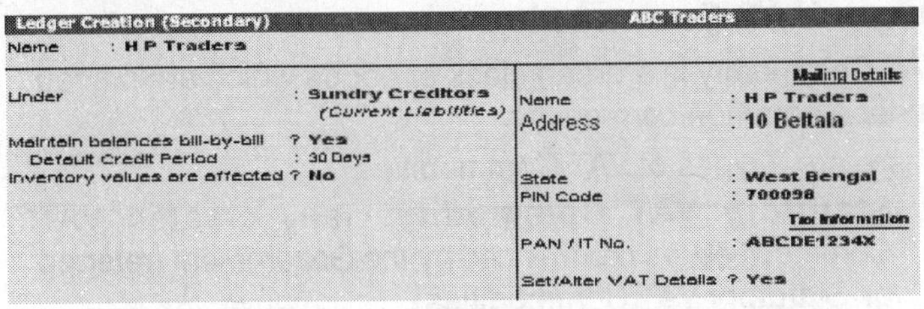

F-7A: Creation of VAT Dealer (Supplier) Ledger

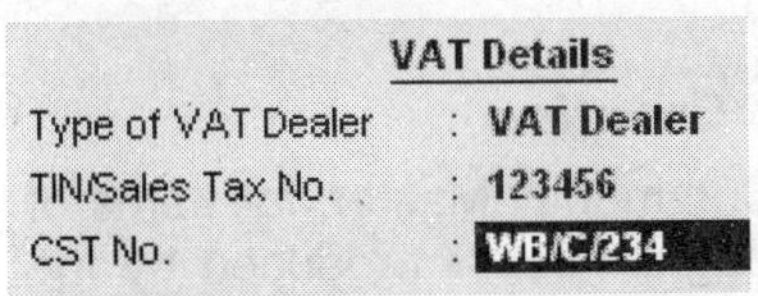

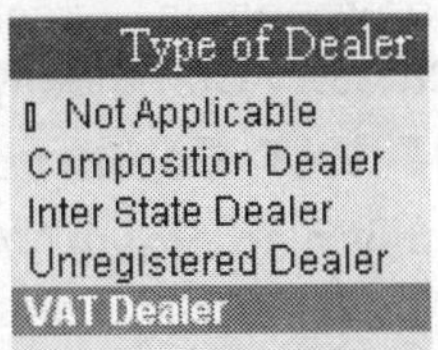

F-7B: VAT details of Supplier F-7C: Dealer Type List

At *Ledger Creation / Alteration* screen (F-7A / F-8A):

- **Ledger Name**: At *Name*, enter the Party Account Ledger Name (Supplier: F-7A, Customer F-8A)
- **Parent Group**: At *Under*, select the Parent Group (*Sundry Debtors* for Customer: F-8A, *Sundry Creditors* for Supplier: F-7A)
- **Inventory Value Link:** At *Inventory Values are Affected*, set *No*
- **Mailing Details & Tax Information**: Enter the Party Mailing Details & PAN as explained earlier (§05/03-01)
- **VAT Class**: At *Set Alter VAT Class*, set *Yes* to get *VAT details screen* (F-7B, F-8B):
    - o **VAT Details**: At *VAT details* screen (F-7B, F-8B):
    - o **VAT Dealer Type**: At *Type of VAT Dealer*, select from the Dealer Type list (F-7C), as follows:
        - *VAT Dealer* for Regular VAT Registered Parties within the same State
        - *Unregistered Dealer* for Parties not Registered under VAT
        - *Composition Dealer* for VAT Composition Registered Parties within the same State
        - *Inter State Dealer* for Parties outside the State, Registered under CST
    - o **TIN / Sales Tax No:** At *TIN / Sales Tax No*, enter the VAT TIN Registration Number (for VAT Dealer / VAT Composition Dealer)
    - o **CST Number**: At CST No, enter CST Registration Number (for Inter Sate Dealer)

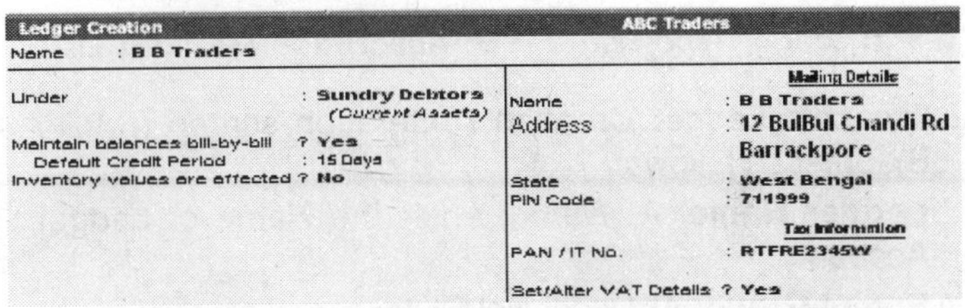

F-8A: Creation of VAT Dealer (Customer) Ledger

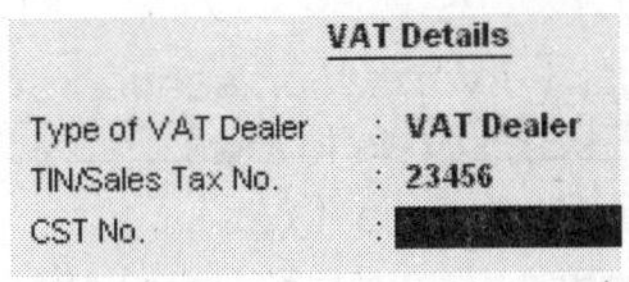

F-8B: VAT details of Customer F-8C: Dealer Type list

04.04 Other Ledger Accounts

Apart from Sales / Purchase & VAT Input / VAT Output Ledgers, some other charges are used for addition / deduction of charges (normally of the type Direct / Indirect Income / Expenses) in the Invoice. You have to specify how such charges are treated in computation of assessable value of Item.

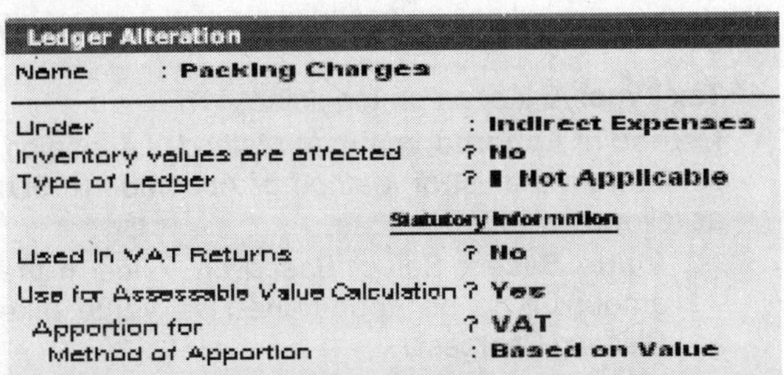

F-9A: Other Ledger Accounts creation (Used for Assessable Value)

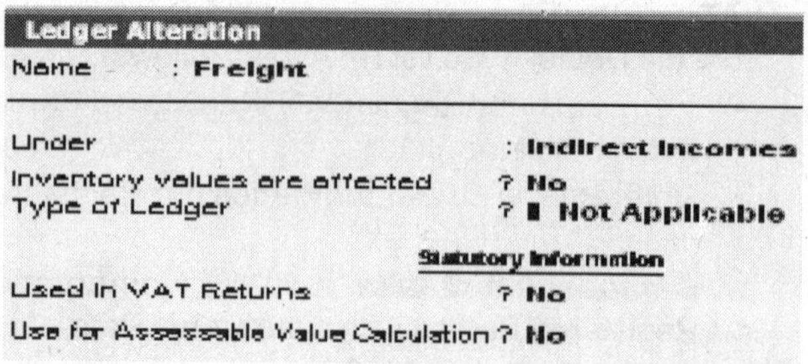

F-9B: Other Ledger Accounts creation (NOT Used for Assessable Value)

F-9C: Ledger Type List F-9D: Absorbtion Methods List

At Accounts Ledger Creation / Alteration screen (F-9A / F-9B), enter as follows:

- **Ledger Name**: At *Name*, enter the Name of Ledger Account
- **Parent Group: At** *Under*, select the parent account group (should be under Direct / Indirect Income / Expenses)
- **Ledger Type**: At *Type of Ledger*, select *Not Applicable* from the Ledger Type list (F-9C)

Statutory Information: At *Statutory Information* section of Ledger Creaion screen (F-9A & F-9B), set as follows

- **VAT Returns**: At *Used in VAT Returns*, set *No*
- **Assessable Value Calculation**: At *Used for Assessable Value Calculation*:
  - o Set *Yes* if the amount is to be proportioned for computation of Assessable Value of VAT (normally when some materials cost is added like Packing Materials etc, which is subject to VAT),
  - o Set *No* (for various expenses like Freight, Handling Charges, Clearing Charges etc).
- **Assessable Value Apportionment**: When you set Yes at *Used for Assessable Value Calculation*, you further set the following options fro apportionment of Assessable Value:
  - **Tax Type**: At *Apportion for*, select *VAT*
  - **Method of Apportionment**: At *Method of Apportion*, select from the list of *Method of Apportion* (F-9D) as follows:
    - ***Value Based***: Select *Based on Value*, if the amount is to be apportioned on Value (like Clearing Charges)
    - ***Quantity Based***: Select *Based on Quantity*, if the amount is to be apportioned on Quantity (like Freight, which is charged on Quantity)

Note:

- **Type of Ledger**: You select *Not Applicable* at Type of Ledger except for Discount Ledger Account, in which case, you select *Discount* at Type of Ledger
- **Used in VAT Return**: Set Yes for *Sales / Purchase Ledgers* & *VAT Input / Output Ledgers* as these are included in VAT Return, to select applicable VAT Class from the list of VAT Class. In all other ledger accounts, set *No*
- **Used for Assessable Value Calculation**: Set *Yes*, if the ledger amount is used for computation of VAT assessable value (otherwise set No). You should set Yes at *Use for Assessable Value Calculation* where Expense / Incomes added in the VAT Invoice is to be apportioned to Items for computation of Assessable Value. Set *No* at *Sales / Purchase Ledger* & *VAT Input / Output Ledger*,

You should normally NOT set YES to both the options (*Used in VAT Return & Use for Assessable Value Calculation)* in same Ledger Accounts. These options are normally mutually exclusive to each other.

05 VAT Commodity

VAT Commodity is a broad class of goods which are placed under a common commodity.

There are 2 types of VAT Commodities:

- **Statutory VAT Commodity**: Tally created VAT Commodities, as pronounced by the Government (referred as Statutory VAT Commodities).
- **General VAT Commodity**: User created VAT Commodities, which must be mapped to one of the Statutory Commodity

05.01 VAT Commodity Creation

You may also create VAT Commodity Master, for Items of each Commodity Class, bought / sold / produced by the organization. This helps you to conveniently manage Stock Items having similar VAT details. You may copy VAT Details / Accounting Allocation from a Stock Item to all the Stock Items belonging to a VAT Commodity (§06)

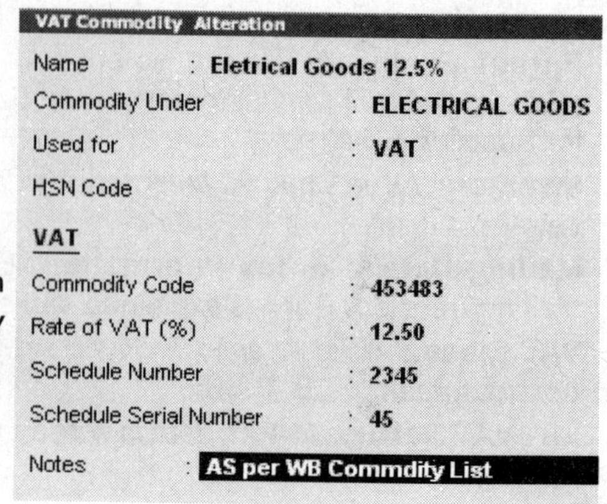

F-10A: Creation of Commodity

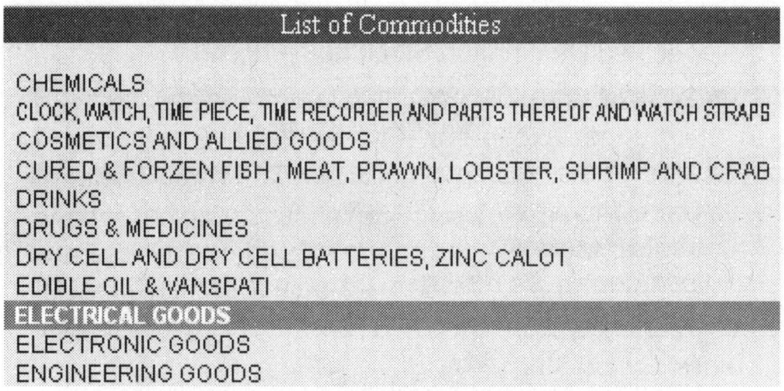

F-10B: Selection of Statutory VAT Commodity

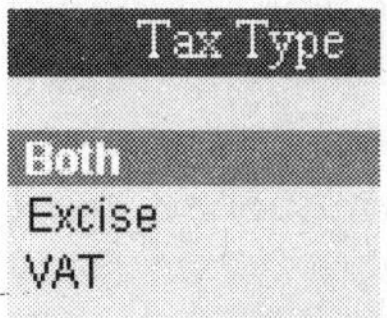

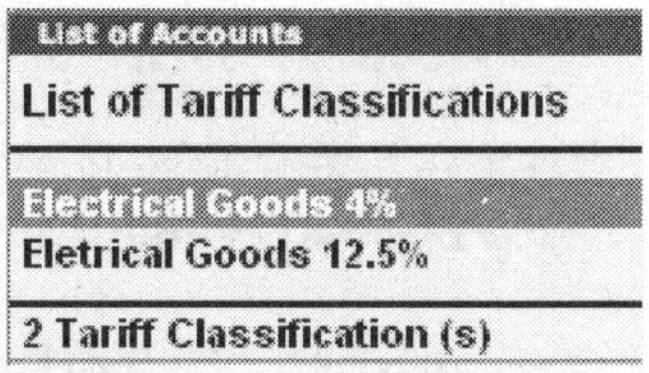

F-10C: List of Tax Type F-10D: Tariff Classification List

At Gateway, select *Inventory Info>VAT Commodity>Create* to get *VAT Commodity entry* screen (F-10A). At *VAT Commodity entry* screen (F-10A), enter as follows:

- **Commodity Name:** At *Name,* enter the Name of VAT Commodity
- **Statutory Commodity:** At *Commodity Under*, select the parent Statutory VAT Commodity from the list of Statutory VAT Commodities (F-10B). Thus a VAT Commodity must belong to one of the Statutory Commodity. Thus you may create multiple VAT Commodities belonging to a Statutory VAT Commodity. However, you cannot create a subordinate VAT Commodity under a created VAT Commodity.
- **Tax Type:** At *Used for*, select from the list (F-10C) as follows:
  - o **VAT:** Select *VAT* if the Commodity is chargeable under VAT rules only. This is applicable for organization registered under VAT only.
  - o **Excise**: Select *Excise* if the Commodity is chargeable under Excise rules only. This is applicable for organization registered under Central Excise only.
  - o **Both**: Select *Both* if the Commodity is chargeable both under VAT as well as Excise rules. This is applicable for organization registered under VAT as well as under Central Excise.
- **VAT details**: At *VAT Commodity entry* screen (F-10A), under the section *VAT*, enter the following details:
  - o **Commodity Code**: At *Commodity Code*, enter the Commodity Code, if any (you may leave blank)
  - o **VAT %**: At *Rate of VAT %*, enter the Rate of VAT (in %)
  - o **Schedule Number**: At *Schedule Number*, enter the VAT Schedule Number, if any (you may leave blank)
  - o **Schedule Serial Number:** At *Schedule Serial Number*, enter the serial number of the Commodity in VAT Schedule, if any (you may leave blank)
  - o **Notes:** At *Notes,* you may enter some Note to record the reference of the Commodity. For your own information / memorandum.

05.02 VAT Commodity List

To get the list of Commodities created (F-10D), at Gateway, select *Display>List of Accounts* and click *F:Tariff Classification* button, The list (F-10D) shows only the Name of Commodities (other details are not shown)

06 VAT Details in Stock Item Master

At the time Stock Item creation / Alteration, you have to enter VAT Details (VAT Commodity, VAT Rate etc) for the Stock Item (F-11A).

Consequently, during Invoice Entry, VAT Classification Code & the corresponding VAT Rate are automatically carried from the Stock Item Master. Otherwise, you have to enter VAT Classification Code and the VAT rate for each Item during Invoice entry (not recommended)

We already explained Stock Item Creation (§05/04-02). Here we explain about mapping of VAT Commodity with the Stock Item

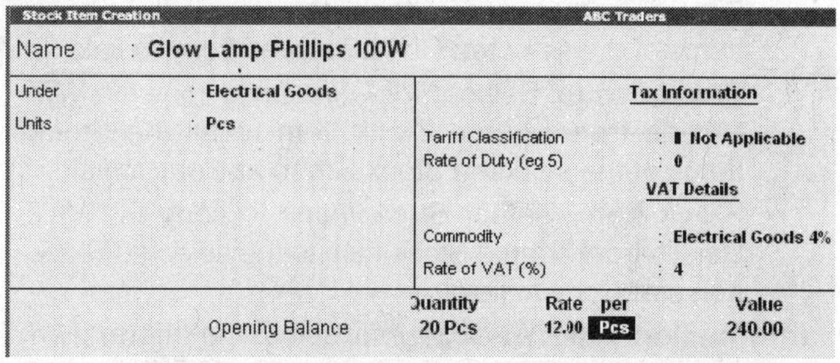

F-11A: VAT chargeable Stock Item Creation

F-11B:Selection of VAT Commodity

At the *VAT Details* section at the right part of the Stock Item entry screen (F-11A), enter as follows:

- **Commodity**: At *Commodity*, select the Commodity from the VAT Commodity list (F-11B) displayed (select Not Applicable for Stock Items in which VAT is not applicable)
- **Rate of VAT (%)**: Enter the Rate of VAT Applicable (Enter Zero for VAT exempted Item)

This way, specify the VAT details for each Stock Item created.

07 VAT Info Updation

Most of the Info of VAT info between the Stock Items are similar. So, instead of typing the VAT details for each Stock Item, you may copy the VAT details from a Stock Item of similar VAT details entered.

Select *GoT>Inventory Indo>Update VAT Info* to get *Update VAT Details* screen (F-12A)

ABC Traders

Update VAT Details

Copy From	: **Glow Lamp Phillips 100W**
Destination Type	: **Stock Groups**
Copy Info.	: **Default Accounting Allocation**
Copy To	: **Electrical Goods**

F-12A: VAT details Updation

List of Items

Glow Lamp Phillips 100W
Lamp Shades

F-12B: Stock Item List

Destination Types

Commodity
Stock Groups
Stock Items

F-12C: Destination Type List

Copy Info.

All Items
Commodity
Default Accounting Allocation

F-12D: Info Type List Destination

List of Groups

All Items
Electrical Goods

F-12E: Group List

- **Source Item**: At *Copy From*, select the Stock Item from Stock Item List (F-12B) for which the VAT Info are to be copied.
- **Destination Type**: At *Destination Type,* select the Destination Type from the list (F-12C) as follows:
  - o **Commodity**: Select *Commodity* to copy the VAT Details from source Stock Item to all the Stock Items of the selected Commodity at *Copy to* field
  - o **Stock Group**: Select *Stock Groups* to copy the VAT Details from source Stock Item to all the Stock Items of the selected Stock Group at *Copy to* field
  - o **Stock Item**: Select *Stock Items* to copy the VAT Details from source Stock Item to the selected Stock Items at *Copy to* field
- **Information Type**: At *Copy Info*, select the Information to be copied from Source Stock Item to the Destination Stock Items, from the list (F-12D) as follows:
  - o **Commodity:** Select *Commodity* to copy the Commodity Details
  - o **Default Accounting Allocation**: Select *Default Accounting Allocation* to copy the Accounting Allocation Details of the Stock Item, if default Stock Item Allocation (F-12F) has been specified in the Stock Item selected at *Copy From* field.
- **Destination**: At Copy To field, select the Commodity, Stock Group or Stock Item, as the case may be, depending on the selection made at Destination Type field.

After entering the details, you get a confirmation screen *Proceed to Set Default VAT Details* (F-12G). Type Y (Yes) to copy the specified information from Source Stock Item, to the specified Destination Stock Items (F-12F).

ABC Traders

Name of Item : **Glow Lamp Phillips 100W**

Default Accounting Allocations for Sales Invoice

Ledger Name	VAT/TAX Class	Percentage %	Rounding Method	Rounding Limit
Sales @4%	Sales @ 4%	100 %		

Default Accounting Allocations for Purchase Invoice

Ledger Name	VAT/TAX Class	Percentage %	Rounding Method	Rounding Limit
Purchase @4%	Purchases @ 4%	100 %		

F-12F: Default Allocation type Info

Proceed to Set Default Vat Details ?
Yes or No

F-12G: VAT details Copy Confirmation

FAQ: Frequently Asked Question

FAQ01: How I set up VAT for the Company

Ans: At *Statutory & Taxation features* screen (F-1A). set Yes at *Enable Value Added Tax (VAT)* to activate VAT and then set Yes at *Set Alter / VAT* to get VAT details screen (F-1B), to set Up VAT details for the Company. At VAT details screen (F-1B), select the State for which the Company is registered under VAT Rules and enter the respective particulars

FAQ-2: For a VAT Registered Company, what are the Ledger Accounts in which VAT related options are to be set Up.

Ans: You have to set up VAT related options for following Ledger Accounts

- Sales Ledgers
- Purchase Ledgers
- Output VAT Ledgers (VAT Ledger related to Sales)
- Input VAT Ledgers (VAT Ledger related to Purchases)
- Any Other ledgers related with VAT Computation

FAQ-3: For a VAT registered organization, what are the VAT rated options to be set up in Stock Item master

Ans: At the *VAT Details* section of the Stock Item entry screen (F-11A), set as follows:

- **Commodity**: Select the Commodity from the VAT Commodity list displayed (select Not Applicable for Stock Items in which VAT is not applicable: F-11B)
- **Rate of VAT (%):** Enter the Rate of VAT Applicable (Enter Zero for VAT exempted Item)

This way, specify the VAT details for each Stock Item created.

VAT Invoice Entry

01 VAT Invoice

Having set the Statutory Info & options (§02/04-02) and having created the VAT related Masters (§04/04-02), you may now proceed to create Sales & Purchase Invoice, Debit Note & Credit Note with VAT. The steps & process of entry, specifically related to VAT are explained here.

01.01 VAT Invoice Configuration set up

At Invoice Entry Configuration (*GoT>F12:Configure>Invoice / Orders Entry)*, set as follows:

- **Sales / Purchase Account**: At *Use Common Ledger for Item Allocation*:
  - o Set *Yes* to select Sales / Purchase Ledger Account at header (useful when the value of all the Items is to be posted to ONE Sales / Purchase Account)
  - o Set *No* to select Purchase Ledger Account at Item Details for each Stock Item (useful when the value of each Stock Items is to be posted to different Sales / Purchase Account
- **VAT Tax Class**: At *Allow selection of VAT Class during Entry*:
  - o Set *Yes* to allow entry of VAT Class (or change of default VAT Class carried, as set in the Stock Item), during Invoice Entry (useful for Multiple VAT Class Invoice entry: §01/04-06)
  - o Set *No*, The default VAT Class carried, as set in the Stock Item would be auto carried (§04/04-02), and the VAT Class entry field would be skipped during Invoice Entry, displaying the carried VAT Class (useful for Single VAT Class Invoice entry)
- **VAT Rate %**: At *Warn in Mismatch of VAT Rates*:
  - o Set *Yes* to get a warning message if the VAT specified in the Invoice mismatches with the Rate % specified in the selected Ledger / VAT Class, so that you may rectify mistake in entry, if any. Useful when standards VAT rate as carried from Master is NOT to be changed in Invoice.
  - o Set *No* to warning message will be triggered if there is any mismatch of VAT Rate % as entered with that specified in Ledger / VAT Class. Useful when standards VAT Rate as carried from Master may be changed in Invoice.

02 Purchase Invoice

Purchase Invoice Entry has been explained in earlier chapters (§05.02/ 03-02/S1). Here, we describe only the VAT related entry features of Purchase Invoice creation (F-1A).

Voucher Header: At Voucher Header (F-1A)., enter as follows:

- **Purchase Ledger Account**: At *Purchase Ledger*, select the Purchase Ledger Account from the list of Accounts, as per configuration options set for *Sale / Purchase* Account (§03/03-01/S1).
- **VAT / Tax Class**: The corresponding *Input VAT Class* as defined in the Purchase Ledger Account is auto carried (§04.01/04-02), as per configuration options set for *VAT Class*

Stock Item Details

Enter the Stock Item details as usual, for each Item.

- **Purchase Ledger Account**: At *Purchase Ledger*, you may select the common Purchase ledger Account for the Stock Item, as per configuration options set for *Sale / Purchase* Account (§04.01/04-02),.
- **Input VAT Class**: At *VAT / Tax Class*, You may select Input VAT Class for the Stock Item, as per configuration options set for *VAT Class* (§04.01/04-02)

Now enter Stock Item details as usual

Ledger Accounts: After entry of Stock Items, select the Ledger Accounts:

- **Input VAT Ledger:** After entry of all Stock Items, select the respective Input VAT Ledger. The VAT is computed as per VAT Rate specified and shown in the Amount Column.
- **Other Ledger Accounts**: Select Other ledger Accounts, if any, as usual and enter the Amount

VAT Details: At *Show Statutory Details* (F-1A):

- Set Yes to get the *Statutory Details* screen (F-1B) to view the Assessable Value / VAT details.
- At *Statutory Details* screen:
  - o Click *F1:Condensed* toggle button to get details of Assessable value / VAT for the Invoice (F-1B)
  - o Click *F1:Detail* toggle button to get Itemwise details of Assessable value/ VAT for each Item in the Invoice (F-1C)

Now enter Voucher Narration & save the Voucher, as usual.

Accounting Voucher Creation Ctrl + M

Purchase No. 3 — 1-Jun-2009, Monday

Supplier Invoice No. : 345 Date : 30-May-2009

Party's A/c Name : B.K.Services

Purchase Ledger : Purchase @12.5%
VAT/Tax Class : Purchases @ 12.5%

Name of Item	Quantity	Rate	per	Amount
Glow Lamp Philips 100W	20 Pieces	122.00	Pieces	2,440.00
Anchor CFL Lamp 12W	5 Pieces	142.00	Pieces	710.00
				3,150.00
Input VAT 12.5%		12.50	%	406.25
FReight Charges				100.00
Goshala Donation		0.50	%	16.00
Cess				30.00

Show Statutory Details ? Yes

Narration: 25 Pieces 3,702.25

F-1A: Purchase Invoice with VAT

ABC Electrical

Statutory Details

Particulars	VAT
Assessable Value	3,250.00
VAT Amount	406.25

F-1B: Assessable Value & VAT figures

Statutory Details

Particulars					VAT
Assessable Value					3,250.00
Glow Lamp Philips 100W					2,520.00
Item Value					*2,440.00*
FReight Charges					*80.00*
Anchor CFL Lamp 12W					730.00
Item Value					*710.00*
FReight Charges					*20.00*
VAT Amount					406.25
Input VAT 12.5%				12.50 %	406.25
Glow Lamp Philips 100W	@	12.50 %	On	2,520.00	315.00
Anchor CFL Lamp 12W	@	12.50 %	On	730.00	91.25

F-1C: Assessable Value & VAT figures (Detailed)

02.01 Purchase Invoice Printing

Purchase Invoice is normally not printed, as it is created by the supplier. However, you may need to print it for your internal record (or when the Supplier's Invoice is changed in your Purchase Voucher entry for some reason).

Printing of Purchase Voucher is explained earlier (§04/03-03). The printed Purchase Invoice (with VAT) entered is shown (Simple Format: F-2A, Normal Format: F-2B).

03 Sales Invoice

Sales Invoice Entry has been explained in earlier (§06.02/03-02/S1). Here, we describe only the VAT related entry features. Enter the Sales Invoice with VAT as follows (F-3A):

Voucher Header

- **Sales Ledger Account**: At *Sale Ledger*, select the Sales Ledger Account from the list of Accounts, as per configuration options set for *Sale / Purchase* Account (§04.01/04-02)
- **VAT / Tax Class**: The corresponding *Output VAT Class* as defined in the Sales Ledger Account is auto carried. as per configuration options set for *VAT Class* (§04.01/04-02).

SUBJECT TO KOLKATA JURISDICTION

Invoice No. 3 Dated 1-Jun-2009
Ref. No. : 345

B.K.Services

Tax Invoice

Party : ABC Electrical
27/C, Rasbihari Road
3rd Floor, Suit No.305
Kolkata-700019
Contact :03312345678,9876543210
E-Mail :nomail@kmail.com

Sl No.	Description of Goods	Quantity	Rate	per	Amount
1	Glow Lamp Philips 100W	20 Pieces	122.00	Pieces	2,440.00
2	Anchor CFL Lamp 12W	5 Pieces	142.00	Pieces	710.00
					3,150.00
	Input VAT 12.5%		12.50	%	406.25
	FReight Charges				100.00
	Goshala Donation		0.50	%	16.00
	Total	25 Pieces			₹ 3,702.25

Amount Chargeable (in words) E. & O.E
Indian Rupees Three Thousand Seven Hundred Two and Twenty Five paise Only

Company's TIN/Sales Tax No. :
Buyer's VAT TIN : 1234567890
Company's CST No. :
Buyer's CST No. : 86531240

for B.K.Services

Authorised Signatory

F-2A: Purchase Invoice (Simple Format)

Tax Invoice

B.K.Services

Invoice No. 3 — Dated 1-Jun-2009
Supplier's Ref. 345 — Other Reference(s)

Consignee
ABC Electrical
27/C, Rasbihari Road
3rd Floor, Suit No.305
Kolkata-700019
Contact :03312345678,9876543210
E-Mail :nomail@kmail.com

Sl No.	Description of Goods	Quantity	Rate	per	Amount
1	Glow Lamp Philips 100W	20 Pieces	122.00	Pieces	2,440.00
2	Anchor CFL Lamp 12W	5 Pieces	142.00	Pieces	710.00
					3,150.00
	Input VAT 12.5%		12.50	%	406.25
	FReight Charges				100.00
	Goshala Donation		0.50	%	16.00
	Cess				30.00
	Total	25 Pieces			₹ 3,702.25

Amount Chargeable (in words) E. & O.E
Indian Rupees Three Thousand Seven Hundred Two and Twenty Five paise Only

Company's TIN/Sales Tax No. :
Buyer's VAT TIN : 1234567890
Company's CST No. :
Buyer's CST No. : 86531240

for B.K.Services

Authorised Signatory

SUBJECT TO KOLKATA JURISDICTION

F-2B: Purchase Invoice (Normal Format)

Stock Item Details: Enter the Stock Item details as usual, for each Item (F-3A).

- **Item Level Ledger Accounts**: After enrty of each Stock Item you may enter the Sales Ledger Accounts details in respect of each Item, as follows:
    - o **Sales Ledger Account**: You may select the Sales ledger Account for the Stock Item, as per configuration options set for *Sale / Purchase* Account.
    - o **Output VAT Class**: You may select Output VAT Class for the Stock Item, as per configuration options set for *VAT Class*

Ledger Accounts: After entry of Stock Items, select the Voucher Ledger Accounts (F-3A):

- **Output VAT Ledger:** After entry of all Stock Items, select the respective Output VAT Ledger. The VAT is computed as per VAT Rate specified and shown in the Amount Column.
- **Other Ledger Accounts**: Select Other ledger Accounts, if any, as usual and enter the Amount

VAT Details: At *Show Statutory Details* (F-3A):

- Set Yes to get the *Statutory Details* screen (F-3B) to view the Assessable Value / VAT details.
- At *Statutory Details* screen (F-3B),
    - o Click *F1:Condensed* toggle button to get details of Assessable value / VAT for the Invoice (F-3B)
    - o Click *F1:Detail* toggle button to get Itemwise details of Assessable value/ VAT for each Item in the Invoice (F-3C)

Accounting Voucher Creation — Ctrl + M

Sales No. 2 — 30-Jun-2009, Tuesday

Ref.:

Party's A/c Name : P.K.Motors

Sales Ledger : Sales 12.5%

VAT/Tax Class : Sales - Works Contract @ 12.5%

Name of Item	Quantity	Rate	per	Amount
Glow Lamp Philips 100W	18 Pieces	160.00	Pieces	2,880.00
Anchor CFL Lamp 12W	4 Pieces	180.00	Pieces	720.00
				3,600.00
Output VAT 12.5%		12.50	%	450.00
Goshala Donation		0.50	%	18.00
Cess				50.00

Show Statutory Details ? Yes (Yes / No: No, Yes)

Narration: 22 Pieces 4,118.00

F-3A: Sales Invoice entry (with VAT)

Statutory Details

Particulars	VAT
Assessable Value	3,600.00
VAT Amount	450.00

F-3B: Statutory Details (condensed)

Statutory Details

Particulars		VAT
Assessable Value		3,600.00
Glow Lamp Philips 100W		2,880.00
Item Value		*2,880.00*
Anchor CFL Lamp 12W		720.00
Item Value		*720.00*
VAT Amount		450.00
Output VAT 12.5%	12.50 %	450.00

F-3C: Statutory Details (Detailed)

Voucher Narration as usual (F-3A) and save the Voucher

03.01 Sales Invoice Printing

Printing of Sales Invoice is explained earlier (§03/03-03). The printed format of the above Sale Invoice entered are shown (Simple Format: F-4A & Normal Format: F-4B).

SUBJECT TO KOLKATA JURISDICTION

Invoice No. 2 — Dated 30-Jun-2009

Ref. No. :

ABC Electrical
27/C, Rasbihari Road
3rd Floor, Suit No.305
Kolkata-700019
Contact :03312345678,9876543210
E-Mail :nomail@kmail.com

Tax Invoice
Sales Bill

Party : P.K.Motors

Sl No.	Description of Goods	VAT %	Quantity	Rate	per	Amount
1	Glow Lamp Philips 100W	12.50	18 Pieces	160.00	Pieces	2,880.00
2	Anchor CFL Lamp 12W	12.50	4 Pieces	180.00	Pieces	720.00
						3,600.00
	Output VAT 12.5%			12.50	%	450.00
	Goshala Donation			0.50	%	18.00
	Total		22 Pieces			₹ 4,118.00

Amount Chargeable (in words) — E. & O.E

Indian Rupees Four Thousand One Hundred Eighteen Only

VAT Amount (in words)

Indian Rupees Four Hundred Fifty Only (₹ 450.00)

VAT %	Assessable Value	VAT Amount
12.50 %		450.00

Company's VAT TIN : 1234567890
Company's CST No. : 98531240

Declaration
We declare that this invoice shows the actual price of the goods described and that all particulars are true and correct.

for ABC Electrical

Authorised Signatory

This is a Computer Generated Invoice

F-4A: Sales Invoice (Simple Format)

04 Debit / Credit Notes

Debit Credit Notes may be issued for:

- **Goods Returns:** Bought goods are returned by Buyer to the vendor for some reason, the Party Returning the goods issues a Debit Note and the Party Receiving back the goods issues a Credit Note. Such Debit / Credit Note affect stock.

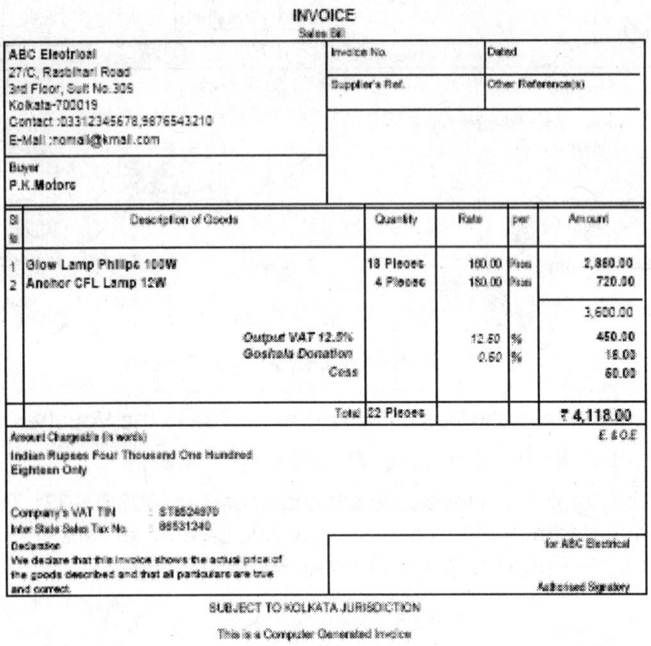

INVOICE
Sales Bill

ABC Electrical 27/C, Rashbihari Road 3rd Floor, Suit No.305 Kolkata-700019 Contact :03312345678,9876543210 E-Mail :nomail@kmail.com	Invoice No.	Dated
	Supplier's Ref.	Other Reference(s)
Buyer P.K.Motors		

Sl No	Description of Goods	Quantity	Rate	per	Amount
1	Glow Lamp Philips 100W	18 Pieces	160.00	Pcs	2,880.00
2	Anchor CFL Lamp 12W	4 Pieces	180.00	Pcs	720.00
					3,600.00
	Output VAT 12.5%		12.50	%	450.00
	Goshala Donation		0.50	%	18.00
	Cess				50.00
	Total	22 Pieces			₹ 4,118.00

Amount Chargeable (in words) E. & O.E
Indian Rupees Four Thousand One Hundred Eighteen Only

Company's VAT TIN : 878524870
Inter State Sales Tax No. : 86531240

Declaration
We declare that this invoice shows the actual price of the goods described and that all particulars are true and correct.

for ABC Electrical

Authorised Signatory

SUBJECT TO KOLKATA JURISDICTION

This is a Computer Generated Invoice

F-4B: Sales Invoice (Normal Format)

- **Other Value Adjustments:** Apart from Goods Returns, Debit / Credit Notes may b ssued for Rate Difference, supplementary charges, Rebates or any other value adjustment between the Parties. Such Debit / Credit Note do not affect stock (only Ledger Accounts get affected)

We discuss the process of Debit / Credit Note entry for both the cases

05 Debit Note for Sales Returns

Debit Note Entry has been explained in earlier chapters (§11/03-02/S1). Here, we describe Debit Note Entry (F-5A) only for the VAT related points.

Voucher Header

- **Debit Note Type**: At *Used for* field, select the option from the list as follows (F-5C):
  - o **Return of Taxable Goods**: Select it when Taxable Goods are returned to supplier. In such case, VAT on the returned goods are also adjusted.
  - o **Others**: Select it for other types of Debits (when VAT is not to be charged in the Debit Note)
- **Purchase Ledger Account**: At *Purchase Ledger*, select the Purchase Ledger Account from the list of Accounts, as per configuration options set for *Purchase* Account
- **Input VAT / Tax Class**: The corresponding *Input VAT Class* as defined in the *Purchase* Ledger Account is auto carried. as per configuration options set for *VAT Class.*

Stock Item Details

Enter the Stock Item details as usual, for each Item.

- **Purchase Ledger Account**: You may select the Purchase ledger Account for the Stock Item, as per configuration options set for *Purchase* Account.
- **Input VAT Class**: You may select Input VAT Class for the Stock Item, as per configuration options set for *VAT Class.*

Ledger Accounts

After entry of Stock Items, select the Ledger Accounts:

- **Input VAT Ledger:** After entry of all Stock Items, select the respective Input VAT Ledger. The VAT is computed as per VAT Rate specified and shown in the Amount Column.
- **Other Ledger Accounts**: Select Other Ledger Accounts, if any, as usual and enter the Amount

VAT Details: At *Show Statutory Details*:

- Set Yes to get the *Statutory Details* screen (F-5B) to view the Assessable Value / VAT details.
- At *Statutory Details* screen (F-5B),
  - o Click *F1:Condensed* toggle button to get details of Assessable Value / VAT for the Invoice
  - o Click *F1:Detail* toggle button to get Itemwise details of Assessable value/ VAT for each Item in the Invoice (F-5B)

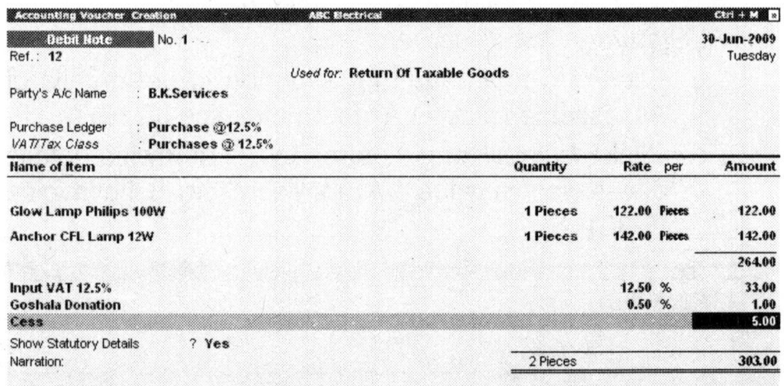

F-5A: Debit Note Entry

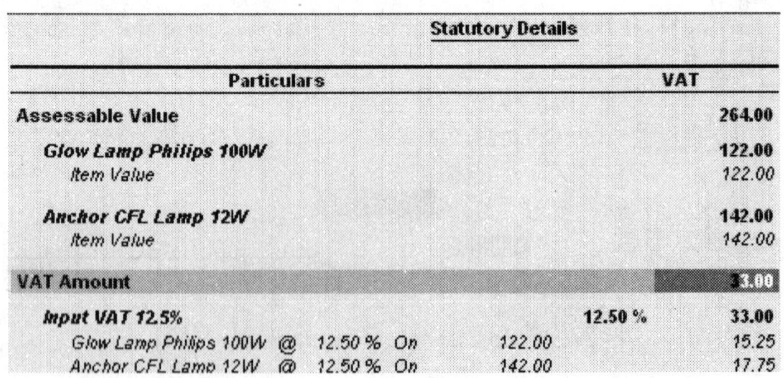

F-5B: Statutory Details sub-screen with computation details

F-5C: List of options at Used for field

Enter *Voucher Narration* and save the Debit Note

05.01 Debit Note Printing

Printing of Debit Note is explained earlier (§05/03-03/S1). The printed format of the above Debit Note entered are shown (Simple Format: F-6A, Normal Format: F-6B).

SUBJECT TO KOLKATA JURISDICTION

Debit Note No. 1 Dated 30-Jun-2009
Ref. No.: 12

ABC Electrical
27/C, Rasbihari Road
3rd Floor, Suit No.305
Kolkata-700019
Contact :03312345678,9876543210
E-Mail :nomail@kmail.com

Debit Note

Party : B.K.Services

Sl No.	Description of Goods	Quantity	Rate	per	Amount
1	Glow Lamp Philips 100W	1 Pieces	122.00	Pieces	122.00
2	Anchor CFL Lamp 12W	1 Pieces	142.00	Pieces	142.00
					264.00
	Input VAT 12.5%		12.50	%	33.00
	Goshala Donation		0.50	%	1.00
	Total	2 Pieces			₹ 303.00

Amount Chargeable (in words) E. & O.E
Indian Rupees Three Hundred Three Only

Company's VAT TIN : 1234567890
Company's CST No. : 86531240

for ABC Electrical

Authorised Signatory

F-6A: Debit Note (Simple Format)

Debit Note

ABC Electrical
27/C, Rasbihari Road
3rd Floor, Suit No.305
Kolkata-700019
Contact :03312345678,9876543210
E-Mail :nomail@kmail.com

Debit Note No.: 1 | Dated: 30-Jun-2009
Supplier's Ref.: 12 | Other Reference(s)

Party :
B.K.Services

Sl No.	Description of Goods	Quantity	Rate	per	Amount
1	Glow Lamp Philips 100W	1 Pieces	122.00	Nos	122.00
2	Anchor CFL Lamp 12W	1 Pieces	142.00	Nos	142.00
					264.00
	Input VAT 12.5%		12.50	%	33.00
	Goshala Donation		0.50	%	1.00
	Cess				5.00
	Total	2 Pieces			₹ 303.00

Amount Chargeable (in words) E. & O.E
Indian Rupees Three Hundred Three Only

VAT %	Assessable Value	VAT Amount
12.50 %	264.00	33.00

Company's VAT TIN : 1234567890
Company's CST No. : 86531240

for ABC Electrical

Authorised Signatory

SUBJECT TO KOLKATA JURISDICTION

Credit Note (Normal Format)

06 Credit Note for Goods Returns

Credit Note Entry has been explained in earlier chapters (§05/03-03). Here, we describe Credit Note Entry (F-7A), specifically describing the VAT related entry points.

Voucher Header

- **Credit Note Type**:At *Used for* field (F-7A), select the option from the list (F-7C) as follows:
  - o **Return of Taxable Goods**: Select it when Taxable Goods are returned to supplier. In such case, VAT on the returned goods are also adjusted.
  - o **Goods Sold Returned:** Select it when Non Taxable goods are returned or VAT is not to be allowed in the Credit Note
  - o **Other Adjustments:** Select it for other adjustments (like Rate Difference etc). VAT is not to be allowed in the Credit Note
  - o **Other s**: Select it for other types of Adjustments (Inter Party Adjustments, etc)
- **Sales Ledger Account**: At *Sales Ledger*, select the Sales Ledger Account from the list of Accounts, as per configuration options set for *Sale / Purchase* Account.
- **Output VAT / Tax Class**: The corresponding *Output VAT Class* as defined in the *Sales* Ledger Account is auto carried. as per configuration options set for *VAT Class*.

Stock Item Details

Enter the Stock Item details as usual, for each Item, as follows

- **Sales Ledger Account**: You may select the Sales ledger Account for the Stock Item, as per configuration options set for *Sale* Account.
- **Output VAT Class**: You may select Output VAT Class for the Stock Item, as per configuration options set for *VAT Class*.

Ledger Accounts

After entry of Stock Items, select the Ledger Accounts:

- **Output VAT Ledger:** After entry of all Stock Items, select the respective Output VAT Ledger. The VAT is computed as per VAT Rate specified and shown in the Amount Column.
- **Other Ledger Accounts**: Select Other ledger Accounts, if any, as usual and enter the Amount

VAT Details: At *Show Statutory Details*:

- Set Yes to get the *Statutory Details* screen (F-5B) to view the Assessable Value / VAT details.
- At *Statutory Details* screen (F-5B),
  - o Click *F1:Condensed* toggle button to get details of Assessable value / VAT for the Invoice
  - o Click *F1:Detail* toggle button to get Itemwise details of Assessable value/ VAT for each Item in the Invoice (F-5B)

Accounting Voucher Creation | ABC Electrical | Ctrl + M

Credit Note No. 1 30-Jun-2009
Ref.: 12 Tuesday
Used for: Return Of Taxable Goods

Party's A/c Name : B.K.Services
Sales Ledger : Sales 12.5%
VAT/Tax Class : Sales - Works Contract @ 12.5%

Name of Item	Quantity	Rate	per	Amount
Glow Lamp Philips 100W	2 Pieces	160.00	Pieces	320.00
Anchor CFL Lamp 12W	1 Pieces	180.00	Pieces	180.00
				500.00
Output VAT 12.5%		12.50	%	62.50
	3 Pieces			562.50

Show Statutory Details ? Yes
Narration:

F-7A: Credit Note entry

Statutory Details

Particulars		VAT
Assessable Value		500.00
Glow Lamp Philips 100W		320.00
Item Value		320.00
Anchor CFL Lamp 12W		180.00
Item Value		180.00
VAT Amount		62.50
Output VAT 12.5%	12.50 %	62.50

F-7B: Statutory Details

F-7C: List of options at Used for field

- Goods Sold Returned
- Other Adjustments
- Others
- Return Of Taxable Goods

06.01 Credit Note Printing

Printing of Credit Note is explained earlier (§05/03-03). The printed format of the above Credit Note entered are shown (Simple Format: F-8A, Normal Format: F-8B)

SUBJECT TO KOLKATA JURISDICTION

Credit Note No. 1 Dated 30-Jun-2009
Ref. No.: 12

ABC Electrical
27/C, Rasbihari Road
3rd Floor, Suit No.305
Kolkata-700019
Contact :03312345678,9876543210
E-Mail :nomail@kmail.com

Credit Note

Party : B.K.Services

Sl No.	Description of Goods	VAT %	Quantity	Rate	per	Amount
1	Glow Lamp Philips 100W	12.50	2 Pieces	160.00	Pcs	320.00
2	Anchor CFL Lamp 12W	12.50	1 Pieces	180.00	Pcs	180.00
						500.00
	Output VAT 12.5%			12.50	%	62.50
	Total		3 Pieces			₹ 562.50

Amount Chargeable (in words) E. & O.E
Indian Rupees Five Hundred Sixty Two and Fifty paise Only

Company's VAT TIN : 1234567890
Company's CST No. : 86531240

for ABC Electrical

Authorised Signatory

F-8A: Credit Note (Simple Format)

07 Debit & Credit Note for value adjustments

We explained the selection of option at *Used For* field in Debit Note / Credit Note for Sales / Purchase Returns, where Assessable Value, VAT Ledger Accounts as well as Stock are affected.

Apart from such Returns, Debit / Credit Notes may be used (for Rate Difference, Rebates for Quality, etc). In such cases, there may be two situations:

Credit Note

ABC Electrical
27/C, Rasbihari Road
3rd Floor, Suit No.305
Kolkata-700019
Contact :03312345678,9876543210
E-Mail :nomail@kmail.com

Credit Note No. 1 Dated 30-Jun-2009
Buyer's Ref. 12 Other Reference(s)

Party :
B.K.Services

Sl No.	Description of Goods	VAT %	Quantity	Rate	per	Amount
1	Glow Lamp Philips 100W	12.50	2 Pieces	160.00	Pcs	320.00
2	Anchor CFL Lamp 12W	12.50	1 Pieces	180.00	Pcs	180.00
						500.00
	Output VAT 12.5%			12.50	%	62.50
	Total		3 Pieces			₹ 562.50

Amount Chargeable (in words) E. & O.E
Indian Rupees Five Hundred Sixty Two and Fifty paise Only

VAT %	Assessable Value	VAT Amount
12.50 %	500.00	62.50

Company's VAT TIN : 1234567890
Company's CST No. : 86531240

for ABC Electrical

Authorised Signatory

SUBJECT TO KOLKATA JURISDICTION

F-8B: Credit Note (Normal Format)

- **The Assessable Value is affected**: The entry would be similar to Debit / Credit Note entered for Sales / Purchase Returns explained above. In quantity column, enter zero and enter the Amount affecting the Assessable Value (e.g Rate Difference). Now enter the VAT as usual. This VAT will be included in VAT Return in the same way as Sales / Purchase Returns discussed above.
- **The Assessable Value not affected**: In cases where assessable value is not affected (e.g Freight or other expenses). At Assessable Value enter zero. It is recommended to create a separate Ledger Accounts for Sales Rebates & Purchase Rebates (under the Group Sales / Purchase as the case may be) and specify No at *Used in VAT Returns* (consequently, you do not need to link with any VAT Class)

It is recommended that you create Ledger Accounts to be used in Debit / Credit Notes as under

Credit Note for Sales

Ledger A/c	Used for VAT Return	Effect
Sales Return (Under Sales Group)	Y	Select it in case of Credit Notes issued for Goods returned by Customers. The Sales Value gets reduced. The assessable value also gets reduced. VAT is added in the Credit Note. Stock also gets affected. Included in VAT Return
Sales Rebate (Under Sales Group)	Y	Select it in case of Credit Notes issued for Sales Value difference due to Price Difference, which affects the Sales Value. The

		assessable value also gets reduced. VAT is added in the Credit Note. Included in VAT Return
Sales Discounts (Under Sales Group, Indirect Expenses Group)	N	Select it in case of Credit Notes issued for various reasons. The Sales Value is affected (if Ledger placed under Sales Group), but assessable value does not get affected. VAT is NOT added in the Credit Note. Not Included in VAT Return.

In the same way, you may create Ledgers for Debit Note for Purchase.

08 VAT in Accounting Vouchers

We have explained entry of Sales / Purchase Invoice entry with Inventory details. However, sometimes, Accounts are maintained without Inventory details (in Accounts only System: §03/01-01/S1), with VAT System. This also happens when Non-Stockable items (for example, Stationery, Repairs materials purchased etc), in which VAT is charged but no stock of such materials are maintained (as these are immediately consumed when purchased). However the purchasing organization is entitled to get Input Credit of VAT paid (included in the Invoice).

In such case, Purchase (05.01/03-02/S1) / Sales Voucher (06.01/03-02/S1) in Accounting Voucher mode is created, as explained earlier. Here we explain the steps exclusively related to VAT.

To enter Sales / Purchase Voucher in Accounts Voucher form (without entering Stock Items), click *V:As Voucher* button at the Voucher Entry screen, to get the Voucher Entry form (F-9A, F-10A)

08.01 Purchase Voucher Entry with VAT

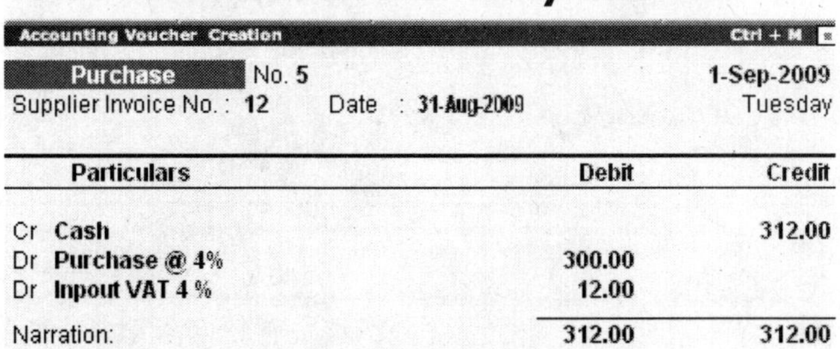

F-9A: Purchase Voucher Entry

At Purchase Voucher entry screen (F-9A), enter as follows:

- **Creditor (Supplier) Account**: At the first ledger account, select the Supplier A/c (Cash for Cash Purchase) and then enter the net Bill Amount.
- **Purchase Account:** Next enter the Purchase Account. At Item allocation screen, press <enter> at the blank input field to skip the Item allocation entry. The linked VAT Class is carried as default in the VAT Class selection screen.. Select the VAT Class for the Purchase Account (F-9B)
- **Input VAT Ledger Account**: Next enter the Input VAT ledger Account. The linked VAT Class is carried as default in the VAT Class selection screen. Select the VAT Class for the Input VAT Ledger Account (F-9C). Enter the Assessable Value.
- **Other Ledger Accounts**: Enter other ledger accounts, if any, charged in the Invoice. If the ledger is linked with any VAT Class, the respective VAT Class will be carried as default in the VAT Class selection screen.

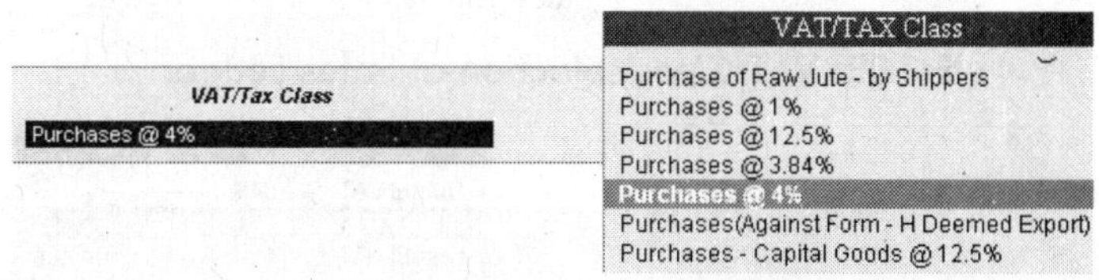

F-9B: VAT Class selection at Purchase Ledger

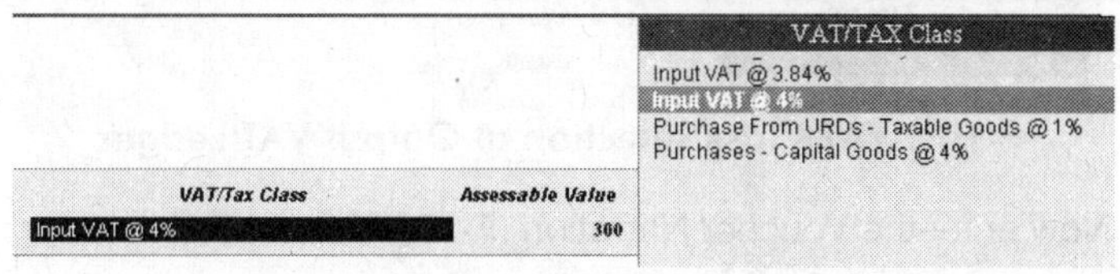

F-9C: VAT Class selection at Input VAT Ledger

Now enter the Voucher Narration (F-9A) & save the voucher.

08.02 Sales Voucher Entry with VAT

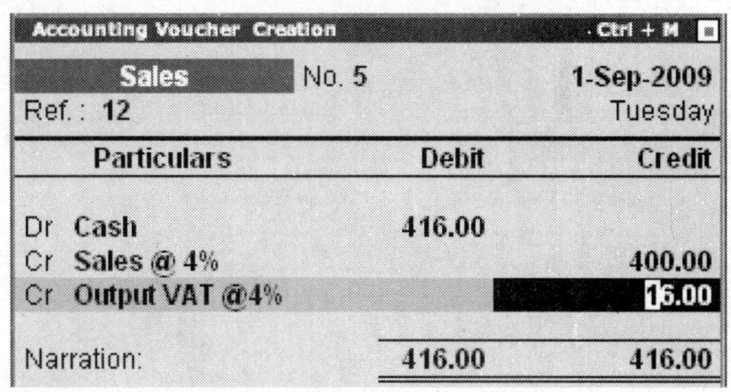

F-10A: Sales Voucher Entry

At Sales Voucher entry screen (F-10A), enter as follows:

- **Debtor Account**: At the first ledger account, select the Customer A/c (Cash for Cash Sale) and then enter the net Bill Amount.
- **Sale Account:** Next enter the Sale Account. At Item allocation screen, press <enter> at the blank input field to skip the Item allocation entry. The linked VAT Class is carried as default in the VAT Class selection screen.. Select the VAT Class for the Sale Account. (F-10B)
- **Output VAT Ledger Account**: Next enter the Output VAT ledger Account. The linked VAT Class is carried as default in the VAT Class selection screen. Select the VAT

Class for the Output VAT Ledger Account (F-10C). Enter the Assessable Value.

- **Other Ledger Accounts**: Enter other ledger accounts, if any, charged in the Invoice (F-10A). If the ledger is linked with any VAT Class, the respective VAT Class will be carried as default in the VAT Class selection screen.

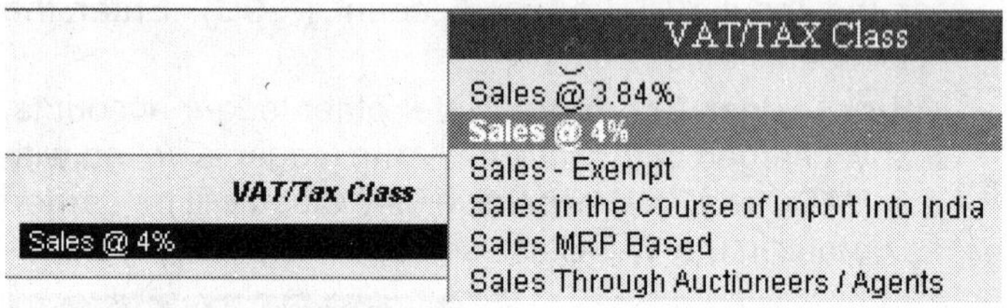

F-10B: VAT Class selection at Sales Ledger

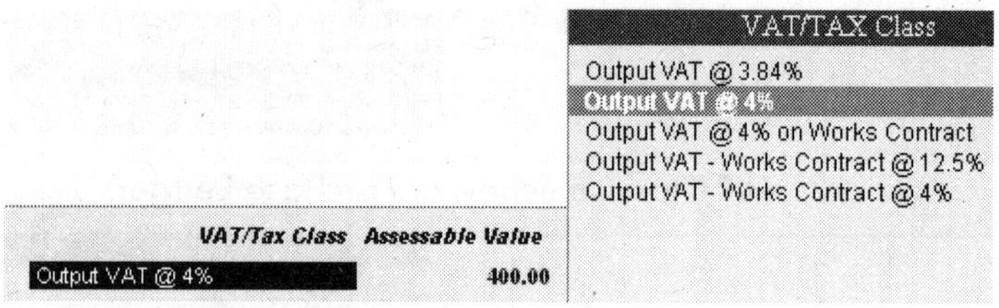

F-10C:VAT Class selection at Output VAT Ledger

Now enter the Voucher Narration (F-10A) & save the voucher.

FAQ: Frequently Asked Question

FAQ-1: How to set up VAT related Invoicing options

Ans: At Invoice Entry Configuration (GoT>F12:Configure> Invoice / Orders Entry), set up the options as follows:

- **Sales / Purchase Account**: At *Use Common Ledger for Item Allocation*:
  - o Set Yes to select Sales / Purchase Ledger Account at header (useful when the value of all the Items is to be posted to ONE Sales / Purchase Account)
  - o Set No to select Purchase Ledger Account at Item Details for each Stock Item (useful when the value of each Stock Items is to be posted to different Sales / Purchase Account
- **VAT Tax Class**: At *Allow selection of VAT Class during Entry*:
  - o Set *Yes* to allow entry (or change of default VAT Class carried, as set in the Stock Item), during Invoice Entry (useful for Multiple VAT Class Invoice entry: §01/04-06)
  - o Set *No*, The default VAT Class carried, as set in the Stock Item would be auto carried (§04/04-02), and the VAT Class entry field would be skipped during Invoice Entry, displaying the carried VAT Class (useful for Single VAT Class Invoice entry)

VAT Reports

04-04

01 VAT Reports

Having entered Sales & Purchase, Debit Note & Credit Note Vouchers, you may now print various reports related to VAT.

At Gateway, select *Display >Statutory Reports>VAT Reports*, to get *VAT Reports* Menu (F-1A) from where you may print various VAT Reports, as explained next.

Gateway of Tally ....
Display Menu ....
Statutory Reports ....

VAT Reports

VAT Computation
VAT Forms
E-VAT Return
VAT Commodity
VAT Register
Quit

F-1A: VAT Reports Menu

VAT Computation — Ctrl + M

Particulars	ABC Traders 1-Apr-2013 to 30-Jun-2013	
	Assessable Value	Tax Amount
Sales		
A. Output Tax		
Output VAT @ 12.5%	690.00	83.33
Output VAT @ 4%	42.00	1.80
Total Output Tax	**732.00**	**85.13**
Purchases		
C. Input Tax		
Excess Input Credit Brought Forward		
Input VAT @ 12.5%	606.00	75.75
Input VAT @ 4%	24.24	0.97
Total Input Credit	**630.24**	**76.72**
VAT Payable		**8.41**

F-2A: VAT Computation Statement

02 VAT Computation Statement

VAT Computation Statement (F-2A) is the summary report of all transactions related to VAT. Select *Display>Statutory Reports>VAT > VAT Computation* (F-1A)

The VAT Computation Report (F-2A) is primarily split into 2 sections, namely Sales and Purchases.

The Sales section shows the details of Output VAT, while the Purchase section shows the details of Input VAT.

If the output VAT is more than Input VAT, the balance is VAT payable. If the Input VAT is more than Output VAT, the balance VAT is to be adjusted in subsequent period. Carried against '*Excess Input Credit Brought Forward*' under the Input Tax section in the VAT Computation Report (F-2A)

03 VAT Classification Vouchers list

At the VAT Computation Report (F-2A), drill down form any Item of under Output Tax / Input Tax to get the Classification Voucher List (F-3A), showing the details in respect of selected VAT Classification.

04 VAT Return & Annexures

The VAT registered organisation has to submit some statutory Returns to the Government. At VAT Reports Menu (F-1A), select *VAT Forms* to get *VAT Forms Menu* (F-4A), showing menu items for printing of VAT Return & Annexures. The contents & format of VAT Return forms & Annexures vary for each State. Tally produces the Report applicable for the State as specified at VAT Set up (§01/04-02)

VAT Classification Vouchers — ABC Traders — Ctrl + M

VAT Classification : **Output VAT @ 12.5%** — **1-Apr-2013 to 30-Jun-2013**

Voucher Date	Particulars	VAT TIN	Voucher Type	Voucher Number	Supplier Inv/ Ref. No. Date	MRP Value	Assessable Value	VAT Amount
20-5-2013	H P Traders	123456	Sales	2	28	666.67	690.00	83.33
	Grand Total					666.67	**690.00**	**83.33**

VAT Classification Vouchers — ABC Traders — Ctrl + M

VAT Classification : **Input VAT @ 12.5%** — **1-Apr-2013 to 30-Jun-2013**

Voucher Date	Particulars	VAT TIN	Voucher Type	Voucher Number	Supplier Inv/ Ref. No. Date	MRP Value	Assessable Value	VAT Amount
7-5-2013	H P Traders	123456	Purchase	1	29/5-May-2013		606.00	75.75
	Grand Total						**606.00**	**75.75**

F-3A: VAT Classification Voucher List in respect of each VAT Classification

VAT Menu (F-4A) contains following reports:

- **VAT Return**: VAT Return (F-8A) shows the Statutory VAT Form for the State with all figures filled up for the specified period.
- **VAT Annexures**: VAT Annexures show the details of figures shown in VAT Return. There may be several VAT Annexures (F-6A).

04.01 VAT Return

Select *GoT>Display>Statutory Reports>VAT>VAT Forms>VAT >VAT Return* to get VAT Return Form printing screen (F-5A). The default Values carried.

- Click *Yes* to print as per the default values shown
- Click *No* to change the default values and then click Yes print

VAT Return Printing Options: At VAT Reports printing screen (F-5A), you may set the following options

- **Period**: Set the Period of the VAT Return (Month / Quarter) at *From*& *To* fields
- **Type of Return**: At *Type of Return*, select the Return Type from the following list
    - o **Original Return**: Select *Original* when you file the VAT Return for the specified period for the first time.
    - o **Revised Return**: Select *Revised* when you file the a Revised VAT return for the specified period subsequent to filing of the Original Return (if there was some mistake in the Original Return)
- **Officer Name**: At *Name*, enter the Name of the designated officer of the Company signing the VAT Return
- **Officer Designation**: At *Status/ Designation*, enter the Designation of the Officer of the Company
- **Place**: At *Place*, enter the Place of signing the Return
- **Date:** At *Date*, enter the Date of signing the Return

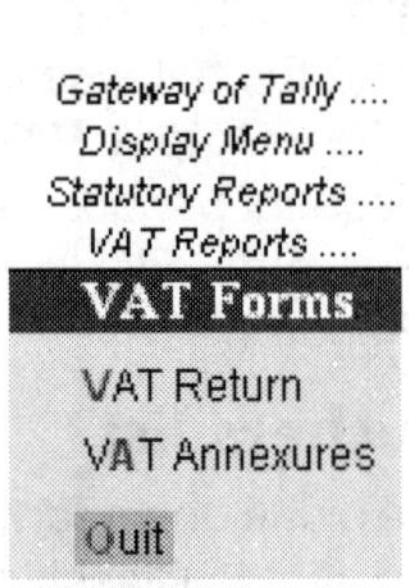

F-4A: VAT Forms Menu

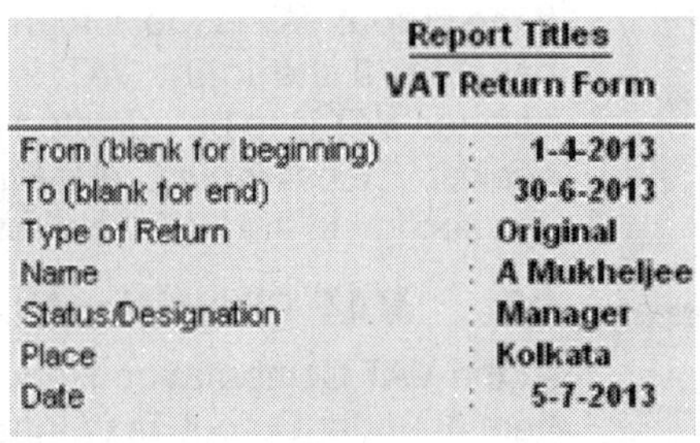

F-5A: VAT Return printing screen

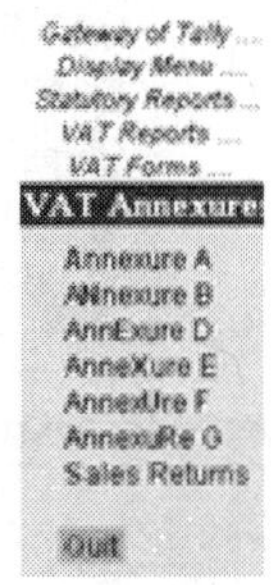

F-6A: VAT Annexure Menu

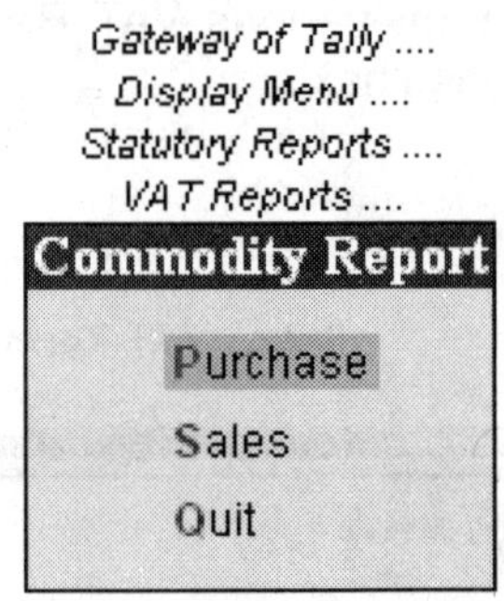

F-7A: VAT Commodity Report Menu

F-8A shows a specimen of VAT Return as per WB VAT rules.

THE WEST BENGAL VALUE ADDED TAX RULES, 2005
FORM 14

[See sub-rule (1) of rule 34]

For dealers not enjoying deferment or tax holiday or remission of tax u/s 118, and not paying tax at compounding rate under sub-section (3), or sub-section (3B) of section 16 or sub-section (4) of section 18

RETURN PERIOD							
From	DD	MM	YY	to	DD	MM	YY
	01	04	2013		30	06	2013

REGISTRATION NUMBER									
1	2	3	4	5	6	7	8	9	0

Name of the	ABC Traders	Trade name, if any	ABC Traders 13-14
Address of the principal place of business	12 Hesham Rd, Kolkata 700999		

invoices and determination of I.T.C.

		Amount (Rs.) A	I.T.C Claimed (Rs.) B
1.	Purchases of goods exempt from tax	Nil	
1a.	Purchases of goods in NEGATIVE LIST appended to Sec.22	Nil	
2.	Purchases of M.R.P goods u/s 16(4)	Nil	
3.	Purchases of goods taxable at the rate of 1%	Nil	Nil
4.	Purchases of goods taxable at the rate of 4 %	24.24	0.97
5.	Purchases of goods taxable at the rate of 12.5%	606.00	75.75
5a.	Purchases of goods taxable at the rate of 14.5%	Nil	Nil
6.	Purchases of goods taxable at the rate of ....%[under section 16(2)(c)]	Nil	Nil
7.	Purchases from dealers paying tax at compounded rate	Nil	
8.	Purchases of capital goods taxable at the rate of 4% see note 4	Nil	Nil
8a.	Purchases of capital goods taxable at the rate of 12.5% (purchase before 15.11.10)	Nil	Nil
8b.	Purchases of capital goods taxable at the rate of 13.5%	Nil	Nil
8X	Adjustment,if any, in respect of I.T.C. shown in column B (+-)		Nil
9.	**Total Purchase from Registered Dealer**	630.24	76.72
9a.	**Purchase from Unregistered Dealer**	**Nil**	
9b.	**Total Purchase from Registered & Unregistered Dealer**	630.24	76.72

Purchases of goods in West Bengal on which purchase tax is payable u/s 11 *or/and u/s 12.

		Amount of purchase (Rs.) A	Purchase tax payable (Rs.) B
10.	Purchases of raw jute ***Shipper of jute only will pay tax u/s 11***	Nil	Nil
11.	Purchases of goods taxable at rate of 1 %	Nil	Nil
12.	Purchases of goods taxable at the rate of 4%	Nil	Nil
13.	Purchases of goods taxable at the rate of 12.5% (purchase before 15.11.10)	Nil	Nil
13a.	Purchases of goods taxable at the rate of 13.5%	Nil	Nil
14.	Purchases of goods taxable at the rate of .....%	Nil	Nil
15.	Total	**Nil**	**Nil**

PART AA

Import of goods from outside the State of West Bengal

		Amount (Rs.)
15A.	Goods purchased within the meaning of section 3 of the Central Sales Tax Act.1956	Nil
15B.	Stock of Goods transferred from other States	880.00
15C.	Goods purchased within the meaning of sub-section(3) of section 5 of the Central Sales Tax Act.1956 from other States	Nil
15D.	Goods imported from outside India within the meaning of sub-section(2) of section 5 of the Central Sales Tax Act. 1956	Nil

PART B

Sales in the return period and calculation of output tax

16.	Aggregate of sale price (excluding VAT)	Rs.	872.00
17.	Sale price of goods, tax on which has been paid on M.R.P u/s 16(4) at the time of purchase or on an earlier occasion [sec.2(55)(a)]	Rs.	Nil
18.	Sales *return/rejection within six months from the date of sale [sec.2(55)(b)]	Rs.	Nil
19.	Turnover of sales (16-17-18)	Rs.	872.00

	Break-up of turnover of sales as arrived at item 19.	Amount (Rs.) A	Output tax (Rs.) B
20.	Sales exempt from tax u/s 21	Nil	
21.	Sales within the meaning of section 3 of the C.S.T Act, 1956	140.00	
22.	Sales in the course of *export/import/last sale preceding export within the meaning of section 5 of the C.S.T Act, 1956	Nil	
23.	Sales which are zero-rated u/s 21 A(1)	Nil	
24.	Sales through auctioneer or agent u/s 16(1)(c) read with rule 27(1)	Nil	
25.	Other Sales u/s 16(1)(c) read with rule(s)....	Nil	
26.	Sales of M.R.P goods u/s 16(4) **[Enclose Annexure A]**	732.00	85.13
27.	Sales of goods (other than M.R.P as in 26) taxable at the rate of 1%	Nil	Nil
28.	Sales of goods (other than M.R.P as in 26) taxable at the rate of 4%	Nil	Nil
29.	Sales of goods (other than M.R.P as in 26) taxable at the rate of 12.5% (purchase before 15.11.10)	Nil	Nil
29a.	Sales of goods (other than M.R.P as in 26) taxable at the rate of 13.5%	Nil	Nil
30.	Sales of goods (other than M.R.P as in 26) taxable at the rate of ...%	Nil	Nil
30a.	Adjustment of output tax on account of sales return, if any		Nil
30b.	Adjustment of output tax, if any other than sales return		Nil
31.	Output tax (26B+27B+28B+29B+30B+30aB+30bb)		85.13

32.	Contractual transfer price (excluding VAT)	Rs.	Nil
33.	Deductions: (a) Contractual transfer price of tax free goods [Sec. 18(2)(a)] (b) Charges towards labour, service and other like charges [Sec. *18(2)(b)read with rule 30(1)/Sec. 18(3) read with rule 30(2)] **[Enclose Annexure D]** (c) Amounts paid to sub-contractors [Sec.18(2)(c)] (d) #Other contractual transfer prices as prescribed in the rule(S)....[Sec. 18(2)(d)]	Rs.	Nil
34.	Taxable contractual transfer price (32-33)		Nil

	Break-up of taxable contractual transfer price arrived at item 34.	Amount (Rs.) A	Output tax (Rs.) B
35.	Taxable contractual transfer price, taxable at the rate of 4%	Nil	Nil
36.	Taxable contractual transfer price, taxable at the rate of 12.5%	Nil	Nil
36a.	Taxable contractual transfer price, taxable at the rate of 13.5%	Nil	Nil
37.	Total	Nil	Nil

PART C

Monthly calculation of output tax, input tax credit , net tax credit, net tax payable, interest, etc.

		1st month (Rs.)	2nd month (Rs.)	3rd month (Rs.)
38.	(a) Output tax **Month-wise break-up of (31B+37B)**	Nil	85.13	Nil
	(b) Amount charged in *short/excess, if any	Nil	Nil	Nil
	(c) Total Output tax [38(a)+38(b)]	Nil	85.13	Nil
39.	(a) Input tax credit B/F (Less refund claimed, if any)	Nil	Nil	Nil
	(b) Input tax credit for the period **Month-wise break-up of III**	Nil	76.72	Nil
	(c) Input tax credit on stock under rule 22	Nil	Nil	Nil
	(d) Input tax credit claimed in *short/excess earlier [Sec.22(17)]	Nil	Nil	Nil
	(e)Reverse credit [Enclose Annexure F]	Nil	Nil	Nil
	(f) Net tax Credit [39[(a+b)+(c)+(d)-(e)]]	Nil	76.72	Nil
40.	(a) Net tax payable [38(c) - 39(f)] or	Nil	8.00	Nil
	(b) Excess input tax credit [39(f)-38(c)]	Nil	Nil	Nil
41.	(a) Out of 40(b), input tax credit/rebate adjustable under Central Sales Tax Act, 1956	Nil	Nil	Nil
	(b) Out of 40(b), input tax credit to be claimed as refund	Nil	Nil	Nil
	(c) Out of 40(b), input tax credit to be carried forward	Nil	Nil	Nil
42.	(a) Tax deducted at source	Nil	Nil	Nil
	(b) Tax paid in appropriate Govt. Treasury, other than 42(a)	Nil	Nil	Nil
	(c) Tax paid in excess in earlier period, now adjusted [Rule 40(2A)]	Nil	Nil	Nil
	(d) Amount credited under Refund Adjustment order RAO Book NO:- Serial NO:- Date:-	Nil	Nil	Nil
43.	Actual tax payable [40(a)-42(a)-42(b)-42(c)-42(d)]Negative amount will be the excess amount	Nil	8.00	Nil
44.	(a) Interest payable, if any u/s 33	Nil	Nil	Nil
	(b) Interest paid in appropriate Govt.Treasury	Nil	Nil	Nil
	(c) Interest *payable/paid in excess [44(a)- 44(b)/44(b) - 44(a)]	Nil	Nil	Nil
44A.	Late Fees Payable(For Extended period set payable value to 0(zero)) Nil	44C.Late Fees Paid		Nil

45. Payment Details								
Date (DD/MM	Challan No.	Bank Name	Branch Name	Treasury Name	Period(YYYY-MM)	Tax Paid (Rs.)	Interest Paid	Late fee Paid

46.	Sale of three main taxable commodities (in terms of sale value) during the return period)		
	Name of the commodity	Rate of Tax	Amount (Rs.)
1	Electrical Goods 12.5%	12.50	690.00
2	Electrical Goods 4%	4	42.00

47.	Information on issue and receipt of tax invoices					
Tax Period	**Tax invoices issued**			**Tax invoices received for purchases from W.B.**		
	From (Serial No)	To (Serial No)		From (No. of Sellers)	Total no.of Invoice	Amount of Purchase (Rs.)

Declaration:

I, [full name in block letters] A Mukherjee declare that the information given in this return is correct and complete.

**Signature with date	5-Jul-2013	Name and Status	A Mukherjee Manager

FOR OFFICE USE ONLY:	
Due date of submission (dd-mm-yyyy)	Date of Receipt (dd-mm-yyyy)
Office Seal	*Signature of the Receiving Officer*

F-8A: VAT Return as per W B VAT Rules

04.02 E-VAT Return

E-VAT Return produces Data in XML format to be uploaded fro e-filing

Select *GoT>Display>Statutory Reports>VAT>E-VAT Return* to get VAT Return exporting screen, similar to VAT Return printing screen (F-5A).The Values in the fields are auto carried

- Click *Yes* to export the data as per the default values shown
- Click *No* to change the default values and then click Yes to export the data

The e-Return data are saved in XML format in the folder as specified in Location of Export Files at the field *Location of Export Files* at *F12:Configure>Data Configuration* (§01/02-25). The file may be used for uploading for e-filing of VAT Return.

04.03 VAT Return Annexures

At VAT Forms Menu (F-4A), select *VAT Annexures* to get *VAT Return Annexures* Menu (like F-6A) showing the list of Annexures, as per the State.

To print the VAT Return Annexures, Select the respective VAT Annexure item from *VAT Return Annexures* Menu (F-4A), to get the respective Annexure printing screen. Set the printing options as described for VAT Report printing options (§04.01)

05 VAT Commodity Report

VAT Commodity Report shows details of Sales / Purchase for each VAT Commodity. Select *GoT>Display>Statutory Reports>VAT* to get VAT Commodity Menu (F-7A)

05.01 VAT Commodity wise Purchase Report

At VAT Commodity Menu (F-8A), select *Purchase* to get VAT Commodity Purchase Report (F-9A), showing the VAT Commodity Codewise figures of each component of Purchases

Commodity wise Purchase — ABC Traders — Ctrl + M

Commodity wise Purchase — 1-Apr-2013 to 30-Jun-2013

Description	Code	Rate	Total Value	Inventory Value	Additions / Deductions	Assessable Value	Tax Amount	Additional Tax
Consignment/Branch Transfer Inward			**880.00**	**880.00**		**880.00**		
Electrical Goods 12.5%	3456987		880.00	880.00		880.00		
Lamp Shades			*880.00*	*880.00*		*880.00*		
Input VAT @ 12.5%			**681.75**	**600.00**	**6.00**	**606.00**	**75.75**	
Electrical Goods 12.5%	3456987	12.50%	681.75	600.00	6.00	606.00	75.75	
Lamp Shades			*681.75*	*600.00*	*6.00*	*606.00*	*75.75*	
Input VAT @ 4%			**25.21**	**24.00**	**0.24**	**24.24**	**0.97**	
Electrical Goods 4%	123456	4%	25.21	24.00	0.24	24.24	0.97	
Glow Lamp Phillips 100W			*25.21*	*24.00*	*0.24*	*24.24*	*0.97*	

F-9A: VAT Commodity wise Purchase Report

Commodity wise Sales — ABC Traders — Ctrl + M

Commodity wise Sales — 1-Apr-2013 to 30-Jun-2013

Description	Code	Rate	Total Value	Inventory Value	Additions / Deductions	Assessable Value	Tax Amount	Additional Tax
Consignment/Branch Transfer Outward			**140.00**	**140.00**		**140.00**		
Electrical Goods 4%	123456		140.00	140.00		140.00		
Glow Lamp Phillips 100W			*140.00*	*140.00*		*140.00*		
Output VAT @ 12.5%			**773.33**	**690.00**		**690.00**	**83.33**	
Electrical Goods 12.5%	3456987	12.50%	773.33	690.00		690.00	83.33	
Lamp Shades			*773.33*	*690.00*		*690.00*	*83.33*	
Output VAT @ 4%			**43.80**	**42.00**		**42.00**	**1.80**	
Electrical Goods 4%	123456	4%	43.80	42.00		42.00	1.80	
Glow Lamp Phillips 100W			*43.80*	*42.00*		*42.00*	*1.80*	

F-9B: Commodity wise Sales Report

05.02 VAT Commoditywise Sale Report

At VAT Commodity Menu (F-8A), select *Sales*, to get *VAT Commodity Sales* Report (F-9B), showing the VAT Commodity Codewise figures of each component of Sales

06 VAT Register

VAT Register is a columnar report showing the complete details of each Voucher, with figures of each component in a separate column, with column totals, for a specified period

At VAT Reports Menu (F-1A), select *VAT Register* to get VAT Register Menu (F-10A)

Gateway of Tally ....
Display Menu ....
Statutory Reports ....
VAT Reports ....

VAT Register

- Vat Purchases
- Vat Sales
- Quit

F-10A: VAT Register Menu

06.01 VAT Purchase Register

At VAT Register Menu (F-10A), select *VAT Purchases* to get VAT Purchase Register (F-11A)

06.02 VAT Sales Register

At VAT Register Menu (F-10A) select *VAT Sales* to get VAT Sales Register (F-12A)

When you drill down from any Voucher from VAT Register (F-11A, F-12A), you get the Voucher in Alteration Mode.

VAT Purchase Register — ABC Traders — Ctrl + M

List of Purchase Vouchers — 1-Apr-2013 to 30-Jun-2013

Date	*Particulars*	Vch No.	TIN No	Gross Total	Assessable Value	MRP Value	Addl. Cost
							2 more ... →
7-May-2013	**H P Traders**	1.	123456	**706.96**	**630.24**		**6.24**
	Glow Lamp Phillips 100W				*24.24*		
	Packing Charges						*0.24*
	Lamp Shades				*606.00*		
	Packing Charges						*6.00*
	Grand Total			**706.96**	**630.24**		**6.24**

F-11A: VAT Purchase Register – Part 1

Ctrl + M

1-Apr-2013 to 30-Jun-2013

VAT/TAX Class	Tax Amount
	76.72
Input VAT @ 4%	*0.97*
Input VAT @ 12.5%	*75.75*
	76.72

Part 2

VAT Sales Register — ABC Traders — Ctrl + M

List of Sales Vouchers — **1-May-2013 to 31-May-2013**

Date	*Particulars*	Vch No.	TIN No.	Gross Total	Assessable Value	MRP Value	Addl. Cost
							2 more ... →
15-May-2013	**H P Traders**	1	123456	**43.80**	**42.00**	**45.00**	
	Glow Lamp Phillips 100W				*42.00*	*45.00*	
20-May-2013	**H P Traders**	2	123456	**773.33**	**690.00**	**750.00**	
	Lamp Shades				*690.00*	*750.00*	
	Grand Total			**817.13**	**732.00**		

F-12A: VAT Sales Register - Part 1

Ctrl + M

1-May-2013 to 31-May-2013

VAT/TAX Class	Tax Amount
	1.80
Output VAT @ 4%	*1.80*
	83.33
Output VAT @ 12.5%	
	85.13

Part 2

FAQ: Frequently Asked Question

FAQ-1: How to get summary report of Output VAT, Input VAT and VAT Payable

Ans: VAT Computation Statement: VAT Computation Statement (F-2A) shows the summary report of all transactions related to VAT.

At Gateway, select *Display>Statutory Reports>VAT > VAT Computation* to get VAT Computation Statement (F-2A), which is primarily split into 2 sections, namely Output VAT (of Sales) and Input VAT (of Purchases).

The Sales section shows the details of Output VAT, while the Purchase section shows the details of Input VAT.

If the output VAT is more than Input VAT, the balance is VAT payable. If the Input VAT is more than Output VAT, the balance VAT is to be adjusted in subsequent period. Carried against '*Excess Input Credit Brought Forward*' under the Input Tax section in the VAT Computation Report (F-2A)

VAT Deposit 04-05

01 VAT Deposit

When the Output Tax is more than Input Tax (together with Input Tax carried forward from previous period), then the difference of Output Tax & Input Tax is payable to the government, as per *VAT Computation Statement* (§02/04-04) discussed earlier

02 VAT Payment Voucher Entry

For payment of VAT to the government, create a Payment Voucher (F-1A). At Gateway, select *Accounting Voucher* and then click *V: VAT Payment* button to get *VAT Payment Details screen* (F-1B)

VAT Payment Details

At *VAT Payment Details screen* (F-1B), enter as follows:

- **Period**: At *Period From*, enter the Period (From & To) for which the VAT payment is made (the period as per VAT Computation Statement: §02/04-04)
- **Tax Type**: At *Payment Towards*, select *VAT* from the Tax Type List (F-1C)
- **Payment Type:** At *Type of Payment*, select from the *Payment Type* list (F-1D), as follows:
    - o **Advance Payment:** Select *Advance Payment*, when VAT Payment is made for the respective period
    - o **Interest:** Select *Interest*, when Interest is paid for delayed VAT Payment, for the respective period
    - o **Late Fees**: Select *Late Fees* for delayed submission of Return, for the respective period
    - o **Penalty:** Select *Penalty* when Penalty amount is paid for any penalty imposed by the VAT authorities
- **Deposit Date**: At *Deposit Date*, enter the Date of Deposit of VAT money to the Bank
- **Challan Number:** At *Challan No.* enter the Challan Number of the Challan issued by Bank
- **Bank Name**: At *Name of Issuing Bank*, select the Bank into which the VAT is deposited, from Bank List (list of Banks Authorised to collect VAT (F-1E)
- **Branch Name**: Select the Name of Branch into which the VAT is deposited, from the list of authorized Branch of the selected Bank.
- **Treasury:** At *Name of Treasury*, enter the Name of Treasury into which the Tax is deposited.
- **Case Number**: At *Case Number,* enter the Case Number when Penalty amount is deposited.
- **Branch Code:** At *Branch Code,* enter the Code of the Bank Branch, as designated by the VAT authorities

Accounting Voucher Creation — Ctrl + M

Payment No. 5 — 31-Mar-2010, Wednesday

	Particulars	Debit	Credit
Dr	Output VAT 12.5% (Cur Bal: 0.00 Dr)	387.50	
Dr	Output VAT @4% (Cur Bal: 0.00 Dr)	16.00	
Cr	Inpout VAT 4 % (Cur Bal: 0.00 Cr)		12.00
Cr	Input VAT 12.5% (Cur Bal: 0.00 Cr)		373.25
Cr	Cash (Cur Bal: 1,510.75 Dr)		18.25
	Narration:	403.50	403.50

Net VAT payabale for the p/e 31.3.10 deposited with Government

F-1A: VAT Payment Voucher

VAT Payment Details

Period From	: 1-Apr-2009 To 31-Mar-2010
Payment towards	: VAT
Type of Payment	: Advance Payment
Deposit Date	: 31-Mar-2010
Challan No.	: 15
Name of the issuing Bank	: BANK OF BARODA
Branch Name	: KIDDERPORE
Name of the Treasury	: Not Applicable
Branch code(remittance)	: 0234

F-1B: VAT Payment details

Having entered the VAT Details at VAT Details entry screen (F-1B), you get back to the VAT Payment Voucher screen (F-1A). Enter the Payment Voucher as usual

At *Voucher Entry* screen (F-1A), enter the Ledger Account details as follows:

- **Output VAT Ledger Accounts**: Select *Output VAT Ledger* Account and enter the VAT Amount in *Debit* Column. This way, select all the Output VAT ledger Accounts for which payment is being made and enter the corresponding VAT amount is *Debit* Column.
- **Input VAT Ledger Accounts**: Select *Input VAT Ledger* Account and enter the VAT Amount in *Credit* Column. This way, select all the Input VAT ledger Accounts for which payment is being adjusted and enter the corresponding VAT amount is *Credit* Column.

- **Cash / Bank Account**: Select the Cash Bank Account and enter the Amount paid (Net of Input & Output VAT amounts) at *Credit* column

Now enter the Voucher Narration (F-1A) and save the Voucher.

Types of Duty/Tax
CST
VAT

F-1C: Selection of Type of Duty

Types of Payment
Not Applicable
Advance Payment
Interest
Late Fees
Penalty

F-1D: Selection of Type of Payment

03 VAT Payment Voucher Printing

At VAT Payment Voucher entry screen (F-1A), click P:*Print* button to get VAT Payment Voucher printing screen (F-2A). Type *Y* to get the voucher in print (F-2B).

Bank List
ALLAHABAD BANK
BANK OF BARODA
BANK OF INDIA
BANK OF MAHARASTRA
CANARA BANK
CENTRAL BANK OF INDIA
DENA BANK
INDIAN BANK
INDIAN OVERSEAS BANK
PUNJAB NATIONAL BANK
RESERVE BANK OF INDIA
STATE BANK OF INDIA
SYNDICATE BANK
UNION BANK OF INDIA
UNITED BANK OF INDIA
UNITED COMMERCIAL BANK

F-1E: Selection of Bank

Report Titles

Payment Voucher

Print as VAT Challan	? **Yes**
Name	: **A Mukheljee**
Status/Designation	: **Manager**
Place	: **Kolkata**
Date	: **1-12-2013**
Assessment Circle (Group)	: **Div 4**

F-2A: VAT Payment Voucher Printing

Payment Voucher

No. : **7** Dated : **31-Mar-2010**

Particulars	Amount
Account :	
Output VAT 12.5%	**387.50**
Output VAT @4%	**16.00**
Less: Inpout VAT 4 %	**(-)12.00**
Less: Input VAT 12.5%	**(-)373.25**
Through :	
Cash	
On Account of :	
Net VAT payabale for the p/e 31.3.10 deposited with Government	
Amount (in words) :	
Indian Rupees Eighteen and Twenty Five paise Only	
	₹ 18.25

F-2B: VAT Payment Voucher in Print

03.01 *Printing of VAT Challan*

At Payment Voucher printing screen (F-2A), set *Yes* at *Print as VAT Challans* and enter the payment details Now type *Y* at *Print Y/N* to print the VAT Challan (F-2C)

ORIGINAL

West Bengal Form No. 2380G (Group Div 4) Challan No. 123

ACCOUNT CODE : 6240000220
Account Head : 0040-00-102-005-03
Under the West Bengal Value Added Tax Act, 2003

Challan of Value Added Tax / Interest / Penalty / Composition Money paid into **ALLAHABAD BANK** (Bank) **MAIN** (Br.)

attached to *Treasury / Reserve Bank of India, Kolkata for the month / quarter / year ending | 3 | 1 | 1 | 2 | 1 | 3 |

Registration certificate no. of the Dealer | 1 | 2 | 3 | 4 | 5 | 6 | 7 | 8 | 9 | 0 | |

Case No.(if any) [ ]

By whom tendered	Name & Address of the Dealer/person on whos behalf money is paid	Amount: Tax including penalty/ composition money		Interest		Total	
		Rs.	P.	Rs.	P.	Rs.	P.
A Mukheljee	ABC Traders 13-14 , 12 Hesham Rd. Kolkata 700999	18	25			18	25

Total Amount(in words)INR Eighteen and Twenty Five paise Only

F-2C: VAT Deposit Challan

04 VAT Ledger Accounts

After the Payment Voucher is created for full VAT Amount payable, the balances of each VAT Ledger account would be NIL

Select *GoT>Display>Accounts Books>Ledger* and then select the VAT Ledger Account to get the Ledger of the selected Ledger Account. F-2A to F-2D show the *Ledger Accounts* of each Input & Output VAT described in earlier examples.

Ledger: **Inpout VAT 4 %** **1-Apr-2009 to 31-Mar-2010**

Date	Particulars	Vch Type	Vch No.	Debit	Credit
1-9-2009	**Cash**	**Purchase**	5	**12.00**	
31-3-2010	**Output VAT 12.5%**	**Payment**	5		**12.00**
		Opening Balance :			
		Current Total :		**12.00**	**12.00**
		Closing Balance :			

F-2A: Input VAT Ledger Account

Ledger: **Input VAT 12.5%** **1-Apr-2009 to 31-Mar-2010**

Date	Particulars	Vch Type	Vch No.	Debit	Credit
1-6-2009	**B.K.Services**	**Purchase**	3	**406.25**	
30-6-2009	**B.K.Services**	**Debit Note**	1		**33.00**
31-3-2010	**Output VAT 12.5%**	**Payment**	5		**373.25**
		Opening Balance :			
		Current Total :		**406.25**	**406.25**
		Closing Balance :			

F-2B: Input VAT Ledger Account

Ledger: **Output VAT 12.5%** **1-Apr-2009 to 31-Mar-2010**

Date	Particulars	Vch Type	Vch No.	Debit	Credit
30-6-2009	**P.K.Motors**	**Sales**	2		**450.00**
30-6-2009	**B.K.Services**	**Credit Note**	1	**62.50**	
31-3-2010	**Inpout VAT 4 %**	**Payment**	5	**387.50**	
		Opening Balance :			
		Current Total :		**450.00**	**450.00**
		Closing Balance :			

F-2C: Output VAT Ledger Account

Ledger: **Output VAT @4%**				1-Apr-2009 to 31-Mar-2010	
Date	Particulars	Vch Type	Vch No.	Debit	Credit
1-9-2009	Cash	Sales	3		16.00
31-3-2010	Inpout VAT 4 %	Payment	5	16.00	
		Opening Balance :			
		Current Total :		16.00	16.00
		Closing Balance :			

F-2D: Output VAT Ledger Account

FAQ: Frequently Asked Question

FAQ-1: How to deposit VAT Payable with Government Account

Ans: If the Output VAT is more than Input VAT (alongwith VAT credit carried forward from previous period),the net VAT is payable to Government, as shown in VAT Computation Summary.

For deposit of VAT payable, create a Payment Voucher. At *Voucher Entry* screen (F-1A), enter the Ledger Account details as follows:

- **Output VAT Ledger Accounts**: Select *Output VAT Ledger* Account and enter the VAT Amount in *Debit* Column. This way, select all the Output VAT ledger Accounts for which payment is being made and enter the corresponding VAT amount is *Debit* Column.
- **Input VAT Ledger Accounts**: Select *Input VAT Ledger* Account and enter the VAT Amount in *Credit* Column. This way, select all the Input VAT ledger Accounts for which payment is being adjusted and enter the corresponding VAT amount is *Credit* Column.
- **Cash / Bank Account**: Select the Cash Bank Account and enter the Amount paid (Net of Input & Output VAT amounts) at *Credit* column

Click *V:VAT Payment* button to get *VAT Payment Details* screen (F-1B), to enter the Payment Particulars. At main voucher entry screen, enter the Voucher Narration (F-1A) and save the Voucher

VAT Special Features

04-06

01 Multi Rate VAT Invoice Entry

Most of the traders deal with same Rate of VAT on all Items in an Invoice, as they deal with one type of Item (e.g, an Electrical Goods Trader deals with Electrical Goods which are charged with same VAT Rate (e.g 4%). Single Rate VAT Invoice is most common. Only large stores, dealing with different kinds of Items (like Super Stores / Departmental Stores, etc) need to create Multi VAT Rate Invoice (Invoices in which different VAT Rates are applied on different Items)

We have already explained Single Rate VAT invoice entry (§02/04-03, §03/04-03). You may make Invoice with Multiple VAT Rates in the same way.

02 Invoice Entry Configuration

At *Other Options* section of *Purchase / Sales Invoice Configuration* screen (§04/03-02/S1), set the following options related to VAT, as required (F-1A):

- **Allow Selection of VAT Class during Entry**: Set *Yes* to get the list of VAT Class to select from, during Voucher Entry, else set No. If the VAT Class are mapped for Sales / Purchase Accounts, then set *No*, as the VAT Classification would be automatically carried from the respective Ledger Accounts & Stock Items.
- **Warn on Mismatch on VAT Rates**: Set Yes to get warning when VAT Rate entered in Voucher differs with the specified VAT Rate as per VAT Classification and other parameters set (to trap mistake in entry of VAT Rates), else set No (No Warning would be shown)
- **Activate E1 / E2 Transaction**: Set *Yes* to enter E1 / E2 Transactions

Statutory	
Calculate Tax on current Sub-Total	? **No**
(else calculations are on Inventory Total only)	
Allow selection of VAT/Tax Class during entry	? **No**
Warn on Mismatch in VAT Rates	? **No**
Activate 'E1' or 'E2' Transaction (VAT)	? **No**

F-1A: Invoice Configuration

03 Multi-Class Purchase Invoice Entry

Purchase Invoice entry has been explained earlier (§02/07-03). Here we discuss about multiple VAT entry (VAT details for each Stock Item).

Stock Items Entry: Enter the Stock Item details in respect of each Item (F-2A)

- **Item detail**: At *Name of Item*, select the Stock Item and enter details (Quantity/ Rate / Value) to get the VAT Class screen for the Stock Item (F-2D). At Accounting Allocation screen for the Item, enter the VAT Class & Item value
    - o **VAT Class:** At VAT Class screen (F-2D), the applicable VAT Class for the Item and the VAT Amount is carried.

This way, enter each Item and the corresponding VAT Class

Ledger Accounts Entry

- **Input VAT Ledger Entry**: After entry of Item Details (F-2A), select the Input VAT ledger. The corresponding VAT amount is carried. This way, enter all the applicable VAT ledger Accounts & Amount one by one
- **Other Ledger Accounts Entry**: Next enter other Ledger Accounts and the Rate / Amount.

Tax Invoice: At *Is Purchase against Tax Invoice* (F-2A):

- Set *Yes* if the Purchase Bill issued by supplier is a Tax Invoice (to avail Input Tax Credit).
- Set *No* if the Purchase Bill issued by supplier is a not a Tax Invoice (Input Tax Credit cannot be availed).

Now enter Voucher Narration (F-2A) and save the Voucher.

Accounting Voucher Creation Ctrl + M

Purchase No. 4 — 31-Jul-2013, Wednesday

Supplier Invoice No. : 7 Date : 31-Jul-2013

Party's A/c Name : B B Traders

VAT/Tax Class : Not Applicable

Name of Item	Quantity	Rate	per	Amount
Glow Lamp Phillips 100W	10 Pcs	12.00	Pcs	120.00
Lamp Shades	5 Pcs	220.00	Pcs	1,100.00
				1,220.00
Input VAT 12.5%		12.50	%	137.50
Input VAT 4%		4	%	4.80

Is Purchase against Tax Invoice ? Yes

Show Statutory Details ? Yes

Narration: 15 Pcs 1,362.30

F-2A: Purchase Invoice with multiple VAT Rate

Accounting Details for : **Glow Lamp Phillips 100W**
Upto: **₹ 120.00 Dr**

Particulars	VAT/Tax Class	Amount
Purchase @4%	Purchases @ 4%	120.00
		120.00

F-2B: Item Allocation for Ledger

Statutory Details

Particulars			VAT
Assessable Value			1,220.00
Glow Lamp Phillips 100W			120.00
Item Value			*120.00*
Lamp Shades			1,100.00
Item Value			*1,100.00*
VAT Amount			142.30
Input VAT 12.5%		12.50 %	137.50
Lamp Shades	@ 12.50 % On 1,100.00		*137.50*
Input VAT 4%		4 %	4.80
Glow Lamp Phillips 100W	@ 4 % On 120.00		*4.80*

F-2C:Stautory Details

VAT/Tax Class	*Assessable Value*
Input VAT @ 12.5%	1,100.00

F-2D: VAT Class for Item

04 Multi-Class Sales Invoice Entry

Single VAT Class Sales Invoice entry has been explained earlier (§03/07-03). Here we discuss about multiple VAT entry (Different VAT Rates for each Stock Item) Sales Voucher entry (F-3A).

Stock Items Entry

- **Item detail**: At *Name of Item* (F-3A), select the Stock Item and enter details (Quantity/ rate / Value) to get the VAT Class screen for the Stock Item (F-3B).
- **VAT Class:** At *VAT Class screen* (F-3C), the applicable VAT Class for the Item and the VAT Amount is carried.

This way, enter each Item and the corresponding VAT Class

Ledger Accounts Entry

- **Output VAT Ledger Entry**: After entry of Item Details, select the Output VAT ledger. The corresponding VAT amount is carried. This way, enter all the applicable VAT ledger Accounts & Amount one by one
- **Other Ledger Accounts Entry**: Next enter other Ledger Accounts, if any, and the Rate / Amount

Accounting Voucher Creation Ctrl + M

Sales No. 1 — **13-May-2013** Monday

Ref. :

Party's A/c Name : **B B Traders**

Name of Item	Quantity	Rate per	Amount
Glow Lamp Phillips 100W	3 Pcs	15.00 Pcs	45.00
Lamp Shades	3 Pcs	250.00 Pcs	750.00
			795.00
Output VAT 4%		4 %	1.80
Output VAT 12.5%		12.50 %	93.75
Show Statutory Details ? **Yes**			
Narration:	6 Pcs		890.55
Sale of Goods			

F-3A: Sale Invoice with multiple VAT Rate

Accounting Details for : **Glow Lamp Phillips 100W**
Upto: ₹ **45.00 Cr**

Particulars	VAT/Tax Class	Amount
Sales @4%	Sales @ 4%	45.00
		45.00

F-3B: Sale Item VAT details

ABC Traders

Statutory Details

Particulars	VAT
Assessable Value	795.00
VAT Amount	95.55

F-3C: Statutory Details of Sale Invoice

Statutory Details: Set Yes at *Show Statutory Details* to view Assessable Value / VAT Amount of the Invoice (Click *F1:Detailed* to view Itemwise Assessable Value / VAT details) Now enter Voucher Narration (F-3A) and save the Voucher.

05 VAT on MRP

For some Items, VAT is to be computed on MRP Rate printed on Pack instead of actual Sale Rate. To compute VAT on MRP, instead of Sales Price, at Stock Item entry screen (F-4A), click *F2:Configure* to get *Stock Item Configuration screen* (F-4B).

MRP Activation: At Stock Item entry / alteration, click F12:Configure to get Stock Item Master *Configuration screen* (F-4B), At *Stock Item Master Configuration screen* (F-4B), set *Yes* at Calculate *VAT on MRP / Marginal* (you must also set *Yes* at *Allow Advanced Entries in Master*)

MRP details at Stock Item Master: Consequently, In Stock Item Master Entry (F-4A), you get additional fields for VAT details for the Stock Item, as follows:

- **MRP Price**: At *MRP / Marginal,* enter the MRP price (on which VAT is to be computed) for the Stock Item
- **Use MRP to print**: At *Use MRP to print,* set *No* to compute Vat on MRP.

Stock Item Alteration — **ABC Traders**

Name : **Glow Lamp Phillips 100W**

↑ ... 3 more | ↑ ... 1 more

Tariff Classification	: **Not Applicable**
Rate of Duty (eg 5)	: **0**
VAT Details	
Commodity	: **Electrical Goods 4%**
Rate of VAT (%)	: **4**
MRP / Marginal	: **15**
Use MRP to print	: **No**
MRP Incl. of VAT	? n

F-4A: VAT Rate specification in Stock Item Master

Now enter the Sale Invoice as usual. The MRP Value would be shown below the Stock Item details for Reference (F-5A)

Stock Item Configuration

Allow ALIASES along with Names	? No
Allow Language ALIASES along with Names	? No
Allow ADVANCED entries in Masters	? Yes
Calculate VAT on MRP/Marginal	? Yes
Use PART NUMBERS for Stock Items	? No
Use Description for Stock Items	? No
Use REMARKS for Stock Items	? No
Specify Default Ledger Allocation for Invoicing	? No
Use ALTERNATE UNITS for Stock Items	? No
Allow Std. Rates for Stock Items	? No
Allow Component list details (Bill of Materials)	? No

F-4B: Stock Item Master Configuration

At *Show Statutory Details*, set Yes to see the details of computation of VAT (F-5A). The Statutory details is only for info and not a part of Sale Invoice). At *Statutory details screen.* click *F1:Details* button to get the complete details of VAT Computation (F-5B)

Accounting Voucher Creation Ctrl + M

Sales No. 1 — 15-May-2013, Wednesday
Ref.: 34
Party's A/c Name : **H P Traders**

Name of Item	Quantity	Rate	per	Amount
Glow Lamp Phillips 100W	3 Pcs	14.00	Pcs	42.00
MRP/ Marginal: 15.00/Pcs				
Output VAT 4%		4	%	1.80
Show Statutory Details ? Yes				
Narration:	3 Pcs			43.80

Sale on MRP Rate

F-5A: Sale Invoice with VAT on MRP

Statutory Details

Particulars			VAT
Assessable Value			42.00
Glow Lamp Phillips 100W	*MRP:45.00*		42.00
Item Value			*42.00*
VAT Amount			1.80
Output VAT 4%		4 %	1.80
Glow Lamp Phillips 100W @ 4 % On 45.00			*1.80*

F-5B: Statutory details for Sale Invoice with VAT on MRP

05.01 MRP Inclusive of VAT

Sometimes, the MRP rate may be inclusive of VAT. If No is set at *Use MRP to print*, at *MRP Incl of VAT*, you may further set

- Yes if the MRP (as entered at MRP / Marginal) is inclusive of VAT
- No if the MRP (as entered at MRP / Marginal) is inclusive of VAT

If MRP Rate is inclusive of VAT, the VAT calculation for the above transaction is explained below:

The effective **VAT%** on VAT inclusive Sale Value is calculated as (100*Rate of VAT)/ (100+Rate of VAT)

For example, the VAT @12.5% on Value inclusive of VAT on MRP is calculated as:

Effective VAT Rate=12.5/112.5 =0.1111=11.11%. So, the effective Rate is 11.11 % on MRP Sale Value inclusive of VAT.

Therefore VAT amount = (Effective VAT % * MRP Value)= (11.11 % on 750) =Rs 83.33.

You may verify it through back calculation from Sale Value. Sale Value @MRP Rate inclusive of VAT = 250x3=750. VAT included is 83.33. So, the net sale value as per MRP, exclusive of VAT is 750.00-83.33 = 666.67. VAT @ 12.5% on 666.67 = (666.67 x 12.5) / 100= 83.33

Note that the MRP (Rs 250) is inclusive of VAT, while the actual sale price (Rs 230) is exclusive of VAT (so VAT is added extra). Here MRP value inclusive of VAT is Rs 750. So, Sale Price exclusive of VAT at MRP is 750-83.33 = 666.67. You may cross check the VAT @ 12.5% on 666.67 = 83.33

Accounting Voucher Creation Ctrl + M

Sales No. 2 — 20-May-2013, Monday
Ref.: 28
Party's A/c Name : **H P Traders**

Name of Item	Quantity	Rate	per	Amount
Lamp Shades	3 Pcs	230.00	Pcs	690.00
MRP/ Marginal: 250.00/Pcs				
Output VAT 12.5%		12.50	%	83.33
Show Statutory Details ? Yes				
Narration:	3 Pcs			773.33

MRP inclusive of VAT

F-6A: Invoice inclusive of VAT on MRP

Stock Item Alteration — ABC Traders

Name : **Lamp Shades**

↑ ... 3 more | ↑ ... 1 more

Tariff Classification	: **Not Applicable**
Rate of Duty (eg 5)	: **0**
VAT Details	
Commodity	: **Electrical Goods 12.5%**
Rate of VAT (%)	: **12.50**
MRP / Marginal	: **250**
Use MRP to print	: **No**
MRP Incl. of VAT	? **Yes**

F-6B: VAT Rate specification in Stock Item Master

Statutory Details

Particulars			VAT
Assessable Value			690.00
Lamp Shades	*MRP:750.00*		690.00
Item Value			*690.00*
VAT Amount			83.33
Output VAT 12.5%		12.50 %	83.33
Lamp Shades @ 12.50 % On 666.67			*83.33*

F-6C: Statutory details of Invoice

In the same way, you may create Purchase Invoice for VAT on MRP and MRP inclusive of VAT.

06 Consignment / Branch Transfers

Consignment / Branch Transfer is just transfer of goods from one place to another. It is not Sales. So, VAT is not charged in such Sales (Transfer) voucher.

Create Ledger Account for:

- *Consignee / Branch Account* (under the Group *Branch / Division*, or its subgroup), like Customer Ledger Account (F-7A), discussed earlier. Enter the VAT details as usual (F-7B)
- *Consignment Outwards Account* (under the Group *Direct Income*, or its subgroup), like Sales Ledger Account (F-8A), discussed earlier. At VAT Classification, select *Consignment / Branch Transfer Outwards* from the list (F-8B).
- *Consignment Inwards Account* (under the Group *Direct Expenses*, or its subgroup), like Purchase Ledger Account)F-9A), discussed earlier. At VAT Classification, select *Consignment / Branch Transfer Inwards* from the list (F-9B).

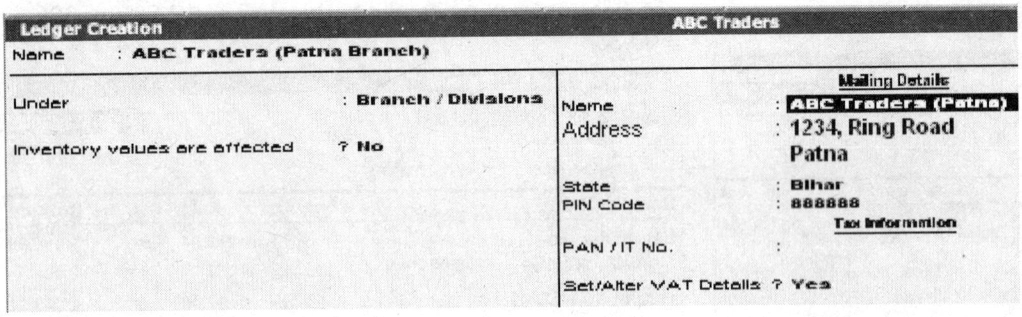

F-7A: Branch / Consignment Agent Ledger creation

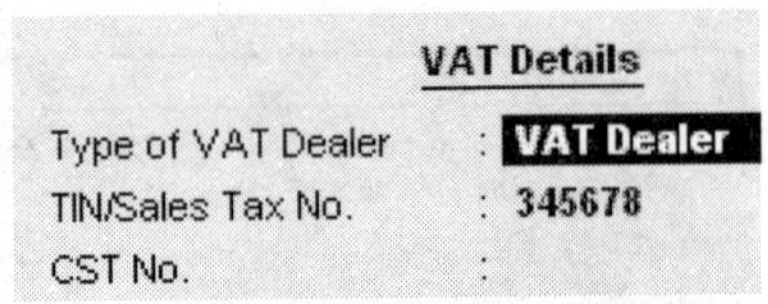

F-7B: VAT details of Branch Ledger Account

06.01 Consignment Outwards for Sales

Now create a Sales Voucher for Transfer to Agent / Branch. At Sales Voucher entry screen, Click *V:As Voucher* button to enter the Sales Voucher in Voucher Mode.

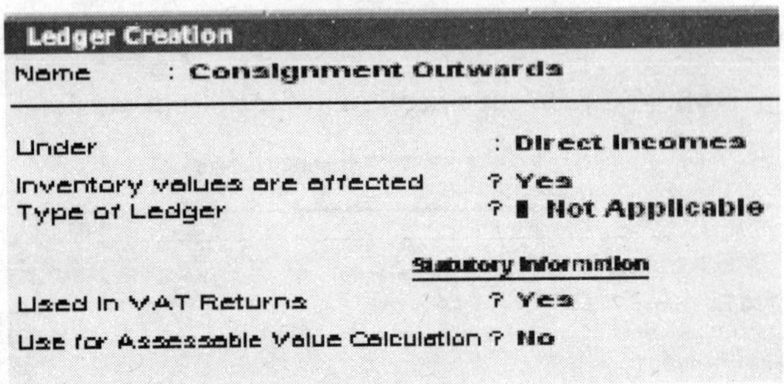

F-8A: Consignment Outwards Ledger Account

Configuration set up: Click *F12:Configure* to get Voucher entry Configuration screen:

- Set *Yes* at *Allow Income Accounts in Sales Voucher* to get the Account Consignment Outwards (under Direct Income Group) in the selection list of Ledger Accounts during Voucher entry
- Set *Yes* at *Show Inventory Details*, to show Inventory details as entered in *Inventory Allocation screen* (F-8D) in main voucher screen (F-8C), else, set *No* (Inventory details will not be shown in main voucher screen)

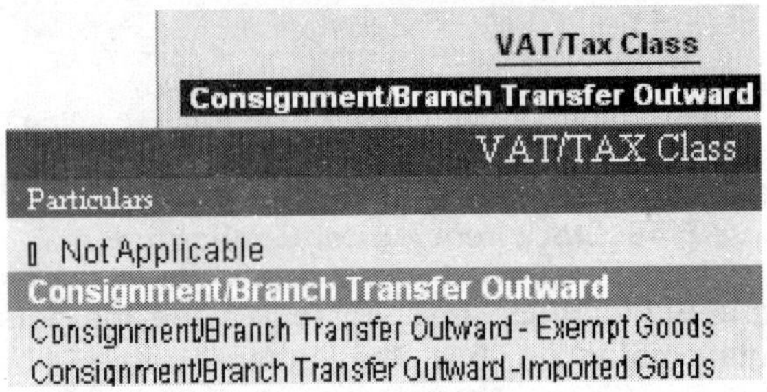

F-8B: VAT Class for Consignment Outwards

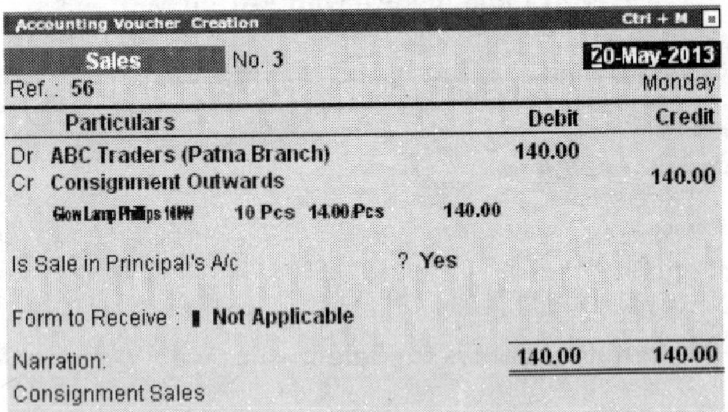

F-8C: Consignment sales Voucher entry

Voucher Entry

In Voucher entry, (F-8C), enter as follows:

- **Ledger Accounts:**
  - o **Consignee Account**: Select the Consignee / Branch Account and enter the Amount (value of Item transferred) at Debit Column
  - o **Consignment Account**: Select the Consignment Outwards Account to get *Inventory Allocation* screen (F-8D).

- **Item Allocation:** At *Inventory Allocation* screen, select the Item, enter Quantity & Rate. You get the VAT Class Allocation screen (the default VAT Class as set for the Consignment Outwards Account (F-8E) is carried, which you may change if needed.

  This way, enter the details of all the Stock Items transferred. After Item details entry, you get back to the main voucher entry screen.

- **Sale Type**: At *Is Sale on Principal Account* (F-8C), set *Yes*
- **Tax Forms:**At *Forms to Receive* (F-8C), select the applicable form to be received, if any (else select *Not Applicable*) from the list of Forms (F-10C).
- **Voucher Narration**: Enter Voucher Narration and save the Voucher

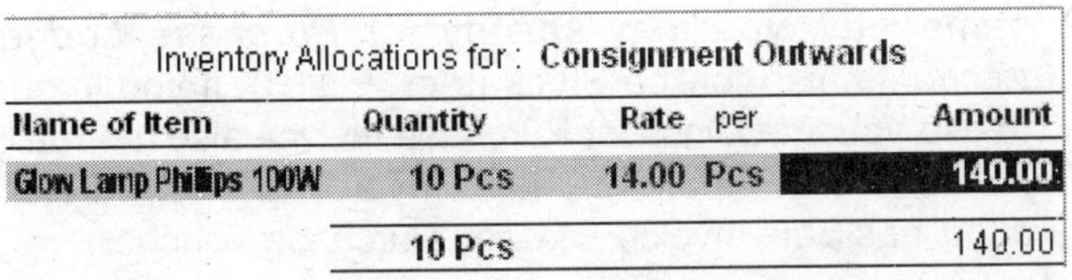

F-8D: Item Allocation in Consignment Outwards Ledger

F-8E: VAT Class for Consignment Outwards

06.02 Consignment Inwards for Purchase

In the same way, you may create Purchase Voucher for Purchase Inwards, for Transfer from Agent / Branch. At Purchase Voucher entry screen, Click *V:As Voucher* button to enter the Purchase Voucher in Voucher Mode. Click *F12:Configure* to get *Voucher entry Configuration* screen.

Configuration Set Up: At Voucher entry Configuration screen, set as follows:

- Set *Yes* at *Allow Expenses / Fixed Assets Accounts in Purchase Voucher* to get the *Consignment Inwards* Account (under Direct Expenses Group) in the selection list of Ledger Accounts during Voucher entry (F-9B)
- Set *Yes* at *Show Inventory Details* to show the Stock Item Details in main voucher screen (F-10A), else set *No* (Inventory details as entered in *Inventory Allocation screen* will not be shown in main voucher screen)

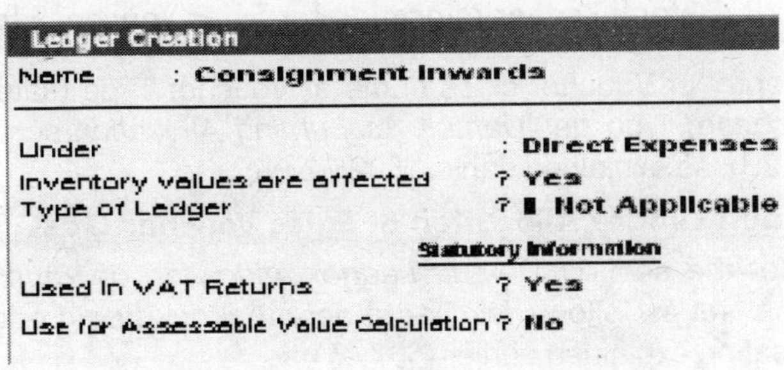

F-9A: Consignment Outwards Ledger Account

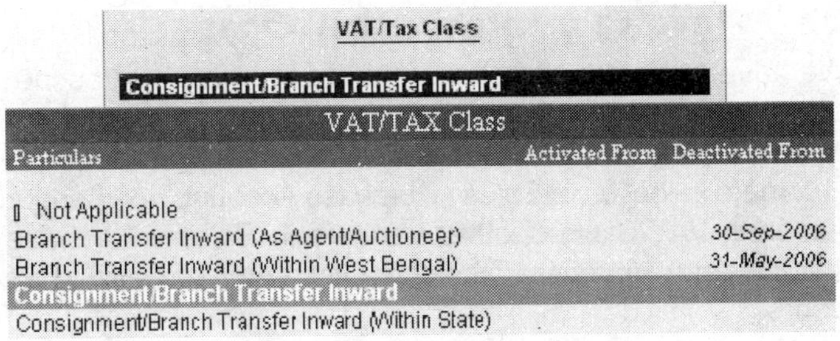

F-9B: VAT Class for Consignment Inwards Ledger Account

Voucher Entry: In Voucher entry screen (F-10A):

- **Ledger Accounts:**
  - o **Consignee Account**: Select the Consignee / Branch Account and enter the Amount (value of Item transferred), at Credit Column
  - o **Consignment Account**: Select the *Consignment Inwards* Account to get *Inventory Allocation* screen.
    - **Item Allocation:**At *Inventory Allocation* screen, select the Item, enter Quantity & Rate. You get the VAT Class Allocation screen (the default VAT Class as set for the Consignment Inwards Account (F-10B) is carried, which you may change if needed.

      This way, enter the details of all the Stock Items transferred. After Item details entry, you get back to the main voucher entry screen.

- **Tax Forms**:At *Forms to Issue* (F-10A), select the applicable form to be received, if any (else select *Not Applicable*) from the list of Forms (F-10C)
- **Voucher Narration**: Enter Voucher Narration and save the Voucher

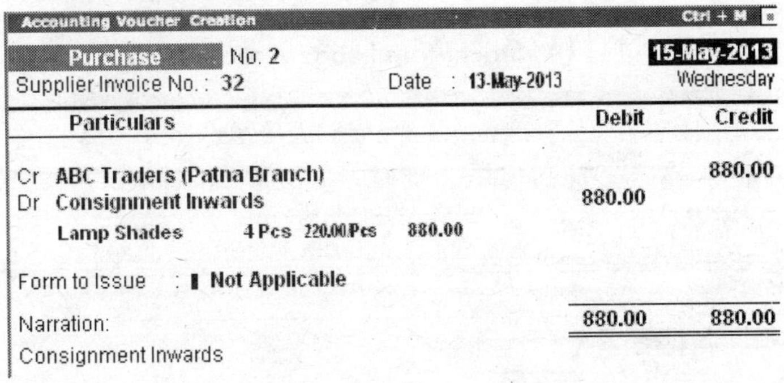

F-10A: Purchase Voucher for Consignment Inwards

F-10B: VAT Class at Voucher entry

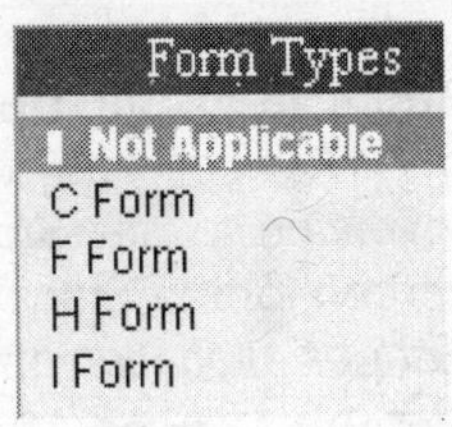

F-10C: Form selection

07 Invoice using Voucher Class

We have explained the concept and advantage of Voucher Class for Sales / Purchase Invoice (§01/08-01). For Invoicing with VAT, use of Voucher Class considerably helps to automate selection of Sales / Purchase Account, VAT Ledger Account, VAT Class & other Ledgers in Sales / Purchase Invoice entry. Voucher Class expedites entry and eliminates errors.

Through Voucher Class, you may enter prices inclusive of VAT and auto allocate internally the apportioned amount of VAT into respective Sales / Purchase Ledgers and Input / Output VAT ledgers. This dramatically simplifies the VAT Invoice entry for retailers, eliminating the process of VAT details entry

Here we explain the process of setting up Masters & Voucher Class VAT Class and entry process of Sales / Purchase Invoice using VAT Class.

07.01 Stock Item Master set up

- **Stock Item Master *Configuration* Set Up**: At respective Stock Item Master Entry / Edit, click *F12:Configure* to get *Stock Item Master Entry configuration screen* (§01/02-01/S2). At *Stock Item Master Entry configuration screen*, set *Yes* at *Specify default ledger allocation for Invoicing*.

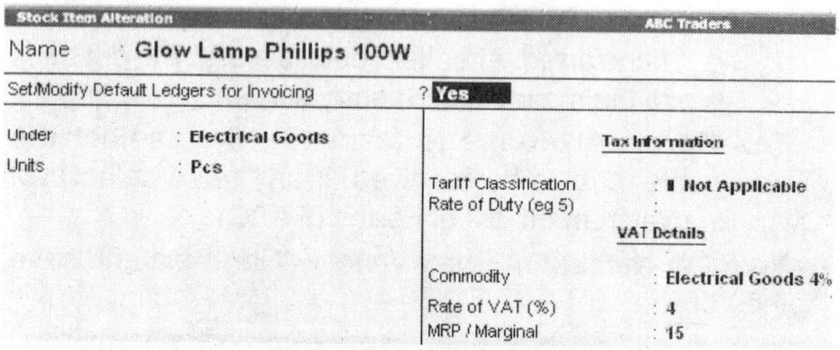

F-11A: Stock Item Ledger creation

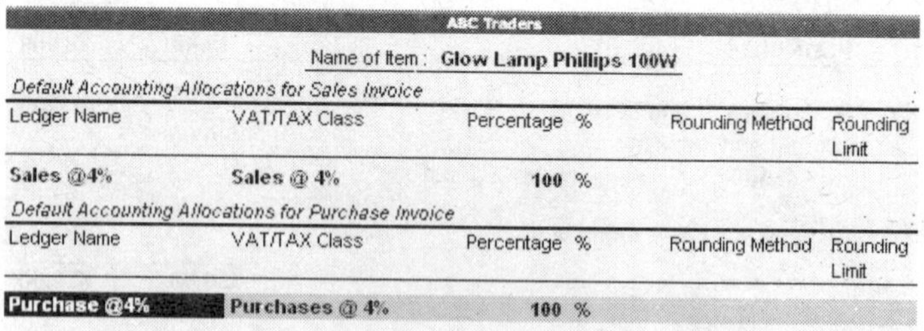

F-11B: Default Stock Item Ledger allocation at Voucher Class

- **Stock Item Set Up**: At *Stock Item Master entry/ edit* (F-11A), set *Yes* at *Set/Modify Default Ledgers for Invoicing* to get *Stock Item default Ledger Allocation* screen for the Stock Item (F-11B). specify under *default Ledger Allocation* as follows:
- **Default Ledger Allocation for Sales Invoice:** Under the head *default Accounting Allocation for Sales Invoice* (F-11B), specify as under:
    - o **Ledger Name**: At *Ledger Name* column, select the Sales ledger to which the Item Sales Value would be posted.
    - o **VAT/Tax class**: At *VAT Clas* column, select the VAT Class applicable
    - o **Percentage**: Enter the percentage of Sales value allocable to Ledger
    - o **Rounding Method**: Enter the Rounding Method (if the allocation is not 100%),
    - o **Rounding Limit**: Enter the Rounding Limit for the Rounding Method Specified

  You may allocate the Item Value in multiple ledgers (if the Sales Value is to be allocated o other ledger accounts also), the total of the percentages of all ledger accounts would be 100.
- **Default Ledger Allocation for Purchase Invoice** In the same way, you may specify for *Purchase Ledger* Accounts also for the Stock Item (F-11B), if you intend to use Voucher Class for Purchase Invoice also (normally not recommended, Purchase Invoice is entered from supplier's Sale Invoice, through Purchase Voucher)

07.02 VAT Voucher Class Set Up

Voucher Class set up is explained earlier (§02/05-05). Here we specify the steps related to VAT only

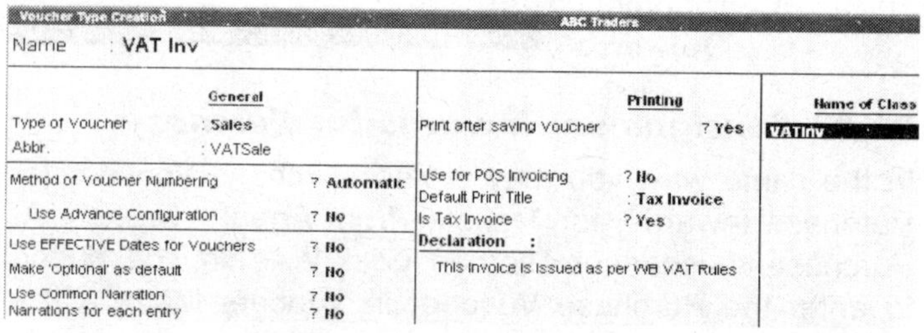

F-12A: Sales Voucher Class creation

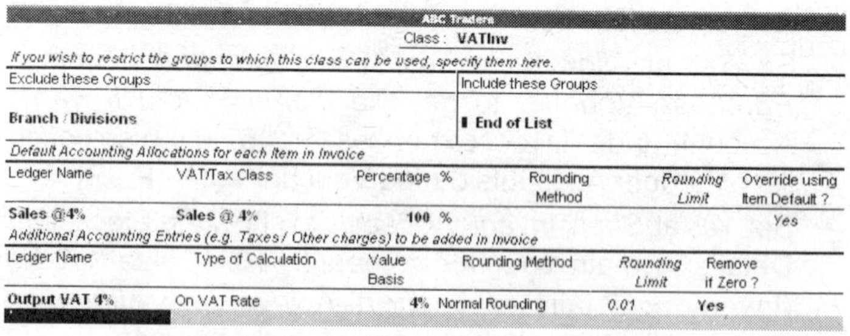

F-12B: Default Ledger Allocation for Sales Voucher Class

On entry of Voucher class name at Voucher Type (sales / Purchase), you get *Default Accounting Allocation* screen (F-12B), as explained earlier (§02/02-05)

Default Ledger Allocation of Sales Voucher Class

Under the section *Default Ledger Allocation of Voucher Class*, set as follows (similar to default Stock Item Ledger Allocation explained earlier (§07.01):

Ledger Name At *Ledger Name* column, select the Sales ledger to which Item Sales Value would be posted

VAT/TAX Class At *VAT/Tax class* column, select the applicable VAT/Tax class

Percentage % At *Percentage* column, enter the percentage. In case of single ledger / VAT class, enter 100% here. In case the sales amount is to be apportioned amongst multiple ledgers / VAT classes, enter the percentage at which the sales proceeds will be apportioned. The total percentage of all allocated ledgers must be 100.

Rounding Method In case of multiple ledger / VAT class, at *Rounding Method* column, select the round off by method from the list (except for the last one).

Rounding Limit On choosing for rounding off, at *Rounding Limit column,* enter the rounding limit, e.g.,.5 for 50 paise, 1 for rounding off to the rupee.

Override using Item default At *Override using Item default* column, set as follows:

- Set Yes to override (allow changes) the sales Ledger and VAT class specified as above in the Voucher Class, during voucher entry.
- Set *No* to post the sale value of the Item to sales ledger and VAT class specified in Stock Item master (F-11B),

Additional Accounting Entries: At *Additional Accounting Entries* section, enter the details of VAT and other ledgers accounts which may be entered in Sales Invoice. If any other billing terms, (e.g discount ledgers) are applicable for the VAT class, select them prior to the VAT ledger.

When you enter Invoice using Voucher Class, the VAT will be automatically computed. However, if Assessable Value is dependent on any other ledger also, such ledger should appear prior to the output VAT ledger to prompt for input of Assessable value, if multiple VAT classes are involved in the Invoice

07.03 Invoice Entry using Voucher Class

The Invoice entry through VAT Class is similar to normal Invoice Entry explained earlier (§03/04-03). The advantage is the VAT Class etc are auto selected and values for all Ledger Accounts are auto computed as per rules / computation method specified. So, Invoicing becomes secured (amounts cannot be edited), correct and fast.

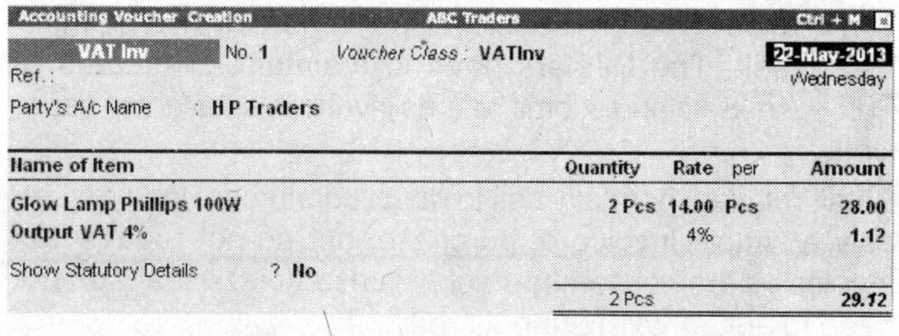

F-13A: Invoice creation using VAT Class

FAQ: Frequently Asked Question

FAQ: How to create a Sales Invoice with multiple VAT Class

Ans: At *Other Option* section of Purchase / Sales Invoice Configuration screen (§04/03-02), set *Yes* at *Allow selection of VAT Class during Entry* to select Voucher Class against each Stock Item, during Voucher Entry.

During Voucher Entry, on selection of a Stock Item, select the Sales Account, and then select the corresponding VAT Class, enabling entry of multiple VAT Class for different Stock Items in one Invoice

After entry of all Stock Items, in the Invoice, select Output VAT ledger Account and select the respective VAT Class. The VAT Amount for the respective liked VAT Class is auto carried.

Thus you enter a Sales Invoice with multiple VST Class in the same Invoice.

VAT Composition

04-07

01 VAT Composition

So far we discussed VAT for registered dealers, who issue Tax Invoice. Traders (Buyers) use VAT Tax invoice for Input VAT credit. The Dealers have to maintain all records of Purchase, Sale and submit returns involving substantial paper work.

Small retailers normally sell to direct consumers who require only a simple invoice of purchase, but do not require Tax Invoice as their buyers (personal consumers) usually do not need to adjust VAT for input credit.

To reduce the Tax burden and the onerous task of maintaining numerous records and returns, the law provides a simple to work *VAT composition scheme* for small retailers.

01.01 Eligibility for VAT Composition scheme

- Small Retailers (with turnover not more than 50 Lacs) may opt for VAT Composition Scheme.
- Manufacturers, Dealers, Inter Sate traders, Importers / Exporters etc., are not eligible for Composition Scheme

Dealers under Composition Scheme pay Tax at much lower

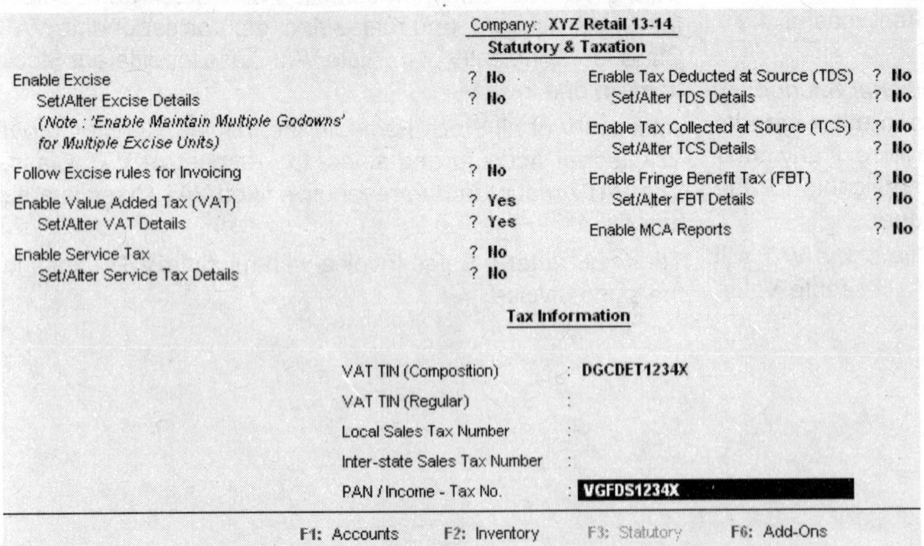

Company: XYZ Retail 13-14

Statutory & Taxation

Enable Excise	? No	Enable Tax Deducted at Source (TDS)	? No
Set/Alter Excise Details	? No	Set/Alter TDS Details	? No
(Note : 'Enable Maintain Multiple Godowns' for Multiple Excise Units)		Enable Tax Collected at Source (TCS)	? No
		Set/Alter TCS Details	? No
Follow Excise rules for Invoicing	? No	Enable Fringe Benefit Tax (FBT)	? No
Enable Value Added Tax (VAT)	? Yes	Set/Alter FBT Details	? No
Set/Alter VAT Details	? Yes	Enable MCA Reports	? No
Enable Service Tax	? No		
Set/Alter Service Tax Details	? No		

Tax Information

VAT TIN (Composition) : DGCDET1234X
VAT TIN (Regular) :
Local Sales Tax Number :
Inter-state Sales Tax Number :
PAN / Income - Tax No. : VGFDS1234X

F1: Accounts F2: Inventory F3: Statutory F6: Add-Ons

F-1A: Statutory & Taxation set up for VAT Composition

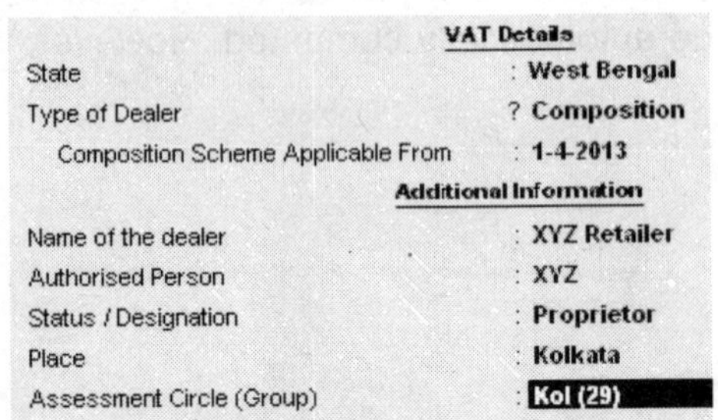

VAT Details

State : West Bengal
Type of Dealer ? Composition
Composition Scheme Applicable From : 1-4-2013

Additional Information

Name of the dealer : XYZ Retailer
Authorised Person : XYZ
Status / Designation : Proprietor
Place : Kolkata
Assessment Circle (Group) : Kol (29)

F-1B: VAT details set up for VAT Composition

rate but cannot avail the VAT input credit, cannot charge VAT and cannot issue Tax Invoice.

The dealers opting for VAT composition have to maintain all records of sales & purchase and file VAT Composition returns. Normally, the returns are to be submitted monthly, but in some states, small dealers may submit return quarterly or half yearly as per applicable rules of the state.

02 VAT Composition Features set up

At *Statutory & Taxation* screen (F-1A), as explained earlier (§02/07-02), set up as follows:

- At *Statutory & Taxation* screen (F-1A), enter VAT TIN at *VAT TIN (Composition)* field
- At VAT details screen (F-1B), enter as follows:
  - o At *Type of Dealer*, select *Composition.*
  - o At *Composition Scheme applicable from.* the Date from which the dealer become registered under Composition scheme,
  - o Under the section, *Additional* Information, enter the respective details as explained (§02/04-02).

03 VAT Composition related Ledgers

Ledger creation have already been explained (§04/04-02). We now explain the additional info to be entered relating to VAT Composition

03.01 VAT Composition Tax Ledger

At Ledger creation of VAT Ledger, as explained (§04.02/04-02), enter as follows (F-2A),

- At *Under*, select *Duties & Taxes* as parent Group
- At Type of Duty / Tax, select *Others*
- At *Use for Assessable Value for Calculation,* set No
- At *Percentage of Calculation*, enter 0 (zero), as no tax is to be charged for Composite Tax sales invoices.

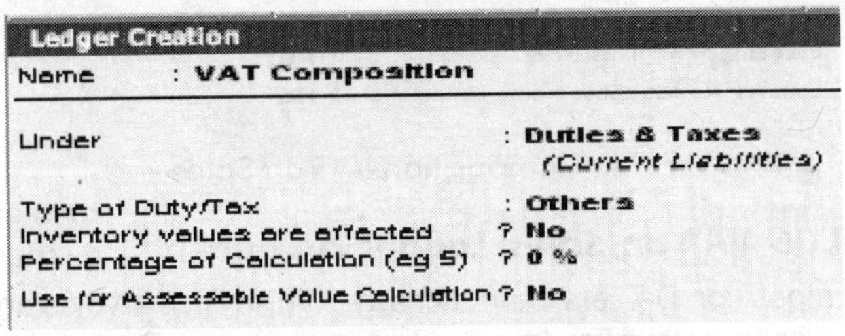

F-2A: VAT Composition Tax Ledger

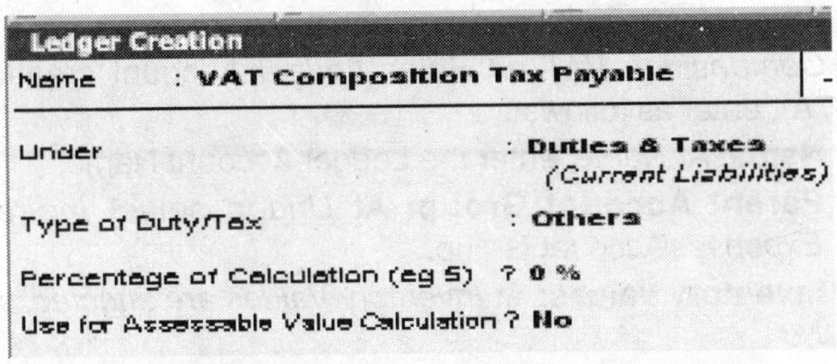

F-2B: VAT Composition Tax Payable Ledger

03.02 VAT Composition Tax Payable Ledger

The VAT Composition Tax Payable ledger represents the Composite VAT including Interest Payable u/s 33

At Ledger Accounts creation screen (F-2B), setas follows (similar to *VAT Composition Tax Ledger* as explained above (§03.01)

- At *Under*, select *Duties & Taxes* as parent Group at *Under* field.
- At Type of Duty / Tax, select *Others*
- At *Use for Assessable Value for Calculation*, Set No
- At Rate of Duty, enter 0 (zero) (as no tax is to be charged for Composite Tax sales invoices)

03.03 VAT Composition Purchase Ledger

In the same way, create Purchase Ledger as explained (04.01/04-02), At Purchase Ledger Accounts creation screen (F-3A)

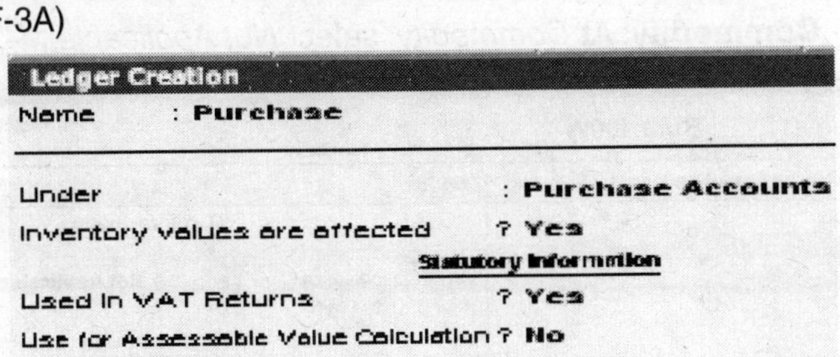

F-3A: Purchase Ledger (VAT Composition)

- At *Under* field, select *Purchase Account* as parent Group
- At *Inventory Values are affected,* set *Yes*
- At *Used in VAT Returns*, set *Yes* to get VAT Tax Class screen (F-3B),
  - o **VAT Tax class**: AT VAT Tax Class screen (F-3B), select the default VAT Class.

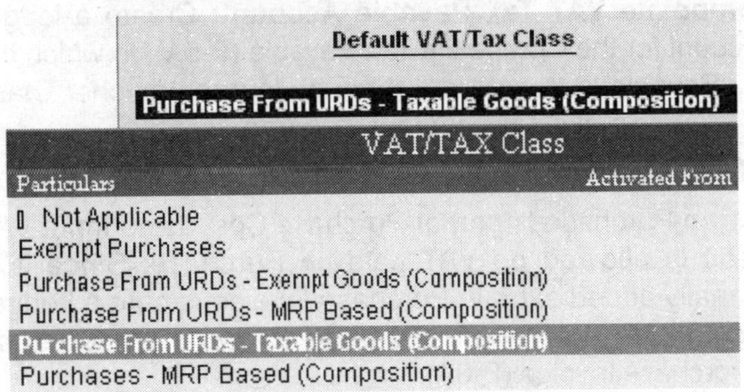

F-3B: VAT Class for Purchase

03.04 VAT Composition Sales Ledger

Similarly, create Sales Ledger as explained (04.01/04-02), At Sales Ledger Accounts creation screen (F-4A), set as follows:

- At *Under*, select *Sales Account* as parent Group
- Set *Yes* at *Inventory Values are affected*
- Set *Yes* at *Used in VAT Returns* to get VAT Tax class screen (F-4B)
  - o **VAT Tax class:** At *VAT Tax class* screen (F-4B), select the VAT composition Tax Class from the list.

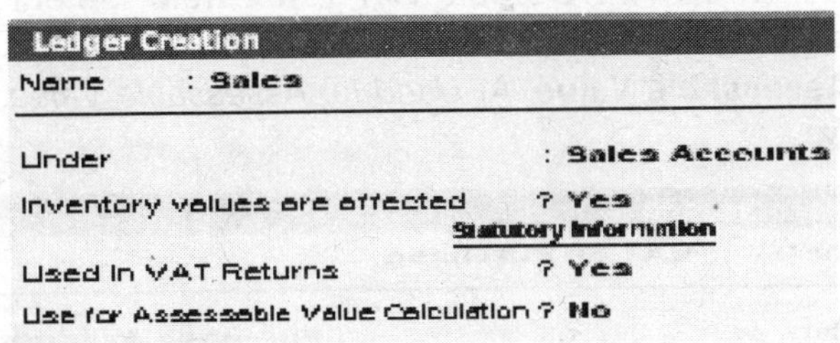

F-4A: Sales Ledger Creation

F-4B: VAT Class selection

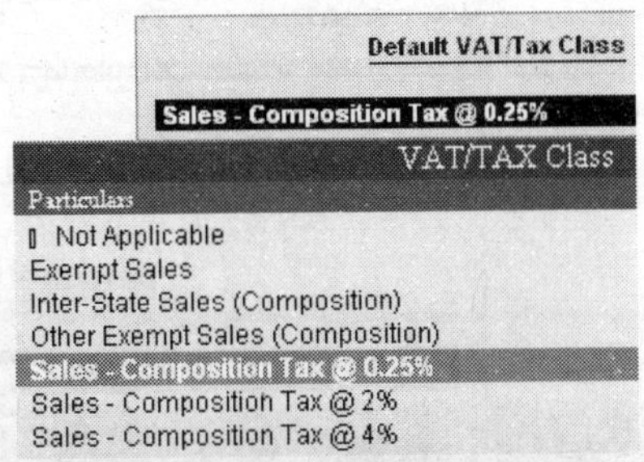

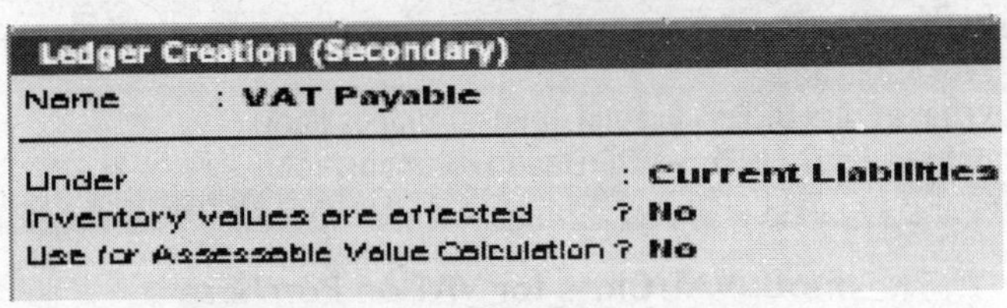

F-5A: VAT Payable Ledger Creation

> **Note:** *At VAT Tax Class screen (F-3B, F-4B), You may select* Not Applicable. *In that case, you will be prompted to select VAT Class during voucher entry, every time.*

Composite VAT Tax Payable Account: Create a ledger Account for the Composite Tax Payable (F-5A), to which the Tax Payable is transferred through Journal Voucher Class (F-13D), to make Tax payment therefrom

03.05 VAT on Purchase Ledger Account

VAT on Purchase is part of Purchase Cost as no Input VAT credit is allowed on VAT paid on Purchase. Since it is normally added extra in Purchase Invoice, create a Ledger Account (e.g *VAT on Purchase*) to enter the VAT Charged in Purchase Invoice (F-6A).

At *VAT on Purchase Ledger Account* creation (F-6A), enter as follows:

- **Name**: Enter the Name of Account
- **Parent Group**: At *Under* field Select *Direct Expenses / Indirect Expenses / Purchase* Account Group
- **Inventory Values are affected**: Since this is common expense on various purchase, there is no need to link it to individual Stock Item (treated as common cost of purchase). Set *No* at this field
- **Used for VAT Returns:** At *Used for VAT Returns*, set *Yes* to get *VAT Tax Class selection* screen (F-6B).
    - o **VAT Tax Class***:* At *VAT Tax Class selection* screen (F-6B), at *Default VAT / Tax* field, select the respective VAT / Tax Class
- **Assessable Value**: At *Used for Assessable Value*, set *No*

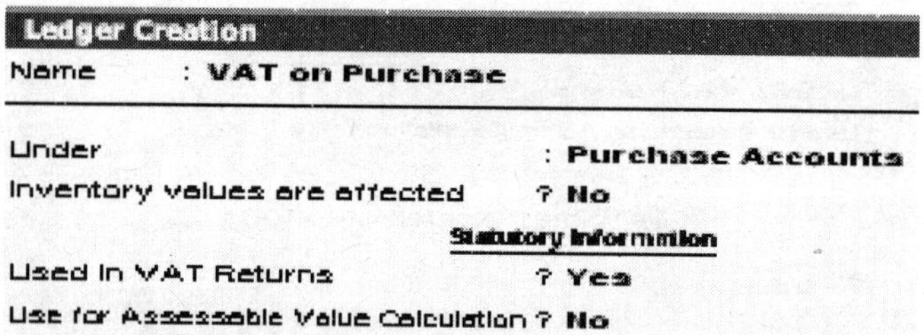

F-6A: VAT on Purchase Ledger Account

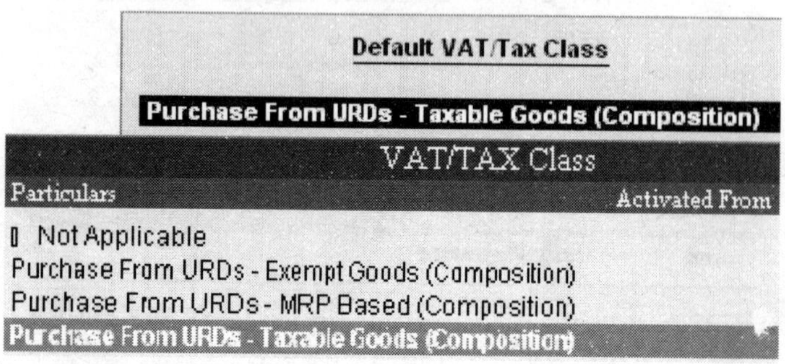

F-6B: VAT Class for VAT on Purchase

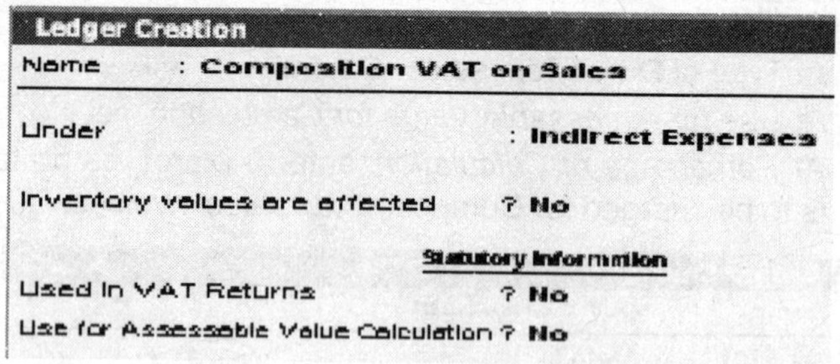

F-7A: Composition VAT on Sales

03.06 VAT on Sales Ledger Account

Composition Dealers cannot charge VAT in Sale Invoice and they cannot issue Tax Invoice. They have to pay Composition VAT at a low rate on total sales. So, for Composition VAT Dealers, VAT on Sales is an expense.

At *Composition VAT on Sales Ledger* Account creation (F-7A), enter as follows:

- **Name**: At *Name*, enter the Ledger Account Name
- **Parent Account Group:** At *Under*: select *Indirect Expenses* Account Group..
- **Inventory Values:** At *Inventory Values are affected*, set *No*
- **VAT Returns:** At *Used for VAT Returns*, **s**et *No*
- **Assessable Value**: At *Used for Assessable Value*, set *No*

03.07 Party Ledger Account

Create Customer & Supplier Ledger (F-9A) as discussed (§04.03/07-02).There is no additional info to be entered in Party Ledgers, relating to VAT. Set *No* at *Set / Alter VAT Details* at Party Ledger (F-9A).

04 Stock Item

The Stock Item creation is similar as described earlier (F-8A). At *Set Modify Default Ledgers* for Inventory,

- Set *Yes* to specify Voucher Class for Sales / Purchase, as explained earlier
- Set *No*, if you do not use Voucher Class for Sales / Purchase.

VAT Details of Stock Item: At *VAT details* section of Stock Item creation (F-8A):

- **Commodity**: At *Commodity*, select *Not Applicable*.

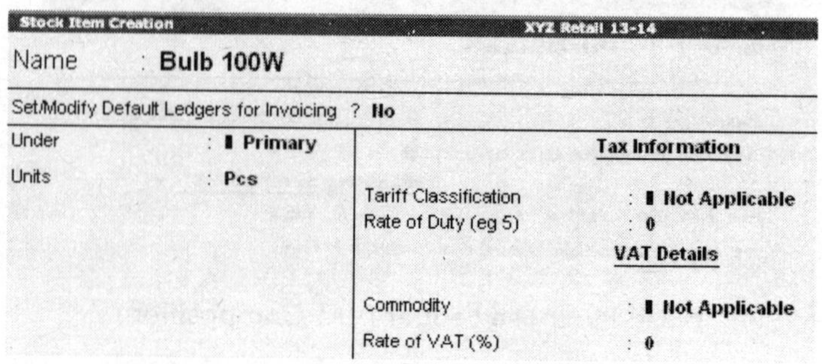

F-8A: Stock Item creation

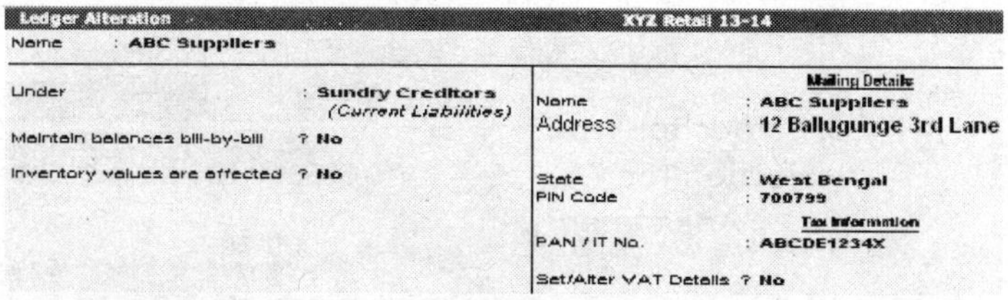

F-9A: Supplier Ledger

- **VAT Rate**: At *Rate of VAT*, enter zero, as VAT Composite Tax cannot be charged extra in the Sales Invoice, but is to be paid separately by the seller to the Government, as expense.

05 Purchase Invoice

Creation of Purchase Invoice has been explained earlier (§02/04-03). Here we explain Purchase Voucher creation (F-10A) by VAT composition Dealer

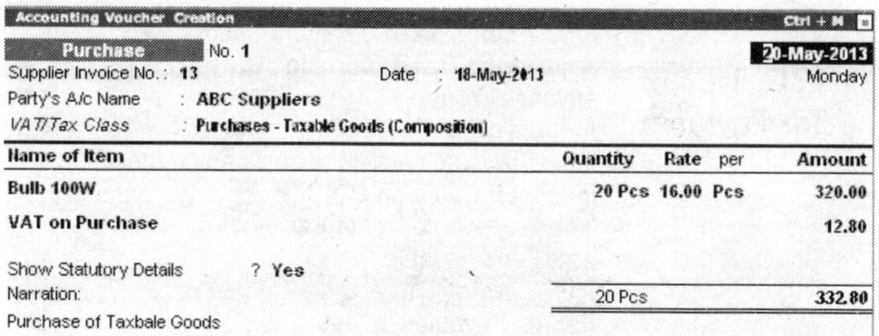

F-10A: Purchase of Taxable Goods from Registered Dealers

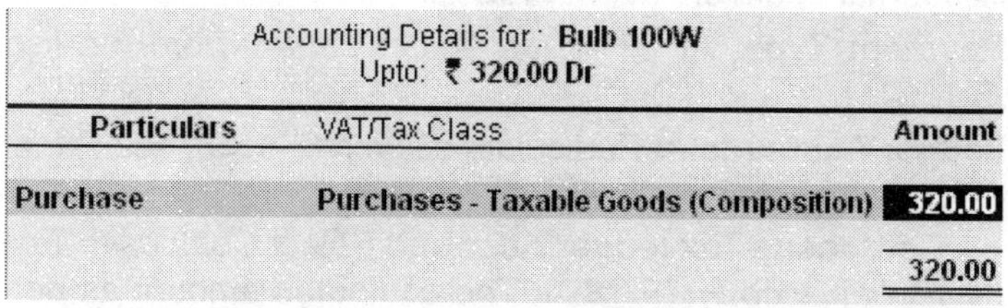

F-10B: Item Allocation screen

At Purchase Voucher creation screen (F-10A), enter as follows:

- **VAT / Tax Class**: At *VAT / Tax Class* field, select the VAT Class from the list
- **Item Details**: Select the Items and enter the Quantity, Rate/ Value for each Item to get Accounting Allocation screen for the Item (F-10B).
    - o **Accounting Allocation**: At *Accounting Allocation* screen (F-10B), at *Particulars*, select the Purchase Ledger Account. At *VAT / Tax Class*, the default VAT Class & at *Amount*, the Item Value is carried.

  This way, enter the Item details for all the Items and Accounting Allocation for each Item.
- **Ledger Accounts**: After entry of Item details, enter VAT Ledger and other Accounts (if any), as per the Purchase Invoice (i.e Sale Invoice of the Supplier) and enter the respective amount for each Ledger Account
- **Voucher Narration**: Enter Voucher Narration, if any.

Save the Voucher.

06 Sales Invoice

Creation of Sales Invoice has been explained (§03/04-03). Here we explain Sales Voucher creation (F-11A) by VAT composition Dealer

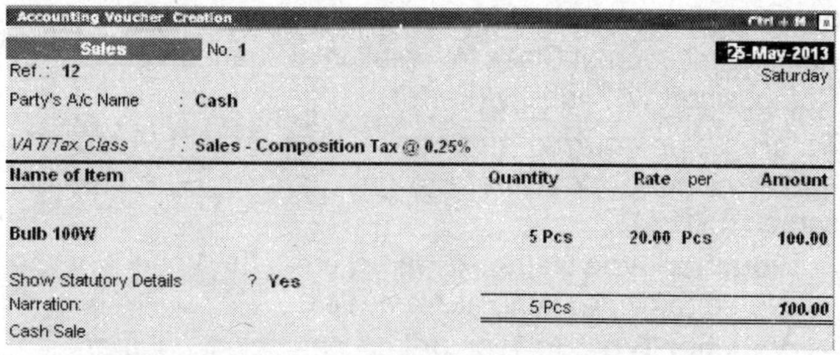

F-11A: Sales Invoice of Composition Dealer

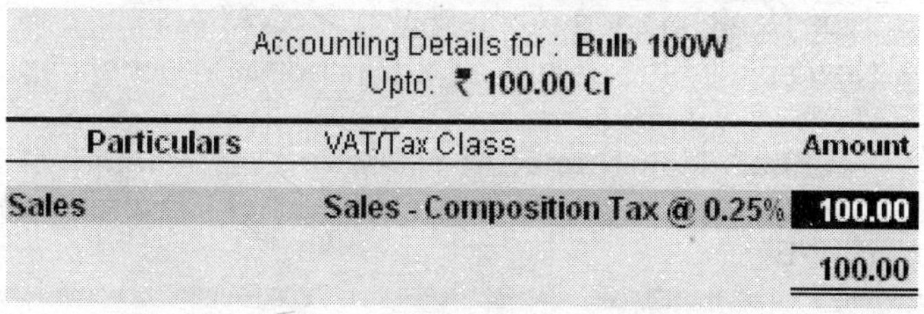

F-11B: Accounting Allocation screen

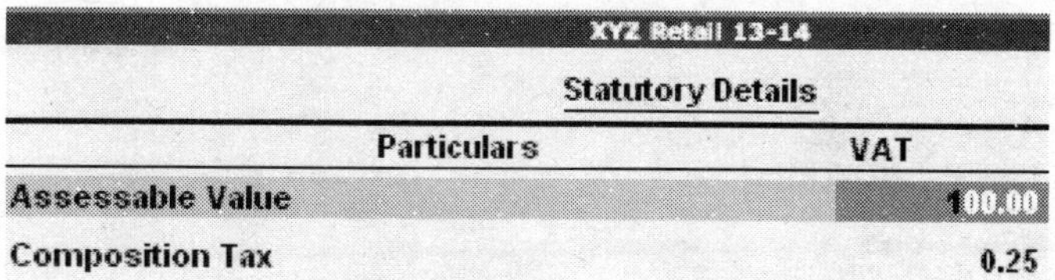

F-11C: Statutory details of Sales Invoice

At Sales Voucher creation screen (F-11A), enter as follows:

- **VAT / Tax Class**: At *VAT / Tax Class* field, select the VAT Class from the list
- **Item Details**: Select the Items and enter the Quantity, Rate/ Value for each Item. You get *Item Allocation* screen (F-11B).
    - o **Item Allocation**: At *Item Allocation* screen (F-11B), select the Sales Ledger Account. The default VAT Class & Item Value is carried (F-11B).

  This way, enter the Item details for all the Items and Accounting Allocation for each Item.
- **Other Ledger Accounts**: After entry of Item details, enter other Ledger Accounts, if any.
- **Statutory Details**: At *Show Statutory Details* (F-11A), set Yes to Statutory Details screen (F-11C) showing Assessable Value / Tax Amount for the Invoice. Click *F1:Detailed* Toggle Button to get Itemwise details of Assessable Value / Tax Amount.

- **Voucher Narration:** Enter Voucher Narration, if any.

Save the Voucher

In the same way, you may create Debit Note / Credit Note Vouchers.

07 VAT Adjustment Voucher Class

You need to make Journal Voucher entry for creating Liability for Composition VAT, through a Journal Voucher Class.

Creation of Journal Voucher class has been described (§02/02-08/S1). Here we describe the points related to VAT Adjustment Journal Class for creation of Journal Voucher for Composition VAT liability (F-12A).

To create a *Journal Voucher Class*, select *Accounts Info>Voucher Type>Create* to get Voucher Type creation screen (F-12A)

- **Voucher Type Name**:At *Name*, enter the Voucher Type Name (e.g. *VAT Adjt)* at *Name* field.
- **Voucher Type:** At *Type of Voucher*, select *Journal*
- **Voucher Type Abbreviation:** At *Abbr*, enter Voucher Type Name in short (Abbreviation, e.g VAT Adj)

  Now specify the details as explained for Voucher Type creation
- **Voucher Clas Name**: At *Name of Class*, enter *VAT Adjmt Class* to get the Journal Voucher Class screen (F-12B)

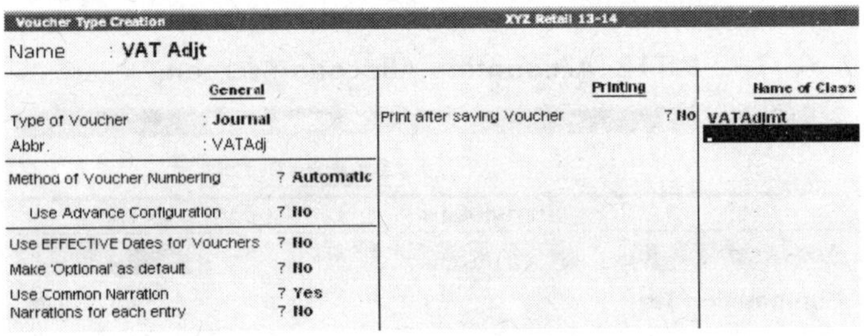

F-12A: Journal Class creation for VAT Adjustment

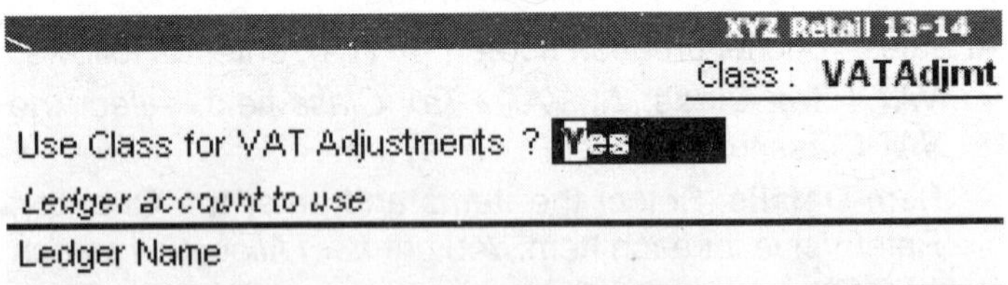

F-12B: Journal Voucher Class set up

At the Journal Voucher Class screen (F-12B), set *Yes* at *Use Class for VAT Adjustment* to use the Voucher Class for VAT Adjustments.

08 Composition VAT Payable Voucher

Through Journal Voucher (F-13D), the Composite Tax payable as per VAT Composition Computation Statement (§10) is transferred to Composite Tax Payable account (F-5A).

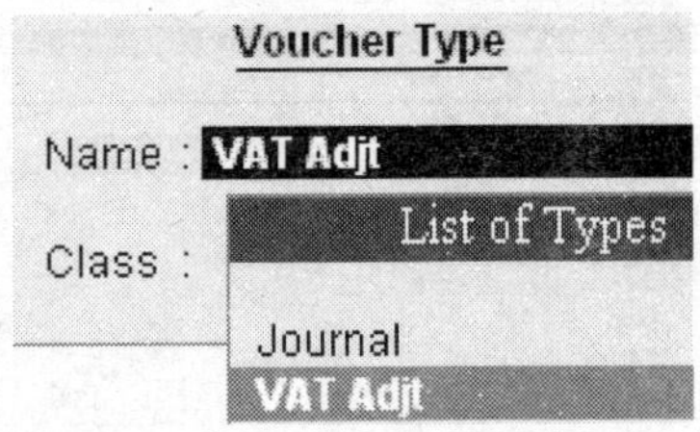

F-13A: Voucher Type selection for VAT Adjustment

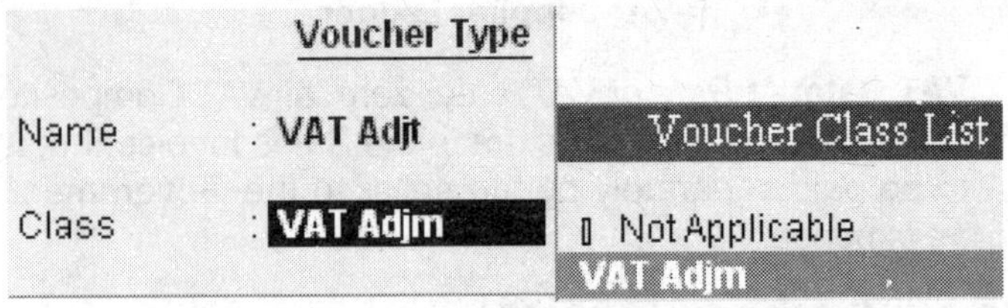

F-13B: Voucher Class selection for VAT Adjustment

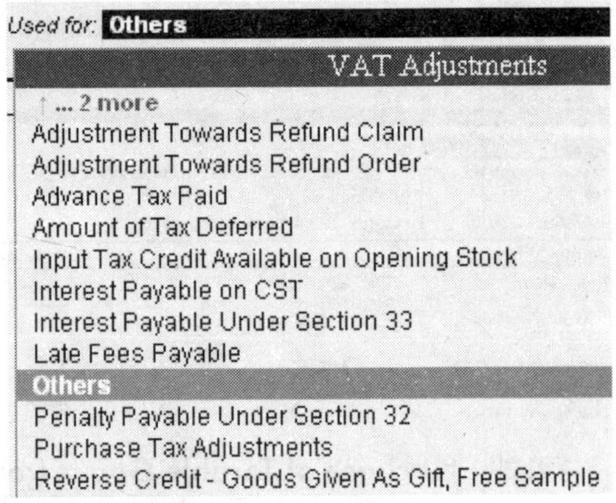

F-13C: Type of Tax Payment

At Journal Voucher entry (F-13D),:

Payment Type: At *Used for*, select *Others* from the list (F-13C)

Ledger Accounts:At Particulars column (F-13D), select the ledger accounts as follows:

- **Composite Tax ledger Account**: Select *Composite Tax ledger Account* (F-13D). The computed amount as per VAT Composition Computation (F-18A) is shown at *Debit* Column
- **VAT Payable Ledger Account**: Select *Composite Tax ledger Account* (F-13D). The Amount is shown at *Credit* Column
- **VAT Tax Class**: Select the VAT Tax Class (F-13F) from the list (F-13E).

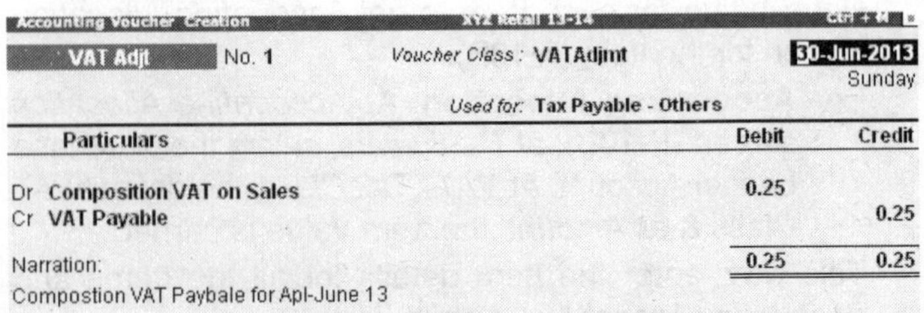

F-13D: Journal Voucher for VAT Liability

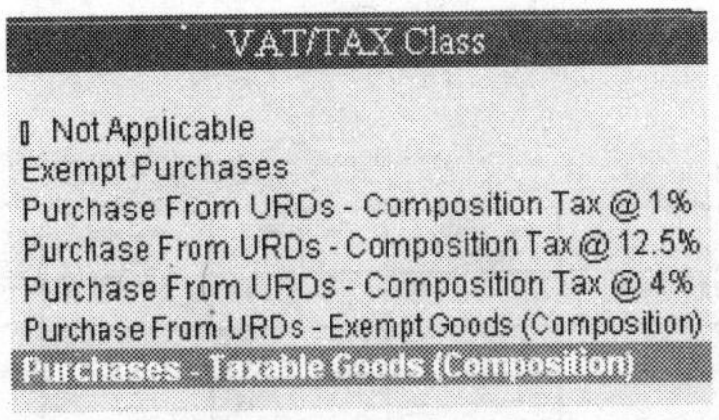

F-13E: VAT Tax Class List for VAT on Purchase

F-13F: VAT Tax Class for VAT onPurchase

09 VAT Composition Reports

At *Gateway of Tally,* select *Display > Statutory Reports* to get *Statutory Reports* menu (F-14A)

At *Statutory Reports* menu (F-14A), select *VAT Composition* to get *VAT Composition Reports* Menu (F-16A).

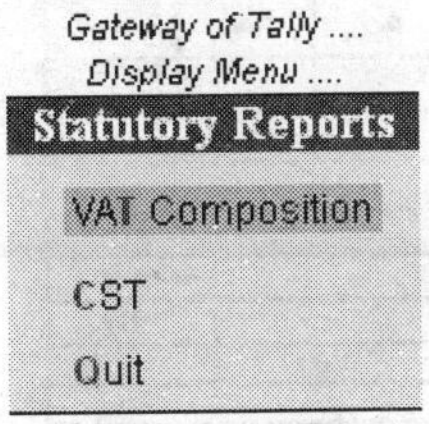

F-14A: Statutory Reports Menu

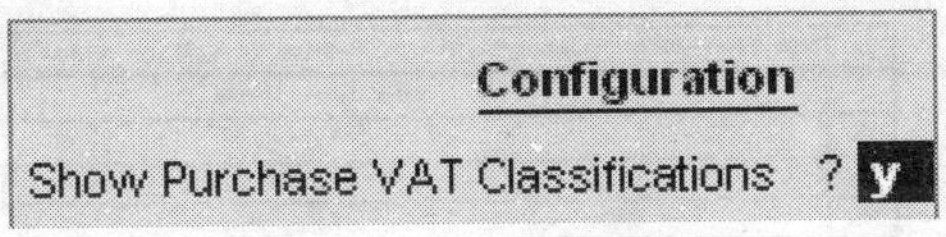

F-15A: Configuration

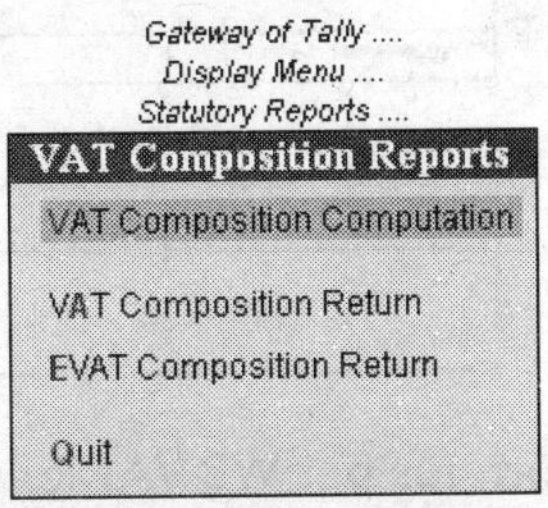

F-16A: VAT Composition Reports Menu

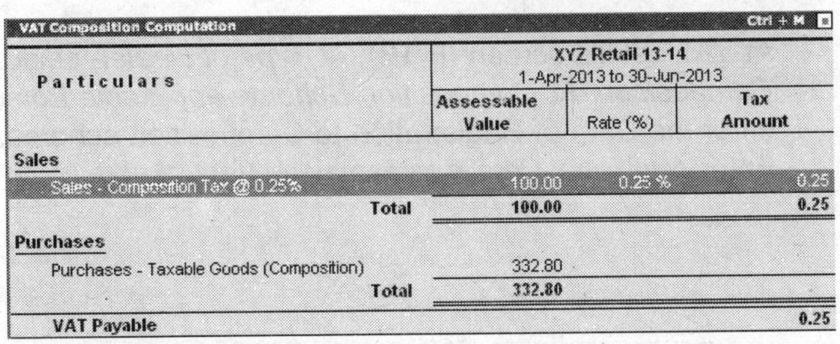

VAT Composition Computation

Particulars	XYZ Retail 13-14 1-Apr-2013 to 30-Jun-2013 Assessable Value	Rate (%)	Tax Amount
Sales			
Sales - Composition Tax @ 0.25%	100.00	0.25 %	0.25
Total	100.00		0.25
Purchases			
Purchases - Taxable Goods (Composition)	332.80		
Total	332.80		
VAT Payable			0.25

F-17A: VAT Composition Computation Statement

10 VAT Composition Computation Statement

At *VAT Composition Reports* menu (F-16A), select *VAT Composition Computation* to get VAT Composition Computation Statement (F-17A), for the selected period.

The *VAT Composition Computation* Statement (F-17A) shows the figures of Sales & Purchase, Assessable Value and the Amount of Composition Tax Payable on Sales.

10.01 VAT Composition Computation Configuration

At *VAT Composition Computation Statement* (F-17A), click *F12:Configure* to get *Configuration* screen (F-15A). Set *Yes* at *Show Purchase VAT Classifications* to get the Composition Purchase details also (F-17A).

11 VAT Composition Return

At *VAT Reports* menu (F-16A), select *VAT Composition Return* to get *VAT Composition Return* Printing screen (F-18A). At VAT Composition Return Printing (F-18A), set the options:

- **Period**: Enter the period at *From* & *To* field
- **Name**: At *Name*, enter the Name of the person responsible for Payment of Tax
- **Designation**: At *Status / Designation*, enter the Designation of the Person
- **Place:** At *Place*, enter the Place
- **Date**: At *Date*, enter the Date of submission of Form

Type Y to print the *VAT Composition Return* (F-20A)

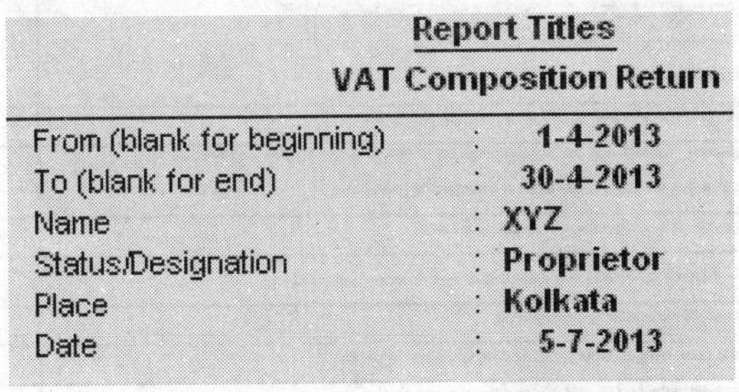

F-18A: VAT Return Printing Screen

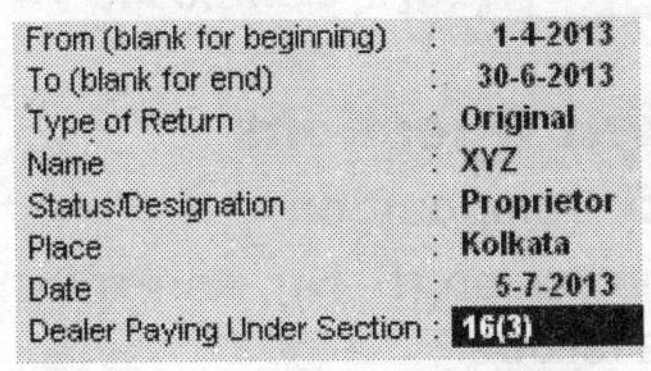

F-19A: e-VAT Return Screen

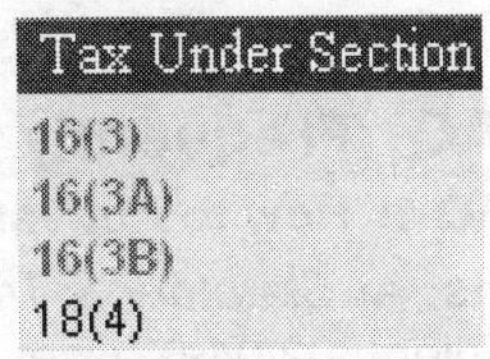

F-19B: List of Tax Section

The VAT Composition Return (F-20A) is State specific.

11.01 E-VAT Composition Return

E-VAT is VAT report Return filed electrically through NET. The e-Return, data is saved in XML file, in the specified folder, which may be used to file e-VAT Return.

At VAT Composition Reports menu (F-16A), select *EVAT Return* to get *EVAT Return* printing screen (F-19A), similar to VAT Composition Return printing screen (F-18A). Set the options (F-19A) similar to VAT Composition Return (F-18A).

At *EVAT Return* printing screen (F-19A), at Dealer Paying under section, select the respective section number applicable for the Dealer, from the list (F-19B)

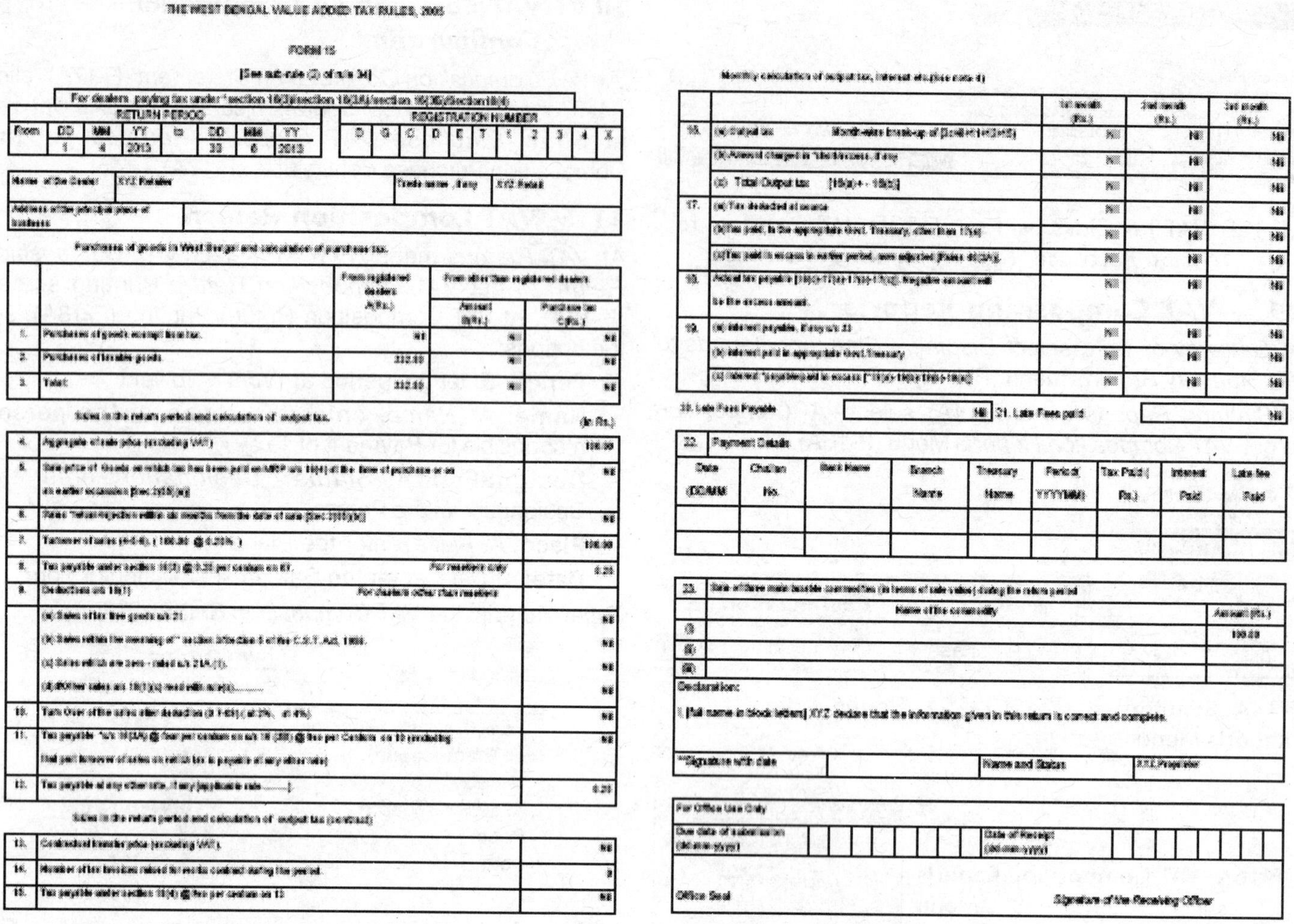

THE WEST BENGAL VALUE ADDED TAX RULES, 2005

FORM 15

RETURN PERIOD							
From	DD	MM	YY	to	DD	MM	YY
	1	4	2013		[illegible]	6	2013

REGISTRATION NUMBER										
D	G	C	D	E	T	1	2	3	4	X

Name of the Dealer	XYZ Retailer	Trade name, if any	XYZ Retail

F-20A: Composite VAT Return (as per WB VAT Rules)

FAQ: Frequently Asked Questions

FAQ-1: How to Activate VAT Composition

Ans: At *Statutory & Taxation* screen (F-1A), as explained earlier (§02/04-02), set up as follows:

- At *Statutory & Taxation* screen (F-1A), at *VAT TIN (Composition)*, enter VAT TIN
- At VAT details screen (F-1B), At *Type of Dealer*, select *Composition*. At *Composition Scheme applicable from*. enter the Date of Registration to Composition scheme. Enter *Additional Details* as explained (§02/04-02).

Part 5

Central Sales Tax

In this Part we describe the process of Invoicing, maintenance, Compliance of records & filing of Returns under Central Sales Tax Act & Rules

- **Central Sales Tax** describes the salient Features of CST Act & Rules and activation of CST for the Company.
- **Inter State Transactions** describes trade Transactions that attract CST Rules
- **CST Deposit** describes the Voucher entries for deposit of CST to the Government Account.
- **CST Reports** describes various reports related to CST & CST Forms.
- **CST Returns** describes filing of CST Statutory Returns and Annexures

Central Sales Tax

05-01

01 Central Sales Tax

Central Sales Tax (CST) is Sales Tax arising from inter-state sales (when goods sold move from one state to another). However, consignments to agents or transfers of goods to branch or other offices is not a *Sale* as per CST Act and so do not attract CST. Similarly, a Sale where goods pass through another state en-route but ultimately reaches to a place in the same State, is also not considered as Sales under CST Act. CST is collected, retained and administered by the state where the goods are sold and moved from.

02 CST Declaration Forms

In case of Inter State Sales Registered dealers (dealers registered under CST), a prescribed CST declaration Form must be issued to buyers/sellers, as described below. The buyer can claim concessional Rate of Sales Tax if the appropriate CST Form is submitted by the registered Buyer.

- **Form C:** Issued by registered buyer to registered seller for specified goods sold as covered in the registration certificate of the purchasing dealer. On submission of Form C, a concessional CST Rate (currently 4% or local ST Rate, whichever is lower) is charged, otherwise, CST is charged at double of local Sales Tax Rate.
- **Form D:** Issued by Government Departments (for goods bought for its own use) to registered seller for goods sold covered in the registration certificate of the selling dealer. On submission of Form D, a concessional CST Rate (currently 4% or local ST Rate, whichever is lower) is charged, otherwise, CST is charged at double of local Sales Tax Rate.
- **Form E1:** Issued by the dealer making first Inter-State Sale, on transfer of document of title (during movement of gods) to enable his purchaser to claim the benefit of exemption from C.S.T. on the second inter-State sale effected by him during the movement of goods. This form is required to be obtained from the Sales Tax Officer.
- **Form E2:** Issued by the second or the subsequent seller (during movement of goods) on transfer of documents of title, to enable the purchaser to claim benefit of exemption of C.S.T, on second or subsequent sale effected by him. This form is to be obtained from the Sales Tax Officer.
- **Form F:** Issued on dispatch of goods to another state as Consignment / Transfer, to claim CST exemption on the goods moved.
- **Form H:** Issued by Exporter, on Inter State Purchase of goods (from another state) to be exported, to claim exemption from CST
- **Form I:** Issued by a dealer located in a Special Economic Zone (SEZ) to claim exemption from CST for goods purchased.

Example:

"A" of Delhi sends goods to "B" of Bangalore, a register dealer. While the goods are in movement from Delhi to Bangalore, "B" sells the goods transferring of documents of title to "M" of Mumbai, who is also registered dealer."M" in turn transferred the Documents to "G" of Ahmedabad, who is also a registered dealer. "G" takes the delivery of goods at Ahmedabad and sold the same to "J" of Jaipur.

Here, the first inter-state sale has been made by "A" to "B". the subsequent sales "B" to "M" and "M" to "G" to the registered dealers during the course of movement of goods from one state to another and shall therefore, be exempt from central sales tax.

However, sale by "G" to "J" is not in the course of same movement of goods as "G" has taken delivery of goods and then made inter state sale. This sale will be chargeable to CST.

03 Activation of CST

CST feature is activated only when VAT feature is activated. At Statutory & Taxation Features (F11:Features> Statutory & Taxation), at *Inter-State Sales Tax Number*, enter the CST Registration Number of the Company (F-1A)

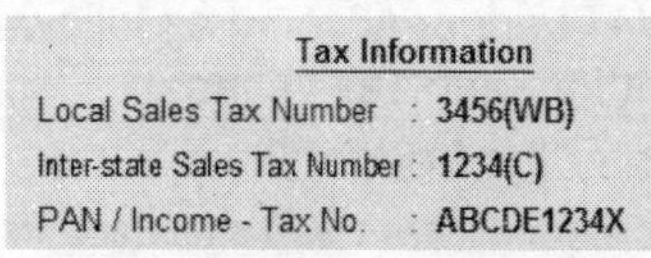

F-1A: CST Regn No of Company

F-2A: CST Regn No of Party

04 CST related Ledgers creation

Now cerate the following Ledger Accounts related to a CST related Transaction.

04.01 Party Ledger Account creation

At Party Ledger Account creation / alteration (of CST Registered Customer / Supplier), at CST No (under *Tax*

Information section) enter the CST Registration Number of the Party (F-2A)

04.02 Inter State Purchase Account creation

Purchase Ledger Creation has been explained earlier. Create separate Purchase Ledger accounts for Inter State Purchase (F-3A). Set *Yes* at *Used in VAT Returns* and then select the applicable VAT / Tax Class (F-3B).

- **Method of Calculation:** At *Method of Computation*, the applicable Method (on *VAT Rate)* is auto carried, implying that CST would be applicable on Assessable Value)
- **Rounding Method**: At *Rounding Method*, select the Rounding Method from the list (and then enter *Rounding Amount*, as applicable).

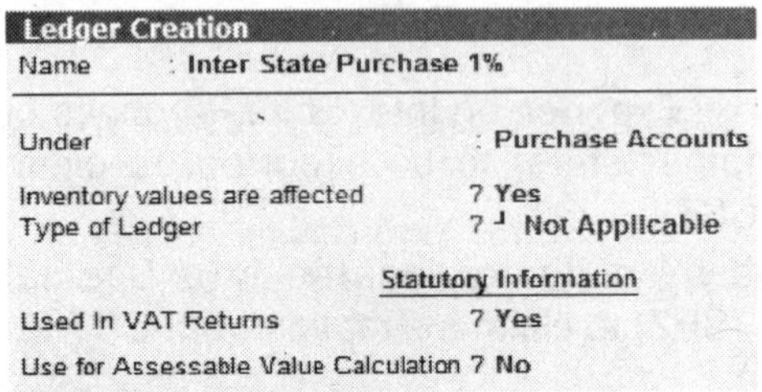

F-3A: Inter State Purchase Ledger Creation

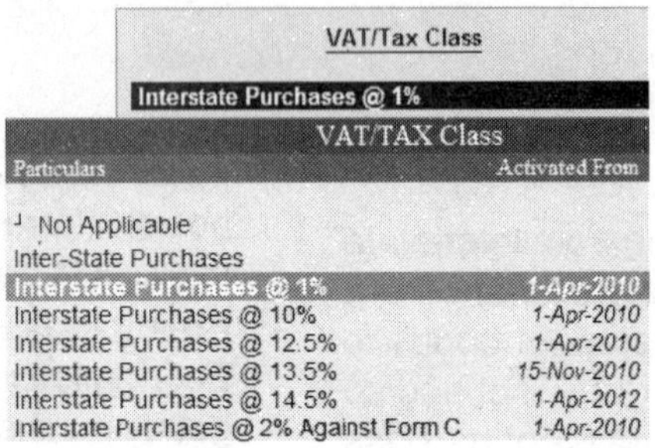

F-3B: VAT / Tax Class in Inter State Creation

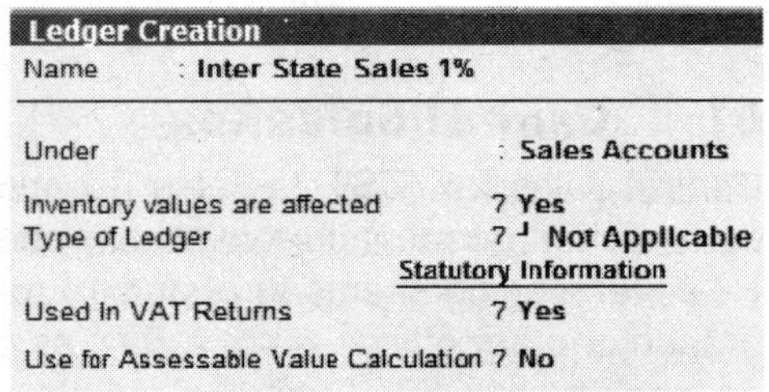

F-4A: Inter State Sales Ledger Purchase Ledger

04.03 Inter State Sales Account creation

Create separate Sales Ledger accounts for Inter State Sales, in the same way as VAT Sales Ledger (F-4A). Set *Yes* at *Used in VAT Returns* (F-4A) and then select the applicable VAT / Tax Class (F-4B).

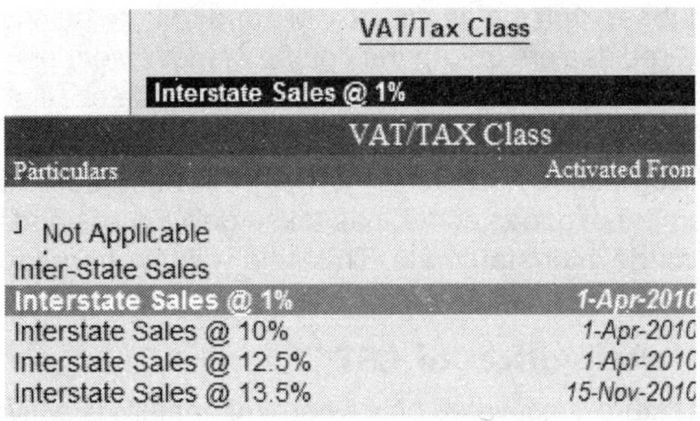

F-4B: VAT / Tax Class in Inter State Sales Ledger

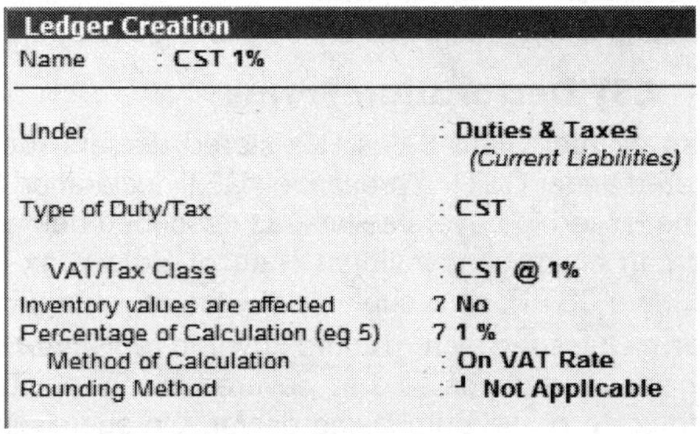

F-5A: CST Ledger Account

04.04 CST Ledger Account creation

Create CST Ledger (F-5A) like VAT Ledger Account as follows (create separate ledger account for each Tax / Class)

- **Ledger Name**: At *Name*, enter the Ledger Name
- **Parent Group**: At *Under*, select *Duties & Taxes* (or its Sub Group)
- **Tax Type:** At *Type of Duty / Tax*, select CST from the list (F-5B)
- **Tax Class**: At *VAT/ Tax Class*, select the VAT Tax Class from te list (F-5C)
- **Inventory Link**: At *Inventory Values are affected*, set *No*
- **Tax Rate:** At *Percentage of Calculation*, the Value is auto carried as per Tax Class selected

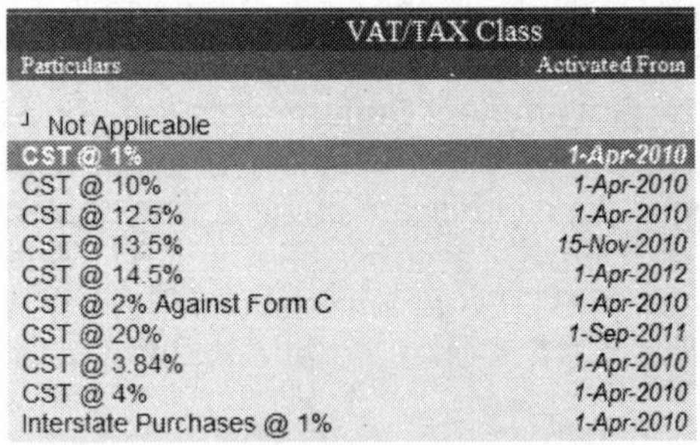

F-5B: Tax Type

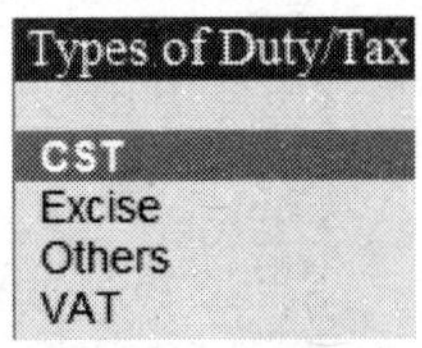

F-5C: Tax Class

FAQ: Frequently Asked Questions

FAQ-1: How do I activate CST System for the Company

Ans: On activation of VAT feature for the Company, at Statutory & Taxation Features screen (F-1A), at *Inter-State Sales Tax Number*, enter the CST Registration Number of the Company.

Further, at Party Ledger Account (CST Registered Customers / Suppliers) creation / alteration, at *CST No* (under *Tax Information* section), enter the CST Registration Number of the Party (F-2A).

Inter State Transactions

05-02

01 Inter State Purchase Voucher entry

Purchase Voucher entry has been explained earlier. Here, we describe points exclusively related to CST (F-1A)

- **Purchase Ledger A/c**: At *Purchase Ledger*, select the respective Purchase Ledger Account.
- **Tax Class**: At *VAT /Tax Class*, the linked Tax Class is carried (or you select the Tax Class)
- **Form Type**: At *Form to Issue column*, enter the Type of the CST Form
- **Form Series**: At *Form Series No. column,* enter the Form Series Number (as printed on the Form)
- **Form No**: At *Form No, column* enter the Form Number (if received / issued at the time of voucher entry) else leave blank

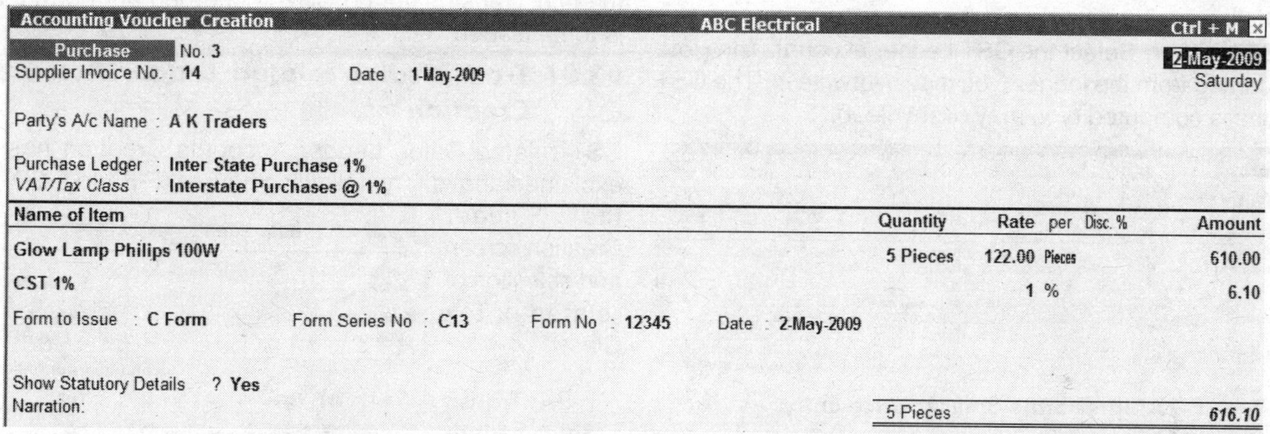

F-1A: Inter State Purchase Invoice Entry

- **Item Details**: Enter the Item details at the respective columns (at Name of Item, Quantity, Rat columns. The computed amount is shown at Amount column) as usual
- **Ledger Accounts**: Select the CST Ledger account. The Rate is carried from the ledger (you may overwrite it). The CST value is computed (you may overwrite it). Next, slect Other Ledger Accounts, if any and enter the Rate / Amount.

Statutory Details

Particulars	VAT
Assessable Value	616.10
Glow Lamp Philips 100W	616.10
Item Value	*610.00*
CST 1%	*6.10*

F-1B: Statutory Details of CST

CST Form Details: After entry of all ledger account details, enter the CST Form Details (Issued / Received / Issuable/ Receivable), as follows (F-1A):

- **Form Date**: If the Form Number is entered, at *Date column*, enter the Form Date also

Statutory Details: At *Show Statutory Details* (F-1A), set *Yes* to view *Statutory Details* screen (F-1B), showing the Details of Assessable Value & CST (Click *F1:Detailed* button to get Details)

02 Inter State Sales Voucher entry

Sales Voucher entry has been explained earlier. Here, we describe Sales Voucher (F-2A) entry points exclusively related to CST

- **Sales Ledger A/c**: At *Sales Ledger*, select the respective Sales Ledger Account.
- **Tax Class**: At *VAT /Tax Class*, the linked Tax Class is carried (or you select the Tax Class)
- **Item Details**: Enter the Item details at the respective columns (at Name of Item, Quantity, Rat columns. The computed amount is shown at Amount column) as usual
- **Item Purchase Details** ; After entry of each Item details, you get Purchase Details screen (F-2B) to enter the

Purchase Details of the Item sold, in the respective columns, as below:

- o **Supplier:** At *Supplier*, select the Supplier Ledger Account
- o **Purchase Invoice:** At *Purchase Invoice No.* enter the Purchase Invoice Number through which the sold Item was Purchased
- o **Purchase Invoice Date:** At *Date*, enter the corresponding Purchase Invoice Date
- o **Purchase Quantity:** At *Qty*, enter the Purchase Quantity of the Item as per the Purchase Invoice referred
- o **Purchase Value:** At *Purchase Value*, enter the Purchase Value of the Item as per the Purchase Invoice referred

This way, enter the details in respect of each Item sold in the Sales Invoice (and then respective Purchase Details).

- **CST Ledger:** Select the CST Ledger account. The Rate is carried from the ledger (you may overwrite it). The CST value is computed (you may overwrite it).

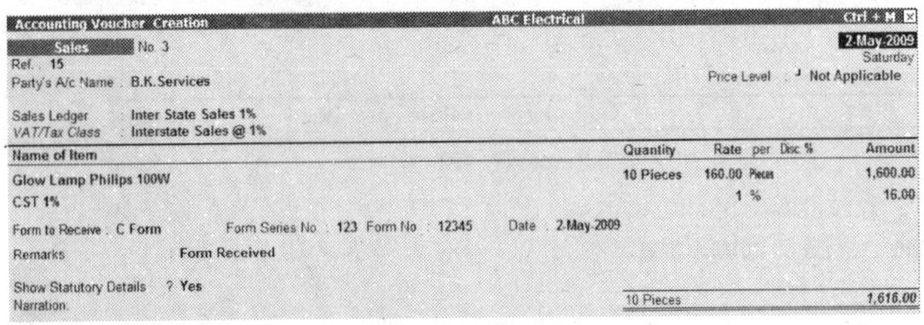

F-2A: Inter State Sales Invoice Entry

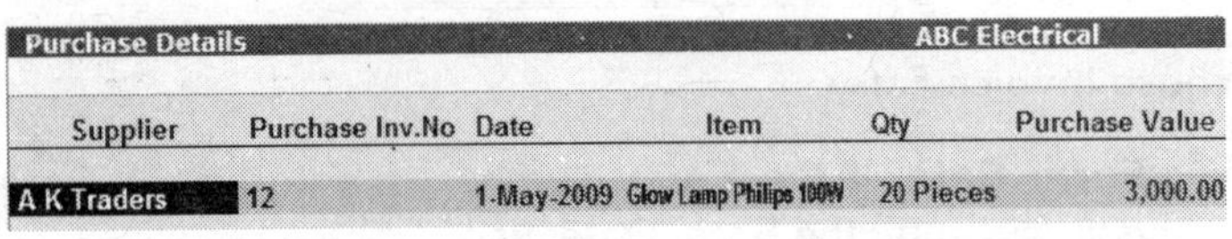

F-2B: Purchase Details of sold Item

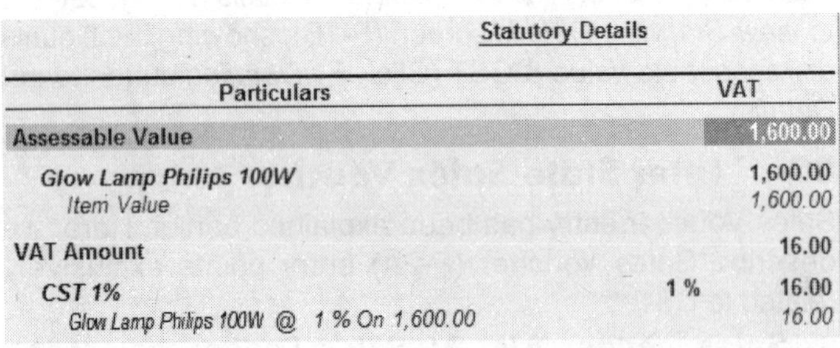

F-2C: Statutory Details of Sales Invoice

- **CST Form Details:** After entry of all ledger account details, enter the CST Form Details (Received / Receivable), as follows:
  - o **Form Type:** At *Form to Receive*, enter the Type of the CST Form Received / Receivable
  - o **Form Series:** Enter the Form Series Number (as printed on the Form)
  - o **Form No:** Enter the Form Number (if received / issued at the time of voucher entry) else leave blank
  - o **Form Date:** If the Form Number is entered, enter the Form Date also
- **Remarks:** At *Remarks*, enter any Remarks (as memorandum), regarding CST Form or other matter (else leave blank)
- **Statutory Details:** At *Show Statutory Details*, set *Yes* to view *Statutory Details* screen (F-2C), showing the Details of Assessable Value & CST (Click *F1:Detailed* button to get Details)

03 Inter State Transit Sales

Transit Sales means where a Party sells the Documents of Title of Goods (a Negotiable Instrument, like Carrier's Receipt, Delivery Order etc pertaining), when the goods are in transit, before the delivery of goods is taken from the Carrier.

In such Transit sale, no CST is charged but Form E1 / E2 is to be issued

03.01 Transit sales related Ledger Accounts Creation

CST related Sales Ledger Accounts Creation has been explained above. The following figures (F-3A to F-3D) show the Ledger Creation screen and selection of related Tax Class

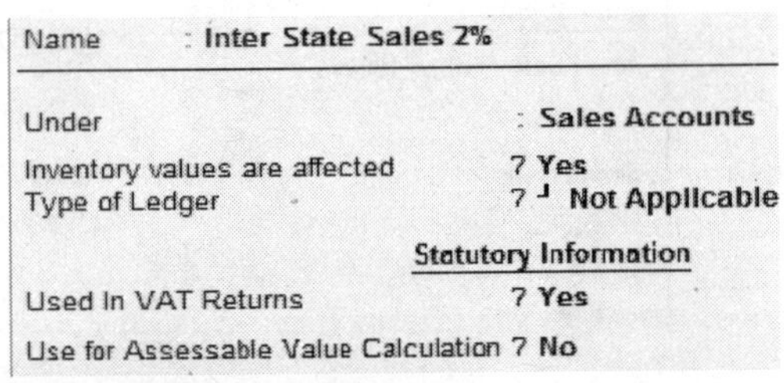

F-3A: Transit Sales Ledger

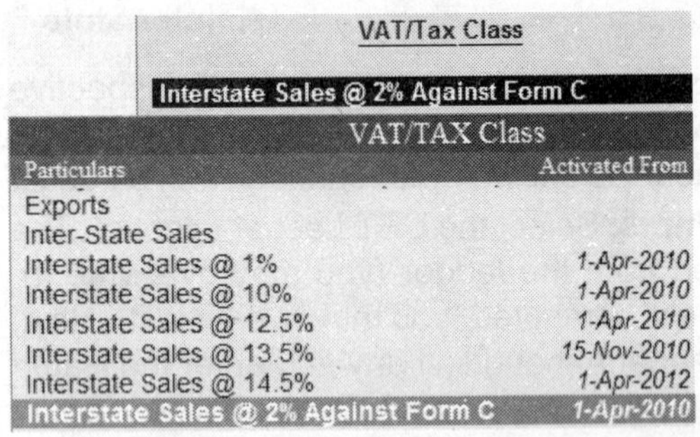

F-3B: Tax Class for Sales Ledger

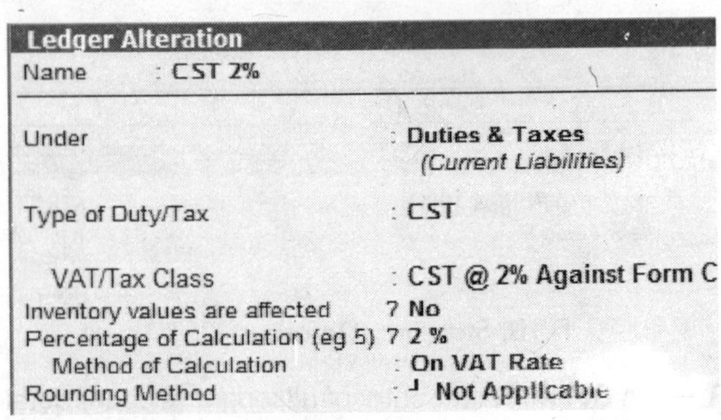

F-3C: CST Ledger

VAT/TAX Class	
Particulars	Activated From
┘ Not Applicable	
CST @ 1%	1-Apr-2010
CST @ 10%	1-Apr-2010
CST @ 12.5%	1-Apr-2010
CST @ 13.5%	15-Nov-2010
CST @ 14.5%	1-Apr-2012
CST @ 2% Against Form C	1-Apr-2010
CST @ 20%	1-Sep-2011
CST @ 3.84%	1-Apr-2010
CST @ 4%	1-Apr-2010

F-3D: CST Ledger Tax Class

03.02 Configuration for Transit Sales

At Sales Invoice entry screen, click *F12:Configure* and set the following *Configuration* Options:

- **Supplementary Details**: At Accept Supplementary Details, set Yes to enter various details of transaction (F-4B)
- **Consignor / Consignee Details**: At *Separate Buyer & Consignee Name*, set Yes to enter the Name, Address & other particulars of both Buyer & Consignee (F-4B) to be printed in Invoice
- **E1/E2 Declaration Form**: At *Activate E1 or E2 Transaction*, set *Yes* to enter E1/ E2 Form details

04 Sales Invoice Entry for Transit Sales

Sales Invoice entry has been explained earlier. Here we will discuss points exclusively related to CST (F-4A)

Accounting Voucher Creation — ABC Electrical — Ctrl + M

Sales No. 4 — 2-May-2009 Saturday
Ref. : 67
Party's A/c Name : A K Traders — Price Level : Retail
Sales Ledger : Inter State Sales 2%
VAT/Tax Class : Interstate Sales @ 2% Against Form C

Name of Item	Quantity	Rate	per	Disc %	Amount
Glow Lamp Philips 100W	10 Pieces	170.00	Pieces		1,700.00
CST 2%		2	%		34.00

Form to Receive : C Form — Form Series No : 25 Form No : 12345 Date : 1-May-2009
Form to Issue : E1 Form — Form Series No : Form No : Date :

Remarks : E1 Form to Be Issued

Show Statutory Details ? Yes
Narration: — 10 Pieces — *1,734.00*

F-4A: Inter State Transit Sales Invoice

Buyer Details

At *Supplementary Details* screen (F-4B), at Buyer Section, enter the Buyer& Consignee Details as follows:

Despatch Details

Delivery Note No(s) :	Despatch Doc. No.	: 12345
	Despatched through	: ETC Transport
┘ **Not Applicable**	Destination	: Bangalore

Order Details

Order No(s) :	Mode/Terms of Payment	: 30 Days
┘ **End of List**	Other Reference(s)	: Owner's Risk
	Terms of Delivery	: Ex Godown

Buyer's Details

Consignee	: **B P Traders**	Buyers	: **A K Traders**
Address	: 56.M.G.Road Bangalore	Address	: Victoria Terminus Mumbai
TIN/Sales Tax No.	: **KA/12345**	TIN/Sales Tax No.	: **MH/98775**
CST Number	: **76453/KA**	CST Number	: **78654/MH**
		Type of Dealer	: **Inter State Dealer**

F-4B: Supplementary Details of Sales Invoice

- **Consignee**: At *Consignee*, enter the Consignee Name (whom the Goods have been despatched to), Address, Tax Details etc.

Type of Dealer
┘ Not Applicable
Composition Dealer
Inter State Dealer
Unregistered Dealer
VAT Dealer

F-4C: Dealer Type List

Statutory Details

Particulars		VAT
Assessable Value		**1,700.00**
Glow Lamp Philips 100W		**1,700.00**
Item Value		*1,700.00*
VAT Amount		**34.00**
CST 2%	**2 %**	**34.00**
Glow Lamp Philips 100W @ 2 % On 1,700.00		*34.00*

F-4D: Statutory Details

- **Buyer Name**: At *Buyers,* enter the Buyer Name (whom goods have been sold), Address, Tax Details etc.
  - o **Buyer Dealer Type**: At Buyer column, at Typ of Dealer, select the Dealer Type from the list

Declaration Form Details

The Invoice would be raised in Buyer Name. The Sale becomes Inter State Sales. So, the Seller would receive Form C from the Buyer and will issue E1 Form.

At Forms Details section (F-4A), enter the Form details, as explained earlier. The Form E1 in the Forms list in the second line would be available only when you set the Configuration (set Yes at *Activate E1 or E2 Transaction* and enter the Form Details in First line)

FAQ: Frequently Asked Questions

FAQ-1: How do I enter E1 / E2 Form details in Inter State Transit sales

Ans: In case of Inter State Transit Sale, where documents are transferred while the goods are in transit, the Seller would receive Form C from the Buyer and the seller will issue E1 Form (First seller) / E2 Form (subsequent seller).

To activate E1 / E2 Form details entry also in Invoice, at Invoice entry click F12:Conigure to get Sales Invoice Configuration screen. At get Sales Invoice Configuration screen, set Yes at *Activate E1 or E2 Transaction*

During Invoice Entry, at Forms Details section (F-4A), enter the Form details, (for ' C 'Form and for 'E1 / E2' Form) as usual (F-4B).

CST Deposit

01 CST Deposit to Government

Having entered the Sales Invoice, you have to periodically deposit the CST to Government within stipulated time.

02 CST payable Ledger Account

Create the CST payable Ledger Account under:

- Current Liabilities or its Sub Group (F-1A), or
- Duties & Taxes or its Sub Group (F-1B).

Ledger Creation

Name : CST Paybale

Under	: Current Liabilities
Inventory values are affected	? No
Use for Assessable Value Calculation	? No

F-1A: CST Payable Ledger under Current Liabilities

Ledger Creation

Name : CST Paybale

Under	: Duties & Taxes (Current Liabilities)
Type of Duty/Tax	: Others
Inventory values are affected	? No
Percentage of Calculation (eg 5)	? 0 %
Use for Assessable Value Calculation	? No

F-1B: CST Payable Ledger under Duties & Taxes

03 Journal Voucher for CST Payable

Now create a Journal Voucher (F-2A) to transfer the Amount of CST (on Sales) to CST Payable.

- **CST Ledger:** Select the CST Ledger Account in which CST was credited through Sales Bills and enter the amount Payable for the period, in Debit Column. The Balance of Ledger, after the entry should be zero
  This way, enter the Ledger Account for all CST Ledgers (e.g CST 1%, CST 4% etc)
- **CST Payable Ledger:** Select the CST Payable Ledger Account to which CST Payable is to be credited. The total amount Payable (total of all CST Ledgers entered) is carried in Credit Column.

Enter the Voucher Narration and save the Journal Voucher (F-2A)

Accounting Voucher Creation Ctrl + M

Journal No. 3 — 1-Jul-2009, Wednesday

Particulars	Debit	Credit
Dr CST 1% (Cur Bal: 0.00 Dr)	16.00	
Cr CST Paybale (Cur Bal: 16.00 Cr)		16.00
Narration:	16.00	16.00

F-2A: CST Journal Voucher

Accounting Voucher Creation ABC Electrical Ctrl + M

Payment No. 1 — 1-Sep-2014, Monday

Statutory Payment for : CST

Account : HDFC Bank

Particulars	Amount
CST Paybale	16.00
Provide Details : Yes	
Narration: CSR paid	16.00

F-3A: CST Payment Voucher

Statutory Payment

		Types of Duty/Tax
Type of Duty/Tax	: CST	CST
Auto Fill Statutory Payment	? No	VAT

F-3B: Statutory Payment details

VAT Payment Details

Period From	: 1-Apr-2009 To 1-Jul-2009
Type of Payment	: Not Applicable
Deposit Date	: 2-Jul-2009
Challan No.	: 12
Name of the issuing Bank	: ALLAHABAD BANK
Branch Name	: MAIN
Name of the Treasury	: Not Applicable
Case No.(if Any)	:
Branch code(remittance)	:

F-3C: CST Payment details

F-3D: S:Stat Payment button — S: Stat Payment

04 Payment Voucher for deposit of CST to Government

Having created the Journal Voucher for CST Payable (F-2A), you may now make the payment Voucher for depositing of

CST to designated Bank (F-3A). The process is similar to VAT Deposit to Government.

Statutory Payment Details: At Payment Voucher (in Single Mode) entry screen (F-3A). Click *S:Stat Payment* button to get *Statutory Payment* screen (F-3B). At *Statutory Payment* screen (F-3B), select CST at *Type of Duty /Tax.* At *Auto Fill Statutory Payment*, select *No.*

Enter the Voucher Narration and save the Voucher (F-3A)

At payment voucher enter screen,

- **Cash / Bank Account**: At Header, select the Cash / Bank Account from which the money is being paid.
- **CST Payable Account:** At *Particulars* column, select the *CST Payable* Account. The Balance of Ledger, after the entry should be zero.

CST Payment Details: Having entered the Ledger Accounts (F-3A), set Yes at *Provide Details* to get *CST Payment Details* screen (F-3C). At *CST Payment Details* screen (F-3C), enter as follows:

- **Accounting Period**: At *Period*, enter the period (of the month / quarter) at *From* & *To* fields, for which the CST is being deposited.
- **Payment Type**: At *Type of Payment*, select *Not Applicable*
- **Deposit Date**: At *Deposit Date*, enter the Date of Deposit of the amount to the Bank
- **Challan Number**: At *Challan No*, enter the Challan Number as specified by the Bank on the receipted challan.
- **Bank Name**: Select the designated Bank from the list
- **Branch Name**: Having selected the designated Bank from the list, select the designated Branch of the Bank from the list (or select *Not Applicable* to deposit through Treasury and then enter Treasury Name at the next field *Name of the Treasury*
- **Case No**: If the money is being deposited against any Order of CST authority, at *Case No*, enter the Case Number
- **Branch Code**: At *Branch Code (remittance),* enter the Branch Code of the remittance Branch, as specified by the CST Authority (stamped on the receipted Challan)

05 Direct Payment of CST to Govt through Payment Voucher

Instead of creating a Journal Voucher (F-2A) to transfer the CST amount to a CST payable and then make Payment Voucher through CST Payable voucher (F-3A), you may create a Payment Voucher (F-4A) using the CST Accounts.

- **Statutory Payment Details**: At Payment Voucher (in Single Mode) entry screen (F-4A). Click *S:Stat Payment* button to get *Statutory Payment* screen. At *Statutory Payment* screen, select CST at *Type of Duty /Tax.* At *Auto Fill Statutory Payment*, select *No.*

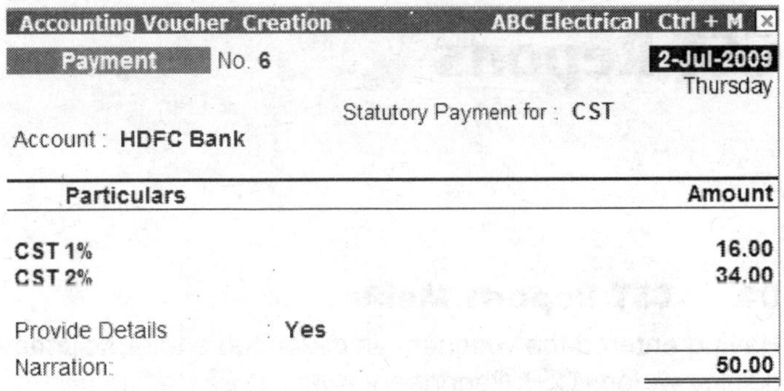

F-4A: Direct CST payment Voucher

- **Cash / Bank Account**: At Header, select the Cash / Bank Account from which the money is being paid.
- **CST Account:** At *Particulars* column, select the *CST Payable* Account and enter the amount of CST Paybale. The Balance of Ledger, after the entry should be zero

  This way, enter the Ledger Account for all CST Ledgers (e.g CST 1%, CST 4% etc)
- **CST Payment Details**: Having entered the Ledger Accounts (F-4A), set Yes at *Provide Details* to get *CST Payment Details* screen. At *CST Payment Details* screen, enter as described earlier

Enter the Voucher Narration and save the Voucher (F-4A).

FAQ: Frequently Asked Questions

FAQ-1: How do I make payment for CST to the Government

Ans. You may create a Payment Voucher (F-4A) to deposit the CST into Government Account. At payment Voucher entry screen in single mode (F-4A), enter as follows:

- **Statutory Payment Details**: Click *S:Stat Payment* button to get *Statutory Payment* screen. At *Statutory Payment* screen, select CST at *Type of Duty /Tax.* At *Auto Fill Statutory Payment*, select *No.*
- **Cash / Bank Account**: At Header, select the Cash / Bank Account from which the money is being paid.
- **CST Account:** At *Particulars* column, select the *CST Payable* Account and enter the amount of CST Paybale. The Balance of Ledger, after the entry should be zero

  This way, enter the Ledger Account for all CST Ledgers (e.g CST 1%, CST 4% etc)
- **CST Payment Details**: Having entered the Ledger Accounts (F-4A), set Yes at *Provide Details* to get *CST Payment Details* screen. At *CST Payment Details* screen, enter as described earlier

Enter the Voucher Narration and save the Voucher (F-4A).

CST Reports 05-04

04 CST Reports Menu

Having entered the vouchers as described earlier, you may display various CST Reports

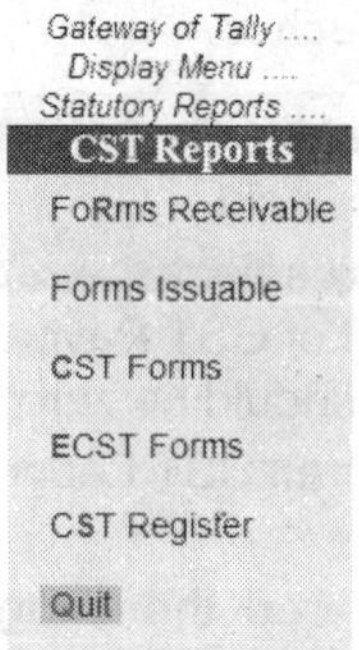

F-1A: CST Reports menu

F-2A: Form Receivable Menu

F-2B: Form Issuable Menu

F-3A: CST Forms Menu

F-4A: CST Register Menu

Select *GoT>Display>Statutory Reports> CST Reports* to get *CST Reports* Menu (F-1A) showing the list of various CST reports, as described next

02 CST Forms Outstanding Reports Menu

Normally CST Forms are issued later on. One Form may be issued against several bills of a Party. So, it is necessary to track the Forms to be Issued and Received, otherwise the concessional rate of CST will not be available and the extra CST will have to be paid by the buyer or seller (normally the seller).

03 CST Forms Receivable

At CST Reports Menu (F-1A), select *Form Receivable*, to get Forms Receivable Menu (F-2A)

03.01 CST Accounts Group Forms Receivable

At CST Forms Receivable Menu (F-2A), select *Group* and then select an Account Group for which you like to display the outstanding Forms Receivable (F-5A)

03.02 CST Accounts Ledger Forms Receivable

At *CST Forms Receivable* Menu(F-5A), select *Ledger* and then select an Account Ledger for which you like to display the outstanding Forms Receivable, to get the list of Vouchers related to the selected Party. The contents of the Report is similar to *CST Accounts Groups Forms Receivable*, explained above.

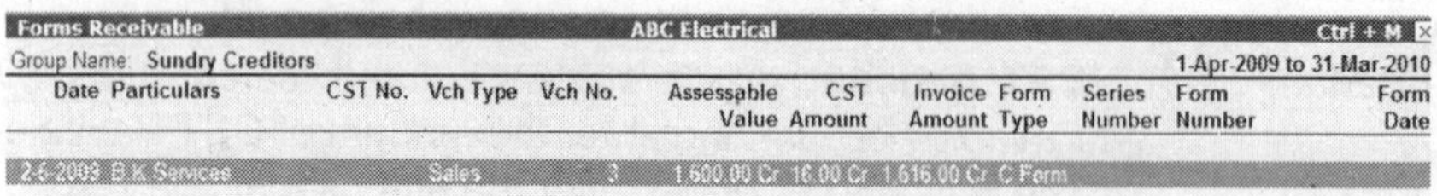

F-5A: Account Group Forms Receivable

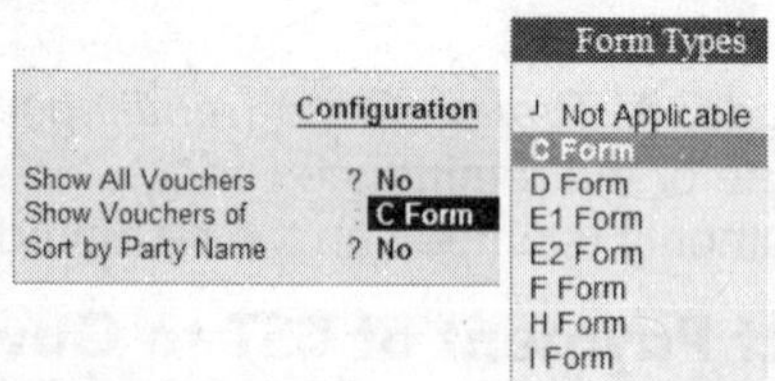

F-5B: Configuration

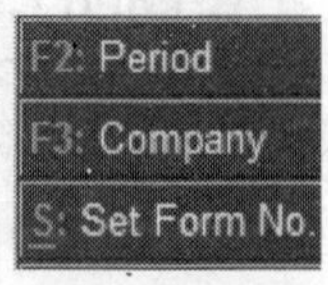

F-5C: Buttons

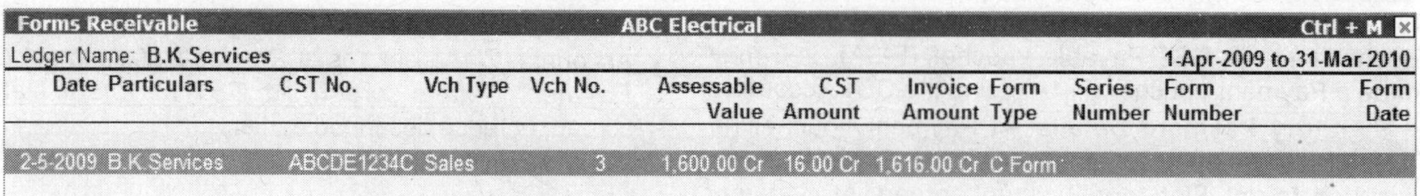

F-6A: Account Ledger Forms Receivable

04 CST Forms Issuable

At CST Reports Menu (F-1A), select *Form Issuable*, to get *Forms Issuable* Menu (F-2B)

04.01 CST Accounts Group Forms Issuable

At CST Forms Issuable Menu (F-2B), select *Group* and then select an Account Group for which you like to display the outstanding Forms Issuable (F-7A)

- **Sorting Order**: At *Sort by Party Name*, set:
- Yes to sort by Party Name to get the list as sorted by Party Name. This is useful to enter From details of Form Received from a Party.
- No to Show Vouchers in default sequence (Voucher Date)

Sorting button is available at *Account Group Forms Receivable / Issuable Report*

Form Issuable — **ABC Electrical** — Ctrl + M

Group Name: **Sundry Creditors** — **1-Apr-2009 to 31-Mar-2010**

Date	Particulars	CST No.	Vch Type	Vch No.	Reference	Effective Date	Assessable Value	CST Amount	Invoice Amount	Form Type	Series Number	Form Number	Form Date
2-5-2009	B.K.Services	ABCDE1234C	Sales	3	15	2-5-2009	1,600.00 Cr	16.00 Cr	1,616.00 Cr	E1 Form			

F-7A: Account Group Forms Issuable

Forms Issuable — **ABC Electrical** — Ctrl + M

Ledger Name: **B.K.Services** — **1-Apr-2009 to 31-Mar-2010**

Date	Particulars	CST No.	Vch Type	Vch No.	Reference	Effective Date	Assessable Value	CST Amount	Invoice Amount	Form Type	Series Number	Form Number	Form Date
2-5-2009	B.K.Services	ABCDE1234C	Sales	3	15	2-5-2009	1,600.00 Cr	16.00 Cr	1,616.00 Cr	E1 Form			

F-8A: Account Ledger Forms Issuable

04.02 CST Accounts Ledger Forms Issuable

At CST Forms Issuable Menu (F-2B), select *Ledger* and then select an Account Ledger for which you like to display the outstanding Forms Issuable, to get the list of Vouchers related to the selected Party (F-8A). The contents of the Report is similar to *CST Accounts Group Forms Issuable* (F-7A), explained above.

05 Forms Receivable / Issuable Configuration

At *Account Group Forms Receivable* (F-6A) */ Issueable* (F-7A), click *F12:Configure* to get *Account Group Forms Receivable Configuration* (F-5B), to set the following Configuration options.

- **Voucher Range**: At *Show All Vouchers*, set:
  - o Yes to Show all Vouchers
  - o No to Show Vouchers related for which Forms is Receivable
- **Forms Type**: At *Show Voucher of,* select the Form Type from the list (select Not Applicable where no Form is Receivable)

06 CST Forms Receivable / Issuable Buttons

At CST Forms Receivable / Issuable Reports (F-5A to F-8A), you get following Buttons (F-5C)

- **S:Set Form Number:** To set the Form Number issued / received against the respective Sale / Purchase Bills, as described later (§09)

07 CST Register

CST Register shows the list of Sales / Purchase Vouches in which CST has been charged

At CST Reports Menu (F-1A), select *CST Register*, to get *CST Register* Menu (F-4A)

07.01 CST Purchase Register

At *CST Register* Menu (F-4A), select *CST Purchases* to get *CST Purchases Register* showing the complete Particulars of each CST Purchase Voucher (F-9A) for the specified period.

07.02 CST Sales Register

At *CST Register* Menu (F-4A), select *CST Sales* to get *CST Sales Register* showing the complete Particulars of each CST Sales Voucher for the specified period (F-10A)

CST Purchase Register — **ABC Electrical** — Ctrl + M

List of Purchase Vouchers — **1-Apr-2009 to 31-Mar-2010**

Date	Particulars	Supplier Invoice No. & Dt.	Vch No	TIN No	CST No	Quantity	Rate	Value
2 May 2009	**A K Traders**	14 / 1-5-2009	3	ANGDC4356	123(C)			**610.00**
	Glow Lamp Philips 100W					*5 Pieces*	*122.00/Pieces*	*610.00*
	CST 1%							
	Grand Total							**610.00**

F-9A: CST Purchase Register (Part 1)

ABC Electrical — Ctrl + M

1-Apr-2009 to 31-Mar-2010

Gross Total	Assessable Value	MRP Value	Addl. Cost	VAT/TAX Class	Tax Amount
616.10	**616.10**		**6.10**		
	616.10			*Interstate Purchases @ 1%*	
			6.10		
616.10	**616.10**		**6.10**		

CST Purchase Register (Part 2)

CST Sales Register | ABC Electrical | Ctrl + M

List of Sales Vouchers | 1-Apr-2009 to 31-Mar-2010

Date	Particulars	Voucher Ref.	Vch No.	TIN No.	CST No.	Quantity	Rate	Value
2-May-2009	**B.K.Services**	15	3	1234(WB)	ABCDE1234C			**1,600.00**
	Glow Lamp Philips 100W					*10 Pieces*	*160.00/Pieces*	*1,600.00*
	Grand Total							**1,600.00**

F-10A: CST Sales Register (Part 1)

ABC Electrical | Ctrl + M

1-Apr-2009 to 31-Mar-2010

Gross Total	Assessable Value	MRP Value	Addl. Cost	VAT/TAX Class	Tax Amount
1,616.00	**1,600.00**				**16.00**
	1,600.00			*CST @ 1%*	*16.00*
1,616.00	**1,600.00**				**16.00**

CST Sales Register (Part 2)

07.03 Contents of CST Invoice Register

The CST Sales / Purchase Register (F-9A / F-10A) contains following columns showing Invoice Data for the selected Period.

- **Date**: Voucher Date
- **Particulars**: Party Name. In details mode, the Item details is shown in next line
- **TIN No**: Sales Tax Number
- **CST No**: CST Regn Number
- **Assessable Value**: Assessable Value on which CST is computed
- **Gross Total**: Total Assessable Value of Materials
- **MRP Value**: MRP value of Materials
- **VAT/Tax Class**: Applicable CST Tax Class
- **Tax Amount**: CST Amount in case of Sales Invoice

In addition to the above, the details as per configuration options set as described next, are also shown.

07.04 CST Register Configuration

Configuration

Show Voucher Number	? Yes
Show Supplier Invoice No. & Dt.	? Yes
Show CST No.	? Yes
Show Quantity Details	? Yes
Show Rate Details	? Yes
Show Item Value	? Yes
Show Additional Cost	? Yes
Show Party from supplementary	? Yes

F-11A: Configuration

F1: Detailed

F2: Date

F2: Period

F-11B: Buttons

At *CST Purchase Register* (F-9A) / *CST Sales Register* (F-10A), click *F12:Configure* to get *Configuration* screen (F-11A), to set the Configuration options as described below:

- **Voucher Number**: At *Show Voucher Number*, set:
  - o *Yes* to show the Voucher Number *Vch No* column
  - o *No*. The Voucher Number is not shown
- **Supplier Invoice Number**: At *Show Supplier Invoice No. & Dt,* set:
  - o *Yes* to show the Supplier Invoice Number & Date at *Supplier Invoice No. & Dt* column
  - o *No*. The Supplier Invoice Number is not shown

  This option appears only in CST Purchase Register
- **CST Number**: At *Show CST Number*, set:
  - o *Yes* to show the Party's CST Number at *CST No* column
  - o *No*. The CST Number column is not shown
- **Item Quantity**: At *Show Quantity Details*, set:
  - o *Yes* to show the Item Quantity / UoM at *Quantity* Column
  - o *No*. The Quantity column is not shown
- **Item Rate**: Having set Yes at *Show Quantity Details*, at *Show Rate Details*, set:
  - o *Yes* to show the Item Rate / UoM at *Rate* Column
  - o *No*. The Rate column is not shown
- **Item Value**: At *Show Item Value*, set:
  - o *Yes* to show the Item Value at *Value* Column
  - o *No*. The Item Value is not shown
- **Additional Cost**: At *Show Additional Cost*, set:
  - o *Yes* to show the Additional Cost at *Addl Cost* column
  - o *No*. The Additional Cost is not shown
- **Party Details**: At *Show Party from Supplementary*, set:
  - o *Yes* to show the Party Details using Party List button in Party Details screen in Cash Invoice
  - o *No*. The Party Details from Supplementary / Party details screen is not shown

08 CST Computation Report

We have already discussed about *VAT Computation* Report. In *VAT Computation* Report, you may optionally also get the CST Computation details.

At *VAT Computation* Report (F-12A), click *F12:Configure* to get *VAT Computation Configuration* (F-12B). At *VAT Computation Configuration* (F-12B), set *Yes* at *Show CST Details* to get CST Computation figures also in VAT /CST Computation Report (F-12A).

09 Forms Received / Issued Entry

Most of the times, the Forms are received subsequent to Invoice creation. To get correct and updated Forms Receivable / Payable report, you should enter the details of Forms as and when you receive / issue the Form.

At Forms Receivable / Issuable Report click *S:Set Form No* button. Select the Voucher against which you like to enter the details of Form received. At the following blank fields, enter respective details of Form Received / Issued as follows (F-13A):

- **Form Series**: At *Series Number*, enter the Series of the Form (shown in Form)
- **Form Number**: At *Form Number*, enter the Form Number of the Form (shown in Form)
- **Form Date**: At Form Date, enter the Date of the Form

A Form may be issued against several Invoices (of same Purchase Order). In that case, enter the same particulars against each Invoice

FAQ: Frequently Asked Questions

FAQ-1: Our Parties (Customers Supplier) are grouped into geographical multiple levels (according to State, District & Towns), for convenience & better organization. How I can get CST Declaration Forms Receivables for all the Parties of a specified geographical location (e.g for a State/ District / Town) for better tracking.

VAT Computation — Ctrl + M

Particulars	ABC Electrical TIN : ABDFE1234C 1-Apr-2009 to 31-Mar-2010	
	Assessable Value	Tax Amount
Sales		
A. Output Tax		
CST @ 1%	1,600.00	16.00
Output VAT @ 12.5%	3,100.00	387.50
Output VAT @ 4%	400.00	16.00
Total Output Tax	**5,100.00**	**419.50**
Purchases		
C. Input Tax		
Excess Input Credit Brought Forward		
Input VAT @ 12.5%	2,986.00	373.25
Input VAT @ 4%	300.00	12.00
Total Input Credit	**3,286.00**	**385.25**
VAT Payable		**34.25**

F-12A: VAT / CST Computation Report

F-12B: VAT / CST Computation Configuration

Configuration

Show All VAT Classifications	? No
Show CST Details	? Yes
Show VAT Analysis	? No

Forms Receivable — **ABC Electrical** — Ctrl + M

Group Name: **Sundry Creditors** — **1-Apr-2009 to 31-Mar-2010**

Date	Particulars	CST No.	Vch Type	Vch No.	Assessable Value	CST Amount	Invoice Amount	Form Type	Series Number	Form Number	Form Date
2-5-2009	B.K.Services		Sales	3	1,600.00 Cr	16.00 Cr	1,616.00 Cr	C Form	AC	123456	1-Jul-2009

F-13A:Forms Received Data entry

Ans: Since the Parties are grouped into multiple levels in State / District / Town, you may print Forms receivable for a specified Location, by selecting the respective Group of Customers (Sundry Debtor).

At CST Forms Receivable Menu (F-2A), select *Group* and then select an Account Group for which you like to display the outstanding Forms Receivable (F-5A) for all the Parties under the selected Account Group.

CST Returns

05-05

01 CST Statutory Returns

A Registered Party has to file CST periodically. Here, we describe about printing of CST Returns and its annexures

Gateway of Tally ....
Display Menu ....
Statutory Reports ....
CST Reports ....

CST Forms

- CST Return
- Annexures
- Quit

F-1A CST Returns Menu

Gateway of Tally ....
Display Menu ....
Statutory Reports ...
CST Reports ....
CST Forms ....

CST Annexures

- Annexure A
- ANnexure B1
- AnnExure B2
- AnneXure C
- AnnexUre D
- AnnexuRe E
- Annexure F
- Annexure G
- Sales Return
- Quit

F-1B:CST Annexures Menu

Report Titles

WBCSTReturn

From (blank for beginning)	:	1-4-2009
To (blank for end)	:	1-7-2009
Type of Return	:	**Original**
Name	:	**Manab Basu**
Status/Designation	:	**Proprietor**
Place	:	**Kolkata**
Date	:	2-7-2009

F-2A: CST Returns Printing screen

02 CST Returns Menu

At *GoT>Display>Statutory Reports>CST Reports, select CST Forms* to get *CST Returns Menu* (F-1A) to print CST Statutory Returns and its Annexures.

03 CST Return

CST Return (F-2B) is a Statutory Return to be submitted at the end of specified period, in the prescribed Form along with all specified Annexures. The Format & contents of CST Return and its Annexures vary according to State. Here, we have show an example of West Bengal CST Return Form (F-2B).

At *CST Returns Menu (*referred as CST Form Menu in Tally Menu: F-1A), select *CST Return* to get *CST Return Printing* screen (F-2A).

At *CST Return Printing screen* (F-2A), enter the Tax Period of the Return and other details (carried from the CST details at Company Statutory details), which you may change. Enter the Report Date (F-2A) and type *Y* to print the Report (F-2B).

FORM - 1

[See rule 8 of the Central Sales Tax (West Bengal) Rules, 1958]

Return of sales tax payable under the Central Sales Tax Act, 1956, for the period form

From:01/04/2009	Registration Certificate No.86531240	To:01/07/2009
	Whether original or revised return ?	Original

1.	Transfer of goods otherwise than by way of sales as referred to in section 6A the Act	
(a)	Value of goods transferred to the assessee's place of principal in other States[Details to be furnished in Annexure A]	NIL
(b)	Value of goods transferred to the assessee's agent or principal in other States (Details to be furnished in Annexure A)	NIL
2.	Gross amount payable to the dealer as consideration for the sales of goods made during the above period in respect to	
(a)	Sales in the course of Inter-State Trade or Commerce including all sales u/s 2(g)	1,616.00
(b)	Sales of goods outside the State (as provided in section 4 of the Act)	NIL
(c)	Sales of goods in the course of export outside India [as provided in section 5(1) of the Act]	NIL
(d)	Sales of goods in the course of import into India [as provided in section 5(2) of the Act]	NIL
(e)	Last sales of goods preceding the sales occasioning the export of those goods outside India [as provided in section 5(3) of the Act] (Details to be furnished in annexure B)	NIL
(f)	Sales of Aviation Turbine Fuel to designated Indian Carriers [as provided in section 5(5) of the Act]	NIL
(g)	Sales effected at place inside West Bengal	3,100.00
Total:	2((a) + (b) + (c) + (d) + (e) + (f) + (g))	4,716.00
3	Gross amount payable to the dealer as consideration for the sales of goods made in the course of Inter-State Trade or Commerce as per SL. No. 2(a) during the above period	1,616.00
4.	Less:	
(a)	Cost of freight,delivery or installation separately charged on customers and includend in SL. No. 3	NIL
(b)	Cash discount allowed according to the practice normally prevailing in the trade and included in SL. No. 3	NIL
(c)	Sale price refunded to purchasers in respect of goods returned by them according to section 8A(1)(b) of the Act,[Statement to be furnished in Annexure Sales Return (CST)]	NIL
Total	of 4(a), 4(b) and 4(c) :	NIL
5.	Balance (3-4): total turnover or inter-State sales.	1,616.00
6.	Deduct :	
(a)	Sale prices received or receivable by the dealer in respect of subsequent sales under section 6(2) of the Act against prescribed certificate(s) and included in SL. No 5 [Details to be furnished in Annexure E & Annexure G]	NIL
(b)	Sale prices received or receivable by the dealer in respect of sales to any official, personnel, consular or diplomatic agent of any foreign diplomatic mission or consulatein India or the United Nations or any other similar international body under section 6(3)of the Act and included in Sl. No. 5	NIL

F-2B: CST Return (PART -1)

(c)	Sale prices received or receivable by the dealer in respect of sales made to a registered dealer of special economic zone under section 8(6) of the Act and included in Sl. No. 5(Details to be furnished in Annexure C)	NIL
(d)	Sale prices received or receivable by the dealer in respect of sales exempt under section8(5) of the Act and included in Sl. No. 5 [Details to be furnished in Annexure E & Annexure G]	NIL
(e)	Any other sales eligible for exemption and included in SL. No 5	NIL
(f)	Total : 6 [(a) + (b) + (c) + (d) + (e)]	NIL
7.	Balance 'X' > [(5) - (6)(f)]	1,616.00

Break up of Balance X as in Sl. No. 7 [If there is no claim of sales return in Sl. No. 4(c)] Break up of Aggregate of Sale Price as in column(1) of Annexure Sales Return (CST) [If sales return is claimed in sl. no. 4(c)]	Amount (1)	Deduction u /s 8A(1a) not claimed earlier (2)	Balance(1-2) (3)	Tax Payable on balance as in col. (3)(4)
(a) Sales in the course of inter-State trade or commerce of goods, the sales of which are free of tax, under section 21 of the West Bengal Value Added Tax Act, 2003 or under section 24 of the West Bengal Sales Tax Act, 1994				

(b) Sales of goods referred to in sub-section (1) of section 8 ofthe Act to registered dealers against prescribed declarationforms (Details to the furnished in Annexure D)				
(i) Taxable at the rate of 2 per centum				
TOTAL				
(c) Sales of goods notified under sub-section (5) of section 8 ofthe Act not included in any other item-				
(i) Taxable at the rate of 1 per centum	1,616.00	16.00	1,600.00	16.00
(d) Other sales of goods [not included in SL.No. 8(a), SL.No.8(b) and Sl.No. 8(c)], referred to in sub -section (2) of section 8, taxable at the rate applicable to sale or purchase of such goods inside the State under the sales tax law of the State -	Amount (1)	Deduction u /s 8A(1a) not claimed earlier (2)	Balance(1-2) (3)	Tax Payable on balance as in col. (3)(4)
(e) Total : [Total of columns of (a), (b), (c), & (d)]	1,616.00	16.00	1,600.00	16.00
9.				
(a) Total tax payable as in column (4) of 8(e)				16.00
(b) Adjustment, if any, in respect of tax payable on account of sales return				NIL
(c) Adjustment, if any, in respect of tax payable other than sales return				NIL
(d) Net amount of tax liability [(a)-(b)+/-(c)]				16.00
10				
(a) Break up of total tax payable as in column (2) of 9(c)			16.00	
(b) Less: amount of tax deferred / remitted, if any				
(c) Less: adjustment of input tax credit or input tax rebate as referred to in rule 8D of the CST (WB) Rules, 1958				
(d) Add: amount of deferred tax payable, if any(Only for dealers whose deferment of tax has expired)				

CST Return (PART - 2)

(e) Net amount of tax payable [(a)-(b)-(c)+(d)]		16.00	
11 (a) Tax paid in excess earlier within the year, now adjusted			
(b) Tax paid for the period into government treasury			
(c) Amount credited under Refund Adjustment Order RAO Book No. SL.No. Date			
(d) Tax short paid / Tax paid in excess. [10(e) -11(a) -11(b) -11(c)] :[use (-) for excess]		16.00	
12 (a) Interest payable as referred to in section 9(2B) of the Act read with section 33 of the West Bengal Value Added Tax Act, 2003 or section 31 of the West Bengal Sales Tax Act, 1994.			
(b) Interest paid for the period into government treasury			
(c) Interest short paid / paid in excess : [(a) - (b)] [use (-) for excess]			

13.(a) Late fee, referred to in section 32(2) of the West Bengal Value Added Tax Act, 2003, payable for late submission of return (For Extended period set payable value to 0 (zero))								
13.(b) Late fee, referred to in section 32(2) of the West Bengal Value Added Tax Act, 2003, paid into government treasury								
Payment Details								
Date (dd/mm/yyyy)	Challan no	Bank/Treasury			Period (yyyymm)	Amount		
		Name	Branch	Code		Tax	Interest	Late Fee
					TOTAL			
14.Goods purchased within the meaning of section 3 of the Central Sales Tax Act, 1956 and for which Form C is required. [Details to be furnished in Annexure E]								618.10
15.Receipt of goods on stock transfer from other States within the meaning of section 6A of Central Sales Tax Act,1956 and for which Form F is required. [Details to be furnished in Annexure F]								
16. I declare that the information given in this return is correct and complete								

Date:-2-Jul-2009

Signature
Name:-Manab Basu
Status:-Proprietor

CST Return (PART -3)

04 CST Return Annexures

The CST Return is to be submitted along with its Annexures. At *CST Returns Menu (*referred as CST Form Menu in Tally Menu: F-1A), select *Annexures* to get *CST Annexures.Menu* (F-1B) The Annexure Menu (F-1B) may vary according to the State in which the Company is registered for CST. Here, we show the specimen Annexures related to West Bengal CST Return (F-1B).

At *CST Annexures Menu*(F-1B)*,* select the Annexure to get the respective Annexure printing screen, similar to CST Return Printing screen (F-2A).

Enter the Report date and type *Y* to print the Annexure (F-3A).

ANNEXURE-SALE-RETURN

Details of subsequent sales u/s 6(2) of the CST Act, 1956 as shown in serial no. 6(a) in Form 1

CST Registration No: 86531240 — **From Date : 01-04-2009** / **To Date : 01-07-2009**

Nature of interState sale from W.B.	Aggrgate of Sale Price(Rs.)	Amount of Sale Return(Rs.)	Net Sale Turnover(Rs.)	Tax involvement in Sales Return(Rs.)
(I) Sales of exempted goods				
(II) Sales exempt u/s 5 of CST Act,1956				
(III) Sales taxable @ 1%	1,600.00		1,600.00	
(IV) Sales taxable @ 4%				
(V) Sales taxable @ 10%				
(VI) Sales taxable @ 12.5%				
(VII) Sales taxable @ 2%				
(VIII) Sales taxable @ 3.84%				
TOTAL	1,600.00		1,600.00	

Date: 2-Jul-2009 **Signature**

F-3A: Annexure of Sales

FAQ: Frequently Asked Questions

FAQ: How do I print CST Return

Ans: At *CST Returns Menu (*referred as *CST Form Menu* in Tally Menu: F-1A), select *CST Return* to get *CST Return Printing* screen (F-2A).

At *CST Return Printing screen* (F-2A), enter the Tax Period of the Return and other details (these are carried from the CST details at Company Statutory details), which you may change. Enter the Report Date (F-2A) and type *Y* to print the Report (F-2B).

Part 6
Excise Duty

In this Part, we describe the process of Set Up, Masters Creation, Invoicing, maintenance & Compliance of records & filing of Returns under by organisations registered under Central Excise rules

Excise Duty explains the definition & explanation of Excise Related Terms, Excisable Goods and Statutory Returns & Forms

Excise Set Up for Manufacturers, describes the process of Activation & et Up of Statutory Information & Masters creation related o Excise Duty, for Manufacturers

Excise Voucher Entry for Manufacturers describes creation of Excisable Goods Purchase & Invoicing and Excise related transactions for Manufacturers.

Excise Duty Payment explains payment of Duty to the Government

Excise Set Up for Dealers, describes the process f Activation & et Up of Statutory Information & Masters creation related to Excise Duty, for Dealers

Excise Voucher Entry for Dealers describes creation of Excisable Goods Purchase & Invoicing and Excise related transactions for Dealers.

Excise Duty Reports for Dealers describes various Excise related Reports

Excise Duty for Manufacturers describes Reports for Manufacturers.

Customs Duty describes the process of Imports and payment of Customs Duty on ustoms clearance

Special Cases describes various exceptional & special situations related to Excise Duty

Excise Duty 06-01

01 Excisable Goods

Excisable Goods means certain marketable goods (capable of being bought & sold) specified in the schedule to the Central Excise Tariff Act, 1985 as being subject to a Duty of Excise.

02 Excise Duty

Excise Duty is a Tax on certain specified goods (called *Excisable Goods*) manufactured or produced in India and intended for domestic consumption (i.e. Sale in India). The Excise Duty is payable at the time of production or manufacture. However, for administrative convenience, duty is paid at the time of removal of goods.

Excise Duty is an *Indirect Tax*. The liability of payment of Excise Duty is of manufacturers or producers (which is passed on to the ultimate consumer). The levy and collection of duty of Excise is provided under authority of the Central Excise Act, 1944 at the rates specified under Central Excise Tariff Act, 1985.

03 Excise Duty Chargeability

Excise Duty chargeability of Various Excise Duties are summarised in the following Table

Type of Duty		Computed on
Basic Excise Duty (BED)	Excise	On Assessable Value
Special Excise Duty (SED)	Excise	On Assessable Value
AED (GSI)	Excise	On Assessable Value
AED (TTA)	Excise	On BED + SED
AED (TTW)	Excise	On BED + SED
AED (PM&T)	Excise	On BED + SED
NCCD (GSI)	Excise	On BED + SED + AED
Special AED	Excise	On Quantity
AED on High Speed Diesel	Excise	On Quantity
Educational Cess	Excise	On Total Excise Duty
SHE Cess on Excise duty	Excise	On Total Excise Duty
Countervailing Duty) (CVD	CVD	On Assessable Value
SED of CVD	CVD	On Assessable Value
AED (GSI) of CVD	CVD	On Assessable Value
AED (TTA) of CVD	CVD	On CVD + SED of CVD
AED (TTW) of CVD	CVD	On CVD + SED of CVD
AED (PM&T) of CVD	CVD	On CVD + SED of CVD
NCCD of CVD	CVD	On CVD + SED of CVD + AED (GSI) of CVD
Special AED of CVD	CVD	On Quantity
AED on High Speed Diesel of CVD	CVD	On Quantity
Educational Cess on CVD	CVD	On Total CVD
SHE Cess on CVD	CVD	On Total CVD

04 Excise Duty Types

Excise Duty may of various types and may have several components into it, as described below:

- **Basic Excise Duty**: Basic Excise Duty is charged on all excisable goods (other than salt) produced or manufactured in India.
- **Special Excise Duty**: Special excise Duty is charged on all excisable goods where Basic excise Duty is applicable
- **Education Cess on excise duty**: Education cess is *Duty on Excise*. It is calculated on aggregate of all duties of excise including special excise duty or any other duty of excise, but excluding education cess on excisable goods.
- **Excise duty in case of clearances by EOU**: The EOU units are expected to export all their production. However, if they clear their final product in DTA (domestic tariff area), the rate of excise duty will be equal to customs duty on like article if imported in India.
- **National Calamity contingent Duty (NCCD)**: A 'National Calamity Contingent Duty' (NCCD) is Charged on Tobacco Products like Pan Masala, chewing tobacco and cigarettes.
- **Additional Duty on goods of special importance** - Additional Duties of Excise is charged on some goods of special importance (like cotton fabrics, silk and wool fabrics, man-made fibres, terry fabrics, metallised yarn, embroidery; sugar, branded tobacco, pan masala

containing tobacco and cigarettes). The 'Additional Duty' is in addition to Excise Duty.

- **Duty on Medical and Toilet preparations**: This is imposed on medical preparations
- **Additional duty on mineral products** – This is also an Additional duty charged on mineral products (like motor spirit, kerosene, diesel and furnace oil)
- **Additional Customs Duty (countervailing Duty -CVD)**: Countervailing duty (CVD) is imposed on the Imports.
- **Special Additional Duty of Customs (Special CVD)**: Special CVD is being imposed on items bound under the Information Technology Agreement (except information technology software), and also on specified inputs/raw materials for manufacture of electronics/IT goods.
- **Additional Duties of Excise (Textiles and Textile Articles) [AED (TTA)]:** This is applicable on specified Textile & Textile Articles
- **Additional Duty of Excise (Tea and Tea Waste) [AED (TTW)]** This is applicable on specified Tea Products
- **Secondary Higher Education Cess:** This is charged on Excise Duty / CVD

Duties under other Acts: Some Duties and Cesses are levied on manufactured products under other Acts. The administrative machinery of central excise is used to collect those taxes. Provisions of Central Excise Act and Rules have been made applicable for levy and collection of these Duties / Cesses.

05 Valuation Methods

Value of the excisable goods (called Assessable Value) has to be determined to levy the duty

- **Ad valorem/ Transaction Value**: Transaction value means the value of goods which are sold at the time and place of removal. In addition to Product Price, it includes any amount that the Buyer is liable to pay for advertising or publicity, marketing and selling, organization expenses, storage, outward handling, servicing, warranty, commission or any other matter.
- **Ad Quantum**: In case of Ad Quantum, the duty is Payable on the basis of UoM (Unit of Measure, like Weight, Length, Volume etc). For example, Duty on cigarette is payable on the basis of length of the cigarette, duty on Sugar is based on per Kg.
- **Value determined on the basis of Maximum Retail Sale Price**: In such case, Assessable Value is computed on Retail Sale price (MRP) of the goods (irrespective of transaction value). It also includes all taxes local or otherwise, freight, transport charges, commission payable to dealers, and all charges towards advertisement, delivery, packing, forwarding etc.

06 CENVAT Credit

A manufacturer or producer of final product is allowed to take CENVAT credit of duties specified in the Cenvat Credit Rules, 2002.

The duties specified under Cenvat Credit Rules, 2002 are:

- Basic Excise Duty on inputs specified in the First Schedule to Central Excise tariff Act (corresponding CVD on imported goods is allowable).
- Special Excise Duty on goods specified in the Second Schedule to the Tariff Act (corresponding CVD on imported goods is allowable).
- Additional Excise Duty paid under Additional Duties of Excise (Textile and Textile Article).
- Additional Excise Duty paid under Additional Duties of Excise (Goods of Special Importance).
- National Calamity Contingent duty (NCCD).
- Education Cess and Secondary and Higher Education Cess on Excise Duty.
- Additional custom duty leviable under Customs Tariff Act (Spl. CVD)
- Education Cess and Secondary and Higher Education Cess on CVD
- Additional Excise Duty paid under Clause 85 of Finance Bill,2005 on Pan Masala and Certain other Tobacco products.
- Service Tax on Input Services.
- Education Cess and Secondary & Higher Education Cess paid on service tax. This credit can be utilised only for payment of education Cess on final product or output services.

07 Excise System in Tally

The entire Excise System in Tally may be divided into following steps & components

- Activation of Excise Duty Features for each Company
- Masters creation
- Voucher Entry
- Reports & Filing of Returns

07.01 Activation of Excise

At Company Features, activate Excise Duty at Company Features menu (Inventory & Statutory)

07.02 Masters creation

Creation of Various types of Masters and special features for maintenance & compliance of Excise System as per statutory Rules

Depending on applicable Excise Duty Type & components, you may need to create the following:

a. Ledgers
   - o Basic Excise Duty Ledger
   - o Education Cess Ledger
   - o Secondary and Higher Education (SHE) Cess Ledger
   - o Expenses Ledger

b. Voucher Types
   - o Excise Voucher Types

c. Tariff Classification
d. Stock Item Group
  o Raw materials
  o Finished Goods (MRP)
  o Finished Goods (Quantum)
  o Finished Goods (Ad Valorem)

07.03 Vouchers Creation

Create the following types of special transaction relating to Excise

a. Purchase Voucher
  o Excise Purchase Voucher – Not Availing CENVAT Credit
  o Excise Purchase Voucher – Availing CENVAT Credit
  o Debit Note (Purchase Returns) – Rule 11 invoice
b. Manufacturing Voucher
  c. Sales Voucher
  o Rule 11 Invoice
  o Rule 11 Invoice for Stock Items Falling Under Different Valuation
  o Rule 11 Invoice for Stock Items with Expenses
d. Journal Voucher – CENVAT Credit Adjustment
e. Payment Voucher – GAR 7 Payment

07.04 Excise Reports for Manufacturers

You may get following Excise Reports for manufacturer from *Gateway of Tally > Display > Statutory Reports > Excise Reports > Manufacturer*

- **Excise Computation**: Excise Computation report displays complete information about excise transactions for a period.
- **Daily Stock Register**: Daily Stock Register is a record of stock maintained on daily basis by every assessee
- **PLA Register**: Personal Ledger Account (PLA) is an account current in which particulars of duty paid to the Government is recorded. It shows the particulars of Duty Payable, PLA & CENVAT Credit & Balance in the PLA account.
- **Form ER 1**: Form ER 1 is a monthly return for production, removal of Goods, other relevant particulars and CENVAT Credit to be filed by assesses.
- **CENVAT Credit Register**: It displays the details of CENVAT credit availed of Principal Input or Capital Goods.

08 Central Excise Tariff 2012-13

THE FIRST SCHEDULETo the Central Excise Tariff Act, 1985 (5 of 1986) and Exemption Notifications (other than general)

Section-I Live Animals; Animal Products	
Chapters 1-4	Chapter 1: Live Animals Chapter 2: Meat and edible meat offal Chapter 3: Fish and crustaceans, molluscs and other aquatic invertebrates Chapter 4: Dairy produce; birds' eggs; natural honey; edible products of animal origin, not elsewhere specified or included
Chapters 5-6	Chapter 5: Products of animal origin, not elsewhere specified or included
Section-II Vegetable Products	
Chapters 1-4	Chapter 1: Live Animals
Chapter 6	Live trees and other plants; bulbs, roots and the like; cut flowers & ornamental foliage
Chapter 7	Edible vegetables and certain roots and tubers
Chapter 8	Edible fruit and nuts; peel of citrus fruit or melons
Chapter 9	Coffee, tea, mate and spices
Chapter 10	Cereals
Chapter 11	Products of the milling industry; malt; starches; inulin; wheat gluten
Chapter 12	Oil seeds and oleaginous fruits, miscellaneous grains, seeds and fruit; industrial or medicinal plants; straw and fodder
Chapter 13	Lac; gums; resins and other vegetable saps and extracts
Chapter 14	Vegetable plaiting materials; vegetable products, not elsewhere specified or included
Section-III Animal or Vegetable Fats and Oils & their Cleavage Products; Prepared Edible Fats; Animal or Vegetable Waxes.	
Chapter 15	Animal or vegetable fats and oils and their cleavage products; prepared edible fats; animal or vegetable waxes
Section-IV Prepared Foodstuffs; Beverages & Vinegar; Tobacco & Manufactured Tobacco Substitutes	
Chapter 16	Preparations of meat, of fish or of crustaceans, molasses or other aquatic invertebrates
Chapter 17	Sugar and sugar confectionery.
Chapter 18	Cocoa and cocoa preparations
Chapter 19	Preparations of cereals, flour, starch or milk; pastrycooks' products
Chapter 20	Preparations of vegetables, fruit, nuts or other parts of plants.

Chapter 21	Miscellaneous edible preparations
Chapter 22	Beverages, vinegar and spirits
Chapter 23	Residues and wastes from the food industries; prepared animal fodder
Chapter 24	Tobacco and manufactured tobacco substitutes
Section-V Mineral Products	
Chapter 25	Salt; sulphur; earths and stone; plastering materials, lime and cement
Chapter 26	Ores, slag and ash
Chapter 27	Mineral fuels, mineral oils and products of their distillation; bituminous substances, mineral waxes
Section-VI Products of the Chemical or Allied Industries	
Chapter 28	Inorganic chemicals; organic or inorganic compounds of precious metals, of rare earth metals, of radioactive elements or of isotopes
Chapter 29	Organic chemicals
Chapter 30	Pharmaceutical products
Chapters 31-32	Chapter 31: Fertilizers Chapter 32: Tanning or dyeing extracts; tannins and their derivatives; dyes, pigments and othercolouring matter; paints and varnishes; putty and other mastics; inks
Chapters 33-34	Chapter 33: Essential oils and resinoids; perfumery, cosmetics or toilet preparations Chapter 34: Soap, organic surface-active agents, washing preparations, lubricating preparations, artificial waxes, prepared waxes, polishing or scouring preparations, candles and similar articles, modelling pastes, dental waxes and dental preparations with a basis of plaster
Chapters 35-37	Chapter 35: Aluminoidal substances; modified starches; glues; enzymes Chapter 36: Explosives; pyrotechnic products; matches; pyrophoric alloys; certain combustible preparations Chapter 37: Photographic or cinematographic goods Chapter38: Miscellaneous chemical products
Section-VII Plastics & Articles thereof: Rubber & Articles thereof	
Chapter 39	Chapter 39: Plastics and articles thereof
Chapter 40	Rubber and articles thereof
Section-VIII Raw Hides & Skins, Leather, Furskins & Articles Thereof; Saddlery & Harness; Travel Goods, Handbags & Similar Containers; Articles of Animal Gut (Other Than Silk - Worm Gut)	
Chapter 41	Raw Hides and Skins (other than Furskins) and Leather
Chapters 42-43	Chapter 42: Articles of leather; saddlery and harness; travel goods, handbags and similar containers; articles of animal gut (other than silk-worm gut) Chapter 43: Fur skins and artificial fur; manufacturers thereof
Section-IX Wood And Articles of Wood; Wood Charcoal; Cork And Articles of Cork; Manufactures of Straw,of Esparto or of Other Plaiting materials; Basket ware & Wicker work	
Chapters 44-45	Chapter 44: Wood and articles of wood, wood charcoal Chapter 45: Cork and articles of cork
Chapter 46	Manufactures of straw, of esparto or of other plaiting materials; Basket-ware and wickerwork
Section-X Pulp of Wood or of other Fibrous cellulosic Material; Recovered (Waste and scrap) Paper Or Paper- Board; Paper & Paper-Board & Articles thereof	
Chapters 47-48	Chapter 47: Pulp of wood or of other fibrous cellulosic material; recovered (waste and scrap) paper or paperboard Chapter 48: Paper and paperboard; articles of paper pulp, of paper or of paperboard
Chapters 49-51	Chapter 49: Printed books, newspapers, pictures and other products of the printing industry, manuscripts, typescripts and plans
Section-XI Textiles & Textile Articles	
	Chapter 50: Silk Chapter 51: Wool, fine or coarse animal hair; horsehair yarn and woven fabric
Chapter 52	Cotton
Chapter 53	Other vegetable textile fibres; paper yarn and woven fabrics of paper yarns
Chapter 54	Man-made filaments; strip ɘ like of man-made textile materials
Chapter 56	Man-made staple fibres

Chapters 56-58	Chapter 56: Wadding, felt and nonwovens; special yarns; twine, cordage, ropes and cables and articles thereof Chapter 57: Carpets and other textile floor coverings Chapter 58: Special woven fabrics; tufted textile fabrics; lace; tapestries; trimmings; embroidery
Chapter 59	Impregnated, coated, covered or laminated textile fabrics; textile articles of a kind suitable for industrial use
Chapter 60	Knitted or crocheted fabrics
Chapters 61-62	Chapter 61: Articles of apparel and clothing accessories, knitted or crocheted Chapter 62: Articles of apparel and clothing accessories, not knitted or crocheted
Chapters 63-68	Chapter 63: Other made up textile articles, sets, worn clothing and worn textile articles; rags
Section-XII Footwear, Headgear, Umbrellas, Sun Umbrellas, Walking sticks, Seat-Sticks, Whips, Riding - Crops And Parts Thereof, Prepared Feathers & Articles made therewith; Artificial Flowers, Articles of Human Hair	
	Chapter 64: Footwear gaiters and the like; parts of such articles Chapter 65: Headgear and parts thereof Chapter 66: Umbrellas, sun umbrellas, walking-sticks, seat-sticks, whips, riding-crops and parts thereof Chapter 67: Prepared feathers and down and articles made of feather or of down - artificial flowers; articles of human hair
Section-XIII Articles Of Stone, Plaster, Cement, Asbestos, Mica or Similar Materials: Ceramic Products, Glass And Glassware	
Chapters 69-71	Chapter 68: Articles of stone, plaster, cement, asbestos, mica or similar material Chapter 69: Ceramic products Chapter 70: Glass and glassware
Section-XIV Natural or Cultured Pearls, Precious or Semi-Precious Stones, Precious Metals, Metals Clad With Precious Metal, And Articles thereof, Imitation Jewellery, Coin	
Chapter 71	Natural or cultured pearls, precious or semi-precious stones, precious metals, metals clad with precious metal, and articles thereof; imitation jewellery; coin.
Section-XV Base Metals & Articles of Base Metal	
Chapter 72	Iron and steel
Chapter 73	Articles of iron or steel
Chapter 74	Copper and articles thereof
Chapters 75-76	Chapter 75: Nickel and articles thereof Chapter 76: Aluminium and articles thereof
Chapters 77-78	Chapter 77: Blank Chapter 78: Lead and articles thereof
Chapter 79	Zinc and articles thereof
Chapter 80	Tin and articles thereof
Chapters 81-83	Chapter 81: Other base metals; cermets; articles thereof Chapter 82: Tools, implements, cutlery, spoons and forks of base metal; parts thereof of base metal Chapter 83: Miscellaneous articles of base metal
Section-XVI Machinery & Mechanical Appliances, Electrical Equipments; Parts thereof; Sound Recorders & Reproducers, Television Image & Sound Recorders & Reproducers, & Parts & Accessories of such Articles	
Chapter 84	Nuclear reactors, boilers, machinery and mechanical appliances; parts thereof
Chapter 85	Electrical machinery and equipment and parts thereof; sound recorders and re-producers, television image and sound recorders and reproducers, and parts and accessories of such articles
Section-XVII Vehicles, Aircraft, Vessels & Associated Transport Equipment	
Chapters 86-87	Chapter 86: Railway or tramway locomotives, rolling-stocks and parts thereof; railway or tramway track fixtures and fittings and parts thereof; mechanical (includingelectro mechanical) traffic signalling equipment of all kinds Chapter 87: Vehicles other than railway or tramway rolling-stocks, and parts and accessories thereof
Chapter 88	Aircraft; spacecraft and parts thereof
Chapter 89	Ships, boats and floating structures

Section-XVIII Optical, Photographic, Cinematographic, Measuring, Checking, Precision, Medical Or Surgical Instruments & Apparatus; Clocks & Watches; Musical Instruments; Parts And Accessories thereof	
Chapter 90	Optical, photographic, cinematographic, measuring, checking, precision, medical or surgical instruments and apparatus; parts and accessories thereof
Chapters 91-92	Chapter 91: Clocks and watches and parts thereof Chapter 92: Musical instruments; parts and accessories of such articles
Section-XIX Arms & Ammunition, Parts & Accessories thereof	
Chapters 93-95	Chapter 93: Arms and ammunition; parts and accessories thereof
Section-XX Miscellaneous Manufactured Articles	
	Chapter 94: Furnitures; bedding, mattresses, mattress supports, cushions and similar stuffed furnishings; lamps and lighting fittings, not elsewhere specified or included; illuminated signs, illuminated name-plates and the like; prefabricated buildings Chapter 95: Toys, games and sports requisites; parts and accessories thereof
Chapter 96	Chapter 96: Miscellaneous manufactured articles
Section XXI Works Of Art, Collectors' Pieces & Antiques	
Chapters 97-98	Chapter 97: Blank Chapter 98: Blank

General Exemptions Central Excise Tariff 2012-13

Second Schedule and Third Schedule-Central Excise Act, 1944

Appendix - I and II	Appendix-I: The Additional Duties of Excise (Goods of Special Importance) Act, 1957Appendix-II: The Additional Duties of Excise (Textiles and Textile Articles) Act, 1978
Appendix - III	National Calamity Contingent Duty (NCCD)
Appendix – IV and IVA	Appendix-IV: Cess on various commodities collected as central excise duty
Appendix-IVA:	Clean Energy Cess, Clean Energy Cess Rules, 2010
Appendix – V, VI and VII	Appendix-V: Assessment on the basis of MRP (abatement as a percentage of retail sale price) Additional duty of excise on pan-masala and certain tobacco products
Appendix-VII:	Provisions of Finance Bill, 2007 relating to levy of Secondary & Higher Education Cess on excisable goods.
Appendix A and B	Appendix-A: Year-wise index of main notifications in force as on 17.3.2012 and Clean Energy CessAppendix-B: list of central excise notifications (tariff/non tariff) rescinded/Superseded/validity expired during the period 10.7.2004 to 17.3.2012

List of Forms

Form of application	Settlement Commission - Form of application for settlement of a case under section 32E
GAR 7 Challan (Front II Reverse)	G.A.R.-7 Proforma for Central Excise Tax Payments (Receipt & Payment Rules 26)
FORM A-1	New Central Excise Registration form. To fill this form Please see Instruction-1 and Instruction-2
FORM A-2	Application form for central excise registration of powerloom weavers / hand processors / Dealers of Yarns and Fabrics/manufacturers of ready-made Garments
FORM A-3	Application form for central excise registration of manufacturers of hand rolled cheroots of tobacco falling under sub-heading no. 2402.00 of central excise tariff act, 1985.
FORM RC	Central Excise Registration Certificate
Surrender of FORM RC	Surrender of Registration Certificate
Declaration FORM	Declaration FORM
FORM for New ECC No.	Format for application for obtaining new excise control code number
FORM B-2	General Bond (Surety/Security)
PLA	Personal Ledger Account
Pass out document	For removal of Liquid gases
Monthly return for	Proforma for monthly return under

CENVAT	rule 7 of the CENVAT Credit Rules, 2001
FORM AC-1	Account of Removals from FTZ, EOU and SEZ to Domestic Tariff Area
FORM E.R.- 1	Monthly return for production and removal of goods and other relevant particulars and CENVAT credit
FORM E.R.-2	Monthly Return for hundred percent EOUs in respect of goods manufactured, goods cleared and receipt of inputs and capital goods
FORM E.R. - 3	Quarterly return for production and removal of goods and other relevant particulars and CENVAT credit
FORM E.R. - 4	Annual financial information statement
FORM E.R. - 5	CENVAT - Annual return of information relating to principal inputs
FORM E.R. - 6	CENVAT - Monthly return of information relating to principal inputs
Form ER - 7	Annual Installed Capacity Statement
Form E.R.- 8	Simplified form for quarterly return of excisable goods cleared @ 1% duty
Quarterly Return Form	Quarterly Return for the Registered Dealers (Under Rule 7 of the CENVAT Credit Rules, 2002)
FORM A.R.E.-1	Application for removal of excisable goods for export by air/sea/post/land
FORM UT-1	Letter of undertaking for removal-for export of excisable goods without payment of duty
FORM B-1	General bond with surety/security for removal for export of excisable goods without payment of duty
FORM CT-1	Certificate for procurement of excisable goods for export without payment of duty
FORM CT-1	Certificate for procurement of excisable goods for export without payment of duty from EOU
Proforma for B-1 Bond	Proforma of Running Bond Account in respect of B-1 Bond
Statement	Statement regarding Export of excisable goods without duty
Return	Return for manufacturers following simplified Export procedure
Invoice	Invoice for goods transmitted to Nepal under Central Excise Seal
	(Also see Notification No. 20/2004-C.E. (N.T.), dated 06-09-2004)
Invoice	Invoice for goods transmitted to Nepal or Bhutan under Central Excise Seal (Also see Notification No. 45/2001-C.E. (N.T.), dated26-06-2001)
Bank Certificate	Bank Certificate for bills covering exports to Nepal / Bhutan
FORM A.R.E.-2	Combined application for removal of goods for export under claim for rebate of duty
Rebate Form	Form of declaration for availing benefit of rebate of Central Excise Duty paid on export of goods
FORM A.R.E.-3	Application for removal of goods from a factory or a warehouse to another warehouse
FORM B-3	General Bond (security)
Proforma of B-3 Bond	Proforma of Running Bond Account in respect of B-3 Bond
FORM C.T.-2	Certificate for procurement of excisable goods under Procedure for Export Warehousing
FORM C.T.-3	Certificate for removal of excisable goods under bond
FORM A.S.P. II (Appendix-I)	Application for permission to avail of the special procedure relating to stainless steel pattis/pattas or aluminium circles
Appendix-II	Removal of stainless steel patties/ pattas under special procedure
ASP I	Application for permission to avail of the special procedure relating to embroidery
Production register	Production register to be maintained by the manufacturer of embroidery working under special procedure
FORM No. E.A. - I	Form of Appeal to the Commissioner (Appeals) under section 35 of the Act
FORM No. E.A.- 2	Form of Application to the Commissioner (Appeals) under sub-section (4) of section 35E of the Act
FORM No. E.A.- 3	Form of Appeal to Appellate Tribunal under sub-section (1) of section 35B of the Act
FORM No. E.A.- 4	Form of Memorandum of Cross-Objections to the Appellate Tribunal under sub-section (4) of section 35B of the Act

FORM No. E.A.- 5	Form of appeal or application to Appellate Tribunal under sub-section (2) of section 35B or under sub-section (1) of section 35E of the Act
FORM No. E.A.- 6	Form of Application to the High Court under sub-section (1) of section 35H of the Act
FORM No. E.A.- 7	Form of Memorandum of Cross-Objections under sub-section (3) of section 35H of the Act
FORM No. E.A.- 8	Form of revision application to the Central Government under section 35EE of the Act
FORM AAR (CE-I)	Form of application for seeking Advance Ruling under section 23C of the Central Excise Act,1944
Form A	Application for refund of CENVAT credit under rule 5 of the CENVAT Credit Rules, 2004
Proforma	Proforma of Challan and Textile Quaterly Statement Form
Application Form	Application to avail the facility of filing excise returns electronically
Application Form	Application for Compounding of Offence
Application Form	Application for permission to avail of the special procedure relating to pan masala and pan masala containing tobacco (Gutkha) (Appendix - I) and Intimation of payment of duty (Appendix - II)
Form- A	Quarterly return for production and removal of goods under area based exemption

FAQ: Frequently Asked Questions

FAQ-1: What are the different Valuation methods of Computation of Assessable Value under Excise Duty Rules

Ans: Value of the excisable goods (called Assessable Value) has to be determined to levy the duty, as follows:

- **Ad Valorem/ Transaction Value**: Transaction value means the value of goods which are sold at the time and place of removal. In addition to Product Price, it any amount that the Buyer is liable to pay for advertising or publicity, marketing and selling, organization expenses, storage, outward handling, servicing, warranty, commission or any other matter.
- **Ad Quantum**: In case of Ad Quantum, the duty is Payable on the basis of UoM (Unit of Measure, like Weight, Length, Volume etc). For example, Duty on Sugar is based on per Kg.
- **Composite Method:** In case of Composite Method, Duty is chargeable partly *Ad Valorem* (on Value of Goods) and Partly Ad Quantum (on Quantity). For example Ad Valorem @ 5% and Ad Quantum @ Rs 2 per Kg.
- **Maximum Retail Sale Price**: Sometimes, Excise Duty may be charged on declared Maximum Retail Price Retail Sale price (MRP) at which the goods may be sold, instead of Actual Price at which the goods is sold. It also includes all taxes local or otherwise, freight, transport charges, commission payable to dealers, and all charges towards advertisement, delivery, packing, forwarding etc.

Excise Duty Set Up

06-02

01 Excise Set Up

There are two types of Registration of Excise Duty according to the type of Business operation

- **Manufacturer**: *Manufacturer* is a person who actually manufactures or produces excisable goods (i.e. one that actually brings into existence new and identifiable product)
- **Dealers**: A *Trader/Dealer* is someone who purchases and sells excisable goods and maintains an inventory of goods. A Dealer may classified as:
    - o **First Stage Dealer**: *Dealer* who buys excisable goods directly from Manufacturer (or Manufacturer's Agent), Importer (or Importer's Agent), Consignment Agent, etc
    - o **Second Stage Dealer:** *Dealer* who buys excisable goods from First Stage Dealer

02 Activation for Excise Duty

At Gateway, click *F11:Features> Statutory & Taxation* to get *Statutory & Taxation Set Up* screen (F-1A). At *Statutory & Taxation* screen, set *Yes* at *Enable Excise* (F-1A)

F-1A: Excise Activation for Company

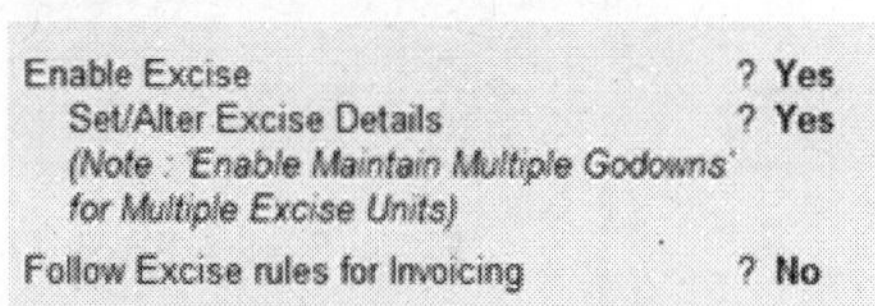

Enable Excise ? Yes
Set/Alter Excise Details ? Yes
(Note : 'Enable Maintain Multiple Godowns' for Multiple Excise Units)
Follow Excise rules for Invoicing ? No

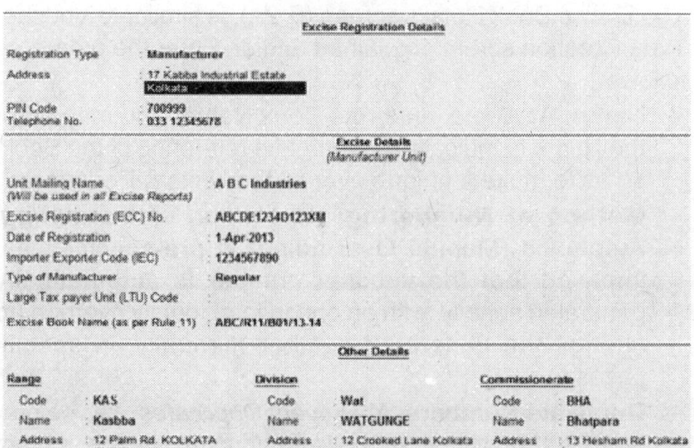

Excise Registration Details

Registration Type : Manufacturer
Address : 17 Kabba Industrial Estate
Kolkata
PIN Code : 700999
Telephone No. : 033 12345678

Excise Details
(Manufacturer Unit)

Unit Mailing Name : A B C Industries
(Will be used in all Excise Reports)
Excise Registration (ECC) No. : ABCDE1234D123XM
Date of Registration : 1-Apr-2013
Importer Exporter Code (IEC) : 1234567890
Type of Manufacturer : Regular
Large Tax payer Unit (LTU) Code :
Excise Book Name (as per Rule 11) : ABC/R11/B01/13-14

Other Details

Range		Division		Commissionerate	
Code	: KAS	Code	: Wat	Code	: BHA
Name	: Kasbba	Name	: WATGUNGE	Name	: Bhatpara
Address	: 12 Palm Rd. KOLKATA 700909	Address	: 12 Crooked Lane Kolkata 700987	Address	: 13 Hesham Rd Kolkata 700988

F-1B: Excise Registration Details (Mfrs)

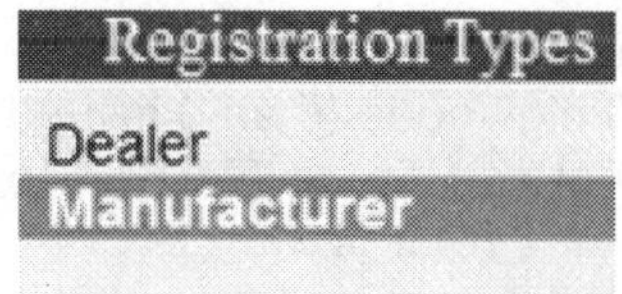

Registration Types
Dealer
Manufacturer

F-1C: Registration Type List

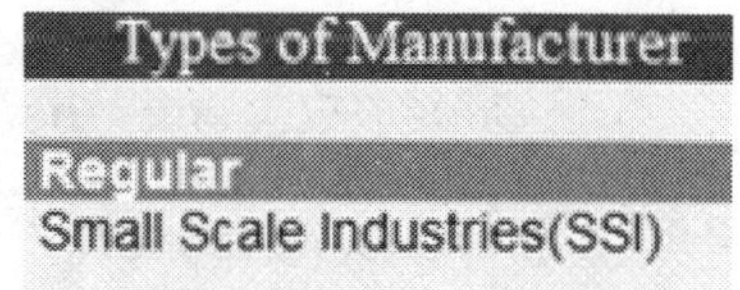

Types of Manufacturer
Regular
Small Scale Industries(SSI)

F-1D: Manufacturer Type List

03 Set up for Excise Duty

Having activated Excise Duty (set *Yes* at *Enable Excise)*, you have to set up Excise Particulars of the Company.

At *Statutory & Taxation Set Up* screen (F-1A), at *Set / Alter Excise Details*, set *Yes* to get Excise *Registration Detail* screen (F-1B). The *Excise Registration Detail* screen (F-1B) is divided in 3 major parts. Enter the respective details as follows:

a. **Excise Registration Detail:** At the upper part of *Excise Registration Detail* screen (F-1B), enter *Excise Registration Details* as follows:
    - **Assessee Type**: At *Registration Type*, select *Manufacturer*, from the list (F-1C)
    - **Address**: At *Address*, enter the complete postal address of the Dealer. The Company Address as entered at Company Creation is carried (you may change it here). This address is printed in all Excise Reports.
    - **PIN Code**: At *PIN Code*, enter the PIN of the postal address of the Dealer. The PIN as entered at Company Creation is carried (you may change it here). This PIN is printed at Company Address in all Excise Reports.
    - **Telephone Number:** At *Telephone No.,* enter the PIN of the postal address of the Dealer. The PIN as entered at Company Creation is carried (you may change it here). This PIN is printed at Company Address in all Excise Reports.

b. **Unit Excise Detail:** At the Middle Part of *Excise Registration Detail* screen (F-1B), enter *Excise Details* of the *Manufacturer* Unit, as follows:
    - **Unit Name**: Enter the Unit Name (it may be different from Company Legal Name, for different units). The Company Main Name is carried as default (you may change it here). The name entered here is printed at Unit Name in all Excise Reports.

- **Excise Registration Number**: At *Excise Registration (ECC) No*, enter the 15 digit Registration Number of the Company. The first 10 digit of ECC Number is the I Tax PAN, the next 5 digit is the unique Number allotted by Excise Deptt (this part indicates Dealer / Manufacturer. e.g XD – For Excise Dealer, XM – For Manufacturer etc).
- **Registration Date:** At *Date of Registration,* enter the Date of Registration of the Excise (date of issue of Excise Registration Certificate)
- **Importer Exporter Code (IEC)**: At *Importer Exporter Code (IEC)*, enter the 10 digit code (if any) issued by Director General of Foreign Trade (DGFT), to Importer / Exporter
- **Excise Book Name:** At *Excise Book Name (as per Rule 11),* select *New Number* to get *Excise Book Details* screen (F-2A) to enter Book Details, as explained next. You may enter multiple Book Numbers here in multiple lines (F-2C), to enter the details of each Book Number (F-2A).

  The following additional options are to be set up for *Manufacturers*
- **Manufacturer Type:** At *Type of Manufacturer*, select the appropriate Manufacturer Type from the list of Types of Manufacturer (F-1D), e.g. Regular / SSI (for SSI Units)
- **Large Tax Payer Unit Code:** At *Large Tax Payer Unit (LTU) Code*, enter the LTU Code for LTU Units (if applicable), else leave blank.

c. **Excise Authorities Details:** At the Bottom Part (F-1B), at *Other Details*, enter *Details* of the Excise Authorities related to the Dealer
- **Range Details**: Enter the details of the related Central Excise Range
  - o **Code:** Enter the Code of the Range under which the company is registered.
  - o **Name:** Enter the Name of the range under which your company is registered.
  - o **Address:** Enter the address of the Range under which your company is registered.
- **Division Details**: Enter the details of the related Central Excise Division, as follows:
  - o **Code:** Enter the code of the division under which your company is registered.
  - o **Name:** Enter the name of the division under which your company is registered.
  - o **Address:** Enter the address of the division under which your company is registered.
- **Commissionerate Details**: Enter the details of the related Central Excise Commissionerate, as follows:
  - o **Code:** Enter the code of the Commissionerate under which your company is registered.
  - o **Name:** Enter the name of the Commissionerate under which your company is registered.
  - o **Address:** Enter the address of the Commissionerate under which your company is registered.

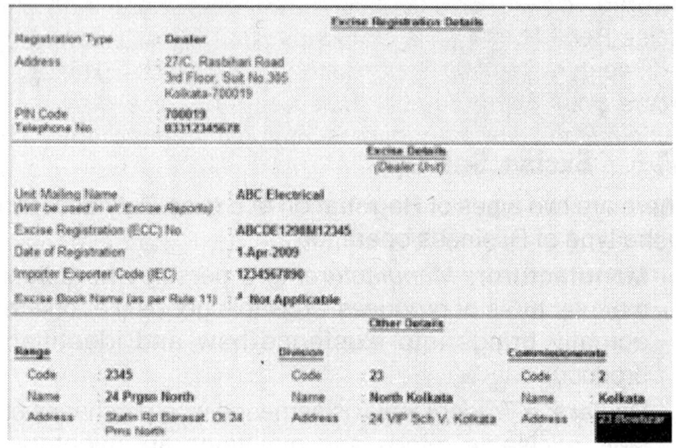

F-1E: Excise Registrtion details (Dealers)

03.01 Excise Book Series Entry

You get the *Excise Book Series Entry screen* (F-2A), when you select *New Number* at Excise Book Name (F-1B), as explained above. Here, enter Book Series Details of Excise Invoice.

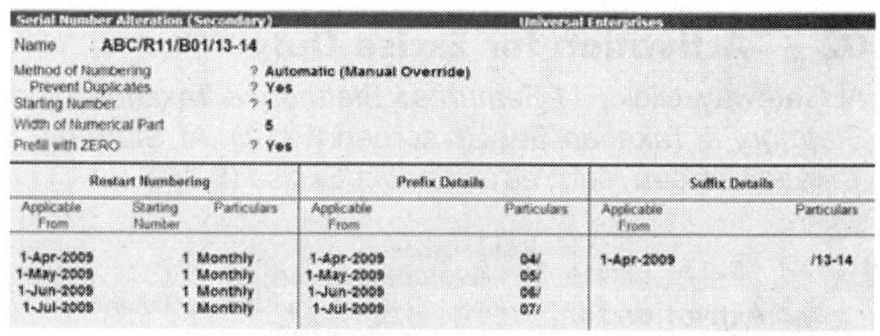

F-2A:Excise Book Details

The Excise Book Details screen (F-2A), is similar to Voucher Type Creation screen explained earlier. Enter the details as follows:

- **Name:** At *Name*, enter the Book Name. You may enter the Name to indicate the complete reference of the Book, so as to make it unique over all the Units & Periods.
- **Method of Numbering:** At *Method of Numbering*, Automatic (Manual Over-riding) is pre-specified as, implying that the voucher number is automatically generated serially, with an option to manually override (to change the generated number manually, in special cases).
- **Duplicate Numbers**: At *Prevent Duplicates, Yes* os pre-specified implying that Duplicate Voucher Number cannot be allotted (even by manual over-riding)
- **Number Width:** At *Width of Numerical Part*, you may specify width of numeric part

- **Zero Fill:** At *Prefill* with Zero, you may specify zero pre-fill for fixed width number (recommended)

Next enter the details at the columns *Re Start Numbering, Prefix Details & Suffix Details*, as usual, as explained for Voucher Type Creation.

Multiple Excise Books: You may create more than one Excise Book Name for a Company /Unit (when allowed by the Deputy/Assistant Commissioner of Central Excise). At *Excise Book Name (as per Rule 11:* F-1B*)*, you may enter multiple Book Numbers here in multiple lines, to enter the details of each Book Number (F-2A).

This way, you may create more serial numbers. At Excide Book Name (as per Rule 11), in the next line select New Number and create a new Serial Number.

For *Manufacturers*, you may also select *GoT>Account Info>Serial Number* (F-2B), select *Create* to get *Excise Book Details* (F-2A) to directly create the Serial Numbers

Even if multiple books are specified, as per Rule 11, only one invoice book shall be in use at a time.

04 Multiple Excise Units Creation

Some times, a Company may have several Excise Units. Multiple Excise Units may be created for a Company.

- Activation for Multiple Excise Units: At *F11: Features > F2: Inventory Feature, set Yes at Maintain Multiple Godowns / Excise Units.*
- **Creation of Multiple Godowns / Excise Units**: Godown Creation has been explained earlier. Here we describe about additional details related to Excise Duty, for Godowns / Excise Units in which Excisable Goods are stored.

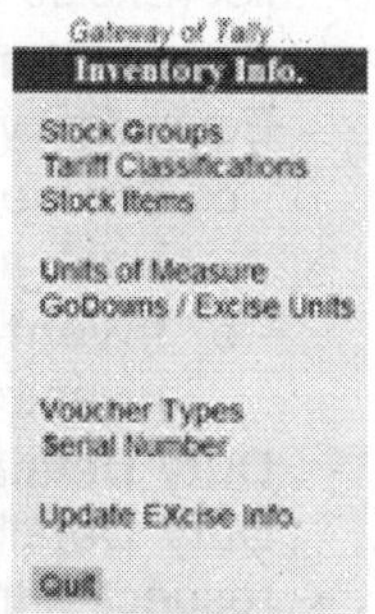

F-2B: Inventory Info Menu with Excise options

F-2C: Excise Book Serial Numbers

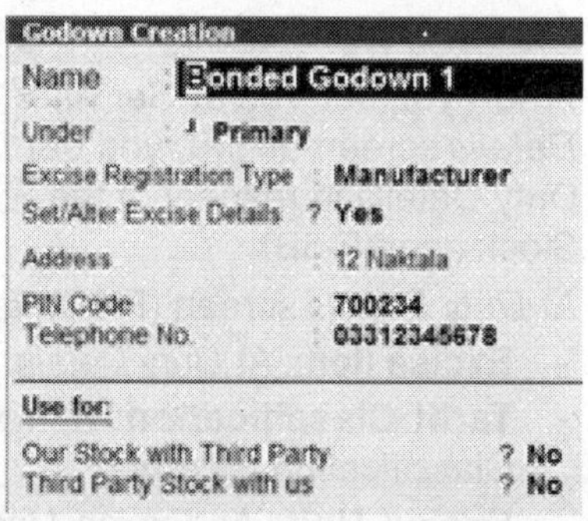

F-3A: Excise Godown creation

At Godown Excise Unit Entry screen (F-3A), enter as follows:

- **Excise Registration Type:** At *Excise Registration Type*, select the Excise Registration Type from the list, as follows:
    - o **Dealer:** Select *Dealer* If the Assessee is Excise Goods Dealer
    - o **Manufacturer:** Select *Manufacturer* If the Assessee is Excise Goods Manufacturer
    - o **Non Excise Godown:** Select *Not Applicable*, if Excisable Goods are not stored in the Godown.
- **Excise Details:** At *Set / Alter Excise details*, set *Yes* to get Excise Details entry screen (F-3B) with information similar to Excise Details entry screen for the Company (F-1B, F-1E), described above. Enter the details in respect of the Godown / Unit, in same way

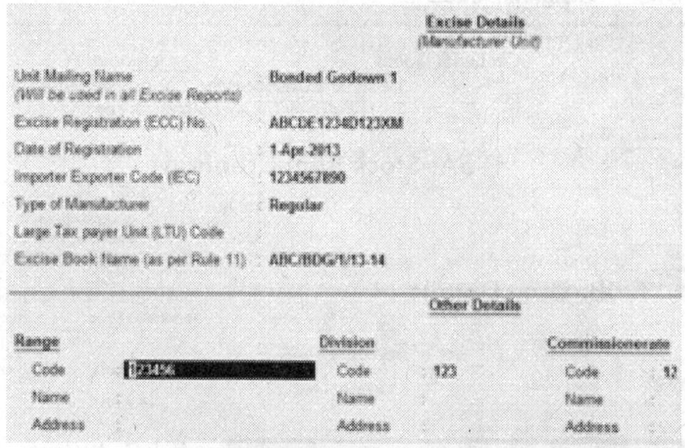

F-3B: Godown Excise Details

05.01 Excise Tariff Group Creation

The Excisable Items are classified as per Tariff Classification. First, create the Tariff Classifications which are dealt with by the Company.

F4A: Tariff Classification Menu

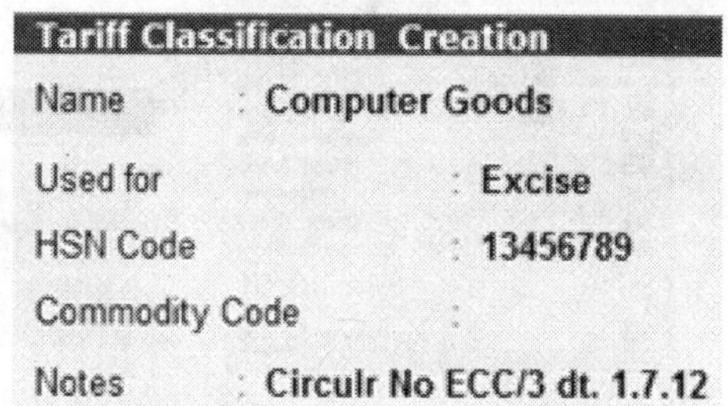

F-4B: Tariff Classification Entry

At Inventory Info Menu (GoT>Inventory Info:F-2B), select *Tariff Classification*, to get *Tariff Classification* Menu (F-4A). At *Tariff Classification* Menu (F-4A), select *Create* to get *Excise Tariff Classification creation* screen (F-4B), to create *Excise Tariff Classification.* At *Excise Tariff Classification creation* screen (F-4B), enter as follows

- **Tariff Name:** At *Name*, enter the Tariff Classification Name
- **Tax Type**: At *Used For*, 'Excise' is Auto carried
- **HSN Code**: Enter the HSN Code (as specified by authorities) of the Tariff Classification
- **Notes**: Enter any internal memo in respect of the Tariff Classification

06 Excisable Stock Items creation

Stock Item creation as been explained earlier. Here, we describe the additional steps relating to Excise Duty. At *Stock Item Entry screen* (F-5A), enter the following particulars in respect of the Stock Item:

- **Tariff Classification**: At *Tariff Classification,* select the Tariff Classification from the list (F-5F)
- **Item Excise Details**: At *Set / Alter Excise Details*, set Yes to get *Excise Item Details* screen (F-5H)

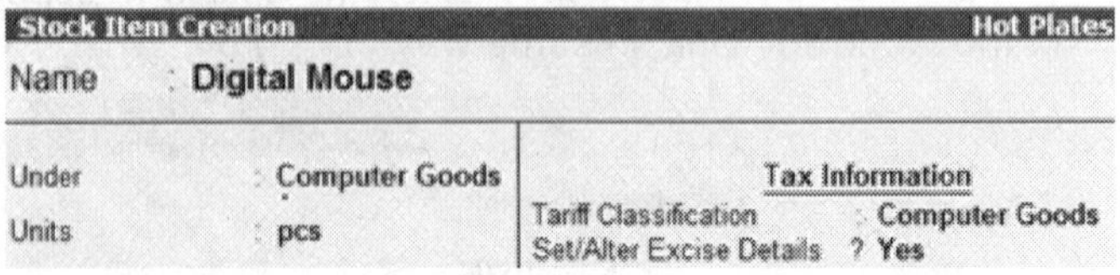

F-5A: Stock Item Creation

F-5B: Duty Details

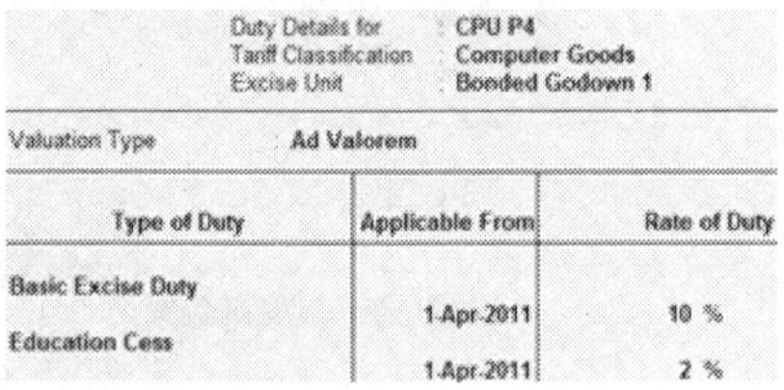

F-5C: List of Excise Units / Godowns

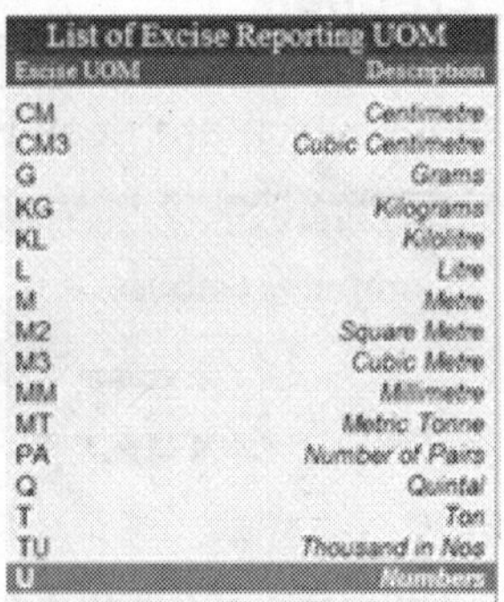

F-5D: Excise UoM List

F-5E: Excise Item Types List

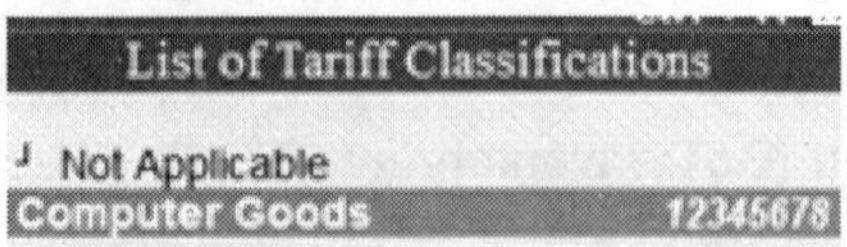

F-5F Tariff Classification List

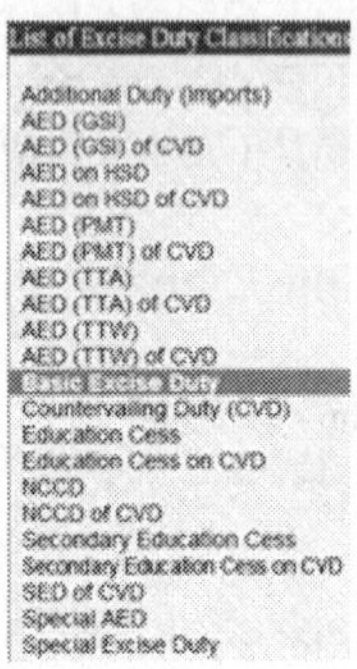

F-5G: Excise Duty Classification

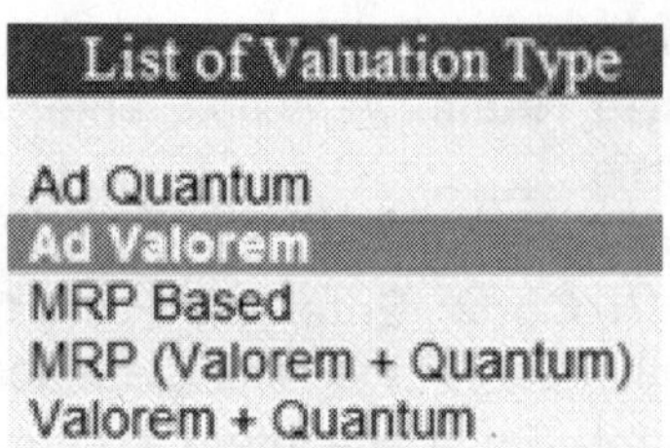

F-5I: Valuation Type List

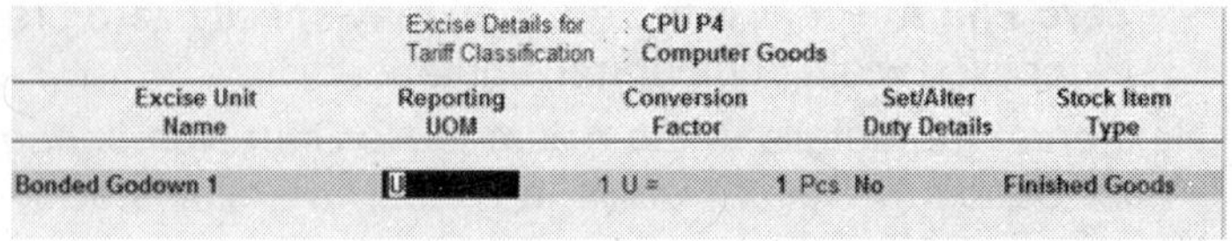

F-5H: Item Excise Details

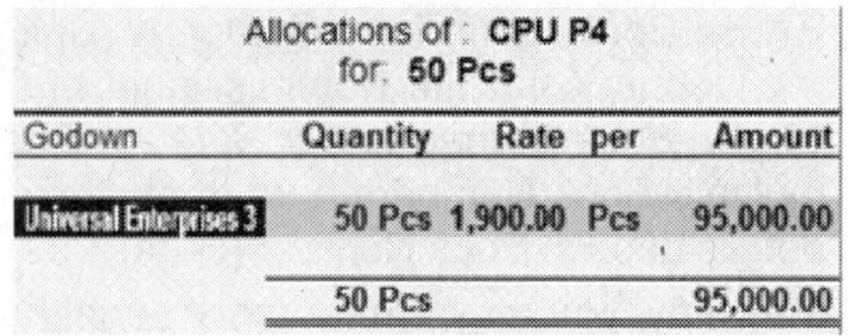

F-5J: Opening Stock Details

06.01 Excise Item Details

At *Excise Item Details* screen (F-5H), enter the following details:

- **Excise Item**: At *Excise Details for,* the Item Name is carried
- **Tariff Classification**: At *Tariff Classification*, the selected Tariff Classification is carried

Now enter the details as follows in respect of each Excise Unit (F-5H)

Excise Unit Name: Select the Excise Unit / Godown from the list

- **Excise UoM**: At *Reporting UoM,* select the UoM from the list (Excise UoM list is internally created by Tally:F-5D)
- **Conversion Factor**: At *Conversion Factor*, enter the Equivalent values of:
    - o **Excise UoM**: Enter the Equivalent Units in Excise UoM, at the left of = sign
    - o **Inventory UoM**: Enter the Equivalent Units in Inventory UoM, at the Right of = sign
- **Duty Details**: At *Set Alter Duty Details*, set *Yes* to get Duty Details screen (F-5B) to enter Duty Details in respect of the Excise Unit / Godown

06.02 Duty Details

When you set *Yes* at *Set Alter Duty Details* at *Excise Item Details* screen (F-5F), you get *Duty Details screen* to enter Duty Details in respect of the Excise Unit / Godown, for the Stock Item (F-5B)

At *Duty Details* screen (F-5B), enter the following details:

- **Excise Item**: At *Duty Details for,* the Item Name is carried
- **Tariff Classification**: At *Tariff Classification*, the Tariff Classification is carried
- **Excise Unit:** At *Excise Unit*, the selected Excise Unit Name is carried
- **Duty Computation Method:** At *Valuation Type*, select the *Duty Computation Method* from the list of Valuation Type (F-5I), as follows:
    - o **On Value:** Select *Ad Valorem* if the Duty is computed as % of Assessable value
    - o **On Quantity:** Select *Ad Quantum* if the Duty is computed on the Quantity

- o **MRP Based:** Select *MRP Based* if the Duty is computed on the MRP Value
- o **MRP (Value & Quantity):** Select *MRP (Valorem + Quantum)* if the Duty is computed on MRP Value as well as Quantity
- o **Value & Quantity:** Select *MRP (Valorem + Quantum)* if the Duty is computed on Assessable value as well as on Quantity

Now enter the details of each *Type of Duty* (component), as follows (F-5B):

- **Duty Component:** At *Type of Duty*, select the *Duty Component* from the *Duty Classification* List (F-5G)
- **Applicable Date**: At *Applicable From*, enter the Date from which the Duty on the Item becomes applicable
- **Rate of Duty**: Enter the rate of Duty (in % or per Unit)

The following Table shows the list of Duty Types and their computation basis

Type of Duty	Computed on
Basic Excise Duty	Assessable Value
Special Excise Duty	Assessable Value
Countervailing Duty (On Import)	Assessable Value
Additional Excise Duty (GSI)	Assessable Value
NCCD	On Duty Value
Additional Excise Duty (TTW)	On Duty Value
Special Additional Duty	On Duty Value
Additional Excise Duty (TTA)	On Duty Value
Additional Duty on Excise	On Duty Value
Education Cess	On Duty Value

In this way, enter the Duty Details in respect of each Duty Component, in respect of Excise Unit / Godown, for each Excisable Item

06.03 Opening Stock Godown Details

Having entered the details as described above, you get back to the Stock Item main screen (F-5A). Entry of Opening Stock details of a Stock Item has been explained earlier. At Opening Stock Details entry screen (F-5J), at the column Godown, select the Excise Godown and enter the Quantity / Rate / Amount as usual

07 Carrying Stock Item Excise Details

As described above, entry of Excise details for each Stock Item entails considerable data entry, spread over several screens. Normally several Stock Item may have the same Item Duty Details. Instead of entering the same value in each Item, you may instantly carry the details into from one Item to other entities.

At Gateway, select *Inventory Info* (F-2B), select *Update Excise Info* to get *Excise Info Menu* (F-6A).

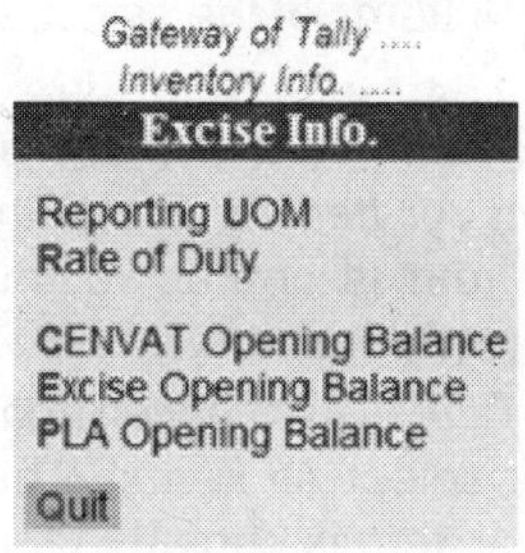

F-6A: Excise Info Menu

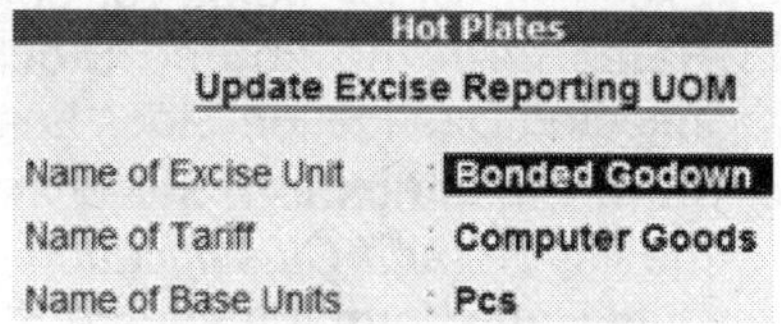

F-6B: Excise Reporting UoM Carrying

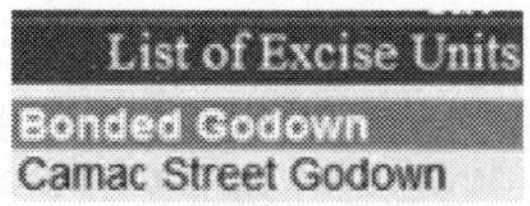

F-6C: Excise Unit List

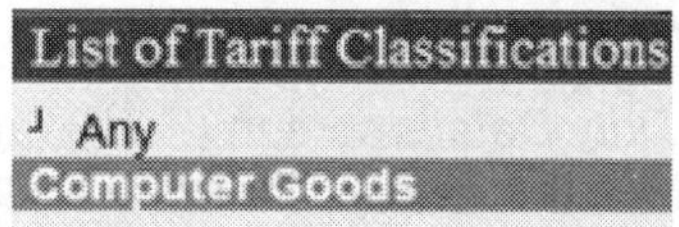

F-6D: Tariff classification List

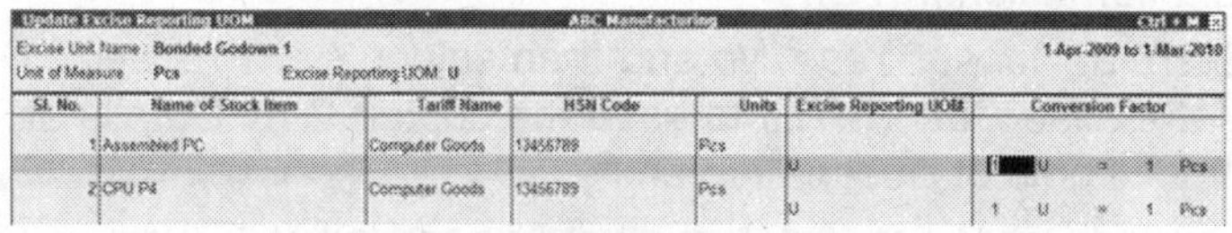

F-6E: Carried UoM Details

07.01 Duty Rate Carrying

Through this process, you may carry the Duty Rates of a Stock Item to other, Stock Item, Stock Items of a Stock Group or Stock Items of a Tariff Classification

At *Excise Info* Menu (F-6A), select *Rate of Duty* to get *Set Excise Rate* screen (F-7A). At *Set Excise Rate* screen, enter as follows:

- **Source Item**: At *Copy From*, select the *Stock Item* (from the list Of Excisable Stock Items) from which the Duty Rates are to be copied.
- **Destination Entity**: At *Destination Type*, select from the list (F-7C):
  - o **Stock Group**: To copy the Duty Type data from selected *Source* Stock Item to the Stock Items under Destination *Group*
  - o **Stock Item**: To copy the Duty Type data from selected *Source* Stock Item to the Destination Stock Item
  - o **Tariff Classification**: To copy the Duty Type data from selected *Source* Stock Item to the Stock Items under Destination *Tariff Classification*
- **Destination:** *At Copy To*, select The Destination Entity as described next.

07.02 Destination Entity Entry

On selection of *Destination Type*, you select the Destination entity of the selected Destination Type, to get *Duty Details screen* (F-7E), as follows:

- o **Stock Group**: Select the *Stock Group* (from the list of *Stock Groups:* F-7D). The Duty Rates form the source

Stock Item is copied to all the Stock Items of the selected Destination Group

- o **Stock Item**: Select the *Stock Item* from the list of Excisable *Stock Items* (or select *All Items*). The Duty Rates form the source Stock Item is copied to the selected Destination Stock Item (or All Items)
- o **Tariff Classification**: Select the *Tariff Classification* from the list of *Tariff Classification* (or select *All Items*). The Duty Rates form the source Stock Item is copied to the Stock Items of the selected Destination *Tariff Classification* (or All Items)

07.03 Excise Duty Details Carrying

At *Duty Details* screen (F-7E), at *Excise Unit Name* column, select the Excise Unit. The Duty details of source Item carried to the Stock Item of Destination entity are displayed for Information (F-7E).

Set Y at *Accept Yes / No* and then select Y at *Proceed to Set Excise Duty* (F-7E) to save the copied Duty Details at Stock Items of Destination entity.

This way, continue to select other Excise Unit at *Excise Unit Name* column, to carry the Duty Details in respect of all Excise Units (F-7E).

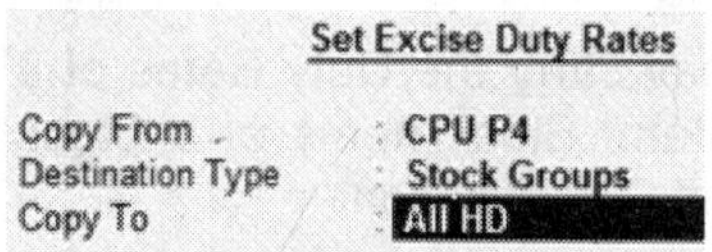

F-7A: Duty Rate Carrying

F-7B: Source Stock Item List

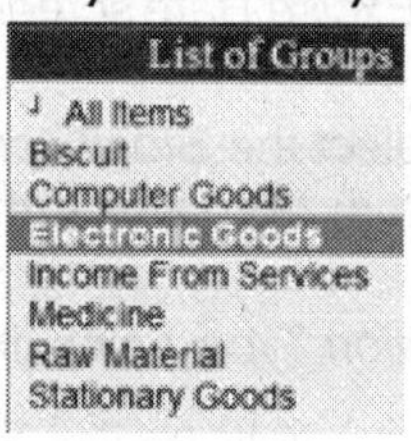

F-7C: Destination Type List

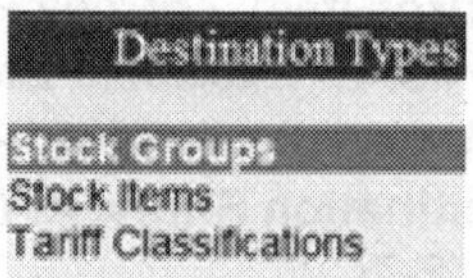

F-7D: Destination Master List

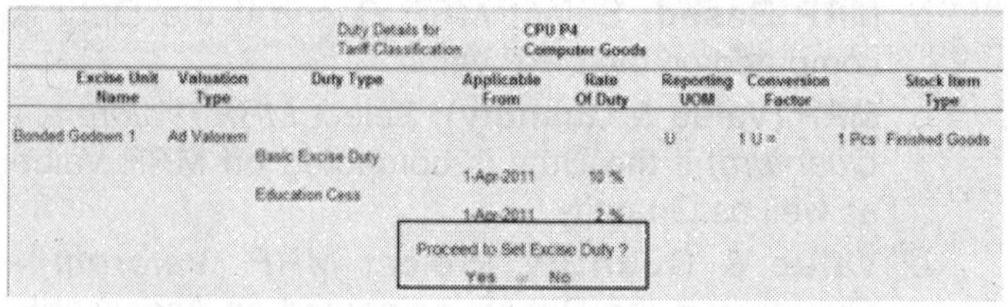

F-7E: Carried Duty Details

07.04 Reporting UoM Carrying

Through this process, you may link the Reporting Excise UoM of each Excisable Stock Item with Item UoM.

At *Excise Info* Menu (F-6A), select *Reporting UoM* to get *Update Excise Reporting UoM* screen (F-6B). At *Update Excise Reporting UoM* screen (F-6B), enter as follows:

- **Excise Unit Name**: At *Excise Unit Name*, select the Excise Unit Name from the *list of Excise Units* (F-6C)
- **Tariff**: At *Name of Tariff*, select the *Tariff Classification* from the list of *Tariff Classifications.* (F-6D)
- **Base Unit**: At *Name of Base Units,* select the UoM from the list of UoMs (or select *Any* for all UoMs) to get *Update Excise Reporting Units* screen (F-6E), to specify the Items for which the Unit / Excise Base Unit would be applied for reporting Quantity in Excise Reports. At *Update Excise Reporting Units,* enter as follows:
- **Stock Item**: At *Name of Stock Item* column, select the Item for which the Unit would be applicable.

The corresponding data in other columns are carried from the Stock Item Master (F-8A), in one stroke

This way, you link all the Items of selected UoM with the Excise UoM.

08 Excise Registered Party Ledger

Party Ledger creation has been discussed earlier. Here we discuss about details exclusively related to Excise Duty.

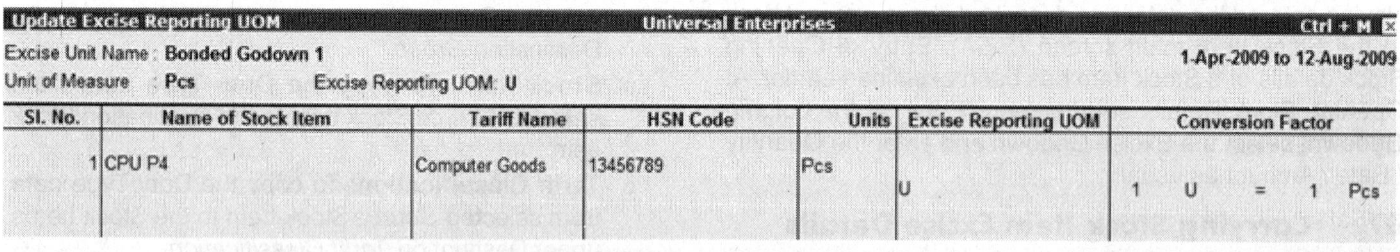

F-8A: UoM Updation

F-9A: Party Ledger Creation

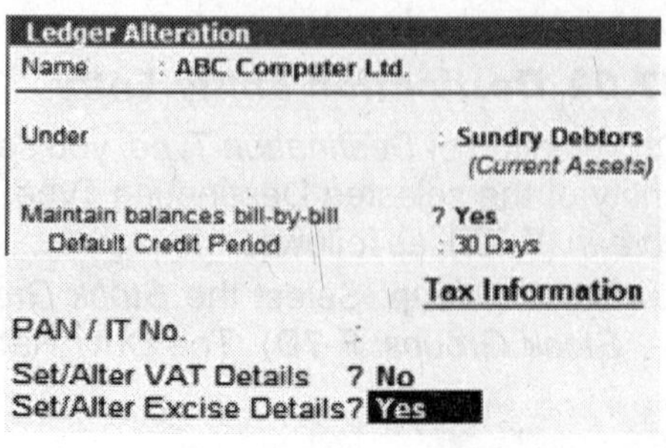

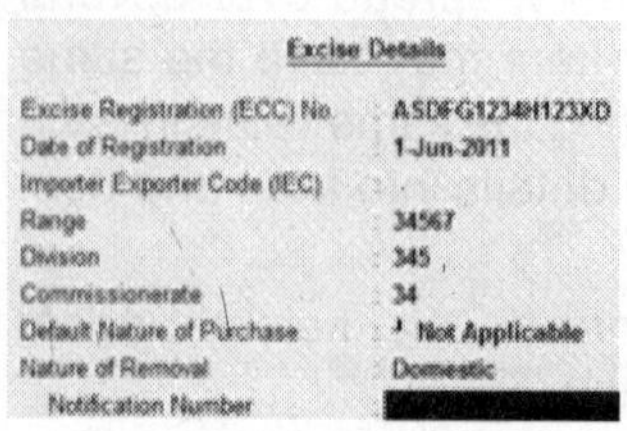

F-9B: Party Excise Details

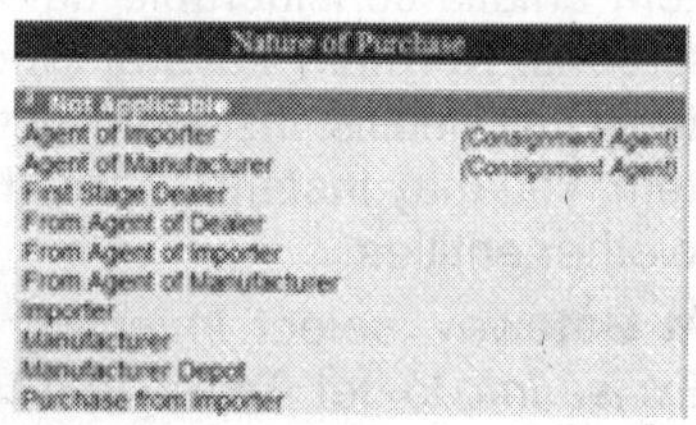

F-9C: Purchaser Type List

At Excise Registered Party Ledger (Ledgers under Sundry Debtor / Creditor Group) creation / alteration screen (F-9A), set *Yes* at *Set / Alter Excise Details*, to get Excise Details screen (F-9B)

Types of Removal
Captive Consumption
Domestic
Exempt
Export
Export - Duty Chargeable
Removal As Such
Special Rate

F-9D: Removal Type List

At *Excise Details* screen (F-9B), enter the following particulars in respect of the Customer / Supplier, as follows:

- **Party Excise Regn. No.:** At *Excise Registration (ECC) No.*, enter the Excise Registration Number of the Party.
- **Party Registration Date**: At *Date of Registration*, enter the Excise Registration Date of the Party.
- **Party Importer Exporter Code.:** At *Importer Exporter Code (IEC),* enter *Importer Exporter Code (IEC)* of the Party, if any, else leave blank.
- **Range:** At *Range*, enter the Range under which the Party is registered.
- **Division:** At *Division*, Enter the Division under which the Party is registered.
- **Commissionerate:** At *Commissionerate*, enter the Commissionerate of the Division under which the Party is Registered.
- **Dealer Type:** At Default *Nature of Purchase*, Select the Default Nature of Dealer from the *Nature of Purchase* list (F-9C). This is carried as default in Voucher Entry, which may be changed in voucher (you may select *Not Applicable*).
- **Removal Type:** At Nature of Removal, select the Removal Type from the list (F-9D)
- **Notification Number:** Enter the relevant Notification number applicable, if any

08.01 Excisable Goods Sales / Purchase Account

The Sales / Purchase Account creation is similar as described for VAT. There is no additional information specific to Excise

09 Excise Duty Ledger Account

You have to create separate Excise Duty Ledger Accounts for Sales / Purchase.

Excise Duty on Purchase may be booked in Purchase Voucher in 2 ways:

- **Inclusive Method**: The Purchase Rate / Purchase Value is inclusive of Excise Duty. The Inclusive Rate / Value is manually calculated and entered during Purchase Voucher entry. In such case, no Excise Duty Ledger Account (on Purchase) is to be created, as the Excise Duty is included in Purchase Rate.

  Dealers normally use Inclusive Method. They do not need to maintain Ledger Accounts of Excise Duty, as duty passed is computed on Assessable Value and not on Purchase Value
- **Exclusive Method**: The Purchase is booked at Basic Rate. The Excise Duty is charged extra and booked o respective ledger. In such case, separate Excise Duty Ledger and related Cess, Surcharge accounts etc, as applicable, are to be created for each duty Types Rates.

Exclusive Method is normally adopted by Manufacturers as they need to keep detailed accounts of Input Credit / Output Duty for CENVAT.

09.01 Basic Excise Duty Ledger Account creation

Ledger Account creation has been described earlier. Here we describe Ledger Account creation, relating to Excise Duty. You should create a separate Ledger Account for each type of Duty and Rate of Duty. At Ledger creation screen, enter as follows (F-10A / F-10B):

- **Parent Group**: At *Under*, select *Duties & Taxes* or its Sub Group
- **Duty Type**: At *Type of Duty / Tax*, select *Excise* from the list of *Types of Duty / Tax* (F-10F)
- **Excise Accounting Code**: At *Excise Accounting Code*, enter the *Excise Accounting Code* for the Duty, as allotted by Excise Duty authorities (this is printed in Excise Returns)
- **Duty Head**: At *Duty Head*, select the *Duty Head* from the list of *Duty Head* (F-10G)
- **Duty Rate**: At *Percentage of Calculation*, enter the applicable Duty Rate
- **Method of Calculation**: Having entered *Duty Rate*, at *Method of Calculation*, select *Method of Calculation* from the list (F-10D).

Ledger Creation	
Name	: Excise Duty on Purchase 16%
Under	: Duties & Taxes (Current Liabilities)
Type of Duty/Tax	: CENVAT
Excise Accounting Code	: 100456
Duty Head	: Basic Excise Duty
Inventory values are affected	? No
Activate Interest Calculation	? No
Percentage of Calculation (eg 5)	? 16 %
Method of Calculation	: On Assessable Value
Rounding Method	: Normal Rounding
Rounding Limit	: 0

F-10A: Basic Excise on Purchase Ledger

Ledger Creation	
Name	: Basic Excise Duty 16%
Under	: Duties & Taxes (Current Liabilities)
Type of Duty/Tax	: Excise
Excise Accounting Code	: 0380003
Duty Head	: Basic Excise Duty
Inventory values are affected	? No
Activate Interest Calculation	? No
Percentage of Calculation (eg 5)	? 16 %
Method of Calculation	: On Assessable Value
Rounding Method	: Normal Rounding
Rounding Limit	: 0

F-10B: Basic Excise on Sales Ledger

Ledger Alteration	
Name	: Education Cess 2%
Under	: Duties & Taxes (Current Liabilities)
Type of Duty/Tax	: Excise
Excise Accounting Code	: 100324
Duty Head	: Cess On Duty
Maintain balances bill-by-bill	? No
Inventory values are affected	? No
Cost centres are applicable	? No
Percentage of Calculation (eg 5)	? 2 %
Method of Calculation	: Additional Duty
Rounding Method	: Not Applicable

F-10C: Excise Cess Ledger

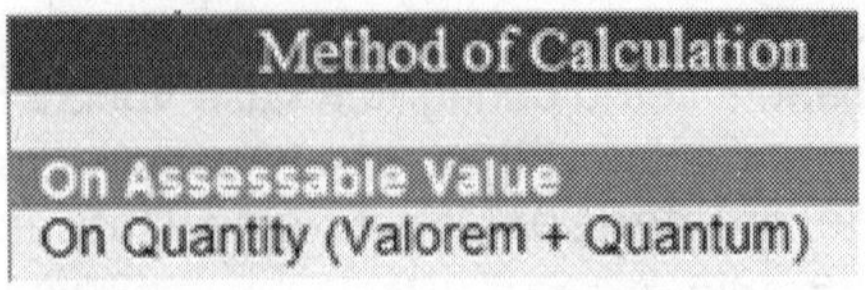

F-10D: Duty Computation Method

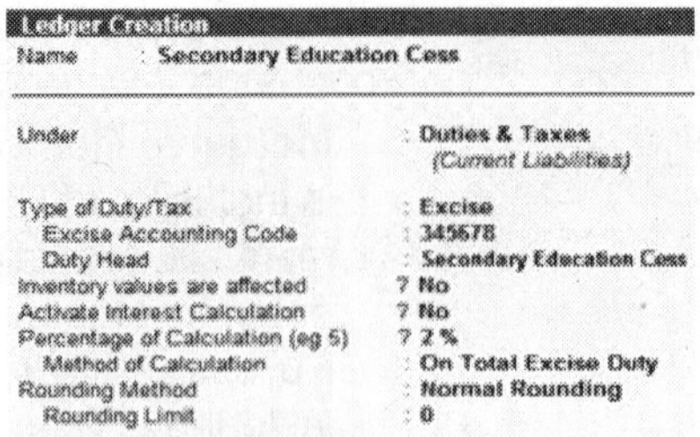

F-10E: Education Cess on Sales Ledger

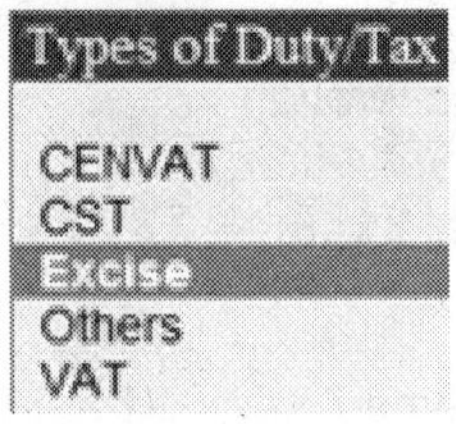

F-10F: Duty Type List

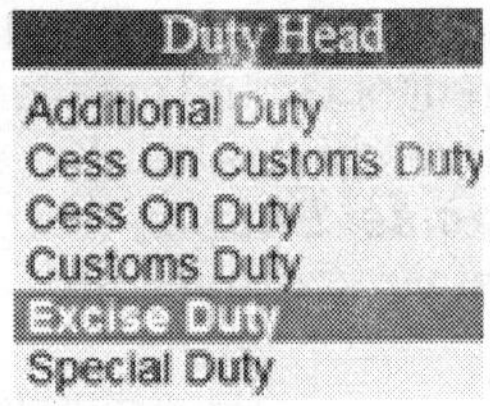

F-10G: Duty Head List

09.02 Education Cess

In the same way, you may create other Excise Duty related ledger accounts like Education Cess (F-10C) etc. The process is similar to creation of Excise Ledger Account. However, set as follows for following fields:

- **Duty Head**: At *Duty Head*, select *Cess on Duty*, as Cess is computed on Excise Duty
- **Method of Calculation**: At *Method of Calculation*, select *Additional Duty* so that amount is computed on Duty (not on Assessable Value)

09.03 Secondary Education Cess

In the same way, you may create Ledger Account for *Secondary Education Cess* as follows (F-10E):

- **Duty Head**: At *Duty Head*, select *Cess on Duty*, as Secondary Education Cess is computed on Excise Duty.
- **Method of Calculation**: At *Method of Calculation*, select *Surcharge on Tax*, as it is Additional Cess and the amount is computed on Duty (not on Assessable Value)

10 Excise Voucher Types

You should create separate *Voucher Types* for the following Excisable Goods:

- Sales Voucher (F-11A)
- Purchase Voucher (F-11B)
- Commercial Voucher (F-11C)

To record Assessable Value & Excise Duty details in Sales / Purchase Voucher, create new Voucher Types for Excisable Goods Sales & Purchase. Such Voucher Types only should be used for Sales / Purchase transactions of Excisable Goods

10.01 Excise Voucher Types creation

Excise related Transactions (like Sales / Purchase) etc should be made through Vouchers excusively created for such transactions, rather than normal Voucher Types used for other (Non Excise related transactions). So, Excise related Voucher Types should be created.

Creation of Voucher Type has been explained earlier. Here, we describe points relating to Excise Voucher Type

- At *Type of Voucher* select *Purchase* (for Purchase) or *Sales* (for Sales)
- Set *Yes* at *Use for Excise*
- At *Default Excise Unit*, select the Excise Unit / Godown from the list

At Right Part (F-1D) of the Voucher Type entry screen, set the options for Printing, Declaration & Excise Information (F-11D)

In the same way, you may create Excise Voucher Types for Debit & Credit Notes also.

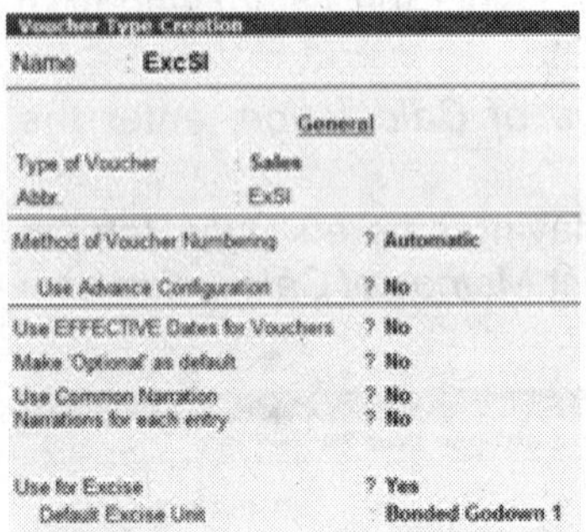

F-11A: Excise Sales Voucher Type

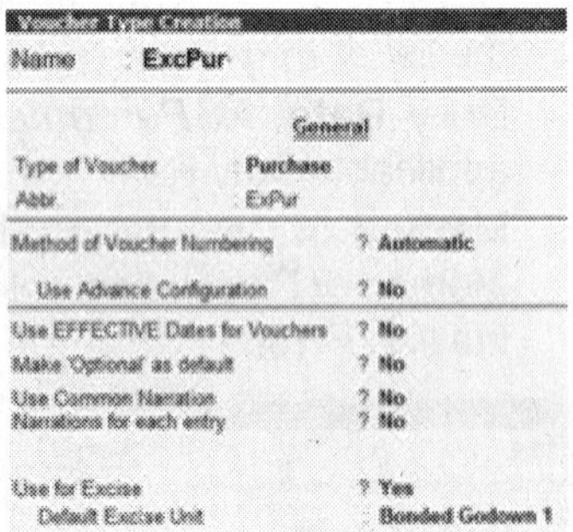

F-11B: Excise Purchase Voucher Type

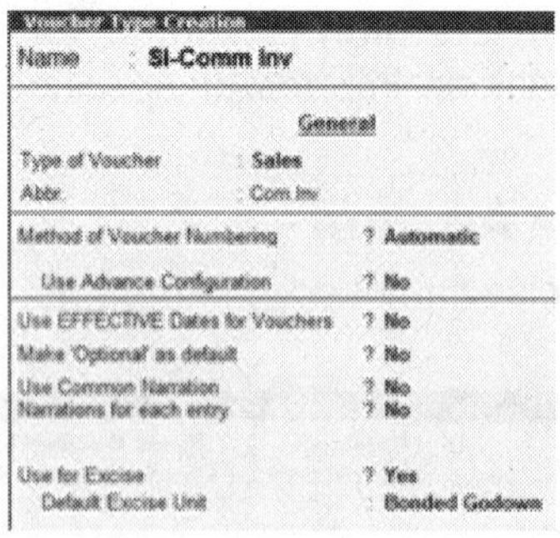

F-11C: Excise Sales (Commercial Invoice) Voucher Type

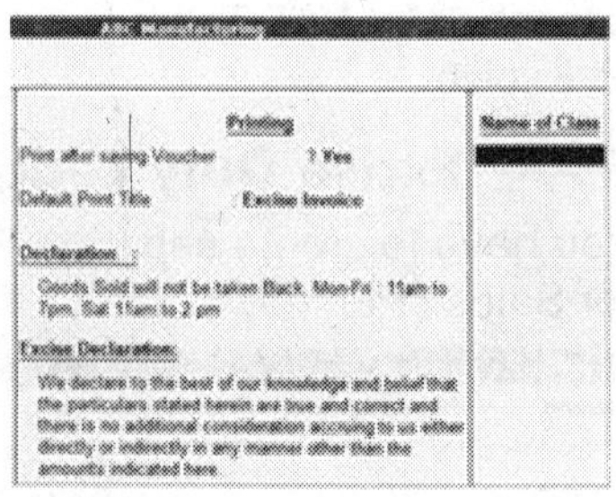

F-11D: Voucher Type set up (Right Part)

Excise Voucher Entry for Manufacturers 06-03

01 Excise Accounts Opening Balance

Having created Masters, you should first enter the Opening Balance on various accounts, before proceeding to Voucher Entry through Excise Info Menu (*GoT>Inventory Info>Update Excise Info*: F-6A/06-02):.

- CENVAT Opening Balance
- Excise Opening Balance
- PLA Opening Balance

The Excise Opening Balances are entered like voucher

02 CENVAT Opening Balance

At Excise Info Menu, (*GoT>Inventory Info>Excise Info*: F-6A/06-02), select *CENVAT Opening Balance* to get *Opening Balance of CENVAT entry screen* to enter details of Opening Balance of CENVAT. The screen is similar to Excise Invoice entry (of Journal Voucher type).

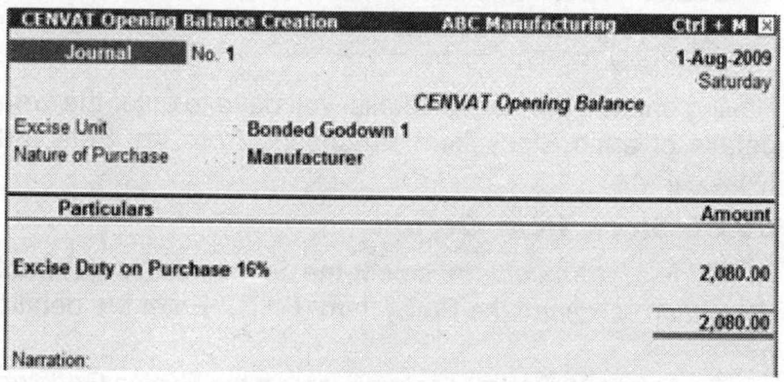

F-1A: CENVAT Opening Balance Entry

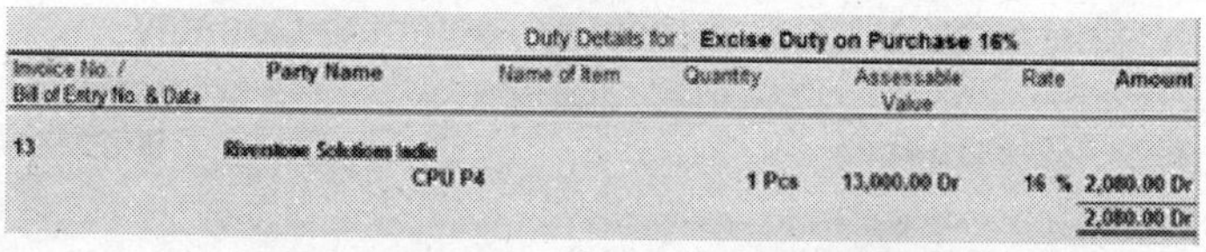

F-1B: CENVAT Opening Balance details Entry

F-1C: Excise Unit List

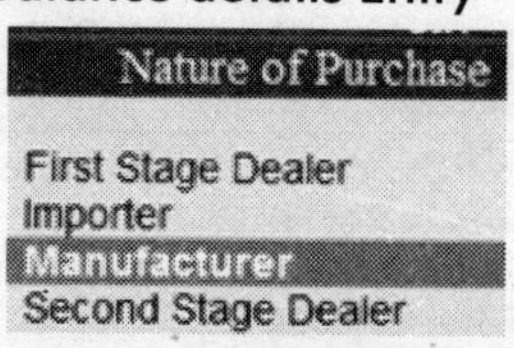

F-1D: Purchase Nature List

The *Opening Balance of CENVAT entry screen* (F-1A), looks like a Journal Voucher Entry screen, in format similar to Invoice Entry screen. The label *CENVAT Opening Balance* appears in the Entry Screen heading, indicating that it is *CENVAT Opening Balance* entry screen. Now enter the details as follows (F-1A):

- **Date**:Enter the Opening Balance Date, (*Financial Year Start Date / Books Beginning Date)*
- **Excise Unit**: At *Excise Unit*, select the Excise Unit from the list (F-1C)
- **Purchase Type**: At *Nature of Purchase*, select the *Nature of Purchase* (e.g Manufacturer) from the list (F-1D)
- **CENVAT Ledger**: At *Particulars* column (F-1A), Select the CENVAT Ledger (Ledger Accounts for which CENVAT is selected at Type of Duty / Tax: F-5A/5B), from the list of CENVAT Ledger Accounts, to get the CENVAT Opening Balance details Entry screen (F-1B)

At *CENVAT Opening Balance Details Entry* screen (F-1B), the CENVAT Ledger Name entered is carried for information. Enter the Invoice wise details of CENVAT credit Opening Balance details, as follows:

- **Invoice Number**: At *Invoice Number / Bill of Entry No & Date* column, enter the Invoice Number & Date against which CENAT Credit is available
- **Supplier Name**: At *Party Name*, select the Supplier Name (Sundry Creditor) from the list
- **Stock Item Name**: Select the Stock Item Name from the list
- **Purchase Quantity**: Enter the Purchase Quantity
- **Assessable Value**: Enter the Assessable Value
- **Duty Rate:** Enter the Duty Rate for the selected Duty Type
- **Duty Amount:** The computed amount of Duty is shown (which you may change, if necessary)

This way, enter the CENVAT Credit details for each Invoice, for each Duty Type. Save the Voucher of CENVAT Opening Balance.

03 Excise Opening Balance

At *Excise Info Menu* (*GoT>Inventory Info>Excise Info*: F-6A/06-02), select *Excise Opening Balance* to get *Excise Opening Balance entry screen* (F-2A) to enter details of Opening Balance of Excise Duty in Opening Sales Invoice. The screen is similar to *CENVAT Opening Balance Entry* (F-1A)

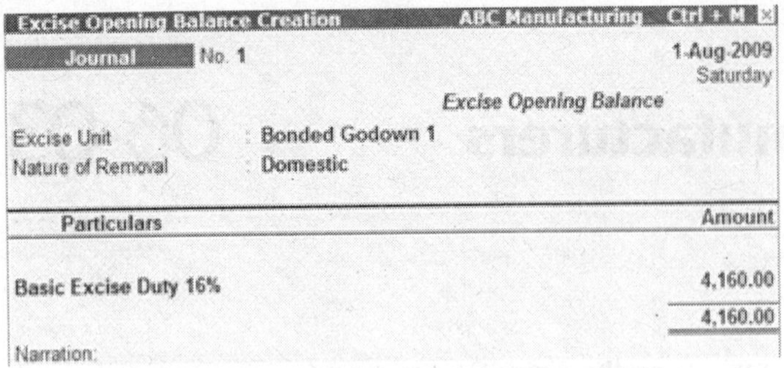

F-2A: CENVAT Opening Balance Entry

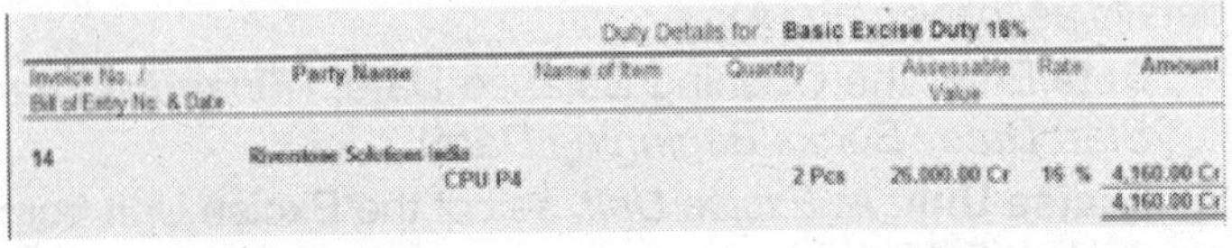

F-2B: Excise Opening Balance details Entry

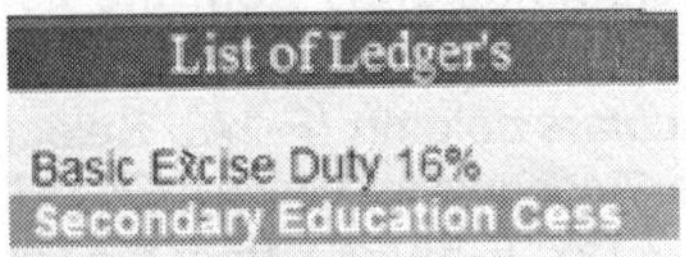

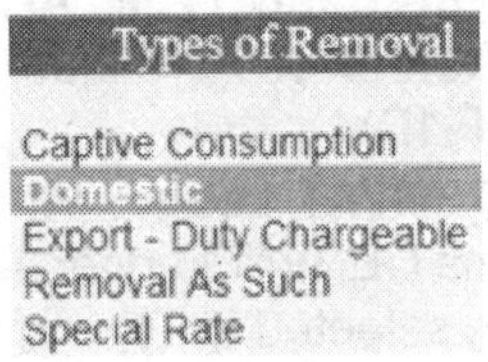

F-2C: Ledger Account List F-2D: Removal Type List

In the same way, you may enter Opening Balance details in respect of other types of Excise Duty Ledger Accounts (like Cess Accounts).

04 PLA Opening Balance

At Excise Info Menu (*GoT>Inventory Info>Excise Info*: F-6A/ 06-02), select *PLA Opening Balance* to get *PLA Opening Balance entry screen* (F-3A) to enter details of Opening Balance of PLA. The screen is similar to *CENVAT Opening Balance Entry*, described earlier (F-1A)

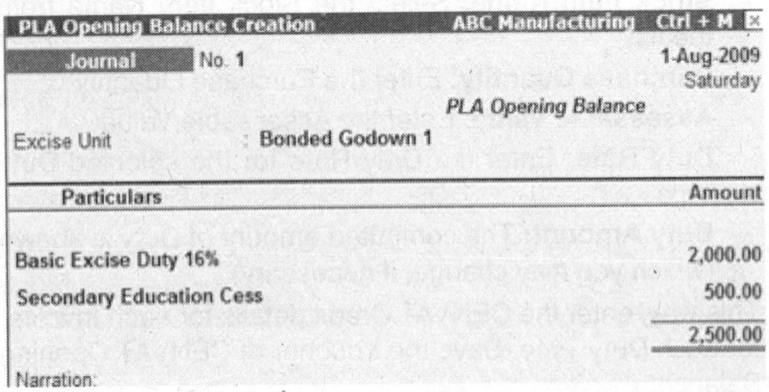

F-3A: PLA Opening Balance entry

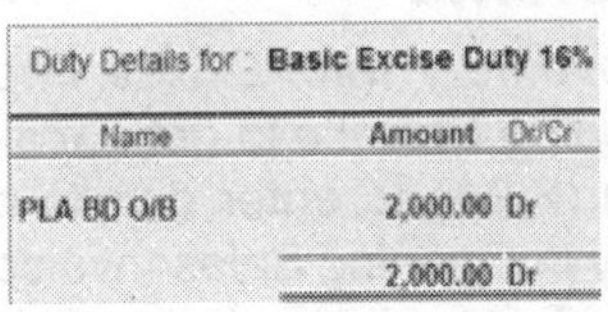

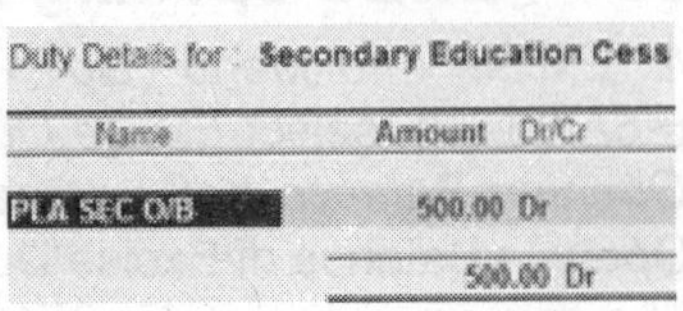

F-3B: Basic ED Details F-3C: Cess details

At *PLA Opening Balance entry* screen (F-3A), at particulars column, select the respective ledger account to get duty details subscreen for the selected Duty Ledger. Enter the Opening Balance (F-3B / F-3C). This way, select the Duty Ledger Accounts and enter the PLA Opening Balance. Save the Voucher (F-3A).

Having created the Masters & Excise Duty Opening Balance, you may enter Excise Sales / Purchase Voucher Entry. Here, we discuss about Voucher Entry for Manufacturers

05 Excisable Goods Purchase Invoice (Not Availing CENVAT) Entry

We have explained Purchase Invoice Entry earlier. Here we discuss about additional details to be entered relating to Excise Duty.

We first explain Purchase Invoice entry, in which CENVAT Credit has not been availed (F-4A).

- **Excise Unit**: At *Excise Unit*, select the Excise Unit from the list, where the Stock is stored
- **Party Name**: At *Party Account Name*, select the Party Ledger from the list of Parties.
- **Supplementary Details:** Now you get the Supplementary details screen showing data carried from Party Ledger and Purchase Invoice. Enter other details of the Purchase Invoice.
- **Dealer Type**: At *Nature of Purchase*, select the Dealer Type (e.g Manufacturer) from the list of *Nature of Purchase* (F-1D)

Having entered the above details, you have to enter the Item details of each Stock Item Purchased from the Selected Dealer (F-4A)

05.01 Stock Item Details

At *Name of Item column*, select the *Stock Item* to get *Item Allocation* screen of the Stock Item (F-4C). Enter the details as follows:

- **Godown**: At *Godown* column, select the Excise Godown from the list.
- **Quantity**: At *Quantity* column, enter the Quantity

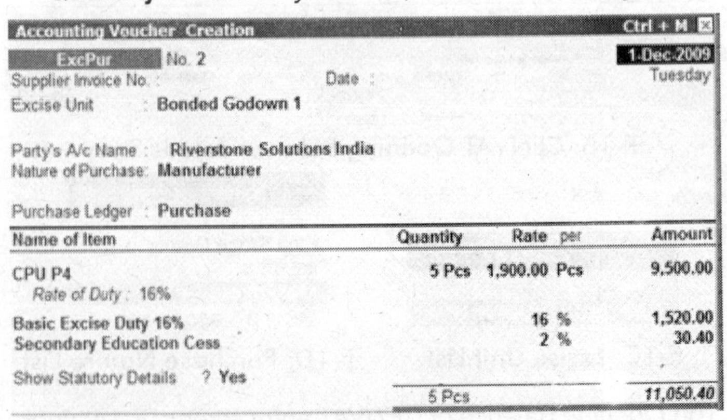

F-4A: Excise Purchase Invoice (Exclusive Method)

- **Item Rate**: At Rate, enter the Purchase Rate (Basic Item Rate)
- **Amount**: the Computed Amount as per Quantity & Rate is shown at Amount Column, which you may change

F-4B: Duty Ledger details

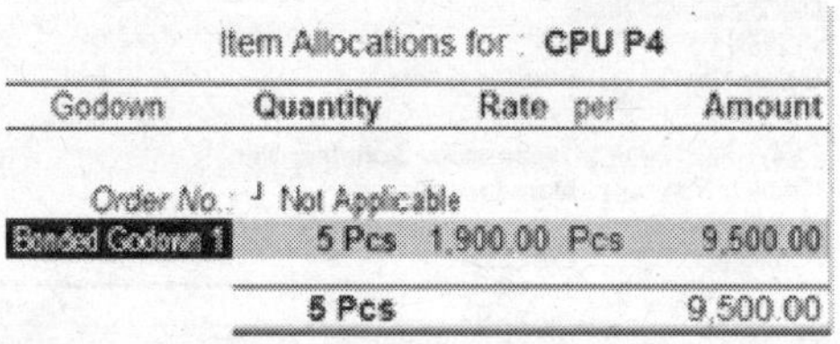

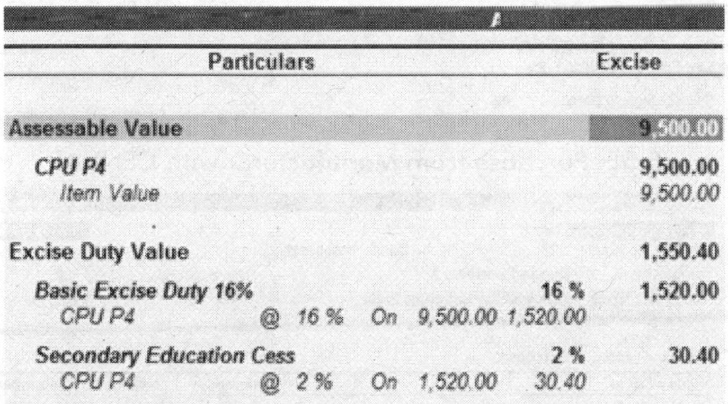

F-4C: Stock Item AllocationF-4D: Statutory Details

05.02 Supplementary Details

After selection of Party Ledger (if Supplementary Details is set on), you get Party Details (F-4E) screen to enter Supplier Details, as follows:

- **Order Details:** Order Number & Order Date, as described earlier
- **Supplier Details:** Consignee (if separate Buyer activated) and Supplier Details, as explained earlier
- **Manufacturer/ Importer / Consignee Details:** Now enter the following details of the of the Manufacturer/ Importer, for record and printing in Invoice
  - o **Name**: At *Name*, enter the Name of the Manufacturer / Importer
  - o **Address**: At *Address*, enter the Address of the Manufacturer / Importer.
  - o **Excise Regn**: At *Excise Regn No.*, enter the 15 digit Excise Regn number of the Manufacturer / Importer.
  - o **Importer / Exporter Code**: At *Importer / Exporter Code,* enter the IEC of the Manufacturer / Importer.
  - o **Excise Range**: At *Range*, enter the Range jurisdiction of the Excise Range, the Manufacturer / Importer belongs to.
  - o **Excise Division:** At Division, enter the Division jurisdiction of the Excise Division, the Manufacturer / Importer belongs to.
  - o **Excise Commissionerate**: At *Commissionerate*, enter the Commissionerate jurisdiction of the Excise Commissionerate, the Manufacturer / Importer belongs to.
  - o **Invoice Number:** Enter the Invoice Number of the Manufacturer / Importer
  - o **Invoice Date:** Enter the Invoice Number of the Manufacturer / Importer

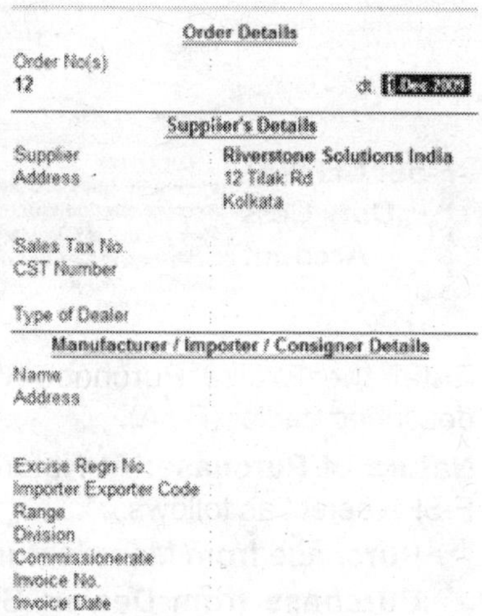

F-4E: Party (Supplementary Details)

05.03 Excise Duty Details

Now, in main voucher screen (F-4A), select the Excise related accounts (like Basic Duty, Cess etc), one by one and enter the details in respect of each ledger account (F-4B), as follows,

- **Ref Number**: At Ref Number, the Bill Ref Number is carried.
- **Item**: At name of Item column, select the Stock Item.
- **Assessable Value**: The Assessable Value of the Item is carried and shown
- **Duty Rate**: The Duty Rate (for the selected Duty Ledger), as specified s shown
- **Duty Amount**: The computed Duty Amount is shown

The Duty Amount shown is carried against the Ledger Account and shown in the main entry screen (F-4A).

This way, enter the Duty details for all the Stock Items

05.04 Statutory Details

After entry of all Ledger Accounts (Duty and other ledger Accounts) at main screen (F-4A), At *Show Statutory Details*, set *Yes* to show the Duty Ledger Accounts and the corresponding Amount (F-4D). Click *F1:Details* to get Stock Item wise break up of each Duty Amount

06 Purchase Invoice with CENVAT Credit

First create the CENVAT Ledger Account for each Type of Excise Duty, in the same way as Excise Duty ledger Accounts, for each Duty (F-5A) and Cess (F-5B), described earlier.

At *Type of Duty/ Tax,* (F-5A / F-5B), select CENVAT

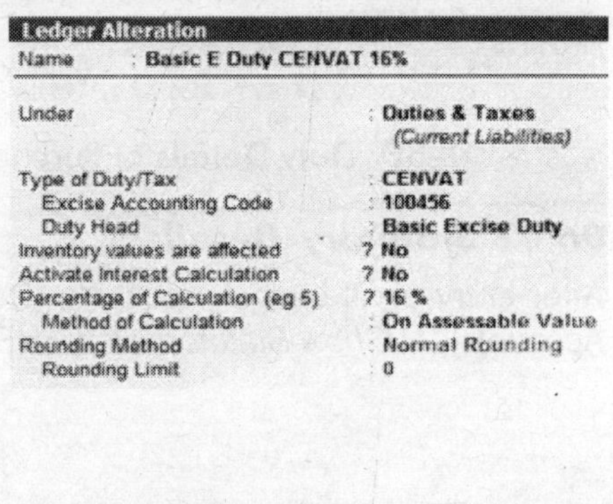

F-5A: CENVAT Basic Duty Account

Ledger Creation

Name	: Sec Ed Cess CENVAT 2%
Under	: Duties & Taxes *(Current Liabilities)*
Type of Duty/Tax	: CENVAT
Excise Accounting Code	: 100456
Duty Head	: Secondary Education Cess
Inventory values are affected	? No
Activate Interest Calculation	? No
Percentage of Calculation (eg 5)	? 2 %
Method of Calculation	: On Total Excise Duty
Rounding Method	: Normal Rounding
Rounding Limit	: 0

F-5B: CENVAT Duty Cess Account

Enter the Excise Purchase Voucher (F-5E / F-5F), as described earlier (F-4A).

Nature of Purchase: At Nature of Purchase field (F-5E / F-5F), select as follows

- **Purchase from Manufacturer**: Select *Manufacturer*
- **Purchase from Dealer**: Select *First Stage Dealer / Second Stage Dealer*, as the case may be

06.01 CENVAT Ledger Details

After entry of Item details, at the main voucher entry screen (F-5E), select the CENVAT Ledger Accounts to get the Duty Details entry screen (F-5D). Enter the details (these are carried & shown). In This way, select each of the CENVAT accounts.

Particulars					Excise
Assessable Value					6,000.00
CPU P4					6,000.00
Item Value					*6,000.00*
Basic E Duty CENVAT 16%					*960.00*
Sec Ed Cess CENVAT 2%					*19.20*
Excise Duty Value					979.20
Basic E Duty CENVAT 16%				16 %	960.00
CPU P4	@ 16 %	On	6,000.00	960.00	
Sec Ed Cess CENVAT 2%				2 %	19.20
CPU P4	@ 2 %	On	960.00	19.20	

F-5C: Statutory details of Purchase Voucher

Duty Details for : **Basic E Duty CENVAT 16%**

Type of Ref	Name / Name of Item	Assessable Amount	Rate	Duty Amount
New Ref	23 / 1-2009			
	CPU P4	6,000.00	16 %	960.00 Dr
				960.00 Dr

Duty Details for : **Sec Ed Cess CENVAT 2%**

Type of Ref	Name / Name of Item	Assessable Amount	Rate	Duty Amount
New Ref	23 / 1-2009			
	CPU P4	960.00	2 %	19.20 Dr
				19.20 Dr

F-5D: Duty Details of Purchase Voucher

06.02 Statutory Details

After entry of all Ledger Accounts (Duty and other Ledger Accounts), At *Show Statutory Details* (F-5E), set *Yes* to show the CENVAT Duty Ledger Accounts and the corresponding Amount (F-5C). Click *F1:Details* to get Stock Item wise break up of each CENVAT Account Amount (F-5C).

Accounting Voucher Creation Ctrl + M

ExcPur No. 1 — 1-May-2009 Friday

Supplier Invoice No. : 23 Date : 1-Apr-2009

Excise Unit : Bonded Godown 1

Party's A/c Name : Riverstone Solutions India

Nature of Purchase: Manufacturer

Purchase Ledger : Purchase

Name of Item	Quantity	Rate	per	Amount
CPU P4	3 Pcs	2,000.00	Pcs	6,000.00
Rate of Duty : 16%				
Basic E Duty CENVAT 16%		16 %		960.00
Sec Ed Cess CENVAT 2%		2 %		19.20
Show Statutory Details ? No				
	3 Pcs			6,979.20

F-5E: Purchase from Manufacturer with CENVAT

Accounting Voucher Creation Ctrl + M

ExcPur No. 1 — 1-May-2009 Friday

Supplier Invoice No. : 23 Date : 1-Apr-2009

Excise Unit : Bonded Godown 1

Party's A/c Name : Riverstone Solutions India

Nature of Purchase: First Stage Dealer

Purchase Ledger : Purchase

Name of Item	Quantity	Rate	per	Amount
CPU P4	3 Pcs	2,000.00	Pcs	6,000.00
Rate of Duty : 16%				
Basic E Duty CENVAT 16%		16 %		960.00
Sec Ed Cess CENVAT 2%		2 %		19.20
Show Statutory Details ? Yes				
	3 Pcs			6,979.20

F-5F: Purchase from Excise Dealer with CENVAT

06.03 Item purchased under multiple Invoice

Sometimes, in a Purchase invoice may relate to multiple manufacturer with different Assessable Value & Different Duty Rate. At Purchase Invoice entry:

- Party Details screen,
    - o Supplier: At *Supplier Details* section, enter the details of Supplier.
    - o Manufacturer / Importer At Manufacturer / Importer section, press Alt+M (or click M:Manual) button and enter the manufacturer details (or select the account if already created).
- Excise Details screen (F-5D):
    - o Assessable Value: Enter the Assessable value manually.
    - o Duty Details: The Duty would be computed accordingly for Manufacturer / First Stage dealer.

This way, select enter separately for each Manufacturer / Importer

07 Modification of Duty Amount

During Voucher entry, the default Rate of Duty as specified in Master, is carried. To Allow Modification in Duty for Purchase from Manufacture to change the Duty amount as necessary, you should set Yes at *Allow Modification of All entries* at the configuration option (Click *F12:Configure* at Invoice entry screen) In that case you may overwrite the computed Duty Amount.

08 Excisable Goods Sales Invoice Entry

We have explained Sales Invoice Entry earlier. Here we discuss about additional details to be entered relating to Excise Duty.

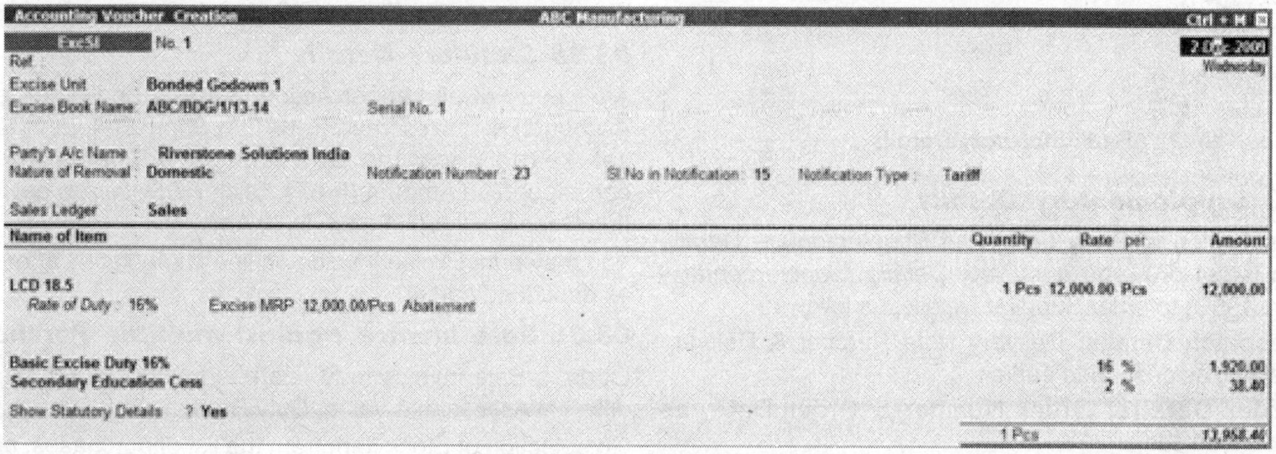

F-6A: Sales Invoice Entry

Voucher Type: At Voucher entry screen, Click *F8:Sales* and then select the Excise Sales Voucher Type to get Sales Voucher (F-6A) entry screen (Click *V:As Invoice* toggle button to enter in Invoice Mode).

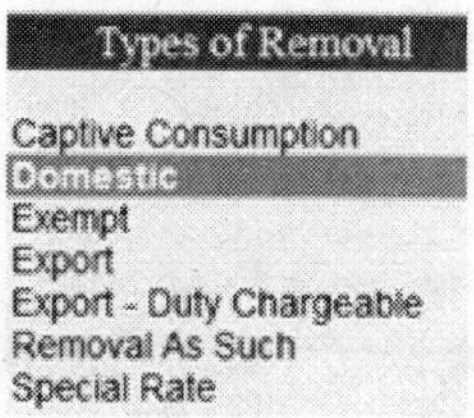

F-6B: Removal Type List

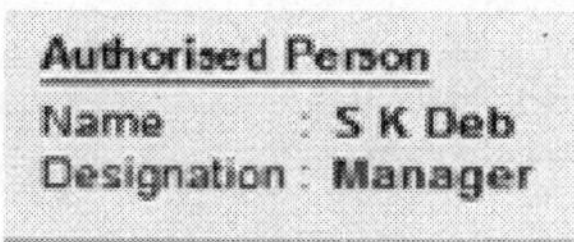

F-6C: Excise Invoice Priting screen

08.01 Excise Details

At the Voucher Header part, enter following details (F-6A)

- **Excise Unit**: At *Excise Unit*, select the Excise Unit from the list, where the Stock is stored
- **Excise Book Name:** At *Excise Book Name*, the default Book Name is carried (select Book Name from the list, in case of multiple books)
- **Party Name**: At *Party Account Name*, select the Party Ledger from the list of Parties.
- **Supplementary Details:** Now you get the Supplementary details screen (F-6D) showing data carried from Party Ledger and Purchase Invoice. Enter other details of the Sales Invoice.
- **Removal Type**: At *Nature of Removal*, select the Removal Type from the Removal Type list (F-6B)

Having entered the above details at Voucher Header, enter the Item details of each Stock Item sold (F-6A)

08.02 Stock Item Details

At *Name of Item column* (F-6A) select the *Stock Item* to get *Item Allocation* screen of the Stock Item (F-6E). Enter the details as follows:

- **Godown**: At *Godown* column, select the Excise Godown from the list.
- **Quantity**: At *Quantity* column, enter the Quantity
- **Item Rate**: At *Rate*, enter the Purchase Rate (Basic Item Rate)
- **Amount**: the Computed Amount as per Quantity & Rate is shown at Amount Column, which you may change

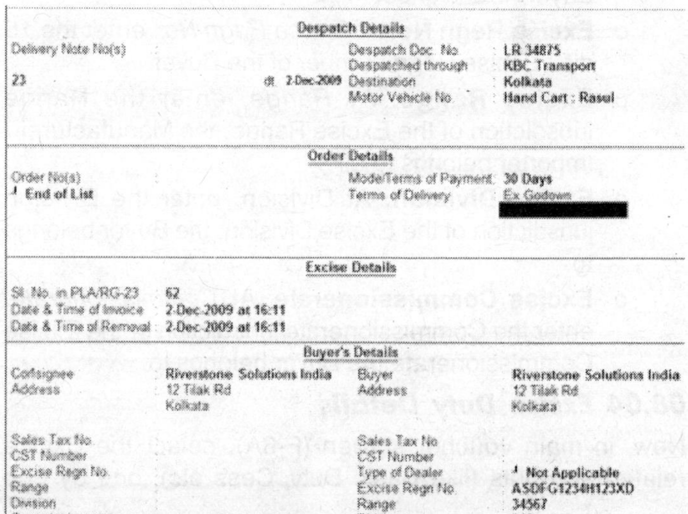

F-6D: Party (Supplementary) Details

F-6E: Item Allocation details

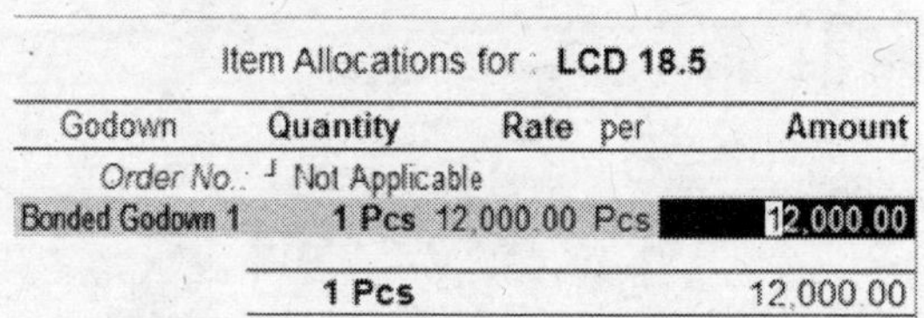

ABC Manufacturing

Statutory Details

Particulars					Excise
Assessable Value					12,000.00
LCD 18.5	On 1 Pcs @ 12,000.00/Pcs Abatement : 10%				12,000.00
Item MRP					
Basic Excise Duty 16%					1,920.00
Secondary Education Cess					38.40
Excise Duty Value					1,958.40
Basic Excise Duty 16%				16 %	1,920.00
LCD 18.5	@ 16 %	On	12,000.00	1,920.00	
Secondary Education Cess				2 %	38.40
LCD 18.5	@ 2 %	On	1,920.00	38.40	

F-6F: Statutory Details

08.03 Supplementary Details

After selection of Party Ledger (if Supplementary Details option is set on), you get *Party Details (Supplementary)* screen (F-6D) to enter Supplier Details, as follows:

- **Despatch Details:** Delivery Note Number & Delivery Details, as described earlier
- **Order Details:** Order Number & Order Date, as described earlier
- **Excise Details**: PLA Entry Number, Date & Time of Invoice & Removal of goods
- **Buyer / Consignee Details:** Now enter the following details of the of the Manufacturer/ Importer, for record and printing in Invoice
    - o **Name**: At *Buyer/ Consignee*, enter the Name of the Buyer / Consignee (if Different)
    - o **Address**: At *Address*, enter the Address of the Buyer / Consignee.
    - o **Excise Regn No**: At *Excise Regn No.*, enter the 15 digit Excise Regn number of the Buyer.
    - o **Excise Range**: At *Range*, enter the Range jurisdiction of the Excise Range, the Manufacturer / Importer belongs to.
    - o **Excise Division:** At Division, enter the Division jurisdiction of the Excise Division, the Buyer belongs to.
    - o **Excise Commissionerate**: At *Commissionerate*, enter the Commissionerate jurisdiction of the Excise Commissionerate the Buyer belongs to.

08.04 Excise Duty Details

Now, in main voucher screen (F-6A), select the Excise related accounts (like Basic Duty, Cess etc), one by one and enter the details in respect of each ledger account (F-4B), as follows,

- **Duty Rate**: At *Rate* column, The Duty Rate (for the selected Duty Ledger), as specified, is shown
- **Duty Amount**: At *Amount* column, the computed Duty Amount is shown.

This way, enter the Duty details for all the Stock Items

08.05 Statutory Details

After entry of all Ledger Accounts (Duty and other ledger Accounts) at main screen (F-6A), At *Show Statutory Details*, set *Yes* to show the Duty Ledger Accounts and the corresponding Amount (F-6F). Click *F1:Details* to get Stock Item wise break up of each Duty Amount

You may print Excise Invoice on line immediately after entry as described earlier

08.06 Sale Invoice against multiple Purchases

Often, a Sale Invoice may relate to multiple purchase with different Assessable Value, Duty Rate

On selection of Stock Item from the list of purchases, at Part Details screen, at Manufacturer / Importer details, enter the respective details

08.07 Excise Invoice in Print

After entry of Invoice, click *P:Print* button to get Invoice Printing screen. Type Y to print the Invoice (F-7A).

Excise Invoice

(ISSUE OF INVOICE UNDER RULE 11 OF CENTRAL EXCISE RULES 2002)

Bonded Godown 1

Excise Regn No. : ABCDE1234D123XM

Range : 123456
Division : 123
Commissionerate : 12

Consignee	Invoice No.	Dated
Riverstone Solutions India 12 Tilak Rd Kolkata	1	
	Buyer's Order No.	Dated
	Delivery Note 23	Dated 2-Dec-2009
	Supplier's Ref.	Despatch Document No. LR 34875
Buyer (if other than consignee) Riverstone Solutions India 12 Tilak Rd Kolkata	Despatched through KBC Transport	Destination Kolkata
	Date & Time of issue of invoice 2-Dec-2009 at 16:11	Motor Vehicle No. Hand Cart : Rasul
Excise Regn No. : ASDFG1234H123XD Range : 34567 Division : 345 Commissionerate : 34	Date & Time of Removal of Goods 2-Dec-2009 at 16:11	Authenticated By *for Bonded Godown 1*
Notification No. : 23	Mode/Terms of Payment 30 Days	*Authorised Signatory*

Sl No.	Description of Goods	Tariff / HSN Classification	Quantity.	Rate	per	Amount
1	LCD 18.5	13456789	1 Pcs	12,000.00	Pcs	12,000.00
	Basic Excise Duty 16%			16	%	1,920.00
	Secondary Education Cess			2	%	38.40

F-7A: Excise Invoice as per Rule 11

Excise Duty Payment

01 Advance Payment to PLA

Excise Duty is paid in advance to keep sufficient balance in the PLA to allow removal of goods.

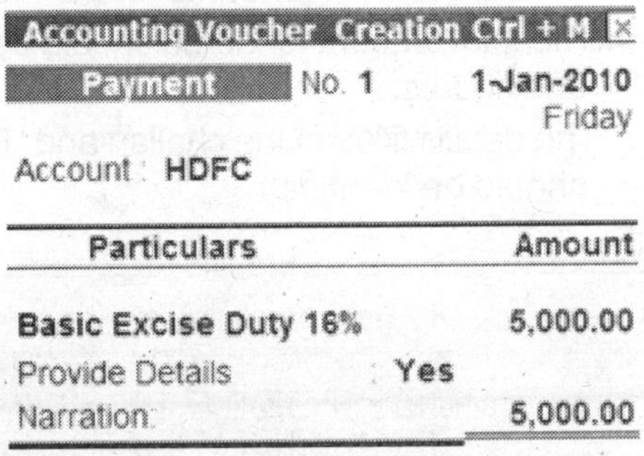

F-1A: Excise Duty Payment

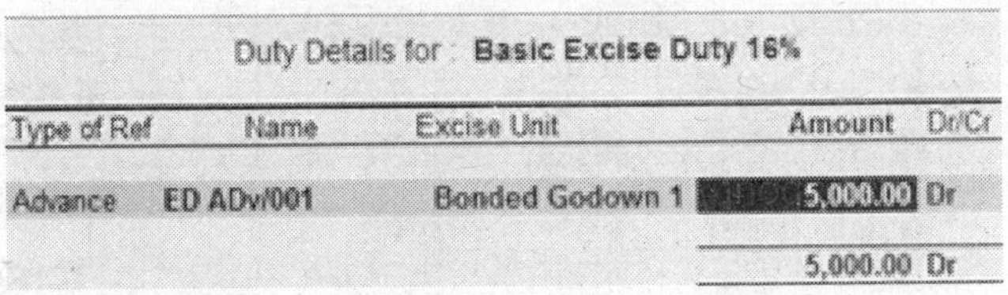

F-1B: Duty Details

The Deposit of Duty is to be entered through Payment Voucher. Payment Voucher entry in single mode has been described earlier. Here we describe the entry steps specific to Excise Duty

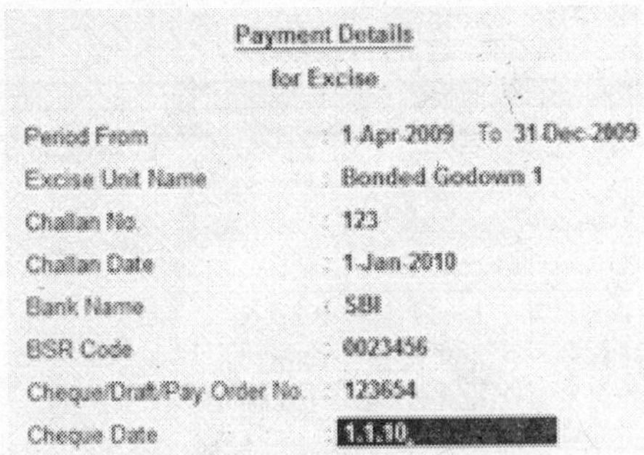

F-1C: Payment Details

At *Main Voucher entry* screen (F-1A), at Particulars column, select Excise Duty Account to get *Duty Details* screen (F-1B).

Duty Details: Here enter as follows:

- o **Payment Type**: At *Type of Ref* column, select *Advance*.
- o **Reference Number**: At *Name* column, the Reference of Advance Payment (by default, the Voucher number prefixed by ED Adv) is carried which you may change.
- o **Excise Unit**: At *Excise Unit* column, select the Excise Unit
- o **Amount**: At Amunt column, enter the amount of Advance paid

The Amount entered is carried at the main Voucher screen (F-1A) against the Excise Duty Ledger Account.

Payment Details: At *Provide Details* (F-1A), set Yes to get Payment Details entry screen (F-1C). Enter the respective details.

02 GAR – 7 Payment

The Excise Duty payable as per Computation Statement for the Period is to be paid. At Payment Voucher screen (F-2A), click *S:Stat Payment* button to get Statutory Payment screen (F-2B). Enter the details:

- **Duty Type**: At *Type of Duty/ Tax*, select *Excise* from the list
- **Amount Fill**: At *Auto Fill Statutory Payment,* set,
  - o **Auto Fill**: *Yes* to get the amount of duty Payable for each duty account, carried in the main voucher screen. This helps payment of exact amount of duty
  - o **Manual Fill**: No. The Duty Account and Amount is to be entered
- **Duty Period**: At *Period From / To*, enter the Period for which the Duty is being paid. The Duty Amount will be carried (in case of Auto Fill),accordingly
- **Excise Unit**: At *Excise Unit*, select the Excise Unit from the list.

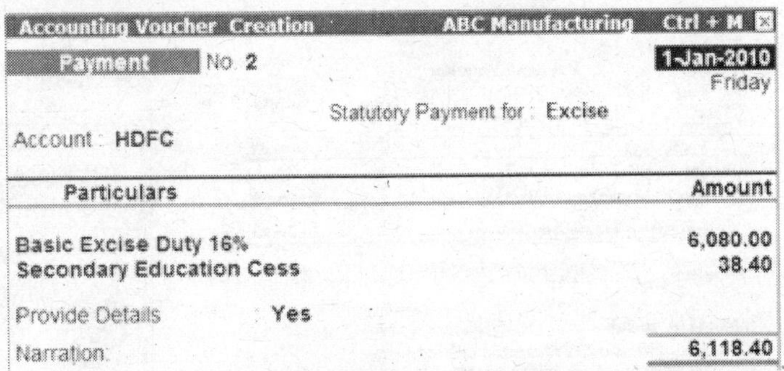

F-2A: Excise Payment Voucher

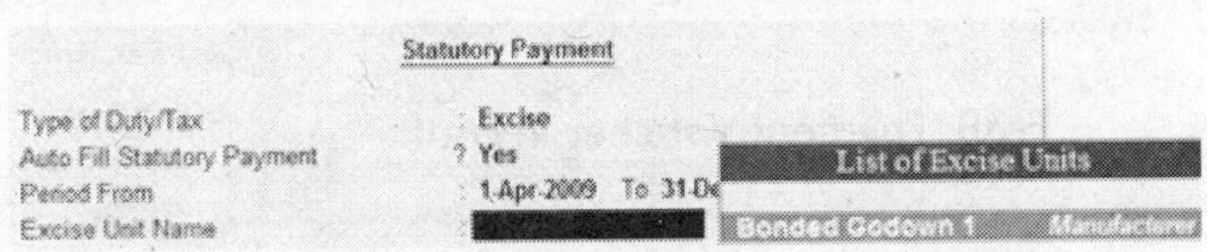

F-2B: Excise Payment Details (Auto Fill)

Payment Details: At *Provide Details* (F-2A), set *Yes* to get Payment Details screen (F-2C).to enter the respective details of Payment.

Payment Details
for Excise

Period From	: 1-Apr-2009 To 31-Mar-2010
Excise Unit Name	: Bonded Godown 1
Challan No	: 13
Challan Date	: 2-Apr-2009
Bank Name	: 2.1.10
BSR Code	: 456789
Cheque/Draft/Pay Order No	: 324567
Cheque Date	: 2.1.10

F-2C: Payment Details

03 Printing of GAR - 7 Challan

Having completed Payment Voucher entry (F-2A), click P:Print to get Payment Voucher Printing screen. At Print GAR-7 Challan (F-3A),:

- Set *Yes* to Print GAR-7 Challan
- Set *No* to Print Payment Voucher

03.01 GAR -7 Form (Instructions)

Instructions for filling up G.A.R-7 Challan Form

1. Name, Address, 15 digit Assessee Code, Commissionerate Name and 8 digit Accounting code is mandatory.
2. The Assessee Code, Commissionerate Code, Division Code and Range Code can be verified from the website http://exciseandservicetax.nic.in
3. The Accounting codes for Duty/Cess are provided in the table below. The total amount tendered should tally with the sum total of amounts for each accounting code.
4. The total amount tendered should be written both in words and figures.
5. The details filled in the challan and 'Taxpayer's Counterfoil' should be identical.

Report Titles
Payment Voucher

Print G.A.R.-7 Challan	: Yes
Print Payment Advice	: No
Payment Advice Date	: 1-Jan-2010
Print Due Date	? No
Print Company's PAN/IT Number	? No

F-3A: Payment Voucher / GAR-7 Printing screen

ABC Manufacturing
201-202, Phase II,
SIDCO Industrial Estate
Bangalore
E-Mail : sales@universal.com

Payment Voucher

No. : 2 Dated : 1-Jan-2010

Particulars	Amount
Account :	
Basic Excise Duty 16%	6,080.00
Secondary Education Cess	38.40
Through :	
HDFC	
Amount (in words) :	
Indian Rupees Six Thousand One Hundred Eighteen and Forty paise Only	₹ 6,118.40

Receiver's Signature Authorised Signatory
Checked by Verified by

F-3B: Payment Voucher in Print

For payments from April 2007 onwards **G.A.R.-7 Proforma for Central Excise Tax Payments** (Receipts & Payment Rules 26)

Full Name: Bonded Godown 1
Complete Address: 12 Naktala
Telephone No: 080-445544 Pincode: 560068
Assessee Code No: ABCDE1234D123XM
Commissionerate Name:
Commissionerate Code: 12 Division Code: 12 Range Code: 12

Accounting Code of the Duty / Cess	Amount Tendered in Rupees
0380003	6080
345678	38
Total	6118

RECEIVING BANK BRANCH STAMP

(In words) Rupees Six Thousand One Hundred Eighteen Only tendered by
Cash/Cheque/Draft/Pay Order No. 324567 Dated 2-Jan-2010 Drawn on 2.1.10
Signature of the Tenderer with date

TAX PAYER'S COUNTERFOIL

Accounting Code of the Duty / Cess	Amount Tendered in Rupees
0380003	6080
345678	38
Total	6118

RECEIVING BANK BRANCH STAMP

Received from Assessee Code No. ABCDE1234D123XM
(In words) Rupees Six Thousand One Hundred Eighteen Only
By Cash/Cheque/Draft/Pay Order No. 324567 Dated 2-Jan-2010 Drawn on 2.1.10
on account of Union Central Excise Duties as detailed in this taxpayer's counterfoil and on stamp affixed and signed therein

F-3C: GAR-7 Challan in Print

6. The Receiving Bank Branch Stamp should contain the following:
   i. BSR code of the receiving Bank Branch (7 digits)
   ii. Date of Deposit of Challan (DDMMYYYY) (8 digits)
   iii. Challan Serial Number (5 digits)

The above information is collectively called the Challan Identification Number (20 digit CIN), which will have to be quoted in the return.

Shareable Duties

1 Basic Excise Duties 00380003
2 Patent & Proprietary Medicines 00380007
3 Auxiliary Duties of Excise 00380010
4 Addl. Duties On Mineral Products 00380012
5 Special Excise Duties 00380013
6 Duties on Motor Vehicle Parts 00380016
7 Other Receipts 00380087

Duties Assigned to States

01 Addl. Duties in lieu of Sales Tax 00380018
02 Duty on Generation of Power 00380020
03 Auxiliary Duties 00380023
04 Special Excise Duties 00380025
05 Addl. Duties on Textile 00380027
06 Addl. Duties on TV Sets 00380028
07 Addl. Duties on Motor Spirit 00380101
08 Addl. Duty on High Speed Diesel 00380102
09 National Calamity Contingent Duty 00380106
10 Special Addl. Duty on Motor Spirit 00380107
11 Other Duties 00380031
12 Cess on Jute 00380037
13 Cess on Tea 00380039
14 Cess on Copra 00380041
15 Cess on Oil 00380042
16 Cess on Cotton 00380044
17 Cess on Rayon &Artsilk Fabrics 00380046
18 Cess on Woollen Fabrics 00380048
19 Cess on Cotton Fabrics 00380050
20 Cess on Bidi 00380056
21 Welfare Cess on Bidis 00380057
22 Cess on Tobacco 00380059
23 Cess on Rubber 00380061
24 Cess on Crude Oil 00380062
25 Cess on Coffee 00380064
26 Cess on Sugar 00380065
27 Cess on Manmade Fabrics 00380070
28 Cess on Paper 00380072
29 Cess on Straw Board 00380074
30 Cess on Vegetable Oil 00380076
31 Cess on Automobiles 00380078
32 Cess on Matches 00380082
33 Cess on other Commodities 00380084
34 Education Cess 00380111

Instructions for Receiving Branches

Receiving Branch should ensure the following:

i. The seal of the receiving branch should contain the CIN information and along with name of the bank branch, date of realization, amount received in Rs. and signature of the authorised signatory. The seal should be affixed in the space provided on the challan and the Taxpayer's Counterfoil.

ii. Challans should be arranged according to the serial number of the entry of the item in the scroll under each scroll. Each day's scrolls should be given a running serial number separately for each Major Head, prefixed by the numeral denoting the Major Head of Account namely, 0038 for the

financial year from 1st April to 31st March to facilitate detection of any omission in submitting the daily scrolls. (Refer RBI's Revised Memorandum of Instruction for Receiving Banks). Instructions for Focal Point Branch Focal Point Branch (FPB) should ensure the following:

i. Amount of remittance received by it through the inter-branch account tallies with the challans and the scrolls.
ii. All challans have been attached with the scroll and amounts in the scrolls tally with the physical challan and electronic data.

Excise Duty Set Up for Dealer

06-05

01 Registered Dealer

A Registered Excise Dealer is a dealer of excisable goods, registered under Central Excise rules,

- **First Stage Dealer:** A registered dealer who purchases Excisable goods directly from Manufacturer or Importer, their depot or consignment agent for re-sale
- **Second Stage Dealer**: A registered dealer who purchases excisable goods from First Stage Dealer, for re-sale.

A registered Excise Dealer (Seller) can issue CENVAT Sales Invoices which can be used as Input Credit for Excise Duty by the Registered Dealer (Buyer).

01.01 Activation for Excise Duty

At Gateway, click *F11:Features> Statutory & Taxation* to get *Statutory & Taxation Set Up* screen (F-1A). At *Statutory & Taxation* screen, set *Yes* at *Enable Excise* (F-1A)

Enable Excise	? Yes
Set/Alter Excise Details	? Yes
(Note : 'Enable Maintain Multiple Godowns' for Multiple Excise Units)	
Follow Excise rules for Invoicing	? No

F-1A: Excise Activation for Company

Registration Types

Dealer
Manufacturer

F-1C: Registration Type List

Excise Registration Details

Registration Type	Dealer
Address	27/C, Rasbihari Road 3rd Floor, Suit No.305 Kolkata-700019
PIN Code	700019
Telephone No.	03312345678

Excise Details *(Dealer Unit)*

Unit Mailing Name *(Will be used in all Excise Reports)*	ABC Electrical
Excise Registration (ECC) No.	ABCDE1298M12345
Date of Registration	1-Apr-2009
Importer Exporter Code (IEC)	1234567890
Excise Book Name (as per Rule 11)	Not Applicable

Other Details

Range		Division		Commissionerate	
Code	2345	Code	23	Code	2
Name	24 Prgsn North	Name	North Kolkata	Name	Kolkata
Address	Statin Rd Barasat. Dt 24 Prns North	Address	24 VIP Sch V. Kolkata	Address	23 Bowbzar

F-1D: Excise Registrtion details

02 Excise Duty Activation for Dealer

At Statutory Features screen (F-1A), set Yes at *Set / Alter Excise Details* to get *Excise Registration Details Screen* (F-1D).

At *Excise Registration Details Screen* entry has been explained earlier. Here we discuss about points specific to Dealers

- **Assessee Type**: At *Registration Type*, select *Dealer*, from the list (F-1C)

03 Excise Tariff Commodity Creation

The Excisable Items are classified as per Commodity Code. Creation of Tariff Commodity has been explained earlier. Accordingly Create Tariff Commodity Codes dealt with by the Excise registered unit.

First, create the Commodity Codes which are dealt with by the Company

Tariff/VAT Commodity Alteration

Name	Computer Goods
Commodity Under	ELECTRONIC GOODS
Used for	Excise
HSN Code	12345678
VAT	
Commodity Code	
Rate of VAT (%)	0
Schedule Number	
Schedule Serial Number	
Notes	Circular No 345 dt 1.12.09

F-2A: Excise Commodity Code Entry

Godown Creation

Name	Bonded Godown
Under	Primary
Excise Registration Type	Dealer
Set/Alter Excise Details	? Yes
Address	123 Burdwan Rd Kolkata
PIN Code	700111
Telephone No	9999999998
Allow Storage of materials	? Yes
Set Job/Project Name for Job Costing	Not Applicable
Use for:	
Our Stock with Third Party	? No
Third Party Stock with us	? No

F-3A: Excise Godown creation

04 Excise Units / Godown Creation

Excise Godown Creation has been explained earlier.

At Godown creation screen, at *Excise Registration Type*, select *Dealer* (F-3A)

05 Excisable Stock Items creation

The Stock Item entry is explained earlier. Fig F-4A to F-4G shows the various steps and components of Stock Item Master entry as described earlier.

Stock Item Creation — Hot Plates

Name : **Digital Mouse**

		Tax Information	
Under	Computer Goods	Tariff Classification	Computer Goods
Units	pcs	Set/Alter Excise Details	? Yes

F-4A: Stock Item Creation

Duty Details for : Digital Mouse
Tariff Classification : Computer Goods
Excise Unit : Camac Street Godown

Valuation Type : Ad Valorem

Type of Duty	Applicable From	Rate of Duty	Per	Method of Calculation
Basic Excise Duty	1-Apr-2006	10 %		On Assessable Value
Secondary Education Cess	1-Apr-2006	2 %		On Duty Value

F-4B: Duty Details

F-4C: List of Excise Units / Godowns

List of Excise Units

Bonded Godown	Dealer
Camac Street Godown	Dealer

Excise Details for : Digital Mouse
Tariff Classification : Computer Goods

Excise Unit Name	Reporting UOM	Conversion Factor	Set/Alter Duty Details	Stock Item Type	Set/Alter Reporting BOM
Bonded Godown	U		Yes		

F-4D: Item Excise Details

List of Valuation Type

Ad Quantum
Ad Valorem

F-4E: Valuation Type List

List of Excise Reporting UOM

Excise UOM	Description
CM	Centimetre
CM3	Cubic Centimetre
G	Grams
KG	Kilograms
KL	Kilolitre
L	Litre
M	Metre
M2	Square Metre
M3	Cubic Metre
MM	Millimetre
MT	Metric Tonne
PA	Number of Pairs
Q	Quintal
T	Ton
TU	Thousand in Nos
U	Numbers

F-4F: Excise UoM List

List of Tariff Classifications

┘ Not Applicable
Computer Goods 12345678

F-4G: Tariff Classification List

At *Tariff Classification* (F-4A), select from the list of Tariff Classification List (F-4G) of Excise Commodity created (F-2A)

At *Set Alter Excise Details*, set *Yes* to get tem Excise Details screen (F-4D)

List of Excise Duty Classifications

Additional Duty (Imports)
AED (GSI)
AED (GSI) of CVD
AED on HSD
AED on HSD of CVD
AED (PMT)
AED (PMT) of CVD
AED (TTA)
AED (TTA) of CVD
AED (TTW)
AED (TTW) of CVD
Basic Excise Duty
Countervailing Duty (CVD)
Education Cess
Education Cess on CVD
NCCD
NCCD of CVD
Secondary Education Cess
Secondary Education Cess on CVD
SED of CVD
Special AED
Special Excise Duty

F-4H: Excise Duty Classification

06 Excisable Goods Party Ledger

Party Ledger creation (Customer / Supplier) has been discussed earlier.

Dealer Type: At *Excise Details Screen* (F-5B), *at Default Nature of Dealer*, select the Default Nature of Dealer (First Sage / Second Stage) from the *Nature of Purchase* list (this may be changed in voucher).

Ledger Alteration

Name : ABC Computer Ltd.

Under : Sundry Debtors *(Current Assets)*

Maintain balances bill-by-bill ? Yes
Default Credit Period : 30 Days

Tax Information

PAN / IT No. :
Set/Alter VAT Details ? No
Set/Alter Excise Details? Yes

F-5A: Party Ledger Creation

Excise Details

Excise Registration (ECC) No. : ASDFG1234-XD-1
Date of Registration : 1-Apr-2006
Importer Exporter Code (IEC) : 1234565432
Range : 1234
Division : 123
Commissionerate : 12
Default Nature of Purchase : First Stage Dealer

F-5B: Party Excise Details

Nature of Purchase

┘ Not Applicable
Agent of Importer *(Consignment Agent)*
Agent of Manufacturer *(Consignment Agent)*
First Stage Dealer
From Agent of Dealer
From Agent of Importer
From Agent of Manufacturer
Importer
Manufacturer
Manufacturer Depot

F-5C: Dealer Type List

07 Excisable Goods Sales / Purchase Account

The Sales / Purchase Account is similar as described for VAT. There is no additional information specific to Excise

08 Excise Duty Ledger Account

The Excise Duty Ledger Accounts (including Cess Accounts) creation has been explained earlier

Ledger Alteration

Name : Excise-Purch 10%

Under : Duties & Taxes *(Current Liabilities)*

Type of Duty/Tax : Excise
Excise Accounting Code : 12345
Duty Head : Excise Duty
Maintain balances bill-by-bill ? No

Inventory values are affected ? No
Cost centres are applicable ? No
Percentage of Calculation (eg 5) ? 10 %
Method of Calculation : On Total Sales
Rounding Method : ┘ Not Applicable

F-6A: Basic Excise on Purchase Ledger

Ledger Creation (Secondary)

Name : Excsie Duty 10%

Under : Duties & Taxes *(Current Liabilities)*

Type of Duty/Tax : Excise
Excise Accounting Code : 123456
Duty Head : Excise Duty
Maintain balances bill-by-bill ? No

Inventory values are affected ? No
Cost centres are applicable ? No
Percentage of Calculation (eg 5) ? 10 %
Method of Calculation : On Total Sales
Rounding Method : ┘ Not Applicable

F-6B: Basic Excise on Sales Ledger

Ledger Alteration

Name	: **Education Cess 2%**
Under	: **Duties & Taxes** *(Current Liabilities)*
Type of Duty/Tax	: **Excise**
Excise Accounting Code	: **100324**
Duty Head	: **Cess On Duty**
Maintain balances bill-by-bill	? **No**
Inventory values are affected	? **No**
Cost centres are applicable	? **No**
Percentage of Calculation (eg 5)	? **2 %**
Method of Calculation	: **Additional Duty**
Rounding Method	: ┘ **Not Applicable**

F-6C: Excise Cess Ledger

Types of Duty/Tax

CENVAT
CST
Excise
Others
VAT

F-6D: Duty Type List

Type of Duty

On Total Sales
Tax based on Item Rate

F-6E: Duty Computation

Duty Head

Additional Duty
Cess On Customs Duty
Cess On Duty
Customs Duty
Excise Duty
Special Duty

F-6F: Duty Head List

Fig F-6A to F-6F shows the various steps & components of Basic Excise Duty & Cess Ledger Accounts

09 Excise Opening Stock Entry

Having created the Masters described so far, you are ready to enter Excise Vouchers, but, first you should enter the details of Opening Stock of Excisable Goods, as described earlier

At Voucher Opening Stock Entry screen (F-7A), at *Nature of Purchase*, the default Nature of Purchase is carried as per Party Ledger Account, which you may change from the *Nature of Purchase* list (F-7B)

Dealer Excise Opening Stock Creation — **Hot Plates** — Ctrl + M

Purch-Exc No. 1 — As on **1-Apr-2009**
Supplier Invoice No. : 12
Excise Unit : **Bonded Godown**

Excise Opening Stock

Party's A/c Name : **ABC Computer Ltd.**
Nature of Purchase : **First Stage Dealer**
Purchase Ledger : **Purchase**

Name of Item	Quantity	Rate per	Amount
Digital Mouse	5 pcs	154.28 pcs	771.40
Narration:	5 pcs		771.40

F-7A: Opening Stock Entry

Nature of Purchase

┘ Not Applicable
Agent of Importer
Agent of Manufacturer
First Stage Dealer
From Agent of Dealer
From Agent of Importer
From Agent of Manufacturer
Importer
Manufacturer
Manufacturer Depot
Purchase from Importer
Second Stage Dealer

F-7B: Purchase Nature List

Item Allocations for : **Digital Mouse**

Godown	Quantity	Rate per	Amount
Bonded Godown	5 pcs	154.28 pcs	771.40
	5 pcs		771.40

F-7C: Item Allocation screen

Fig F-7A to F-7D shows the various steps & components of Stock Item Opening Stock Entry.

Excise Details for : **Digital Mouse**
(Tariff Classification : 12345678)

RG 23D Entry No. : **1234**

Supplier Invoice Details

Supplier Invoice No. : **12**
Supplier Invoice Date : **1-Apr-2009**
Supplier RG 23D Entry No. : **3456**
Excise Opening Stock : **5 pcs**
Assessable Value : **700.00**

Manufacturer / Importer Invoice Details

Name :
Invoice No. :
Invoice Date :
PLA/RG 23 Entry No. :
Billed Qty : **5 pcs**
Assessable Value : **700.00**

Type of Duty	Rate of Duty Per	Duty Amount	Mfgr / Importer Duty Amount
Basic Excise Duty	10 %	70.00	70.00
Secondary Education Cess	2 %	1.40	1.40
Total		**71.40**	**71.40**

F-7D: Opening Stock Item Details

10 Excise Voucher Types

You should create separate voucher types for Excisable Goods. Create separate Voucher Type for each type of transaction (sales , Purchase, Debit Note, Credit Note), as discussed earlier

Voucher Type Alteration

Name	: **Sale-Excise**
General	
Type of Voucher	: **Sales**
Abbr.	: SL-EXC
Method of Voucher Numbering	? **Automatic**
Use Advance Configuration	? **No**
Use EFFECTIVE Dates for Vouchers	? **No**
Make 'Optional' as default	? **No**
Use Common Narration	? **Yes**
Narrations for each entry	? **No**
Use for Excise	? **Yes**
Default Excise Unit	: **Bonded Godown**

F-8A: Excise Sales Voucher Type

Voucher Type Alteration

Name	: **Purch-Exc**
General	
Type of Voucher	: **Purchase**
Abbr.	: PR-EXC
Method of Voucher Numbering	? **Automatic**
Use Advance Configuration	? **No**
Use EFFECTIVE Dates for Vouchers	? **No**
Make 'Optional' as default	? **No**
Use Common Narration	? **Yes**
Narrations for each entry	? **No**
Use for Excise	? **Yes**
Default Excise Unit	: **Bonded Godown**

F-8B: Excise Purchase Voucher Type

Voucher Type Creation

Name	: **Sl-Comm Inv**
General	
Type of Voucher	: **Sales**
Abbr.	: Com.Inv
Method of Voucher Numbering	? **Automatic**
Use Advance Configuration	? **No**
Use EFFECTIVE Dates for Vouchers	? **No**
Make 'Optional' as default	? **No**
Use Common Narration	? **No**
Narrations for each entry	? **No**
Use for Excise	? **Yes**
Default Excise Unit	: **Bonded Godown**

F-8C: Excise Sales (Commercial Invoice) Voucher Type

Fig F-8A to F-8C shows the various steps & components of Voucher Type Entry.

11 Excise Ledger Accounts Opening Balance

Having created Masters, you should first enter the Opening Balance on various accounts, before proceeding to Voucher Entry through Excise Info Menu (*GoT>Inventory Info>Update Excise Info*: F-6A/12-02):.

- CENVAT Opening Balance
- Excise Opening Balance
- PLA Opening Balance

The Excise Opening Balances are entered like voucher.

11.01 CENVAT Opening Balance

The process of entry has been explained earlier. At Nature of Purchase (F-9A), select the Type of Dealer (First Stage Dealer / Second Stage Dealer) from the list (F-9D).

Fig F-9A to F-9D shows the various steps & components of CENVAT Opening Balance Entry.

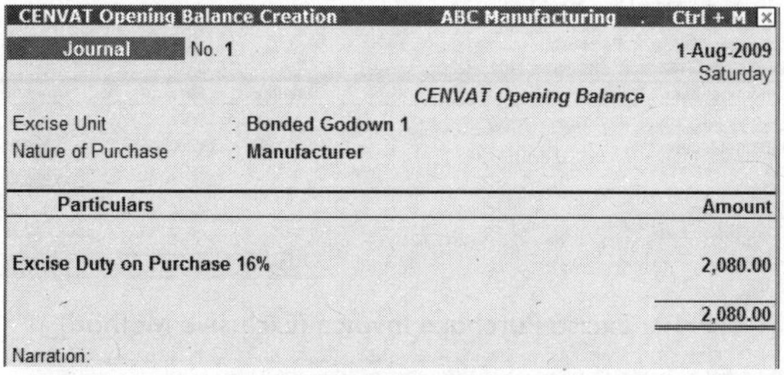

F-9A: CENVAT Opening Balance Entry

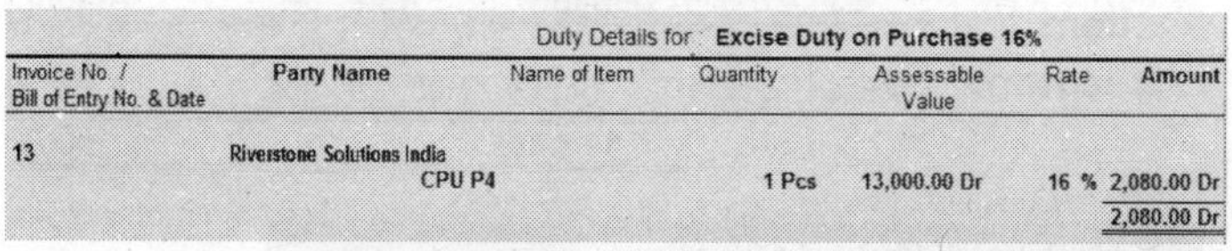

F-9B: CENVAT Opening Balance details Entry

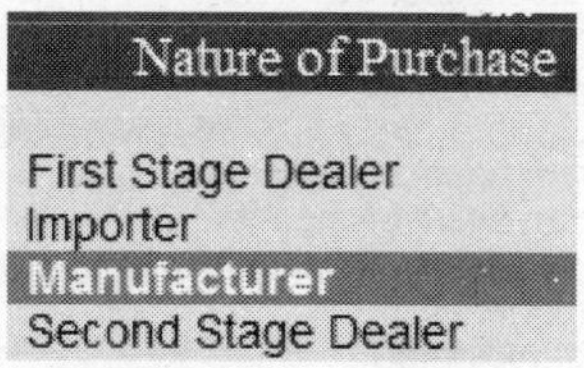

F-9C: Excise Unit List F-9D: Purchase Nature List

11.02 Excise Duty Opening Balance

The process of *Excise Duty Opening Balance* entry has been explained earlier.

Fig F-10A to F-10D shows the various steps & components of *Excise Duty Opening Balance* Entry.

In the same way, you may enter Opening Balance details in respect of other types of Excise Duty Ledger Accounts (like Cess Accounts).

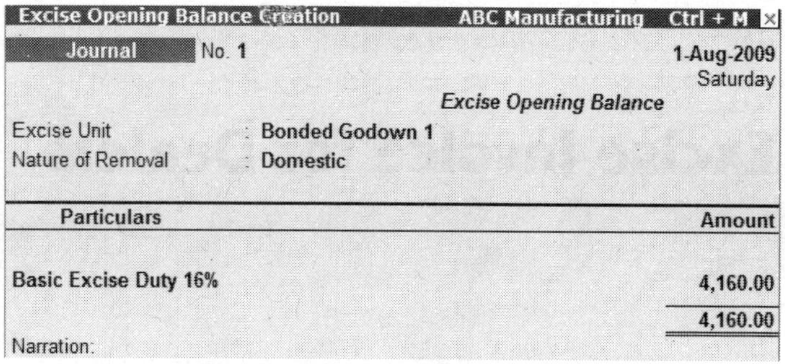

F-10A: Excise Duty Opening Balance Entry

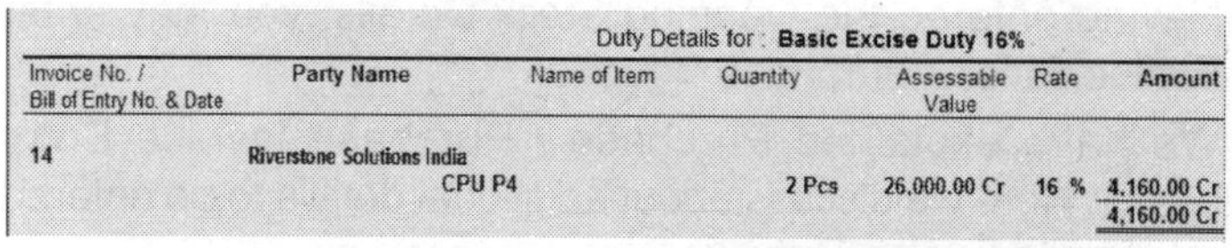

F-10B: Excise Opening Balance details Entry

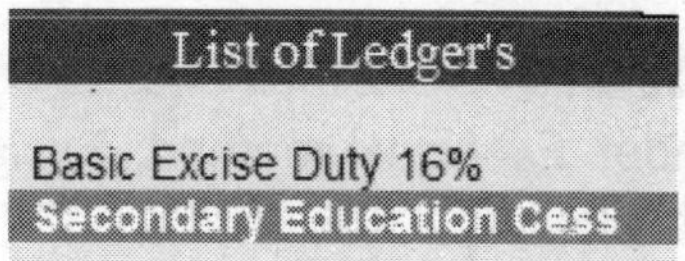

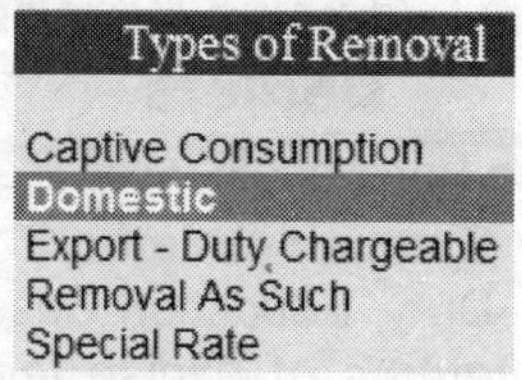

F-10C: Ledger Account List F-10D: Removal Type List

11.03 PLA Opening Balance

The process of *PLA Opening Balance* entry has been explained earlier.

Fig F-11A to F-11D shows the various steps & components of *Excise Duty Opening Balance* Entry.

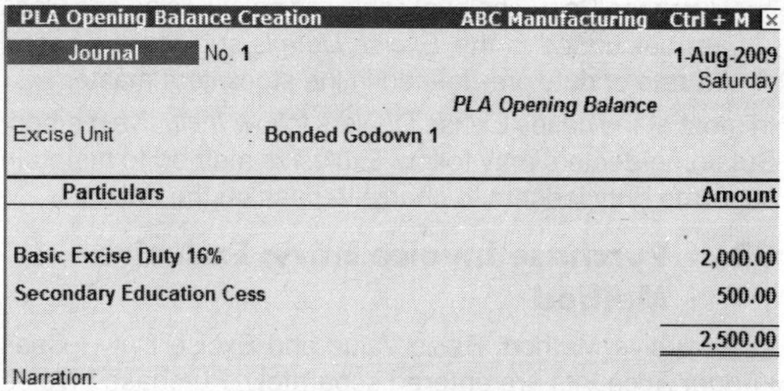

F-11A: *PLA Opening Balance entry*

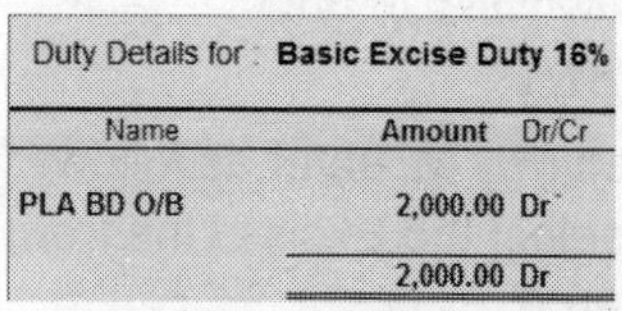

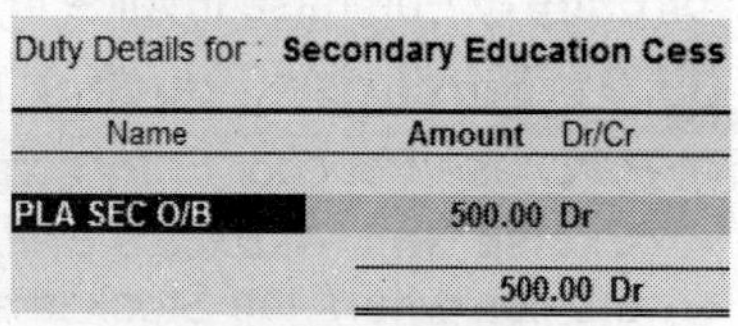

F-11B: Basic ED Details F-11C: Cess details

Excise Invoice for Dealers

01 Excise Sales / Purchase Invoice Entry

Having entered the Opening Stock Details, you may enter Excise Sales / Purchase Voucher.

We have explained Purchase / Purchase Invoice Entry earlier. Here we discuss about additional details to be entered relating to Excise Duty.

02 Excise Purchase Invoice Entry for Dealers

The Purchase Invoice may be entered in 2 methods:

- **Exclusive Method**: Under *Exclusive* method, Excise Duty, Education Cess, Higher Education Cess & other duties of excise ledgers are created and itemised separately in the Purchase Invoice (F-1A). and as a result the excise amount paid is available separately in the respective ledgers.
- **Inclusive Method**, the Excise Duty is clubbed up with Basic Value and the combined value is shown in Invoice (F-2A). The value of Excise Duty and other cess amount is debited to Purchase Accounts i.e., apportioned to the Purchase Cost. The applicable Duties of Excise and Cess are calculated in the *Excise Details* sub screen based on rate of duty pre-defined in the stock item master.

In most of the cases Excise Dealers follow *Inclusive* method. But some dealers may follow *Exclusive* method to maintain separate duty ledgers to charge & pass on the duties.

03 Purchase Invoice Entry: Exclusive Method

In Exclusive Method, Basic Value and Excise Duty / Cess Ledger Accounts are entered separately. Purchase Invoice Entry has been explained earlier. Here we describe steps for Entry of Purchase Invoice in Exclusive Method.

03.01 Purchase Voucher Entry

At *Purchase Voucher Entry* screen (F-1A), enter as follows:

- **Excise Unit**: At *Excise Unit*, select the Excise Unit from the list, where the Stock is stored
- **Party Name**: At *Party's A/c Name*, select the Party Ledger from the list of Parties.
- **Supplementary Details:** Now you get the Supplementary details screen showing data carried from Party Ledger and Purchase Invoice. Enter other details of the Purchase Invoice (F-1D), as explained next (§03.02).
- **Dealer Type**: At *Nature of Purchase*, select the Dealer Type from the *Nature of Purchase* list (F-1C)

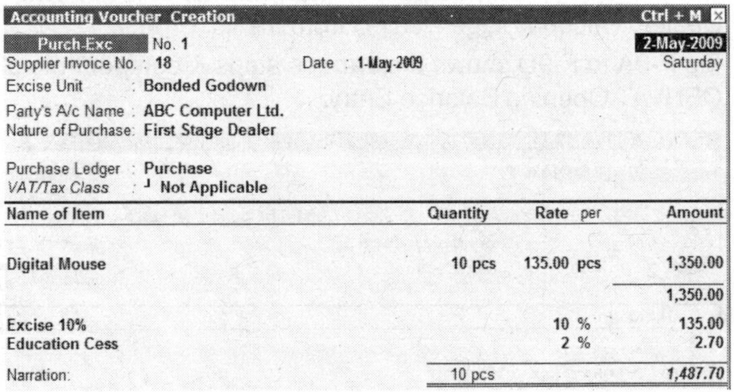

F-1A: Excise Purchase Invoice (Exclusive Method)

F-1B: Stock Item Allocaton

Item Allocations for : **Digital Mouse**

Godown	Quantity	Rate	per	Amount
Bonded Godown	10 pcs	135.00	pcs	1,350.00
	10 pcs			1,350.00

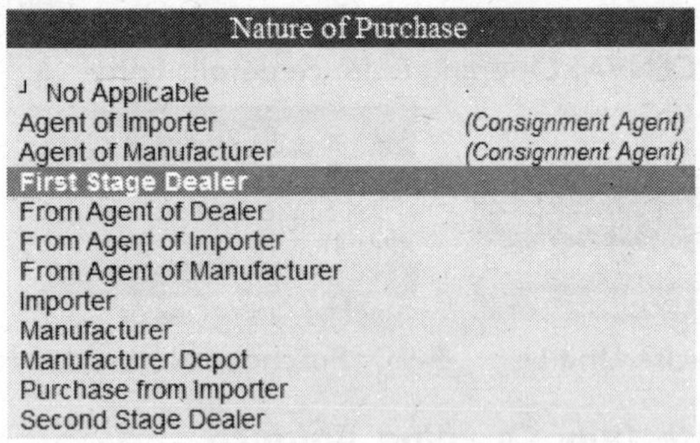

F-1C: Nature of Purchase List

03.02 Party Details

After selection of Party Ledger, you get Party Details screen (F-1D) to enter:

- **Delivery Document Details:** Here enter the following particulars of the delivery document
  - o **Delivery Ref**: At *Despatch Doc No*, enter the supplier's reference of the Delivery Document of the materials and the Date of the Delivery Document.
  - o **Carrier:** At *Despatched Through*, enter the Carrier

Name through whom the materials were delivered by the supplier.

- **Destination:** At *Destination*, enter the Destination of the materials where to be delivered.

- **Supplier Details:** Now enter the following details of Supplier of the materials:
  - **Name**: At *Supplier*, enter the Name of the Supplier. This is carried from the selected Party (Supplier) Ledger Account (you may change it here).
  - **Address**: At *Address*, enter the Address of the Supplier. This is carried from the Party Ledger (you may change it here).
  - **Sales Tax /VAT Regn**: At *TIN / Sales Tax Number*, enter the TIN/ VAT Regn number of the Supplier (if any). This is carried from the Party Ledger Statutory details (you may change it here).
  - **CST Regn**: At *CST Number*, enter the CST Regn number of the Supplier (if any). This is carried from the Party Ledger Statutory details (you may change it here).
  - **VAT Dealer Type**: At *Type of Dealer*, select the Dealer Type from the list (if the Party is a Registered VAT dealer), else select *Not Applicable.*
  - **Excise Regn**: At *Excise Regn No.*, enter the 15 digit Excise Regn number of the Supplier. This is carried from the Party Ledger Statutory details (you may change it here).
  - **Importer / Exporter Code**: At *Importer / Exporter Code,* enter the IEC of the Supplier. This is carried from the Party Ledger Statutory details (you may change it here).
  - **Excise Range**: At *Range*, enter the Range jurisdiction of the Excise Range, the Supplier belongs to. This is carried from the Party Ledger Statutory details (you may change it here).
  - **Excise Division:** At *Division*, enter the Division jurisdiction of the Excise Division, the Supplier belongs to. This is carried from the Party Ledger Statutory details (you may change it here).
  - **Excise Commissionerate**: At *Commissionerate*, enter the Commissionerate jurisdiction of the Excise Commissionerate, the Supplier belongs to. This is carried from the Party Ledger Statutory details (you may change it here).

- **Manufacturer/ Importer Details:** Now enter the following details of the of the Manufacturer/ Importer from whom the 1st Stage Dealer purchased materials under the current Purchase Invoice being entered.
  - **Name**: At *Name*, enter the Name of the Manufacturer / Importer
  - **Address**: At *Address*, enter the Address of the Manufacturer / Importer.
  - **Excise Regn**: At *Excise Regn No.*, enter the 15 digit Excise Regn number of the Manufacturer / Importer.
  - **Importer / Exporter Code**: At *Importer / Exporter Code,* enter the IEC of the Manufacturer / Importer.
  - **Excise Range**: At *Range*, enter the Range jurisdiction of the Excise Range, the Manufacturer / Importer belongs to.
  - **Excise Division:** At Division, enter the Division jurisdiction of the Excise Division, the Manufacturer / Importer belongs to.
  - **Excise Commissionerate**: At *Commissionerate*, enter the Commissionerate jurisdiction of the Excise Commissionerate, the Manufacturer / Importer belongs to.
  - **Invoice Number:** Enter the Invoice Number of the Manufacturer / Importer
  - **Invoice Date:** Enter the Invoice Number of the Manufacturer / Importer

03.03 Common Purchase Ledger Details

You may enter Purchase Ledger Account (in case of Common Purchase Ledger Account) at the header area, as described earlier.

Having entered the above details, you have to enter the Item details of each Stock Item Purchased from the Selected Dealer

03.04 Stock Item Details

At *Particulars* column (F-1A), select the *Stock Item* to get *Item Allocation* screen of the Stock Item (F-1B). Enter the details as follows (F-1B):

- **Godown**: At *Godown* column, select the Excise Godown from the list.
- **Quantity**: At *Quantity* column, enter the Quantity
- **Item Rate**: At Rate, enter the Purchase Rate (Basic Item Rate)
- **Amount**: the Computed Amount as per Quantity & Rate is shown at Amount Column, which you may change

03.05 Excise Duty Details

After entry of Stock Item details at *Item Allocation* screen (F-1B), you get *Duty Details* screen (F-1D) to enter the Duty Details of the Item.

At *RG-23D Entry details*, enter the respective reference number of RG-23D entered previously at the time of Receipt of he goods.

03.06 Duty Details

Duty Details screen (F-1E) is divided into following major sections.

a. **Supplier Invoice Details:** At the upper part, enter the *Supplier* details, if the Item is Purchased from Excise Goods Dealer.

   - **Manufacturer / Importer Invoice Details**: A the lower potion, enter the *Manufacturer / Importer*

Details, from whom the Item is Purchased by the 1st Stage Dealer.

- **Supplier Details:** If the Item is Purchased from Excise Goods Dealer. Enter the following details (F-1E):
    - o **Invoice Number**: At *Supplier Invoice Number*, enter the reference of supplier Invoice under which the Item in stock was purchased
    - o **Invoice Date**: At *Supplier Invoice Date*, enter the Date of supplier Invoice under which the Item in stock was purchased
    - o **RG-23D Entry Reference**: At *RG-23D Entry No*, enter the Reference Number provided by the Supplier in their Supply Invoice
    - o **Assessable Value**: At *Assessable Value*, the Item Amount as entered at Amount column at *Item Allocation screen* is carried (which you may change)

b. **Manufacturer / Importer Details:** Enter the details of the supply by the Manufacturer / Importer, to the 1st Stage Dealer, as follows (where the Manufacturer is the supplier, i.e. the Item is ought from Manufacturer the details may be omitted as I is same as Supplier)

- **Name**: If the Manufacturer / Importer Leger Account is existing, then you may select it from the list (or pres Alt+C to create it), else select Not Applicable (the Supplier Name is already entered at Party Details screen).
- **Invoice Number**: At *Supplier Invoice Number*, enter the reference of supplier Invoice under which the Item in stock was purchased
- **Invoice Date**: At *Supplier Invoice Date*, enter the Date of supplier Invoice under which the Item in stock was purchased
- **RG-23D Entry Reference**: At *RG-23D Entry No*, enter the Reference Number provided by the Supplier in their Supply Invoice
- **Assessable Value**: At *Assessable Value*, the Item Amount as entered at Amount column at *Item Allocation screen* is carried (which you may change)

03.07 Duty Particulars

After entry of Supplier / *Manufacturer / Importer* Details, the Duty Particulars screen showing the Particulars of Excise Duty of the Item are shown as follows:

- **Duty Type**: At *Type of Duty*, the Duty Type is shown
- **Duty Rate**: At *Rate of Duty*, the Duty Rate is shown
- **Duty Amount**: At *Duty Amount,* the Dealer Duty Amount is shown
- **Mfg / Importer Duty Amount**: At Mfg / Importer *Duty Amount,* the Mfg / Importer Duty Amount is shown

This way, enter the details of each Stock Item at Particulars column of the main voucher entry screen and then the corresponding details at Item Allocation screen (F-1B) and Duty details (F-1E).

Despatch Doc. No.	: 23	dt. 1-May-2009
Despatched through	: ABC Carriers	
Destination	: Kolkata	

Supplier's Details

Supplier	: ABC Computer Ltd.
Address	: 27/3 Jorabagan Kolkata 700 999
TIN/Sales Tax No.	: 1234(WB)
CST Number	: 456(C)
Type of Dealer	: ┘ Not Applicable
Excise Regn No.	: ASDFG1234-XD-1
Importer Exporter Code	: 1234565432
Range	: 1234
Division	: 123
Commissionerate	: 12

Manufacturer / Importer Details

Name	: XYZ Mfg Co
Address	: Mumbai
Excise Regn No.	: FDREW1234-XM-1
Importer Exporter Code	: 345678902
Range	: 5671
Division	: 567
Commissionerate	: 56
Invoice No.	: 345
Invoice Date	: 2.4.2009

F-1D: Supplier's Details (1st Stage Dealer)

Excise Details for : Digital Mouse
(Tariff Classification : 12345678)

RG 23D Entry No.	: 345

Supplier Invoice Details

Supplier Invoice No.	: 18
Supplier Invoice Date	: 2-May-2009
Supplier RG 23D Entry No.	: 234
Assessable Value	: 1,350.00

Manufacturer / Importer Invoice Details

Name	: ┘ Not Applicable
Invoice No.	: 457
Invoice Date	: 2-Apr-2009
PLA/RG 23 Entry No.	: 825
Billed Qty	: 10 pcs
Assessable Value	: 1,350.00

Type of Duty	Rate of Duty	Per Duty Amount	Mfgr / Importer Duty Amount
Basic Excise Duty	10 %	135.00	135.00
Secondary Education Cess	2 %	2.70	2.70
Total		137.70	137.70

F-1E: Excise Duty Details

03.08 Excise Ledger Accounts

Having entered the details of all Stock Items, enter the details of Ledger Accounts at the main Voucher Entry screen (F-1A).

Select the Excise Ledger Account. The Duty Amount for all the Items entered for the specified ledger is carried by default

This way, enter other Duty Heads (like AED, Cess etc) and enter the amount in the same way.

Enter Other Charges Ledger Accounts (if any) and the Amount

Finally enter the Narration and save the voucher. Fig F-1A to F-1E shows various stages & components of Voucher Entry.

04 Purchase Invoice Entry: Inclusive Method

In *Inclusive Method*, the Excise Duty is clubbed up with Basic Value and the combined value is shown in Invoice (F-2A).

The entry process in *Inclusive Method* is mostly similar to *Exclusive Method* discussed above (F-1A). The differences are explained below:

On section of Stock Item, at Item allocation screen (F-2B), after the Quantity, enter the Rate inclusive of Tax.

This way, enter the details of each Stock Item. At Item allocation screen, enter the Rate inclusive of Duty (manually calculate it). Enter the Supplier's Details (F-2C), Duty Details (F-2E) etc, as described above. After entry of Item details (and related sub-screens), do not select Duty Ledger Accounts (as the Duty, Cess etc are already included in the Rate). Save the Purchase voucher.

Accounting Voucher Alteration (Secondary) Ctrl + M

Purch-Exc No. 1 — 2-May-2009, Saturday

Supplier Invoice No. : 18 Date : 1-May-2009

Excise Unit : Bonded Godown

Party's A/c Name : ABC Computer Ltd.

Nature of Purchase: First Stage Dealer

Purchase Ledger : Purchase

VAT/Tax Class :

Name of Item	Quantity	Rate	per	Amount
Digital Mouse	10 pcs	148.77	pcs	1,487.70
Narration:	10 pcs			*1,487.70*

F-2A: Excise Purchase Invoice (Inclusive Method)

Item Allocations for : **Digital Mouse**

Godown	Quantity	Rate	per	Amount
Bonded Godown	**10 pcs**	148.77	pcs	1,487.70
	10 pcs			1,487.70

F-2B: Item Allocation

All the Excise record will be maintained and reports be displayed in same manner, irrespective of *Method* of entry of Purchase Vouchers (*Exclusive or Inclusive)*

Henceforth, we will discuss about *Inclusive* Method, as the data entry is simpler and faster.

Party Details

Despatch Doc. No. : 34 dt. 31-Jul-2009

Despatched through : Komal

Destination : Kolkata

Supplier's Details

Supplier : ABC Mfg Co

Address : 1235, Chetal Rd, Kolkata 700 987

TIN/Sales Tax No. :

CST Number :

Type of Dealer : ┘ Not Applicable

Excise Regn No. : GFDSE1234C/XM-01

Importer Exporter Code : 345679021

Range : 4567

Division : 456

Commissionerate : 45

Manufacturer / Importer Details

Name : ┘ Not Applicable

Address :

Excise Regn No. :

Importer Exporter Code :

Range :

Division :

Commissionerate :

Invoice No. :

Invoice Date :

F-2C: Party Details

Accounting Voucher Creation Ctrl + M

Purch-Exc No. 2 — 1-Oct-2009, Thursday

Supplier Invoice No. : 34 Date : 31-Jul-2009

Excise Unit : Bonded Godown

Party's A/c Name : ABC Mfg Co

Nature of Purchase: Manufacturer

Purchase Ledger : Purchase

VAT/Tax Class : ┘ Not Applicable

Name of Item	Quantity	Rate	per	Amount
Digital Mouse	10 pcs	150.00	pcs	1,500.00
Narration:	10 pcs			*1,500.00*

F-2D: Purchase Invoice

Excise Details for : Digital Mouse

(Tariff Classification : 12345678)

RG 23D Entry No. : 4567

Supplier Invoice Details

Supplier Invoice No. : 34

Supplier Invoice Date : 1-Oct-2009

PLA/RG 23 Entry No. : 12

Assessable Value : 1,500.00

Type of Duty	Rate of Duty	Per	Duty Amount
Basic Excise Duty	10	%	150.00
Secondary Education Cess	2	%	3.00
Total			153.00

F-2E: Duty Details

Fig F-2A to F-2E shows various stages & components of Voucher Entry

05 Purchases from Manufacturer

The process of Purchases from Manufacturer (F-2D) is similar to Purchases from First Stage Dealer. Here we explain only those points which differ.

- **Party Ledger:** Purchase Ledger creation has been explained earlier. Create the Party Ledger Account of the Manufacturer supplier of the materials. At *Excise Details* screen of the Supplier Ledger creation, select *Manufacturer* (F-2E)
- **Purchase Voucher**: Enter the details as follows (F-2D):
  - o **Dealer Type**: At Voucher Entry main screen (F-2D), at *Nature of Purchase,* select *Manufacturer* from the list
  - o **Party Details**: You need not enter the details again at Manufacturer / Importer section (F-2C), as the Supplier & Manufacturer is same (as the materials are Purchased from Manufacturer direct).
  - o **Excise Duty Details**: At *Excise Duty Details* (F-2E),
    - ▪ **Buyer RG-23 Reference**: At Duty Details screen, at *RG-23D Entry Number*, enter the entry reference number of the receipt of goods in the buyer's excise books
    - ▪ **Supplier *PLA/ RG-23* Reference**: Under *Supplier Invoice Details* section, at *PLA/ RG-23 Entry No.,* enter the respective entry reference in the Excise Records of the delivery under which the goods were delivered by the Supplier/ Manufacturer / Importer.

06 Dealer to Dealer Sale of Goods bought from Manufacturer

Sales Invoice entry has been described earlier. The process exclusively related to Dealers Excise Invoice entry of Goods bought from Manufacturer only are described here.

Voucher Type: At Voucher entry screen, Click *F8:Sales* and then select the Excise Sales Voucher Type to get Sales Voucher entry screen (Click *V:As Invoice* toggle button to enter in Invoice Mode: F-3A).

Excise Unit: At *Excise Unit* (F-3A), the Excise Unit linked with the selected Voucher Type is displayed in voucher entry screen.

Accounting Voucher Creation Ctrl + M

Sale-Excise No. 1 — 1-Oct-2009, Thursday

Ref. : 45

Excise Unit : **Bonded Godown**

Party's A/c Name : **ABC Computer Ltd.**

Sales Ledger : **Sales**

Name of Item	Quantity	Rate	per	Amount
Digital Mouse	3 pcs	170.00	pcs	510.00
Show Statutory Details ? **Yes**				
Narration:	3 pcs			*510.00*

F-3A: Sales Invoice entry

Item Purchase details: After selection of Stock Item, you get the list of Pending Stock Items of Purchase (F-3D). Select the Purchase Bill Reference against which the Sales is mad ein the current Sale Invoice.

Supplier Details: After selection of Purchase Reference, you get the Supplier Details screen of the selected Purchase Reference (F-3E) for the selected Sale Item. Enter the Sale Quantity of the Item (F-3E) against the selected Purchase Reference.

This way you may select more Purchase Reference for the Item sold (if the Item sold is against different Purchase Documents)

Party Details — Hot Plates

Despatch Details

Delivery Note No(s) :
Despatch Doc. No. :
Despatched through :
Destination :
Motor Vehicle No. :

Order Details

Order No(s) :
Mode/Terms of Payment: **30 Days**

VAT/Excise Details

Date & Time of Invoice : **1-Oct-2009 at 10:56**
Date & Time of Removal : **1-Oct-2009 at 10:56**

Buyer's Details

Buyer : **ABC Computer Ltd.**
Address : 1234, Garia
TIN/Sales Tax No. :
CST Number :
Type of Dealer : **Not Applicable**
Excise Regn No. : ASDFG1234-XD-1
Range : 1234
Division : 123
Commissionerate : 12

F-3B:Party Details

Item Allocations for : **Digital Mouse**

Godown	Quantity	Rate	per	Amount
Bonded Godown	3 pcs	170.00	pcs	510.00
	3 pcs			510.00

F-3C: Item Allocation details

List of Purchases

Supplier Invoice	Invoice Date	Supplier Name	Nature of Purchase	Pending Qty	Rate of Duty	Duty / Uni
12	*1-Apr-2009*	*ABC Mfg Co*	*Manufacturer*	*5 pcs*	*10 %*	*14.28 / pcs*
18	*2-May-2009*	*ABC Traders*	*First Stage Dealer*	*10 pcs*	*10 %*	*13.77 / pcs*
34	*1-Oct-2009*	*ABC Mfg Co*	*Manufacturer*	*10 pcs*	*10 %*	*15.30 / pcs*

F-3D: Pending Purchases List of Stock Item

Supplier Details for : **Digital Mouse**
(Tariff Classification : 12345678)

Supplier Invoice Number / Date	Supplier Name / Nature of Purchase	Quantity Utilised
12 *1-Apr-2009*	ABC Mfg Co *Manufacturer*	3 pcs
	Total	**3 pcs**

F-3E: Sale Item details

Item Allocation Details: After entry of Sale Item details against Purchase Reference for an Item, you get the Item

Allocation screen (F-3C). Enter the details as usual (select an Item of Stock purchased from Manufacturer: F-3D). Rest of the pat of Entry is similar to Excise Sale Entry described earlier.

Statutory Details

Particulars	Excise	VAT
Assessable Value	510.00	510.00
Digital Mouse	510.00	510.00
Item Value	*510.00*	*510.00*

F-3F: Statutory Details

Fig F-3A to F-3F shows various stages & components of Voucher Entry

07 Dealer to Manufacturer Sale of Goods bought from Manufacturer

Sales Invoice entry has been described earlier. The process exclusively related to Manufacturer's Excise Invoice entry of Goods bought from Manufacturer only are described here.

Accounting Voucher Creation (Secondary) Ctrl + M

Sale-Excise No. 2 — 1-Nov-2009, Sunday

Ref. : 45
Excise Unit : Bonded Godown
Party's A/c Name : ABC Mills
Sales Ledger : Sales

Name of Item	Quantity	Rate	per	Amount
Digital Mouse	2 pcs	180.00	pcs	360.00
Show Statutory Details ? Yes				
Narration:	2 pcs			*360.00*

F-4A: Sales Invoice Entry

List of Purchases

Supplier Invoice No.	Invoice Date	Supplier Name	Nature of Purchase	Pending Qty	Rate of Duty	Duty / Unit
12	1-Apr-2009	ABC Mfg Co	Manufacturer	2 pcs	10 %	14.28 / pcs
18	2-May-2009	ABC Traders	First Stage Dealer	10 pcs	10 %	13.77 / pcs
34	1-Oct-2009	ABC Mfg Co	Manufacturer	10 pcs	10 %	15.30 / pcs

F-4B: Pending Purchases List of Stock Item

F-4C: Sale Item details

Supplier Details for : **Digital Mouse**
(Tariff Classification : 12345678)

Supplier Invoice Number / Date	Supplier Name / Nature of Purchase	Quantity Utilised
12 *1-Apr-2009*	ABC Mfg Co *Manufacturer*	2 pcs
	Total	2 pcs

The process of entry is similar to sale of Goods bought from Manufacturer to a Dealer, described above

Fig F-4A to F-4C shows various stages & components of Sales Invoice Entry.

08 Dealer to Manufacturer Sale of Goods bought from Dealer

Sales Invoice entry has been described earlier. The process exclusively related to Manufacturer's Excise Invoice entry of Goods bought from Dealer only are described here.

Accounting Voucher Creation Ctrl + M

Sale-Excise No. 3 — 2-Nov-2009, Monday

Ref. : 56
Excise Unit : Bonded Godown
Party's A/c Name : ABC Mills
Sales Ledger : Sales

Name of Item	Quantity	Rate	per	Amount
Digital Mouse	4 pcs	175.00	pcs	700.00
Show Statutory Details ? Yes				
Narration:	4 pcs			*700.00*

F-5A: Sales Invoice Entry

List of Purchases

Supplier Invoice No.	Invoice Date	Supplier Name	Nature of Purchase	Pending Qty	Rate of Duty	Duty / Unit
18	2-May-2009	ABC Traders	First Stage Dealer	10 pcs	10 %	13.77 / pcs
34	1-Oct-2009	ABC Mfg Co	Manufacturer	10 pcs	10 %	15.30 / pcs

F-5B: Pending Purchases List of Stock Item

F-5C: Sale Item details

Supplier Details for : **Digital Mouse**
(Tariff Classification : 12345678)

Supplier Invoice Number / Date	Supplier Name / Nature of Purchase	Quantity Utilised
18 *2-May-2009*	ABC Traders *First Stage Dealer*	4 pcs
	Total	4 pcs

Item Allocation Details: After entry of Sale Item details against Purchase Reference for an Item, you get the Item Allocation screen. Enter the details as usual (select an Item of Stock purchased from First Stage Dealer: F-5B). Rest of the part of Entry is similar to Excise Sale Entry described earlier.

Fig F-5A to F-5C shows various stages & components of Voucher Entry

09 Sale by Dealer to Dealer of Goods Purchased from Dealer

Sales Invoice entry has been described earlier. The process exclusively related to Dealer's Excise Invoice entry for sale to another Dealer, of Goods bought from Dealer only are described here.

Accounting Voucher Creation Ctrl + M

Sale-Excise No. 4 — 1-Dec-2009, Tuesday

Ref. : 67
Excise Unit : Bonded Godown
Party's A/c Name : ABC Computer Ltd.
Sales Ledger : Sales

Name of Item	Quantity	Rate	per	Amount
Digital Mouse	7 pcs	190.00	pcs	1,330.00
				1,330.00
Show Statutory Details ? Yes				
Narration:	7 pcs			*1,330.00*

F-6A: Sales Invoice Entry

Item Allocations for : **Digital Mouse**

Godown	Quantity	Rate per	Amount
Bonded Godown	7 pcs	190.00 pcs	1,330.00
	7 pcs		1,330.00

F-6B: Item Allocation details

List of Purchases

Supplier Invoice No.	Invoice Date	Supplier Name	Nature of Purchase	Pending Qty	Rate of Duty	Duty / Unit
18	2-May-2009	ABC Traders	First Stage Dealer	2 pcs	10 %	13.77 / pcs
34	1-Oct-2009	ABC Mfg Co	Manufacturer	3 pcs	10 %	15.30 / pcs

F-6C: Pending Purchases List of Stock Item

Supplier Details for : **Digital Mouse**
(Tariff Classification : 12345678)

Supplier Invoice Number / Date	Supplier Name / Nature of Purchase	Quantity Utilised
18 *2-May-2009*	ABC Traders *First Stage Dealer*	7 pcs
	Total	7 pcs

F-6D: Sale Item details

Item Allocation Details: After entry of Sale Item details against Purchase Reference for an Item, you get the Item Allocation screen. Enter the details as usual (select an Item of Stock purchased from First Stage Dealer: F-6C). Rest of the part of Entry is similar to Excise Sale Entry described earlier.

Fig F-6A to F-6D shows various stages & components of Voucher Entry

10 Commercial Invoice

Where the dealer sells excisable goods to direct consumers or dealers, who do not claim CENVAT Credit (or pass CENVAT credit to next Purchasing Dealer), the sale of excisable goods is to be recorded through a *Commercial* Invoice.

At Sales Voucher Type, select Commercial Invoice (you should have created a Commercial Invoice Type as described earlier) Voucher Type.

Accounting Voucher Creation — Ctrl + M

Sl-Comm Inv No. **1** — **1-Oct-2009** Thursday

Ref. :
Excise Unit : **Bonded Godown**
Party's A/c Name : **A.K.Corporation**

Sales Ledger : **Sales**
VAT/Tax Class : **Sales - Exempt**

Name of Item	Quantity	Rate per	Amount
Digital Mouse	**4 pcs**	**177.00 pcs**	**708.00**
Show Statutory Details ? **Yes**			
	4 pcs		*708.00*

F-7A: Commercial Sales Invoice

The process of entering Commercial Invoice entry is similar as explained. Fig F-7A tp F-7F shpws he various components & steps of Commercial Invoice Entry.

Party Details — **Hot Plates**

Despatch Details

Delivery Note No(s) :		Despatch Doc. No.	: **15**
		Despatched through	: **TCP Carriers**
16	dt. **1-Oct-2009**	Destination	: **N Delhi**
		Motor Vehicle No.	: **1234**

Order Details

Order No(s) : Mode/Terms of Payment :

VAT/Excise Details

Date & Time of Invoice : **1-Oct-2009 at 16:05**
Date & Time of Removal : **1-Oct-2009 at 16:05**

Buyer's Details

Buyer	**A.K.Corporation**
Address	: 1234 Barakhamba Rd New Delhi
TIN/Sales Tax No.	:
CST Number	:
Type of Dealer	: **Not Applicable**
Excise Regn No.	:
Range	:
Division	:
Commissionerate	:

F-7B: Customer Details

List of Purchases

Supplier Invoice No.	Invoice Date	Supplier Name	Nature of Purchase	Pending Qty	Rate of Duty	Duty / Unit
18	2-May-2009	ABC Traders	First Stage Dealer	6 pcs	10 %	13.77 / pcs
34	1-Oct-2009	ABC Mfg Co	Manufacturer	3 pcs	10 %	15.30 / pcs

F-7C: List of Pending Purchases

Supplier Details for : **Digital Mouse**
(Tariff Classification : 12345678)

Supplier Invoice Number / Date	Supplier Name / Nature of Purchase	Quantity Utilised
18 *2-May-2009*	ABC Traders *First Stage Dealer*	4 pcs
	Total	4 pcs

F-7D: Supplier Details

Item Allocations for : **Digital Mouse**

Godown	Quantity	Rate per	Amount
Bonded Godown	4 pcs	177.00 pcs	708.00
	4 pcs		708.00

F-7E: Sales Item Allocation

Statutory Details

	Excise	VAT
Assessable Value	708.00	**708.00**
Digital Mouse	**708.00**	**708.00**
Item Value	*708.00*	*708.00*

F-7F: Statutory Details

In Commercial Invoice, the Excise Duty Details are not printed.

11 Charging Duty in Excise Sales Invoice

In the above examples, in Dealers Invoice (other than Commercial Invice), the Duty amount is not included in the Bill Amount, but the details of Duty Charged & Input Credit is shown in the printed Invoice under Rule 11. However some Dealers may issue Excise Sales invoice by charging the duty in the Invoice.

In such case, after entry of Stock Items details, select the Ledger Account for Duty / Cess. The amount of Duty is auto computed for the respective Duty Ledger Account.

The **Excise Duty/Cess** paid on purchase of the stock item based on the Supplier Invoice selected is shown in the Duty amount in Sales Invoice (not the amount calculated on the Sales Amount).

12 Excise Invoice Printing

You may print Excise Invoice on line immediately after entry as described earlier. At Voucher entry screen, click P:print to get Excise Invoice Printing screen (F-8B). At report title, you get a default sub heading (ISSUE OF INVOICE UNDER RULE 11 OF CENTRAL EXCISE RULES 2002), which you may change if necessary.

Excise Sales Invoice Printing Configuration: At *Excise Sales Invoice Printing* screen (F-8B), click *F12:Configure* to get Invoice Printing Configuration (F-8A). Set the options as explained earlier

We now show the printed Invoice f various sales Invoice entry described above.

13 Excise Sales Invoice by Dealer to Dealer, of Goods bought from Manufacturer

F-9A shows Excise Invoice under Rule 11, as shown in Fig F-3A to F-3F

Hot Plates

Invoice Printing Configuration

Title of Document : EXCISE INVOICE
(for Optional Voucher): PROFORMA INVOICE
Sub Title (if any) :

Height of Normal Invoice (inches) : 10 Simple: 10
Width of Normal Invoice (inches) : 7.50 Simple: 7.50
Space to leave on top (default 0.25) : 0.25 Simple: 0.25
Space to leave on left (default 0.5) : 0.50 Simple: 0.50

Print as Commercial Invoice	? No	Print Serial No.	? Yes
		Print Part No.	? No
		Print Quantity Column	? Yes
Print Voucher Reference	? Yes	Print Alternate Quantity	? No
Print Order Details	? Yes	Print as separate Column	? No
Print Terms of Payment and Delivery	? Yes	Print Actual Quantity Column	? No
Print details of Despatch	? Yes	Print Rate Column	? Yes
Print Authenticated By	? Yes	Print VAT/CST % Column	? No
Print Item Taxable Values	? No	Print Date & Time	? Yes
Print Tax Analysis of Items	? No		
Print VAT/CST Analysis of Items	? No	Print Batch Details	? No
Print Company's PAN / Income Tax No.	? Yes	Print Rate of Duty with Items	? Yes
Print Company's Tax Regn. Numbers	? Yes		
Print Buyer's Tax Regn. Number	? Yes	Print Sub-Totals after each line	? No
Print Buyer's CST Regn. Number	? Yes	Print Narration	? No
Print Declaration	? Yes	Print Narration for each entry	? No
Print Excise Declaration	? No	Print Base Currency Symbol for Total	? Yes
		Print Passed On Duty Assessable Value	? Yes
		Print Trader Supplier Info	? Yes
		Print Multi Page Excise Invoice	? Yes
		Print Supplier Name and Address	? Yes
		Print Mfgr / Importer Name and Address	? Yes
		Print Mfgr / Importer PLA RG 23 No.	? Yes
		Print Purchase Excise Duty Details	? Yes
		Print Purchase Assessable Value	? Yes
		Print Mfgr / Importer Excise Duty Details	? Yes
		Print 'Removal as Such' (If applicable)	? No

Method to use for Party Name : Name Only
Place : Kolkata
Date : 1-10-2009
Method to use for Stock Item Name : Name Only
Print Bank Details ? No

Jurisdiction : Kolakata

Generated by : This is last line of Invoice

Authorised Person
Name : A K Ghosh
Designation: Manager

F-8A: Excise Sales Invoice Printing Configuration

Report Titles

EXCISE INVOICE
(ISSUE OF INVOICE UNDER RULE 11 OF CENTRAL EXCISE RULES 2002)

F-8B: Invoice Printing screen

EXCISE INVOICE
(ISSUE OF INVOICE UNDER RULE 11 OF CENTRAL EXCISE RULES 2002)
First Stage Dealer

Bonded Godown
123 Burdwan Rd, Kolkata
Phone : 9999999998 / E-mail : hot@yahoo.com

Excise Regn No.: **ABCDE1234X-001**
Importer Exporter Code : **1234567890**

Buyer		
ABC Computer Ltd. 1234, Garia Excise Regn No.: **ASDFG1234-XD-1** Range : **1234** Division : **123** Commissionerate : **12**	Invoice No. **1**	Dated **1-Oct-2009**
	Buyer's Order No.	Dated
	Delivery Note	Dated
	Supplier's Ref. **45**	Despatch Document No.
	Despatched through	Destination
	Date & Time of issue of Invoice **1-Oct-2009 at 10:56**	Motor Vehicle No.
	Date & Time of Removal of Goods **1-Oct-2009 at 10:56**	Authenticated By ***for Bonded Godown***
	Mode/Terms of Payment **30 Days**	*Authorised Signatory*

Sl No.	Description of Goods	Tariff / HSN Classification	Quantity	Rate	per	Amount
1	Digital Mouse	12345678	3 pcs	170.00	pcs	510.00
	Total		**3 pcs**			**₹ 510.00**

Amount Chargeable (in words): **Indian Rupees Five Hundred Ten Only**

Sl No.	Description of Goods	Assessable Value	Rate of BED	BED Amount	Rate of Sec Ed Cess	Sec Ed Cess Amount
1	Digital Mouse	420.00	10 %	42.00	2 %	0.84
	Total	**420.00**		**42.00**		**0.84**

Amount of Duty (in words): **Indian Rupees Forty Two Only**
Amount of Cess (in words): **Indian Rupees and Eighty Four paise Only**

Name & Address of Supplier of goods if he is not a Manufacturer/Importer .	Excise Regn No.	Division	Invoice No. / Date	Seller RG 23D No. 1234
	Range	Commissionerate		
Name & Address of the Manufacturer/Importer : **ABC Mfg Co**	Excise Regn No **GFDSE1234C/XM-01**	Division **456**	Invoice No. / Date 12 / 1-Apr-2009	Mfg/Impr PLA/RG 23 No. 3456
	Importer Exporter Code 1234565432	Commissionerate 45		
	Range 4567			

Manufacturer/Importer Duty Details

Sl No.	Description of Goods	Tariff Classification	Quantity	Assessable Value	BED Amount	Sec Ed Cess Amount	Total Duty Amount	Duty per Unit
1	Digital Mouse	12345678	5 pcs	700.00	70.00	1.40	71.40	14.28
	Total		**5 pcs**	**700.00**	**70.00**	**1.40**	**71.40**	

Amount of Duty (in words) : **Indian Rupees Seventy Only**
Amount of Cess (in words) : **Indian Rupees One and Forty paise Only**

Declaration : We declare that this invoice shows the actual price of the goods described and that all particulars are true and correct.

for Bonded Godown

Name : A K Ghosh
Designation: Manager Authorised Signatory

SUBJECT TO KOLAKATA JURISDICTION E & O.E

This is last line of Invoice

F-9A: Excise Invoice under Rule 11

14 Excise Sales Invoice by Dealer to Manufacturer, of Goods Purchased from Manufacturer

Fig F-10A shows Invoice for Sale by Dealer to Manufacturer, of Goods Purchased from Manufacturer, as described at F-4A to F-4C

15 Excise Sale Invoice by Dealer to Manufacturer, of Goods bought from Dealer

Fig F-11A shows the printed Invoice for Sale by Dealer to Manufacturer, of Goods Purchased from Dealer (with Declaration), as described at F-5A to 5C

EXCISE INVOICE
(ISSUE OF INVOICE UNDER RULE 11 OF CENTRAL EXCISE RULES 2002)
First Stage Dealer

Bonded Godown
123 Burdwan Rd, Kolkata
Phone : 9999999998 / E-mail : hot@yahoo.com
Excise Regn No.: **ABCDE1234X-001**
Importer Exporter Code : **1234567890**

Buyer		
ABC Mills 4567 Baghbazar Visakhapatnam Excise Regn No.: **KJHGF1234C-XM-1** Range : **5678** Division : **567** Commissionerate : **56**	Invoice No. 2	Dated **1-Nov-2009**
	Buyer's Order No.	Dated
	Delivery Note	Dated
	Supplier's Ref. 45	Despatch Document No.
	Despatched through	Destination
	Date & Time of issue of Invoice **1-Nov-2009 at 13:04**	Motor Vehicle No.
	Date & Time of Removal of Goods **1-Nov-2009 at 13:04**	Authenticated By ***for Bonded Godown***
	Mode/Terms of Payment **60 Days**	*Authorised Signatory*

Sl No	Description of Goods	Tariff / HSN Classification	Quanity	Rate	per	Amount
1	Digital Mouse	12345678	2 pcs	180.00	pcs	360.00
	Total		**2 pcs**			**₹ 360.00**

Amount Chargeable (in words) : **Indian Rupees Three Hundred Sixty Only**

Sl No	Description of Goods	Assessable Value	Rate of BED	BED Amount	Rate of Sec Ed Cess	Sec Ed Cess Amount
1	Digital Mouse	280.00	10 %	28.00	2 %	0.56
	Total	**280.00**		**28.00**		**0.56**

Amount of Duty (in words): **Indian Rupees Twenty Eight Only**
Amount of Cess (in words): **Indian Rupees and Fifty Six paise Only**

Name & Address of Supplier of goods if he is not a Manufacturer/Importer :	Excise Regn No	Division	Invoice No. / Date	Seller RG 23D No.
	Range	Commissionerate		1234

Name & Address of the Manufacturer/Importer :	Excise Regn No.	Division	Invoice No. / Date	Mfgr/Impr PLA/RG 23 No
ABC Mfg Co	GFDSE1234C/XM-01	456	12 / 1-Apr-2009	3456
	Importer Exporter Code 1234565432	Commissionerate 45		
	Range 4567			

Manufacturer/Importer Duty Details

Sl No.	Description of Goods	Tariff Classification	Quantity	Assessable Value	BED Amount	Sec Ed Cess Amount	Total Duty Amount	Duty per Unit
1	Digital Mouse	12345678	5 pcs	700.00	70.00	1.40	71.40	14.28
	Total		**5 pcs**	**700.00**	**70.00**	**1.40**	**71.40**	

Amount of Duty (in words) : **Indian Rupees Seventy Only**
Amount of Cess (in words) : **Indian Rupees One and Forty paise Only**

Declaration : We declare that this invoice shows the actual price of the goods described and that all particulars are true and correct.

for Bonded Godown
Name : A K Ghosh
Designation : Manager
Authorised Signatory

SUBJECT TO KOLAKATA JURISDICTION E. & O.E

This is last line of Invoice

F-10A: Sale by Dealer to Manufacturer, of Goods Purchased from Manufacturer

EXCISE INVOICE
(ISSUE OF INVOICE UNDER RULE 11 OF CENTRAL EXCISE RULES 2002)
Second Stage Dealer

Bonded Godown
123 Burdwan Rd, Kolkata
Phone : 9999999998 / E-mail : hot@yahoo.com
Excise Regn No.: **ABCDE1234X-001**
Importer Exporter Code : **1234567890**

Buyer		
ABC Mills 4567 Baghbazar Visakhapatnam Excise Regn No.: **KJHGF1234C-XM-1** Range : **5678** Division : **567** Commissionerate : **56**	Invoice No. 3	Dated **2-Nov-2009**
	Buyer's Order No.	Dated
	Delivery Note	Dated
	Supplier's Ref. 56	Despatch Document No.
	Despatched through	Destination
	Date & Time of issue of Invoice **2-Nov-2009 at 13:40**	Motor Vehicle No.
	Date & Time of Removal of Goods **2-Nov-2009 at 13:40**	Authenticated By ***for Bonded Godown***
	Mode/Terms of Payment **60 Days**	*Authorised Signatory*

Sl No.	Description of Goods	Tariff / HSN Classification	Quantity	Rate	per	Amount
1	Digital Mouse	12345678	4 pcs	175.00	pcs	700.00
	Total		**4 pcs**			**₹ 700.00**

Amount Chargeable (in words) : **Indian Rupees Seven Hundred Only**

Sl No.	Description of Goods	Assessable Value	Rate of BED	BED Amount	Rate of Sec Ed Cess	Sec Ed Cess Amount
1	Digital Mouse	540.00	10 %	54.00	2 %	1.08
	Total	**540.00**		**54.00**		**1.08**

Amount of Duty (in words): **Indian Rupees Fifty Four Only**
Amount of Cess (in words): **Indian Rupees One and Eight paise Only**

Name & Address of Supplier of goods if he is not a Manufacturer/Importer :	Excise Regn No.	Division	Invoice No / Date	Seller RG 23D No.
ABC Traders	FREWS1234V-XD-01	456	18 / 2-May-2009	345
	Importer Exporter Code 1234565432	Commissionerate 45		
	Range 4567			

Supplier Duty Details

Sl No.	Description of Goods	Tariff Classification	Quantity	Assessable Value	BED Amount	Sec Ed Cess Amount	Total Duty Amount	Duty per Unit
1	Digital Mouse	12345678	10 pcs	1,350.00	135.00	2.70	137.70	13.77
	Total		**10 pcs**	**1,350.00**	**135.00**	**2.70**	**137.70**	

Amount of Duty (in words) : **Indian Rupees One Hundred Thirty Five Only**
Amount of Cess (in words) : **Indian Rupees Two and Seventy paise Only**

Name & Address of the Manufacturer/Importer :	Excise Regn No.	Division	Invoice No / Date	Mfgr/Impr PLA/RG 23 No
	FDREW1234-XM-1	567	457 / 2-Apr-2009	825
	Importer Exporter Code 345678902	Commissionerate 56		
	Range 5671			

Manufacturer/Importer Duty Details

Sl No.	Description of Goods	Tariff Classification	Quantity	Assessable Value	BED Amount	Sec Ed Cess Amount	Total Duty Amount	Duty per Unit
1	Digital Mouse	12345678	10 pcs	1,350.00	135.00	2.70	137.70	13.77
	Total		**10 pcs**	**1,350.00**	**135.00**	**2.70**	**137.70**	

Amount of Duty (in words) : **Indian Rupees One Hundred Thirty Five Only**
Amount of Cess (in words) : **Indian Rupees Two and Seventy paise Only**

Declaration : We declare that this invoice shows the actual price of the goods described and that all particulars are true and correct.

Excise Declaration
Certified that the goods covered under this invoice were :- (A) imported directly by us or Received directly from M/s. .... who have imported the goods (B) Received directly from Factory/Depot/Consignment Agent /Authorized Premises of M/s. .... (C) Received from M/s. ABC Traders who are the First Stage Dealer of M/s. Place : Kolkata Date : 2-Nov-2009

for Bonded Godown
Name : A K Ghosh
Designation : Manager
Authorised Signatory

SUBJECT TO KOLKATA JURISDICTION E. & O.E

This is last line of Invoice

F-11A; Sale by Dealer to Manufacturer, of Goods Purchased from Dealer (with Declaration)

16 Sale by Dealer to Dealer, of Goods Purchased from Dealer

Fig F-12A shows Sale Invoice for Sale by Dealer to Dealer, of Goods Purchased from Dealer, as described in Fig 6A to 6D.

17 Commercial Invoice Printing

When a dealer sells goods to buyer who is not entitled to avail CENVAT credit, it issues a Commercial Invoice (like Normal Sales Invoice), instead of Invoice under Central Excise Rule 11

Configuration set up for Commercial Invoice: After entry of Sales Invoice, click *P:Print* to get Invoice printing screen. Click *F12:Configure* to get Sales *Invoice Printing Configuration*. At *Invoice Printing Configuration*, set *Yes* at *Pint as Commercial Invoice* (F-8A) to print the Invoice in Commercial Invoice Format.

EXCISE INVOICE

(ISSUE OF INVOICE UNDER RULE 11 OF CENTRAL EXCISE RULES 2002)

First Stage Dealer

Bonded Godown
123 Burdwan Rd, Kolkata
Phone : 9999999998 / E-mail : hot@yahoo.com

Excise Regn No.: **ABCDE1234X-001**
Importer Exporter Code : **1234567890**

Buyer		
ABC Computer Ltd. 1234, Garia Excise Regn No.: **ASDFG1234-XD-1** Range : **1234** Division : **123** Commissionerate : **12**	Invoice No. **4**	Dated **1-Dec-2009**
	Buyer's Order No.	Dated
	Delivery Note	Dated
	Supplier's Ref. **67**	Despatch Document No.
	Despatched through	Destination
	Date & Time of issue of Invoice **1-Dec-2009 at 14:26**	Motor Vehicle No.
	Date & Time of Removal of Goods **1-Dec-2009 at 14:26**	Authenticated By ***for Bonded Godown***
	Mode/Terms of Payment **30 Days**	*Authorised Signatory*

Sl No.	Description of Goods	Tariff / HSN Classification	Quantity	Rate	per	Amount
1	Digital Mouse	12345678	7 pcs	190.00	pcs	1,330.00
	Total		**7 pcs**			**₹ 1,330.00**

Amount Chargeable (in words): **Indian Rupees One Thousand Three Hundred Thirty Only**

Sl No.	Description of Goods	Assessable Value	Rate of BED	BED Amount	Rate of Sec Ed Cess	SecEd Cess Amount
1	Digital Mouse	1,050.00	10 %	105.00	2 %	2.10
	Total	**1,050.00**		**105.00**		**2.10**

Amount of Duty (in words): **Indian Rupees One Hundred Five Only**
Amount of Cess (in words): **Indian Rupees Two and Ten paise Only**

Name & Address of Supplier of goods if he is not a Manufacturer/Importer :	Excise Regn No.	Division	Invoice No. / Date	Seller RG 23D No 4567
	Range	Commissionerate		
Name & Address of the Manufacturer/Importer : **ABC Mfg Co** 1235, Chetal Rd, Kolkata 700 987	Excise Regn No. **GFDSE1234C/XM-01**	Division **456**	Invoice No. / Date 34 / 1-Oct-2009	Mfg/Impr PLA/RG 23 No. 12
	Importer Exporter Code **345679021**	Commissionerate **45**		
	Range **4567**			

Manufacturer/Importer Duty Details

Sl No.	Description of Goods	Tariff Classification	Quantity	Assessable Value	BED Amount	Sec Ed Cess Amount	Total Duty Amount	Duty per Unit
1	Digital Mouse	12345678	10 pcs	1,500.00	150.00	3.00	153.00	15.30
	Total		**10 pcs**	**1,500.00**	**150.00**	**3.00**	**153.00**	

Amount of Duty (in words) **Indian Rupees One Hundred Fifty Only**
Amount of Cess (in words) : **Indian Rupees Three Only**

Declaration : We declare that this invoice shows the actual price of the goods described and that all particulars are true and correct.

Excise Declaration
Certified that the goods covered under this invoice were :- (A) Imported directly by us or Received directly from M/s. .... who have imported the goods (B) Received directly from Factory/Depot/Consignment Agent /Authorized Premises of M/s. ABC Mfg Co (C) Received from M/s.................. .... who are the First Stage Dealer of M/s.............................. Place : Kolkata Date : 2-Nov-2009

for Bonded Godown

Name : A K Ghosh
Designation: Manager   Authorised Signatory

SUBJECT TO KOLKATA JURISDICTION   E. & O.E

This is last line of Invoice

F-12A Sale by Dealer to Dealer, of Goods Purchased from Dealer

EXCISE INVOICE

Hot Plates 12 Lenin Sarani Kolkata E-Mail :hot@yahoo.com	Invoice No. **1**	Dated **1-Oct-2009**
	Delivery Note **16**	Mode/Terms of Payment
	Supplier's Ref.	Other Reference(s)
Buyer **A.K.Corporation** 1234 Barakhamba Rd	Buyer's Order No.	Dated
	Despatch Document No. **15**	Dated **1-Oct-2009**
	Despatched through **TCP Carriers**	Destination **N Delhi**
	Terms of Delivery	

Sl No.	Description of Goods	Quantity	Rate	per	Amount
1	**Digital Mouse**	**4 pcs**	177.00	pcs	708.00
	Total	**4 pcs**			**₹ 708.00**

Amount Chargeable (in words)   E. & O.E
Indian Rupees Seven Hundred Eight Only

Company's PAN : **ITFGD1234**   Date & Time of Invoice **1-Oct-2009 at 16:05**

Declaration
We declare that this invoice shows the actual price of the goods described and that all particulars are true and correct.

for Hot Plates

Authorised Signatory

SUBJECT TO KOLKATA JURISDICTION

This is last line of Invoice

F-13A: Commercial Invoice

Fig F-13A shows Commercial Sale Invoice as described in Fig 7A to 7E. In Commercial Invoice, Duty Details are not printed as Buyer does not avail (or pass on) CENVAT Credit.

18 Sales / Purchase Returns

In the normal course of business, customers may return goods to Seller for numerous reasons such as defective quality, price differences, and so on.

- **Debit Note**: The Buyer creates a Debit Note on Vendor whom the bought goods are returned to. Debit Note for Purchase Returns are explained earlier. The process of entry in respect of Excise Details are almost similar to Purchase Invoice.
- **Credit Note**: On the other hand, the Vendor issues a Credit Note in favour of Customer from whom the sold goods are received back. Credit Note for Sales Returns are explained earlier. The process of entry in respect of Excise Details are almost similar to Sales Invoice.

19 Requirements of Excise Invoice

A dealer of excisable goods (First Stage / Second Stage dealer) is required to issue a CENVAT invoice as per Rule 11 of the Central Excise Rules 2002, on sale of excisable goods to registered Excise dealers/ manufacture, to pass the CENVAT Credit to the subsequent dealer/ manufacturer.

The CENVAT Invoice sales affected to CENVAT Customers should be printed in the prescribed format**:** The Registered Location of the dealer is required to issue invoice in the prescribed format containing the following details:

- At least three copies of Invoice are required to be prepared and the copies of the invoice should be marked at the top in the following manner:
  - o *Original* copy should be marked as *Original for Buyer*
  - o *Duplicate* should be marked as *Duplicate for Transporter*
  - o *Triplicate* should be marked as *Triplicate for Assessee*
- Extra copies of the Invoice printed should be marked as *Not for Cenvat purposes.*
- The dealer is required to issue only one invoice in respect of the consignment wherein all the packages are dispatched in one lot. However, in cases where the consignment is dispatched separately either on the same day or different days or loaded on more than one vehicle, a separate invoice shall be made out for each lot or consignment.
- The copies of the invoices issued by a first stage dealer and a second stage dealer shall be marked at the top as *First Stage Dealer* and *Second Stage Dealer* respectively.
- Name, address and Central Excise Registration number of the registered location issuing the invoice, name of the jurisdictional range / Division / Commissionerate and

company's Income Tax Number and Sales Tax Registration Number should be pre-printed on the Invoice.

- Only one invoice book of each type shall be used by the registered location.
- Each CENVAT Invoice issued by the location should bear a printed serial number, beginning from 1st April of the year.
- The serial numbers of the invoices to be used are to be intimated to the respective jurisdictional Assistant Commissioner of Central Excise and obtain a dated acknowledgement of such intimation.
- Records and Invoice generated through computer are also recognized. In that case, the serial number likely to be used in the forthcoming quarter should be intimated to the Asst. Commissioner. As soon as the said serial Nos. are exhausted, a revised intimation may be sent. Such registered Location should also send details of the software used including the format for information of the Asst. Commissioner.

Sales Invoice Entry has been explained earlier. Here we discuss about additional details to be entered relating to Excise Duty.

20 Accounting for Loss of Materials

In any business, loss of goods are likely to occur because of some inherent, natural or unavoidable reasons. Loss of goods may occur during storage, evaporation, shrinkage, leakages, dismantling, piecing, handling, shipping, damage, theft etc

Ledger Creation for Loss of Goods: To account for Loss of goods for any reason, create a ledger Account Loss of Goods under Direct Expenses. Creation of Expenses Ledger Account has been explained earlier. At *Ledger Creation* screen (F-14A), set as follows:

- **Account Group**: At *Under*, select Direct Expenses from the list of Account Groups
- **Inventory Link**: Set *No* at Inventory Values are affected (as you do not make Inventory Allocation for Lost materials)
- **Assessable Value**: Set *No* at Used for Assessable Value Calculations, as this will not be included in Assessable value of sale / purchase

Journal Voucher Class: To account for loss of materials, create a Journal Voucher Class, as explained earlier (F-14B).

Journal Voucher: Journal Voucher creation using Voucher Class has been explained earlier. Select the Voucher Class (F-14C) and enter Journal Voucher (F-14D). At Voucher entry screen (F-14D), at *Used For*, the reason Shortage / damage/ Loss of Excise Stock appears by default.

Ledger Accounts: At Voucher entry screen (F-14D), enter the Ledger Account details as follows:

- **Loss Account**: Select the Loss Ledger account created, as explained earlier and enter the amount of Loss (Quantity * Purchase Cost) at Debit column
- **Purchase Account**: Select the Purchase Ledger Account through which the Purchase was originally Booked and select the pending Purchase Item from the list.
  - o **Item Details**: At Item Allocation screen, select the Item, enter the Quantity of Loss (the balance available quantity under the selected Purchase Refernce is shown by default, which you may change), Purchase Rate. The Amount (of Quantity Lost) is computed.

In Supplier details seen, the shortage quantity is displayed

Save the Journal Voucher. The entry would be reflected in Excise Stock Register, RG-23 Regsiter (under Duty NOT Passed on section), Excise Purchase Bill Register (at Issue section)

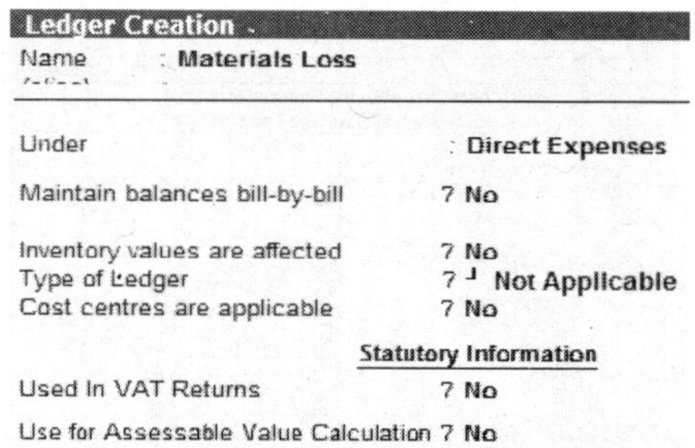

F-14A: Materials Loss Ledger creation

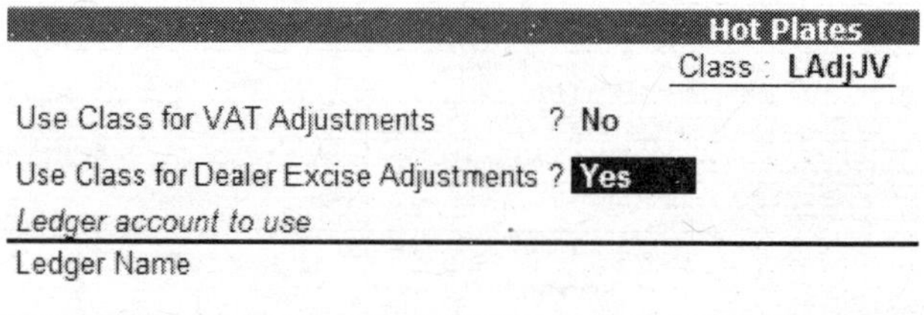

F-14B: Journal Voucher Class creation for Adjustment

F-14C: Journal Voucher Class selection

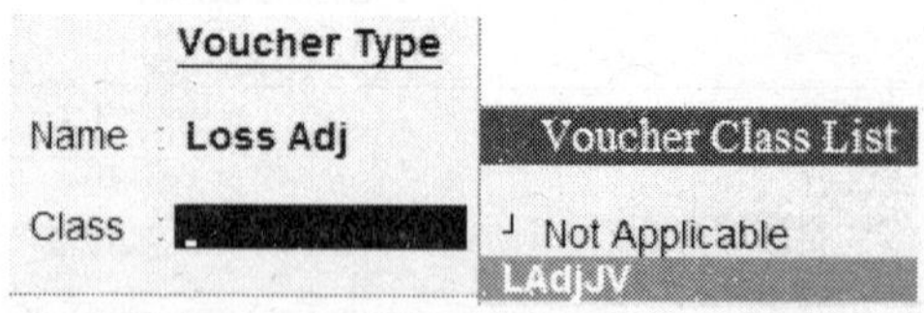

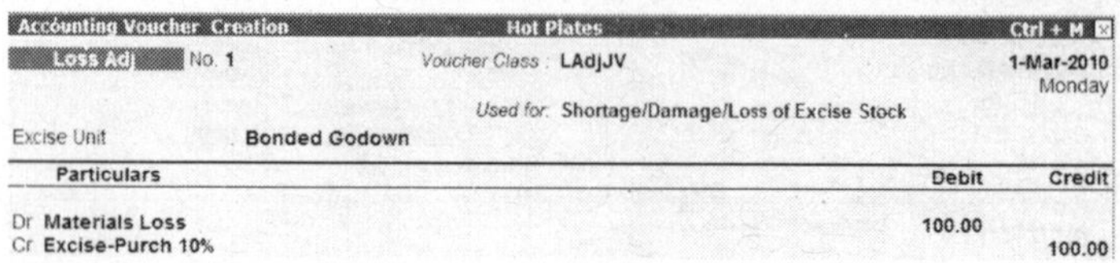

F-14D: Journal Voucher using Adjustment Voucher Class

Dealers Excise Duty Reports

06-07

01 Dealers Excise Reports

Having entered the vouchers as described, you may print the Dealers Excise Reports. Select *GoT>Display> Statutory Repots>Excise> Dealer* to get *Dealers Excise Reports* Menu (F-1A)

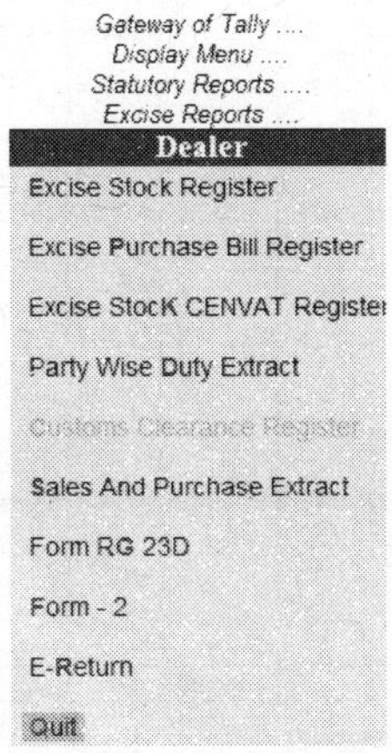

F-1A:Excise Reports Menu

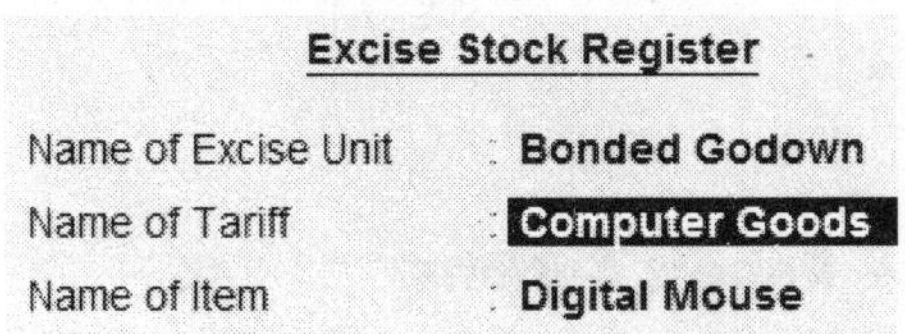

F-2A: Excise Stock Register Display

F-2B: Excise Stock Register Printing

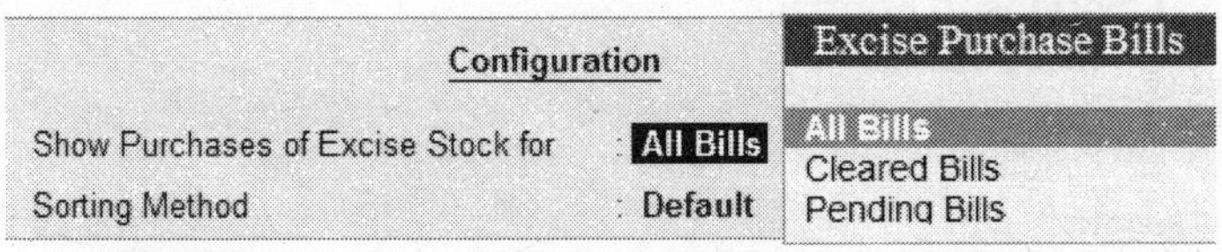

F-2C: Excise Stock / Purchase / Sale Register Configuration

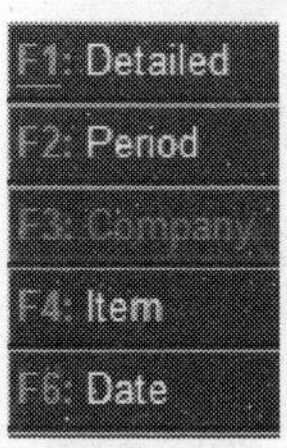

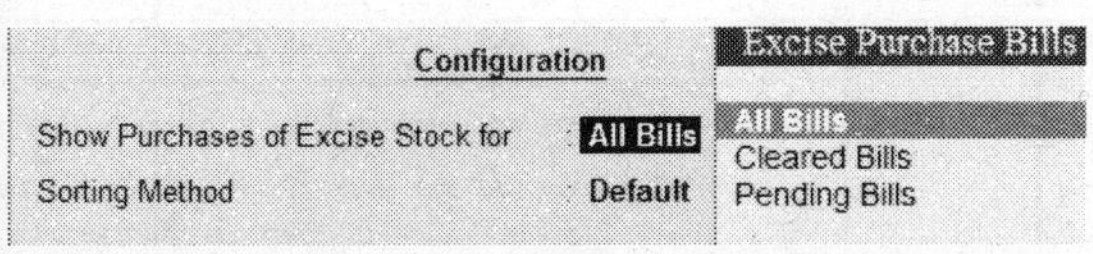

F-2D: Excise Stock Register Buttons

F-2E: Excise Stock Register Configuration

02 Excise Stock Register

Excise Stock Register shows the Quantitative & Duty details of Opening Stock, Receipts, Deliveries & Closing Stock of the selected Excise Unit, Tariff Type of the Stock Item, in chronological order It shows the Duty Amount passed & NOT Passed, and the balance of Duty including Cess.

At *Dealers Excise Reports* Menu (F-1A), select *Excise Stock Register* to get Excise Stock Register display screen (F-2A). Now set as follows:

- **Excise Unit**: At *Name of Excise Unit*, select the Excise Unit
- **Tariff**: At *Name of Tariff*, select the Tariff Type (select Any to get Stock Item of all Tariff Type
- **Stock Item**: At *Name of Item*, select the Stock Item (from the list of Stock Items under the selected Tariff Type), for which you like to display Stock Register (F-2F)

02.01 Contents of Report

The Report is mainly divided into 2 section, Receipt & Issue, containing following columns

Receipt: The Receipt section shows following columns

- **Invoice/Bill of Entry No. with Date**: Purchase invoice number (in case of domestic purchases) or Bill of Entry No. (in case of imports) along with date.
- **Name and Address of the Supplier**: Name and the Address of the Supplier.
- **Nature of Purchase**: Nature of Purchase as specified during the Invoice Entry.
- **Quantity**: Quantity purchased.
- **Rate**: Purchase Rate of the item
- **Assessable value**: Total Assessable Value of the Purchased product.
- **Duty per Unit**: The Total Duty per UoM (Duty amount divided by quantity)
- **Total Duty**: The Total Duty for the Stock Item
- **Cess per Unit**: Cess per UoM (Cess amount divided by quantity)
- **Total Cess**: Total Cess on on the Receipt Quantity

Issue: The Issue section shows following columns

- **Duty Details:** Particulars of Duty (Passes / NOT Passed)
- **Duty Passed On/Duty not Passed on**: Details of the Stock Items on which the duty is passed or not passed.
- **Balance Duty**: Balance available Duty Amount to be passed on
- **Issued Quantity**: The Total Quantity of Items Sold/ Returned
- **Total Duty**: Total Duty utilized for the Quantity Issued/ Returned.
- **Total Cess**: The Total Cess Amount utilized

Bonded Godown
123 Burdwan Rd
Kolkata

Digital Mouse
Excise Stock Register
1-Apr-2009 to 1-Oct-2009

Units : pcs Excise Tariff Classification : 12345678 Page 1

				Receipt							Issue			
Sl. No.	Invoice / Bill of Entry No. with Date	Name and Address of the Supplier	Nature of Purchase	Quantity	Rate	Assessable Value	Duty per Unit	Total Duty	Cess per Unit	Total Cess	Duty Details	Issued Quantity	Total Duty	Total Cess
1	12 1-Apr-2009 Excise Opening Stock	ABC Mfg Co	Manufacturer	5	140.00	700.00	14.00	70.00	0.28	1.40	Duty Passed On Duty Not Passed On	5	70.00	1.40
											Total	5	70.00	1.40
											Balance Duty			
2	18 2-May-2009	ABC Traders	First Stage Dealer	10	135.00	1,350.00	13.50	135.00	0.27	2.70	Duty Passed On Duty Not Passed On	8	108.00	2.16
											Total	8	108.00	2.16
											Balance Duty	2	*27.00*	*0.54*
3	34 1-Oct-2009	ABC Mfg Co 1235, Chetal Rd, Kolkata 700 987	Manufacturer	10	150.00	1,500.00	15.00	150.00	0.30	3.00	Duty Passed On Duty Not Passed On	7	105.00	2.10
											Total	7	105.00	2.10
											Balance Duty	3	*45.00*	*0.90*
			Total	25		3,550.00		355.00		7.10				

F-2F: Dealers Excise Stock Register

02.02 Excise Stock Report Configuration

At *Dealers Excise Stock Register* (F-2F), click *F12:Configuration* to get *Configuration screen* (F-2E), to set as follows:

- **Bill Type**: At Show Purchase of Excise Stock For, select the Bill Type (All Bills/ Cleared Bills/ Pending Bills)

02.03 Excise Stock Report Buttons

At Excise Stock Report (F-2F), following buttons are available (F-2D)

- **F1:Detailed / Condensed**: To get Detailed (additional columns showing Name & Address of the Party)/ Condensed Format

Bonded Godown
123 Burdwan Rd
Kolkata

Excise Purchase Bill Register
1-Apr-2009 to 1-Oct-2009

Page 1

					Receipt						Issue			
Sl. No.	Invoice / Bill of Entry No. with Date	Particulars	Name and Address of the Supplier	Nature of Purchase	Quantity	Rate	Assessable Value	Total Duty	Total Cess	Duty Details	Issued Quantity	Total Duty	Total Cess
1	12 1-Apr-2009 Excise Opening Stock	Digital Mouse 12345678	ABC Mfg Co	Manufacturer	5 pcs	140.00	700.00	70.00	1.40	Duty Passed On Duty Not Passed On	5 pcs	70.00	1.40
										Total	5 pcs	70.00	1.40
										Balance Duty			
2	18 2-May-2009	Digital Mouse 12345678	ABC Traders	First Stage Dealer	10 pcs	135.00	1,350.00	135.00	2.70	Duty Passed On Duty Not Passed On	8 pcs	108.00	2.16
										Total	8 pcs	108.00	2.16
										Balance Duty	*2 pcs*	*27.00*	*0.54*
3	34 1-Oct-2009	Digital Mouse 12345678	ABC Mfg Co 1235, Chetal Rd, Kolkata 700 987	Manufacturer	10 pcs	150.00	1,500.00	150.00	3.00	Duty Passed On Duty Not Passed On	7 pcs	105.00	2.10
										Total	7 pcs	105.00	2.10
										Balance Duty	*3 pcs*	*45.00*	*0.90*
				Total	25 pcs		3,550.00	355.00	7.10				

F-3A: Dealers Excise Purchase Register (Default)

- **F4:** To get Excise Stock Register Display screen (F-2A) to select another Item
- **F6: Date / Purchase Date:**

03 Excise Purchase Register

Excise Purchase Register (F-3A) shows the Quantitative & Duty details of Opening Stock, Receipts, Deliveries & Closing Stock of the selected Excise Unit, Tariff Type & Stock Item. It shows the Duty Amount passed & NOT Passed, and the balance of Duty including Cess.

At *Dealers Excise Reports Menu* (F-1A), select *Excise Stock Register* to get Excise Stock Register display screen. At *Name of Excise Unit*, select the Excise Unit

03.01 Contents of Report

Like Excise Stock Register (F-2F), Excise Purchase Register also contain 2 main sections, Receipt & Issue, containing similar columns as follows (F-3A):

a. **Receipt**

- **Invoice/ Bill of Entry No with Date**: Shows *Purchase Invoice number* (incase of domestic Purchase) / *Bill of Entry number* (in case of Imports) and Date.
- **Particulars**: Shows Stock Item purchased, with Tariff Number.
- **Name and Address of the Supplier**: Name and the Address of the Supplier.
- **Nature of Purchase**: Nature of Purchase as specified during the Invoice Entry.
- **Quantity**: Quantity purchased.
- **Rate**: **Rate** at which the item is purchased.
- **Assessable Value**: Total Assessable Value of the Item
- **Total Duty**: Total Duty for the Stock item

Bonded Godown
123 Burdwan Rd
Kolkata

Excise Purchase Bill Register
1-Apr-2009 to 1-Dec-2009

Page 1

	Receipt									Issue				
Sl. No.	**Invoice / Bill of Entry No. with Date**	**Particulars**	**Name and Address of the Supplier**	**Nature of Purchase**	**Quantity**	**Rate**	**Assessable Value**	**Total Duty**	**Total Cess**	**Vch Type / Invoice No. / Date**	**Name and Address of the Party**	**Issued Quantity**	**Total Duty**	**Total Cess**
1	12 1-Apr-2009 Excise Opening Stock	Digital Mouse 12345678	ABC Mfg Co	Manufacturer	5 pcs	140.00	700.00	70.00	1.40	Sale-Excise 1 / 1-Oct -2009	ABC Computer Ltd. 1234, Garia	3 pcs	42.00	0.84
										Sale-Excise 2 / 1-Oct -2009	ABC Mills 4567 Baghbazar, Visakhapatnam	2 pcs	28.00	0.56
											Duty Passed On		**70.00**	**1.40**
											Duty Not Passed On			
											Total	**5 pcs**	**70.00**	**1.40**
											Balance Duty			
2	18 2-May-2009	Digital Mouse 12345678	ABC Traders	First Stage Dealer	10 pcs	135.00	1,350.00	135.00	2.70	St-Comm Inv 1 / 1-Oct -2009	A.K. Corporation 1234 Barakhamba Rd	4 pcs	54.00	1.08
										Sale-Excise 3 / 2-Nov -2009	ABC Mills 4567 Baghbazar, Visakhapatnam	4 pcs	54.00	1.08
											Duty Passed On		**108.00**	**2.16**
											Duty Not Passed On			
											Total	**8 pcs**	**108.00**	**2.16**
											Balance Duty	*2 pcs*	*27.00*	*0.54*
3	34 1-Oct-2009	Digital Mouse 12345678	ABC Mfg Co 1235, Chetal Rd, Kolkata 700 987	Manufacturer	10 pcs	150.00	1,500.00	150.00	3.00	Sale-Excise 4 / 1-Dec -2009	ABC Computer Ltd. 1234, Garia	7 pcs	105.00	2.10
											Duty Passed On		**105.00**	**2.10**
											Duty Not Passed On			
											Total	**7 pcs**	**105.00**	**2.10**
											Balance Duty	*3 pcs*	*45.00*	*0.90*
				Total	**25 pcs**		**3,550.00**	**355.00**	**7.10**					

F-3B: Dealers Excise Purchase Register (Detailed)

- **Total Cess**: Total Cess Amount on the purchased quantity

b. **Issue:** This section displays the Sales/Credit Note/Debit Note details.
- **Duty Details**: Details of Duty Passed On, Duty Not Passed On and Balance Duty on the Quantity sold.
- **Issued Quantity**: Total Quantity of Items Sold/ Returned
- **Total Duty**: Total Duty Utilized in respect of the quantity Issued/Returned.
- **Total Cess**: Total Cess Amount in respect of Stock items Issued/Returned

Below the Issue line, the Balance (Quantity, Duty & Cess) is also shown.

03.02 Excise Stock Report Configuration

At *Dealers Excise Stock Register* (F-3A), click *F12:Configuration* to get *Configuration screen* (F-2E), to set as follows:

- **Bill Type**: At *Show Purchase of Excise Stock For*, select the Bill Type (All Bills/ Cleared Bills/ Pending Bills)

03.03 Buttons

At *Excise Stock* Report (F-2F), following buttons are available (F-2D)

- **F1:Detailed / Condensed**: To get Detailed (additional column showing Name & Address of the Party:F-3B) / Condensed Format (F-3A)

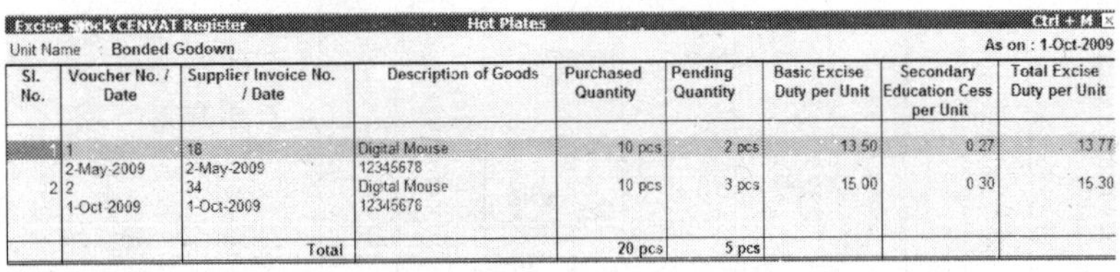

Excise Stock CENVAT Register — Hot Plates — Ctrl + M

Unit Name : Bonded Godown — As on : 1-Oct-2009

Sl. No.	Voucher No. / Date	Supplier Invoice No. / Date	Description of Goods	Purchased Quantity	Pending Quantity	Basic Excise Duty per Unit	Secondary Education Cess per Unit	Total Excise Duty per Unit
1	1 2-May-2009	18 2-May-2009	Digital Mouse 12345678	10 pcs	2 pcs	13.50	0.27	13.77
2	2 1-Oct-2009	34 1-Oct-2009	Digital Mouse 12345678	10 pcs	3 pcs	15.00	0.30	15.30
		Total		20 pcs	5 pcs			

F-4A: Excise Stock CENVAT Register (Default)

04 Excise Stock CENVAT Register

Excise Stock CENVAT Register shows the CENVAT details of Goods Purchased. Using this report, Excise Dealer can ascertain the pending quantity and CENVAT duty per unit which he can pass on to the subsequent buyers.

Excise Stock CENVAT Register display Menu: At Dealers Excise Reports Menu (F-1A), select *Excise Stock CENVAT Register* to get Excise Stock CENVAT Register display Menu (F-4D)., with following options

- **CENVAT Register for All Items:** To get the report for all Items
- **CENVAT Register for One Item:** To get the report for one selected Item

At CENVAT Register display Menu (F-4D),

- **All Items**: select All Items. At *Name of Excise Unit*, select the Excise Unit.
- **One Item**: Select as follows:
  - o **Excise Unit Name**: At *Name of Excise Unit*, select the Excise Unit.
  - o **Tariff**: At *Name of Tariff*, select the Tariff Type (select Any to get Stock Item of all Tariff Type
  - o **Stock Item**: At *Name of Item*, select the Stock Item (from the list of Stock Items under the selected Tariff Type), for which you like to display Stock Register to get *Excise Stock CENVAT Register* (F-4A)

04.01 Contents of Report

Excise Stock CENVAT Register (F-4A) shows the details of Quantity & Duty per UoM of Stock In hand and the corresponding Purchase Details

04.02 Excise Stock CENVAT Register Configuration

At *Excise Stock CENVAT Register* (F-4A), click *F12:Configure* to get Excise Stock CENVAT Register Configuration Screen (F-4B), to set the options as follows:

- **Purchase Bills:** At *Show Purchases of Excise Stock for,* select the required type of Purchase bills - All Bills, Cleared bills & Pending Bills. According to the option selected, the Bills are filtered in the Report.
- **Supplier Name and Address**: At *Show Supplier Name and Address*, set *Yes* to view Name & Address of the Supplier.

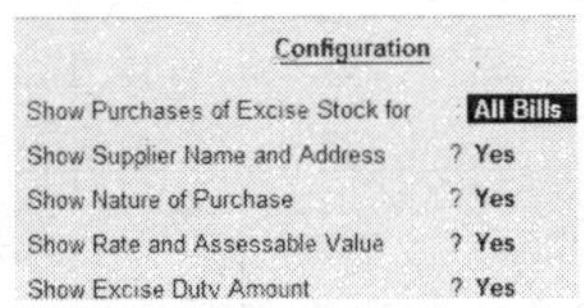

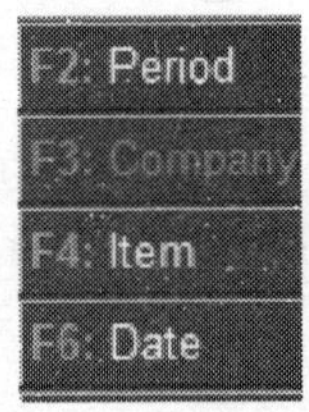

F-4B: Configuration F-4C: Button F-4D: Menu

- **Nature of Purchase**: At *Show Nature of Purchase*, set *Yes* to get the Nature of Purchase (like Manufacturer, First Stage Dealer etc) column in the Report.
- **Rate and Assessable Value**: At *Show Rate and Assessable Value*, set *Yes* to get columns showing Rate & Assessable Value of the Excise Stock.
- **Excise Duty Amount**: At *Show Excise Duty Amount*, set *Yes* to get Total excise duty paid on the excise stock (by default *Duty per Unit* is shown)

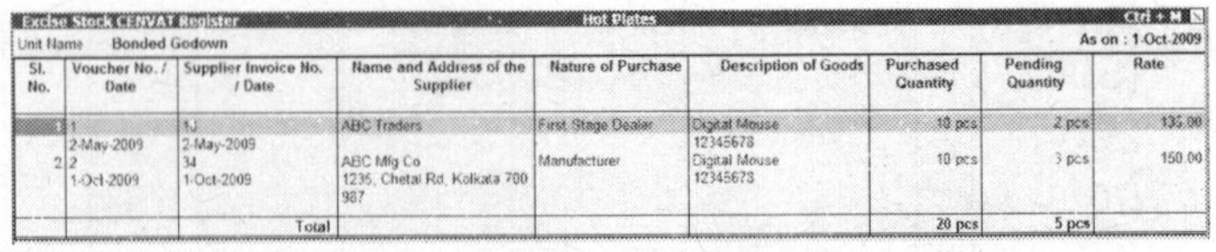

Excise Stock CENVAT Register — Hot Plates — Ctrl + M

Unit Name Bonded Godown — As on : 1-Oct-2009

Sl. No.	Voucher No. / Date	Supplier Invoice No. / Date	Name and Address of the Supplier	Nature of Purchase	Description of Goods	Purchased Quantity	Pending Quantity	Rate
1	1 2-May-2009	18 2-May-2009	ABC Traders	First Stage Dealer	Digital Mouse 12345678	10 pcs	2 pcs	135.00
2	2 1-Oct-2009	34 1-Oct-2009	ABC Mfg Co 1235, Chetal Rd, Kolkata 700 987	Manufacturer	Digital Mouse 12345678	10 pcs	3 pcs	150.00
		Total				20 pcs	5 pcs	

F-4E: Excise Stock CENVAT Register (Part – 1)

Hot Plates — Ctrl + M

As on : 1-Oct-2009

Assessable Value	Basic Excise Duty per Unit	Basic Excise Duty	Secondary Education Cess per Unit	Secondary Education Cess	Total Excise Duty per Unit	Total Excise Duty
1,350.00	13.50	135.00	0.27	2.70	13.77	137.70
1,500.00	15.00	150.00	0.30	3.00	15.30	153.00
2,850.00		285.00		5.70		290.70

F-4F: Excise Stock CENVAT Register (Part – 2)

04.03 Buttons

At Excise Stock Report (F-4A), following buttons are available (F-4C)

- **F4:Item:** To get the Excise Stock Register Display screen (F-2A) to select another Item
- **F6: Date / Purchase Date:**

Fig F-4E / F-4F shows the various columns as respective Configuration options set (F-4B)

Configuration

Show Separate Special Excise Duty Column	? Yes
Show CETSH No. Column	? Yes
Range of Transactions to show	? Purchase

F-5C: Configuration

F1: Condensed
F2: Period
F3: Company
F4: Change

F-5D: Buttons

Hot Plates

Party Wise Duty Extract

Name of Excise Unit	: Bonded Godown
Name of Group	: Sundry Creditors
Name of Ledger	: ABC Mfg Co

F-5E: Partywise Duty Extract

05.01 Contents of Report

Party Wise Duty Extract (F-5A / F-5B) displays shows following:

Party Wise Duty Extract — Hot Plates — Ctrl + M

Unit Name : Bonded Godown — 1-Apr-2009 to 1-Dec-2009
Group : Sundry Creditors
Ledger : ABC Mfg Co

Sl. No.	Voucher No. with Date / Supplier Invoice No. with Date	Particulars	Voucher Type	CETSH No.	Quantity	Assessable Value	Excise Duty	Special Excise Duty	Education Cess	Secondary Education Cess	Duty per Unit	Total Duty
1	1 / 1-Apr-2009 / Excise Opening Stock	Purchase	Purch-Exc		5 pcs	700.00	70.00			1.40	14.28	71.40
	12 / 1-Apr-2009	*Digital Mouse*		*12345678*	*5 pcs*	*700.00*	*70.00*			*1.40*	*14.28*	*71.40*
2	2 / 1-Oct-2009	Purchase	Purch-Exc		10 pcs	1,500.00	150.00			3.00	15.30	153.00
	34 / 1-Oct-2009	*Digital Mouse*		*12345678*	*10 pcs*	*1,500.00*	*150.00*			*3.00*	*15.30*	*153.00*
			Total		15 pcs		220.00			4.40		224.40

F-5A: Party Wise Duty Extract – Creditors (Detailed)

Party Wise Duty Extract — Hot Plates — Ctrl + M

Unit Name : Bonded Godown — 1-Apr-2009 to 31-Mar-2010
Group : Sundry Debtors
Ledger : ABC Computer Ltd.

Sl. No.	Voucher No. with Date / Supplier Invoice No. with Date	Particulars	Voucher Type	Quantity	Assessable Value	Excise Duty	Education Cess	Secondary Education Cess	Duty per Unit	Total Duty
1	1 / 1-Oct-2009	Sales	Sale-Excise	3 pcs	420.00	42.00		0.84	14.28	42.84
2	4 / 1-Dec-2009	Sales	Sale-Excise	7 pcs	1,050.00	105.00		2.10	15.30	107.10
			Total	10 pcs		147.00		2.94		149.94

F-5B: Party Wise Duty Extract – Debtors (Condensed)

05 Party Wise Duty Extract

Party Wise Duty Extract (F-5A / F-5B) displays details of **Purchases /Sales** for the selected Party.

At *Dealers Excise Reports* Menu (F-1A), select *Party Wise Duty Extract* to get *Party Wise Duty Extract* display screen (F-5E). Now set as follows:

- **Excise Unit**: At *Name of Excise Unit*, select the Excise Unit
- **Group**: At *Name of Group*, select the Account Group (Sundry Debtors / Sundry Creditors)
- **Ledger:** At *Name of Ledger*, select the Party Ledger (from the list of Party Ledger Account (or *All Items* for All Ledgers), under the selected Account Group), for which you like to display Party Wise Duty Extract (F-5A / F-5B)

- **Header**
  - o **Excise Unit Name**: Selected **Excise Unit** is dispayed(F-5E)
  - o **Group**: The selected Account Group (F-5E) is displayed
  - o **Ledger**: The Party ledger selected (F-5E) is displayed
- Transaction Details: In the Table, the details of each voucher is displayed in the columns as follows:
  - o **Voucher No. with Date/ Supplier Invoice No. with Date**: In this column by default the voucher Number and Date will be displayed. On viewing the report in detailed mode (Click *F1:Detailed* button) the supplier Number & Date will be displayed
  - o **Particulars**: Sales ledger used in the invoice will be displayed

- o **Voucher Type**: Name of the voucher type used to record the excise transactions
- o **Quantity**: Quantity of goods sold to customer or returned by the customer.
- o **Assessable Value**: Assessable value of the stock item sold on which the duty is passed on.
- o **Excise Duty**: Excise duty passed on
- o **Education Cess**: Education cess passed on
- o **Secondary Education Cess**: Secondary education cess passed on
- o **Duty per Unit**: Total duty per unit passed on the stock item
- o **Total Duty**: Total duty (Excise Duty + Education Cess + Secondary Education Cess) passed on.

05.02 Party Wise Duty Extract Configuration

At *Party Wise Duty Extract* **(**F-5A), click *F12:Configure* to get *Party Wise Duty Extract report Configuration* screen (F-5C), to set the options as follows:

- **Special Excise Duty:** At *Show Separate Special Excise Duty Column*, set *Yes* to display the *Special Excise Duty* in separate column
- **Central Excise Tariff Sub Heading Number:** At *Show CETSH No.* Column, set *Yes* to display Central Excise Tariff Sub Heading Number of the stock item.
- **Transaction Type:** At *Range of Transaction to Show,* select *the Transaction Type (Sales for Sales, Purchase for Purchase, Both for Sales & Purchase*

Note

- o HSN code (Tariff Number) will be displayed in Party Wise Duty Extract only in Detailed Mode.
- o For *Sundry Creditors* Group Purchase and Debit Note are shown by default, while For *Sundry Debtors* Group, Sales and Credit Note are shown by default,

05.03 Party Wise Duty Extract Configuration Buttons

At *Party Wise Duty Extract* (F-5A), following Buttons are available

- **F1:Detailed / Condensed**: To show the Report in Detailed / Condensed format
- **F4:Change:** To get the selection screen (F-5E) to select the Report Option

06 Sales & Purchase Extract

Sales and Purchase Extract (F-6A) shows the details of purchase and sales transactions of all excisable goods (Excise & Commercial Invoice).

At Dealers Excise Reports Menu (F-1A), select *Sales and Purchase Extract* to get Sales and Purchase Extract Printing screen (F-6B). Set the details to get *Sales and Purchase Extract* Report (F-6A)

Sales And Purchase Extract
Quarterly Return under Rule 9 of the CENVAT Rules, 2004 for the Registered Dealers

Return for the Quarterly Ending 31-Dec-2009

Page 1

1. Name of the First Stage / Second Stage Dealer : **Bonded Godown**
2. Excise Registration Number : **ABCDE1234X-001**
3. Address : **123 Burdwan Rd, Kolkata**
4. **Particulars of Invoice issued by First Stage / Second Stage Dealer**

Sl. No.	Invoice Number with Date	For all the Items in the Document					
		Description of the Goods	Central Excise Tariff Heading	Quantity	Amount of Duty	Amount of Ed Cess	Amount of Sec Ed Cess
1	1 / 1-Oct-2009	Digital Mouse	12345678	3 pcs	42.00		0.84
2	2 / 1-Oct-2009	Digital Mouse	12345678	2 pcs	28.00		0.56
3	1 / 1-Oct-2009	Digital Mouse	12345678	4 pcs	54.00		1.08
4	3 / 2-Nov-2009	Digital Mouse	12345678	4 pcs	54.00		1.08
5	4 / 1-Dec-2009	Digital Mouse	12345678	7 pcs	105.00		2.10
			Total	20 pcs	283.00		5.66

5. **Particulars of the Documents based on which the Credit is Passed on**

S-l.	Invoice / Bill of Entry Number with Date	Name and Address of the First Stage / Second Stage Dealer / Manufacturer / Importer Depot	Name and Address of the Manufacturer / Importer	For all the Items in the Document					
				Description of the Goods	Central Excise Tariff Heading	Quanti-ty	Amount of Duty	Amount of Ed Cess	Amount of Sec Ed Cess
1	12 / 1-Apr-2009		ABC Mfg Co	Digital Mouse	12345678	5 pcs	70.00		1.40
2	18 / 2-May-2009	ABC Traders		Digital Mouse	12345678	10 pcs	135.00		2.70
3	34 / 1-Oct-2009		ABC Mfg Co 1235, Chetal Rd, Kolkata 700 987	Digital Mouse	12345678	10 pcs	150.00		3.00
					Total	25 pcs	355.00		7.10

Place : **Kolkata**
Date : **1-Dec-2009**

Signature of the Registered Person or the Authorised Signatory

Seal of the Registered Dealer

F-6A: Sales & Purchase Extract

Report Titles

Sales And Purchase Extract
Quarterly Return under Rule 9 of the CENVAT Rules, 2004 for the Registered Dealers

Excise Unit : **Bonded Godown**
From : **1-4-2009**
To : **31-12-2009**
Place : **Kolkata**
Date : **31-12-2009**

F-6B: Sales & Purchase Extract Printing

06.01 Contents of Report

The Report contains 2 main sets of data:

- Particulars of Invoice Issued by First Stage/Second Stage Dealer
- Particulars of Documents based on which the Duty Credit is passed on

a. **Report Header:** At top of the Report, following info are displayed
   - o **Name of the First Stage/Second Stage Dealer**: At *Name of the First Stage/Second Stage Dealer***, the** Name of the Company specified in the Company Creation screen.
   - o **Excise Registration Number**: At *Excise Registration Number*, the Excise Registration Number specified at Company Statutory details
   - o **Address**: At *Address*, Company address specified in the Company Creation screen

b. **Particulars of Invoice issued by First Stage / Second Stage Dealer**: Under the section *Particulars of Invoice* *issued by First Stage / Second Stage Dealer*, the Table shows the Details of Sales Invoices under following columns:

- o **Invoice Number with Date**: The Date and the Invoice Number
- o **Description of the Goods**: Stock Items sold
- o **Central Excise Tariff Heading**: The Tariff Number of the Stock Item
- o **Quantity**: The total number of Stock items sold is printed in this column.
- o **Amount of Duty**: Total amount of Excise Duty passed on for the Stock Item
- o **Amount of Ed Cess**: Total amount of Education Cess passed on for the Stock Item
- o **Amount of Sec Ed Cess**:Total amount of Sec Education Cess passed on for the Stock Item

c. **Particulars of the Documents based on which the credit is passed on**: Under the section *Particulars of the Documents based on which the credit is passed on*, the Table shows the details of Purchase Invoices under following columns:

- o **Invoice / Bill of Entry Number with Date**: Purchase Invoice number and date
- o **Name and Address of the First Stage /Second Stage Dealer**: First Stage /Second Stage Dealer details specified in the Purchase Entries.
- o **Name and Address of the Manufacturer / Importer**: Manufacturer / Importer details specified in the Purchase Entries.
- o **Description of the Goods**: Description of Goods
- o **Central Excise Tariff Heading**: The Tariff number of the Stock Items
- o **Quantity**: The quantity of goods purchased
- o **Amount of Duty**: Total duty passed on for the Stock Items purchased.
- o **Amount of Ed Cess**: Total amount of Education Cess passed on for the Stock Items purchased.
- o **Amount of Sec Ed Cess**: Total amount of Sec Education Cess passed on for the Stock Items

FORM RG 23D All Items
Performa for records of receipts of duty paid goods and issue thereof
1-Apr-2009 to 1-Dec-2009

1. Name	: **Bonded Godown**	3. Excise Regn. No.	: **ABCDE1234X-001**	5. Range	:
2. Address	: **123 Burdwan Rd, Kolkata**	4. Commissionerate	:	6. Division	:
		7. Importer Exporter Code	: **1234567890**		

Page 1

Invoice / Bill of Entry Number with Date	RG 23D No.	Name and Address of Manufacturer / Importer including Central Excise Regn. No. / Importer Exporter Code / Range / Division / Commissionerate	Particulars	Quantity	Rate	Assessable Value	Basic Excise Duty	Secondary Education Cess	Excise Duty per Unit	Total Excise Duty
12 1-Apr-2009 / Excise Opening Stock	**1234**	**ABC Mfg Co**	**Digital Mouse 12345678**	**5 pcs** *5 pcs*	**140.00**	**700.00**	**70.00**	**1.40**	**14.28**	**71.40**
Duty Passed On										
1 1-Oct-2009 / Sale-Excise		*ABC Computer Ltd. 1234, Garia*		*3 pcs*			*42.00*	*0.84*	*14.28*	*42.84*
2 1-Oct-2009 / Sale-Excise		*ABC Mills 4567 Baghbazar, Visakhapatnam*		*2 pcs*			*28.00*	*0.56*	*14.28*	*28.56*
		Total		**5 pcs**			**70.00**	**1.40**		**71.40**
		Balance Duty								

18 2-May-2009 / Purch-Exc	345	ABC Traders	Digital Mouse 12345678	10 pcs	135.00	1,350.00	135.00	2.70	13.77	137.70
Duty Passed On										
1 *1-Oct-2009 /* *Sl-Comm Inv*		*A.K.Corporation* *1234* *Barakhamba Rd*		*4 pcs*			*54.00*	*1.08*	*13.77*	*55.08*
3 *2-Nov-2009 /* *Sale-Excise*		*ABC Mills* *4567* *Baghbazar,* *Visakhapatnam*		*4 pcs*			*54.00*	*1.08*	*13.77*	*55.08*
		Total		8 pcs			108.00	2.16		110.16
		Balance Duty		2 pcs			27.00	0.54		27.54
34 1-Oct-2009 / Purch-Exc	4567	ABC Mfg Co 1235, Chetal Rd, Kolkata 700 987	Digital Mouse 12345678	10 pcs	150.00	1,500.00	150.00	3.00	15.30	153.00
Duty Passed On										
4 *1-Dec-2009 /* *Sale-Excise*		*ABC Computer Ltd.* *1234, Garia*		*7 pcs*			*105.00*	*2.10*	*15.30*	*107.10*
		Total		7 pcs			105.00	2.10		107.10
		Balance Duty		3 pcs			45.00	0.90		45.90

F-7A: Form RG-23D

07 Form RG-23D

Form **RG-23D** shows the details the **Excise Purchases** and the **corresponding Sales** Transactions.

At Dealers Excise Reports Menu (F-1A), select *RG-23D* to get RG-23D to get RG 23-D Printing menu (F-7E).

07.01 RG 23-D for All Items

At *RG 23-D Printing menu* (F-7E), select *All Items.* At Name of Excise Unit, select the Excise Unit from the list to get RG-23D for all Items (F-7A).

a. **Contents of the Report:** The Report shows the details of Purchase Invoices under following columns:
   - o **Invoice / Bill of Entry Number with Date**: The Purchase Invoice number (in case of Domestic Purchase) or Bill of Entry Number (in case of Imports)
   - o **RG 23D No.**: **RG 23 Entry No**: Entry reference number of transaction in the relevant page of **RG 23 D Register**.
   - o **Name and Address of Manufacturer/ Importer including Central Excise Regn No/ Range/ Division/ Commissionerate**: The Manufacturer/ Importer details entered at Party the Party details of the Purchase voucher
   - o **Quantity**: The **quantity** of items purchased
   - o **Rate**: The **Rate (per UoM)** of the Stock Item purchased
   - o **Assessable Value**: The Assessable Value of the Stock Items
   - o **Basic Excise Duty**: The Excise Duty on the **Assessable Value**
   - o **Education Cess**: The total Education Cess
   - o **Secondary Education Cess**: Total amount of Secondary and Higher Education Cess paid
   - o **Excise Duty per Unit**: Excise Duty paid per unit
   - o **Total Excise Duty**: Total Duty paid

b. Duty Passed on

   This section lists the corresponding details of Duty Passed on Sales.

07.02 RG 23-D for One Item

At RG 23-D Printing menu (F-7E), select *One Item.* Now set as follows:

- **Excise Unit**: At *Name of Excise Unit*, select the Excise Unit
- **Tariff**: At *Name of Tariff*, select the Tariff Type (select Any to get Stock Item of all Tariff Type
- **Stock Item**: At *Name of Item*, select the Stock Item (from the list of Stock Items under the selected Tariff Type), for which you like to display Stock Register (F-2F)

The Report Contents are similar a described above

07.03 Form RG-23D (Sale Bill Wise)

This report shows Purchases made during the Report and corresponding Sales against the Purchases.

At RG 23-D Printing menu (F-7E), select *Sale Billwise.* Now set as follows:

- **Excise Unit**: At *Name of Excise Unit*, select the Excise Unit

- **Tariff**: At *Name of Tariff*, select the Tariff Type (select Any to get Stock Item of all Tariff Type
- **Stock Item**: At *Name of Item*, select the Stock Item (from the list of Stock Items under the selected Tariff Type), for which you like to display Stock Register (F-7B)

The Report is divided into main sections, Receipt & Issue details of the transactions.

FORM RG 23D — Hot Plates — Ctrl + M

Unit Name: Bonded Godown — 1-Apr-2009 to 1-Dec-2009

Item Name: Digital Mouse — Excise Tariff Classification 12345678

RECEIPT

1	2	3	4	5	6			7
Sl. No.	Manufacturer or Importer Invoice No. or Bill of Entry No. and Date	Name and Address of Manufacturer or Importer including Central Excise Range, Division and Commissionerate, Custom House and His New Excise Control Code (Manufacturer) or Importer Exporter Code (IEC)	Rate and Amount of Duty (both in words and figures)	Quantity	Total Amount (both in words and figures)			Description of Goods
					Excise Duty	Education Cess	Secondary Higher Education Cess	
1	[illegible] 2-Apr-2009		10%, 2%		135.00 (Indian Rupees One Hundred Thirty Five only)		2.70 (Indian Rupees Two and Seventy paise only)	Digital Mouse
2	34 1-Oct-2009	ABC Mfg Co 1235, Chetal Rd, Kolkata 700 987	10%, 2%	10 pcs	150.00 (Indian Rupees One Hundred Fifty only)		3.00 (Indian Rupees Three only)	Digital Mouse
3	12 1-Apr-2009 / Excise Opening Stock	ABC Mfg Co	10%, 2%	5 pcs	70.00 (Indian Rupees Seventy only)		1.40 (Indian Rupees One and Forty paise only)	Digital Mouse
		Total		15 pcs	355.00		7.10	

F-7B: Form RG-23D (Sale Bill Wise) - Part 1

Hot Plates — Ctrl + M

Bonded Godown — 1-Apr-2009 to 1-Dec-2009

Digital Mouse — Excise Tariff Classification 12345678

8	9	10	11	12			13
Invoice No. and Date or Bill of Entry No. and Date of Supplier if he is not Manufacturer or Importer	Name and Address of Supplier including Central Excise Range, Division and Commissionarate, Custom House or Importer Exporter Code (IEC)	Quantity	Tariff Heading or Sub Heading	Total Amount (both in words and figures)			Invoice No. and Date
				Excise Duty	Education Cess	Secondary Higher Education Cess	
18 2-May-2009	ABC Traders	10 pcs	12345678	135.00 (Indian Rupees One Hundred Thirty Five only)		2.70 (Indian Rupees Two and Seventy paise only)	1 1-Oct-2009 / Sl -Comm Inv
							3 2-Nov-2009 / Sale -Excise
			12345678				4 1-Dec-2009 / Sale -Excise
			12345678				1 1-Oct-2009 / Sale -Excise
							2 1-Oct-2009 / Sale -Excise
		10 pcs		135.00		2.70	

F-7B: Form RG-23D (Sale Bill Wise) - Part 2

Hot Plates — Ctrl + M

1-Apr-2009 to 1-Dec-2009

Excise Tariff Classification : 12345678

ISSUE

14	15	16			17
Name of the Customers to whom goods are sold including Central Excise Range, Division and Commissionerate, Customs House	Quantity	Total Amount (both in words and figures)			Balance Quantity
		Excise Duty	Education Cess	Secondary Higher Education Cess	
A K Corporation	4 pcs	54.00 (Indian Rupees Fifty Four only)		1.08 (Indian Rupees One and Eight paise only)	6 pcs
ABC Mills 4567 Baghbazar, Visakhapatnam	4 pcs	54.00 (Indian Rupees Fifty Four only)		1.08 (Indian Rupees One and Eight paise only)	2 pcs
ABC Computer Ltd. 1234, Gana	7 pcs	105.00 (Indian Rupees One Hundred Five only)		2.10 (Indian Rupees Two and Ten paise only)	3 pcs
ABC Computer Ltd 1234, Gana	3 pcs	42.00 (Indian Rupees Forty Two only)		0.84 (Indian Rupees and Eighty Four paise only)	2 pcs
ABC Mills 4567 Baghbazar, Visakhapatnam	2 pcs	28.00 (Indian Rupees Twenty Eight only)		0.56 (Indian Rupees and Fifty Six paise only)	0 pcs
	20 pcs	283.00		5.66	

F-7B: Form RG-23D (Sale Bill Wise) - Part 3

Configuration

Show Separate Special Excise Duty Column	? No
Show Opening Balance	? No
Include Excise Credit Note and Debit Note	? No
Include Normal Sales and Credit Note	? No

F-7C: Form RG-23D (Sale Bill Wise) – Configuration

F1: Detailed
F2: Period
F3: Company
F4: Item

F-7D: Form RG-23D (Sale Bill Wise) – Buttons

Gateway of Tally ....
Display Menu ....
Statutory Reports ...
Excise Reports ....
Dealer ....

Form RG 23D

All Items
One Item
Sales Bill Wise
Quit

F-7E: Form RG-23D Menu

08 Excise Form 2

Excise Form 2 is the Quarterly Return to be submitted by Registered Dealer. At Dealers Excise Reports Menu (F-1A), select *Form 2* to get the Form 2 Printing screen (F-8B). Set the details to get the Report.

Form - 2

Quarterly Return under Rule 9 of the CENVAT Rules, 2004 for the Registered Dealers

Return for the Quarterly Ending **31-Mar-2010**

Page 1

1. Name of the First Stage / Second Stage Dealer : **Bonded Godown**
2. Excise Registration Number : **ABCDE1234X-001**
3. Address : **123 Burdwan Rd, Kolkata**

4. Particulars of Invoice issued by First Stage / Second Stage Dealer

Sl. No.	Invoice Number with Date	For the Main Item in the Document					
		Description of the Goods	Central Excise Tariff Heading	Quantity	Amount of Duty	Amount of Ed Cess	Amount of Sec Ed Cess
1	1 / 1-Oct-2009	Digital Mouse	12345678	4 pcs	54.00		1.08
2	1 / 1-Oct-2009	Digital Mouse	12345678	3 pcs	42.00		0.84
3	2 / 1-Oct-2009	Digital Mouse	12345678	2 pcs	28.00		0.56
4	3 / 2-Nov-2009	Digital Mouse	12345678	4 pcs	54.00		1.08
5	4 / 1-Dec-2009	Digital Mouse	12345678	7 pcs	105.00		2.10
			Total	20 pcs	283.00		5.66

5. Particulars of the Documents based on which the Credit is Passed on

S-l.	Invoice / Bill of Entry Number with Date	Name and Address of the First Stage / Second Stage Dealer / Manufacturer / Importer Depot	Name and Address of the Manufacturer / Importer	For the Main Item in the Document					
				Description of the Goods	Central Excise Tariff Heading	Quanti-ty	Amount of Duty	Amount of Ed Cess	Amount of Sec Ed Cess
1	12 / 1-Apr-2009		ABC Mfg Co	Digital Mouse	12345678	5 pcs	70.00		1.40
2	18 / 2-May-2009	ABC Traders		Digital Mouse	12345678	10 pcs	135.00		2.70
3	34 / 1-Oct-2009		ABC Mfg Co 1235, Chetal Rd, Kolkata 700 987	Digital Mouse	12345678	10 pcs	150.00		3.00
					Total	25 pcs	355.00		7.10

Place : **Kolkata**
Date : **1-Apr-2010**

Signature of the Registered Person or the Authorised Signatory

Seal of the Registered Dealer

F-8A: Form 2 in Print

Report Titles

Form - 2
Quarterly Return under Rule 9 of the CENVAT Rules, 2004 for the Registered Dealers

Excise Unit	: **Bonded Godown**
From	: **1-10-2009**
To	: **31-12-2009**
Place	: **Kolkata**
Date	: **1-12-2009**

F-8B: Form -2 Printing screen

F-8C: Form -2 Configuration

Configuration

Show All Items	? **Yes**
Show Separate Special Excise Duty Column	? **Yes**
Show Purchase Reference(s)	? **Yes**

08.01 Form 2 Configuration

At *Form 2 Printing screen* (F-8B), click *F12:Configure* to get *Form 2 Configuration* screen (F-8C),to set the following options:

- **Items Range**: At *Show All Items*, set *Yes* to show All Items, else set *No* to show only the transacted Items
- **Special Duty**: At *Show separate Special Duty column*, set *Yes* to show *Special Duty* in a special column.
- **Purchase Reference:** At *Show Purchase References*, set Yes to show the correspsnding Purchase Entry Reference

Manufacturers Excise Duty Reports 06-08

01 Manufacturers Excise Duty Reports Menu

At Excise Reports Menu, select *Manufacturer* (this option gets selected only when you select *Manufacturer* at *Registration Type* at *Excise Registration Details*, discussed earlier) to get *Manufacturers Excise Reports* Menu (F-1A).

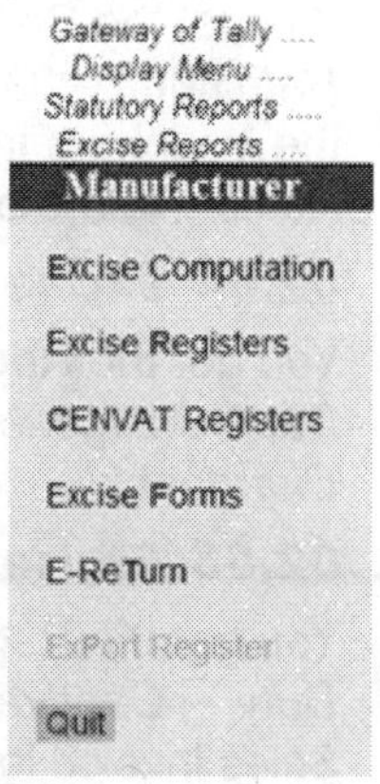

F-1A: Manufacturers Excise Reports Menu

02 Excise Computation Report

Excise Computation report (F-2A) shows a comprehensive account of all key figures related to Excise in concise & summarised form.

At *Manufacturers Excise Reports* Menu (F-1A), select *Excise Computation* to get ***Excise Computation*** report (F-2A).

02.01 Contents of the Report

Excise Computation report is divided into following main sections, which are further sub divided into several elements as shown below:

- **Excise Duty Payable**: This section displays the details of Excise Sales, Payable from previous period and Excise Duty Payments/ Credit Adjustment.
  - o **Excise Sales**: This section displays Excise details *Removals* on account of:
    - **Regular Rate Sales**
    - **Exempt Sales**
    - **Exports Sales**
    - **Export Sales** (duty chargeable)
    - **Captive Consumption**
    - **Removal as such**
    - **Special Rate**
  - o **Payable from previous period**: Duty amount payable for previous period.

Excise Computation — ABC Manufacturing — Ctrl + M

Particulars			Bonded Godown 1 ABC Manufacturing 1-Apr-2009 to 31-Mar-2010 Assessable Value	Duty Amount
Excise Duty Payable				
A. Excise Sales				
Regular Rate			64,890.00	10,149.85
Special Rate			1,900.00	310.08
Export - Duty Chargeable			1,900.00	310.08
Captive Consumption			300.00	37.08
Removal as such			300.00	37.08
Stock Transfer and Duty Liability Booked			9,500.00	1,550.40
	Assessable Value	***Duty Amount***		
Total Stock Transfer for the current period where duty is liable to be booked	*12,500.00*	*1,910.40*		
Less: Liability booked for the current period	***9,500.00***	***1,550.40***		
Balance Stock Transfer where duty is liable but not booked (a)	*3,000.00*	*360.00*		
Previous Stock Transfer where duty is liable but not booked (b)				
Total Stock Transfer where duty is liable but not booked till now (a+b)	***3,000.00***	***360.00***		
Total Excise Sales (A)			**78,790.00**	**12,394.57**
B. Payable from previous period				
Total Excise Duty Payable (A+B)				**12,394.57**
C. Excise Duty Payments / Credit Adjustments				
G.A.R. 7 Payments				6,118.40
Total Excise duty paid / Adjusted (C)				**6,118.40**
Balance Excise Duty Payable ((A+B)-C)				**6,276.17**
Balance Input Credit				
CENVAT Credit on Inputs				3,875.20
CENVAT Credit on Capital Goods				300.00
Excise Duty Advance Paid				17,000.00
Total Available CENVAT credit				**21,175.20**

F-2A: Excise Computation Report

- **Excise Duty Payments/ Credit Adjustments**: Duty amount adjusted for the period
  - o **G.A.R. 7 Payments**: Duty amount paid for the period using G.A.R. 7 Challan.
  - o **Credit Adjustment**: Duty amount adjusted with CENVAT Credit for the period.
  - o **Other Charges**: Other charges (e.g Interest, Penalty, etc), if paid during the period.

The Total of Excise Duty payable (on Current period + Previous Period) is shown in next line

- **Balance Input Credit**: At the end of Report, Balances available for Input Credit, on account of:
  - o **CENVAT Credit on Inputs**: CENVAT Credit on Inputs
  - o **CENVAT Credit on Capital Goods**: CENVAT Credit on Capital Goods
  - o **Service Tax Input Credit**: Service Tax Input Credit.
  - o **Excise Duty Advance Paid**: Duty paid in advance.

The total figures of CENVAT Credit available is shown at the end of Report

From ***Excise Computation*** report (F-2A), you may further drill down through the respective element, to get further details of the related transactions and finally reach to the respective vouchers, as shown next.

Detail Reports

You may further drill down form following figures in Excise Computation Report, to get the detailed voucher lists in respect of each section.

On further drill down from the detailed report, through any Voucher, you get the Voucher alteration screen of the Voucher.

02.02 Excise Vouchers: Regular Rate

You get the Report (F-3A) when you drill down from *Regular Rate* figures (under Excise Duty Payable section). It shows the Vouchers in respect of Sales under Regular Rates of Excise Duty charged (Nature of Removal – *Domestic*).

02.03 Excise Vouchers: Special Rate

You get the Report (F-4A) when you drill down from *Special Rate* figures (under Excise Duty Payable section). It shows the Vouchers in respect of Sales, charging duty at Special Rates (Nature of Removal – *Special Rate*).

02.04 Excise Vouchers: Duty Chargeable

You get the Report (F-4B) when you drill down from *Excise Duty- Chargeable* figures (Nature of Removal – *Excise – Duty Chargeable*).

02.05 Excise Vouchers: Captive Consumption

You get the Report (F-5A) when you drill down from *Excise Duty – Captive Consumption* figures, showing the Excise Sales Invoice for Captive Consumption (Nature of Removal – *Captive Consumption*).

02.06 Excise Vouchers: Removal as such

You get the Report (F-6A) when you drill down from *Excise Duty – Removal as such* figures (Nature of Removal – *Removal As Such*).

Excise Vouchers: Regular Rate — 1-Apr-2009 to 31-Mar-2010

Date	Excise Invoice No	Particulars	Vch Type	Vch No.	Assessable Amount	Duty Value	Amount
1-Jul-2009	9	Riverstone Solutions India	ExcSI	1	19,800.00	3,231.36	15,231.36
1-Jul-2009	10	Riverstone Solutions India	ExcSI	2	5,000.00	459.00	5,459.00
1-Aug-2009		Basic Excise Duty 16%	Journal	1	26,000.00	4,160.00	4,160.00
1-Nov-2009	2	Riverstone Solutions India	ExcSI	6	2,090.00	341.09	2,431.09
2-Dec-2009	1	Riverstone Solutions India	ExcSI	7	12,000.00	1,958.40	13,958.40
				Total:	64,890.00	10,149.85	41,239.85

F-3A : Excise Vouchers : Regular Rate

Excise Vouchers: Special Rate — 1-Apr-2009 to 31-Mar-2010

Date	Excise Invoice No	Particulars	Vch Type	Vch No.	Assessable Amount	Duty Value	Amount
1-Oct-2009	3	Riverstone Solutions India	ExcSI	5	1,900.00	310.08	2,210.08
				Total:	1,900.00	310.08	2,210.08

F-4A: Excise Vouchers : Special Rate

Excise Vouchers: Export - Duty Chargeable — 1-Apr-2009 to 31-Mar-2010

Date	Excise Invoice No	Particulars	Vch Type	Vch No.	Assessable Amount	Duty Value	Amount
1-Jan-2010	5	Global Computers	ExcSI	8	1,900.00	310.08	2,210.08
				Total:	1,900.00	310.08	2,210.08

F-4B: Excise Vouchers – Duty Chargeable

Excise Vouchers: Captive Consumption							1-Apr-2009 to 31-Mar-2010
Date	Excise Invoice No	Particulars	Vch Type	Vch No.	Assessable Amount	Duty Value	Amount
1-Sep-2009	6	ABC Manufacturing	ExcSI	4	300.00	37.08	337.08
				Total:	300.00	37.08	337.08

F-5A: Excise Vouchers – Captive Consumption

Excise Vouchers							Ctrl + M
Excise Vouchers: Removal as such							1-Apr-2009 to 31-Mar-2010
Date	Excise Invoice No	Particulars	Vch Type	Vch No.	Assessable Amount	Duty Value	Amount
1-Sep-2009	4	Riverstone Solutions India	ExcSI	3	300.00	37.08	337.08
				Total:	300.00	37.08	337.08

F-6A: Excise Vouchers – Removal as such

Excise Vouchers: Stock Transfer and Duty Liability Booked							1-Apr-2009 to 31-Mar-2010
Date	Excise Invoice No	Particulars	Vch Type	Vch No.	Assessable Amount	Duty Value	Amount
1-Mar-2010	ABC/BDG/1/13-148	Behala Branch	ExJrnAdj	1	9,500.00	1,550.40	11,050.40
				Total:	9,500.00	1,550.40	11,050.40

F-7A: Excise Vouchers – Stock Transfer & Duty Liability Booked

02.07 Excise Vouchers: Stock Transfer & Duty Liability Booked

You get the Report (F-7A) when you drill down from *Stock Transfer & Duty Liability Booked,* showing the Stock Journals for Transfer of Goods (Used For – *Excise Duty on Movement of Goods*).

When you further drill down through any Voucher, you get the Voucher alteration screen of the Voucher.

02.08 Excise Vouchers: Stock Transfer & Duty Liability to be Booked

You get the Report (F-8A) when you drill down from *Excise Duty –Total Transfer for current period where duty is liable to be booked.* It shows Stock Transfer Out Vouchers (Nature of Removal – *Domestic*).

02.09 Excise Vouchers: Liability Booked for Current period

You get the Report (F-9A) when you drill down from *Liability Booked for the Current period.* It shows Journal Vouchers (Used For – *Excise Duty on Movement of Goods*). This figure is reduced from the previous figures of *Stock Transfer & Duty Liability to be Booked.*

This figure (shown in Bold) is already included for computation of Excise Sales under section A of the Computation Details screen (Details of *Removals*), as described above (F-2A).

Excise Vouchers: Stock Transfer and Duty Liability Booked							1-Apr-2009 to 31-Mar-2010
Date	Excise Invoice No	Particulars	Vch Type	Vch No.	Assessable Amount	Duty Value	Amount
1-Dec-2009	7	Behala Branch	Exc Stock Trf Out	1	3,000.00	360.00	3,360.00
1-Mar-2010	8	Behala Branch	Exc Stock Trf Out	2	9,500.00	1,550.40	11,050.40
				Total:	12,500.00	1,910.40	14,410.40

F-8A: Stock Voucher- Current period where duty is liable to be booked

Excise Vouchers: Stock Transfer and Duty Liability Booked							1-Apr-2009 to 31-Mar-2010
Date	Excise Invoice No	Particulars	Vch Type	Vch No.	Assessable Amount	Duty Value	Amount
1-Mar-2010	ABC/BDG/1/13-148	Behala Branch	ExJrnAdj	1	9,500.00	1,550.40	11,050.40
				Total:	9,500.00	1,550.40	11,050.40

F-9A: Stock Vouchers- Liability Booked for Current Period

Excise Vouchers			Manufacturing			Ctrl + M
Excise Vouchers: G.A.R. 7 Payments						
Date	Vch No.	Challan Date	Total Duty	Challan Details		
				Challan No.	Cheque No / DD No	Bank Name
1-1-2010	2	2-4-2009	6,118.40 Dr	13	324567	2.1.10
Total			6,118.40 Dr			

F-10A: GAR -7 Payment Details

02.10 GAR 7 Payment Details

You get the Report (F-10A) when you drill down from *GAR-7 Payments* under *GAR Payments / Credit Adjustments* section. This shows all Payments made under GAR-7 Challan.

02.11 CENVAT Credit on Inputs

You get the CENVAT Credit on Inputs Report (F-11A) when you drill down from *CENVAT Credit on Inputs* from (under Balance Input Credit section), showing the list of Vouchers in which CENVAT credit has been availed

Excise Vouchers: CENVAT Credit on Inputs		1-Apr-2009 to 31-Mar-2010	
Date	Ref. No.	Total Credit	Balance Credit
1-Aug-2009	13	2,080.00	2,080.00
1-May-2009	23 / 1-2009	979.20	979.20
	Total:	3,059.20	3,059.20

F-11A: CENVAT Credit on Inputs

02.12 Advance Excise Duty Payments

You get the Advance *Excise Duty Payments* Report (F-12A), when you drill down from *Excise Duty Advance Paid* under *Balance Input Credit*, showing the list of Vouchers of advance duty payments.

Excise Vouchers: Excise Duty Advance Paid		1-Apr-2009 to 31-Mar-2010	
Date	Ref. No.	Total Credit	Balance Credit
1-Aug-2009	12	12,000.00	12,000.00
1-Jan-2010	ED ADv001	5,000.00	5,000.00
	Total:	17,000.00	17,000.00

F-12A: Advance Excise Duty payments

03 Excise Registers

At *Manufacturers Excise Reports* Menu (F-1A), select *Excise Registers* to get *Excise Registers Menu* (F-13A).

Gateway of Tally ....
Display Menu ....
Statutory Reports ....
Excise Reports ....
Manufacturer ....

Excise Registers

Daily Stock Register

PLA Register
PLA Summary

Quit

F-13A: Excise Registers Menu

04 Daily Stock Register

At *Excise Registers* Menu (F-13A), select *Daily Stock Registers* to get *Daily Stock Account* Menu (F-14A), which provides for 2 types of Reports: Summary & Day Wise. Under each section, you may get report for a selected Item (One Item), Items for a selected Tariff (Multiple Items).

Gateway of Tally ....
Display Menu ....
Statutory Reports ....
Excise Reports ....
Manufacturer ....
Excise Registers ....

Daily Stock Account

Summary
One Item
Multi Item
Tariff Wise

Day Wise
ONe Item
Multi Item
Tariff Wise

Quit

F-14A: Daily Stock Account Menu

04.01 Stock Register Summary

Summary Reports available under Summary section of the *Daily Stock Account* Menu (F-14A), shows the transactions in the selected period, for only the days in which transactions has occurred for the Item.

04.02 Stock Register (Summary) for One Item

At Daily Sock Account Menu under *Summary* section, select *One* Item (F-14A), to get Stock Summary printing for One Item (F-15A) screen to display the report for a selected Stock Item.

Daily Stock Register

Name of Excise Unit	:	**Bonded Godown 1**
Name of Tariff	:	**Computer Goods**
Name of Item	:	**Assembled PC**
From	:	**1-12-2009**
To	:	**31-12-2009**

F-15A: Stock Register (Summary) printing for One Item

At Stock Summary printing for One Item (F-15A) screen, select as follows

- **Excise Unit Name:** At *Name of Excise Unit*, select the Excise Unit from the list
- **Tariff Classification:** At *Name of Tariff*, select the *Tariff Classification* from the list
- **Item Name:** At *Name of Item*, select the *Stock Item* from the list of Stock Items under the selected Tariff Classification
- **Period:** At *From* & *To* enter the period. The report would be shown for Stock on the period end Date of the selected Period.

Assembled PC
Daily Stock Register
1-Apr-2009 to 31-Dec-2009

Units U Excise Tariff Classification Computer Goods - [illegible]

Page 1 (A) / Page 1 (B)

Date	Document Reference	Opening Balance	Quantity Manufactured	Total Quantity	Issued for Further Products-on u/n 67/95	Issued for repacking	Issued for Home Clearance	Issued for Export /SEZ under Bond	Issued for Export /SEZ under LUT	Issued for Export / SEZ Under Rebate	Issued for Exempt (To 100% EOU and Others)	To Other Factories or Warehouse under Bond	Assessable Value	Excise Duty	Education Cess	Secondary Education Cess	Balance Quantity	Excise Notification	Remarks
1-Jul-2009	ExcSR / 10						1						10,000.00	450.00		9.00	(-)1	45	
	Total						1						10,000.00	450.00		9.00	(-)1		

F-16A: Daily Stock Register (Summary) for One Item

To get Stock Summary printing for *One Item* Report (F-16A). At the Report Header, the *Stock Item Name, Report Period, Excise UoM* & *Tariff Classification ID* of the selected Item is printed.

04.03 Stock Register Summary for Multiple Items

At *Daily Sock Account* Menu, under Summary section, select *Multi Item* (F-14A) to get Stock Register Summary printing screen for Multi Items, to get the Report (F-17A) for all Items of a selected Tariff classification. Now select as follows:

F-17A: Daily Stock Register (Summary) printing for Multiple Items

Daily Stock Register

Name of Excise Unit	: Bonded Godown 1
Name of Tariff	: Any
From	: 1-12-2009
To	: 31-12-2009

- **Excise Unit Name:** At *Name of Excise Unit*, select the Excise Unit from the list
- **Tariff Classification:** At *Name of Tariff*, select the *Tariff Classification* from the list
- **Period**:At *From* & *To* enter the period. The report would be shown for Stock on the period end Date of the selected Period.

LCD 18.5
Daily Stock Register
1-Dec-2009 to 31-Dec-2009

Units U Excise Tariff Classification Computer Goods : 0A8700

Page 1 (A)

Date	Document Reference	Opening Balance	Quantity Manufactured	Total Quantity	Issued for Further Production u/s 67 / 95	Issued for repacking	Issued for Home Clearance	Issued for Export /SEZ under Bond	Issued for Export /SEZ under LUT	Issued for Export / SEZ Under Rebate	Issued for Exempt (To 100% EOU and Others)	To Other Factories or Warehouse under Bond	Assessable Value	Excise Duty	Education Cess	Secondary Education Cess
2-Dec-2009	ExcSI / 1	(-)1		(-)1			1						19,800.00	1,920.00		38.40
	Total	(-)1		(-)1			1						19,800.00	1,920.00		38.40

Page 1 (B)

Balance Quantity	Excise Notification	Remarks
(-)2	23	
(-)2		

F-18A: Daily Stock Register (Summary) for Multiple Items

The Report is similar to Stock Report for Single Item. The report is shown for each Stock Item for the Selected Tariff Classification, one after another

F-19A: Daily Tariff Wise Stock Register Summary printing

Daily Stock Register

Name of Excise Unit	: Bonded Godown 1
Name of Tariff	: Computer Goods
Reporting UOM	: U
From	: 1-4-2009
To	: 31-12-2009

04.04 Stock Register Tariff Wise Summary

At *Daily Sock Account Menu*, under *Summary* section (F-14A), select *Tariff wise* to get Tariff wise Stock Register Summary printing screen (F-19A) for Tariff Wise, to get the Report (F-20A) for all Items of a selected Tariff classification and Reporting UoM

Now select as follows (F-19A):

- **Excise Unit Name:** At *Name of Excise Unit*, select the Excise Unit from the list
- **Tariff Classification:** At *Name of Tariff*, select the *Tariff Classification* from the list
- **Reporting UoM:** At *Reporting UoM*, select the *Reporting UoM* from the list of Reporting UoM
- **Period**:At From & To enter the period.

The Tariff wise Stock Register Summary (F-20A) would be shown as per selected option

04.05 Day Wise Stock Register

We have described the *Stock Summary* Reports available under *Summary* section of *Daily Stock Reports* Menu. Now we discuss about similar Reports available, under Day Wise section.

In Day wise Reports, consecutive records for each Date within the Report period appears, even if no transaction occurred for the day (showing blank figures).

04.06 Day Wise Stock Register for One Item

At *Daily Sock Account* Menu (F-14A), under *Day Wise* section, select *One* Item to get Stock Register Summary printing screen for a selected Stock Item, similar to that for

Computer Goods
Daily Stock Register
1-Apr-2009 to 31-Dec-2009

Units U Excise Tariff Classification Computer Goods

Page 1 (A)

Date	Document Reference	Description of Goods	Opening Balance	Quantity Manufactured	Total Quantity	Issued for Further Production u/s 67 / 95	Issued for repacking	Issued for Home Clearance	Issued for Export /SEZ under Bond	Issued for Export /SEZ under LUT	Issued for Export / SEZ Under Rebate	Issued for Exempt (To 100% EOU and Others)	To Other Factories or Warehouse under Bond
1-Jul-2009	ExcSI / 10	Assembled PC	10		10			1					
1-Jul-2009	ExcSI / 8	LCD 18.5	9		9			1					
2-Dec-2009	ExcSI / 1	LCD 18.5	8		8			1					
	Total		16		16			3					

F-20A : Tariff wise Stock Register Summary (Part 1)

Computer Goods
Daily Stock Register
1-Apr-2009 to 31-Dec-2009

Page 1 (B)

Assessable Value	Excise Duty	Education Cess	Secondary Education Cess	Balance Quantity	Excise Notification	Remarks
10,000.00	480.00		9.60	9	46	
19,800.00	3,168.00		63.36	8	13	
12,000.00	1,920.00		38.40	7	23	
41,800.00	6,528.00		110.76	7		

Tariff wise Stock Register Summary (Part 2)

Assembled PC
Daily Stock Register
1-Jul-2009 to 2-Jul-2009

Name of the Company	: Bonded Godown 1	Range	:
Central Excise Regn.No	: ABCDE1234D123XM	Division	:
Excise Tariff Classification	: Computer Goods - 13456789	Commissionerate	:
Unit of Measurements	: U		

Page 1 (A)

Date	Document Reference	Opening Balance	Quantity Manufac-tured	Total Quantity	Issued for Further Producti-on u/n 67 / 95	Issued for repacking	Issued for Home Clearance	Issued for Export /SEZ under Bond	Issued for Export /SEZ under LUT	Issued for Export / SEZ Under Rebate	Issued for Exempt (To 100% EOU and Others)	To Other Factories or Warehou-se under Bond	Assessable Value	Excise Duty
1-Jul-2009							1						10,000.00	450.00
	ExcSI / 10						1						10,000.00	450.00
2-Jul-2009		(-)1		(-)1										
-	Total						1						10,000.00	450.00

F-21A : Day Wise Stock Register for One Item (Part 1)

Summary Report discussed above, to get *Day Wise Stock Register for One Item* (F-21A)

Range	:
Division	:
Commissionerate	:

Page 1 (B)

Education Cess	Second-ary Educati-on Cess	Balance Quantity	Excise Notification	Remarks
	9.00	(-)1		
	9.00	(-)1	45	
		(-)1		
	9.00	(-)1		

Day Wise Stock Register for One Item (Part 2)

04.07 Day Wise Stock Register for Multiple Items

At *Daily Sock Account* Menu (F-14A), under *Day Wise* section, select *Multiple* Item to get Stock Register Summary printing screen for a selected *Tariff Classification*, similar to that for Summary Report discussed above, to get *Day Wise Stock Register for Multiple Items* (F-22A).

Range	:
Division	:
Commissionerate	:

Page 2 (B)

Education Cess	Second-ary Educati-on Cess	Balance Quantity	Excise Notification	Remarks
	63.36	(-)1		
	63.36	(-)1	13	
		(-)1		
	63.36	(-)1		

Day Wise Stock Register for Multiple Items (Part 2)

04.08 Day Wise Stock Register Tariff wise

At *Daily Stock Account* Menu (F-14A), under *Day Wise* section, select *Tarff Wise* to get Stock Register Summary

Assembled PC
Daily Stock Register
1-Jul-2009 to 2-Jul-2009

Name of the Company	: Bonded Godown 1	Range	:
Central Excise Regn.No	: ABCDE1234D123XM	Division	:
Excise Tariff Classification	: Computer Goods - 13456789	Commissionerate	:
Unit of Measurements	: U		

Page 1 (A)

Date	Document Reference	Opening Balance	Quantity Manufac-tured	Total Quantity	Issued for Further Producti-on u/n 67 / 95	Issued for repacking	Issued for Home Clearance	Issued for Export /SEZ under Bond	Issued for Export /SEZ under LUT	Issued for Export / SEZ Under Rebate	Issued for Exempt (To 100% EOU and Others)	To Other Factories or Warehou-se under Bond	Assessable Value	Excise Duty
1-Jul-2009							1						10,000.00	450.00
	ExcSI / 10						1						10,000.00	450.00
2-Jul-2009		(-)1		(-)1										
	Total						1						10,000.00	450.00

F-22A: Day Wise Stock Register for Multiple Items (Part 1)

Computer Goods
Daily Stock Register
1-Jul-2009 to 2-Jul-2009

Name of the Company	: Bonded Godown 1	Range	:
Central Excise Regn.No	: ABCDE1234D123XM	Division	:
Excise Tariff Classification	: Computer Goods	Commissionerate	:
Units	: U		

Page 1 (A)

Date	Document Reference	Description of Goods	Opening Balance	Quantity Manufactu-red	Total Quantity	Issued for Further Production u/n 67 / 95	Issued for repacking	Issued for Home Clearance	Issued for Expoft /SEZ under Bond	Issued for Export /SEZ under LUT	Issued for Export / SEZ Under Rebate	Issued for Exempt (To 100% EOU and Others)	To Other Factories or Warehouse under Bond
1-Jul-2009			10		10			2					
	ExcSI / 9	*LCD 18.5*	10		10			1					
	ExcSI / 10	*Assembled PC*	9		9			1					
2-Jul-2009			8		8								
	Total		10		10			2					

F-23A: Day Wise Stock Register Tariff wise – Part 1

printing screen for a selected *Tariff Classification*, similar to that for Summary Report discussed above, to get *Day Wise Stock Register – Taif Wise* (F-23A).

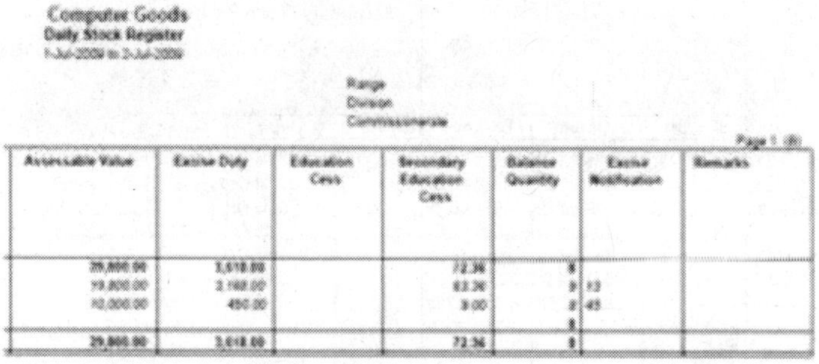

Day Wise Stock Register Tariff wise – Part 2

Contents of Stock Register: Contents of all the Stock Reports discussed above are quite similar, as described below:

Header: The following fields appear at the Report Header

- **Unit Name**: Displays the selected Unit Name for which the Daily Stock Register is displayed.
- **Stock Item**: Displays the selected Stock Item
- **Units**: Displays the Reporting UOM of the stock item
- **Excise Tariff Classification**: Displays the Excise Tariff Classification Name and Tariff Code of the Stock Item

Table Area: The following columns appear at the Report Header

- **Date**: Displays the date of transaction (Voucher)
- **Document Reference**: Displays the reference of the transaction (Voucher)
- **Opening Balance**: Opening Stock Quantity of the selected, as on the Start Date of the Report. In **Tariff Wise Daily Stock Register** report, total Opening Quantity of the Items under selected Tariff will be shown.
- **Quantity Manufactured**: Quantity manufactured (as recorded in Production side *of Excise* ***Manufacturing Journal*** and ***Stock Journal*** for which the option ***Use as Manufacturing Journal*** is enabled).
- **Total Quantity**: Shows Total Quantity (Opening Balance + Quantity Manufactured)
- **Issued for Further production u/n 67/95**: Quantity issued for further production under notification number 67/ 95, as recorded in Consumption side ***of Excise Manufacturing Journal*** and Excise ***Sales*** transactions with ***Captive Consumption*** recorded at ***Nature of Removal***
- **Issued for Repacking**: Quantity of Item Issued for repacking.
- **Issues for Home Clearance**: Quantity issued for Domestic Sales (Sales Vouchers with ***Domestic, Special Rate, or Removal As Such*** **at** ***Nature of Removal*).**
- **Issued for Export/SEZ under Bond**: Quantity issued for Export Sales under Bond (Sales Vouchers with ***Export*** and ***SEZ/Bond*** at ***Nature of Removal***).
- **Issued for Export/SEZ under LUT**: Quantity issued for export sales under LUT (Sales Voucher with ***Export/LUT*** and ***SEZ/LUT*** **at** ***Nature of Removal***).
- **Issued for Export/SEZ under Rebate**: Quantity for Export Sales under Rebate (Sales Vouchers with ***SEZ/ Rebate*** **at** ***Nature of Removal***).
- **Issued for Exempt (To 100% EOU or Others)**: Quantity for Exempt Sales (Sales Vouchers with ***Exempt*** at ***Nature of Removal*).**
- ***To Other factories*** **or Warehouses under Bond**: Quantity for Sales to a Warehouse with CT2 form issued by the warehouse.
- **Assessable value**: Shows Assessable Value on which the duty is calculated
- **Excise Duty**: Shows Excise Duty Amount
- **Education Cess**: Shows Education Cess Amount
- **Secondary Education Cess**: Shows Secondary Education Cess amount
- **Balance Quantity**: Shows Balance Quantity.
- **Excise Notification**: Excise Notification Number entered in case of Exempt, Export transactions or any notification issued by the Central Board of Excise & Customs.

05 PLA Register

PLA (Personal Ledger Account) is an account through which Assessee pays duty to the Government. The PLA is CREDITED when the duty is liable to pay and DEBITED when the Duty is discharged (by CENVAT Credit /Payment).

F-24A: *PLA Register* Display

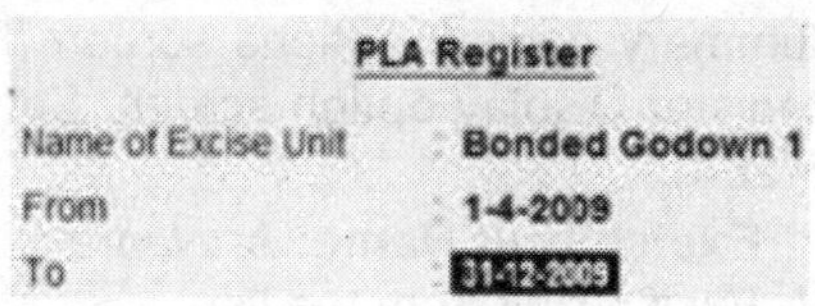

At *Excise Registers* Menu (F-13A),, select *PLA Register* to get PLA Register Display option screen (F-24A), to set as follows:

- **Excise Unit Name:** At *Name of Excise Unit*, select the Excise Unit from the list
- **Period**: At From & To, enter the Period.

To get the PLA Register (F-25A) for the selected period

Report Contents: The Report shows the following columns:

- **Particulars of Credit/Debit Document / Description of Documents With name of treasury Where necessary**: Displays the description of the documents (Invoices)
- **Document No./ Date**: Document Reference and Date
- **Central Excise Tariff Sub-heading Number**: Displays the tariff classification number of the Stock item.
- **ECC no. of the Buyer**: Displays the Excise Control Code of the buyer.
- **Basic Excise Duty**: Displays the Credit, Debit and Balance Duty amount.

PLA Register | ABC Manufacturing | Ctrl + M

Excise Unit Name: **Bonded Godown 1** | 1-Apr-2009 to 31-Dec-2009

Particulars of Credit / Debit Document Description of Documents with name of treasury where necessary	Document No. / Date	Central Excise Tariff Sub-heading Number	Central Excise Regn. No. of the Buyer	Basic Excise Duty			Secondary Education Cess		
				Credit	Debit	Balance	Credit	Debit	Balance
ExcSI	9 / 1-Jul-2009	13456789	ASDFG1234H123XD		3,168.00 Dr	3,168.00 Dr		63.36 Dr	63.36 Dr
ExcSI	10 / 1-Jul-2009	13456789	ASDFG1234H123XD		450.00 Dr	3,618.00 Dr		9.00 Dr	72.36 Dr
ExcSI	4 / 1-Sep-2009	13456789	ASDFG1234H123XD		36.00 Dr	3,654.00 Dr		1.08 Dr	73.44 Dr
ExcSI	6 / 1-Sep-2009	13456789			36.00 Dr	3,690.00 Dr		1.08 Dr	74.52 Dr
ExcSI	3 / 1-Oct-2009	13456789	ASDFG1234H123XD		304.00 Dr	3,994.00 Dr		6.08 Dr	80.60 Dr
ExcSI	2 / 1-Nov-2009	13456789	ASDFG1234H123XD		334.40 Dr	4,328.40 Dr		6.69 Dr	87.29 Dr
ExcSI	1 / 2-Dec-2009	13456789	ASDFG1234H123XD		1,920.00 Dr	6,248.40 Dr		38.40 Dr	125.69 Dr
Payment	1 / 1-Jan-2010			5,000.00 Cr		1,248.40 Dr			125.69 Dr
Payment	2 / 1-Jan-2010	13456789		6,080.00 Cr		4,831.60 Cr	38.40 Cr		87.29 Dr

F-25A: PLA Register

- **Education Cess**: Displays the Credit, Debit and Balance Education Cess amount.
- **Secondary Education Cess**: Displays the Credit, Debit and Balance Secondary Education Cess amount.

06 PLA Summary

PLA Summary (F-27A), displays the summary figures of **Advance Duty paid to the Government, Adjusted towards Duty Payable & the Balance amount available in PLA for adjustment**

PLA Summary

Name of Excise Unit	:	**Bonded Godown 1**
From	:	**1-4-2009**
To	:	**31-3-2010**

F-26A: PLA Summary Display options

At Excise Registers Menu, select PLA Summary to get PLS Summary display options screen (F-26A), similar ot PLA Register Display option screen. Set the options as follows (F-26A):

- **Excise Unit Name:** At *Name of Excise Unit*, select the Excise Unit from the list
- **Period**: At From & To, enter the Period.

To get the PLA Summary (F-27A)

Contents of the Report

At PLA Summary **Report** (F-27A) **Header, the selected Excise Unit Name is shown. Each column in the report is described below**

- **Particulars of Credit/Debit Document / Description of Documents With name of treasury Where necessary**: Shows the Name of the Bank through which the duty is paid as advance to the government.
- **Document No./ Date**: Displays the Challan Number and the Date of payment
- **Central Excise Tariff Sub-heading Number** and **ECC no. of the Buyer**: Respective details are shown where available.
- **Basic Excise Duty**: Displays the Credit, Debit and Balance of Basic Excise Duty amount.
- **Education Cess**: Displays the Credit, Debit and Balance of Education Cess amount.
- **Secondary Education Cess**: Displays the Credit, Debit and Balance of Secondary Education Cess amount.

07 CENVAT Registers

At *Manufacturers Excise Reports* Menu (F-1A), select *CENVAT Registers* to get CENVAT Registers Menu (F-28A).

08 Credit Summary

Credit Summary Report (F-30A) initially shows the Monthly figures of **Opening Balance, Credit for the Month, Utilised** and **Closing Balance** of CENVAT Credit**,** for each element of Excise Duty, in separate columns.

At CENVAT Register Menu (F-28A), select *Credit Summary* to get *CENVAT Credit Summary* options (F-29A), as described below:

PLA Summary | ABC Manufacturing | Ctrl + M

Excise Unit Name: **Bonded Godown 1** | 1-Apr-2009 to 31-Mar-2010

Particulars of Credit / Debit Document Description of Documents with name of treasury where necessary	Document No. / Date	Central Excise Tariff Sub-heading Number	Central Excise Regn. No. of the Buyer	Basic Excise Duty			Secondary Education Cess		
				Credit	Debit	Balance	Credit	Debit	Balance
SB	123/1-Jan-2010			5,000.00		5,000.00			

F-27A: PLA Summary

Gateway of Tally ....
Display Menu ....
Statutory Reports ....
Excise Reports ....
Manufacturer ....

CENVAT Registers

Credit Summary
Credit Availed

RG23 Part I

RG23 Part II
Annexure - 10
ABstract

RuLe 16 Register

Quit

F-28A: CENVAT Register Menu

CENVAT Credit Summary

Name of Excise Unit	: **Bonded Godown 1**
Name of Tariff	: **Computer Goods**
Stock Item Type	: **Principal Input**
Stock Item Name	: **All Items**

F-29A: CENVAT Credit Summary options

List of Item Types

Capital Goods
Principal Input
Rule 16-Returned Goods

F-29B: Item Type List

List of Stock Items

All Items
CPU P4
Mother Board Port

F-29C: Stock Item List

Set the Options to get *CENVAT Credit Summary* (F-30A)

- **Excise Unit Name:** At *Name of Excise Unit*, select the Excise Unit from the list
- **Tariff Classification:** At *Name of Tariff*, select the *Tariff Classification* from the list
- **Stock Item Type:** At *Stock Item Type*, select the *Stock Item Type* from the list
- **Stock Item Name:** Select the *Stock Item Name* from the list of Stock Items under the selected Tariff Classification & Stock Item Type.

Buttons: At *CENVAT Credit Summary* (F-30A),you get the following buttons (F-30B)

- **F1: Detailed / Summary:** Click the toggle button to show *Condensed* (showing only the Opening & Closing figures for the month) / *Detailed* (showing the break up of Credits & Utilisation also for each month: F-30C).
- **F2: Period**:At From & To enter the period. The report would be shown for the period

F4: Item: Select the Stock Item from the list of Stock Items

09 CENVAT Credit Availed

CENVAT Credit Availed report displays the details of CENVAT credit availed.

At *CENVAT Register* Menu (F-28A), select *Credit Availed* to get *CENVAT Credit Availed* selection option (F-31A)

At *CENVAT Credit Availed* selection option (F-31A), set the options to get *CENVAT Credit Availed* Report (F-31B), as per selection option, described below:

- **Excise Unit Name:** At *Name of Excise Unit*, select the Excise Unit from the list
- **Tariff Classification:** At *Name of Tariff*, select the *Tariff Classification* from the list
- **Stock Item Type:** At *Stock Item Type*, select the *Stock Item Type* from the list
- **Stock Item Name:** Select the *Stock Item Name* from the list of Stock Items (select *All Items* for All Items) under the selected Tariff Classification & Stock Item Type.
- **Period**: At Period, enter *From* & *To* enter the Period.

10 RG-23 Part-1

Form RG 23 Part I displays Quantitative account of input goods on which CENVAT credit is availed, showing the details

CENVAT Credit Summary — ABC Manufacturing — Ctrl + M

Unit Name : Bonded Godown 1 — 1-Apr-2009 to 31-Mar-2010

Excise Tariff Classification : Computer Goods Stock Item Type Principal Input Stock Item : CPU P4

Month	Particulars	Basic Excise Duty	Secondary Education Cess	Total
January-2010	Opening Balance	960.00 Dr	19.20 Dr	979.20 Dr
	Closing Balance	1,760.00 Dr	35.20 Dr	1,795.20 Dr
February-2010	Opening Balance	1,760.00 Dr	35.20 Dr	1,795.20 Dr
	Closing Balance	1,760.00 Dr	35.20 Dr	1,795.20 Dr
March-2010	Opening Balance	1,760.00 Dr	35.20 Dr	1,795.20 Dr
	Closing Balance	1,760.00 Dr	35.20 Dr	1,795.20 Dr

F-30A: CENVAT Credit Summary (Condensed)

F1: Detailed
F2: Period
F3: Company
F4: Item

F-30B: Buttons

CENVAT Credit Summary — ABC Manufacturing — Ctrl + M

Unit Name : Bonded Godown 1 — 1-Apr-2009 to 31-Mar-2010

Excise Tariff Classification : Computer Goods Stock Item Type : Principal Input Stock Item : CPU P4

Month	Particulars	Basic Excise Duty	Secondary Education Cess	Total
January-2010	Opening Balance	960.00 Dr	19.20 Dr	979.20 Dr
	Credit for the Month	800.00 Dr	16.00 Dr	816.00 Dr
	Utilised for Duty			
	Utilised for Service Tax			
	Closing Balance	1,760.00 Dr	35.20 Dr	1,795.20 Dr
February-2010	Opening Balance	1,760.00 Dr	35.20 Dr	1,795.20 Dr
	Credit for the Month			
	Utilised for Duty			
	Utilised for Service Tax			
	Closing Balance	1,760.00 Dr	35.20 Dr	1,795.20 Dr
March-2010	Opening Balance	1,760.00 Dr	35.20 Dr	1,795.20 Dr
	Credit for the Month			
	Utilised for Duty			
	Utilised for Service Tax			
	Closing Balance	1,760.00 Dr	35.20 Dr	1,795.20 Dr

F-30C: CENVAT Credit Summary (Detailed)

CENVAT Credit Availed

Name of Excise Unit	: **Bonded Godown 1**
Name of Tariff	: **Computer Goods**
Stock Item Type	: **Principal Input**
Stock Item Name	: **All Items**
From	: **1-4-2009**
To	: **31-3-2010**

F-31A: CENVAT Credit Availed

CENVAT Credit Availed			ABC Manufacturing				Ctrl + M
Unit Name	: Bonded Godown 1					1-Apr-2009 to 31-Mar-2010	
Stock Item Type	: Principal Input						
Date of Entry	**Invoice / Adj Reference**	**Type of Document**	**Supplier Name**	**Supplier ECC No.**	**Assessable Value**	**Basic Excise Duty**	**Secondary Education Cess**
1-May-2009	23 / 1-2009	ExcPur	Riverstone Solutions India	ASDFG1234H123XD	6,000.00	960.00	19.20
1-Jan-2010	DN/2	DNExVcl	Riverstone Solutions India	ASDFG1234H123XD	5,000.00	800.00	16.00
			Total CENVAT			1,760.00	35.20
			Total Adjusted				
			Balance			1,760.00	35.20

F-31B: CENVAT Credit Availed Report

of Receipt of inputs (Principal Input /Capital goods) & Consumption / Deliveries for manufacture of Excisable Goods & Closing Stock.

At *CENVAT Register* Menu (F-28A), select *RG-23 Part-1* to get *RG-23 Part-1* Menu (F-32A).

Gateway of Tally . Display Menu .... Statutory Reports . Excise Reports .. Manufacturer .... CENVAT Registers

RG23 Part-1

One Item
Multi Item
Tariff Wise
Quit

F-32A: RG-23 Part-1 Menu

10.01 RG-23 Part-1 for One Item

At *RG-23 Part-1 Menu* (F-32A), select *One Item*, to get the following Options (F-32B):

FORM R.G.23

Name of Excise Unit	: Bonded Godown 1
Stock Item Type	: Principal Input
Stock Item Name	: Mother Board Port
From	: 1-4-2009
To	: 31-3-2010

F-32B: RG-23 Part-1 Display for One Item

- **Period:** At *From* & *To* enter the period.

Set the Options (F-32B) to get RG-23 Part-1 Register (One Item) Report (F-32C).

10.02 RG-23 Part-1 for Multi Item

At *RG-23 Part-1 Menu* (F-32A), select *Multi Item*, to get the Report Printing options (F-33A) to set the respective options, as described, to get RG-23 Part1 Register for Multi Item(F-33B)

In RG-23 Part1 Register for Multi Item Report (F-33B), the details in respect of each Item as per selected options are shown, one after another. To print the details of each Item in separate Page, at Report Printing Screen (F-33A), set *Yes* at *Start Fresh Page at each Item*

10.03 RG-23 Register Tariff wise

At *RG-23 Part-1 Menu*, select *Tariff Wise*, to get the Report Printing Screen to set the respective options, as described.

FORM R.G.23.A PART - I

QUANTITATIVE ACCOUNT OF INPUTS ON WHICH CENVAT CREDIT AVAILED

[Under Rule 9 of Cenvat Credit Rules, 2004]

Name of the Company	: Bonded Godown 1		Commissionerate	:
Central Excise Regn. No.	: ABCDE1234D123XM		Division	:
Description of Input	: Mother Board Port		Range	:
Unit of Measurements	: U		For the month of	: March 2010

Page 1

Date	Opening Balance	Receipt of Input					Issued for Manufacture of final product		Issued for Clearance as such		Closing (2 +3B-4B-5B)	Central Excise Officer's Initial and Date	Remarks
		Sr.No. of Input Credit Register(Cross reference)	Quantity Received	Particulars of Invoice /BOE/Other Approved Doc and Date	Name & Address of the Manufacturer/Importer/Stock yard and ECC number	Range and Division from where goods are received	Requisition No and Date	Quantity Issued	Invoice No and Date	Quantity Issued			
1	2	3A	3B	3C	3D	3E	4A	4B	5A	5B	6	7	8
1-Sep-2009									3 /1-Sep -2009	10	(-)10		
1-Jan-2010	(-)10						1/1-Jan -2010	8			(-)18		
1-Mar-2010	(-)18						1/1-Mar -2010	80			(-)98		
Total								88		10			

F-32C: RG-23 Part-1 Register (One Item)

- **Excise Unit Name:** At *Name of Excise Unit*, select the Excise Unit from the list
- **Stock Item Type:** At *Stock Item Type*, select the *Stock Item Type* from the list
- **Stock Item Name:** Select the *Stock Item Name* from the list of Stock Items (select *All Items* for All Items) under the selected Tariff Classification & Stock Item Type.

Excise Unit	: Bonded Godown 1
Stock Item Type	: Principal Input
Name of Tariff	: Computer Goods
Reporting UOM	: U
Start fresh page for each Item	: No
From	: 1-4-2009
To	: 31-3-2010

F-33A: RG-23 Register Printing for Multi Items

Page 1

Date	Opening Balance	Receipt of Input					Issued for Manufacture of final product		Issued for Clearance as such		Closing (2+3B-4B-5B)	Central Excise Officer's Initial and Date	Remarks
		Sr.No. of Input Credit Register(Cross reference)	Quantity Received	Particulars of Invoice /BOE /Other Approved Doc and Date	Name & Address of the Manufacturer /Importer/Stock yard and ECC number	Range and Division from where goods are received	Requisition No and Date	Quantity Issued	Invoice No and Date	Quantity Issued			
1	2	3A	3B	3C	3D	3E	4A	4B	5A	5B	6	7	8
Description of Input : CPU P4													
Unit of Measurements : U					Tariff Classification	: Computer Goods							
1-May-2009	30	1	3	23/1 -Apr -2009	Riverstone Solutions India 12 Tilak Rd, Kolkata ASDFG1234H1-23XD	34567 345					33		
1-Aug-2009	33										33		
Total			3										
Description of Input : Mother Board Port													
Unit of Measurements : U					Tariff Classification	: Computer Goods							
1-Sep-2009									3/1 -Sep -2009	10	(-)10		
1-Jan-2010	(-)10						1/1 -Jan -2010	8			(-)18		
1-Mar-2010	(-)18						1/1 -Mar -2010	80			(-)98		
Total								88		10			

F-33B: RG-23 Register for Multi Items

Set the printing options (F-34A) to get RG-23 Part 1 Register – Tariff wise (F-34B)

RG23 Part1 Register

Name of Excise Unit	: **Bonded Godown 1**
Stock Item Type	: **Principal Input**
Name of Tariff	: **Computer Goods**
Reporting UOM	: **U**
From	: **1-4-2009**
To	: **31-3-2010**

F-34A: RG-23 Part 1 Register – Tariff wise

- **Excise Unit Name:** At *Name of Excise Unit*, select the Excise Unit from the list
- **Stock Item Type:** At *Stock Item Type*, select the *Stock Item Type* from the list
- **Tariff Classification:** At *Name of Tariff*, select the *Tariff Classification* from the list
- **Reporting UoM**: Select the Reporting UoM from the list
- **Period**: At Period, enter *From* & *To* enter the Period.

Condensed Format

FORM R.G.23.A PART - I

QUANTITATIVE ACCOUNT OF INPUTS ON WHICH CENVAT CREDIT AVAILED

[Under Rule 9 of Cenvat Credit Rules, 2004]

Name of the Company	: Bonded Godown 1		Commissionerate	:
Central Excise Regn. No.	: ABCDE1234D123XM		Division	:
Excise Tariff Classification	: Computer Goods		Range	:
Unit of Measurements	: U		For the month of	: March 2010

Page 1 (A)

Date	Opening Balance	Description of Inputs received	Receipt of Input				
			Sr.No. of Input Credit Register(Cross reference)	Quantity Received	Particulars of Invoice/BOE Other Approved Doc and Date	Name & Address of the Manufacturer/ Importer/Stock yard and ECC number	Range and Division from where goods are received
1	2	3	3A	3B	3C	3D	3E
1-May-2009	30	CPU P4	1	3	23/1-Apr-2009	Riverstone Solutions India	34567
1-Sep-2009	33	Mother Board Port					
1-Jan-2010	23	Mother Board Port					
1-Mar-2010	15	Mother Board Port					
Total	30			3			

F-34B: RG-23 Register Part 1– Tariff wise: Left Part

FORM R.G.23.A PART - I

QUANTITATIVE ACCOUNT OF INPUTS ON WHICH
CENVAT CREDIT AVAILED

[Under Rule 9 of Cenvat Credit Rules, 2004]

Name of the Company	: Bonded Godown 1		Commissionerate	:
Central Excise Regn. No.	: ABCDE1234D123XM		Division	:
Excise Tariff Classification	: Computer Goods		Range	:
Unit of Measurements	: U		For the month of	: March 2010

Page 1 (B)

Date	Opening Balance	Issued for Manufacture of final product		Issued for Clearance as such		Closing Balance (2+3B-4B-5B)	Central Excise Officer's Initial and date	Remarks
		Requisition No and Date	Quantity Issued	Invoice No and Date	Quantity Issued			
1	2	4A	4B	5A	5B	6	7	8
1-May-2009	30					33		
1-Sep-2009	33			3, 1-Sep-2009	10	23		
1-Jan-2010	23	1/1-Jan-2010	8			15		
1-Mar-2010	15	1/1-Mar-2010	80			(-)65		
Total	30		88		10	(-)65		

RG-23 Register Part 1 – Tariff wise: Right Part

FORM R.G.23.A PART - I

QUANTITATIVE ACCOUNT OF INPUTS ON WHICH
CENVAT CREDIT AVAILED

[Under Rule 9 of Cenvat Credit Rules, 2004]

Name of the Company	: Bonded Godown 1		Commissionerate	:
Central Excise Regn. No.	: ABCDE1234D123XM		Division	:
Excise Tariff Classification	: Computer Goods		Range	:
Unit of Measurements	: U		For the month of	: March 2010

Page 1 (A)

Date	Opening Balance	Description of inputs received	Receipt of input				
			Sr.No. of Input Credit Register(Cross reference)	Quantity Received	Particulars of Invoice/BOE Other Approved Doc and Date	Name & Address of the Manufacturer/ Importer/Stock yard and ECC number	Range and Division from where goods are received
1	2	3	3A	3B	3C	3D	3E
1-May-2009	30	CPU P4	1	3	23/1-Apr-2009	Riverstone Solutions India 12 Tilak Rd, Kolkata ASDFG1234H123XD	34567 346
1-Sep-2009	33	Mother Board Port					
1-Jan-2010	23	Mother Board Port					
1-Mar-2010	15	Mother Board Port					
Total	30			3			

F-34C: RG-23 Register Part 1-Tariff wise: Detailed – Left Part

FORM R.G.23.A PART - I

QUANTITATIVE ACCOUNT OF INPUTS ON WHICH
CENVAT CREDIT AVAILED

[Under Rule 9 of Cenvat Credit Rules, 2004]

Name of the Company	: Bonded Godown 1		Commissionerate	:
Central Excise Regn. No.	: ABCDE1234D123XM		Division	:
Excise Tariff Classification	: Computer Goods		Range	:
Unit of Measurements	: U		For the month of	: March 2010

Page 1 (B)

Date	Opening Balance	Issued for Manufacture of final product		Issued for Clearance as such		Closing Balance (2+3B-4B-5B)	Central Excise Officer's Initial and date	Remarks
		Requisition No and Date	Quantity Issued	Invoice No and Date	Quantity Issued			
1	2	4A	4B	5A	5B	6	7	8
1-May-2009	30					33		
1-Sep-2009	33			3, 1-Sep-2009	10	23		
1-Jan-2010	23	1/1-Jan-2010	8			15		
1-Mar-2010	15	1/1-Mar-2010	80			(-)65		
Total	30		88		10	(-)65		

RG-23 Register Part 1-Tariff wise: Detailed- Right Part

Detailed Format: At RG-23 Register Part 1– Tariff wise Report (F-34B), click F1:Detailed button to get RG-23 Register Part 1– Tariff wise Report in Detailed Format (F-34C)

Configuration: At RG-23 Register – Part 1: Tariff wise Report Display, click *F12:Configure* to get *Configuration* screen (F-34E), to set options as follows:

- **Item Description**: At *Show Item Description*, set *Yes* to show Item Description also in the Report

Buttons: At RG-23 Register – Tariff wise Report Display (F-34B, F-34C), you get buttons (F-34D) as follows:

F2: Period
F3: Company
F1: Detailed
F2: Period
F12: Configure
F4: Change Tariff

F-34D: Buttons

Configuration

Show Item Description ? **Yes**
Sorting Method : **Default**

F-34E: Configuration screen

- **F2: Period**: To set the Report Period (Alt+F2)
- **F1:Detailed / Condensed**: To toggle between the Condensed (F-34B) & Detailed Format (F-34C)
- **F2: Period**: To set the Report Period
- **F12:Configure**: To get the Report Configuration screen, to set the Configuration options
- **F4: Change Tariff**: To select another Tariff Classification

11 RG-23 Register Part II

RG 23 Part II Report displays the details of **Fresh Credit allowed, Available & Credit Adjusted** for the selected Period.

At CENVAT Register Menu (F-28A), select RG-23 Part II to get At RG-23 Part II Display Options (F-35A).

FORM R.G.23

Name of Excise Unit : **Bonded Godown 1**
Stock Item Type : **Principal Input**
From : **1-4-2009**
To : **31-3-2010**

F-35A: RG-23 Part II Display Options

At RG-23 Part II Display Options (F-35A), to set the Printing options.

- **Excise Unit Name:** At *Name of Excise Unit*, select the Excise Unit from the list
- **Stock Item Type:** At *Stock Item Type*, select the *Stock Item Type* from the list
- **Period**: At *From* & *To* enter the period.

At RG-23 Part II Display Options (F-35A), set the options to get RG-23 Part II Register (F-35B)

12 Annexure – 10

Annexure- 10 is a monthly return showing the details of **CENVAT credit availed**. Though this return is officially discontinued by Excise Department notification (w.e.f 1-10-2003), many organisations still use it for submission of Monthly Return for CENVAT Credit availed.

At CENVAT Register Menu (F-28A), select Annexure 10 to

Bonded Godown 1
12 Naktala Road, Kolkata

Page 1 (A)

FORM R.G.23A PART II
ENTRY BOOK OF DUTY CREDIT

Central Excise Reg.No. : ABCDE1234D123XM
Range :
For the month of : March 2010

Sl. No.	Name of Supplier	Date	Opening Balance of Duty in Credit				Fresh Credit Allowed			Fresh Credit Allowed Amount of Duty Credit			
			CENVAT	Education Cess	Secondary Education Cess	Additional-Duties	Invoice No. /Bill of Entry No. & Date	C.E.RegNo /IEC Code No. of the Supplier & Range /Customs house from where received	Folio & Entry No. in Part I	CENVAT	Education Cess	Secondary Education Cess	Additional-Duties
1	Riverstone Solutions India	14-May-2009					23/14-May-2009	ASDFG1234H123XD 34567	1	960.00		19.20	
2	Riverstone Solutions India	1-Jan-2010	960.00		19.20		DN/2	ASDFG1234H123XD 34567	DN/2	800.00		16.00	

Date : 1-Apr-2010 Place : Kolkata Signature of Assessee

F-35B: RG-23 Register Part II: Left Part

Bonded Godown 1
12 Naktala Road, Kolkata

Page 1 (B)

FORM R.G.23A PART II
ENTRY BOOK OF DUTY CREDIT

Central Excise Reg.No. : ABCDE1234D123XM
Range :
For the month of : March 2010

Sl. No.	Name of Supplier	Date	Total Credit Available				Debit						
			CENVAT	Education Cess	Secondary Education Cess	Additional-Duties	Invoice No. & Date	C.E.Tariff Heading /Sub-Heading	C.E.Reg.No. of the Buyer	CENVAT	Education Cess	Secondary Education Cess	Additional-Duties
1	Riverstone Solutions India	14-May-2009	960.00		19.20								
2	Riverstone Solutions India	1-Jan-2010	1,760.00		35.20								

Date : 1-Apr-2010 Place : Kolkata Signature of Assessee

RG-23 Register Part II: Middle Part

Bonded Godown 1
12 Naktala Road, Kolkata

Page 1 (C)

FORM R.G.23A PART II — Central Excise Reg.No. : ABCDE1234D123XM

ENTRY BOOK OF DUTY CREDIT — Range :

For the month of : March 2010

Sl. No.	Name of Supplier	Date	Balance Credit: CENVAT	Education Cess	Secondary Education Cess	Additional-Duties	Remarks
1	Riverstone Solutions India	1-May-2009	960.00		19.20		
2	Riverstone Solutions India	1-Jan-2010	1,760.00		35.20		

Date : 1-Apr-2010 Place : Kolkata Signature of Assessee

RG-23 Register Part II: Right Part

get Annexure-10 display options screen (F-36A), to set the following options:

- **Excise Unit Name:** At *Name of Excise Unit*, select the Excise Unit from the list
- **Stock Item Type:** At *Stock Item Type*, select the *Stock Item Type* from the list (F-36B)
- **Period**: Enter the Dates at *From* & *To*, to set the Report Period to get Annexure 10 Report display (F-36C)

Annexure - 10

Name of Excise Unit	: **Bonded Godown 1**
Stock Item Type	: **Principal Input**
From	: **1-4-2009**
To	: **31-3-2010**

F-36A: Annexure- 10

List of Item Types

Capital Goods
Principal Input

F-36B: Input Type List

Contents of Annexure- 10

At Annexure 10 Report (F-36C), at **the header, the selected Excise Unit Name & Stock Item Type is displayed. The Table contains the following columns:**

- **Type of Document**: Voucher Type of document of the transaction
- **No. and Date of Document**: Voucher Number & Date
- **Name of the Supplier**: Shows Name of the supplier and the Type
- **C.E.No. of the Supplier**: Suppliers Excise Control Code (ECC)
- **Date on which principal inputs/Capital Goods received**: Voucher Date of the Document.
- **Value**: Total Value on which Credit is availed.
- **CENVAT**: CENVAT Credit availed.
- **Education Cess**: Education Cess availed.
- **Secondary Education Cess**: Secondary Education Cess availed
- **For the Main item Details**: **Details under the following columns:**
  - o **Description**: **Name** of the Main item.
  - o **Sub-Heading**: **Tariff sub-heading** of the Main Item
  - o **Qty**: **Quantity** of the Main Item

Configuration

At *Annexure-10* Display (F-36B), click *F12:Configure* to get Configuration screen, to set the following options:

Annexure - 10 — ABC Manufacturing — Ctrl + M

Unit Name : Bonded Godown 1 — 1-Apr-2009 to 31-Mar-2010

Stock Item Type : Principal Input

Type of Document	No. and Date of Document	Name of the Supplier	C.E.No. of the Supplier	Date on Which Principal Input received	Value	CENVAT	Secondary Education Cess	For the main Item in the document: Description	Sub - Heading	Qty
ExcPur	23 / 1-2009 1-May-2009	Riverstone Solutions India *(First Stage Dealer)*	ASDFG1234H1Z3XD	1-May-2009	6,000.00	960.00	19.20	CPU P4	13456789	3 Pcs
DNExVcl	DN/2	Riverstone Solutions India *(Manufacturer)*	ASDFG1234H1Z3XD	1-Jan-2010	5,000.00	800.00	16.00	CPU P4	13456789	1 Pcs
		Total				1,760.00	35.20			

F-36C: Annexure- 10

- **Supplier Nature Option**: At *Show Nature of Supplier*, set *Yes* to display also the *Nature of Supplier* under Supplier Name. Set *No*. Supplier Nature option list will not be displayed
- **Supplier Nature:** Having set Nature of Supplier, at *Select Nature of Supplier*, you may further select the Nature of Supplier (select *All Items* for all) from the list (F-36D) to display the report for the selected Nature of Supplier.

Configuration

Show Nature of Supplier	? Yes
Select Nature of Supplier	? All Items

F-36C: Configuration

Nature of Purchase

All Items
First Stage Dealer
Importer
Manufacturer
Second Stage Dealer

F-36D: Supplier Nature List

13 CENVAT Abstract

The Abstract report shows the summary figures of **Credit Availed, Credit Utilised** with **Opening** and **Closing Balance** of Credit, for the selected Item Type

ABSTRACT

Name of Excise Unit	: Bonded Godown 1
Stock Item Type	: Principal Input
From	: 1-4-2009
To	: 31-3-2010

F-37A: Abstract Display

List of Item Types

Capital Goods
Principal Input

F-37B: Stock Item Type List

At *CENVAT Registers* Menu (F-28A), select *Abstract* to get Abstract display option screen (F-37A), to set the following options:

ABSTRACT — ABC Manufacturing — Ctrl + M

Unit Name : Bonded Godown 1 — 1-Apr-2009 to 31-Mar-2010

Stock Item Type : Principal Input

	Opening Balance	Credit Availed on Principal Input	Other Credit	Credit Availed on Input Services	Total Credit Availed	Credit Utilised for Payment of Duty on goods	Credit Utilised when Inputs goods are removed as such	Credit Utilised Payment of Duty on Services	Closing Balance
CENVAT		1,760.00			1,760.00				1,760.00
Secondary Education Cess		35.20			35.20				35.20
Service Tax									
Cess on Taxable Services									
Total		1,795.20			1,795.20				1,795.20

F-37C: CENVAT Abstract

- **Excise Unit Name:** At *Name of Excise Unit*, select the Excise Unit from the list
- **Stock Item Type:** At *Stock Item Type*, select the *Stock Item Type* from the list (F-37B)
- **Period**: At Period, enter *From* & *To* enter the Period.

At Abstract Display option screen (F-37A), set the options to get Abstract Report (F-37C).

Contents of Abstract Report

- **Opening Balance**: Opening Balance at the Start Date of the Period, for respective Duty Head
- Amount for the Period: The following columns shows the figures in respect of the selected Period
  - o **Credit Availed on Principal Input**: Displays the details of duty credit availed on principal Input goods, for respective Duty Head
  - o **Other Credit**: Displays other credit details, for respective Duty Head
  - o **Credit Availed on Input Services/Capital Goods**: Displays the duty head wise credit availed on Input Services/ Capital Goods, for respective Duty Head
  - o **Total Credit Availed**: Displays the total credit availed against different duty heads
  - o **Credit Utilised for Payment of Duty on Goods**: Displays the Credit Amount utilised for the payment of duty on goods.
  - o **Credit Utilised When Inputs are Removed as such**: Credit Amount utilised for Goods *Removed As Such*
  - o **Credit Utilised for payment of Duty on services:** Credit Amount utilised for payment of duty on services
- **Closing Balance**: Duty head wise Closing Balance, as at the Report end Date

14 Rule 16 Register

The Rule 16 Register shows the Sales Returns of excisable goods and goods sent for further processing (manufacturing), sales etc. The contents are quite similar to RG 23.

At *CENVAT Registers* Menu, select *Rule 16 Register* to get *Rule 16 Register* display screen, to set the following options:

Rule 16 Registers

Name of Excise Unit	: Bonded Godown 1
Stock Item Name	:
From	: 1-3-2010
To	: 31-3-2010

F-38A: Rule-16 Register display

Rule 16 Register

Name of the Company : Bonded Godown 1
Central Excise Regn. No. : [illegible]
Description of Input : LCD 18.5
Unit of Measurements : [illegible]

Commissionerate :
Division :
Range :
For the month of : March 2010

Page 1

S.No.	Particulars of Invoice / BOE other Approved Doc and Date	Rejection Invoice Details: Own Invoice No. / Date	Party's Invoice No. / Date	Description of goods	Quantity Rejected	Reason for Rejection	Amount of credit Availed	Inspection Report No/Date	Action taken on the rejected stock: Scrap	Qty. issued for Re-work or manufacture	Work Order reference	Qty. issued for Clearance as Such	Clearance Invoice no. / Date	Closing Balance
1	2	3	4	5	6	7	8	9	10	11	12	13	14	15
1	1/1-Aug-2009	9/1-Jul-2009	13/31-Jul-2009	LCD 18.5	1	Goods Defective	3,231.36	1234/1-Aug-2009		1				
	Total				1					1				

F-38B: Rule 16 Register

- **Excise Unit Name:** At *Name of Excise Unit*, select the Excise Unit from the list
- **Stock Item Type:** At *Stock Item Type*, select the *Stock Item Type* from the list
- **Period**: At Period, enter *From* & *To* enter the Period to get Rule-16 Register Report display screen

Contents of the Report

At the Rule-16 Register, at the Header, the Excise Unit Name, selected Stock Item Name and corresponding Reporting Unit is displayed, with following columns:

- **Sl. No**: Running serial number of the transaction in the report, starting from 1.
- **Particulars of Invoice / BOE other approved Doc and Date**: The voucher number / Reference Number of the Voucher
- **Own Invoice No./Date**: The original excise sales invoice number & date against which the credit note is recorded. If the goods are returned, the details of party who has returned the goods against this invoice may also be shown in detailed mode.
- **Party's Invoice No./Date**: The Excise Debit Note number & Date raised by the party returning the goods.
- **Description of goods**: Stock item name in excise credit note.
- **Quantity Rejected**: Quantity returned.
- **Reason for Rejection**: The reason of Return (as entered in Item Allocation screen of Excise Credit Note).
- **Amount of credit Availed**: Amount of Excise Credit availed through the Excise Credit Note
- **Inspection report No/date**: Inspection report or document Reference & Date of the Excise Credit Note will be captured here.
- **Scrap**: The quantity entered in Scrap column, if any, in Item Allocation screen of Excise Credit Note.
- **Qty. issued for Re-work or manufacture**: This quantity entered in Excise manufacturing journal by selecting the **Nature of Process** as **Reprocessing** is captured here.
- **Work order reference**: The reference number entered in excise manufacturing journal is captured here.
- **Qty. issued for Clearance as Such**: Out of the stock item recorded in excise credit note, the quantity entered in excise sales invoice by selecting **Removal as Such** as the Nature of Removal is captured here.
- **Clearance Invoice no./Date**: The invoice number and date entered for resale of goods in excise sales invoice by selecting **Removal as Such** as the Nature of Removal is captured here.
- **Closing Balance**: The closing balance of stock which is neither sold as Removal as such nor sent for manufacturing is captured here.

15 Excise Forms

Gateway of Tally ...
Display Menu ....
Statutory Reports ..
Excise Reports ....
Manufacturer ....

At *Excise Manufacturer* Reports Menu (F-1A), select Excise Forms to get *Excise Forms* Menu (F-39A)

Excise Forms

Form ER 1
Form ER 3
Form ER 5
Form ER 6
Form ER 8
Quit

F-39A: Excise Forms Menu

15.01 ER-1 Form

Form ER 1 is a **Monthly** return for production, removal of Goods, other relevant particulars and CENVAT Credit, to be submitted by **Excise Manufacturing Units.**

At *Excise Forms* Menu (F-39A), select *Form ER-1* to get ER-1 Form printing screen (F-40A).

At ER-1 Form printing screen (F-40A), set the options to get ER-1 Form (F-40B) as per options set.

Report Titles

Form ER 1

Excise Unit	: **Bonded Godown 1**
From (blank for beginning)	: **1-4-2009**
To (blank for end)	: **31-3-2010**
Include Export/Exempt Quantity	? **Yes**
Include Export/Exempt Assessable Value	? **Yes**
Show Export and Captive Consumption	? **Yes**
Show All Items	? **Yes**
Show Excise Duty Amount Round Off	? **Yes**
Place	: **Kolkata**
Date	: **1-4-2010**
Assessee Name	: **ABC MFG**

F-40A: Form ER-1 printing

ANNEXURE-12

Monthly return for production and removal of goods and other relevant particulars and CENVAT credit
Form E.R.-1

Original/Duplicate

[See rule 12 of the Central Excise Rules, 2002 and rule 9(7) of CENVAT Credit Rules,2004]

Return of excisable goods and availment of CENVAT credit for the Month	MM YYYY 04 2009
Large Taxpayer Unit opted for (name of the city)*:-	

1. Registration number :- ABCDE1234D123XM

2. Name of the Assessee :- Bonded Godown 1

3. Details of the manufacture, clearance and duty payable:-

CETSH No	Description of goods	Unit of quantity	Opening balance	Quantity manufactured	Quantity cleared	Closing balance	Assessable Value (Rs.)
					Domestic		Domestic
(1)	(2)	(3)	(3A)	(4)	(5A)	(5D)	(6A)
13456789	Computer Goods	U	10	2	3	9.00	36,800.00
	Total		10	2	3	9.00	36,800.00

Duty	Notification availed	Serial number in Notification	Rate of duty (adv)	Rate of duty (specific)	Duty Payable	Provisional assessment number (if any)
(7)	(8)	(9)	(10)	(11)	(12)	(13)
Secondary Education Cess					111.00	
Basic Excise Duty					5,538.00	

4. Clearance details of inter unit transfer of intermediate goods without payment of duty under sub-rule (1) of rule 12BB*:-

Registration number of the recipient unit	Name and address of the recipient premises	CETSH NO	Description of goods sent	Unit of Quantity	Quantity cleared
(1)	(2)	(3)	(4)	(5)	(6)

5. Receipt details of intermediate goods received from other premises under sub-rule (1) of rule 12BB*:-

Registration number of sender premises	Name and address of the sender premises	CETSH NO	Description of goods received	Unit of Quantity	Quantity received
(1)	(2)	(3)	(4)	(5)	(6)

6. Details of duty paid on excisable goods:-

Duty Code	Credit Account (Rs.)	Account Current (Rs.)	Challan		BSR code	Total duty paid (2+3)
			No.	Date		
(1)	(2)	(3)	(4A)	(4B)	(5)	(6)
Basic Excise Duty		6,080.00				6,080.00
Secondary Education Cess		38.00				38.00

F-40B: ER-1 Form – Page 1

7. Abstract of ACCOUNT-CURRENT (Cash payment):-

Summary particulars	Amount in Rs.
(1)	(2)
Opening Balance	12,000.00
Add: TR-6/GAR-7 Challan payments made in the month (in aggregate)	11,118.00
Add*: Adjustment of the excess duty paid during previous period under sub-rule(2) of rule 12BB (in case of LT)	
Total amount available	23,118.00
Less: Utilization towards Payment of duties on excisable goods during the month [vide Details furnished under col.no. 3 in Sl.No. (6) of the Return]	6,118.00
Less: Utilization towards Other Payments made during the month [vide Details furnished under Sl.No. (9) of the Return]	
Closing balance	17,000.00

8. Details of CENVAT credit taken and utilised:-

Sl. No.	Details of credit	CENVAT (Rs.)	AED (TTA) (Rs.)	NCCD (Rs.)	ADE levied under clause 85 of Finance Act, 2005 (Rs.)	Additional duty of cus -toms levied under section 3 (5) of the Customs Tariff Act, 1975	Education Cess on excisable goods (Rs.)	Seconda-ry and Higher Education Cess on Excisable goods (Rs.)	Service Tax (Rs.)	Education Cess on taxable services (Rs.)	Seconda-ry and Higher Education Cess on taxable services (Rs.)
	(1)	(2)	(3)	(4)	(5)	(6)	(7)	(8)	(9)	(10)	(11)
1	Opening balance										
2	Credit taken on inputs on invoices issued by manufa-cturers	800.00						16.00			
3	Credit taken on inputs on invoices issued by Ist or IInd stage dealers	960.00						19.00			
4	Credit taken on imported inputs										
5	Credit taken on capital goods on invoices issued by manufa-cturers or by Ist or IInd stage dealers	300.00									

ER-1 Form – Page 2

	(1)	(2)	(3)	(4)	(5)	(6)	(7)	(8)	(9)	(10)	(11)
6	Credit taken on imported capital goods										
7	Credit taken on input services										
8	Credit taken from inter-unit transfer of credit by a large taxpayer										
9	Credit taken under sub-rule (2) of rule 12BB of Central Excise Rules, 2002*										
10	Total credit available	2,060.00						35.00			
11	Credit utilised for payment of duty on goods										
12	Credit utilised when inputs or capital goods are removed as such										
13	Credit utilised for payment of amount in terms of Rule 6 of CENVAT Credit Rules, 2004.										
14	Credit utilised for other payment										
15	Credit utilised for payment of tax on services										
16	Credit utilised towards inter unit transfer of credit by a large taxpayer *										
17	Closing balance	2,060.00						35.00			

ER-1 Form – Page 3

9. Details of other payments made:-

Payments	Amount paid (Rs.)		Challan		BSR code	Source document	
	Account current	Credit Account	No.	Date		No.	date
(1)	(2A)	(2B)	(3A)	(3B)	(4)	(5A)	(5B)
Arrears of duty under rule 8							
Other arrears of duty							
Interest payment under rule 8							
Other interest payments							
Misc. payments							
[Total]							

10. Self-Assessment Memorandum:-

(a) I hereby declare that the information given in this return is true, correct and complete in every respect and that I am authorised to sign on behalf of the assessee.

(b) During the month, total Rs. 11,118.40 was deposited vide TR-6 Challans (copies enclosed).

(c) During the month, invoices bearing Sl.No. **9 to 5 of ABC/BDG/1/13-14 were issued.**

(d) During the month, transfer challans under rule 12BB of the Central Excise Rules, 2002 bearing S.No. ____to____, and transfer challan under rule 12A of the CENVAT Credit Rules, 2004 bearing S.No. ____to____were issued.*

ABC MFG

(Authorised signatory)

Place : **Kolkata**
Date : **1-Apr-2010**

*Applicable only for large taxpayers defined under Rule 2(ea) of the Central Excise Rule,2002 and who has opted to operate as Large Taxpayer.

ACKNOWLEDGMENT

	MM	YYYY
Return of excisable goods and availment of CENVAT credit for the month of	04	2009

	DD	MM	YYYY
Date of Receipt			

ER-1 Form – Page 4

Contents of ER-1 Form

1. **Registration Number:** Registration Number of the Manufacturing Unit
2. **Name of the Assessee**: Name of the Excise Unit
3. **Details of the manufacture, clearance and Duty payable**: This section displays following details of manufacture, clearance of stock and duty payable on clearance of goods, in tabular form
   - **CETSH No.** – Central Excise Tariff Sub Heading Number of the Stock item.
   - **Description of the Goods**: Tariff Classification of the stock Item.
   - **Unit of Quantity**: Reporting UOM of the Stock Item.
   - **Opening Balance**: Opening Stock for the selected period.
   - **Quantity Manufactured**: Quantity of Stock Item manufactured during the period.
   - **Quantity Cleared**: Quantity of Stock Item cleared during the period.
   - **Closing Balance**: Closing Stock Balance of the stock item for the period.
   - **Assessable Value**: Assessable Value of the stock Item, on which the duty is calculated.
   - **Duty**: Duty Type applicable for the Tariff Classification.
   - **Notification Availed**: Notification Number applicable, if any (e.g tariff classification regarding duty exemption, special rates etc).
   - **Serial Number in Notification**: Line number of the tariff classification in the notification.
   - **Duty Payable**: Total Duty payable for the period

4. **Clearance details of inter unit transfer of intermediate goods without payment of Duty under sub-rule (1) of rule 12BB**: This section shows the details of inter unit transfer of intermediate goods without payment of goods.
5. **Receipt details of intermediate goods received from other premises under sub-rule (1) of rule 12BB**: This section shows details of intermediate goods received from other premises.
6. **Details of duty paid on excisable goods**: Displays the details of duty paid
   - **Duty Code**: Duty code towards which the duty is paid.
   - **Credit Account**: CENVAT credit amount adjusted for the period
   - **Account Current**: Duty Amount paid for the period.
   - **Challan No and Date**: Challan Number and Date of Payment of duty.
   - **BSR Code**: BSR code of the bank through which the duty is paid.
   - **Total Duty paid**: Total of CENVAT Credit availed and the net Duty paid for the period.
7. **Abstract of ACCOUNT-CURRENT (Cash Payment)**: This section shows the details of all the payments made during the period using G.A.R.7 Challan
8. **Details of CENVAT credit taken and utilised**: This section shows the details of CENVAT credit taken and utilised during the period.
9. **Details of other payment made**: This section shows the details of other payments (e.g arrears, penalty, interest and miscellaneous payments) during the period.
10. **Self-Assessment memorandum**: In this section assessee makes necessary declaration
11. **ACKNOWLEDGMENT**: This portion will be returned to the assessee, after being sealed and signed by the Range officer.

Instructions For ER-1

The following are the guidelines issued by Excise Department for preparation of ER-1

1. The large taxpayer may indicate the Large Taxpayer Unit authority viz. Delhi, Mumbai,
   Kolkata, Bangalore or Chennai under which the large taxpayer has opted. Indicate the 15-digit PAN based registration number and the name as appearing in the Registration Certificate
2. In case more than one item is manufactured, additional row may be inserted in each table, wherever necessary. For giving information about the details of production and clearance, payment of duty and CENVAT credit availed and utilised month wise, the respective tables may be replicated.
3. If a specific product attracts more than one rate of duty, then all the rates should be mentioned separately. For example: If a product is cleared at full rate of duty to the local market and at a concessional /nil rate of duty for earthquake relief, then the details for each category of clearance must be separately mentioned.

3A. The term 'CENVAT' used at serial numbers 3,6 and 8 refer to the Basic Excise Duty and the term 'Other duties' refers duties including AED, SED, NCCD, Cesses, etc.

4. In case the goods are cleared for export under Bond or Letter of undertaking, the details of clearance may be mentioned separately. Under the columns (8) and (9) of table at serial number 3, the words 'Export under Bond' may be mentioned.
5. In case the intermediate goods are cleared by a large taxpayer under sub rule (1) of rule 12BB, the details of such clearances may be mentioned separately. Under columns (8) and (9) of the table at serial number 3, the words 'inter unit transfer by large taxpayer under rule 12BB (1) ' may be mentioned. There is no need to give the value for such inter unit transfers.
6. Details at serial number 4 and 5 are to be provided only by a large taxpayers defined under sub-rule (ea) of rule 2 of the Central Excise Rules, 2002 who have opted to operate as large taxpayer to provide break up of the intermediate goods that are either transferred or received.
7. If a specified product attracts different rates of duty, within the same month, then such details should be separately mentioned.

   For example: On the 10th of a month, the effective rate of duty leviable for the product is changed, then the details relating to production, clearance and payment of duty need to be mentioned separately for the period up to 9th of the month and from 10th to the end of the month.
8. 8-digit CETSH Number may be indicated without any decimal point.
9. Wherever quantity codes appear, indicate relevant abbreviations
10. Where the duty is specific and is charged based on specified unit quantity, the same quantity code must be used for showing clearance figures.
11. In column (6) of Table at serial number 3, the assessable value means,
    (a) where goods attract advalorem rate of duty, the value under section 4 of Central Excise Act, 1944 (1 of 1944);
    (b) where goods are covered under section 4A of the Act, the assessable value as worked out under MRP after allowing deductions as provided under section 4A of the Act;
    (c) in case of goods for which the tariff value is fixed, such tariff value;
    (d) in case of specific rated goods, the aggregated invoice value of the goods excluding all taxes;

(e) in case of combination of advalorem and specific duties, the transaction value under section 4 of the Act;

(f) in case of exports under Bond, the ARE-1/ARE-2/ invoice value.,

12. In Tables at serial numbers 3 and 6 the 'Other duties' paid/payable, as applicable, may be mentioned
13. In column (10) in Table at serial number 3, indicate the effective rates of duty. Columns which are not applicable, may be left blank.
14. Goods cleared under compounded levy scheme, indicate the aggregate duty payable in column (12) of Table at serial number 3 as per the compounded levy scheme. The columns not applicable may be kept blank.
15. In case the goods are assessed provisionally, the details may be given separately in Table at serial number 3. In column (13) of Table at serial number 3, specify the Unique Identification number mentioned in the order for Provisional Assessment.
16. The details of the challans for duty payment should be mentioned in Table at Sr.No. 6. In Table at S.No.9, separate challans should be used for pre-deposit of duty for the purpose of appellateremedy, for paying dues for approaching Settlement Commission and for other payments.
17. In column (5) of Table at serial number 9, specify the Order-in-Original number and date relating to the payment of arrears of duty and of interest, the period for which the said interest has been paid. For other miscellaneous payments, mention the source document number and date. Miscellaneous payment includes penalty, redemption fine, and pre-deposit.
18. In the Tables at serial numbers 6 and 9, the BSR codes of the Bank branch should be indicated when the instructions to this effect are issued.
19. Additional information required to be given only by a large taxpayer defined under sub-rule (ea) of rule 2 of the Central Excise Rules 2002, who has opted to operate as large taxpayer has been indicated with an asterix (*)

15.02 Form ER-5

ER-5 is an Annual Return relating to Principal Inputs (Quantity) used in the manufacture of Finished Goods.

At *Excise Forms* Menu (F-39A), select ER-5 to get ER-5 Form printing screen (F-41A). At ER-15 Form printing screen (F-41A), Set the options to get ER-5 Form (F-41B) as per options set.

F-41A: ER-5 Form printing

Form ER 5	
Excise Unit	: Bonded Godown 1
From (blank for beginning)	: 1-4-2009
To (blank for end)	: 31-3-2010
Place	: Kolkata
Date	: 1-4-2010
Assessee Name	: ABC MFG

Contents of Form ER-5

- **Name of the Manufacturer**: Name of the manufacturer (as entered at *Unit Mailing Name* at **Statutory & Taxation screen)**
- **Pan based Registration Number**: **Registration Number** of the **Excise Unit** (as entered at Statutory & Taxation screen) of the Excise Unit.
- **Annual Declaration**: Tick the appropriate Box indicating whether the declaration is new or amended.
- **New Declaration**: Tick New declaration box If the Form for the period is submitted first time
- **Amendments to the declaration already filed**: Tick the box If the Form ER 5 is a amended
- **Declaration for the Year**: The year for which the Form relates to.
- **Principal inputs used in the manufacture of Finished Goods:**The Table below shows the detail of principal inputs used in the manufacture of Finished Goods.
    - o **Description of Principal Inputs**: Name of the Principal Inputs used in the production of finished goods
    - o **Central Excise Tariff Sub-Heading No. of Principal Inputs**: HSN code of the Principal Inputs
    - o **Quantity Code**: Reporting UOM of the Principal Inputs
    - o **Description of Finished goods in which principal input mentioned in column (2) is used**: Name of the finished goods produced using the principal inputs
    - o **Central Excise Tariff Sub-heading No. of finished goods**: HSN code of the Finished goods.
    - o **Quantity code**: Reporting UOM of the Finished Goods
    - o **Quantity of Principal units mentioned in column (2) required for use in the manufacture of unit quantity of finished goods mentioned in column (5)**: Quantity of the principal inputs used in the production of the finished goods.
- **Place & Date**: Place & Date of preparation of Report

FORM ER - 5
[Sub-rule (1) of rule 9A of CENVAT Credit Rules,2004]

1. Name of the Manufacturer : Bonded Godown 1
2. PAN based Registration Number : ABCDE1234D123XM
3. Annual Declaration
(i) New Declaration :
(ii) Amendments to declaration already filed :
(Please tick the appropriate box)
4. Declaration for the Financial Year : 2009

Sr.No.	Description of Principal Inputs	Central Excise Tariff Sub-Heading No. of Principal inputs	Quantity Code	Description of finished goods in which principal input mentioned in column (2) is used	Central Excise Tariff Sub-Heading No.of finished goods	Quantity Code	Quantity of Principal input mentioned in column (2) required for use in the manufacture of unit quantity of finished goods mentioned in column (5)
(1)	(2)	(3)	(4)	(5)	(6)	(7)	(8)
1	Mother Board Port	13456789	U				
				Mother Board	13456789	U	8
				Monitor	13456789	U	8
				Mother Board Port	13456789	U	80

NOTE :-

Please indicate the abbreviation referred to in Instruction No.7 mentioned in Form E.R.-1 and Form E.R.-3 specified in the Government of India, Ministry of Finance (Department of Revenue) vide No.25/2004 -Central Excise (N.T.), dated the 27th September,2004 published vide G.S.R.No.643(E) dated the 25th September,2004.

5. (i) I/We ABC MFG hereby declare that the information given above is true, correct and complete in every respect to the best of my/our knowledge and belief.

(ii) I/We/am/are authorized to sign this return.

(Name in capital letters and Signature of the Authorized

Place : **Kolkata**
Date : **1-Apr-2010**

ACKNOWLEDGMENT

Declaration for the Financial Year :			**2009**
	DD	**MM**	**YYYY**
Date of Receipt			

F-41B: Form ER-5

15.03 ER-6 Form

ER- 6 is a **Monthly** Return showing the quantitative details of **Opening Balance, Receipts** and **Consumption** of Principal inputs and finished goods manufactured.

At *Excise Forms* Menu (F-39A), select ER-6 to get ER-6 Form printing screen (F-42A). At ER-6 Form printing screen (F-42A), set the options to get ER-6 Form (F-42B) as per options set.

Report Titles

Form ER 6

Excise Unit	:	**Bonded Godown 1**
From (blank for beginning)	:	**1-4-2009**
To (blank for end)	:	**31-3-2010**
Place	:	**Kolkata**
Date	:	**1-4-2010**
Assessee Name	:	**ABC MFG**

F-42A: Form ER-6 Printing

FORM ER - 6

[Sub-rule (3) of rule 9A of CENVAT Credit Rules, 2004]

1. Name of the Manufacturer	Bonded Godown 1
2. PAN based Registration Number	ABCDE1234D123XM
3. Month to which the return relates	04 2009

4. Details of receipt and consumption of principal inputs and finished excisable goods :

Sr.No.	Description of Principal inputs	Quantity Code	Opening Balance	Receipt	Taken for use in the manufacture of dutiable and exempted finished goods	Removed as such for export or for home consumption	Closing Balance	Finished goods manufactured out of inputs		Quantity Code finished goods	Quantity of finished goods manufactured
								Sr.No.	Description		
(1)	(2)	(3)	(4)	(5)	(6)	(7)	(8)	(9 A)	(9 B)	(10)	(11)
1	CPU P4	U	30	3			33				
2	[illegible]	U			8	10	(-)18				
								1	Mother Board	U	1
								1	Monitor	U	1

5. Details of waste and scrap arising during manufacture and cleared/destroyed :

Sr.No.	Description of Waste and Scrap	Quantity Code	Quantity	
			Cleared	Destroyed
(1)	(2)	(3)	(4 A)	(4 B)

NOTE:-

(1) Finished Goods mentioned in Column 9(B) should be stated in respect of each of the inputs mentioned in Column (2) and (6).

(2) Please indicate the abbreviation referred to in instruction No.7 mentioned in Form E.R.-1 and Form E.R.-3 specified in the Government of India, Ministry of Finance (Department of Revenue) vide No.25/2004 Central Excise (N.T), dated 27th Sepetember, 2004 published vide G.S.R.No.643 (E)dated the 25th of September, 2004.

6. (i) I/We ABC MFG declared that the particulars declared above have been compared with the records and books of my/our factory/warehouse and the same are true and Correct to the best of my/our knowledge.

(ii) I/We/am/are authorized to sign this return.

(Authorised signatory)

Place : **Kolkata**
Date : **1-Apr-2010**

ACKNOWLEDGMENT

	MM	YYYY
Return of excisable goods and availment of CENVAT credit for the month of	04	2009

	DD	MM	YYYY
Date of Receipt			

F-42B: Form ER-6

Contents of ER-6

- **Name of Manufacturer**: Name of the manufacturing unit
- **PAN based Registration Number**: **Registration Number** of the **Excise Unit.**
- **Month to which the return relates**: Month for which the declaration is generated.
- **Details of receipt and consumption of principal inputs and finished excisable goods**: The Table displays the details of principal inputs used in the manufacture of finished goods.
  - o **Description of Principal Inputs**: Name of the Principal Inputs used in the production of finished goods.
  - o **Quantity Code**: **Reporting UOM** of the Principal Inputs.
  - o **Opening Balance**: Opening Stock as on the Start Date of the specified period the report at the beginning of the month.
  - o **Receipt**: Principal inputs purchased and received during the month.

- o **Taken for use in the manufacture of dutiable and exempted finished goods**: Quantity of goods taken for manufacture of dutiable and exempted finished goods.
- o **Removed as such for Export or for Home Consumption**: Principal Inputs removed as such for Export and home (domestic) consumption.
- o **Closing Balance**: Closing Balance of principal inputs as on the Report End Date.
- o **Finished goods Manufactured out of inputs**: Shows the Serial Number and Name of the Finished goods manufactured.
  - **Serial Number**: Manufacturing Journal Voucher number of related to manufacture finished goods.
  - **Description**: Name of the finished goods manufactured
- o **Quantity Code of finished goods**: Reporting UOM defined in the finished goods manufactured
- o **Quantity of finished goods manufactured**: Quantity of Finished Goods manufactured

- **Details of waste and scrap arising during manufacture and cleared/destroyed:**
- **Place & Date**: Place & Date of report preparation

15.04 ER-8

***ER-8* is a Quarterly Return** to be filed by the manufactures who are neither availing input credit nor clearing the goods which are charged at excise over 1%.

Report Titles	
Form ER 8	
Excise Unit	: **Bonded Godown 1**
From (blank for beginning)	: **1-1-2010**
To (blank for end)	: **31-3-2010**
Place	: **Kolkata**
Date	: **1-4-2010**
Assessee Name	: **ABC MFG**

F-43A: ER- 8 Return printing screen

Form ER - 8

[See rule 12 of the Central Excise Rules, 2002]

Original

[To be submitted by the assessee falling under sixth proviso to rule 12(1) of the Central Excise Rules, 2002]

Return of excisable goods cleared @ 1% duty for the quarter			
From	Apr 2009	To	Mar 2010

1 Registration No : ABCDE1234D123XM

2 Name of the Assessee : Bonded Godown 1

3 Details of the manufacture, clearance and duty payable :

Sr. No	CETSH NO.	Description of goods	Unit of Quantity	Serial Number in notification no: 1/2011	Opening Balance	Quantity Manufactured	Quantity cleared	Closing balance	Assessable Value (Rs.)	Excise duty payable @ 2 %	Education cess & Secondary Education Cess (2%+1 %)	Total Duty payable
1	2	3	4	5	6	7	8	9	10	11	12	13

4. Details of duty paid on excisable goods :

Duty Code	Amount(Rs.)	Challan No:	Date	Bank Code	Branch Code
1	2	3	4	5	6
Cenvat	6,060.00	123	1-Jan-2010	0023456	
Edu. Cess & Sec & Higher Education cess		13	2-Apr-2009	456789	
Total duty paid	6,060.00				

5. Details of other payments made :

Payment	Amount (Rs.)	Challan No:	Date	Bank Code	Branch Code	Remark
1	2	3	4	5	6	7
Arrears						
Penalty						
Interest						
Others						

6. Self- assessment memorandum :

a) I hereby declare that the information given in this Return is true, correct and complete in every respect and that I am authorised to sign on behalf of the assessee.

b) During the quarter, total Rs. 6,060.00 was deposited vide GAR7 Challans (copies enclosed).

c)

Date : Kolkata

Place : 31-Mar-2010

ABC MANUFCATURING

Name and signature of Assessee or Authorised Signatory

ACKNOWLEDGEMENT

Return of excisable goods cleared @ 1% duty for the quarter

From ______ To ______

DD MM YYYY

Date of Receipt

Name and Signature of the Range Officer with Official Seal

F-43B: ER-8 Return

At *Excise Forms* Menu (F-39A), select ER-8 to get ER-8 Form printing screen (F-43A). Set the options to get ER-8 Form (F-43B) as per options set.

Contents of ER-8

1. **Registration No**: 15-digit PAN based the Excise Registration number of the Company.
2. **Name of the Assessee**: Name as appearing in the Registration Certificate (as entered at ***Unit Mailing Name*** at *Excise Registration Details* screen).
3. **Details of the Manufacture, Clearance and duty payable**: Details of goods under following columns.
   - Serial Number: Running serial number, starting from 1, under the sub heading
   - **CETSH**: 8 digit CETSH Number (Tariff Code) of the goods manufactured/cleared.
   - **Description of Goods**: Tariff Classification Name.
   - **Unit of Quantity**: Reporting UOM of the excisable goods Manufactured /cleared.
   - **Sr. No in Notification no: 1/2011CE**: Serial number in the notification
   - **Opening Balance**: Opening Stock Quantity at he start of the Reporting period
   - **Quantity Manufactured**: Quantity of goods manufactured during the reporting period (Quarter).
   - **Quantity Cleared**: Quantity cleared during the reporting period (Quarter)
   - **Closing Balance**: This column displays the Closing Balance Quantity of the Excisable Goods
   - **Assessable Value**: This column displays the assessable value on which the excise duty is calculated.
   - **Excise Duty payable @ 1%**: Displays the Excise Duty payable on the goods removed during the Quarter.
   - **Education Cess and Secondary Education Cess (2% +1%)**: This column displays the education cess and secondary education cess amount payable on the goods removed during the Quarter.
   - **Total Duty Payable**: This column displays the total duty payable during the Quarter.

5. **Details of Duty paid on excisable goods**: under this serial number, details of duty paid on the excisable goods will be captured.
6. **Duty Code**: This column displays the Type of Duty paid on excisable goods during the Quarter.
7. **Amount**: Displays the amount of duty paid during the Quarter.
8. **Challan No.**: Displays the Challan Number of the duty payments made during the Quarter. If duty is paid more than once during the Quarter, the first 3 payments challan Number will be captured in Challan number column.
9. **Date**: Displays the data of payment of duty to government entered in Challan.
10. **Bank Code**: Displays the BSR Code of the Bank through which the excise duty is paid to the Government.

6. **Details of other payments made**: Under this serial number, details of other payments like penalty, interest etc. paid during the Quarter will be captured.
7. **Payment**: This column displays the other payments type.
8. **Amount**: capture the amount of other payment made during the Quarter
9. **Challan no.**: The Challan number through which the other payments are made Government will be captured in this column.
10. **Date**: Displays the data of payment of other payments to government entered in Challan.
11. **Bank Code**: Displays the BSR Code of the Bank through which the other payments are made to the Government.
12. **Remarks**: Captures the details of remarks, if any.

7. **Self-assessment Memorandum**: Under this section details of self assessment of the assessee along with the total amount of duty paid during the Quarter and the invoice number under which the excisable goods are cleared will be captured.
8. **Date**: This field displays the date on which Form ER- 8 is generated. In this field, date mentioned in **Date** field of **Excise ER8 Print Configuration** screen will be captured.
9. **Place**: This field displays the place of generating Form ER- 8. In this field, place mentioned in **Place** field of **Excise ER8 Print Configuration** screen will be captured.
10. **Name & Signature of Assessee or Authorised Signatory**: Displays the name of Authorised Signatory mentioned in **Assessee Name** field of **Excise ER8 Print Configuration** screen.

Instructions For ER-8: The following are the instructions given by Excise Department for filing ER-8 Form

1. Indicate the 15-digit PAN based registration number and the name as appearing in the Registration Certificate.
2. In case more than one item is manufactured, additional row may be inserted in each table, wherever necessary.
3. In case the goods are cleared for export under Bond, the details of clearance may be mentioned separately.
4. 8-digit CETSH Number may be indicated under the column CETSH.
5. Wherever quantity codes appear, indicate relevant abbreviations

01 Goods Imports

So far, we have discussed about normal transactions Domestic Dealer / Manufacturer. Now we discuss cases relating to Importer

01.01 Customs Duty

In case of Imports, goods imported will be first stored in Customs Bonded Warehouse. Imported goods will be released from the bonded warehouse only on payment of Customs duty. In practice Importers withdraw the goods (partially or wholly) from the bonded warehouse as and when required. CENVAT Credit is availed only on clearance from Customs Bonded Warehouse on payment of Duty.

So, in case of Imports, instead of Excise Duty & Cess; Customs Duty, CVD & Cess on CVD is charged

01.02 Customs Duty Computation

The following example shows the various components of Customs Duty and Duty Computation

Example: Imported Gods of 5000 Pcs@ 150 =Rs.7,50,000 (Assessable Value)

Duty Head	Computation Formula	Computation Details	Amount
Customs Duty	On Assessable Value	30% on 7,50,000	2,25,000
CVD	On (Assessable Value + Customs Duty)	10% on (7,50,000 + 2,25,000) = 10% on 9,75,000	97,500
Ed Cess on CVD	On CVD	2% on 97,500	1,950
Sec. Ed Cess on CVD	On CVD	1% on 97,500	975
Ed Cess on Cust Duty	On (Customs Duty + CVD + Ed Cess on CVD + Sec. Ed Cess on CVD)	2% on (2,25,000 + 97,500 + 1,950+ 975) = 2% on 3,25,425	6,509
S. Ed Cess on Cust Duty	On (Customs Duty + CVD + Ed Cess on CVD + Sec. Ed Cess on CVD)	1% on (2,25,000 + 9,750 + 1,950+ 975) = 1% on 3,25,425	3,254
Additional Duty on Imports	On (Assessable Value + Customs Duty + CVD + Ed Cess on CVD + Sec. Ed Cess on CVD)	4% on (7,50,000+ 2,25,000 + 1,950+ 975 + 6,509+3,254) = 4% on 10,85,188	43,408

02 Customs Duty for Manufacturers

First, we discuss the process of recording for Manufacturers for Imort of Materials

02.01 Duty Ledger Accounts Creation

Ledger Account creation has been explained earlier. Create the Duty Ledger Accounts for each of the Accounts as described earlier. At Ledger Creation / Alteration screen, at *Duty Head*, select from the list as follows

- CVD on Import
- Customs Duty
- Cess on Duty
- Cess on Customs Duty
- Additional Duty

Customs Duty Ledger Accounts: Customs Duty (including Cess on Customs Duty) are like expenses for Purchase of Imported goods. So, such accounts (F-1A) are to be treated as Purchase Expenses and to be allocated to Stock Items.

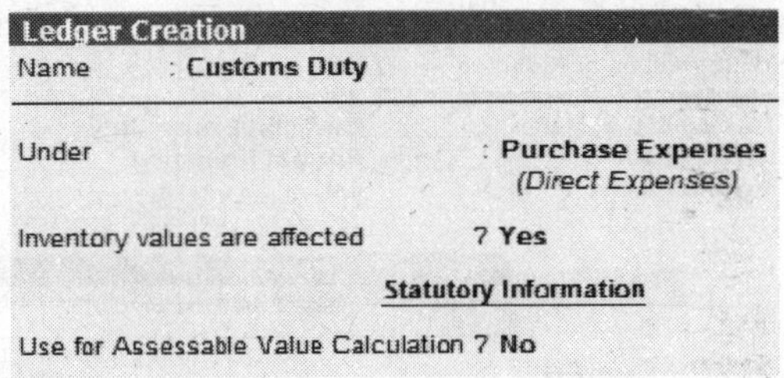
Ledger Creation
Name : Customs Duty
Under : Purchase Expenses (Direct Expenses)
Inventory values are affected ? Yes
Statutory Information
Use for Assessable Value Calculation ? No

F-1A: Customs Duty

In this way, create other Purchase Expenses ledger accounts also.

Such expenses are to be allocated to the respective Stock Item. So, set Yes at *Inventory Values are affected* (F-1A) to get Ledger Allocation details screen during voucher entry involving such ledger accounts.

Duty Ledger Accounts

In case of Imports, CVD (and Cess on CVD) and Special Duty on Imports are to be paid. CVD (Counter Veiling Duty) is like an alternate Excise Duty on Import. Like Excise Duty, Cess on CVD is also applicable. So, CENVAT credit is available on CVD and Cess on CVD,.

Ledger Creation

Name	: **CVD on Imports**
Under	: **Current Assets**
Type of Duty/Tax	: **CENVAT**
Excise Accounting Code	:
Duty Head	: **Basic Excise Duty**
Inventory values are affected	? **No**
Percentage of Calculation (eg 5)	? **10 %**
Method of Calculation	: **On Assessable Value**
Rounding Method	: **Normal Rounding**
Rounding Limit	: **0.01**

F-2A: CVD Ledger Account Creation

So, create the Ledger Accounts (F-2A to F-2D) in same way as CENVAT Ledger Accounts explained earlier.

Ledger Creation

Name	: **Edu Cess on CVD**
Under	: **Current Assets**
Type of Duty/Tax	: **CENVAT**
Excise Accounting Code	:
Duty Head	: **Education Cess**
Inventory values are affected	? **No**
Percentage of Calculation (eg 5)	? **2 %**
Method of Calculation	: **On Total Excise Duty**
Rounding Method	: **Normal Rounding**
Rounding Limit	: **0.01**

F-2B: Ed Cess on CVD Ledger Account Creation

Ledger Creation

Name	: **Sec Edu Cess on CVD**
Under	: **Current Assets**
Type of Duty/Tax	: **CENVAT**
Excise Accounting Code	:
Duty Head	: **Secondary Education Cess**
Inventory values are affected	? **No**
Percentage of Calculation (eg 5)	? **1 %**
Method of Calculation	: **On Total Excise Duty**
Rounding Method	: **Normal Rounding**
Rounding Limit	: **0.01**

F-2C: Sec Ed Cess on CVD Ledger Account Creation

- **Type of Duty**: At *Type of Duty*, select CENVAT, as CENVAT is allowed on these accounts.
- **Duty Head**: At *Duty Head*, select the respective duty head from the list.
- **Method of Calculation**: At *Method of Calculation*, the respective option is auto carried depending on the Type of Duty selected.

Ledger Creation

Name	: **Add Import Duty**
Under	: **Current Assets**
Type of Duty/Tax	: **CENVAT**
Excise Accounting Code	:
Duty Head	: **Special Excise Duty**
Inventory values are affected	? **No**
Percentage of Calculation (eg 5)	? **4 %**
Method of Calculation	: **On Assessable Value**
Rounding Method	: **Normal Rounding**
Rounding Limit	: **0.01**

F-2D: Special Excise Duty on Imports Ledger Account Creation

02.02 Stock Item Creation

Stock Item Creation has been explained earlier. At Stock Item creation screen (F-3A), at *Duty Details* screen (F-3C), enter the Duty Heads & Applicable Rates, on which CENVAT credit is available, as described earlier

- CVD
- Ed Cess on CVD
- Sec. Ed Cess on CVD
- Additional Duty on Imports

Stock Item Creation — **ABC Manufacturing**

Name : **Item (Imported)**

Set/Modify Default Ledgers for Invoicing ? **No**

		Tax Information	
Under	: **Primary**		
Units	: **Pcs**	Tariff Classification	: **Computer Goods**
Alternate Units	: **Not Applicable**	Set/Alter Excise Details	? **Yes**

F-3A: Stock Item creation

At Stock Item creation screen (F-3A), set Yes at *Set / Alter Excise Details* to get *Excise Details* entry screen (F-3C)

Excise Details for : **Item (Imported)**
Tariff Classification : **Computer Goods**

Excise Unit Name	Reporting UOM	Conversion Factor	Set/Alter Duty Details	Stock Item Type
Bonded Godown 1	**U**	**1 U = 1 Pcs**	**Yes**	**Principal Input**

F-3B: Excise Details for Stock Item creation

Duty Details for : **Item (Imported)**
Tariff Classification : **Computer Goods**
Excise Unit : **Bonded Godown 1**

Valuation Type : **Ad Valorem**

Type of Duty	Applicable From	Rate of Duty
Basic Excise Duty	**1-Apr-2009**	**10 %**
Education Cess	**1-Apr-2009**	**2 %**
Secondary Education Cess	**1-Apr-2009**	**1 %**
Special Excise Duty	**1-Apr-2009**	**4 %**

F-3C: Duty Details for Stock Item creation

At get *Excise Details* entry screen (F-3C), enter the respective duty details

02.03 Debit Note Voucher Class

To claim CENVAT credit, create a Debit Note Voucher Class (F-4A), as explained earlier.

Voucher Type Creation — **ABC Manufacturing**

Name : **CVClm**

General		**Printing**		**Name of Class**
Type of Voucher	: **Debit Note**	Print after saving Voucher	? **Yes**	**CvclmCl**
Abbr.	: Cvclm			
Method of Voucher Numbering	? **Automatic**			
Use Advance Configuration	? **No**			
Use EFFECTIVE Dates for Vouchers	? **No**			
Make 'Optional' as default	? **No**			
Use Common Narration	? **Yes**			
Narrations for each entry	? **No**			
Use for Excise	? **No**			

F-4A: Debit Note Voucher Type creation

ABC Manufacturing	
	Class : CvclmCl
Use Class for Excise / CENVAT Adjustments	? Yes
Use Class for Interest Accounting	? No

F-4B: Debit Note Voucher Class set up

At *Debit Note Voucher Class* (F-4A), set *No* at *Use for Excise* (don't be confused with the text of the prompt). At name of Class (F-4A), enter the Voucher Class Name, to get *Voucher Class Set Up* screen (F-4B)

At the *Voucher Class Set Up* screen (F-4B), set *Yes* at *Use Class for Excise / CENVAT Adjustments* (you get this field only when you set *No* at *Use for Excise* at main voucher entry screen: F-4A),

02.04 Purchase Invoice

Often, the whole lot is cleared on payment of duty at a time. Sometimes, materials are cleared in installments, as and when required, on payment of customs duty on the cleared materials only.

- **Clearance of Full materials**: When full materials are cleared at a time, you may enter a Purchase Voucher for the entire import quantity, without any pending Tracking Number.
- **Partial Clearance**: When materials are cleared in instalments, you have to create Purchase Invoice with Pending Tracking Number, and subsequently, create Receipt Notes for the quantity release, as explained later in this Chapter.

Here, we explain the creation of Purchase Voucher for the entire quantity, at a time

Purchase Voucher Entry: Create a purchase voucher, either as Normal Purchase Voucher (F-5A) or Excise Purchase Voucher (F-5B), as described earlier.

In case of Normal Purchase Voucher, at *Party Details* screen, at *Supplier Details* section, enter the details of supplier as described earlier.

In case of Excise Purchase Voucher, at ***Manufacturer / Importer Details*** section (F-5C), you may specify your company details with excise details, since you can declare as Self Importer (equivalent to Manufacturer). To avoid entry of self details, you may create a Party Ledger in the name of your own company.

Accounting Voucher Creation — Ctrl + M

Purchase No. 5 — 1-Jul-2009 Wednesday
Supplier Invoice No. : 23 — Date : 1-Jul-2009

Party's A/c Name : Szbroad Technology Co.,Ltd
Purchase Ledger : Purchase

Name of Item	Quantity	Rate per	Amount
Item (Imported)	5,000 Pcs	150.00 Pcs	7,50,000.00
Narration:	5,000 Pcs		7,50,000.00

Item imported

F-5A: Purchase (Import): Normal Purchase Mode

At *Nature of Purchase* (F-5A, F-5B), *Importer* will be carried as default. At Purchase Ledger (F-5A, F-5B), select the applicable Purchase Ledger.

Accounting Voucher Creation — Ctrl + M

ExcPur No. 3 — 1-Jul-2009 Wednesday
Supplier Invoice No. : 23 — Date : 1-Jul-2009
Excise Unit : Bonded Godown 1

Party's A/c Name : Szbroad Technology Co.,Ltd
Nature of Purchase: Importer
Current Balance :
Purchase Ledger : Purchase

Name of Item	Quantity	Rate per	Amount
Item (Imported)	5,000 Pcs	150.00 Pcs	7,50,000.00
Rate of Duty : 10%			
	5,000 Pcs		7,50,000.00

F-5B: Purchase (Import): Excise Purchase Mode

In the Import Purchase Invoice (F-5A, F-5B), there will be no entry for Excise Duty etc. Customs Duty (and Cess on Customs Duty) will be paid to Customs Deptt to make clearance of the goods from Customs.

Order Details
Order No(s) :

Supplier's Details
Supplier : Szbroad Technology Co.,Ltd
Address :
Sales Tax No. :
CST Number :
Type of Dealer : Not Applicable

Manufacturer / Importer / Consigner Details
Name : ABC Mfg
Address :
Excise Regn No. :
Importer Exporter Code :
Range :
Division :
Commissionerate :
Invoice No. :
Invoice Date :

F-5C: Party Details for Excise Purchase Mode

02.05 Customs Duty Payment

At the time of payment of Customs Duty, you may create a payment voucher (F-6A) charging customs duty paid. Payment voucher creation for expenses have been explained earlier.

Payment No. 1 — 2-Jul-2009 Thursday

Particulars		Debit	Credit
Dr Customs Duty		2,34,763.00	
Item (Imported)	2,34,763.00		
Cr HDFC			2,34,763.00
Narration:		2,34,763.00	2,34,763.00

Customs Duty & Cess 225000+6509+3254 paid

F-6A: Customs Duty Payment Voucher

Item Allocations for : **Item (Imported)**

Godown	Quantity	Rate per	Amount
Order No.: Not Applicable			
Bonded Godown 1			2,34,763.00
			2,34,763.00

F-6B: Item Allocation for Ledger Account of Payment Voucher

As you have set *Yes* at *Inventory Values are affected* at Customs Duty (and Cess on Customs Duty) Ledger Accounts creation (F-1A), on selection of these Ledger Accounts in Payment voucher (F-6A), you will get Item Allocation screen (F-6B) for each of the ledger account.

At the respective Item allocation screen (F-6B), select the Item and specify only the Amount (do not enter Quantity, as the stock will again be increased by the Quantity entered).

This way, you may create Payment Voucher for other Purchase expenses also.

02.06 Debit Note for CENVAT Claim

Now, you have to create Debit Note for CENVAT Claim to be reflected in relevant Excise Returns. Debit Note entry using Voucher Class has been explained earlier

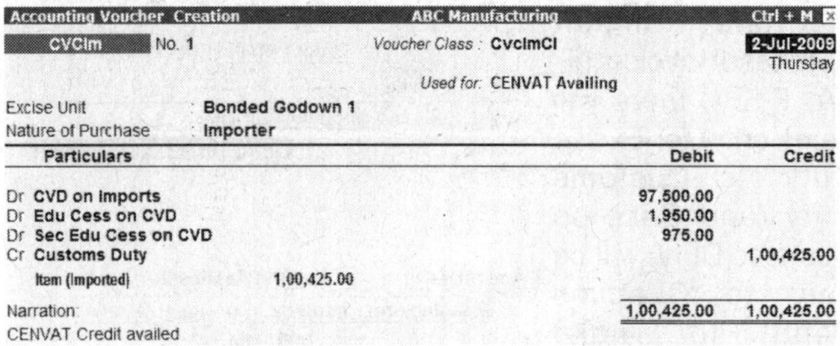

F-7A: Debit Note for CENVAT creation

At Debit Note entry screen (F-7A), select the CVD Account and enter the CENVAT amount for CVD to get Duty Details screen for CVD (F-7B). Enter the respective details as explained earlier.

CVD Account Details: Next select the Education Cess on CVD Account and enter the CENVAT amount for CVD to get Education Cess on CVD Details screen for CVD (F-7C).

Education Cess on CVD Account Details: At Voucher entry screen (F-7A), next select the Education Cess on CVD Account and enter the respective CENVAT amount to get Education Cess on CVD Details screen for CVD (F-7C).

At Duty Details screen for Education Cess on CVD (F-7C), set *Yes* at *Copy Details for Previous Duty Ledgers* to carry the relevant details as entered at previous ledger screen (F-7B), to the current screen (F-7C), so that you do not have to enter the details again. The figures are auto computed for Education Cess on CVD (F-7C), as per applicable Rate specified at Duty Details screen (F-3C) of Stock Item creation screen

Secondary Education Cess on CVD Account Details:: In the same way, at Voucher entry screen (F-7A), next select the Secondary Education Cess on CVD Account and enter the respective CENVAT amount to get Education Cess on CVD Details screen for CVD (F-7D).

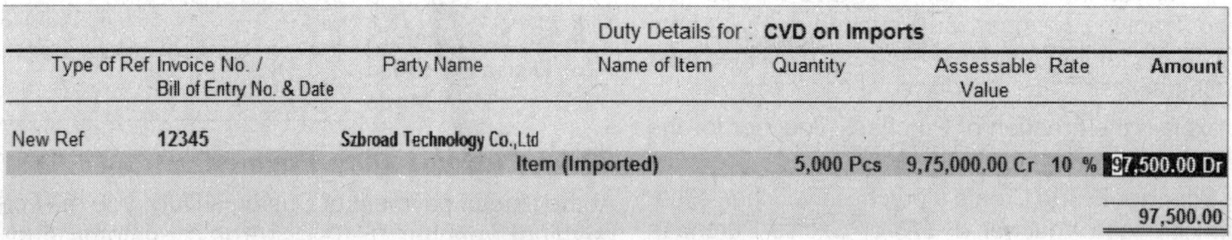

F-7B: Duty details for CVD

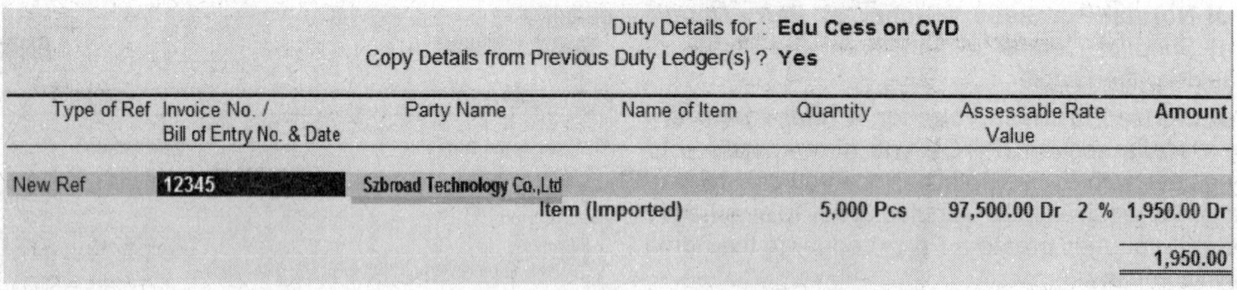

F-7C: Duty details for CVD

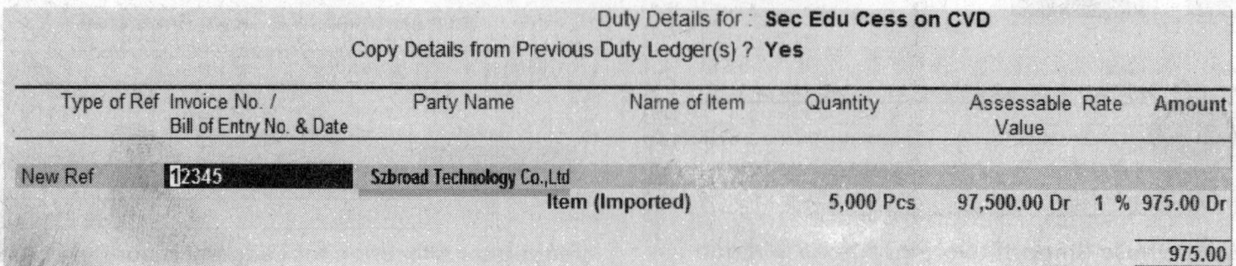

F-7D: Duty details for CVD

In the same way, At Duty Details screen for Secondary Education Cess on CVD (F-7D), set *Yes* at *Copy Details for Previous Duty Ledgers* to carry the relevant details entered at previous ledger screen (F-7C), to the current screen (F-7D). The figures are auto computed for Secondary Education Cess on CVD (F-7D), as per applicable Rate specified at Duty Details screen (F-3C) of Stock Item creation screen

Item Allocations for : **Item (Imported)**

Godown	Quantity	Rate	per	Amount
Order No.: ▯ Not Applicable				
				1,00,425.00
				1,00,425.00

F-7E: Duty details for CVD

03 Customs Duty for Dealers

We have described Import Purchase Voucher entry for manufacturers and availing of CENVAT credit on such Imports. Now we discus about Purchase Invoice entry for Imports for Dealers

03.01 Stock Item Creation

We have described Stock Item creation for Imported Item, manufacturers (organizations who have set *Manufacturer* at *Registration Type* at *Excise Registration Details* screen: F-1B/06-02) earlier (F-3A).

Stock Item Creation — Hot Plates

Name : **Item (Imported)**

Set/Modify Default Ledgers for Invoicing ? **No**

		Tax Information	
Under	: **Computer Goods**		
Units	: **Pcs**	Tariff Classification	: **Computer Goods**
Alternate Units	: ▯ **Not Applicable**	Set/Alter Excise Details	? **Yes**

F-8A: Import Stock Item creation screen

Registered Dealer (organizations who have set *Dealer* at *Registration Type* at *Excise Registration Details* screen: F-1B/06-02), should create Stock Item Masters (F-8A), in the same way as described earlier(F-3A)

Excise Details for : **Item (Imported)**
Tariff Classification : **Computer Goods**

Excise Unit Name	Reporting UOM	Conversion Factor	Set/Alter Duty Details	Stock Item Type
Bonded Godown	**U**		**Yes**	

F-8B: Excise Details for Import Stock Item

The entry screen for Excise Details of Stock Item (F-8B) is similar to that as shown at F-3B.The *Stock Item Type* column (F-8B) is not activated as shown in F-3B

However, in case of Dealer, at Duty details screen (F-8C), you have to specify the CVD Duty heads instead of Excise Duty heads as shown in case of Manufacturer (F-3C)

Duty Details for : **Item (Imported)**
Tariff Classification : **Computer Goods**
Excise Unit : **Bonded Godown**

Valuation Type : **Ad Valorem**

Type of Duty	Applicable From	Rate of Duty	Method of Calculation
Countervailing Duty (CVD)	1-Apr-2009	10 %	On Assessable Value
Education Cess on CVD	1-Apr-2009	2 %	On Duty Value
Secondary Education Cess on CVD	1-Apr-2009	1 %	On Duty Value
Additional Duty (Imports)	1-Apr-2009	4 %	On Duty Value

F-8C: Duty Details for Import Stock Item

03.02 Supplier Ledger Creation

Supplier Ledger creation (F-9A) has been described earlier.

Ledger Creation — Hot Plates

Name : **Szboad Technology Co Ltd**

Under	: **Sundry Creditors** *(Current Liabilities)*	**Mailing Details**	
		Name	: **Szboad Technology Co Ltd**
		Address	
Maintain balances bill-by-bill	? **Yes**		
Default Credit Period	:		
Inventory values are affected	? **No**		
Cost centres are applicable	? **No**	State	: ▯ **Not Applicable**
		PIN Code	
		Provide Bank Details	: **No**
		Tax Information	
		PAN / IT No.	:
		Set/Alter VAT Details	? **No**
		Set/Alter Excise Details?	**Yes**

F-9A: Supplier Ledger creation

At Supplier Ledger creation screen (F-9A), set Yes at Set / Alter Excise Details to get *Excise Details* screen(F-9B)

Excise Details

Excise Registration (ECC) No.	: **ABCDE5678001D**
Date of Registration	: **1-Apr-2004**
Importer Exporter Code (IEC)	: **123457**
Range	: **1234**
Division	: **123**
Commissionerate	: **12**
Default Nature of Purchase	: **Importer**

F-9B: Excise Details screen of Supplier

Nature of Purchase

▯ Not Applicable
Agent of Importer *(Consignment Agent)*
Agent of Manufacturer *(Consignment Agent)*
First Stage Dealer
From Agent of Dealer
From Agent of Importer
From Agent of Manufacturer
Importer
Manufacturer
Manufacturer Depot
Purchase from Importer
Second Stage Dealer

F-9C: Supply Nature list

At *Excise Details* screen(F-9B), enter the details as described earlier. At *Default Status of Purchase*, select *Importer* from the list (F-9C)

03.03 Purchase Invoice creation

Purchase Invoice (Excise goods Purchase) has been

explained earlier. Here we explain points related to Purchase Invoice for Imports, by Registered Dealer (F-10A)

Purch-Exc No. 2 — 1-Jul-2009 Wednesday
Supplier Invoice No. : 2 Date : 1-Jul-2009
Excise Unit : Bonded Godown

Party's A/c Name : Szboad Technology Co Ltd
Nature of Purchase: Importer

Purchase Ledger : Purchase
VAT/Tax Class : Not Applicable

Name of Item	Quantity	Rate per	Amount
Item (Imported)	5,000 Pcs	150.00 Pcs	7,50,000.00
	5,000 Pcs		7,50,000.00

Narration:
Import of materials

F-10A: Purchase Invoice entry

At Purchase Invoice entry screen (F-10A), on selection of Party Ledger Account, you get Despatch details screen (F-10B) to enter the relevant details of the dispatch of materials

Despatch Doc. No. : 12 dt. 1-Jun-2009
Despatched through : Vessel
Destination : Kolkata

Supplier's Details

Supplier	: Szboad Technology Co Ltd
Address	: Switzeland
TIN/Sales Tax No.	:
CST Number	:
Type of Dealer	: Not Applicable
Excise Regn No.	: ABCDE5678001D
Importer Exporter Code	: 123457
Range	: 1234
Division	: 123
Commissionerate	: 12

Manufacturer / Importer Details

Name	: ABC Co Ltd
Address	:
Excise Regn No.	: ABCDE1234001D
Importer Exporter Code	: 123456
Range	: 1234
Division	: 123
Commissionerate	: 12
Invoice No.	: 3456
Invoice Date	: 1-Jun-2009

F-10B: Despatch details of Purchase Invoice

On selection of Stock Item at Main Voucher entry screen (F-01A), you get the Item Allocation screen (F-10C)

Item Allocations for : **Item (Imported)**

Godown	Quantity	Rate per	Amount
Bonded Godown	5,000 Pcs	150.00 Pcs	7,50,000.00
	5,000 Pcs		7,50,000.00

F-10C: Item Allocation screen

After entry of details at Item allocation screen (F-10C), you get the Excise derails screen (F-10D).

Excise Details for : Item (Imported)
(Tariff Classification : 12345678)

RG 23D Entry No. : 123

Supplier Invoice / Bill of Entry Details

Invoice / Bill of Entry No. : 2
Invoice / Bill of Entry Date : 1-Jul-2009
PLA/RG 23 Entry No. : 234
Assessable Value : 7,50,000.00

Type of Duty	Rate of Duty	Duty Amount
Countervailing Duty (CVD)	10 %	75,000.00
Education Cess on CVD	2 %	1,500.00
Secondary Education Cess on CVD	1 %	750.00
Additional Duty (Imports)	4 %	33,090.00
Total		1,10,340.00

F-10D: Excise Details screen

Excise Details: Excise Details entry in Purchase Invoice has been explained earlier. In ***Excise Details*** screen (F-10D), enter as follows:

- **RG-23D#**: At ***RG 23D Entry No***, enter the RG 23D entry number of the purchase in your books
- **Supplier Invoice**: ***Supplier Invoice Number*** will be carried form the Supplier Invoice No. field (if entered), other wise enter the supplier Invoice number
- **Voucher Date**: *Supplier Invoice Date*, as entered in main voucher entry screen (F-10A), is carried by default as the ***Supplier Invoice Date*, which you may change**
- **PLA: PLA/ RG 23D Entry no.** is not required for Dealers.
- **Assessable Value**: At *Assessable Value*, the materials Assessable Value is carried, which you may change

Next, the Duty figures are computed and shown as default (F-10D), as per Duty Rates specified in Stock Item Master, which you may change, if required

04 Partial Customs Clearance

Often, the Buyer clears the goods from Customs Bonded Warehouse, as and when required, paying the Customs Duty.

In such case, each time some material is cleared, a Receipt Note is created for the Quantity cleared,

04.01 Excise Receipt note Voucher Type creation

Voucher Type creation has ben explained earlier. Create a *Receipt Note* Voucher Type (F-11A).

Voucher Type Creation

Name : **RcpNoteExc**

General

Type of Voucher	: Receipt Note
Abbr.	: RcpNotExs
Method of Voucher Numbering	? Automatic
Use Advance Configuration	? No
Use EFFECTIVE Dates for Vouchers	? No
Make 'Optional' as default	? No
Use Common Narration	? Yes
Use for Excise	? Yes
Default Excise Unit	: Bonded Godown

F-11A: Receipt Note Voucher Type for Excise Goods

At *Receipt Note* Voucher Type creation screen (F-11A), set *Yes* at *Use for Excise* to activate the Excise Duty related Options. At *Default Excise Unit* (F-11A), select the Excise Unit from the list.

04.02 Purchase Voucher Entry

If full quantity is not released from Customs, the Buyer will still make the Purchase Voucher entry (F-12A), as described earlier, but with pending Tracking Number.

We have already explained the concept of Pending Tracking Number (Purchase Bills Pending), for Purchase Invoice Made but Receipt Note not made.

At Purchase Voucher entry screen (F-12A), after selection of Party Ledger, you get *Receipt Details* entry screen (F-12B).

Purch-Exc No. 3 — 1-Jul-2009 Wednesday
Supplier Invoice No. : 23 Date : 1-Jun-2009
Excise Unit : Bonded Godown

Party's A/c Name : Szboad Technology Co Ltd
Nature of Purchase: Importer

Purchase Ledger : Purchase
VAT/Tax Class : Not Applicable

Name of Item	Quantity	Rate per	Amount
Item (Imported)	5,000 Pcs	150.00 Pcs	7,50,000.00
Narration:	5,000 Pcs		7,50,000.00

F-12A: Purchase Voucher entry

Receipt Details

Receipt Note No.(s) : Despatch Doc. No. : 23 dt. 1-Jun-2009
Despatched through : Vessel
Pd/1 dt. 1-Jul-2009 Destination : Kolkata

Supplier's Details

Supplier : Szboad Technology Co Ltd
Address
TIN/Sales Tax No. :
CST Number :
Type of Dealer : Not Applicable
Excise Regn No. : ABCDE5678001D
Importer Exporter Code : 123457
Range : 1234
Division : 123
Commissionerate : 12

Manufacturer / Importer Details

Name : ABC Co Ltd
Address

Excise Regn No. :
Importer Exporter Code :
Range :
Division :
Commissionerate :
Invoice No. :
Invoice Date :

F-12B: Receipt Details of Purchase Voucher

List of Tracking Numbers

- End of List
- New Number
- Not Applicable

F-12C: Tracking Number option list

New Number

Pd/1

F-12D: Tracking Number entry

At *Receipt Details* entry screen (F-12B), enter as follows:

- **Tracking Number:** At Receipt Note Numbers, select *New Number* from the list (F-12C), and then enter the new Tracking Number (F-12D) in the input box.
- **Supplier / Importer details**: At *Receipt Details* entry screen (F-12B), the supplier Details are carried as default, which you may change. At Manufacturer / Importer detail, enter the name of the Company (as it is the Self-importer), or create a Ledger Account of the Company Name and select it.

List of Tracking Numbers

Name	Godown	Date	Balance	Rate
New Number				
Not Applicable				
Pd/1				

F-12E: Pending Tracking Number list

Next, select the pending Tracking reference from the list of Pending Tracking Numbers (F-12E) to get *Item Allocation* screen (F-12F).

Item Allocations for : **Item (Imported)**

Godown	Quantity	Rate per	Amount
Tracking No. : Pd/1			
Bonded Godown	5,000 Pcs	150.00 Pcs	7,50,000.00
	5,000 Pcs		7,50,000.00

F-12F: Item Allocation screen

At *Item Allocation* screen (F-12F), select the Godown, Quantity & Rate for the Purchase Invoice. The computed value is shown at Amount column and you get the Excise Details screen (F-12G)

Excise Details for : Item (Imported)
(Tariff Classification : 12345678)

Customs Clearance Pending ? No

RG 23D Entry No.
Supplier Invoice / Bill of Entry Details
Invoice / Bill of Entry No. : 23
Invoice / Bill of Entry Date : 1-Jun-2009
PLA/RG 23 Entry No.
Assessable Value : 7,50,000.00

Type of Duty	Rate of Duty	Duty Amount
Countervailing Duty (CVD)	10 %	75,000.00
Education Cess on CVD	2 %	1,500.00
Secondary Education Cess on CVD	1 %	750.00
Additional Duty (Imports)	4 %	33,090.00
Total		1,10,340.00

F-12G: Excise Details screen (initial)

Excise Details for : Item (Imported)
(Tariff Classification : 12345678)

Customs Clearance Pending ? Yes

RG 23D Entry No. :
Supplier Invoice / Bill of Entry Details
Invoice / Bill of Entry No. :
Invoice / Bill of Entry Date :
PLA/RG 23 Entry No. :
Assessable Value :

Type of Duty	Rate of Duty	Duty Amount
Countervailing Duty (CVD)	0	
Education Cess on CVD	0	
Secondary Education Cess on CVD	0	
Additional Duty (Imports)	0	
Total		

F-12H: Excise Details screen for Pending clearance

At Excise Details screen (F-12G), the Excise Duty computed for the Quantity as entered in Purchase Invoice, as per applicable Rates as entered at Stock Item Excise Details, is shown (F-12G). Now, set *Yes* at *Customer Clearance Pending*, to blank out (set zero) the Duty Details section (F-12H).

This way, enter the details of each Stock Item.

Save the Purchase Voucher (F-12A).

04.03 Receipt Note Entry

When some materials are released form Customs, after Payment of Duties on the released quantity, a *Receipt Note*

Voucher (F-13A) is created, against the Pending Tracking Number (F-13C).

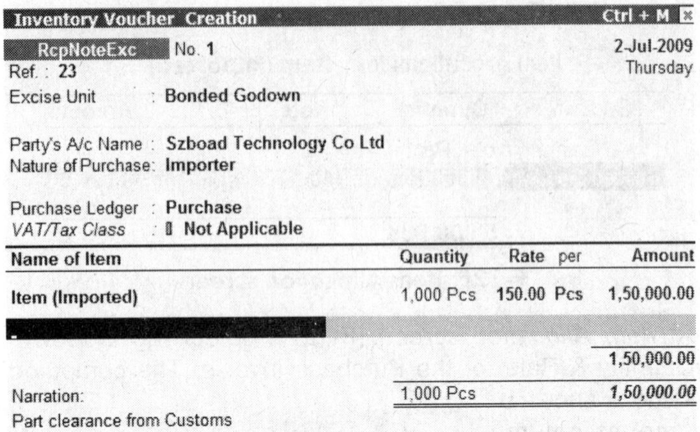

F-13A: Receipt Note Entry

At *Receipt Note* Entry screen (F-13A), on selection of Supplier Ledger account, you get *Receipt* details entry screen (F-13B), to enter the supplier details.

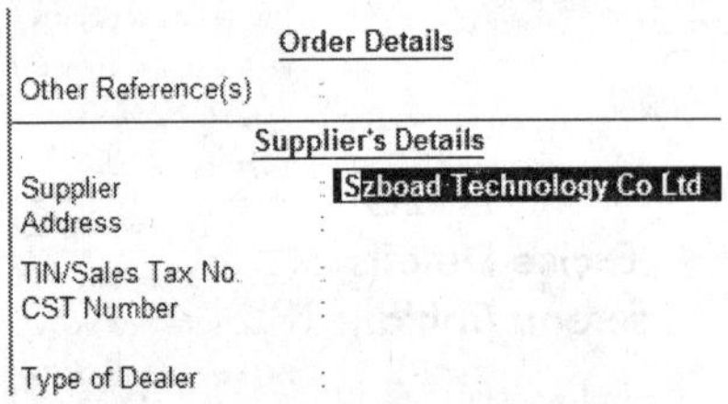

F-13B:Supplier Details

F-13C: Pending Tracking list

On entry of Receipt Details (F-13B), you get the list of Pending Tracking Number (F-13C), to select from. Select the Pending Tracking Number against which the Receipt Note is being created, from the list (F-13C), to get *Item Allocation* screen (F-13D).

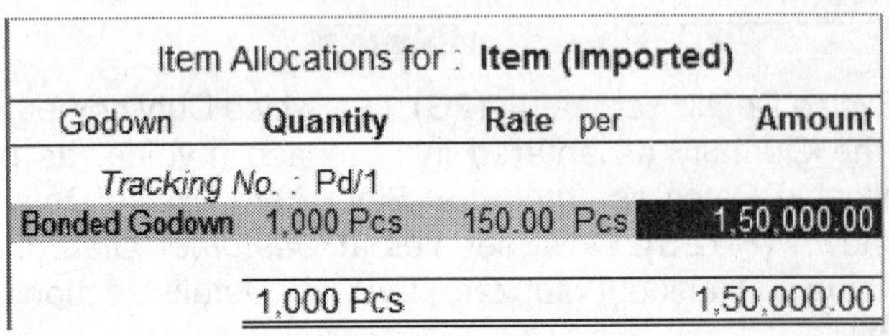

F-13D: Item Allocation

At *Item Allocation* screen (F-13D), enter the Quantity & Rate. The computed Amount is shown at *Amount* column to get Excise Details entry screen (F-13E).

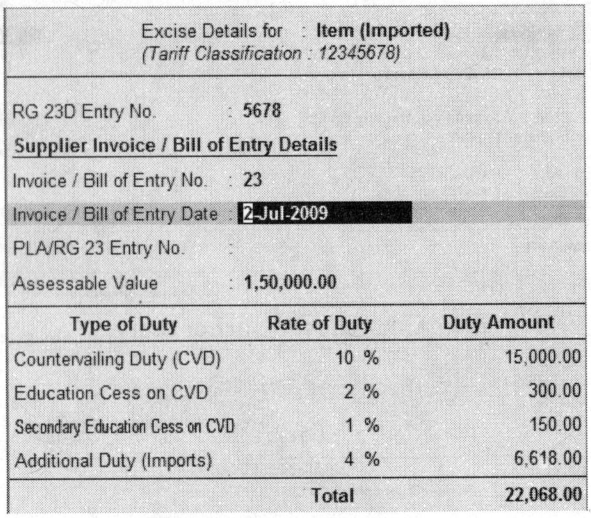

F-13E: Excise Details screen

At Excise Details screen (F-13E), enter the RG 23 D Entry Number, The supplier Bill details are carried as default (which you may change). The computed Duty details for the Receipt Quantity, as per Duty Rates specified at Stock Item Duty details are shown, which you may change.

This way, enter all the Items in the Receipt Note (F-13A) and finally save the Receipt Note.

This way, create the Receipt Notes as and when materials are released from Customs, against the Pending Purchase Invoice, till the entire materials are cleared.

05 Conditional Passing of Additional Duty (Imports)

Additional Duty paid on Imports may be conditionally (optionally) passed.

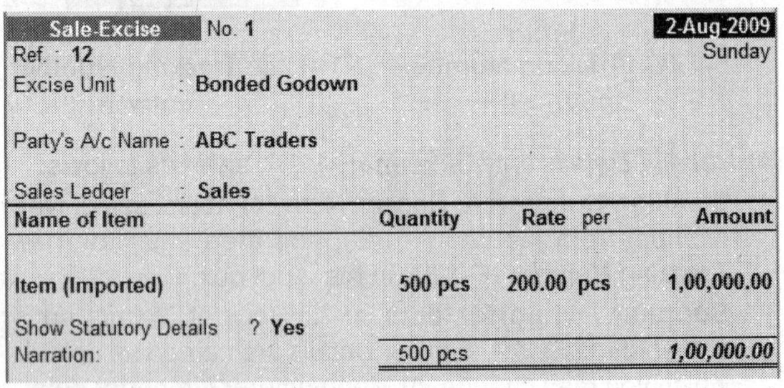

F-14A: Sales Invoice

During Sales Voucher entry for sale of an Imported Item (F-14A), on sale of Item on which Additional Duty (Imports) have been paid at the time of Purchase, you may opt to pass the duty credit to buyer Here we show the relevant screen where you set the options to pass the additional duty paid on Imports.

List of Purchases						
Supplier Invoice No.	Invoice Date	Supplier Name	Nature of Purchase	Pending Qty	Rate of Duty	Duty / Unit
2	1-Jul-2009	Szboad Technology Co Ltd	Importer	5,000 pcs	10 %	22.07 / pcs
23	2-Jul-2009	Szboad Technology Co Ltd	Importer	1,000 pcs	10 %	22.07 / pcs

F-14B: Pending Purchase document selection

Supplier Details for : **Item (Imported)**
(Tariff Classification : 12345678)

Supplier Invoice Number / Date	Supplier Name / Nature of Purchase	Quantity Utilised	Is Additional Duty Imports (SAD) Not Pass On
2 *1-Jul-2009*	Szboad Technology Co Ltd *Importer*	500 pcs	Yes
	Total	500 pcs	

F-14C: Supplier Details screen

At Sales Invoice Entry select the Item (F-14A), and then select the Import Purchase Invoice (for which Additional Duty has been paid) from the list of Pending Purchases (F-14B), to get *Supplier Details* screen (F-14C)

At *Supplier Details* screen (F-14C), at *Is Additional Duty Imports (SAD) not Pass On*, set as follows:

- Not Passing the Credit to Buyer: Set *Yes* (F-15A)
- Passing the Credit to Buyer: Set *No* (F-15B)

EXCISE INVOICE
(ISSUE OF INVOICE UNDER RULE 11 OF CENTRAL EXCISE RULES 2002)
Importer

Bonded Godown
123 Burdwan Rd, Kolkata
Phone : 9999999998 / E-mail : hot@yahoo.com

Excise Regn No. : **ABCDE1234X-001**
Importer Exporter Code : **1234567890**

Buyer	Invoice No.	Dated
ABC Traders 9876 BoHoogly Excise Regn No. : **FREWS1234V-XD-01** Range : **4567** Division : **456** Commissionerate : **45**	**1**	**2-Aug-2009**
	Delivery Note	Dated
	Despatched through **Rail**	Despatch Document No. **12**
	Date & Time of issue of Invoice **2-Aug-2009 at 01:27**	Destination **Delhi**
	Date & Time of Removal of Goods **2-Aug-2009 at 01:27**	Motor Vehicle No.
		Authenticated By ***for Bonded Godown*** *Authorised Signatory*

Sl No.	Description of Goods	Tariff / HSN Classification	Quantity	Rate	per	Amount
1	Item (Imported)	12345678	500 pcs	200.00	pcs	1,00,000.00
		Total	**500 pcs**			**₹ 1,00,000.00**

Amount Chargeable (in words) : **Indian Rupees One Lakh Only**

Description of Goods	Assessable Value	Rate of CVD	CVD Amount	Rate of Ed Cess on CVD	Ed Cess on CVD Amount	Rate of Sec Ed Cess on CVD	Sec Ed Cess on CVD Amount
Item (Imported)	75,000.00	10 %	7,500.00	2 %	150.00	1 %	75.00
Total	**75,000.00**		**7,500.00**		**150.00**		**75.00**

Amount of Duty (in words) : **Indian Rupees Seven Thousand Five Hundred Only**
Amount of Cess (in words) : **Indian Rupees Two Hundred Twenty Five Only**

Name & Address of Supplier of goods if he is not a Manufacturer/Importer :	Excise Regn No.	Division	Invoice No. / Date	Seller RG 23D No.
	Range	Commissionerate		123
Name & Address of the Manufacturer/Importer : **ABC Co Ltd**	Excise Regn No. **ABCDE1234001D**	Division **123**	Invoice/BOE No. & Date **2 / 1-Jul-2009**	Mfgr/Impr PLA/RG 23 No.
	Importer Exporter Code **123456**	Commissionerate **12**		
Manufacturer/Importer Duty Details	Range **1234**			

Description of Goods	Tariff Classification	Quantity	Assessable Value	CVD Amount	Addl Duty (Imports) Amount	Ed Cess on CVD Amount	SecEd Cess on CVD Amount	Total Duty Amount	Duty per Unit
Item (Imported)	12345678	5,000 pcs	7,50,000.00	75,000.00	33,090.00	1,500.00	750.00	1,10,340.00	22.07
Total		**5,000 pcs**	**7,50,000.00**	**75,000.00**	**33,090.00**	**1,500.00**	**750.00**	**1,10,340.00**	

Amount of Duty (In words) : **Indian Rupees One Lakh Eight Thousand Ninety Only**
Amount of Cess (In words) : **Indian Rupees Two Thousand Two Hundred Fifty Only**

SAD Declaration : In Respect of Goods Covered therein, No Credit of the Additional Duty of Customs levied under Sub Section (5) of the Customs Tariff Act, 1975 shall be admissible.

Certified that the goods covered under this invoice were :- (A) Imported directly by us or Received directly from M/s. ABC Co Ltd who have imported the goods (B) Received directly from Factory/Depot/Consignment Agent/Authorized Premises of M/s........................ (C) Received from M/s........................ .... who are the First Stage Dealer of M/s........................
Place : Kolkata Date : 2-Aug-2009

for Bonded Godown
Name : A B Ghosh
Designation : Sales Officer
Authorised Signatory

SUBJECT TO KOLKATA JURISDICTION — E. &OE
This is a Computer Generated Invoice

F-15A: Sales Invoice (without Passing Additional Duty)

EXCISE INVOICE

(ISSUE OF INVOICE UNDER RULE 11 OF CENTRAL EXCISE RULES 2002)

Importer

Bonded Godown
123 Burdwan Rd, Kolkata
Phone : 9999999998 / E-mail : hot@yahoo.com

Excise Regn No. : **ABCDE1234X-001**
Importer Exporter Code : **1234567890**

Buyer	Invoice No.	Dated
ABC Traders 9876 BoHoogly	**1**	**2-Aug-2009**
Excise Regn No. : **FREWS1234V-XD-01**	Delivery Note	Dated
Range : **4567**	Despatched through **Rail**	Despatch Document No. **12**
Division : **456**	Date & Time of issue of Invoice **2-Aug-2009 at 01:27**	Destination **Delhi**
Commissionerate : **45**	Date & Time of Removal of Goods **2-Aug-2009 at 01:27**	Motor Vehicle No.
		Authenticated By ***for Bonded Godown*** Authorised Signatory

Description of Goods	Assessable Value	Rate of CVD	CVD Amount	Rate of Addl Duty (Imports)	Addl Duty (Imports) Amount	Rate of Ed Cess on CVD	Ed Cess on CVD Amount	Rate of Sec Ed Cess on CVD	Sec Ed Cess on CVD Amount
Item (Imported)	75,000.00	10 %	7,500.00	4 %	3,309.00	2 %	150.00	1 %	75.00
Total	**75,000.00**		**7,500.00**		**3,309.00**		**150.00**		**75.00**

Amount of Duty (In words) : **Indian Rupees Ten Thousand Eight Hundred Nine Only**
Amount of Cess (In words) : **Indian Rupees Two Hundred Twenty Five Only**

Name & Address of Supplier of goods if he is not a Manufacturer/Importer :	Excise Regn No.	Division	Invoice No. / Date	Seller RG 23D No. 123
	Range	Commissionerate		

Name & Address of the Manufacturer/Importer :	Excise Regn No.	Division	Invoice/BOE No. & Date	Mfgr/Impr PLA/RG 23 No.
ABC Co Ltd	**ABCDE1234001D**	**123**	2 / 1-Jul-2009	
	Importer Exporter Code **123456**	Commissionerate **12**		
Manufacturer/Importer Duty Details	Range **1234**			

Description of Goods	Tariff Classification	Quantity	Assessable Value	CVD Amount	Addl Duty (Imports) Amount	Ed Cess on CVD Amount	Sec Ed Cess on CVD Amount	Total Duty Amount	Duty per Unit
Item (Imported)	12345678	5,000 pcs	7,50,000.00	75,000.00	33,090.00	1,500.00	750.00	1,10,340.00	22.07
Total		**5,000 pcs**	**7,50,000.00**	**75,000.00**	**33,090.00**	**1,500.00**	**750.00**	**1,10,340.00**	

Amount of Duty (In words) : **Indian Rupees One Lakh Eight Thousand Ninety Only**
Amount of Cess (In words) : **Indian Rupees Two Thousand Two Hundred Fifty Only**

Certified that the goods covered under this invoice were :- (A) Imported directly by us or Received directly from M/s. ABC Co Ltd who have imported the goods (B) Received directly from Factory/Depot/Consignment Agent/Authorized Premises of M/s.............................. (C) Received from M/s.......................... .... who are the First Stage Dealer of M/s...
Place : Kolkata Date : 2-Aug-2009

for Bonded Godown

Name : A B Ghosh
Designation : Sales Officer Authorised Signatory

SUBJECT TO KOLKATA JURISDICTION E. &OE

This is a Computer Generated Invoice

F-15B: Sales Invoice (Passing Additional Duty)

Save the Voucher and print the Invoice

F-15 A shows the Sales Invoice not passing the Additional Duty. F-15 B shows the Sales Invoice passing the Additional Duty.

06 Customs Clearance Register

Customs Clearance Register shows the list of import bill report displaying the details of imports of Excisable goods having stock pending for Clearance.

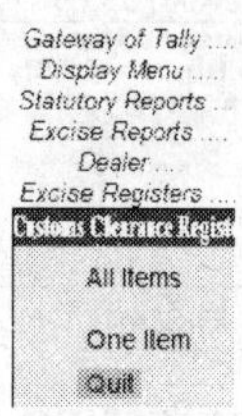

F-16A: Customs Clearance Register Menu

At Dealers Excise Registers Menu (F-1A/06-03), select *Customs Clearance Register* to get *Customs Clearance Register* Menu (F-16A), with following options

- **All Items**: At *Name of Excise Unit*, select the Excise Unit.
- **One Item**: Select as follows:
  - o **Excise Unit Name**: At *Name of Excise Unit*, select the Excise Unit.
  - o **Tariff**: At *Name of Tariff*, select the Tariff Type (select Any to get Stock Item of all Tariff Type

- **Stock Item**: At *Name of Item*, select the Stock Item (from the list of Stock Items under the selected Tariff Type), for which you like to display Stock Register to get Customs Clearance Register (F-16B).

Contents of Report: The *Customs Clearance Register* (F-16B) shows the details of Quantity Purchased, Cleared & Pending Quantity of Imported Items.

Customs Clearance Register — Hot Plates — Ctrl + M

Unit Name : **Bonded Godown** — 1-Apr-2009 to 1-Dec-2009

Sl. No.	Invoice No. / Date	Bill of Entry No. / Date	Voucher Type	Particulars	Name and Address of the Supplier	Tracking No.	Purchased Quantity	Cleared Quantity	Pending Quantity
1	23 1-Jul-2009		Purch Exc	Item (Imported) 12345678	Szboad Technology Co Ltd	Pd/1	5,000 Pcs		5,000 Pcs
	Clearance Made								
	23 2-Jul-2009	23 2-Jul-2009	RcpNoteExc	Item (Imported) 12345678	Szboad Technology Co Ltd	Pd/1		1,000 Pcs	4,000 Pcs
						Total	5,000 Pcs	1,000 Pcs	4,000 Pcs

F-16B: Customs Clearance Register

Special Cases

01 Partial CENVAT Credit on Purchase

We have so far described the normal cases applicable for all Registered Excise Manufacturers. Here we explain special cases applicable for some specific dealers, or arising in some special cases for Manufacturers.

In some cases, the CENVAT Credit may be available only on part of the Purchase Value. In such case, first create a Purchase Voucher without availing CENVAT Credit (for the Purchase Value) and then create a Debit Note availing the CENVAT credit (for the Partial Amount).

01.01 Purchase Voucher Creation without CENVAT Credit

Purchase Voucher entry without CENAT Credit has been explained earlier. The respective screens are shown (F-1A to F-1D). As CENVAT credit has not been availed, Excise Duty accounts have been selected instead of CENVAT accounts in the purchase voucher (F-1A).

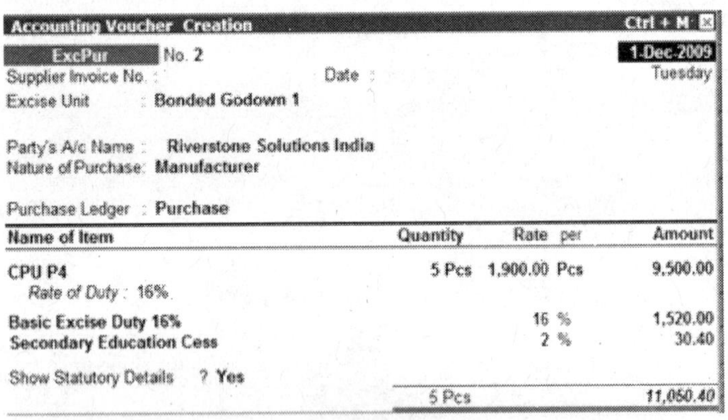

Accounting Voucher Creation — Ctrl + M

ExcPur No. 2 — 1-Dec-2009 Tuesday

Supplier Invoice No. : Date :

Excise Unit : Bonded Godown 1

Party's A/c Name : Riverstone Solutions India

Nature of Purchase: Manufacturer

Purchase Ledger : Purchase

Name of Item	Quantity	Rate per	Amount
CPU P4 Rate of Duty : 16%	5 Pcs	1,900.00 Pcs	9,500.00
Basic Excise Duty 16%		16 %	1,520.00
Secondary Education Cess		2 %	30.40
Show Statutory Details ? Yes			
	5 Pcs		11,050.40

F-1A: Excise Purchase Invoice (No CENVAT Credit)

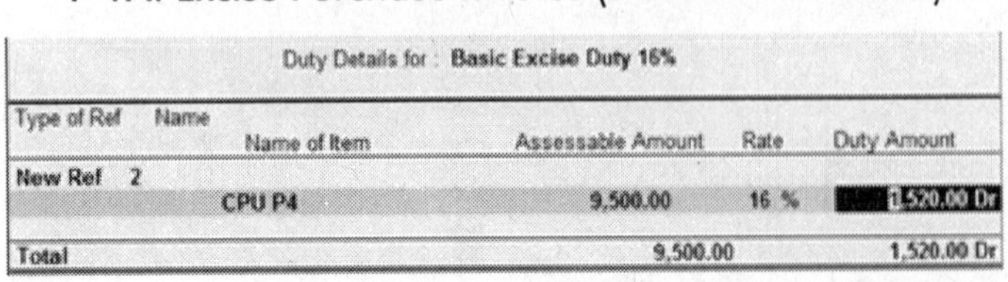

Duty Details for : Basic Excise Duty 16%

Type of Ref	Name	Name of Item	Assessable Amount	Rate	Duty Amount
New Ref	2				
		CPU P4	9,500.00	16 %	1,520.00 Dr
Total			9,500.00		1,520.00 Dr

F-1B: Duty Ledger details

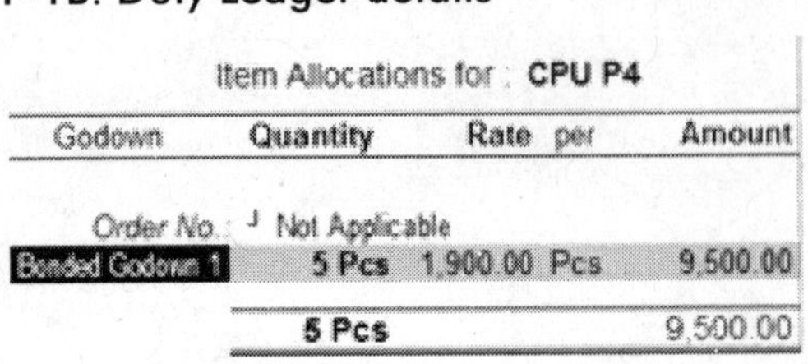

Item Allocations for : CPU P4

Godown	Quantity	Rate per	Amount
Order No. : Not Applicable			
Bonded Godown 1	5 Pcs	1,900.00 Pcs	9,500.00
	5 Pcs		9,500.00

F-1C: Stock Item Allocation

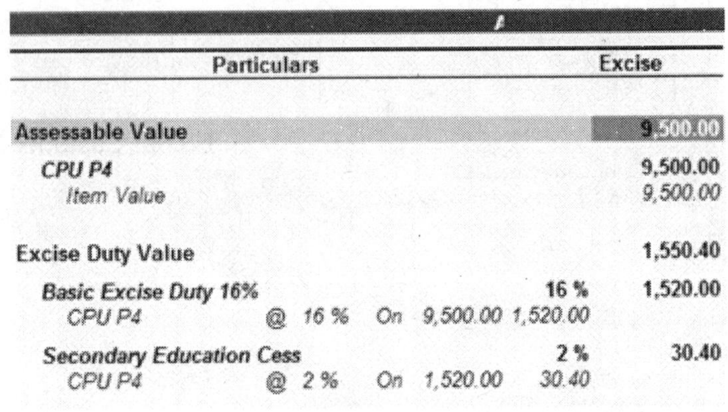

Particulars						Excise
Assessable Value						9,500.00
CPU P4						9,500.00
Item Value						*9,500.00*
Excise Duty Value						1,550.40
Basic Excise Duty 16%					16 %	1,520.00
CPU P4	@ 16 %	On	9,500.00	1,520.00		
Secondary Education Cess					2 %	30.40
CPU P4	@ 2 %	On	1,520.00	30.40		

F-1D: Statutory Details

01.02 Debit Note Voucher Class

Now create a Debit Note to avail CENVAT credit. To do that, you must have created a Debit Note Voucher Type for Excise, to create Debit Note Voucher Class for Excise Duty (F-2A). At VAT Class definition screen (F-2B), set Yes at *Use Class for Excise / CENVAT Adjustments.*

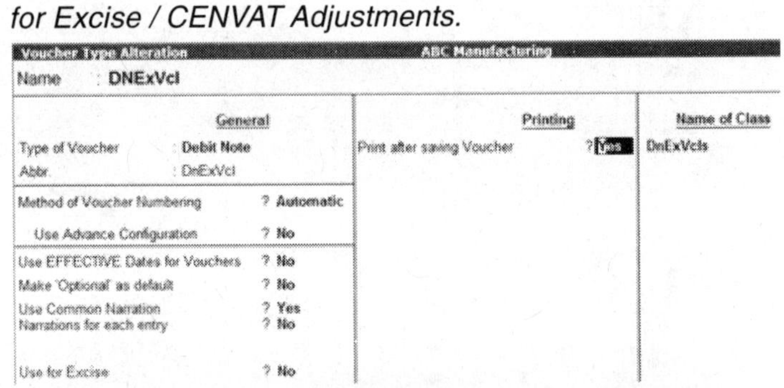

Voucher Type Alteration — ABC Manufacturing

Name : DNExVcl

General

Type of Voucher : Debit Note

Abbr. : DnExVcl

Method of Voucher Numbering ? Automatic

Use Advance Configuration ? No

Use EFFECTIVE Dates for Vouchers ? No

Make 'Optional' as default ? No

Use Common Narration ? Yes

Narrations for each entry ? No

Use for Excise ? No

Printing

Print after saving Voucher ? Yes

Name of Class

DnExVcls

F-2A: Debit Note Voucher Class for Excise Adjustments

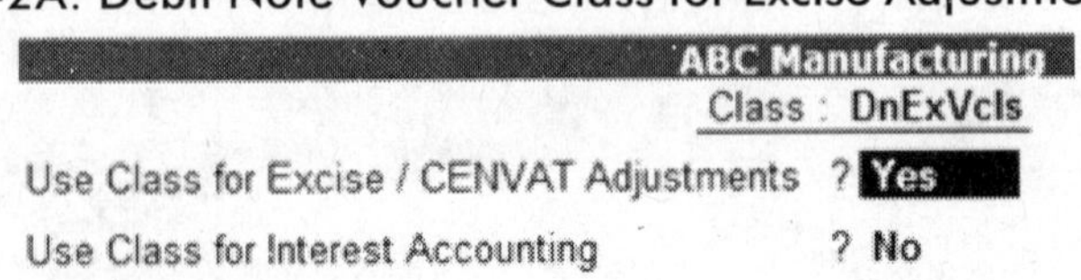

ABC Manufacturing

Class : DnExVcls

Use Class for Excise / CENVAT Adjustments ? Yes

Use Class for Interest Accounting ? No

F-2B: Excise Adjustment Voucher Class set up

Having created the Debit Note Voucher class (F-2A), create a Debit Note Voucher using the Voucher class for Excise / CENVAT Adjustment.

01.03 Debit Note Entry for CENVAT Credit

Now create a Debit Note to avail CENVAT credit. Debit Note entry has been explained earlier. At Debit Note entry screen

(F-3B), select the Voucher Type / Voucher Class (F-3A) to get the Debit Note Voucher Class entry screen (F-3B)

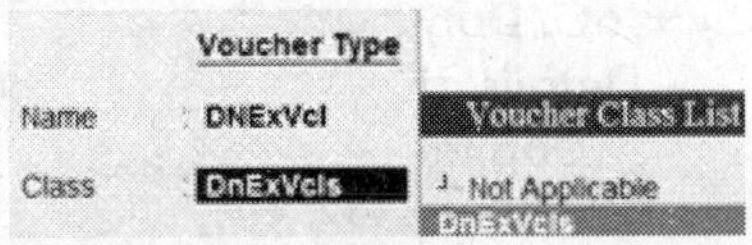

F-3A: Voucher Class Selection

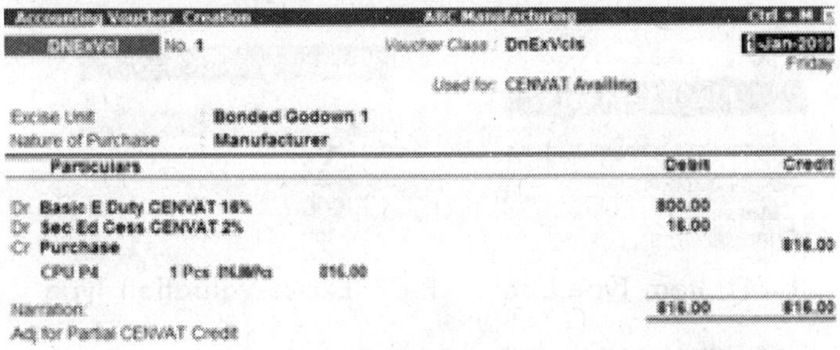

F-3B: Debit Note for Excise Adjustments (Partial CENVAT Credit)

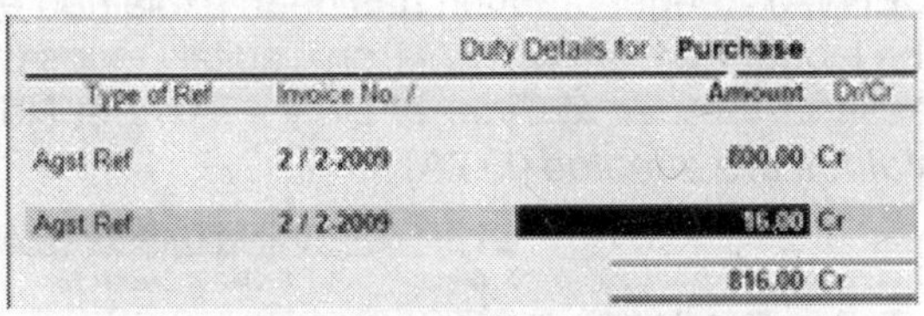

F-3C: Duty Details

F-3A to F-3F shows the various steps of entry of Debit Note as explained earlier (out of Purchase of Rs 9500: F-1A, CENVAT Credit for Rs 5000 (F-3E) has been availed in Debit Note (F-3B)

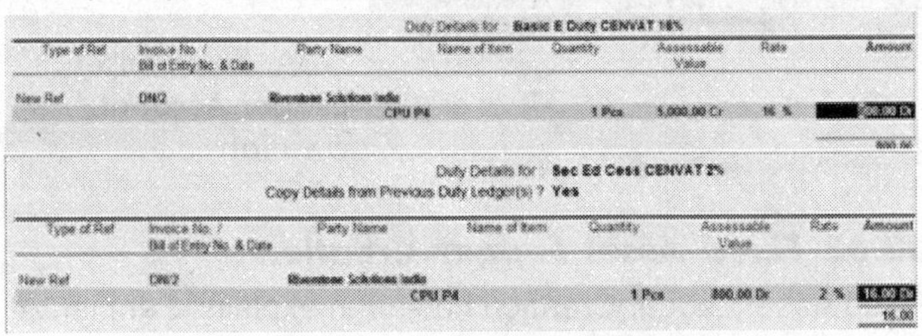

F-3E: Duty details for each Duty Type

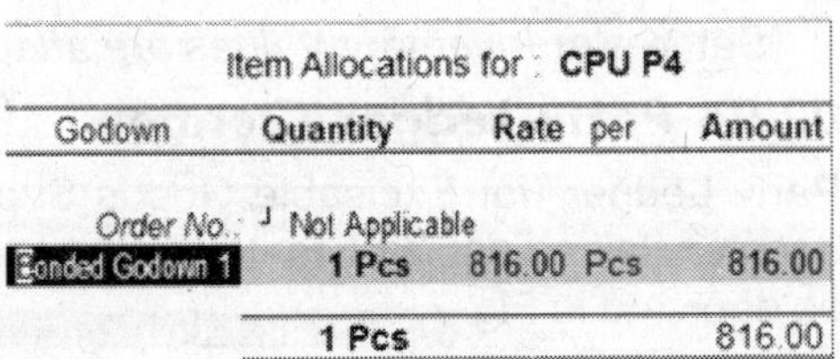

F-3F: Item Allocation for Debit Note

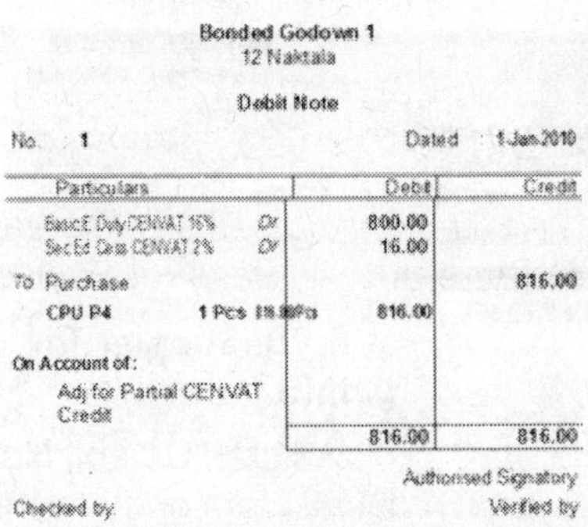

F-4A: Debit Note in Print (for CENVAT Adjustments)

Now print the Debit Note (F-4A), as explained earlier

02 Purchase Order with Excise Duty Details

Purchase Order entry and subsequent voucher entry (Receipt Note / Purchase Invoice) linking the Purchase Order has been explained earlier. Since Purchase Order is just a business contract and no transaction happens on creation of an Order, entry of Excise Details in Purchase Order, makes no effect on any Ledger Account or any Excise Report / Returns. If you have entered Excise details in Purchase Ordr, the Purchase Order is valued properly showing the details of Excise Duty. The Excise parameters specified in the Order are carried by default in next stage voucher (like Delivery / Receipt Notes, Invoices etc), to reduce data entry again and avoid mistakes.

02.01 Excise Purchase Order Voucher Type

To enter Purchase Order with Excise Details, you must create a separate Voucher Type (F-5A) for Purchase Order. Creation of Voucher Type has been explained earlier

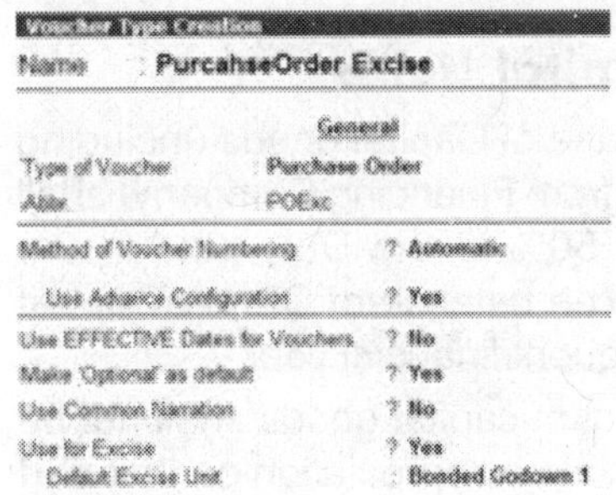

F-5A: Purchase Order Voucher Type (Excise)

F-5B: Voucher Type selection

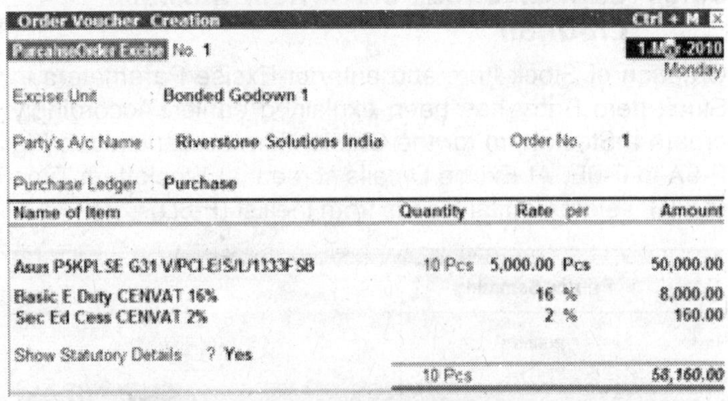

F-5C: Purchase Order Entry with Excise Details

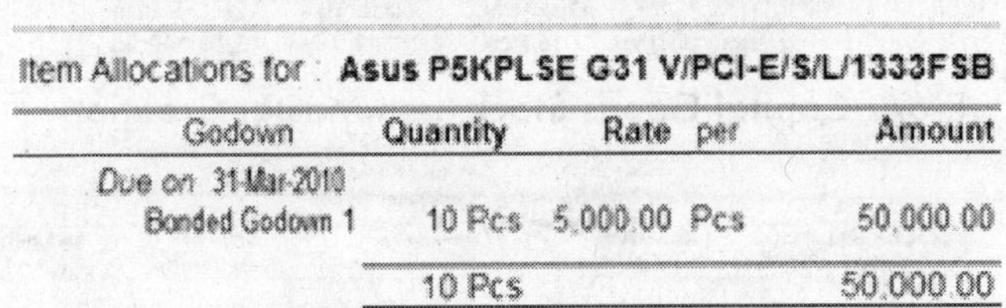

F-5D: Item Details screen

At *Voucher Type Creation* screen (F-5A), set as follows for Excise Duty:

Particulars	Excise
Assessable Value	
Asus P5KPLSE G31 WPG-E/S/L/1333FSB	
Item Value	
Basic E Duty CENVAT 16%	
Sec Ed Cess CENVAT 2%	
Excise Duty Value	8,160.00
Basic E Duty CENVAT 16% 16 %	
Sec Ed Cess CENVAT 2% 2 %	

F-5E: Stautory Details

- **Excise Applicability**: Set *Yes* at *Use for Excise*. Consequently, you may enter Excise Detail in the Voucher, using the Voucher Type
- **Default Excise Unit**: Select the Default Unit from the list of Excise Units, This will be carried by default at subsequent during voucher entry using the Voucher Type, which you may change during voucher entry.

02.02 Purchase Order Entry with Excise Details

Having created the Purchase Order Voucher Type, you may create Purchase Order. Purchase Order has been explained earlier. Fig F-5A to F-5E shows the steps of Order Entry with Excise details.

03 Purchase of Capital Items

CENVAT credit on the purchase of Capital goods (including Lease / Hire Purchase, Loan from Financing Company) shall be availed to the extent of 50% of the Duty paid in the financial year of Purchase. The balance of CENVAT credit may be availed in any subsequent financial year.

The CENVAT credit in respect of capital goods shall not be allowed if the manufacturer claims depreciation on that part of the value of such capital goods that represents the amount of duty on such capital goods.

03.01 Capital Goods Stock Item Master Creation

Creation of Stock Item and entry of Excise Parameters in Stock Item Entry has been explained earlier. Accordingly create a Stock Item for the Capital Item as depicted in Fig F-6A to F-6E. At Excise Details screen, at Stock Item Type (F-6B), select Capital Goods from the list (F-6D).

Stock Item Alteration — ABC Manufacturing

Name : **Printer Samsung**

Under : Printer
Units : Pcs

Tax Information
Tariff Classification : Computer Goods
Set/Alter Excise Details ? Yes

	Quantity	Rate	per	Value
Opening Balance	15 Pcs	38,000.00	Pcs	5,70,000.00

F-6A: Capital Goods Stock Item Master Creation

Excise Details for : Printer Samsung
Tariff Classification : Computer Goods

Excise Unit Name	Reporting UOM	Conversion Factor		Set/Alter Duty Details	Stock Item T
Bonded Godown 1	U	1 U =	1 Pcs	No	Capital Goods

F-6B: Excise details of Capital Goods

Duty Details for : Printer Samsung
Tariff Classification : Computer Goods
Excise Unit : Bonded Godown 1

Valuation Type : Ad Quantum

Type of Duty	Applicable From	Rate per Unit
Basic Excise Duty	1-Apr-2008	300 /U

F-6C: Duty Details of Capital Goods

List of Item Types
Capital Goods
Finished Goods
Others
Principal Input

F-6D: Item Type List

List of Valuation Type
Ad Quantum
Ad Valorem
MRP Based
MRP (Valorem + Quantum)
Valorem + Quantum

F-6E: Excise Valuation Type

03.02 CENVAT on Capital Goods ledger account creation

CENVAT Ledger creation has been explained earlier. Create the ledger Account CENVAT on Capital Goods (under Current Assets). Set *No* at *Type of Duty / Tax*. Set No at *Inventory Values are affected* (F-7A)

Ledger Alteration
Name : CENVAT Credit for Capital Goods
Under : Current Assets
Type of Duty/Tax : Not Applicable
Inventory values are affected ? No

F-7A: CENVAT on Capital Goods Ledger

Ledger Alteration
Name : Computer Accesories
Under : Fixed Assets
Inventory values are affected ? Yes

F-8A: Fixed Asset Ledger Account creation

03.03 Fixed Asset Ledger Creation

Fixed Asset Ledger Creation has been explained earlier. At Fixed Asset Leger Account creation (F-8A):

- Select Fixed Asset Group at *Under*
- Set *Yes* at *Inventory Values are affected.*

03.04 Party Ledger Creation

Party Ledger (for Excisable Goods Supplier) creation has been explained earlier. Create Fixed Asset Supplier Account as depicted in Fig F-9A to F-9C.

Ledger Alteration
Name : Digitech Infosys
Under : Sundry Creditors (Current Liabilities)
Maintain balances bill-by-bill ? Yes
Default Credit Period : 30 Days
Inventory values are affected ? No

F-9A: Fixed Asset Supplier account

Tax Information
PAN / IT No. : WERTY1234F
Sales Tax No. :
CST No. :
Set/Alter Excise Details? Yes

F-9B: Suppler Tax Info

Excise Details

Excise Registration (ECC) No.	: WERTY1234F123XD
Date of Registration	: 1-Apr-2010
Importer Exporter Code (IEC)	:
Range	: 34567
Division	: 3456
Commissionerate	: 34
Default Nature of Purchase	: First Stage Dealer
Nature of Removal	: Domestic
Notification Number	:

F-9C: Suppler Duty Info

03.05 Purchase Voucher Creation

Purchase Voucher creation of Excisable Goods has been explained earlier. Here we explain points specific of Purchase Voucher creation of Capital Goods with CENVAT Credit as per rules.

Voucher Configuration set up fo Fixed Asset Purchase: At Purchase Voucher creation screen (F-10A), Click *F12:Confgure* to get Purchase Voucher Entry Configuration (F-10B). At *Purchase Voucher Entry Configuration* (F-10B), set *Yes* at *Allow Expenses / Fixed Assets for Accounting Allocation.*

At Purchase Voucher Entry (F-10A), at Purchase Ledger, select the Fixed Asset ledger account

Accounting Voucher Alteration (Secondary) Ctrl + M

ExcPur No. 4 — 1-Dec-2009, Tuesday

Supplier Invoice No. : 34 Date : 1-Dec-2009

Excise Unit : Bonded Godown 1

Party's A/c Name : Digitech Infosys

Nature of Purchase : First Stage Dealer

Purchase Ledger : Computer Accesories

Name of Item	Quantity	Rate per	Amount
Printer Samsung *Rate per Unit : 300/U*	1 Pcs	40,000.00 Pcs	40,000.00
Basic Excise Duty Ad Quantum			300.00
Handling Charges			200.00
Freight			250.00
Show Statutory Details ? Yes			
	1 Pcs		40,750.00

F-10A: Capital Goods Purchase Voucher Entry

Purchase Invoice Configuration

Accept Supplementary Details *(Address Details, Despatch Details etc.)*	? No
Print Default Name & Address of Party	? No
Allow Separate Buyer and Consignee Names	? No
Use Common Ledger A/c for Item Allocation	? Yes
Allow Expenses/Fixed Assets for Accounting Allocations	? Yes

F-10B: Purchase Voucher Entry Configuration

Statutory Details

Particulars	Excise
Assessable Value	
Excise Duty Value	300.00

F-10C: Capital Goods Purchase Statutory Details

Fig F-10A to F-10E shows the various stages & comments of Purchase Voucher entry as explained earlier. In the Capital Goods Purchase Voucher (F-10A), CENVAT has not been claimed.

Duty Details for : Basic Excise Duty 16%

Type of Ref	Name	Name of Item		Assessable Amount	Rate	Duty Amount
New Ref	34-4-2009					
		Printer Samsung	On	1 U	300 /U	300.00 Dr
Total						300.00 Dr

F-10D: Capital Goods Purchase Duty details

Item Allocations for : **Printer Samsung**

Godown	Quantity	Rate per	Amount
Bonded Godown 1	1 Pcs	40,000.00 Pcs	40,000.00
	1 Pcs		40,000.00

F-10E: Item Allocation

03.06 Journal Voucher for CENVAT Credit Adjustment on Fixed Asset Purchase

The Purchase Voucher for Fixed Asset Purchase as described above (F-10A) is created without CENVAT Credit. Now you have to create a Journal Voucher for CENVAT Credit on Purchase of Fixed Asset (F-11A).

Ledger Creation

Name : Cenvat Credit for Capital Gods

Under : Current Assets

Type of Duty/Tax : Not Applicable

Inventory values are affected ? No

Types of Duty/Tax: Not Applicable, CENVAT

F-10F: Ledger Account creation for CENVAT Credit Control Ledger Account

First create a CENVAT Credit control Account (F-10F).

Accounting Voucher Creation Ctrl + M

Journal No. 1 — 1-Dec-2009, Tuesday

Particulars				Debit	Credit
Dr **CENVAT Credit for Capital Goods**				300.00	
Cr **Computer Accesories**					300.00
Printer Samsung	1 Pcs	300.00/Pcs	300.00		
Narration:				300.00	300.00

CENVAT Credit on Fixed Asset Purchase availed

F-11A; Journal Voucher for CENVAT Credit on Fixed Asset Purchase

Inventory Allocations for : **Computer Accesories**

Name of Item	Quantity	Rate per	Amount
Printer Samsung	1 Pcs	300.00 Pcs	300.00
	1 Pcs		300.00

F-11B: Purchase Account allocation

Item Allocations for : **Printer Samsung**

Godown	Quantity	Rate per	Amount
Bonded Godown 1	1 Pcs	300.00 Pcs	300.00
	1 Pcs		300.00

F-11C: Stock Item Allocation

Fig F-11A to F-11C shows the various steps & components of Journal Voucher for CENVAT Credit Adjustment for entire amount of CENVAT.

03.07 Debit Note Voucher Class for availing CENVAT Credit on Fixed Asset Purchase

Having created Journal Voucher for CENVAT Credit, you will have to create an Excise Debit Note for availing CENVAT Credit (50% in current year and balance in next year).

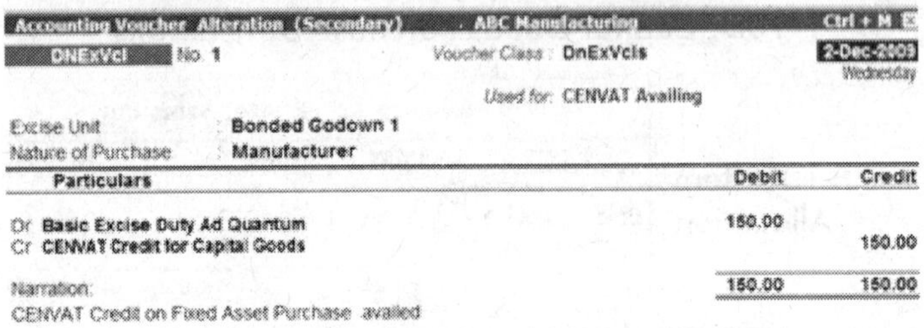

F-12A: Debit Note for CENVAT Credit

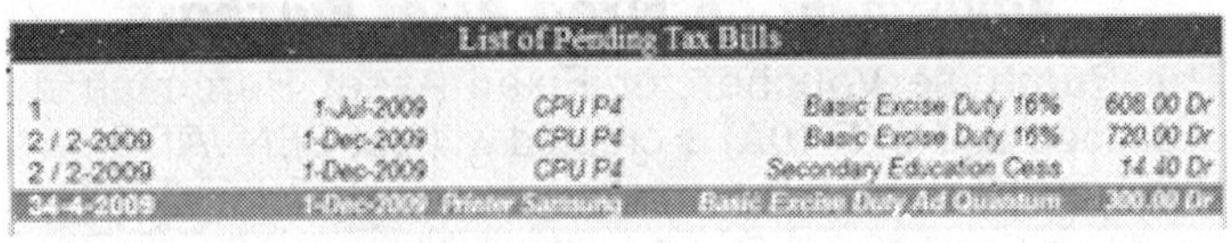

F-12B: Selection of Pending Bill Reference

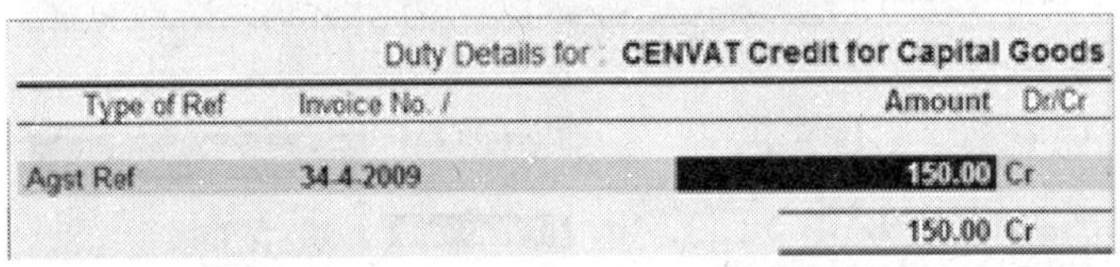

F-12C: Ledger Account Allocation

In the current year Create a Debit Note (F-12A) using Excise Duty Adjustment Debit Note Class (you have to create a Debit Note Voucher Class for Excise Duty as explained)

At Debit Note for CENVAT Credit, at *Used For* (F-12A), select *CENVAT Availing*.

Ledger Accounts: At Particulars column, select the Ledger Accounts details as follows:

- ***Excise Duty* ledger**: Select the *Excise Duty* Ledger Account to get Duty Details screen. Enter the 50% of the Duty at Debit Column
- **CENVAT Control Ledger**: Select the *CENVAT Credit* Control Ledger Account (which was debited in Journal Voucher explained earlier) to get Duty Details screen (F-12C). Select *Agnst Ref* to get the list of Pending Tax Bills (F-12B). Select the entry from the list (F-12B) and enter of the Duty Amount to avail CENVAT Credit in the current year.

Save the voucher. Now, there will a balance of 50% amount in the CENVAT Ledger account, which is to be adjusted through Debit Note in next year. So, in next year, you do not have to create any further Journal Voucher (like F-11A), but create Debit Note using Debit Note Voucher (like F-12A).to avail the balance amount of ENVAT Credit

04 Excisable Goods Production

We have so far explained Trading of Excisable Goods, on which the Goods Purchased is sold. In Manufacturing, Raw Materials are Purchased (recorded through Purchase Voucher), which undergo a manufacturing process to produce finished goods (recorded through Manufacturing Journal). The finished goods are sold (recorded through sales Voucher). The Item purchased and Items sold are different.

We describe the process of creation of Masters & Vouchers involved in Manufacturing Process

04.01 Production Process Stock Item Creation

Excisable Stock Item creation has been explained earlier. Here we show Stock Item creation for Input Raw Materials (F-13A & F-13B) and Output Produced Item (14A & F-14B), involved in the manufacturing process.

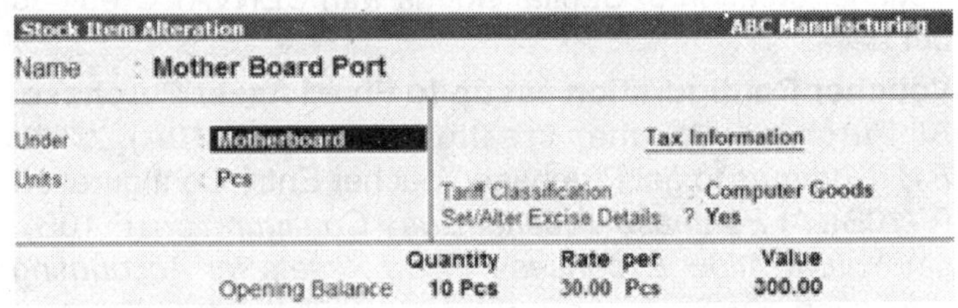

F-13A: Raw Materials Stock Item creation

F-13B: Raw Materials Stock Item Duty details

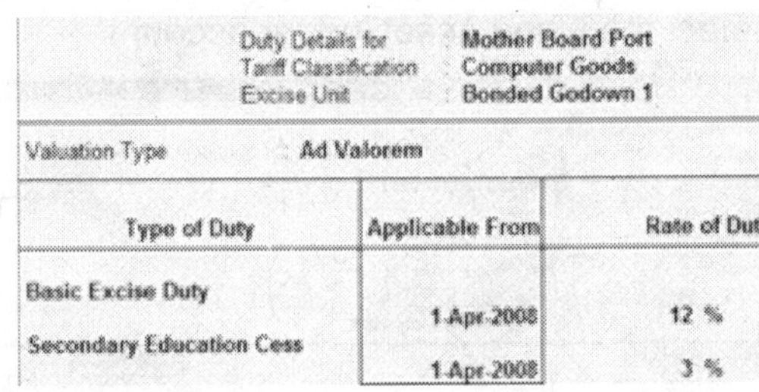

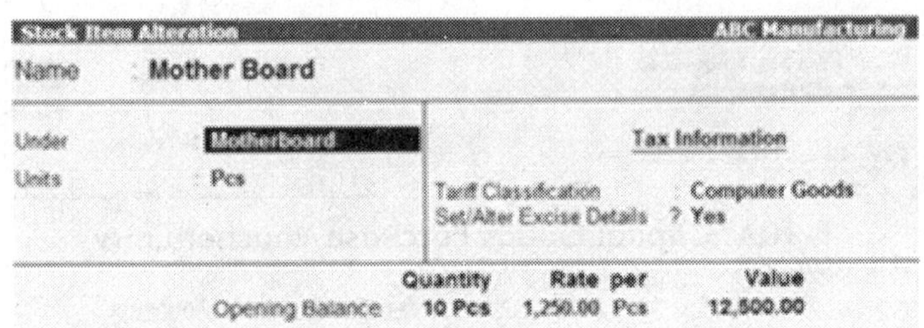

F-14A: Produced Material Stock Item creation

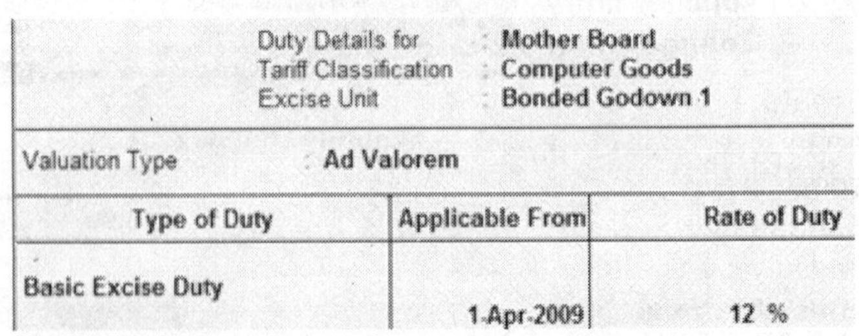

F14B: Produced Stock Item Duty details

04.02 Manufacturing Journal Voucher Creation

Creation of Manufacturing Journal Voucher Type & Manufacturing Journal has been explained earlier.

Having created the Stock Item Masters, you have to create Manufacturing Journal Voucher Type (F-15A) to create Manufacturing Journal (F-15B).

At Voucher Entry screen (F-15B), enter as follows:

- **Finished Products details**: At the header, enter the details of Finished Products. At the left part, enter the details of Input Materials Consumed. At the Right part, enter he details of manufacturing expenses.
- **Consumption Materials details**: At Left part, enter the details of input consumed materials
- **Products:** At the left part, enter the details of Input Materials Consumed. At the Right part, enter he details of manufacturing expenses.
- **Co-Products / By Products:** In case of Co-Products / By Products, you may enter the details at the Right Part of Stock Journal (F-15B). In case of multiple products (both main product), you may create a use a Excise Stock Journal.
- **Manufacturing Expenses:** At Right Part, enter the manufacturing expenses details

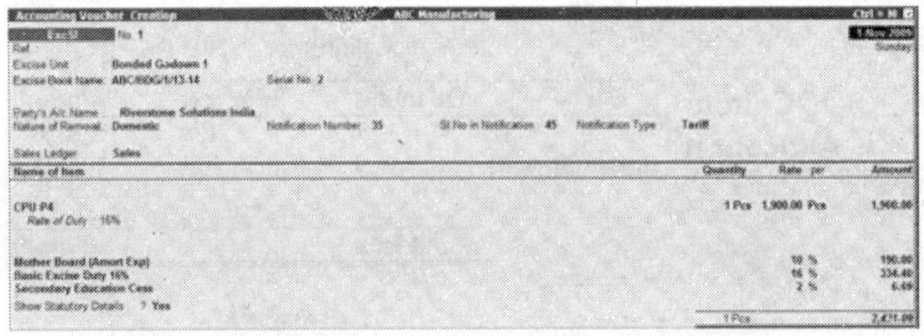

F-19A: Sales Invoice with Amortised Expenses

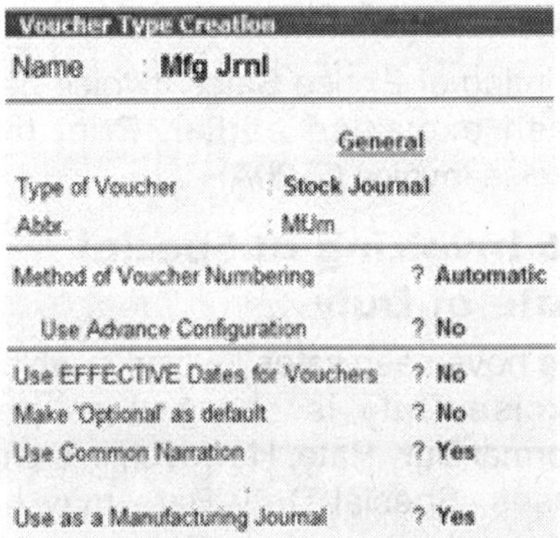

F-15A: Mfg Journal Type creation

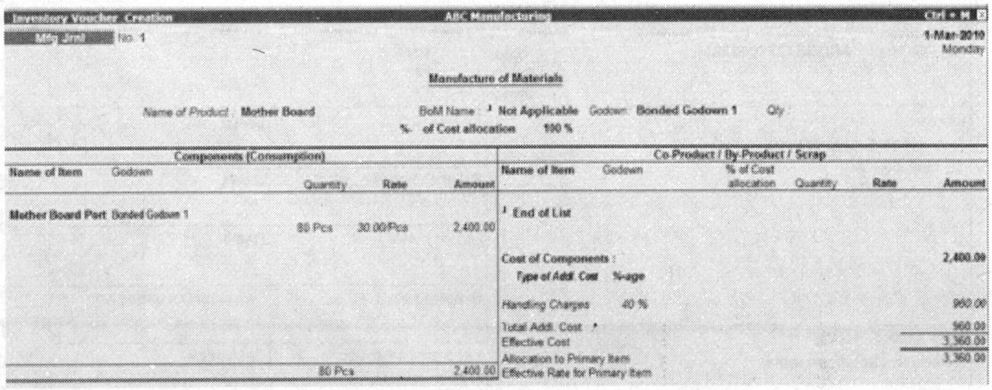

F-15B: Manufacturing Journal

05 Sales Invoicing including Manufacturing Expenses

All *Amortised Costs* (e.g Cost of Tools, Dies, Designs etc. spread over its useful life) are to be added for the computation of cost of Items for the purpose of Excise Duty.

05.01 Creation of Amortisation Cost Ledger Account

Create a Ledger Account exclusively for the Stock Item for Amortised cost to be added in Sales Invoice & Assessable Value for Duty Computation.

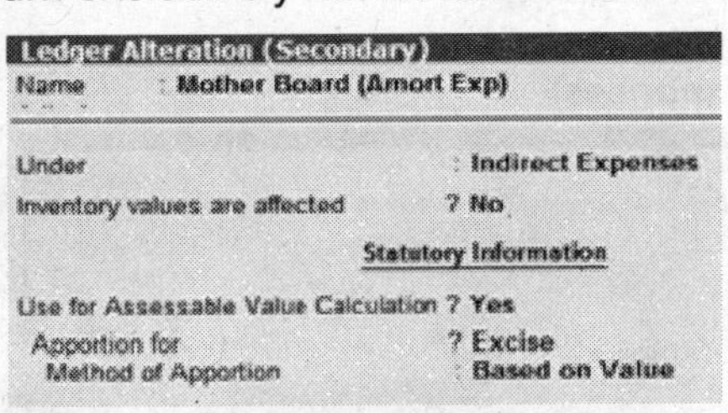

F-18A: Expense Ledger Creation

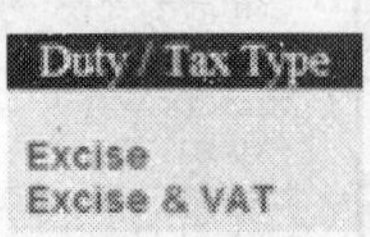

F-18B: Tax Type List F-18C: Apportion Method

Account Leger creation has been explained earlier. At *Account Leger creation* screen for Amortisation Expenses (F-18A), set as follows:(

- **Account Group**: At *Under*, select *Indirect Expenses*
- **Statutory Information**: Under *Statutory Information* section, set as follows (F-18A):
  - o **Assessable Value**: At *Use for Assessable Value*, set *Yes*
  - o **Duty Type**: At *Apportion For*, select *Excise* (select *Excise & VAT* if it is to be apportioned for both), from the list (F-18B)
  - o **Apportionment Method**: At Method of Apportion, select the applicable Apportionment method form the list (F-18C)

05.02 Sales Invoice creation with Amortised Cost

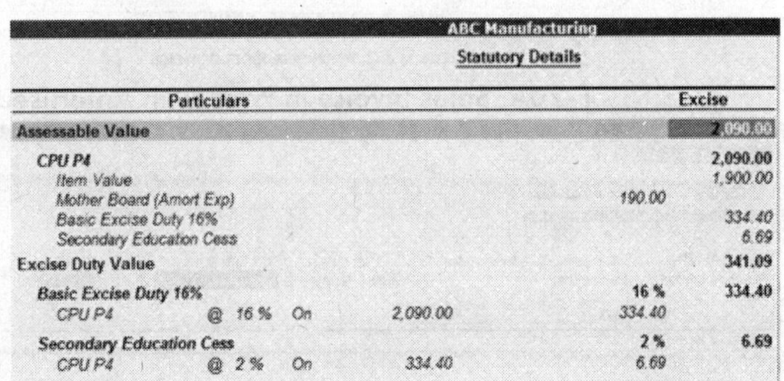

F-19B: Sales Invoice Statutory Details

Item Allocations for : **CPU P4**

Godown	Quantity	Rate	per	Amount
Bonded Godown 1	1 Pcs	1,900.00	Pcs	1,900.00
	1 Pcs			1,900.00

F-19C: Item Allocation

Excise Sales Invoice Creation as been explained earlier. At Sales Invoice Creation screen (F-19A), after Item details entry, select the Amortisation Expenses Ledger, enter the Rate in % (if Based on Value) or in per UoM (if Based on Quantity).

Now enter the Excise Ledger Account, Cess & Other Ledger Account as usual (F-19A)

Excise Invoice

(ISSUE OF INVOICE UNDER RULE 11 OF CENTRAL EXCISE RULES 2002)

Bonded Godown 1
12 Naktala
Phone : 03312345678 / E-mail : sales@universal.com

Excise Regn No. : **ABCDE1234D123XM**
Range : **123456**
Division : **123**
Commissionerate : **12**

Consignee	Invoice No.	Dated
Riverstone Solutions India 12 Tilak Rd Kolkata	2	**1-Nov-2009**
	Buyer's Order No.	Dated
	Delivery Note	Dated
	Supplier's Ref.	Despatch Document No.
Buyer (if other than consignee) **Riverstone Solutions India** 12 Tilak Rd Kolkata	Despatched through	Destination
	Date & Time of issue of Invoice **1-Nov-2009 at 09:52**	Motor Vehicle No.
Excise Regn No. : **ASDFG1234H123XD** Range : **34567** Division : **345** Commissionerate : **34** Notification No. : **35**	Date & Time of Removal of Goods **1-Nov-2009 at 09:52** Mode/Terms of Payment **30 Days**	Authenticated By ***for Bonded Godown 1*** *Authorised Signatory*

Sl No.	Description of Goods	Tariff / HSN Classification	Quantity	Rate	per	Amount
1	CPU P4	13456789	1 Pcs	1,900.00	Pcs	1,900.00
	Mother Board (Amort Exp)			10	%	190.00
	Basic Excise Duty 16%			16	%	334.40
	Secondary Education Cess			2	%	6.69
	Total		**1 Pcs**			**₹ 2,431.09**

Amount Chargeable (in words) : **Indian Rupees Two Thousand Four Hundred Thirty One and Nine paise Only**

Amount of Duty (in words) : **Indian Rupees Three Hundred Thirty Four and Forty paise Only**
Amount of Cess (in words) : **Indian Rupees Six and Sixty Nine paise Only**

Serial No. in PLA/RG-23 :

VAT Declaration : Goods Sold will not be taken Back. Mon-Fri : 11am to 7pm, Sat 11am to 2 pm

Excise Declaration
We declare to the best of our knowledge and belief that the particulars stated herein are true and correct and there is no additional consideration accruing to us either directly or indirectly in any manner other than the amounts indicated here.

for Bonded Godown 1
Name : S K Deb
Designation : Manager
Authorised Signatory

SUBJECT TO KOLKATA JURISDICTION — E.& O.E

This is a Computer Generated Invoice

F-20A: Sales Invoice in Print (with Amortised Expenses)

05.03 Printing of Sales Invoice with Amortised Expenses

Printing of Excise Sales Invoice has been explained earlier. Print the Excise Invoice (F-20A)

06 Invoicing at Special Rate of Duty

We have seen sales Invoice in which Excise Duty is charged as per Normal Duty Rate. However, in some cases, Special Duty Rate may be applicable, as per Government Notification. The process of Invoicing with Special Rate is almost similar to Normal Rate Sales Invoice.

At Sales Invoice entry screen (F-21A), at *Nature of Removal*, select *Special Rate* and enter the Notification details (Notification Number, Serial Number in Notification & Notification date) in which the Special Rate has been notified. of Special Duty Rate.

At Duty Ledger Accounts, at Rate of Duty, enter the applicable Special Duty Rate for the Invoice. The Duty would be computed accordingly.

Fig F-21A to F-21D shows the various components of Sales Invoice Entry screen as explained earlier.

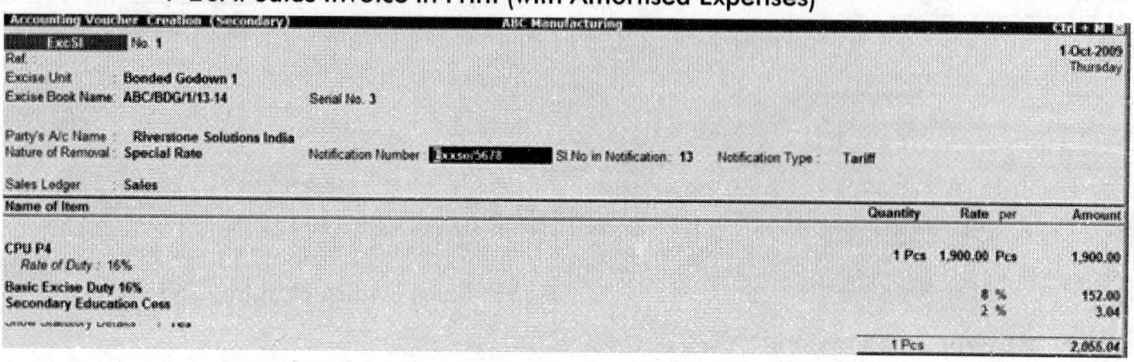

F-21A: Sales Invoice Entry with Special Duty Rate

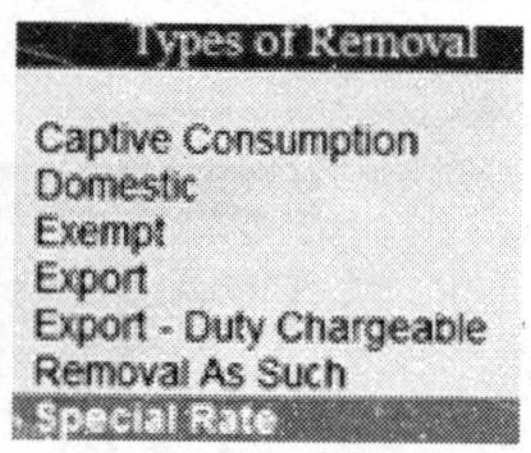

F-21B: Removal Type List

ABC Manufacturing

Statutory Details

Particulars				Excise
Assessable Value				1,900.00
CPU P4				1,900.00
Item Value				*1,900.00*
Basic Excise Duty 16%				*152.00*
Secondary Education Cess				*3.04*
Excise Duty Value				155.04
Basic Excise Duty 16%			8 %	152.00
CPU P4	@ 8 %	On 1,900.00	152.00	
Secondary Education Cess			2 %	3.04
CPU P4	@ 2 %	On 152.00	3.04	

F-21C: Statutory Details

Duty Details for : **Basic Excise Duty 16%**

Type of Ref	Name / Name of Item	Assessable Amount	Rate	Duty Amount
New Ref	ABC/BDG/1/13-143			
	CPU P4	1,900.00	8 %	152.00 Cr
				152.00 Cr

F-21D: Duty Details

07 Stock Item Removals

Sometimes Raw Materials for Production / Capital Goods are removed for Sale without being used into Production, on payment of duty. Removals are entered in Sales Voucher.

Accounting Voucher Creation Ctrl + M

ExcSl No. 1 1-Sep-2009 Tuesday

Ref. :
Excise Unit : **Bonded Godown 1**
Excise Book Name : ABC/BDG/1/13-14 Serial No. 4

Party's A/c Name : **Riverstone Solutions India**
Nature of Removal : **Removal As Such**

Sales Ledger : **Sales**

Name of Item	Quantity	Rate per	Amount
Mother Board Port	10 Pcs	30.00 Pcs	300.00
Rate of Duty : 12%			
Basic Excise Duty 16%		12 %	36.00
Secondary Education Cess		2 %	1.08
Show Statutory Details ? Yes			
	10 Pcs		*337.08*

F-22A: Excise Sale Invoice of Removals

Duty Details for : **Basic Excise Duty 16%**

Type of Ref	Name / Name of Item	Assessable Amount	Rate	Duty Amount
New Ref	ABC/BDG/1/13-144			
	Mother Board Port	300.00	12 %	36.00 Cr
				36.00 Cr

Duty Details for : **Secondary Education Cess**

Type of Ref	Name / Name of Item	Assessable Amount	Rate	Duty Amount
New Ref	ABC/BDG/1/13-144			
	Mother Board Port	36.00	3 %	1.08 Cr
				1.08 Cr

F-22B: Invoice Excise Details

The Sale Voucher entry is similar to Sales Invoice Entry described earlier. Fig F-2A to F-22D shows the various components of Invoice Entry.

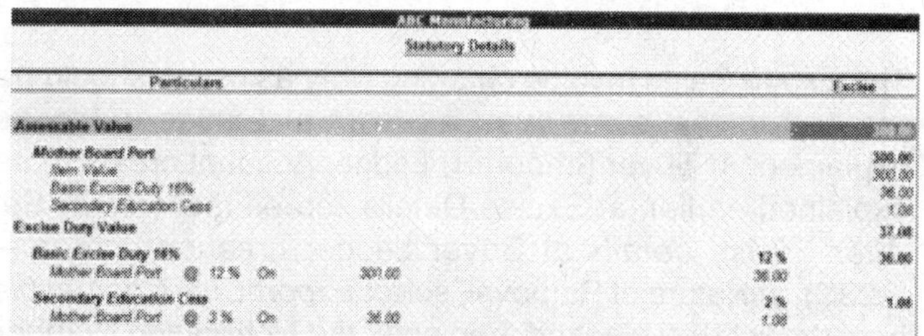

F-22C: Invoice Duty Details

F-22D: Item Allocation

Item Allocations for : **Mother Board Port**

Godown	Quantity	Rate per	Amount
Bonded Godown 1	10 Pcs	30.00 Pcs	300.00
	10 Pcs		300.00

08 Export with Payment of Duty

Sometimes Export is done with Payment of Duty and then Duty Refund is claimed. In such case, the Sale is made as *Export – Duty Chargeable*

Accounting Voucher Creation ABC Manufacturing Ctrl + M

ExcSl No. 5 1-Jan-2010 Friday

Ref. :
Excise Unit : **Bonded Godown 1**
Excise Book Name : ABC/BDG/1/13-14 Serial No. 5

Party's A/c Name : **Global Computers**
Nature of Removal : **Export - Duty Chargeable** Notification Number : **23456** Sl.No in Notification : **12** Notification Type : **Tariff**

Sales Ledger : **Export Sales**

Name of Item	Quantity	Rate per	Amount
CPU P4	1 Pcs	1,900.00 Pcs	1,900.00
Rate of Duty : 16%			
Basic Excise Duty 16%		16 %	304.00
Secondary Education Cess		2 %	6.08
Show Statutory Details ? No			
	1 Pcs		2,210.08

F-23A: Export Invoice with Duty paid

Notification Type

Non Tariff
Tariff

F-23B: Notification Type List

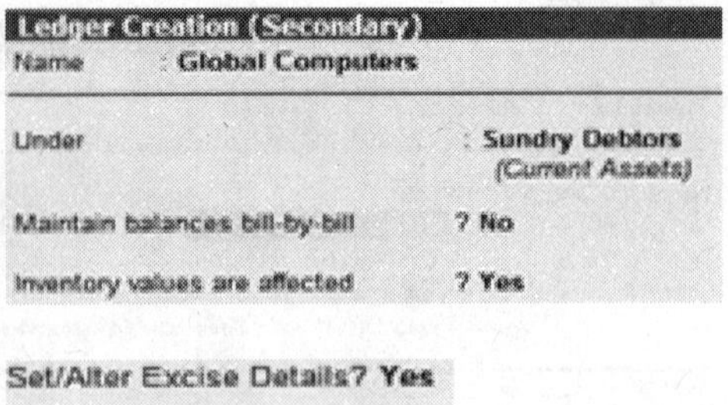

F-23C: Importer Ledger

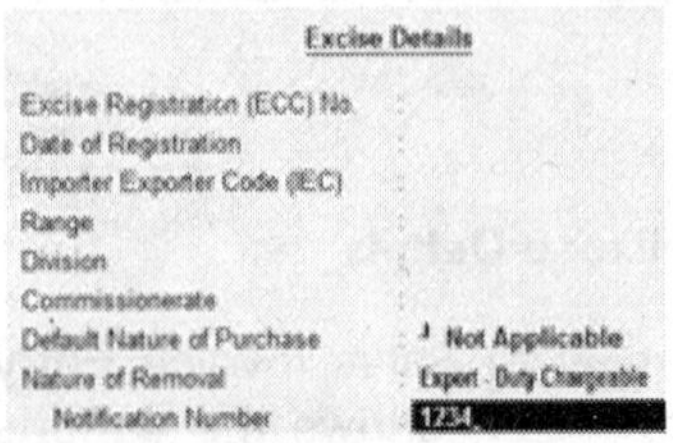

F-23D: Importer Excise Details

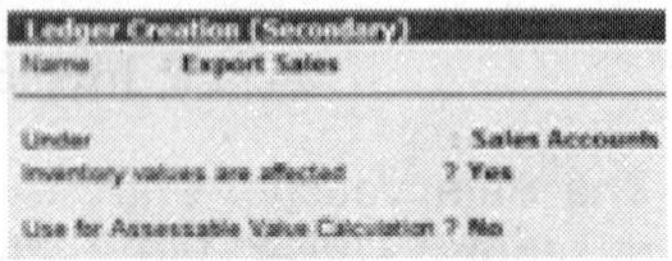

F-23E: Export Sales Ledger

The Export Sales Invoice charging Duty as usual, should be created in the same way as Normal Excise sales as explained. At Buyer (Importer) Ledger Account creation, as explained earlier, at Excise Details screen (set *Yes* at *Set Alter Excise details* at Buyer Ledger creation screen – F-23C), at Nature of Removal, select *Export-Duty Chargeable* from the list (F-21B), and then enter the Notification Number (F-23D).

At Sales Voucher entry screen (F-23A), at Nature of removal, select *Export-Duty Chargeable* from the list (F-21B), and at *Notification Type*, select Tariff from Notification Type list (F-23B).

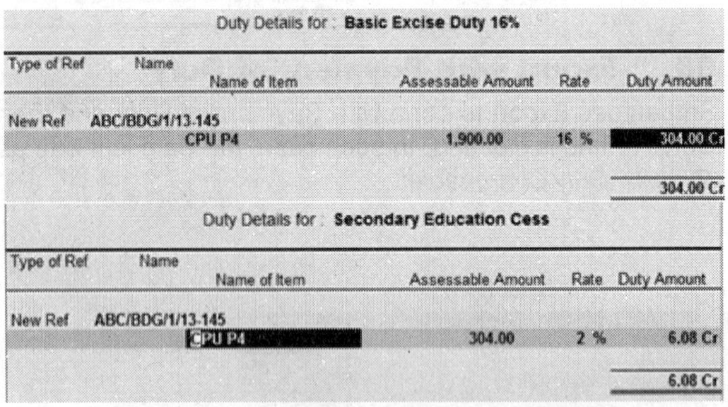

F-23G: Excise Ledger Accounts Details

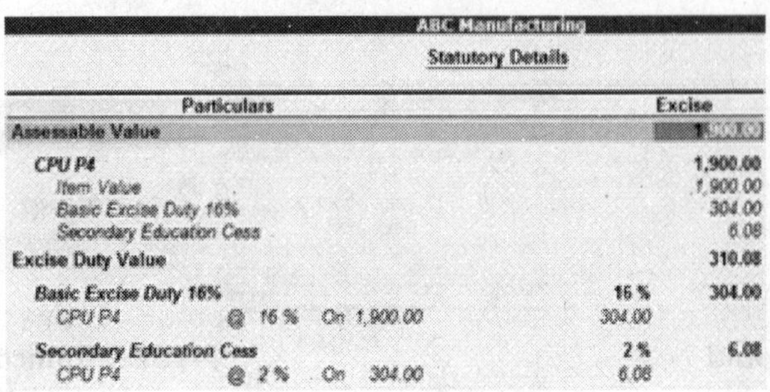

F-23H: Statutory Details

Later on. to adjust the duty refundable, enter a Journal Voucher, as described earlier.

Fig F-23A to F-23H shows the various components of Export Sales Invoice entry charging Excise Duty.

09 Captive Consumption

For Captive (Internal) consumption of Duty Chargeable Items, which are consumed for Production of Duty Exempted goods, Duty is to be paid. Such internal (captive) consumption is entered as Sales Voucher with the Company as Seller as well as Buyer. So, create a Party Ledger (Buyer) in the name of the Company.

09.01 Ledger Account for Captive Consumption

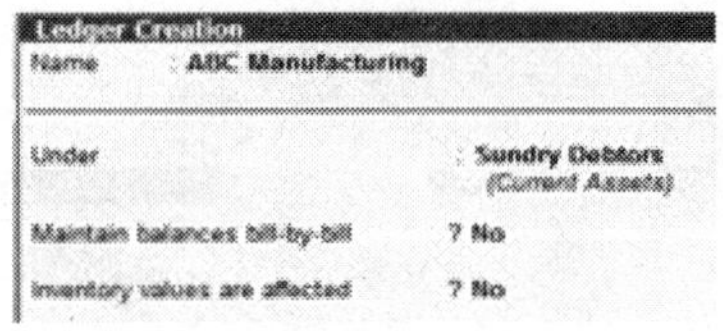

F-24A: Own Ledger creation

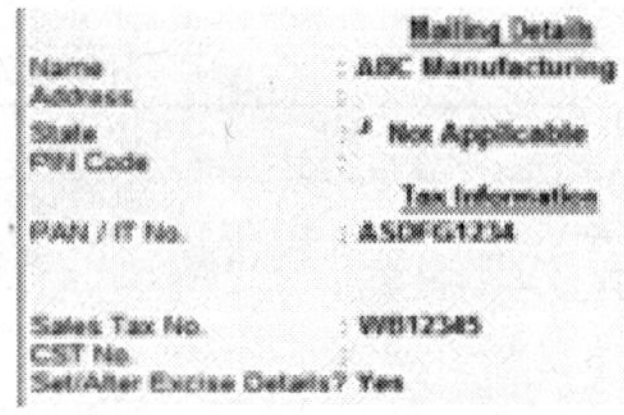

F-24B: Ledger Details

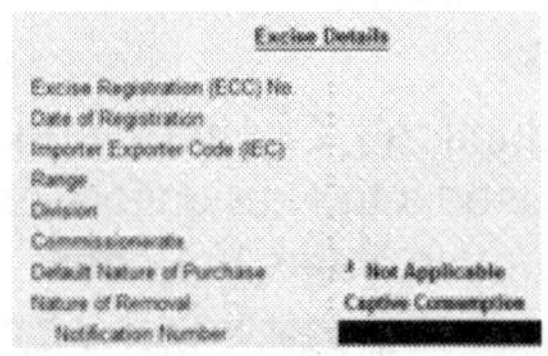

F-24C: Excise Details of Ledger

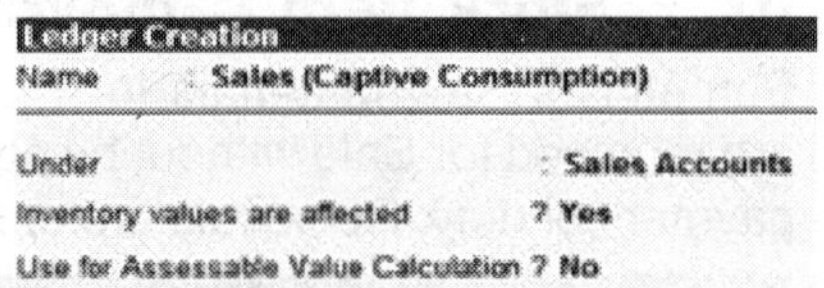

F-24D: Sales Ledger for Captive Consumption

Create a Party Ledger in the Company's Name (F-24A), and set the relevant details (F-24B & F-24C). Create a Sales Ledger Account for Captive Consumption, to create a Sales Invoice on the Company itself.

09.02 Sales Invoice for Captive Consumption

Fig 24E to F-24H shows the Sale Invoice for Captive Consumption and its various components

10 Excise Stock Transfer

When Excisable goods are moved from the Excise Godown (Bonded Warehouse) to another Godown / Branch, it is called ***Stock Transfer***. The Company is liable to pay duty on the transfer of stock to another godown. To enable Inter Godown Stock Transfer, you have to:

- Activate Multiple Godown
- Create Godown Masters
- Create Stock Transfer Voucher Type
- Create Stock Transfer Voucher
- Create Branch Ledger

10.01 Multiple Godown Activation

At *F11:Features>Inventory Features*, under *Order Processing*, set *Yes* at *Job Order Processing* (F-25A) to activate Multiple Godowns Feature for the Company.

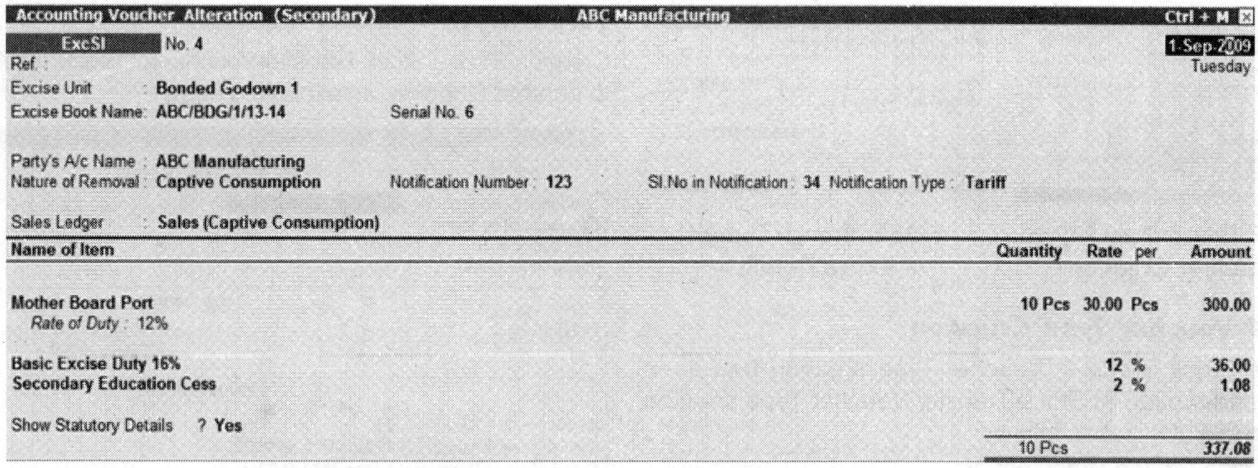

Accounting Voucher Alteration (Secondary) ABC Manufacturing Ctrl + M

ExcSI No. 4 1-Sep-2009 Tuesday

Ref. :

Excise Unit : Bonded Godown 1

Excise Book Name: ABC/BDG/1/13-14 Serial No. 6

Party's A/c Name : ABC Manufacturing

Nature of Removal : Captive Consumption Notification Number : 123 Sl.No in Notification : 34 Notification Type : Tariff

Sales Ledger : Sales (Captive Consumption)

Name of Item	Quantity	Rate	per	Amount
Mother Board Port *Rate of Duty : 12%*	10 Pcs	30.00	Pcs	300.00
Basic Excise Duty 16%		12 %		36.00
Secondary Education Cess		2 %		1.08
Show Statutory Details ? Yes				
	10 Pcs			337.08

F-24E: Captive Consumption Invoice

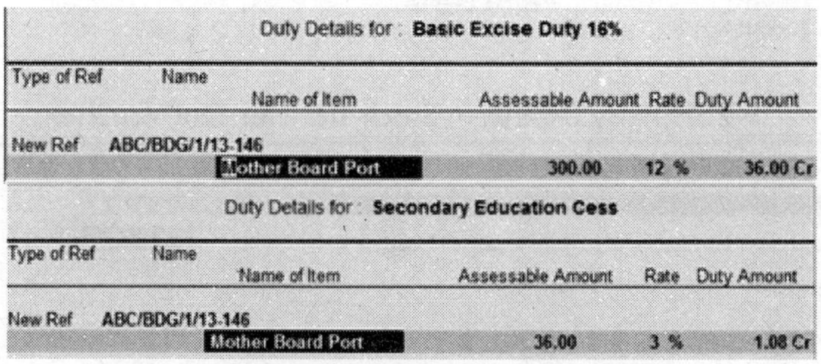

Duty Details for : **Basic Excise Duty 16%**

Type of Ref	Name	Name of Item	Assessable Amount	Rate	Duty Amount
New Ref	ABC/BDG/1/13-146				
		Mother Board Port	300.00	12 %	36.00 Cr

Duty Details for : **Secondary Education Cess**

Type of Ref	Name	Name of Item	Assessable Amount	Rate	Duty Amount
New Ref	ABC/BDG/1/13-146				
		Mother Board Port	36.00	3 %	1.08 Cr

F-24F:Duty details of Sales Invoice

F-24F: Duty Details of Sales Invoice

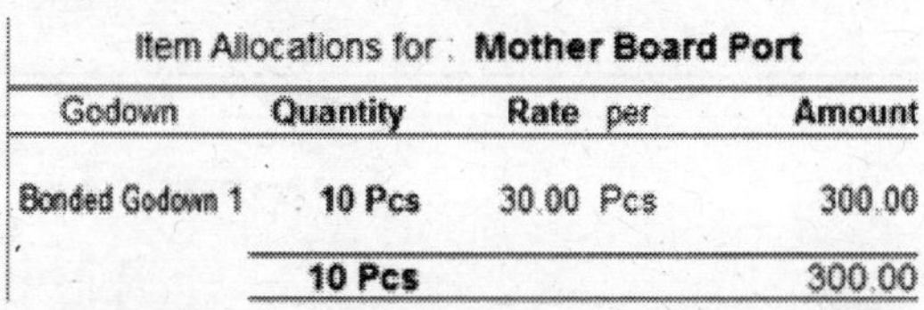

Item Allocations for : **Mother Board Port**

Godown	Quantity	Rate	per	Amount
Bonded Godown 1	10 Pcs	30.00	Pcs	300.00
	10 Pcs			300.00

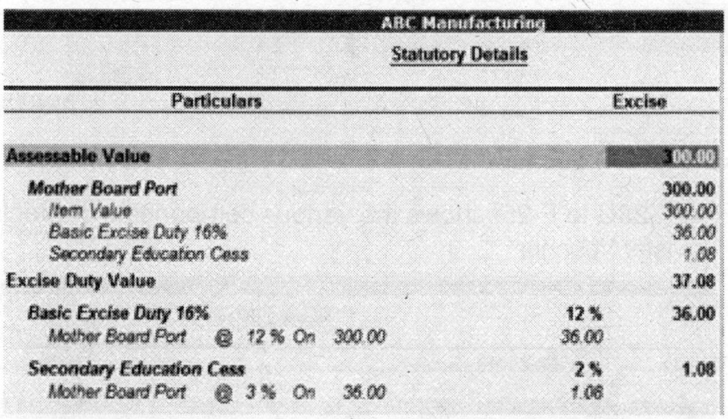

ABC Manufacturing

Statutory Details

Particulars		Excise
Assessable Value		300.00
Mother Board Port		300.00
Item Value		300.00
Basic Excise Duty 16%		36.00
Secondary Education Cess		1.08
Excise Duty Value		37.08
Basic Excise Duty 16%	12 %	36.00
Mother Board Port @ 12 % On 300.00	36.00	
Secondary Education Cess	2 %	1.08
Mother Board Port @ 3 % On 36.00	1.08	

24H: Statutory details of Sales Invoice

Godown Creation: Having activated Multiple Godowns, create the Godown where the excisable goods will be transferred (F-25B), as explained earlier. Set as Follows:

- **Our Stock**: At *Our Stock with Third party*, set *Yes*
- **Third Party Stock**: At *Third party Stock with Us*, set *No*

10.02 Branch Ledger Creation

Ledger Account creation has been explained earlier. Create Ledger Account for Branch (F-25D).

- At *Under*, select *Branch / Division* as Parent Group.
- At *Set / Alter Excise details*, set Yes to get Ledger Excise Details screen (F-25E).
  - o At *Nature of Removal*, select *Domestic* from *Removal Type* list (F-21B)

10.03 Excise Duty Payable Ledger Creation

Create Excise Payable Ledger Account (F-25F). At *Statutory Information* section, set as follows:

- At *Use for Assessable Value Calculation*, set Yes
- At *Apportion for*, select *Excise* from Tax Type List (F-18B)
- At *Method of Apportion*, select the appropriate method of Apportion from the list (F-18C)

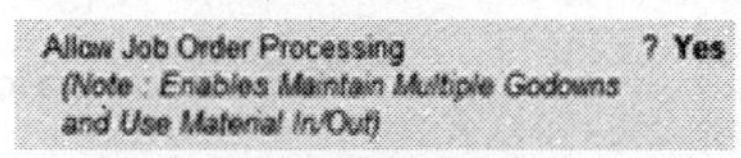

Allow Job Order Processing ? Yes

(Note : Enables Maintain Multiple Godowns and Use Material In/Out)

F-25A: Multiple Godown Activation

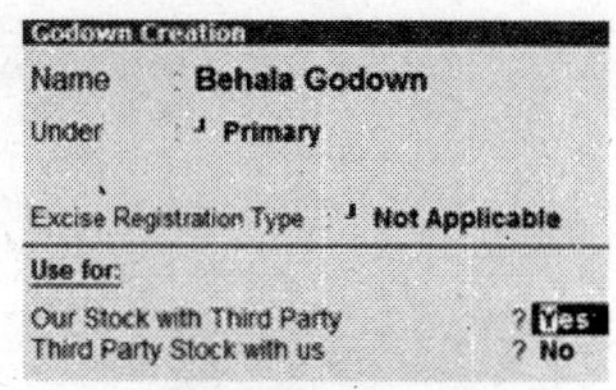

Godown Creation

Name : Behala Godown

Under : Primary

Excise Registration Type : Not Applicable

Use for:

Our Stock with Third Party ? Yes

Third Party Stock with us ? No

F-25B: Godown Creation

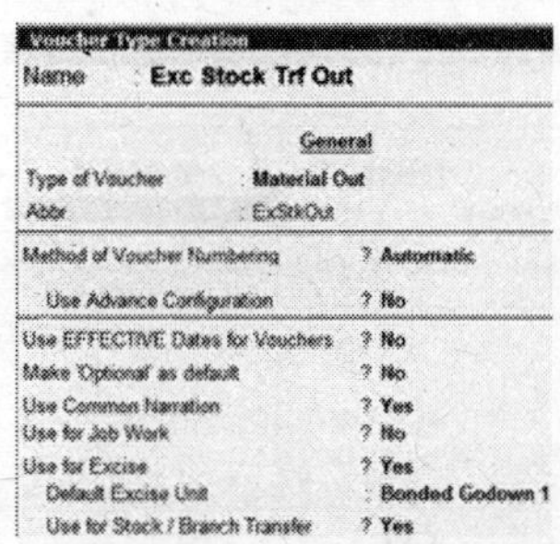

Voucher Type Creation

Name : Exc Stock Trf Out

General

Type of Voucher : Material Out

Abbr : ExStkOut

Method of Voucher Numbering ? Automatic

Use Advance Configuration ? No

Use EFFECTIVE Dates for Vouchers ? No

Make 'Optional' as default ? No

Use Common Narration ? Yes

Use for Job Work ? No

Use for Excise ? Yes

Default Excise Unit : Bonded Godown 1

Use for Stock / Branch Transfer ? Yes

F-25C: Stock Transfer Voucher Type

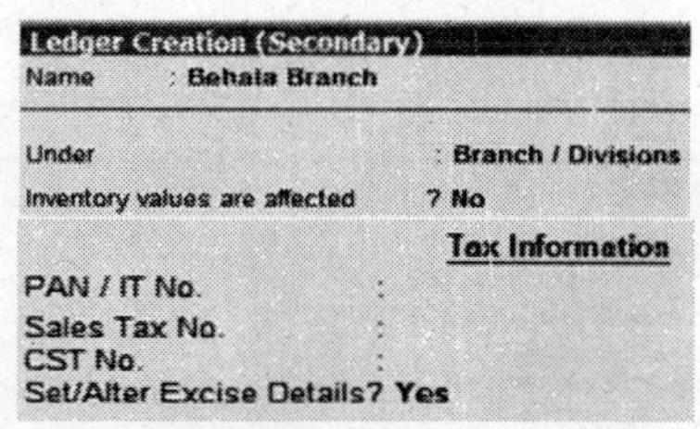

Ledger Creation (Secondary)

Name : Behala Branch

Under : Branch / Divisions

Inventory values are affected ? No

Tax Information

PAN / IT No. :

Sales Tax No. :

CST No. :

Set/Alter Excise Details? Yes

F-25D: Branch Ledger Creation

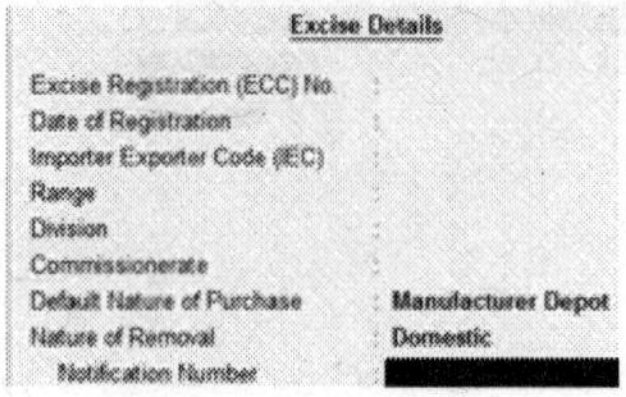

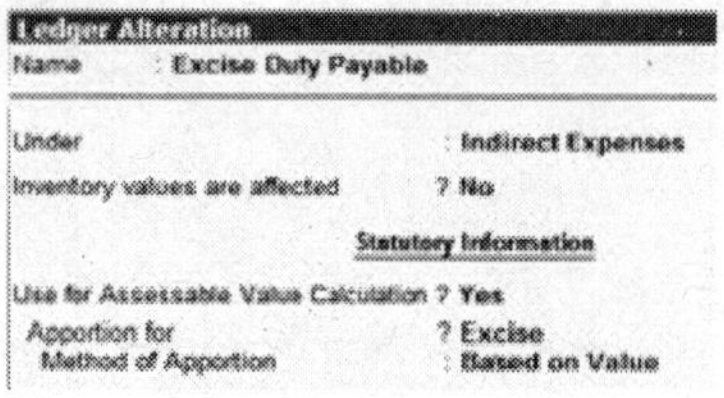

F-25F: Excise Duty Payable Ledger Creation

F-25E: Branch Ledger Excise Details

10.04 Voucher Type Creation

Excise Stock Transfer Voucher Type creation has been explained earlier, At Stock Transfer Voucher Type creation screen (F-25C), set as follows:

- At *Use for Job Work*, set *No*
- At *Use for Excise*, set *Yes*, as explained earlier
- At *Default Excise Unit*, set the default Excise Godown, as explained earlier

10.05 Journal Voucher Class Creation

Create a *Journal Voucher Class* for Excise / CENVAT Adjustment (F-25F), as explained earlier. At Voucher Class set up screen (F-25G), set *Yes* at *Use Class for Excise / CENVAT Adjustment.*

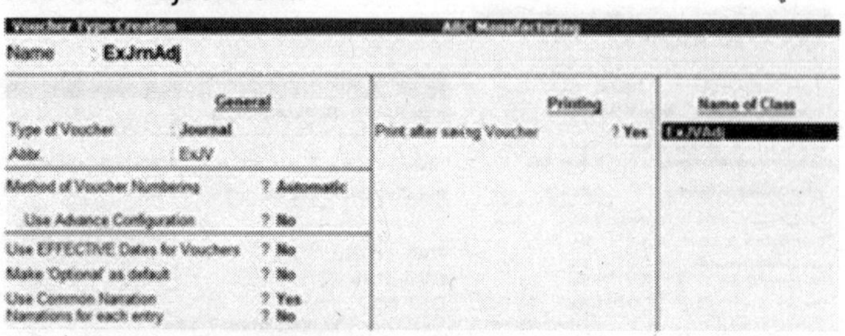

F-25F: Excise Adjustment Journal Voucher Class creation

F-25G: Voucher Class Set Up

10.06 Stock Transfer Voucher

Create a Excise Stock Transfer Voucher for Stock Transferred to another Godown, as explained earlier.

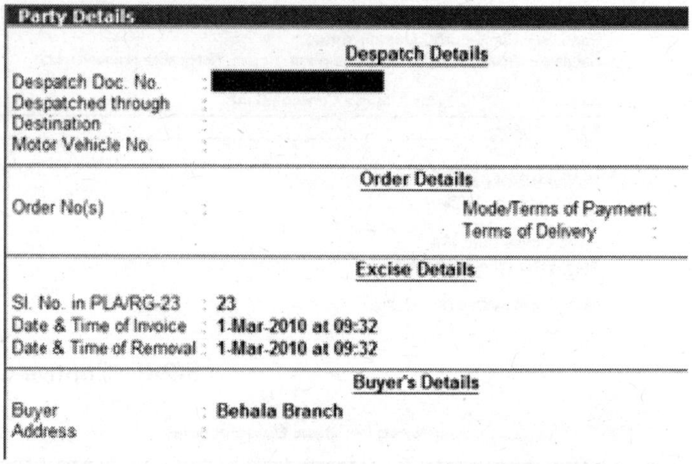

F-25H:Party Details in Stock Transfer Out Voucher

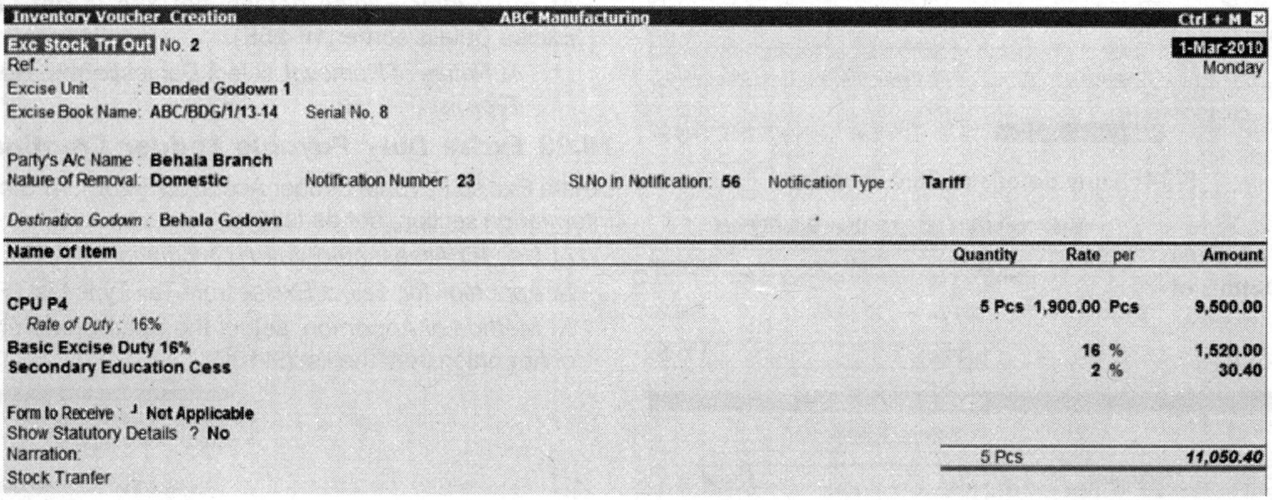

F-25G: Excise Stock Transfer Voucher

Fig F-25G to F-25I shows the various components of Stock Transfer Voucher

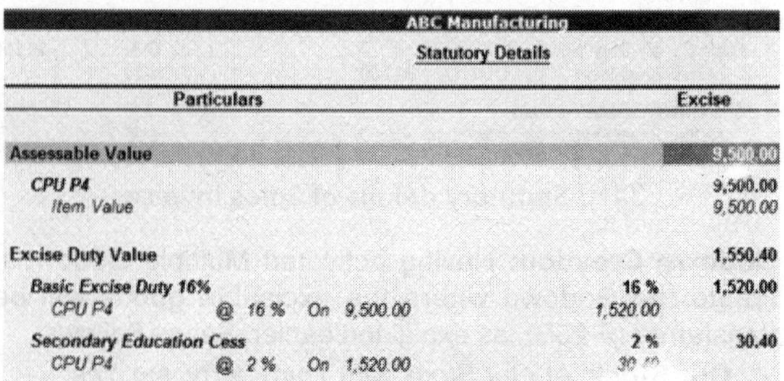

F-25I: Statutory Details in Stock Transfer Out Voucher

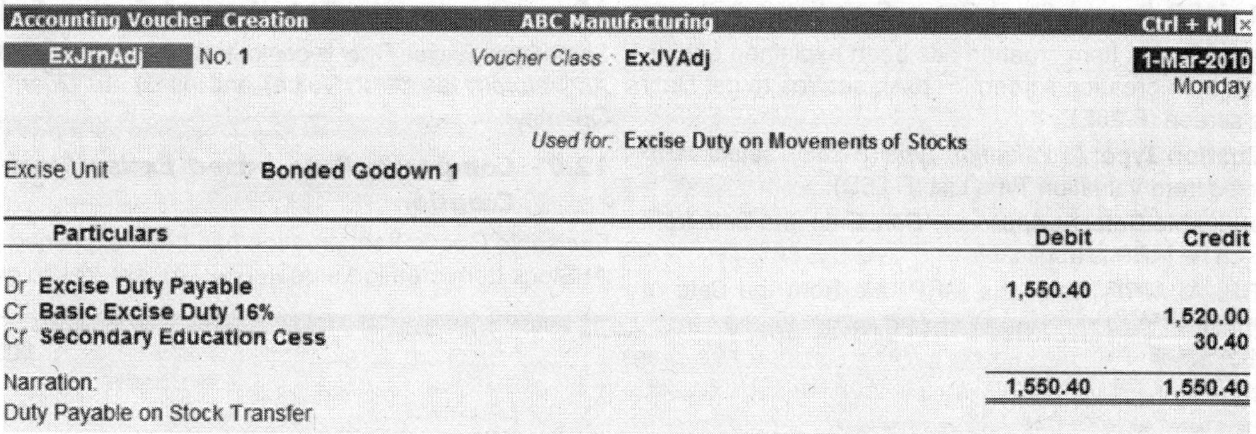

F-25J:Duty Adjustment Journal for Stock Transfer

10.07 Journal Voucher for Stock Transfer Duty Liability

The Stock Transfer Voucher is a pure Inventory Voucher which does not have any effect in Accounts. To create the Liability for Excise Duty Payable, create a Journal Voucher using the CENVAT / EXCISE Voucher Class.

At *Used For*, select *Excise Duty for Movements of Stock* from *Excise Adjustment Nature* List (F-25M).

At *Journal Voucher* Entry screen, click *L:Excise Helper* button to get Excise Adjustment Helper screen (F-25K). Enter as follows:

- **Excise Unit**: At *Excise Unit*, select the Excise Unit from which the materials is being transferred
- **Expenses Ledger**: At Expenses Ledger, select the Excise Duty payable Ledger Account
- **Period**: At period enter the period for which the Liability of Duty on Transfers are being ceated through the Journal Voucher.

A confirmation screen (*Proceed to Availing Debit Excise Duties on Movement of Stock*) appears for computation of Duty Liability creation (F-25L). Set *Yes* to get the Journal Voucher Entry screen (F-25J).

At *Journal Voucher* Entry screen (F-25J), select the Ledger Accounts, enter the Amount and save the Voucher.

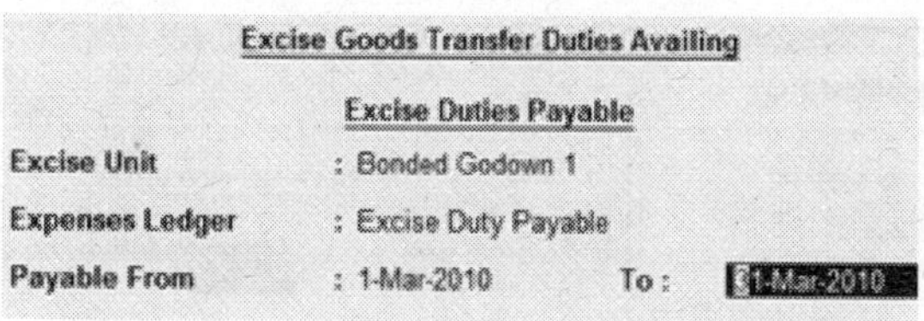

F-25K: Excise Adjustment Helper screen

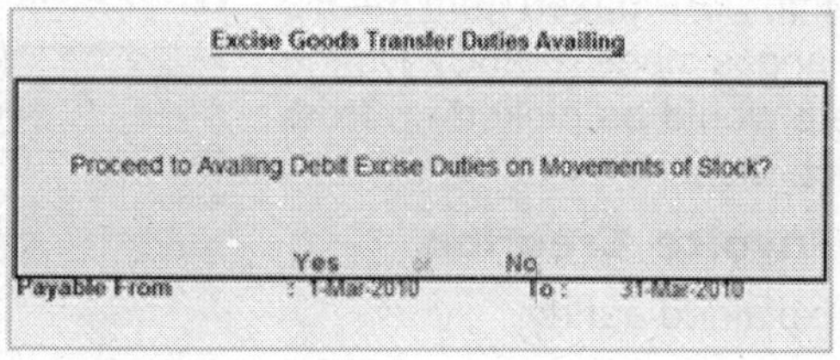

F-25L: Excise Adjustment confirmation

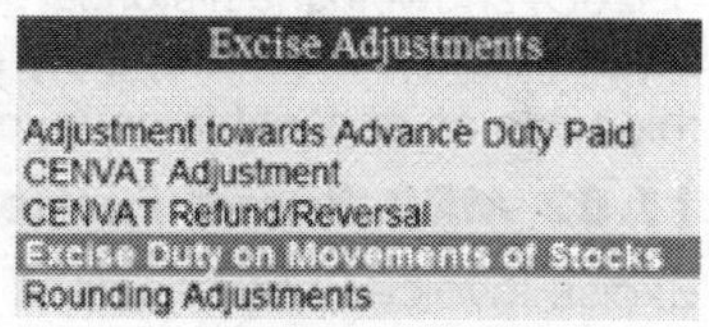

F-25M: Excise Adjustment nature

11 Sale with MRP Based Duty

In some products (like Tobacco Products), the Excise Duty is charged on declared MRP (Maximum Retail Price) of the goods irrespective of actual sale price.

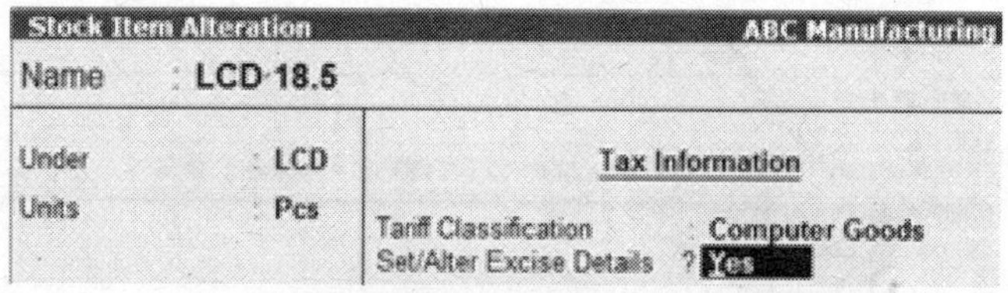

F-26A: Stock Item creation

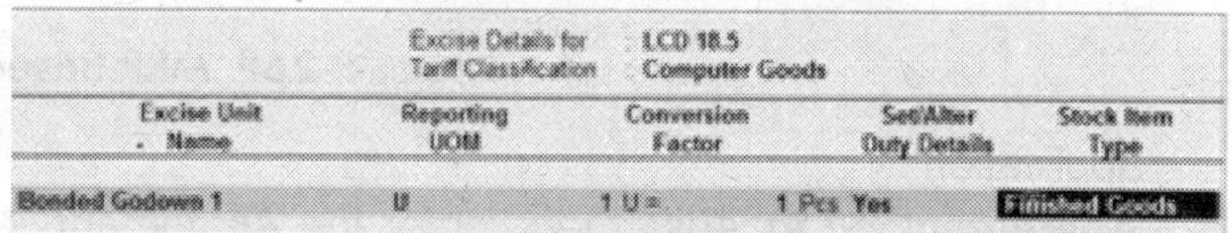

F-26B: Item Duty Details

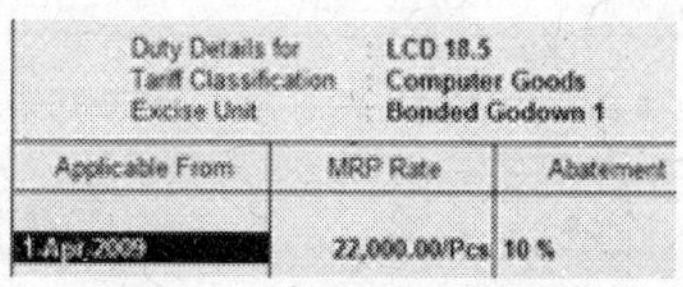

F-26C: MRP Based Item Details

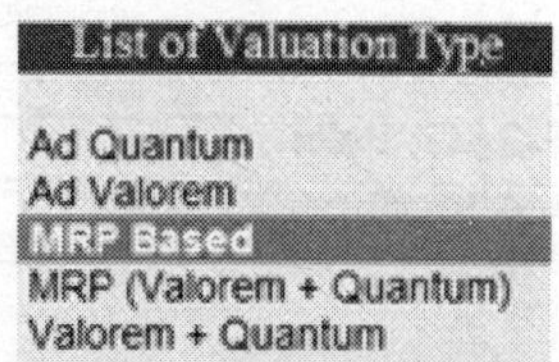

F-26D: Valuation Type List

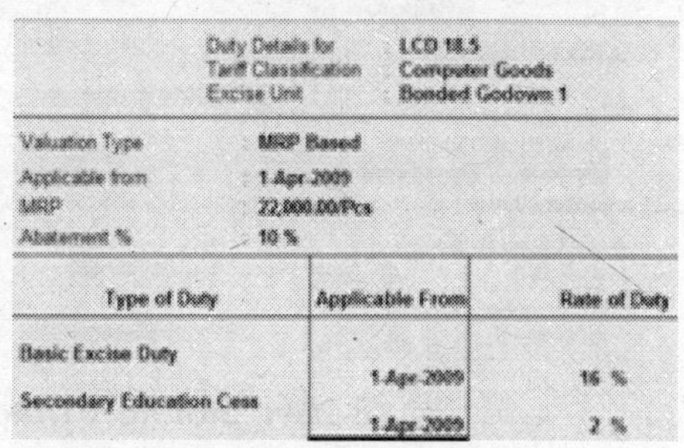

F-26E: MRP Based Item Duty Details

11.01 MRP Based Stock Item Creation

Excisable Goods Item creation has been explained earlier. At Stock Item creation screen (F-26A), set Yes to get Duty details screen (F-26E).

- **Valuation Type**: At *Valuation Type* (F-26E), select *MRP Based* from Valuation Type List (F-26D).
- **Applicable Date**: At *Applicable Date* Enter the Date from which he MRP is applicable
- **MRP:** At *MRP*, Enter the MRP rate from the date of application
- **Abatement %**: At *Abatement*, enter the Abatement % (Abatement is now withdrawn)

Next you get the details carried into MRP based Item details (F-26C) showing the historical changes made.(F-26C). During Invoice Entry, the Rate, Duty etc would be picked up from this table as applicable on Invoice Date

11.02 MRP Based Excise Invoice Creation

Excise Invoice Entry has been explained earlier.

Fig F-26F to F-26G shows the various components of MRP Based Invoice

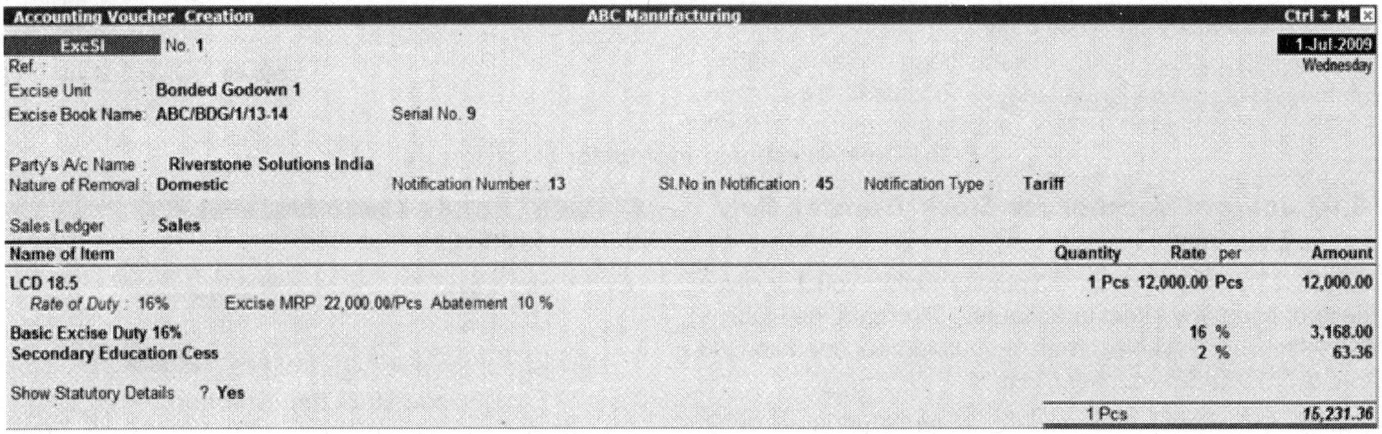

Accounting Voucher Creation — ABC Manufacturing — Ctrl + M

ExcSI No. 1 — 1-Jul-2009 Wednesday

Ref. :

Excise Unit : Bonded Godown 1

Excise Book Name: ABC/BDG/1/13-14 Serial No. 9

Party's A/c Name : Riverstone Solutions India

Nature of Removal : Domestic Notification Number : 13 Sl.No in Notification : 45 Notification Type : Tariff

Sales Ledger : Sales

Name of Item	Quantity	Rate	per	Amount
LCD 18.5	1 Pcs	12,000.00	Pcs	12,000.00
Rate of Duty : 16% Excise MRP 22,000.00/Pcs Abatement 10 %				
Basic Excise Duty 16%		16	%	3,168.00
Secondary Education Cess		2	%	63.36
Show Statutory Details ? Yes				
	1 Pcs			15,231.36

F-26F: MRP Based Excise Sale Invoice

F-26G: Item Allocation

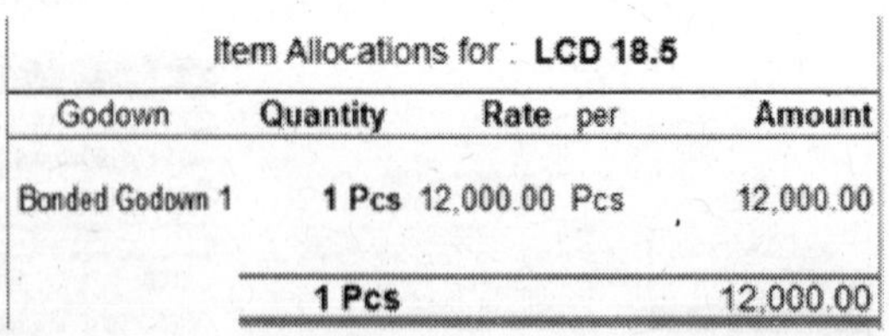

Item Allocations for : LCD 18.5

Godown	Quantity	Rate	per	Amount
Bonded Godown 1	1 Pcs	12,000.00	Pcs	12,000.00
	1 Pcs			12,000.00

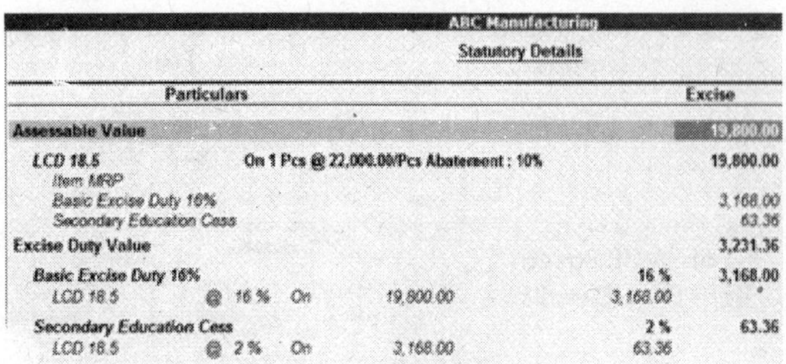

ABC Manufacturing

Statutory Details

Particulars				Excise
Assessable Value				19,800.00
LCD 18.5	On 1 Pcs @ 22,000.00/Pcs Abatement : 10%			19,800.00
Item MRP				
Basic Excise Duty 16%				3,168.00
Secondary Education Cess				63.36
Excise Duty Value				3,231.36
Basic Excise Duty 16%			16 %	3,168.00
LCD 18.5	@ 16 % On	19,800.00	3,168.00	
Secondary Education Cess			2 %	63.36
LCD 18.5	@ 2 % On	3,168.00	63.36	

F-26H: Statutory Details

12 Composite Rate based Excise Sale

Sometimes Excise Duty is computed on combination of partly *Ad Valorem* (as % on Value) and partly *Ad Quantum* (on Quantity).

12.01 Composite Rate based Excise Stock Item Creation

Excisable Goods Item creation has been explained above. At Stock Item creation screen (F-27A), set *Yes* to get Duty details screen (F-27B). At *Valuation Type* (F-27B), select *Valorem + Quantum* from Valuation Type List (F-26D). At Rate of Duty / Rate per unit columns, enter the Ad Valorem (in%) & Ad Quantum (Rs Unit).

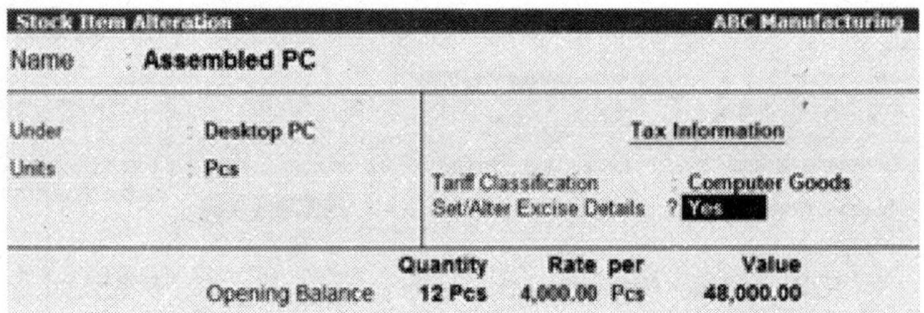

Stock Item Alteration — ABC Manufacturing

Name : Assembled PC

Under : Desktop PC

Units : Pcs

Tax Information

Tariff Classification : Computer Goods

Set/Alter Excise Details ? Yes

	Quantity	Rate	per	Value
Opening Balance	12 Pcs	4,000.00	Pcs	48,000.00

F-27A: Stock Item for Ad Valorem & Ad Quantum Duty

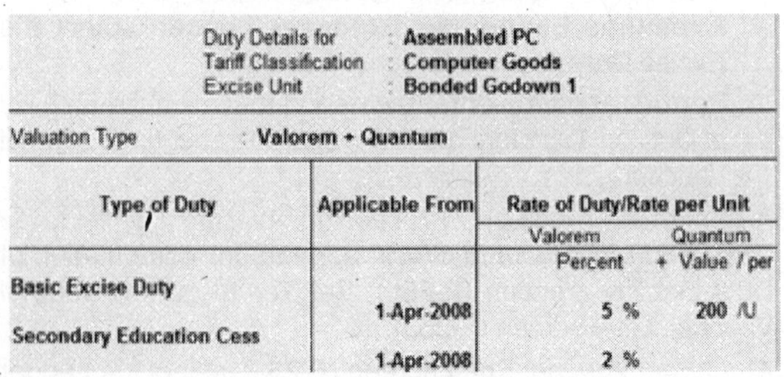

Duty Details for : Assembled PC

Tariff Classification : Computer Goods

Excise Unit : Bonded Godown 1

Valuation Type : Valorem + Quantum

Type of Duty	Applicable From	Rate of Duty/Rate per Unit: Valorem Percent	+ Quantum Value / per
Basic Excise Duty	1-Apr-2008	5 %	200 /U
Secondary Education Cess	1-Apr-2008	2 %	

F-27B: Stock Item Duty details

Excise Details for : Assembled PC
Tariff Classification : Computer Goods

Excise Unit Name	Reporting UOM	Conversion Factor		Set/Alter Duty Details	Stock Item Type
Bonded Godown 1	U	1 U =	1 Pcs	Yes	Finished Goods

F-27C: Stock Item Excise Details

Allocations of : **Assembled PC**
for: **12 Pcs**

Godown	Quantity	Rate	per	Amount
Universal Enterprises 3	12 Pcs	4,000.00	Pcs	48,000.00
	12 Pcs			48,000.00

F-27D: Opening Stock Details

12.02 Composite Rate based Excise Duty Ledgers Creation

Creation of Duty Ledger Account has been explained earlier. You have to create separate ledger accounts for Ad Valorem (F-27E) & Ad Quantum (F-27F) Ledger Accounts as follows:

Method	Percentage of Calculation	Method of Calculation
Ad valorem (F-27E)	Enter the % Rate	On Assessable Value
Ad Quantum (F-27F)	Enter any value (e.g 1%)	On Quantity (Valorem + Quantum)

In case of *Ad Quantum* (F-27E), the Rate entered is not considered. The Rate as specified at Item Master Duty Details (F-27B) will be applicable.

Ledger Creation
Name : **Basic Excise Duty 5%**

Under : **Duties & Taxes**
(Current Liabilities)

Type of Duty/Tax : **Excise**
Excise Accounting Code : **300500**
Duty Head : **Basic Excise Duty**
Inventory values are affected ? **No**
Percentage of Calculation (eg 5) ? **5 %**
Method of Calculation : **On Assessable Value**
Rounding Method : **Not Applicable**

F-27E: Ad valorem Duty Ledger Account

Ledger Creation
Name : **Basic Excise Duty (Fixed)**

Under : **Duties & Taxes**
(Current Liabilities)

Type of Duty/Tax : **Excise**
Excise Accounting Code : **450001**
Duty Head : **Basic Excise Duty**
Inventory values are affected ? **No**
Percentage of Calculation (eg 5) ? **1 %**
Method of Calculation : **On Quantity (Valorem + Quantum)**
Rounding Method : **Normal Rounding**
Rounding Limit : **0**

F-27F: Ad Quantum Duty Ledger Account

12.03 Value & Quantity based Excise Sale Invoice

Excise Sales Invoice has been explained earlier.

At Sales Invoice entry (F-27G), on selection of Item, the Duty Rate is shown below the Item for information. On selection of Duty Ledger Account, the respective duty amount is carried automatically. At *Show Statutory Details*, set *Yes* to get the Statutory Details (showing the detailed computation of Duty.

12.04 Composite Duty Excise Invoice

Having entered the Invoice, click P:*Print* to print the Invoice (F-18A)

In Printed Invoice, the Rate for Fixed Component is not printed as it is irrelevant and misleading.

Accounting Voucher Creation ABC Manufacturing Ctrl + M
ExcSI No. 2 1-Jul-2009
Ref. : Wednesday
Excise Unit : Bonded Godown 1
Excise Book Name: ABC/BDG/1/13-14 Serial No. 10
Party's A/c Name : Riverstone Solutions India
Nature of Removal : Domestic Notification Number : 45 Sl.No in Notification : 4 Notification Type : Tariff
Sales Ledger : Sales

Name of Item	Quantity	Rate	per	Amount
Assembled PC	1 Pcs	5,000.00	Pcs	5,000.00
Rate of Duty : 5% *Rate per Unit : 200/U*				
Basic Excise Duty 5%		5 %		250.00
Basic Excise Duty (Fixed)		1 %		200.00
Secondary Education Cess		2 %		9.00
Show Statutory Details ? **Yes**				
	1 Pcs			5,459.00

F-27G: Value & Quantity based Excise Sale Invoice creation

ABC Manufacturing

Statutory Details

Particulars						Excise
Assessable Value						5,000.00
Assembled PC						
Item Value						5,000.00
Basic Excise Duty 5%						250.00
Basic Excise Duty (Fixed)						200.00
Secondary Education Cess						9.00
Excise Duty Value						**459.00**
Basic Excise Duty 5%					5 %	250.00
Assembled PC	@ 5 %	On	5,000.00	1 U	250.00	
Basic Excise Duty (Fixed)					1 %	200.00
Assembled PC	@ 200/U	On	1 U		200.00	
Secondary Education Cess					2 %	9.00
Assembled PC	@ 2 %	On	450.00	1 U	9.00	

F-27H: Statutory Details

Item Allocations for : **Assembled PC**

Godown	Quantity	Rate	per	Amount
Bonded Godown 1	**1 Pcs**	5,000.00	Pcs	5,000.00
	1 Pcs			5,000.00

F-27I: Item allocation

Excise Invoice

(ISSUE OF INVOICE UNDER RULE 11 OF CENTRAL EXCISE RULES 2002)

Bonded Godown 1
12 Naktala
Phone : 03312345678 / E-mail : sales@universal.com

Excise Regn No. : **ABCDE1234D123XM**

Range : 123456
Division : 123
Commissionerate : 12

Buyer	Invoice No.	Dated
Riverstone Solutions India 12 Tilak Rd Kolkata	**10**	**1-Jul-2009**
	Buyer's Order No.	Dated
	Delivery Note	Dated
	Supplier's Ref.	Despatch Document No.
	Despatched through	Destination
	Date & Time of issue of Invoice **1-Jul-2009 at 12:09**	Motor Vehicle No.
	Date & Time of Removal of Goods **1-Jul-2009 at 12:09**	Authenticated By ***for Bonded Godown 1***
Notification No. : **45**	Mode/Terms of Payment **30 Days**	*Authorised Signatory*

Description of Goods	Tariff / HSN Classification	Quantity	Rate	per	Amount
Assembled PC	13456789	1 Pcs	5,000.00	Pcs	5,000.00
Basic Excise Duty 5%			5	%	250.00
Basic Excise Duty (Fixed)					200.00
Secondary Education Cess			2	%	9.00
Total		**1 Pcs**			**₹ 5,459.00**

Amount Chargeable (in words) : **Indian Rupees Five Thousand Four Hundred Fifty Nine Only**

Description of Goods	Assessable Value	Rate of BED	BED Amount	BED on Qty	Rate of Sec Ed Cess	Sec Ed Cess Amount
Assembled PC	5,000.00	5 %	250.00	200.00	2 %	9.00
Total	**5,000.00**		**250.00**	**200.00**		**9.00**

Amount of Duty (in words) : **Indian Rupees Four Hundred Fifty Only**
Amount of ED Cess (in words) :
Amount of SHE Cess (in words) : **Indian Rupees Nine Only**

Serial No. in PLA/RG-23 : **38**

VAT Declaration : Goods Sold will not be taken Back. Mon-Fri : 11am to 7pm, Sat 11am to 2 pm

Excise Declaration
We declare to the best of our knowledge and belief that the particulars stated herein are true and correct and there is no additional consideration accruing to us either directly or indirectly in any manner other than the amounts indicated here.

for Bonded Godown 1

Name : S K Deb
Designation : Manager

Authorised Signatory

SUBJECT TO KOLKATA JURISDICTION

E. & O.E.

This is a Computer Generated Invoice

F-28A: Value & Quantity based Excise Sale Invoice

Section 4

Payroll

Part 1
Payroll Masters

In this Part, we explain the process of Pay roll Activation, Statutory Information set up & creation of various Payroll Masters to implement the Payroll System

- **Payroll Set Up** explains activation of Payroll & Statutory Fetaures and Configurtaion set up for Payroll System
- **Pay Heads** explains Ratio of various Pay Head Maser records, their computation rules & formulas
- **Employee Masters** explains Employee Group, Employee Category & Employee Personal records creation, specifying Pay Structure and various Employee Set Ups

Payroll Set up

01 Payroll Activation

To maintain Payroll System, first you should activate Payroll Features for the respective Company. You may maintain Payroll for any type of Company (*Accounts Only Company* or *Accounts with Inventory*).

At *Gateway of Tally,* Click *F11: Features >Accounting Features* to get Accounting Features screen. Under the Cost / Profit Centres Management section (F-1A), set as follows to activate Payroll Features:

- Set *Yes* at *Maintain Payroll features* (F-1A)
- For simplicity, Set *No* at *Maintain Cost Centres* (consequently other options under Cost Centre will not get activated (these are discussed in later part of the book).

F-1A: Accounting Features Set Up

Cost/Profit Centres Management	
Maintain Payroll	? Yes
Maintain Cost Centres	? No

Consequently, several options related to Payroll get activated at Menus and other relevant places. Now you may start creating Masters &Transaction data for Payroll as described in later chapters. The options to activate Statutory Features of Payroll are discussed in later part of the Book.

02 *Features at a Glance*

Tally Payroll is fully integrated Payroll module of Tally ERP 9 system. The salient features o the system are listed below:

User definable unlimited Earnings & Deductions heads: You may create your own Pay Heads for Earnings & Deductions appearing in Payslip. Apart from that, you may also create Pay Heads for accounts that are not part of Payslip but are affected with employee payments, like Employer's Contribution, Administration charges payable for PF, DLI, ESI etc, Gratuity or any other deferred payments, other employee benefits etc.

Pay Heads Linked with Ledger Accounts: Each Pay Head is linked with a distinct ledger account

User definable Pay Head Names: You may specify alternate Pay Head names to appear in Payslip and other Pay reports, which may be different from the respective ledger heads. This way, you may customize Pay reports in your own way

Employee Groups: Employees belonging to similar computation rules may be grouped so that similar rules may be applied to them, offering operational ease and organised reports. Pay slips/ pay reports, pay processing etc may be done for a specific employee or employee group, or can be done for all employees at a stroke. Such flexibility allows to process payroll for small organization of a few employees to large organization with multi level divisions, departments & sections, with equal ease.

Employee Category: Apart from Employee Groups, employees may be classified into independent Categories. In this way, you may get multi level multi directional filtering facility for reporting and pay processing

Employee Specific Computation rules: All rates & applicability rules for each pay head can be distinctly defined for each employee, or group of employees, providing enormous flexibility to define specific rules for any employee / employee group

Pay Computation rules: You get enormous flexible pay computation rules to set up independently for each employee and each pay head like:

- **Attendance based direct computation**: Pay may be computed on attendance on Daily / Hourly rates, for any period.
- **Absenteeism based indirect computation**: Pay may be indirectly computed after deducting for absenteeism / without pay days, from the monthly rates.
- **Slab based based computation**: Uniform or multi staged slab based rates may be coupled with any computation rule, to adapt to more complex rules. The rates may be discreet specific amount or percentage based, or even a mix of them within same slab.
- **Inter head dependency rules**: You may set up rules to compute pay from the result of other pay heads. For example, PF may be computed on Basic & DA as per specific rules, while Basic & DA gets computed through other independent data, parameters & rules.
- **Fixed Rate based computation**: You may specify monthly fixed rates to be applied uniformly without any regard to attendance, leave or absenteeism.
- **Variable amount figures:** For pay heads where the amount varies each month, it may be entered in each pay slip for each employee, on post processing of pay.

User definable Time & Production heads: Any number of heads for time recording (like Attendance, Leave, OT,

Absenteeism etc) or production units, may be created & organized into multi level groups

Time & Production entry Form: For quick & easy data entry, the Time & Production entry Form may be set for One Employee, Group of Employees or All Employees at a time with employee names carried from Employee Master, in a tabular format with free navigation among Employee Names / Heads for fast entry.

Time & Production based Pay computation: Any head may be computed based on time unit (Month, Day, Hour etc) or production units.

Overtime Computation: You may set several types of Overtime (like Normal, Holiday etc) & applicable rates

User defined simple & compound Time units: You may create simple time units (like days, Hours) or compound units (like month of 30 days, Day of 7.5 hours etc) for computation involving dual time units.

User defined simple & compound Production units: You may create simple Production Units (like Pcs, Kg) or compound units (like Box of 24 Pcs) for computation involving dual Production units.

Complete Pay Rate History: On Pay revision, the revised Rates are appended (old rates are NOT overwritten) keeping all past history records. So, the lifetime pay rate history is available at any point of time.

Attendance Sheet & Production Register: Provides all sorts of attendance & production reports for a specified period and for specified employee.

Loan & Salary Advance: Multiple Loans may be disbursed and recovered simultaneously, maintaining separate account and loan balances for each employee

Loan Interest recovery: Loan interest also may be recovered for each loan account from each employee, on total loan amount or reducing balance, in instalments

Pay Advise through Bank Account Transfers: Bank advise may be printed to disburse Pay through bank transfers

Manual & Automated Pay voucher: Pay is auto computed and Pay voucher created. However, Pay vouchers may also be manually created, if needed.

Pay Slips: Pay slips may be printed in Vertical & Horizontal formats with YTD figures for each Head. The contents of Payslip and Pay Reports may be configured as desired.

Employee Ledger: Employee Ledger may be printed with Headwise & Employeewise details breakup

Columnar Employee Pay Sheet: Employee Pay sheet may be printed in columnar format with separate columns for each pay head and space for Revenue Stamp so that pay sheet itself may be used for Pay disbursement.

Provident Fund: The reports for Employees contribution (Statutory & Voluntary), DLI, Administration Charges etc, including all Statutory Forms as per P F Rules may be printed.

ESI: The reports for Employees & Employer's contribution etc., including all Statutory Forms as per ESI Rules may be printed.

Deposit of PF & ESI Contribution: Simple Auto Fill voucher entry for Deposit of all sorts of Employer's & Employees Contribution to Bank

Gratuity: You may specify the Gratuity computation rules, get Gratuity provision figures at any point of time and create vouchers for Gratuity provision and payment. Print Gratuity Reports

Bonus: You may specify the Bonus computation rules, get Bonus provision figures at any point of time and create vouchers for Bonus provision and payment. Print Bonus Reports

Production wages: Specify Production Wages Rates for each Product and Employee, enter Production data and get Production Wages computed in Pay voucher. Print Production Wages Report

Pay Revision: You may create Pay Structure to give effect of Pay Revision, even with retrospective effect. In same way, you may record prospective pay revision as per scale and effective date

Arrears Pay: In case of Pay Revision with retrospective effect, you may process and create Arrears Pay voucher auto computed. Alternatively, you may include headwise Arrear Pay in the current period voucher. A great time saving feature, extremely useful in Government departments and PSU organizations, where Pay revision often take place with retrospective effect.

Employee Joining & Leaving: The First Pay voucher (on Joining) and Last Pay voucher (on Leaving) is computed as per Date of Joining & Leaving.

Expatriate Reports: Various reports containing info in respect of Expatriates (like VISA, Contract Details) are available

03 Payroll System

The entire Payroll System of Tally ERP 9 may be divided into following major Components

- Employee Masters
- Payroll Masters
- Pay Head Masters
- Salary particulars
- Payroll Processing

Pay Heads

01 Pay Heads

A Pay Head is an element of Earnings (like Basic, DA, HRA etc) / Deduction (PF, ESI, P Tax, Loan Recovery, Fines, etc) and other payments made by employer / benefits (like Employer's Contribution to PF, DLI expenses etc) etc.

For each Pay Head created, a Ledger Account is auto created and linked with the Pay Head. A Pay Head may appear in Pay Slip (like Basic Salary, DA, OT, PF, ESI, P. Tax etc) or may not be a part of Payslip (like Bonus, Gratuity, Employer's Contribution to PF, ESI, DLI etc) but take part in Payroll computation.

So, first plan and make a comprehensive list of all Pay Heads before you start creating them.

Classify the Pay Heads as (because you will have to enter these attributes while creating the Pay Head)

Pay Head Creation

Name : **Basic Salary**

Pay Head Info

Pay Head Type	: **Earnings for Employees**
Income Type	: **Fixed**
Under	: **Employe Expenses** *(Indirect Expenses)*
Affect Net Salary	? **Yes**
Name to appear in Payslip	: **Basic**
Use for Gratuity	? **Yes**
Calculation Type	: **On Attendance**
Attendance / Leave with Pay	: ┘ **Not Applicable**
Leave without Pay	: **Absent**
Calculation Period	: **Months**
Per Day Calculation Basis	: **As Per Calendar Period**

Rounding Info

Rounding Method : **Normal Rounding** Limit : **1**

Opening Balance (on 1-Apr-2015) :

F-1A: Pay Ledger Creation

List of Pay Head Types

- ┘ Not Applicable
- Deductions from Employees
- **Earnings for Employees**
- Employees' Statutory Deductions
- Employer's Statutory Contributions
- Gratuity
- Loans and Advances
- Reimbursements to Employees

F-1B: Pay Head Type List

Income Type

- **Fixed**
- Variable

F-1C: Income Type List

List of Calculation

- As Computed Value
- As User Defined Value
- Flat Rate
- **On Attendance**
- On Production

F-1D: Calculation Type List

List of Attendance Types

- ┘ **Not Applicable**
- Attendance ┘ *Primary*

F-1E: Attendance Type List

List of Leave Types

- **Absent** ┘ *Primary*

F-1F: Leave Type List

List of Calculation Periods

- Days
- Fortnights
- **Months**
- Weeks

F-1G: Calculation Period List

Calculation Basis

- **As per Calendar Period**
- User defined
- User Defined Calendar Type

F-1H: Calculation Basis List

02 Pay Head Creation

At *Gateway of Tally,* Select *Payroll Info > Pay Heads> Create* to create a Pay Head as described below:

- **Pay Head Name:** At *Name*, enter the Name of Pay Head. A Ledger Account of this Name would be automatically created on saving the Pay Head. The name should be such that you can easily identify the related Pay Head. The name may be same or different from the Pay Head appearing in Pay Slip / Pay Reports.
- **Head Alias:** At *Alias*, enter **the** alternative Name or code for the Pay Head/ Ledger Account, (if alias is activated. You may enter the ledger code (if any) here.
- **Pay Head Type:** At *Pay Head Type*, select the Pay Head Type from the list (F-1B), as explained later
- **Income Type:** This field appears only when you select *Earnings from Employees* or *Reimbursement to Employees* (*Incomes* for Employee) at *Pay Head Type*. Select the *Income Type* from the list, as explained later.
- **Account Group:** At *Under*, select the parent Account Group under which the Pay Head Ledger is placed in Chart of Accounts, from the List as explained later (press *Alt+C* at *Under* field, to get Account Group Creation screen to create a new Account Group and select it as Parent Account Group). The selectable Account Group

depends on Pay Head type selected (F-1B). The Ledger Account created & linked with the Pay Head is placed under the selected Account Group.

- **Pay Head Nature:** At *Affect Net Salary*, set:
  - o *Yes* for Cash Heads which affect Net Pay in Pay Slip (like Basic, DA, I Tax, P tax, P F Deduction, ESI Deduction etc). These Pay Heads appear in Pay Slip / Pay Register as they are part of regular periodical Pay
  - o *No* for Non Cash Heads (Fringe Benefits) which do not affect Net Pay in Pay Slip. This option do not appear for Non Cash Pay Head Types like *Employer's Statutory Contribution*, etc.(F-1B). These Pay Heads normally do not appear in Pay Slip / Pay Register as they are not part of regular periodical Pay
- **Pay Head Title:** At *Name to Appear in Payslip*, the Pay Head Name is carried as default. You may change it to enter the Name of the Head as it should appear in the Payslip & other Pay Reports. Keep it brief so as to fit nicely in the column heading of Pay Register
- **Gratuity Includible:** At *Use for Gratuity* (this appears only when you select Earnings for Employees at Pay Head Type (F-1B):
  - o Set *Yes* for those Earnings Pay Heads which are included in Gratuity computation (such as Basic Salary, HRA, etc.).
  - o Set *No* for those Earnings Pay Heads which are NOT included in Gratuity computation (such as Overtime).

Calculation Type: At *Calculation Type*, select the Calculation Type for the Pay Head, from the list (F-1D), as explained later

Rounding Info: At *Rounding Method*, select the *Rounding Method* and then select the Rounding Limit as described earlier.

03 Pay Head elements

The process of selection of Pay Head elements of Pay Head entry screen (§02) are described below

03.01 Pay Head Types

Pay Head Types are class of elements of Earnings & Deductions that are used in Pay Computation. Pay Head Types also include Pay Heads exclusively related to Employee Expenses incurred in Payroll System, like Gratuity, Pension, Employer's Contribution to PF, ESI, DLI, Administration charges paid to statutory authorities, which are not normal part of Employee Pay.

At *Pay Head Types*, following Pay Types appear in the list of Pay Head Types (F-1B), to select from:

- **Earnings for Employees:** The amount for such Pay Head Type is added to compute Employee's Nat Pay (normally set *Yes* at *Affect Net Salary* field for such Pay Heads in Pay Head Entry screen: F-1A)
- **Deductions from Employees:** The amount for such Pay Head Type is Deducted to compute Employee's Nat Pay (normally set *No* at *Affect Net Salary* field for such Pay Heads in Pay Head Entry screen: F-1A)
- **Employees' Statutory Deductions**: These are computed as per Rules at prevailing Rates from the eligible employees and deducted to compute the Net Pay (like PF, ESI, P tax, I Tax etc). Amount of such heads are included in the respective Statutory Reports. Though these heads are Deductions, these heads should NOT be specified as *Deductions from Employees* as mentioned above
- **Employer's Statutory Contributions**: These are computed as per Rules and paid separately by the Employer with Appropriate Statutory Authorities. (like Employer's Contribution to PF, ESI, DLI, Administration charges paid to statutory authorities). Amount of such heads are included in the respective Statutory Reports. These are normally not included to compute Net Pay of the Employee (normally set *No* at *Affect Net Salary* field for such Pay Heads in Pay Head Entry screen: F-1A)
- **Gratuity:** Select *Gratuity* for Gratuity Pay Head, which is computed and paid on retirement from / cessation of employment with the Company, as explained later.
- **Loans & Advances:** Select *Loans & Advances* for Loans disbursement & Loan Recovery Heads.
- **Expenses Reimbursement:** Select *Reimbursement to Employees* for Heads in respect of Loans disbursement & Loan Recovery Heads.

03.02 Calculation Type

At *Calculation Types*, following Calculation Types appear in the list of *Calculation Types* (F-1D), to select from:

- o **On Attendance**: Select *On Attendance*, for computation on the basis of Paid Attendance Days. Normally Basic, DA, etc are paid on Attendance Basis. The amount under such head is deducted for Without Pay Days. For example, if the Computation period is Calendar Month, Basic Pay 3000 per month, Actual Attendance is 24 days, Leave With Pay is 4 days and Leave without Pay is 3 days, then his Basic Pay for May (31 calendar days), would be 3000-(3000*3) / 31 = 2709.68
  - ▪ **Attendance Type:** On selection of *On Attendance* Calculation Type, at the option *Attendance / Leave with Pay*, further select the Attendance Type from the list of Attendance Types (on which the amount under the Pay Head would be computed), or select *Not Applicable* (F-1E)
    - **Calculation Period:** On selection of *Attendance Type*, at the option *Attendance / Leave with Pay*, at *Calculation Period*, further select the Calculation Period from the list of Calculation Period (F-1G).

- o **Calculation Basis:** On selection of *Calculation Period*, at the option *Calculation Basis*, further select the Calculation Basis from the list of Calculation Basis (F-1H).
- o **On Production**: Select *On Production*, for computation on the basis of Paid Attendance Days. Normally Basic, DA, etc are paid on Attendance Basis, as explained later
  - **Production Type:** On selection of *On Production* Calculation Type, at the option *Production Type* further select the Production Type from the list of Production Types (on which the amount under the Pay Head would be computed), or select *Not Applicable* (F-1E)
- o **Flat Rate:** Select *Flat Rate* when the fixed amount is to be paid in every Pay Period, as selected at *Calculation Period.*
- o **User Defined Value:** Select *As User Defined Value*, when the Amount of the Head is to be input at the time of Attendance entry at each PaySlip generation.
- o **Computed Value:** Select *As Computed Value*, when the Amount of the Head is computed on other Pay Heads.
  - **Computation Rules:** On selection of *As Computed Value*, at *Calculation Type*, set the Rules of Computation at Computation Info section, described later.

03.03 Income Type

At *Income Type*, select (F-1C):

- **Fixed:** If the Amount form a part of Employees Gross Salary (e.g Basic Pay)
- **Variable:** If the Amount is part of Net Pay (like Overtime)

03.04 Computation Rules

At *Calculation Type*, on selection of As Computed Value from the list, you get Computation Info screen to enter the Computation Rules / Parameters, as follows

Computation Info

Compute : **On Current Earnings Total**

Effective From	From Amount	Amount Upto	Slab Type	Value Basis
1-Apr-2015				
		10,000.00	Value	300
	10,000.00	15,000.00	Percentage	8 %
	15,000.00		Value	1,000

F-2A: Computation Info

Computation On

- On Current Deductions Total
- **On Current Earnings Total**
- On Current SubTotal
- On Specified Formula

F-2B: Computation Basis List

Additional Computations for

- End of List
- **Add Pay Head**
- Divide by Attendance
- Multiply with Attendance
- Subtract Pay Head

F-2C: Computation Rule

Compute : **On Specified Formula**

Function	Pay Head
Add Pay Head	Basic Salary

F-2D: Computation Formula

03.05 Computation Basis

At *Compute* (F-2A), select the option from the list of *Computation On* (F-2B) as follows. On the Basis as selected from the list (F-2C), the computation is done as per Slabs / Rates specified at the Table described next.

- **On Deductions**: Select *On Current Deductions Total*, if the amount is to be computed on sum of all Deduction Heads (Pay Heads for which *Deductions for Employees* is selected at Pay Head Types)
- **On Earnings**: Select *On Current Earnings Total*, if the amount is to be computed on sum of all Earnings Heads (Pay Heads for which *Earnings for Employees* is selected at Pay Head Types)
- **Current Sub Total**: Select *On Current Sub Total*, if the amount is to be computed on cumulative sub total prior to the computation of current head, as per sequence of appearance of the Head in Pay Slip
- **Specified Pay Heads**: Select *On Current Sub Total*, if the amount is to be computed on the current period total amount other Pay Heads., as described later

03.06 Specified Computation Formula

- **Computation Function**: At *Function* column (F-2D), select the Computation Rule from the list of *Additional Computation For,* as follows:
  - **Add Pay Head:** Select it to apply the rule on any selected Pay Head (it is automatically selected as the first option) and add the amount computed ti include it in Net Pay
  - **Subtract Pay Head:** Select it to apply the rule on any selected Pay Head and add the amount computed ti include it in Net Pay
  - **Divide by Attendance**: Select it to divide the amount of the prior selected Pay Head by Attendance (this is usually selected to apply per day Rate for Monthly Pay etc)
  - **Multiply by Attendance**: Select it to multiply the amount of the prior selected Pay Head by Attendance (this is usually selected to apply per day Rate for Monthly Pay etc)
- **Pay Head**: At Pay Head, select the Pay Head on which the Computation Rule as specified above would be applied to.

03.07 User Defined Pay Heads

User Defined Pay Head are special Pay Heads, which are not applicable for all Employees. You process the Payroll separately before Pay roll processing to update the Pay Computation.

Like other Pay Heads creation as described earlier, create User Defined Pay Heads (F-3A) At *Calculation Type*, select User Defined Value from the list of Calculation Type (F-1D).

04 User Defined Pay Head Processing

Like Other Pay Heads, as described earlier, you may link

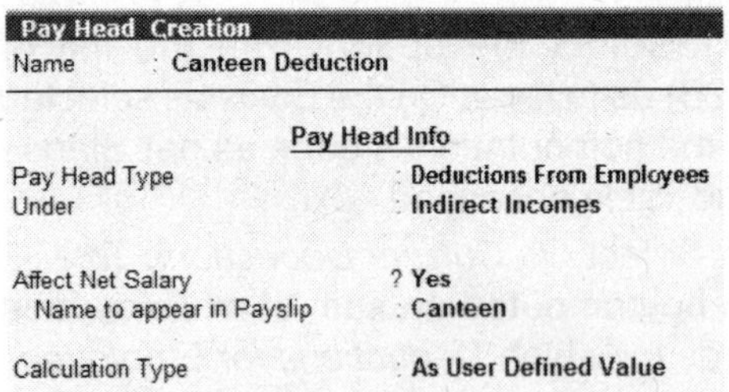

Pay Head Creation
Name : Canteen Deduction

Pay Head Info
Pay Head Type : Deductions From Employees
Under : Indirect Incomes
Affect Net Salary ? Yes
Name to appear in Payslip : Canteen
Calculation Type : As User Defined Value

F-3A: Creation of User Defined Pay Head

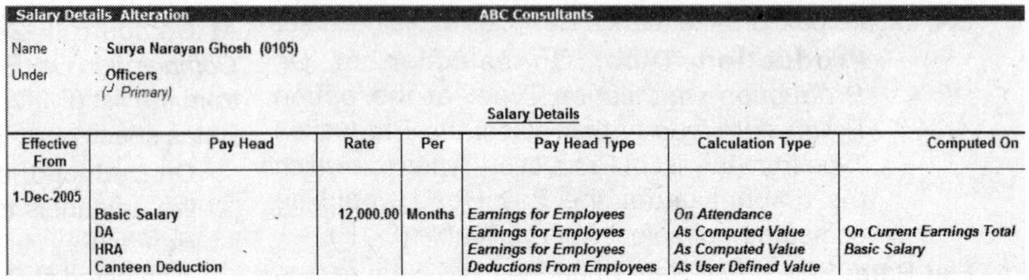

Salary Details Alteration — ABC Consultants
Name : Surya Narayan Ghosh (0105)
Under : Officers (Primary)

Salary Details

Effective From	Pay Head	Rate	Per	Pay Head Type	Calculation Type	Computed On
1-Dec-2005	Basic Salary	12,000.00	Months	Earnings for Employees	On Attendance	
	DA			Earnings for Employees	As Computed Value	On Current Earnings Total
	HRA			Earnings for Employees	As Computed Value	Basic Salary
	Canteen Deduction			Deductions From Employees	As User Defined Value	

F-3B: Salary Structure with User Defined Head

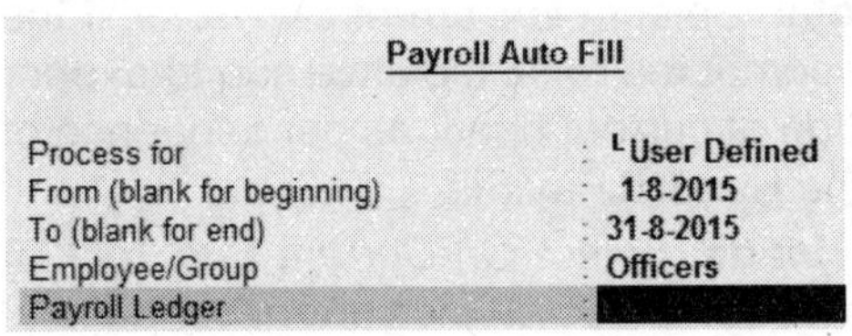

Payroll Auto Fill
Process for : User Defined
From (blank for beginning) : 1-8-2015
To (blank for end) : 31-8-2015
Employee/Group : Officers
Payroll Ledger :

F-4A: Payroll Process for User Defined Head

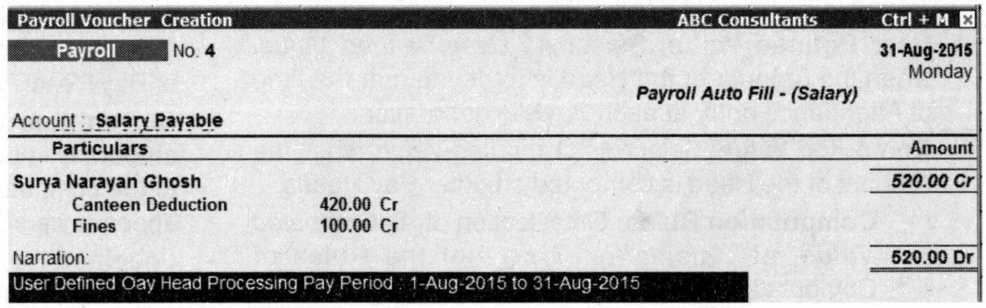

Payroll Voucher Creation — ABC Consultants — Ctrl + M
Payroll No. 4 — 31-Aug-2015 Monday
Payroll Auto Fill - (Salary)
Account : Salary Payable

Particulars		Amount
Surya Narayan Ghosh		520.00 Cr
Canteen Deduction	420.00 Cr	
Fines	100.00 Cr	

Narration: 520.00 Dr
User Defined Oay Head Processing Pay Period : 1-Aug-2015 to 31-Aug-2015

F-4B: Payroll Voucher for User Defined Head

the *User Defined Pay Head* to Pay Structure of selective Employee Group or selective Employee (F-3B)

During *Auto Fill* Payroll Voucher, as described earlier, first process the User Defined Head before processing Salary. At *Procedure For*, select *User Defined* (F-4A).

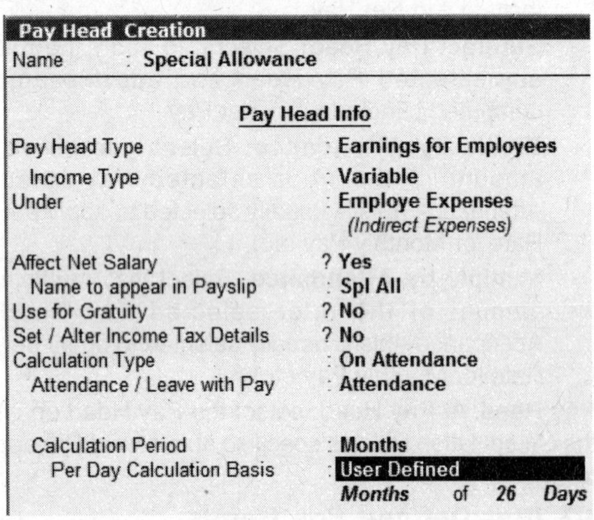

Pay Head Creation
Name : Special Allowance

Pay Head Info
Pay Head Type : Earnings for Employees
Income Type : Variable
Under : Employe Expenses (Indirect Expenses)
Affect Net Salary ? Yes
Name to appear in Payslip : Spl All
Use for Gratuity ? No
Set / Alter Income Tax Details ? No
Calculation Type : On Attendance
Attendance / Leave with Pay : Attendance
Calculation Period : Months
Per Day Calculation Basis : User Defined
Months of 26 Days

F-5A: Pay Head (User Defined Attendance Period)

Consequently, at Payroll Voucher Entry screen (F-4B), on selection of Employee, all the User Defined Pay Heads as specified in the Pay Structure are listed (F-4B). Enter the Value for each such Pay Head. The Debit Credit sign will be auto selected as per Earnings / Deduction Type of the Head.

05 User Defined Attendance Period

Calculation Type: When you select *On Attendance* at Calculation Type (F-5A), at Calculation Basis (5A), select from the list (F-5B):

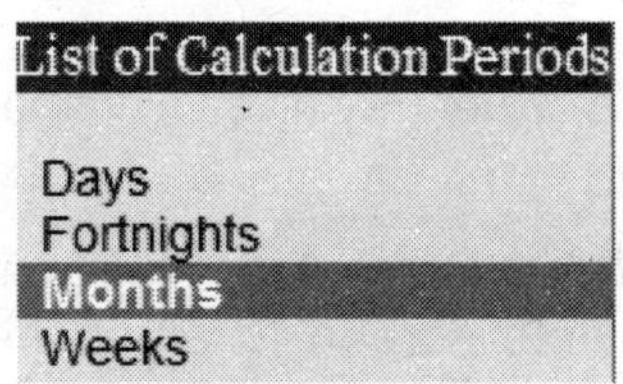

List of Calculation Periods
Days
Fortnights
Months
Weeks

F-5B:Calculation Period List

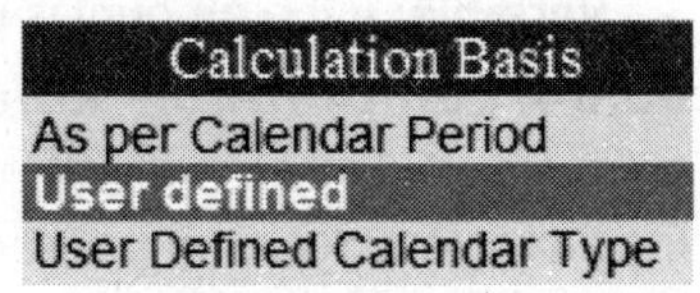

Calculation Basis
As per Calendar Period
User defined
User Defined Calendar Type

F-5C: Calculation Basis List

Select the Calculation Period from the list of Calculation periods (F-5B) Period. Select *User Defined* from the Calculation Basis List (F-5C).

F-5D: Pay Head (User Defined Calendar Based)

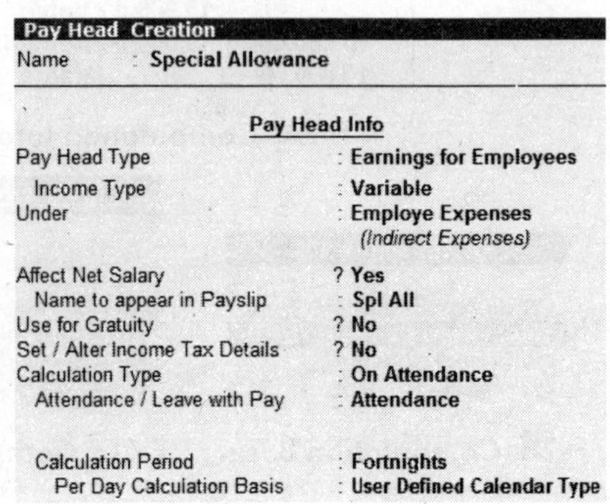

Pay Head Creation
Name : Special Allowance

Pay Head Info
Pay Head Type : Earnings for Employees
Income Type : Variable
Under : Employe Expenses (Indirect Expenses)
Affect Net Salary ? Yes
Name to appear in Payslip : Spl All
Use for Gratuity ? No
Set / Alter Income Tax Details ? No
Calculation Type : On Attendance
Attendance / Leave with Pay : Attendance
Calculation Period : Fortnights
Per Day Calculation Basis : User Defined Calendar Type

On selection of Calculation Period from the list (F-5B). At *Per Day Calculation Basis*, select:

- **User Defined Calculation Period**: *User Defined* from Calculation Basis list (F-5C) and then at Select the Calculation Period from the list (F5C). On selection of Calculation Period, at Per Day Calculation Basis (F-5A), enter the number of Days for the selected Calculation Period (e.g Week of 6 Days, Month of 26 Days etc)
- **User Defined Calendar Type:** *User Defined Calendar Type* from the Calculation Basis List (F-5C)

06 Expenses Reimbursements

Sometimes employees incur expenses by them, which, the employer should have borne. Such expenses are reimbursed to the Employee through Payroll system. As, these are not real income for the employee, such reimbursement should not be considered for I Tax computation

Expenses Reimbursements Pay Head: Pay Head creation has been explained earlier. Here, we discuss about creation of Reimbursement Head Type (F-6A).

- **Pay Head Type**: At *Pay Head Type*, select *Reimbursement to Employees* from the list of Pay Head Types (F-6B).
- **Income Type**: Select *Variable* as it is not regular item of Payroll for each period
- **Parent Account Group**: At *Under* select Indirect Expenses, as the expenses are to be borne by the employer.
- **Net Salary Effect**: At *Affect Net Salary*, set *Yes* (if it is paid through Pay Sheet), else set *No* (if it paid through separate voucher)
- **Income Tax Details**: Set *Yes* to get *Income Tax Details* screen (F-6C) and set as follows:
    - o **Income Tax Component:** At *Income Tax Component*, select *Other Earnings / Allowances (Fully Exempted)*, as it is just reimbursement of expenses incurred by the Employee and Not Income for Employee)
    - o **Tax Calculation Basis:** At *Tax Calculation Basis*, select on Actual value, as such figures are not regular.
    - o **TDS Deduction:** At *Deduct TDS across Periods*, select *No* as such amount is not to be considered for Income Tax
- **Calculation Type**: At *Calculation Type*, As User Defined Value, as the value is to be input by User during Payroll Processing

Pay Head Creation

Name	: **Laundry Exp**

Pay Head Info

Pay Head Type	: **Reimbursements to Employees**
Income Type	: **Variable**
Under	: **Indirect Expenses**
Affect Net Salary	? **Yes**
Name to appear in Payslip	: **Ldry**
Set / Alter Income Tax Details	? **Yes**
Calculation Type	: **As User Defined Value**

F-6A: Reimbursement Pay Head creation

List of Pay Head Types

- Not Applicable
- Bonus
- Deductions from Employees
- Earnings for Employees
- Employees' Statutory Deductions
- Employer's Other Charges
- Employer's Statutory Contributions
- Gratuity
- Loans and Advances
- **Reimbursements to Employees**
- Tax paid by Employer on Perquisites

F-6B: Pay Head Type List

Income Tax Details

Income Tax Component	: **Other Earnings/Allowances (Fully Exempt)**
Tax Calculation Basis	: **On Actual Value**
Deduct TDS Across Period(s)	: **No**

F-6C: Income Tax details

Employee Masters

Having created the Pay Heads Ledgers, create each Employee Record.

01 Employee Group

Employee Group refers to a Group Class of Employees whose pay Structure is quite similar. You may set the Pay Heads which are common to all Employees of an Employee Group, to be carried by to each Employee under the Employee Group, so that these heads need not be specified for each Employee Group.

At Gateway, select *Payroll Info>Employee Group* to get *Employee Group Menu* (F-1A). At *Employee Group Menu* (F-1A), select *Create* to get *Employee Group Creation* screen (F-2A).

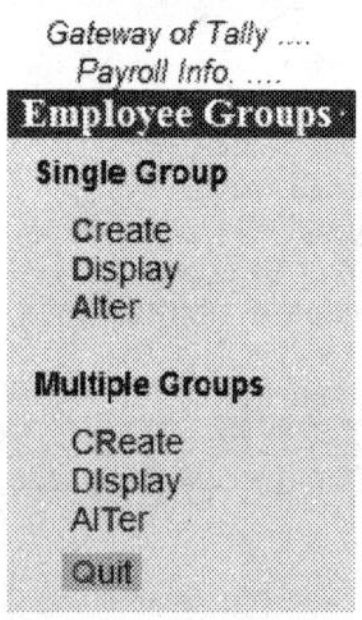

F-1A Employee Group Menu

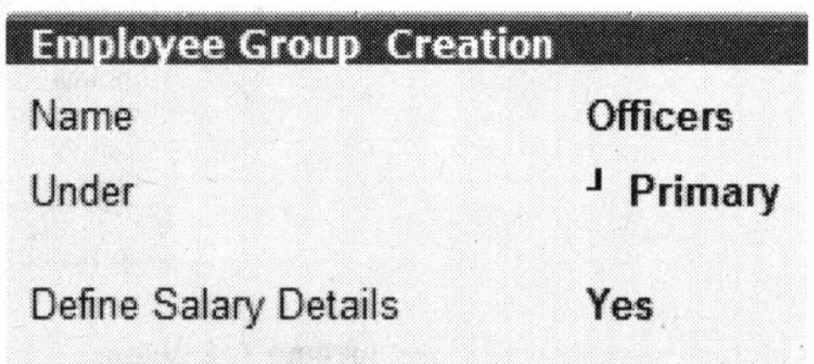

F-2A: Employee Group Entry

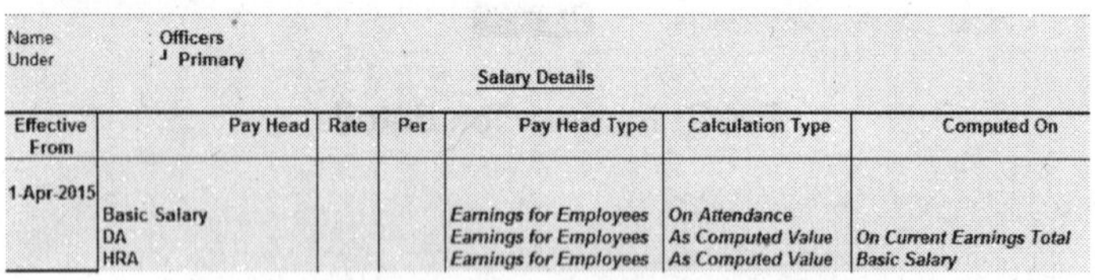

Name : Officers
Under : ┘ Primary

Salary Details

Effective From	Pay Head	Rate	Per	Pay Head Type	Calculation Type	Computed On
1-Apr-2015						
	Basic Salary			*Earnings for Employees*	*On Attendance*	
	DA			*Earnings for Employees*	*As Computed Value*	*On Current Earnings Total*
	HRA			*Earnings for Employees*	*As Computed Value*	*Basic Salary*

F-2B: Employee Group Salary Definition

F-3A: Copying Structure from another Employee Group

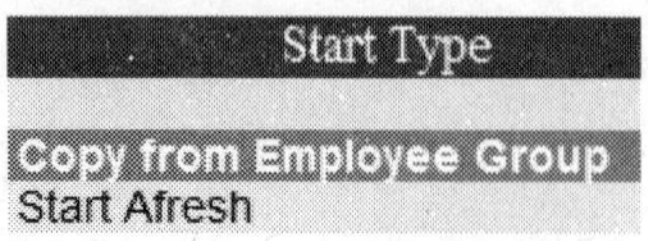

01.01 Employee Group Creation

At Employee Group Creation screen (F-2A), enter as follows to create a new Employee Group

- **Employee Group Name**: At *Name*, enter the name of Employee Group
- **Parent Group:** At *Under*, select the parent Employee Group from the list of existing Employee Groups (select *Primary* for top level Employee Group or the first created Employee Group). You may press Alt+C to get a Employee Group creation screen to create the new Parent Employee Group and select it at *Under* field of the current Employee Group being created.
- **Salary Definition:** At *Define Salary Details*, set *Yes* to defines Salary details for the Employee Group, to get *Employee Group Salary Definition* screen (F-2B), to set the particulars as described next (§01.02), else set *No* (no Salary Details are set for the Employee Group)

01.02 Employee Group Salary Definition

When you set *Yes* at *Define Salary Details* at Employee Group Entry screen (F-2A), you get *Employee Group Salary Definition* screen (F-2B), to enter the Employee Group Salary

- **Employee Group**: At *Name*, The current Employee Group Name as entered at Employee Group creation screen (F-2A) is shown
- **Parent Employee Group**: At *Under*, the Parent Employee Group Name as entered at Employee Group creation screen (F-2A) is shown
- **Salary Structure:** Next you get a Table to define the various common Pay Head elements of the Employee Group (§01.03), as described below.

01.03 Employee Group Salary Structure

At *Employee Group Salary Definition screen* (F-2B), under the section Salary Details, enter the Pay Structure of the current Employee Group as follows:

- **Effective Date**: At *Effective From* column, enter the Start Date of the Pa Period, from which the Rate structure is Applicable. This Date should be from beginning o a Pay Period. For example, for Monthly paid employees, the Date should be from Start of a Month (and not from the middle of a month).
- **Pay Head**: At *Pay Head* column, select the common Pay Head for the Employee Group from the list of Pay Heads
- **Rate:** At *Rate* column, enter the Rate fro the Pay Head, if it is uniformly applicable for all employees under the Employee Group, else leave blank. If *Rate* is entered, then at *Per* column, the *Computation Period* is carried from the Pay Head Master for information.

Consequently, the information in rest of the columns are carried from the respective Pay Head (you cannot change it).

01.04 Copying from another Employee Group

Having created at least one Employee Group record, at the time of creation of rest of the Employee Groups, to create furher new Groups, at the column *Pay Head*, you get option list to (F-3A):

- Copy from another Group
- Start Afresh to create a new group

Select *Copy from Employee Group* and then select the Employee Group from the list of Employee Groups. All the details are carried from the selected Employee Group to the current Employee Group being created

01.05 Alteration of Employee Group

At Employee Group Menu, select *Alter* and select the Employee. Now you may alter any data of Employee Group in the same way as you enter data.

01.06 Display of Employee Group

At Employee Group Menu, select *Display* and select the Employee to display the contents of Employee Data. You can just view and can not alter any data

01.07 Nesting of Employee Group

You may create a Group belonging to an Existing Group. At *Under* field (F-2A), select the parent Group to which the current Group being created belongs to. This way, you may several levels of Group like, Division, Department, Section etc.

On creation of Employee Group, you may select a specific sub Group at Employee Filter, Attendance Filter, Pay sheet, Attendance sheet etc, tp process / get reports of a subordinate Group, as desired.

02 Employee Master

At *Payroll Info* Menu, select *Employees* to get *Employee Master Menu* (F-1A). At *Employee Master Menu* (F-1A), select *Create* to get *Employee Creation* screen (F-2A).

02.01 Employee Master Creation

At *Employee Menu* (F-4A), select *Create* to get Employee Master screen. Now enter as follows:

Employee Master creation is composed of 3 parts:

Gateway of Tally ....
Payroll Info. ....
Employees
Single Employee
Create
Display
Alter
Multiple Employees
CReate
DIsplay
AlTer
Quit

F-4A: Employee Master Menu

- Employee Particulars (F-5A)
- Pay Structure Creation Options (F-6A)
- Employee Pay Structure (F-6B)

02.01.01 Employee Particulars

At Employee Particulars screen (F-5A), enter the details in 3 sections (F-5A)

- Employee General Info
- Employee Bank Details
- Employee Statutory Details

Employee Creation — ABC Consultants

Name	: Surya Narayan Ghosh
Display Name in Reports	: S N Ghosh
Under	: Officers (┘ Primary)
Date of Joining	: 1-Dec-2005
Define Salary Details	: Yes

General Info

Employee Number	: 0105
Designation	: Sales Manager
Function	: North Div
Location	: Sales Deptt
Gender	: Male
Date of Birth	: 1-May-1980
Blood Group	: O Positive
Father / Mother Name	: B B Ghosh
Spouse Name	: Namita Ghosh
Address	: 12 Crooked Lane Kolkata 700999
Contact Numbers	: 9898989898
E-Mail ID	: skg123456789@nomail.com

Payment Details

Bank Name	:
Branch	:
Bank A/c Number	:
IFS Code	:
MICR Code Number	:

Statutory Details

Income Tax Number (PAN)	: ABCDE1234X
PF Account Number	: WB/1467/1234567
ESI Number	: 1234-56789

F-5A: Employee Master creation screen

Employee Particulars: The *Employee Particulars* screen (F-5A), contain various Employee details, as follows:

Gender
┘ Unknown
Female
Male
Transgender

F-5B: Employee Gender List

- **Employee Full Name**: At *Name*, enter the complete Name of the Employee. Employee Name must be unique. If two names are similar, you must distinguish them by some distinctive letters.
- **Alias:** If Alias name is activated, then you may enter alternative name, code or Employee Number at this field, else leave blank. Alias Name must be unique.
- **Employee Short Name**: At Display Name in Reports, enter the short Name of the Employee, for unique identification, which is printed in all Payroll Reports
- **Under**: Select the parent Employee Group(not account group) of the Employee (or select *Primary)*
- **Date of Joining:** Enter the Date of Joining in dd-mm-yyyy format (like 1-4-1976). This is an important field used for first payslip computation and for computation of length of service for the purpose of Gratuity.
- ***Pay Structure:*** *At* Define Salary Details, *set* Yes *to get the Pay Structure screen (F-5B, F-5C), else set* No *(if Pay Structure is not readily available, to be filled up later on, through Alteration Mode), to move to enter Employee Particulars as described next (General Info, Bank Details & Statutory Details).*

Employee General Info

In this section, enter the following details.

- **Employee Number**: At *Employee Number*, enter the Employee Number (may be duplicate), if any, or leave blank. It is recommended that you should have unique alphanumeric Employee Number.

- **Designation**: At *Designation*, enter the Designation (like Pay Clerk), as applicable, or leave blank
- **Function**: At *Function*, enter the Function Name (like Time & Attendance Recording), if any, or leave blank.
- **Location**: In case of multi location company, at *Location*, enter the location. You may also enter the Department / Section, or leave blank.
- **Gender**: At *Gender*, select the Gender from the list (F-5C). Select *Unknown* if the Info is not available at the time Master entry, which you may change later on through Modification.
- **Date of Birth**: At *Date of Birth*, enter the Date of Birth. This is an important piece of data and should be normally filled up.
- **Blood Group**: At Blood Group, enter the blood group, an important piece of information, or leave blank if the info is not available.
- **Father's/Mother's Name:** Enter the Father's or Mother's (or both together in one line) This is important info and is required in some Statutory Returns.
- **Spouse Name:** Enter the Spouse Name. This is important info and is required in some Statutory Returns.
- **Address**: Enter the local & permanent address in multiple lines. Write both Local & Permanent address (if different) separately, one after another. As you type one line, cursor moves to next line of the address field where you may write the next line. To terminate address data entry, press <enter> at the blank line.
- **Contact Number**: Enter the Telephone Number, mobile number of the employee, if any (or the emergency telephone number of the neighbourhood, nearest relative etc)
- **E-Mail ID**: Enter the e-mail id of the employee, if any, (or of the neighbourhood, nearest relative etc) or leave blank.

Employee Bank Details

After entering Employee Particulars (at *General Info* section), you may enter Employee Bank Details (at *Payment Details* section), as follows. These details are useful to make Salary Payment through Bank. You may leave any or all of these fields blank, if not required (where paymn is not made through Bank Transfers)

- **Bank Name**: At *Bank Name*, enter the Name of the Bank of the Employee Bank Account
- **Branch Name:** At Branch, enter the Name of the Bank Branch where the employee account is held.
- **Bank A/c Number**: At *Bank Account Number*, enter the Bank Account Number to which the Net Salary Payable would be credited.
- **IFS Code**: At *IFS Code*, enter the IFS Code of the Bank Branch
- **MICR Code**: At *MICR Code Number,* enter the MICR Code of the Bank Branch

02.02 Employee Statutory Details

Under Statutory Details section (F-5A), enter the respective details, which are relevant only when you have activated the Statutory Info for the Company. These are discussed at the relevant place. You may leave blank, if these are not relevant in your case

02.03 Employee Pay Structure

At Employee Master screen (F-5A), set *Yes* at *Define Salary Details*, you get *Employee Master Pay Structure* screen (F-6B), to enter the Pay Heads applicable for each Employee. At the header, the Employee Name & Parent Group are carried from Employee Master as entered (F-5A).

Pay Head Details: Now enter Pay Head Details of Pay Structure, at following columns (F-6B):

- **Effective Date**: At *Effective Date* column, the Date of Join is carried (which you cannot change).
- **Entry Method**: At the outset, at *Pay Head* column, select the option from *Start Type* List (F-6A), as follows:
  - o **Copying from Any Employee Group**: Select *Copying from Employee Group* it if you like to Copy Pay Heads details, as defined from a selected Account Group and then select the Account group from the list. This is useful when the applicable Pay Head is already defined in any Employee Group, as explained earlier
  - o **Copying from Parent Employee Group**: Select *Copying from Parent Value* if you like to Copy Pay Heads details, as defined from the Parent Employee Group (as specified at *Under* field).

Start Type

Copy from Employee Group
Copy From Parent Value
Start Afresh

F-6A: Employee Master Creation option

Name : Surya Narayan Ghosh
Under : Officers
(↲ Primary)

Salary Details

Effective From	Pay Head	Rate	Per	Pay Head Type	Calculation Type	Computed On
1-Dec-2005	Basic Salary	12,000.00	Months	*Earnings for Employees*	*On Attendance*	
	DA			*Earnings for Employees*	*As Computed Value*	*On Current Earnings Total*
	HRA			*Earnings for Employees*	*As Computed Value*	*Basic Salary*

F-6B: Employee Master

- o **Fresh Entry**: Select *Start Afresh* to enter the *Pay Structure*, as explained at entry of *Pay Head Structure* of Employee Group.

> **Note:** *If you do not like to enter Historical Pay Structure from the Date of Joining, at the first line (where Date of Joining is carried at 'Effective From' column, select* 'Start Afresh' *from the Option List and at Pay Head, select 'End of List' from the list of Pay Heads. Now at next record line, at Effective Date column, enter the Date from which you like to start entry of Pay Structure and enter the Pay Structure data.*

03 Alteration of Employee Master

At Employee Menu (F-4A), select *Alter* and select the Employee. Now you may alter (enter data of blank fields left at the time of Entry), any data of Employee level, Employee Details or Pay Structure in the same way as you enter data.

04 Display of Employee Master

At Employee Master Menu (F-4A), select *Display* and select the Employee to display the contents of Employee Data. You can just view and can not alter any data

05 Salary Structure Updation

Often, the Salary details of Employee need to be changed (due to Salary Increment, promotion etc). addition / alteration of Pay element etc. To change the Salary Structure, instead of modifying the Employee Master Records (Employee Group / Employee), at *Payroll Info* menu, select *Salary Details*, to get Salary Details Menu (F-7A).

Gateway of Tally ...
Payroll Info. ....

Salary Details

Define

Display

Quit

F-7A: Salary Details Menu

Salary Details Display — **ABC Consultants**

Name : **Officers**

Under : **Primary**

Salary Details

Effective From	Pay Head	Rate	Per	Pay Head Type	Calculation Type	Computed On
1-Apr-2015	Basic Salary			*Earnings for Employees*	*On Attendance*	
	DA			*Earnings for Employees*	*As Computed Value*	*On Current Earnings Total*
	HRA			*Earnings for Employees*	*As Computed Value*	*Basic Salary*

F-8A: Salary Details of Employee Group

Entry / Modification of Salary Structure: At Salary Details Menu (F-7A), select *Define*:

- **Salary Structure of Employee Group**: Select he desired Account Group and enter / change the respective data as explained at Salary Structure of Employee Group.
- **Salary Structure of Employee:** Select the desired Account Group and enter / change the respective data as explained at Salary Structure of Employee.

06 Employee Profile

Employee Profile is list of Employee Records showing the details of Employee Particulars.

At Gateway, select *Display>Pay Roll Reports >PayRoll Reports> Employee Profile* to get *Employee Profile* menu (F-9A).

Gateway of Tally ....
Display Menu ....
Payroll Reports ....
Statements of Payroll ....

Employee Profile

All Employees

Single Employee

Group of Employees

Quit

F-9A: Employee Profile Menu

All Employees Profile — **ABC Consultants** — Ctrl + M

Under Employee Group : **All Items**

S.No	Name of the Employee	Under	Employee Number	Joining Date	Designation	Function
		Basic Details				5 more ... →
1	Aloke Kumar Ghosh	Officers	2014/07	1-May-2014	Sales Officer	Sales

F-10A: Employee Profile List

At *Employee Profile* menu (F-9A):

- **All Employees**: Select *All Employees* to get the *Employee Profile* list showing All Employees (F-10A).
- **Group of Employees:** Select the *Employee Group* to get the *Employee Profile* list of Employees of selected Employee Group, similar to list of Al Employees (F-10A).
- **Single Employee:** Select the Employee to get the *Employee* Profile of the selected Employee (F-11A)

07 Employee Category

Employee Category is a parallel classification of employees independent of Employee Group. For example, you may treat Departments as Employee Group, Sections as Employee Sub Group. Further you may create an independent cross cutting Category like Directors, Executive, Officers & Clerks. Using Categories, you get Categorywise summarized Reports and drill down to next level summary figures.

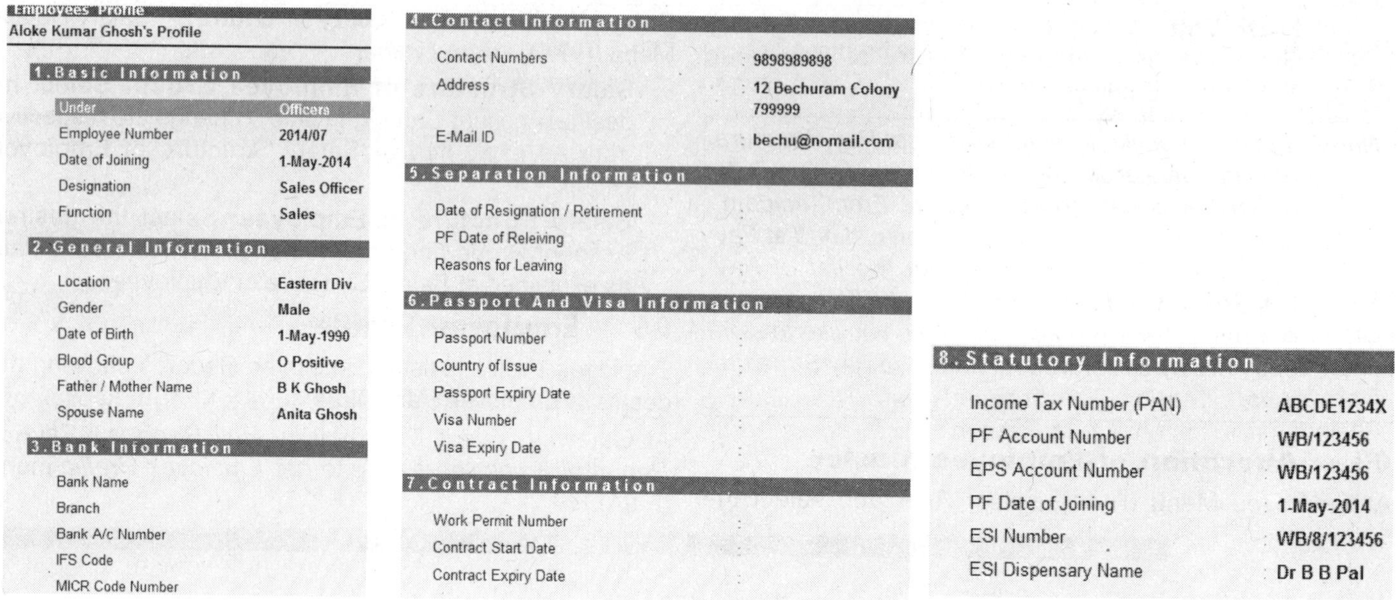

F-11A: Employee Profile

07.01 Employee Category Activation

To enable creation of new Categories, at Gateway click *F11:Features > Accounting Features*. At *Accounting Features* screen, Under *Cost / Profit Centres Management*, set *Yes* at *More than ONE Payroll / Cost Category* (F-12A).

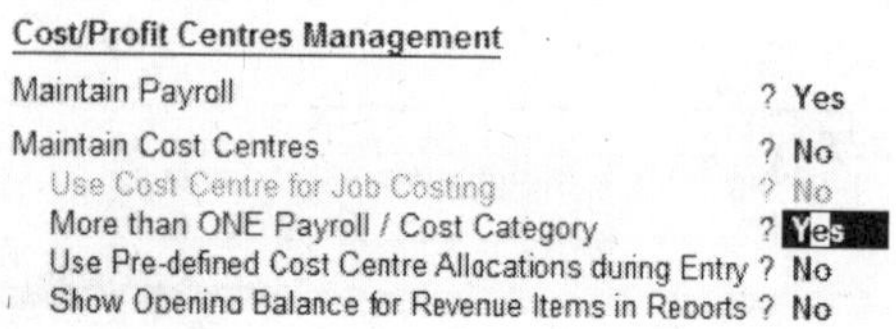

F-12A: Employee Category option set up

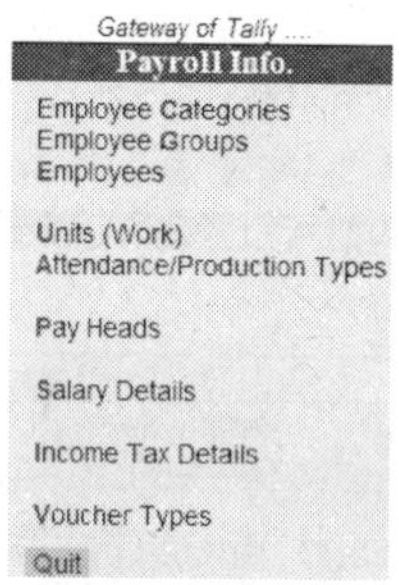

12B: Payroll Info Menu with Employee Category opion

Consequently, *Employee Category* option gets activated at *Employee Info Menu* (Gateway>Employee Info: F-12B),). A default Category named *Primary Cost Category* is auto created (F-14B). Now, you may create new Employee Categories

07.02 Employee Category Creation

To create a new Employee Category, at *Gateway,* select *Payroll Info>Employee Category* to get Employee Category creation Menu (F-13A). At Employee Category Menu (F-13A), select *Create* to get Employee Category creation screen (F-14A). Employee Category Creation is very similar to Cost Category creation explained earlier

F-13A: Employee Category Menu

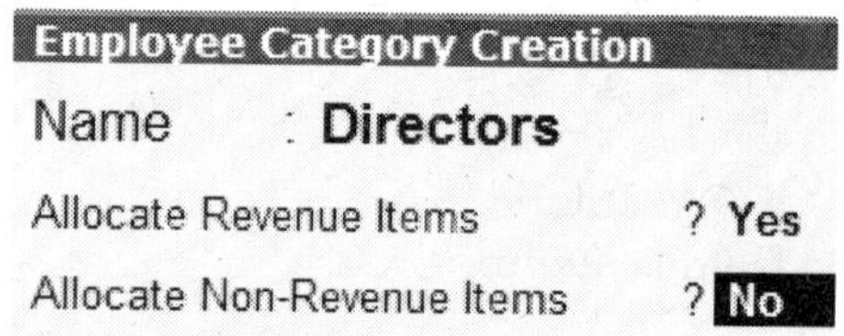

F-14A: Employee Category creation

07.03 Employee Grouping & Categorisation

If Category is activated for the Company, during Employee Master creation (F-14A), at *Category*, select the Category (F-14A) from the list of Employee Categories (F-14B)

F-14A: Category selection in Employee Master

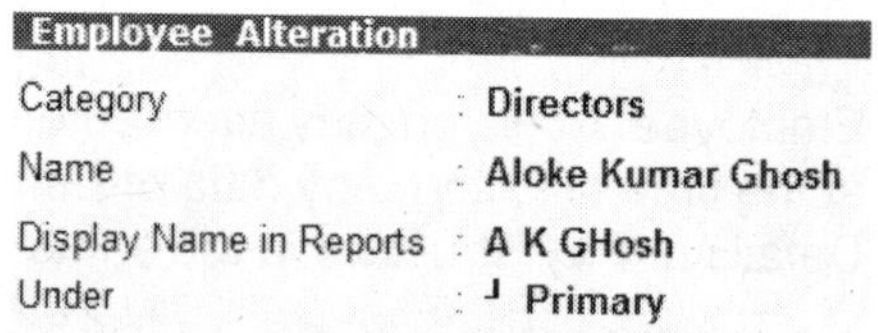

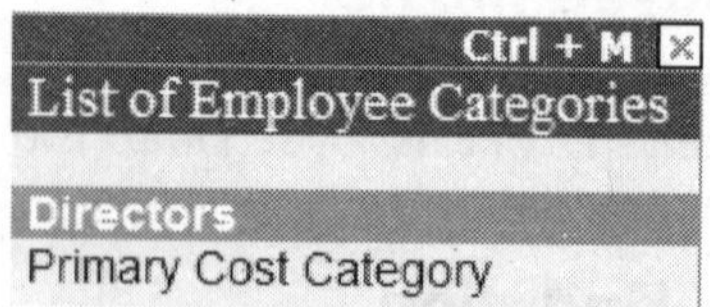

F-14B: Employee Category selection list

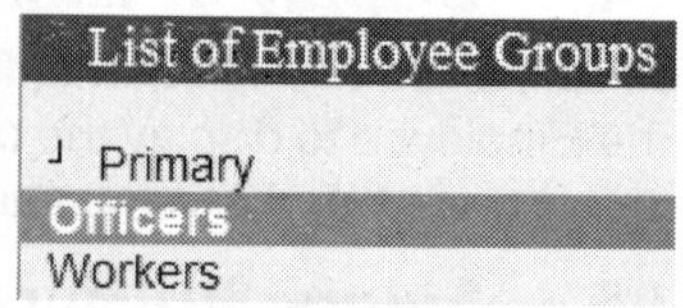

F-14C: Employee Group selection list

Parent Category: At *Under*, select the parent Employee Group (F-14A) from Employee Group selection list (F-14C), as explained earlier.

You must select the auto created *Primary* Employee Group at *Under*, or select the auto created *Primary* Cost Category at Category. You can not select a newly created Group at *Under* as well as a newly Created Employee Category at Category. You must select either the default *Primary* Employee Group or default *Primary Cost Category* (F-14A) fro an Employee.

08 Employment Cessation

On leaving the Company, alter the Employee Master, as described earlier. At *Employee Alteration* screen (F-15A), at *Date of Resignation / Retirement*, enter the Date of Resignation / Retirement. At *Reason of Leaving*, select the Reason from the list (F-15B)

The Period of Service for computation of Gratuity is considered from the *Date of Joining* & *Date of Leaving*.

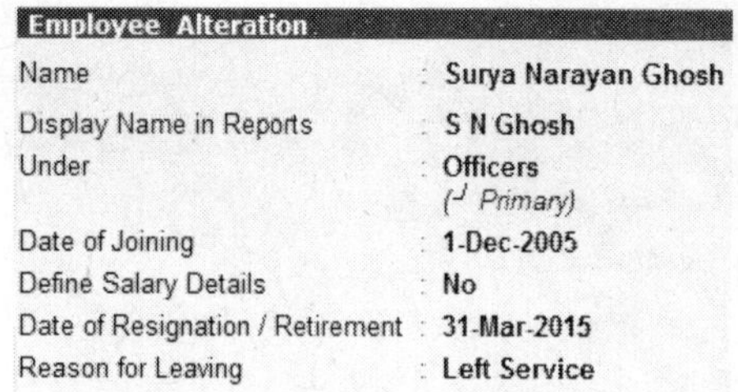

F-15A: Employee Particulars

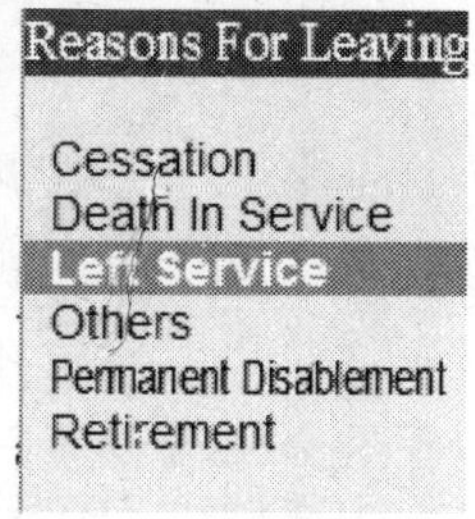

F-15B: Reason of Leaving List

Part 2
Payroll Vouchers

In this Part, we describe the process of manual entry and Auto fill (auto computed) process of creation of Payroll Vouchers

Payroll Voucher describes creation of Payroll Voucher through manual Entry and & auto computation process

Employee Loan explains disbursement of Loan to Employee, regular deduction of instalments & Interest from Pay, modification of deduction amount.

Payroll Voucher Class explains creation of Voucher classes for various Payroll voucher creation processes to auto fill the voucher with specified computation formula, rules & Payhead / Ledger Accounts

Pay Revision & Arrears explains Pay Revision & re-computation of Pay with retrospective effect, computation & payment of Arrears Pay on account of such Pay Revision.

Payroll Voucher 02-01

01 Payroll Voucher

Payroll Vouchers may be entered in 2 modes:

- **Manual Mode:** In this mode, enter the computed value of each Pay Head. Tally does not make any computation whatsoever. It helps to maintain complete Pay Head details of each employee, and is suitable for small organisation having few employees, due to simplicity of its implementation and data entry.
- **Auto Fill Mode:** In this mode, the amount for each element of Pay Head is auto computed from Pay Rates, Attendance, Production and other computation formula as specified in the system. This method is mostly used as it computes Payroll correctly and quickly, maintaining all supporting data

02 Payroll Voucher Manual Entry

At Gateway, select Payroll Vouchers *to get Payroll Voucher Entry screen (F-1A), which looks like a Payment Voucher entry screen in single mode. Accounts Voucher entry in Single Mode has been entry has been explained earlier. Here we disciss about features specific to Payroll Voucher*

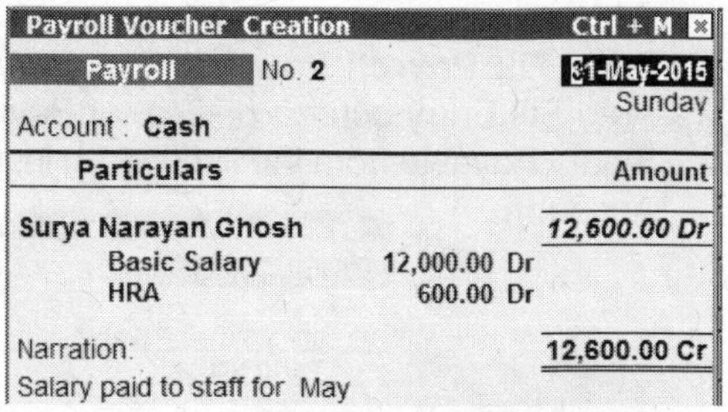

F-1A: Payroll Voucher Manual Entry

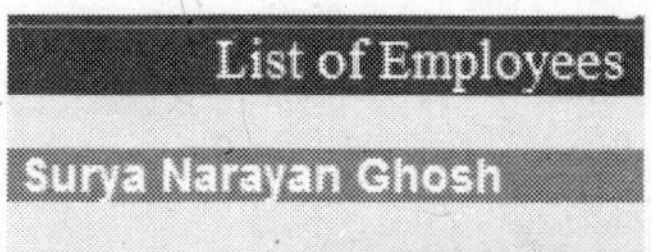

F-1B: Employee selection

F-1C: Pay Head selection

At Payroll Voucher Entry screen (F-1A), enter as follows:

- **Header Account**: At the Header, select the Account (Cash / Bank or Salary Payable) from the list of Ledger Accounts.
- ***Employee Account**: At* Particulars *column, select the Employee from list of Employees, in the same way as Attendance Entry.*
  - o **Pay Head Details**: Now enter the Pay Head details of the employee, as follows:
    - **Pay Head**: Having selected the Employee, at Particulars column, select a Pay Head for which you like to enter the amount for the Employee
    - **Amount**: Now enter the Amount for the Account Head. The Dr / Cr will be auto set according to the Type (Earnings / Deductions) as defined in the Pay Head Master.

    This way, select the Heads one by one, for which amount is to be entered in respect of the employee. Finally select End of List *from the list of Pay Heads to terminate he Pay Head entry*

  This way, select the Employees one by one, and enter the respective Pay Head details as explained above. Finally select End of List *from the list of Employees to terminate the Employee selection.*
- ***Voucher Narration**: Enter* Voucher Narration *and save the Voucher.*

03 Payroll Voucher Auto Fill

Instead of manually entering Amount for each Employee, you may get the Voucher Auto filled. At Payroll Voucher Entry screen (F-2B), click A:Auto Fill *button to get* Payroll Auto fill *Screen (F-2A). At Payroll Auto fill Screen (F-2A). enter as follows:*

- ***Salary Process**: At* Process For, *select* Salary *from the Process List (F-2A), to Process Salary*
- ***Pay Period**: At* From & To, *enter the Start & End Date of Pay Period, as follows:*
  - o ***Period Start Date**: At* From, *enter the Start Date of Pay Period*
  - o ***Period End Date**: At* To, *enter the End Date of Pay Period*
- ***Employee Range**: At* Employee Group, *Select from the List (F-2D) as follows:*
  - o **Employee Group**: Select the Employee Group. The Payroll will be processed for all Employees of the selected Employee Group.
  - o **One Employee**: Select an Employee. The Payroll will be processed for the selected Employee
  - o ***All Employees**: Select* All Items *to process the Payroll for All Employees*

- ***Account Ledger**: At* Payroll Ledger, *select Cash / Bank or Salary Payable Ledger from the list of Ledgers (F-2C)*

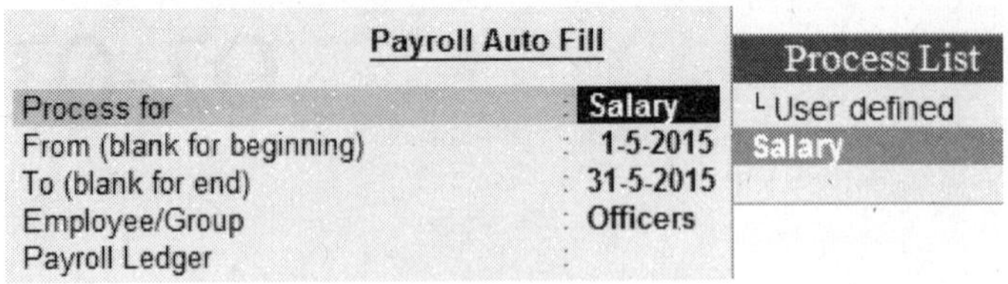

F-2A: Payroll Auto Fill

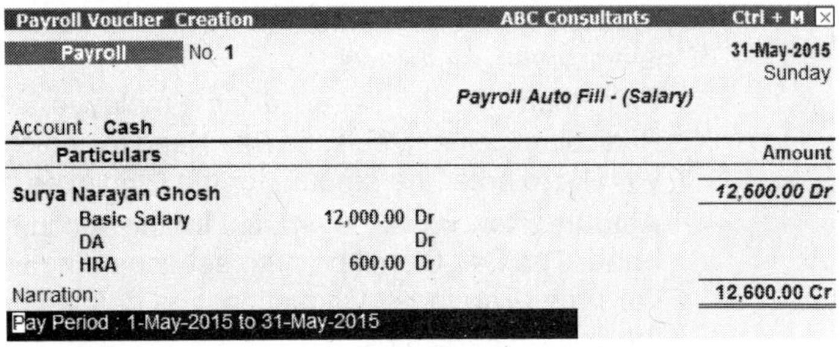

F-2B: Payroll Voucher (Auto Fill)

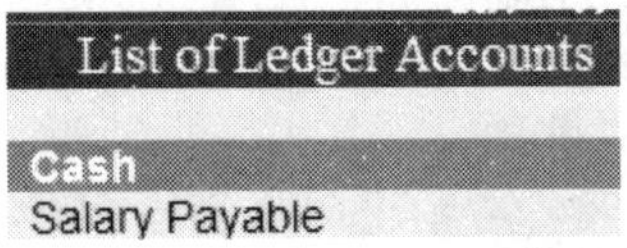

F-2C: Ledger Account List

F-2D: List Employee / Employee Grou

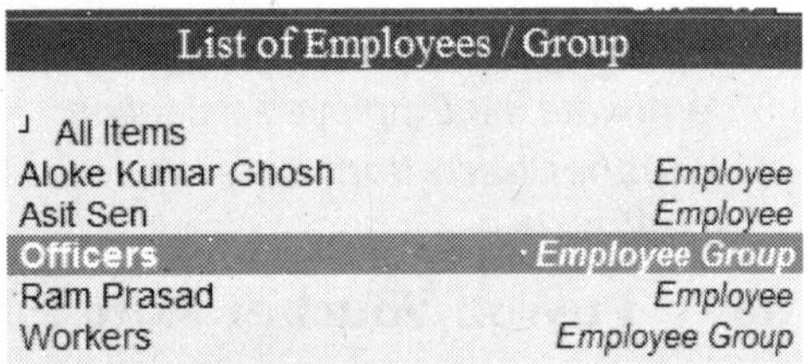

04 Salary Payable Ledger

As explained above, you may create a Payroll Voucher in 2 ways:

- **Direct Debit to Cash / Bank**: By direct payment Crediting Cash / Bank Account at the Header Account,
- **Salary Payable Ledger**: Create a Journal entry crediting Salary Payable Account (under Current Liabilities). Through the Payroll Voucher, first create provision for Salary payment an then create a Payment Voucher at the time of Payment, debiting the Salary Payable Voucher This is much better method as the entire Salary may be processed together and then paid to the respective employees in stages

It is always advisable to create a Payroll voucher to credit the Net Pay amount to Salary Payable account. So, you create a Pay Head (F-3A), as described earlier. Select *Not Applicable* at Pay Head type (F3B), because it is neither a *deduction* nor an *earning*. At *Under* (F-3A), select the Account Group from the list (F-3C).

You may also create the Salary Payable Account from Payroll Auto Fill screen (F-2A). At Payroll Ledger press Alt+C to get Pay Head Creation screen (F-3A) and create the Salary Payable:Ledger as described.

F-3A: Salary Payable Pay Head

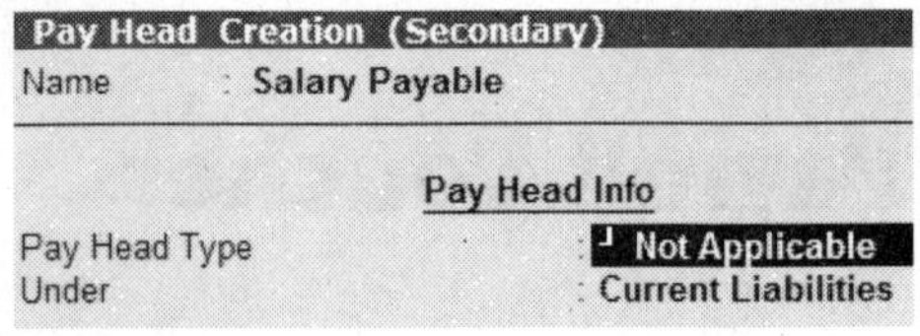

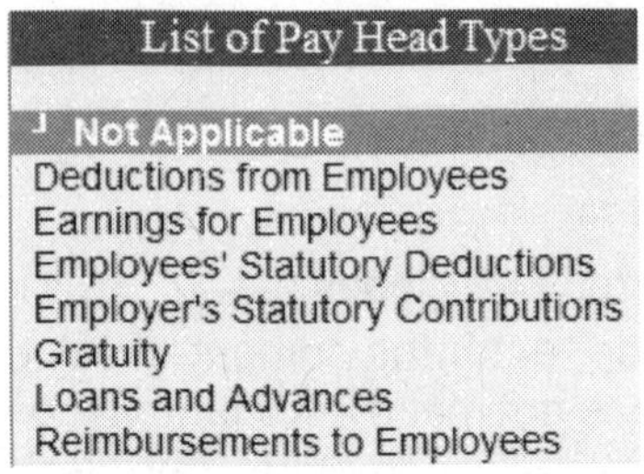

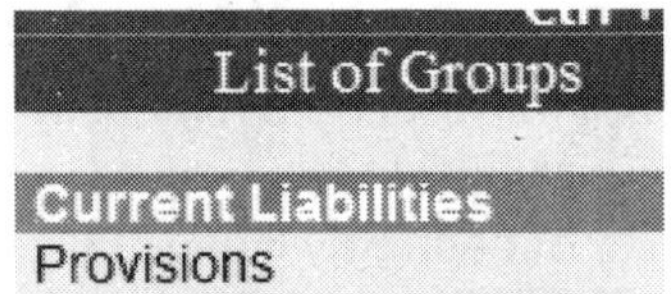

F-3B: Pay Head Type F-3C: Account Group

The Accounting effect of the Payroll Voucher is:

Account Head	Debit	Credit
Pay Account Head	Amount	
Deduction Account Head		Amount
Cash Bank / Salary Payable		Net Pay Amount

05 Salary Payable Voucher creation

To create provision for Salary Payable, create Auto Fill Payroll Voucher *as described,*

- **Manual Payroll Voucher Entry:** At Manual Payroll Voucher Entry screen (F-1A), at Header Account, select Salary Payable from the list (F-2C), instead of Cash Bank Account.
- **Auto Fill Payroll Voucher Entry:** At Payroll Voucher Auto Fill Entry screen (F-2A), at Payroll Ledger, select Salary Payable from the list (F-2C), instead of Cash Bank Account.

F-4A: Payroll Voucher Manual

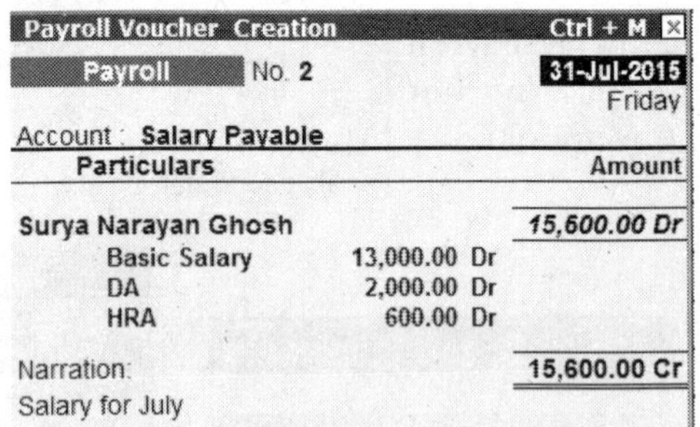

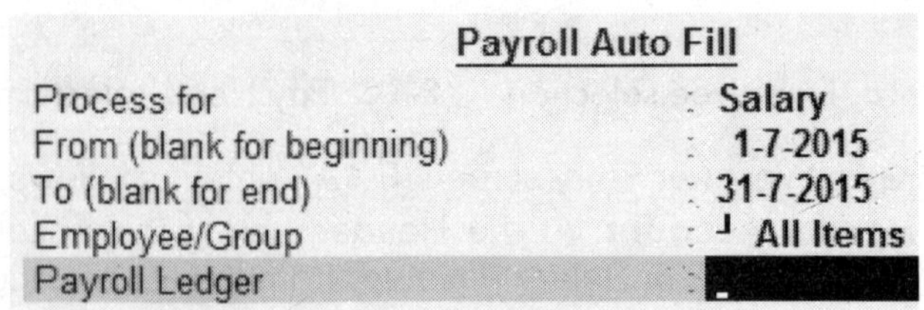

F5A: Payroll Voucher Auto Fill

Payroll Voucher Creation — ABC Consultants — Ctrl + M

Payroll No. 4 — 31-Jul-2015, Friday

Payroll Auto Fill - (Salary)

Account : Salary Payable

Particulars		Amount
		10,600.00 Cr
Surya Narayan Ghosh		
Basic Salary	(-)14,000.00 Dr	
DA	(-)4,000.00 Dr	
HRA	(-)600.00 Dr	
		10,600.00 Dr

Narration:
Pay Period : 1-Jul-2015 to 31-Jul-2015

F-6A: Payroll Voucher Auto Fill

06 User Defined Pay Head Values

We have discussed Auto Fill computation through which the amount of each Pay Head in Payroll Voucher is computed as per rules defined in Pay Structure and Pay Head definitions described later. However, for User Defined Pay Heads (for which User Defined is selected as Calculation Type), the amount is to be entered in respect of each Pay for each Employee.

Pay Head Alteration

Name : Canteen Deduction

Pay Head Info

Pay Head Type	: Deductions From Employees
Under	: Indirect Incomes
Affect Net Salary	? Yes
Name to appear in Payslip	: Canteen
Calculation Type	: As User Defined Value

F-7A: User Defined Pay head creation

Salary Details Alteration — ABC Consultants

Name : Aloke Kumar Ghosh (2014/07)
Under : Officers
(Primary)

Salary Details

Effective From	Pay Head	Rate	Per	Pay Head Type	Calculation Type
1-Jul-2015					
	Basic Salary	12,000.00	Months	*Earnings for Employees*	*On Attendance*
	Canteen Deduction			*Deductions From Employees*	*As User Defined Value*

F-8A: Employee Pay Structure

To enter Amount for User Defined Heads included in Pay Structure of respective employees, during Payroll creation, at Payroll Auto Fill, select *User Defined* at *Process For* (F-9B), and process the Payroll Voucher. The Voucher will show the User Defined fields in respect of respective Employee (F-9A) and you have to fill up the amount for such Head for each Employee and save the Voucher (F-9A).

Payroll Voucher Creation — Ctrl + M

Payroll No. 3 — 31-Jul-2015, Friday

Account : Salary Payable

Particulars		Amount
Aloke Kumar Ghosh		120.00 Cr
Canteen Deduction	120.00 Cr	
		120.00 Dr

Narration:
Pay Period : 1-Jul-2015 to 31-Jul-2015

F-9A: User Defined Pay Head value entry in Payroll Voucher

Process List

- User defined
- ESI Contribution
- PF Contribution
- Salary

F-9B: User Defined Payroll Process

On entry of User Defined Values, process the Payroll for Computed Heads. The Payroll voucher is now complete with all Computed Pay Heads and User Defined Pay Heads, as shown in Payslip (F-10A)

However, to use Auto Fill Voucher, you should create Pay Structure and define computation rules as described later. You should also create Attendance / Production heads and specify the computation rules. Having defined hem, you may create Payroll Voucher using Auto Fill process.

Pay Slip — ABC Consultants — Ctrl + M

Pay Slip for July-2015

Aloke Kumar Ghosh

Employee Number	: 2014/07	Income Tax Number (PAN)	: ABCDE1234X
Function	: Sales	PF Account Number	: WB/KOL/1234567/123/WB/1234
Designation	: Sales Officer	ESI Number	: WB/8/123456
Location	: Eastern Div		
Bank Details	:		
Date of Joining	: 1-May-2014		

Attendance Details	Value
Absent	1 Days
Attendance	30 Days

Earnings	Amount	Gross Salary
Basic Salary	11,613.00	12,000.00
Total Earnings	11,613.00	12,000.00
Deductions	**Amount**	**Gross Salary**
Canteen	120.00	120.00
Total Deductions	120.00	120.00
Net Amount	₹ 11,493.00	₹ 11,880.00

F-10A: Pay Slip with User Defined values

Employee Loans 02-02

01 Employee Loans & Recoveries

Often, employees take Loan / Advance from Employer, which is deducted from their Salary. To record Loan/ Advance to employees and recover in Payslip, create Loan / Advance Pay head. You may create several types of Loan Payheads to keep balance for each of them (like Salary Advance, Housing Loan, Furniture Loan, Vehicle Loan, Marriage Loan, Medical Treatment Loan etc). Tally maintains employee wise balances of loans and advances within a Loan or Advance ledger. So, no need not create individual employee wise loan or advance account.

More than one type of Loan may be paid to and recovered from an employee simultaneously. Loan Interest may also be recovered optionally, where applicable

02 Loan Pay Head Creation

Loan is recovered from Pay in Instalments while Salary Advance is recovered is recovered fully from current month Pay. Normally, same Ledger Account may be used both for Salary Advance & Loan Disbursement. Similarly, same Pay Head may be used both for recovery of Salary Advance & Loan, from Salary.

To deduct Loan from Pay, you should create a Pay Head for Loan Deduction. Pay Head creation as been explained earlier.

Pay Head Creation

Name : **Employee Loan**

Pay Head Info

Pay Head Type	: **Loans and Advances**
Under	: **Loans & Advances (Asset)** *(Current Assets)*
Affect Net Salary	? **Yes**
Name to appear in Payslip	: **Loan Dedn**
Calculation Type	: **Flat Rate**
Calculation Period	: **Months**

Rounding Info

Rounding Method : ┘ **Not Applicable**

F-1A: Loan Deduction Pay Head Creation

Creation of Loan Pay Head (F-1A) is described below:

- **Pay Head Name:** At *Name*, enter the Pay Head Name (e.g Employee Loan). A Ledger Account of this name will be auto created. The Loan Disbursement would be done through this Ledger account

List of Pay Head Types

┘ Not Applicable
Bonus
Deductions from Employees
Earnings for Employees
Employees' Statutory Deductions
Employer's Other Charges
Employer's Statutory Contributions
Gratuity
Loans and Advances
Reimbursements to Employees
Tax paid by Employer on Perquisites

F-1B:Pay Head Type List

- **Pay Head Type**: At *Pay Head Type*, select *Loans & Advances* from the list of Pay Head Types (F-1B).
- **Parent Account Group**: At *Under* select the respective Account Group (e.g Loans & Advances or any Sub Group under it) from the Account Group list
- **Pay Slip Inclusion**: Set *Yes* to Deduct the Loan Recovery in Pay Slip. Loan Instalment will be auto deducted in Pay Slip.
- **Pay Head in Reports**: At *Name to appear in Pay Slip*, enter the Name of the Pay Head that would appear in Pay Slip / Pay Reports (e.g Loan Dedn).
- **Calculation Type:** Normally Lon Recovery is made in fixed instalment in every month. So, specify *Fixed* at Calculation Type (preferred way). Alternatively, you may set *User Defined Value*. In that case, the Loan Amount would not be auto filled in Pay Slip. You have to enter the Loan Recovery Amount in each month, till the Loan is fully recovered.

In case of Salary Advance (where the amount paid is to be recovered in full in one instalment), then you may set *User Defined Value* and then enter the amount to be deducted at the time of Payroll Processing.

03 Loan Payment Voucher entry

When Loan is disbursed to Employee, create a Payment Voucher.

Payment Voucher creation hs been explained earlier. At Gateway, select Accounts Voucher. Click *F5:Payment* button (or press F5 function key) to get Payment Voucher (F-2A).

Select the Loan Account (F-2A) to get Employee Allocation screen (F-2B).

- **Employee Name**: At *Name of Employee* column, select the Employee to whom the Loan is Paid.

- **Loan Amount**: At Amount column, enter the Loan Amount paid to the Employee

This way, you may select Multiple Employees, when Loan is paid to multiple Employees in ONE Voucher

Accounting Voucher Creation — Ctrl + M

Payment No. 1 — 1-Oct-2015 Thursday

Particulars		Debit	Credit
Dr Employee Loan		10,000.00	
Aloke Kumar Ghosh	10,000.00 Dr		
Cr Cash			10,000.00
Narration:		10,000.00	10,000.00

Loan Paid recoverable @ 1000 pm from Nov Salary

F-2A: Payment Voucher for Loan Disbursement

F-2B: Employee Allocation

Employee Allocations for : **Employee Loan**
Upto: ₹ 10,000.00 Dr

Name of Employee	Amount
Aloke Kumar Ghosh	10,000.00
	10,000.00

1-10-14 (so enter 1-10-14 at *Effective From* column). Now enter all the Pay heads and the details and add the Loan details in the Pay Structure as follows (F-3B)

- At *Pay Head* column select the Loan Head which you have debited in the Loan Payment Voucher.
- At *Rate* column, enter the monthly instalment to be deducted
- At *Calculation Type* column select *Flat Rate*

Now when you create the Payroll voucher, the loan instalment will get deducted

Payroll Voucher Creation — ABC Consultants — Ctrl + M

Payroll No. 5 — 31-Dec-2015 Thursday

Payroll Auto Fill - (Salary)

Account : **Salary Payable**
Cur Bal: 30,680.00 Cr

Particulars			Amount
Surya Narayan Ghosh			
Surya Narayan Ghosh			12,400.00 Dr
Basic Salary	12,000.00 Dr		
DA	Dr		
HRA	600.00 Dr		
Employee Loan	200.00 Cr		
Narration:			12,400.00 Cr

F-4A: Payroll Voucher with Loan Recovery

Salary Details Alteration — ABC Consultants — Ctrl + M

Name : Aloke Kumar Ghosh (2014/07)
Under : Officers
(Primary)

Salary Details

Effective From	Pay Head	Rate	Per	Pay Head Type	Calculation Type	Computed On
1-Oct-2015						
	Basic Salary	12,000.00	Months	*Earnings for Employees*	*On Attendance*	
	HRA			*Earnings for Employees*	*As Computed Value*	*Basic Salary*
	Employer's Cont to ESI			*Employer's Statutory Contributions*	*As Computed Value*	*(Basic Salary + HRA) + DA*
	Employees Cont to ESI			*Employees' Statutory Deductions*	*As Computed Value*	*Basic Salary + HRA*
	Employees P F Cont			*Employees' Statutory Deductions*	*As Computed Value*	*On Current Earnings Total*
	Employer's Contribution to PF			*Employer's Statutory Contributions*	*As Computed Value*	*Employees P F Cont - Employer's Cont to Pension Fund*
	Employer's Cont to Pension Fund			*Employer's Statutory Contributions*	*As Computed Value*	*On Current Earnings Total*
	Professional Tax			*Employees' Statutory Deductions*	*As Computed Value*	*On Current Earnings Total*
	Employee Loan	200.00	Months	*Loans and Advances*	*Flat Rate*	

F-3B: Loan Recovery entry in Pay Structure

The total amount allocated at Employee Allocation screen (F-2B) must match with the loan amount entered in the main screen of the voucher (F-2A).

Enter Narration and save the voucher (F-2A)

04 Loan Recovery set up in Pay Structure

Having created the loan payment voucher, enter the deduction details in Pay Structure of the Employee, as described earlier.

Select *GoT>Payroll Info>Salary Details>Define* and then select the Employee to get *Salary Details Alteration* screen At Pay Structure, enter the Pay Head Employee Loan to include the Loan Deduction. For example, if you have paid the loan in Sep and like to deduct the loan instalment from Oct salary, then you should create a new Pay Structure w.e.f

05 Loan Report

To see the Loan Recovery & outstanding balance for each Employee, at Gateway, select *Display>Payroll Report> Statement of Payroll > Employee Payhead Breakup*. and then Select the Pay head from the list (F-5B) to get the Employee wise break up of the Loan (F-5A).

By setting the period, you may get the report for any specified Pay period or for a period comprising several Pay period (e.g for a Quarter, Half Year or Annual).

06 Loan Recovery Stoppage

If you set up *Flat Rate* at *Calculation Type* at Employee Loan Pay Head (F-1A) and include it in the Employee Pay Structure (F-3B), the Loan Recovery would continue as per Pay Structure, even if the Loan has been fully recovered and the balance is zero. You have to keep track of the balance

Employee Breakup of Pay Head Ctrl + M

Particulars	Pay Head: Employee Loan ABC Consultants 1-Apr-2015 to 1-Oct-2015			
	Opening Balance	Transactions Debit	Transactions Credit	Closing Balance
Primary Cost Category		*10,000.00*		10,000.00 Dr
Officers		10,000.00		10,000.00 Dr
Aloke Kumar Ghosh		*10,000.00*		10,000.00 Dr

F-5A: Employee Loan Report

ABC Consultants
Name of Pay Head

List of Pay Heads
Basic Salary
Canteen Deduction
DA
Employee Loan
Employees Cont to ESI
Employees P F Cont
Employees Volutary P F Deduction
Employer's Contribution to PF
Employer's Cont to Pension Fund
Fines
HRA
Income Tax From Employees
Professional Tax
Salary Payable

F-5B: Loan Pay Head seletion

Salary Details Alteration ABC Consultants

Name : Surya Narayan Ghosh (0105)
Under : Officers
(*Primary*)

Salary Details

Effective From	Pay Head	Rate	Per	Pay Head Type	Calculation Type	Computed On
1-May-2015						
	Basic Salary	12,000.00	Months	*Earnings for Employees*	*On Attendance*	
	DA			*Earnings for Employees*	*As Computed Value*	*On Current Earnings Total*
	HRA			*Earnings for Employees*	*As Computed Value*	*Basic Salary*
	Canteen Deduction			*Deductions From Employees*	*As User Defined Value*	
	Fines			*Deductions From Employees*	*As User Defined Value*	
	Employee Loan	200.00	Months	*Loans and Advances*	*Flat Rate*	
1-Dec-2015	Copy From Previous Value					
	Basic Salary	12,000.00	Months	*Earnings for Employees*	*On Attendance*	
	DA			*Earnings for Employees*	*As Computed Value*	*On Current Earnings Total*
	HRA			*Earnings for Employees*	*As Computed Value*	*Basic Salary*
	Canteen Deduction			*Deductions From Employees*	*As User Defined Value*	
	Fines			*Deductions From Employees*	*As User Defined Value*	
	Employee Loan			*Loans and Advances*	*Flat Rate*	

F-6A: Pay Structure Revision

Start Type
Copy From Parent Value
Copy From Previous Value
Start Afresh

F-6B: Start Option

every month and when the balance becomes zero for any employee, you should create a new loan structure removing the Loan account from the Pay Structure or modify the Loan Deduction amount in Pay Structure and make it zero.

To revise Pay Structure, you have to create a Pay Structure with new Effective Date. At Pay Roll Info Menu, select *Salary Details* and select the Employee to get the salary Details Alteration screen showing the Salary Structure.

Now enter the Date from which the Loan Recovery is to be stopped and then select the Option *Copy from Previous Value* from *Start Type* list.

All the Heads will be copied from the previous period. Now edit the value in Rate column for Employee Loan Pay head and enter zero at Rate column. Consequently, Employee Loan will not be deducted form the salary from the period specified at Effective Date.

07 Loan Recovery Amount Modification

Sometimes an Employee may request not to deduct instalment (or deduct more or less amount) in a particular month. If the request is acceded by management, then after the Payroll voucher is created, modify the Amount.

To modify such Payroll voucher, you have to drill down through any report (like Balance Sheet, P L Account, Trial Balance, ledger etc) to reach to the voucher and then modify the Loan deduction Amount (F-7A).

You may also create a new Pay structure for the current month (eliminating the loan deduction) and insert the loan deduction for the next month as usual, to stop / reduce loan deduction for current month only. In that case, you will have to again change the structure for the next pay period to resume the Loan Recovery. So, alteration of a single voucher is more convenient to take care of exceptional situations, rather than modifying the Pay Structure

Payroll Voucher Alteration (Secondary) Ctrl + M

Payroll No. 3 31-Jul-2015 Friday

Account : Salary Payable
Cur Bal: 520.00 Dr

Particulars		Amount
Surya Narayan Ghosh		*15,600.00 Dr*
Basic Salary	13,000.00 Dr	
DA	2,000.00 Dr	
HRA	600.00 Dr	
Employee Loan	Cr	
		15,600.00 Cr

Narration:
Salary for July

F-7A: Payroll voucher Modification

08 Transfer of Loan Balance

When you give a fresh loan, you create a payment voucher as described and the loan amount is reflected in Employee Ledger Breakup report.

Tally does not allow Employee wise allocation of the Opening Balance of a Payroll Head (like Opening balance of

Employee Loan Head), to Employees So, you cannot enter the Opening Balance in the Payroll Head (a Ledger Account is also auto created for the Payroll Head and auto linked with the Payroll Head). So create another ledger account and enter the Opening Balance in that Ledger Account (but not at Opening Balance of Payroll Head).

So, you create another Ledger Account for Loan Account and enter the Opening Balance (F-8A). You should create a common Employee Loan Account and enter the total Opening Balance (no need to create individual Employee Loan Ledger Account).

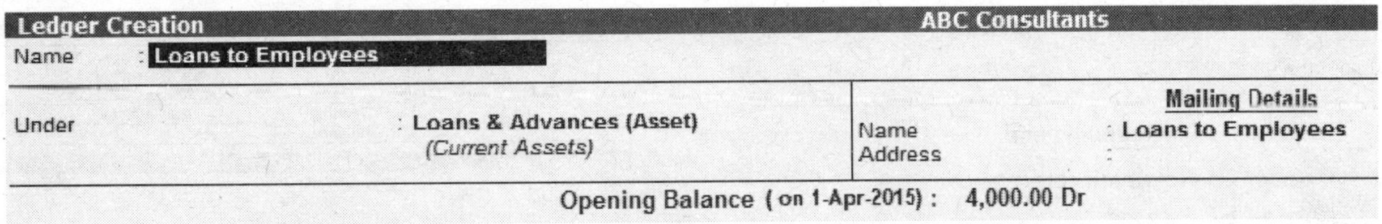

F-8A: Employee Loan Ledger Account for Opening Balance

In respect of Opening Balance of loan already given prior to start of Payroll system, loan is lying outstanding in individual loan ledger account of each employee (under the Group Loan & Advances). So, the Ledger Balance shows the outstanding amount of loan in respect of each Employee.

08.01 Loan Transfer Journal Voucher

Now create a Journal Voucher to Transfer the Ledger balances to the respective Loan account, as on the start date of the Payroll System

	Ledger A/c	Amount
Dr	Employee Loan A/c	Total of loan outstanding as on starting date, in respect of all employees
Cr	Loan to Employee (the Pay Head linked Ledger Account)	Outstanding amount in respect of each employee

Journal Voucher entry has been explained earlier. Here we show Journal Voucher (F-9A) to transfer the Opening Outstanding Loan to individual Employee Account.

At first Ledger Account, Debit the Loan Pay Head Ledger Account to get Employee Allocation screen (F-9B). Select the Employee and enter the enter the outstanding Opening Loan Amount in respect of all the employees. The Total Amount is carried in the main screen of the Voucher at Debit column(F-9A).. Next, Credit the Loan Ledger (in which you entered the Opening balance),

The total Amount allocated to Employees (F-9B) should match with the Amount Debited to Loan Account in main screen (F-9A).

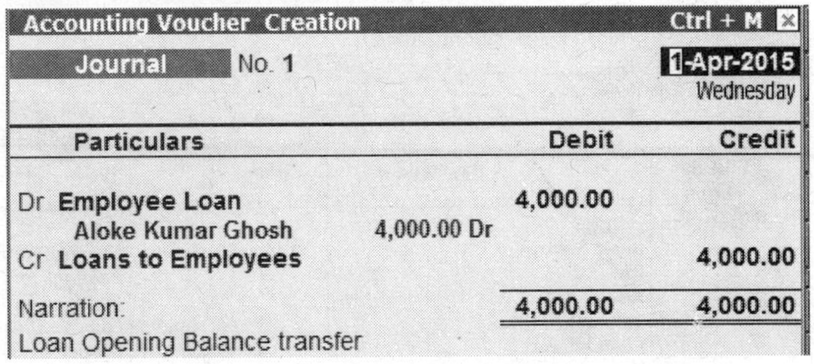

F-9A: Journal Voucher for transferring Opening Loan balances

F-9B: Employee Allocation

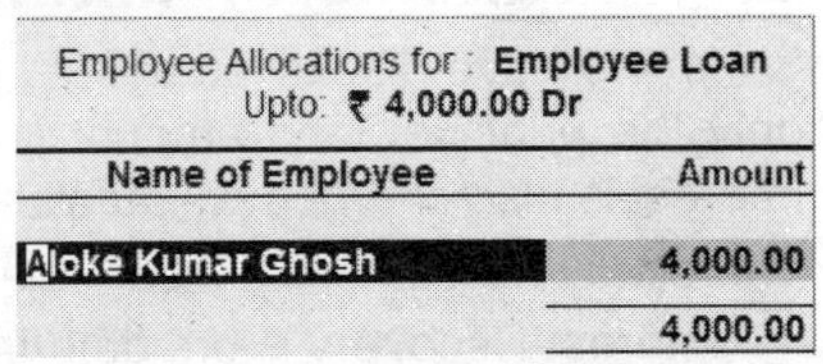

09 Loan Report

At *Statement of Payroll Menu*, select *Employee Pay Head Breakup*, as explained earlier. Set the Period and select the Employee Loan Pay Head to get Employee Wise details of Loan Payments (at Debit Column), Recoveries (at Credit Column) & Balance for the specified Period (F-10A).

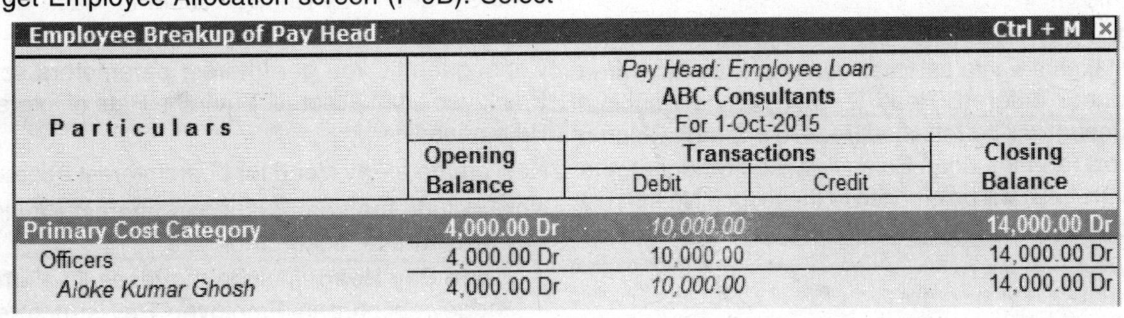

F-10A: Loan Report

Pay Head Creation

Name : **Loan Interest**

Pay Head Info

Pay Head Type : **Deductions From Employees**
Under : **Indirect Incomes**

Affect Net Salary ? **Yes**
Name to appear in Payslip : **Loan Int**

Calculation Type : **Flat Rate**
Calculation Period : **Months**

Rounding Info

Rounding Method : **Not Applicable**

F-11A: Loan Interest Pay Head

Payroll Voucher Creation Ctrl + M

Payroll No. 3 31-Oct-2015 Saturday

Account : **Salary Payable**
Cur Bal: 716.35 Dr

Particulars		Amount
Aloke Kumar Ghosh		**12,080.00 Dr**
Basic Salary	12,000.00 Dr	
HRA	300.00 Dr	
Employee Loan	200.00 Cr	
Loan Interest	20.00 Cr	

Narration: **12,080.00 Cr**
Salary for Oct 15

F-13A: Payroll Voucher

Employee Breakup of Pay Head Ctrl + M

Particulars	Pay Head: Employee Loan ABC Consultants 1-Oct-2015 to 31-Oct-2015			
	Opening Balance	Transactions Debit	Transactions Credit	Closing Balance
Primary Cost Category	4,000.00 Dr	10,000.00	200.00	13,800.00 Dr
Officers	4,000.00 Dr	10,000.00	200.00	13,800.00 Dr
Aloke Kumar Ghosh	4,000.00 Dr	10,000.00	200.00	13,800.00 Dr

F-14A: Loan Statement

Salary Details Alteration ABC Consultants Ctrl + M

Name : **Aloke Kumar Ghosh (2014/07)**
Under : **Officers**
(Primary)

Salary Details

Effective From	Pay Head	Rate	Per	Pay Head Type	Calculation Type	Computed On
1-May-2014						
	Basic Salary	12,000.00	Months	*Earnings for Employees*	*On Attendance*	
	DA			*Earnings for Employees*	*As Computed Value*	*On Current Earnings Total*
	HRA			*Earnings for Employees*	*As Computed Value*	*Basic Salary*
	Employee Loan	200.00	Months	*Loans and Advances*	*Flat Rate*	
	Loan Interest	20.00	Months	*Deductions From Employees*	*Flat Rate*	

F-12A: Pay Structure change for Loan Interest

10 Loan Interest Recovery

So far we have discussed about Interest Free Loan where only the principal loan amount is recovered. Sometimes, Interest is also charged on Outstanding Loan Account.

There may 2 instances of Loan Interest Computation:

- Interest Recovery is pre determined at the time of Loan sanction
- Interest is computed through Payroll system on Reducing Balance Method

10.1 Fixed Interest

In such case create another Pay Head Loan Interest. Now include the Loan Interest Recovery in the Employee Pay Structure (F-12A), in the same way as Loan Instalment Recovery (F-6A).

Now create the Payroll Voucher as explained earlier (F-13A). The Loan Instalment & Interest Instalment would be recovered separately under different Head (F-13A). While Principal Instalment amount will be reflected (F-14A) in Credit Column of Loan Report (and the Loan Balance will be reduced), the Loan Interest (F-14B) will be credited to the respective Interest Income Ledger (Loan Balance will not get affected) as defined.

Employee Breakup of Pay Head Ctrl + M

Particulars	Pay Head: Loan Interest ABC Consultants 1-Oct-2015 to 31-Oct-2015	
	Nett Transactions	Closing Balance
Primary Cost Category	20.00 Cr	20.00 Cr
Officers	20.00 Cr	20.00 Cr
Aloke Kumar Ghosh	20.00 Cr	20.00 Cr

F-14B: Loan Interest Statement

10.2 Interest on Outstanding Balance

If Interest is to be computed on each month's outstanding balance, then you have to create a separate Loan Account for each employee and set the Interest Rate.

Create a Loan Pay Head Account for each Employee. Set *Yes* at Activate Interest Calculation

Consequently, you get Interest parameters screen for the Employee Loan account. Enter the Rate of interest & Interest Rate period.

Now create a Pay Head for Loan Interest Account

Now include the Loan and Loan Interest Pay Heads in the Pay Structure for each Employee

- **Loan Pay Head**: Include the respective employee loan ledger account in Employee Pay structure. Since the Principal Loan Recovery is in equal instalments, set it As *Flat Rate* and set the Loan Instalment Amount at

Value column.

- **Loan Interest Pay Head**: As the Loan Interest varies for each month (as it is computed on each month's balance), set it as *User Defined value*.

10.3 Loan Interest Computation

Print the Loan Interest for the current month. Select *Display>Statement of Accounts>Interest Calculations> Interest Receivable* and print the Interest Report for the Month

10.4 Loan Interest Recovery in Payroll Voucher

Now create an Auto Fill Pay Voucher. The Loan Recovery gets filled up automatically as per Pay Structure, but the Loan Interest field is blank as it is set as User Defined Value in Pay Structure

In the Pay Voucher, place the cursor at the Loan Interest field and enter the Interest Recovery Amount for the respective employee as per Loan Interest Statement

Having entered the Loan Interest Amount, save the voucher.

You see the Interest on Reducing balance Method is quite complicated to operate as you will have to do a lot of manual work and create separate ledger account for Loan to each Employee.

Payroll Voucher Class

01 Payroll Voucher Class

Tally uses 3 Voucher Types related to Payroll (viz, Payment, Payroll & Attendance). You may create template of these Voucher Types to create Voucher Class.

Voucher Class helps to automate and control usage of ledger accounts and computed values to be posted. However, Voucher Class is not mandatory. It only provides additional flexibility & convenience.

Voucher Class enables you to define the rules of voucher entry for a particular voucher type. It also helps in speeding up the process and minimises data entry for posting a voucher.

Voucher Type / Voucher Class creation / alteration *(Payroll Info>Voucher Type)* has been explained earlier. At Voucher Type creation / alteration screen (F-1A), select the Voucher Type from the list, to create Payroll related Voucher Type / Voucher Class.

02 Voucher Class Creation

To create a Voucher Class, at Voucher creation / alteration screen (F-1A), at *Name of Class*, enter the Voucher Class Name to get Voucher Class set up screen (F-1B).

Account Groups: Set the Account Groups:

- At Voucher Class set up screen (F-1B), set as follows:

  Exclude Account Groups: At the left part, at *Exclude these Groups*, select the Accounts Groups to b excluded to exclude the subordinate Ledger Accounts to be entered in the Voucher), else select *End of List.*
- **Include Account Groups**: Having set the Exclude Groups, you may select Groups out of the excluded Groups to be included (else select *End of List*)

Account Ledger: At *Ledger Name*, select the Ledger that will be auto selected in the Voucher

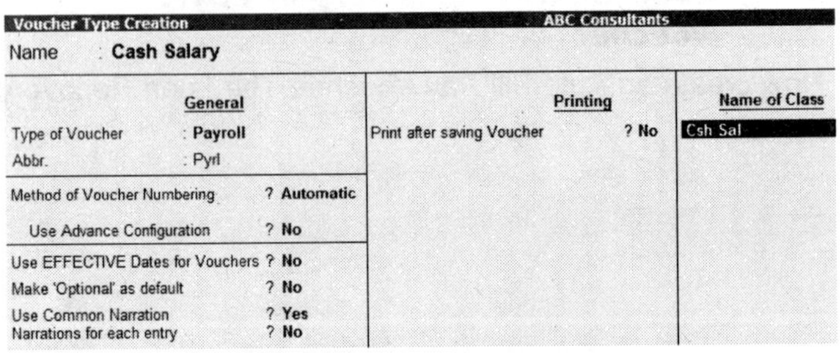

F-1A: Voucher Class creation

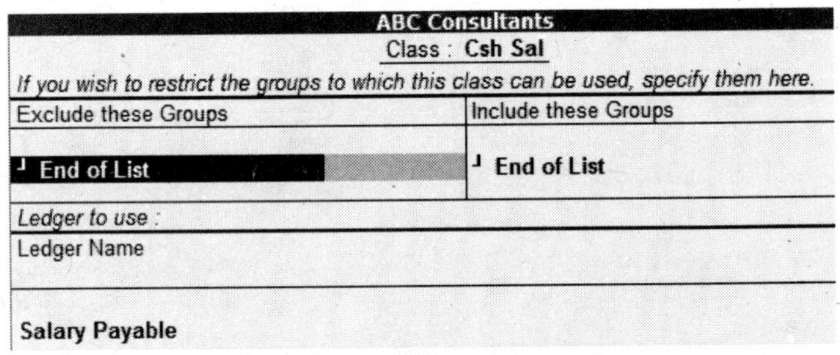

F-1B: Voucher Class set Up

F-1C: Voucher Type List

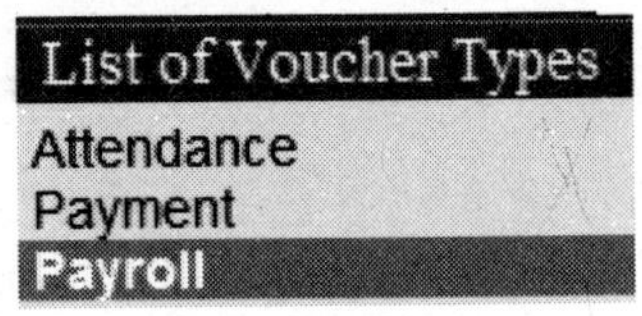

03 Payroll Voucher through Voucher Class

At Gateway, select Accounting Voucher, click F5:Payment Button and select the voucher class (e.g Sal Bank Pmt). Click *Payroll Auto-Fill* (or Press *CTRL+F7*) to bring up Employee Filters pop-up. Select appropriate employee group (for whom the respective Bank Voucher is applicable, or *All Items* (for all employees) and select *Salary Payable* in the Payroll Ledger field.

Tally will fill the Payment voucher with employee wise Net salary in the Salary Payable account F-2A)

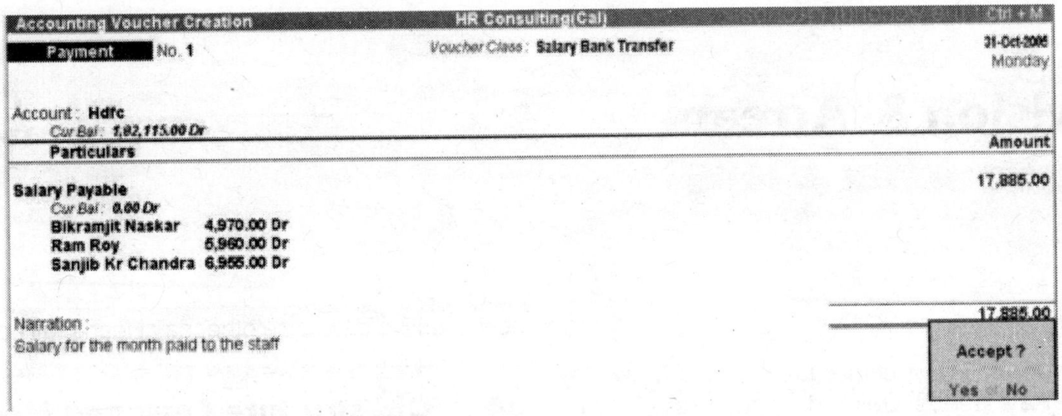
Accounting Voucher Creation HR Consulting(Cal) Ctrl + M

Payment No. 1 Voucher Class : Salary Bank Transfer 31-Oct-2006 Monday

Account : Hdfc
Cur Bal : 1,02,115.00 Dr

Particulars	Amount
Salary Payable Cur Bal : 0.00 Dr Bikramjit Naskar 4,970.00 Dr Ram Roy 5,960.00 Dr Sanjib Kr Chandra 6,955.00 Dr	17,885.00
	17,885.00

Narration :
Salary for the month paid to the staff

Accept ?
Yes or No

F-2A: Salary Payment Voucher through Voucher Class

Pay Revision & Arrears 02-04

01 Pay Revision

When any change in Pay structure takes place (new Pay Heads added, Pay Heads Deleted or the Rate or any parameter changed), you have to add a new Pay Structure from the effective Date of change. This also enables to maintain a history of all revision of Pay Structure of each Employee

02 Pay Structure Revision

There are 2 ways of Modifying Pay Structure

- Adding New Pay Structure
- Copying Old Structure & Modifying
    - o Copying from Pay Structure of Previous Period
    - o Copying from Pay Structure of Parent Employee Group

new effective date, else other pay Heads will not be computed in the Payroll Voucher.

04 Old structure Copy and Modify

Instead of entering all the Pay Heads again afresh, it is much easier to copy the previous Pay Structure at the new Effective Date and modify the elements as desired to get the new Pay structure

- At *Effective From* column, enter the Date from which the new Pay Structure takes effect (F-1A)
- At Start Type List, Select:
    - o *Copy From Previous Value* to copy the previous Pay Structure of the Employee (F-1B), or
    - o *Copy From Parent Value* to copy the Pay Structure of the Parent Employee Group of the Employee

Salary Details Alteration — **ABC Consultants**

Name : Surya Narayan Ghosh (0105)

Under : Officers
(↲ Primary)

Salary Details

Effective From	Pay Head	Rate	Per	Pay Head Type	Calculation Type	Computed On
1-Dec-2015						
	Basic Salary	12,000.00	Months	Earnings for Employees	On Attendance	
	DA			Earnings for Employees	As Computed Value	On Current Earnings Total
	HRA			Earnings for Employees	As Computed Value	Basic Salary
	Canteen Deduction			Deductions From Employees	As User Defined Value	
1-Jan-2016	Copy From Parent Value					
	Basic Salary	13,000.00	Months	Earnings for Employees	On Attendance	
	DA			Earnings for Employees	As Computed Value	On Current Earnings Total
	HRA			Earnings for Employees	As Computed Value	Basic Salary
	Employee Loan	200.00	Months	Loans and Advances	Flat Rate	
	Canteen Deduction			Deductions From Employees	As User Defined Value	

F-1A: Pay Revision

Start Type

Copy From Parent Value
Copy From Previous Value
Start Afresh

F-1B:Pay Revision Methods

At *GoT>Payroll Info>Salary Details>Define* and then select the Employee Group / Employee to get the Salary Details Alteration screen (F-1A) of the selected Employee Group / Employee to, modify the Pay Structure.

03 Adding New Pay Structure

In this method, all the elements (Pay Heads) of the revised Pay Structure is typed again against the new effective date.

- At *Effective From* column, enter the Date from which the new Pay Structure takes effect (F-1A)
- Select *Start Afresh* from the *Start Type* list (F-1B).

Even if there is a change in one head or addition of one head, you must enter all the heads that are applicable from the

Against the new *Effective Date*, enter / modify the Pay Head and values, as explained for creation of Pay Structure:

- **Insert New Pay Head**: Select the new Pay Head from he list of Pay Heads and enter the respective values / computation rules
- **Modify Pay Head**: Select the desired pay Head and modify the values
- **Delete Pay Head**: Select the Pay Head to be deleted and select *End of List* from the list of Pay Head to remove the Pay Head from the Pay Structure

Irrespective of the method (start Afresh or Copy / Modify) used, the end result in the Pay Structure is same.

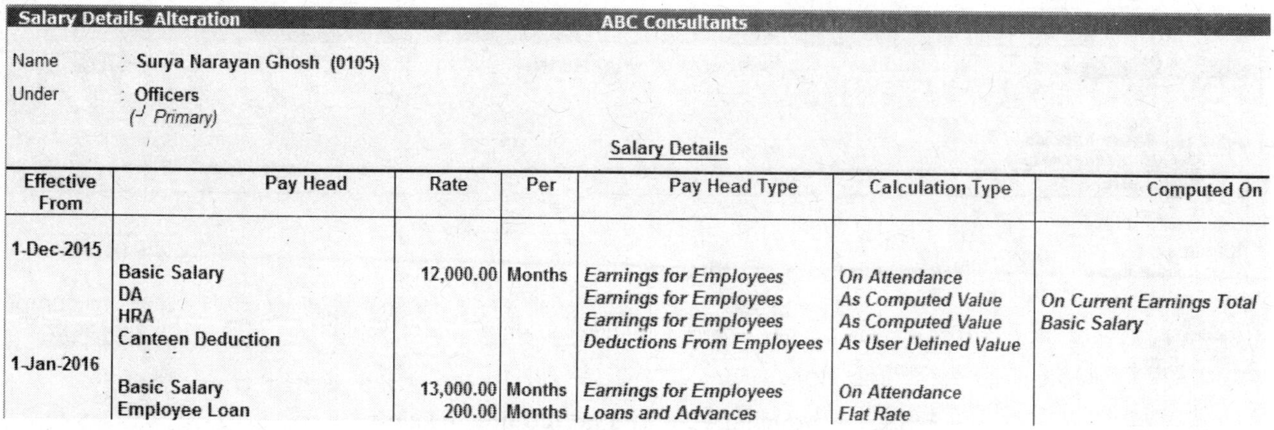

Salary Details Alteration — ABC Consultants

Name : Surya Narayan Ghosh (0105)

Under : Officers (↲ Primary)

Salary Details

Effective From	Pay Head	Rate	Per	Pay Head Type	Calculation Type	Computed On
1-Dec-2015						
	Basic Salary	12,000.00	Months	*Earnings for Employees*	*On Attendance*	
	DA			*Earnings for Employees*	*As Computed Value*	*On Current Earnings Total*
	HRA			*Earnings for Employees*	*As Computed Value*	*Basic Salary*
	Canteen Deduction			*Deductions From Employees*	*As User Defined Value*	
1-Jan-2016						
	Basic Salary	13,000.00	Months	*Earnings for Employees*	*On Attendance*	
	Employee Loan	200.00	Months	*Loans and Advances*	*Flat Rate*	

F-2A: Pay Revision – Wrong way

For example, if you enter the modified / new heads only (F-2A), only the heads entered in the revised pay structure will be applied and the omitted heads will not be considered in subsequent Pay Roll processing, resulting wrong Pay Computation

05 Mid Period Pay Revision

If the Pay Revision takes place in a middle of month, sometimes the revised Pay may not get computed correctly, when (in such cases, you may have to enter or Edit the Pay Voucher):

- The Employee Pay Structure includes has a Pay head with calculation type *Mth Rate-Deduct on Attd*, having compound Month unit (e.g Mnth of 30 days) and the calendar days in the month is different (say 31 days) from the number of days in the defined compound unit
- The Employee Pay Structure includes has a Pay head with calculation type *As Monthly Flat Rate*

Mth Rate-Deduct on Attd

In this case, Tally would compute the value to be reduced from the Monthly Salary by dividing value by the specified days (e.g 30), and then multiplying it with the number of days present in the 2nd part of the pay period.

For example, the Basic pay was 4000 / m and is revised to 9000 / m from 2-5- 2006 (F-3A) The Unpaid Days is 1d (unit 30 day month) for May 06 (F-4A), then the Basic Pay for May would be computed as Rs 8400.

This is computed as:

The full Pay is first computed for the 2nd part of the revision (i.e 2-5-2006 to 31-5-2006), ignoring the first part period (1-5-2006 to 1-5-2006) as Rs (9000) – (9000/30)x1 = 8700

Then it deducts for one day, i.e, deducts Rs 300 (9000/30)x4

So, the Pay is computed as Rs 8400 (8700- 300).

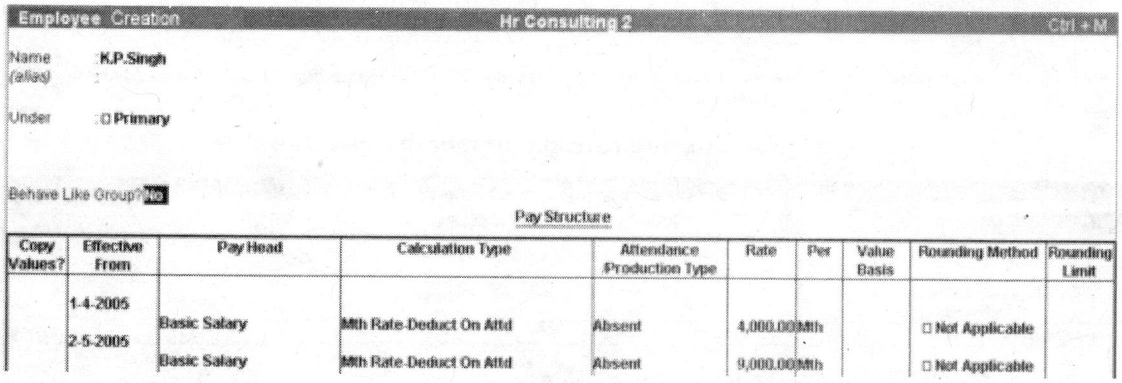

Employee Creation — Hr Consulting 2 — Ctrl + M

Name : K.P.Singh

(alias) :

Under : □ Primary

Behave Like Group? No

Pay Structure

Copy Values?	Effective From	Pay Head	Calculation Type	Attendance /Production Type	Rate	Per	Value Basis	Rounding Method	Rounding Limit
	1-4-2005								
		Basic Salary	Mth Rate-Deduct On Attd	Absent	4,000.00	Mth		□ Not Applicable	
	2-5-2005								
		Basic Salary	Mth Rate-Deduct On Attd	Absent	9,000.00	Mth		□ Not Applicable	

F-3A: Mid period Pay structure Revision

Let us suppose that the unpaid days for May is 4 days. Then the pay would be computed as:

The full Pay is first computed for the 2nd part of the revision 2-5-2006 to 31-5-2006, ignoring the period 1-5-2006 to 1-5-2006 as Rs (9000) – (9000/30)x1 = 8700

Then it deducts for 4 days, i.e, deducts Rs 1200 (9000/30)x4

So, the Pay is computed as Rs 7500 (8700- 1200).

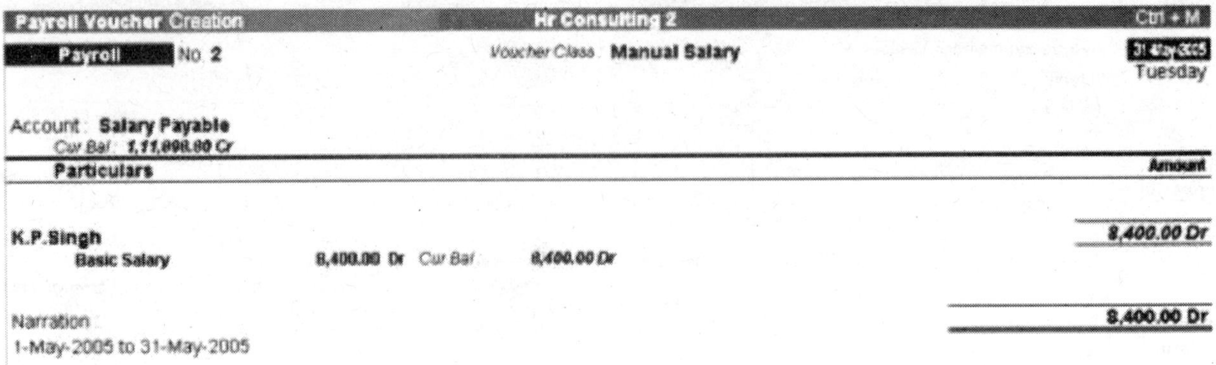

F-4A: Pay voucher with mid period pay revision

Monthly Flat Rate

Tally would add up the value for both Parts of the Month.

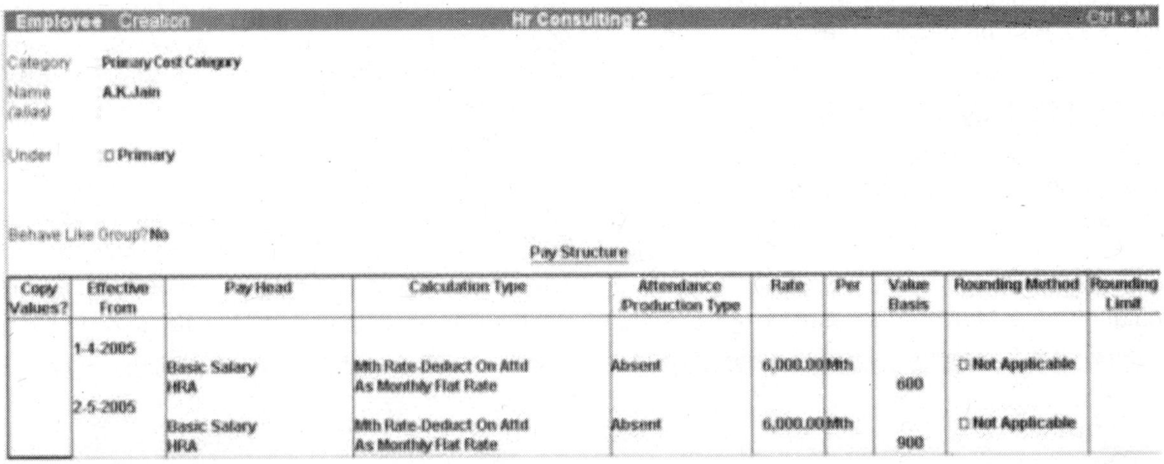

F-5A: Pay structure revision for Monthly Flat rate

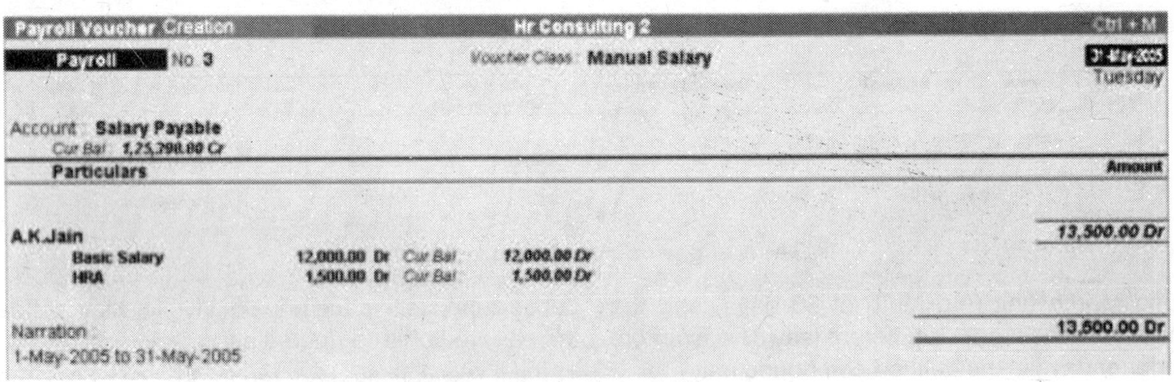

F-6A: Revision Pay voucher monthly flat rate

For example, HRA was Rs 600 /m and is revised from 2-5-2006 to 900 / month (Fig 25-7). Then the HRA would be computed as Rs 1500 (Rs 900+600) for May (Fig 25-8)

06 Pay Revision with retrospective effect

When you create a Pay voucher second time, Tally computes the Pay again with current effective rates after deducting the amount in previous voucher. This property can be effectively used to prepare a supplementary Pay voucher for *Arrears Pay* due for the back period (for the period for which pay voucher has already been prepared).

On Pay Revision, Revise the Pay Structure as explained above. For example, if the Pay is revised on 1.10.2015, w.e.f 1.7. 2015, then in the Pay Period, the Pay for October 2015 should include the Pay for 1.10.2010 to 31.10. 20 and also the difference (arrears) for the period 1.7.201 to 30.9.2015, in respect of each Head of Earnings & Deductions (including Statutory Deductions). The Arrears will also affect the Employer's Statutory Contribution

Name : Surya Narayan Ghosh (0105)
Under : Officers
(✓ Primary)

Salary Details

Effective From	Pay Head	Rate	Per	Pay Head Type	Calculation Type	Computed On
1-Apr-2015						
	Basic Salary	13,000.00	Months	*Earnings for Employees*	*On Attendance*	
	DA			*Earnings for Employees*	*As Computed Value*	*On Current Earnings Total*
	HRA			*Earnings for Employees*	*As Computed Value*	*Basic Salary*
1-Jul-2015	Copy From Previous Value					
	Basic Salary	15,000.00	Months	*Earnings for Employees*	*On Attendance*	
	DA			*Earnings for Employees*	*As Computed Value*	*On Current Earnings Total*
	HRA			*Earnings for Employees*	*As Computed Value*	*Basic Salary*

F-7A: Pay Revision

06.01 Arrears processing for Payment by separate voucher

Normally Arrear is paid separately. In such case, you may create new ledger account *Arrears Payable* (or may use the *Salary Payable* account

Create a new Payroll voucher Class named *Arrears Payment* using *Arrears Payable* (or *Salary Payable*).

Now create Payroll Voucher selecting the Voucher Class (voucher Date must be different from Normal Pay Voucher), click on *Auto-Fill* button. At *From* and *To* dates, enter the dates to cover the entire period of retrospective effect for which Payroll already processed, i.e. excluding current month period.

Tally would create the Arrear voucher with only the Arrears amount (F-8A), to be paid due to the change in the Pay Structure for the selected period, as follows:

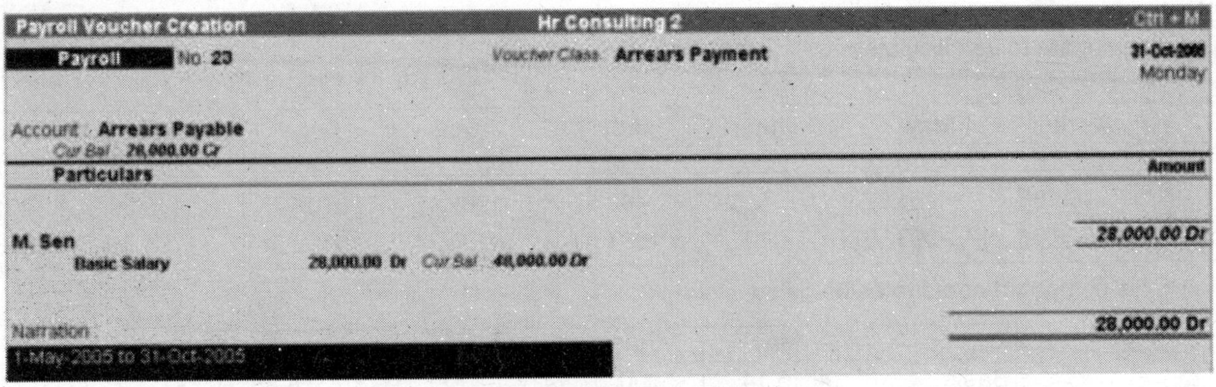

F-8A: Arrears Payment voucher

- First Pay for the covered period would be computed with revised Rates.
- The amount of all the vouchers already created for the covered period would be added up.
- Now the differential amount would be shown in the Arrear Voucher (total amount as per revised rate -amount already paid)

While printing the Arrear Payslip (F-9A), set the *From* and *To* date (F-9B). Tally would put the Period in Report Title (which you may change)

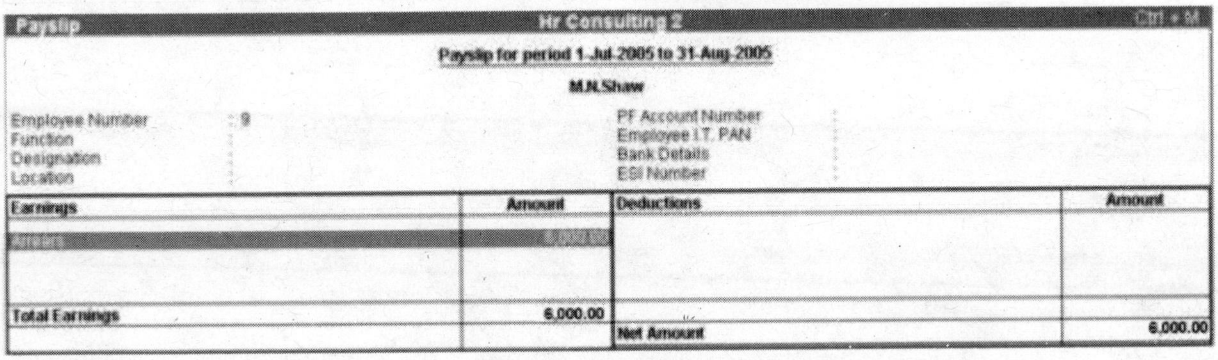

F-9A: Arrear Pay slip

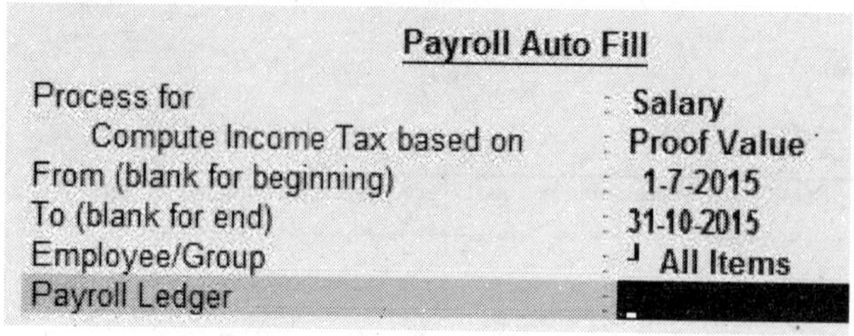

F-9B: Auto Fill Payroll

06.02 Arrears Payment included in current Payroll Voucher

If the Arrear payment is also included in the current Payroll Voucher, there is no need of separate processing and Payroll voucher and printing of Arrears Paysheet

In such case, using the Auto-Fill functionality, change the Period tp cover the Arrear Period (e.g 1.7.201 tp 31.1.0.2015). Click F2:Period and enter the dates to cover entire period for which the arrears are to be calculated

Tally would consider the new Pay Structure, the attendance data during the period and compute the current Pay Head values inclusive of the Arrears amount.

As discussed, Arrear Pay computation may not be accurate in specified cases of mid-period revision. Such cases should be scrutinized and rectified manually.

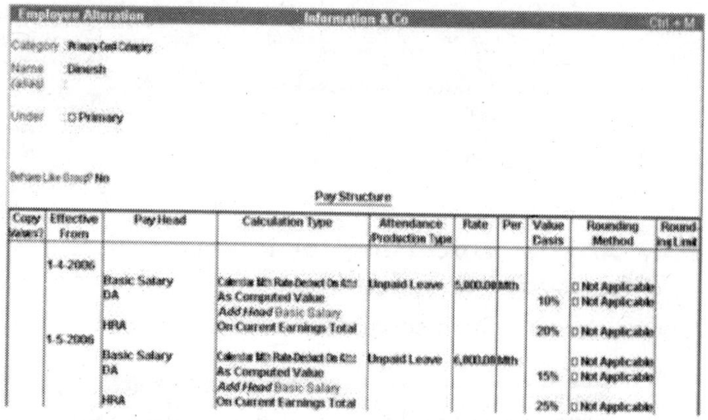

F-10A: Pay Revision with retrospective effect

	April	May	June	July	Total	Aug	Arrear	Paid in Aug
Basic	4666.67	4516.14	5000	4838.71	19021.52	5806.44	2870.97	8677.41
DA	466.66	451.62	500	483.87	1902.15	870.97	1148.39	2019.36
HRA	1026.67	993.55	1100	1064.52	4184.74	1669.35	1794.35	3463.70

Initially the Pay is computed at old rates as below:

	May	June	July	Total
Basic	4516.14	5000.00	4838.71	14354.85
DA	451.62	500.00	483.87	1435.49
HRA	993.55	1100.00	1064.52	3158.07
Total	5961.31	6600	6387.10	

Arrear is computed as below:

	Revised				Already paid				Arrear
	May	June	July	Total	May	June	July	Total	
Basic	5419.35	6000.00	5806.45	17225.80	4516.14	5000.00	4838.71	14354.85	2870.97
DA	812.90	900.00	870.96	2583.86	451.62	500.00	483.87	1435.49	1148.39
HRA	1558.06	1725.00	1669.35	18952.41	993.55	1100.00	1064.52	3158.07	1794.35

Part 3
Payroll Reports

In this Part we describe display / printing of Payslip and various Payroll Reports.

Pay Disbursements describes printing of Paylip, Pay advices etc in respect of payment to individual employees

Pay Reports describes various Pay reports in respect of each Employee and each Pay Head.

Bonus describes computation of Bonus or each employee for each Pay Period, processing of Bonus and preparation of Bonus Voucher for payment of Bonus to Employees

Gratuity describes set up for Gratuity and Gratuity Computation formula. Provision of Gratuity in respect of each financial year and Payment of Gratuity on cessation of Employment.

Expat Reports describes various reports containing the special information in respect of Expatriate Employees.

Pay Disbursements

01 Pay slip Menu

Having entered the Pay Voucher as described, you are now ready to print Pay Slip & Pay Advice for disbursement of Pay

At Gateway of Tally, select *Display >Payroll Reports>Statement of Payroll* to get *Statement of Payroll* Menu (F-1A). At *Statement of Payroll* Menu, select Payslip to get *Payslip Menu* (F-2A)

Gateway of Tally ....
Display Menu ....
Payroll Reports ....

Statements of Payroll

Pay Slip
Pay Sheet

PaYroll Statement
PayMent Advice

PayRoll Register

Employee ProFile

Employee Head Count

Employee Pay Head Breakup
Pay Head EmpLoyee Breakup

Quit

F-1A: Statement of Payroll Menu

Gateway of Tally ....
Display Menu ....
Payroll Reports ....
Statements of Payroll ..

Pay Slip

Single Pay Slip

Multi Pay Slip

E-Mail IDs

Quit

F-2A: Payslip Menu

02 Pay Slip

Pay Slip (F-3A) contains the details of Pay & Deduction for the Employee for the Pay Period. It is delivered to the concerned employee at each Pay Period, as complete record of Pay for the Employee.

Single Payslip: At Payslip Menu (F-2A), select *Single Payslip* and then select the Employee to get the Payslip for the selected Employee (F-3A). This is useful to print the Payslip for a specific Employee.

Pay List: At *Payslip Menu* (F-2A), select *Multiple Payslip* and then select the Employee / Employee Group (F-4D) to get the *Pay List* (Multi Payslip) for the selected Employee / Employee Group (F-4A). *Pay List* (Multi Payslip) shows the details of Bank Account Details and Net Pay. It is a statement of Employee wise Net Pay and is useful for disbursement of Pay (in Cash) / to send advice to Bank for credit of Net Pay Amount to the respective Employee Bank Account

02.01 Payslip Configuration

Single Pay Slip Configuration: You get the Single Payslip format for the selected employee, with currently set Configuration. To change the Configuration options, at Payslip display screen, Click F12 to get *Payslip Configuration* screen (F-3A), to set the options as follows:

- **Pay Slip Format:** At *Show Vertical Pay Slip,* set to Yes to align Deduction Part below the Earning. Set *No* to align them side-by-side (F-3A)
- **Employee Details:** At *Show Employee Details*, set *Yes* to display Employee Details as entered in the employee master.

  Having set *Yes* at *Show Employee details*, you may further set as follows:

Pay Slip | ABC Consultants | Ctrl + M

Pay Slip for May-2015

Aloke Kumar Ghosh

Employee Number : 2014/07
Function : Sales
Designation : Sales Officer
Location : Eastern Div
Bank Details :
Date of Joining : 1-May-2014

Income Tax Number (PAN) : ABCDE1234X
PF Account Number : WB/KOL/1234567/123/WB/1234
ESI Number : WB/8/123456

Attendance Details	Value
Absent	1 Days
Attendance	22 Days
Leave with Pay	8 Days

Earnings	Amount	Gross Salary	Deductions	Amount	Gross Salary
Basic Salary	11,613.00	12,000.00	PF	780.00	780.00
HRA	580.65	600.00	P Tax	50.00	50.00
Total Earnings	12,193.65	12,600.00	Total Deductions	830.00	830.00
			Net Amount	₹ 11,363.65	₹ 11,770.00

F-3A: Employee Pay Slip Display

Configuration

Show Vertical Pay Slip	? No
Show Employee Details	? Yes
Show Joining Date	? Yes
Show Attendance/Production Details	? Yes
Show Attendance/Production Groups	? Yes
Display Production Types in Tail Units	? No
Show Year To Date Values	? No
Show Gross Salary	? Yes
for Deduction's also	? Yes
Remove Zero Entries	? Yes
for Attendance/Production also	? Yes
Appearance of Employee Names	: Name Only
Appearance of Pay Head Names	: Payslip Name

F-3B: Pay Slip Configuration

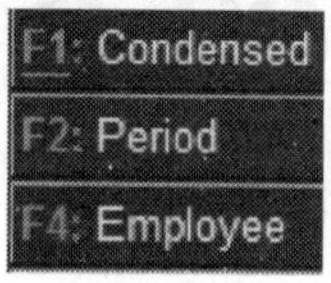

F-3C: Buttons

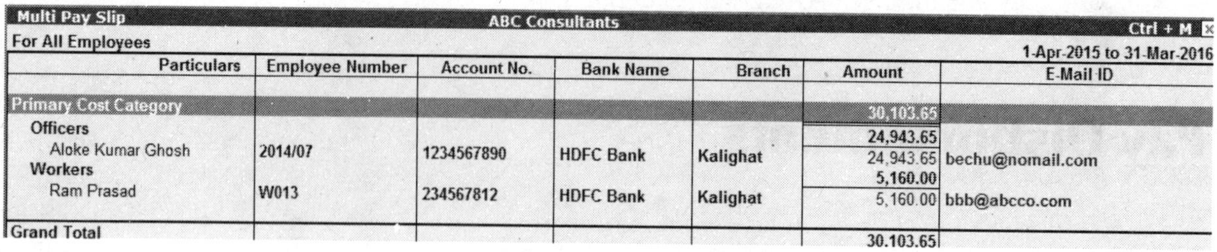

Multi Pay Slip — ABC Consultants — Ctrl + M

For All Employees — 1-Apr-2015 to 31-Mar-2016

Particulars	Employee Number	Account No.	Bank Name	Branch	Amount	E-Mail ID
Primary Cost Category					30,103.65	
Officers					24,943.65	
Aloke Kumar Ghosh	2014/07	1234567890	HDFC Bank	Kalighat	24,943.65	bechu@nomail.com
Workers					5,160.00	
Ram Prasad	W013	234567812	HDFC Bank	Kalighat	5,160.00	bbb@abcco.com
Grand Total					30,103.65	

F-4A: Pay List (Multiple Pay Slip) Display

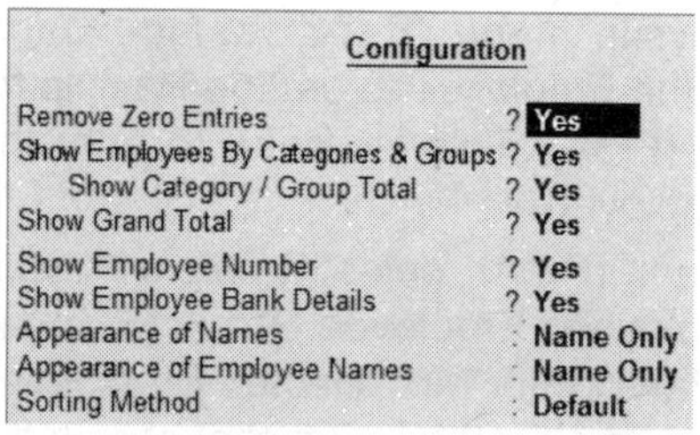

F-4B: Multi Pay Slip Configuration

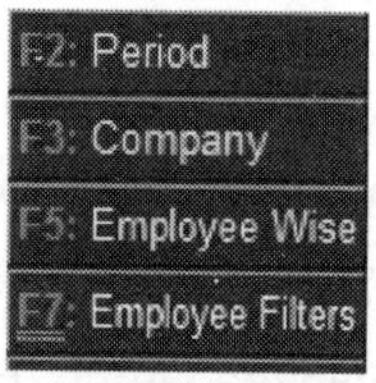

F-4C: Multi Pay Slip Button

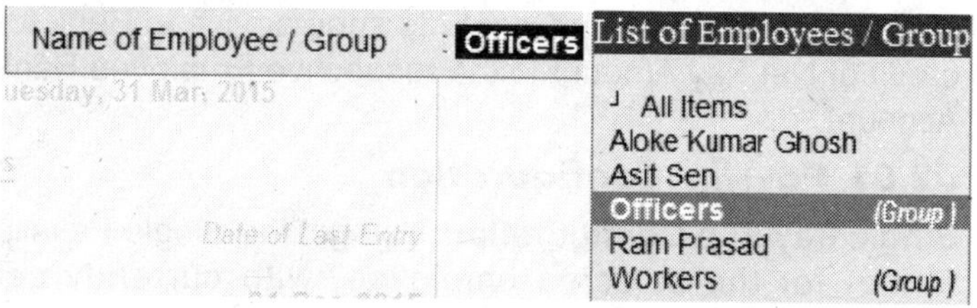

F-4D: Multi Payslip Employee Selection

- o **Passport Details:** At *Show Passport Details*, set *Yes* to display the Passport Details (applicable for expatriates)
- o **Visa Expiry Date:** At *Show Visa Expiry Date:* set ***Yes*** to display the Visa Expiry Date (applicable for expats)
- o **Joining Date:** At *Show Joining Date* set *Yes* to display the Employee Joining Date.

- **Attendance/Production Details**: At *Show Attendance/ Production Details,* set *Yes* to display Attendance/ Production data.
  - o **Attendance / Production Groups**: Having set *Yes* at *Show Attendance/Production Details,* set *Yes* at *Show Attendance / Production Groups* to display the respective Attendance/ production Groups (as defined in Attendance Types creation).
- **Compound Production Units:** For Compound Units used in Attendance / Production Type, set Yes at *Display Production Type in Tail Units*, to display value of the Attendance/Production Data in *Tail Unit*, else set No, to show in *Main unit.*
- **Year To Date Values**: At *Show Year To Date values*, set *Yes* to display cumulative value of attendance/production data or Earning and Deduction data for the current Financial Year.
- **Gross Salary Details**: At *Show Gross Salary,* set *Yes* to display the Gross Salary details for each component in the Salary Details.
  - o **Deduction Details:** Having set *Yes* at *Show Gross Salary*, you may further set Yes at *For Deduction* also, to display the Details for each Deduction component.
- **Hide Zero Entries**: At *Remove Zero Entries*, set *Yes* to hide Zero value Pay Head from the Pay Slip
  - o **For Attendance/Production Also**: Having set *Yes* at *Remove Zero Entries*, At *For Attendance/ Production Also,* you may further set *Yes* to hide zero value Attendance Head from the Pay Slip.

02.02 Drill Down

At *Multiple Pay Slip*, select any Employee and press <Enter> to get *Single Pay slip* of the selected Employee.

02.03 Pay List Configuration

You get the Pay List (Multiple Payslip) as per currently set Configuration. To change the Configuration options, at Multiple Pay Slip Display (F-6A), click *F12:Configure* to get *Multiple Payslip Configuration* screen (F-4B), to set the options as described above

02.04 Buttons

At *Pay Slip Display*, you get following buttons:

- **Single Payslip Buttons:** At Single *Pay Slip Display* (F-3A), you get following buttons:
- **F1: Detailed / Condensed**: To toggle between detailsed & condensed mode, as follows:
  - o **Detailed**: Click *F1: Detailed* to view Voucher details of individual Attendance and Pay Head values. This may be useful when multiple attendance/payroll vouchers are entered during the same payroll period. You may drill down to the corresponding voucher directly from the Pay Slip screen.
  - o **Condensed:** Click *F1: Condensed* to view head wise values without Voucher Details
- **F4: Employee:** To select another Employee to view the Pay Slip of the selected Employee
- **Multiple Single Payslip Buttons***: At Single Pay Slip Display (F-3A), you get following buttons:*
  - o **F5:Employee / Category wise:** To get the Report in sequence of Employee Name / Employee

Category and then Employee under the respective Category.

- o **F7:Employee Filter:** To select the Employee, Employee Group or *All Items* filter (F-4D) to show Filtered Report.

02.05 Payslip Printing

At *Payslip Display* (F-3A / F-4A), Click *P:Printing* button to get *Payslip Printing* screen (F-5A), to set the printing options (these options are relevant only for Single Payslip)

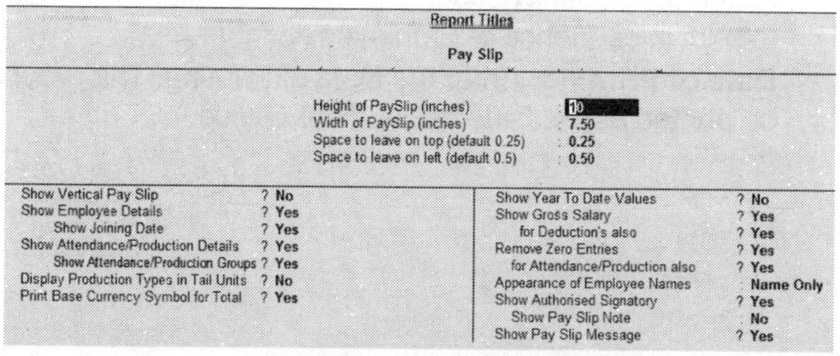

F-5A: Pay Slip Printing Screen

03 Employee e-mail ID

At *Pay Slip* Menu (F-2A), select *e-mail ID* to get Employee e-mail ID display screen (F-6A) showing the List of Employees and e-mail ID entered in the Employee Master as described earlier

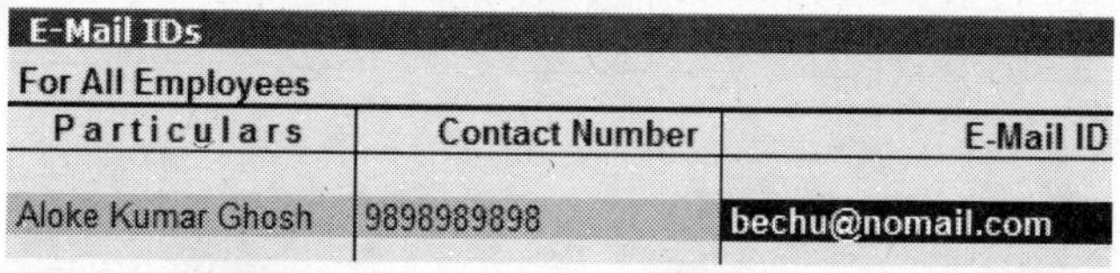

F-6A: Employee e-mail ID Display

F-6B: Buttons F-6C: Employee Filters

The Employee e-mail ID list (F-6A) shows the Employee Name, Contact Number & e-mail ID (as entered at Employee Master). You may enter / modify the e-mail IDs at the e-mail ID column for the respective Employees.

03.01 Buttons

At the email-Id Display, you get following Buttons (F-6B):

- **F5: All Item / Exceptions**: Click *F5:All Item / Exceptions*, toggle button to:
  - o **F5:All Item**: To show list of all employees (whether the emil ID are filled up or not. This helps to enter / update e-mal ids of all employees
  - o **F5:Exceptions**: To show list of only those employees whose e-mail ID are not filled up (blank), to enter e-mail IDs of those employees quickly.

  At e-mal ID column, enter / modify the e-mal ID directly in the list.
- ***F7: Employee Filters***: To get Employee Filter screen (F-6C) to select the option to show All Employees (select All Items), select an *Employee Group* or *Employee* from the list of Employees / Employee Group (F-4D), to show the filtered list of Employees in Employee e-mail ID list (F-6A).

04 Bank Payment Advice

Normally Employees open bank accounts in the same bank where the Company has its account. In such case, instead of issuing individual cheque to each employee, a bank advice may be sent to the bank to credit the Net Pay amount to the respective employee's account.

If all employees do not have accounts in the same bank, then you will have to create a Group for employees for each bank account. The payment advice can be printed either for *All Employees* of the company or for *All Employees* of a Group. So, you should create Employee Groups accordingly to print pay Advice.

To print Payment Advice, at Gateway, select *Display > Payroll Reports > Statement of Payroll> Payment Advice* to get the Payment Advice Printing screen (F-8A).

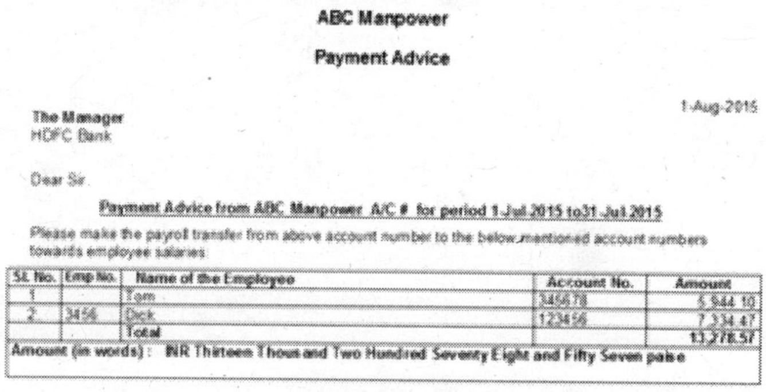

ABC Manpower

Payment Advice

1-Aug-2015

The Manager
HDFC Bank

Dear Sir

Payment Advice from ABC Manpower A/C # for period 1-Jul-2015 to31-Jul-2015

Please make the payroll transfer from above account number to the below mentioned account numbers towards employee salaries

Sl. No.	Emp No.	Name of the Employee	Account No.	Amount
1		Tom	345678	5,944.10
2	3456	Dick	123456	7,334.47
		Total		13,278.57

Amount (in words) : INR Thirteen Thousand Two Hundred Seventy Eight and Fifty Seven paise

F-7A Payment Advice

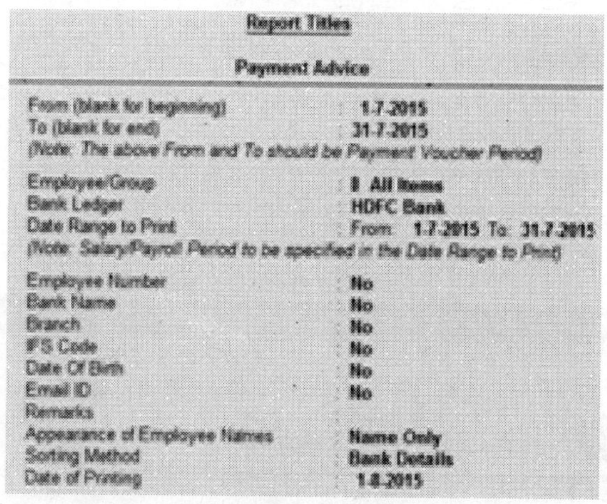

F-8A Payment Advice Printing screen

Now set up as follows:

- **Period:** At *From & To*, enter the Range of voucher date for which to print the Pay advice
- **Employee Group**: At *Employee Group*, select the Employee Group / Employee (or *All Items* for *All Employees*) for whom the Bank Advice is to be printed.
- **Bank Ledger**: At *Bank Ledger*, select the Bank Ledger Account from which the amount would be debited. The Name & Address of the Bank as per Ledger Account Master of the selected Bank Account, would be printed at the header of the Advice.
- **Date Range to Print**: At Date Range to Print, enter the Salary Period for which to print the Pay advice
- **Employee Particulars**: Now Set Yes (to print) / No (to omit) against each field to print the respective details in the Pay Advice
  Employee Number, Bank Name, Branch, IFS Code, Date of Birth, e-mail ID, from the Employee Master record.
- **Remarks**: Enter any message that would be printed against each employee at the last column.
- **Sorting Method**: Select *Default* to print in alphabetical order of Employee Name, *Bank Details* to print in sequence of Bank account Number & *Employee Number* to print in sequence of Employee Number
- **Date of Printing:** Enter the Date of Printing. This would be printed as the Date of Payment Advice.

Pay Reports 03-02

01 Pay Sheet

Pay Sheet is compact columnar report showing Pay headwise details of each employee.

At Statement of Payroll Menu (F-1A/04-05), select *Pay Sheet* and then select the Employee Filter from list (F-4D/04-05) to get Pay Sheet for the selected Employee / Group of Employees (F-1A)

Pay Sheet shows the complete details of each element of Pay Head and Net Pay amount, as they appear in Pay Slip.

01.01 Pay Sheet Configuration

At Pay Sheet display (F-1A), click *F12:Configure* button to get *Pay Sheet Configuration* screen (F-3A) to set the Configuration options, as described below:

- **Pay Head Columns**: At *Appearance of Name*, select from the list (F-3B)
    - o *All Columns*: *All Items* to show all columns of Earnings & Deduction Heads
    - o *Deductions Columns*: *Deductions* to show all columns of Deduction Heads
    - o *Earning Columns*: *Earnings* to show all columns of Earnings Heads only
- **Net Pay:** At *Show Net Pay Column,* set *Yes* to display the *Net Amount* Column (F-1A), else set *No* (the Net Pay Column is not shown).
- **Column Subtotals**: At *Show Column Subtotals,* set *Yes* to display the total Earnings & total *Deduction* columns in separate Columns, else set *No* (the Total columns are not shown)
- **Pay Head Name:** At *Show Payslip Names for Ledgers*, set *Yes* to display Pay Ledger Name, else set *No* to display Pay Heads the Name.
- **Gross Salary:** At *Show Gross Salary Details*, set *Yes* to display Fixed Income Type Pay Heads, else set *No*.
- **Show Grand Total**: Set *Yes* to display Grand Total at the bottom of the report, else set *No*

PaySheet — ABC Consultants
For All Employees

Employee Name	Basic Salary	HRA	Canteen	PF	VPF 4%
Aloke Kumar Ghosh	11,613.00	580.65		780.00	
Grand Total	11,613.00	580.65		780.00	

F-1A: Pay Sheet (Part 1)

Ctrl + M
1-Apr-2015 to 31-Mar-2016

P Tax	Net Amount
50.00	11,363.65
50.00	11,363.65

Pay Sheet (Part 2)

F1: Condensed
F2: Period
F3: Company
F7: Employee Filters

F-2A:Buttons

Configuration

Appearance of Pay Head Types	All Items
Show 'Net Amount' Column	? Yes
Show Column SubTotals	? No
Show Payslip Names for Ledgers	? Yes
Show Gross Salary Details	? No
Show Grand Total	? Yes
Show Attendance Details	? No
Display Production Types in Tail Units	? No
Show Employees By Categories & Groups	? No
Show Category / Group Total	? No
Show Category / Group in Columns	? No
Remove Zero Entries Employees	? Yes

F-3A: Paysheet Configuration (part 1)

Format	: Detailed
Show Employee Number	? No
Show Employee Bank Details	? No
Show Income Tax Number (PAN)	? No
Show Employee PF Account Number	? No
Show Employee ESI Number	? No
Show Employee Designation	? No
Show Employee Function	? No
Show Date of Joining & Resignation	? No
Expand all levels in Detailed Format	? Yes
Appearance of Employee Names	: Name Only
Sorting Method	: Default

Paysheet Configuration (part 2)

Appearance
All Items
Deductions
Earnings

F-3B: Appearance List

Format
Condensed
Detailed

F-3C: Format List

- **Attendance Details**: At Show *Attendance Details*, set *Yes* to *Show details of Attendance* also, else set *No* (*Attendance* details are not shown).
- **Compound Unit Production Details**: Having set Yes at Show *Attendance Details*. You may further set Yes at *Production Types in Tail Units*, to show the Production figures in Tail Unit, else set *No* to show Production figures in Compound Units.
- **Employee Group / Category**: At *Show Employees by Categories & Groups* set Yes to show the Category & Groups Rows also, else set *No* to show only Employee details
  - o **Group / Category Total:** Having set *Yes* at *Show Employees by Categories & Groups*, you may further set *Yes* at *Show Category / Group Total* to show the total figures of each Category / Group, else set No (the Category / Group Total would not be shown).
  - o **Group / Category Columns:** Having set *No* at *Show Employees by Categories & Groups*, you may further set *Yes* at *Show Category / Group in Column* to show the total figures of each Category / Group, else set No (the Category / Group Columns would not be shown).
- **Zero Amount**: At *Remove Zero Entries Employees*, set *Yes* to hide the Names of Employees of Zero Earnings & Deductions.
- **Format** – At *Format*, select *Detailed* (F-3C) to get voucher break up, select *Condensed* (F-3C) to get Employee wise totals. You may also click *F1:Detailed / Condensed* toggle button (F-2A) at button bar to get *Detailed / Condensed* report.
- **Detailed Format options:** On selection of *Detailed* Format, you may further set for the following Options
  - o **Employee Number** – At *Show Employee Number*, set *Yes* to display Employee Number along with the Name, else set No (the Employee Number is not shown).
  - o **Employee Bank Details** – At *Show Employee Bank Details*, set *Yes* to display Employee Bank Details, else set No (the Employee Bank Details is not shown).
  - o **Employee I Tax PAN** – At *Show Income Tax PAN*, set *Yes* to display Employee I Tax PAN, else set No (the Employee I Tax PAN is not shown).
  - o **Employee PF Account Number** – At *Employee PF Account Number*, set *Yes* to display Employee PF Account Number, else set No (the Employee PF Account Number is not shown).
  - o **Employee ESI Number** – At *Employee ESI Number*, set *Yes* to display Employee ESI Number, else set No (the Employee ESI Number is not shown).
  - o **Employee Designation** – At *Employee Designation*, set *Yes* to display Employee Designation, else set No (the Employee Designation is not shown).
  - o **Employee Function** – At *Employee Function*, set *Yes* to display Employee Function, else set No (the Employee Function is not shown).
  - o **Employee Date of Joining / Resignation** – At *Employee Date of Joining / Designation*, set *Yes* to display Employee Date of Joining / Designation, else set *No* (the Employee Date of Joining / Designation is not shown).
  - o **Expand all levels in Detailed format** – At *Expand all levels in Detailed format*, set *Yes* to get complete details of each Employee / Voucher.

01.02 Pay Sheet Buttons

At *Employee Pay Sheet*, you get following Buttons (F-2A):

- ***F1:Detailed / Condensed***: To toggle to get *Detailed / Condensed* report.
- ***F7: Employee Filters***: To filter Employee / Employee Group from the Employee Filter list (F-4D/04-05)

01.03 Additional Columns in Pay Sheet

To show any additional column for any other pay Head (not displayed in default Pay Sheet, e.g Employer's Contribution to PF), at Paysheet (F-1A), click *New Column* button (or press ALT+C) to get Column Details screen (F-4A), to select the Pay Head from list of Pay Heads(F-4B). The selected Pay Head is added as an additional Column (New Column) in the Pay Sheet.

F-4A: Additional Pay Head inclusion

- **Alteration of Additional Column**: To change the contents of the newly created column as described above, place the cursor on the column (e.g EPF) and click *Alter Column* button (or press ALT+A) and select the head which you like to replace at the currently specified column.

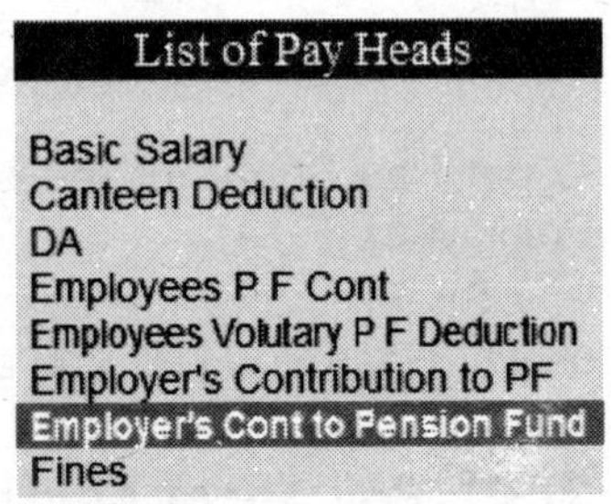

F-4B: Additional Pay Head selection

- **Deletion of Additional Column**: To Delete any of the newly created column (as explained here), place the cursor on the column to be Deleted (the new column created by you) and click Delete Column button or (press ALT+D).

This way, you may fully customize the contents of Paysheet.

01.04 Pay Sheet Printing

To print the Pay Sheet, at Pay Sheet Display screen (F-1A), Click *P:Print* button (or press ALT+P) at Pay get Pay Sheet Printing screen (F-5A) to set the printing options (F-5A), as follows:

Report Titles
Pay Sheet
Increase Line Height for Signature / Stamp ? No

F-5A: Pay Sheet Printing screen

Stamp Space in Pay Sheet: To fix Revenue Stamp and put Employee Signature on receipt of Pay by Employees on the Pay Sheet, at Pay Sheet Printing screen (F-5A), set *Yes* at *Increase Line Height for Signature / Stamp* to increase the line height (to increase vertical space between Employee Lines.

Type Y to print the Pay Sheet.

Payroll Statement	Ctrl + M
For All Employees	1-Apr-2015 to 31-Mar-2016
Particulars	Basic Salary
Primary Cost Category	23,613.00
Officers	23,613.00
Aloke Kumar Ghosh	23,613.00

F-6A: Payroll Statement

Configuration	
Show Payslip Names for Ledgers	? Yes
Show Grand Total	? Yes
Show Employees By Categories & Groups	? No
Show Category / Group Total	? No
Show Category / Group in Columns	? Yes
Remove Zero Entries Employees	? Yes

Format	: Detailed
Show Employee Number	? No
Show Employee Bank Details	? No
Show Income Tax Number (PAN)	? No
Show Employee PF Account Number	? No
Show Employee ESI Number	? No
Show Employee Designation	? No
Show Employee Function	? No
Show Date of Joining & Resignation	? No
Expand all levels in Detailed Format	? Yes
Appearance of Employee Names	: Name Only
Sorting Method	: Default

F-6B: Configuration Options

- F1: Condensed
- F2: Period
- F3: Company
- F7: Employee Filters

F-6C:Buttons

02 Payroll Statement

While Pay Sheet gives Pay Headwise details of Payroll vouchers, Payroll Statement gives employee wise listing of a specific Pay Head. It is like Pay Ledger for the selected Pay Head.

At Gateway of Tally, select *Display > Payroll Reports > Statement of Payroll>Payroll Statement* and then selected the Pay Head (you may select only ONE Pay Head) to get Payroll Statement for the selected Pay Head (F-6A). The total amount for the Pay Head in respect of each Employe is shown under the column of selected Pay Head

Payroll Statement Configuration: At Payroll Statement (F-6A), Click F12:Configure button to get Payroll statement Configuration screen (F-6B). The Configuration options are almost similar to Paysheet Configuration options, described earlier.

Payroll Statement Buttons: At Payroll Statement (F-6A), you get Buttons similar to Pay Sheet (F-6C), described earlier.

03 Payroll Voucher Register

Payroll Voucher Register (F-7A) shows the list of Payroll Vouchers for a specified Period

At *Gateway of Tally*, select *Display > Payroll Reports > Statement of Payroll > Payroll Register* to get Payroll Register (F-7A). Initially the Payroll Register shows the number of Payroll Vouchers for each Month. Select any Month to get Voucher Register showing the list of Payroll Vouchers for the selected month.

Payroll Voucher Register Configuration: At *Payroll Voucher Register*, click *F12:Configure* to get Payroll Voucher Register Configuration screen (F-7B). The options are similar to Accounts Voucher Register discussed earlier.

Payroll Voucher Register Buttons: At *Payroll Voucher Register*, you get the buttons similar to Accounts Voucher Register discussed earlier.

Voucher Register — Ctrl + M

List of All Payroll Vouchers — 1-May-2015 to 31-May-2015

Date	Particulars		Vch Type	Vch No.	Debit Amount	Credit Amount
31-5-2015	Basic Salary		Payroll	1	11,613.00	
	HRA	580.65 Dr				
	Employees P F Cont	780.00 Cr				
	Professional Tax	50.00 Cr				
	Salary Payable	11,363.65 Cr				

F-7A: Payroll Voucher Register

Configuration	
Show Extract of Register	? No
Format	: Detailed
Show Narrations also	? No
Show Billwise Details also	? No
Show Employee Details also	? No
Show Inventory Details also	? No
Show Bank Details also	? No
Appearance of Names	: Name Only
Sorting Method	: Default

F-7B: Payroll Voucher Register Configuration

- F1: Condensed
- F2: Date
- F2: Period
- F3: Company
- F4: Chg Vch
- F5: Columnar
- F6: Extract

F-7C: Buttons

Payroll Voucher Extract: It shows the Ledger Account wise summary of Vouchers listed in Payroll Voucher Register. To get Payroll Voucher Extract:

- At *Payroll Voucher Configuration* (F-7B), set Yes at *Show Extract of Register*
- At *Payroll Voucher Buttons* (F-7C), click *F6:Extract*

04 Salary Payment Summary

At *Gateway of Tally,* select *Display > Payroll Reports > Statement of Payroll > Employee Head Count* to get Salary / Wages Payment Summary (F-8A)

Salary Payment Summary Configuration

At *Salary Payment Summary Configuration,* click *F12: Configure* to get Salary Payment Summary Configuration to set the options as follows:

- **Head Count**: At *Show Head Count* set Yes to show the figures to get the columns of Head Count (F-8A), else set *No*, to suppress the Head Count Columns.

the Date of Birth, else set No (Date of Birth column is not shown).

- **Date of Joining:** At ***Show Date of Joining***, set *Yes* to display the Date of Joining, else set No (Date of Joining column is not shown).
- **Date of Leaving:** At *Show Date of Leaving*, set *Yes* to display the date of leaving for Employees having left, else set *No* (Date of Leaving column is not shown).
- **Employee Designation:** At *Show Employee Designation*, set *Yes* to display the Employee's Designations, else set *No* (Employee Designation column is not shown).

Salary/Wages Payments — ABC Consultants — Ctrl + M

Salary / Wages Payment Summary — 1-May-2015 to 31-May-2015

Particulars	Head Count				Earnings	Deductions	Nett Salary	Salary Paid	Balance Salary
	Opening Balance	Newly Joined	Resigned / Retired	Closing Balance					
May	1			1	12,193.65	830.00	11,363.65		11,363.65
Grand Total					12,193.65	830.00	11,363.65		11,363.65

F-8A: Salary Payment Summary

Configurations

Show Head Count	? Yes
Show Earnings and Deductions Breakup	? No
Show Salary Paid & Balance Amount	? Yes

F-9A: Salary Payment Summary Configuration

Head Count Details — ABC Consultants — Ctrl + M

For All Employees — 1-May-2015 to 31-May-2015

Particulars	Employee Number	Head Count				Date of Birth	Date of Joining	Date of Leaving	Employee Designation	Location
		Opening Balance	Newly Joined	Resigned / Retired	Closing Balance					
Primary Cost Category		1			1					
Officers		1			1					
Aloke Kumar Ghosh	2014/07					1-May-1990	1-May-2014		Sales Officer	Eastern Div

F-10A: Head Count Details

Configuration

Show Employee Number	? No
Show Date of Birth	? No
Show Date of Joining	? No
Show Date of Leaving	? No
Show Employee Designation	? No
Show Location	? No
Appearance of Names	: Name Only

F-10B: Head Count Details Configuration

- **Earnings & Deduction Break Up:** Having set *No* at *Show Head Count*, you may further set *Yes* to get columns of Earnings & Deduction Heads, else set No.
- **Salary Paid & Balance:** At *Salary Paid & Balance* set *Yes* to get columns of Salary Paid & Balance also (F-8A), else set No (these 2 columns are not shown)

05 Head Count Details

At Salary / Wages Payment Summary (F-8A), drill down through any Month record, to get the Head Count Details for the month, showing the Name & Particulars of each Employee (F-10A)

Head Count Details Configuration: At *Head Count Details* (F-10A), click *F12: Configure* to get F-10B: Head Count Details Configuration screen to set the Configuration options as below:

F1: Condensed
F2: Period
F7: Employee Filters

F-10C: Buttons

- **Employee Number:** At *Show Employee Number*, set Yes to display the Employee Number, else set No (Employee Number column will not be shown)
- **Date of Birth:** At *Show Date of Birth*, set *Yes* to display

- **Location:** At *Show Location*, set *Yes* to display the Location of Employees, else set *No* (Employee Location column is not shown).

Head Count Details Buttons: At *Head Count Details* (F-10A), you get the following Buttons

- **F7: Employee Filter:** To get Employee Filter option list (F-4D/04-05), to select All Employees, Group or Employee or specific Employee, to show the list of respective Employee.

Employee Breakup of Pay Head — Ctrl + M

Particulars	Pay Head: Basic Salary ABC Consultants 1-Sep-2015 to 31-Mar-2016			
	Opening Balance	Transactions Debit	Transactions Credit	Closing Balance
Primary Cost Category		12,000.00		12,000.00 Dr
Officers		12,000.00		12,000.00 Dr
Aloke Kumar Ghosh		*12,000.00*		12,000.00 Dr
Asit Sen				

F-11A: Employee Pay Head Break Up

06 Employee Pay Head Breakup

At Gateway, select *Display>Payroll Reports>Statement of Payroll>Employee Pay Head Break Up* and then select a Pay

Head to get *Employee Pay Head Break Up* Report for selected Pay Head. This report shows the details of employee wise Account Ledger figures for the selected Pay Head.

Configuration	
Show Opening Balances	? Yes
Show transactions	? Yes
Nett transactions only	? No
Show Closing Balances	? Yes
Show Percentages	? No
Appearance of Names	: Name Only
Scale Factor for Values	: Default
Expand all levels in Detailed Format	? Yes

F-11B: Employee Pay Head Break Up Configuration

F1: Condensed
F2: Period

F-11C: Buttons

Employee Pay Head Break Up Configuration: At *Employee Pay Head Break Up*, click *F12:Configure* to get *Employee Pay Head Break Up Configuration,* similar to *Account Group Summary* described earlier.

07 Pay Head Employee Breakup

At Gateway, select *Display>Payroll Reports>Statement of Payroll> Pay Head Employee Break Up* and then select an Employee to get *Pay Head Employee Break Up* Report for selected Employee. This report shows the Account Group/ Ledger Account Summary (like Extract), in respect of Pay Roll Vouchers.

Pay Head Employee Break Up Configuration: At *Pay Head Employee Break Up* (F-12A), click *F12:Configure* to get *Pay Head Employee Break Up Configuration* (F-12B), similar to *Employee Pay Head Break Up Configuration* (F-11B).

Breakup of Employee — Ctrl + M

Employee: Aloke Kumar Ghosh
ABC Consultants
1-Apr-2015 to 1-Oct-2015

Particulars	Opening Balance	Transactions Debit	Transactions Credit	Closing Balance
Current Liabilities			13,693.65	13,693.65 Cr
Duties & Taxes			50.00	50.00 Cr
Professional Tax			*50.00*	50.00 Cr
Bonus Payable			1,500.00	*1,500.00 Cr*
Employees P F Cont			780.00	*780.00 Cr*
Salary Payable			11,363.65	*11,363.65 Cr*
Direct Expenses		*11,613.00*		**11,613.00 Dr**
Basic Salary		11,613.00		*11,613.00 Dr*
Indirect Expenses		*2,080.65*		**2,080.65 Dr**
Employe Expenses		2,080.65		2,080.65 Dr
Bonus		*1,500.00*		1,500.00 Dr
HRA		*580.65*		580.65 Dr
Grand Total		***13,693.65***	***13,693.65***	

F-12A: Pay Head Employee Break Up

Configuration	
Show Opening Balances	? Yes
Show transactions	? Yes
Nett transactions only	? No
Show Closing Balances	? Yes
Show Percentages	? No
Appearance of Names	: Name Only
Scale Factor for Values	: Default
Sorting Method	: Default
Expand all levels in Detailed Format	? Yes

F-12B: Pay Head Employee Break Up Configuration

F1: Condensed
F2: Period
F4: Group
F5: Led-wise
F6: Monthly
F7: Vouchers

F-12C: Buttons

Pay Head Employee Break Up Buttons: At *Pay Head Employee Break Up* (F-12A), you get Buttons (F-12C), similar to *Account Group Summary* described earlier

Bonus

03-03

01 Bonus Pay Head

Bonus is extra Payment at a certain interval (normally Yearly) and is paid separately.

Create a Pay Head for Bonus. Pay Head creation has been explained earlier. Here we explain creation of Bonus Head

At Gateway, select *Payroll Info>Pay Heads> Create* to create the Pay Head for Bonus (F-1A).

- **Pay Head Type**: At *Pay Head Type*, select *Bonus* from the list of Pay Head Types.
- **Parent Account Group**: At *Under* select Employee Expenses from the Account Group list
- **Inclusion in Pay:** At *Affect Net Salary*, set Yes as the Bonus becomes payable to Employee
- **Calculation Type**: At *Calculation Type*, select *As Computed Value,*as Bonus is normally computed as % of specified Pay Heads (e.g Basic & DA)

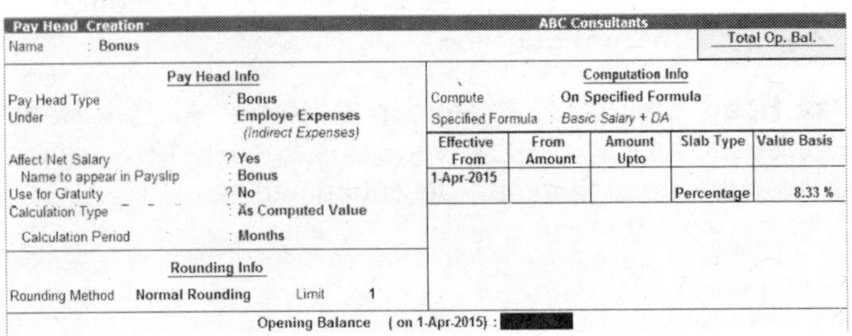

F-1A: Pay Head Creation

F-1B: Pay Head Computation

Compute : On Specified Formula	
Function	**Pay Head**
Add Pay Head	Basic Salary
Add Pay Head	DA

01.01 Bonus Computation Info

At the right Part of Bonus Pay Head entry csreen (F-1A), you get Computation Info screen. The process of entry of Computation Info has been explained earlier. Here we discuss about set up details for *Bonus* Head.

- **Computation Method**: Bonus is normally paid on some specified earnings only.

  So, at *Compute*, select *on Specified Formula* from the list to get Specified Formula screen to specify the Computation Formula
- At Function column select the function *Add Pay Head* and select the Pay Head on which Bonus is computed. This way, select Add pay Head and select other Pay Head on which Bonus is to be computed.
- Consequently, the formula showing the Pay Heads selected appear at Specified Formula at the entry screen (F-1B)
- **Effective Date**: At *Effective From* column, the Financial Start Date is carried by default, at the first instance
  - o **Slab Range & Rate**: Now enter the Range & corresponding rates for each Slab, as follows:
  - o **Slab Lower Amount**: At *From Amount*, enter the Slab *Lower* range amount in first slab, this is skipped, indicating zero as Starting Range of first slab)
  - o **Slab Limit**: If there is upper limit on Bonus, At Amount Upto, enter the upper limit amount

    If there is no limit for Bonus Amount, then leave blank at *From Amount & Amount Upto* columns so that Bonus is computed on the entire amount as per computation formula.
  - o **Computation Method:** At *Slab Type*, select *Percentage* from List of Slabs
  - o **Rate:** At *Value Basis*, enter Bonus % Rate

02 Bonus Payable Head

Bonus Payable Pay Head (F-2A) is required to facilitate creation of Liabilities for Bonus Payment

(like Salary Payable) explained earlier.

F-2A: Bonus Payable

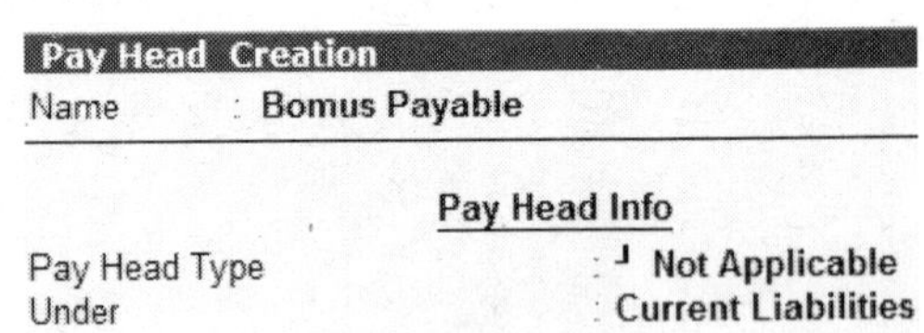

03 Bonus Voucher

Now create the Bonus voucher (F-3A) to Compute Bonus and create the Bonus Liability for the Employees. At Gateway, Select Payroll Voucher>Payroll Voucher:

Payroll Voucher Class: To use Payroll Voucher Class, if created, Click F4:Payroll button and select the respective Voucher Type to get the Payroll Voucher entry screen

You may enter the Bonus Voucher as explained earlier and as shown (F-3A)

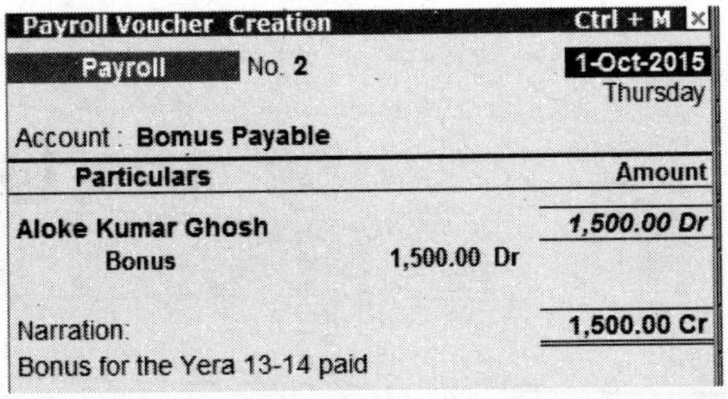

F-3A: Bonus Voucher (Manual)

04 Bonus Report

Having created the Bonus Voucher, to get details of Bonus for each Employee, at Gateway, At *Display>Payroll Reports> Statement of Payroll*, select

- Employee Payhead Breakup
- Payroll Statement

and select Bonus Payable (or Bonus Pay Head) from the list.to get the Employee wise list of Bonus Report (F-4A).

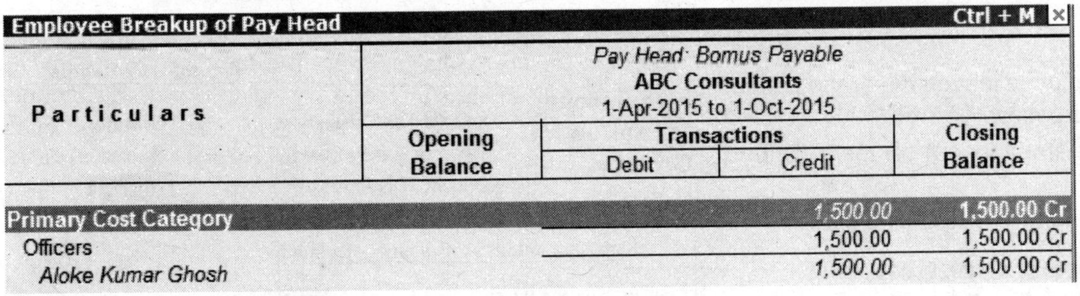

Employee Breakup of Pay Head — *Pay Head: Bomus Payable* — ABC Consultants — 1-Apr-2015 to 1-Oct-2015

Particulars	Opening Balance	Transactions Debit	Transactions Credit	Closing Balance
Primary Cost Category			*1,500.00*	1,500.00 Cr
Officers			1,500.00	1,500.00 Cr
Aloke Kumar Ghosh			*1,500.00*	1,500.00 Cr

F-4A: Bonus Report

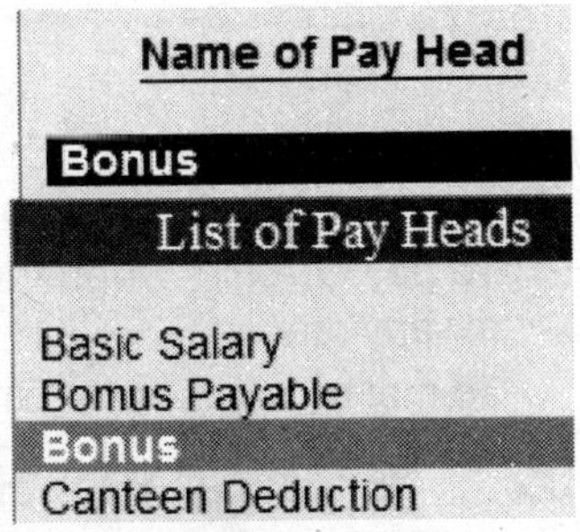

F-4B: Bonus Pay Head selection

01 Gratuity

Gratuity is paid when an Employee leaves the organization. Gratuity is computed for 2 purposes:

- To pay Gratuity when the employment comes to an end for any reason
- To make provision for Gratuity on continuing basis

02 Gratuity Pay Head Creation

Pay Head creation has been explained earlier. Here we explain creation of Gratuity Pay Head

At Gateway, select *Payroll Info>Pay Heads> Create* to create the Pay Head for Gratuity (F-1A).

- **Pay Head Type**: At *Pay Head Type*, select *Gratuity* from the list of Pay Head Types.
- **Parent Account Group**: At *Under* select *Provisions* from the Account Group list

Pay Head Creation

Name : Gratuity

Pay Head Info

Pay Head Type : Gratuity
Under : Provisions
(Current Liabilities)

F-1A: Gratuity

F-1B: Income Tax set up for Gratuity

Income Tax Details

Income Tax Component : Gratuity
Tax Calculation Basis : On Actual Value
Deduct TDS Across Period(s) : No

Slab Rate details for Gratuity Calculation

Gratuity Days of a Month : 26

Number of Months From:	To:	Eligibility days for Gratuity Calculation per year
1	60	0
61	0	15

F-1C: Gratuity Slab Set Up

In the Table area, enter the following figures

Months Slab: At *From* & *To* enter the slab as follows:

- Normally for 1 to 60 Months, as Gratuity is not payable (enter zero at *Eligibility Days for Gratuity Computation per Year)*
- After 60 months (5 Year) and enter the days credited per year (e.g enter 15 at *Eligibility Days for Gratuity Computation per Year)*

Salary Details Alteration ABC Consultants Ctrl + M

Name : Aloke Kumar Ghosh (2014/07)
Under : Officers
(√ Primary)

Salary Details

Effective From	Pay Head	Rate	Per	Pay Head Type	Calculation Type	Computed On
1-May-2014						
	Basic Salary	12,000.00	Months	*Earnings for Employees*	*On Attendance*	
	DA			*Earnings for Employees*	*As Computed Value*	*On Current Earnings Total*
	HRA			*Earnings for Employees*	*As Computed Value*	*Basic Salary*
	Employees Cont to ESI			*Employees' Statutory Deductions*	*As Computed Value*	*Basic Salary + HRA*
	Employees P F Cont			*Employees' Statutory Deductions*	*As Computed Value*	*On Current Earnings Total*
	Employer's Contribution to PF			*Employer's Statutory Contributions*	*As Computed Value*	*Employees P F Cont - Employer's Cont to Pension Fund*
	Employer's Cont to Pension Fund			*Employer's Statutory Contributions*	*As Computed Value*	*On Current Earnings Total*
	Professional Tax			*Employees' Statutory Deductions*	*As Computed Value*	*On Current Earnings Total*
	Gratuity			*Gratuity*		

F-2A: Gratuity set up in Pay Structure

Gratuity Days of a Month: At *Gratuity Days of a Month*, enter the number of Days in a month that would be considered to compute the Per Day Rate applicable for Gratuity computation. Normally it is 26.

03 Gratuity Head set up in Pay Structure

To get Gratuity computed as on going provision, enter the Gratuity Pay head also in Pay structure as described.

04 Gratuity Summary

Gratuity Summary (F-3A) shows the accrued Gratuity figures for each employee.

Gratuity Summary — Ctrl + M

For All Employees						1-Mar-2015 to 31-Mar-2015
Particulars	Employee Number	Date of Birth	Date of Joining	Date of Leaving	Gratuity Eligible Salary	Gratuity Amount
Primary Cost Category					12,000.00	577.00
Officers					12,000.00	577.00
Aloke Kumar Ghosh	2014/07	1-5-1990	1-5-2014		12,000.00	577.00
Grand Total						577.00

F-3A: Gratuity Summary

Configuration

Show Employee Number	? Yes
Show Date of Birth	? Yes
Show Zero Valued Employees also	? No

F-3B: Gratuity Summary Configuration

F1: Condensed
F2: Period
F5: Employee Wise
F6: Till Date
F7: Employee Filters

F-3C: Buttons

Select *Display> Payroll Reports>Statutory Reports> Gratuity* (or Display> *Statutory Reports> Payroll Reports* > Gratuity) to get *Gratuity Summary* (F-3A).

Gratuity Summary Configuration: At *Gratuity Summary* (F-3A), click *F12:Configure* to get *Gratuity Summary Configuration* (F-3B).

- **Employee Number:** At *Show Employee Number*, set Yes to show Employee Number also, else set No (Employee Number is not shown).
- **Employee Birth Date**: At *Show Date of Birth,* set *Yes* to show *Date of Birth* also, else set No (Employee Birth Date is not shown).
- **Zero Valued Employees:** At *Show Zero Valued Employees*, set *Yes* to show Employees whose Gratuity Provision is *zero* (All Employee names are listed), else set No (Zero Valued Employees are not listed)

Gratuity Summary Buttons: At *Gratuity Summary* (F-3A), you get following Buttons (F-3C).

- **F1: Condensed / Details:** To get Summary Figures at Employee Group/ Category Level (Condensed) / Employee wise Details (Detailed) for each Employee.
- **F5:Employee Wise / Category Wise:** To get the Report in sequence of Employee Category / Employee Name
- **F6:Till date / Show Period:** To Show the Period / As On date at the Report Header and show the Periodical / Cumulative Gratuity Period
- **F7:Employee Filter:** To get Employee Filter to select Employee Group / All Employees / Specified Employee

05 Gratuity Details

At *Gratuity Summary* (F-3A), drill down through an employee to get Gratuity computation details of the Employee

The Gratuity is computed as follows:

Applicable Daily Rate = Last Month Salary / Gratuity Days in Month

Number of Days paid for = (No of Months worked for /12) x Eligibility Days for Gratuity per year

Amount of Gratuity = Number of days paid for x Applicable Daily Rate

Example

Last basic Salary: 6000 / month, DA – 2000 / month. Gratuity is applicable on Basic & DA

Date of Joining: 1-4-1999. Gratuity Days in a month = 30, Eligibility Days of Gratuity per year = 15

Gratuity for the period till 31-5-2006 would be computed as:

Number of Months worked for (completed months from date of Joining, i.e 1-4-1999 to date of Leaving, i.e 31.5.2006) = 86

Applicable Daily rate = (6000+2000)/ 30 = Rs.266.667

Number of Days paid for = (86/12)x15 = 107.50 Days

Amount of Gratuity = 107.50 x 266.67 = Rs 28667.03

The following consolidated formula gives you the Gratuity computation

(Last Salary / Gratuity Days in a month) x (No of Months worked for) / 12) x Gratuity Days in Month

The Gratuity is computed even for the period for which Eligibility Days for Gratuity is zero, for Provision purpose

06 Date of Leaving

When the employee leaves, at Date of Resignation, enter the date of Resignation. The Number of Days paid for and consequently, the Gratuity Amount will be computed accordingly from the length of Service (Date of Leaving – Date of Joining)

Accounting Voucher Creation — ABC Consultants — Ctrl + M

Payment No. 1 — 1-Oct-2015 Thursday

Particulars				Debit	Credit
Dr **Gratuity**				10,000.00	
Aloke Kumar Ghosh	10,000.00 Dr				
Cr **HDFC Bank**					10,000.00
Gratuity	Cheque	10,000.00			
Cheque Range : Not Applicable	*Inst. No.* : 12345	*Inst. Date* : 1-Oct-2015	*Cross Using* : A/c Payee		
Bank Date :					
Narration: Gratuity paid to Aloke Kr Ghosh				10,000.00	10,000.00

F-4A: Gratuity Payment Voucher

Employee Allocations for : **Gratuity**
Upto: **₹ 10,000.00 Dr**

Name of Employee	Amount
Aloke Kumar Ghosh	10,000.00
	10,000.00

F-4B: Gratuity Allocation

07 Gratuity Payments

Create a Payment Voucher (F-4A), to Pay Gratuity. Payment Voucher entry has been explained earlier.

At *Particulars* column, select Gratuity Ledger Account to get Employee Allocation screen (F-4B)

08 Accounting of Gratuity

There are 2 ways of charging Gratuity as expenses in Accounts:

- Gratuity on Cash basis
- Gratuity Provision

08.01 Gratuity on Cash Basis

Gratuity is charged on Cash basis when it is paid. So, the full amount of Gratuity is charged to P L Account during the year it is paid, as explained above.

So, the P L account would show the amount of Gratuity paid debiting Gratuity Account.

08.02 Gratuity Provision

However, most of the organizations make provision of Gratuity on continuing basis. The actual Gratuity is paid to the leaving employee out such Gratuity Provision.

Let us take an example:

As on 1.4.2015 the Opening balance of *Provision for Gratuity* was Rs 1,75,000 Cr (under Provision)

One employee left during the year whom a sum of Rs 32000 was paid as Gratuity

As on 31.3.2016,

The total gratuity amount as on 31-3-2016, as per Gratuity statement is Rs 1,82,000 (excluding the employee who has left during the year).

Make a payment voucher of Rs 32000 at the time of payment of Gratuity, debiting *Provision for Gratuity.*

On 31.3.2016, you should make a Journal voucher of Rs 1,82,000- (1,75,000-32,000) = Rs. 39,000. to make adequate provision for Gratuity.

Gratuity A/c Dr 39,000

Provision for Gratuity Cr 39,000

The P L Account would now show Rs 39,000 as charge to Gratuity Account for FY 15-16

And the Balance Sheet would show Rs 1,82,000 under Provision foe Gratuity

In case of Gratuity Provision, the Payment is made debiting Gratuity Provision Account. The P L Account does not show Gratuity actually paid, instead the Gratuity paid account is shown at Balance Sheet under Provision for Gratuity and is reduced from Gratuity Provision

Expat Reports 03-05

01 Expat Reports

Expat Reports contains details of employees of Foreign Nationalities. So, Expats Reports are relevant only when foreign nationals (Expats) are employed in the organization. The Expat Reports show the details of such Foreign Nationals (Passport, VISA, Work Contract, etc)

02 Expat Configuration set up

To maintain Passport / VISA / Work Contract details of Expatriate employees and their contract details (F-2A), at Gateway, click *F12:Configure* to get Configuration Menu. At Configuration Menu, select *Payroll Configuration* to get *Payroll Configuration* screen (F-1A). At *Payroll Configuration* screen (F-1A):

- At *Show Passport / VISA detail,* set *Yes* to enable entry of *Passport /Visa Details* for Expat Employees.

Payroll Configuration

Add NOTES for Employees	? Yes
Show Statutory Details	? Yes
Show Passport & Visa Details	? Yes
Show Contract Details	? Yes
Show Resigned / Retired Employees	? No
Show Employee Display Name	? y

F-1A: Payroll Configuration

- At *Contract details*, set *Yes* to enable entry of *Contract Details* for Expat Employees.

03 Expat Details in Employee Master

Employee Master entry has been explained earlier. Having set the Configuration option for Expat Details (F-1A), you get the additional fields in Employee Master entry (F-2A) for entry of Expat details as follows (F-2A):

Passport & VISA Details

Enter the Passport / VISA details when you set *Yes* at *Use Passport /VISA details.*

- Passport Number
- Country of Issue
- Passport Expiry Date
- VISA Number
- VISA Expiry Date

Contract Details

Enter Work Contract details when you set Yes at *Use Contract details.*

- Work Permit Number
- Contract Start Date
- Contract Expiry Date

Employee Alteration — ABC Consultants

Name : Aloke Kumar Ghosh
Display Name in Reports : A K GHosh
Under : Officers (↲ Primary)
Date of Joining : 1-May-2014
Define Salary Details : No
Date of Resignation / Retirement :

General Info

Employee Number	2014/07
Designation	Sales Officer
Function	Sales
Location	Eastern Div
Gender	Male
Date of Birth	1-May-1990
Blood Group	O Positive
Father / Mother Name	B K Ghosh
Spouse Name	Anita Ghosh
Address	12 Bechuram Colony 799999
Contact Numbers	9898989898
E-Mail ID	bechu@nomail.com

Payment Details

Bank Name	
Branch	
Bank A/c Number	
IFS Code	
MICR Code Number	

Statutory Details

Income Tax Number (PAN)	ABCDE1234X
PF Account Number	WB/123456
EPS Account Number	WB/123456
PF Date of Joining	1-May-2014
PF Date of Relieving	
ESI Number	WB/8/123456
ESI Dispensary Name	Dr B B Pal

Passport & Visa Details

Passport Number	A123456
Country of Issue	United Kingdom
Passport Expiry Date	1-May-2020
Visa Number	123456
Visa Expiry Date	1-Dec-2017

Contract Details

Work Permit Number	67890
Contract Start Date	1-Apr-2014
Contract Expiry Date	31-Mar-2016

F-2A: Entry of EXPAT details

04 Expat Reports Menu

Having entered the Expat Details, you may get the relevant Expat Reports.

At *Gateway of Tally,* select *Display > Payroll Reports > Expat Reports* to get Expat Reports Menu (F-3A).

F-3A Expat Reports Menu

05 Passport Expiry

At *Expat Reports Menu* (F-3A), select *Passport Expiry* to get Passport Expiry Report (F-4A), showing the Passport Details.

05.01 Passport Expiry Configuration

At *Passport Expiry Report* Display (F-4A), click *F12:Configuration* to get the Passport Expiry Display Configuration screen (F-4B).

- **Show Employee Email Id:** At *Show Employee Email Id,* set *Yes* to view the e-mail id, set *No* to suppress this column.

05.02 Passport Report Buttons

At Passport Expiry Report, you get the following buttons:

- **F5:Employeewise / Categorywise**: Toggle button to get the Report in sequence of Employee Name / Category
- **F7:Employee Filter**: To select a specific Employee, Employee Group or Employee Category

06 Visa Expiry

Like Passport Expiry Report (F-4A), VISA Expiry Report (F-5A) shows VISA details

At *Expat Reports Menu* (F-3A), select *VISA Expiry* to get VISA Expiry Report (F-5A), showing the Employee VISA Details

The Configuration options (F-5B) and Buttons (F-5C) are similar to that of Passport Expiry Report discussed above.

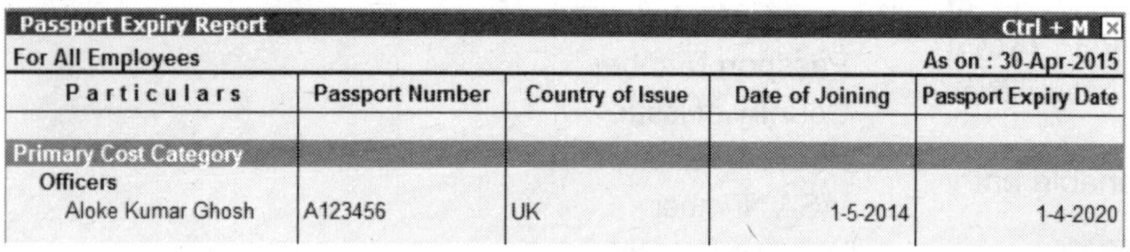

F-4A: Passport Expiry Report (Default)

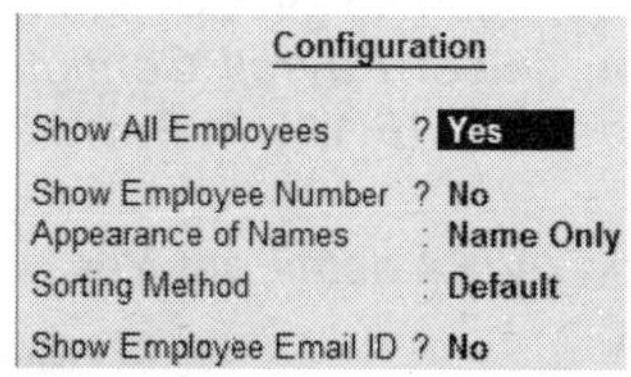

F-4B: Configuration

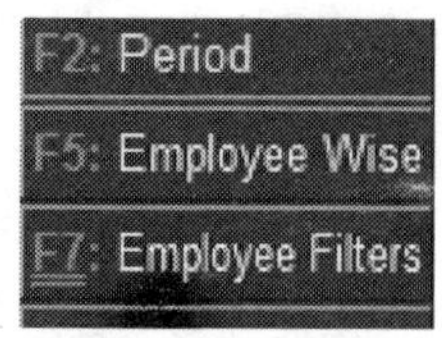

F-4C: Button

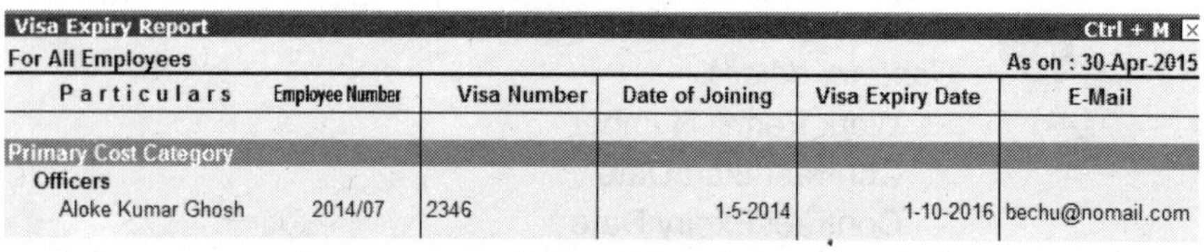

F-5A: VISA Expiry Report

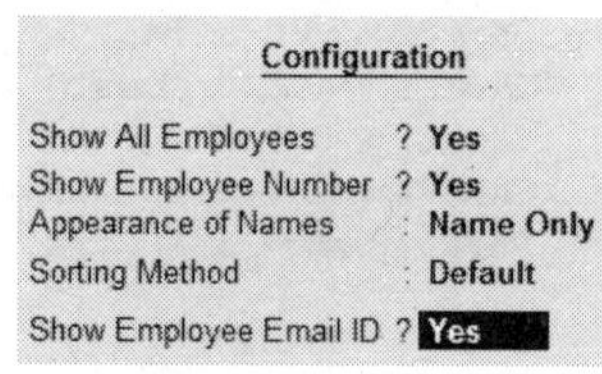

F-5B: Configuration

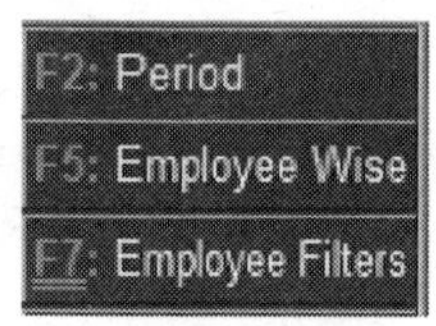

F-5C: Buttons

Now set the Passport Expiry Report Configuration options as follows:

- **Employee Status Filter:** At *Show All Employees,* set *Yes* to view all the employee passport details (Expired & Unexpired), set *No* to view only employees for which Passport is still not Expired
- **Employee Number:** At *Show Employee Number,* set *Yes* to display the Employee Number in the report, set *No* to suppress this column.

07 Contract Expiry

This report gives the details of Contracted Employees.

At Expat Reports Menu (F-3A), select *Contract Expiry* to get Contract Expiry Report (F-6A), showing the Contract Details (F-6A)

The Configuration options (F-6B) and Buttons (F-6C) are similar to those of Passport Expiry Reports as discussed below

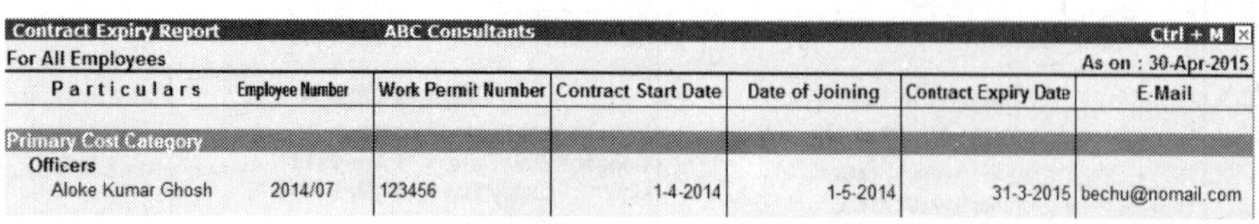

F-6A: Contract Expiry Report

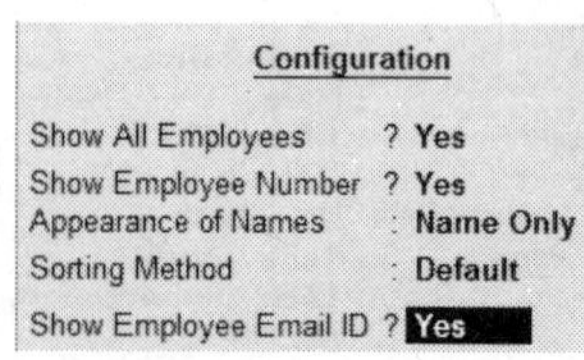

F-6B: Configuration

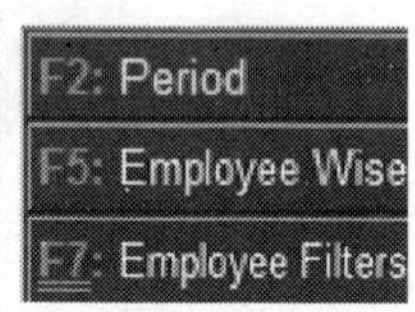

F-6C: Buttons

Part 4

Payroll Statutory Deductions

In this Part, we describe the set up of various Statutory Deduction features in relation to Pay Computation, processing during Payroll Voucher to effect the deductions, Voucher & Challan for deposit of Statutory Deduction with government authorities

Professional Tax describes set up for P Tax deductions, Statutory information, P Tax Rates, Deduction of P Tax from Pay, deposit of P Tax with Government, Printing & filing of various P Tax Returns.

Income Tax describes set up for I Tax deductions, Statutory information, I tax components set up, I Tax Declarations, I Tax Exemption set up, etc. for computation of Tax Liability for each Employee. It also covers Tax Payment Voucher, Deposit of I Tax, Printing of Tax Challans etc. for Payment of Tax.

Income Tax Reports describes Tax Computation Reports, Tax Projection and various Periodical Returns to be filed with Income Tax Authorities

Employees State Insurance describes activation & Set Up of ESI Features, ESI Heads creation and Computation Formula setup, Processing of ESI Deduction, ESI payment Voucher & Challan, Display & Printing of ESI Reports & Returns.

Provident Fund describes activation & Set Up of P F Features, PF related Heads creation and Computation Formula setup, Processing of PF Deduction, PF payment Voucher & Challan, Display & Printing of PF Reports & Returns.

Statutory Reports Summary shows the details of all types of Statutory Deduction from Employee Pay (like I Tax, P Tax, ESI & PF) and the amount payable to the Government. It provides top level summary report with drill down details for each Account Head & Employee.

Professional Tax

04-01

01 Professional Tax

Professional Tax (P Tax) is a State imposed Tax on Professions & Employment. A specified amount is deducted for P Tax from the salary of Employee.

02 Professional Tax Pay Head

To deduct P Tax from Employee Salary, you have to create Pay Head. Pay Head creation has been explained earlier. The specific points exclusively related to P Tax head creation are described below (F-1A):

- **Pay Head Type**: At *Pay Head Type*, select *Employees' Statutory Deductions* from the list of Pay Head Types (F-1A).
- **Statutory Pay Type**: Having selected the *Pay Head Type* as above, at *Statutory Pay Type*, select *Professional Tax* from the list
- **Registration Number**: At Registration Number, enter the P Tax Registration Number of the organization, with the P Tax Authorities. This is printed in P Tax Statutory Reports
- **Parent Account Group**: At *Under*, select *Current Liabilities* from the Account Group list

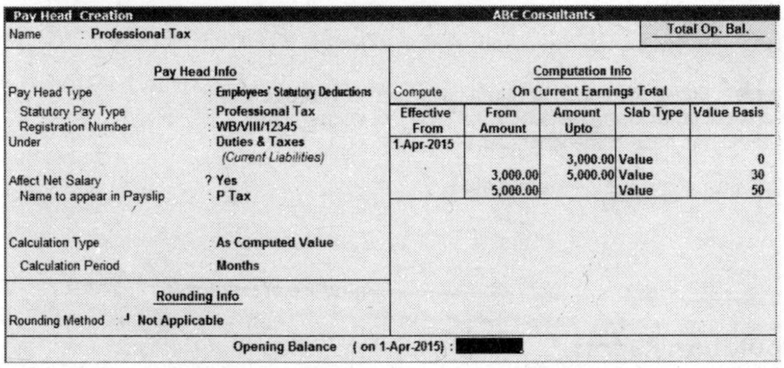

F-1A: Professional Tax Head

P Tax Computation Info: At the right Part of the screen (F-2A), you get Computation Info section. The process of entry of Computation Info has been explained earlier. Here we discuss about set up details for P Tax Account:

Computation Method: At *Compute*, select *on Current Earnings Total* from the list (as P Tax is computed on Earnings).

- **Effective Date**: *At Effective From* column, the Financial Start Date is carried by default, at the first instance
- **Slab Range & Rate**: Now enter the Range & corresponding rates for each Slab, as follows:
  - o **Slab Lower Amount**: At *From Amount*, enter the Slab *Lower* range amount. In first slab, this is skipped, indicating zero as Starting Range of first slab)
  - o **Slab Upper Limit**: At *Amount Upto*, enter the Slab *Upper* limit amount. In the last slab, the Upper Limit is left blank.
- **Computation Method:** At Slab Type, select *Value* from List of Slabs, as Fixed Amount of P Tax is deducted as per Total Earnings.
- **Rate:** At *Value Basis*, enter the Amount of P Tax deductible for the respective Slab

This way, enter the second slab and the applicable Rates

Round Off: Set Round Off rules as *Not Applicable* as P Tax is fixed amount and need not be Rounded Off

03 P Tax Reports

After creation of Salary Voucher, you may get the P Tax Report to get the amount of Tax to be deposited and then submit the P Tax Report with Challan details. At Payroll Reports (Select *GoT>Display>Statutory Reports>Payroll Reports*), select *Professional Tax* to get *Professional Tax* Reports Menu (F-2A)

F-2A: P Tax Report Menu

PROFESSIONAL TAX - Monthly Statement
(Professional Tax)

Name & Address of the Factory or Establishment : **ABC Consultants**
12 Pitambar Rd
Kolkata

Statement for the Period : 1-Apr-2015 to 31-Mar-2016

Sl.No	Employee No.	Employee Name	Worked Days	Gross Wages	Value
1	2014/07	Aloke Kumar Ghosh	364	26,952.65	100.00
		Total		26,952.65	100.00

F-2B: P Tax Statement

Report Titles		
Professional Tax		
Professional Tax Monthly Statement		
From (blank for beginning)	:	**1-4-2015**
To (blank for end)	:	**31-3-2016**
Employee/Group	:	**┘ All Items**
Sorting Method	:	**Employee Name**
Appearance of Employee Names	:	**Name Only**

F-2C: P Tax Statement Printing

03.01 P Tax Computation Report

P Tax Computation Report (F-3A) shows the Number of Employees & P Tax Deducted as per P Tax Slab.

At *P Tax Menu* (F-2A), select *Computation Report* (at Gateway, select *Display>Payroll Reports>Professional Tax>Computation Report*) and then select P Tax Ledger Account from the list of Ledgers to get P Tax Computation Printing screen (F-3B). Enter the relevant details (these are printed in P Tax Reports) to get the *P Tax Computation* Report (F-3A).

Report Titles		
PROFESSIONAL TAX PAYABLE BY EMPLOYER		
From (blank for beginning)	:	**1-4-2015**
To (blank for end)	:	**31-3-2016**
Employee/Group	:	**┘ All Items**
Place	:	**Kolkata**
Date of Printing	:	**31-3-2016**
Authorised Signatory Name	:	**S Ghosh**
Print Payment Details	:	**Yes**

F-3B: P Tax Computation Printing

PROFESSIONAL TAX PAYABLE BY EMPLOYER

Return of Tax payable for the period	:	**1-Apr-2015 to 31-Mar-2016**
Name of the Employer	:	**ABC Consultants**
Address	:	12 Pitambar Rd Kolkata
Registration Certificate No.	:	**WB/VIII/12345**

Number of employees during the month in respect of whom the tax is payable as under :

SNo.	Employees whose monthly salaries / wages / both are				Number of Employees	Rate of tax per month Rs.	Amount of Tax Deducted Rs.
1	Rs	0	to	3,000.00		0.00	
2	Rs	3,000.00	to	5,000.00		30.00	
3	Rs	5,000.00	and above		1	50.00	100.00
				TOTAL	1.00		100.00

Amount Paid : **100.00**

Amount in Words : **INR One Hundred Only**

I certify that all employees who are liable to pay the tax in my employment during the period of return have been covered by the forgoing particulars. I also certify that the necessary revision in the amount of tax deductable from the salary or wages of the employees on account of variation in the salary or wages earned by them has been made wherever necessary.

I, Shri S Ghosh solemnly declare that above statements are true to the best of my knowledge and belief.

Place : **Kolkata**

Date : **31-Mar-2016** **Signature of Employer**

F-3A: P Tax Computation Report

03.02 P Tax Statement

P Tax Statement (F-2B) shows the Employee wise details of Working Days, Wages & P Tax deducted for the specified Report Period (normally Monthly)

At *P Tax Menu* (F-2A), select *Statement* (at Gateway, select *Display>Payroll Reports>Professional Tax>Statement*) and then select P Tax Ledger Account from the list of Ledgers, to get *P Tax Statement* Printing screen (F-2C). Enter the relevant details (these are printed in P Tax Reports) to get the *P Tax Statement* (F-2B).

04 Professional Tax Payment

The Professional Tax is to be paid to prescribed authority, through Payment Voucher

Payment Voucher entry has been explained earlier. At Payment Voucher entry screen, Click *A:Payroll Auto Fill* button to get Payment Auto Fill screen (F04B). At *Payment Auto Fill* screen (F-4B), enter the details:

- At *Process For*, select *Professional Tax Payment* from the list

- At *Payroll Ledger*, select *Professional Tax Ledger* account from the list

Accounting Voucher Creation	ABC Consultants	Ctrl + M
Payment No. 2		31-Mar-2016 Thursday
	Payroll Auto Fill - (Professional Tax Payment)	
Account : HDFC Bank		

Particulars		Amount
Professional Tax		50.00
Aloke Kumar Ghosh	50.00 Dr	
Asit Sen		
Ram Prasad		
Provide Details : Yes		
Narration:		50.00

F-4A: Professional Tax Payment Voucher

F-4B: Payment Auto Fill Screen

Payment Auto Fill

Process for	: Professional Tax Payment
From (blank for beginning)	: 1-3-2015
To (blank for end)	: 31-3-2015
Voucher Date	: 31-3-2015
Employee/Group	: All Items
Bank / Cash Ledger	: HDFC Bank
Payroll Ledger	:

Payment Details

Cheque / DD No	: 123456
Cheque / DD Date	: 31-Mar-2016
Depositor Name	: A K Bose
Bank Name	: HDFC Bank
BSR Code	: 123456
Challan Date	: 31-Mar-2016
Challan Number	: 1234

(Note : All the Above Details Will Be Used in Challan, Forms & Returns)

F-4C: Payment Details screen

The Name sof Employes and Amount are auto filled, showinh the amount of P Tax deducted. as per Payroll Voucher

Professional Tax Payment Details: At *Provide Details* (F-4A), set Yes to get Payment Details sreen (F-4C). Enter the relevant details of P Tax payment.

Save the Voucher.

Income Tax on Salary

04-02

01 Payroll Statutory Details

So, far we have explained various normal *Pay Heads* of Earnings & Deductions. However, there are some Statutory Deductions, like PF, ESI, I Tax, P Tax etc. Here we discuss about activation of Statutory Deductions.

At Gateway, click *F12:Configure* to get *Configuration Menu*. At *Configuration Menu*, select Payroll Configuration to get Payroll Configuration screen (F-1A). At *Payroll Configuration screen* (F-1A), at *Show Statutory Details*, set *Yes* to capture, compute & show data of Statutory Heads like (PF, ESI, I Tax).

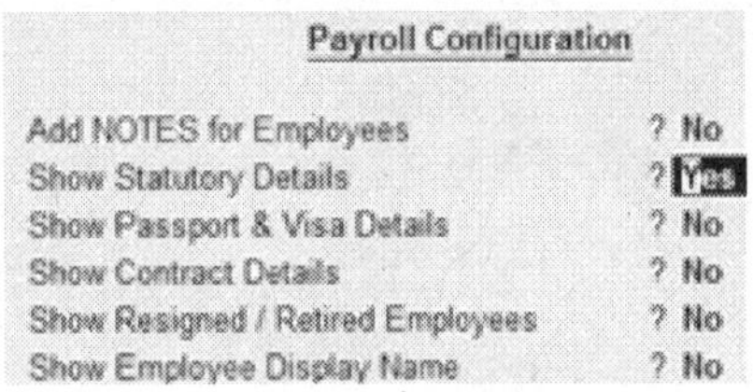

F-1A: Payroll Configuration

F-2A: Payroll Statutory Features Activation

01.01 Payroll Statutory Features Activation

Click *F11:Fetaures* to get Company Features Manu. At Company Features Menu, select Statutory Features to get *Statutory Features screen.*

At *Enable Payroll Statutory*, set *Yes* to activate Statutory Features (PF, ESI, I Tax).

01.02 Income Tax Statutory Details

Having activated Statutory Features (F-1A), at further set *Yes* at *Set / Alter Payroll Statutory Details* to get *Payroll Statutory Details* screen. At *Payroll Statutory Details*, enter the relevant details for Income Tax (F-1B), as follows:

- **TAN:** At *Tax Deduction & Collection Account Number,* enter the TAN (4 Alpha, 5 numeric & 1 Alpha) as allotted by Income Tax Department. TAN is printed in Income Tax Challans & Statutory Reports
- **Income Tax Circle/ Ward:** At *Income Tax Circle/ Ward,* enter the name of the Income Tax Ward Jurisdiction. This is printed in ESI Statutory Reports
- **Organsiation Type:** At *Deductor Type*, select the Organisation Type from list of *Company Type* (F-1C)
- **Officer Name:** At *Name of Person responsible*, enter the name pf the officer responsible for Deduction & Deposit of Income Tax
- **Officer's Father's Name:** At *Son / Daughter of*, enter the Father's name of the officer mentioned above
- **Designation:** At *Designation*, enter the Designation of the Officer specified above

F-1B: Income Tax Details

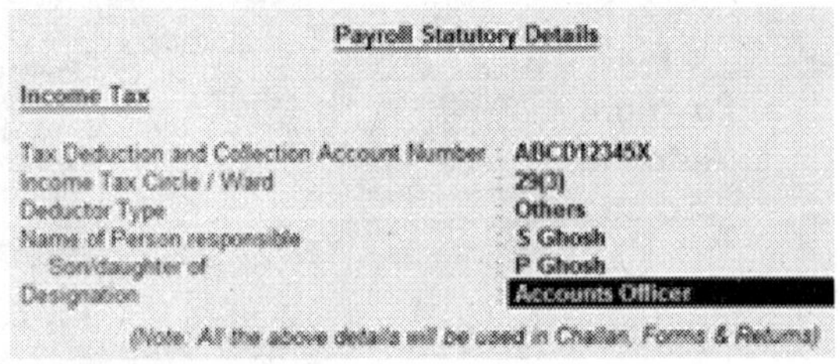

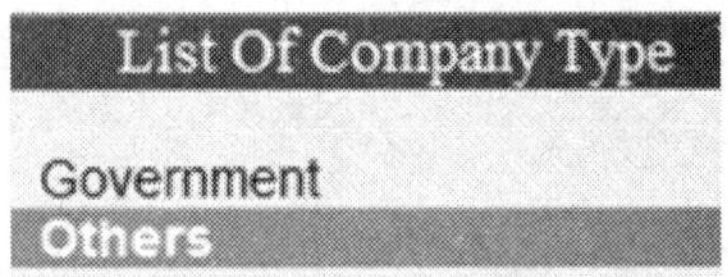

F-1C:Compnay Type List selection

02 Income Tax Head

For some employees, whose Taxable Income exceeds the Income Tax exemption limit, TDS is deducted from the salary and deposited with the Government.

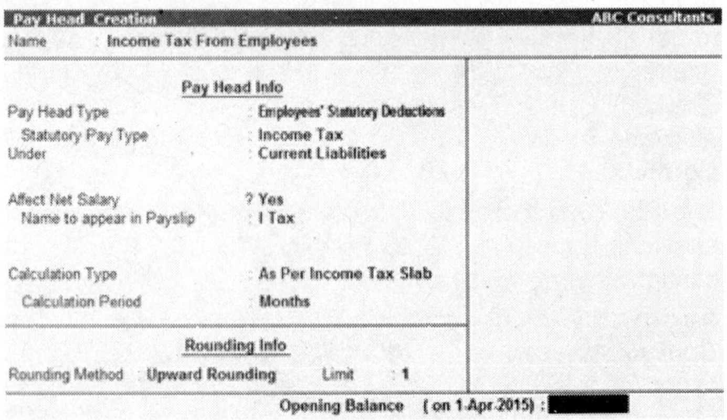

F-2A: Employees' ESI Deduction Pay Head

So, Income Tax Pay Head is to be created for I Tax deducted from Employee Salary. Pay Head creation has been explained earlier. The process of creation of Income Tax Head, is described below (F-2A):

- **Pay Head Type:** At *Pay Head Type*, select *Employees' Statutory Deductions* from the list of Pay Head Types (F-4B).

- **Statutory Pay Type:** Having selected the *Pay Head Type* as above, at *Statutory Pay Type*, select *Income Tax* from the list.
- **Parent Account Group:** At *Under* select Current Liabilities (or Provision) from the Account Group list
- **Calculation Type**: At *Calculation Type*, *As per Income Tax Slab* is auto carried.
- **Round Off**: At *Round Off*, set Normal Rounding of Rs 1.00

03 Income Tax Menu

The various process relating to set up of I Tax are provided in I Tax Menu. Select *Payroll Info>Income Tax* details to get Income Tax Menu (F-3A).

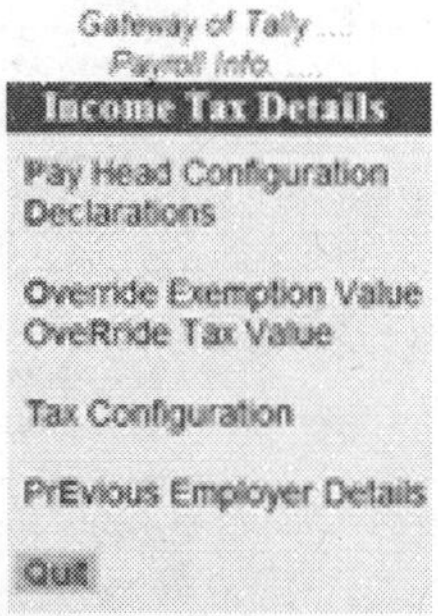

F-3A: Income Tax Menu

- **Head Type:** At *Master Type*, he Master Type (Pay Head / Ledger) is displayed for information
- **Income Tax Head:** At *Income Tax Component*, select the respective Income Tax head from the list (F-5B)
- **Calculation Basis:** At Tax Calculation Basis, select the Calculation Basis from the list (F4B), as follows:
  - o **Projected:** Select *On Projected Value* to take the value (as monthly amount) from Salary Details for each month coputing the rojected value on the basis of the amount.
  - o **Atual:** Select *On Actual Value* to consider the latest amount which will get included in the Projected Amount (like Bonus)
- **TDS Applicability:** At *TDS Deduct Across Periods*, set *Yes* where TDS eduction is to be spread over the eprod. Set No, to dedcut TDS in the current month itself

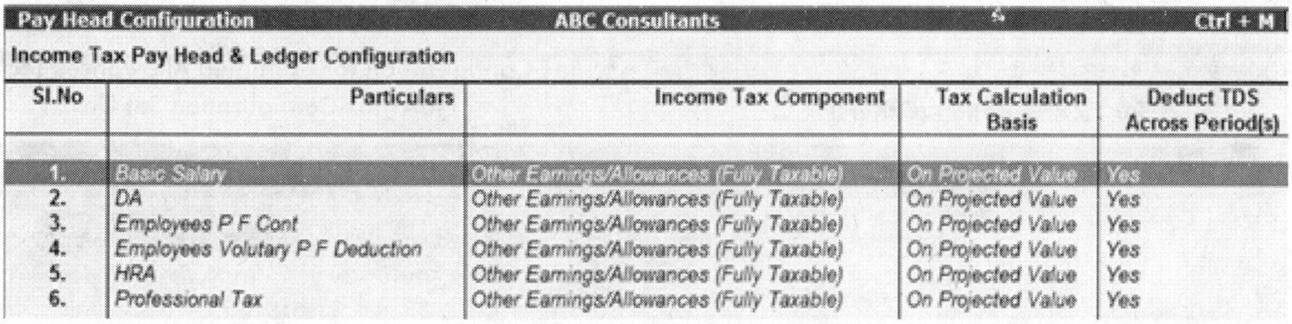

Pay Head Configuration — ABC Consultants — Ctrl + M

Income Tax Pay Head & Ledger Configuration

Sl.No	Particulars	Income Tax Component	Tax Calculation Basis	Deduct TDS Across Period(s)
1.	*Basic Salary*	*Other Earnings/Allowances (Fully Taxable)*	*On Projected Value*	*Yes*
2.	*DA*	*Other Earnings/Allowances (Fully Taxable)*	*On Projected Value*	*Yes*
3.	*Employees P F Cont*	*Other Earnings/Allowances (Fully Taxable)*	*On Projected Value*	*Yes*
4.	*Employees Volutary P F Deduction*	*Other Earnings/Allowances (Fully Taxable)*	*On Projected Value*	*Yes*
5.	*HRA*	*Other Earnings/Allowances (Fully Taxable)*	*On Projected Value*	*Yes*
6.	*Professional Tax*	*Other Earnings/Allowances (Fully Taxable)*	*On Projected Value*	*Yes*

F-4A: Income Tax Configuration

04 Income Tax Component Set Up

At *Income Tax Menu* (F-3A), select *Pay Head Configuration* to get *Pay Head Configuration* screen (F-4A), to configure the Income Tax Components for all the existing Pay Heads. The Ledgers which are used for making the Payroll payments also can be configured for the respective **Income Tax Component.**

The Pay Heads already configured for the Income Tax are shown in bold, while the Pay Heads which are not yet configured are shown in *Italics*.

Adding / Re-configuring Pay Head: At *Pay Head Configuration* screen (F-4A). Press <Enter> at any Pay head to get *Income Tax Configuration* screen (F-5A), to Configure / Reconfigure the Pay Head

At *Income Tax Configuration* screen (F-5A), enter as follows:

- **Pay Head / Ledger Name:** At *Name of Pay Head / Ledger*, the Pay Head / Ledger Name is displayed.

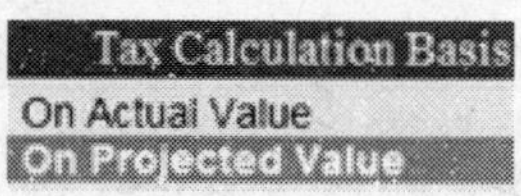

F-4B: Tax Calculation Basis List

F-4C: Buttons

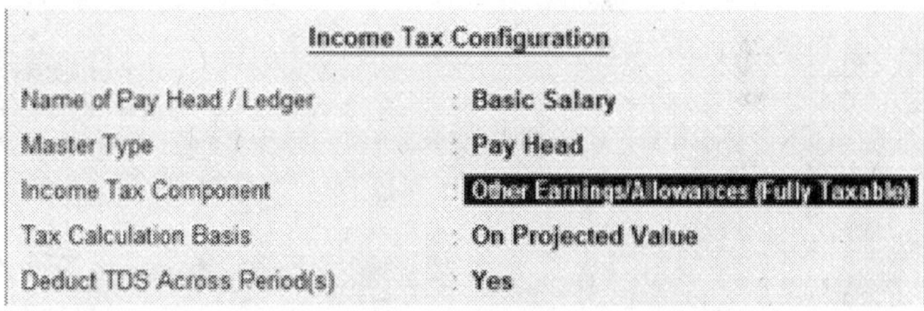

Income Tax Configuration

Name of Pay Head / Ledger	: **Basic Salary**
Master Type	: **Pay Head**
Income Tax Component	: **Other Earnings/Allowances (Fully Taxable)**
Tax Calculation Basis	: **On Projected Value**
Deduct TDS Across Period(s)	: **Yes**

F-5A: Income Tax Configuration screen

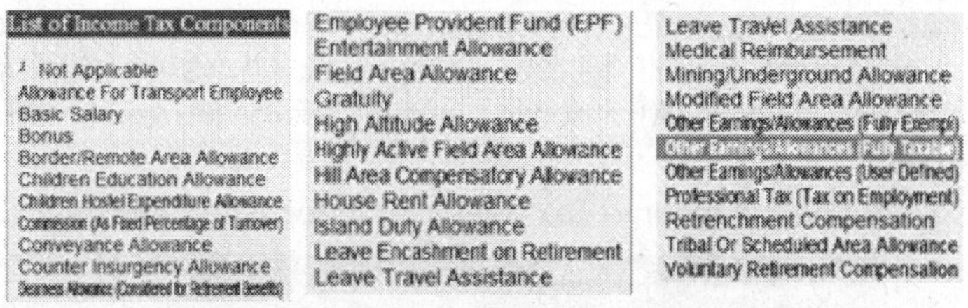

F-5B: List of Income Tax Components

05 Income Tax Configuration

At *Pay Head Configuration* (F-4A), click *T:Tax Config* button to get Tax Configuration set up screen (F-6A) listing the various heads for Tax Configuration

Tax Configuration	Ctrl + M
Tax Configuration	1-Apr-2015 to 31-Mar-2016
Particulars	**Status**
Gross Salary	
Salary as per provisions contained in Sec 17(1)	✓ Not Applicable
Value of Perquisites u/s 17(2) (as per Form 12BA)	✓ Not Applicable
Profits in lieu of Salary u/s 17(3) (as per Form 12BA)	✓ Not Applicable

Tax Configuration for Gross Salary section

Particulars	Status
Deductions U/s 16	
Entertainment Allowance	Not Configured
Professional Tax (Tax on Employment)	Not Configured
Other Income declared by Employee	
Other Income (House Property / Other Source) / Interest on Housing Loan	✓ Not Applicable
Deductions under Chapter VI-A	
Investments (U/s 80C, 80CCF, 80CCG, etc.)	✓ Not Applicable
Others (U/s 80D, 80DD, 80E, etc.)	✓ Not Applicable
Relief	
Relief (U/s 89,90 & 91)	✓ Not Applicable
Tax deduction Details	
Advance Tax Declared by Employee	✓ Not Applicable
Tax deducted by previous Employer	✓ Not Applicable
Tax Deducted other than Salary	✓ Not Applicable
Self Assessment Tax Declared by Employee	✓ Not Applicable

Tax Configuration (Others)

Allowance to the extent exempted U/s 10	
Allowance For Transport Employee	Not Configured
Border/Remote Area Allowance.	Not Configured
Children Education Allowance	Not Configured
Children Hostel Expenditure Allowance	Not Configured
Conveyance Allowance	Not Configured
Counter Insurgency Allowance	Not Configured
Field Area Allowance	Not Configured
Gratuity	Not Configured
High Altitude Allowance	Not Configured
Highly Active Field Area Allowance	Not Configured
Hill Area Compensatory Allowance	Not Configured
House Rent Allowance	Not Configured
Island Duty Allowance	Not Configured
Leave Encashment on Retirement	Not Configured
Leave Travel Assistance	Not Configured
Medical Reimbursement	Not Configured
Mining/Underground Allowance	Not Configured
Modified Field Area Allowance	Not Configured
Other Earnings/Allowances (Fully Exempt)	Not Configured
Other Earnings/Allowances (User Defined)	Configured
Retrenchment Compensation	Not Configured
Tribal Or Scheduled Area Allowance	Not Configured
Voluntary Retirement Compensation	Not Configured

Tax Configuration for Exempted Allowances section

F-6A: Tax Configuration Set Up

IncomeTax Allowance Setup — ABC Consultants

Children Education Allowance

Masters

Defining Children Education Allowance Component

Configure Pay heads / Ledgers for computing Income Tax by linking Income Tax Component, Basis of Tax Calculation & Frequency of Tax Deduction.

(Allowance provided to Employees to meet the expenses for their children education, exemption allowed for maximum to two children)

Define Values

Declaration of Number of Children

Declaration for Number of Children to avail Children Education Allowance benefit. Exemption is allowed up to a maximum of two children.

Quit

F-7A: Income Tax Allowance Set Up screen

06 Income Tax Allowance Set Up

At *Tax Configuration Set Up* screen (F-6A), select any Head and press <enter> to get *Income Tax Allowance Set Up* screen (like F-7A), showing the details of corresponding head

To define the Income Tax heads, at Income Tax Allowances Set Up screen (F-7A), press <enter> at the respective Head, to get the Pay Head Configuration screen (F-7B). At Pay Head Configuration screen (F-7B). Press Enter to get Pay Head Configuration screen (F-5A). At Pay Head Configuration screen, press <enter> to get Income Tax Configuration screen (F-5A), to set Pay Head Configuration as explained earlier.

Pay Head Configuration — ABC Consultants — Ctrl + M

Income Tax Pay Head & Ledger Configuration

Sl.No	Particulars	Income Tax Component	Tax Calculation Basis	Deduct TDS Across Period(s)
1.	*Bonus*	*Other Earnings/Allowances (Fully Taxable)*	*On Projected Value*	Yes
2.	*HRA*	*Other Earnings/Allowances (Fully Taxable)*	*On Projected Value*	Yes
3.	*Production Wages*	*Other Earnings/Allowances (Fully Taxable)*	*On Projected Value*	Yes
4.	*Professional Tax*	*Other Earnings/Allowances (Fully Taxable)*	*On Projected Value*	Yes

F-7B: Pay Head Configuration

07 Income Tax Declarations

While computing the Taxable Income, certain *Exemptions* (u/s 10) and *Deductions* (under Chapter VIA) are allowed to employees, as per statements and declarations submitted by them to the employer. The process of entry of these particulars of Exemptions & Deductions are described here

At *Income Tax Menu* (F-3A), select *Declarations* to get the *Income Tax Declarations* showing the Heads for Exemptions (F-8A) and Deductions (F-10A)

07.1 Income Tax Exemption Heads

The process of entry of Declaration for Income Tax Heads for each type of Exemption is similar. At Income Tax

Income Tax Declaration

Exemption

R : **House Rent Allowance**
Details of Rent paid (payable) by the employee(s) and place (Metro & Non-Metro) where such accommodation is situated.
(Is an allowance specifically granted to meet expenditure actually incurred on payment of rent in respect of residential accommodation)

L : **Leave Travel Assistance**
Define Exemption Amount for Leave Travel Assistance.
(Value of any travel concession or assistance provided in connection with proceeding on leave to any place in India)

A : **Conveyance Allowance**
Employee's Physical Status (Blind or orthopedically handicapped) Declaration.
(Transport allowance provided for traveling (expenditure) between residence and place of duty)

C : **Children Education Allowance**
Declaration for Number of Children to avail Children Education Allowance benefit. Exemption is allowed up to a maximum of two children.

X : **Children Hostel Expenditure Allowance**
Declaration of Number of Children availing Children Hostel Expenditure Allowance benefit, exemption allowed up to a maximum of two children.

Income declared by Employee

I : **Single Employee Multi Component**

N : **Multi Employees Single Component**
Define Employee(s) Declaration and Proof/Eligible amount for the other income (including loss from House Property (Interest on Housing Loan)) other than income under the head 'Salaries' offered for TDS.

F-8A: Income Tax Declarations for Exemptions

House Rent Declaration — ABC Consultants — Ctrl + M

Employee / Group : All Items
Type of Allowance : House Rent Allowance
Financial Year : 1-Apr-2014 to 31-Mar-2015

Employee Name	Employee Number	Effective From	Monthly Rent		Place of Residence
			Declared	Proof	
Surya Narayan Ghosh	0105	1-5-2015	1,200.00	1,200.00	Metro

F-9A: Income Tax Declaration for Exemption

Declaration screen (F-8A), select the Exemption Head to get Employee Selection list (list of Employee Group, Employee, or All Items) for selection of Employee (F-9B). On selection from Employee list, you get the Declaration screen for the respective Head The selected Employees are listed, showing Employee Name & Employee Number, and other particulars of Declarations (F-9A), which vary according the Exemption Head selected at Income Tax Declaration screen (F-8A)

07.2 Income Tax Exemption Declaration

At Income Tax Declaration screen for Exemption (F-9A), enter the respective Details (which vary according the Exemption Heads).

F-9B: Employee Selection List

List of Employees / Group
All Items
Officers (Group)
Surya Narayan Ghosh

The summarised description of Declaration to be entered for each type Exemption Head are shown listed in the Table below.

Hot Key	Exemption Head	Declaration Details
Exemption for Allowances		
R	House Rent Allowance	*Declared* (Monthly Amount Declared as paid), *Proof* (Monthly Amount paid for which supporting documents submitted), *Place of Residence* (Metro / Non Metro)
L	Leave Travel Assistance	*Income Tax Component* (select from the list: F-5B), *Ledger Name* (select from the list), *Override For* (Exempted is auto selected), *Exemption* (Amount Exempted for LTA)
A	Conveyance Allowance	*Employee Status* (Physically Challenged / Others)
C	Children Education Allowance	*Number of Children*
X	Children Hostel Expenditure Allowance	*Number of Children*
Income Declared by Employees		
I	Single Employee Multi Component	*Particulars of Income Other than Salary*(Select from the list of Other Income Heads), Declare (Annual Declared Amount), Proof (Annual Amount paid for which supporting documents submitted)
N	Multi Employee Single Component	*Type of Income* (select from the list of Income Heads), Declare (Annual Declared Amount), Proof (Annual Amount paid for which supporting documents submitted), *Qualifying Amount* (Amount Allowable under I Tax Rule)

07.3 Income Tax Deduction Declaration

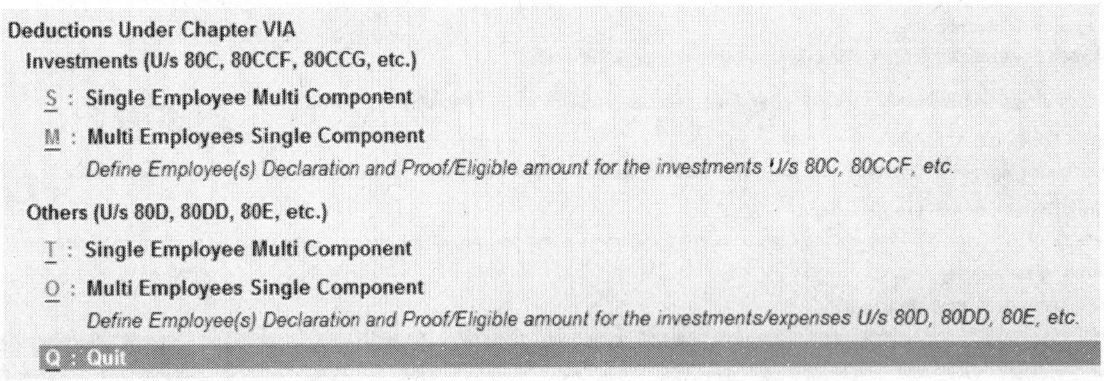

F-10A: Income Tax Declarations for Deductions

The summarised description of Declaration to be entered for each type of Deduction Head are shown listed in the Table below.

Hot Key	Deduction Head	Declaration Details
Deductions		
a. Investments		
S	Single Employee Multi Component	*List of Investments* (Select from the list of Eligible Investment Types), *Declared* (Annual Amount Declared as paid), *Proof / Eligible* (Annual Amount paid for which supporting documents submitted / Annual Eligible Amount)
M	Multi Employee Single Component	*List of Investments* (Select from the list of Eligible Investment Types), *Declared* (Annual Amount Declared as paid), *Proof / Eligible* (Annual Amount paid for which supporting documents submitted / Annual Eligible Amount)
b. Others		
T	Single Employee Multi Component	*List of Investments* (Select from the list of Eligible Investment Types), Condition (select from List, e.g Senior Citizen, Severe Disability, Others), *Declared* (Annual Amount Declared as paid), *Proof / Eligible* (Annual Amount paid for which supporting documents submitted / Annual Eligible Amount), Qualifying Amount (Amount allowable as per I Tax Act)

O	Multi Employee Single Component	*List of Investments* (Select from the list of Eligible Investment Types), Condition (select from List, e.g Senior Citizen, Severe Disability, Others), *Declared* (Annual Amount Declared as paid), *Proof / Eligible* (Annual Amount paid for which supporting documents submitted / Annual Eligible Amount), Qualifying Amount (Amount allowable as per I Tax Act)

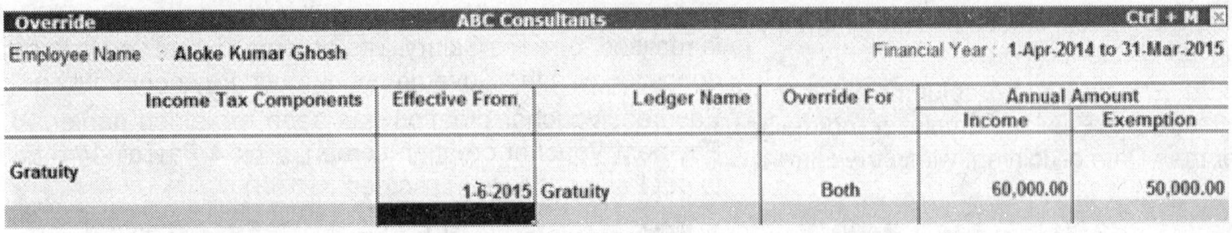

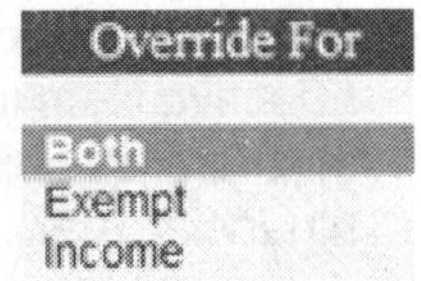

F-11A: Override entry screen

11-B:Override List

08 Tax Exemption Override

Using Override Exemption Value, you may override Income / Exemption Amount for any Allowance Head. In such case, the Voucher Amount is disregarded, instead the amount specified in Override For is considered instead

To specify the Override Details, at *Income Tax Menu* (F-3A), select *Override Exemption Value* and then select the Employee Name from the List of Employees to get Override entry screen (F-11A)

At Override entry screen (F-11A), enter as follows:

- **Income Tax Allowance Head:** At *Income Tax Components*, select the Allowance Head from the list of *Income Tax Components* (F-5B).
- **Effective Date:** At *Effective From*, specify the Date from when the Override details are applicable (normally the Financial Year Beginning Date or Date of Joining / Date of Applicability, whichever is later)
- **Ledger Name:** At *Ledger Name*, select the Ledger / Pay Head from the *List of Ledgers*
- **Override Type:** At *Override for*, select the *Override Type* from the list (F-11B).
- **Amount:** Enter the amount in the *Income / Exemption* column, as the case may be.

At *Income Tax Menu* (F-3A), select *Tax Configuration*, to get Tax Configuration screen (F-6A) as explained earlier.

On selecting any head from Tax Configuration (F-6A), you get Income Tax Allowance Set up screen (F-7A) as explained earlier.

10 Previous Employer Details

When a new Employee Joins in idle of Financial Year, you have to enter the details of emoluments received from his previous employer, and Tax Deducted there from, which are to be considered to compute Taxable Income / Income Tax for the current Financial Year.

The joining employee gets Form 16 from the previous employer giving the details in respect of employment period part (of current financial year), with previous employer. The details are to be entered from the Form 16 submitted by previous employer.

At *Income Tax Menu* (F-3A), select *Previous Employer Details* to get *Previous Employer Details* Menu (F-12A).

10.1 Previous Employer Income / Exemption Details

At *Previous Employer Details* Menu (F-12A), select *Income Exemption Details* and then select the Employee from List

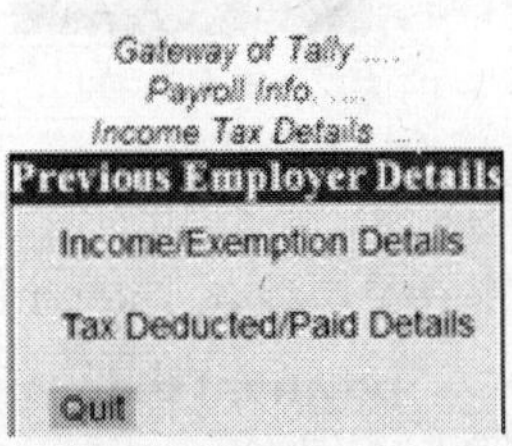

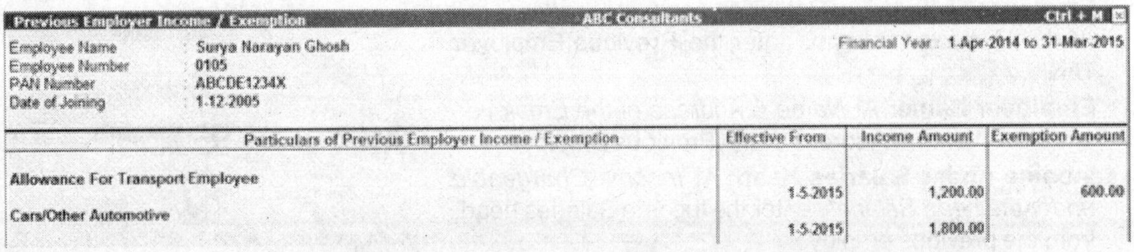

F-12A: Previous Employer Details Menu

F-13A: Previous Employer Income / Exemption details

of Employees to get *Income Exemption details entry screen* (F-13A), for entry of Amount of Income / Exemption allowable to the Employee in respect of earlier period of employment with the previous employer for the period falling within the current Financial Year.

09 Income Tax Quick Set Up

Instead of configuring individual Heads as explained, you may Configure Income Tax related changes from one central screen

At *Previous Employer Income Exemption* entry *screen* (F-13A), at the header, the Employee Name, Employee Number, I Tax PAN & date of Joining of the Employee is carried and shown for Information

Now enter the details as follows:

- **Income / Exemption Heads:** At *Particulars of Previous Employer Income / Exemption*, select the Head from the list of *Income Tax Components* (F-5B).
- **Effective Date:** At *Effective From* column, enter the Effective Date in respect of Previous Employer (normally this date is earlier than Date of Joining, within the current Financial Year).

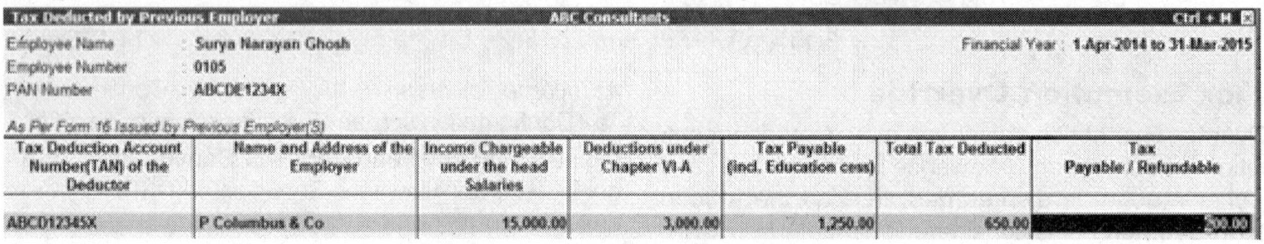

F-14A: Previous Employer Tax details

- **Income Amount:** At *Income Amount* column, enter the Income Amount in respect of part of the Previous Employment within the current Financial Year
- **Exemption Amount:** At *Exemption Amount* column, enter the corresponding Exemption Amount

10.2 Previous Employer Tax details

At *Previous Employer Details* Menu (F-12A), select Tax Deducted / Paid Details and then select the Employee from List of Employees to get *Tax Deducted / Paid details entry screen* (F-14A), for entry of Taxable Amount, Allowance & Tax Deducted.

At *Tax Deducted by Previous Employer* screen (F-14A), at the header, the Employee Name, Employee Number, I Tax PAN of the Employee is carried and shown for Information

Now enter the details as follows, as as per Form 16 submitted by the previous employer:

- **Employer TAN:** At *Tax Deduction Account Number (TAN) of the Deductor* column, enter the Previous Employer TAN.
- **Employer Name:** At *Name & Address of the Employer,* enter the Name & Address of the Previous Employer.
- **Income under Salaries Head:** At *Income Chargeable under the head Salaries*, enter the Income Salaries head, from the previous employer
- **Deductions:** At *Deductions under Chapter VIA*, enter the amount of total deductions allowable
- **Tax Payable:** At *Tax Payable*, enter the Amount of Tax Payable
- **Tax Deducted:** At *Total Tax Deducted*, enter the Amount of Tax Deducted
- **Tax Payable / Refundable:** At *Tax Payable / Refundable* enter the balance amount of Tax Payable / Refundable

11 Income Tax Payment

During Salary Payroll Voucher creation, the Income Tax (TDS) is realised form the Salary. The amount so realised is to be deposited with the Government, through Payment Voucher Payment Voucher creation has been explained earlier. At Payment Voucher creation screen, click *A:Payroll Auto Fill* to get Payment Auto Fill screen (F-15B).

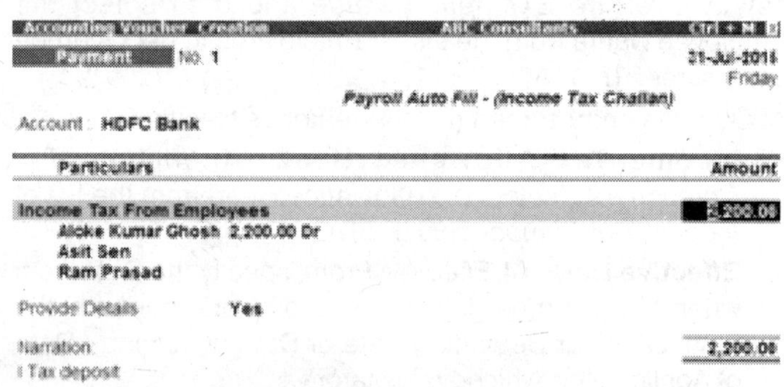

F-15A: I Tax payment Voucher

F-15B: I Tax payment Auto Fill screen

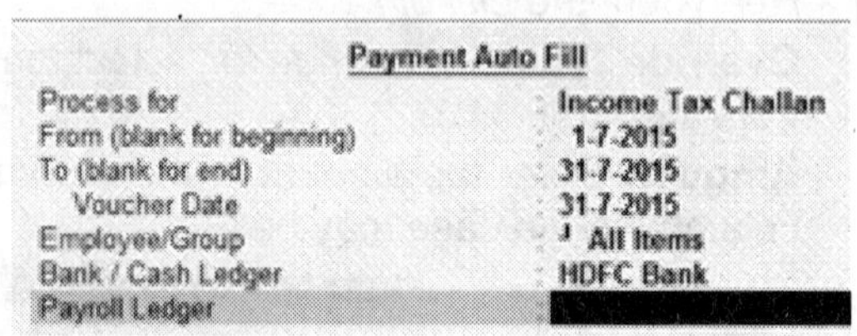

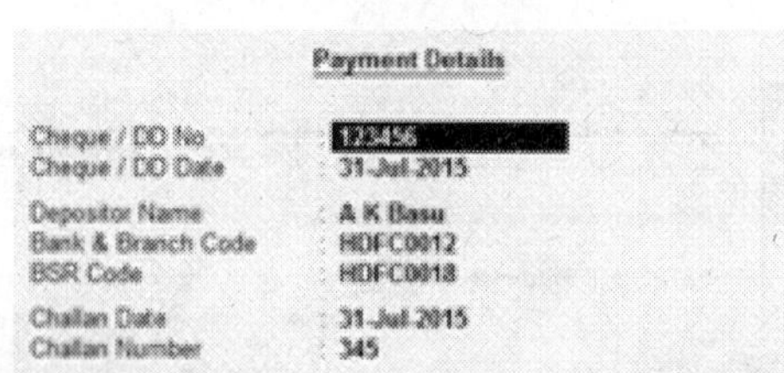

F-15C: I Tax payment details

At *Payment Auto Fill screen* (F-15B), enter as follows:

- **Process:** At *Process For*, select *Income Tax Challan* from the list

- **Period:** At *From / To*, enter the period Dates
- **Voucher Date:** Enter the Voucher Date of the Payment Voucher
- **Employee Group:** At Employee Group, select the Employee Group from the list
- **Cash / Bank Ledger**: Select the Cash / Bank Ledger from which the payment is made
- **Payroll Ledger:** Select Income Tax Ledger from the list of Ledger Accounts

Now you get the Income Tax Payment Details screen (F-15C) to enter the respective details of Payment

The Payment Voucher (F-15A) now gets auto created showing the Income Tax amount paid in respect of each Employee.

12 Income Tax Challan

To deposit the Income Tax (TDS) Amount Payable, you have to print the Income Tax Challan with relevant details of payment (F-16A). To print the Income Tax Challan (F-16A), having created the Income Tax Payment Voucher as explained above, at Income Tax Payment Voucher entry screen (F-15A), click *P:Print* button to get *Income Tax Payment Voucher* printing screen (F-16A)

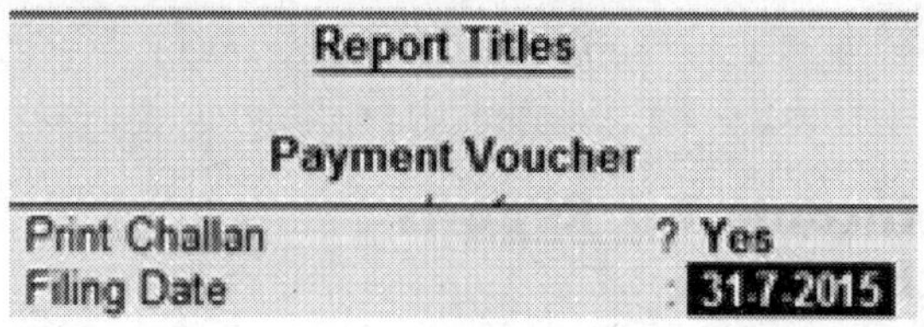

F-16A: I Tax Payment Voucher printing screen

Click Yes to print the Income Tax Challan (P-16B), containing all the relevant details, for deposit of Income Tax (TDS) to the Government, No to print PaymentVoucher

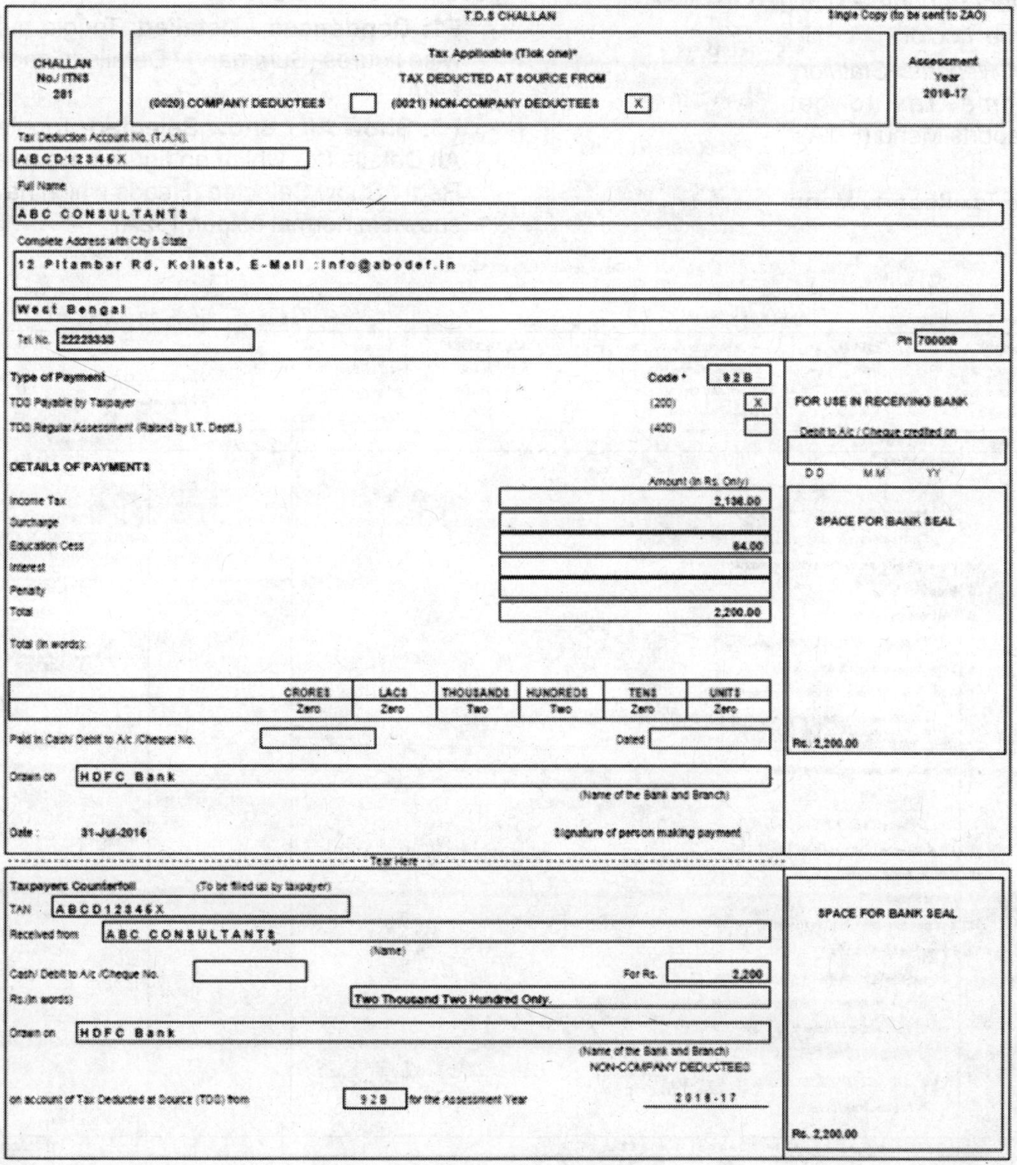

T.D.S CHALLAN — Single Copy (to be sent to ZAO)

CHALLAN No./ ITNS 281

Tax Applicable (Tick one)*
TAX DEDUCTED AT SOURCE FROM
(0020) COMPANY DEDUCTEES [ ] (0021) NON-COMPANY DEDUCTEES [X]

Assessment Year 2016-17

Tax Deduction Account No. (T.A.N): ABCD12346X

Full Name: ABC CONSULTANTS

Complete Address with City & State: 12 Pitambar Rd, Kolkata, E-Mail :info@abcdef.in

West Bengal

Tel No. 22223333 Pin 700009

Type of Payment — Code * 92B
TDS Payable by Taxpayer (200) [X]
TDS Regular Assessment (Raised by I.T. Dept.) (400) [ ]

FOR USE IN RECEIVING BANK
Debit to A/c / Cheque credited on
DD MM YY

DETAILS OF PAYMENTS

	Amount (in Rs. Only)
Income Tax	2,136.00
Surcharge	
Education Cess	64.00
Interest	
Penalty	
Total	2,200.00

Total (in words):

CRORES	LACS	THOUSANDS	HUNDREDS	TENS	UNITS
Zero	Zero	Two	Two	Zero	Zero

SPACE FOR BANK SEAL — Rs. 2,200.00

Paid in Cash/ Debit to A/c /Cheque No. Dated

Drawn on HDFC Bank
(Name of the Bank and Branch)

Date : 31-Jul-2016 Signature of person making payment

Tear Here

Taxpayers Counterfoil (To be filled up by taxpayer)

TAN ABCD12346X

Received from ABC CONSULTANTS
(Name)

Cash/ Debit to A/c /Cheque No. For Rs. 2,200

Rs.(in words) Two Thousand Two Hundred Only.

Drawn on HDFC Bank
(Name of the Bank and Branch)
NON-COMPANY DEDUCTEES

on account of Tax Deducted at Source (TDS) from 92B for the Assessment Year 2016-17

SPACE FOR BANK SEAL — Rs. 2,200.00

P-16B: Income Tax Challan

Income Tax Reports 04-03

01 Income Tax Reports Menu

Having recovered Income Tax from Employee Salary, you may get various Income Tax Reports, available a Income Tax Reports menu (F-1A)

At Gateway, select:

- *Display>Statutory Reports>Payroll Reports>Income Tax,* or
- *Display>Payroll Reports> Statutory Reports>Income Tax* to get Income Tax Reports Menu (F-1A)

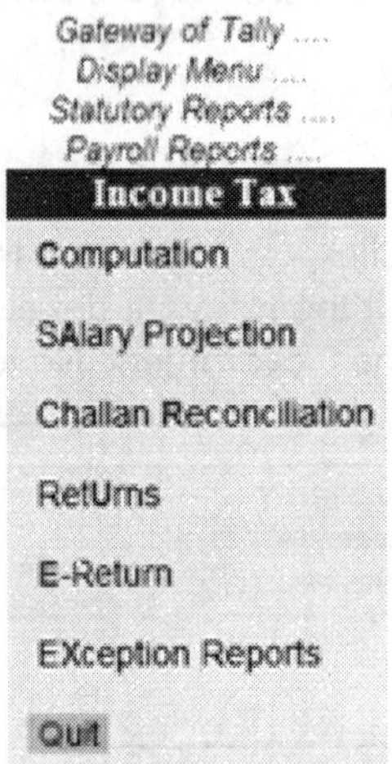

F-1A: Income Tax Reports Menu

02 Income Tax Computation

At *Income Tax Reports* Menu (F-1A), select *Computation* and select the Employee from list of Employees, to get the Income Tax Computation statement (F-2A), showing the elements of Earnings, Deduction, Exemption, Tax Liability, Tax Paid and I Tax payable in respect of selected Employee

Buttons: At *Income Tax Computation* statement (F-2A), you get the following Buttons:

- **F1: Condensed / Detailed**: Toggle button to get head wise figures (Summary) / Details of each head (Detailed: F-2A)
- **F3: Show All / Show Selected**: Toggle Button to show All Details (for which no figures are available, shown in Red) / Show Selected (Heads which have been defined, shown in normal colour: F-2A)

Income Tax Computation

Page 1

Income Tax Computation for	: Aloke Kumar Ghosh			Financial Year	: 1-Apr-2015 to 31-Mar-2016
Employee No.	: 2014/07	PAN Number	: ABCDE1234X	Total Income Tax	: NIL
Gender	: Male	Computed based on	: Proof Value	Less: Deducted till May-2015	: 2,200.00
Date of Joining	: 1-5-2014	Computed for the month	: May - 2015	Balance Deductible	: NIL
Date of Birth	: 1-5-1990	Assessment Year	: 2016 - 2017	Tax Per Month from Jun-2015	: NIL

S.No	Particulars	Amount	Amount
1.	**Gross Salary**		1,38,193.65
	Salary as per provisions contained in Sec 17(1)	1,38,193.65	
	Value of Perquisites u/s 17(2) (as per Form 12BA)		
	Profits in lieu of Salary u/s 17(3) (as per Form 12BA)		
2.	**Less: Allowance to the extent exempted U/s 10**		
3.	**Balance (1 - 2)**		1,38,193.65
4.	**Deductions U/s 16**		550.00
	Professional Tax (Tax on Employment)	550.00	
5.	**Total Income from Salary (3 - 4)**		1,37,643.65
6.	**Add: Other Income declared by Employee**		
	Other Income (House Property / Other Source) / Interest on Housing Loan		
7.	**Gross Total Income (5 + 6)**		1,37,643.65
8.	**Deductions under Chapter VI-A**		8,580.00
	Investments (U/s 80C, 80CCF, 80CCG, etc.)	8,580.00	
	Others (U/s 80D, 80DD, 80E, etc.)		
9.	**Total Income chargeable to Tax (7 - 8)**		1,29,060.00
10.	**Tax on Total Income**		
11.	**Less: Relief**		
12.	**Tax payable after Relief (10 - 11)**		
13.	**Less: Tax Deducted**		2,200.00
	a) Advance Tax declared by Employee		
	b) Tax deducted by the previous Employer		
	c) Tax Deducted other than Salary		
	d) Tax paid by the Employer		
	e) Self Assessment Tax declared by Employee		
	f) Tax deducted till date	2,200.00	
	Balance Tax Payable/ Deductible (12 - 13)		(-)2,200.00

F-2A:Income Tax computation statement

- **F4: Employee**: To select another Employee to show the Report for the selected Employee

- F1: Condensed
- F3: Show All
- F4: Employee
- F5: Proof Value
- A: Employee Alter

F-2B: Buttons

- **F5:Proof Value / Declared Value:** Toggle button to consider the Proof Value / Declared Value as entered in various declaration statement.
- **A: Employee Alter**: To get Employee Master Alteration screen, to alter any Employee Master Data

03 Salary Projection

At *Income Tax Statutory Reports* Menu (F-1A), select *Salary Projection* and select the Employee from list of Employees, to get the *Salary Projection Report* (F3A), showing the projected Earnings & Deductions for each month, for the selected Employee

04 Income Tax Challan Reconciliation

At the time of entry of Payment Voucher for I Tax, the Challan Details are not available. The Challan Dtaa are to be entered after the Challan is received from Bank, through Challan Reconciliation.

At *Income Tax Statutory* Reports Menu (F-1A), select *Challan Reconciliation* to get the Income *Tax Challan Reconciliation* Display (F-4A), showing the Payment Details of Income Tax (TDS from Employees)

At *Challan Reconciliation* Display (F-4A), clickF5:Challn Reconcile to get *Challan Reconciliation* screen to enter data of Challan in the following columns (F-4B) to reconcile the Challan

Cheque / DD NO., Name of Bank, BSR Code, Challan No, Chalan date

Alternately, at Income Tax Challan Reconciliation screen (F-4B), you may click S:Set Challan Details to get Challan

Gross Salary Projection
1-Apr-2015 to 31-Mar-2016

Page 1

Employee Name : **Aloke Kumar Ghosh**
Employee No. : **2014/07**

Particulars	Total	Actuals '0	Actuals May' 2015	Actuals '0	Projection Jul' 2015	Projection Aug' 2015	Actuals '0	Projection Oct' 2015	Actuals '0	Projection Dec' 2015	Projection Jan' 2016	Actuals '0	Projection Mar' 2016
Earnings													
Basic Salary	83,613.00		11,613.00		12,000.00	12,000.00		12,000.00		12,000.00	12,000.00		12,000.00
HRA	4,180.65		580.65		600.00	600.00		600.00		600.00	600.00		600.00
Total Earnings	87,793.65		12,193.65		12,600.00	12,600.00		12,600.00		12,600.00	12,600.00		12,600.00
Deductions													
Employees P F Cont	5,460.00		780.00		780.00	780.00		780.00		780.00	780.00		780.00
Professional Tax	350.00		50.00		50.00	50.00		50.00		50.00	50.00		50.00
Total Deductions	5,810.00		830.00		830.00	830.00		830.00		830.00	830.00		830.00
Total Nett Earnings	81,983.65		11,363.65		11,770.00	11,770.00		11,770.00		11,770.00	11,770.00		11,770.00

F-3A: Salary Projection

P: Print | E: Export | M: E-Mail | O: Upload | S: Shop | G: Language | K: Keyboard | K: Control Centre | H: Support Centre | H: Help

Income Tax Challan Reconciliation — **ABC Consultants** — Ctrl + M

Income Tax Challan Reconciliation **1-Apr-2015 to 31-Mar-2016**

Date	Particulars	Period From	Period To	Cheque/DD No.	Name of Bank	BSR Code	Challan No.	Challan Date	Vch No.	Amount
31-7-2015	HDFC Bank	1-7-2015	31-7-2015						1	2,200.00

F-4A: Income Tax Challan Reconciliation Display

Income Tax Challan Reconciliation — **ABC Consultants** — Ctrl + M

Income Tax Challan Reconciliation **1-Apr-2015 to 31-Mar-2016**

(Reconciliation)

Date	Particulars	Period From	Period To	Cheque/DD No.	Name of Bank	BSR Code	Challan No.	Challan Date	Vch No.	Amount
31-7-2015	**HDFC Bank**	1-7-2015	31-7-2015	123456	HDFC	HDFC--12	234		1	**2,200.00**

F-4B: Income Tax Challan Reconciliation

No Buttons are available at Salary Projection Report (F-3A). The report is auto set for Current Period.

Details entry screen (F-4C) to enter the respective data of Challan. The data entered is shown at F-4B: Challan Reconciliation screen (F-4B)

Challan Details

From Date	: 1-7-2015
To Date	: 31-7-2015
Bank Name	: HDFC
BSR Code	: HDFC0012
Bank Challan No.	: 234
Challan Date	1-8-15

F-4C: Challan data entry

Gateway of Tally ...
Display Menu ...
Payroll Reports ...
Statutory Reports ...
Income Tax ...

Return

Quarterly

FOrm 24Q
ANnexure I to 24Q
AnnExure II to 24Q

Annual

Form 16
Form 12BA
ITR - 1
Quit

F-5A: Income Tax Returns Menu

Report Titles

ITForm24 Quarterly

Name	S Ghosh	Quarter Period for	Q2 - [July - September]
Designation	Accounts Officer	Type of deductor	Others
Address		Place	Kolkata
Flat No.	12 Pitambar Rd	Date	1-10-2015
Name of the premises/building	Kolkata		
Road/Street/Lane			
Area/Location			
Town/City/District			
State	West Bengal		
Pin Code	700009		
Telephone No.	22223333		
E-mail	info@abcdef.in		

F-6B: Form 24Q Return

05 Income Tax Returns

At Income Tax Statutory Reports Menu (F-1A), select *Returns* to get Income Tax Returns Menu (F-5A).

FORM NO. 24Q
(See section 192 and rule 31A)

Quarterly statement of deduction of tax under sub-section (3) of section 200 of the Income-tax Act, 1961 in respect of salary for the quarter ended 0

1. (a) Tax Deduction Account No. : ABCD12345X
   (b) Permanent Account No. :
   (c) Financial year : 2014 - 2015
   (d) Assessment year : 2016 - 2017
   (e) Has any statement been filed earlier for this quarter (Yes/No) :
   (f) If answer to (e) is 'Yes' then Provisional Receipt No. of original statement :

2. Particulars of the deductor (employer)
   (a) Name : ABC Consultants
   (b) Type of deductor : Others
   (c) Branch/Division (if any) :
   (d) Address
   Flat No. : 12 Pitambar Rd
   Name of the premises/building : Kolkata
   Road/street/lane :
   Area/location :
   Town/City/District :
   State : West Bengal
   Pin code : 700009
   Telephone No. : 22223333
   E-mail : info@abcdef.in

3. Particulars of the person responsible for deduction of tax
   (a) Name : S Ghosh
   (b) Address
   Flat No. : 12 Pitambar Rd
   Name of the premises/building : Kolkata
   Road/street/lane :
   Area/location :
   Town/City/District :
   State : West Bengal
   Pin code : 700009
   Telephone No. : 22223333
   E-mail : info@abcdef.in

4. Details of tax deducted and paid to the credit of Central Government ?

Sr.No	TDS Rs.	Surcharge Rs.	Education Cess Rs.	Interest Rs.	Others Rs.
(301)	(302)	(303)	(304)	(305)	(306)

Sr.No	Total tax deposited (302 + 303 + 304 + 305 + 306) Rs.	Cheque / DD No. (if any)	BSR Code	Date on which tax deposited	Transfer Voucher / Challan serial No.	Whether TDS deposited by Book entry? Yes/No
(301)	(307)	(308)	(309)	(310)	(311)	(312)

5. Details of salary paid and tax deducted thereon from the employees as per Annexure I enclosed.

Verification

I, S Ghosh hereby certify that all the particulars furnished above are correct and complete.

Place : Signature of person responsible for deducting tax at source

Date : 1-Jul-2015 Name : S Ghosh,Designation : Accounts Officer

F-6A: I Tax Form 24Q

06 Form 24Q

Form 24Q (F-6A) is a Quarterly statement which contains the details of the salary paid and tax deducted from the employees.

At Income Tax Return Menu (F-5A), select *Form 24Q* to get Form 24 Q Printing screen (F-6B). Set the Printing options to get the Form 24Q Return (F-6A).

06.01 Form 24Q – Annexure I

Form 24Q – Annexure I is the annexure to be enclosed to Form 24 Q Quarterly Return, in each of the 4 Quarters.

At *Income Tax Return Menu* (F-5A), select *Annexure I to Form 24Q* to get Form 24 Q Annexure I Printing screen (F-7B). Set the Printing options to get the Form 24Q Annexure I (F-7A).

ANNEXURE I

Deductee wise break-up of TDS

(Please use separate Annexure for each line - item in the table at S.No. 04 of main Form 24Q)

Details of salary paid and tax deducted thereon from the employees

BSR code of the branch where tax is deposited	: 123456	Name of Employer	: ABC Manpower
Date on which tax deposited	: 31-Oct-2015		
Challan Serial No.	: 1234		
Section (which payment made)	: 92B	TAN	: ABCD12345X
Total TDS to be allocated	: 400.00		
Interest	: 0.00		
Others	: 0.00		
Total of the above	: 400.00		

Sr. No	Employee reference No. provided by employer	PAN of the employee	Name of the employee	Date of payment /credit	Taxable amount or which tax deducted Rs.	TDS
(313)	(314)	(315)	(316)	(317)	(318)	(319)
1		[illegible]	Tom	31-10-2015	7,583.10	194.00
	Total				7,583.10	194.00

Sr. No	Surcharge	Education Cess	Total Tax Deducted (319 +320 +321)	Total tax deposited Rs.	Date of deduction	Date of deposit	Reason for nondeduction/lower deduction*
(313)	(320)	(321)	(322)	(323)	(324)	(325)	(326)
1		6.00	200.00	400.00	31-10-2015	31-10-2015	
	Total	6.00	200.00	400.00			

Verification

I, A K Ghosh hereby certify that all the particulars furnished above are correct and complete.

Place : Signature of person responsible for deducting tax at source

Date : 31-Oct-2015 Name : A K Ghosh,Designation : Secretary

F-7A: 24Q Annexure – I

Report Titles

ITForm24 Quarterly

Name	S Ghosh	Quarter Period for	Q2 - [July - September]
Designation	Accounts Officer	Type of deductor	Others
Address		Place	Kolkata
Flat No.	12 Pitambar Rd	Date	1-10-2015
Name of the premises/building	Kolkata		
Road/Street/Lane			
Area/Location			
Town/City/District			
State	West Bengal		
Pin Code	700009		
Telephone No.	22223333		
E-mail	info@abcdef.in		

F-7B: 24Q Annexure – I Printing

06.02 Form 24Q – Annexure II

Form 24Q – Annexure II is the annexure to be enclosed to Form 24 Q Quarterly Return, only in the last Quarter (Jan – Mar)

ABC Manpower

Form 24Q - Annexure II

1-Apr-2015 to 31-Mar-2016

Page 1 (A)

ANNEXURE II

Details of salary paid/credited during the Financial Year (2015 - 2016) and net tax payable

Serial Number	Permanent Account Number (PAN) of the employee	Name of the Employee	Write (W) for woman, (S) for senior citizen and (G) for others	Date from which employed with current employer		Total amount of salary (See note 4 appearing at the end of the main Form)
(327)	(328)	(329)	(330)	(331)		(332)
				Date From	Date To	
1.	ABCDE5679X	Dick	G	1-4-2015	31-3-2016	42,548.42
2.	ASDGF1234X	Harry	S	2-10-2015	31-10-2015	
3.	QWERT1234X	Tom	G	1-4-2015	31-3-2016	28,620.10

Place : Signature of person responsible for paying salary

Date : 31-Mar-2016 Name : A K Ghosh;Designation : Secretary

F-7C: 24Q Annexure – II

At *Income Tax Return Menu* (F-5A), select *Annexure II to Form 24Q* to get Form 24 Q Annexure II Printing screen (F-7B). Set the Printing options to get the Form 24Q Annexure I (F-7A).

Report Titles

Form 24Q - Annexure II

Name	S Ghosh	Quarter Period for	Q4 - [January - March]
Designation	Accounts Officer	Place	Kolkata
Appearance of Employee Names	Name Only	Date	1-7-2015

F-7D: 24Q Annexure – II Printing

07 Form 16

Form 16 (F-8A) is Annual statement which contains the Computation & Tax deducted details in respect of each Employee, whose Total Income exceeds the I Tax threshold limit

Name	S Ghosh	Quarter	Acknowledgement
Son/Daughter	P Ghosh	Apr-Jun	Apr-Jun
Designation	Accounts Officer	Jul-Sep	Jul-Sep
From (blank for beginning)	1-4-2015	Oct-Dec	Oct-Dec
To (blank for end)	31-3-2016	Jan-Mar	Jan-Mar
Challan Date till	31-3-2016	CIT(TDS) Details	
Type of Copy	Default	Address	Aykar Bhavan
Place		City	Rabindra Sarani
Date of Printing	2-4-2014	Pin Code	700081
Appearance of Employee Names	Name Only		
Include Previous Employer Income	? No		

F-8A: Form 16 Printing

FORM NO. 16

[See rule 31(l)(a)]

PART A

Certificate under section 203 of the Income-tax Act, 1961 for Tax deducted at source on Salary

Name and Address of the Employer ABC Consultants 12 Pitambar Rd Kolkata		Name and Designation of the Employee Aloke Kumar Ghosh Sales Officer		
PAN of the Deductor	TAN of the Deductor ABCD12345X	PAN of the Employee ABCDE1234X		
CIT (TDS) Address : CIT Rd Sch VIIM City : Kolkata Pincode : 700054		Assessment Year	Period	
			From	To
		2016 - 2017	1-Apr-2015	31-Mar-2016

Summary of tax deducted at source

Quarter	Receipt Numbers of original statements of TDS under sub-section(3) of section 200	Amount of tax deducted in respect of the employee	Amount of tax deposited / remitted in respect of the employee
Quarter 1			
Quarter 2			
Quarter 3			
Quarter 4			
Total			

F-8B: Form 16 Part 1

FORM NO. 16

[See rule 31(l)(a)]

PART A

Certificate under section 203 of the Income-tax Act, 1961 for Tax deducted at source on Salary

Name and Address of the Employer **ABC Consultants** 12 Pitambar Rd Kolkata		**Name and Designation of the Employee** **Aloke Kumar Ghosh** Sales Officer		
PAN of the Deductor	**TAN of the Deductor** ABCD12345X	**PAN of the Employee** ABCDE1234X		
CIT (TDS) **Address** : Aykar Bhavan **City** : Rabindra Sarani **Pincode** : 700081		**Assessment Year**	**Period**	
			From	**To**
		2016 - 2017	**1-Apr-2015**	**31-Mar-2016**

Summary of tax deducted at source

Quarter	Receipt Numbers of original statements of TDS under sub -section(3) of section 200	Amount of tax deducted in respect of the employee	Amount of tax deposited / remitted in respect of the employee
Quarter 1		100.00	
Quarter 2	Jul-Sep	2,200.00	2,200.00
Quarter 3	Oct-Dec	60.00	60.00
Quarter 4			
Total		2,360.00	2,260.00

F-8B: Form 16 (Part A)

	PART B			
	Details of Salary paid and any other income and tax deducted			
1.	**Gross Salary**			
a)	Salary as per Provisions contained in sec.17(1)	*41,993.65*		
b)	Value of perquisites u/s 17(2) (as per Form No.12BA. wherever applicable)			
c)	Profits in lieu of salary under section 17(3) (as per Form No.12BA, wherever applicable)			
	Total		**41,993.65**	
2.	**Less: Allowance to the Extent u/s 10**			
3.	**Balances (1-2)**			**41,993.65**
4.	**Deductions**			
	Professional Tax (Tax on Employment)	*50.00*		
5.	**Aggregate of deductions**		**50.00**	
6.	**Income Chargable under the head 'salaries' (3-5)**			**41,943.65**
7.	**Add: Any other income reported by the employee**			
	Income From House Property			
	Income From Other Sources			
	Interest on Housing Loan - Self Occupied			
8.	**Gross total income (6+7)**			**41,943.65**
9.	**Deductions under Chapter VIA**			
	(A) Section 80C, 80CCC and 80CCD			
	i) Section 80C		**780.00**	
	Employee Provident Fund (EPF)	780.00		
	ii) Section 80CCC: Contribution to Certain Pension Funds			
	iii) Section 80CCD: Contribution to Notified Pension Scheme			
	Total of 80C, 80CCC & 80CCD (Max 1,00,000.00)			**780.00**
	(B) Other Sections (e.g. 80E, 80G etc.,) Under Chapter VI-A			
	Total of Other Sections 80E, 80G etc.,			
10.	**Aggregate of deductible amount under Chapter VIA**			**780.00**
11.	**Total Income (8-10)**			**41,160.00**
12.	**Tax on total income**			
13.	**Education cess @ 3% (on tax computed as S.No.12)**			
14.	**Tax Payable (12 + 13)**			
15.	**Less: Relief under section 89 (attach details)**			
16.	**Tax Payable (14-15)**			

F-8C: Form 16 (Part B)

Verification	
I S Ghosh son/daughter of P Ghosh Working in the capacity of Accounts Officer (designation) do hereby certify that a sum of Rs. 2,260.00 [INR Two Thousand Two Hundred Sixty (in words)] has been deducted at source and paid to the credit of the Central Government. I further certify that the information given above is true and correct based on the books of account,documents and other available records.	
Place :	
Date : **2-Apr-2014**	**Signature of person responsible for deduction of tax**
Designation : **Accounts Officer**	**Full Name : S Ghosh**

ANNEXURE-B
DETAILS OF TAX DEDUCTED AND DEPOSITED IN THE CENTRAL GOVERNMENT ACCOUNT THROUGH CHALLAN
(The Employer to provide the payment wise details of tax deducted and deposited with respect to the employee)

S.No.	**Tax Deposited in respect of the employee (Rs.)**	**Challan identification number (CIN)**		
		BSR Code of the Bank Branch	**Date on which tax deposited (dd/mm/yyyy) Statement**	**Challan Serial Number**
1	100.00	HDFC0012	1-Jul-2015	678
2	2,200.00	HDFC-12	1-Aug-2015	234
3	60.00	HDFC0018	2-Nov-2015	456
Total	**2,360.00**			

F-8D: Form 16 (Verification, Annexure B)

At Income Tax Return Menu (F-5A), select Form 16 to get Form 16 Printing screen (F-8A). Set the Printing options to get the Form 16 (F-8B to F-8D).

08 Form 12 BA

Form 12 BA is Annual statement (F-9A) showing the particulars of Non-Cash benefits like Perquisites, Other benefits or amenities, Profits in lieu of Salary, etc.

FORM No.12BA

[See rule 26A(2)(b)]

Statement showing particulars of perquisites, other fringe benefits or amenities and profits in lieu of salary with value thereof

1. Name and Address of Employer : ABC Manpower
2. TAN : ABCD12345X
3. TDS Assessment Range of the Employer : 36(2)
4. Name, designation and PAN of employee : Dick ABCDE5679X
5. Is the Employee a director or a person with substantial interest in the company (where the Employer is a Company) : No
6. Income under the head 'Salaries' of the Employee other than from perquisites : 41,548.42
7. Financial year : 2015 - 16
8. Valuation of Perquisites

S.No.	Nature of perquisites (see rule 3)	Value of perquisite as per rules (Rs.)	Amount, if any, recovered from the employee (Rs.)	Amount of perquisite chargeable to tax Col.(3) - Col.(4) (Rs.)
(1)	(2)	(3)	(4)	(5)
1	Any Other Benefit/Amenity/Service/Right/Privilege			
2	Any Specified Security/sweat Equity Shares Alloted Or Transferred			
3	Cars/Other Automotive			
4	Club Expenses			
5	Credit Card Expenses			
6	Employer Contribution to NPS	4,154.84		4,154.84
7	Free Education			
8	Free Meals	2,000.00	1,000.00	1,000.00
9	Free Or Concessional Travel			
10	Gas, Electricity, Water			
11	Gifts, Vouchers, Etc.			
12	Holiday Expenses			
13	Interest Free Or Concessional Loans			
14	Other Benefits Or Amenities			
15	Rent Free Accommodation			
16	Sweeper, Gardener, Watchman Or Personal Attendant			
17	Transfer of Assets to Employees			
18	Use of Movable Assets by Employee			
19	Total value of perquisities	6,154.84	1,000.00	5,154.84
20	Total value of profits in lieu of salary as per section 17(3)			

F-9A: Form 12BA

At Income Tax Return Menu (F-5A), select Form 12BA to get Form 12BA Printing screen (F-9B). Set the Printing options to get Form 12BA(F-9A).

Report Titles

Form 12BA

From (blank for beginning)	1-4-2015	Name	: S Ghosh
To (blank for end)	: 31-3-2016	Son/Daughter	: P Ghosh
Employee/Group	: All Items	Designation	: Accounts Officer
Appearance of Employee Names	: Name Only	Is Employee a Director	: No
Place	:	TDS Assessment Range	: 292
Date of Printing	: 1-4-2016		

F-9B: Form 12BA Printing screen

09 Form ITR-I

Form ITR-1 is used to file the Income Tax return, by Employee

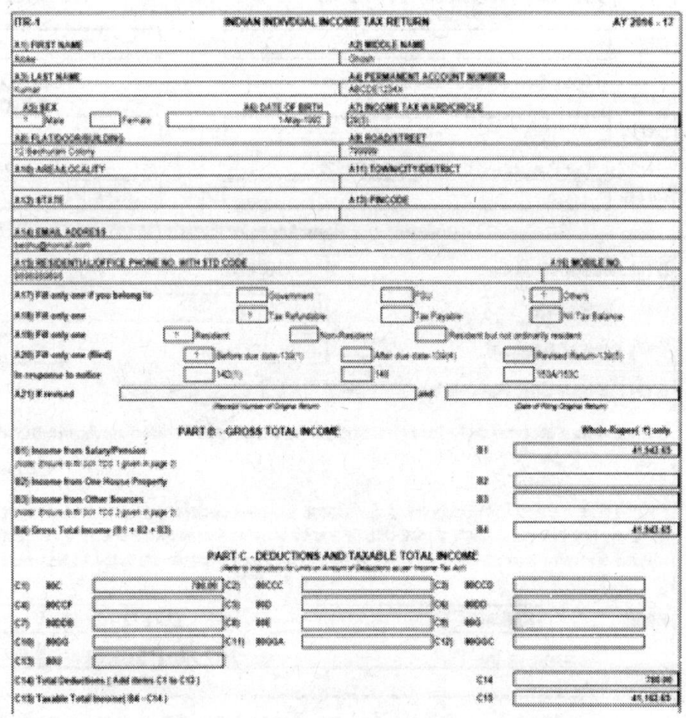
ITR-1 INDIAN INDIVIDUAL INCOME TAX RETURN AY 2016 - 17

PART B - GROSS TOTAL INCOME

PART C - DEDUCTIONS AND TAXABLE TOTAL INCOME

F-10A: Form ITR- I (Part 1)

At Income Tax Return Menu (F-5A), select Form ITR – I and the Employee to get Form ITR-I Printing screen (F-10D). Form ITR-I Printing screen (F-10D)., set the printing options to get IRT-I in print (F-10A to F-10C)

10 Income Tax Exception Reports

At Income Tax Statutory Reports Menu (F-1A), select *Exception Report* to get Income Tax Exception Reports Menu (F-11A)

PERMANENT ACCOUNT NUMBER: ABCDE1234X

PART D - TAX COMPUTATION AND TAX STATUS

D1)	Tax Payable on Total Income (C15)	D2)	Secondary & Higher Education Cess	D3)	Total Tax & Cess (D1 + D2)
D4)	Relief U/s 89	D5)	Relief U/s 90/91	D6)	Balance Tax after Relief (D3-D4-D5)
D7)	Total Interest U/s 234A/234B/234C	D8)	Total Tax and Interest (D6+D7)	D9)	Total Advance Tax Paid
D10)	Total Self Assessment Tax Paid	D11)	Total TDS Deducted (D9+D10+D11) 2,360.00	D12)	Total Prepaid Taxes 2,360.00
D13)	Tax Payable (D8-D12, If D8>D12)	D14)	Refund (D12-D8, If D12>D8)		

Bank Account Details (Mandatory in all cases irrespective of refund due or not)

D15) Account Number: 1234567890

D16) MICR Code: HDFC0012

D17) Type of Account: [ ] Current [?] Savings

D18) Fill only one: Refund by [ ] Cheque [ ] deposited directly in to your bank account

D19) Exempt Income only for reporting purposes (From Dividends, Agricultural Income < Rs 5000/-)

VERIFICATION

I Aloke Kumar Ghosh son/daughter of B K Ghosh solemnly declare that to the best of my knowledge and belief, the information given in the return is correct and complete and that the amount of total income and other particulars shown therein are truly stated and are in accordance with the provisions of the Income-tax Act, 1961, in respect of income chargeable to Income-tax for the previous year relevant to the Assessment Year 2016 - 17

Place: Kolkata Date: 2-Apr-2014 SIGN HERE ->

Name of the TRP	TRP PIN [10 Digit]	Amount to be paid to TRP	TRP Signature

Sch IT - DETAILS OF ADVANCE TAX AND SELF ASSESSMENT TAX PAYMENTS

BSR Code (Col.i)	Date of Deposit (Col.ii)	Challan No. (Col.iii)	Tax Paid (Col.iv)

Sch TDS1 - DETAILS OF TAX DEDUCTED AT SOURCE FROM SALARY

TAN (Col.i)	Name of the Employer (Col.ii)	Income Under Salary (Col.iii)	Tax Deducted (Col.iv)
ABCD12345X	ABC Consultants	41,943.65	2,360.00

Sch TDS2 - DETAILS OF TAX DEDUCTED AT SOURCE FROM INCOME OTHER THAN SALARY

TAN (Col.i)	Name of the Deductor (Col.ii)	Tax Deducted (Col.iii)	Amt out of (iii) claimed this YR (Col iv)

F-10B: Form ITR- I (Part 2)

ITR - V	ACKNOWLEDGEMENT	AY 2016 - 17

Received with thanks from Aloke Kumar Ghosh a return of income in

ITR No. [?] 1(SAHAJ) [ ] 2 [ ] 3 [ ] 4S(SUGAM) [ ] 4 [ ] 5 [ ] 6 for assessment year 2016 - 17 , having the following particulars

A1) FIRST NAME	**A2) MIDDLE NAME**
Aloke	Ghosh
A3) LAST NAME	**A4) PERMANENT ACCOUNT NUMBER**
Kumar	ABCDE1234X
A5) SEX [?] Male [ ] Female **A6) DATE OF BIRTH** 1-May-1990	**A7) INCOME TAX WARD/CIRCLE** 29(3)
A8) FLAT/DOOR/BUILDING	**A9) ROAD/STREET**
12 Bechuram Colony	799999
A10) AREA/LOCALITY	**A11) TOWN/CITY/DISTRICT**
A12) STATE	**A13) PINCODE**

A20) Fill only one (filed) [?] Before due date-139(1) [ ] After due date-139(4) [ ] Revised Return-139(5)

In response to notice [ ] 142(1) [ ] 148 [ ] 153A/153C

COMPUTATION OF INCOME AND TAX RETURN

Whole-Rupee(₹) only.

B1) Gross Total Income	B1	41,943.65
B2) Deductions under Chapter VI-A	B2	780.00
B3) Total Income	B3	41,163.65
B4) Current Loss If any	B4	
B5) Net Tax Payable	B5	
B6) Interest Payable	B6	
B7) Total Tax and Interest Payable	B7	
B8) Total Advance Tax Paid	B8	
B9) Total Self Assessment Tax Paid	B9	
B10) Total TDS Deducted	B10	2,360.00
B11) Total TCS Deducted	B11	
B12) Total Prepaid Taxes (B8+B9+B10+B11)	B12	2,360.00
B13) Tax Payable (B7-B12, If B7 > B12)	B13	
B14) Refund (B12-B7, If B12 > B7)	B14	

F-10C: Form ITR- I (Part 3)

Report Titles

INDIAN INCOME TAX RETURN

From (blank for beginning)	: 1-4-2015
To (blank for end)	: 31-3-2016
Place	: Kolkata
Date of Printing	: 2-4-2014
Appearance of Employee Names	: Name Only
Print Acknowledgement	? Yes

F-10D: Form ITR- I Printing

Gateway of Tally ....
Display Menu ....
Payroll Reports ....
Statutory Reports ....
Income Tax ....

Exception Reports

PAN Not Available
Other Records
TDS Variance
Quit

F-11A: I Tax Exception Reports Menu

10.01 PAN Not Available

At I Tax Exception Reports Menu (F-11A), select *PAN Not Available* to get PAN Not Available Display (F-12A), showing the list of Employees for which PAN is not entered inn their Master Record.

At *PAN Not Available* Display(F-12A), at *Income Tax Number (PAN)* column, you may enter the PAN directly & quickly, which will get updated at the Master Record (you need not *Alter* Master of each Employee)

Buttons: At *PAN Not Available* Display (F-12A), you get the following Button:

- **F5:All Items / Exceptions:** Toggle button to show only the Employees whose PAN is not entered (Exceptions) / to show the records of all Employees (All Employees, PAN filled up or Blank).

10.02 Other Reports

At I *Tax Exception* Reports Menu (F-11A), select *Other Reports* to *get Employees Other Reports Display (F-13A)*, showing the list of Employees, each field in separate column,

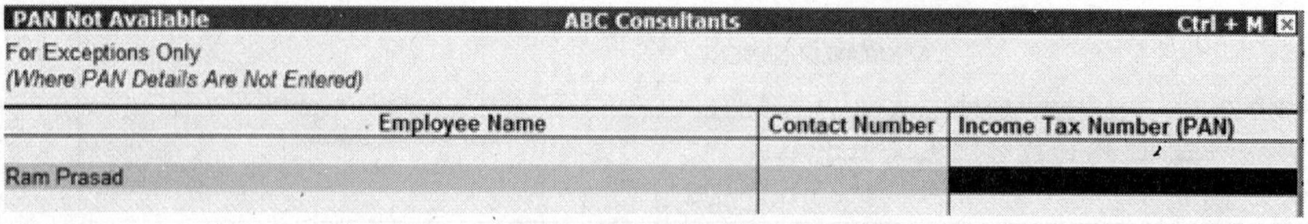

PAN Not Available — ABC Consultants — Ctrl + M

For Exceptions Only
(Where PAN Details Are Not Entered)

Employee Name	Contact Number	Income Tax Number (PAN)
Ram Prasad		

F-12A: PAN Not Available Report

F5: All Items

F-12B:Buttons

Employees Other Records — ABC Consultants — Ctrl + M

For All Employees

Name of the Employee	Employee Number	Joining Date	Date of Resignation / Retirement	Date of Birth	Gender	Designation
						6 more ... →
Primary Cost Category						
Officers						
Aloke Kumar Ghosh	2014/07	1-May-2014		1-May-1990	Male	Sales Officer
Asit Sen		1-Jul-2000				
Workers						
Ram Prasad	W013	1-Apr-2000			Male	Cutter

F-13A: Other Reports

F7: Employee Filters

F-13B: Buttons

in Tabular Form. Place the cursor at the desired field (you have Pan Left / Right to get the desired field) to update any field of the Employee quickly, which will get updated at the Master Record (you need not *Alter* Master of each Employee)

Buttons: At **Buttons:** At *PAN Not Available* Display (F-13A), you get the following Button (F-13B):

- **F7:Emloyee Filter:** To select a specific Employee, Employee Group or Employee Category to get the list Employees as per selection

10.03 TDS Variance

The TDS Variance report provides the Details of TDS amount short Deducted from Employees, as per estimated I Tax Payable. This Report helps to deduct the balance amount to be recovered within the Financial Year, from their Salary

At I Tax Exception Reports Menu (F-11A), select *TDS Variance* and then select the Employee Group (or All Items) to *get TDS Variance Display* (F-14A), showing the monthwise break up of Variance. Drill down through any Month to get the Employeewise details of Variance

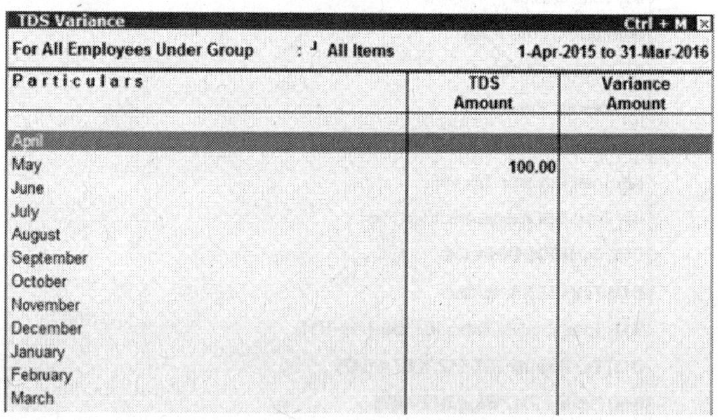

TDS Variance — Ctrl + M

For All Employees Under Group : All Items — 1-Apr-2015 to 31-Mar-2016

Particulars	TDS Amount	Variance Amount
April		
May	100.00	
June		
July		
August		
September		
October		
November		
December		
January		
February		
March		

F-14A: TDS Variance Report

Employees State Insurance

04-04

01 ESI Contribution

Employees' Sate Insurance (ESI) contribution is a statutory deduction from pay of an Employee. Employer also contribute and both the Employer's & Employees' contribution is deposited to the ESI authority

01.01 ESI Statutory Details

We have explained activation of Statutory Features earlier. Having activated Statutory Features, further set *Yes* at *Set / Alter Payroll Statutory Details* to get *Payroll Statutory Details* screen. At *Payroll Statutory Details*, enter the relevant details for ESI (F-1A), as follows:

- **Company ESI Code**: At *Company Code*, enter the ESI Code as allotted by ESI Department. This Code is printed in ESI Statutory Reports
- **ESI Branch Office**: At ESI Branch Office, enter the name of the ESI Branch Office as per jurisdiction. This is printed in ESI Statutory Reports
- **Standard Working days (per Month)**: Enter the name of Standard Working Days (e.g 26), which is used for per day earnings computation for the purpose of ESI

F-1A: Company ESI Particulars

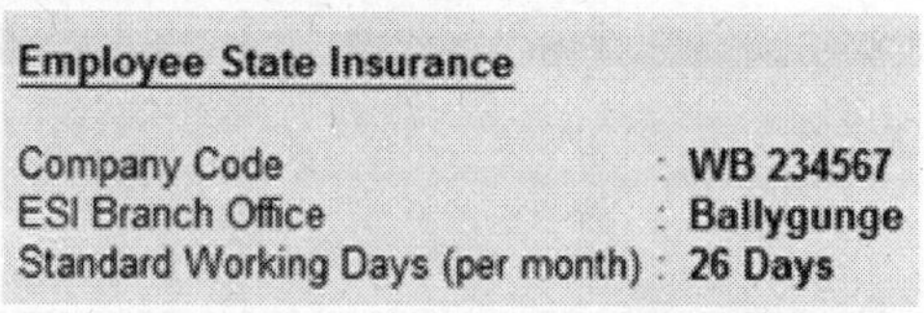

02 Employees' ESI Deduction Pay Head

Some amount is deducted towards Employees Contribution to ESI, under ESI Rules. So, you have create Pay Head to deduct the amount of ESI Contribution from Employee Salary. Pay Head creation has been explained earlier. The process of creation of Employees' ESI Deduction Pay Head, is described below (F-2A):

- **Pay Head Type**: At *Pay Head Type*, select *Employees' Statutory Deductions* from the list of Pay Head Types (F-4B).
- **Statutory Pay Type**: Having selected the *Pay Head Type* as above, at *Statutory Pay Type*, select *Employees State Insurance* from the list
- **Parent Account Group**: At *Under* select Current Liabilities (or Provision) from the Account Group list
- At *Calculation Type*, As Computed Value is auto selected (you cannot change it).

ESI Computation Info: At the right Part of the screen (F-2A), you get Computation Info section. The process of entry of Computation Info has been explained earlier. Here we discuss about set up details for *Employees' Contribution to ESI* Account:

Computation Method: At *Compute*, select *on On Specified Formula,* from the list (as ESI is computed on some specified Earnings Heads), to get Specified Formula screen (F-2B). At Specified Formula screen (F-2B), at Function column, select *Add Pay Head* (F-2C) and then at column Pay Head, select the Head on which ESI is deductible. This way, select Add pay option and selecte all the pay Heads one by one, on which ESI is to be computed.

At *Specified Formula*, the arithmetical computation Formula showing the Pay Heads is displayed for Info.

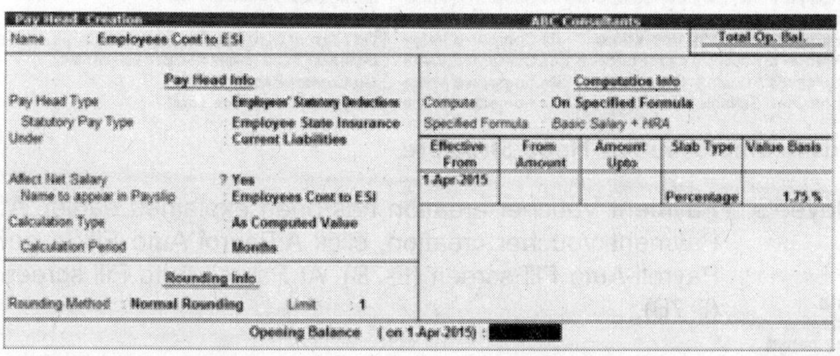

F-2A: Employees' ESI Deduction Pay Head

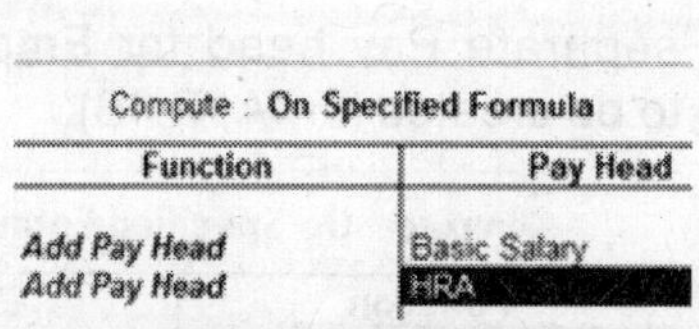

F-2B: Computation Formula screen

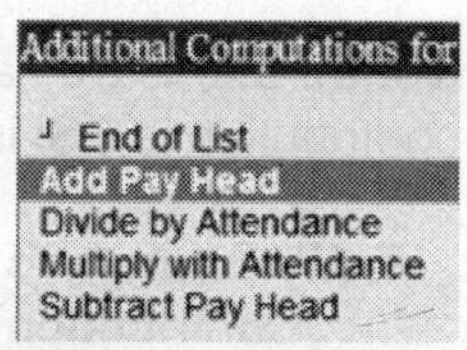

F-2C: Computation Option list

Effective Date: At Start From, the Financial Start Date is carried by default, at the first instance

Slab Range & Rate: Now enter the Range & corresponding rates for each Slab, as follows:

- **Slab Amount:** At *From Amount* & *Amount Upto*, at leave blank as ESI is computed on the amount arrived at as per Formula specified
- **Computation Method:** At *Slab Type*, select *Percentage* from List of Slabs, as ESI Contribution is computed as Percentage on amount computed as per specified formula.
- **Rate:** At Value Basis, enter the Rate of Percentage of ESI Deduction (1.75%) from Employees Salary.

Round Off: Set Round Off rules for Normal Rounding of Rs 1.00, as per ESI Rules

03 Employer's Contribution to ESI

Pay Head Creation — ABC Consultants

Name : Emploer's Cont to ESI — Total Op. Bal.

Pay Head Info

Pay Head Type : Employer's Statutory Contribution
Statutory Pay Type : Employee State Insurance
Under : Indirect Expenses

Affect Net Salary ? No

Calculation Type : As Computed Value
Calculation Period : Months

Rounding Info

Rounding Method : Normal Rounding Limit : 1

Computation Info

Compute : On Specified Formula
Specified Formula : (Basic Salary + HRA) + DA

Effective From	From Amount	Amount Upto	Slab Type	Value Basis
1-Apr-2015			Percentage	4.75 %

Opening Balance (on 1-Apr-2015) :

F-4A: Employer's Contribution to ESI Head

While Employee's contribution to ESI is deducted from Employee salary and deposited with ESI Authorities, Employer also pay specified amount along with Employer's Contribution. So, a separate Pay head for Employee's contribution to ESI is to be created (F-4A, F-4B).

Compute : On Specified Formula

Function	Pay Head
Add Pay Head	Basic Salary
Add Pay Head	HRA
Add Pay Head	DA

F-4B: Employer's Contribution Computation Formula

04 ESI Payable Ledger

ESI Deductions made form Employees Salary and Employer's Contribution to ESI are to be deposited to ESI Authority. So, these amount are credited to a ESI Payable Ledger Account and the Payment is made by debiting the ESI Payable Ledger Account. So, you have to create ESI Payable Ledger Account (like Salary Payable Ledger Account discussed earlier).

Pay Head Creation

Name : **ESI Payable**

Pay Head Info

Pay Head Type : **Not Applicable**
Under : **Current Liabilities**

F-5A: ESI Payable Head

05 ESI Heads in Employee Payroll Structure

Now include the ESI PayHeads (or modify the Pay Structure) as described earlier (F-6A).

06 ESI Processing

During Salary Payroll processing, the Employees Contribution is deducted from the Employee Pay. However, the Employer's contribution is paid alongwith Employer's Contribution to the Government authorities. To compute and provide for Employer's Contribution to ESI, you have to create a Payroll Voucher

Salary Details Alteration — ABC Consultants — Ctrl + M

Name : **Aloke Kumar Ghosh (2014/07)**
Under : **Officers**
(*Primary*)

Salary Details

Effective From	Pay Head	Rate	Per	Pay Head Type	Calculation Type	Computed On
1-Jul-2015						
	Basic Salary	12,000.00	Months	*Earnings for Employees*	*On Attendance*	
	HRA			*Earnings for Employees*	*As Computed Value*	*Basic Salary*
	Employer's Cont to ESI			*Employer's Statutory Contributions*	*As Computed Value*	*(Basic Salary + HRA) + DA*
	Employees Cont to ESI			*Employees' Statutory Deductions*	*As Computed Value*	*Basic Salary + HRA*
	Employees P F Cont			*Employees' Statutory Deductions*	*As Computed Value*	*On Current Earnings Total*
	Employer's Contribution to PF			*Employer's Statutory Contributions*	*As Computed Value*	*Employees P F Cont - Employer's Cont to Pension Fund*
	Employer's Cont to Pension Fund			*Employer's Statutory Contributions*	*As Computed Value*	*On Current Earnings Total*
	Professional Tax			*Employees' Statutory Deductions*	*As Computed Value*	*On Current Earnings Total*

F-6A: ESI Pay Heads in Employee Pay Head Structure

Payment Voucher creation has been explained earlier. At Payment Voucher creation, click A:Payrol Auto Fill to get Payroll Auto Fill screen (F-7B). At Payroll Auto Fill screen (F-7B).:

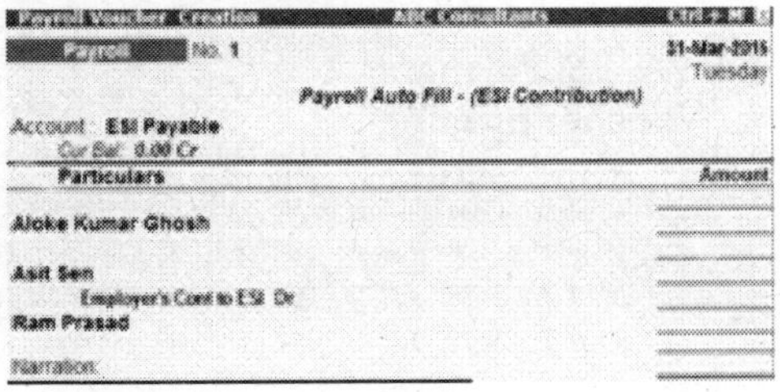

F-7A: Payroll Voucher for ESI Processing

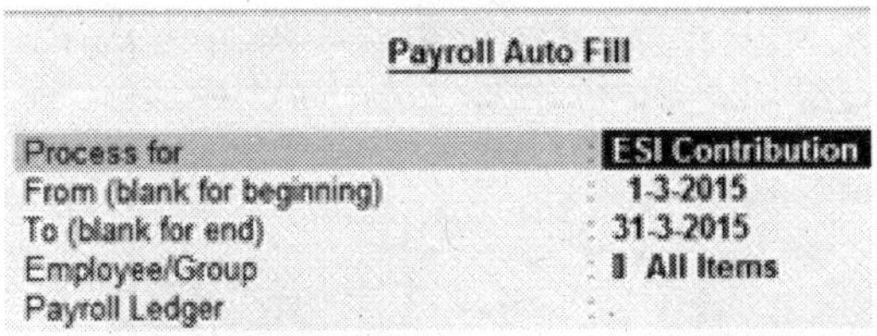

F-7B: ESI Process

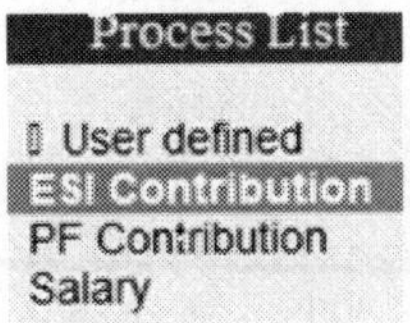

F-7C: Process selection list

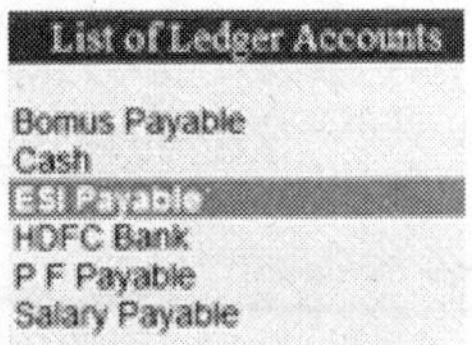

F-7D: Payables Ledger selection list

At *Payroll Auto Fill screen* (F-7B), enter as follows:

- **Process**: At *Process For*, select *ESI Contribution* from the list (F-7C)
- **Period:** At From / To enter the period Dates
- **Employee Group**: At Employee Group, select the Employee Group from the list
- **Payroll Ledger**: At Payroll Ledger, select *ESI Payable* Ledger Account, from the list of all Payable Ledger Accounts (F-7D)

Payment Details: At Payment Voucher entry screen (F-7A), set *Yes* at *Provide Details* to get *Payment Details* screen, where enter the details of ESI payment, which are printd in ESI Challan & ESI Reports

Save the Voucher

07 ESI Payment

Having completed the ESI Process, you may now make payment for ESI in respect of Employers & Employees Contribution to ESI, through Payment Voucher (F-8A).

Payment Voucher creation has been explained earlier. At *Payment Voucher* creation screen, click *A:Payroll Auto Fill* to get *Payment Auto Fill* screen (F-8B).

At *Payroll Auto Fill screen* (F-8B), enter as follows:

- **Process:** At *Process For*, select *ESI Challan* from the list
- **Period:** At *From / To*, enter the period Dates
- **Voucher Date**: Enter the Voucher Date of the Payment Voucher
- **Employee Group**: At Employee Group, select the Employee Group from the list

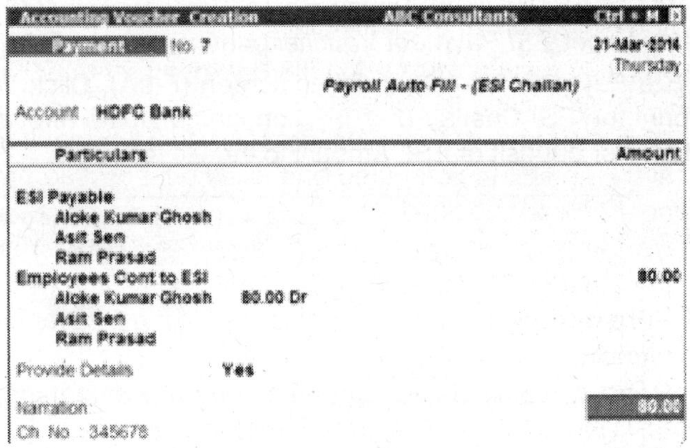

F-8A: ESI payment Voucher

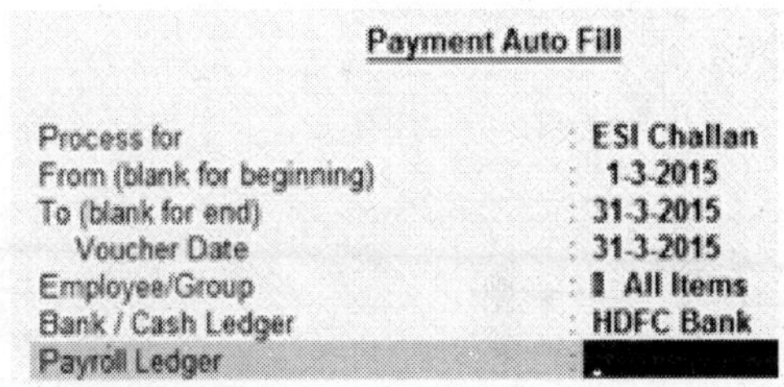

F-8B: Payroll Auto Fill

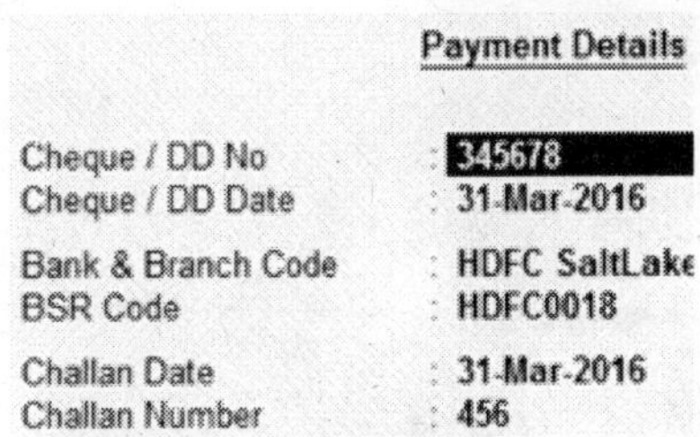

F-8C: ESI payment details

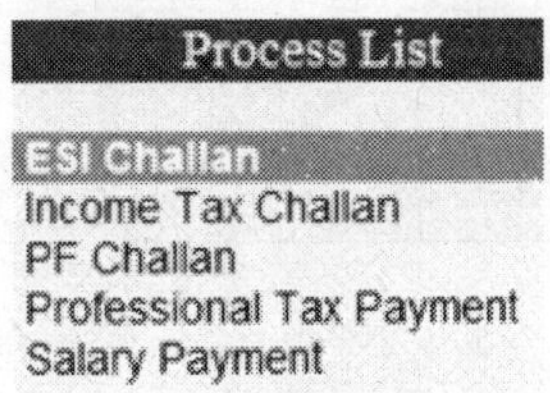

F-8D: Process selection List

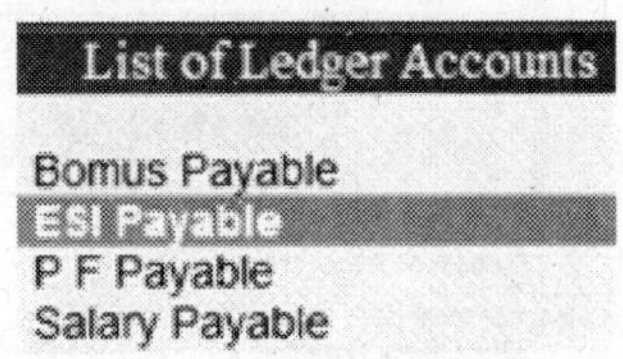

F-8E: ESI Payable Account selection

- **Cash / Bank Ledger**: Select the Cash / Bank Ledger from which the payment is made
- **Payroll Ledger:** Select *ESI Payable* Ledger from the list of Payable Ledger Accounts

Now you get the ESI Payment Details screen (F-8C) to enter the respective details of Payment

The Payment Voucher (F-12A) now gets auto created showing the ESI amount paid in respect of each head in respect of each Employee.

08 ESI Challan

To deposit the ESI Amount Payable, you have to print the ESI Challan with relevant details of payment. To print the ESI Challan, having created the ESI payment Voucher entry

(F-8A), at ESI Payment Voucher entry screen, click *P:Print* button to get *ESI Payment Voucher* printing screen (F-9A)

At *ESI Payment Voucher* printing screen (F-9A), Click Yes to print the ESI Challan (F-10A), containing all the relevant details, for deposit of ESI. Amount to the Government.

F-9A: ESI Payment Voucher printing screen

Report Titles

Payment Voucher

Print Challan ? **Yes**

EMPLOYEES' STATE INSURANCE CORPORATION

Challan Form for Deposit in A/C No.1

Original
For Bank

Employer's Code :

Date	Month	Year
31	03	2015

Bank & Branch Code : **HDFC Salt Lake**

Name & Address of the Factory or Establishment **ABC Consultants, 12 Pitambar Rd, Kolkata, E-Mail :info@abcdef.in**

Mode of Payment [Tick mode used] Cash ☐ Cheque ☐ DD ☐

Cheque/DD No. : 345678 Dated 31 | 03 | 2015

Drawn on (Name of the Bank) HDFC Bank Period of Contribution Month 03 Year 2015

Nature of Payment [Tick] Regular Contribution ☐ Interest ☐ Damages ☐ Others ☐

No. of Employees Total Wages Rs. Ps.

Employees' Contribution	80.00
Employer's Contribution	
Interest	
Damages	
Others	
Total	80.00

Total Amount (in words) **INR Eighty Only.**

R.O. Demand Letter No. & Date

Date of Presentation	Date of Clearing
BANK SEAL	BANK SEAL

Signature

Name & Designation-Seal of Authorised Signatory

(Acknowledgement)

(to be filled by Depositor)

Received Rs. 80.00

(INR Eighty Only.)

For use in Bank

Bank Scroll No.

Date

Authorised signature & seal of the Receiving Bank

In cash/by Cheque/DD No. 345678 Dated 31-Mar-2015

(subject to realisation) drawn on HDFC Bank (Bank) in favour of ESIC A/C No.1

(For Bank Branch Code see on reverse)

Note:Please put cross (x) mark in blank boxes

F-10A: ESI Challan

Provident Fund

01 P F Statutory Details

Having activated Payroll Statutory Features (F-2A/04-02), further set *Yes* at *Set / Alter Payroll Statutory Details* to get *Payroll Statutory Details* screen (F-1A). At *Payroll Statutory Details*, enter the relevant details, as follows:

Payroll Statutory Details

Provident Fund

Company Code	: WBKOL1234567123
Company Account Group Code	: 123456
Company Security Code	: 567890

F-1A: P F Statutory Details Entry

- **Company PF Code:** At *Company Code*, enter the 15 letter PF Code (2+3+7+3) as allotted by P F Department. This Code is printed in P F Statutory Reports
- **Company Group Code:** At *Company Account Group Code*, enter P F *Company Group Code*, as allotted by P F Department, if any. This Code is printed in P F Statutory Reports
- **Company Security Code:** At *Company Account Group Code*, enter P F *Company Group Code*, as allotted by P F Department, if any. This Code is printed in P F Statutory Reports

02 Employees' P F Deduction Pay Head

Some amount is deducted towards Employees Contribution to PF, under PF Rules. So, you have create Employees P F Contribution Pay Head (F-2A) to deduct the amount of PF Contribution from Employee Salary Pay Head creation has been explained earlier. The process of creation of Employees' P F Deduction Pay Head (P-2A), is described below

- **Pay Head Type:** At *Pay Head Type*, select *Employees' Statutory Deductions* from the list of Pay Head Types (F-3A).
- **Statutory Pay Type:** Having selected the *Pay Head Type* as above, at Statutory Pay Type, select *P F Account No 1* from the list (F-4A)
- **Parent Account Group:** At *Under* select Current Liabilities (or Provision) from the Account Group list
- At *Calculation Type*, As Computed Value is auto selected (you cannot change it).

Pay Head Creation — ABC Consultants

Name : Employees P F Cont — Total Op. Bal.

Pay Head Info

Pay Head Type	: Employees' Statutory Deductions
Statutory Pay Type	: PF Account (A/c No. 1)
Under	: Current Liabilities
Affect Net Salary	? Yes
Name to appear in Payslip	: PF
Calculation Type	: As Computed Value
Calculation Period	: Months

Rounding Info

Rounding Method : Normal Rounding — Limit : 1

Computation Info

Compute : On Current Earnings Total

Effective From	From Amount	Amount Upto	Slab Type	Value Basis
1-Apr-2015		6,500.00	Percentage	12 %
	6,500.00		Value	780

Opening Balance (on 1-Apr-2015) :

F-2A: Employees' P F Deduction (A/c 1) Pay Head

List of Pay Head Types

- Not Applicable
- Bonus
- Deductions from Employees
- Earnings for Employees
- **Employees' Statutory Deductions**
- Employer's Other Charges
- Employer's Statutory Contributions
- Gratuity
- Loans and Advances
- Reimbursements to Employees
- Tax paid by Employer on Perquisites

F-3A; Pay Head Type List

Computation On

- On Current Deductions Total
- **On Current Earnings Total**
- On Current SubTotal
- On Specified Formula

F-2B: Computation Method List

Employees' Statutory Deductions

- Employee State Insurance
- Income Tax
- **PF Account (A/c No. 1)**
- Professional Tax
- Voluntary PF (A/c No. 1)

F-4A: Employees Statutory Deduction List

02.1 P F Computation Info

At the right Part, you get Computation Info screen. The process of entry of Computation Info has been explained earlier. Here we discuss about set up details for *Employees P F Contribution* Account:

Computation Method: At *Compute*, select *on Current Earnings Total* from the list (F-2B), as P F is computed on Earnings.

Effective Date: At Start From, the Financial Start Date is carried by default, at the first instance

Slab Range & Rate: Now enter the Range & corresponding rates for each Slab, as follows:

- **Slab Lower Amount:** At *From Amount*, enter the Slab *Lower* range amount in first slab, this is skipped, indicating zero as Starting Range of first slab)

- **Slab Upper Limit:** At *Amount Upto*, enter the Slab *Upper* limit amount. In the last slab, the Upper Limit is left blank
- **Slab Type:** At *Slab Type*, select *Percentage* from List of Slabs, as P F Contribution is computed as Percentage on Total Earnings.
- **Rate:** At *Value Basis*, enter the Rate of Percentage of P F Deduction on Earnings
    - o **Ceiling on P F Contribution:** However, there is ceiling on P F Contribution. P F is deductible upto Earnings of Rs 6500. So, in the 2nd slab, for the Range above 6500, specify Value and enter Rs 780 (12.5% on 6500 max).

03 Employees Voluntary P F Account

Some P F Schemes offer additional contribution by employees to Provident Fund (Employer's Contribution remain same). Create *Employees Voluntary P F Head* (F-5A), In the same way, as *Employees P F Account* (F-2A to F-4A) as explained above. If there are several Rates of Voluntary Contribution, you have to create separate Head for each of them

- **Pay Head Type:** At *Pay Head Type*, select *Employees' Statutory Deductions* from the list of Pay Head Types (F-4B).
- **Statutory Pay Type:** Having selected the *Pay Head Type* as above, at Statutory Pay Type, select *Voluntary P F (A/c No 1)* from the list (F-4A)
- **Parent Account Group:** At *Under* select *Current Liabilities* from the Account Group list
- **Calculation Type:** At *Calculation Type*, *As Computed Value* is auto selected (you cannot change it).

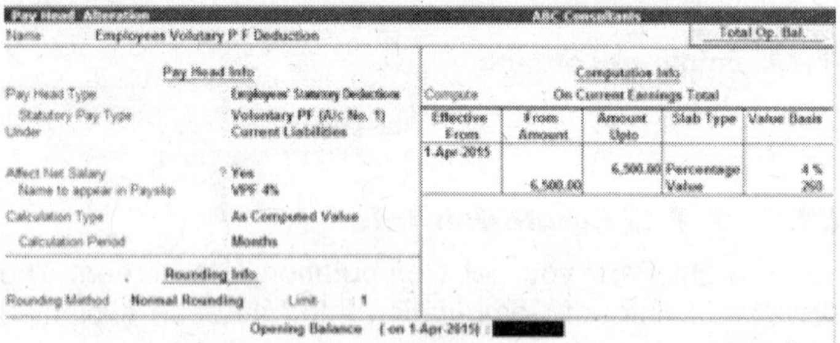

F-5A: Employees P F Voluntary Deduction Head

P F Computation Info: At the right Part, you get Computation Info screen. The process of entry of Computation Info has been explained earlier. Here we discuss about set up details for *Employees Voluntary P F Contribution* Account:

Computation Method: At *Compute*, select *on Current Earnings Total* from the list (F-2B), as Voluntary P F is computed on Earnings.

Effective Date: At Start From, the Financial Start Date is carried by default, at the first instance

Slab Range & Rate: Now enter the Range & corresponding rates for each Slab, as follows:

- **Slab Lower Amount:** At *From Amount*, enter the Slab *Lower* range amount in first slab, this is skipped, indicating zero as Starting Range of first slab)
- **Slab Upper Limit:** At *Amount Upto*, enter the Slab *Upper* limit amount. In the last slab, the Upper Limit is left blank
- **Computation Method:** At *Slab Type*, select *Percentage* from List of Slabs, as P F Contribution is computed as Percentage on Total Earnings.
- **Rate:** At Value Basis, enter the Rate of Percentage of P F Deduction on Earnings
    - o **Ceiling on P F Contribution:** However, there is ceiling on Voluntary P F Contribution. P F is deductible upto Earnings of Rs 6500. So, in the 2nd slab, for the Range above 6500, at *Slab* Type, specify *Value* and enter the upper limit (e.g Rs 260, being 4% on 6500 max, where the Voluntary P F Rate is 4%).

04 Employer's Contribution to Pension Fund

Like Employee's Contribution to PF, Employer has also to contribute an amount to Pension Fund. This is an additional amount contributed directly to Employees P F Account and so do not appear in Pay Slip / Pay, so set *No* at *Affect Net Salary*

- **Pay Head Type:** At *Pay Head Type*, select *Employees' Statutory Deductions* from the list of Pay Head Types (F-4B).
- **Statutory Pay Type:** Having selected the *Pay Head Type* as above, at *Statutory Pay Type*, select *E P S Account No 10* from the list (F-7B)
- **Parent Account Group:** At *Under* select Eploye Expenses from the Account Group list
- At *Calculation Type*, *As Computed Value* is auto selected (you cannot change it).

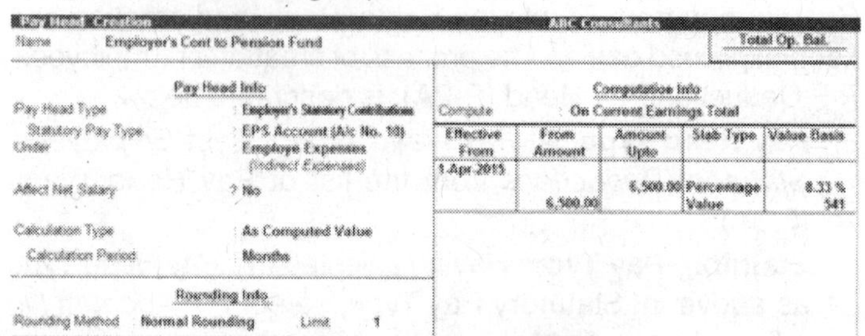

F-7A: Employer's Pension Fund Contribution Head

F-7B: Statutory Contribution Type List

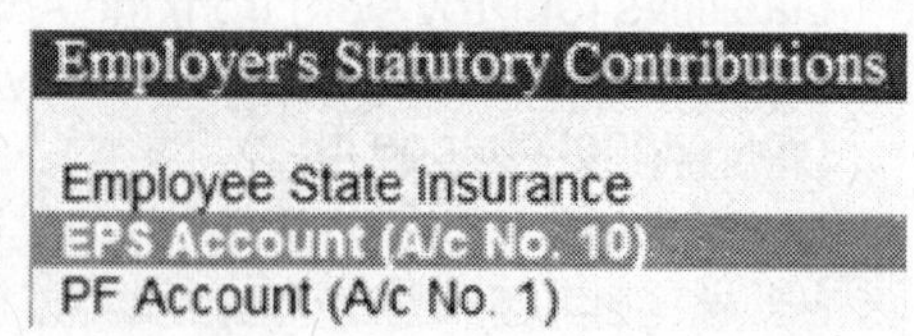

P F Computation Info: At the right Part, you get Computation Info screen. The process of entry of Computation Info has been explained earlier. Here we discuss about set up details for *Employer's Pension Fund Contribution* Account:

Computation Method: At *Compute*, select *on Current Earnings Total* from the list(F-2B), as Pension Fund Computation is computed on Earnings.

Effective Date: At Start From, the Financial Start Date is carried by default, at the first instance

Slab Range & Rate: Now enter the Range & corresponding rates for each Slab, as follows:

- **Slab Lower Amount:** At *From Amount*, enter the Slab *Lower* range amount in first slab, this is skipped, indicating zero as Starting Range of first slab)
- **Slab Upper Limit:** At *Amount Upto*, enter the Slab *Upper* limit amount. In the last slab, the Upper Limit is left blank
- **Computation Method:** At Slab Type, select *Percentage* from List of Slabs, as P F Contribution is computed as Percentage on Total Earnings.
- **Rate:** At Value Basis, enter the Rate of Percentage of P F Deduction on Earnings
  - o **Ceiling on P F Contribution:** However, there is ceiling on Voluntary P F Contribution. P F is deductible upto Earnings of Rs 6500. So, in the 2nd slab, for the Range above 6500, at *Slab* Type, specify *Value* and enter the upper limit (e.g Rs 541, being 8.33% on 6500 max, where the Voluntary P F Rate is 8.33%).

05 Employer's Contribution to Provident Fund

Like Employee's Contribution to PF, Employer has also to contribute an amount to Pension Fund. The Balance part of total employers contribution after the Contribution towards Pension Fund, is contributed to this account. For Example, if the Salary is 5000, the total contribution payable is 625 (12.5% of 5000). If 8.33%, i.e $s 417) has been deducted in Pension Fund, then te Balance Amount Rs 208 (i.e 625-417), payable by Employer to this account

Since it is directly contributed directly to Employees Pension Fund Account, it does do not appear in Pay Slip / Pay, so set *No* at *Affect Net Salary*

- **Pay Head Type**: At *Pay Head Type*, select *Employees' Statutory Deductions* from the list of Pay Head Types (F-4B).
- **Statutory Pay Type**: Having selected the *Pay Head Type* as above, at Statutory Pay Type, select *P F Account No 1* from the list (F-4C)
- **Parent Account Group**: At *Under* select Current Liabilities from the Account Group list
- **Calculation Type**: At *Calculation Type*, *As Computed Value* is auto selected (you cannot change it).

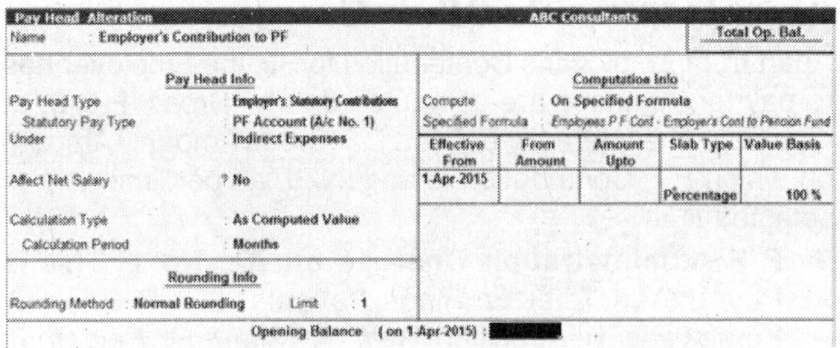
Pay Head Alteration — ABC Consultants
Name : Employer's Contribution to PF — Total Op. Bal.
Pay Head Info
Pay Head Type : Employer's Statutory Contributions
Statutory Pay Type : PF Account (A/c No. 1)
Under : Indirect Expenses
Affect Net Salary ? No
Calculation Type : As Computed Value
Calculation Period : Months
Rounding Info
Rounding Method : Normal Rounding Limit : 1
Computation Info
Compute : On Specified Formula
Specified Formula : Employees P F Cont - Employer's Cont to Pension Fund

Effective From	From Amount	Amount Upto	Slab Type	Value Basis
1-Apr-2015			Percentage	100 %

Opening Balance (on 1-Apr-2015) :

F-6A: Employer's P F Contribution Head

Compute : **On Specified Formula**

Function	Pay Head
Add Pay Head	Employees P F Cont
Subtract Pay Head	Employer's Cont to Pension Fund

F-6B: Computation Formula set up

P F Computation Info: At the right Part, you get Computation Info screen. The process of entry of Computation Info has been explained earlier. Here we discuss about set up details for *Employer's Contribution to PF* Head.

Computation Method: Contribution to PF is the Balance of Total Contribution Payable over the contribution to Pension Fund). As the Employer contributes equal the Employees Contribution, the Employer's Contribution to P F may be computed as Employees Contribution to PF – Employers Contribution to Pension Fund.

So, at *Compute*, select *on Specified Formula* from the list to get Specified Formula screen to specify the Computation Formula

At Function column select the function at Pay Head (it is auto selected) and select the Pay Head *Employees Contribution to P F* Head, from the list of Pay Heads Next, select Subtract Pay Head and select *Employees Cont to Pension Fund,* from the list of Pay Heads.

Consequently, the formula *Employees P F Cont – Employees Cont to Pension Fund* appear at Specified Formula at the entry screen (F-6A)

Effective Date: At Start From, the Financial Start Date is carried by default, at the first instance

Slab Range & Rate: Now enter the Range & corresponding rates for each Slab, as follows:

- **Slab Lower Amount:** At *From Amount*, enter the Slab *Lower* range amount in first slab, this is skipped, indicating zero as Starting Range of first slab)
- **Slab Limit:** At *Amount Form & Amount Upto*, leave blank
- **Computation Method:** At Slab Type, select *Percentage* from List of Slabs
- **Rate:** At Value Basis, enter 100% as the Amount thus Computed is to be contributed towards Employer's Contribution to PF

06 Employer's Other Charges

Apart from Employer's Contribution to PF, the Employer has to pay for, As these are computed on *P F Gross* (F-8A), at *Compute*, the internally defined P F Gross Amount (Amount on which P. F Contribution is deducted, as per limit set), is selected

- **P F Administration Charges on A/c No 1:** This is Payable on Total Earnings Payable, like P F for all Employees, at specified Rate. At *Statutory Pay Head* Type, select *Admin Charges A/c No 2* (F-8B)
- **Contribution to Deposit Linked Insurance:** This is payable on Total Earnings Payable, like P F for all Employees, at specified Rate. At *Statutory Pay Head* Type, select *EDLI Contribution A/c No 21*(F-8B)
- **Deposit Linked Insurance Administration Charges:** This is payable on Total Earnings Payable, like P F for all Employees, at specified Rate. At *Statutory Pay Head* Type, select *EDLI Administration Charges A/c No 22.* (F-8B)

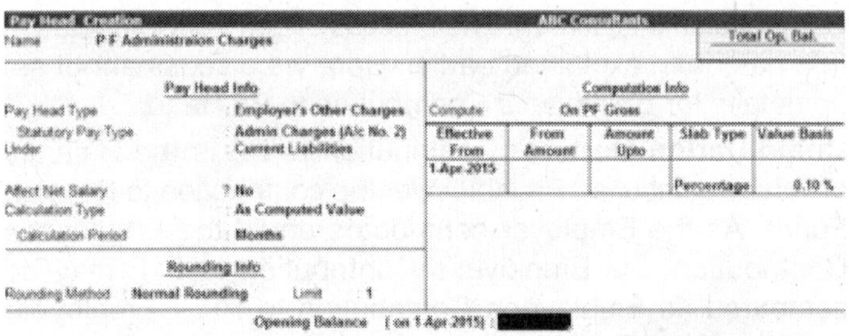

F-8A: Employer's P F Administration Charges Head

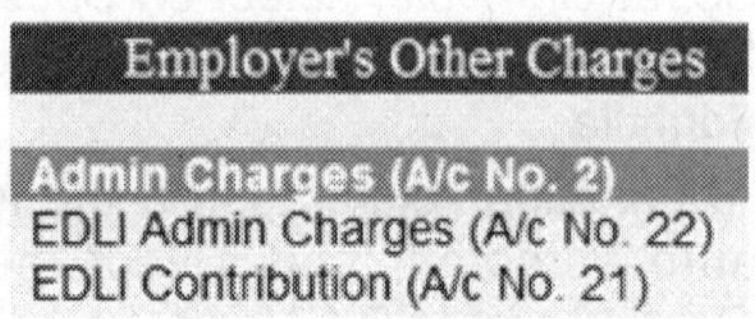

F-8B: Employer's P F Other Charges List

07 P F Payable Ledger

The deductions made form Employees Salary (Statutory & Voluntary), Employer's Contribution (to PF & Pension Fund) and employer's charges (Administration Charges etc) are to be deposited to P F Authority. So, these amount are credited to a P F Payable Ledger Account and the Payment is made by debiting the P F Payable Ledger Account. So, you have to create a P F Payable Ledger Account (like Salary Payable Ledger Account discussed earlier).

F-9A: P F Payable Head

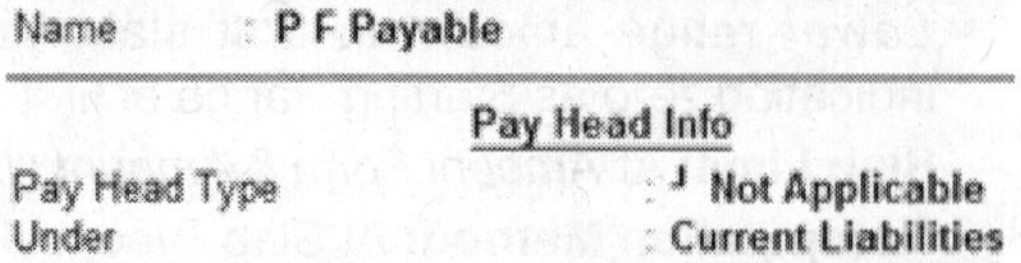

08 Employer's P F Contribution Process

During Pay roll Voucher processing, the Employees P F Contribution is deducted from Employee Salary. Apart from that Employer has to contribute their share. So, you have to process the Employer's P F Payable to compute the figures of various PF related heads and credit the P F Payable Ledger Account.

Payroll Voucher creation has been explained earlier. At Payroll Voucher entry screen (F-10A), click *A:Auto Fill* to get *Payroll Auto Fill screen* (F-10B).

At *Payroll Auto Fill screen* (F-10B), enter as follows:

- **Process:** At *Process For*, select P F Contribution.
- **Period:** At *From / To* enter the period Dates
- **Employee Group:** At Employee Group, select the Employee Group from the list
- **Payroll Ledger:** At Payroll Ledger, select P F Payable Ledger Account, from the list of all Payable Ledger Accounts (F-10C)

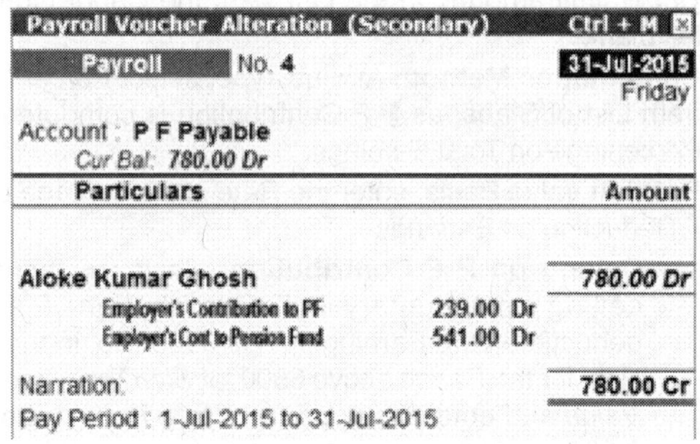

F-10A: P F Contribution Payable Voucher

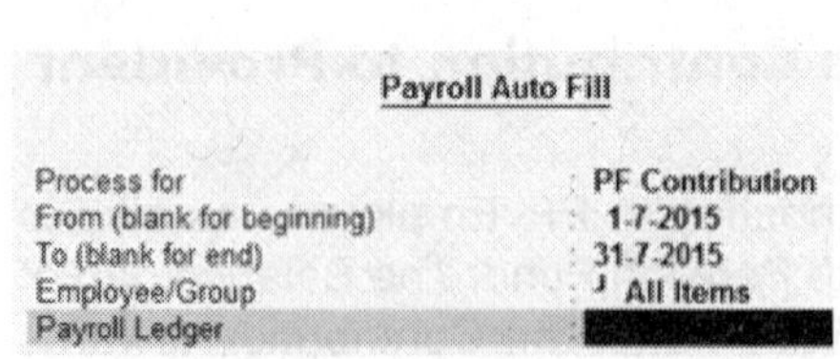

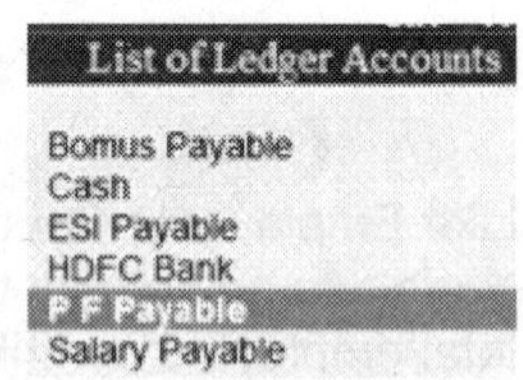

F-10B: P F Voucher Auto Fill

F-10C: P F Payable Ledger selection

You will get the Payroll Voucher auto filled with Employers Contribution (to P F & EPS Fund) figures.

09 P F Administration Charges Processing

During Salary Voucher processing, the Employees P F Contribution is deducted from Employee Salary. Further, during Employer's Contribution Processing, Employer's Contribution Payable are computed and a voucher is created. Further, the Employer has to Pay:

- PF Administration Charges
- Employer's Cont to DLI
- DLI Administration Charges

So, a Journal Voucher is to be created to computing the amount payable on the above 3 accounts

Journal Voucher creation has been explained earlier. At Journal Voucher entry screen, click A:*Other Charges Auto Fill* to get *Other Charges Auto Fill* screen

At *Other Charges Auto Fill screen* (F-11B), enter as follows:

- **Period:** At From / To enter the period Dates
- **Employee Group:** At Employee Group, select the Employee Group from the list
- **P F Admn Ch Ledger:** At *Expense Ledger*, select P F Administration Charges Ledger Account, from the list of Ledger Accounts.
- **Administration Charges (A/c No 2):** At *Administration Charges (A/c No 2)*, select the respective expense Ledger Account for *P F Administration Charges*, from the list of Employer's Statutory Expense Ledger Accounts
- **EDLI Cont A/c (A/c No 21):** At EDLI Contribution *(A/c No 21)*, select the respective expense Ledger Account for *Employer Contribution to EDLI A/c,* from the list of Employer's Statutory Expense Ledger Accounts
- **EDLI Admin. Charges (A/c No 22):** At EDLI Administration *Charges (A/c No 22)*, select the respective expense Ledger Account for *EDLI Administration Charges*, from the list of Employer's Statutory Expense Ledger Accounts

Journal No. 4 — 31-Oct-2015, Saturday

Particulars		Debit	Credit
Dr **P F Adm Ch**		75.00	
Dick	40.00 Dr		
Tom	30.00 Dr		
Harry	5.00 Dr		
Cr **P F Admn Exp**			75.00
Narration:		75.00	75.00
P F Adm Ch			

F-11A: P F Administration Charges Journal Voucher

Accounting Voucher Creation — Ctrl + M

Journal No. 4 — 31-Oct-2015, Saturday

Particulars		Debit	Credit
Dr **DLI Ch**		20.00	
Dick	8.00 Dr		
Tom	8.00 Dr		
Harry	4.00 Dr		
Dr **DLI Adm Ch**		6.00	
Dick	2.00 Dr		
Tom	2.00 Dr		
Harry	2.00 Dr		
Cr **P F Admn Exp**			26.00
Narration:		26.00	26.00
P F Admn Exp payable			

F-11B: DLI charges

The Voucher shows the amount computed in respect of each Pay Head in respect of each Employee

10 P F Payment Voucher

Having completed the above 3 processes and created the respective Vouchers, you may now create Payment Voucher for deposit of PF Payable to government account an print the Challan with respective details

To deposit the P F Payable with prescribed authorities, create Payment Voucher (F-12A).

Payment No. 1 — 31-Mar-2015, Tuesday

Payroll Auto Fill - (PF Challan)

Account : **HDFC Bank**

Particulars		Amount
P F Payable		4,488.00
Dick	2,250.00 Dr	
Tom	2,238.00 Dr	
Employees P F Dedn		1,488.00
Dick	750.00 Dr	
Tom	738.00 Dr	
Employees V P F		260.00
Dick	260.00 Dr	
Provide Details : **Yes**		
Narration:		6,236.00

F-12A: P F Payment Voucher

Payment Auto Fill

Process for	PF Challan
From (blank for beginning)	1-3-2015
To (blank for end)	31-3-2015
Voucher Date	31-3-2015
Employee/Group	Officers
Bank / Cash Ledger	HDFC Bank
Payroll Ledger	

F-12B: Payment Auto Fill

List of Ledger Accounts

Bomus Payable
ESI Payable
P F Payable
Salary Payable

F-12C:P F Payment Details

Process List

ESI Challan
Income Tax Challan
PF Challan
Professional Tax Payment
Salary Payment

F-12D:Process List

Payment Details

Cheque / DD No	345678
Cheque / DD Date	31-Mar-2015
Depositor Name	A K Ghosh
Bank Name	HDFC
BSR Code	HDFC0018
Challan Date	31-Mar-2015
Challan Number	4567

F-12E Payment details

Payment Voucher creation has been explained earlier. Here we explain the steps for P F Payment. At payment Voucher entry screen, click *A:Payroll Auto Fill* button to get Auto Fill screen (F-12B). The Payment Voucher (F-12A) gets auto filled showing the P F amount paid in respect of each head in respect of each Employee.

At *Payroll Auto Fill screen* (F-12B), enter as follows:

- **Process:** At *Process For*, select *P F Challan* from the list
- **Period:** At *From / To*, enter the period Dates
- **Voucher Date:** Enter the Voucher Date of the Payment Voucher
- **Employee Group:** At Employee Group, select the Employee Group from the list
- **Cash / Bank Ledger:** Select the Cash / Bank Ledger from which the payment is made
- **Payroll Ledger:** Select P F Payable Ledger from the list of Payable Ledger Accounts (F-12C)

At Provide Details (F-12A), set Yes to get the P F Payment Details screen (F-12E) to enter the respective details of Payment

11 P F Combined Challan

To deposit the P F Amount (in respect of all accounts in one Challan), you have to print the PF Challan with relevant details of payment. To print the PF Challan, having created the P F payment Voucher, at P F payment Voucher entry screen (F-12A), click P:*Print* button to get *P F Payment Voucher* printing screen (F-13A)

At *P F Payment Voucher Printing* screen (F-13A), the total Number of Employees for each account is computed on the basis of Employees for whom P F Account Number is entered in the Employee Master. Click Yes to print the P F Challan (P-13B), containing all the relevant details, for deposit of PF. Amount to the Government.

Report Titles	
Payment Voucher	
Print Challan	? Yes
Total No. of Subscribers (A/c.1)	: 2
Total No. of Subscribers (A/c.10)	: 2
Total No. of Subscribers (A/c.21)	: 2

F-13A: P F Payment Voucher printing screen

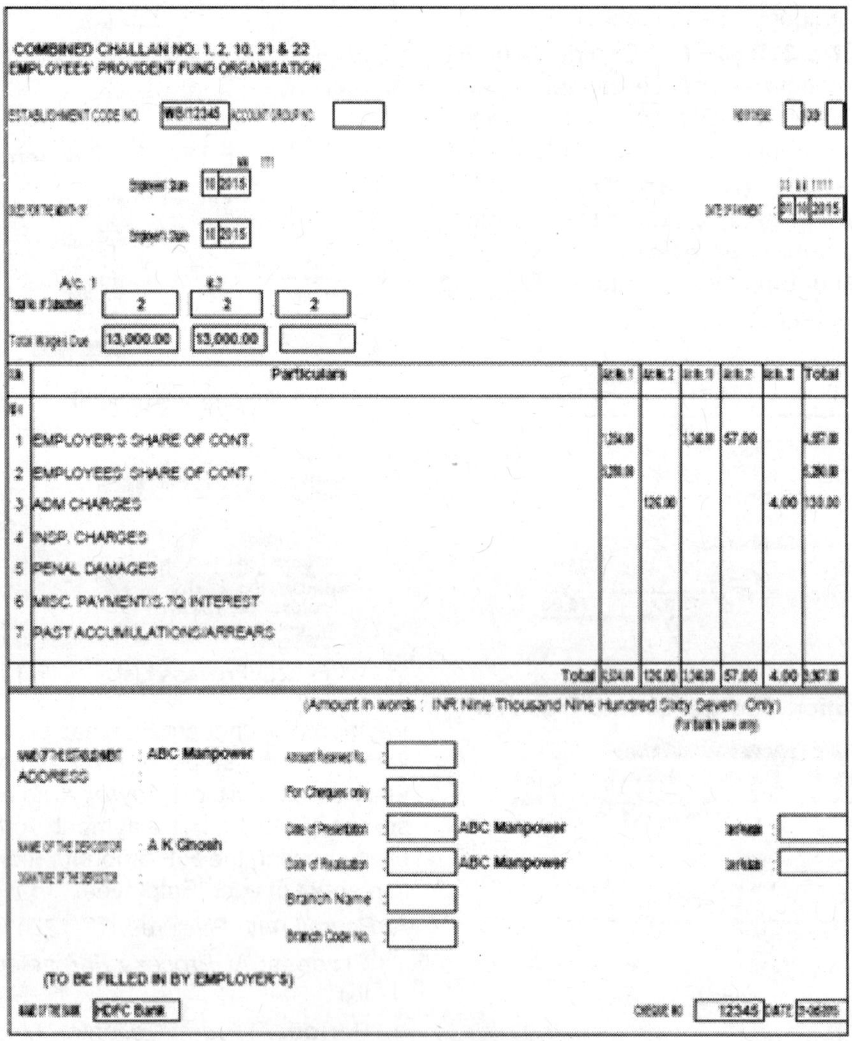
COMBINED CHALLAN NO. 1, 2, 10, 21 & 22
EMPLOYEES' PROVIDENT FUND ORGANISATION

ESTABLISHMENT CODE NO. WB/12345 ACCOUNT GROUP NO.

A/c. 1

Total No. of Subscribers	2	2	2
Total Wages Due	13,000.00	13,000.00	

Sl.	Particulars	A/c 1	A/c 2	A/c 10	A/c 21	A/c 22	Total
1	EMPLOYER'S SHARE OF CONT.	[illegible]		[illegible]	57.00		[illegible]
2	EMPLOYEES' SHARE OF CONT.	[illegible]					[illegible]
3	ADM CHARGES		126.00			4.00	130.00
4	INSP. CHARGES						
5	PENAL DAMAGES						
6	MISC. PAYMENT(S.7Q INTEREST						
7	PAST ACCUMULATIONS/ARREARS						
	Total	[illegible]	126.00	[illegible]	57.00	4.00	[illegible]

(Amount in words : INR Nine Thousand Nine Hundred Sixty Seven Only)

NAME OF THE ESTABLISHMENT : ABC Manpower
ADDRESS :
NAME OF THE DEPOSITOR : A K Ghosh
SIGNATURE OF THE DEPOSITOR :

For Cheques only :
Date of Presentation : ABC Manpower
Date of Realisation : ABC Manpower
Branch Name :
Branch Code No. :

(TO BE FILLED IN BY EMPLOYER'S)

NAME OF THE BANK HDFC Bank CHEQUE NO 12345

F-13B: P F Combined Challan

Payroll Statutory Pay Head Details — ABC Consultants — Ctrl + M

Pay Head Type: Employees' Statutory Deductions — 1-Apr-2015 to 31-Mar-2016

Particulars	Gross Amount	Statutory Details		Payable Amount	Paid Amount
		Percentage	A/c No.		
Employees P F Cont	6,500.00	12%	A/c No.1	780.00	
Grand Total				780.00	

F-14A: P F Statutory details Summary

Employee Breakup of Pay Head — Ctrl + M

Pay Head: Employees P F Cont — 1-Apr-2015 to 31-Mar-2016

Employee Name	Gross Amount	Payable
Aloke Kumar Ghosh	6,500.00	780.00
Grand Total	6,500.00	780.00

F-14B: Employee P F Summary

12 P F Statutory Head Details

At *Statutory Summary* (*Display>Payroll Reports>Statutory Reports>Summary*) drill down through Account Heads under P F Details, to get the *P F Summary* of selected PF Account (F-14A).

PF Employee Details: At *P F Summary* (F-14A), drill down through any head to get Employeewise details of P F Head.

13 Provident Fund Statutory Returns

At Gateway, select *Display>Payroll Reports>Statutory Reports>Provident Fund*, to get Provident Fund Returns Menu (F-15A)

Gateway of Tally ....
Display Menu ....
Payroll Reports ....
Statutory Reports ....

Provident Fund

Monthly

Form 5
Form 10
Form 12A
Monthly Statement
E-Challan Return (ECR)

Annual

Form 3A
Form 6A

E-Return

Quit

F-15A: P F Reports Menu

14 PF Form -5

This Form shows the employees who newly joined the Fund during the Report Period

At PF Reports Menu (*GoT>Display>Payroll Reports>Statutory Reports>Provident Fund:* F-15A*)*, select *Form 5* to get P F Form 5 Return (F-17A) printing screen. Enter the relevant details and type *Y* to print the Form -5 Monthly Return (F-16A).

FORM 5

THE EMPLOYEES' PROVIDENT FUNDS SCHEME, 1952
[Paragraph 36(2)(a) & THE EMPLOYEES PENSION SCHEME, 1995 Paragraph 20(2)]

Return of Employees' qualifying for membership of the Employees' Provident Fund, Employees' Pension Fund & Employees' Deposit Linked Insurance Fund for the first time during the month of October 2015 (To be sent to the Commissioner with Form2 (EPF & EPS))

Name and Address of the Factory / Establishment : ABC Manpower

Code No. of the Factory / Establishment : WB/12345

Sl No.	Account No.	Name of Employee (In block letters)	Father's Name or Husband's Name (in case of married women)	Date of Birth	Sex	Date of Joining the Fund	Total period of previous service as on the date of joining the Fund (Enclose Scheme Certificate if applicable)	Remarks
1	2	3	4	5	6	7	8	9
1	WBKOL/4567	HARRY	JOHN		Male	2-10-2015		

Date : 31-10-2015

Signature of the employer or other authorised Officer of the Factory /Establishment & Stamp of the Factory /Establishment

F-16A: P F Form 5

Report Titles
Form 5

From (blank for beginning)	:	1-7-2015
To (blank for end)	:	31-7-2015
Employee/Group	:	All Items
Sorting Method	:	Account Number
Appearance of Employee Names	:	Name Only
Date of Printing	:	31-7-2015

F-17A: P F Form 5 Printing screen

15 PF Form -10

This Form shows the Employees who left the Fund during the Report Period

FORM 10

THE EMPLOYEES' PROVIDENT FUNDS SCHEME, 1952
[Paragraph 36(2) (a) & (b) EMPLOYEES' PENSION SCHEME, 1995 (Paragraph 20(2))]

Return of the members leaving service during the month of : October 2015

Name and Address of the Factory / Establishment : ABC Manpower

Code No. of the Factory / Establishment : WB/12345

Sl No.	Account No.	Name of the Member (in block letters)	Father's Name or husband's Name (in case of married women)	Date of leaving service	Reason for leaving service	Remarks
1	2	3	4	5	6	7
1	WBKOL/4567	HARRY	JOHN	31-10-2015	Retirement	

Date : 31-10-2015

Signature of the employer or the authorised Officer
Stamp of the Factory/Establishment

Please state whether the member is (a)retiring according to para(69), (i) (a) or (b) of the scheme (b) leaving India for permanent settlement abroad (c) retrenchment (d) Pt. & total disablement due to employment injury (e) discharged (f) resigning from or leaving service (g) taking up employment elsewhere (The name and address of the Employers should be stated) (h) death; (i) attained the age of 58 years.

Certified that the member mentioned at serial No.__________ Shri__________ was paid/not paid retrenchment compensation of Rs__________ under the Industrial Dispute Act, 1947.

F-18A: P F Form 10

Report Titles	
Form 10	
From (blank for beginning)	: **1-7-2015**
To (blank for end)	: **31-7-2015**
Employee/Group	: **↵ All Items**
Sorting Method	: **Account Number**
Appearance of Employee Names	: **Name Only**
Date of Printing	: **31-7-2015**

F-18B: P F Form 10 Printing screen

At Gateway of Tally, select *Display>Payroll Reports>Statutory Reports>Provident Fund>Form 10* to get *P F Form 10 Return Printing* screen (F-18B). Enter the relevant details and type *Y* to print the Form -10 Monthly Return (F-18A).

16 PF Form -12A

This Monthly report shows the summary figures of amount of Employer's & Employees Contribution & Employers Charges deposited nto Government Account.

At Gateway of Tally, select *Display>Payroll Reports>Statutory Reports>Provident Fund>Form 10* to get P F Form 10 Return printing screen (F-19B). Enter the relevant details and type *Y* to print the *Form -10 Monthly Return* (F-19A).

(Only for Un-exampted Establishments)

EMPLOYEES' PROVIDENT FUNDS AND MISC. PROVISIONS ACT, 1952 EMPLOYEES' PENSION SCHEME[PARA 20 (4)]
FORM 12 - A (R)

(To be filled by the EPFO)

Group Code
Establishment status

Name and Address of the Establishment : ABC Manpower

Code No. : WB/12345

Currency period from : 1-Apr-2015 to 31-Mar-2016

Statement of Contribution for the month of : Oct-2015

	Wages on which Contributions are	Amount of Contribution		Amount of contribution remitted		Amount of Administrative charges due	Amount of Administrative charg-	Date Of Remittance (enclose triplicate copies of Challan)
		Recovered from the Employee	Payable by the Employer	Employee's Share	Employer's Share			
E.P.F. A/c No. 01	13,000.00	5,280.00	1,254.00	5,280.00	1,254.00	126.00	126.00	31-Oct-2015
Pension Fund A/c No. 10	13,000.00	NIL	3,246.00	NIL	3,246.00	NIL	NIL	31-Oct-2015
E.D.L.I A/c No. 21		NIL	57.00	NIL	57.00	4.00	4.00	31-Oct-2015

Total No. of Employees : 3
(a) Contract : 0
(b) Rest : 0
(c) PF Subscribers : 3

Name & Address of the Bank in which the amount is remitted : HDFC Bank

Details of Subscribers	E.P.F.	Pension Fund	E.D.L.I.
No. of Subscribers as per last month (vide Form 12A)	2	2	2
No. of New Subscribers (vide Form 5)	1	1	1
No. of Subscribers left service (vide Form 10)			
Net Total Number of Subscribers	3	3	3

Signature of the Employer with Official (Seal)

F-19A: PF Form 12A Monthly Return

Report Titles	
Form 12A	
From (blank for beginning)	: 1-7-2015
To (blank for end)	: 31-7-2015
Employee/Group	: ↵ All Items
Name & Address of the Bank	: HDFC Bank Salt Lake SEctor 1 Kolkata
Include VPF Account	: Yes
Number of Contract Employees	: 0
Number of Rest(Temporary Employees)	: 0

F-19B: PF Form 12A Monthly Return Printing

17 PF Monthly Statement

The monthly report shows employee wise details of P F Contribution for each head, for the Report Period.

At Gateway of Tally, select *Display>Payroll Reports>Statutory Reports>Provident Fund>Monthly Statement* to get P F Monthly Statement printing screen (F-20B). Enter the relevant details and type *Y* to print the P F Monthly Statement (F-20A).

EMPLOYEE PROVIDENT FUND SCHEME - Monthly Statement

Name & Address of the Factory or Establishment : **ABC Consultants**
12 Pitambar Rd
Kolkata

Statement for the Period : 1-Jul-2015 to 31-Jul-2015

S. No.	E-mp No	PF Number	Employee Name	Worked Days	Earned Wages	Employee's Contribution			Employer's Contribution		
						PF 12%	VPF	Total	EPS 8.33%	EPF 3.67%	Total
1	[illegible]	WB/123456	Aloke Kumar Ghosh	30	6,500.00	780.00		780.00	541.00	239.00	780.00
				Total	6,500.00	780.00		780.00	541.00	239.00	780.00

F-20A: P F Monthly Statement

Report Titles	
PF Monthly Statement	
From (blank for beginning)	: 1-7-2015
To (blank for end)	: 31-7-2015
Employee/Group	: ↵ All Items
Sorting Method	: Account Number
Appearance of Employee Names	: Name Only

F-20B: P F Monthly Statement Printing

FORM 3 A [REVISED]
EMPLOYEE'S PROVIDENT FUND ORGANISATION
THE EMPLOYEE'S PROVIDENT FUND SCHEME, 1952 [Paras 35 & 42]
AND THE EMPLOYEES' PENSION SCHEME, 1995 [Para 19]

Contribution Card for currency period from 1-Apr-2015 to 31-Mar-2016

1. Account No. : 45678
2. Name/Surname (in block letters) : DICK
3. Father's / Husband's Name :
4. Statutory Rate of Contribution : 12 %
5. Voluntary Higher Rate of Employee's contribution if any : 1,040.00
6. Name & Address of the Factory / Establishment : ABC Manpower
7. Code Number : WB/12345

Month	WORKER'S SHARE			EMPLOYER'S SHARE		Refund of Advance	No. of days period of non contributing service (if any)	Remarks
	Amount of Wages	E.P.F.12%	Rate of higher voluntary contribution (if any)	E.P.F. Difference between 12 % & 8.33% if any	Pension Fund Contribution 8.33%			
1	2	3	3a	4a	4b	5	6	7
April 2015 Paid in May 2015								
June 2015	6,500.00							
July 2015								
August 2015	6,500.00							
September 2015	6,500.00							
October 2015								
November 2015	6,500.00	3,000.00	1,040.00	627.00	1,623.00			
December 2015								
January 2016								
February 2016								
March 2016								
March 2016 Paid in April 2016								
Total	26,000.00	3,000.00	1,040.00	627.00	1,623.00			

Certified that the total amount of contribution (both shares) indicated in this Card i.e. Rs.4,667.00 has already been remitted in full in E.P.F. A/c No.1 & Pension Fund A/c No.10 Rs.1,623.00

Certified that the difference between the total of the contribution shown under Cols. 3, 3a, 4a & 4b of the above table and that arrived at on the total wages shown in column 2 at the prescribed rate is solely due to rounding off the contributions to the nearest rupee under the rules.

F-21A: PF Form 3A

Report Titles

Form 3A

From (blank for beginning)	:	1-7-2015
To (blank for end)	:	31-7-2015
Employee/Group	:	┘ All Items
Include VPF Account	:	Yes
Sorting Method	:	Account Number
Appearance of Employee Names	:	Name Only
Date of Printing	:	31-7-2015

F-21B: PF Form 3A printing

18 PF Form 3A

P F Form 3A is annual Contribution Card for each Employee.

At Gateway of Tally, select *Display>Payroll Reports> Statutory Reports>Provident Fund>Form 3A* to get Form 3A printing screen (F-21B). Enter the relevant details and type *Y* to print Form 3A (F-21A).

19 PF Form 6A

This is annual statement showing the summary of Contribution for each Employee

At Gateway of Tally, select *Display>Payroll Reports>Statutory Reports>Provident Fund>Form 6A* to get Form 6A printing screen (F-22B). Enter the relevant details and type *Y* to print Form 3A (F-22A).

FORM 6 A

THE EMPLOYEE'S PROVIDENT FUND SCHEME, 1952. [Paragraph 43]
AND THE EMPLOYEES' PENSION SCHEME, 1995 [Paragraph 20(4)]

Annual Statement of contribution for the currency period from 1-Apr-2015 to 31-Mar-2016

Name & Address of the Establishment	:	ABC Consultants 12 Pitambar Rd Kolkata
Statutory Rate of Contribution	:	12 %
Code No. of the Establishment	:	WBKOL1234567123
No. of members voluntarily contributing at a higher rate	:	0

SlNo.	Account Number	Name of the Member (in block letters)	Wages, retaining allowance (if any) & DA including cash value of food concession paid during the currency period	Amount of Worker's Contributions deducted from the wages on 12 % E.P.F.	Employer's Contribution E.P.F. Difference between 12 % & 8.33 %	Employer's Contribution Pension Fund 8.33 %	Refund of Advance	Rate of higher voluntary Contribution (if any)	Remarks
1	2	3	4	5	6	7	8	9	10
1	WB/123456	ALOKE KUMAR GHOSH	6,500.00	780.00	239.00	541.00			

F-22A: P F Form 6A

Report Titles

Form 6A

From (blank for beginning)	:	1-4-2015
To (blank for end)	:	31-3-2016
Employee/Group	:	┘ All Items
Sorting Method	:	Account Number
Appearance of Employee Names	:	Name Only

F-22B: P F Form 6A Printing

Statutory Reports Summary 04-06

01 Statutory Dues

We have so far described various Statutory Deduction from Employee Salary like Income Tax, PF, ESI, P Tax etc., which are to be deposited to Government Account. Here we describe a summary report of all dues payable to Government, to facilitate Payment to Government.

02 Statutory Dues Summary

The *Statutory Dues Summary* shows the summary of Statutory Deduction for each Statutory Heads (PF, ESI, P tax & Income Tax) for a specified period.

Payroll Statutory Summary Ctrl + M

Payroll Statutory Computation 1-Apr-2015 to 31-Mar-2016

Particulars	Payable Amount	Paid Amount
Provident Fund		
Employees' Statutory Deductions	7,028.00	7,028.00
Employer's Statutory Contributions	8,988.00	8,988.00
Employer's Other Charges	195.00	199.00
Employee State Insurance		
Employees' Statutory Deductions	1,069.00	1,069.00
Employer's Statutory Contributions	2,780.75	2,780.75
National Pension Scheme		
Employees' Statutory Deductions	10,952.00	16,240.00
Employer's Statutory Contributions	6,819.36	6,819.36
Professional Tax		
Employees' Statutory Deductions	200.00	200.00
Income Tax		
Employees' Statutory Deductions	400.00	400.00
Grand Total	38,432.11	43,724.11

F-1A: Statutory Summary

At Gateway of Tally, select *Display>Payroll Reports>Statutory Reports>Summary* to get Statutory Summary (F-1A).

Configuration

Format	: Condensed
Show Provident Fund Details	? Yes
Show Employee State Insurance Details	? Yes
Show Professional Tax Details	? Yes
Show TDS Details	? Yes

F-1B: Statutory Summary Configuration

F1: Detailed

F2: Period

F-1C: Buttons

Statutory Summary Configuration: At Statutory Summary (F-1A), click *F12:Configure* to get *Statutory Summary Configuration* screen (F-1B), to set the Configuration options as follows:

- **Format:** At *Format*, select Detailed to show the headwise computation details of each of the 4 Statutory Accounts, select Condensed (F-1A), to get only the headwise figures of Amount Payable & Amount Paid (F-1A).
- **P F Details**: At *Show Provident Fund Details*, set *Yes* to get the P F Account details, else set No, the PF Account details are not shown
- **ESI Details**: At *Show Employees State Insurance Details*, set *Yes* to get the ESI Account details, else set No, the ESI Account details are not shown
- **P Tax Details**: At *Show P Tax Details*, set *Yes* to get the P Tax Account details, else set No, the P Tax Account details are not shown
- **Income Tax Details**: At *Show TDS Details*, set *Yes* to get the Income Tax Deduction details, else set No, the Income Tax Deduction details are not shown

Drill Down: At Statutory Summary (F-1A), Drill Down through any of the heads to get Payroll Statutory Head details, of the respective Head.

Part 5

Attendance & Production

This Part describes the work measurement, Attendance & Production, the basis of computation of Pay for each Employee. It describes creation of various Units for Production, Attendance, Overtime & Leave types, entry of Production, Attendance & Leave in respect of each Employee, and computation of Pay based on Attendance, Leave, Overtime & Production.

Attendance & Production describes creation of various types of Attendance, Leave, Production & Overtime heads.

Attendance Heads explains creation of various Attendance, Leave, Production & Overtime heads and related Pay Heads

Attendance Entry describes creation of Attendance Voucher for entry of Attendance, Leave, Production & Overtime data.

Attendance Reports describes Display of reports relating to Attendance, Leave, Production & Overtime heads and Pay

Production Wages describes Production Wages reports of each employee bases on Production.

Overtime describes entry of Overtime Work, computation and display of Overtime Wages for each Employee

Attendance Heads 05-01

01 Attendance Heads

You may keep Attendance, Leave & OT records for each Employee and also compute Pay based on Attendance.

To keep Attendance, Leave & OT data, you have to first create respective Attendance Heads.

The following Table shows a typical example of various of Attendance Types, like

- Attendance
- Paid Leave
- Unpaid Leave
- Holidays
- Overtime etc.

02 Attendance Head Entry

At *Payroll Info* Menu, select *Attendance / Production Types* to get *Attendance Master* Menu (F-1A).

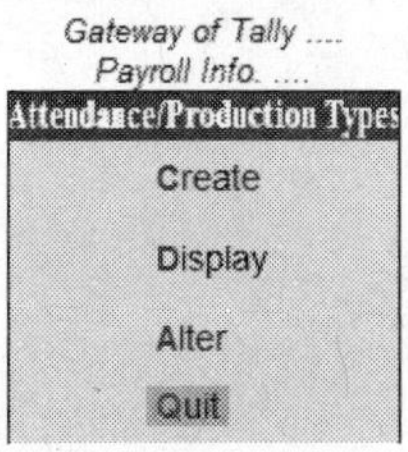

F-1A: Attendance Master Menu

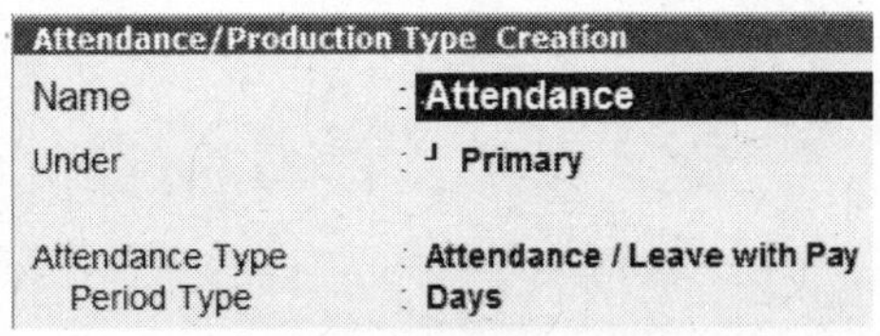

F-2A: Attendance Heads (With pay)

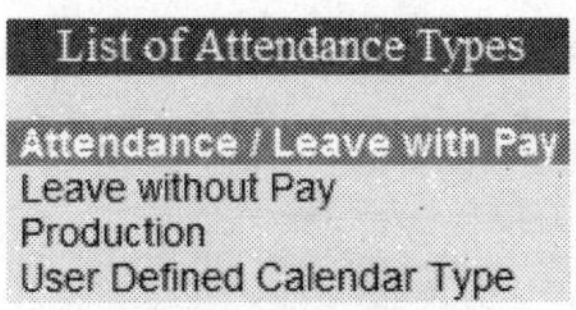

F-2B: Attendance Type List

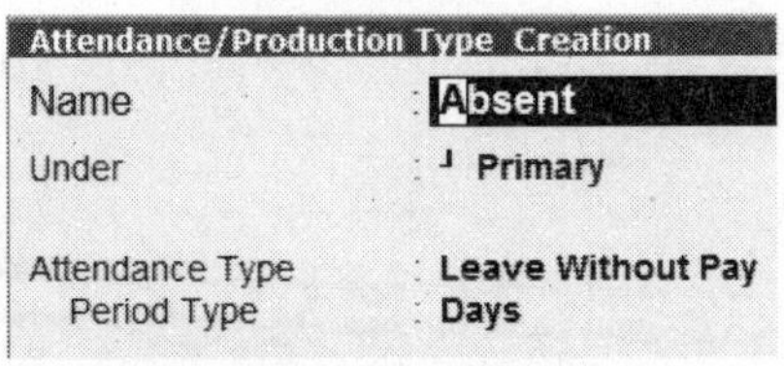

F-2C: Attendance Heads (Without pay)

You may also create Attendance Heads under a created Attendance Heads to create several Attendance Heads under an Attendance Head Group, to organise Attendance / Production Heads as per your own needs.

At *Attendance / Production Types* Menu (F-1A) select *Create* to get *Attendance / Production* Head creation screen (F-2A). Now enter as follows:

- **Name**: At *Name*, enter the *Attendance Type* Head, e.g Paid Leave
- **Parent Head**: At *Under,* select the Parent Attendance Type Group. For First head, you must select *Primary* (Attendance Type Group is explained later)
- **Attendance Type**: Select the Attendance Type from the list (F-2B)
  - o **Production Type:** Select *Production* for Production Type Head as explained later under Production Section
  - o **Attendance & Leave Type:** In case of heads for *Attendance / Leaves*, select from the list (F-2B) as follows:
    - **Attendance & Leave with Pay:** Select *Attendance & Leave with Pay* for Attendance / Leave Heads with pay (e.g for Actual Attendance & Leave with Pay).
    - **Leave without Pay:** Select *Leave without Pay* for Leave Days with Pay
    - **User Defined Calendar Type:** Select *User Defined Calendar Type*, for specific user Defined Attendance Period, as explained later

03 Attendance Group

To organize Attendance heads organized in structured manner, you may create Attendance Group and then create Attendance Head under such Groups. Attendance Groups are created in the same as creation of Attendance Types as explained (F-3A). To create next level Attendance Types under the Attendance Group, select the Attendance Group at *Under* field (F-3B)

F-3A: Attendance Head Group creation

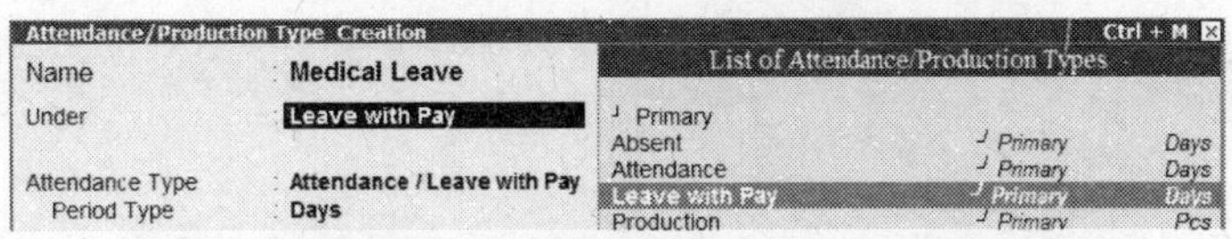

F-3B: Attendance Head under Attendance Group

We give some common examples of Attendance Groups and the child Attendance Heads normally used by Industrial & Commercial organizations:

Attendance

- **In-Office Attendance (IA)**: Physical attendance at office
- **Out-Office Attendance (OA)**: Out of office duty attendance. This is normally required to include / exclude any allowance which is given or disallowed for Out of Office Duty. For example, an employee gets Daily Allowance OA and Tiffin Allowance for IA.

Paid Leave

- **Privilege Leave (PL)**: Pre sanctioned Long leave (more than 3 days in a stretch)
- **Casual Leave (CL)**: Sudden emergency short leave, pre/post sanctioned (upto 3 days in a stretch)
- **Sick Leave (SL)**: Leave due to sickness, may be pre/post sanctioned
- **Maternity Leave (ML)**: Pre sanctioned Leave for pregnant female employees during pre / post natal period.
- **Education Leave (EL)**: Pre sanctioned Leave for Education / Training

Holidays

- **Weekly Holidays (WH)**: Weekly off days for employee (like Sunday, Saturday or any specified weekly off day).
- **Festival Holidays (FH)**: Other holidays (like Independence Day, Republic Day etc and other declared holidays for religious functions etc.)

Leave Without Pay

- **Unpaid Leave**: Sanctioned Without Pay Leave
- **Absent:** Without Pay Absent without official sanction.

Overtime

- **Normal OT (NOT)**: Over time work on Normal Working Days
- **Holiday OT (HOT)**: Over time work on weekly off days or holidays.

The two kinds of OT allows OT pay computation based on different rates, e.g: Normal OT may be based on 1.5 times of Normal Pay Rate while Holiday OT may be twice the Normal Pay Rate.

Having different kind of Attendance, Leave & Holidays, you may apply separate computation formulas & rules for each of them, as well as get better analysis of Attendance & Absenteeism.

Attendance Entry 05-02

01 Attendance Voucher Entry

Having created the Attendance Heads, you can now enter the Attendance data in respect of Attendance, Leave & OT Time for each specified Attendance Head.

While generating the Payroll voucher through Auto Fill, Tally uses Attendance Voucher data

Attendance Voucher Creation — Ctrl + M

Attendance No. 1 — 1-May-2014, Thursday

Employee Name	Employee Number	Attendance/Production Type	Value	Unit
Surya Narayan Ghosh	0105	Attendance	28	Days
Surya Narayan Ghosh	0105	Leave with Pay	2	Days
Surya Narayan Ghosh	0105	Absent	1	Days

F-1A:Employee selection for Attendance entry

List of Attendance/Production Types

Absent	Primary	Days
Attendance	Primary	Days
Leave with Pay	Primary	Days
Production	Primary	Pcs

F-1B:Attendance Type List

At Gateway, select *Payroll Voucher* to get Payroll Voucher Entry screen. At Payroll Voucher Entry screen, click *F5:Attendance* to get *Attendance Entry* screen (F-1A).

Now enter as follows (F-1A):

- **Employee:** At *Employee Name*, select the Employee from the list of Employees. The corresponding Employee Number is displayed at *Employee Number* column, for information
- **Attendance Type**: At *Attendance / Production Head Type* column, select the Attendance Head from list (F-1B)
- **Attendance**: At *Value* column, enter the number of Days for the selected Attendance Type

The Attendance Unit (e.g Days) is displayed at Unit Column

This way, you select Employee & Attendance Head and enter the value for each Attendance Head and each Employee. Each time the Employee Name is to be selected even while continuing entry for the same employee.

02 Attendance Entry Auto Fill

In manual entry as explained above (F-1A), you have to select Attendance Head & Employee Name each time, which takes considerable time for Attendance Entry. To enter values for a specific Attendance Head, for All Employees or Group of Employees, at Attendance Voucher entry screen as described above, click *A:Attd Auto Fill* button to get *Attendance Auto Fill* screen (F-2B)

Attendance Voucher Creation — Ctrl + M

Attendance No. 1 — 31-Jul-2015, Friday

Employee Name	Employee Number	Attendance/Production Type	Value	Unit
Surya Narayan Ghosh	0105	Attendance	22	Days

Narration: Attendance for July

F-2A Attendance Entry Auto Fill

Attendance Auto Fill

Voucher Date	: 31-7-2015
Employee/Group	: All Items

Auto Fill Values

Attendance/Production Type	: Attendance
Default Value to Fill	: 0
(Value entered above will be prefilled for all the Employees)	
Sort by	: Employee Name

F-2B: Auto Fill Screen

At *Attendance Auto Fill* screen (F-2B), enter as follows:

- **Voucher Date**: Enter the Date of Attendance Voucher (normally the last date of relevant Pay Period)
- **Employee Range:** At *Employee Group*, Select from the List (F-2C) as follows:
    - o **Employee Group:** Select the Employee Group, to make Attendance Entry for all Employees of the selected Employee Group.
    - o **One Employee:** Select an Employee to make Attendance Entry for the selected Employee
    - o **All Employees:** Select All Items to make Attendance Entry for All Employees
- **Attendance Type**: At *Attendance / Production Type*, select the Attendance Type for which you like to make Attendance Entry from the list of Attendance Types (F-2D). You have to enter data for each Attendance Type separately. In one entry session, you can enter data for one selected Attendance Type only.
- **Default Carrying Value:** Enter the default value (is most common for the Attendance Type) that would be carried by default for each employee, to reduce data entry time. For Example:

    22 for Attendance if there are 22 working days in the month

6 for Holidays, if there are 6 Holidays (including Sundays) in the month

0 for Absent

- **Employee Sorting Order**: At *Sort By*, select the Sorting Order from the list (F-2E), as you like the Employee Names for Attendance Entry to appear during Attendance Entry, to facilitate faster entry.

Attendance Entry: Now you will get the Attendance Entry screen similar to manual Attendance entry screen described earlier (F-1A).

At *Employee Name* column, select the Employee from the list (as per selection of Employee Group – F-2C). The Employee Number and the selected Attendance Type (F-2D) are displayed beside at the respective columns. At *Value* column the default value for the Attendance Type as set (F-2B) is carried, which you may change as necessary.

This way, select Employee on by one and enter the respective Attendance Values.

This way, enter the data for each Attendance Type. Though, you have to enter Attendance in several process (separately for each Attendance Tye), instead of ONE compact grid type Form, from practical point of view, this method is useful if the input document often is available for each type of Attendance separately.

List of Employees / Group	
All Items	
Officers	*Employee Group*
Surya Narayan Ghosh	*Employee*

F-2C:Employe Group

List of Attendance/Production Types		
Absent	*Primary*	*Days*
Attendance	*Primary*	*Days*
Leave with Pay	*Primary*	*Days*
Production	*Primary*	*Pcs*

F-2D: Attendance Type

Sorting Methods
Employee Name
Employee Number

F-2E: Sorting Method

Attendance Reports

01 Attendance Reports

At Payroll Reports Menu you get the following reports related to Attendance:

- Attendance Sheet
- Attendance Register

02 Attendance Sheet

The Attendance Sheet is similar to Pay Sheet, with columns created for each Attendance Heads

At *Gateway of Tally,* select *Display > Payroll Reports > Attendance Sheet* to get Attendance Sheet (F-1A)

Attendance Sheet — Ctrl + M

For All Employees — 1-Apr-2015 to 31-Mar-2016

Particulars	Rod Cutting	Production	Absent	Attendance	Leave with Pay
Primary Cost Category	230 Pcs	230 Pcs	2 Days	52 Days	8 Days
Officers			2 Days	52 Days	8 Days
Aloke Kumar Ghosh			2 Days	52 Days	8 Days
Workers	230 Pcs	230 Pcs			
Ram Prasad	230 Pcs	230 Pcs			

F-1A: Attendance Sheet

Configuration

Remove Zero Entries	? Yes
Show Employees By Categories & Groups	? Yes
Show Category / Group Total	? Yes
Include Group Attendance/Production Types	? Yes
Display Production Types in Tail Units	? No
Format	: Detailed
Show Employee Number	? No
Expand all levels in Detailed Format	? Yes
Appearance of Names	: Name Only
Sorting Method	: Default

F-1B: Attendance Sheet Configuration

- F1: Condensed
- F2: Period
- F3: Company
- F7: Employee Filters

F-1C: Buttons

02.01 Attendance Group

At *Attendance Sheet Configuration* screen (F-1B), set *Yes* at *Include Group Attendance/Production Types* to print Group Attendance/Production Types in Attendance Sheet report

02.02 Attendance Units

At *Attendance Sheet Configuration* screen (F-1B), set *No* at *Display Attendance/Production Types in Tail Units* to display the Attendance in Compound Units (Fig 16-5), set *Yes* to Display Attendance in Compound Units in Tail units only.

03 Attendance Voucher Register

Attendance Voucher Register shows the details of Attendance Vouchers for the selected Period.

At *Gateway of Tally,* select *Display > Payroll Reports > Attendance Register* to get the monthwise break up of number of Attendance Voucher for the Current Period. Select any Month and set the Period to get Attendance Voucher Register (F-2A).

Voucher Register — Ctrl + M

List of All Attendance Vouchers — 1-Apr-2015 to 31-Mar-2016

Date	Particulars			Vch Type	Vch No.	Debit Amount	Credit Amount
31-5-2015	Aloke Kumar Ghosh - Attendance			Attendance	1		
	Aloke Kumar Ghosh	Attendance	22				
	Aloke Kumar Ghosh	Leave with Pay	8				
	Aloke Kumar Ghosh	Absent	1				
31-7-2015	Aloke Kumar Ghosh - Attendance			Attendance	2		
	Aloke Kumar Ghosh	Attendance	30				
	Aloke Kumar Ghosh	Absent	1				
31-12-2015	Ram Prasad - Rod Cutting			Attendance	3		
	Ram Prasad	Rod Cutting	230				

F-2A: Attendance Voucher Register

Configuration

Format	: Detailed
Show Narrations also	? No
Show Billwise Details also	? No
Show Cost Centre Details also	? No
Show Inventory Details also	? No
Show Bank Details also	? No
Appearance of Names	: Name Only
Sorting Method	: Default

F-2B: Attendance Voucher Register Configuration

- F1: Condensed
- F2: Date
- F2: Period
- F4: Chg Vch

F-2C: Buttons

Attendance Voucher Register Configuration: At *Attendance Voucher Register* (F-2A), click *F12:Configure* to get *Attendance Voucher Register Configuration* screen (F-2B) similar to Voucher Register. The Configuration options are not normally relevant to Payroll (these relate to Accounts & Inventory) and *Buttons* (F-2C) are similar.

Attendance Voucher Register Buttons: At *Attendance Voucher Register* (F-2A), you get Buttons similar to Voucher Register

Production Wages 05-04

01 Production

Workers' Wages may be computed on following basis:

- On Attendance
- On Production
- Both on Attendance & Production

We have discussed about Attendance. Now we discuss about Production Entry and computation of Production Wages.

02 Work Unit

Labour / Production may be measured in various Units. Often Pay is computed in various work units of time of work (Time units like Hr, Min) or Physical Units of Production (like Pcs, Kg etc), to pay for Normal Attendance, Overtime, Piece Rated Wages etc.

To create Work Unit, at Payroll Info Menu, select *Units (Work),* to get *Work Unit* menu (F-1A).

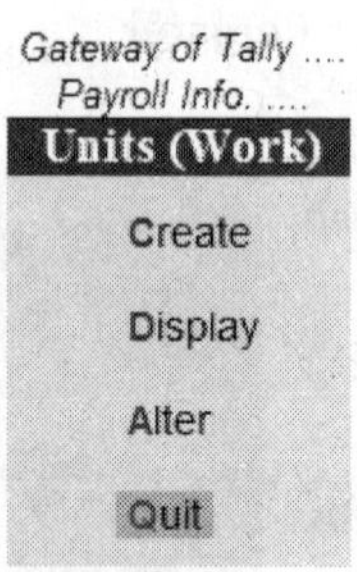

F-1A:Work Units Menu

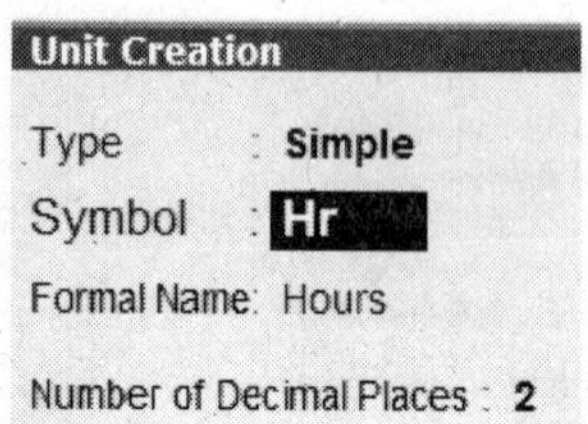

F-2A: Work Unit Creation

03 Simple Work Unit Creation

At Work Unit menu (F-1A), select *Create* to get Work Unit Creation screen (F-2A). Now enter as follows:

- **Type**: Select *Simple* to create a Simple Unit (if the cursor skips this field, press Shift+Tab to get the cursor here, if necessary).
- **Symbol**: Enter the symbol as will be printed in all Payroll reports (e.g: Hr for Hours)
- **Formal Name**: Enter the Formal Name of the Unit (this is only for reference to understand the Symbol and must be unique & different from Symbol)
- **Number of Decimal Places**: Enter the number of decimal places, e.g 2 so that you may enter days in fractional figures, like 1.50. If you enter zero, you will not be able to enter fractional number in the Attendance / Production entry using this Unit.

03.01 Simple Work Unit Alteration

To change the data of any Work Unit, at Unit Menu (F-1A), select *Alter* and then select the Unit to get Work Unit Alteration screen similar to Entry screen. Now change the data of any field. However, you cannot change the Unit Type data (the cursor skips this field). You cannot change Number of Decimal Places after you have entered Attendance / Production Data.

03.02 Work Unit Display

To Display the data of any Work Unit, at Work Unit Menu (F-1A), select *Display* and then select the Work Unit to Display the selected Work Unit record for information. Through *Display*, you cannot change any data.

04 Production Type

Now create Production Types (F-3A) & Production Head (F-3B) in the same way as Attendance Heads for each product / process.

Attendance / Production Type Master creation (*GoT>Payroll Info>Production/ Attendance Type)* has been described earlier. First create the *Production Type* (F-3A) Master. At *Under*, select Primary. At *Attendance Type*, select *Production* from *Attendance Type* List (F-3C).

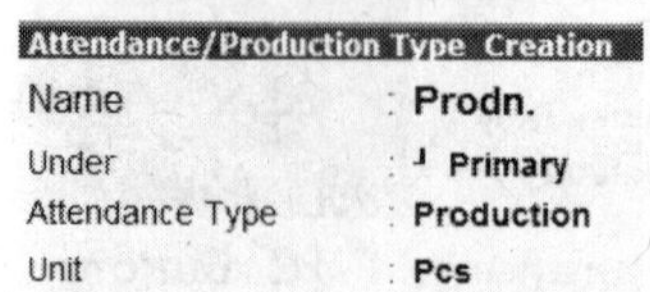

F-3A: Production Type creation

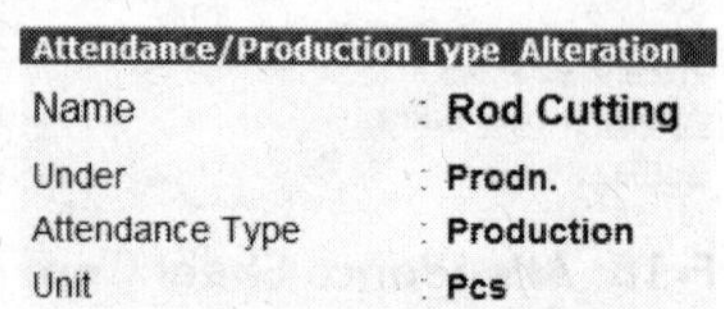

F-3B: Production Head

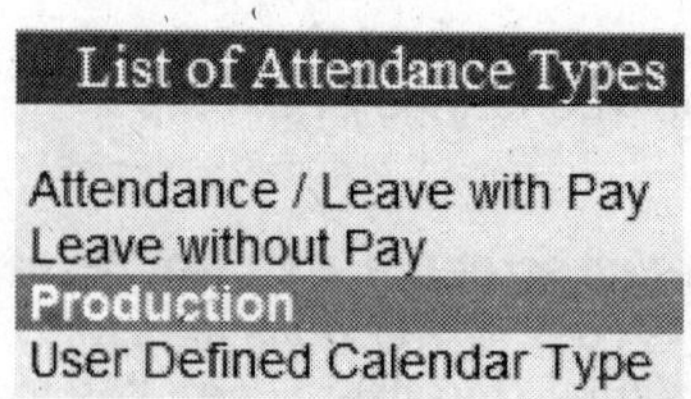

F-3C:Attendance / Type List

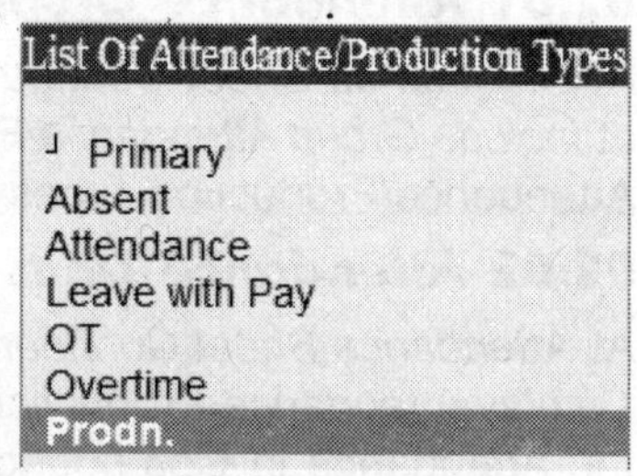

F-3D:Attendance / Production Type List

Now create Production Head (F-3B).At *Under*, select the parent Production Type head created (F-3A) from the list

(F-3D), as described (you may select *Primary*). At *Attendance Type*, select *Production* from *Attendance / Production Type* List (F-3C).

05 Production Pay Head

Now set the Production Pay heads (F-4A) as described earlier

Pay Head Creation — ABC Consultants

Name : **Production Wages**

Pay Head Info

Pay Head Type	: **Earnings for Employees**
Income Type	: **Fixed**
Under	: **Direct Expenses**
Affect Net Salary	? **Yes**
Name to appear in Payslip	: **P Wage**
Use for Gratuity	? **No**
Set / Alter Income Tax Details	? **No**
Calculation Type	: **On Production**
Production Type	? **Rod Cutting**

Rounding Info

Rounding Method : **Normal Rounding** Limit : **1**

Opening Balance (on 1-Apr-2015) :

F-4A: Production Wages Pay Head

List of Calculation

As Computed Value
As User Defined Value
Flat Rate
On Attendance
On Production

F-4B: Computation Type List

List of Production Types

Production	*Primary*	*Pcs*
Rod Cutting	*Production*	*Pcs*

F-4C: Production Type List

At *Calculation Type* (F-4A), select *On Production* from the Calculation Type List (F-4B), At *Production Type* (F-4A), select from the Production Type list (F-4C).

06 Employee Master

Employee Creation has been explained earlier. Here we explain Employee Master do define the Pay Structure of an Employee in which a Productio Py Head is included to compute Pay on Production basis.

Employee Creation

Name	**Ram Prasad**
Display Name in Reports	**R Prasad**
Under	**Workers** (*Primary*)
Date of Joining	**1-Apr-2000**
Define Salary Details	**Yes**

F-5A: Employee Master

Name : **Ram Prasad**
Under : **Workers** (*Primary*)

Salary Details

Effective From	Pay Head	Rate	Per	Pay Head Type	Calculation Type	Computed On
1-Apr-2000	Production Wages	10.00	Pcs	*Earnings for Employees*	*On Production*	

F-5B Employee Production Pay Structure

Employee Pay Structure: At *Define Salary* Details, set *Yes* to get Salary Details screen (F-5B) and set the Pay Structure as explained earlier. At *Pay Head* column, select the Production Pay. At *Rate* column, enter the Rate. The Unit is carried from the respective Production Type Master for the selected Pay Head (F-3B). Now add other Pay Heads as described earlier.

07 Production Voucher

Now enter the Production in Attendance voucher (F-7A), as described earlier. At *Attendance Production Type* column (F-7A), select the *Production Type* from the list (F-7B)

Attendance Voucher Creation — Ctrl + M

Attendance No. 3 — 31-Dec-2015, Thursday

Employee Name	Employee Number	Attendance/Production Type	Value	Unit
Ram Prasad	W013	Rod Cutting	230	Pcs

Narration:
Production Voucher for Oct 15

F-7A: Production Voucher

List of Attendance/Production Types

Absent	*Primary*	*Days*
Attendance	*Primary*	*Days*
Leave with Pay	*Primary*	*Days*
Production	*Primary*	*Pcs*
Rod Cutting	*Production*	*Pcs*

F-7B: Attendance / Production Type List

08 Payroll Voucher

Now create the Payroll voucher as described earlier. Set the *Auto Fill* details (F-8B). The Payroll Voucher (F-8A) gets generated with amount computed and auto filled.

Payroll Voucher Creation — Ctrl + M

Payroll No. **4** — **31-Dec-2015**, Thursday

Account : **Salary Payable**

Particulars		Amount
Ram Prasad		
Production Wages	Dr	
Ram Prasad		***2,300.00 Dr***
Production Wages	2,300.00 Dr	
Narration:		**2,300.00 Cr**

Pay Period : 1-Dec-2015 to 31-Dec-2015

F-8A: Payroll Voucher with Production wages

Payroll Auto Fill

Process for	: **Salary**
Compute Income Tax based on	: **Declared Value**
From (blank for beginning)	: **1-12-2015**
To (blank for end)	: **31-12-2015**
Employee/Group	: **Workers**
Payroll Ledger	:

F-8B: Payroll Voucher Auto Fill

09 Compound Work Unit

If the Work Unit of Pay Head is different from the Unit of Work (e.g for Unpaid days), you have to create a Compound Unit for Attendance Head also (after creating the Simple Unit – e.g Days), establishing a relationship between the two Units (Days & Hrs), For example, if the Pay Rate is per Day and the Overtime is in Hrs, then to compute Pay, you have to create a Compound Unit to establish the relationship between Days & Hours.

09.1 Compound Work Unit Creation

Work Unit creation has been described above (*GoT>Payroll Info>Units (Work):* §02). *At* Unit Creation screen (F-9A), if the cursor skips *Type* field, press Shift+Tab to get back to the *Type* field and select *Compound* at Type field (F-9A), to create the Compound Unit, specifying the relationship between the Unit Components of Compound Unit, as follows. Creation of *Compound Work Unit* is similar to creation of *Compound Unit of Measurement* (UoM) explained at Inventory section.

- **Compound Unit:** At *First Unit*, select the Compound Unit (larger Unit, like Days), from the list of Simple Units (F-9B),
- **Conversion Factor:** At *Conversion*, enter the conversion factor
- **Tail Unit:**At *Second Unit*, select the smaller Unit (Hrs) from the list of Simple Units (F-9B) to create the Compound Work Unit (e.g Days of 7.5 Hrs).

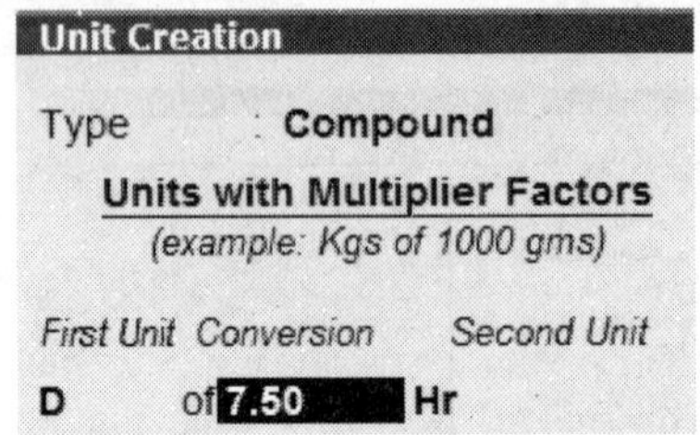

F-9A: Compound Work Unit creation

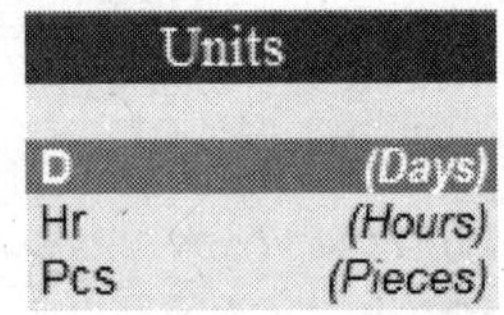

F-9B: Primary Unit selection list

Overtime Pay

05-05

01 Overtime Work

If Overtime Work and Over Time Pay is applicable, you have to create Heads for Overtime Pay and also Work Units (Overtime is normally recorded in Hours instead of Days).

Overtime Work Unit: Create Overtime Work Unit (e.g Hours), as described earlier

02 Overtime Attendance Head

As described for creation of Production Type, create Overtime Attendance / Production Head (F-1A). At *Under*, select Primary. At *Attendance Type*, select *Production* (to compute it as Production Pay), or *Attendance / Leave with Pay* (to compute it as Attendance Pay, the preferred way)., from the list of Attendance Type (F-1C). At *Unit*, select the Work Unit from Work Unit List (F-1B)

Attendance/Production Type Creation	
Name	: **Overtime**
Under	: ┘ **Primary**
Attendance Type	: **Production**
Unit	: **Hr**

F-1A: OT Attendance / Production Type Head

Units	
D	(Days)
D of 7.50 Hr	
Hr	**(Hours)**
Pcs	(Pieces)

F-1B: Work Unit selection

List of Attendance Types
Attendance / Leave with Pay
Leave without Pay
Production
User Defined Calendar Type

F-1C: Attendance Type List

03 Overtime Pay Head

Pay Head creation has been explained earlier. Create Pay Head for Overtime Pay (F-2A), as described earlier. At *Calculation Type*, select *On Production / On Attendance* (as the case may be) from Calculation Type list (F-2B). At Production Type, select *Over Time* Head created as described above, from the list (F-2C)

Pay Head Creation ABC C

Name : **Overtime Wages**

Pay Head Info

Pay Head Type	: **Earnings for Employees**
Income Type	: **Fixed**
Under	: **Employe Expenses** *(Indirect Expenses)*
Affect Net Salary	? **Yes**
Name to appear in Payslip	: **OT Wages**
Use for Gratuity	? **No**
Calculation Type	: **On Production**
Production Type	? **Overtime**

Rounding Info

Rounding Method : **Normal Rounding** Limit : **1**

Opening Balance (on 1-Apr-2015) :

F-2A: Overtime Pay Head

List of Calculation
As Computed Value
As User Defined Value
Flat Rate
On Attendance
On Production

F-2B: Calculation Type List

List of Production Types		
Overtime	┘ *Primary*	*Hr*
Production	┘ *Primary*	*Pcs*
Rod Cutting	*Production*	*Pcs*

F-2C: Production Type List

04 Employee Pay Structure

Employee Master creation has been explained earlier. Create / Modify the Employee Master / Define Pay Structure to include Overtime Wages in the Employee Master and enter the Rates at Pay Structure (F-3B).

Employee Alteration	
Name	: **Ram Prasad**
Display Name in Reports	: **R Prasad**
Under	: **Workers** (┘ *Primary*)
Date of Joining	: **1-Apr-2000**
Define Salary Details	: **Yes**

F-3A: Employee Pay Head

Name : **Ram Prasad (W013)**
Under : **Workers** (┘ *Primary*)

Salary Details

Effective From	Pay Head	Rate	Per	Pay Head Type	Calculation Type
1-Apr-2000					
	Production Wages	10.00	Pcs	*Earnings for Employees*	*On Production*
	Overtime Wages	20.00	Hr	*Earnings for Employees*	*On Production*

F-3B: Employee Pay Head Structure

05 Overtime Work Entry

Attendance Voucher entry for Attendance / Production has been explained earlier. Having created the Pay Structure including Overtime (F-3B), enter the Overtime Work in Attendance Voucher (F-4A). At *Attendance / Production Type* (F-4A), select from the list (F-4B).

Attendance Voucher Creation — Ctrl + M

Attendance No. 3 — 31-Jul-2015, Friday

Employee Name	Employee Number	Attendance/Production Type	Value	Unit
Ram Prasad	W013	Rod Cutting	240	Pcs
Ram Prasad	W013	Overtime	23	Hr

Narration:
Attd for Workers for Jul 15

F-4A: Attendance Voucher Entry

List of Attendance/Production Types

Absent	Primary	Days
Attendance	Primary	Days
Leave with Pay	Primary	Days
OT	Primary	Days
Overtime	Primary	Hr
Production	Primary	Pcs
Rod Cutting	Production	Pcs

F-4B: Attendance Type List

06 Payroll Voucher

Pay Voucher creation with Auto Fill has been explained earlier. Now create the Payroll Voucher with Auto Fill (F-5A) showing the computed overtime as per Overtime work and Rate as per Pay Structure. Fill up the Auto Fill screen (F-5B) as explained earlier. At *Payroll Ledger* (F-5B) select the Ledger Account from the list (F-5C). The Payroll voucher (F-5A) is generated.

Payroll Voucher Creation — Ctrl + M

Payroll No. 2 — 31-Jul-2015, Friday

Account : **Salary Payable**
Cur Bal: 25,743.65 Cr

Particulars		Amount
Ram Prasad		***2,860.00 Dr***
Production Wages	2,400.00 Dr	
Overtime Wages	460.00 Dr	
Narration:		**2,860.00 Cr**

Pay Period : 1-Jul-2015 to 31-Jul-2015

F-5A: Payroll Voucher with OT / Production

Payroll Auto Fill

Process for	: Salary
Compute Income Tax based on	: Declared Value
From (blank for beginning)	: 1-7-2015
To (blank for end)	: 31-7-2015
Employee/Group	: Workers
Payroll Ledger	:

F-5B: Payroll Voucher Auto Fill

List of Ledger Accounts

Bomus Payable
Cash
HDFC Bank
Salary Payable

F-5C: Salary Ledger selection

Index

D

S